Critical to Remember

Drug Guides

Communication Dialogues

Additional copies of the companion pocket book can be purchased through your local bookstore, or you can order directly by calling 1-800-544-6678. Ask for *Keys to Clinical Practice: Maternal-Newborn Nursing*, ISBN 0-7216-5194-1.

Foundations of Maternal Newborn Nursing

Foundations of Maternal Newborn Nursing

Trula Myers Gorrie, M.N., R.N.,C.
Formerly, Professor of Nursing
Golden West College
Huntington Beach, California

Emily Slone McKinney, M.S.N., R.N.,C.
Associate Professor of Nursing
Tarrant County Junior College
Fort Worth, Texas

Sharon Smith Murray, M.S.N., R.N.,C.
Professor of Nursing
Golden West College
Huntington Beach, California

W. B. SAUNDERS COMPANY
A Division of Harcourt Brace & Company
Philadelphia • London • Toronto • Montreal • Sydney • Tokyo

W. B. SAUNDERS COMPANY
A Division of Harcourt Brace & Company

The Curtis Center
Independence Square West
Philadelphia, Pennsylvania 19106

Library of Congress Cataloging-in-Publication Data

Gorrie, Trula.
Foundations of maternal-newborn nursing/Trula Myers Gorrie,
Emily Slone McKinney, Sharon Smith Murray.—1st ed.
p. cm.
Includes index.
ISBN 0–7216–4033–8
1. Maternity nursing. I. McKinney, Emily Slone. II. Murray, Sharon Smith. III. Title.
[DNLM: 1. Maternal-Child Nursing. 2. Family Health.
WY 157.3 G673f 1994]
RG951.G668 1994
610.73′67—dc20
DNLM/DLC 93–32193

Foundations of Maternal-Newborn Nursing ISBN 0–7216–4033–8

Printed in the United States of America.

Last digit is the print number: 9 8 7 6 5 4 3 2 1

To Clayton and Brian, for encouragement and joy.

T.M.G.

For all that you do, Michael, with my love.
To my mother and late father, for giving me a firm foundation.
To my daughters, Cathy and Amy.

E.S.M.

To my husband Skip, my daughters Vicki, Holly, and Shannon, and my mother, Clare, with love and thanksgiving.

S.S.M.

Consultants

Betty W. Hamlisch, B.S.N., M.S., R.N.
Professor of Nursing, Tompkins Cortland Community College, Dryden, New York

Patricia Dillon Montpas, M.S.N., Ed.D., R.N.
Professor of Nursing, Mott Community College, Flint, Michigan

Carrie Russell Pierce, B.S., M.S., R.N.
Assistant Chairperson, Evening Division; and Associate Professor, Maria College, Albany, New York

Nancy Rooker, M.S.N., R.N.
Nursing Instructor, Elgin Community College, Elgin, Illinois

Carol A. Rusin, A.A.S., B.S. Ed.D., R.N.
Professor, Trocaire College, Buffalo, New York

Roselena Thorpe, Ph.D., R.N.
Professor and Department Chairperson, Community College of Allegheny County, Allegheny Campus, Pittsburgh, Pennsylvania

Elizabeth J. Tipping, M.S.N., R.N.,C.
Maternal Infant Coordinator, Greenville Technical College, Greenville, South Carolina

Reviewers

Barbara Blizzard, C.N.M.
University of Texas, Austin, Texas

Mary K. Bourgeois-Harris, M.S.N., C.F.N.P., R.N.
Kaiser Permanente Medical Group, Huntington Beach, California

Loretta Faye Crawford, M.S., R.N.
College of Eastern Utah, Price, Utah

Joan Dauphinee, M.S., R.N.,C.
Magee-Women's Hospital, Pittsburgh, Pennsylvania

Kathryn Deitch, Ph.D., R.N.,C.
California State University, San Bernardino, California

Carole Linda DeMaio, M.A., R.N.,C.
Central Florida Infertility Specialists, Winter Park, Florida

Gretchen Stone Dimico, Pd.D., R.N.,C.
Intercollegiate Center for Nursing Education, Spokane, Washington

Kathleen K. Furniss, M.S.N., R.N.,C.
Wayne Obstetrics Group, Wayne, New Jersey; and Saint Barnabas Medical Center, Livingston, New Jersey

Sandra Gale, C.N.M., M.P.H.
Austin-Travis County Health and Human Services, Austin, Texas

Laura R. Garcia-Romero, M.S., C.N.M., R.N.
East Los Angeles College, Monterey Park, California

Linda R. Goodwin, M.Ed., R.N.,C.
Tokos Medical Corporation, Seattle, Washington

C. Anne Green, M.S.N., Ed.D., R.N.
Solano Community College, Suisun City, California

Lynn Grommet, B.S.N., R.N.,C.
East Arkansas Community College, Forrest City, Arkansas

Linda Coburn Hildenbrand, B.S., M.S., R.N.
Hagerstown Junior College, Hagerstown, Maryland

Nancy G. Hinzman, M.S.N., R.N.,C.
Northern Kentucky University, Highland Heights, Kentucky

Linda Howard-Glenn, M.N., R.N.,C.
Memorial-Miller Children's Hospital, Long Beach, California

Marilyn Hurt, M.S.N., R.N.
McLennan Community College, Waco, Texas

Dorothy J. Insolera, M.S.N., R.N.,C.
College of Saint Mary, Omaha, Nebraska

Gail H. Jones, B.S.N., M.S.N., R.N.
George C. Wallace Community College, Dothan, Alabama

Mary F. King, M.S.N., R.N.
Phillips County Community College, Helena, Arkansas

Cynthia Kirbie, C.R.N.A.
John Peter Smith Hospital, Fort Worth, Texas

Glenda LeMaitre, M.S.N., R.N.,C.
University of District of Columbia, Washington, DC

Mira L. Lessick, Ph.D., R.N.
College of Nursing, Rush University, Chicago, Illinois

Janet Llewellyn, S.R.N., S.C.M., R.N.
Utah Valley Community College, Orem, Utah

Judy Wright Lott, M.S.N., N.N.P., D.S.N.(C), R.N.
Children's Hospital of Cincinnati, Cincinnati, Ohio

Mary Ann Lush, M.S.N., R.N.
Abington Memorial Hospital, Abington, Pennsylvania

Gloria Matsuura, M.S., C.N.M., A.C.C.E.
North Memorial Medical Center, Robbinsdale, Minnesota

Linda May Mayer, M.S.N., R.N.
Umpqua Community College, Roseburg, Oregon

Arlene M. McMahon, M.S.N., R.N.
Gwynedd-Mercy College, Gwynedd Valley, Pennsylvania; and Hospital of the University of Pennsylvania, Philadelphia, Pennsylvania

Joan M. Millett, B.S., M.A., R.N.
Springfield Technical Community College, Springfield, Massachusetts

Sally Morgan, M.S.N. Candidate, R.N.
Golden West College, Huntington Beach, California

Joyce J. Morris, M.S., A.R.N.P., R.N.
College Hospital Clinic, Tampa, Florida

Irene E. Muth, R.D., C.N.S.D.
Temple University, Philadelphia, Pennsylvania

Mary O'Pray, M.A., R.N.,C.
Sante Fe Community College, Gainesville, Florida

Josanne M. Paxton
University Medical Center, Arizona Health Science Center, Tucson, Arizona

Tena B. Payne, M.S.N., R.N.
Paducah Community College, Paducah, Kentucky

Kathy Lynn Plummer, B.S.N., O.G.N.P., R.N.,C.
Rose Medical Center, Denver, Colorado

Janet F. Pope, Ph.D., R.D.
College of Human Ecology, Louisiana Technical University, Ruston, Louisiana

Elizabeth Ann Quill, M.S., F.N.P., R.N.
Cochise College, Douglas, Arizona

Gloria S. Riemenschneider, B.S.N., M.S.N., C.N.M.
Formerly: University of Texas Health Science Center, San Antonio, Texas

Cheryl Ann Sassack, B.S.N., M.S.N., R.N.
Allen Memorial Hospital, Waterloo, Iowa

Patricia A. Schlecht, M.S.N., R.N.,C.
University of Cincinnati, Raymond Watters College, Cincinnati, Ohio

Jeanne K. Stotler, M.S.N., R.N.,C.
Planned Parenthood of the Rocky Mountains, Aurora, Colorado

Barbara R. Stright, M.S.N., R.N.
Clarion University of Pennsylvania, Venango Campus, Oil City, Pennsylvania

Nancy H. Sullivan, M.S., C.N.M., R.N.
Healthy Start, Inc., Hillsboro, Oregon; and Department of Family Nursing and Obstetrics and Gynecology, Oregon Health Sciences University, Portland, Oregon

Eunice Warren, M.S., R.N.
Baylor University, Atlanta, Georgia

Diane Welch, M.S.N., R.N.,C.
Sacramento City College, Sacramento, California

Grace R. Whitis, Ph.D., R.N.
Arkansas State University, State University, Arkansas

Donna Wilsker, M.S., R.N.
Lamar University, Beaumont, Texas

Anna Wingate, B.S.N., M.S.Ed., R.N.
Rockingham Community College, Wentworth, North Carolina

Catherine Witt, M.S., N.N.P., R.N.,C.
P/SL Medical Center, Women's and Children's Services, Denver, Colorado

Illustrators

Illustrations by *Rosemarie D'Alba*

Photography by *Eric Woodward*

Preface

The Challenge of Maternity Nursing Education

Nurses play an important role during a family's birth experience. Today, nurses are challenged to support birth as a natural physical, emotional, and social experience in an increasingly complex technological setting. Nurses promote the family—in whatever way the client defines "family"—and help strengthen emotional bonds among family members.

Today's maternity nurse must be flexible to accommodate diversity among clients, birth attendants, and care settings. Consumers of maternity nursing care vary in age, ethnicity, language, culture, marital status, and attitude toward health care. Women may rely on nurse-midwives or physicians for maternity care. Their prenatal care (if indeed they receive it) and birth may occur in public clinics or hospitals, private hospitals, birth centers, or the home. Moreover, hospitals may provide maternity services in single-room (labor-delivery-recovery-postpartum: LDRP) environments or may have specialized areas for labor, birth and recovery. The nurse not only gives safe and effective nursing care but also helps each family achieve a unique and satisfying childbirth experience.

Nursing students are as diverse as their clients. Today's nursing student may be an older adult with family responsibilities or a traditional young high school graduate; a female or a male; a person with a degree in a different field who wants to change careers; or a person for whom English is a second language and who devotes extra time and effort to reading. Learning skills and experiences differ from student to student. Consequently, a textbook needs to present content that can be read with ease, yet is thorough and comprehensive to enrich the learning of the most dedicated student. Summaries and use of visual cues, such as illustrations, tables, and highlights, are proven learning aids and are used generously throughout this text.

Themes

Our purpose in writing this book has been to help the nursing student achieve competency in maternity nursing as a novice working within the realities of the learning environment. The book has grown out of our rich experiences as practicing maternity nurses and seasoned nursing educators.

The five themes we consider most important are the nursing process, scientific base, communication, client teaching, and cultural diversity.

The Nursing Process

The nursing process is the common thread joining students, teachers, and nurses in practice. It is a logical framework for client assessment, analysis of client needs, planning and provision of nursing care, and evaluation of the client's response to care. Critical analysis of client needs allows the nurse to most appropriately apply scientific knowledge and technical and interpersonal skills.

Client needs are often a mixture of those for which nurses have the primary responsibility and those for which another discipline provides definitive therapy, yet which have an overlapping nursing component. Thus, when analyzing theoretical client needs, we have chosen either a ***nursing diagnosis*** or a ***collaborative problem***, depending on whether nurses have the primary responsibility for helping the client meet those needs. Nursing diagnoses are drawn from the most recent list of those approved by the North American Nursing Diagnosis Association (NANDA).

Two methods are used to show the student how the nursing process might be applied to maternity care, depending on the nature of the topic: in narrative text and in nursing care plans. We lead the reader through the five steps of the nursing process in chapters that present nursing care, using one or both approaches.

In the narrative, basic knowledge and theory are discussed and nursing care is then presented, organized by ***steps of the nursing process,*** augmented by collaborative problems, and supported by rationales. In addition, because students often have difficulty transferring nursing knowledge to the care of a specific client, we have created **"Nursing Care Plans"** based on scenarios of ***client situations*** frequently encountered in maternity nursing. Nursing care plans are in easy-to-read tabular format and present a variety of ages, families, and cultural groups that add interest and realism to learning.

Sometimes, medical care is the overriding client need. For topics such as complications of labor or obstetrical emergencies, we present the condition, its medical therapy, and related nursing considerations to help students obtain the needed information quickly.

Scientific Base

Safe and effective nursing care is based on a firm understanding of the physiological and pathophysiological bases for medical treatments and nursing interventions. Although an anatomy and physiology course is part of every nursing curriculum, the direct applicability of this course to the nursing content varies from school to school. The diverse backgrounds and learning styles of contemporary nursing students add yet another challenge to provide nursing education on a strong scientific base. Because of these needs, we have incorporated sound principles of physiology and pathophysiology throughout this book. We have presented these scientific concepts in a clear and understandable manner so that the reader can best understand the forces that underlie both health and dysfunction.

Chapters 4, 5, and 6 give a thorough introduction to reproductive physiology, genetics, and the process of conception and fetal development. Chapters 7, 12, 17, and 19 cover physiological adaptation during pregnancy, birth, and the post partum period and in the newborn.

The entire high-risk unit, Part V, Families at Risk During the Childbearing Period, carefully describes the physiological bases of complications in the mother and in the newborn.

Communication

Communication skills are rarely named as core content in maternal-newborn courses; yet nurses must be able to communicate effectively to enable comprehensive client assessment, reduce anxiety in the client and her family, teach needed self-care and infant care skills, and evaluate the client's responses to care. Throughout the text, we reinforce the student's previous learning and give practical examples of ***applied communication skills in the maternity setting.***

The theme of communication is presented in three ways:

- In Chapter 2, guidelines for therapeutic communication and examples of effective communication and potential blocks can serve as an introduction to communication or as a convenient review and refresher, depending on individual student needs.
- Color-highlighted ***communication cues*** in the text give tips on how to interact with clients or suggest possible interpretations of a client's behavior. Tips include ways to avoid potentially embarrassing situations, role modeling of effective communication styles, and reading non-verbal behavior. Communication cues are listed in the index for easy access.
- Nurse-client dialogues, using an informal tone and ordinary words, present realistic possible nurse-client interactions. As the conversation develops, we identify therapeutic ***communication techniques*** that nurses use. Because no one is perfect, we occasionally insert communication blocks, identify them, and suggest alternate responses. Nurse-client dialogues are especially helpful for role modeling and can enliven classroom discussions.

Client Teaching

Nurses in all settings are challenged to provide care in a short time frame, because a woman rarely stays at the birth facility more than 24 hours following an uncomplicated birth. In addition, many consumers of health care today expect comprehensive information about their health, their care, and management of any problems. Nurses often must teach in less than ideal circumstances and must be well prepared and well organized.

Client teaching is presented in three ways:

- In Chapter 2, principles and a review of the teaching-learning process are presented.
- ***Key content chapters*** are organized so that the student can gather information and translate it into client teaching. For example, Chapter 9, Nutrition for Childbearing, lays a foundation of basic nutritional facts, discusses diversity of cultural food practices, presents assessment of nu-

tritional status, and offers nursing interventions devoted to effective teaching so that the client can better care for herself. Chapter 22, Parenting During the Early Weeks, helps prepare the student to provide anticipatory guidance to new parents, because questions are often asked of the maternity nurse.

- Specific client teaching guidelines are highlighted in "**Want to Know**" features, which give practical advice or answer frequent client questions. Many boxed features relate to home management. For example, the feature "How to Overcome the Common Discomforts of Pregnancy" in Chapter 7 addresses the learning needs of the woman experiencing nausea, fatigue, or other discomfort. The conversational tone in these features has been carefully constructed—it shows students how to present technical information in everyday language so that women and their families will better understand teaching.

Cultural Diversity

To understand the implications of culture on nursing practice, nurses need a basic understanding of diverse values and beliefs. Effective nursing care requires nurses to consider their own cultural values and to examine how these values may create conflict with those whose values are different.

Chapter 1 offers an overview of Western cultural values and contrasts these with four major cultural groups in the United States. Additional information is integrated throughout the book as it relates to specific areas such as pregnancy, nutrition, birth, and the puerperium. "Cultural diversity" is indexed so that the student can easily find information, but content is integrated into discussions so that cultural diversity is understood as a norm, not the exception.

Organization of the Book

Foundations of Maternal-Newborn Nursing is divided into six parts, with content generally progressing from normal to complicated and from general to specific. Part I, Foundations for Nursing Care of Childbearing Families, presents an ***overview of contemporary maternity care***, including the nurse's role. Current ethical, social, and legal issues are addressed as well. A review of reproductive anatomy and physiology is included, which is especially important for the student who has not recently completed a full anatomy and physiology course. The hereditary and environmental factors that impact childbearing are presented, with many illustrations included to clarify content.

Part II, The Family Before Birth, covers conception and fetal development throughout pregnancy. Chapters on both ***physiological*** and ***psychosocial adaptations to pregnancy*** address the changes the pregnant woman and her family experience during this time. Because adequate nutrition is essential to the expectant mother's health and that of her fetus and newborn, we have devoted a chapter to this important subject. To cover this topic most efficiently, we also include nutritional care of the woman after birth and during lactation.

Part III, The Family During Birth, covers the ***physiologic processes of birth and nursing care during labor and birth.*** Intrapartum fetal monitoring, pain management, and obstetrical procedures, such as cesarean birth, are discussed. Nursing considerations for specific obstetrical procedures also are presented.

Part IV, The Family Following Birth, discusses ***care of the new mother and infant.*** Infant nutrition and a chapter on parenting during the early weeks appear in this portion of the book.

Part V, Families at Risk During the Childbearing Period, includes a chapter on the family with special needs and covers age-related concerns, ***childbearing in a substance-abusing environment***, responses to infants with congenital anomalies, ***pregnancy loss***, the ***relinquishing mother***, and ***violence against women.*** Additional chapters describe common complications encountered during pregnancy, labor and birth, and the postpartum and neonatal periods.

Part VI, Other Reproductive Issues, includes chapters on family planning, care of infertile couples, and ***women's health care.*** With these topics organized into three concise chapters, maximum flexibility is allowed for reading assignments.

Features to Enhance Teaching and Learning

We have included many features designed to enhance the student's mastery of basic maternity nursing content and to develop the student's ability to think critically about client situations. These features represent methods that we have found especially useful to strengthen student understanding of content.

Visual Appeal. Illustrations and photographs express visually what is difficult to express in words. Illustrations are designed especially for this book and are used to clarify concepts, expand upon text, and reinforce learning.

Objectives and Definitions. Each chapter begins with a list of educational objectives for that chapter. A list of key terms with their definitions follows the objectives. A **glossary** at the back of the book summarizes key terms from all chapters.

Check Your Reading Questions. At intervals throughout each chapter, we have included questions about the material presented so that students can monitor their comprehension and keep their study time focused. A student can check the ***answers*** in Appendix F for immediate feedback. Because **Check Your Reading** questions cover core content, the student should find the questions and answers a ***convenient review outline.***

Relevance to Clinical Practice. Many chapters include sample **Clinical Situations** to help the student apply theoretical knowledge to a hypothetical client situation. Each situation provides a scenario and asks pertinent questions to reinforce learning. Answers are provided below the questions.

Procedures and Drug Guides. Maternity nursing procedures are included in appropriate chapters. These are listed on the inside front cover for easy access. Guides are included for drugs commonly administered in maternity nursing and women's health care. In some cases, drug information is presented in a table rather than in a **Drug Guide.**

Use of Summary Methods. Tables are used to summarize or compare complex content. In some cases, *tables are used instead of a more lengthy narrative discussion*. Students should be aware that tables contain important material.

Critical to Remember features are brief lists appearing in most clinical chapters. These alert the nurse to danger signs, or they reinforce specific clinical points. Examples include signs associated with fetal compromise and hazards of neonatal cold stress.

Infection Control. Avoidance of infection is an essential part of nursing practice. Two related components are involved in safeguarding nurses and their clients from exposure to infectious organisms:

- Protection from blood-borne pathogens such as human immunodeficiency virus and hepatitis B virus (universal precautions)
- Protection from other potentially infectious organisms

△ A logo in the margin emphasizes the need to use personal protective equipment as a barrier to the very serious pathogens that may be transmitted in blood and other specific body fluids to which universal precautions apply. In Appendix B, we have listed these fluids and summarized guidelines from the Centers for Disease Control and Prevention for preventing blood-borne pathogens.

The body fluids cited in universal precautions do not include other potential sources of infection often encountered in maternity and women's health care. Therefore, Appendix B also alerts the reader to common situations in which both types of pathogens may be encountered and for which personal protective equipment is appropriate.

Use of the logo in this book is reserved for discussion of situations in which there is a high likelihood of exposure to substances included in universal precautions. The logo is not used with discussion of every instance of possible exposure to infectious organisms, including both blood-borne and other pathogens.

Color Photographs. One family's birth experience is beautifully illustrated in 24 color pictures that help prepare students to participate in maternal-newborn nursing. This color story appears in Chapter 13, which discusses nursing care during labor and birth. An additional color insert in Chapter 20 shows the birth sequence and depicts anomalies that may occur in newborns.

Each chapter closes with **Summary Concepts** to further reinforce essential points. These concepts relate to the objectives stated in the beginning of the chapter.

Keys to Clinical Practice

The realities of nursing education sometimes dictate that students begin their clinical experience before they have had the opportunity to discuss all theory in the classroom. We have developed a small pocket-sized handbook for students to take to the clinical setting that will help them supplement their classroom preparation. Use of this handbook should decrease student anxiety, especially during the early days of their clinical practice. Several components of this handbook are also included in Appendix E.

The clinical components in *Keys to Clinical Practice* include:

- Care guides for the woman in labor, for meeting her physiological and psychological needs during the postpartum period, and for care of the neonate during admission and thereafter
- Drug guides describing the most common medications encountered in maternity care
- How to individualize nursing care plans, a task found to be difficult by many students

- Client teaching on key topics, for example, assisting the inexperienced mother to breastfeed and answering common questions asked by parents

Instructor's Materials

The *Instructor's Manual* was written by Nancy Morgan, an experienced educator in maternity nursing. Suggestions for teaching-learning activities in both classroom and practicum settings promote learning, application, and retention of the content. Options for extra-credit activities are given for the student who desires the experience or who perhaps must make up an absence. Various group activities promote development of analytical thinking skills and provide alternatives for days when the client census may be low. The answers to group activities, with rationales, are given.

Several experienced nursing educators have contributed to the test bank. Questions within each chapter are distributed over the content and relate to the chapter's objectives. Each item is assigned a cognitive level of knowledge, comprehension, or application. The test bank is supplied in a ***computer version,*** "ExaMaster," which offers the instructor numerous options in test construction, and a ***printed version*** in the *Instructor's Manual.*

A transparency package of 70 illustrations that we believe to be most useful in classroom teaching is part of the instructor's materials. Many transparencies feature two colors to emphasize important concepts. In addition, 40 color slides are available for qualified adopters that will allow the instructor to present a pictorial overview of childbirth. These slides illustrate the multiple roles that nurses play in family-centered maternity care.

Acknowledgments

Foundations of Maternal-Newborn Nursing would not have been possible without the contributions of many people. First, we want to thank the educators and clinicians who participated as Consultants and Reviewers; their names are listed on a separate page. We have been most fortunate to work with a group of consultants who have read manuscript, shared their experiences and insights, and been wonderful supports and motivators. We also want to thank Fountain Valley Regional Hospital and Medical Center and Saddleback Memorial Medical Center for helping us meet our needs for photographs as well as the many nurses, nursing students, and new parents who were so gracious in posing for them.

Ilze Rader, Senior Nursing Editor at W.B. Saunders, brought us together and guided our first tentative steps as we began the book. She stimulated us to think creatively, yet critically, by asking, "What do you think about . . . ? or "What if you did it this way?"

Developmental Editor Miriam McCauley consistently gave us gentle and patient guidance. Her constructive comments were always given in a most encouraging manner. Miriam's attention to detail helped refine and organize this complex project.

Most illustrations were created by Rosemarie D'Alba. Her talent and training were evident as she converted our rough drawings into sensitive and accurate illustrations.

Eric Woodward worked long hours at all times of day and night in sometimes less than ideal settings to take the photographs that would best capture the concepts we were trying to convey to students.

The work of two people at W. B. Saunders supplemented the illustration and photographic art. Mechanical artist Risa Clow created the charts and graphs that amplify the narrative text, and Cecilia Roberts coordinated the many different types of art.

Other talented and hard-working people helped mold our manuscript into a beautiful book. Marie Thomas and Eileen Mann helped keep the volumes of manuscript and reviews flowing. Three manuscript editors, Carol Robins, Jodi von Hagen, and Mary Ellen Johansen, smoothed out our writing. Book designer Karen O'Keefe pulled all the narrative, tables, illustrations and photographs into an attractive format for learning. Finally, Peter Faber was the production manager who oversaw the physical production of the book from manuscript through the final bound volume.

TRULA MYERS GORRIE
EMILY SLONE MCKINNEY
SHARON SMITH MURRAY

Brief Contents

Detailed Contents

Part I

Foundations for Nursing Care of Childbearing Families, 1

Part II

The Family Before Birth, 89

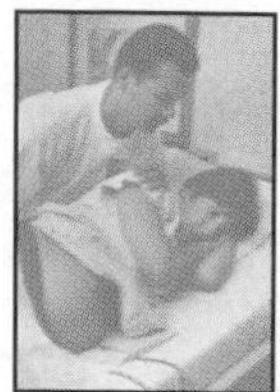

Part III

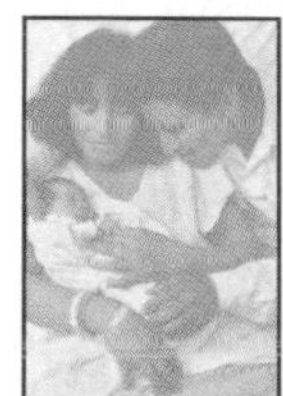

Part IV

The Family Following Birth, 413

Part V

Families at Risk During the Childbearing Period, 613

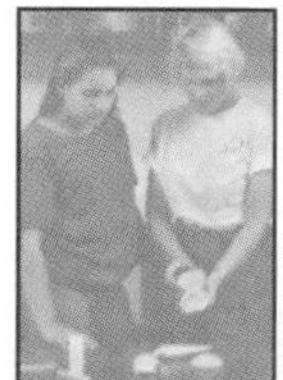

Part VI

Foundations for Nursing Care of Childbearing Families

1

Maternity Care Today

Objectives

1. Describe changes in maternity care from home birth with lay midwives to the emergence of medical management, including the impact of federal involvement and consumer demands.
2. Compare current settings for childbirth both within and outside the traditional hospital setting.
3. Identify trends that have led to the development of family-centered maternity care.
4. Discuss the downward trends in infant and maternal mortality rates, and compare current infant mortality rates for specific ethnic groups and nations.
5. Explain changes in family structure and their impact on family functioning.
6. Compare Western cultural values with those of differing cultural groups, and describe the effect of cultural diversity on nursing practice.

Definitions

Culture • Sum of values, beliefs, and practices of a group of people that are transmitted from one generation to the next.

Ethnic • Pertaining to religious, racial, national, or cultural group characteristics, especially speech patterns, social customs, and physical characteristics.

Ethnicity • Condition of belonging to a particular **ethnic** group; also refers to ethnic pride.

Ethnocentricism • Opinion that one's own ethnic group is superior as related to beliefs and customs.

Infant mortality rate • Number of deaths per 1000 live births that occur within the first 12 months of life.

Maternal mortality rate • Number of maternal deaths per 100,000 live births as a direct result of the reproductive process.

Neonatal mortality rate • Number of deaths per 1000 live births occurring at birth or within the first 28 days of life.

Post-neonatal mortality rate • Number of deaths between 28 days and 1 year of life per 1000 live births.

Maternity care has undergone major changes in the last decades, resulting in a progressive decline in maternal and infant mortality rates. However, there is room for improvement, as the United States ranks far below other industrialized countries in infant mortality rates and there continues to be wide variation among ethnic groups. Moreover, nursing care must take into account the changes in family structure and function as well as differing cultural beliefs and customs that have occurred.

Historical Perspectives on Childbearing

"Granny" Midwives

Prior to the twentieth century, childbirth occurred most often in the home and the delivery was accomplished by a "granny" midwife who had little education beyond that obtained by an apprenticeship with a more experienced granny midwife. These lay midwives were regarded not as a part of the medical establishment but as a separate profession with a unique role. Physicians were involved in childbirth only if there were serious problems.

Although many women and infants fared well when a lay midwife assisted with birth in the home, maternal and infant death rates resulting from childbearing were high. The primary causes of maternal death were postpartum hemorrhage; postpartum infection, also known as puerperal sepsis (or "childbed fever"); and toxemia, now known as pregnancy-induced hypertension. The primary causes of infant death were prematurity, dehydration resulting from diarrhea, and contagious diseases.

Emergence of Medical Management

In the late nineteenth century, developing technology led to a decline in home births, with an increase in physician-assisted hospital births. Significant discoveries that set the stage for change in maternity care have included:

- The development of forceps to facilitate difficult births by physicians
- The discovery of chloroform, which was used to control pain
- The discovery by Semmelweis that puerperal infection could be prevented by hygienic practices
- Advances in operative procedures such as cesarean birth
- The use of drugs to start labor (induction) or to increase uterine contractions (augmentation of labor)

Consequently, hospitals hurried to develop policies and procedures to prevent infection and to meet the needs of physicians.

In the hospital setting, maternity care became highly regimented. All prenatal, intrapartum, and postpartum care was managed by physicians. Lay midwifery became illegal, and nurse-midwifery was not well established. By 1960, 90 per cent of all births occurred in hospitals. The nurse's primary functions were to assist the physician in delivery of the infant and to follow prescribed medical orders following childbirth. Teaching and counseling were not valued nursing functions at that time.

Unlike at-home births, hospital births hindered bonding between parents and infant. During labor, the woman received medication, such as "twilight sleep," a combination of scopalamine and morphine that provided pain relief but left her disoriented, confused, and heavily sedated. Because of this and because little was known of the importance of early contact between parents and child, many mothers did not see the infant for several hours after the delivery. The father was relegated to a waiting area and not allowed to see the mother until some time after the birth of the infant.

Despite technological advances, maternal and infant mortality declined slowly. This was primarily due to preventable problems, such as poor nutrition, infectious diseases, and inadequate prenatal care. These stubborn problems remained because of inequalities in health care delivery. Whereas affluent families could afford comprehensive medical care that began early in the pregnancy, poor families had very limited access to care or to information. Two concurrent trends, federal involvement and consumer demands, led to additional changes in maternity care.

Federal Involvement in Maternal-Newborn Care

The high rates of maternal and infant mortality among indigent women provided the impetus for the first federal involvement in maternity care. The Sheppard-Towner Act of 1921, the first federally sponsored program, provided funds for state-managed programs in maternal-child health. Although this act was later repealed, it set the scene for future allocation of federal funds. In 1935, Title V of the Social Security Act was amended to provide funding for maternal-child health programs. Today, the federal government provides several programs to support maternal-child health (Table 1–1).

Table 1–1. FEDERAL PROJECTS FOR MATERNAL-CHILD CARE

Program	Purpose
Title V of Social Security Act	Provides funds for maternal-child health programs
National Institute of Health and Human Development	Supports research and education of personnel needed for maternal and child health programs
Title V Amendment of Public Health Service Act	Established the Maternal and Infant Care (MIC) projects to provide comprehensive prenatal and infant care in public clinics
Title XIX of Medicaid Program	Provides funds to facilitate access to care by pregnant women and young children
Head Start	To provide educational opportunities for low-income children of preschool age
National Center for Family Planning	A clearinghouse for contraceptive information
Women, Infants, and Children (WIC)	Provides supplemental food and nutrition information

Although government funds partially solved the problem of maternal and infant mortality, the *distribution* of health care remained inequitable. Most physicians practiced in urban or suburban areas where the affluent could afford to pay for medical services, but women in rural or inner city areas had difficulty obtaining care. Distribution of health care is a problem that persists today.

The ongoing problem of providing health care for poor women and children has left the door open for nurses to expand their roles, and advanced programs of education prepared nurses as nurse-midwives, nurse practitioners, and clinical specialists. Chapter 2 provides a more complete description of the nurse's role in current maternal-child care.

Impact of Consumer Demands

In the early 1950s, consumers of health care began to insist on their right to be involved in the care they receive. Pregnant women were no longer willing to accept just what was offered. They wanted information about planning and spacing their children, and they wanted to know what to expect during pregnancy. Along with the mother, the father, siblings, and grandparents wanted to be part of the extraordinary events of pregnancy and childbirth. Moreover, families wanted some say in how delivery was accomplished. Dr. Grantly Dick-Read proposed a method of childbirth that allowed the mother to control her fear and thus to control her pain during labor so that birth without pharmacological intervention was possible. Additional methods, such as Lamaze and Bradley, quickly gained favor. (See Chapter 11.)

There was a growing consensus among child psychologists and nurse researchers that the benefits of early extended parent-infant contact far outweighed the risks of infection. As a result, some parents began to insist that the infant remain with them at all times and the practice of separating the infant from the family was gradually abandoned. Two new concepts resulted: rooming-in, whereby the infant remained with the mother throughout the hospital stay, and mother-baby coupling, whereby care was provided for the mother-infant dyad rather than separately to the mother and to the infant. These changes gradually led to the development of family-centered maternity care.

Development of Family-Centered Maternity Care

Family-centered maternity care is the term used to describe safe, quality care that recognizes and adapts to both the physical and psychosocial needs of the family, including those of the newborn, with emphasis on fostering family unity while maintaining physical safety.

The basic principles of family-centered care are as follows:

- Childbirth is usually a normal, healthy event in the life of a family.
- Childbirth impacts on the entire family, and restructuring of family relationships is required.
- Families are capable of making decisions about care, provided that they are given adequate information and professional support.

Family-centered care greatly increased the responsibilities of nurses in hospitals. It is no longer enough for nurses to provide only physical care and to assist physicians. Nurses now assume a major role in teaching, counseling, and supporting families in their decisions.

Current Settings for Childbirth

Desire for more natural approaches and more family involvement has brought about changes in how and where childbirth occurs. The traditional hospital setting gradually gave way to alternative settings in many areas.

Traditional Hospital Setting

In the traditional setting, a woman is admitted to a labor room that resembles a typical functional hospital room. Procedures and protocols depend on the hospital; however, many hospitals require continuous electronic fetal monitoring (see Chapter 14) and administration of intravenous fluids. Analgesia and anesthesia are frequently administered (see Chapter 15). Labor occurs in one room, and when birth is imminent, the mother is moved to a delivery area similar to an operating room. Following childbirth, the mother is transferred to a recovery area for 1 to 2 hours of observation, then to the postpartum unit, which resembles a standard hospital room. The infant is often transferred to the newborn nursery when the mother is moved to the recovery area. Mother and infant are usually reunited when the mother is transferred to the postpartum unit. The father or another significant support person usually remains with the mother throughout labor, delivery, and recovery.

Although care in the traditional setting is very safe, the rooms seem impersonal and "sterile" and having to move from one room to another disrupts family time together. In years past, the mother saw her newborn briefly in the delivery room and then only at feeding times. Fathers saw their infants only through the windows of the nursery. However, efforts to make the hospital experience more family-centered have changed this. Mothers keep the infants with them for longer periods of time, and fathers are encouraged to hold the infants and to remain with the mothers. Visiting hours are expanded, and visitors may now see and hold the baby in the mother's room. Fathers are encouraged to visit for extended hours. Early discharge is common practice. Mothers often go home on the second morning after a vaginal delivery and on the fourth morning after a cesarean birth at the latest.

Alternative Settings Within Hospitals

LABOR, DELIVERY, AND RECOVERY ROOMS

Today, more than 80 per cent of hospitals offer alternative settings in some form (Mathews and Zadak, 1991). The most common alternative setting is the labor, delivery, and recovery room (LDR), where all of labor, childbirth, and recovery from childbirth occur in one room. Some LDR rooms are quite luxurious, with hardwood floors, paintings, refrigerators, television, and video players; in some facilities, whirlpool baths are available. However, the furniture can quickly be transformed into a well-equipped delivery room. Paintings slide to the side, revealing suction and oxygen apparatus, ceiling spotlights are activated, and wood chests open to reveal fetal monitors and all equipment necessary for the birth. A typical LDR room is illustrated in Figure 1–1.

During labor, the woman's significant others are allowed to remain with her in the LDR room. This may include a variable number of relatives, friends, and even her other children, depending on the policies of the agency and the mother's desires. Once she has given birth, the mother typically remains in the LDR room for 1 to 2 hours, after which she is transferred to the postpartum unit. The infant may remain with the mother throughout her stay in the LDR room. When she is transferred to the postpar-

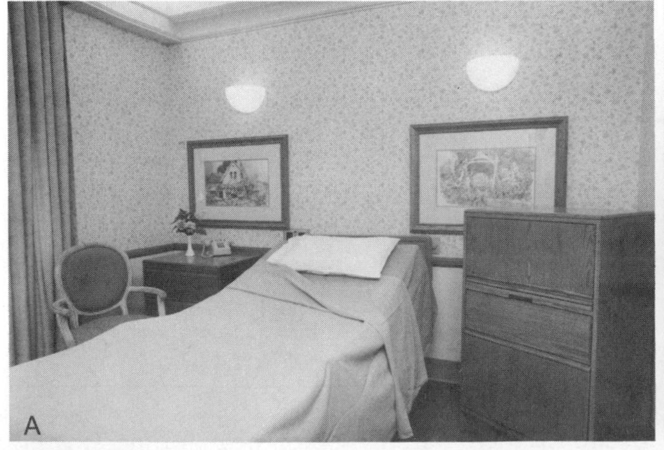

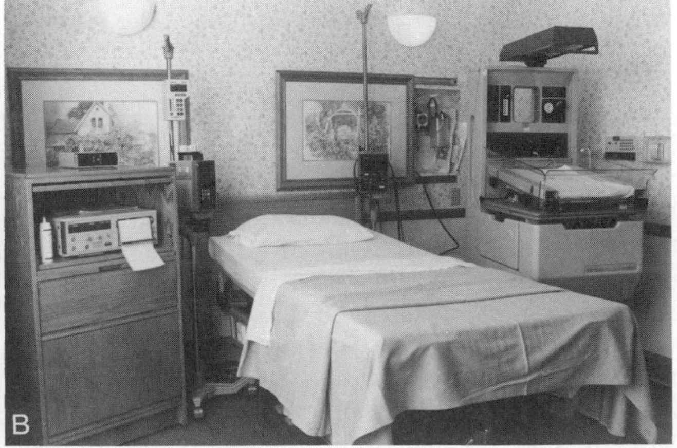

Figure 1–1

A, A typical labor, delivery, and recovery room. **B**, Home-like furnishings can quickly be adapted to needed technical equipment.

tum unit, the infant may be transferred to the nursery for assessments or may remain with the mother.

The amount of technology used in an LDR room varies. In some settings, electronic fetal monitoring provides initial assessment of the fetus and is used only periodically unless complications develop. In other settings, monitoring is a standard part of care. The use of medication and anesthesia for pain relief varies widely and depends on the mother's wishes, the philosophy of the physician, and hospital policy.

LABOR, DELIVERY, RECOVERY, AND POSTPARTUM ROOMS

Some hospitals offer rooms that are similar to LDR rooms in layout and in function but the mother is not transferred to a postpartum unit. She and the infant remain in the LDR postpartum room until discharge, often within 12 to 24 hours following childbirth.

Birth Centers

Free-standing birth centers are designed to provide maternity care to low-risk women outside the hospital setting. Women attend the centers for prenatal care, birth, and postpartum follow-up by physicians or certified nurse midwives. Although birthing centers are separate from hospitals, they have arrangements with hospitals and obstetricians so that if complications develop, the mother can be referred for care.

Although there were some early birth centers in rural areas, the first birth center for urban women opened in 1975 in New York City. Many centers are privately owned, although a few hospitals operate birthing centers as a method of reducing costs for uncomplicated pregnancies and for providing education for residents and nurses. Delivery is often performed by certified nurse midwives who have been providing care for the woman throughout her pregnancy. Should unforeseen difficulties develop during labor, the woman is transferred by ambulance to a nearby hospital to the care of a back-up obstetrician who has agreed to perform this role.

The cost of care in a birth center may be as little as one-half that of traditional care by an obstetrician with delivery in a hospital. In addition to care during the birth, prenatal care is offered throughout the pregnancy. The mother may attend classes there to prepare her for childbirth, breastfeeding, and infant care. The mother and infant continue to receive follow-up care at the birthing center during the first 6 weeks. This may include help with breastfeeding problems, a postpartum examination at 4 to 6 weeks, family planning information, and examination of the newborn.

In the future, the free-standing birth center may become the standard for providing care for low-risk maternity clients. Because of the high costs of care in hospitals that offer advanced technology that may be unnecessary for low-risk women and infants, interest in this method of birthing is increasing. In addition, the satisfaction rate among women who want a safe, home-like birth is very high.

Home Births

Although some home births are attended by physicians, certified nurse midwives conduct most deliveries in the home. They provide prenatal care for the women they attend as well as education about the birth and how to prepare for it. Midwives spend a great deal of time with each woman and have established a relationship of trust by the time birth occurs. During birth, the midwife is with the mother throughout active labor and, after birth, provides follow-up care for the mother and the infant.

Only a small number of women have their babies at home today. Because of the high cost and lack of availability of malpractice insurance for midwives doing home births, the number of midwives who offer this service has decreased greatly. Many have moved their practices to hospitals or birth centers. Mothers who once sought home births have found that they can have many of the advantages of family-centered care in the safe environment of a hospital LDR room or a birth center while avoiding the disadvantages and potential dangers of home birth.

CHOOSING HOME BIRTH

Advantages. Home birth provides the advantages of keeping the family together in their own familiar environment throughout the childbirth experience. When all goes well, birth at home can be a growth-enhancing experience for every family member. Young siblings do not face separation from their mothers and are able to establish positive relationships with the new baby immediately after birth. Mothers do not have to worry about how their other children are faring in their absence. Fathers are an integral part of all aspects of the birth. Bonding with the infant is unimpeded by hospital routines, and breastfeeding is highly encouraged and supported. Women who have their babies at home maintain a feeling of control because they actively plan and prepare for each detail of the birth.

Disadvantages. Women who plan a home birth must be carefully screened to make sure that they have a very low risk for complications. Opponents for home birth cite the need for immediate highly technological care of the woman or fetus if complications develop. Even when transfer is to a nearby hospital, the time needed may be too long. Other problems of home birth include the need for the parents to provide a setting and adequate supplies for the birth. Moreover, the mother must take care of herself and the infant without the professional help she would have in a hospital setting.

✔ Check Your Reading

1. What two trends created change in maternity care in the last four decades?
2. How does family-centered maternity care differ from previous maternity care?
3. What are the advantages and disadvantages of childbirth in birthing centers and within the home?

Statistics of Maternal and Infant Health

Statistics provide a broad perspective about the relationship between numbers. Statistics related to infant and maternal health often focus on mortality rates as a representation of health. However, statistics are just numbers unless one thinks about the people and situations they represent. When one thinks about the tragedy of even one maternal or infant death, the numbers become more meaningful.

Mortality Rates

Mortality rates indicate the number of deaths that occur each year by different categories. They are important sources of information about the health of groups of people within a country. They may also be an indication of the value a society places on health care and the kind of health care available to the people.

Throughout history, the number of deaths of women and infants has been high, especially around the time of childbirth. Fatalities were often due to poor health of the mother, poor sanitation, and lack of knowledge about causes and treatment of diseases. In 1910, one of every 154 women having a baby in the United States died of causes related to pregnancy and childbirth. In that same year, 13 of every 100 children succumbed before reaching their first birthday (Simkin, 1989).

Infant and maternal mortality rates began to fall when the health of the general population improved, basic principles of sanitation were applied, and medical knowledge increased. By 1940, major improvements in care reduced the infant mortality rate to half that of 1910. A further large decrease over the next 10 years was a result of the widespread availability of antibiotics, improvement in public health, and increased prenatal care (Simkin, 1989). Today, mothers seldom die in childbirth because of the advanced understanding of infection and the technology available. Infant mortality rates continue downward, although at a more gradual pace than that between 1940 and 1950. The downward trend in maternal and infant mortality rates, however, is greater for some ethnic groups than for others.

MATERNAL MORTALITY

Because few women today die in childbirth, the maternal mortality rate is determined by the number of deaths per 100,000 live births instead of per 1000 live births. In 1989, the rate was 7.9 for all women in the United States, with 320 women dying from pregnancy or birth-related causes. African-American women currently are more likely to die from birth-related causes than Caucasian women. The maternal mortality rate for African-American women is 18.4, or more than three times the 5.6 rate for Caucasian women (National Center for Health Statistics, 1991).

INFANT MORTALITY

Infant mortality rates are often said to be a major indicator of the health of the children of a nation. Unlike maternal rates, these rates are calculated by the number of deaths per 1000 live births. The provisional infant mortality rate in the United States is 9.1 infants who die before they reach the age of 1 year for every thousand infants born alive each year (National Center for Health Statistics, 1992). Although there has been a decline in infant mortality rates for Americans overall, the decline among Caucasians has remained significantly greater than that for African-Americans. Figure 1–2 compares the rates of infant mortality among Caucasians and African-Americans for the last 50 years.

African-American infants die at more than twice the rate of Caucasian infants. In 1989 the infant death rate was 18.6 for African-American infants but 8.1 for infants born to Caucasian mothers. Latino infants fare better than African-American infants but not as well as Caucasians. The infant mortality rate for Latino infants is 8.5 (National Center for Health Statistics, 1992).

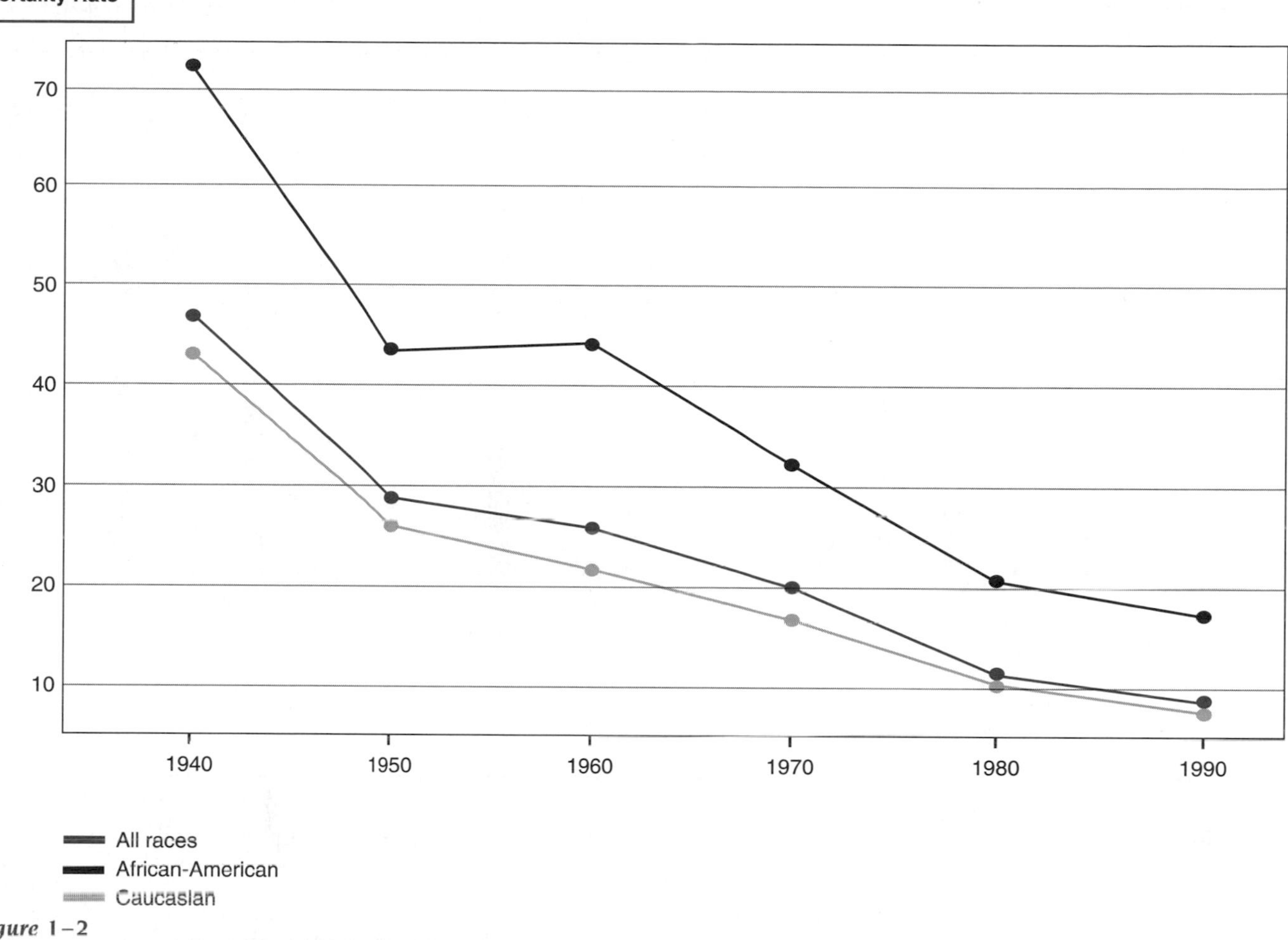

Figure 1–2

Comparison of infant mortality rates from 1940 to 1990. (Data from National Center for Health Statistics [1992, Jan. 7]. Advance report on final mortality statistics, 1989. *Monthly Vital Statistics Report*, 40 [Suppl. 2]).

NEONATAL MORTALITY

Infant mortality rates are subdivided into neonatal and post-neonatal. Neonatal rates refer to the number of infants in each 1000 live births who die before they reach 28 days of life. The rate gives an indication of how many infants are born with conditions so serious that they could sustain life for only a short time. The total neonatal mortality rate for the 12 months ending November 1990 was 5.7 (National Center for Health Statistics, 1991). Again, there is a difference according to ethnic group, the rate being 5.2 for Caucasian, 11.9 for African-American, and 5.4 for Latino infants (National Center for Health Statistics, 1992).

POST-NEONATAL MORTALITY

Post-neonatal mortality rates refer to the number of infants who die between 28 days and 11 months of age for each 1000 live births. This eliminates causes that were fatal during the first 4 weeks of life; it includes some that were present at birth and others, like sudden infant death syndrome (SIDS), that occurred later. The rate has remained consistent during recent years. From 1985 to 1989, it was 3.6 for all infants. Rates by ethnic groups are 2.9 for Caucasians, 6.7 for African-Americans, and 3.1 for Latinos (National Center for Health Statistics, 1992). Figure 1–3 illustrates neonatal, post-neonatal, and infant mortality rates for Caucasians, African-Americans, and Latinos.

REASONS FOR ETHNIC DISPARITY

The discrepancy between ethnic groups is most likely due to socioeconomic status (Simkin, 1989). The rate of poverty is higher for non-Caucasians in the United States. Poor people are unlikely to be in

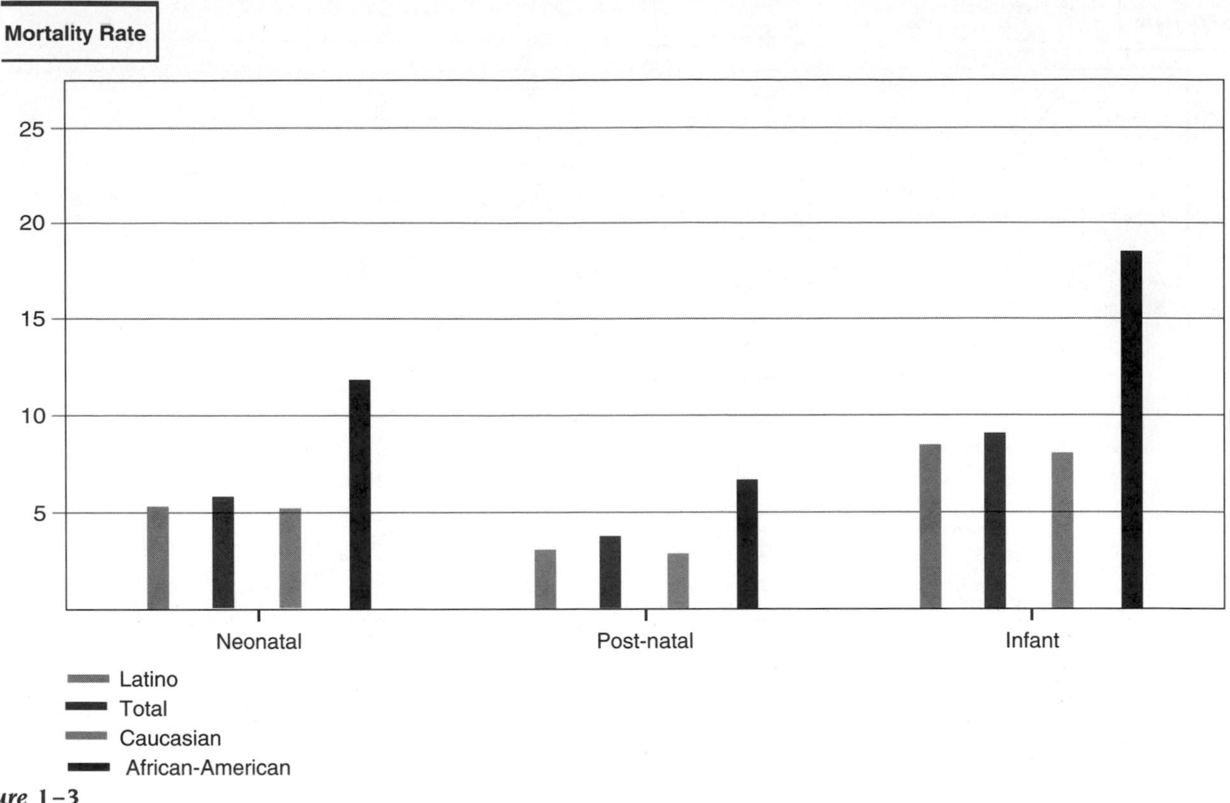

Figure 1–3

Comparison of current neonatal, post-neonatal, and infant mortality rates. (Data from National Center for Health Statistics [1992, Jan. 7]. Advance report on final mortality statistics, 1989. *Monthly Vital Statistics Report*, 40 [Suppl. 2]).

good health or to get the health care they need. Obtaining care becomes vital during pregnancy and infancy and is reflected in the high mortality rates in all categories.

COMPARISON OF INFANT MORTALITY AMONG NATIONS

Japan, Sweden, Finland, Switzerland, Singapore, and Canada have the lowest infant mortality rates in the world. One would expect that a country such as the United States, which has one of the highest gross national products in the world, would have one of the lowest infant mortality rates. Yet in 1990 the infant mortality rate in the United States was higher than that of 20 other countries (*Population and Vital Statistics Report*, 1992). See Table 1–2.

The major reasons for this poor showing are:

1. Unequal access to health care for women of all socioeconomic levels. In other countries, such as Sweden, Switzerland, and Canada, prenatal care is provided free for all women.

2. A high rate of adolescent pregnancy, which is associated with higher levels of low birth weight and infant mortality.

Table 1–2. INFANT MORTALITY RATES FOR SELECTED COUNTRIES, 1990

Country	Infant Mortality (Per 1,000 Live Births)
Japan	4.8
Sweden	5.8
Finland	6.1
Switzerland	6.8
Singapore	7.0
Canada	7.3
Hong Kong	7.4
Ireland	7.4
The Netherlands	7.5
France	7.7
Austria	8.1
Denmark	8.3
German Federal Republic	8.3
Norway	8.4
German Democratic Republic	8.5
Spain	8.5
United Kingdom	8.8
Australia	9.2
Belgium	9.7
Italy	9.9
United States	9.9

From *Population and Vital Statistics Report of 1990* (1992). Series A *44*(1). New York: United Nations.

Table 1–3. MAJOR CAUSES OF INFANT DEATHS AND THEIR RANK FOR CAUCASIAN AND AFRICAN-AMERICAN INFANTS

Cause	Total	Caucasian	African-American
Congenital anomalies	1	1	3
Sudden infant death syndrome	2	2	2
Prematurity and low-birth-weight disorders	3	4	1
Respiratory distress syndrome	4	3	4
Maternal complications of pregnancy affecting infant	5	5	5
Accidents	6	7	6
Complications of placenta, cord, and membranes	7	6	8
Infections	8	8	7
Intrauterine hypoxia and birth asphyxia	9	9	9
Pneumonia and influenza	10	10	10

From National Center for Health Statistics (1992, Jan. 7). Advance report on final mortality statistics, 1989. *Monthly Vital Statistics Report, 40*(8) (Suppl. 2).

3. Four disorders, accounting for more than half of all deaths in infants:

- Congenital anomalies
- Sudden infant death syndrome
- Disorders related to short gestation or low birth weight
- Respiratory distress syndrome.

When the causes are analyzed by race, African-American infants are more likely to die from prematurity or low birth weight; the most common cause of death in Caucasian infants is congenital anomalies (National Center for Health Statistics, 1992). Table 1–3 lists the most common causes of infant mortality and their ranking for Caucasian and African-American infants.

✔ Check Your Reading

4. Why is the infant mortality rate so much lower today than at the beginning of the twentieth century?
5. Why are African-American women and infants more likely to die than Caucasian women and children?
6. How does the infant mortality rate in the United States compare with the rates in Japan, Switzerland, and Canada?

The Family

The traditional definition of family—that is, a group of two or more persons related by blood, marriage, or adoption and residing together—is no longer adequate for the variety of family structures that nurses encounter today. This definition does not take into account persons who live in the same household but who are not related by blood, marriage, or adoption. Nor does it consider persons who are closely related but do not share the same household. For instance, a biological father remains a father even though he may live in a different place and have limited contact with his children. A more current definition might be that a family is a group of at least two persons (one of whom must be an adult), with strong emotional ties who live in close proximity. Regardless of the definition, the term family is used in this book to indicate the relationship that exists between dependent children and the adult or adults who provide primary care for them.

Table 1-4 provides a summary of family types.

Redefining "Family"

It may be helpful for nurses to examine social trends that have made it necessary to redefine the American family. For instance, early sexual activity and unplanned pregnancy among adolescents are common and one of three marriages now ends in divorce. As a result, the number of single-parent families and the number of three-generation families living in the same household have greatly increased. Additional factors, such as poverty, substance abuse, and family violence, have altered the traditional definition of families. Homeless families, for instance, fit the definition of "family," but they are families

Table 1–4. GENERAL FAMILY TYPES

Family Type	Definition
Traditional	
Nuclear	Mother, father, and subadult children (either natural or adopted) living in same household
Non-traditional	
Extended	Nuclear family plus relatives of either or both spouses living in same household
Communal	Several households of adults and their children living in a common geographical area, working together in a common way to achieve the group's goals
Blended	A parent, stepparent, children, and stepchildren living in same household
Single-Parent	A never-married, divorced, or widowed adult and his or her natural or adopted children
Foster	Care provided by family other than biological or adoptive parents

without households. Foster families are becoming more common, as alternative caretakers are required when substance abuse or family violence is identified and alternative care must be obtained for the children.

Families are sometimes categorized into three groups: traditional, nontraditional, and high-risk. Kagan and Seitz (1988) use the term "mainstream" rather than "traditional" to convey that both family structure and circumstances affect family functioning. In theory, mainstream, or traditional, family structures require care that differs from that needed by nontraditional or high-risk families.

MAINSTREAM FAMILIES

Mainstream families (also called nuclear families) are headed by a husband and wife who view parenting as the major priority in their lives and whose energies are not depleted by extraneous conditions, such as poverty, illness, or substance abuse. Generally speaking, mainstream families are motivated to learn all they can about pregnancy, childbirth, and parenting. These families are best served by providing information as the need arises.

Mainstream families can be single-income or dual-income.

Single-Income Families. In the 1950s and 1960s, the idealized single-income American family was epitomized in several long-running television series, such as "Leave It to Beaver." This family was composed of a father who was the sole provider, a mother who was homemaker and caregiver, and two children. Today it is critical to realize that this family structure represents only 8 per cent of the nation's families (National Center for Health Statistics, 1991).

Dual-Income Families. Most two-parent families are now dependent on dual incomes. This has created a great deal of stress on these mainstream families, subjecting them to many of the same problems that single-parent families face. For instance, reliable, competent child care has become a major issue and has increased the stress on mainstream families.

NONTRADITIONAL FAMILIES

Nontraditional families are defined by their unique structure and may be single-parent, blended, or extended. As with mainstream families, nontraditional families require information and they benefit from referral to meet specific needs, for instance, single-parenting classes, classes for mothers with twins, or group classes for adoptive families.

Single-Parent Families. More than 15 million families are now headed by a single parent, most often the mother, who not only must function as homemaker and caregiver but also is often the major provider for the family's financial needs (National Center for Health Statistics, 1991). Divorce is the most common cause of single-parent families, although childbirth among unmarried women is also a major factor.

Single-parent families are more likely to live below the poverty level and are vulnerable to a variety of problems. Parents may feel overwhelmed by the prospect of assuming all childrearing responsibilities and may be less prepared for illness or loss of a job than mainstream families.

When dealing with single-parent families, nurses are concerned because they cannot change the reality of the situation. However, nurses can support and encourage single-parent families by listening to the unique problems of each family. Nurses are also the primary source of information about health care for many of these families and are often instrumental in initiating the necessary referrals.

Blended Families. Blended families are formed when divorced or widowed parents remarry and bring children from a previous marriage into the new relationship. Many times the couple desires children with each other, creating a contemporary family structure commonly described as "yours, mine, and ours." These families may have difficulty forming a cohesive family unit unless they can overcome differences in parenting styles and values. Differing expectations of children in terms of behavior and development as well as differing beliefs about discipline often cause family conflict.

Extended Families. The extended family includes members from three generations living under one roof. This family structure is becoming increasingly common in the United States and has given rise to the term "boomerang" families. This refers to adult children who return to the parents' home, either because they are unable to support themselves or because they want the additional support that the grandparents provide for the grandchildren. Extended families are vulnerable to generational conflicts and may require education and referral to prevent disintegration of the family unit.

Homosexual Families. Although homosexual families are relatively uncommon, they are recognized increasingly in the United States. Children in homosexual families may be offspring of previous heterosexual unions, or they may be adopted children or children conceived by artificial inseminination of one or both members of a lesbian couple. This couple may face a great many challenges from a community that is unaccustomed to alternative lifestyles.

Adoptive Families. Persons who adopt a child may have problems that biological parents do not face. Biological parents have the long period of gestation and the gradual changes of pregnancy to help them adjust emotionally and socially to the birth of a child. The needs of adoptive parents may be overlooked following the adoption process. Adoptive parents as well as biological parents need information, support, and guidance that prepare them to care for the infant and to maintain their own relationship.

HIGH-RISK FAMILIES

High-risk families include those below the poverty level, those headed by a single teen-age parent, and those with unanticipated stress, such as an infant who is preterm, ill, or handicapped. In addition, families with lifestyle problems such as alcoholism, use of illicit drugs, or family violence are considered at high risk for problems in providing adequate care for the infant.

Many high-risk families require specialized services. In such cases, the major responsibility of staff nurses is to refer families in need to agencies that can provide comprehensive care. Some of the most common referrals are to social service agencies for financial assistance, crisis intervention, home visits, or drug rehabilitation programs. Chapters 3 and 23 provide additional information about substance abuse, teenage parenting, and the effect of poverty on family structure and function.

✔ *Check Your Reading*

7. How do structures of mainstream and nontraditional families differ?
8. What are four reasons why families might be identified as "high-risk"?

Family Function

The family provides the emotional support and nurturing that are required by all human beings if they are to grow and develop to their highest potential. Ideally, the family not only provides for survival and for the physical development of children but also serves as a sanctuary where members gain strength and understanding so that they can continue to function in a highly industrialized and complex society.

CHARACTERISTICS OF A HEALTHY FAMILY

In general, healthy families are able to adapt to changes that occur in the family unit. Pregnancy and childbirth create some of the most powerful changes that a family experiences. The relationship between adults must change to include the care of a helpless infant. Children must learn to share the attention of parents with a new sibling. The healthy, viable family is able to adapt to these changes without undue stress, but the family that is unprepared for change may suffer conflict.

Healthy families exhibit some common characteristics that provide a framework for assessing how all families function:

1. Healthy families communicate openly with each other to express the concerns and needs of each family member.
2. Healthy families remain flexible in role assignment so that if one person is not able to complete the assigned tasks, another member will offer assistance.
3. Adults in healthy families agree on the basic principles of parenting so that there is minimal discord about such things as discipline and sleep schedules.
4. Healthy families are adaptable and are not overwhelmed by changes that occur in the home and in relationships as a result of childbirth. For instance, adaptable families can tolerate less than perfect housekeeping, an irregular schedule of meals, and interrupted sleep, which are common experiences when an infant is added to the family structure.
5. Members of a healthy family volunteer assistance without waiting to be asked. Some young parents feel guilty if they must ask for help with the tasks of parenting but are relieved when assistance is offered.

FACTORS THAT INTERFERE WITH FAMILY FUNCTIONING

It is important for nurses to recognize factors that interfere with the family's ability to provide for the individual needs of family members. These factors include lack of financial resources, absence of adequate family support, birth of an infant who requires specialized care, unhealthy habits such as smoking or abuse of other substances, and inability to make mature decisions that are necessary to provide care for an infant.

✔ Check Your Reading

9. What are the characteristics of a healthy family?
10. What factors interfere with family functioning?

Cultural Perspectives in Childbearing

To provide effective care, nurses must be aware of the impact of cultural diversity on health care. First, nurses must examine their own beliefs and how they may generate conflict with cultures that hold different opinions. A brief overview of Western cultural values and those of four major culturally diverse groups is presented in this chapter. Additional information is presented throughout the book as it relates to specific areas such as nutrition, pregnancy, birth, and the postpartum period.

Implications of Culture on Nursing Practice

To understand the implications of culture on nursing practice, nurses must have a basic understanding of diverse values. Leininger (1985) defines cultural values as a desirable or preferred way of acting or knowing something that is reinforced by the social structure and ultimately governs one's actions or decisions. Culturally diverse nursing care refers to variations nurses must make in their approaches in order to provide appropriate nursing care. Effective nursing care must take into account divergent thinking that can lead to misunderstanding and a failure in health care delivery.

Examples of culturally divergent thinking include:

- How time is measured (in minutes and seconds or by more flexible methods)
- Personal space and the emotion experienced when someone enters that space
- Communication style (verbal and nonverbal)
- Views of life and death, including predestination and fatalism
- Modesty and the implications when it is violated
- "Face" and the effects of loss of face on families
- Shame and pride
- "Hot and cold" practices and their effects on recovery
- Family hierarchies (who plays the active role in defining illness and seeking health care)
- Dietary practice
- Confrontational versus passive behaviors
- Male and female roles
- Power and authority and its meaning for behaviors (Roessler, 1989).

Western Cultural Values

Nursing practice in the United States is based on Western beliefs and demonstrates clearly defined roles and functions that differ from those in other societies. It is imperative that nurses recognize the beliefs that form the basis of their practice and acknowledge that other groups have far different values. Moreover, nurses must acknowledge that many individuals believe their cultural values and methods of reacting are superior. This belief is termed *ethnocentrism,* and it is the basis for many conflicts that occur when persons from different societies have frequent contact.

Leininger (1978) identified seven dominant Western cultural values that greatly influence the thinking and action of nurses in the United States but which may not be shared by their clients:

1. Democracy is a cultural value that is not shared by many families who believe that decisions are made by higher authorities in the cultural group. Decision makers may be the elders in the group or the oldest man in the family. Members of this family would need to obtain permission to follow instructions from health care personnel.
2. Individualism conflicts with many cultural groups in which individual goals and needs are subordinated to the greater good of the group.
3. Cleanliness is an American "obsession" viewed with amazement by many who are quite comfortable with having some dirt on their person and in their environment.
4. Preoccupation with time seems to be emphasized more in societies that are technologically advanced. In some cultures, time is marked by seasons or by body needs and not by minutes and seconds. This cultural difference gives rise to serious conflicts between health care workers who schedule appointments in minutes and families for whom the concept of time is very different.
5. Emphasis on technology during pregnancy and childbearing and reliance on machines and equipment often intimidate and frighten families who have not reached even minimal comfort with technology.
6. Optimal health is considered to be a right in this society. Yet this thinking is in direct contrast to many cultures in the world where health is not a major emphasis or even an expectation. This is par-

ticularly true as it relates to children. Many families expect that a certain number of their children will die, and they will have a large number of offspring in preparation for this event.

7. Self-sufficiency for Americans means that they value financial success and admire the "good provider" and the "take charge" person. This may conflict with cultures that place less value on financial success and put more value on less tangible things such as spirituality.

Cultural Variations

It is not possible to predict how a specific family will behave solely on the basis of cultural background. There are variations among individuals in all cultures. For instance, people from many culturally diverse groups have lived in the United States for generations and their beliefs and customs have been diluted by their exposure to other customs.

This discussion is not meant to stereotype families; however, it is important to become familiar with some of the cultural variations and to validate how this information applies to individual families. Four of the largest cultural groups are briefly discussed.

SOUTHEAST ASIANS

Southeast Asians make up the largest groups of recent immigrants to the United States. The vast majority are of childbearing age, and their first exposure to the U.S. health care system is likely to be through obstetrics.

Communication. Language is the greatest barrier to health care for those from Southeast Asia (Mattson and Lew, 1992). Besides the national languages of Vietnam, Cambodia, and Laos, numerous tribal languages are spoken in each country. In addition, most immigrants have little knowledge of anatomy, physiology, germ theory, or family planning and may fail to understand information presented in unfamiliar terms. In general, people from Southeast Asia speak softly and avoid prolonged eye contact, which is considered rude, in contrast to the Western belief that eye contact denotes honesty and forthrightness.

Health Care Beliefs. When health care is needed, the family is likely to seek assistance from elders and family members before obtaining care from the health care team. Folk traditions are rich in the knowledge and use of herbal medicines. Dermabrasion, the rubbing or irritation of the skin to relieve discomfort, is a common health care practice. The most popular form is *coining*, in which the affected area is covered with ointment and the edge of a coin is rubbed over the area. All dermabrasion methods leave marks resembling bruises or burns on the skin and may be mistaken for signs of physical abuse (Mattson, 1992). Non-medical remedies include prayer, offerings to spirits, and consultation with faith healers.

Health Beliefs That Affect Childbearing. Many health beliefs of Southeast Asians affect childbearing practices. For instance, because pregnancy is not considered an illness, the concept of early, regular prenatal care is unfamiliar to new immigrants. Moreover, Southeast Asian women are extremely modest and the American practice of pelvic examinations is distressing for them. Surgery is seen as mutilation of the body that involves loss of the spirit. If a cesarean birth is necessary, it is essential that a fluent interpreter be located to explain the necessity and to alleviate the fear the family feels.

Southeast Asians have a strong belief in a "hot-cold" balance, and women who have recently given birth believe they must keep warm. They may refuse to take baths, shampoo, or drink cold liquids for fear of upsetting the hot-cold balance. Many have special "hot" foods, such as soup with rice or noodles.

Although many Southeast Asian women breastfeed, they may be embarrassed to nurse the infant in the presence of others and many may not want to begin breastfeeding until the milk comes in.

Spiritual and Family Values. Southeast Asians have a strong belief in fate, or *Karma*, and Buddhism, which encourages tolerance and suffering, is a prominent religion. As a result, many do not seek medical attention because they perceive that pain is something that must be endured rather than something that can be alleviated. This has implications for nurses who care for Southeast Asian women during labor, when nurses must be particularly sensitive to nonverbal signs of pain.

Southeast Asians have a strong belief in male authority. The grandfather is the head of the family, and this position of authority carries down to the oldest son. The extended family is highly valued, and these bonds are an important part of their culture.

The prevailing fatalistic attitudes derived from spiritual beliefs and the soft manner of speaking often result in Southeast Asian people being viewed by Americans as passive and possibly unwilling to assume responsibility for their own illness and recoveries.

LATINOS

A second large group of recent immigrants includes families from Mexico, Central America, and South

America. Many Latinos have been in the United States for generations, and their beliefs have been tempered by long association with other Americans. Recent immigrants, however, tend to share some of the same values.

Communication. As with other new immigrants, language is a major problem in providing care although many nurses speak Spanish. Latinos tend to be polite and gracious in conversation. Preliminary social interaction is particularly important, and Latinos may be insulted if a problem is addressed directly without taking time for "small talk." This is counter to the American value of "getting to the point" and may cause frustration for the client as well as the health care worker.

Health Care Beliefs. When a family member is ill, rituals such as promise making, offering candles, and visiting shrines are performed. Some Latinos also believe in witchcraft and *cuaranderismo*, which reflects the belief that natural folk illness can be cured by a *curandero(a)*, a folk healer, who has been chosen for this work by God. These illnesses do not carry an evil connotation, and they include indigestion, evil eye, and fright. Many Latinos have some knowledge of witchcraft, depending on their degree of mixing with other cultural groups. However, many Latinos are reluctant to share information or to discuss their beliefs with persons outside their own culture.

Health Beliefs That Affect Childbearing. Hot and cold have symbolic significance during reproduction. When the terms are applied to foods, they have nothing to do with temperature but denote qualities of the food itself. A pregnant woman may be advised not to consume "hot" foods because she is thought to have an especially warm body. She should bathe often and take short walks. On the other hand, after childbirth a woman might be told to avoid "cold" foods or taking a bath. Cold is believed to diminish milk flow, whereas warmth is thought to increase the flow (Cherry and Giger, 1991).

Spiritual and Family Values. The welfare of the family unit is a primary consideration, and individual needs are subordinated to the family. Closely associated with this is the cultural value of family hierarchy. The dominant pattern is "the older command the younger and the men command the women." This illustrates the two dimensions around which family relationships are ordered. Compare this with the dominant American ideals of individualism and egalitarianism. Most Latinos are Catholic, and their religion is felt to be a personal relationship between themselves and God. Common religious practices are baptism, confirmation, and communion. During times of crisis, Latinos may rely on the priest and family for prayers and for support.

Next is the cultural value of the present. Latinos are usually characterized as having a present orientation to time and being reluctant to incorporate the future into their plans. Time orientation may conflict with the rigorous schedule maintained by health care workers who often take little time to experience the moment-by-moment happenings of the day and, in fact, may be irritated by a culture that tolerates a lot of spontaneous interruptions that may result in missing or being late for appointments.

AFRICAN-AMERICANS

It is particularly difficult to characterize African-Americans by looking at their cultural beliefs because many are not recent immigrants. They may have lived in the Western culture for generations. Therefore, an attempt is made to select a few of the most frequently described behaviors and beliefs that may assist nurses in planning and implementing nursing care.

Communication. Sociologists have noted that African-Americans sometimes have a communication style that may cause conflict when they seek health care (see Chapter 8). Some African-Americans use idioms or colloquial expressions that differ significantly from those used by many health care workers. Their unique speech patterns develop within neighborhoods and serve as a unifying factor in maintaining cultural and ethnic identity (Cherry and Giger, 1991). Nurses must often clarify what is being said so that misunderstandings can be avoided and so that teaching can be effective.

Health Care Beliefs. African-Americans have a long and rich heritage of health beliefs developed over generations by people who found themselves in need of ways to cope with a wide variety of experiences. Folk beliefs provide a predictable structure for the causes and effects of various behaviors and events and were invaluable to a people living amid great changes. For example:

- Food cravings during pregnancy should be satisfied
- Putting the arms over the head may cause the cord to strangle the fetus
- Some teas have healing powers
- Pica (eating non-food substances such as starch) may make the birth easier

Spiritual and Family Values. Religion, spirituality, and the church serve as major resources for health, education, political activity, and emotional comfort. This aspect of culture is particularly important for nurses to observe when caring for African-American families. Time and opportunity must be provided for meeting spiritual needs.

Family relationships, both immediate and extended, have high value for African-Americans. Within these families, there are strong kinship bonds, a strong work and achievement ethic, and adaptability in family roles (Sue and Sue, 1990). Community members and other non-related African-Americans may be regarded as brothers and sisters, resulting in a close-knit community. Sharing good and bad is natural, and this includes helping one another in the childbearing experience.

African-American families are often oriented around women, who are responsible for protecting the health of family members. Nurses must recognize the importance of the African-American woman in disseminating information and in assisting the family members to make decisions. However, it is also essential to include the men in the decision-making process.

African-Americans value harmonious relationships, and there is greater emphasis on harmony than on competition. This need for harmony may not always work for the good of the childbearing family. In some instances, health teaching may be ignored because it is poorly understood or because it is in disagreement with other beliefs, yet the family may not express the difference or probe for reasons that would make the teaching meaningful.

MIDDLE-EASTERN IMMIGRANTS

More people are migrating to the United States and Canada because of political unrest in countries that include Lebanon, Syria, Jordan, Arabia, Egypt, Turkey, Iran, and Palestine.

Communication. In the Middle East, communication is an elaborate system. However, it may be difficult to obtain information because Islam (the primary religion) dictates that family affairs should remain family affairs and not be shared. Personal information is shared only with personal friends, and health assessment must be done gradually. When interpreters are used, they should be of the same country and religion, if possible, because of regional differences and hostilities. Because Muslim society tends to be paternalistic, it is wise to ask the man's permission or opinion when family members require health care.

Health Care Beliefs. Many Middle Eastern people have home cures for common health problems. These include herbs, concentrated sugar preparations (used extensively for newborns), and "hot" or "cold" foods. Although most believe in the superiority of Western medicine, they often practice home remedies side by side with modern medical practices.

Children are viewed as a blessing to the family; however, parents are more concerned with weight gain, health, and normality of their children rather than with cognitive skills (Samiezadi-Yazd, 1989).

Health Beliefs That Affect Childbearing. Middle Eastern women possess a feeling of fatalism; they do not plan for future events but leave them to the will of God. As a result, many women do not seek prenatal care in the Middle East but wait until the baby is ready to be born to go to the birth facility or to call a midwife to assist with the birth. Many women do not plan the layette or select a name until after the infant is born. Most women breastfeed for extended periods of time.

Spiritual and Family Values. Nurses who provide care for Middle Eastern families should be familiar with some of the precepts of Islam, one of the major religions in the world. Islam is based on submission to the will of Allah (God). Muslims (members of Islam) follow the dictates of the Koran, resulting in a fluid feeling of time and a sense of fatalism. In line with the teaching of the Koran, Muslims do not eat pork, gamble, drink intoxicants, use illicit drugs, or engage in unlawful sexual practices such as premarital sex or infidelity.

Family is a great comfort in times of illness, and praying with a group is strengthening; however, the Muslim has no priest or minister. Muslims pray five times a day, generally on rising, at midday, in the afternoon, in the early evening, and before retiring. Prayer is accompanied by ritual cleansing of the face, arms, top of the head, and feet before each prayer.

Modesty is very important. Women dress differently outside the home than they do inside the home. The body tends to be covered, and only the eyes, hands, and feet are visible outside the home. This manner of dress is usually modified for Muslim women residing in the West, but protecting the modesty of Muslim women is a major concern for health care workers.

✔ *Check Your Reading*

11. Why is it important for nurses to examine their own cultural values and beliefs?
12. How does the Western cultural value of time result in conflict with other cultural groups?
13. How might a fatalistic view of life impact on childbearing?

Summary Concepts

- Changes in maternity care in the United States came about as a result of technological advances, increased knowledge, government involvement, and consumer demands.

- Alternative settings for childbirth are now available within hospitals and in free-standing birth centers; home births are less frequently selected as an alternative.
- Family-centered maternity care, based on the principle that families can make decisions about health care if they have adequate information, has greatly increased the role of nurses.
- Infant and maternal mortality rates have declined dramatically in the last 50 years; however, the United States continues to rank well below other industrialized nations and there is still wide variation in different ethnic groups.
- Social trends such as poverty, early unplanned pregnancy, and the increased rate of divorce have altered family structure and function and have increased the need for information and support provided by nurses.
- To provide culturally appropriate care, nurses must examine their own beliefs and become familiar with diverse values and customs.

References and Readings

Anderson, J.M. (1990). Health care across cultures. *Nursing Outlook*, 38(3), 136–139.

Cabral, H., Fried, L.E., Levenson, S., et al. (1990). Foreign-born and U.S.-born black women: Differences in health behaviors and birth outcomes. *American Journal of Public Health*, 80(1), 70–72.

Cherry, B., & Giger, J.N. (1991). Black Americans. In J.N. Giger, & R.E. Davidhizar (Eds.), *Transcultural nursing: Assessment intervention*. St. Louis: Mosby Year Book.

Inglis, A.D. (1991). United States maternal and child health services. Part I: Right or privilege? *Neonatal Network*, 9(8), 35–43.

Kagan, S.L., & Seitz, V. (1988). Family support programs for new parents. In G.Y. Michaels, & W.A. Goldberg (Eds.), *The transition to parenthood: Current theory and research* (pp. 311–341). Cambridge, England: Cambridge University Press.

Leininger, M. (1978). *Transcultural nursing: Concepts, theories, practices*. New York: John Wiley & Sons.

Leininger, M. (1985). Transcultural care diversity and universality: A theory of nursing. *Nursing and Health Care*, 6(4), 209–212.

Manio, E.B., & Hall, R.R. (1987). Asian family traditions and their influence in transcultural health care delivery. *Children's Health Care*, 15(3), 172–177.

Mathews, J.J., & Zadak, K. (1991). The alternative birth movement in the United States: History and current status. *Women and Health*, 17(1), 39–56.

Mattson, S., & Lew, L. (1992). Culturally sensitive prenatal care for Southeast Asians. *Journal of Obstetric, Gynecologic, and Neonatal Nursing*, 21(1), 48–54.

National Center for Health Statistics. (1991, April 8). Births, marriages, divorces, and deaths for 1990. *Monthly Vital Statistics Report*, 39(12).

National Center for Health Statistics. (1992, Jan. 7). Advance report on final mortality statistics, 1989. *Monthly Vital Statistics Report*, 40(8) (Suppl. 2).

Pakizegi, B. (1990). Emerging family forms: single mothers by choice—demographic and psychosocial variables. *Maternal-Child Nursing Journal*, 19(1), 1–17.

Population and Vital Statistics Report 1990 (1992). Series A, 44(1). New York: United Nations.

Roessler, G. Cultural perspective (1989). In T.M. Gorrie (Ed.), *Guide to the nursing of childbearing families* (pp. 23–27). Baltimore: Williams & Wilkins.

Rooks, J.P. Weatherby, N.L., Ernst, E.K.M., Stapleton, S., Rosen, D., & Rosenfield, A. (1989). Outcomes of care in birth centers: The national birth center study. *New England Journal of Medicine*, 321, 1804–1811.

Samiezadi-Yazd, C. (1989). Middle-Eastern culture. In R.B. Murray & J.P. Zenter (Eds.), *Nursing assessment and health promotion strategies through the life span*, (4th ed., pp. 16–21). Norwalk, Conn.: Appleton & Lange.

Simkin, P. (1989). Childbearing in social context. *Women and Health*, 15(3), 5–21.

Sue, D.W., & Sue, D. (1990). *Counseling the culturally different: Theory and practice* (2nd ed.). New York: John Wiley & Sons.

Tripp-Reimer, T., & Anna, L. (1989). Cross-cultural perspectives on patient teaching. *Nursing Clinics of North America*, 24(3), 613–619.

2

The Nurse's Role in Maternity Care

Objectives

1. Explain the expanded roles for nurses in maternal-newborn nursing.
2. Discuss the implications for new roles for nurses in maternal-newborn nursing.
   a. Review purpose, principles, and techniques for therapeutic communication.
   b. Identify the principles of teaching and learning, and describe factors that influence learning.
3. Describe the steps of the nursing process, and relate them to maternal-newborn nursing.
4. Compare nursing diagnosis with collaborative problems in terms of goals, outcomes, and nursing interventions.

Definitions

Baseline data • Information that describes the status of the client before treatment begins.

Cesarean birth • Surgical delivery of the fetus through an incision in the lower abdominal wall and uterus.

Delegated nursing interventions • Physician-prescribed nursing actions that require nursing judgment because nurses are accountable for correct implementation.

Diagnostic statement • A phrase that describes a health problem; usually consists of a category label plus the etiology or contributing factors. It may describe manifestations.

Fetus • The developing baby from 9 weeks after conception until birth. In everyday practice, the term is often used to describe a developing baby during pregnancy, regardless of age.

Independent nursing interventions • Nurse-prescribed actions used in both nursing diagnoses and collaborative problems.

Validate • To make certain that the information collected during assessment is true.

In 1983 the American Nurses' Association defined "nursing" as the diagnosis and treatment of human responses to actual or potential health problems. Maternal-neonatal nursing is devoted to the delivery of care to childbearing families and is based on a family-centered approach, as described in Chapter 1. Thus, maternal-neonatal nursing can be defined as the diagnosis and treatment of the responses of childbearing women, their infants, and their families to actual or potential health problems that may develop. As maternity care changed from regimented care of the mother and newborn to a family-centered approach, maternity nursing evolved to a new era of autonomy and independence.

Important aspects of maternal-newborn nursing include:

- Caring for families during periods of transition, such as pregnancy and childbirth
- Providing basic nursing care that includes surveillance, regulation of the environment, and preventing infection
- Providing comfort and security
- Functioning in a major role as health educator for childbearing families

Nurses who work with childbearing families must be able to communicate effectively and to use nursing process to develop a plan of care that meets the unique needs of each family. Moreover, many nurses complete advanced programs of education that allow them to provide primary care in expanded roles.

Expanded Roles for Nurses

The gradual change to family-centered maternity care and the persistent challenge of providing health care for indigent women have led to an expanded role for nurses. Nurses have taken advantage of advanced programs of education to become prepared as certified nurse midwives, nurse practitioners, and clinical specialists.

Certified Nurse-Midwives

Certified nurse-midwives are registered nurses who have completed an extensive program of study and clinical experience. They must pass a certification test administered by the American College of Nurse-Midwives. Certified nurse-midwives are qualified to take complete health histories and to perform physical examinations. They can provide complete care during pregnancy, labor and delivery, and the postpartum period. They attend both the mother and the infant as long as the mother's progress is normal. The certified nurse-midwife also provides gynecological services as well as family planning information and counseling.

The effectiveness of care provided by nurse-midwives has a long history. In the 1930s, the Maternity Center Association, founded to provide care for indigent women, began to educate public health nurses in midwifery. At almost the same time, Mary Breckinridge, a nurse-midwife from England, founded the Frontier Nursing Service to provide primary care (including midwifery services) for destitute families in the remote mountains of Kentucky.

Despite the proven effectiveness of care provided by nurse-midwives, physicians opposed the widespread use of nurse-midwives. As a result, many restrictions were placed on the scope and location of their practice.

In 1970 many restrictions were alleviated when the American College of Obstetricians and Gynecologists, together with the Nurses Association of the American College of Obstetricians and Gynecologists (now known as the Association of Women's Health, Obstetric, and Neonatal Nurses), issued a joint statement, which admitted nurse-midwives as part of the health care team. In 1981, Congress authorized Medicaid payments for the services of certified nurse-midwives. This has greatly increased use of nurse-midwives, particularly in health maintenance organizations (HMOs) in birth centers and in some hospitals.

Nurse Practitioners

Nurse practitioners are registered nurses with advanced preparation that allows them to provide primary care for specific groups of patients. They can take a complete health history, perform physical examinations, order and interpret laboratory and other diagnostic studies, and provide primary care for health maintenance and health promotion. All nurse practitioners collaborate with physicians for treatments and medications that are beyond their scope of practice.

The nurse practitioner movement in the United States began in 1961 at Massachusetts General Hospital, and nurse practitioner programs have grown rapidly since then (Grippando and Mitchell, 1989). The responsibilities of nurse practitioners continue to expand as they provide care in many settings. Many work in group practice with physicians, in neighborhood and community agencies, in nursing clinics, in hospital outpatient departments, in schools, and in industry.

Restrictions against direct third-party payment to nurse practitioners, however, has limited the extent of their practice. The issue of direct payment is being debated at national and state levels as the crisis in health care continues to escalate.

The approach of nurse practitioners is *holistic*; that is, the emphasis is on the interrelatedness of parts and wholes and the patient is treated as a part of a family and a community. Nurse practitioners now specialize in many areas of practice, including maternal-child care.

The maternity nurse practitioner, or women's health practitioner, can assess the pregnant woman at prenatal appointments and evaluate the progress of the pregnancy. In addition, the nurse practitioner provides information and manages the common discomforts of pregnancy. Women's health practitioners are particularly concerned with health promotion and health maintenance of women throughout their life span.

Family nurse practitioners are prepared to provide care for all family members. They also provide care for women during uncomplicated pregnancies as well as follow-up care for the mother and infant following birth. Unlike certified nurse-midwives, they do not deliver the baby.

Pediatric nurse practitioners provide health maintenance care for infants and children who do not require the services of physicians.

Family planning nurse practitioners often work in family planning clinics or with physicians in private practice. Major responsibilities include performing pelvic examinations and screening procedures for sexually transmitted diseases as well as providing family planning services.

Clinical Nurse Specialists

Maternity clinical specialists are registered nurses at the Masters level who provide in-depth interventions for many problems encountered in maternity care. These specialists frequently serve as consultants to assist other nurses in planning care for difficult problems encountered in the maternity unit. Examples include the birth of an infant with anomalies and care of a pregnant woman who is hypertensive or diabetic or who has a history of substance abuse. Although clinical specialists are involved in staff education or in schools of nursing, they also provide direct services to patients in their area of specialty.

Implications of New Roles for Maternal-Newborn Nurses

As maternity care has changed, so have the roles of maternal-newborn nurses. Nurses now work in a variety of highly specialized areas, such as fetal diagnostic centers and infertility clinics and in genetic counseling. Moreover, nurses have assumed primary responsibilities for client education in preparation for childbirth, breastfeeding, and infant care.

Most maternal-newborn nurses continue to work in the hospital setting, and the role of hospital-based nurses has also changed to keep pace with rapid developments in care of the childbearing family. Before 1960, nurses served primarily in dependent roles; that is, they assisted physicians with childbirth, carried out medical orders, and provided basic physical care for mothers and infants. Nurses are now responsible for independent functions, such as teaching, counseling, and intervening for a wide variety of non-medical problems that trouble the childbearing family.

The added responsibilities of teaching and counseling make it necessary for all nurses to develop and maintain additional intrapersonal skills. These skills include communication, effective teaching, and the use of nursing process to identify and intervene for a variety of problems.

Therapeutic Communication

Therapeutic communication is a vital part of all nursing, and communication techniques are taught early in all curricula. Communication is emphasized in this chapter for three reasons: (1) to review the process, (2) to emphasize the importance of communication in maternal-newborn nursing, and (3) to provide examples of how to use therapeutic communication with childbearing families.

Therapeutic communication, unlike social communication, is purposeful, goal-directed, and focused. Therapeutic communication is directed toward meeting the client's (family's) needs, and conscious effort and considerable practice are required. To fulfill the roles now expected, nurses must understand and use the techniques of effective communication. They must be aware of verbal as well as non-verbal messages. Moreover, nurses must be aware of their own feelings before they can recognize the feelings of others.

GUIDELINES FOR THERAPEUTIC COMMUNICATION

Although therapeutic communication requires great flexibility and cannot depend on a particular set of learned techniques, certain guidelines may prove helpful:

1. A calm setting that provides privacy, reduces distractions, and minimizes interruptions is essential.

2. Interactions should begin with introductions and clarification of the nurse's role: "My name is Claudia Lyall; I am here to complete the discharge teaching that was started yesterday." This acknowledges the purpose of the interaction and sets the scene to discuss concerns about what happens when the parents are discharged from the hospital.

3. Therapeutic communication should be focused because it is directed toward meeting the needs expressed by the family. Beginning the interaction with an open-ended question is one method of focusing the interaction: "How do you feel about going home today?" It may also be necessary to redirect the conversation: "Thanks for showing me the beautiful pictures of the baby; I understand you are having a bit of trouble getting him to nurse."

4. Non-verbal behaviors may communicate more powerful messages than the spoken word. For example, facial expressions and eye movements can confirm or contradict what the woman says. Repetitive hand gestures, such as finger tapping or twirling a lock of hair, may indicate frustration, irritation, or boredom. Body posture, stance, and gait can convey energy, depression, or discomfort. Voice tone, pitch, rate, and volume may indicate joy, anger, or fear. Grooming also conveys messages about how the woman feels about herself. If she is tired or depressed, she may neglect grooming, although some may not verbalize the problem.

5. Active listening necessitates that the nurse "attend" to what is being said as well as to the non-verbal clues. Attending behaviors that convey interest and a sincere desire to understand include:

- Eye contact, which signals a readiness to interact
- Relaxed posture, with the upper portion of the body inclined toward the client
- Encouraging cues, such as nodding, leaning closer, and smiling; verbal cues include "Uh huh, Go on," "Tell me about that," or "Can you give me an example?"
- Touch, which can be a powerful response when words would break a mood or fail to convey the depth of feeling experienced between the woman and the nurse

6. Cultural differences influence communication. In some cultures (Chinese, Southeast Asian), prolonged eye contact is confrontational and initiates a great deal of concern. Some people from other cultures (Middle Eastern, Native Americans) are sometimes uncomfortable with touch and would be disturbed by unsolicited touching.

7. Communication consists of the message sent and the message received, and it is often necessary for the nurse to clarify what the woman or family member meant by the statement: "I'm not sure I understand." "So you are undecided about breastfeeding?"

8. Emotions are part of communication, and nurses must often reflect feelings that are expressed verbally or non-verbally: "You looked forward to delivery in a birth center and are disappointed that you needed a cesarean birth?"

THERAPEUTIC COMMUNICATION TECHNIQUES

Therapeutic communication involves responding as well as listening, and nurses must learn to use responses that facilitate rather than block communication. These facilitative responses, often called communication techniques, focus on both the content of the message and the feeling that accompanies the message. Communication techniques include clarifying, reflecting, silence, questioning, and directing. For a brief review of these and other communication techniques, see Table 2–1.

In addition to being aware of effective communication techniques, nurses must be aware of blocks to communication. These are listed with examples and alternatives in Table 2–2.

✔ *Check Your Reading*

1. How does therapeutic communication differ from social communication?
2. What are the major blocks to communication?
3. What are the major communication techniques?

The Nurse's Role in Teaching and Learning

Nurses can be the most significant teacher on the health care team because of the nature of the relationship that exists between nurses and clients and because they have more contact with clients than any other member of the team. Moreover, clients often perceive nurses as less threatening than physicians and as having time to respond to concerns that the physician may find trivial. Nurses are often the primary teachers in public clinics as well as in the private practice of obstetricians. Nurses teach in a variety of settings, in one-to-one interactions, in formal classes, and in group discussions. Nurses are responsible for antepartum, intrapartum, and postpartum teaching.

Teaching is a basic function of perinatal nurses because the first aim of maternal-newborn nursing is to promote and maintain the optimal health of each individual and the family unit. This means that nurses must be familiar with principles of teaching

Table 2–1. COMMUNICATION TECHNIQUES

Definition	Examples
Clarifying	
Clearing up or following up to understand both content and feelings expressed; to check the accuracy of how the nurse perceives the message.	"I'm confused about your plans; could you explain?" "Tell me what you mean when you say you don't feel like yourself." "Are you saying that ______?" "Can you tell me more about ______?"
Paraphrasing	
Restating in words other than those used by client what the client seems to express; this is a form of clarification.	Example No. 1. Client: "My boyfriend won't even come into the room for the birth. I am furious with him." Nurse: "You want him with you and you are angry because he won't be here?" Example No. 2. Client: "I watch my diet, but I am gaining too much weight anyway." Nurse: "You want to control your weight, but your diet isn't working."
Reflecting	
Verbalizing comprehension of what the client said and what she seems to be feeling. It is important to link content and feeling and to reflect the client as a mirror reflects a person. The opinion, values, and personality of the nurse should not be in the reflected image.	Example No. 1. Client: "I don't know what to do. My husband doesn't think a cesarean is needed, but the doctor says the baby is showing some stress." Nurse: "You're confused and frightened because they don't agree." Example No. 2. Woman in early labor: "It was my husband's idea for me to become pregnant. I wasn't too excited about it at first." Nurse: "I'll bet the dad will be a pushover as a father." This reflects the nurse's opinion and fails to acknowledge the mother's statement. A better response might be: "Your husband was more excited early in the pregnancy than you?"
Silence	
Waiting and allowing time for the client to continue; verbal communication need not be constant.	The nurse waits quietly for the client to continue.
Structuring	
Creating guidelines or setting priorities.	"You said you don't know how to take care of the baby and also that you are afraid of getting pregnant again. What should we talk about first?"
Pinpointing	
Calling attention to differences or inconsistencies in statements.	"You say you feel wonderful, but I see some tears."
Questioning	
Eliciting information directly; using open-ended questions to avoid yes or no answers and to prevent controlling the answers.	"How do you feel about being pregnant?" instead of "Are you happy to be pregnant?"
Directing	
Using non-verbal responses or succinct comments to encourage the client to continue.	Nodding. "Um mm." "You were saying ______." "Please go on."
Summarizing	
Reviewing the main themes or issues that were discussed.	"You had two major concerns today ______." "We have talked about breastfeeding and how to bathe the baby today."

Table 2–2. BEHAVIORS THAT BLOCK COMMUNICATION

Behavior	Example	Alternative
Conveying lack of interest	Looking away, fidgeting	Attending behaviors such as eye contact, nodding.
Conveying sense of haste	Checking the time, standing near the door	Sitting at bedside.
Closed posture	Arms crossed over chest, holding clip board in front of body	Arms relaxed, leaning forward
Interrupting, finishing sentences	Woman: "I'm not sure how ____." Nurse: "We will have a bath demonstration later."	"Go on ____." "You were saying ____."
Providing false reassurance	"You're going to be O.K."	"I sense you are concerned about how to care for the baby. I will help you give the bath today."
Inappropriate self-disclosure	To woman in labor, "I was in labor 12 hours, then had a cesarean."	"What concerns you most about labor?"
Giving advice	"You should ____." "If I were you, I would ____."	"How do you feel about that?" "What do you think is most important?"
Failure to acknowledge comments or feelings	Woman: "I'm sick of being pregnant; I feel like an incubator." Nurse: "You will soon have a beautiful baby."	"You're ready for this to be over?"

and learning. These principles can serve as guides for structuring learning so that teaching can be more efficient and effective.

PRINCIPLES OF TEACHING AND LEARNING

Application of eight major principles will help nurses become effective teachers in the childbearing setting.

1. Real learning depends on the readiness of the family to learn and the relevance of the content. Fortunately, childbearing families are highly motivated to learn. The parents want to be effective, and any content that is relevant to the health of either mother or child is eagerly sought.

2. Active participation increases learning. Whenever possible, the learner should be an active participant in the educational process rather than a passive listener or viewer. Therefore, learning is enhanced when goals are mutually developed by the family and the nurse and when ample time is allowed for questions and explanations. Moreover, a discussion format in which all can participate stimulates more learning than a straight lecture.

3. Repetition of a skill increases retention as well as a feeling of competence. For example, parents experience real learning when they are allowed to bathe, feed, and diaper the infant more than once before discharge from the hospital or birth center.

4. Praise and positive feedback are powerful motivators for learning. They are particularly important when the family is trying to master a frustrating task such as breastfeeding an unresponsive infant.

5. Role modeling is an effective method for demonstrating behavior. Parents benefit greatly from watching a competent nurse respond to the infant. Nurses must be aware that their behavior is carefully scrutinized at all times and that it may be copied later.

6. Conflicts and frustration impede learning, and they should be recognized and resolved for learning to progress. For instance, couples are sometimes not in agreement about how the infant should be fed (breastfeeding versus formula feeding). This issue and the feelings it generates must be acknowledged before teaching about breastfeeding can be effective.

7. Learning is enhanced when teaching is structured to present simple tasks before more complex material is presented, for instance, teaching umbilical cord care, which is simple, before teaching how to bathe and shampoo the infant, which is more difficult.

8. A variety of teaching methods are necessary to maintain interest and to illustrate concepts. Posters, videos, and printed materials supplement lectures and discussion. Models may be especially useful for teaching family planning or the processes of labor.

FACTORS THAT INFLUENCE LEARNING

A variety of factors influence learning. Some of the most important are the developmental level of the family, their primary language, their cultural orientation, and previous experiences.

Developmental Level. It is not surprising that teenaged parents have different concerns than those of the older couple; to be effective, the nurse must acknowledge this and the teaching-learning sessions

In the prenatal clinic, the nurse teaches a woman one-to-one.

must be structured to meet the primary concerns of each. For example, very young parents often do not benefit from printed material to the same degree as older parents.

Language. The ability to understand the language determines how much the family learns. Although many newly arrived immigrants speak English fairly well, they do not understand the idioms, nuances, medical words, or slang terms that are frequently used. It is critical to create a climate in which families feel free to ask questions when they do not understand.

It is often difficult to determine how much a person has understood. This is particularly true of Asians, who fear the instructor may "lose face" if members of the group indicate that they do not understand. It is sometimes helpful to ask those who speak a different language to describe what they have learned and how they plan to use the information. It may also be helpful to determine whether the information conflicts with what they have learned previously.

Culture. Background and culture influence learning. People tend to forget content with which they disagree. For instance, if the family is from a culture that believes certain foods should be eaten by the mother after childbirth, they may not remember different foods recommended by the nurse. Also, if there are conflicts between what elders in the family recommend and what nurses or physicians teach, many young parents follow the advice of the elders. Therefore, it is wise for the nurse to determine the cultural beliefs and attempt to reach an understanding about what information will be useful before beginning to teach.

Previous Experiences. Parents who already have children have concerns unique to their situation. These families may not need instruction in how to care for a newborn; however, they may be very concerned about how older children will accept a new infant.

Physical Environment. Learning is also influenced by the physical environment. The hospital room is generally suitable for individual teaching. If group instruction is planned, it is helpful to arrange comfortable chairs in a circle so that all persons can hear and participate in face-to-face communication. To decrease interruptions, the nurse should restrict visitors and telephone calls during the teaching session.

Organization and Skill of the Instructor. The instructor must determine the objectives of the class, develop a plan for meeting the objectives, and gather all material before beginning the teaching session. If the objective is that all parents present will observe a bath demonstration, the nurse must decide how to demonstrate the bath, when care of the umbilical cord and circumcision will be presented, and which major principles should be addressed.

It is also very helpful to summarize the major principles that were discussed. For example, after a bath demonstration, the nurse might conclude by saying: "The important points to remember are how to prevent the baby from becoming chilled; how to be sure the infant doesn't fall; and to start at the face, which is the cleanest area, and to bathe the bottom last."

EFFECTS OF EARLY DISCHARGE

Although the principles of teaching and learning should be used whenever possible, early discharge of the mother and infant makes this difficult. Many mothers now leave the hospital within 24 hours after childbirth, and a great deal of teaching must be compressed into a few hours. As a result, there is not enough time for repetition and return demonstrations of infant care. Many families leave the hospital before they have attained any degree of comfort with infant care.

Nurses have developed innovative methods to provide the necessary teaching in the time allowed (see Chapter 17). In addition, nurses have been actively involved in developing methods for supplementing teaching that takes place in the hospital at birth. Follow-up teaching is available on many hospital "hotlines" or "baby lines," which concerned parents can call at any time to ask questions, to verbalize their concerns, or simply to validate how to do something. In many geographical areas, nurses

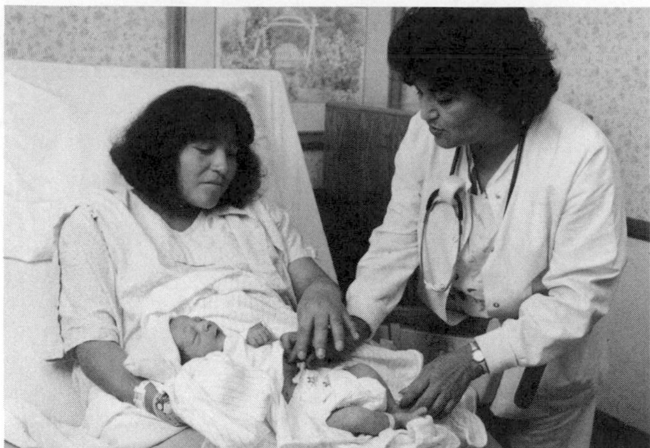

Often, the nurse must condense teaching into a few hours because many mothers and infants leave the birth facility within 24 hours following childbirth.

conduct prenatal parenting classes as well as childbirth education classes. These parenting classes focus on growth and development of the infant, what to do about crying, and how to respond to the infant's needs. Parenting classes are also conducted for families in the weeks after childbirth when parents often have individual problems (see Chapter 22).

✔ Check Your Reading

4. What are the major principles of teaching and learning?
5. What factors affect learning?

Application of Nursing Process to Maternal-Newborn Nursing

Nursing process forms the basis for maternal-newborn nursing, as it does for all of nursing. In maternal-newborn nursing, however, nursing process must be adapted to a population that is generally healthy and that is experiencing a life event that holds the potential for growth as well as for problems. Much maternal-newborn nursing activity is devoted to assessing and diagnosing client strengths and healthy functioning. Interventions often focus on promoting and enhancing these strengths to help families achieve the highest level of wellness. This differs somewhat from providing care for clients who are ill and presents some difficulty for maternal-newborn nurses when they use the list of largely problem-oriented nursing diagnoses provided by the North American Nursing Diagnosis Association (NANDA).

Nursing process consists of five distinct steps: (1) assessment, (2) analysis, (3) planning, (4) implementation, and (5) evaluation. Each step is considered separately, with special emphasis on application to maternal-newborn nursing.

Assessment

Nursing assessment is accomplished in a systematic, deliberate manner and includes not only physiologic data but also information related to other life processes that involve psychological, social, and cultural considerations. Thus, although the mother or the infant may be the primary client, nurses must assess the belief systems, available support, perceptions, and plans of other family members in order to provide the best nursing care.

Two types of nursing assessments are used to collect comprehensive data: (1) the data base assessment, and (2) focus assessments.

DATA BASE ASSESSMENT

The data base assessment is usually performed at the initial contact with the woman and the purpose is to gather information about all aspects of her health. This information, called "baseline" data, describes the client's health status before interventions begin. This information forms the basis for identifying strengths as well as for identifying problems.

In many facilities, the data base assessment centers on body systems, such as cardiovascular, respiratory, and reproductive. In other facilities, assessment is organized around nursing models that are based on nursing theory. Examples include Roy's Adaptation to Stress Theory or Orem's Self-Care Deficit Theory. Regardless of how data are organized, the physiological status of the woman and infant must be determined, and the psychological, social, and cultural factors that affect the childbearing family must be evaluated.

FOCUS ASSESSMENT

A focus assessment is used to gather information that is specifically related to an actual health problem or a problem that the client or family is at high risk for acquiring. A focus assessment directs attention to the specific condition of the patient. It is often performed at the beginning of a shift and centers on areas relevant to childbearing. For instance, in maternal-newborn nursing, one should assess the breasts and nipples because the mother is at risk for problems if she does not have adequate information about breastfeeding or care of the nipples.

A focus assessment is also used to determine the cause of problems that are identified. For example, if the new mother has sore, cracked nipples, the nurse must observe the mother breastfeeding to see whether the nipple trauma is caused by breastfeeding techniques that should be corrected.

Analysis

The data gathered during assessment must be analyzed so that problems or potential problems and their causes can be identified. Some problems, such as ineffective breastfeeding or ineffective thermoregulation (maintenance of temperature), do not require medical intervention but can be treated by independent nursing actions. Problems that do not require medical intervention are termed *nursing diagnoses* because they describe problems that the nurse can legally identify and for which the nurse is legally accountable.

NURSING DIAGNOSES

Nurses have always been aware that they provide care for clients with a variety of health problems that are not addressed by other health professionals. However, nurses did not have a formal method for communicating their independent functions for many years. They needed a method to describe problems for which they are responsible, and they needed a clear, consistent language to communicate and share information in a formalized manner. This provided the impetus for the formation of North American Nursing Diagnosis Association (NANDA).

NANDA is composed of a group of nurses actively involved in the identification and classification of health states that they can legally diagnose and treat. At present, more than a hundred such health problems (nursing diagnoses) have been identified. Each health problem identified by NANDA as a nursing diagnosis consists of three components:

1. The *title* offers a concise description of the health problem.
2. *Defining characteristics* refer to a cluster of signs and symptoms that are often seen with that particular diagnosis.
3. *Etiological and related factors* are factors that can cause or contribute to the problem. The etiology may be pathophysiological, situational, or maturational.

THE DIAGNOSTIC STATEMENT

A nursing diagnosis may be either a two-part or a three-part statement, depending on whether the problem exists now or whether the client is at risk for the problem later.

Actual Nursing Diagnoses. Actual nursing diagnoses exist at the time and can be validated by the presence of defining characteristics or clusters of clinical signs and symptoms. A three-part statement identifies the problem, etiology, and clinical manifestations of the problem or the signs and symptoms. This is sometimes referred to as the "PES format" (Gordon, 1987); P stands for problem, E represents etiology, and S indicates signs and symptoms that validate the presence of the problem. Although the three-part statement requires that existing signs and symptoms be listed, in clinical practice this part of the statement is often omitted.

It is not realistic to expect that the nurse can always determine the cause of a problem. In that case, it is appropriate for the nurse to list the problem and to state that the etiology is unknown. This alerts the nursing staff to continue the assessments until the cause is known so that interventions can be developed. Table 2–3 provides examples of actual nursing diagnoses.

High-Risk Nursing Diagnoses. When an individual or family is more likely to be affected by a problem

Table 2–3. EXAMPLES OF ACTUAL AND HIGH-RISK NURSING DIAGNOSES

Actual Nursing Diagnoses		
Problem	***Etiology***	***Signs and Symptoms***
Alteration in Nutrition: Less Than Body Requirement	Knowledge deficit of nutritional needs during lactation	Weight loss of 5 kg and daily caloric intake <1500 calories
Ineffective Breastfeeding	Nipple trauma	Cracked nipples and reports of discomfort during nursing

High–Risk Nursing Diagnoses	
Problem	***Risk Factors***
High Risk for Ineffective Breastfeeding	Lack of knowledge of correct positioning of infant and appropriate breast care
High Risk for Alteration in Nutrition: Less Than Body Requirements	Knowledge deficit of nutritional needs during lactation

than other people in the same or a similar situation, the diagnostic label begins with the words "high risk." Until 1992, these diagnoses began with the phrase "potential for"; however, terminology changed to emphasize that these diagnoses should be used only when the person is more vulnerable than others in a similar situation (McCourt and Carroll-Johnson, 1992). For example, mothers who undergo cesarean birth have a potential for infection because the incision breaks the protective barrier of the skin. Nursing care for cesarean birth is usually stated in standards of care for cesarean delivery or in a generic nursing care plan. An *individual* nursing diagnosis would not be necessary unless additional risk factors are present. If the mother has additional factors that increase her risk for infection, such as an abnormally low hemoglobin level or hematocrit value and/or prolonged rupture of membranes, which allows bacteria from the vagina to ascend into the uterus, she is especially vulnerable to infection and an individual nursing diagnosis would be appropriate.

High-risk nursing diagnoses consist of a two-part statement: (1) the problem, and (2) the risk factors. The cluster of signs and symptoms (defining characteristics) is not a present factor and, of course, is not part of the statement (see Table 2–3).

Possible Nursing Diagnoses. It is sometimes difficult to distinguish "possible" nursing diagnoses from "high-risk" nursing diagnoses; however, there is a slight difference. Possible nursing diagnoses indicate that a problem may exist but that there are not sufficient data to be sure and risk factors are not clearly demonstrated. Possible nursing diagnoses alert the nursing staff to focus their assessment in a particular area in the coming hours to determine whether a problem does exist or whether risk factors are present, for example, "Possible Alteration in Parenting related to rapidly changing roles of teenaged parents." This nursing diagnosis is based on the knowledge that adolescent parents sometimes have difficulty with parenting because of their own lack of maturity. Additional risk factors have not been identified, and there have been no signs of problems in parent-infant interaction. Additional data are needed before a high-risk diagnosis can be made.

Any nursing diagnosis may be appropriate for maternal-newborn nursing; however, some nursing diagnostic categories are particularly common (Table 2–4).

Table 2–4. COMMON NURSING DIAGNOSES IN MATERNAL-NEWBORN NURSING

Anxiety
Body Image Disturbance
Breastfeeding, Effective
Breastfeeding, Ineffective
Communication, Impaired Verbal
Constipation
Decisional Conflict
Family Coping: Potential for Growth
Family Processes: Altered
Health Maintenance, Altered
Health Seeking Behaviors
Infection, High Risk for
Nutrition, Altered: Less than Body Requirements
Nutrition, Altered: More than Body Requirements
Pain
Parental Role Conflict
Parenting, Altered
Role Performance, Altered
Self-Esteem, Situational Low
Sexuality Patterns, Altered
Sleep Pattern Disturbances
Thermoregulation, Ineffective
Urinary Elimination, Altered

Planning

The third step in nursing process involves planning care for problems that were identified during assessment and that are reflected in the nursing diagnoses. During this step, nurses develop goals, objectives, or outcomes that state what is to be accomplished by a certain time and plan interventions that help to accomplish the goals.

ESTABLISHING GOALS AND EXPECTED OUTCOMES

Although the terms "goals," "objectives," and "outcomes" are often used interchangeably, there are differences. Generally, broad goals or objectives do not state the specific outcome criteria and are less measurable than outcome statements. If broad goals are developed, it is suggested that they be linked with more specific and measurable outcome criteria, for example, *goal*—the parents will demonstrate effective parenting by discharge as evidenced by *outcome criteria*—prompt, consistent responses to infant signals and competence in bathing, feeding, and comforting the infant.

Regardless of which term is used, certain rules for setting goals and outcomes are followed:

1. Goals must be stated in client terms; this identifies who is expected to achieve the goal.
2. Measurable verbs must be used. For example, "identify," "demonstrate," "express," "walk," "relate," and "list" are verbs that are observable and measurable. Examples of verbs that are difficult to measure

are "understand," "appreciate," "feel," "accept," "know," and "experience." For instance, "Ms. Brown will experience less anxiety about assuming care of her infant" poses a problem because it is difficult to determine whether or not she experiences less anxiety. This outcome can be reworded as: "Ms. Brown will *report* decreased anxiety." This goal is easier to validate. The statement can also be rewritten to include more specific outcome criteria: "Ms. Brown will experience less anxiety about assuming care of her infant, as demonstrated by participating in infant care (umbilical cord, circumcision, bathing) before discharge."

3. Goals must have a time frame. When is the person expected to perform the action? By the first postpartum day? By discharge? Within the second trimester?

4. Goals must be realistic and attainable. For instance, if a nursing diagnosis of "pain related to uterine contractions and lack of knowledge of the processes of labor" is formulated, a realistic goal or outcome might be: "Will use learned relaxation and breathing techniques during contractions to reduce discomfort." Other goals, such as "will remain free of pain throughout labor" are not attainable by nursing interventions only.

5. Goals and outcomes are worked out in collaboration with the client and family to ensure their participation in the plan of care.

DEVELOPING NURSING INTERVENTIONS

Once the goals and outcomes are developed, it is necessary to write nursing interventions that will help the client meet the established outcomes.

Planning Interventions for Actual Nursing Diagnoses. Nursing interventions for actual nursing diagnoses are aimed at reducing or eliminating the causes or related factors. For instance, suppose the nursing diagnosis is "Altered Parenting related to interruption of bonding process secondary to illness of infant as manifested by absences of attachment behaviors (eye contact, holding)." The desired outcome might be that the parents will demonstrate progressive attachment behaviors, such as touching, palming, eye contact, and participation in infant care within 1 week. Nursing interventions would focus on increasing contact between parents and infant and on facilitating attachment behaviors.

A second example may help to clarify the process. Suppose the nursing diagnosis is "Constipation related to insufficient fluid and fiber intake and inadequate exercise as manifested by painful defecation of small, hard stools." The desired outcome is that the patient will establish a pattern of soft, painless stools of more than three times per week. Appropriate nursing interventions seek to bring about increased fluid and fiber intake and to initiate a realistic exercise regimen.

Planning Interventions for a High-Risk Nursing Diagnosis. Interventions are aimed at (1) monitoring for onset of the problem, (2) reducing or eliminating risk factors, and (3) preventing the problem. For example, suppose the nursing diagnosis for an infant is "High Risk for Impaired Skin Integrity related to frequent, loose stools." The planned outcome is that the skin will remain intact, with nursing interventions to include monitoring the condition of the skin at prescribed times for signs and symptoms of skin impairment and initiating measures to keep the skin clean and dry.

Planning Interventions for Possible Nursing Diagnoses. Nursing interventions identify methods of collecting additional data to determine whether clinical manifestations or contributing factors are present. The purpose is to confirm or rule out the diagnosis.

Implementing Nursing Interventions

Planning and implementation are closely related: In planning, nursing interventions are written to direct nursing care; in implementation, nursing interventions or orders are carried out. Implementing interventions may involve (1) performing an activity for a client, (2) assisting the client in performing an activity, (3) demonstrating a skill, (4) counseling the client or family about health care resources, (5) assessing the client for potential complications or for a change in status, or (6) providing information.

A major problem with implementing nursing interventions occurs because written interventions are often not specific and do not clearly spell out exactly what should be done. Nursing interventions should be as specific as physician's orders. When a physician orders "morphine sulfate, 10 mg IM every 3 hours prn for pain," the order specifies what is to be given, how much is to be given, how it is to be administered, at what time, and why it is necessary. A well-written nursing intervention is equally specific: "Provide 200 ml of fluid (water or juice of choice) q2h while the woman is awake."

Conversely, poorly written interventions, such as "assist with breastfeeding" provide generalizations rather than specific steps to follow. Spelling out exactly how the nurse should assist the mother to breastfeed is more effective: "Demonstrate correct positioning in cradle and football hold at first attempt to breastfeed. Teach mother to elicit rooting reflex by stroking infant's lips with nipple. Demonstrate how to latch infant to nipple, and request a return demonstration before mother is discharged."

Nursing interventions should include the following:

- The date on which the intervention is written
- An action verb ("demonstrate," "assist," "instruct," "provide"); avoid verbs that do not clearly state what action is to be performed ("encourage," "support," "facilitate") unless additional direction is provided
- A phrase that describes the action (how often, when, where, how long, how much)
- The signature of the person writing the interventions

Evaluation

The evaluation determines how well the plan worked or if the goals were met. To evaluate how well the plan worked, the nurse must assess the status of the client and compare the current status with the goals or outcome criteria that were developed during the planning step. The nurse then judges how well the client is progressing toward goal achievement and makes a decision. Should the plan be continued? Modified? Abandoned? Are the problems resolved

Table 2–5. DEVELOPING INDIVIDUALIZED NURSING CARE PLANS

Although nursing process is the foundation for maternal-newborn nursing, initially it is a challenging process to apply in the clinical area. It requires proficiency in focus assessments of the new mother and infant as well as the ability to analyze data and formulate nursing care plans for individual clients and families. It may be helpful to pose questions at each step of the nursing process.

Assessment

1. Were there data that were not within normal limits or expected parameters? For example, the client states that she feels "dizzy" when she tries to ambulate.
2. If so, what else should be assessed? (What else should I look for? What might be related to this symptom?) For instance, what are the blood pressure, pulse, skin color, temperature, and amount of lochia if the client feels "dizzy"?
3. Did the assessment identify the cause of the abnormal data? What are the hemoglobin count, hematocrit value, and estimated blood loss during childbirth?
4. Are there other factors? What medication is the client taking? How long since she has eaten? Is the environment a related factor (crowded, warm, unfamiliar)? Is she reluctant to ask for assistance?

Analysis

1. Are adequate data available to reach a conclusion? What else is needed? (What do you wish you had assessed? What would you look for next time?)
2. What is the major concern? (On the basis of the data, what are you worried about?) The client who is "dizzy" may fall as she ambulates to the bathroom.
3. What might happen if no action is taken? (What might happen to the client if you do nothing?) She may suffer an injury or a complication.
4. Is there a NANDA-approved diagnostic category that reflects your major concern? How is it defined? Suppose during analysis you decide the major concern is that the patient will faint and suffer an injury. What diagnostic category most closely reflects this concern? High Risk for Injury? Definition: The state in which an individual is at risk for harm because of a perceptual or physiological deficit, a lack of awareness of hazards, or maturational age.
5. Do this category and definition "fit" this client? Is she at greater risk for a problem than others in a similar situation? Why? What are the additional risk factors?
6. Is this a problem that nurses can manage independently? Are medical interventions also necessary?
7. If the problem can be managed by nurses, is it an actual problem (defining characteristics are present), high-risk (risk factors are present), or possible (you have a "hunch" and some data but not enough).

Planning

1. What outcomes are desired? That the client will remain free of injury during hospital stay? That she will demonstrate position changes that reduce the episodes of vertigo?
2. Would the outcomes be clear, specific, and measurable to anyone reading them?
3. What nursing interventions should be initiated and carried out to accomplish these goals or outcomes?
4. Are your written interventions specific and clear? Are action verbs used ("assess," "teach," "assist")? After you have written the interventions, look them over. Do they define exactly what is to be done (when, what, how far, how often)? Will they prevent the client from suffering an injury?
5. Are the interventions based on sound rationale? For instance, dehydration that may occur during labor causes weakness that may result in falls; loss of blood during delivery often exceeds 500 ml, which results in hypotension that is aggravated when the client stands suddenly.

Implementing Nursing Interventions

1. What are the expected effects of the prescribed intervention? Are there potential adverse effects? What are they?
2. Are the interventions acceptable to the client and family?
3. Are the interventions clearly written so that they can be carefully followed?

Evaluation

1. What is the status of the client right now?
2. What were the goals and outcomes? Are they specific? Can they be measured?
3. Compare the current status of the client with the stated goals and outcomes.
4. What should be done now?

Abbreviation: NANDA, North American Nursing Diagnosis Association.

or the causes diminished? Is another nursing diagnosis more relevant?

Nursing process is dynamic, and evaluation frequently results in expanded assessment and additional or modified nursing diagnoses and interventions. Nurses are cautioned not to view lack of goal achievement as a failure. Instead, it is simply time to reassess and to begin the process anew.

Table 2–5 summarizes the procedure for creating a nursing care plan.

✔ Check Your Reading

6. How does data base assessment differ from focus assessment?
7. How do actual nursing diagnoses differ from high-risk nursing diagnoses?
8. How should goals and outcomes be stated?
9. Why are interventions sometimes difficult to implement? How can this be corrected?

Collaborative Problems

In addition to nursing diagnoses that describe problems that respond to independent nursing functions, nurses must also deal with problems that are beyond the scope of independent nursing practice. These are sometimes termed "collaborative problems"— physiological complications that usually occur in association with a specific pathology or treatment. They are unlike medical diagnoses, in that they represent situations that are the primary responsibility of nurses. Nurses monitor to detect the onset of the complication and collaborate with physicians to manage changes in client status. Both physician-prescribed and nursing-prescribed interventions are necessary to minimize complications (Carpenito, 1992). Examples of collaborative problems in maternal-newborn nursing include excessive bleeding following childbirth or labor that begins before the fetus is fully developed.

Stating Collaborative Problems

The words "Potential Complication" should precede each collaborative problem. For example, Potential Complication: Fetal Distress or Potential Complication: Postpartum Hemorrhage. It is not necessary to identify the cause, although it may be written if it is known. "Potential Complication" alerts nurses that nurse-prescribed as well as physician-prescribed interventions are needed.

Planning

Goals for collaborative problems differ from those for nursing diagnoses. According to NANDA, nursing diagnoses provide the basis for a selection of nursing interventions to achieve goals for which the nurse is accountable. Goals for nursing diagnoses are stated in client terms and describe a favorable change in client status as a result of nursing interventions (Alfaro, 1990). *It is inappropriate to identify client-centered goals for a collaborative problem because the goals cannot be achieved by independent nursing action.* Client-centered goals for collaborative problems incorrectly imply accountability for problems that nurses cannot independently manage (Carpenito, 1992).

Collaborative problems should reflect the nurse's responsibility in situations requiring physician-prescribed interventions. The responsibility includes:

- Monitoring for signs of complications
- Consulting standing orders, protocols, and physicians if signs of complications are observed
- Performing specific actions to minimize the severity of an event or situation (Carpenito, 1992)

Interventions

Nursing interventions for collaborative problems include (1) performing frequent assessments to monitor the status of the client and to detect signs and symptoms of complications, (2) communicating with the physician when signs and symptoms of complications are noted, (3) performing physician-prescribed interventions to prevent or correct the complication, and (4) performing nursing interventions described in the standards of care or policy and procedure manuals.

Evaluation

Although client-centered goals or outcomes are not developed for collaborative problems, the nurse collects and compares data to established norms and judges whether the data are within normal limits. If data are not within normal limits, the nurse communicates with the physician for additional direction and implements physician-prescribed interventions as well as nursing interventions.

✔ Check Your Reading

10. How do nursing diagnoses differ from collaborative problems?

11. Why are client-centered goals inappropriate for collaborative problems?

Summary Concepts

- Registered nurses with advanced education are prepared to provide primary care for women and children as certified nurse-midwives and nurse practitioners.
- Registered nurses, prepared at the Masters level as clinical nurse specialists, provide in-depth interventions for many problems encountered in maternity care.
- As maternity care has changed, so has the role of nurses, who must be adept at communication techniques and blocks to communication to meet their responsibilities as educators and counselors.
- A primary responsibility of nurses is to provide information to childbearing families; nurses must know the principles of teaching and learning to fulfill the role of educator.
- Nursing process begins with assessment and includes analysis of data that may result in nursing diagnoses. These are problems that nurses are legally accountable for identifying and managing independently.
- Collaborative problems are usually physiological complications that require both physician-prescribed and nurse-prescribed interventions.

References and Readings

Alfaro, R. (1990). *Applying nursing diagnosis and nursing process: A step by step guide* (2nd ed.). Philadelphia: J.B. Lippincott.

Arnold, E., & Boggs, K. (1989). *Interpersonal relationships: Professional communication skills for nurses.* Philadelphia: W.B. Saunders.

Avant, K.C. (1990). The art and science in nursing diagnosis development. *Nursing Diagnosis,* 1(2), 51–56.

Carlson, J.H., Craft, C.A., McGuire, A.D., & Popkess-Vawter, S. (1991). *Nursing diagnoses: A case study approach.* Philadelphia: W.B. Saunders.

Carpenito, L.J. (1991). *Nursing care plans and documentation: Nursing diagnoses and collaborative problems.* Philadelphia: J.B. Lippincott.

Carpenito, L.J. (1983). *Nursing diagnosis: Application to clinical practice.* Philadelphia: J.B. Lippincott.

Carpenito, L.J. (1992). *Nursing diagnosis: Application to clinical practice* (4th ed.). Philadelphia: J.B. Lippincott.

Carpenito, L.J. (1993). *Nursing diagnosis: Application to clinical practice* (5th ed.). Philadelphia: J.B. Lippincott.

Cox, H.C., Hinz, M.D., Lubno, M.A., et al. (1989). *Clinical application of nursing diagnosis.* Baltimore: Williams & Wilkins.

Gordon, M. (1987). *Nursing diagnosis: Process and application* (2nd ed.). New York: McGraw-Hill Book.

Gorrie, T.M. (1989). *A guide to the nursing of childbearing families.* Baltimore: Williams & Wilkins.

Grippando, G.M., & Mitchell, P.R. (1989). *Nursing perspectives and issues* (4th ed.). Albany: Delmar Publishers, Inc.

Hendrikson, M., Wall, G., Lethbridge, D., & McClurg, V. (1992). Nursing diagnosis and obstetric, gynecologic, and neonatal nursing: Breastfeeding as an example. *Journal of Obstetric, Gynecologic, and Neonatal Nursing,* 21(6), 446–456.

Iyer, P.W., Taptich, B.J., & Bernocchi-Losey, D. (1991). *Nursing process and nursing diagnosis* (2nd ed.). Philadelphia: W.B. Saunders.

Maas, M., Hardy, M., & Craft, M. (1990). Some methodologic considerations in nursing diagnoses. *Nursing Research,* 1(1), 24–30.

McCourt, A., & Carroll-Johnson, R.M. (Eds.) 1992 Classification of Nursing Diagnoses: Proceedings of the Ninth NANDA National Conference. Philadelphia: J.B. Lippincott.

McFarland, G.K., & McFarlane, E.A. (1989). *Nursing diagnosis and intervention.* St. Louis: C.V. Mosby.

Weber, E. (1992). Making nursing diagnosis work for you and your client. *Nursing and Health Care,* 12(8), 424–430.

3

Ethical, Social, and Legal Issues

Objectives

1. Apply theories and principles of ethics to ethical dilemmas.
2. Describe how the steps of the nursing process can be applied to ethical decision making.
3. Discuss ethical conflicts related to reproductive issues such as elective abortion, forced contraception, and infertility.
4. Relate how major social issues, such as poverty and access to health care, affect maternal-newborn nursing.
5. Describe the legal basis for nursing practice.
6. Identify measures to prevent malpractice claims.

Definitions

Bioethics • Rules or principles that govern right conduct, specifically that related to health care.

Deontological theory • Ethical theory holding that the right course of action is the one dictated by ethical principles and moral rules.

Ethical dilemma • A situation in which no solution seems completely satisfactory.

Ethics • Rules or principles that govern right conduct and distinctions between right and wrong.

Malpractice • Negligence by a professional person.

Negligence • Failure to act in the way a reasonable, prudent person of similar background would act in similar circumstances.

Nurse practice acts • Laws that determine the scope of nursing practice in each state.

Standard of care • Level of care that can be expected of a professional. This is determined by laws, professional organizations, and health care agencies.

Standardized procedures • Procedures determined by nurses, physicians, and administrators that allow nurses to perform duties usually part of the medical practice.

Utilitarian theory • Ethical theory stating that the right course of action is the one that produces the greatest good for the largest number of people.

When ethical and social issues affect nursing practice, many questions arise, but few answers are easy or acceptable to everyone. Maternal-newborn nurses often must grapple with ethical and social dilemmas that affect childbearing families. Nurses must know how to approach these issues in a knowledgeable and systematic manner. Some ethical and social issues result in the passage of laws that regulate reproductive practice. It is important for nurses to understand the legal basis for their scope of practice to decrease the risk of involvement in malpractice claims.

Ethics and Bioethics

Ethics involves determining the best course of action in a certain situation. It is the analysis of what is morally right and reasonable. Bioethics is the application of ethics to health care. Ethical behavior for nurses is discussed in various codes, such as the American Nurses' Association Code of Ethics. Ethical issues have increased as developing technology has allowed more options in health care. Ethical issues are often controversial because there is lack of agreement over what is right or best and because moral support is possible for more than one course of action. Ethical dilemmas, approaches for solving them, and some current ethical issues are discussed next.

Ethical Dilemmas

An ethical dilemma is a situation in which no solution seems completely satisfactory. There may be more than one opposing course of action that seems equally desirable, or all possible solutions may seem undesirable. Nurses find ethical dilemmas to be among the most difficult situations in their practice. Finding solutions involves applying ethical theories and principles and determining the burdens and benefits of any course of action.

ETHICAL THEORIES

Two major theories guide ethical decision making. Very few people use one theory exclusively; instead, they make decisions by examining both theories and trying to determine which one is most appropriate for the circumstances.

Deontological Theory. The deontological approach determines what is right by applying ethical principles and moral rules. It does not vary the solution according to individual situations. For example, consider the rule, "life must be maintained at all costs and in all circumstances." Strictly used, the deontological approach would not consider the quality of life or weigh the use of scarce resources against the likelihood that the life maintained would be near normal.

Utilitarian Theory. The utilitarian theory approaches ethical dilemmas by analyzing the benefits and burdens of any course of action to find one that will result in the greatest amount of good for the largest number of people. With this theory, the appropriate actions may vary according to the situation. It is a pragmatic approach that is concerned with the consequences of actions more than the actual actions themselves. In its simplest form, this is an "end justifies the means" approach. If the outcome is positive, the method of arriving at that outcome is less important.

ETHICAL PRINCIPLES

Ethical principles are also important in solving ethical dilemmas. Four of the most important principles are beneficence, non-maleficence, autonomy, and justice (Table 3–1). Although principles guide decision making, in some situations it may be impossible to apply one without conflicting with another. In such cases, one principle may outweigh another in importance.

For example, treatments designed to do good may also cause some harm. A cesarean birth may be good when a fetus in distress is delivered before permanent harm occurs; however, the surgery that saves the fetus also harms the mother, in that it causes pain and temporary disability and may impose a financial hardship. However, both the mother and caregivers may decide that the principle of beneficence outweighs the principle of non-maleficence. If the mother does not want surgery, the principles of autonomy and justice must also be considered. Is the mother's right to determine what happens to her body more or less important than the right of the fetus to be treated fairly and equally with the mother?

Table 3–1. ETHICAL PRINCIPLES

Beneficence: One is required to do or promote good for others.

Non-maleficence: One must avoid risking or causing harm to others.

Autonomy: People have the right to self-determination. This includes the right to respect, privacy, and information necessary to make decisions.

Justice: All people should be treated equally and fairly regardless of disease or social or economic status.

APPLICATION OF ETHICAL THEORIES AND PRINCIPLES

Ethical theories and principles can be applied to the question of whether or not it is acceptable to use the organs from a newborn with anencephaly (congenital absence of brain tissue) who has no chance to survive to save the lives of other infants. The deontological view is that it is wrong to take organs necessary for life from one human being to give to another, even when the dying infant cannot survive more than a few days or weeks. This view would also disapprove of aggressive treatment necessary to maintain perfusion to the organs until a recipient is located because this treatment does not help the dying infant and may increase suffering. This invokes the principle of non-maleficence.

The utilitarian viewpoint argues that the anencephalic infant cannot survive but that organ transplants provide great benefit to other infants (beneficence). The family of the anencephalic infant may believe very strongly that helping other infants to live allows good to come from their own tragedy. Therefore, the greatest good would be for an organ transplant. At present, this dilemma is unresolved. Although transplants have been done in the past, they are not currently practiced because of the ethical concerns.

These considerations bring up other potential problems. If such transplants became routine, might parents of anencephalic infants some day be required to donate organs, even against their will (autonomy)? Would the mother be required to carry an anencephalic fetus to term so that the organs could be harvested, even if she would rather terminate the pregnancy? If anencephalic infants are used for organ donation, would people with profound mental retardation or persistent vegetative states eventually be placed in the same situation? Who would determine this? How will infants to benefit be chosen, and who will choose (justice)?

SOLVING ETHICAL DILEMMAS

There are many approaches to solving ethical dilemmas. Although an approach does not guarantee that the right decision is chosen, it provides a logical, systematic method for going through the steps of decision making. Because the nursing process is also a method of problem solving, a similar approach can be used for solving ethical dilemmas (Table 3–2).

Table 3–2. APPLYING NURSING PROCESS TO SOLVE ETHICAL DILEMMAS

Assessment: Gather data to clearly identify the problem and the decisions necessary. Obtain viewpoints of all who will be affected by the decision as well as legal, policy, and common practice standards that may apply.

Analysis: Decide whether or not an ethical dilemma exists. Analyze the situation using ethical theories and principles. Determine whether and how these conflict.

Planning: Identify as many options as posisble, their advantages and disadvantages, and which are most realistic. Predict what is likely to happen if each option is followed. Include the option of doing nothing. Choose the solution.

Implementation: Carry out the solution. Determine who will implement the solution and how. Identify all interventions necessary and what support is needed.

Evaluation: Analyze the results. Determine whether further interventions are necessary.

The steps to decision making in ethical dilemmas may seem straightforward, but they do not necessarily result in one answer that is obvious and agreeable to everyone involved. Many hospitals have instituted bioethics committees to help in making decisions in specific cases as well as to provide education and formulate policies regarding ethical situations. These committees include professionals from many backgrounds, such as physicians, nurses, social workers, ethicists, and clergy. The client and family also participate, if possible. There is a greater chance that a satisfactory solution to ethical dilemmas will be reached when a variety of people work together.

✔ Check Your Reading

1. What is the difference between ethics and bioethics?
2. How does the utilitarian theory of ethics differ from the deontological theory of ethics?
3. When might one ethical principle conflict with another?
4. How do the steps of the nursing process apply to ethical decision making?

Ethical Issues in Reproduction

Reproductive issues often involve conflicts in which a woman behaves in a way that may cause harm to her fetus or in a way that is disapproved of by some or most members of society. Conflicts between mother and fetus occur when the mother's needs, behavior, or wishes may injure the fetus. The most obvious instances are those involving abortion, substance abuse, or a mother's refusal to follow the advice of caregivers. Health care workers and society in general may respond to such a woman with anger rather than support. However, the rights of both mother and fetus must be examined.

ELECTIVE ABORTION

Abortion has been a volatile legal, social, and political issue ever since the *Roe v. Wade* decision by the U.S. Supreme Court in 1973. (Before that, states could prohibit abortion, making the procedure illegal). This decision declared that abortion was legal anywhere in the United States and that existing state laws prohibiting abortion were unconstitutional because they interfered with the mother's constitutional right to privacy. The Supreme Court decision stipulated that (1) a woman could obtain an abortion at any time during the first trimester, (2) the state could regulate abortions during the second trimester only to protect the woman's health, and (3) the state could regulate or prohibit abortion during the third trimester except when the mother's life might be jeopardized by continuing the pregnancy.

For many, the woman's constitutional right to privacy conflicts with the fetus's constitutional right to life. However, the Supreme Court did not rule on when life begins. This omission provokes debate between those who believe life begins at conception and those who believe life begins when the fetus is viable, or capable of living outside the uterus. Those who believe life begins at conception may be opposed to abortion at any time during pregnancy. Those who believe life begins when the fetus is viable (20 to 26 weeks of gestation) may oppose abortion after that time.

It is important that nurses be knowledgeable about past Supreme Court decisions related to abortion and about the conflicting beliefs that divide society on this issue.

Conflicting Beliefs About Abortion. Perhaps no issue creates greater division or incites more powerful emotions among Americans than that of elective abortion. Simply stated, some people believe abortion should be illegal at any time because it deprives the fetus of life; in contrast, some people believe that women have the right to control their reproductive function and that political discussion of reproductive rights is an invasion of the most private decisions of women.

Belief That Abortion Is a Private Choice. At the heart of political action to keep abortion legal is the conviction that women have the right to make decisions about their reproductive function on the basis of their own ethical and moral beliefs and that the government has no place in these decisions. Many women who support this movement state that they would not choose abortion for themselves. However, they support the right of each woman to make her own decision and view government action as interference in a very private part of the lives of women. Many people who support legal abortions prefer to call themselves "pro-choice" rather than "pro-abortion," as they believe that term expresses their philosophical and political position more accurately.

Each year since 1985, there have been more than 1.5 million abortions in the United States. Of this number, 12 per cent (182,000) were obtained by minors (Henshaw, 1992). Advocates of the legal right to abortion point out that abortion, either legal or illegal, has always been a reality of life and will continue regardless of legislation or judicial rulings. Advocates express concern about the unsafe conditions that accompany illegal abortion, citing the deaths that occurred as a result of illegal abortions performed before the *Roe v. Wade* decision.

Belief That Abortion Is Taking a Life. Many people believe that legalized abortion condones taking a life and feel morally bound to protect the lives of fetuses. Many people who feel this way call their position "pro-life." This term has become emotionally charged, in that others feel it polarizes opinions and implies that those who do not agree with the anti-abortion position are not concerned about life or are "anti-life."

Those persons opposed to abortion have demonstrated their commitment by organizing to become a potent political force and by their willingness to be arrested for civil disobedience when they attempt to block admissions to clinics that perform abortions.

Legal Aspects of *Roe v. Wade*. Abortion has been a complex legal issue since 1973, and the U.S. Supreme Court has made major decisions that affect abortion law since that time. Some decisions have strengthened the original *Roe v. Wade* ruling, and others have weakened it. Because nurses should know about the legal history of abortion, some of these decisions are enumerated here.

1. In 1976 the Supreme Court held that states could not give a husband veto power over his spouse's decision to have an abortion.
2. In 1977 the Court ruled that states do not have an obligation to pay for abortions as part of government-funded health care programs. Advocates of legal abortions objected to this ruling as unfair discrimination against poor women who are unable to pay for an abortion and are penalized by this ruling.
3. In 1979 the Court allowed physicians broad discretion in determining fetal viability and gave states leeway to restrict abortions of viable fetuses.
4. The issue of minors seeking abortions was addressed in 1979, when the Court ruled that states may require parental consent for abortion as long as an alternative, such as the minor getting a judge's approval, was also available. In 1990 the Court allowed states to require notification of both parents before a woman under the age of 18 years has an

abortion. A judicial bypass process to permit a judge to authorize the abortion without parental consent was also mandated.

5. In 1989 the Court upheld a Missouri law barring abortions performed in public hospitals and clinics or performed by public employees. The ruling also required physicians to conduct tests for fetal viability at 20 weeks of gestation.

6. In 1992 the Court validated the power of states to impose restrictions on abortions when it upheld all but one of the restrictions of a Pennsylvania law. The restrictions upheld are as follows:

- A woman must be told about fetal development and alternatives to abortion
- She must wait at least 24 hours after this explanation
- Unmarried women under the age of 18 must obtain consent from their parents—or a judge
- Physicians must keep detailed records of each abortion, subject to public disclosure

The Court struck down only one requirement of the Pennsylvania law: that a married woman must inform her husband before having an abortion.

The so-called "gag" rule, which restricted counseling that health care professionals (with the exception of physicians) could provide at federally funded family planning clinics, was rescinded in 1993.

Political Aspects of Abortion. The abortion question is one of the primary issues confronting political candidates. It is not unusual for the question to be asked: "How does the candidate stand on abortion?" Abortion rights advocates are emphasizing that their message is to keep government out of the daily lives of citizens and that it is unconstitutional to abridge women's rights to abortion. Anti-abortion leaders will probably continue confrontational strategy to bring attention to their point of view. In addition, they may attempt to get legislation passed that would require complicated tests to determine fetal viability before abortion is allowed.

Implications for Nurses. As health care professionals, nurses are involved in the conflict between differing beliefs about abortion. Nurses have several responsibilities that cannot be ignored. First, nurses must be informed about the complexity of the abortion issue from a legal and ethical standpoint and know the exact regulations and laws in their state. Second, they must realize that, for many, abortion is an ethical dilemma that results in confusion, ambivalence, and personal distress. Next, they must also recognize that the issue is not a dilemma for many but is a fundamental violation of the personal or religious views that give meaning to their lives. Finally, it is absolutely essential that nurses acknowledge the sincere convictions and the strong emotions of all sides of the issue.

Personal Values. A nurse's values often have a profound effect on the quality of care given to a client, and nurses must think through their own beliefs about abortion and come to their own conclusions. Nurses respond to abortion in several ways that illustrate the complexity of the issue and the ambivalence that it produces in many people. For instance, some nurses have no objection to participating in abortion. Others do not assist with an abortion but may care for the woman following the procedure. Some nurses may assist with a first-trimester abortion but may object to a second-trimester abortion. Many nurses are comfortable assisting in abortion if the fetus has severe anomalies but are uncomfortable in other circumstances. Other nurses feel that they could not provide care before, during, or after an abortion and that they would be bound by their conscience to try to dissuade women from their decision.

Professional Obligations. Nurses have no obligation to support a position with which they disagree. Many states have laws that allow nurses to refuse to assist with the procedure if abortions violate ethical, moral, or religious beliefs. Nurses are obligated, however, to disclose this information before they are employed in an institution that performs abortions. It would be unethical for a nurse to withhold this information until assigned to care for a woman having an abortion and then refuse to provide care. As always, nurses must be prepared to respect the decisions of women who look to nurses for care. If nurses feel that they are not able to provide compassionate care because of personal convictions, they must acknowledge this to a supervisor so that appropriate care can be arranged.

✔ Check Your Reading

5. How did the *Roe v. Wade* ruling affect state laws related to abortion in the United States?
6. What are the major conflicting beliefs about abortion?
7. What are some Supreme Court decisions that have modified the *Roe v. Wade* ruling?
8. What are nurses' responsibilities if they are morally opposed to abortion?

COURT-MANDATED CONTRACEPTION

The recent availability of long-term contraceptive devices that can be implanted under the skin has caused speculation about whether certain women should be forced to use them. In fact, the procedure has already been used as a condition of probation to avoid jail terms for women accused of child abuse.

Other controversial suggestions include requiring women who receive Aid to Families with Dependent Children (AFDC) to use the implants; a refusal might result in AFDC payments being decreased or stopped.

Some consider the advantage of forced contraception to be its potential for preventing the birth of additional children to women thought to be unsuitable parents. The implants are also viewed as a means of decreasing government expenses for dependent children. However, this is a punitive approach to social and ethical problems that does not provide long-term solutions to the problems. In addition, coercing the poor to use birth control to limit the money spent supporting them is questionable both legally and ethically.

Forcing any woman to undergo such a medical procedure interferes with her constitutional rights to privacy, to reproduction, to refusal of medical treatment, and freedom from cruel and unusual punishment (Rhodes, 1991). Although the state has the right to protect children from abuse, contraceptive implants would not protect children already born. In addition, the implants may pose health risks to the woman. Other methods of limiting unwanted pregnancies, such as access to free or low-cost information on family planning, would be more appropriate.

FETAL INJURY

When a fetus is injured, as in an assault, the courts have held the person causing the injury to be liable. When a mother's actions cause injury to her fetus, the question of whether she should be restrained or prosecuted has both legal and ethical implications. In some instances, courts have issued jail sentences to women who have caused or who may cause injury to the fetus. The sentence serves to punish the woman and to place her in a situation in which she cannot do further harm to the fetus. In other cases, women have been forced to undergo cesarean births against their will when physicians testified that such a procedure was necessary to prevent injury to the fetus (Rhodes, 1990a).

The state has an interest in protecting children, and the Supreme Court has ruled that children have the right to begin life with sound mind and body (Rhodes, 1990b). Although there is no specific law against use of drugs during pregnancy, women have been charged with negligence, involuntary manslaughter, delivering drugs to a minor, and child endangerment (Rhodes, 1992).

Forcing a woman to behave in a certain way against her will goes against the principles of autonomy, self-determination of competent adults, bodily integrity, and personal freedom. If this practice became widespread, it might impede health care during pregnancy instead of advancing it. Fear of prosecution could jeopardize prenatal care as well as treatment of addiction. Women are unlikely to seek prenatal care or treatment for substance abuse unless they feel safe. The American Nurses' Association is one of a number of professional groups who oppose criminalization of substance abuse in pregnancy, considering it to be counterproductive ("Opposition," 1992).

The issue of the punitive approach also raises the question of how much control the government should have over a pregnant woman in an effort to protect the fetus. Laws could be passed not only against substance abuse during pregnancy but also against refusal to follow any advice from physicians. This might include advice for cesarean birth, fetal tests, or intrauterine surgery to correct fetal defects, or even making sure that the woman gains the desired weight and eats the right foods. It would be hard to draw the line between just how much control should be allowed in the interests of fetal safety.

The state's interest in protecting the health of the fetus is carried out only with great interference with the autonomy of the mother. In addition, such restrictions would be difficult or impossible to enforce. They would place the woman and her physician in adversarial positions as well as deprive the woman of her civil rights. The final result would be more likely to prevent women from seeking prenatal care than to ensure that they received it (Field, 1989).

FETAL THERAPY

Fetal therapy is in the early phases of use but may become more widespread as techniques improve. Although intrauterine blood transfusions are relatively standard practices in some geographical areas, other therapy is very new. Surgery in the fetus, such as that done for abnormal accumulation of cerebrospinal fluid in the brain (hydrocephalus) or obstructions in urinary tract, is still at the research stage.

The risks and benefits of surgery for major fetal anomalies must be considered in every case. Even when surgery can correct a condition, not every fetus survives. Those that do survive may have other serious problems. Preterm labor is a frequent result of surgery, often requiring weeks of bed rest for the mother. Although the risk to future childbearing appears to be minimal, cesarean birth is necessary and the mother will have undergone two surgical procedures in one pregnancy (Longaker et al, 1991). Preterm birth may mean long hospitalization of the infant. Yet in spite of the risks, successful surgery may result in birth of an infant who otherwise could not have survived.

Parents need help in balancing the potential risks to the mother with the best interests of the fetus. There is a danger that mothers might feel pressured to have surgery or other fetal treatment that they do not understand. As with any situation involving informed consent, women need adequate information to make their decision. They should understand whether procedures are still experimental and should be advised about chances of success and alternative options.

ISSUES IN INFERTILITY

Infertility Treatment. Perinatal technology has found ways for some infertile couples to bear children (see Chapter 31). There are many happy results from such practices when an infertile couple is finally able to give birth, but there have been some ethical concerns as well.

Some of the concerns are the high cost and overall low success rate of various treatments. A couple may spend thousands of dollars for each attempt to achieve pregnancy. Because the costs are usually not covered by insurance, their use is limited to the wealthy. The high price of research on techniques that will benefit only a few has also been questioned. Some think that the money should be spent on research that will help a greater number of people.

Even with highly technological infertility treatment, many couples will never meet their goal to give birth to a healthy infant because the overall success rate for these procedures is still low. Some women will remain unable to become pregnant, and some may experience problems once they become pregnant. Even when a birth does result, there have been a large number of multiple births and premature infants, leading to extensive complications and expensive care associated with preterm birth.

Other ethical concerns focus on the fate of embryos that are not used. Should they be frozen for later use by the woman or someone else? Should the embryos be used in research on genetics? In multiple pregnancies with more fetuses than can be expected to survive intact, reduction surgery may be used to destroy one or more fetuses for the benefit of those remaining. The ethical and long-term psychological implications of this are also controversial.

Surrogate Parenting. In surrogate parenting, a woman agrees to bear an infant for another woman. Conception may take place outside the body using ova and sperm from the couple who wish to become parents. These "test-tube babies" are then implanted into the surrogate mother, or the surrogate may be artificially inseminated with sperm from the intended father.

There have been widely publicized cases in which the surrogate mother wanted to keep the child. There are no standard regulations governing these cases, which are decided on an individual basis. Ethical concerns involve who should be a surrogate mother, what her role should be after birth, and who should make these decisions. Screening of parents as well as surrogates may be necessary to determine whether they are suitable for their roles. But who should do the screening? Should it be left to the private interests of those involved, or should the government become involved? There are no definite answers to these questions at this time.

✔ Check Your Reading

9. What dangers are involved in punitive approaches to ethical and social problems?
10. How could punishment of mothers for fetal injury lead to decreased prenatal care?

Social Issues

Nurses are exposed to many social issues that influence health care in their daily work. These issues often have ethical implications as well. Some of the issues that affect maternity care include poverty, homelessness, access to care, and allocation of funds.

Poverty

Poverty is the underlying factor that causes many other problems, such as inadequate access to health care and homelessness. Of all children in the United States, 20 per cent are poor. Minority children are more likely to be poor: 43 per cent of African-American children and 37 per cent of Latino children live in poverty (Inglis, 1991a). Because of adverse living conditions and poor health care, infants born to low-income women are more likely to have health problems such as low birth weight. Poverty affects the health of women and children throughout their lives because all types of health care are less available to the poor.

Poverty tends to breed poverty. In poor families, children may leave the educational system early, making them less likely to learn skills necessary to obtain good jobs. Childbearing at an early age is common and interferes with education and the abil-

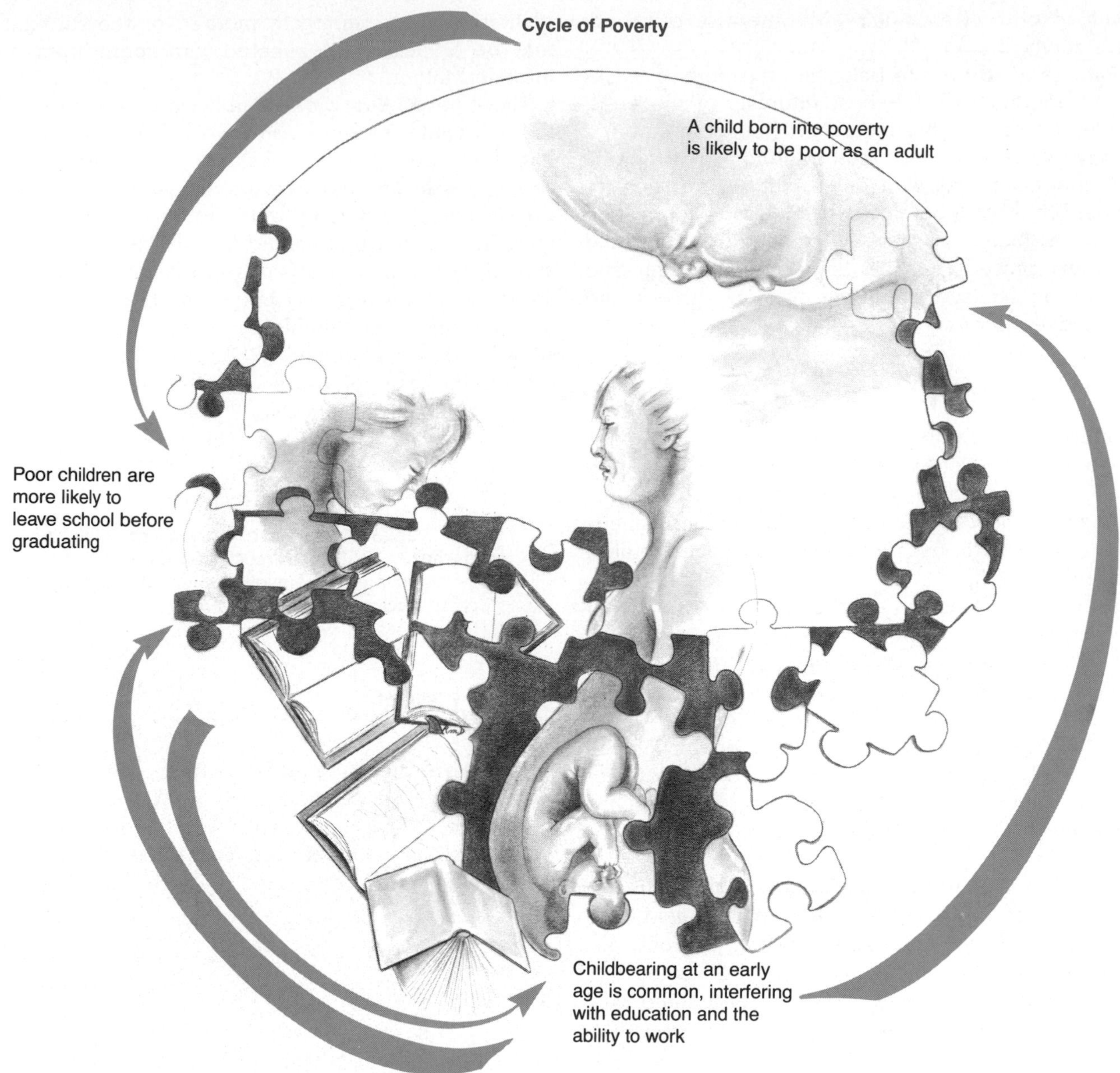

Figure 3–1

The cycle of poverty.

ity to work. The cycle of poverty may continue from one generation to another as a result of hopelessness and apathy (Fig. 3–1).

People who are not considered to be at the poverty level may still be poor when it comes to ability to pay for health care. The working poor have jobs but receive wages that barely meet their day-to-day needs. They have little opportunity to save for improvements or to meet emergencies.

More than 35 million people in the United States have no health insurance. Millions of others have only limited insurance and would not be able to survive financially should serious illness occur. People without insurance seek care only when absolutely necessary. Prenatal care may seem too costly and unnecessary to them. Some receive no health care during pregnancy until they arrive at the hospital for delivery.

Various government programs help the poor. One is AFDC, which provides money for basic living costs of poor children and their families. Eligibility requirements, however, vary among the states, and many families, although poor, have incomes too high to meet the requirements.

Homelessness

Homelessness is an extension of poverty, and the problem of homelessness is increasing in this affluent nation. Families, many composed of single women and their children, are the fastest-growing group of homeless people. Their health problems are immense. Some of the women are substance abusers. Both women and children are poorly nourished and are exposed to diseases such as tuberculosis, acquired immunodeficiency syndrome (AIDS), and sexually transmitted diseases. Rape and assault are always a problem, with a high rate of pregnancy among homeless girls. Such infants have a lower average birth weight, and the neonatal mortality rate is higher than the norm (Rafferty, 1989b).

Pregnancy and birth may be one of the many contributing causes of becoming homeless, as may having a first baby before age 18 (Weitzman, 1989). Pregnancy interferes with a woman's ability to work and may decrease her income to the point where she loses her housing. Without child care or a home address, she may have less chance of obtaining and keeping employment. In addition, her children are more likely to be sick without adequate food and shelter. Without money to pay for early health care, there is an increased chance that children will need hospitalization.

Access to Health Care

As noted in Chapter 1, the United States ranks 21st in infant mortality rate compared with other countries. For every thousand births each year in the United States, 9.1 infants die before they reach their first birthday. Many of these deaths are related to low birth weight and other prenatal factors.

PRENATAL CARE IN THE UNITED STATES

Prenatal care is widely accepted as an important element in improving pregnancy outcome. However, in the United States, not every woman obtains adequate prenatal care. Approximately 16 per cent of all American women have less than adequate prenatal care. This means that they fail to begin prenatal care before the fifth month of pregnancy or have less than half the 13 prenatal visits recommended by the American College of Obstetricians and Gynecologists (Witwer, 1990). The United States is the only industrialized nation except South Africa that does not provide free basic health care for pregnant women and children of all socioeconomic levels (Inglis, 1991b).

This lack of access to care is a major reason for the high infant mortality rate and the large number of low-birth-weight infants born each year in the United States. Adequate prenatal care could eliminate between two thirds and three quarters of all premature births (Thompson and Thompson, 1989). Because preterm infants form the largest category of those needing intensive care, millions of dollars could be saved each year by ensuring adequate prenatal care. Even a slight improvement in an infant's birth weight decreases complications of prematurity and time spent in the hospital.

Some of the factors that interfere with access to care are summarized in Table 3–3. Many of them overlap. For example, poverty is often associated with the other characteristics listed. Minority women are more likely to be poor, less likely to obtain adequate prenatal care, and more likely to die in childbirth when compared with Caucasian women in the United States. The percentage of teenagers giving birth is higher in the United States than in any other industrialized country (Inglis, 1991a).

In some situations, women can obtain prenatal care but choose not to do so. These include women who do not understand the importance of the care or who are in a state of denial of the pregnancy. Some women have had such unsatisfactory past experiences with the health care system that they avoid it as long as possible. Others want to hide substance use or other habits from disapproving health care workers. Language and cultural differences also play a part in whether or not a woman seeks prenatal care. Although these are not access issues as such, they must be addressed to improve health care.

Table 3–3. FACTORS RELATED TO LACK OF ACCESS TO HEALTH CARE

Poverty
Unemployment
Lack of medical insurance
Adolescent
Minority group
Inner city area
Rural area
Unmarried mother
Less than high school education
Inability to speak English

GOVERNMENT PROGRAMS FOR HEALTH CARE

Medicaid. More than 50 per cent of all money spent on health care is publicly funded (McCarron, 1991). One government program that increases access to health care is Medicaid, which has existed since 1965. Medicaid provides health care for the poor, aged, and disabled, with pregnant women and young children especially targeted. Medicaid is funded by both the federal and state governments. The states administer the program and determine which services are offered. Although all states provide a certain level of funding, there is great variation between them in just how poor one must be to qualify for assistance. To be eligible in many states, incomes must be less than half the federal poverty level (Brecht, 1989).

In addition to the variations in eligibility requirements, there are other problems with Medicaid. It often takes weeks for a client to go through the process to become eligible. The woman must fill out lengthy, complicated forms, provide documentation of income, then wait for determination of eligibility. If a woman is not already enrolled at the beginning of her pregnancy, she is unlikely to finish the process in time to receive early prenatal care.

Many physicians are unwilling to care for Medicaid clients who are likely to be at high risk. This is especially true when the reimbursement rate for physicians and hospitals may be as little as half the usual rate. With their continual concern about malpractice suits, physicians are less inclined to accept high-risk, low-paying clients.

Medicaid clients may receive care in clinics rather than from private physicians. However, clinics are often understaffed and attended by large numbers of clients. The clinic may not be located in an area easily accessible to a pregnant woman who has transportation problems. Long waits for appointments may necessitate taking time off from work. A mother may not have anyone to care for other children while she visits the clinic. These problems all decrease the chances that women who do not understand the importance of prenatal care will be willing to go through the difficulties involved in obtaining care.

Shelters and Health Care for the Homeless. Federal funding has provided assistance for homeless people with shelter and health care. Health care has been provided in clinics specifically for the homeless or by integrating them into other care settings. However, homeless people have the same difficulties as other poor people in obtaining essential health care. Lack of transportation, inconvenient hours, and lack of continuity of care continue to be problems.

Quality as well as quantity of care in clinics may be poor because of inadequate funding. There are too few health professionals to attend the numbers of people who need care. The homeless have serious medical and social problems that some nurses and physicians may not have experienced previously in caring for more affluent clients. Nurse practitioners often play a major role in these clinics. Nurses have also been instrumental in opening and staffing shelters, clinics, and outreach services. They help to inform the public and legislatures about the needs of the homeless.

Innovative Programs. Innovative programs to see that all women receive good prenatal care are necessary. Many different programs are available in various areas of the country, but there are not enough to meet the need. Some include outreach programs designed to improve health in women who traditionally do not seek prenatal care. Bilingual health care workers and bilingual educational classes are part of some programs. Many programs employ nurse practitioners and are located in schools, shopping centers, workplaces, or neighborhoods so that clients have easy access. More such programs will be necessary if adequate health care for women and children is to become a reality.

Allocation of Health Care Resources

In 1991, the United States spent $738 billion on health care. This figure is expected to double by the year 2000 to $1.5 trillion because of the rapid increase in health care costs (Greene, 1992). Methods of reforming health care financing have drawn increasing attention in recent times and major changes may occur in the near future. How to provide care for the poor, the uninsured or underinsured, and those with long-term care needs are some of the areas that must be addressed. The distribution of the limited funds available for health care among all the needs is a major concern.

CARE VERSUS CURE

One problem to be addressed is whether the focus of health care should be on preventive and caring measures or on cure of disease. Medicine has traditionally centered more on treatment and cure than on prevention and care. Yet prevention not only avoids suffering: it also is less expensive than treating diseases once they occur. However, it involves not only care of the healthy to prevent illness but also broader social issues, such as providing adequate food and housing for the poor.

The focus on cure has resulted in great technological advances (such as lung or kidney transplants) that have enabled some people to live longer, healthier lives. Conditions that were once invariably fatal are now treatable. However, technology is very expensive, and costs must be balanced against the benefits obtained when financial resources are limited. Indeed, the cost of one organ transplant would pay for prenatal care for more than 100 low-income mothers (Styles, 1990). Where the money should be spent to provide the greatest benefit is an issue.

Although low-birth-weight infants make up a small percentage of all infants born, they require a large percentage of total hospital expenditures (Swartz, 1989). The expenses of one preterm infant for a single day in an intensive care nursery are more than enough to pay for care of the mother throughout her pregnancy and delivery. Yet, if the mother had received prenatal care, the infant might not have needed intensive care.

In addition, "quality of life" issues are important in regard to technology. Neonatal nurseries are able to keep very-low-birth-weight babies alive because of advances in knowledge. Some of these infants go on to lead normal or near-normal lives, but others may gain quantity but not quality of life. Families and health care workers must face difficult decisions about when to treat, when to terminate treatment, and when suffering outweighs the benefits.

Neonatal intensive care units are among the most costly uses of the health care dollar. Although survival of low-birth-weight infants is very good, the overall infant mortality rate has not been favorably affected by high technology (Inglis, 1991b). This will happen only when prenatal care in the United States improves.

HEALTH CARE RATIONING

Although no one would advocate abandoning technological progress, modern technology has had a great impact on health care rationing. Some might argue that such rationing does not exist, but it does occur when some people have no access to care and there is not enough money for all people to share equally in the health technology available. Our advanced medical care often benefits only a small number of people, but at great cost.

Health care is also rationed when it is more freely given to those who have money to pay for it than to those who do not. For example, one study compared sick newborns of families with and without insurance. The infants of uninsured families experienced hospital stays an average of 2.5 days less and received fewer hospital services than newborns with similar conditions whose families were insured (Braveman et al, 1991).

Many questions will need answers in the years ahead as the costs of health care increase faster than the funds available. Is health care a fundamental right? Should a certain level of care be guaranteed to all citizens? What should that care entail? Should the cost of treatment and its effectiveness be considered when one is deciding what government or third-party payers will cover? Should those with private insurance have access to more advanced health care than those whose care is government-funded? Nurses will be instrumental in finding solutions to these vital questions.

✔ Check Your Reading

11. How do poverty and inadequate prenatal care affect infant mortality and morbidity?
12. How does a decision to spend money on technology sometimes conflict with issues of prevention?

Legal Issues

The legal foundation for the practice of nursing provides safeguards for health care and sets standards by which nurses can be evaluated. Nurses need to understand how the law applies specifically to them. When nurses do not meet the standards expected, they are at risk for being involved in legal action.

Safeguards for Health Care

Three categories of safeguards determine how the law views nursing practice: (1) nurse practice acts, (2) standards of care set by professional organizations, and (3) rules and policies set by the institution employing the nurse.

NURSE PRACTICE ACTS

Every state has a nurse practice act that determines the scope of practice of registered nurses in that state. Nurse practice acts define what the nurse is and is not allowed to do in caring for clients. Some parts of the law may be very specific; others are stated broadly enough to allow interpretation of the law that permits flexibility in the role of nurses. Nurse practice acts vary from one state to another, and nurses must be knowledgeable about these laws wherever they practice.

Laws relating to nursing practice also delineate methods, called *standardized procedures*, by which nurses may assume certain duties commonly consid-

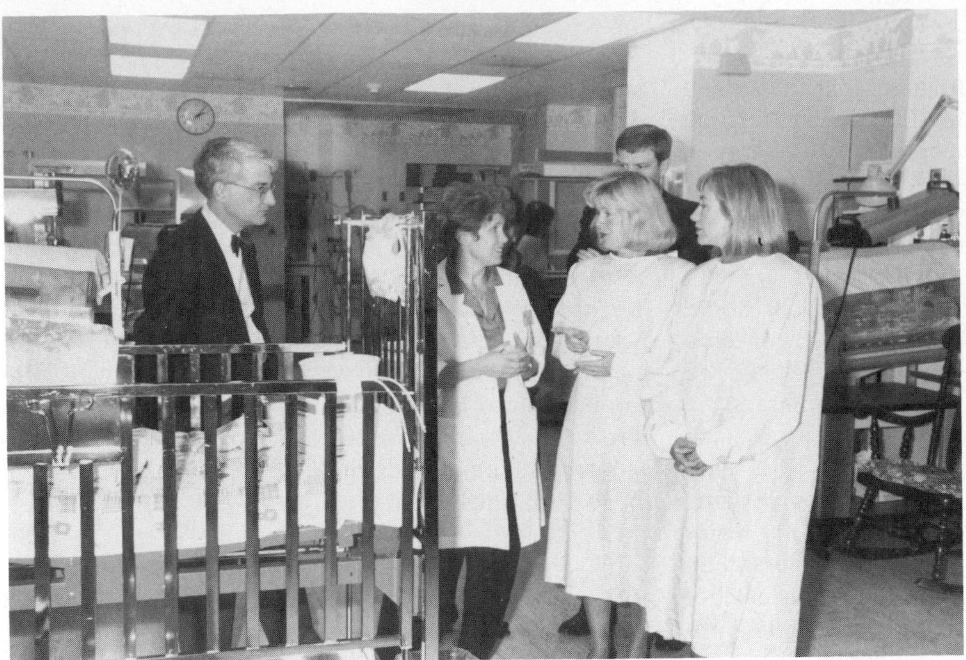

Government leaders recognize the important role that nurses play in the delivery of maternal and neonatal care. Here, Tipper Gore and Hillary Rodham Clinton visit the neonatal intensive care unit at the University of Colorado Health Sciences Center to learn about effects of prenatal care on the incidence of preterm birth. (Courtesy of Trish Beachy, M.S., R.N., Perinatal Program Coordinator, University of Colorado Health Sciences Center, Denver.)

ered part of medical practice. The procedures are written by committees of nurses, physicians, and administrators. They include specific instructions about which nurses are qualified to practice the procedure, in what situations, and the education required. Standardized procedures allow for changing the role of the nurse to meet the needs of the community and of expanding knowledge.

STANDARDS OF CARE

Although courts do not have the force of laws, they have generally held that nurses must practice according to established standards and hospital policies. Standards of care are set by professional associations and describe the level of care that can be expected from practitioners. For example, maternity nurses are held to the standards published by the Association of Women's Health, Obstetric and Neonatal Nurses (AWHONN), since it is a widely respected organization for nurses in this field. Formerly known as the Organization for Obstetric, Gynecologic, and Neonatal Nurses (NAACOG), AWHONN publishes national standards for nursing care as well as specific practice resources on subjects when a consistent minimum standard of care is desirable. These standards are based on research and the agreement of experts. (See Appendix A.)

AGENCY POLICIES

Each health care agency sets specific policies governing nursing care. Some policies apply to all nurses working for the agency; others apply only to those working on certain units or with certain types of clients. For example, policies for nurses working in labor and delivery units differ from those for nurses in neonatal intensive care units. All nurses should be familiar with the policies in the agencies in which they work. Nurses are frequently involved in writing nursing policies and in changing them when necessary.

Malpractice

Negligence is the failure to perform the way a reasonable, prudent person of similar background would act in a similar situation. Negligence may consist of doing something that should not be done or failing to do something that should be done.

Malpractice is negligence by professionals, such as nurses or physicians, in the performance of their duties. Nurses may be accused of malpractice if they do not perform according to established standards of care and in the manner of a reasonable, prudent nurse with similar education and experience.

Four elements must be present to prove negligence. See Critical to Remember: Elements of Negligence.

Prevention of Malpractice Claims

Malpractice claims have escalated in recent years. As a result of awards from such claims, malpractice in-

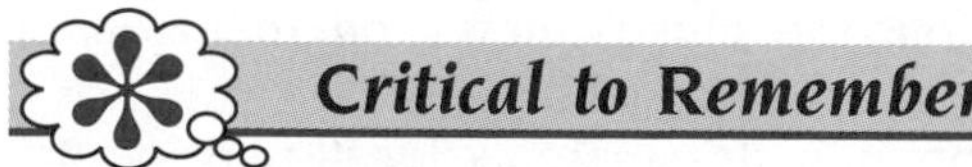

Critical to Remember

Elements of Negligence

Duty. The nurse must have a duty to act or give care to the client. It must be part of the nurse's responsibility.

Breach of duty. A violation of that duty must occur; the nurse fails to conform to established standards in performing that duty.

Proximate cause. It must be proved that the nurse's breach of duty is the cause of harm to the client.

Damage. There must be actual injury or harm to the client as a result of the nurse's breach of duty.

surance has risen for all health care workers. In addition, more health care workers practice defensively, accumulating evidence that they are acting in the client's best interest. Physicians may order more diagnostic tests, and nurses are careful to include detailed data when they chart. This is especially true in maternity care, since this is the area in which most suits occur.

Health care agencies and individual nurses have reason to try to prevent malpractice claims. Hospitals have paid millions of dollars for lawsuits claiming malpractice. Although nurses are not often sued, there has been an increase in the number of nurses named in lawsuits. Prevention of claims is sometimes referred to as "risk management" or "quality assurance." Nurses can help prevent malpractice claims by following guidelines for informed consent, refusal of care, and documentation and by maintaining their level of expertise.

INFORMED CONSENT

Informed consent is an ethical concept that has been enacted into law. Clients have the right to decide whether to accept or reject treatment options as part of their right to function autonomously. In order for them to decide wisely, clients need full information about the treatment offered.

Competence. Certain requirements must be met before consent can be considered "informed." The first is that the client be competent, or able to think through a situation and make rational decisions. A client who is comatose or severely mentally retarded or who is a newborn is incapable of making such decisions. A client who has been medicated with drugs that interfere with ability to think is temporarily incompetent. In these cases, another person would be appointed to make decisions for the client.

Full Disclosure. The second requirement is that of full disclosure of information, including what the treatment entails and the expected results. The risks, side effects, and benefits as well as other treatment options must be explained to clients. The client must also be informed as to what would happen if no treatment were chosen.

Understanding of Information. The client must comprehend information about proposed treatment. Health professionals must explain the facts in terms the person can understand. If a client does not speak English, an interpreter may be necessary. Nurses may find that a client does not fully understand a treatment or has questions about it. The nurse must be a client advocate in such cases. If it is a minor point, the nurse may be able to clarify; otherwise, the nurse must inform the physician so that the client's misconceptions can be clarified.

Voluntary Consent. Clients must be allowed to make choices voluntarily without undue influence or coercion from others. Although others can give information, the client alone makes the decision. Clients should not feel pressured to choose in a certain way or that their future care is dependent on their decision (NAACOG, 1987).

REFUSAL OF CARE

Sometimes clients decline treatment offered by health care workers. This may be as simple as refusing to take a bath, and no action would be required. Or it may be more serious, such as declining to take needed medication or to have surgery. Clients refuse treatment when they believe that the benefits of treatment are not sufficient to balance the burdens of the treatment or the life they will have after that treatment. Clients do have this right, and they can withdraw agreement to treatment at any time. When this occurs, a number of steps should be taken. Some of them involve the nurse, and some involve the physician.

First, it should be established by the physician or nurse that the client understands the treatment and the results of refusal. The physician, if unaware of the client's decision, should be notified by the nurse. The nurse documents the refusal, explanations given the client, and notification of the physician on the chart. If the treatment is considered vital to the client's well-being, the physician discusses the need with the client and documents the results. Opinions by other physicians may be offered to the client as well.

Clients may be asked to sign a form indicating that they understand the possible results of rejecting treatment. This is to prevent a later lawsuit in which a client claims lack of knowledge of the possible

Critical to Remember

Requirements of Informed Consent

- Client's competence to consent
- Full disclosure of information needed
- Client's understanding of information
- Client's voluntary consent

results of a decision. If there is no ethical dilemma, the client's decision stands.

If an ethical dilemma exists, a referral may be made to the hospital ethics committee. In rare situations, the physician may seek a court ruling to force treatment, for an example, when a woman's refusal of a cesarean birth is likely to cause grave harm to the fetus. However, this action is discouraged by the American College of Obstetricians and Gynecologists (ACOG), as it places the woman and her caregiver in adversarial positions.

Coercion is illegal (as well as unethical) in obtaining consent. Even though the nurse may strongly believe that the client should receive the treatment, the client should not feel forced to submit to unwanted procedures. Nurses must be sure that personal feelings do not adversely affect the care they give. Clients have the right to good nursing care, regardless of their decision to accept or reject treatment.

DOCUMENTATION

Documentation is the best evidence that a standard of care has been maintained. All information recorded about a client should reflect that standard of care. This includes not only nurses' notes but also fetal monitoring strips, flow sheets, nursing care plans, and any other data recorded in the chart. In many instances, notations on hospital records, such as the chart or fetal monitor strip, are the only proof that care has been given. When documentation is not present, juries tend to assume that care has not been given. Statutes of limitations vary in different states. However, in regard to newborns, more than 20 years could elapse before a suit is brought. Charting must be specific enough so that nurses do not have to rely on memory.

Fetal monitor strips are important sources of information about the mother and fetus during labor and delivery. Nurses record a great deal of information about nursing care on the monitor strip. Sometimes the client requires the nurse's full attention and completion of charting must be temporarily delayed. In this situation, the nurse's notes on the monitor strip provide the basis for later charting.

Although monitor strips are a legal part of the chart, they may become lost. This makes it particularly important that all information from the strip be recorded in the nurse's notes. Complete, detailed charting ensures that the nurse's actions will be clear many years later in a court of law even without the monitor strip.

Another form of documentation is the *incident report*, sometimes called a "quality assurance report" or an "unusual occurrence report." The nurse completes a report whenever something has occurred that might result in injury to a client. The report warns the hospital legal department that there may be a problem. The incident report also provides a way of keeping track of situations that might endanger clients in the future. Finding a remedy to such a situation can prevent future problems. Incident reports are not a part of the client's chart and should not be referred to on the chart. When an incident occurs, documentation on the chart should include the same type of factual information on the client's condition that would be recorded in any other situation.

CONTINUING EDUCATION

It is the duty of nurses to maintain their knowledge and skills at the level necessary to ensure their ability to give safe care. Two ways to ensure that nurses are performing in the way a reasonably prudent peer would perform include attending classes or conferences and reading nursing journals. These activities serve to update nurses and keep them abreast of new developments. Most states require proof of continuing education for renewal of nursing licenses.

Employers often provide continuing education classes for their nurses. There are also many workshops and seminars available on a wide variety of nursing subjects. Membership in a professional nursing organization, such as state branches of the American Nurses' Association, and in a specialty organization, like AWHONN, gives nurses access to new information through publications as well as educational offerings.

THE NURSE AS CLIENT ADVOCATE

Nurses are ethically and legally bound to act as the client's advocate. This means that the nurse must act in the client's best interests at all times. When nurses feel that the client's best interests are not being served, they are obligated to seek help for the patient from appropriate sources. This usually involves taking the problem through the normal chain of command. The nurse consults a supervisor and the client's physician. If the results are not satisfactory, the nurse continues through administrative channels to the director of nurses and the chief of the medical staff, if necessary.

In seeking help for clients, nurses must document their efforts. For example, when postpartum patients are experiencing excessive bleeding, nurses document what they have done to control the bleeding; they document each time they call the physician, what information was given the physician, and the response received. When nurses cannot contact the physician or do not receive adequate instructions, they should document their efforts to seek instruction from others, such as the supervisor. They should also complete an incident report.

✔ Check Your Reading

13. How do standards of care and agency policies, which are not laws, influence judgments about malpractice?
14. What is the difference between negligence and malpractice?
15. How can nurses help to prevent malpractice claims?

Summary Concepts

- Ethical dilemmas are a difficult area for nurses and are best solved by applying ethical theories and principles as well as the steps of the nursing process.
- When ethical principles of beneficience, non-malefience, autonomy, and justice result in ethical dilemmas, nursing process may be used to guide ethical decision making.
- Elective abortion is a controversial issue that generates strong feelings in two opposing factions in the United States and has resulted in several decisions by the Supreme Court that limit or uphold the right of states to impose restrictions on abortion.
- Nurses must examine their beliefs and come to a personal decision about abortion before they are faced with the situation in their own practice.
- Punitive approaches to ethical and social problems may prevent women from seeking adequate prenatal care.
- Issues in fetal therapy include weighing the risks and benefits for the mother versus those for the fetus and determining whose rights should prevail.
- Poverty is a major social issue that leads to questions about allocation of health resources, access to prenatal care, government programs to increase health care to indigent women and children, and health care rationing.
- Issues in infertility concern the high cost and low success rate of some treatments, the fate of unused embryos and multiple fetuses, and the rights of surrogate parents.
- Nurses are expected to perform in accordance with nurse practice acts, standards of care, and agency policies to provide expected care and to avoid malpractice claims.
- Nurses can help to prevent malpractice claims by following guidelines for informed consent, refusal of care, and documentation and by maintaining their level of expertise.
- To give informed consent, the client must be competent, must receive full information, must understand that information, and must consent voluntarily.
- Documentation is the best evidence of the standard of care received by a client. Therefore, nurses must ensure that their documentation accurately reflects the care given.

References and Readings

American Academy of Pediatrics Committee on Bioethics (1988). Fetal therapy: Ethical considerations. Pediatrics, 81(6), 898–899.

American Medical Association Board of Trustees (1992). Requirements or incentives by government for the use of long-acting contraceptives. *Journal of the American Medical Association*, 267(13), 1818–1821.

Blum, R.W., Resnick, M.D., & Stark, T. (1990). Factors associated with the use of court bypass by minors to abortions. *Family Planning Perspectives*, 22(4), 158–160.

Braveman, P.A., Egerter, S., Bennett, T., & Showstack, J. (1991). Differences in hospital resource allocation among sick newborns according to insurance coverage. *Journal of the American Medical Association*, 266(23), 3300–3308.

Brecht, M.C. (1989). The tragedy of infant mortality. *Nursing Outlook*, 37(1), 18–22.

Bushy, A., Rauh, J.R., & Matt, B.F. (1989). Ethical principles: Application to an obstetric case. *Journal of Obstetric, Gynecologic, and Neonatal Nursing*, 18(3), 207–212.

Doblin, B.H., Gelberg, L., & Freeman, H.E. (1992). Patient care and professional staffing patterns in McKinney Act clinics providing primary care to the homeless. *Journal of the American Medical Association*, 267(5), 698–701.

Donley, R. (1991). Forging connections: The consumer connection. *Maternal-Child Nursing Journal*, 16, 299–304.

Erlen, J.A. (1989). Anencephalic infants as sources of organs. *Journal of Obstetric, Gynecologic, and Neonatal Nursing*, 19(3), 249–253.

Field, M.A. (1989). Controlling the woman to protect the fetus. *Law, Medicine and Health Care*, 17(2), 114–129.

Grady, C. (1989). Ethical issues in providing care to human immunodeficiency virus-infected populations. In Fry, S.T. (Ed.); Issues in nursing. *Nursing Clinics of North America*, 24(2), 523–535.

Greenberger, M.D. & Connor, K. (1991). Parental notice and consent: Out of step with family law principles and policies. *Family Planning Perspectives*, 23(1), 31–35.

Greene, J. (1992, March 9). Systems geared up for coming reforms. *Modern Healthcare*, 22(10), 24–28.

Greenlaw, J.L. (1990). Treatment refusal, noncompliance, and substance abuse in pregnancy: Legal and ethical issues. *Birth* 17(3), 152–156.

Henshaw, S.K. (1992). Abortion trends in 1987 and 1988: Age and race. *Family Planning Perspectives*, 24(2), 85–86.

Infant mortality—United States, 1989. (1992). *Journal of the American Medical Association*, 267(9), 1182–1183.

Inglis, A.D. (1991a). United States maternal and child health services. I. Right or privilege? *Neonatal Network*, 9(8), 35–43.

Inglis, A.D. (1991b). United States maternal and child health services. II. A comparison with Western Europe and strategies for change. *Neonatal Network*, 10(1), 7–13.

Longaker, M.T., Golbus, M.S., Filly, R.A., Rosen, M.A., Chang, S.W., & Harrison, M.R. (1991). Maternal outcome after open fetal surgery. *Journal of the American Medical Association*, 265(6), 737–741.

McCarron, L. (1991). Equal access to health care: Ethical issues in determining public policy. *Journal of Professional Nursing*, 7(2), 71.

Murphy, P. (1989). The role of the nurse on hospital ethics committees. In Fry, S.T. (Ed.)., Issues in nursing. *Nursing Clinics of North America*, 24(2), 551–556.

NAACOG (1987). *Ethical Decision Making in Obstetric, Gynecologic and Neonatal Nursing Practice*. Washington, D.C.

NAACOG (1991). *Standards for the Nursing Care of Women and Newborns* (4th ed.). Washington, D.C.

Opposition to the criminal prosecution (1992). Birth, 19(1), 43.

Rafferty, M. (1989a). How nurses are helping the homeless. *American Journal of Nursing*, 89(12), 1618–1619.

Rafferty, M. (1989b). Standing up for America's homeless. *American Journal of Nursing*, 89(12), 1614–1617.

Rhodes, A.M. (1992). Criminal penalties for maternal substance abuse. *Maternal-Child Nursing Journal*, 17(1), 11.

Rhodes, A.M. (1990a). Legal alternatives for fetal injury. *Maternal-Child Nursing Journal*, 15(2), 111.

Rhodes, A.M. (1990b). Maternal liability for fetal injury? *Maternal-Child Nursing Journal*, 15(1), 41.

Rhodes, A.M. (1991). Norplant and the "coerced conception" controversy. *Maternal-Child Nursing Journal*, 16(5), 277.

Shearer, M.H. (1988). Some effects of assisted reproduction on perinatal care. *Birth*, 15(3), 131–133.

Stone, R., & Waszak (1992). Adolescent knowledge and attitudes about abortion. *Family Planning Perspectives*, 24(2), 52–58.

Styles, M.M. (1990). Challenges for nursing in this new decade. *Maternal-Child Nursing Journal*, 15(6), 347–352.

Swartz, R.M. (1989). What price prematurity? *Family Planning Perspectives*, 21(4), 170–174.

Thompson, J.E., & Thompson, H.O. (1991). Ethical decision making: Process and models. *Neonatal Network*, 9(1), 69–70.

Thompson, J.E., & Thompson, H.O. (1989). Let's be practical. *Neonatal Network*, 7(6), 84–85.

Weitzman, B.C. (1989). Pregnancy and childbirth: Risk factors for homelessness? *Family Planning Perspectives*, 21(4), 175–178.

Witwer, M.B. (1990). Prenatal care in the United States: Reports call for improvements in quality and accessibility. *Family Planning Perspectives*, 22(1), 31–35.

4

Reproductive Anatomy and Physiology

Objectives

1. Explain female and male sexual development from prenatal life through sexual maturation.
2. Describe normal anatomy of the female and male reproductive systems.
3. Explain normal function of the female and male reproductive systems.
4. Explain normal structure and function of the female breast.

Definitions

Amenorrhea • Absence of menstruation. **Primary amenorrhea** is a delay of the first menstruation. **Secondary amenorrhea** is cessation of menstruation after its initiation.

Cilia • Hair-like processes on the surface of a cell. Cilia beat rhythmically to move the cell or to move fluid or other substances over the cell surface.

Climacteric • Endocrine, body, and psychic changes occurring at the end of a woman's reproductive period. Also informally called **menopause.**

Coitus • Sexual union between a male and a female.

Fornix (pl. fornices) • An arch or pouch-like structure at the upper end of the vagina. Also called a **cul-de-sac**.

Gamete • Reproductive cell. The female gamete is an **ovum**; the male gamete is a **spermatozoon.**

Genetic sex • Sex determined at conception by union of two X chromosomes (female) or an X and a Y chromosome (male). Also called **chromosomal sex**.

Gonad • Reproductive (sex) gland that produces gametes and sex hormones. The female gonads are **ovaries**; the male gonads are **testes**.

Gonadotropic hormones • Secretions of the anterior pituitary gland that stimulate the gonads, specifically follicle-stimulating hormone (FSH) and luteinizing hormone (LH). Chorionic gonadotropin is secreted by the placenta during pregnancy.

Graafian follicle • A small sac within the ovary that contains the maturing ovum.

Menarche • Onset of menstruation; average age is 12.8 years.

Menopause • Permanent cessation of menstruation during the climacteric.

Puberty • Period of sexual maturation accompanied by development of secondary sex characteristics and the capacity to reproduce.

Ruga (pl. rugae) • Ridge or fold of tissue, as on the male's scrotum and in the female's vagina.

Secondary sex characteristics • Physical differences between mature males and females that are not directly related to reproduction.

Somatic sex • Gender assignment as male or female on the basis of form and structure of the external genitalia.

Spermatogenesis • Formation of male **gametes** (sperm) in the testes.

Spinnbarkeit • Clear, slippery, stretchy quality of cervical mucus during ovulation.

To understand women's health care and normal childbearing, the nurse needs to know the female and male reproductive organs. This chapter reviews basic prenatal development, sexual maturation, and structure and function of the female and male reproductive systems. Because of its emphasis in this book, the female reproductive system is discussed more extensively.

Sexual Development

Sexual development begins at conception with determination of the child's genetic sex. During childhood, the sex organs are quiescent, but they become active during puberty to bring about sexual maturation.

Prenatal Development

When the ovum is fertilized by a spermatozoon at conception, the genetic sex of the fetus is determined. The mother's ovum carries a single X chromosome. The father's sperm carries either an X chromosome or a Y chromosome. If an X-bearing spermatozoon fertilizes the ovum, the child's genetic sex is female. If a Y-bearing spermatozoon fertilizes the ovum, a male offspring results.

Although the genetic sex of the fetus is determined at the moment of conception, the reproductive system of both males and females is similar, or sexually undifferentiated, for the first 6 weeks of prenatal life. During the 7th week, differences between males and females begin to appear.

The basic tendency for prenatal sexual development is to be female. The presence of a Y chromosome changes this pattern and directs the primitive sex cells to become testes and to produce testosterone. The absence of a Y chromosome causes the primitive sex cells to continue on their course of becoming ovaries. Prenatal development of the reproductive organs is detailed in Chapter 6.

During fetal life, both ovaries and testes actively secrete their primary hormones, estrogen and testosterone, respectively. Estrogen causes development of female internal sex organs and external genitalia; testosterone causes development of male sex organs and external genitalia.

Childhood

The sex glands of both girls and boys are quiet during infancy and childhood and do not produce significant amounts of sex hormones. The child's gonads are capable of producing sex hormones and forming gametes if the proper stimulus is present. However, the child's immature hypothalamus does not normally secrete adequate amounts of stimulating hormones to cause sexual development until puberty. Secretion of even tiny quantities of sex hormones before puberty is enough to suppress the hypothalamus from stimulating sexual development.

Sexual Maturation

Puberty refers to the time during which the reproductive organs become fully functional. It is not a single event, but a series of changes occurring over several years during late childhood and early adolescence. Primary sex characteristics develop as the organs directly responsible for reproduction mature. Examples of primary sex characteristics are maturation of ova in the ovaries and production of sperm in the testes. Secondary sex characteristics are changes in other systems that differentiate females and males. Table 4–1 cites examples of female and male secondary sex characteristics.

Table 4–1. COMPARISON OF SECONDARY SEX CHARACTERISTICS IN MALES AND FEMALES

Females	Males
Development of glandular and ductal systems in the breast; deposition of fat selectively in the breast, buttocks and thighs, resulting in a rounded figure	Muscle mass 50% greater
Wide, round pelvis	Narrow, upright, and heavier pelvis
Pubic and axillary hair	Pubic and axillary hair; facial and chest hair; increased amount of hair on upper back in some males; male-pattern baldness, beginning on top of head
Soft, smooth skin texture	Coarser skin
Higher-pitched voice	Deeper voice

INITIATION OF SEXUAL MATURATION

The exact factors that initiate sexual maturation are not known. Hormones secreted in the hypothalamus, the anterior pituitary, and the gonads all play a part. The hypothalamus is capable of secreting hormones that initiate puberty even during infancy and childhood, but it does not do so until late childhood (at about 10 years of age). Maturation of another brain area, as yet unknown, probably triggers the hypothalamus to initiate puberty (Guyton, 1991).

The maturing child's hypothalamus gradually becomes less sensitive to negative feedback of sex hormones and secretes increasing quantities of gonadotropin-releasing hormone (GnRH). GnRH is transported to the anterior pituitary via the hypophyseal portal system, where GnRH stimulates the anterior pituitary to secrete two gonadotropic hormones: (1) follicle-stimulating hormone (FSH), and (2) luteinizing hormone (LH). The target glands of FSH and LH are the female ovaries and male testes, where they influence development of gametes and secretion of sex hormones. The sex hormones, in turn, induce development of primary and secondary sex characteristics. Table 4–2 presents the major hormones that play a role in reproduction.

The age at which puberty begins varies among individuals and in different geographical areas. Nutritional state can also determine when puberty begins, occurring earlier when the child is well nourished. Girls begin puberty about 6 months earlier than boys, although the early growth spurt in girls makes it seem that she begins puberty about 2 years before the boy (Kreipe and McAnarney, 1990). Changes of puberty occur in an orderly sequence in both sexes, regardless of the age when puberty begins. Girls complete puberty changes in about 3 years; males complete them in about 4 years.

FEMALE PUBERTY CHANGES

Puberty begins at about 9 to 10 years in girls, as the anterior pituitary gland secretes increasing amounts of FSH and LH. These two pituitary secretions stimulate secretion of estrogens and progesterone by the ovary, which cause maturation of the reproductive organs and breasts and development of secondary sex characteristics. The first menstrual period (menarche) marks the most obvious change and occurs rather late in puberty, when the girl is about 13 years old in the United States (Buyalos, 1992, p. 511; Guyton, 1991).

Breast Changes. The earliest outward changes of puberty occur in the breasts. First, the nipple enlarges and protrudes. The areola surrounding the nipple enlarges and becomes somewhat protuberant, although less so than the nipple. These changes are followed by growth of the ductal and glandular tissue. Fat is deposited in the breasts to give them the characteristic rounded female appearance. During puberty, it is not unusual for a girl's breasts to develop at different rates, resulting in a lopsided appearance until one catches up with the other.

Body Contours. The pelvis widens and assumes a rounded, basin-like shape that is favorable for passage of the fetus during childbirth. Fat is deposited selectively in the hips, giving them a rounder appearance than that of the male.

Body Hair. Pubic hair appears, downy at first, but becoming thicker as puberty progresses. Axillary hair appears near the time of menarche. The texture and quantity of pubic and axillary hair vary among women and in different ethnic groups. Women of African descent usually have body hair that is coarser and curlier than that of Caucasian women. Asian women often have sparser body hair than women of other racial groups.

Skeletal Growth. A girl's adolescent growth spurt occurs at about the same time as breast development and pubic hair growth. As the ovaries secrete estrogen, girls grow rapidly in height for several years during early puberty. However, estrogen also causes the epiphyses (growth areas of the bone) to unite with the shaft of the long bones, limiting mature height. The height-limiting effect of estrogen is stronger than the similar effect of testosterone in the male.

Reproductive Organs. The girl's external genitalia enlarge as fat is deposited in the mons pubic, labia majora, and labia minora. The vagina, uterus, fallopian tubes, and ovaries increase in size. Additionally, her vaginal mucosa becomes more resistant to trauma and infection in preparation for sexual activity. Cyclic changes in her reproductive organs occur during each female reproductive cycle (see p. 60).

Menarche. Two to three years after a girl's breasts begin developing, she experiences her first menstrual period. Early menstrual periods are often irregular and scant. These early menstrual cycles are not usually fertile because ovulation occurs inconsistently. Fertile reproductive cycles require preparation of the uterine lining precisely timed with ovulation. However, ovulation may occur during any female reproductive cycle, including the first. The sexually active girl can conceive even before her first menstrual period.

Onset of menstruation may be delayed (*primary amenorrhea*) or may stop after it begins (*secondary amenorrhea*) in females who are extremely thin and have a low percentage (under 16 per cent) of body fat. Girls and women who are competitive athletes or

Table 4–2. MAJOR HORMONES IN REPRODUCTION

Produced by	Target Organs	Action in Female	Action in Male
Gonadotropin-Releasing Hormone (GnRH)			
Hypothalamus	Anterior pituitary	Stimulates release of FSH and LH, initiating puberty and sustaining female reproductive cycles; release is cyclic in female	Same as female, except that release is relatively constant
Follicle-Stimulating Hormone (FSH)			
Anterior pituitary	Ovaries (female) Testes (male)	1. Stimulates production of estrogens, progesterone 2. Stimulates growth and maturation of graafian follicles before ovulation	Stimulates sperm formation in testes
Luteinizing Hormone (LH)			
Anterior pituitary	Ovaries (female) Testes (male)	1. Stimulates final maturation of follicle 2. Surge of LH about 14 days before next expected menstrual period causes ovulation 3. Stimulates transformation of graafian follicle into corpus luteum, which continues secretion of estrogens and progesterone for about 12 days if ovum is not fertilized. If fertilization occurs, placenta gradually assumes this function	Stimulates Leydig cells of testes to secrete testosterone
Estrogens			
1. Ovaries and corpus luteum (female) 2. Placenta (pregnancy) 3. Formed in small quantities from testosterone in Sertoli cells of testes (male)	Female: Internal and external reproductive organs; breasts Male: Testes	1. Reproductive organs a. Maturation at puberty b. Stimulation of endometrium prior to ovulation 2. Breasts: Induces growth of glandular and ductal tissue; initiates deposition of fat at puberty 3. Stimulates growth of long bones, but causes closure of epiphyses, limiting mature height 4. Pregnancy: Stimulates growth of uterus, breast tissue; inhibits active milk production	Necessary for normal sperm formation

ballet dancers or who suffer from eating disorders (such as anorexia nervosa or bulimia) may have too little fat to produce enough sex hormones to stimulate ovulation and menstruation.

MALE PUBERTY CHANGES

Puberty in the male begins at approximately age 11 to 16 years. FSH and LH from the anterior pituitary enable spermatogenesis and secretion of testosterone in the male. Testosterone stimulates development of a boy's reproductive organs and secondary sex characteristics.

Growth of the Testes and Penis. The first observable evidence of male sexual maturation is growth of the testes. Growth and lengthening of the penis follow about a year after testicular growth begins.

Nocturnal Emissions. Often called "wet dreams" by the adolescent, nocturnal emissions commonly occur during the teens. The boy experiences a spon-

Table 4–2. MAJOR HORMONES IN REPRODUCTION *Continued*

Produced by	Target Organs	Action in Female	Action in Male
		Progesterone	
Ovary, corpus luteum, placenta	Uterus, breasts	1. Stimulates secretion of endometrial glands; causes endometrial vessels to become highly dilated and tortuous in preparation for possible embryo implantation 2. Pregnancy: Induces growth of cells of uterine lining to nourish embryo; decreases contractions of uterus; prepares breasts for lactation	Not applicable
		Prolactin	
Anterior pituitary	Female breasts	Stimulates secretion of milk (lactogenesis); estrogen and progesterone from placenta have an inhibiting effect on milk production until after placenta is expelled at birth; suckling of newborn stimulates prolactin secretion to maintain milk production	Not applicable
		Oxytocin	
Posterior pituitary	Uterus, female breast	1. Uterus: stimulates contractions during birth and stimulates postpartum contractions to compress uterine vessels 2. Stimulates let-down, or milk-ejection reflex during lactation	Not applicable
		Testosterone	
Testes (male) Adrenal glands (female)	Sexual organs (male) Male body conformation after puberty	Small quantities of androgenic (masculinizing) hormones from adrenal glands cause growth of pubic and axillary hair at puberty	1. Induces development of male sex organs in fetus 2. Induces growth and division of the cells that form sperm 3. Induces development of male secondary sex characteristics

taneous ejaculation of seminal fluid during sleep, often accompanied by dreams with sexual content. It is important to prepare boys for this normal occurrence so that they do not feel abnormal.

Body Hair. As in the female, pubic hair is the first to grow, beginning at the base of the penis. Gradually, the hair coarsens and growth spreads upward and in the midline of the abdomen. In about 2 years, axillary hair appears. Facial hair begins as a fine, downy mustache and progresses to the characteristic beard of the adult male. In most boys, chest hair develops, and some boys have increased hair on their upper backs. The amount and character of body hair vary among men of different racial groups, with Asian and Native American men often having less than Caucasian or African men. There is substantial variation in the quantity and character of body hair among men of the same racial group as well.

Body Composition. Under the influence of testosterone, the male develops a greater average muscle mass than the female. At maturity, the man's muscle mass exceeds the woman's by 50 per cent. This explains why a man has a biological advantage over a woman in tasks that require great muscle strength.

Skeletal Growth. Testosterone causes boys to undergo a rapid growth spurt, especially in height. A boy's linear growth begins about a year later than a girl's and lasts for a longer time. Testosterone also causes the epiphyses of the long bones to unite with their shafts. However, the effect of testosterone is not as strong as that of estrogen in females, so boys grow in stature for several years longer than do females. The male's greater height at maturity is the combined result of beginning the growth spurt at a later age and continuing it for a longer time.

A boy's shoulders broaden as his height increases. His pelvis assumes a more upright shape, with narrower diameters and heavier composition than the female's. A man's pelvis is structurally suited for tasks requiring load bearing.

Voice Changes. Hypertrophy of the laryngeal mucosa and enlargement of the larynx cause the male's voice to deepen. Prior to reaching its bass tones at maturity, many boys experience an embarrassing "cracking" or "squeaking" of their voice when they speak.

Decline in Fertility

A marked difference exists between the decline in fertility for women and for men. A woman's ability to reproduce gradually decreases over a period of years called the climacteric. In most women, the climacteric occurs between the ages of 45 and 50. At this time, maturation of ova and production of ovarian hormones slowly decline. The external and internal reproductive organs atrophy somewhat as well. Menstruation ceases, and menopause is the term used to describe the final menstrual period. However, "menopause" and "climacteric" are often used interchangeably to describe the entire gradual process of change.

Males do not experience a distinct marker event like menopause. Their production of testosterone and sperm gradually declines, but men in their 50s, 60s, and beyond may still be able to father children.

✔ Check Your Reading

1. What are the first noticeable changes of puberty in girls and in boys?
2. What are common differences in body hair characteristics among mature people of different races?
3. What are basic differences between the mature male and female pelves?
4. Why do males generally attain greater height than females?
5. What are common male and female secondary sex characteristics?

Female Reproductive Anatomy

The nurse needs a basic knowledge of the structure and function of the external and internal reproductive organs to understand their role in pregnancy and childbirth. The functions of the female reproductive and accessory organs are summarized in Table 4–3.

Table 4–3. FUNCTIONS OF FEMALE REPRODUCTIVE AND ACCESSORY ORGANS

Organ	Function
Vagina	1. Female organ for coitus: receives male penis. 2. Passageway for the menstrual flow and for the fetus during birth.
Uterus	Houses and nourishes fetus until sufficiently mature to function outside the mother's body; uterine muscle propels fetus to outside.
Fallopian tube	1. Provides passageway for ovum as it travels from ovary to uterus. 2. Site of fertilization.
Ovaries	1. Endocrine glands that secrete estrogens and progesterone. 2. Contain ova within follicles for maturation during the woman's reproductive life.
Breasts	
Alveoli	Acinar cells within alveoli secrete milk after childbirth.
Lactiferous ducts and sinuses	Collect milk from alveoli and conduct it to the outside.

External Female Reproductive Organs

Collectively, the external female reproductive organs are called the *vulva.* These structures include the mons pubis, labia majora and minora, clitoris, structures of the vestibule, and perineum (Fig. 4–1).

MONS PUBIS

The mons pubis is the rounded, fleshy prominence over the symphysis pubis that forms the anterior border of the external reproductive organs. It is covered with varying amounts of pubic hair.

LABIA MAJORA AND LABIA MINORA

The labia majora are two rounded, fleshy folds of tissue that extend from the mons pubis to the perineum. They have slightly deeper pigmentation than surrounding skin and are covered with pubic hair.

The labia minora run parallel to and within the labia majora. The labia minora extend from the clitoris anteriorly and merge posteriorly to form the fourchette, or posterior rim of the vaginal introitus, or opening. The labia minora do not have pubic hair.

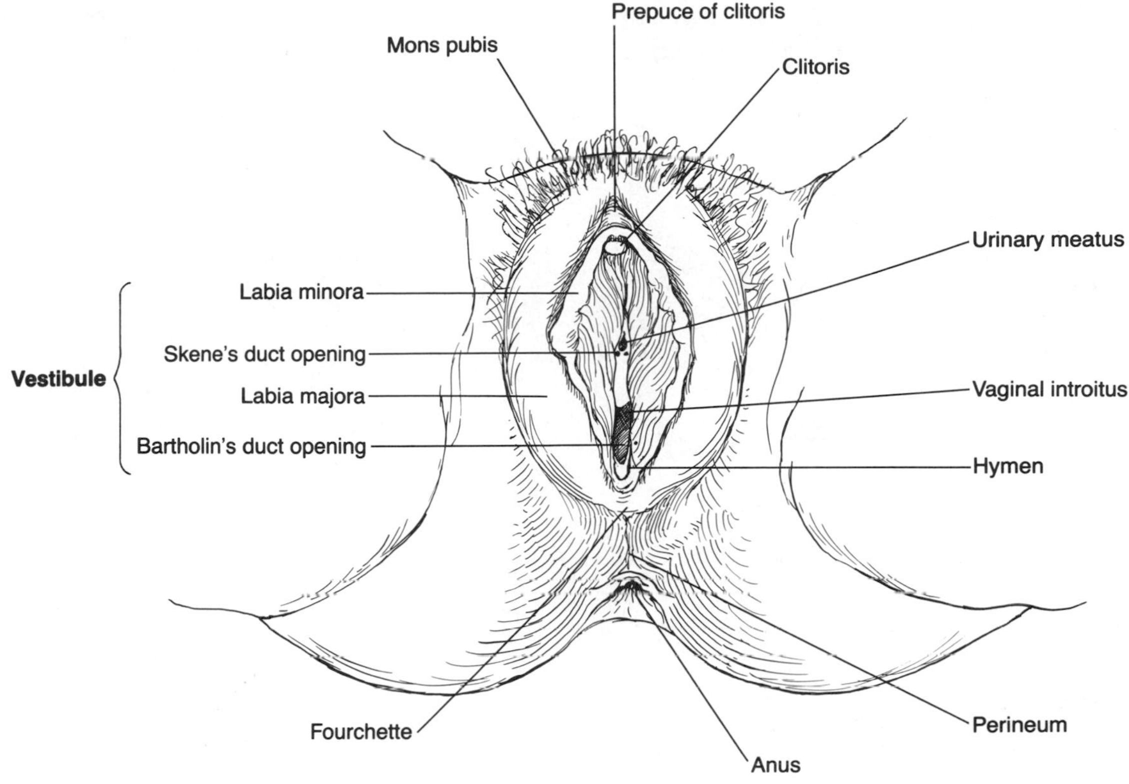

Figure 4–1

External female reproductive structures.

CLITORIS

The clitoris is a small projection at the anterior junction of the two labia minora. This structure is composed of highly sensitive erectile tissue that is similar to that of the male penis.

VESTIBULE

The vestibule refers to structures enclosed by the labia minora. The urinary meatus, vaginal introitus, and the ducts of Skene's and Bartholin's glands lie within the vestibule. Skene's, or periurethral, glands provide lubrication for the urethra. Bartholin's glands provide lubrication for the vaginal introitus, particularly during sexual arousal.

The vaginal introitus is surrounded by erectile tissue. During sexual stimulation, blood flows into the erectile tissue, allowing the introitus to tighten around the penis. This adds a massaging feeling that heightens the male's sexual sensations, encouraging release of semen.

The hymen is a thin fold of mucosa closing the vagina from the vestibule to various degrees. Neither the presence nor absence of the hymen is a criterion of virginity. The intact hymen may be broken with injury, with the use of tampons, and during intercourse or childbirth.

PERINEUM

The perineum is the most posterior part of the external female reproductive organs. The perineum extends from the fourchette anteriorly to the anus posteriorly. It is composed of fibrous and muscular tissues that provide support for pelvic structures. The perineum may be lacerated during childbirth, or it may be incised to enlarge the vaginal opening in a procedure called *episiotomy*.

Internal Female Reproductive Organs

The internal reproductive structures are the vagina, uterus, fallopian tubes, and ovaries (Figs. 4–2 and 4–3). These organs are supported and contained within the bony pelvis (see p. 59).

VAGINA

The vagina is a tube of muscular and membranous tissue about 8 to 10 cm long, lying between the bladder anteriorly and the rectum posteriorly. The vagina connects the uterus above with the vestibule below. The vaginal lining has multiple folds, or rugae, and a muscular layer that are capable of marked distention during childbirth. The vagina is

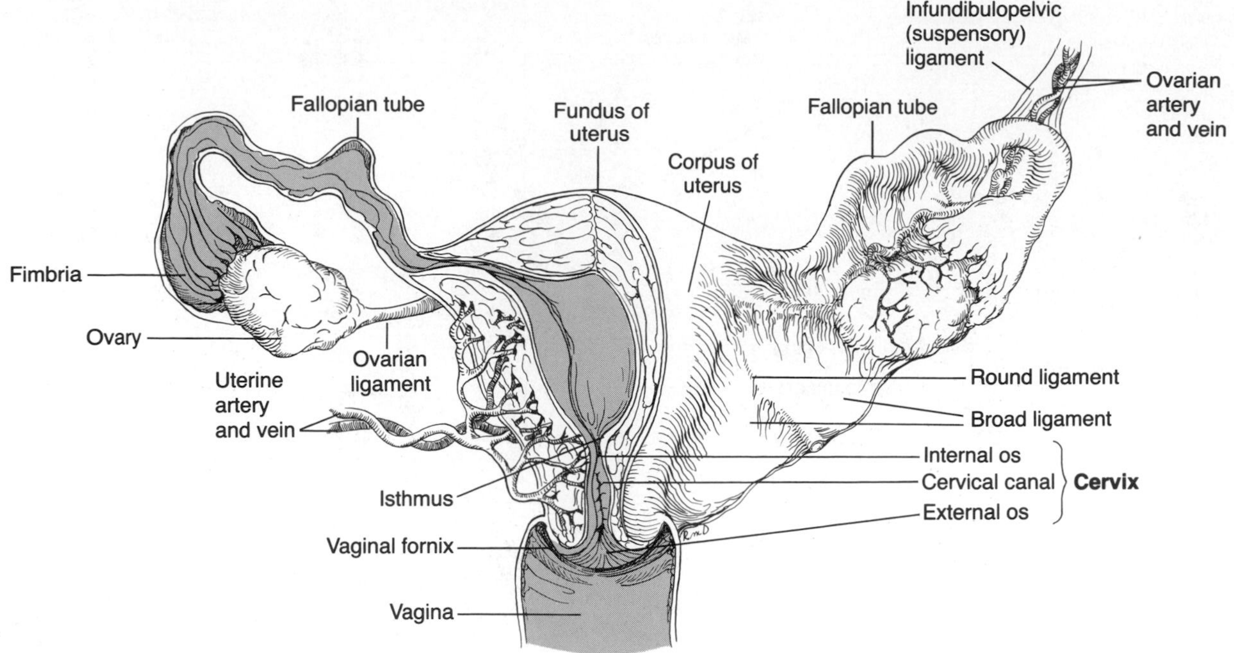

Figure 4–2

Internal female reproductive structures, anterior view.

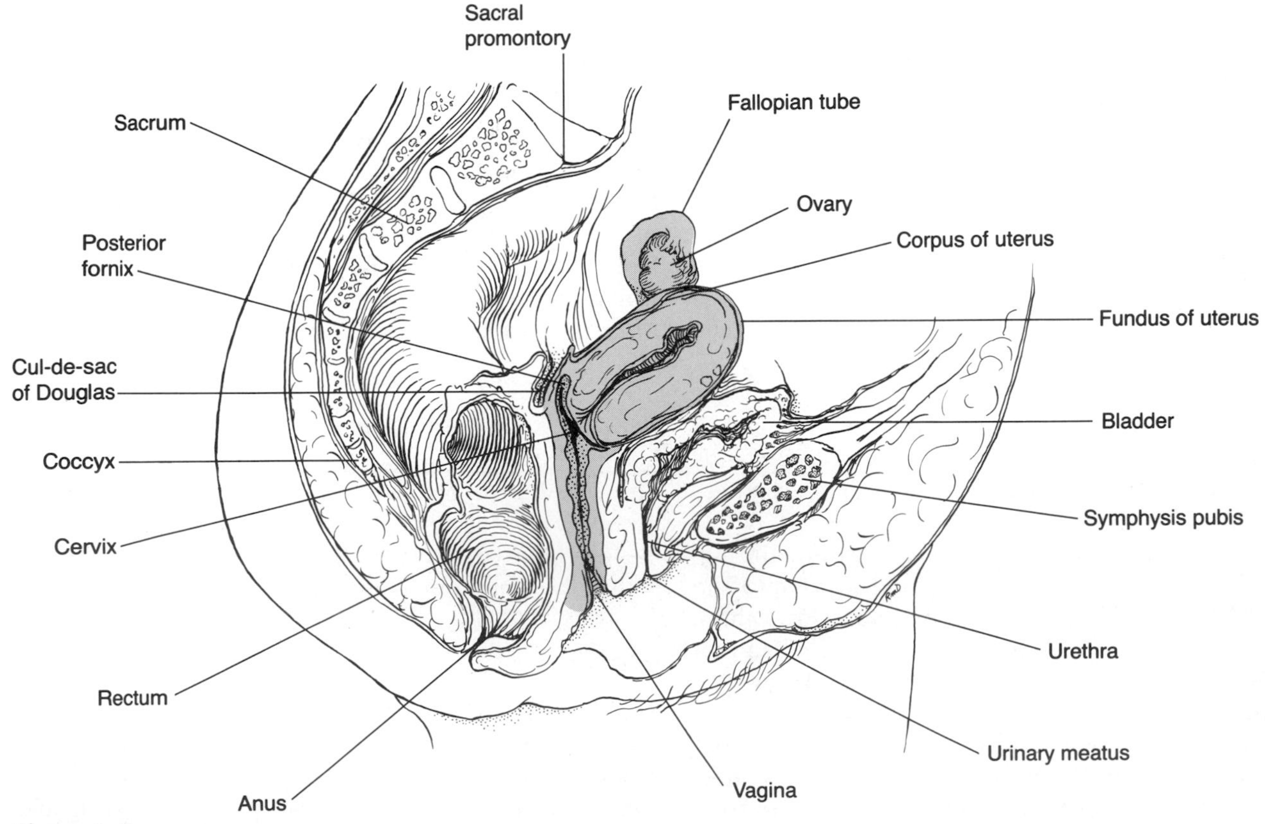

Figure 4–3

Internal female reproductive structures, mid-sagittal view.

lubricated by secretions of the cervix, the lowermost part of the uterus.

The vagina does not end abruptly at the uterine opening but arches to form a pouch-like structure, the vaginal fornix, or cul-de-sac. The fornix is described by its location: anterior, posterior, or lateral. The posterior fornix is important because it allows access to the peritoneal cavity from the vagina with a needle or an endoscope (instrument for visual inspection) to diagnose disorders such as ovarian cysts.

The vagina has three major functions: (1) it provides a means for discharge of the menstrual flow; (2) it is the female organ of coitus; and (3) during childbirth, it allows passage of the fetus from the uterus to the outside.

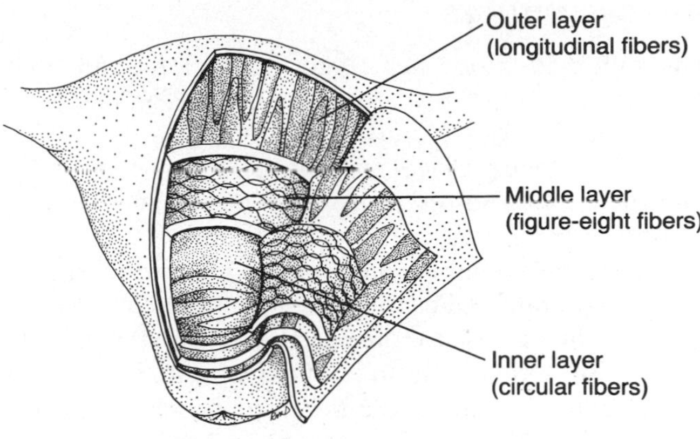

Figure 4–4

Layers of the myometrium, showing the three types of smooth muscle fiber.

UTERUS

The uterus is a hollow, thick-walled, muscular organ that is shaped like a flattened upside-down pear. The uterus houses and nourishes the fetus until birth, then contracts rhythmically during labor to expel the fetus. Each month, the uterus is prepared for a pregnancy, whether or not conception occurs.

The uterus measures about 7.5 × 5 × 2.5 cm. It is suspended above the bladder and anterior to the rectum. Its normal position is anteverted (rotated forward) and slightly anteflexed (flexed forward).

Divisions of the Uterus

The uterus has three divisions.

Corpus. The upper uterus is the corpus, or body. The uppermost part of the uterine corpus is the fundus, above the area where the fallopian tubes enter the uterus.

Isthmus. A narrower transition zone, the isthmus, is between the corpus of the uterus and cervix. During late pregnancy, the isthmus elongates and is known as the lower uterine segment.

Cervix. The cervix is the tubular "neck" of the lower uterus, and is about 2 to 3 cm long. During labor, the cervix effaces (thins) and dilates (opens) to allow passage of the fetus (see p. 267). The upper part of the cervix is marked by the internal os, and the lower cervix is marked by the external os. The external os of a childless woman is round and smooth. After childbirth, the external os has an irregular, slit-like shape and may have tags of scar tissue.

Layers of the Uterus

The uterus has three layers.

Perimetrium. The perimetrium is the outer peritoneal layer that covers the uterus, except at the anterior isthmus, just above the bladder. Laterally, the peritoneal layer of the uterus is continuous with the broad ligaments on either side of the uterus.

Myometrium. The myometrium is the middle layer of thick muscle. The myometrium contains three types of smooth muscle fibers, each suited to specific functions in childbearing (Fig. 4–4).

1. *Longitudinal fibers* are found mostly in the fundus and are designed to expel the fetus efficiently toward the pelvic outlet during birth.
2. *Interlacing fibers* in a figure-eight design make up the middle layer. These fibers contract after birth to compress blood vessels that pass between them to limit blood loss.
3. *Circular fibers* form constrictions where the fallopian tubes enter the uterus and surround the internal cervical os. Circular fibers prevent reflux of menstrual blood and tissue into the fallopian tubes, promote normal implantation of the fertilized ovum, and retain the fetus until the appropriate time of birth.

Endometrium. The endometrium is the inner layer of the uterus. It is responsive to the cyclic variations of estrogen and progesterone during the female reproductive cycle (see p. 60). The endometrium has two layers:

- The *basal layer*, the area nearest the myometrium that regenerates the functional layer of the endometrium after each menstrual period and after childbirth.
- The *functional layer*, which lies above the basal layer and contains the endometrial arteries, veins, and glands; this layer is shed during each menstrual period and after childbirth in the *lochia*, the vaginal discharge (see p. 417).

FALLOPIAN TUBES

The fallopian tubes are 10 to 14 cm long and quite narrow (0.6 cm). They are a pathway for the ovum between the ovary and the uterus. If fertilization occurs, it takes place in the fallopian tubes. The fallopian tubes enter the upper uterus at the *cornu*, or horn, of the uterus.

The fallopian tubes are lined with folded epithelium containing cilia that beat rhythmically toward the uterine cavity to propel the ovum through the tube. The rough, folded surface of the lining combined with the small diameter makes the fallopian tube vulnerable to blockage from infection or scar tissue. Tubal blockage may result in sterility or a tubal pregnancy because the fertilized ovum cannot enter the uterus for proper implantation.

The tubes have four divisions:

- The *interstitial* portion, which runs into the uterine cavity and lies within the uterine wall
- The *isthmus*, the narrow part adjacent to the uterus
- The *ampulla*, the wider area of the tube lateral to the isthmus, where fertilization occurs
- The *infundibulum*, the wide, funnel-shaped terminal end of the tube. *Fimbria* are finger-like processes surrounding the infundibulum.

The fallopian tubes are not directly connected to the ovary. At ovulation, the ovum is expelled into the abdominal cavity. Wave-like motions of the fimbria draw the ovum into the tube. The tubal isthmus, however, remains contracted until 3 days after conception to allow the fertilized ovum to develop within the tube. Growth of the fertilized ovum within the fallopian tube promotes its normal implantation in the upper, fundal portion of the uterus.

OVARIES

The ovaries are the female gonads, or sex glands. They have two functions: (1) hormone production, and (2) maturation of an ovum during each reproductive cycle.

The ovaries secrete estrogen and progesterone in varying amounts during a woman's reproductive cycle to prepare the uterine lining for pregnancy. Ovarian hormone secretion gradually declines to very low levels after menopause.

At birth, the ovary contains all the ova that it will ever have. About one million ova are present at birth. Many of these degenerate until puberty, when 300,000 to 400,000 remain. Many ova begin the maturation process, but most never reach maturity. During the course of a woman's reproductive life, only about 400 of the ova ever mature enough to be fertilized. By the time a woman reaches the climacteric, almost all of her original ova have been released during ovulation or have regressed. The few remaining ova are unresponsive to stimulating hormones and do not mature.

✔ Check Your Reading

6. What is the location of each of these external female reproductive organs: Labia majora and minora? Clitoris? Urinary meatus? Vaginal introitus? Hymen? Perineum?
7. What are the three divisions of the uterus?
8. Describe the location of the three layers of the uterus.
9. How do the fallopian tubes conduct the ovum from the ovary to the uterus?
10. What are the two functions of the ovaries?

Support Structures

The bony pelvis supports and protects the lower abdominal and internal reproductive organs. Muscles and ligaments provide added support for the internal organs of the pelvis against the downward force of gravity and increases in intra-abdominal pressure.

PELVIS

The bony pelvis is a basin-shaped structure at the lower end of the spine. Its posterior wall is formed by the sacrum. The side and anterior pelvic walls are composed of three fused bones: *ilium*, *ischium*, and *pubis*. Figure 4–5 illustrates important anatomic landmarks on the pelvis.

The linea terminalis is an imaginary line that divides the upper, or false, pelvis from the lower, or true pelvis. The false pelvis provides support for the internal organs and the upper part of the body. The true pelvis is most important during childbirth, and its divisions and measurements are discussed in Chapter 12.

MUSCLES

Six pairs of muscles enclose the lower pelvis and provide support for internal reproductive, urinary, and bowel structures (Fig. 4–6). Additionally, a fibromuscular sheet, the *pelvic fascia*, provides support for the pelvic organs. Vaginal and urethral openings are in the pelvic fascia.

The *levator ani* is a collection of three pairs of muscles: the *pubococcygeus*, which is also called the *pubovaginal* muscle in the female; the *puborectal*; and the *iliococcygeus*. These muscles support internal pelvic structures and resist increases in the intra-abdominal pressure.

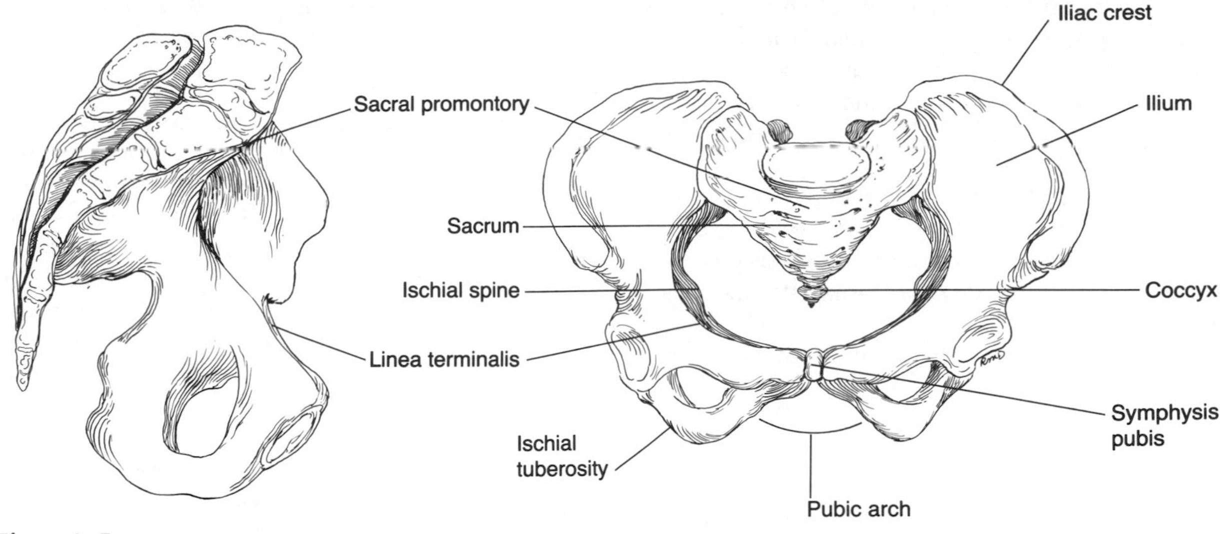

Figure 4–5

Structures of the bony pelvis, shown in lateral and anterior views.

The *ischiocavernosus* muscle extends from the clitoris to the ischial tuberosities on each side of the lower bony pelvis. The two *transverse perineal muscles* extend from fibrous tissue of the perineum to the two ischial tuberosities, stabilizing the center of the perineum.

LIGAMENTS

Seven pairs of ligaments maintain the internal reproductive organs, with their nerve and blood supplies, in their proper positions within the pelvis (see Fig. 4–2).

Lateral Support. Four pairs of ligaments stabilize the uterus and ovaries laterally and keep them in the midline of the pelvis. The *broad ligament* is a sheet of tissue extending from each side of the uterus to the lateral pelvic wall. The round ligament and fallopian tube mark the upper border of the broad ligament, and the lower edge is bounded by the uterine blood vessels. Within the two broad ligaments are the ovarian ligaments, blood vessels, and lymphatics.

The right and left *cardinal ligaments* provide support to the lower uterus and vagina. They extend from the lateral walls of the cervix and vagina to the side walls of the pelvis.

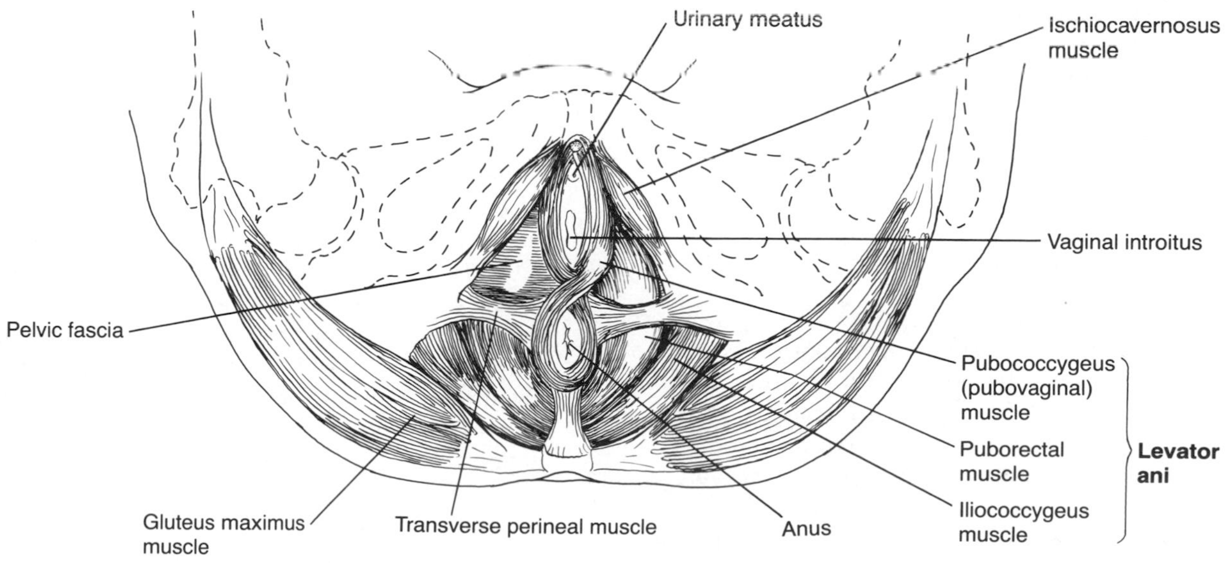

Figure 4–6

Muscles of the female pelvic floor.

The two *ovarian ligaments* connect the ovaries to the lateral uterine walls. The *infundibulopelvic (suspensory) ligaments* connect the lateral ovary and distal fallopian tubes to the pelvic side walls. The infundibulopelvic ligament also carries the blood vessel and nerve supply for tne ovary.

Anterior Support. Two pairs of ligaments provide anterior support for the internal reproductive organs. The *round ligaments* connect the upper uterus to the connective tissue of the labia majora. These ligaments maintain the uterus in its normal anteflexed position and help direct the fetal presenting part against the cervix during labor.

The *pubocervical ligaments* support the cervix anteriorly. They connect the cervix to the interior surface of the symphysis pubis.

Posterior Support. The *uterosacral ligaments* provide posterior support, extending from the lower posterior uterus to the sacrum. These ligaments also contain sympathetic and parasympathetic nerves of the autonomic nervous system.

BLOOD SUPPLY

The uterine blood supply is carried by the *uterine arteries*, which are branches of the internal iliac artery. Blood drains into the *uterine veins* and from there into the internal iliac veins. These vessels enter the uterus at the lower border of the broad ligament, near the isthmus of the uterus. The vessels branch, downward to supply the cervix and vagina and upward to supply the uterus. The upper branch also supplies the ovaries and fallopian tubes. The vessels are coiled to allow for elongation as the uterus enlarges and rises out of the pelvis during pregnancy.

The ovarian blood supply is carried by the *ovarian artery*, which arises from the abdominal aorta. The ovarian blood supply drains from the two *ovarian veins*. The left ovarian vein drains into the left renal vein, but the right ovarian vein drains directly into the inferior vena cava.

NERVE SUPPLY

Many functions of the reproductive system are not under voluntary, or conscious, control. Nerves of the autonomic nervous system from the uterovaginal plexus and inferior hypogastric plexus control automatic functions of the reproductive system.

Sensory and motor nerves that innervate the reproductive organs enter the spinal cord at the T-12 through L-2 levels. These nerves are most important during childbearing in terms of pain management (see Chapter 15).

Female Reproductive Cycle

The female reproductive cycle describes the regular and recurrent changes in the anterior pituitary hormones, ovaries, and uterine endometrium that are designed to prepare the body for pregnancy. Additionally, changes in the characteristics of cervical mucus are designed to promote fertilization. The female reproductive cycle is often called the *menstrual cycle* because menstruation provides an obvious marker for each cycle's beginning and end if pregnancy does not occur. Figure 4–7 illustrates these interrelated changes during the cycle.

The female reproductive cycle is driven by a *feedback loop* between the anterior pituitary and the ovaries; that is, as levels of one or more hormones fall, levels of others rise. The reverse is also true.

The duration of the cycle is about 28 days, although it may range from 20 to 45 days (Guyton, 1991). Significant deviations from the "ideal" 28-day cycle are associated with reduced fertility. The first day of the menstrual period is counted as day 1 of the woman's cycle. The cycle is further divided into two cycles that reflect changes in the ovaries and uterine endometrium.

Ovarian Cycle

In response to GnRH from the woman's hypothalamus, the anterior pituitary secretes FSH and LH. FSH and LH stimulate the ovaries to mature an ovum, release it, and secrete hormones that will prepare the endometrium for implantation of a fertilized ovum. The ovarian cycle consists of three phases: the follicular phase, ovulation, and the luteal phase.

FOLLICULAR PHASE

The follicular phase is the period during which an ovum matures. It begins with the first day of menstruation and ends about 12 to 14 days later. The fall in estrogen and progesterone secretion by the ovary just before menstruation stimulates secretion of FSH and LH by the anterior pituitary. As the FSH and LH levels rise, six to 12 graafian follicles, each containing an immature ovum, begin growing. The follicles secrete estrogen, which accelerates their maturation. Eventually, one follicle outgrows all the others to reach maturity. All other follicles recede entirely and cannot be matured again.

OVULATION

Near the middle of a woman's reproductive cycle, about 2 days before ovulation, a surge of LH, accom-

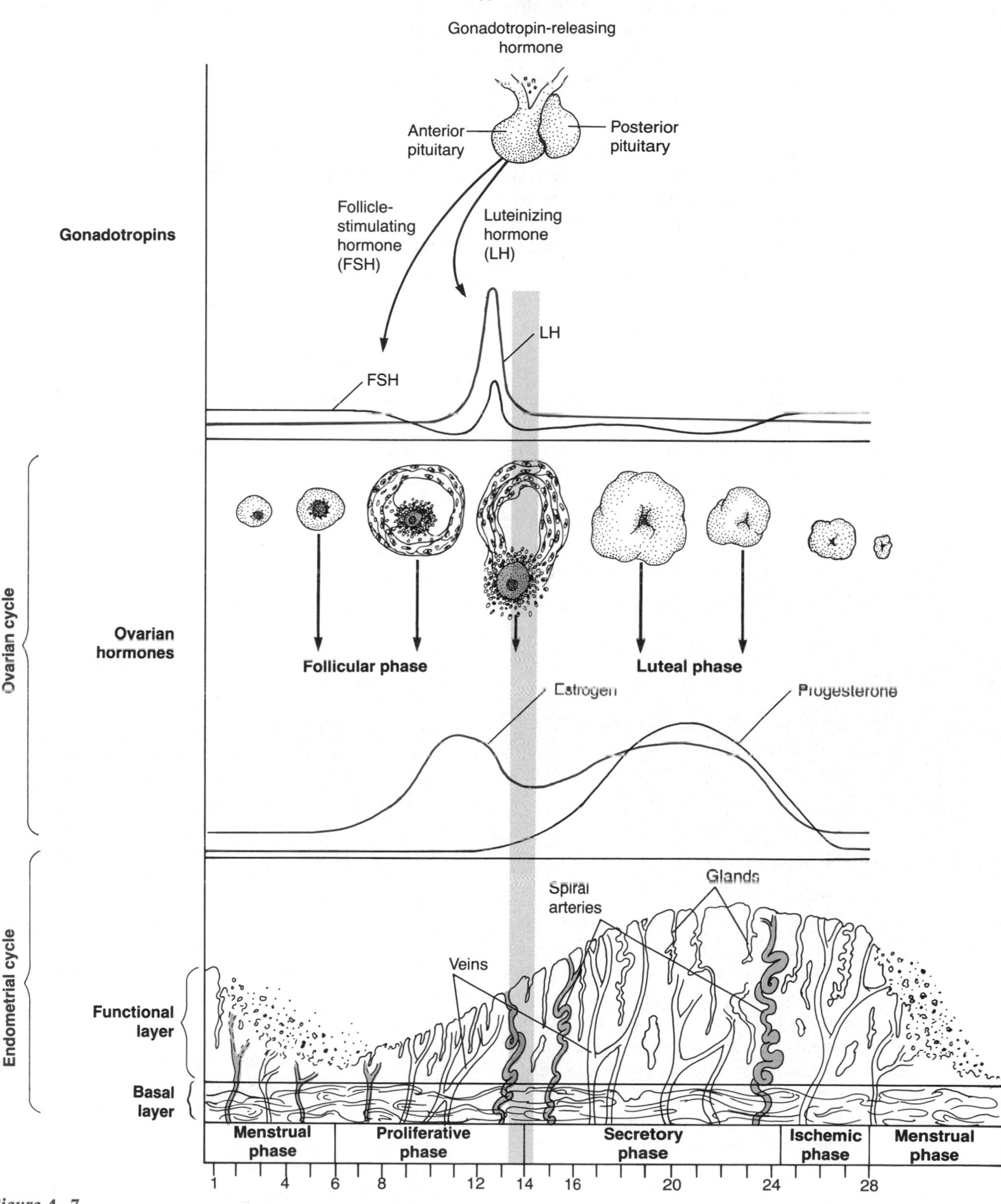

Figure 4–7

The female reproductive cycle showing the changes in hormone secretion from the anterior pituitary and interrelated changes in the ovary and uterine endometrium.

panied by a slight fall in estrogen production, stimulates full maturation of a single follicle. Occasionally, more than one follicle is matured and its ova released, which can lead to a multifetal pregnancy.

The mature follicle is a mass of cells with a fluid-filled chamber. A smaller mass of cells houses the ovum within this chamber. At ovulation, a blister-like projection forms on the wall of the follicle (a *stigma*), the follicle ruptures, and the ovum with its surrounding cells is released from the surface of the ovary, where it is picked up by the fimbriated end of the fallopian tube. (See Chapter 6 for further discussion of ovulation and ovum transport to the uterus.)

LUTEAL PHASE

After ovulation and under the influence of LH, the remaining cells of the old follicle persist for about 12 days as a *corpus luteum*. The corpus luteum secretes large amounts of estrogen and progesterone to prepare the endometrium for a fertilized ovum. FSH and LH levels decrease during this phase. If the ovum is not fertilized, the fall in FSH and LH levels causes the corpus luteum to regress, resulting in menstruation. The old corpus luteum is replaced by fibrous tissue called the *corpus albicans*.

Endometrial Cycle

The uterine endometrium responds to ovarian stimulation with cyclic changes. Three phases mark the changes in the endometrium: the proliferative phase, the secretory phase, and menstrual phase.

PROLIFERATIVE PHASE

The proliferative phase occurs during the follicular and ovulatory phases of the ovarian cycle, lasting about 11 days. After completion of a menstrual period, the endometrium is very thin. The basal layers of the endometrium remain after menstruation and begin to proliferate to form new endometrial epithelium and endometrial glands under the influence of rising estrogen secretion by the ovary. Endometrial spiral arteries and endometrial veins increase in length to accompany thickening of the endometrial layer and to nourish the proliferating cells.

SECRETORY PHASE

The secretory phase occurs during the luteal phase of the ovarian cycle as the uterus is prepared to receive a fertilized ovum; this phase lasts about 12 days. The endometrium continues to thicken under the influence of estrogen and progesterone, reaching its maximum thickness of 5 to 6 mm (Guyton, 1991). The blood vessels and endometrial glands become twisted and dilated.

The endometrial glands secrete substances to nourish a fertilized ovum. Large quantities of glycogen, proteins, lipids, and minerals are stored within the endometrium, awaiting arrival of the ovum.

MENSTRUAL PHASE

If fertilization does not occur, the corpus luteum regresses and its production of estrogen and progesterone falls. About 2 days before the onset of the menses, vasospasm of the endometrial blood vessels causes the endometrium to become ischemic and necrotic. The necrotic areas of endometrium separate from the basal layers, resulting in the menstrual flow. The duration of the menstrual phase is about 5 days.

During a menstrual period, women lose about 40 ml of blood (Guyton, 1991). Because of the recurrent loss of blood, many women are anemic during their reproductive years, especially if their diets are low in iron.

Changes in Cervical Mucus

During most of the female reproductive cycle, the mucus of the cervix is scant, thick, and sticky. Just before ovulation, cervical mucus becomes thin, clear, and elastic to promote passage of sperm into the uterus and fallopian tube, where they can fertilize the ovum. Spinnbarkeit refers to the elasticity of cervical mucus. At its maximum elasticity near ovulation, a drop of cervical mucus can be drawn out to a length of at least 6 cm (Meldrum, 1992). A woman may assess the elasticity of her cervical mucus to avoid conception (see Chapter 30) or to identify the cause of infertility (see Chapter 31).

✔ Check Your Reading

11. Where is the true pelvis located?
12. What are the purposes of the muscles of the pelvis?
13. Which ovarian structure secretes estrogen and progesterone?
14. What ovarian changes occur during each female reproductive cycle?
15. How does the uterine endometrium change during a woman's reproductive cycle?
16. Why does the cervical mucus become thin, clear, and elastic around the time of ovulation?

The Female Breast

Structure

The breasts, or mammary glands, are not directly functional in reproduction, but they secrete milk after childbirth to nourish the infant. The small, raised nipple is at the center of each breast (Fig. 4–8). The nipple is composed of sensitive erectile tissue and may respond to sexual stimulation. Surrounding the nipple is a larger circular areola. Both the nipple and areola are darker than surrounding skin. Montgomery tubercles are sebaceous glands in the areola. They are inactive except during pregnancy and lactation, when they enlarge and secrete a substance that keeps the nipple soft. Women often ask about the Montgomery tubercles during pregnancy or after birth because they have never noticed them before.

Within each breast is the glandular tissue that secretes milk, arranged like spokes of a wheel around the hub. Fifteen to 20 of these lobes are arranged around and behind the nipple and areola. Fibrous tissue and fat in the breast support the glandular tissue, blood vessels, lymphatics, and nerves. The amount of fat is the major determinant of breast size. All women have about the same amount of glandular tissue to secrete milk. Thus, breast size is unrelated to the quantity or quality of milk secreted.

Alveoli are small sacs that contain acinar cells to secrete milk. The acinar cells of the alveoli extract substances needed from the rich mammary blood supply to manufacture milk when the breasts are properly stimulated. Myoepithelial cells surround the alveoli to contract and eject the milk into the ductal system when signaled by secretion of the hormone oxytocin from the posterior pituitary gland.

The alveoli drain into lactiferous ducts, which connect to drain milk from all areas of the breast. The lactiferous ducts become wider under the areola and are called *lactiferous sinuses* in this area. The lactiferous sinuses narrow again into ducts as they open to the outside in the nipple. (See Chapter 21 for further information on breastfeeding.)

Function

The breasts are inactive until puberty, when rising estrogen levels stimulate growth of the glandular tis-

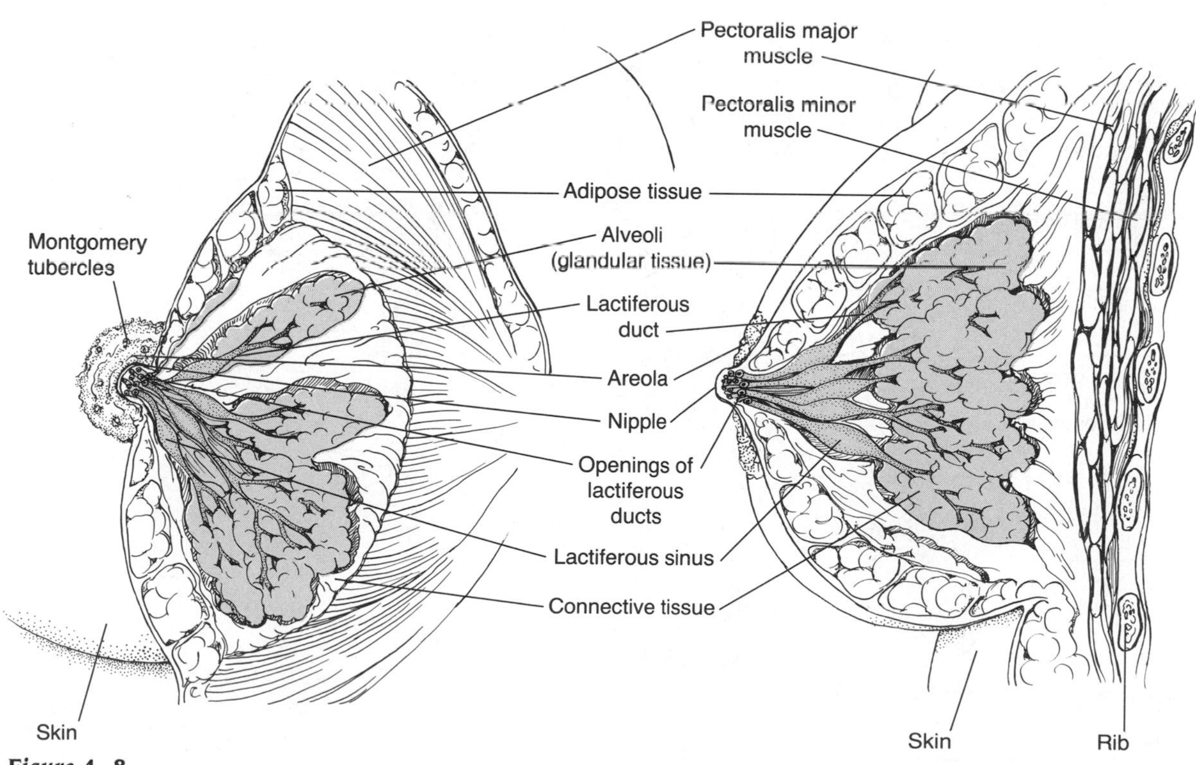

Figure 4–8

Structures of the female breast.

sue. In addition, fat is deposited in the breasts, resulting in the mature female contour.

During pregnancy, high levels of estrogen and progesterone, produced by the placenta, stimulate growth of the alveoli and ductal system to prepare them for lactation. Prolactin secretion by the anterior pituitary gland stimulates milk production during pregnancy, but this effect is inhibited by estrogen and progesterone produced by the placenta. Inhibiting effects of estrogen and progesterone stop when the placenta is expelled after birth, and milk production occurs unless the mother chooses to suppress it (see Chapter 17).

✔ Check Your Reading

17. What is the function of Montgomery's tubercles?
18. How is a woman's breast size related to the amount of milk she can produce?
19. Why is milk not actively secreted during pregnancy?

Male Reproductive Anatomy and Physiology

External Male Reproductive Organs

The male has two external organs of reproduction, the penis and scrotum (Fig. 4–9).

PENIS

The penis has two functions. As part of the urinary tract, it carries urine from the bladder to the exterior during urination. As a reproductive organ, the penis deposits semen into the female vagina during sexual intercourse (coitus).

The penis is composed mostly of erectile tissue, spongy tissues with many small spaces inside. There are three areas of erectile tissue: (1) the corpus spongiosum, which surrounds the urethra on the un-

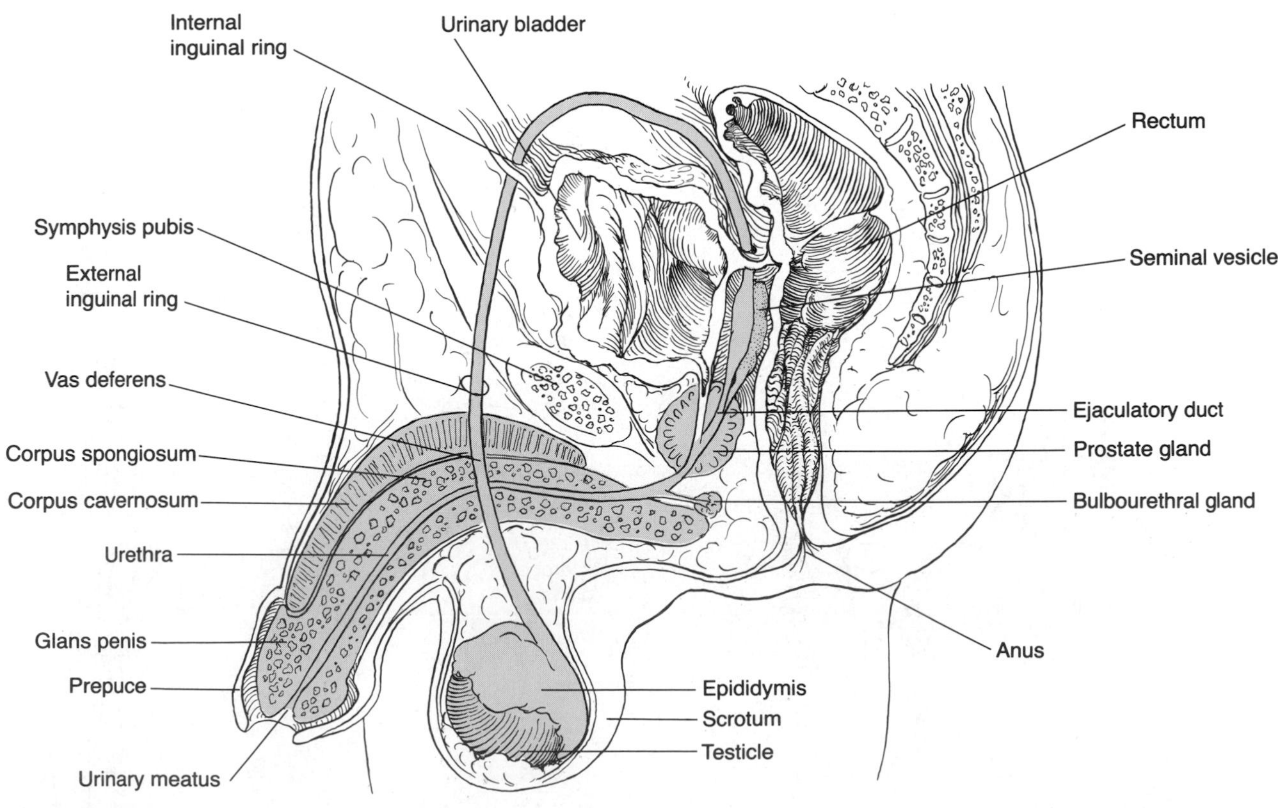

Figure 4–9

Structures of the male reproductive system (mid-sagittal view).

derside of the penis, and (2) two columns of the corpus cavernosum on each side of the penis.

The penis is flaccid most of the time because the small spaces within the erectile tissue are collapsed. During sexual stimulation, the arteries within the penis dilate and veins are partly occluded, trapping blood in the spongy tissue. Entrapment of blood within the penis causes erection and enables the man to penetrate the vagina during sexual intercourse.

The glans is the distal end of the penis. The urinary meatus is centered in the end of the glans. Covering the glans is the loose skin of the prepuce, or foreskin. The prepuce is surgically removed during *circumcision*, a surgical procedure usually performed on the newborn (see p. 532), although it may be performed later. The glans is very sensitive to tactile stimulation, adding to a man's external sensation during intercourse.

Table 4–4. FUNCTIONS OF MALE REPRODUCTIVE AND ACCESSORY ORGANS

Organ	Function
Penis	1. Conduit for urine from bladder. 2. Male organ of sexual intercourse.
Scrotum	Houses testes and maintains their temperature at a level cooler than the trunk of the body, thus promoting normal sperm formation.
Testes	1. Endocrine glands that secrete the primary male sex hormone testosterone. 2. Growth and maturation of sperm.
Vas deferens	Conduction of sperm from testes to urethra.
Seminal vesicles, prostate, bulbourethral glands	Secretion of seminal fluids that carry sperm and provide for: 1. Nourishment of sperm. 2. Protection of sperm from hostile acidic environment of vagina. 3. Enhancement of motility of sperm. 4. Washing of all sperm from urethra.

SCROTUM

The scrotum is a pouch of thin skin and muscle that is suspended behind the penis. The skin color of the scrotum is somewhat darker than the surrounding skin and is covered with small ridges called rugae. The scrotum is divided internally by a septum. One of the male gonads (testicle) is contained within each pocket of the scrotum.

The scrotum's main purpose is to keep the testes cooler than the core body temperature. Formation of the male gametes (sperm) requires that the testes not be too warm. A cremaster muscle is attached to each testicle to draw them closer to the body and warm them, or to relax, allowing the testes to fall away from the body and become cooler.

Internal Male Reproductive Organs

The functions of the male external and internal organs are summarized in Table 4–4.

TESTES

The male gonads, or testes, have two functions: (1) they serve as endocrine glands, and (2) they produce male gametes, or sperm, also called spermatozoa. Androgens (male sex hormones) are the primary endocrine secretions of the testes. Androgens are produced by the Leydig cells of the testes. The primary androgen produced by the testes is testosterone.

Unlike the female, who experiences a cyclic pattern of hormone secretion, the male secretes testosterone in a relatively even pattern. A feedback loop with the hypothalamus and anterior pituitary keeps testosterone levels stable. A small amount of testosterone is converted to estrogen in the male and is necessary for sperm formation.

Sperm production (spermatogenesis) occurs within the seminiferous tubules of the testes. The Sertoli cells of the testes nourish and support sperm during their production and maturation. Unlike the female, who has a lifetime supply of ova in her gonads at birth, the male does not begin producing sperm until puberty. The normal male continues to produce new sperm throughout life.

At ejaculation, about 400 million sperm are deposited in the vagina. This tremendous number is necessary for normal fertility, although a single spermatozoon fertilizes the ovum. Only a few sperm ever reach the fallopian tube where an ovum may be available for fertilization. When the first spermatozoon penetrates the ovum, changes within the ovum prevent other sperm from also fertilizing it. (See Chapter 6 for further discussion of sperm formation and conception.)

ACCESSORY DUCTS AND GLANDS

From the seminiferous tubules, sperm pass into the epididymis within the scrotum for storage. The epididymis empties into the vas deferens, which leads upward into the pelvis, then back down toward the penis through the internal and external inguinal rings. Within the pelvis, the vas deferens joins the ejaculatory duct before connecting to the urethra.

Three glands—the *seminal vesicles*, the *prostate*, and the *bulbourethral glands*—secrete seminal fluids that carry sperm into the vagina during intercourse. The seminal fluid (1) nourishes the sperm; (2) protects the sperm from the hostile pH environment of the vagina; (3) enhances the motility of the sperm; and (4) washes the sperm out of the urethra so that the maximum number are deposited in the vagina.

✔ Check Your Reading

20. What is the purpose of the penis?
21. What two types of erectile tissue are in the penis? What is their function?
22. Why is it important for the testes to be contained within the scrotum?
23. What are the two functions of the testes?

Summary Concepts

- Initial prenatal development of the reproductive organs is similar for both males and females. Unless a Y chromosome is present, female reproductive structures will develop.
- Puberty is the time during life when the reproductive organs become fully functional and secondary sex characteristics develop.
- Puberty begins about 6 months earlier in girls than in boys, although the girl's early growth spurt makes it seem that she begins puberty much earlier than the boy.
- Females are generally shorter than males because they begin their growth spurt at an earlier age and complete it more quickly than boys.
- The onset of menstruation is an obvious marker of puberty in girls.
- Girls often do not ovulate in early menstrual cycles, although they can ovulate even before the first one. Therefore, a girl can become pregnant before her first menstural period if she is sexually active.
- The onset of puberty in boys is more subtle than in girls, beginning with growth of the testes and penis.
- Boys may have nocturnal emissions of seminal fluid; this may be distressing unless they are educated that these events are normal and expected.
- A woman's reproductive organs are designed to promote the conception, nourishment, and birth of a baby.
- At birth, a woman has all the ova she will ever have. New ova are not formed after birth. Almost all ova are depleted when a woman reaches the climacteric.
- The female reproductive cycle is often called the menstrual cycle. It includes changes in the anterior pituitary gland, ovaries, and uterine endometrium to prepare for a fertilized ovum. The character of cervical mucus also changes to encourage fertilization.
- Breast size is unrelated to the quantity or quality of milk a woman can produce for her infant after childbirth.
- For normal sperm formation, a man's testes must be cooler than his core body temperature.
- Seminal fluids secreted by the seminal vesicles, prostate, and bulbourethral glands nourish and protect the sperm, enhance their motility, and ensure that most sperm are deposited in the vagina during sexual intercourse.

References and Readings

Blackburn, S.T., & Loper, D.L. (1992). *Maternal, fetal, and neonatal physiology.* Philadelphia: W.B. Saunders.

Buyalos, R.P. (1992). Puberty and precocious puberty. In N.F. Hacker & J.G. Moore (Eds.), *Essentials of obstetrics and gynecology* (2nd ed., pp. 511–521). Philadelphia: W.B. Saunders.

Deitch, K.V. (1992a). Reproductive anatomy and physiology. In S. Mattson & J.E. Smith (Eds.), *Core curriculum for maternal-newborn nursing* (pp. 3–16). Philadelphia: W.B. Saunders.

Deitch, K.V. (1992b). Endocrinology and pregnancy. In S. Mattson & J.E. Smith (Eds.), *Core curriculum for maternal-newborn nursing* (pp. 17–28). Philadelphia: W.B. Saunders.

Guyton, A.C. (1991). *Textbook of medical physiology* (8th ed.). Philadelphia: W.B. Saunders.

Jacob, S.W., & Francone, C.A. (1989). *Elements of anatomy and physiology* (2nd ed.). Philadelphia: W.B. Saunders.

Kreipe, R.E., & McAnarney, E.R. (1990). Adolescent medicine. In R.E. Behrman & R. Kliegman (Eds.), *Nelson essentials of pediatrics* (pp. 207–240). Philadelphia: W.B. Saunders.

Meldrum, D.R. (1992). Infertility. In N.F. Hacker & J.G. Moore (Eds.), *Essentials of obstetrics and gynecology* (2nd ed., pp. 551–562). Philadelphia: W.B. Saunders.

Moore, J.G. (1992). Female reproductive anatomy. In N.F. Hacker & J.G. Moore (Eds.), *Essentials of obstetrics and gynecology* (2nd ed., pp. 3–11). Philadelphia: W.B. Saunders.

Moore, K.L. (1983). *Before we are born.* Philadelphia: W.B. Saunders Co.

Toot, P.J., Surrey, E.S., & Lu, J.K.H. (1992). In N.F. Hacker & J.G. Moore (Eds.), *Essentials of obstetrics and gynecology* (2nd ed., pp. 36–51). Philadelphia: W.B. Saunders.

5

Hereditary and Environmental Influences on Childbearing

Objectives

1. Describe structure and function of normal human genes and chromosomes.
2. Give examples of ways genes and chromosomes are studied.
3. Describe transmission of single gene traits from parent to child.
4. Relate chromosome abnormalities to spontaneous abortion and to birth defects in the infant.
5. Explain characteristics of multifactorial birth defects.
6. Identify environmental factors that can interfere with prenatal development and how their effects can be avoided or reduced.
7. Describe the process of genetic counseling.
8. Explain the role of the nurse in caring for individuals or families with concerns about birth defects.

Definitions

Allele • An alternate form of a gene.

Autosomes • Any of the 22 pairs of **chromosomes** other than the **sex chromosomes.**

Birth defect • An abnormality of structure, function, or body metabolism that often results in a physical or mental handicap, shortens life, or is fatal (according to the March of Dimes Birth Defects Foundation).

Congenital • Present at birth.

Diploid • Having a pair of chromosomes (46 in humans). The diploid number of chromosomes represents one copy of every chromosome from each parent and is the number normally present in body cells other than **gametes.**

Familial • Presence of a trait or condition in a family more often than would be expected by chance alone.

Gamete • Reproductive cell. The female gamete is an **ovum**; the male gamete is a **spermatozoon.**

Genetic • Pertaining to the genes or the chromosomes.

Genotype • Genetic make-up of an individual.

Haploid • Having one copy of each chromosome pair (23 in humans). **Gametes** normally have a haploid number of chromosomes.

Heterozygous • Having two different **alleles** for a genetic trait.

Homozygous • Having two identical **alleles** for a genetic trait.

Karyotype • A photomicrograph of a cell's chromosomes, arranged from largest to smallest.

Monosomy • Presence of only one of a chromosome pair in every body cell.

Mutation • A permanent and transmissible change in a gene.

Pedigree • A graphic representation of a family's medical and hereditary history and the relationships among the family members. May be called a **genogram.**

Phenotype • The outward expression of one's genetic constitution.

Polyploidy • Having additional sets of chromosomes.

Sex chromosome • The X and Y chromosomes. Females have two X chromosomes; males have one X and one Y chromosome.

Somatic cells • Body cells other than the **gametes**, or germ cells.

Teratogen • An agent that can cause defects in a developing baby during pregnancy.

Translocation • Attachment of all or part of a chromosome to another chromosome.

Trisomy • Presence of three copies of a chromosome in each body cell.

Hereditary and environmental forces influence one's development from before conception until death and can affect development positively or negatively. The nurse needs a basic understanding of these important factors to better understand disorders evident at birth and those that develop later in life.

A nurse may be the first professional whom people consult for concerns about birth defects, disorders that seem to "run in the family," or potentially harmful agents. These concerns are often heightened just before and during pregnancy, but they may arise any time.

Hereditary Influences

Hereditary influences on development are those resulting from the directions provided by genes that make up the 46 chromosomes in every cell other than the gametes. If there is too much or too little genetic material in the cells, or if one or more genes are abnormal and provide incorrect directions, disease can result.

Structure of Genes and Chromosomes

A review of the structure of genes and chromosomes aids in understanding how disorders may result if they are abnormal. Chromosomes are composed of genes that in turn are composed of DNA (Fig. 5–1).

DNA

DNA (deoxyribonucleic acid) is the basic building block of genes and chromosomes. It has three units: (1) a sugar (deoxyribose), (2) a phosphate group, and (3) one of four nitrogen bases (adenine, thymine, guanine, and cytosine).

DNA resembles a spiral ladder, with a sugar and a phosphate group forming each side of the ladder, and a pair of nitrogen bases forming each rung. The four bases of the DNA molecule pair to each other in a fixed way, allowing the DNA to be accurately duplicated during each cell division.

- Adenine pairs with thymine
- Guanine pairs with cytosine

The sequence of bases within the DNA determines which amino acids will be assembled to form a protein and the order in which they will be assembled. Some of these proteins form the structure of body cells, whereas many others are enzymes that control metabolic processes within the cell. If the sequence of nitrogen bases in the DNA is incorrect, or if some bases are missing or added, a defect may be present in body structure or function.

GENES

A gene is formed from a segment of DNA that directs the production of a specific product needed for body structure or function. There may be long segments of non-functional DNA between each gene. Humans may have as many as 100,000 genes, but not all genes function at the same time. Some are active only during prenatal life; others become functional at various times after birth.

Genes that code for the same trait often have two or more alternate forms (alleles). These alleles are usually normal, such as those that code for a person's blood type. Normal alleles provide genetic variation and sometimes a biological advantage. However, alleles can be harmful, such as those that cause the production of abnormal hemoglobin in sickle cell disease. Sometimes a single change in the sequence of bases within the gene's DNA is enough to cause an allele to be harmful rather than normal.

Genes are too small to be seen under a microscope, but they can be studied by tissue analysis in several ways:

- By measuring the products that they direct cells to produce, such as an enzyme
- By direct study of the gene's DNA if its exact location is known
- By analyzing its close association (linkage) with another gene that can be studied

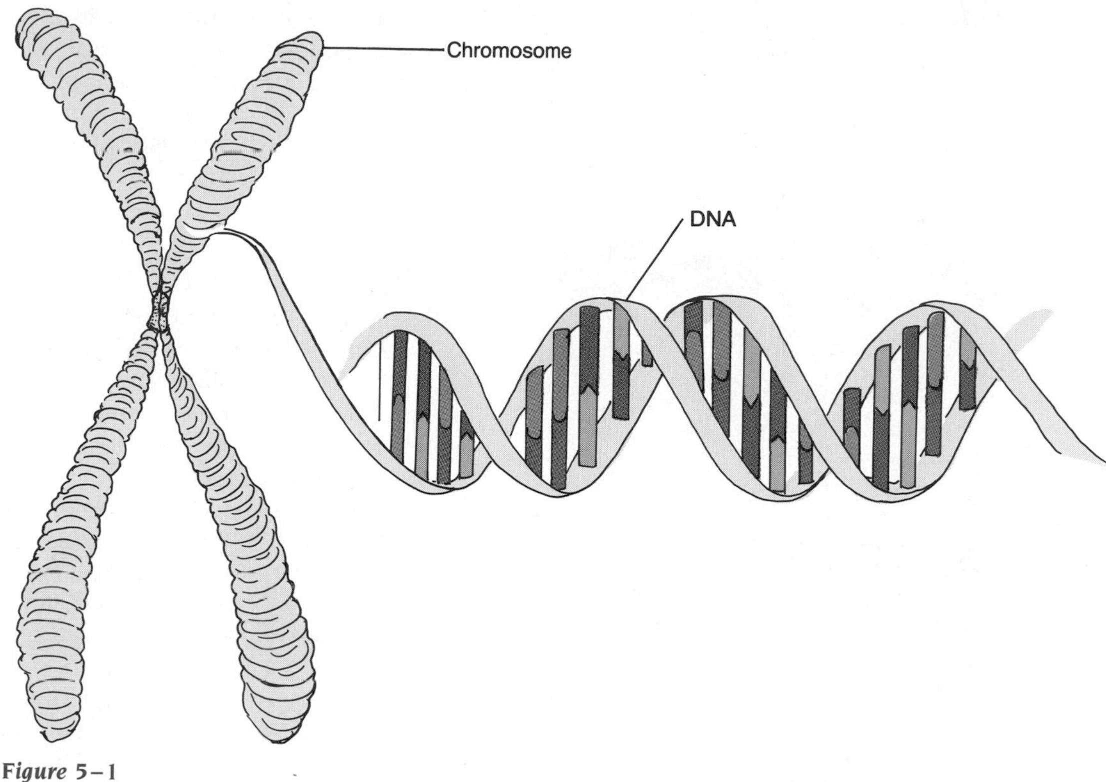

Figure 5–1

Diagrammatic representation of the DNA helix, which is the building block of genes and chromosomes.

The tissue used for study of a gene depends on where the gene product is present in the body and on the available technology. These tissues may include blood, skin cells, hair follicles, and fetal cells from the amniotic fluid or chorionic villi. Genes that can be studied by direct analysis of DNA can be studied in any body tissue, even if the gene product is not present in that tissue.

CHROMOSOMES

Genes are organized into 46 paired chromosomes in the nucleus of body (somatic) cells. A gene can be described as a single bead; the chromosome represents a string of beads. Each chromosome is composed of varying numbers of genes. Twenty-two chromosome pairs are autosomes, and the 23rd pair makes up the sex chromosomes. Added or missing chromosomes or structurally abnormal chromosomes are usually harmful.

Mature gametes have half the chromosomes (23) of other body cells. When the ovum and sperm unite at conception, the total is restored to 46 paired chromosomes. Each gamete receives about half its chromosomes (and thus half its genes) from the mother and half from the father. One chromosome from each pair is distributed randomly in the gametes, allowing variation of genetic traits among people.

Chromosomes can be studied using any of several types of cells: white blood cells, skin fibroblasts, bone marrow cells, and fetal cells from the chorionic villi (future placenta) or those suspended in amniotic fluid. Newer technology may enable some disorders to be routinely diagnosed from fetal cells recovered from the mother's blood.

Cells for chromosome analysis must have a nucleus and must be living. Unlike genes, chromosomes can be seen under the microscope, but only during division of live cells. Specimens must be obtained and preserved carefully to provide enough living cells for chromosome analysis. Temperature extremes, clotting of blood, and addition of improper preservatives can kill the cells and render them useless for analysis.

Chromosomes look jumbled when viewed under a microscope (Fig. 5–2). Organizing the chromosomes from a photomicrograph into the organized array of a karyotype (Fig. 5–3) allows systematic study. In a karyotype, autosome pairs are arranged from largest to smallest. Letters describe groups that have similar size and appearance.

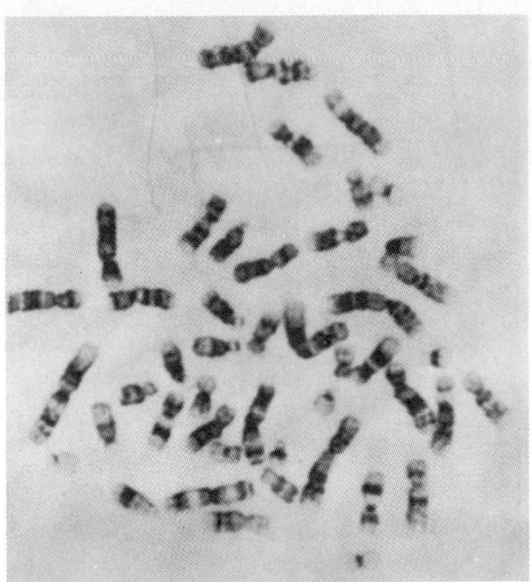

Figure 5–2

When viewed under a microscope, chromosomes appear jumbled. (From Thompson, M.W., McInnes, R.R., & Huntington, F.W. [1991]. *Thompson and Thompson genetics in medicine* [5th ed., p. 16]. Philadelphia: W.B. Saunders. Courtesy of R.G. Worton, The Hospital for Sick Children, Toronto.)

A person's karyotype is abbreviated by a combination of numbers and letters. A number is used to describe the total number of chromosomes, followed by either an XX to indicate sex chromosomes of a female or XY to indicate those of a male. Thus, the chromosome complement of a normal male is abbreviated 46,XY and a normal female, 46,XX. If the chromosome number is abnormal, such as Down syndrome, which has an extra 21 chromosome, the abbreviation indicates the abnormality: 47 (total number of chromosomes), XY (male), +21 (the number that describes the added chromosome). Other abbreviations describe karyotypes having missing or structurally altered chromosomes.

✔ Check Your Reading

1. What is the relationship between genes and chromosomes?
2. Can genes be studied by examining them under a microscope? What are the methods used to study them?
3. Why is it important to keep cell specimens for chromosome analysis alive?
4. What do each of these abbreviations mean? 46,XY? 46,XX?

Transmission of Traits by Single Genes

Inherited characteristics are passed from parent to child by the genes on each chromosome. These traits are classified according to whether they are dominant (strong) or recessive (weak) and whether the gene is located on one of the autosome pairs or on the sex chromosomes. Both normal and abnormal hereditary characteristics can be transmitted by these mechanisms.

ALLELES

Because human beings have a pair of matched chromosomes (except the sex chromosomes in the male), they have one allele for a gene at the same location on each member of the chromosome pair. The paired alleles may be identical (homozygous) or different (heterozygous).

Some alleles, both normal and abnormal, occur more frequently in certain groups than they do in the population as a whole. For example, the gene that causes Tay-Sachs disease is carried by about one of every 27 Ashkenazi Jews, whose families have their roots in eastern Europe. However, only one of every 150 people outside this group carries the gene. Because the abnormal gene occurs more frequently in this group, the incidence of Tay-Sachs disease is also higher. Other disorders that are prevalent in certain ethnic groups are cystic fibrosis (Caucasians) and sickle cell disease (primarily people of African descent).

A new trait (harmful, harmless, or sometimes beneficial) may occur because of a mutation in the gene. When a mutation occurs, the DNA in the gamete is different from that in the person's other body cells. The infant who receives the new version of the gene can then pass it on to future generations unless the mutation is lethal or does not allow reproduction.

DOMINANCE

The observable results of genetic traits result in a person's phenotype. One's phenotype can be observed in characteristics such as outward appearance, internal structure, and body function or by laboratory studies.

Dominance describes how the genetic composition is translated into the phenotype. Some genes are stronger than others, or dominant. In this case, one copy of the gene is enough to cause the trait to be expressed. For example, in the ABO blood system, groups A and B are dominant. Therefore, a single copy of one of these genes is enough to be expressed in the person's blood type.

Other genes are weak or recessive, and two identical copies of the gene are required for the trait to

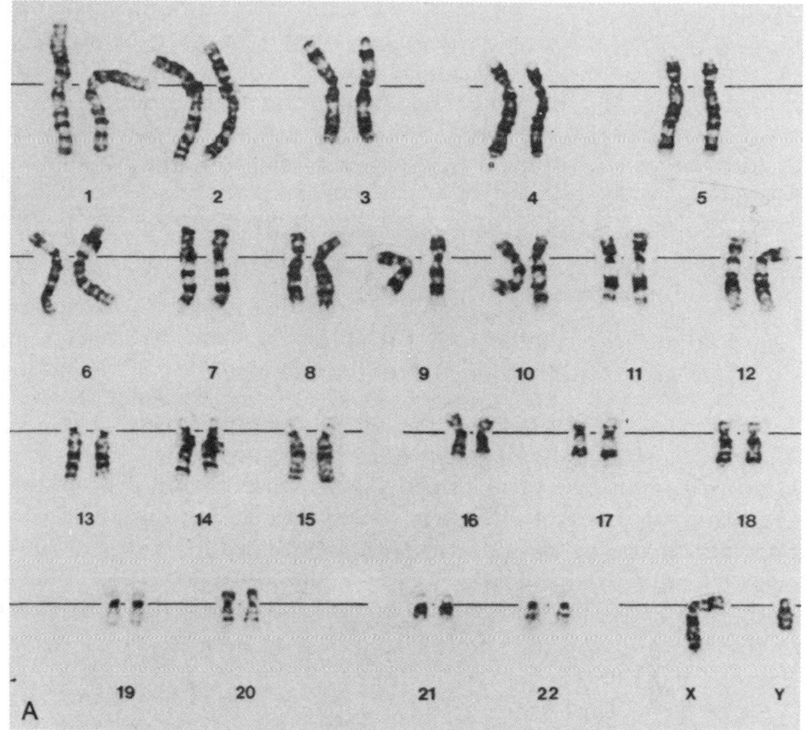

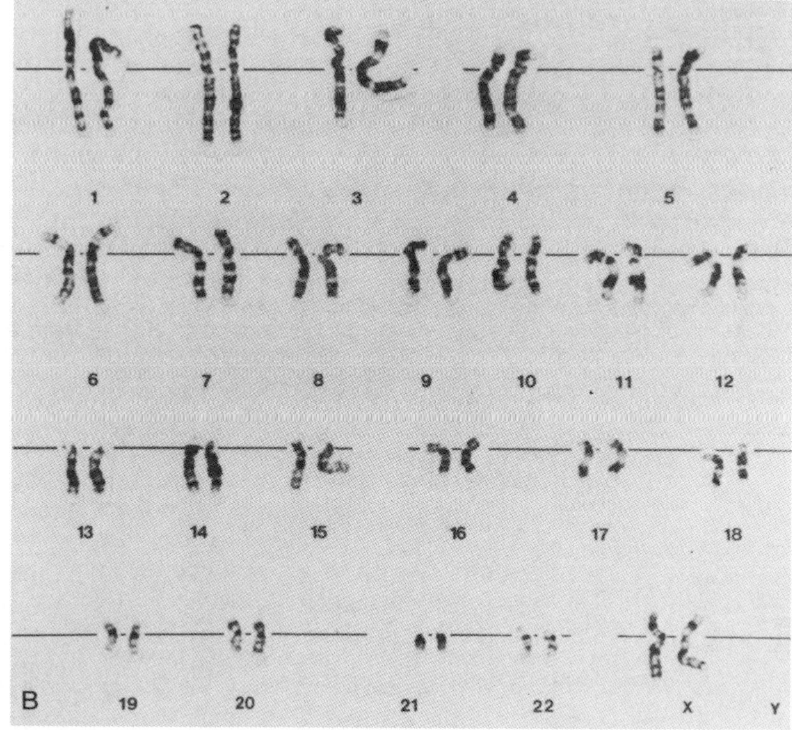

Figure 5–3

Chromosomes arranged in karyotypes. **A,** Normal male karyotype: 46,XY. **B,** Normal female karyotype: 46,XX. (From Knuppel, R.A., & Drukker, J.E. [1986]. *High-risk pregnancy:* A *team approach* [p. 519]. Philadelphia: W.B. Saunders. Courtesy of The Children's Hospital, Denver.)

be expressed. The gene that codes for blood group O is recessive. If a person receives a gene for group O from one parent and group A from the other parent, group A will be expressed in laboratory blood typing. Only if the person receives a gene for group O from both parents will laboratory testing identify his blood group as O.

On the basis of dominant and recessive forms of a gene, a person with group A blood can have one of two possible combinations of gene alleles:

- Two group A alleles
- One group A allele and one group O allele

Dominance and recessiveness are not absolute for all genes. Some people having a single copy of an abnormal recessive gene (carriers) may have a lower than normal level of the gene product (such as an enzyme) that can be detected by laboratory methods. These people usually do not have disease because the normal copy of the gene produces enough of the required product to allow normal or near-normal function.

Some gene alleles are equally dominant. The person who receives a gene for blood group A from one parent and group B from the other will have type AB blood because both forms of the gene (alleles) are equally dominant.

CHROMOSOME LOCATION

Genes located on autosomes are either autosomal dominant or autosomal recessive, depending on the number of identical copies of the gene needed to produce the trait. However, genes located on the X chromosome are paired only in females because males have one X and one Y chromosome.

A female with an abnormal recessive gene on one of her X chromosomes usually has a normal gene on the other X chromosome that compensates and maintains relatively normal function. However, the male is at a disadvantage if his only X chromosome has an abnormal gene. The male has no compensating normal gene because his other sex chromosome is a Y. The abnormal gene will be expressed in the male because it is unopposed by a normal gene.

Patterns of Single Gene Inheritance

Three important patterns of single gene inheritance are (1) autosomal dominant, (2) autosomal recessive, and (3) X-linked. Each pattern of inheritance has characteristics that distinguish it from the other two. Table 5–1 summarizes characteristics and transmission of each pattern. The inheritance patterns are

Table 5–1. SINGLE GENE TRAITS

Pedigree Symbols

A pedigree is a way to symbolically represent a family's medical history and their relationships to each other. It can help identify patterns of inheritance that may help distinguish one type of disorder from another.

Male

Female

2 Sex not specified (number indicates the number of persons represented by the symbol)

Affected

Carriers (heterozygous) for an autosomal recessive trait

Female carrier of an X-linked recessive trait

Deceased

Mating/marriage

Consanguineous mating/marriage

I Roman numerals indicate generations

Autosomal Dominant

Characteristics

A single copy of the gene is enough to produce the trait.

Males and females are equally likely to have the trait.

Often appears in every generation of a family, although family members having the trait may have widely varying manifestations of it.

May have multiple and seemingly unrelated effects on body structure and function.

Transmission of Trait from Parent to Child

A parent with the trait has a 50% (1 in 2) chance of passing the trait to the child.

The trait may arise as a new mutation from an unaffected parent. The child who receives the mutated gene can then transmit it to future generations.

Examples

Normal traits: Blood groups A and B; Rh-positive blood factor.

Abnormal traits: Huntington's disease; neurofibromatosis.

Pedigree

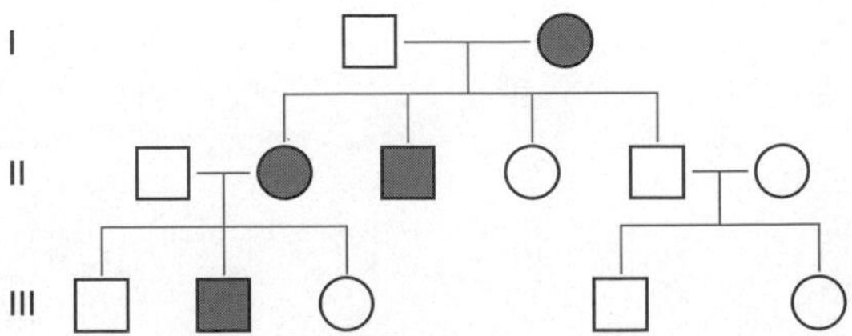

graphically illustrated with a pedigree to represent a family's history and the relationships among family members.

Single gene traits have mathematically predictable and fixed rates of occurrence. For example, if a couple has a child with an autosomal recessive disorder, the risk that their future children will have the same disorder is 1 in 4 (25 percent) at every conception. It is not important how many of their children are or are not affected; the risk is the same at every conception.

AUTOSOMAL DOMINANT TRAITS

An autosomal dominant trait is produced by a dominant gene on a non–sex chromosome. The expression of some autosomal dominant genes may result in multiple and seemingly unrelated effects in the person. The gene's effects also may vary substantially in severity, leading a family to believe incorrectly that a trait "skips a generation." A careful physical examination may reveal subtle evidence of the trait in each generation. Or, some people may carry the dominant gene but may have no apparent expression of it in their physical makeup. In some autosomal dominant disorders, such as Huntington's disease, the person having the gene will always have the disease. In others, only a portion of those carrying the gene will exhibit the disease.

New mutations account for the introduction of some abnormal autosomal dominant traits into a family that has no prior history. In this case, parents

Table 5–1. SINGLE GENE TRAITS *Continued*

Autosomal Recessive

Characteristics

Two autosomal recessive genes are required to produce the trait.
Males and females are equally likely to have the trait.
There is often no prior family history of the disorder before the first affected child.
If more than one family member is affected, they are usually full siblings.
Consanguinity (blood relationship) of the parents increases the risk for the disorder.
Disorders are more likely to occur in groups isolated by geography, culture, religion, or other factors.
Some autosomal recessive disorders are more common in specific ethnic groups.

Transmission of Trait from Parent to Child

Unaffected parents are carriers of the abnormal autosomal recessive trait.
Children of carriers have a 25% (1 in 4) chance for receiving both copies of the defective gene and thus having the disorder.
Children of carriers have a 50% (1 in 2) chance of receiving one copy of the gene and being carriers like the parents.
Children of carriers have a 25% (1 in 4) chance of receiving both copies of the normal gene. They are neither carriers nor affected.

Examples

Normal traits: Blood group O; Rh-negative blood factor.
Abnormal traits: Tay-Sachs disease; sickle cell disease; cystic fibrosis.

Pedigree

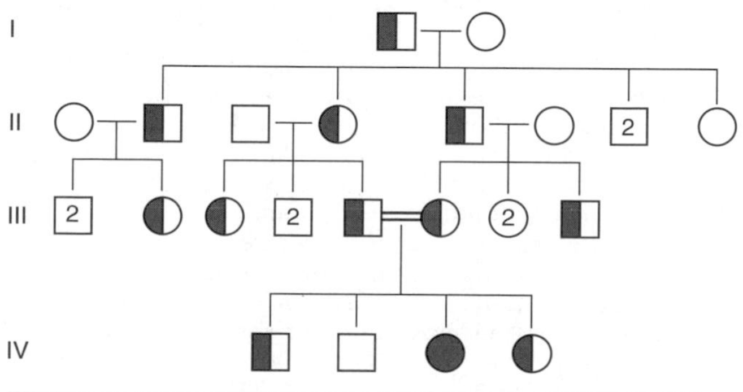

X-Linked Recessive

Characteristics

Although recessive, only one copy of the gene is needed to cause the disorder in the male who does not have a compensating X without the trait.
Males are affected, with rare exceptions.
Females are carriers of the trait, but not usually adversely affected.
Affected males are related to each other through carrier females.
Affected males do not transmit the trait to their sons.

Transmission of Trait from Parent to Child

Males who have the disorder transmit the gene to
100% of their daughters.
None of their sons.
Sons of carrier females have a 50% (1 in 2) chance of being affected. They also have a 50% chance of being unaffected.
Daughters of carrier females have a 50% (1 in 2) chance of being carriers like their mothers. They also have a 50% chance of being neither affected nor carriers.
An abnormal X-linked recessive gene also may arise by mutation.

Examples

Colorblindness; Duchenne muscular dystrophy; hemophilia A

Pedigree

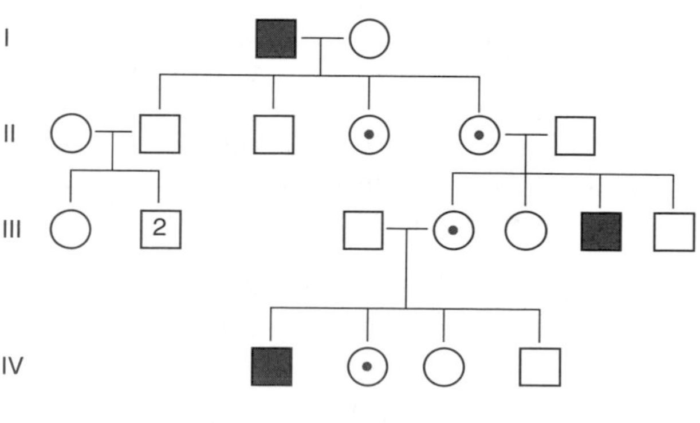

Critical to Remember

Single Gene Abnormalities

- A person affected with an autosomal dominant disorder has a 50 per cent chance of transmitting the disorder to his or her children.
- Two healthy parents who carry the same abnormal autosomal recessive gene have a 25 per cent chance of having a child affected with the disorder.
- Parental consanguinity increases the risk for having a child with an autosomal recessive disorder.
- One copy of an abnormal X-linked recessive gene is enough to produce the disorder in a male.
- Abnormal genes can arise as new mutations that are then transmitted to future generations.

of the child will be normal because their body cells do not have the altered gene. Men who father children in their fifth decade or later are more likely to have offspring with a new autosomal dominant mutation.

The person who is affected with an autosomal dominant disorder is usually heterozygous for the gene. That is, the person has a normal gene on one chromosome and an abnormal gene on the other chromosome of the pair. However, the abnormal gene overrides the influence of the normal gene. Occasionally, a person receives two copies of the same abnormal autosomal dominant gene. Such an individual is usually much more severely affected than someone with only one copy.

AUTOSOMAL RECESSIVE TRAITS

An autosomal recessive trait occurs if a person receives two copies of a recessive gene carried on one of the autosomes. Everyone carries about six abnormal autosomal recessive genes without manifesting the disorder because they have a compensating normal gene. Because the probability that two unrelated people will share even one of the same abnormal genes is low, the incidence of autosomal recessive diseases is relatively uncommon in the general population.

Situations that increase the likelihood that two parents will share some of the same abnormal autosomal recessive genes are:

- Consanguinity (blood relationship of the parents).
- Populations that are isolated by culture, geography, religion, or other factors. Inbreeding allows abnormal genes to become concentrated and occur in a greater frequency than they do in groups that are not genetically isolated.

Many autosomal recessive disorders are severe, and affected persons may not live long enough to reproduce. Two exceptions are those with phenylketonuria (PKU) and cystic fibrosis. Improved care of people with these disorders has allowed them to live into the reproductive years. If one of the couple has the autosomal recessive disorder, all of their children will be carriers. Their risk for having similarly affected children is higher as well, depending on the prevalence of the abnormal gene in the general population.

X-LINKED TRAITS

X-linked recessive traits are more common than X-linked dominant ones, and they are the only X-linked pattern discussed here. Sex differences in the occurrence of X-linked recessive traits and the relationship of affected males to each other are important factors that distinguish these disorders from autosomal dominant or recessive disorders. In general, males are the only ones who show full effects of an X-linked recessive disorder because their only X chromosome has the abnormal gene on it. Females can show the full disorder in two uncommon circumstances:

- If a female has a single X chromosome (Turner's syndrome, p. 75)
- If a female child is born to an affected father and a carrier mother

X-linked recessive disorders can be relatively mild, such as colorblindness, or they may be severe, such as hemophilia. Additionally, those having the disorder may be affected with varying degrees of severity.

✔Check Your Reading

5. If a parent has an autosomal dominant disorder, what is the chance that the child will have the same disorder?
6. Why are parents who are related by blood more likely to have a child with an autosomal recessive disorder?
7. If each member of a couple carries a gene for an autosomal recessive disorder, what is the chance that the children will have the disorder? What is the chance that the children will be carriers? What is the chance that the children will not receive the abnormal gene from either parent?
8. Why are males more often affected with X-linked recessive disorders? If a female carries an X-linked recessive disorder such as hemophilia, what are the chances that her sons will have the disorder? What is the chance that her daughters will be carriers?

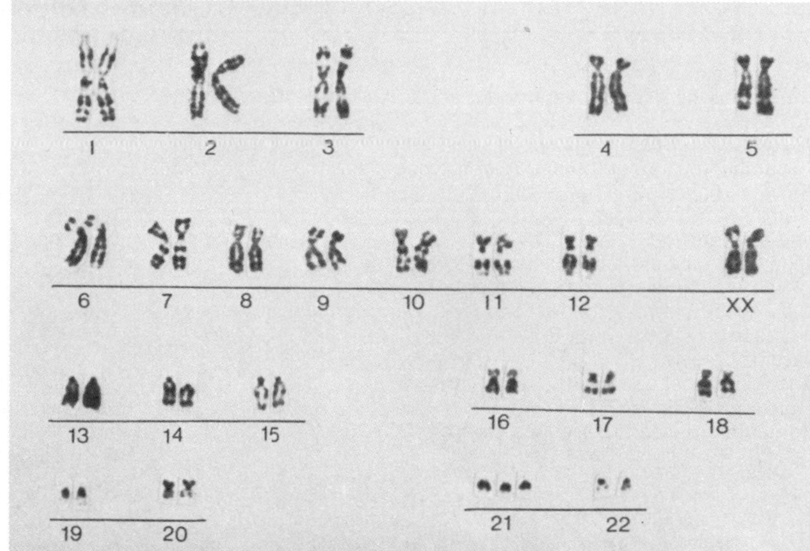

Figure 5–4

Karyotype of a female with trisomy 21 (Down syndrome: 47,XX +21). (From Hacker, N., & Moore, J.G. [1992]. *Essentials of obstetrics and gynecology* [2nd ed., p. 95]. Philadelphia: W.B. Saunders.)

Chromosome Abnormalities

Chromosome abnormalities can be numerical or structural. They are quite common (50 per cent or more) in the embryo or fetus that is spontaneously aborted. Chromosome abnormalities often cause major structural and functional abnormalities because they involve many added or missing genes.

NUMERICAL ABNORMALITIES

Numerical chromosome abnormalities are those involving added or missing single chromosomes or those with multiple sets of chromosomes. Trisomy and monosomy are numerical abnormalities of single chromosomes. Polyploidy describes abnormalities involving whole sets of chromosomes.

Trisomy. A trisomy exists when each body cell contains an extra copy of one chromosome, bringing the total number to 47 (Fig. 5–4). Each chromosome is normal, but there are too many of them. The most common trisomy is *Down syndrome*, or trisomy 21. In Down syndrome, each cell has three copies of chromosome 21. Trisomies of chromosomes 13 and 18 are less common, and have more severe effects. The incidence of trisomies increases with maternal age, so that most women who are 35 years old or older are offered prenatal diagnosis to determine whether the fetus has Down syndrome or another trisomy.

Infants with Down syndrome have characteristic features that are usually noticed shortly after birth (Table 5–2). Chromosome analysis is done during the neonatal period to confirm the diagnosis and to determine whether Down syndrome is caused by trisomy 21 or a rarer chromosome anomaly that involves a structural rather than a numerical abnormality.

Children with Down syndrome reach developmental milestones more slowly than normal children. They are mentally retarded, although the severity varies, just as intelligence varies in the general population. Early intervention programs and regular medical care help these children to reach their full ability and manage physical problems associated with Down syndrome. (See a pediatric nursing text for more complete discussion of Down syndrome.)

Monosomy. A monosomy exists when each body cell has a missing chromosome, with a total number of 45. The only monosomy that is compatible with postnatal life is *Turner's syndrome*, or monosomy X (Fig. 5–5). People with Turner's syndrome have a single X chromosome and are always female. Turner's syndrome, like other chromosome abnormalities, is very common in fetuses lost to spontaneous abortion.

Live-born infants have excess skin around the neck and edema that is most noticeable in the hands and feet (Table 5–3). If Turner's syndrome is not identified and treated during infancy or childhood, an affected girl will remain very short and will not have menstrual periods or develop secondary sex characteristics. Children with Turner's syndrome usually have normal intelligence, although they may have difficulty with spatial relationships or solving visual problems, such as reading a map. Table 5–3 shows an infant with Turner's syndrome and lists additional characteristics that may be present at birth or later in life.

Table 5–2. CHARACTERISTICS ASSOCIATED WITH DOWN SYNDROME (TRISOMY 21)

Poor muscle tone at birth
Short, wide head with a flat occiput and a flat face
Upslanting eyes
Speckled iris (Brushfield's spots)
Epicanthal folds near the bridge of the nose
Short flat nose with a flat nasal bridge
Prominent or protruding tongue
Low-set ears
Wide, short fingers, often incurving toward the radius
Simian crease (single transverse palmar crease)
Wide space between the first two toes, with a prominent plantar crease
Cardiac defects
Gastrointestinal defects (duodenal atresia)
Prone to infections
Mental retardation (Intelligence Quotient [IQ] 25–70)

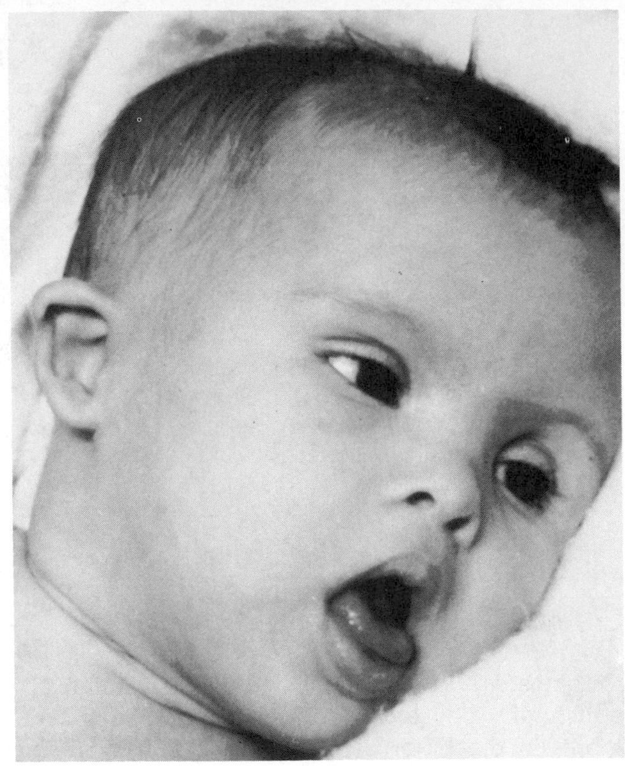

Infant with characteristic features of Down syndrome. (From Simpson, J.L., & Golbus M.S.: [1992]. *Genetics in obstetrics and gynecology* [2nd ed., p. 62]. Philadelphia: W.B. Saunders.)

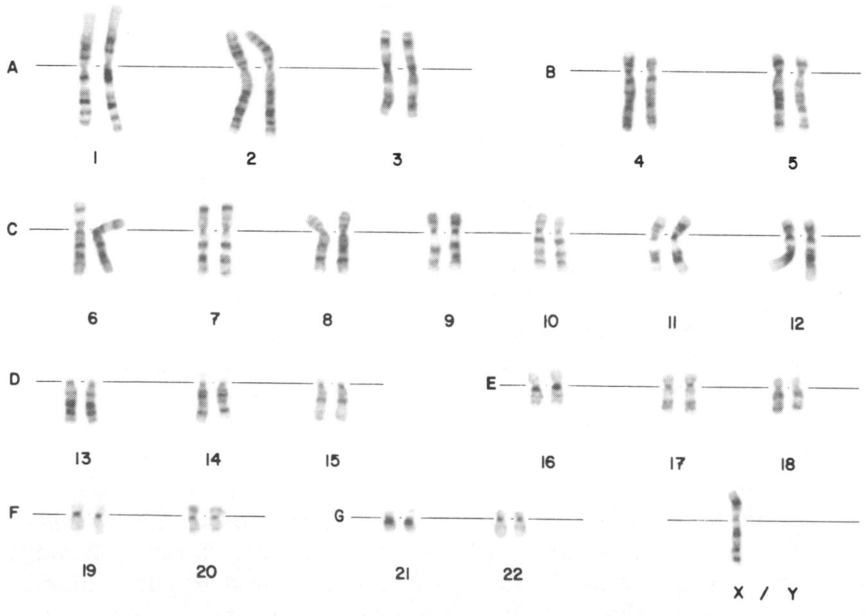

Figure 5–5

Karyotype of a female with monosomy X (Turner's syndrome: 45,X). (Courtesy of Dr. Mary Jo Harrod, University of Texas Southwestern Medical Center.)

Table 5–3. CHARACTERISTICS ASSOCIATED WITH TURNER'S SYNDROME (MONOSOMY X)

Decreased birth weight
Edema at birth, noticeable on hands and feet
Short broad neck, with excess webbed skin
Low posterior hairline
Broad shield-shaped chest with widely spaced nipples
Cardiac anomalies (coarctation of the aorta)
Renal anomalies (horseshoe kidneys)
Permanently sexually immature with infantile appearance
Short adult height
Intelligence Quotient (IQ) normal, but difficulty with spatial relationships a possibility

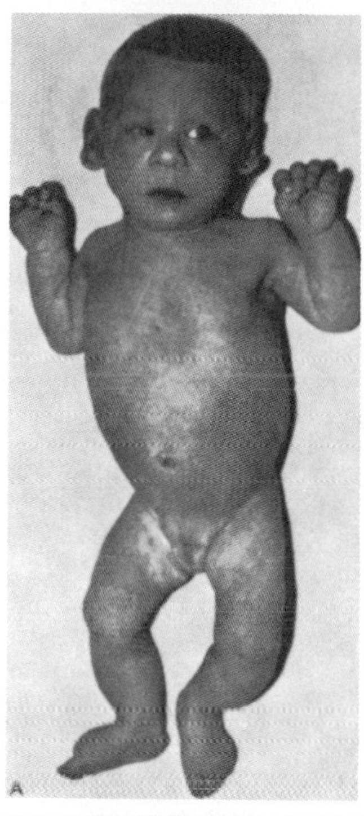

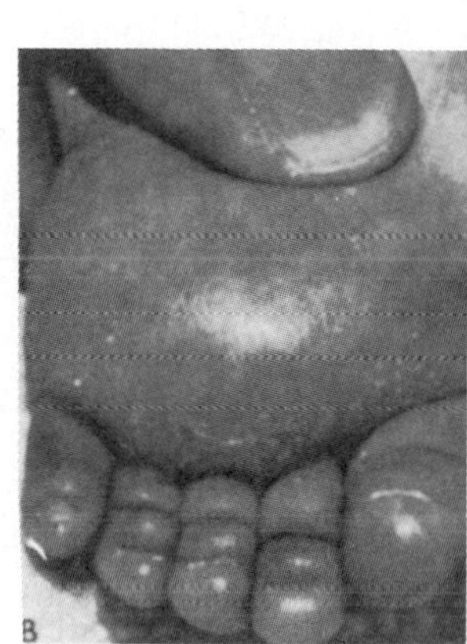

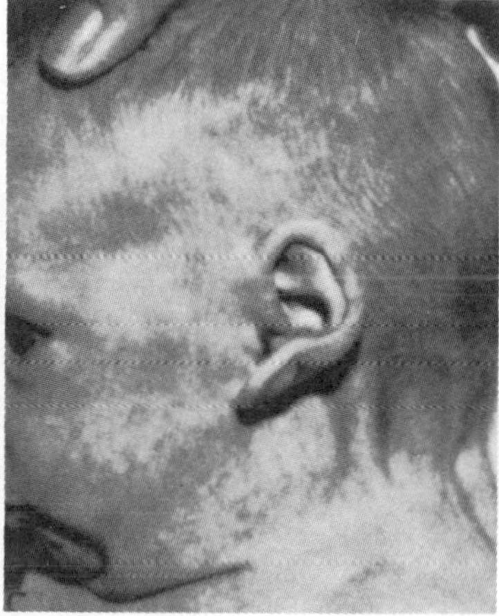

Infant with characteristic features of Turner's syndrome. (From Lemli, L., & Smith, D.W. [1963]. The XO syndrome: A study of the differentiated phenotype in 25 patients. *Journal of Pediatrics, 63*, 577.)

Early identification of Turner's syndrome and treatment with growth hormone or anabolic steroids may help a girl grow taller, although she is still likely to be shorter than her peers. Estrogen may be given to induce development of secondary sex characteristics so that a girl will have a more mature appearance.

Polyploidy. Polyploidy may occur when gametes do not halve their chromosome number during meiosis and retain both members of the pair or if two sperm fertilize an ovum simultaneously. The result is an embryo with one or more entire extra sets of chromosomes. The total number of chromosomes is a multiple of the haploid number of 23 (69 or 92 total chromosomes). Polyploidy almost always results in an early spontaneous abortion but may occasionally be seen in a live-born infant. This abnormality may be found in chorionic villus sampling (see p. 223) and may reflect an abnormality of the chorionic villi rather than the fetus.

STRUCTURAL ABNORMALITIES

Chromosome abnormalities may involve the structure of one or more chromosomes. Part of a chromosome may be missing or added, or DNA within the chromosome may be rearranged. Some of these abnormalities may reflect common benign variations. However, many are harmful because important genetic material is lost or duplicated in the structural abnormality, or the position of the genes in relation to other genes is altered so that it cannot function properly.

Another structural abnormality occurs when all or part of a chromosome is attached to another (*translocation*). Many people with a translocation chromosome abnormality are clinically normal because the total of their genetic material is normal, or balanced (Fig. 5–6). If a parent has a balanced translocation, the offspring may have completely normal chromosomes or may have a balanced translocation like the

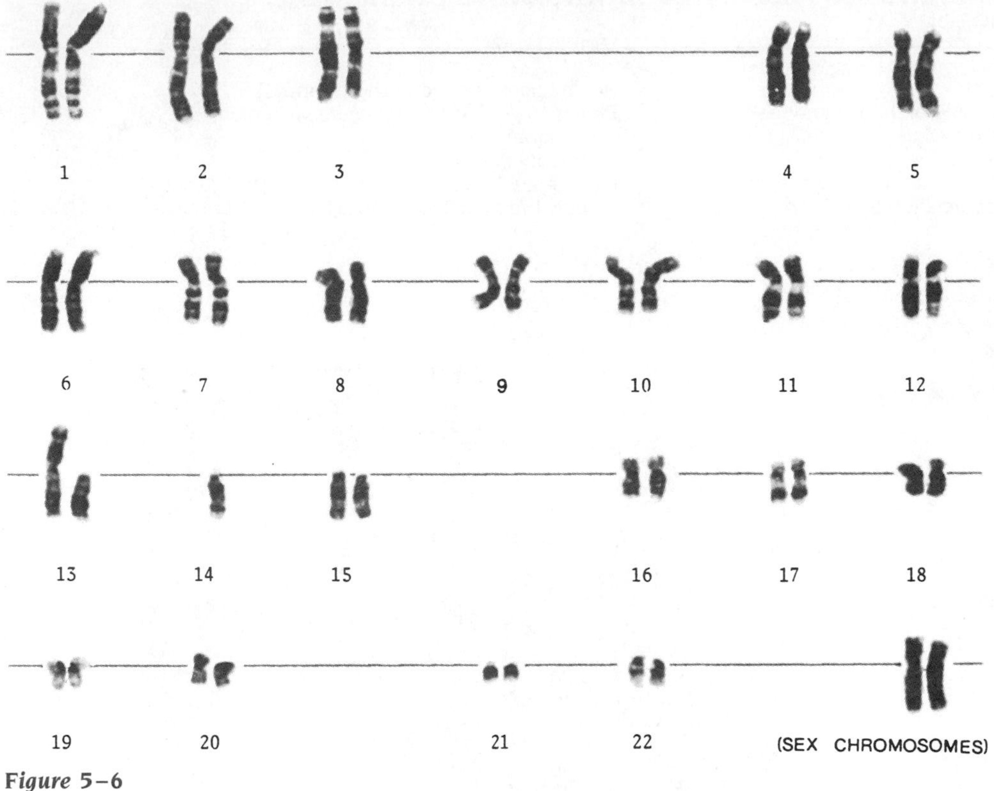

Figure 5–6

Karyotype of a balanced chromosome translocation. One of the 14th chromosome pair is attached to one of the 13th pair. (From Creasy, R.K., & Resnik, R. [1989]. *Maternal-fetal medicine: Principles and practice* [2nd ed., p. 37]. Philadelphia: W.B. Saunders.)

parent. However, the offspring may receive too much or too little chromosome material and may be spontaneously aborted or may have birth defects.

Balanced translocations are usually discovered when a pregnant woman undergoes amniocentesis and a translocation in the fetus is revealed, or they may be found during infertility evaluations if there is a history of recurrent spontaneous abortions. Either balanced or unbalanced chromosome translocations may occur spontaneously in the offspring of parents in whom translocation is absent.

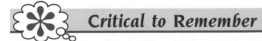

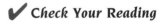

Critical to Remember

Chromosome Abnormalities

Chromosome abnormalities are either numerical or structural.

Numerical	Structural
Entire single chromosome added (trisomy)	Part of a chromosome missing or added
Entire single chromosome missing (monosomy)	Rearrangements of material within chromosome(s)
One or more added sets of chromosomes	Two chromosomes that adhere to each other

✔ Check Your Reading

9. What is a chromosome trisomy? Name a common trisomy.
10. What is a chromosome monosomy? Which monosomy is compatible with life?
11. Why are structural chromosome abnormalities often harmful?
12. What are the possible outcomes of the offspring of a parent who with a balanced chromosome translocation?

Multifactorial Disorders

Disorders resulting from interaction of genetic and environmental factors are termed multifactorial. The action of genetic factors (those pertaining to a person's genes and chromosomes) may vary with environmental influences. These interactions may influence prenatal and postnatal development either positively or negatively. For example, two embryos may have an equal genetic susceptibility for development of a disorder like spina bifida (open spine). However, the disorder will not occur unless an environment that favors its development also exists.

Characteristics

Multifactorial disorders have two characteristics that distinguish them from other types of birth defects. They are typically (1) present and detectable at birth, and (2) isolated defects rather than occurring with other unrelated abnormalities.

A multifactorial defect may *cause* a secondary defect, however. For example, infants with spina bifida often have hydrocephalus (abnormal collection of spinal fluid within the brain) as well. The hydrocephalus is not a separate defect, but occurs because abnormal development of the spine and spinal cord disrupts spinal fluid circulation, allowing it to build up within the brain's ventricular system.

The infant who has spina bifida plus defects other than those associated with disrupted central nervous system development probably does *not* have a multifactorial disorder. In this case, the spina bifida is more likely to be part of a syndrome that may pose a much different risk for recurrence in a future child.

Multifactorial disorders represent some of the most common birth defects that a maternal-child nurse encounters. Examples include (1) many heart defects, (2) neural tube defects such as anencephaly (absence of most of the brain and skull) and spina bifida, (3) cleft lip and cleft palate, and (4) pyloric stenosis.

Risk for Occurrence

Unlike single gene traits, multifactorial disorders are not associated with a fixed risk of occurrence or recurrence in a family. The risks are an average rather than a constant percentage. Factors that may vary the risk are as follows.

Number of affected close relatives. Risk increases as the number of affected close relatives (parent, sibling, and/or child) increases.

Severity of the disorder in affected family members. For example, unilateral cleft lip is associated with a lower risk for recurrence in a close relative than is a bilateral cleft lip.

Sex of affected person(s). For example, pyloric stenosis occurs five times as often in males than females. The couple who has a daughter with pyloric stenosis faces a higher risk for recurrence with subsequent children because there is a greater genetic influence for development of the defect.

Geographical location. The risk for some disorders, such as neural tube defects, is higher in some locations than others.

Seasonal variations. With some multifactorial disorders seasonal variations are noted.

If multifactorial disorders had no environmental component, the risk for occurrence and recurrence would be a precise percentage rather than a range. However, if there were no genetic component (that is, if the disorder were totally related to environment), there would be little ability to predict the risk for occurrence or recurrence.

Environmental Influences

Environmental influences on childbearing are those that do not have an identified genetic component. At one time, the placenta was thought to be a shield against harmful agents within an expectant mother's body. Now we recognize that most agents can cross the placenta and affect the developing fetus.

Environment may influence prenatal development positively, such as good nutrition that supplies all necessary raw materials for fetal growth. However, some environmental influences are harmful, for example, teratogens and mechanical forces that disrupt development.

Critical to Remember

Multifactorial Birth Defects

- Multifactorial defects are some of the most common birth defects encountered in maternity and pediatric nursing practice.
- They are a result of interaction between one's genetic susceptibility and environmental factors during prenatal development.
- These are usually single, isolated defects, although the primary defect may cause secondary defects.
- Some occur more often in certain geographical areas.
- A greater risk of occurence exists if:

  Several close relatives have the defect, whether mild or severe.
  One close relative has a severe form of the defect.
  The defect occurs in a child of the less frequently affected sex.

Infants who have several major and/or minor defects that are not directly related probably *do not* have a multifactorial defect, but have another syndrome, such as a chromosome abnormality.

Teratogens

Teratogens are agents in the fetal environment that either cause or increase the likelihood that a birth defect will occur. People often ask whether a certain drug or other substance will harm the baby. Some drugs have been definitely established as safe or harmful. For most agents, it is not clear how harmful they are to the fetus. Several factors make it difficult to establish the teratogenic potential of an agent.

Retrospective study. Investigators must rely on the mother's memory about substances she ingested or was exposed to during pregnancy. Only when many cases are collected that have a similar exposure history and similar birth defects is it possible to conclude that an agent is harmful and what the nature of that harm is.

Timing of exposure. Agents may be harmful at one stage of prenatal development but not at another.

Different susceptibility of organ systems. Some agents affect only one fetal organ system, or they affect one system at one stage of development and another at a different stage of development.

Non-controlled fetal exposure. Exposures cannot be controlled to eliminate extraneous agents or to ensure a consistent dose. Interactions with other agents may reduce or compound the fetal effects. An agent that is toxic at one dose may have no apparent effects at another.

Placental transfer. Agents vary in their ability to cross the placenta.

Individual variations. Fetuses show varying susceptibility to harmful agents.

Non-transferability of animal studies. Results of animal studies cannot always be transferred to humans. Agents that do not harm animal fetuses may damage the human embryo or fetus.

Teratogens typically cause more than one defect, which distinguishes teratogenic defects from multifactorial disorders. However, children affected by single gene and chromosome defects are also likely to have multiple defects. Therefore, clinicians consider single gene disorders, chromosome abnormalities, and effects of teratogenic agents when trying to diagnose an infant born with multiple anomalies.

Hundreds of individual agents are either known or suspected teratogens. Types of teratogens include:

- Maternal infectious agents (viruses or bacteria) that cross the placenta and damage the embryo or fetus
- Drugs and other substances used by the expectant mother (therapeutic agents, tobacco, alcohol, illicit drugs).
- Pollutants, chemicals, or other substances to which the mother is exposed in her daily life
- Ionizing radiation
- Maternal disorders, such as diabetes mellitus or phenylketonuria.

Table 5–4. ENVIRONMENTAL AGENTS KNOWN OR SUSPECTED TO HARM THE FETUS

Alcohol
Aminoglycosides
Antineoplastic agents
Antithyroid drugs
Cocaine
Diethylstilbesterol
Diphenylhydantoin (phenytoin)
Folic acid antagonists
Infections
Cytomegalovirus
Herpes simplex virus
Human immunodeficiency virus
Rubella
Syphilis
Toxoplasmosis
Varicella
Lithium
Mercury
Retinoic acid
Tetracycline
Tobacco
Trimethadione
Valproic acid
Warfarin

Table 5–4 lists some of the most common known or suspected teratogens.

It is theoretically possible to eliminate all or some of the risk to the developing fetus by avoiding exposure to the agent or changing the fetal environment in some way.

AVOIDING FETAL EXPOSURE

Ideally, avoiding exposure to harmful influences begins before conception because all major organ systems develop early in pregnancy (see Chapter 6), often before a woman realizes that she is pregnant. To avoid some agents, such as alcohol or illicit drugs, pregnant women must be committed to make substantial lifestyle changes.

Infections. Rubella immunization at least 3 months before pregnancy virtually eliminates the risk that the mother will contract this infection, which can severely damage the fetus. For infections that cannot be prevented by immunization, the mother should avoid situations in which acquiring the disease is more likely. (See Chapters 25 and 29 for other infections that may harm the fetus.)

Drugs and Other Substances. The U.S. Food and Drug Administration has established pregnancy categories for therapeutic drugs based on their potential to harm the fetus. The categories range from A through D, and X. Class A drugs have no demonstrated fetal risk in well-controlled studies. At the opposite extreme, pregnancy category X drugs are well established as being harmful. For about 80 per cent of therapeutic drugs, it is unknown whether they are definitely safe or definitely unsafe (See Appendix D for a list of common drugs and other substances that may adversely affect the fetus.)

Drug abuse is a problem in our society. It is especially difficult to establish whether a specific illicit drug can cause prenatal damage, because women who use drugs often have other factors that complicate analysis of fetal effects. For example, these women often use multiple drugs and often have poor nutrition, untreated sexually transmitted diseases, inadequate prenatal care, and a stressful life. Additionally, because the purity of illicit substances is often questionable, substances used to dilute illicit drugs may in themselves be teratogenic.

The expectant mother's best action is to eliminate use of non-therapeutic drugs and other substances such as alcohol. If she takes therapeutic drugs, the physician may be able to prescribe an alternate drug with a lower risk to the fetus or may eliminate therapeutic drugs that are not essential, such as acne medications. The pregnant woman who abuses drugs presents a complicated picture because maintenance of her drug habit takes priority over other needs. (See Chapter 23 for discussion of the special needs of drug-dependent women.)

Ionizing Radiation. Non-urgent radiological procedures may be done during the first 2 weeks after the menstrual period begins. This is usually before ovulation and thus before conception is possible. For urgent procedures, the lower abdomen should be shielded with a lead apron if possible. The radiation dose is kept as low as possible to reduce fetal exposure.

MANIPULATING THE FETAL ENVIRONMENT

Appropriate medical therapy can help a woman avoid fetal damage that could result from her illness. For example, the woman who has diabetes should try to keep her blood glucose levels normal and stable before and during pregnancy for the best possible fetal outcomes. A woman with phenylketonuria should return to her special low-phenylalanine diet before conception to avoid buildup of toxic metabolic products that may damage the fetus. (See Chapter 25 for further discussion of maternal disorders.)

Occasionally, a pregnant woman is given a drug to medicate her fetus, for example, digitalis for fetal cardiac arrhythmias. In these cases, it is the fetus who has the disorder, not the mother. The mother is the conduit for medicating the fetus to allow normal development and function.

Mechanical Disruptions to Fetal Development

Mechanical forces that interfere with normal prenatal development include oligohydramnios and fibrous amniotic bands.

Oligohydramnios, an abnormally small volume of amniotic fluid, reduces the cushion surrounding the fetus and may result in deformations such as clubfoot. Prolonged oligohydramnios can interfere with fetal lung development. Oligohydramnios may not be the primary fetal problem, but it is associated with other fetal anomalies. Oligohydramnios is usually unlikely to recur during another pregnancy, depending on its cause.

Fibrous amniotic bands may result from tears in the inner sac (amnion) of the fetal membranes and can result in fetal deformations or intrauterine limb amputation. Fibrous bands are usually sporadic and unlikely to recur. Because these bands can cause multiple defects, they may be confused with birth defects from other causes such as chromosome or single gene abnormalities.

✔ Check Your Reading

13. What are the usual characteristics of multifactorial disorders?
14. What are some factors that can vary the likelihood that a multifactorial disorder will occur or recur?
15. What are some ways in which a woman can avoid exposing her fetus to teratogens?
16. Why should a woman with phenylketonuria adhere to a low-phenylalanine diet before and during pregnancy?

Genetic Counseling

Genetic counseling helps people to better understand the disorder they are concerned about and the risk that it will occur in their family. The services provided at most centers are more inclusive than the term genetic counseling implies. Those concerned about multifactorial or environmental hazards can also receive up-to-date information at most centers.

Availability

Genetic counseling is usually available through university medical centers. State departments of mental health and mental retardation or rehabilitation services also may provide counseling services. Local chapters of the March of Dimes are an important source of information about birth defects and counseling sites. Additionally, organizations that focus on specific birth defects provide valuable support and assistance in obtaining needed services for individuals and families affected by that defect.

Focus on the Family

Unlike many areas of health care, genetic counseling focuses on the family rather than on an individual. One family member may have a birth defect, but study of the entire family is often needed for accurate counseling. This may involve obtaining medical records or performing physical examinations or laboratory studies on numerous family members, who may live far apart. Counseling is impaired if family members are unwilling to provide their medical records or agree to examinations or laboratory studies. Moreover, those who seek counseling may be unwilling to request cooperation from other family members.

Process of Genetic Counseling

Genetic counseling is often a slow process that is not always straightforward. Several visits spread over months may be needed. Additionally, some tests may be performed at only one or a few laboratories in the world, and several weeks may be required to complete them. Despite a comprehensive evaluation, a diagnosis may not be established, which is quite frustrating to those involved. An accurate diagnosis is crucial for providing families with correct information about the risks for a specific birth defect, the prognosis, and options available to avoid or manage the disorder. Advances in knowledge about birth defects may allow a definite diagnosis later, and families are encouraged to contact the center, as needed, for updates. Table 5–5 lists examples of procedures that may be used before conception, prenatally, and after birth to establish an accurate diagnosis related to birth defects.

Individuals or families may request genetic counseling before or during pregnancy or after a child has been born with a defect. The process of genetic counseling is individualized and may include a comprehensive evaluation to establish a diagnosis:

- A complete medical history, including prenatal and perinatal history
- The medical history of other family members
- Laboratory, imaging, or other studies
- Physical assessment of the child with the birth defect and other family members as needed
- Examination of photographs, particularly for family members who are deceased or unavailable
- Construction of a pedigree to identify relationships among family members and their relevant medical history

If a diagnosis is established, genetic counseling educates the family about the following:

- What caused the disorder
- The natural course of the disorder
- Options for care of an affected person
- The likelihood that the disorder will occur or recur
- Whether prenatal diagnosis is available for the disorder
- How a couple may be able to avoid having an affected child
- Availability of treatment and services for the person with the disorder

Table 5–5. DIAGNOSTIC METHODS THAT MAY BE USED IN GENETIC COUNSELING

Pre-conception Screening
Family history to identify hereditary patterns of disease or birth defects
Examination of family photographs
Physical examination for obvious or subtle signs of birth defects
Carrier testing
Persons from ethnic groups with a higher incidence of some disorders
Persons with a family history suggesting that they may carry a gene for a specific disorder
Chromosome analysis
Prenatal Diagnosis for Fetal Abnormalities
Chorionic villus sampling
Amniocentesis
Ultrasonography
Percutaneous umbilical blood sampling
Postnatal Diagnosis for an Infant with a Birth Defect
Physical examination and measurements
Imaging procedures (ultrasonography, radiography, echocardiography)
Chromosome analysis
Tests for metabolic disorders (phenylketonuria, cystic fibrosis)
Hemoglobin analysis for disorders such as sickle cell disease
Immunological testing for infections
Autopsy

Genetic counseling is non-directive; that is, the counselor does not tell the individual or parents what decision to make but educates them about options for dealing with the disorder. However, families often interpret the counseling subjectively. Some parents may regard a 50 per cent risk of occurrence or recurrence as low, whereas others may think that a 1 per cent risk is unacceptably high. Additionally, the family's values and beliefs influence whether they will seek counseling and what they will do with the information that is provided.

Supplemental Services

Comprehensive genetic counseling includes services of professionals from many disciplines, such as biology, medicine, nursing, social work, and education. They provide added support for families and may offer referral to parent support groups, grief counseling, and intervention for problems that often accompany the birth of a child with a birth defect, such as socioeconomic or family dysfunction.

Nursing Care of Families Concerned About Birth Defects

Nurses have an important role in helping families who are concerned about birth defects. Some nurses work directly with families who are undergoing genetic counseling. Many more nurses are generalists and may bring their knowledge about birth defects and their prevention to the public.

Nurses As Part of a Genetic Counseling Team

Many genetic counseling teams include nurses. With additional education, nurses can provide some counseling. Examples of such care include:

- Guiding a woman or couple through prenatal diagnosis
- Helping parents make decisions in regard to abnormal prenatal diagnostic results
- Assisting parents who have had a child with a birth defect to locate needed services and support
- Providing support to help the family deal with the emotional impact of a birth defect
- Coordinating services of other professionals, such as social workers, physical and occupational therapists, psychologists, and dietitians
- Helping families find appropriate lay support groups to help them cope with the daily stresses associated with a child who has a birth defect

Parents Want To Know

About Birth Defects

How can this birth defect be genetic? No one else in our family has ever had anything like this.

Autosomal recessive disorders are carried by parents who themselves are unaffected. The abnormal gene may have been passed down through many generations, but there is no risk for an affected child until *two* carrier parents mate.

Isn't there only a one-in-a-million chance that this birth defect will happen to another of our children?

Autosomal recessive disorders have a 25 per cent (1 in 4) chance to recur in children of the same parents. Autosomal dominant disorders may pose a 50 per cent risk for recurrence unless they resulted from a new mutation in the parental germ cells.

Isn't this birth defect very likely to recur? We'd better not have any more children.

Some birth defects are associated with a relatively high risk of recurrence. However, prenatal diagnosis may offer parents a way to avoid having an affected child or to treat some disorders before birth.

Since we've already had a child with this birth defect [an autosomal recessive one], will the next three be normal?

If both parents are carriers for an autosomal recessive disorder, there is a 25 per cent (1 in 4) risk that is constant with *each* conception. There is an equal chance that their children will be neither affected nor carriers.

If I have an amniocentesis or other prenatal diagnostic test, can the test detect all birth defects?

Although many disorders can be prenatally diagnosed, not all can be diagnosed in the same fetus. Testing is offered for one or more specific disorders after a careful family history is taken to determine appropriate tests.

If the prenatal test is normal, will my baby be normal?

Normal results from prenatal testing exclude those disorders that were specifically tested. Every healthy couple has about a 5 per cent risk for having a child with a birth defect, some of which are not obvious at birth. This baseline risk remains, even if all prenatal test results are normal.

Will I have to have an abortion if my prenatal tests show that my baby is abnormal?

Abortion may be an option for parents whose fetus is affected with a birth defect, but most parents are reassured by normal test results. If results are abnormal, some parents appreciate the time to prepare for a child with special needs. For some birth defects, better medical management can be planned for a newborn who is expected to have problems. Prenatal diagnosis gives many parents the confidence to have children despite their increased risk for having a child with a birth defect.

Nurses in General Practice

Nurses who work in antepartum, intrapartum, newborn, or pediatric settings often encounter families who are concerned about birth defects. These families may include a member who has a birth defect. Other families may believe that they have an increased risk for having a child with a birth defect. The nurse is often the first person to whom the family expresses their concerns. Generalist nurses provide care and support that may parallel or complement that of nurses who work on a genetic counseling team.

ANTEPARTUM NURSES

During the initial antepartum interview, the nurse often identifies the pregnant woman or family who may benefit from genetic counseling. The antepar-

Therapeutic Communication

Paula Crandall is a 41-year-old Caucasian woman who is 8 weeks pregnant with her first child after more than 10 years of infertility. Barbara Glenn is a nurse who works with Paula's obstetrician.

Paula: I know all about the risks at my age. I'm not so much worried about my own health, but the baby's.

Barbara: You're concerned that the baby might not be all right?

Clarifying

Paula: Sure, what woman wouldn't be? I know the baby is more likely to have Down syndrome and be mentally retarded if the mother is older . . . and I certainly qualify as older!

Barbara: Yes, you're right. The risks of chromosome abnormalities do increase after the mother is 35 years old. Have you considered having prenatal diagnosis to see if the fetus has this kind of problem?

Paraphrasing and giving information. Barbara also uses a closed-end question that tends to block communication because it can be answered with a simple "yes" or "no."

Paula: Oh, yes. I know all about what's available. When I became 35 and wasn't yet pregnant, I just assumed that if I ever did get pregnant, I'd automatically have amniocentesis or whatever tests were recommended. I just don't know . . .

Barbara: You're reconsidering prenatal testing?

Reflecting

Paula: Well, not exactly reconsidering. It's just that I've waited so long for a baby, and this is probably the only one I'll ever have.

Barbara: It sounds as if you're worried about the risks of prenatal diagnosis.

Clarifying

Paula: I am. I know amniocentesis has a low risk, but what if it causes me to lose a normal baby? It took me so long to finally get pregnant, and I'm running out of time. I don't think I'll get another chance.

Barbara: It must be a very difficult decision.

Reflecting

Paula: It is. Even if I have testing and the baby has Down syndrome, I'm not so sure I'd have an abortion. The outlook for people with Down syndrome is much better than it used to be. On the other hand, I worry about who would care for a handicapped child when I am no longer able to. Why even have prenatal testing if I wouldn't do anything about an abnormal baby?

Barbara: You certainly have some valid concerns. How does your husband feel about testing?

Questioning using an open-ended question

Paula: Oh, Bill is all for it. He keeps reminding me that the baby is probably normal and that I probably won't have a miscarriage if I have amniocentesis. But his cousin had a child with Down syndrome, and Bill doesn't think we should knowingly bring a child with a serious birth defect into the world. What would you do if you were in my place?

Barbara: I can't answer that question because I'm not in your place and I don't have to live with the decision. Let's review some of the issues so you can make the best decision for yourself and your family.

First, you know you have an increased risk for having a baby with a chromosome defect such as Down syndrome because of your age. Second, the odds that the baby will be normal are much higher than the risk that the baby will be abnormal. Third, amniocentesis poses a small but real risk of causing a miscarriage. Fourth, you are undecided abut whether you would terminate a pregnancy if the fetus is abnormal. Another issue that you haven't specifically mentioned is time. If you choose prenatal diagnosis, amniocentesis is done between 16 and 17 weeks gestation and chorionic villus sampling must be done within the next 2 weeks.

Summarizing

Paula: I know. I'm running out of time in more ways than one.

Barbara: If you like, I can set up an appointment with a genetic counselor. The counselor can provide you with the most accurate assessment of your risk for having a child with a birth defect and also the risks of any indicated prenatal diagnosis procedure. Then you can decide whether or not to have testing.

Paula: I think I'd like that, as long as I don't have to be committed to a particular decision before I go.

tum nurse also assists families with decision making, teaching, and emotional support.

Identifying Families for Referral. Nurses in antepartum settings often identify a woman or family who is appropriately referred for genetic counseling. The personal and family history of the woman and her partner may identify factors that increase their risks for having a child with a birth defect. In addition to the usual medical history about disorders such as hypertension or diabetes, the woman should be questioned about a family history of birth defects, diseases that seem to "run in the family," mental retardation, or developmental delay. Table 5–6 lists common reasons for referral to a genetic counselor.

Some people are reluctant to disclose that they have a family member with mental retardation or a birth defect. The nurse can gently probe for sensitive information by asking questions about whether there are family members who have learning problems or who are "slow." Using words that are lay-oriented often elicits more information than using clinical terms that may seem harsh to the woman and her partner.

Helping the Family Decide About Genetic Counseling. If genetic counseling is appropriate, the physician usually discusses it with the client and offers to refer her and her partner to an appropriate center. However, the final decision rests with the clients. The nurse can help the family decide whether they want genetic counseling at all and weigh issues that are important to them.

Genetic counseling can raise issues that are uncomfortable, such as whether to undergo prenatal diagnosis, what to do if a condition cannot be prenatally diagnosed, and what options are acceptable if prenatal diagnosis shows abnormal results. Counseling may open family conflicts if information from other family members is needed or if family values differ on issues such as abortion of an abnormal fetus. Additionally, there can be unexpected results (Table 5-7). The nurse must be careful not to allow personal values to influence the family's decision. It is the family who must live with the decision they make.

Table 5–6. REASONS FOR REFERRAL TO A GENETIC COUNSELOR

- Pregnant women who will be older than 35 years of age when the infant is born
- Men who father children after age 40
- Members of a group with an increased incidence of a specific disorder
- Carriers of autosomal recessive disorders
- Women who are carriers of X-linked disorders
- Couples related by blood (consanguineous relationship)
- Family history of birth defect or mental retardation
- Family history of unexplained stillbirth
- Women who experience multiple spontaneous abortions
- Pregnant women exposed to known or suspected teratogens or other harmful agents, either before or during pregnancy
- Pregnant women with abnormal prenatal screening results, such as alpha-fetoprotein, or suspicious ultrasound findings

Table 5–7. PROBLEMS ENCOUNTERED IN GENETIC COUNSELING AND PRENATAL DIAGNOSIS

- Inadequate medical records
  - Family members' refusal to release records
  - Records that are incomplete, vague, or uninformative
- Inconclusive testing
  - Too few family members available when family studies are needed
  - Inadequate number of live fetal cells obtained during amniocentesis
  - Failure of fetal cells to grow in culture
  - Ambiguous prenatal test results that are neither clearly normal nor clearly abnormal
- Unexpected results from prenatal diagnosis
  - Finding an abnormality other than the one tested
  - Non-paternity revealed
- Inability to determine the severity of a prenatally diagnosed disorder
- Inability to rule out all birth defects

Teaching About Lifestyle. Nurses can teach a pregnant woman about harmful factors in her lifestyle that can be modified to reduce the risk of defects to offspring. The nurse can support the woman in making lifestyle changes that may be difficult, such as stopping alcohol consumption, reducing or eliminating smoking, or improving her diet. Using liberal praise can motivate a client to continue her efforts to promote an optimal outcome. However, a negative attitude from nurses or other professionals may make her feel like a failure, and she may abandon her efforts to create a healthier lifestyle.

Providing Emotional Support. The antepartum nurse is a significant source of emotional support for the woman who seeks genetic counseling and prenatal diagnosis. The time between prenatal testing and the results may span several difficult weeks. In the meantime, the pregnancy is becoming more obvious and the client may begin to feel fetal movement. Many women delay telling their friends or family about their pregnancy until they know that prenatal test results are normal. When results are abnormal, women face difficult decisions about whether to terminate or continue the pregnancy.

Helping the Family Deal with Abnormal Results. Because prenatal diagnostic tests are performed to detect disorders involving serious physical and often mental effects, the woman or couple whose test results are abnormal must confront painful decisions. For most of these disorders, no effective prenatal or postnatal treatment exists. In many cases, there are only two choices: continue the pregnancy or terminate it. In addition, the decision to terminate a pregnancy must be made in a short time. Arriving at "no decision" is essentially a decision to continue the pregnancy. Although the physician or genetic counselor is the one who discusses abnormal results and the available options, the nurse can reinforce the information given to these anxious families.

When test results are abnormal, nurses can expect the couple to grieve. Even if a pregnancy was unplanned, the woman who reaches the stages of prenatal diagnosis has usually already made the initial decision to continue the pregnancy. If results are abnormal, a client must decide all over again about terminating the pregnancy. Women who continue their pregnancies grieve over the expected normal infant.

INTRAPARTUM AND NEONATAL NURSES

Nurses working in these settings encounter families who have given birth to an infant with a birth defect that was often unexpected. Stillborn infants sometimes have birth defects that contributed to their intrauterine death. Besides the loss of their baby, these parents face added pain because of the associated abnormality. An autopsy may be performed to document all anomalies and to establish the most accurate diagnosis of the birth defect for future counseling. Nursing care for families experiencing a perinatal loss, whether a result of the infant's death or the loss of the expected normal infant, is addressed in Chapter 23.

Nurses who care for these families in the intrapartum and neonatal settings will find the clients anxious, depressed, and sometimes hostile because of the unexpected event. The family's usual coping mechanisms may be inadequate for the situation, yet they have not developed new ones. Various diagnostic studies are often recommended soon after the birth of an abnormal infant to establish a diagnosis and to give parents accurate information about the disorder and options. However, a high anxiety level reduces the ability to understand the often massive amount of information received. The nurse is in the best position to evaluate the family's perception of the problem, help them understand the diagnostic tests, reinforce correct information, and correct misunderstandings. Moreover, the nurse is often most therapeutic by just being an available, active listener, helping to ease the family's pain over the event.

Nurses should encourage families to contact lay support groups. These groups are a significant source of support because they fully understand the daily problems encountered when caring for a child with a birth defect. They can help the parents deal with the stress and chronic grief associated with prolonged care of these children. Support groups can also help the parents see the positive aspects and victories when caring for their special-needs child.

PEDIATRIC NURSES

Children with birth defects typically have numerous recurrent medical problems. They usually are hospitalized more often and for longer periods than children without birth defects. They may have to travel to specialized hospitals for care, adding to the family's stress. Their families often have large expenses for medical care and equipment that are not covered by insurance or public assistance programs. There may be lost income because one parent, usually the mother, stops working to care for the child. Insurance benefits may be depleted when the maximum limits are reached, commonly $1,000,000.

Family dysfunction is common, and the strain of having a child with a serious birth defect may lead to divorce. Siblings of the child often feel left out of their parents' attention because the needs of the sick child demand so much of their care.

The pediatric nurse can reduce the family's stress by helping them locate appropriate support services. The nurse can contact social services departments to help the family find financial and other resources needed to care for the child. If parents have not connected with a lay support group, the pediatric nurse can encourage them to do so.

Summary Concepts

- The 46 human chromosomes are long strands of DNA, each containing up to several thousand individual genes.
- With the exception of those genes located on the X and Y chromosomes in males, genes are inherited in pairs that may be identical or different. Some genes are dominant, and some are recessive.
- Many, but not all, genes can be analyzed in one of three ways: the products they produce, their DNA, and their close association with another gene that is more easily analyzed.
- Cells for chromosome analysis must be living. Specimens must be handled carefully to preserve their viability.
- Chromosome abnormalities are either numerical, with the addition or deletion of entire chromo-

some(s), or structural, with deletion, addition, or rearrangement of the chromosome material.

- Single gene disorders are associated with a fixed risk of occurrence or recurrence. The type of single gene abnormality (autosomal dominant, autosomal recessive, or X-linked) determines the risk.
- Multifactorial disorders occur because of a genetic predisposition combined with environmental factors.
- The risk for occurrence or recurrence of multifactorial disorders is not fixed, but varies according to the number of close relatives that are affected, the severity of the defect in affected persons, the sex of the affected person, and geographical locale. Seasonal variations may affect the risk for some disorders.
- Few agents that can enter the fetal environment are definitely known to be teratogenic or to be safe.
- The risk for fetal damage from environmental agents can be decreased by reducing exposure to the agent or manipulating the fetal environment.
- The purpose of genetic counseling is to educate individuals or families with accurate information so they can make informed decisions about reproduction and appropriate care for affected members.
- The nurse cares for clients with concerns about birth defects by identifying those needing referral, by teaching, by coordinating services, and by offering emotional support.

References and Readings

Amato, S.S. (1990). Genetic and metabolic disorders. In R.E. Berhman & R. Kliegman (Eds.), *Nelson essentials of pediatrics* (pp. 122–152). Philadelphia: W.B. Saunders.

American Academy of Pediatrics and American College of Obstetricians and Gynecologists. (1992). *Guidelines for perinatal care* (3rd ed., pp. 56–62). Elk Grove Village, Ill., and Washington, D.C.

Bernhardt, J.H. (1990). Potential workplace hazards to reproductive health: Information for primary prevention. *Journal of Obstetric, Gynecologic, and Neonatal Nursing, 19*(1), 53–62.

Boehm, C.D., & Kazazian, H.H. (1991). Prenatal diagnosis by DNA analysis. In M.R. Harrison, M.S. Golbus, & R.A. Filly (Eds.), *The unborn patient: Prenatal diagnosis and treatment* (pp. 82–91). Philadelphia: W.B. Saunders.

Farrell, C.D. (1989). Genetic counseling: The emerging reality. *Journal of Perinatal and Neonatal Nursing, 2*(4), 21–33.

Haddow, J.E. (1991). Alpha-fetoprotein. In M.R. Harrison, M.S. Golbus, & R.A. Filly (Eds.), *The unborn patient: Prenatal diagnosis and treatment* (2nd ed., pp. 63–74). Philadelphia: W.B. Saunders.

Hall, J.G. (1987). Impact of genetic disease on pediatric health care. In *Report of the 92nd Ross conference on pediatric research* (pp. 1–7). Columbus, Ohio: Ross Laboratories.

Jones, K.L. (1989). Effects of chemical and environmental agents. In R.K. Creasy & R. Resnick, *Maternal-fetal medicine: Principles and practice* (pp. 180–192). Philadelphia: W.B. Saunders.

Jones, O.W. (1989). Basic genetics and patterns of inheritance. In R.K. Creasy & R. Resnick, *Maternal-fetal medicine: Principles and practice* (pp. 3–77). Philadelphia: W.B. Saunders.

Kuller, J.M. (1990). Effects on the fetus and newborn of medications commonly used during pregnancy. *Journal of Perinatal and Neonatal Nursing, 3*(4), 73–87.

Lemons, P.K., & Brock, M.J. (1990). Prenatal diagnosis and congenital disease: Role of the clinical nurse specialist. *Neonatal Network, 9*(3), 15–22.

McCloy, E.C. (1989). Work, environment and the fetus. *Midwifery, 5*(2), 53–62.

Meyers, C.M., & Elias, S. (1990). Genetic screening for mendelian disorders. *Contemporary OB/Gyn, 35*(8), 56–82.

Moore, K.L. (1988). *The developing human: Clinically oriented embryology* (4th ed.). Philadelphia: W.B. Saunders.

Morgan, C.D., & Elias, S. (1989). Prenatal diagnosis of genetic disorders. *Journal of Perinatal Neonatal Nursing, 2*(4), 1–12.

Myhre, C.M., Richards, T., & Johnson, J. (1989). Maternal serum α-fetoprotein screening: An assessment of fetal well being. *Journal of Perinatal and Neonatal Nursing, 2*(4), 13–20.

Mueller, L. (1991). Second-trimester termination of pregnancy: Nursing care. *Journal of Obstetric, Gynecologic, and Neonatal Nursing, 20*(4), 284–289.

Osband, B.A. (1989). Multifactorial inheritance: Implications for perinatal and neonatal nurses. *Journal of Perinatal and Neonatal Nursing, 2*(4), 43–52.

Pletsch, P.K. (1990). Birth defect prevention: Nursing interventions. *Journal of Obstetric, Gynecologic, and Neonatal Nursing, 19*(6), 482–488.

Rhodes, A.M. (1989). Minimizing the liability risks of genetic counseling. *MCN: American Journal of Maternal Child Nursing, 14*(5), 313.

Simpson, J.L., & Elias, S. (1989). Prenatal diagnosis of genetic disorders. In R.K. Creasy & R. Resnick, *Maternal-fetal medicine: Principles and practice* (pp. 78–107). Philadelphia: W.B. Saunders.

Simpson, J.L., & Golbus, M.S. (1992). *Genetics in obstetrics and gynecology*. Philadelphia: W.B. Saunders.

Steele, S. (1989). Phenylketonuria: Counseling and teaching functions of the nurse on an interdisciplinary team. *Issues in Comprehensive Pediatric Nursing, 12*(5), 395–409.

Stringer, M., Librizzi, R., & Weiner, S. (1991). Establishing a prenatal genetic diagnosis: The nurse's role. *MCN: American Journal of Maternal Child Nursing, 16*(3), 152–156.

Thompson, M.W., McInnes, R.R., & Willard, H.F. (1991). *Thompson and Thompson genetics in medicine* (5th Ed.). Philadelphia, W.B. Saunders.

Thomson, E.J., & Cordero, J.F. (1989). The new teratogens: Accutane and other vitamin-A analogs. *MCN: American Journal of Maternal Child Nursing, 14*(4), 244–248.

Wells, P.W., & Meghdadpour, S. (1988). Research yields new clues to cystic fibrosis. *MCN: American Journal of Maternal Child Nursing, 13*(3), 187–190.

Welshimer, K.J., & Earp, J.A.L. (1989). Genetic counseling within the context of existing attitudes and beliefs. *Patient Education and Counseling, 13*(3), 237–255.

Williams, J.K. (1989). Screening for genetic disorders. *Journal of Pediatric Health Care, 3*(3), 115–121.

Williams, J.K. (1986). Genetic counseling in pediatric health care. *Pediatric Nursing, 12*(4), 287–290.

Williamson, R.A. (1989). Understanding consanguinity. *Contemporary OB/Gyn, 34*(5), 31–34.

Zacharias, J.F. (1990). The new genetics. *Journal of Obstetric, Gynecologic, and Neonatal Nursing, 19*(2), 122–128.

Zamula, E. (1989). Drugs and pregnancy: Often the two don't mix. *FDA Consumer, 23*(5), 7–10.

Part II

The Family Before Birth

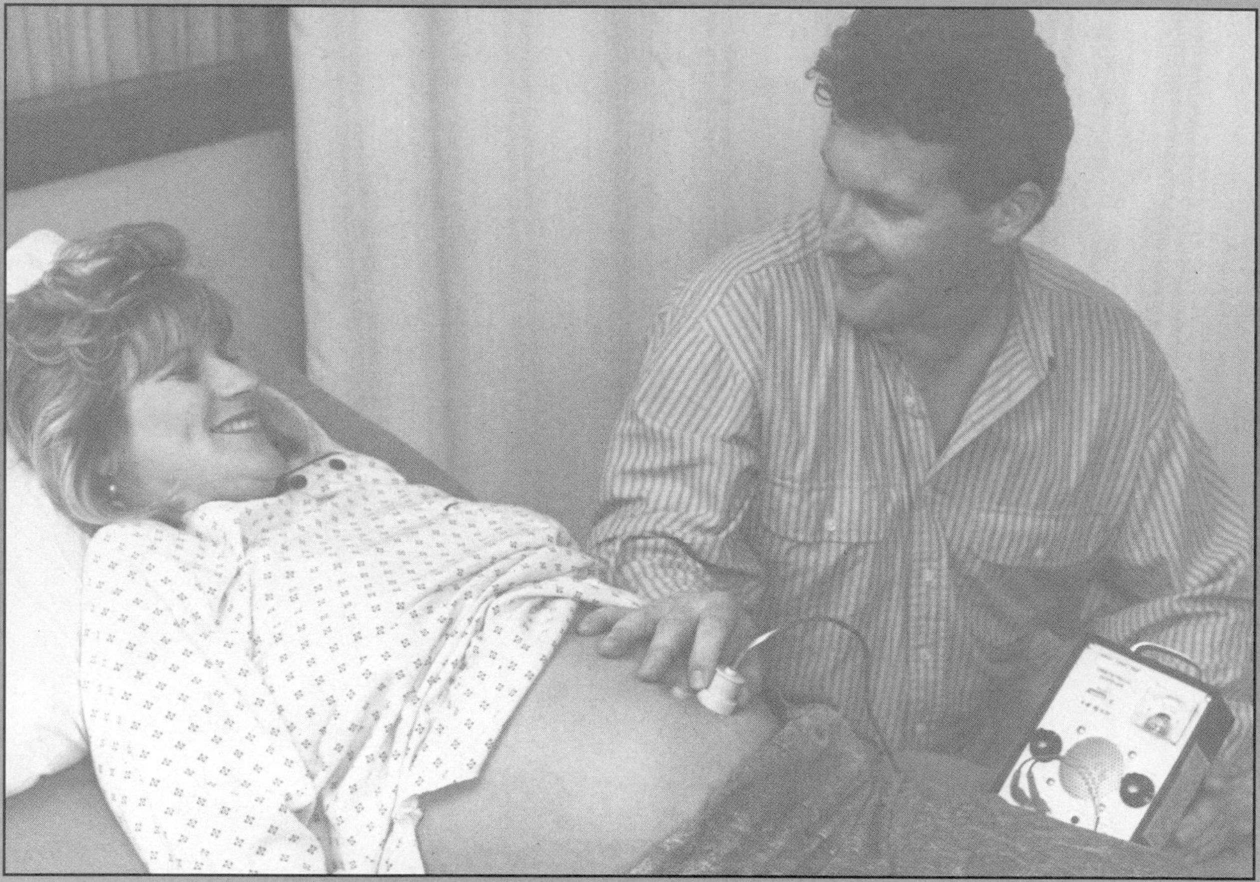

6

Conception and Prenatal Development

Objectives

1. Describe formation of the female and male gametes.
2. Relate ovulation and ejaculation to the process of human conception.
3. Explain implantation and nourishment of the embryo before development of the placenta.
4. Describe normal prenatal development from conception through birth.
5. Explain structure and function of auxiliary fetal structures.
6. Describe how common deviations from usual conception and prenatal development occur.
7. Relate prenatal circulation and the circulatory changes after birth.
8. Describe how multifetal pregnancies can occur.

Definitions

Autosome • Any of the 22 pairs of **chromosomes** other than the **sex chromosomes.**

Conceptus • Cells and membranes resulting from fertilization of the ovum.

Corpus luteum • Graafian follicle cells remaining after ovulation that produce estrogen and progesterone.

Diploid • Having a pair of chromosomes (46 in humans). The diploid number of chromosomes represents one copy of every chromosome from each parent and is the number normally present in body cells other than **gametes.**

Ejaculation • Expulsion of **semen** from the penis.

Embryo • The developing baby from the 8th day through the 8th week after conception.

Endometrium • Lining of the uterus.

Fertilization age • Prenatal age of the developing baby calculated from the date of conception. Also called **post-conceptional age.**

Fetus • The developing baby from 9 weeks after conception until birth. In everyday practice, this term is often used to describe a developing baby during pregnancy, regardless of age.

Gamete • Reproductive cell. The female gamete is an **ovum;** the male gamete is a **spermatozoon.**

Gestational age • Prenatal age of the fetus (measured in weeks) calculated from the first day of the woman's menstrual period. Also called **menstrual age.** About 2 weeks longer than the **fertilization age.**

Graafian follicle • A small sac within the ovary that contains the maturing ovum.

Haploid • Having one copy of each chromosome pair (23 in humans). **Gametes** normally have a haploid number of chromosomes.

Meiosis • Reduction cell division in **gametes** that halves the number of chromosomes in each cell.

Mitosis • Cell division in body cells other than the **gametes.**

Nidation • Implantation of the fertilized ovum **(zygote)** in the uterine endometrium.

Oogenesis • Formation of **gametes (ova)** in the female.

Ovulation • Release of the mature ovum from the ovary.

Placenta • Fetal structure that provides nourishment and removes wastes from the developing baby and secretes hormones necessary for the pregnancy to continue.

Sex chromosomes • The X and Y **chromosomes.** Females have two X chromosomes; males have one X and one Y chromosome.

Somatic cells • Body cells other than the **gametes,** or sex cells.

Spermatogenesis • Formation of male **gametes** (sperm) in the testes.

Teratogen • An agent that can cause defects in a developing baby during pregnancy.

Zygote • The developing baby from conception through the first week of prenatal life.

The maternity nurse needs a basic understanding of conception and prenatal development to provide care to parents during normal childbearing and to better understand problems such as infertility or birth defects. Knowledge of normal prenatal development enables the nurse to counsel pregnant women about factors that can enhance or hamper normal prenatal development.

This chapter addresses formation of the gametes, the process of conception, prenatal development, and important auxiliary structures that support normal prenatal development. A short discussion of how multifetal pregnancy, such as twinning, occurs is also included.

Gametogenesis

Gametogenesis is the process of gamete formation: ova in the woman and sperm in the man. Production of gametes requires a different process than formation of ordinary body cells (somatic cells). Somatic cells reproduce by a process called mitosis. Each somatic cell has 46 paired chromosomes (the diploid number): 22 pairs of autosomes and one pair of sex chromosomes. During mitosis the cell divides into two new cells, with each having 46 chromosomes, like the parent cell.

Gametogenesis requires a special reduction division called meiosis. Unlike mitosis, whereby the diploid number of chromosomes is retained in the new cells, meiosis halves the number of chromosomes (haploid number). Only one of each chromosome pair is directed to the gamete, 22 autosomes and one sex chromosome. When the sperm and ovum unite at conception, these "halves" form a new cell and restore the chromosome number to 46. See Table 6–1 for a summary of human gametogenesis and differences between males and females.

Table 6–1. COMPARISON OF FEMALE AND MALE GAMETOGENESIS

	Oogenesis	Spermatogenesis
Time during which primary germ cells are produced	Fetal life. No others develop after about 30 weeks of gestation.	Continuously after puberty
Hormones controlling process	GnRH FSH LH Estrogen	GnRH FSH LH Testosterone Estrogen (small amounts converted from testosterone) Growth hormone
Number of mature germ cells that develop from each primary cell	One	Four
Quantity	One during each reproductive cycle of about 28 days.	200–600 million are released with each ejaculation.
Size	Large. Visible to naked eye. Abundant cytoplasm to nourish embryo until implantation.	Tiny compared to ovum. Little cytoplasm. Head is almost all nuclear material (chromosomes).
Motility	Relatively non-motile. Carried along by action of cilia and currents within fallopian tubes.	Independently motile by means of whip-like tail. Mitochondria in middle piece provide energy for motility.
Chromosome complement	23 total: 22 autosomes plus one X sex chromosome.	23 total: 22 autosomes, plus either an X or a Y sex chromosome.

Abbreviations: GnRH, gonadotropin-releasing hormone; FSH, follicle-stimulating hormone; LH, luteinizing hormone.

Oogenesis

Oogenesis is the formation of female gametes (Fig. 6–1,A), within the ovary. Oogenesis begins during prenatal life when primitive ova (oogonia) multiply by mitosis, like all other cells. The oogonia contain 46 chromosomes (22 pairs of autosomes and a pair of X chromosomes) as do other body cells. Before birth, these oogonia enlarge to form primary oocytes with a layer of follicular cells surrounding each one. These are called *primary follicles.* They still contain 46 chromosomes and remain dormant until puberty.

The female fetus has all the ova she will ever have by the 30th week of gestation. Many of these ova regress during childhood. When a girl's reproductive cycles begin during puberty, some of the primary follicles present at birth begin maturing. The process of gamete maturation continues throughout her reproductive years until the ova are depleted at the climacteric.

When the oocyte matures, two meiotic divisions reduce the chromosome number from 46 paired to 23 unpaired chromosomes: 22 autosomes and an X. Shortly before ovulation, the primary oocyte undergoes its first meiotic division, dividing the chromosomes in half and forming a secondary oocyte. The primary cell's cytoplasm is divided unequally with this division, with most being retained by the secondary oocyte. The remainder of cytoplasm, plus the other half of the chromosomes go into a tiny, nonfunctional polar body that soon degenerates.

At ovulation, the secondary oocyte begins dividing again (second meiotic division) to form a mature ovum. The second meiotic division is prolonged, and

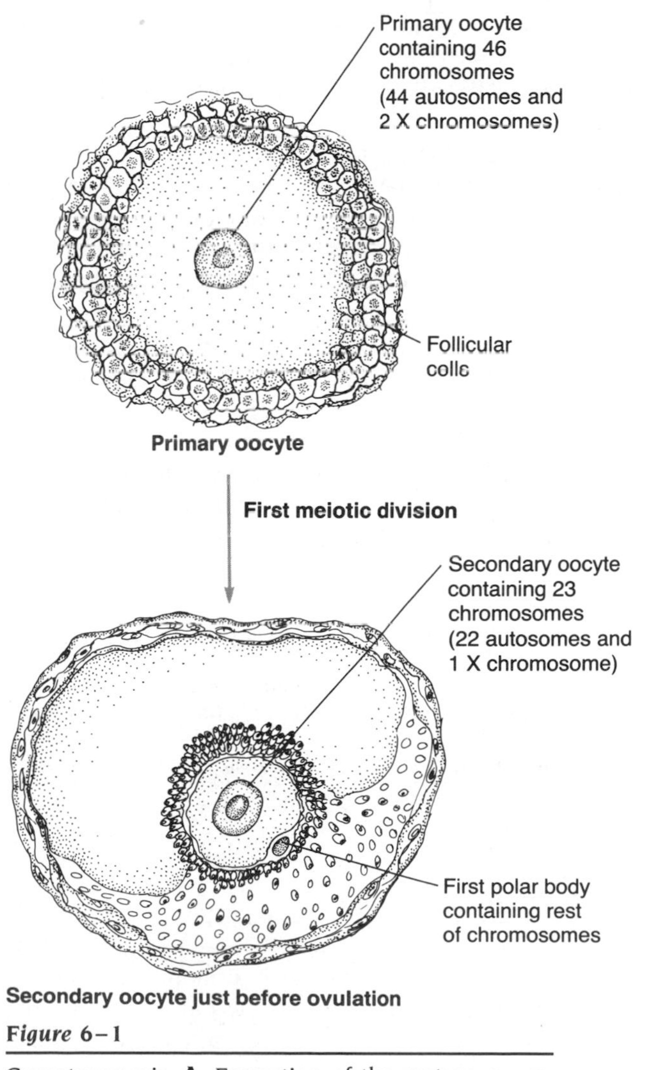

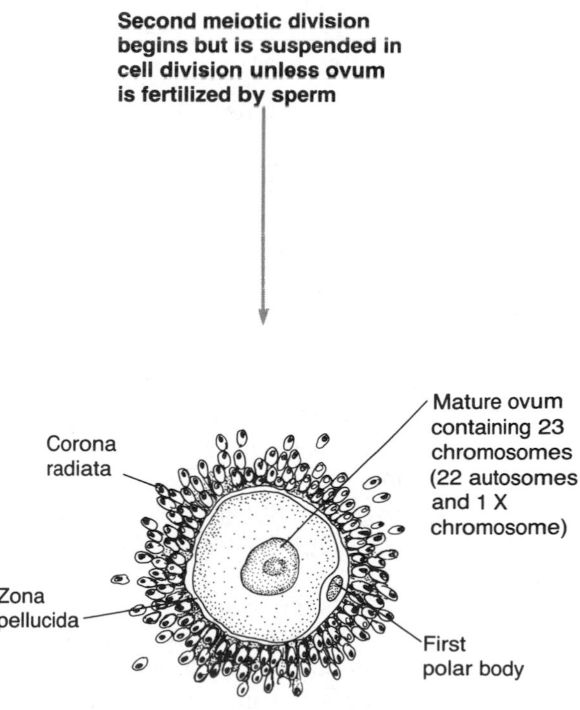

Figure 6–1

Gametogenesis. **A,** Formation of the mature ovum.

Illustration continued on following page

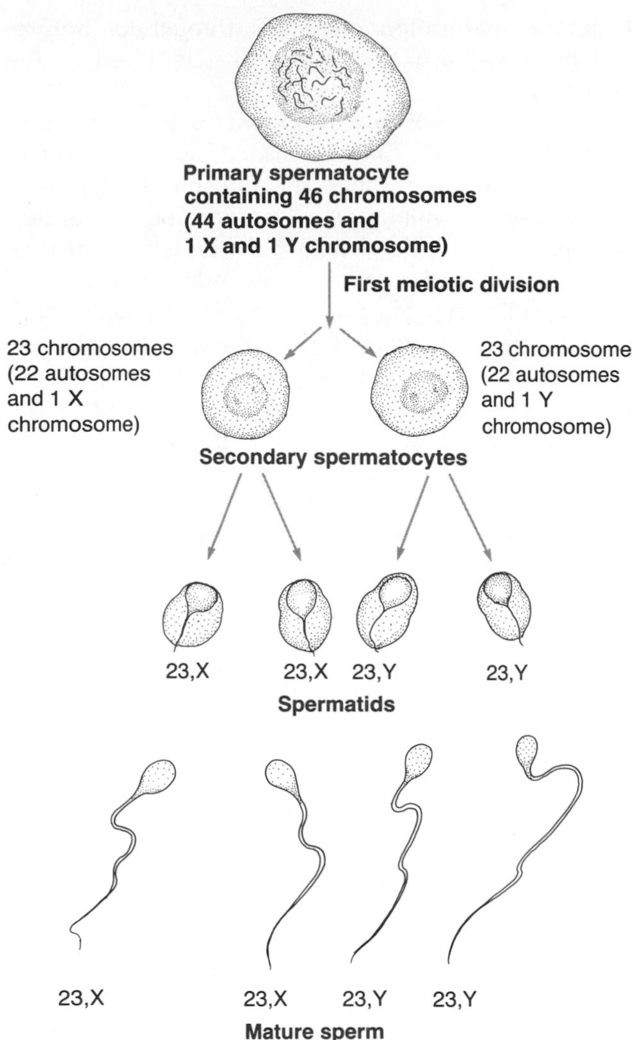

Figure 6–1 Continued

B, Formation of mature sperm.

the mature ovum remains suspended in metaphase, the middle part of cell division. If fertilization occurs, the second meiotic division is then completed, resulting in a mature ovum containing 23 chromosomes and a second tiny polar body that degenerates. If the ovum remains unfertilized, it will not complete the second meiotic division and will degenerate. In oogenesis, one primary oocyte results in a single mature ovum.

When released from the ovary, the mature ovum is surrounded by two layers, the zona pellucida and the cells of the corona radiata. These layers protect the ovum and prevent fertilization by more than one sperm. For fertilization to occur, the sperm must penetrate these two layers to reach the ovum's cell nucleus.

Spermatogenesis

Spermatogenesis (Fig. 6–1,B) begins during puberty in the male. Primitive sperm cells (*spermatogonia*) develop during the prenatal period and begin multiplying by mitosis during puberty. Unlike the female, the male continues producing new spermatogonia that can mature into sperm throughout his lifetime. Although male fertility gradually declines with age, men can father children in their 50s, 60s, and beyond.

Each spermatogonia contains 46 paired chromosomes, like other body cells. In the mature male, each spermatogonium enlarges to become a primary spermatocyte, still containing all 46 chromosomes. The first meiotic division forms two secondary spermatocytes and reduces the number to 23 unpaired chromosomes: 22 autosomes and one sex chromosome, either an X or a Y.

Each secondary spermatocyte divides again to form two spermatids. Half of the spermatids carry an X chromosome, and half carry a Y. The spermatids gradually evolve into mature sperm. Thus the original spermatogonium produces a total of four mature sperm.

The gamete from a male determines the sex of the new baby. Each mature sperm contains 23 chromosomes: 22 autosomes and either an X or a Y. If an X-bearing spermatozoon fertilizes the ovum, the baby will be a girl. If a Y-bearing spermatozoon fertilizes the ovum, the baby will be a boy.

The mature sperm has three major sections: a head, a middle portion, and a tail (Fig. 6–2). The head is almost entirely a cell nucleus. The head contains the male chromosomes that will join the chromosomes of the ovum. The middle portion supplies energy for the tail's whip-like action. The movement of the tail propels the sperm toward the ovum.

✔ Check Your Reading

1. What is the purpose of meiosis in the gametes?
2. How many mature ova can be produced by each oogonium?
3. How many mature spermatozoa can be produced by each spermatogonium?

Conception

Conception occurs when a spermatozoon and an ovum unite. Conception of a new baby requires precise timing between release of a mature ovum at

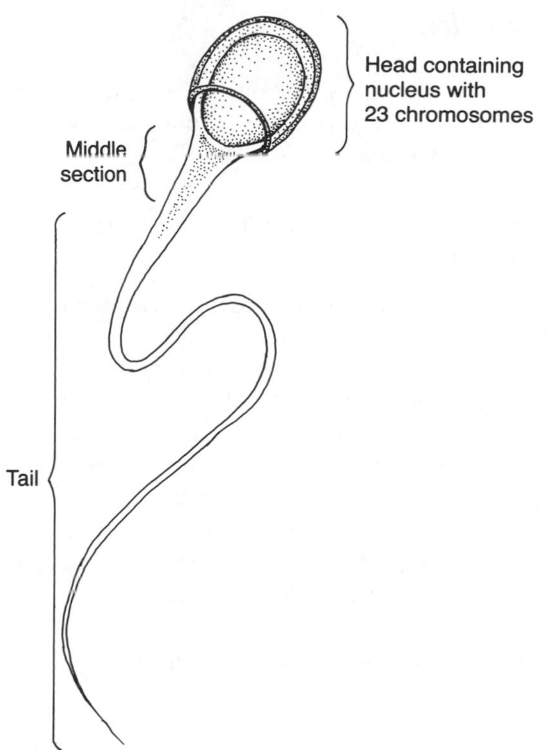

Figure 6–2

Mature sperm.

ovulation and ejaculation of enough healthy, motile sperm into the vagina. The ovum degenerates 24 hours after its release at ovulation, and most sperm do not survive more than 24 hours in the female reproductive tract. This allows approximately 48 hours during which the sperm and ovum can unite. Considering these narrow time constraints, it is remarkable that conception ever occurs.

Preparation for Conception in the Female

Before ovulation, several oocytes begin maturing under the influence of follicle-stimulating hormone (FSH) and luteinizing hormone (LH) from the female's anterior pituitary gland. The maturing oocytes are contained within a sac called the graafian follicle, which produces estrogen and progesterone to prepare the endometrium for a possible pregnancy. Eventually, one follicle outgrows the others. The less mature oocytes regress and cannot mature again. (See Chapter 4 for discussion of the simultaneous changes in the ovary and uterus during the female reproductive cycle.)

RELEASE OF THE OVUM

Ovulation occurs about 14 days before a woman expects her next menstrual period to begin. The follicle develops a weak spot on the surface of the ovary and ruptures at this spot, releasing the mature ovum with its surrounding cells on the surface of the ovary. The collapsed follicle is transformed into the corpus luteum, which maintains high estrogen and progesterone secretion necessary to make final preparation of the uterine lining for a fertilized ovum.

OVUM TRANSPORT

The mature ovum is released on the surface of the ovary, where it is picked up by the fimbriated (fringed) ends of the fallopian tube as they sweep back and forth over the ovary. The ovum is transported through the tube by muscular action of the tube and movement of cilia within the tube. Fertilization normally occurs in the distal third of the fallopian tube, near the ovary. The ovum, fertilized or not, enters the uterus about 3 to 4 days after its release from the ovary.

Preparation for Conception in the Male

The male preparation for fertilizing the ovum consists of ejaculation, movement of the sperm in the female reproductive tract, and preparation of the sperm for actual fertilization.

EJACULATION

When a male ejaculates during sexual intercourse, 200 to 600 million sperm are deposited in the upper vagina and over the cervix. The sperm are suspended in seminal fluid, which nourishes and protects the sperm from the hostile acidic environment of the vagina.

TRANSPORT OF SPERM IN THE FEMALE REPRODUCTIVE TRACT

Whip-like movement of the tails of spermatozoa propels them through the cervix, uterus, and fallopian tubes. Uterine contractions induced by prostaglandins in the seminal fluid enhance movement of the sperm toward the ovum. Only sperm cells enter the cervix. The seminal fluid remains behind in the vagina.

Many sperm are lost along the way. Many are digested by vaginal enzymes and phagocytes in the female reproductive tract, while others simply lose their way, moving into the wrong tube, or past the ovum and out into the peritoneal cavity. Only a few hundred reach the area of the fallopian tube where the ovum is located.

PREPARATION OF SPERM FOR FERTILIZATION

Sperm are not immediately ready to fertilize the ovum when they are ejaculated. While making the trip to the ovum, the sperm undergo changes that enable one of them to penetrate the protective layers surrounding the ovum. The sperm that reach the ovum release enzymes to digest a pathway through the cells of the corona radiata. Their tails beat harder to propel them toward the center of the ovum. Eventually, one spermatozoon penetrates the ovum.

Fertilization

Fertilization occurs when one spermatozoon enters the ovum and the two nuclei containing the parents' chromosomes merge (Fig. 6–3).

ENTRY OF ONE SPERMATOZOON INTO THE OVUM

Entry of a spermatozoon into the ovum has two results. First, changes in the zona pellucida surrounding the ovum prevent other sperm from entering. Second, the ovum, which has been suspended in the middle of its second meiotic division since ovulation, completes meiosis. This results in a nucleus with 23 chromosomes and expulsion of a second non-functional polar body. The mature ovum now contains 23 unpaired chromosomes, 22 autosomes, and one X chromosome in its nucleus.

FUSION OF THE NUCLEI OF SPERM AND OVUM

Once a spermatozoon has penetrated the ovum, fusion of their nuclei begins. The sperm head enlarges, and the tail slowly degenerates. The nuclei of the gametes move toward the center of the ovum, where

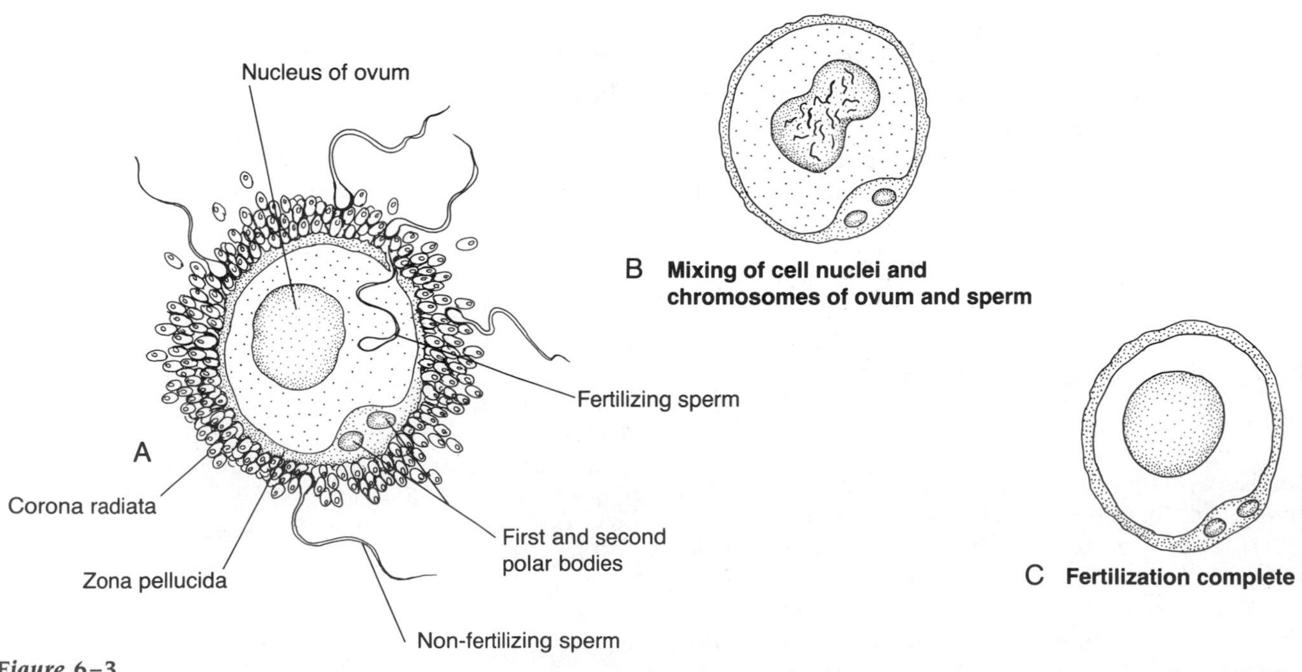

Figure 6–3

Process of fertilization. **A,** A sperm enters the ovum. **B,** The 23 chromosomes from the sperm mingle with the 23 chromosomes from the ovum, restoring the diploid number to 46. **C,** The fertilized ovum is now called a zygote and is ready for the first mitotic cell division.

the membranes surrounding their nuclei touch and dissolve. The 23 chromosomes from the sperm mingle with the 23 from the ovum, restoring the diploid number to 46 as in all other body cells. Fertilization is complete, and cell division can begin when the nuclei of the sperm and ovum unite.

✔ Check Your Reading

4. Where does fertilization usually occur?
5. What are the purposes of the seminal fluid?
6. What occurs when a spermatozoon penetrates the ovum?
7. When is fertilization complete and a new human conceived?

Pre-Embryonic Period

Prenatal development begins in the fallopian tube for the first 2 days after fertilization. On the 3rd day the zygote enters the uterus. Figure 6–4 illustrates fertilization through implantation.

Initiation of Cell Division

The zygote divides into two cells, then four, then eight cells. Up to the 16-cell stage, the cells become smaller with each division, so they occupy about the same amount of space as the original ovum. When the conceptus is a solid ball of 12 to 16 cells, it is called a *morula* because it resembles a mulberry.

The outer cells of the morula secrete fluid, forming a sac of cells with an inner cell mass placed off-center within the sac (blastocyst). The inner cell mass will develop into the fetus. Part of the outer layer of cells will eventually develop into the placenta and fetal membranes. (See p. 107 for information on these structures that are crucial for normal prenatal growth and development.)

Entry of the Zygote into the Uterus

The zygote enters the uterus about 3 days after conception, when it contains a total of about 100 cells. It

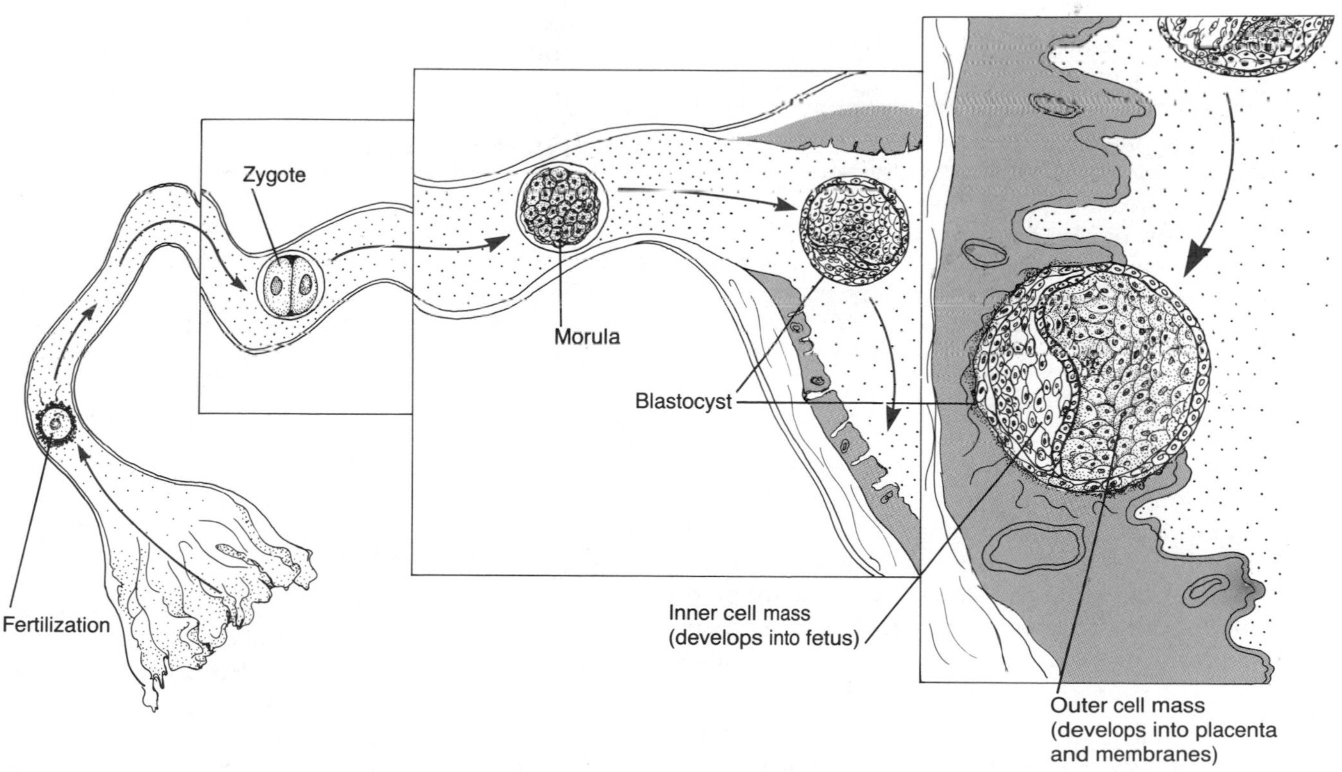

Figure 6–4

Prenatal development from fertilization through implantation of the blastocyst. Implantation gradually occurs from the sixth through the tenth day. Implantation is complete on the tenth day.

lingers in the uterus another 2 to 4 days before beginning implantation. The endometrium is now in the secretory phase of the reproductive cycle, 1½ weeks before the woman would otherwise begin her menstrual period. The endometrial glands are secreting at their maximum, providing rich fluids to nourish the conceptus before placental circulation is established. The endometrial spiral arteries are well developed in the secretory phase, providing easy access for developing the placental blood supply.

Implantation in the Endometrium

The zygote carries a small supply of nutrients for early cell division. However, implantation at the proper time and location in the uterus is critical for continued normal development. Implantation (nidation) is not sudden, but is a gradual process beginning 6 days after conception. Implantation is complete on the 10th day. During the relatively long process of implantation, embryonic structures also are developing.

Maintaining the Endometrium

Implantation and survival of the conceptus are critically dependent on a continuing supply of estrogen and progesterone to maintain the endometrium in the secretory phase. The zygote secretes human chorionic gonadotropin (hCG) to signal the woman's body that a pregnancy has begun. With continued hCG production by the conceptus, the corpus luteum will persist and continue secreting estrogen and progesterone.

Location of Implantation

The conceptus must be in the right place at the right time for normal implantation to occur. The site of implantation is important because that is where the placenta will develop. Normal implantation occurs in the upper uterus (fundus), often in the anterior or posterior fundus. The fundus is the best area for implantation and placental development for three reasons:

- The fundus is richly supplied with blood for optimum fetal gas exchange and nutrition.
- The uterine lining is thick in the fundus, preventing the placenta from attaching so deeply that it cannot be easily expelled after birth.
- Fundal implantation limits blood loss after birth because strong muscle fibers in this area compress open vessels after the placenta detaches.

Mechanism of Implantation

Enzymes produced by the conceptus erode the endometrium, tapping maternal sources of nutrition. At this early stage, nutritive fluid passes to the embryo by *diffusion* (see Table 6–3) because no circulatory system is yet established. The conceptus is fully embedded within the mother's thick uterine endometrium by 10 days, and the site of implantation is almost invisible.

As the conceptus implants, usually near the time of the next expected menstrual period, there may be a small amount of bleeding ("spotting") from the site. Implantation bleeding may be confused with a normal menstrual period, particularly if menstrual periods are usually light. Implantation bleeding may cause inaccurate calculation of a pregnancy's duration if it is counted as a normal menstrual period.

✔ Check Your Reading

8. When does implantation occur?
9. What are the advantages of implantation in the uterine fundus?
10. How is the embryo nourished before the placenta develops?

Embryonic Period

The embryonic period begins during implantation at 8 days after conception and continues through the 8th week. Basic structures of all major body organs are completed during the embryonic period. Table 6–2 presents major developments in body systems during prenatal life. Figure 6–5 illustrates the external appearance of the embryo from the 3rd through the 8th weeks after conception.

Differentiation of Cells

Early embryonic cells are undifferentiated and can follow several possible pathways of development. The embryo progresses from having cells with essentially identical functions (undifferentiated) to differentiated, or specialized, body cells. By the end of the 8th week, all major organ systems are in place and many are functioning, although in a simple way.

Development of the specialized structures is controlled by three factors: (1) the genetic content of the chromosomes received from the parents, (2) in-

Table 6–2. TIMETABLE OF PRENATAL DEVELOPMENT BASED ON FERTILIZATION AGE*

Nervous/Sensory System	Cardiorespiratory System	Digestive System	Genitourinary System	Musculoskeletal System	Integumentary System
3 Weeks: 1.5 mm CRL					
Flat neural plate begins closing to form neural tube. Neural tube still open at each end.	Heart consists of 2 parallel tubes. Chorionic villi of early placenta connect with heart.	Endoderm (inner) germ layer will become digestive tract.		Cube-shaped swellings (somites) appear and will form most of the head and trunk skeleton.	Epidermis (outer skin layer) will develop from ectoderm (outer germ layer). Dermis (deep skin layer) will develop from mesoderm (middle germ layer).
4 Weeks: 4.0 mm CRL					
Neural tube closed at each end. Cranial end of neural tube will form brain, caudal end will form spinal cord. Eye development begins as an outgrowth of forebrain. Nose development begins as two pits.	Heart begins partitioning into 4 chambers and begins beating. Blood circulating through embryonic vessels and chorionic villi. Tracheal development begins as a bud on the upper gut and branches into two bronchial buds.	Development of primitive gut as embryo folds laterally. Stomach begins as a widening of the tube-shaped primitive gut. Liver, gallbladder and biliary ducts begin as a bud from primitive gut.	Primordial germ cells are present on embryonic yolk sac.	Upper limb buds are present and look like flippers. Lower limb buds appear.	
6 Weeks: 13 mm CRL					
Development of pituitary gland and cranial nerves. Head sharply flexed because of rapid brain growth. Eyelid development beginning. Ear development begins in neck region as six swellings.	Blood formation primarily in liver. Three right and two left lung lobes develop as outgrowths of the right and left bronchi.	Most intestines are contained within the umbilical cord because the liver and kidneys occupy most of the abdominal cavity. Stomach nearing final form. Development of upper and lower jaws.	Kidneys are near bladder in the pelvis. Kidneys occupy much of the abdominal cavity Primordial germ cells incorporated into developing gonads. Male and female gonads are identical in appearance.	Arms paddle-shaped, fingers webbed. Feet and toes develop similarly, but a few days later than arms and hands. Bones cartilaginous, but ossification of skull begins.	Mammary glands begin development. Tooth buds for primary (deciduous) teeth begin developing.
8 Weeks: 30 mm CRL					
Spinal cord stops at end of vertebral column. Taste buds begin developing.	Heart partitioning into 4 chambers complete. Heart beat detectable with ultrasound. Additional branching of bronchi.	Stomach has reached final form. Lips are fused.	Testes begin developing under influence of Y chromosome. Ovaries will develop if a Y chromosome is not present. External genitalia begin to differentiate, but still appear quite similar.	Fingers and toes still webbed, but distinct by end of eighth week. Bones begin to ossify.	

* Fertilization age is about 2 weeks less than gestational age.
Abbreviation: CRL, crown-rump length.

Table continued on following page

Table 6–2. TIMETABLE OF PRENATAL DEVELOPMENT BASED ON FERTILIZATION AGE* *Continued*

Nervous/Sensory System	Cardiorespiratory System	Digestive System	Genitourinary System	Musculoskeletal System	Integumentary System
		10 Weeks: 61 mm CRL Weight 14 g			
Head flexion still present, but straighter. Eyelids closed and fused. Top of external ear is slightly below eye level.	May be possible to detect heart beat with Doppler transducer. Blood produced in spleen.	Intestines contained within abdominal cavity as growth of this cavity catches up with digestive system development. Digestive tract patent from mouth to anus.	Kidneys are in their adult position. Male and female external genitalia have different appearance, but still easily confused.		Fingernails begin developing. Tooth buds for permanent teeth begin developing below those for primary teeth.
		12 Weeks: 87 mm CRL Weight 45 g			
Surface of brain is smooth, without sulci (grooves) or gyri (convolutions). Nasal septum and palate complete development.	Heart beat should be detected with Doppler transducer.	Sucking reflex present.	Kidneys begin producing urine. Male and female external genitalia can be distinguished by appearance.	Limbs are long and thin. Involuntary muscles of viscera develop.	Downy lanugo begins developing at end of this week.
		16 Weeks: 140 mm CRL Weight 200 g			
	Pulmonary vascular system developing rapidly.	Fetus swallows amniotic fluid and produces meconium (bowel contents).	Urine excreted into amniotic fluid.	Lower limbs reach final relative length, longer than upper limbs. A woman who has been pregnant before may begin to feel fetal movements.	External ears have enough cartilage to stand away from head somewhat. Blood vessels easily visible through the delicate skin.
		20 Weeks: 160 mm CRL Weight 460 g			
Myelination of nerves begins, and continues through first year of postnatal life.	Heartbeat should be detectable with regular fetoscope.	Peristalsis well developed.	Over 40% of nephrons are mature and functioning. Testes contained in abdomen, but begin descent toward scrotum. Primordial follicles of ovary develop.	Fetal movements felt by mother and may be palpable by an experienced examiner.	Skin covered with vernix caseosa. Brown fat production complete. Nipples begin development.

Table 6–2. TIMETABLE OF PRENATAL DEVELOPMENT BASED ON FERTILIZATION AGE* *Continued*

Nervous/Sensory System	Cardiorespiratory System	Digestive System	Genitourinary System	Musculoskeletal System	Integumentary System
24 Weeks: 230 mm CRL Weight 820 g					
Spinal cord ends at level of first sacral vertebra because of more rapid growth of vertebral canal.	Primitive thin-walled alveoli (air sacs) have developed and are surrounded by capillary network. Surfactant production begins in lungs to reduce surface tension within alveoli. Respiration possible, but most fetuses die if born at this time.			Fetus is active. Fetal movements become progressively more noticeable to both mother and examiner.	Body appearance lean. Skin wrinkled and red. Fingerprints and footprints develop. Fingernails present. Eyebrows and lashes present.
28 Weeks: 270 mm CRL Weight 1300 g					
Major sulci and gyri are present. Eyelids no longer fused after 26 weeks. Responds to bitter substances on tongue.	Blood formation shifts to bone marrow. Sufficient alveoli, surfactant, and capillary network to allow respiratory function, although respiratory distress syndrome is common. Many infants born at this time will survive with intensive care.		Testes begin descent into scrotum.		Skin slightly wrinkled, but smoothing out as subcutaneous fat is deposited under it.
32 Weeks: 300 mm CRL Weight 2100 g					
			Testes enter scrotum.		Skin smooth and pigmented. Large vessels visible beneath skin. Fingernails reach fingertips. Lanugo disappearing.
38 Weeks: 360 mm CRL Weight 3400 g					
Sulci and gyri developed. Visual acuity about 20/600 at birth	Newborn infant has about one-eighth to one-sixth the number of alveoli as an adult. Well-developed ability to exchange gas.		Both testes usually palpable in scrotum at birth. The newborn girl's ovaries contain about 1 million follicles. No new ones are formed after birth.		Fetus plump and skin smooth. Vernix caseosa present in major body creases. Lanugo present on shoulders and upper back only. Fingernails extend beyond the fingertips. Ear cartilage firm.

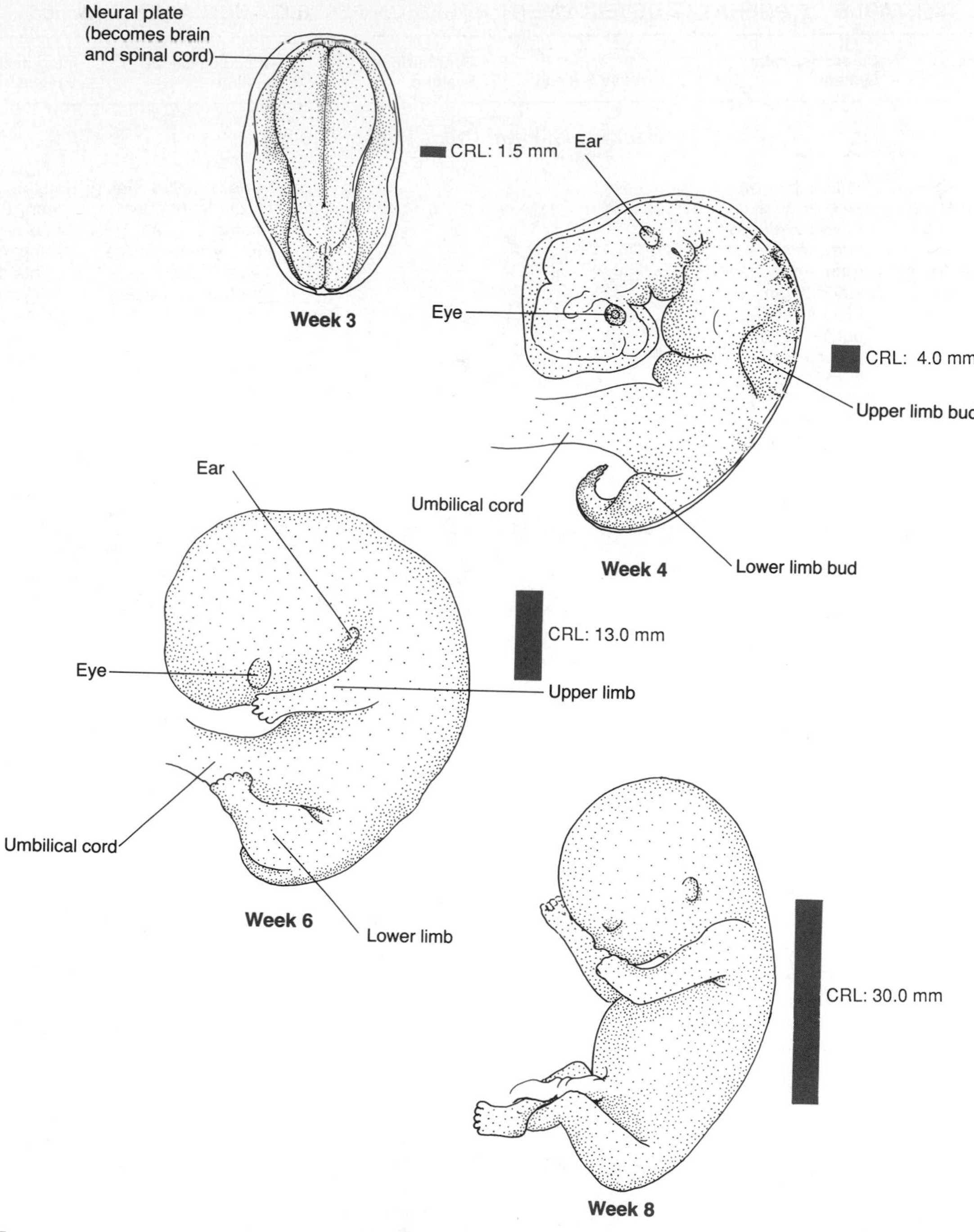

Figure 6–5

Embryonic development from 3 weeks through the eighth week after fertilization. CRL, crown-to-rump length.

teraction between adjacent tissues, and (3) timing. Although basic instructions are within the chromosomes, one tissue may induce change toward greater specialization in another, but only if signal between the two tissues occurs at a specific time during development. In this way, structures develop with appropriate size and relationships to each other.

During the embryonic period, structures are vulnerable to damage from teratogens because they are developing rapidly and normal development of one structure may depend on normal and properly timed development of another. Unfortunately, a woman may not even realize that she is pregnant at this sensitive time. For this reason, the possibility of pregnancy should be explored with her before drugs or diagnostic procedures, such as x-rays, are prescribed. Some agents may be damaging at one time during pregnancy, but not at another. Others may be damaging at any time during pregnancy. Appendix E contains information about substances that may cause prenatal damage.

Weekly Developments

Development occurs simultaneously in all of the embryonic organ systems. Changes beginning the 2nd week after conception are described next. Development of the embryo and fetus proceeds in a cephalocaudal (head-to-toe) and a central to peripheral direction. This developmental pattern continues after birth.

SECOND WEEK

Implantation is complete by the end of the 2nd week. The most growth occurs in the outer cells (*trophoblast*), which eventually becomes the placenta. The inner cell mass that will develop into the baby becomes flattened into the *embryonic disc*. Cells that will eventually form part of the fetal membranes develop.

THIRD WEEK

Many women will miss their first menstrual period during the 3rd week of pregnancy. The embryonic disc develops three layers (germ layers) that, in turn, give rise to major organ systems of the body.

The central nervous system begins developing during the 3rd week. A thickened flat neural plate appears, extending toward the cranial end of the embryonic disc. The neural plate develops a longitudinal groove that folds to form the neural tube. At the end of the 3rd week, the neural tube is fused in the middle but is still open at each end.

Early heart development consists of a pair of parallel heart tubes that run longitudinally in the embryo. Vessels developing in the chorionic villi and membranes join the heart tubes. Primitive blood cells arise from the endoderm lining the distal blood vessels.

FOURTH WEEK

The shape of the embryo changes. It folds at the head and tail end and laterally. The embryo resembles a C-shaped cylinder by the end of the 4th week. A "tail" is apparent during the embryonic period because the brain and spinal cord develop more rapidly than other systems. The tail becomes less prominent and finally disappears as the rest of the body catches up with growth of the central nervous system.

The neural tube completes closure during the 4th week. If the neural tube does not close, defects such as spina bifida or anencephaly will result.

Formation of the face and upper respiratory tract begins. Beginnings of the internal ear and the eye are apparent. The upper extremities appear as buds on the lateral body walls.

Because the embryo is sharply flexed anteriorly, the heart is near the embryo's mouth. The heart, still tubular at the beginning of the 4th week, begins contracting. Partitioning of the heart into four chambers begins during the 4th week and is completed by the end of the 6th week.

The lower respiratory tract begins development as a branch off the upper digestive tract. Gradually, the esophagus and trachea completely separate. The trachea branches to form the right and left bronchi. These bronchi in turn branch to form the three lobes of the right lung and two lobes of the left lung. Continued branching of the bronchi eventually forms the terminal air sacs (*alveoli*). The alveoli proliferate and become surrounded by a rich capillary network that enables oxygen and carbon dioxide exchange at birth.

FIFTH WEEK

The brain develops rapidly during the 5th week. The heart is beating and developing four chambers. Upper limb buds are paddle-shaped with obvious notches between the fingers. Lower limbs form slightly later than upper ones. Lower limbs are also paddle-shaped, but the area between the toes is not as well defined as the division between the fingers.

SIXTH WEEK

The head is prominent because of rapid development and is bent over the chest. The heart reaches its final four-chambered form. Upper and lower extremities continue to become more defined.

The eye continues to develop, and the beginning of the external ear is apparent as six small bumps near each side of the neck. Facial development begins with eyes, ears, and nasal pits widely separated, aligned with the body walls. Gradually, the embryo grows so that the face comes together in the midline.

SEVENTH WEEK

General growth and refinement of all systems occurs. The face becomes more human-looking. The eyelids begin to grow, and the extremities become longer and better defined. The trunk elongates and straightens, although a C-shaped spinal curve is still present in the newborn at birth.

The intestines have been growing faster than the abdominal cavity during the embryonic period. The relatively large liver and kidneys also occupy much of the abdominal cavity. Therefore, most of the intestines are contained within the umbilical cord while the abdominal cavity grows to accommodate them. The abdomen is large enough to contain all its normal contents by 10 weeks.

EIGHTH WEEK

The embryo has a definite human form, and refinements to all systems continue. The ears are low-set, but approaching their final form. The eyes are pigmented, but not yet fully covered by eyelids. Fingers and toes are stubby, but well defined. The external genitalia begin to differentiate, but male and female characteristics are not distinct until after the 10th week.

✔ Check Your Reading

11. Why is the embryo particularly susceptible to damage from teratogens?
12. How does the lower respiratory tract develop?
13. Why are the intestines mostly contained within the umbilical cord until the 10th week?

Fetal Period

The fetal period represents the longest segment of prenatal development. It begins 9 weeks after conception and ends with birth. All major systems are present in their basic form. Dramatic growth and refinement in the structure and function of all organ systems occurs during the fetal period. Teratogens may damage already formed structures but are less likely to cause major structural alterations. The central nervous system is vulnerable to damaging agents through the entire pregnancy. Figure 6–6 illustrates growth and development during the fetal period.

Weeks 9 Through 12

At the beginning of this period, the head is quite large, almost half the total length of the fetus. The body begins growing faster than the head. The extremities approach their final relative lengths, although the legs remain proportionally shorter than the arms. The first fetal movements begin but are too slight for the mother to detect.

The face is broad, with a wide nose and widely spaced eyes. The eyes close at 9 weeks and will reopen by 28 weeks. The ears appear low-set because the mandible is still small.

The intestinal contents that were partly contained within the umbilical cord enter the abdomen as the capacity of the abdominal cavity catches up with them in size. Blood formation occurs primarily in the liver during the 9th week but shifts to the spleen by the end of the 12th week. The fetus begins producing urine during this period, excreting it into the amniotic fluid.

Internal differences in males and females begin to be apparent in the 7th week. External genitalia look similar until the end of the 9th week. By the end of the 12th week, the fetal sex can be determined by the appearance of the external genitalia.

Weeks 13 Through 16

The fetus grows rapidly in length, so the head becomes smaller in proportion to the total length. Movements become stronger, and some women, particularly those who have been pregnant before, may be able to detect them (*quickening*).

The face looks human because the eyes face fully forward. The ears reach their final position, in line with the eyes.

Weeks 17 Through 20

The mother should feel fetal movements if she has not felt them before. Early fetal movements feel like fluttering or "butterflies." Some women may not recognize these subtle sensations for what they are. If

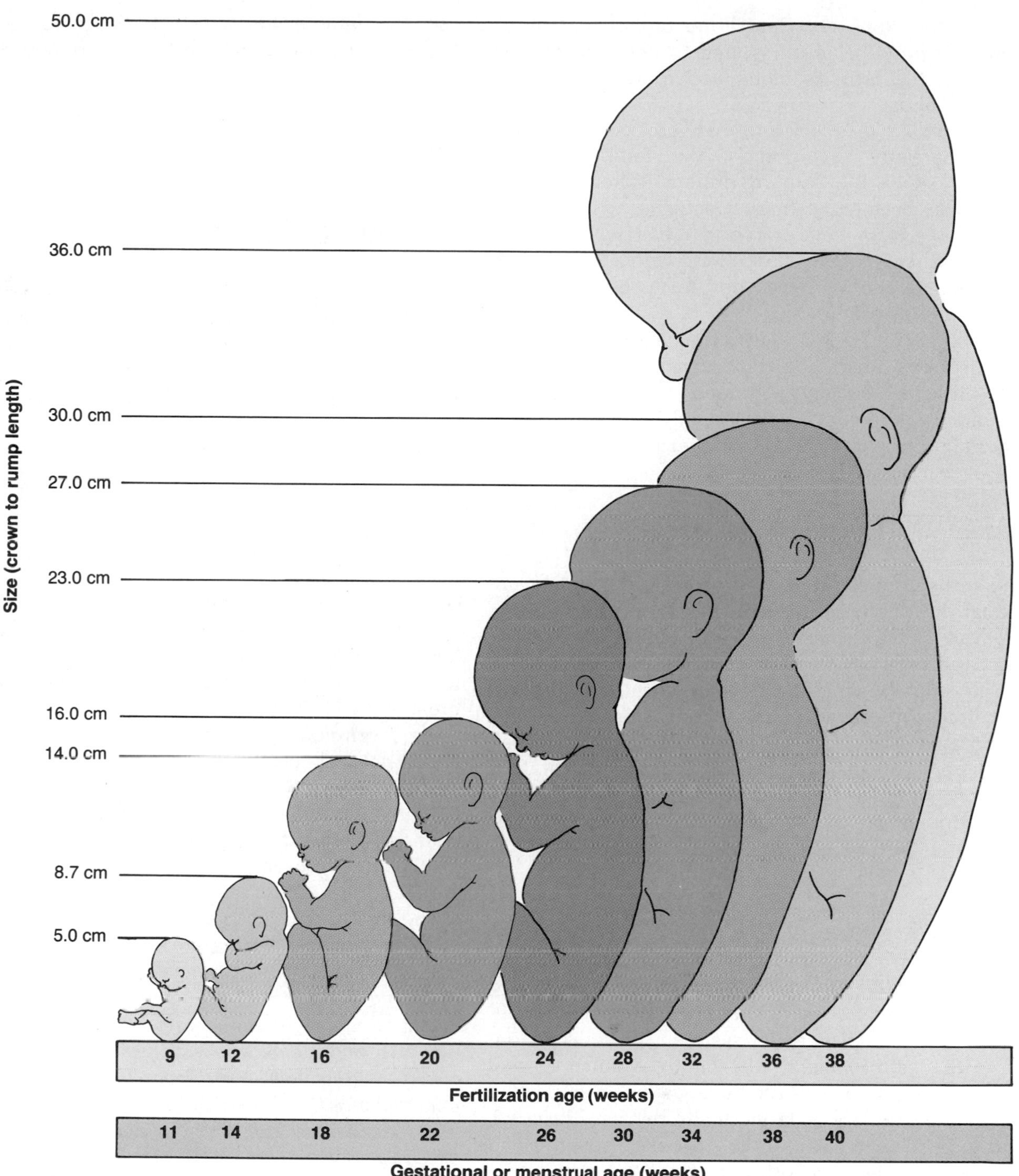

Figure 6–6

Fetal development from 9 weeks of fertilization age through 38 weeks of fertilization age. The gestational age, measured from the first day of the last menstrual period, is 2 weeks longer than fertilization age.

the mother does not detect movement, the physician may perform an ultrasound examination to confirm that the fetus is living and to re-evaluate the gestational age.

Changes in the skin and hair are evident. *Vernix caseosa*, a fatty secretion of the fetal sebaceous glands, covers the skin to protect it from constant exposure to amniotic fluid. *Lanugo* is a fine, downy hair that covers the fetal body. Lanugo helps the vernix adhere to the skin. Both vernix and lanugo diminish as the fetus reaches term. Eyebrows and head hair appear.

Brown fat is a special heat-producing fat that begins to be deposited during this period. It is located on the back of the neck, behind the sternum, and around the kidneys. Brown fat will help the neonate maintain temperature stability after birth (see p. 482).

Weeks 21 Through 24

The fetus continues growing and gaining weight, although he or she is thin and has little subcutaneous fat. The skin is translucent and looks red because the capillaries are close to its fragile surface.

The lungs begin to produce *surfactant*, a surface-active lipid substance that makes it easier for the baby to breathe after birth because it keeps the lung alveoli from collapsing with each breath. The capillary network surrounding the alveoli is increasing but is still very immature, although gas exchange is possible.

Weeks 25 Through 28

The fetus may survive if born during this period because of maturation of the lungs, pulmonary capillaries, and central nervous system. The fetus continues to gain weight, becoming plumper and smoother-skinned as subcutaneous fat is deposited under the skin. The skin gradually becomes less red. The eyes, closed since about 9 weeks, reopen. Head hair is abundant. Blood formation shifts from the spleen to the bone marrow.

During early pregnancy, the fetus floats relatively freely within the amniotic sac. However, the fetus usually assumes a head-down position in the uterus during this time. The head-down position is most common for two reasons:

- The uterus is shaped like an inverted egg. The overall shape of the fetus in flexion is similar, with the head being the small pole of the egg shape and the buttocks, flexed legs, and feet being the larger pole.
- The fetal head is heavier than the feet, and gravity causes the head to drift downward in the pool of amniotic fluid.

The head-down position is most favorable for normal birth as well.

Weeks 29 Through 32

The skin is pigmented according to race and is smooth. Larger vessels are visible over the abdomen, but small capillaries cannot be seen. Toenails are present, and fingernails extend to the fingertips. The fetus has more subcutaneous fat, rounding the body contours. If the fetus is born during this period, chances of survival are good.

Weeks 33 Through 38

Growth of all body systems continues until birth, but the rate of growth slows as full term approaches. The fetus is mainly gaining weight. The pulmonary system matures to enable efficient and unlabored breathing after birth.

The well-nourished term fetus is rotund, with abundant subcutaneous fat. At birth, boys are slightly heavier than girls. The skin is pink to brownish-pink, depending on race. Lanugo may be present over the forehead, upper back, and upper arms. Vernix is often present in major creases, such as the groin and axillae.

The testes are in the scrotum. Breasts of both male and female infants are enlarged, and there is palpable breast tissue beneath the areola and nipple.

Full term ranges from 36 to 40 weeks of fertilization age, or 38 to 42 weeks of gestational age. *Because conception occurs about 2 weeks after the first day of the last menstrual period, the fertilization age is about 2 weeks shorter than the gestational age. However, gestational age is the most commonly used because the last menstrual period provides a known marker, whereas most women do not know exactly when they conceived.*

✔ Check Your Reading

14. What is the purpose of each of these fetal structures or substances: Vernix caseosa? Lanugo? Brown fat? Surfactant?
15. Why does the fetus usually assume a head-down position in the uterus?
16. What is the difference between fertilization age and gestational age? Which term is more commonly used and why?

Auxiliary Structures

Two major auxiliary structures sustain the pregnancy and promote normal prenatal development: the placenta, and the fetal membranes. These structures develop simultaneously with the baby's development.

Placenta

The placenta is a thick, disc-shaped organ that is necessary to support prenatal growth and development. The placenta has two components, maternal and fetal (Fig. 6–7). Its major functions are (1) metabolic, (2) transfer of substances between mother and fetus, and (3) endocrine. The fetal side is smooth, with branching vessels covering the membrane-covered surface. The maternal side is rough where it was attached to the uterus (see Color Plate IX).

The umbilical cord is normally inserted on the fetal side of the placenta, near the center. However, it may insert off-center or even out on the fetal membranes. Figure 6–8 illustrates the normal configuration and variations from normal.

During early pregnancy, the placenta is larger than the embryo or fetus. However, the fetus grows faster than the placenta, so that the placenta is about one-sixth the weight of the fetus at the end of a term pregnancy.

MATERNAL COMPONENT

Development. When conception occurs, cells of the endometrium undergo changes that promote early nutrition of the embryo and enable most of the uterine lining to be shed after birth. These changes convert endometrial cells into the *decidua*. Not all functions of the decidua are known. In addition to providing nourishment for the embryo, the decidua may protect the mother from uncontrolled invasion of trophoblast into the uterus.

There are three decidual layers:

- The *decidua basalis* underlies the developing embryo and forms the maternal side of the placenta.
- The *decidua capsularis* overlies the embryo and bulges into the uterine cavity as the embryo and fetus grows.
- The *decidua parietalis* lines the rest of the uterine cavity. By about 22 weeks of gestation, the decidua capsularis fuses with the decidua parietalis, filling the uterine cavity.

Circulation. Eighty to 100 spiral arteries arise from the endometrium and carry oxygenated and nutrient-bearing blood into the placenta. Endometrial veins drain deoxygenated blood containing waste products from the placenta and return it to the maternal circulation for excretion.

Maternal and fetal blood do not mix in the placenta. Exchange of substances between mother and fetus occurs within the *intervillous spaces* of the placenta. While in the intervillous space, maternal blood is temporarily outside her circulatory system. About 150 ml of maternal blood is contained within the intervillous space, and it is changed about three or four times per minute.

FETAL COMPONENT

Development. The fetal side of the placenta develops from the outer cell layer (trophoblast) of the blastocyst at the same time the inner cell mass develops into the embryo and fetus.

Circulation. The umbilical cord contains the umbilical arteries and vein to transport blood between the fetus and placenta. Tiny finger-like projections (*chorionic villi*) are bathed by oxygen-rich and nutrient-rich maternal blood in the intervillous spaces. Each chorionic villus is supplied by a tiny fetal artery carrying deoxygenated blood and waste products from the fetus. The vein of the chorionic villus returns oxygenated blood and nutrients to the embryo and fetus.

Capillaries in the chorionic villi are separated from actual contact with the mother's blood by the membranes of each villus. This arrangement allows contact close enough for exchange while preventing gross mixing of maternal and fetal blood. The closed fetal circulation is important because the blood types of mother and fetus may not be compatible.

The placental arteries and veins converge in the blood vessels of the umbilical cord. Two umbilical arteries and one umbilical vein transport blood between the fetus and the fetal side of the placenta. Blood is circulated to and from the fetal side of the placenta by the fetal heart.

METABOLIC FUNCTIONS

The placenta produces some nutrients needed by the embryo and for its own functions. Substances synthesized include glycogen, cholesterol, and fatty acids (Moore, 1988).

TRANSFER FUNCTIONS

Transfer of oxygen, nutrients, and waste products across the placental membrane occurs by several

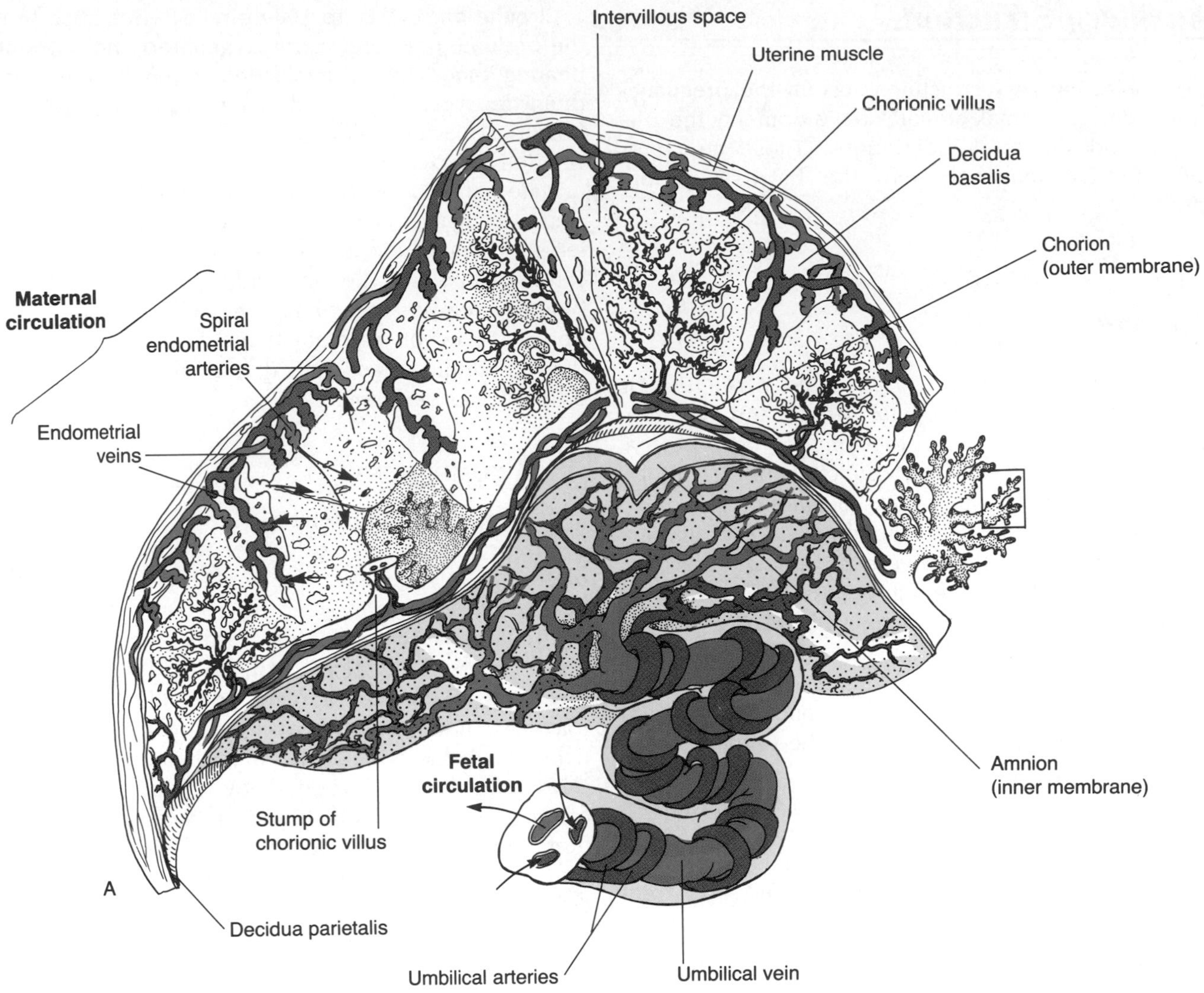

Intervillous space
Uterine muscle
Chorionic villus
Decidua basalis
Chorion (outer membrane)
Maternal circulation
Spiral endometrial arteries
Endometrial veins
Amnion (inner membrane)
Fetal circulation
Stump of chorionic villus
A
Decidua parietalis
Umbilical arteries
Umbilical vein

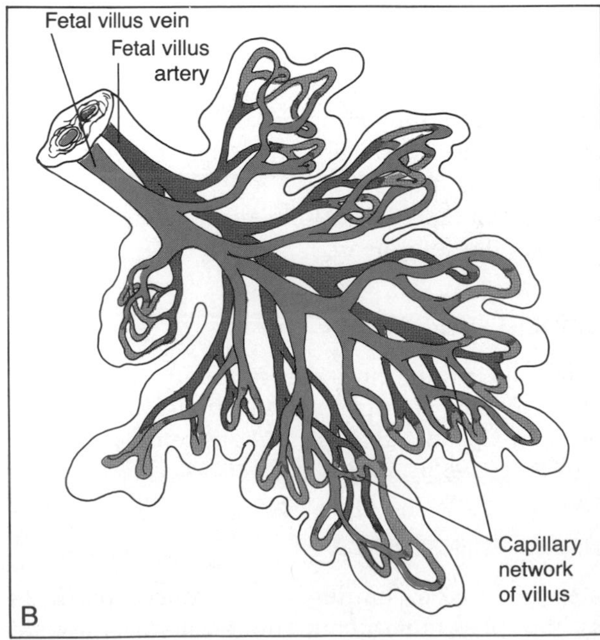

Figure 6–7

A, Placental structure showing relationship of placenta, fetal membranes, and uterus. Arrows indicate the direction of blood flow between the woman's circulation and the placenta through the endometrial arteries and veins and between the fetus and placenta through the umbilical arteries and vein. Blood from the woman bathes the fetal chorionic villi within the intervillous spaces to allow exchange of oxygen, nutrients, and waste products without gross mixing of maternal and fetal blood. **B,** Structure of a chorionic villus showing its fetal capillary network.

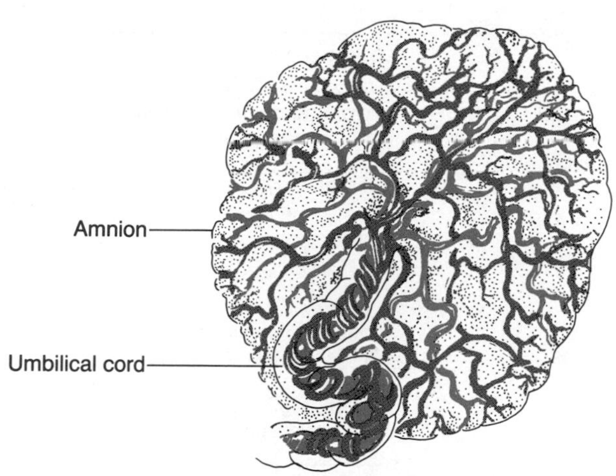

Normal placenta, with insertion of umbilical cord near center and branching of fetal umbilical vessels over surface

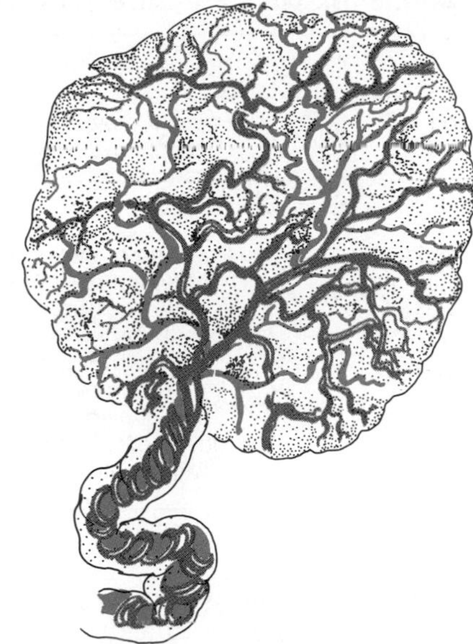

Placenta with cord inserted near margin of placenta

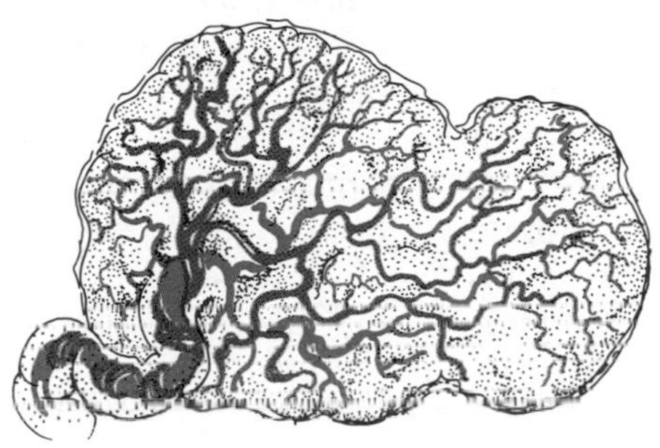

Placenta with a small accessory lobe

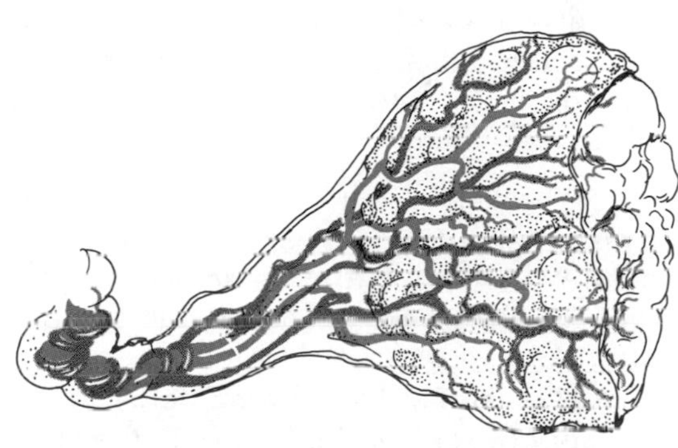

Velamentous insertion of umbilical cord. Cord vessels branch far out on membranes. When membranes rupture, fetal umbilical vessels may be torn and the fetus can hemorrhage.

Figure 6–8

Placental variations.

methods. Transfer may be a complex process involving more than a single method. Table 6–3 presents examples of how substances are transferred between the mother and the developing fetus. The placenta's transfer abilities may be used to deliver therapeutic medications to the fetus. For example, the mother may be given digitalis to benefit the fetus affected with heart failure.

Placental transfer of harmful substances may occur as well. Most substances that enter the mother's blood stream can enter the fetal circulation, and many agents enter it almost immediately.

Gas Exchange. A key function of the placenta is respiration. Oxygen and carbon dioxide pass through the placental membrane by simple diffusion. The average oxygen partial pressure (Po_2) of maternal blood in the intervillous space is 50 mmHg. The average blood Po_2 in the umbilical vein is about 30 mmHg.

The fetus can thrive in this low oxygen environment for three reasons:

- Fetal hemoglobin can carry 20 to 30 per cent more oxygen than adult hemoglobin.
- The fetus has a higher oxygen-carrying capacity because of a higher average hemoglobin (about 18 g) and hematocrit value (about 55 per cent).
- Hemoglobin can carry more oxygen at low carbon dioxide partial pressure (Pco_2) levels than it can at high ones (Bohr effect). Blood entering

Table 6–3. MECHANISMS OF PLACENTAL TRANSFER

Mechanism	Description	Example
Simple diffusion	Passive movement of substances across a cell membrane from an area of higher concentration to one of lower concentration	Oxygen and carbon dioxide Carbon monoxide Water Urea and uric acid Most drugs and their metabolites
Facilitated diffusion	Passage of substances across a cell membrane by binding with carrier proteins that assist transfer	Glucose
Active transport	Transfer of substances across a cell membrane against a pressure gradient, or from an area of lower concentration to one of higher concentration	Amino acids Water-soluble vitamins Minerals: Calcium, iron, iodine
Pinocytosis	Movement of large molecules by ingestion within cells	Maternal IgG class antibodies. Some passage of maternal IgA antibodies

the placenta from the fetus has a high Pco_2, but carbon dioxide diffuses quickly to the mother's blood, where the Pco_2 is lower, reversing the levels of carbon dioxide in maternal and fetal bloods. Therefore, the fetal blood becomes more alkaline and the maternal blood becomes more acidic. This allows the mother's blood to give up oxygen and the fetal blood to combine with oxygen readily.

Fetal Pco_2 is only about 2 to 3 mmHg higher than that of maternal blood. However, carbon dioxide is very soluble, allowing it to pass across the placental membrane into maternal blood at this low pressure gradient.

Nutrient Transfer. The growing fetus requires a constant supply of nutrients from the pregnant woman. Glucose, fatty acids, vitamins, and electrolytes pass readily across the placenta. Glucose is the major energy source for fetal growth and metabolic activities.

Waste Removal. In addition to carbon dioxide, urea, uric acid, and bilirubin are readily transferred from the fetus to the mother for disposal. Because the normal placenta removes wastes for the fetus, metabolic defects such as phenylketonuria (PKU) are usually not evident until after birth.

Antibody Transfer. Many of the immunoglobulin G (IgG) class of antibodies are passed from mother to fetus through the placenta. This confers passive (temporary) immunity to the fetus against diseases such as diphtheria and measles if the mother is immune to them. Passage of antibodies against disease is beneficial because the newborn does not produce them for several months after birth. The preterm infant has little protection from maternal antibodies because they are transferred during late pregnancy.

Passage of antibodies from expectant mother to fetus is not always beneficial. If maternal and fetal blood types are not compatible, the mother either may already have or may produce antibodies against fetal erythrocytes. The mother's antibodies may then destroy the fetal erythrocytes, causing anemia or even fetal death. This situation may occur if the mother is Rh-negative and the fetus is Rh-positive. (See p. 691 for a discussion of Rh isoimmunization and its prevention and treatment.)

Transfer of Maternal Hormones. Most maternal protein hormones do not reach the fetus in significant amounts. The female fetus exposed to androgenic hormones may have masculinization of her genitalia, and her gender may be difficult or impossible to determine at birth.

One instance of adverse effects from fetal exposure to hormones is that of "DES daughters." In the late 1940s through the early 1960s, diethylstilbestrol (DES) was prescribed to prevent spontaneous abortion. The drug was ineffective for this purpose, and its use was abandoned. However, as the females who were prenatally exposed to DES reached their teens and early 20s, researchers noted an association between exposure to the DES and reproductive system problems. Vaginal carcinoma was noted in a few adolescent and young adult females. DES daughters have a higher incidence of infertility, spontaneous abortion, and preterm labor compared with unexposed women. Although the effects on males have been less publicized than the effects on females, some sons of women who took DES also showed reproductive abnormalities.

ENDOCRINE FUNCTIONS

The placenta produces several hormones necessary for normal pregnancy. Human chorionic gonadotropin causes the corpus luteum to persist and secrete estrogens and progesterone. As the placenta develops further, it produces estrogens and progesterone and the corpus luteum gradually regresses after 20 weeks. When a Y chromosome is present in the male fetus, hCG also causes the fetal testes to secrete testosterone necessary for normal development of male reproductive structures.

Human chorionic somatomammotropin (hCS) is a placental hormone that promotes normal nutrition and growth of the fetus and maternal breast development for lactation. The hormone decreases maternal insulin sensitivity and utilization of glucose, making more glucose available for fetal nutrition.

Fetal Membranes and Amniotic Fluid

The two fetal membranes are the *amnion* (inner membrane) and the *chorion* (outer membrane). The two membranes are so close as to be one (the "bag of waters"), but they can be separated. If the membranes rupture in labor, amnion and chorion usually rupture together, releasing the amniotic fluid within the sac.

The amnion is continuous with the surface of the umbilical cord, joining the epithelium of the fetus' abdominal skin. Chorionic villi proliferate over the entire surface of the gestational sac for the first 8 weeks after conception. If the conceptus is observed at this time, it looks like a shaggy sphere with the embryo suspended inside. As the embryo grows, it bulges into the uterine cavity. The villi on the outer surface gradually atrophy and form the smooth-surfaced chorion. The remaining villi continue to branch and enlarge to form the fetal side of the placenta.

Amniotic fluid protects the growing fetus and promotes normal prenatal development. Amniotic fluid protects the fetus by:

- Cushioning against impacts to the maternal abdomen
- Providing a stable temperature

Amniotic fluid promotes normal prenatal development by:

- Allowing symmetrical development as the major body surfaces fold toward the midline
- Keeping the membranes from adhering to developing fetal parts
- Allowing room and buoyancy for fetal movement

Amniotic fluid is derived from two sources: (1) fetal urine; and (2) fluid transported from the maternal blood across the amnion. Cast-off fetal epithelial cells and vernix are suspended in the amniotic fluid. The water of the amniotic fluid changes by absorption across the amnion, returning to the mother. The fetus also swallows amniotic fluid, where it is absorbed by the digestive tract, and waste products are returned to the placenta via the umbilical arteries.

The volume of amniotic fluid increases during pregnancy, until it is about 1000 ml at 37 weeks (Moore, 1988). An abnormally small quantity of fluid (under 400 ml in the third trimester) is called *oligohydramnios* and may be associated with poor fetal lung development and malformations that result from compression of fetal parts. Oligohydramnios may occur because the kidneys fail to develop, urine excretion is blocked, or because the placental blood flow is inadequate. *Hydramnios* (also called *polyhydramnios*) is the opposite situation, when the quantity may exceed 2000 ml. Hydramnios may occur when the fetus has a severe malformation of the central nervous system or gastrointestinal tract that prevents normal ingestion of amniotic fluid.

Fetal Circulation

The course of fetal blood circulation is from the fetal heart, to the placenta for exchange of oxygen and waste products, and back to the fetus for delivery to fetal tissues (Fig. 6–9,A)

Umbilical Cord

The fetal umbilical cord is the lifeline between the fetus and placenta. It has two arteries that carry blood away from the fetus and one vein that returns blood to the fetus. The umbilical arteries and vein are coiled within the cord to allow them to stretch and prevent obstruction of blood flow through them. The entire cord is cushioned by a soft substance called *Wharton's jelly* to prevent obstruction due to pressure.

The two fetal arteries carry deoxygenated blood and waste products away from the fetus to the placenta, where these substances are transferred to the mother's circulation. The umbilical vein carries freshly oxygenated and nutrient-laden blood from the placenta back to the fetus.

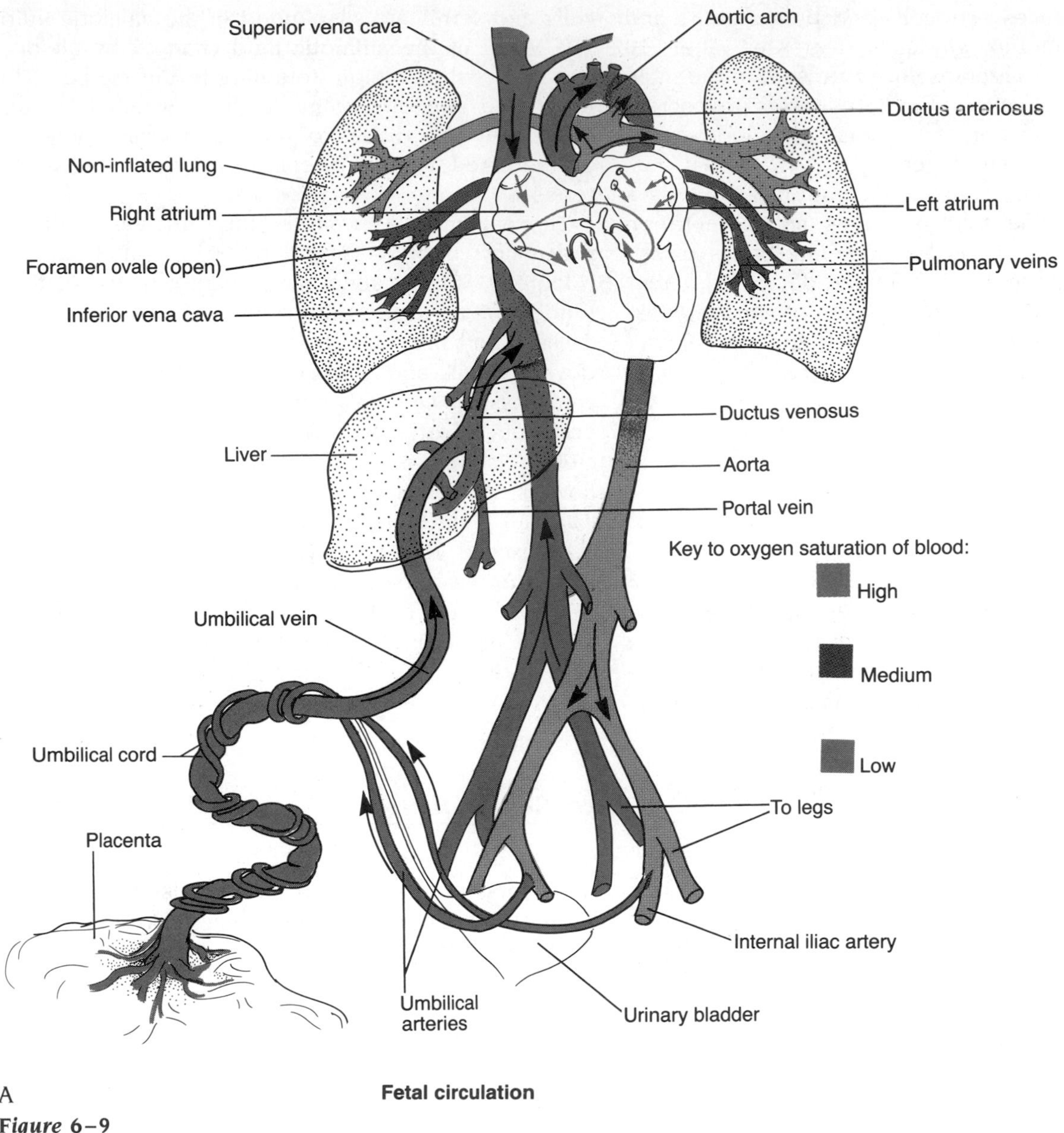

Figure 6–9

A, Fetal circulation. Three shunts exist to allow most blood from the placenta to bypass the fetal lungs and liver, the ductus venosus, the ductus arteriosus, and the foramen ovale.

Fetal Circulatory Circuit

Because the fetus does not breathe, several variations of the post-birth circulatory route are needed (Fig. 6–9,B). Three shunts exist in the fetal circulatory system that divert most circulating blood from the lungs. At birth, the infant's lungs begin oxygenating the blood, so the need to bypass the lungs no longer exists. Shortly after birth, all three shunts will be converted to functions unrelated to circulating the blood.

Oxygenated blood enters the fetal body through the umbilical vein. About half the blood goes through the liver, and the rest bypasses the liver and enters the inferior vena cava through the first shunt, the *ductus venosus*. The blood then enters the right atrium. Most of the blood passes directly into the left atrium through the second shunt, the foramen ovale, where it mixes with the small amount of blood returning from the lungs. Blood is pumped from the left ventricle into the aorta to nourish the body, especially the upper body. A small amount of

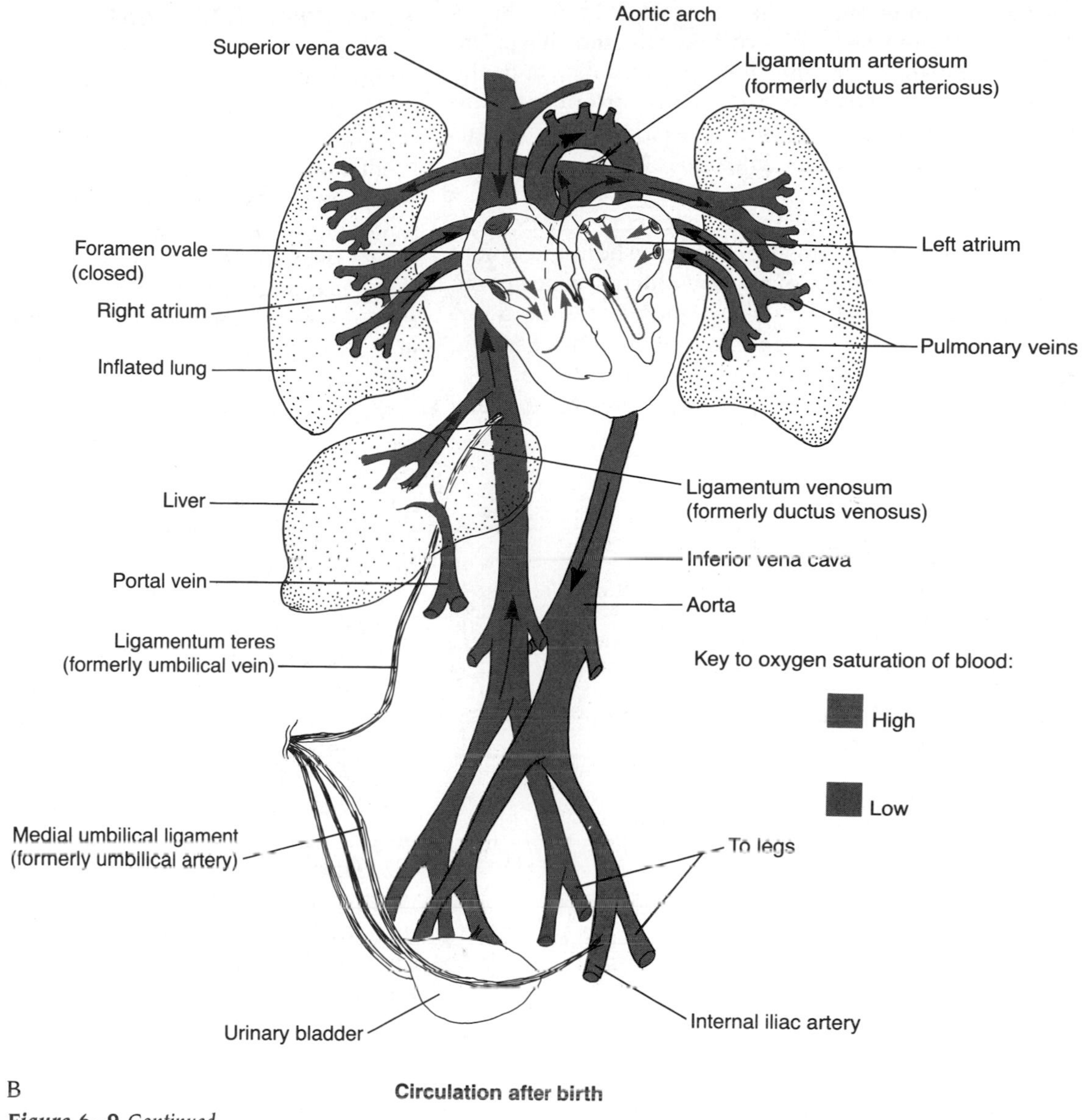

Figure 6–9 *Continued*

B, Circulation after birth. Note that the fetal shunts have closed. The umbilical vessels, the ductus venosus and ductus arteriosus, have been converted to ligaments.

blood from the right ventricle is circulated to the lungs to nourish the lung tissue. The rest of the blood from the right ventricle joins oxygenated blood in the aorta through the third shunt, the *ductus arteriosus*. The head and upper body receive the greatest amount of oxygenated blood.

The muscle wall of the right side of the fetal heart is thicker than the left because resistance to blood flow through the uninflated lungs is high. When the infant begins breathing after birth, resistance to pulmonary blood flow falls dramatically and the right side of the heart does not need to be so thick. During infancy, the thickness of the right heart gradually decreases because its workload decreases.

Changes in Blood Circulation After Birth

Fetal circulatory shunts are not needed after birth because the infant oxygenates blood in the lungs and is not connected to the placenta (Fig. 6–9,B). As the infant breathes, blood flow to the lungs increases, pressure in the right heart falls, and the foramen ovale closes. The ductus arteriosus constricts as the arterial oxygen level rises. The ductus venosus constricts when infusion of blood from the umbilical cord stops.

Transition to the postnatal circulatory pattern is gradual. Functional closure occurs when the infant breathes. The foramen ovale and ductus venosus are permanently closed as tissue proliferates in these structures. The ductus venosus becomes a ligament, as do the umbilical vein and arteries. Table 19–1 (see p. 480) lists the changes from fetal to neonatal circulation.

✔ Check Your Reading

17. Which structure takes over functions of the corpus luteum?
18. What is the purpose of the intervillous space?
19. Why is it important that fetal and maternal blood do not actually mix?
20. What factors enable the fetus to thrive in a low oxygen environment?
21. What are the purposes of the fetal membranes and amniotic fluid?
22. Trace the path of fetal circulation from the placenta, through the fetal body, and its return to the placenta.

Multifetal Pregnancy

Multifetal pregnancy (multiple gestation) is a deviation from the usual course of gestation. The process of conception and implantation is presented next. (See Chapter 26 for a discussion of the intrapartum management.)

Twins occur spontaneously about once in 90 pregnancies, triplets about once in 8100 pregnancies, quadruplets once in 729,000 pregnancies, and quintuplets only once in more than 65 million pregnancies (Moore, 1988).

Twinning is the most common form of multifetal pregnancy. The same processes that occur in twin pregnancies also may occur in other multiple gestations. Twins are often called "identical" or "fraternal" by lay people. They are more accurately described by their genetic origin, or the number of ova and sperm involved. The two types of twins are monozygotic and dizygotic. Figure 6–10 illustrates these two mechanisms of twinning.

Monozygotic Twinning

Monozygotic twins are conceived by the union of a single ovum and spermatozoon, with later division of the conceptus into two. Monozygotic twins have identical genetic complements and are of the same sex. They may not always look identical at birth, however, because one twin may have grown much larger than the other, or one may have a birth defect, such as a cleft lip. Monozygotic twinning occurs essentially at random (1 in 250 births), and there is not a well-established hereditary component (Simpson and Golbus).

Monozygotic twinning occurs when a single conceptus divides early in gestation. In most cases (70 per cent), when the *blastocyst* is formed, it has two inner cell masses instead of one. If this occurs, the fetuses will have two amnions (inner membranes) but a single chorion (outer membrane).

If the conceptus divides earlier, two separate but identical morulas (and then blastocysts) will develop and implant separately. These monozygotic twins will have two amnions and two chorions. Although their placentas develop separately, they may fuse and appear as one at birth. Their chorions also may fuse during prenatal development. Therefore, examining the placenta and membranes after birth cannot always establish whether twins are monozygotic or dizygotic.

Late separation of the inner cell mass may result in twins having a single amnion and a single chorion. These twins often die because their umbilical cords become entangled. Incomplete separation of the inner cell mass may result in conjoined (formerly called "Siamese") twins.

Dizygotic Twinning

Dizygotic twins arise from two ova that are each fertilized by different sperm. Dizygotic twins are like any other siblings: they may be the same or different sex, and they may or may not have similar physical characteristics.

Dizygotic twining may be hereditary in some families, presumably because of an inherited tendency of the females to release more than one ovum per cycle. Women of some races are more likely to have dizygotic twins as well:

- African: 1 in 20 births
- Asian: 1 in 150 births
- United States Caucasian: 1 in 80 births

There is an increased incidence of dizygotic twin births in women who conceive after age 40. Fertility

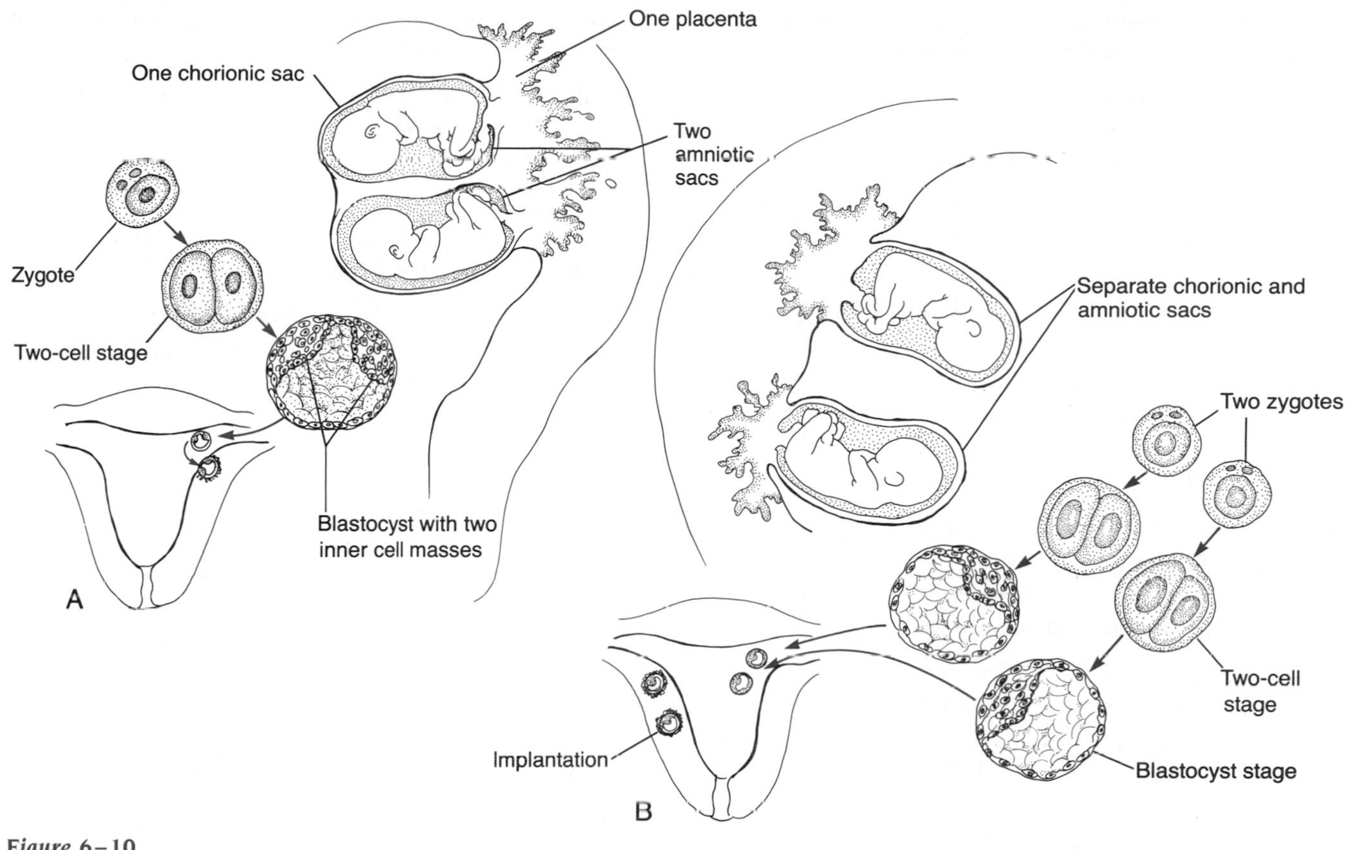

Figure 6–10

A, Monozygotic twinning. The single inner cell mass divides into two inner cell masses during the blastocyst stage. These twins have a single placenta and chorion, but each twin develops in its own amnion. **B,** Dizygotic twinning. Two ova are released during ovulation, and each is fertilized by a separate spermatozoon. The ova may implant near each other in the uterus, or they may be far apart.

treatments that induce ovulation also lead to an increased incidence of dizygotic multifetal gestations.

Because dizygotic twins arise from two separate zygotes, their membranes and placentas are separate. The membranes and/or placentas may fuse during development if they implant closely. Dizygotic twins are not conjoined because they do not involve division of a single cell mass into two, but arise from two separate conceptions.

Other Multifetal Gestations

Pregnancies resulting in more offspring than twins may arise from a single zygote or a combination of a single and mutliple zygotes, or each may arise from a separate zygote. These pregnancies pose much greater hazards to both expectant mother and fetuses. The incidence of long-term handicaps is higher as the number of fetuses increases.

✔ Check Your Reading

23. How do monozygotic twins occur?
24. Why can examination of the placenta and membranes in a multifetal pregnancy not always establish whether they are monozygotic or dizygotic?
25. Why are dizygotic twins often of different sex?

Summary Concepts

- The purpose of gametogenesis is to produce ova and sperm that have half the full number of chromosomes, or 23 unpaired chromosomes. When an ovum and sperm unite at conception, the number is restored to 46 unpaired chromosomes.
- The female has all the ova she will ever have at 30 weeks of prenatal gestation. No other ova are formed after this time.
- One primary oocyte can mature into one mature

ovum that contains 23 unpaired chromosomes (22 autosomes and an X chromosome).

- A male can continuously produce new sperm from puberty through the rest of his life, although fertility declines somewhat after age 40.
- One primary spermatocyte can result in production of four mature sperm. Two of the mature sperm will have 22 autosomes and an X sex chromosome. Two will have 22 autosomes and a Y sex chromosome.
- The male determines the baby's sex because only sperm carry either an X or an Y sex chromosome. The female can contribute only an X chromosome to the baby.
- The basic structure of all organ systems occurs during the first 8 weeks of pregnancy. Teratogens during this period may cause major structural and functional damage to the developing organs.
- The fetal period is one of growth and refinement of already established organ systems. Teratogens can still damage the fetus, but are less likely to cause major structural damage. They may still cause major functional damage.
- The placenta is an embryonic or fetal organ with metabolic, respiratory, and endocrine functions.
- Transfer of substances between mother and embryo or fetus occurs by four mechanisms: simple diffusion, facilitated diffusion, active transport, and pinocytosis.
- Most substances in the maternal blood can be transferred to the fetus.
- The fetal membranes contain the amniotic fluid, which cushions the fetus, allows normal prenatal development, and maintains a stable temperature.
- The umbilical cord is the lifeline between the fetus and the placenta. Two umbilical arteries carry deoxygenated blood and waste products to the placenta for transfer to the mother's blood. One umbilical vein carries oxygenated and nutrient-rich blood to the fetus. Coiling of the vessels and enclosure in Wharton's jelly reduces the risk that the umbilical vessels will be obstructed.
- Three fetal circulatory shunts are needed to partially bypass the fetal liver and lungs: the ductus venosus, the foramen ovale, and the ductus arteriosus. These structures close functionally after birth but are not closed permanently until several weeks or months later.
- Multifetal pregnancy may be monozygotic or dizygotic. Twins are the most common form of multifetal pregnancy.
- Examination of the placenta and membranes alone cannot conclusively establish whether multiple fetuses are monozygotic or dizygotic.
- Dizygotic twins are more likely to occur in certain families and racial groups and especially in mothers over 40 years old and in women who take fertility treatments to induce ovulation.

References and Readings

Arnold-Aldea, S.A., & Parer, J.T. (1991). Fetal-maternal circulation. In M.Y. Divon (Ed.), *Abnormal fetal growth* (pp. 29–46). New York: Elsevier.

Benirschke, K. (1989). Multiple gestation: Incidence, etiology and inheritance. In R.K. Creasy & R. Resnick (Eds.), *Maternal-fetal medicine: Principles and practice* (pp. 565–579). Philadelphia: W.B. Saunders.

Benirschke, K. (1989). Normal development. In R.K. Creasy & R. Resnick (Eds.), *Maternal-fetal medicine: Principles and practice* (pp. 116–127). Philadelphia: W.B. Saunders.

Blackburn, S.T., & Loper, D.L. (1992). *Maternal, fetal, and neonatal physiology: A clinical perspective*. Philadelphia: W.B. Saunders.

Brace, R.A. (1989). Amniotic fluid dynamics. In R.K. Creasy & R. Resnick (Eds.), *Maternal-fetal medicine: Principles and practice* (pp. 128–135). Philadelphia: W.B. Saunders.

Glass, R.H. (1989). Sperm and egg transport, fertilization, and implantation. In R.K. Creasy & R. Resnick (Eds.), *Maternal-fetal medicine: Principles and practice* (pp. 108–115). Philadelphia: W.B. Saunders.

Guyton, A.C. (1991). *Textbook of medical physiology*. Philadelphia: W.B. Saunders.

Jacob, S.W., & Francone, C.A. (1989). *Anatomy and physiology*. Philadelphia: W.B. Saunders.

MacLennan, A.H. (1989). Multiple gestation: clinical characteristics and management. In R.K. Creasy & R. Resnick (Eds.), *Maternal-fetal medicine: Principles and practice* (pp. 580–591). Philadelphia: W.B. Saunders.

Moore, K.L.(1988). *The developing human: Clinically oriented embryology* (4th ed.). Philadelphia: W.B. Saunders.

Moore, K.L. (1989). *Before we are born* (3rd ed.). Philadelphia: W.B. Saunders.

Noller, K.L. (1990). In utero DES exposure. In E.J. Quilligan & F.P. Zuspan (Eds.), *Current therapy in obstetrics and gynecology* (pp. 136–138). Philadelphia: W.B. Saunders.

Simpson, J.L., & Golbus, M.S. (1992). *Genetics in Obstetrics and Gynecology*, 2nd ed. Philadelphia, W.B. Saunders.

Sparks, J.W., & Cetin, I. (1991). Fetal growth: Energy and substrate requirements. In M.Y. Divon (Ed.), *Abnormal fetal growth* (pp. 1–27). New York: Elsevier.

Toot, P.J., Surrey, E.S., & Lu, J.K.H. (1992). The menstrual cycle, ovulation, fertilization, implantation, and the placenta. In N.F. Hacker & J.G. Moore (Eds.), *Essential of obstetrics and gynecology*, 2nd. ed. (pp. 36–51). Philadelphia: W.B. Saunders.

7

Physiological Adaptations to Pregnancy

Objectives

1. Describe the physiological changes that occur during pregnancy.
2. Differentiate presumptive, probable, and positive signs of pregnancy.
3. Compute gravida, para, and estimated date of delivery.
4. Discuss cultural assessment and negotiation that may improve nursing care during the antepartum period.
5. Identify the components and purpose of initial and subsequent antepartum assessments.
6. Describe nursing care for the most common nursing diagnoses of pregnancy.

Definitions

Amenorrhea • Absence of menses. **Primary amenorrhea** is a delay of the first menstruation. **Secondary amenorrhea** is cessation of menstruation after its initiation.

Braxton-Hicks contractions • Irregular, mild uterine contractions that occur throughout pregnancy; they become stronger and more evident in the last trimester.

Chadwick's sign • Bluish discoloration of the cervix, vagina, and labia during pregnancy as a result of increased vascular congestion.

Chloasma • Brownish pigmentation of the face during pregnancy; "mask of pregnancy."

Colostrum • Breast fluid secreted during pregnancy and the first 2 to 3 days following childbirth.

Diastasis recti • Separation of the longitudinal muscles of the abdomen (rectus abdominis) during pregnancy.

Goodell's sign • Softening of the cervix, a probable indication of pregnancy.

Physiologic anemia of pregnancy • Decrease in hematocrit values caused by dilution of erythrocytes by expanded plasma volume rather than by an actual decrease in erythrocytes or hemoglobin.

Striae gravidarum • Irregular reddish streaks resulting from tears in connective tissue; during pregnancy, they generally appear on the woman's abdomen, breasts, or thighs.

△ Alert for a high risk of exposure to substances to which universal precautions apply. See Appendix B for additional information about infection control.

From the moment of conception, significant changes occur in the expectant mother's body that are necessary to support and nourish the fetus, to prepare her for childbirth and lactation, and to maintain her health. Pregnant women are often puzzled by the physical changes and unprepared for the discomforts that sometimes accompany them. Many pregnant women rely on nurses to provide accurate information and compassionate guidance throughout their pregnancies. To respond effectively, nurses must understand not only the physiological changes but also how these changes affect the daily lives of expectant mothers.

Changes in Body Systems

Pregnancy challenges each body system to adapt to increasing demands of the fetus. The most obvious changes are in the reproductive system but other profound adaptations occur as well.

Reproductive System

UTERUS

Perhaps the most dramatic change during pregnancy occurs in the uterus, which, before conception, is a small, pear-shaped organ entirely contained in the pelvic cavity. Before pregnancy, it weighs approximately 60 g (2 ounces) and has a capacity of about 10 ml (one third of an ounce). At the end of pregnancy, the uterus extends to the level of the xiphoid process, weighs approximately 1000 g (2.2 pounds), and has sufficient capacity for the fetus, placenta, and amniotic fluid, usually about 5000 ml.

Uterine growth occurs as the result of both hyperplasia and hypertrophy. During the first trimester, growth is due mainly to hyperplasia and the formation of new cells that result from stimulation of the myometrium by estrogen (Resnick, 1989). During the second and third trimesters, uterine growth is due to hypertrophy as the muscle fibers stretch in all directions to accommodate the growing fetus. Muscle fibers in the myometrium increase in both length and width. As a result, by the third trimester the uterine walls are thin and the fetus can be easily palpated through the abdominal wall. The uterus gradually rotates toward the right and displaces the intestine as it expands into the abdominal cavity.

The uterus grows in a predictable pattern that provides information about fetal growth and helps to confirm the expected date of delivery (EDD)(Fig. 7–1). For instance, by 12 weeks of gestation, the uterus extends out of the maternal pelvis and can be palpated above the symphysis pubis; at 16 weeks, the fundus reaches midway between the symphysis pubis and the umbilicus; and at 20 weeks, the fundus is palpable at the umbilicus. By 36 weeks, the fundus reaches its highest level at the xiphoid process; it pushes against the diaphragm, and the expectant mother may experience shortness of breath even during rest. By 40 weeks, the fetal head descends into the pelvic cavity and the uterus sinks to a lower level. This descent of the fetal head is called *lightening* because it reduces pressure on the diaphragm and makes breathing easier.

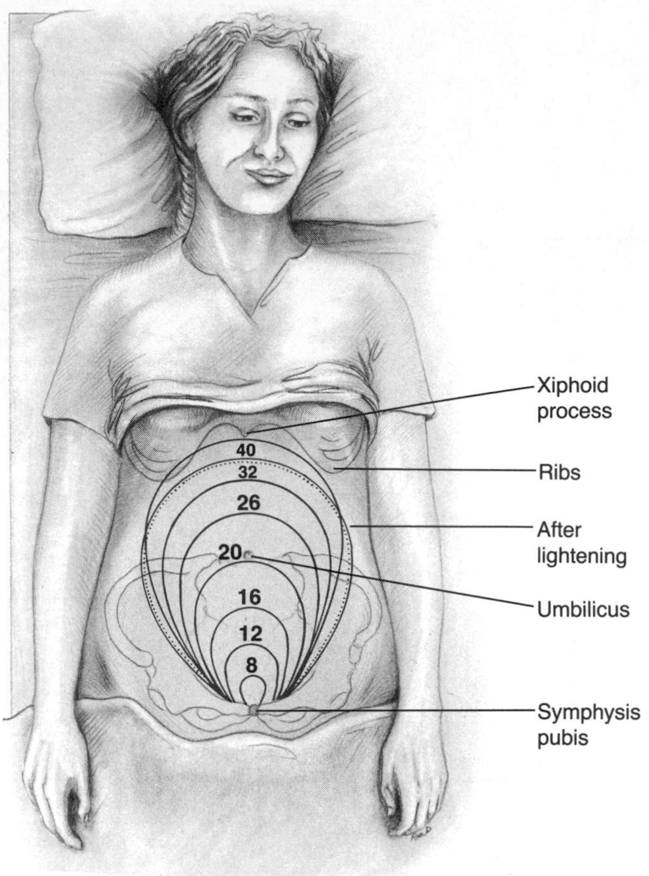

Figure 7–1

Uterine growth pattern during pregnancy.

CERVIX

The cervix also undergoes significant changes following conception. The most obvious changes occur in color and consistency. In response to the increasing levels of estrogen, the cervix becomes congested with blood (hyperemic), resulting in the characteristic bluish color that extends to include the vagina and labia. This discoloration, referred to as Chadwick's sign, is one of the earliest signs of pregnancy.

The cervix is largely composed of connective tissue that softens when the collagen fibers become swollen and loosely connected as a result of increased vascularity. Before pregnancy, the cervix has a consistency that is similar to that of the tip of the nose. Following conception, the cervix feels more like the lobe of the ear. The cervical softening is referred to as Goodell's sign. A less obvious change occurs as the cervical glands proliferate during pregnancy and the glandular walls become thin and widely separated. As a result, the endocervical tissue resembles a honeycomb that fills with mucus that is secreted by the cervical glands. The mucus forms a plug in the cervical canal; this is important because it blocks the ascent of bacteria from the vagina into the uterus during pregnancy and thus protects the membranes and fetus from infection (Fig. 7–2). The mucus plug remains in place until the onset of labor, when the cervix begins to thin and dilate, allowing the mucus plug to be expelled. One of the earliest signs of labor is "bloody show," which consists of the mucus plug plus a small amount of blood that results from disruption of the cervical capillaries as the mucus plug is dislodged.

VAGINA

Changes in the vagina are due to increased vascularity and are similar to those of the cervix. The vaginal walls appear bluish and there is a gradual softening of the connective tissue that allows the vagina to distend during childbirth. The mucosa thickens, and vaginal rugae (folds) become very prominent. Vaginal cells contain increasing amounts of glycogen, which results in rapid sloughing and increased vaginal discharge. Although increased vaginal discharge is normal, it should be assessed for the presence of blood or for a foul odor, which indicates infection.

The pH of the vagina decreases, and the acidic condition works to prevent growth of harmful bacteria that are found in the vagina. The glycogen-rich environment, however, favors the growth of *Candida albicans*, and persistent yeast infections (candidiasis) are common during pregnancy.

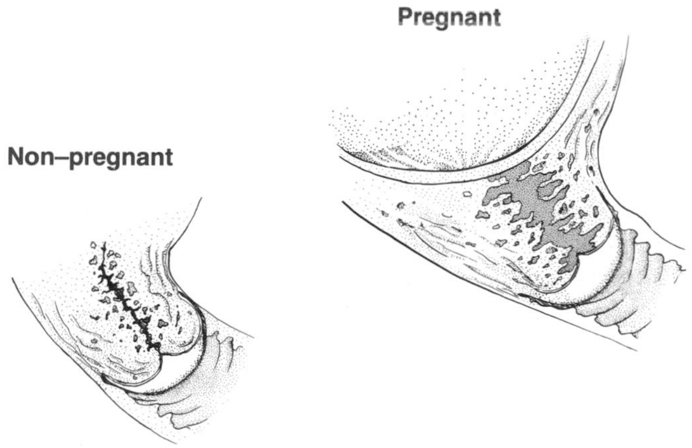

OVARIES

Once conception occurs, the major function of the ovaries is to secrete progesterone for the first 6 to 7 weeks of the pregnancy. Progesterone (from Latin, *pro*, for; *gestare*, bearing or reproduction) is called the "hormone of pregnancy," and if the pregnancy is to be maintained, adequate progesterone must be available from the earliest stages. The corpus luteum secretes progesterone until the placenta is developed. Once developed, the placenta secretes progesterone throughout pregnancy and the corpus luteum disintegrates because it is no longer needed.

Ovulation ceases during pregnancy because the circulating levels of estrogen and progesterone are high, inhibiting the release of follicle-stimulating hormone (FSH) and luteinizing hormone (LH), which are necessary for ovulation. (See Chapter 6 for information on ovarian function following conception.)

Figure 7–2

Cervical changes that occur during pregnancy. Note enlargement of spaces in cervical mucosa, which are filled with a thick mucus plug.

Breasts

During pregnancy, the breasts change in both size and appearance (Fig. 7–3). The increase in size is due to the effects of estrogen and progesterone. Estrogen stimulates the growth of mammary ductal tissue; progesterone promotes the growth of lobes, lobules, and alveoli. The breasts become highly vascular, and a delicate network of veins is often visible just beneath the surface of the skin. If the increase in breast size is extensive, striations ("stretch marks") similar to those that occur on the abdomen may develop.

Characteristic changes in the nipples and areolae occur during pregnancy. The nipples increase in size and become more erect, and the areolae become larger and more pigmented. The degree of pigmentation varies with the complexion of the expectant mother. Women with very light complexions exhibit less change in pigmentation than those who have

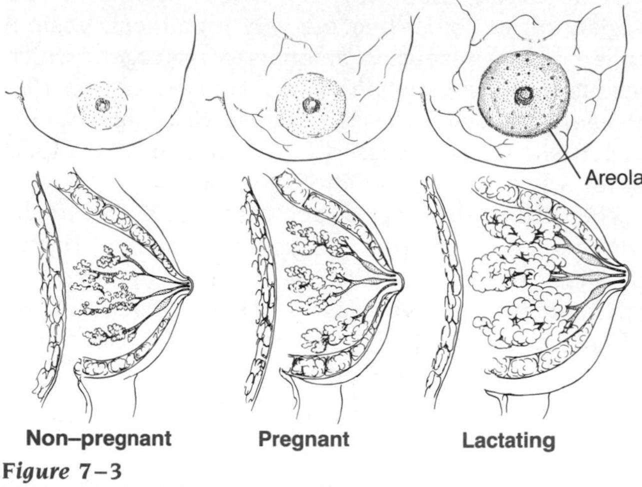

Figure 7–3

Breast changes that occur during pregnancy. The breasts increase in size and become more vascular, the areolae become darker, and the nipples become more erect.

darker skin. Sebaceous glands, called *tubercules of Montgomery*, become more prominent during pregnancy and secrete a substance that lubricates the nipples.

Breast changes are often the first indications of pregnancy. Many women experience tingling, feelings of fullness, and tenderness soon after the first missed menstrual period. In addition, a thin, yellowish breast fluid (*colostrum*) is present in greater or lesser amounts throughout pregnancy and can readily be expressed by the third trimester. (See Chapter 21 for a complete discussion of lactation.)

✔ *Check Your Reading*

1. What is the expected uterine growth at 20 weeks compared with that at 36 weeks?
2. How does the cervical mucus plug protect the fetus?
3. How do the breasts change during pregnancy in terms of size and appearance?

Cardiovascular System

During pregnancy, the cardiovascular system undergoes significant changes to provide for the additional demands on the mother's body, to transport nutrients and oxygen to the fetus, and to remove fetal wastes. Alterations occur in heart size and position as well as in blood volume, blood flow, and blood components.

HEART SIZE AND POSITION

Cardiac changes are slight, and they reverse soon after childbirth. The muscles of the heart (myocardium) enlarge slightly during pregnancy. Growth of the heart is due to the increased work load and is similar to heart enlargement that follows endurance training (Brinkman, 1989). The heart is pushed upward and toward the left as the uterus elevates the diaphragm during the third trimester. As a result of the change in position, the locations for auscultating (listening to) heart sounds may be shifted upward and laterally in late pregnancy.

BLOOD VOLUME

One of the earliest and perhaps the most noteworthy change in the cardiovascular system is the rapid increase in blood volume to 50 per cent over the prepregnant volume (Wasserstrum, 1992). Blood volume starts to increase during the first trimester, expands rapidly during the second trimester, and rises at a much slower rate during the third trimester.

The cause of blood volume expansion is poorly understood; however, the increased volume (hypervolemia) is clearly needed for two reasons: (1) to transport nutrients and oxygen to the placenta, where they become available for the growing fetus, and (2) to meet the demands of the expanded maternal tissue in the uterus and breasts. An additional benefit of hypervolemia is that it protects the pregnant woman from the adverse effects of blood loss that occurs during childbirth.

One negative consequence of hypervolemia can be a condition called physiologic anemia, or pseudoanemia, of pregnancy. This occurs because blood plasma volume expansion is more pronounced and occurs earlier than the increase in red blood cells (*erythrocytes*), resulting in a *dilution* of hemoglobin concentration rather than inadequate hemoglobin. Reduced levels of hemoglobin and hematocrit during pregnancy often reflect the dilution of solutes in greatly expanded volume. Although not true anemia, this physiologic anemia should not be dismissed as unimportant. Frequent laboratory examinations may be needed to distinguish physiologic anemia from true anemia. Generally, iron deficiency anemia does not exist unless the hematocrit value is less than 33 per cent or the hemoglobin is lower than 10 g/dl of blood (Nuwayhid and Khalife, 1992).

Cardiac Output. A major consequence of increased vascular volume during pregnancy is an increase in cardiac output. Cardiac output is the amount of blood discharged from the heart each minute. It is based on stroke volume (the amount of blood pumped from the heart with each contraction) and heart rate (the number of times the heart beats each minute). Cardiac output increases rapidly during the first trimester and remains elevated throughout pregnancy. During pregnancy, the increase in cardiac output is primarily due to an increase in stroke volume; however, there is a rise in heart rate of about 10 beats per minute (BPM).

Blood Pressure. Despite the increase in blood volume, blood pressure (BP) remains stable during pregnancy. During the second trimester, there is a slight decrease in both systolic and diastolic BP. The decrease is due to three factors: vasodilation that occurs in response to progesterone, decreased sensitivity of the blood vessels to angiotensin II, resulting in decreased vascular resistance, and the addition of the uteroplacental unit, which provides a greater area for circulation. During the third trimester, BP increases slightly; however, it should remain at or near the normal levels of early pregnancy.

Effect of Position on Blood Pressure. Arterial BP is affected by position during pregnancy. Pressure is highest when the pregnant woman is sitting and lowest when she is in a lateral recumbent position. Therefore, it is important to assess maternal blood pressure in the same position each time and to document the position as well as the pressure so that the site of evaluation remains consistent. If two positions are used, for instance both sitting and reclining or both the right and left arms, each position should be clearly documented.

Supine Hypotension. When the expectant mother is in the supine position, particularly in the second and third trimesters, the weight of the *gravid (pregnant)* uterus partially occludes the vena cava and the descending aorta (Fig. 7–4). This impedes return of blood from the lower extremities and, as a consequence, reduces cardiac return, cardiac output, and arterial BP. This supine hypotensive syndrome is also called *vena caval syndrome*; however, occlusion of the aorta also causes decreased blood pressure in the lower extremities, and thus a more precise term is *supine hypotensive syndrome*. Symptoms include faintness, lightheadedness, dizziness, and agitation. Some may experience syncope, a brief lapse in con-

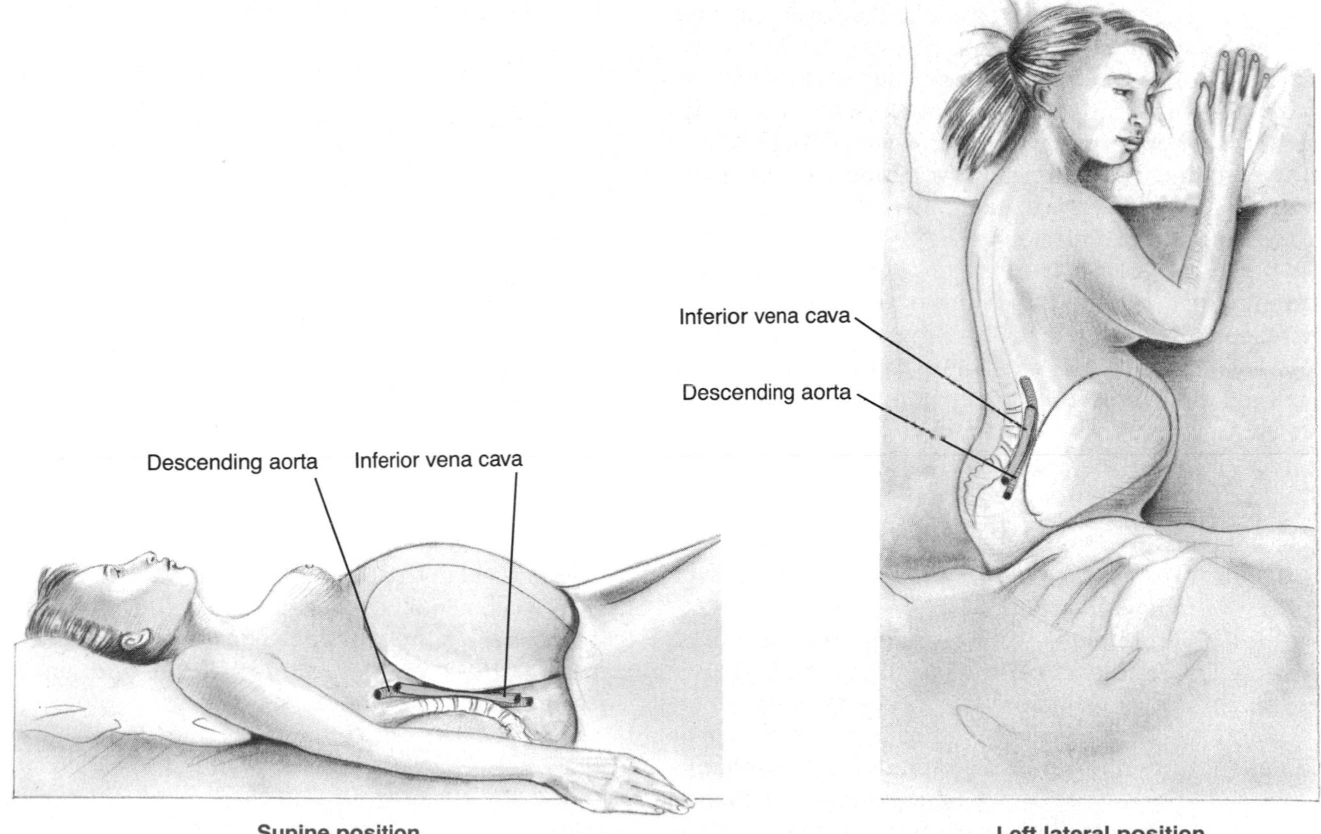

Figure 7–4

Vena caval syndrome, or supine hypotensive syndrome. When the woman is in the supine position, the weight of the gravid uterus partially occludes the vena cava and the descending aorta. Turning to a lateral recumbent position corrects supine hypotension.

sciousness. Blood flow through the placenta is also decreased if the woman remains in the supine position for a prolonged period of time, and this could result in fetal hypoxia.

Turning to a lateral recumbent position frees the pressure on the blood vessels and quickly corrects supine hypotension. Women should be advised to rest in a side-lying position to prevent supine hypotension from occurring as well as to correct it when it does occur.

Blood Flow

Four major changes in blood flow occur during pregnancy.

1. Blood flow is altered to include the uteroplacental unit, which requires 300 to 800 ml/minute to adequately perfuse the placenta and thus to provide oxygen and nutrients to the developing fetus.
2. Approximately 30 per cent more blood must circulate through the maternal kidneys to remove the increased metabolic wastes that are generated by mother and fetus.
3. The woman's skin requires increased circulation to dissipate heat that is generated by increased metabolism during pregnancy.
4. Venous pressure increases in the lower extremities as pregnancy progresses. The weight of the expanding uterus on the vena cava and iliac veins partially obstructs blood return from veins in the legs and blood pools in the deep and superficial veins of the legs. The resulting stasis of blood exerts pressure on the veins and may cause the veins to become distended. This leads to feelings of fullness in the legs and often results in "dependent edema" (edema that occurs only in the feet or ankles). It increases markedly when the pregnant woman sits or stands for long periods of time. On the other hand, periodic elevation of the legs, resting in a lateral recumbent position, or walking increases blood return and enhances circulation to the lower legs and thus reduces dependent edema.

Prolonged engorgement of the veins of the lower legs may also result in varicose veins of the legs, vulva, or rectum (hemorrhoids).

Blood Components. During pregnancy, there is an increase in red blood cells, white blood cells (leukocytes) and clotting factors. Erythrocytes increase by as much as 33 per cent if sufficient iron, which is necessary for hemoglobin formation, is available. Hemoglobin is an important part of erythrocytes, and maintaining adequate hemoglobin is a major concern during pregnancy because it transports oxygen to all maternal and fetal cells.

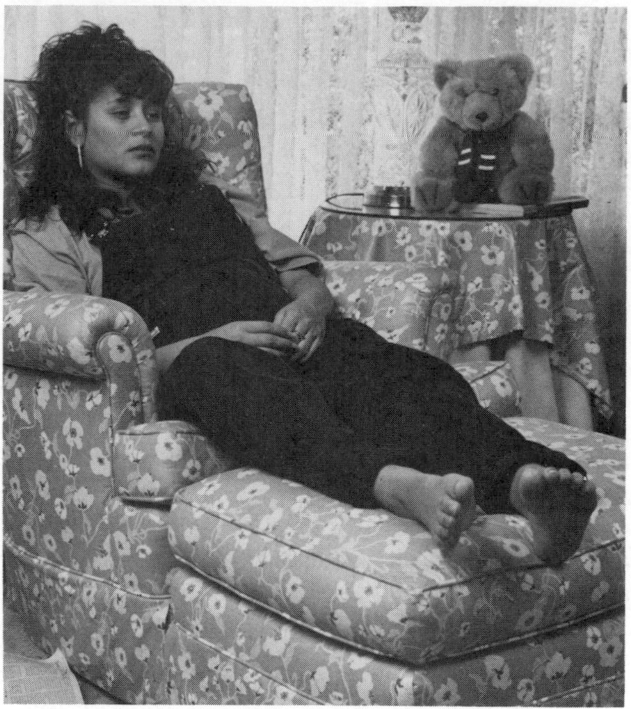

Dependent edema increases when the pregnant woman sits or stands for long periods. Periodic elevation of the legs helps to reduce dependent edema.

Although iron absorption and iron-binding power are increased during pregnancy, sufficient iron is not always supplied by diet. Iron supplementation is necessary to promote hemoglobin synthesis and thus to ensure that erythrocyte production is sufficient to prevent the development of iron deficiency anemia. (See Chapter 9 for additional information about iron requirements during pregnancy.)

Leukocytes increase from an average prepregnant level of 5000 cells/mm^3 to approximately 12,000 to 16,000 cells/mm^3 (Blackburn and Loper, 1992). Leukocytes increase further during labor as a result of exertion and may reach 25,000 by the early postpartum period.

Several clotting factors are elevated during pregnancy, particularly plasma fibrinogen (factor I), which rises by about 50 per cent. Elevated fibrinogen levels increase the ability to form clots, and this creates both a protective mechanism and an increased risk for the mother. It offers some protection from hemorrhage during childbirth; however, it also increases the risk of clot formation (*thrombus*) in the legs and the development of thrombophlebitis. This is particularly true if the woman must stand or sit for prolonged periods of time, and there is stasis of blood in the veins of the legs. See Appendix D for additional changes in blood components.

✔ Check Your Reading

4. How does physiologic anemia or pseudoanemia differ from iron deficiency anemia in terms of cause?
5. Why is circulation to the kidneys and skin increased during pregnancy?
6. Why do some pregnant women feel faint when they are in a supine position?

Respiratory System

PHYSICAL CHANGES

Estrogen causes edema and hyperemia of mucous membranes of the upper respiratory tract, and some women experience nasal stuffiness or epistaxis (nosebleeds) as a result. By the third trimester, the enlarging uterus lifts the diaphragm by about 4 cm (1.6 inches), which prevents the lungs from expanding as fully as they normally do. To compensate for the reduced space, the ribs flare, the substernal angle widens, and the circumference of the chest increases by about 6 cm (~ 2.5 inches). Breathing becomes thoracic rather than abdominal, causing some women to experience shortness of breath as pregnancy progresses. Vital capacity (the amount of air that can be moved with maximum effort) increases slightly; however, tidal volume (amount of air that is inhaled and exhaled during quiet respiration) increases by 30 to 40 per cent.

CHEMICAL CHANGES

The growth of fetal, placental, and maternal tissue creates a greater demand for oxygen. High levels of progesterone raise the sensitivity of the breathing center of the brain (medulla oblongata) to carbon dioxide, thereby stimulating an increase in both the depth and rate of respiration. Although the rise in rate is slight (approximately two breaths per minute) the enlarged respiratory depth results in a decrease in the partial pressure of carbon dioxide ($Paco_2$) and a mild respiratory alkalosis (an increase in arterial pH) during pregnancy.

Gastrointestinal System

The gastrointestinal system undergoes changes that are clinically significant because they may cause discomfort for the expectant mother.

MOUTH

Elevated levels of estrogen cause hyperemia of the tissues of the mouth and gums that may lead to gingivitis and bleeding gums. Some women experience *ptyalism*, or excessive salivation that is unpleasant and embarrassing. The cause of ptyalism is unknown, and interventions are often unsuccessful. Small, frequent meals, gum chewing, and oral lozenges offer limited relief for some women (Van Dinter, 1991). The teeth are unaffected by pregnancy; contrary to common beliefs, they do not lose minerals to the fetus.

STOMACH AND SMALL INTESTINE

More than 50 per cent of all women experience nausea and vomiting during the first trimester. The problem usually begins at 4 to 6 weeks of gestation and continues until the early part of the second trimester. This is related to several factors, including increased levels of hormones, such as human chorionic gonadotropin (hCG), estrogen, and progesterone. The relative hypoglycemia that most women experience during early pregnancy as a result of altered carbohydrate metabolism is also believed to be related to "morning sickness."

The increased levels of progesterone also relax all smooth muscle, which leads to decreased tone and motility of the gastrointestinal tract. The stomach and small intestine take longer to empty, which allows additional time for nutrients to be absorbed. This benefits the growing fetus, but it may exacerbate nausea in the expectant mother. Moreover, the cardiac sphincter (the circular muscle that controls the opening between the esophagus and the stomach) works less efficiently and acidic stomach secretions may reflux into the esophagus and produce heartburn (*pyrosis*).

LARGE INTESTINE

Decreased motility in the large intestine allows time for more water to be absorbed, which tends to make the stool hard and may lead to constipation. Constipation is one of the most common complaints of pregnancy, and hemorrhoids may be caused or exacerbated by constipation if the expectant mother must strain to have bowel movements.

LIVER AND GALLBLADDER

Although the size of the liver and gallbladder remain unchanged during pregnancy, functional changes occur largely as a result of the effects of progesterone. The gallbladder becomes hypotonic and emptying time is prolonged, resulting in thicker bile that can predispose to the development of gallstones.

Liver function is altered during pregnancy; serum alkaline phosphatase and serum cholesterol levels are almost doubled by the end of pregnancy, whereas levels of serum albumin fall gradually.

Urinary System

BLADDER

The urinary bladder undergoes changes in size and muscle tone. During the first trimester, the uterus begins to expand within the pelvic cavity. This applies pressure to the bladder, causing the woman to experience frequency and urgency of urination. During the second trimester, the uterus extends into the abdominal cavity, which relieves pressure on the bladder and the urge to void decreases. In addition, bladder capacity almost doubles as the bladder, like all smooth muscle, relaxes in response to increasing levels of progesterone.

In the last 2 weeks of pregnancy, the fetus settles into the pelvis (lightening) and presses against the bladder. Once again, the woman experiences frequency, urgency, and nocturia. Although frequency and urgency are normal during early and late pregnancy, they are also signs of infection; if they are accompanied by burning sensations or pain, the client should be assessed for urinary tract infection.

KIDNEY AND URETER

During pregnancy, the kidneys change in both size and shape because dilation of the renal pelves, calyces, and ureters occurs above the pelvic brim. The dilation is caused by (1) the effect of progesterone, which relaxes the walls of the ureters and makes them more distensible, and (2) compression of the ureters between the enlarging uterus and the bony pelvic brim. As the flow of urine through the ureters is obstructed, particularly on the right side (the left ureter is cushioned by the sigmoid colon), the ureters dilate and apply hydrostatic pressure against the renal pelvis, which also dilates. The resulting stasis of urine is clinically significant because it allows time for bacteria to multiply and increases the risk of urinary tract infection during pregnancy.

Functional changes also occur in the kidneys throughout pregnancy. Both the renal plasma flow (RPF)—the total amount of plasma to flow through the kidneys—and the glomerular filtration rate (GFR)—the rate that water and disolved substances are filtered in the glomerulus—increase by as much as 50 per cent. The increase is necessary to excrete additional metabolic waste from the mother and fetus; however, it also affects the excretion of glucose. As GFR increases, the filtered load of glucose exceeds the ability of the renal tubules to reabsorb it and glucose spills into the urine. Therefore, glycosuria is not uncommon during pregnancy, particularly after consumption of foods, such as candy or cookies, that are high in simple sugars. Furthermore, small quantities of amino acids and water-soluble vitamins are excreted. Bacteria thrive in urine that is rich in nutrients, and this is one reason why the incidence of urinary tract infections is increased during pregnancy.

Tests of renal function may be misleading during pregnancy. As a result of increased GFR, plasma concentrations of both creatinine and urea normally decline.

✔ Check Your Reading

7. How does the respiratory system compensate for the pressure exerted on the diaphragm by the enlarging uterus?
8. Why do some pregnant women experience nausea and vomiting in the first trimester?
9. Why are expectant mothers at increased risk for urinary tract infection?

Integumentary System

SKIN

There is increased circulation to the skin during pregnancy, which encourages activity of the sweat and sebaceous glands. Expectant mothers also experience an increased feeling of warmth and more perspiration, particularly during the last trimester. Accelerated activity by the sebaceous glands fosters the development of facial blemishes, which are usually reduced by careful cleansing of the face several times each day. Additional changes include hyperpigmentation and vascular changes in the skin.

Hyperpigmentation. Increased pigmentation may begin as early as the 2nd month, when levels of melanocyte-stimulating hormone (MSH) become elevated because of the effects of estrogen and progesterone. Brunettes and dark-skinned women exhibit more hyperpigmentation than women with very light skin. Areas of pigmentation include brownish patches, called *chloasma*, which usually involve the forehead, cheeks, and the bridge of the nose. This is commonly called the "mask of pregnancy." A dark line of pigmentation (*linea nigra*) may also extend from the umbilicus to the symphysis pubis. Pre-existing moles become darker, and, as previously stated, the areolae become darker as pregnancy progresses.

Hyperpigmentation usually disappears following childbirth, when the levels of estrogen and progesterone decline; however, pregnant women should be advised to avoid prolonged exposure to the sun and to use a sunscreen with a protective factor of at least 15.

Cutaneous Vascular Changes. Changes in surface blood vessels are common in Caucasian women during pregnancy. These include angiomas that appear as tiny, red elevations that branch in all directions. Commonly called *vascular spiders*, or telangiectasis, they appear most often on the face, neck, upper chest, and arms. Redness of the palms or soles of the feet, known as *palmar erythema*, also occurs in many Caucasian women and in some African-American women. Many times, vascular changes occur simultaneously, and although they may be emotionally distressing for the expectant mother, they are clinically insignificant and usually disappear shortly after childbirth.

CONNECTIVE TISSUE

There may be linear tears in the connective tissue. These occur most often on the abdomen, breasts, and buttocks, appearing as slightly depressed, pink to purple streaks called *striae gravidarum*, or "stretch marks" (Fig. 7–5). Women are concerned about striae because although the marks fade to silvery lines, they do not disappear following childbirth. Many women insist that striae can be prevented by massage with oil or vitamin E; however, this has not been documented. Antipruritic ointments may be effective in controlling the itching that accompanies severe striae.

HAIR AND NAILS

Hair grows more rapidly and less hair falls out during pregnancy because there are fewer follicles in the resting phase. Following childbirth, hair follicles return to normal activity and many women become concerned at the rate of hair loss. They need reassurance that more follicles have returned to the normal resting phase and that excessive hair loss will not continue.

Nail growth increases during pregnancy, although many women notice thinning and softening of the nails as pregnancy progresses. Reasons for this are unclear.

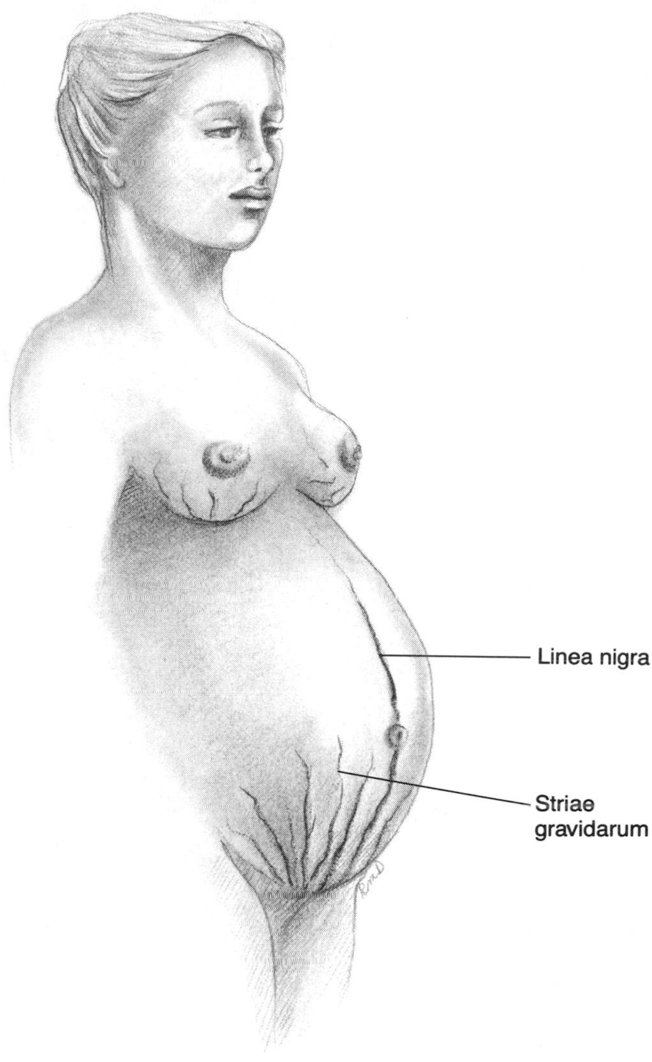

Figure 7–5

Striae gravidarum are linear tears that may occur in the connective tissue. Linea nigra, a dark line of pigmentation from the umbilicus to the symphysis pubis, may also appear.

Musculoskeletal System

POSTURAL CHANGES

Musculoskeletal changes are progressive. They begin in the second trimester, when maternal hormones (relaxin and progesterone) initiate gradual softening of the pelvic ligaments and joints to facilitate passage of the fetus through the pelvis at the time of birth. Relaxation of the pelvic joints creates pelvic instability, and the pregnant woman assumes a wide stance and the so-called "waddling" gait of pregnancy to compensate for a changing center of gravity.

During the third trimester, as the uterus increases in size, it becomes necessary for the expectant

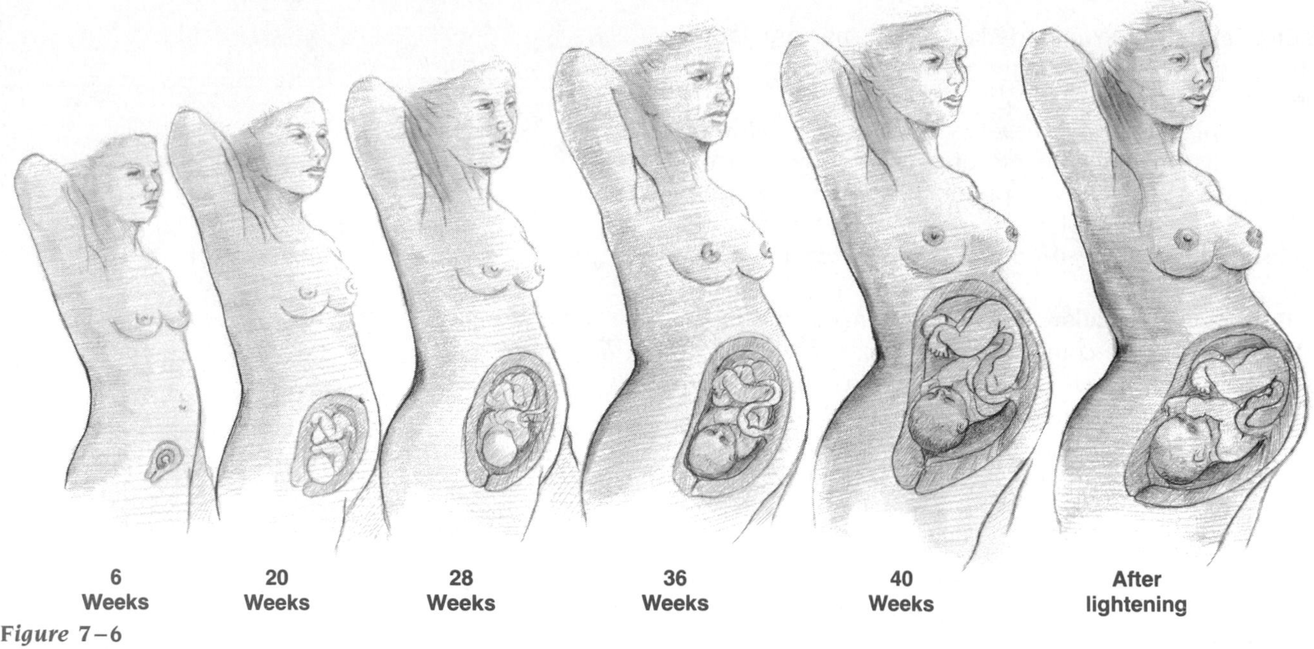

Figure 7–6

As pregnancy progresses, obvious changes in posture occur and lordosis increases.

mother to lean backward to maintain her balance. This creates a progressive *lordosis*, or curvature of the lower spine (Fig. 7–6).

ABDOMINAL WALL

Pregnancy also affects the abdominal muscles, which may be stretched beyond their capacity during the third trimester, causing the rectus abdominus muscles to separate (*diastasis recti*). The extent of the separation varies from slight, which is not clinically significant, to severe, when a large portion of the uterine wall is covered only by skin and fascia. (See Chapter 17.)

Endocrine System

PITUITARY GLAND

Most hormones from the pituitary gland are suppressed during pregnancy. The only hormone from the *anterior* pituitary that increases in amount is prolactin, which prepares the breasts to produce milk. FSH and LH, normally produced to stimulate ovulation in the non-pregnant woman, are unnecessary during pregnancy, and the growth hormone from the anterior pituitary also appears to decrease during pregnancy.

The *posterior* pituitary gland secretes oxytocin, a second hormone that is involved in lactation. Oxytocin stimulates the milk-ejection reflex following childbirth. Oxytocin also stimulates contractions of the uterus; however, during pregnancy this action is inhibited by progesterone, which relaxes smooth muscle fibers that compose the uterus. Following childbirth, progesterone levels decline and oxytocin plays an important role in keeping the uterus contracted.

THYROID GLAND

Early in the first trimester, there is an increase in total thyroxine (T_4) along with a corresponding increase in thyroxine-binding protein. The increased amounts of T_4 bind readily with the thyroxine-binding proteins, and the serum level of unbound T_4 remains stable. Thyroid changes do produce a slight increase in the size of the thyroid gland and an increase in basal metabolic rate (BMR). The increased BMR results in greater cardiac output, pulse rate, and heat intolerance. BMR returns to normal within a few weeks after childbirth.

PARATHYROID GLANDS

Metabolism of calcium and phosphorus depends on the secretion of parathyroid hormone. During pregnancy, fetal demands for calcium and phosphorus increase and the maternal parathyroid glands respond by producing additional parathyroid hormone.

PANCREAS

Pregnant women have increased insulin needs, particularly during the second and third trimesters, when nausea and vomiting have subsided and maternal tissue becomes increasingly resistant to insulin. The pancreas of a healthy woman is able to produce additional insulin to meet maternal needs. Insulin does not cross the placental barrier, and the fetus produces insulin to metabolize the glucose it receives from the mother. Changes in insulin production are discussed later in the chapter and in Chapter 25.

ADRENAL GLANDS

The adrenal glands enlarge only slightly during pregnancy, but they produce a significant increase in two adrenal hormones: cortisol and aldosterone. The unbound level of cortisol is elevated during pregnancy, although the specific plasma protein (transcortin) that binds to cortisol is also elevated. Cortisol regulates carbohydrate and protein metabolism and stimulates gluconeogenesis (formation of glycogen from nonprotein sources such as amino or fatty acids).

Aldosterone regulates the absorption of sodium from the distal tubules of the kidneys and has been called the "great sodium saver." Aldosterone production is increased during pregnancy to overcome the salt-wasting effects of pregnancy and thereby maintains the necessary level of sodium in the greatly expanded blood volume. Aldosterone is closely related to water metabolism (see p. 128). Table 7–1 summarizes the major hormones related to pregnancy.

CHANGES CAUSED BY PLACENTAL HORMONES

hCG. In early pregnancy, hCG is produced by the trophoblastic cells that surround the developing embryo. The primary function of hCG in early pregnancy is to stimulate the corpus luteum to produce progesterone and estrogen until the placenta is developed sufficiently to assume that function.

Estrogen. Although estrogen is produced by the ovaries during the menstrual cycle and by the corpus luteum for the first few weeks of pregnancy, it is produced primarily by the placenta after the 6th or 7th week of pregnancy. Estrogen has numerous functions during pregnancy: (1) it stimulates uterine growth and increases blood supply to uterine vessels; (2) it aids in developing the ductal system in

Table 7–1. HORMONES RELATED TO PREGNANCY

Hormone	Source	Major Effects
Estrogen	Ovary, placenta	Stimulates uterine development to provide environment for fetus and stimulates breast to prepare for lactation
Progesterone	Ovary, placenta	Maintains uterine lining for implantation, relaxes all smooth muscle, including uterus; develops acini cells and lobes to prepare breasts for lactation
Human placental lactogen	Placenta	Stimulates metabolism of glucose and converts it to fat; antagonistic to insulin
Human chorionic gonadotropin	Trophoblasts (placenta)	Prevents involution of corpus luteum, thus maintaining production of progesterone until placenta is formed
Relaxin	Ovary, placenta	Softens muscles and joints of pelvis
Follicle-stimulating hormone	Anterior pituitary	Initiates maturation of ovum, necessary for conception; suppressed during pregnancy
Luteinizing hormone	Anterior pituitary	Stimulates ovulation of mature ovum in nonpregnant state
Melanocyte-stimulating hormone	Anterior pituitary	Increased during pregnancy; produces hyperpigmentation
Oxytocin	Posterior pituitary	Stimulates uterine contractions to initiate labor; stimulates milk-ejection reflex
Prolactin	Anterior pituitary	Primary hormone of milk production
Aldosterone	Adrenals	Increased during pregnancy to conserve sodium and maintain fluid balance
Cortisol	Adrenals	Increased during pregnancy; active in metabolism of glucose and fats; anti-inflammatory effect *may* be helpful in preventing rejection of pregnancy
Thyroxine	Thyroid	Increased during pregnancy to stimulate basal metabolic rate

the breasts in preparation for lactation; and (3) it is associated with hyperpigmentation, vascular changes in the skin, increased activity of the salivary glands, and hyperemia of the gums and nasal mucous membranes (discussed earlier).

Progesterone. Progesterone is produced first by the corpus luteum and then by the fully developed placenta. Progesterone is the most important hormone of pregnancy: it maintains the endometrial layer for implantation of the fertilized ovum; it prevents spontaneous abortion; it stimulates the development of the lobes and lobules in the breast in preparation for lactation; and it is responsible for maternal fat stores to be deposited in the subcutanteous tissue over the abdomen, back, and upper thighs. The additional adipose tissue serves as a reserve of energy for pregnancy and lactation.

Progesterone relaxes not only the smooth muscle of the uterus but all smooth muscle. As a consequence, it is associated with decreased motility of the bowel, dilation of the ureters, and increased bladder capacity. Progesterone lowers the respiratory sensitivity to carbon dioxide and thus stimulates increased respiratory effort.

Human Placental Lactogen (HPL). Also called human chorionic somatomammotropin (hCS), this hormone is present in early pregnancy and increases steadily throughout pregnancy. A primary function of hPL is to increase the availability of glucose for the fetus, who needs a constant supply for growth and development. hPL does this by decreasing the sensitivity of maternal cells to insulin, which decreases maternal metabolism of glucose, thereby freeing glucose for transport to the fetus. In addition, under the influence of hPL, free fatty acids are quickly metabolized to provide energy for the pregnant woman.

Relaxin. Relaxin is produced by the corpus luteum and by the placenta. It is present by the first missed menstrual period. Relaxin inhibits uterine activity, softens connective tissue in the cervix, relaxes pelvic joints, and stimulates growth of the breasts.

Changes in Metabolism

WEIGHT GAIN

Attitudes about weight gain have changed over the years. At one time, maternal weight gain was restricted as a means of controlling fetal size so that labor would be easier. In recent times, the correlation between infant mortality and low birth weight has been documented. As a result, the number of pounds acceptable for maternal weight gain have increased. See Table 9–1 (p. 184) for the recommended weight gain for women of normal weight, women who are underweight, and those who are overweight prior to conception, and for women expecting twins.

The normal composition of weight gain is illustrated in Figure 9–1 (see p. 185). The fetus, placenta, and amniotic fluid make up less than half the recommended weight gain. The remainder is found in the increased size of the uterus and breasts, increased blood volume, increased interstitial fluid, and maternal stores of subcutaneous fat.

WATER METABOLISM

Fluid volume balance is dependent on adequate concentrations of sodium; therefore, the kidneys must compensate for the many factors that favor excretion of sodium during pregnancy. For example, increased GFR, decreased concentration of plasma proteins, and increased progesterone levels all result in an increase in sodium excretion. On the other hand, increased concentrations of estrogen, cortisol, prolactin, and aldosterone all tend to promote the reabsorption of sodium.

The net effect of the combined hormonal action is that sodium balance is maintained; however, there is a slight decrease in colloid osmotic pressure, which favors the development of edema during pregnancy. Edema is further increased toward term, when the weight of the uterus compresses the veins of the pelvis. This delays venous return, causing the veins of the legs to become distended. This increases venous pressure and results in additional fluid shifting from the vascular compartment to interstitial spaces. Edema of the feet and ankles is obvious at the end of the day, particularly if a pregnant woman stands for prolonged periods, and the force of gravity contributes to the pooling of blood in the veins of the legs. Dependent edema is clinically insignificant; however, if edema of the face or hands is noted, further assessment for hypertension or proteinuria is essential to determine whether signs of pregnancy-induced hypertension are developing.

Fluid retention is also associated with *carpal tunnel syndrome*, believed to result when edema compresses the median nerve at the point where it goes through the carpal tunnel of the wrist. Symptoms include soreness, weakness, and tenderness of the muscles of the thumb. The condition is usually resolved when the pregnancy ends.

CARBOHYDRATE METABOLISM

Carbohydrate metabolism changes markedly during pregnancy because more insulin is required. Reasons for this are complicated, but it is believed that three placental hormones (estrogen, progesterone, hPL) cause maternal tissue to be resistant to insulin. Moreover, insulinase, an enzyme produced by the placenta, speeds up the breakdown of insulin.

Insulin is essential for the metabolism of glucose and for maintenance of proper blood glucose levels. Decreasing the mother's ability to use insulin is a species-sparing (protective) mechanism that allows an ample supply of glucose for transfer to the fetus. However, her pancreas must produce more insulin so that she can continue to metabolize enough glucose to meet her own energy needs and to prevent hyperglycemia. Hyperglycemia occurs when blood glucose levels exceed available insulin needed to transport glucose into cells.

For most women, this is not a problem and insulin production is increased, particularly during the second and third trimesters. In some women, however, insulin production cannot be increased and these women experience periodic hyperglycemia. This condition is called *pregnancy-induced glucose intolerance*, or gestational diabetes (see Chapter 25). The effects of hyperglycemia on the fetus are discussed in Chapter 29.

✔ Check Your Reading

10. What causes the progressive changes in posture and gait during pregnancy?
11. Why is progesterone called the hormone of pregnancy?
12. Why do maternal needs for insulin change during pregnancy?

Table 7–2. INDICATIONS OF PREGNANCY AND OTHER POSSIBLE CAUSES

Sign	Other Possible Causes
Presumptive Indications	
Amenorrhea	Emotional stress, strenuous physical exercise, endocrine problems, chronic disease, early menopause
Nausea and vomiting	Gastrointestinal virus, food poisoning, emotional stress
Fatigue	Illness, stress, sudden changes in lifestyle
Urinary frequency	Urinary tract infections
Breast and skin changes	Premenstrual changes, use of oral contraceptives
Quickening	Abdominal gas, peristalsis, or pseudocyesis (false pregnancy)
Probable Indications	
Abdominal enlargement	Abdominal or uterine tumors
Cervical changes	Infection or hormonal imbalance
Ballottement	Uterine or cervical polyps
Braxton-Hicks contractions	Soft uterine fibroids (myomas)
Palpation of fetal outline	Large myomas may feel like the fetal head; small soft myomas may simulate small parts of the fetus
Pregnancy tests	Certain medications (antianxiety or anticonvulsant drugs), premature menopause, blood in urine, or malignant tumors that produce human chorionic gonadotropin may result in false-positive findings

Confirmation of Pregnancy

Confirmation of pregnancy has become much simpler since the development of ultrasonography, which makes it possible to view the fetal outline and to observe the fetal heartbeat very early in pregnancy. Traditionally, however, the diagnosis of pregnancy has been based on symptoms experienced by the expectant mother as well as on signs a physician, certified nurse-midwife, or nurse practitioner observes. These signs and symptoms are grouped into three classifications: presumptive, probable, or positive indications of pregnancy. A diagnosis of pregnancy cannot be made solely on the presumptive or probable signs. Table 7–2 lists other possible causes for these signs.

Presumptive Indications

Presumptive indications can also be termed *subjective* changes because they are what the expectant mother experiences and reports. Presumptive changes are the least reliable indicators of pregnancy because any one of them can be caused by conditions other than pregnancy.

AMENORRHEA

Absence of menstruation in a woman who regularly menstruates is one of the first changes noted and strongly suggests that conception has occurred in a sexually active woman. Menses cease after conception because progesterone and estrogen, secreted from the corpus luteum, maintain the endometrial lining in preparation for implantation of the fertilized ovum.

NAUSEA AND VOMITING

Most women experience nausea and vomiting during early pregnancy, generally beginning at the first missed menstrual period and lasting for about 10 weeks. This phenomenon is called "morning sickness" because it is more acute on arising; however, it can occur at any time of the day and may continue throughout the day. Nausea and vomiting are believed to be caused by the increased levels of hormones (hCG, estrogen), decreased gastric motility, and relative hypoglycemia that results from nightlong fasting. It may be aggravated by cooking odors or fatigue.

FATIGUE

Many pregnant women experience extraordinary fatigue and drowsiness during the first trimester. The direct cause is unknown, but it may be related to periodic hypoglycemia that occurs because glucose is transferred from the mother to the fetus to provide energy for rapid development.

URINARY FREQUENCY

Urinary frequency is first noticed by the expectant mother in the first few weeks of pregnancy when the urge to void is caused by the pressure exerted on the bladder by the expanding uterus. This symptom abates during the second trimester, when the uterus expands into the abdominal cavity. Late in the third trimester, the fetus settles into the pelvic cavity, and once again the woman experiences frequency and urgency of urination because the uterus presses against the bladder.

BREAST AND SKIN CHANGES

Breast changes occur early, at about the 6th week of pregnancy. The expectant mother experiences breast tenderness, feelings of fullness, and increased size and pigmentation of the areolae. Breast changes are due to the influence of estrogen and progesterone, which stimulate the lobes and ducts to prepare for lactation.

Many women observe increased pigmentation of the skin (chloasma, linea nigra, darkening of the areolae of the breasts) during pregnancy. These skin changes are due to increased levels of melanocyte-stimulating hormone, one of the effects of estrogen.

FETAL MOVEMENT

Unlike other presumptive indications of pregnancy, the expectant mother does not observe fetal movement (quickening) until the second trimester. Between 16 to 20 weeks of gestation, she first notices subtle fetal movements that gradually increase in intensity.

Probable Indications

Probable indications of pregnancy are *objective findings* that can be documented by an examiner. They are primarily related to physical changes in the reproductive organs. Although they are stronger indicators of pregnancy, a positive diagnosis of pregnancy cannot be made on this basis.

ABDOMINAL ENLARGEMENT

Enlargement of the abdomen during the childbearing years is a fairly reliable indication of pregnancy, particularly if it corresponds to a slow, gradual increase in uterine growth (see Fig. 7–1). Evidence of pregnancy is even more reliable when uterine growth is accompanied by amenorrhea.

CHANGES IN THE CERVIX

Color. The cervix changes from pink to a dark bluish-violet. The color change, called *Chadwick's sign*, extends to the vagina and labia as well as the cervix. The bluish color is due to increased vascularity of the pelvic organs during pregnancy.

Consistency. The cervix also becomes softer as a result of pelvic vasocongestion (Goodell's sign). This is noted by the examiner during pelvic examination. At about the 6th week of pregnancy, the lower uterine segment is so soft that it can be compressed to the thinness of paper. This is called *Hegar's sign* (Fig. 7–7). Because of the softening, the uterus can be easily flexed against the cervix (*McDonald's sign*).

CHANGES IN THE UTERUS

Ballottement. A sudden tap on the cervix during vaginal examination may cause the fetus to rise in the amniotic fluid and then rebound to its original position (Fig. 7–8). Ballottement is a strong indication of pregnancy; however, it may also be caused by other factors such as uterine or cervical polyps.

Braxton-Hicks Contractions. Irregular, painless contractions occur throughout pregnancy, although many expectant mothers do not notice them until the third trimester. Braxton-Hicks contractions are not positive signs of pregnancy because similar contractions may occur with other conditions, such as soft uterine myomas (fibroids).

Palpation of the Fetal Outline. An experienced practitioner is able to palpate (feel) the outlines of the fetal body by the second half of pregnancy. Outlining the fetus becomes easier as the pregnancy progresses, and the uterine walls thin to accommodate the growing fetus. Occasionally, large myomas

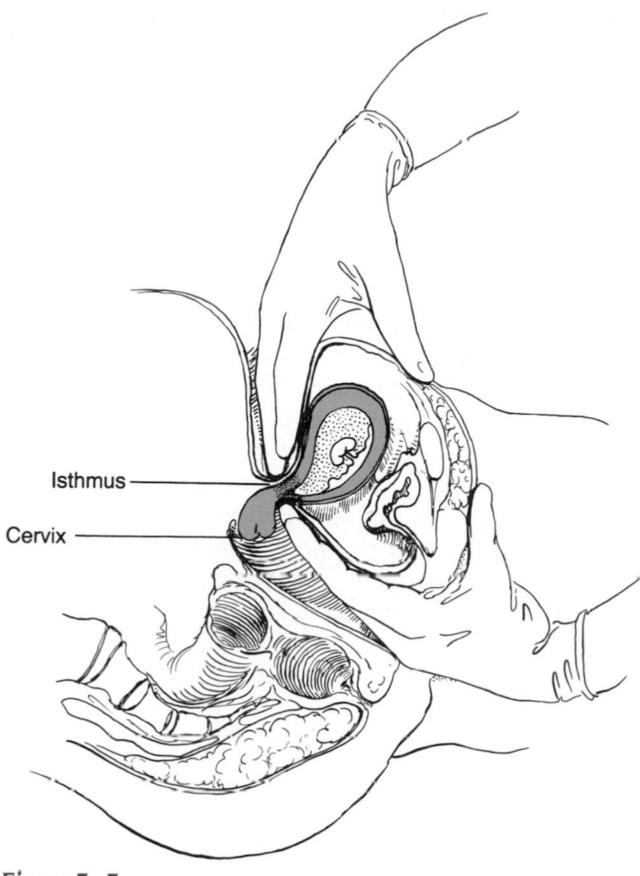

Figure 7–7

Hegar's sign demonstrates softening of the isthmus of the cervix.

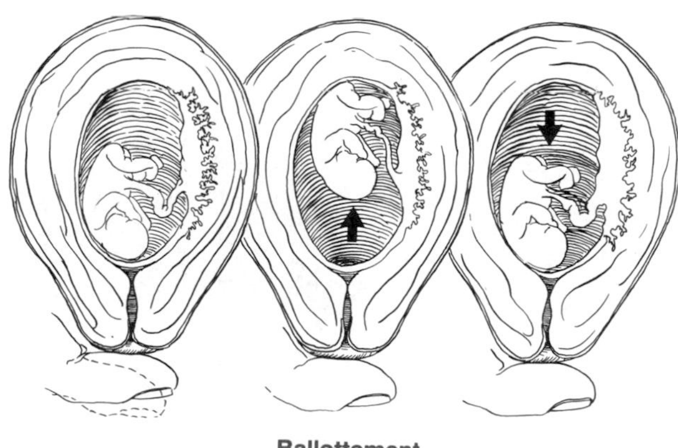

Figure 7–8

When the cervix is tapped, the fetus floats upward in the amniotic fluid. A rebound is felt by the examiner when the fetus falls back.

may feel like the fetal head, or small soft myomas may simulate small parts of the fetus and may result in a false diagnosis of pregnancy.

Uterine Souffle. A soft, blowing sound that corresponds to the maternal pulse may be auscultated over the uterus. This is due to blood circulating through the placenta, and it corresponds to the maternal pulse. Therefore, the rate of the maternal pulse must be checked simultaneously to identify uterine souffle. Uterine souffle differs from *funic souffle,* the soft purring sound heard over the umbilical cord and corresponding to the fetal heart rate.

PREGNANCY TESTS

Home Pregnancy Tests. In recent years, pregnancy tests have been greatly improved. They are based on the presence of hCG in maternal urine, and they may be used as early as 3 days after a missed menstrual period. Pregnancy tests are available for purchase over the counter, and they are uncomplicated and convenient. The test requires the first voided urine in the morning because the urine is most concentrated at that time. If used as directed, the tests are accurate 90 per cent of the time.

Pregnancy tests are considered probable indications of pregnancy because false-negative and false-positive results may occur. A result may be false negative because

- The test may be performed too soon, before hCG is produced by the cells surrounding the blastocyst (developing embryo)
- The woman may fail to use the first voided specimen of the day; as a consequence, the urine is too dilute
- The specimen may be allowed to stand longer than the recommended time

Professional Tests. Blood or urine may be tested for the presence of hCG as part of the initial physical examination. Blood (serum) pregnancy tests are performed in laboratory, clinic, or office settings as part  of a comprehensive evaluation. They may also be performed as a single service at minimal charge by women's health centers. Serum tests are more sensitive than urine tests and provide early, accurate results.

Positive Indications

Only three signs are accepted as positive confirmation of pregnancy: auscultation of fetal heart sounds, fetal movement felt by an examiner, and visualization of the fetus by sonography.

AUSCULTATION OF FETAL HEART SOUNDS

Fetal heart sounds can be heard with a fetoscope by 18 to 20 weeks of gestation. The electronic Doppler scan amplifies fetal heart sounds so that they are audible by 10 to 12 weeks. Both the fetoscope and the Doppler transducer are illustrated in Chapter 14.

To make a positive diagnosis of pregnancy, it is necessary not only to hear the fetal heart beat but also to distinguish it from the maternal pulse. The fetal heart rate is generally between 110 and 160 BPM and should be auscultated while the brachial pulse of the expectant mother is being assessed. The fetal heart rate is muffled by amniotic fluid, and the sound has been likened to that of a clock ticking behind a pillow. The location changes because the fetus moves freely in the amniotic fluid.

FETAL MOVEMENTS FELT BY EXAMINER

Fetal movements vary from faint flutterings in early pregnancy to the characteristic kick or thrust of later pregnancy. These movements are considered a positive sign of pregnancy when felt by an experienced examiner who is not likely to be deceived by similar sensations produced by peristalsis in the large intestine.

VISUALIZATION OF THE FETUS

Transabdominal ultrasound examination is frequently used to confirm pregnancy as early as 5 to 6 weeks of gestation. This involves placing an ultrasound transducer, or "probe," on the lower abdomen to detect the gestational sac, which is readily identifiable in the maternal pelvis; movements of the fetal heart are also discernible. By the 14th week, the fetal head and thorax can be identified.

Positive confirmation of pregnancy is possible even earlier when transvaginal ultrasound is used. An ultrasound probe is placed in the vagina, and the gestational sac is obvious by 10 days following implantation. This corresponds to 16 days following ovulation or 2 days following a missed menstrual period (Cunningham et al, 1989).

Figure 7–9 summarizes fetal and maternal changes that occur throughout pregnancy.

Figure 7–9. Fetal Growth and Development and Maternal Responses

Gestational age, computed from the last menstrual period, is 2 weeks greater than fertilization age, which is the time from conception.

Gestational age 1–4 weeks

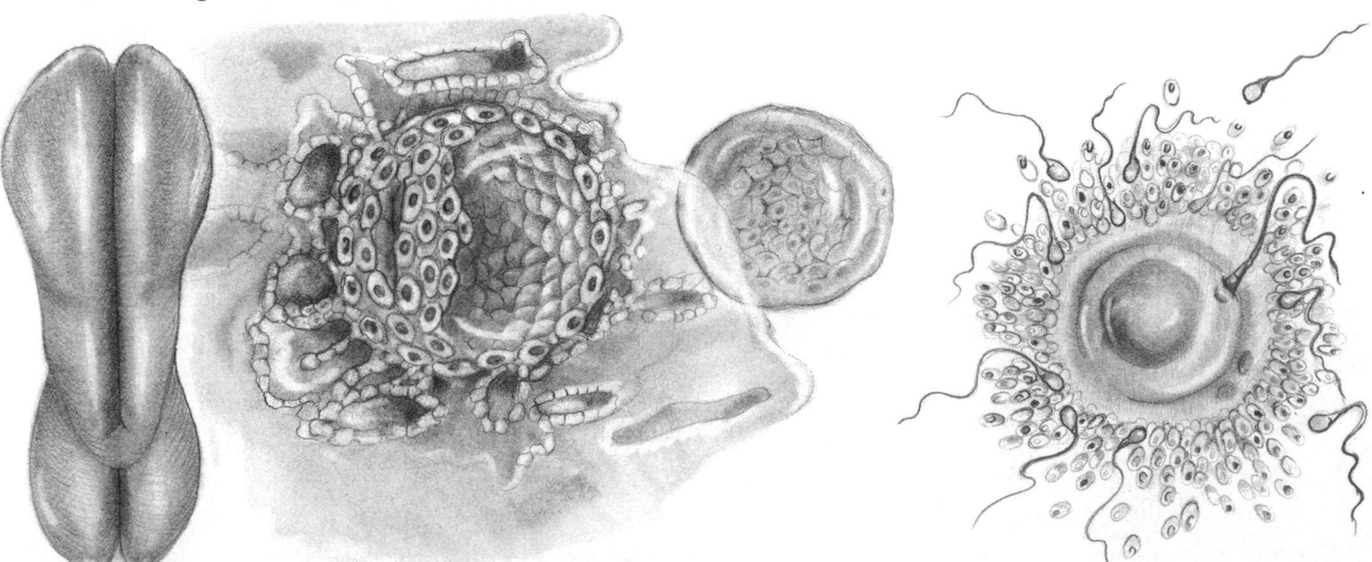

Crown-to-rump length 4 mm. Fertilization, implantation. Pre-embryonic stage.

Woman's basal body temperature elevated. hCG elevated; pregnancy tests positive.

Figure 7–9. Fetal Growth and Development and Maternal Responses *Continued*

Gestational age 5–8 weeks

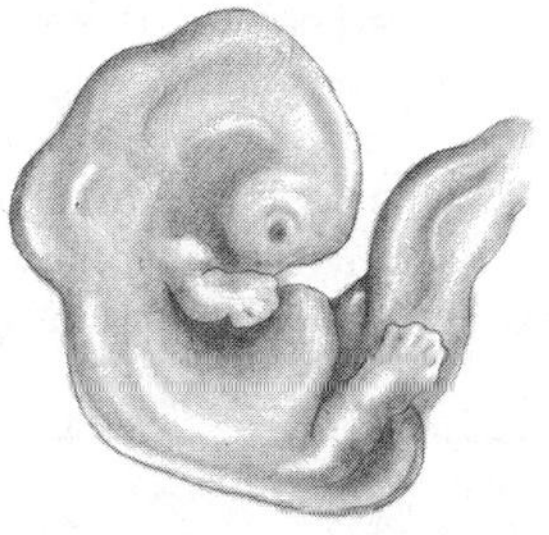

Crown-to-rump length 13 mm. Embryonic stage. Heart developed, beginning to pump. Arm and leg buds present. Head large, with facial features beginning to form.

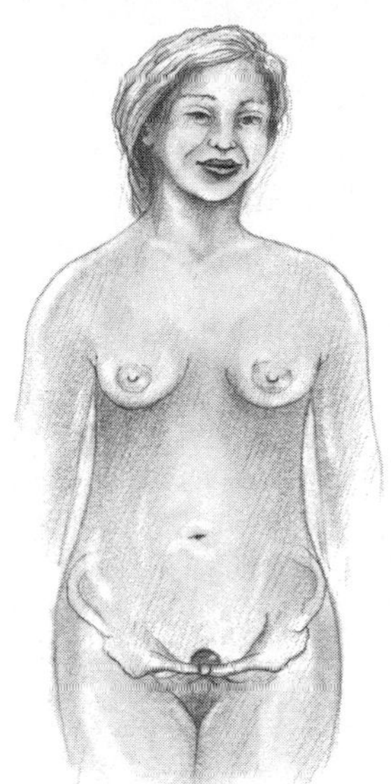

Woman misses menstrual period. Nausea; fatigue. Tingling of breasts. Uterus is size of a lemon; positive Chadwick's, Goodell's and Hegar's signs. Urinary frequency as enlarging uterus presses on the bladder; increased vaginal discharge.

Gestational age 9–12 weeks

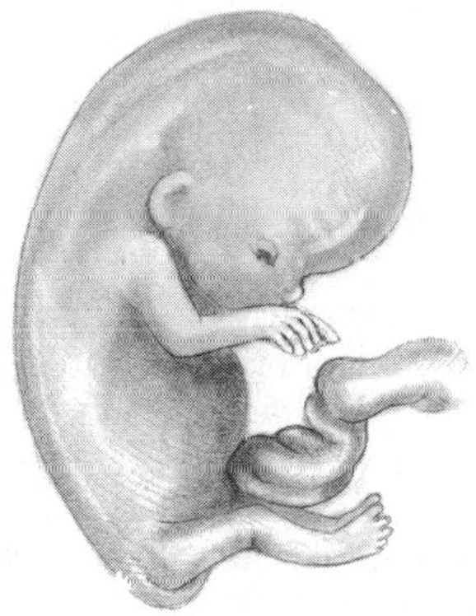

Crown-to-rump length 6–7 cm. Fetal stage begins at 10 weeks after last menstrual period. Extremities developed; fingers and toes differentiated; external genitalia show signs of male or female sex. Weight 14 g (0.5 oz).

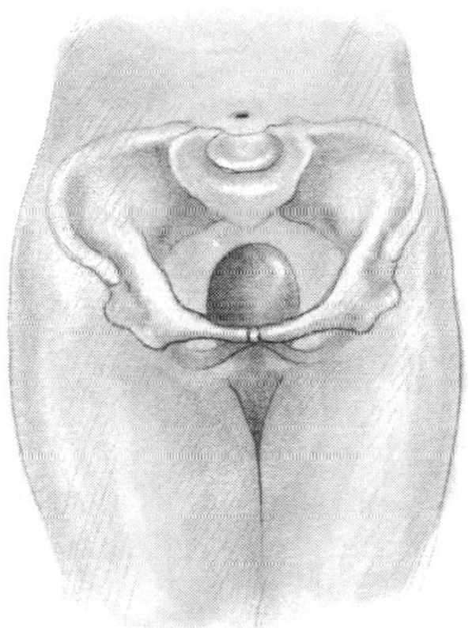

Nausea decreases after 12 weeks. Uterus is size of an orange; palpable above symphysis pubis. Vulvar varicosities may appear.

Gestational age 13–16 weeks

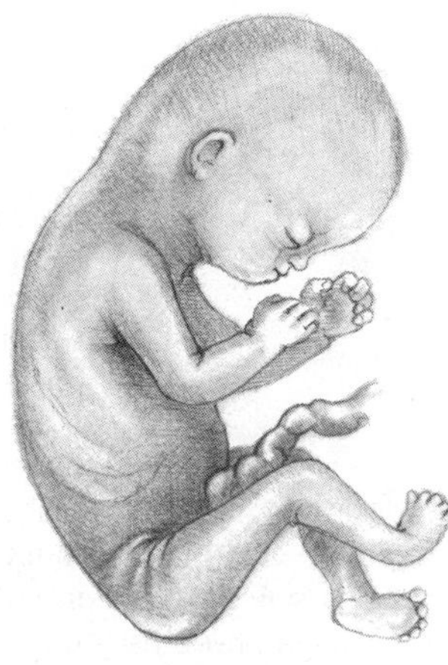

Crown-to-rump length 12 cm. Weight 110 g. Fetus begins to move. Head and thorax can be identified by ultrasound; sexual organs formed. Urine formation begins.

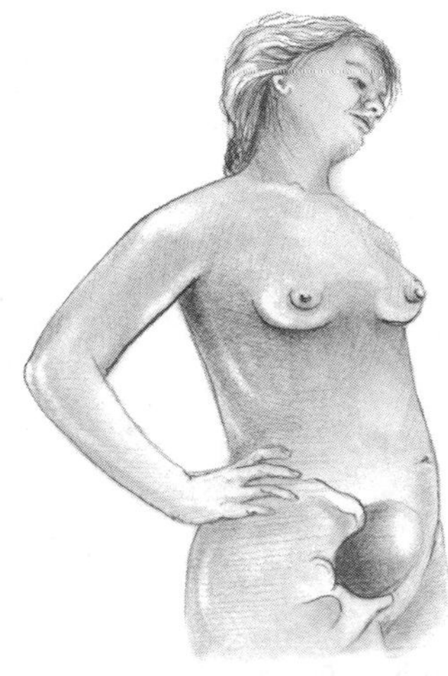

Fetal movements may be felt. Uterus has risen into the abdomen; fundus midway between symphysis pubis and umbilicus. Urinary frequency decreases; blood volume increases; uterine souffle heard.

Illustration continued on following page

Figure 7–9. Fetal Growth and Development and Maternal Responses *Continued*

Gestational age 17–20 weeks

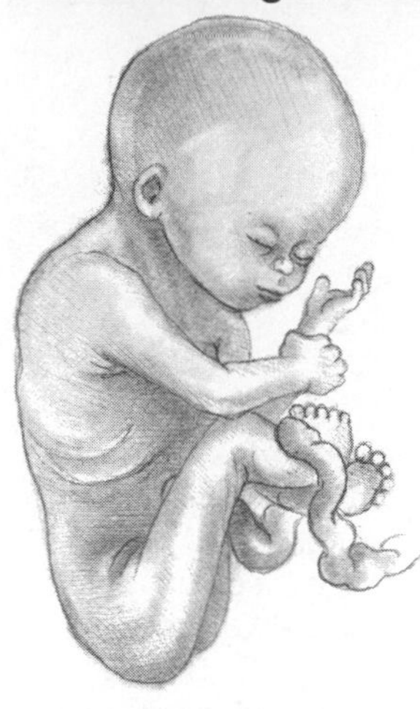

Crown-to-rump length 16 cm. Weight 320 g. Heart beat can be heard with fetoscope or electronic device. Meconium begins collecting in bowel. Period of very rapid growth.

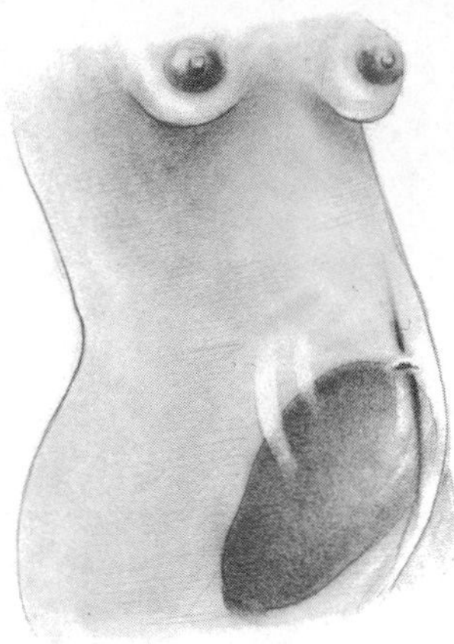

Skin pigmentation increases: areolae darken; chloasma and linea nigra may be obvious. Colostrum may be expressed. Braxton-Hicks contractions palpable. Fundus at level of umbilicus.

Gestational age 21–24 weeks

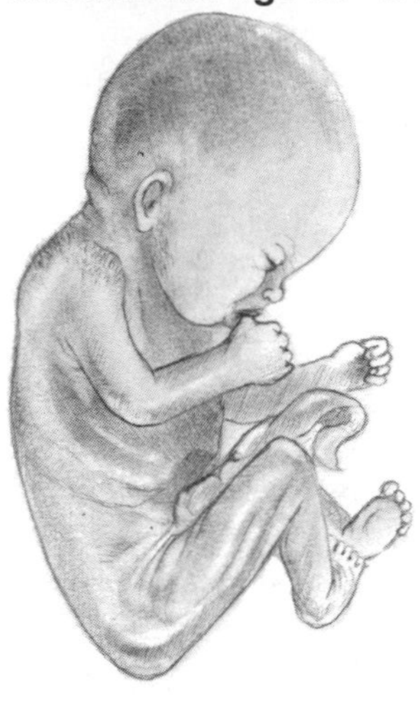

Crown-to-rump length 21 cm. Weight 630 g. Skin wrinkled and red; vernix present; head and body covered with lanugo.

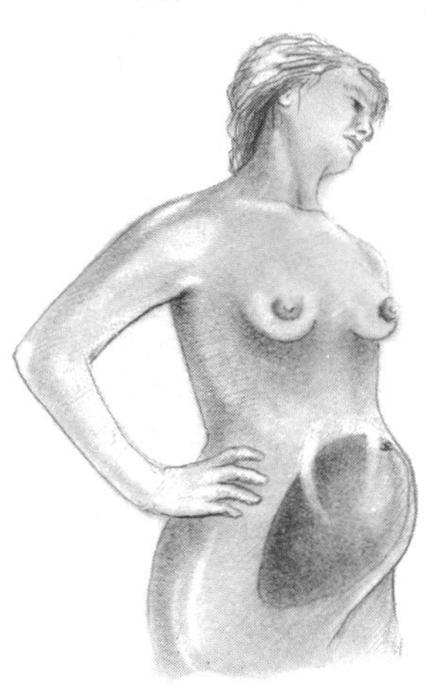

Relaxation of smooth muscles of veins and bladder increases the chance of varicose veins and urinary tract infections. Woman is more aware of fetal movements.

Gestational age 25–28 weeks

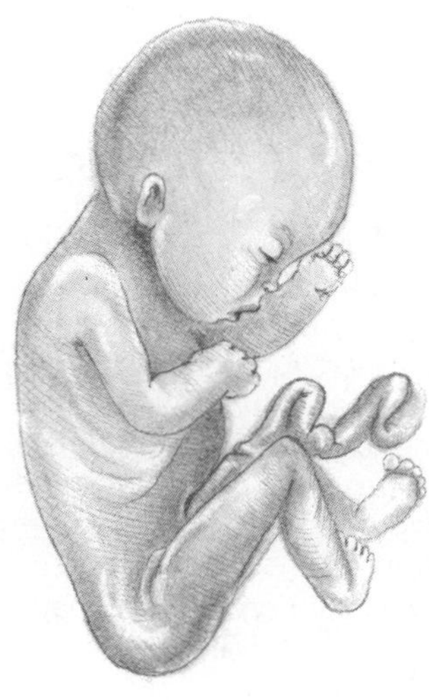

Crown-to-rump length 25 cm. Weight 1000 g. Eyes partially open; eyelashes present. Skin covered with vernix. Respiratory system immature, but fetus may survive if born.

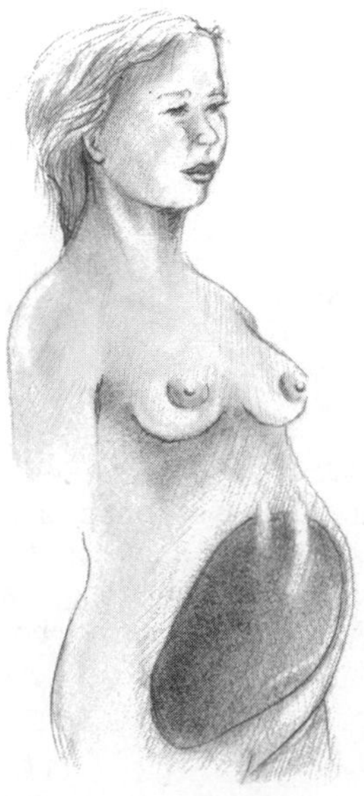

Period of greatest weight gain and lowest hemoglobin level begins. Fundal height is 3 to 4 fingerbreadths above umbilicus. Lordosis may cause backache.

Figure 7–9. Fetal Growth and Development and Maternal Responses *Continued*

Gestational age 29–32 weeks

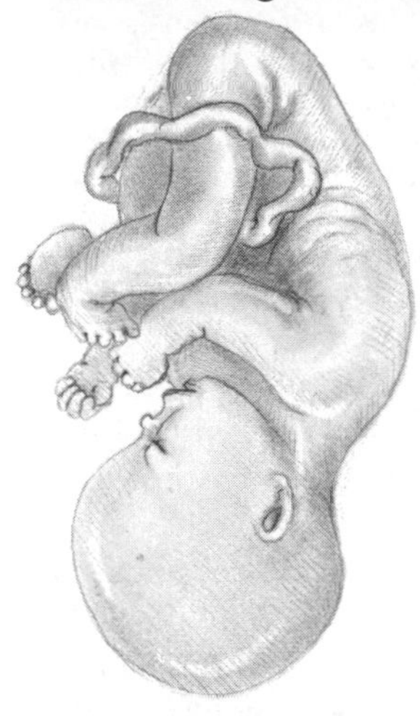

Crown-to-rump length 28 cm. Weight 1700 g. Toenails resent. Body filling out, testes descending. Iron, nitrogen, calcium stored. Vernix covers body. Chances of survival improving.

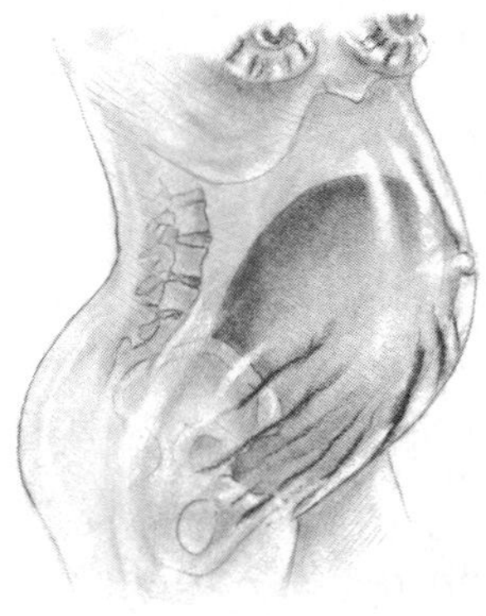

Heartburn common as uterus presses on diaphragm and displaces stomach. Braxton-Hicks contractions mre noticeable. Lordosis increases; waddling gait develops as relaxin softens pelvic joints.

Gestational age 33–36 weeks

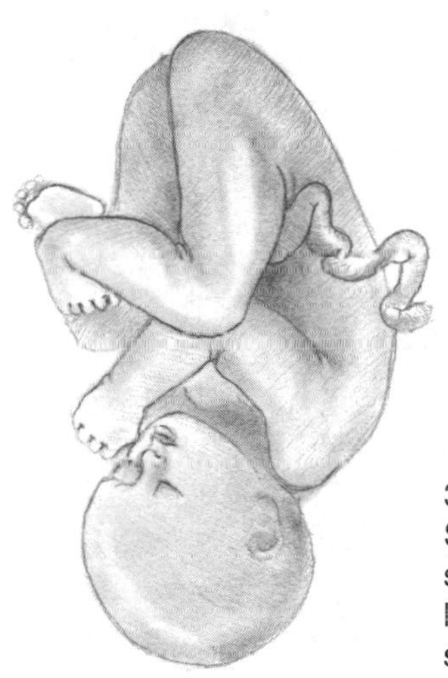

Crown-to-rump length 30–32 cm. Weight 2000–2500 g. Skin thicker, less wrinkled as subcutaneous fat accumulates. Excellent chance for survival.

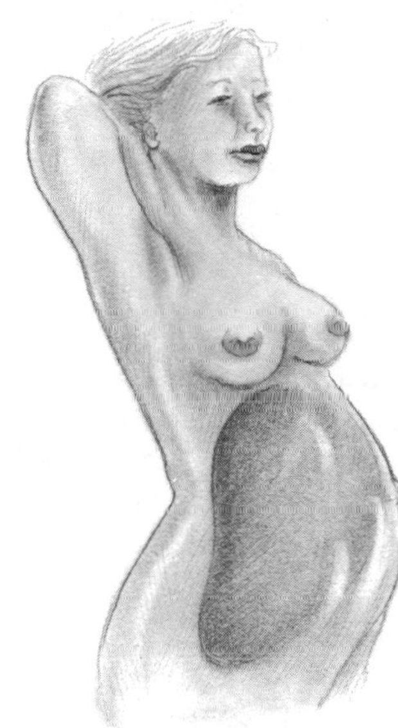

Shortness of breath caused by upward pressure on diaphragm; woman may have difficulty finding a comfortable position for sleep. Umbilicus protrudes. Varicosities more pronounced; pedal or ankle edema may be present. Urinary frequency noted following lightening when presenting part settles into pelvic cavity.

Gestational age 37–40 weeks

Crown-to-rump length 36 cm. Weight 3400 g. Body plump; lanugo remains only over shoulders; nails extend beyond nail beds; testes within scrotum; female labia well developed; labia majora cover labia minora.

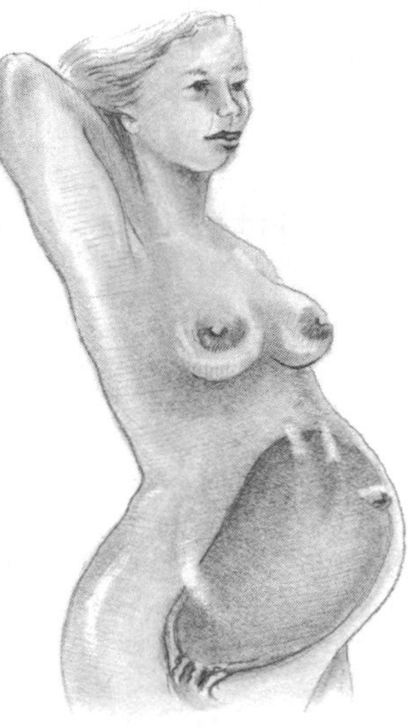

Woman is uncomfortable; looking forward to birth of baby. Cervix softens, begins to efface; mucus plug is often lost.

✔ Check Your Reading

13. How do presumptive and probable indications of pregnancy differ?
14. Why is "fetal" movement felt by the expectant woman not a positive sign of pregnancy?
15. What are the most common causes of false-negative pregnancy tests?

Cultural Considerations

Although the physical changes of pregnancy are fairly universal, culture often determines the health beliefs, values, and expectations of the family when a woman becomes pregnant. When a family and the health care professionals are from different cultures, they often hold different health beliefs and rely on health practices that are specific to their culture. Conflict may result from these variations in beliefs about what constitutes appropriate behaviors. To overcome the conflict and provide effective care, nurses must understand the family's way of thinking, feeling, and acting during pregnancy.

Cultural Assessment

Cultures are so diverse nurses cannot know all the specific aspects of each. Instead, they must become adept at performing cultural assessment. Some specific questions may elicit information that helps to understand the family's beliefs, for instance:

- How do you expect to feel during pregnancy?
- How will you and your family prepare for the baby?
- What makes you most concerned about the pregnancy?
- What would provide the greatest assistance?
- What do you and your family expect from the health care team during pregnancy?
- Where do you obtain most health care information?
- What foods are encouraged? Curtailed?
- Where will the baby be born? Who will assist in delivery of the baby?

Cultural Negotiation

Negotiation involves providing information while acknowledging that the family may hold different views. If the family indicates that the information would be helpful, it can be incorporated into the teaching plan.

If the family indicates that the information is not helpful or is harmful in their opinion, the conflict must be acknowledged openly and clarified. "I sense that you are unsure of this." "Help me understand your reluctance to try it." The nurse then explains reasons why the recommendation is valid and allows the family to continue to express their beliefs until a compromise is worked out.

An example of negotiating is the following. A Middle Eastern woman who is fatalistic does not plan for future events but rather leaves them to the will of God. Therefore, agreeing to regular prenatal examinations involves a major change in her expectations of care. She may be convinced by explanations that problems can often be identified and managed if detected early in pregnancy. If she is not convinced, it may be helpful to determine the patterns of kinship and decision making and seek approval from that family member to initiate a plan of care. This is particularly true in the Latino community, where women are viewed as weaker and in need of protection. The advice and counsel of the husband or father is often necessary to convince the woman that the plan of care has value.

Application of Nursing Process

Before beginning an assessment, it is essential to know the terms that are unique to maternity nursing.

Abortion–In the United States, this refers to spontaneous or elective termination of pregnancy before the 20th week of gestation, based on the date of the last menstrual period. Spontaneous abortion is frequently termed "miscarriage" by the lay public.

Gravida–A woman who is or has been pregnant, regardless of the duration of the pregnancy.

Primigravida–A woman who is pregnant for the first time.

Multigravida–A woman who has been pregnant more than once.

Para–Number of pregnancies that have progressed past 20 weeks. The term does not indicate whether the fetus was born alive or was stillborn. Parity does not reflect the number of fetuses or infants; a multiple gestation (twins, triplets) is considered to be one parous experience.

Nullipara–A woman who has never completed a pregnancy beyond 20 weeks of gestation.

Primipara–A woman who has given birth after a pregnancy of at least 20 weeks of gestation.

Multipara–A woman who has given birth two or more times at more than 20 weeks of gestation.

Preterm–A delivery that occurs after the 20th week and before the start of the 38th week of gestation.

Term–A delivery that occurs between the 38th and 42nd weeks of gestation.

Postterm–Delivery that occurs after 42 weeks of gestation.

Trimester–A division of pregnancy into three equal parts of 13 weeks each.

It is essential to know how to calculate gravida and para; however, incomplete information is obtained when only gravida and para are counted. Table 7–3 provides examples of the TPAL method for obtaining complete information.

Nurses must exercise caution when discussing gravida and para with the expectant mother in the presence of her family or significant other. Although the prenatal record indicates a previous pregnancy or childbirth, she may not have shared this information with her family and her right to privacy could be jeopardized by probing questions. The pregnancy may have terminated in elective or spontaneous abortion or in the birth of an infant who was placed for adoption. In either instance, the confidentiality of the pregnant woman must be protected.

Assessment

A thorough history as well as a thorough physical examination must be completed at the first antepartum visit. Increasing numbers of nurses are prepared to obtain health histories and to perform physical examinations. Nurses who have not fully developed these skills are responsible for assisting the nurse practitioner, certified nurse-midwife, or physician who is the primary health care provider. Although each agency has its own specific forms, the forms differ only in format because both medical and nursing practice are governed by standards and similar data are obtained by all agencies. The essential information that must be obtained is called the data base assessment.

The primary objectives of the first antepartum examination are to:

- Verify or rule out pregnancy
- Evaluate the pregnant woman's physical health relevant to childbearing
- Assess the growth and health of the fetus
- Establish baseline data for comparison with future observations
- Establish trust and rapport with the childbearing family
- Evaluate the psychosocial needs of the woman and her family
- Assess the need for counseling or teaching
- Negotiate a plan of care to ensure a healthy mother and a healthy baby.

Table 7–3. CALCULATING GRAVIDA AND PARA

A useful method for calculating gravida and para is to divide para into number of term pregnancies, preterm pregnancies, abortions, and living children. The acronym TPAL is helpful: T = Term, P = Preterm, A = Abortions, L = Living children.

The following examples illustrate how to use this method to obtain complete information.

Rosalie Beeman gave birth to twins at 36 weeks; she gave birth to a stillborn infant at 24 weeks; 2 years later, she suffered a spontaneous abortion at 12 weeks. If pregnant now, she is gravida IV, para II. T = 0, P = 3, A = 1, L = 2. The birth at 24 weeks is counted in the para, although the infant was stillborn. The termination of pregnancy before 20 weeks is counted in the gravida but not in the para. The twins are counted as one pregnancy and one delivery.

Louise Elam is pregnant for the fifth time. She had two elective abortions in the first trimester; she has a son who was born at 40 weeks of gestation and a daughter who was born at 36 weeks. She is gravida V, para II. T = 1, P = 1, A = 2 L = 2. The two abortions are counted in the gravida but are not included in the para because they occurred before 20 weeks.The daughter born at 36 weeks is preterm.

HISTORY

A complete history is taken, usually at the initial visit to the clinic or practitioner's office. Information is sought about previous pregnancies, menstruation, use of contraceptives, medical-surgical history, and the family's and partner's health.

Obstetric History. This provides essential information about prior pregnancies that may alert the physician or nurse-midwife to possible problems in the present pregnancy. The usual components are:

- Gravida, para, abortions, living children
- Weight of infants at birth, length of gestation
- Labor experience, type of delivery, location of birth, name of attending physician or midwife
- Type of anesthesia and any difficulties
- Maternal complications, such as hypertension, diabetes, infection, bleeding
- Complications with the infant
- Method of infant feeding planned (breast or formula)
- Special concerns

Menstrual History. A complete menstrual history is necessary to establish the EDD. It is common practice to estimate the EDD based on the first day of the last menstrual cycle, although ovulation and conception occur approximately 2 weeks after the beginning of menstruation. The average duration of pregnancy from the first day of the last normal menstrual period is 40 weeks, or 280 days. N*agele's rule* is often used to establish EDD. To use this method, subtract three months, and add 7 days to the first day of the last normal menstrual period (LNMP) and correct the year.

For example: LNMP—June 30, 1993
Subtract 3 months = March 30, 1993
Add 7 days and change the year = April 6, 1994.

A gestational calculator, or "wheel," also permits care providers to calculate EDD accurately and quickly.

Contraceptive History. Some forms of contraception may impose a risk on the fetus, the mother, or both; therefore, a detailed history of contraceptive methods is needed. Very recent use of oral contraceptives before pregnancy or continued use during early unrecognized pregnancy remains a source of concern, although some authorities report little, if any, risk of birth anomalies. Some physicians advise women in preconception counseling to stop taking oral contraception and to use alternative methods (condoms, diaphragm) to prevent conception for 3 months before conceiving.

Although intrauterine devices (IUDs) are not widely used in the United States, if pregnancy occurs with an IUD in place, there are serious risks of abortion, premature delivery, or puncture of the uterus.

Medical and Surgical History. Chronic conditions, such as diabetes mellitus, hypertension, or renal disease, can affect the outcome of the pregnancy and must be investigated. Infections, such as hepatitis or pyelonephritis, as well as surgical procedures or trauma that may complicate the pregnancy or delivery must be documented. The history includes:

- Age, race, ethnic background (relevant for groups at high risk for specific genetic problems, such as sickle cell anemia, thalassemia, or Tay-Sachs disease.)
- Childhood diseases and immunizations
- Chronic illnesses, such as asthma or heart disease (onset, treatment)
- Previous illnesses, surgical procedures, injuries (particularly of the pelvis or back)
- Previous infections: hepatitis, sexually transmitted diseases
- History of anemia and how it was treated
- Medications: prescription, over-the-counter, reasons for use
- Bladder, bowel function (problems or changes)
- Amount of caffeine consumed each day (coffee, tea, chocolate, colas)
- Tobacco use (number of years and number of packs per day)
- Use of drugs (name, amount, date and time of last use)
- Overall health and energy
- Appetite, general nutrition
- Contact with domestic pets, particularly cats, which increases the risk of infections such as toxoplasmosis
- Allergies or drug sensitivities

Family History. A family history provides valuable information about the general health of the family and the major causes of death. Moreover, information about patterns of genetic or congenital anomalies may be revealed. Major components include:

- Health status of parents, and siblings (living and well; cause of death if they are deceased)
- Chronic diseases (tuberculosis, heart disease, diabetes)
- Recent contagious infections in family members
- Pregnancy complications experienced by family members
- Occurrence of multiple births
- Cesarean births in relatives
- Congenital anomalies or genetic defects in relatives

Partner's Health History. Determine whether the father of the expected child or his family has a history of significant health problems. These might include genetic abnormalities, chronic diseases, or infections. Use of drugs, such as cocaine or alcohol may affect the ability of the family to cope with pregnancy and childbirth. Tobacco use by the father is important because both the mother and infant are at risk for upper respiratory complications as a result of passive smoking (inhaling smoke that is exhaled by another).

In addition, the blood type and Rh factor of the father are important if the mother is Rh-negative and there is the possibility of a blood incompatibility between the mother and the fetus.

Complete a psychosocial history at the same time (see Chapter 8).

PHYSICAL EXAMINATION

Because many women have never had a physical examination until they become pregnant, a thorough evaluation of all body systems is necessary to detect previously undiagnosed physical problems that may affect the pregnancy outcome. A complete examination also allows the examiner to establish baseline levels that will guide the treatment of the expectant mother and fetus throughout pregnancy.

Clinical Situation

Wilma Turner gave birth to twin girls at 38 weeks of gestation 3 years ago. She had a spontaneous abortion last year at 12 weeks of gestation and thinks she may be pregnant now because she has missed a menstrual period and is experiencing morning sickness. Wilma's last normal menstrual period began June 22, 1993.

Q:
1. If Wilma is pregnant now, what would be the gravida and para?
2. Explain to Wilma why amenorrhea and morning sickness are not positive indications of pregnancy.
3. Use Nagele's rule to compute the EDD.

A:
1. If pregnant now, Wilma is gravida 3, para 1 (the twin birth counts as one parous experience). If the acronym TPAL is used, more complete information can be recorded. T = 2 (twin infants born at term), P = 0 (no preterm infants), A — 1 (one pregnancy ended before 20 weeks' gestation), L = 2 (living twins).
2. Amenorrhea and nausea and vomiting are only presumptive (subjective) indications of pregnancy because they can be caused by conditions other than pregnancy.
3. Count back 3 months to March 22, and add 7 days. This brings the date to March 29. Correct the year to 1994. Wilma's EDD is March 29, 1994.

Vital signs

Blood Pressure. Obtaining a baseline BP is one of the most important assessments during the initial visit. Systolic BP should be in the region of 100 to 125 mmHg and should remain relatively stable throughout pregnancy. Diastolic BP normally decreases during the second trimester to 60 to 70 mmHg and returns to a prepregnancy level in the third trimester.

Any increase over baseline pressure of 30 mmHg in systolic BP or 15 mmHg in diastolic BP indicates pregnancy-induced hypertension and warrants medical evaluation and management (see Chapter 24).

Pulse. The normal pulse rate is from 60 to 90 BPM and may increase by 10 BPM as the pregnancy progresses. Tachycardia is associated with anxiety, hyperthyroidism, or infection and should be investigated. Apical pulse should be assessed for at least 1 minute to determine the amplitude and regularity of the heart beat. Pedal pulses are assessed to determine if there are circulatory problems in the legs. Pedal pulses should be strong, equal, and regular.

Respiratory Rate. Respiratory rate during pregnancy is in the region of 16 to 24 breaths per minute. Tachypnea may indicate respiratory infection or cardiac disease.

Temperature. Normal temperature during pregnancy is 36.2 to 37.6°C (98 to 99.6°F). Increased temperature suggests infection that may require medical management.

Cardiovascular System

Venous Congestion. Additional assessment of the cardiovascular system includes observation for venous congestion, which can develop into varicosities. Venous congestion is most commonly noted in the legs, vulva, or rectum.

Edema. Edema of the legs may be a benign condition that reflects pooling of blood in the extremities, which results in a shift of intravascular fluid into interstitial spaces. Edema of the face or hands may indicate serious problems involving pregnancy-induced hypertension and should be carefully evaluated by a physician.

Respiratory System

Assess the nose for edema of the nasal mucosa and for nasal stuffiness or epistaxis (nosebleeds).

In addition to counting the respiratory rate, auscultate the lung fields. Breath sounds should be equal bilaterally, chest expansion should be symmetrical, and lung fields should be free of all abnormal breath sounds.

Musculoskeletal System

Posture and Gait. Observe body mechanics as well as changes in posture and gait that may produce strain on the muscles of the lower back and legs.

Height and Weight. An initial weight is needed to establish a baseline for weight gain throughout pregnancy. Compare weight to the ideal-weight-for-height charts to determine whether the expectant mother is underweight or overweight and to identify nutritional needs. Preconception weight below 45 kg (100 pounds) or height under 150 cm are associated with preterm labor and low-birth-weight infants. Preconception weight above 90 kg (200 pounds) is associated with increased incidence of pregnancy-induced glucose intolerance (gestational diabetes) and pregnancy-induced hypertension (pre-eclampsia).

Pelvic Measurements. Early in pregnancy, the bony pelvis is evaluated to determine whether the diameters are adequate to permit vaginal delivery. (For pelvic measurements, see Chapter 12.)

Abdomen. Assess the abdomen for contour, size, muscle tone, separation of abdominal muscles (dias-

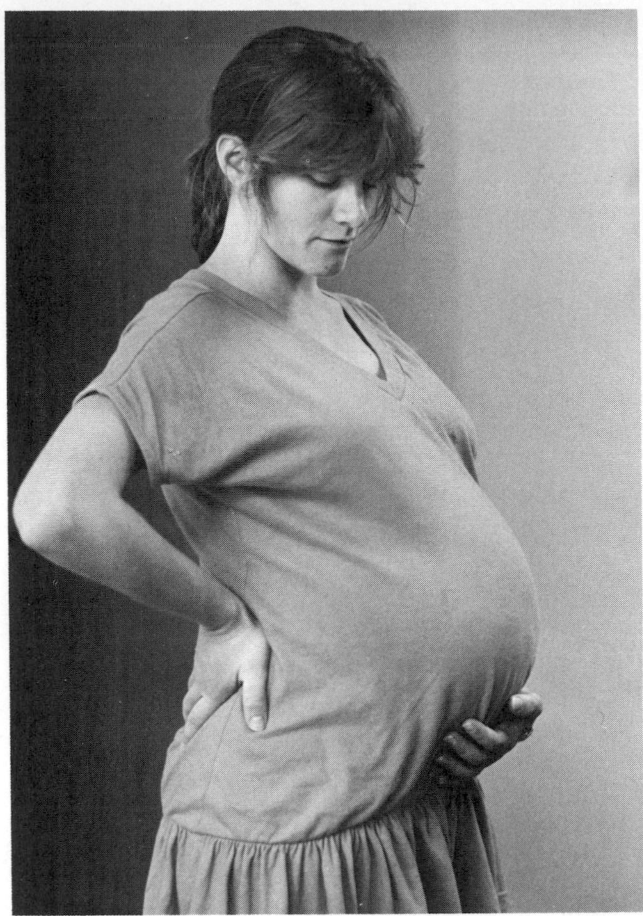

As the uterus increases in size, progressive lordosis causes strain on the muscles of the lower back and legs.

tasis recti), and location of uterine fundus. If the fundus is located above the symphysis pubis, measure the distance between the upper border of the symphysis pubis and the top of the fundus (Fig. 7–10). Fundal height in centimeters roughly equals gestational age in weeks. This is particularly true between 16 and 36 weeks. For example, at 20 weeks

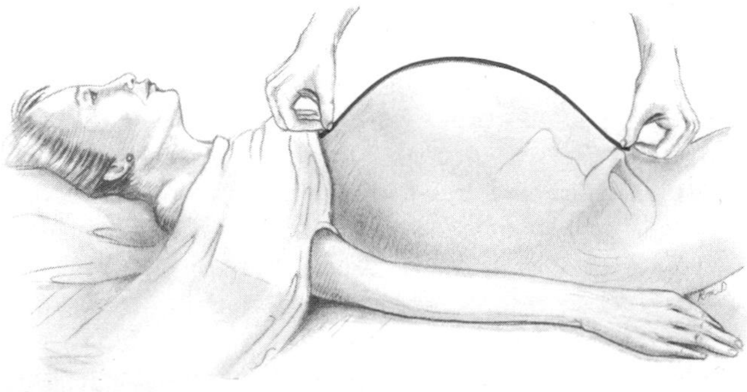

Figure 7–10

Measuring the uterus includes the distance between the upper border of the symphysis pubis and the top of the fundus.

of gestation, the fundal height should measure approximately 20 cm; at 28 weeks, it should measure approximately 28 cm.

If fundal height exceeds weeks of gestation, additional assessment is necessary to investigate the cause for the unexpected uterine size. It may be that the EDD is incorrect and the pregnancy is farther advanced than previously thought; perhaps the EDD is correct, but more than one fetus is present; or the cause may be excessive amniotic fluid or hydatidiform mole, which must be investigated (see Chapter 24).

If fundal height is less than expected on the basis of gestational age, confirm the EDD. If dates are accurate, further assessment may be necessary to determine whether the fetus is experiencing intrauterine growth retardation (IUGR).

If the pregnancy is advanced far enough to hear fetal heart tones, count and document the fetal heart rate. In addition, document the area where heart tones were located.

Neurologic System

Assess deep tendon reflexes for hyperreflexia, which is associated with pregnancy-induced hypertension. If hyperreflexia is noted, perform careful assessments for edema, hypertension, and proteinuria. (See Procedure 24–1, p. 688, for assessment of deep tendon reflexes.)

Integumentary System

Skin and Nails. Skin color should be consistent with racial background. Pallor may indicate anemia; jaundice may indicate hepatic disease. Examine the skin carefully for lesions, bruising, or areas of hyperpigmentation (chloasma, linea nigra) that are related to pregnancy. Observe the breasts, abdomen, and thighs for striae. Nail beds should be pink with instant capillary return.

Endocrine System

The thyroid enlarges slightly during the second trimester; however, gross enlargement or tenderness may indicate hyperthyroidism and requires further medical evaluation.

Gastrointestinal System

Mouth. Check the condition of the mouth and teeth. Mucous membranes should be pink, smooth, glistening, and uniform. The lips should be free of ulcerations; the gums may be red, tender, and edematous as a result of the effects of increased estrogen, which produces hyperplasia. The teeth should be in good repair.

Intestine. Use a warm stethoscope and light pressure to assess bowel sounds. Bowel sounds may be diminished because of the effects of progesterone on smooth muscle. This is an excellent time to ask if there are problems with constipation. Bowel sounds are often increased if a meal is overdue or if diarrhea is present.

Urinary System

Obtain a midstream urine sample at each prenatal appointment to test for glucose and protein. The presence of glycosuria necessitates additional assessment for pregnancy-induced glucose intolerance; the presence of proteinuria may reflect contamination of the specimen by vaginal discharge or may indicate pregnancy-induced hypertension. Medical follow-up is required to make a diagnosis.

Reproductive System

Breasts. Check breasts for size, symmetry, condition of nipples, and presence of colostrum. Examine the breasts for lumps, dimpling of the skin, or asymmetry of the nipples at the initial assessment. (See Chapter 32 for a complete description of breast assessment.)

External Reproductive Organs. The skin and mucous membranes of the perineum, vulva, and anus should be free of excoriations, growths, ulcerations, lesions, varicosities, warts, chancres, or perineal scars. Enlargement, tenderness, redness, or discharge of Bartholin's glands or Skene's glands may indicate gonorrheal or chlamydial infections. The examiner should obtain a specimen for culture of any discharge from lesions or inflamed glands to determine the causative organisms and to provide effective care.

Internal Reproductive Organs. A speculum, inserted into the vagina, permits the examiner to visualize the walls of the vagina and the cervix. The cervix should be pink in a non-pregnant woman, however, bluish discoloration (Chadwick's sign) may be observed during pregnancy. The external cervical os is closed in primigravidas, but one finger tip may be admitted in multiparas. The cervix feels relatively firm except during pregnancy, when marked softening is noted (Goodell's sign). If lesions or unusual discharge is observed, the examiner obtains a specimen of the discharge so that infections can be diagnosed. The examiner also collects a specimen for a Papanicolaou (Pap) smear, a screening test for cervical cancer.

A bimanual examination involves using both hands to palpate the internal genitalia. The examiner palpates the uterus for size, contour, tenderness, and position. The uterus should be movable between the two examining hands and should feel smooth. The ovaries, if palpable, should be about the shape and size of almonds and should not be tender. (See Chapter 32 for additional information on pelvic examinations.)

Laboratory Data

A complete blood count and determinations of hemoglobin, hematocrit, blood type, and Rh factor are essential for all expectant mothers. If the blood is Rh-negative, determine whether there are antibodies to Rh-positive blood that may cause fetal problems. If antibodies are not present, the administration of Rh_o (D) immune globulin (RhoGam) at 28 weeks of gestation and within 72 hours following the birth of an Rh-positive infant prevents future fetal complications. (Chapter 24 provides more complete information about Rh incompatibility.)

Hemoglobin electrophoresis, to assess for sickle cell trait, is recommended for African-American women. See Table 7–4 for a complete list of recommended laboratory tests.

ASSESSMENT FOR THE COMMON DISCOMFORTS OF PREGNANCY

Many women experience discomforts of pregnancy that are not serious in themselves, but their presence detracts from the mother's feeling of comfort and well-being.

Nausea and Vomiting. Women need reassurance that nausea and vomiting, however distressing, are common and that the condition is temporary. "Morning sickness" must be distinguished from *hyperemesis gravidarum*, a severe state of vomiting that is accompanied by weight loss, dehydration, electrolyte imbalance and ketosis. (See Chapter 24.)

Although the cause of nausea and vomiting is unknown, it is believed to be related to increased levels of hCG and estrogen. Emotional factors may also be implicated; it is known that women under emotional stress are more likely to experience nausea.

Heartburn. Heartburn is described as an acute burning sensation in the epigastric and sternal regions. It may be associated with other gastrointestinal symptoms, such as eructation, nausea, or epigastric pressure.

Heartburn occurs when reverse peristaltic waves cause regurgitation of acidic stomach contents into

Table 7–4. LABORATORY TESTS ROUTINELY PERFORMED DURING PREGNANCY

Test	Purpose	Significance
Hemoglobin, hematocrit	To detect anemia	If < 11 g/dl, supplementation with iron is necessary
Complete blood count (CBC)	To determine blood abnormalities or signs of infection	Follow-up for additional signs if necessary
ABO and Rh typing	To identify mothers with type O or Rh-negative blood	If mother is Rh-negative, check for presence of anti-Rh antibodies. Check partner's blood type; if positive, repeat maternal antibody titers throughout pregnancy; may be a candidate for Rh immune globulin at 28 weeks of gestation.
Hemoglobin electrophoresis	To screen for sickle cell trait if client is African-American	If mother is positive, check partner; fetus is at risk only if both partners are sickle cell–positive
VDRL/FTA	To identify untreated syphilis	Initiate immediate therapy to prevent congenital syphilis
Rubella titer	To determine immunity to rubella	If titer is <1:10, mother is not immune and should be cautioned to avoid contact with crowds or with children with infections of unknown origin, immunization offered in immediate postpartum period
TB skin test	To screen high-risk populations (homeless, indigent)	If mother is positive, refer for additional testing or therapy
Urinalysis	To screen for renal disease or diabetes	If glycosuria present, initiate follow-up blood glucose test; protein, hematuria, or casts indicate renal disease
Gonorrhea culture (discharge from vagina or urethra)	To screen for untreated gonorrhea	Refer for treatment
Papanicolaou (Pap) (cervix)	To screen for cervical neoplasia	Rescreen or refer for additional treatment

Abbreviations: VDRL/FTA, Veneral Disease Research Laboratory/fluorescent treponemal antibody; TB, tuberculosis.

the esophagus. The underlying causes are diminished gastric motility and displacement of the stomach by the enlarging uterus. Improper diet and nervous tension may be precipitating factors.

Backache. Backache is a common complaint during the third trimester. A primary focus is to prevent backache by teaching correct posture and body mechanics. Figure 7–11 illustrates correct and incorrect posture. Stooping or bending puts a great deal of strain on the muscles of the lower back. Figure 7–12 illustrates correct and incorrect methods for lifting.

Urinary Frequency. During the first weeks of pregnancy, urinary frequency occurs because the expanding uterus exerts pressure on the bladder. Late in the third trimester, urinary frequency and urgency again become a problem when the fetus settles into the pelvic cavity and exerts pressure on the bladder.

Varicosities. Varicosities are common during pregnancy. They are usually confined to the legs, however, they may involve the veins of the vulva or rectum (hemorrhoids). They occur most often in women with a family history of varicose veins and are more likely to be a problem in women who are obese or who are multiparas. Symptoms depend on the degree of engorgement, from barely noticeable blemishes with minimal discomfort at the end of the day to large tortuous veins that produce severe discomfort with any activity.

Varicosities are common in pregnancy because the weight of the uterus partly compresses the veins that return blood from the legs. As blood pools, the vessels dilate and the valves in the veins become stretched and incompetent. This results in even more pooling, and, in time, the veins may become engorged, inflamed, and painful. Varicose veins are exacerbated by prolonged standing when the force of gravity makes blood return more difficult.

Hemorrhoids. Hemorrhoids are varicosities of the rectum; they may be external (outside the anal sphincter) or internal (above the sphincter). Some of the most common causes of hemorrhoids are vascular engorgement of the pelvis, constipation, straining at stool, and prolonged sitting or standing. Pushing during the second stage of labor exacerbates the problem, which may continue into the postpartum period.

Constipation. Occasional constipation is not harmful, although it can cause a feeling of abdominal

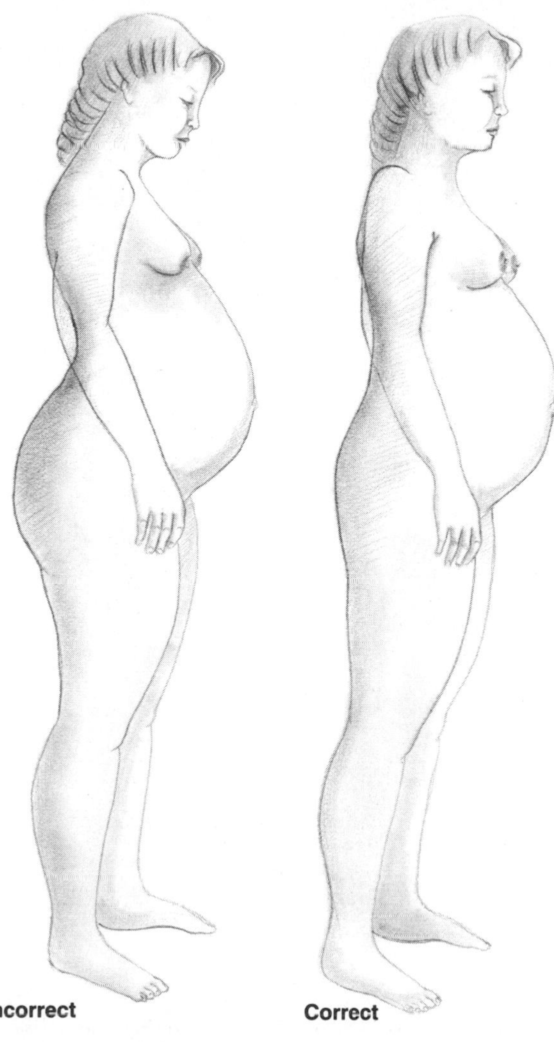
Incorrect
The neck is jutting forward, the shoulders are slumping, and the back is sharply curved, creating back pain and discomfort.
Correct
The neck and shoulders are straight, the back is flattened, and the pelvis is tucked under and slightly upward.

Figure 7–11

Posture during pregnancy may cause or alleviate backache.

fullness and flatulence and can aggravate painful hemorrhoids. Intestinal motility is reduced during pregnancy as a result of progesterone. This benefits the expectant mother and the fetus by allowing additional time for nutrients to be absorbed. It also adds time for water to be absorbed from the large intestine, which can result in hard dry stools and decreased frequency of bowel movements. Iron supplementation also causes constipation in some women.

Leg Cramps. Painful contraction of the muscles of the lower legs occur most often during sleep when the muscles are relaxed. They are also likely to occur when the woman stretches and extends her foot. Leg cramps are believed to be caused by an imbalance of serum calcium and phosphorus. A 1:1 ratio of calcium to phosphorus is desired; however, this is difficult to achieve in pregnancy, when many women consume large amounts of dairy products that are high in calcium. Venous congestion in the legs during the third trimester also contributes to leg cramps.

RISK ASSESSMENT

Use the initial assessment to identify the factors that put the expectant mother or the fetus at high risk to experience complications and thus to need specialized care. Since not all factors present equal threats, a risk-scoring tool is used by many agencies to determine degree of risk. Although risk scoring is a valuable method for identifying the high-risk pregnancy, it cannot be counted on to predict problems or the absence of complications 100 per cent of the time. Many women, identified as being at high risk, give birth to healthy term infants. Furthermore, risk factors change as pregnancy progresses, and risk assessment must be updated throughout pregnancy because gestations that are categorized as low-risk at the initial assessment may become high-risk later. Table 7–5 lists the major risk factors and identifies maternal and fetal-neonatal implications.

✔ *Check Your Reading*

16. What is the relationship between gestational age and expected fundal height?
17. How does progesterone contribute to constipation during pregnancy?
18. Why is a bimanual examination necessary at the initial physical examination?

SUBSEQUENT ASSESSMENTS

Ongoing prenatal care is important to the successful outcome of pregnancy. The recommended schedule for prenatal assessment in an uncomplicated pregnancy is as follows:

Conception to 28 weeks—every 4 weeks
29 to 36 weeks—every 2 weeks
37 weeks to delivery—weekly

The major components of subsequent assessments are described next.

Vital Signs. To obtain accurate information, measure BP using the same arm with the mother in the same position each time. Report significant deviations from the baseline value, pulse, or respiratory rate to the physician, nurse-midwife, or nurse practitioner. Temperature should remain within normal limits.

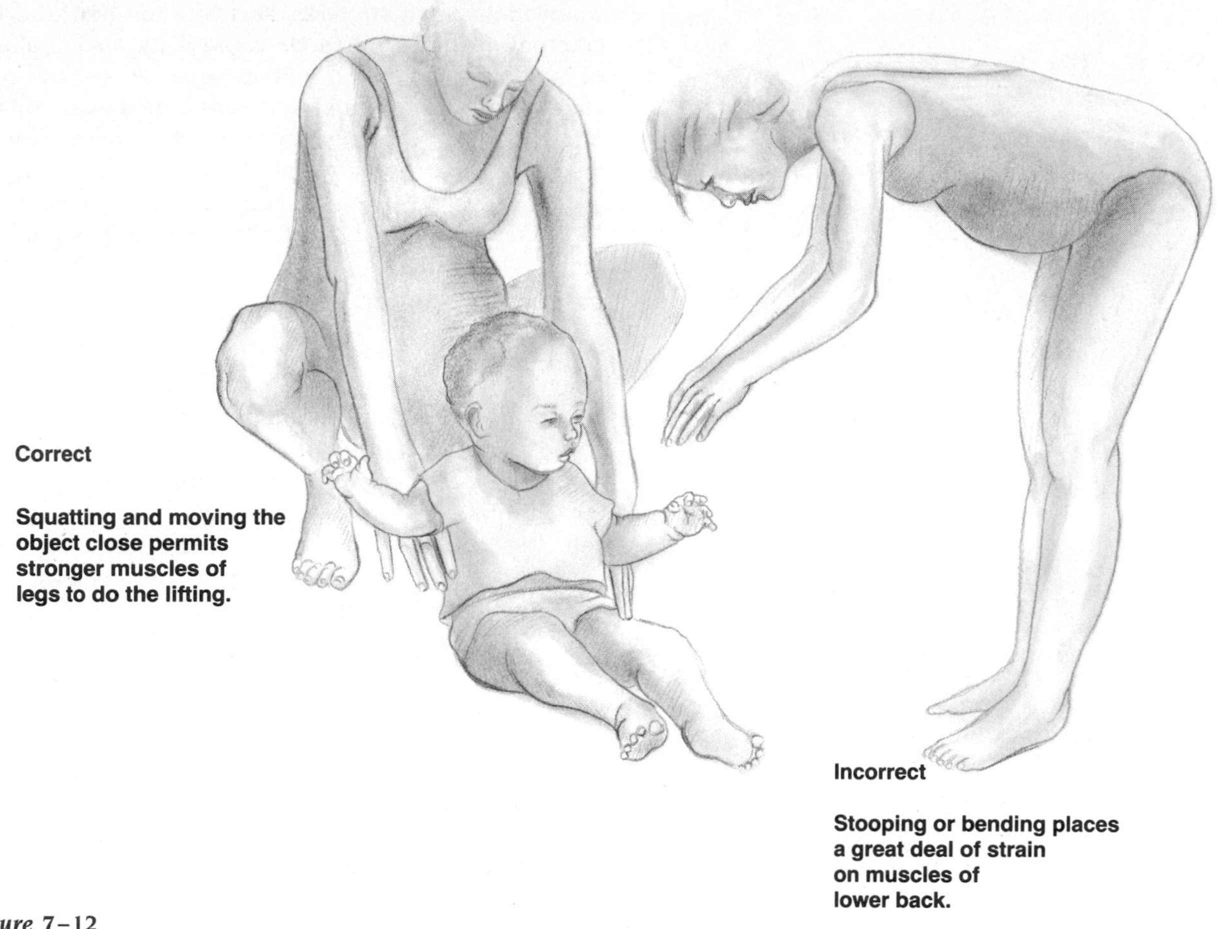

Correct
Squatting and moving the object close permits stronger muscles of legs to do the lifting.
Incorrect
Stooping or bending places a great deal of strain on muscles of lower back.

Figure 7–12

Techniques for lifting. Squatting places less strain on the back.

Weight. Report weight loss; plot weight gain to validate that the expected pattern of weight gain is being attained. Inadequate weight gain may signify that the pregnancy is not as advanced as first thought; sudden, rapid weight gain may indicate fluid retention, and further assessment for pregnancy-induced hypertension is indicated. (See Chapter 9 for a thorough discussion on the desired pattern of weight gain.)

Urinalysis. Test urine for protein and glucose levels; proteinuria may indicate contamination of the specimen by vaginal secretions, or it may be an indication of pregnancy-induced hypertension (see Chapter 24). Glycosuria may be due to alterations in the glomerular filtration rate and consequent "spilling" of glucose into the urine, but the client should be referred for further evaluation.

Fundal Height. From 22 weeks until near term, the fundal height, measured in centimeters from the symphysis pubis to the top of the fundus, is equivalent to the gestational age of the fetus in weeks. If fundal height does not correlate roughly with weeks of gestation, additional assessment is needed to confirm EDD, to rule out or confirm more than one fetus, or to determine whether intrauterine growth retardation of the fetus is a possibility. To be accurate, the bladder must be empty before the measurement is taken. The woman lies on her back with knees slightly flexed; the top of the fundus is palpated, and a tape is stretched from the top of the symphysis pubis over the abdominal curve to the top of the fundus. See Figure 7–10.

Leopold's Maneuvers. A systematic method for palpating the fetus through the abdominal wall, these maneuvers provide valuable information about the fetus. (See Chapter 13.)

Fetal Heart Rate. The fetal heart rate may be heard in early pregnancy with a Doppler examination or, in later pregnancy, with a fetoscope. Figure 14–1A and 14–1B illustrate fetoscopic and Doppler techniques. The fetal heart rate should be between 110 and 160 BPM; the site provides information that may help determine in what position the fetus is entering the pelvis. For instance, fetal heart tones heard in an upper quadrant of the abdomen suggest that the fetus is in a breech presentation.

Table 7–5. SUMMARY OF HIGH-RISK FACTORS IN PREGNANCY

Factors	Implications
Demographic Factors	
< 16 years or > 35 years	Increased risk for preterm labor, pregnancy-induced hypertension, congenital anomalies
Low socioeconomic status or dependent on public assistance	Increased risk for preterm labor, low-birth-weight infants
Non-Caucasian race	Incidence of infant and maternal death twice that of Caucasians
Multiparity: > 4 pregnancies	Increasing parity increases risk of pregnancy loss, antepartum or postpartum hemorrhage, and cesarean birth
Social-Personal Factors	
Weight < 45 kg (100 pounds)	Associated with low-birth-weight infant
Weight > 90 kg (200 pounds)	Increased risk for pregnancy-induced hypertension, difficult labor, large-for-gestational-age infant, and cesarean birth
Height < 154 cm (5 feet)	Increased incidence of cesarean birth due to cephalopelvic disproportion
Smoking	Associated with low-birth-weight infant, increased risk for preterm birth
Use of alcohol or addicting drugs	Increased risk of congenital anomalies, neonatal withdrawal syndrome, and fetal alcohol syndrome
Obstetric Factors	
Birth of previous infant > 4000 g (8.5 pounds)	Increased need for cesarean birth; increased risk for infant birth injury, neonatal hypoglycemia, and maternal gestational diabetes.
Previous stillborn infant	Maternal psychological distress
Rh sensitization	Fetal anemia, erythroblastosis fetalis, kernicterus
Existing Medical Conditions	
Diabetes mellitus	Increased risk of pregnancy-induced hypertension, cesarean birth, infant either small or large for gestational age, neonatal hypoglycemia, fetal or neonatal death; increased incidence of congenital anomalies
Thyroid disorder	
Hypothyroidism	Increased incidence of spontaneous abortion, congenital anomalies, congenital hypothyroidism
Hyperthyroidism	Maternal risk of pregnancy-induced hypertension, thyroid storm, or postpartum hemorrhage; neonatal risk of thyrotoxicosis
Cardiac disease	Maternal risk for cardiac decompensation and increased death rate; increased risk for fetal and neonatal death
Renal disease	Maternal risk for renal failure and preterm delivery; fetal risk for intrauterine growth retardation
Concurrent Infections	Severe fetal implications (heart disease, blindness, deafness, bone lesions) if maternal disease occurred in the first trimester
	Increased incidence of spontaneous abortion or congenital anomalies are associated in the same infections (see Chapter 25)

Fetal Activity. First noticed by the expectant mother at 16 to 20 weeks of gestation, fetal movements gradually increase in both frequency and strength. In the last trimester, the woman may be asked to count fetal body movements. To do this, she lies on her left side following a meal and notes how long it takes for ten fetal movements to occur. If more than 2 hours is required, additional assessments are necessary (McCaul and Morrison, 1990). (See Chapter 10 for additional information about fetal movement counts.)

Maternal Serum. Many physicians check the serum at 16 to 18 weeks for the presence of abnormal levels of alpha-fetoprotein, which may indicate fetal anomalies. (See Chapter 10 for a complete discussion of alpha-fetoprotein.)

Glucose Screen. Many health providers order a 50-g glucose screen at 24 to 28 weeks. If the plasma glucose level is elevated, a follow-up glucose tolerance test is usually recommended.

Analysis

Each family has unique responses to the physiological changes of pregnancy, and a variety of nursing diagnoses can be made. (See the three nursing care plans.) Some of the most common are:

1. Fatigue, related to increased need for sleep during early pregnancy.
2. Potential Alteration in Nutrition: Less than Body Requirement related to nausea and vomiting.
3. Constipation, related to insufficient fluid and fiber intake, and lack of exercise, and
4. Pain or backache, related to muscular strain secondary to change in balance and knowledge deficit of measures that reduce strain.

Nursing diagnoses that are relevant to most women during the prenatal period do not address the intense desire of most families to protect the health of the unborn child and the well-being of the mother. Perhaps the most encompassing nursing diagnosis for this period is *Health Seeking Behaviors: Prenatal care and health practices that provide optimum benefit to the fetus and mother.*

Planning

Goals for this nursing diagnosis are that the expectant mother (and/or the family) will:

- Demonstrate knowledge of practices that promote the safety and well-being of the mother and fetus throughout pregnancy.
- Describe measures that provide relief from the common discomforts of pregnancy.
- Describe a realistic plan during the first trimester to modify behaviors or habits that do not promote the health of the mother and fetus.

Interventions

Following the initial assessment, the woman is usually not seen by the health care provider for 4 weeks. She and her family must be instructed about the signs and symptoms that indicate the presence of a serious danger; any such signs or symptoms should be reported immediately. (See Critical to Remember: Danger Signs of Pregnancy.)

Although it is crucial that the expectant mother be made aware of the danger signs of pregnancy, the nurse must take care not to frighten her. Avoid the term "danger signs" when talking to the woman or her family. It is less frightening to say, "The signs I am about to tell you are rare, but if you see them notify the physician (or nurse-midwife) at once because they require immediate attention."

Critical to Remember

Danger Signs of Pregnancy

- Vaginal bleeding, with or without discomfort
- Rupture of membranes (escape of fluid from the vagina)
- Swelling of the fingers (rings become tight) or puffiness of the face or around the eyes
- Continuous pounding headache
- Visual disturbances (blurred vision, dimness, spots before the eyes)
- Persistent or severe abdominal pain
- Chills or fever
- Painful urination
- Persistent vomiting
- Change in frequency or strength of fetal movements

TEACHING HEALTH BEHAVIORS

Bathing. Daily bathing protects pregnant women from potential infection if bacteria normally present on the skin are allowed to remain and multiply. Bathing also promotes comfort by dissipating heat that is produced by increased metabolism. Tub baths are acceptable until the last trimester, when balance is altered by a changing center of gravity and the chance of falling or slipping is increased. Bathing in hot tubs should be avoided because it increases body temperature, which may cause fetal anomalies.

Douching. In spite of increased vaginal discharge, there is no hygienic need for douching before, during, or after pregnancy. The only exception is a physician's order to treat a specific problem. In that case, guidelines must be carefully followed to prevent the possibility of injury (Cunningham et al, 1989).

- Bulb-type syringes have been associated with deaths caused by air embolism and should never be used.
- Douche bags should not be elevated more than 2 feet above the hips to prevent excessive force of the fluid.
- The nozzle should not be inserted more than 3 inches into the vagina.

Breast Care. Instruct the expectant mother to wash her breasts and nipples with clear water and to avoid soap, which removes the natural lubricant that forms on the nipples. Advise all clients to wear a well-made bra that supports the breasts and prevents loss of muscle tone that can occur as the breasts become heavier during pregnancy. Wide bra straps distribute the weight evenly across the shoulders and provide greater comfort. Inform the couple that breast stimulation, which increases oxytocin secretion and thus initiates uterine contractions, is unsafe if there has been a history of preterm labor or if signs of preterm labor exist; these signs include uterine contractions that increase in frequency or intensity, rhythmic pelvic pressure, or uterine contractions that assume a regular pattern.

Clothing. Recommend practical, comfortable, nonconstricting clothing. Tight jeans or panty hose that may constrict venous circulation should be worn for short periods of time. Low heels are preferred because they do not interfere with balance and because high heels increase the curvature of the lower spine (lordosis) that is prevalent during the last trimester.

Exercise. Exercise during pregnancy is generally beneficial; however, the amount of exercise recommended depends on the condition of the woman and the stage of pregnancy. Walking is perhaps the ideal exercise because it stimulates muscular activity of the entire body, gently increases respiratory and cardiovascular effort, and does not result in fatigue or strain. Potential dangers arise when pregnant women engage in strenuous aerobic exercises because pregnancy imposes additional physiological demands. Pregnant women should pay particular attention to avoiding dehydration and hyperthermia, meeting increased nutritional needs resulting from exercise, and elevating legs after exercising because of decreased venous return (Fishbein, 1991). Additional exercise guidelines (ACOG, 1985) include:

1. The maternal heart rate should not exceed 140 BPM.
2. Strenuous exercise should not exceed 15 minutes in duration.
3. No exercise should be performed in the supine position after the 4th month of gestation is completed.
4. Exercises that employ the Valsalva maneuver should be avoided.
5. Maternal core temperature should not exceed 38°C (100.4°F).

Concerns About Safety. A major concern is the possibility that vigorous exercise will divert blood supply from the placenta to maternal muscles and thus deprive the fetus of needed oxygen. Vigorous exercise also increases circulating catecholamines, which cause visceral vasoconstriction and decreased placental circulation.

Recommend that women not begin strenuous exercise programs or intensify training during pregnancy. As pregnancy progresses, it may be necessary to reduce the level of exercise to prevent physiological stress. Teach the client to take her pulse every 10 to 15 minutes and not to exceed a target heart rate that has been determined in consultation with the physician or midwife.

Pregnant women must avoid becoming overheated because heat is transmitted to the fetus. Women should allow a cool-down period of mild activity after exercising. Emphasize the importance of taking liquids before and after exercising to prevent dehydration and the possible necessity of interrupting the exercise program to replace fluids.

Expectant mothers should curtail any activity that causes undue fatigue or that poses the threat of injury. This may mean that activity that is safe in the first trimester may not be safe in the third trimester. Suggest that the expectant mother avoid sports that require balance and that she postpone undertaking a totally new sport until after childbirth.

Sleep and Rest. Finding a comfortable position for rest becomes a problem in the third trimester. Figure 7–13 illustrates how pillows can be used to support the abdomen and back and provide the best opportunity for sleep.

Employment. Most women of childbearing age in the United States are employed outside the home, and most continue to work during pregnancy. Whether the expectant mother can or should work depends on the presence of environmental toxins, industrial hazards, and physical activity involved.

Maintaining Maternal Safety. Work should not lead to undue fatigue. Frequent rest periods, with feet

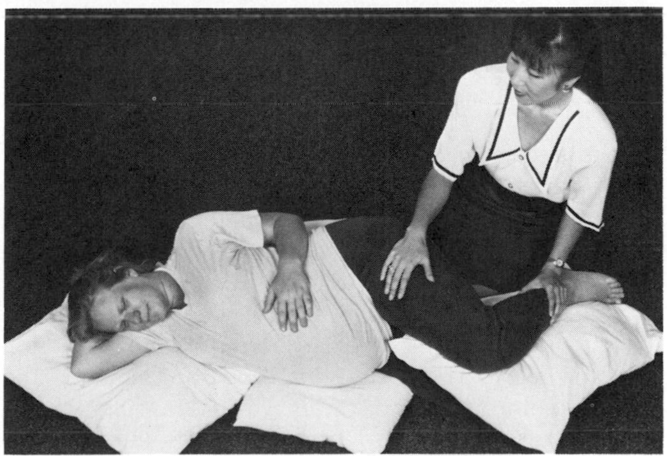

Figure 7–13

During the third trimester, pillows supporting the abdomen and back provide a comfortable position for rest.

elevated, are essential. Jobs that require constant standing or sitting are very tiring, and it is necessary to plan ways to change positions or to walk briefly to stimulate circulation and reduce fatigue. Jobs that require balance may be hazardous because the uterus enlarges and the center of gravity shifts. Suggest that these jobs be curtailed during the last trimester.

Avoiding Exposure to Teratogens. Problems of intrauterine exposure to toxic substances is a major concern in many industries. Advise women to take the initiative to investigate their own particular situations. For example, hairdressers are exposed to toxic substances in hair dyes and aerosol sprays; painters and printers may be exposed to benzene, lead, or toluene; nurses and hospital personnel may be exposed to radiation, anesthetic gases, and hexachlorophene; and laundry and dry cleaning workers may be exposed to fetotoxic compounds. In addition, some women are exposed to passive smoking in the workplace, and this is known to be harmful to both mother and fetus.

Sexual Activity. In spite of the need for information, most couples are reluctant to initiate a discussion about sexual activity. Furthermore, most health professionals do not introduce the topic for a number of reasons: they may fear offending the client; they may be uncomfortable with their own sexuality and feel embarrassed to begin a discussion; or they may lack time for any but the most pressing assessments. The result may be that an important aspect of care is ignored.

It may be helpful to use a broad opening statement to initiate a discussion about sexual activity. For example, "Many women tell me it is difficult to find a comfortable position for intercourse during pregnancy." Or "Sometimes couples are concerned about having sex during pregnancy." Broad opening statements provide a method of introducing the subject in such a way that the woman feels comfortable to pursue it or to let it drop.

It is generally agreed that sexual intercourse does no harm to the healthy pregnant woman and that maternal comfort is the watchword for couples during pregnancy. Position may need to be altered during the last 4 to 6 weeks, when supine hypotensive syndrome may result from a male-superior position. Alternate positions include side-lying, female-superior, or rear-entry. The side-lying position may be the most comfortable and require the least amount of energy during the third trimester. It is important to view sexuality in its broadest sense, since fatigue, ligament pain, urinary frequency, or shortness of breath may also interfere with vaginal intercourse. Hugging, kissing, mutual massage, and cuddling are pleasurable expressions of affection that do not always lead to intercourse.

Advise the couple to curtail all sexual activity if the client is at risk for preterm labor because uterine contractions may be initiated by orgasm. Emphasize that if membranes have ruptured or if there is bleeding, intercourse should be restricted.

Travel. Although travel by car is generally safe, it may cause discomfort or fatigue. Frequent stops are necessary to allow the expectant mother to empty her bladder and walk around. She must fasten the seat belt snugly, with the lap belt under the abdomen. This is uncomfortable for some women, and it causes concern about internal injuries should a collision occur, however, it is much safer to wear the belt than to leave it off and risk being ejected from the car during an accident.

Travel by plane and train are also safe and allow more freedom to move about. During travel to remote locations, a major concern is that adequate medical care be available at the destination.

Immunizations. In general, immunizations that use live virus vaccines are contraindicated during pregnancy because of teratogenic effects on the fetus. These include measles, mumps, and rubella. Inactivated virus or bacterial vaccines are used to meet travel requirements or as postexposure prophylaxis. Advise the woman to divulge that she is pregnant before a vaccine is administered.

TEACHING ABOUT THE COMMON DISCOMFORTS OF PREGNANCY

Although pregnancy is a state of health, the numerous physiological changes that occur during pregnancy often cause physical discomfort. No medical cures exist for these discomforts. Relief depends on self-help measures that well-qualified nurses are expected to teach. Figure 7–14 illustrates prenatal exercises that help prevent and relieve backache during pregnancy. In addition, measures to prevent or alleviate other discomforts are detailed in Women Want to Know: How to Overcome the Common Discomforts of Pregnancy.

TEACHING NECESSARY LIFESTYLE CHANGES

Many expectant parents are willing to make changes in a lifestyle that might adversely affect the fetus. For example, use of tobacco, alcohol, or illegal drugs should be curtailed during pregnancy. Over-the-counter medications and prescription drugs should be taken only with permission from the physician or nurse-midwife.

Figure 7–14. Exercises to Prevent Backache

Shoulder circling

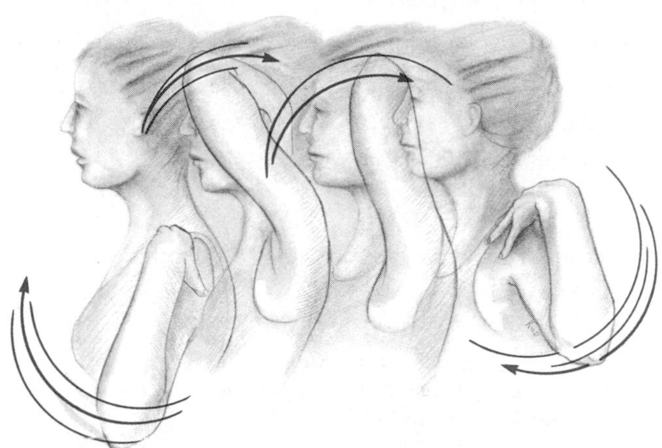

The fingertips are placed on the shoulders, then brought forward and up during inhalation, back and down during exhalation. Repeat 5 times.

Tailor sitting

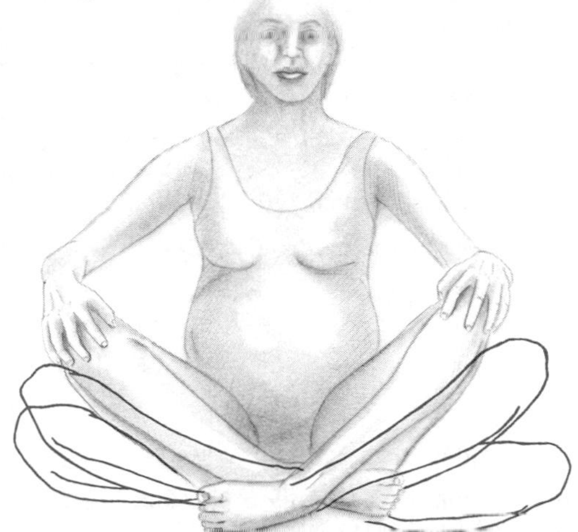

The woman uses her thigh muscles to press her knees to the floor. Keeping her back straight, she should remain in the position for 5 to 15 minutes.

Pelvic tilt or pelvic rocking

This exercise can be performed on hands and knees, with the hands directly under the shoulders and the knees under the hips. The back should be in a neutral position, not hollowed. The head and neck should be aligned with the straight back. The woman then presses up with the lower back and holds this position for a few seconds, then relaxes to a neutral position. Repeat 5 times. The exercise may also be done in a standing or lying position.

Women Want To Know

How to Overcome the Common Discomforts of Pregnancy

Nausea and Vomiting: This condition is *temporary, and here are some remedies*:

- Eat dry crackers or toast before arising in the morning, then get out of bed slowly.
- Eat dry crackers every 2 hours to prevent an empty stomach, or eat five to six small meals a day rather than three full meals.
- Take fluids separately from meals.
- Avoid fried, greasy, or spicy foods and foods with strong odors, such as onion and cabbage.

Heartburn

- Eat several small meals daily, and avoid fatty foods.
- Curtail smoking and coffee drinking, which stimulate acid formation in the stomach.
- Sitting upright reduces reflux and relieves symptoms.
- At night, sleep with an extra pillow under your head and shoulders.
- Deep breathing and sipping water may help relieve the burning sensation.
- Antacids—a combination of aluminum hydroxide and magnesium hydroxide (Maalox, Alumid) is recommended. Avoid antacids that are high in sodium (Alka-Seltzer, baking soda, or sodium bicarbonate) because excessive sodium may result in fluid retention and electrolyte imbalance. Antacids high in calcium (Tums, Alkamints) provide relief but may cause rebound hyperacidity.

Backache

- Maintain correct posture, with head up and shoulders back.
- To pick up objects, squat rather than bend from the waist.
- When sitting, use foot supports, arm rests, and pillows behind your back.
- Exercises, such as the tailor position, shoulder circling and pelvic rocking, will strengthen your back and help prepare you for labor.

Urinary Frequency: Performing Kegel's exercises helps to maintain bladder control:

- You can identify the muscles to be exercised when you stop the flow of urine midstream. However, do not perform the exercise while urinating because you might become susceptible to infection.
- Contract the muscles around the vagina, and hold for 5 seconds. Relax.
- Repeat the contraction-relaxation cycle ten times, slowly contracting and relaxing the muscles.

Varicosities: The key to treatment is preventing pooling of blood in the large veins of the legs. You can:

- Avoid wearing constricting clothing, and refrain from crossing your legs at the knees because this impedes blood return from the legs.
- Take frequent rest periods with your legs elevated above the level of your hips.
- You may obtain relief by wearing support hose or elastic stockings. Stockings should reach above the varicosities, and they should be applied before you get out of bed each morning. Putting them on later makes them less effective because pooling begins as soon as you arise.
- If you must work in one position for prolonged periods, walk around for a few minutes at least every 2 hours. This stimulates blood flow and relieves discomfort.

Hemorrhoids

- To prevent hemorrhoids, try to establish a regular pattern of bowel elimination that does not require straining. Drink plenty of water, eat foods rich in fiber, and exercise regularly.
- To relieve existing hemorrhoids, take frequent, tepid sitz baths or warm soaks, apply cool witch hazel compresses or anesthetic ointments, or lie (on your side) with your hips elevated on a pillow.
- Gently push the hemorrhoids back into the rectum. To do so, put on a latex glove and lubricate your index finger. Maintain pressure for 1 to 2 minutes.
- If you have persistent pain or bleeding, call your physician or midwife.

Over-the-Counter Drugs. Advise the pregnant women to remind her pharmacist that she is pregnant before taking any over-the-counter drugs. Drugs are frequently sought for "colds" and nasal congestion; however, there is little information about the effects of these during pregnancy. Some laxatives interfere with absorption of nutrients and should be taken only when other methods are ineffective. Fecal wetting agents, such as docusate calcium (Surfak) and docusate sodium (Colace), as well as bulk-forming laxatives (Metamucil) are sometimes recommended.

Although morning sickness is one of the most common complaints of pregnancy, medications are not recommended for relief because of possible harmful effects.

Tobacco. Make every effort to motivate the expectant mother to stop smoking and to avoid contact with others who smoke. It is well documented that

Women Want To Know

How to Overcome the Common Discomforts of Pregnancy *Continued*

Constipation: Self-care measures generally are as effective as using laxatives, but they are most beneficial because they do not interfere with absorption of nutrients or lead to laxative dependency.

- Drink at least eight glasses of water each day. This should not include coffee, tea, or carbonated drinks because of the diuretic effect. If you do drink one of these beverages, adding a glass of water afterward may counteract their diuretic effect.
- Additional fiber in your diet helps to maintain bowel elimination. Foods high in fiber include unpeeled fresh fruits and vegetables, whole grain cereals, bran muffins, oatmeal, baked potatoes with skins, and fruit juices. Four pieces of fruit plus a large salad provide enough fiber requirements for 1 day.
- Restrict cheese consumption, which causes constipation.
- Curtail your intake of sweets, which increase bacterial growth in the intestine and can lead to flatulence.
- Do not discontinue taking iron supplements if they have been prescribed. If constipation persists, consult your health care provider for advice about bulk-forming laxatives or fecal wetting agents.
- A brisk walk of at least one mile per day is one of the best exercises to stimulate peristalsis and improve muscle tone. Swimming and riding a stationary bicycle are also helpful.
- Establish a regular pattern by allowing a consistent time each day for elimination. One hour after meals is ideal to take advantage of the gastrocolic reflex (the peristaltic wave in the colon that is induced by taking food into the fasting stomach). Using a footrest during elimination provides comfort and decreases straining.

Leg Cramps

- To relieve cramps, extend the affected leg, keeping the knee straight; bend your foot toward you; or ask someone to help you flex the foot. If you are alone, stand and apply pressure on the affected leg. Either measure lengthens the affected muscles and relieves cramping.
- To prevent cramps, frequently elevate your legs during the day to improve circulation.
- Restricting milk intake and taking supplemental calcium may provide relief, but these measures should be initiated only with permission of the physician or certified nurse-midwife.
- For frequent leg cramps, your physician or nurse-midwife may suggest aluminum hydroxide gel capsules. These absorb phosphorus and thus raise the level of calcium in the blood.

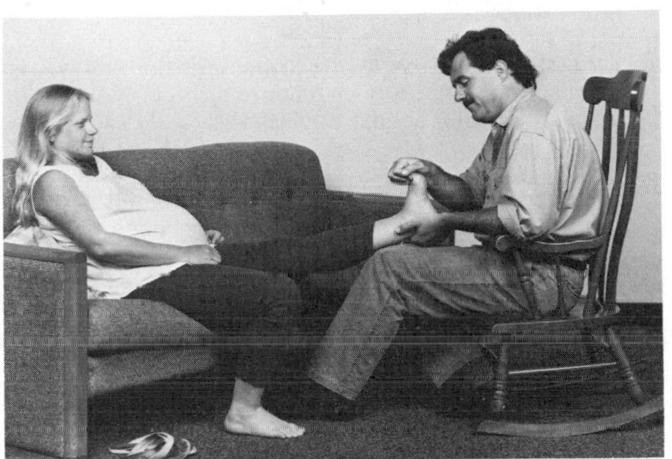

pregnant women who smoke have smaller infants and an increased incidence of preterm births. Moreover, developmental problems, such as short attention span and lower cognitive skills, are also more common in children when the mother continues to smoke during pregnancy.

Smoking tobacco affects fetal development for several reasons:

- Nicotine causes vasoconstriction of vessels in the placenta
- Carbon monoxide, released in tobacco smoke, inactivates maternal and fetal hemoglobin, which is essential to transport oxygen to the fetus
- Maternal appetite is decreased, causing inadequate intake of calories
- Plasma volume, needed to transport nutrients and oxygen to the fetus, is decreased

Alcohol. Alcohol is a known teratogen, and maternal alcohol use is one of the leading causes of mental retardation in the United States. Alcohol produces a characteristic cluster of developmental anomalies known as *fetal alcohol syndrome* (FAS). Children with FAS exhibit a typical pattern of prenatal and postnatal growth retardation with characteristic facial, cardiovascular, and limb defects (See Figure 23–1). These children also exhibit cognitive and fine motor dysfunction that is tragic and irreversible.

There has been some controversy about the effects of social or moderate drinking on the fetus, and conclusive data are not available. Therefore, the best advice for women who are pregnant or who plan to become pregnant is to abstain from all alcohol.

Illegal Drugs. Use of so-called street drugs, such as cocaine, heroin, and methamphetamines, are harmful to the fetus. Cocaine and crack cocaine use

Text continued on page 157

Nursing Care Plan 7–1

Discomfort During Early Pregnancy

Assessment: Maria Gomez, a primigravida of 8 weeks' gestation, states at the initial office visit that she is experiencing nausea with occasional vomiting throughout the day. She reports the nausea is intensified by the odor of cooking food and that she has little appetite.

Nursing Diagnosis: High Risk for Alteration in Nutrition: Less than Body Requirements related to nausea, vomiting, and anorexia.

Goals:

The client will:

1. Maintain adequate intake of calories and nutrients to meet her needs, as evidenced by sufficient energy to carry on the activities of daily living, and a continuous pattern of weight gain during pregnancy. (See Chapter 9 for recommended pattern of weight gain.)
2. Verbalize less nausea and a decrease in the episodes of vomiting.
3. Demonstrate no signs nor symptoms of dehydration.

Intervention:	Rationale:
1. Recommend that the expectant mother eat two dry crackers half an hour before arising in the morning and that she get out of bed slowly.	1. This counteracts the hypoglycemia that occurs as a result of night-long fasting and prevents an initial episode of nausea that may become difficult to control.
2. Suggest that she consume a bedtime snack that is high in protein, such as cottage cheese or half a tuna fish sandwich on whole wheat bread.	2. Proteins are metabolized at a slower rate, and this helps to prevent morning hypoglycemia.
3. Instruct her to eat small, dry meals five to six times a day rather than three large ones.	3. This prevents the stomach from becoming empty, which increases the feeling of nausea.
4. Suggest that fluids be taken separately.	4. This prevents overstretching the stomach, which might precipitate vomiting.
5. Recommend that she eat a dry cracker, unbuttered popcorn, or dry toast every 2 hours.	5. Nausea is more intense when the stomach is empty.
6. Suggest that she avoid fried or greasy foods, foods that are highly seasoned, and foods that have strong odors.	6. Odors and greasy textures are associated with nausea and increased episodes of vomiting.
7. Teach her to keep a record of daily intake of food and fluids, episodes of vomiting, and measures that reduce nausea.	7. It is essential to determine whether adequate nutrients and fluids are being retained and to identify the most helpful measures to control nausea.
8. Suggest that she experiment with soups, eggnogs, or vegetable drinks.	8. These foods are high in nutrients and are often tolerated well when taken separately.
9. Reassure her that nausea and vomiting usually disappear by the beginning of the second trimester and that they do not indicate a problem with the pregnancy.	9. It reduces anxiety to know the condition is self-limiting and that it does not threaten the fetus.
10. Assess the mother's weight at each prenatal visit, and compare weight gain with that expected for the weeks of gestation.	10. If weight gain compares favorably with that expected, the focus remains on relieving the discomfort of nausea and vomiting. If weight gain is less than it should be, or if signs of dehydration are present, refer her for medical management.

Nursing Care Plan 7–1 *Continued*

Discomfort During Early Pregnancy

Evaluation:
Periodic nausea and vomiting continued throughout the first trimester but ceased during the second trimester. At 20 weeks, Maria appears well hydrated and has gained 4.5 kg. (~10 pounds).

Assessment: Maria also says that she is often very sleepy during the day even though she is sleeping many hours at night. This concerns her because she is employed and must keep her mind on her work.

Nursing Diagnosis: Fatigue related to inadequate rest periods to accommodate the physiological demands of pregnancy.

Goals:
The client will:

1. Identify methods to cope with fatigue, such as negotiating a flexible work schedule or negotiating time for short rest periods while continuing employment during pregnancy.
2. Verbalize increased energy by the end of the first trimester.

Intervention:	Rationale:
1. Acknowledge the fatigue and reassure Maria that this is self-limiting and a common experience during the first months because of the change in hormone levels.	1. Reassurance helps to alleviate the concern that this indicates a problem with her pregnancy.
2. Recommend that she lie down or sit comfortably with feet elevated for a few minutes every 2 hours and consciously relax the muscles of the legs, abdomen, and shoulders.	2. This renews energy even though sleep is not possible.
3. Suggest that she try deep breathing, visualizing a favorite location or pastime whenever possible. Progressive relaxation, conscious tensing, and relaxing groups of muscles—beginning with those in the feet and working upward toward the head—may be helpful.	3. These exercises relieve physical tension that adds to fatigue and also provide mental distraction.
4. Recommend that she get as much sleep as she feels she needs when possible; this may involve curtailing social activities and tasks that can be postponed.	4. Although recreation is important, the need for sleep is overwhelming for some women during the first weeks of pregnancy.
5. Encourage her to explore a flexible schedule or routine with her employer.	5. Often a very short nap in the morning or afternoon is all that is needed to continue to function effectively.
6. Recommend that she enlist the assistance of family, significant other, and friends with home responsibilities.	6. This can free her of all but the most essential tasks during this time.

Evaluation:
Maria was able to negotiate two short rest periods each day and, at 12 weeks gestation, continues to use learned techniques to renew energy. Maria relates increased energy at the third prenatal visit (16 weeks).

Additional Nursing Diagnoses to Consider:

Fluid Volume Deficit
High Risk for Activity Intolerance
Diversional Activity Deficit
Altered Sexuality Patterns
Altered Family Processes

Nursing Care Plan 7–2

Self-Care During Pregnancy

Assessment: Paula Orne, a primigravida of 28 weeks' gestation, has numerous questions about self-care. She is a courier and drives many hours each day. She is concerned about safety while driving. She also asks what sexual activity is allowed, and she is concerned because her partner continues to smoke.

Nursing Diagnosis: Health-Seeking Behaviors: Prenatal Care related to travel, sexual activity, and effects of passive smoking.

Goals:

The client will:

1. Describe measures to reduce discomfort and promote safety when traveling.
2. Continue mutually satisfying sexual activity during pregnancy.
3. Modify the environment to eliminate exposure to passive smoking

Intervention:	Rationale:
1. Recommend that she use both the lap and shoulder restraints throughout pregnancy. Suggest that she keep the lap restraint under the abdomen.	1. This prevents ejection from the car in case of an accident. The most serious injuries are sustained when a person is ejected at impact.
2. Suggest that she stop the car at least every 2 hours and walk for a few minutes and perform some gentle shoulder and upper body stretches. She should also empty the bladder at each stop.	2. To improve circulation and to relieve the muscles involved in prolonged sitting and driving. Frequent voiding promotes comfort and prevents bladder infection due to stasis of urine.
3. Suggest that she drink a glass of water at each stop but that she avoid sweet drinks or those that contain caffeine.	3. Sweet drinks increase thirst, and caffeine drinks act as a diuretic and increase thirst. Water refreshes and prevents dehydration.
4. Assess the client's specific concerns about sexuality, and respond to those in particular.	4. Concerns vary from couple to couple. Some couples worry about harming the fetus or causing discomfort for the mother.
5. Reassure her that sexual activity poses no harm to either the mother or the fetus in a normal pregnancy; explain the anatomy of the vagina, cervix, and uterus; if necessary, use a plastic model; and suggest she bring her husband to the next visit if he has concerns.	5. Knowledge of the separation between the vagina and the fetus may relieve concern about the safety of vaginal intercourse during pregnancy.
6. Suggest that alternate positions, such as side-lying, woman superior, or rear-entry, be used during the third trimester.	6. The male-superior position becomes uncomfortable for the woman when the uterus is large and heavy, and it increases the risk of supine hypotension.
7. Acknowledge the danger of passive smoking, and recommend that the partner curtail smoking in the house, car, or other enclosed areas. This is important during pregnancy and also after the infant is born.	7. Toxins in cigarette smoke affect those in the vicinity as well as the one who is smoking.

Evaluation:
Paula uses both shoulder and lap restraints and says she feels more comfortable while driving. She relates mutually satisfying sexual experiences. Her partner agrees to curtail smoking in Paula's presence.

Additional Nursing Diagnoses to Consider:

High Risk for Injury
Altered Sexuality Patterns
Altered Health Maintenance

Nursing Care Plan 7–3

Discomfort During Late Pregnancy

Assessment: Ann Reeves is a multipara of 32 weeks' gestation. She states that she is constipated and plans to discontinue taking the iron supplement, which she believes causes the problem. Further assessment reveals that she "doesn't drink water" and that her diet contains very few vegetables or fruits. She is a secretary and has a very sedentary lifestyle.

Nursing Diagnosis: Constipation related to insufficient dietary intake of fiber and fluid and inadequate exercise to stimulate peristalsis.

Goals:

The client will:

1. Establish a regular pattern of soft, formed bowel elimination of more than three stools per week.
2. Continue to supplement iron intake as recommended.

Intervention:	Rationale:
1. Instruct Ann to drink eight glasses of water per day and not to count tea, coffee, or colas as part of this.	1. Drinks that contain caffeine and carbonation act as diuretics and do little to maintain the necessary fluid increase. Sufficient water is important during pregnancy, when motility in the bowel is decreased and the additional water is absorbed from the large intestine, leaving the stool dry and hard.
2. Provide a list of foods that are high in fiber (bran, unpeeled fresh fruit and vegetables, whole grain, oatmeal, and dried fruits, such as prunes and figs). Suggest that she choose at least four servings of fruit plus a large salad each day and that she use whole wheat breads and cereals.	2. Fiber has a water-holding capacity that increases stool bulk, which has a stretching effect on the colon and increases the urge to defecate.
3. Suggest that she substitute fruit for sweets and sugar in the diet.	3. Sugar stimulates the growth of bacteria, leading to flatulence and increased discomfort.
4. Recommend a program of walking, starting with two or three blocks each day and gradually increasing the distance to a mile a day.	4. Exercise increases circulation, peristalsis, and muscle tone.
5. Suggest that she establish a regular pattern of elimination. She chooses a time that fits her schedule but, if possible, selects a time that follows a meal. She allows adequate time that is free from interruptions.	5. Circadian rhythms may be considered in assisting defecation at a regular time. The gastrocolic reflex stimulates mass peristalsis two or three times a day, most often following meals.
6. Emphasize that she should not ignore the urge to defectate.	6. Repeated lack of response to the urge to defectate desensitizes the nerves in the rectum to feelings of pressure.
7. Recommend that she continue to take the iron supplement; however, she may decrease the dose of iron while increasing the frequency of taking the iron.	7. It is not possible to obtain adequate iron from the diet during pregnancy, and iron supplementation is necessary for adequate hemoglobin synthesis. Constipation may be lessened if less iron is taken at one time, but the frequency is increased until the total recommended dose is taken each day.
8. Instruct her to avoid laxatives unless they are prescribed by the physician, nurse-midwife, or nurse practitioner.	8. Laxatives can interfere with absorption of nutrients from the intestine. Laxatives that contain oil prevent absorption of fat-soluble vitamins and nutrients. Bulk-forming laxatives may increase intestinal motility and interfere with absorption of nutrients. Use for more than 1 week can lead to laxative dependency.

Nursing Care Plan continued on following page

Nursing Care Plan 7–3 Continued

Discomfort During Late Pregnancy

Evaluation:
Ann relates that she regularly has a soft, formed stool at least three times per week and continues to take iron supplements as recommended.

Assessment: Ann also states that she has persistent backache and seeks information to alleviate it. She demonstrates marked lordosis and is observed to bend to pick up her toddler. She stands with shoulders slumping and head forward.

Nursing Diagnosis: Pain: Backache related to muscular strain that is secondary to change in balance and knowledge deficit of measures to reduce strain.

Goals:
The client will:

1. Demonstrate body mechanics that prevent muscle strain when lifting.
2. Demonstrate correct posture to relieve muscle strain.
3. Verbalize increased comfort at next clinic visit.

Intervention:	Rationale:
1. Teach correct posture: stand erect with shoulders back and neck straight; contract abdominal muscles to flatten the back; tuck pelvis under and slightly forward; and distribute weight through the center of the feet.	1. Further muscle strain occurs when the shoulders slump forward and the lower back curve is exaggerated.
2. Demonstrate proper body mechanics for stooping and lifting: squat and move the object to be lifted close to the body and use the thigh muscles to stand and lift.	2. These motions prevent muscle strain in the lower back by using the stronger muscles of the legs. Stooping lowers the center of gravity and prevents muscle strain that occurs when one bends and lifts.
3. Demonstrate prenatal exercises: pelvic rocking, shoulder circling, and tailor sitting (see Fig. 7–14).	3. Shoulder circling strengthens muscles of the shoulders and helps to prevent slumping that exacerbates lordosis. Tailor sitting and pelvic rocking strengthen muscles of the thighs and back and help maintain posture as well as relieve discomfort.
4. Recommend that Ann vary activities frequently, avoid prolonged standing, and use a foot rest when sitting.	4. Prolonged standing or sitting in an unsupported position causes one group of muscles to become fatigued and strained.

Evaluation:
Ann demonstrates correct posture and body mechanics to relieve muscle strain; however, backache continues. Ann demonstrates pelvic rocking and agrees to practice this prenatal exercise several times a day.

Additional Nursing Diagnoses to Consider:

High Risk for Activity Intolerance
High Risk for Injury
Sleep Pattern Disturbance

has escalated dramatically in the past decade (Lynch and McKeon, 1990). The pregnant woman should be advised to discontinue all illicit drug use.

Cocaine produces increased levels of catecholamines in the blood, resulting in maternal hypertension, poor placental perfusion, and increased incidence of premature separation of the placenta (abruptio placentae). There is an increased incidence of preterm labor and impaired fetal growth. The newborn exhibits signs of central nervous system dysfunction that are believed to be due to toxicity rather than withdrawal. In addition, cocaine users typically ingest alcohol to mediate the side effects of cocaine and the fetus thus suffers a double physiological insult.

Intravenous drug users are also at high risk for exposure to hepatitis and human immunodeficiency virus (HIV); both conditions are transmitted across the placental barrier to the fetus. (For more information about substance abuse, see Chapter 23.)

Evaluation

Interventions can be judged to be effective to meet the goals established if the mother and her family: (1) verbalize or demonstrate knowledge of self-care practices that promote her safety and health and that of the fetus, (2) identify a plan early in pregnancy (first trimester) to modify habits that do not promote health, such as curtailing the use of alcohol or tobacco, and (3) verbalize knowledge of measures that provide relief from the common discomforts of pregnancy.

If interventions are ineffective, collaborate with the family to define new plans and work out additional interventions.

Summary Concepts

- Pregnancy causes a predictable pattern of uterine growth that provides information about fetal growth and helps to confirm the expected date of delivery. In general, the uterus can be palpated at the level of the umbilicus at 20 weeks of gestation and at the xiphoid process by 36 weeks.
- Thick mucus fills the softened connective tissue in the cervical canal and protects the fetus from infection resulting from ascending bacteria from the vagina.
- Plasma volume expands faster and to a greater extent than red blood cells, resulting in a dilution of hemoglobin concentration. This is referred to as physiologic (pseudo) anemia because the low levels of hemoglobin and hematocrit are due to dilution and do not reflect inadequate red blood cells.
- Blood flow is altered during pregnancy to include the uteroplacental unit; increased renal plasma flow results in increased glomerular filtration rate, which effectively removes additional metabolic wastes produced by the mother and the fetus but often results in "spilling" of glucose and other nutrients in the urine; increased blood flow to the skin attempts to reduce the additional heat generated by the increased maternal metabolic rate.
- The gravid uterus partially occludes the vena cava and the descending aorta when the mother rests in a supine position. This causes supine hypotensive syndrome, which can be prevented or corrected when she assumes a lateral position.
- During the last trimester, the uterus pushes the diaphragm upward, which can result in decreased lung capacity. To compensate, the ribs flare, the substernal angle widens, and the circumference of the chest increases.
- Alterations in hormones during pregnancy may result in discomfort for the mother: Increased hCG and estrogen are associated with nausea in early pregnancy. Increased progesterone is associated with relaxation of all smooth muscle, including those of the ureters, bladder and bowel. Resulting stasis of urine that is rich in nutrients increases the risk of urinary tract infections. Decreased bowel motility is a major cause of constipation during pregnancy.
- Alterations in hormones are also responsible for cutaneous changes, such as hyperpigmentation.
- The expanding uterus plus the hormone relaxin results in progressive changes that can lead to muscle strain and backache during the last trimester.
- Progesterone is called the hormone of pregnancy because it maintains the uterine lining for implantation of the blastocyst; prevents uterine contractions during pregnancy, which could result in spontaneous abortion; and helps to prepare the breasts for lactation.
- Presumptive and probable signs of pregnancy may be caused by conditions other than pregnancy, and thus they cannot be considered positive or diagnostic signs.

- A complete history and physical examination are necessary at the initial antepartum visit to determine the potential risks to the mother and fetus and to obtain baseline data so that a plan of care can be developed.
- Families require information related to self-care and health promotion as well as information to deal with the common discomforts of pregnancy, which do not require or respond to medical management. Nurses provide a great deal of the information and assist the parents in making necessary changes in lifestyle.

References and Bibliography

Aaronson, L.S., & Macnee, C.L. (1989). Tobacco, alcohol, and caffeine use during pregnancy. *Journal of Obstetric, Gynecologic, and Neonatal Nursing*, 18(4), 279–287.

American College of Obstetricians and Gynecologists (ACOG) (1985). *Exercise during pregnancy and the postnatal period*. Washington, D.C.

American Nurses Association (1987). *Access to prenatal care: Key to preventing low birthweight*. Report of Consensus Conferences. Kansas City, Kansas.

Anderson, J.M. (1990). Health care across cultures. *Nursing Outlook*, 38(3), 136–139.

Baddeley, S. (1991). Exercise in pregnancy. *Nursing Time*, 87(48), 66–67.

Bernhardt, J.H. (1990). Potential workplace hazards to reproductive health. *Journal of Obstetric, Gynecologic, and Neonatal Nursing*, 19(1), 53–62.

Blackburn, S.T., & Loper, D.L. (1992). *Maternal, fetal, and neonatal physiology*. Philadelphia: W.B. Saunders.

Brinkman, C.R. (1989). Biologic adaptation to pregnancy. In R.K. Creasy & R.R. Resnik (Eds.), *Maternal fetal medicine: Principles and practice* (2nd ed., pp. 734–735). Philadelphia: W.B. Saunders.

Cox, H.C., Hinz, M.D., Lubno, M.A., et al. (1989). *Clinical applications of nursing diagnosis*. Baltimore: Williams & Wilkins.

Cunningham, F.G., MacDonald, P.C., & Gant, N.F. (1989). *Williams obstetrics* (18th ed.). Norwalk, Conn.: Appleton & Lange.

Cyr, M.G., & Moulton, A.W. (1990). Substance abuse in women. *Obstetrics and Gynecology Clinics of North America*, 17(4), 905–925.

Fishbein, E.G., & Phillips, M. (1990). How safe is exercise during pregnancy? *Journal of Obstetric, Gynecologic, and Neonatal Nursing*, 19(1), 45–49.

Gorrie, T.M. (1990). *A guide to the nursing of childbearing families*. Baltimore: Williams & Wilkins.

Hacker, N.F., & Moore, J.G. (1992). *Essentials of obstetrics and gynecology*. Philadelphia: W.B. Saunders.

Hammond, T.L., Mickens-Powers, B., Strickland, K., et al. (1990). The use of automobile safety restraint systems during pregnancy. *Journal of Obstetric, Gynecologic, and Neonatal Nursing*, 19(4), 239–243.

Iyer, P.W., Taptich, B.J., & Bernocchi-Losey, D (1991). *Nursing Process and Nursing Diagnosis* (2nd ed.). Philadelphia: W.B. Saunders.

Karb, V.B., Queener, S.F., & Freeman, J.B. (1989). *Handbook of drugs for nursing practice*. St. Louis: C.V. Mosby.

Krozy, R.E., & McColgan, J.J. (1985). Auto safety: Pregnancy and the newborn. *Journal of Obstetric, Gynecologic, and Neonatal Nursing*, 14(1), 11–15.

Lynch, M., & McKeon, V.A. (1990). Cocaine use during pregnancy: Research findings and clinical implications. *Journal of Obstetric, Gynecologic, and Neonatal Nursing*, 19(4), 285–292.

Mahan, L.K., & Arlin, M. (1992). *Krause's food, nutrition, and diet therapy* (8th ed.). Philadelphia: W.B. Saunders.

Matthews, A.K. & Smith, A.C.M. (1993). Genetic counseling. In R.A. Knuppel & J.E. Drukker (Eds.), *High-risk pregnancy: A team approach* (2nd ed., pp. 664–703). Philadelphia: W.B. Saunders.

McCaul, J.F., & Morrison, J.C. (1990). Antenatal fetal assessment: An overview. *Obstetrics and Gynecology Clinics of North America*, 17(1), 1–16.

Mills, J.L. (1993). Moderate caffeine use and the risk of spontaneous abortion and intrauterine growth retardation. *Journal of American Medical Association* 269(5), 593–597.

Nuwayhid, B., & Khalife, S. (1992). Medical complications of pregnancy. In N.F. Hacker & J.G. Moore (Eds.), *Essentials of obstetrics and gynecology* (2nd ed., pp. 197–222). Philadelphia: W.B. Saunders.

Resnik, R. (1989). Anatomic changes in the reproductive tract. In R.K. Creasy & R. Resknik (Eds.), *Maternal-fetal medicine: Principles and practice* (2nd ed., pp. 136–140). Philadelphia: W.B. Saunders.

Spector, R.E. (1991). *Cultural diversity in health and illness* (3rd ed.). Norwalk, Conn.: Appleton & Lange.

Tripp-Reimer, T., & Afifi, L.A. (1989). Cross-cultural perspectives on patient teaching. *Nursing Clinics of North America*, 24(3), 613–619.

Van Dinter, M.C. (1991). Ptyalism in pregnant women. *Journal of Obstetric, Gynecologic, and Neonatal Nursing*, 20(3) 206–209.

Nurses Association of the American College of Obstetrics and Gynecology (1991). *Standards for the nursing care of women and newborns* (4th ed.). Washington, D.C.

Wasserstrum N. (1992). Maternal Physiology. In N.F. Hacker & J.G. Moore (Eds.), *Essentials of obstetrics and gynecology* (2nd ed., pp. 61–81). Philadelphia: W.B. Saunders.

8

Psychosocial Adaptations to Pregnancy

Objectives

1. Describe the psychological responses of the expectant mother to pregnancy.
2. Identify the process of role transition and explain the maternal tasks of pregnancy.
3. Discuss the developmental processes that a man completes to make the transition to the role of father.
4. Describe the responses of prospective grandparents and siblings.
5. Explain how multiparity affects the maternal response to pregnancy.
6. Identify the socioeconomic and cultural factors that affect pregnancy, and describe how these factors affect nursing practice.

Definitions

Ambivalence • Simultaneous conflicting emotions, attitudes, ideas, or wishes.

Attachment • Development of strong affectional ties as a result of interaction between infant and significant other (mother, father, sibling, caretaker).

Body image • Subjective image of one's physical appearance and capabilities; derived from own observations and from the evaluation of significant others.

Bonding • Development of a strong emotional tie to a newborn; also called **claiming** or **binding in.**

Couvade • Pregnancy-related rituals or a cluster of symptoms experienced by some prospective fathers during pregnancy and childbirth.

Developmental task • A necessary step in growth and maturation that one must complete before additional growth and maturation are possible.

Disturbance in body image • Negative feelings about characteristics, functions, or limits of one's body.

Fantasy • Mental images formed to prepare for the birth of a child.

Introversion • Inward concentration on oneself and one's body.

Mimicry • Copying the behaviors of other pregnant women or mothers as a method to "try on" the role of advanced pregnancy or motherhood.

Narcissism • Undue preoccupation with oneself.

Role transition • Changing from one pattern of behavior and one image of self to another.

Becoming a parent, capable of loving and caring for a totally dependent infant, is more than a biological event. It is a process that begins before conception and involves major changes in the expectant mother, her partner, and the total family. Although each couple adapts to pregnancy in a unique manner, it is known that the psychological responses of the prospective parents change as the pregnancy progresses. Thus, although the initial reaction may be one of uncertainty, by the time the infant is born, the woman and her partner complete developmental tasks that make it possible for them to become parents in the true sense of the word. Moreover, both social and cultural factors influence the way the woman adjusts to pregnancy.

Maternal Psychological Responses

A pregnant woman experiences a wide variety of responses to the changes caused by pregnancy. Initially, she may feel ambivalent about her condition and focus only on herself. Later, when the pregnancy becomes evident to her and those around her, the woman's focus changes from self to the fetus she is carrying. As pregnancy progresses, she must adapt her self-image, sexual identity, and sense of independence.

First Trimester

UNCERTAINTY

Uncertainty is one of the major emotional responses during the early weeks of pregnancy. The woman is unsure whether she is pregnant and spends a great deal of time trying to confirm it. She observes her body carefully for changes that indicate she is pregnant. She may confer with family and friends about the probability and may use an over-the-counter pregnancy test kit for validation.

Reaction to the possibility of pregnancy depends on the individual. A woman may be eager to find confirming signs, or she may dread the possibility and hope for signs that indicate she is not pregnant at this time. Usually, she will seek confirmation from a physician, certified nurse-midwife, or nurse practitioner within 12 weeks of the first missed menstrual period.

AMBIVALENCE

Once the pregnancy is confirmed, almost all women have conflicting feelings or ambivalence about being pregnant. Feelings fluctuate between acceptance and rejection of the pregnancy. There is often a feeling that this is not the right time even if the pregnancy is wanted and planned. Even women who had planned to become pregnant often say they thought it would take longer for the pregnancy to become a reality and are unprepared for it. Many pregnancies are desired but unplanned, and these women often say they wish they had not become pregnant until some specific goals were met or plans were completed.

Many women examine what the pregnancy means in terms of changes that must be made in their lives and what they must give up as a result of the pregnancy. If it is a first pregnancy, a woman may worry about the added responsibility and feel unsure of her ability to be a good parent. Some women worry about how this pregnancy will affect their relationship with other children or with the father.

SELF AS PRIMARY FOCUS

Throughout the first trimester, the woman's primary focus is on herself, not the fetus. Early physical responses to pregnancy, such as nausea and fatigue, confirm that something is happening to her, but the fetus remains vague and unreal. Because she has not gained weight that would confirm that a fetus is growing and developing, she will probably say "I am pregnant," rather than "I am going to have a baby."

Physical changes and increased hormone levels may cause emotional lability (unstable moods). Her mood can change quickly from contentment to irritation or from optimistic planning to an overwhelming need for sleep when all plans will be temporarily abandoned. This may be confusing to her partner, who is accustomed to a more stable relationship. The nurse should tell the couple that mood changes are normal and expected and that they do not necessarily indicate unresolved problems.

Second Trimester

PHYSICAL EVIDENCE OF PREGNANCY

During the second trimester, physical changes occur in the expectant mother that make the fetus "real." The uterus grows rapidly and can be palpated in the abdomen; weight increases and clothing becomes tighter; breast changes are obvious. Most importantly, she feels the fetus move (quickening). This is an important event because the gentle fetal movement confirms that a life is developing within the uterus. As a result, she no longer sees the fetus as simply a part of her body but now perceives it as separate, although entirely dependent on her. Now she might say, "I am going to have a baby."

THE FETUS AS PRIMARY FOCUS

The major focus during the second trimester becomes the fetus. The pregnant woman usually feels well, the discomforts of the first trimester are fewer, and her size does not alter her activity. She is concerned about how she can produce a big, healthy infant. She generally seeks information about diet and feels a sense of accomplishment when her weight increases. She is fascinated with information about the growth and development of the fetus and experiences a feeling of creative energy and satisfaction.

NARCISSISM AND INTROVERSION

Many women become increasingly concerned about their bodies and their ability to protect and provide for the fetus. This concern is often manifested as narcissism and introversion. Selecting exactly the right foods to eat, the right clothes to wear, or the most comfortable environment may assume more importance than ever before. Some women may lose interest in their jobs because the work seems alien to the events taking place in their bodies. They may be less interested in current events as they concentrate on their pregnancy, or they may become fearful that world events threaten them and therefore present a danger to the fetus. If she is a primigravida, the expectant mother wonders what the infant is like. She looks at baby pictures of herself and her mate and wants to hear stories about them as infants. Although multiparas know what infants are like, they are interested in *this* infant and think about how this child will be accepted by siblings and grandparents.

BODY IMAGE

During the second trimester, rapid and profound changes take place in the body. There is a noticeable change in body size and contour, with obvious bulging of the abdomen, thickening of the waist, and enlargement of the breasts. The changes are often welcomed because they signify growth of the fetus, and this creates pride in the woman and her partner. However, not only the change in body size, shape, and contour but also hyperpigmentation of the skin and striae gravidarum (stretch marks) may contribute to a negative body image. Moreover, some women report unexpected changes in body function that include altered balance, less physical endurance, or discomfort in the pelvis and lower back areas.

CHANGES IN SEXUALITY

The way a woman and her partner view body changes affect their sexuality during pregnancy. A number of women react positively to the body changes of pregnancy. They experience increased sensitivity of the labia and clitoris and increased vaginal lubrication as a result of pelvic vasocongestion. This, coupled with not having to deal with the concern about getting pregnant, may increase the sexual responsiveness of many women. On the other hand, the large abdomen and general discomfort may inhibit sexual activity, which can lead to feelings of guilt and frustration.

Although many men feel more positively about the physical changes of pregnancy than their partners, sexual response varies widely among males. Some report heightened feelings of sexual interest; however, some men perceive the woman's body in late pregnancy as unattractive and erotic feelings decrease. Moreover, for some men, fear of harming the fetus or causing discomfort during pregnancy interferes with sexual activity.

The expectant couple should be made aware of the normal changes in sexual desire that occur during pregnancy and the importance of communicating their feelings openly with each other so that solutions to problems can be found. The nurse can suggest alternative positions (see Chapter 7) and reassure the couple that their feelings are normal.

Third Trimester

VULNERABILITY

The sense of well-being and contentment that dominates the second trimester gives way to increasing feelings of vulnerability during the third trimester, particularly during the 7th month of pregnancy. Pregnant women often feel that the precious baby may be lost or harmed if not protected at all times. Many mothers have fantasies or nightmares about harm coming to the infant and become vary cautious as a result. They may avoid crowds because they feel unable to protect the infant from infectious diseases that may be present. They may become anxious if children are actively playing near them and become concerned that the children could cause them to fall and injure the fetus.

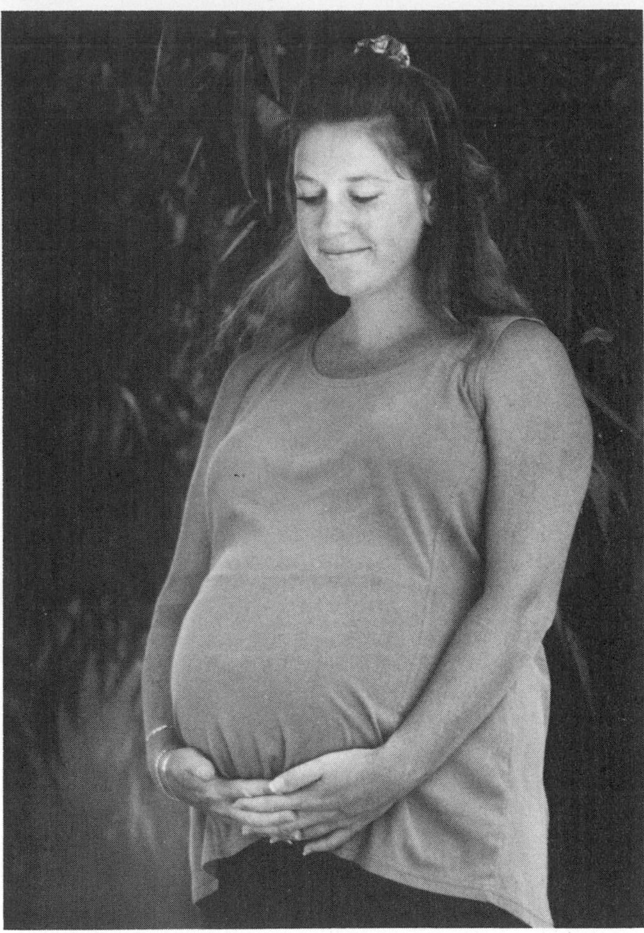

During the third trimester, the mother feels increasingly vulnerable; she cradles her fetus to signify her protectiveness.

INCREASING DEPENDENCE

The expectant mother often becomes increasingly dependent on her partner in the last weeks of pregnancy. She may insist that he carry a beeper so he can be summoned if labor begins or she may call his place of work several times during the day just to be sure he is available. Her need for love and attention from her partner are even more pronounced in late pregnancy. She needs to be certain of his support and availability. When she is assured of his concern and willingness to provide assistance, she feels more secure and able to cope.

Although the woman may not be able to explain the increasing dependence, she expects her partner to understand the feeling and may become angry if he is not sympathetic and available. The nurse can encourage couples to discuss their fears and feelings openly so that misunderstandings can be avoided.

PREPARATION FOR BIRTH

Gradually, the feelings of vulnerability are partially resolved as the woman comes to terms with her situation. The fetus continues to grow, and fetal movements are no longer gentle; pokes, jabs, and kicks are intrusive expressions of the baby's crowded condition and increasing activity. The woman's relationship with the fetus changes as she acknowledges that although she and the fetus are interrelated, the baby is not a part of herself but is a pervasive presence. Although she may not consciously acknowledge the increasing feelings of separateness, she longs to *see* the baby and to become acquainted with her child.

Most pregnant women are concerned with their ability to determine when they are in labor. They review the signs of labor that are taught in childbirth education classes and question friends and family members who have given birth. Many couples worry that they will not get to the hospital or clinic in time for the birth, and they may be concerned about how they will cope with labor.

During the last several weeks, the woman becomes increasingly concerned with her expected date of delivery (EDD) and with the experience of labor and delivery. Some women fear labor and dread the EDD, whereas some are so uncomfortable that they look forward to that day as the *exact* day the birth will occur.

During the third trimester, an expectant mother may say, "I am going to be a mother," as she prepares for the infant. Clothing, a place for the infant to sleep, and negotiating how household tasks will be shared with her partner are examples of plans that are made. In addition, many couples complete childbirth education classes at this time. Table 8–1 summarizes the progressive changes in maternal responses during pregnancy.

✔ Check Your Reading

1. Why might an expectant mother say "I am pregnant" during the first trimester, but "I am going to be a mother" late in pregnancy?
2. How might changes in body image affect sexual responses during pregnancy?

Maternal Role Transition

Becoming a mother involves more than giving birth and providing physical care for the newborn. Mothering also involves intense feelings of love, tenderness, and devotion that endure over a lifetime. Mothers give comfort, food, protection, and love. But

Table 8–1. PROGRESSIVE CHANGES IN MATERNAL RESPONSES TO PREGNANCY

First Trimester	Second Trimester	Third Trimester
	Emotional Response	
Uncertainty, ambivalence, focus on self	Fetus becomes focus	Vulnerability Increased dependence Acceptance that fetus is separate but totally dependent
	Physical Validation	
No obvious signs of fetal growth	Quickening Obvious fetal growth	Discomfort Decreased maternal activity
	Role	
May begin to seek safe passage for self and fetus	Seeks acceptance of fetus and her role as mother	Prepares for birth
	"Self" Statement	
"I am pregnant."	"I am going to have a baby."	"I am going to be a mother."

how does one learn to be a mother, make the transition from woman without a child to mother?

The transition into mothering is not automatic; it takes time and requires that previous roles be re-examined or given up. Lederman (1984) described two factors that are important to the woman's ability to assume a motherhood role: (1) how motivated she is to assume the role, and (2) the extent of preparation for the role. Motivation reflects the resolution that she feels to excel at mothering. Preparation includes envisioning herself as a mother and contemplating her life as a woman with a child. She thinks about what characteristics she wishes to have as a mother and anticipates life changes that will be necessary.

Steps in Maternal Role Taking

Rubin (1984) observed specific steps that provide a framework for understanding the process of maternal role taking: mimicry, role play, fantasy, finding a role "fit," and grief work.

MIMICRY

Mimicry involves observing and copying the behavior of other women who are pregnant or who are already mothers. It is an earnest attempt to discover what it is like to begin the role. Mimicry often begins in the first trimester, when the woman may wear maternity clothes before they are needed to see how women in more advanced pregnancy feel and to see how people react to her. She may also mimic the waddling gait or posture of a woman who is close to delivery long before this is necessary for her.

ROLE PLAY

Role play consists of acting out some aspect of what mothers actually do. The pregnant woman searches for opportunities to hold infants or to provide care for infants in the presence of another person. She does this to evaluate not only her comfort in the situation but also the response of the observer. Role playing gives her an opportunity to "practice" the expected role and to receive validation from the observer that she has functioned well. She is particularly sensitive to the responses of her partner and her mother.

FANTASY

Fantasy takes place in the mind rather than in behavior. Many fantasies have to do with how the infant will look and what characteristics he or she will have. Fantasies allow the woman to try out a variety of possibilities and to daydream or to "try on" a variety of behaviors. She may daydream about taking her daughter to the park or how she will hold the child and read or play music.

At times, fantasies are fearful. What happens if there is something wrong with the infant? What if the baby cries and won't stop? Fearful fantasies often provoke a pregnant woman to respond to the fears by seeking information or reassurance. For instance, she may ask her partner if he will love the baby even if it is not perfect, or she may strive to learn all she can about how to care for a baby that is difficult to console.

LOOKING FOR A FIT

This is a process that occurs once the woman has built up a set of role expectations for herself. She has internalized a view of how a "good" mother behaves. She then observes the behaviors of mothers and compares them to her own expectations of herself. She imagines herself acting in the same way and either rejects or accepts the behaviors, depending on how well they fit her sense of what is right. This implies that the woman has explored the role of mother long enough to have developed a sense of herself in the role and to be able to select behaviors that reaffirm her sense of how she wants to fulfill the role.

GRIEF WORK

At first, grief work seems incongruous in a discussion of maternal role taking. However, there is often a sense of sadness when the expectant mother realizes that she must give up certain aspects of her previous self and that she can never go back. She will never again be a carefree girl without a child. She will have to relinquish some of her old patterns of behavior so that she can move into the new identity as mother of an infant. Even simple things such as going shopping or going to the movies will require planning to include the infant or to find alternate care. Changes may be particularly difficult for the adolescent who is not used to planning ahead and who may have to give up or change school plans as well.

Maternal Tasks of Pregnancy

It is obvious that pregnant women spend a great deal of time and energy learning new behaviors in order to become mothers. Moreover, as a woman works to establish a relationship with the infant, she must also reorder the relationship with her partner and family. This psychological work of pregnancy has been grouped into four maternal tasks of pregnancy (Rubin, 1984): (1) seeking safe passage for self and baby through pregnancy, labor, and delivery; (2) securing acceptance of the baby and herself by her partner and family; (3) learning to give of herself; and (4) developing attachment and interconnection with the unknown child.

Seeking Safe Passage

Seeking safe passage for herself and her baby is the woman's priority task. If she cannot be assured of that safety, she cannot move on to the other tasks. Behaviors that ensure safe passage include seeking the care of a physician or certified nurse-midwife and following his or her recommendations about diet, vitamins, rest, and subsequent visits to the office or clinic.

In addition to following medical advice, the pregnant woman must also adhere to cultural practices that will ensure the safety of herself and the infant. For instance, Korean-American women may refrain from eating eggs, peaches, or duck because these are believed to affect the unborn child adversely (Choi, 1986).

Securing Acceptance

Securing acceptance is a process that begins in the first trimester and continues throughout pregnancy. It involves reworking relationships so that the important persons in the family accept the woman in the role of mother and welcome the baby into the family constellation. For example, she and the father of the baby must give up an exclusive relationship and make a place in their lives for a child. When the partner expresses pride and joy in the pregnancy, the woman feels valued and comforted. This is so important that many women retain a memory of the partner's reaction to the announcement of pregnancy for many years.

Women are also concerned how their family and friends will react to the pregnancy. Securing the acceptance of her own mother is particularly important to a pregnant woman, who gains energy and contentment when acceptance is freely given and support is offered by her mother.

Problems may occur if the family strongly desires a child with particular characteristics and if the woman feels that the family may reject an infant who does not meet the criteria. For example, if family members wish for a boy, will they accept a girl? Women who gain unconditional acceptance experience the least anxiety (Mercer, 1990).

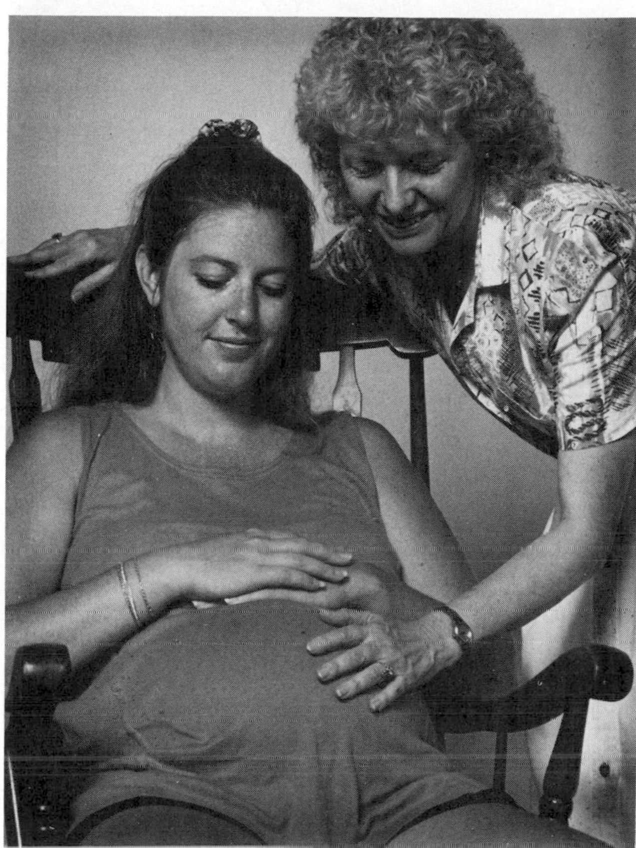

The bond between a pregnant woman and her own mother is particularly important to the young mother.

Learning to Give of Self

Giving is one of the most idealized components of motherhood but one that must be learned. Learning to give begins in pregnancy when the woman allows her body to give space and nurturing to the fetus. She also observes giving in others and then tests her own ability to derive pleasure from giving. This most often takes the form of providing food or care for her family. If they accept and enjoy the "gift," this enhances her pleasure and the role is strengthened. She explores further by making and giving small gifts to friends, especially those who are pregnant, and she feels pride and delight when the gift is appreciated.

Pregnant women also learn to give by receiving. Gifts received at "baby showers" are more than needed items; they also confirm continued interest and commitment from friends and family and enhance the ability of the woman to give. Intangible gifts from others, such as companionship, attention, and support help to increase her energy and affirm the importance of giving.

Commitment to the Unknown Child

Developing attachment to the unborn baby does not end in pregnancy but continues throughout the neonatal period (Lederman, 1984; Rubin, 1984). The process begins in early pregnancy when the woman accepts or "binds-in" to the idea she is pregnant, although the baby is not yet real to her. During the second trimester, the baby becomes real and feelings of love and attachment surge. There is a special, exclusive relationship between woman and fetus that simulates a secret, romantic love. She fantasizes about the special characteristics of this baby and endeavors to know all its qualities. Love of the infant becomes possessive and leads to the feelings of vulnerability described earlier. The woman integrates the role of mother into her image of herself. She becomes comfortable with the idea of herself as mother and finds pleasure in contemplating the new role.

✔ Check Your Reading

3. What does "looking for a fit" mean in role transition?
4. Why is grief work part of maternal role transition?
5. How does the pregnant woman seek safe passage for herself and the baby?

Paternal Adaptation

Although expectant fathers do not experience the biological processes of pregnancy as women do, they must also make major psychosocial changes to adapt to their new role. Moreover, the changes may be more difficult because the male partner is often neglected by the health care team as well as by his peer group as attention is focused on the woman.

Variations in Paternal Adaptation

There are wide variations in the types of involvement that men work through. Some are emotionally invested and comfortable as full partners and wish to explore every aspect of pregnancy, childbirth, and parenting. Others are more task-oriented and see themselves as managers. They may direct the diet and rest periods of the pregnant partner and act as coaches during childbirth but remain detached from the emotional components. Other men are more comfortable as observers and prefer not to participate. Some men are culturally stereotyped to see pregnancy and childbirth as "women's work" and they may not be able to express their true feelings about pregnancy and fatherhood.

Factors such as age, the relationship with his partner, the influence of his own father, his own personality, and the effect of other stresses in his life determine how a man adapts to pregnancy and childbirth.

Developmental Processes

As with the responses of the expectant mother, the responses of the expectant father are not static but progress through phases that are subject to individual variation. Jordan (1990) described three developmental processes that he must work through:

- He must grapple with the reality of pregnancy and the new child
- He must struggle for recognition as a parent from his family and social network
- He must make an effort to be seen as relevant to childbearing.

GRAPPLING WITH THE REALITY OF PREGNANCY AND THE CHILD

The pregnancy and the child must become real before a man can take on the identity of father. The process requires time, and it is often incomplete until the father meets the child face to face at birth. Initially, the pregnancy is a diagnosis only and changes in the expectant woman's behavior, such as nausea and fatigue, are perceived as symptoms of illness that have little to do with having a baby.

A man's initial reaction to the announcement of pregnancy may be pride and joy, but he often experiences the same ambivalence that his partner experiences. This is particularly true if he is unprepared for the added responsibility or commitment.

Various experiences act as catalysts or "reality boosters" that make the child more real. The most frequently mentioned experiences are hearing the baby's heart beat, feeling the infant move, and seeing the fetus on a sonogram. Once they can feel the fetus move, many expectant fathers invent a nickname and invest the fetus with special characteristics. The fetus is now a potential baby and not just a diagnosis of pregnancy.

Preparing the nursery or a space in the home and accumulating supplies for the new addition also reinforce the reality of the forthcoming child. These

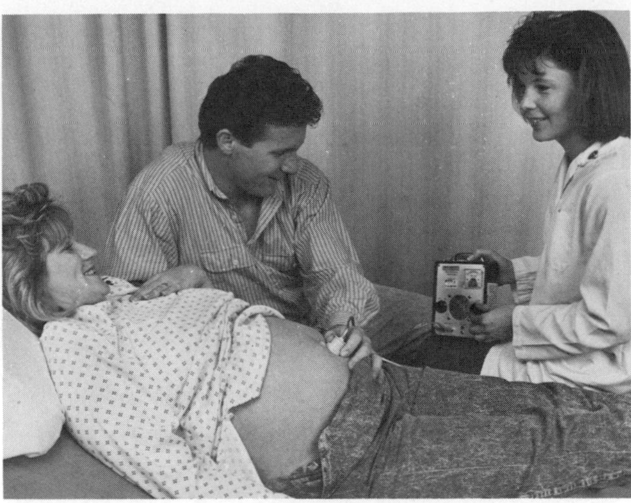

The existence of the fetus becomes real for the father when he hears the fetal heart beat through the transducer.

tasks often represent the first time the expectant father has the opportunity to do something for the child directly. The birth itself is the most powerful "reality booster," and the infant becomes real to the father when he has an opportunity to see and hold the infant.

STRUGGLING FOR RECOGNITION AS A PARENT

Men tend not to be perceived as parents in their own right by their mates, co-workers, friends, or family. They are often viewed as helpmates but not as co-parents. Their primary responsibilities are to act as a support person for their partners as they progress through pregnancy and childbirth.

Many men find it upsetting that there is often little validation of their feelings or recognition that they want to be considered as a parent as well as a helper. Some men accept that the focus should be on the woman, but some men find it frustrating that there is so little understanding of what the experience is like for them.

Expectant mothers play an important role in helping their partners gain recognition as parents. Women who openly share the physical sensations and emotions that they experience help the expectant father to feel that he is part of the process. These women often refer to it as "our" pregnancy and "our" child rather than as "my" pregnancy or "my" child. They also insist that the man be included in all discussions and decisions.

Nurses must learn to view the mother-father-child as the client and not focus exclusively on the mother and fetus. Men are reported to worry more than women about physical symptoms experienced by expectant mothers (Bothamley, 1990). The nurse should encourage the man to ask questions about his partner's pregnancy. These men are entitled to as much advice and reassurance as expectant women.

CREATING THE ROLE OF INVOLVED FATHER

Often men have no clear-cut role model whose parenting behaviors can be copied. Many view their own fathers as being distanced from parenting, particularly during the early years of childhood. This view is often confirmed by their co-workers and friends who leave infant care to their partners. The lack of a role model leaves many expectant fathers in the position of having to create a new role when they want to become actively involved in infant care.

Moreover, men often believe they do not have the knowledge, skills, or support to care for a newborn and they lack confidence to try. Many see the mother as the expert in child care and they are often frustrated because they feel incapable in this endeavor.

Men use various means to create a parenting role that is comfortable for them. They may seek closer ties with their own fathers to reminisce about their own childhood. They also observe men who are already fathers and "try on" fathering behaviors to determine whether they are comfortable and fit their own concept of the father role. Moreover, many men assertively seek information about infant care and growth and development so that they will be prepared when the infant arrives.

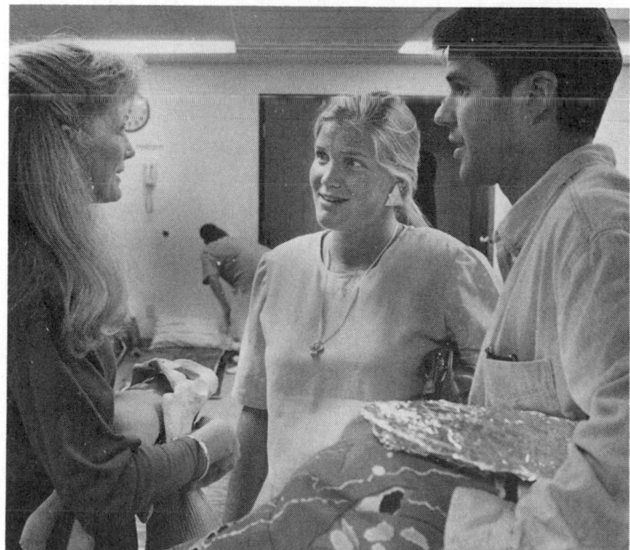

The nurse who views the mother/father/child as a client provides parents with the greatest opportunity to learn infant care and parenting skills.

Nurses are the primary providers of childbirth and parenting education and have many opportunities to provide recognition for fathers and to provide them opportunities to learn infant care and parenting skills. The nurse can arrange appointments for antepartum care or parenting classes when the father is available to accompany the expectant mother. Weekends or evenings may be the only possibility for including expectant fathers who may not feel free to request time off to participate in the instruction the woman receives.

Couvade

The term couvade refers to pregnancy-related symptoms and behavior in expectant fathers. In primitive cultures, couvade took the form of rituals involving special dress, confinement, limitations of physical work, avoidance of certain foods, sexual restraint, and, in some instances performance of "mock labor."

In modern practice, expectant fathers sometimes experience a cluster of physical symptoms similar to those experienced by women during pregnancy: loss of appetite, nausea and vomiting, headache, fatigue, and weight gain (Broude, 1988). Couvade symptoms are more likely to occur in early pregnancy and diminish as the pregnancy progresses. Symptoms may be caused by stress, anxiety, or empathy for the pregnant partner. They are usually harmless but may persist and result in nervousness, insomnia, restlessness, and irritability. Although the symptoms are almost always unobserved by the health care team, it is believed that anticipatory guidance would prove beneficial for both partners.

✔ Check Your Reading

6. What are reality boosters? Why are they important for the expectant father's adjustment?
7. How can nurses help men in their struggle for recognition as parents?

Adaptation of Grandparents

Factors That Influence Emotional Responses

Grandparents are often the first persons told of the pregnancy, and their initial reaction depends on several factors, including their ages, the number and spacing of other grandchildren, and the perception of the role of grandparents.

AGE

Age is a major factor in determining the emotional responses of prospective grandparents. By the time they become grandparents, many people have already dealt with their feelings about aging and react with joy when they find they are to become grandparents. They look forward to being able to love grandchildren, who signify the continuity of life and family.

Other prospective grandparents are in their mid-40s and may not be happy with the stereotype of grandparents as old persons. They may experience a great deal of conflict when they must resolve their self-image with the stereotype. Furthermore, people in their 40s and 50s often have career responsibilities and may not be accessible because of the continuing demands of their own lives.

NUMBER AND SPACING OF OTHER GRANDCHILDREN

The number and spacing of other grandchildren also determine how grandparents feel. A first grandchild may be an exciting event that creates great joy. However, if the grandparents already have several young grandchildren, the birth of another may be welcomed but the excitement is often less than that experienced with the birth of the first grandchild. The subdued reaction may be disappointing to the couple, who may desire the same excited reaction as that expressed for the first grandchild.

PERCEPTION OF THE ROLE OF GRANDPARENTS

Beliefs about how important grandparents are to grandchildren vary widely. Many grandparents see their relationship with the grandchild as second in importance only to the parent-child relationship. They want to be involved in the pregnancy, and grandmothers often engage in rituals such as shopping and gift-giving showers that confirm their role as important participants. Many grandparents look forward to being intimately involved in child care and offer unconditional love to the child.

As pregnancy progresses, grandparents often have concerns about the health of mother and baby. The last few weeks of pregnancy pass slowly, and grandparents often say, "I will be glad when the baby is born, and then I'll know everything is all right." During this time, they make plans about how they can assist the new parents. Many grandparents offer to care for older children while the mother gives birth, and they assist during the first weeks following childbirth.

In the past, grandparents were often looked to for advice about childbearing and childrearing. Health care workers have now become the "experts," and many grandparents have difficulty adjusting to this. If the issue is not recognized, distance may develop as the grandparents withdraw, sensing that their participation is no longer desired.

On the other hand, some contemporary grandparents hold different beliefs about the role of grandparents and plan much less participation in pregnancy or child care. A comment frequently heard is, "I have raised my children and I don't plan to do it again." This often results in conflict with the parents, who are hurt by the attitude and wish that the grandparents were around to help during the third trimester and following the birth.

Nurses may be able to help defuse a potentially disruptive process by clarifying the situation and assisting the families to verbalize their feelings.

"It may seem that the grandparents aren't interested in the child; however, that may not be the actual message." "Perhaps they are uneasy about being responsible for care of the child. Reassure them that you are responsible but that you want them to share in the joy the child brings."

Parents and grandparents may need to negotiate how the grandparents can be involved without feeling they must assume care of the child. For instance, the couple may need suggestions that will help the grandparents participate in family gatherings that do not involve babysitting or child care.

Education for Grandparenting

Although there has been little research in the adaptation of grandparents, in some areas grandparenting classes and groups have formed to prepare people to enter what can be a very rewarding experience. The nurse should explain changes in birthing and parenting practices that have taken place so that the grandparents can be supportive of these unfamiliar practices. Classes often provide tips for being a welcome grandparent. These include:

- Taking over some of the mother's responsibilities (meals, laundry) so that she has more time and energy for the infant
- Offering praise and support for the parents' efforts
- Not criticizing childrearing patterns
- Respecting the privacy of the parents
- Praising the child and being aware that comments can be misinterpreted
- Respecting the parents' wishes regarding permitted foods, naps, and bedtimes

- Avoiding comparing one child with another (ages when they slept through the night, walked, began to talk)

Adaptation of Siblings

Toddlers

How siblings adapt to the birth of an infant depends largely on the age and developmental level. Very young children, 2 years of age or younger, are unaware of the maternal changes that occur during pregnancy and are unable to understand that a new brother or sister is going to be born. An only child is accustomed to being the focus of attention and may feel threatened and abandoned when that attention must be shared. It is easy to imagine that the young child feels intense anger and fear but is unable to put those feelings into perspective. The child may become "clingy" and revert to infantile behaviors such as thumb sucking or bedwetting.

Although it is difficult to prepare very young children for the birth of a baby, the nurse can make suggestions that may prove helpful. First, any change in sleeping arrangements should be made several weeks before the birth so that the child does not feel displaced by the new baby. Second, parents must be certain that family and friends give as much time and attention to the child as they give to the new baby. Each parent should frequently arrange time alone with the older child, perhaps a picnic or a trip to the park. Additional time should be allowed for reading, listening to music, and cuddling the older child before bedtime. It is wise to keep a supply of small gifts available so that when friends bring a gift to the new baby, the child will also receive a present.

Until children feel that their place in the affection of their parents is secure, it is not realistic to expect the 2-year-old to welcome the new "stranger." Frequent reassurances of parental love and affection are of primary importance. Hugs, kisses, and statements such as "we love you all the time" help to provide the security that the toddler needs. The parents can be taught to accept strong feelings the toddler expresses, such as anger, jealousy, or frustration without judgment and to continue to reinforce the lovability of the child.

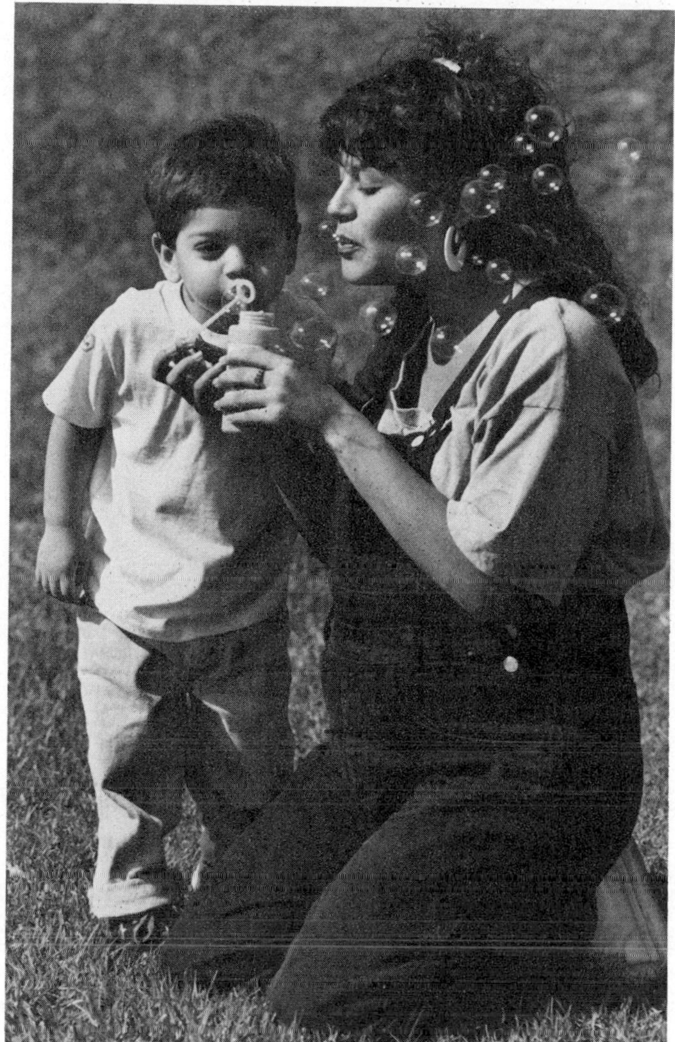

A pregnant woman who spends time with an older child can provide affection and a sense of security.

Older Children

The older child, from 3 to 12 years of age, is more aware of changes in the mother's body and may be aware that a baby is to be born. These children may be interested in observing the mother's abdomen and feeling the fetus move. They enjoy listening to the heart beat and may have questions about how the fetus develops, how it started, and how it will get out of the abdomen. They often understand that the baby will be a brother or sister and look forward to its arrival. However, they may expect that the infant will be a full-fledged playmate and so are shocked when the infant is small and helpless.

School-aged children benefit from being included in preparations for the new baby. They often enjoy recording the size and development of the fetus on a calendar. They are interested in preparing space for the infant to sleep and accumulating supplies the infant will need. The children should be encouraged to feel the fetus move, and many will come close to the mother's abdomen and talk to the fetus, who begins to take on unique characteristics.

Children as young as 3 years benefit from sibling classes. They are encouraged to bring a doll so that they can simulate care that an infant will need. The classes also provide an opportunity for them to discuss what changes the new baby will mean for the family. (See Chapter 11 for additional information about sibling classes.)

In some areas, children as young as 5 years are permitted to be with the mother during childbirth. If this is to be the case, it is recommended that they attend a class that will prepare them for the event. A familiar person should be available to explain what is taking place and to comfort them or to remove them if the birth becomes overwhelming for them.

Adolescents

The response of adolescents also depends on their developmental level. Some adolescents may be embarrassed because the pregnancy confirms the continued sexuality of their parents. They may be repelled by the obvious physical changes. Many adolescents are immersed in their own developmental tasks that involve loosening ties to their parents and coming to terms with their own sexuality. They may be indifferent to the pregnancy unless it directly affects them or their activities. Some adolescents, on the other hand, become very involved and want to help with preparations for the baby.

✔ Check Your Reading

8. What determines the response of grandparents to the pregnancy?
9. Explain the effect of a new baby on a toddler.
10. How can parents prepare siblings for the addition of a newborn to the family?

Factors That Influence Psychosocial Adaptations

Multiparity

One might assume that a multipara needs less help than a first-time mother; however, this is not the case. Pregnancy tasks are actually much more complex for the multipara than they are for the primigravida (Mercer, 1990). When dealing with the task of negotiating safe passage for self and infant, the multipara does not have time to take special care of herself as she did during the first pregnancy. Multiparas report more fatigue, and significantly fewer report feeling very well or excellent. Moreover, more multiparas report having serious worries, such as how the children will accept the infant and how to find time and energy for additional responsibilities. When seeking acceptance of the new baby, the multipara may find the family less excited than they were for the first child and the couple's celebration is also more subdued. She spends a great deal of time working out a new relationship with the first child, who often becomes demanding. This may foster feelings of guilt as she tries to expand her love to include the second child. Developing attachment for the coming baby is hampered by feelings of loss between her and the first child. She senses that the child is growing up and away from her, and she may grieve for the loss of their special relationship.

Nurses must remember that multiparas may need more help and understanding than primigravidas. The nurse cannot assume that the process is "old hat" and that there is no need to provide information about labor, breastfeeding, and infant care. Special assistance may be necessary to help a multipara integrate a second (or more) infant into the family structure.

Socioeconomic Status

One of the greatest influences on childbearing practices is the socioeconomic status of the family into which the child is born. Socioeconomic status refers to the resources that the family has to meet the needs for food, shelter, and health care. Socioeconomic status and social class are closely related. Social class is roughly divided into upper, middle, and lower class.

UPPER CLASS

Upper class families have resources to provide for their needs and to purchase health care. They have a good income, secure shelter in a safe neighborhood, and the education and reserves to protect themselves from economic fluctuations. They are able to provide an enriched environment for children, and they can pay for health care either from private means or through insurance.

The attitudes related to health care reflect the ability of upper class families to pay. They know that they deserve the best in health care and believe that they deserve respect from health care providers. They insist on being active participants in their care and they are future-oriented, which means that they value preventive care. In general, they seek early, regular antepartum care and comply with recommendations of the health care providers.

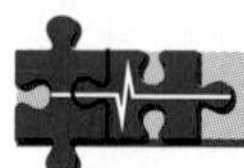

Clinical Situation

Emma H., a 24-year-old multipara of 32 weeks' gestation, appears apathetic and tired when she arrives at the prenatal clinic. She states that she is concerned about how her 2-year-old son will acccept the new baby and sometimes feels guilty that she is having this baby so soon.

Q:
1. How does multiparity affect the maternal tasks of pregnancy?
2. How should the nurse respond to her concerns?
3. What measures can the client take to prepare the 2-year-old before the new baby arrives? After the infant is born?

A:
1. The tasks of pregnancy are more complex than for a primigravida; there is not enough time; there is more fatigue; there is less excitement; the client must work out a new relationship with the first child, who has had her undivided time.
2. Respond by acknowledging her concerns and reflecting her feelings so that she can fully express how she feels. "You worry that your son will be upset when the new baby is born, and you feel guilty that he will have to share your time and energy with the baby."
3. Suggest that the client make any changes in sleeping arrangements now so that her son will not feel displaced by the infant. Recommend that she plan ways to have time alone with the older child when the baby arrives, and review measures to reduce sibling rivalry. The mother can tell the 2-year-old how much she loves him, hug and cuddle him frequently, and arrange his bedtime to allow time together for favorite activities, such as reading, listening to music, or watching his favorite videos. The mother can remind others to pay attention to him as well as to the baby.

MIDDLE CLASS

The middle class makes up the largest group of families in the United States; indeed, most health care workers fit into this class. Although they do not have the reserves of the upper class, they generally have adequate income to rent or own their homes in relatively safe neighborhoods. There is an adequate supply of good food, and they have either education or skills that assist them in getting and in keeping jobs for long periods of time. They often share child care with family and neighbors and develop a network of people who can rely on each other for support and assistance.

Health care is expensive, and middle class families rely on group insurance, obtained as part of their salaries, to shield themselves from exorbitant costs. A major concern is loss of a job that will result in loss of health care insurance. Middle class values emphasize the importance of hard work, saving for the future, and taking care of oneself. Middle class families express some ambivalence in their attitudes toward health care. They believe that health care should be a right for all citizens, but this belief conflicts with the belief that families must earn the right to health care by their ability to support themselves.

Middle class families are future-oriented; they seek health care early in pregnancy so that the mother and infant will have the best chance for a healthy outcome. They prepare for the birth and make plans to provide as much as possible for children in terms of security and education.

LOWER CLASS

The lower class is composed of unskilled workers who live with a great deal of uncertainty. They work for low wages, are often the last hired and the first fired. They often live below the poverty level and barely have enough to survive. Many have difficulty meeting the basic needs for food and shelter, and the number of homeless families is growing in the United States. The very poor have no financial resources, and their limited skills give them no bargaining power or sense of optimism. They desire better things for their children but see no opportunity to improve their lot. Many live in a perpetual state of despair and develop a resigned and fatalistic outlook on life.

Attitudes related to health care differ from those of the more affluent classes. Because of the economic uncertainty, they place more emphasis on meeting the needs of the present rather than on future goals. As a result, they place less value on preventive care, which requires an orientation toward the future. This is particularly obvious during pregnancy, when prenatal care may be postponed until the pregnancy is near term or even until labor begins.

NEW POOR

The new poor comprise an expanding group of individuals and families who were previously self-sufficient but who, because of circumstances, such as loss of a job and loss of health care insurance, are now without resources or health insurance. These people must find their way into a health care system that is unfamiliar and frightening.

The values of the new poor are those of the middle class: self-sufficiency, hard work, and pride in their ability to succeed. It is very difficult for this group to seek public assistance. These families are

Table 8–2. IMPACT OF SOCIOECONOMIC FACTORS ON FAMILY'S RESPONSE TO PREGNANCY

Upper Class	Middle Class	Lower Class
	Resources	
Confident of ability Financial reserves protect family from economic fluctuations Own or rent home in a safe neighborhood Have health insurance or can pay for health care Able to provide enriched environment	Relative security, but fewer reserves and more debt Own or rent home in relatively safe neighborhood Health insurance depends on employment	Lack skills, bargaining power Most vulnerable to economic fluctuations Struggle for basic needs
	Value Placed on Health Care	
Value preventive care	Value health care but must rely on health insurance related to employment	May value health care but often do not see a way to improve situation
	Time Orientation	
Seek prenatal care early	Future oriented and seek early prenatal care Make plans to provide best possible care and education for children	Priority is to meet needs of present Often seek prenatal care late Uncertain future

devastated when they encounter the lack of respect and rudeness that are prevalent among health care workers when they deal with families who are unable to pay for health care. Table 8–2 summarizes the impact of socioeconomic status on the family's response to pregnancy.

Unsympathetic Attitude: A Barrier to Prenatal Care

One of the biggest barriers to health care results from the unsympathetic attitude of health care workers toward poor people who are unable to pay for medical care. This is due to conflicting values between many health professionals and poor families with whom they come in contact. Health care professionals generally accept the middle class values of "rugged individualism" and the belief that poor people would improve their lives if they worked harder and planned for the future. It is difficult for many physicians and nurses to understand the sense of despair and hopelessness that many poor people experience.

The lack of sympathy affects the care given to poor families, who often experience long delays, hurried examinations, rudeness, and arrogance from members of the health care team who work in public clinics and who are responsible for providing government-sponsored care. Many pregnant women report waiting 3 to 4 hours for an examination that lasts only a few minutes. Many never see the same health care provider more than once. Many pregnant women fail to keep clinic appointments because they do not see the importance of the hurried examinations. Additional reasons may be that no one is available to watch other children, the woman cannot afford to take time off from work, or no transportation is available. These obstacles might be difficult to overcome if, when the woman arrives, care is perceived as unsupportive and judgmental. Failure to return for subsequent appointments reinforces the attitude that many poor people do not help themselves, and the cycle of misunderstanding continues.

Rather than help the most vulnerable families obtain care so that they will have healthier babies, prevailing attitudes and policies frequently stigmatize poor families and make it harder for them to obtain care (*Access to Prenatal Care*, 1987). Nurses must examine their social values and recognize that these values are often not those of the families that need health care the most. Nurses must understand the importance of treating each family with respect and consideration, and they must insist that poor families who are unable to pay receive the same standard of care as that received by families who can pay. (See Chapters 3 and 23.)

Cultural Influences on Childbearing

The United States has been called a "melting pot," which means that there are more different cultural groups in this country than anywhere else in the world. Each culture has its own health and healing belief system that offers explanation and provides order during major life events such as pregnancy and childbirth. Belief systems vary from culture to culture, and the success of health care depends on how well it fits in with the beliefs of those being served. Therefore, ignorance of culturally divergent beliefs may lead to failure in health care delivery.

CULTURALLY DIVERGENT GROUPS

The newest large group of immigrants comes from Southeast Asia, and includes Cambodians, Vietnamese, Laotians, and Hmong. Latinos also make up a large group. In this chapter Latino encompasses individuals living in the United States who come from, or are of ancestry from, Mexico, Puerto Rico, Cuba, El Salvador, the Dominican Republic, and other Latin American countries. The term is not accepted by all groups; some prefer Hispanic, Mexican-American, Chicano, or La Raza (the race); however, the term as used here indicates common background in Spanish language and customs.

The term African-American includes those with a common background in African languages and customs. It is particularly difficult to describe cultural aspects of pregnancy for African-Americans. Many have been in the United States for generations, and their health beliefs do not differ significantly from those held by Caucasians. New immigrants from Africa, however, often retain some of the cultural beliefs of their country of origin.

Other groups that differ significantly in their cultural beliefs are Native Americans, Hindus (largely from India), Muslims from the Middle East, and Filipinos.

DIFFERENCES WITHIN CULTURES

There are wide variations of beliefs and practices within each culture, and nurses must recognize that not everyone in a culture has identical beliefs. Those who have been in Western societies for years or even for generations often do not follow behaviors prescribed by their culture. Nurses must be careful not to stereotype families or expect a certain set of behaviors from every family in a particular cultural group. Individual differences are as important as cultural variations.

NURSES' RESPONSIBILITIES

Nurses must be knowledgeable about cultural differences and sensitive to the effect these differences have on the health of women during pregnancy. Nurses must be able to identify cultural beliefs that (1) promote health during pregnancy, (2) provide a sense of security but do not affect the outcome of pregnancy, and (3) may prove harmful during pregnancy.

Examples of health beliefs that promote health during pregnancy include practices that provide all the needed nutrients or that maintain activity. Examples of beliefs that provide comfort or security but do not affect the outcome of pregnancy include wearing special articles of clothing, such as the "muneco," which is believed by some Latinas to ensure a safe delivery and to prevent morning sickness.

An example of a health belief that may prove harmful is ingestion of non-food substances (*pica*), described in Chapter 9.

CULTURAL DIFFERENCES THAT CAN CAUSE CONFLICT

Cultural differences that cause conflict between health care workers and families during pregnancy are observed most often in the areas of communication, time orientation, dietary practices, and health care beliefs.

Communication Techniques

Language. Language is a major barrier to health care. Not only are the national languages different but there are numerous tribal languages and dialects in most languages, often making it difficult to find a competent translator. Those who came to the United States as children may speak English well and can translate for their parents and grandparents. Other family members or friends as well as co-workers in the clinic or hospital may be helpful, but many are not fluent and can misunderstand instructions, particularly if medical jargon is used. For example, when a newly arrived immigrant from Vietnam was told that a prescription for iron supplementation would prevent anemia, she understood that the written prescription protected her, but she did not have the prescription filled to obtain the needed iron.

English is spoken by most African-Americans; however, variations in pronunciation, grammar, and sentence structure may make communication difficult. The dialect spoken by African-Americans is sometimes labeled "Black English" (Cherry and Giger, 1991). Nurses who work with African-Americans must bear in mind that English as spoken by African-Americans cannot be viewed as an unacceptable form of English, and nurses must avoid labeling and stereotyping those who speak a different dialect.

Nurses must also clarify the meaning of slang terms. For example, "tripped out" may be interpreted to be related to taking drugs when it may actually mean the woman became excited and energetic.

Communication Style. Styles in communication differ among cultures. Nodding and smiling do not necessarily denote agreement or even understanding by Asians but simply, "Yes, I hear you." When presenting information, the nurse should validate how much the person understands by requesting him or her to repeat the information. "Tell me what you understood, and show me what you learned."

Latinos are traditionally diplomatic and tactful; they frequently engage in "small talk" before bringing up questions they may have about their care. Nurses must remember that small talk is a valuable use of time, as it establishes rapport and often helps to accomplish the goals of care.

Eye Contact. Native Americans and Southeast Asians believe that it is rude to make eye contact or to indicate they do not understand what has been said. This sometimes frustrates health care personnel who believe that eye contact denotes honesty.

Eye behavior is important especially when nurses deal with Latino infants and children. *Mal ojo* (evil eye) is a condition that occurs when an individual attributed with special power looks at a child but does not touch the child. The child may become feverish or ill unless the individual, such as the nurse, touches as well as looks at the child (Andrews, 1991). Eye contact between unmarried men and women is considered taboo by Hindus, who may view prolonged eye contact as seductive.

Touch. Touch is also an important component of communication. Some Native Americans avoid shaking hands but will lightly touch the hand of the person they are greeting. In some cultures (Hindu and Muslim), touch by a woman other than the wife is offensive. In contrast, women from Haiti find touch supportive and reassuring, and gentle touch is particularly important during labor and birth. Nurses must remain sensitive to the response of the person being touched and refrain from touching if the person indicates that touch is not welcomed.

Time Orientation

Time orientation can create conflict between health care professionals, who parcel out care in discrete units of time that is measured in minutes, and groups who keep time by the progress of the sun or even by the seasons. Middle Eastern women, Latino women (Latinas), and African-American women tend to see time in terms of what is important at the moment rather than what is important in the future. This causes conflicts in a health care setting where tests or appointments are scheduled at particular times. If a woman does not place the same importance on keeping appointments, she may encounter anger and frustration in the health care setting that leaves her bewildered and shamed.

Dietary Practices

Southeast Asians and Latinos are likely to believe in the hot/cold theory of health and diet. This theory has nothing to do with temperature of the food but describes intrinsic properties of the foods and their effect on the body. The person strives for a balance between hot and cold.

The Chinese believe that a balance between the two elements of yin and yang maintains harmony in the universe. Yin represents female, cold, and darkness, whereas yang represents male, hot, and light (Andrews, 1989). The terms yin and yang are often, although somewhat inaccurately, translated into cold and hot. The balance of yin and yang in the diet is considered essential to good health. See Chapter 9 for additional information related to dietary practices.

Dietary practices may present problems during pregnancy. Some Asian and Latino diets tend to be high in salt, which is associated with an increase in blood pressure. Some African-Americans believe that pregnant women must avoid meats and high-calorie foods to protect themselves from too much blood in the body ("high blood"). Nurses must be aware that some African-American women assume that high blood pressure is due to too much blood, and will decrease their already depleted protein intake and increase their consumption of salt to counteract the high blood pressure (Andrews, 1989).

Health Practices

Belief in Fate. Health practices are affected by cultural beliefs. For example, in cultures where there is a strong belief in fate (Southeast Asia, the Middle East) women often believe that the only way in which they can affect the outcome of pregnancy is by eating correctly and observing the taboos of their culture. Because of this belief, it is sometimes difficult to get women to seek early and regular prenatal care.

Folk Medicine. Folk medicine plays a role in pregnancy. The Chinese use health foods and herb tonics to prevent and cure illness. Garlic, for instance, is used for hypertension, and herbal teas are used for gastrointestinal upset. Latinas often consult with *curanderas* (faith healers) who work with women to keep a balance between hot and cold and to relieve them of their sins, which may be the basis for illness. Some rely on folk medicine that includes witchcraft, voodoo, and magic (Africans, Haitians).

To be certain that all essential information about folk medicine is obtained, nurses should inquire whether the client is taking folk remedies. "What do pregnant women take to protect themselves and the baby?" "How often and how much of this do you take?" "Tell me about special foods and drinks that are important."

Modesty

Fear, modesty, and a desire to avoid examination by males may keep some women from seeking health care during pregnancy. In many cultures (Muslim, Hindu, Latino), exposure of the genitals to males is considered demeaning. Nurses must remember that the reputation of women from these cultures depends on their demonstrated modesty. If necessary, female physicians or nurse practitioners can perform the examinations. If this is not possible, the woman should be carefully draped, with the legs completely covered. A female nurse needs to remain with the woman at all times. It may be necessary to obtain permission from the husband before any examination or treatment can be performed.

Infibulation. Female circumcision (excision of the clitoris and parts of the labia minora) and infibulation (scraping and bringing together the labia minora) are widely practiced in parts of Northern Africa (Lightfoot-Klein and Shaw, 1990). The practice has been associated with premarital chastity, and in some African cultures it is a prerequisite for marriage.

Women who have been infibulated express hope that physicians and nurses would be knowledgeable about the custom and be prepared for how the genitals look. Pelvic examination provokes two major concerns: (1) exposure of the genitals and (2) inescapable pain because the introitus is so small and inelastic scar tissue makes the area especially sensitive to pain.

Nurses must make sure that pelvic examinations are as comfortable as possible, maintaining utmost privacy, draping the woman to provide maximum coverage, and assisting her in locating a health care provider with whom she is comfortable. The infibulated woman may not give any verbal or nonverbal sign of pain, but this does not indicate an absence of pain.

✔ *Check Your Reading*

11. Why do many poor women delay seeking health care until the second or third trimester?
12. How do the attitudes of health care workers affect the care of poor families?

Application of Nursing Process

Assessment

The purpose of a psychosocial assessment is to monitor the adaptation of the family to pregnancy, which has been termed a maturational "crisis" that requires a major transition in role function and relationships. Whether one agrees that pregnancy is a crisis, there is no doubt that it initiates change and stress. How the family copes is a primary concern. For some families, pregnancy offers the potential for growth; for others, there is an alteration in family processes that requires guidance and information. Other women or families have more specific needs that are discovered during a thorough psychosocial assessment.

Some data required for a psychosocial assessment can be obtained from the physical assessment. For example, age, gravida, para, and general health status provide important information in both areas. Table 8–3 identifies areas for assessment, provides sample questions, and indicates nursing implications.

Analysis

Nursing diagnoses are made on the bases of analysis of data obtained during individual assessments and thus vary from family to family. Pregnancy is a time of transition for all families, whether it is the first pregnancy or one of several. When pregnancy occurs, most families strive to maintain the health of the expectant mother and fetus and to complete developmental tasks that allow the couple to become parents of one child or more than one child. The most encompassing nursing diagnosis related to psychosocial adaptation is *Family Coping: Potential for Growth related to readiness and desire to meet added family needs and to assume parenting roles.*

Planning

Goals for this Nursing Diagnosis are as follows:

- The family will verbalize emotional responses that are appropriate to each trimester.
- The family will verbalize methods that assist the expectant parents to complete the developmental processes of pregnancy.
- The family will identify cultural factors that may produce conflicts and collaborate to reduce those conflicts.

Table 8–3. PSYCHOSOCIAL ASSESSMENT

Findings (Normal and Unusual)*	Sample Questions	Nursing Implications
	Psychologic Response	
Excitement, ambivalence (fear, anger, apathy)	"How do you/partner feel about being pregnant?" "How will your lives change as a result of being pregnant?" "How do you feel about the changes in your body?" "What preparations have you made for the baby?"	Use active listening and reflection to establish a sense of trust; re-evaluate negative responses (fear, ambivalence, anger) in subsequent assessments
	Availability of Resources	
Financial concerns (lack of funds, or insurance)	"What are your plans for prenatal care and birth?"	Determine if there are adequate funds or if family needs help to find a public clinic that will provide care
Response and availabiity of grandparents, friends, family (family geographically or emotionally unavailable)	"How do your parents feel about being grandparents?" "What do they want to be called?" "Who else can you depend on besides the family?" "Who provides strength when there is a conflict?"	It may be necessary to help the couple discover alternative resources if the family is unavailable; early identification of family conflicts allows time for resolution
	Changes in Sexual Practices	
Mutual satisfaction with changes (concern with comfort or safety)	"How have sexual patterns or satisfaction changed?" "How do you cope with the changes?" "What concerns you most?"	Offer reassurance that intercourse is usually safe; suggest alternative positions and open communication
	Educational Needs	
Many questions about pregnancy, childbirth, and infant care (no questions, absence of interest in educational programs)	"How do you feel about caring for an infant?" "What are your major concerns?" "Whom do you count on for information?" "What would be most helpful?"	Respond to priority needs that are expressed; refer couple to appropriate child- and parenting classes
	Cultural Influences	
Either the woman or her family is able to speak English or fluent interpreters are available; cultural influences support a healthy pregnancy and infant (unable to communicate verbally, some cultural beliefs or health practices may prove harmful)	"What foods are recommended during pregnancy?" "What practices are recommended?" "What is forbidden?" "How can we provide the best care?" "What is most important in your care?" "How do your religious beliefs affect pregnancy?"	Locate fluent interpreters if necessary; avoid labeling beliefs as superstitions; reinforce beliefs that promote a good pregnancy outcome; assess accepted source of information; elicit help of this person to overcome practices that may prove harmful

* Findings that require additional assessment or intervention are shown in parentheses.

Interventions

PROVIDING INFORMATION

Provide information and anticipatory guidance about:

- The emotional changes that occur during pregnancy (ambivalence, introversion, increased feelings of vulnerability)
- The developmental tasks of the mother (seeking safe passage, securing acceptance, forming attachment with the unknown baby)
- Role transition (mimicry, role playing, fantasy, grief work)
- The developmental processes of the prospective father (grappling with the reality, struggling for recognition as a parent, creating the role of involved father).

Guidance is necessary to prepare prospective parents for the progressive changes that occur during pregnancy and to reassure them that their feelings and behaviors are normal. This also gives them an opportunity to ask questions and explore their feelings.

DISCUSSING RESOURCES

Initiate a discussion of the adequacy of the financial situation and support systems. The nurse may have to help couples who have no financial resources or insurance coverage to find the most convenient location to obtain prenatal care and to determine where the client will give birth. This is particularly important for the new poor, who have little idea of how to gain access to government-sponsored care. Emotional resources include those that assist the new family to adjust to the demands of pregnancy and parenting.

Discuss the responses and participation of the grandparents. Although emotional responses vary, the family unit is strengthened and the attachment of the grandparents to the child is enhanced when grandparents actively participate in the pregnancy.

If family members, who traditionally offer support in times of stress, are unavailable, refer the prospective parents to community resources, such as childbirth education classes, support groups, sibling classes, and later to breastfeeding and new parenting classes.

HELPING THE FAMILY PREPARE FOR THE BIRTH

During the last trimester, it is helpful to discuss lifestyle changes that will occur when the infant is born. Unanticipated changes that accompany this dramatic life event may add stress and lead to disruption in family processes. Help the prospective parents make practical plans for the infant, such as obtaining clothing, finding a place to sleep, and choosing the method of feeding. Siblings should also be prepared several weeks or even months before the birth. The response of children depends on their ages and developmental levels. Older children (above 3 to 4 years) often benefit from participating in prenatal care and planning for the baby; younger children do not grasp the concept of time and can be prepared for the arrival of a new baby shortly before the birth.

Discuss with expectant parents how they will work out the division of household and parenting tasks. Ask them to consider how they will manage the care of the newborn if the mother must return to work following childbirth. If these issues are not dealt with, the couple can experience frustration and anger as one parent, usually the mother, assumes total care of the infant and attempts to complete all household tasks. Moreover, exhaustion and frustration can overwhelm the joys of parenting when one parent must provide all care.

MODELING COMMUNICATION TECHNIQUES

When disagreements are evident, it is often helpful to discuss and model therapeutic communication techniques that include all significant family members as the family prepares for the birth. Techniques that clarify, summarize, and reflect feelings, can defuse negative feelings that might result in family disruption. (See Chapter 2.)

IDENTIFYING CULTURAL FACTORS THAT COULD CAUSE CONFLICT

Discuss possible areas of conflict related to cultural beliefs and health practices that affect pregnancy.

It is reassuring to expectant mothers when nurses support health beliefs and dietary practices that are beneficial before confronting them with health care beliefs that cause concern. For example, "It is so good for you and the baby when you eat so many vegetables, but I am worried because you missed your last appointment."

If there is conflict as a result of differences in time orientation, acknowledge the problem, convey understanding of the differences and emphasize the importance of calling when appointments cannot be kept. Many families do not realize that when they miss their appointment, another family misses the opportunity for health care.

Evaluation

When the family verbalizes concerns and emotions throughout pregnancy, the initial goal is met. Continued interest and involvement of the partner and significant family members is evidence that the family has completed the developmental tasks of pregnancy. Participation of the family with health care workers to find a compromise when differing cultural beliefs cause conflict confirms that the family will identify and initiate measures to reduce conflicts.

Summary Concepts

- Maternal psychological responses progress during pregnancy from uncertainty and ambivalence to feelings of vulnerability and preparation for the birth of the infant.

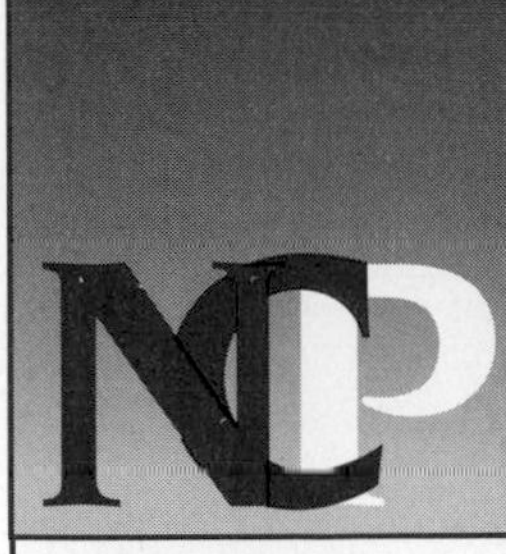

Nursing Care Plan 8–1

Socioeconomic Problems During Pregnancy

Assessment: Theresa Matheny, a 19-year-old primigravida, is seen for initial prenatal care at 24 weeks of gestation. She took the day off from work in a laundry and rode the bus to the clinic. She is currently living with an unmarried sister who receives Aid to Families with Dependent Children. During the interview, Ms. Matheny states that she will not be able to keep clinic appointments because she cannot afford to take more time off until the baby comes. She is unmarried and states that the father of the baby "is gone." She says that she is healthy and only needs to find someone to deliver the baby.

Nursing Diagnosis: High Risk for Altered Health Maintenance related to lack of a plan to obtain regular prenatal care and knowledge deficit of the importance of care.

Goals:

The client will:

1. Verbalize a plan for regular prenatal care at the initial prenatal visit.
2. Describe the benefits of regular prenatal care by the end of the initial prenatal visit.

Intervention:	Rationale:
1. Assist Theresa in devising a plan to obtain regular prenatal care. a. Provide her with a list of prenatal clinics near her home or place of work and the hours they are open. b. Provide alternative bus schedules or transportation services. c. Determine whether there are family members or friends who can help her keep prenatal appointments. d. Explore dates, times, and alternatives until she finds a schedule that will work for her. e. Obtain a list of phone numbers where she can be reached for follow-up. Include the numbers of friends, family, and the employer.	1. Some clinics are open weekends and evenings to accommodate working women. Unreliable transportation is a major reason for failure to keep scheduled appointments, and clinic schedules that allow some flexibility are helpful. Moreover, interest in a client's individual situation is highly motivating for her to find a way to continue prenatal care.
2. Emphasize reasons why regular prenatal care is essential to: a. Monitor the growth and development of the baby (maternal pattern of weight gain, fundal height, fetal heart tones, fetal activity. b. Evaluate Theresa's health, which directly affects the health of the fetus (blood pressure, urinalysis, weight gain). c. Detect problems, and intervene before they become severe.	2. Preventive care is often not a priority when the client has conflicting needs for food and shelter. Moreover, many women are unaware that some complications, such as pregnancy-induced hypertension or glucose intolerance (gestational diabetes), which may be detected and treated in early pregnancy, are serious hazards if they remain undetected.

Evaluation:

Verbalized knowledge of the benefits of prenatal care, a plan for transportation, and the development of a schedule to attend a prenatal clinic on a regular basis meet the original goals. If a client misses scheduled appointments, follow-up phone calls to arrange alternative appointments may be necessary.

Additional Nursing Diagnoses to Consider:

Altered Family Processes
Impaired Home Maintenance Management
High Risk for Injury
Altered Role Performance

Nursing Care Plan 8–2

Body Image During Pregnancy

Assessment: Dolores White is a 34-year-old primigravida in the 26th week of pregnancy. Both she and her husband have been runners for several years. She stopped running 6 months ago and reports that she now walks "like other old ladies." She verbalizes concern about how much bigger she will get and says she feels "awkward and ugly." She states, "I hate the way I look; I can't wait to get back into shape."

Nursing Diagnosis: Body Image Disturbance related to changes in body size, contour, and function.

Goals:

The client will:

1. Make statements that indicate acceptance of expected body changes during pregnancy.
2. Express her feelings about body changes to her husband as well as to the health care team by (date).
3. Set realistic goals for weight loss and the resumption of running program following childbirth.

Intervention:	Rationale:
1. Acknowledge Dolores's feelings. "I can see you are disappointed at not being able to run, and I sense you are concerned about how your body has changed as a result of pregnancy."	1. Feelings must be acknowledged, reflected, and dealt with before the underlying cause can be addressed.
2. Clarify her concerns. "You have always been an athlete. Are you wondering how much permanent change will result from pregnancy?"	2. An underlying, unvoiced concern may be that pregnancy and childbirth will change the woman from athlete to mother. This altered perception of herself causes fear and/or grief.
3. Suggest that she share her feelings with her husband and seek his support. It may be necessary to model this interaction. "I am feeling awkward and left out of a big part of our lives. I need some reassurance from you now."	3. Although one may assume that the partner observes and understands when negative feelings exist, this may not be true.
4. Demonstrate the expected pattern of weight gain from 26 weeks to term gestation, and correlate this with the growth and development of the fetus.	4. Many women achieve satisfaction from the knowledge that weight gain indicates that the fetus is growing. Moreover, knowledge of how much weight gain is expected may allay unexpressed fears of excessive weight gain.
5. Help Dolores make realistic plans to lose weight and recover her strength and endurance following childbirth. a. Discuss the expected pattern of weight loss following childbirth: an initial weight loss of 4.5 to 5 kg or 10 to 12 pounds. An additional 2.5 kg or 5.5 pounds may be lost in the first few postpartum days. By the end of 8 weeks, many women return to their pre-pregnancy weight. b. Demonstrate graduated exercises that increase muscle tone and strength. c. Explain the purpose of adipose tissue gained during pregnancy, and discuss a diet that provides sufficient calories to meet the client's needs, taking into account the calories required for breastfeeding following childbirth.	5. Adipose tissue provides a needed source of energy following childbirth and during lactation. Many women are relieved to know that there is a purpose and that the added weight will be lost gradually. Breastfeeding requires at least 500 additional calories per day.

Nursing Care Plan continued on following page

Nursing Care Plan 8–2 Continued

Body Image During Pregnancy

Evaluation:
Statements by Dolores indicating acceptance of body changes during pregnancy are important signs that the interventions have been successful. Increased communication between the partners about the concerns of the client reduce her frustration. It may be necessary to monitor her plans for weight loss and for exercise after childbirth so that unrealistic goals are not made.

Additional Nursing Diagnoses to Consider:
High Risk for Situational Low Self-Esteem
Personal Identity Disturbance
Knowledge Deficit
Altered Family Processes

Nursing Care Plan 8–3

Language Barrier During Pregnancy

Assessment: Ms. Thuy Nguyen, a young Vietnamese primipara of 26 weeks' gestation, speaks very little English. She listens quietly to health care instructions, and although she appears confused, she asks no questions. Her husband is more familiar with English; however, he has difficulty responding to questions about his wife's health. Both speak with a pronounced accent.

Nursing Diagnosis: Impaired Verbal Communication related to foreign language barriers.

Goals:
The family will:
1. Keep scheduled appointments, demonstrate ability to follow health care instructions, and verbalize basic needs and concerns.
2. Verbalize feelings of support from the health care team throughout prenatal care and childbirth.

Intervention:	Rationale:
1. Assess the couple's ability to speak, read, or write in English, and determine the languages in which each is fluent.	1. Although the client may not be fluent in speaking a language, at times she may be more adept at reading. Many Vietnamese also speak Chinese or French; this knowledge is important when you are seeking a translator.
2. Obtain the assistance of a fluent translator. a. Establish a list of bilingual staff members in all areas of the facility (business office, housekeeping, maintenance) who are willing to translate. b. Enlist the aid of family members or friends who can accompany the client and who can translate. c. Engage an interpreter to develop colorful cards that have common questions and answers printed in languages that are most frequently spoken. d. Develop printed instructions in the most commonly spoken languages.	2. A fluent translator is essential because Vietnamese do not always reveal when they do not understand instructions and it is essential that follow-up questions can be asked. Communication cards convey interest in communicating and provide a means of eliciting basic information. Printed instructions reinforce information that was given verbally and may answer unasked questions.
3. Speak quietly, and use the same interpreter whenever possible.	3. This protects the privacy and modesty of the patient. A natural response when people do not understand is to raise the voice; this does not facilitate understanding but may convey impatience or anger.

Nursing Care Plan 8–3 *Continued*

Language Barrier During Pregnancy

4. Consider nonverbal factors when communicating.
   a. Speak slowly and softly; smile.
   b. Keep an open posture. Avoid crossing the arms over the chest or turning away from the family.
   c. Assess the client's response to light touch on the arm, and either use or avoid touch, depending on her response.
   d. Attend carefully to what the family says by nodding, leaning forward, or encouraging continued talk with frequent "uh huhs."
   e. Avoid foot shuffling or fidgeting.
   f. Do not expect prolonged eye contact.

4. Even subtle body language can indicate interest and empathy or impatience, annoyance, or a desire to escape. Touch and eye contact are sensitive cultural variables, and nurses must be aware that they are not always welcomed.

Evaluation:
Continued regular prenatal care and compliance with recommended health care indicate progress in communication. Continued attempts of the family to share specific concerns indicate a feeling of support from the staff.

Additional Nursing Diagnoses to Consider:
Knowledge Deficit
Noncompliance
High Risk for Altered Health Maintenance

- As the fetus becomes real, usually in the second trimester, maternal focus shifts from self to the fetus and the woman turns inward to concentrate on the processes going on in her body.
- Changes in the maternal body during pregnancy may result in a negative body image that affects sexual responses. This may be especially troubling if the couple does not discuss emotions and concerns related to the changes in sexuality.
- It takes time for a woman to make the transition to the role of mother, and the process involves mimicking the behavior of other mothers, fantasizing about the baby, grieving for the loss of previous roles, and developing a sense of self as mother.
- To complete the maternal tasks of pregnancy, the woman must take steps to seek safe passage for herself and the infant, gain acceptance of significant persons, and form an interconnection and attachment to the unknown child.
- Paternal responses change throughout pregnancy and depend on the ability to perceive the fetus as real, to gain recognition for the role of parent, and to create a role as involved father
- The most powerful reality boosters for the expectant father during pregnancy are hearing the fetal heart beat, feeling the fetus move, and viewing the infant on a sonogram.
- In primitive cultures, couvade refers to pregnancy-related rituals performed by the man; in modern society, it often refers to a cluster of pregnancy-related signs and symptoms experienced by the man.
- The response of grandparents to the announcement of pregnancy depends on their age, number and ages of other grandchildren, and their perception of the role of grandparents.
- The response of siblings to pregnancy depends on their ages and developmental levels. Toddlers may feel displaced in their parents' affection unless measures are taken to reassure them.
- It is more difficult for multiparas to complete the developmental tasks of pregnancy because they have less time, experience more fatigue, and must negotiate a new relationship with the older child or children.
- Socioeconomic status is a major factor in determining health practices during pregnancy. Poor families have competing priorities for food and shelter and seek prenatal care late in pregnancy.
- Cultural differences can create major conflicts be-

tween expectant families and health care workers. Language, time orientation, dietary practices, and health beliefs are the areas where conflicts are most likely to occur.

References and Readings

American Nurses Association (1987). *Access to prenatal care: Key to preventing low birth weight* (p. 52). Report of Consensus Conference. Kansas City, Kansas.

Andrews, M.M. (1989). Culture and nutrition. In J.S. Boyle & M.M. Andrews (Eds.), *Transcultural concepts in nursing care* (pp. 333–355). Glenview, Ill.: Scott, Foresman/Little, Brown, College Division.

Bothamley, J. (1990). Are fathers getting a fair deal? *Nursing Times*, 86(36), 68–69.

Broude, G.J. (1988). Rethinking the couvade: Cross-cultural evidence. *American Anthropologist*, 90(6), 902–911.

Cherry, B., & Giger, J.N. (1991). Black Americans. In J.N. Giger & R.E. Davidhizar (Eds.), *Transcultural nursing* (pp. 147–182). St. Louis: Mosby Year Book.

Choi, E.C. (1986). Unique aspects of Korean-American mothers. *Journal of Obstetric, Gynecologic, and Neonatal Nursing*, 15(5), 394–400.

Fortier, J.C., Carson, V.B., Will, S., & Shubkagel, B.L. (1991). Adjustment to a newborn: Sibling preparation makes a difference. *Journal of Obstetric, Gynecologic, and Neonatal Nursing*, 20(1), 73–79.

Gann, P., Nghiem, L., & Warner, S. (1989). Pregnancy characteristics and outcomes of Cambodian refugees. *American Journal of Public Health*, 79(9), 1251–1257.

Greener, D.L. (1989). Transcultural nursing care of the childbearing woman and her family. In JS Boyle & M.M. Andrews (Eds.), *Transcultural concepts in nursing care* (pp. 95–118). Glenview, Ill.: Scott, Foresman/Little, Brown, College Division.

Jordan, P.L. (1990). Laboring for relevance: Expectant and new fatherhood. *Nursing Research*, 39(1), 11–16.

Lederman, R.P. (1984). *Psychosocial adaptation in pregnancy* (p. 36). Englewood Cliffs, N.J.: Prentice-Hall,

Lightfoot-Klein, H. (1989). Prisoners of ritual: *An odyssey into female genital circumcision in Africa*. New York: Haworth Press.

Lightfoot-Klein, H., & Shaw, E. (1990). Special needs of ritually circumcised women patients. *Journal of Obstetric, Gynecologic, and Neonatal Nursing*, 20(2), 102–106.

Manio, E.B., & Hall, R.R. (1987). Asian family traditions and their influence in transcultural health care delivery. *Children's Health Care*, 15(3), 172–177.

Mattson, S., & Lew, L. (1991). Culturally sensitive prenatal care for Southeast Asians. *Journal of Obstetric, Gynecologic, and Neonatal Nursing*, 21(1), 48–54.

May, K. (1982). Three phases in the development of father involvement in pregnancy. *Nursing Research*, 31(6), 377–379.

McAvoy, B.R., & Donaldson, L.J. (1990). *Health care for Asians*. New York: Oxford University Press.

McClanahan, P. (1992). Improving access to and use of prenatal care. *Journal of Obstetric, Gynecologic, and Neonatal Nursing*, 21(4), 280–284.

Mercer, R. (1986). *First-time motherhood*. New York: Springer.

Mercer, R.T. (1990). *Parents at risk*. New York: Springer.

Murray, R.B., & Zenter, J.P. (1989). *Nursing assessment and health promotion strategies through the life span* (4th ed.). Norwalk, Conn.: Appleton & Lange.

Norbeck, J.S., & Anderson, N.J. (1989). Psychosocial predictors of pregnancy outcomes in low-income black, Hispanic, and white women. *Nursing Research*, 38(4), 204–209.

Qureshi, B. (1990). Diet and nutrition. In B.R. McAvoy & L.J. Donaldson (Eds.), *Health care for Asians* (pp. 117–129). New York: Oxford University Press.

Rubin, R. (1984). *Maternal identity and the maternal experience*. New York: Springer.

Rubin, R. (1975). Maternal tasks in pregnancy. *Maternal-Child Nursing Journal*, 4(3), 143–153.

Sue, D.W., & Sue, D. (1990). *Counseling the culturally different: Theory and practice*. New York: John Wiley & Sons.

Tripp-Reimer, T., & Afifi, L.A. (1989). Cross-cultural perspectives on patient teaching. *Nursing Clinics of North America*, 24(3), 613–619.

9

Nutrition for Childbearing

Objectives

1. Explain the importance of adequate nutrition and weight gain during pregnancy.
2. Compare the nutrient needs of the pregnant woman to those for the woman who is not pregnant.
3. Describe common factors that influence a woman's nutritional status and choices.
4. Describe common nutritional risk factors, and explain how they affect nutritional requirements during pregnancy.
5. Compare the nutritional needs of the postpartum woman who is breastfeeding with those of one who is not breastfeeding.
6. Apply nursing process to nutrition during pregnancy, the postpartum period, and lactation.

Definitions

Anorexia nervosa • Refusal to eat because of a distorted body image and a feeling of obesity.

Bulimia • Eating disorder characterized by ingestion of large amounts of food, followed by purging behavior such as induced vomiting or laxative abuse.

Complete protein food • Food containing all the essential amino acids.

Essential amino acids • Amino acids that cannot be synthesized by the body and that must be obtained from foods.

Gynecologic age • The number of years since menarche.

Heme iron • Iron obtained from meat, poultry, or fish sources; the form most usable by the body.

Incomplete protein food • Food that does not contain all the essential amino acids.

Kilocalorie • The amount of heat necessary to raise the temperature of 1 gram of water 1 degree Celsius. Commonly called **calorie.**

Lacto-ovovegetarian • A **vegetarian** whose diet includes milk products and eggs.

Lactose intolerance • Inability to digest most dairy products because of a lack of the enzyme lactase.

Lactovegetarian • A **vegetarian** whose diet includes milk products.

Non-heme iron • Iron obtained from plant sources.

Nutrient density • The degree to which a food contains protein, vitamins, and minerals per 1000 calories.

Ovovegetarian • A **vegetarian** whose diet includes eggs.

Pica • Ingestion of a non-food substance, such as laundry starch, dirt, or ice.

Recommended Dietary Allowances (RDA) • Levels of nutrient intake considered to meet the needs of healthy individuals.

Vegan • A complete **vegetarian** who does not eat any animal products.

Vegetarian • An individual whose diet consists wholly or mostly of plant foods and who avoids animal food sources.

At no other point in a woman's life is nutrition as important as it is during pregnancy and lactation. At this time, her food intake must nourish not only her own body but also that of her baby. There can be longstanding effects on both the infant and the mother if nutrition is deficient. Nutrition may affect the size of the fetus and whether or not it has adequate stores of nutrients after birth. If the expectant mother fails to consume sufficient nutrients, her own stores may be depleted to meet the needs of the fetus, who may be deprived of essential nutrients as well.

Because the nurse may have ongoing contact with women during office or clinic visits throughout the childbearing period, education about nutritional needs can be offered on a continuing basis. Nurses can begin nutrition counseling even before conception for the woman who is considering becoming pregnant. This increases the chances that she will understand and practice good nutrition during pregnancy and may increase her ability to meet the nutritional needs of her entire family. Therefore, nutritional education is an essential part of nursing care.

Nutritional care is accomplished by a team of health care workers. Although the nurse can do much of the counseling necessary for normal pregnancy, the registered dietician counsels the woman who has complex nutritional problems.

Weight Gain During Pregnancy

Weight gain during pregnancy, especially after the first trimester, is an important determinant of fetal growth. Low birth weight due to growth retardation in the fetus, increased risk of fetal and newborn mortality, and possible long-term neurobehavioral effects in the infant are associated with insufficient weight gain during pregnancy.

Excessive weight gain is also a problem. It is associated with large-for-gestational-age infants and may lead to prolonged labor, difficulty or failure of the infant to fit through the birth canal, birth trauma, and operative delivery. The amount of weight gained is important in itself, but even more important is the nutrient intake that makes up the gain. Weight gain from food lacking in essential nutrients will not be as beneficial as gain from a balanced diet.

Recommendations for Total Weight Gain

Recommendations for weight gain during pregnancy have changed considerably over the years. In the late nineteenth century, rickets, a disease of the bones from calcium and vitamin D deficiency, caused some women to have small, distorted pelves. Restricted weight gain kept the fetus small so that it could be delivered more easily. Beginning in the 1920s, weight gain was limited because of the view that large gains caused pregnancy-induced hypertension, a belief now known to be inaccurate. Recommendations for weight gain gradually increased from approximately 15 pounds to 20–25 pounds during the 1970s.

The recommended weight gain during pregnancy is now 25 to 35 pounds (11.5 to 16 kg) for the woman who begins pregnancy at normal weight for her height. This amount is believed to reduce intrauterine growth retardation caused by inadequate maternal and therefore fetal nutrition. A range is given to provide for individual differences because there is no precise weight gain appropriate for every woman. The range provides a target, while allowing for variations in individual needs.

Suggested gains vary according to the woman's weight before pregnancy, as shown in Table 9–1. Women who are 10 per cent below normal weight for their height should gain more during pregnancy to bring their weight up to normal, in addition to meeting the needs of pregnancy. For overweight women (20 per cent above normal weight for height), the gain can be somewhat less. In the past, obese

Table 9–1. RECOMMENDED WEIGHT GAIN DURING PREGNANCY

Weight Before Pregnancy	Total Gain	Total Gain (First Trimester)	Weekly Gain (Second and Third Trimesters)
Normal weight	25–35 lb (11.5–16 kg)	3.5 lb (1.6 kg)	0.97 lb (0.44 kg)
Underweight (10% below normal for height)	28–40 lb (12.5–18 kg)	5 lb (2.3 kg)	1.07 lb (0.49 kg)
Overweight (20% over normal for height)	15–25 lb (7–11.5 kg)	2 lb (0.9 kg)	0.67 lb (0.3 kg)
Twin pregnancies	35–45 lb (16–20.5 kg)	3.5 lb (1.6 kg)	1.5 lb (0.75 kg)

Based on data from *Nutrition during pregnancy, Part I: Weight gain.* © 1990 by the National Academy of Sciences. Published by National Academy Press, Washington, D.C.

women, more than 35 per cent over their normal weight, were told to gain little or even to lose weight during pregnancy. However, it is now thought that a gain of at least 15 pounds, which is equivalent to the weight of the products of conception, should be encouraged so that the fetus can receive sufficient nutrients.

Other variations include the woman who is pregnant with more than one fetus; she is encouraged to gain more weight because fetal needs are increased and low birth weight is a persistent problem with multifetal pregnancies. Women who are shorter than 62 inches (157 cm) tall may not need to gain as much as taller women and are advised to gain only to the lower limits of the recommended range. Young adolescents, who have not completed their own growth, may need to gain to the upper end of the range, or more. This allows nutrients for their own growth during the pregnancy and provides for the needs of the fetus.

Pattern of Weight Gain

The pattern of weight gain is as important as the total increase. Early and adequate prenatal care allows assessment of adequacy of gain on a week-to-week basis throughout pregnancy. The general recommendation is for an increment of about 3.5 pounds (1.6 kg) during the first trimester, when the mother may be nauseated and the fetus needs fewer nutrients for growth. During the rest of the pregnancy, the expected weight gain is just under a pound (0.44 kg) a week.

Although slight variations from the recommended weight gain have little significance, possible reasons for larger differences should be examined carefully. For women of normal weight, a monthly gain of less than 2 pounds (1 kg) should lead to a discussion of diet and possible problems in food intake. A gain of more than 6.5 pounds (3 kg) per month may signify a serious problem such as pregnancy-induced hypertension (see Chapter 24). However, errors in calculation of gestation may also cause a pattern of weight gain different from expected.

✔Check Your Reading

1. How does weight gain in the mother relate to the birth weight of the infant?
2. How much weight should the average woman gain during pregnancy? What factors might change this?
3. What pattern of weight gain is recommended for the average woman?

Maternal and Fetal Distribution

Women often wonder why they should gain so much weight when the fetus weighs only 7 to 8 pounds. Explaining the distribution of weight helps them understand this (Fig. 9–1). The nurse should also explain the dangers of poor weight gain by the mother.

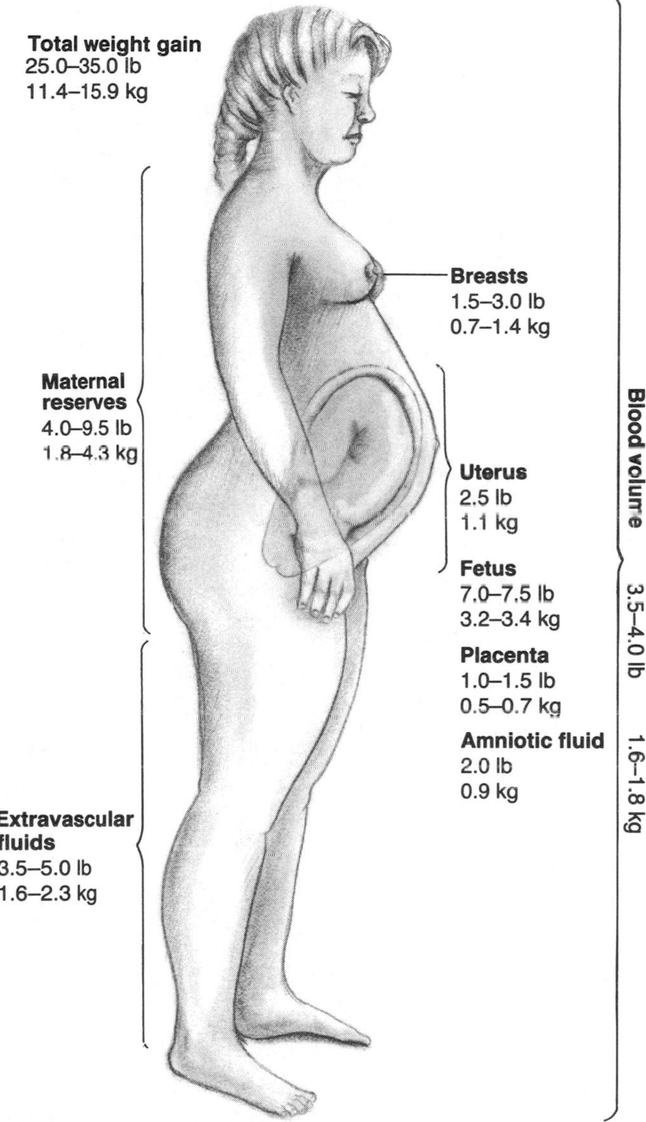

Figure 9-1

Distribution of weight gain in pregnancy. The figures represent a general distribution, as there is a great deal of variation between women. The area with the greatest fluctuation is the amount of weight increase attributed to extravascular fluids (edema) and maternal reserves or fat.

Table 9–2. EXAMPLES OF FOOD AMOUNTS NEEDED DAILY TO MEET NUTRIENT NEEDS OF PREGNANCY

Adult Female RDA*	Pregnancy RDA	Extra Amounts Needed	Total Amount Needed
		Protein	
Age 11–14: 46 g Age 15–18: 44 g Age 19–24: 46 g Age 25–50: 50 g	60 g	2 oz meat, fish, poultry or 2 c milk or 2 oz cheddar cheese or ½ c cottage cheese or 1 c rice + 1 c beans or 1 block (4 oz) tofu	6 oz meat, fish, poultry + 1 oz hard cheese + 1 c noodles + ½ c peas + 1 slice bread
		Calcium	
Age <25: 1200 mg Age >25: 800 mg	1200 mg	1⅓ c milk or 1 c yogurt, or 2 oz hard cheese or 3 oz salmon with bones + 1 c peanuts + 1 c broccoli or 1 oz cheese and 5 corn tortillas or 2 pieces tofu (2.5 × 2.75 ×1 inch) + 1 c sunflower seeds	4 c milk or 3 oz sardines with bones + 1 c broccoli + 1 oz cheese + ⅓ c sunflower seeds or 1 block tofu (2.5 × 2.75 × 1 inch) + 1 c almonds + 2 T molasses + 1½ c kale + 1½ c broccoli
		Iron	
15 mg	30 mg	3 oz red meat + 2 eggs + 1 c lima beans + ½ c bran flakes with raisins + ½ c cooked spinach + 2 slices bread	Iron supplements usually needed to meet recommended amounts
		Vitamin A	
800 RE (retinol equivalents) 1 RE = 3.33 IU	800 RE	No increase	⅔ c broccoli or ⅓ raw carrot or 2 peaches or ½ c raw spinach or ¼ baked sweet potato or 1⅓ c tomato juice or 2 eggs and 4 c milk (any type)
		Thiamin	
1.1 mg	1.5 mg	1 c bran flakes or 1 c peanuts or 2 T sunflower seeds or 3 oz liver or pork or 1 c kidney beans and 1 c rice or barley or macaroni	1 c wheat flakes and 3 oz pork and ¼ c sunflower seeds or 1 c bran flakes and 1 c rice and 1 c black-eye peas and 1 c peanuts
		Riboflavin	
1.3 mg	1.6 mg	¾ c milk or yogurt or cottage cheese or enriched cereal or 2 eggs or 5 oz poultry or meat or 1 c broccoli or 1 c spinach and ½ c macaroni	4 c milk and 1 oz cheese or 6 oz meat or poultry and 1 c cottage cheese and 1 c enriched cereal and ½ c spinach or 1 c macaroni and 1 c sunflower seeds and 1 c broccoli and 1 c enriched cereal and 1 c peanuts
		Niacin	
15 mg	17 mg	1 T peanut butter or 3 slices bread or 1½ oz meat Also made by body from tryptophan	3 oz meat and 3 oz white poultry or ⅔ c peanuts or 1 c enriched cereal and 1 c noodles and 1 c navy beans and 1 c sunflower seeds
		Vitamin C	
60 mg	70 mg	⅓ c cabbage or ⅓ c lima beans or 1 c looseleaf lettuce	⅔ c orange juice or 1¾ c tomato juice or 1 orange or 1 c strawberries

Data from Mahan, L. K., & Arlin, M. (1992). *Krause's food, nutrition, and diet therapy* (8th ed.) Philadelphia: W. B. Saunders Co.

* Unless otherwise specified, values are for adult females aged 19–24 years.

Factors That Influence Weight Gain

Factors that may have a positive influence on weight gain include the expectant mother's understanding of the importance of her diet for fetal growth. This is an area in which the nurse may have great influence. Discussing the reasons why maternal intake is important for fetal growth and storage of nutrients after birth often motivates women to improve their nutrition. Knowledge of factors that may have a negative influence on nutrient intake and weight gain helps the nurse devise plans for improving nutrition.

Women at risk for inadequate weight gain include those who are young, unmarried, in the low-income group, poorly educated, or of short stature. The causes of inadequate weight gain may include poverty, lack of education, insufficient prenatal care, poor general health, and other factors. African-American, Southeast Asian, and Latino women are more at risk for low weight gains during pregnancy than are Caucasian women. Adequate weight gain is especially important for African-Americans and teenagers, who tend to have smaller infants even when they gain weight in the same amount as Caucasian or older mothers. The reasons for this are not fully understood (Institute of Medicine, 1990). Multiparas are at higher risk for low weight gain than women in their first pregnancy. Smoking or substance abuse may interfere with food intake and weight gain.

Women who experience large weight gains may give birth to large infants. This increases risk to both mother and infant for birth complications such as injuries, need for forceps or cesarean delivery, and lacerations of the birth canal. These women are also likely to retain more weight following pregnancy than women who gain within the recommended range.

Infants born of a multifetal pregnancy are often born before term and tend to weigh less than infants born of single pregnancies. Therefore, a higher weight gain in the mother is suggested in hopes of promoting fetal weight gain.

Nutritional Requirements During Pregnancy

Nutrient needs during pregnancy increase to meet the demands of the mother and fetus. The amount of increase for each nutrient varies. In most cases, the increases are not large and are relatively easy to obtain through the diet. Table 9–2 gives examples of foods that meet the increases recommended for some of the major nutrients.

Recommended Dietary Allowances

Studies have determined the amounts of specific nutrients necessary in the diet to meet the needs of people at different ages and during pregnancy and lactation. In the United States, these recommended dietary allowances (RDAs) are determined by the Food and Nutrition Board of the National Research Council. The RDA refers to the intake of major nutrients necessary for healthy individuals to meet daily nutrient needs. Except for calories, the recommendations are about 30 per cent higher than amounts essential to maintain health. This provides a safety margin to allow for individual differences and the fact that most people do not meet the need for every nutrient every day.

Tables of recommendations are based on a "reference individual," a hypothetical person used to calculate nutrient needs based on age, sex, and size. The reference individual is of median size when compared with others in the United States of the same age and sex. For example, the reference woman from age 19 to 24 years is 65 inches (164 cm) tall and weighs 128 pounds (58 kg), whereas the woman between the ages of 25 and 50 years is slightly smaller at 64 inches (163 cm) and 138 pounds (63 kg). Actual needs of individuals (particularly for calories and protein) may vary according to body size, previous nutritional status, and usual activity level. Table 9–3 shows the 1989 RDAs.

Recommendations are revised when new information becomes available. Some of the differences between the 1979 and 1989 versions reflect a different method of calculating requirements rather than actual changes in nutrient needs. Other differences have resulted from research showing that some nutrients are needed in lower amounts than previously thought.

Energy

The energy provided by foods for body processes is calculated in kilocalories, the amount of heat necessary to raise the temperature of 1 g of water 1°C. Kilocalories (used interchangeably with the term calories) are obtained primarily from carbohydrates, which provide 4 kcal in each gram, and fats, which provide 9 kcal in each gram.

CARBOHYDRATES

Carbohydrates may be simple or complex. The most common simple carbohydrate is sucrose, or table sugar, which is a source of energy but does not pro-

Table 9–3. RECOMMENDED DIETARY ALLOWANCES

	Non-pregnant (15–23 Years)	Non-pregnant (19–24 Years)	Non-pregnant (25–50 Years)	Pregnant	Lactating (1st 6 Months)	Lactating (2nd 6 Months)
Protein (g)	44	46	50	60	65	62
Vitamin A (μg RE)*	800	800	800	800	1300	1200
Vitamin D μg†	10	10	5	10	10	10
Vitamin E (mg)‡	8	8	8	10	12	11
Vitamin K (μg)	55	60	65	65	65	65
Vitamin B_6 (mg)	1.5	1.6	1.6	2.2	2.1	2.1
Vitamin B_{12} (μg)	2.0	2.0	2.0	2.2	2.6	2.6
Folate (μg)	180	180	180	400	280	260
Thiamin (mg)	1.1	1.1	1.1	1.5	1.6	1.6
Riboflavin (mg)	1.3	1.3	1.3	1.6	1.8	1.7
Niacin (mg NE)§	15	15	15	17	20	20
Vitamin C (mg)	60	60	60	70	95	90
Iron (mg)	15	15	15	30	15	15
Calcium (mg)	1200	1200	800	1200	1200	1200
Phosphorus (mg)	1200	1200	800	1200	1200	1200
Zinc (mg)	12	12	12	15	19	16
Magnesium (mg)	300	280	280	300	355	340
Iodine (μg)	150	150	150	175	200	200

Reprinted with permission from *Recommended Dietary Allowances,* 10th ed. © 1989 by the National Academy of Sciences. Published by National Academy Press, Washington, D.C.

* Retinol equivalents. 1 retinol equivalent = 1 μg retinol or 6 μg beta-carotene.

† As cholecalciferol. 10 μg cholecalciferol = 400 IU of vitamin D.

‡ Alpha-tocopherol equivalents. 1 mg, *d*-alpha-tocopherol = 1 alpha-TE.

§ 1 NE (niacin equivalent) = 1 mg of niacin or 60 mg of dietary tryptophan.

vide other nutrients. Fruits and vegetables also contain simple sugars. Complex carbohydrates are found in starches, such as cereals. They supply vitamins, minerals, and fiber.

Another type of carbohydrate is fiber, the nondigestible product of plant foods. It is an important source of bulk in the diet. Fiber absorbs water and stimulates peristalsis, causing food to pass more quickly through the intestines. This helps prevent constipation. It also slows gastric emptying, causing a sensation of fullness.

FATS

Fats provide energy as well as fat-soluble vitamins. When caloric intake needs to be decreased, intake of simple carbohydrates and fat should be reduced but not eliminated. If carbohydrate and fat intake provides insufficient calories, the body uses protein to meet energy needs. This decreases protein available for building and repairing tissue.

CALORIES

Approximately 60,000 to 80,000 additional kilocalories are needed during pregnancy (Williams, 1993). These extra calories furnish energy for production and maintenance of the fetus, placenta, added maternal tissues, and increased basal metabolic rate.

The RDA for calories for women of childbearing age is 2200 calories per day. Although there is little need for additional calories during the early weeks of pregnancy, another 300 kcal are necessary each day after that time. A 300-kcal increase can be achieved relatively easily with a variety of foods.

Nutrient density, the degree to which foods contain essential nutrients such as vitamins, minerals, and protein per 1000 kcal, must be considered when adding calories. During pregnancy, the increased need for most nutrients may not be met unless the increased calories are selected carefully. The term "empty calories" is often used for foods that are high in calories but low in other nutrients. Many snack foods not only contain excessive calories and low nutrient value but also are high in fat and sodium. Increased calories should be "spent" on foods that provide the nutrients needed in increased amounts during pregnancy.

Protein

Protein is necessary for metabolism, tissue synthesis, and tissue repair. Adults require 0.8 g/kg of body weight daily. This averages to a daily need of 44 to 50 g for females, depending on age and size. During pregnancy, a protein intake of 60 g is recommended each day for expansion of blood volume and growth of maternal and fetal tissues. This is an increase of 10 to 16 g over non-pregnant needs.

Protein is generally abundant in diets in most industrialized nations, and many women obtain more than the required amount of this nutrient. However, diets that are low in caloric intake may also be low in protein. If calories are low and protein is used to provide energy, fetal growth may be impaired.

The nurse should counsel women at risk for poor protein diets about how to determine protein intake and ways to increase food sources of protein. When a woman needs to increase her protein intake, she should eat more high-protein foods rather than using high-protein powders or drinks, which may increase protein but not other nutrients that are provided by food.

Vitamins

Although most people do not eat as much of every vitamin each day as they should, true deficiency states are uncommon in North America. During pregnancy, dietary intakes of vitamin A, vitamin C, thiamin, riboflavin, niacin, and vitamin B_{12} are usually within recommended range. However, women may not eat enough foods high in vitamins B_6, D, or E and folate to obtain the recommended levels. Food sources of the major vitamins are summarized in Table 9–4.

FAT-SOLUBLE VITAMINS

The fat-soluble vitamins include A, D, E, and K. Because they can be stored in the liver, deficiency states are not as likely to occur as with the water-soluble vitamins (B and C). However, excessive intakes of fat-soluble vitamins can be toxic.

Vitamin A. Vitamin A is important for vision and cell reproduction, growth, and functioning, especially of epithelial tissues, such as skin and mucous membranes. There are two types of vitamin A. Preformed vitamin A, or retinoid, is found in animal sources, such as liver, whole milk, fortified low-fat milk or skim milk, eggs, butter, and fish oils. Provitamin A, or carotenoid, is found in plant sources, such as dark yellow vegetables and fruits and green leafy vegetables.

During pregnancy, vitamin A is important for fetal growth and cellular differentiation. Vitamin A is stored in the liver, and most women have enough accumulated stores to meet the small increases needed by the fetus. Therefore, the RDA for vitamin A does not increase during pregnancy.

Table 9–4. COMMON SOURCES OF VITAMINS AND MINERALS

Vitamin A: Liver, whole or fortified low-fat or skim milk, eggs, butter, fish oils, dark-yellow vegetables and fruits, green leafy vegetables

Vitamin D: Fortified milk, cereals, soy products

Vitamin E: Vegetable oils, whole grains, nuts, green leafy vegetables

Vitamin K: Green leafy vegetables, dairy products, meat, eggs

Vitamin C: Citrus fruit, strawberries, cantaloupe, cabbage, green and red peppers, tomatoes, potatoes, green leafy vegetables

Vitamin B_6: Chicken, fish, liver, pork, eggs, peanuts, whole grains

Vitamin B_{12}: Meats, eggs, dairy products

Thiamin: Whole and enriched grain products, brewers yeast, organ meats, lean pork, legumes, corn, peas, seeds, nuts

Riboflavin: Dairy products, meats, poultry, fish, enriched (but not whole) grain products, green vegetables (broccoli, turnip greens, asparagus, spinach)

Niacin: Meats, legumes, enriched grains; can be made by the body from tryptophan, an amino acid

Folates: Green leafy vegetables, asparagus, green beans, fruits, whole grains, liver, legumes, yeast

Iron: Meats, chicken, fish, liver, legumes, green leafy vegetables, whole or enriched grain products, nuts, blackstrap molasses, tofu, eggs, dried fruits, foods cooked in cast iron pans.

Calcium: Dairy products, canned salmon or sardines with their bones, tofu processed with calcium sulfate, leafy green vegetables (kale, mustard, collard, turnip greens), bok choy, broccoli, legumes, nuts, dried fruits, blackstrap molasses

Zinc: Meat, poultry, fish, eggs, seeds, legumes, yogurt, whole grains

Magnesium: Nuts, seeds, legumes, whole grains, green vegetables, scallops, oysters; occurs in many foods in small amounts

Excessive intake of vitamin A may cause spontaneous abortion and serious defects in the fetus. Women who take the vitamin or synthetic forms, such as isotretinoin (Accutane) for acne, should avoid pregnancy until they are no longer using the drug. Because of the possible hazard, the nurse should inquire about any medications, including vitamins, taken by pregnant women and counsel them about the dangers of vitamin A excess.

Vitamin D. Vitamin D is necessary for metabolism of calcium and prevention of rickets. Inadequate amounts in pregnancy may result in abnormally low levels of calcium, hypoplasia of tooth enamel, and maternal osteomalacia, a softening of the bones. Vitamin D is found in few foods but is synthesized in the skin when exposed to sunlight. In the winter, or in areas where sunlight is limited, skin synthesis is decreased. In the United States, milk is fortified with vitamin D. Soy and cereal products may also be fortified. Strict vegetarians may need to take vitamin D supplements if they are not exposed to the sun and do not eat foods fortified with the vitamin. Excessive amounts of vitamin D can be dangerous, causing hypercalcemia and possible fetal deformities. Therefore, supplementary vitamin D should be taken only by those who do not obtain adequate amounts from the diet or exposure to the sun.

Vitamin E. This vitamin is important for tissue growth and integrity of cells, particularly red blood cell membranes. People deficient in vitamin E have anemia and neuromuscular and reproductive abnormalities. Sources of vitamin E include vegetable oils, whole grains, nuts, and green leafy vegetables. The recommendation for vitamin E is increased 25 per cent, to a total of 10 mg during pregnancy. Although many women do not get enough vitamin E, the increased need can be obtained by diet alone for most women.

Vitamin K. Necessary for clotting, vitamin K is best obtained from green leafy vegetables, with smaller amounts available in dairy products, meat, and eggs. It can also be produced by normal bacterial flora in the small intestine. The RDA for pregnancy is the same as for nonpregnant adults. Normal dietary intake meets the need for vitamin K. Because newborns are temporarily deficient in vitamin K, they receive one dose by injection at birth to prevent hemorrhage (see Chapter 19).

WATER-SOLUBLE VITAMINS

Water-soluble vitamins include vitamin B_6, vitamin B_{12}, folate, thiamin, riboflavin, niacin, and vitamin C. Because these vitamins are easily transferred from food to water in cooking, foods should be steamed, microwaved, or prepared in only small amounts of water, with the remaining water used in other dishes, such as soups. Water-soluble vitamins are not stored in the body as well as fat-soluble vitamins. Therefore, they should be included in the daily diet. Because excess amounts are excreted in the urine, there is less chance of toxicity from excessive amounts.

Vitamin B_6. Important in carbohydrate, fat, and especially amino acid metabolism, vitamin B_6 needs increase during pregnancy along with these nutrients. Vitamin B_6 also plays a role in blood, hormone and immune function. Some of the vitamin is transferred to the fetus late in pregnancy. The usual dietary intake of vitamin B_6 may fall below the RDA of 2.2 mg daily for pregnancy, but a woman can meet her requirement if she eats adequate amounts of chicken, fish, liver, pork, eggs, peanuts, and whole grains. Women at risk for diets low in vitamin B_6, such as vegetarians, should take supplements.

Vitamin B_{12}. Cell division and protein synthesis, both important in pregnancy, require vitamin B_{12}. It is present in meat, fish, eggs, and milk, and most adults take in adequate amounts. Women who take in no foods from animal sources (vegans) may use vitamin B_{12}-fortified soy and cereal products. Long-term vegans may need supplements during pregnancy to ensure adequate intake.

Folate. Folate is important for cell replication and metabolism and for prevention of megaloblastic anemia. During pregnancy, the requirement for folate more than doubles to provide for expanded blood volume and growth of maternal and fetal tissue. Lack of folate may have a role in spontaneous abortion and neural tube defects. It is excreted in the urine in greater amounts during pregnancy, and absorption rate does not change to meet this increased loss.

Folate is present in green leafy vegetables, whole grains, fruit, liver, dried peas and beans, and yeast, but it may be lost in cooking. Eating raw fruits and vegetables ensures better availability. The dietary intake in pregnant women is commonly below the recommended levels, but true deficiency states are rare in the United States. Pregnant women at risk for inadequate diets should take supplemental folate to meet recommended levels.

Thiamin, Riboflavin, and Niacin. These three B vitamins form coenzymes necessary to release energy. Pregnancy increases the requirement for thiamin, riboflavin, and niacin because they are needed to use the greater intake of calories to meet the energy needs of pregnancy. Most adult women more than meet their need for these nutrients. Thiamin is found in whole or enriched grain products, legumes, and organ meats. Riboflavin is in dairy products, lean meats, poultry, fish, enriched grains, and leafy vegetables. Niacin is present in meats, legumes, and enriched grains and can be made by the body from tryptophan, an amino acid.

Vitamin C. Ascorbic acid is important in collagen formation, tissue integrity, healing, immune response, and metabolism. The result of severely inadequate intake is scurvy with red, swollen bleeding gums, petechiae, and joint pain. The 10-mg increase for pregnancy is usually easy to obtain through the diet. Smokers, drug and alcohol abusers, women who have taken oral contraceptives before pregnancy, aspirin users, and those with multifetal pregnancy need supplemental vitamin C to meet increased needs. Sources include citrus fruit, strawberries, cantaloupe, cabbage, green and red peppers, tomatoes, potatoes, and green leafy vegetables. Vitamin C may be destroyed by heat and oxidation on exposure to air, or it may be lost in water used for cooking.

✔ Check Your Reading

4. How many more kilocalories should a woman eat each day during pregnancy?
5. How much protein is recommended during pregnancy?
6. Which vitamins are most likely to be low in the diets of pregnant women?
7. Which vitamins are included in the fat-soluble and water-soluble groups? What is the difference in the way they are stored in the body?

Minerals

Although most minerals are supplied in adequate amounts in normal diets, the intake of iron, calcium, zinc, and magnesium may drop below recommended levels for pregnancy (Institute of Medicine, 1990). Generally, only iron may be supplemented for women during pregnancy. Food sources of the major minerals are summarized in Table 9–4.

IRON

Iron is important in the formation of hemoglobin to carry oxygen throughout the body and helps form some enzymes necessary for metabolism. During pregnancy, added iron is needed for the approximately one third increase in maternal red blood cells and for transfer to the fetus for storage and production of red blood cells. Full-term infants are seldom anemic at birth. However, anemia may develop later if adequate iron to last 4 to 6 months after birth was not stored during fetal life.

Iron is probably the only nutrient that cannot be supplied completely and easily from the diet during pregnancy. Food sources include meat, chicken, fish, liver, legumes, green leafy vegetables, whole or enriched grain products, nuts, blackstrap molasses, tofu (soybean curd), and foods cooked in cast iron pans. Table 9–5 contains a list of common foods and the amount of iron they contain.

Iron is present in many foods, but it takes large amounts of these foods to provide enough iron for pregnancy needs by diet alone. The average American diet contains only about 6 mg of iron for each 1000 kcal of food. Therefore, the non-pregnant woman would have to eat approximately 2500 kcal daily whereas the pregnant woman would need as much as about 5000 kcal to take in enough dietary iron to meet her needs (Worthington-Roberts, 1993). In addition, some women restrict their intake of meats and grains in an effort to cut down on fat and calories. Thus, many adult women do not meet their daily non-pregnancy requirement for iron and begin pregnancy already anemic or with low iron stores.

Table 9–5. FOODS HIGH IN IRON CONTENT

Food and Amount	Average Amounts Supplied Iron (mg)
Meats (3 oz)	
Liver	5.3
Red meats (avg)	2.5
Poultry	
Chicken	0.9
Turkey	1.4
Legumes (1 c)	
Kidney beans	4.6
Lentils	4.2
Peanuts	2.8
Sunflower seeds	15.2
Chickpeas (garbanzo beans)	4.9
Blackeye peas	3.6
Lima beans, baby	3.5
Peas	2.5
Eggs	
Eggs (each)	1.0
Grains (1 c)	
Rice	1.8
Bran flakes	6.8
with raisins	9.0
Oatmeal	1.6
Bread (slice)	0.9
Fruits	
⅓ c raisins	1.0
4 prunes	1.2
½ c dried apricots	3.0
Vegetables (1 cup)	
Asparagus, (frozen)	1.2
Broccoli	1.8
Collards	1.9
Spinach	
Raw	1.5
Cooked (frozen)	2.9
Other	
Tofu (2.5 × 2.75 × 1 inch)	2.3

Data from Mahan, L.K. & Arlin, M. (1992). *Krause's food, nutrition, and diet therapy* (8th ed.) Philadelphia: W. B. Saunders.

The Recommended Daily Allowance for iron during pregnancy is 30 mg daily. While many women do not eat enough iron-containing foods in their daily diet to meet this need and take supplements, iron in foods is often better absorbed. Therefore, the nurse should suggest ways a woman can increase her dietary iron.

Absorption of iron is affected by many other substances. Calcium and phosphorus in milk and tannin in tea decrease iron absorption from plant sources (called non-heme iron) if consumed during the same meal. Coffee binds iron (prevents it from being fully absorbed), but foods cooked in iron pans contain more iron. Foods containing ascorbic acid and meats eaten with other iron-containing foods increase absorption. Iron from meat, fish, and poultry (called heme iron) is more readily absorbed than that from plants and is less affected by other foods.

Physicians and nurse practitioners often prescribe iron supplements of 30 mg daily during pregnancy because of the difficulty of obtaining enough iron in the diet. Supplementation should begin during the second trimester, when the need increases. Since morning sickness is usually finished by this time, the expectant mother tolerates the iron better. Iron taken on an empty stomach is absorbed more completely, and it may be tolerated better if taken at bedtime. Women should not take iron with milk, but taking it with orange juice may increase absorption. Side effects occur more often with higher doses and include nausea, vomiting, heartburn, epigastric pain, constipation, or diarrhea. Women who experience discomfort from side effects when taking iron on an empty stomach may take it 1 to 2 hours after meals more comfortably. (Anemia during pregnancy is discussed on p. 202.)

CALCIUM

Calcium is necessary for bone formation, maintenance of cell membrane permeability, coagulation, and neuromuscular function. It is transferred to the fetus, especially in the last trimester, and is important for mineralization of fetal bones and teeth. Calcium absorption increases during the second trimester. The pregnant woman's diet must provide enough calcium for her own and fetal needs to avoid loss from her bones. Since the total amount of calcium required is only a small part of that stored in the bones, mineralization of her bones is not usually reduced significantly; however in women with poor diets, with more than one fetus, or with closely spaced pregnancies, stores may be depleted. A common myth is that calcium is removed from the teeth during pregnancy, leading to excessive decay. However, calcium in the teeth is stable and is not affected by pregnancy.

Calcium is found in greatest amounts in dairy products. Whole, low-fat, or skim milk all contain the same amounts of calcium and may be used interchangeably to reduce calorie intake. However, women with lactose intolerance (lactase deficiency resulting in gastrointestinal problems when dairy products are consumed) need other sources for calcium. Calcium is also present in legumes, nuts, dried fruits, dark-green leafy vegetables (kale, cabbage, collards, turnip greens), and broccoli. Although spinach contains calcium, it also contains oxalates that decrease calcium availability; thus, it cannot be considered a good source. Canned salmon or sardines with bones also provide calcium. Tofu processed with calcium sulfate and blackstrap molasses are sources for vegans. Caffeine increases the excretion of calcium. Table 9–6 lists foods high in calcium.

In the past, calcium supplements and decreased milk intake were recommended to prevent leg cramps. This was thought to improve the balance of calcium and phosphorus, both occurring in high amounts in milk. However, the effectiveness of this treatment has not been proven. Because milk provides a large number of nutrients, it generally should not be limited during pregnancy (Worthington-Roberts, 1993; Mahan and Arlin, 1992).

Table 9–6. CALCIUM SOURCES APPROXIMATELY EQUIVALENT TO 1 CUP OF MILK*

1 c yogurt
1½ oz hard cheese
2 c low-fat cottage cheese
1¾ c ice cream or ice milk
3 c sherbet
11 eggs
2½ c peanuts
1 c almonds
9 oz sunflower seeds
2 c refried beans
3 pieces (2.5 × 2.75 × 1 inch) tofu (soybean curd)
1¾ c broccoli
1½ c cooked kale
1 c collards
1⅓ c oysters
4 oz salmon with bones
2½ oz sardines with bones
7 corn tortillas
5 tsp blackstrap molasses

Data from Mahan, L.K. & Arlin, M. (1992). *Krause's food, nutrition, and diet therapy* (8th ed.). Philadelphia: W. B. Saunders.

* This list can be used to counsel women who are vegans or lactose-intolerant. Lactose-intolerant women can often tolerate yogurt and cheese without distress. Although the amounts of some foods listed are more than would be likely to be eaten within a day, they serve for comparison.

The 1200-mg daily calcium requirement for pregnancy is a 50 per cent increase over the RDA for the non-pregnant woman over 25 years but the same as that for the woman below age 25. Women who eat few or no dairy products for cultural reasons, because of lactose intolerance, because they avoid animal products, or for other reasons should receive supplements. Women under 25 years with diets low in calcium may need supplements during pregnancy because their bone density is not complete; lack of available calcium may interfere with adequate bone formation in the mother. To ensure absorption of calcium, women should take supplements with meals, separately from when they take iron supplements.

PHOSPHORUS

A 1-to-1 ratio of calcium to phosphorus intake is needed in both the non-pregnant and pregnant state because these minerals work together. Phosphorus combines with calcium for bone formation and is involved in cell metabolism. Phosphorus is present in dairy products and lean meats. It is added to many processed foods, snacks, and carbonated beverages. This may cause an excessive intake of phosphorus in relation to calcium, resulting in binding of calcium in the intestines, which prevents calcium absorption. For this reason, women should avoid "junk" foods with high phosphorus content, or they should eat them in moderation.

ZINC

Zinc is necessary for cell differentiation and reproduction as a part of DNA and RNA synthesis. It is also important for metabolism and maintenance of acid-base balance. Intake of zinc is commonly below the RDA. Sources include meat, poultry, seafood, and eggs. Vegetarians may need to take zinc if they eat no animal products, although nuts, seeds, legumes, wheat germ, and whole grains are also sources. Excessive intake of zinc interferes with metabolism of copper and iron, whereas high doses of iron decrease zinc and copper absorption. When women with anemia require supplementation with more than 60 mg of iron, zinc and copper should also be supplemented.

MAGNESIUM

Magnesium activates enzymes needed for metabolism of energy and protein, and it is important for cell growth and neuromuscular function. The best sources are whole grains, nuts and legumes, and dark-green vegetables. The usual magnesium intake is below the RDA for many pregnant women. When amounts in the diet are low, absorption and retention are increased, which explains why deficiency states do not occur in healthy people eating normal diets. Magnesium supplementation is not considered necessary during pregnancy. Added magnesium may interfere with absorption of iron.

COPPER

Copper constitutes a part of many enzymes that are important in metabolic processes. Because there is less information about copper than some of the other minerals, the RDA has not been set. Instead, estimated safe and adequate daily dietary intakes have been determined until more research is done. When women require high levels of zinc supplementation, they may not absorb copper as well. Therefore, supplementary copper is also given.

IODINE

Iodine is important for thyroid function. Lack of iodine can cause abortion, stillbirth, congenital hypothyroidism, and neurological conditions. Added needs for iodine are met by normal diets, especially because of the widespread use of iodized salt in North America.

SODIUM

Women were once told to restrict sodium in hopes of preventing pregnancy-induced hypertension, but it is now known that excessive amounts do not cause this condition (see Chapter 24). Sodium is necessary in increased amounts during pregnancy because of the expanded fluid volume as well as fetal requirements. However, most women use salt in amounts high enough to make sodium deficiency unlikely. Pregnant women should salt foods to taste but should avoid large amounts of excessively salty foods. Because many women are not aware of the sodium content of various foods, the nurse should teach them what foods to avoid, particularly canned, snack, or other processed foods. Table 9–7 lists common high-sodium foods.

Supplementation

PURPOSE

Food is the best source for nutrients. The Institute of Medicine Subcommittee on Nutritional Status and Weight Gain During Pregnancy (Institute of Medicine, 1990) recommends that women not receive routine vitamin and mineral supplements during pregnancy unless there is reason to believe that the diet is inadequate. The exception is iron, which is unlikely to be obtained in adequate amounts through normal food intake. Expectant mothers who are vegetarians

Table 9–7. HIGH-SODIUM FOODS*

Products that contain the word salt or sodium, such as table salt, onion salt, monosodium glutamate, bicarbonate of soda (baking soda)
Foods that taste salty, including snack foods like popcorn, potato chips, pretzels, crackers
Condiments and relishes, like catsup, horseradish, mustard, soy sauce, bouillon cubes, pickles, green and black olives
Smoked, dried, or processed foods, such as ham, bacon, lunch meats, corned beef
Canned soups, meats, and vegetables unless label states low in sodium
Packaged mixes for sauces, gravies, cakes, and other baked foods

*During pregnancy, foods high in sodium should be consumed in moderation. Expectant mothers should be taught to read labels and to avoid products in which sodium is listed among the first ingredients.

or lactose-intolerant or who have special problems in obtaining nutrients through diet alone may need vitamin mineral supplements to maintain the pregnancy and provide for fetal needs. Assessment of each woman's individualized needs determines whether or not supplementation is appropriate.

DISADVANTAGES AND DANGERS

Routine supplementation with vitamin-mineral capsules or tablets is very common during pregnancy, but this practice has been questioned because of the problems it may cause. Commonly used vitamin-mineral supplements contain from 50 per cent to 150 per cent of the RDA for the vitamins and minerals they contain. In some cases, the interaction between certain nutrients may interfere with their absorption or use. For example, a high calcium intake decreases absorption of iron and zinc. Excessive intake of vitamin C inhibits absorption and metabolism of vitamin B_{12}.

Because many people think of vitamin-mineral supplements as harmless ways to improve their diets, some women take them without consulting a physician or take them in addition to those prescribed. Women should be advised that taking extra vitamins and minerals may cause them to be deficient in others. The physician or nurse-midwife or practitioner can advise them how to increase intake if necessary and still maintain a balance.

The use of supplements, in addition to food, may increase the intake of some nutrients to doses much higher than the recommended amounts. Excessive amounts of some vitamins and minerals may be toxic to the fetus. Vitamin A can cause fetal defects such as hydrocephalus or microcephaly when taken in large amounts. Other nutrients that may cause harm in excessive amounts include vitamins C, B_6, and D and the minerals iron and zinc. The consequences of excessive intake of some nutrients on the fetus are not fully understood at this time, and future research may discover other effects.

Another disadvantage of vitamin-mineral supplements is that some women may develop a false sense of reassurance because they think that their nutrient needs can be met in pill form. Therefore, they may be unconcerned about their food intake. Supplements do not contain protein or calories and and may be lacking many necessary nutrients. Nurses must emphasize that supplements are not food substitutes and do not contain all the nutrients needed during pregnancy. In fact, we may not even know all the nutrients that are important to pregnancy and provided by foods.

Water

Water is important during pregnancy to meet the needs for expanded blood volume (see Chapter 7) and as a part of the fetal and increased maternal tissues. Women should drink approximately eight to ten 8-ounce glasses of fluids each day, with water constituting the majority of fluid intake. Fluids low in nutrients should be limited because they are filling and take the place of other more nutritional foods and drinks. These include carbonated beverages, coffee, tea, and "juice" drinks that contain high amounts of sugar and little real juice.

Food Groups

Most adults are familiar with the four food groups and can keep track of their nutritional intake more easily using them. The United States Department of Agriculture's (USDA) food pyramid is often used as a guide for healthy eating for adults and children, and it can serve as a guide during pregnancy as well. Foods at the base should be eaten in greatest quantity. Foods closer to the top should be eaten in smaller amounts. Table 9–8 lists the servings of each food group needed during pregnancy.

Grain Products. At the base of the pyramid are whole grains and cereal products, upon which a healthy diet is based. They provide complex carbohydrates and fiber as well as vitamins and minerals. Whole grains provide more nutrients than processed grain products. Although foods can be enriched to replace some of the nutrients lost during processing, zinc, vitamin B_6, magnesium, and vitamin E may not be replaced by enrichment. The USDA recommends a minimum of six servings of this group for healthy adults over age 25; the recommendation during pregnancy and lactation is seven.

Fruits and Vegetables. Fruits and vegetables form the next layer of the pyramid and are important sources of vitamins, minerals, and fiber. At least one food that provides vitamin C and one that provides vitamin A are important in selecting from the fruit and vegetable group each day. Healthy adults should have at least five servings of fruits and vegetables. The recommendation is the same for pregnancy and lactation.

Dairy Foods. Dairy foods and protein sources make up the next level of the food pyramid. Dairy products contain approximately the same nutrient values whether they are whole (4 per cent fat), lowfat (2 per cent fat) or nonfat (skim), but the calories and fat are lower in the latter two. Dairy products are especially good sources of calcium. The minimum

Table 9–8. DAILY FOOD PLAN*

Food Group	No. Servings: Non-pregnant Women	No. Servings: Pregnant and Lactating Women
Whole grain products (1 slice bread or ½ c)	<Age 25: 7 >Age 25: 6	7 7
Vegetables and fruits (1 piece or ½ c): Total	5	5
Vitamin C source	1	1
Deep yellow or dark-green leafy	1	1
Other fruits and vegetables	3	3
Dairy products (equivalent to 1 c milk)	<Age 25: 3 >Age 25: 2	3 3
Protein sources (meat, fish, poultry, eggs, or equivalent in vegetable protein)	5–7 (1 oz each)	7 (1 oz each)
Unsaturated fats	3 tsp	3 tsp

* Nurses can use this table as a guide when counseling women about nutrient needs during pregnancy and lactation. Consuming at least the number of servings listed will meet the minimum for nutrients needed during pregnancy. Additional calories may be necessary to meet individual requirements.

recommendation is two servings for adults over age 25 and three servings for pregnant or lactating women.

Protein. Many adults think of meat, poultry, fish, and eggs as the only sources of protein. However, legumes (dried beans and peas), nuts, and soybean products such as tofu are also good sources. Adults should consume at least 5 to 7 ounces; pregnant or lactating women need 7 ounces of protein foods. Three ounces is about the size of a deck of playing cards.

Other Elements. The tip of the pyramid represents fats, oils, and concentrated sugars, which should be used most sparingly. They provide calories for energy but few other nutrients. (Critical to Remember: What Is One Serving? shows serving sizes.)

Critical to Remember

What Is One Serving?

Whole grains
1 slice bread
1 small tortilla
1 ounce (¾ cup) cold cereal
½ cup cooked cereal, rice, or pasta

Fruits and vegetables
1 medium piece
½ cup cooked or chopped raw
1 cup lettuce
¾ cup juice

Dairy products
1 cup milk or yogurt
2 cups cottage cheese
1½ ounces (⅓ cup grated) hard cheese

Protein—1 ounce equals:
¼ cup meat, poultry, fish
1 egg
3 ounces tofu
½ cup legumes
2 tablespoons peanut butter

✔ Check Your Reading

8. Which minerals are likely to be below the recommended amounts in the diets of pregnant women?
9. Why is routine use of vitamin-mineral supplements unnecessary and possibly dangerous?
10. How much fluid should a woman drink each day during pregnancy?
11. How many servings of each food group are recommended during pregnancy?

Factors That Influence Nutrition

Cultural background, age, and knowledge about nutrition influence the food choices women make and their nutritional status. Because these factors are unlikely to change during pregnancy, the nurse must take them into consideration when counseling women about their diets.

Culture

Food is important in all cultures and often has special meaning during illness or childbirth, when certain foods may be favored or discouraged. Before making assumptions about the influence of a woman's culture on her diet, the nurse must assess each client individually. Not all women follow food practices thought to be typical for their culture. Variations among members of a culture may be due to diverse practices found in different areas within their country of origin.

The nurse should also assess how assimilated the woman has become into her present culture. Her age and length of time in the United States may affect her eating habits. Younger members of a culture are more exposed to the prevailing diet practices and may adapt more rapidly than older relatives. Some women usually eat a diet that is different from the traditional diet of their culture but follow some aspects of their own cultural dietary practices during pregnancy to "be sure" that they do not harm the fetus.

Many cultures are characterized by the belief that foods, conditions, and medicines are "hot" or "cold" and that the balance between the two must be maintained to preserve health. In Asian cultures, this is referred to as "yin" (cold) and "yang" (hot) and may influence what the mother eats during pregnancy and the postpartum period. Table 9–9 lists common hot and cold foods.

Nurses often use pamphlets as a part of nutritional teaching and may be able to obtain them in various languages.

The nurse should be certain the woman can read her own language before giving her written materials. People who cannot read may not readily admit it. In addition, the material may be written in language too complicated for the client with little education to understand.

Having a translator discuss the material with the woman helps to discover whether she can read and also helps with other teaching.

There is enormous variety in cultural preferences for foods. For example, some African-Americans may follow a diet that is similar to that of people living in the southeastern United States, with foods such as okra, mustard greens, and hominy or grits. However, the diet of other African-Americans may depend more on the geographical area in which they live. Many African-Americans eat a diet deficient in iron and fresh fruits and vegetables, especially if they have low incomes. Lactose intolerance is common, resulting in lack of calcium if other sources are not present in the diet.

Jewish women may follow no dietary restrictions, or they may adhere to a strictly kosher diet in which meat is processed to remove all blood, only animals with cloven hooves can be eaten, and milk and meat are never consumed in the same meal.

Table 9–9. COMMON HOT AND COLD FOODS: SOUTHEAST ASIAN AND LATINO DIETS*

Southeast Asian	
"Hot" (Yang) Foods	***"Cold" (Yin) Foods***
Peppers, onions	Most fruits and juices
Meat and poultry	Flour
Fish and fish sauce	Cold fluids
Broth	Sour foods
Eggs	
Spices, sweets	
Latino	
"Hot" Foods	***"Cold" Foods***
Potatoes, peas, onions, chili peppers	Most fruits and vegetables
Cheese, evaporated milk	Milk
Chicken, lamb	Fish
Flour tortillas	Corn tortillas
Chickpeas and kidney beans	Green and red beans

Although there are variations within cultural groups, foods considered "hot" are used for conditions thought to be "cold" and vice versa. This influences what clients are willing to eat during childbirth or illness, and these customs must be respected as part of nursing care.

The diet of Native American (or American Indian) women may be low in calcium because lactose intolerance is common. Iron intake may be deficient because of a low intake of meats. Fat intake is often high, whereas fruits and vegetables are lacking. Poor Native American women who live on a reservation may receive foods distributed by the government, such as white flour, cornmeal, white rice, and processed meats. Potatoes and pinto beans may be an important part of the diet (Teufel and Dufour, 1991).

Food preferences for two cultures, Southeast Asian and Latino, are discussed in detail as examples of the influence of culture on diet. Immigrants and refugees from Southeast Asia are the newest large group of people to come into the United States. They are likely to continue diets similar to those from their homelands. Latinos are a large minority group in the United States, making up about 11 per cent of the population (U.S. Department of Commerce, 1992). Nurses throughout the United States are likely to need information about Latino food preferences.

SOUTHEAST ASIAN DIETARY PRACTICES

The term Southeast Asian refers to people from Cambodia, Laos, and Vietnam who came to the United States beginning in the mid-1970s. The majority settled in western states, but smaller numbers found homes throughout the country. Many formed groups with others from their country of origin and maintain many of their dietary customs, opening markets and restaurants to provide foods important to their culture.

Southeast Asian cooking methods include searing fresh vegetables quickly with a small portion of meat, poultry, or fish in a little oil over high heat. Meals cooked in this manner are low in fat and retain vitamins. Most meals are accompanied by rice, which increases the intake of complex carbohydrates. A salty fish sauce called *nuoc mam* and fresh vegetables are part of most meals.

Many Southeast Asians have adapted their dietary habits to more American ways. Increased intake of meats, poultry, eggs, fruit, and bread have added nutrients but also fat to the diet. Coffee, soft drinks, and fast foods have been less favorable influences because they are low in nutrients but high in fat. Their intake of fish, a low-fat source of protein has decreased (Williams, 1989).

Effect of Culture on Diet During Childbearing

In the Southeast Asian culture, pregnancy, especially the third trimester, is considered "hot" and the woman is encouraged to eat "cold" foods to maintain a balance of hot and cold. During pregnancy, more sour foods, fruits, noodles, and sweets are eaten and fish, salty foods, and rice are avoided.

The postpartum period is considered "cold," partly because of the loss of blood, which is "hot." Mothers try to avoid losing more heat, which would have ill effects on their health. They avoid becoming cold physically (and may refuse to shower for fear of exposure to cold). They choose "hot" foods to eat. These include rice with fish sauce, broth, salty meats, fish, and eggs. They refuse cold drinks but will take hot fluids. Tea or even plain hot water is often requested. Families frequently bring in food to the mother while she remains in the hospital because hospital food may not meet her preferences.

The diet of Southeast Asians, especially those with low incomes, may be below recommended levels for energy, calcium, iron, zinc, magnesium, and vitamins B_6 and D but high in sodium (Newman and Norcross, 1991). This may be of special concern during pregnancy. The woman can often increase her intake of needed nutrients without deviating greatly from her usual diet.

Increasing Nutrients with Traditional Foods

Milk products are not part of the traditional Southeast Asian diet, and lactose intolerance is common. However, increasing intake of commonly used dark-green leafy vegetables, such as mustard greens, bok choy, or broccoli, increases levels of calcium, iron, magnesium, and folates. Tofu contains good amounts of calcium and iron. A broth made from pork or chicken bones soaked in vinegar (which removes calcium from the bones) is frequently taken. One tablespoon of the broth contains calcium equal to ¼ cup of milk (Williams, 1989). If no fortified milk is taken, the mother may need vitamin D supplementation. Increasing the intake of meats or poultry elevates levels of vitamin B_6 and zinc.

LATINO DIETARY PRACTICES

Spanish-speaking people, such as Mexican Americans, Puerto Ricans, and Cuban Americans, are often referred to as Latinos or Hispanics. This is a major minority group in the United States and continues to grow. Mexican Americans make up the largest share of the group. Although large numbers live in the southwestern United States and Florida, they are located throughout the country. Like Asians, Latinos follow the theories of "hot" and "cold" foods and conditions. They also consider pregnancy to be "hot" and the postpartum period to be "cold" and adjust the diet accordingly.

Dried beans (especially pinto beans) are a staple of the Mexican American diet and are part of most meals either alone, as refried beans, or mixed with other foods, such as rice. The most common meats are beef and chicken. The major cereal is corn, which is ground and made into a dough called *masa* to make corn tortillas. The corn is treated with lime and is a good source of calcium. Corn or flour tortillas are fried in lard and eaten with most meals. Rice is also an important grain. Although milk is not commonly used except for infants, cheese is a part of many dishes.

Corn, tomatoes, and chili peppers are the most common vegetables used; others include beets, cabbage, chayotes, bell peppers, and string beans. Dark-green and yellow vegetables are seldom used. Oranges, bananas, canned peaches, pumpkin, and avocado are common fruits.

Foods are often hot and spicy and frequently fried. Thus, the diet tends to be high in calories and fat, leading many Mexican Americans to become overweight. The diet may be low in iron, calcium, and vitamins A and D, which should be increased through foods or supplemented during pregnancy (Institute of Medicine, 1990).

The Puerto Rican and Cuban diets are similar to that of the Mexican American, with the addition of tropical fruits and vegetables from the homeland, when available. Viandas, which are starchy fruits and vegetables like plantain, green bananas, sweet potatoes, yams, and breadfruit are common. They may be cooked with codfish and onion. Guava, papaya, mango and eggplant are also used when available.

✔ Check Your Reading

12. When the nurse assesses cultural influences on nutrition during pregnancy, what factors must be considered?
13. Compare the diet of the Southeast Asian woman with that of the Latina woman.

Age

Extremes of age may have an influence on the nutritional needs of pregnancy. The adolescent may not be fully mature and will need nutritional support for her own growth (see nutritional risk factors following). The older woman who is in good health otherwise should have the same nutritional requirements as any other pregnant woman. She may have more knowledge about nutrition though life experiences or may need as much teaching as the younger woman. She is more likely to be financially secure than the very young woman.

Nutritional Knowledge

Some women are very interested in nutrition and methods of ensuring a good dietary intake of nutrients. Books and magazine articles about nutrition are common in the popular press. Even women who have not been especially attentive to their diets before pregnancy often try to increase their knowledge about the relationship between what they eat and the effect on the fetus, once pregnancy is confirmed. Other women may not have a sound basic knowledge about nutrition. Although they know they should "eat well" when they become pregnant, they may have little idea of what that means. They may have many misconceptions based on common food myths that interfere with good nutritional choices. These expectant mothers need more help from nurses in learning about nutrition.

Nutritional Risk Factors

Factors that present risk that the woman will be unable to meet the nutritional needs of pregnancy include poverty, adolescence, vegetarianism, lactose intolerance, nausea and vomiting of pregnancy, anemia, abnormal prepregnancy weight, eating disorders, pica, multiparity, and substance abuse.

Socioeconomic Status

POVERTY

Low-income women tend to have deficient diets because of insufficient financial resources and lack of nutritional education. Carbohydrate foods are often less expensive than meats, dairy products, fruits, and vegetables. Therefore, the diet may be high in calories but lacking in vitamins and minerals. The woman's usual intake should be assessed and a referral made to Aid to Families with Dependent Children or the Special Supplemental Food Program for Women, Infants and Children (WIC) if it appears that her food intake is inadequate because of lack of money. Vitamin and mineral supplementation may be important for her, especially if her diet is likely to be inconsistent.

FOOD SUPPLEMENT PROGRAMS

The WIC program is administered by the USDA to provide nutritional assessment, counseling, and education to poor pregnant or lactating women and their children up to age 5 years. The program is designed to improve the diets of women during pregnancy and lactation in hopes of preventing low-birth-weight infants and the resulting long-term health problems and high cost of treatment. The program also provides foods such as milk, cheese, eggs, iron-fortified cereal, fruit juice, and dried beans to qualified women and their children. Eligibility is based on an income at or below 185 per cent of the federal poverty level or as determined by individual states, but funding problems prevent everyone entitled to benefits from receiving them. Although the program has been in existence since 1974, changing priorities for government funds often put it at risk.

Adolescence

Adolescent pregnancies are generally considered to be associated with higher risk for complications for both the expectant mother and the fetus. Adolescents at greatest risk for problem pregnancies are those who are the youngest in terms of gynecologic age (number of years since menarche). Girls who become pregnant less than 2 years after menstruation begins are not anatomically and physiologically mature, and they require more nutrients to meet their needs than older adolescents. Those with a gynecologic age of 4 years are physically mature and have nutritional demands similar to those of older women (Rees and Worthington-Roberts, 1993). (See also Chapter 23, p. 616.)

The adolescent must consume nutrients adequate to support her own growth and maturation as well as that of the fetus. Adequate weight gain is especially important because teenagers less than 2 years postmenarche tend to have smaller infants even with good weight gains. In determining what is appropriate weight gain for an individual teenager, the nurse considers the weight that would be gained during next 9 months if she were not pregnant. (Growth charts for children and adolescents are found in pediatrics textbooks.) This amount is added to the usual amount for pregnancy. Because growth slows after menarche, the girl of youngest gynecologic age must gain the most weight to meet growth needs. An example of weight gain to allow for the girl's growth needs follows. Just as for the older adult, the underweight teenager should gain an added amount to place her at normal weight for her age and height. The overweight girl must still gain, but 15 to 25 pounds may be adequate for her.

For a 13-year-old girl:

Pre-pregnancy height: 61.75 inches (157 cm)
Pre-pregnancy weight: 101 pounds (46 kg)
Expected weight gain for age over 40 weeks: 6.5 pounds (3 kg)
Weight gain for pregnancy (upper limits suggested for adolescents): 35.0 pounds (16 kg)
Total during pregnancy: 41.5 pounds (19 kg)

NUTRIENT NEEDS

In the past, it was usual to add the RDA for pregnancy to the nutritional requirements for the adolescent. The 1989 RDAs list absolute amounts for each nutrient, based on a woman aged 19 to 24 years. These amounts are adequate for most adolescents, but individualized assessment of gynecologic age, nutritional status, and daily diet may indicate the need for increases in some areas. Energy, protein, and calcium are nutrients that are commonly increased to meet growth needs for the younger teen.

COMMON PROBLEMS

The diets of teenagers, both before and during pregnancy, are often low in vitamin A, vitamin D, vitamin B_6, folic acid, riboflavin, calcium, and iron (Rees and Worthington-Roberts, 1993). Although supplements may be prescribed, the adolescent may not take them regularly. This combination of poor intake and unreliable supplementation may further deplete nutrient stores and general nutrition.

Peer pressure is an important part of the way adolescents respond to the nutritional needs of pregnancy. They are often concerned about their body image. If weight is a major focus for a teenager and her peers, she is more likely to restrict calories to avoid weight gain during pregnancy.

Teenagers tend to skip meals and snack frequently. The meal most frequently missed is breakfast. Because the fetus requires a steady supply of nutrients, the expectant mother's stores may be used. If intake is not sufficient to meet energy needs, the result is use of stored fats.

Because snacks provide as much as a quarter of the caloric intake of the adolescent girl, they should be high in nutrient density (Rees and Worthington-Roberts, 1993). Fast foods from restaurants or snack machines are a significant part of many teenagers' diets. Although occasional consumption of these

Pregnant Adolescents Want To Know

How Can I Eat Fast Foods and Still Maintain a Good Diet?

- Eat cheeseburgers instead of hamburgers to increase calcium as well as protein intake. Add lettuce and tomato for vitamins A and C.
- Avoid dressings on hamburgers because they tend to be high in calories and fat.
- Choose foods that are broiled, roasted, or barbecued to cut down on fat and calories. Examples are barbecued or broiled chicken breast or roast beef.
- Cut down on fried foods (french fries, fried zucchini, onion rings) because they are high in fat and the high heat may destroy some of the vitamins. Breaded foods like chicken nuggets or breaded clams are also high in calories and tend to absorb more of the oil if they are fried.
- Baked potatoes with broccoli, cheese, or meat fillings provide better nutrition than french fries or even baked potatoes with sour cream and butter.
- Pizza is fairly high in calories but provides protein and calcium because of the cheese. Adding vegetables to the topping or adding a salad increases vitamins.
- Salad bars are often available at fast food restaurants and provide vitamins and minerals while avoiding too many calories. Use only a small amount of salad dressing, which is high in fat.
- Milk, a milkshake, or orange juice provides more nutrients than carbonated beverages, which are high in sodium, phosphorus, and calories. Too much sodium may increase swelling of the ankles; too much phosphorus may lead to leg cramps.
- Avoid pickles, olives, and other salty foods. Add only small amounts of salt to foods to prevent or decrease swelling.

foods is not harmful, they are often high in calories, fat, and sodium, yet low in vitamins and fiber. Choosing fast foods that will not make her appear different to her peers, yet will meet her added nutrient needs, is important. (See Pregnant Adolescents Want to Know: How Can I East Fast Foods and Still Maintain a Good Diet?)

TEACHING THE ADOLESCENT

Teaching the adolescent about nutrition can be a challenge for nurses. It is essential to establish an accepting, relaxed atmosphere and show willingness to listen to the teenager's concerns. Her lifestyle, pattern of eating, and food likes and dislikes should be explored first. The nurse must consider these in determining whether changes are necessary in the diet.

The adolescent's home life may affect her nutritional status. She may live at home with a mother who does the cooking, and the whole family may eat together; or, she may eat with the rest of the family only occasionally because she is often away at mealtimes. Some pregnant adolescents are homeless or in unstable situations. The number of other people in the home and whether there is enough food for all alter the dietary intake.

In making suggestions, the nurse should suggest only those changes that are necessary. If an adolescent believes that she must eliminate all her favorite foods, she is likely to rebel. Suggestions should be kept to a minimum, and snacks should be included in the meal plan. Asking for the adolescent's input frequently increases the likelihood that she will follow suggestions. When changes are suggested, the nurse should explain the reasons why they are necessary to the needs of the fetus as well as to the expectant mother. Teenagers, like other pregnant women, often make changes for the sake of their unborn child that they would not consider for themselves alone.

The need to be like her peers is of major importance to the adolescent, especially at this time, when she is going through the changes of pregnancy. With some education about what foods to choose, she can eat fast foods with her friends and still maintain a nourishing diet. Giving her plenty of examples of alternatives from which she can choose should be very helpful. Table 9–10 and Pregnant Adolescents Want to Know provide suggestions for nutritional foods that can be selected from snack dispensers or fast food restaurants that will allow the teenager to feel part of her group.

Table 9–10. NUTRITIONAL CHOICES FROM SNACK MACHINES*

Food	Nutrients Provided
Yogurt, white or chocolate milk	Protein, calcium
Fruit juices or fresh fruits (usually apples or oranges)	Vitamins, fiber
Popcorn (best without butter or salt)	Fiber
Peanuts	Protein
Granola or granola bars	Fiber, protein
Crackers and cheese	Protein, calcium
Crackers and peanut butter	Protein

* Snack machines generally dispense foods that are high in calories, fats, and sodium and low in nutrients needed during pregnancy. The foods listed here, although somewhat high in calories, also provide other worthwhile nutrients.

Vegetarianism

Although the knowledgeable vegetarian may eat a highly nutritional diet, she is at higher risk during pregnancy when her nutrient intake must nourish the fetus as well as herself. If she is new to vegetarian food practices, uninformed about pregnancy needs, or careless with her diet, she could become deficient for a number of nutrients.

Vegetarianism occurs in a variety of forms. Vegans avoid all animal products and may have the most difficulty meeting their nutrient needs. Their diet may be lacking in adequate iodine, calcium, iron, zinc, riboflavin and vitamins D and B_{12} (Poleman and Peckenpaugh, 1991). Vegans must pay particular attention to obtaining these nutrients in food or supplement form. Lactovegetarians, ovovegetarians, and lacto-ovovegetarians will have less difficulty meeting their nutrient needs.

While not true vegetarianism, elimination of red meats from the diet to decrease intake of saturated fats and cholesterol is a growing trend. Women who follow this type of diet usually eat small amounts of chicken, fish, and dairy products. The needs of women who follow any form of vegetarianism are different during pregnancy.

MEETING THE NUTRITIONAL REQUIREMENTS OF PREGNANCY

Energy. All of the vegetarian diets are low in calories and fat and may not meet energy needs of pregnancy. In addition, the diets are high in fiber, causing a feeling of fullness before enough calories are eaten. A pregnant woman can increase caloric intake by eating foods with higher calorie content and by increasing between-meal snacks. If carbohydrate and fat intake are inadequate, proteins may be used for energy, making it unavailable for other purposes.

Protein. Protein intake is a concern in all vegetarian diets. Foods are sources of "complete" protein when they contain all the essential amino acids the body cannot synthesize from other sources. Because the body must have these amino acids, they are an indispensable part of the diet. Animal proteins are complete, but vegetable proteins lack one or more of the essential amino acids. Combining incomplete plant proteins with other plant foods that have complementary amino acids allows intake of all essential amino acids. This requires knowledge of how to mix foods to ensure adequate intake of essential amino acids. Dishes that combine beans with rice or tofu with rice are examples. Table 9–11 lists combinations of foods that provide complete proteins.

Incomplete proteins can also be combined with small amounts of complete protein foods like cheese to provide all amino acids. Therefore, women who include even small amounts of animal products have less difficulty meeting their protein needs.

Calcium. Vegetarians who include milk products in their diet may take in sufficient calcium to meet their pregnancy needs. Vegans obtain calcium from vegetables, but their high-fiber diet may interfere with calcium absorption. Calcium-fortified soy products, such as soy milk or tofu, may meet the requirements, or calcium supplements may be necessary. Vitamin D may also need to be added through supplementing if the woman drinks no milk and has little exposure to sunlight. Soy milks may be enriched with vitamin D.

Iron. Iron in the vegetarian diet may be poorly absorbed because of the lack of heme iron (from meats), which improves absorption. Iron is available in green leafy vegetables, grains, legumes, dried fruits, and molasses. Absorption is enhanced by addition of foods containing vitamin C taken at the same time. Because of the large amount of iron required during pregnancy, iron supplementation is often recommended for women whether or not they are vegetarians.

Zinc. Because the best sources of zinc are meat and fish, vegans may be deficient in this mineral. Other sources include whole grains, fortified cereals, legumes, and nuts and seeds. However, vegans usually need supplements to meet their needs for zinc.

Vitamin B_{12}. Vitamin B_{12} is obtained only from animal products. Vegans may eat foods fortified with the vitamin, such as soy products, or may take supplements. Because vegetarian diets contain large amounts of folates, the development of anemia from inadequate intake of vitamin B_{12} may not be apparent at first. Vitamin B_{12} may be deficient in the milk of lactating vegans, and their infants often must receive supplementation.

Vitamin A. Vitamin A is generally abundant in the vegetarian diet. If a pregnant woman receives a multiple vitamin–mineral supplement, she may ingest excessive amounts of vitamin A, resulting in toxicity with anorexia, irritability, hair loss, and dry skin. Supplementation should be individualized for each woman on the basis of her diet and her needs.

Table 9–12 presents guidelines on vegetarian foods during pregnancy. This scheme is similar to the use of food groups for the non-vegetarian and

Table 9–11. FOOD COMBINATIONS TO PROVIDE COMPLETE PROTEINS

Food	Served with
Grains	
Wheat	Beans
	Soybeans and sesame
	Soybeans and rice
	Soybeans and rice and peanuts
Rice	Soybeans and rice
	Soybeans and peanuts and wheat
	Soybeans and wheat
	Sesame
	Beans (other types)
	Peas
Corn	Beans
Legumes	
Soybeans	Wheat and sesame
	Rice and wheat
	Peanuts and sesame
	Peanuts and wheat and rice
Beans (other types such as garbanzo, navy, peas)	Rice
Nuts and Seeds	
Peanuts	Sunflower seeds
	Soybeans and sesame
	Soybeans and wheat and rice
Brazil nuts	Lima beans
	Sprouts
	Cauliflower
	Broccoli
Sesame	Soybeans and wheat
	Soybeans and peanuts
	Beans
	Rice
	Lima beans
	Sprouts
	Cauliflower
	Broccoli
Sunflower	Peanuts

Based on data from Lappé, F.M. (1982). *Diet for a small planet.* New York: Ballantine.

Table 9–12. FOOD PLAN FOR PREGNANT VEGETARIANS

Food	No. of Servings
Whole and enriched grains	7
Green and yellow vegetables	3–5
Fruits, including vitamin C	3
Dairy products	3
Legumes, soy products, meat substitutes	2–3

Vitamin and mineral supplements may be necessary according to individual needs. Those who do not use dairy products need to increase sources of calcium and may need supplementation.

easy to remember when one is planning the daily diet.

Lactose Intolerance

Intolerance to lactose results from an absence of the small-intestine enzyme lactase, necessary for absorption of the milk sugar lactose. Some degree of lactose intolerance is the norm for most of the world's population after early childhood. This includes many African-American, Latina, Asian, Native American, and Middle Eastern women. Although women with lactose intolerance are often able to tolerate cultured or fermented milk products, such as aged cheese, buttermilk, or yogurt, symptoms may occur after drinking as little as a cup of milk (Mahan and Arlin, 1992). Symptoms include nausea, bloating, flatulence, diarrhea, and intestinal cramping.

Although a woman's ability to tolerate lactose may increase during pregnancy, women who do not eat dairy foods are at risk for consuming less than the recommended levels of calcium unless they get enough calcium from other sources. Most women can tolerate small amounts of milk, and they should increase their intake of cheese, yogurt, and other foods that provide calcium. Low-lactose milk is available, or the enzyme lactase (LactAid) can be added to milk. Table 9–6 lists additional sources of calcium.

Nausea and Vomiting of Pregnancy

Morning sickness usually occurs during the mornings of the first trimester and disappears soon afterward, although some women experience nausea at other times of the day and for longer than 12 weeks. However, most women are able to consume enough food to maintain nutrition sufficiently. They are usually able to manage frequent, small meals better than three large meals. Protein and complex carbohydrates are often tolerated best, but fatty foods increase nausea. Drinking liquids between meals instead of with meals often helps. At bedtime, a protein snack, such as cheese, helps to maintain glucose levels through the night. Eating a carbohydrate food like the traditional dry toast or crackers before getting out of bed in the morning helps to prevent nausea.

Anemia

Anemia is a common concern during pregnancy. Although the normal hemoglobin level for non-pregnant women is 13.5 g/dl, hemoglobin values during the second trimester of pregnancy average 11.6 g/dl as a result of the dilution of the blood caused by plasma increases. This is often called *physiologic anemia* because it is normal (see Chapter 7). During the third trimester, hemoglobin levels generally rise to 12.5 g/dl because of increased absorption of iron from the gastrointestinal tract, even though iron is transferred to the fetus primarily during this time. Fetal iron stores during the third trimester are sufficient to prevent anemia in the newborn for the first 4 to 6 months after birth.

Iron stores may be measured by determining the serum ferritin level of the blood. A ferritin level less than 12 micrograms per liter (μg/L) indicates that anemia is due to iron deficiency. A woman may begin pregnancy with anemia, or it may develop during pregnancy. Pregnant women are considered anemic if the hemoglobin level drops below 10.0 g/dl (Herbert et al, 1993).

The most common cause of anemia is insufficient intake of iron. Anemic women need help in choosing foods high in iron (see Table 9–5). They also need to take iron supplements, since diet alone is unlikely to provide adequate amounts of iron. When the pregnant woman takes an iron supplement, she should take it between meals with a dietary source

Pregnant Women Want To Know
About Vitamins and Minerals

- Take only vitamin and mineral supplements prescribed by a physician, nurse practitioner, or certified nurse-midwife. Over-the-counter supplements may not be formulated to meet your individual needs and could be harmful to you and your baby.
- Take iron on an empty stomach, if possible. If you have nausea, heartburn, constipation, or diarrhea, try taking your iron at different times of the day, such as at bedtime or 1 to 2 hours after meals. To increase absorption, take it with orange juice or another source of vitamin C. Do not take iron with calcium supplements, milk, tea, or coffee because these substances decrease absorption.

of vitamin C to increase absorption. Because high intakes of iron inhibit use of zinc and copper, she may also need to take these minerals.

Abnormal Pre-pregnancy Weight

The need for adjustments in the caloric intake according to pre-pregnancy weight has been described under weight gain. In addition to teaching about dietary changes, the nurse should be alert for other problems associated with abnormal pre-pregnancy weight. The woman who is below normal weight may not have enough money for food or may have an eating disorder. An obese woman may have other health problems, such as hypertension, that may affect the nurse's nutritional counseling plan.

Eating Disorders

Eating disorders include anorexia nervosa (refusal to eat due to a distorted body image and feeling of obesity) and bulimia (overeating, sometimes followed by induced vomiting). If a weight loss of more than 10 to 15 per cent of normal weight for height occurs, these women are amenorrheic (do not have menstrual periods) and therefore do not become pregnant until they are in recovery (Bowles and Williamson, 1990). If they do achieve pregnancy, old fears about obesity may be reactivated by the normal weight gain of pregnancy and they may return to their previous eating patterns. These clients need a great deal of individual counseling to be sure they meet the increased nutrient needs of pregnancy.

Pica

The practice of eating substances not normally thought of as food is called pica. Clay or dirt and solid laundry starch are the most common materials involved, but other items, such as chalk, ice, burnt matches, hair spray, or ashes may be included. Pica is more common in the southeastern United States but is not limited to any one socioeconomic or geographic area. The cause of pica is not known, although cultural values may make pica a common practice. Pica may be related to beliefs about the effect of the material eaten on labor or the baby. For example, some women believe that starch gives the skin a lighter tone or helps the baby to be born more easily.

Iron deficiency was once thought to be a cause of pica but is now considered a result. The major concern is that eating non-food substances decreases the intake of foods and, therefore, essential nutrients. Clay and dirt may decrease absorption of other nutrients, or it may be contaminated with organisms. The nurse should routinely ask about pica because clients will probably not mention the subject themselves.

Multiparity

The number and spacing of pregnancies as well as the presence of more than one fetus influences the nutritional requirements. The woman who has had more than five pregnancies may begin a pregnancy with a nutritional deficit if she did not eat well during or between the previous pregnancies. In addition, she may be too busy meeting the needs of her family to be attentive to her own nutritional needs.

Closely spaced pregnancies may not allow a woman to make up any nutritional deficits originating during a previous pregnancy. Thus, she begins a new pregnancy with inadequate nutrient stores to maintain her own needs and fetal requirements. She will not be able to draw from those stores, as is usual during pregnancy, and must meet nutritional needs from her daily diet and supplementation alone. The development of morning sickness from a new pregnancy soon after delivery may further interfere with an expectant mother's ability to eat an adequate diet.

The woman with a multifetal pregnancy must provide enough nutrients to meet the needs of each fetus without depleting her own stores. This increases her need for nutrients, but no specific amounts are recommended at this time. The expectant mother definitely needs more calories to meet her weight gain and energy needs. Suggested weight gain for women pregnant with twins is 10 to 20 pounds more than for women with single pregnancies. Calcium, iron, and folate may need to be added through supplementation.

Substance Abuse

The deleterious effects of smoking, alcohol, and drug use on the fetus are discussed in Chapter 23. This part of the chapter describes the effects of substance abuse on the nutritional requirements for pregnancy. In addition to direct consequences on nutritional status, substance abuse often goes along with a lifestyle that is unlikely to promote good nutritional habits. The expense of supporting a substance abuse habit may decrease money available for purchase of food. Therefore, nutrition in pregnant women who abuse substances should be explored fully. Usually, more than one substance is involved, and the effects on nutrition of various combinations are not fully understood.

SMOKING

Cigarette smoking increases maternal metabolic rate and decreases appetite, which may result in a lower weight gain. Infant birth weight decreases in spite of adequate diet as the amount of smoking increases. This may be due to the vasoconstriction that occurs with smoking and interferes with blood flow through the placenta. The many chemicals found in cigarette smoke may also retard fetal growth. Smokers may require more vitamins B_{12} and C, folate, iron, zinc, and amino acids because smoking decreases the availability of these nutrients to both the pregnant woman and the fetus. Women may benefit from counseling to help them stop smoking or at least decrease the number of cigarettes smoked during pregnancy. Vitamin and minerals in tablet form may be necessary to meet their needs during pregnancy.

CAFFEINE

The effect of caffeine on nutrition during pregnancy is not fully understood, but it may change calcium, zinc and iron absorption or excretion. Caffeine should be limited during pregnancy until more is known about its results on nutrition and the fetus. Because many women think that caffeine is present only in coffee and tea, the nurse should discuss other sources of caffeine; these include chocolate, some carbonated beverages, and some medications.

ALCOHOL ABUSE

Because of the association between drinking and fetal alcohol syndrome (see Chapter 23, p. 630) a woman should avoid alcohol completely during pregnancy. Alcohol interferes with absorption and use of some nutrients (protein, thiamin, folates, and zinc), impairs metabolism, and often takes the place of food in the woman's diet. Multivitamin-mineral supplementation may be necessary for women who had large intakes of alcohol before pregnancy, even if they stop drinking after conception, because their nutrient stores may be depleted.

DRUG ABUSE

The use of drugs other than those prescribed during pregnancy increases danger to the fetus and may interfere with nutrition. Women should be warned that no medications of any kind (including cold medicines, vitamins, and diet pills) should be taken during pregnancy without consulting the physician or nurse-midwife first. Often drug abusers use a combination of various drugs. The interaction of various drugs with nutrients is not fully understood.

Marijuana increases appetite, but women may not satisfy their hunger with foods of good nutrient quality. Heroin interferes with insulin response to glucose and metabolism. Cocaine acts as an appetite suppressant, interfering with nutrient intake. The vasoconstriction that results from cocaine use decreases nutrient flow to the fetus. Cocaine users tend to drink more alcohol- and caffeine-containing beverages. Amphetamines depress appetite and have been used for this purpose. Women who have used amphetamines for dieting should be warned that the drugs should be discontinued during pregnancy.

Other Risk Factors

Oral contraceptives interfere with use of vitamins A, B_6, and B_{12} and folates, copper, iron, and zinc (Williams, 1989). Long-term use of oral contraceptives may decrease a woman's stores and result in an increased daily need for these nutrients during pregnancy.

Women who follow food fads may be at risk for not meeting the requirements for pregnancy. Each diet must be carefully analyzed to determine its nutrient content. If a woman has followed a severely restricted diet for a long period of time, she may have depleted her stores of some nutrients. The nurse can help these women understand nutrition during pregnancy and what diet changes they need to make to ensure a successful pregnancy.

Women with complications of pregnancy, such as diabetes, heart disease, or pregnancy-induced hypertension, may require dietary alterations (see Chapters 24 and 25). Those with other medical conditions, such as extreme obesity and celiac disease, also need dietary adjustments.

✔ Check Your Reading

14. What nutritional problems should the nurse assess for when caring for women who are poor?
15. What nutritional problems may the adolescent have during pregnancy?
16. What suggestions can the nurse give the vegan about diet during pregnancy?
17. How can lactose-intolerant women increase their intake of calcium?
18. What other conditions present nutritional risk factors during pregnancy?

Nutrition After Birth

Nutritional requirements after birth vary according to whether or not the mother is breastfeeding her infant. If she plans to breastfeed, the nurse teaches her how to adapt her diet to meet the needs of lactation. If she plans to use formula, the nurse can review the woman's nutritional knowledge as she returns to her pre-pregnancy diet.

Nutrition for the Lactating Woman

The lactating mother must continue to nourish both herself and her baby as she did during pregnancy. Therefore, she continues to need a highly nutritional diet. The RDAs for lactating women are significantly increased after birth for calories, protein, magnesium, zinc, and vitamins A and C. They are lower than RDAs for pregnant women for iron and folates and remain the same for calcium. They are higher for almost every nutrient when compared to the needs of the non-pregnant adult woman (see Table 9–3). These recommendations are based on the assumption the mother will produce approximately 750 to 800 ml of breast milk daily. However, the amount of milk produced varies according to the infant's age and whether or not the infant is taking formula or solid foods in addition to breast milk.

The lactating mother is most likely to consume calcium, zinc, magnesium, vitamin B_6, and folate in amounts below the RDAs for nursing women (Institute of Medicine, 1991). A woman is able to produce milk that is adequate for her infant for at least the first 4 to 6 months even when her own diet is less than optimal. However, this depletes her own nutrient stores.

ENERGY

Approximately 640 kcal/day are required over non-pregnancy needs to produce milk during the first 6 months of lactation. The RDA during lactation is for 500 kcal each day over normal needs for women according to age, weight, and height. For the average adult woman, this represents a total caloric intake of 2700 calories each day. The remainder of the calories needed to produce breast milk are drawn from maternal stores, aiding in weight loss over a period of time. Women who were underweight before pregnancy and/or had inadequate weight gain during pregnancy need more calories. The recommendation for them is 650 calories each day, depending on their overall nutritional status.

PROTEIN

The RDA for protein during lactation is 65 g each day during the first 6 months and slightly less during the second 6 months. This is 5 g above that needed during pregnancy and 15 to 21 g above that required by non-pregnant women, depending on age. This small increase is easily met. A small (5-ounce) glass of milk supplies the amount of protein needed in addition to that required during pregnancy and provides calcium as well.

VITAMINS AND MINERALS

Lactating women who take in at least 1800 calories (which is well below the energy intake recommended) will probably consume adequate amounts of other essential nutrients to meet the infant's and her own needs. Although the quality of the milk is not affected by the mother's intake of most minerals, the vitamin content may be decreased if her diet is consistently low in vitamins. Nutrient levels in the milk may remain constant because some nutrients, such as calcium and folates, are drawn from the mother's stores if her intake is poor. Routine vitamin-mineral supplements are not necessary unless there is concern that the diet is lacking.

SPECIFIC CONCERNS

Some women are unlikely to regularly consume all the nutrients they require, and they need special counseling. This group includes women who are dieting, adolescents, complete vegetarians, women who avoid dairy products, or those who eat an inadequate diet for other reasons. Women who cannot obtain adequate nutrition from foods will need vitamin-mineral supplements.

Women Who Are Dieting

Women who are concerned about losing weight after pregnancy need special consideration. After the initial losses in the first month, the average weight loss for the lactating woman is approximately a pound or two each month. This gradual decrease in weight occurs because maternal fat is used to meet a portion of the energy needs of lactation. Gradual weight loss is preferable and should be accomplished by a combination of moderate exercise and a diet high in nutrients with at least 1800 kcal/day.

Dieting should be postponed for a minimum of 3 weeks after birth to allow the mother to recover fully from childbirth. Although moderate dieting does not affect the quantity of the milk, the mother should evaluate the infant's apparent satisfaction with feedings. She should not use liquid diet drinks or diets that severely restrict any nutrient because she will not consume adequate nutrients to meet her needs. Nursing mothers should avoid appetite suppressants, which may pass into the milk and may harm the infant. Weight loss of more than 4.5 pounds a month or intakes below 1500 kcal/day are likely to interfere with milk production and the mother's nutrient stores (Institute of Medicine, 1991).

Adolescents

The problems of the adolescent diet continue to be of concern during lactation. The adolescent may be deficient in the same nutrients listed for other mothers during lactation, and she may also be lacking in iron. If she is poor, she may have an inadequate vitamin A intake because of low intake of fruits and vegetables.

Vegetarians

Vegetarians who eat no animal products may need a supplement to ensure adequate intake of vitamin B_{12}, which is found primarily in animal foods. The milk of the vegan mother may contain inadequate vitamin B_{12}, and her infant will need supplementation. Vegans can meet their need for other nutrients during lactation by diet alone with careful planning. Those who are not knowledgeable about nutrition need supplementation.

Women Who Avoid Dairy Products

The recommendation for calcium remains the same for pregnancy and lactation, and the calcium content of milk is not affected by maternal intake. However, prolonged lactation with inadequate calcium intake may cause removal of calcium from the mother's bones. Women who do not eat dairy products should obtain calcium from other sources (see Table 9–6) or take a calcium supplement. Unless they consume foods fortified with vitamin D or have exposure to sunlight, they may also require supplementation with vitamin D because it is necessary for calcium absorption.

Women with Inadequate Diets

Women who have cultural or other food prohibitions may need help choosing a diet adequate for lactation. Those with inadequate income may need referral to agencies such as WIC. If the mother must take medications that interfere with absorption of certain nutrients, her diet should be high in foods containing those nutrients.

Alcohol

Alcohol intake during lactation is another concern. Although it was once thought that the relaxing effect of alcohol would be helpful to the nursing mother, the deleterious effects of alcohol are too important to consider this suggestion appropriate today. An occasional single glass of an alcoholic beverage may not be harmful, but larger amounts may interfere with the milk-ejection reflex. Mothers who are alcoholics generally do not breastfeed their infants.

Caffeine

Foods high in caffeine should also be limited. The mother should restrict her caffeine intake to two cups of coffee or equivalent each day. Caffeine in excessive amounts can make the infant irritable and may decrease the iron content of the milk.

Fluids

Nursing mothers should drink fluids sufficient to relieve thirst, which often increases in the early breastfeeding period. Eight to ten glasses of fluid, other than those containing caffeine, are adequate. There is no need to drink larger quantities of fluids, as was once recommended.

Breastfeeding Mothers Want To Know

How Can I Tell Which Foods Are Affecting My Baby?

- Keep a list of any new foods you eat (those different from your usual diet).
- Observe for signs that the baby may be reacting to something you ate. These include excessive irritability, crying as if in pain, passing gas, diarrhea, or rash. Remember, these happen for other reasons besides a reaction to your diet, so consider other causes as well.
- When your baby has a fussy period, note whether you ate anything new during the previous 8 to 12 hours.
- Note the baby's reaction after you have eaten any of the foods that sometimes cause problems for infants. These include foods in the cabbage family, foods that are highly allergenic (wheat, eggs, cow's milk) or acidic (orange juice), spicy foods, nuts, and chocolate.
- If you think there may be a connection between something you ate and distress in your baby, do not eat that food again for several days to a week. Then eat a small amount of the food again. If the baby seems to be affected, eliminate that food from your diet.
- Eat all foods in moderation. Avoid large amounts of any food. Babies often tolerate small amounts of any food in the mother's diet but react to large amounts.

FOODS TO AVOID

Lactating mothers are often concerned about whether they should avoid certain foods that might have an adverse effect on the infant. Except for foods to which the mother is allergic, there are no foods that must be restricted in every case. Most mothers find that there are few foods that affect the infant and that fussiness is related to other factors. (See Breastfeeding Mothers Want to Know: How Can I Tell Which Foods Are Affecting My Baby?)

Nutrition for the Non-lactating Mother

The postpartum woman who is not breastfeeding can return to her pre-pregnancy diet, provided that it meets the RDA for the adult woman. She should plan her diet so that it contains enough protein and vitamin C foods to promote healing. If the mother was taking vitamin-mineral supplements, many nurse practitioners and obstetricians suggest that she continue to take them until her supply is finished. This ensures adequate intake during the early weeks, when involution occurs, and helps renew nutrient stores.

The nurse should assess the mother's understanding of the number of servings she needs from each food group. A review of important nutrient sources for calcium and iron may be relevant. If a woman was anemic during pregnancy, she should continue to take an iron supplement until hemoglobin levels return to normal.

When her baby is born, a mother can expect to lose about 12 pounds immediately. She will lose approximately another 8 pounds during the first 6 weeks and probably all but about 2 pounds by the end of the first year if she follows a well-balanced diet. She should take in 300 kcal/day less than she did during pregnancy to avoid retaining weight.

Some women are impatient with a slow weight loss and are disappointed that they do not lose all their pregnancy weight gain as soon as the baby is born. New mothers should wait at least 3 weeks to start dieting to lose weight, as they need energy to meet the demands of infant care. Suggestions about sensible calorie reduction combined with exercise may be appropriate. The mother who has gained a large amount of weight beyond that recommended during pregnancy may have more difficulty losing it after birth, and it will take a longer period of time. She may require help from a dietitian in planning a weight loss program.

Mothers are sometimes so involved with the needs of the infant during the early days that they fail to eat properly. They may snack instead of planning meals for themselves, especially if they are home alone with the baby during the day. The nurse should remind the mother that snacking often involves high caloric intake without meeting nutritional needs. This is a time when a mother needs to ensure her own good health so that she will be able to care for her baby.

✔ Check Your Reading

19. How do the nutritional needs of the lactating mother compare with those of the woman who is not lactating? With those of the woman who is pregnant?
20. What should the breastfeeding woman avoid in her diet?
21. What changes should the woman who is not breastfeeding make after the birth of her baby?

Application of Nursing Process

The nursing process focuses on determining the factors that might interfere with the woman's ability to meet the nutrient needs of pregnancy and lactation and on finding solutions to any problems identified. This primarily involves education of the client.

Assessment

The nurse uses a number of methods to assess for nutritional problems. They are similar to those used for assessment of other problems.

INTERVIEW

The interview provides an opportunity to develop rapport and to determine whether there are specific problems that affect dietary intake.

Appetite. The interview can begin with a discussion of the client's appetite. Has it changed during the pregnancy, and how does it compare to her appetite before pregnancy? Morning sickness may decrease her food intake during the first trimester. Determine the severity and duration of nausea and vomiting. For some women, the discomfort is mild and occurs only during the mornings or when they are fatigued. For others, severe nausea continues throughout the day and beyond the first trimester. Hyperemesis gravidarum is the most serious form of this problem, requiring hospitalization to correct fluid and electrolyte imbalance. (See Chapter 24, p. 678.)

Eating Habits. Assess the usual pattern of meals to discover poor food habits, such as skipping breakfast or eating only snack foods for lunch. Whether or not the pregnant woman does the cooking may be important. The teenager whose mother cooks for her may have little choice about what she eats when at home. In that case, discuss nutritional needs during pregnancy with her mother. If the woman does the cooking herself, the likes and dislikes of other family members may influence what she serves, especially if she has little understanding of her own needs during pregnancy.

Food Preferences. Ask about her food preferences and dislikes. The mother who dislikes all fruits and vegetables needs another source of vitamins. During pregnancy, some women experience an aversion to certain foods, like meats, that they do not have at other times. Careful counseling helps to work around dislikes or aversions to find ways of obtaining the nutrients needed.

Discussing likes and dislikes provides an opening to ask about food cravings and pica. Cravings may be for nutritional foods or for foods that are low in nutrient density and eaten in amounts that interfere with intake of other foods. Ask about pica in a matter-of-fact way to avoid giving an impression of disapproval. Food items such as ice are sometimes included in pica, so be sure to ask about it as well. Also ask if the mother eats large amounts of any one particular food or group of foods.

In assessing for pica, the nurse might say, "Have you had any cravings for special things to eat during your pregnancy?" This can be followed by, "Women sometimes like to eat things like clay or starch during their pregnancy. Is that something you are fond of?" Or "Do you like to eat things that are not usually considered food—like clay or starch?"

Psychosocial Influences. Ascertain whether there are cultural or religious considerations that affect the diet. Do these apply only during pregnancy, or are they present at all times? Assess whether the client follows them completely or whether she observes only some of the usual restrictions. Determine the effect on her nutrient intake.

The interview may reveal other factors that interfere with adequate nutrition. Women with low incomes may not know about sources of help. Question the vegetarian to determine how long she has followed the practice and her awareness of changes necessary during pregnancy. Smoking, alcohol intake, and other substance abuse may become obvious during the interview. Ask about prescription drugs, and determine whether medications she takes interfere with nutrient absorption. Include questions about the amount of time she has for food preparation and the frequency of eating fast foods.

Ask the client if she has any special concerns about her diet. This may bring out fears about weight gain leading to obesity or concerns that specific foods could hurt the fetus. It also allows her to discuss issues the nurse has not yet addressed.

At the end of this part of the initial interview, the nurse should have information about the client as well as factors that may alter her dietary intake. Determining her actual intake of foods is next.

DIET HISTORY

Diet histories provide information about a woman's usual intake of nutrients. Twenty-four hour diet histories, food intake records, and food frequency questionnaires can form a basis for counseling about any changes required to meet pregnancy needs. They also help the woman become more aware of what she is eating.

Twenty-Four Hour Diet History. Ask the woman to recall what she ate at each meal and for between meal snacks during the previous 24 hours. Use specific questions about the size of the portions and how they were prepared to include all ingredients. Take each meal individually, and then ask about anything eaten before the next meal. Ask about beverages as well as snacks between meals and at bedtime. Determine whether this is typical of her usual daily food intake; if not, ask which foods are more representative. Analyze the 24-hour diet history to determine whether the client has met the recommendations for specific food groups, calories, and protein. Detailed analysis for individual nutrients is unnecessary because it is time-consuming and there may be a daily variation in intake.

The food history may be inaccurate if the client cannot remember what she ate or is mistaken about the amounts of food. Models of food items or using measuring utensils may be helpful. The expectant mother may wish to please the nurse and alter her reported intake to make it appear that she is eating better than she is. She may be embarrassed about her inability to follow the diet prescribed because of lack of money or cooking facilities. The atmosphere set by the nurse is important in helping mothers feel free to be honest.

Food Intake Records. Food intake records are used to register what is eaten over one or more days. Ask the client to list everything she eats throughout the day. The list is more accurate if she writes down each food immediately after eating. This method avoids the problems of forgetfulness, but some women eat more nutritional foods during the recording period, when they are concentrating on good diet, then go back to a less wholesome diet later.

Food Frequency Questionnaires. Food frequency questionnaires may provide information about diet over a longer time. They contain lists of common foods. Review the questionnaire with the client, and ask her how often she eats each food. Foods consumed daily or weekly are her most common source of nutrients. Analyze the list to determine whether foods from each food group are eaten in adequate amounts to meet pregnancy needs. Determine whether there are any major groups omitted.

PHYSICAL ASSESSMENT

Physical assessment provides further information about nutritional status. It includes measurement of weight and assessment for signs of nutritional deficiency. This should be done at each prenatal visit.

Weight at Initial Visit. Weigh the woman at the first prenatal visit to get a baseline value for future comparison. Ask the client if this is her usual weight or if weight gain has already occurred. Take her height at the same time. Measure her height without shoes instead of relying on her reported height because she may not have had an accurate recent measurement.

Determine her weight for height before pregnancy begins, and compare it to tables of normal values to help draw conclusions about her pre-pregnancy nutritional status. If weight is low for height, nutritional reserves are marginal. If it is high, the client may be overweight or obese.

Weight at Subsequent Visits. Assessment of weight gain at each prenatal visit provides an easy method of estimating whether or not nutrition is adequate and serves as a basis for counseling about nutrition. Weigh the woman at each visit on the same scale with approximately the same amount of clothing. To obtain an accurate measurement, have the mother remove her shoes and coat.

Weight should be plotted on a weight grid at each visit throughout the pregnancy. This allows the pattern as well as the total gain to date to be examined. It also helps keep track of the amount of gain between individual visits.

Figure 9–2 is an example of a weight gain grid. Measurement of skinfold thickness is often used in research to determine body fat changes, but its use in clinical practice is generally not helpful, as there are no standardized recommendations for pregnancy.

Be careful to avoid overemphasizing weight gain. In some instances, a woman may be afraid that caregivers will be disapproving if she gains weight and, consequently, she may diet or fast a day or two before her prenatal visit.

Signs of Nutrient Deficiency. Other indications of nutritional status include any signs of deficiency. For example, bleeding gums might indicate inadequate intake of vitamin C. However, actual deficiency states are not likely to occur in women in most industrialized countries. Even though nutritional intake may not be enough to allow for optimum health and storage of nutrients, most women obtain enough nutrients to avoid signs of deficiency. The most important exception is nutritional anemia, which is common in a mild form. Signs and symptoms include pallor, low hemoglobin level, fatigue, and increased susceptibility to infection.

LABORATORY TESTS

Laboratory tests are generally impractical for in-depth analysis of nutrient intake. Analysis of specific nutrients is expensive and may be inaccurate because physiological changes of pregnancy, rather than true deficits of nutrients, may be demonstrated. Although tests are available for various nutrients, they are more useful for research studies than for general assessment during pregnancy. In addition, the normal laboratory values during pregnancy have not been determined for all laboratory tests. Hemoglobin, hematocrit, and in some cases serum ferritin are the tests used most often to determine anemia and particularly iron-deficiency anemia.

Analysis

Although some women may eat more calories than they need during pregnancy and risk obesity as a result, more women are likely to eat less of various nutrients than is recommended. The problem may be related to many factors, but the most common factor is general lack of knowledge. Therefore, the most important nursing diagnosis concerning nutrition is: *Alteration in Nutrition: Less Than Body Requirements related to lack of understanding about the nutrient needs of pregnancy.*

Planning

Goals for this nursing diagnosis are as follows:

- The woman will consume a diet containing the RDAs for nutrients throughout her pregnancy, as demonstrated by eating the recommended servings of each food group each day.
- The woman (of normal weight for height before pregnancy) will gain weight at the rate of approximately 3 to 4 pounds during the first tri-

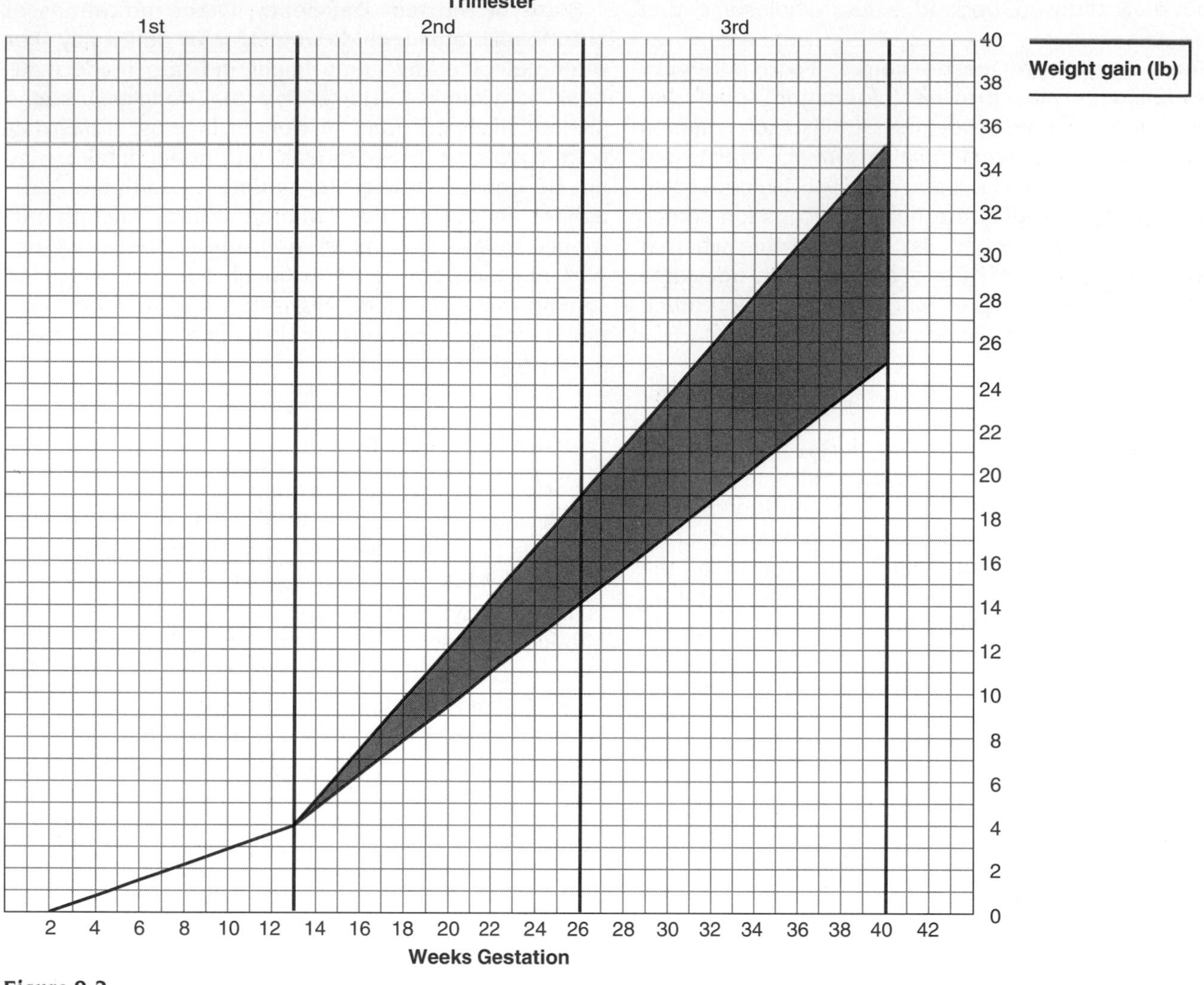

Figure 9-2

Weight gain grid for pregnancy. The normal range for weight gain is 25 to 35 pounds. Adolescents often need to gain in the higher end of the range, whereas women who are shorter than 62 inches should gain in the lower portion.

mester and a pound a week during the second and third trimesters, for a total gain between 25 and 35 pounds.

Interventions

IDENTIFYING PROBLEMS

After analysis of food likes and dislikes and a 24-hour diet history, determine whether there are obvious areas of potential deficiency. Examples might be the client who eats little meat, avoids vegetables, is lactose-intolerant, or is following a vegetarian or other diet. Determine also the woman's knowledge about the nutrient needs of pregnancy.

EXPLAINING NUTRIENT NEEDS

Use the woman's diet history as a basis to introduce information about nutrition during pregnancy. Explain the recommended servings from each food group. Help the woman analyze her own diet so that she understands the process and its importance. Determine whether she meets the number of servings recommended for each food group. Explain which important nutrients are provided in each food group and why they are necessary for her and the fetus.

Make a rough estimate of calories, protein, iron, and calcium in the diet for a general idea of maternal intake of these nutrients. Compare the usual sources of these major nutrients with her diet history and favorite foods to help her determine whether or not she is likely to eat enough of these foods on a

Women often make changes in their diets for the sake of their unborn child that they would not consider for themselves alone.

regular basis. Suggest ways in which she can increase nutrients lacking.

PROVIDING REINFORCEMENT

Give frequent positive reinforcement when the client is eating appropriately. Assist her in evaluating where changes in her diet might be necessary, and plan ways to overcome weaknesses in her present diet. Ask her what problems she foresees in obtaining the nutrients she needs. Determine whether this will affect the rest of the family. Perhaps the changes she needs to make for her own needs would be beneficial for the entire family. Explore a variety of ideas with her on how she can overcome expected problems.

If the client can read, give her written materials on nutrition during pregnancy and review these with her. If she can take the information home, she can review it often to ensure she is eating what she should. A small pamphlet with pictures might be placed on the refrigerator to help her remember what foods she needs each day.

EVALUATING WEIGHT GAIN

Compare the expectant mother's weight to a weight gain grid to ascertain whether she has gained the appropriate amount of weight for this point in her pregnancy. Discuss the importance of weight gain, and share with her the expected pattern of weight gain for her. Explain the importance of eating foods high in nutrient density when she is increasing calories. If she is greatly outside of normal ranges, discuss with her primary health care provider what modifications of her diet may be necessary. For example, a very obese woman is expected to gain weight, but the amount must be individualized according to her particular needs.

REASSESSING NUTRITIONAL STATUS AT EACH VISIT

At each office or clinic visit for prenatal care, reassess dietary status. Ask the client how she is doing with the diet and if she has had any difficulty. Check weight gain to see if she is within the expected pattern. Evaluate hemoglobin and hematocrit levels to detect anemia. Explain which assessments are being made and why.

ASSESSING SUPPLEMENT INTAKE

If vitamin-mineral supplements have been prescribed, determine whether she is taking them regularly. If she is not taking the supplements, explore the reasons and possible solutions. Iron supplements often cause constipation, but dietary changes, such as increasing fluids and fiber, can help avoid this problem (Table 9–13). If the problem is forgetfulness, suggest that she take vitamin-mineral supplements with meals or iron supplements with orange juice at bedtime just before she brushes her teeth. If she avoids iron supplements because of side effects such as nausea, suggest that she take them with meals or a snack. Even though this decreases the absorption of the iron, it is preferable to not using the supplements at all. Let her know that black stools are a harmless side effect of iron.

REFERRING WHEN NECESSARY

The nurse can give nutritional counseling that is more than adequate for most women, but there may be some situations that warrant referral to other sources. Women with other health problems that may affect nutrition may need an initial consultation

Table 9–13. COMMON SOURCES OF DIETARY FIBER

Fruits and vegetables, with skins when possible
- Apples, strawberries, pears, carrots, corn, potato with skin, cabbage, broccoli

Whole grains and whole grain products
- Whole wheat bread, bran muffins, bran cereals, oatmeal, brown rice, whole wheat pasta

Legumes
- Peas, lentils, kidney beans, lima beans, baked beans, peanuts

Nursing Care Plan 9–1

Nutrition for the Pregnant Adolescent

Assessment: Vicki, age 15, is 20 weeks pregnant and has gained 10 pounds. She attends school and lives at home, but usually cooks for herself because "I don't like the stuff my mom cooks." She generally skips breakfast and eats from snack machines during breaks at school. She often joins her friends at fast food restaurants for lunch and after school. Vicki states she is disgusted with how heavy she looks and wants to go on a diet to lose some weight or "I'm going to look like a blimp!" Her diet history shows a high intake of calories and fat, but low intake of vegetables, fruits, and grain products. She does not like most vegetables and fruits and avoids breads and cereals to save calories. She likes milk, but usually drinks diet soda. Her hemoglobin level is 10.4 g/dl. She listens with interest when the nurse discusses nutrition, especially when weight is mentioned. She makes statements that show concern about her baby's needs. Vicki was at normal weight before her pregnancy, and it is determined that a weight gain of approximately 35 pounds is appropriate for her.

Nursing Diagnosis: Alteration in Nutrition: Less Than Body Requirements related to concern about weight gain and diet choices inadequate to meet nutrient requirements of adolescent pregnancy.

Goals:

Vicki will:

1. Explain the weight gain pattern and intake from each food group optimal for adolescent pregnancy.
2. List foods she can choose at fast food restaurants that will meet her nutrient needs and allow her to feel part of her peer group.
3. Gain approximately 1 to 1¼ pounds (0.44 to 0.57 kg) a week for the rest of her pregnancy.
4. Maintain a hemoglobin level above 10 g/dl throughout her pregnancy.

Intervention:	Rationale:
1. Praise Vicki for her interest in nutrition and her concern about gaining too much weight.	1. Praise helps foster rapport and may focus attention on learning.
2. Discuss the reasons for appropriate weight gain during pregnancy and its effect on the fetus. Focus on the needs of the adolescent who is not finished growing and on the importance of preventing low birth weight in the infant. Explain the problems involved in low birth weight.	2. Adolescents may not understand how diet affects the fetus and themselves during pregnancy.
3. Assist Vicki in comparing her food intake to the recommended servings from each food group. Point out areas of strength, and praise her for these.	3. Active involvement of the learner and positive reinforcement help increase motivation.
4. Ask Vicki what problems she sees in her diet. Point out areas she may have missed. Explain the effect continued lack of specific nutrients might have on the fetus.	4. Adolescents learn best when they see how the material applies to them.
5. Discuss the high caloric intake of fast foods in relation to her present diet, and explain the concept of nutrient density in terms of "spending calories" to buy nutrients needed during pregnancy.	5. Relating information to concepts already understood increases understanding.
6. Determine, from a list of Vicki's food likes and dislikes, foods that she could eat to meet her nutrient needs, yet are low in calories. Point out fruits and vegetables high in vitamins A and C, yet low in calories.	6. Emphasizing the positive increases compliance.
7. Suggest nutritional foods that Vicki could choose at fast food restaurants, and ask which ones are acceptable to her.	7. This adolescent needs to feel that she is part of her peer group. Including her input on what she likes to eat may increase her compliance.

Nursing Care Plan 9–1 Continued

Nutrition for the Pregnant Adolescent

Intervention:	Rationale:
8. Discuss the importance of breakfast during pregnancy. Explain that the fetus needs a steady supply of nutrients and will need food in the morning after the long fast during the night.	8. Prolonged periods without maternal food intake can lead to a state of ketosis that is hostile to the fetus.
9. Discuss breakfast foods that Vicki might like. Point out the nutrients found in whole grain breads and cereals (protein, iron, B vitamins) and their importance.	9. Whole grains are often a part of a well-balanced breakfast.
10. Suggest that Vicki eat foods not usually considered breakfast foods if she prefers. For example, cold pizza provides calcium and protein.	10. Non-traditional methods of meeting the adolescent's nutritional needs may be very effective.
11. Suggest foods high in nutrient density that are available from snack dispensers. Ask which of these are acceptable to Vicki.	11. Adolescents are unlikely to give up foods that help them feel part of their peer group.
12. Ask Vicki if she is willing to eat more dairy products after explaining their importance to her and her baby. Ask her to help plan which ones she will eat to meet her needed intake.	12. Compliance is increased when clients maintain a feeling of control.
13. Ask Vicki if she is taking her vitamin-mineral supplements and how she is tolerating them. Offer suggestions on how to deal with any problems she is having in this area. Reinforce the importance of consistent intake.	13. Adolescents may be inconsistent in taking supplements, especially if they experience side effects.
14. Ask Vicki to bring in another 24 hour diet history on her next visit.	14. Reassessment of dietary intake identifies new or continuing problems.
15. Ask Vicki to tell you of other ways she has found to meet her diet needs that you could share with other teenagers. Ask for feedback on the methods discussed.	15. It is important for the adolescent to feel that her thoughts and ideas are valued by the nurse.

Evaluation:
Vicki gains 4 to 6 pounds a month throughout the rest of her pregnancy, for a total weight gain of 33 pounds. Her reported dietary intake shows that she is meeting the recommendations for each food group. She brings back ideas about how to eat fast foods healthfully and seems to like "educating" the nurse about teenage diet preferences. Her hemoglobin level rises to 11 g/dl. A healthy 7½-pound baby girl is born at term.

Additional Nursing Diagnoses to Consider:

Body Image Disturbance
Situational Low Self-Esteem

with a dietitian and follow-up with the nurse. The new diabetic, the woman with celiac disease, or a client with extreme weight problems falls within this category. Women with inadequate financial resources to buy enough food can be referred to public assistance programs such as Aid to Families with Dependent Children or the WIC program. At the next visit, ask the woman about the results of the referral to determine follow-up and need for other assistance.

Evaluation

Ongoing evaluation of diet and pattern of weight gain throughout the pregnancy determines whether or not the goals have been met. The client should meet the RDA for pregnancy by eating the recommended number of servings of each food group and should gain 3 to 4 pounds during the first trimester and a pound a week for the second and third trimester. Total weight gain should fall within 25 to 35 pounds.

Summary Concepts

- Nutritional education during the childbearing period may have long-term positive effects on the mother, the infant, and the entire family.
- Weight gain during pregnancy is an important determinant of fetal growth. Poor weight gain in pregnant women is associated with low birth weight in infants; however, excessive weight gain may lead to large-for-gestational-age infants.
- The recommended weight gain during pregnancy is 25 to 35 pounds. The amount is greater for women who are underweight or who carry more than one fetus, and it is lower for obese women.
- The pattern of weight gain is as important as the total increase in weight. The average should be 3 to 4 pounds during the first trimester and a pound a week thereafter.
- The recommended increase in energy intake during pregnancy is 300 kcal daily. Calorie increases should be attained by choosing foods high in nutrient density to meet the other needs of pregnancy.
- Protein should be increased to 60 g daily during pregnancy, an increase of 10 to 16 g over nonpregnant needs. Although most North American women obtain enough protein, the nurse should teach the woman high-protein foods if necessary.
- Women may not eat enough foods high in vitamins B_6, D, and E and folate to meet recommendations. The nurse should encourage clients to eat more foods containing these vitamins.
- Fat-soluble vitamins (A, D, E, and K) are stored in the liver. Excess consumption may result in toxicity.
- Daily intake of water-soluble vitamins (B and C) is necessary because excesses are not stored but excreted.
- Minerals most likely to be consumed below recommended amounts in pregnancy are iron, calcium, zinc, and magnesium. Iron is often added as a supplement, while calcium is added for women with low intake. The nurse can suggest foods high in iron and calcium.
- Routine use of vitamin-mineral supplements is unnecessary and may lead to excessive intake and toxicity. Increased intake of some nutrients interferes with use of others and may result in deficiencies.
- Pregnant women should drink eight to ten 8-ounce glasses of fluids each day. They should eat at least seven servings of whole grains, five servings of fruits and vegetables, three servings of dairy products, and seven 1-ounce servings of protein foods.
- Culture can influence a woman's diet during pregnancy. The nurse should learn whether she follows traditional dietary practices and whether her food practices are consistent with good nutrition.
- Both Southeast Asian and Latino dietary practices include the importance of balancing yang and yin or hot and cold. The nurse must know which foods are acceptable at what times.
- Poor women may not have enough money or knowledge to meet the nutrient needs of pregnancy. The nurse should refer them for financial assistance and nutritional counseling.
- Adolescents may skip meals, eat snacks and fast foods of low nutrient density, and are subject to peer pressure that may decrease their nutritional intake.
- Pregnant vegetarians may need help in choosing an adequate diet that includes non-animal sources of energy, protein, iron, calcium, vitamin B_{12}, and other nutrients. Vegetarians may need vitamin-mineral supplements during pregnancy.
- Lactose-intolerant women need to increase calcium intake from foods other than milk, like calcium-rich vegetables.

- Abnormal pre-pregnancy weight, anemia, eating disorders, pica, grand multiparity, substance abuse, having closely spaced pregnancies, and multifetal pregnancy are all nutritional risk factors that warrant adaptations of diet during pregnancy.
- Lactating women need more of almost every nutrient than women who are not lactating. The increased calories needed for milk production can be met by an added intake of 500 calories, and the rest can come from maternal fat stores.
- During lactation, mothers should avoid alcohol, caffeine, and foods that seem to cause distress in the infant.
- The postpartum woman who does not breastfeed should decrease her calorie intake by 300 but should eat a well-balanced diet to enhance recovery from childbirth. Weight loss should be accomplished slowly and sensibly.

Readings and References

Abrams, B. (1989). Maternal nutrition. In R.K. Creasy & R. Resnik (Eds.), *Maternal-fetal medicine: Principles and practice* (2nd ed.). Philadelphia: W.B. Saunders.

Bowles, B.C., & Williamson, B.P. (1990). Pregnancy and lactation following anorexia and bulimia. *Journal of Obstetric, Gynecologic, and Neonatal Nursing*, 19(3), 243–254.

Calhoun, M.A. (1986). Providing health care to Vietnamese in America: What practitioners need to know. *Home Healthcare Nurse*, 4(5), 14–22.

California Department of Health Services (1990). *Nutrition during pregnancy and the postpartum period: A manual for health care professionals, summary*. Sacramento.

Cerrato, P.L. (1993). Nutrition support: Suggest diets with a difference. RN, 56(2), 67–72.

Cunningham, F.G., MacDonald, P.C., & Gant, N.F. (1989). *Williams obstetrics* (18th ed.). Norwalk, Conn.: Appleton & Lange.

D'Avanzo, C.E. (1992). Bridging the cultural gap with Southeast Asians. MCN: *American Journal of Maternal Child Nursing*, 17(4), 204–208.

Herbert, W.N.P., Dodds, J.M., & Cefalo, R.C. (1993). Nutrition in pregnancy. In R.A. Knuppel, & J.E. Drukker (Eds.), *High-risk pregnancy: A team approach* (2nd ed.). Philadelphia: W.B. Saunders.

Holm, L.D., Schendt, C.A., & Rayburn, W.F. (1991). Advising patients on prenatal vitamins. *Contemporary OB/Gyn*, 36(4), 144–150.

Horner, R.D., Lackey, C.J., Kolasa, K., & Warren, K. (1991). Pica practices of pregnant women. *Journal of the American Dietetic Association*, 91(1), 34–38.

Institute of Medicine, National Academy of Sciences, Food and Nutrition Board. (1991). *Nutrition during lactation*. Washington, D.C.: National Academy Press.

Institute of Medicine, National Academy of Sciences, Food and Nutrition Board. (1990). *Nutrition during pregnancy*. Part I: *Weight gain*. Part II: *Nutrient supplements*. Washington, D.C.: National Academy Press.

Knuppel, R.A., & Drukker, J.E. (1993). High-risk pregnancy: A *team approach* (2nd ed.). Philadelphia: W.B. Saunders.

Lappé, F.M. (1982). *Diet for a small planet*. New York: Ballantine.

Lawrence, R.A. (1989). *Breastfeeding: A guide for the medical profession* (3rd ed.). St. Louis: C.V. Mosby.

Mahan, L.K., & Arlin, M. (1992). *Krause's food, nutrition, and diet therapy* (8th ed.). Philadelphia: W.B. Saunders.

Merlin, R. (1992). Understanding bulimia and its implications in pregnancy. *Journal of Obstetric, Gynecologic, and Neonatal Nursing*, 21(3), 199–205.

Messina, M., & Messina, V. (1991). Increasing use of soyfoods and their potential role in cancer prevention. *Journal of the American Dietetic Association*, 91(7), 836–840.

Mohs, M.E., Watson, R.R., & Leonard-Green, T. (1991). Nutritional effects of marijuana, heroin, cocaine and nicotine. *Journal of the American Dietetic Association*, 91(9), 1261–1267.

National Research Council (1989). *Recommended dietary allowances*. (10th ed.). Washington, D.C.: National Academy Press.

Newman, V., & Norcross, W. (1991). Nutrient intake of low-income Southeast Asian pregnant women. *Journal of the American Dietetic Association*, 91(7), 793–799.

Poleman, C.M., & Peckenpaugh, N.J. (1991). *Nutrition essentials and diet therapy* (6th ed.). Philadelphia: W.B. Saunders.

Rees, J.M., & Worthington-Roberts, B.S. (1993). Nutritional needs of the pregnant adolescent. In B. Worthington-Roberts & S.R. Williams (Eds.), *Nutrition in pregnancy and lactation* (5th ed.). St. Louis: Times Mirror/Mosby.

Samolsky, S., & Hynak-Hankinson, M.T. (1990). Feeding the Hispanic hospital patient: Cultural considerations. *Journal of the American Dietetic Association*, 90(12), 1707–1710.

Spector, R.E. (1991). *Cultural diversity in health and illness* (3rd ed.). Norwalk, Conn.: Appleton & Lange.

Symposium: Advising pregnant women about nutrition. (1991). *Contemporary OB/Gyn*, 36(1), 80–97.

Teufel, N.I., & Dufour, D.L. (1991). Patterns of food use and nutrient intake of obese and non-obese Hualapai Indian women of Arizona. *Journal of the American Dietetic Association*, 90(9), 1229–1235.

Trouba, P.H., Okereke, N., & Splett, P.L. (1991, November). Summary document of nutrition intervention in prenatal care. *Journal of the American Dietetic Association* (Suppl.), pp. S21–S26.

U.S. Department of Agriculture. (1992, April). USDA's food guide pyramid. *Home and Garden Bulletin*, No. 249.

U.S. Department of Agriculture and U.S. Department of Health and Human Services. (1990, November). Nutrition and your health: Dietary guidelines for Americans (3rd ed.). *Home and Garden Bulletin*, No. 232.

U.S. Department of Commerce (1992). *Summary population and housing characteristics* United States. Washington, D.C.

Wilkerson, N.N. (1988). Nutrition. In F.H. Nichols & S. S. Humernick (Eds.), *Childbirth education: Practice, research, and theory*. Philadelphia: W.B. Saunders.

Williams, S.R. (1989). *Nutrition and diet therapy* (6th ed.). St. Louis: Times Mirror/Mosby.

Williams, S.R. (1993). Nutrition assessment and guidance in prenatal care. In B. Worthington-Roberts & S.R. Williams (Eds.), *Nutrition in pregnancy and lactation* (5th ed). St. Louis: Times Mirror/Mosby.

Worthington-Roberts, B.S. (1993). Prenatal nutrition—general issues. In B. Worthington-Roberts & S.R. Williams (Eds.), *Nutrition in pregnancy and lactation* (5th ed). St. Louis: Times Mirror/Mosby.

10

Fetal Diagnostic Tests

Objectives

1. Identify indications for fetal diagnostic procedures.
2. Discuss the purpose, procedure, advantages, and risks of specific diagnostic procedures:
   - Ultrasound
   - Doppler ultrasound blood flow assessment
   - Alpha-fetoprotein testing
   - Chorionic villus sampling
   - Amniocentesis
   - Non–stress test
   - Vibroacoustic stimulation test
   - Contraction stress test
   - Biophysical profile
   - Percutaneous umbilical blood sampling
   - Maternal assessment of fetal movement
3. Provide information for some of the most common questions parents have about procedures.

Definitions

Alpha-fetoprotein (AFP) • Plasma protein produced by the fetus that crosses from amniotic fluid to maternal blood.

Amniocentesis • Transabdominal puncture of the amniotic sac to obtain a sample of amniotic fluid that contains fetal cells and biochemical substances for laboratory examination.

Biophysical profile (BPP) • Method for evaluating fetal status during the antepartum period based on five variables originating with the fetus: *fetal heart rate, breathing movements, gross movements, muscle tone*, and *amniotic fluid volume*.

Chorionic villus sampling • Transcervical or transabdominal sampling of chorionic villi (projections of the outer fetal membrane) for analysis of fetal cells.

Contraction stress test (CST) • Method for evaluating fetal status during the antepartum period by observing response of the fetal heart to the stress of uterine contraction.

Late deceleration • Slowing of the fetal heart rate after the onset of a uterine contraction that persists after the contraction ends.

Lecithin/sphingomyelin ratio (L/S ratio) • The ratio of two phospholipids in amniotic fluid that is used to determine lung maturity; an L/S ratio greater than 2:1 indicates fetal lung maturity.

Meningocele • Protrusion of the meninges through a defect in the bony spine; a form of neural tube defect.

Neural tube defect • A congenital defect in closure of the bony encasement of the spinal cord or of the skull. Includes **anencephaly, spina bifida, meningocele,** and **myelomeningocele.**

Non–stress test • A method for evaluating fetal status during the antepartum period by observing the response of the fetal heart rate to fetal movement.

Percutaneous umbilical blood sampling (PUBS or **cordocentesis)** • Procedure for obtaining fetal

△ Alert for a high risk of exposure to substances to which universal precautions apply. See Appendix B for additional information about infection control.

blood through ultrasound-guided puncture of an umbilical cord vessel to detect fetal problems such as inherited blood disorders, acidosis, or infection.

Phosphatidylglycerol (PG) • A major phospholipid of **surfactant**; its presence in amniotic fluid indicates fetal lung maturity.

Phosphatidylinositol (PI) • A phospholipid of **surfactant**; produced and secreted in increasing amounts as the fetal lungs mature.

Placenta previa • Abnormal implantation of the placenta in the lower uterus.

Spina bifida • Defective closure of the bony spine that encloses the spinal cord; a type of **neural tube defect.**

Surfactant • Combination of lipoproteins produced by the lungs of the mature fetus to reduce surface tension in the alveoli, thus promoting lung expansion after birth.

Ultrasonography • Technique for visualizing deep structures of the body by recording the reflections (echoes) of sound waves directed into the tissue.

Vibroacoustic stimulation test • Using sound stimulation to elicit acceleration (speeding up) of the fetal heart rate.

Until recently, only primitive methods were available to assess the condition of the fetus. Fundal height was measured to estimate fetal growth, the fetal heart rate was auscultated, and fetal movements were noted. In recent years, however, the development of a variety of sophisticated methods has made it possible to detect physical abnormalities in the fetus and to monitor the fetal condition with a great deal of accuracy. The ability to predict fetal outcome offers reassurance for some parents but not for all. If fetal anomalies are ruled out and if the fetus is determined to be in good condition, the parents often experience a feeling of relief and reduced anxiety. However, if fetal health is uncertain, the tests are repeated frequently, causing parents anxiety throughout the pregnancy. If fetal anomalies are identified, parents are then faced with the choice of whether to continue or to terminate the pregnancy. This can create emotional conflict as well as ethical dilemmas that impose a great deal of stress on the family.

Indications for Fetal Diagnostic Tests

Fetal diagnostic procedures are reserved for pregnancies that are termed *high-risk*; that is, those in which there is reason to believe the fetus may experience developmental or physical problems. They are not performed in all pregnancies.

In general, there are two reasons for performing diagnostic procedures: to detect congenital anomalies and to evaluate the condition of the fetus. Some procedures, such as amniocentesis and ultrasonography, are used for both purposes. They are used in early and mid-pregnancy to detect congenital defects, but they are used in the latter half of pregnancy to evaluate the condition of the fetus.

Many factors increase the risk for the fetus during pregnancy, for example, *maternal medical conditions*, such as diabetes or hypertension. *Demographic factors*, such as age and poverty, as well as *obstetric factors*, such as prior birth of a stillborn infant or an infant with congenital anomalies, increase the risk to the current pregnancy. Table 10–1 provides a more complete list of indications for fetal diagnostic procedures.

Ultrasonography

When high-frequency sound waves are aimed in a direction, they are deflected by objects that are in their path and return as echoes. The amount of energy returned as an echo depends on the density of the object that deflected the ultrasonic wave. In obstetrics, when ultrasonic waves are directed through the maternal abdomen, they are deflected by tissue and returned as two-dimensional images showing structures of different densities. (Fig. 10–1).

Almost all ultrasound procedures in obstetrics now use real-time scanning. A rapid sequence of fixed images is displayed on the screen and shows movement as it happens. This technique allows the observer to detect fetal heart beat, fetal breathing activity, and fetal body movement.

Emotional Responses

As might be expected, the parents' response to ultrasound (ultrasonography) varies widely. Some expectant mothers exhibit excitement and pleasure and report feelings of love and protectiveness when they view the fetus and observe fetal movement. Others, however, report increased feelings of vulnerability and anxiety about the fetus. Some mothers state that they fear something will be found wrong, and they dread the experience for this reason. Expectant fathers are often fascinated by fetal movement and insist that the fetus "waved" at them or that they could see the facial expression as the fetus looked directly at them. Some couples wish to be told if the fetus is male or female and are either

Table 10–1. INDICATIONS FOR FETAL DIAGNOSTIC PROCEDURES

Medical Conditions
Pre-existing diabetes mellitus or gestational diabetes
Hypertension (chronic or pregnancy-induced)
Chronic infections (such as pyelonephritis)
Sexually transmitted diseases
Anemia
Parents carry or exhibit genetic disorder (such as sickle cell anemia, cystic fibrosis)

Demographic Factors
Maternal age <16 or >35 years
Poverty
Non-Caucasian (twice the risk of neonatal or infant death)
Inadequate prenatal care (initial visit after 20 weeks' gestation or fewer than five prenatal visits to physician or nurse-midwife)

Obstetric Factors
History of low-birth-weight infant (<2500 g)
Multiple gestation
Malpresentation (breech, shoulder)
Previous fetal loss or birth of infant with congenital anomaly
Previous infant (>4000 g at birth)
Hydramnios (>2000 ml at term)
Oligohydramnios (<500 ml at term)
Decrease or absence in fetal movements
Uncertainty about gestational age
Suspected intrauterine growth retardation
Postmaturity (>42 weeks)
Preterm labor (>20 weeks or <38 weeks of gestation)
Grandmultiparity (>5 pregnancies)

Concurrent Maternal Factors
Less than ideal-weight-for-height at conception
More than 20% above ideal-weight-for-height at conception
Inadequate weight gain or poor pattern of weight gain
Excessive weight gain
Use of drugs, alcohol, tobacco

disappointed or pleased with the news. Others do not want to know the sex of the child, even if it is obvious, and prefer to wait and "be surprised."

Purpose

Clinically, ultrasound evaluation is often referred to as Level I (basic) or Level II (targeted).

BASIC ULTRASONOGRAPHY (LEVEL I)

Although ultrasound is not yet a standard of care for all women, it is widely used because a great deal of information can be obtained with minimum risk to mother or fetus. Ultrasound may be used during any trimester, but the reasons for its use vary.

First Trimester. During the first trimester, basic ultrasound is most frequently used to:

- Confirm pregnancy
- Verify the location of the pregnancy (uterine or ectopic)
- Detect multifetal gestations
- Determine gestational age
- Confirm fetal viability
- Determine the position of the uterus, cervix, and area of placental formation for transcervical chorionic villus sampling (CVS)
- Guide the needle insertion for transabdominal chorionic villus sampling

During the first trimester, gestational age is based on visualization of the gestational sac (accurate to within 0.5 to 3 days at 6 to 8 weeks of pregnancy) and crown-to-rump (CRL) of the fetus (accurate to within 0.5 to 3 days at 8 to 14 weeks of pregnancy) (Manning, 1989).

Fetal viability is confirmed by observation of fetal heart beat, which is clearly visible by the 7th week following the last menstrual period. In addition, gross structural anomalies, such as anencephaly, may be visualized as well as maternal abnormalities, such as bicornate uterus, uterine fibroids, and ovarian cysts.

Figure 10–2 illustrates a pregnancy of 12 weeks' gestation.

Second and Third Trimesters. Level I ultrasound is used throughout the second and third trimesters to:

- Confirm gestational age
- Locate the placenta when there is vaginal bleeding and a placenta previa is suspected
- Determine fetal presentation
- Determine amniotic fluid volume
- Evaluate amniotic fluid index (depth of fluid in all four quadrants surrounding the maternal umbilicus)

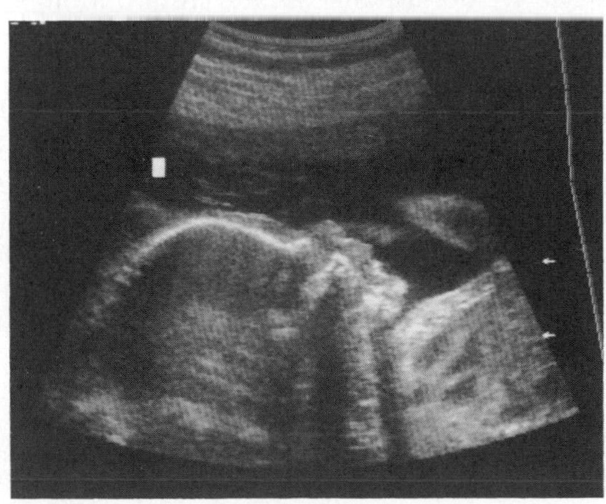

Figure 10–1

Sonogram showing fetal structures. Profile of fetal facial structures. (Courtesy of Karin Buxton.)

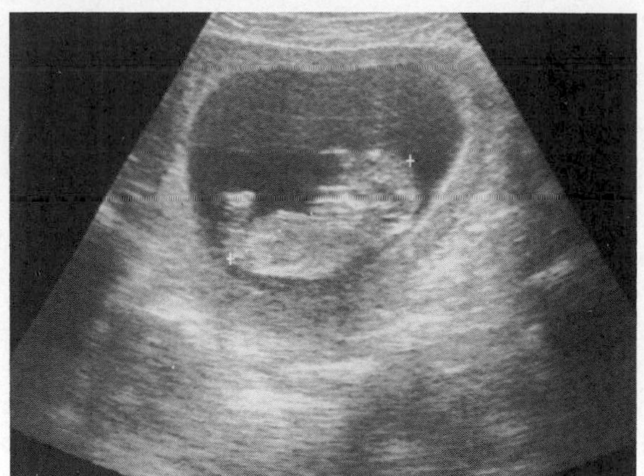

Figure 10–2

Sonogram of a 12-week fetus showing a crown-to-rump length of 5.5 cm.

- Monitor and document fetal movements
- Guide needle placement when amniocentesis or percutaneous umbilical blood sampling is necessary

Various measurements are used to determine gestational age during the last half of pregnancy. These include biparietal diameter, femur length, and abdominal circumference. The biparietal diameter is most accurate (±7 days) from 12 to 20 weeks (Manning, 1989). After 30 weeks, estimation of gestational age is often based on abdominal circumference, biparietal diameter, and femur length and is accurate to ±14 to 21 days.

Determination of gestational age must be accurate when maternal levels of serum alpha-fetoprotein, (AFP) a protein that is altered by the age of the fetus, are abnormal. Accurate gestational age is also important if intrauterine growth retardation is suspected or if there is a question about the expected date of delivery (EDD).

Assessment of fetal movements is important because coordination of whole body movement requires complex neurological control that indicates the nervous system is functioning well. On the other hand, a lower than expected number of body movements may predict fetal compromise, especially if placental perfusion is suspected to be inadequate, which may result in fetal hypoxia and acidosis.

TARGETED ULTRASONOGRAPHY (LEVEL II)

In the second trimester, ultrasound may be targeted toward specific evaluation of fetal anatomy and physiology when there is increased risk for fetal abnormalities, for example, a maternal history of giving birth to an infant with anomalies or a history of abnormal clinical findings, such as *hydramnios* (excessive amniotic fluid), *oligohydramnios* (insufficient amniotic fluid), or abnormal levels of AFP. In Level II ultrasound, the fetal anatomy is carefully and systematically examined in order to identify major system and organ anomalies, such as neural tube defects (incomplete closure of the neural folds from which the brain and spinal cord are formed, allowing herniation of meninges, spinal cord, and/or brain tissue). Protrusion of intestine through the intestinal wall, malformed kidneys, hydrocephalus, obstruction in fetal bowel or urinary system, as well as cleft lip and palate, and cardiac defects can be detected with targeted ultrasound.

Targeted ultrasound is also used to evaluate placental maturity based on the identification and distribution of calcium deposits within the placenta and the increasing delineations that occur as the placenta matures.

Procedure

Two approaches are used during pregnancy: transabdominal and transvaginal. With the transabdominal approach, a transducer is passed over the abdomen to obtain images of the uterus and its contents. When a transvaginal approach is selected, the transducer is placed in the vagina to obtain the images.

TRANSABDOMINAL ULTRASONOGRAPHY

Transabdominal ultrasound may be used during any trimester, but it is used most frequently during the second and third trimesters, when the uterus extends out of the pelvis and clear visualization of the fetus and placenta is possible because the view is not obstructed by pelvic bones.

If transabdominal ultrasound is used during the first trimester, when the uterus remains in the pelvis and visualization may be difficult, it is necessary to perform the test when the woman has a full bladder. This provides a "window" through which the uterus and its contents can be viewed. The woman must be instructed to drink 1 to 2 quarts of clear fluid an hour before the time of the examination, and she should be instructed not to void until the examination is completed.

Ultrasound requires minimal time and produces very little discomfort (other than the distended bladder, which many women say is distinctly uncomfortable). The expectant mother is positioned on her back with the head and knees supported by pillows. If she desires, the display panel can be positioned so that she (and the father) can see the images on the screen. Her head should be elevated slightly, and she should be turned slightly to one side to prevent supine hypotension. A wedge or rolled blanket is placed under one hip to help her maintain the position comfortably. Positioning is particularly important during the latter half of pregnancy, when the uterus expands out of the pelvis and may compress the vena cava when the woman is in a supine position. Warm mineral oil or transmission gel is spread over her abdomen and the sonographer (nurse, physician, or ultrasound technician) slowly moves a transducer over the abdomen to obtain a picture (Fig. 10–3). The woman may experience discomfort as the transducer is moved over the distended bladder. The procedure takes 10 to 30 minutes. The sonographer can "freeze" a picture and copy it for permanent records or for the parents if they wish. Many new ultrasound systems offer videotaping of the evaluation, and some facilities provide a small section of videotape for the parents.

TRANSVAGINAL ULTRASONOGRAPHY

Transvaginal ultrasound allows clear visualization of the uterus, gestational sac, and embryo in early pregnancy; it also allows visualization of deep pelvic structures, such as the ovaries and fallopian tubes. For that reason, this modality is used when an ectopic pregnancy or ovarian cyst is suspected. Transvaginal ultrasound is not an uncomfortable procedure, although it may provoke feelings of embarrassment in some women. The woman is placed in lithotomy position. A transvaginal probe, which is encased in a disposable cover and coated with a gel that provides lubrication and promotes conductivity, is inserted into the vagina. The woman may feel more comfortable if she is allowed to insert the probe. The procedure generally takes about 10 to 15 minutes.

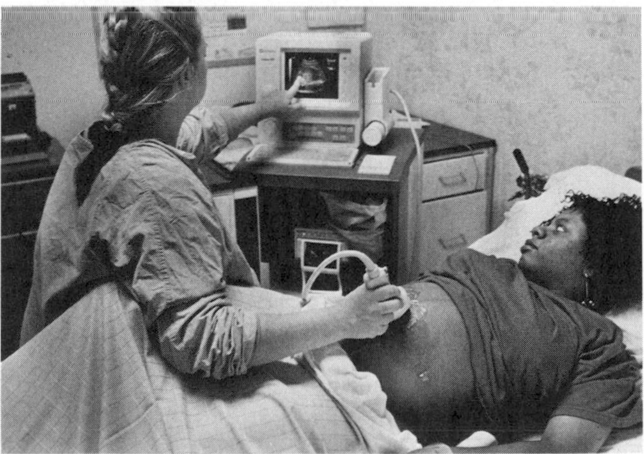

***Figure* 10–3**

The nurse moves an ultrasound transducer over the mother's abdomen to obtain an image.

Advantages

Ultrasound is one of the most important tools in modern obstetrical care. It allows clear visualization of the fetus and surrounding structures, and it is safe. No clinically significant adverse effects have been reported (Veille et al, 1993). It is noninvasive and relatively comfortable; moreover, results are obtained immediately. It is widely available, and, finally, it is portable and can be moved to the area of need.

Disadvantages

Cost can be a problem for a woman who does not have insurance or who does not have access to prenatal care in the first trimester of pregnancy.

Doppler Ultrasound Blood Flow Assessment

A new advance in perinatal medicine is the ability to study blood flow in the fetus and the placenta. When an ultrasound wave is directed at an acute angle to a moving target, as with blood flowing through a vessel, the frequency of echoes is changed as the cardiac cycle goes through systole and diastole. This change, referred to as the *Doppler shift*, indicates forward movement of blood within a vessel.

Doppler ultrasound blood flow studies have been used most extensively to study blood flow through the umbilical vessels and the placenta. This modality is particularly useful when maternal conditions, such as hypertension, are suspected of creating uteroplacental insufficiency, which can result in fetal hypoxemia and acidosis.

✔ *Check Your Reading*

1. What are the major reasons why Level I ultrasonography is performed during the first trimester?
2. Why is Level II ultrasonography called "targeted" ultrasound?

Alpha-fetoprotein Testing

Although alpha-fetoprotein (AFP) is a protein that is synthesized by all normally developing fetuses, unusual concentrations may indicate serious fetal anomalies. AFP is shed by the fetus into surrounding amniotic fluid. From there, it crosses the placental barrier and thus gains access to maternal serum. Therefore, AFP levels can be measured in maternal serum (MSAFP) as well as in amniotic fluid (AFAFP).

Purpose

Although several conditions are associated with abnormal findings, the primary reason for the evaluation of MSAFP is to determine whether the fetus has an open neural tube defect, that is, whether the embryonic neural tube has not closed properly. If the neural tube is "open," neural tissue may be exposed totally or covered with only a very thin layer of tissue, allowing high levels of AFP to seep into amniotic fluid and to enter maternal serum.

The most common open neural tube defects are: (1) anencephaly, in which the cranial vault is absent and the brain is undeveloped, and (2) spina bifida. Spina bifida ranges in severity from spina bifida occulta, which is barely noticeable, to meningocele, in which the meninges protrude from the spinal canal, and meningomyelocele, in which not only the meninges but also the spinal cord protrude through the defect and extensive nerve damage may be expected. (See Chapter 29 for additional information on neural tube defects.)

Other conditions associated with abnormal levels of MSAFP are listed in Table 10–2. Low levels as well as elevated levels are associated with fetal anomalies. Expected levels of AFP are related to the gestational age of the fetus. The most common cause of an abnormal level is incorrect estimation of gestational age.

Procedure

Between 15 and 18 weeks of gestation the physician offers the woman the option of having blood drawn to evaluate the concentration of AFP in her serum. She is informed that MSAFP is only a screening test and that further tests are required to investigate abnormal concentrations. Figure 10–4 shows recommended diagnostic procedures associated with abnormal levels of AFP. If MSAFP levels are elevated, Level I ultrasound is recommended to determine

Table 10–2. CONDITIONS ASSOCIATED WITH ABNORMAL MATERNAL SERUM ALPHA-FETOPROTEIN LEVELS

Elevated Levels of AFP
- Open neural tube defects
- Esophageal obstruction
- Abdominal wall defects (omphalocele, gastroschisis)
- Increased amount leaked by fetal kidney (hydronephrosis)
- Threatened abortion
- Undetected fetal demise
- Normal fetus in conjunction with one or more of the following:
  - Amniotic fluid contaminated with fetal blood
  - Underestimation of fetal age
  - Multifetal gestation
  - Decreased maternal weight
  - Maternal insulin-dependent diabetes

Low Levels of AFP
- Chromosomal trisomies (eg, Down syndrome)
- Gestational trophoblastic disease
- Normal fetuses in conjunction with:
  - Overestimation of gestational age
  - Increased maternal weight

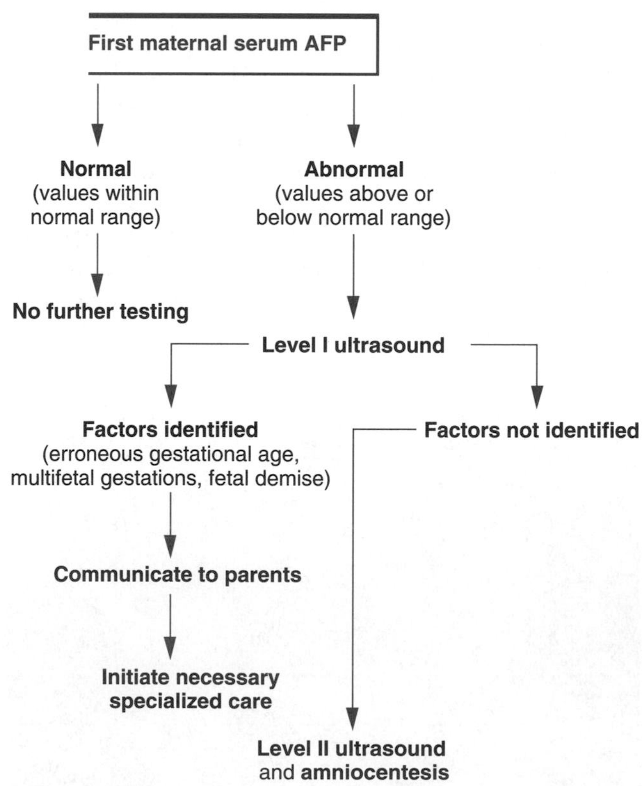

Figure 10–4

Abnormal levels of maternal serum alpha-fetoprotein (MSAFP) indicate the need for further testing to identify the fetal causative factor.

whether the abnormal concentration is due to multifetal gestation, inaccurate gestational age, or fetal demise.

If Level I ultrasound fails to explain the abnormal levels of AFP, Level II ultrasound with amniocentesis should be the next step. Amniotic fluid is analyzed for elevated levels of AFP and for acetylcholinesterase (AChE). Elevations of AChE have been noted in association with open neural tube defects; however, AChE assessment is not a primary diagnostic tool but is used as a secondary measure to reduce the number of false-positive results when AFAFP is elevated.

Advantages

There are several advantages to MSAFP evaluation:

- It is a simple procedure that requires only a sample of maternal blood.
- It is the least invasive and most economical procedure to screen for an open neural tube defect, a defect that occurs in 1 to 2 infants per 1000 live births and that may produce serious, lifelong, neurological disability.
- Prenatal diagnosis allows parents time to examine their options or to prepare for the birth of an infant who will require special care.

Limitations

There are some major limitations to MSAFP:

- MSAFP evaluation is a screening test only and must be viewed as the first step in a series of diagnostic procedures that are necessary if abnormal concentrations are found.
- Because many other conditions, such as overestimation or underestimation of gestational age, can result in apparent abnormal levels, the parents may experience a great deal of anxiety when follow-up tests are necessary.
- Timing also imposes some limits. MSAFP evaluation is performed between the 15th and 18th weeks of pregnancy; however, many women do not seek prenatal care until after the 18th week and miss the opportunity for MSAFP screening.
- Because closed neural tube defects do not produce elevated levels of AFP, normal levels of AFP do not guarantee a perfect baby.

✔ Check Your Reading

3. Why is MSAFP called a screening test?
4. What are the possible causes for an elevation in AFP levels?

Chorionic Villus Sampling

Purpose

Chorionic villus sampling (CVS) is used primarily to diagnose genetic or chromosomal abnormalities in the fetus. Chorionic villi are microscopic projections from the outer membrane (chorion) that proliferate and burrow into endometrial tissue as the placenta is being formed. The villi are fetal in origin and reflect the chromosomes and genetic makeup of the fetus. Fetal villous tissue can be obtained as early as 8 weeks of gestation and is analyzed directly for chromosomal and genetic abnormalities.

Indications

CVS is recommended only for women who are at high risk to give birth to an infant with genetic anomalies. Its use is restricted because of reported complications, such as spotting or bleeding, uterine cramping, or fetal loss. Women past the age of 35 years or those with a history of a previous fetus with anomalies, or couples who are carriers of or who exhibit genetic defects are the most at risk, and CVS would be an option to consider.

Procedure

Although transabdominal CVS is possible, transcervical aspiration under the direct visualization of real-time ultrasound is the most widely used technique. The woman is placed in lithotomy position. Both the vagina and cervix are washed with an antiseptic germicidal agent, and strict aseptic technique is critical  to decrease the chance of infection. A flexible catheter is inserted through the cervix, and a sample of chorionic villi is aspirated through the catheter into a syringe (Fig. 10–5).

Advantages

CVS can be performed between 9 and 12 weeks of gestation; since first-trimester cells divide rapidly, results can be known within 24 to 48 hours. Unlike amniocentesis, which is performed during the second trimester and necessitates 2 to 4 weeks for culture of fetal cells that have been shed into amniotic fluid, CVS does not impose the burden of a long, anxious wait on the prospective parents for data to be available. As a result, CVS offers access to prenatal diag-

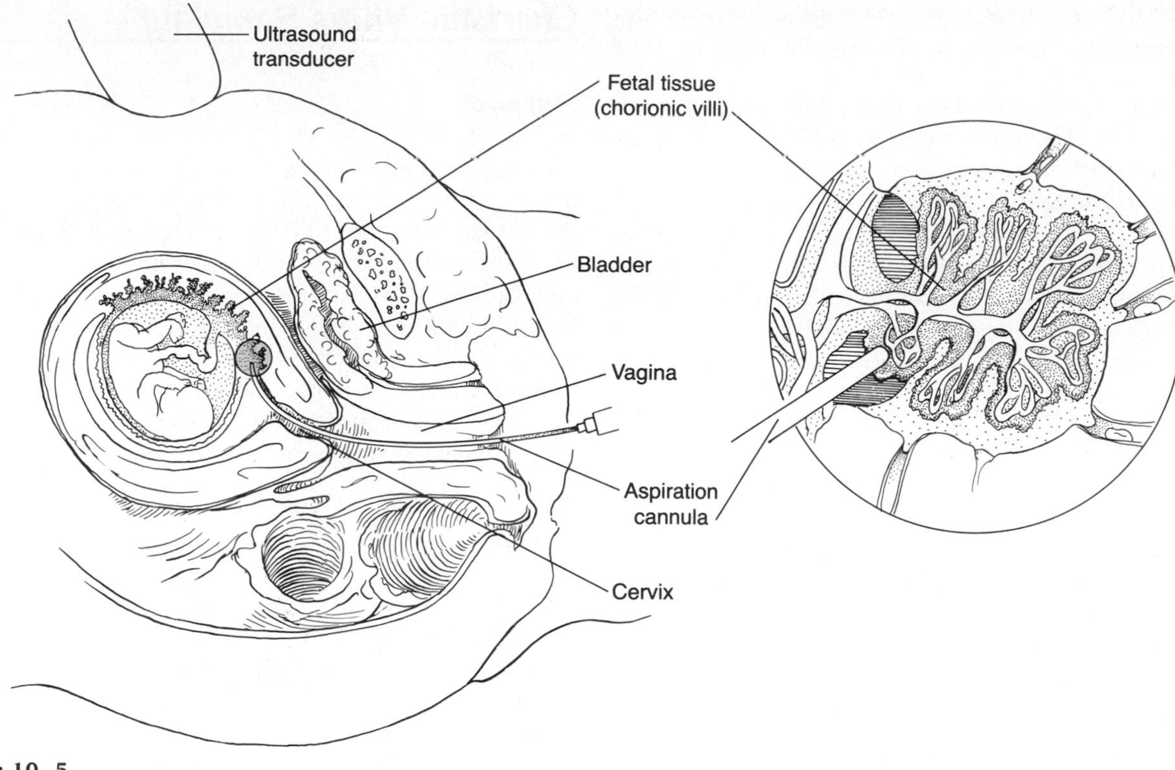

Figure 10–5

In chorionic villus sampling (CVS), a sample is aspirated to detect the presence of genetic defects in the fetus.

nosis to women who find second-trimester procedures unacceptable. Furthermore, it may save women carrying affected fetuses from the physical and emotional trauma of a second-trimester abortion.

Risks

Because CVS is a relatively new procedure, there are not enough data to list the risks with certainty. However, prospective parents and physicians remain concerned that the risks may outweigh the benefits. The rate of pregnancy loss varies from 2 to 5 per cent (Hogge, 1990) to between 5 and 12 per cent (Hogge et al, 1986). When compared to the pregnancy loss following amniocentesis described next, the CVS procedure–related pregnancy loss was 0.6 per cent higher than that for women undergoing amniocentesis for prenatal diagnosis (National Institutes of Health, 1989). Like amniocentesis, CVS increases the risk of Rh sensitization, and Rh_0 (D) immune globulin should be administered to all unsensitized Rh-negative women following the procedure.

In addition, there is concern about risks that are theoretically possible but have not been reported. These include prematurity, placental abnormalities, and birth defects (Hogge, 1990).

False or misleading diagnostic results are also possible because of maternal cell contamination; however, the incidence is unknown.

Maternal infection is a risk, and the procedure is contraindicated if endocervicitis, active genital herpes, pelvic inflammatory process, or a positive culture for *Neisseria gonorrhoeae* has been documented.

As with all diagnostic procedures, the couple should receive genetic counseling prior to the test. The ,risks and benefits of the procedure should be carefully explained and a signed consent obtained. The woman should be informed that the actual procedure takes about half an hour, but up to 2 hours should be allotted in case of delays.

After the procedure, maternal vital signs are assessed and the woman is allowed to void. A small amount of vaginal spotting may appear; however, heavy bleeding or the passage of amniotic fluid, clots, or tissue should be reported. The client will need to rest at home for several hours after the procedure.

✔ *Check Your Reading*

5. What is the major advantage of CVS over amniocentesis?
6. What are the major risks associated with CVS?

Amniocentesis

Amniocentesis involves inserting a needle through the abdominal wall, the uterine wall, and the amniotic sac of the expectant woman to withdraw a small sample of amniotic fluid for study of cells that have been shed from the fetus.

Purpose

Amniocentesis can be performed either during the second or third trimester. The timing of the procedure depends on the reason it is being done.

During the second trimester, the primary purpose is to examine fetal cells that are present in amniotic fluid to determine whether chromosomal abnormalities exist. Before disorders of the chromosomes can be detected, the cells must be allowed to grow in a culture medium from 2 to 4 weeks; they are then harvested for karyotyping. Abnormal number and structure of chromosomes are readily identified from the karyotype. (See Chapter 5 for detailed information about karyotyping and specific chromosomal abnormalities.)

In addition to detecting chromosomal abnormalities, amniocentesis is often used to evaluate the pregnancy when the woman is Rh-sensitized, to diagnose amnionitis, and to investigate amniotic fluid AFP when the maternal serum AFP level is elevated. Indications for mid-trimester amniocentesis are listed in Table 10–3.

During the third trimester, amniocentesis is most often performed to determine fetal maturity or to diagnose fetal hemolytic disease (Rh incompatibility). Several tests are used to estimate fetal maturity.

Table 10–3. INDICATIONS FOR SECOND-TRIMESTER AMNIOCENTESIS

Maternal age 35 years or more
Chromosomal abnormality in close family member
Sex determination for maternal carrier of X-linked disorder (such as hemophilia or Duchenne's muscular dystrophy)
Birth of previous infant with chromosomal abnormalities or neural tube defect
Pregnancy after three or more spontaneous abortions
Elevated levels of maternal serum alpha-fetoprotein
Maternal Rh sensitization

TESTS TO DETERMINE FETAL LUNG MATURITY

A test for fetal lung maturity is recommended when delivery is contemplated prior to 38 weeks' gestation. The lecithin/sphingomyelin (L/S) ratio is the best known test for estimating fetal lung maturity. Lecithin and sphingomyelin are lipoproteins that make up pulmonary surfactant that is necessary to keep the alveoli patent and prevent respiratory distress syndrome in the newborn. The proportion of lecithin to sphingomyelin does not differ markedly until about the 30th week of gestation, when the level of spingomyelin stops rising but lecithin continues to rise and surpasses that of sphingomyelin. An L/S ratio greater than 2 : 1 generally indicates that surfactant (lipoproteins that reduce surface tension and prevent alveolar collapse in the newborn) is adequate and the fetal lungs are mature; however, this is not always true, particularly if the client has diabetes mellitus. Therefore, amniotic fluid is also tested for the presence of phosphatidylglycerol (PG) and phosphatidylinositol (PI), phospholipids that boost the properties of lecithin. Their presence confirms fetal lung maturity.

The *foam stability index*, or "shake test," is sometimes used to evaluate fetal lung maturity. Exact amounts of 95 per cent ethanol, isotonic saline, and amniotic fluid are mixed, and the test tube is shaken. If a ring of bubbles develops and persists after 15 minutes, the test is termed positive, signifying lung maturity.

ADDITIONAL TESTS FOR FETAL MATURITY

Amniocentesis can provide other barometers of fetal maturity, such as fetal fat cells, creatinine, and bilirubin; however, tests for these components are seldom used at the present time for assessing fetal maturity.

TEST FOR FETAL HEMOLYTIC DISEASE

An amniocentesis is also performed to determine bilirubin concentration if the mother is Rh-negative and is isoimmunized (has been exposed to the Rh antigen and has developed antibodies). The level of bilirubin in amniotic fluid reflects the amount of fetal red blood cell destruction that occurs when antibodies destroy Rh-positive fetal red blood cells, leaving the fetus vulnerable to erythroblastosis fetalis and hydrops fetalis.

Erythroblastosis is marked by excessive destruction of *erythrocytes* (mature red blood cells that are capable of carrying oxygen) and the proliferation of *erythroblasts* (immature red blood cells, incapable of carrying oxygen). Because of the rapid hemolysis of erythrocytes, *bilirubin* (a waste product of red blood cell breakdown) increases markedly. The fetus will become anemic, jaundiced, and edematous (hydrops fetalis).

(See Chapter 24 for a more complete description of Rh incompatibility.)

Procedure

Amniocentesis involves aspiration of amniotic fluid from the amniotic sac (Fig. 10–6). Before the examination, the woman is asked to void so that the bladder is empty and out of the field. She is placed in a supine position and is draped with her abdomen exposed. A rolled towel is placed under the right buttock to shift the weight of the uterus slightly to the left and off the vena cava and aorta. Maternal blood pressure and fetal heart tones are assessed for baseline levels.

Ultrasound is used to locate the fetus and placenta and to identify the largest pockets of amniotic fluid that can safely be sampled. Next, the skin is prepared with antiseptic solution. A small amount of local anesthetic is injected in the skin. This causes the only pain the woman will experience, although she may experience the sensation of pressure as the needle is inserted and mild cramping as the needle enters the myometrium.

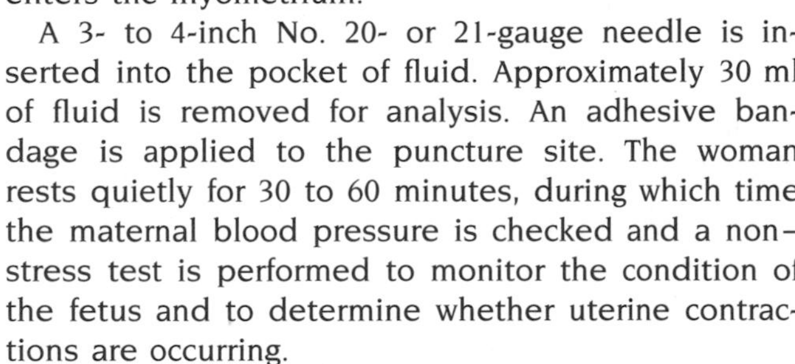

A 3- to 4-inch No. 20- or 21-gauge needle is inserted into the pocket of fluid. Approximately 30 ml of fluid is removed for analysis. An adhesive bandage is applied to the puncture site. The woman rests quietly for 30 to 60 minutes, during which time the maternal blood pressure is checked and a non–stress test is performed to monitor the condition of the fetus and to determine whether uterine contractions are occurring.

After the procedure, the client may experience some mild cramping. The nurse should advise her to rest until the cramping subsides. The woman is instructed to report any complications, such as increased vaginal discharge; persistent, severe cramping; or fever. Rh_o (D) immune globulin is administered to non-sensitized Rh-negative women following amniocentesis to prevent isoimmunization. (See Chapter 24, Drug Guide for Rh_o (D) immune globulin.)

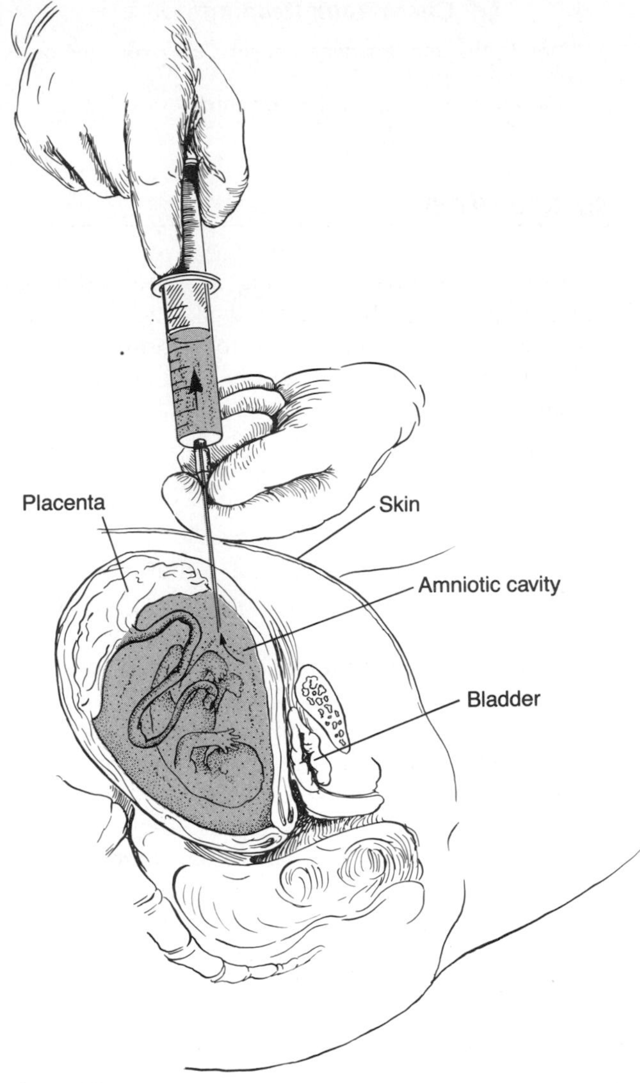

Figure 10–6

In amniocentesis, a needle is inserted through the expectant mother's abdomen to aspirate fluid from the amniotic sac. The fluid can then be tested to determine fetal maturity, chromosome abnormalities, or other fetal abnormalities.

Advantages

There are several advantages to amniocentesis:

- It is a simple, safe procedure that permits the diagnosis of many fetal anomalies and confirms fetal maturity.
- It is an outpatient procedure that can be performed in the physician's office.
- It is a relatively painless procedure that takes only a short time.
- It has been done for many years with few reported complications.

Risks

The use of ultrasound has greatly reduced the risks once associated with amniocentesis:

- The risk of injury to the fetus or umbilical cord

is minimal when ultrasound is used to guide needle insertion.

- A second puncture at a different site may be necessary if enough fluid cannot be obtained for analysis.
- The risk of spontaneous abortion associated with amniocentesis is 0.5 per cent or less (Simpson and Elias, 1989).
- Hemorrhage can result from perforation of the placenta or vessels in the umbilical cord; however, this is unlikely when ultrasound visualization is used to guide needle insertion.
- Accidental transfer of fetal blood to maternal circulation may occur, resulting in isoimmunization of the Rh-negative mother carrying an Rh-positive fetus.

As with all fetal diagnostic procedures, amniocentesis cannot guarantee the birth of a perfect infant. Parents need to be counseled that not all defects are detectable by amniocentesis.

✔ Check Your Reading

7. What factors make a pregnant woman a candidate for second-trimester amniocentesis?
8. Why is amniocentesis sometimes performed during the third trimester?

Non–Stress Test

Purpose

One way to assess fetal well-being is to evaluate the ability of the fetal heart to accelerate (speed up) either spontaneously or in association with fetal movement. An increase in fetal heart rate (FHR) when the fetus moves indicates adequate oxygenation of the fetus and a fetal heart that is capable of responding to stimuli. On the other hand, if the fetal heart does not accelerate, there may be concern about fetal hypoxemia and acidosis. When the fetal heart does

Therapeutic Communication

Margaret Kitchner is a 37-year-old primigravida. She has postponed pregnancy to complete her education and to establish a law practice. The pregnancy is at 16 weeks, and she has been referred for an amniocentesis. Counseling has already been provided by a specialist in genetics, and the risks and benefits have been discussed.

Margaret: I'm here, but I'm not thrilled to be here.

Nurse: You wish you were somewhere else?

Clarifying without attempting to lead

Margaret: The place isn't the problem really, but what about this test?

Nurse: You have some questions you'd like to ask about the amniocentesis?

Seeking information, staying with the woman's comments by paraphrasing

Margaret: Well, my mother believes that if one thinks bad thoughts, bad things will come to pass.

Nurse: Bad thoughts?

Knowing that the intergenerational belief system is powerful, the nurse focuses and seeks clarification

Margaret: Yes, you know, if we think something could be wrong with the baby, it's more likely to be true.

Nurse: I'd like to hear more—

"I" statement conveys interest and invites more discussion

Margaret: Well, my mother is not familiar with the tests, and she's just afraid that the test could hurt the baby.

Nurse: *Notes that Margaret identifies her mother as the person who is concerned, avoids her own feelings.* She must be very anxious about this test. How do you feel?

Acknowledging mother's feeling; focusing to woman's feeling by open-ended question

Margaret: She's anxious, and to tell you the truth, I'm anxious too.

Nurse: You would rather not be having the test.

This makes an assumption, she only said she was anxious. It might be more therapeutic to say "tell me more about that."

Margaret: No, I want the test. I know the reason is because of my age, but I want this baby so much.

Nurse: *"Hears" the anxiety that Margaret didn't put into words:* So the anxiety is really about the test results—

Summarizing concerns and helping the woman identify and focus on what seems unclear to her

Margaret: That's for sure. It will be so hard to wait for the results, and I don't know what I would do if the news is bad.

Nurse: Waiting is difficult, but chances are that the news will be good.

It is therapeutic to acknowledge the difficulty but offering reassurance blocks the interaction instead of focusing on the uncertainty expressed. The nurse might have said instead: "And it's very hard to imagine something is wrong with the baby." This would have kept the interaction going and focused on the patient's feelings. Instead, the blocking comment ended the interaction without allowing a full expression of feelings.

Margaret: You think so? Oh, I hope so.

not accelerate in response to fetal movements, additional tests, such as the contraction stress test (CST) or the biophysical profile, are necessary to determine the metabolic condition of the fetus.

Procedure

The test (also called an NST) takes about 30 to 40 minutes. It is conducted by a nurse with special preparation in a hospital or in an obstetrician's office. Prior to the test, the nurse instructs the patient in how the test is to be conducted and provides information and emotional support when further testing is considered necessary (Fig. 10–7). The test is termed "non–stress" because it consists of monitoring only; the fetus is not challenged or stressed by uterine contractions to obtain the necessary data.

The woman sits in a reclining chair in a semi-Fowler's position or in a left lateral position to prevent supine hypotension. Her blood pressure is checked before the test and every 10 to 15 minutes throughout the test. If hypotension occurs, her position is changed to maintain the baseline pressure.

The nurse applies external electronic monitoring equipment. First, an ultrasound transducer, to record fetal heart activity, is secured over the spot on the clients abdomen, where the fetal heart is heard most clearly. Next, a tocotransducer, which detects uterine activity and fetal movement, is secured to the maternal abdomen. The client may also be given a remote event marker to press each time she senses movement. Fetal heart activity and fetal movements are recorded on the same moving strip of paper.

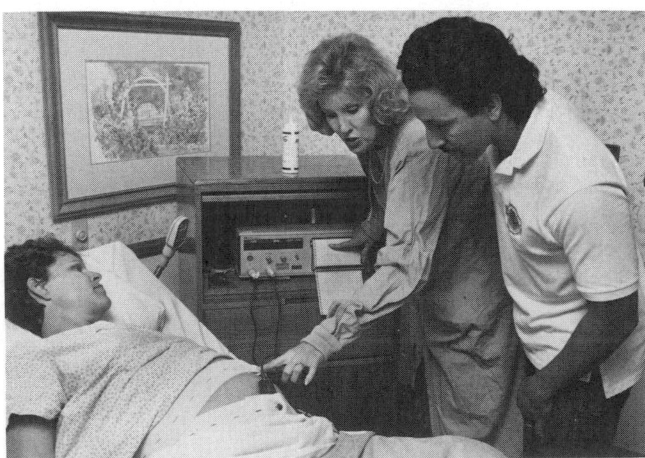

Figure 10–7

A non–stress test is a non-invasive test that measures fetal heart rate accelerations in response to fetal movements. An external fetal monitor measures fetal heart rate, and a tocotransducer measures uterine activity with fetal movements.

(See Chapter 14 for more information about fetal monitoring.)

Interpretation

Results are judged to be reactive (normal), nonreactive (abnormal), or equivocal.

To be considered *reactive*, there must be two or more FHR accelerations of at least 15 beats per minute (BPM), each with a duration of at least 15 seconds, in a 20-minute interval (Fig. 10–8) (Devoe, 1990).

A finding is considered *non-reactive* if it does not meet the criteria in a minimum time of 40 minutes and requires further evaluation.

At times the data are conflicting or difficult to interpret, and results are judged to be *equivocal*. For example, fewer than two fetal movements in a 20-minute period, accelerations of fewer than 15 BPM, an abnormal fetal heart rate baseline (>160 or <120 BPM). In this case, further follow-up is essential. Moreover, if decelerations (slowing down), either late or variable occur, further testing is necessary (Parer, 1989).

Advantages

The NST is non-invasive and painless and is believed to be without risk to mother or fetus. As a consequence, it is the primary means of fetal surveillance in pregnancies that are at increased risk for uteroplacental insufficiency and consequent fetal hypoxia. The NST is easy to administer and is often repeated weekly or even daily if necessary. In addition, results are available immediately.

Disadvantages

A major disadvantage is the large number (80 per cent) of nonreactive findings that are termed false-positive (Key and Resnick, 1988). That is, a normal, well-oxygenated fetus may not exhibit movement for more than 20 minutes. This is primarily due to the sleep-wake cycle of the fetus. If the test is administered during a sleep cycle, the fetus may not move during the time allotted and the test may be interpreted as nonreactive when, in fact, the fetus is healthy but merely asleep. Testing is usually continued for a minimum of 40 minutes before a pattern is called nonreactive (McCaul and Morrison, 1990). Waiting for the fetus to awaken prolongs the time required for testing, and efforts may be made to stimulate the fetus to move.

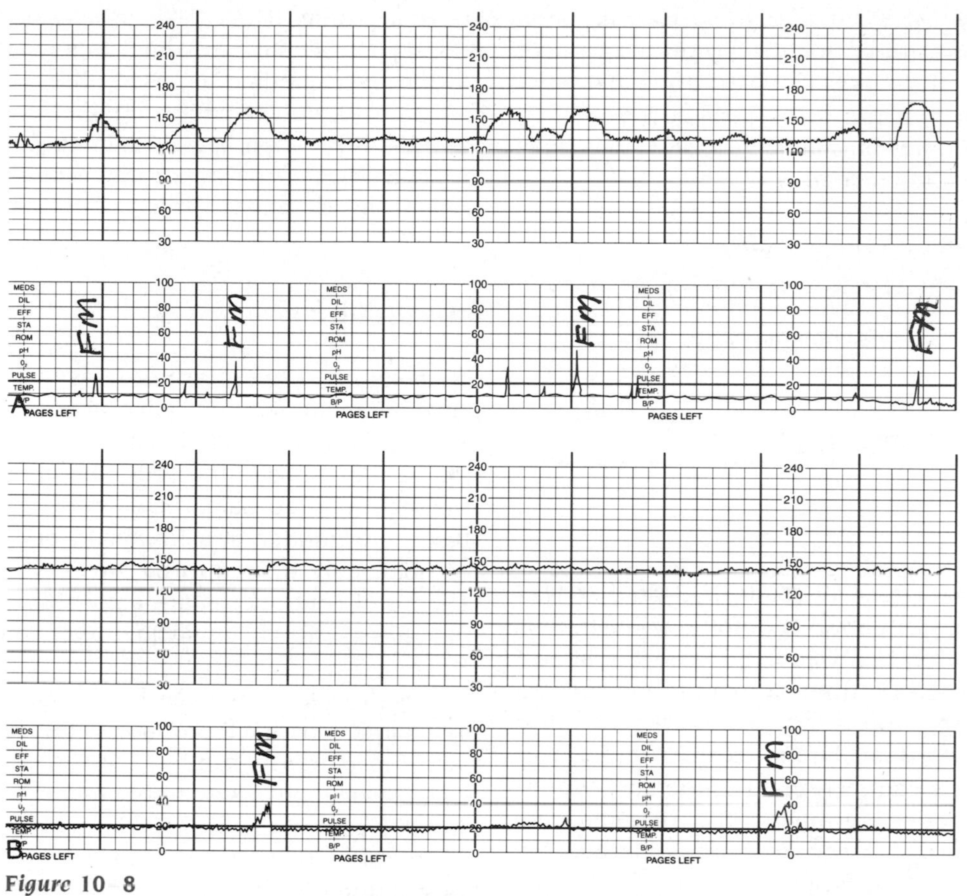

Figure 10-8

A, In this reactive non–stress test, fetal heart rate accelerates by 25 to 30 beats per minute (BPM) in response to fetal movement. **B,** In this non-reactive non–stress test, accelerations are absent following fetal movement (FM). (**A** and **B**, Courtesy of Graphic Controls, Buffalo, N.Y.)

Although there are no guidelines for stimulation techniques, several methods have been used with varying success. Stroking the client's abdomen or having her drink orange juice to raise her blood glucose level, are successful at times in eliciting fetal movement. The fetus may respond when the woman drinks cold water, and this may be preferable if the client has diabetes mellitus. It may be necessary to schedule an NST after a snack or meal, when many fetuses are more active.

Vibroacoustic Stimulation Test

Purpose and Procedure

In recent years, the vibroacoustic stimulation test (VST) has been used to confirm nonreactive NST findings or to shorten the time required to obtain NST data of good quality. The procedure for the VST is similar to that for the NST. Electronic fetal monitoring equipment is used to obtain an FHR baseline. Then an artificial larynx is applied to the maternal abdomen over the area of the fetal head for 1 second. The fetus is stimulated by the sound emitted as well as the vibration created. If there is no acceleration within 10 seconds, stimulation may be repeated (Auyeung and Goldkrand, 1991). A review of the literature reveals that FHR accelerations in response to vibroacoustic stimulation are indicative of fetal health and correlate well with other methods of fetal assessments (Sleutel, 1990).

Potential Risks

Although no known risks exist, there is speculation that repeated use of the artificial larynx may cause fetal hearing loss. Additional long-term studies are necessary to document the safety of this procedure.

In addition, prolonged fetal tachycardia has been noted in some instances, but the significance is not known. Moreover, if the test is used frequently, there is some question that the fetus may become habituated to the stimulus and not respond. This may make the test results unclear.

✔ Check Your Reading

9. What is a non–stress test, and why is it so named?
10. How does a VST differ from an NST?

Contraction Stress Test

Purpose

A contraction stress text (CST) is indicated if NST findings are nonreactive or if fetal oxygenation is only marginally adequate when the uterus is at rest and will be decreased further during uterine contractions. As the name implies, a CST involves recording the response of the fetal heart rate to stress that is induced by uterine contractions. Uterine contractions compress the arteries supplying the placenta with oxygenated maternal blood, further reducing the amount of oxygen to the fetus.

The fetus with adequate oxygen reserves can tolerate the temporary hypoxia and the FHR will remain unchanged. If the fetus has inadequate reserves, contractions, which further deplete oxygen, cause late decelerations in the FHR. Late decelerations are associated with a poor fetal outcome in about 50 per cent of the cases (Key and Resnick, 1988). If FHR variability is also decreased in the presence of persistent late decelerations, the correlation with fetal compromise is increased. (Chapter 14 reviews FHR monitoring and abnormal FHR patterns.)

Procedure

The procedure for the CST is similar to that for NST. The client is positioned in the same manner, and external electronic fetal monitoring devices are applied to record both uterine activity and the FHR. Uterine contractions must be initiated. Two methods are used to accomplish this.

The *breast self-stimulation test* (BSST) is based on the knowledge that stimulation of the breasts and nipples causes the release of oxytocin from the posterior pituitary and that oxytocin causes uterine contractions.

The *oxytocin challenge test* (OCT) involves the intravenous infusion of dilute oxytocin to stimulate uterine contractions. The OCT is usually performed if the BSST is not effective in stimulating contractions.

Whichever method is used, the objective is to stimulate three palpable uterine contractions, 40 seconds in duration, in a 10-minute period. Interpretation of data is based on this number of contractions of this duration in this amount of time.

Interpretation

CST results may be interpreted as negative (normal), positive (abnormal), or equivocal.

A *negative* test result indicates that there were no late decelerations in the FHR, although the fetus was stressed by three palpable contractions of at least a 40-second duration in a 10-minute period.

Findings are judged to be *positive* when 50 per cent or more of contractions are accompanied by late decelerations (those persisting after the contraction ends).

A result is *equivocal* when fewer than 50 per cent of the contractions have produced late decelerations or when the uterus is hyperstimulated, that is, contractions closer than every 2 minutes or duration longer than 90 seconds (McCaul, 1990).

See Table 10–4 for a summary of CST interpretations and implications.

Advantages

There are several advantages to the CST:

- The test allows follow-up of a non-reactive NST result.
- If findings are negative, the CST offers reassurance that the uteroplacental unit will continue to support life for at least a week longer (Cunningham et al, 1989).
- A positive CST result allows the physician to analyze available options and to make plans for the birth of an infant who may be compromised as a result of decreased placental functioning during labor.

Disadvantages

The CST is associated with four major disadvantages:

- The test is time-consuming, usually requiring about 2 hours.
- It is tedious, necessitating either the participation of the client in the BSST or careful infusion of oxytocin to obtain an adequate contraction

Table 10–4. SUMMARY OF CONTRACTION STRESS TEST (CST) INTERPRETATIONS

Result	Interpretation	Implications
Negative	No late decelerations	Reassuring that the fetus can tolerate labor
	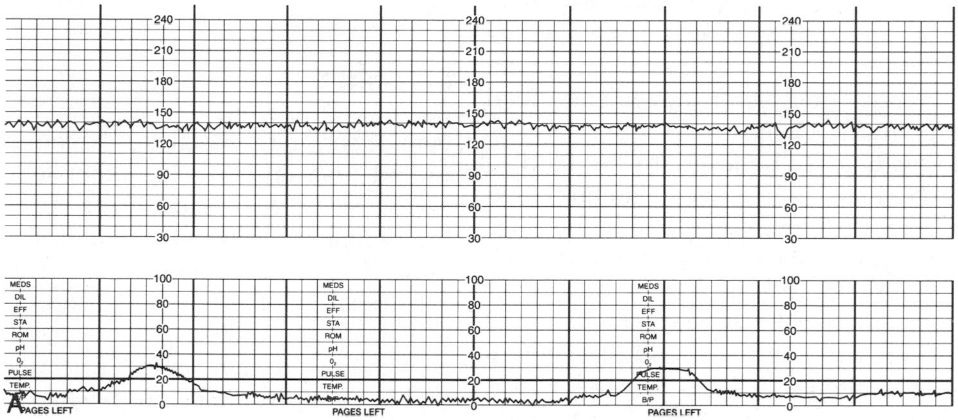	
Positive	Consistent late decelerations in 50% of the contractions	Indicates UPI and fetal compromise during contractions
	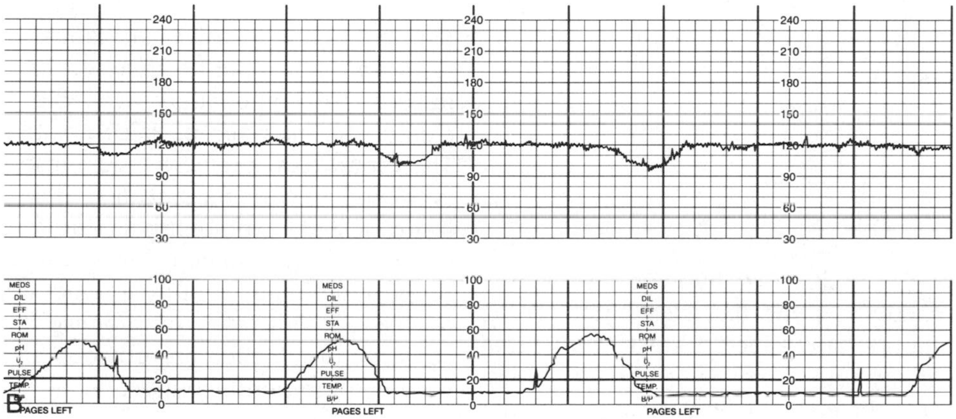	
Equivocal	Late decelerations with < 50% of the contractions	A second CST should be repeated within 24 hours
Hyperstimulation	Late decelerations with excessive uterine activity (contractions closer than every 2 minutes or lasting longer than 90 seconds)	Repeat CST within 24 hours with careful monitoring of the situation
Unsatisfactory	Test cannot be interpreted; either not enough data or unsatisfactory tracing	Repeat CST with careful attention to maternal position, oxytocin infusion, and placement of tocotransducer

Source: Graphs courtesy of Graphic Controls, Buffalo, N.Y.
UPI, Uteroplacental insufficiency and inadequate fetal reserves during contractions.

pattern without causing hyperstimulation of the uterus.

- Errors in interpretation are common. These may be due to technical difficulties in obtaining tracings or problems in interpreting the data. For example, there may be FHR acceleration with fetal movement as well as late decelerations with contractions (a reactive NST but a positive CST). Such an interpretation would require further testing, such as a biophysical profile, to confirm the well-being of the fetus.
- The cost is high. A CST is usually done in a hospital setting. A prolonged period of time with a nurse who is educated to administer the test is necessary, and preliminary interpretations must be made.

✔ Check Your Reading

11. Why is it necessary to initiate contractions in a CST?
12. In a CST, what do late decelerations of fetal heart rate indicate?

Biophysical Profile

It is believed that fetal well-being can be most accurately predicted if several parameters are evaluated. Unlike the NST and CST, which assess only fetal heart activity, the biophysical profile assesses five parameters of fetal activity: fetal heart rate, fetal breathing movements, gross fetal movements, fetal tone, and amniotic fluid volume.

Amniotic fluid volume is believed to be particularly important because decreased amniotic fluid volume is associated with long-term fetal hypoxemia. During periods of hypoxemia the fetus has a remarkable ability to shunt blood from areas that are not critical to fetal life (kidneys, lungs, and intestine) and toward the vital organs (heart, brain, and placenta). If the hypoxemia is prolonged, there may be virtual cessation of blood flow to the fetal kidneys and lungs that contribute to the production of amniotic fluid. Therefore, oligohydramnios indicates prolonged fetal hypoxia and is a strong indication of fetal compromise.

Purpose

The underlying premise of the biophysical profile is that centers in the fetal central nervous system respond to hypoxia in a gradual way. For instance, the fetal heart is most sensitive to hypoxia and a decrease in FHR reactivity is the first sign noted. Fetal breathing movements are affected next, with fetal movement and finally fetal tone being the last areas affected. Therefore, absence of fetal tone would indicate advanced asphyxia and acidosis. Figure 10–9 illustrates the cascade effect of gradual hypoxia on the central nervous system of the fetus.

Modified Biophysical Profile

Although biophysical profile is relatively new, it has already been modified. Some physicians now elect to assess the fetus only by ultrasound and to omit the NST if all parameters are normal. In other medical centers, the test is modified to include only two parameters: amniotic fluid index (quantity in all four quadrants) and an NST. Conversely, some physicians now include a sixth parameter, placental grading.

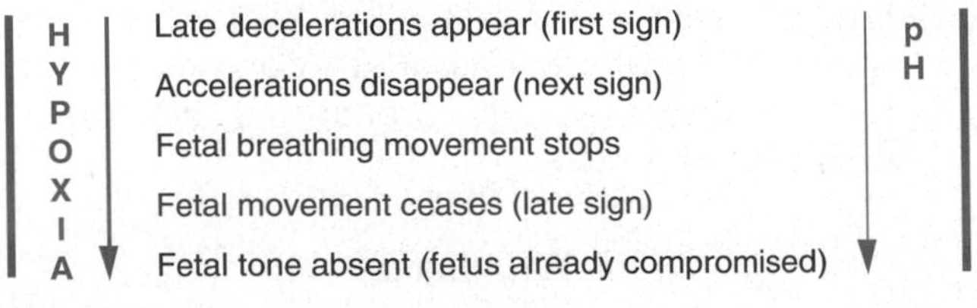

Figure 10–9

Cascade effect of gradual hypoxia.

Procedure

Fetal heart rate reactivity is measured and interpreted from an NST. The other four parameters are measured by real-time ultrasound scanning. A scoring technique is used to interpret the data, with each of the five parameters contributing either 2 or zero points. A score of 10 is perfect; a score of zero is the worst possible. A total score of 8 to 10 is considered normal *unless oligohydramnios is present* (Table 10–5) (Huddleston, 1993).

Advantages

The test is non-invasive and is less costly than some tests because it can be done on an outpatient basis. Results are immediately available, and it may decrease the number of false-positive NST findings. The biophysical profile allows conservative treatment of high-risk patients because delivery can be delayed if fetal well-being is indicated. The test is often used to monitor for signs of fetal infection when membranes rupture prematurely. The changes associated with fetal compromise occur before clinical signs of infection are obvious and may give early warning of impending infection.

Table 10–5. SCORING THE BIOPHYSICAL PROFILE

	Points	
Criterion	**None**	**Present**
Reactive non–stress test	0	2
Fetal breathing movements (at least one episode of 30 seconds in 30 minutes)	0	2
Gross body movements (at least 3 body or limb movements in 30 minutes)	0	2
Fetal tone (at least 1 episode of extension with return to flexion)	0	2
Amniotic fluid volume (at least one pocket of fluid that measures at least 1 cm in two perpendicular planes)	0	2

Key: Normal = 8 to 10 points (if amniotic fluid volume is adequate); equivocal = 6; abnormal = <4 and delivery may be considered (Manning, 1990).

Disadvantages

Additional research is needed to refine interpretation of the test. For example, each variable is given equal weight, although some variables are more important. At present, not enough research has been done to determine the meaning of low scores to long-term development of the child. Furthermore, although the test is valid in some instances, it may not accurately predict continued fetal well-being.

✔ Check Your Reading

13. What is the relationship between loss of fetal tone and hypoxia?
14. Why is amniotic fluid volume an important parameter in the biophysical profile?

Percutaneous Umbilical Blood Sampling

Percutaneous umbilical blood sampling (PUBS), also called cordocentesis, involves the aspiration of fetal blood from the umbilical cord for prenatal diagnosis or therapy (Fig. 10–10). Major indications for PUBS include diagnosis and intrauterine management of Rh disease, genetic studies, diagnosis of abnormal blood clotting factors, and acid-base status of the fetus. High-resolution ultrasound scanning is used to locate the umbilical cord, and the sample is drawn from near the site of insertion of the umbilical cord into the placenta.

It is predicted that PUBS will become a widely used procedure in the future; however, it is not risk-free. Additional data are needed to determine the actual loss rate. In the meantime, the procedure should remain confined to those medical centers that offer accumulated experience in invasive intrauterine procedures.

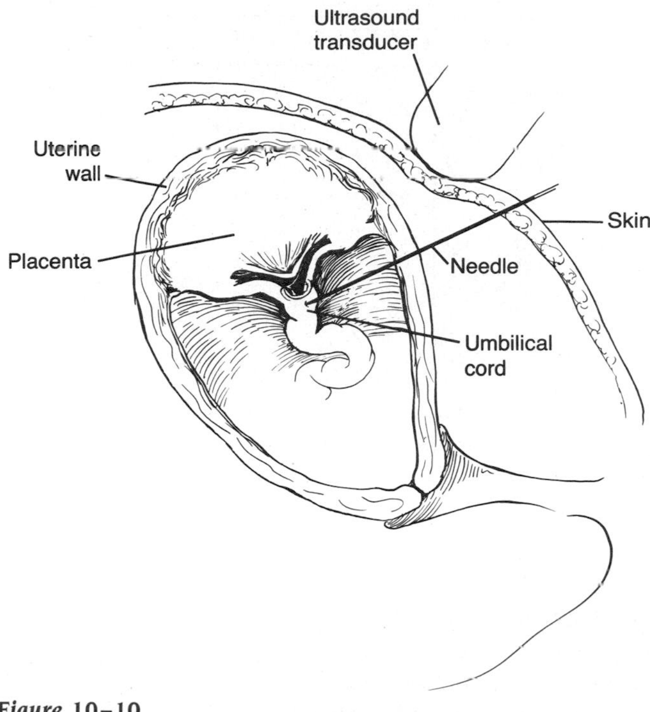

Figure 10–10

Percutaneous umbilical blood sampling allows diagnosis and intrauterine management of some hematopoietic disorders. A needle is inserted through the expectant mother's abdomen and into the umbilical vein to withdraw a sample of fetal blood.

Maternal Assessment of Fetal Movement

Movements by the fetus, as assessed by the mother, are sometimes referred to as "kick counts." Fetal movement is associated with fetal condition, and daily evaluation of these movements provides an inexpensive, non-invasive way of evaluating the fetus.

Procedure

Protocols for assessment of fetal movement by the client vary. In general, women are advised to count fetal movements for 30 to 60 minutes three times a day (usually after meals when the fetus is more active). The client lies down on the left side. She places her hands on the largest part of her abdomen and concentrates on fetal movements. She uses a clock or timer and records the number of movements felt during that time (Fig. 10–11).

Women should notify their health care provider in certain cases:

- If they do not feel a movement at least four times in any counting period
- If the number of total movements for the day is less than 12
- If there is any change in the type or character of the movements

Dates: 11-14-93 to 11-20-93

Time of day	Sunday	Monday	Tuesday	Wednesday	Thursday	Friday	Saturday
Morning 8-9 a.m.	𝍸 𝍸	𝍸 ||	𝍸 ||||				
Afternoon 1-2 p.m.	𝍸 |	𝍸 |||	𝍸				
Evening 9-10 p.m.	𝍸 || 𝍸	𝍸 ||||					
Total	28	24					

***Figure* 10–11**

Daily fetal movement record in use. The mother counts the number of fetal movements, or "kicks," within a specified period several times a day and indicates each movement on a chart. She reports any abnormality to her health care provider.

Advantages

Counting fetal movement is one of the oldest methods for evaluating the condition of the fetus. There are some obvious advantages:

- It is inexpensive
- It is non-invasive
- It is convenient for the client

Disadvantages

Many variables make interpretation of fetal movement counts difficult:

- Fetal resting state when movements are decreased
- Maternal glucose load, which affects fetal reactivity
- Maternal perception of movement
- Time of day (lower in the morning, higher in the evening)
- Drugs (methadone, heroin, cocaine, alcohol, tobacco), which affect fetal activity

Estriol Assays

The production of estriol (a form of estrogen) is controlled by the fetus and the expectant mother. Normally, maternal serum and urine levels rise as the pregnancy progresses, reflecting the status of the fetoplacental unit. Estriol assays were of more use before the development of ultrasonography and electronic fetal monitoring. Currently, the test has no clinical use in high-risk pregnancy and is mentioned only for historical purposes.

Application of Nursing Process

The role of the nurse in fetal diagnostic procedures depends on the place of employment and the nurse's expertise in the field. Many perinatal nurses with special education are actively involved in fetal diagnostic procedures. Nurses perform NSTs, CSTs, and biophysical profiles. Many nurses who work in clinics or with physicians in private practice do basic ultrasonographic examinations. Regardless of the level of the nurse's involvement in actual testing, nursing process is the organizing framework for providing care. Nurses are expected to provide information about the testing procedures and what can be determined from the tests. Nurses also provide emotional support and coordinate the series of procedures that are necessary.

Assessment

Nurses who are actively involved in fetal diagnostic procedures must collect as much information as possible about the client and her reasons for having the tests because the information may be important to conducting the tests or may be helpful to the physician interpreting the tests. Necessary information includes:

- Gravida, para, living children, gestation (in weeks)
- Maternal health problems (hypertension, diabetes, heart disease)

- Current obstetrical problems (vaginal bleeding, decreased fetal movement, multifetal gestation, intrauterine growth retardation, malpresentation, polyhydramnios, oligohydramnios)
- Prior obstetrical problems (birth of stillborn infant or infant with congenital anomalies, birth of low-birth-weight infant or large-for-gestation infant)
- History of substance abuse, including alcohol and tobacco
- Knowledge of reasons for the test and the procedure to be performed: "Do you have any questions before we start the test?"
- Knowledge of surveillance regimen if additional testing is necessary: "Do you have questions about the need to repeat the test every week?"
- Emotional response to the tests: "What are your major concerns?" "What can we do to make the tests easier for you?"
- Expectations of the diagnostic tests. Many couples think that the tests can guarantee a perfect baby but must be told what the test actually reveals.

Analysis

Women who are at increased risk for problems during pregnancy are the ones who require fetal diagnostic procedures. Clients' responses vary, depending on their knowledge and on their usual response to stressful situations. However, many women are concerned not only with the tests themselves but also with the condition of the fetus. The Nursing Diagnosis relevant to this woman is: *Anxiety* related to lack of knowledge of diagnostic procedures and uncertain condition of the fetus.

Planning

Goals for this nursing diagnosis are that the woman (and her family) will:

- Verbalize knowledge of how, when, and why she is to be tested before testing procedures are initiated
- Verbalize concerns about the condition of the fetus and seek information from health care team at each appointment.

Interventions

PROVIDING INFORMATION

Even nurses who do not work in antepartum testing must understand reasons for the tests and should be able to describe in general terms what the procedures entail. Many parents want to know how safe the tests are and how much discomfort they will cause. Parents want to know why some of the tests must be repeated. Many parents become very concerned when a screening test, such as an AFP assessment, is abnormal, and they need to know that the findings may be due to an error in estimation of gestational age and do not necessarily indicate a problem. Moreover, nurses often need to interpret technical information that may confuse the parents and cause them undue anxiety.

Provide simple, clear explanations of what the tests measure and the purpose and frequency of the tests. Explain how long the test will take, and describe the procedure so that anxiety caused by lack of knowledge can be reduced. Instruct the client and her family about follow-up care and events that should be reported to the health care team.

PROVIDING SUPPORT

It is critical that nurses identify and respond to feelings expressed by prospective parents when antepartum testing procedures are recommended or when fetal problems are confirmed. The woman often experiences frustration with the discomfort, limitations, and time-consuming demands of the pregnancy and the regimen of fetal testing. Skill in therapeutic communication is never more important than when counseling about fetal diagnostic tests. *Active listening* conveys interest and concern. *Paraphrasing* allows for interpretation because it expresses in different words what concerns the family. The art of *reflecting* back to the family what they convey about feelings helps them "hear" what their feelings are. *Clarifying* helps the woman "see" what the issues are and what options are available. Comforting measures, such as touch, convey empathetic concern and are especially important during difficult procedures. Although nurses offer caring concern and careful reflection of feelings, they do not offer advice. The decisions must be made by the family; however, nurses frequently help the family make contact with those persons to whom they turn in troubled times, perhaps a member of the clergy or a close relative.

HELPING CLIENTS SET REALISTIC GOALS

Women benefit from knowing that compliance with the testing regimen is beneficial for the fetus. Each day in the uterus allows time for growth and development and increases the chance that the infant will be strong and healthy. The fetus has an improved chance of surviving as long as the testing remains reassuring.

SUPPORTING THE WOMAN'S DECISION

Nurses must examine their own ethical beliefs before they become involved in fetal diagnostic testing. They must be prepared to support whatever decision is made, even if it is not one they would have made. For example, when a woman decides to continue or terminate a pregnancy, she is entitled to compassionate care regardless of whether the decision is one the nurse would make.

Evaluation

Interventions are successful if the woman verbalizes knowledge of why tests are recommended, an idea of how and when they will be performed, and her concerns about the condition of the fetus and whether she actively seeks information to relieve her anxiety.

Summary Concepts

- Basic and targeted ultrasonography is used during pregnancy to estimate a variety of fetal and placental conditions that may make it necessary for nurses to assist the family to cope with anxiety that is created.
- Alpha-fetoprotein assessment, a screening test performed on maternal serum or amniotic fluid, is used primarily to detect open neural tube defects; additional tests are required if AFP levels are abnormal.
- Chorionic villus sampling can be performed as early as 8 to 9 weeks of gestation; it provides parents with information about chromosomal defects in the first trimester of pregnancy. It is also used to obtain specimens for other analyses, such as DNA and enzymes; however, it cannot be used to determine neural tube defects.
- Amniocentesis can be performed in the second or third trimester to determine congenital defects or to evaluate fetal maturity.
- The non–stress test is used to determine acceleration of the fetal heart rate, which is a reassuring sign associated with adequate fetal oxygenation and the ability of the fetus to respond to stimuli such as fetal movement.
- Contraction stress tests are used to determine the ability of the fetal heart to respond to uterine contractions that decrease placental blood flow and may result in fetal hypoxemia.
- With ultrasonography, it is now possible to guide needle placement and to aspirate blood from umbilical vessels (PUBS or cordocentesis) for diagnosis and management of fetal disease.
- Maternal assessment of fetal movement ("kick counts") provides an inexpensive and non-invasive method of evaluating the fetus.
- The role of the nurse depends on her expertise and on the primary location of employment.
- All perinatal nurses must be prepared to offer clear explanations of diagnostic procedures and to provide support for the family requiring fetal diagnostic tests.

References and Readings

Auyeung, R.A., & Goldkrand, J. (1991). Vibroacoustic stimulation and nursing intervention in the nonstress test. *Journal of Obstetric, Gynecologic, and Neonatal Nursing*, 20(3), 232–238.

Barth, W.H., Frigoletto, F.D., Krauss, C.M., et al. (1991). Ultrasound detection of fetal aneuploidy in patients with elevated maternal serum alpha-fetoprotein. *Obstetrics and Gynecology*, 77(6), 897–900.

Chez, B.F. (1990). Interpretations of nonstress tests by obstetric nurses. *Journal of Obstetric, Gynecologic, and Neonatal Nursing*, 19(3), 227–230.

Cohen, F.L. (1987). Neural tube defects: Epidemiology, detection, and prevention. *Journal of Obstetric, Gynecologic, and Neonatal Nursing*, 16(2), 105–115.

Cunningham, F.G., MacDonald, P.C., & Gant, N.F. (1989). *Williams obstetrics* (18th ed.). Norwalk, Conn.: Appleton & Lange.

Devoe, L.D. (1990). The nonstress test. *Obstetrics and Gynecology Clinics of North America*, 17(1) 111–128.

Fresquez, M.L., & Collins, D.E. (1992). Advancement of the nursing role in antepartal fetal evaluation. *Journal of Perinatal Neonatal Nursing*, 5(4), 16–22.

Gaffney, S.E., Salinger, L., & Vintzileos, A.M. (1990). The biophysical profile for fetal surveillance. MCN: *American Journal of Maternal Child Nursing*, 15(6), 356–360.

Gebauer, C.L., & Lowe, N.K. (1993). Biophysical profile: Antepartal assessment of fetal well-being. *Journal of Obstetrical, Gynecologic, and Neonatal Nursing*, 22(2), 115–127.

Gegor, C.L., Paine, L.L., & Johnson, T.R. (1992). Antepartum fetal assessment techniques: An update for today's perinatal nurse. *Journal of Perinatal Neonatal Nursing*, 5(4) 1–15.

Green, M.F., & Benacerraf, B.R. (1991). Prenatal diagnosis in diabetic gravidas: Utility of ultrasound and maternal serum alpha-fetoprotein screening. *Obstetrics and Gynecology*, 77(4), 520–523.

Haddow, J.E. (1990). Alpha-fetoprotein. In M.R. Harrison, M.S. Golbus, & R.A. Filly (Eds.), *The unborn patient* (2nd ed.). Philadelphia: W.B. Saunders.

Heidrich, S.N., & Cranley, M.S. (1989). Effect of fetal movement, ultrasound scans, and amniocentesis on maternal-fetal attachment. *Nursing Research*, 38, 81–84.

Hogge, J.S., Hogge, W.A., & Globus, M.S. (1986). Chorionic villus sampling. *Journal of Obstetric, Gynecologic, and Neonatal Nursing*, 15(1), 24–28.

Hogge, W.A. (1990). Chorionic villus sampling. In M.R. Harrison, M.S. Globus, & R.A. Filly (Eds.). *The unborn patient: Prenatal diagnosis and treatment* (2nd ed., pp. 53–58). Philadelphia: W.B. Saunders.

Huddleston, J.F., Williams, G.S., & Fabbri, E.L. (1993). Antepartum assessment of the fetus. In R.A. Knuppel & J.E. Drukker (Eds.), *High-risk pregnancy: A team approach* (2nd ed., pp. 62–75). Philadelphia: W.B. Saunders.

Key, T.C., & Resnik, R. (1988). Obstetric management of the high-risk patient. In G.N. Burrow & T.F. Ferris (Eds.), *Medical complications during pregnancy* (pp. 95–116). Philadelphia: W.B. Saunders.

Manning, F.A. (1989). General principles and application of ultrasound. In R.K. Creasy & R. Resnik (Eds.), *Maternal-fetal medicine: Principles and practice* (2nd ed., pp. 195–253). Philadelphia: W.B. Saunders.

Manning, F.A. (1990). The Fetal Biophysical Profile Score: Current status. *Obstetrics and Gynecology Clinics of North America*, 17(1). 147–161.

Maulik, D., Yarlagadda, P., & Downing, G. (1990). Doppler velocimetry in obstetrics. *Obstetrics and Gynecology Clinics of North America*, 17(1), 163–186.

Mayberry, L.J., & Inturrisi-Levy, M. (1987). Use of breast stimulation for contraction stress tests. *Journal of Obstetric, Gynecologic, and Neonatal Nursing*, 16(2), 121–124.

McCaul, J.F., & Morrison, J.C. (1990). Antenatal fetal assessment *Obstetrics and Gynecology Clinics of North America*, 17(1) 1–16.

Miller-Slade, D., Gloeb, D.J., Bailey, S., Bendell, A., Interlandi, E., Kline-Kaye, V., & Kroesen, J. (1991). Acoustic stimulation-induced fetal response compared to traditional nonstress testing. *Journal of Obstetric, Gynecologic, and Neontal Nursing*, 20(2), 160–167.

National Institute of Health CVS Study Group (1989). The safety and efficacy of chorionic villus sampling compared to amniocentesis for prenatal diagnosis. *New England Journal of Medicine*, 320(10), 609–617.

Parer, J.T. (1989). Fetal heart rate. In R.K. Creasy & R. Resnik (Eds.), *Maternal-fetal medicine* (2nd ed., pp. 314–343). Philadelphia: W.B. Saunders.

Pircon, R.A. & Freeman, R.K. (1990). The contraction stress test. *Obstetrics and Gynecology Clinics of North America*, 17(1), 129–146.

Simpson, J.L., & Elias, S. (1989). Prenatal diagnosis of genetic disorders. In R.K. Creasy & R. Resnik (Eds.), *Maternal-fetal medicine: Principles and practice* (2nd ed., pp. 78–107). Philadelphia: W.B. Saunders.

Sleutel, M.R. (1989). An overview of vibroacoustic stimulation. *Journal of Obstetric, Gynecologic, and Neonatal Nursing* 18(6), 447–452.

Sleutel, M.R. (1990). Vibroacoustic stimulation and fetal heart rate in nonstress tests. *Journal of Obstetric, Gynecologic, and Neonatal Nursing*, 19(3), 199–204.

Smith, C.V. (1990). Amniotic fluid assessment. *Obstetrics and Gynecology Clinics of North America*, 17(1), 187–200.

Stringer, M., Librizzi, R., & Weiner, S. (1991). Establishing a prenatal genetic diagnosis: The nurse's role. MCN: *American Journal of Maternal-Child Nursing*, 16(3), 152–156.

Veille, J.C., Deviney, M., & Hanson, R. (1993). Ultrasound in pregnancy. In R.A. Knuppel & J.E. Drucker (Eds.), *High-risk pregnancy: A team approach* (pp. 78–96). Philadelphia: W.B. Saunders.

11

Education for Childbearing

Objectives

1. List the goals of childbearing education.
2. Explain choices in childbearing and the effect of education on these choices.
3. Describe the various types of education for childbearing families.
4. Compare and contrast specific methods of childbirth education.
5. Describe techniques for pain relief taught in Lamaze childbirth classes.
6. Explain the components frequently included in a birth plan.

Definitions

Birth plan • A plan that a couple makes during pregnancy to identify their preferences for their birth experience.

Cleansing breath • A deep breath taken at the beginning and end of each labor contraction.

Effleurage • Massage on the abdomen or other body part performed during labor contractions.

Habituation • Decreased response to a repeated stimulus.

Paced breathing • Learned breathing technique used during labor contractions to promote relaxation and increase **pain tolerance**.

Psychoprophylaxis • Method of prepared childbirth that emphasizes concentration and relaxation to increase **pain tolerance**.

Valsalva's maneuver • Increasing pressure within the abdomen and thorax by holding the breath and pushing against a closed glottis.

Western society places much importance on individuals learning how to become and remain healthy. One of the results of this focus on self-help is the development of classes, often taught by nurses, to educate childbearing families. Nurses who work with families should know what their clients are learning so that they can assist them to have positive childbearing experiences.

Although the focus of this chapter is on classes for childbearing, such education may be presented in settings other than the classroom. Nurses in offices, clinics, and birth sites often educate women in an informal manner as part of routine care. Some nurses use the time women spend waiting for clinic appointments to discuss childbearing topics and concerns. Education is an ongoing process and can occur in any setting.

Goals of Education for Childbearing

The goals of education for childbearing are to help parents become knowledgeable consumers, take an active role in maintaining health during pregnancy and birth, and learn coping techniques to deal with pregnancy, childbirth, and parenting. Meeting these goals increases parents' ability to make the many decisions necessary regarding childbirth with confidence and satisfaction.

Providers of Education

Although most childbearing education classes are taught by registered nurses, physical therapists or others who have taken special courses may also be childbirth educators. Many instructors are certified by organizations such as the American Society for Psychoprophylaxis in Obstetrics (ASPO) or the International Childbirth Education Association (ICEA). Certification ensures that the instructors have received special preparation and that they will provide sound education that adheres to the certifying organization's general philosophy. Teachers must be versed in adult education theory and techniques, and they must be skillful in handling groups of people from backgrounds that may be diverse.

Classes may be sponsored by community agencies such as schools, health departments, or community organizations; by health care providers such as medical groups or hospitals; or by private individuals. Teachers may be employed by any of these sponsoring agencies or may be self-employed. Classes may be located in offices, clinics, hospitals, schools, churches, or homes.

Class Participants

Participants in classes about childbearing have traditionally been middle-income couples who are older and better educated than those who do not take classes. Low-income women may not have money to pay for classes. Although inexpensive classes are available in some areas, women who obtain little or no prenatal care may not be aware of classes or of possible options in childbearing. Classes in languages other than English have become more readily available in areas where there is a need.

People take classes for a variety of reasons. Many have a strong desire to participate actively in all aspects of childbearing. For these people, making decisions about what will happen to them is important, and they want the education to help them decide wisely. Others are looking for coping strategies to deal with their fear of childbirth or of pain. When women feel informed and feel that they have some control over what happens to them, they are more likely to expect birth to be satisfying and fulfilling and to experience it as such (Green et al, 1990).

Choices for Childbearing

Many of the changes in childbearing practices during the last 40 years have occurred in response to consumer desire for more input and control over the birth experience. The family-centered approach, designed to make birth seem less institutionalized and more personalized, is one response to this consumer movement. Choices about the use and types of pain relief available, the inclusion of the father or other support person, and early discharges have resulted from the work of concerned consumers and health care providers.

One of the purposes of any childbearing educational program is to help parents learn what options are available so that they can make adequate choices. Knowledgeable parents can talk to health care providers about their choices in a positive yet assertive manner. They learn that there are many ways of birthing and that no one method is the only right way. General choices are discussed here, and more specific choices for labor and delivery are discussed under Parents Want to Know: What Options Should We Consider for Our Birth Plan? (See p. 256).

Health Care Professional

A major decision that must be made by the couple involves who will provide care during the pregnancy and birth. They may choose a certified nurse midwife (CNM), a nurse practitioner, an obstetrician, or a family practice physician. They need to know what to expect from each of these practitioners.

A CNM cares for women who are at low risk for complications and refers them to a "back-up" physician should problems develop. CNMs, nurse practitioners, and physicians follow women during pregnancy and the postpartum period, but nurse practitioners do not usually perform deliveries. A family practice physician may care for the newborn as well. The CNM may be present through most of labor and birth, whereas a physician generally arrives near the end of labor for the birth. Couples may make appointments with several different care providers to discuss their plans for birth before choosing the one they feel will be best for them.

Setting

Couples in areas where more than one type of birth setting is available will need to choose which they prefer and select a care provider who practices in that setting. Hospitals are the most frequent setting for birth in North America. They may have a traditional labor and delivery suite, or they may offer birthing suites that provide a home-like atmosphere. A free-standing birth center provides an atmosphere that is less institutional than that of the hospital. Home birth allows the woman to be in her own surroundings and to feel a greater sense of control over the birth. Delivery is often managed by a nurse midwife, who has followed the couple throughout pregnancy. (More information about these birth settings is presented in Chapter 1.)

Support Person

During labor, it is important for the woman to have someone who stays with her to help her through the experience. The support person is most often the father of her baby. However, if the father is unable to be with her or if the mother prefers, a relative or friend takes this role (Fig. 11–1). Some women wish to share the birth experience with several close friends or relatives. The number of support people allowed during labor and birth varies. If the area is small and the setting traditional, often only one person is permitted to be with her. In less traditional settings, more support people are usually allowed.

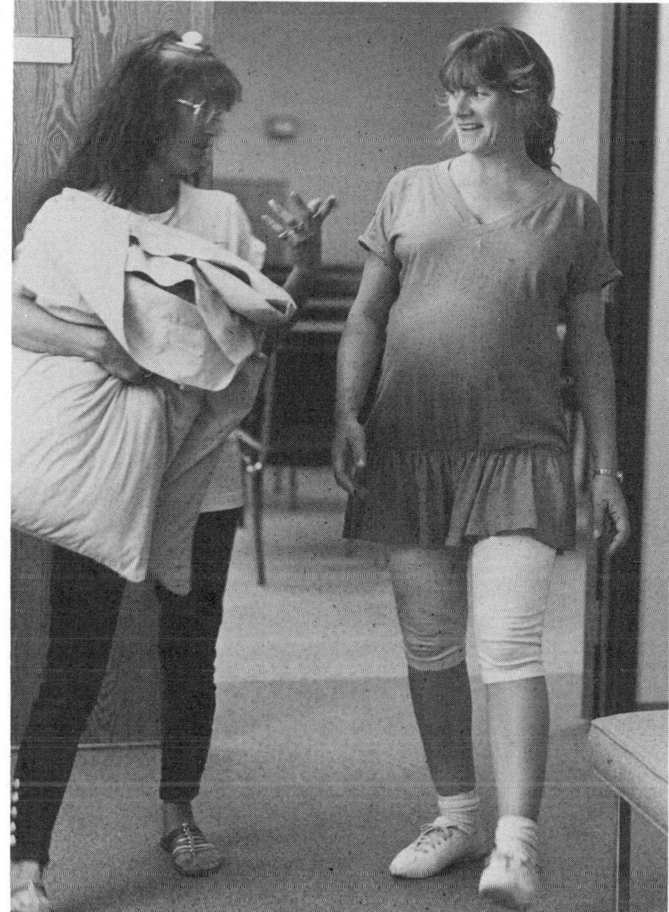

Figure 11-1

This expectant mother has asked her friend to be her labor partner. They are attending classes together.

Siblings

The presence of children at birth is a controversial topic. Some feel that children become closer to their new sibling when they are present at the birth. Others think that seeing the birth process, the blood, and the mother in pain may be too frightening for children. Some of the debate centers on what age it is most appropriate to include the child.

Regardless of the controversy, some parents believe that their other children should participate in the birth. They may wish them to attend all or part of the labor and birth or to join the parents just after the birth to be included in the immediate celebration. In some areas, sibling participation takes place only in home births. In others, siblings are allowed in hospitals or birth centers under certain circumstances.

When sibling presence is permitted, an adult support person stays with the child throughout the experience. The support person should have no role other than to attend to the child. This role includes gauging the child's response, giving the child explanations and reassurance, and taking the child out of the room as needed. Because labor generally is lengthy, children often come and go during the labor process but are present when birth is imminent or just after the actual birth.

Education

One of the decisions that the expectant mother must make is whether to take prenatal education classes, based on what is available in her area, costs, and the kinds of information she needs. In some areas, there is a vast array of different classes from which to choose. In others, the selection is limited to childbirth preparation classes only.

Small classes of a few women and their partners are ideal, but they may be too expensive or unavailable. If the class includes more than ten to 12 couples, the teacher should have an assistant to help with individual instruction. There is some variety in teacher qualifications. The educator may or may not be a registered nurse, have experience in some area of maternity nursing, or be certified by a nationally known organization. Classes based in hospitals include detailed information on what to expect in that particular hospital but may not cover options not available there. Hospital classes have sometimes been criticized for teaching clients to be "good" or compliant patients. A woman may wish to talk to the instructor before taking the class to ask about the size of the class, the teacher's philosophy of childbirth and background, teaching methods used, and any other questions that she may have about the classes.

✔ Check Your Reading

1. What are the goals of education for childbearing?
2. What are some of the major decisions couples must make in preparation for childbirth?

Types of Classes Available

Although most people think of education for childbearing primarily in terms of preparation for the birth experience, classes are available in all areas of pregnancy, childbirth, and parenting. Some of the more common educational offerings are discussed here.

Early Pregnancy Classes

Early pregnancy classes focus on the first two trimesters. First-trimester classes are sometimes called "Early Bird" or "Right Start" classes. They cover information on adapting to pregnancy, dealing with early discomforts such as morning sickness and fatigue, and understanding what to expect in the months ahead. Emphasis is on how to have a healthy pregnancy by obtaining prenatal care and avoiding hazards to the fetus.

During second-trimester classes, the focus is on changes that occur during middle pregnancy and preparing for birth. Information on body mechanics in relation to an enlarging abdomen, working during pregnancy, and what to expect during the third trimester is included. Teachers discuss childbirth choices and information to help students become more knowledgeable consumers. Mothers may attend classes alone or with a support person. A complete list of topics for early pregnancy classes is in Table 11–1.

Exercise Classes

Exercise classes help women keep fit and healthy during pregnancy. Some classes continue into the postpartum period as well. A woman may need her physician's consent to be certain that she is able to participate safely. The instructor should understand the special needs of pregnancy. Exercises should be

Table 11–1. EARLY PREGNANCY CLASSES

Pregnancy
- Anatomy and physiology
- Physiological and psychological changes
- Fetal development
- Hazards to the mother or fetus (drugs, alcohol, cigarettes, environmental)
- Medical care (what to expect at each visit, importance)
- Prenatal screening tests

Self-Care
- Hygiene
- Nutrition
- Exercise and body mechanics
- Discomforts of pregnancy
- Sexuality
- Working and pregnancy

Infant Care
- Preparation for the newborn
- Choosing a pediatrician
- Infant development and care
- Infant feeding
- Preparation for breastfeeding

Birth
- Birth options (birth plan, costs)
- Danger signs
- Preterm labor

low impact and preceded by warm-up routines. Women should avoid excessive heart rate elevation to prevent diversion of blood away from the uterus. An added benefit of the classes is the opportunity for women to meet others with similar concerns.

Childbirth Preparation Classes

Women and their support persons learn self-help measures and what to expect during labor and birth in childbirth preparation classes (Fig. 11–2). Although once referred to as "natural childbirth" classes, they are now called "prepared childbirth" classes to denote that women are prepared for all aspects of childbirth, including complications. Couples learn coping methods that help them approach childbirth in a positive manner. Although teachers do not promise prevention of all pain in labor, the increased confidence gained in prepared childbirth classes is associated with a decreased perception and increased tolerance of pain during labor (Lowe, 1991).

Classes include information about phases and stages of labor and often a tour of the birth setting. The teacher describes pharmacologic and non-pharmacologic methods of pain relief. Supervised practice of relaxation and coping strategies in "labor rehearsals" is part of every class. Films of labor and birth assist women to develop a realistic picture of the birth process.

Advantages and disadvantages of various options in birthing are discussed. For example, couples may learn that epidural anesthesia generally removes most pain but may increase the length of labor, may make pushing less effective, and may make catheterization and administration of oxytocin more likely. On the other hand, use of relaxation techniques may avoid the need for analgesic drugs and the disadvantages of anesthesia but will probably not remove all discomfort. When women have a balanced view of their options, they are able to discuss them intelligently with caregivers and make better decisions.

Class series range from four to nine, depending on the content included. Because these may be the only classes a woman attends, information about the third trimester of pregnancy is often presented. Some classes also include discussion of the postpartum period, breastfeeding, and infant care. Table 11–2 contains a list of the usual prepared childbirth class topics.

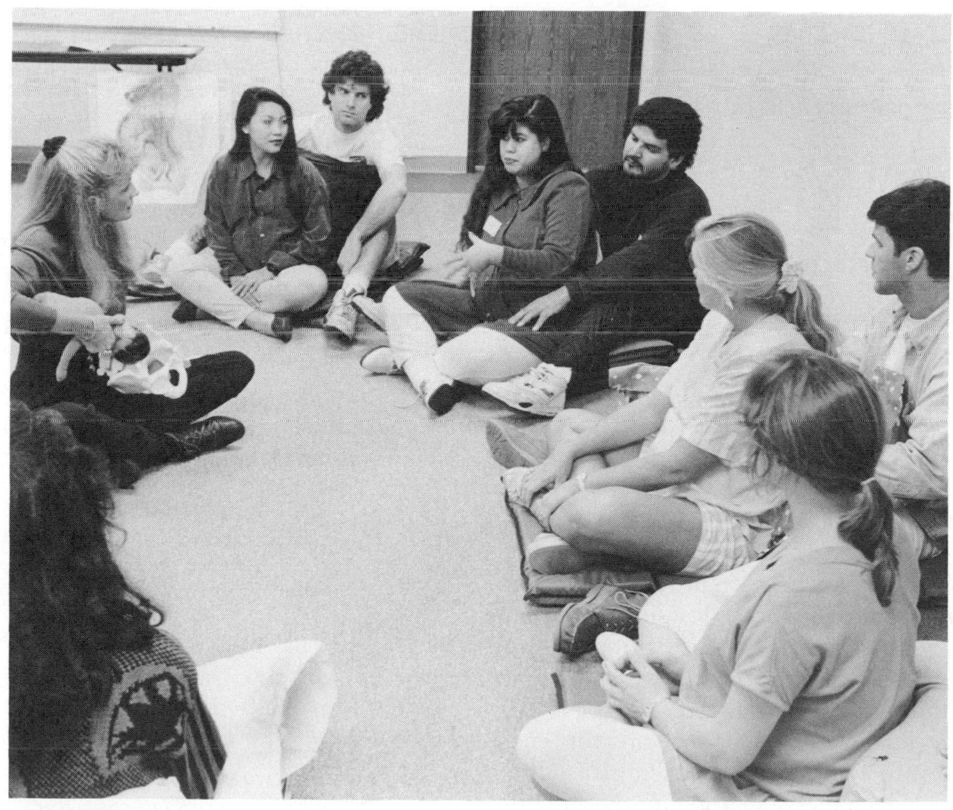

Figure 11-2

The nurse teaching the class discusses movement of the fetus through the pelvis.

Table 11–2. PREPARED CHILDBIRTH CLASSES

Third Trimester
Anatomy and physiology
Physical and psychological changes
Common discomforts and concerns
Nutrition
Exercise and body mechanics
Sexuality
Antepartum Testing
Ultrasound examination
Stress and non–stress tests
Amniocentesis
Labor and Birth
Anatomy and physiology of labor
Planning for the birth (consumerism, options, birth plan)
Signs of labor and when to go to the hospital
Admission to the hospital
Common procedures
Labor variations (back labor, long or short labor, etc.)
Delivery room occurrences
Recovery
Tour
Coping Techniques for Labor
Relaxation
Breathing techniques
Comfort measures
Labor rehearsals
Pain relief: pharmacologic and non-pharmacologic
Complications
Danger signs
High-risk pregnancy
Reasons for cesarean birth
Support Person
Role
Coaching techniques
Postpartum Period
Physiological and psychological changes
Hospital stay
Postpartum "blues"
Role adaptation
Normal Newborn
Characteristics
General care
Feeding
Safety

Refresher Courses

When more than 2 or 3 years has elapsed between a prepared childbirth class and a subsequent pregnancy, a refresher course is recommended to provide couples an update on new developments and to review techniques. Classes consist of one to three sessions in which supervised practice is the major focus. Basic information is omitted or briefly reviewed to clarify misconceptions and answer questions. Teachers often include a discussion of sibling adjustment and role changes in the family after the birth of another infant because these are major concerns of many parents.

Cesarean Birth Preparation Classes

Education about cesarean birth may take place in general childbirth classes or may be conducted separately for those planning a cesarean delivery. A full list of subjects included in cesarean birth classes is included in Table 11–3.

GENERAL CLASSES

Because one fourth of all births are cesarean deliveries, being prepared for this possibility is important for all women. Unanticipated cesarean delivery is discussed during prepared childbirth classes. Some teachers show films of both vaginal and cesarean births. Topics include indications, options, surgical procedure, and postoperative course.

Reasons for cesarean births should be discussed in detail. A woman might view the terms "failed induction" or "failure to progress" as casting blame on her. She may believe that if she had used relaxation techniques better or been more tolerant of pain, she might have avoided the need for surgery. Teachers often point out that the causes of cesarean births are not ones over which the woman has control.

Couples are sometimes inattentive during discussions about cesarean birth because they feel that "it can't happen to me." Pointing out the number of couples in the class who may have cesarean births (based on an average of 25 per cent) may catch their attention. Providing written materials may be helpful for later review should the need for surgery develop.

PLANNED CESAREAN BIRTH CLASSES

Women who know they will have a cesarean birth may attend planned cesarean birth classes. For those who had a cesarean delivery previously, the class offers an opportunity to share experiences and feelings and to clarify misconceptions. Often these women remember little of the preparation for the

Table 11–3. CESAREAN BIRTH CLASSES

Indications
Prenatal tests
Preparation (such as NPO, shave, Foley catheter)
Surgical procedure
Role of support person during surgery
Options
Postsurgical care
Anesthesia
Postoperative pain relief
Relaxation techniques
Postpartum course
Future birth options

procedure because they were frightened and exhausted. Women anticipating their first cesarean birth may appreciate hearing from others who have had the experience. The support person who will accompany the woman during surgery can learn from others who have filled this role.

Class content includes information on indications for cesarean births, preoperative and postsurgical care, and possible tests that might be necessary. An anesthesiologist may talk about pain relief. The woman and her support person may learn relaxation techniques to use during and after surgery. A discussion of options is included as well. A woman may want to watch the birth and can ask that a mirror be positioned so that she can see it. A woman who wishes to go into labor to ensure maturity of the fetus and who wants to experience labor should discuss this with her caregiver. Class discussion helps couples feel that they have some control over what happens and provides a basis for discussion with caregivers.

Vaginal Birth After Cesarean Birth (VBAC)

Vaginal birth is encouraged for women who have had a previous cesarean birth, whenever possible. These women may take a VBAC class. Content includes explanations of when a VBAC is possible, the extra precautions taken and their reasons, what to expect during labor and birth, and coping techniques. Although the focus is on positive expectations, situations that might make another cesarean delivery necessary are covered. Discussion includes the emotional aspects of a "failed VBAC" as well.

Breastfeeding Classes

Classes on breastfeeding help to increase a woman's confidence in her ability to breastfeed successfully and provide her with sources of help should she encounter difficulties. They include information on physiology of lactation, feeding techniques, establishing a milk supply, and prevention and solutions to common problems (Table 11–4). Women generally take the class during the last trimester. Partners who attend learn methods of providing support during breastfeeding. Some teachers hold additional sessions after the birth to provide ongoing counseling at a time when mothers may experience unexpected problems alone. This allows discussion of problems as they occur and preparation for later events such as weaning.

Table 11–4. BREASTFEEDING CLASSES

Anatomy and physiology of the breast	Problems
Preparation for breastfeeding	Prevention
Flat or inverted nipples	Engorgement
Breast shells	Sore nipples
Physiology of lactation	Mastitis
Positioning	Insufficient milk supply
Types	Use of bottles
Latch on	Storing breast milk
Establishing milk supply	Nipple confusion
Frequency of feedings	Breast pumps
Length of feedings	Types
Nutrition	Use
	Working and breastfeeding
	Weaning

Infant Care Classes

Instruction on newborn care may be included in prepared childbirth classes or given separately. Content typically includes general care and common concerns, such as the crying infant and advantages and disadvantages of circumcision. Baby equipment, such as various types of infant car seats, is often available for parents to examine. The teacher may discuss concepts of infant stimulation to help parents learn its importance and methods of stimulating infants during pregnancy and after birth. Table 11–5 lists topics usually covered in infant care classes.

Postpartum Classes

Although the topic of the postpartum period is often covered in prepared childbirth classes, there are also classes that the mother can attend when she

Table 11–5. INFANT CARE CLASSES

Characteristics of the normal newborn	Safety
Marks and rashes	Car seats
Normal behavior	"Baby proofing" the home
General care	Baby equipment
Diapering	How to choose
Cord care	Safety features
Circumcision care	Toys appropriate for age
Laundering baby clothes	Early growth and development
Bathing	Expectations
Feeding methods and possible problems	Infant stimulation
Schedules	Immunization
Night feedings	Illness
Colic	Signs
Other concerns	How to take a temperature
Crying	Calling the physician
Sleeping through the night	Common conditions
	First aid
	Infant cardiopulmonary resuscitation (CPR)

Table 11-6. POSTPARTUM CLASSES

Physiological changes	Nutrition
Involution	Exercise and weight loss
Psychological changes	Sexuality
"Baby blues"	Resumption of intercourse
Role changes	Contraception
Siblings	Working and parenting
Self-care	

returns home after birth. Content may include the physiological and psychological changes of the postpartum period, role transition, sexuality, and nutrition. The class may be in lecture format or may be an informal support group led by a knowledgeable professional. Some classes focus primarily on exercise for the postpartum period and cover other information only briefly. Because so many women return to work soon after childbirth, classes are often held at night or on weekends, and the problems involved in being a working mother are discussed (Table 11-6).

Classes for Other Family Members

SIBLINGS

Children who take sibling classes usually range from age 2 to 10 years. The classes help them develop a realistic understanding of newborn characteristics and decrease their anxiety about the approaching birth (Fig. 11-3). Parents learn ways of helping children adjust to the birth of a new baby. Such preparation of children and parents can improve family interaction, reduce conflicts, and decrease sibling rivalry (Fortier et al, 1991).

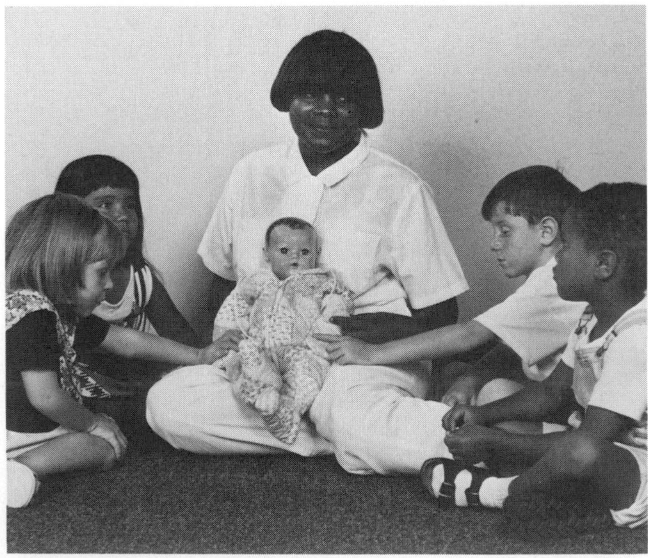

***Figure* 11-3**

During sibling classes, children learn about the new baby coming into their lives.

Many young children have never seen a newborn infant and are expecting an older child to be their playmate. A tour of the nursery or a visit with a newborn infant allows them to see newborns at close range and learn to be safe helpers. The teacher may explain the birth process in terms suitable for the ages of the children. Videos promote discussion about normal feelings of jealousy and anger. Emphasis is placed on the important role of big brothers and sisters and the fact that a baby could not take their place. Other teaching techniques include stories, dolls, drawings, coloring books, and models of fetal development.

A separate discussion for parents may provide suggestions for further preparation and methods of assisting siblings in the transition period after birth. Concerns about sibling rivalry and meeting the needs of more than one child are common topics. The importance of sibling visitation during hospitalization is another topic. Seeing the mother in the hospital decreases a child's anxiety about why she is not at home.

Special sibling classes may be held for children who will be present at the birth. These help prepare the child for the sights and sounds of birth. The child's support person also attends the class.

GRANDPARENTS

Classes for grandparents provide an update about changes in childbirth and parenting practices in the years since they became parents. Lack of understanding about new ways of childbearing may cause conflict between young couples and their parents. An explanation of these developments improves communication between the generations. Grandparents learn about their own importance in providing assistance to young parents and compare parenting in the past and present in a supportive environment with others in similar situations.

Topics generally focus on family-centered childbirth, infant care, and the art of grandparenting. Because grandfathers were not allowed to participate in labor and delivery when they became fathers, grandparents may have many questions about this change. Infant care discussions review current thinking about care and feeding. Early growth and development and accident prevention are also included.

Particularly emphasized is the importance of the role of grandparents. Without help in understanding the vital part that they play in the developing new family, they may feel shut out. After classes, grandparents often express pleasure about the changes that have occurred and develop practical ways of helping the entire family adjust to their new roles.

✔ Check Your Reading

3. What is included in classes women take in early and later pregnancy?
4. Why should all women learn about cesarean childbirth?
5. Why are sibling and grandparent classes important?

Education for Childbirth

Many studies have attempted to determine whether or not education for childbirth affects the outcome in regard to client satisfaction, pain relief, length of labor, and frequency of complications. The results of these studies vary. Some report shorter labors with fewer complications and less need for pharmacologic pain relief measures, whereas others report no difference between prepared and unprepared women. Most studies agree that couples receiving prenatal preparation for childbirth are more satisfied with their birth experiences and have a greater feeling of control, even when there are unexpected complications.

Causes of Pain in Labor

The pain of childbirth results from hypoxia of uterine muscle, dilation and stretching of the cervix, pressure and pulling on adjacent organs, and pressure from the presenting part on the vagina and perineum during birth (Blackburn and Loper, 1992). Many other factors can increase pain. Fetal size and position influence length of labor as well as pain. Vaginal examinations and use of oxytocin increase the strength of contractions. A woman's expectations, level of fatigue, anxiety, and availability and actions of a support person also affect her perception of pain.

Methods of Pain Management

EDUCATION

One of the most important aspects of any childbirth preparation class is education to increase the woman's confidence in her ability to cope with birth. Women who are confident about their coping abilities report less pain during labor than women who lack confidence (Lowe, 1991). Confidence may be increased by attending classes that provide knowledge about what will happen, vicarious experiences such as films or reports of others' births, and techniques to increase coping ability during labor. All methods of prepared childbirth today include education to reduce anxiety and fear of the unknown.

By learning what to expect during labor and birth, women have a chance to rehearse the experience in their minds to prepare for the actual event. They practice using coping techniques during simulated contractions. It is essential that class information is realistic and valid and that possible variations are discussed. If women find labor or birth greatly different from what they learned in classes, they may feel that none of the information they received will be beneficial in helping them.

RELAXATION

Tension during labor causes tightening of abdominal muscles, impeding contractions, and increasing pain by stimulation of nerve endings that heighten awareness of pain. Prolonged muscle tension causes fatigue and increased pain perception (Shrock, 1988). When anxiety and tensions are high, uterine contractions are less effective and length of labor increases. A woman who is able to remain relaxed is likely to labor more efficiently and with less pain and to be better able to use other techniques to help herself. Many different techniques are taught to enhance relaxation during labor.

CONDITIONING

Many of the techniques used for prepared childbirth are partially based on theories of conditioned response, in which certain responses to stimuli become automatic through frequent association. Women learn to associate uterine contractions with relaxation by practicing relaxation techniques with a mental image of a contraction. Because conditioning requires a great deal of practice to make it effective, women are encouraged to practice their techniques daily. For some women, the intensity of real uterine contractions is surprisingly different from what they experienced during practice sessions. They may have difficulty with relaxation as a result and will need to use other methods along with conditioning.

GATE CONTROL THEORY

According to gate control theory, transmission of impulses is controlled by a neural mechanism in the dorsal horn of the spinal cord. Transmission is affected by stimulation of large- or small-diameter sensory nerve fibers and descending impulses from the brain. This mechanism opens or closes the "gate" to pain sensation by allowing or preventing some impulses from reaching the brain, where they are recognized as pain.

Pain is transmitted through small-diameter sensory nerve fibers. Stimulation of large-diameter fibers interferes with conduction through small-diameter fibers, thus "closing the gate" and decreasing the amount of pain felt. Firm massage, heat, cold, and pressure on the palms or fingertips stimulate large-diameter nerve fibers. Relief is temporary because stimulation of these fibers results in habituation, or decreased response to stimuli. Periodically changing the type or area of stimulation increases effectiveness. Because impulses from the brain have a similar ability to impede transmission through the dorsal horn, mental stimulation techniques, such as breathing and imagery, that increase concentration are also useful in labor (Blackburn and Loper, 1992). Although these methods may not completely prevent pain, they may decrease the severity of perceived pain.

Methods of Childbirth Education

Although all methods of prepared childbirth education use some combination of the pain management techniques discussed above, each has some unique aspects. There are some differences in types of classes and class content, depending on geographical area. Many of the classes have a somewhat eclectic approach, providing a variety of techniques from which couples can choose those that work best for them.

Dick-Read Childbirth Education

Grantly Dick-Read was an English physician who was one of the first to use education and relaxation techniques to help women through childbirth. His theory was that fear of childbirth resulted in tension and pain. The method involves slow abdominal breathing in early labor and rapid chest breathing in advanced labor. His methods were the first to be called "natural childbirth."

Bradley Childbirth Education

The Bradley method was the first to include the father as support person for "husband-coached childbirth." Slow abdominal breathing and relaxation are taught in these classes. There may be an emphasis on avoidance of medication or other interventions.

LeBoyer Method of Childbirth

LeBoyer childbirth, sometimes called "birth without violence," is not a method of childbirth but a view that birth is a traumatic experience for the neonate. To decrease the trauma at birth, lights are dimmed and noise is decreased to help the newborn adapt to extrauterine life more easily. The infant receives a warm bath immediately after birth to help relaxation.

Lamaze Childbirth Education

The Lamaze method is often called the "psychoprophylaxis" method because it uses the mind to prevent pain. It involves the mind in concentration and uses conditioning to help the woman respond to contractions with relaxation and various techniques to decrease pain. It is the most popular method used today.

CLASS CONTENT

Content of specific Lamaze classes may differ, but most follow a similar pattern. Although the focus is on the childbirth experience, other topics such as exercise in pregnancy, the postpartum period, and infant care are often included. Techniques for increasing coping in labor are directed at education to prevent fear of the unknown and activities that promote relaxation during labor.

Teachers of the Lamaze method acknowledge that labor is painful and do not promise that techniques will produce a pain-free birth. Instead, the techniques are used to increase the woman's ability to cope with pain by relieving some of the distress that accompanies it. The gate theory of pain relief and the importance of practice for conditioning are emphasized.

EXERCISES

Women learn exercises to tone and condition muscles to prepare for childbirth and help prevent discomfort in late pregnancy. Because the classes are taken during the third trimester of pregnancy, selection of exercises must take into consideration the changes in center of gravity and joint stability that occur at that time. Exercises often include the pelvic rock (or tilt), tailor sit, Kegel exercise, and various stretching exercises (see Chapter 7).

RELAXATION TECHNIQUES

The ability to relax during labor is one of the most important components for coping effectively with childbirth. Women learn a variety of exercises to help them recognize and release tension. The labor partner or coach assists the woman by providing feedback during exercise sessions as well as during labor. Because the coach knows the woman well and how she responds to strain, he or she is alert to ways in which the woman shows tension. For example, she may tighten her shoulders, wrinkle her forehead, or jiggle her foot when stressed. The coach helps her focus on areas that she finds difficult to relax.

Like other techniques, relaxation exercises are partially based on conditioning and must be practiced frequently to be useful during labor. Couples begin practice sessions in a quiet, comfortable setting. Later they practice in other places that simulate the noise and unfamiliar setting of the hospital. Relaxation exercises may also be combined with other techniques such as imagery or massage (Fig. 11–4).

Progressive Relaxation. Progressive relaxation involves contracting and then consciously releasing different muscle groups. The exercise is repeated throughout the body until all voluntary muscles are relaxed. By doing this, the woman learns to differentiate the feeling of tense muscles from that of relaxation. With this knowledge, she can systematically assess and then free muscle tension throughout her body.

Neuromuscular Dissociation. Neuromuscular dissociation helps the woman learn to relax her body even when one group of muscles is strongly contracted. This helps prepare her to relax during the powerful uterine contractions of labor. The woman contracts an area such as an arm or leg, then concentrates on letting tension go from the rest of her body. After a short time of contracting one area, she relaxes it and moves on to another. Her coach checks for unrecognized tension by gently moving areas to see that they are limp.

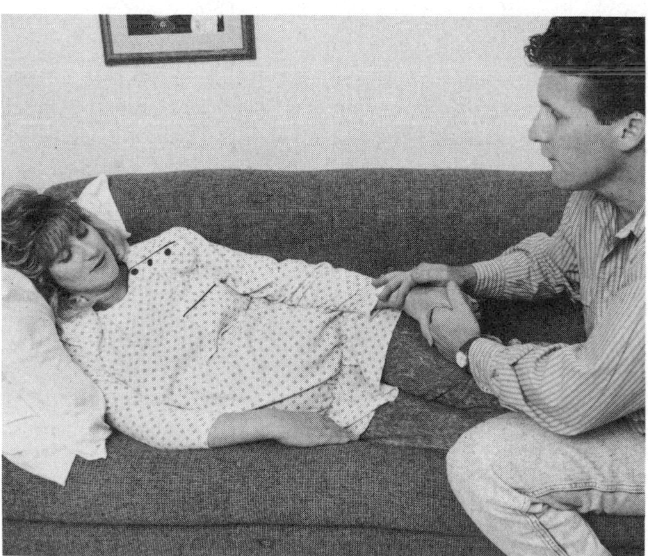

Figure 11-4

The coach checks for areas of tension while his partner practices relaxation techniques for labor.

Touch Relaxation. The purpose of this exercise is to help the woman learn to loosen taut muscles when they are touched by her partner. The woman tenses an area and then relaxes it as her partner strokes or massages it. By frequent practice of this exercise, the woman becomes conditioned to respond to touch with relaxation. During labor, her partner's touch is a signal that causes automatic release of tension.

Relaxation Against Pain. Because it is difficult to imagine the pain and strength of labor contractions for the first-time mother, women may occasionally practice use of relaxation against pain. The pain is caused by her partner, who exerts pressure against a tendon or large muscle of the arm or leg. The pressure is applied gradually to simulate the gradual increase, peak, and decrease of a uterine contraction.

OTHER TECHNIQUES

All of the other techniques taught in prepared childbirth classes aid the woman in relaxation. They can be divided into those that involve touch or cutaneous stimulation and those that involve mental stimulation. Various methods of touch stimulate large-diameter sensory nerve fibers and interfere with transmission of pain impulses to the brain through small-diameter sensory nerve fibers. Mental focusing or distraction also interferes with pain messages reaching the brain.

Cutaneous Stimulation Techniques

Effleurage. Effleurage is massage usually performed on the abdomen during contractions (Fig. 11–5). It is most effective if firm pressure is applied because light pressure stimulates small-diameter nerve fibers, the same ones over which pain impulses travel. Therefore, light massage may actually increase pain. Firm pressure stimulates large-diameter nerve fibers of the abdomen as well as those in the palms and fingertips.

Women learn to do effleurage of the abdomen using both hands in a circular motion. If external

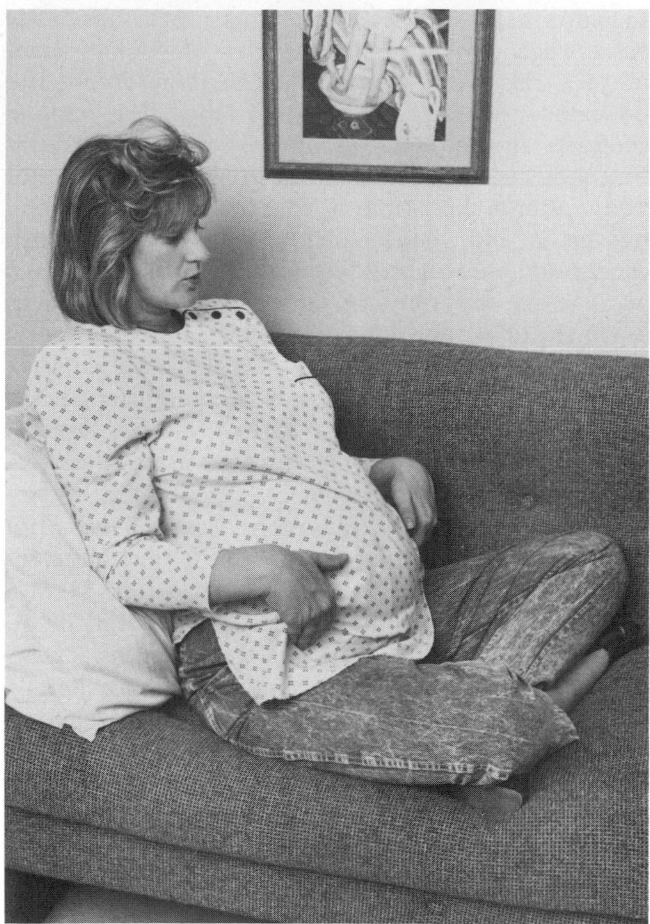

Figure 11-5

The woman begins effleurage with the hands at the symphysis and then slowly moves around the sides and down the center to the symphysis again. As an alternative, she can go up the center of the abdomen and around the sides. Using firm pressure is important.

fetal monitor belts cover the abdomen during labor, the woman can massage between the belts. When she lies on her side, she uses only one hand to massage her abdomen. In the sidelying position, she may find it more comfortable to make smaller movements on her abdomen or massage her thigh so that her arm and shoulder can remain relaxed.

Because habituation results in loss of effectiveness, effleurage should be varied periodically. The woman can massage her thigh instead of her abdomen or use her fingertips to trace circles or a figure-8 on the bed. When a specific pattern of effleurage is used, it provides a source of concentration and increased input into the brain. This may also interfere with transmission of pain impulses.

Other Massage. Some women like having the support person perform massage. Massage of the temples or shoulders may help the women relax these areas. The palms and soles of the feet are particularly sensitive to touch, and firm massage of these areas may be helpful. Having the woman and the coach alternate application of massage provides more variety in sensory input and decreases habituation. Types of stimuli should be changed whenever they no longer seem effective, generally every 15 to 30 minutes.

Sacral Pressure. Firm pressure against the sacrum may be helpful if the woman experiences the majority of her pain in her back. During contractions, the coach begins to increase pressure on the sacrum as soon as the contraction begins. If a fetal monitor is in place, the coach can watch the line depicting the contraction to determine when to begin and end the pressure. The hand may be moved slowly over the area or remain positioned directly over the sacrum, but pressure should be continuous and firm throughout the contraction.

Between contractions, the woman should give her coach feedback about hand placement. Often moving the hands a fraction of an inch will increase effectiveness. This technique can be combined with thermal stimulation to increase effectiveness. Tennis balls may also be used to apply pressure to the back.

Thermal Stimulation. Application of heat or cold stimulates thermoreceptors and may decrease pain sensation. Cool cloths used to wipe the woman's face, ice in a glove covered with a washcloth applied to the woman's lower back, or even ice chips offered to the woman for eating may be effective. Alternating cold with heat prevents habituation. In early labor, a shower with warm water directed against the back may be soothing. A warm bath blanket or a glove filled with warm water can be held against the sacrum for pressure and warmth. Heat and cold should never be applied to any area that is anesthetized, as injury could result.

Positioning. Position changes during labor also provide cutaneous stimulation. Women are taught to practice their techniques using a variety of positions and to change position frequently during labor. Ambulation in early labor makes contractions more efficient yet less painful. Changing from lying on one side to another or using a sitting position enhances ability to relax. Position changes approximately every 30 to 60 minutes increase comfort and decrease muscle fatigue.

Mental Stimulation Techniques

A variety of methods decrease pain by increasing mental concentration. These may modify pain perception as a result of interference with pain impulses in the spinal cord or in the brain itself.

Focal Point. A focal point is an object on which the woman focuses her attention during contractions. It helps her direct her thoughts away from the contractions. During the contraction, she not only looks at the focal point but thinks about the shape, size, and gradations of colors of the focal point. Women often bring pictures of infants or a restful scenic landscape to focus on. The picture may bring back pleasant memories of a happy experience. If a video player will be available during labor, a videotape of scenery, perhaps combined with music, may increase interest in the focal point (Fig. 11–6).

Women who do not bring their own focal point to the birth setting may use anything near their line of vision, such as a picture in the room or a pattern on the wallpaper. Because the fetal monitor is directly next to the bed, many women focus on it. Watching the contraction pattern on the monitor is usually not soothing and tends to focus increased attention on the strength of the contraction. Focusing on a button or knob may be more helpful.

Some women prefer closing their eyes during contractions and using an internal focal point. This allows them to shut out light and movement around them and focus on a mental picture. Women who are familiar with meditation techniques may be more comfortable with this method of focusing.

Imagery. Another technique to enhance relaxation is imagery. During imagery exercises, childbirth educators often talk about a pleasant scene or experience while the woman imagines herself in that setting. The teacher may portray a walk through a meadow by describing the flowers, the warmth of the sun, the sound of birds, and a feeling of peacefulness. Couples are encouraged to practice imagining themselves in scenes of their own choosing. While practicing breathing techniques, the woman can picture oxygen entering her body to nourish her baby with every inhalation and tension leaving each time she exhales.

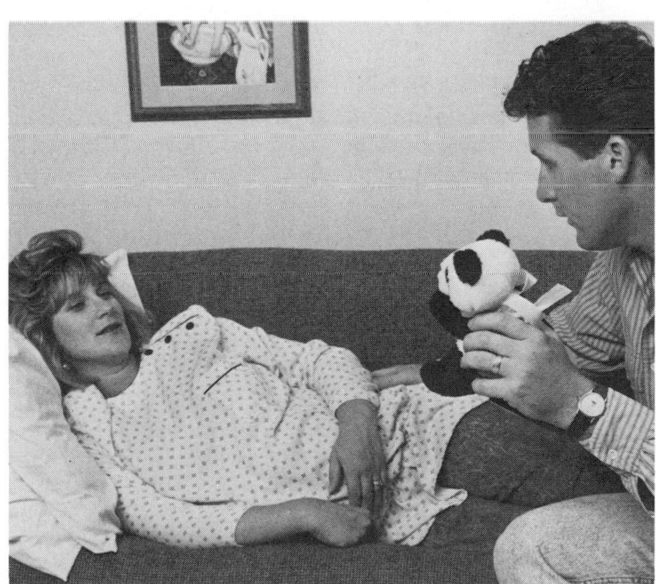

Figure 11-6

A stuffed toy or any other object can serve as a focal point on which the expectant mother can fix her attention during labor.

Other imagery suggestions are given for use during labor. The woman might picture a flower opening from a bud into full bloom to simulate opening of the cervix. She can imagine the cervix pulling over the infant's head or the infant moving lower in the pelvis with each contraction. Teachers usually advise women to save images of cervical dilation and childbirth until labor actually begins.

Music. Some women find that music or other sounds, like rainfall or waves at the seashore, help them relax. They may use tapes during practice and bring them, with headphones, when they come to the birth setting in labor. Using the tapes in practice makes them more effective for use in labor. Use of headphones has the added benefit of obscuring surrounding noise. The rhythm of the music may assist the woman in pacing her breathing.

BREATHING TECHNIQUES

As with other coping strategies, the primary purpose of breathing techniques is to enhance relaxation and decrease the number of pain impulses that are recognized by the brain. Although childbirth educators sometimes use different terms for breathing methods, the techniques are fairly similar among Lamaze classes.

The woman and her partner must practice the techniques frequently to gain comfort with them. If they become too complicated or if the woman has not practiced, they may not be helpful during labor. In labor, breathing should not be started until it is actually needed. This is usually when the woman can no longer walk or talk during a contraction. If techniques are used too early, the woman tends to move through the different types too quickly and she may stop using them.

First-Stage Breathing

Breathing in the first stage of labor consists of a cleansing breath and various breathing techniques known as paced breathing. The method begins with a very simple technique used as long as possible.

When it is no longer effective, breathing that requires more concentration is added.

Cleansing Breath. Each contraction begins and ends with a deep inspiration and expiration known as the cleansing breath. Like a sigh, a cleansing breath helps the woman release tension. It provides oxygen to help prevent myometrial hypoxia, one cause of pain in labor. The cleansing breath also helps the woman clear her mind to focus on relaxing and signals her support person that the contraction is beginning or ending. The woman may inhale through the nose and exhale through the mouth or may take her cleansing breath in any way comfortable.

Slow Paced Breathing. The first breathing used to cope with labor is slow paced breathing. It is a slow, deep breathing that increases relaxation. The woman should concentrate on relaxing her body rather than on regulating the rate of her breathing. This naturally brings about slower breathing, similar to that which occurs during sleep. She can use nose, mouth, or combination breathing, depending on which is most comfortable.

The woman uses slow paced breathing as long as possible during labor because it promotes relaxation and sufficient oxygenation. Labor nurses often teach the technique to women who enter labor unprepared. It is easy to learn between contractions and, with the support of the nurse, helps even a frightened woman become calm and able to work with her contractions.

As with all techniques, there needs to be some variety introduced to prevent habituation. Adding other pain relief approaches such as effleurage may help prolong the effectiveness of slow paced breathing. Using another type of breathing for a short time may allow the woman to return to slower breathing again later.

Although a specific rate may or may not be taught, slow paced breathing should be *no slower than half* the woman's usual respiratory rate to ensure adequate oxygenation. This is generally about six to nine breaths a minute.

Modified Paced Breathing. When slow paced breathing is no longer effective, the woman begins modified paced breathing. This upper chest breathing at a faster rate matches the natural tendency to use more rapid breathing during stress or physical work, such as labor. Although modified paced breathing is more shallow than slow paced breathing, the faster rate allows oxygen intake to remain about the same. As with slow paced breathing, the focus is on release of tension rather than on the actual number of breaths taken.

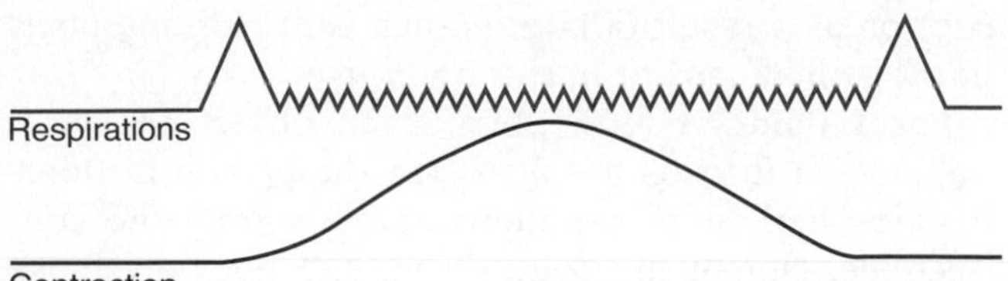

The pattern for modified paced breathing should be comfortable to the woman, and *no faster than twice* her normal respiratory rate, to prevent hyperventilation or interference with relaxation.

Women sometimes learn to combine slow and modified paced breathing during the course of a contraction. They begin slowly and use shallow, faster breathing over the peak of the contraction. During labor, women often do this naturally and may not need to practice beforehand. The most important concern is that the breathing not interfere with relaxation but enhance it.

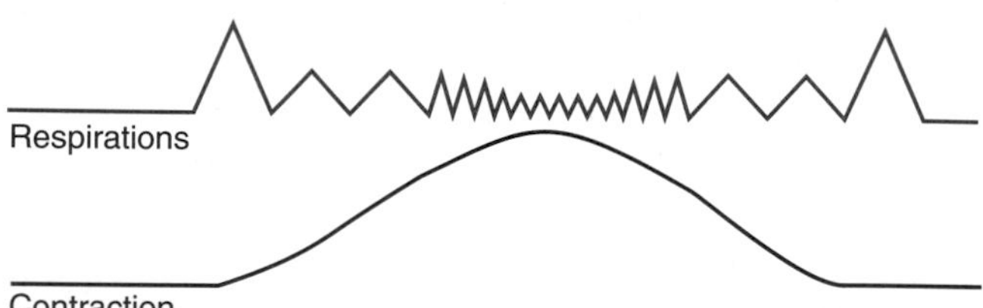

Slow and modified paced breathing can be combined by using the slower breathing at the beginning and end of the contraction and the more rapid breathing over the peak of the contraction.

Patterned Paced Breathing. Patterned paced breathing (sometimes called pant blow, "hee hoo," or "hee blow" breathing) involves focusing on the pattern of breathing. It is similar to modified paced breathing; after a certain number of breaths, however, the woman exhales with a slight emphasis or blow, then begins the modified paced breathing again. This addition causes her to focus more on her breathing and reduces habituation. Some educators teach women to make a sound such as "hee" during this breathing and to blow through pursed lips with a "hoo" sound. Others avoid special sounds, which tighten the vocal cords and may decrease relaxation.

The number of breaths before the increased exhalation may remain constant (usually between two and six) or may change in a pattern. Variations include a

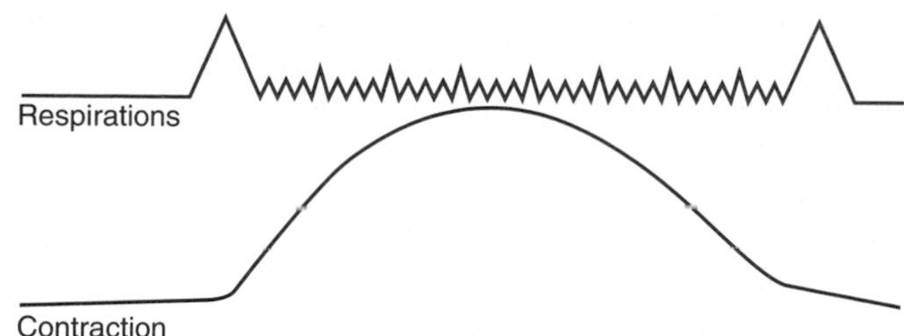

Patterned paced breathing adds a slight emphasis or "blow" on the exhalation in a pattern. The diagram shows the emphasis after every third inhalation.

set pattern such as "3-1, 6-1, 3-1" or a decreasing pattern such as "6-1, 5-1, 4-1, 3-1." Some couples use a random pattern determined by the coach, who uses hand signals to show the number of breaths the woman should take before each blow. The coach may hold up fingers to show the total breaths to be taken or a single finger for each breath. This may help the woman maintain a steady pattern. However, use of the random pattern may be ineffective without sufficient practice to enable the couple to work together well.

Breathing to Prevent Pushing. If a woman pushes strenuously before the cervix is completely dilated, there is a risk of injury to the cervix and the fetal head. Instructors teach women to blow when they have a premature urge to push. This prevents closure of the glottis and breath holding, which are a part of strenuous pushing. The woman learns to blow repeatedly using short puffs during the time the urge to push is strong. The support person may learn to blow along with her to help the woman concentrate.

Common Problems. Common problems that occur during breathing techniques include hyperventilation and dryness of the mouth. Hyperventilation occurs when breathing is incorrectly performed; that is, rapid deep breathing causes excessive loss of carbon dioxide, eventually resulting in respiratory alkalosis. The woman may feel dizzy or lightheaded and have impaired thinking. Vasoconstriction leads to tingling and numbness in fingers and lips. If hyperventilation continues, tetany due to decreased calcium in tissues and blood may result in stiffness of the face and lips and carpopedal spasm.

Women are taught to blow into a paper bag or their own cupped hands if they begin to feel dizzy. This increases carbon dioxide levels. Coaches learn that hyperventilation is a sign of incorrect breathing and help the woman make changes in her breathing as necessary.

Dryness of the mouth occurs when the woman uses prolonged mouth breathing. To avoid dryness, she can place her tongue gently against the roof of her mouth to moisturize entering air. The support person can offer ice, mouthwash, sour suckers, or liquids if they are allowed.

Second-Stage Breathing

Breathing in the second stage of labor includes the traditional method of pushing, as well as methods that involve less breath holding. The childbirth educator should be knowledgeable about the methods practiced in the surrounding communities so that the mother and her support person can learn those that they will actually use during labor (Fig. 11–7). The couple is encouraged to discuss second-stage

***Figure* 11-7**

The teacher helps each couple, individually and together, with pushing.

breathing techniques with the physician or nurse midwifc.

Traditional Pushing. In traditional pushing, the woman takes one or more cleansing breaths at the beginning of the contraction and then holds her breath, pushing as hard as she can for as long as possible. Generally, the coach counts slowly to ten while the woman holds her breath. She then quickly exhales, takes another breath, and pushes again, repeating the process until the contraction is over. The concern of those who oppose this method is that pushing against a closed glottis, the Valsalva maneuver, results in an increase in intrathoracic pressure and a decrease in blood pressure and blood return to the heart. The final result may be impaired blood flow to the uterus (Nelsson-Ryan, 1988). Proponents feel that breath holding is important in order to complete the second stage as quickly as possible, because this may be a time of danger for the fetus.

Other Pushing Methods. Other methods involve exhalation of small amounts of air through an open glottis during pushing. The woman may push in short bursts only when the urge is very strong instead of using prolonged expulsive efforts. If she holds her breath at all, it is for very short intervals only. Proponents feel that this method allows better oxygenation of both expectant mother and fetus.

✔ Check Your Reading

6. How can education, relaxation, and conditioning decrease pain?
7. How do cutaneous stimulation and imagery help reduce pain?
8. What is the purpose of breathing methods in labor?

The Support Person

Almost all methods of childbirth preparation encourage participation of someone who remains with the woman throughout labor. This person may be called a support person, coach, labor partner, or labor companion. The terms are often used interchangeably. Having someone with the woman during labor has been shown to help her cope more effectively and to decrease distress, duration of labor, and need for medication. The overall result is greater satisfaction with the childbirth experience (Butler et al, 1988). Emotional support has also been shown to reduce hospital stay and need for cesarean birth (Kennell et al, 1991).

The person who takes on this role may be the father of the baby, a friend or relative, or even a hired professional labor coach. They generally attend classes with the mother to learn about labor and delivery as well as techniques of coaching. By practicing together, the woman and her support person learn to work smoothly as a team during labor. Classes may increase self-esteem for support persons, who learn specific techniques to use during labor. When the support person is the father, practice sessions and working together may increase communication and a sense of closeness between the couple.

Role of the Support Person

Not all support persons play identical roles during labor. Whereas some take a major part in assisting the mother with relaxation and breathing techniques, others provide support in less active ways. They may confine their coaching to verbal encouragement or to giving physical care such as back rubs only when asked. Still others feel most comfortable with passive support—"being there" but not participating actively. Even with education, the support person may feel somewhat helpless and look to others to provide help to the laboring woman. Some men believe that active involvement in labor is not an acceptable role for them, perhaps because of cultural values. Nurses should encourage whatever role support persons choose.

It is important that coaches do not feel responsible for more than is included in the role. Teachers should discuss the duties of the labor nurse and encourage support persons to seek assistance when they are uncertain. The labor nurse may have suggestions or adaptations of techniques that may be very helpful. Class discussion of complications should include the role of the support person. For example, coaches should understand circumstances that would allow or preclude their presence during a cesarean birth.

Support Techniques

Support persons need practical methods to help the woman in labor. They learn how to time contractions at home and how to work with the fetal monitor, if used, in the hospital. Telling the woman when the monitor shows that the peak of the contraction is over can be particularly helpful. In advanced labor, the monitor may show a contraction beginning before the woman feels it. The coach can alert her to begin her techniques before the contraction becomes strong. The coach makes suggestions to make the environment less stressful. These might include lis-

Table 11–7. ITEMS FOR THE "GOODIE BAG"

Focal point
Lotion or powder to make massage more comfortable
Warm socks for cold feet
Several washcloths for washing face (ones from home smell better than hospital washcloths; colored, not white, which might get lost)
Hand-held fan
Tennis balls in sock for sacral pressure
Sugarless sour lollipop for dry mouth
Mouthwash for dry mouth
Lip balm
Instruction sheets or reminder checklists
Paper and pencil
Playing cards or simple games for early labor
Camera
Snack for coach
Tape player with headphones and tapes
Change for telephone and telephone numbers of important people to call after birth
Pillows

tening to tapes with headphones to obscure surrounding noise or turning down the lights to promote rest between contractions.

Some coaches learn a "panic technique" to use when the woman is finding coping with labor particularly difficult. This includes making eye contact and breathing along with her to help pace the breathing, helping her move to a more advanced level of breathing, and remaining calm. Having some direction for what to do if the woman loses control may make the support person feel more secure.

Providing comfort measures is an important role of the support person. These measures include offering ice chips, wiping the woman's face with a cold cloth, or helping her change positions. The coach applies sacral pressure or gives back rubs or other types of massage. During classes, couples learn breathing and relaxation techniques together. Coaches learn how to provide feedback and make suggestions during practice sessions as well as in labor. They discover the importance of encouragement and making suggestions in a positive manner.

The woman and her support person may pack a "goodie bag" of things that may aid in comforting the expectant mother during labor. As labor progresses, the coach uses each article as it seems appropriate. A list of common items for the "goodie bag" is given in Table 11–7.

✔ *Check Your Reading*

9. How does having someone with her help the woman in labor?
10. What are the various roles that the support person might take?
11. What specific techniques do coaches learn to help the woman in labor?

Application of Nursing Process

The nursing process will focus on assisting the woman and her partner to attain knowledge necessary to plan for a birth experience that is realistic and meets their individual needs. This will ensure that each family progresses through the childbearing experience as knowledgeable consumers and full participants in their own health care.

Assessment

Assessment includes determining the educational needs of the woman and her partner. The nurse may find that the couple is quite knowledgeable about available prenatal classes and childbirth options or that they need direction in this area. They may need help in choosing classes that will be right for them. The couple may come to the nurse with a birth plan already made, or they may need help in thinking through their expectations and desires.

Determine whether there are special factors that require adaptation of the usual educational approaches. Examples are the pregnant adolescent, the woman older than age 35 years, or the woman with a high-risk pregnancy. Cultural factors may be very influential in determining individual educational needs.

Assess the needs of support persons as well as the degree of participation they wish to have in the birth. They may have concerns about their role, especially during labor and delivery. These must be addressed to decrease their anxiety and to help them to be more effective in supporting their partner.

Analysis

The nursing diagnosis in this section pertains to the couple who is not unusually anxious about childbirth but desires more information: *Health Seeking Behaviors related to desire for education about pregnancy, childbirth, and/or parenting.*

Planning

The goals for this nursing diagnosis are that the woman and her partner will:

- Write a birth plan that is realistically based on available options and will meet their needs

- Verbalize a plan for obtaining education for pregnancy, childbirth, and parenting
- Report a feeling of increased confidence in their ability to cope with pregnancy, childbirth, and parenting after educational preparation is completed

Interventions

MAKING A BIRTH PLAN

Help couples write out a plan for their birth experience if they wish. The birth plan helps women and their partners look at the options that they have and take an active part in planning their birth experience. It is a tool for expanding communication with health professionals and ensures that the couple's wishes are known before labor begins. The plan may help the couple choose a provider, a setting, and classes that are most conducive to meeting their needs.

Help the couple learn about what choices are actually available in their locale. Making a plan to have a midwife assist at the birth in a free-standing birth center is unrealistic if such a center is not available near the couple's home. Explain any other restrictions that may be placed on their choices. For example, their insurance coverage may affect their length of stay or the type of facility that they can use. Low-income women may find that the kind of room or anesthesia that they receive for normal deliveries is dependent on their ability to pay. In addition, the health care provider or birth agency may have set policies on certain issues. Complications during labor or birth may necessitate changes in the plan.

Parents Want To Know

What Options Should We Consider for Our Birth Plan?

Whether or not the following options are available may depend on the policies of the birth facility and the health care provider. Discuss them with your provider to learn more about what is available to you.

Monitoring: Do you have strong feelings about using electronic fetal monitoring? Some women find it reassuring because it provides continuous information about the fetus. Others feel that it interferes with their ability to remain active during labor. Intermittent use of monitoring may be possible if there are no complications.

Intravenous Fluids: Some health care professionals consider intravenous fluids necessary to replace fluids lost during labor and for giving pain medications or emergency drugs. Some women find them painful and intrusive, whereas others do not mind them. Alternatives include waiting until active labor to begin intravenous fluids, avoiding them unless there are complications, or using a heparin lock so that you can move about more freely.

Food and Oral Fluids: Other than ice chips, food and fluids are generally not allowed during active labor because of decreased gastric motility, vomiting, and the possibility of aspiration if general anesthesia were suddenly needed. Clear fluids may be an option.

Shaving and Enemas: A very-small-volume enema and shaving just around the episiotomy area may or may not be routine. You may wish to make your preferences known.

Position: Walking, taking a shower, or otherwise remaining active rather than staying in bed throughout labor may or may not be important to you. Some women prefer a squatting, kneeling, or side-lying position for delivery. A birthing bed or chair may allow a comfortable and effective delivery position.

Episiotomy: Although an episiotomy is frequently performed, you may wish to avoid it unless absolutely necessary. Discuss the use of massage to stretch the perineal tissue as an alternative to an episiotomy.

Pain Relief: You may plan to avoid medication for pain relief completely, use it only if absolutely necessary, or wish to take it as soon as possible to avoid all pain. You may expect to use relaxation techniques throughout labor or only until you can receive anesthesia. Specific ideas about kinds of pain relief available should also be considered.

Support Person: You may wish only the infant's father, a relative, or a close friend to be with you during labor and birth, or you may prefer a number of people present for some or all of the experience.

Breastfeeding: You may wish to begin breastfeeding immediately after birth or within the first hour. You may prefer that no water or formula be given to your baby unless a problem develops. In order that they can sleep, some mothers ask that the nursery staff feed the baby during the night.

Siblings: You may want your other children present at the birth or to visit you while you are in the hospital.

Care of the Newborn: It may be possible to have your baby stay with you at all times to promote bonding. To get more rest, you may prefer to care for the baby only during the day and evening hours. The infant may spend the night in the nursery or return to you for night feedings.

Discharge: Although insurance coverage often determines the time of discharge, you may wish to leave the hospital even earlier, such as 12 hours after birth. Some women want to stay as long as possible to rest before assuming full care of the newborn along with their other responsibilities.

Some couples interview several physicians or nurse midwives to learn about the provider's usual practices, what exceptions are made, and the options available. With discussion, the couple and the provider can work out a plan that all find satisfactory. Some frequently considered alternatives for birth plans are discussed in Parents Want to Know: What Options Should We Consider for Our Birth Plan?

CHOOSING CLASSES

Help the woman and her partner find classes suited to their educational needs. Give them a list of classes in the community and a description of each. Suggest that they talk to others who have taken various classes to learn how well their needs were satisfied. Suggest that they interview teachers to learn about their preparation and philosophy. They should choose classes that include a wide range of information. Prepared childbirth classes should include discussion of complications as well as normal births. Some couples may want classes that make avoidance of pain medication a primary goal of childbirth. Many will prefer those that consider many tools, including medication, for coping with pain.

SUGGESTING CLASSES FOR SPECIAL NEEDS

Women with special needs may need referral to courses specifically for them. If none are available, make suggestions about how they can adapt what they learn in regular classes to their own situation.

Adolescents. Although adolescents may attend regular prenatal classes, those designed especially to meet their needs are most effective. Adolescents who attend special educational programs during pregnancy have been found to have fewer complications during and after birth (Slager-Earnest et al, 1987). Courses may be offered by high schools with programs for school-aged mothers, hospitals, clinics, or community agencies. Separating teenagers from adults results in a more comfortable environment in which girls can learn with peers who have similar problems and concerns. Fathers or other support persons may also attend.

Education for pregnant adolescents is similar to that for adults, but it focuses on the teenager's perceptions of childbearing. Clarification of misconceptions in a non-judgmental manner makes classes more meaningful. The girls need information about the importance of prenatal care, nutrition, weight gain, body image, and contraception, as well as labor and delivery. The effects of substance abuse and sexually transmitted diseases on pregnancy and the fetus are important topics for discussion.

Although the decision about whether to keep or relinquish the infant is often made before classes begin, the girls may discuss their options. Adolescents have a greater need for information about infant care than older mothers because of their lack of experience and unrealistic expectations of infants. Classes provide an opportunity for discussion of how an infant will affect their lives, future goals, and schooling.

Teenagers with academic problems may have difficulty with reading material or understanding abstract concepts. The effective teacher uses concrete terms and simple language to ensure understanding. Models, videos, and hearing from those who have previously taken classes make the course more relevant.

Mature Women. Although women older than age 35 may have special needs, classes specifically for them are seldom available. They generally take regular prenatal classes, but they may feel "different" from the younger women in their class as well as isolated from their friends who have completed childbearing. However, because delaying parenthood is quite common today, classes may provide older couples an opportunity to make friends with others with similar backgrounds. Older couples may want more sophisticated information than is usually included in regular prenatal classes, and they have many questions about the chances of complications related to age. Offer realistic reassurance, and direct them to books and articles that meet their need for in-depth information.

Women with High Risk Pregnancies. The woman with a high-risk pregnancy may miss regular prenatal classes because she must spend her last months of pregnancy confined to bed. If possible, help her arrange for individual instruction at home or in the birth facility. Audio and video tapes, written materials, or phone contact with an instructor are ways for her to learn and practice techniques without attending classes. In addition to helping her to prepare for childbirth, this will help decrease the boredom of bed rest and decrease her anxiety about what lies ahead.

Women Who Must Make Cultural Adaptations. Women from other cultures, especially those who do not speak English, are at a disadvantage when they enter birth settings in the United States. Classes in other languages are often available in communities where there are large groups with this need. Although these classes contain the same basic information as the English versions, the content and process must be adapted to meet the cultural and learning needs of the students.

The instructor discusses childbirth in the United States and compares it with that in the couples'

Nursing Care Plan 11–1

Planning for Childbirth

Assessment: Carmen Sanchez, age 19, is 4 months pregnant with her first baby and in good health. She and her husband Ramon "want to be the best parents possible." Carmen works as a bilingual teacher's aide in a primary school. Ramon, age 26, manages a small restaurant. Both Carmen and Ramon are the youngest in their families and have little actual experience with infants. Carmen plans to deliver her baby at the local hospital in a labor, delivery, recovery room (LDR).

Carmen tells the nurse that Ramon tends to favor the "old ways" and is unsure whether or not he should be involved during childbirth. She is most anxious for him to participate during her labor. Ramon seems embarrassed and says, "Having a baby is for women." He seems very loving toward Carmen and later says, "I want to help Carmen, but I don't know anything about these things. I'd just be in the way."

Nursing Diagnosis: Decisional Conflict related to father's ambivalence toward his anticipated role in childbirth.

Goals:

Ramon will:

1. Explore various options regarding his role during Carmen's labor and the birth of his baby.
2. Make a decision about his role during childbirth by 1 month before the baby is expected.

Intervention:	Rationale:
1. Explore Ramon's concerns before beginning discussion of educational opportunities with Carmen.	1. In some cultures, the man is the head of the family and makes many of the decisions. It is important to show respect for his authority if health teaching is to be accepted.
2. Use therapeutic communication techniques (such as reflection or paraphrasing) to help Ramon discuss his feelings about participating in childbirth.	2. Use of these techniques shows the nurse is willing to listen and thinks that the client's feelings are important.
3. Ask Ramon how he pictures childbirth and the role of the support person during labor and birth.	3. Teaching should begin at the client's level of knowledge.
4. Explain the various roles of the labor support person. Include the options of acting as "coach" or merely being present for the labor, the delivery, both, or neither.	4. The nurse must encourage and accept whatever role the support person chooses.
5. Ask Ramon what the advantages and disadvantages of each role might be. Clarify misinformation and discuss additional advantages and disadvantages if necessary.	5. Participation increases learning.
6. Present all information in a non-judgmental atmosphere.	6. If the nurse remains non-judgmental, the client will not feel pressured to make a particular decision.
7. Encourage Ramon to discuss this new information with his friends and family. If possible, refer him to other men who have played various roles during labor and delivery.	7. Discussion with family and friends is important when making decisions and provides a source for other viewpoints.
8. Suggest that Ramon think about his options and make a decision at a later date. Provide written information for Ramon and Carmen to review at home.	8. It takes time to digest new information and make decisions. Written information provides a readily available source for review.
9. Include Carmen throughout the discussion.	9. A couple may be unaware of each other's concerns and feelings. Hearing the partner talk about them will help each understand the other's point of view.

Nursing Care Plan 11–1 Continued

Planning for Childbirth

Evaluation:
Ramon reports 2 months later that he has decided to go with Carmen to classes to learn more about childbirth. He is unsure whether he will remain in the room during the actual delivery and says that he will decide how he feels about it when the time arrives. Carmen says that she feels comfortable with Ramon's decision and is glad he will go to prepared childbirth classes with her.

Assessment: Carmen has many questions about various options for childbirth. She is anxious to start classes with Ramon and asks about classes available on preparation for childbirth and parenting.

Nursing Diagnosis: Health Seeking Behaviors related to desire for education about pregnancy, childbirth, and parenting.

Goals:
1. Carmen and Ramon will identify what areas of information they need and how they will obtain that information.
2. Carmen will make a birth plan that satisfies them both.
3. After attending classes, they will both report a feeling of confidence in their ability to cope with pregnancy, childbirth, and parenting.

Intervention:	Rationale:
1. Give Carmen information about classes available in the community. Include types of classes, location, material covered, and costs. If this information is not available, refer Carmen to appropriate sources.	1. Providing a wide range of resources allows the client to choose classes that are most appropriate for her.
2. If there are many classes available, discuss what to look for and how to choose between classes. Discuss class size, number of classes in a series, and what information is covered in each.	2. Discussion of how to choose between options helps the client to become a more knowledgeable consumer.
3. Determine if Carmen has special educational needs. For example, would classes in Spanish or English be best for Carmen? If Ramon plans to attend classes, discuss his needs as well.	3. A couple may be more comfortable taking classes in their native language, if available. If Ramon attends classes, he may feel more at home with other men who may share his language, background, and concerns.
4. Suggest that they talk to other couples that they know who have attended various classes.	4. Talking to other couples helps couples learn from the experience of others.
5. Discuss various options for childbirth with Carmen. Discuss common practices of the physician and the birth setting Carmen has chosen. Give or refer Carmen to written material on the subject and answer questions. Suggest that as she reads, she list other questions to be discussed at a future visit.	5. A woman needs information about realistic options. Written material can be reviewed later and will stimulate other questions to increase her understanding.

Evaluation:
Carmen decides to take an early pregnancy class and an exercise class in English. She and Ramon will take a preparation for childbirth class that also includes breastfeeding and infant care. They will take this class in Spanish so that Ramon feels supported by other fathers in the class. After taking the classes, they report that they are anticipating a positive childbirth experience. Carmen is very pleased with her birth plan and shares it with the nurse and her physician.

Additional Nursing Diagnoses to Consider:
Anxiety related to lack of knowledge about childbirth
Ineffective Individual Coping related to extreme worry about childbirth

country of origin. Students learn the importance of prenatal care, which may not have been emphasized in their own culture. Misconceptions about needs and care throughout the childbearing period are clarified. It is important that the instructor not disparage customs that may seem very different from those practiced in the United States. Couples need to learn what to expect of health care providers and what will be expected of them during the birthing experience. The teacher for these classes usually has the same cultural background as the students. This ensures fluency in their language, understanding of their needs, and increases the chances that the instructor will be accepted.

Women with Other Needs. Refer the woman and her support person to classes that address other specific needs if necessary. Pre-conception classes are available for those just considering having a baby. They provide information about health before conception, choosing a caregiver, and the effect of pregnancy and childbirth on a woman's relationships and career. There may be classes for adoptive couples or women with multifetal pregnancies or handicaps. Those who have concerns about continuing their careers after birth may enroll in courses for working mothers to help them choose child care and learn to balance the needs of family and work. Classes for fathers only may provide a comfortable environment for discussion of fathering, sexuality, and role during labor and delivery, breastfeeding, and the postpartum period in the company of other men with similar concerns.

Evaluation

If goals have been achieved, the woman and her partner will:

- Write a realistic birth plan and attend classes that are appropriate for their needs.
- Verbalize satisfaction with the education they have received.
- Verbalize increased confidence in coping with pregnancy, childbirth, and parenting.

Summary Concepts

- Education for childbearing helps parents become knowledgeable consumers and active participants in pregnancy and childbirth.
- Women must make many decisions about childbirth. Some of the most important include choosing a birth attendant, a birth setting, a support person for labor, and the type of educational classes to attend.
- Many classes are available for pregnant women and their support persons. Those offered in early pregnancy emphasize having a healthy pregnancy. Those conducted in later pregnancy focus on preparing for childbirth, breastfeeding, and early parenting.
- Because one fourth of all births are cesarean, women in all prepared childbirth classes should be made aware of this possibility and learn about the procedure.
- Classes for siblings and grandparents help all family members prepare for the birth. Classes are designed to improve communication by discussing feelings and role change.
- Education, relaxation, and conditioning are used to increase coping ability for childbirth. Other techniques act to decrease transmission of pain impulses from the spinal cord to the brain, based on the gate control theory.
- Exercises in relaxation help women recognize and learn to reduce tension during labor.
- Cutaneous and mental stimulation techniques act to reduce pain perception. Techniques need to be varied to prevent habituation.
- Women learn a variety of breathing techniques for labor. Their purpose is to increase relaxation. Breathing should be no slower than half a woman's normal rate and no faster than twice her normal respiratory rate.
- Having a support person increases a woman's satisfaction with childbirth. The educated support person may find labor less stressful and feel increased self-esteem.
- The support person may participate in labor actively, minimally, or only by being present. All roles taken by the support person should be accepted by the nurse.
- Specific support techniques include assisting with relaxation and breathing, encouragement, sacral pressure, massage, and comfort measures.

References and Readings

Bernat, S.H., Powhatan, J.W., Marecki, M., & Snell, L. (1992). Biofeedback-assisted relaxation to reduce stress in labor. *Journal of Obstetric, Gynecologic, and Neonatal Nursing*, 21(4), 295–303.

Blackburn, S.T., & Loper, D.L. (1992). *Maternal, fetal, and neonatal physiology: A clinical perspective*. Philadelphia: W.B. Saunders.

Broussard, A.B., & Rich, S.K. (1990). Incorporating infant stimulation concepts into prenatal classes. *Journal of Obstetric, Gynecologic, and Neonatal Nursing*, 19(5), 381–387.

Butler, M., Luther, D., & Frederick, E. (1988). Coaching: The labor companion. In F.H. Nichols & S.S. Humenick (Eds.), *Childbirth education: Practice, research, and theory*. Philadelphia: W.B. Saunders.

Cahill, C.A. (1989). Beta-endorphin levels during pregnancy and labor: A role in pain modulation? *Nursing Research*, 38(4), 200–203.

Chapman, L.L. (1992). Expectant fathers' roles during labor and birth. *Journal of Obstetric, Gynecologic, and Neonatal Nursing*, 21(2), 114–119.

Crowe, K., & VonBaeyer, C. (1989). Predictors of a positive childbirth experience. *Birth*,16(2), 59–63.

Degenhart-Leskosky, S.M. (1989). Health education needs of adolescent and nonadolescent mothers. *Journal of Obstetric, Gynecologic, and Neonatal Nursing*, 18(3), 238–243.

Dick-Read, G. (1959). *Childbirth without fear*. New York: Harper & Row.

Evans, C.J. (1991). Description of a home follow-up program for childbearing families. *Journal of Obstetric, Gynecologic, and Neonatal Nursing*, 20(2), 113–118.

Fortier, J.C., Carson, V.B., Will, S., & Shubkagel, B.L. (1991). Adjustment to a newborn: Sibling preparation makes a difference. *Journal of Obstetric, Gynecologic, and Neonatal Nursing*, 20(1), 73–79.

Green, J.M., Coupland, V.A., & Kitzinger, J.V. (1990). Expectations, experiences, and psychological outcomes of childbirth: A prospective study of 825 women. *Birth*, 17(1), 15–24.

Guyton, A. (1991). *Textbook of medical physiology* (3rd ed.). Philadelphia: W.B. Saunders.

Hetherington, S.E. (1990). A controlled study of the effect of prepared childbirth classes on obstetric outcomes. *Birth*, 17(2), 86–90.

Kennell, J., Klaus, M., McGrath, S., Robertson, S., & Hinkley, C. (1991). Continuous emotional support during labor in a U.S. hospital: A randomized controlled trial. *Journal of the American Medical Association*, 265(17), 2197–2202.

Leventhal, E.A., Leventhal, H., Shacham, S., & Easterling, D.V. (1989). Active coping reduces reports of pain from childbirth. *Journal of Consulting and Clinical Psychology*, 57(3), 365–371.

Lowe, N.K. (1991). Maternal confidence in coping with labor: A self-efficacy concept. *Journal of Obstetric, Gynecologic, and Neonatal Nursing*, 20(6), 457–463.

NAACOG (1990). Childbirth classes support pregnant teens. NAACOG *Newsletter*, 17(8), 1, 7.

NAACOG Ad Hoc Committee. (1987). *Competencies and program guidelines for nurse providers of childbirth education*. Washington, D.C.

Nelsson-Ryan, S. (1988). Positioning: Second stage labor. In F.H. Nichols & S.S. Humenick (Eds.), *Childbirth education: Practice, research, and theory*. Philadelphia: W.B. Saunders.

Shrock, P. (1988). The basis of relaxation. In F.H. Nichols & S.S. Humenick (Eds.), *Childbirth education: Practice, research, and theory*. Philadelphia: W.B. Saunders.

Slager-Earnest, S.E., Hoffman, S.J., & Beckmann, C.J.A. (1987). Effects of a specialized prenatal adolescent program on maternal and infant outcomes. *Journal of Obstetric, Gynecologic, and Neonatal Nursing*, 16(6), 422–429.

Spadt, S.K., Martin, L.R., & Thomas, A.M. (1990). Experiential classes for siblings-to-be. MCN: *American Journal of Maternal Child Nursing*, 15(3), 184–186.

Sturrock, W.A., & Johnson, J.A. (1990). The relationship between

Part III

The Family During Birth

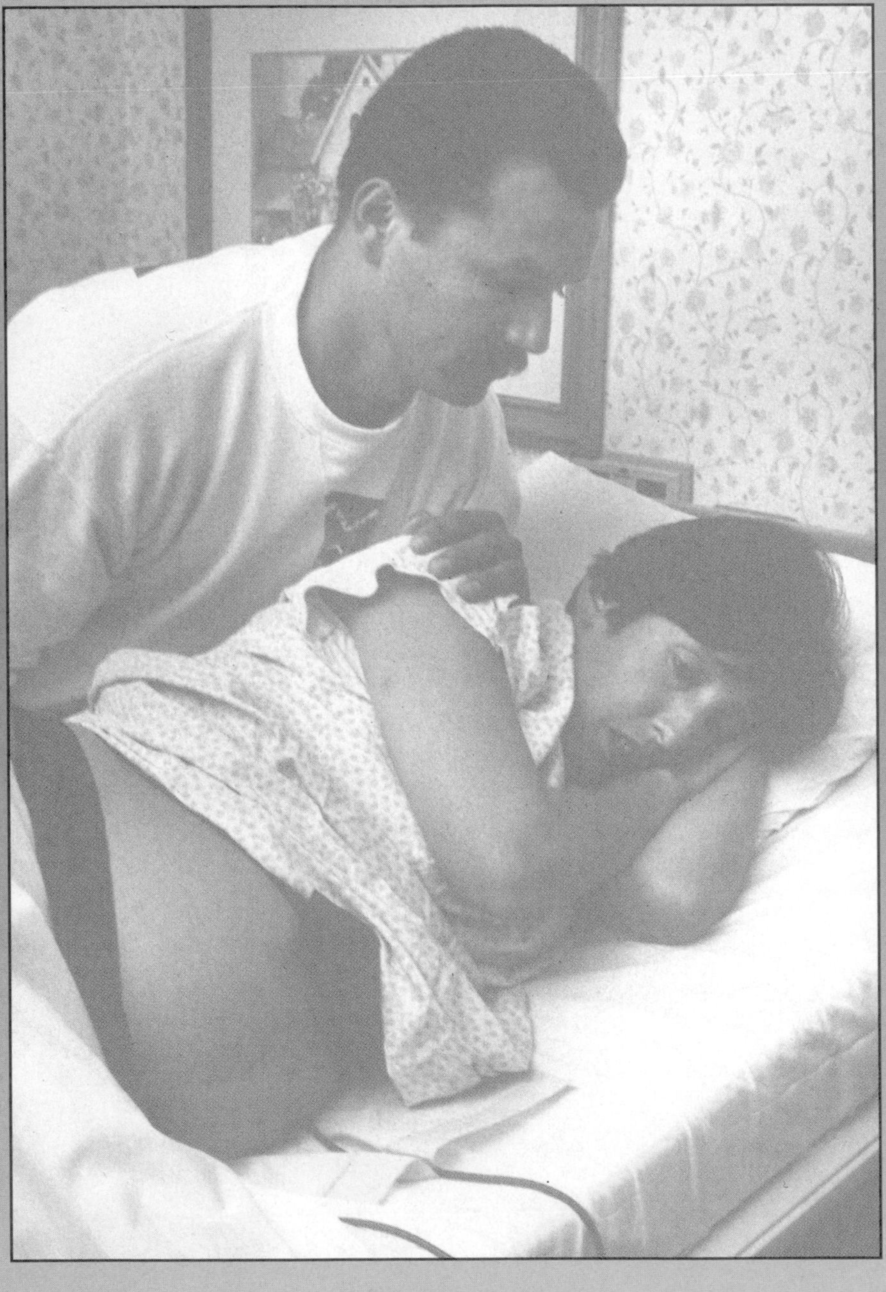

12

The Processes of Birth

Objectives

1. Describe the physiological effects of labor on the mother and fetus.
2. Explain how each component of the birth process affects the course of labor and birth and how the components are interrelated.
3. Relate each mechanism of labor to the process of vaginal birth.
4. Explain premonitory signs indicating that the onset of labor may be near.
5. Compare true labor with false labor.
6. Describe common differences in the labors of nulliparous and parous women.
7. Compare each stage and phase of labor.

Definitions

Acme • Peak, or period of greatest strength, of a uterine contraction.

Attitude • Relationship of fetal body parts to each other.

Bloody show • Mixture of cervical mucus and blood from ruptured capillaries in the cervix; often precedes labor and increases with cervical dilation.

Braxton Hicks contractions • Irregular, mild uterine contractions that occur throughout pregnancy; they become stronger and more evident in the last trimester.

Decrement • Period of decreasing strength of a uterine contraction.

Duration • Period from the beginning of a uterine contraction until the end of the same contraction.

Engagement • Descent of the fetal presenting part to at least a zero **station** (the level of the ischial spines in the maternal pelvis).

Fontanelle • Space at the intersection of sutures connecting fetal or infant skull bones.

Frequency • Period from the beginning of one uterine contraction until the beginning of the next.

Increment • Period of increasing strength of a uterine contraction.

Intensity • Strength of a uterine contraction.

Interval • Period between the end of one uterine contraction and the beginning of the next.

Lie • Relationship of the long axis of the fetus to the long axis of the pregnant woman.

Lightening • Descent of the fetus toward the pelvic inlet preceding labor.

Lochia • Vaginal drainage after birth.

Molding • Shaping of the fetal head during movement through the birth canal.
Myometrium • Uterine muscle.
Nullipara • A woman who has not completed a pregnancy to at least 20 weeks of gestation.
Para • A woman who has given birth after a pregnancy of at least 20 weeks of gestation. Also, the number of pregnancies that have ended after at least 20 weeks of gestation.
Position • Relation of a fixed reference point on the fetus to the quadrants of the maternal pelvis.
Presentation • Fetal part that enters the pelvic inlet. Also, the presenting part.
Station • Measurement of fetal descent in relation to the ischial spines of the maternal pelvis. See also *Engagement*.
Sutures • Narrow areas of flexible tissue that connect fetal skull bones, permitting slight movement during labor.
VBAC • Acronym for vaginal birth after cesarean birth.

Physiologic Effects of the Birth Process

The process of birth affects the physiologic systems of both the pregnant woman and fetus. These effects may occur in many body systems but are striking in the maternal reproductive system and those related to fetal and neonatal oxygenation.

Maternal Response

The most obvious effects of labor occur in the expectant mother's reproductive system, but her other systems respond in various ways as well. Important responses during labor may be noted in her cardiovascular, respiratory, gastrointestinal, urinary, and hematopoietic systems.

REPRODUCTIVE SYSTEM

Characteristics of Contractions

Normal labor contractions are coordinated, involuntary, and intermittent.

Coordinated. The uterus can contract and relax in a coordinated way, as can other smooth muscle such as the heart. Contractions during pregnancy are of low intensity and not coordinated. As the woman approaches full term, contractions become progressively better organized and gradually assume a regular pattern of increasing frequency, duration, and intensity during labor. Coordinated labor contractions begin in the uterine fundus and spread downward toward the cervix to propel the fetus through the pelvis.

Involuntary. Uterine contractions are involuntary, in that they are not under conscious control, as are skeletal muscles. The mother cannot cause labor to start or stop by conscious effort. However, walking or other activity may stimulate labor contractions that have already begun.

Intermittent. Labor contractions are intermittent rather than sustained, allowing relaxation of the uterine muscle and resumption of blood flow to the placenta.

Contraction Cycle

Each contraction consists of three phases that may be likened to a hill (Fig. 12–1):

The increment occurs as the contraction begins

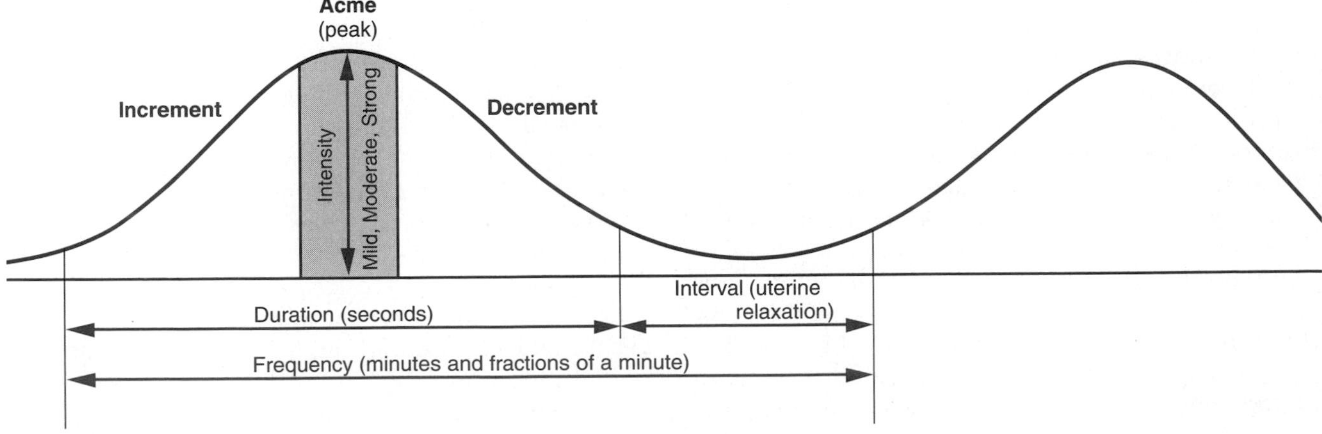

Figure 12–1

Contraction cycle.

and spreads throughout the uterus. The acme, or peak, is the period during which contraction is the most intense.

The decrement is the period of decreasing intensity as the uterus relaxes.

The contraction cycle and the overall pattern of contractions are also described in terms of:

Frequency, the period from the beginning of one uterine contraction to the beginning of the next; it is expressed in minutes and fractions of minutes.

Duration, the length of each contraction from beginning to end; it is expressed in seconds.

Intensity, the strength of the contractions. The terms "mild," "moderate," and "strong" describe contraction intensity as palpated by the nurse.

Interval, the period between the end of one contraction and the beginning of the next.

Uterine Body

Two levels of uterine activity occur during labor. The upper two thirds of the uterus contracts actively; the lower one third is relatively inactive.

The myometrial cells of each segment behave in opposite ways as well. Myometrial cells in the upper segment do not return to their original length at the end of each contraction but remain shorter. This quality enables the uterine muscle to maintain tension between contractions, aiding downward passage of the fetus through the pelvis.

The lower uterine segment is the lower third of the uterus. The cervix is similar to the lower uterine segment in that it is also passive. Myometrial cells in the lower segment become stretched with each contraction and do not return to the shorter length between contractions.

The opposing characteristics of myometrial contraction in the upper and lower segments cause changes in the thickness of the uterine wall during labor. The upper segment becomes thicker while the lower segment becomes thinner and pulled upward during labor. The physiologic retraction ring marks the division between the upper and lower segments of the uterus (Fig. 12–2).

The internal size of the uterine cavity decreases because muscles in the upper segment thicken, and it becomes narrower. These two characteristics straighten the fetal body and direct it downward in the pelvis as room at the top and sides of the uterus decreases.

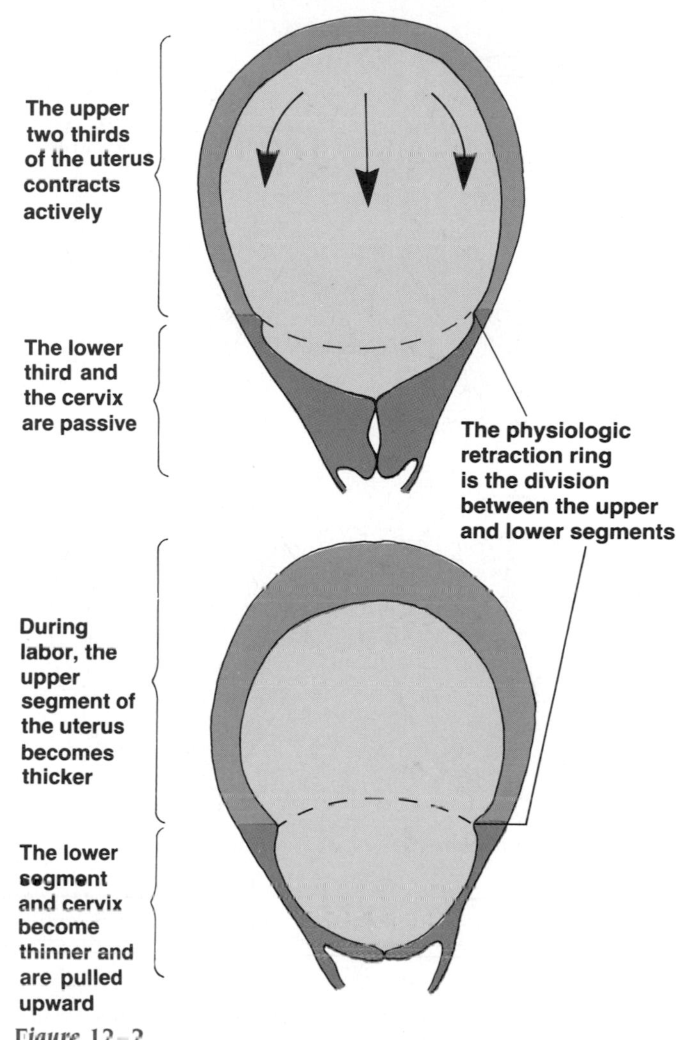

Figure 12–2

Opposing characteristics of uterine contraction in the upper and lower segments of the uterus.

Cervical Changes

Effacement (thinning and shortening) and *dilation* (opening) constitute the major cervical changes during labor. Dilation and effacement occur simultaneously during labor but not at the same rates. The cervix of a nullipara (a woman who has not given birth to a viable infant) completes more effacement before the rate of dilation increases. The parous woman usually has a thicker cervix at all degrees of cervical dilation.

Effacement. Before labor, the cervix is a thick, cylindrical structure about 2 cm long at the lower end of the uterus. Labor contractions push the fetus downward against the resistance of the cervix as they simultaneously pull the cervix upward. If the membranes have not ruptured, hydrostatic (fluid) pressure of the amniotic sac adds to the force of the presenting part on the cervix. The cervix becomes shorter and thinner as it is drawn over the fetus and amniotic sac (Fig. 12–3). The cervix gradually merges

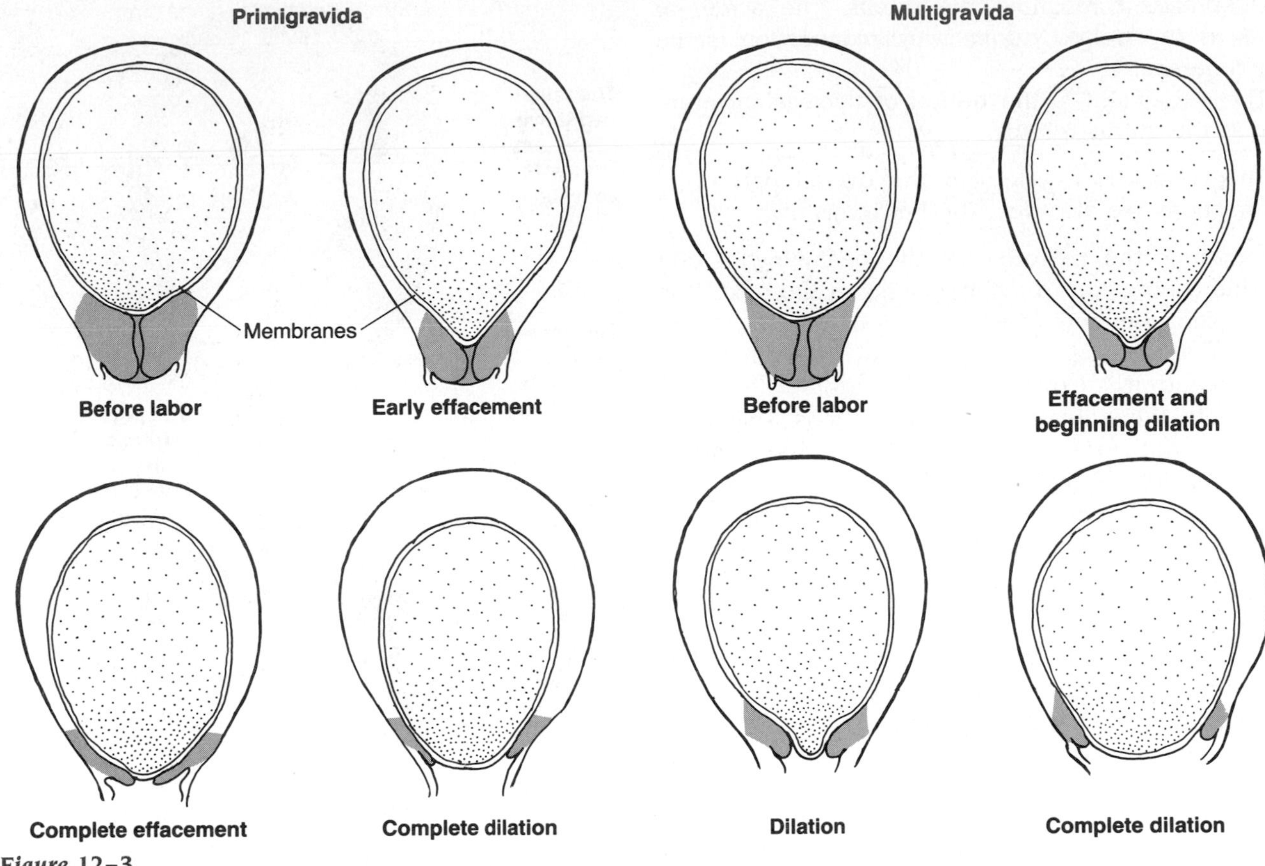

Figure 12–3

Cervical dilation and effacement. During labor, the multigravida's cervix remains thicker than the nullipara's.

with the thinning lower segment of the uterus rather than remaining a distinct cylindrical structure. Effacement is expressed as a percentage, with a fully thinned cervix being 100 per cent effaced, or as the approximate length in centimeters.

Dilation. As the cervix is pulled upward and the fetus is forced downward, the cervix dilates. The action during dilation can be likened to pushing a small ball out the cuff of a sock. Dilation is expressed in centimeters, with approximately 10 cm being full dilation and large enough to allow passage of the average-sized term fetus.

CARDIOVASCULAR SYSTEM

During uterine contractions, blood flow to the placenta temporarily stops, causing a relative increase in the mother's blood volume. This temporary change increases her blood pressure slightly and slows her pulse. Therefore, *the mother's vital signs are best assessed during the interval between contractions because of slight alterations in her blood pressure and pulse that may occur during a contraction.* Although it is more likely to occur during the antepartal period, supine hypotension (see p. 121) also may occur during labor if the mother lies on her back. *The mother should be discouraged from resting in the supine position because it may reduce blood return to her heart and reduce placental blood flow and fetal oxygenation.*

RESPIRATORY SYSTEM

For most women in labor, depth and rate of respirations increase, especially if they are anxious or in pain. A woman who breathes rapidly and deeply may experience symptoms of hyperventilation if she blows off too much carbon dioxide and respiratory alkalosis occurs. She may feel tingling of her hands and feet, numbness, and dizziness.

GASTROINTESTINAL SYSTEM

Some authorities believe that peristalsis in the gastrointestinal tract is slower during labor, but others disagree (Broach and Newton, 1988; Douglas, 1988). The main concern is that any woman may need general anesthesia for delivery and might regurgitate and aspirate food remaining in her stomach. Therefore, facilities may differ on what oral intake is routinely permitted during labor. Ice chips are commonly offered to relieve discomfort from a dry mouth. Other clear liquids, juices, popsicles, or hard candy also may be permitted.

URINARY SYSTEM

The most common renal change during labor is a reduced sensation of a full bladder. Because of the intensity of contractions or effects of regional anesthesia, the woman may be unaware that her bladder is full. A full bladder may inhibit fetal descent because it occupies space in the pelvis.

After birth, fluid retention that is normal during pregnancy is quickly reversed and large quantities of urine are excreted. The bladder may fill rapidly during the first few days after birth (see p. 421).

HEMATOPOIETIC SYSTEM

Most authorities recognize 500 ml as the maximum blood loss during vaginal birth. Most women tolerate this loss well because the blood volume increases during pregnancy. A woman who is anemic at the beginning of labor has less reserve for normal blood loss and a poor tolerance for excess bleeding. A hemoglobin of 11 g/dl and a hematocrit of 33 per cent or higher gives most women an adequate margin of safety for blood loss associated with normal birth. The leukocyte count may be as high as 25,000 to 30,000 during active labor, a level that might otherwise suggest infection (Blackburn and Loper, 1992).

Levels of several clotting factors are elevated during pregnancy and continue to be elevated during labor and post partum. Although the elevation of clotting factors provides protection from hemorrhage, it also increases the mother's risk for a venous thrombosis during pregnancy and post partum.

Fetal Response

Three major fetal systems react during labor. Responses are most notable in the placental circulation, the cardiovascular system, and the pulmonary system.

PLACENTAL CIRCULATION

Chapter 6 (see p. 107) explains the functions of the placenta during prenatal life. As a review, exchange of oxygen and waste products between mother and fetus occurs in the intervillous spaces without actual mixing of maternal and fetal blood. During labor contractions, the maternal blood supply gradually stops as the spiral arteries supplying the intervillous space are compressed by the contracting uterine muscle. Therefore, most maternal-fetal exchange occurs during the interval between contractions.

The placenta usually has enough reserve over fetal basal needs to tolerate the intermittent interruption of blood flow well. In conditions associated with reduced placental function, such as maternal diabetes or hypertension, the fetus may not tolerate labor contractions well.

CARDIOVASCULAR SYSTEM

The fetal cardiovascular system reacts quickly to events during labor. Alterations in the rate and rhythm of the fetal heart may be the result of normal stress on the fetus, or they may suggest that the fetus is not tolerating the stress of labor. The fetal heart rate is rapid, averaging 110 to 160 beats per minute (BPM). (See Chapter 14 for further discussion of the fetal response to labor.)

PULMONARY SYSTEM

During labor and vaginal birth, the fetal chest is compressed as it passes through the birth canal (the "thoracic squeeze"). Compression helps remove excess fluid in the fetal airways in preparation for air breathing at birth. The infant born by cesarean delivery may have more fluid in the airways because chest compression has not occurred.

Catecholamines, primarily epinephrine and norepinephrine, produced by the fetal adrenal glands in response to the stress of labor, appear to contribute to the infant's adaptation to extrauterine life. Catecholamines speed clearance of fluid that remains in the lungs after birth and aid in temperature regulation. Catecholamine levels increase as the fetus adapts to the stress of normal labor and birth. Infants born by elective (ie, not preceded by labor) cesarean birth are more likely to have transient breathing difficulty (see Chapter 29, p. 843).

✔ Check Your Reading

1. How do labor contractions cause the cervix to efface and dilate?
2. What differences in effacement are expected between the parous woman and the woman who has not previously given birth?
3. What changes occur in these maternal systems during labor? Cardiovascular? Respiratory? Gastrointestinal? Renal? Hematopoietic?

4. Why is it important that uterine contractions be intermittent rather than sustained?
5. How does the normal process of vaginal birth benefit the newborn after birth?

Components of the Birth Process

Many forces may influence childbirth, but four major variables interact during normal childbirth. These are often called the "four P's." They are the powers, the passage, the passenger, and the psyche.

Powers

The two powers of labor are:

Uterine contractions. During the first stage of labor (see p. 280), uterine contractions are the primary power that moves the fetus through the maternal pelvis.

Maternal pushing efforts. During the second stage of labor, uterine contractions continue to propel the fetus through the pelvis. In addition, the woman feels an urge to push or bear down as the fetus distends her vagina and puts pressure on her rectum. She adds her voluntary pushing efforts to the force of uterine contractions in second-stage labor.

Passage

The passage for birth of the fetus consists of the maternal pelvis and the soft tissues. The bony pelvis is usually more important to the outcome of labor than the soft tissue because the bones and joints do not readily yield to the forces of labor, although there is softening of the cartilage linking the pelvic bones at term.

The bony pelvis is divided by the linea terminalis (or pelvic brim) into the false pelvis above and the true pelvis below. (See pp. 58–59). for a review of the structure of the pelvis.) The true pelvis is most important in childbirth. The true pelvis has three subdivisions: (1) the *inlet*, or upper pelvic opening; (2) the *midpelvis*, or pelvic cavity; and (3) the *outlet*, or lower pelvic opening. During birth, the true pelvis functions like a curved cylinder with different dimensions at different levels. See Table 12–1 for discussion and illustrations of important pelvic measurements.

The pelvis is most often assessed clinically during a vaginal examination. Therefore, measurements are estimates rather than exact. X-ray measurement of the pelvis (pelvimetry) was once common but is seldom used today.

Passenger

The passenger is the fetus plus the membranes and placenta. As in other components of the birth process, many fetal anatomical and positional variables influence the course of labor.

FETAL HEAD

Because the fetus enters the birth canal in the cephalic presentation 96 per cent of the time, one must understand the structures and diameters of the fetal head. The fetal shoulders are also important because of their width, but they are usually movable to adapt to the pelvis.

Bones, Sutures, and Fontanelles. The bones of the fetal head most involved in the birth process are the two frontal bones on the forehead, the two parietal bones at the crown of the head, and the occipital bone at the back of the head (Fig. 12–4). The five major bones are not fused but are connected by sutures, composed of strong but flexible fibrous tissue. The fontanelles are wider spaces at the intersection of the sutures.

The *anterior fontanelle* is diamond shaped and formed by the intersection of four sutures: the two coronal, the frontal, and the sagittal. The *posterior fontanelle* is very small, often more like a small indentation in the skull. The posterior fontanelle has a triangular shape formed by the intersection of three sutures: one sagittal and two lambdoid. These sutures connect the two parietal bones and the occipital bone. The sutures and fontanelles allow the bones to move slightly, changing the shape of the fetal head so that it can adapt to the size and shape of the pelvis by molding. *The sutures and the different shapes of the fontanelles provide important landmarks to determine fetal position and head flexion during vaginal examination.*

Fetal Head Diameters. Most fetuses enter the pelvis in the cephalic presentation, but there are several possible variations. The major transverse diameter of the fetal head is the biparietal, measured between the two parietal bones. The biparietal diameter averages 9.5 cm.

The anterior-posterior diameter of the head varies with how much it is flexed. In the most favorable situation, the head becomes fully flexed during labor and the anterior-posterior diameter is the suboccipitobregmatic, averaging 9.5 cm. See Figure 12–4 for

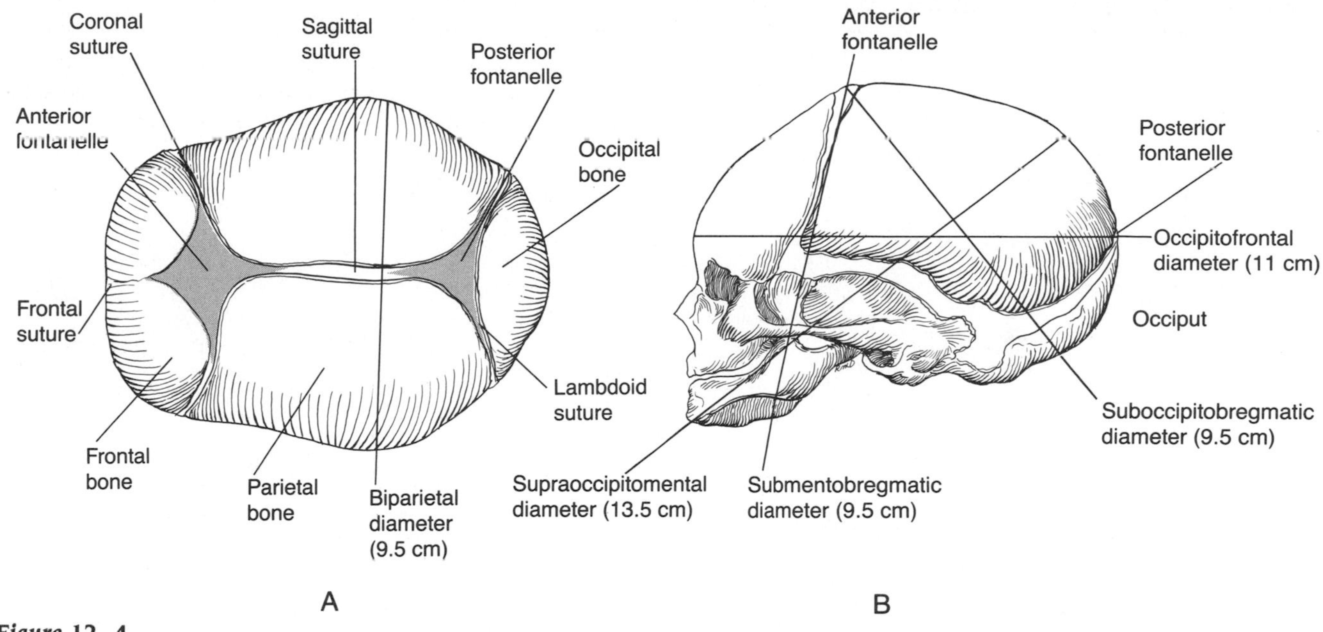

Figure 12–4

A, Bones, sutures, and fontanelles of the fetal head. Note that the anterior fontanelle has a diamond shape whereas the posterior fontanelle is triangular. **B,** Lateral view of the fetal head demonstrating how anterior-posterior diameters vary with the amount of flexion or extension.

anterior-posterior head diameters in different degrees of flexion or extension.

VARIATIONS

Fetal Lie

The orientation of the long axis of the fetus to the long axis of the mother is the fetal lie (Fig. 12–5). In more than 99 per cent of pregnancies, the lie is longitudinal, or parallel to the long axis of the mother. In the *longitudinal lie,* either the head or buttocks of the fetus enter the pelvis first.

A *transverse lie* exists when the long axis of the fetus is at right angles to the mother's long axis and occurs in fewer than 1 per cent of births. A fetal shoulder enters the pelvis first.

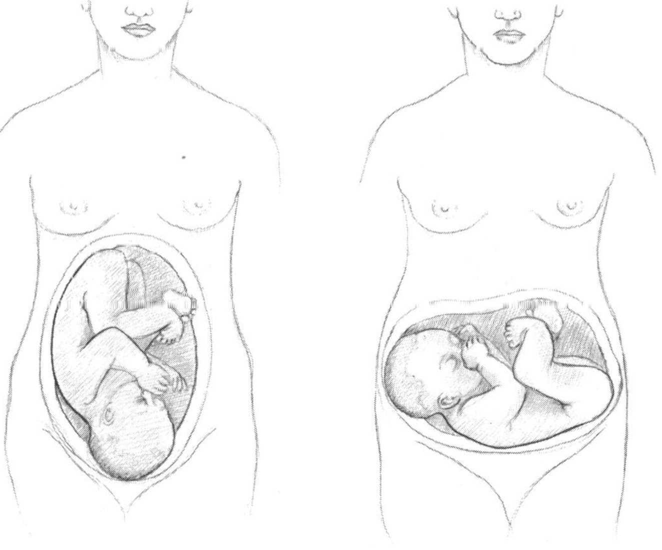

Figure 12–5

A, Lie. In a longitudinal lie, the long axis of the fetus is parallel to the long axis of the expectant mother. **B,** The long axis of the fetus is at right angles to the long axis of the mother in a transverse lie. The uterus usually has a wide, short appearance.

Attitude

The relation of fetal body parts to each other is the attitude of the fetus (Fig. 12–6). The normal fetal attitude is one of flexion, with the chin flexed on the chest and the arms and legs flexed over the thorax. The back is curved in a convex C shape. Flexion remains a characteristic feature of the neonate after birth.

Table 12–1. PELVIC DIVISIONS AND MEASUREMENTS

Inlet

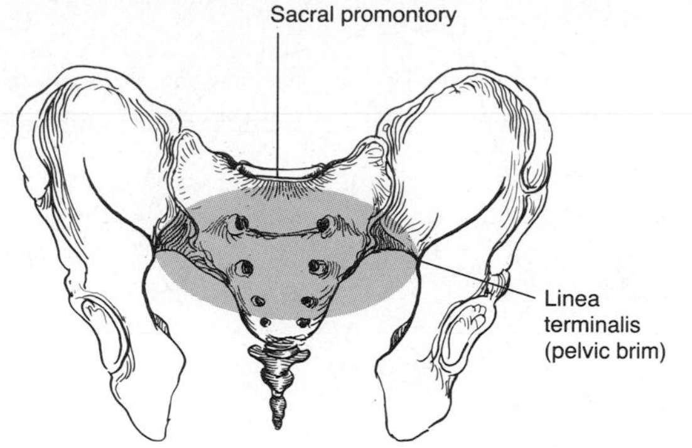

Frontal view, cutaway

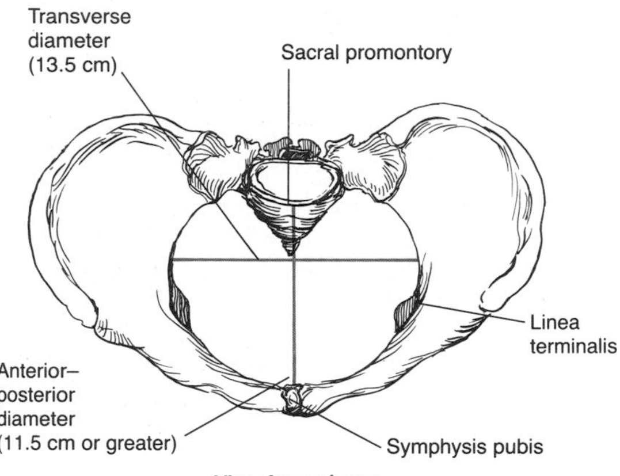

View from above

Sacral promontory

True conjugate
(1.5 cm less than
diagonal conjugate)

Diagonal conjugate
(11.5 cm or greater)

Symphysis pubis

Side view, cutaway

The boundaries of the inlet are the symphysis pubis anteriorly, the sacral promontory posteriorly, and the linea terminalis on each side. The inlet is slightly wider in its transverse diameter (13.5 cm) than its anterior-posterior or diagonal conjugate diameter (11.5 cm or greater). The diagonal conjugate is slightly larger than the true conjugate.

The true conjugate cannot be directly measured during a vaginal examination. It is estimated by deducting approximately 1.5 cm from the diagonal conjugate measurement.

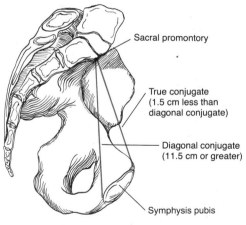

If the inlet is small, the fetal head may not be able to enter it. Because it is almost entirely surrounded by bone, except for cartilage at the sacroiliac joint and symphysis pubis, the inlet cannot enlarge much to accommodate the fetus. The bony measurements are essentially fixed.

Midpelvis

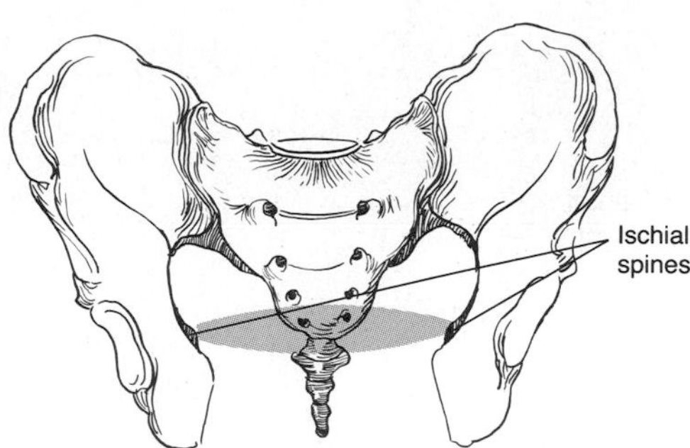

Frontal view, cutaway

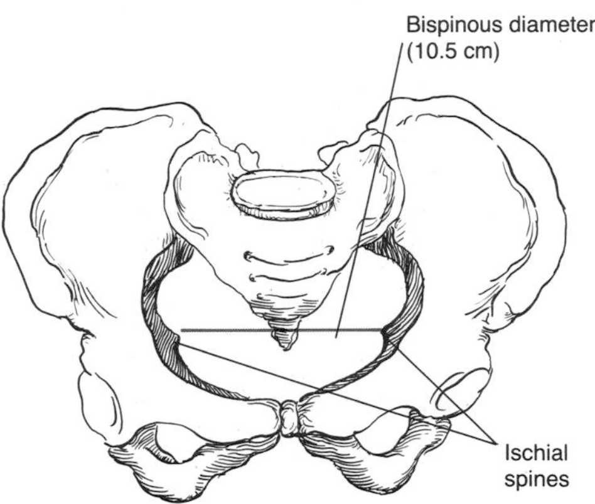

View from above, with pelvis tilted anteriorly

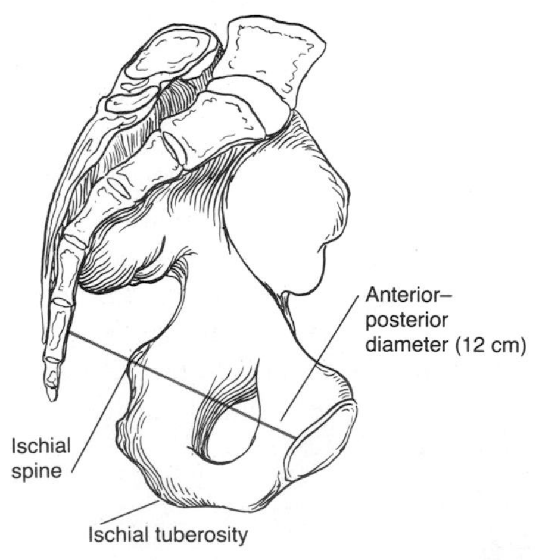

Side view, cutaway

The midpelvis, or pelvic cavity, is the narrowest part of the pelvis through which the fetus must pass during birth. Midpelvic diameters are measured at the level of the ischial spines. The anterior-posterior diameter averages 12 cm.

The transverse diameter (bispinous or interspinous) averages 10.5 cm. Prominent ischial spines that project into the pelvic cavity can reduce the bispinous diameter.

Table 12–1. PELVIC DIVISIONS AND MEASUREMENTS *Continued*

Outlet

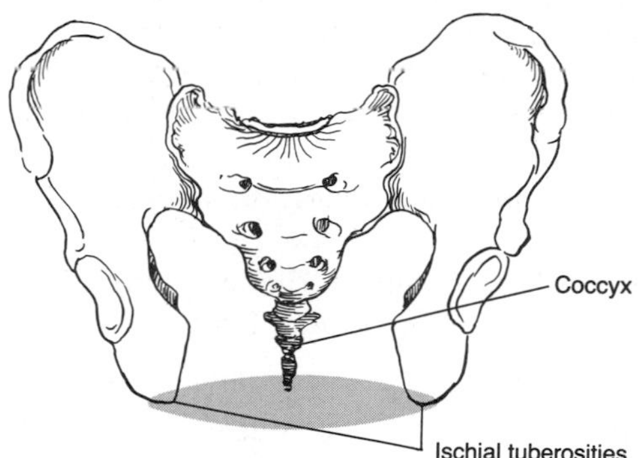

Frontal view, cutaway

Three important diameters of the pelvic outlet are (1) the anterior-posterior, (2) the posterior sagittal, and (3) the transverse (bi-ischial or intertuberous). The anterior-posterior diameter ranges from 9.5 to 11.5 cm, varying with the curve between the sacrococcygeal joint and the tip of the coccyx. The anterior-posterior diameter can increase if the coccyx is easily movable.

The transverse diameter is the bi-ischial or intertuberous diameter. This is the distance between the ischial tuberosities and averages 11 cm.

Narrower outlet diameters are less likely to interfere with fetal descent because the outlet has more soft tissue surrounding it and the coccyx can move.

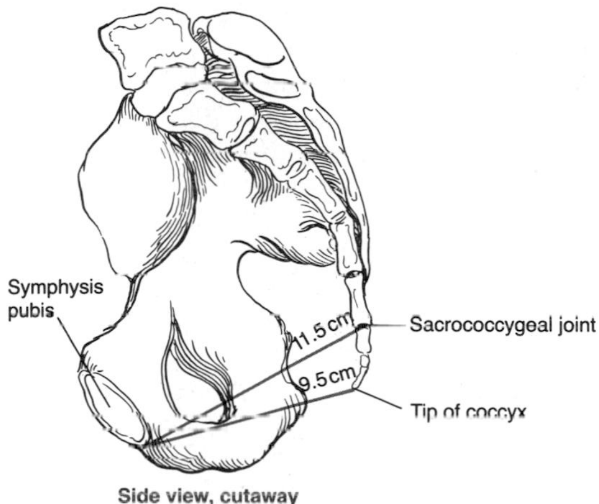

Side view, cutaway

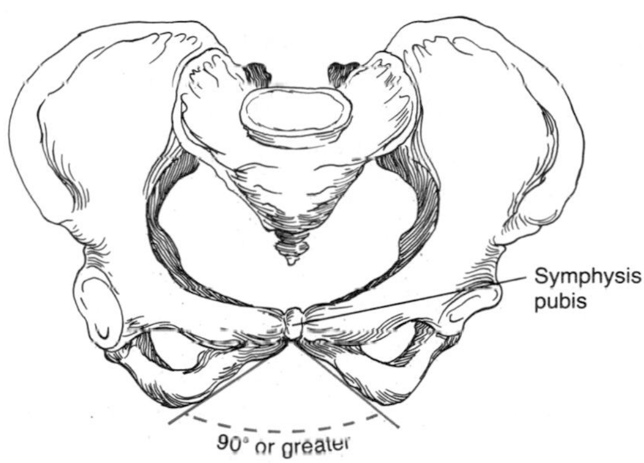

Frontal view, with pelvis tilted anteriorly

The angle of the pubic arch is important because it must be wide enough for the fetus to pass under. The angle should be least 90 degrees. A narrow pubic arch displaces the fetus posteriorly toward the coccyx as it tries to pass under the arch.

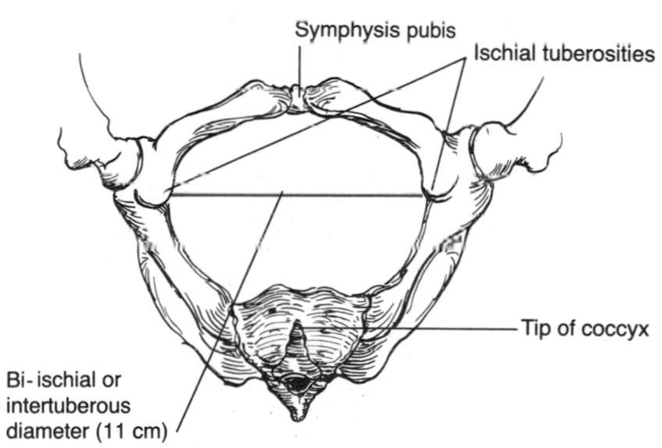

View from below (woman is in lithotomy position)

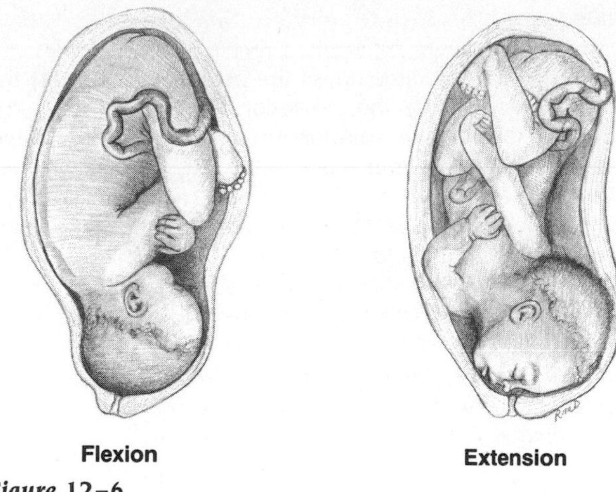

Figure 12–6

A, Attitude. The fetus is in the normal attitude of flexion, with the head, arms, and legs flexed tightly against the trunk. **B,** The fetus is in an abnormal attitude of extension. The head is extended, and the right arm is extended. A face presentation is illustrated.

Presentation

The fetal part that enters the pelvis first is the presenting part. There are three categories of presentation: (1) cephalic, (2) breech, and (3) shoulder. The cephalic presentation with the fetal head flexed is the most common (Fig. 12–7). Other presentations are associated with prolonged labor or other abnormalities and are more likely to necessitate a cesarean birth.

Cephalic Presentation. The cephalic presentation is more favorable than others for several reasons:

- The fetal head is the largest single fetal part, although the breech (buttocks), with the legs and feet flexed on the abdomen, is collectively larger than the head. After the head is born, the smaller parts follow easily as the extremities unfold.
- During labor, the fetal head can gradually change shape, molding to adapt to the size and shape of the maternal pelvis.

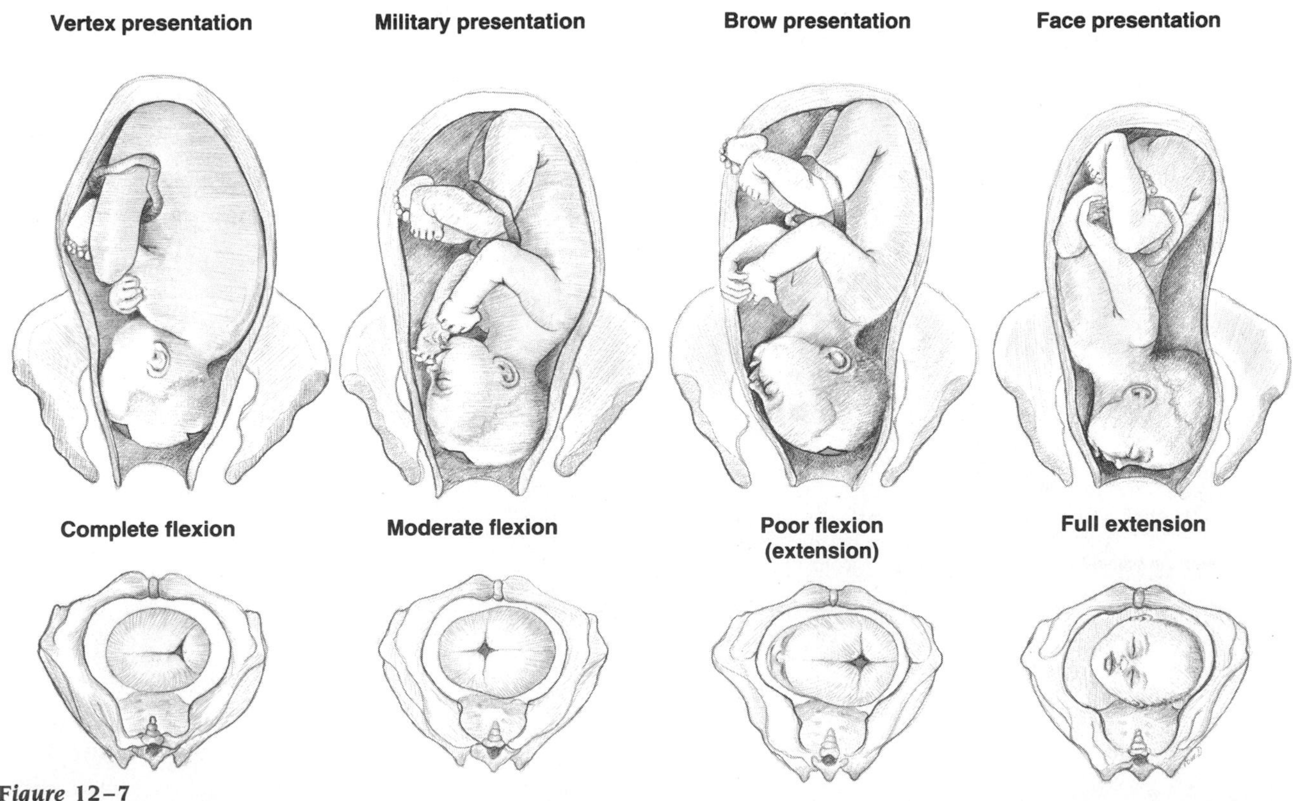

Figure 12–7

Four types of cephalic presentation. The vertex presentation is normal. Note positional changes of the anterior and posterior fontanelles in relation to the maternal pelvis.

- The fetal head is smooth and round, making it a more efficient fetal part to dilate the cervix, which is also round.

There are four variations of the cephalic presentation (Fig. 12–7).

Vertex. This is the most common presentation, with the fetal head fully flexed. It is often simply called a "vertex presentation" in everyday usage. The smallest suboccipitobregmatic diameter is presenting. This presentation is the most favorable for normal labor progress.

Military. The head is in a neutral position, neither flexed nor extended. The occipitofrontal diameter is presenting.

Brow. The fetal head is partly extended. The brow presentation is usually unstable, converting to a vertex if the head flexes or to a face presentation if it extends. The longest supraoccipitomental diameter is presenting.

Face. The head is fully extended, and the fetal occiput is near the fetal spine. The submentobregmatic diameter is presenting.

Breech Presentation. A breech presentation occurs when the fetal buttocks enter the pelvis. This presentation is more common in preterm births or when there is a fetal abnormality such as hydrocephalus (enlargement of the head with fluid) that prevents the head from entering the pelvis.

Breech presentations are associated with several disadvantages:

- The buttocks are not smooth like the head, and they are less efficient at dilating the cervix.
- The fetal head is the last part to be born. By the time the fetal head is deep in the pelvis, the umbilical cord is outside the mother's body and is subject to compression between the head and maternal pelvis.
- Because the umbilical cord can be compressed after the fetal thorax is born, the head must be delivered quickly to allow the infant to breathe. This does not permit gradual molding of the fetal head as it passes through the pelvis.

There are three variations of breech presentation, depending on how the legs are flexed (Fig. 12–8):

Frank Breech. This is the most common variation, occurring when the fetal legs are extended across the abdomen toward the shoulders.

Full (or Complete) Breech. This is a reversal of the usual vertex presentation. The head is flexed, and the legs are flexed at the knee and hip but the buttocks are presenting.

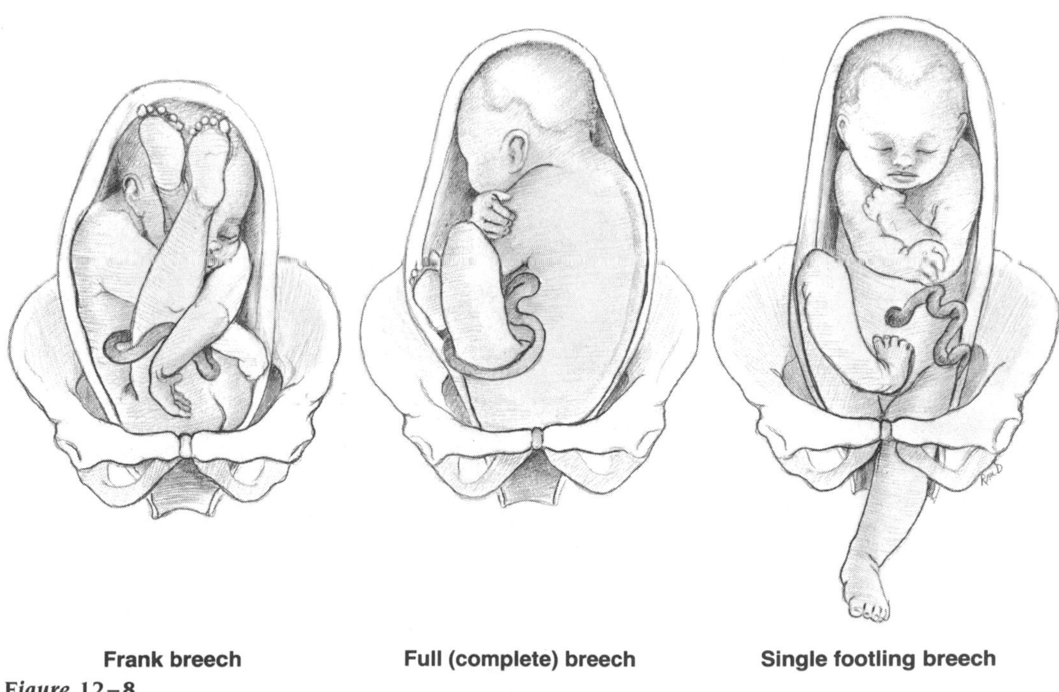

Figure 12–8

Three variations of a breech presentation. Frank breech is the most common variation. Footling breeches may be single or double.

Footling Breech. This occurs when one or both feet are presenting.

Shoulder Presentation. The shoulder presentation is the same as a transverse lie and is more common in preterm birth, high parity, if the membranes have ruptured prematurely, or in placenta previa (placenta low in the uterus). In practice, variations of the shoulder presentation are less important because a cesarean birth is necessary.

✔ *Check Your Reading*

6. What are the powers of labor during the first stage of labor? In the second?
7. What are the three divisions of the true pelvis?
8. Why is the vertex presentation best during birth?

Position

The location of a fixed reference point on the fetal presenting part in relation to the four quadrants of the maternal pelvis is the fetal position (Fig. 12–9). The four quadrants are the right and left anterior and the right and left posterior. The actual fetal position is not static, but it changes during labor as the fetus moves downward and adapts to the changing pelvic contours.

Abbreviations are used to signify the relationship between the fetal presenting part and the maternal pelvis:

Right (R) or Left (L). The first letter of the abbreviation describes whether the fetal reference point is in the right or left of the mother's pelvis. If the fetal point is neither to the right nor left of the pelvis, this letter is omitted.

Occiput (O), Mentum (M), or Sacrum (S). The second letter of the abbreviation refers to the fixed fetal reference point, which varies with the presentation. The occiput is used in a vertex presentation. The chin, or mentum, is the reference point in a face presentation. The sacrum is used for breech presentations.

Anterior (A), Posterior (P), or Transverse (T). These letters describe whether the fetal reference point is in the anterior or the posterior quadrant of the mother's pelvis. If the fetal point is neither in the anterior nor in the posterior quadrant, it is described as transverse.

If the fetal occiput is located in the left anterior quadrant of the mother's pelvis, the position is described as left occiput anterior (LOA). If the occiput is directly in the mother's anterior pelvis, neither to the right nor the left, it is described as occiput anterior (OA). If the fetal sacrum is located in the mother's right posterior pelvis, the abbreviation is R (right) S (sacrum) P (posterior). See Figure 12–10 for different fetal presentations and positions.

✔ *Check Your Reading*

9. For each fetal position listed, describe the fetal landmark. Where is this landmark located in relation to the mother's pelvis: ROP? OA? RSA? LMA?
10. If the fetus is in a face presentation, why is it not possible to use the occiput to determine position within the pelvis?

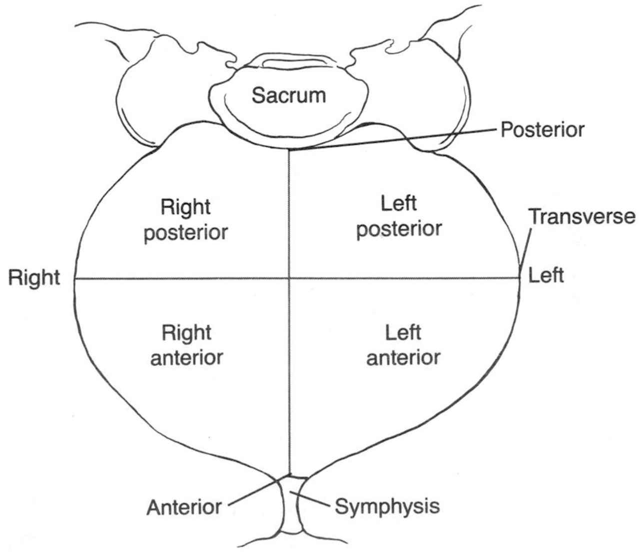

Figure 12–9

Four quadrants of the maternal pelvis, used to describe fetal position.

Psyche

In the past, only three physiologic "P's" were considered important during childbirth—the passage, the passenger, and the powers. More recently, the psyche has been recognized as a unique and crucial part of the process. For example, marked anxiety or fear decreases a pregnant woman's ability to cope with pain in labor. Maternal catecholamines—stress hormones secreted when the woman is anxious or fearful—inhibit uterine contractility and placental blood flow. Relaxation, however, augments the natural process of labor.

INDIVIDUAL AND CULTURAL VALUES

A woman in childbirth is more than a physical being. She is a blend of her experiences, her present status, and her future expectations. She is an individual, a member of a family and cultural group, and part of her larger society.

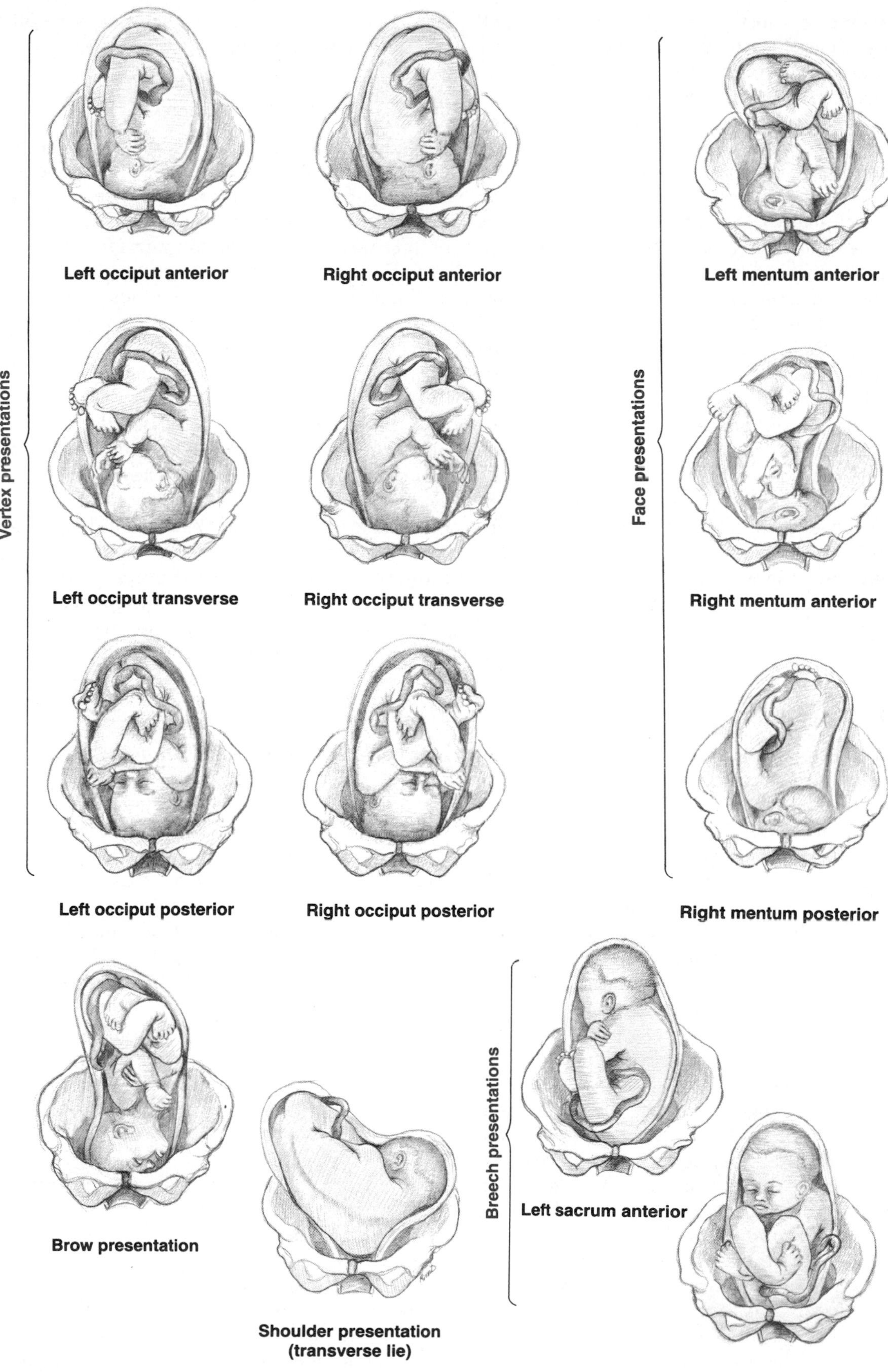

Figure 12–10

Fetal presentations and positions.

A family's culture affects one's views of birth and the ordinary practices that surround it. Culture shapes the values that people hold and their expectations of the birth experience. A woman's culture gives her cues about how she should behave and react to labor and how she should interact with her newborn. If the woman, her family, and caregivers have similar values, little conflict in their values and expectations are likely. However, if these individuals hold markedly different values, they may be perplexed because each expects something different of the other. The effects of cultural differences are most obvious when newly immigrant women give birth. After time and exposure to other cultural groups, the distinctive cultural practices and values often become blurred.

Within a culture, people are individuals. Knowledge of the values of cultural groups commonly encountered in an area provides a framework for assessment and care of the woman and her family; however, nurses should avoid making assumptions on knowing the basis of common values of the culture. The nurse must individually assess each woman and her family about their expectations and values surrounding birth.

BIRTH AS AN EXPERIENCE

Childbirth is both a physical and an emotional experience. It is an irrevocable event that changes a woman forever. Families discuss the births of their children in the same terms that they use to describe other significant events in their life: marriages, anniversaries, religious events, or even deaths. They do not talk about childbirth in the factual way they might discuss an illness or surgery. With the declining birth rate and the prevalence of smaller families, parents have greater expectations about the *experience* of childbirth than in the past. The more realistic a woman's expectations about the birth are, the more likely she is to have an experience that is consistent with those expectations (Stolte, 1987).

Novice nurses are caught up in the excitement and significance of childbirth. They are interested in the technical and anatomical aspects of the process but more often focus on the humanness and emotion of the experience. They rarely discuss a birth in the same detached way as they might discuss a surgical procedure. Participation in a family's birth bonds the nurse to that family in a unique way unparalleled in other areas of nursing practice.

One nursing role is to promote a positive childbearing experience for the woman and her family. Nursing measures to increase her sense of control and mastery during birth enrich her perception that the birth was a positive event.

IMPACT OF TECHNOLOGY

The goal of maternity care is to protect the health of the expectant mother, the fetus, and the newborn and to support and enrich family ties. New technology assists caregivers to understand and intervene to protect the health of mother and fetus quickly. However, the hazard of sophisticated technology is that it may make maternity care seem less personal. Some women may feel that they are less important than the monitors and infusion pumps attached to them.

Normal labor and birth do not warrant sophisticated technology. However, many women giving birth in the United States subordinate their desire for a peak emotional experience to their desire for maximum safety for their baby. They accept and even seek "high-tech" interventions because they believe that these interventions best assure them of having a healthy child. The intrapartum nurse is in a unique position to bridge the gap between technology and the humanness of the birth experience. The nurse can maintain the focus on the woman and her family while using technology to observe the maternal and fetal well-being.

Interrelationships of Components

The four "P's" have been discussed separately, but in reality they are an interrelated whole. For instance, a woman with a small pelvis (passage) and a large fetus (passenger) may experience a normal labor and birth if the fetus is ideally positioned and the uterine contractions and maternal bearing down efforts (powers) are vigorous. The nurse's supportive attitude strengthens psychological elements (psyche) and enhances the processes of birth. The nurse can act as an advocate for the laboring woman and her family to increase their sense of control and mastery of labor.

Normal Labor

Theories of Onset

Despite research on the subject, the reason labor begins is still unknown. Labor normally starts when the fetus is mature enough to adjust smoothly to extrauterine life but before the fetus becomes so large that vaginal birth is impossible. This stage

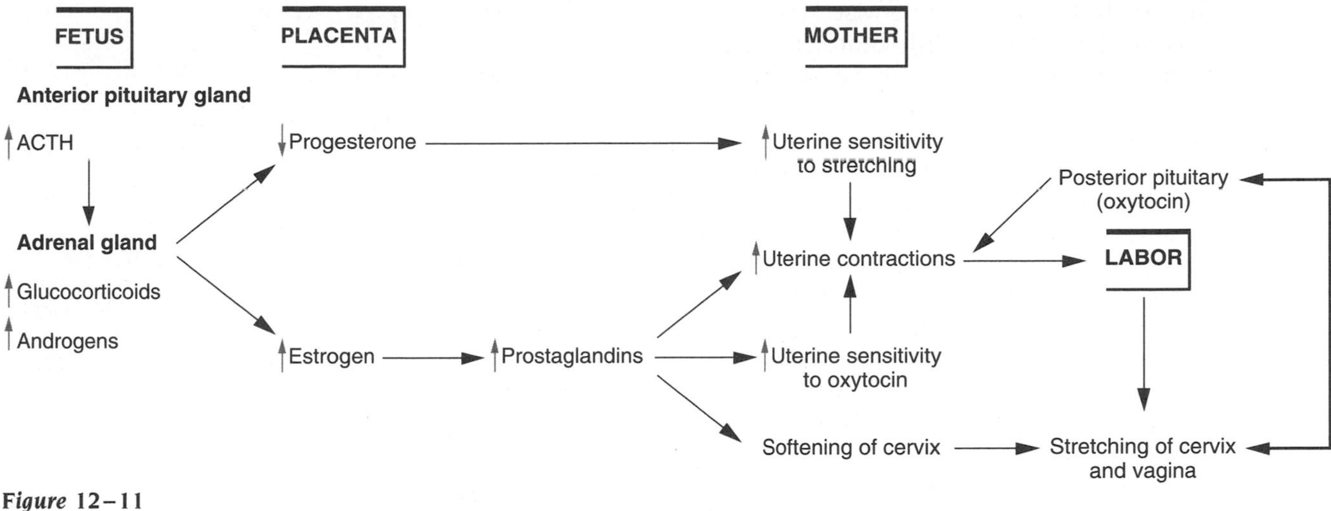

Figure 12–11

Schematic representation of factors believed to have a role in starting labor.

(term gestation) occurs between 38 and 42 weeks after the first day of the last menstrual period.

The onset of labor is a result of many interrelated factors (Fig. 12–11). Labor begins when forces favoring continuation of pregnancy are offset by forces favoring its end. Four elements are thought to have a role in starting labor:

- Increased production of glucocorticoids and androgens by the fetal adrenals
- Decreased placental production of progesterone
- Increased placental production of estrogen
- Increased maternal production of and uterine sensitivity to prostaglandins and oxytocin

Premonitory Signs

Before labor begins, women usually notice one or more premonitory, or warning, signs that labor is about to begin.

Braxton Hicks Contractions. The contractions are irregular and mild, occurring throughout pregnancy. As term approaches, contractions become more noticeable and even painful. Parous women often describe more uterine activity preceding labor than nulliparous women.

Increased perception of Braxton Hicks contractions often makes sleep difficult at the end of pregnancy. The contractions may become regular at times, only to decrease spontaneously. Because contractions are often uncomfortable and at times regular, the woman may be confused and frustrated because she does not know whether labor has really begun.

Lightening. As the fetus descends toward the pelvic inlet, the woman notices that she breathes more easily because upward pressure on her diaphragm is diminished. However, increased pressure on her bladder causes her to urinate more frequently. Many women say that the baby has "dropped" when they describe lightening. Pressure of the fetal head in the pelvis also may cause leg cramps and edema of the lower extremities. Lightening is most noticeable in nulliparas, occurring about 2 to 3 weeks before the onset of labor.

Increased Vaginal Mucous Secretions. An increase in clear and non-irritating vaginal secretions occurs as fetal pressure causes congestion of the vaginal mucosa. The woman may need to wear a perineal pad because of the quantity of mucus.

Bloody Show. As full term approaches, the cervix begins to soften, dilate, and efface slightly ("ripening") so that it yields more easily to labor contractions. These cervical changes cause expulsion of the mucus plug that sealed the cervix during pregnancy, rupturing small cervical capillaries in the process. Bloody show is a mixture of mostly thick mucus and pink or dark brown blood. It may begin several days to a few weeks before labor's onset, especially in the nulliparous woman.

A recent vaginal examination or sexual intercourse also may result in small amounts of bloody show. Bloody show increases during labor as the cervix completes dilation and effacement. Women who have previously had a vaginal birth often have less bloody show than nulliparas because their cervix stretches more easily.

Rupture of Membranes. In some women at or near term, the amniotic sac ruptures before labor (premature rupture of the membranes). Unless her physician or nurse-midwife directs otherwise, the woman should go to the hospital or birth center for evaluation after the membranes rupture because (1) infection is more likely, since the seal that isolated the unsterile vagina from the uterine cavity is broken, and (2) the cord may drop between the fetal presenting part and the maternal pelvis, where it may be compressed, interrupting blood flow and fetal oxygenation.

Energy Spurt. Some women have a sudden increase in energy ("nesting"). They should be cautioned to conserve their energy so that they will not be exhausted when labor actually begins.

Weight Loss. A small weight loss of about 1 to 3 pounds may occur because of changing levels of estrogen and progesterone. These changes cause excretion of excess fluid that accumulates during pregnancy.

True Labor and False Labor

False labor may be called "prelabor" or "prodromal labor" because the exact time when spontaneous labor begins is rarely known. False labor is a concern because women frequently enter the hospital thinking labor has started, only to be disappointed when it has not.

Several characteristics distinguish true labor from false labor: contractions, discomfort, and cervical change. The conclusive distinction between true and false labor is that contractions of true labor cause *progressive change in the cervix.* Effacement, dilation, or both occur with true labor contractions. See Women Want to Know: How to Know If Labor Is "Real."

Mechanisms of Labor

The mechanisms (cardinal movements) of labor are the changes that occur as the fetus is passively moved through the pelvis during birth. To adapt most effectively to the changing size and shape of the mother's pelvis, the fetus, in a vertex presentation, undergoes several positional changes (Table 12–2). The mechanisms of labor are different in other presentations, but the reason is the same: efficient use of available space in the pelvis. Although the mechanisms of labor are discussed separately, some occur simultaneously.

✔ Check Your Reading

11. Why does the fetus enter the pelvis with the sagittal suture aligned with the transverse diameter of the expectant mother's pelvic inlet?
12. Why does the fetal head turn during labor until the sagittal suture aligns with the anterior-posterior diameter of the mother's pelvic outlet?
13. What are some of the signs and symptoms that a woman might experience before labor begins?
14. What are the differences between true and false labor? Which is the most important?

Women Want To Know

How to Know If Labor is "Real"

True labor differs from false labor in three categories.

FALSE LABOR	TRUE LABOR
Contractions	
Inconsistent in frequency, duration, and intensity.	A consistent pattern of increasing frequency, duration, and intensity usually develops.
A change in activity, such as walking, does not alter contractions, or activity may decrease them.	Walking tends to increase contractions.
Discomfort	
Felt in the abdomen and groin.	Begins in lower back and gradually sweeps around to lower abdomen like a girdle.
May be more annoying than truly painful.	Back pain may persist in some women. Early labor often feels like menstrual cramps.
Cervix	
No change in effacement; dilation of the cervix.	Effacement and/or dilation of cervix should occur. Progressive effacement and dilation of cervix is most important characteristic.

Stages and Phases of Labor

Labor is divided into at least three stages. Each has attributes that set it apart from the other stages. In addition, a fourth stage represents the early recovery and bonding stage following birth. These descriptions of the typical physiologic characteristics and maternal behaviors are average. Individual women vary in normal labor patterns and responses to labor. Use of regional anesthetics, such as the epidural block, is likely to modify the typical maternal behaviors. Table 12–3 summarizes characteristics of each stage of labor.

FIRST STAGE

Cervical effacement and dilation occur in the first stage, or *stage of dilation.* It begins with the onset of true labor contractions and ends with complete dilation (10 cm) and effacement (100 per cent) of the cervix.

Table 12–2. MECHANISMS (CARDINAL MOVEMENTS) OF LABOR

Descent, Engagement, and Flexion

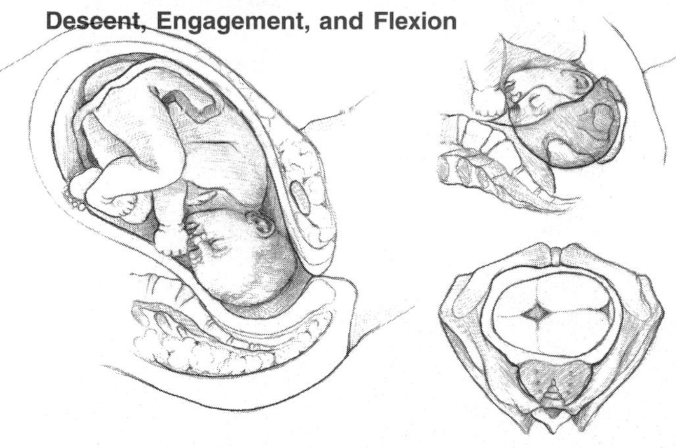

Descent of the fetus is a mechanism of labor that accompanies all the others. Without descent, none of the other mechanisms will occur.

Station

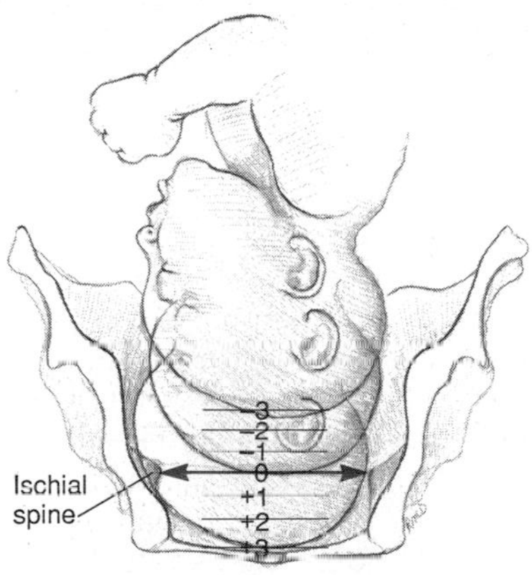

Station represents the measurement of fetal descent. The ischial spines are the reference point for estimating station. The level of the ischial spines is a zero station. If the fetal presenting part is above the ischial spines, a negative number describes station. If the fetal presenting part is below the ischial spines, a positive number is assigned to the station. The upper pelvis, from the inlet (linea terminalis or pelvic brim) to the ischial spines is represented by negative stations such as −3, −2, or −1. The lower pelvis, from the ischial spines to the pelvic floor, is represented by positive stations (+1, +2, +3). Sometimes the terms "floating" or "ballotable" may describe a fetal presenting part so high that it is easily displaced during abdominal or vaginal examination, similar to tossing a ball upward.

Engagement

Engagement occurs when the largest diameter of the fetal presenting part (normally the head) has passed the pelvic inlet and entered the pelvic cavity. Engagement is presumed to have occurred when the station of the presenting part is zero or lower. Engagement often takes place before onset of labor in nulliparous women. In many parous women and in some nulliparas, it does not occur until after labor begins.

Flexion

As the fetus descends, the fetal head is flexed further as it meets resistance from the soft tissues of the pelvis. Head flexion presents the smallest anterior-posterior diameter (suboccipitobregmatic) to the pelvis.

Internal Rotation

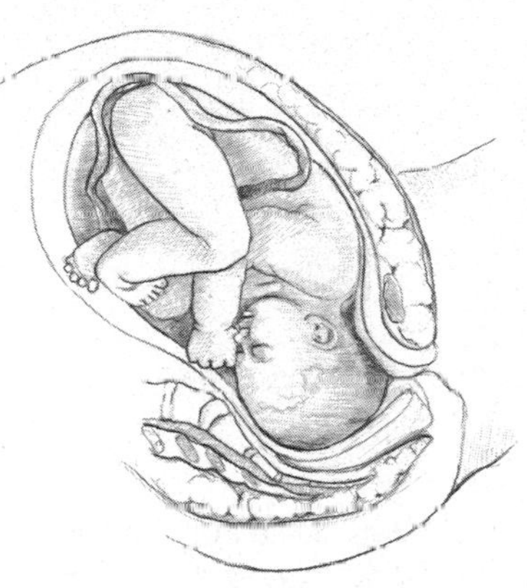

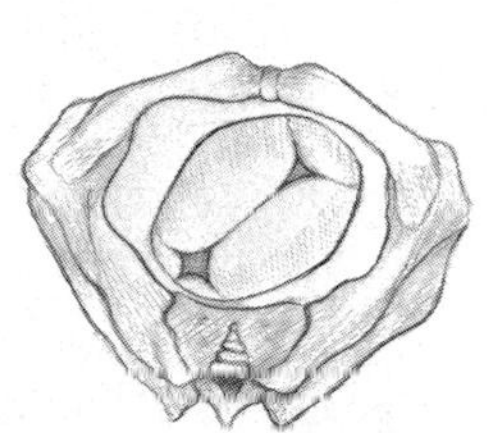

The fetus enters the pelvic inlet with the sagittal suture in a somewhat transverse orientation to the maternal pelvis because that is the widest inlet diameter. Internal rotation allows the longest fetal head diameter (the anterior-posterior) to conform to the longest diameters of the maternal pelvis.

The longest pelvic outlet diameter is the anterior-posterior. As the head descends to the level of the ischial spines, it gradually turns so that the fetal occiput is in the anterior of the pelvis (OA position, directly under the maternal symphysis pubis). When internal rotation is complete, the sagittal suture is oriented in the anterior-posterior pelvic diameter (OA). Less commonly, the head may turn posteriorly so that the occiput is directed toward the hollow of the mother's sacrum.

Table continued on following page

Extension

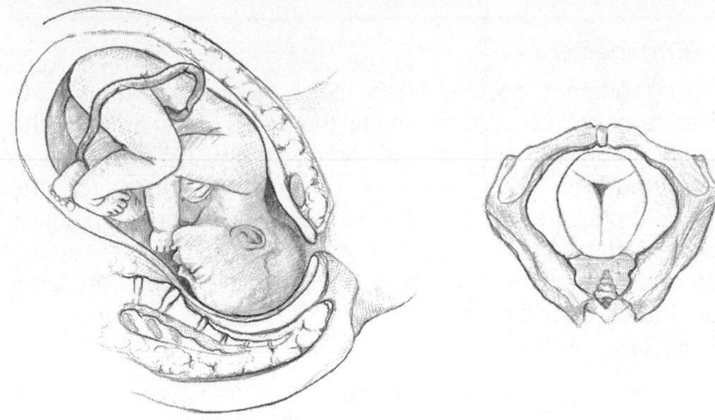

Extension beginning (internal rotation complete)

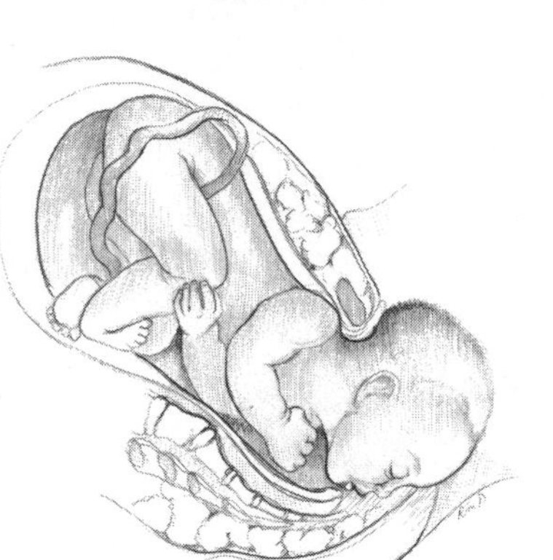

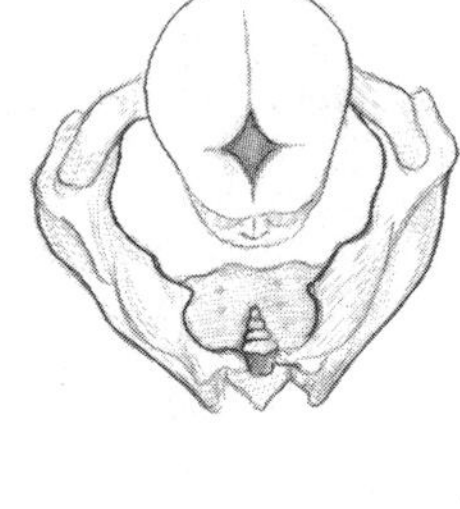

Extension complete

Because the true pelvis is shaped like a curved cylinder, the fetal head is directed posteriorly toward the rectum as it begins its descent. To negotiate the curve of the pelvis, the fetal head must change from an attitude of flexion to one of extension.

While still in flexion, the fetal head meets resistance from the tissues of the pelvic floor. At the same time, the fetal neck stops under the symphysis, which acts as a pivot. The combination of resistance from the pelvic floor and the pivoting action of the symphysis causes the fetal head to swing anteriorly, or extend, with each maternal pushing effort. The head is born in extension, with the occiput sliding under the symphysis and the face directed toward the rectum. The fetal brow, nose, and chin slide over the perineum as the head is born.

External Rotation

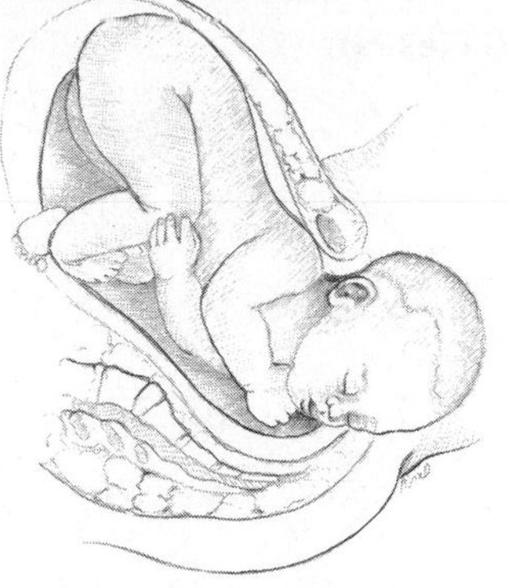

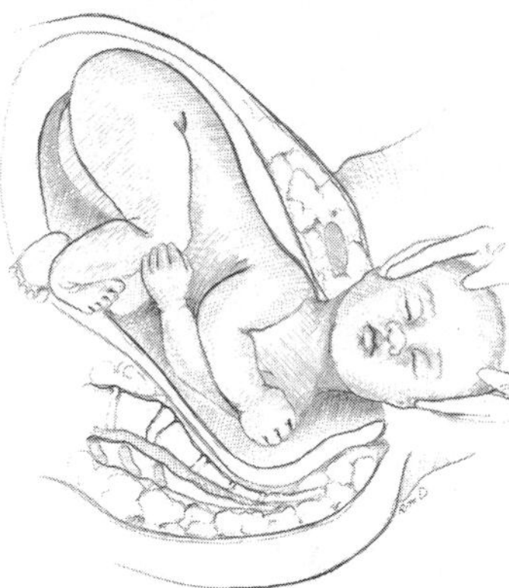

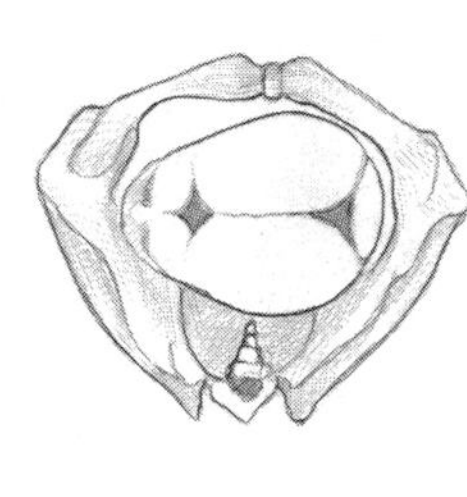

When the head is born with the occiput directed anteriorly, the shoulders are positioned somewhat transversely in the pelvis. The shoulders must rotate internally so that they align with the anterior-posterior diameter of the pelvis.

After the head is born, it spontaneously turns to the same side as it was in utero as it realigns with the shoulders and back (restitution). The head then turns further to that side in external rotation as the shoulders internally rotate and are positioned with their transverse diameter in the anterior-posterior diameter of the pelvic outlet. External rotation of the head accompanies internal rotation of the shoulders.

Expulsion

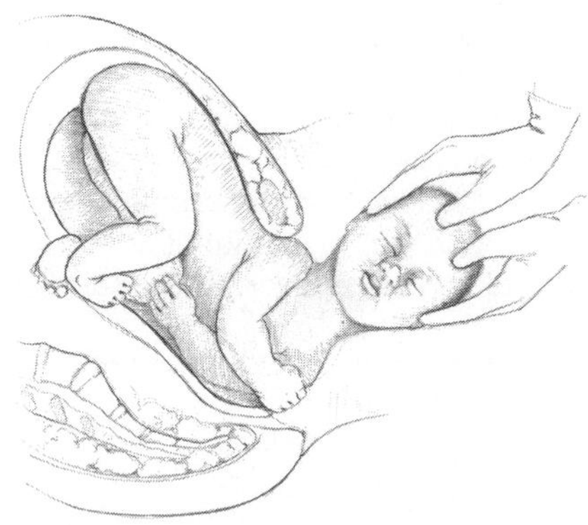

Expulsion occurs first as the anterior, then the posterior, shoulder passes under the symphysis. After the shoulders are born, the rest of the body follows.

Table 12–3. CHARACTERISTICS OF NORMAL LABOR

	First Stage	Second Stage	Third Stage	Fourth Stage
Work accomplished	Effacement and dilation of cervix	Expulsion of fetus	Separation of placenta	Physical recovery and bonding with newborn
Forces	Uterine contractions	Uterine contractions and voluntary bearing-down efforts	Uterine contractions	Uterine contraction to control bleeding from placenta site
Average duration				
Nullipara	8–10 hr; after reaching active phase, dilation averages 1.2 cm/hr	1–1½ hours	5–10 minutes; up to 30 minutes is normal for unassisted placental separation	1–4 hr after birth
Multipara	6–8 hr; after reaching active phase, dilation averages 1.5 cm/hr	20–45 minutes	Same as for nullipara	Same as for nullipara
Cervical dilation	Latent phase: 0 to about 4 cm Active phase: 4 cm to 7 cm Transition phase: 8–10 cm	10 cm (complete)	Not applicable	Not applicable
Uterine contractions	*Latent phase* Initially mild, every 10–20 minutes; progress to moderate strength, about every 5 minutes with a regular pattern; duration increases to about 30 seconds by end of latent phase *Active phase* Increase in frequency, duration, and intensity until every 3–5 minutes, 45 seconds, moderate to strong intensity *Transition phase* Strong, every 2–3 minutes, 60 seconds, with some lasting up to 90 seconds	Strong, every 3 minutes, 50–70 seconds; contractions sometimes slightly less intense than during transition	Firmly contracted	Firmly contracted

Table continued on following page

Table 12–3. CHARACTERISTICS OF NORMAL LABOR *Continued*

	First Stage	Second Stage	Third Stage	Fourth Stage
Discomfort	Often begins with a low backache and sensations similar to those of menstrual cramps; back discomfort gradually sweeps to the lower abdomen in a girdle-like fashion, discomfort intensifies as labor progresses	Urge to push or bear down with contractions, which becomes stronger as fetus descends; distention of vagina and vulva may cause a stretching or splitting sensation	Little discomfort; sometimes slight cramp is felt as placenta is passed	Discomfort varies; some women have afterpains, more common in multigravidas or those who have had a large baby; as anesthesia wears off, perineal discomfort may become noticeable
Maternal behaviors	Sociable, excited, and somewhat anxious during early labor; becomes more inwardly focused as labor intensifies; may lose control during transition	Intense concentration on pushing with contractions; often oblivious to surroundings and appears to doze between contractions	Excited and relieved after baby's birth; usually very tired; often cries	Tired, but may find it difficult to rest because of excitement; eager to become acquainted with her newborn

The first stage of labor is the longest for both nulliparous and parous women. Duration of first-stage labor is about 8 to 10 hours for the nullipara and about 6 to 8 hours for the parous woman (Kilpatrick and Laros, 1989). The rate of labor progress is also important. Once the active phase begins, the cervix of the nullipara usually dilates about 1.2 cm/hour, that of the multipara about 1.5 cm/hour.

First-stage labor consists of three phases: latent, active, and transition. Each phase is characterized by changing maternal behaviors. These phases vary with the woman's preparation, use of coping skills, and use of medication.

Latent Phase. The latent phase lasts from the beginning of labor until about 4 cm of cervical dilation. Much cervical effacement occurs during this phase.

Contractions gradually increase in frequency, duration, and intensity. The interval between contractions shortens until contractions are about 5 minutes apart as the woman progresses to the active phase. Duration increases to about 30 seconds by the end of the latent phase. Intensity begins with mild contractions, when the contracting uterus can be easily indented with the fingertips, progressing to moderate contractions, in which the uterine muscle can be indented with more difficulty.

During early labor, the woman may notice discomfort in her back with each contraction. As labor progresses, back discomfort encircles the lower abdomen. Many women describe the discomfort as similar to menstrual cramps, especially during early labor.

The expectant mother is usually sociable and excited, but cooperative. She is anxious as she realizes that this is the "real thing" and there is no turning back. Women having their first baby often arrive at the hospital accompanied by several friends or family, not realizing that labor is likely to last several more hours and that they will not be as interested in visiting when they enter the active phase.

Active Phase. The active phase of labor is aptly named because the pace of labor increases. The cervix dilates from 4 to 7 cm and at a more rapid rate than in the latent phase. Any remaining effacement of the cervix occurs during the active phase. The cervix of the multipara may never be as effaced as that of the nullipara, remaining thicker even when the cervix is near full dilation. The fetus descends in the pelvis, and internal rotation begins.

Contractions continue to increase in frequency, duration, intensity, and regularity. They average 3 to 5 minutes apart, with a duration of about 45 seconds, and range from moderate to strong intensity.

As contractions intensify, discomfort also increases. The site of discomfort during the active phase is similar to the location during the latent phase. Many women who want pain medication request it during this phase.

The expectant mother's behavior changes. She becomes more anxious and may feel helpless as the contractions intensify. The sociability that characterized the early part of labor is gone, replaced with a more inward focus. She is still cooperative but is less likely to initiate interactions with others unless she has specific requests. Her behaviors are typical of one concentrating intently on a difficult task.

Transition Phase. The cervix dilates from 8 to 10 cm, and the fetus descends further into the pelvis. Bloody show often increases with completion of cervical dilation. Transition is a short but intense phase.

Contractions are very strong. Their frequency is 2 to 3 minutes apart, about the same as the active phase, and the duration of some may be almost 90 seconds. Strong contractions combined with fetal descent may cause the woman to have an urge to push or bear down at the peak of each contraction. Leg tremors, nausea, or vomiting are common.

The expectant mother often finds the transition phase to be the most difficult. She may be very irritable and lose control. Her partner may be confused because actions that were helpful just a short time ago now annoy her. However, if she and her partner have attended childbirth classes, her partner may be encouraged by these behaviors because they mean that the end of labor is close. Transition is usually short, and she can look forward to coping better with the next stage.

Clinical Situation

After examining a woman in labor, the nurse midwife gives you the following information:

"Mrs. Saenz is about 2 to 3 cm, 75 per cent, and 0. The baby is vertex and ROP."

Q: What is the correct interpretation of this information?

A: Mrs. Saenz's cervix is about 2 to 3 cm dilated and has effaced to about one fourth of its original length (about 1.5 cm). The leading edge of the fetal head is at the level of the ischial spines (0 station). (A zero station means that the head is most probably engaged or that its largest diameters have passed the pelvic inlet.)

The vertex presentation means that the fetal head is well flexed, which is most favorable because it presents the smallest anterior-posterior diameter to the maternal pelvis. ROP means that the fetal occiput is in Mrs. Saenz's right posterior pelvic quadrant.

SECOND STAGE

The second *stage of expulsion* begins with complete (10 cm) dilation and full (100 per cent) effacement of the cervix and ends with the birth of the baby. The duration is about 1½ hours in nulliparas and about 20 to 45 minutes in parous women (Kilpatrick and Laros, 1989).

Contractions may occur slightly less frequently than during transition, but they are still about 3 minutes apart. They are very strong, with a duration of about 50 to 70 seconds.

As the fetus descends, pressure of the presenting part on the rectum and the pelvic floor causes the mother to have an involuntary pushing response. She may say that she needs to have a bowel movement or "the baby's coming." Her voluntary pushing efforts augment involuntary uterine contractions. As the fetus descends low in the pelvis and the vulva distends with crowning of the fetal head, she may feel a sensation of stretching or splitting even if no trauma has occurred.

The woman often regains a feeling of control during the second stage of labor. Although contractions are strong, she may feel more in control, as if she is doing something to complete the process. "Labor" is a fitting word to describe the second stage. The woman exerts intense physical effort to push her baby out. Between contractions, she may be oblivious to her surroundings and may appear asleep. She feels tremendous relief and excitement as the second stage ends with the birth of the baby.

THIRD STAGE

The third (*placental*) stage begins with the birth of the baby and ends with the expulsion of the placenta. This stage is the shortest, lasting up to 30 minutes, with an average length of 5 to 10 minutes. There is no difference in duration for nulliparas and paras.

As soon as the infant is born, the uterine cavity becomes much smaller. The reduced size decreases the size of the placenta site, causing it to separate. Externally, four signs suggest probable placenta separation:

- The uterus has a spherical shape.
- The uterus rises upward in the abdomen as the placenta descends into the vagina and pushes the fundus upward.
- The cord descends further from the vagina.
- A gush of blood appears as blood trapped behind the placenta is released as it separates.

The placenta may be expelled from the vagina in one of two ways. In the more common *Schultze mechanism*, the placenta is expelled with the shiny fetal side first. The *Duncan mechanism* is less common, with the rough fetal side presenting.

The uterus must contract firmly and remain contracted after the placenta is expelled to compress open vessels at the implantation site. Inadequate uterine contraction after birth may result in profuse hemorrhage.

Pain during the third stage of labor results from uterine contractions and the brief stretching of the cervix as the placenta passes through it. The woman may experience more pain if the physician vigorously massages her uterus to speed placental detachment.

FOURTH STAGE

The fourth stage of labor is the *stage of physical recovery* for the mother and infant. It lasts from the delivery of the placenta through the first 1 to 4 hours post partum.

The firmly contracted uterus can be palpated through the abdominal wall as a firm, rounded mass. The firm uterus is about 10 to 15 cm in diameter immediately after birth, with variation among women. Uterine size varies with the size of the infant and parity of the mother, being larger when the infant is large or if the mother is a multipara. A full bladder or a blood clot in the uterus interferes with uterine contraction, increasing blood loss. A soft (boggy) uterus and increasing uterine size are associated with postpartum hemorrhage because large blood vessels at the placenta site are not compressed (see Chapter 27).

The vaginal drainage after delivery is called *lochia*. There are three stages: lochia rubra, lochia serosa, and lochia alba (see p. 417). Lochia rubra is present in the fourth stage.

Many women have a chill after birth. The cause of this reaction is unknown but probably relates to the sudden decrease in effort, loss of heat that had been produced by the fetus, a decrease in intra-abdominal pressure, and fetal blood cells that enter the maternal circulation. The chill lasts for about 20 minutes and subsides spontaneously.

Discomfort during the fourth stage results from birth trauma, such as lacerations, an episiotomy, edema, or a hematoma. The localized discomfort from birth trauma is evident as the effects of local or regional anesthetics diminish.

Afterpains are intermittent uterine contractions that occur after birth as the uterus begins the process of involution (a return to the pre-pregnancy state). The discomfort is similar to that of menstrual cramps. They are more prominent in multiparas and in women who breastfeed or when something interferes with proper uterine contraction, such as a full bladder.

The mother is simultaneously excited and tired after birth. She may be exhausted, but too excited to rest. The fourth stage of labor is an ideal time for bonding of the new family because the interest of both parents and newborn is high. The baby is alert and seeks to make eye contact with the new parents. These infant behaviors provide a powerful reinforcement for the parents' attachment to their newborn.

✔ Check Your Reading

15. How do maternal behaviors change during each phase of first-stage labor and during the second stage?
16. What are the typical characteristics of contractions during each phase of first-stage labor and second-stage labor?
17. What four signs may indicate that the placenta has separated?
18. What complications may occur if the uterus does not contract firmly and remain contracted after the placenta is expelled?

Duration of Labor

Duration of labor is significantly different for women who have never given birth and for those who have previously given birth vaginally. The parous woman usually delivers more quickly than does the nulliparous woman. However, the nurse must realize that women are individuals. Some nulliparas progress through labor very quickly, whereas labor for some parous women is more like that of women who have never given birth. If a woman has experienced a long labor with her first child, she may not have a long labor with every baby. If she has a history of rapid labor, however, later births are often rapid as well.

Because vaginal birth after cesarean (VBAC) is becoming more common, it is not unusual for a parous woman to have had no vaginal births. In this situation, the woman is likely to have a labor more like that of the nullipara, particularly if she did not labor before her previous cesarean birth.

Summary Concepts

- Labor contractions are intermittent, allowing for resumption of placental blood flow and exchange of oxygen and waste products between maternal and fetal circulations.
- The upper uterine segment contracts actively during labor, maintaining tension to pull the more passive lower uterine segment and cervix over the fetal presenting part. These actions bring about cervical effacement and dilation.

- Maternal vital signs are best assessed between contractions because slight alterations in her blood pressure and pulse may occur during a contraction.
- Hyperventilation may occur if the woman breathes deeply and rapidly. Its manifestations include tingling of the hands and feet, numbness, and dizziness.
- The fetal heart rate and rhythm respond rapidly to events that occur during labor.
- Fetal chest compression during labor and increased catecholamines aid the newborn in making respiratory adaptations to extrauterine life.
- Four interrelated components affecting the process of birth are the powers, the passage, the passenger, and the psyche. Presentation and position further describe the relation of the fetus (passenger) to the maternal pelvis.
- The mechanisms of labor favor the most efficient passage of the fetus through the mother's pelvis.
- The exact reasons labor begins are unknown, but several maternal and fetal factors seem to have a role. These include fetal production of glucocorticoids and androgens, changes in placental production of estrogen and progesterone, and increased maternal production of prostaglandins and oxytocin. Additionally, the woman's uterus becomes more sensitive to those factors that cause uterine contractions.
- As labor approaches, the woman may notice one or more premonitory signs that precede its onset: Braxton Hicks contractions, lightening, increased vaginal secretions, a bloody show, rupture of the membranes, a spurt of energy, or weight loss.
- The conclusive difference between true and false labor is progressive dilation and effacement of the cervix.
- Multiparas usually give birth more rapidly than women who have never delivered a baby, but each woman should be evaluated individually.
- The four stages and phases of labor are characterized by different physiological events and maternal behaviors: first stage, cervical dilation and effacement; second stage, expulsion of the fetus; third stage, expulsion of the placenta; fourth stage, maternal physiological stabilization and parent-infant bonding.
- Normal labor is characterized by consistent progression of uterine contractions, cervical dilation and effacement, and fetal descent.

References and Readings

Blackburn, S.T., & Loper, D.L. (1992). *Maternal, fetal, and neonatal physiology: A clinical perspective.* Philadelphia: W.B. Saunders.

Bochner, C. (1992). Anatomic characteristics of the fetal head and maternal pelvis. In N.F. Hacker & J.G. Moore (Eds.), *Essentials of obstetrics and gynecology* (pp. 109–118). Philadelphia: W.B. Saunders.

Bowes, W.A. (1989). Clinical aspects of normal and abnormal labor. In R.K. Creasy & R. Resnick, *Maternal-fetal medicine: Principles and practice* (pp. 510–546). Philadelphia: W.B. Saunders.

Broach, J., & Newton, N. (1988a). Food and beverages in labor. Part I: Cross-cultural and historical practices. *Birth*, 15(2), 81–85.

Broach, J., & Newton, N. (1988b). Food and beverages in labor. Part II: The effects of cessation of oral intake in labor. *Birth*, 15(2), 88–92.

Brown, S.T., Campbell, D., & Kurtz, A. (1989). Characteristics of labor pain at two stages of cervical dilation. *Pain*, 38(3), 289–295.

Cohen, W. (1990). Labor and delivery. In R. Eden & F. Boehm (Eds.), *Assessment and care of the fetus: Physiological, clinical, and medicolegal principles* (pp. 823–833). Norwalk, Conn.: Appleton & Lange.

Cooper, R.L., & Goldenberg, R.L. (1990). Catecholamine secretion in fetal adaptation to stress. *Journal of Obstetric, Gynecologic, and Neonatal Nursing*, 19(3), 223–226.

Cunningham, F.G., MacDonald, P.C., & Gant, N.F. (1989). *Williams obstetrics.* Norwalk, Conn.: Appleton & Lange.

Davis, L.K. (1992). Protocol for fetal heart rate monitoring. In L.K. Mandeville & N.H. Troiano (Eds.), *High risk intrapartum nursing* (pp. 305–308). Philadelphia: J.B. Lippincott.

Douglas, M.J. (1988). Commentary: The case against a more liberal food and fluid policy in labor. *Birth*, 15(2), 93–94.

Faxelius, G., Hägnerik, K., Lagercrantz, H., Lundell, B., & Irestedt, L. (1983). Catecholamine surge and lung function after delivery. *Archives of Disease in Childhood*, 58(4), 262–265.

Gennaro, S. (1988). The childbirth experience. In F.H. Nichols & S.S. Humenick (Eds.), *Childbirth education: Practice, research and theory* (pp. 52–68). Philadelphia: W.B. Saunders.

Kilpatrick, S.H., & Laros, R.K. (1989). Characteristics of normal labor. *Obstetrics and Gynecology*, 74(1), 85–87.

Korones, S.B. (1986). *High-risk newborn infants: The basis for intensive nursing care.* St. Louis: C.V. Mosby.

Lagercrantz, H., & Slotkin, T.A. (1986). The "stress" of being born. *Scientific American*, 254(7), 100–107.

Murray, M. (1988). *Antepartal and intrapartal fetal monitoring.* Washington, D.C.: NAACOG.

NAACOG. (1990). *Fetal heart rate auscultation.* Washington, D.C.

Parer, J.T. (1989). Fetal heart rate. In R.K. Creasy & R. Resnick (Eds.), *Maternal-fetal medicine: Principles and practice* (pp. 314–343). Philadelphia: W.B. Saunders.

Quilligan, E.J. (1989). Breech delivery. In R.K. Creasy & R. Resnick (Eds.), *Maternal-fetal medicine: Principles and practice* (pp. 204–205). Philadelphia: W.B. Saunders.

Resnik, R. (1989). Anatomic alterations in the reproductive tract. In R.K. Creasy & R. Resnik (Eds.), *Maternal-fetal medicine: Principles and practice* (pp. 136–140). Philadelphia: W.B. Saunders.

Rose, A.T., & Hilbers, S.M. (1988). Relaxation: Paced breathing techniques. In F.H. Nichols & S.S. Humenick (Eds.), *Childbirth Education: Practice, research and theory* (pp. 216–233). Philadelphia: W.B. Saunders.

Ross, M.G., Hobel, C.J., & Murad, S.H.N. (1992). Normal labor, delivery, and the puerperium. In N.F. Hacker & J.G. Moore (Eds.), *Essentials of obstetrics and gynecology* (pp. 119–133). Philadelphia: W.B. Saunders.

Stolte, K. (1987). A comparison of women's expectations of labor with the actual event. *Birth*, 14(2), 99–103.

13

Nursing Care During Labor and Birth

Objectives

1. Analyze issues that may face the inexperienced nurse who cares for women during the intrapartum period.
2. Explain guidelines for going to the hospital or birth center.
3. Describe admission and continuing intrapartum nursing assessments.
4. Apply the nursing process to care for the woman experiencing false labor.
5. Apply the nursing process to care of the woman and her family during the intrapartum period.
6. Describe common nursing procedures used when caring for women during the intrapartum period.
7. Identify nursing priorities when assisting the woman to give birth under emergency circumstances.
8. Relate therapeutic communication skills to care of the childbearing family.

Definitions

Abortion • A pregnancy that ends before 20 weeks' gestation, either spontaneously or electively. **Miscarriage** is a lay term for a spontaneous abortion.

Amniotomy • Artificial rupture of the amniotic sac (fetal membranes).

Caput succedaneum • Area of edema over the presenting part of the fetus or newborn resulting from pressure against the cervix. Often called simply "caput."

Crowning • Appearance of the fetal scalp or presenting part at the vaginal opening.

EDD • Abbreviation for estimated date of delivery; also called EDC (estimated date of confinement).

Episiotomy • Surgical incision of the perineum to enlarge the vaginal opening.

Ferning or fern test • Microscopic appearance of amniotic fluid that resembles fern leaves when the fluid is allowed to dry on a microscope slide.

Gravida • A woman who is or has been pregnant, regardless of the duration of the pregnancy(ies). Also refers to the number of pregnancies, including the one in progress, if applicable.

Multipara • A woman who has given birth after two or more pregnancies of at least 20 weeks of gestation. Also may be used informally to describe a woman before the birth of her second child.

Nitrazine paper • Paper to detect pH; it helps to determine whether the amniotic sac has ruptured.

Nuchal cord • Umbilical cord around the fetal neck.

Nullipara • A woman who has not completed a pregnancy to at least 20 weeks' gestation.

Para • A woman who has given birth after a pregnancy of at least 20 weeks of gestation. Also, the number of pregnancies that have ended after at least 20 weeks of gestation.

Primipara • A woman who has given birth after a pregnancy of at least 20 weeks of gestation.

△ Alert for a high risk of exposure to substances to which universal precautions apply. See Appendix B for additional information about infection control.

Nursing care of the woman and her family during labor and birth can be one of the most satisfying of nursing roles. Far more than a physiological event, the birth of a new baby has deep personal and social significance for the family. Their roles and relationships are forever altered by this event.

While caring for laboring women is usually satisfying, it is often demanding. The nurse must support natural physical processes, promote a satisfying experience for the family, and be vigilant for complications. Additionally, there are two clients to watch—and the fetus cannot be seen.

The intrapartum unit is typically a happy place, and good outcomes for mothers and infants are usual. Most women have accepted their pregnancy and look forward to holding their infant. Yet some women have had stressful pregnancies because of physical or substance abuse, economic hardship, non-supportive personal relationships, or other problems. Nursing care for women in labor with uncomplicated pregnancies is presented here. Nursing care for women with special needs is described in Chapter 23.

Issues for Nurses

Inexperienced nurses often approach care of laboring women with apprehension. Some of the following are common issues that new nurses face when caring for families during birth.

Pain Associated with Birth. Working with people in pain is difficult, and most nurses feel compelled to relieve the client's distress promptly. Yet, pain is a normal and expected part of labor and cannot be completely relieved. The nurse must accept that some pain in labor is normal. Helping the woman master the pain is an essential part of nursing care.

Inexperience or Negative Experiences. The nurse who has never given birth may feel inadequate to care for laboring women, although he or she rarely feels it necessary to experience a fractured leg to care for a client with that problem. Nursing skills needed by the intrapartum nurse are basic: problem solving, therapeutic communication, comfort measures, observation, empathy, and common sense.

Nurses who have children may be apprehensive because of their own difficult experiences during birth. These nurses must be careful not to convey negative attitudes to the laboring woman.

Unpredictability. Some nurses find the unpredictable nature of an intrapartum unit disturbing. The number of women needing care may change dramatically and within a few minutes. Some situations simply are not predictable or easily explained and may be frustrating for some nurses.

Intimacy. The intimate nature of intrapartum care and its sexual overtones may make nurses uncomfortable. They may feel that they are intruding on a private marital time.

The male nurse often finds this aspect of intrapartum care most anxiety-provoking. Although he may have cared for other female clients, care has not been this focused on the reproductive system. He often wonders how the woman's husband or partner will accept him as a care provider.

The best approach for both male and female nurses is to maintain a professional demeanor. The nurse can take cues from the couple. If they want to be alone, the nurse can provide as much private time as possible, intruding only as needed to assess the woman and fetus. In later labor, both partners often welcome the presence of a competent, caring nurse of either sex.

Admission to the Birth Facility

The Decision to Go to the Hospital or Birth Center

During the last trimester, the woman needs to know when she should go to the hospital or birth center. Many factors are considered, such as:

- Number and duration of any previous labors
- Distance from the hospital
- Available transportation
- Child care needs

Nurses should teach women differences between false and true labor and should offer guidelines for going to the birth facility (see Women Want to Know: When to Go to the Hospital or Birth Center). Because not everyone will have a typical labor, women should be encouraged to go the hospital or birth center for evaluation if they are uncertain or have other concerns.

Nursing Responsibilities During Admission

In most hospitals, a woman is admitted directly to the intrapartum unit for evaluation of any pregnancy concerns. The intrapartum nurse has two priorities when the woman arrives: (1) establishing a therapeutic relationship and (2) determining the condition of

Women Want To Know

When to Go to the Hospital or Birth Center

Facilities, nurse-midwives, and physicians may have different recommendations than those given here; also, women have varying needs. Consider these to be only guidelines for providing individualized instruction to each woman about when to enter the hospital or birth center.

Contractions

A pattern of increasing regularity, frequency, duration, and intensity.

- *Nullipara*: Regular contractions, 5 minutes apart, for 1 hour
- *Multipara*: Regular contractions, 10 minutes apart, for 1 hour

Ruptured Membranes

Either a gush or trickle of fluid from the vagina should be evaluated, whether or not you have contractions.

Bleeding

Bright-red bleeding that is not mixed with mucus is not expected in labor and should be evaluated. Normal bloody show is thicker, pink or dark red, and is obviously mixed with mucus.

Decreased Fetal Movement

If you notice a substantial decrease in fetal movement, notify your physician or nurse-midwife so that the fetus can be evaluated.

Other Concerns

These guidelines cannot cover all situations. Therefore, please go to the hospital for evaluation of any concerns or feelings that something may be wrong.

---

the mother and fetus. Table 13–1 provides details about the initial intrapartum assessment.

ESTABLISHING A THERAPEUTIC RELATIONSHIP

The nurse must quickly establish a therapeutic relationship with the woman and her partner or family. For many women, childbirth is their first hospital admission. Their first impression is an important influence on how they feel about the quality of their birth experience. The nurse who admits the woman lays the groundwork for a therapeutic relationship during the birth and post partum. If families are treated in a rude or hurried manner, it may be difficult or impossible for later caregivers to overcome the initial poor impression. Interpersonal nursing skills are as important as technical competence (Kintz, 1987).

Making the Family Feel Welcome

Greeting the woman and her family warmly when they arrive conveys that they are valued. Because of the fluctuations in the number of women needing care, nurses are often very busy. Even if the unit is busy, the nurse should convey a sense of interest and caring. Families usually understand if the nurse is busy; they do not understand rudeness or insensitivity to their needs.

When caring for the woman who has not had prenatal care or childbirth classes—behaviors most nurses value—one must not be judgmental in either words or actions. The woman's priorities and values may not be the same as those of the nurse, but she deserves the same respect and care as the woman who made every preparation for her baby's birth.

Determining Family Expectations About Birth

Regardless of how many children they have, women and their partners enter the birth unit with certain expectations about the upcoming birth. Today's childbearing family is often well educated and goal-directed. They have often studied their options in birth and have planned a birth that best fits their ideals. The family who has not made specific plans also has expectations about the birth, shaped by their contact with relatives and friends who have children.

Previous childbirth experience may enable the couple to be assertive so that they can achieve their goals for this birth. They may want to repeat a previous satisfying experience, but it is more likely that they want to avoid repeating an unsatisfying experience. Sometimes only one part of their past birthing experience did not meet their expectations but has colored their impression of the entire process.

Cultural values shape the family's expectations about the birth. Groups that view pregnancy and birth as normal processes find the usual interventions of many hospitals puzzling. Other groups believe that childbirth is risky, thus warranting a variety of scientific and/or folk remedies to ensure safety for the mother and baby.

Conveying Confidence

From the first encounter, the nurse should convey a sense of confidence in the woman's ability to give birth and her partner's ability to support her. As labor progresses, the woman's labor contractions and

Text continued on page 297

Table 13–1. INTRAPARTUM ASSESSMENT GUIDE

Women who have had prenatal care will have much of this information available on their prenatal record. The nurse needs only to verify it or update it as needed.

Assessment, Method (Selected Rationales)	Common Findings	Significant Findings, Nursing Action
	Interview	
Purpose: To obtain information about the woman's pregnancy, labor, and conditions that may affect her care. The interview is curtailed if she seems to be in late labor.		
Introduction: Introduce yourself and ask the woman how she wants to be addressed. Ask her if she wants her partner and/or family to remain during the interview and assessment. (These courtesies show respect for the woman and give her control over those she wants to remain with her.)	Many women prefer to be addressed by their first names during labor.	The surname (family name) precedes the given name in some cultures. Clarify which name is used to properly address the woman and to properly identify both mother and newborn.
Culture/language: If she is from another culture, ask what her preferred language is and what language(s) she speaks, reads, or verbally understands. (Using the woman's primary language enables the most accurate data collection.)	Common non-English languages of women in the United States are Spanish or one of the Asian dialects. The most common non-English language varies with location.	Try to secure a translator fluent in the woman's primary language. Ask her if there are people who are not acceptable to her as translators (for example, males or one from a group in conflict with her culture). Family members may not be the best translators because they may translate selectively, adding or subtracting information as they see fit.
Communication: Ask the woman to tell you when she has a contraction, and pause during the interview and physical assessment. (Shows the nurse is sensitive to her comfort and allows her to concentrate more fully on the information the nurse requests.)	Women in active labor have difficulty answering questions or cooperating with a physical examination while they are having a contraction.	If contractions are very frequent, assess the woman's labor status promptly rather than continuing the interview. Ask only the most critical questions.
Non-verbal cues: Observe the woman's behaviors and interactions with her family and the nurse. (Permits estimation of her level of anxiety. Identifies behaviors indicating that she should have a vaginal examination to determine whether birth is imminent.)	*Latent phase:* Sociable and mildly anxious. *Active phase:* Concentrating intently with contractions; often uses prepared childbirth techniques if she has attended classes.	The unprepared or extremely anxious woman may breathe deeply and rapidly, displaying a tense facial and body posture during and between contractions. These behaviors may indicate that birth is imminent: 1. Her statement that the baby is coming. 2. Grunting sounds (low-pitched, guttural sounds). 3. Bearing down with abdominal muscles. 4. Sitting on one buttock. Euphoria, combativeness, or sedation may indicate recent illicit drug ingestion.
Reason for admission: "What brings you to the hospital/birth center today?" (Open-ended question promotes more complete answer.)	Labor contractions at term are the usual reason. Observation for false labor is another common reason for admission.	Bleeding, preterm labor, pain other than labor contractions. Report these findings to the physician or nurse-midwife promptly.
Prenatal care: "Did you see a doctor or nurse-midwife during your pregnancy?" "Who is your doctor or nurse-midwife?" "How far along were you in your pregnancy when you saw the physician or nurse-midwife?" (Enables location of prenatal record.)	Early and regular prenatal care promotes maternal and fetal health.	No prenatal care or care that was irregular or begun in late pregnancy means that complications may not have been identified.
Estimated date of delivery (EDD): "When is your baby due?" (Determines if gestation is term.) "When did your last menstrual period begin?" (For estimation of EDD if woman did not have prenatal care.)	*Term gestation:* 38–42 weeks. The woman's gestation may have been confirmed or adjusted during pregnancy with an ultrasound or other clinical examination.	Gestations earlier than 38 weeks (preterm) or later than the end of the 42nd week (post-term) are associated with more fetal or neonatal problems.

Table 13–1. INTRAPARTUM ASSESSMENT GUIDE *Continued*

Women who have had prenatal care will have much of this information available on their prenatal record. The nurse needs only to verify it or update it as needed.

Assessment, Method (Selected Rationales)	Common Findings	Significant Findings, Nursing Action
Interview		
Gravidity, parity, abortions: "How many times have you been pregnant?" "How many babies have you had? Were they full-term or premature?" "How many children are now living?" "Have you had any miscarriages or abortions?" "Were there any problems with your babies after they were born?" (Helps estimate probable speed of labor and anticipate neonatal problems.)	Labor may be faster for the woman who has given birth before than for the nullipara. Miscarriage is used to describe a spontaneous abortion because many lay people associate the term "abortion" with only induced abortions.	Parity of 5 or more (grand multiparity) may be associated with placenta previa or postpartum hemorrhage (see p. 780). Women who have had several spontaneous abortions or who have given birth to infants with abnormalities may face a higher risk for an infant with a birth defect.
Pregnancy history—identifies problems that may affect this birth:		
Present pregnancy: "Have you had any problems during this pregnancy, such as high blood pressure, diabetes, or bleeding?"	Complications are not expected.	Women having diabetes or hypertension may have poor placental blood flow, possibly resulting in fetal distress. Some complications of past pregnancies, such as diabetes, may recur in another pregnancy. The woman who plans a VBAC may need more support and reassurance to give birth vaginally.
Past pregnancies: "Were there any problems with your other pregnancy(ies)?" "Were your other babies born vaginally or by cesarean birth?"	Women who had previous cesarean birth(s) often have a trial of labor and vaginal birth (VBAC).	
Other: "Is there anything else you think we should know about your pregnancy so that we can better care for you?"	This open-ended question gives the woman a chance to share information that may not be elicited by other questions.	
Labor status: "When did your contractions become regular?" "What time did you begin to think you might really be in labor?" (Facilitates a more accurate estimation of the time labor began.)	Varies among women. Many women go to the birth facility when contractions first begin. Others wait until they are reasonably sure that they are really in labor.	Women who say they have been "in labor" for an unusual length of time (for example, "for two days") have probably had false labor. These women may be very tired from the annoying, non-productive contractions.
Contractions: "How often are your contractions coming?" "How long do they last?" "Are they getting stronger?" "Tell me if you have a contraction while we are talking." (Obtains the woman's subjective evaluation of her contractions. Alerts the nurse to palpate contractions that occur during the interview.)	Varies according to her stage and phase of labor. Labor contractions are usually regular and show a pattern of increasing frequency, duration and intensity.	Irregular contractions or those that do not increase in frequency, duration, or intensity are more likely to represent false labor. Contractions with a duration of longer than 90 seconds or intervals of full uterine relaxation shorter than 60 seconds can reduce placental blood flow.
Membrane status: "Has your water broken?" "What time did it break?" "What did the fluid look like?" "About how much fluid did you lose—was it a big gush or a trickle?" (Alerts the nurse of the need to verify whether the membranes have ruptured if it is not obvious. Identifies possible prolonged rupture of membranes.)	Most women go to the birth facility for evaluation soon after their membranes rupture. If a woman is not already in labor, contractions usually begin within a few hours after the membranes rupture at term.	If the woman's membranes have ruptured and she is not in labor or if she is not at term, a vaginal examination is often deferred. Labor may be induced if she is at term with ruptured membranes.
Allergies: "Are you allergic to any foods or medicines?" "What kind of reaction do you have?" "Have you ever had a problem with anesthesia when you had dental work?" (Determines possible sensitivity to drugs that may be used.)	Record any known allergies to food and medication. As needed, describe how they affected the woman.	Allergy to seafood, iodized salt, or x-ray contrast media may indicate iodine allergy. Because iodine is used in many "prep" solutions, alternative ones should be used. Allergy to dental anesthetics may indicate possible allergy to the drugs used for local or regional anesthetics. These drugs usually end in the suffix -caine.

Table continued on following page

Table 13–1. INTRAPARTUM ASSESSMENT GUIDE *Continued*

Women who have had prenatal care will have much of this information available on their prenatal record. The nurse needs only to verify it or update it as needed.

Assessment, Method (Selected Rationales)	Common Findings	Significant Findings, Nursing Action
Interview		
Food intake: "When was the last time you had something to eat or drink?" "What did you have?" (Promotes safer general anesthesia, if needed.)	Record the time of the woman's last food intake and what she ate. Include both liquids and solids.	Recent food intake may be delayed in emptying from the stomach, which could pose a risk for regurgitation and aspiration if the woman needs general anesthesia. If she says she has not had any intake for an unusual length of time, question her more closely: "Is there any food you may have forgotten, such as a snack or a drink of water?"
Recent illness: "Have you been ill recently?" "What was the problem?" "What did you do for it?" "Have you been around anyone with a contagious illness recently?"	Most pregnant women are healthy. An occasional woman may have had a minor illness such as an upper respiratory infection.	Untreated urinary tract infections are associated with preterm labor. The woman who has had contact with someone having a communicable disease may become ill and possibly infect others in the facility.
Medications: "What drugs do you take that your doctor or nurse-midwife has prescribed?" "Are there any over-the-counter drugs that you use?" "I know this may be uncomfortable to discuss, but we need to know about any illegal substances that you use to more safely care for you and your baby." (Permits evaluation of the woman's drug intake and encourages her to disclose non-prescribed use.)	Prenatal vitamins and iron are commonly prescribed. Record all drugs the woman takes, including time and amount of last ingestion. Women who use illegal substances often conceal or diminish the extent of their use because they fear reprisals.	Drugs may interact with other medications given during labor, especially analgesics and anesthetics. Substance abuse is associated with complications for the mother and infant (see Chapter 23). If the woman discloses that she uses illegal drugs, ask her what kind and the last time she ingested them (often referred to as a "hit"). A non-judgmental approach is more likely to result in honest information.
Tobacco or alcohol: "Do you smoke or use tobacco in any other form? About how many cigarettes a day?" "Do you use alcohol? About how many drinks do you have each day (or week)?" (Evaluates use of these legal substances.)	As in substance abuse, women often underreport the extent of their use of tobacco or alcohol.	Infants of heavy smokers are often smaller and may have reduced placental blood flow during labor. Infants of women who use alcohol may show fetal alcohol effects (see Chapter 23).
Birth plans (shows respect for the woman and her family as individuals and promotes achievement of their expectations. Enables more culturally appropriate care):		
Coach or primary support person: "Who is the main person you want to be with you during labor?" Ask that person how he or she wants to be addressed, such as "Mr. Smith" or "Bob."	This is usually the woman's husband or the baby's father, but it may be her mother, sister, or a friend, especially if she is single.	The woman who has little or no support from significant others will probably need more intense nursing support during labor and after the birth. These clients are more likely to have problems with parent-infant attachment.
Other support: "Is there anyone else you would like to be present during labor?"	Women often want another support person present.	
Preparation for childbirth: "Did you attend prepared childbirth classes?" "Did someone go with you?"	Ideally, the woman and a partner have had some preparation in formal classes or self-study. Women who attended classes during previous pregnancies do not always repeat the classes during subsequent pregnancies.	The unprepared woman may need more support with simple relaxation and breathing techniques during labor. Her partner may need to learn techniques to assist her.
Preferences: "Are there any special plans you have for this birth?" "Is there anything you want to avoid?" "Did you plan to record the birth with pictures or a video?"	Some women or couples have strong feelings regarding certain interventions. Common ones are: (1) analgesia or anesthesia; (2) intravenous lines; (3) fetal monitoring; (4) preparatory shave or enema; or (5) use of episiotomy or forceps.	Conflict may arise if the woman has not previously discussed her preferences with her physician or nurse-midwife or if she is unaware of what services are available where she will give birth. Most conflicts arise if the woman wants no intervention and the clinician is not comfortable with this approach.
Cultural needs: "Are there any special cultural practices that you plan when you have your baby?" "How can we best help you to fulfill these practices?"	Women from Asian and Hispanic cultures often subscribe to the "hot/cold" theory of illness and will want specific foods after birth, such as soft-boiled eggs. They may not want their water iced.	Try to incorporate all positive or neutral cultural practices. If a practice is harmful, explain why and try to find a way to work around it if the family does not want to give it up.

Table 13–1. INTRAPARTUM ASSESSMENT GUIDE *Continued*

Women who have had prenatal care will have much of this information available on their prenatal record. The nurse needs only to verify it or update it as needed.

Assessment, Method (Selected Rationales)	Common Findings	Significant Findings, Nursing Action
	Fetal Evaluation	
Purpose: To determine if the fetus seems to be healthy and tolerating labor well.		
Fetal heart rate (FHR): Assess by intermittent auscultation, or apply an external fetal monitor if that is the facility's policy (most common in the United States). Document FHR at least this often for the fetus at low risk for complications: 1. Every hour during the latent phase 2. Every 30 minutes during active and transition phases 3. Every 15 minutes during second stage	Average is 110–160 BPM. Rate should increase when the fetus moves.	These signs may indicate fetal stress and should be reported to the physician or nurse-midwife: 1. Rate outside the normal limits 2. Slowing of the rate that persists after the contraction ends 3. No increase in rate when the fetus moves More frequent assessments should be made of the FHR.
	Labor Status	
Purpose: To identify whether the woman is in labor and if birth is imminent. If she displays signs of imminent birth, this assessment is done as soon as she is admitted.		
Contractions (Can yield objective information about labor status): In addition to asking the woman about her contraction pattern, assess the contractions by palpation with the fingertips of one hand. A guideline is to assess: 1. Hourly during the latent phase 2. Every 30 minutes during the active phase 3. Every 15 minutes during transition and second stage	See Interview section earlier in table	See Interview section earlier in table. Women who have intense contractions or who are making rapid progress need to be assessed more frequently.
 *Vaginal examination:* Done by the experienced nurse. (Determines cervical dilation and effacement; fetal presentation, position, and station; bloody show; and status of the membranes.)	Varies according to the stage and phase of labor. It may not be possible to determine fetal position by vaginal examination when membranes are intact and bulging over the presenting part.	A vaginal examination is not performed if the woman reports or has evidence of active bleeding (not bloody show). Report reasons for omitting a vaginal examination to the physician or nurse-midwife.
Status of membranes: During a vaginal examination a flow of fluid indicates ruptured membranes. A Nitrazine test and/or fern test may be done. (Test needed only if it is not obvious that the membranes have ruptured.)	Amniotic fluid should be clear, possibly containing flecks of white vernix. Its odor is distinctive but not offensive. Nitrazine test with a color change to blue-green to dark blue (pH > 6.5) suggests true rupture of the membranes but is not conclusive. Fern test is more diagnostic of true rupture of membranes.	A greenish color indicates meconium staining, which may be associated with fetal distress or postterm gestation. Thick meconium with much particulate matter ("pea soup") is most significant (see p. 844). Thick green-black meconium may be passed by the fetus in a breech presentation and is not necessarily associated with fetal distress. Cloudy, yellowish, strong- or foul-smelling fluid suggests infection. Bloody fluid may indicate partial placental separation (p. 670).
Leopold's maneuvers: Often done before assessing the FHR because they help locate the best place to assess the FHR. (Identifies fetal presentation and position. Most accurate when combined with information from vaginal examination.)	A cephalic presentation with the head well flexed (vertex) is normal. The fetal head is often easily displaced upward ("floating") if the woman is not in labor. When the head is engaged, it cannot be displaced upward with Leopold's maneuvers.	A hard, round, freely movable object in the fundus suggests a fetal head, meaning the fetus is in a breech presentation. Less commonly, the fetus may be cross-wise in the uterus: a transverse lie.
Pain: Note discomfort during and between contractions. Note tenderness when palpating contractions. (Distinguishes between normal labor pain and abnormal pain that may be associated with a complication.)	There may be verbal or non-verbal evidence of pain with contractions, but the woman should be relatively comfortable between contractions. The skin around the umbilicus is often sensitive.	Constant pain or a tender, rigid uterus may indicate a complication, such as abruptio placentae (separated placenta) or, less commonly, uterine rupture (see p. 766).

Table continued on following page

Table 13–1. INTRAPARTUM ASSESSMENT GUIDE *Continued*

Women who have had prenatal care will have much of this information available on their prenatal record. The nurse needs only to verify it or update it as needed.

Assessment, Method (Selected Rationales)	Common Findings	Significant Findings, Nursing Action
Physical Examination		
Purpose: To evaluate the woman's general health and identify conditions that may affect her intrapartum and postpartum care.		
General appearance: Observe skin color and texture, nutritional state, and appearance of rest or fatigue. Examine the woman's face, fingers, and lower extremities for edema. Ask her if she can take her rings off and on.	Women are often fatigued if their sleep has been interrupted by Braxton Hicks contractions, fetal activity, or frequent urination. Mild edema of the lower extremities is common in late pregnancy.	Pallor suggests anemia. Edema of the face and fingers or extreme (pitting) edema of the lower extremities is associated with pregnancy-induced hypertension (see p. 679).
Vital signs: Take the woman's temperature, pulse (P), respirations (R), and blood pressure (BP). Reassess the temperature every 4 hours (every 2 hours after membranes rupture or if elevated); repeat BP, P, R every hour.	*Temperature:* 35.8°–37.3°C (96.4°–99.1°F). *Pulse:* 60–100/minute *Respirations:* 12–20/minute, even and unlabored. BP near baseline levels established during pregnancy. Transient elevations of BP are common when the woman is first admitted, but they return to baseline levels within about ½ hour.	Report abnormalities to physician or nurse-midwife. Temperature of 38°C (100.4°F) or higher suggests infection. Pulse and respirations may also be elevated. Pulse and BP may be elevated if the woman is extremely anxious or in pain. A BP of 140/90 or higher or an elevation of 30 mmHg systolic or 15 mmHg diastolic over the mother's pregnancy baseline is considered hypertensive. For women who did not have prenatal care, there is no baseline to compare.
Heart and lung sounds: Auscultate all areas with a stethoscope.	Heart sounds should be clear with a distinct S_1 and S_2. A physiologic murmur is common because of the increased blood volume and cardiac output. Breath sounds should be clear, with respirations even and unlabored.	The woman who is breathing rapidly and deeply may have symptoms of hyperventilation: tingling and spasm of the fingers, numbness around the lips.
Breasts: Palpate for a dominant mass.	Breasts are full and nodular. Areola is darker, especially in dark-skinned women. Breasts may leak colostrum (clear, sticky, straw-colored fluid) during labor.	Report a dominant mass to the physician or nurse-midwife.
Abdomen: Observe for scars at the same time Leopold's maneuvers and the FHR are assessed. It is usually sufficient to assess the fundal height by observing its relation to the xiphoid process.	Striae (stretch marks) are common. If scars are noted, ask the woman what surgery she had. The fundus at term is usually slightly below the xiphoid process.	Report a previous cesarean birth to the physician or nurse-midwife. Transverse uterine scars are least likely to rupture if the woman is in labor (see p. 406). Measure the fundal height (see p. 140) if the fetus seems small or if the gestation is questionable.
Deep tendon reflexes: Assess patella reflex (see p. 121).	Brisk knee jerk without spasm or sustained muscle contraction is normal. Some women normally have hypoactive reflexes.	Report absent (uncommon unless the woman is receiving magnesium sulfate) or hyperactive reflexes. Hyperactive reflexes and clonus (repeated tapping when the foot is dorsiflexed) are associated with pregnancy-induced hypertension and often precede a seizure (see p. 688).
Midstream urine specimen: Assess protein and glucose levels with a dipstick if these procedures are routine in the facility. Follow instructions on the package for waiting times. Send for urinalysis if ordered.	Negative or trace of protein; negative glucose.	Proteinuria is associated with pregnancy-induced hypertension but may also be associated with urinary tract infections or a specimen that is contaminated with vaginal secretions. Glucosuria is associated with diabetes.
Laboratory tests: Women who have had prenatal care may not need additional tests. Common tests include:		
1. Complete blood count (or hematocrit done on unit)	1. Hemoglobin at least 11 g/dl; hematocrit at least 33%	1. Values lower than these reduce maternal reserve for normal blood loss at birth.

Nursing Care: The Childbirth Story

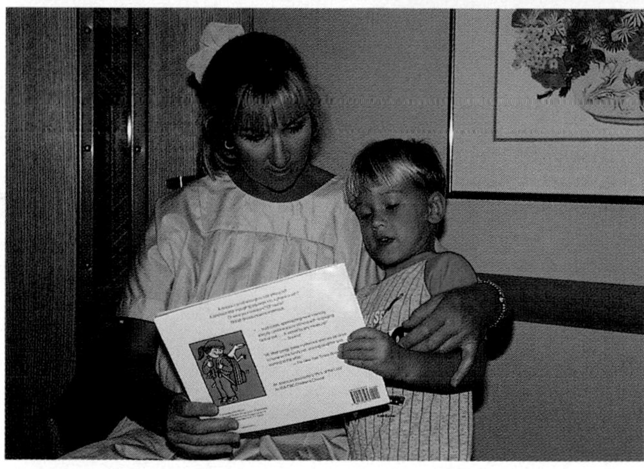

1. Shari, in early labor with her second child, spends time with her 5-year-old son in the labor-delivery-recovery room.

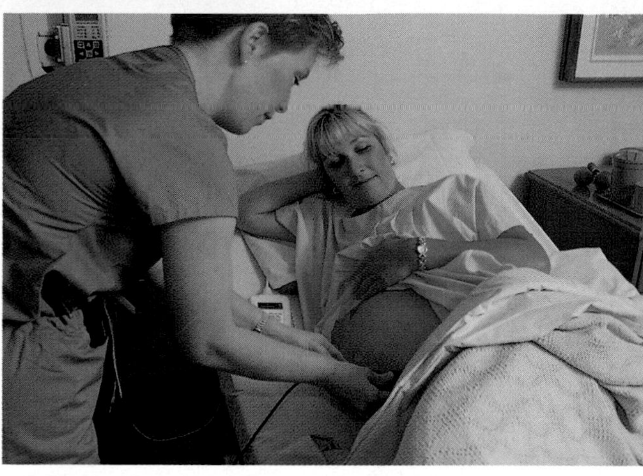

2. The nurse frequently assesses the condition of both the mother and the fetus. Here she listens to fetal heart tones.

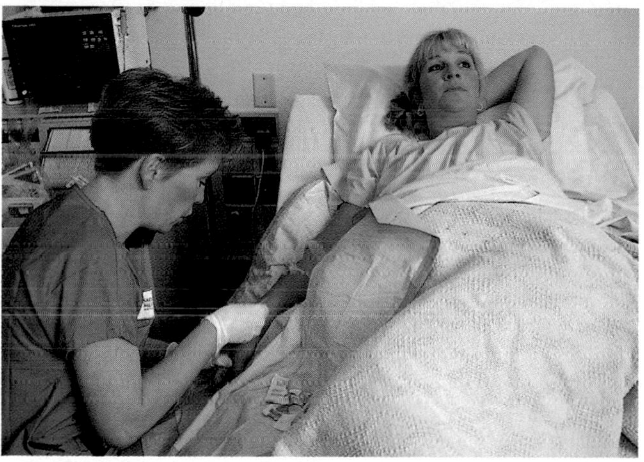

3. Although intravenous fluids are not always necessary, most physicians order them to prevent dehydration and for access to a vein in case an emergency develops.

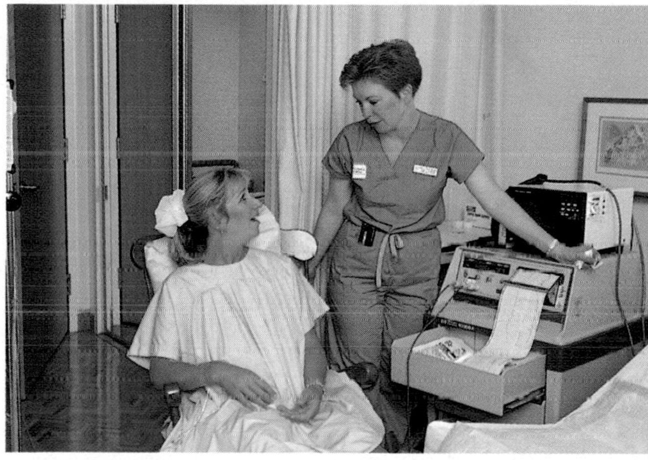

4. The nurse establishes a relationship of trust by assisting Shari into a position of comfort and explaining information obtained by electronic monitoring.

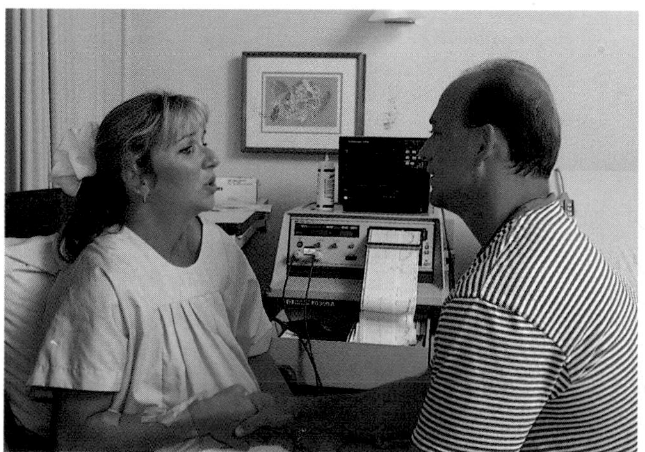

5. Shari plans a childbirth without anesthesia, and the father, Darren, uses skills learned in childbirth education classes to help her cope with discomfort.

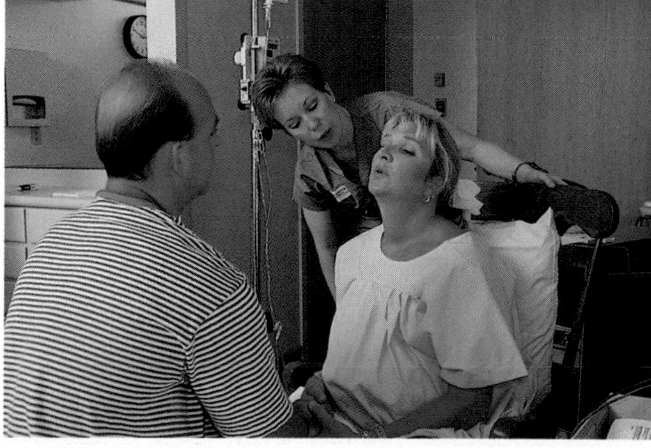

6. It is more difficult for the couple to maintain control as the contractions become stronger. The nurse praises their efforts and reviews measures to reduce discomfort.

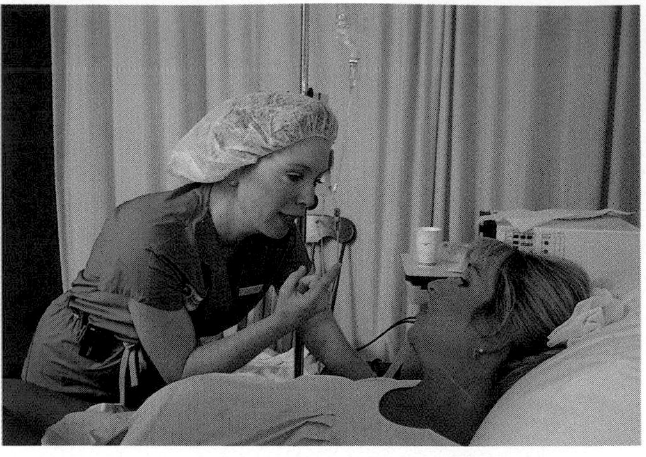

7. During transition, often the most painful phase of labor, the nurse remains in close contact with Shari and assists her through each contraction.

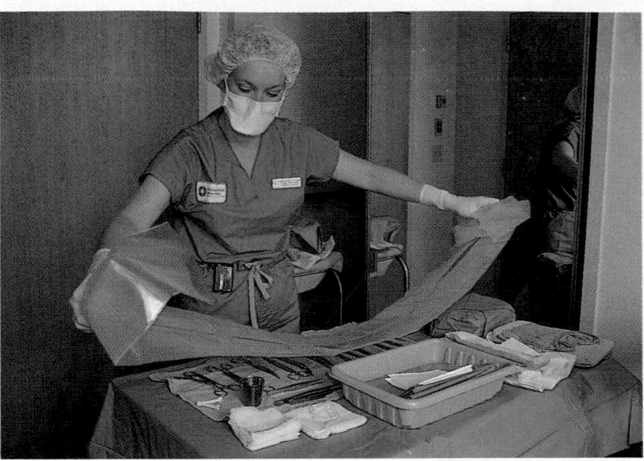

8. The nurse prepares the sterile instruments that will be used during the birth.

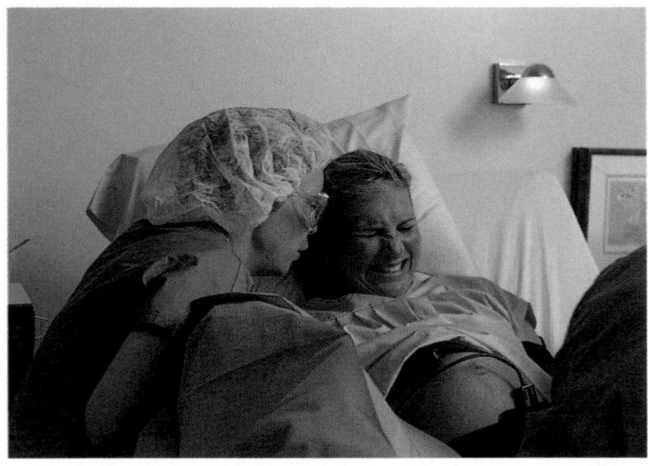

9. As birth approaches, the nurse positions Shari and assists her to push with each contraction. Note the nurse now wears protective glasses.

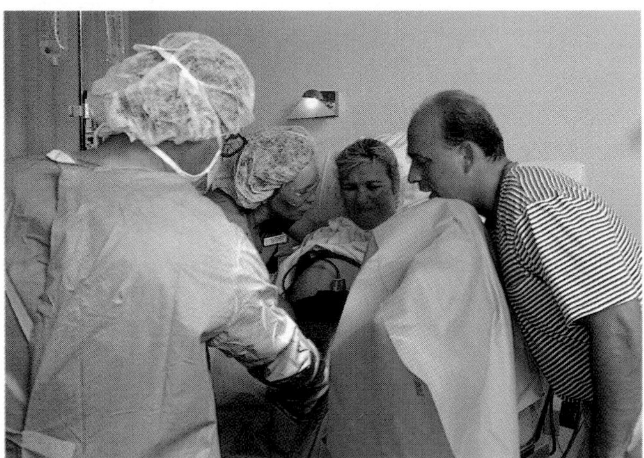

10. The nurse also encourages Darren to remain in close contact with the mother and continue to participate in the birth.

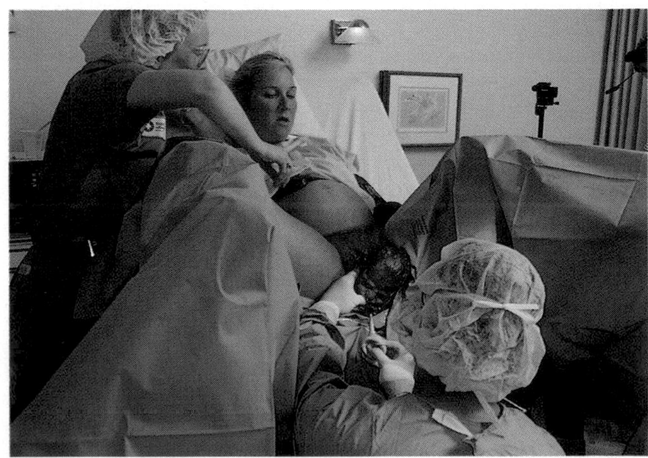

11. The physician suctions secretions from the nose and mouth of the infant when the head is delivered.

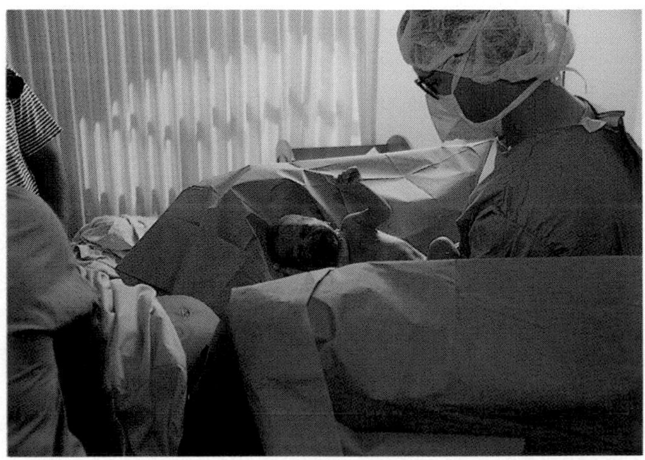

12. The physician holds the infant so the parents can get their first look at their newborn son.

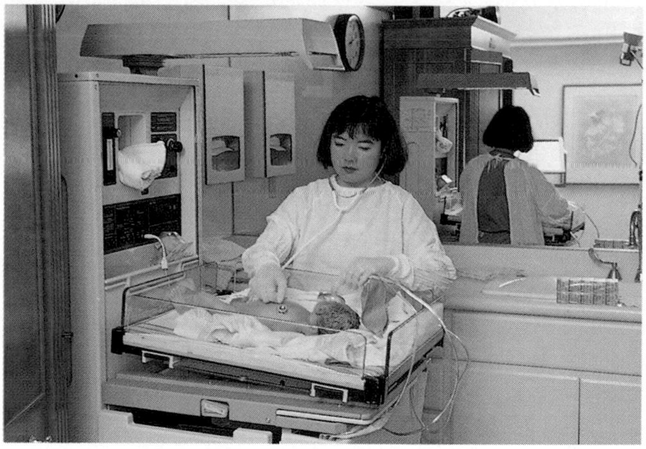

13. A nurse counts the apical pulse and observes the newborn's pink color, which makes the administration of oxygen unnecessary.

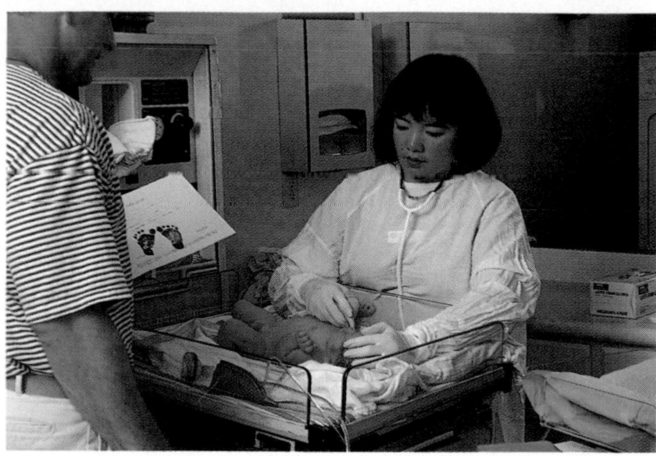

14. The father observes as the nurse suctions secretions from the newborn's nose and mouth and completes identification procedures, such as footprinting.

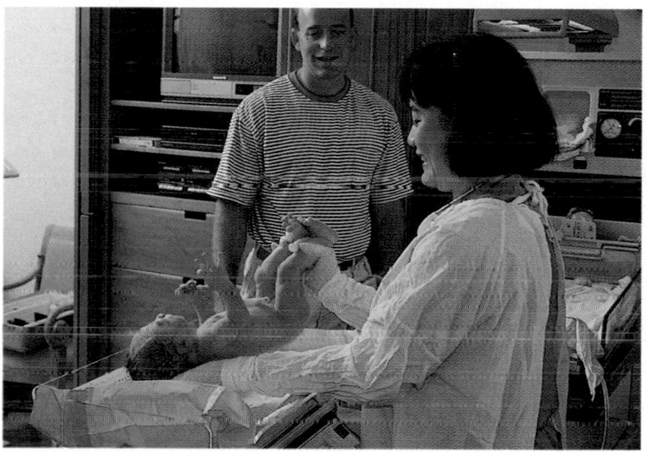

15. The father is an interested observer as the nurse weighs and measures the newborn.

16. Nurses are aware of the importance of early contact, and as soon as possible after birth, the mother, father, and newborn are brought together.

17. Although Adam was not present at the birth, within a short time he meets the wide-eyed baby who gazes intently at his older brother.

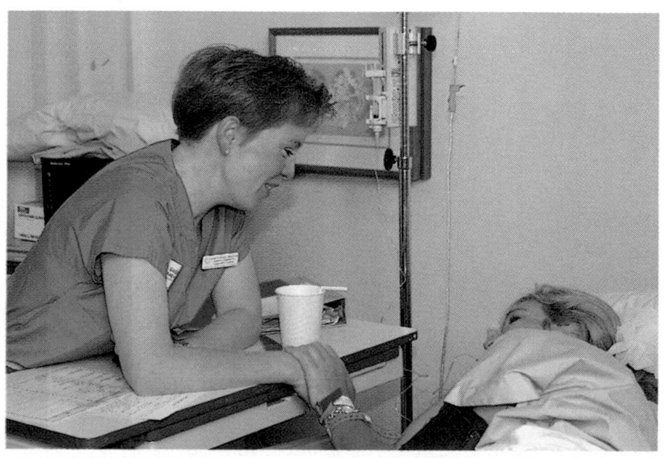

18. Shari and the nurse demonstrate the mutual regard that developed as they shared the intense experience of labor and birth.

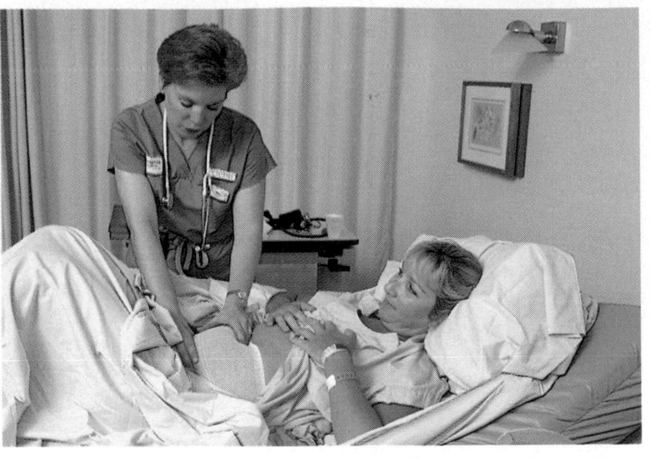

19. The nurse palpates the fundus frequently the first hour following childbirth to confirm that the uterus is firmly contracted and thus to prevent excessive bleeding.

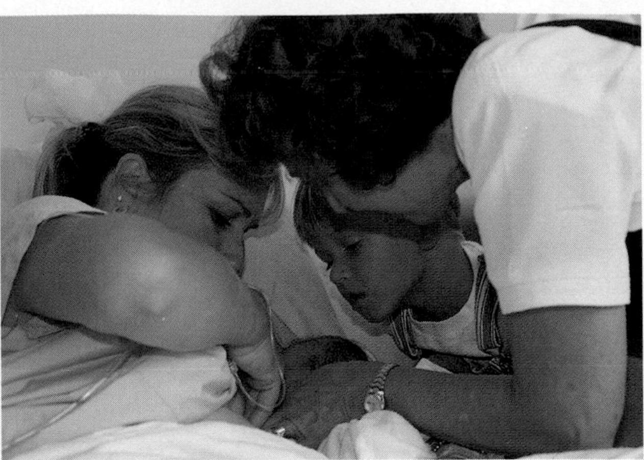

20. Adam watches intently as his mother and grandmother put the baby to breast for the first time.

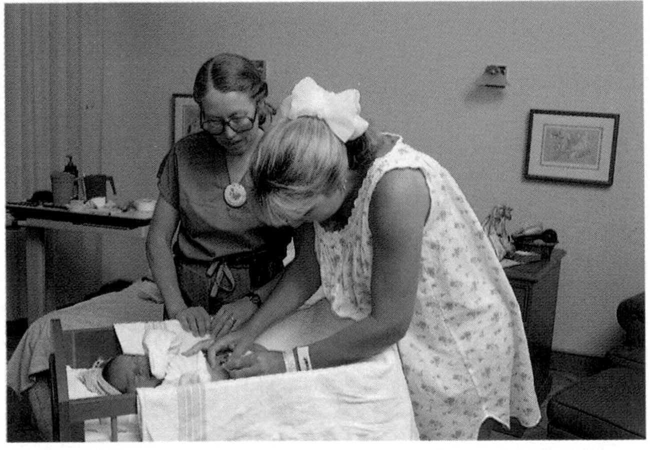

21. Nurses must teach mothers how to care for themselves and the infant within a very short time. Here the nurse instructs Shari in cord care.

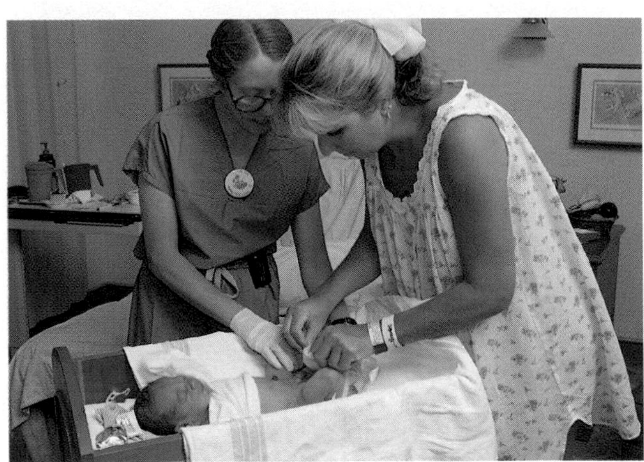

22. Shari gains confidence in circumcision care when the nurse allows for a return demonstration.

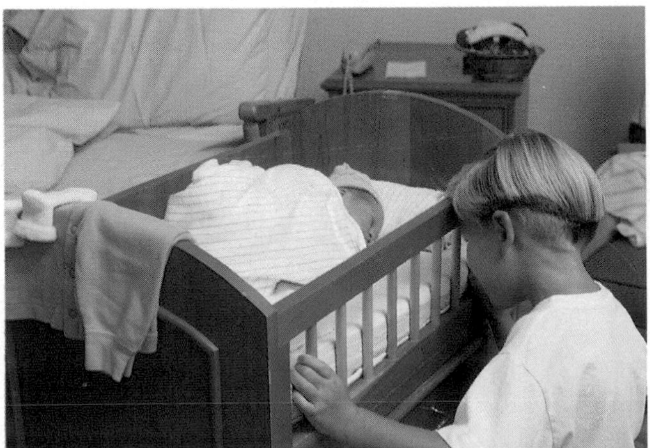

23. Adam peeks at his baby brother while the family receives additional instructions.

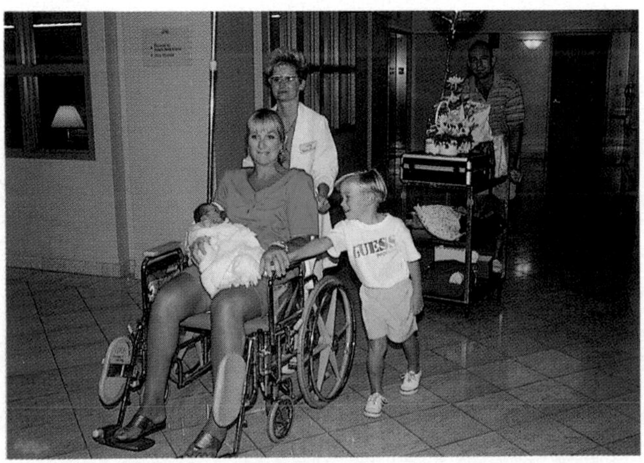

24. Twenty-four hours after her admission, Shari and the infant are discharged from the postpartum unit.

Table 13–1. INTRAPARTUM ASSESSMENT GUIDE *Continued*

Women who have had prenatal care will have much of this information available on their prenatal record. The nurse needs only to verify it or update it as needed.

Assessment, Method (Selected Rationales)	Common Findings	Significant Findings, Nursing Action
Physical Examination		
2. Blood type and Rh factor	2. The woman who is Rh-negative usually has received Rh immune globulin at about 28 weeks' gestation to prevent formation of anti-Rh antibodies	2. Rh-negative mothers will need Rh immune globulin if their infant is Rh-positive.
3. Serologic tests for syphilis	3. Negative	3. A positive test may indicate that the baby will be infected and need treatment after birth. The mother should be treated if she has not been treated already.

discomfort become more intense. She and her partner will need reassurance that labor is progressing as expected. Women having their first baby find the power of normal labor contractions surprising and even overwhelming. The experienced nurse can reassure these women that intense contractions are normal in active labor while also watching for problems.

Consider the different attitudes conveyed by the phrases "give birth" and "be delivered." When a woman *gives birth*, she is an active and able participant. However, when her baby *is delivered*, the language implies that she is passive. Try asking the woman who will attend her when she gives birth rather than asking her who will deliver her baby.

Assigning a Primary Nurse

Ideally, an expectant mother should have a primary nurse during labor to provide a continuing relationship. This is unrealistic, but it is helpful to reduce the number of different nurses who care for a client. Introduce the woman to others who will be caring for her, such as anesthetists and nursing students, and inform her about what care to expect from each. For example, the primary nurse may explain that the nursing student will be assisting in her care but will not be providing independent care. Common roles of students in the intrapartum area include providing comfort measures, emotional support, and helping the primary nurse observe for maternal or fetal complications.

Using Touch for Comfort

Touch is a powerful communication technique that conveys acceptance and provides physical and emotional comfort. The nurse's touch is comforting and reassuring to many laboring women. Women who do not ordinarily welcome physical contact may appreciate it when they are giving birth. Cultural influences also determine whether a woman is comfortable with touch from a stranger. One must not generalize; ask the woman if she welcomes or benefits from touch. As labor progresses, her desire for touch may change; during late labor, it may become an irritant rather than a comfort measure.

Respecting Cultural Values

Birth is an event of deep significance in all cultures. Most cultural groups have specific practices related to childbearing. The nurse should incorporate a family's cultural practices into care as much as possible if they are beneficial or neutral. Cultural beliefs and practices give structure and meaning to a family's birth experience.

If a family's cultural practices are potentially harmful, the nurse should explain how they are harmful and should encourage the family to abandon these practices. If the practice is not crucial, the family may agree. If not, the nurse must try to work around potentially harmful practices.

People naturally believe that their own cultural values are the best. The nurse should avoid treating people from a different culture with a superior attitude or one that diminishes the validity of their cultural beliefs.

ADMISSION ASSESSMENT

Women who have had prenatal care have a record on file in the birth facility. The record is begun in the physician's office or antepartum clinic and is sent to the birth facility where the woman plans to deliver. Updates to this record are sent in late pregnancy as well. These records are filed until the woman enters the birth facility, at which time they are added to her chart.

Much admission information can be obtained from the prenatal record and verified or updated as needed. Women who have not had prenatal care will need a more extensive assessment by both the nurse and physician. A variety of forms are available to collect important data. See Table 13–1 for common assessments, usual findings, significant findings, and appropriate nursing actions.

Focus Assessment

In the intrapartum unit, perform a focus assessment before the more comprehensive data base assessment, opposite of the usual order. Two priorities of the focus assessment are to determine the condition of the mother and fetus, and determine whether birth is impending.

Fetal Heart Rate. After admission, promptly use Leopold's maneuvers (Procedure 13–1) to locate fetal heart and assess fetal heart rate (FHR). A rate of 110 to 160/minute without slowing that persists after the end of contractions provides reassurance of fetal health (NAACOG, 1990). Repeat assessments of the fetal heart rate throughout labor identify trends in the rate or signs suggesting that the fetus is not tolerating labor well. See Procedure 13–2 for assessment of the FHR with the fetoscope or Doppler transducer. See Procedure 14–1 for application of the external fetal monitor.

Maternal Vital Signs. Assess maternal vital signs primarily for signs of hypertension or infection. Hypertension during pregnancy is defined as a blood pressure of 140/90 and/or an elevation of 30 systolic or 15 diastolic pressure over her pregnancy baseline levels.

Impending Birth. Occasionally a woman enters the intrapartum unit almost ready to give birth. The nurse abbreviates the initial assessment and collects other needed information after birth. The woman may be about to give birth if she says the baby is coming or if she is making grunting sounds or bearing down.

If initial focus assessments of mother and fetus are normal and birth is not imminent, complete the admission assessment in a relaxed yet efficient way. If the initial assessments are not normal or birth is near, another nurse notifies the physician or nurse-midwife. The primary nurse gathers other information and prepares for birth.

✔ Check Your Reading

1. What communication skills can the nurse use to establish a therapeutic relationship when the woman and her family enter the hospital or birth center?
2. How can the nurse incorporate a couple's cultural practices into intrapartum care?
3. What are the assessment priorities when a woman comes to the hospital or birth center?

Data Base Assessment

In addition to the focus admission assessment, assess the expectant mother and fetus and available support (Table 13–1).

Basic Information. A woman who has had prenatal care has most of this information in her records. Interview her for information such as:

- Her reason for coming to the hospital or birth center
- Whether she has had prenatal care
- Her estimated date of delivery
- Number of pregnancies, births, and abortions
- Medical, surgical, and pregnancy history
- Allergies
- Food intake
- Recent illness
- Medications, including over-the-counter drugs, abused substances, tobacco, and alcohol
- Her subjective evaluation of her labor
- Birth plans

Use caution when asking about prior pregnancies and births. The woman may have had an abortion or relinquished a baby for adoption, and her family may not know about it. A status board is often visible to visitors, and the staff must be careful not to reveal sensitive information. Even if the woman's partner knows about previous pregnancies, her family and friends may not.

Many women want their family to remain during the admission assessment but may not admit substance abuse in their presence. Non-verbal cues, such as a too-quick denial, avoidance of eye contact, or vague responses, are clues that the woman may have practiced substance abuse of some kind. The nurse should follow up on maternal behaviors privately.

Fetal Assessments. Assess the FHR, presentation and position, and the color of the amniotic fluid if the membranes have ruptured. 

Labor Status. Assess the woman's labor status by evaluating her contraction pattern and performing a vaginal examination. Assess the contraction pattern 

Procedure 13–1 Leopold's Maneuvers

Purpose: To determine presentation and position of the fetus.
To aid in location of the fetal heart sounds.

1. **Explain procedure to woman and the rationale for each step as it is done. Tell her what is found at each step.** *Gives information and teaches woman. Reassures her when the assessment findings are normal.*

2. **Ask the woman to empty her bladder if she has not recently voided. Have her lie on her back with her knees flexed slightly. Place a small pillow or folded towel under one side.** *Decreases discomfort of a full bladder during abdominal palpation and improves ability to feel fetal parts in the suprapubic area. Knee flexion helps the woman relax her abdominal muscles to enhance palpation. Uterine displacement prevents supine hypotension (see p. 121).*

3. **Wash your hands with warm water.** *Prevents transmission of microorganisms. Warm hands are more comfortable during palpation and prevent tensing of abdominal muscles.*

4. **Stand beside woman, facing her head, with dominant hand nearest her.** *First three maneuvers are most easily performed in this position.*

FIRST MANEUVER

5. **Palpate the uterine fundus. The breech feels softer and more irregular in shape than the head. Moving the breech will also move the trunk. The head is harder, with a round, uniform shape. The head will move without moving the entire trunk.** *Distinguishes between a cephalic and a breech presentation. If the fetus is in a cephalic presentation, the breech will be felt in the fundus. If the presentation is breech, the head will be felt in the fundus.*

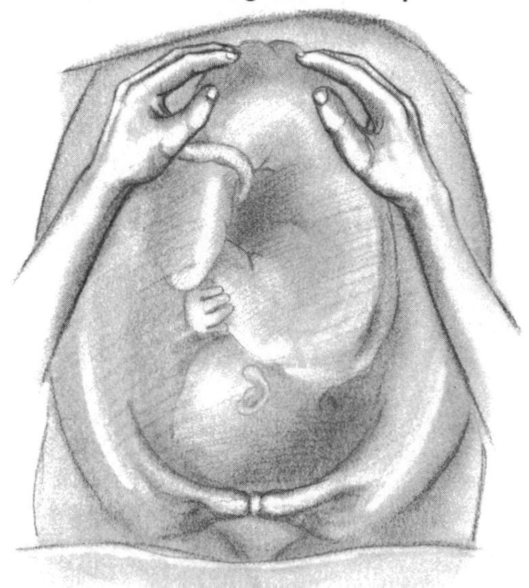

SECOND MANEUVER

6. **Hold the left hand steady on one side of the uterus while palpating the opposite side of the uterus with the right hand. Then hold the right hand steady while palpating the opposite side of the uterus with the left hand. The fetal back is a smooth convex surface. The fetal arms and legs feel nodular and the fetus will often move them during palpation.** *Determines which side of the uterus the back is on, and which side the fetal arms and legs ("small parts") are on.*

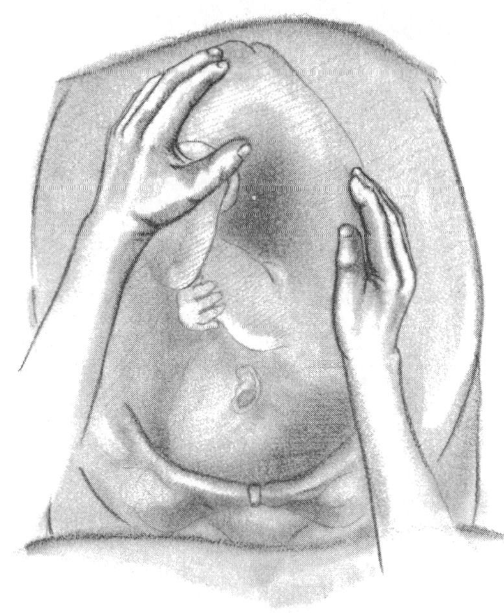

Procedure continued on following page

Leopold's Maneuvers *Continued*

THIRD MANEUVER

7. **Palpate the suprapubic area. If a breech was palpated in the fundus, expect a hard, rounded head in this area. Attempt to grasp the presenting part gently between the thumb and fingers. If the presenting part is not engaged, the grasping movement of the fingers will easily move it upward in the uterus.** *Confirms the presentation determined in the first maneuver. Determines whether the presenting part is engaged (at or below a zero station) in the maternal pelvis.*

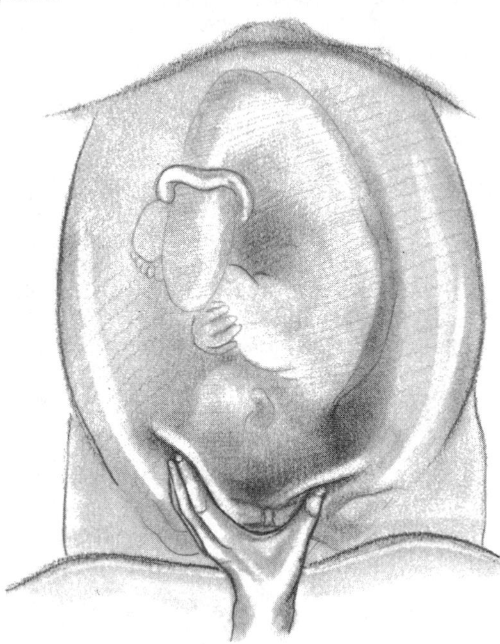

8. **Omit the fourth maneuver if the fetus is in a breech presentation.** *Is done only in cephalic presentations to determine whether the fetal head is flexed.*

FOURTH MANEUVER

9. **Turn so that you face the woman's feet.** *Is most easily performed in this position.*

10. **Place your hands on each side of the uterus with fingers pointed toward the pelvic inlet. Slide hands downward on each side of the uterus. On one side, your fingers will easily slide to the upper edge of the symphysis. On the other side, your fingers will meet an obstruction, the cephalic prominence.** *Determines whether the head is flexed (vertex) or extended (face). The vertex presentation is normal. If the head is flexed, the cephalic prominence will be felt on the opposite side from the fetal back. If the head is extended, the cephalic prominence will be felt on the same side as the fetal back.*

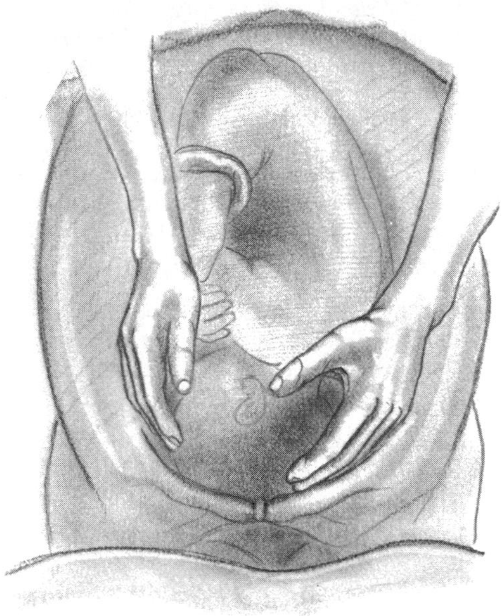

Procedure 13–2 Auscultating Fetal Heart Rate

Purpose: To evaluate the fetal condition and tolerance of labor.

1. **Explain the procedure, and wash your hands with warm water.** *Gives information to the woman. Reduces transfer of microorganisms to her. Warm hands are more comfortable.*

2. **Use Leopold's maneuvers to identify the fetal back (see Procedure 13–1). Illustrations show approximate locations of the FHR in different presentations and positions.** *The FHR is most easily heard through the fetal back because it usually lies closest to the surface of the maternal abdomen.*

3. **Assess the FHR with a fetoscope, Doppler transducer, or external fetal heart monitor. (Application of the external fetal monitor is discussed in Chapter 14.)** *The FHR can be assessed using any of these instruments.*

4. ***Fetoscope (Fig. 14–1):* Place the bell of the fetoscope over the fetal back with the head plate pressed against your forehead. Move the fetoscope until you locate where the sound is loudest. Use your forehead to maintain pressure during auscultation.** *The head plate adds bone conduction to the sound coming through the earpieces. The FHR is faint with the fetoscope because sounds pass through several layers of maternal and fetal tissue.*

5. ***Doppler transducer (Fig. 14–1):* Review manufacturer's instructions for operating the transducer. Place water-soluble conducting gel over the transducer, and turn the instrument on. Place the transducer over the fetal back, and move it until you clearly hear the sharp double sounds of the fetal heart.** *The Doppler transducer uses sound waves reflected off the moving fetal heart to create the audible signal. Gel makes a liquid interface to allow clear transmission of the signals. The fetal heart has a distinct double sound similar to that of galloping horses.*

6. **With one hand, palpate the mother's radial pulse. If her pulse is synchronized with the sounds from the fetoscope or Doppler transducer, try another location for the fetal heart.** *The nurse must be sure that the FHR is what is actually heard. Other sounds that may be heard are the funic souffle (blood flowing through the umbilical cord) or uterine souffle (blood flowing through the uterine vessels). The funic souffle is synchronized with the fetal heart; the uterine souffle is synchronized with the mother's pulse.*

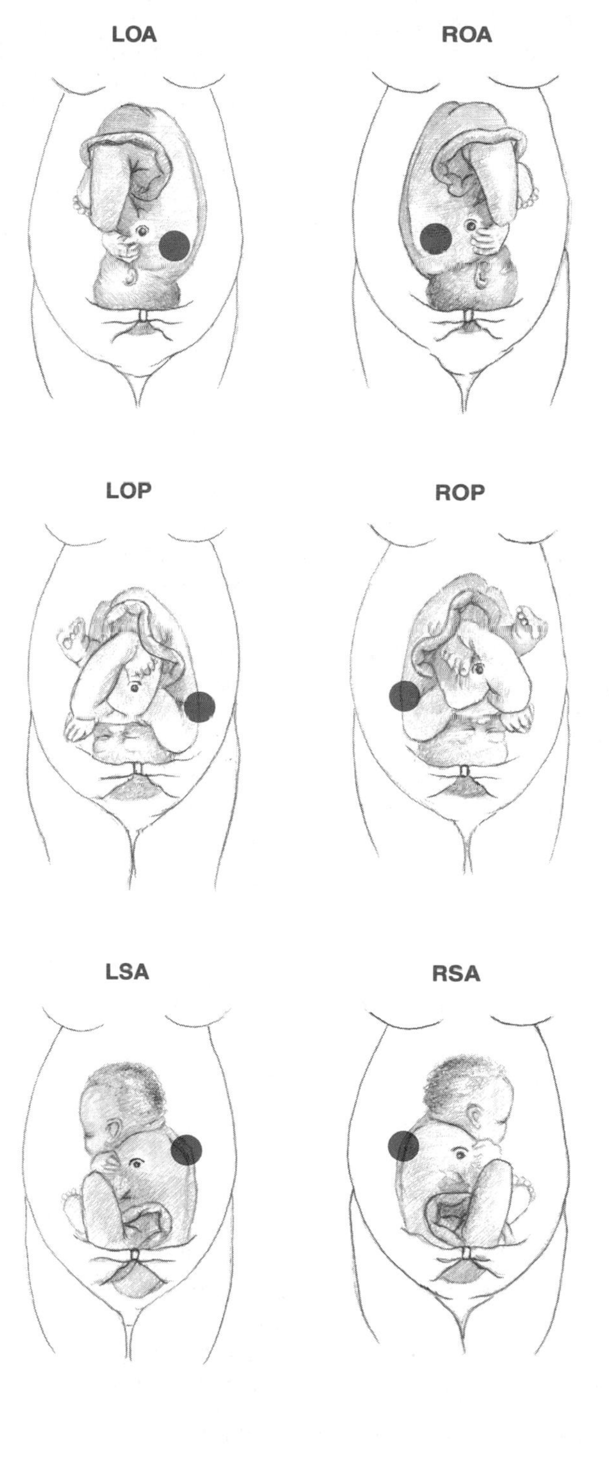

Procedure continued on following page

Auscultating Fetal Heart Rate *Continued*

7. **Assess the FHR before, during, and after a contraction. Count the baseline FHR for 30–60 seconds between contractions. Note accelerations and slowing of the rate.** *Allows fetal assessment through a contraction cycle: increment, acme, decrement, and interval.*

8. **Note reassuring signs:**
   a. Average rate 110–160/minute (some healthy term fetuses may have a rate 10/minute lower).
   b. Accelerations when the fetus moves. *These signs indicate that the fetus seems to be tolerating labor well.*

9. **Note non-reassuring signs, and make more frequent assessments (apply the fetal monitor if that is policy). Notify the physician or nurse-midwife.**
   a. FHR outside normal limits (110–160).
   b. Slowing of the FHR that persists after the contraction ends. *These signs do not necessarily indicate fetal compromise but should be further evaluated by the nurse and physician or nurse-midwife. (See Chapter 14 for discussion of fetal response and appropriate nursing actions.)*

by palpation and/or with the fetal monitor (Procedure 13–3). The experienced nurse performs a vaginal examination to determine the woman's cervical dilation and effacement and to determine the fetal station, presentation, and position. The vaginal examination may also reveal whether the membranes have ruptured or if they are still intact. *However, a vaginal examination is not performed if the woman has active bleeding other than bloody show because the procedure may increase bleeding.*

Physical Examination. Perform a brief physical examination to evaluate the woman's overall health. Pay special attention to presence of edema, abdominal scars, and height of the maternal fundus.

✔ Check Your Reading

4. What is the average fetal heart rate?
5. Which two tests may be done if the nurse is not certain whether the woman's membranes have ruptured?
6. Which characteristics of contractions may reduce blood flow to the placenta?

ADMISSION PROCEDURES

Notifying the Birth Attendant

After assessment, the nurse notifies the woman's physician or nurse-midwife and reports on her status. The birth attendant then gives orders to admit or observe the woman and gives other needed orders. The nurse includes the following data in the report:

- Gravidity, parity, and abortions
- Estimated date of delivery (EDD)
- Contraction pattern
- Fetal presentation and position
- Cervical dilation and effacement; station of the presenting part
- Fetal heart rate
- Maternal vital signs
- Any identified abnormalities
- Pain, anxiety, or other reactions to labor

If the physician or nurse-midwife admits the woman, several routine procedures may be done. Some are done only for specific indications.

Permits

At the birth facility, the woman signs permits for care during labor, anesthesia, vaginal birth, and possible cesarean birth. Permits for newborn care are often completed as well.

Laboratory Tests

Women who had regular prenatal care may not need laboratory work on admission unless there are specific indications. Simple tests are often done on the unit, such as:

- Hematocrit obtained by finger stick 
- Midstream urinalysis for protein and glucose levels by reagent strip (dipstick), sometimes done before the nurse notifies the physician or nurse-midwife.

Procedure 13–3 Palpating Contractions

Purpose: To determine whether a contraction pattern is typical of true labor.
To identify abnormal contractions that may jeopardize the health of the mother or fetus.

1. **Assess at least three contractions in a row, but preferably more. Guidelines for minimum frequency of assessments are:**
   a. Hourly during latent phase.
   b. Every 30 minutes during active phase and transition.
   c. Every 15 minutes during second stage.
   Assess more frequently if abnormalities are identified. *Assessment of at least three sequential contractions permits better evaluation of the pattern. Palpate contractions periodically when an external fetal monitor is used because it is less accurate for intensity as a result of thickness of the abdominal fat pad, maternal position, and fetal position.*

2. **Place fingertips of one hand on uterine fundus. Keep fingertips relatively still rather than moving them over uterus.** *The fingertips are more sensitive to the first tightening of the uterus. Contractions usually begin in the fundus although the mother usually feels them in her lower abdomen and back. Moving the examining hand over the uterus may stimulate contractions and give a false assessment of their true pattern.*

3. **Note the time when each contraction begins and ends.**
   a. Determine frequency by calculating average time that elapses from beginning of one contraction until beginning of next one.
   b. Determine duration by noting average time in seconds from beginning to end of each contraction.
   c. Determine interval by noting average time between end of one contraction and beginning of the next one. *Contractions are expected to increase in frequency, duration, and intensity as labor progresses. False labor is usually characterized by contractions that are irregular and do not increase in frequency, duration, and intensity.*

4. **Estimate the average intensity of contractions by noting how easily the uterus can be indented during the acme (peak) of the contraction:**
   a. Mild contractions are easily indented with the fingertips. They feel similar to the tip of the nose.
   b. Moderate contractions can be indented with more difficulty. They feel similar to the chin.
   c. Firm contractions feel "woody" and cannot be readily indented. They feel similar to the forehead. *Contractions during labor are expected to intensify progressively. If they do not, the woman may not be in true labor, or she may be experiencing dysfunctional labor (see Chapter 26).*

5. **Report hypertonic contractions:**
   a. Durations longer than 90 seconds
   b. Intervals shorter than 60 seconds
   c. Incomplete relaxation of the uterus between contractions. *Hypertonic contractions reduce placental blood flow by compressing the vessels that supply the intervillous space.*

Intravenous Fluids

Intravenous (IV) fluids are usually started with at least an 18-gauge catheter to maintain adequate hydration and permit drug administration. A heparin lock may be used, or the woman may receive continuous infusion of fluids. The heparin lock eases walking during early labor and is less associated with one's being sick. It can be converted to a continuous infusion if needed.

Intravenous fluids are individualized for each pregnant woman and her fetus. In general, dextrose-containing solutions are limited because the infant may react with hypoglycemia after birth. A rate of 60 to 125 ml/hr is adequate for most women.

Preparatory Shave (Shave Prep)

Once thought to reduce risk of infection from microorganisms harbored in the pubic hair, use of a shave prep has declined. It is rarely needed, and women are usually uncomfortable when the hair regrows. The prep is done if perineal hair is in the immediate area of an episiotomy. It may be done at the time of admission but is often delayed until just before birth. A minimal amount of hair is removed by shaving or by simply clipping the hair close to the skin with the shaver or scissors (sterile or disposable).

Enema

An enema was once thought to prevent fecal contamination of the baby or episiotomy during birth, but its routine use is uncommon. The woman may need an enema if she has not had a recent bowel movement or if a large amount of stool is felt in her rectum during a vaginal examination. Small-volume enemas (such as Fleets) are most common. The woman can expel the enema in the bathroom if there is no contraindication to walking. Because many women in labor have hemorrhoids, use extra lubricant on the tip when giving an enema.

ASSESSMENTS AFTER ADMISSION

Some women do not have typical labor patterns even when they are in true labor. Most facilities allow an observation period if it is unclear whether the woman is in true labor after the initial assessment. After 1 or 2 hours, progressive cervical change (effacement and/or dilation) indicates true labor. During the observation period, assess the woman and fetus as if she were in labor.

After the admission nursing assessment, laboring women and their fetuses need similar routine assessments. Women who have risk factors or who have needed some medical interventions require more frequent or additional assessments. Facilities have specific policies for the frequency of these assessments, but general guidelines are listed here.

Fetal Assessments

The nurse assesses the fetus for signs of well-being and for signs that may indicate compromise. The principal fetal assessments include the fetal heart rate and the character of the amniotic fluid. Abnormalities revealed in these assessments may be associated with impaired fetal oxygenation or infection.

Fetal Heart Rate. Assess the FHR using either intermittent auscultation or continuous electronic fetal monitoring. Intermittent auscultation is usually done with a Doppler transducer but may be done with a fetoscope. Continuous monitoring is used for most women who give birth in hospitals in the United States. Intermittent monitoring allows the woman to be up and walking, especially during early labor. (See Chapter 14 for a discussion of fetal monitoring.)

For the fetus at low risk for complications, guidelines for frequency of assessments (by either intermittent auscultation or continuous monitoring) and documentation are:

Table 13–2. ASSESSMENT AND DOCUMENTATION OF FETAL HEART RATE

Low-Risk Patients	High-Risk Patients
First stage of labor	First stage of labor
Every 1 hour in latent phase	Every 30 minutes in latent phase
Every 30 minutes in active phase	Every 15 minutes in active phase
Second stage of labor	Second stage of labor
Every 15 minutes	Every 5 minutes

Labor Events

Assess fetal heart rate before:
- Initiation of labor-enhancing procedures (such as artificial rupture of membranes)
- Periods of ambulation
- Administration of medications
- Administration or initiation of analgesia or anesthesia

Assess fetal heart rate following:
- Rupture of membranes
- Recognition of abnormal uterine activity patterns, such as increased basal tone or tachysystole (excessive frequency)
- Evaluation of oxytocin (maintenance, increase, or decrease of dosage)
- Administration of medications (at time of peak action)
- Expulsion of enema
- Urinary catheterization
- Vaginal examination
- Periods of ambulation
- Evaluation of analgesia and/or anesthesia (maintenance, increase, or decrease in dosage)

From NAACOG. (1990). *Fetal heart rate auscultation.* Washington, D.C.

First-stage labor: every 1 hour during the latent phase and every 30 minutes during active and transition phases.

Second-stage labor: every 15 minutes.

Table 13–2 presents other times for documenting the FHR.

Amniotic Fluid. The membranes may rupture spontaneously, or the physician or nurse-midwife may rupture them artificially (see the description of amniotomy, Chapter 16). When the membranes rupture, assess the FHR for at least 1 minute. The umbilical cord could be displaced in a large fluid gush, resulting in compression and interruption of blood flow through it.

Amniotic fluid should be clear and may include bits of vernix, the creamy fetal skin lubricant. Green fluid indicates that the fetus passed meconium before birth. Meconium passage may have been in response to transient hypoxia, although the cause may remain unknown. At birth, the newborn's airway is suctioned thoroughly to remove meconium. Cloudy, yellow, or foul-smelling amniotic fluid suggests infection.

Describe quantity in approximate terms; for example, a "large" amount is more than about 1000 ml; a "moderate" amount is about 500 ml; and a "scant" amniotic fluid is only a trickle, barely enough to detect. If the fetus is well down into the pelvis when the membranes rupture, a small amount of fluid in front of the fetal head may be discharged (forewaters), with the rest lost at birth.

Maternal Assessments

Several maternal assessments also relate to the health of the fetus, such as blood pressure and contractions.

Vital Signs. Assess maternal vital signs according to the facility's policy or by the guidelines in Table 13–1. A temperature of 38°C (100.4°F) or higher suggests infection.

Contractions. Assess contractions by palpation or with the electronic fetal monitor (see Chapter 14) according to the facility's policy or guidelines in Table 13–1.

Progress of Labor. The experienced nurse and physician or nurse-midwife perform a vaginal examination periodically to determine cervical dilation and effacement and fetal descent (Table 13–3). There are no specific guidelines for frequency of vaginal examinations. The frequency depends on the woman's parity and the overall speed of her labor. The experienced nurse relies heavily on the woman's behavioral changes to estimate how advanced her labor is. Vaginal examinations should be limited because microorganisms from the perineal area can be introduced into the uterus.

Intake and Output. Record the woman's approximate intake by IV and oral routes. Although urine output does not routinely need to be measured in the woman without complications, record each time she urinates. She may not feel the urge to void, so assess her suprapubic area for bladder distention.

The woman may have a bowel movement even if she has had an enema. Pressure of the fetal head on the rectum in late labor makes many women feel the need to defecate. If she is in advanced labor or progressing rapidly, look at her perineum. An experienced nurse may perform a vaginal examination if the woman says she needs to have a bowel movement.

Response to Labor. Observe the woman's behavioral responses as labor intensifies. She withdraws from interactions, but needs more nursing presence as labor progresses. Labor is physically and psychologically stressful. The woman may become more anxious or fearful because of discomfort and fear of bodily injury, unknown outcome, loss of control, unresolved psychological issues that influence her readiness to give birth, or unexpected occurrences during labor.

Because women vary in how they handle pain (see Chapter 15), be alert to their need for additional pain control measures, including pharmacological relief. An expectant mother may need assistance with pain control if she:

- Cannot use breathing techniques she has learned
- Tenses her muscles or arches her back during contractions
- Has muscle tension persisting between contractions
- Has a tense facial expression
- States that she "can't take it anymore"
- Requests pain medication or other measures to help her cope with pain

The Partner's Response

Intrapartum nursing includes the woman's partner, usually the child's father. Labor is stressful for the partner. He may become anxious, fearful, or tired like anyone else. He feels a deep responsibility to protect and support the woman and baby but may have limited resources for doing so. It is very difficult for him to watch the woman he loves in pain, even if labor is progressing normally. The father may respond to stress in many ways. He may be quiet, suffering silently, or he may react with pacing or anger. The father may respond by leaving the room frequently.

Consider their cultural background when assessing the woman and her partner. Most nurses encourage and value the father's presence during labor and birth. However, this may be disturbing to families in which birthing is a strictly female activity. The father may be pulled in two directions. He may want to be actively involved in the labor and birth, but may be hesitant because it is not customary to be present at birth in his culture. Respect the values of each couple, and respect their wishes about father involvement.

✔ *Check Your Reading*

7. Why should the FHR be assessed after the membranes rupture?
8. What is the significance of greenish amniotic fluid?
9. Why are frequent vaginal examinations undesirable during labor?
10. What behaviors indicate that the mother may not be tolerating labor pain well?

Table 13–3. VAGINAL EXAMINATION DURING LABOR

Purposes

To determine whether membranes have ruptured.
To determine cervical effacement and dilation.
To determine fetal presentation, position, and station.

Method

Vaginal examination is not performed by the inexperienced nurse except when training for graduate nursing practice in the intrapartum area.

Equipment

Sterile gloves, sterile lubricant. If Nitrazine paper is being used to test for ruptured membranes, lubricant is not used to avoid altering the test paper.

Hand Position

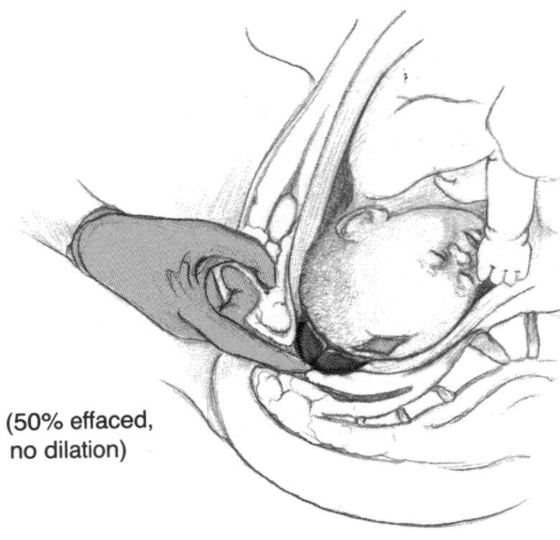

(50% effaced, no dilation)

The nurse usually uses the index and middle fingers of the dominant hand for vaginal examination. The thumb and other fingers are kept out of the way to avoid carrying microorganisms into the vagina.

Determining Whether Membranes Have Ruptured:

Intact membranes feel like a slippery membrane over the fetal presenting part.

If the membranes are *bulging,* they feel like a slippery, fluid-filled balloon over the presenting part. It may be difficult to feel the fetal presentation clearly if the membranes are bulging tensely.

If the membranes have ruptured, fluid will often drain from the vagina as the nurse manipulates the cervix and presenting part.

Determining Cervical Effacement and Dilation

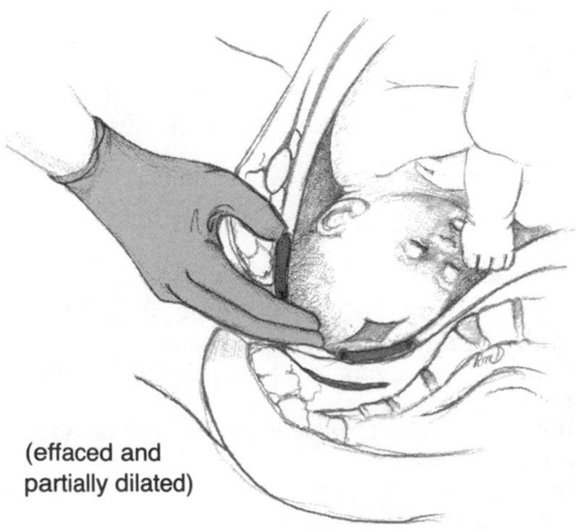

(effaced and partially dilated)

The nurse determines *effacement* by estimating the thickness of the cervix. The uneffaced cervix is about 2 cm long. If it is 50% effaced, it is about 1 cm long. Effacement is expressed as a percentage from 0% to 100%, or it may be described as the length in centimeters.

Dilation is determined by sweeping the fingertips across the cervical opening. The average woman's index finger is about 1.5 cm in diameter.

Determining the Presenting Part

The fetal skull feels smooth, hard, and rounded in a cephalic presentation. The fetal buttocks are softer and more irregular in a breech presentation. If the membranes are ruptured, the fetus in a breech presentation may expel thick, green-black meconium. (Presence of meconium in a breech presentation is *not* necessarily a sign of fetal distress. The nurse must evaluate other signs of fetal condition.)

Determining the Fetal Position

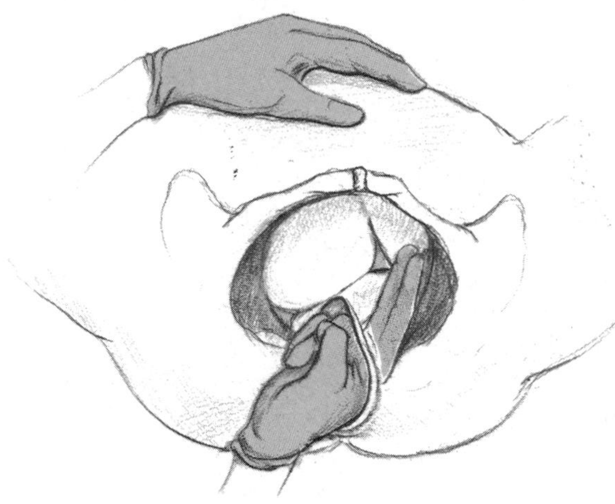

In a cephalic presentation, the nurse feels for the distinctive features of the fetal skull. The posterior fontanelle is usually felt in a vertex presentation and is triangular with three suture lines (two lambdoid and one sagittal) leading into it. The anterior fontanelle is not felt unless the head is poorly flexed. It feels like a diamond-shaped depression with four suture lines (one frontal, two coronal, and one sagittal) leading into it.

Determining the Station

The nurse locates the ischial spines on either side of the pelvis and estimates how far the leading edge of the fetal presenting part is above or below them. If the leading edge is at the same level as the ischial spines, the station is zero (0).

Documenting the Examination

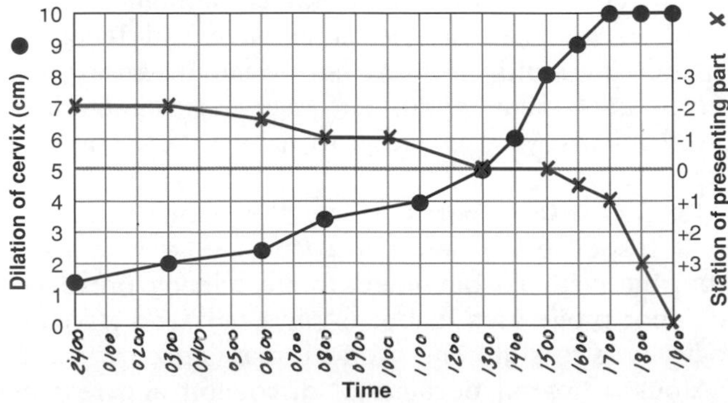

Findings of the vaginal examination may be recorded on a labor flow sheet, narrative, or on a graph. The graph may be termed a Friedman curve, a partogram, or a labor curve.

False Labor: Application of Nursing Process

Assessment

After assessment, it may be apparent that the woman is not in true labor or is in very early labor. If findings are normal and her membranes are intact, she is usually discharged home. The woman who is in early labor may be discharged to await active labor, especially if she is a nullipara and does not live a long distance from the facility.

Analysis

Sleep pattern disturbance is a nursing diagnosis that would apply to the woman who is weary because of contractions, fetal movement, or frequent urination that interrupts her sleep. Many women are frustrated because they cannot tell whether labor is real. They often say that they will not return until they are absolutely sure labor has begun, possibly causing them to delay care needlessly. A nursing diagnosis that applies to many women with false labor is: *High Risk for Altered Health Maintenance related to lack of knowledge about characteristics of true labor.*

Planning

An appropriate goal for this nursing diagnosis is that before discharge home, the woman will describe reasons for returning to the intrapartum unit for evaluation.

Interventions

Providing Reassurance. A woman sent home after observation often feels foolish and frustrated. Reassure her that she is not foolish. Remind her that the reason for having an observation period is that professionals cannot always be sure that she is in true labor after the initial assessment. Tell her that symptoms of false labor and early true labor are often similar.

Teaching. Although the client may have been taught during her prenatal visits about when to go to the hospital or birth center, review the guidelines with her. Explain that these are guidelines and that she should return if she has any concerns. It is better

Therapeutic Communication

Sandra Hall is a student nurse assigned to the intrapartum unit today. A woman walks to where Sandra is standing, leaning on her partner and breathing rapidly. She says to Sandra, "I think I'm in labor, and my water broke on the way to the hospital. I'm Amy James and my nurse-midwife is Donna Moore."

Sandra: It sounds like today's the day! I'm Sandra Hall, a student nurse at Valley Community College. Let's find you a room.

Sandra asks the charge nurse what room to escort Amy to and they walk to it.

Sandra: What name do you want us to call you and your husband?

Questioning for information. Shows respect by not assuming how the couple wants to be addressed.

Amy: Amy, and my husband is Jeff.

Sandra: Is this your first baby Amy, or have you had others?

Questioning in a way that avoids yes or no answers.

Amy: It's my second, but the first took forever! I've been having contractions since midnight, but they didn't get regular till about 6 this morning. They are coming every 3 minutes now and starting to hurt a lot. [*It is now* 9:00 *a.m.*]

Sandra begins preparing the external fetal monitor to check the FHR, *but she does not follow up on Amy's implied concern about having a long labor.*

Amy: Oh no . . . the monitor . . .

Sandra: You have a problem about the monitor?

Clarifying the non-specific remark that Amy made about the monitor.

Amy: I hated having that thing on with my last baby. I had to lay the same way all the time or they couldn't hear the baby. I know it's best for the baby, though.

Sandra: You seem to have mixed feelings about the monitor.

Reflecting what Amy seems to be feeling.

Amy: Yes, I didn't like it, but I do feel more secure knowing the baby's OK.

Sandra: We can usually find ways so it doesn't bother you much. We don't want you to feel tied down because it makes you more uncomfortable.

Sandra has observed that Amy's contractions are every 3 minutes and strong. She finds an experienced nurse to help evaluate Amy. Sandra wisely sought help from an experienced nurse because Amy seems to be in active labor and this is her second baby. The fact that Amy's first labor "took forever" does not necessarily mean that this labor will be long.

for her to return with another false alarm than to remain at home while complications develop.

Evaluation

The woman will have met the established goal if she can describe guidelines for returning to the birth center:

- Contraction pattern
- Ruptured membranes
- Bleeding
- Decreased fetal movement
- Other concerns.

The most precise evaluation is to ask the woman to describe the guidelines rather than having her verbally indicate that she understands them.

Normal Labor: Application of Nursing Process

The admission assessment may confirm the woman is in true labor, or true labor may be evident after observation. Nursing diagnoses and collaborative problems change during labor because the intrapartum period is a dynamic, evolving process. Common ones encountered in most laboring women who do not have high-risk factors or complications relate to fetal oxygenation, maternal discomfort, and prevention of maternal injury.

Fetal Oxygenation

Assessment

Refer to assessments listed in Tables 13–1 and 13–3 for intrapartum fetal assessments.

Analysis

Because of complete dependence on the mother's physiological systems, the fetus is the more vulnerable of the mother-fetal pair. Any number of factors may reduce fetal oxygenation and waste removal, such as maternal hypotension, excessively strong or long contractions, or compression of the umbilical cord. The healthy fetus usually tolerates labor well, and the nurse simply needs to be alert for unexpected problems. The collaborative problem selected is: *Potential complication: fetal compromise*. The focus of this chapter is normal labor. For a more complete discussion of this collaborative problem, see Chapter 14.

Planning

Client-centered goals are inappropriate for this collaborative problem because nurses cannot manage fetal distress independently. Planning includes nursing responsibilities to (1) promote normal placental function and (2) observe for and report problems to the physician or nurse-midwife.

Interventions

Positioning the Woman. The woman can use any position she desires, but she should avoid the supine position, which may cause compression of her inferior vena cava. If she must be in the supine position for a procedure such as catheterization, a small pillow or wedge under one side displaces the uterus enough to maintain normal blood flow.

Observing for Conditions Associated with Fetal Compromise. Maternal and fetal circumstances listed in Critical Things to Remember: Conditions Associated with Fetal Compromise do not indicate or cause fetal distress but are sometimes associated with it. If they occur, assess the fetus more frequently and notify the physician or nurse-midwife.

Evaluation

Evaluation of client goals does not apply to a collaborative problem because no goals are established for the woman. However, throughout labor, the nurse compares actual data to the norms for the mother and fetus.

Discomfort

Assessment

See Table 13–1 and p. 304 for continuing assessments of the expectant mother's status.

Analysis

Labor is painful, and women vary in how they respond to pain. Even if a woman uses highly effective pharmacological pain relief methods, labor is well established before these measures are begun.

Critical to Remember

Conditions Associated with Fetal Compromise

- FHR outside the normal range of 110–160 BPM
- Slowing of the fetal heart rate (FHR) persisting after contraction ends
- Meconium-stained amniotic fluid
- Cloudy, yellowish, or foul odor to amniotic fluid (suggests infection)
- Contractions lasting longer than 90 seconds
- Incomplete uterine relaxation or intervals shorter than 60 seconds between contractions
- Maternal hypotension (may shunt blood flow away from placenta to ensure adequate perfusion of the maternal brain and heart)
- Maternal hypertension (may be associated with vasospasm in spiral arteries, which supply the intervillous spaces)
- Maternal fever (38°C or 100.4°F or higher)

The woman who successfully masters the pain and other physical sensations of labor is more likely to view her entire birth experience as positive. If her partner succeeds at supporting her, he is likely to feel more satisfaction with the experience as well.

Nursing diagnoses that are often related are pain, anxiety, or sensory-perceptual alterations. Of these, the nursing diagnosis selected for this chapter is: *Pain related to effects of uterine contractions.* (See Chapter 15 for other pain relief techniques, pharmacological methods of pain control, and nursing diagnoses that may apply.)

Clinical Situation

Chloe Green is in labor with her second baby. The baby is in a left occiput anterior (LOA) position and Chloe's cervix is 5 cm dilated and completely effaced. Her membranes rupture at the end of a strong contraction. You note that the fluid is green and watery.

Q: What are the most important nursing actions?

A: Assess the fetal heart rate for at least 1 minute for an abnormal rate. Note the odor and approximate amount of amniotic fluid. Report the findings to the physician or nurse-midwife because green, meconium-stained amniotic fluid may be associated with fetal compromise. Reassess the fetal heart rate more frequently.

Planning

Eradication of pain is not realistic for the laboring woman. Appropriate goals addressing the needs of the woman and her partner are as follows:

- During labor, the woman will state that she is able to tolerate pain satisfactorily.
- By the end of labor, the woman's partner will express satisfaction at his ability to support her.

Interventions

Labor pain management includes general measures to promote comfort as well as specific techniques such as patterned breathing, analgesia, or anesthesia. (See Chapters 11 and 15 for other pain management techniques.)

PROVIDING COMFORT MEASURES

Every discussion of pain management should include ordinary comfort measures to reduce irritating surroundings that impair a woman's ability to relax and use coping skills.

Lighting. Soft, indirect lighting is soothing, whereas a bright overhead light may be a source of vague irritation. Bright lights imply a hospital ("sick") atmosphere rather than the normal life event that birth is. Turn on the overhead light only when needed. A penlight or small flashlight is handy for the woman who wants her room dark.

Temperature. Labor is work. Women in labor are often hot and diaphoretic. Cool, damp washcloths on the woman's face, neck, or other parts of her body make her feel more comfortable. Keep an ample supply of damp washcloths available, and change them regularly to keep them cool.

An electric fan circulates air in the labor room and directs a breeze on the mother. A hand-held fan can be used, but this is fatiguing and diverts the partner's and nurse's attention. A package of gloves or the cardboard back of chart forms can be used if there is no electric fan.

Encourage the woman to wear socks if her feet are cold.

Cleanliness. Bloody show and amniotic fluid leak from the woman's vagina during labor. Change the sheets and gown as needed to keep her dry and comfortable. Let her preferences be the guide because she may not want to be disturbed by extensive linen changes during late labor. Change the disposable underpad regularly to reduce microorganisms that may ascend into the vagina. A folded towel absorbs larger quantities of amniotic fluid.

Mouth Care. Many women experience a dry mouth during labor from mouth breathing. If permissible, give her ice chips, popsicles, or hard candy. If the woman must remain on NPO status,* she can use lemon-glycerine swabs to moisten her mouth. She may brush her teeth or rinse her mouth at intervals, but caution her not to swallow the water if her status is NPO. Many women appreciate a moist washcloth to their lips, even if they are taking ice chips.

Bladder. A full bladder is a source of discomfort during labor and can delay fetal descent. Remind the woman to empty her bladder about every 2 hours or more often if she has taken large quantities of IV fluids.

Positioning. Occasionally, a specific maternal position is recommended to reduce discomfort or to facilitate the labor process. Otherwise, encourage the woman to assume any position she finds comfortable (other than the supine). Frequent changes reduce discomfort from constant pressure and help the fetus adapt to the pelvic contours. Table 13–4 lists various maternal positions for labor.

Water. Water in the form of a shower, tub, or whirlpool is comforting to many women because it is relaxing and improves their tolerance of contractions.

TEACHING

Teaching the woman in labor is a constant task. This intervention changes as her needs change.

First Stage

Many women feel discouraged when their cervix dilates to about 4 or 5 cm because several hours are usually required to have reached that point. They believe the last 5 cm will take as long as the first 5 cm. From a time standpoint, 5 cm is more like two thirds of the way to full dilation rather than half of the way because the rate of dilation increases. Explain that labor usually speeds up when she reaches the active phase.

As the woman nears the second stage, the fetus may descend enough to give her an urge to push before she is fully dilated. If she pushes before full dilation, her cervix may become edematous and impede progress. Pushing against an incompletely dilated cervix also may cause a cervical laceration. These potential problems are more likely with the nullipara because her cervix does not dilate as readily as the multipara's. Most of the time, however, the urge to push occurs when the cervix is fully dilated and effaced. Teach the woman to blow out in short, forceful breaths if she should not push.

Second Stage

During the second stage, many women need help to push effectively. The woman usually feels a strong urge to push when her cervix dilates fully and the fetal presenting part reaches a +1 station or lower.

Time Limit. Two hours was once considered the upper limit for the duration of the second stage. More recently, it has been recognized that a second stage longer than 2 hours is safe as long as the mother and fetus show no signs of distress.

Some women are tired and do not immediately feel the urge to push when their cervix is fully dilated. If assessments are normal, it is not necessary to coach them to push before they feel the urge. Women push most effectively when they feel the reflex urge to bear down.

Positions. The mother can push in any position she prefers. Many women prefer semi-sitting and side-lying. Squatting enlarges the pelvic outlet slightly; this is an advantage if the woman has a small pelvis or the fetus is large.

When she pushes, teach her to keep her head flexed, with her chin on her chest. She should keep her body curled around her uterus in a "C" shape. For most effectiveness, teach her to pull on her flexed knees, hand-holds on the bed, or a squatting bar.

Many nurses encourage the woman to push as if she were having a bowel movement. However, this may cause the woman who is modest or fears losing control to inhibit her best pushing efforts. A pleasing and anatomically correct image is to teach the woman to push down and forward under her symphysis, following the pelvic curve. Seeing a diagram of the pelvis helps her visualize the curve. Give her instructions such as, "Push toward the end of the bed."

Method and Breathing Pattern. Regardless of which position is chosen, the basic method is similar. The woman should push with her abdominal muscles while she relaxes her perineum. Teach her to take a deep breath and exhale to begin. Have her take another breath and exhale while she pushes for about 5 to 6 seconds at a time. Sustained pushing and closing her glottis (the Valsalva maneuver) can decrease blood flow to the placenta.

PROVIDING ENCOURAGEMENT

Nothing breeds success like success. Let the woman know when her labor is progressing. If she can see that her efforts are successful, she has more courage and motivation to continue. Let her touch or see the baby's head with a mirror as crowning occurs.

Praise the woman and her coach when they use

* NPO = nothing by mouth.

Table 13–4. MATERNAL POSITIONS FOR LABOR

Walking

Advantages
Adds gravity to force of contractions to promote fetal descent.
Contractions less uncomfortable and more efficient.
Disadvantages
Tiring over long periods.
Continuous fetal monitoring is not possible unless unit has telemetry.
Nursing Interventions
If the woman has an intravenous line, give her a rolling pole.
Encourage her to alternate walking with more restful positions whenever she feels the need.
Remind the woman and her partner when she should return for evaluation of the fetal heart rate.

Standing, Leaning Forward with Support

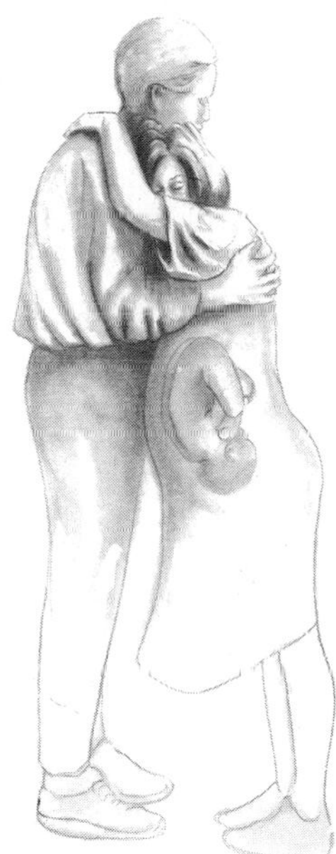

Advantages
Adds gravity to force of contractions to promote fetal descent.
Reduces back pain because fetus falls forward, away from sacral promontory.
Good position during contractions for the expectant mother who is walking.
Promotes intimacy between the woman and her partner.
Disadvantages
Tiring over a long time.
Continuous fetal monitoring is not possible if the woman is also walking; if she is remaining at bedside, continuous monitoring is possible, although external leads tend to slip downward.
Nursing Interventions
Same as for walking if the woman is alternating walking and standing.
Reposition fetal monitoring leads if they slip.

Sitting Upright

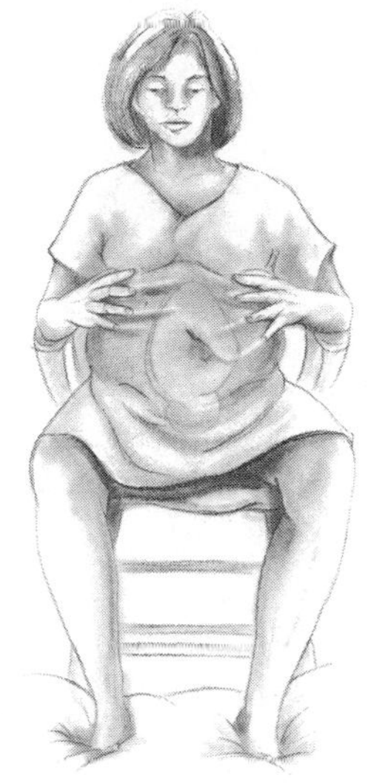

Advantages
Uses gravity to aid fetal descent.
Can be done when sitting on side of bed or in a chair.
Can be used with continuous fetal monitoring.
Avoids supine hypotension.
Disadvantages
May increase suprapubic discomfort.
Contractions are the most efficient when the expectant mother alternates sitting with other positions.
Nursing Interventions
A rocking chair is soothing.
Place a pillow on a chair with a disposable underpad over the pillow to absorb secretions.
Use pillows or a foot stool to keep the short woman's legs from dangling.
Encourage the expectant mother to alternate positions periodically; for example, she can alternate walking with sitting or sitting with side lying.

Sitting, Leaning Forward with Support

Advantages
Same as for sitting.
Reduces back pain because fetus falls forward, away from sacral promontory.
Partner or nurse can rub back or give sacral pressure to relieve back pain.
Disadvantages
Same as for sitting.
Nursing Interventions
Same as for sitting.

Semi-sitting

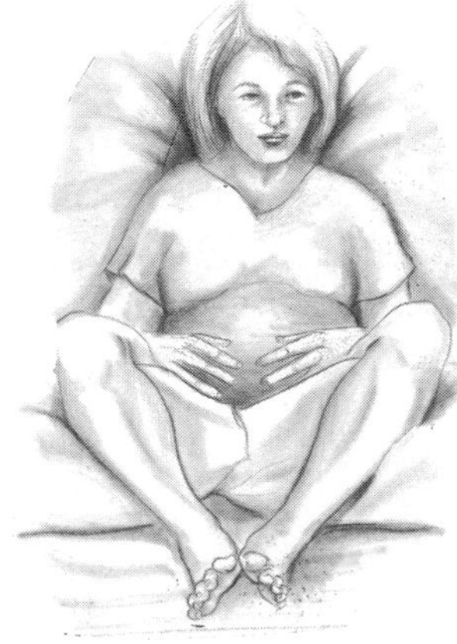

Advantages
Same as for sitting.
Aligns long axis of uterus with pelvic inlet, which applies contraction force in the most efficient direction through pelvis.
Disadvantages
Same as for sitting.
Does not reduce back pain as well as the forward-leaning positions.
Nursing Implications
Same as for sitting.
Raise bed to about a 30- to 45-degree angle.
Encourage the woman to use sitting (leaning forward) or side lying if she has back pain so that the caregiver can rub her back or apply sacral pressure.

Table continued on following page

Table 13-4. MATERNAL POSITIONS FOR LABOR *Continued*

Side-Lying

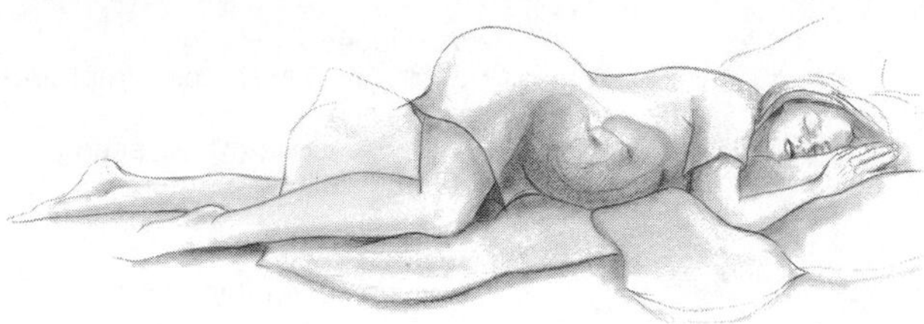

Advantages

Is a restful position.

Prevents supine hypotension and promotes placental blood flow.

Promotes efficient contractions, although they may be less frequent than with other positions.

Can be used with continuous fetal monitoring.

Disadvantages

Does not use gravity to aid fetal descent.

Nursing Implications

Teach the pregnant woman and her partner that although the contractions are less frequent, they are more effective.

This position offers a break from more tiring positions.

Use pillows, as needed, for support and to prevent pressure: at her back, under her superior arm, and between her knees. Use disposable underpads to protect the pillow between the woman's knees from secretions.

Some expectant mothers like to put their superior leg on the bed rail. If the woman wants this variation, pad the bed rail with a blanket to prevent pressure.

If she wants to remain recumbent, she should use this position to promote placental blood flow.

Kneeling, Leaning Forward with Support

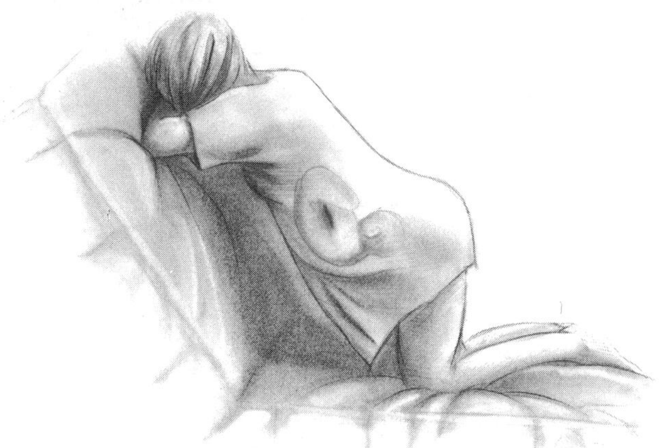

Advantages

Reduces back pain because fetus falls forward, away from sacral promontory.

Adds gravity to force of contractions to promote fetal descent.

Can be used with continuous fetal monitoring.

Caregivers can rub her back or apply sacral pressure.

Promotes normal mechanisms of birth.

Disadvantages

Knees may become tired or uncomfortable.

Tiring if used for long periods.

Nursing Implications

Raise the head off the bed, and have the woman face the head of the bed while she is on her knees.

Another method is for the partner to sit in a chair, with the woman kneeling in front, facing her partner, and leaning forward on him or her for support.

Use pillows under the knees and in front of the woman's chest, as needed, for support.

Encourage her to change positions if she becomes tired.

Hands and Knees

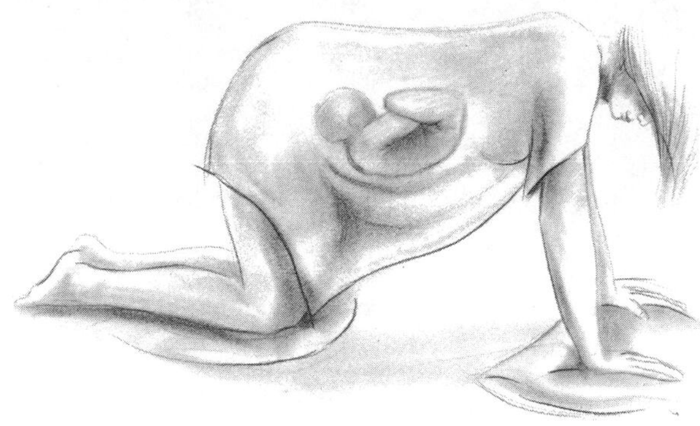

Advantages

Reduces back pain because the fetus falls forward, away from the sacral promontory.

Promotes normal mechanisms of birth.

The woman can use pelvic rocking to decrease any back pain.

Caregivers can rub the woman's back or apply sacral pressure easily.

Disadvantages

The expectant mother's hands (especially wrists) and knees can become uncomfortable.

Tiring when used for a long time.

Some women are embarrassed to use this position.

Nursing Implications

Encourage the expectant mother to change to less tiring positions occasionally.

Ensure privacy when encouraging the reluctant woman to try this position if she has back pain.

A second hospital gown with the opening in front covers her back and hips but may be too warm.

Table 13–4. MATERNAL POSITIONS FOR LABOR *Continued*

Positions for Pushing in Second Stage
Squatting

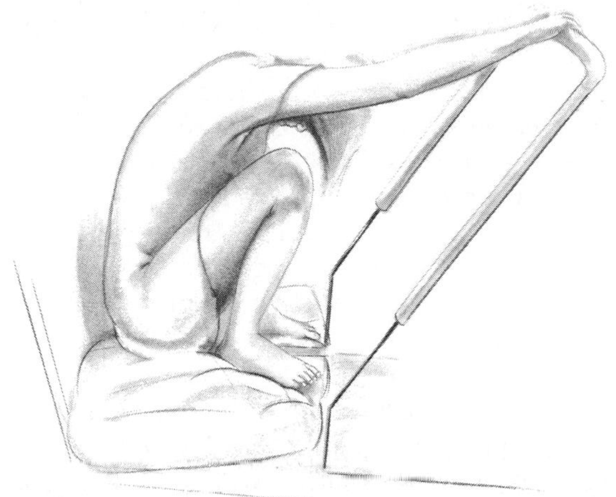

Advantages
Adds gravity to force of contractions to promote fetal descent.
Straightens the pelvic curve slightly for more direct fetal descent.
Increases dimensions of pelvis slightly.
Promotes effective pushing efforts in the second stage.
Caregivers can rub back or provide sacral pressure.

Disadvantages
Knees and hips may become uncomfortable because of prolonged flexion.
Tiring over a long time.

Nursing Implications
Provide support with a squat bar attached to the bed or by two people standing at each side of the woman.
If she becomes tired or between contractions, she can lean back into the semi-sitting or upright sitting position.

Adaptations of Positions for Pushing
Standing
This position may be tiring, and access to the woman's perineum is difficult. Because the infant could fall to the ground if birth occurs rapidly, provide padding under the mother's feet. Gravity aids fetal descent.

Semi-sitting

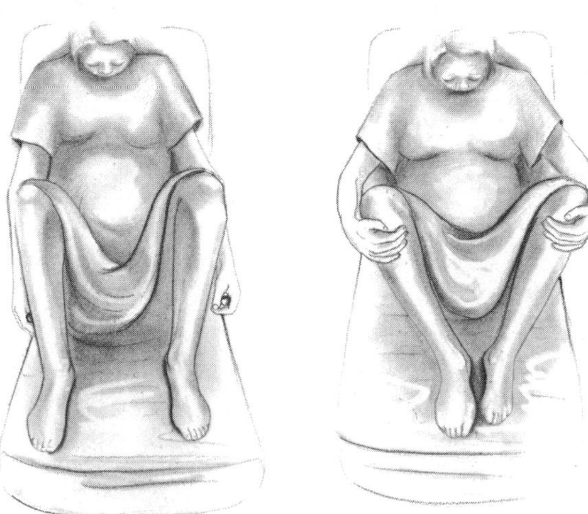

Many women prefer this position because they have the security of a back rest; it is also familiar to caregivers and allows easy observation of the perineum. Elevate the woman's back at least 30 to 45 degrees so that gravity aids fetal descent. The woman pulls on her flexed knees (behind or in front of them) as she pushes. She should keep her head flexed and her sacrum flat on the bed to straighten the pelvic curve.

Side-Lying
The woman flexes her chin on her chest and curls around her uterus as she pushes. She pulls on her flexed knees or the knee of the superior leg only as she pushes.

Hands and Knees
Advantages and disadvantages are similar to those during first-stage labor. Additionally, caregivers must reorient themselves because the landmarks are upside down from their usual perspective.
A variation is for the mother to kneel and lean forward against a beanbag or the side of the bed. This variation reduces some of the strain on her wrists and hands.

breathing or other coping techniques effectively. This reinforces their actions and conveys the respect and support of the nurse to them. If one technique is not helpful after a reasonable trial (about three to five contractions), encourage them to try other techniques.

GIVING OF SELF

The nurse's caring presence is a crucial element in labor support. Even women who are very independent usually become dependent during labor and need human contact. Many times the woman simply requires reassurance that all is going well and that the nurse is there for her when needed. The nurse's presence helps to allay her fears of abandonment and conveys acceptance, support, and comfort.

Although the woman and her partner may have had prepared childbirth classes, they often welcome suggestions and affirmation from the nurse. The nurse's presence, coaching, and encouragement helps the woman have confidence in her own body and her fitness to give birth.

OFFERING PHARMACOLOGIC MEASURES

Some women need no pharmacologic pain relief during labor, but others need varying amounts (see Chapter 15). Some request analgesia readily, but others are reluctant to do so. Inform the woman about medications available to her.

Most women have an open mind about using analgesia or anesthesia, but some may have a firm goal of not using any pain medication during labor. They may then feel let down or guilty if they need pharmacologic relief. Allow the woman to ventilate her feelings about her experience. Although the experience may not be what she wanted, expression of her feelings will help her put it into perspective.

CARING FOR THE PARTNER

The woman's partner is an integral part of pain and anxiety management during labor. Her partner can provide care and comfort, which increase the woman's ability to tolerate childbirth. However, do not expect too much of him or make assumptions about what kind of involvement he and the woman desire.

Some partners are coaches in the true sense of the word, actively leading the woman through labor. Other men want the woman and nurse to lead them and tell them how to help. They are eager to do what they can but may expect instructions about how and when to do it. Many couples see the partner's role as one of encouragement, moral support, and just being there for the woman. Moreover, not every woman wants her partner to take an active role; she may expect only his presence and concern (Chapman, 1992).

To impose unrealistic expectations of leadership, care, and comfort on the partner makes the birth experience unnecessarily stressful on him. Accept whatever pattern of support he is able and willing to provide and whatever the couple finds comfortable to ensure a positive experience for both. Without taking over or diminishing his role, provide support that the partner cannot provide.

Encourage the partner to conserve physical strength. He may have missed sleep during the hours of early labor. He may need a break or may want to sit down for a while. A comfortable tall stool at the bedside helps him conserve strength while he supports the woman during contractions. If the woman has been in labor a long time, ask if he has eaten. Many men are hesitant to leave even briefly to take a break and eat. Bring him a snack if he is reluctant to leave the room. Remind him that he can be a more effective support if he takes care of his own needs. Fathers who do not eat for a long time are more likely to faint during the birth.

Evaluation

The first goal is met if the woman indicates that she is able to tolerate the pain of labor satisfactorily. The second goal is achieved if her partner says that he is satisfied with his support during labor. This nursing diagnosis and goal are constantly re-evaluated during labor.

Preventing Injury

Assessment

Nursing assessments of the mother and fetus continue as the woman nears birth. During the second stage, observe for signs of impending birth (see p. 298). Observe the woman's perineum for bulging or crowning, which indicates that it is time to position her in the birthing bed or transfer her to the delivery room.

The exact time for final birth preparations varies according to the woman's parity, the overall speed of labor, and the fetal station. Final preparations are usually completed when crowning in the nullipara reaches a diameter of about 3 to 4 cm. The multipara is prepared sooner, usually when her cervix is fully dilated but before crowning has occurred.

If the infant's head has scalp edema (caput), the woman may need to push longer before final preparations are made. The nurse waits until the leading edge of the fetal skull (not the edematous scalp) has descended enough to get the woman ready for birth.

Analysis

The woman is vulnerable to injury immediately before birth for several reasons: (1) physical sensations of intense contractions and pressure, (2) positional changes for birth, and (3) the ever-present possibility of rapid progress. Women who have had epidural anesthesia also experience diminished sensation, and some may have decreased ability to move as a result of blockade of motor nerves. A nursing diagnosis that applies to many laboring women near the time of birth is: *High Risk for Injury (maternal) related to positional changes or an unexpected rapid birth.*

Planning

The nurse's primary objective is to avoid or minimize injuries that can occur because of birth positioning or a sudden birth. An appropriate goal for this nursing diagnosis is that the woman will not have an avoidable injury, such as muscle strains, thrombosis, or lacerations, during birth.

Interventions

Transport of the woman to the delivery site or positioning her in the birthing bed is the first step in the sequence of events that culminates in delivery of the infant (Table 13–5). During this period, the nurse must reduce factors that may contribute to maternal injuries. However, these injuries may occur despite nursing actions to avoid them and are not always related to events during the intrapartum period. See color plates for more photographs of birth.

TRANSFER TO A DELIVERY ROOM

Many births occur in a combination labor, delivery, and recovery room (LDR); in other circumstances, the woman must be transferred to a separate delivery room. The experienced nurse will transfer the woman early enough to avoid rushed, last-minute preparations that cause anxiety for the woman and her partner. Do not transfer her too early because it is tiring for her to remain in the birthing position for a long time.

POSITIONING FOR DELIVERY

Elevate the woman's back, shoulders, and head with a large wedge cushion (on a delivery table), or raise the head of the birthing bed to promote more effective pushing and take advantage of gravity.

Stirrups or foot rests may be used to support the woman's legs and feet. To avoid strain on her muscles and ligaments when stirrups are used, raise and lower her legs together and do not separate them too widely.

Pad the surfaces of stirrups to avoid pressure on the legs; otherwise, this may impede venous blood return and may lead to thrombus formation. Pay special attention to padding the popliteal space behind the knee because the veins are close to the surface there.

OBSERVING THE PERINEUM

The exact time at which a woman is ready to give birth is an educated guess at best. The woman who has had a long labor unexpectedly may make rapid progress, which can catch even the experienced nurse by surprise. Birth is near when the fetal head swings anteriorly in the mechanism of extension as the occiput slips beneath the symphysis pubis. Observe the woman's perineum, especially when she is pushing.

A *classic sign of imminent birth occurs when she says, "The baby's coming!"* Look at her perineum, and if the baby will be born before the physician or nurse-midwife arrives, remain calm and support the infant's body with gloved hands as it emerges (Table 13–6).

Evaluation

The goal for this nursing diagnosis is evaluated throughout the postpartum period because muscle strains or thrombus formation will not be evident until later. The physician or nurse-midwife notes lacerations after the baby's birth. (Degrees of lacerations are provided in Table 17–2, p. 419.)

✔ Check Your Reading

11. How may maternal hypotension or hypertension affect the fetus?
12. What position should the woman avoid during labor?
13. What are some general measures that can make her more comfortable during labor?
14. Why is it important to watch the perineum as she pushes?

Table 13–5. SEQUENCE FOR DELIVERY

Transfer and Positioning for Birth

Action: When the woman is almost ready to give birth, transfer her to the delivery room or position the birthing bed. The exact time varies with several factors (such as overall speed of labor and rate of fetal descent). *Rationale:* Rushed, last-moment preparations are anxiety-producing for the woman, her partner, and the nurse. Remaining in the position for delivery for a long time can be tiring.

Action: Continue observing her perineum while making final preparations for birth. *Rationale:* Birth may occur unexpectedly, and the nurse should be prepared to "catch" the infant if the physician or nurse-midwife is not in the room.

Action: Continue observing the fetal heart rate (FHR) with continuous monitoring or intermittent auscultation. *Rationale:* Detects changes in fetal condition that may require interventions by the physician or nurse-midwife to speed birth.

Action: Elevate the woman's back, shoulders, and head with a wedge (on a delivery table) or by raising the head of the birthing bed. *Rationale:* Allows more effective maternal pushing and uses gravity to aid fetal descent.

Action: Stirrups or foot rests to support the woman's legs and feet may be used on a birthing bed. If using stirrups, do not separate the woman's thighs widely. Pad the surface. *Rationale:* Padding reduces pressure, preventing venous stasis and possible thrombus formation.

Action: When placing the woman's legs in stirrups, elevate them and remove them simultaneously. Do not separate her legs widely. *Rationale:* Reduces strain on muscles and ligaments.

"Prepping" and Draping

Action: After the woman is in position, cleanse the perineal area with a sterile iodophor and water preparation unless she is allergic. Use warm water to dilute the iodophor scrub. *Rationale:* Removes secretions and feces from perineal area.

Action: After handwashing, apply sterile gloves for the prep procedure. Take a fresh sponge to begin each new area, and do not return to a clean area with a used sponge. Six sponges are needed. The proper order and motions are as follows:

1. Use a zig-zag motion from clitoris to lower abdomen just above the pubic hairline.

2., 3. Use a zig-zag motion on the inner thigh from the labia majora to about halfway between the hip and knee. Repeat for the other inner thigh.

4., 5. Apply a single stroke on one side from clitoris over labia, perineum, and anus. Repeat for the other side.

6. Use a single stroke in the middle from the clitoris over the vulva and perineum.

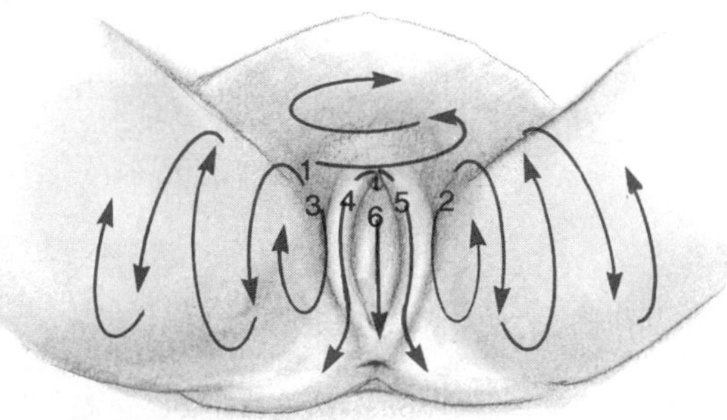

Rationale: Prevents cross-contamination or recontamination of an area that is already clean.

Action: Either the physician or nurse-midwife may apply sterile drapes if desired. *Rationale:* A vaginal birth is a clean procedure rather than a sterile one because the vagina is not sterile. Sterile drapes are unnecessary, but some attendants may prefer to use them.

Birth of the Head

Action: If an episiotomy is needed, the physician or nurse-midwife will perform it when the head is well crowned (see Chapter 16). *Rationale:* Minimizes blood loss from the episiotomy.

Action: As the vaginal orifice encircles the fetal head, the physician or nurse-midwife applies gentle pressure to the woman's perineum with one hand while applying counterpressure to the fetal head with the other hand (Ritgen's maneuver). The attendant may ask the mother to blow so that she avoids pushing, or to push gently. *Rationale:* Controls the exit of the fetal head so that it is born gradually rather than popping out; this minimizes trauma to the maternal tissues.

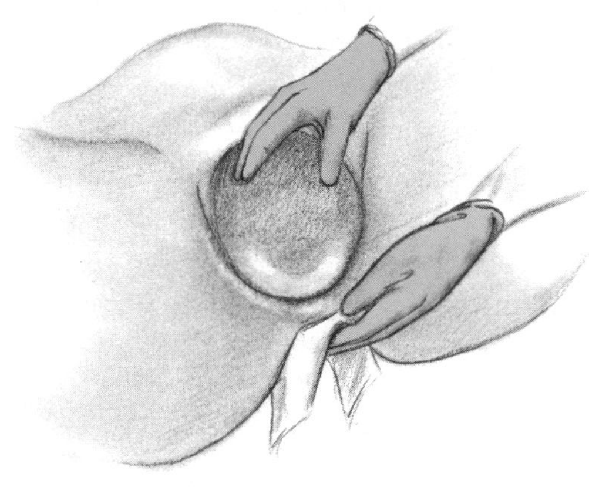

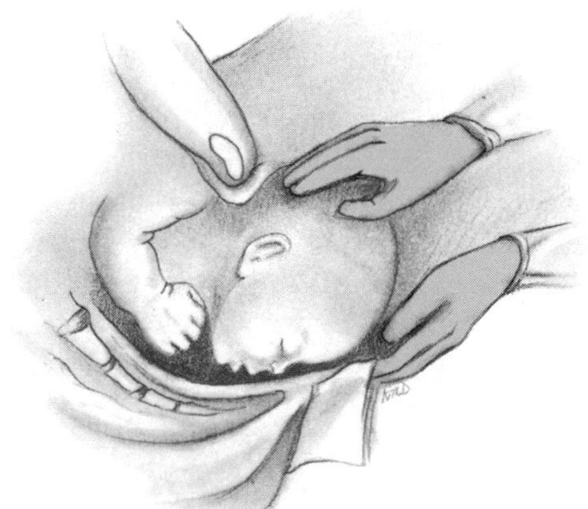

Table 13–5. SEQUENCE FOR DELIVERY *Continued*

Action: The attendant wipes secretions from the infant's face and suctions the nose and mouth with a bulb syringe. *Rationale:* Removes blood and secretions, preventing the infant from aspirating them with the first breaths.

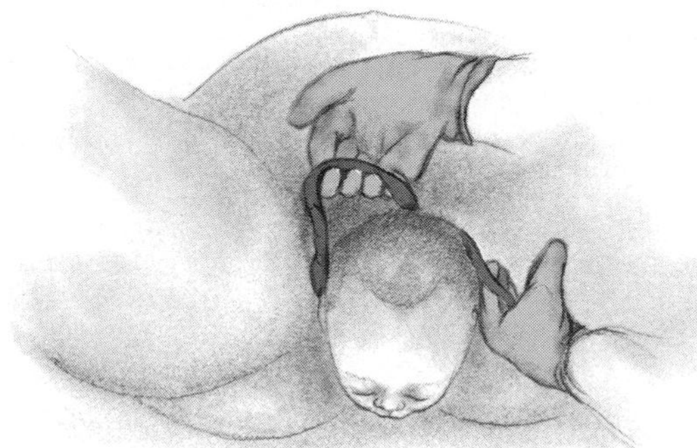

Action: The physician or nurse-midwife feels for a cord around the fetal neck (nuchal cord). If it is loose, it is slipped over the head. If tight, it is clamped and cut between two clamps before the rest of the baby is born. *Rationale:* Allows the rest of the birth to occur and prevents stretching or tearing the cord.

Birth of the Shoulders

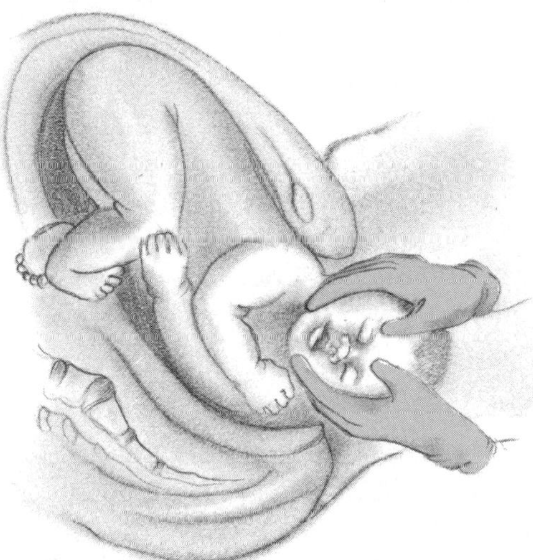

Action: After external rotation, the physician or nurse-midwife applies gentle traction on the fetal head in the direction of the mother's perineum. *Rationale:* External rotation allows the shoulders to rotate internally and aligns their transverse diameter with the anterior-posterior diameter of the mother's pelvic outlet. Traction on the head in the direction of her perineum allows the anterior fetal shoulder to slip under the symphysis pubis.

Action: The attendant then lifts the head toward the mother's symphysis pubis. *Rationale:* Permits the posterior fetal shoulder to be eased over the perineum, minimizing trauma to the maternal tissues.

Clearing the Infant's Airway and Cutting the Cord

Action: The rest of the infant's body is born quickly after the shoulders are born. The physician or nurse-midwife maintains the infant in a slightly head-dependent position while suctioning excess secretions with a bulb syringe. The infant is often placed on the mother's abdomen. *Rationale:* Gravity aids spontaneous drainage of secretions and prevents aspiration of oral mucus and secretions.

Action: The physician or nurse-midwife clamps the cord. Either the father or the attendant cuts the cord above the clamp. *Rationale:* Allows parents to interact more freely with their infant. Prevents flow of blood between placenta and infant, which might result in anemia (if infant is higher than placenta) or polycythemia (if infant is below the placenta).

Delivery of the Placenta

Action: After the placenta separates, it can usually be delivered if the mother bears down. The attendant may pull gently on the cord. *Rationale:* Excess traction on the cord may cause it to break, making the placenta harder to deliver.

Action: The physician or nurse-midwife inspects both sides of the placenta. *Rationale:* Ensures that no fragments remain inside the uterus that might cause hemorrhage and infection.

After the infant and placenta are born, the physician or nurse-midwife inspects the birth canal for injuries. If needed, any injuries and the episiotomy (if one was done) are repaired.

Table 13–6. ASSISTING WITH AN EMERGENCY BIRTH

The inexperienced nurse rarely must deliver a baby in the hospital or birth center, but occasionally helps the more experienced nurse do so. Unplanned out-of-hospital births are not common, but they do occasionally occur.

Nursing Priorities for an Emergency Birth in Any Setting

Prevent or reduce injury to the mother and infant.

Maintain the infant's airway and temperature after birth.

Preparing for an Emergency Birth

Study the delivery sequence in Table 13–5.

Locate the emergency delivery tray ("precip" tray) on the unit.

During the Birth

Remain with the woman to assist her in giving birth. Use the call bell, or ask her partner to call for help. Stay calm to reduce the couple's anxiety.

Put on gloves, preferably sterile, to prevent contamination with blood and other secretions. Sterile gloves reduce transmission of environmental organisms to the mother and infant. The nurse will be "catching" the infant in this situation. No invasive procedure is done.

After the Birth

Observe the infant's color and respirations for distress. Suction excess secretions with a bulb syringe.

Dry the infant, and place skin-to-skin with the mother or cover with warmed blankets to maintain warmth.

Put the infant to the mother's breast, and encourage sucking to promote uterine contraction, facilitating expulsion of the placenta and controlling bleeding.

Nursing Care During the Late Intrapartum Period

Responsibilities During Birth

The nurse has responsibilities during the birth in addition to the nursing care discussed previously. These responsibilities, which may vary among institutions, include:

- Preparation of a sterile delivery table with gowns, gloves, drapes, solutions, and instruments
- Perineal prep
- Initial care and assessment of the newborn
- Administration of medications, usually oxytocin, to contract the uterus and control blood loss (see Drug Guide 16–1)

An anesthesiologist or nurse anesthetist may give all medications. A nurse from the nursery is often present if there is an increased risk for newborn problems such as respiratory depression.

Occasionally, the woman will be ready to give birth before the physician or nurse-midwife arrives. In such an event, experienced maternity nurses are prepared to assist. Table 13–6 presents appropriate actions for nurses helping under emergency circumstances.

△ At birth, the newborn will be covered with blood, amniotic fluid, vernix, and other body substances. All personnel involved in infant care should wear gloves and other protective equipment until after the first bath to avoid contact with potentially infectious secretions.

Responsibilities After Birth

Intrapartum nursing care extends through the fourth stage of labor and includes care of the infant, mother, and the family unit. (See Table 13–7 for a summary of nursing care through all the stages of labor.) Nursing care during the recovery period is briefly addressed in this chapter. (For complete discussion of post-birth care of the mother and infant, see Part IV, Chapters 17 through 22.)

CARE OF THE INFANT

Nursing care of the infant addresses maintaining adequate cardiopulmonary function, thermoregulatory function, and identifying the infant. In addition, the nurse assesses the infant for approximate gestational age (see p. 535) and observes for obvious anomalies or birth injuries.

Maintaining Respiratory Function

Assess the infant's Apgar score for a rapid evaluation of immediate cardiopulmonary adaptation (Table 13–8) at 1 and 5 minutes after birth. If the Apgar score is 8 or higher, usually no intervention other than promoting normal respiratory efforts is needed.

Keep the infant in a flat or slight Trendelenburg position while secretions drain. After the infant cries vigorously and has minimal secretions, position him or her tilted to one side with the head of the crib flat or slightly elevated. Keeping the baby in a Trendelenburg position longer than needed may limit diaphragm movement because of upward pressure from the intestines. The parents may hold the infant after respirations are established. Suction the infant's mouth and nose with a bulb syringe as needed (see p. 521).

Supporting Thermoregulation

Dry the infant thoroughly to reduce evaporative heat loss. Dry the head well because damp hair may be a continuing source of evaporative loss. Because it is

Table 13–7. SUMMARY OF INTRAPARTUM NURSING CARE

Assess maternal and fetal conditions during first- and second-stage labor (see guidelines in Tables 13–1 and 13–2). Assess the mother during the fourth stage.

First Stage

Latent Phase

1. On entry to the birth center, greet the woman and her partner or family. Orient them to the environment.
2. Reinforce breathing and coping skills that the couple may have learned during childbirth classes. Teach the unprepared woman simple breathing and relaxation techniques (see Chapters 11 and 15).
3. If there is no contraindication, encourage the woman to walk as much as she desires.
4. Initiate needed procedures such as signing permits and laboratory work. Insertion of an intravenous (IV) line may be delayed until she is in active labor or needs fluids or medication.
5. Maintain her modesty, which may be a high priority in many cultural groups.

Active Phase

1. Provide general comfort measures, such as linen or underpad changes, cool washcloths, back rubs, and ice chips.
2. Encourage frequent position changes (every 30 minutes or as desired).
3. Observe the woman's bladder, and remind her to void every 2 hours if she does not sense the urge to void. Encourage more frequent voiding if she receives a large quantity of IV fluids.
4. Assist the woman and her partner or coach to use breathing and relaxation techniques.
5. Provide ordered analgesics as needed. Specifically ask the woman about her pain and how she is managing it. Women from cultural groups that place a high value on restraint may avoid showing non-verbal signs of pain until it is intolerable.
6. Encourage and reassure her. Tell her when she makes progress. Praise her efforts to manage her labor.
7. Support the partner or coach so that he or she can better support the mother. Encourage the partner or coach to take a break or have a snack.

Transition Phase

1. Provide general comfort measures as needed or desired. Linens may be damp from perspiration or soiled with bloody show or amniotic fluid, yet the woman may not want a linen change. Provide clean underpads, and wash her perineal area and thighs as needed.
2. Minimize distractions, and do not try to engage her in conversation.
3. If she has trouble using breathing techniques, breathe with her to help her focus on the technique (or have the partner or coach do so).
4. Observe for signs that are associated with onset of the second stage of labor: grunting sounds, bearing down, a statement that the baby is coming, or that she needs to push.
5. The multipara may be prepared for birth at about 9 to 10 cm dilation, but usually before the fetal head crowns. The time for final preparations varies according to the overall speed of labor and the rate of fetal descent.

Second Stage

1. Observe the woman's perineum for crowning of the fetal head.
2. Encourage her spontaneous bearing-down efforts, but advise her not to hold her breath for prolonged periods (longer than 5 to 6 seconds).
3. Help the woman push most effectively by having her:
   a. Push in the position she finds most comfortable.
   b. Push downward toward vaginal outlet with the abdominal muscles.
   c. Keep her head flexed with her chin on her chest with her body curled in a "C" position around her uterus.
   d. She should concentrate on keeping the perineum relaxed.
4. Be encouraging.
   a. Tell her about progress. ("Your bottom is bulging now, so we should see the baby's head soon." "I can see a little of the baby's head now.")
   b. Let her touch the baby's head when crowning occurs, or let her see it with a mirror.

Third Stage

1. Have the physician's or nurse-midwife's usual oxytocin dosage prepared, and administer it when ordered.

2. Observe maternal blood loss, and note firm uterine contraction.
3. Observe the infant's Apgar scores at 1 and 5 minutes (see Table 13–8).
4. Maintain the infant's temperature by drying quickly and placing under a radiant warmer. Put a cap on the infant's dry head once he or she is out of the warmer.

5. Assess the infant for obvious abnormalities and approximate gestational age (see p. 535).

6. Perform infant identification procedures according to policy.
7. Promote parent-infant attachment while completing infant care.
   a. Move the radiant warmer so that the parents can see the baby.
   b. Encourage parents to hold the infant's hand or otherwise touch the infant.
   c. Complete care quickly, then wrap the infant in warmed blankets and give to the parents to hold.
   d. Make positive comments about the infant, but be aware of cultural differences. Some cultural groups (often Asian) may believe that positive comments about the infant will cause spirits to make him or her ill or to be taken away. These women may seem apathetic about their infants because of their cultural beliefs.

Fourth Stage

1. Assess the mother's vital signs, fundus, bladder, perineal condition, and lochia (see guidelines, pp. 320–321).
2. Place an ice pack on the mother's perineum if she had an episiotomy or laceration or if ecchymoses are noted.

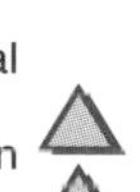

3. Provide warm blankets and liquids to decrease chilling. Women from Asian cultures often want hot water, soups, or a soft-cooked egg.
4. Provide analgesics, as needed, for afterpains or perineal pain.
5. If the infant remains with the parents, observe for respiratory problems, as evidenced by tachypnea, grunting, or retractions with respirations (p. 478), or cyanosis. Suction secretions as needed with a bulb syringe.

6. Maintain the infant's warmth with a radiant warmer, warm blankets, or skin-to-skin contact with the parents.
7. Encourage the mother to nurse her baby if she is breastfeeding. Women from some cultures do not nurse their infants until the milk "comes in" because they believe colostrum is "dirty" or "old." Modesty also may make them reluctant to nurse the baby when others are present.
8. Observe for signs of parent-infant attachment.
   a. Eye contact with the infant (observe how infant responds also).
   b. Enfolding or holding infant close.
   c. Making positive comments about the infant (see note above about different cultures).
9. Promote family integration when the parents are ready. Invite other family members and younger siblings as the parents desire. Help younger siblings hold or see the infant by raising them up to the infant's level or bringing the infant down to their level. Toddlers are more interested in contact with their mother than in the new baby.

Table 13–8. APGAR SCORE*

Assessment	Points 0	1	2
Heart rate	Absent	Below 100/minute	100/minute or higher
Respiratory effort	No spontaneous respirations	Slow respirations or weak cry	Spontaneous respirations with a strong, lusty cry
Muscle tone	Limp	Minimal flexion of extremities; sluggish movement	Flexed body posture; spontaneous and vigorous movement
Reflex response	No response to suction or gentle slap on soles	Minimal response (grimace) to suction or gentle slap on soles	Responds promptly to suction or a gentle slap to the sole with cry or active movement
Color	Pallor or cyanosis	Bluish hands and feet	Pink (light-skinned) or absence of cyanosis (dark-skinned)

*The Apgar score is a method of rapid evaluation of the infant's cardiorespiratory adaptation after birth. The nurse scores the infant at 1 minute and 5 minutes in each of five areas. The assessments are arranged from most important (heart rate) to least important (color). The infant is assigned a score of 0 to 2 in each of the five areas and the scores totaled. General guidelines for the infant's care are based on three ranges of 1 minute scores:

0 1 2 3	4 5 6 7	8 9 10
Infant needs resuscitation	Gentle stimulation by rubbing the infant's back while administering oxygen; determine if mother received narcotics, which may have depressed infant's respirations. Have naloxone (Narcan) available for administration	No action other than support of the infant's spontaneous efforts and continued observation

about one quarter of the total surface area, substantial heat loss can occur from the infant's head. A stockinette cap can further reduce heat loss if placed on the baby's *dry* head.

Place the infant in a pre-warmed radiant warmer to reduce heat loss (see p. 521). Avoid coming between the infant and the heat source. A cap is not worn in the warmer because the cap slows transfer of heat to the baby. When the infant is out of the warmer, wrap in warm blankets. Skin-to-skin contact with the parents is another intervention that maintains the baby's temperature and promotes attachment.

Identifying the Infant

Arm and leg bands having matching numbers and identifying information are the primary means of ensuring that the right baby goes to the right mother. The identification bands must be applied securely. Apply two bands on the infant, one on an arm and another on a leg. The bands are applied more tightly than they would be if worn by an adult: about one adult fingerwidth of slack in the bands. Apply the larger band to the mother's wrist. In some facilities, a fourth band is worn by the father or other primary support person.

In most facilities, an identification record is completed, including the band numbers, the infant's footprints, and the mother's thumb or index fingerprint. The physician or nurse-midwife, delivery room nurse, and nursery nurse sign the record to confirm proper identification. The mother signs the form when she and the baby are discharged.

CARE OF THE MOTHER

Nursing care of the mother during the fourth stage of labor focuses on observing for hemorrhage and relieving discomfort.

Observing for Hemorrhage

Important observations related to possible hemorrhage are checks of the woman's vital signs, uterine fundus, bladder, and lochia. The routine frequency of these assessments varies, depending on the birth facility. Mothers who are more at risk for postpartum hemorrhage should be checked more often. For additional information about these Assessments, see Chapter 17. For nursing Care related to postpartum hemorrhage, see Nursing Care Plan 27–1.

Vital Signs. Check the woman's temperature on admission. Check blood pressure, pulse and respirations every 15 minutes during the first hour. A rising pulse is an early sign of shock.

Fundus. Excessive bleeding may occur if the uterus does not contract and compress open vessels at the placental site. Other sources of bleeding are

Critical to Remember

Problems During Fourth Stage of Labor

Sign	Potential Problem
Rising pulse rate	An early sign of hypovolemic shock, probably due to hemorrhage (visible or concealed)
Soft (boggy) uterus	An uncontracted uterus that does not adequately compress large open vessels at placental site, resulting in hemorrhage
High uterine fundus, often displaced to one side	A full bladder that can interfere with uterine contraction and result in hemorrhage
Lochia exceeding one saturated perineal pad per hour during fourth stage	May indicate hemorrhage; however, perineal pads vary in their absorbency, and this must be considered
Intense pain, poorly relieved with analgesics.	Hematoma, usually of vaginal wall or perineum; signs of shock may occur with substantial blood loss into tissues

lacerations and hematomas of the birth canal. Check the firmness, height, and positioning of the uterine fundus with each vital sign assessment. The fundus should be firm and in the midline, about halfway between the symphysis pubis and the umbilicus during the first hour. If the fundus is firm, no massage is necessary; if it is soft (boggy), massage it until it is firm. To maintain firm uterine contraction and control bleeding, oxytocin is often added to the intravenous solution after the placenta is expelled.

Bladder. A full bladder interferes with contraction of the uterus and may lead to hemorrhage. Suspect a full bladder if the fundus is above the umbilicus or is displaced to one side, usually the right side. If there is no contraindication, such as sedation or altered sensation, the mother can walk to the bathroom. Measure the first two voidings, or record output until she is voiding regularly, without difficulty, and empties her bladder completely. Each voiding will usually be at least 300 to 400 ml if she is emptying her bladder.

Lochia. Assess lochia with each vital sign and fundal check. Lochia rubra is present during the recovery period, and the amount seems large to the inexperienced nurse. Perineal pads vary in their absorbency, but saturation of one pad within the first hour is a guideline for the maximum normal lochia flow. Observe for lochia that pools under the mother's buttocks and back. Small clots may be present, but the presence of large clots is not normal and the physician or nurse-midwife should be notified. A continuous trickle of bright-red blood when the fundus is firm suggests a laceration in the birth canal.

Relieving Discomfort

Uterine contractions (afterpains) and perineal trauma are common causes of pain after birth. The pain is usually mild and readily relieved. Notify the physician or nurse-midwife if pain is intense or does not respond to relief measures.

Warmth. A warm blanket is comforting and can shorten the chill that is common after birth. An portable radiant warmer provides warmth to both the mother and infant. The mother may enjoy warm drinks if there is no contraindication to oral intake.

Ice Packs. Apply an ice pack to her perineum to reduce edema and limit hematoma formation. Small hematomas are common, but a rapidly enlarging hematoma may cause substantial blood loss and pain. Some perineal pads have chemical cold packs incorporated in them. Because these pads do not absorb as much lochia, this should be considered when pad saturation is estimated.

Analgesics. Afterpains and perineal pain respond well to mild oral analgesics. Keeping the bladder emptied reduces the severity of afterpains because the uterus contracts more effectively.

PROMOTING EARLY FAMILY ATTACHMENT

The first hour after birth is an ideal time for parent-infant attachment because the infant is alert and responsive. Usually the nurse only needs to stay out of the way while the family gets acquainted. Provide privacy while unobtrusively observing the parents and infant. It is unnecessary to remove the infant from the parent's arms to take a temperature or suction small amounts of secretions.

Encourage the mother to breastfeed during the recovery period. The infant is usually alert and will nurse briefly. Even if the baby does not suck actively, early nipple stimulation helps initiate milk production.

When the parents are ready, allow siblings, other family members, and friends to visit. Help siblings to see and touch their new brother or sister by putting a stool at the bedside or letting them sit on the bed.

Nursing Care Plan 13–1

Normal Labor and Birth

Assessment: Cathy Taggart, 17 years old, is a gravida I, para 0, who has just been admitted in early labor. Her cervix is 3 cm dilated, completely effaced, and the fetus is at a 0 station. Her membranes are intact. Cathy's husband Tim is with her. They did not attend childbirth classes. Cathy is holding Tim's hand tightly and breathing rapidly with each contraction. She says in a shaky voice, "I'm so scared. I've never been in a hospital before. I just don't know if I can do this."

Nursing Diagnosis: Anxiety (moderate) related to unfamiliar environment and lack of labor preparation as evidenced by Cathy's verbal remarks and non-verbal behaviors.

Goals:
Cathy will:

1. Express a reduction in her anxiety after admission procedures are completed.
2. Have a relaxed facial and body posture between contractions.

Intervention:	Rationale:
1. Maintain a calm and confident manner when caring for Cathy.	1. Provides non-verbal reassurance that labor is normal and that Cathy can manage it.
2. Use therapeutic communication when talking with Cathy. Adapt communication to the changing situation, simplifying explanations and directions as labor intensifies.	2. Identifies Cathy's dominant concerns so they can be appropriately addressed. Intense physical sensations reduce her ability to comprehend complex information.
3. Determine the couple's plans for birth and work within them as much as possible.	3. Enhances Cathy's sense of control and helps the couple to have a more satisfying birth experience.
4. Stay with Cathy as much as possible during labor.	4. Provides reassurance of human contact and reduces Cathy's fears of abandonment.
5. Orient Cathy to the labor room and explain all procedures and equipment.	5. Reduces fear of the unknown.

Evaluation:
Cathy relaxes a bit after talking with the nurse and slows her breathing. She still holds Tim's hand, but not as tightly. Cathy says, "I feel a little better now. I hope I can have my baby before you go home."

Assessment: Cathy's admission vital signs are all normal: Temperature 98.8, pulse 88, respirations 20, and blood pressure 112/70. The FHR averages 140–146. Her contractions are every 4 minutes, duration of 50 seconds, and moderate intensity.

Potential Complication: Fetal compromise.

Goals:
Goals are not formulated for a potential complication because the nurse cannot independently manage fetal compromise. The nurse will:

1. Take actions to promote normal placental function.
2. Observe for and report signs associated with fetal compromise.

Intervention:	Rationale:
1. Encourage Cathy to use any position she desires except the supine.	1. The supine position can cause aortocaval compression, reducing blood flow to the placenta.

Nursing Care Plan 13–1 Continued

Normal Labor and Birth

Intervention	Rationale
2. Assess and document the FHR using the guidelines in Table 13–3. Report rates outside the normal 110–160 or slowing that persists after contractions. Assess the FHR more frequently if deviations from normal are identified.	2. Allows prompt identification of changes in the rate or of abnormal rates. FHR assessments that are outside average parameters should be reported for possible medical intervention.
3. When the membranes rupture, observe the color, odor, and approximate amount of fluid.	3. Normal amniotic fluid is clear and does not have a strong or foul odor. Meconium-stained fluid may be associated with fetal compromise and should be reported.
4. Assess contractions using guidelines in Table 13–1. Report contraction durations longer than 90 seconds, or intervals shorter than 60 seconds.	4. Most placental exchange occurs during the interval between contractions. Contractions that are too long or an inadequate interval between them decreases the time available for the intervillous spaces of the placenta to refill with oxygenated blood.
5. Assess Cathy's blood pressure, pulse, and respirations every hour. Assess her temperature every 4 hours until her membranes rupture, then every 2 hours.	5. Maternal hypotension can decrease blood flow to the placenta. Maternal fever can increase the fetus' demand for oxygen beyond the mother's ability to supply it.
6. See Nursing Care Plan 14–1 for additional interventions if signs of fetal compromise occur.	6. This nursing care plan addresses corrective actions to increase fetal oxygenation.

Evaluation:
Because no client goal is established for a potential complication, evaluation is not done. The FHR remains at approximately the same rate, and no signs of fetal compromise occur. Cathy finds that sitting in a rocking chair is most comfortable. She has no interest in lying in the supine position.

Assessment: In 1½ hours, Cathy's cervical dilation progresses to 5 cm and the fetus descends to a +1 station. Her contractions are every 3 minutes, 60 seconds long, and of strong intensity. The FHR remains at about its baseline level. Cathy is having difficulty relaxing between contractions and is complaining of back pain. She is relieved that her labor is progressing normally.

Nursing Diagnosis: Pain related to effects of uterine contractions as evidenced by Cathy's statement of pain and inability to relax.

Goal:
Cathy will express that she can satisfactorily manage labor pain.

Intervention:	Rationale:
1. Encourage Cathy to try positions such as standing/sitting and leaning forward, side-lying, leaning over the back of the bed, or hands and knees. Remind her to change positions about every half hour or when she feels the need for a change.	1. These positions shift the weight of the fetus away from the sacral promontory, reducing back pain. Alternating positions relieves strain and constant pressure and also helps the fetus to adapt to the pelvis.
2. Teach Tim to rub Cathy's back. Ask her where the best place is and how hard to press. Apply powder to the area rubbed.	2. Back rubs or firm pressure counteract some of the back pain. Powder decreases friction and promotes skin comfort.
3. Teach Cathy simple breathing and relaxation techniques (see Chapters 11 and 15).	3. Provides distraction from pain sensations and gives her a sense of control. Relaxation enhances ability to manage pain and enhances normal labor processes.

Nursing Care Plan continued on following page

Nursing Care Plan 13–1 *Continued*

Normal Labor and Birth

4. Observe Cathy's suprapubic area and palpate for a full bladder every 2 hours. Remind her to void if she has not done so recently.	4. A full bladder contributes to discomfort and can prolong labor by taking up space in the pelvis and obstructing fetal descent.
5. Tell Cathy about her progress in labor. Explain that she will probably begin to dilate faster now that she has entered active labor.	5. Encouragement and the knowledge that her efforts are having the desired results increases her willingness to continue.
6. Tell Cathy what pharmacologic pain relief measures are available to her.	6. Gives Cathy a sense of control because she has choice about whether she wants to use these measures. Lets her know that additional relief measures are available without pressuring her to use them.
7. See Nursing Care Plan 15–1 for additional interventions.	7. Provides guidance about several non-pharmacologic and pharmacologic pain management measures.

Evaluation:
Cathy continues to have back pain, but says that she is more comfortable sitting on the side of the bed with her head on a pillow on the overbed table. Tim rubs her back during contractions. She says she is able to manage the pain and does not want medication yet.

Assessment: After another 2 hours, Cathy is quite uncomfortable and requests pain medication. A vaginal examination reveals that her cervix is 8 cm dilated and the station is +1. She is occasionally feeling an urge to push. Cathy cries and says she is "losing it" and "can't take it anymore." Tim asks anxiously, "What's wrong? Is Cathy OK? Why is she acting this way?" The FHR remains within the baseline range. Contractions are every 2 minutes, 70 seconds, and strong.

Nursing Diagnosis: Anxiety related to lack of knowledge about the transition phase of labor as evidenced by Cathy's statement and Tim's questions.

Goal:
Tim and Cathy will indicate that they understand why she seems to have lost control.

Intervention:	Rationale:
1. Continue with pain management measures from previous nursing diagnosis. Administer analgesia as ordered by Cathy's physician.	1. Pain beyond Cathy's ability to manage contributes to anxiety and loss of control.
2. Reassure Cathy and Tim that this phase of labor is very intense, but usually short.	2. Lets the couple know that the intensity of this phase of labor is self-limiting and does not last as long as the other two phases.
3. Explain that Cathy's behaviors are typical of this phase of labor and that she will feel more in control when she begins pushing in the second stage.	3. Relieves anxiety due to the unknown and reassures Tim and Cathy of the temporary nature of her behaviors and feelings. Expresses confidence in her ability to regain control.

Evaluation:
Cathy is almost overwhelmed by the intensity of her labor, but she and Tim express relief that this phase of labor should not last long. Butorphanol (Stadol) 0.5 mg IV gave her enough analgesia to regain control and work with her contractions.

Nursing Care Plan 13–1 *Continued*

Normal Labor and Birth

Assessment: Cathy is fully dilated in 45 minutes, and the fetal station is +2. She begins pushing with each contraction, but tends to stiffen her back and push on the bed with her arms with each push. She pushes for about 10 to 15 seconds at a time. She prefers a semi-sitting position.

Nursing Diagnosis: Knowledge Deficit: Effective pushing techniques as evidenced by Cathy's use of inefficient techniques.

Goal:
After instruction in more effective pushing techniques, Cathy will use the techniques until the birth occurs.

Intervention:	Rationale:
1. Observe Cathy's perineum for fetal crowning with each push.	1. Although this is Cathy's first baby, she could still give birth rapidly and unexpectedly. Observation permits the nurse to maintain the safety of Cathy and the baby should an unexpected birth occur.
2. Coach Cathy to hold her breath for no more than 5 to 6 seconds when she pushes. Count to 5 or 6 at a moderate pace to give her a framework for this time if she prefers to push while holding her breath.	2. Prolonged pushing against a closed glottis can reduce blood return to the heart, maternal oxygen saturation, and decrease placental blood flow.
3. As an alternative to breath-holding while pushing, teach Cathy to exhale slowly while she pushes for about 10 seconds at a time.	3. Avoids prolonged breath-holding (see No. 2 above).
4. Teach Cathy techniques to make each push more effective:	4.
a. Flex head with each push, putting her chin on her chest.	a. Directs each push downward into the pelvic cavity.
b. Pull against her flexed knees (or hand holds on the bed) as she pushes.	b. Provides leverage to gain more effective push from abdominal muscles.
c. Push toward the vaginal outlet.	c. Anatomically correct direction.
d. Relax her perineum as she pushes down.	d. Reduces soft tissue resistance to fetal descent.
e. Keep her sacrum flattened against the bed when she pushes.	e. Straightens pelvic curve somewhat (similar to squatting).
4. Do not talk to Cathy unnecessarily between contractions.	4. Allows her to conserve her energy for pushing efforts.

Evaluation:
Cathy pushes more effectively with the nurse coaching her during each contraction. In another hour, she gives birth to a 7-pound, 6-ounce (3346 g) boy. The baby's Apgar scores are 9 at both 1 and 5 minutes. Cathy has a small first-degree laceration that is sutured with a local anesthetic. The new family gets acquainted during the recovery period.

Additional Nursing Diagnoses to Consider:
- Communication, Impaired
- Coping, Ineffective Individual or Family
- Fluid Volume Deficit
- Injury, High Risk for
- Powerlessness
- Sensory-Perceptual Alterations

Toddlers are often upset by separation from their mother and may not be interested in the new baby. With supervision, children of preschool age or older can hold the infant while they sit in a chair. School-aged children are often fascinated by the new baby and surroundings and ask many questions. Adolescents react in various ways. They may be excited and eager to be a substitute parent, or they may be embarrassed about their parents having a new baby "at their age."

Observe for signs of normal early parent-infant attachment. Parent behaviors are tentative at first, progressing from fingertip touch to palm touch to enfolding of the infant. Expect parents to make eye contact with the infant and talk to a baby in higher-pitched, affectionate tones. (See pp. 450 to 452 for a more detailed discussion of parent-infant attachment.)

Summary Concepts

- Not all women will have symptoms typical of true labor. The nurse should encourage them to enter the hospital or birth center for evaluation if they are uncertain or have concerns other than those listed in the guidelines.
- The pregnant woman's initial impression on admission to the intrapartum unit is important for facilitating a therapeutic relationship between her health care providers and herself.
- When a woman enters the intrapartum unit, the most important assessments are for maternal and fetal health and labor status.
- The fetus is the more vulnerable of the maternal-fetal pair because of complete dependence on the mother's physiological systems.
- The normal fetal heart rate averages 110 to 160 BPM at term. To ensure fetal safety, the nurse should report any FHR outside normal limits or slowing of FHR that persists 30 seconds after the contraction ends.
- Persistent contraction durations of longer than 90 seconds or intervals shorter than 60 seconds may reduce placental blood flow and fetal oxygenation.
- Placental blood flow may be reduced if the woman remains in a supine position because the uterus compresses her aorta and inferior vena cava.
- General comfort measures promote the expectant mother's ability to relax and cope with labor.
- Regular changes in position during labor promote maternal comfort and help the fetus adapt to pelvic diameters.
- Because any woman may progress to the point of birth quickly and unexpectedly, the nurse must be alert for signs of impending birth: The woman may state, "The baby is coming," she may make grunting sounds, or she may be bearing down.
- The most critical nursing care of the newborn is to promote normal respirations and maintain normal body temperature.
- The most critical nursing care of the mother after birth consists of assessing for hemorrhage and promoting firm uterine contraction.

References and Readings

Acosta, Y.M., Goodwin, C., Amaya, M.A., Tinkle, M.B., Acosta, E., & Jaquez, I. (1992). HIV disease and pregnancy. Part 2. Antepartum and intrapartum care. *Journal of Obstetric, Gynecologic, and Neonatal Nursing*, 21(2), 97–103.

American Academy of Pediatrics and American College of Obstetricians and Gynecologists (1992). *Guidelines for perinatal care* (3rd ed.). Elk Grove Village, Ill., and Washington, D.C.

American Academy of Pediatrics. Committee on Fetus and Newborn. (1986). Use and abuse of the Apgar score. *Pediatrics*, 78(6), 1148–1149.

Andrews, C.M., & Chrzanowski, M. (1990). Maternal position, labor, and comfort. *Applied Nursing Research*, 3(1), 7–13.

Berry, L.M. (1988). Realistic expectations of the labor coach. *Journal of Obstetric, Gynecologic, and Neonatal Nursing*, 17(5), 354–355.

Bonovich, L. (1990). Recognizing the onset of labor. *Journal of Obstetric, Gynecologic, and Neonatal Nursing*, 19(2), 141–145.

Bowes, W.A. (1989). Clinical aspects of normal and abnormal labor. In R. Creasy & R. Resnik (Eds.), *Maternal-fetal medicine: Principles and practice* (pp. 510–546). Philadelphia: W.B. Saunders.

Broach, J., & Newton, N. (1988). Food and beverages in labor. Part II: The effects of cessation of oral intake during labor. *Birth*, 15(2), 88–92.

Brown, S.T., Campbell, D., & Kurtz, A. (1989). Characteristics of labor pain at two stages of cervical dilation. *Pain*, 38(3), 289–295.

Carty, E.M., & Tier, T. (1989). Birth planning: A reality-based script for building confidence. *Journal of Nurse-Midwifery*, 34(3), 111–114.

Chapman, L.L. (1992). Expectant fathers' roles during labor and birth. *Journal of Obstetric, Gynecologic, and Neonatal Nursing*, 21(2), 114–120.

Crowe, K., & von Baeyer, C. (1989). Predictors of a positive childbirth experience. *Birth*, 16(2), 59–63.

D'Avanzo, C.E. (1992). Bridging the cultural gap with Southeast Asians. *MCN: American Journal of Maternal Child Nursing*, 17(4), 204–208.

Davis, L.K. (1992). Protocol for fetal heart rate monitoring. In L.K. Mandeville & N.H. Troiano (Eds.), *High-risk intrapartum nursing*. Philadelphia: J.B. Lippincott.

Douglas, M.J. (1988). Commentary: The case against a more liberal food and fluid policy in labor. *Birth*, 15(2), 93–94.

Gabbe, S. (1988). Commentary: Current practices of intravenous fluid administration may do more harm than good. *Birth*, 15(2), 73–74.

Grabenstein, J. (1987). Nursing documentation during the perinatal period. *Journal of Perinatal-Neonatal Nursing*, 1(2), 29–38.

Greer, P.S. (1988). Head coverings for newborns under radiant warmers. *Journal of Obstetric, Gynecologic, and Neonatal Nursing*, 17(4), 265–270.

Hacker, N.F., & Moore, J.G. (1986). *Essentials of obstetrics and gynecology*. Philadelphia: W.B. Saunders.

Hodnett, E.D., & Osborn, R.W. (1989). A randomized trial of the effects of monitrice support during labor: Mothers' views two to four weeks post partum. *Birth*, 16(4), 177–183.

Jarvis, C. (1992) *Physical examination and health assessment*. Philadelphia: W.B. Saunders.

Keppler, A.B. (1988). The use of intravenous fluids during labor. *Birth*, 15(2), 75–79.

Kintz, D.L. (1987). Nursing support in labor. *Journal of Obstetric, Gynecologic, and Neonatal Nursing*, 16(2), 126–130.

Kliegman, R.M. (1990). Fetal and neonatal medicine. In R.E. Behrman & R.M. Kliegman (Eds.), *Nelson essentials of pediatrics* (pp. 153–206). Philadelphia: W.B. Saunders.

Korones, S. (1986). *High risk newborn infants: The basis for intensive nursing care*. St. Louis: C.V. Mosby.

Kurokawa, J., & Zilkoski, M. (1985). Adapting hospital obstetrics to birth in the squatting position. *Birth*, 12(2), 87–90.

Leventhal, E.A., Leventhal, H., Shacham, S., & Easterling, D.V. (1989). Active coping reduces reports of pain from childbirth. *Journal of Consulting and Clinical Psychology*, 57(3), 365–371.

Lowe, N.K. (1991). Maternal confidence in coping with labor: A self-efficacy concept. *Journal of Obstetric, Gynecologic, and Neonatal Nursing*, 20(6), 457–463.

Martin, E.J. (1990). *Intrapartal management modules: A perinatal education program*. Baltimore: Williams & Wilkins.

McKay, S., & Roberts, J. (1990). Obstetrics by ear: Maternal and caregiver perceptions of the meaning of maternal sounds during second stage labor. *Journal of Nurse-Midwifery*, 35(5), 266–273.

Murray, M. (1988). *Antepartal and intrapartal fetal monitoring*. Washington, D.C.: NAACOG.

NAACOG. (1990). *Fetal heart rate auscultation*. Washington, D.C.

Nelsson-Ryan, S., Positioning: Second stage labor. In F. Nichols & S.S. Humenick (Eds.), *Childbirth education: Practice, research, and theory* (pp. 256–274). Philadelphia: W.B. Saunders.

Newton, N., Newton, M., & Broach, J. (1988). Psychologic, physical, nutritional, and technologic aspects of intravenous infusion during labor. *Birth*, 15(2), 67–72.

Pavlik, M. (1988). Positioning: First stage labor. In F. Nichols & S.S. Humenick (Eds.), *Childbirth education: Practice, research, and theory* (pp. 234–255). Philadelphia: W.B. Saunders.

Phillips, C.R. (1988). Rehumanizing maternal-child nursing. MCN: *American Journal of Maternal Child Nursing*, 13(5), 313–318.

Roberts, J.E., Goldstein, S.A., Gruener, J.S., Maggio, M., & Mendez-Bauer, C. (1987). A descriptive analysis of involuntary bearing-down efforts during the expulsive phase of labor. *Journal of Obstetric, Gynecologic, and Neonatal Nursing*, 16(1), 48–54.

Romond, J., & Baker, I. (1985). Squatting in childbirth: A new look at an old tradition. *Journal of Obstetric, Gynecologic, and Neonatal Nursing*, 14(5), 406–411.

Stolte, K. (1987). A comparison of women's expectations of labor with the actual event. *Birth*, 14(2), 99–103.

Weaver, D.F. (1990). Nurses' views on the meaning of touch in obstetrical nursing practice. *Journal of Obstetric, Gynecologic, and Neonatal Nursing*, 19(2), 157–161.

14

Intrapartum Fetal Monitoring

Objectives

1. Identify the purposes of fetal surveillance during labor.
2. Explain normal and pathophysiologic mechanisms that influence fetal heart rate.
3. Identify advantages and limitations of each method of intrapartum fetal monitoring: auscultation and electronic monitoring.
4. Explain equipment used for electronic fetal monitoring during labor, including advantages and limitations.
5. Describe interpretation of electronic fetal monitoring data.
6. Explain methods that may be used in addition to electronic fetal monitoring to judge fetal well-being.
7. Describe appropriate responses to non-reassuring fetal heart rate patterns.
8. Use the nursing process to plan care for a woman having intrapartum electronic fetal monitoring.

Definitions

Acidosis • A condition resulting from accumulation of acid (hydrogen ions) or depletion of base (bicarbonate). The pH measures acid-base balance.

Amnioinfusion • Infusion of warmed isotonic saline into the uterine cavity during labor to reduce umbilical cord compression; also done to wash meconium out of the uterus, reducing the risk that the infant will aspirate it at birth.

Asphyxia • A condition in which there is deficient oxygen in the blood and excess carbon dioxide in the blood and tissues.

Baroreceptors • Cells that are sensitive to blood pressure changes.

Chemoreceptors • Cells that are sensitive to chemical changes in the blood, specifically changes in oxygen and carbon dioxide levels, and in acid-base balance.

Hypercapnia • Excess carbon dioxide in the blood, evidenced by an elevated $P{CO_2}$.

Hypertonic contractions • Uterine contractions that are too strong, too frequent, or too long to allow optimum uteroplacental exchange.

Hypoxemia • Reduced oxygenation of the blood, evidenced by a low $P{O_2}$.

Hypoxia • Reduced availability of oxygen to the body tissues.

Intermittent monitoring • A variation of electronic fetal monitoring in which a 20-minute strip is obtained on admission. If patterns are reassuring, the woman is re-monitored for 15 minutes at regular intervals (about every 30 to 60 minutes).

Nuchal cord • Umbilical cord around a fetus' neck.

△ Alert for a high risk of exposure to substances to which universal precautions apply. See Appendix B for additional information about infection control.

Telemetry • Transmission of electronic fetal monitoring data to the bedside monitor unit with radio signals.

Tocolytic • A drug that inhibits uterine contractions.

Transducer • A device that translates one physical quantity to another, such as fetal heart motion to an electrical signal for rate calculation or generation of sound or of a written record.

Uterine resting tone • Degree of uterine muscle tension when the woman is not in labor or during the interval between labor contractions.

Intrapartum fetal monitoring is the process of fetal surveillance to identify signs associated with well-being and signs associated with compromise. Accurate assessment of these signs permits appropriate and timely nursing care to minimize hazards to the fetus. At a minimum, intrapartum fetal monitoring includes assessment of the fetal heart rate and the expectant mother's uterine activity. More comprehensive monitoring adds assessment of fetal activity, fetal response to stimulation, and sometimes evaluation of fetal blood gases and pH.

During labor there are two clients: the expectant mother and her fetus. The purposes of intrapartum fetal monitoring are to evaluate how the fetus tolerates labor and to identify the fetus who may be undergoing hypoxic insult. Fetal surveillance cannot identify every compromised fetus. It cannot prevent fetal distress, neurological dysfunction, or mental retardation.

There are two basic approaches to intrapartum fetal monitoring: a low-intervention approach and electronic fetal monitoring. Each has advantages and limitations. The nurse may use a combination of the two types to assess a fetus during labor.

The low-intervention approach uses auscultation of the fetal heart rate and palpation of uterine activity. In the United States, this type of fetal observation is more commonly used in home births and birth centers. It may also be used during normal births in hospitals.

Electronic fetal monitoring is the second approach to intrapartum fetal surveillance. It is the dominant method used in hospital births in the United States and is the major focus of this chapter. Despite its dominance as a method of intrapartum fetal surveillance, routine use of electronic fetal monitoring remains controversial because its benefits to the fetus are unclear and it has been implicated in the high incidence of cesarean births.

Fetal Oxygenation

Adequate fetal oxygenation requires five related factors:

- Normal maternal blood flow
- Normal oxygen saturation in maternal blood
- Adequate exchange of oxygen and carbon dioxide in the placenta
- An open circulatory path between the placenta and the fetus through vessels in the umbilical cord
- Normal fetal circulatory and oxygen-carrying function

Labor is stressful on a fetus, and several mechanisms exist to compensate for these stresses. One must understand the dynamics of uteroplacental exchange and fetal circulation to understand normal fetal responses during labor. (Also see Chapter 6 for additional discussion of placental functions.)

Uteroplacental Exchange

Oxygen-rich and nutrient-rich blood from the woman enters the intervillous spaces of the placenta via the spiral arteries (see Fig. 6-7). Oxygen and nutrients in the maternal blood pass into the fetal blood that circulates within capillaries in the intervillous spaces. Carbon dioxide and other waste products pass from the fetal blood into the maternal blood simultaneously. Maternal blood that carries fetal waste products drains from the intervillous spaces through endometrial veins and returns to the mother's circulation for elimination by her body. The blood of the woman and her fetus do not mix, but substances pass back and forth through the thin membranes of the fetal capillaries.

During labor, contractions compress the spiral arteries, temporarily stopping maternal blood flow into the intervillous spaces. The fetus depends on the oxygen supply already present in body cells, erythrocytes, and the intervillous spaces during contractions. The oxygen supply in these areas is enough for about 1 to 2 minutes. As each contraction relaxes, fresh oxygenated maternal blood re-enters the intervillous spaces and carbon dioxide–laden blood drains out.

Fetal Circulation

The fetal heart circulates oxygenated blood from the placenta throughout the body and returns deoxygenated blood to the placenta. The umbilical vein carries oxygenated blood to the fetus, and the two umbilical arteries carry deoxygenated blood from the fetus to the placenta (see Fig. 6-9).

Regulation of Fetal Heart Rate

Mechanisms that regulate the heart rate are balanced to maintain cardiac output at a level that keeps the fetal heart and brain oxygenated. Fetal cardiac output increase is primarily accomplished by an increase in the heart rate. Conversely, a marked decrease in fetal heart rate (FHR) decreases the cardiac output.

Five fetal factors interact to regulate the heart rate: (1) autonomic nervous system, (2) baroreceptors, (3) chemoreceptors, (4) central nervous system, and (5) adrenal glands. The balance among forces that increase and those that slow the heart rate result in the characteristic fluctuations in fetal heart rate.

AUTONOMIC NERVOUS SYSTEM

The sympathetic and parasympathetic branches of the autonomic nervous system are balanced forces that regulate the fetal heart rate. Sympathetic stimulation increases the heart rate and strengthens myocardial contractions through release of norepinephrine. The net result of sympathetic stimulation is an increase in cardiac output.

The parasympathetic nervous system, through stimulation of the vagus nerve, decreases the fetal heart rate and maintains short-term variability (see p. 341). The parasympathetic branch becomes dominant as the fetus matures. Therefore, the average FHR in the preterm fetus is usually higher than in the term fetus.

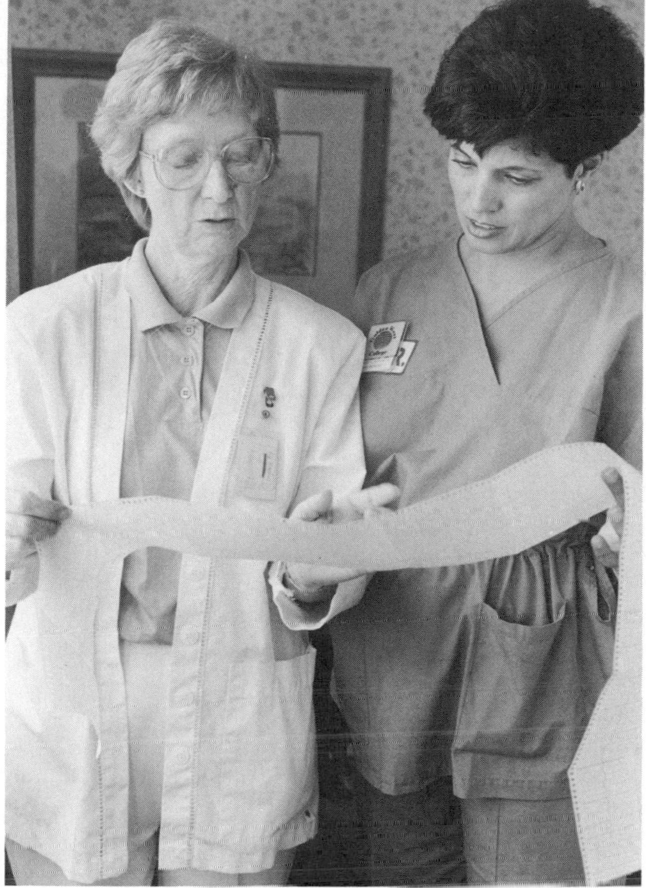

Electronic fetal monitoring is continuous and provides nurses with monitor strips on which uterine activity and fetal heart rate are permanently recorded.

BARORECEPTORS

Cells in the carotid arch and major arteries respond to stretching when the fetal blood pressure increases. The baroreceptors stimulate the vagus nerve to slow the fetal heart rate and decrease the blood pressure.

CHEMORECEPTORS

Cells that respond to changes in oxygen, carbon dioxide, and blood pH affect the fetal heart rate. They are found in the medulla oblongata (central chemoreceptors) and in the aortic and carotid bodies (peripheral chemoreceptors). Decreased oxygen and increased carbon dioxide content in the blood supplying the medulla oblongata trigger an initial increase in the heart rate and blood pressure. Baroreceptors respond to the higher blood pressure by reducing it. If reduced oxygen and high carbon dioxide levels persist, the eventual result is a decreased heart rate.

ADRENAL GLANDS

The adrenal medulla secretes epinephrine and norepinephrine in response to stress. This causes a sympathetic response and accelerates the fetal heart rate. The adrenal cortex responds to a fall in the fetal blood pressure with release of aldosterone and retention of sodium and water. The net result of these responses is to increase the circulating fetal blood volume.

CENTRAL NERVOUS SYSTEM

The fetal cerebral cortex causes the heart rate to increase during fetal movement and decrease when the fetus sleeps. The hypothalamus coordinates the two branches of the autonomic nervous system. The medulla oblongata maintains the balance between stimuli that accelerate and stimuli that decelerate the heart rate.

Pathophysiologic Influences on Fetal Oxygenation

Compromise of fetal oxygenation may occur because of alterations in any of the placental or fetal factors or those of the expectant mother.

MATERNAL CARDIOPULMONARY ALTERATIONS

Actual or relative reductions in the mother's circulating blood volume impair perfusion of the intervillous spaces with oxygenated maternal blood. Hemorrhage causes an actual decrease in her blood volume. Relative reductions in maternal circulating volume involve altered distribution of the blood volume without blood loss. For example, epidural or subarachnoid block anesthesia may result in vasodilation. The volume of the maternal vascular bed is larger with vasodilation. However, the amount of blood available to fill the vessels is unchanged. Hypotension then results, and placental blood flow is less.

Aortocaval compression can occur when a pregnant woman lies in the supine position and the weight of the uterus compresses the aorta and inferior vena cava. Aortocaval compression reduces blood return to her heart, lowers the cardiac output, and can reduce placental perfusion. Supine hypotensive syndrome (see p. 121) may result.

Maternal hypertension may reduce blood flow to the placenta because of vasospasm and narrowing of the spiral arteries. Hypertension may be pregnancy-induced or chronic or may result from ingestion of drugs such as cocaine.

Lowered oxygen tension in the mother's blood reduces the amount available to the fetus. Maternal acid-base alterations that often accompany respiratory abnormalities also can compromise exchange in the placenta. A lower maternal oxygen tension may result from respiratory disorders, such as asthma, or from smoking.

UTERINE ACTIVITY

Hypertonic contractions reduce the time available for the intervillous spaces to refill with oxygenated blood. An elevated uterine resting tone causes constant compression of the spiral arteries. Thus, a lesser amount of freshly oxygenated blood enters the intervillous spaces. Hypertonic contractions may occur spontaneously or with oxytocin administration (see p. 391).

PLACENTAL ALTERATIONS

Conditions such as abruptio placentae (see p. 670) and infarcts reduce the placental surface area available for exchange. The amount of surface area disruption directly relates to the degree of impairment in uteroplacental exchange.

INTERRUPTIONS IN UMBILICAL FLOW

The usual cause of interrupted blood flow through the umbilical cord is compression. Blood flow through the umbilical cord may be reduced by compression between the fetal presenting part and the pelvis, a nuchal cord, or a knot in the cord. It also may occur with oligohydramnios because there is inadequate amniotic fluid to cushion the cord. The umbilical cord also may become entangled between fetal body parts.

The thin-walled umbilical vein is compressed initially, resulting in a reduced inflow of blood to the fetus. This results in initial hypoxia with hypotension. Baroreceptors and chemoreceptors respond by accelerating the fetal heart rate. Flow through the firmer-walled umbilical arteries is reduced as the cord is further compressed, resulting in hypertension. Baroreceptors respond to hypertension by reducing blood pressure and slowing the fetal heart. The fetal heart rate again accelerates as pressure is relieved on the arteries and then on the vein.

FETAL ALTERATIONS

Fetal cells may be hypoxic despite adequate oxygen supply from the woman and adequate exchange within the placenta. A low circulating fetal blood volume, fetal hypotension, or fetal anemia may result in cellular hypoxia. Central nervous system or cardiac abnormalities may cause an abnormal rate or rhythm. For example, a fetus with complete heart block may not respond to stimuli that would normally cause a rate increase.

Rates lower than 50 beats per minute (BPM) may reduce fetal cardiac output enough to impair brain and heart perfusion. However, a fetal heart rate faster than 200 BPM also decreases cardiac output because the ventricles do not have time to fill with blood during diastole.

Risk Factors

When conditions associated with reduced fetal oxygenation exist (Table 14–1), assessments by either

Table 14–1. CONDITIONS ASSOCIATED WITH DECREASED FETAL OXYGENATION

Antepartum Period

Maternal History

Prior stillbirth
Prior cesarean birth
Chronic diseases, such as cardiac disease, hypertension, or diabetes
Drug abuse

Problems that Develop During Pregnancy

Fetal growth retardation
Gestation > 42 weeks
Marked decrease in fetal movement
Multifetal gestation
Pregnancy-induced hypertension
Gestational diabetes
Placenta previa
Maternal severe anemia
Maternal infection

Intrapartum Period

Maternal Problems

Hypotension, usually associated with regional anesthetics, such as epidural block
Induction or augmentation of labor with oxytocin
Tetanic uterine contractions, spontaneous or oxytocin-induced
Abnormal labor: preterm or dysfunctional
Prolonged ruptured membranes
Chorioamnionitis
Fever

Fetal or Placental Problems

Abnormal auscultated fetal heart rate
Meconium-stained amniotic fluid
Abnormal presentation or position
Prolapsed cord
Abruptio placentae

intermittent auscultation and palpation or electronic fetal monitoring are done more often. No absolute indications, including the presence of risk factors, *demand* the use of electronic fetal monitoring during labor. Properly performed auscultation is equivalent to continuous electronic monitoring in detecting fetal compromise (ACOG, 1989a).

In reality, the choice of intermittent auscultation over electronic fetal monitoring in high-risk situations can place a practitioner in legal jeopardy. If intermittent auscultation is used when risk factors are present and the infant is born with neurological damage, defense in a lawsuit could be more difficult. Therefore, most hospitals, physicians, and nurse-midwives specify the use of continuous electronic fetal monitoring for women with risk factors, even if it is not routine for all laboring women. Moreover, the low-risk woman may unexpectedly become at high risk.

✔ Check Your Reading

1. What five factors influence fetal oxygenation?
2. What changes in the fetal heart rate occur when the umbilical cord is compressed?
3. How is the fetal heart rate related to fetal cardiac output?
4. What risk factors indicate that fetal monitoring should be done more frequently?
5. Why is electronic fetal monitoring usually performed if risk factors are present?

Auscultation and Palpation

The nurse may use intermittent auscultation of the fetal heart rate and palpation of uterine activity for intrapartum fetal surveillance. This is a low-intervention approach that allows the expectant mother greater freedom to move around during labor. Intermittent auscultation of the fetal heart rate can be done using either the fetoscope or Doppler ultrasound transducer (Fig. 14–1). Because fetal assessment is an important part of nursing care during labor, several aspects are addressed in Chapter 13. (See Table 13–2 and Procedures 13–2 and 13–3 for discussion of guidelines for frequency of assessment, technique for intermittent auscultation, and palpation of uterine activity.)

Advantages

Mobility is the primary advantage of auscultation and palpation for assessment of fetal heart rate and uterine activity. The expectant mother is free to change position and walk around, which is especially helpful during early labor. She can use methods of pain management that use water, such as whirlpool baths or showers. The perception of a natural atmosphere for the birth is important to some couples.

Limitations

The main disadvantage of auscultation and palpation as the primary method of fetal assessment is that fetal heart rate and uterine activity are assessed for a small percentage of the total labor. The fetus is most stressed during contractions because of normal reduced blood flow to the placenta. Although the fetal heart rate is assessed during some contractions, it is not recorded during every contraction. Moreover, there is no continuous printed record to demonstrate the fetal response throughout labor or to identify subtle trends in the response.

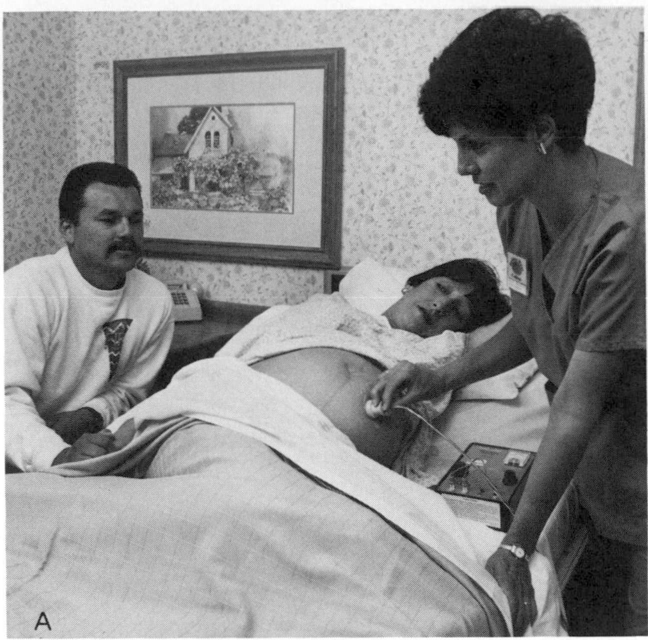

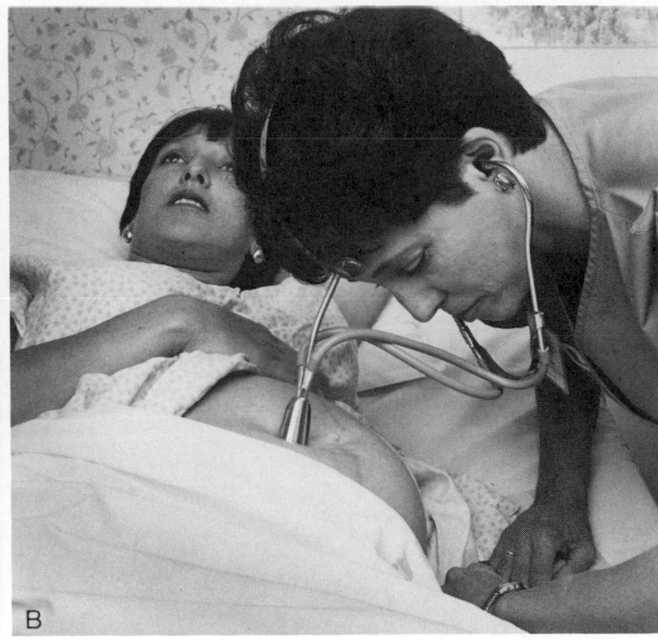

Figure 14–1

Low-intervention methods for evaluating the fetal heart rate during labor. **A**, Doppler examination. **B**, Fetoscope, showing head attachment to enhance conduction of faint fetal heart sounds.

Some women feel that interruptions for auscultation are distracting. The pressure of the instrument on the abdomen may be uncomfortable for some, and it may require several moves before locating the best place for auscultation.

Intermittent auscultation is somewhat more staff-intensive than electronic monitoring. For example, the nurse must check the fetal heart rate before, during, and after a contraction. Fetal heart sounds are difficult to hear during a contraction. There is no paper record to see the fetal response to previous contractions. When there are many clients for the number of nurses, auscultation is not a realistic option as the primary method of intrapartum fetal surveillance.

Electronic Fetal Monitoring

Electronic fetal monitoring is the more common method routinely used in United States hospitals for both low-risk and high-risk women during labor. Electronic monitoring may be continuous, starting shortly after the woman is admitted, or intermittent, with a strip taken at regular intervals during labor.

Advantages

The electronic monitor supplies more data about the fetus and prints a permanent record. Gradual trends and possible problems can often be identified because the strip provides a graphic record for review. Continuous electronic fetal monitoring shows how the fetus responds before, during, and after each contraction rather than with occasional contractions. In the United States, most hospitals use electronic fetal monitoring because of the larger amount of printed data with this method.

Many women are reassured by electronic fetal monitoring if they understand its capabilities and limitations. They often expect electronic monitoring and find the constant sound of the fetal heart beat comforting. The tracing of contractions on the monitor strip helps the coach participate in labor by helping the woman anticipate the beginning and end of each contraction.

Electronic monitoring often allows one nurse to observe two laboring women, primarily during first-stage labor. A 1-to-1 nurse-client ratio is needed during the second stage, regardless of the monitoring method used. Electronic monitoring can give the nurse more time for teaching and supporting the laboring woman with breathing and relaxation techniques.

Limitations

Reduced mobility is one limitation of electronic fetal monitoring. Telemetry or intermittent monitoring allows the pregnant woman more freedom of movement than continuous electronic monitoring without telemetry.

Frequent maternal position changes or an active fetus sometimes require constant adjustment of equipment. The belts or stockinette needed to keep sensors for external monitoring positioned properly are uncomfortable for some women.

The electronic fetal monitor imparts a more technical air to the surroundings and may be objectionable to some women. They may feel that the machine interferes with their desire for a natural or home-like birth experience.

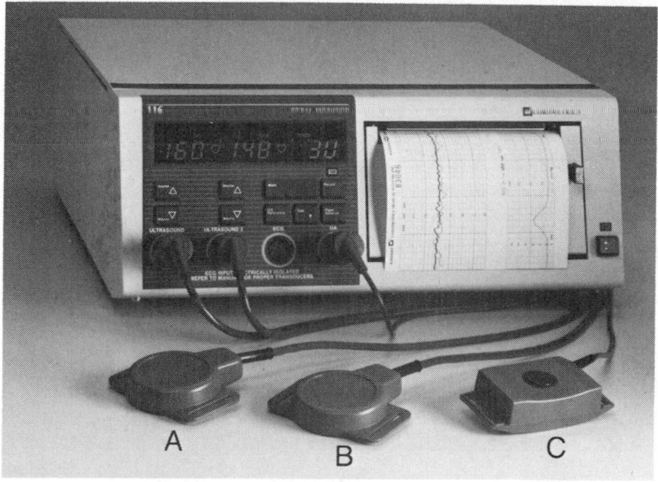

Figure 14–2

Bedside unit for electronic fetal monitoring. **A**, **B**, Doppler ultrasound sensors for external assessment of the fetal heart rate. In this model, twins can be assessed simultaneously. **C**, External uterine activity sensor. Note the pressure-sensitive button in the center. (Courtesy of Corometrics Medical Systems, Inc., Wallingford, Conn.)

Electronic Fetal Monitoring Equipment

Electronic fetal monitoring equipment consists of the bedside monitor unit and sensors for fetal heart rate and uterine activity. Sensors may be either internal or external. Additional equipment may include data entry devices, remote units, and computer interfaces.

Bedside Monitor Unit

The bedside monitor unit receives information about the fetal heart rate and uterine activity from the external or internal sensors. It processes the information and provides output in the form of a digital display and a printed strip (Fig. 14–2). The unit has a channel for the fetal heart rate and one for uterine activity. Many newer models have another channel to record a second fetal heart rate in a twin pregnancy.

Paper Strip

Data about the fetal heart rate and uterine activity are printed on a Z-fold paper strip having a horizontal grid for each set of data (Fig. 14–3). There are minor variations in monitor paper from different suppliers.

The paper speed most commonly used in the United States is 3 cm/minute. A full paper pack contains 8 hours of recording time at this speed. A colored or hatched line between the two grids warns that the paper is nearly gone. When this line appears, about 20 minutes' worth of paper remains, depending on the manufacturer and paper speed.

The fetal heart rate is graphically recorded on the upper strip. The range of rates is from 30 to 240 BPM. The upper grid is divided by horizontal lines into 10-BPM segments, and the lines are labeled every 30 beats. Units with the ability to monitor two fetuses use the upper grid for both heart rates. The tracings are distinguished because one line is darker than the other.

Uterine activity is recorded on the lower grid as bell-shaped curves or small hills. The lower grid is also subdivided horizontally to record contraction intensity and uterine resting tone from 0 to 100 mmHg (using an intrauterine pressure catheter; see p. 339).

Vertical lines on both upper and lower grids are time divisions. At a paper speed of 3 cm/minute, dark vertical lines are 1 minute apart. Lighter lines subdivide the 1-minute divisions into six 10-second segments. The vertical time lines are used for timing contraction frequency and duration and identifying the fetal response in relation to the contractions.

A panel is one segment of paper between perforations, and each panel has 3 or 4 minutes of recording time, depending on the supplier. Each panel is numbered for identification and reassembly of a multipart strip.

Data Entry Devices

Most monitors print some notations automatically, such as the date, time, paper speed, and the devices being used to detect the fetal heart rate and uterine activity. Newer monitors may have data entry devices to enter data and print it on the strip. Small keypads or full keyboards allow information such as

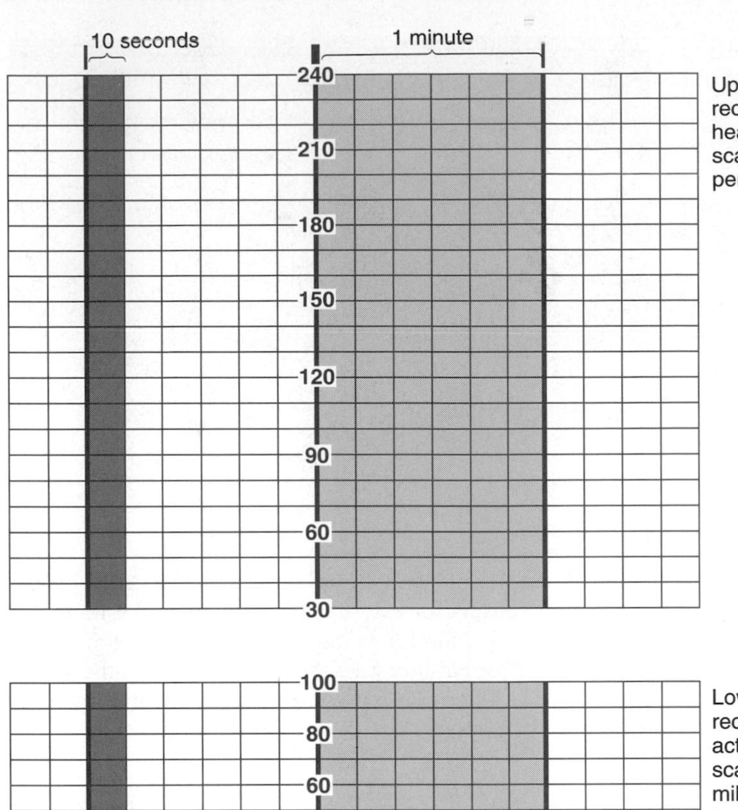

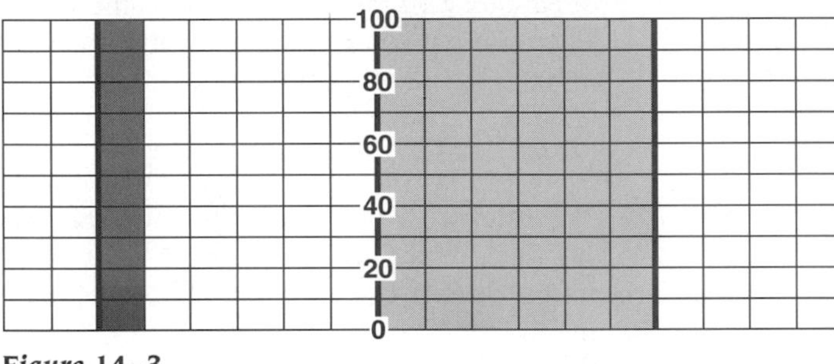

Figure 14–3

Paper strip for recording electronic fetal monitoring data. Each dark vertical line represents 1 minute, and each lighter vertical line represents 10 seconds.

vital signs, labor data, or procedures like vaginal examinations to be printed rather than handwritten.

Remote Surveillance

Some facilities have display units at the nursing station or other locations to allow surveillance when the nurse is not at the bedside. These units display the tracing on a screen and have settings for alerts, such as range of the heart rate, decelerations, or end of the paper.

Computer Interface

Computers are used increasingly with electronic fetal monitoring to help nurses manage the large amount of data generated during birth. Computer systems may alert the nursing staff about abnormal patterns and permanently store recordings. Other functions may include an electronic status board to keep track of all intrapartum clients.

Devices for External Fetal Monitoring 

Both the fetalheart rate and uterine activity can be monitored by external sensing devices, or transducers. External devices are secured on the mother's abdomen by elastic straps, a tube of wide stockinette, or an adhesive ring (Fig. 14–4). External devices are less accurate than internal ones but are non-invasive; they do not require ruptured membranes or cervical dilation. External devices are used in the antepartum period for some fetal tests as well as during the intrapartum period (see Chapter 10). Procedure 14–1 contains instructions for using the external electronic fetal monitor.

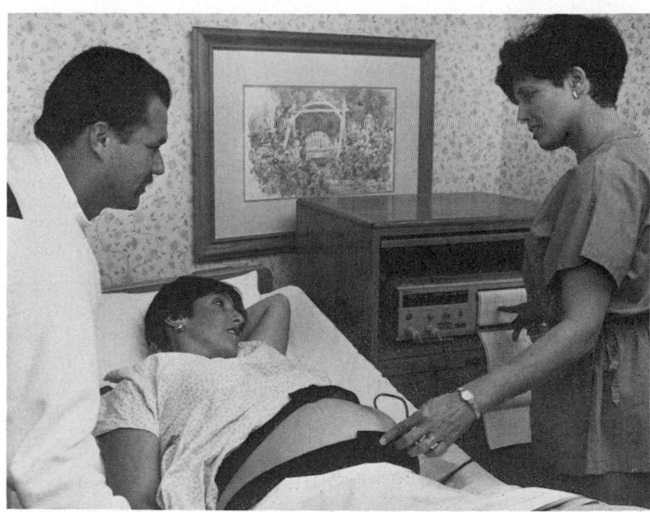

Figure 14–4

The nurse teaches a couple about the external fetal monitor. Note that the uterine activity transducer is on the mother's upper abdomen, in the fundal area. The Doppler transducer for sensing the fetal heart rate is placed on her lower abdomen, the usual site when the fetus is in the cephalic presentation.

FETAL HEART RATE MONITORING WITH AN ULTRASOUND TRANSDUCER

A Doppler ultrasound transducer detects fetal heart movement to calculate the rate. The transducer sends high-frequency sound waves into the uterus. The sound waves are reflected, and the monitor's computer calculates the fetal heart rate based on the movement sensed.

Fetal heart motion does not always correlate with electrical heart activity (the QRS complex on an electrocardiograph). Other movements such as fetal or maternal activity or blood flow through the umbilical cord and the woman's aorta also can be detected. Most monitors today ignore these extraneous sounds to provide a cleaner tracing.

The Doppler transducer produces a two-part muffled sound resembling galloping horses. The two closely linked sounds represent closure of the heart valves during systole (mitral and tricuspid valves) and diastole (aortic and pulmonic valves). Fetal or maternal activity produces a rough, erratic sound rather than the crisp, rhythmic sound characteristic of the fetal heart.

UTERINE ACTIVITY MONITORING WITH A TOCOTRANSDUCER

A tocotransducer (also called a tocodynamometer or simply a "toco") with a pressure-sensitive area detects changes in abdominal contour to measure uterine activity. The uterus pushes outward against the mother's anterior abdominal wall with each contraction. The monitor calculates changes in this signal and prints them as bell shapes on the lower grid of the strip. Uterine activity assessed by external or internal monitors is not accompanied by sound as the fetal heart rate is.

Movement other than uterine activity also registers on the monitor. For example, maternal respirations cause the uterine activity line to have a zigzag appearance. Sudden fetal or maternal movements appear as spikes on the uterine activity tracing.

Because uterine activity is sensed through the woman's abdomen, it is useful for observing the frequency and duration of contractions. It does not accurately measure actual contraction intensity and uterine resting tone. Several factors affect apparent intensity as printed on the strip.

- *Fetal size.* A small fetus prevents the uterus from pushing firmly against the abdominal wall with each contraction, making contractions appear less intense.
- *Abdominal fat thickness.* A thick layer of abdominal fat absorbs energy from uterine contractions, reducing the apparent intensity on the printed strip. The uterine activity recording of a thin woman whose uterus rotates sharply anteriorly with each contraction may appear to be more intense than it actually is.
- *Maternal position.* Different maternal positions may increase or decrease the pressure against the transducer.
- *Location of the transducer.* Uterine activity is best detected where it is strongest and where the fetus lies close to the uterine wall. This is usually over the fundus. Changes in abdominal contour may not be detectable if the transducer is located elsewhere.

Devices for Internal Fetal Monitoring

Accuracy is the main advantage of using internal devices for electronic fetal monitoring. However, their use requires ruptured membranes and about 2 cm of cervical dilation. The devices are invasive, and there is a slightly increased risk of infection. With the exception of the permanent cords used to connect them to the bedside unit, internal fetal monitoring devices are available as disposable, single-use items.

Procedure 14–1 External Fetal Monitor

Purpose: To properly apply the electronic fetal monitor.
To perform a basic evaluation of the fetal heart rate and uterine activity patterns to identify data needing further assessment by the experienced nurse, physician, or nurse-midwife.

1. **Read instruction manual for equipment.** *To become familiar with proper operation of the equipment and identify equipment.*

2. **Perform a function test following manufacturer's instructions. Press TEST button and observe for result. Common correct test results are:**
   a. Fetal heart rate: The monitor prints a line at 120, 150, or 200 BPM, depending on the model.
   b. Uterine activity: The monitor adds 50 to uterine activity display. *A correct function test assures that the bedside monitor unit is calibrated properly so that caregivers are assured of accurate data to interpret. Each manufacturer sets standards for indicators of proper function.*

3. **Explain the basic procedure of electronic fetal monitoring to the woman and her partner or family. Vary instructions according to equipment being used and hospital protocols. A sample is:**
   a. The electronic fetal monitor does not mean that you or the baby has a problem. It is the way we normally assess the baby's response to labor contractions.
   b. Two belts will go around your abdomen, one for the fetal heart rate sensor and one for uterine activity.
   c. Feel free to move with monitor on. If the tracing is poor, we can adjust the sensors. *Knowledge decreases the woman's fear of the unknown. Teaching her that she can move with the monitor in place enhances her comfort and promotes normal labor.*

4. **Apply belts or stockinette:**
   a. Slide both belts under the woman's back without the sensors attached. Be sure to keep belts smooth under her back.
   b. Cut a length of stockinette tubing about 15 to 18 inches long for the average sized woman. Cut a longer length of wide stockinette for a heavier woman. Slide the stockinette up from her feet to her abdomen. *A smooth application of straps or stockinette will enhance a woman's comfort and improve contact of external sensors with her abdomen. Good contact improves the quality of the tracing and may reduce the number of adjustments needed.*

5. **Use Leopold's maneuvers, (see Procedure 13–1) to locate the fetus' back. During early labor, this will usually be in the left or right lower quadrant of the woman's abdomen. During later labor, the fetal back will usually be nearer the woman's abdominal midline.** *The fetal heart rate is best detected through the back of the fetus. If the fetus is not engaged or is in a breech presentation, the fetal heart rate will probably be found higher on the woman's abdomen.*

6. **Apply ultrasound gel to the Doppler ultrasound transducer and place it on the woman's abdomen at the approximate location of the fetus' back. Move the transducer until a clear signal is heard. Most bedside units have a green light or flashing heart shape to indicate a good signal.** *Gel improves transmission and reception of the ultrasound waves to provide more accurate data. The Doppler ultrasound transducer senses fetal heart motion to compute the rate. A clear signal is needed to distinguish the fetal heart movement from other movement.*

7. **Place the uterine activity sensor in the fundus area, or the area where contractions feel the strongest when palpated. This will often be slightly above the umbilicus. When the woman has a contraction, observe the tracing for the bell shape. The line for uterine activity will be jagged because it also senses the rise and fall of the abdomen with breathing. Fetal or maternal movement will cause a spike in the line. Observe through several contractions.** *The external uterine activity monitor senses the change in the abdominal contour as the uterus rotates anteriorly with each contraction. Contractions are usually best perceived in the fundus of the uterus. Observation of the uterine activity line (on the lower paper grid) through several contractions verifies correct placement and identifies needed position changes.*

8. **Observe the strip for baseline fetal heart rate, presence of long-term variability, periodic changes, and uterine activity (contraction duration and frequency). Palpate contractions for intensity and relaxation between contractions. Notify the experienced nurse and physician or nurse-midwife of non-reassuring patterns.** *Identifies reassuring and non-reassuring fetal heart rate patterns (see Table 14–2). Contractions having a frequency greater than every 2 minutes, duration longer than 90 seconds, or incomplete uterine relaxation between contractions may reduce maternal blood flow into the intervillous spaces and impair exchange of oxygen and waste products. The external uterine activity sensor is useful only for contraction frequency and duration. It is not accurate for actual intensity or uterine resting tone.*

FETAL HEART RATE MONITORING WITH A SCALP ELECTRODE

The fetal scalp electrode (or spiral electrode) detects electrical signals from the fetal heart in a manner similar to that of an electrocardiograph (ECG) (Fig. 14–5). The monitor calculates the rate by measuring the time from one R wave of the QRS complex to the next and plots it on the strip. Fetal or maternal movement does not interfere with accuracy because the rate is calculated from electrical events in the fetal heart. The monitor unit generates a beeping sound with each fetal heart beat.

Although called a fetal scalp electrode, it also can be applied to the buttocks in a breech presentation. Areas to avoid for electrode application are the fetal face, fontanelles, and genitals.

Two wires from the electrode protrude from the mother's vagina and are attached to a leg plate to secure them. Older monitors require the use of electrocardiographic paste on the leg plate, which is then attached to the monitor by a cord.

Because it barely penetrates the fetal skin (about 1 mm), the electrode is easily displaced. The tracing will then be erratic or will stop if the electrode is fully detached. Secure attachment of the electrode is often difficult if the fetus has abundant hair. The electrode is removed by turning it counterclockwise about 1½ turns until it detaches.

UTERINE ACTIVITY MONITORING WITH AN INTRAUTERINE PRESSURE CATHETER

Two kinds of intrauterine pressure catheters can be used to measure uterine activity, including contraction intensity and resting tone:

- A hollow, fluid-filled catheter that connects to a pressure transducer on the bedside monitor unit
- A solid catheter with a pressure transducer in its tip (Fig. 14–6); this catheter may have an additional lumen for amnioinfusion.

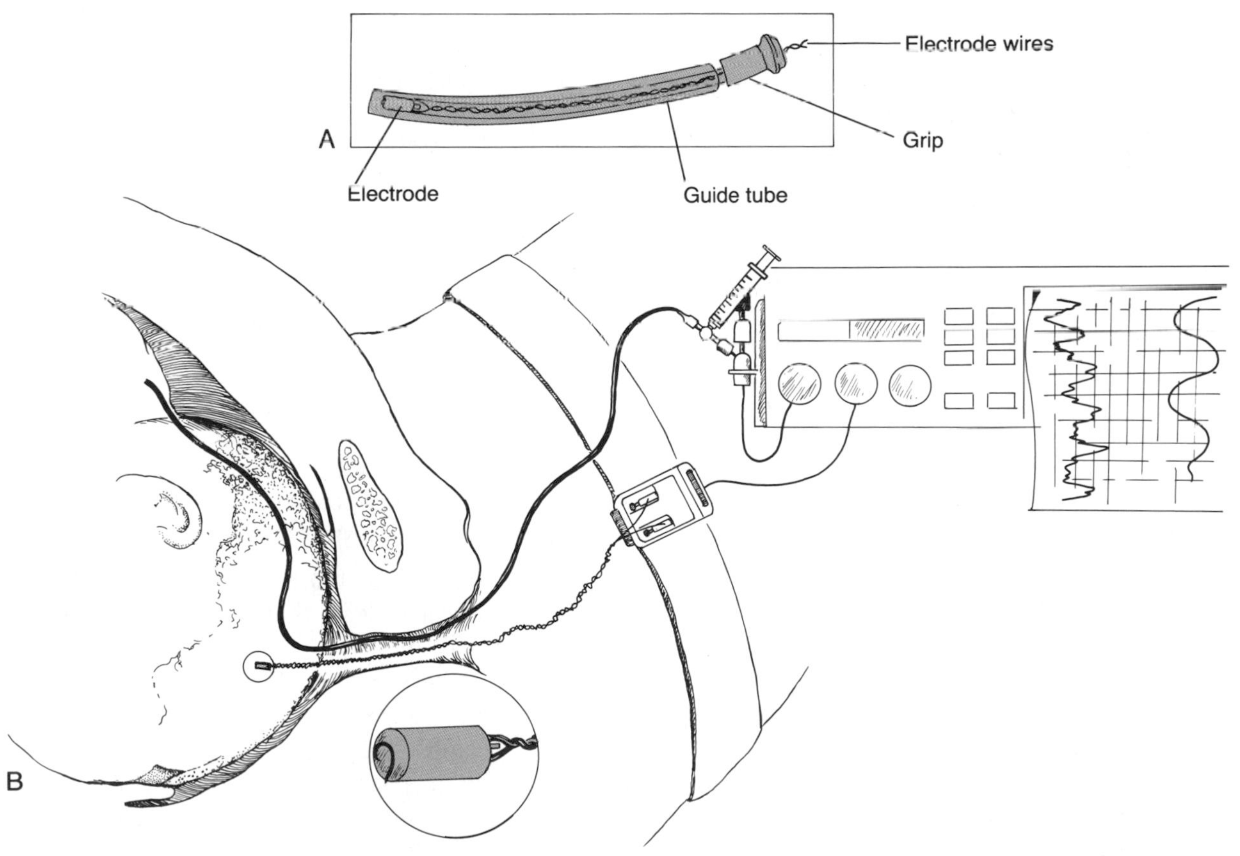

Figure 14–5

Internal spiral electrode and intrauterine pressure catheter. **A**, Parts of the fetal scalp electrode before it is applied. **B**, Fetal scalp electrode and intrauterine pressure catheter in place and connected to the bedside monitor unit.

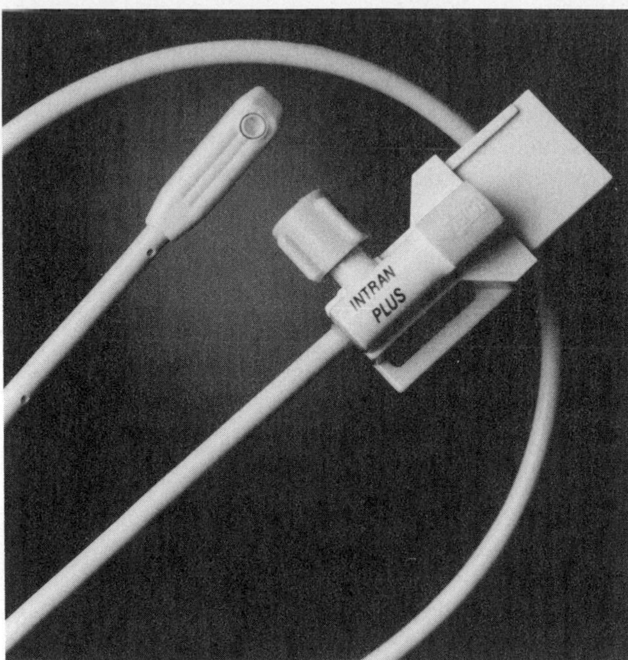

Figure 14–6

Solid intrauterine pressure catheter with transducer in its tip. This model also has a lumen for amnioinfusion. (Courtesy of Utah Medical Products, Midvale, Utah.)

Both types reflect intrauterine pressure and increases in intra-abdominal pressure, such as with coughing or vomiting. They translate these pressures into an electrical signal that is processed and printed on the lower grid of the strip.

The tip of the fluid-filled catheter in the uterus should be at the level of the transducer on the outside for best accuracy. If the tip is lower than the transducer, the recorded pressure will be lower than the actual intrauterine pressure. If the tip is higher, the recorded pressure may be artificially high. Changes in the mother's position may alter the height of the catheter tip, requiring adjustment of the transducer's height.

The solid catheter is not affected by height because its transducer is in the catheter. However, the sensor in its tip measures hydrostatic pressure from the amniotic fluid above the fetal presenting part as well as the pressure from uterine activity. Therefore, intrauterine pressures from the solid catheter may be higher than those from the fluid-filled catheter.

Both catheters must be "zeroed" to compensate for atmospheric pressure. The fluid-filled catheter can be zeroed any time, but the solid catheter must be zeroed before insertion and cannot be calibrated again.

✔ Check Your Reading

6. What are the advantages and limitations of each fetal monitoring method?
7. Which grid on the paper strip of the electronic fetal monitor is used to record the fetal heart rate? Uterine activity?
8. Which electronic fetal monitoring sensor uses heart motion to measure fetal heart rate?
9. What are some variables that can affect the accuracy of the external uterine activity sensor?
10. What are the two types of internal uterine activity catheters? Which one is affected by its height in relation to the mother's position?

Evaluating Electronic Fetal Monitoring Strips

A consistent, organized approach to the analysis of fetal monitor patterns ensures completeness. The nurse evaluates the fetal heart rate for baseline, variability, and presence of periodic changes. Uterine activity is evaluated by determining the frequency, duration, and intensity of contractors, and by assessing uterine resting tone. Fetal heart rate and uterine activity patterns must be evaluated together.

Other data are relevant to strip interpretation, such as maternal vital signs, maternal position, drug or oxygen administration, character of the amniotic fluid, labor status, and procedures performed. These are customarily recorded on the strip as well as in the labor record.

Fetal Heart Rate Baseline

The fetal heart rate baseline is the most consistent heart rate, excluding segments occurring during contractions or periodic (temporary and recurrent) changes. It is composed of rate and variability. The baseline rate is classified as:

- *Normal*: 110 to 160 BPM (NAACOG, 1990)
- *Bradycardia*: less than 110 BPM, persisting at least 10 minutes
- *Tachycardia*: greater than 160 BPM, persisting at least 10 minutes

Some healthy term fetuses have bradycardia between 100 and 110 BPM with no other signs of compromise. A normal preterm fetus may have a baseline rate slightly higher than a term fetus (about 130 to 170 BPM) because the parasympathetic nervous system is immature.

Baseline Fetal Heart Rate Variability

Variability is defined as the fluctuations in the fetal heart rate that cause the printed line to have a rough, rather than smooth, appearance (Fig. 14–7). The presence of variability is reassuring because it suggests that multiple inputs that speed and slow the heart rate are balanced. Variability has both long-term and short-term components. It is most accurately assessed with the fetal scalp electrode because the ultrasound seeks movement and tends to exaggerate the appearance of variability.

Variability is a significant component of the fetal heart rate tracing on the electronic monitor for two reasons:

- Adequate oxygenation promotes normal function of the autonomic nervous system and helps the fetus adapt to the stress of labor
- Variability is an important indicator of fetal oxygenation because it indirectly reflects the function of the fetal autonomic nervous system

LONG-TERM VARIABILITY

Long-term variability describes the rhythmic waves of the entire printed line. There are normally three to five waves per minute. The difference between the lowest and highest rates is the range of long-term variability. A long-term variability range of 3 to 25 BPM is reassuring and suggests that the fetus does not have metabolic acidosis (Murray, 1988). There is no universal agreement for classifying long-term variability, and birth facilities should develop classifications for their staff to use consistently. One system uses four levels:

Range of Variability	Classification
0–2 BPM	Absent
3–5 BPM	Minimal
6–25 BPM	Moderate
>25 BPM	Marked

Long-term variability is normally decreased during fetal sleep, which usually lasts no longer than 20 to 30 minutes at a time.

SHORT-TERM VARIABILITY

Short-term variability, or beat-to-beat variability, describes changes in the fetal heart rate from one beat to the next, or rate changes on a beat-to-beat basis. It can be confirmed only with a fetal scalp electrode. A common guideline is this: A pattern that does not

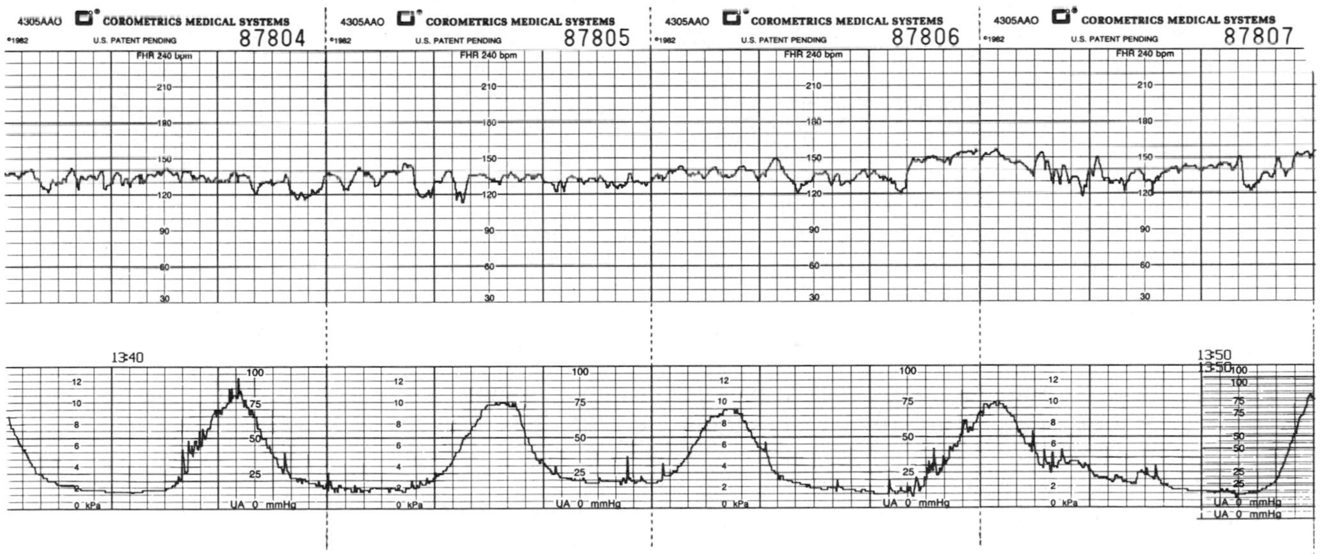

Figure 14–7

Electronic fetal monitor strip showing a reassuring pattern of fetal heart rate (FHR) and uterine activity. The FHR baseline is 130 to 140 beats per minute (BPM), variability is about 10 BPM. There are no periodic changes in this strip. Contraction frequency is about every 2 to 3 minutes, intensity is 75 to 90 mmHg with the internal spiral electrode, and uterine resting tone is about 10 mmHg. (Courtesy of Corometrics Medical Systems, Inc., Wallingford, Conn. Redrawn with permission.)

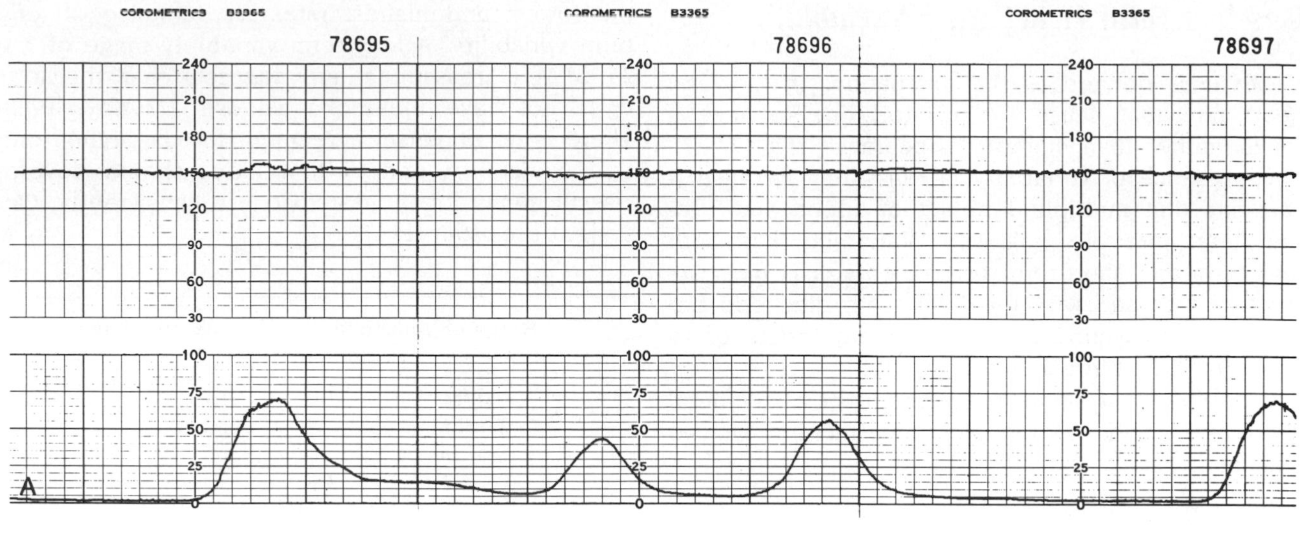

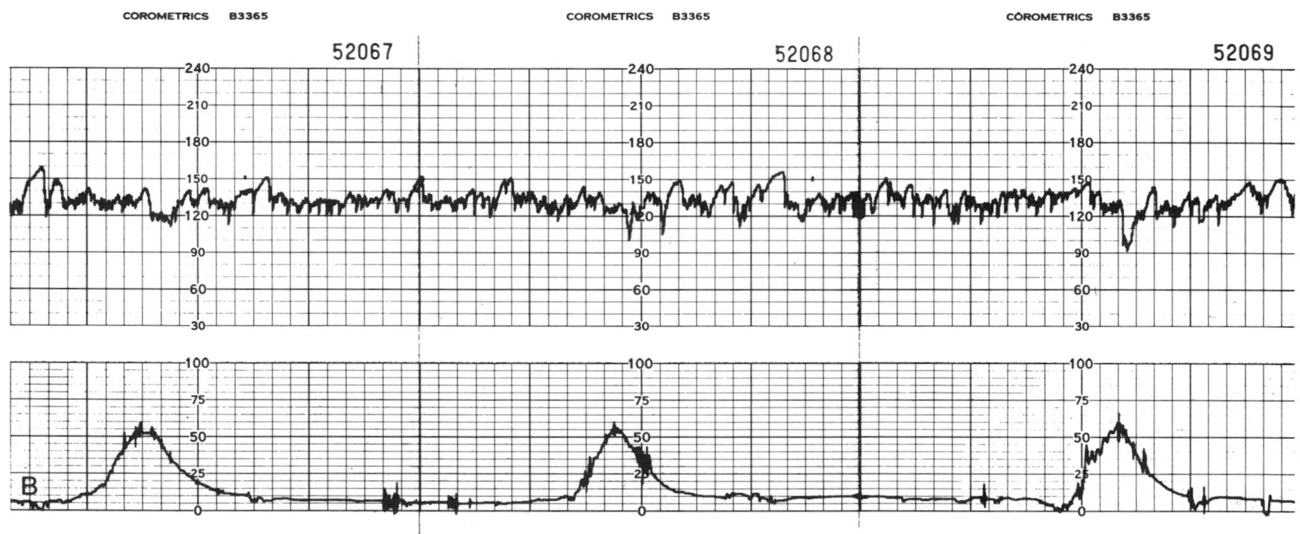

Figure 14–8

Contrasts in fetal heart rate variability. A fetal scalp electrode is being used. **A**, Minimal to absent variability (less than 3 BPM). Note the smooth, flat line in the FHR channel. **B**, Increased variability (about 20 BPM). Note the marked zigzag appearance of the fetal heart rate line. (Courtesy of Corometrics Medical Systems, Inc., Wallingford, Conn. Redrawn with permission.)

look reassuring with the external fetal heart rate monitor is probably less reassuring when an internal device is used. Figure 14–8 illustrates strips having absent and increased variability.

A normal (3 to 7 BPM) or increased (more than 7 BPM) range of short-term variability reassures one of fetal well-being. Evaluation of short-term variability is an important way to clarify how a fetus is responding to the stress of labor. Presence of short-term variability (at least 3 BPM) suggests that a fetus is compensating for the stresses and maintaining normal oxygenation and acid-base balance (ACOG, 1989a; Chez et al, 1990; Davis, 1992).

Periodic Patterns in the Fetal Heart Rate

Periodic patterns are transient and recurrent changes from the baseline rate associated with uterine contractions. They include accelerations and decelerations.

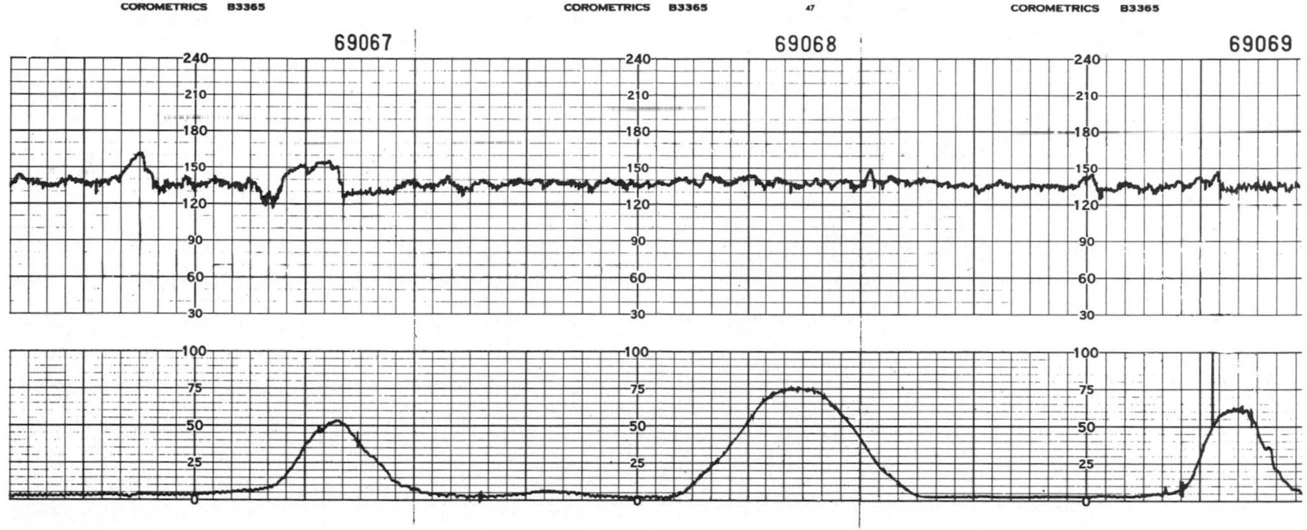

Figure 14–9

Accelerations of the fetal heart rate. (Courtesy of Corometrics Medical Systems, Inc., Wallingford, Conn. Redrawn with permission.)

ACCELERATIONS

An acceleration is a brief, temporary increase in the fetal heart rate of at least 15 beats above the baseline, usually lasting 15 to 20 seconds (Chez et al, 1990; ACOG, 1989a). Accelerations usually occur with fetal movement. They may be non-periodic (having no relation to contractions) as well as periodic. They may occur with vaginal examinations, uterine contractions, and mild cord compression and when the fetus is in a breech presentation. Accelerations are a reassuring sign, reflecting a responsive, non-acidotic fetus (Fig. 14–9).

DECELERATIONS

Periodic decelerations are classified into three types based on their relationship to uterine contractions.

Early Decelerations. Fetal head compression alters cerebral blood flow, causing the vagus nerve to slow the heart rate. Early decelerations are not associated with fetal compromise and require no intervention. They occur *during* contractions, usually during the active phase of labor, as the fetal head is pressed against the woman's pelvis or soft tissues, such as the cervix.

Early decelerations are consistent in appearance; they are uniform in that one early deceleration looks

Critical to Remember

Differences Between Early and Late Decelerations

Early Decelerations

- Occur only during contractions as the fetal head is compressed
- Return to the baseline fetal heart rate by the end of the contraction
- Are mirror images of the contraction (brief contraction = brief early deceleration)
- Are not associated with fetal compromise and require no added interventions

Late Decelerations

- Look similar to early decelerations but begin well after the contraction begins (often near the peak)
- Do not return to baseline until after the end of the contraction
- Reflect impaired placental exchange or uteroplacental insufficiency
- The degree of fall in rate from baseline is not related to the amount of uteroplacental insufficiency
- Should be addressed by nursing interventions to improve placental blood flow and fetal oxygen supply

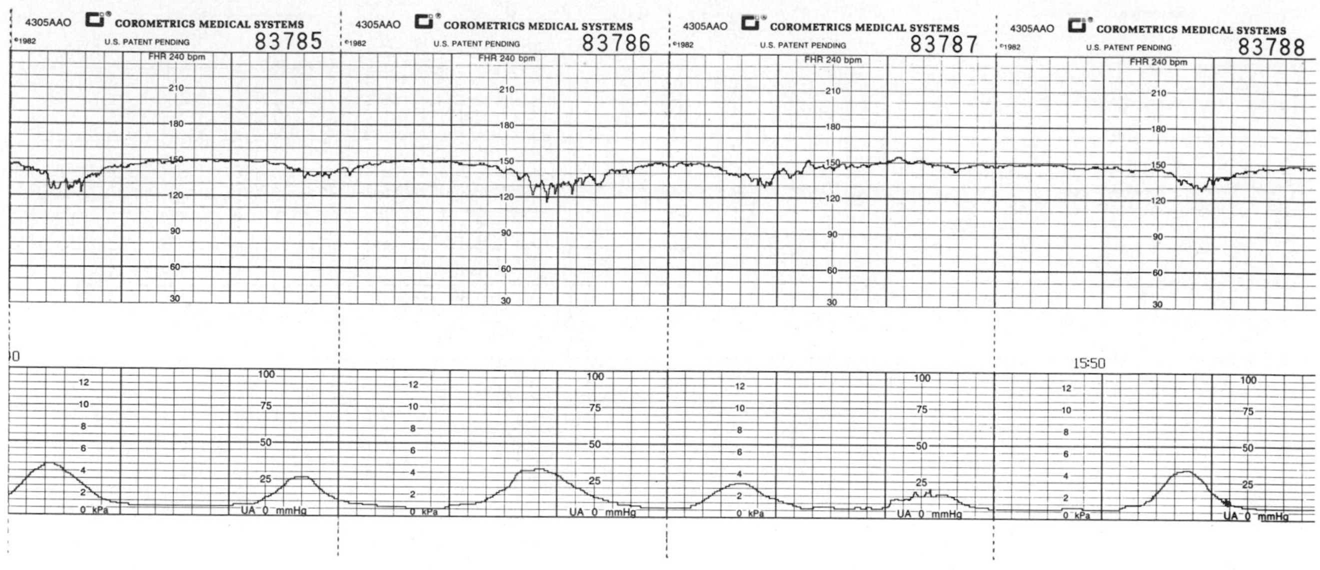

***Figure* 14–10**

Early decelerations. Note that the slowing of the fetal heart rate mirrors the contraction. It begins near the beginning of the contraction and returns to the baseline by the end of the contraction. Cause: fetal head compression. (Courtesy of Corometrics Medical Systems, Inc., Wallingford, Conn.)

similar to others. They mirror the contraction, beginning near its onset and returning to the baseline by the end of the contraction (Fig. 14–10). The rate at the lowest point of the deceleration usually remains above 100 BPM.

Late Decelerations. Deficient placental exchange (uteroplacental insufficiency) may result in a pattern of late decelerations. The cause of uteroplacental insufficiency may be acute, such as maternal hypotension secondary to regional block anesthesia (see p. 372). It may also occur with chronic conditions that impair placental exchange, such as maternal hypertension or diabetes. Repeated late decelerations or those accompanied by decreased variability or an increasing baseline rate are more likely to be associated with fetal compromise (ACOG, 1989a).

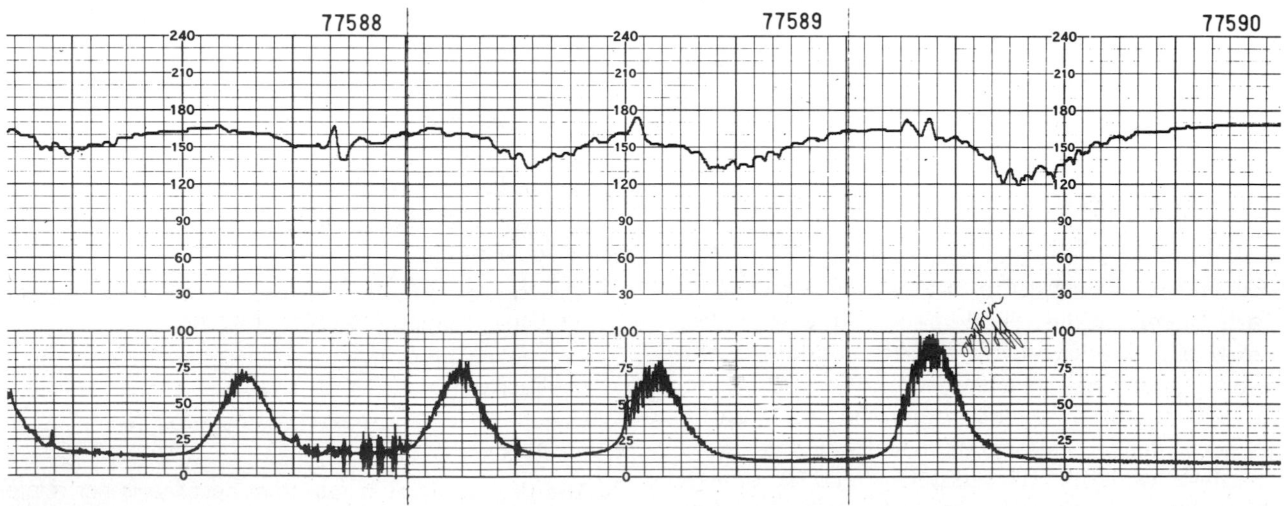

***Figure* 14–11**

Late decelerations. Note that the decelerations look similar to early decelerations but are offset to the right. They begin at about the peak of the contraction and do not return to the baseline until after the contraction ends. Cause: uteroplacental insufficiency. (Courtesy of Corometrics Medical Systems, Inc., Wallingford, Conn. Redrawn with permission.)

Late decelerations look similar to early decelerations but are shifted to the right in relation to the contraction. They return to baseline after the end of the contraction (Fig. 14–11). They have a consistent appearance. The fetal heart rate may remain in the normal range and may not fall much below its baseline level. The amount of rate decrease from the baseline does not indicate how much uteroplacental insufficiency exists.

Variable Decelerations. Conditions that restrict flow through the umbilical cord may result in variable decelerations. These decelerations do not have the uniform appearance of early and late decelerations. Their shape, duration, and degree of fall below baseline rate is variable. They fall and rise abruptly with the onset and relief of cord compression, unlike the gradual fall and rise of early and late decelerations (Fig. 14–12). Variable decelerations also may be non-periodic, occurring at times unrelated to contractions.

Short (under 30 seconds) rate accelerations that precede and follow variable decelerations are a reassuring sign. These "shoulders" represent a fetus' ability to compensate for the hemodynamic changes occurring with umbilical cord compression. Prolonged, smooth-appearing accelerations after variable decelerations ("overshoot") are not reassuring because they suggest that the fetus is not compensating for the changes occurring with cord compression.

Several methods are used to classify variable decelerations according to depth and duration, but there is no uniform agreement. One guideline suggests that variable decelerations are significant when the fetal heart rate repeatedly decreases to less than 70 BPM and persists at that level for at least 60 seconds (ACOG, 1989a).

Uterine Activity

Assessment of uterine activity has four components: frequency, duration, and intensity of the contractions, and uterine resting tone. Contraction frequency may be measured with the electronic monitor the same way as with palpation (beginning of one contraction to beginning of the next) or from peak to peak. Duration is calculated from the beginning to end of each contraction.

Assessing contraction intensity depends on the method of monitoring. Palpation is used to estimate intensity and resting tone when an external uterine activity monitor is used (see Procedure 13-3). Contraction intensity is described as mild, moderate, or strong. The uterus should relax fully between contractions for 60 seconds or longer.

With the intrauterine pressure catheter, the scale on the paper is used to describe intensity and resting tone. Intensity increases as labor progresses.

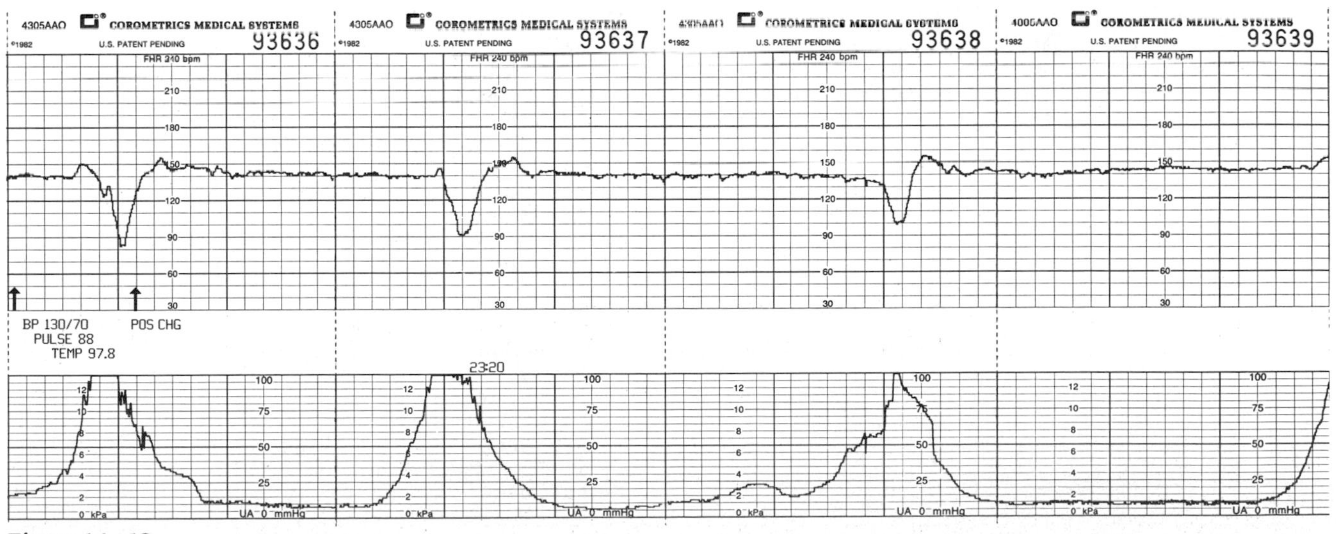

Figure 14–12

Variable decelerations. The decelerations are sharp in onset and offset. Note slight rate accelerations (shoulders) after each variable deceleration. Cause: umbilical cord compression. (Courtesy of Corometrics Medical Systems, Inc., Wallingford, Conn. Redrawn with permission.)

Table 14–2 REASSURING AND NON-REASSURING FETAL HEART RATE PATTERNS

Reassuring Patterns

Baseline rate: Stable between 110 and 160 BPM
Long-term variability: Variation in rate between 3 and 25 BPM with at least 3 cyclic changes/minute
Short-term variability (fetal scalp electrode): At least 3 BPM
Accelerations with fetal movement: At least 15 BPM above the baseline for at least 15 seconds
Uterine activity:
- Contraction frequency: no more frequent than every 2 minutes
- Contraction duration: no longer than 90 seconds
- Interval between contractions: at least 60 seconds
- Uterine resting tone: uterus relaxed between contractions (with external monitor); uterine resting tone <20 mmHg (with intrauterine pressure catheter)

Non-reassuring Patterns

Pattern and Description	Possible Etiology
Tachycardia	
Baseline FHR >160 BPM for at least 10 minutes Mild: 161–180 BPM Severe: Greater than 181 BPM	Maternal or fetal fever (fetal tachycardia may be the first sign of an intrauterine infection) Maternal dehydration Maternal or fetal hypoxia Fetal acidosis Maternal or fetal hypovolemia Fetal cardiac arrhythmias Maternal severe anemia Maternal hyperthyroidism Drugs administered to mother (such as terbutaline)
Bradycardia	
Baseline FHR <110 BPM for at least 10 minutes Baseline rates between 100 and 110 BPM are usually not associated with fetal compromise if there are no non-reassuring patterns	Fetal head compression Fetal hypoxia Fetal acidosis Fetal heart block Umbilical cord compression Second-stage labor with maternal pushing
Decreased or Absent Variability	
FHR baseline has a smooth, flat appearance Long-term variability: range of fluctuations <3 BPM or fewer than three cyclic changes/minute Short-term variability (fetal scalp electrode): <3 BPM	Fetal sleep (usually decreases long-term variability and lasts no longer than 30 minutes at a time) Fetal hypoxia with acidosis Drug effects: CNS depressants Local anesthetic agents
Late Decelerations	
Recurrent decelerations with a uniform appearance and a consistent relation to the contraction; begin after the contraction starts (usually at the peak) and do not return to baseline until after the contraction ends	Uteroplacental insufficiency, which may be secondary to: Maternal hypotension Excess uterine activity Placental interruption, such as abruptio placentae or placenta previa Pregnancy-induced or chronic hypertension Maternal diabetes Maternal severe anemia Maternal cardiac disease
Variable Decelerations	
Sharp in onset and offset Appearance and relationship to contractions is not consistent, may occur as a non-periodic pattern (randomly)	Umbilical cord compression, which may be secondary to: Prolapsed cord Nuchal cord (around fetal neck) Oligohydramnios (abnormally small amount of amniotic fluid) Cord between fetus and mother's uterus or pelvis, without obvious prolapse Cord between fetal body parts Knot in cord

Abbreviations: BPM, beats per minute; FHR, fetal heart rate.

Uterine contraction intensity with the intrauterine pressure catheter is about 50 to 75 mmHg during labor, although it may reach 110 mmHg with pushing during the second stage. If the intensity exceeds 100 mmHg, the printed contraction pattern will have a flat top because the graph stops at 100 mmHg. Average resting tone is 5 to 15 mmHg.

Significance of Fetal Heart Rate Patterns

Fetal heart rate patterns on the electronic monitor are classified as either "reassuring" or "non-reassuring." In between these two classifications are those patterns that are "equivocal"— neither clearly reassuring nor clearly non-reassuring. For equivocal (ambiguous) patterns, several methods may be used to further evaluate the fetal condition. Table 14–2 presents a summary of reassuring and non-reassuring patterns.

Reassuring Patterns

Fetal heart rate patterns are reassuring if they show signs usually associated with fetal well-being. No intervention is necessary because the pattern suggests that the fetus is compensating for intrapartum stressors.

Non-reassuring Patterns

Non-reassuring patterns occur if favorable signs are absent or if signs that are associated with fetal hypoxia or acidosis are present. Non-reassuring patterns do not necessarily indicate that fetal hypoxia or acidosis, or both, have occurred. Electronic fetal monitoring best identifies the well-oxygenated fetus; it less reliably identifies the compromised fetus. Thus, electronic fetal monitoring is a screening rather than a diagnostic tool.

Non-reassuring patterns are more significant if they occur together and are persistent. For example, bradycardia with short-term variability of less than 3 BPM and late decelerations suggests greater fetal compromise than bradycardia alone. The healthy fetus may demonstrate an occasional late deceleration, but a persistent pattern of late decelerations is more likely to represent a fetus that may be compromised. Non-reassuring patterns include but are not limited to tachycardia, bradycardia, decreased or absent variability, late decelerations, variable decelerations falling to less than 70 BPM for longer than 60 seconds, prolonged decelerations, and hypertonic uterine activity.

Non-reassuring patterns do not always indicate that labor should end immediately, usually by cesarean birth. Several medical and nursing interventions may be used to establish the fetal condition, identify the probable cause of the non-reassuring pattern, and increase fetal oxygenation.

CLARIFICATION OF DATA

Fetal heart rate patterns are sometimes ambiguous and do not clearly suggest a healthy, compensating fetus. Four methods may clarify data and establish fetal well-being. Three methods are used during the intrapartum period: (1) fetal scalp stimulation (2) vibroacoustic stimulation, and (3) fetal scalp blood sampling. A fourth method, analysis of umbilical cord blood gases and pH is done immediately after birth.

Fetal Scalp Stimulation. Scalp stimulation evaluates the fetus' response to tactile stimulation (Fig. 14–13). It may be done by the nurse, physician, or nurse-midwife. The examiner applies pressure to the scalp (or other presenting part) with a gloved finger or fingers and sweeps the fingers in a circular motion. A fetal heart rate acceleration of 15 BPM for at least 15 seconds is a reassuring response, suggesting a fetus in normal oxygen and acid-base balance. The acceleration may be delayed rather than immediate.

Fetal scalp stimulation is not done in some cases. These situations are essentially those in which vaginal examination would be limited:

- Preterm fetus (may cause contractions)
- Prolonged rupture of membranes (higher risk of infection)
- Chorioamnionitis (intrauterine infection)
- Maternal fever of unknown origin (with the possibility of introducing microorganisms into the uterus)

Vibroacoustic Stimulation. Acoustic, or vibroacoustic, stimulation may be used by the nurse, physician, or nurse-midwife to supplement fetal scalp stimulation or if scalp stimulation is contraindicated.

An artificial larynx is applied to the mother's lower abdomen, and it is turned on for up to 3 seconds. The reassuring response is the same as with fetal scalp stimulation: acceleration of 15 BPM for 15 seconds. An absent response, however, does not necessarily mean the fetus is hypoxic or acidotic.

Concerns about the loudness of the electronic larynx have led to the use of other methods to induce fetal heart rate accelerations. Methods that have been used include vibration with an electric tooth-

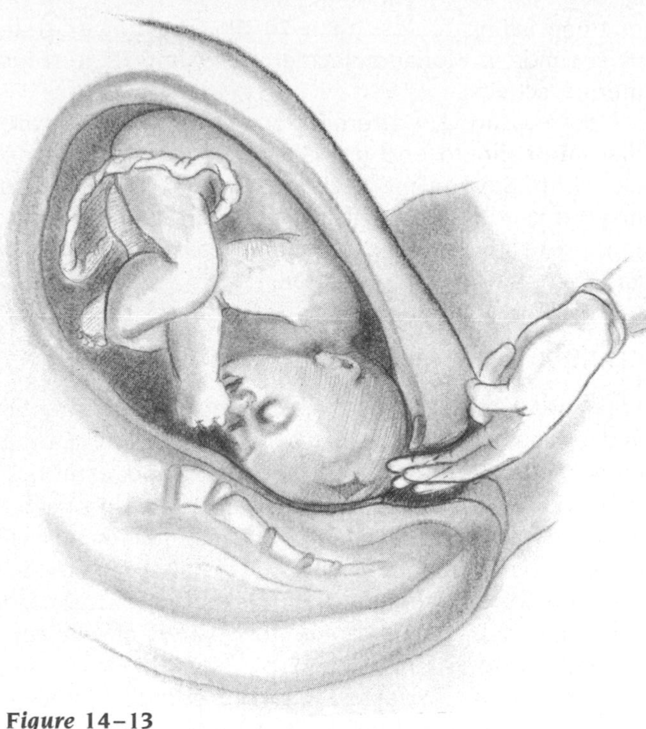

Figure 14–13

Fetal scalp stimulation.

brush and placing radio speakers on the woman's abdomen while playing music.

Fetal Scalp Blood Sampling. Occasionally, the physician may obtain a sample of fetal scalp blood to evaluate the pH. Because this procedure is more complex than scalp stimulation or vibroacoustic stimulation, it is not often done. Normal scalp pH is 7.25 to 7.35. Acidosis is present if the pH is less than 7.2, and the clinician may hasten the birth by using forceps or cesarean delivery. The scalp sample is usually repeated for a borderline pH of 7.2 to 7.24 to verify its accuracy.

Cord Blood Gases and pH. Umbilical cord blood analysis is used to assess the infant's status immediately after birth for oxygenation and acid-base balance. The samples are analyzed for pH, PCO_2, PO_2 and bicarbonate and base deficit. This information helps guide the pediatrician in the most appropriate care of the infant by identifying whether acidosis exists and whether it is respiratory, metabolic, or mixed. Normal cord blood gases and pH can confirm that the fetus was adjusting normally to the stresses of labor, although the fetal monitoring pattern may have been non-reassuring. (See a medical-surgical nursing text for further information about blood gases and acid-base balance.)

The cord is double-clamped and cut to isolate a 10- to 20-cm (4 to 8 inches) segment. Blood samples from an umbilical artery and/or vein are drawn into heparinized syringes to prevent coagulation and are capped to avoid altering values by exposure to room air (Fig. 14–14). Samples kept at room temperature are reliable for up to 60 minutes (ACOG, 1989b). Those kept in ice are reliable for up to 3 hours (Boylan and Parisi, 1989).

INTERVENTIONS FOR NON-REASSURING PATTERNS

Any of several nursing or medical interventions, or both, may be indicated if there is a non-reassuring fetal heart rate pattern. All are directed toward identifying the cause of the non-reassuring pattern and improving fetal oxygenation.

Identifying the Cause of a Non-reassuring Pattern. Careful examination of the strip may suggest a cause for the non-reassuring fetal heart rate pattern and direct the most appropriate interventions. For example, a pattern of late decelerations suggests uteroplacental insufficiency. However, uteroplacental insufficiency may be secondary to a variety of causes, such as maternal hypotension or excessive uterine activity. Different causes require different corrective interventions. Checking the mother's vital signs identifies hypotension, hypertension, or fever. Medications given to the woman may decrease or increase variability.

A vaginal examination may identify a prolapsed cord, which may cause variable decelerations or bradycardia, or both, as it is compressed. A vaginal examination also can determine the woman's labor status, which helps the physician's or nurse-midwife's decisions. For example, the clinician may allow labor

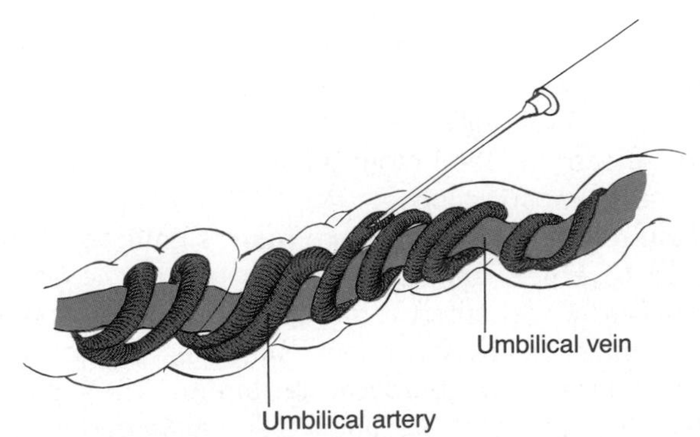

Figure 14–14

Obtaining a blood sample for umbilical cord blood gases and pH. Samples are drawn from the umbilical artery and/or vein. The samples in capped syringes may be kept for up to 60 minutes at room temperature and 3 hours on ice.

to continue or terminate labor with a forceps birth if a non-reassuring pattern occurs during late labor. If the same persistent non-reassuring pattern occurs during early labor, a cesarean birth is more likely to be chosen.

Internal monitoring is usually begun for greater accuracy if a non-reassuring pattern develops when external devices are used. The fetal scalp electrode is needed for a true picture of variability, a strong indicator of fetal condition. The physician or nurse-midwife may rupture the membranes to allow internal monitoring if they have not already ruptured when the non-reassuring pattern occurs.

Increasing Placental Perfusion. The expectant mother is positioned on her side to eliminate aortocaval compression, which may reduce placental blood flow. Increasing non-additive intravenous fluids such as lactated Ringer's solution increases the maternal blood volume to better perfuse the placenta.

Uterine activity reduces blood flow into the intervillous spaces, and a fetus with little reserve for stress may be unable to tolerate even normal contractions. Persistent hypertonic uterine activity may compromise a fetus with normal reserves. If a woman is receiving oxytocin, it is discontinued so that uterine activity is not stimulated. The physician may order an intravenous tocolytic drug to reduce uterine activity, such as magnesium sulfate, 2 g, or terbutaline, 0.25 mg (Staisch, 1992). (See Chapter 26 for discussion of tocolytic drugs.)

Increasing Maternal Blood Oxygen Saturation. Administration of 100 per cent oxygen through a snug face mask makes more oxygen available for transfer to the fetus. Recommendations for the flow rate of oxygen vary, but a commonly suggested rate is 8 to 10 L/minute.

Reducing Cord Compression. If cord compression is suspected, the woman is repositioned. She may be turned from side to side, or her hips may be elevated to shift the fetal presenting part toward her diaphragm. Several position changes may be required before the pattern improves or resolves.

Amnioinfusion increases the fluid around the fetus and cushions the cord. Warmed normal saline is infused into the uterus through an intrauterine pressure catheter. The underpads must be changed regularly because fluid will leak out constantly. Possible complications include overdistention of the uterus and increased uterine resting tone. These complications are relieved by releasing some of the excessive fluid. Amnioinfusion also may be used to wash out and dilute fluid that is stained heavily with meconium so that the infant does not aspirate it at birth.

Critical to Remember

Nursing Responses to Non-reassuring Fetal Heart Rate Patterns

1. Identify the cause of the non-reassuring pattern to plan the most applicable interventions:
   - Evaluate pattern for probable cause (late or variable decelerations, bradycardia or tachycardia, absent variability).
   - Evaluate maternal vital signs to identify hypotension, hypertension, or fever.
   - Perform vaginal examination to identify a prolapsed umbilical cord.
2. Stop oxytocin infusion, if being administered.
3. Reposition the woman, avoiding the supine position, for patterns associated with cord compression; repositioning may improve other non-reassuring patterns as well.
4. Increase the rate of a non-additive IV fluid to expand the mother's blood volume and improve placental perfusion.
5. Administer oxygen by face mask at 8 to 10 L/minute, or as directed by the birth facility's policy to increase her blood oxygen saturation, making more oxygen available to the fetus.
6. Initiate continuous electronic fetal monitoring with internal devices if safe and if permitted by physician, nurse-midwife, and facility policy.
7. Notify physician or nurse-midwife as soon as possible. Report and document the following:
   - The pattern that was identified.
   - Nursing interventions taken in response to the pattern.
   - The fetal response after nursing interventions.
   - The response of the physician or nurse-midwife (orders, other response).
8. If the non-reassuring pattern is severe, other staff members should begin preparing for immediate delivery (usually cesarean birth unless vaginal birth is imminent).

✔ Check Your Reading

11. What is the significance of fetal heart rate accelerations?
12. What are the differences between early and late decelerations? Which pattern is non-reassuring?
13. What do variable decelerations look like? What is their cause?
14. What is the rationale for performing fetal scalp stimulation or vibroacoustic stimulation? What is the expected fetal response to these actions?
15. What is the purpose for blood gas and pH determinations on cord blood samples?
16. What nursing actions are appropriate for a non-reassuring fetal heart rate pattern? Why are they done?
17. Why might a tocolytic drug increase oxygen supply to the fetus?
18. What are the two purposes of amnioinfusion?

Application of Nursing Process

The novice nurse usually provides care in the form of applying the external monitor, recording maternal vital signs, and assisting in position changes and ambulation. The novice nurse notifies the experienced intrapartum nurse if basic non-reassuring patterns, such as an abnormal fetal heart rate, occur unexpectedly. Interpretation of electronic fetal monitoring patterns requires additional education in the specialty area of intrapartum nursing.

The nurse may identify several problems if a woman has had electronic fetal monitoring. The woman or couple who prefer a non-technical environment for birth may encounter a decision conflict if electronic fetal monitoring is recommended. Anxiety is likely if the woman does not understand the electronic monitor or if complications develop. Altered comfort may accompany reduced mobility.

Two nursing care needs related to intrapartum fetal monitoring are the woman's (or couple's) learning needs and an expansion of nursing care related to fetal oxygenation. Care related to fetal monitoring by either electronic means or auscultation should be combined with that for normal or complicated intrapartum nursing as needed.

Learning Needs

Assessment

Determine what the woman and her partner already know about the electronic fetal monitor. Women who have attended prepared childbirth classes or have given birth before may have a basic understanding of the purpose and limitations of the fetal monitor. Identifying what they already know allows the nurse to build on it appropriately and allows correction of inaccurate information.

If the woman is not familiar with electronic fetal monitoring, assess her perception of it. For example, does she believe that use of the monitor indicates the development of a complication or does she expect its use? If intermittent auscultation is an option at the birth facility, is the woman comfortable with that approach to intrapartum fetal assessment?

Lack of knowledge contributes to anxiety. Note the parents' anxiety level when the monitor is used. For example, is the woman afraid to move because the fetal heart sounds and tracing skip when she does? Does she place the monitor's data above her own comfort? Note her questions about the monitor and its data. Reassess after teaching to identify information that is still unclear or causing her anxiety.

Analysis

Many women expect to have continuous electronic fetal monitoring during labor, and they have often been introduced to it during prepared childbirth classes. Most women have additional questions, however, and some women know very little about this common mode of fetal surveillance.

The nursing diagnosis is: *Knowledge Deficit: Fetal Monitoring.*

Planning

The goal for this nursing diagnosis is as follows:

After being taught about the fetal monitor, the woman and her partner, through verbal and non-verbal behaviors, will express understanding of:

- The equipment
- The procedures
- The expected data

Interventions

EXPLAINING THE ELECTRONIC FETAL MONITOR

Teaching is continuous as circumstances change. Explain the purposes of the monitor and the equipment to be used. A simple explanation is to tell the parents that the monitor is a tool to assess how the fetus reacts to labor, especially during contractions. If electronic fetal monitoring is routine at the birth facility, assure the woman that its use does not mean something is wrong with her or her baby. Explain why changes in the monitoring mode (external to internal) are done. It may be helpful to explain that her physician or nurse-midwife evaluates many factors during labor and that the monitor strip is only one of those factors.

ADDRESSING PARENTS' SAFETY CONCERNS

Explain how the equipment functions. Some women are afraid of being attached to an electrical device, especially since cords and electrodes are wet with amniotic fluid and vaginal secretions. Reassure the woman that the connections to her and those to the wall current are isolated from each other.

Parents Want To Know
About Electronic Fetal Monitoring

When women have electronic fetal monitoring during labor, they often have questions that the nurse may answer. Here are some commonly asked questions and appropriate answers.

Can I move around with the monitor?

You can move freely with the monitor. If you notice that the machine isn't picking up the fetal heart sounds or contractions as well, call me and I'll readjust it. Make yourself comfortable, then we'll adjust the machine if needed.

What if I need to go to the bathroom?

If you need to go to the bathroom, we'll unplug the cords from the machine and you can walk in there, or we can roll the monitor to the door of the bathroom.

Will the monitor shock me? I don't know if I want to be hooked to an electric outlet, especially since my water has broken.

The part of the monitor that is attached to you and your baby only transmits information into the machine for processing. The sensors on your body are isolated from electrical parts in the monitor.

Why is the baby's heart beating so fast?

A baby's heart normally beats faster than an adult's, both before and after birth. The normal rate is about 110 to 160 BPM. A rate outside these boundaries does not necessarily mean the baby has a problem, but we do look at the monitor strip very closely to see how he or she is doing.

Why do those numbers for the baby's heart rate change so much?

The heart rate of a healthy baby who is awake usually changes by several beats per minute. When the baby moves, the heart speeds up, just as yours does.

What do those numbers for contractions (external monitor) *mean? They change all the time.*

The numbers reflect a change in the pressure that the monitor senses. The monitor senses many changes in pressure other than those from contractions, such as changes from breathing, coughing, or movement of you or the baby.

My contractions don't look very strong, but they sure seem strong to me! (External uterine activity monitor is being used.)

The external monitor senses contractions indirectly, rather than sensing the actual pressure within the uterus. Their appearance on the tracing varies because of many factors, such as your position, the position of the sensor on your abdomen, and the thickness of your abdominal wall.

Will the internal monitor hurt my baby? (The spiral electrode attaches only to the outer layer of skin on the baby's head.)

We are careful to avoid sensitive areas on the head, such as the fontanelles (soft spots), or the face. The uterine catheter slides up beside the baby. In practice, we've had few problems with either of these devices.

Some women are concerned about attachment of the scalp electrode to the fetal presenting part. Emphasize that the electrode is a very fine wire and penetrates the outer layer of skin only (about 1 mm or the thickness of a dime). If she is concerned about the intrauterine pressure catheter, tell her that it lies beside the fetus, between the fetus and the inner wall of the uterus.

COPING WITH MISLEADING DATA

Teach the woman that the monitor may give data that indicate a problem when there is none. For example, the fetal heart rate may suddenly fall to zero and the audible tone stop if the sensor (external or scalp electrode) is displaced. Tell her to call the nurse for adjustment or replacement of the sensor.

The expectant mother may be discouraged because the curves representing contractions do not look as strong on the strip as they feel to her. This is more likely when she has the external tocotransducer. Explain the many factors that may cause the contraction curves to appear more strong or less strong than they really are. Tell her that the strip is used mainly to assess the timing of contractions and the fetus' reaction when an external tocotransducer is used. Explain that the physician or nurse-midwife may use an intrauterine pressure catheter if knowing intrauterine pressure is crucial.

Reassure the woman that her perception of her contractions and discomfort is important. Value the woman-generated data as well as the machine-generated data.

The natural reaction is for the nurse's attention to be drawn to the electronic fetal monitor when entering a woman's room. Stay focused on the woman and her family rather than devoting excessive attention to the monitoring equipment.

INCLUDING THE COACH OR PARTNER

Tell the partner how to identify the onset and peak of contractions. During active labor, some women discover that contractions become intense before they can prepare for them with a cleansing breath (see Chapter 11). If this is the case, have the coach tell the woman when each contraction begins. The coach also can tell her when the peak has passed to encourage her.

ENHANCING COMFORT

Some women feel tied to the electronic fetal monitor and are reluctant to make themselves more comfortable. Nursing care involves finding ways to make the mother comfortable and the monitor as non-intrusive as possible. Teach her ways to improve comfort while still obtaining an adequate tracing.

Explain that staying in one position is uncomfortable and does not promote normal labor. The woman may assume any other position than supine, unless a specific position is needed. Electronic monitoring can be used with many different maternal positions (see Table 13–4), even if telemetry is not available. Encourage the woman to find the position in which she is most comfortable, then adjust the external devices to best detect contractions and the fetal heart beat. Internal devices may be an option if external devices cannot be adjusted to provide useful data.

If the woman finds the sound produced by the electronic fetal monitor distracting or inconsistent with the atmosphere she desires, turn the sound down or off. Remember the auditory cues for rate accelerations and decelerations will be absent.

If there are no other contraindications to walking, the woman may go to the bathroom to urinate or defecate. The machine may be rolled to the door of the bathroom; the cords are usually long enough to remain connected. Alternatively, unplug the sensors at the machine, loop the cords, and let her walk to the bathroom. Reconnect and adjust them when she returns. Document the ambulation and interruption in monitoring on the strip. If the fetus has a nonreassuring pattern, it is preferable not to interrupt the recording.

Evaluation

The evaluation of parental knowledge is continuous because most parents think of other questions after initial explanations. Achievement of the goal is evident if the partners indicate their understanding after each explanation. Their understanding may be accompanied by a decrease in anxiety behaviors as well.

Clinical Situation

LaShonda Blair is in active labor and is having external electronic fetal monitoring for fetal assessment. LaShonda has not had medication, and her labor has been normal so far. Her membranes ruptured about 1 hour ago. Contractions are every 3 minutes, 60 seconds in duration, and of moderate intensity. Her uterus fully relaxes between each contraction.

The student nurse who is supporting LaShonda notes abrupt slowing of the fetal heart rate to 90 BPM during the next two contractions, each time lasting about 30 seconds.

Q: What should the student nurse do?

A: The pattern described is one of variable decelerations, usually associated with cord compression. The student nurse should use the call bell to summon LaShonda's primary nurse, Tanya Clark. At the same time, LaShonda should be asked to change her position; if she is on her left side, she should turn to the right. Changing position may relieve pressure on the cord. Tanya will further evaluate LaShonda and her baby and may perform other interventions.

Tanya should contact the physician or nurse-midwife as soon as possible if the variable decelerations persist or worsen. However, attempting to correct the cause of the variable decelerations is the first priority.

Fetal Oxygenation

Assessment

Use a systematic approach when evaluating a fetal monitoring strip. Assess the fetal heart rate for baseline, variability, and periodic changes. Assess uterine activity for frequency, duration, and intensity of contractions and uterine resting tone. Assessment intervals are the same as those recommended for intermittent auscultation:

- *Low-risk women*: every 30 minutes during the active phase and every 15 minutes during the second stage
- *High-risk women*: every 15 minutes during the active phase and every 5 minutes during the second stage

(See Table 13–2 for other times the fetal heart rate should be evaluated and documented.)

Take the woman's temperature every 4 hours (every 2 hours after membranes rupture). Maternal fever increases the fetal temperature and fetal oxygen requirements. Assess her pulse, respirations, and blood pressure hourly. Hypotension or hypertension may reduce maternal blood flow to the intervillous spaces.

Assessment and evaluation of mother and fetus is continuous during the dynamic process of labor. Compare data about fetal heart rate patterns, uterine activity, and maternal vital signs to baseline data and normal ranges. Observe for subtle trends in the data. Distinguish between patterns having similar appearances, such as early and late decelerations.

Vaginal examination is part of routine labor assessment and may be performed by the experienced nurse to evaluate specific fetal heart rate patterns, for example, to check for a prolapsed cord if a pattern of variable decelerations occurs (see p. 764).

Analysis

A collaborative problem is selected for nursing care related to fetal oxygenation when electronic fetal monitoring is used.

Potential complication: Fetal distress.

Planning

Because the nurse cannot manage fetal distress independently, client (fetal) goals are inappropriate. The nurse's responsibility includes planning to:

- Promote adequate fetal oxygenation
- Take corrective actions to increase fetal oxygenation if non-reassuring patterns are identified
- Report non-reassuring patterns to the physician or nurse-midwife
- Support the woman and her partner if a complication develops
- Document assessments and care

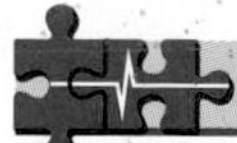

Clinical Situation

Nancy Joe is having her labor induced with oxytocin. Her contractions are every 2.5 minutes, 90 seconds in duration, and reach 75 mmHg on the scale for the intrauterine pressure catheter. Uterine resting tone between contractions is 20 mmHg. The baseline fetal heart rate is 135 to 142 BPM with 7 BPM variability.

Her nurse, Jackie Brown, notes a pattern of uniform decelerations that begin at the peak of each contraction. The rate falls to 125 BPM before returning to the previous baseline about 30 seconds after the contraction ends.

Q: What is the most appropriate nursing response?

A: The pattern described is one of late decelerations, probably caused by hypertonic uterine activity secondary to the use of oxytocin. Jackie's initial action should be to stop the oxytocin infusion and increase the rate of Nancy's non-additive intravenous fluid. Oxygen should be given through a snug face mask at the rate specified by the birth facility's policy (often 8 to 10 L/minute). Nancy should be placed on her side, if she is not already in this position, to increase placental blood flow. After the immediate corrective actions are completed, Jackie should contact Nancy's physician or nurse-midwife, documenting the content of the call.

Interventions

Measures to promote fetal oxygenation have been discussed with the care of the woman in normal labor (see Chapter 13), see also the woman having an epidural or subarachnoid block (Chapter 15).

TAKING CORRECTIVE ACTIONS

If a non-reassuring pattern is noted, take actions to identify its cause and improve fetal oxygenation (see p. 347). Birth facilities should have protocols to give nurses a framework and support for interventions if non-reassuring patterns develop. Nursing interventions may include both independent and delegated actions. Nurses may begin preparing for a cesarean birth, if that seems likely, on the basis of a severe or persistent non-reassuring pattern (see Chapter 16).

REASSURING PARENTS

Parents understandably become anxious when a non-reassuring pattern occurs. Remain at the bedside, and use a calm and supportive manner to avoid increasing their anxiety. Use the call bell to summon other nurses to help with corrective actions and to notify the physician or nurse-midwife if needed.

Explain the problem that was identified and the reason for corrective actions in simple, concise language. Severe anxiety reduces the parents' ability to understand information. Inform them if the fetal heart rate returns to a reassuring pattern. Some corrective actions, such as oxygen administration or positioning, are continued after a reassuring pattern returns. Tell the woman that she may talk with the oxygen mask on.

REPORTING NON-REASSURING PATTERNS

Notify the physician or nurse-midwife of non-reassuring patterns as soon as possible after taking corrective actions. The priority of nursing care is to improve fetal oxygenation. Another nurse may call the physician or nurse-midwife. Document the time and content of all consultations with the physician or nurse-midwife about the mother or fetus and the clinician's response.

Nursing Care Plan 14-1

Intrapartum Fetal Compromise

Assessment: Glenda Brown is a 30-year-old African-American woman. She is a gravida IV, para I who has had two spontaneous abortions. Glenda has been an insulin-dependent diabetic since the age of 15 years. Glenda began seeing Dr. Terry Bloomquist before she became pregnant and has had regular, frequent prenatal care. She had several fetal diagnostic tests during her pregnancy including two normal biophysical profiles. Glenda's labor is being induced with oxytocin (Pitocin) today at 39 weeks' gestation because she had a slight blood pressure elevation at her early morning antepartum care appointment. Baseline pregnancy blood pressure averaged 110 to 120 systolic and 70 to 75 diastolic. Today's blood pressure was 130/80 and repeat assessments have been about the same level. Glenda's fetus is to be monitored with electronic fetal monitoring. Glenda is accompanied by her husband, Paul. Glenda said they did not take classes because she was afraid this pregnancy would be "another disappointment." Chris Lowe will be Glenda's intrapartum nurse.

Nursing Diagnosis: Knowledge deficit: Electronic fetal monitoring.

Goals:
Glenda and Paul will state that they understand the reason for electronic monitoring, related equipment and procedures, and the data that are expected.

Intervention:	Rationale:
1. Assess the parents' present knowledge about electronic fetal monitoring.	1. Allows the nurse to build on existing accurate knowledge and to correct misunderstandings.
2. Explain information about the monitor to Glenda and Paul:	2. Reassure Glenda and Paul that the use of the electronic fetal monitor does not mean something is wrong with Glenda or the baby.
a. Purposes: To provide an audible and written record of the fetal response to labor and to guide caregivers in appropriate interventions if non-reassuring patterns are identified.	a. Provides a realistic explanation of how the monitor is used.
b. Safety: The monitoring sensors are electrically isolated from the wall current. The fetal scalp electrode (if used) penetrates the outer layer of skin, about a dime's thickness. The intrauterine pressure catheter will lie between the baby and the wall of the uterus.	b. Answers safety concerns that parents often express.
c. Misleading data: Encourage Glenda to call for assistance if she cannot hear the fetal heart beat or if she notices that her contractions do not seem to be evident on the strip.	c. Sensors, especially external devices, can easily be displaced and stop picking up data. Preparing Glenda and Paul for this possibility reduces their fears if they should stop hearing the fetal heartbeat.
d. Encourage Glenda to move about freely. Tell her that a nurse will readjust her monitor if it stops recording properly. Explain that she should urinate about every 2 hours and that the nurse can help her roll the monitor to the bathroom door or temporarily disconnect the sensors.	d. Maternal movement and regular urination enhance normal labor processes. Glenda is likely to become anxious and uncomfortable if she concentrates more on maintaining data from the monitor than on coping with labor.

Evaluation:
Glenda and Paul say that they did not go to classes but expected electronic fetal monitoring during labor. Glenda is familiar with the external monitor because it was used for the biophysical profile. She says she prefers not to have internal monitors if they are not needed but understands that their greater accuracy is especially important because of her higher risk status. She agrees to have internal monitoring if needed.

Assessment: Chris applies the external fetal monitor because Glenda's membranes are intact. She is having occasional spontaneous contractions, but no regular contractions. The fetal heart rate baseline averages 125 to 135 BPM and accelerates when the fetus moves. The nurse begins an oxytocin infusion to induce labor. Glenda's blood pressure is 145/90.

Nursing Care Plan 14–1 *Continued*

Intrapartum Fetal Compromise

Potential Complication: Fetal compromise.

Goals:

Client goals for the fetus are inappropriate because nurses cannot independently manage fetal distress. Chris' planning for Glenda should reflect the need to:

1. Compare fetal heart rate and uterine activity data with baseline levels before oxytocin induction.
2. Promote normal fetal oxygenation.
3. Take immediate corrective actions for non-reassuring patterns.
4. Notify Glenda's physician if non-reassuring patterns develop.

Intervention:	Rationale:
1. Identify relevant risk factors for fetal compromise.	1. Women who have risk factors that could reduce fetal oxygenation should have fetal assessments more frequently. In Glenda's case, there are three identified risk factors: diabetes mellitus, pregnancy-induced hypertension, and labor induced with oxytocin.
2. Encourage Glenda to assume any comfortable position other than the supine position.	2. The supine position may reduce blood return to Glenda's heart by compressing the inferior vena cava. Compression of the aorta and reduced cardiac output will reduce placental perfusion.
3. Evaluate the tracing at the following times, signing or initialing the strip each time. Document a summary of the evaluation on Glenda's labor record.	3. Documents that assessment was done. Documenting on both strip and labor record allows each to stand alone.
a. Every 15 minutes during the first stage and every 5 minutes during the second stage.	a. Provides a framework for regular assessment of the fetal response to labor. Glenda has a high-risk pregnancy and the fetus should be evaluated by those guidelines.
b. Before and after procedures such as amniotomy, medications, epidural anesthesia.	b. Rupture of membranes (spontaneously or by amniotomy) may result in cord compression. Medications may alter the rate or variability of the fetal heart beat. Epidural anesthesia may cause hypotension, which can decrease uteroplacental perfusion.
c. With changes of activity, such as urination or repositioning.	c. Changes in activity or position could alter the uterine or umbilical cord blood flow. Also, external sensors may slip and need adjustment.
4. Use a four-step approach to evaluate the strip:	4. Provides a systematic framework to evaluate the fetal response to labor.
a. Baseline fetal heart rate.	a. Tachycardia may be an early response to hypoxia. Bradycardia may occur in response to vagal stimulation or prolonged hypoxia.
b. Variability (primarily if fetal scalp electrode is used).	b. Normal variability suggests that the fetus is well oxygenated and not in acidosis. Normal short-term variability (more than 3 BPM) is a sensitive indicator of adequate fetal oxygenation and normal acid-base balance. Variability is most accurate with a fetal scalp electrode because external Doppler ultrasound tends to cause a tracing that shows more variability than is really present.
c. Periodic changes: Accelerations, decelerations. Note relationship of periodic changes to fetal movement, contractions, the woman's status and activity. Note non-periodic (random) accelerations or variable decelerations.	c. Accelerations are a reassuring sign of fetal well-being and are accompanied by fetal movement. Early decelerations are a normal response to head compression. Late (uteroplacental insufficiency) and variable (umbilical cord compression) decelerations are non-reassuring. The nurse should attempt to identify their cause, correct it, and take steps to improve fetal oxygenation.

Nursing Care Plan 14–1 *Continued*

Intrapartum Fetal Compromise

Intervention	Rationale
d. Uterine activity: Evaluate frequency and duration using either external or internal devices. Estimate intensity with an external device by palpating three or more contractions. Note if the uterus relaxes between contractions for at least 60 seconds. If an intrauterine pressure catheter is used, read contraction intensity and uterine resting tone from scale on strip.	d. Contractions that are too long (more than 90 seconds duration) or too frequent (more than every 2 minutes), a resting interval of less than 60 seconds, or intrauterine pressure of more than 20 mmHg can reduce the time available for normal uteroplacental exchange. Because of Glenda's high-risk problems (specifically diabetes and pregnancy-induced hypertension), uteroplacental exchange may be less before labor begins. Oxytocin also can stimulate excess uterine activity.
5. If non-reassuring patterns develop, take appropriate corrective actions such as discontinuing the oxytocin, increasing the rate of the non-additive intravenous solution, positioning Glenda on her side, and administering oxygen. Notify Dr. Bloomquist of non-reassuring patterns, corrective actions taken, and the fetal response. Document Dr. Bloomquist's response and any orders.	5. The first priority is to identify the cause of the non-reassuring pattern and increase fetal oxygenation. Dr. Bloomquist should be notified to keep abreast of the status of Glenda and her fetus and for needed medical orders or interventions.

Evaluation:
Goals are not established for collaborative problems. Chris compared data from the fetal monitor and other nursing evaluations to the baseline before Glenda started having oxytocin or contractions. For the first 4 hours of the oxytocin induction, the fetal heart rate continued near its baseline of 125 to 135 RPM, with long-term variability averaging 10 BPM. Fetal heart rate accelerations with fetal movement continue. No non-reassuring patterns were noted.

Assessment: Dr. Bloomquist ruptures Glenda's membranes and inserts internal devices for the fetal heart rate and uterine activity. Glenda's blood pressure remains near 145/90 and her oxytocin infusion continues. She is having contractions every 4 minutes; they are of 50 seconds duration, 50 mmHg intensity, and she has a uterine resting tone of 10 mmHg. One hour after Glenda's membranes are ruptured, Chris notes the baseline fetal heart rate has risen to approximately 145 to 150 BPM and that short-term variability averages 3 BPM. A pattern of repeated late decelerations develops. Chris stops the oxytocin infusion and increases the rate of non-additive intravenous fluid, positions Glenda on her left side, and administers oxygen at 10 L/minute with a snug face mask. Dr. Bloomquist is notified. Baseline variability improves to 5 BPM, but late decelerations with most contractions continue. Glenda is holding Paul's hand tightly and breathing rapidly. Her vital signs are blood pressure, 145/90; pulse, 90; respirations, 32. Uterine activity is unchanged.

Nursing Diagnosis: Anxiety related to unexpected development of complications.

Goals:
1. Glenda will have a reduced respiratory rate (14 to 22/minute) after interventions.
2. Glenda will have a more relaxed face and body posture after interventions.

Intervention:	Rationale:
1. Maintain a calm demeanor while performing corrective actions and notifying Dr. Bloomquist.	1. Non-verbally communicates to Glenda and Paul that woman and fetus are receiving competent care. Anxious behavior on the part of caregivers tends to increase the parents' anxiety.
2. Use simple, concise language for all explanations.	2. High anxiety or intense physical sensations impair one's ability to comprehend explanations.

Nursing Care Plan 14–1 *Continued*

Intrapartum Fetal Compromise

3. Explain the following to Glenda and Paul: a. The problem that was identified. b. The usual cause for the problem. c. Reasons for corrective actions. d. Expected results. e. Glenda can talk with oxygen mask on.	3. If Glenda and Paul understand what is happening and why the corrective actions are taken, they are more likely to comply with the care. Knowledge decreases fear of the unknown. Assuring Glenda that she can talk with the oxygen mask on allows her to ask questions and ventilate feelings to reduce anxiety and fear.
4. Inform Glenda and Paul if the pattern improves or is resolved. For example, tell them when baseline variability improves.	4. Decreases anxiety about the fetus' condition.
5. Allow Glenda and Paul to ventilate their feelings about the labor and birth during the postpartum period. Explain any gaps in their understanding about what happened.	5. Helps Glenda and Paul accept and put unexpected occurrences in perspective. Decreases the possibility that one or both parents will feel like "a failure" if emergency intervention (cesarean birth) becomes necessary.

Evaluation:
Over the next hour, the fetal heart rate pattern gradually improves. The baseline rate becomes lower (130 to 140 BPM), and late decelerations are sporadic. Baseline short-term variability improves to about 8 BPM. Glenda gradually relaxes her grip on Paul's hand and her body relaxes. Her respiratory rate slows to 22/breaths/minute. Glenda requires a cesarean birth, however, because her cervix does not dilate to greater than 7 cm.

DOCUMENTING ASSESSMENTS AND CARE

Record data related to fetal well-being in the labor record and on the monitor strip. Both are permanent records, although they may be stored separately. Each should be complete and able to document care independently of the other; reconstructing the events of labor should be possible using either. Table 14–3 shows guidelines for documentation on the monitor strip and labor record. Documentation can demonstrate good nursing care and show that the standard of care has been met.

Write the woman's name, the date, and the time on the strip when electronic fetal monitoring begins. An adhesive label is supplied with fetal monitoring paper to identify the strip and record relevant information. These labels are usually stamped with her permanent chart number, which may not be available when monitoring begins. When there is a break in the strip, such as to change paper, label the new strip with the woman's name, the date, and the time. Record the last panel number of the previous strip on the new strip so that the entire record can be reassembled sequentially.

Continue documenting the heart rate and maternal observations in the delivery or birthing room until vaginal birth occurs. If a cesarean birth occurs, continue monitoring by auscultation or electronic means as long as practical while preparing the woman for surgery. Remove internal devices before securing her legs to the operating table with a strap. Document the time at which monitoring is stopped and the time of abdominal incision.

Evaluation

Client-centered goals are not formulated for a collaborative problem. The nurse compares data to established standards to determine whether they are within normal limits. If non-reassuring patterns are identified, the nurse:

- Takes measures to increase fetal oxygenation
- Notifies the physician or nurse-midwife
- Documents all relevant data

Table 14–3. DOCUMENTING ELECTRONIC FETAL MONITORING

Documentation When Monitoring Initiated

Monitor Strip

Woman's name
Physician's or nurse-midwife's name
Date and time of admission
Date and time electronic monitoring is begun; (verify date and time if this information is automatically printed by monitor)
Gravidity, parity, abortions, living children
Gestation in weeks
Presence of identified risk factors
Character of amniotic fluid (if membranes are ruptured)
Function test of monitor accuracy
Initial mode of monitoring (external or internal devices)

Labor Record

Same information as on monitor strip
First panel number when strip is begun

Continuing Documentation

Monitor Strip

Maternal vital signs
Vaginal examinations, including cervical dilation and effacement and fetal station
Rupture of membranes (spontaneously or artificially)
Color, quantity, and character (such as foul odor) of amniotic fluid
Maternal position changes
Maternal or fetal movement
Maternal vomiting, coughing, or other movement that affects tracing
Adjustment of equipment
Medication and anesthesia, including related interventions
Changes of equipment mode (such as external to internal device)
Interventions for non-reassuring patterns
Temporary interruptions in strip, such as woman walking

Labor Record

Same information as on monitor strip
Periodic summary of the baseline rate, variability, periodic changes, and uterine activity (frequency, duration, and intensity of contractions and uterine resting tone)

Summary Concepts

- The purpose of intrapartum fetal surveillance is to identify fetal well-being and to identify the fetus who may be having hypoxic stress beyond the ability to compensate for it. It cannot prevent fetal distress, neurological dysfunction, or mental retardation.
- The two approaches to intrapartum fetal monitoring are intermittent auscultation with palpation of uterine activity and electronic fetal monitoring. Because each type has distinct advantages and limitations, neither approach can be considered superior to the other.
- Fetal oxygenation depends on a normal flow of oxygenated maternal blood into the placenta, normal uteroplacental exchange, patent umbilical cord vessels, and normal fetal circulatory and oxygen-carrying function.
- Stimulation of the sympathetic nervous system increases the fetal heart rate and strengthens the heart contraction. Stimulation of the parasympathetic nervous system slows the heart rate and maintains short-term variability.
- External electronic fetal monitoring is less accurate for fetal heart rate and uterine activity patterns than internal monitoring, but it is non-invasive.
- Greater accuracy is the main advantage of internal electronic fetal monitoring devices.
- A non-reassuring pattern on the external fetal monitor may look worse with an internal fetal scalp electrode because the Doppler sensor tends to exaggerate variability slightly.
- Non-reassuring electronic fetal monitoring patterns are not diagnostic of fetal hypoxia or acidosis. The physician or nurse-midwife should be notified of non-reassuring patterns for further evaluation and treatment.
- Nursing responsibilities related to intrapartum fetal monitoring include promoting fetal oxygenation, identifying and reporting non-reassuring findings, supporting parents, communicating with the physician or nurse-midwife, and documenting all care.

References and Readings

American Academy of Pediatrics and American College of Obstetricians and Gynecologists (1992). *Guidelines for perinatal care* (3rd ed.). Elk Grove Village, Il.

American College of Obstetricians and Gynecologists (ACOG) (1989a). ACOG *Technical Bulletin*, No. 132. Intrapartum fetal heart rate monitoring. Washington, D.C.

American College of Obstetricians and Gynecologists (ACOG) (1989b). ACOG *Technical Bulletin*, No. 127. Assessment of fetal and newborn acid-base status. Washington, D.C.

Boehm, F. (1990). Fetal distress. In R. Eden & F. Boehm (Eds.), *Assessment and care of the fetus: Physiological, clinical, and medicolegal principles* (pp. 809–821). Norwalk, Conn.: Appleton & Lange.

Boylan, P., & Parisi, V. (1989). Fetal acid-base balance. In R. Creasy & R. Resnik (Eds.). *Maternal-fetal medicine: Principles and practice* (pp. 362–374). Philadelphia: W.B. Saunders.

Chez, B.F., Harvey, C.F., & Murray, M.L. (1990). *Critical concepts in fetal heart rate monitoring: Resources, guidelines, documentation.* Baltimore: Williams & Wilkins.

Davis, L.K. (1992). Protocol for fetal heart rate monitoring. In L.K. Mandeville & N.H. Troiano (Eds.), *High-risk intrapartum nursing* (pp. 305–308). Philadelphia: J.B. Lippincott.

Divoll, M. (1987). The role of the perinatal and neonatal nurse in risk management. *Journal of Perinatal Neonatal Nursing*, 1(2), 1–8.

Doig, J. (1990). In N. Nelson (Ed.), *Current therapy in neonatal-perinatal medicine–2*, (pp. 80–81). Philadelphia: B.C. Decker.

Eganhouse, D.J. (1992). Fetal monitoring of twins. *Journal of Obstetric Gynecologic, and Neonatal Nursing*, 21(1), 17–27.

Ellison, P.H., Foster, M., Sheridan-Pereira, M., & MacDonald, D. (1991). Electronic fetal heart monitoring, auscultation, and neonatal outcome. *American Journal of Obstetrics and Gynecology*, 164 (3, Part 1), 1281–1287.

Fields, L. (1987). Electronic fetal monitoring: practices and protocols for the intrapartum patient. *Journal of Perinatal Neonatal Nursing*, 1(1), 5–12.

Galvan, B., van Mullem, C., & Broekhuizen, F. (1989). Using amnioinfusion for relief of repetitive variable decelerations during labor. *Journal of Obstetric, Gynecologic, and Neonatal Nursing*, 19(3), 222–229.

Grabenstein, J. (1987). Nursing documentation during the perinatal period. *Journal of Perinatal Neonatal Nursing*, 1(2), 29–38.

Harvey, C. (1987). Fetal scalp stimulation: Enhancing the interpretation of fetal monitor tracings. *Journal of Perinatal Neonatal Nursing*, 1(1), 13–21.

Harvey, C. (1989). Interpreting the electronic fetal monitor: Strategies for management. *Journal of Nurse-Midwifery*, 34(2), 75–84.

Haubrich, K. (1989). Amnioinfusion: A technique for the relief of variable decelerations. *Journal of Obstetric, Gynecologic, and Neonatal Nursing*, 19(4), 299–303.

Hobel, C., & Bochner, C. (1990). Meconium staining of amniotic fluid. In R. Eden & F. Boehm (Eds.), *Assessment and care of the fetus: Physiological, clinical, and medicolegal principles* (pp. 801–808). Norwalk, Conn.: Appleton & Lange.

Knorr, L. (1989). Relieving fetal distress with amnioinfusion. *MCN: American Journal of Maternal Child Nursing*, 14(5), 346–350.

Lowdermilk, D. (1990). Ask the experts. *NAACOG Newsletter*, 17(9), 9, 16.

Marieskind, H. (1989). Cesarean section in the United States: Has it changed since 1979? *Birth*, 16(4), 196–202.

McCusker, J. (1988). Association of electronic fetal monitoring during labor with cesarean section rate and with neonatal morbidity and mortality. *American Journal of Public Health*, 78(9), 1170–1174.

McMullen, P. (1990). Liability in obstetrical nursing. *Nursing Connections*, 3(2), 61–63.

Merlo, C. (1990). Ask the experts. *NAACOG Newsletter*, 17(5), 6, 10.

Miller, F. (1990). Fetal scalp stimulation. In E. Quilligan & F. Zuspan (Eds.), *Current therapy in obstetrics and gynecology* (pp. 332–333). Philadelphia: W.B. Saunders.

Murray, M. (1988). *Antepartal and intrapartal fetal monitoring*. Washington, D.C.: NAACOG.

NAACOG (1988a). *Nursing responsibilities in implementing intrapartum fetal heart rate monitoring*. Washington, D.C.

NAACOG (1988b). *Practice competencies and educational guidelines for nurse providers of intrapartum care*. Washington, D.C.

NAACOG (1990). *Fetal heart rate auscultation*. Washington, D.C.

O'Brien-Abel, N.E., & Benedetti, T.J. (1992). Saltatory fetal heart rate pattern. *Journal of Perinatology*, 12(1), 13–17.

Painter, M., Painter, M.J., Scott, M., Hirsch, R.P., O'Donoghue, P., & Depp, R. (1988). Fetal heart rate patterns during labor: Neurologic and cognitive development at six to nine years of age. *American Journal of Obstetrics and Gynecology*, 159(4), 854–858.

Parer, J. (1989a). Fetal heart rate. In R. Creasy & R. Resnik (Eds.), *Maternal-fetal medicine: Principles and practice* (pp. 314–343). Philadelphia: W.B. Saunders.

Parer, J. (1989b). Fetal heart rate monitoring. In J. Parer (Ed.), *Antepartum and intrapartum management* (pp. 167–183). Philadelphia: Lea & Febiger.

Peacock, W. (1989). Parental expectations of a perfect baby. In J. Parer (Ed.), *Antepartum and intrapartum management* (pp. 225–233). Philadelphia: Lea & Febiger.

Pheigaru, J.L. (1988). Keeping staff up on electronic fetal monitoring. *MCN: American Journal of Maternal Child Nursing* 13(5), 334–335.

Quilligan, E. (1989). Fetal heart rate monitoring in the prevention of fetal neurologic damage. In J. Parer (Ed.), *Antepartum and intrapartum management* (pp. 216–221). Philadelphia: Lea & Febiger.

Roberts, J. (1989). Managing fetal bradycardia during second stage of labor. *MCN: American Journal of Maternal Child Nursing* 14(6), 394–398.

Sarno, A., Sarno, A.P., Ahn, M.O., Phelan, J.P., & Paul, R.H. (1990). Fetal acoustic stimulation in the early intrapartum period as a predictor of subsequent fetal condition. *American Journal of Obstetrics and Gynecology*, 162(3), 762–767.

Schifrin, B. (1990). Fetal monitoring during labor. In N. Nelson (Ed.), *Current therapy in neonatal-perinatal medicine-2* (pp. 3–6). Philadelphia: B.C. Decker.

Schmidt, J. (1989). Ask the experts. *NAACOG Newsletter*, 16(8), 7, 12.

Sleutel, M.R. (1989). An overview of vibroacoustic stimulation. *Journal of Obstetric, Gynecologic, and Neonatal Nursing*, 18(6), 447–452.

Sleutel, M.R. (1990). Vibroacoustic stimulation and fetal heart rate in nonstress tests. *Journal of Obstetric, Gynecologic, and Neonatal Nursing*, 19(3), 199–204.

Staisch, K.J. (1992). Identification and management of fetal distress during labor. In N.F. Hacker & J.G. Moore (Eds.), *Essentials of obstetrics and gynecology* (pp. 250–260). Philadelphia: W.B. Saunders.

Strong, T. (1990). Fetal distress in the intrapartum period. In E. Quilligan & F. Zuspan (Eds.), *Current therapy in obstetrics and gynecology* (pp. 318–321). Philadelphia: W.B. Saunders.

Syndal, S. (1988). Responses of laboring women to fetal heart rate monitoring: a critical review of the literature. *Journal of Nurse-Midwifery*, 33(5), 208–216.

Tucker, S.M. (1988). *Pocket guide to fetal monitoring*. St. Louis: C.V. Mosby.

Verny, T. (1985). The psycho-technology of pregnancy and labor. *Neonatal Network*, 3(5), 12–22.

15

Pain Management During Childbirth

Objectives

1. Compare childbirth pain to other types of pain.
2. Describe how excessive pain can affect the laboring woman and her fetus.
3. Examine how physical and psychological forces interact in the laboring woman's pain experience.
4. Describe use of non-pharmacological pain management techniques in labor.
5. Describe how medications may affect a pregnant woman and the fetus or neonate.
6. Identify benefits and risks of specific pharmacological pain relief methods.
7. Explain nursing care related to different types of intrapartum pain management.

Definitions

Agonist • A drug or natural substance that causes a physiological effect.

Analgesic • A systemic agent that relieves pain without loss of consciousness.

Anesthesia • Loss of sensation, especially to pain, with or without loss of consciousness.

Anesthesiologist • A physician who specializes in administration of anesthesia.

Antagonist • A drug that blocks the action of another drug or of body secretions.

Aspiration pneumonitis • A chemical injury to the lungs that may occur with regurgitation and aspiration of acidic gastric secretion.

Cerebrospinal fluid (CSF) • The clear fluid that bathes and cushions the brain and spinal cord.

Endorphins • Morphine-like substances that occur naturally in the central nervous system and modify pain sensations.

Epidural space • The area outside the dura, between the dura mater and the vertebral canal.

General anesthesia • Systemic loss of sensation with loss of consciousness.

Motor block • Loss of voluntary movement caused by regional anesthesia.

Nurse anesthetist • A registered nurse who has advanced education and certification in administration of anesthetics. Also certified registered nurse anesthetist (CRNA).

Pain threshold (or pain perception) • The lowest level of stimulus one perceives as painful. Pain threshold is relatively constant under different conditions.

Pain tolerance • Maximum pain one is willing to endure. Pain tolerance may increase or decrease under different conditions.

Regional anesthesia • Anesthesia that blocks pain impulses in a localized area without loss of consciousness.

△ Alert for a high risk of exposure to substances to which universal precautions apply. See Appendix B for additional information about infection control.

Sensory block • Loss of sensation caused by **regional anesthesia.**

Subarachnoid space • Space between the arachnoid mater and the pia mater containing **cerebrospinal fluid.**

Each woman has unique expectations about birth, including expectations about pain and her ability to control it. The woman who masters the pain of labor is more likely to view her experience as a positive life event. A woman's experience with labor pain varies with several physical and psychological elements, and each woman responds differently.

Management of labor pain interests most pregnant women and motivates many to attend childbirth classes. This chapter provides an overview of techniques to help laboring women manage pain successfully. Nonpharmacological and pharmacological methods give the nurse and laboring woman a wide selection of pain management techniques to choose from.

The Unique Nature of Pain During Birth

Pain is a universal experience but is difficult to define. It is an unpleasant sensation of distress resulting from stimulation of sensory nerves. Pain is subjective and personal; no one can feel another's pain. Childbirth pain, however, differs from other pain in several important respects:

- *It is part of a normal process.* Childbirth pain is part of a normal process, whereas other types of pain usually signify an injury or illness. Pain is useful in labor, causing a woman to seek shelter and help from others. Pain also may cause her to assume different positions in labor, favoring descent of the fetus through her pelvis.
- *There is time for preparation.* The pregnant woman has several months to prepare for labor, including acquiring skills to help manage pain. Realistic preparation and knowledge about the birth process help her develop skills to cope with labor pain.

  The woman and her partner have a chance to talk with others about their birth experiences. They may encounter a variety of responses about labor pain, ranging from it being unbearable to being mild or even non-existent.
- *It is self-limiting.* Labor pain has a foreseeable end. A woman can expect her labor to end in hours, rather than days, weeks, or months. Other kinds of pain may also be brief, but the baby's birth brings a rapid decrease in pain.

  Labor pain is not constant but intermittent. A woman may describe little discomfort with contractions during early labor. Even during late labor, a woman may be relatively comfortable during the short rest period between contractions.
- *Labor ends with the birth of a baby.* The emotional significance of her child's birth cannot be ignored when trying to understand a woman's response to pain. Concern about her fetus often motivates a woman to tolerate more pain during labor than she otherwise might be willing to endure.

Adverse Effects of Excessive Pain

Although expected during labor, unrelieved pain that exceeds a woman's tolerance may have harmful effects on her and the fetus.

Physiological Effects

A woman may react to pain with a stress response that diverts blood flow from the uterus, compromising fetal oxygen supply. Moreover, she breathes fast, resulting in respiratory alkalosis, which may be accompanied by vasoconstriction. The fetus also may have acidosis because of a reduced oxygen supply and the expectant mother's altered acid-base balance.

Labor may be longer when a woman has excessive pain. The release of epinephrine in response to pain inhibits efficient uterine activity, resulting in prolonged labor.

Psychological Effects

Poorly relieved pain lessens the pleasure of this extraordinary life event. The mother may find it difficult to interact with her infant because she is depleted from a painful labor. Unpleasant memories of the birth may affect her response to sexual activity or another labor. Additionally, her partner may feel inadequate as a support person for the laboring woman.

✔ Check Your Reading

1. How may the pain of labor be useful?
2. How does the pain of childbirth differ from other kinds of pain?
3. How can excessive pain adversely affect a laboring woman and her fetus?

Variables in Childbirth Pain

The nurse must identify factors that modify childbirth pain and influence a woman's response to intervene effectively. Physiological and psychosocial factors contribute to her response.

Physical Factors

SOURCES OF PAIN

Four potential sources of labor pain exist in most labors. Other physical factors may modify labor pain, increasing or decreasing it.

Cervical Dilation. Dilation and stretching of the cervix and lower uterine segment stimulate nerve ganglia and are a major source of pain. Pain stimuli from cervical dilation travel through the hypogastric plexus, entering the spinal cord at the T10, T11, and T12 levels and the L1 level (Fig. 15–1).

Uterine Ischemia. The blood supply to the uterus decreases during contractions. Ischemic uterine pain has been likened to ischemic heart pain.

Pressure and Pulling on Pelvic Structures. Some pain results from pressure and pulling on pelvic structures, such as ligaments, fallopian tubes, ovaries, bladder, and peritoneum. The pain is deep and a woman may feel it in her back and legs.

Distention of the Vagina and Perineum. Marked distention of the vagina and perineum occurs with fetal descent, especially during the second stage.

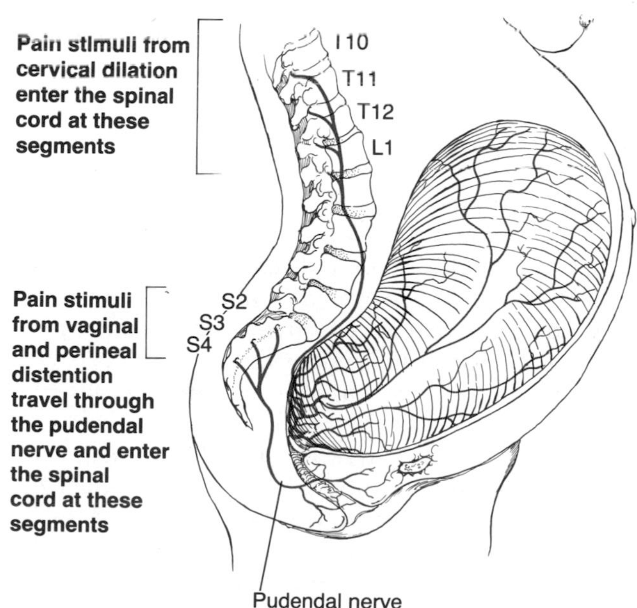
Pain stimuli from cervical dilation enter the spinal cord at these segments
T10
T11
T12
L1
Pain stimuli from vaginal and perineal distention travel through the pudendal nerve and enter the spinal cord at these segments
S2
S3
S4
Pudendal nerve

Figure 15–1

Pathways of pain transmission during labor.

The woman may describe a sensation of burning, tearing, or splitting. Pain from vaginal and perineal distention and pressure and pulling on adjacent structures enters the spinal cord at the S2, S3, and S4 levels (see Fig. 15–1).

FACTORS INFLUENCING PERCEPTION OR TOLERANCE OF PAIN

Although physiological processes cause labor pain, a woman's tolerance of pain may be affected by other physical influences.

Intensity of Labor. The woman who has a short, intense labor often complains of severe pain because each contraction does so much work (dilation, effacement, and fetal descent). A rapid labor frequently limits her options for pharmacological pain relief as well.

Cervical Readiness. If pre-labor cervical changes (softening, with some dilation and effacement) are incomplete, the cervix will not yield as readily. More contractions will be needed to achieve dilation and effacement, resulting in a longer labor and greater fatigue in the laboring woman.

Fetal Position. Labor is likely to be longer and more uncomfortable when the fetus is in an abnormal position. An occiput posterior position is a common variant. In this position, each contraction pushes the fetus' occiput against the woman's sacrum. She experiences intense back discomfort (back labor) that persists between contractions. Few women can deliver an infant in the occiput posterior position. The fetal head must therefore rotate a wider arc before the mechanisms of extension and expulsion occur, so labor is usually longer. Back pain often decreases dramatically when a fetus rotates into an occiput anterior position. The rate of labor progress usually increases as well.

Characteristics of the Pelvis. The size and shape of a woman's pelvis influence the course and length of her labor. Abnormalities may cause a difficult and longer labor. Abnormalities in the pelvis also may contribute to fetal malpresentation or malposition.

Fatigue. A woman's ability to tolerate pain and her ability to use coping skills she has learned are diminished with fatigue. She may lack the energy to focus on relaxation and breathing techniques that would otherwise help her tolerate labor. An extremely fatigued woman may have an exaggerated response to contractions, or she may be unable to respond to sensations of labor such as the urge to push.

Many women find that sleep is difficult during the last weeks of pregnancy. A woman's shortness of breath when lying down, frequent urination, and fetal activity interrupt sleep so that she often begins labor with a sleep deficit. If labor begins late in the evening, she may have been awake more than 24 hours by the time she gives birth. Even if a woman begins labor well rested, slow progress may result in fatigue or even exhaustion.

Intervention of Caregivers. Although they may be appropriate for the safety and well-being of a woman and fetus, some interventions add discomfort to the natural pain of labor.

Intravenous lines cause pain when they are inserted and remain noticeable to many women during labor. Fetal monitoring equipment is uncomfortable to some women. Both may hamper a woman's mobility, which she might otherwise use to assume a more comfortable position.

A woman whose labor is induced or augmented often reports more pain and increased difficulty coping with it (see p. 391). Vaginal examinations and amniotomy also increase a woman's discomfort temporarily.

Psychosocial Factors

Several psychosocial variables influence a woman's experience of pain. Psychological distress decreases her ability to tolerate pain because she cannot work with the labor process as effectively.

CULTURE

A woman's sociocultural roots influence how she perceives, interprets, and responds to pain during childbirth. Some cultures encourage loud and vigorous expression of pain, whereas others value self-control. However, women are individuals within their cultural groups. The experience of pain is unique, and one should not make assumptions about how a woman from a specific cultural or ethnic group will behave during labor.

Women should be encouraged to express themselves in any way they find comforting, and the diversity of their expressions must be respected. *Accepting a woman's individual response to labor and pain promotes a therapeutic relationship.*

The nurse should avoid praising some behaviors (such as stoicism) while belittling others (such as noisy expression). This is sometimes difficult because noisy, expressive women can be challenging to work with and may disturb other laboring women.

Women's diverse expressions make nursing management of childbirth pain complex. The nurse can miss important cues if the woman is either stoic, having little outward expression of pain, or expresses herself loudly and constantly. With either extreme, the nurse may not readily identify critical information such as impending birth or symptoms of a complication.

Clinical Situation

Truc Pham is a Vietnamese-American in labor with her first baby. Her cervix is dilated 6 cm, effacement is 100 per cent, and the fetus is at a +1 station. Truc's contractions are every 3 minutes, 50 to 60 seconds, and of strong intensity. She smiles at the nurse each time the nurse talks to her but does not talk much herself. Truc stiffens her body during contractions but otherwise does not indicate that she is uncomfortable.

Q: What are appropriate nursing actions for this situation?

A: Do not assume that Truc does not need pain relief because she smiles and has not requested pain medication. Asian women usually value stoicism and are concerned with harmonious relationships. Truc may be smiling to please the nurse rather than because she is comfortable.

Truc's labor progress and pattern of contractions plus her tension indicate she may need medication. However, do not assume that she needs or wants medication either. Non-pharmacological actions, such as breathing techniques, may be adequate.

The best course of action is to discuss Truc's needs for pain relief with her, sharing observations about her body posture during contractions. If Truc does not speak English well, try to get an interpreter to assess her needs for pain relief. Demonstrate non-pharmacological actions, such as breathing techniques, for Truc to use with or without medication.

ANXIETY AND FEAR

Mild and moderate anxiety can have a positive effect by heightening attention and enhancing learning. However, excess anxiety and fear intensify sensitivity to pain and impair a woman's ability to tolerate it. They consume energy she needs to use non-pharmacological pain management techniques.

Anxiety and fear increase muscle tension, diverting oxygenated blood to the brain and skeletal muscles. Tension in pelvic muscles counters the expulsive forces of uterine contractions and the laboring woman's pushing efforts during the second stage. Prolonged tension results in general fatigue, increased pain perception, and reduced ability to use skills to cope with pain.

If a previous pregnancy had a poor outcome, such as a stillborn infant or one with abnormalities, a woman will probably be more anxious during labor and for a time after birth. She will probably examine and re-examine her infant to assure herself that this baby is normal.

PREVIOUS EXPERIENCES WITH PAIN

Early in life a child learns that pain is a symptom of bodily injury. Consequently, fear and withdrawal are a woman's natural reactions to pain during labor. Learning about the normal sensations of labor, including pain, helps a woman suppress her natural reactions of fear and withdrawal, allowing her body do the work of birth.

A woman who has given birth previously has a different perspective. If she has had a vaginal delivery, she is probably aware of normal labor sensations and is less likely to associate them with injury or abnormality. A woman who had a regional anesthetic for her previous labor may not have felt much pain and may be more vulnerable to the effects of pain during subsequent labors. Also, time has a way of blunting the memory of painful experiences.

A woman who had a child by cesarean birth and has never experienced labor may be particularly anxious. The experience of cesarean birth is known to her, whereas labor is unknown. A subsequent cesarean delivery may seem like the quick and less painful option. She may have difficulty allowing her body to do the work of labor, particularly if she is not highly motivated to give birth vaginally.

A woman who has had a previous long and difficult labor is more likely to be anxious about the result of the present one. If she had a cesarean birth following the difficult labor, she may doubt her ability to deliver vaginally.

Previous experiences do not always adversely affect a woman's ability to deal with pain. She may have learned ways to cope with pain during other episodes of pain or during other births. She may use these skills adaptively during labor.

PREPARATION FOR CHILDBIRTH

A pain-free labor is not ensured by preparation for childbirth. A woman should be prepared for pain realistically, including reasonable expectations about analgesia and anesthesia (Stolte, 1987). Otherwise, she may feel that her entire preparation is invalid if what she expects does not happen when she is in labor. She may then be unable to use other pain control methods that she learned during her preparation.

Preparation reduces anxiety and fear of the unknown. It allows a woman to rehearse for labor and

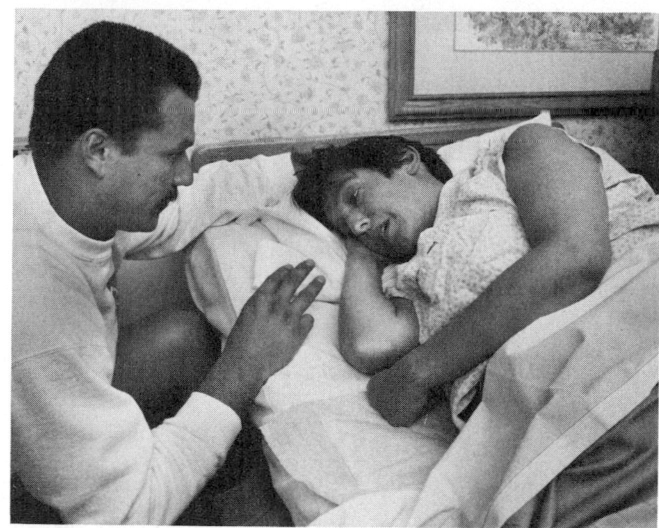

A woman and her partner who are prepared for labor have learned a variety of skills to master pain as labor progresses. The coach uses hand signals to tell the woman how to change her pattern of paced breathing.

learn a variety of skills to master pain as labor progresses. She and her partner learn about expected behavioral changes during labor, which decreases their anxiety when they occur.

SUPPORT SYSTEM

An anxious partner is less able to provide the support and reassurance that the woman needs during labor. Additionally, anxiety in others can be contagious, increasing her anxiety. She may assume that if they are worried, something is probably wrong.

The birth experiences of a woman's family and friends cannot be overlooked. These individuals can be an important source of support if they convey realistic information about labor pain and its control. If they describe labor as intolerable, however, she may have needless distress. It is equally detrimental for a woman to hear that labor was painless. No two labors are alike, even in the same woman.

✔ *Check Your Reading*

4. How may physical and psychological factors interact in a woman's labor pain experience?
5. What four sources of pain are present in most labors?
6. How can each of these physical factors influence the pain a woman experiences during childbirth? a. Labor intensity? b. Cervical readiness? c. Fetal position? d. Maternal pelvis? e. Fatigue?
7. Which psychosocial factors influence a woman's experience with labor pain?

Non-pharmacological Pain Management

The nurse who cares for women in labor and birth can offer two major types of pain management: non-pharmacological and pharmacological methods. Non-pharmacological methods require no medical order. Education about non-pharmacological pain management is the foundation of prepared childbirth classes (see Chapter 11, pp. 248–254, for discussion of specific techniques).

The intrapartum nurse should know methods taught in local childbirth classes to be most helpful to women and their partners. Teaching techniques that conflict with what a woman learned and practiced may confuse her. Other techniques can be reserved for use if a woman finds learned techniques ineffective.

Advantages. Non-pharmacological techniques are both an alternative to pharmacological methods and an adjunct to them. Most women use a combination of the two. The woman who chooses analgesia will need alternate pain management until it is given, usually after labor is well established. Also, pharmacological methods may not eliminate labor pain, and a woman will need non-pharmacological methods to control the pain that remains.

Non-pharmacological methods may be the only realistic option for a woman who enters the hospital in advanced, rapid labor. In this case, the drugs might not have enough time to take effect. Also, the newborn might have respiratory depression if the drug reaches its peak action about the time of birth.

Non-pharmacological methods have several advantages over pharmacological methods *if* pain control is adequate. They are harmless to the woman and fetus, do not slow labor, and have no side effects or risk of allergy.

Limitations. Non-pharmacological methods also have limitations, especially as the sole method of pain control. Many women will not achieve satisfactory pain control using these methods alone. Because of the many variables related to pain, a well-prepared and highly motivated woman may have a difficult labor and need analgesia or anesthesia.

Preparation for Pain Management

The ideal time to learn non-pharmacological pain control is before labor. During the last few weeks of pregnancy, the woman learns about labor, including its painful aspects, in childbirth classes. She can prepare to confront the pain, learning a variety of skills to use during labor. Her partner learns specific methods to encourage and support her. After admission, the nurse can review and reinforce what the partners learned in class.

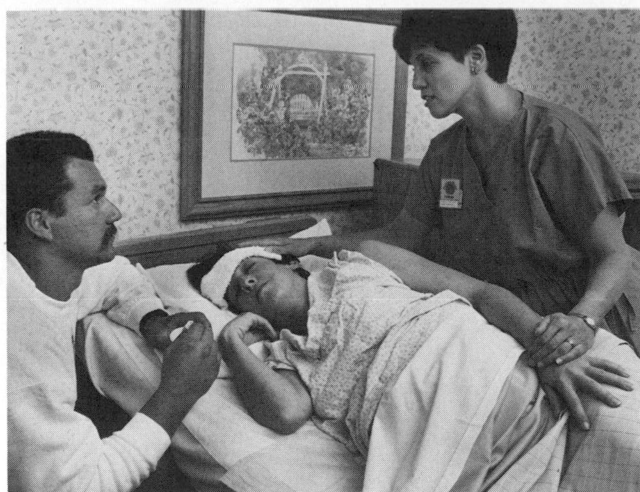

The nurse can best teach or reinforce non-pharmacological pain control during the latent phase of labor, when the woman is comfortable enough to understand the teaching.

The nurse can teach the unprepared woman and her support person non-pharmacological techniques. The latent phase of labor is the best time for intrapartum teaching because the woman is usually anxious enough to be attentive and interested, yet comfortable enough to understand. Late labor is a difficult time to teach because the woman cannot focus well on learning.

No one method or combination of methods will help every woman. Many methods may become less effective (habituation) after prolonged use. A woman needs to alternate techniques to reduce the effect of habituation. The nurse who knows a variety of methods can select those that are most helpful to an individual woman.

Application of Non-pharmacological Techniques

Four kinds of techniques discussed in Chapter 11 that can be applied to intrapartum care are addressed in this chapter: relaxation techniques, cutaneous stimulation, mental stimulation, and breathing techniques.

RELAXATION

Promoting relaxation provides a base for all other methods, both non-pharmacological and pharmacological. Relaxation is good in labor because it:

- Promotes uterine blood flow, improving fetal oxygenation.
- Promotes efficient uterine contractions.
- Reduces tension that increases pain perception and decreases pain tolerance.
- Reduces tension that can inhibit fetal descent.

Environmental Comfort. Comfortable surroundings support a woman's ability to relax. The nurse can promote environmental comfort by reducing irritants such as bright lights and by adjusting the room temperature.

Taped music masks outside noise and provides a background for use of imagery and breathing techniques. Television may have the same effect for many women. They are not paying attention to the program as much as using its sound to mask other disturbing sounds. Many individuals already have a conditioned response to television because they fall asleep with it on each evening.

Personal Comfort. Promoting the expectant mother's personal comfort helps her focus on pain management techniques during labor. This includes actions to increase comfort and reduce the effect of intrusive actions.

Reducing Anxiety and Fear. The nurse may reduce a woman's anxiety and increase her self-control by providing accurate information and focusing on the normality of birth. Most individuals associate hospitals with illness or injury, situations that are anxiety-provoking. Yet hospitals are the most common site for the basic physiological and emotionally unique event of birth.

Simple nursing actions keep the focus on the normality of childbirth, regardless of the setting. For example, referring to a woman as a patient reinforces the atmosphere of illness associated with being in a hospital, whereas calling her a woman or mother promotes a wellness approach.

Implementing Specific Relaxation Techniques. The techniques discussed in Chapter 11 are most successful if practiced before labor. However, during labor, caregivers can watch a woman for signs of tension and help her focus on relaxing tense muscles. Her partner often recognizes subtle signs of tension and can be taught to massage the area or call attention to the tension and guide the laboring woman to release it.

CUTANEOUS STIMULATION

Cutaneous stimulation has several variations that are often combined with each other or with other techniques.

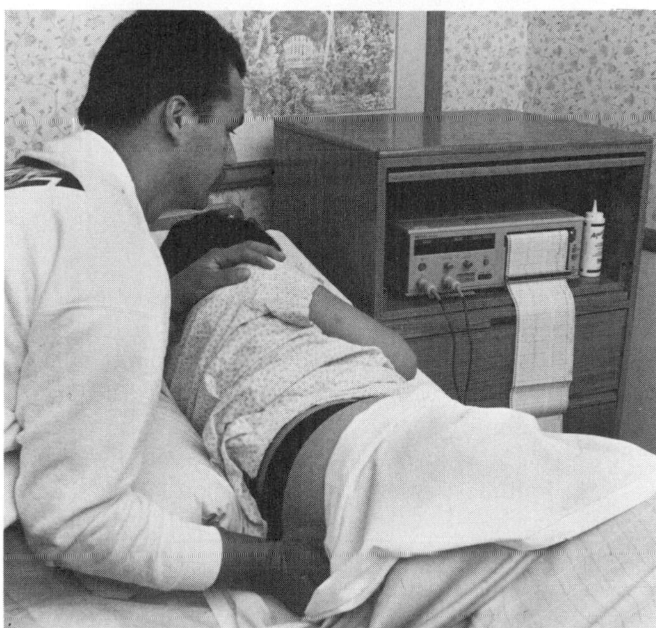

The coach applies sacral pressure and watches the contraction pattern on the monitor strip in order to know when to apply pressure.

Self-massage. The woman may rub her abdomen, legs, or back during labor (effleurage) to counteract discomfort. Some women find abdominal touch irritating, especially near the umbilicus. Effleurage traditionally uses light stroking, but women in labor often find firmer stroking most helpful (see Fig. 11–5).

Some women benefit from firm palm or sole stimulation during labor. They may like to have their palms rubbed vigorously by another, rub their hands or feet together, or bang their palms on, or grip, the cool bed rail. They may grip another's hand tightly during a contraction. The main point is to determine if these behaviors signify excess pain or if they are simply a woman's way of countering pain and therefore useful.

Massage by Others. The partner or the nurse can rub the woman's back, shoulders, or legs, or any area where she finds massage helpful. Sacral pressure is a variation that may help when the woman has back pain, which is usually most intense when the fetus is in an occiput posterior position. Sacral pressure may be applied, using the palm of the hand, the fist or fists, or a firm object such as two tennis balls in a sock.

Thermal Stimulation. Many women appreciate warmth to their back during labor. A warmed disposable bottle of solution can be used to provide both warmth and pressure on the back. A warm shower or tub bath is relaxing and provides thermal stimulation. Cool, damp washcloths may be comforting, especially in later labor when a woman may be hot. She may put them on her head, throat, abdomen, or anyplace she wants. She also may want to put them in her mouth to relieve dryness.

MENTAL STIMULATION

Mental techniques occupy the woman's mind and compete with pain stimuli. They also aid relaxation by providing a tranquil imaginary atmosphere.

Imagery. If the woman has not practiced a specific imagery technique, the nurse can help her evoke a relaxing mental scene. Most women find images of warmth, softness, security, and total relaxation most comforting.

Imagery can help the woman dissociate herself from the painful aspects of labor. For example, the nurse can help her visualize the work of labor: the cervix opening with each contraction or the fetus moving down toward the outlet each time she pushes. This technique is like visualizing success or movement toward a goal with each contraction.

Focal Point. When using non-pharmacological techniques, a woman may prefer to close her eyes or may want to concentrate on an external focal point. She may bring a picture of a relaxing scene or an object to use as a focal point and to aid the use of imagery. She can use any point in the room as a focal point.

BREATHING TECHNIQUES

Breathing techniques give a woman a different focus during contractions, interfering with pain. They begin with simple patterns and progress to more complex ones as needed. There is no single right time to change patterns during labor. However, complex patterns are fatiguing to use for a prolonged time.

The nurse can teach an unprepared woman these breathing techniques. Latent labor is the ideal time for teaching, but she can learn each technique as she needs to use it (see Chapter 11 for discussion of breathing techniques).

✔ Check Your Reading

8. Why should the nurse ensure relaxation during labor?
9. What are some nursing actions to promote relaxation during labor?
10. How can the nurse reduce a laboring woman's anxiety or fear?
11. What touch techniques may help the woman during labor? What actions may reduce back pain during labor?

Pharmacological Pain Management

Pharmacological methods for pain management include analgesics, adjunctive drugs, and anesthesia. These are further divided into systemic drugs and regional methods. The intrapartum nurse gives analgesics and most adjunctive drugs. Depending on the type, the attending physician or nurse-midwife, an anesthesiologist, or a nurse anesthetist may give anesthetics. Licensing laws and policies of individual hospitals or birth centers determine what anesthetics each clinician may administer.

Special Considerations When Medicating a Pregnant Woman

Medicating a woman when she is pregnant is not as straightforward as when she is not pregnant:

- Any drug (therapeutic or abused) given to the expectant mother may affect the fetus.
- Drugs may have different effects in pregnancy.
- Some analgesics and anesthetics can affect the course and length of labor.
- Complications may limit pharmacological pain management methods.
- Women who require other therapeutic drugs or who practice substance abuse may have fewer safe choices for pain relief.

EFFECTS ON THE FETUS

Effects on the fetus of drugs given to the mother may be direct, resulting from passage of the drug or its metabolites across the placenta to the fetus. An example of a direct effect on the fetus is decreased fetal heart rate variability following administration of a narcotic analgesic to the woman.

Effects on the fetus may be indirect, or secondary to drug effects in the expectant mother. For example, if a drug causes maternal hypotension, blood flow to the placenta is reduced. Fetal hypoxia and acidosis may then occur. Although not directly affected by the drug, a fetus is affected by the mother's response to it.

MATERNAL PHYSIOLOGICAL ALTERATIONS

Normal pregnancy changes in four body systems carry the greatest implications for pharmacological pain management methods.

Cardiovascular Changes. Compression of the aorta and inferior vena cava (aortocaval compression) by the uterus can occur when a woman lies in the supine position (see Fig. 7–4). However, some anesthetics require that she assume the supine position temporarily. In such a case, the uterus is displaced to one side with the hands or with a small wedge under her right hip.

Respiratory Changes. A pregnant woman's full uterus reduces her respiratory capacity. To compensate, she breathes more rapidly and deeply. As a result, she is more vulnerable to reduced arterial oxygenation during induction of general anesthesia and is more sensitive to inhalational anesthetic agents.

Gastrointestinal Changes. A pregnant woman's stomach is displaced upward by her large uterus; the stomach's interior also has a higher pressure within. Progesterone slows peristalsis and reduces the tone of the sphincter at the junction of the stomach and esophagus. These changes make a pregnant woman more vulnerable to regurgitation and aspiration of acidic gastric contents during general anesthesia.

Nervous System Changes. During pregnancy and labor, circulating levels of endorphins are high. Endorphins modify pain perception and reduce requirements for analgesia and anesthesia.

The epidural and subarachnoid spaces are smaller during pregnancy, enhancing the spread of anesthetic agents used for epidural or subarachnoid blocks. Cerebrospinal fluid (CSF) pressure is higher, reaching a peak during the second stage of labor. Nerve fibers are more sensitive to local anesthetic agents, probably because of acid-base or hormonal alterations. High intra-abdominal pressure causes engorgement of the epidural veins, increasing the risk for intravascular injection of anesthetic agents. The net result of these changes is that a reduced volume of local anesthetic is needed to achieve satisfactory epidural or subarachnoid block.

EFFECTS ON THE COURSE OF LABOR

Most analgesics are not given until labor is well established because they may slow progress if given too early. However, caregivers must consider the adverse effects of excessive pain on labor's progress when helping a woman choose methods of pain relief. Regional anesthetics, primarily the epidural block, may slow progress during the second stage because they can impair the laboring woman's natural urge to push.

EFFECTS OF COMPLICATIONS

Complications during pregnancy may limit the choices of analgesia or anesthesia. For example, infusion of large volumes of intravenous fluids is done to prevent hypotension with regional anesthesia. If a pregnant woman has heart disease or pregnancy-induced hypertension, this fluid load could be detrimental. Yet without it, she is vulnerable to hypotension.

INTERACTIONS WITH OTHER SUBSTANCES

A woman who ingests drugs (therapeutic, over-the-counter, or abused) or other substances may have fewer options because of interactions between these substances and analgesics or anesthetics. For example, alcohol increases the depressant effects of narcotics, making both the mother and newborn susceptible to respiratory depression.

✔ *Check Your Reading*

12. How can drugs taken by the expectant mother affect the fetus?
13. How do changes in four maternal body systems affect pharmacological pain management?
14. How do endorphins influence the mother's need for pharmacological pain relief during labor?
15. Why is it important to know all drugs or abused substances that a laboring woman has ingested?

Analgesics and Adjuncts

NARCOTICS

Analgesics are systemic agents that reduce perception of pain without loss of consciousness. Injectable narcotic analgesics are the systemic drugs of choice in labor. Common analgesics for intrapartum use are butorphanol (Stadol), nalbuphine (Nubain), and meperidine (Demerol). Table 15–1 summarizes common drugs used for intrapartum pain relief.

Butorphanol and nalbuphine have mixed narcotic agonist and antagonist effects. These drugs should not be given to a woman who is opiate-dependent (heroin) to avoid withdrawal effects. They should not be given if she has already received a pure narcotic, such as meperidine, or some analgesic effect of the first drug will be reversed.

Table 15–1. DRUGS COMMONLY USED FOR INTRAPARTUM PAIN MANAGEMENT

Drug/Dose	Comments
Narcotic (Opiate) Analgesics	
Meperidine (Demerol) 12.5–50 mg every 2–4 hours	Respiratory depression (primarily in the neonate) is the main side effect
Butorphanol (Stadol) 1 mg every 3–4 hours; range 0.5–2 mg	Has some narcotic antagonist effects; should not be given to the opiate-dependent woman (may precipitate withdrawal) or after other narcotics such as meperidine (may reverse their analgesic effects); also a respiratory depressant
Nalbuphine (Nubain) 10 mg every 3–6 hours IV	Same as butorphanol
Adjunctive Drugs	
Promethazine (Phenergan) 12.5–25 mg every 4–6 hours	Duration of action is longer than most narcotics; enhances respiratory depressant effects of narcotics
Propiomazine (Largon) 20 mg (range 10–40 mg) every 3–4 hours	See promethazine
Diphenhydramine (Benadryl) 25–50 mg IV	Given to relieve pruritus from epidural narcotics
Narcotic Antagonists	
Naloxone (Narcan) Adult: 0.4–2 mg IV To reverse pruritus from epidural narcotics: 0.04–0.2 mg IV or IV infusion 0.2–0.6 mg/hour Neonate: 0.1 mg/kg IV (umbilical vein) or intratracheal	Action shorter than most narcotics it reverses; must observe for recurrent respiratory depression and be prepared to give additional doses
Naltrexone (Trexan): 6 mg p.o. × 1 dose	Long-acting drug to relieve pruritus from epidural narcotics (investigational when used for this purpose)

IV = intravenously; p.o. = orally.

The primary side effect of narcotic analgesics is respiratory depression, which is more likely to occur in the newborn. Timing of narcotic administration is important to reduce neonatal respiratory depression. An infant who is born 1 to 4 hours after the mother receives meperidine is more likely to have respiratory depression than if born earlier or later. Additionally, metabolites of meperidine are active for a prolonged time in the newborn and can cause delayed respiratory depression (Endler and Bhatia, 1990).

Butorphanol and nalbuphine also produce respiratory depression, but it does not increase markedly as the dose increases. These two drugs are becoming more popular for intrapartum analgesia because of the more limited respiratory depression seen with them than with meperidine (see Drug Guide 15–1 on butorphanol).

Narcotics are usually given in small, frequent doses by the intravenous route during labor to provide a rapid onset and shorten the duration of action. A woman benefits from rapid onset of analgesia, with less likelihood of neonatal respiratory depression. Starting the injection at the beginning of the contraction, when blood flow to the placenta is normally reduced, limits transfer to the fetus (Endler and Bhatia, 1990).

NARCOTIC ANTAGONIST

Naloxone (Narcan) reverses narcotic-induced respiratory depression. Naloxone does not reverse respiratory depression from other causes, such as barbiturates, anesthetics, non-narcotic drugs, or pathological conditions. Naloxone has a shorter duration of action than most of the narcotics it reverses. In an opiate-dependent woman or newborn, naloxone may induce withdrawal symptoms. Naloxone is used with other measures as needed to support cardiopulmonary function. (See Chapter 29 for discussion of neonatal resuscitation.)

The usual routes for naloxone administration are intravenous or intratracheal. Although naloxone may be given by the sublingual, subcutaneous, or intramuscular routes, absorption may be erratic. The adult dose is 0.4 to 2 mg. The neonatal and pediatric dose is 0.1 mg/kg by the intravenous or intratracheal route (American Academy of Pediatrics Committee on Drugs, 1989). Intravenous naloxone is given to the neonate through the umbilical vein.

Drug Guide

BUTORPHANOL (Stadol)

Classification: Narcotic analgesic.

Action: Narcotic analgesic with some narcotic agonist-antagonist effects. Exact mechanism of action is unknown. Produces respiratory depression that does not increase markedly with larger doses.

Indications: Systemic pain relief during labor.

Dosage and Route: Intravenous: 1 mg every 3 to 4 hours; range 0.5 to 2 mg. May be given undiluted.

Absorption: Onset of analgesia almost immediate with intravenous administration, peaks about 30 minutes, and lasts about 3 hours. Faster acting and shorter duration of action than meperidine or morphine.

Excretion: Excreted in urine. Crosses placental barrier. Secreted in breast milk.

Contraindications and Precautions: Contraindicated in persons who are hypersensitive. Do not use in opiate-dependent persons because antagonist activity of the drug may cause withdrawal symptoms in the woman or newborn. Use cautiously during labor and delivery of preterm infants. Drug is potentiated (enhanced) by barbiturates, phenothiazines, cimetidine, and other tranquilizers.

Adverse Reactions: Respiratory depression or apnea (woman or newborn), anaphylaxis. Dizziness, lightheadedness, sedation, lethargy, headache, euphoria, mental clouding, fainting, restlessness, excitement, tremors, delirium, insomnia. Nausea, vomiting, constipation, increased biliary pressure, dry mouth, anorexia. Flushing, altered heart rate and blood pressure, circulatory collapse. Urinary retention. Sensitivity to cold.

Nursing Considerations: Assess the woman for allergies and opiate dependence. Observe vital signs and respiratory function in woman (12/minute or more) and newborn (30/minute or more). Have naloxone and resuscitation equipment available for respiratory depression in woman and neonate. Report nausea or vomiting, or both, to the physician or nurse-midwife for a possible order for an antiemetic. Antiemetics or other central nervous system depressants may enhance the respiratory depressant effects of butorphanol.

ADJUNCTIVE DRUGS

Adjunctive drugs during the intrapartum period include antiemetics and sedatives. Although these drugs do not relieve pain, they may reduce other discomfort (see Table 15–1).

Promethazine (Phenergan) relieves nausea and vomiting, which may occur when narcotic drugs are given. The narcotic dose is usually reduced because promethazine augments the action of the narcotic drug, including its depressant effects on maternal and newborn respirations. Promethazine has a longer duration of action than most narcotics and is not always repeated with every dose of narcotic.

Barbiturates, such as secobarbital (Seconal), are not routinely given because they have prolonged depressant effects on the neonate. The newborn may be sleepy, hypoventilate, feed poorly, and have poor muscle tone for up to 2 days. However, a small dose of a short-acting barbiturate may be given to a woman who is fatigued from false labor.

✔ Check Your Reading

16. What is the primary adverse effect of narcotic administration? How can this effect be reduced?
17. What should the nurse watch for after birth in the infant who received naloxone?
18. What is the correct dose of naloxone for an infant weighing 7 pounds (3178 g)?

Anesthetics

The two types of anesthesia used in intrapartum care are regional blocks and general anesthesia. The most popular regional blocks are the local, pudendal, epidural, and subarachnoid (spinal) blocks. The local and pudendal blocks are given in the vaginal-perineal area. The epidural and subarachnoid blocks anesthetize sensory nerves as they enter the spinal canal.

REGIONAL ANESTHESIA

Regional blocks use a local anesthetic agent to block conduction of pain impulses without loss of consciousness. Although they are classified as anesthetics, regional blocks are more accurately described as analgesics. They do not block all sensation, because the woman feels pressure, and sometimes reduced pain, in the anesthetized area.

The major advantage of all types of regional anesthesia is that the woman can remain awake and participate at birth and still have satisfactory pain relief. She can interact with her infant and partner immediately and does not lose her protective airway reflexes (see p. 377). Disadvantages vary with the type of block, as discussed further on. With most types of regional anesthesia, the effects on the fetus depend on how the woman responds rather than on direct drug effects.

LOCAL INFILTRATION

The physician or nurse-midwife infiltrates the perineum with a local anesthetic agent to numb the area before performing an episiotomy or suturing a laceration (Fig. 15–2). Local infiltration does not alter pain from uterine contractions or distention of the vagina. The local agent provides anesthesia in the immediate area of the episiotomy or laceration. There is a short delay between anesthetic injection and onset of numbness, and the drug burns before its anesthetic action begins. A woman will feel pain unless the physician or nurse-midwife allows time for the anesthetic action to begin. Local infiltration rarely has adverse effects on either mother or infant.

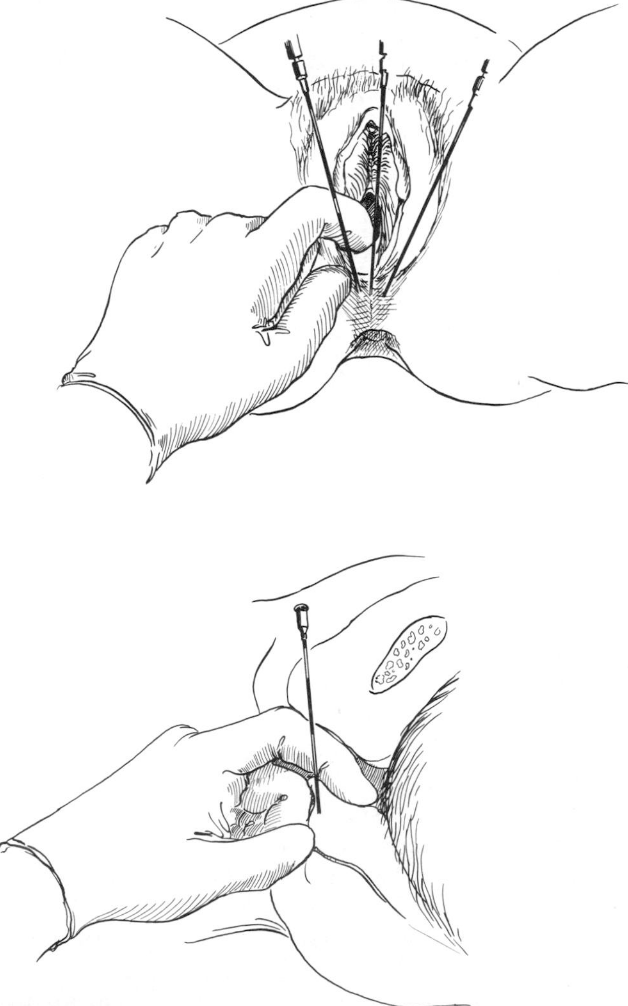

***Figure* 15–2**

Local infiltration anesthesia numbs the perineum just before birth for an episiotomy or after birth for suturing of a laceration. The physician or nurse-midwife protects the fetal head by placing a finger inside the vagina while injecting the perineum in a fan-like pattern.

PUDENDAL BLOCK

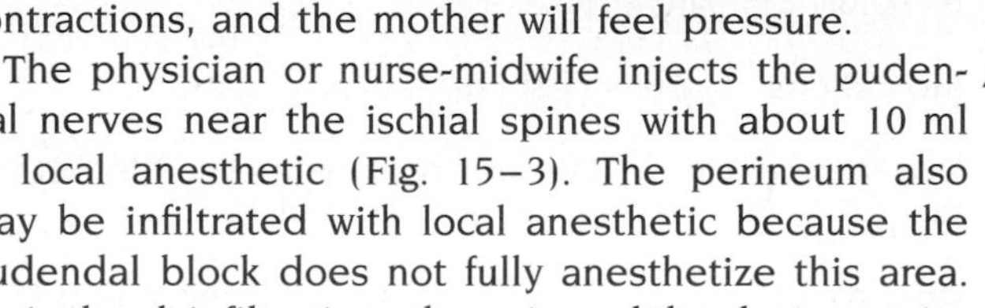

A pudendal block anesthetizes the lower vagina and part of the perineum to provide anesthesia for an episiotomy and a birth using low forceps if needed. A pudendal block does not block pain from uterine contractions, and the mother will feel pressure.

The physician or nurse-midwife injects the pudendal nerves near the ischial spines with about 10 ml of local anesthetic (Fig. 15–3). The perineum also may be infiltrated with local anesthetic because the pudendal block does not fully anesthetize this area. As in local infiltration, there is a delay between injection and onset of numbness. Possible maternal complications include a toxic reaction to the anesthetic, rectal puncture, hematoma, and sciatic nerve block. If maternal toxicity is avoided, the fetus is usually not affected.

EPIDURAL BLOCK

The lumbar epidural block is a popular regional block because it can provide pain relief for labor and birth without sedation of the woman and fetus. It is used for both vaginal and cesarean births.

The epidural space is outside the dura mater, between the dura and the spinal canal. It is loosely filled with fat, connective tissue, and epidural veins that are dilated during pregnancy (Fig. 15–4).

The epidural is more difficult than other regional blocks. It is done by injecting local anesthetic into the epidural space and can provide almost complete relief of pain from contractions and perineal pain. The level of the epidural block can be extended upward to provide anesthesia for a cesarean birth or tubal ligation after birth. The woman usually retains motor function when lower concentrations of anesthetic are used. She also may feel the urge to push during the second stage of labor. Higher concentrations used for abdominal surgery result in loss of both motor and sensory function.

Technique. The epidural block is started after labor is well established or just before cesarean birth. The physician or nurse anesthetist enters the epidural space at about the L3–L4 interspace (below the end of the spinal cord) and passes a catheter through the needle into the epidural space (Fig. 15–5). The catheter allows intermittent injection or continuous infusion of medication to maintain pain relief during labor and delivery or cesarean birth.

Epidural anesthesia requires a larger amount of anesthetic agent than the subarachnoid block. The physician or nurse anesthetist injects a small (3 ml)

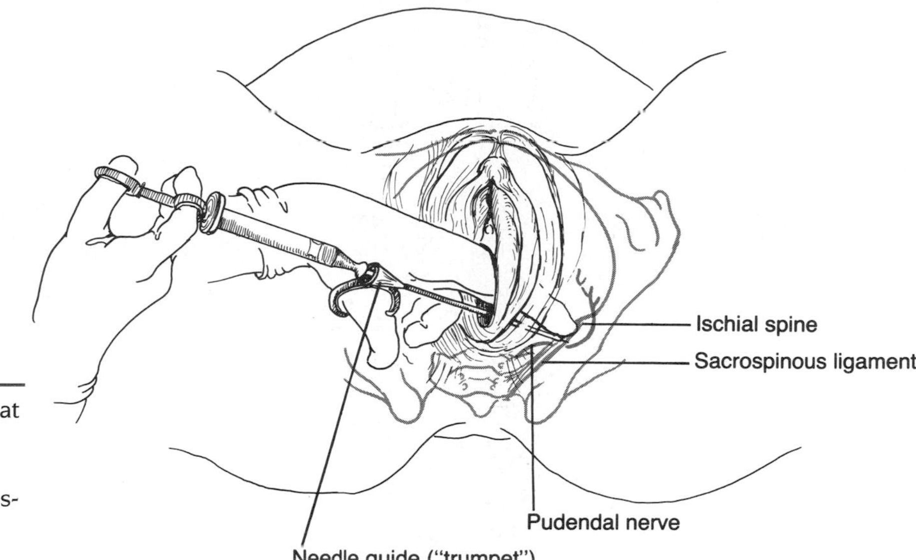

***Figure* 15–3**

Pudendal block provides anesthesia that is adequate for an episiotomy and use of low forceps. A needle guide ("trumpet") protects the maternal and fetal tissues from the long needle needed to reach the pudendal nerve.

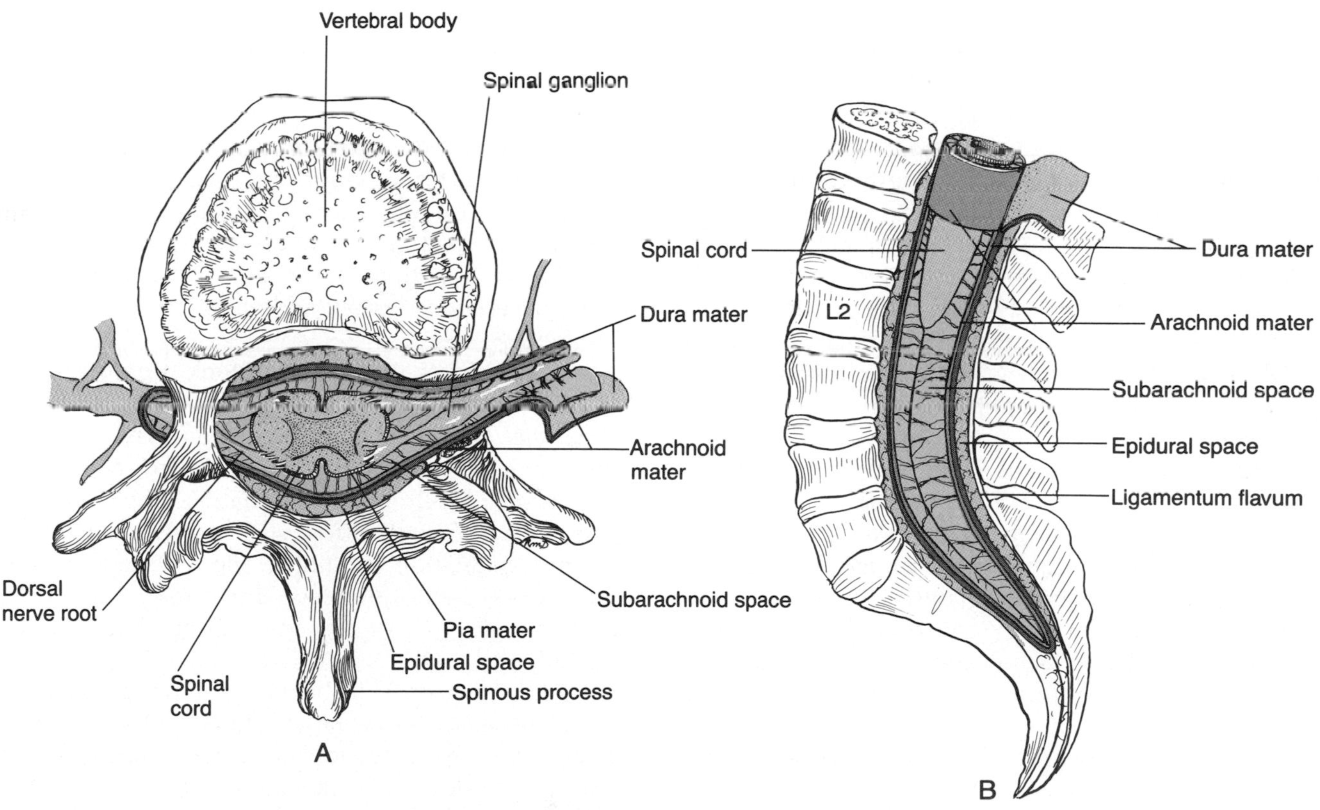

***Figure* 15–4**

A, Cross section of spinal cord, meninges, and protective vertebra. The dura and arachnoid lie close together. The pia mater is the innermost of the meninges and covers the brain and spinal cord. The subarachnoid space is between the arachnoid and pia mater. **B,** Sagittal section of spinal cord, meninges, and vertebrae. The epidural and subarachnoid spaces are illustrated. Note that the spinal cord ends at the L-2 vertebra.

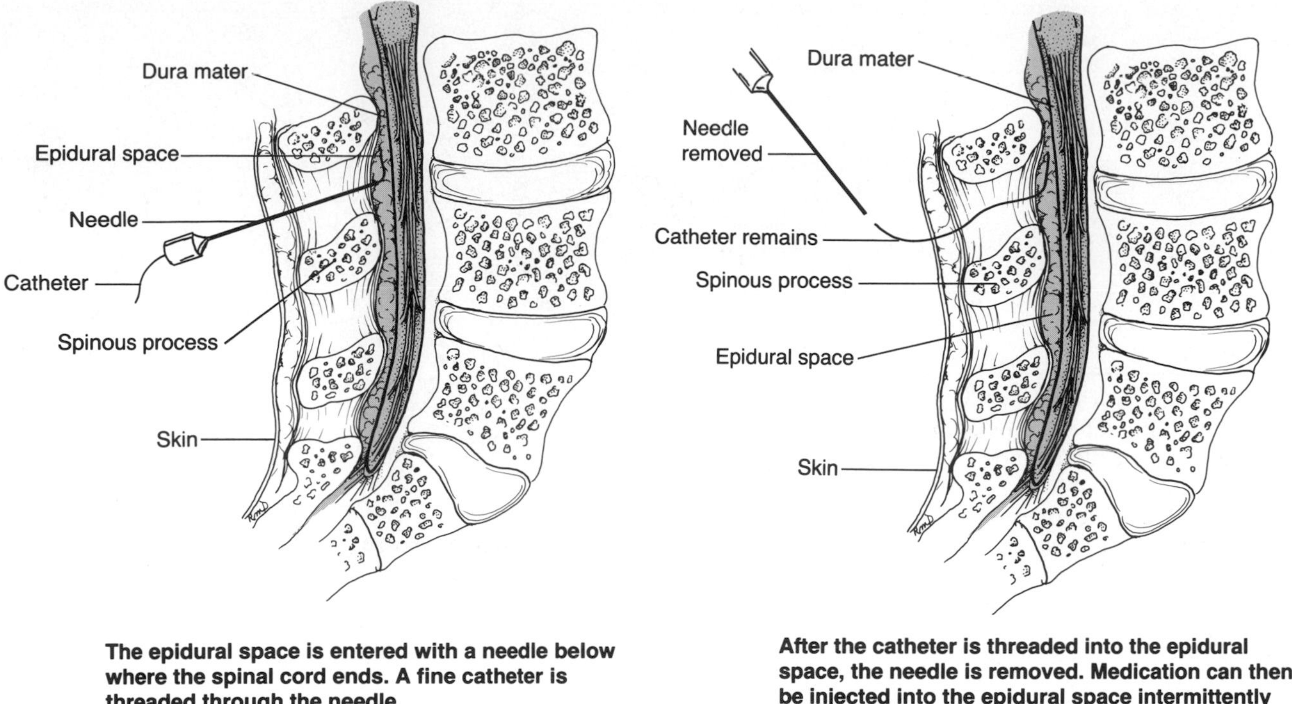
Dura mater
Epidural space
Needle
Catheter
Spinous process
Skin
The epidural space is entered with a needle below where the spinal cord ends. A fine catheter is threaded through the needle.
Dura mater
Needle removed
Catheter remains
Spinous process
Epidural space
Skin
After the catheter is threaded into the epidural space, the needle is removed. Medication can then be injected into the epidural space intermittently or by continuous infusion for pain relief during labor and birth.

Figure 15–5

Technique for epidural block.

test dose of local anesthetic before giving the full dose and before subsequent intermittent doses. If the catheter is in the subarachnoid space instead of the epidural space, the woman will have rapid, intense motor and sensory block. The test dose also can detect accidental intravascular injection. The woman will have numbness of the tongue and lips, lightheadedness, dizziness, and tinnitus with intravascular injection. Epinephrine in the test dose will produce tachycardia if injected intravascularly.

Dural Puncture. Because the tough dura and the fragile web-like arachnoid membranes lie close together, dural puncture also punctures the arachnoid. If the dura is unintentionally punctured with the large-gauge needle used to introduce the catheter, substantial leakage of CSF can occur, which may result in a spinal headache (see p. 376). Dural puncture and spinal headache also can occur without obvious CSF leakage.

Local anesthetics may be used alone in the epidural block or combined with a very small dose of a narcotic analgesic such as fentanyl (Sublimaze). The drug combination provides quicker and longer lasting pain relief for labor with a lower total dose of local anesthetic. Epidural narcotics are also given after cesarean birth to provide long-acting postoperative analgesia with a low narcotic dose.

Contraindications and Precautions. Epidural block is not suitable for all laboring women, and many do not want it. Contraindications include a woman's refusal, major coagulation defects, uncorrected hypovolemia, an infection in the area of insertion or a severe systemic infection, and allergy (Nicholson and Ridolfo, 1989).

Adverse Effects of Epidural Block. Epidural anesthesia can have adverse effects.

Maternal Hypotension. Hypotension may occur because sympathetic nerves are blocked along with pain nerves, resulting in vasodilation. Rapid infusion of an intravenous solution such as Ringer's lactate offsets vasodilation by filling the vascular system, reducing hypotensive effects. Ephedrine, 5 to 15 mg, intravenously, may be given for hypotension (McMorland, 1988).

Bladder Distention. A woman's bladder may fill quickly because of the large quantity of intravenous solution, yet her sensation to void is often reduced. Bladder distention may cause pain that remains after initiation of the block.

Prolonged Second Stage. If a woman does not have a spontaneous urge to push, the second stage of labor may be prolonged. However, the nurse can coach her to push with each contraction.

Catheter Migration. After accurate placement, the

catheter may move. A woman may then have symptoms of intravascular injection, an intense block or one that is too high, absence of anesthesia, or a unilateral block.

Adverse Effects of Epidural Narcotics. If epidural narcotics are used, the woman may have adverse effects in addition to those related to the epidural block alone.

Delayed Respiratory Depression. The possibility of late respiratory depression exists for up to 24 hours after the administration of epidural narcotics, depending on the drug used.

Pruritus. Itching of the face and neck is an annoying side effect of many epidural narcotics. Although she may not specifically complain of itching, a woman may rub or scratch her face and neck frequently. Diphenhydramine (Benadryl), naloxone (Narcan), or naltrexone (Trexan) may relieve pruritus (see Table 15–1).

SUBARACHNOID (SPINAL) BLOCK

A subarachnoid block is a simpler procedure than the epidural block. It can be done more quickly than the epidural block but not as quickly as general anesthesia. The shorter time needed to establish adequate anesthesia is more critical when a quick cesarean birth is necessary.

The physician or nurse anesthetist injects local anesthetic into the subarachnoid space in a single dose just before birth occurs. The subarachnoid block is most often used for cesarean section. It does not provide pain relief for labor.

Technique. The anesthesiologist or nurse anesthetist introduces a 25- to 26-gauge spinal needle into the subarachnoid space. Appearance of CSF at the needle hub assures correct needle placement, and the local anesthetic is injected (Fig. 15–6).

The level of anesthesia for both epidural and subarachnoid blocks is determined by the volume, concentration, and density of the drug (Fig. 15–7). For vaginal birth, the level is usually at the T10–T12 level. For cesarean birth, a T4–T6 level is needed (Ramanathan, 1988). The woman loses both sensory and motor function below the level of the subarachnoid block, with complete relief of perineal pain and pain from contractions.

Contraindications and Precautions. These are similar to those for epidural block: the woman's refusal, major coagulation defects, uncorrected hypo-

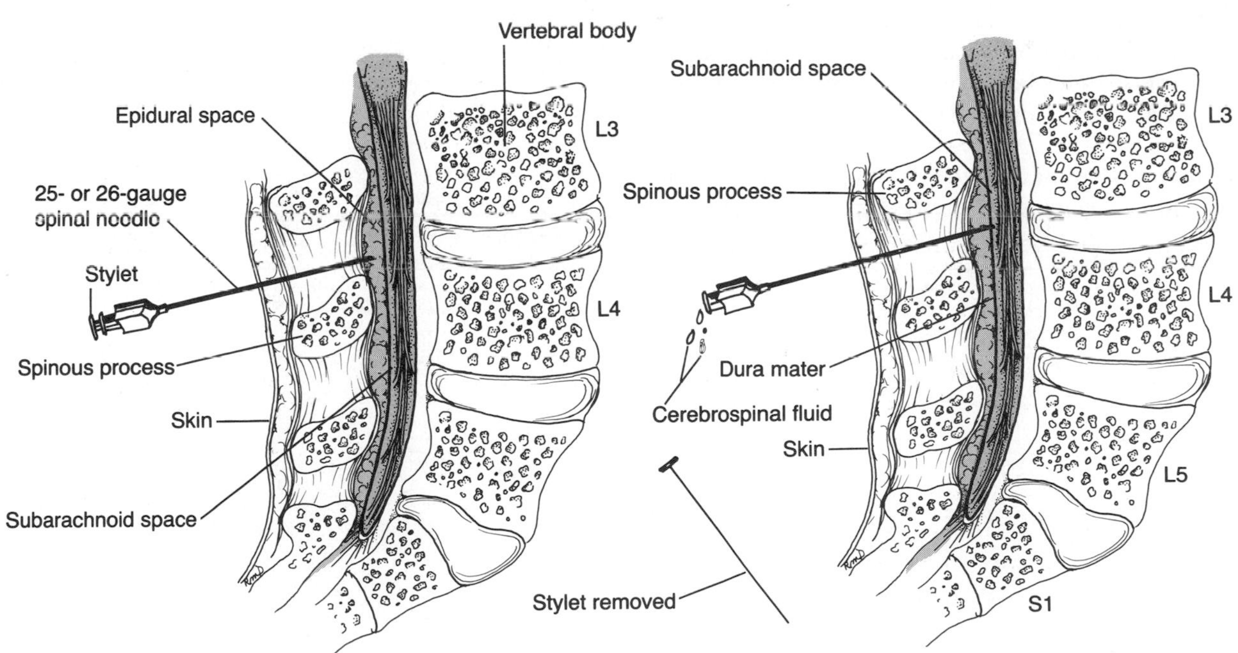
Vertebral body
Epidural space
25- or 26-gauge spinal needle
Stylet
Spinous process
Skin
Subarachnoid space
L3
L4
A 25- or 26-gauge spinal needle with a stylet occluding its lumen is passed into the subarachnoid space below where the spinal cord ends.
Subarachnoid space
Spinous process
Dura mater
Cerebrospinal fluid
Skin
Stylet removed
L3
L4
L5
S1
The stylet is removed, and one or more drops of clear cerebrospinal fluid at needle hub confirm correct needle placement. Medication is then injected, and the needle is removed.

Figure 15–6

Technique for subarachnoid block.

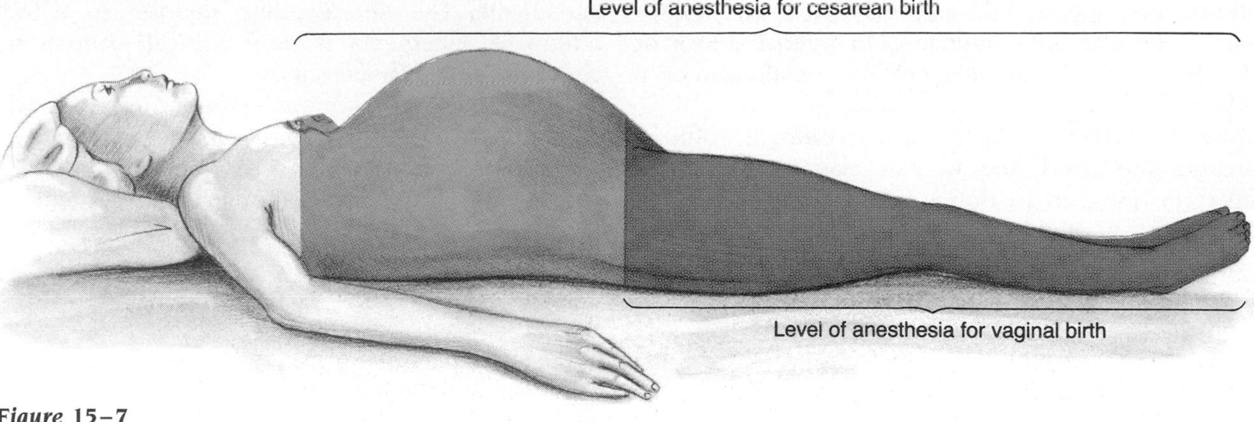

Figure 15–7

Levels of anesthesia for epidural and subarachnoid blocks. A level of T10-12 is adequate for vaginal birth. A higher level of T4-6 is needed for cesarean birth.

volemia, infection in the area of insertion, systemic infection, and allergy.

Adverse Effects. Three adverse effects of a subarachnoid block include maternal hypotension and bladder distention (see Epidural Block) and spinal headache. Hypotension is more likely with the subarachnoid block than with the epidural block.

Post-spinal headache may occur after subarachnoid block in some women because of CSF leakage at the site of dural puncture. A spinal headache is postural; it is worse when a woman is upright, yet may disappear entirely when she is lying flat. The incidence of spinal headache is lower if a small-gauge needle is used.

Bed rest with oral or intravenous hydration helps relieve the post-spinal headache. A blood patch often gives dramatic, definitive relief. The blood patch is done by injecting 10 to 15 ml of the woman's blood (obtained with sterile technique) into the epidural space. The blood forms a gelatinous seal over the hole in the dura, stopping spinal fluid leakage (Fig. 15–8). The blood patch can be repeated if needed.

OLDER REGIONAL BLOCKS

The use of caudal, paracervical, and saddle blocks is infrequent today because of their limitations or adverse effects and because of the success of continuous lumbar epidural anesthesia.

GENERAL ANESTHESIA

General anesthesia is rarely given for vaginal births, but it still has a place in cesarean birth. Some women either refuse or are not good candidates for epidural or subarachnoid block. In other cases, it may be necessary to perform a cesarean birth quickly, and there is not time to establish either type of regional block.

Technique. Before induction of anesthesia, a woman breathes oxygen for 3 to 5 minutes, or at

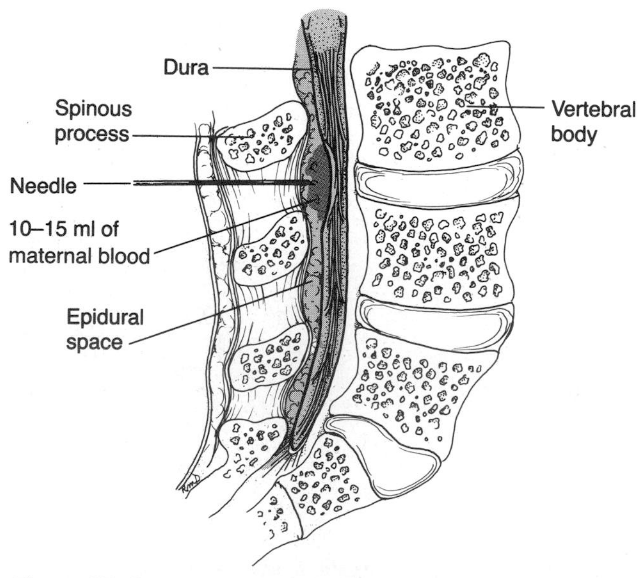

Figure 15–8

Blood patch for relief of spinal headache. Ten to 15 ml of the woman's blood is injected into the epidural space to seal a dural puncture.

least four deep breaths, to increase her oxygen stores and those of her fetus for the short period of apnea during anesthesia induction. The expectant mother has a wedge under her right side (or the operating table is tilted toward her left side) to reduce aortocaval compression and increase placental blood flow.

Adverse Effects. Major adverse effects are possible with the use of general anesthesia.

Maternal Aspiration of Gastric Contents. Regurgitation with aspiration of acidic gastric contents is a potentially fatal complication of general anesthesia. Aspiration of food particles may result in airway obstruction. Aspiration of acidic secretions results in a chemical injury to the airways—aspiration pneumonitis. Infection often occurs after the initial lung injury.

Respiratory Depression. This condition may occur in either the mother or the infant but is more likely in the baby.

Uterine Relaxation. Some inhalational anesthetics may cause uterine relaxation. This characteristic is desirable for some complications, such as replacing an inverted uterus (see p. 768). However, postpartum hemorrhage may occur if the uterus relaxes after birth.

Methods to Minimize Adverse Effects. Measures to reduce the risk of maternal aspiration or of lung injury if aspiration occurs include:

- Restricting intake to clear fluids.
- Administering drugs to raise the gastric pH and make secretions less acidic, such as sodium citrate and citric acid (Bicitra), ranitidine (Zantac), or cimetidine (Tagamet).
- Administering drugs to reduce secretions, such as glycopyrrolate (Robinul).
- Administering drugs to speed gastric emptying, such as metoclopramide (Reglan).
- Use of cricoid pressure (Sellick's maneuver) to block the esophagus by pressing the rigid trachea against it (Fig. 15–9).

Neonatal respiratory depression may be averted by:

- Reducing the time from induction of anesthesia until the cord is clamped.
- Keeping the anesthesia level as light as possible until the cord is clamped.

To reduce the time from induction of anesthesia to cord clamping, the woman is prepared and draped and the physicians are ready before anesthesia is begun. Before cord clamping, the anesthesia is so light that it is more accurately described as amnesia with profound analgesia. She may move on the operating table as the incision is made, but she rarely remembers the experience. If a hazy memory remains, she does not usually remember it as painful. The anesthesia level is deepened after the cord is clamped.

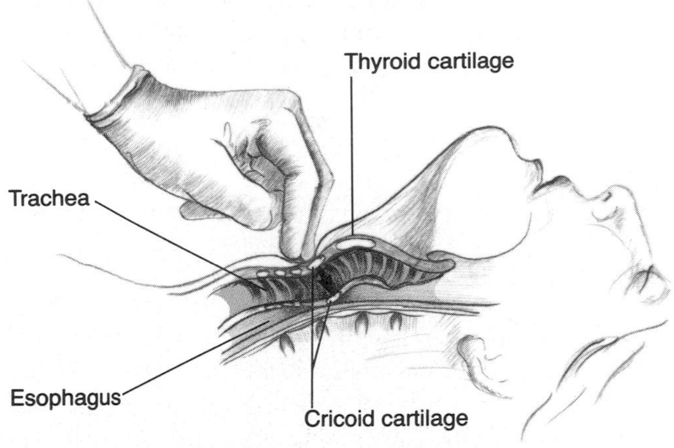

***Figure* 15–9**

Sellick's maneuver to prevent vomitus from entering the woman's trachea while she is being intubated for general anesthesia. An assistant applies pressure to the cricoid cartilage to obstruct the eosphagus. Once the woman is successfully intubated with a cuffed endotracheal tube, gastric secretions cannot enter the trachea.

✔ *Check Your Reading*

19. What are two major advantages of using regional anesthetics during childbirth?
20. What is the major adverse effect of the epidural or subarachnoid block? How can the fetus be affected? How may this effect be reduced?
21. What are the major adverse effects of general anesthesia? What measures reduce the risk?

Application of Nursing Process

The nurse assists laboring women with both nonpharmacological and pharmacological methods of pain control as needed. Nursing care related to pain management should be combined with that for normal labor and any complications that arise. Care of the fetus remains a priority and is discussed in

Chapters 13 and 14. Two problems that commonly affect the woman are pain and her potential for respiratory compromise if she needs general anesthesia.

Pain

Assessment

Pain assessment begins at admission and continues throughout labor. The assessments discussed on pp. 298–302 and in Table 13–1 guide the nurse in obtaining data related to pain management. Pain-related assessments include:

- Plans for pain management
- Maternal vital signs
- Fetal heart rate and monitor patterns
- Allergies, focusing especially on allergy to narcotics, dental anesthetics, and iodine (used in most "prep" solutions)
- Food intake
- Evidence of pain: verbal—statement, requests for pain relief measures, crying, moaning; and non-verbal—tense, guarded posture or facial expression
- Labor status

In addition to these routine assessments, ask the woman if she needs help with pain management. A stoic woman may give little outward evidence of pain, yet may say she wants medication or other pain control if asked.

Asking a woman to rate her pain on a scale of 0 to 10 helps make a subjective experience more objective. Zero represents no pain, whereas 10 is the worst possible pain. Ask the woman to rate her pain on this scale before and after pain relief measures for most accurate evaluation of their effectiveness.

The woman who remains tense between contractions may be having difficulty coping with pain. Moaning, crying, thrashing, and an inability to use learned non-pharmacological techniques suggest that she needs pharmacological pain relief.

Evaluate the woman's labor status to help her choose the most appropriate method of pain control. If she has reached a point in labor when she needs to decide for or against a specific pharmacological method, inform her. This is not an exact time or an exact amount of cervical dilation, but is estimated according to when she is likely to give birth, the time needed to establish a specific method, and the pharmacology of the drug or drugs.

Avoid making assumptions about the amount of pain a woman is having on the basis of her rate of labor progress, cervical dilation, or apparent intensity of contractions. It is tempting to assume that a woman whose cervix is 2 cm dilated has little pain and that a woman whose cervix is dilated 8 cm has intense pain. An obese woman's contractions may be strong, but they may seem mild if they are assessed by palpation or an external monitor. Labor progress or contraction intensity cannot be equated with a woman's pain perception or tolerance.

Neither should a woman's need for pain relief be based on her outward expression only. A quiet woman may need medication but may be reluctant to ask, whereas the expressive woman may be quite satisfied with only non-pharmacological measures. Since women who do not speak the prevailing language may not be aware of what is available, seek an interpreter to communicate.

Observe for pain that is not typical of labor. Although labor pain is often intense, it should not be constant but should come and go with each contraction. The uterus should not be tender or board-like between contractions. Report atypical pain to the physician or nurse-midwife. (See Chapter 26 for complications of labor.)

Analysis

Because pain is an expected part of normal childbirth, most laboring women will have nursing needs that relate to its management. The nursing diagnosis is: *Pain related to effects of uterine contractions and fetal descent.*

Planning

Because pain is a subjective experience, and labor is not expected to be painless, two goals are realistic. The woman will:

- Describe pain relief measures as satisfactory during labor.
- Use breathing and relaxation techniques during labor.

Interventions

The main points of nursing care related to intrapartum pain management are to reduce factors that hinder the woman's pain control and to enhance those that benefit it. Refer to Chapter 13 for the following general nursing measures that should be included in the care of all laboring women: Positioning, teaching, encouragement, and care of the partner.

PROMOTING RELAXATION

Simple attention to details can help the woman relax. Adjust her environment so that it is more comfortable. If noise is a problem, suggest music or television to mask it. Small earphones further mask outside noise and keep her choice of music from disturbing others.

A warm blanket or a cool cloth provides tangible comfort and conveys the nurse's caring attitude. Change the linens or underpads as needed to keep the woman reasonably clean and dry.

Offer the woman a warm shower or bath, especially if she is tense or having difficulty with back pain and if there are no contraindications (Table 15–2). In general, walking is good during early labor and water therapy is better during active labor. Newer birth units may have large tubs or whirlpools to use during labor. The baby may even be born in the water and brought to the surface right after birth. The mild nipple stimulation that occurs in a whirlpool or shower may intensify contractions in a woman whose labor has slowed because it causes her posterior pituitary gland to secrete oxytocin.

Reduce intrusions as much as possible. For example, wait until a contraction is over before asking questions or doing a procedure. Longer assessments and procedures may span several contractions, but try to stop during a contraction.

Table 15–2. USE OF WATER THERAPY DURING LABOR

Use of water therapy has accompanied trends toward a low-intervention approach to intrapartum care. Water therapy can be delivered in several ways:
- Shower
- Standard tub
- Whirlpool

Benefits
- Associated with a more natural, home-like atmosphere
- Gives a woman greater control over her labor
- Upright position facilitates progress of labor
- Faster labor progress if contractions are frequent when entering the tub
- Buoyancy relieves tired muscles
- Facilitates fetal rotation from occiput posterior or transverse positions to the occiput anterior; the woman can also assume different positions to aid rotation
- Many women report a perception of less pain
- Reduction in the mean arterial pressure, edema, and increased diuresis; this is especially helpful if the woman has pregnancy-induced hypertension

Disadvantages
- May reduce frequency of contractions and dilation during the latent phase of labor
- Fetus must be assessed with intermittent auscultation rather than electronic fetal monitoring, which requires more nursing time

Contraindications-Precautions
- No specific contraindications if the woman can safely be out of bed
- Thick meconium in the amniotic fluid is an indication for continuous electronic fetal monitoring in most birth facilities and would preclude use of water therapy
- Bleeding
- Oxytocin induction or augmentation; use of both oxytocin and water therapy could cause excess uterine activity

REDUCING OUTSIDE SOURCES OF DISCOMFORT

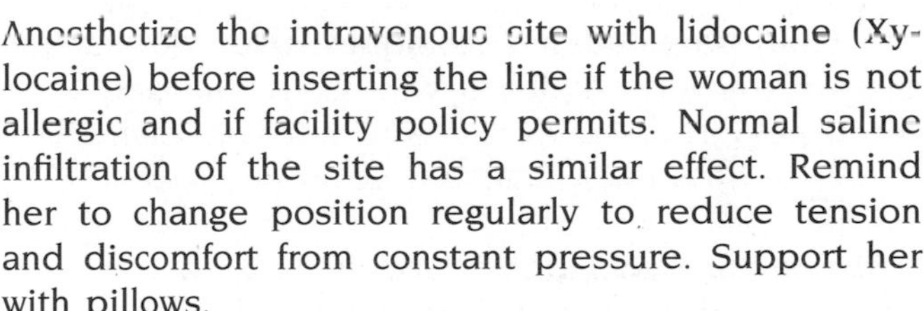

Anesthetize the intravenous site with lidocaine (Xylocaine) before inserting the line if the woman is not allergic and if facility policy permits. Normal saline infiltration of the site has a similar effect. Remind her to change position regularly to reduce tension and discomfort from constant pressure. Support her with pillows.

Observe the woman's bladder for distention hourly, and encourage her to void every 2 hours or more often if she has received a large quantity of intravenous fluids. Obtain an order to catheterize her if she cannot void and her bladder is full.

REDUCING ANXIETY AND FEAR

Accurate information reduces the negative psychological impact of the unknown. Tell the woman about her labor and its progress. It is impossible to predict when she will give birth, but tell her if labor progress is or is not on course. Sometimes she only needs the reassurance from an experienced nurse that her intense contractions are indeed normal. The woman may be willing to endure more discomfort than she otherwise would if she is making progress.

All persons caring for a woman should introduce themselves and tell her what she may expect from them. Inform her about procedures and medications, including the rationale and expected results. Be honest if problems do occur. A woman usually knows if there is a problem and is more anxious if she does not know what it is. Explain all measures taken to correct the problem and keep her informed about the results.

HELPING THE WOMAN USE NON-PHARMACOLOGICAL TECHNIQUES

If the non-pharmacological method is safe for the woman and fetus, and if it is effective, do not interfere with its use. Try not to distract the woman from whatever technique she is using. Avoid standing in front of her focal point. Ask, if it is not obvious, what she is using as a focal point.

Massage Techniques. Fetal monitor belts may hinder abdominal effleurage. Encourage a woman to do effleurage on uncovered areas of her abdomen or to stroke her thighs. Consider using intermittent fetal monitoring if this method is appropriate (see p. 334).

During massage, baby powder reduces friction and skin irritation. The woman needs to tell the person who is providing sacral pressure or other massage how much pressure helps and where the best location for it is. Since this information may change during labor, or massage may become uncomfortable rather than helpful, seek the woman's feedback regularly.

Mental Stimulation Techniques. Use a low, soothing voice when helping a woman use imagery. It is often helpful to speak close to her ear when trying to create a tranquil imaginary scene or trying to calm her.

Breathing Techniques. Women learn a variety of breathing techniques in prepared childbirth classes and often modify them or invent some of their own during labor. Encourage the woman to change techniques when she needs to, avoiding the complex ones during early labor. If she has trouble maintaining her concentration, the nurse or her partner can make eye contact and breathe the pattern with her.

Symptoms of hyperventilation (dizziness, tingling and numbness of the fingers and lips, carpopedal spasm) are likely if a woman breathes fast and deep, whether or not she is using patterned breathing techniques. If she hyperventilates, have her breathe into her cupped hands, a paper bag, or a washcloth placed over her nose and mouth.

Teach breathing techniques to the unprepared woman when she is admitted. Review them when she seems to need a different method. Many women make up their own breathing techniques.

When teaching the woman who is in advanced labor non-pharmacological pain management techniques, follow these guidelines:

- **Teach only one method at a time.**
- **Demonstrate the method between contractions.**
- **Use breathing techniques with the woman while maintaining eye contact.**

INCORPORATING PHARMACOLOGICAL METHODS

Many, if not most, women will need pharmacological pain management during labor. All pharmacological methods require collaboration with medical personnel for orders. Many physicians or nurse-midwives leave orders when the woman is admitted. Tell the woman soon after admission what medication is available if she needs it. This is done not to undermine her self-confidence but so that she can better understand when she needs to make a choice about medication. Also, analgesia is most effective if it is given before pain is severe.

Tell her that her preferences about pain relief methods will be honored if possible, but it is impossible to predict the course of her labor. Her preferred method of pain management may be inappropriate if labor has unexpected developments. Assure her, however, that no pharmacological method will be given without her understanding and consent (see Parents Want to Know: How Will This Medicine Affect Our Baby?).

If a woman finds non-pharmacological methods inadequate, try other ones or offer her available medication. Contact the physician or nurse-midwife if there is no medication order or if the medication that is administered is ineffective. When reporting, tell the physician or nurse-midwife about the fetal and maternal status (fetal heart rate and vital signs), labor status, and her request for medication. If she has a continuous epidural block, contact the person who inserted it if problems occur. Observe special nursing considerations associated with the method used (Table 15–3).

Parents Want To Know

How Will This Medicine Affect Our Baby?

Women and their partners often ask whether pain medication or anesthesia will harm their baby. The nurse can help parents to choose wisely from available options by providing honest information.

- Pain that is beyond your ability to tolerate is not good for you or your baby, and it reduces the pleasure of this special event.
- Some risk is associated with every type of pain medication or anesthesia, but careful selection and use of preventive measures will minimize this risk. If complications occur, there are corrective measures to reduce the risk to you and your baby.
- Narcotics can cause your baby to be slow to breathe at birth, but carefully controlling the timing and dose of the medication reduces the likelihood that this will occur. We can use another medication to reverse this effect if needed.
- Epidural or spinal anesthesia can cause your blood pressure to fall, which can reduce the blood flow to your baby. However, we give you lots of intravenous fluids to reduce this effect. We can use other medications to increase your blood pressure if the fluids are not enough.
- General anesthesia can cause your baby to be slow to breathe at birth. To reduce this risk, the anesthesia will not be started until everything is ready for the surgery and the doctors will clamp the baby's umbilical cord as quickly as possible.

Table 15–3. PHARMACOLOGICAL METHODS OF INTRAPARTUM PAIN MANAGEMENT

Method and Uses	Nursing Considerations
Narcotics	
Systemic analgesia during labor and for postoperative pain after cesarean birth. May be combined with adjunctive drug such as promethazine to reduce nausea and vomiting that sometimes occur with narcotic use.	1. Assess the woman for drug use at admission. Women who are opiate-dependent should not receive narcotics having mixed narcotic and narcotic-antagonist actions (butorphanol and nalbuphine). 2. Observe neonate for respiratory depression, especially if the mother had narcotics within 4 hours of birth: Delay in initiating or sustaining respirations Rate < 30/minute Poor muscle tone: limp, floppy 3. Use of adjunctive drugs, such as promethazine, enhances respiratory depressant effects. 4. Have naloxone available in both infant and adult doses. Observe for recurrent respiratory depression after administration of naloxone. Repeat at 20- to 60-minute intervals as needed.
Epidural Narcotics	
Labor: Mixed with a local anesthetic agent to give better pain relief with less motor block. *Postoperatively:* Gives long-acting analgesia without sedation, allowing the mother and infant to interact more easily.	1. Observe same nursing implications as with epidural block. 2. Do not give additional narcotics or other CNS depressants except as ordered by the anesthesia clinician. 3. Respiratory depression may be delayed up to 24 hours. Observe respiratory rate, depth, and arousability hourly for 24 hours. Notify anesthesia clinician for rate < 12/minute, oxygen saturation < 95% on pulse oximeter, reduced respiratory effort, or difficulty arousing. Cyanosis is a late sign. 4. Have naloxone, 0.4 mg, readily available. 5. Observe for pruritus or rubbing of the face and neck. Notify anesthesia clinician for relief measures. 6. Urinary retention may occur. After cesarean birth, women have an indwelling catheter for about 24 hours. Observe for adequate voiding (if the woman does not have a catheter). 7. Notify anesthesia clinician for relief of nausea or vomiting. 8. Assess sensation and mobility before allowing ambulation.
Local Infiltration Anesthesia	
Numbs perineum for episiotomy or repair of laceration at vaginal birth. No relief of labor pain because it is done just before or after birth. Not adequate for forceps-assisted birth.	1. Assess for drug allergies, especially to dental anesthetics because they are related to those used in maternity care. 2. Apply ice to perineum to reduce edema and hematoma formation and to increase comfort.
Pudendal Block	
Numbs the lower vagina and perineum for vaginal birth. No relief of labor pain because it is done just before birth. Provides adequate anesthesia for many forceps-assisted births.	1. Same as local infiltration. A woman may be alarmed by the long needle (about 6 inches). Teach her that it must be long to reach the pudendal nerve and that it will only be inserted about 0.5 inch into her tissue. Tell her that a guide ("trumpet") will be used to avoid damaging her or her fetus' tissue.
Epidural Block	
Labor: Insertion of catheter provides pain relief for labor and vaginal birth (T10–T12 level). *Cesarean birth:* If epidural was used during labor, level of block can be extended upward (T4–T6 level). Also used for planned cesarean birth and post-birth tubal ligation.	1. Prehydrate the woman with non-glucose crystalloid solution such as Ringer's lactate. Common amounts: 500–1000 ml for labor and vaginal birth; 1500–2000 ml for cesarean birth. Keep solutions for rapid infusion in a solution warmer to reduce chilling. 2. Displace uterus to left manually or with a wedge under woman's right side to enhance placental perfusion. 3. Assess for hypotension at least every 5 minutes after block is begun and with each new dose until vital signs are stable. Report to anesthesia clinician: systolic BP < 110 mmHg or a fall of 20% or more from baseline levels, pallor, or diaphoresis. 4. Assess FHR for signs of impaired placental perfusion and report to anesthesia clinician and nurse-midwife: Tachycardia (> 160/minute), bradycardia (< 110/minute), late decelerations (see Table 14–2). 5. If hypotension or signs of impaired placental perfusion occur: increase rate of non-additive IV fluid; turn woman to her left side, administer oxygen by face mask 8–10 L/minute. Have ephedrine available (usually included in epidural tray). 6. Observe for bladder distention. Get an order to catheterize woman if she cannot void. 7. Turn woman from side to side hourly when a continuous infusion is used to avoid unilateral block. 8. If block is being given by intermittent injection, notify anesthesia clinician for reinjection when pain recurs. 9. Observe progress of labor. Coach woman to push if she cannot feel the urge during second stage.

Table continued on following page

Table 15–3. PHARMACOLOGICAL METHODS OF INTRAPARTUM PAIN MANAGEMENT *Continued*

Method and Uses	Nursing Considerations
	10. Observe for signs of catheter migration: unilateral or absent pain relief, too intense motor and sensory block, signs of intravascular injection (numbness of tongue and lips, lightheadedness, dizziness, and tinnitus). 11. Transfer carefully because the woman may not have full use of her legs. Assess for return of sensation and movement before ambulation.
Subarachnoid Block	
Cesarean birth. Is simpler and can be established more quickly than epidural block. May rarely be used for complicated vaginal birth. Does not provide pain relief for labor because it is done just before birth.	1. See Epidural Block for these interventions: a. IV prehydration b. Uterine displacement c. Observation of blood pressure and FHR d. Care for hypotension or signs of impaired placental perfusion e. Bladder distention f. Transfer and ambulation precautions 2. Have the woman keep head flat as instructed by anesthesia clinician. 3. Observe for post-spinal headache: a headache that is worse when woman is upright and that may disappear when she is lying flat. Notify anesthesia clinician if it occurs (a blood patch may be done). 4. Nursing interventions for post-spinal headache: keep woman in bed with head flat; increase oral fluids if not contraindicated; give analgesics as ordered.
General Anesthesia	
Cesarean birth if epidural or spinal block is not possible or if the woman refuses regional anesthesia. May be required for emergency procedures such as replacement of inverted uterus.	1. Determine type and time of last food intake on admission. 2. Restrict oral intake to clear liquids or as ordered. Consult with physician or nurse-midwife if surgical intervention is likely. 3. Report to anesthesia clinician: oral intake before and during labor, vomiting. 4. Displace uterus (see Epidural Block). 5. Give ordered drugs such as sodium citrate and citric acid (Bicitra). 6. Maintain cricoid pressure (Sellick's maneuver) while anesthesia clinician intubates woman. 7. Maintain in a side-lying position (after surgery) until protective (gag) reflexes have returned. 8. Interventions for postoperative respiratory depression: give oxygen by face mask; observe oxygen saturation with pulse oximeter until woman is awake and alert; have woman take several deep breaths if oxygen saturation falls below 95%.

Abbreviations: CNS, central nervous system; BP, blood pressure; FHR, fetal heart rate; IV, intravenous.

Evaluation

Labor is not expected to be painless, even with the most effective pharmacological methods. The first goal is achieved if the woman is satisfied with her ability to tolerate and cope with pain. Many women have occasional difficulty using breathing or other techniques, even if they have practiced faithfully. They achieve the second goal if they use coping skills somewhat consistently during labor.

Respiratory Compromise

Assessment

General anesthesia may be needed any time during birth, most often for cesarean birth. Document the type (solids or liquids) and time of the woman's last food intake. Ask again about food intake before she has anesthesia because she may recall other intake. Question her closely if she reports an unusually long interval since her last oral intake. Anesthesia clinicians can anticipate and prevent problems better if they know the actual oral intake. Note allergies as well.

Analysis

Aspiration is a short-term risk if the woman has general anesthesia. Nursing care of laboring women includes this risk because it is impossible to predict every woman who will require general anesthesia. The nursing diagnosis is: *High risk for Aspiration related to impaired protective laryngeal reflexes.*

Planning

The goal for this nursing diagnosis is that the woman will not aspirate gastric contents into her trachea during the perioperative period.

Nursing Care Plan 15–1

Intrapartum Pain Management

Assessment: Beth Anderson is a 28-year-old gravida I, para 0 who was admitted 1 hour ago in early labor. Vaginal examination reveals that Beth is 3 cm dilated and 100% effaced, and the station is −2. Contractions are every 3 minutes, last 40 to 50 seconds, and are of moderate intensity. The fetal heart rate averages 135 to 145 BPM and has no abnormal patterns on the monitor. Although relatively comfortable when admitted, Beth is becoming more uncomfortable. She says that back pain is most troubling. Beth and her husband, Sam, had prepared childbirth classes and are using breathing techniques they learned.

Nursing Diagnosis: Pain related to effects of uterine contractions and pressure on pelvic structures as evidenced by Beth's statement.

Goals:
During labor, Beth will:
1. Continue to use techniques she learned in prepared childbirth classes.
2. Have a relaxed facial and body posture between contractions.

Intervention:	Rationale:
1. Adjust the environment for comfort: a. Adjust room thermostat. b. Add warm blankets and socks for warmth. c. Offer small electric fan or hand fan if Beth is hot.	1. A comfortable environment is conducive to relaxation. Relaxation underlies all other interventions because it increases a woman's ability to tolerate discomfort and use her coping skills.
2. Reduce distractions: a. Close door to reduce outside noise. b. Play music of Beth's choice to mask external noise. c. Do not stand in front of her focal point. d. Try to delay assessments such as vaginal examinations, fetal assessments, or questions until after a contraction is over.	2. Distractions interfere with Beth's ability to use the skills for pain management that she learned in her prepared childbirth classes.
3. Reduce irritating stimulants. a. Keep sheets and underpads dry. b. Lower lights as Beth desires, especially bright overhead lights. Use bright lights only when necessary. c. Do all procedures and nursing interventions as gently as possible. d. Avoid bumping the bed.	3. Irritating stimulants are a distraction that decrease Beth's ability to use her prepared childbirth skills. They are a source of discomfort themselves, adding to labor's discomfort.
4. Encourage Beth to assume positions she finds most comfortable and to change positions regularly (about every 30 to 60 minutes). If there is no contraindication, she may walk around or sit in a chair at the bedside. She should avoid the supine position.	4. Frequent position changes favor fetal descent by encouraging the fetal head to adapt to the pelvic diameters most efficiently and reduce muscle tension and unrelieved pressure. Upright positions enhance descent with gravity. The supine position is uncomfortable to most women and may cause aortocaval compression with decreased placental perfusion.
5. Check for bladder distention hourly. Encourage Beth to try to empty her bladder at least every 2 hours. Catheterize her if her bladder is full and she cannot void (get order).	5. Beth's sensation to void may be decreased during labor. A full bladder contributes to overall discomfort and may impede fetal descent and prolong labor.
6. If permitted by medical orders and Beth's condition, give her small amounts of clear fluids such as ice chips. If oral intake is prohibited, moisten her mouth with a damp washcloth or have her rinse her mouth with water.	6. Prepared childbirth breathing techniques often use rapid mouth breathing, resulting in a dry mouth. These methods may relieve some of the discomfort associated with a dry mouth. Clear liquids limit the risk of aspiration if general anesthesia is needed.

Nursing Care Plan continued on following page

Nursing Care Plan 15–1 *Continued*

Intrapartum Pain Management

7. Offer a back rub or firm, constant sacral pressure. Ask Beth where and how firm pressure should be. Use baby powder when rubbing the back. Have her tell caregivers if this technique becomes uncomfortable or if the location on her back needs to be changed. If Sam is rubbing her back, offer to relieve him occasionally and encourage him to take a break.	7. Back rubs may reduce discomfort associated with back labor somewhat by stimulating large-diameter fibers and interfering with transmission of the pain impulse to the brain. As labor continues, back rubs may later become less effective or even uncomfortable. Powder reduces friction, which could be another source of discomfort. Sam needs a break from the exertion of rubbing her back to conserve energy and be able to help Beth in later labor.
8. Keep Beth and Sam informed about the progress of labor and their baby's condition.	8. Reduces anxiety and fear of the unknown. Anxiety and fear increase pain perception and reduce pain tolerance.

Evaluation:
Beth concentrates on her breathing techniques with each contraction but has a relaxed body posture between them. Beth continues to use learned skills effectively for about 2 hours, when she begins to have more difficulty coping with her contractions. Interventions for pain continue but are revised to include those for pharmacological pain management.

Assessment: Three hours after admission, Beth's vaginal examination shows that she is 4 cm dilated and 100% effaced, and the station is −1. Contractions are every 2 to 3 minutes, last 50 seconds, and are firm. Fetal heart rate and monitor patterns are essentially unchanged. Back discomfort persists, and she is having difficulty relaxing between contractions and is discouraged that labor is not progressing as quickly as she expected. She is no longer able to use prepared childbirth techniques effectively. Beth reluctantly requests an epidural block, which will be given by continuous infusion.

Potential Complication:
Fetal compromise.

Goals:
Client goals are inappropriate for a collaborative problem because the nurse cannot independently manage fetal compromise. Planning reflects the nurse's responsibilities to:

1. Observe Beth's response to the epidural block.
2. Observe for signs of fetal compromise.
3. Take steps to reduce the risk of fetal compromise.
4. Report abnormalities to the physician or nurse-midwife and the anesthesia clinician.

Intervention:	Rationale:
1. Take Beth's blood pressure, pulse, and respiration hourly before the epidural block. Take blood pressure at least every 5 minutes until stable when epidural block is initiated, or according to protocol. An automatic blood pressure monitor makes frequent assessments easier.	1. Establishes a baseline to compare to blood pressures after the epidural block is established. Hypotension in the woman is the most common side effect of epidural block.
2. With medical order, infuse 500 to 1000 ml of warm Ringer's lactate or other dextrose-free crystalloid solution.	2. Expands the blood volume to compensate for the vasodilation resulting from sympathetic block associated with epidural block.
3. Keep Beth tilted slightly to her side with a wedge placed under her opposite side. Tilting to the left is usually the first position. Change her position from side to side every 30 to 60 minutes.	3. Prevents aortocaval compression, which might reduce placental perfusion and fetal oxygenation. Changing position from side to side reduces the possibility of a one-sided block and relieves pressure.

Nursing Care Plan 15–1 *Continued*

Intrapartum Pain Management

Intervention	Rationale
4. Assess fetus for tachycardia (fetal heart rate $>$160/minute), bradycardia (fetal heart rate $<$110/minute), or for a pattern of late decelerations on the monitor.	4. Maternal hypotension may reduce placental perfusion. These fetal heart rate changes are associated with impaired placental perfusion, although they may occur for reasons other than maternal hypotension (see Chapter 14).
5. If maternal hypotension or changes in fetal heart rate (as in No. 4) occur, notify anesthesia clinician and physician or nurse-midwife and:	5. Medical assistance may be needed if nursing measures do not correct hypotension or non-reassuring fetal heart rate changes occur. Measures to increase placental perfusion:
a. Increase the rate of non-additive intravenous fluid	a. Fills vascular system
b. Position Beth farther on side	b. Prevents aortocaval compression
c. Give Beth oxygen by face mask at 8 to 10 L/minute	c. Increases maternal oxygen saturation making more available to her fetus
d. Have ephedrine available for administration	d. Ephedrine is a centrally acting vasopressor that restores normal arterial tone

Evaluation:
Because client-centered goals are not developed for collaborative problems, the nurse compares data to baseline data. For this situation, the nurse is reassured by signs that Beth and her fetus are tolerating the effects of epidural block. Specific indicators are:

1. Beth's blood pressure remains greater than 100 mmHg systolic and does not fall 20% or more below her baseline level.
2. The fetal heart rate remains at its baseline range of 135 to 145 BPM without late decelerations.

Assessment: Beth is more comfortable after the epidural block takes effect. She cannot feel most of her contractions. She is able to move her legs but does not have full voluntary control.

Nursing Diagnosis: High risk for injury related to altered sensation as evidenced by reduced sensation and movement of her lower extremities.

Goals:

1. Beth will not fall or suffer other injury until effects of epidural block are gone.
2. The fetus will not be born in an uncontrolled manner.

Intervention:	Rationale:
1. Keep Beth in bed while block is in progress. Assist her to change positions, supporting her lower extremities as needed.	1. The epidural block causes a varying degree of motor block. Because Beth cannot accurately sense her position and may be unable to move independently, she is at risk for muscle strains.
2. Observe for signs of labor progress: a. Contractions increase in frequency, duration, and intensity b. Increase in bloody show c. Statement reflecting urge to push (may *not* be present)	2. Beth's sensation is altered and she may be unable to detect rectal pressure associated with fetal descent. Although unlikely, because this is Beth's first birth, the fetus could be born unattended because of her altered sensation.
3. If Beth cannot feel the urge to push during the second stage, tell her when to push during contractions.	3. Epidural block may alter Beth's reflex urge to push. Coaching her about when to push aids fetal descent.
4. After birth, do not allow Beth to ambulate until sensation and movement have returned to her lower extremities. Ask another nurse to assist when she first ambulates.	4. Prevents falls due to weakness and inability to sense where her feet are. Having assistance prevents injury to Beth if she is unexpectedly weak when she ambulates.

Nursing Care Plan continued on following page

Nursing Care Plan 15–1 *Continued*

Intrapartum Pain Management

Evaluation:
Beth is satisfied with her pain relief after the epidural block. She has minimal motor block and is able to turn herself with assistance. Her blood pressure and the fetal heart rate remain within expected limits. Vaginal dilation progresses to 10 cm (complete) without injury to Beth or her fetus.

Assessment: Despite Beth's adequate pushing efforts, the fetal station remains at 0. Beth has a cesarean birth, delivering an 8 pound, 10 ounce girl.

Nursing Diagnosis: (Preoperative and intraoperative):
High risk for aspiration related to impaired laryngeal reflexes secondary to possible general anesthetic.*

Goal:
Beth will not aspirate gastric contents during general anesthesia. (Although an epidural block is in place, general anesthesia may become necessary.)

Intervention:	Rationale:
1. Record Beth's last oral intake before admission and all oral intake after admission. Record all instances of emesis: quantity, character (liquid or with food particles), number of times. Notify anesthesia clinician of these observations.	1. Advance knowledge allows anesthesia clinician to prepare for respiratory complications more accurately.
2. Allow Beth nothing by mouth when operative intervention seems likely. Consult with the physician, nurse-midwife, or anesthesia clinician for questions about oral intake.	2. Keeps volume of gastric contents as low as possible, minimizing the risk of regurgitation and aspiration.
3. Give sodium citrate and citric acid (Bicitra) or other medication as ordered or according to hospital protocol.	3. Reduces gastric acidity. If regurgitation and aspiration occur, less lung damage is likely if the aspirate is less acidic.

Evaluation:
Beth does not require general anesthesia and thus retains all her protective laryngeal reflexes. The nursing diagnosis relating to general anesthesia is discontinued. The nursing diagnosis relating to pain made during labor is also discontinued. The nursing diagnosis relating to altered sensation is retained until the effects of the block are gone.

Additional Nursing Diagnoses to Consider:
Anxiety
Powerlessness
Situational low self-esteem
Urinary retention

* Only nursing diagnoses related to pain relief during and immediately after surgery are discussed here. For other intraoperative and postoperative nursing care, see Nursing Care Plan 16–1 and Chapter 17.

Interventions

Aspiration of gastric contents may occur despite careful medical and nursing interventions to prevent it. Nursing interventions relate to (1) identifying factors that may increase a woman's risk for aspiration, and (2) collaborative and nursing measures to reduce the risk of aspiration or lung injury.

IDENTIFYING RISK FACTORS

Report oral intake both before and after admission to the anesthesia clinician. Consult the physician or nurse-midwife about oral intake during labor. In general, oral intake is restricted to clear liquids or hard candies to reduce anesthetic risk while relieving a woman's dry mouth. Chart all oral intake during labor. Most women are not hungry during labor but find small amounts of ice chips or a Popsicle refreshing.

Vomiting is a common discomfort during normal labor, regardless of the mother's oral intake. If vomiting occurs, chart the time, quantity, and character (amount, color, presence of undigested food). Report emesis to the anesthesia clinician.

REDUCING RISK OF ASPIRATION OR LUNG INJURY

Nursing and medical personnel collaborate to reduce a woman's risk for pulmonary complications.

Perioperative Care. Discontinue oral intake until consulting the physician or nurse-midwife if surgical intervention seems likely because the woman may need general anesthesia. Check the unit's policy and medical orders for what drugs should be given. The nurse usually gives oral medications such as sodium citrate and citric acid (Bicitra). Either the nurse or anesthesia clinician may give parenteral drugs, depending on when they are administered.

Provide cricoid pressure (Sellick's maneuver) to assist the anesthesia clinician during intubation. Maintain pressure until instructed to release it. Cricoid pressure is done by an experienced nurse, usually the circulating nurse, or other assistant.

Postoperative Care. Following general anesthesia, the woman will not be extubated until her protective laryngeal reflexes have returned and she is unlikely to aspirate any vomitus. Position her on her side until she is awake to allow gravity to drain her secretions.

Birth facility protocols guide routine postoperative care. Administer oxygen by mask or face tent until the woman is awake and alert because general anesthesia is a respiratory depressant. A pulse oximeter allows continuous observation of oxygen saturation. If her oxygen saturation falls below 95 per cent have her take several deep breaths. Deep breathing also helps her eliminate inhalational anesthetics and reduces stasis of pulmonary secretions.

Assess the woman's pulse, respiration, and blood pressure every 15 minutes for 1 hour or until stable. Observe her color for pallor cyanosis, which may indicate shock or a late sign of hypoventilation.

Evaluation

Interventions for this nursing diagnosis are preventive and short-term because it is a temporary high-risk situation. The goal is met if the woman does not aspirate gastric contents during the perioperative period.

Summary Concepts

- Childbirth pain is unique because it is normal and self-limiting, can be prepared for, and ends with a baby's birth.
- Excess or poorly relieved pain may be harmful to the mother and fetus.
- Pain is a complex physical and psychological experience. It is subjective and personal.
- Four sources of pain are present in most labors, but other physical and psychological factors may increase or decrease the pain felt from these sources. These sources are cervical dilation, uterine ischemia, pressure and pulling on pelvic structures, and distention of the vagina and perineum.
- Relaxation enhances other pain management techniques.
- Physiological alterations of pregnancy may affect a woman's response to medications.
- Any drug that the expectant mother takes, whether therapeutic or abused, also may affect the fetus. Fetal effects may be direct or indirect.
- The nurse should observe for respiratory depression, primarily in the newborn, when the mother has received narcotics during labor.
- The major advantages of regional anesthesia are that the woman can participate in the birth and that she retains her protective airway reflexes.

- The nurse should observe for maternal hypotension with the epidural or subarachnoid blocks.
- The nurse should observe for impaired placental perfusion if the expectant mother is at risk for hypotension, such as with epidural or subarachnoid blocks.
- The main nursing observations for the woman who receives epidural narcotics are for delayed respiratory depression and pruritus.
- Regurgitation with aspiration of acidic gastric contents is the greatest risk for a woman who receives general anesthesia.

References and Readings

Abboud, T.K., Afrasiabi, A., Davidson, J., Zhu, J., Reyes, A., Khoo, N., & Steffens, A. (1990a). Prophylactic oral naltrexone with epidural morphine: Effect on adverse reactions and ventilatory responses to carbon dioxide. *Anesthesiology*, 72(2), 233–237.

Abboud, T.K., Lee, K., Zhu, J., Reyes, A., Afrasiabi, A., Mantilla, M., Steffens, Z., & Chai, M. (1990b). Prophylactic oral naltrexone with intrathecal morphine for cesarean section: Effects on adverse reactions and analgesia. *Anesthesia and Analgesia*, 71(2), 367–370.

Aderhold, K.J., & Perry, L. (1991). Jet hydrotherapy for labor and postpartum pain relief. MCN: *American Journal of Maternal Child Nursing*, 16(2), 97–99.

American Academy of Pediatrics Committee on Drugs (1988). Emergency drug doses for infants and children. *Pediatrics*, 81(3), 462–465.

American Academy of Pediatrics Committee on Drugs (1989). Emergency drug doses for infants and children and naloxone use in newborns: Clarification. *Pediatrics*, 83(5), 803.

Bowes, W.A. (1989). Clinical aspects of normal and abnormal labor. In R.K. Creasy & R. Resnik (Eds.), *Maternal-fetal medicine: Principles and practice* (pp. 510–546). Philadelphia: W.B. Saunders.

Cahill, C.A. (1989). Beta-endorphin levels during pregnancy and labor: A role in pain modulation? *Nursing Research*, 38(4), 200–203.

Clark, R.B. (1990). Regional anesthesia. In N.M. Nelson (Ed.), *Current therapy in neonatal-perinatal medicine* 2 (pp. 128–130). Philadelphia: B.C. Decker.

Corke, B.C. (1988). Complications of obstetric anesthesia. In F.M. James, A.S. Wheeler, & D.M. Dewan (Eds.), *Obstetric anesthesia: The complicated patient* (2nd ed.) (pp. 113–130). Philadelphia: F.A. Davis.

Diaz, J.H. (1991). The physiological changes of pregnancy have anesthetic implications for both mother and fetus. In J.H. Diaz (Ed.), *Perinatal anesthesia and critical care* (pp. 24–50). Philadelphia: W.B. Saunders.

Eakes, M. (1990). Economic considerations for epidural anesthesia in childbirth. *Nursing Economics*, 8(5), 329–332.

Endler, G.C., & Bhatia, R.K. (1990). Analgesia and anesthesia. In R. Eden & F. Boehm (Eds.), *Assessment and care of the fetus: Physiological, clinical, and medicolegal principles* (pp. 839–858). Norwalk, Conn.: Appleton & Lange.

Evans, A.T., & Gillogley, K. (1991). Drug use in pregnancy: Obstetric perspectives. *Clinics in perinatology*, 18(1), 23–32.

Gahart, B.L. (1991). *Intravenous medications* (7th ed.) St. Louis: C.V. Mosby.

Geden, E.A., Lower, M., Beattie, S., & Beck, N. (1989). Effects of music and imagery on physiologic and self-report of analogued labor pain. *Nursing Research*, 38(1), 37–41.

Glosten, B., & Rosen, M.A. (1989). Obstetrical anesthesia: Alternatives to epidural analgesia for labor. In J.T. Parer (Ed.), *Antepartum and intrapartum management* (pp. 184–203). Philadelphia: Lea & Febiger.

Henrikson, M.L., & Wild, L.R. (1988). A nursing process approach to epidural analgesia. *Journal of Obstetric, Gynecologic, and Neonatal Nursing*, 17(5), 316–320.

Hetherington, S.E. (1990). A controlled study of the effect of prepared childbirth classes on obstetric outcomes. *Birth*, 17(2), 86–90.

Hoegerman, G., & Schnoll, S. (1991). Narcotic use in pregnancy. *Clinics in Perinatology*, 18(1), 51–76.

Horowitz, J. (1988). Anesthetic implications of substance abuse in the parturient. *Journal of the American Association of Nurse Anesthetists*, 56(6), 510–514.

Inturrisi, M., Camenga, C.F., & Rosen, M. (1988). Epidural morphine for relief of postpartum, postsurgical pain. *Journal of Obstetric, Gynecologic, and Neonatal Nursing*, 17(4), 238–243.

Isenor, L., & Penny-MacGillivray, T. (1993). Intravenous meperidine for obstetric analgesia. *Journal of Obstetric, Gynecologic, and Neonatal Nursing*, 22(4), 349–356.

Jimenez, S.L.M. (1988). Supportive pain management strategies. In F.H. Nichols & S.S. Humenick (Eds.), *Childbirth education: Practice, research, and theory* (pp. 97–117). Philadelphia: W.B. Saunders.

Kenepp, N.B., & Hamilton, P.R. (1991). Substance abuse. In S. Datta (Ed.), *Anesthetic and obstetric management of high-risk pregnancy* (pp. 564–595). St. Louis: C.V. Mosby.

Leventhal, E.A., Leventhal, H., Shacham, S., & Easterling, D.V. (1989). Active coping reduces reports of pain from childbirth. *Journal of Consulting and Clinical Psychology*, 57(3), 365–371.

Loebl, S., Spratto, G.R., Woods, A.L., & Matejski, M. (1991). *The nurse's drug handbook*. Albany, N.Y.: Delmar.

McMorland, G.H. (1988). Anesthetic alternatives for obstetrics. In F.M. James, A.S. Wheeler, & D.M. Dewan (Eds.), *Obstetric anesthesia: The complicated patient* (2nd ed.) (pp. 93–111). Philadelphia: F.A. Davis.

NAACOG (1988). *Practice competencies and educational guidelines for nurse providers of intrapartum care*. Washington, D.C.

Nicholson, C. (1990). Nursing considerations for the parturient who has received epidural narcotics during labor or delivery. *Journal of Perinatal Neonatal Nursing*, 4(1), 14–26.

Nicholson, C. (Speaker). (1992). *Current concepts of obstetric anesthesia*, NAACOG Ninth National Meeting (Cassette Recording OGN-207). Chicago: Teach'em, Inc.

Nicholson, C., & Ridolfo, E. (1989). Avoiding the pitfalls of epidural anesthesia in obstetrics. *Journal of the American Association of Nurse Anesthetists*, 57(3), 220–230.

O'Grady, J.P., & Youngstrom, P. (1990). Must epidurals always imply instrumental delivery? *Contemporary OB/Gyn*, 35(8), 19–27.

Powell, A.H., & Bova, M.B. (1989). How do you give continuous epidural fentanyl? *American Journal of Nursing*, 89(9), 1197–1200.

Ramanathan, S. (1988). *Obstetric anesthesia*. Philadelphia: Lea & Febiger.

Rosenthal, M.J. (1991). Warm-water immersion in labor and birth. *The Female Patient*, 16(8), 35–37, 40–41, 44, 46–47.

Sharts-Engel, N.C. (1991). Naloxone review and pediatric dosage update. MCN: *American Journal of Maternal Child Nursing*, 16(3), 182.

Stampone, D. (1990). The history of obstetric anesthesia. *Journal of Perinatal-Neonatal Nursing*, 4(1), 1–13.

Steiner, S.H., & Steiner, J.F. (1988). In F.H. Nichols & S.S. Humenick (Eds.), *Childbirth education: Practice, research, and theory* (pp. 291–302). Philadelphia: W.B. Saunders.

Stolte, K. (1987). A comparison of women's expectations of labor with the actual event. *Birth*, 14(2), 99–103.

Sturrock, W.A., & Johnson, J.A. The relationship between childbirth education classes and obstetric outcome. *Birth*, 17(2), 82–85.

Taylor, T. (1993). Epidural anesthesia in the maternity patient. MCN: *The American Journal of Maternal-Child Nursing*, 18(2), 86–93.

Thorp, J.A., Parisi, V.M., Boylan, P.C., & Johnston, D.A. (1989). The effect of continuous epidural analgesia on cesarean section for dystocia in nulliparous women. *American Journal of Obstetrics and Gynecology*, 161(3), 670–675.

Vertommen, J.D., & Schnider, S.M. (1989). Refining epidural anesthesia in labor: Use of low-dose bupivicaine with opiates. *Current Reviews for Nurse Anesthetists*, 11(26), 202–208.

Weisenberg, M., & Caspi, Z. (1989). Cultural and educational influences on pain of childbirth. *Journal of Pain and Symptom Management*, 4(1), 13–19.

Wild, L., & Coyne, C. (1992). The basics and beyond: Epidural analgesia. *American Journal of Nursing*, 92(4), 26–36.

Zuspan, K. (1990). Anesthesia and analgesia. In F.P. Zuspan & E.J. Quilligan (Eds.), *Current therapy in obstetrics and gynecology* (Vol. 3, pp. 194–198). Philadelphia: W.B. Saunders.

16

Nursing Care During Obstetrical Procedures

Objectives

1. Identify clinical situations in which obstetrical procedures are appropriate.
2. Explain risks, precautions, and contraindications of each procedure.
3. Identify nursing responsibilities for each procedure.
4. Identify methods to provide effective emotional support to the woman having an obstetrical procedure.
5. Apply the nursing process to plan care for the woman having a cesarean birth.

Definitions

Abruptio placentae • Premature separation of a normally implanted placenta.

Amniotomy • Artificial rupture of the amniotic sac (fetal membranes).

Augmentation of labor • Artificial stimulation of uterine contractions that have become ineffective.

Cephalopelvic disproportion • Fetal size that is too large to fit through the maternal pelvis at birth. Also called **fetopelvic disproportion.**

Cesarean birth • Surgical delivery of the fetus through an incision in the lower abdominal wall and uterus.

Chignon • Newborn scalp edema created by a vacuum extractor.

Chorioamnionitis • Inflammation of the amniotic sac (fetal membranes) usually caused by bacterial or viral infections. Also called **amnionitis.**

Dystocia • Difficult or prolonged labor, often associated with abnormal uterine activity and **cephalopelvic disproportion.**

Episiotomy • Surgical incision of the perineum to enlarge the vaginal opening.

Hydramnios • Excessive volume of amniotic fluid (more than 2000 ml at term). Also called **polyhydramnios.**

Iatrogenic • An adverse condition resulting from treatment.

Induction of labor • Artificial initiation of labor.

Laminaria • Slender cones of prepared seaweed or a similar substance inserted into the cervix to dilate it as the cones absorb water.

Nuchal cord • Umbilical cord around the fetal neck.

Oligohydramnios • Abnormally small quantity of amniotic fluid (less than 500 ml at term).

Placenta previa • Abnormal implantation of the placenta in the lower uterus.

Premature rupture of the membranes • Spontaneous rupture of the membranes before the onset of labor. The gestation may be term, preterm, or postterm.

Version • Turning the fetus from one presentation to another before birth, usually from breech to cephalic.

△ Alert for a high risk of exposure to substances to which universal precautions apply. See Appendix B for additional information about infection control.

Although labor is a normal physiological process, some women require special procedures to help them. Some procedures may be necessary to protect the life and health of an expectant mother and fetus. Although a physician or nurse-midwife performs these procedures, nursing interventions for each are addressed.

Amniotomy

Indications

Amniotomy is a common procedure in both spontaneous and induced labors. Amniotomy may be performed to induce labor, stimulate labor, or allow internal electronic fetal monitoring and fetal scalp blood sampling (see Chapter 14).

Risks

Amniotomy is performed by the physician or nurse-midwife. It is not a nursing procedure because the nurse is not qualified to respond medically to an emergency that may arise related to this procedure. (NAACOG, 1988b). Three risks of amniotomy are described.

Prolapse of the Umbilical Cord. The primary risk is that the umbilical cord will slip down in the gush of fluid (see p. 764). The cord can be compressed between the fetal presenting part and the expectant mother's pelvis, obstructing blood flow to and from the placenta.

Infection. With interruption of the membrane barrier, vaginal organisms have free access to the uterine cavity and may cause infection there (chorioamnionitis). The organisms may not be pathogenic in the vagina but may cause infection within the uterine cavity. The risk is low at first but increases as the interval between membrane rupture and birth increases. There is no absolute time when infection will occur. Performance of an amniotomy commits the physician or nurse-midwife to delivery because of the risk of infection.

Abruptio Placentae. If the uterus is distended with excessive amniotic fluid when the membranes rupture, abruptio placentae (see p. 670) may occur. As the uterus collapses with discharge of the amniotic fluid, the area of placental attachment shrinks. The placenta then no longer fits its implantation site. Reduced fetal oxygenation may result if a large area of placental surface is disrupted.

Technique

A disposable plastic hook (Amnihook) is commonly used to perforate the amniotic sac (Fig. 16–1). The physician or nurse-midwife does a vaginal examination to determine cervical dilation and effacement, fetal station, and the fetal presenting part. Amniotomy is usually delayed if the fetal presenting part is high or if the presentation is other than vertex because the risk of a prolapsed cord is higher.

After determining that amniotomy is safe and appropriate, the physician or nurse-midwife passes the hook through the cervix, snagging the membranes with the hook. The hole is enlarged with the finger, allowing fluid to drain.

Nursing Care

OBTAINING BASELINE INFORMATION

Assess the fetus before amniotomy for reassuring fetal heart rate patterns (see Table 14–2) and for a baseline to compare later assessments. A minimum of 20 to 30 minutes is needed for adequate fetal evaluation.

ASSISTING WITH AMNIOTOMY

Before the amniotomy, place two or three underpads under the woman's buttocks to absorb the fluid, overlapping them to extend from her waist to her knees. A folded bath towel under the buttocks absorbs a larger quantity of amniotic fluid.

Supplies needed are a disposable plastic hook, a sterile glove, and an individual packet of sterile lubricant. Drop lubricant on the physician's or nurse-midwife's gloved examining fingers without touching the lubricant package to the sterile gloves. Peel the package containing the plastic hook partly open at the handle end, holding the package ends back until the physician or nurse-midwife takes the hook.

PROVIDING CARE AFTER AMNIOTOMY

Nursing care after amniotomy is the same as that following spontaneous membrane rupture.

Identifying Complications. Assess and document the fetal heart rate for at least 1 full minute following amniotomy. Report non-reassuring patterns to the physician or nurse-midwife (see Table 14–2). Cord compression is usually accompanied by a rate under 100 beats per minute (BPM), which worsens during contractions.

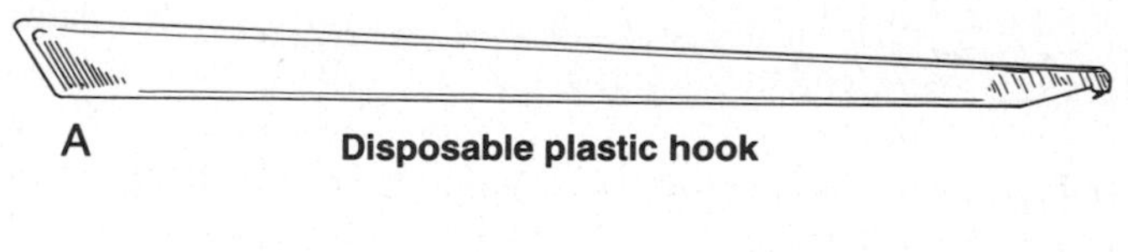

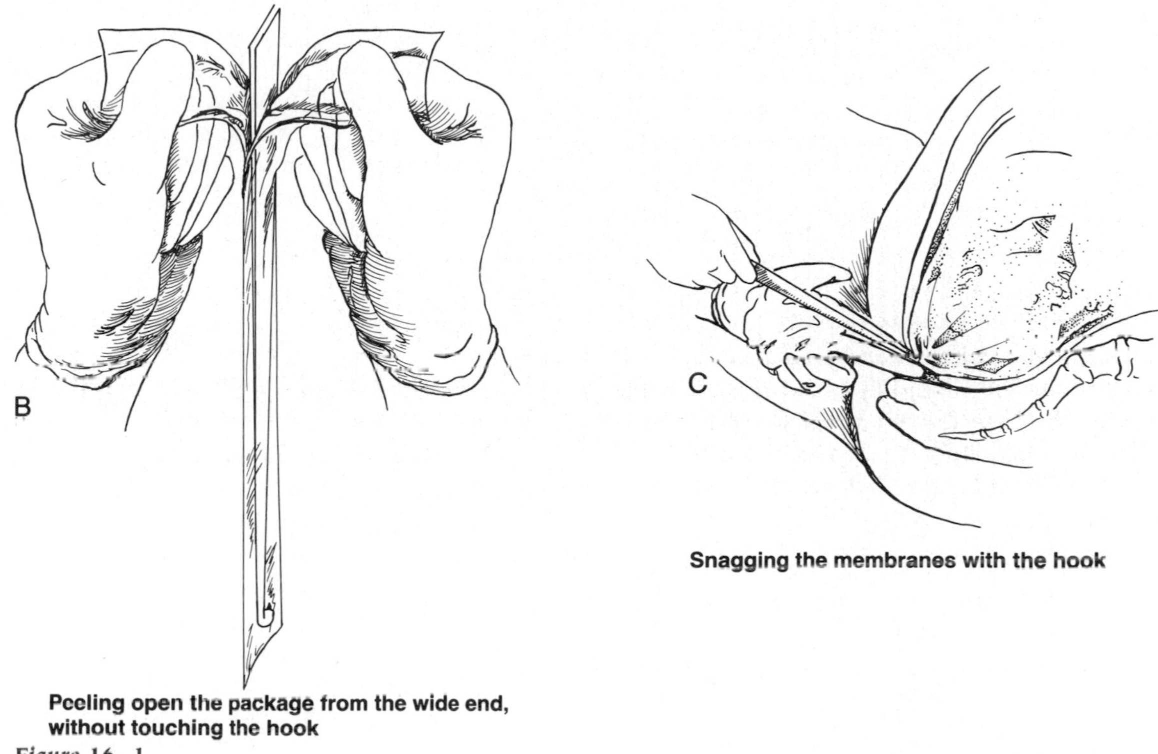

B
C
Snagging the membranes with the hook
Peeling open the package from the wide end, without touching the hook

Figure 16–1

A, Disposable plastic membrane perforator. **B,** Correct method to open the package. **C,** Technique for artificial rupture of membranes.

Document the quantity, color, and odor of the amniotic fluid. The fluid should be clear (possibly containing bits of vernix) and free of foul odor. A large amount of vernix in the fluid suggests that the fetus may be preterm. Greenish meconium-stained fluid is more often seen in postterm gestation or placental insufficiency. Fluid having a foul or strong odor, cloudy appearance, or a yellow color suggests chorioamnionitis. Hydramnios is associated with some fetal abnormalities. Oligohydramnios may be associated with placental insufficiency or fetal urinary tract abnormalities.

Take the woman's temperature every 2 hours after the membranes rupture. Report elevations above 38°C (100.4°F). Observe for fetal tachycardia (above 160 BPM), as this sign may precede maternal fever.

Promoting Comfort. After the membranes rupture, amniotic fluid will continue to leak from the woman's vagina. Change underpads regularly to keep her drier and reduce the moist environment that favors bacterial growth.

✔ Check Your Reading

1. What are three risks associated with amniotomy?
2. Why is the fetal heart rate assessed after the membranes rupture?
3. What is the significance of green amniotic fluid?
4. What maternal and fetal signs are associated with chorioamnionitis?

Induction and Augmentation of Labor

The induction and augmentation of labor use artificial methods to stimulate uterine contractions. Most techniques and nursing care are similar for both induction and augmentation.

Indications

Induction of labor is considered by the physician or nurse-midwife when continuing the pregnancy is

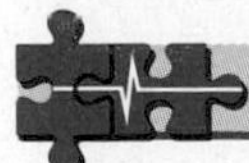

Clinical Situation

A physician performs an amniotomy. When the fluid is released, it has a strong odor. The fetal heart rate is 170 BPM.

Q: 1. What do these two findings suggest?
2. What assessments should you perform?

A:
1. These findings suggest chorioamnionitis, or infection of the amniotic sac.
2. Continue to assess the fetus for tachycardia. Assess the expectant mother's temperature at least every 2 hours for temperature of 38°C (100.4°F) or higher. Report abnormalities to the physician or nurse-midwife.

likely to be detrimental to the health of the expectant mother or fetus and when labor and vaginal birth are considered reasonably safe.

Specific conditions that may be an indication for induction are:

- Pregnancy-induced hypertension, associated with impaired placental perfusion and resolved by birth (see p. 679)
- Premature rupture of the membranes without spontaneous labor
- Chorioamnionitis
- Maternal medical conditions that may worsen with continuation of the pregnancy (diabetes, renal disease, pulmonary disease)
- Conditions in which the intrauterine environment is hostile to fetal well-being (intrauterine fetal growth retardation, postterm gestation, maternal-fetal blood incompatibility)
- Fetal death

Convenience for the family or physician is not an indication for labor induction. However, logistical factors, such as a history of rapid labors or living a long distance from the hospital, may be valid reasons to induce labor when there is a real risk a woman would give birth without assistance.

Contraindications

There are several relative contraindications to induction of labor. Labor and vaginal birth, whether spontaneous or induced, may be too hazardous to the woman or fetus in several circumstances, including:

- Placenta previa, which may result in hemorrhage during labor
- Umbilical cord prolapse or compression
- Abnormal fetal presentation (vaginal birth is often more hazardous; also, the fetus may turn to a normal position in time if there is no other reason to induce labor)
- Fetal presenting part above the pelvic inlet, suggesting cephalopelvic disproportion or a preterm fetus
- Active genital herpes infection, which the fetus may acquire during birth (see p. 723)
- Maternal pelvic structural abnormalities that may contribute to cephalopelvic disproportion
- Previous classic (vertical) cesarean incision, which is more likely to rupture during labor than the more common low transverse incision (see p. 405)

Risks

Induction and augmentation of labor, as with spontaneous labor, are associated with risks.

- Hypertonic uterine activity that may reduce placental perfusion and fetal oxygenation
- Uterine rupture (see p. 766)
- Maternal water intoxication with oxytocin infusion, more likely with use of dextrose and water intravenous solutions and with rates greater than 20 mU/minute (Cunningham and MacDonald, 1989).

Technique

Induction or augmentation may be accomplished by either surgical or medical methods, or the two may be combined. Amniotomy is the method of surgical induction and augmentation because rupturing membranes stimulates uterine contractions. Medical induction or augmentation involves drugs such as prostaglandin or intravenous oxytocin (Pitocin) to stimulate contractions.

DETERMINING WHETHER INDUCTION IS INDICATED

The physician or nurse-midwife first evaluates whether labor and birth are less hazardous to the expectant mother or fetus than continuing the pregnancy. Labor is infrequently induced if the fetus is younger than 39 weeks' gestational age unless there is a compelling reason, such as intrauterine growth retardation. Also, the uterus becomes more sensitive to oxytocin at term gestation, increasing the drug's effectiveness.

The physician or nurse-midwife will evaluate the cervix to determine how favorable it is for induction. The Bishop scoring system (Table 16–1) is used to

Table 16–1. BISHOP SCORING SYSTEM* TO EVALUATE THE CERVIX

Factor	Score			
	0	*1*	*2*	*3*
Dilation	0 cm	1–2 cm	3–4 cm	5–6 cm
Effacement	0–30%	40–50%	60–70%	80% or more
Station	−3	−2	−1 or 0	+1 or +2
Cervical consistency	Firm	Medium	Soft	
Cervical position	Posterior	Middle	Anterior	

Adapted from Bishop, E. H. (1964). Pelvic scoring for elective induction. *Obstetrics and Gynecology, 24*(2), 266–268.

* This system is used to estimate how easily a woman's labor can be induced. Higher scores are associated with a greater likelihood of successful induction because her cervix has undergone prelabor changes, often called ripening. A woman who has given birth before usually has a successful induction when her Bishop score is 5 or higher. A woman who is having her first baby is most successfully induced if her score is 7 or higher.

estimate cervical readiness for labor with five factors: cervical dilation, effacement, consistency, position, and fetal station. Higher Bishop scores indicate that induction is more likely to be successful in starting uterine contractions.

CERVICAL RIPENING

Procedures to soften the cervix and make it more receptive to uterine contractions are a common adjunct to labor induction. They are usually done the day before an induction. If there is no other reason for hospitalization, the woman returns home after the procedure.

Prostaglandin E_2 (PGE_2) gel (dinoprostone cervical gel, Prepidil), 0.5 mg, may be inserted in the woman's cervical canal by the physician to facilitate cervical ripening. The major adverse reactions relate to hypertonic uterine contractions. The drug should not be given to women who are hypersensitive to prostaglandins. It should not be given, or should be given cautiously, to women who have asthma, glaucoma, or raised intraocular pressure. The gel should be administered in a hospital that is equipped to deal with emergencies related to hypertonic uterine contractions. Women who cannot receive prostaglandin gel may be given dilute oxytocin over a 2- or 3-day period (serial induction) to prepare the cervix and start labor.

An alternative to using pharmacological means to prepare the cervix is the use of a mechanical method. Insertion of a laminaria into the cervix allows it to absorb water and swell, thus softening and dilating the cervix. Lamicel is a synthetic sponge that contains 450 mg of magnesium sulfate and is used in a manner similar to that of the laminaria.

OXYTOCIN ADMINISTRATION

Oxytocin is a powerful drug (Drug Guide, p. 394), and it is impossible to predict a woman's response to it. Birth facilities establish policies for administration of oxytocin during induction and augmentation of labor. These policies include techniques for oxytocin administration, maternal and fetal assessments, emergency nursing actions for adverse reactions, and physician availability.

Several precautions reduce the chance of adverse reactions in the expectant mother or the fetus, or both.

- Oxytocin is diluted and given as a secondary (piggyback) infusion to allow it to be stopped quickly if complications develop (Fig. 16–2).
- The oxytocin line is inserted into the primary (nonadditive) intravenous line as close as possible to the venipuncture site so that there is a small amount remaining in the tubing if the solution must be stopped. 
- Oxytocin is started slowly at 0.5 to 1 mU/minute, regulated with an infusion pump.
- Oxytocin is increased gradually in increments of 1 to 2 mU/minute every 30 to 60 minutes.
- Oxytocin is usually started at the lower dose (0.5 mU/minute) if labor is being augmented because the uterus is expected to be more sensitive of the drug's effects. A lower maximum rate is usually effective for these women.

The woman's uterus becomes more sensitive to oxytocin as labor progresses. Therefore, the rate of oxytocin infusion may be gradually reduced when she is well into the active phase of labor, about 5 to 6 cm cervical dilation.

Nursing Care

The nurse monitors the expectant mother and fetus for complications and takes corrective actions if abnormalities are noted. In addition, the nurse provides general intrapartum care for a woman. The same nursing care applies if a woman has a cervical ripening procedure until she is discharged home.

OBSERVING THE FETAL RESPONSE

Most hospitals in the United States specify electronic fetal monitoring for clients having risk factors, including oxytocin administration (see Table 14–1). Oxytocin may cause hypertonic contractions, which may result in uteroplacental insufficiency. Before induction or augmentation of labor, observe a baseline strip for reassuring fetal heart rate patterns and to

Drug Guide

OXYTOCIN (Pitocin)

Classification: Oxytocic.

Action: Synthetic compound identical to the natural hormone from the posterior pituitary. Stimulates uterine smooth muscle, resulting in increased strength, duration, and frequency of uterine contractions. Has vasopressive and antidiuretic properties. Uterine sensitivity to oxytocin increases gradually during gestation.

Indications: Induction or augmentation of labor at or near term. Promotes firm contraction of the uterus after birth to control postpartum bleeding. Management of inevitable or incomplete abortion.

Dosage and Route:

Induction or Augmentation of Labor:

1. *IV infusion* via a secondary (piggyback) line. Dilute 10 units (1 ml) of oxytocin in 1000 ml of a balanced electrolyte solution such as Ringer's lactate, resulting in a concentration of 10 milliunits (mU) of oxytocin per ml.
2. Using an infusion pump, begin oxytocin infusion at 0.5 to 1 mU/minute. Increase dose by 1 to 2 mU/minute increments according to uterine response and absence of adverse effects at 30- to 60-minute intervals. Most women respond to 16 mU/minute or less and seldom require a dose higher than 20 to 40 mU/minute. A lower starting dose is usually required when augmenting labor.
3. After an adequate contraction pattern is established and the laboring woman's cervix is dilated 5 to 6 cm, the oxytocin may be reduced by similar increments.

Control of Postpartum Bleeding: *IV infusion*—Dilute 10 to 40 units in 1000 ml of IV solution (see previously). Rate of infusion must control uterine atony. Begin at a rate of 10 to 20 mU/minute, increasing or decreasing rate according to uterine response. *IM:* 10 units after delivery of placenta.

Inevitable or Incomplete Abortion: Same as postpartum bleeding.

Absorption: IV: immediate; IM: 3 to 5 minutes.

Excretion: Liver and urine.

Contraindications and Precautions: Include, but are not limited to, placenta previa, vasa previa, abnormal fetal presentation, prolapsed umbilical cord, presenting part above the pelvic inlet, previous classic uterine incision, active genital herpes infection, pelvic structural deformities, invasive cervical carcinoma.

Adverse Reactions: Most result from hypersensitivity to drug or excessive dosage. Adverse reactions include hypertonic uterine activity, impaired uterine blood flow, uterine rupture, and abruptio placentae. Uterine hypertonicity may result in fetal bradycardia, tachycardia, reduced fetal heart rate variability, late decelerations. Fetal asphyxia may occur with diminished uterine blood flow. Fetal and/or maternal trauma, or both, may occur from rapid birth. Prolonged administration may cause maternal fluid retention leading to water intoxication. Hypertension, tachycardia, cardiac dysrhythmias, and subarachnoid hemorrhage are other adverse reactions.

Nursing Implications:

Intrapartum: Assess fetal heart rate for 20 minutes before induction to identify reassuring or non-reassuring patterns. Perform Leopold's maneuvers or vaginal examination, or both, to identify fetal presentation. Do not begin induction and notify physician if non-reassuring fetal heart rate patterns are identified or if fetal presentation is other than cephalic.

Observe uterine activity for establishment of effective labor pattern: contraction frequency every 2 to 3 minutes, duration 45 to 90 seconds, intensity 50 to 80 mmHg (using intrauterine pressure catheter). Observe for hypertonic uterine activity: contractions less than 2 minutes frequency, rest interval shorter than 60 seconds, duration longer than 90 seconds, or an elevated resting tone greater than 20 mmHg with an intrauterine pressure catheter. Observe fetal heart rate for non-reassuring patterns such as tachycardia, bradycardia, decreased variability, or late decelerations.

If uterine hypertonicity or a non-reassuring fetal heart rate pattern occurs, intervene to reduce uterine activity and increase fetal oxygenation: stop oxytocin infusion; increase rate of non-additive solution; place woman in side-lying position; administer oxygen by snug face mask at 8 to 10 L/minute. Notify physician of adverse reactions, nursing interventions, and response to interventions. Record maternal blood pressure every 30 to 60 minutes. Record intake and output.

Post Partum: Observe uterus for firmness, height, and deviation. Massage until firm if uterus is "boggy." Observe lochia for color, quantity, and presence of clots. Notify physician or nurse-midwife if uterus fails to remain contracted or if lochia is bright red or contains large clots. Assess for cramping. Assess vital signs every 15 minutes or according to protocol. Monitor intake and output to identify fluid retention or bladder distention.

Inevitable or Incomplete Abortion: Observe for cramping, vaginal bleeding, clots, and passage of products of conception. Observe maternal vital signs, intake and output as noted under postpartum nursing implications.

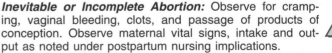

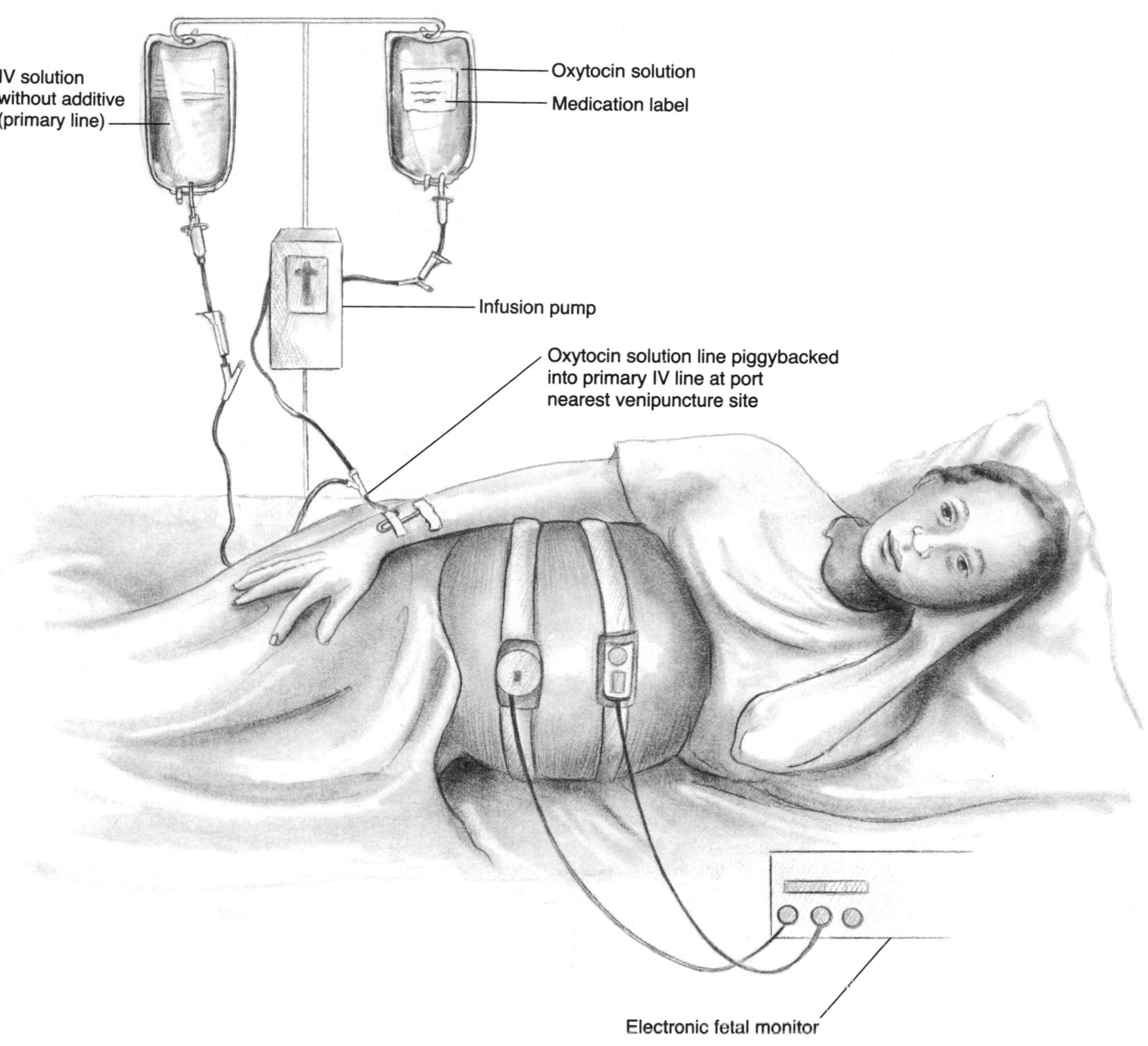

Figure 16–2

Intravenous oxytocin setup for induction or augmentation of labor.

rule out nonreassuring patterns. Document the fetal heart rate in the labor record every 15 minutes during first-stage labor and every 5 minutes during the second stage.

Observe the fetus during the induction or augmentation for non-reassuring fetal heart rate patterns. The patterns that are more likely to occur are associated with impaired placental exchange (uteroplacental insufficiency), for example, fetal bradycardia (rate less than 110 BPM), tachycardia (rate more than 160 BPM), late decelerations, and decreased fetal heart rate variability. Uteroplacental insufficiency may have causes other than hypertonic uterine activity, such as maternal hypotension. Assess the woman and fetus carefully to identify the most likely cause of the problem and the indicated corrective actions.

If non-reassuring patterns occur, take steps to reduce uterine activity and increase fetal oxygenation:

1. Stop the oxytocin infusion and increase the rate of the non-additive infusion.
2. Keep the woman on her side to increase placental blood flow.
3. Give 100 per cent oxygen by snug face mask at 8 to 10 L/minute to increase the expectant mother's oxygen saturation, making more available for the fetus.

Notify the physician for medical orders that may include administration of terbutaline (Brethine) or magnesium sulfate to reduce uterine activity (see p. 685).

OBSERVING THE MOTHER'S RESPONSE

Women who have a laminaria or prostaglandin for cervical ripening may begin labor before their scheduled induction. Teach these women signs of labor's onset (see p. 291) and tell them to return to the birth facility if these signs occur.

Observe uterine activity for hypertonus that may reduce fetal oxygenation and contribute to uterine rupture (Critical to Remember: Signs of Hypertonic Uterine Activity). Assess contractions for frequency, duration, and intensity. Assess uterine resting tone for relaxation of at least 60 seconds between contractions. Document observations with the same frequency as the fetal heart rate. Corrective actions for hypertonic uterine activity are the same as those listed in the discussion of the fetal response.

At a minimum, take the woman's blood pressure and pulse every 30 to 60 minutes, each time the oxytocin dose is evaluated for change or maintenance. Take her temperature every 4 hours, every 2 hours if the membranes are ruptured.

Although water intoxication is uncommon when oxytocin is given by the preceding guidelines, observe the woman for this complication. Record her intake and output to identify fluid retention, which may precede water intoxication. Signs and symptoms of water intoxication include headache, blurred vision, behavioral changes, increased blood pressure and respirations, decreased pulse, rales, wheezing, and coughing.

After birth, observe the mother for postpartum hemorrhage caused by uterine atony (see Chapter 27). Uterine atony is more likely if she has received oxytocin for a long time because the uterine muscle becomes fatigued and does not contract effectively to compress vessels at the placental site. It is manifested by a soft fundus and excess amounts of lochia, usually with large clots. Hypovolemic shock may occur with hemorrhage.

Clinical Situation

A woman is having labor induced with oxytocin. The nurse notes that the fetal heart rate is 100 to 110 BPM and contractions are every 2 minutes and last 95 seconds.

Q:
1. What is the status of uterine activity?
2. What are appropriate nursing actions in this situation?

A:
1. The woman is having hypertonic uterine activity because the duration of contractions is longer than 90 seconds. It is probably caused by oxytocin.
2. The first action is to stop the oxytocin infusion to reduce stimulation of contractions. The primary (non-additive) intravenous infusion should be increased to maintain adequate circulating volume. The woman should be maintained in a lateral position (usually left side) to reduce aortocaval compression and maximize placental blood flow. Oxygen at 8 to 10 L/minute (or by facility protocol) with a snug face mask increases her blood oxygen saturation, making more available to the fetus. (See Chapter 14 for further information about fetal responses to reduced placental perfusion.)

Critical to Remember

Signs of Hypertonic Uterine Activity

- Duration longer than 90 seconds
- Frequency greater than every 2 minutes or less than 60 seconds relaxation between contractions
- Uterine resting tone above 20 mmHg (with intrauterine pressure catheter)
- Peak pressure higher than 90 mmHg during first-stage labor (with intrauterine pressure catheter)
- A fetal heart rate pattern of late decelerations may accompany hypertonic uterine activity

Nursing actions for hypertonic uterine activity:

- Stop the oxytocin infusion
- Increase the rate of the primary non-additive infusion
- Keep the laboring woman in a lateral position
- Give oxygen by face mask, 8 to 10 mL/minute
- Notify the physician or nurse-midwife

✔ Check Your Reading

5. What four precautions are taken to enhance the safety of oxytocin administration for the expectant mother and fetus?
6. How may oxytocin administration differ if labor is being augmented rather than induced?
7. What signs may indicate an abnormal fetal response to oxytocin?
8. What are the signs of hypertonic uterine activity?
9. How can induction of labor with oxytocin contribute to postpartum hemorrhage?

Version

There are two methods used to change fetal presentation: external or internal version. Each has different indications and technique.

Indications

External Version. The fetal presentation can be changed from a breech to a cephalic presentation by the use of external version. A transverse lie also may be changed to the cephalic presentation. Because vaginal breech birth is associated with more fetal risk, cesarean birth is often performed if the abnormal presentation persists.

Successful external version can reduce a woman's chances of having a cesarean birth without exposing the fetus to undue risk. On the basis of several studies, external version was about 70 percent successful, with a net reduction in cesarean births of about 50 per cent (Bowes, 1989). Few fetal complications were noted.

Internal Version. Malpresentation in twin gestations is usually managed by cesarean birth, but internal version is sometimes used in vaginal twin births. Multifetal gestations of more than two fetuses almost always result in a cesarean delivery. After the first twin is born, the presentation of the second twin may be a transverse lie, in which birth cannot occur vaginally. Internal version changes the presentation to one in which birth can occur vaginally. External version also may be done for the second twin.

Risks

There are few risks to the laboring woman. The principal risk is that the fetus may become entangled in the umbilical cord, compressing its vessels and resulting in hypoxia. Abruptio placentae also may occur. The fetus may revert to the abnormal presentation, although this is not a risk of the procedure. Cesarean birth may be required for fetal distress during the version or later because the fetus returns to the abnormal presentation.

Contraindications

The expectant mother or fetus may have a condition that is a contraindication for version. If vaginal birth is contraindicated or unlikely, version is also contraindicated, since that is its goal. There is no reason to expose the fetus to even the low risks of external version in that situation. Some of these contraindications are relative rather than absolute. The woman's birth attendant will weigh the potential benefits against the risk to her and her fetus. Another consideration is parity, as external version is easier to perform in a multipara because her abdominal and uterine walls are more relaxed than in a nulliparous woman.

There are several maternal conditions that contraindicate external version:

- Uterine malformations. These limit the amount of space to perform the version. The uterine malformation also may be the reason the fetus is in the abnormal presentation.
- Previous cesarean birth or other uterine surgery. Manipulation of the fetus within the scarred uterus may put undue strain on the old incision, contributing to uterine rupture. Additionally, the prior surgery may be a contraindication for vaginal birth.
- Disproportion between fetal size and maternal pelvic size.
- Maternal conditions that constitute a contraindication for using tocolytic drugs, such as terbutaline (Brethine) or ritodrine (Yutopar).

Fetal contraindications to version are primarily those that put the fetus at higher risk for hypoxia:

- Placenta previa, unless it is marginal. Manipulation of the fetus within the uterus may cause hemorrhage, endangering both mother and fetus.
- Multifetal gestation. This reduces available room to turn the fetus or fetuses.
- Oligohydramnios or a nuchal cord. This may lead to umbilical cord compression and fetal hypoxia. Either condition limits the ability to turn the fetus.
- Uteroplacental insufficiency. Uterine contractions occurring during the version or labor may worsen the insufficiency and cause fetal compromise. Labor also may be contraindicated.

Internal version of the second twin is not a planned procedure like external version. Basically, contraindications to internal version are the same. Any contraindication to continuing labor for birth of the second twin is also a contraindication to internal version.

Technique

External Version. A non–stress test (see p. 227) is done before external version to evaluate fetal health and placental function. If the test is non-reactive or if there are other non-reassuring signs, the version is not done. Version would add stress to the fetus already functioning with reduced physiological reserve. An ultrasound examination confirms fetal gestational age and the abnormal fetal presentation.

External version is attempted after 37 weeks of gestation but before the woman is in labor because:

- The fetus is more likely to return to an abnormal presentation if version is attempted before 37 weeks.
- As term nears, the fetus may spontaneously turn to a cephalic presentation, eliminating the need for version.
- If fetal distress or onset of labor occurs, a fetus born after 37 weeks is unlikely to have major problems, such as respiratory distress syndrome, associated with preterm birth.

Most physicians give the woman a tocolytic drug such as terbutaline or ritodrine to relax the uterus before and during version. (See Chapter 26 for discussion of the effects and side effects of these drugs.)

Ultrasound guides fetal manipulations during external version. After the uterus is relaxed, the physician gently pushes the breech out of the pelvis and toward the mother's side. The fetal head is pushed downward and to the opposite side (Fig. 16–3). The tocolytic drug is stopped after the fetus is turned to the cephalic presentation or if the version attempt is abandoned.

Rh-negative women should receive Rh immune globulin after external version. Small disruptions in the placenta may allow fetal blood to leak into the expectant mother's circulation, possibly resulting in production of anti-Rh antibodies (see p. 691)

Internal Version. The physician reaches into the uterus with one hand and, with the other hand on the maternal abdomen, maneuvers the fetus into a cephalic position or a footling breech (Fig. 16–4).

Nursing Care

The nurse provides information, assesses the expectant mother and fetus, and helps to reduce her anxiety.

PROVIDING INFORMATION

The indications and risks for version should be explained to the woman by her physician before the procedure. After admission, she may have additional questions about the procedure. A signed informed consent is needed for external version.

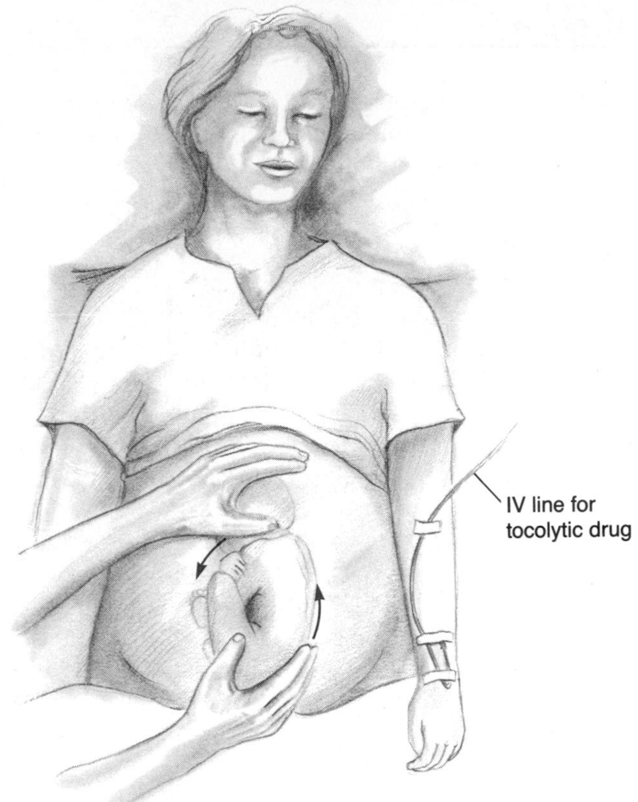

Figure 16–3

External version.

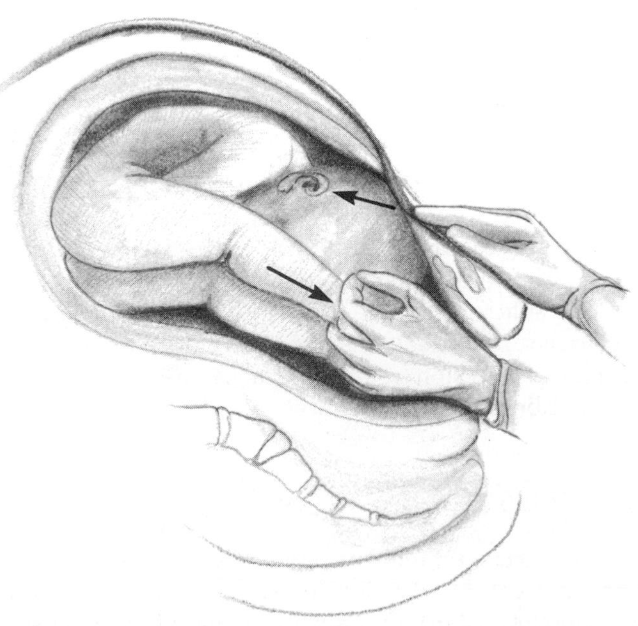

Figure 16–4

Internal version for vaginal birth of a second twin.

Teach about possible side effects of the tocolytic drug planned. Tachycardia and tremors are noticeable to the mother and usually stop shortly after discontinuing the medication at the end of the procedure.

PROMOTING MATERNAL AND FETAL HEALTH

At admission, obtain all information needed as if the woman were in labor or having a cesarean birth because the need for operative intervention may arise unexpectedly. The woman should have nothing by mouth during this short procedure.

Take baseline maternal vital signs, and begin a fetal monitor strip for baseline values and the initial non–stress test. Observe and report abnormalities and non-reassuring fetal heart rate patterns (see Table 14–2).

Administer the tocolytic drug as ordered. During the version, take the woman's blood pressure and pulse every 5 minutes. Observe for tachycardia, tremors, and hypotension.

Monitor the fetus as continuously as possible during abdominal manipulations with Doppler auscultation or with real-time ultrasound. Record all fetal heart rates. Fetal bradycardia may occur during the version, but the rate usually returns to normal when manipulation ceases.

After the version, assess the expectant mother and fetus for a return of their vital signs to the baseline at admission. Use electronic fetal monitoring to assess the fetus for 1 hour after the version. Reassuring signs are a fetal heart rate about the same range as on admission, resolution of bradycardia, and the presence of rate accelerations with movement.

Assess maternal vital signs every 15 minutes until they return to their baseline level. Observe for regular contractions that may indicate onset of labor. Spontaneous rupture of membranes occasionally occurs, so check for leakage of fluid from the mother's vagina.

Because the woman having external version is near term, review the signs of true labor with her (see p. 280). Explain guidelines for coming to the hospital (see p. 291).

REDUCING ANXIETY

The woman may be anxious before version because its success is not certain and sudden complications may require rapid operative delivery. After version, she may still be anxious because the fetus may return to its previous position. Remain with her, and keep her informed about what is occurring during the version to reduce her fear of the unknown.

She is probably concerned about the fetal condition. Show her signs that the fetus is tolerating the version if that is true. Point out reassuring fetal monitor patterns, such as a normal rate and rate accelerations. If problems develop, such as bradycardia, tell her what has happened and what steps are being done to relieve it.

✔ *Check Your Reading*

10. Which type of version is used during vaginal birth?
11. Why is it important to observe the fetal heart rate during and after external version?
12. Why should the uterine activity be monitored after external version?

Episiotomy

The physician or nurse-midwife may do an episiotomy just before birth when the fetal presenting part has crowned. Routine use of episiotomy has come under scrutiny in the last few years. Many women want to have natural births, avoiding procedures that are not clearly helpful to them or the fetus. Many physicians and nurse-midwives try to avoid episiotomy unless there are clear indications for doing it.

Indications

Indications for episiotomy may pertain to the fetus, the laboring woman, or both.

Fetal indications are similar to those for forceps or vacuum extraction (see p. 400). An additional indication is to reduce pressure on the delicate head when a small preterm infant is born.

Maternal indications, in addition to those for forceps or vacuum extraction, include:

- To control the direction and extent the vaginal opening is enlarged. This is an advantage if the woman has a short perineum (a short distance between her lower vaginal opening and anus) because a tear is likely to extend into or through the anal sphincter.
- A clean surgical incision that is simpler to repair and heals well. This is controversial, because a perineal laceration may be smaller than the episiotomy and thus may lend itself better to repair and healing.

Risks

Infection is the primary risk of episiotomy. The woman has more pain with episiotomy than she would with no perineal trauma. However, pain from episiotomy is not necessarily greater or less than that from a laceration.

Technique

There are two types of episiotomies, each with advantages and disadvantages: *median* or midline and *mediolateral* (Table 16–2). The physician or nurse-midwife uses blunt-tipped scissors to cut the perineum so that the tissues of the woman and fetus are protected.

Nursing Care

Nursing interventions begin during the recovery period and are the same for both episiotomy and perineal laceration. Observe the perineum for hematoma and edema. Cold applications reduce pain, edema, and hematoma formation (see Chapter 17 for additional nursing interventions.)

Forceps and Vacuum Extraction

Forceps help the woman's expulsive efforts by providing traction to extract the fetal head, assisting rotation of the fetal head from the occiput posterior or transverse position to the occiput anterior, or both. Vacuum extraction is similar but is used only for extraction of the fetal head.

Forceps are curved metal instruments that can be locked in the center. Several types of forceps are used for different needs. They have curved blades shaped to grasp the fetal head (Fig. 16–5). The blades may be closed, such as Tucker-McClean forceps, or open (fenestrated), such as Simpson's forceps. Disposable foam pads are available to cushion the fetal head from the blades. Piper forceps are a special type that may be needed to assist expulsion of the head in a breech vaginal birth. Forceps or a vacuum extractor also may be used during cesarean birth.

The vacuum extractor uses suction to grasp the fetal head while traction is applied (Fig. 16–6). It cannot be used to deliver the aftercoming head in a breech presentation.

Table 16–2. TYPES OF EPISIOTOMIES

Median or Midline		Mediolateral	
		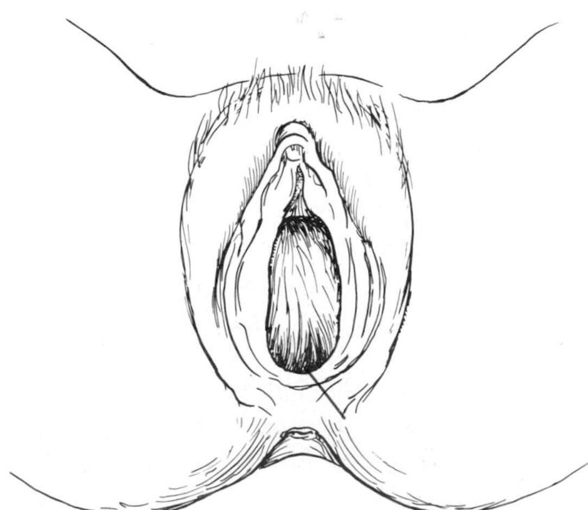	
Advantages	***Disadvantages***	***Advantages***	***Disadvantages***
Minimal blood loss Neat healing with little scarring Less postpartum pain than the mediolateral epistomy	An added laceration may extend the median episiotomy into the anal sphincter Limited enlargement of the vaginal opening because perineal length is limited by the anal sphincter	More enlargement of the vaginal opening Little risk that the episiotomy will extend into the anus	More blood loss Increased postpartum pain More scarring and irregularity in the healed scar Prolonged dyspareunia (painful intercourse)

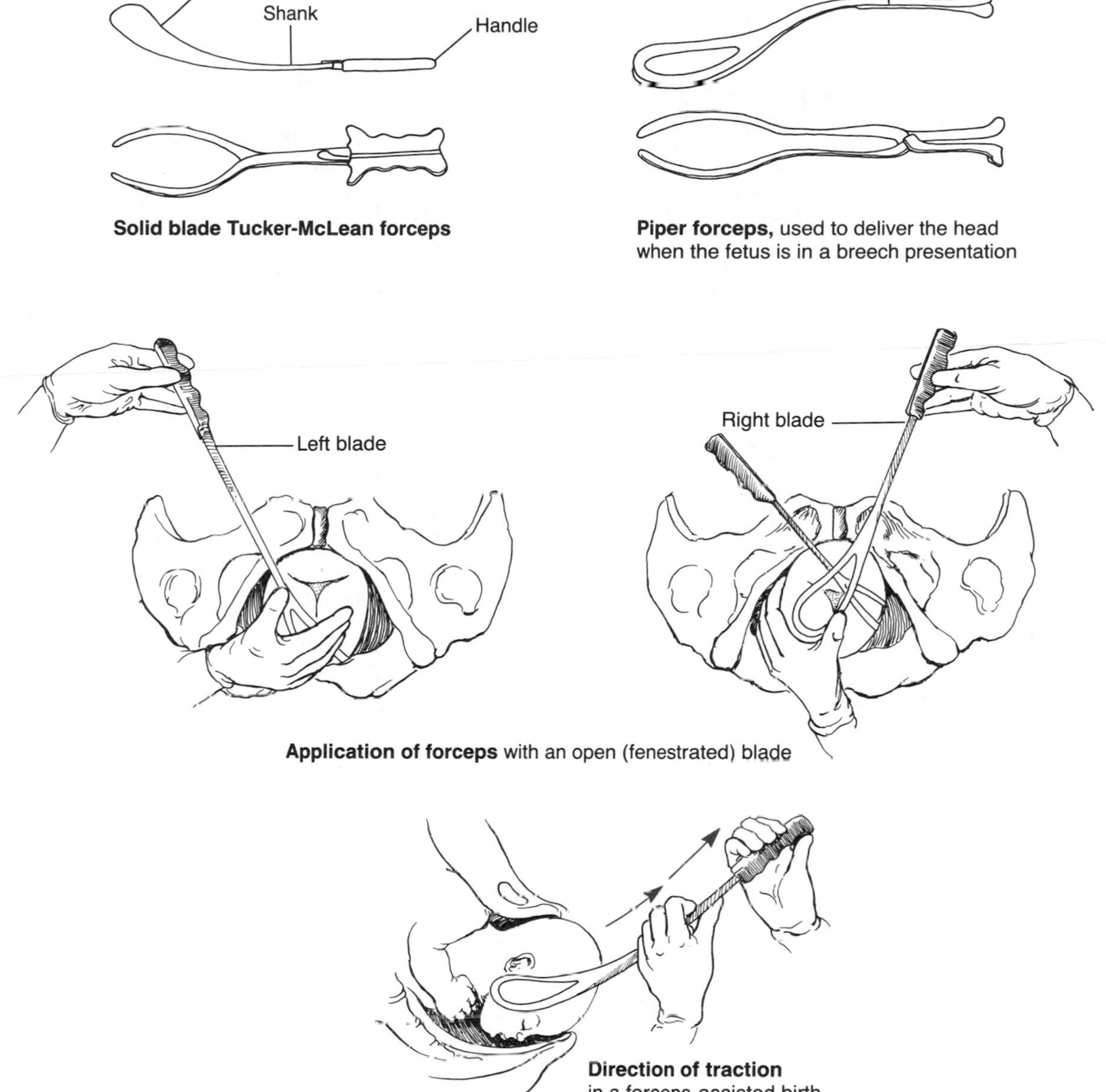

Figure 16–5

Obstetrical forceps and their application.

Indications

Indications for forceps or vacuum extraction exist if the second stage should be shortened for the well-being of the expectant mother, fetus, or both, and if vaginal birth can be accomplished quickly without undue trauma.

Maternal indications, include exhaustion, inability to push effectively, cardiac or pulmonary disease, and intrapartum infection.

Fetal indications may include a prolapsed cord, premature separation of the placenta, and non-reassuring fetal heart rate patterns.

Contraindications

Cesarean birth is preferable if the maternal or fetal condition mandates a more rapid birth than can be accomplished with forceps or vacuum extractor or if the procedure would be too traumatic. Examples of these conditions are fetal distress; maternal distress,

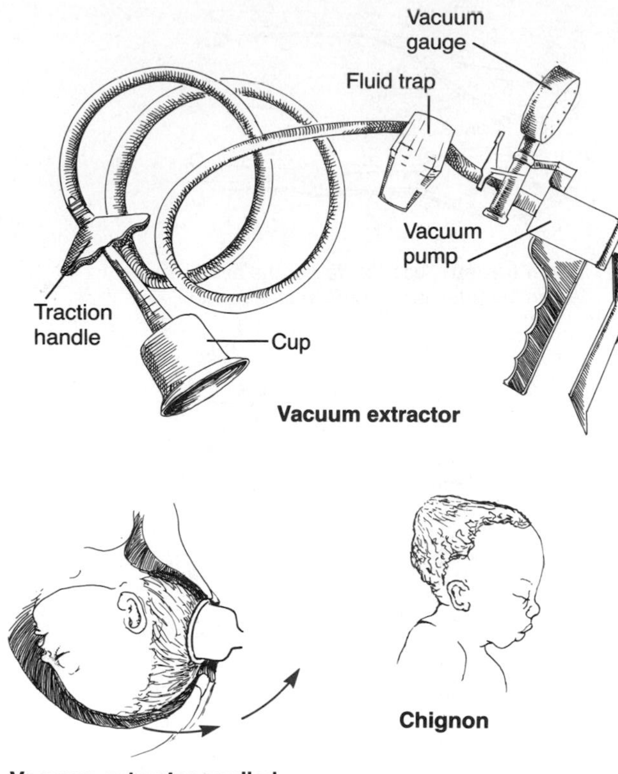

Figure 16–6

Vacuum extractor.

such as congestive heart failure or pulmonary edema; a high fetal station, and disproportion between the size of the fetus and maternal pelvis.

Risks

The main risk of forceps or vacuum extraction is trauma to maternal or fetal tissues. More serious trauma to the mother or fetus is likely if the forceps or vacuum extractor birth is difficult. For this reason, and because of the relative safety of cesarean birth, most physicians abandon an attempted forceps or vacuum extractor birth if the fetal head does not easily descend.

Maternal risks include vaginal wall laceration and vaginal wall hematoma (see Chapter 27).

The infant can have ecchymoses, facial and scalp lacerations or abrasions, cephalhematoma, subgaleal hemorrhage, and intracranial hemorrhage. The vacuum extractor creates circular edema, called a *chignon*, at the application area (Fig. 16–6).

Technique

Preparation for forceps or vaginal extraction is the same as for any vaginal birth. In addition, the woman is catheterized to provide more room in the pelvis and reduce bladder trauma that may occur with instrumental birth. Membranes must be ruptured and the cervix completely dilated for forceps or vacuum extraction. The woman must have adequate anesthesia (see Chapter 15).

Forceps and vacuum extractor are classified according to how far the fetal head has descended into the pelvis when they are applied (American Academy of Pediatrics and American College of Obstetricians and Gynecologists, 1992):

Outlet–the fetal head is on the perineum, with the scalp visible at the vaginal opening.
Low–the leading edge of the fetal skull is at station +2 or more.
Mid-forceps (rare)–the leading edge of the fetal skull is between a 0 and a +2 station.

The physician determines the presentation, position, and station of the fetal head and the amount of cervical dilation. The left side of the forceps is inserted on the mother's left, and the right blade is applied on her right side. They are properly applied if the long axis of the blade lies over the fetal cheeks and parietal bones. The physician checks proper application and makes sure the maternal tissues are not pinched, then locks the two blades in the center. The physician pulls gently on the forceps, following the curve of the pelvis. An episiotomy is usually done as the fetal head distends the perineum.

The physician may keep the forceps on until the head is born or may unlock and remove the blades just before full expulsion. If the blades are removed before the head is born, the physician applies upward pressure to the fetal chin through the perineum (Ritgen's maneuver, see p. 316) to complete extension and expulsion. The rest of the fetus is born in the conventional way.

For vacuum extraction, the cup is applied to the midline of the fetal occiput over the posterior fontanelle. The cup is connected to tubing and a suction machine that creates a vacuum that holds the cup on the fetal head. The physician applies traction intermittently, as in forceps birth. An episiotomy may be performed when the head distends the perineum.

Forceps also may be used to rotate a fetus that remains in an occiput posterior or transverse position. Application is similar to that discussed before.

Before traction is applied, however, the fetal head is rotated to the occiput anterior position. The forceps are taken off and reapplied to assist head expulsion.

Nursing Care

When anticipating a forceps or vacuum extraction birth, add a catheter to the delivery instrument table. The physician specifies what type of forceps or vacuum cup is needed on the table. Assess the fetal heart rate with continuous monitoring or Doppler auscultation until birth at recommended intervals (see Table 13–2). Tell the physician if the rate is lower than 100 BPM.

After birth, observe the mother and infant for trauma. Undetected vaginal wall lacerations bleed continuously and are bright red in the presence of a firm fundus. Women with vaginal wall hematomas complain of severe and unrelenting pain. Observe for edema and discoloration of the labia and perineum. Cold applications reduce pain by numbing

the area and limit bruising and edema of the tissues. (See Chapter 27 for further discussion of these maternal complications.)

The infant will often have reddening and mild bruising of the skin where the blades were applied. These areas do not require treatment. The infant does not receive cold treatment because of the possibility of inducing hypothermia. Observe for skin breaks that are a portal of entry for infectious orga-

nisms and keep the area clean. Facial asymmetry, most obvious when the infant cries, suggests facial nerve injury. (See Chapter 29 for further information on neonatal complications.)

After a forceps birth, a parent may ask why the baby's cheeks are reddened or bruised. A good response is to explain that the pressure of the forceps on the baby's delicate skin may cause minor bruising that usually resolves without treatment. Point out improvement in the area during the postpartum stay.

✔ Check Your Reading

13. What are the similarities in the uses of forceps and vacuum extractors? What are the differences?
14. A physician expects to use forceps during a birth. Why should the nurse add a urinary catheter to the instrument table?
15. A woman has a forceps birth with a median episiotomy. What nursing interventions can make her more comfortable?
16. What injury is suggested by an asymmetrical facial appearance when the infant cries?

Table 16–3. GUIDELINES FOR VAGINAL BIRTH AFTER CESAREAN BIRTH

- The practice of a routine repeat cesarean birth should be replaced by a specific indication for the repeat surgical birth
- The previous uterine incision or incisions should be low transverse
- A previous classic uterine incision is a contraindication to labor
- Normal activity should be encouraged during the latent phase of labor
- A physician capable of evaluating labor and performing a cesarean delivery should be readily available

Data from American College of Obstetricians and Gynecologists *(1988). Guidelines for vaginal delivery after a previous cesarean birth: ACOG committee opinion, 64.*

Cesarean Birth

In 1965, the cesarean rate was 4.5 per cent of all births, rising to 23 per cent in 1989 (Centers for Disease Control, 1992). The increased safety of the surgery and recognition that vaginal breech births and use of mid-forceps are hazardous account for part of this rise. Continuous electronic fetal monitoring has been implicated in the increase because it permits identification of subtle abnormalities in the fetal condition and labor pattern.

Maternity care professionals are trying to reduce the cesarean rate without compromising outcomes for mother or infant. Efforts include (1) promoting vaginal birth after cesarean (VBAC) (Table 16–3), (2) selection of some women to deliver their infants in the breech presentation, and (3) careful evaluation of dystocia (difficult or prolonged labor). Moreover, greater experience with electronic fetal monitoring has strengthened knowledge of normal fetal responses to the stress of labor, enabling more appropriate interventions for the fetus' benefit. Nurses, nurse-midwives, and physicians increasingly recognize that simple interventions, such as squatting during the second stage, may facilitate normal labor progress and prevent a cesarean birth.

Indications

Cesarean birth is performed when delaying birth would compromise the mother, fetus, or both, yet when awaiting vaginal birth is not safe. Common indications for cesarean birth include, but are not limited to:

- Dystocia
- Cephalopelvic disproportion

- Pregnancy-induced hypertension
- Maternal diseases such as diabetes, heart disease, or cervical cancer
- Active genital herpes
- Some previous uterine surgical procedures, such as a classic cesarean incision
- Fetal distress
- Prolapsed umbilical cord
- Fetal malpresentations, such as breech or transverse lie
- Hemorrhagic conditions, such as abruptio placentae or placenta previa

Contraindications

There are few absolute contraindications to cesarean birth, but there are conditions in which it may not be desirable: intrauterine fetal death, a fetus that is too preterm to survive, maternal coagulation defects.

Risks

Cesarean birth is one of the safest major surgical procedures; however, it poses greater risk for the mother than does vaginal birth. Maternal mortality is less than 1 in 1000 cesarean births in the United States. The woman's death sometimes may be attributed to the problem that led to the cesarean delivery rather than to the surgery itself. Maternal mortality may result from factors related to anesthesia, such as aspiration of gastric contents (see p. 377). Other maternal risks include

- Infection
- Hemorrhage
- Urinary tract trauma
- Thrombophlebitis
- Paralytic ileus

Risks of cesarean birth to the fetus or neonate include

- Inadvertent preterm birth
- Transient tachypnea of the newborn caused by delayed absorption of lung fluid (see p. 843)
- Persistent fetal circulation (see p. 807)
- Injury, such as laceration, bruising, or other trauma as the fetus is pulled through the uterine incision

The greatest risk to the neonate is an iatrogenic preterm birth if the gestation is miscalculated. Physicians may use several criteria to assure that the fetus is born at term when the cesarean birth is planned (see Chapter 10).

Technique

PREPARATION

A general anesthetic (see p. 376) may be needed unexpectedly for cesarean birth even if a regional block is planned. Institution of the regional block may not be possible, or an inadequate anesthetic block may require the use of supplemental general anesthesia. The woman receives nothing by mouth, and 30 ml of a clear non-particulate antacid, such as sodium citrate and citric acid (Bicitra), is given to reduce gastric acidity before surgery. Women in labor are often offered only clear fluids because of the possible unexpected need for general anesthesia during cesarean birth. The woman does not usually have pre-medication other than drugs to control gastric and respiratory secretions.

Common laboratory studies include complete blood count, clotting studies such as prothrombin and partial thromboplastin times, and blood typing and screening. The physician may order 1 or more units of blood typed and cross-matched to have available for transfusion if the woman's hemoglobin and hematocrit values are low and if she is at greater risk for hemorrhage, such as grand multiparity (five or more births that occurred after 20 weeks' gestation).

The woman's abdomen is shaved from just above the umbilicus to the mons pubis, about where her legs come together. If a Pfannenstiel (transverse, or "bikini") skin incision is planned, the upper border of the shave begins about 3 inches above the pubic hairline. An indwelling catheter, inserted before the cesarean delivery, keeps the bladder away from the operative area, reducing the risk for injury. The catheter also allows accurate estimation of urine output during and after surgery, which helps evaluate circulatory status.

If general anesthesia is required, preoperative preparations are completed before anesthesia is begun to reduce neonatal exposure to anesthesia. The team scrubs, dons gowns and gloves, and drapes the woman before anesthesia is induced. Although there is less need to rush when regional anesthesia is used, the infant is still delivered as quickly as possible.

The circulating nurse does an abdominal scrub just before draping. As in other surgical skin preparations, the direction is circular, from the center of the operative area outward.

Prophylactic antibiotics are usually ordered for cesarean births. Some physicians may flush the operative area with an antibiotic solution before abdominal closure.

Table 16–4. SKIN (ABDOMINAL WALL) INCISIONS FOR CESAREAN BIRTH

Vertical	Pfannenstiel
	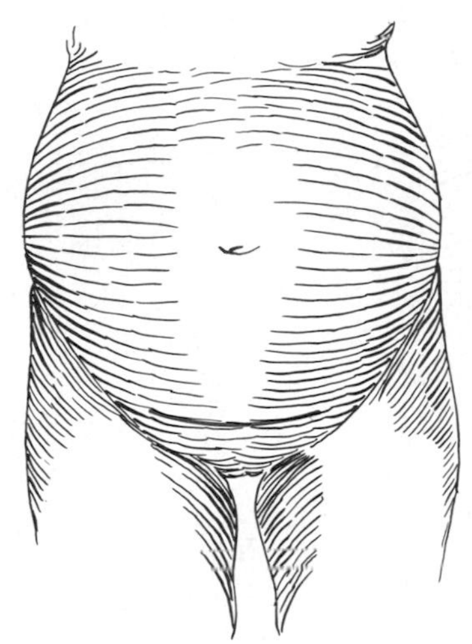
Advantages Quicker to perform Better visualization of the uterus Can quickly extend upward for greater visualization if needed Often more appropriate for obese women	***Advantages*** Less visibility when healed and the pubic hair grows back Less chance of dehiscence or formation of a hernia
Disadvantages Easily visible when healed Greater chance of dehiscence and hernia formation	***Disadvantages*** Less visualization of the uterus Cannot be done as quickly, which may be important in an emergency cesarean birth Cannot easily be extended to give greater operative exposure Re-entry at a subsequent cesarean birth may require more time

INCISIONS

Two incisions are made: one in the abdominal wall and the other in the uterine wall. Either of two skin (abdominal wall) incisions are used: a midline vertical incision below the umbilicus and above the symphysis or a Pfannenstiel incision just above the pubic hairline. Table 16–4 presents advantages and disadvantages of each type.

There are three types of uterine incisions (Table 16–5), each with different indications and limitations: (1) low transverse, (2) low vertical, and (3) classic, a vertical incision into the upper uterine segment. The low transverse uterine incision is preferred. The uterine incision does not always match the skin incision. For example, a woman may have a vertical skin incision and a low transverse uterine incision.

The low transverse incision may not be suitable if the fetus is very large. The location of the uterine artery and vein at the lower sides of the uterus limits the length of this incision. It may not be large enough to deliver a large fetus through without tearing these large vessels.

A classic uterine incision is rarely made but must occasionally be used when the other two incisions are not advisable. The vertical uterine incision, especially the classic one, is more likely to rupture during later pregnancies.

SEQUENCE OF EVENTS IN CESAREAN BIRTH

The sequence of events in cesarean birth is similar to that in a vaginal birth. When the woman is adequately anesthetized and draped, the physician makes the skin incision. After the bladder is dissected away from the uterine wall, it is held downward with a wide bladder retractor. The uterus is incised, usually in a low transverse incision.

If the membranes are intact, they are ruptured with a sharp instrument, such as an Allis clamp, and amniotic fluid is suctioned from the operative field. As in vaginal births, the color, odor, and approximate quantity of the amniotic fluid are noted.

The physician lifts the fetal head (or breech) through the uterine incision. An assistant may push on the uterine fundus to help deliver the fetus through the abdominal incision. Forceps or a vacuum extractor may be needed to facilitate birth of the fetal head, usually if the mother has been in labor and the fetal head is in the pelvis.

The infant's face is wiped and the mouth and nose are suctioned to remove secretions that would impair breathing. The cord is quickly clamped and cut. The physician collects cord blood for analysis.

Following the infant's birth, the physician again reaches through the incision and scoops out the placenta. Oxytocin is given IV to contract the uterus firmly. The physician then closes the uterine and abdominal incisions, approximating each layer separately.

Nursing Care

Nursing care for a woman who has a cesarean birth may vary according to the situation. She may be planning a cesarean birth, or a surgical birth may be

Table 16–5. UTERINE INCISIONS FOR CESAREAN BIRTH*

Low Transverse	Low Vertical	Classic
	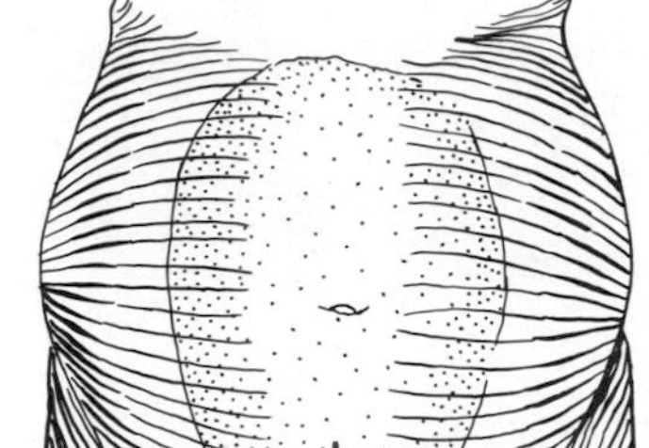 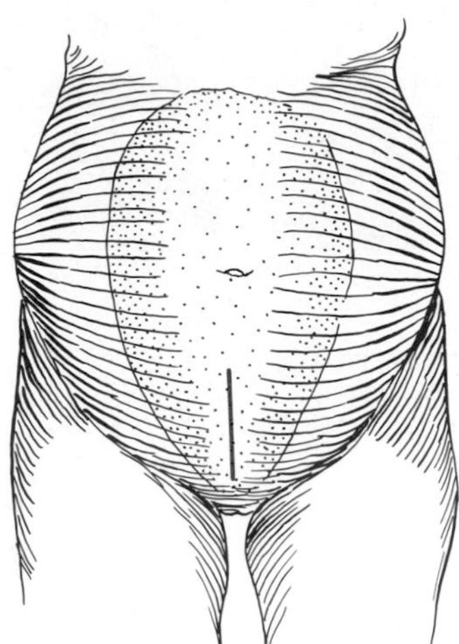	
Advantages Unlikely to rupture during a subsequent birth Makes VBAC possible for subsequent pregnancy Less blood loss Easier to repair Less adhesion formation	***Advantage*** Can be extended upward to make a larger incision if needed	***Advantages*** May be the only choice in these situations: Implantation of a placenta previa on the lower anterior uterine wall Presence of dense adhesions from previous surgery Transverse lie of a large fetus with the shoulder impacted in the mother's pelvis
Disadvantages Limited ability to extend laterally to enlarge the incision	***Disadvantages*** More likely to rupture during a subsequent birth A tear may extend the incision downward into the cervix	***Disadvantages*** Most likely of the uterine incisions to rupture during a subsequent birth Eliminates VBAC as an option for birth of a subsequent infant

* The abdominal and uterine incisions do not always match.
Abbreviation: VBAC, Vaginal birth after cesarean.

unexpected. Even within these two situations, women differ. For example, is the planned cesarean her first? Or has she had a cesarean birth before? The unexpected cesarean delivery may arise after many hours of unsuccessful labor or may be needed in an emergency.

Nursing care for women having cesarean childbirth may be similar, but the approach in each situation is different. Adapt nursing interventions to fit the circumstances. For example, although preoperative teaching is important, it must be abbreviated or even omitted in a true emergency. Table 16–6 presents a summary of nursing care for women having cesarean birth.

PROVIDING EMOTIONAL SUPPORT

Emotional support may begin well before the birth and extend well after it. A mother who has had a previous cesarean may harbor unresolved feelings of grief, guilt, or inadequacy because she perceives that she somehow failed in her expected birth experience. Use therapeutic communication techniques to identify stressors and misunderstanding. For example, the nurse in the prenatal setting can open the subject with a broad lead such as, "Tell me about when you had your other baby."

Anxiety is an expected and normal reaction to surgery and, within limits, is functional. For example, mild anxiety may prompt the woman who plans a cesarean to learn more about her upcoming experience. If anxiety is high, however, she may have difficulty concentrating. The woman who has an unplanned cesarean birth is more likely to have high levels of anxiety, but the woman who expects the surgery is also vulnerable.

The staff's behavior can either reduce or increase the woman's anxiety. A calm and confident attitude

Table 16–6. SUMMARY OF NURSING CARE FOR A WOMAN HAVING CESAREAN BIRTH

Before the Cesarean Birth

1. Assess time of last oral intake and what was eaten.
2. Assess for allergies.
3. Have woman sign a consent form.
4. Obtain ordered laboratory work.
5. Do preoperative teaching: what to expect in the operating and recovery rooms.

6. Start ordered intravenous infusion.
7. Do abdominal shave and cleansing preparation.
8. Insert an indwelling catheter.
9. Administer ordered antacid.
10. Administer antibiotics if ordered.
11. Apply a grounding pad for electrocautery.

During the Recovery Period

1. Begin anesthesia-related interventions: pulse oximeter, oxygen administration, cardiac monitor.
2. Assess the woman's vital signs every 15 minutes the first hour, every 30 minutes the second hour, and hourly until she is transferred to the postpartum area.
3. Assess the fundus gently for firmness, height, and deviation with each vital sign check. Massage the fundus if it is poorly contracted.
4. Assess the lochia for color, quantity, and presence of clots with each vital sign check.
5. Assess urine output for color and quantity as well as patency of catheter and tubing with each vital sign check.
6. Assess the abdominal dressing for drainage or bleeding with vital sign checks.
7. Assess the need for analgesia. Administer medication as ordered.
8. Change woman's position hourly if there is no contraindication. Have her breathe deeply and cough when assessing vital signs.

helps her feel that she is being cared for by competent professionals. Speak in a quiet, low voice. There is little reason to shout, even in an emergency.

The nurse and the woman's significant others are important sources of emotional support. Remain with her, and let her express her fears. Help her identify her concerns, and provide explanations that may reduce her fear of the unknown.

Encourage the father or other support person to remain with her during surgery if she has a regional anesthetic. In some hospitals, the father may come into the operating room when the mother receives a general anesthetic after she is successfully intubated. In this case, the purpose of having the support person present is to foster attachment with the infant and help the mother integrate the cesarean experience after birth. Other facilities encourage the father to accompany the newborn to the nursery for bonding.

Although the primary focus of care is on the mother and baby, nurses also support her partner and significant others during the cesarean experience. The partner may be as anxious as the mother but may be afraid to express it because the mother needs much support. The partner may be physically exhausted after hours of labor support. Do not expect more support from the partner than he or she can provide.

Although cesarean births are a common event in the intrapartum unit, they are not routine to women who undergo them or to their families. Avoid belittling their fears by telling women and their families not to worry or that everything will be all right.

After the birth, it is helpful to visit the mother and her family to answer questions about the surgery and fill in any gaps in their understanding. This helps them integrate the experience and promotes a positive perception of the birth.

TEACHING

Knowledge helps to dispel fear of the unknown and increases the woman's sense of control over her infant's birth. Do not assume that a woman who has had a previous cesarean birth already knows what will happen and why. If her previous surgery was done after a long labor or in an emergency, she may recall only bits and pieces and may not understand what she does remember. Teaching should be in simple language that she can understand. Include her partner in all teaching if possible.

Explain all preoperative procedures, such as the abdominal shave preparation, indwelling catheter, intravenous lines, and dressings, and their purposes. Tell her about how long the catheter and intravenous lines will remain (usually no longer than 24 hours after birth). The anesthesia clinician explains anesthesia-related procedures, but the nurse may reinforce the information.

Women who have regional anesthesia, such as epidural or subarachnoid block, often fear that they will be able to feel pain during surgery. Explain that they will feel pressure and pulling, but that these sensations do not mean the anesthesia is wearing off.

If a woman is having general anesthesia, explain why all operative preparations are done before she is anesthetized. Assure her that surgery will not begin until she is asleep and that she will not wake up during the procedure.

Describe the operating room and all individuals who will be present. The operating room is usually very cool, and the surgery table is narrow. The intrapartum nurse is usually the circulating nurse during surgery, so the mother will see a familiar face.

Tell the father or support person who plans to attend the birth when he or she can expect to come into the operating room. If it is not already in place, an epidural anesthetic is usually administered when

Nursing Care Plan 16–1

Cesarean Birth

Assessment: Christina Cole is 22 years old and is expecting her first baby. Her due date is 1 week from today. The baby is in a complete (full) breech presentation. A previous attempt at version was unsuccessful, and the fetus did not turn spontaneously. She is in early labor and expecting a cesarean birth. Although her physician discussed cesarean birth with her, Christina is anxious and has many questions about what will happen to her and her baby. She says she is very nervous about the upcoming surgery. Christina's mother and husband Bruce are with her.

Nursing Diagnosis:
Anxiety related to unfamiliarity with procedures for cesarean birth.

Goals:
1. Christina will state that she feels less apprehensive about surgery following interventions.
2. She will indicate adequate anxiety control and learning by:
   a. Verbalizing understanding of preoperative and postoperative care
   b. Return demonstration of postoperative techniques for coughing and deep breathing

Intervention:	Rationale:
1. Assess level of anxiety: mild, moderate, severe, or panic. Mild to moderate levels of anxiety are expected.	1. Assessment enables the nurse to approach preoperative care of the woman in the most appropriate manner. Mild to moderate anxiety may facilitate learning. However, severe or panic levels impair or prevent learning.
2. Remain with Christina as much as possible. Allow her to express her fears. Encourage her mother and Bruce to remain with her.	2. Reduces Christina's fears of abandonment and helps the nurse to understand what is really bothering her. Helps the nurse most appropriately to answer her concerns. Christina may draw strength from family support.
3. Elicit Christina's feelings about surgery by using broad leads, such as: "What were your thoughts when you found out you might have your baby by cesarean?"	3. Identifies sources of anxiety and misunderstandings and possible feelings of inadequacy or anger. Identifies Christina's expectations of her birth experience so that actions can be taken to make it a positive one. The closer her expected and actual experience match, the more satisfied Christina is likely to feel.
4. Explain preoperative preparations using simple language: a. Visit by anesthesiologist or nurse anesthetist to explain anesthesia b. Enema, if applicable. c. Shave preparation: just above umbilicus to mons pubis (lower if a Pfannenstiel incision is planned) d. Indwelling urinary catheter, which is usually inserted after shave preparation and epidural anesthesia is begun e. The epidural anesthetic is given in the operating room f. Operating room: appearance, narrow table, cool temperature, equipment g. People who will be in the operating room: circulating nurse (usually the nurse who cares for Christina before surgery), scrub nurse, surgeon's assistant, nursery staff, pediatrician Verify Christina's understanding, and give her the opportunity to ask questions.	4. Knowledge decreases anxiety and fear of the unknown. Simple language facilitates understanding because Christina's attention is narrowed from anxiety. Shows respect for Christina and gives her a greater sense of control.

Nursing Care Plan 16–1 *Continued*

Cesarean Birth

5. Explain what to expect postoperatively, demonstrating as needed.
   a. Oxygen mask may be used
   b. Pulse oximeter on finger
   c. Frequent checks of her vital signs, fundus, and lochia. Emphasize that nurses will be as gentle as possible when assessing her fundus
   d. Catheter will remain in place about 24 hours
   e. She will be asked to move and change position several times
   f. Demonstrate effective coughing (splinting the abdomen with a pillow) and deep breathing techniques; have Christina return demonstrate each.

5. Reduces anxiety and fear of the unknown. Promotes understanding and acceptance of care that will be painful.

   Return demonstration verifies that Christina has learned material and identifies the need for any additional teaching.

6. Reduce unnecessary stimulation:
   a. Keep lights low and noise to a minimum
   b. Limit unnecessary visitors and staff
   c. Plan operative preparations so that they are done efficiently
   d. Maintain calm behavior

6. Promotes relaxation and allows Christina to devote her attention to coping with the new experience.

Evaluation:
Christina discusses her disappointment that the baby did not turn before she went into labor. However, she believes that a cesarean birth is best for her baby. Christina asks a few other questions, then states that she understands preoperative and postoperative care. She return demonstrates effective coughing and deep breathing techniques.

Assessment: Christina had soup and a sandwich about 2 hours before admission. She will have epidural anesthesia for her birth. Her vital signs are temperature 99°F, pulse 90 BPM, respirations 22 breaths per minute, blood pressure 122/70. The fetal heart rate is 130 to 140 BPM and accelerates with fetal movement.

Nursing Diagnosis:
High Risk for Aspiration related to presence of food in stomach and possible altered protective reflexes.

Goals:
Christina will not aspirate secretions or gastric contents after surgery.

Intervention:	Rationale:
1. Determine what Christina last ate and when. Give her nothing orally, other than ordered medications such as antacid.	1. Although Christina plans epidural anesthesia, general anesthesia may be unexpectedly required. The anesthesia clinician can better anticipate complications with an accurate history of food intake. Restricting food and fluids avoids adding to her stomach contents.
2. Give Christina a non-particulate antacid, such as 30 ml of sodium citrate with citric acid as ordered.	2. Raises gastric pH to reduce lung damage if gastric aspiration does occur.

Evaluation:
Christina does not need general anesthesia and does not aspirate.

Nursing Care Plan continued on following page

Nursing Care Plan 16–1 Continued

Cesarean Birth

Assessment: Christina is transferred to the operating room and epidural anesthesia is begun. She gives birth to an 8-pound, 8-ounce (3856 g) baby. Christina is transferred to the recovery room for postoperative care.

Nursing Diagnosis:
High risk for injury related to altered sensation from epidural anesthesia and use of electrical equipment during surgery.

Goals:
Christina will not have injury, such as pressure areas, muscle strains, or electrical injury, during the perioperative period.

Intervention:	Rationale:
1. Pad the operating table carefully, particularly under Christina's bony prominences. Be careful to avoid obstruction of her popliteal area.	1. Reduces potential for tissue damage caused by pressure. Avoiding pressure at the popliteal space reduces venous stasis with possible thrombus formation.
2. Transfer Christina to and from the operating table carefully, using enough staff members to keep her body in alignment. Brace the bed and operating table to keep them from separating.	2. Reduces risk of fall or muscle strains in both Christina and the staff.
3. After anesthesia is begun, position Christina on the operating table and secure her legs with a safety strap.	3. Prevents falls or displacement of legs, which have lost sensation.
4. Apply grounding pad if electrocautery is to be used.	4. Prevents electrical shock or burn.

Evaluation:
During surgery, Christina's body was secured in proper alignment, with proper padding of all her bony prominences. The grounding pad ensured electrical safety when the electrocautery was used. Christina was transferred to the recovery room without incident. During the recovery period, she showed no signs of pressure, electrical, or musculoskeletal injury.

Additional Nursing Diagnoses to Consider:
Pain
High Risk for Altered Respiratory Function
Hypothermia
Family Coping, Potential for Growth

Note: Only nursing diagnoses related to the preoperative and intraoperative care of the woman are discussed here. See Chapter 14 for nursing care related to fetal oxygenation. See Chapter 15 for care related to anesthesia. See Chapters 13 and 17 for nursing care of the mother during recovery and post partum.

the woman goes to the operating room. The partner is not usually brought in until the regional anesthetic is completed. It may be as long as 30 to 45 minutes before the father or support person is summoned. Assure the support person that he or she will not be forgotten and that the apparent delay does not indicate a problem but that it takes that long to achieve adequate surgical anesthesia and make other operative preparations.

Describe to the woman the recovery room and any equipment that will be used, such as a pulse oximeter. Explain nursing assessments and interventions such as fundus and lochia checks (see p. 320), coughing, and deep breathing. Explain to the woman that simple exercises promote normal circulation in her legs. Reassure her that every effort will be made to promote her comfort with medication, positioning, and other interventions.

PROMOTING SAFETY

Assume that the woman will need general anesthesia. Assess her food intake for type and time on admission. Note oral intake and emesis during labor. Be certain that she receives whatever oral antacid is ordered. Give her nothing by mouth except ordered medications once a cesarean birth is planned or is a high probability.

Transfer and position the woman carefully to prevent injury. The woman who has received regional anesthesia has reduced motor control and sensation. Check to be sure that her bony prominences are well padded. Secure her position on the operating table with a safety strap placed across her thighs. Place a wedge under her right side, or tilt the operating table to avoid aortocaval compression and reduced placental blood flow. When postioning, ensure that the indwelling catheter has free drainage. The catheter bag is usually placed near the head of the table so that the anesthesia clinician can monitor urine output. After the birth, smoothly transfer the mother to a bed to avoid undue pain and hypotension.

The circulating nurse or anesthesia clinician applies leads for the cardiac monitor and pulse oximeter. Apply a grounding pad for safe use of the electrocautery equipment. Check function of all machines such as suction, monitors, and electrocautery to be sure they are functioning properly.

PROVIDING POSTOPERATIVE CARE

In the recovery room, care for the mother who has had a cesarean birth is similar to that for one who has had a vaginal birth, with additional interventions. Assess her fundus for height, firmness, and position every 15 minutes during the first hour. This will be painful after regional anesthesia wears off, but the post-cesarean mother can also have uterine atony. To reduce pain from fundal checks, help her relax her abdominal muscles by slightly flexing their knees and taking slow deep breaths. Gradually approach her fundus from the side by gently "walking" the fingers from the side toward the midline. If the fundus is firm, there is no need to massage it. Assess the lochia and urine output with each fundal check.

Assess her pulse, respirations, and blood pressure. Assess temperature on admission and according to protocol thereafter. If using a pulse oximeter, note oxygen saturation below 95 per cent and have her take several deep breaths. Have her breathe deeply and cough to move secretions out of the lungs. Change her position to improve ventilation and decrease discomfort from constant pressure if there is no contraindication.

Assess the dressing for drainage with each fundal check. Also check the intravenous site and flow rate and the patency of the catheter. Observe the mother's level of consciousness for signs of excessive sedation from medications or for restlessness and anxiety that may accompany pain or shock.

Analgesia may be given by intermittent injections or a patient-controlled analgesia (PCA) pump. Many women who receive epidural blocks may have epidural injection of a narcotic to provide long-lasting analgesia. Observe for respiratory depression that may be delayed for up to 24 hours, depending on the narcotic used. Have naloxone immediately available if the respiratory rate falls below 12 breaths per minute. Do not give other parenteral analgesics unless specifically ordered by the anesthesiologist. (See Chapter 15 for more information about anesthesia and analgesia for cesarean birth.)

✔ *Check Your Reading*

17. Why is the low transverse uterine incision preferred for cesarean birth? What is the main risk of a classic uterine incision?
18. What should a woman who expects a cesarean birth be taught about the operating room? The recovery room?
19. How should the nurse modify recovery room care of the mother who had a cesarean birth from that of the mother who had a vaginal delivery?

Summary Concepts

- Prolapse and compression of the umbilical cord is the primary risk of amniotomy. As the fluid gushes out, the cord can become compressed between the fetal presenting part and the expectant woman's pelvis.
- Infection is more likely to occur when membranes have been ruptured for a long time, usually thought to be about 24 hours.
- Induction of labor may be done if continuing the pregnancy is more hazardous to the maternal or fetal health than is the induction. It is not done if there is a maternal or fetal contraindication to labor or vaginal birth.
- Oxytocin-stimulated uterine contractions may be hypertonic, decreasing placental perfusion.
- External version is done to promote vaginal birth by changing the fetal presentation from a breech or transverse lie to cephalic. Internal version may be used to change presentation of a second twin, following the birth of the first twin.
- The median episiotomy is less painful but more likely to extend into the rectum. The mediolateral

episiotomy is more painful but is not likely to extend into the rectum.

- Trauma to maternal and fetal tissue is the primary risk associated with use of forceps and vacuum extractor. Possible trauma to the mother includes vaginal wall laceration or hematoma. Trauma to the infant may include ecchymoses, lacerations, abrasions, or intracranial hemorrhage.
- The preferred uterine incision for cesarean birth is the low transverse incision because it is least likely to rupture in a subsequent pregnancy. The skin incision does not always match the uterine incision and is unrelated to the risk of later uterine rupture.
- Some women may have feelings of guilt or inadequacy if they have a cesarean delivery. Therapeutic communication and sensitive, family-centered care are essential to help them achieve a positive perception of their birth experience.

References and Readings

Afriat, C.I. (1990). Vaginal birth after cesarean section: A review of the literature. *Journal of Perinatal-Neonatal Nursing*, 3(3), 1–13.

American Academy of Pediatrics and American College of Obstetricians and Gynecologists (1992). *Guidelines for perinatal care* (3rd ed.). Elk Grove Village, Il.

Baruffi, G., Strobino, D.M., & Paine, L.L. (1990). Investigation of institutional differences in primary cesarean birth rates. *Journal of Nurse-Midwifery*, 35(5), 274–281.

Bishop, E.H. (1964). Pelvic scoring. *Obstetrics and Gynecology*, 24(2), 266–268.

Blackburn, S.T., & Loper, D.L. (1992). *Maternal, fetal, and neonatal physiology: A clinical perspective*. Philadelphia: W.B. Saunders.

Bowes, W.A. (1989). Clinical aspects of normal and abnormal labor. In R. Creasy & R. Resnik (Eds.), *Maternal-fetal medicine: Principles and practice* (pp. 510–546). Philadelphia: W.B. Saunders.

Boylan, P., & Macdonald, D. (1988). Commentary: Oxytocin: The need to distinguish between induction and augmentation and between multiparas and primiparas. *Birth*, 15(4), 203–205.

Brodsky, P.L., & Pelzar, E.M. (1991). Rationale for the revision of oxytocin administration protocols. *Journal of Obstetric, Gynecologic and Neonatal Nursing*, 20(6), 440–444.

Centers for Disease Control (1992). Rates of cesarean delivery and vaginal birth after a previous cesarean (VBAC) by selected maternal and infant characteristics—reporting areas, 1989. *Morbidity and Mortality Weekly Report*, 41(30), 561.

Chenia, F., & Crowther, C.A. (1987). Does advice to assume the knee-chest position reduce the incidence of breech presentation at delivery? A randomized clinical trial. *Birth*, 14(2), 75–78.

Cunningham, F.G., & MacDonald, P.C. (1989). *Williams obstetrics* (18th ed.). Norwalk, Conn.: Appleton & Lange.

Curtis, P., & Safransky, N. (1988). Rethinking oxytocin protocols in the augmentation of labor. *Birth*, 15(4), 199–202.

Garite, T.J. (1990). Amnionitis. In R. Creasy & R. Resnik (Eds.), *Maternal-fetal medicine: Principles and practice* (pp. 190–192). Philadelphia: W.B. Saunders.

Kearney, M., & Cronenwett, L.R. (1989). Perceived perinatal complications and childbirth satisfaction. *Applied Nursing Research*, 2(3), 140–142.

Kozak, L.J. (1989). Surgical and nonsurgical procedures associated with hospital delivery in the United States: 1980–1987. *Birth*, 16(4), 209–213.

Loebl, S., Spratto, G.R., Woods, A.L., & Matejski, M. (1991). *The nurse's drug handbook*. Albany, N.Y.: Delmar.

Lumley, J. (1987). Commentary: How to find out if assuming the knee-chest position is superior to external cephalic version in turning the breech. *Birth*, 14(2), 79–80.

Marieskind, H.I. (1989). Cesarean section in the United States: Has it changed since 1979? *Birth*, 16(4), 196–202.

Martin, E.J. (1990). *Intrapartum management modules*. Baltimore: Williams & Wilkins.

Murray, M. (1988). *Antepartal and intrapartal fetal monitoring*. Baltimore: Williams & Wilkins.

NAACOG (1988a). The nurse's role in induction/augmentation of labor. Washington, D.C.

NAACOG (1988b). Practice competencies and educational guidelines for nurse providers of intrapartum care. Washington, D.C.

Nageotte, M. How can we lower the C/S rate? (1990). *Issues in OB/Gyn*, 35, 63–88.

Nager, C.W., Key, T.C., & Moore, T.R. (1987). Cervical ripening and labor outcome with preinduction intracervical prostaglandin E_2 (Prepidil) gel. *Journal of Perinatology*, 7(3), 189–193.

National Center for Health Statistics data line. (1992) *Public Health Reports*, 107(4), 484–485.

Newnham, J.P., & Hoebel, C.J. (1992). Operative delivery. In N.F. Hacker & J.G. Moore (Eds.), *Essentials of obstetrics and gynecology* (pp. 308–315). Philadelphia: W.B. Saunders.

O'Grady, J.P. (1990). A role exists for vaginal instrumental delivery. *Issues in OB/Gyn*, 35, 49–50, 52, 54, 56, 58.

Perez, P.G. (1989). The patient observer: What really led to these cesarean births? *Birth*, 16(3), 130–139.

Porreco, R.P. (1990). Commentary: The twice-wounded uterus. *Birth*, 17(3), 150–151.

Rayburn, W.F. (1989). Prostaglandin E_2 gel for cervical ripening and induction of labor: A critical analysis. *American Journal of Obstetrics and Gynecology*, 160(30), 529–534.

Reichert, J.A., Baron, M., & Fawcett, J. (1993). Changes in attitudes toward cesarean birth. *Journal of Obstetric, Gynecologic, and Neonatal Nursing*, 22(2), 159–167.

Resick, L.K., & Erlen, J.A. (1990). Vaginal birth after cesarean: Issues and implications. *Journal of the American Academy of Nurse Practitioners*, 2(3), 100–106.

Schifrin, B.S. (1988). Polemics in perinatology: Disengaging forceps. *Journal of Perinatology*, 8(3), 242–245.

Shields, J.R., & Medearis, A.L. (1992). Fetal malpresentations. In N.F. Hacker & J.G. Moore (Eds.), *Essentials of obstetrics and gynecology* (pp. 230–240). Philadelphia: W.B. Saunders.

Stafford, R.S. (1990). Cesarean section use and source of payment: An analysis of California hospital discharge abstracts. *American Journal of Public Health*, 80(3), 313–315.

Tighe, D., & Sweezy, S.R. (1990). The perioperative experience of cesarean birth: Preparation, considerations, and complications. *Journal of Perinatal-Neonatal Nursing*, 3(3), 14–39.

Wilcox, L.S., Strobino, D.M., Baruffi, G., & Dellinger, W.S. Episiotomy and its role in the incidence of perineal lacerations in a maternity center and a tertiary hospital obstetric service. *American Journal of Obstetrics and Gynecology*, 160(5, Part I), 1047–1052.

Part IV

The Family Following Birth

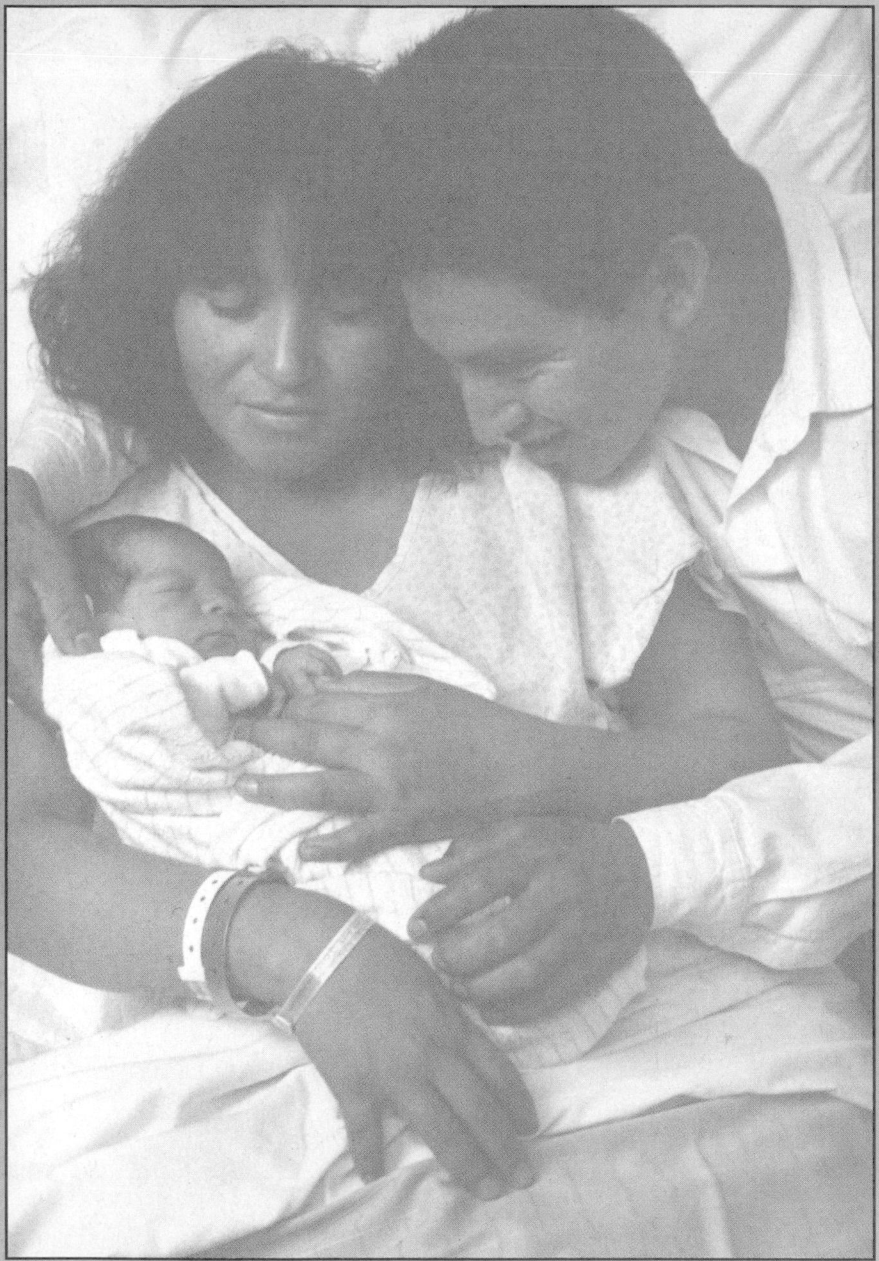

17

Postpartum Physiological Adaptations

Objectives

1. Explain the physiological changes that occur during the postpartum period.
2. Identify nursing assessments that are necessary during the postpartum period.
3. Describe the nurse's responsibility for providing care and instruction that protect the health of the new mother.
4. Recount nursing interventions for the most common nursing diagnoses during the postpartum period.
5. Describe the nurse's responsibility for patients who choose early discharge from the birth facility.
6. Compare cesarean birth and vaginal birth in terms of nursing assessments and care.

Definitions

Afterpains • Cramping pain following childbirth caused by alternate relaxation and contraction of uterine muscles.

Atony • Absence or lack of usual muscle tone.

Catabolism • A destructive process that converts living cells into simpler compounds; process involved in involution (changes) of the uterus after childbirth.

Diastasis recti • Separation of the longitudinal muscles of the abdomen (rectus abdominus) during pregnancy.

Dyspareunia • Difficult or painful coitus in women.

Engorgement • Swelling of the breasts resulting from increased blood flow and presence of milk.

Episiotomy • Surgical incision of the perineum to enlarge the vaginal opening.

Fundus • Part of the uterus farthest from the cervix, above the openings of the fallopian tubes.

Involution • Retrogressive changes that return the reproductive organs, particularly the uterus, to their pre-pregnancy size and condition.

Kegel exercises • Alternate contracting and relaxing of the pelvic muscles; these movements strengthen the pubococcygeus muscle, which surrounds the urinary meatus and vagina.

Lactation • Secretion of milk from the breasts; also describes the time in weeks or months during which a child is breastfed.

Lochia alba • Whitish or clear vaginal discharge that follows **lochia serosa;** occurs when the amount of blood is decreased and the number of leukocytes is increased.

Lochia rubra • Reddish vaginal discharge that occurs immediately after childbirth; composed mostly of blood.

Lochia serosa • Pinkish or brown-tinged vaginal discharge that follows **lochia rubra** and precedes **lochia alba;** composed largely of serous exudate, blood, and leukocytes.

△ Alert for a high risk of exposure to substances to which universal precautions apply. See Appendix B for additional information about infection control.

Oxytocin • Hormone produced by the posterior pituitary gland that stimulates uterine contractions and the **milk-ejection reflex**; also prepared synthetically.

Prolactin • Anterior pituitary hormone that promotes growth of breast tissue and stimulates production of milk.

Puerperium • Period from the end of childbirth until **involution** of the uterus is complete; approximately 6 weeks.

REEDA • Acronym for redness, edema, ecchymosis, discharge, and approximation; useful for assessing wound healing or the presence of inflammation or infection.

The first 6 weeks following the birth of an infant are known as the postpartum period, or puerperium. During this time, mothers experience numerous physiological and psychosocial changes. In order to make the theoretical concepts clear, psychosocial changes and their implications are presented separately in Chapter 18, although in actual practice physiological and psychosocial assessments are made at the same time.

Many of the physiological changes are retrogressive in nature; that is, changes that occurred in body systems during pregnancy are reversed as the body returns to the pre-pregnancy state. Progressive changes also occur, most obviously in the initiation of lactation and the restoration of normal menstrual cycles.

Reproductive System

Involution of the Uterus

Involution refers to the changes that the reproductive organs, particularly the uterus, undergo after childbirth to return to their pre-pregnancy size and condition. Involution depends on two processes: (1) catabolism and (2) contraction of muscle fibers. After childbirth, the muscle cells of the uterus, which increased greatly during pregnancy, undergo catabolic changes in protein cytoplasm that cause a reduction in cell size. The products of the catabolic process are absorbed by the blood stream and are excreted in urine as nitrogenous waste. The uterus also decreases in size when muscle fibers, which have been stretched for many months, contract and gradually regain their former contour and size.

Involution begins immediately following delivery of the placenta; uterine muscle fibers contract firmly around maternal blood vessels at the area where the placenta was attached. This controls bleeding from the area left denuded when the placenta separated.

The placental site, which is about 7 cm (2.7 inches) in diameter, heals by a process of *exfoliation* (scaling off of dead tissue). New endometrium is generated at the site from glands and tissue that remain in the lower layer of the decidua after separation of the placenta. This process leaves the endometrial layer smooth and spongy, as it was before pregnancy, and leaves the uterine lining free of scar tissue, which would interfere with implantation of future pregnancies (Cunningham et al, 1989).

DESCENT OF THE UTERINE FUNDUS

Contraction of uterine muscles reduces the size of the uterus. Immediately following delivery, the uterus is about the size of a large grapefruit and can be palpated midway between the symphysis pubis and umbilicus. Within an hour, the fundus rises to the level of the umbilicus and should remain at this level for about 24 hours. Although there are individual differences related to body size and type, the uterus now weighs approximately 1000 g (2.2 pounds).

After 24 hours, the fundus begins to descend by approximately 1 cm, or one fingerbreadth, per day, so that by the 10th day it is in the pelvic cavity and cannot be palpated abdominally. Within a week, the weight of the uterus decreases to about 500 g (1 pound); at 6 weeks, the uterus weighs 60 g (2 ounces), which is roughly the pre-pregnancy weight. Figure 17–1 illustrates descent of the fundus as involution occurs.

If the mother breastfeeds, suckling by the infant stimulates the production of oxytocin, which stimulates uterine contraction, and thus involution occurs more quickly in breastfeeding mothers.

AFTERPAINS

Intermittent uterine contractions, known as afterpains, are a source of discomfort for many women. The discomfort is more acute for a multipara because of loss of muscle tone, which results in alternate contraction and relaxation of the uterus; the uterus of a primipara tends to remain contracted. Primiparas may also experience severe afterpains if the uterus has been overdistended by twins, a large infant, hydramnios (excess of amniotic fluid), or retained blood clots.

Afterpains are particularly severe during breastfeeding, when oxytocin, released from the posterior pituitary to stimulate the milk-ejection reflex, also

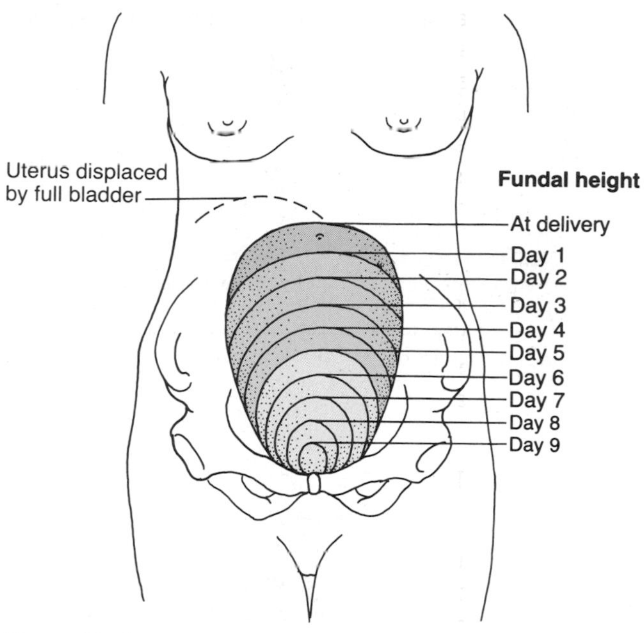

Figure 17–1

Involution of the uterus. Height of the uterine fundus decreases by approximately 1 cm/day.

stimulates strong contractions of uterine muscles.

Nursing Considerations. Analgesics are frequently used to lessen the discomfort of afterpains. If the mother is breastfeeding, she will achieve maximum relief by taking the medication at least ½ hour before nursing the infant. Many breastfeeding mothers are reluctant to take medication for fear the infant will get the medication in breast milk. There is general agreement, however, that analgesics may be used for short-term pain relief without harm to the infant. The benefits of pain relief, such as comfort and relaxation, which facilitate the milk-ejection reflex, usually outweigh the negligible effects of the medication on the infant. Some mothers also find that lying in a prone position, with a small pillow or folded blanket under the abdomen, provides relief. It is also beneficial to reassure the mother that afterpains are self-limiting and that they decrease rapidly after 48 hours.

LOCHIA

The endometrial lining (decidua) of the uterus separates into two layers during the first 3 days following delivery. The outer layer is sloughed off in a vaginal discharge (lochia). The inner layer remains attached to the endometrium and serves as the foundation from which a new layer of endometrium will be formed. The endometrial layer is formed by the third postpartum week except at the site of placental attachment, where regeneration takes about 6 weeks.

The odor of lochia is usually described as fleshy, earthy, or musty. The odor should not be offensive or foul. If a foul odor is noted, endometrial infection should be suspected and additional assessments should be made. These include obtaining maternal temperature and pulse to detect fever or tachycardia and palpating the abdomen for uterine tenderness or pain. Table 17–1 summarizes the characteristics of normal and abnormal lochial discharge.

Changes in Lochia. For the first 3 days following delivery, lochia consists almost entirely of blood, with small particles of decidua and mucus. Because of its red color it is termed lochia rubra. The amount of blood decreases by about the 4th day, when leukocytes begin to invade the area as they do any healing surface. The color of lochia changes from red to pinkish in color (lochia serosa). Lochia serosa is composed of serous exudate, erythrocytes, leukocytes, and cervical mucus. By about the 11th day, the erythrocyte component decreases. The discharge becomes clear and colorless or white (lochia alba). Lochia alba contains leukocytes, decidual cells, epithelial cells, fat, cervical mucus, and bacteria. It is present in most women until the third week following childbirth but may persist for 6 weeks.

Amount. Because it is difficult to estimate the amount of lochia, nurses frequently document lochia in terms that are difficult to quantify, such as "scant," "moderate," or "heavy." Luegenbiehl et al (1990)

Table 17–1. CHARACTERISTICS OF LOCHIA

Time and Type	Normal Discharge	Abnormal Discharge
Days 1–3: lochia rubra	Bloody; small clots; fleshy, earthy odor	Large clots; saturated perineal pads; foul odor
Days 4–10: lochia serosa	Decreased amount; serosanguineous; pink or brown	Excessive amount; foul smell; continued or recurrent reddish color
Days 11–21; lochia alba	Creamy, yellowish color; decreasing amounts	Persistent lochia serosa; return to lochia rubra, foul odor; discharge continuing

proposed the following terms, which include a description as well as an estimation in milliliters for the amount of lochia in 1 hour:

Scant–Less than a 2-inch (5-cm) stain on the peripad (~10 ml).
Small–Less than a 4-inch (10-cm) stain (~10 to 25 ml).
Moderate–Smaller than a 6-inch (15-cm) stain (25 to 50 ml).
Large–Larger than a 6-inch stain (50 to 80 ml).

Figure 17–2 illustrates lochial discharge for 1 hour and quantifies the amount in milliliters.

Lochia is often heavier when the new mother first gets out of bed because gravity allows blood that pooled in the vagina during the hours of rest to flow freely when she stands.

Cervix

Immediately after childbirth, the cervix is formless, flabby, and open wide enough to admit the entire hand. This allows manual extraction of the placenta, if necessary, and manual examination of the uterus. Small tears or lacerations may be present, and the cervix is often edematous. Rapid healing takes place, and by the end of the first week the cervix feels firm and the external os is the width of a pencil. The internal os will close as before pregnancy, but the shape of the external os is permanently changed. It remains slightly open and appears slit-like rather than round, as in the nulliparous woman (Fig. 17–3).

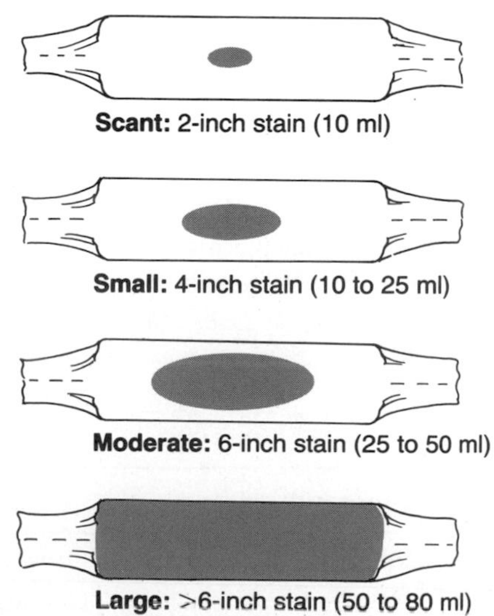

Figure 17–2

Guidelines for assessing the volume of lochia based on amount of stain on the perineal pad.

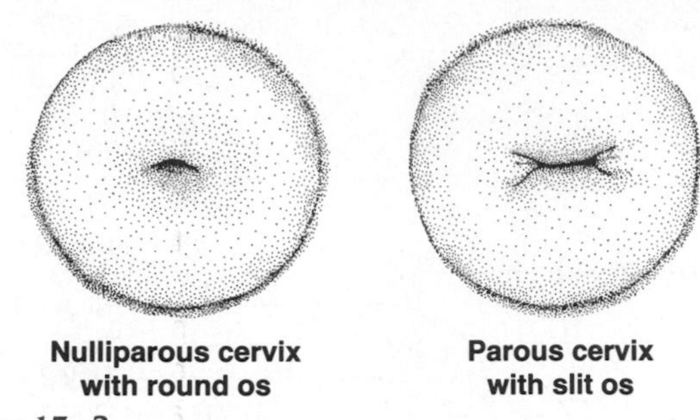

Figure 17–3

A permanent change occurs in the cervical os following childbirth.

Vagina

The vagina and vaginal introitus are greatly stretched during birth to allow passage of the fetus and placenta. Soon after childbirth, the vaginal walls appear edematous and multiple small lacerations may be present. Very few vaginal rugae (folds) are present. The hymen is permanently torn and heals with small, irregular tags of tissue visible at the vaginal introitus.

Although the vaginal mucosa heals and rugae are regained by 3 weeks, it takes the entire postpartum period (6 weeks) for the vagina to complete involution and to gain approximately the same size and contour it had before pregnancy; however, the vagina does not entirely regain the nulliparous size.

Effect of Breastfeeding on Vaginal Mucosa. During the postpartum period, vaginal mucosa becomes atrophic and vaginal walls do not regain their thickness until estrogen production by the ovaries is reestablished. Because ovarian function, and therefore estrogen production, is not well established during lactation, breastfeeding mothers are likely to experience vaginal dryness and may experience discomfort during intercourse (dyspareunia) for 4 to 6 months (Fischman et al, 1986). Although many of the concerns about changes in the vagina are unexpressed, a woman and her sexual partner may have numerous questions. Nurses must be sensitive to unasked questions and should try to provide anticipatory guidance. Nursing Care Plan 17–2 presents the nursing diagnosis, Altered Sexuality Patterns.

Perineum

The muscles of the pelvic floor stretch and thin greatly during the second stage of labor, when the fetal head applies pressure as it descends, rotates, and then extends to be delivered. After delivery, the perineum may be edematous and bruised. In the United States, some women who give birth also have a surgical incision (episiotomy) of the perineal area.

Generally, the episiotomy is median or midline; that is, it extends straight back from the lower edge of the introitus toward the anus. Occasionally, mediolateral incisions, begun at the introitus and directed laterally and downward away from the rectum to either the right or left side, are made to provide additional room for birth of the infant.

Lacerations of the perineum may also occur during delivery. Lacerations and episiotomies are classified according to tissue involved (Table 17–2). (See further discussions of episiotomy and lacerations in Chapters 13 and 16.)

Discomfort. Although the episiotomy is relatively small, the muscles of the perineum are involved in many activities (walking, sitting, stooping, squatting, bending, defecating). An incision in this area can cause a great deal of discomfort. In addition, many pregnant women are affected by hemorrhoids (distended rectal veins), which are pushed out of the rectum during the second stage of labor.

Nursing Considerations. Hemorrhoids, as well as perineal trauma, episiotomies, or lacerations, can make physical activity or bowel elimination difficult during the postpartum period. Relief of perineal discomfort is a nursing priority that includes teaching self-care measures, such as sitz baths, perineal care, and topical anesthesia. (See Nursing Care Plan 17–1 for discussions of Perineal Pain and Constipation.)

Table 17–2. LACERATIONS OF THE BIRTH CANAL

Perineum

Perineal lacerations are classified in degrees to describe the amount of tissue involved. Some physicians or nurse-midwives also use degrees to describe the extent of median episiotomies.

First-degree: Involves the superficial vaginal mucosa or perineal skin.

Second-degree: Involves the vaginal mucosa, perineal skin, and deeper tissues, which may include muscles of the perineum.

Third-degree: Same as second-degree lacerations but involves the anal sphincter.

Fourth-degree: Extends through the anal sphincter into the rectal mucosa.

Periurethral Area

A laceration in the area of the urethra. Women with periurethral lacerations may have difficulty urinating after birth. They may require an indwelling catheter for a day or two.

Vaginal Wall

A laceration involving the mucosa of the vaginal wall.

Cervix

Tears in the cervix may be a source of significant bleeding after birth.

✔ Check Your Reading

1. Which two processes are involved in involution?
2. How is the fundus expected to descend following childbirth?
3. What are the differences between lochia rubra, lochia serosa, and lochia alba in terms of appearance and expected duration?

Cardiovascular System

Blood Volume

Following delivery, despite 300 to 400 ml of blood loss during a normal vaginal delivery, excess blood volume, which was necessary during pregnancy, remains in the intravascular compartment and in interstitial spaces. The body rids itself of the fluid, which is no longer necessary, in two ways:

- *Diuresis* (increased excretion of urine) is facilitated by a decline in the adrenal hormone aldosterone, which was increased during pregnancy to counteract the salt-wasting effect of progesterone. As aldosterone production decreases, sodium retention declines and fluid excretion is accelerated. A urinary output of 3000 ml/day is not uncommon for the first few days of the postpartum period.
- *Diaphoresis* (profuse perspiration) also rids the body of excess fluid; although it is not clinically significant, diaphoresis can be uncomfortable and unsettling for the mother who is not prepared for it. Explanations of the cause and comfort measures, such as showers and dry clothing, are generally sufficient.

Coagulation

Besides the dramatic remobilization and excretion of excess circulating plasma volume that take place during the postpartum period, significant changes that occurred during pregnancy also affect the body's ability to coagulate blood and form clots post partum. During pregnancy, plasma fibrinogen (necessary for coagulation) increased as a protection against postpartum hemorrhage. As a result, the mother's body has a greater ability to form clots and thus prevent excessive bleeding. She does not, however, have an increased ability to eliminate clots because a corresponding increase in plasminogen (necessary for lysis of clots) has not occurred during pregnancy. The net result is that she is at risk for thrombus (clot) formation.

Although the incidence of thrombophlebitis has declined greatly in recent years, probably as a result of early postpartum ambulation, new mothers are still at increased risk for thrombus formation. Women who have varicose veins, who have a history of thrombophlebitis, or who have experienced a cesarean birth are at further risk, and the lower extremities should be monitored closely. Anti-emboli hosiery is often applied before a cesarean birth or if the mother is at particular risk because of a history of previous phlebitis or the presence of varicosities. (See Chapter 27 for further discussion of thromboembolic disorders.)

Blood Values

Besides clotting factors, other components of the blood change during the postpartum period. There is marked leukocytosis, with the white blood cell count increasing from the non-pregnancy normal range of 5,000 to 10,000/mm up to 20,000 or even 30,000/mm. Neutrophils, which increase in response to inflammation, pain, and stress to protect against invading organisms, account for the major increase in white blood cells.

Maternal hemoglobin and hematocrit values are difficult to interpret during the first few days after birth because of the remobilization and rapid excretion of excess body fluid. The hematocrit is low when plasma (the liquid part of blood) increases and thus dilutes the concentration of blood cells and other substances carried by the plasma. As excess fluid is excreted the dilution is gradually reduced. Hematocrit should return to normal limits within 3 to 7 days unless there has been excessive blood loss.

Vital Signs

Because all vital signs are usually assessed together, temperature and respirations are included with vital signs that assess the cardiovascular system.

Temperature. A temperature of 38°C (100.4°F) is common the first 24 hours following childbirth and may be caused by dehydration or normal postpartum leukocytosis. If the elevated temperature persists for longer than 24 hours or if it exceeds 38°C, infection should be suspected and reported to the physician or nurse-midwife.

Blood Pressure. Blood pressure should remain near the pre-pregnancy level during the puerperium. Postpartum blood pressure should be compared with that of the pre-delivery period so that deviations from the parameters that are normal for the mother can be quickly identified. An increase from the baseline suggests pregnancy-induced hypertension; a decrease may indicate dehydration or hypovolemia resulting from excessive bleeding.

Orthostatic Hypotension. Although normal blood pressure is expected, orthostatic hypotension may occur during the postpartum period because of decreased vascular resistance in the pelvis, which results, first, in a decreased cardiac return and, subsequently, in a decrease in cardiac output, which produces inadequate circulation to the brain when the new mother stands. A drop of 20 mmHg or more in systolic pressure when she moves from a supine to sitting position indicates orthostatic hypotension. As a result of the sudden drop in blood pressure, mothers often say that they feel dizzy, lightheaded, or faint when they stand. The Nursing Diagnosis: Potential for Injury is applicable to women with orthostatic hypotension. (See Nursing Care Plan 17–2 for application of this nursing diagnosis.) Hypotension may also indicate hypovolemia and careful assessments for hemorrhage (location and firmness of the fundus, amount of lochia, pulse rate for tachycardia) should be made if the postpartum blood pressure is significantly less than the prenatal baseline blood pressure.

Pulse. Bradycardia, defined as a pulse rate of from 50 to 60/minute, is expected and reflects the increased amount of blood that returns to the central circulation following delivery of the placenta. The increase in central circulation results in increased cardiac output and allows a slower heart rate to provide adequate maternal circulation.

Tachycardia may indicate excitement, fatigue, dehydration, or hypovolemia. If tachycardia is noted, additional assessments should include blood pressure, location and firmness of the uterus, amount of lochia, estimated blood loss at delivery, hemoglobin, and hematocrit values. The objective of the additional assessments is to rule out excessive bleeding or to intervene at once if hemorrhage is suspected.

Respirations. A normal respiratory rate of 16 to 20/minute should be maintained. It is not necessary to assess breath sounds if the mother has had a normal vaginal delivery, is ambulatory, and is without signs of respiratory distress. Breath sounds should always be auscultated if the birth has been cesarean, if she is a smoker, if she has a history of frequent or recent upper respiratory infections, or if she has a history of asthma.

✔ Check Your Reading

4. What are two possible reasons, other than infection, for increased temperature during the first 24 hours after delivery?

5. What are three possible causes of tachycardia?
6. What are the typical cause, onset, and symptoms experienced by the mother with orthostatic hypotension?

Gastrointestinal System

Soon after delivery, digestion begins to be active and the new mother experiences hunger because of the energy expended in childbirth. Moreover, she is usually thirsty because of the long period of fluid restriction during labor, the fluid loss from exertion, and the beginning diaphoresis.

Changes in Patterns of Bowel Elimination

Constipation is a common problem during the postpartum period for a variety of reasons. First, bowel tone, which was diminished during pregnancy as a result of progesterone, remains sluggish for several days and intestinal motility is decreased. Dehydration often occurs during labor and food intake is restricted for several hours, resulting in small, hard stools. Perineal trauma, episiotomies, and hemorrhoids cause discomfort and interfere with effective bowel elimination. In addition, many women anticipate pain when they attempt to defecate and are unwilling to exert pressure on the perineum.

Temporary constipation is not harmful, although it can cause a feeling of abdominal fullness and flatulence. Many women become extremely concerned about constipation, and nursing interventions are aimed at prevention and promoting comfort. (The Nursing Diagnosis: Constipation is discussed in Nursing Care Plan 17–1). Stool softeners and laxatives are frequently prescribed to prevent or treat constipation. See Table 17–3 for a summary of the most commonly recommended laxatives.

Urinary System

Physical Changes

As a result of multiple changes that occur during pregnancy, the bladder of the postpartum woman has an increased capacity and has lost some of its muscle tone. Moreover, during the delivery the urethra, bladder, and tissue around the urinary meatus may become edematous and traumatized as the fetal head passes on the bladder's underside. This often results in diminished sensitivity to fluid pressure, and many mothers have no sensation of needing to void even when the bladder is distended. This makes it important to remember that the bladder fills rapidly as a result of the diuresis that follows childbirth.

As a consequence, the mother is at risk for overdistention of the bladder, incomplete emptying of the bladder, and retention of residual urine. Women who have received regional anesthesia are at particular risk for bladder distention and for difficulty voiding until feeling returns.

Urinary retention and overdistention of the bladder may be the causes of two complications: (1) urinary tract infection as urinary stasis allows time for bacteria to multiply, and (2) postpartum hemorrhage, which can occur because uterine ligaments were stretched, allowing the uterus to be displaced upward and laterally by the full bladder and resulting in excessive bleeding from the placental site (Fig. 17–4).

CHEMICAL CHANGES

Both protein and acetone may be present in the urine in the first few postpartum days. Acetone suggests dehydration that occurred during the exertion of labor. Mild proteinuria may occur briefly as a result of the catabolic processes involved in uterine involution.

Table 17–3. COMMONLY RECOMMENDED LAXATIVES FOR THE POSTPARTUM PERIOD

Generic Name	Examples	Comments
Fecal wetting agents	Docusate calcium (Surfak) Docusate sodium (Colace)	Detergent-like action, permit easier mixing of fats and fluids with fecal mass; produce softer, more easily passed stools
Saline laxatives	Milk of magnesia	Work by osmotic action drawing water through the intestinal wall to soften stool
Stimulant laxatives	Bisacodyl	Should not be taken within 1 hour of taking antacid or milk products
Suppositories	Glycerine, bisacodyl	Contain stimulant for defecation

Data from Karb, V.B., Queener, J.B., & Freeman, J.B. (1989). *Handbook of drugs for nursing practice.* St. Louis: C.V. Mosby.

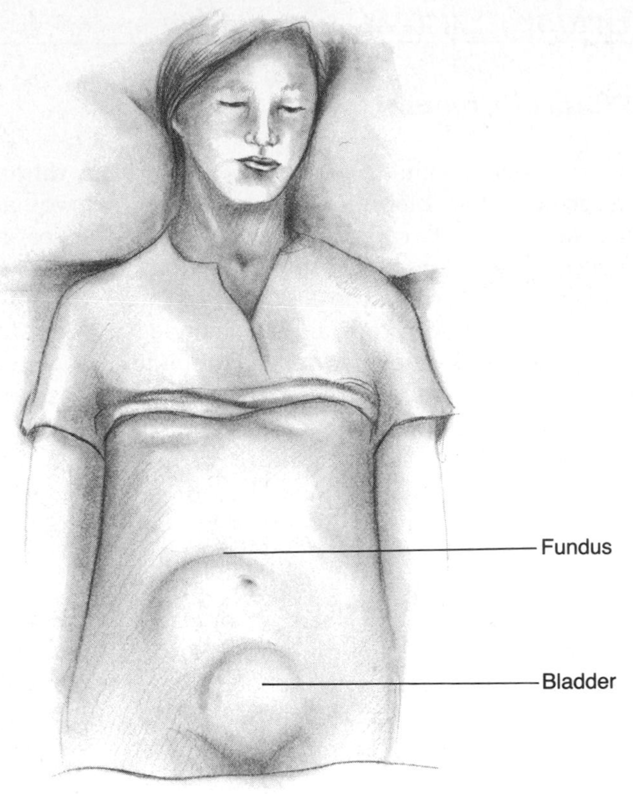

Figure 17–4

A full bladder displaces and prevents contraction of the uterus.

Abdominal Wall

During pregnancy, the abdominal walls stretch to accommodate the growing fetus and muscle tone is diminished. Many women, expecting that the abdominal muscles will return to the pre-pregnancy condition immediately after childbirth, are dismayed to find the abdominal muscles weak, soft, and flabby.

The longitudinal muscles of the abdomen may also separate (diastasis recti) during pregnancy (Fig. 17–5). The separation may be minimal or severe. The mother may benefit from special exercises to strengthen the abdominal wall. Figure 17–6 illustrates exercises that help to correct diastasis recti.

Integumentary System

Many skin changes that occur during pregnancy are caused by an increase in hormones; when the hormone levels decline following childbirth, the skin gradually reverts to the pre-pregnancy state. For example, levels of melanocyte-stimulating hormone (MSH), which caused hyperpigmentation during pregnancy, decrease rapidly after childbirth and pigmentation begins to recede. This is particularly noticeable when the "mask of pregnancy" (*chloasma*) and linea nigra disappear. In addition, spider nevi and

Musculoskeletal System

Muscles and joints

In the first 1 to 2 days following childbirth, many women experience muscle fatigue and aches, particularly of the shoulders, neck and arms, as a result of exertion during labor. Warmth and gentle massage increase circulation to the area and provide comfort and relaxation.

During the first few days, levels of the hormone relaxin gradually subside and ligaments and cartilage of the pelvis begin to return to their pre-pregnancy position. This can cause hip or joint pain that interferes with ambulation and exercise. It is helpful if the mother understands that the discomfort is temporary and does not indicate a medical problem. Good body mechanics and correct posture are extremely important during this time to prevent low back pain and injury to the joints. (See Figures 7–11 and 7–12 for correct and incorrect posture and body mechanics.)

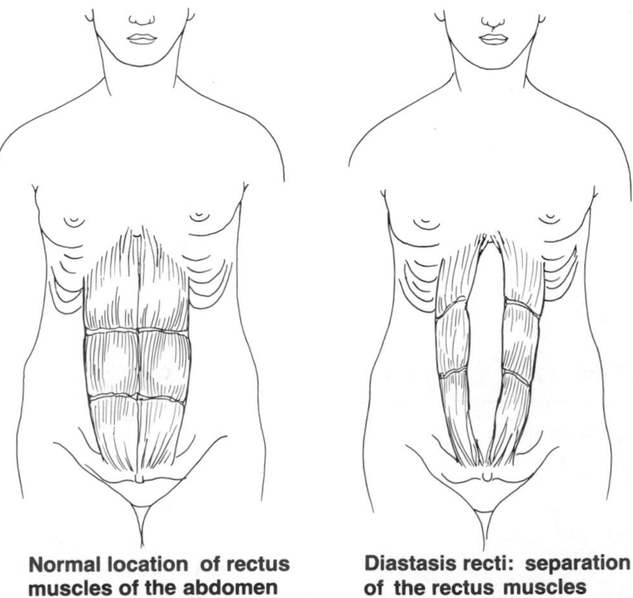

Normal location of rectus muscles of the abdomen
Diastasis recti: separation of the rectus muscles

Figure 17–5

Diastasis recti occurs when the longitudinal muscles of the abdomen separate during pregnancy.

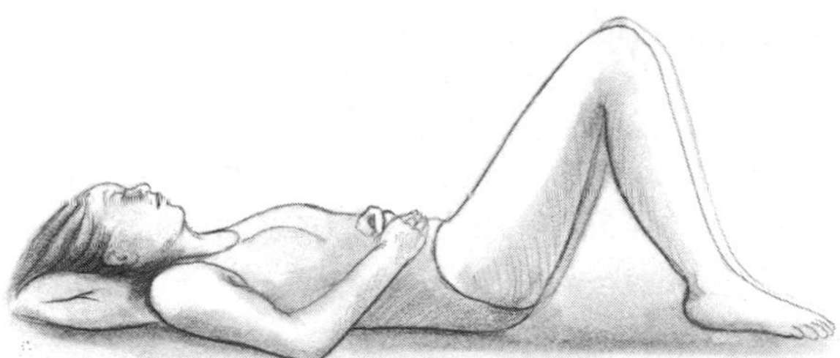

The woman inhales and supports the abdominal wall firmly with her hands

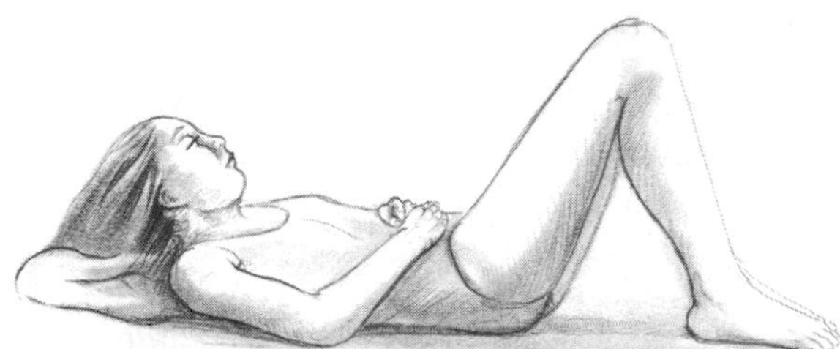

Exhaling, the woman raises her head as she pulls the abdominal muscles together

Figure 17–6

Abdominal exercises for diastasis recti.

palmar erythema, which may develop during pregnancy as a result of increased estrogen levels, gradually disappear.

Striae gravidarum (stretch marks), which develop during pregnancy when connective tissue in the abdomen and breasts is stretched, gradually fade to silvery lines but do not disappear altogether.

Endocrine Function

Following delivery of the placenta, there is a fairly rapid decline in hormones that were secreted by the placenta during pregnancy: estrogen, progesterone, human placental lactogen (hPL), and human chorionic gonadotropin (hCG). Adrenal hormones, such as aldosterone, return to pre-pregnancy levels. If the mother is not breastfeeding, the pituitary hormone prolactin, which stimulates milk secretion, disappears in about 2 weeks.

Resumption of Ovulation and Menstruation

Most non-nursing mothers resume menstruation within 7 to 9 weeks after childbirth, although times vary widely. Of these, approximately half ovulate during the first cycle (Resnik, 1989).

Breastfeeding delays return of both ovulation and menstruation. The length of the delay depends on the duration of lactation and the frequency of breastfeeding. Women who breastfeed for less than 28 days ovulate at approximately the same time as non-nursing mothers. The longer the period of lactation, the longer the average time to the first menstrual period. Women who breastfeed six or more times daily are also likely to ovulate and menstruate later than women who breastfeed less often.

Most lactating women resume menstruation within 12 weeks, although a few do not menstruate for the entire lactation period. *Breastfeeding is not an effective form of contraception because ovulation may occur before menstrual cycles are established.*

Lactation

During pregnancy, estrogen and progesterone prepare the breasts for lactation. Following childbirth, levels of these hormones decline but levels of prolactin increase. Prolactin initiates milk production 2 to 3 days following childbirth. New mothers often experience breast engorgement when lymphatic and vascular circulation increases prior to milk production. The nipples may become sore during the first days following childbirth when the mother begins breastfeeding. (The process of lactation and measures to prevent discomfort are described in detail in Chapter 21.)

If the mother chooses not to breastfeed, measures should be initiated to suppress lactation. The safest method is to prevent breast distention by either binding the breasts or by having the mother wear a tight-fitting bra. If breast engorgement does occur, discomfort can usually be managed by application of ice, which reduces vasocongestion, and by administration of analgesics.

Bromocriptine (Parlodel) is still recommended by some health practitioners to suppress lactation; however, problems of rebound engorgement when the drug is discontinued, gastrointestinal upsets, and central nervous system side effects (depression, drowsiness) have been reported. As a result, many physicians no longer prescribe Parlodel for suppression of lactation.

Weight Loss

From 7.5 to 9 kg (17 to 20 pounds) is usually lost following childbirth. This includes the weight of the fetus, placenta, amniotic fluid, and blood lost during the birth. It also includes the weight lost by diuresis and diaphoresis during the first few postpartum days as well as weight lost as the reproductive organs undergo the process of involution.

Adipose (fatty) tissue that was gained during pregnancy to meet the energy requirements of breastfeeding is not lost initially, and the usual rate of loss is quite slow. This may be frustrating for many mothers who desire an immediate return to prepregnancy weight. Nurses must be prepared to provide information about diet and exercise that will produce an acceptable weight loss but that does not deplete the energy or impair the health of the mother.

✔ Check Your Reading

7. How much weight is lost as a result of childbirth and involution? What makes up the weight loss?
8. Why does hyperpigmentation decrease following childbirth?
9. How does breastfeeding affect the resumption of ovulation and menstruation?
10. How is lactation suppressed when the mother elects not to breastfeed?

Application of Nursing Process

A major focus of nursing care during the postpartum period is on physical restoration of the mother. Nurses' responsibilities include physical assessment, history taking, and knowledge of self-care measures. Health education is an integral part of nursing care. *Because of the high risk for coming into contact with body fluids (colostrum, breast milk, amniotic fluid, and lochia from the mother as well as urine, stool, and blood from the infant) when caring for postpartum patients, the recommendations of the Centers for Disease Control for universal blood and body fluid precautions must be diligently maintained.* (See Appendix B.)

Assessment

INITIAL ASSESSMENT

Initial assessment of the mother takes place when she is transferred from the labor, delivery, recovery unit, usually within 1 to 2 hours following childbirth. She should be quickly examined to determine whether she is physically stable. Initial assessment includes:

- Skin color
- Level of consciousness
- Level of feeling and ability to move if regional anesthesia was administered
- Location and firmness of the fundus
- Amount and color of lochia
- Presence and location of pain
- Intravenous infusions (type of fluid)
- Added medications (type and amount)
- Patency of the intravenous (IV) line
- Examination of the intravenous site for redness, pain, or edema
- Time and amount of last voiding
- Presence of a urinary catheter

CHART REVIEW

When the initial assessment confirms that the mother's physical condition is stable, review the chart to obtain pertinent information and to determine if there are factors that increase the risk that she will experience complications during the postpartum period. Relevant information includes:

- Gravida, parity
- Time and type of delivery
- Anesthesia or medications administered during labor
- Significant medical and surgical history, such as diabetes, heart disease, or hypertension
- Medications routinely taken and reasons why they are needed
- Food and drug allergies
- Chosen method of infant feeding
- Condition of the baby

Laboratory data must also be examined. Of particular interest are the prenatal hemoglobin and hematocrit values, the blood type and Rh factor, hepatitis B surface antigen, and a syphilis screen, or VDRL (Veneral Disease Research Laboratory).

Need for Rh_o(D) Immune Globulin. Check prenatal and neonatal records to determine whether Rh_o(D) immune globulin should be administered. Rh_o(D) immune globulin may be necessary if the mother is Rh-negative and the newborn is Rh-positive.

In many facilities, it is the responsibility of nurses to remind the health care provider that Rh_o(D) immune globulin should be ordered. *Rh_0(D) immune globulin should be administered within 72 hours after childbirth to prevent the development of maternal antibodies that would affect subsequent pregnancies.* (See also Chapter 24 for a discussion of maternal-fetal Rh incompatibility.)

Need for Rubella Vaccine. A prenatal rubella antibody screen is done on each pregnant woman to determine if she is immune to rubella. If she is not immune, rubella vaccine is offered following delivery to prevent her from acquiring rubella during subsequent pregnancies, when it can cause serious fetal anomalies. Rubella vaccine is a live virus that can produce serious consequences for the fetus if the mother becomes pregnant soon after it is adminis-

Critical to Remember

Postpartum High-Risk Factors

Hemorrhage

- Multiparity (> 3)
- Overdistention of the uterus (large baby, twins, hydramnios)
- Precipitous labor (< 3 hours)
- Retained placenta
- Placenta previa or abruptio placentae
- Induction or augmentation of labor
- Administration of tocolytics to stop uterine contractions
- Operative procedures (vacuum extraction, forceps, cesarean birth)

Infection

- Operative procedures (cesarean birth, forceps, vacuum extraction)
- Multiple cervical examinations
- Prolonged labor (>24 hours)
- Manual extraction of placenta
- Diabetes
- Indwelling catheter
- Anemia (hemoglobin >10 mg/dl)

tered. Before administration, some agencies require that she sign a statement indicating that she understands the risks of becoming pregnant again within 3 months following the injection.

Risk Factors for Hemorrhage and Infection. Be aware of conditions that increase the risk of hemorrhage and infection, the two most common complications of the puerperium. See Critical to Remember: Postpartum High-Risk Factors.

FOCUS ASSESSMENT FOLLOWING VAGINAL BIRTH

Focus assessments are completed at the change of the nurse's shift or more often if the mother is experiencing problems. The assessment for women whose infants were delivered vaginally differs from that performed for post-cesarean mothers. (See p. 443 for the more complete assessment required for cesarean birth.)

Although assessments vary, depending on the particular problems experienced by the mother, in general a focus assessment for vaginal delivery includes vital signs, breasts, fundus, bladder elimination, lochia, perineum, bowel elimination, and lower extremities. In addition, note dietary practices and sleep patterns so that interventions can be planned.

Vital Signs. *Temperature* should be between 36.2° to 38°C (98° to 100.4°F). Temperature above 38°C (100.4°F) after the first 24 hours may indicate infection.

Pulse should be between 50 and 90 BPM. Tachycardia may indicate hemorrhage, pain, fever, or dehydration.

Respirations should be between 16 and 24 per minute. Tachypnea may indicate respiratory dysfunction.

Blood pressure should be consistent with baseline pressure during pregnancy. Elevations may be due to pregnancy-induced hypertension, anxiety, or chronic hypertension. Hypotension may be due to hemorrhage.

Orthostatic hypotension may be present for 24 hours. Observe the mother when she gets out of bed for unsteadiness, when there are subjective symptoms of weakness or dizziness, or when she feels that she is going to faint. Interventions for orthostatic hypotension appear in Nursing Care Plan 17–2, under the Nursing Diagnosis: High Risk for Injury related to physiological effects of orthostatic hypotension.

Breasts. For the first day or two after delivery, the breasts should be soft and non-tender. After that, breast changes depend largely on whether the mother is breastfeeding or is taking measures to prevent lactation. Assess the breasts even if she chooses formula feeding because the breasts may become engorged despite preventive measures. Observe the breasts for size, symmetry, and shape. Reassure mothers that breast size has no relationship to successful breastfeeding. Inspect the skin for dimpling or thickening, which, although very rare, can indicate breast tumor.

Inspect the areola and nipple carefully for potential problems, such as flat or retracted nipples, which sometimes make breastfeeding more difficult. Signs of nipple trauma (redness, blisters, or fissures) are often noted during the first days of breastfeeding, especially if the mother needs assistance in positioning the infant correctly. (For full details, see Chapter 21.)

Palpate the breasts for firmness and tenderness, which may indicate primary engorgement (increased vascular and lymphatic circulation) that precedes milk production. The breasts may feel "lumpy" as various lobes begin to produce milk.

The breast assessment provides an excellent opportunity to provide information or reassurance about breast care and breastfeeding techniques.

Fundus. Assess the uterine fundus for firmness and location. Procedure 17–1 illustrates how to locate and palpate the fundus. If the fundus is difficult to locate or is soft or "boggy," use uterine massage to contract the uterus. *The non-dominant hand must support and gently anchor the lower uterine segment if it is*

Procedure 17–1 Assessing the Uterine Fundus

Purpose: To determine location and firmness of the uterus

1. **Explain the procedure and rationale for each step before beginning the procedure.** *Reduces anxiety and elicits cooperation.*

2. **Have the mother empty her bladder if she has not voided recently.** *A distended bladder lifts and displaces the uterus.*

3. **Place the mother in a supine position with her knees slightly flexed.** *Relaxes the abdominal muscles and permits accurate location of the fundus.*

4. **Put on clean gloves, and lower the perineal pads to observe lochia as the fundus is palpated.** *Gloves are recommended anytime there is the possibility of coming into contact with body fluids.*

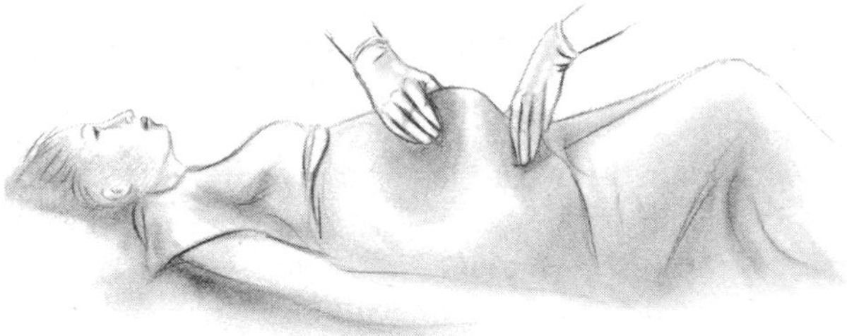

5. **Place the non-dominant hand above the symphysis pubis.** *Supports and anchors the lower uterine segment during palpation or massage of the fundus.*

6. **Use the flat part of the fingers (not the fingertips) for palpation.** *The larger surface provides more comfort; palpation is essential, but it may be painful, particularly for the mother who had a cesarean birth; locating the fundus is more difficult if the woman is obese or if the abdomen is distended.*

7. **Begin palpation at the umbilicus, and palpate gently until the fundus is located. Note firmness and location of the fundus. The fundus should be firm, in midline, and approximately at the level of the umbilicus.** *The most common cause of uterine displacement is a distended bladder, which lifts the uterus and promotes uterine atony (loss of muscle tone) that could result in excessive bleeding.*

8. **If the fundus is difficult to locate or is soft or "boggy," keep the non-dominant hand above the symphysis pubis and massage the fundus with the dominant hand until the fundus is firm.** *The non-dominant hand anchors the lower segment of the uterus and prevents trauma while the uterus is massaged. The uterus contracts in response to tactile stimulation; contraction is essential to control excessive bleeding.*

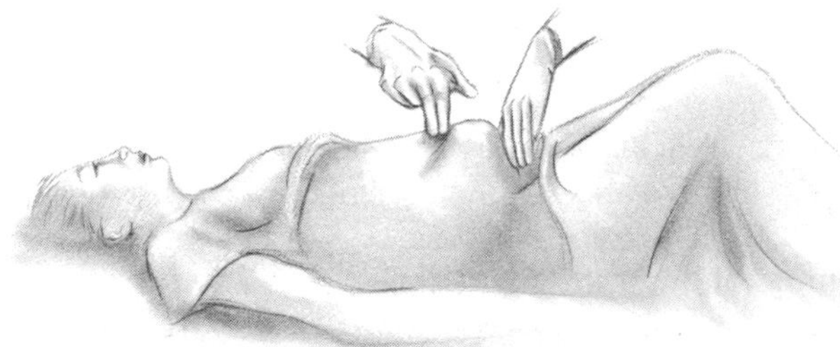

9. **Document the consistency and location of the fundus. Consistency is recorded as "fundus firm," "firm with massage," or "boggy." Fundal height is recorded in fingerbreadths above or below the umbilicus. For example, "fundus firm, midline, U-2" (two fingerbreadths below umbilicus). As another example, "Fundus firm with light massage, U + 2" (two fingerbreadths above umbilicus), displaced to right.** *Promotes accurate communication and identifies deviations from expected so that potential problems can be identified early*

Table 17–4. OBSERVATIONS OF THE UTERINE FUNDUS REQUIRING NURSING ACTIONS

Normal Findings	Abnormal Findings	Nursing Actions
Fundus firmly contracted	Fundus soft, "boggy," uncontracted, or difficult to locate	Support lower uterine segment; massage until firm
Fundus remains contracted when massage is discontinued	Fundus becomes soft and uncontracted when massage is stopped	Continue to support lower uterine segment; massage until firm and apply pressure to fundus to express clots that may be accumulating in uterus; notify health care provider and begin oxytocin administration, as prescribed, to maintain a firm fundus
Fundus located at level of umbilicus and midline	Fundus above umbilicus and/or displaced from midline	Assess bladder elimination; assist mother in urinating or catheterize, if necessary, to empty bladder

necessary to massage an uncontracted uterus. Uterine massage is not necessary if the uterus is firmly contracted. Table 17–4 describes normal and abnormal findings and includes follow-up nursing actions for abnormal findings.

Drugs are sometimes needed to assist uterine contraction. Drugs frequently used to maintain contraction of the uterus and thus to prevent postpartum hemorrhage are methylergonovine (Methergine) and oxytocin (Pitocin, Syntocinon). See Table 17–5 for drugs commonly administered post partum.

Lochia. Observe lochia while the uterus is being palpated or massaged so that the amount of blood expressed from the uterus during these procedures can be documented. Assess lochia for amount, color, and odor. It is difficult for students and inexperienced nurses to estimate the volume of lochia. Refer to Figure 17–2 for criteria to determine the amount of lochia, and to Table 17–1, for the characteristics of lochia as well as abnormal observations that must be reported. Note these two important guidelines:

1. A *constant trickle of lochia indicates excessive bleeding and requires immediate attention.*
2. *Excessive lochia in the presence of a contracted uterus suggests lacerations of the birth canal and the health care provider must be notified so the laceration can be located and repaired.*

The odor of lochia is usually described as "fleshy," "earthy," or "musty." A foul odor suggests endometrial infection, and additional assessments should be made. These include maternal temperature for fever or tachycardia and palpation of the abdomen for uterine tenderness and pain.

Absence of lochia, like the presence of a foul odor, may also indicate infection. Lochia may be scant, particularly if the birth was cesarean or when the cavity of the uterus is wiped by sponges, which removes some of the endometrial lining; however, lochia should not be entirely absent.

Bladder Elimination. Because the mother may not experience the urge to void even if the bladder is full, nurses must rely on physical assessment to determine whether the bladder is distended. Bladder distention often produces an obvious or palpable bulge that feels like a soft, movable mass above the symphysis pubis. Other signs include an upward and lateral displacement of the uterine fundus and frequent voidings of less than 150 ml, which suggests urinary retention with overflow.

Measure the first two voidings. When the mother is able to void at least 300 to 400 ml, the bladder is usually empty. Assess the fundus, however, to confirm that the bladder is completely empty. Subjective symptoms of urgency, frequency, or dysuria suggest urinary tract infection and should be reported to the health care provider.

Perineum. The acronym REEDA is used as a reminder that the site of episiotomy or a perineal laceration should be assessed for five signs: redness (R), edema (E), ecchymosis (bruising) (E), discharge (D), and approximation (A) (the edges of the wound should be close as though stuck or glued together).

Redness of the wound may indicate the usual inflammatory response to injury; however, if it is accompanied by pain or tenderness, it may indicate

Critical to Remember

Signs of a Distended Bladder

- Location of fundus above *baseline* level, which is obtained when the bladder is empty
- Fundus displaced from midline
- Excessive lochia
- Bladder discomfort
- Bulge of bladder above symphysis
- Frequent voidings of less than 150 ml of urine, which indicates urinary retention with overflow

Table 17–5. COMMONLY USED DRUGS DURING THE POSTPARTUM PERIOD

Indications	Usual Dosage	Nursing Considerations
	Methylergonovine Maleate (Methergine)	
Prevention and treatment of hemorrhage due to uterine atony	0.2 mg IM or p.o. q 6–12 hr	Monitor and record blood pressure, pulse rate, and uterine response; report any sudden change in vital signs, continued uterine relaxation, or excessive lochia.
	Oxytocin (Pitocin, Syntocinon)	
Reduction of bleeding after expulsion of the placenta	10–40 units in 1000 ml of 5% dextrose in normal saline solution IV at a rate to control bleeding (usually 20 to 40 mU/minute, or 10 units IM)	Administer by infusion, not by bolus (a concentrated mass); monitor and record uterine contraction, heart rate, and blood pressure every 15 minutes; assess and record amount of lochia
	Simethecone (Mylicon)	
Flatulence, abdominal distention	40–80 mg after each meal and at bedtime	Must be chewed; assess for bowel activity
	Ibuprofen (Motrin, Advil)	
Mild to moderate pain	400 mg p.o. q 4–6 hr	Assess for nausea, vomiting, diarrhea
	Acetaminophen (Tylenol, Panadol)	
Mild to moderate pain	325–650 mg p.o. q 4–6 hr	Side effects rare; assess for allergic reaction, such as skin rash
	Percocet (325 mg Acetaminophen and 5 mg Oxycodone)	
Moderate pain	1–2 tablets p.o. q 4 hr	Determine sensitivity to acetaminophen or oxycodone; observe for signs of respiratory depression; do not administer with sedatives
	Empirin No. 3 (325 mg of Aspirin with 30 mg Codeine)	
Moderate pain	1–2 tablets q 4 hr	Assess for sensitivity to aspirin or codeine; administer with food to prevent gastric upset
	Rho(D) Immune Globulin (RhoGAM, Gamulin Rh, HypRho-D)	
Prevention of sensitization to Rh factor in Rh-negative mothers who gave birth to Rh-positive infants	One vial IM within 72 hr following childbirth	Confirm that administration is necessary; check with second licensed personnel that medication is cross-matched for the specific woman.
	Rubella Virus Vaccine, Live (Meruvax II)	
To stimulate active immunity against rubella virus	Single-dose vial; administer SC in outer aspect of upper arm	Advise the mother to avoid pregnancy for 3 months; signed informed consent usually required; do not administer if mother is sensitive to neomycin or if she has had a transfusion within the last 3 months

Abbreviations: q, every; p.o., orally (per os); IM, intramuscularly; IV, intravenously; mU, milliunit; SC, subcutaneously.

beginning localized infection. Ecchymosis or edema indicates soft tissue damage that can delay healing. There should not be discharge from the wound. Rapid healing necessitates that the edges of the wound be closely approximated. Procedure 17–2 describes the perineal examination.

Bowel Elimination. Bowel movement is expected by the 2nd or 3rd postpartum day. Constipation is common and may be due to a sluggish bowel, inadequate fluid intake during labor, a painful perineum, or hemorrhoids. Diarrhea is uncommon and may be caused by multiple factors, including medications or gastroenteritis.

Lower Extremities. Examine the legs for signs or symptoms of thrombophlebitis, such as localized areas of redness, heat, edema, or tenderness. Pedal pulses may be obstructed by thrombophlebitis; palpate with each assessment.

Homans' Sign. Discomfort behind the knee on sharp dorsiflexion of the foot (Fig. 17–7) has been viewed as an indicator of deep vein thrombosis. Although the sign is of limited value (Sternbach, 1989),

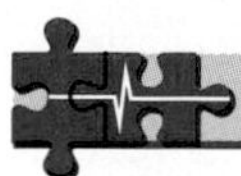

Clinical Situation

Linda Welker, a 22-year-old multipara, was admitted from the Labor, Delivery, and Recovery Unit 2 hours following the birth of an 8-pound (3600 g) baby boy. Her fundus is firm, located three fingerbreadths above the umbilicus and displaced to the right; her perineal pads, which are changed just before transfer, are saturated.

Q:
1. What is the priority nursing action?
2. What is the probable cause of the increased lochia?
3. Why doesn't the new mother experience an urge to void?

A:
1. The nurse should assist Linda in emptying her bladder. If she is able to ambulate, she can be assisted to the bathroom; if she cannot ambulate or if she is unable to urinate, she must be catheterized.
2. Lochia is heavy because the bladder has lifted and displaced the uterus, making it difficult for Linda's uterus to remain contracted. This allows excessive bleeding from the site of placental attachment.
3. Linda does not experience the urge to void because the bladder has not regained the muscle tone lost during pregnancy and the sensitivity to pressure is decreased.

it continues to be part of the assessment of the lower extremities in the postpartum period. A negative Homans' sign indicates the absence of discomfort. A positive Homans' sign indicates the presence of discomfort and should be reported to the physician or nurse-midwife.

Edema and Deep Tendon Reflexes. Pedal, or pre-tibial, edema may be present for the first day or two, until excess interstitial fluid is remobilized and excreted. Deep tendon reflexes should be 1+ to 2+. Report brisker than average and hyperactive reflexes (3+ to 4+), which suggest pregnancy-induced hypertension.

The reflexes are defined as follows (NAACOG, 1991):

1+ = low normal; somewhat diminished
2+ = average, normal
3+ = brisker than average; possible indication of disease
4+ = very brisk, hyperactive; often associated with clonus

(See p. 688 for a description of how to assess deep tendon reflexes.)

Comfort Level. Comfort is essential to postpartum recovery; however, some new mothers are too excited by the birth of their child to complain of discomfort. Nurses must remain alert to covert signs of afterpains, perineal discomfort, or breast tenderness. Signs of discomfort include inability to relax or sleep, a change in vital signs, restlessness, irritability, and facial grimaces.

Analgesics, such as acetaminophen (Tylenol, Panadol), and nonsteroidal anti-inflammatory drugs, such as ibuprofen (Motrin, Advil) are frequently prescribed to provide relief for mild to moderate discomfort. Empirin No. 3 and Percocet are often prescribed for more severe discomfort. See Table 17–5 for adverse effects and nursing considerations for drugs commonly used in the postpartum period.

Rest and Sleep. Perform an assessment to determine the degree of fatigue and to discover whether a significant other is available to share responsibilities for infant care when the mother goes home. Single mothers, mothers with little outside support, and mothers with young preschool children are especially vulnerable to extreme fatigue during the first weeks after childbirth.

The mother who is fatigued appears worn out and lethargic with slumping posture and often verbalizes a generalized decrease in energy and strength.

The postpartum assessment includes four factors that increase the risk that the mother will experience severe fatigue (Gardner and Campbell, 1991):

- Labor lasting longer than 30 hours, a high-exertion labor and delivery, or perceptions of severe pain during labor
- Pathological factors, including hemoglobin < 10 g/dl, a documented postpartum hemorrhage, any secondary disease (diabetes, heart disease, pregnancy-induced hypertension), or evidence of substance abuse
- Psychological factors, including sleeping difficulties, absence of a supportive partner, or a small or ill newborn
- Situational factors, such as dependent children at home, no help with child care or household tasks, or family crisis (loss of job, death in the family).

Assess the mother's perception of the number of hours of sleep needed and her ability to go back to sleep when she is awakened at night.

Dietary Practices. An assessment of dietary practices is particularly important for three reasons: (1) breastfeeding requires additional calories, (2) many new mothers are concerned about losing weight gained during pregnancy, and (3) an adequate supply of nutritious food may not be available.

Nutrients Needed for Breastfeeding. At least 500 ad-

Text continued on page 434

Procedure 17–2 Assessing the Perineum

Purpose: To observe perineal trauma and the state of healing.

1. **Provide privacy, and explain the purpose of the procedure.** *Elicits cooperation and reduces anxiety about the procedure.*

2. **Put on clean gloves.** *Implements Universal Precautions to provide protection from possible contact with body fluids.*

3. **Request the mother to assume a Sims position and flex her upper leg; lower the perineal pads, and lift the superior buttocks; use a flashlight to inspect the perineal area.** *Position provides an unobstructed view of the perineum; light allows better visualization.*

4. **Note the extent and location of edema or bruising.** *Extensive bruising or asymmetrical edema may indicate formation of a hematoma.* (See also Chapter 27.)

5. **Examine the episiotomy or laceration for redness, ecchymosis, edema, discharge, and approximation (REEDA).** *Redness, edema, or discharge may indicate infection of the wound; extensive bruising may delay healing; wound edges must be in direct contact for uncomplicated healing to occur.*

6. **Note number and size of hemorrhoids.** *Swollen, painful hemorrhoids interfere with activity and bowel elimination.*

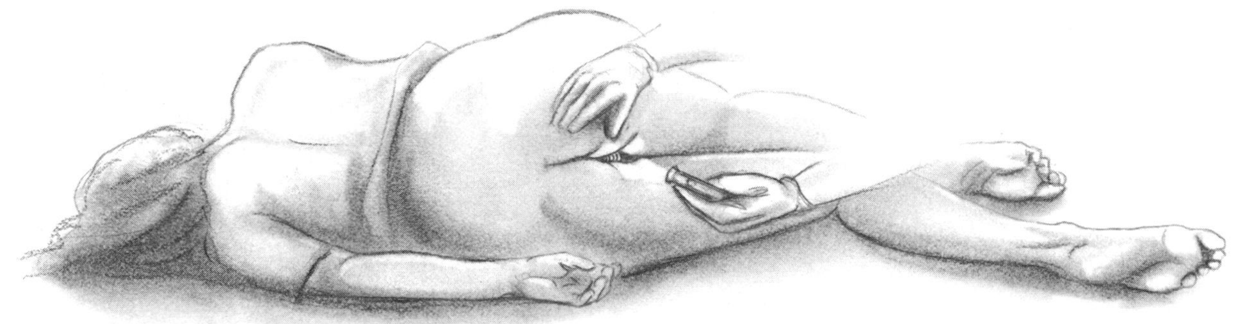

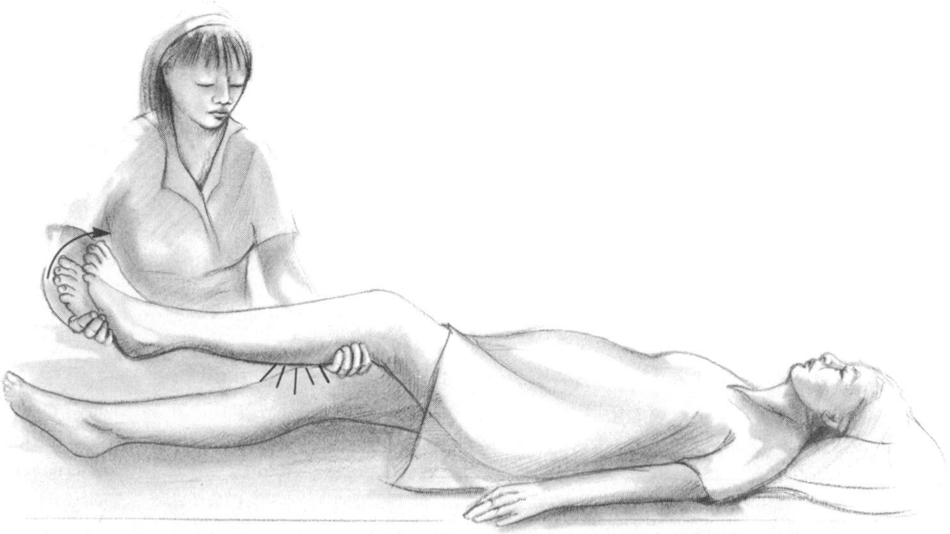

Figure 17–7

Homans' sign is positive when the mother experiences discomfort behind the knee on sharp dorsiflexion of the foot.

Nursing Care Plan 17–1

Perineal Trauma

Assessment: Four hours after she gave birth to a baby boy weighing 4200 g, Elba Salazar, a primipara, states that it is difficult to find a comfortable position because of perineal pain. The second stage of labor lasted more than 2 hours, and Elba had a third-degree extension of a midline episiotomy. There is marked edema and bruising of the perineum, and a cluster of four hemorrhoids is observed.

Nursing Diagnosis:
Pain related to perineal trauma and hemorrhoids.

Goals:

1. Elba will verbalize increased comfort by (time).
2. She will demonstrate self-care measures to promote comfort before discharge.

Intervention:	**Rationale:**
1. Apply ice packs for the first 12 hours following delivery. Use chemical ice packs or a glove filled with ice and tied at the cuff. Wrap the ice pack in disposable paper or a washcloth before applying it to the perineum. Leave the ice pack in place until the ice melts. Remove the pack for 10 minutes, and reapply fresh ice pack.	1. Ice causes vasoconstriction and is most effective if applied soon after delivery to *prevent* formation of edema. Ice numbs the area and provides comfort in this manner.
2. Instruct the mother in the use of benzocaine analgesic sprays (Americaine, Dermoplast). The nozzle is held 6 to 12 inches from her body and directed toward the perineum. The spray can be used following perineal care and before clean pads are applied.	2. Anesthetic sprays decrease surface discomfort and allow more comfortable ambulation. Because local anesthetic sprays are absorbed by mucous membranes of the labia and vagina, the lowest concentration should be used. The spray is discontinued as soon as the mother can tolerate the discomfort (Karb et al, 1989).
3. Demonstrate the use of topical agents, such as prepackaged witch hazel astringent compresses or ointments that have been ordered. Emphasize that the mother must wash her hands thoroughly before and after applying compresses or ointments.	3. Witch hazel and some topical ointments have a cooling effect on the burning pain of hemorrhoids; hand washing is essential to prevent bacterial contamination.
4. Instruct the mother to squeeze her buttocks together before sitting and to lower her weight slowly onto the buttocks.	4. Prevents stretching of the perineal muscles and avoids sharp impact on the traumatized area.
5. Initiate sitz baths according to physician or facility protocol; either cool or warm water may be used (LaFoy and Geden, 1989).	5. Continuous circulation of water cleanses and promotes comfort of the traumatized perineum. Cool water reduces pain caused by edema and may be most effective within the first 24 hours; warm water increases circulation and promotes healing; it may be most effective after 24 hours.
6. Test water temperature and help the mother sit in the sitz bath; be sure the emergency call bell is within easy reach.	6. Prevents injury caused by slipping or by water that is too hot. An emergency call bell provides for immediate response if the mother feels faint.

Evaluation:
Interventions can be judged effective if the mother verbalizes increased comfort and if she demonstrates self-care measures that reduce discomfort.

Nursing Care Plan continued on following page

Nursing Care Plan 17–1 Continued

Perineal Trauma

Assessment: At the next assessment, the fundus is two fingerbreadths above the umbilicus and displaced to the right. Baseline bladder assessment following catheterization 4 hours ago revealed that the fundus was firm, in the midline, and at the umbilicus. She has voided small amounts twice; however, there is a palpable bulge above the symphysis pubis.

Nursing Diagnosis:
Altered Patterns of Urinary Elimination related to temporary loss of sensation and decreased muscle tone of the bladder.

Goals:
Elba will empty her bladder completely at least every 3 to 4 hours, as demonstrated by voiding more than 400 ml and by a return of fundus to the level that was palpated following catheterization.

Intervention:	Rationale:
1. Place a measuring device (Pilgrim's hat) on the toilet to measure the amount voided until urine retention is no longer a problem; remember to deduct the amount of water used in perineal care from the amount in the measuring device to determine the actual amount of urine.	1. Less than 150 ml voided may indicate overflow from a distended bladder rather than an empty bladder; more than 300 to 400 ml usually indicates the bladder is empty. However, the fundus must be evaluated to confirm this.
2. Assist the mother to the bathroom as soon as she is able to ambulate safely; provide privacy and allow adequate time.	2. Privacy and time promote relaxation, which sometimes facilitates urination.
3. Use selected measures to initiate urination: a. Run water, place the mother's hands in water, pour water over the vulva. b. Ask the mother to blow bubbles through a straw. c. Encourage voiding in the shower or a sitz bath. d. Provide hot tea or fluids of choice; recommend fluid intake is at least 2500 ml/day.	3. Promotes relaxation of the perineal muscles and stimulates the sensation of needing to void. Although it is not possible to measure the amount voided in the shower or sitz bath, the nurse can determine whether the bladder was emptied by palpating the area over the symphysis and can also determine the location of the fundus.
4. Assess the bladder, fundus, and lochia if the mother is able to void.	4. A non-palpable bladder and a firm fundus at the umbilicus and in the midline confirms that the bladder is empty; this rules out urinary retention with overflow.
5. Catheterize the mother if she is unable to void, if the amount voided is less than 150 ml, or if the fundus is elevated from the baseline or displaced.	5. Urinary retention is a major cause of uterine atony (loss of tone), which permits excessive bleeding; stasis of urine in the bladder predisposes to urinary tract infection.
6. Follow the facility's format for repeated catheterizations. Usually, if catheterization is necessary for the third time, an indwelling catheter is inserted for 24 hours.	6. Repeated catheterizations increase the chance of urinary tract infection because bacteria may be pushed into the bladder despite scrupulous aseptic technique.

Evaluation:
Despite measures to stimulate voiding, Elba remains unable to void and an indwelling catheter is inserted. Bladder assessment should resume when the catheter is removed.

Nursing Care Plan 17–1 *Continued*

Perineal Trauma

Assessment: Elba has not had a bowel movement by the morning of the third postpartum day. She is scheduled to go home at noon and says that she is worried that the first bowel movement will be painful. She ambulates slowly and only to the bathroom. She states that she had problems with constipation throughout her pregnancy.

Nursing Diagnosis:
High Risk for Constipation related to fear of painful defecation and lack of knowledge of measures to prevent constipation.

Goals:
Elba will
1. Have a bowel movement before being discharged home.
2. Identify measures to reduce discomfort caused by defecation and to prevent constipation.

Intervention:	Rationale:
1. Teach methods to prevent constipation, such as: a. Drinking eight glasses of water per day (do not count tea or coffee). b. Eating foods high in fiber (unpeeled fresh fruit, vegetables, fruit juices, whole grain cereal, bread). c. Eating four pieces of fruit plus a large salad each day.	1. Adequate fluid prevents the stool from becoming dry and hard; fiber provides bulk, which absorbs fluid in the lower bowel to produce large, soft stool and prevents irritation of hemorrhoids by hard stool.
2. Encourage physical activity, such as walking.	2. Increases peristalsis of the bowel and thus prevents excessive water absorption from the large intestine, which results in hard, dry stool.
3. Encourage the mother to try to establish a schedule of bowel elimination (for instance, following breakfast) to take advantage of gastrocolic reflex (stimulation of peristalsis induced in the colon when food is consumed on an empty stomach).	3. Bowel elimination occurs every 24 to 48 hours and is facilitated by the gastrocolic reflex, which usually follows breakfast when there has been night-long fasting.
4. Instruct the mother to assume a Sims position for at least ½ hour several times a day.	4. Aids in venous return from the rectal area and reduces discomfort of inflamed hemorrhoids.
5. Administer stool softener according to the protocol of the health care provider; most often, stool softeners are started on the first day following delivery. If the mother has not had a bowel movement by the third postpartum day, a mild laxative or suppository may be ordered. *Do not give rectal suppositories if the mother has an episiotomy or laceration that extends into the rectal sphincter.*	5. Promotes comfort during defecation; the rectal sphincter may be injured during insertion of suppositories if laceration extends into the sphincter.
6. Teach measures to reduce perineal and hemorrhoidal pain. (See **Nursing Diagnosis.** Pain related to perineal trauma and hemorrhoids.)	6. Increases the likelihood that defection will be comfortable, and fear of pain should decrease.

Evaluation:
Elba has a formed stool after administration of laxative; she describes measures to prevent constipation and to promote comfort following discharge.

Additional Nursing Diagnoses to Consider:
Altered Health Maintenance
High Risk for Body Image Disturbance

ditional calories are needed to meet the new mother's energy requirements and to produce an adequate supply of milk for the infant. Caution mothers that attempts to lose weight by dieting during pregnancy may result in production of less milk each day.

Rate of Weight Loss. The rate of weight loss after giving birth depends on several factors. Is the mother planning to breastfeed? How active is she? Does she exercise regularly? What type of foods are included in her diet? How are the foods prepared?

If the mother is an adolescent, ask who does the shopping and cooking. Does she usually eat at home? How often does she eat at a fast food restaurant? What are her favorite foods?

Food Supply. It is sometimes appropriate to determine the amount and type of food that is available. This is particularly true for families of low socioeconomic status who might benefit from referral to government-sponsored programs, such as food stamps or Women, Infant, and Children (WIC). It may also be necessary to determine the facilities that are available for cooking and storing food. Sometimes the new family must be referred to a social worker so that the best solutions for their unique problems can be found. (Chapter 9 provides additional information about maternal nutrition during breastfeeding.)

Sexual Patterns. Assess the couple's knowledge about the resumption of sexual intercourse and contraceptive choices. Cultural or religious convictions may restrict the choice of method for some couples, whereas availability of health care or inadequate finances may dictate the choice for others. Plan discussions with the couple regarding their previous experience with contraceptives and their satisfaction with that method. Evaluate the vocabulary that the couple uses and understands, their knowledge of time required for healing of the perineum, and their understanding of the effects of decreased estrogen during lactation.

Many new parents are reluctant to ask about when to resume sexual activity and potential alterations in sexuality resulting from pregnancy and childbirth. If couples do not indicate such concerns, the nurse introduces the topic in a general, nonspecific manner. "You have an episiotomy that may cause some discomfort with intercourse until it is completely healed." "Sometimes couples are not aware that some vaginal dryness occurs as a result of breastfeeding." Such broad opening statements permit the family to pursue the topic as they desire.

Analysis

In general, mothers adapt to the physiological changes following childbirth and nursing care is wellness-oriented. However, many new mothers are at risk for experiencing a disruption in health because of lack of knowledge of self-care measures. Therefore, a nursing diagnosis that is applicable for many women and forms the basis for nursing interventions is High Risk for Altered Health Maintenance related to insufficient knowledge of self-care, signs of complications, and preventive measures. Some of the most common diagnostic categories—Constipation, Altered Patterns of Urinary Elimination, High Risk for Injury, Altered Patterns of Sexuality, and Pain—appear in Nursing Care Plans 17–1 and 17–2.

Planning

Goals for the nursing diagnosis *High Risk for Altered Health Maintenance related to insufficient knowledge of self-care, signs of complications, and preventive measures* are:

- The new mother will verbalize/demonstrate understanding of self-care instructions by day of discharge.
- She and her family will verbalize understanding of practices that promote maternal health by (date).
- She will describe plans for follow-up care and signs and symptoms that should be reported to the physician, nurse-midwife, or nurse practitioner by day of discharge.

Interventions

TEACHING SELF-CARE

Breast Care for Lactating Mothers. Instruct the breastfeeding mother to wash the nipples with clear water and to avoid soaps that remove the natural lubrication secreted by Montgomery's glands. Advise her to feed the infant when the breasts feel full or when the infant indicates hunger rather than to follow a schedule. Explain that she should not restrict the duration of breastfeeding but should allow adequate time for both breasts to be emptied at each feeding. Keeping the nipples dry between feedings helps to prevent tissue damage, and wearing a good bra provides necessary support as breast size increases. (For additional information about breastfeeding, see Chapter 21.)

Breast Care for Non-lactating Mothers. The mother who is not breastfeeding should avoid breast stimulation, and she should not pump the breasts to relieve engorgement. Pumping stimulates more milk production and makes the condition worse. Wearing a snug bra often prevents engorgement. Analgesics and ice may relieve the discomfort of engorgement should it occur.

Perineal Care. Nurses are responsible for teaching some form of perineal cleansing as soon as possible after childbirth. The most common method is to fill a squeeze bottle with warm water and spray the perineal area from the front toward the back. In some facilities, a small amount of cleansing solution is added; in others, only clear, warm water is used. Remind the new mother not to separate the labia during this procedure so that water does not enter the vagina. If a commercial product that includes a nozzle attached to the faucet is used, teach the mother that the nozzle should not touch the perineum during use.

Moist antiseptic towelettes or toilet paper is used in a patting motion to dry the perineum. Teach the mother to dry from front to back to prevent fecal contamination from the anal area toward the vaginal introitus. She should perform perineal cleansing after each voiding or defecation, and she should change perineal pads (peripads) at the same time.

Many women do not use peripads for menstrual protection and must be taught how to use them correctly. Careful handling of the pads is important to prevent localized perineal infection:

Thorough hand washing is a must before and after changing the pads.

Pads should be stored inside their package.

Pads should be applied without touching the side that comes into contact with the perineum.

If a belt is used, the mother can lower the belt to her knees before sitting on the toilet. The tabs are fastened through the belt hooks before she stands; the belt, with the attached peripads, is pulled into place after she stands.

The pads should be applied and removed in a front-to-back direction to prevent contamination of the vagina and perineum.

In some facilities, mesh panties and adhering pads are used instead of belts and perineal pads with tabs. In either case, the same principles apply.

Kegel Exercises. All mothers should become familiar with Kegel exercises. These movements strengthen the pubococcygeal muscle, which surrounds the vagina and urinary meatus. This exercise helps to prevent the loss of muscle tone that can occur following childbirth.

The exercise, which may be started in the postpartum period, involves contracting muscles around the vagina (as though stopping the flow of urine), holding tightly for a few seconds, and then relaxing. The contraction-relaxation cycle is repeated ten times, and the series is repeated five times a day during the postpartum period.

Comfort Measures. Nurses can teach new mothers how to reduce perineal discomfort and how to relieve discomfort when they go home. See Nursing Care Plan 17–1 for the Nursing Diagnosis: Pain related to edema and trauma of the perineum.

PROMOTING REST AND SLEEP

There are several reasons for the extreme fatigue that mothers experience in the puerperium. For one thing, they are tired when they begin the postpartum period; women often do not sleep well during the third trimester, and many are further exhausted by the exertion of labor. Women commonly experience feelings of excitement and euphoria for some time following childbirth and are unable to rest. Numerous visitors during the first few days also interfere with long periods of rest. Hospital routines, an unfamiliar environment, and physical discomfort also make it difficult for the new mother to rest.

Many mothers are discharged from the facility within 24 hours after childbirth, and most go home with a tremendous deficit in sleep and energy. Yet new parents may be unprepared for the conflict between their need for sleep and the infant's need for care and attention. The joys of parenting can easily be overshadowed by the exhaustion and frustration that result.

Rest at the Birth Facility. Hospital routines continue around the clock, making uninterrupted rest difficult and increasing the probability that the mother will be fatigued when she is discharged. Make every attempt to allow adequate time for uninterrupted rest periods. Group assessments and care and try to correlate them with times when the mother would be awake, for instance, just before or after meals, feeding times, or visiting hours. If the room is shared, providing care for both women at the same time also reduces activities that interrupt sleep.

It may be possible to elicit the cooperation of the mother to select a time when phone calls and visitors are restricted so that she can use this time for napping. A quiet, softly lit environment also promotes sleep.

Rest at Home. Help the mother to understand the impact that her physical discomfort and the demands of the newborn will have on her energy during the first few weeks. Emphasize measures that conserve energy, such as:

A relaxed, flexible routine that focuses on care of the mother and infant

Simple meals and flexible meal times

Accepting assistance with food shopping and meal preparation

Postponing major household projects

Involving friends and family to provide care for other children

Nursing Care Plan 17–2

Postpartum Hypotension, Fatigue and Pain

Assessment: Jacqueline Tilden, gravida II, para II, gave birth to a baby girl weighing 3400 g (7.5 pounds) 4 hours ago. She became weak and dizzy and mentioned that "everything was going black" when she attempted to ambulate the first time. Her gait was unsteady, and it was necessary for the nurse to lower her back to bed to prevent her from fainting. Her color was pale, and her pulse was rapid.

Nursing Diagnosis:
High Risk for Injury related to physiological effects of orthostatic hypotension

Goal:
Jacqueline will remain free of injury caused by fainting and falling during the postpartum period.

Intervention:	Rationale:
1. Check the mother's blood pressure in a supine position and in a sitting position; check the blood pressure in the same arm.	1. A decrease of 20 mmHg in systolic pressure in the upright position indicates orthostatic hypotension (a sudden decrease in blood pressure when one moves from a supine to standing position). Measuring from the same arm provides more accurate information because the reading may differ slightly in each arm.
2. Instruct the mother in measures to overcome the sudden drop in blood pressure: a. Elevate the head of the bed for a few minutes before she attempts to stand. b. Help her sit on the side of the bed for several minutes before standing, and help her stand slowly.	2. Allows time for blood pressure to stabilize before she is fully upright, thus maintaining circulation to the brain.
3. Instruct the mother to move her feet constantly when she first stands.	3. Increases venous return from the lower extremities; this maintains cardiac output and increases cerebral circulation.
4. Suggest that she take brief, tepid (not hot) showers and that she bend her knees and "march" during the shower.	4. Hot water dilates peripheral blood vessels, allowing additional blood to remain in the vessels of the legs. Moving the feet and legs increases blood return from the legs and increases blood to the brain.
5. Initiate measures to prevent injuries that could be sustained if she fainted: a. Stay with the mother when she ambulates, and be prepared to assist her in sitting down or in lowering her gently to the floor if she becomes faint. b. Call for assistance before attempting to return her to bed. c. Remind her to call for assistance before trying to ambulate. Check to see that the call light is conveniently located.	5. Lowering her to a sitting or lying position increases blood flow to the brain and prevents fainting. Adequate assistance prevents falling and possible injury during a fainting episode.

Evaluation:
Jacqueline has participated in self-care and has sustained no injury during her hospital stay.

Nursing Care Plan 17–2 *Continued*

Postpartum Fatigue and Pain

Assessment: Jacqueline demonstrates skill in breastfeeding but wonders how she will be able to care for the baby and her older child, an 18-month-old boy, when she gets home. She has a third-degree episiotomy and asks what can be done to prevent the pain she experienced during intercourse for several months after the last child was born.

Nursing Diagnosis:
High Risk for Altered Patterns of Sexuality related to fatigue and dyspareunia (painful intercourse).

Goals:
The couple will:
1. Verbalize measures to promote comfort during sexual activity by (date).
2. Verbalize plan to reduce fatigue, which interferes with interest in, and energy for, sexual activity by (date).

Intervention:	Rationale:
1. Recommend that the parents postpone vaginal intercourse until the perineum is well healed, usually about 3 weeks. Suggest that the mother continue perineal care, sitz baths, and the use of topical agents until the perineum is healed.	1. Promotes rapid healing and reduces pain or fear of pain when sexual activity is resumed.
2. Suggest the use of a water-soluble vaginal lubricant (K-Y jelly, Lubrin, Replens) if the mother is planning to breastfeed for longer than 6 weeks.	2. Breastfeeding delays the resumption of ovarian hormones, including estrogen, which may result in vaginal dryness that is most noticeable after 6 weeks of breastfeeding.
3. Prior to vaginal intercourse, as part of foreplay, suggest that one finger be inserted into the vaginal introitus to determine areas of tenderness or pain.	3. Locates areas of discomfort, and stretches the perineal scar gently.
4. Suggest that the woman assume the superior position during intercourse.	4. Controls the depth and location of penetration, thereby reducing discomfort.
5. Remind parents that sexual arousal may be slower because of decreased hormones and fatigue; more stimulation may be required before the mother is sexually aroused.	5. Knowledge of the physiological changes reduces the anxiety and tension that occur if the parents are unprepared for them.
6. Remind the mother to perform Kegel exercises until she can comfortably do 50 each day. She may gradually work up to performing 100 repetitions twice each day.	6. Strengthens the muscles around the vagina and promotes increased sexual satisfaction.
7. Suggest that the infant be breastfed just prior to initiating sexual activity.	7. Reduces the chance of leaking milk, which interferes with sexual pleasure for some couples; may also allow uninterrupted time while the infant sleeps.
8. Suggest measures that may lessen fatigue: a. Recommend that each partner nap for 30 minutes sometime during the day or evening. b. Suggest that sexual activity be resumed in the morning or afternoon rather than at the end of a tiring day. c. Suggest that parents rest when the infant has long periods of sleep and that they postpone additional home projects that will increase fatigue until the infant is older and is sleeping through the night.	8. Lessens fatigue, which is cited by both mothers and fathers as one of the major causes of decreased interest in sexual activity following childbirth.

Nursing Care Plan continued on following page

Nursing Care Plan 17–2 *Continued*

Postpartum Fatigue and Pain

Intervention:	Rationale:
9. Encourage frank communication between partners about measures that reduce discomfort as well as specific concerns and needs.	9. Facilitates understanding and fosters a feeling of closeness that can enhance sexual interest.

Evaluation:
The couple expresses interest in learning measures that reduce fatigue and discomfort; they verbalize a plan to use the instructions provided.

Additional Nursing Diagnoses to Consider:
- Ineffective Breastfeeding
- Altered Health Maintenance
- High Risk for Infection
- Health-Seeking Behaviors

Explain to the mother that she should delay her return to employment, if possible, until the infant sleeps through the night (usually by 4 months). Advise her to restrict coffee, tea, colas, and chocolate (which all contain the stimulant caffeine) for the first few weeks and to rest whenever the infant sleeps rather than to use this time to catch up on housecleaning tasks.

Infant Sleep and Feeding Schedules. Provide information about infant sleep cycles, frequency of feeding, and probable crying episodes so that the family is aware of some of the demands of infant care during the first weeks. Although newborns sleep 16 to 20 hours per day, they may awaken every 2 to 3 hours for feeding. On average, they spend 2 to 3 hours crying during a 24-hour period. Some infants (particularly those who are small or who have colic) may need to be fed more often, and they may spend more time crying. (See Chapter 22 for a discussion of parenting during the first weeks.)

Relaxation Exercises. Total relaxation exercises (lying quietly, alternately tightening and relaxing the muscles of the neck, shoulders, arms, legs, and feet) are helpful when a nap is not possible. Emphasize to the mother the importance of asking for help when she begins to feel exhausted or overwhelmed and that she share these feelings with family, friends, and other new mothers.

PROVIDING NOURISHMENT AND NUTRITION COUNSELING

After a normal vaginal delivery, the postpartum client is thirsty and hungry. Adequate fluids of her choice should be available, and she should be encouraged to eat a diet that supplies nutrients from the recommended food groups. Nursing management consists largely of educating and counseling families about basic nutrition following childbirth.

Lactating Mothers. Although many women are not satisfied with the slow rate of weight loss, emphasize that moderate to severe restriction of caloric intake during lactation will interfere with the ability to synthesize milk (Mahan and Arlin, 1992). About 85 calories is required to produce 100 ml of milk.

To meet the additional demands imposed by lac-

Therapeutic Communication

Clare Beauchamp gave birth to a baby boy 48 hours ago. Terry Meyer is a nurse preparing to teach Clare self-care measures before discharge from the birth facility.

Clare: Look at me; I still look pregnant, and my husband calls me Tubby.

Terry: You were looking forward to your abdomen being flat after the baby was born?

Clarifying the woman's concern by reflecting content.

Clare: Well, I was always so flat; I am really disappointed.

Terry: Remember it took nine months for those muscles to stretch. You can't expect them to snap back in a few days.

Blocking communication by ignoring the feeling expressed. A more helpful response would be to acknowledge the disappointment and to delay giving information until feelings have been expressed. For example: "It is upsetting, and when you are ready, we can discuss some exercises that will help."

tation, additional servings of foods are recommended. These include 2 cups of milk; 2 ounces of meat, fish, or chicken; two extra servings of dark green or yellow vegetables; one extra serving of citrus fruit; and one additional slice of whole grain bread (Worthington-Roberts et al, 1989).

Non-lactating Mothers. Even if the mother has chosen formula feeding, it is recommended that she not restrict calories severely. Advise her to select foods that provide adequate calories to meet her energy needs, taking into account the time and energy required to care for a newborn. Strict dieting can leave the mother feeling tired and lower her immunity. A balanced, low-fat diet emphasizing adequate protein, complex carbohydrates, fruits, and vegetables provides the energy needed.

PROMOTING REGULAR BOWEL ELIMINATION

Progressive exercise, adequate fluid, and dietary fiber are effective means of preventing constipation. Walking is perhaps the best exercise, and the distance can be increased as strength and endurance increase. At least 8 glasses of water daily helps to maintain normal bowel elimination. Dietary fiber is present in fruits and vegetables, particularly when they are unpeeled. Prunes act as a natural laxative. Additional fiber is found in whole grain cereals, bread, and pasta.

For additional preventive measures, see Nursing Care Plan 17–1 for the Nursing Diagnosis *High Risk for Constipation related to fear of painful defecation and inadequate knowledge of preventive measures.* (Chapter 9 more fully discusses dietary needs of the postpartum woman.)

PROMOTING GOOD BODY MECHANICS

Exercise. Specific exercises can be taught in the early postpartum period to strengthen the abdominal muscles and to firm the waist. The exercises can be started soon after childbirth; to begin, each can be repeated five times twice each day. Gradually, the number is increased as the mother gains strength. Post-cesarean mothers should follow instructions of their health care provider, but they should not begin an exercise program for at least 4 to 6 weeks. Figure 17–8 illustrates recommended postpartum exercises that may begin with approval of the physician, nurse-midwife, or nurse practitioner.

Preventing Back Strain. Back strain can often be prevented if the mother and father find a location for infant care, such as a kitchen table or bathroom counter, that does not require bending or leaning forward. For lifting objects, teach parents to hold the back straight as they squat and use the legs rather than bending at the waist. Figure 7–12 (see p. 144), illustrates this concept.

COUNSELING ABOUT SEXUAL ACTIVITY

Couples often have questions regarding resuming sexual activity, promoting maternal comfort during intercourse, and effective family planning methods. For an example of how the nurse might teach these couples, see Nursing Care Plan 17–2, which provides interventions for the Nursing Diagnosis *High Risk for Altered Patterns of Sexuality related to perineal discomfort, dryness of vaginal mucosa and/or fatigue.*

PROVIDING INSTRUCTION FOR FOLLOW-UP CARE

New parents must be made aware of the available resources for follow-up care. Some facilities follow up with telephone interviews that focus on questions and problems that the new parents have. A few facilities offer home visits by registered nurses if requested by the family. Telephone "hotlines," staffed by registered nurses, are available 24 hours a day in many areas to respond to questions. In addition, breastfeeding and parenting classes as well as "baby and me" walks or exercise sessions are offered by many institutions.

Instruct new mothers to make an appointment for examination by their health care provider at 2 weeks and 6 weeks post partum. General physical and psychological status is assessed at this time, with particular emphasis on the condition of the breasts and uterus, lochia, dietary practices, and elimination patterns. It may be necessary to refer the family for consultations with social workers, lactation specialists, or public health nurses to see that their particular problems receive ongoing interventions.

TEACHING ABOUT SIGNS AND SYMPTOMS THAT SHOULD BE REPORTED

New mothers and at least one member of the family must be taught the physical signs and symptoms that should be reported to the health care provider as soon as possible. These include:

- Fever
- Localized area of redness, swelling, or pain in either breast that is not relieved by support or analgesics
- Persistent abdominal tenderness or feelings of pelvic fullness or pelvic pressure

Figure 17–8. Postpartum Exercises

ABDOMINAL BREATHING

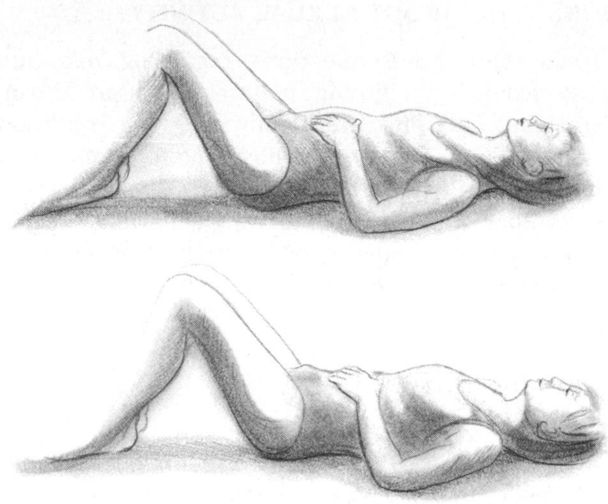

This is one of the simplest exercises and can be started on the first postpartum day. The woman assumes a supine position with knees bent. She inhales through the nose, keeps the rib cage as stationary as possible, and allows the abdomen to expand. She then contracts the abdominal muscles as she exhales slowly through the mouth.

HEAD LIFT

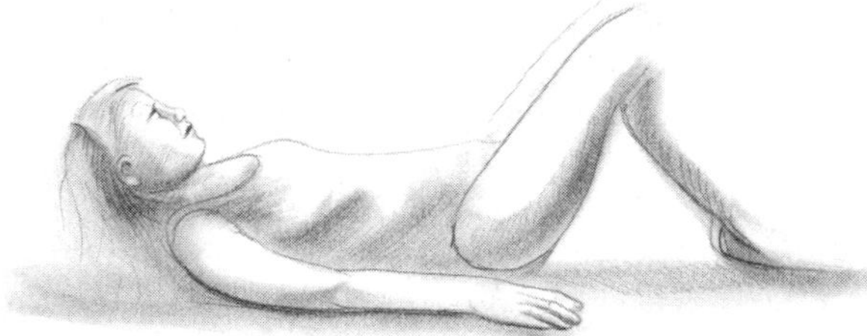

This exercise can be started within a few days after childbirth. The mother is supine with knees bent and arms outstretched at her side. She inhales deeply to begin, then exhales while lifting the head slowly; she holds the position for a few seconds and relaxes.

MODIFIED SIT-UPS

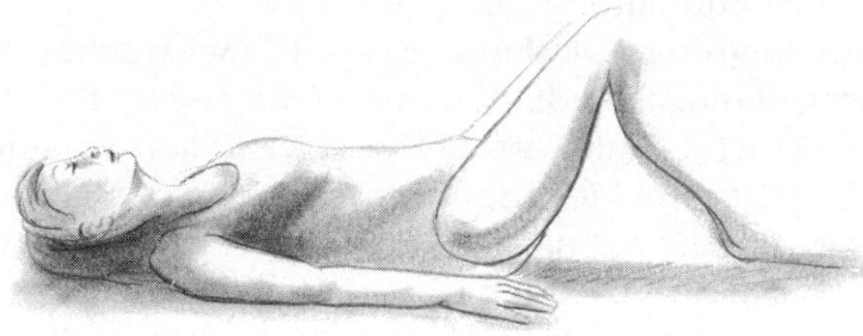

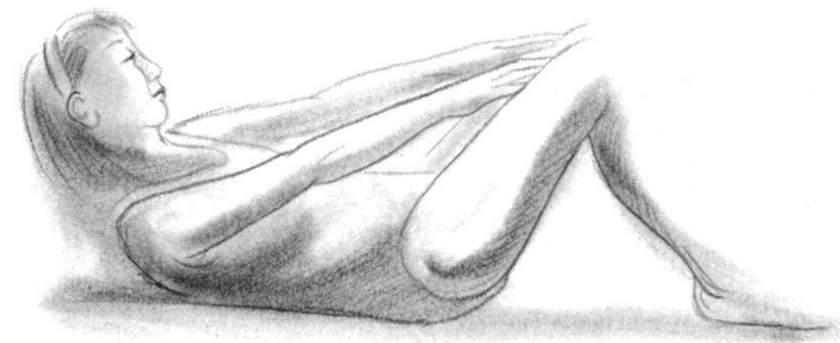

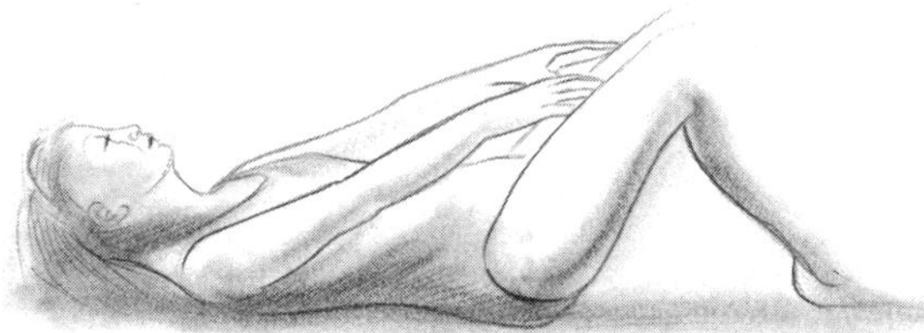

Head-lifts may progress to modified sit-ups with the approval of the health care provider; the mother should follow the advice of the health care provider about number of repetitions.

The exercise begins with the mother supine with arms outstretched. She raises her head and shoulders as her hands reach for her knees. She raises the shoulders only as far as the back will bend; her waist remains on the floor.

KNEE AND LEG ROLLS

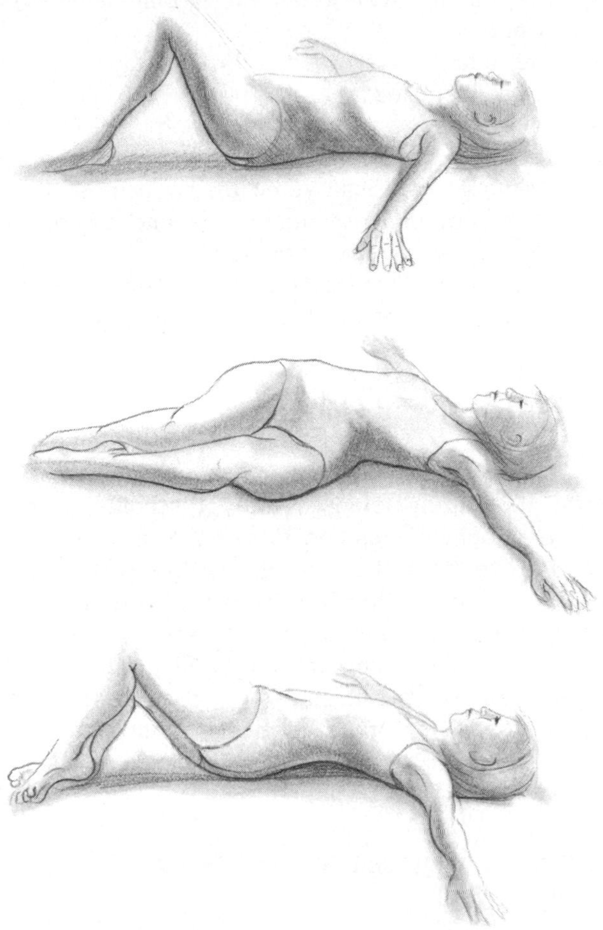

This is an excellent exercise to begin firming the waist. The mother lies flat on her back with knees bent and feet flat on the floor or bed; she keeps the shoulders and feet stationary and rolls the knees to touch first one side of the bed, then the other. She maintains a smooth motion as the exercise is repeated five times. Later, as flexibility increases, the exercise can be varied by the rolling of one knee only. The mother rolls her left knee to touch the right side of the bed, returns to center, and rolls the right knee to touch the left side of the bed.

CHEST EXERCISES

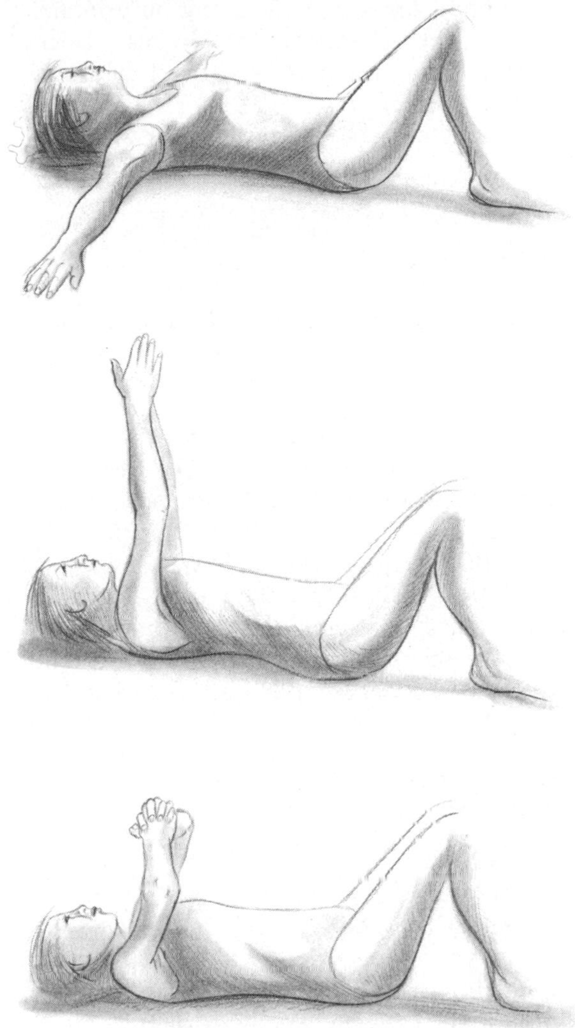

This is an excellent exercise to strengthen the chest muscles. The mother lies flat with arms extended straight out to the side; she brings the hands together above the chest while keeping the arms straight; she holds for a few seconds and returns to the starting position. She repeats the exercise five times initially and follows the advice of the health care provider for increasing the number of repetitions.

Isometric exercises also increase strength and tone; the mother bends her elbows, clasps her hands together above her chest, and presses her hands together for a few seconds. This is repeated at least five times.

- Persistent perineal pain
- Frequency, urgency, or burning on urination
- Change in character of lochia (increased amount, resumption of bright-red color, passage of clots, foul odor)
- Localized tenderness, redness, or warmth of the legs

Evaluation

Demonstration of correct breast and perineal hygiene provides evidence of ability to perform self-care measures.

- The mother's ability to verbalize practices that promote health in the areas of diet, exercise, rest, and sleep confirm understanding of these measures.
- Her ability to list the follow-up resources offered by the facility and a plan for future appointments for examination with the health care provider increase the likelihood that she will experience an uncomplicated recovery.

Early Discharge

Mothers and infants are frequently discharged as early as 24 hours following childbirth. There are several advantages to early discharge: lower hospital costs, reduced contact with hospital pathogens, less time spent in unfamiliar surroundings that may interfere with sleep and rest, and less disruption in family life. Early discharge may also enhance early parent-infant bonding.

Criteria

The mother and infant must be carefully evaluated during the first hours following childbirth. Only low-risk mothers and infants are offered early discharge.

- The mother's vital signs must be stable, and the estimated blood loss during delivery should not exceed expected levels of 300 to 400 ml.
- The fundus must be firm, with lochia rubra scant to moderate and without clots or offensive odor.
- The mother must be able to ambulate and to empty her bladder completely.
- The perineum must be free of signs of infection, and the mother should not experience undue perineal pain.
- The mother must be free of signs of thrombophlebitis (redness, swelling, tenderness of the legs, or positive Homans' sign).
- The infant must weigh more than 2500 g (5.5 pounds).
- The infant must have a lusty, robust cry and normal reflexes.*
- The infant must have voided before discharge.
- Required laboratory tests must be done before discharge, although some tests, such as screening for phenylketonuria (PKU) and thyroid abnormalities may be repeated.
- The umbilical cord and circumcision site must be free of signs of bleeding or infection.

Nursing Care

TEACHING SELF-CARE

When the family chooses early discharge, a great deal of teaching must be done in a short time. Be prepared to teach the mother how to care for herself and the infant. Mothers are expected to demonstrate how to assess the fundus, how to assess lochia, and how to promote comfort and healing of the perineum. Perhaps the greatest need is to help the mother establish competence and confidence in her ability to breastfeed, and this is often a task that requires more than 24 hours.

ENSURING THAT ALL ELEMENTS HAVE BEEN TAUGHT

Nurses are challenged by the responsibility for streamlining and organizing information so that it can be presented in the time available. Group instruction and hospital classes are returning to the postpartum environment. For example, classes that demonstrate infant care or provide breastfeeding instructions are common.

To prevent omissions, many hospitals utilize teaching "check-off" sheets listing the areas that must be covered. For example, care of the umbilical cord and circumcision site, using a bulb syringe, and taking a temperature are part of the infant care teaching that must take place before the mother leaves the hospital.

CASE MANAGEMENT

A case management approach has been suggested as an innovative method for meeting the needs of the postpartum family leaving the hospital within 24 hours (Gillerman and Beckham, 1991). This approach identifies elements that are common to all mothers who had vaginal or cesarean delivery and utilizes a

* See Chapter 19, p. 485

Mother-Baby Care Path to provide care and teaching within a specific time frame. Figure 17–9 illustrates the Mother-Baby Care Path for mothers who gave birth vaginally, and Figure 17–10 illustrates the Mother-Baby Care Path for mothers who had a cesarean birth.

The Mother-Baby Care Path establishes time frames for specific nursing assessments and interventions that prepare the mother and infant for early discharge. It does not eliminate the need to identify nursing diagnoses or to plan nursing interventions when problems are encountered.

With adequate information and consistent follow-up, most low-risk mothers who experienced uncomplicated vaginal deliveries do not experience untoward effects of early discharge. On the contrary, early discharge has been associated with higher maternal attachment scores, fewer maternal concerns, and greater satisfaction with postpartum care (Norr et al, 1989). Careful monitoring of maternal and infant health during the first month is urgently needed. Early discharge, combined with close follow-up may be a more effective use of health care resources than a conventional hospital stay.

✔ *Check Your Reading*

11. What are the criteria for early discharge from the standpoint of the mother? Of the baby?
12. What is the major challenge that early discharge presents to the nurse?

Nursing Care Following Cesarean Birth

Assessment

In addition to the usual postpartum assessments, the post-cesarean mother must also be assessed as any other postoperative patient.

RESPIRATIONS

Assess the respiratory rate more frequently because many mothers receive epidural narcotics that depress the respiratory center. An apnea monitor may be used for 24 hours to detect a decreased respiratory rate. If an apnea monitor is not used, check the respiratory rate and depth for a full minute every 15 minutes for the first hour, every ½ hour for the next 12 hours, and every hour for the next 11 hours, for a total of 24 hours of observation after epidural narcotics are administered (Inturrisi et al, 1988).

Auscultate breath sounds carefully because depressed respirations as well as a longer period of immobility allow secretions to pool in the bronchioles. Note the mother's ability to turn, cough, and expand the lungs by breathing deeply.

ABDOMEN

Palpate the abdomen for distention. Auscultate the abdomen for bowel sounds, which indicate that fluid and air are moving through the intestine; ask the mother if she has begun to expel flatus.

Inspect the surgical dressing for intactness or discharge. Use the acronym REEDA to observe the incision when the dressing is removed. Palpate the fundus gently because of increased discomfort caused by the uterine incision.

INTAKE/OUTPUT

Monitor the intravenous infusion for rate of flow and the condition of the intravenous site; report any signs of infiltration, such as edema or coolness, at the site; report signs of infection, such as edema, redness, or pain. Monitor the amount, color, and clarity of urine. Observe the mother for side effects, such as nausea and vomiting or pruritus (itching), from epidural narcotics.

Interventions

THE FIRST 24 HOURS

The mother who gave birth by cesarean is cared for as one would care for other postoperative clients.

Overcoming Effects of Immobility. The new mother will be on bed rest; help her to turn, cough, and breathe deeply every 2 hours to prevent pooling of secretions in the airway. Splinting the abdomen with a small pillow reduces incisional discomfort when she attempts to cough. Encourage her to flex her legs and to move her feet and legs frequently to improve peripheral circulation. She will need assistance to sit and to dangle her legs 8 to 12 hours following surgery.

Providing Comfort. When the mother is in a side-lying position, place a pillow behind her back and one between her knees to prevent strain and discomfort. Excellent physical care (oral hygiene, pericare, a bed bath, and clean linen) comforts and refreshes her. Pain medication is more effective if it is given before pain becomes severe; encourage the mother to take the medication as needed. Client-controlled anesthesia is commonly used for the first 24 hours, allowing the mother to control the time and amount of medication needed for comfort.

PT. ____________
M.D. ____________
CASE MGR. ____________
DATE DEVELOPED ____________
DATE REVIEWED BY M.D. ____________

Mother-Baby Care Path
Vaginal Birth

DX: Vaginal Delivery without Complicating Dx
DRG: 373
EXPECTED LOS: 24 hours after delivery

	Prenatal/Birth Care Center	By 3rd Hour After Admission to PP Unit	1st Baby Visit or By End of 1st Shift	By End of 2nd Shift After Adm.	2nd Baby Visit or By End of 2nd Shift	By End of 3rd Shift After Adm.	3rd Baby Visit or By End of 3rd Shift	Discharge Shift
Lab	H & H Type and Screen VDRL, HBSAG, Rubella } on prenatal record or drawn	H & H, Type & Screen on computer/chart.		H & H done if AM, results WNL.		Determine Rhogam and Rubella prep. status (if indicated).		Rhogam/Rubella have been given if indicated.
IV	IV	May be discontinued.						
Voiding	Empty bladder at least q 4°. Normal fundal check post-del.	Void/cath if fundus displaced or increased bleeding.		Emptying bladder with each void (criteria = normal fundal exam).				
Anesthesia/ Sensorimotor	Moving legs after delivery.	Able to stand and walk.						
Activity	Transfer to guerney/WC.	Ambulate with assistance.	Positioned for holding baby.	Ambulating without assistance.				
Medications	Pitocin added to IV Analgesic prn.	May be discontinued.	Stool softeners/laxatives, PNV.					Rx filled or given to take home.
Treatments/ Interventions	OB check q 15 min. WNL Pericare by caregiver Ice pack to perineum.	OB check WNL q 1° x 3. Pericare by patient. Bra applied. Assessment tool completed.	Observe bonding process.	OB check q shift WNL. Perineal meds by patient.	Bonding progressing (by observation).	Sitz bath if ordered.		
Teaching/Discharge Plan	Positioning for breastfeeding. Transfer to floor.	Ambulation. Self Pericare. Perineal meds. Involution, bleeding (fundus, lochia). Give booklet, introduce videos.	Handwashing. Supporting the infant's head and extremities. Proper positioning for feeding, burping. If breastfeeding: positioning of baby, rooting, latch-on, timing, removal.	Diet. Activity/rest. Elimination. Medications.	Bonding. Patient concerns. Normal newborn characteristics. Diaper change. Cord care. Frequency/timing of feeding, water, pacifiers, suckling pattern.	Use of sitz bath. Review "danger signals".	Safety: Baby positioning, car seat, always attended, no bottle propping. Reinforce teaching. Answer questions. Return demo: newborn characteristics, diaper change, feeding, circumcision care.	Appropriate time and person to call if problems. Check-out procedure. Baby DC. Reinforce use of booklet. Review health care provider follow-up appointments.
Consults				Evaluate need for consults: MSW, Lactation Specialist.		Lactation Specialist and MSW prn before discharge.		

LBMMC HGMB 1989

Figure 17–9

Mother–baby care path (vaginal birth). (Courtesy of Memorial Women's Hospital, Long Beach Memorial Medical Center, Long Beach, California.)

PT. ______
M.D. ______
CASE MGR. ______
DATE DEVELOPED ______
DATE REVIEWED BY M.D. ______

Mother-Baby Care Path
Cesarean Birth

DX: Cesarean Delivery without Complicating Dx
DRG: 371
EXPECTED LOS: 4 days after delivery

	CNC	Immediate Pre-Op/BCC	By 3rd Hour After Admission to PP	1st Day with Baby	1st PP Day	2nd Day with Baby	2nd PP Day	3rd Day with Baby	3rd PP Day	Discharge Day
Lab Tests	CBC, UA, T&S, VDRL, Rubella, HBSAg (may be on prenatal record).				H & H, WNL. All results on chart. Check Rhogam/ Rubella status.		Rhogam/Rubella have been given if indicated.			
GU		Retention catheter.	Retention catheter draining clear urine 30-60 cc/hour.		Retention catheter discontinued. Emptying bladder with each void (normal fundal exam).					
GI			0 to hypoactive bowel sounds.		Hypoactive to active BS.		+ BS, + Flatus.		+ BS, + Flatus.	
Anesthesia/ Sensorimotor			Resp. rate WNL. Alert/easily awakened. Moves extremities.		Full function, alert and responsive.					
Diet	NPO after MN	NPO	Sips of water/ice chips with no nausea/vomiting.		Clear liquids.		Regular diet - tolerated well.		Regular diet - tolerated well.	
IV		IV started.	IV with Pitocin.		IV w/o Pitocin, may be discontinued.		Discontinued.			
Activity			Bedrest	Positioned for holding baby.	Ambulate with assistance and alone in room. Chair/bed bath.		Amb. alone in hall Chair bath.		Shower, continues to amb. alone.	
Medications		Na citrate taken.	Pain controlled by analgesics IM/PO. Nausea controlled by antiemetic prn.		Pain controlled by PO analgesic.		P.O. Analgesic controls pain.		Decreased need for P.O. analgesics.	Rx filled or given to take home.
Treatments/ Interventions			OB check q 1° x 3 WNL. TCDB with splinting with assist q 1°. Abd. dsg D/I. Pericare by caregiver.	Observe bonding process.	VS q 4° WNL. OB check q shift WNL. TCDB with splinting with min. assist q 2°. Abd. dsg. D/I. Bra applied. Pericare by patient.	Bonding progressing (by observation).	VS + OB check every shift WNL. Dressing changed or removed according to orders.		VS + OB check WNL q shift. Dressing removed if ordered.	VS + OB check WNL. Staples removed, steri-strips applied.
Teaching	Events of day of surgery. Post-op care. Postpartum routine. C/S, anesthesia procedure. Pain control.	C/S, anesthesia procedure.	TCDB, splinting q 1° when awake. Pain control. Involution, bleeding (fundus, lochia).	Handwashing. Supporting infant's head and extremities. Positioning for feeding, burping. If breastfdg: positioning of baby, rooting, latch-on, timing, removal.	Reinforce TCDB. Amb/Body Mechanics/ Positioning. Give booklet, introduce videos. Reinforce involution process.	Bonding. Patient concerns. Normal newborn characteristics. Diaper change. Cord care. Freq/timing of fdgs, water, pacifier, suckling pattern.	Diet. Activity/rest. Elimination. Medications.	Safety: Baby position, car seat, always attended, no propping. Return verb./demo: newborn characteristics, diaper change, feeding, circumcision care.	Self-concept issues related to C-birth. Review "danger signals".	Appropriate time and person to call if problems. Reinforce use of booklet, teaching. Answer questions.
DC Plan					Plans for DC, identification of home maintenance problems.					Check-out procedure. Baby DC. Review health care provider follow-up appointments. schedule.
Consult					MSW prn, Lactation Specialist prn.					

Figure 17–10

Mother–baby care path (cesarean birth). (Courtesy of Memorial Women's Hospital, Long Beach Memorial Medical Center, Long Beach, California.)

AFTER 24 HOURS

Reinstating Normal Activities. After 24 hours, several normal functions return as post-cesarean women are able to participate more actively in their own care:

- Both the indwelling catheter and intravenous infusion are usually discontinued.
- The dressing is usually removed, and often staples or clamps are removed also; Steri-Strips or a small non-stick dressing may be used to cover the incision.
- Mothers are usually helped to ambulate on the first postpartum day and are comfortable sitting in a chair for a brief period of time.
- Clear liquids are allowed once bowel sounds are audible; if abdominal distention is minimal, the diet progresses to soft foods and then to a regular regimen.

Encourage the mother to increase her activity and ambulation each postpartum day. By the second day, she is usually allowed to shower. Some health care providers request that the incision be covered with plastic; others permit showering without covering the incision.

Assisting the Mother with Infant Feeding. Take care to help the mother in finding a comfortable position for holding and feeding her infant. A side-lying position may be most comfortable; however, some mothers prefer sitting with a pillow on the lap to protect the incisional area. The football hold is often the most comfortable position for breastfeeding because the infant is not on the lap and thus does not cause incisional discomfort. (See Chapter 21 for additional information about breastfeeding.)

Preventing Abdominal Distention. Abdominal distention is a major source of discomfort, and measures should be taken to prevent or minimize it. Early, frequent ambulation is perhaps the best method; however, there are some additional measures:

- Pelvic lifts (a flat, supine position with knees bent, lifting the pelvis from the bed) may be repeated up to ten times several times each day.
- Tightening and relaxing the abdominal muscles may also be helpful.
- Carbonated beverages as well as the use of straws, which increase the accumulation of intestinal gas, should be restricted.
- Simethecone may disperse upper gastrointestinal flatulence.
- Rectal suppositories stimulate peristalsis and passage of flatus.

✔ Check Your Reading

13. Which four additional assessments are necessary for the post-cesarean mother?
14. Which three measures are used to prevent or minimize abdominal distention?

Summary Concepts

- Following childbirth, the uterus returns to its prepregnancy size and condition by involution, which involves catabolic processes that reduce enlarged muscle cells and contraction of stretched muscle fibers.
- Involution can be evaluated by measuring the descent of the fundus (about 1 cm/day): by the 10th day post partum, the fundus should be located in the pelvic cavity and no longer palpable abdominally.
- The site of placental attachment heals by a process of exfoliation, which leaves the endometrium smooth and without scars.
- Vaginal discharge (lochia) progresses from lochia rubra (containing mostly blood), to lochia serosa (containing serous exudate, blood, and leukocytes) to lochia alba (containing increased amounts of leukocytes and decidual cells) in a predictable time frame. Lochia should be assessed for volume, type, and odor; foul odor suggests endometrial infection.
- Sexual activity may be resumed when the vagina and perineum are completely healed (approximately 3 weeks); however, contraceptive methods should be discussed with both lactating and non-lactating mothers.
- Breastfeeding mothers are more likely to experience dyspareunia as a result of vaginal dryness that results from inadequate estrogen.
- The excess fluid of pregnancy is remobilized and excreted by diaphoresis and diuresis. The bladder fills quickly, and problems of bladder elimination are common because of increased capacity and decreased sensitivity to pressure.
- A distended bladder lifts and displaces the uterus; this can interfere with uterine contraction and can result in excessive bleeding.
- Increased clotting factors predispose the postpartum woman to thrombus formation. Early, frequent ambulation is the best method for preventing thrombophlebitis.
- The postpartum woman should be afebrile; tem-

perature may be higher the first 24 hours after delivery as a result of exertion, dehydration, and leukocytosis.

- Bradycardia is expected; tachycardia may be due to excitement, dehydration, or hypovolemia. Additional assessments (lochia, fundus) are required to determine whether excessive bleeding is the cause.
- Orthostatic hypotension occurs when the mother goes from a supine to a standing position quickly and may result in injury if precautions to protect her are not initiated.
- Constipation may occur as a result of inadequate fluid intake during labor, reduced activity, decreased muscle tone, or fear of pain during defecation.
- Breastfeeding may delay the return of ovulation and menstruation; however, it is not a reliable method of family planning. Both lactating and non-lactating mothers need information about family planning.
- Lactation may be suppressed by the wearing of a snug bra, by binding of the breasts, and by avoiding stimulation of the breasts; medication is sometimes prescribed also.
- Nurses provide information that permits the mother to perform care of herself and the infant, teaching measures that promote comfort and rest, providing instruction about diet and exercise, teaching the family signs and symptoms that must be reported, and helping the family to plan follow-up care.
- The post-cesarean woman requires postoperative as well as postpartum assessments and care. She is at increased risk for problems associated with immobility and discomfort.
- The common practice of early discharge challenges nurses to streamline information and to develop a plan for teaching self-care and infant care in a short amount of time.

References and Readings

Balkam, J. (1986). Guidelines for drug therapy during lactation. *Journal of Obstetric, Gynecologic, and Neonatal Nursing*, 15 (1), 65–70.

Carr, C. (1989). A four-week observation of maternity care in Finland. *Journal of Obstetric, Gynecologic, and Neonatal Nursing*, 18 (2), 100–105.

Cunningham, F.G., McDonald, P.C., & Gant, N.F. (1989). *Williams obstetrics* (18th ed.). Norwalk, Conn.: Appleton & Lange.

Deglin, J.H., & Vallerand, A.H. (1991). *Davis's drug guide for nurses* (3rd ed.). Philadelphia: F.A. Davis.

Donaldson, N.E. (1991). A review of nursing intervention research on maternal adaptation in the first 8 weeks postpartum. *Journal of Perinatal Neonatal Nursing*, 4 (4), 1–11.

Eaton, J. (1991). Suppressing lactation. *Nursing Times*, 87 (18), 27–30.

Ellis, D., & Hewat, R. (1985). Mother's postpartum perceptions of spousal relationships. *Journal of Obstetric, Gynecologic, and Neonatal Nursing*, 14 (2), 140–146.

Fischman, S., Rankin, E., Soeken, K., & Lenz, E. (1986). Changes in sexual relationships in postpartal couples. *Journal of Obstetric, Gynecologic, and Neonatal Nursing*, 15 (1), 58–63.

Gardner, D.L., & Campbell, B. (1991). Assessing postpartum fatigue. *MCN: American Journal of Maternal Child Nursing*, 16 (5), 264–266.

Gillerman, H., & Beckham, M.H. (1991). The postpartum early discharge dilemma: An innovative solution. *Journal of Perinatal Neonatal Nursing*, 15 (1), 9–17.

Gorrie, T.M. (1986). Postpartal nursing diagnosis. *Journal of Obstetric, Gynecologic, and Neonatal Nursing*, 15 (1), 58–64.

Hampson, S.J. (1989). Nursing interventions for the first three postpartum months. *Journal of Obstetric, Gynecologic, and Neonatal Nursing*, 18 (2), 116–122.

Inturrisi, M., Camegna, C., & Rosen, M. (1988). Epidural morphine for relief of postpartum, postsurgical pain. *Journal of Obstetric, Gynecologic, and Neonatal Nursing*, 17 (4), 238–243.

Jansson, P., (1985). Early postpartum discharge. *American Journal of Nursing*, 85 (5), 547–550.

Karb, V.B., Queener, S.F., & Freeman, J.B. (1989). *Handbook of drugs for nursing practice*. St. Louis: C.V. Mosby.

LaFoy, J., & Geden, E. (1989). Postepisiotomy pain: warm versus cold sitz bath. *Journal of Obstetric, Gynecologic, and Neonatal Nursing*, 18 (5), 399–403.

Lowe, N.K. (1987). Parity and pain. *Journal of Obstetric, Gynecologic, and Neonatal Nursing*, 16 (5), 340–347.

Luegenbiehl, D., Brophy, G., Artigue, G., Phillips, K., & Flack, R. (1990). Standardized assessment of blood loss. *MCN: American Journal of Maternal Child Nursing*, 15 (4), 241–244.

Lukacs, A. (1991). Issues surrounding early postpartum discharge: Effects on the caregiver. *Journal of Perinatal Neonatal Nursing*, 5 (1), 33–42.

Mahan, L.K., & Arlin, M. (1992). *Krause's food, nutrition, and diet therapy*. Philadelphia: W.B. Saunders.

Mercer, R.T., & Ferketich, S.L. (1990). Predictors of family functioning eight months following birth. *Nursing Research*, 39 (2), 76–83.

NAACOG Practice Resource (1991). *Postpartum nursing care: Vaginal delivery*. Washington, D.C.

Nine, S., Bayes, K., Christian, S., & Dillon, B. (1992). Organizing quality assurance in a maternal-child health division. *Journal of Obstetric, Gynecologic, and Neonatal Nursing*, 21 (1), 28–35.

Norr, K., Nacion, K., & Abramson, R. (1989). Early discharge with home follow-up: Impacts on low-income mothers and infants. *Journal of Obstetric, Gynecologic and Neonatal Nursing*, 18 (2), 133–142.

Reichert, J.A., Baron, M., & Fawcett, J. (1993). Changes in Attitudes toward cesarean birth. *Journal of Obstetric, Gynecologic, and Neonatal Nursing*, 22 (2), 159–167.

Resnik, R. (1989). The puerperium. In R.K. Creasy & R. Resnik (Eds.), *Maternal-fetal medicine: Principles and practice* (pp. 149–152). Philadelphia: W.B. Saunders.

Sternbach, G. (1989). John Homans: The dorsiflexion sign. *The Journal of Emergency Medicine*, 7 (5) 287–290.

Weiss, M.E., & Armstrong, M. (1991). Postpartum mothers' preference for nighttime care of the neonate. *Journal of Obstetric, Gynecologic, and Neonatal Nursing*, 20 (4), 290–298.

Wild, L., & Coyne, C. (1992). Epidural anesthesia: The basics and beyond. *American Journal of Nursing*, 92 (4), 26–37.

Williams, L.R., and Cooper, M.K. (1993). Nurse-managed postpartum home care. *Journal of Obstetric, Gynecologic, and Neonatal Nursing*, 22 (1), 25–32.

Worthington-Roberts, B., Vermeersch, R., & Williams, S. (1989). *Nutrition in pregnancy and lactation* (4th ed.). St. Louis: C.V. Mosby.

18

Postpartum Psychosocial Adaptations

Objectives

1. Explain the process of bonding and attachment, including maternal touch and verbal interactions.
2. Describe the progressive phases of maternal adaptation to childbirth and the stages of maternal role attainment.
3. Discuss postpartum blues in terms of cause, manifestations, and interventions.
4. Describe the processes of family adaptation (father, siblings, grandparents) to the birth of a baby.
5. Identify and discuss factors that affect family adaptation.
6. Discuss cultural influences on family adaptation.
7. Identify the components of psychosocial assessments and interventions for specific nursing diagnoses.

Definitions

Attachment • The development of strong affectional ties between an infant and a significant other (mother, father, sibling, caretaker).

Bonding • The development of a strong emotional tie to a newborn; also called "claiming" or "binding in."

En face • Position that allows eye-to-eye contact between the newborn and a parent; optimal distance is 20 to 22 cm (8 to 9 inches).

Engrossment • Intense fascination and close face-to-face observation between father and newborn.

Entrainment • Newborn movement in rhythm to adult speech, particularly high-pitched tones, which are more easily heard.

Finger-tipping • First tactile (touch) experience between mother and newborn; mother explores the infant's body with her finger tips only.

Fourth trimester • The first 12 weeks following birth; a time of transition for parents and siblings.

Letting-go • A phase of maternal adaptation that involves relinquishment of previous roles and assumption of a new role as a parent.

Postpartum blues • Temporary, self-limiting period of weepiness experienced by many new mothers within the first few days following childbirth.

Reciprocal bonding behaviors • Repertoire of infant behaviors that promote attachment between parent and newborn.

Sibling rivalry • Feelings of jealousy and fear of replacement when a young child must share the attention of the parents with a newborn infant.

Taking-hold • Second phase of maternal adaptation during which the mother assumes control of her own care and initiates care of the infant.

Taking-in • First phase of maternal adaptation during which the mother passively accepts care, comfort, and details of the newborn.

Perhaps no other event requires such a rapid change in lifestyle and role function as the birth of a baby. However, many parents are unprepared for the change and are overwhelmed by the needs of the newborn. One young father remarked that the first 6 weeks at home with the new infant were "tougher than boot camp in the Marine Corps." It is acknowledged that too much change can alter the processes of even the healthiest families and that information, anticipatory guidance, and support are necessary to maintain family structure and function following the birth of a child.

The role of maternity nurses has gradually expanded from the care of the mother-infant dyad to include the well-being of the entire family. Nurses are concerned about the family's adjustment to childbearing, not only during the hospital stay but also during the early weeks at home as they make the transition to parenthood.

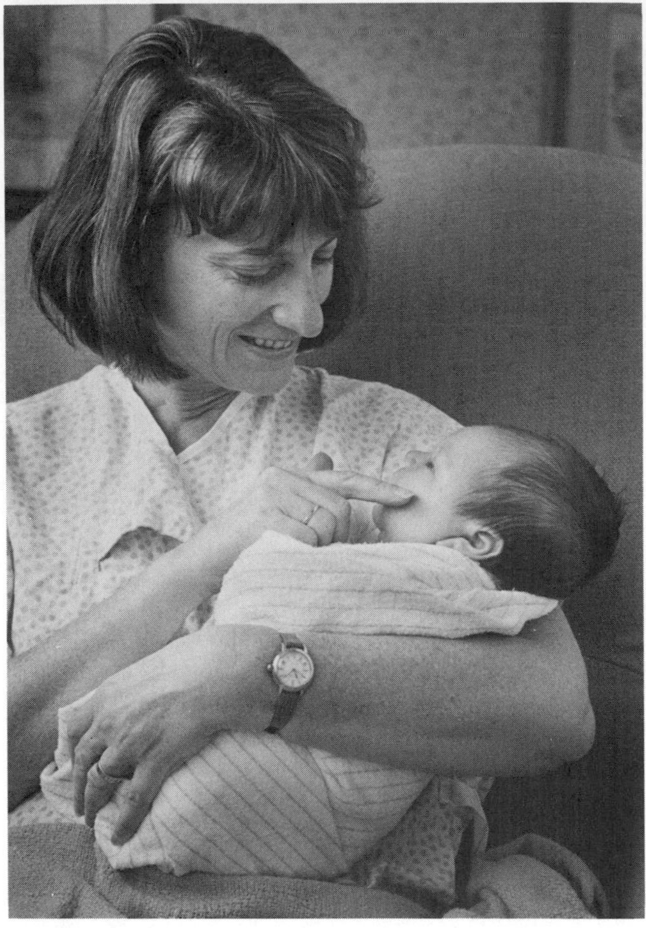

Figure 18–1

The infant is quiet and alert during the initial sensitive period. The newborn gazes at the mother and responds to her voice and touch. This mother is holding her infant in the *en face* position.

The Process of Becoming Acquainted

A great deal of information has appeared in nursing literature in recent years that describes how parents and newborns become acquainted and progress to develop feelings of love, concern, and deep devotion that last throughout life. The terms bonding and attachment are commonly used to describe the initial steps. Although the terms are often used interchangeably, theoretically there is a difference.

Bonding

Bonding has been described as the initial attraction felt by the parent; it is unidirectional, from parent to child, and is initiated and enhanced by eye contact, skin-to-skin contact, and suckling.

Much has been made in recent years of the necessity for parents and infants to have contact during the *sensitive period*—that is, the time when the infant is in a quiet, alert stage and is able to respond to parents and thus elicit the feeling of "falling in love" that has been used to describe bonding. The quiet, alert stage is believed to extend through the first 30 to 60 minutes following birth. During this time, the newborn's eyes are open; he or she seems to gaze directly at the parents and responds physically to parental voice and touch (Fig. 18–1).

Nurses frequently delay procedures that can interfere with this time between parents and newborns. Instillation of prophylactic eye medication, administration of vitamin K injections, and measurements of the head, chest, and length are often postponed so that the parents can have this time with the newborn babies.

Attachment

Regarding the topic of attachment, three concepts must be emphasized:

- Attachment is a process that follows a progressive or developmental course that changes over time. It is rarely instantaneous.
- Attachment is facilitated by positive feedback, either real or perceived; thus, an infant's grasp reflex around a parent's finger means "I love you," to the parent.
- Attachment occurs through mutually satisfying experiences; therefore, if the newly delivered mother is in severe pain or is physically ex-

Critical to Remember

Reciprocal Attachment Behaviors

Newborn infants have the ability to:

- Make eye contact and engage in prolonged, intense, mutual gazing
- Move their eyes and attempt to "track" the parent's face
- Grasp the parent's finger and hold on
- Move synchronously in response to rhythms and patterns of the parent's voice; synchronized movement is called *entrainment*
- Root, suckle, and finally latch on to the breast
- Be comforted by the parent's voice or touch

hausted, pain relief or assistance, or both, are needed for her to enjoy the early experiences with the baby (Mercer & Ferketich, 1990b).

Attachment is reciprocal, that is, going in both directions between parent and infant. For attachment to occur, there must be some response from the infant to parental signals. Infants are not "blank tablets"; instead, they have a whole repertoire of responses called reciprocal attachment behaviors, and they are the infant's part in the process of early attachment that progresses to lifelong mutual devotion.

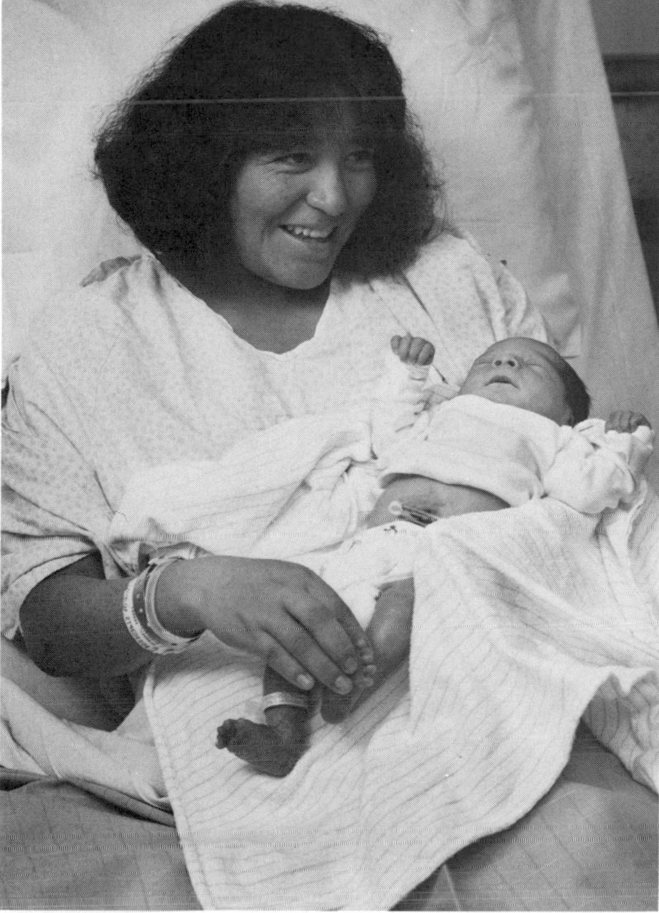

Figure 18–2

The mother's initial touch includes *finger-tipping*, whereby she becomes acquainted with her infant by touching only with her finger tips.

MATERNAL TOUCH

Maternal behavior, particularly maternal touch, changes rapidly as the mother progresses through a discovery phase with her infant. Initially, the mother may not reach for the infant, but if the infant is placed in her arms, she will hold the baby in the cradle hold, with the infant's face in the same vertical plane as her own. This is called the *en face* position, and mothers and infants can be observed to engage in prolonged mutual gazing (see Fig. 18–1).

Initially, the mother needs time to get acquainted with the tiny stranger. She may gently explore the infant's face, fingers, and toes with her finger tips only. This finger-tipping, which is common during the early minutes, is illustrated in Figure 18–2.

Most mothers will "finger-tip" the infant for only a few minutes and then will begin to stroke the chest and legs with the palm. Next, they will use the entire hand to enfold the infant and to bring him or her close to their body. After this, mothers typically reach out with both hands and arms for the infant and no longer wait for the infant to be placed. They hold the newborn closer, stroke the hair, press the cheek against the infant's cheek, and will finally feel comfortable enough to engage in a full range of consoling behaviors.

The mother next begins to identify specific features of the newborn (Fig. 18–3). "Look how big his hands and feet are." Then she begins to relate features to family members. "He has his dad's chin and mouth, but I think his eyes and nose are like mine." This identification process has been termed *claiming*, or *binding-in* (Rubin, 1977). The process is also called bonding (Klaus and Kennell, 1982).

VERBAL BEHAVIORS

Verbal behaviors are also important indicators of maternal attachment. Most mothers speak to the infant in a high-pitched voice and progress from calling the baby "it" to "he or she" and then to using the given name. "I cannot believe it is here" rapidly becomes "Brian is such a good boy." Verbal behaviors may provide clues to a mother's early psycho-

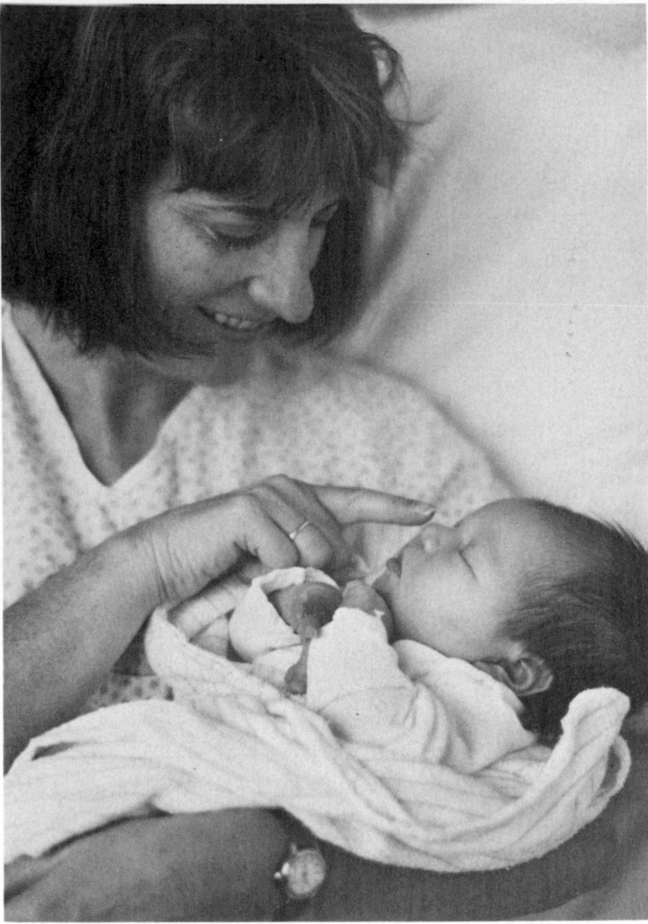

Figure 18–3

The *binding-in* or *bonding* process includes the mother's identification of her baby's specific features, relating them to other family members.

logical relationship to her infant. Mothers with the highest non-verbal attachment behaviors have also been found to be considerably more active in verbal behaviors (Tomlinson, 1990). Nurses are in a position to observe interactions of mothers and their infants and, if necessary, to teach and model interactions that foster early attachment between them.

✔ Check Your Reading

1. What is meant by the "sensitive period"? Why is this important in the attachment process?
2. How does maternal touch change over time?
3. How does verbal interaction change over time?

Process of Maternal Adaptation

Puerperal Phases

Nurses have been aware for many years that adjustment to parenthood is a gradual process and not an instant reaction to the birth of a child. In the early 1960s, Rubin identified restorative phases that the mother must go through to replenish the energy lost during labor and to attain comfort in the role of mother. The phases are called taking-in, taking-hold, and letting-go and for 30 years they have been used to plan and implement nursing care during the postpartum period.

Although many aspects of maternity care have changed and Rubin's original study has been questioned, contemporary investigation tends to support the concept that mothers do progress through fairly discrete phases of recovery—however, at a more rapid rate than was first thought (Martell and Mitchell, 1984; Ament, 1990). It is suggested that the phases provide a useful method to observe progressive change in maternal behavior but should not be used as strict guidelines for maternal assessment; rather, they can be used to anticipate maternal needs and to intervene to meet the needs.

TAKING-IN PHASE

Nurses who are not aware that maternal behaviors progress through phases are sometimes puzzled by the mother's early reaction to childbirth when she seems primarily focused on her own needs rather than on her infant. Her primary needs are for fluid and food and for deep restorative sleep to replenish the energy expended during labor. During this phase, she is often passive and dependent as she takes in food, attention, and physical care. She seldom makes suggestions for care or initiates contact with the infant, although she takes in or absorbs every detail of the neonate. She seems content to allow others to make decisions and complies with the hospital routine.

The mother also begins to integrate her birth experience fully into reality by recounting the details of her labor and delivery over and over. She spends a great deal of time on the telephone describing her labor and the birth of this child. She repeats her experiences for visitors and attempts to piece together all the details from those who were involved. This process helps the mother realize that the pregnancy is over; the infant is born, and is now an individual separate from her. Although Rubin believed the taking-in phase lasted for approximately 2 days, current investigators observed the behaviors for 24 hours or less (Ament, 1990).

The taking-in phase may be prolonged when a cesarean birth has been necessary. Studies suggest that women who had a cesarean birth require continued attention and sensitive care that takes into account their special needs for pain relief and sustained contact with their newborn (Reichert et al, 1993).

TAKING-HOLD PHASE

The mother becomes more independent in the taking-hold phase. She exhibits concern about managing her own body functions, particularly bowel and bladder elimination, and assumes responsibility for her own self-care. When she feels more comfortable and in control of her body, she gradually shifts her attention from her own needs to the performance of the infant. She compares her infant with other infants to validate wellness and wholeness. She welcomes information about the wide variation exhibited by newborns. Parents enjoy learning that the infant can see and hear, and they frequently ask if their infant is stronger, bigger, more alert, calmer, or more active than other infants.

During the taking-hold phase, the mother may verbalize a great deal of anxiety about her competence as a mother (see Therapeutic Communication). She may compare her caretaking skills unfavorably with those of the nurse. *Nurses must be careful not to assume the mothering role but instead allow the mother to perform as much of the caretaking as possible and to praise each attempt, even if the mother's early care is awkwardly performed.*

Therapeutic Communication

Fawn Jackson is a nurse in the postpartum unit. When she enters the room of Tamara Bradley, a new mother, she finds the woman crying.

Tamara: (crying) I can't do anything right. The pediatrician just asked me a bunch of questions, and I couldn't answer any of them.

Fawn: In fact, you are doing a lot right, but it is distressing when you feel you don't have all the answers.

Offering reassurance and acknowledging feelings

Tamara: Well, he just fired the questions at me and I couldn't think so fast.

Fawn: You feel that you're not measuring up because you couldn't answer the questions?

Paraphrasing and focusing on Tamara's feelings

Tamara: Well, I want to be a good mother, but I'm so worried that I won't know what to do.

Fawn: You're concerned that you don't have all the answers.

Reflecting feelings without leading

Tamara: There is just so much to caring for a baby. I don't know where to start.

Fawn: You don't feel confident about how to take care of the baby. What concerns you most?

Reflecting feelings and inviting the mother to describe specific concerns

By allowing Tamara to express her feelings, Fawn has helped dissipate the feelings and set the stage for effective teaching.

Because of early discharge, teaching must be started before the mother has reached this phase; however, this is the ideal time to teach because of a heightened readiness to learn. The taking-hold phase has been called the "teachable, reachable, referrable moment," and the mother will respond enthusiastically to instruction and demonstration of infant care.

LETTING-GO PHASE

The letting-go phase is believed to occur after the mother has returned home, and it is a time of relinquishment for the mother and often for the father. If it is a first child, the couple must give up their previous role as childless couple and acknowledge the loss of a carefree lifestyle. Many mothers must also give up idealized expectations of the birth experience. For example, they may have planned to have a vaginal delivery with minimal or no anesthesia and instead they required a cesarean delivery or regional anesthesia. In addition, some mothers (and fathers) are disappointed in the size, sex, or characteristics of the infant who does not "match up" with the fantasy baby of pregnancy. They must relinquish the infant of their fantasies and accept the real infant. These losses often provoke feelings of grief; the feelings may be so subtle that they are unexamined or unacknowledged. Both parents may benefit, however, if given the opportunity to verbalize feelings that are unexpected and to realize that these feelings are not uncommon. If the mother is very young or the pregnancy was unplanned, the feelings of loss and grief may be acute.

Change in Body Image

Coping with a changing body that is no longer pregnant but has not yet fully returned to pre-pregnancy size causes some mothers additional concern. Many mothers are prepared for the changes in body image, and the temporary alteration in body function is of little concern. Others may grieve for the loss of their pre-pregnant figure (Mercer, 1986). Many mothers begin to ask questions about abdominal exercises, weight loss, and stretch marks, or they may have questions about the effect of pregnancy and breastfeeding on the size and shape of the breasts. In addition, body function, which contributes to body image, is temporarily altered by fatigue, sleep deprivation, and discomfort.

Postpartum Blues

Postpartum blues, also known as "baby blues" or "maternity blues," is a mild, transient condition that affects 75 to 80 per cent of American women who have just given birth. Postpartum blues has an early onset (1 to 10 days after a woman has given birth) and usually lasts no longer than 2 weeks (Ugarriza, 1992). It is characterized by fatigue, weeping, mood instability, anxiety, mild confusion, and hostility toward the husband (Landry et al, 1989). The symptoms are usually unrelated to events, and the condition does not seriously affect the ability of the mother to care for the infant. Typically, the mother will say, "I do not know why I am crying; I do not feel sad." Although the direct cause is unknown, it is generally accepted that postpartum blues is related to the wide hormonal fluctuations that occur during labor, delivery, and the immediate postpartum period. Postpartum blues is self-limiting and requires only support and empathy for full recovery.

This condition is frequently ignored by the health care team because of its self-limiting nature and brief duration. As a result, most postpartum women are not supported during this distressing episode. Many mothers are confused about what causes the weeping and anxious feelings when they thought they would be feeling joy and contentment. It is very helpful if nurses reassure the mother that what she is experiencing is normal; this is frequently enough to allay much of the anxiety caused by lack of knowledge. A few moments of support and focusing on the mother's feelings at this time can be a very meaningful nursing intervention.

Family members, who are frequently baffled by the mood swings of the new mother, may respond by becoming angry or anxious themselves or by ignoring or minimizing the emotional responses of the mother. Family members must be educated about the signs and symptoms and duration of postpartum blues. With adequate information, they are able to respond with supportive techniques such as active listening and empathetic responses to the mother.

Postpartum blues must be distinguished from *postpartum depression* and *postpartum psychosis*. These are separate entities that are disabling and require therapeutic management for full recovery. (See Chapter 27 for a more detailed discussion of postpartum depression and postpartum psychosis.)

Role Attainment

Role attainment is the process by which a mother (or a father) learns parenting behaviors and becomes comfortable in the role of parent. The transition to the maternal or paternal role follows four stages (Mercer, 1985):

1. *The anticipatory stage* begins during the pregnancy when couples choose a physician or nurse-midwife and the location for the infant's birth. Many attend childbirth classes in order to be prepared and to have some control over the birth experience. The expectant mother seeks out role models for learning how to go about assuming the role of mother.
2. *The formal stage* begins with the birth of the infant and continues for approximately 6 to 8 weeks (Mercer, 1990). During this stage, behaviors are largely guided by others: health professionals, close friends, or parents. A major task during this stage is for the parents to become acquainted with their infant so that they can mesh their parenting activities with cues from the infant.
3. *The informal stage* begins after the parents have learned appropriate responses to their infant's cues or signals. They then begin to respond according to the unique needs of the infant rather than following textbook or health professionals' directives.
4. *The personal stage* is attained when the parent feels a sense of harmony in the role, enjoys the infant, sees the infant as a central person in his or her life, and has internalized the parental role. This means that the parent accepts the role of parent and feels comfortable in this role. The range of time for achieving the parental role is highly variable, but most parents feel they have achieved it by 4 months (Mercer, 1986).

✔ Check Your Reading

4. How do maternal behaviors in the taking-in phase differ from those in the taking-hold phase?
5. What does the mother relinquish in the letting-go phase?
6. What causes postpartum blues? How can nurses intervene for this common emotional response?
7. How does the mother progress through the stages of role attainment?

The Processes of Family Adaptation

No matter whether this is the first baby or the fifth, the birth of a new infant creates the need for reorganization of family structure and function. The previously childless couple abruptly and irrevocably becomes a family. Parents with children must now integrate a new member into the family unit, whereas siblings must adapt to a new standing in the family structure.

Paternal Adjustment

At present, most birthing centers and hospitals allow the father to be present throughout labor and childbirth, and many allow siblings to be present if they have taken classes that prepare them for childbirth. It has been thought that fathers who were active participants in the birth experienced early bonding and developed stronger ties to the newborn. Research indicates, however, that other factors, such as readiness for fatherhood, personality traits, an ongoing relationship with the mother, and previous life experiences, are more important variables (May and Perrin, 1985).

Paternal behaviors have been observed to parallel behaviors of the mother during initial contact with the infant. Fathers are fascinated with the infant and respond with concern to infant signals. The term engrossment is frequently used to describe the intense fascination that fathers exhibit when they first interact with the newborn (Fig. 18–4). There is little research that compares attachment behaviors of fathers with those of mothers; however, fathers demonstrate similar attachment behaviors in the early postpartum period and throughout the infant's first year of life (Mercer & Ferketich, 1990b).

Many fathers eagerly look forward to co-parenting their infant with their mate; however, they may lack confidence in providing infant care and are sensitive to being left out of instructions and demonstrations of infant care. Many report that they receive the pervasive message that their major role is to support the mother (Jordan, 1990). One father said he had been treated as a "fifth wheel" and resented patronizing remarks about his awkwardness when he handled the infant.

Nurses must be sensitive to fathers' needs and involve them in teaching sessions and parenting decisions whenever possible.

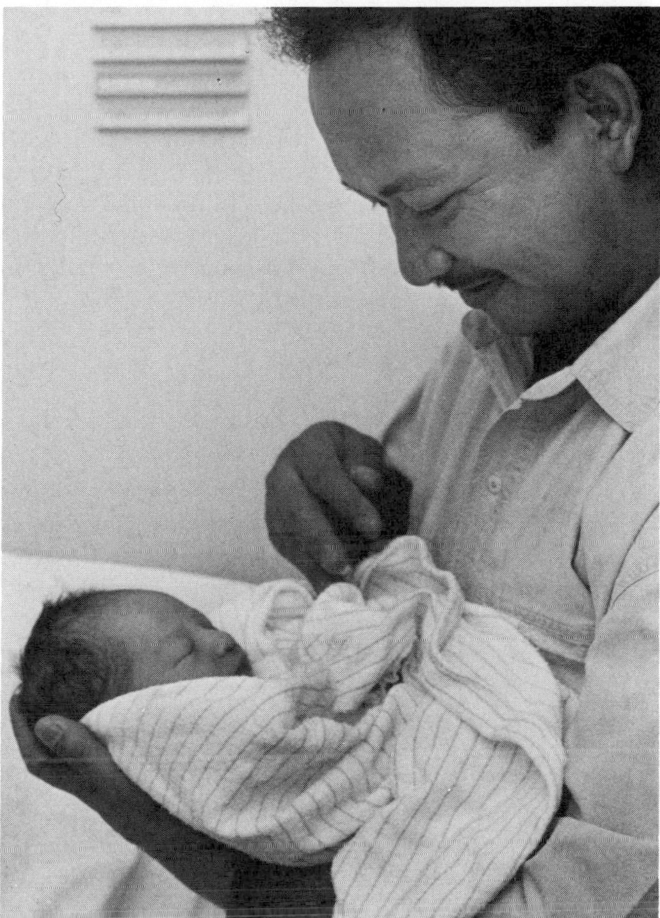

***Figure* 18–4**

Fathers' behaviors at initial contact with their infants often correspond with maternal behaviors. The intense fascination that fathers exhibit is called *engrossment*.

Siblings

Little research has been done on early attachment between siblings and their new brother or sister. Most siblings younger than 5 years of age engage in more looking than touching, and they tend to focus on the infant's head and face. The majority spend at least some time in close proximity to the infant and talk to the mother about the infant; some will kiss or hug the new baby. Girls tend to position themselves closer to the baby than do boys. Prenatal sibling education classes produce no significant difference in behavior (Marecki et al, 1985).

Sibling response to the birth of a new brother or sister depends on age and developmental level. Toddlers are usually not completely aware of the impending birth until they see the infant with either the mother or the father. The birth of an infant can be considered a crisis for young siblings. They may view the infant as competition or fear that they will be replaced in the parents' affection. Negative behaviors may surface and indicate the degree of stress the youngster feels. These behaviors include sleep problems, an increase in attention-seeking efforts, and regression to more infantile behaviors, such as renewed bed-wetting or thumb sucking. Some may exhibit hostile behaviors toward the mother, particularly when she holds or feeds the newborn. These behaviors are manifestations of the jealousy and frustration that young children feel as they observe the mother's attention being given to another. Parents must find opportunities to affirm their continued love and affection for the very vulnerable sibling.

It is recommended that a relaxed, natural setting, without time constraints, may make it easier for young children to interact with the infant. Special care must be taken by the parents and grandparents to pay as much attention to the sibling as to the new baby. Nurses are also urged to acknowledge the visiting sibling, and many hospitals now give small gifts to "big brother" or "big sister."

Grandparents

The involvement of grandparents with grandchildren depends on many factors. One of the most important factors is proximity. Grandparents who live near enough to see the child frequently often develop strong attachment that evolves into unconditional love and a special relationship that brings joy to the grandparents and an added sense of security to the grandchildren.

Often grandparents live hundreds or thousands of miles from grandchildren, and their contact is, of necessity, sporadic. It is more difficult to form a close attachment when there is infrequent contact, and many grandparents spend time trying to devise ways to foster a relationship with grandchildren they seldom see.

Expectations of the role of grandparents is also a factor in how the grandparents adapt to the birth of a grandchild. Many grandparents feel that the grandparents' role is second in importance to the role of parents, and they strive to be fully involved in the care and upbringing of the child. Others desire less involvement, and this may cause some conflict with parents or it may be a comfortable arrangement with both families.

Grandparents are often a major part of the support system that new parents need. Grandmothers, in particular, provide assistance with household tasks and infant care, which allows the mother to recover from childbirth and make the transition to parenthood (Fig. 18–5). The birth of a grandchild allows grandfathers the opportunity to nurture. They may have been too busy providing for their own children to fully enjoy this aspect of parenting, and their sons or daughters may be surprised at this previously undiscovered aspect of their fathers. One young father remarked, "I cannot get over how my father cuddles and plays with the baby; I do not remember that he ever played with me when I was a child."

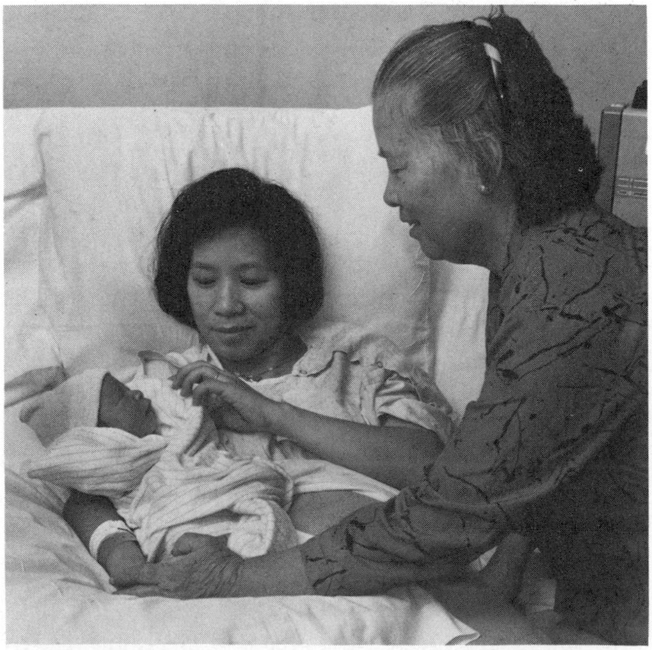

Figure 18–5

Grandmother may ease the mother's adaptation to the new role of parent. She can reinforce cultural customs, help with infant care, and assist with household tasks.

The Fourth Trimester

The first 12 weeks following the birth of an infant have been termed the "fourth trimester," when the family must adapt to changes in family relationships and roles. The couple must renegotiate their relationship while establishing a relationship with the infant. Children must work out their own standing in the family structure and begin to relate to the new infant. Past patterns and past roles must be reordered, and this may produce stress in the family.

REDEFINING ROLES

The mother is particularly concerned about redefining roles and focuses on maintaining a strong, adaptive relationship with her partner. She observes him carefully for any change in behavior and is acutely sensitive to his interaction with the infant. From the father's perspective, anxieties about succeeding in his new role put added pressure on the family. Conflicting demands between work and home, feelings of exclusion, and concerns about his relationship with his partner present additional challenges.

It may be essential for the new parents to agree on a division of tasks and responsibilities that was not necessary before the birth of the infant. This is accomplished quickly and with very little discord in some families. Role assignment in other families is much less flexible, and any change can be a source of tension and frustration.

Nurses must be aware of the need to redefine roles and the stress this process can create within the family. Although nurses are not actively involved in redefining family roles, they can use their skills in communication to assist the family in expressing their feelings and concerns so that the changes can be accomplished with minimum stress.

ROLE CONFLICT

Role conflict occurs when one's perception of role responsibilities differs significantly from reality. For example, if the mother perceives that her responsibility is to provide care and comfort for the infant, but reality dictates that she must place the infant with another caregiver and return to full-time employment, role conflict may occur. Nearly 2 million women face this conflict each year, and many report feelings of guilt for leaving the infant and experience intense "separation grief" when they first leave the infant with a caregiver. Some report feeling jealous of the caregiver and fear that they will be supplanted by him or her in the infant's affection.

Acknowledging the feelings and reassuring the mother that her emotions are normal may be helpful. The mother needs time to re-establish feelings of closeness when she comes home from work, and she needs to develop a schedule that allows maximum time with the infant when she is at home. This may involve negotiating with another family member to take over some of the household tasks until the mother feels more comfortable with the situation.

Many mothers try to do everything and fall into a "superwoman syndrome" as they try to earn needed income to contribute to the family needs, fulfill the role of mother to their satisfaction, and continue to maintain the home and fulfill the role of wife. Attempting to do all this may result in frustration and fatigue and can greatly diminish the joys of parenting.

Factors Affecting Family Adaptation

Numerous factors influence the family's adjustment. Some can be anticipated because they are so common; lingering discomfort and chronic fatigue in the mother are almost universal. Additional factors include knowledge of infant needs, expectations of the infant, previous experience, age of the parents, and the temperaments of the mother and the infant. Unanticipated events, such as cesarean birth, birth of a preterm or ill infant, or the birth of twins, also affect the ease and speed with which the family adjusts.

Lingering Discomfort and Fatigue

Normally, discomfort associated with childbirth, such as breast engorgement, perineal pain, or afterpains, resolve within the first few days following the birth. Although the discomfort is acute, however, it may be difficult for the mother to obtain adequate rest and to focus on the needs of the newborn. Fatigue often remains a problem during the first few weeks, when the infant's schedule is erratic and there is little chance for uninterrupted sleep. When the infant begins to sleep through the night (at about 16 weeks), the parents can once again establish familiar patterns, and fatigue becomes less of a factor.

Knowledge of Infant Needs

Parents experience powerful feelings of protectiveness when they discover that they can console their infants and that the infants respond to their care. First-time parents, in particular, are often unsure of how to care for the newborn and become very anxious if they are unable to comfort or console a crying infant. Moreover, many are concerned about specific procedures, such as care of the umbilical cord or the circumcision. They want to know if the infant is receiving adequate nutrition. Breastfeeding benefits both mother and infant; however, initially it adds to the stress that parents experience. Is the infant getting enough milk? What happens until the milk comes in? How often should one nurse? (Chapter 21 provides detailed information about breastfeeding, and Chapter 22 discusses early parenting.)

Some parents have concerns about spoiling the infant. They are particularly concerned about responding each time the infant cries and believe that this causes the child to cry to get his or her way. It may be necessary to remind the parents that infants cry to indicate a need: they are hungry, cold, or wet, or they need to be cuddled or gently stimulated. It is important to reassure the parents that responding to infant crying does not spoil the child. It is helpful to point out that a prompt, gentle response when the infant cries helps him or her to develop trust that the world is a safe, secure place. This is a basic developmental task of infancy that depends on the child's knowing he or she can trust caregivers to respond consistently and gently.

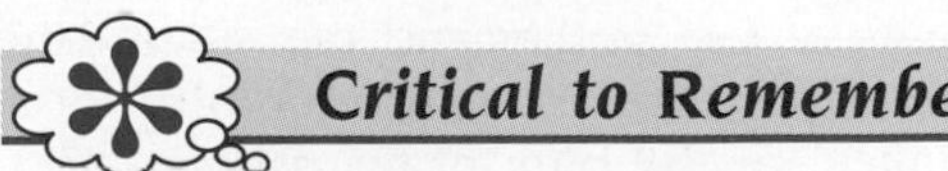

Factors That Affect Adaptation

- Lingering discomfort or pain
- Chronic fatigue
- Knowledge of infant needs
- Available support system
- Expectations of the newborn
- Previous experience with infants
- Maternal personality
- Infant characteristics
- Unanticipated events: cesarean birth, preterm or ill infant, or birth of more than one infant (twins)

Previous Experience

Previous experience with newborns may also affect maternal attachment. As expected, multiparas are more comfortable with infants and exhibit attachment behaviors earlier than do primiparas, who may spend many more hours in the taking-in phase and in the early discovery phase of attachment. Mothers who have previously given birth to infants with anomalies or to infants who did not survive may need more time to feel comfortable with the child.

Expectations for the Newborn

Unrealistic expectations of the infant may also influence adjustment. Many parents have very little experience with newborns and are disappointed at the way a newborn looks. They are unprepared for the normal characteristics of newborns, such as cranial molding, blotchy skin, and blue hands and feet. They may have anticipated that the infant would be able to smile and would sleep through the night.

Nurses must be prepared to teach normal growth and development and to assist the parents in working through their misconceptions. The capacity of an infant's stomach is small, and the infant must be fed frequently. Also, infants are neurologically unable to sleep through the night for several weeks. They begin to smile in about 5 to 6 weeks, but they are able to see and hear from the time of birth.

Some mothers may be very disappointed in the sex of the child, or they may sense that their partners are disappointed. These feelings must be acknowledged and dealt with before attachment can take place. One mother, who already had four sons, was so disappointed when the fifth child turned out to be a boy that she cried for several hours and refused to see the infant. Her grief continued until she held the baby and began to observe differences and make comparisons with her other sons. This began her discovery period with this unique child.

Maternal Age

Adjustment to parenthood requires that a parent of any age reorganize self-perceptions, family roles, and routine activities. These changes are an extra challenge to the teenager who has not completed the developmental tasks of adolescence and must now make the transition to the role of parent.

The maturing adolescent has difficulty maintaining intimate relationships before a secure individual identity is achieved, usually in late adolescence. Intimacy is a necessary component of the parent-infant relationship, and this may make adaptation to the role of parent difficult for young adolescents.

In general, teenagers tend to talk less, respond less, appear more passive, and sometimes appear less affectionate with their children than do adult parents (Comfort et al, 1987). Clearly, teenaged mothers and fathers need special assistance to develop necessary parenting skills that will promote optimal development of the infant. (Additional information regarding teenaged parenting is presented in Chapter 23.)

Maternal Personality

Maternal personality traits are a major influence on attachment. Mothers who are calm, secure in their ability to learn, and free from unnecessary anxiety adjust more easily to the demands of motherhood. Conversely, mothers who are excitable, insecure, and anxious have more difficulty. Mothers who are aware that it takes time for the body to return to its prepregnancy weight and who do not insist on rigorous dieting or an unrealistic exercise regimen adjust more easily.

Temperament of the Infant

The infant is also a factor in maternal adjustment. Infants who are calm, easily consoled, and enjoy cuddling increase parental confidence and feelings of competence. Conversely, irritable infants who are difficult to console and who do not need or respond to cuddling increase parental frustration and interfere with attachment.

Availability of Strong Support System

A strong, consistent support system is a major factor in the adjustment of the new mother. She needs assistance with household tasks such as meal preparation, laundry, and shopping. In addition she needs encouragement, praise, and reassurance that she is a good mother. It is very important to her that others see that the baby is special and that they demonstrate love and affection (see Therapeutic Communication).

Unanticipated Events

Unanticipated events can make parental adjustment more difficult. For example, an unplanned cesarean birth may result in financial strain, a longer recovery time for the mother, additional discomfort, and increased stress for the family. Birth of a preterm or ill infant results in additional concern for the condition of the infant and may necessitate prolonged separation of parents and child. This may delay the process of attachment and create stress on the normally functioning family.

Even if expected, the birth of more than one infant may present problems of attachment. It is believed the process of attachment is structured so that the parents become attached to only one infant at a time, and parents should be encouraged to interact with each child individually, especially in the early getting acquainted period. Nurses must help the parents to relate to each infant as an individual rather than as part of a unit by pointing out the individual responses and uniqueness of each infant. Early, frequent contacts or rooming-in helps the parents gain confidence in caretaking and facilitates the attachment process. Support and instruction should continue when the family goes home. Some nurses assist the mother in making up a specific schedule for infant care that may prove helpful, at least initially. Keeping records of when each infant was fed and bathed or when each voided or had a bowel movement may be helpful when fatigue is a problem and the parents may forget whose turn it is. However, the schedule should be flexible because it is likely to be interrupted frequently.

Breastfeeding should be encouraged, and the mother needs to be reassured that she will produce an ample supply of milk for each infant, since supply increases as demand increases. (For additional information about breastfeeding twins, see Chapter 21.) Parents often benefit from referral to a support group composed of the parents of twins, and nurses should be aware of groups in their community.

Therapeutic Communication

Janet Lawson gave birth to a baby boy 8 days ago. Robin Richards was her nurse following delivery. Robin has called Janet at home to check on the family's adjustments after discharge.

Janet: My life has changed completely, I spend all my time caring for the baby. I don't have time for anything else.

Robin: It feels as if you don't have a free moment?

Paraphrasing content without leading or probing

Janet: Well, Phillip goes to work and his life is just the same. I'm the one who is stuck at home and never gets out.

Robin: You feel confined and wish you could get out more as Phillip does.

Reflecting underlying feeling, encouraging Janet to pursue topic

Janet: Actually, I feel a lot of resentment even though I really want to be home with the baby and love taking care of him.

Robin: It is a dilemma; you want to be home with the baby but feel isolated and resentful. Does Phillip know how you feel?

Paraphrasing and summarizing content and exploring communication between parents

Janet: Well, I haven't told him, but he ought to know; he can see I never get out and I'm tired most of the time.

Robin: You wish he would notice that you're tired and frustrated.

Reflecting content and feelings

Janet: Well, what can he do about it anyway? He has to go to work.

Robin: Sounds like you think you will have to deal with it. What would make you feel better?

Reflecting content and inviting the mother to begin to think of solutions

By reflecting, paraphrasing, and summarizing, Robin assists Janet in expressing and clarifying her feelings before initiating problem solving.

✔ Check Your Reading

8. What does a father mean when he says he feels like a "fifth wheel"?
9. What feelings may siblings experience when a new baby is born into the family?
10. How does the birth of twins affect parental attachment?

Cultural Influences on Adaptation

The major goal of nursing practice in the postpartum period is to provide nursing care that is culture-specific; that is, it fits the health beliefs, values, and practices of a particular culture. This is difficult because of the increasing ethnic diversity in countries such as the United States and Canada. A major challenge for nurses in the postpartum period is to be aware of cultural beliefs and to acknowledge their importance in family adaptation. Many cultural factors that are relevant to the postpartum period can be grouped into communication, dietary practices, and health beliefs.

COMMUNICATION

Verbal communication may be difficult because of the numerous dialects and languages spoken. A translator should be fluent in the language, of the same religion, and of the same country of origin if possible. This is particularly important for Middle Eastern families whose religious orientation may vary widely and who have longstanding social and religious conflicts (Murray and Zentners, 1989).

Respecting the privacy and modesty of all families is important, but modesty is especially important to Latinas, Middle Eastern women, and Asian women.

Tactfulness and warmth are important to remember for health care workers who place a premium on efficiency and feel that they must come directly to the point. This type of communication can be distressing, particularly for Latinas (ancestry from Mexico, Central America, and South America) and Native Americans, who approach a subject only after polite and gracious comments have been exchanged.

When the nurse and the family speak different primary languages, it is important to verify that the family has understood what is being said. An affirmative nod may be a sign of courtesy rather than signifying understanding or agreement. To be certain the message has been received, the nurse should ask the family to repeat in their own words what they have been told.

DIETARY PRACTICES

Dietary practices that are most obvious center around the hot-cold theory of health and diet. Hot-cold has nothing to do with temperature but with intrinsic properties of certain foods. For example, following childbirth Southeast Asians (Cambodians, Vietnamese, Hmongs, and Laotians) believe that the woman should eat only "hot" foods, such as eggs, chicken, and rice. "Hot" foods help to replace blood that was lost during childbirth.

Some Chinese believe that a combination of yin and yang maintains balance. Yin foods include bean sprouts, broccoli, carrots, and cauliflower. Yang foods include broiled meat, chicken, soup, and eggs.

HEALTH BELIEFS

Many cultural beliefs and practices provide a sense of security to new mothers. For example, Muslims believe that the first sounds a child hears should be from the Koran in praise and supplication to God (Allah), and parents want to say a prayer in the newly born child's ears at the time of birth. Allowing this practice will go a long way toward building trust in the relationship with the family.

Many Middle Eastern families believe that compliments should be directed to Allah rather than to the newborn, so the compliment is converted into a blessing so that mistrust or jealousy does not occur. Some Southeast Asians believe the spirit resides in the head and are troubled if someone pats or rubs the head of the newborn.

Health beliefs having to do with breastfeeding and hygiene cause the most conflict in the postpartum period. Southeast Asians and Latinas believe that the mother should be kept warm to avoid upsetting the balance of hot and cold. Some women refuse to take baths or wash their hair during the postpartum period. This practice is upsetting for nurses who are concerned about hygiene. A great deal of tact and sensitivity is required to find a compromise. Many Southeast Asian women believe that colostrum is "unclean" and that they should not breastfeed until the milk comes in. This conflicts with the belief that breastfeeding should start as soon after birth as possible. It may be helpful to determine when the woman believes the milk comes in and how the infant is fed until there is an adequate supply of breast milk.

Application of Nursing Process

Maternal Adaptation

Assessment

Several factors can affect maternal adaptation to the birth. Table 18–1 summarizes the assessment of the mother and nursing considerations related to each assessment.

PROGRESSION THROUGH PUERPERAL PHASES

It is necessary to observe how the mother is progressing through the puerperal phases of taking-in, taking-hold, or letting-go so that appropriate nursing

Table 18–1. ASSESSING MATERNAL ADAPTATION

Assessments	Nursing Considerations
Puerperal Phases	
Taking-in	Passive, dependent on nurses for assistance; recounts birth experience; does not initiate care of infant
Taking-hold	More autonomous, assumes control of own care, actively seeks information, concerned about ability to be a good mother
Letting-go	Relinquishes fantasy baby; begins to adapt to body changes; gives up role as childless person; begins to integrate concept of self as mother
Maternal Mood	
Mood and energy level, eye contact, posture, and comfort	Tense body posture, crying, or anxiety may indicate the beginning of postpartum blues, fatigue, or discomfort
Factors That Affect Maternal Adaptation	
Age of mother	May need additional support if < 18 years of age
Gravida and para status	Primiparas often progress through puerperal phases at a slower pace and may require additional assistance Multiparas often have more experience and knowledge of infant care Previous birth of a child with anomalies, or death of an infant may create anxiety and delay adaptation
Type of delivery	Cesarean birth may result in increased discomfort and longer recovery
Interaction with Infant	
Maternal touch	Mother progresses from "finger-tipping" to enfolding and comforting behaviors
Verbal interaction	Mother may call infant "it" initially but quickly progresses to using given name and identifying specific characteristics
Response to infant cues or signals	Prompt, gentle, consistent response indicates progressive adaptation to parenting role
Preparation for Parenting	
Classes in breastfeeding, parenting, or infant care	Many mothers feel more prepared after completing classes and participate in care sooner

care can be provided. Behaviors that should be noted include the mother's need to rest, her need to recount the details of her labor and childbirth, and her readiness to learn infant care and assume control of her own care.

MOOD

Observations of the general energy level and mood of the mother are also important. Lethargy, mood swings, and weepiness may suggest the onset of postpartum blues or the need for further assessment of the mother's physical comfort as well as factors that affect her adaptation to the birth of this child.

FACTORS AFFECTING ATTACHMENT

Mothers must be assessed for factors that affect maternal adaptation. If the mother is younger than 18 years of age, additional support and information, as well as an assessment of her support system, may be required. Knowledge of infant needs and care must be assessed. What previous experience does she have? How does she respond to infant signals such as crying or fussing? In general, mothers who have had children require less instruction and progress through the puerperal phases more rapidly than do first-time mothers.

The temperaments of both mother and infant affect adaptation. Is the mother anxious? Calm and relaxed? Uncertain of parenting skills? Questions such as, "What concerns you most?" often elicit important information. Does the infant have characteristics that may affect maternal attachment? For instance, is the infant easily consoled? Is the mother successful in quieting the infant?

INTERACTION WITH INFANT

Both verbal and non-verbal responses to the infant provide information about bonding and attachment. Non-verbal behaviors such as how the mother touches the infant (finger-tipping, palming, enfolding) and how she holds the infant (en face, far from the body) are particularly important. Verbal interactions are also important: Does she refer to the baby by name? Does she point out positive or negative characteristics? How is she feeding the infant, and is she satisfied with the method chosen?

UNANTICIPATED EVENTS

It is important to make note of unanticipated events, such as a cesarean birth, birth of a preterm or ill infant, or the birth of more than one infant. Any of these factors can affect maternal adaptation.

Analysis

Parenting involves the ability of the parents to create an environment that nurtures the growth and development of the infant. Parenting may be altered when one or more caregivers experience difficulty creating or continuing a nurturing environment. This occurs most often when there is delayed or inadequate attachment and when the parents lack knowledge of infant care. Therefore, a common nursing diagnosis is: *High Risk for Alteration in Parenting related to impaired maternal-infant attachment secondary to fatigue, discomfort, and lack of knowledge of infant care.*

Planning

For this nursing diagnosis, the mother will:

- Verbalize feelings of comfort and support as she progresses through the phases of recovery.
- Demonstrate progressive attachment behaviors by discharge.
- Participate in care of the newborn before discharge from the health care facility.

Interventions

ASSISTING THE MOTHER THROUGH RECOVERY PHASES

"Mother" the Mother. The early taking-in phase is a time to mother the mother so that she can move on to more complex tasks of maternal adjustment. During the first few hours following childbirth, she has a great need for physical care and comfort. Provide ample fluids and favorite food. Keep linens dry, tuck warm blankets around her until chilling has stopped, and use warm water for perineal care. A warm bath not only cleanses the skin following labor but also induces a feeling of being cared for and comforted.

Monitor and Protect. The new mother is dependent on nurses to monitor and protect her. She must be reminded of the need to void and should be assisted to ambulate. At the first signs of fatigue, she should be positioned for sleep and reassured that this is necessary for her body to recover from the exertion of labor. Nurses must also assess the level of comfort and offer analgesia before discomfort is severe and analgesia is less effective.

Listen to Birth Experience. Be prepared to listen to details of the birth experience and to offer sincere praise for her efforts during labor.

Many mothers spend so much time on the telephone that it is difficult to complete assessments and care. Students are reluctant to interrupt; however, the mother's physical safety is a priority and a request to make an assessment is seldom refused. It is often helpful to offer a choice. "Excuse me for a moment. You do not have to hang up, I just need to check you soon. I can do it now or come back in 5 minutes."

FOSTERING INDEPENDENCE

As the mother becomes more independent, allow her to schedule her care as much as possible. Collaborate with her to plan when procedures, such as sitz baths, will be done. Encourage her to assume responsibility for self-care, and emphasize that the nurse's role at this point is to assist and to teach.

PROMOTING BONDING AND ATTACHMENT

Early, unlimited contact between parents and infants is of primary importance to facilitate the attachment process (Fig. 18–6). Many hospitals and almost all

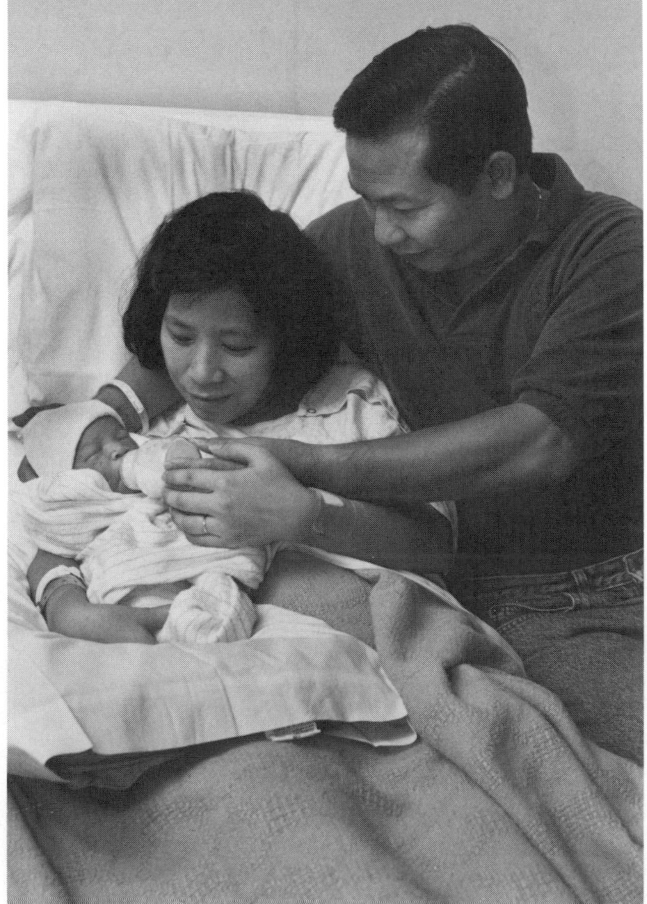

Figure 18–6

Attachment between infant and parents is facilitated when they all spend unlimited amounts of time together.

birth centers provide for rooming-in, which means that the infant remains in the room with the mother (and father) at all times. Some hospitals have a modified rooming-in plan in which infants are with the mothers for long periods but may be returned to a central nursery at night or when the mother wishes to rest. Specific nursing measures to promote bonding and attachment follow:

- Assist the parents in taking the baby out of the blanket and inspecting the toes, fingers, and body. Inspection fosters identification and allows the parents to become acquainted with the "real" baby that must replace the fantasy baby that many parents imagined during the pregnancy.
- Position the infant in an *en face* position; point out that the eyes are open and the infant can see the parent's face; face-to-face and eye-to-eye contact is a first step in establishing mutual interaction between the infant and the parent.
- Point out the reciprocal bonding activities of the infant. "Look how she holds your finger." "He has not taken his eyes off you." "See how the baby moves when you speak in a high-pitched voice."
- Allow the infant to remain with the parents as long as they wish so that they can progress at their own speed through the discovery or getting acquainted phase.
- Assist the mother in putting the infant to the breast if she plans to breastfeed. If necessary reassure her that many infants do not latch on to the breast right away. If she is formula feeding, assist her in positioning the infant securely and reassure her that holding and cuddling the infant provides comfort and security.
- Model behaviors by holding the infant close and speaking in high-pitched, soothing tones.
- Point out the positive characteristics of the infant: "She has the tiniest pink ears and such a lot of dark hair."
- Provide comfort and ample time for rest because the mother must replenish her energy and be relatively free of discomfort before she can progress to initiating care of the infant.

INVOLVING PARENTS IN INFANT CARE

Providing care for the infant fosters feelings of responsibility and nurturing and is an important component of bonding and attachment. Moreover, it allows parents to develop confidence in their ability to care for an infant before they go home.

Demonstrate infant care procedures; begin with the simpler tasks such as care of the cord, and progress to more complicated procedures such as bathing. When the parents receive positive reinforcement for the simple tasks, they are more willing to try the more complicated ones. (See Chapters 20 and 22 for detailed information about the infant care that should be taught before the mother is discharged.)

It is important for the entire staff to agree on how basic care is to be taught. Mothers seek confirmation of information, and they become confused and lose faith in the credibility of the staff if information varies.

- Allow time for practice; mothers become easily discouraged if they think they have failed at some attempt to care for their infants.
- Offer repeated praise and encouragement. Remember, parents are especially vulnerable to criticism.

Suggestions for care must be tactfully phrased to avoid the implication that the parents are inept. "You burped that baby like a professional; there are a couple of little hints I can share about diapering."

Evaluation

Assuming a more independent role in her own care confirms the mother's progression through the phases of recovery:

- Progressive attachment behaviors include enfolding the infant, calling the infant by name, and responding when the infant cries.
- Participation in infant care includes diapering and feeding and care of the umbilical cord and circumcision.

Family Adaptation

Assessment

PATERNAL ADAPTATION

The father's emotional status and interaction with the infant are particularly important because he usually serves as the mother's primary support person. Is the father available? Is he involved with mother and infant? How does he interact with the infant? Does he respond to infant cues? How much information does he have about infant characteristics and care? What are his expectations about his partner's recovery? Unrealistic expectations of the infant (will sleep through the night, smile, be easily consoled) may lead to problems. Moreover, if he expects the mother to recover her energy and libido rapidly, he may become resentful if her recovery takes longer than anticipated.

SIBLINGS

It is important to note the ages of siblings and how they react to the newborn. Are they interested and helpful? Are they hostile and aggressive? How do the parents react to sibling behaviors?

Family members often provide a powerful support system, and their involvement is important to the adaptation of the family. Are grandparents available and invovled? Are there sisters or brothers who live nearby? Are they available to help the new parents? If the family is unavailable, who provides support? What arrangements have been made for assistance?

NON-VERBAL BEHAVIOR

Non-verbal behavior is equally important. Is what the mother or father says congruent with what is being observed. For example, the mother verbalizes satisfaction with her infant's characteristics but re-

Table 18–2. ASSESSING FAMILY ADAPTATION

Assessment	Nursing Considerations
Characteristics of Infant That May Affect Family Adaptation	
Sex and size of infant	The sex of an infant is a factor for some families; disappointment in the sex or concern about the small size may interfere with bonding
Unusual characteristics (cephalohematoma, jaundice, cranial molding, newborn rash)	Be prepared to explain unexpected appearance or behavior in words parents can comprehend
Infant behavior (irritable, easily consoled, cuddles)	Easily consoled, cuddly infant increases bonding and attachment
Paternal Adaptation	
Response to mother and to infant	Mate often provides the most important support for the mother, and his involvement with the infant indicates acceptance of parenting role
Knowledge of infant care	Useful in planning teaching that includes the father
Response to infant cues or signals (crying, fussing)	Many fathers feel awkward handling the infant but want to become proficient in infant care so that they can co-parent
Ages and Developmental Levels of Siblings	
Reaction of siblings	Young children often fear that the newborn will replace them in the affection of parents; anticipatory guidance about sibling rivalry may be needed
Support System	
Interest and availability of family or friends to assist during early weeks	Families benefit from active, nurturing support during the weeks following childbirth; families sometimes need assistance in identifying available support
Plans for first few days at home	How much support will parents have? Plans for obtaining adequate rest? Many hospitals have telephone service to answer questions and give reassurance
Follow-up plans	Appointments should be scheduled at 2 weeks and 6 weeks with clinic or health care provider
Cultural Factors	
Ask family to describe practices that are part of their cultural heritage and beliefs that may affect nursing care; determine expectations of health care team	To determine hygenic practices, dietary preferences, usual care and feeding of infants, and role of mate and family in child care so that culture-specific care can be planned

sponds slowly to infant signals.

Table 18–2 summarizes the family assessment and briefly indicates nursing considerations (see p. 464).

Validate impressions and conclusions that are arrived at during a psychosocial assessment. One of the best ways to do this is to ask, for example, "How much experience have you had with newborns?" "You really thought you were having a girl and a boy is a big surprise?" "How are newborns fed in Vietnam until the mother's milk comes in?" "What are your plans when you go home? How long can your mother stay?"

Analysis

The purpose of the family assessment is to identify family strengths as well as areas in which nursing interventions could promote family adaptation or prevent disruptions in family functioning. The nursing diagnosis *Alteration in Family Processes* occurs when a family that usually functions effectively is unable to cope because of a specific event. In this case, the event is the birth of a baby and the necessity of the family to integrate a newborn into the existing family structure. Therefore, this common nursing diagnosis is *related to lack of knowledge of infant needs and behaviors, methods for reducing stress during the early weeks at home, and coping with sibling rivalry.*

Planning

Goals for this nursing diagnosis include the following:

- Parents will verbalize understanding of infant needs and behaviors before discharge.
- The family will identify methods for reducing stress during the early weeks at home by (date).
- The family will describe measures to reduce sibling rivalry by date of discharge.
- The family will identify external resources before discharge.

Interventions

TEACHING THE FAMILY ABOUT THE NEWBORN

Infant Needs. Some new parents have unrealistic expectations of the newborn, and nurses are in the best position to provide information about what the infant is capable of doing and what the infant needs to thrive (Fig. 18–7). Parents are often thrilled to learn that the infant can see and hear them. They are sometimes surprised to hear that infants sleep 16 to 20 hours/day but must be fed every 2 to 4 hours and that they will not sleep through the night for 12 to 16 weeks. Besides physical care, infants also need cuddling and gentle stimulation. They enjoy looking at mobiles or being with the family. Some infants respond to soothing music or a rocking motion.

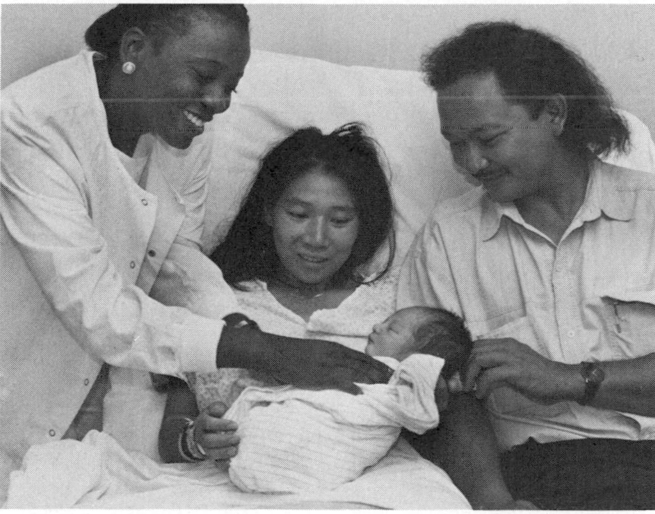

Figure 18–7

By teaching about the newborn and family, the nurse helps parents develop confidence in their ability to provide care for the infant.

Infant Signals. Discuss the importance of responding to infant signals and cues promptly and gently so that the infant can begin to trust that the world is a safe and secure place. This differs from the beliefs of some parents that if one responds when the infant cries, the infant will become "spoiled." Reassure parents that infants do not deliberately cry to exert control over the parents; rather, crying indicates a need, and a prompt response helps the infant learn to trust the world but does not encourage crying.

HELPING THE FAMILY ADAPT

Anticipatory Guidance About Stress Reduction. Nurses can do a great deal to assist by providing information and anticipatory guidance about the first weeks at home, when the family must adjust to the demands of a newborn. At a time when the need for rest is greatest, the opportunity for rest is the least and fatigue is a common problem.

- Recommend that mothers establish a relaxed home atmosphere and a flexible meal schedule because attempts to maintain a rigid schedule

Clinical Situation

Carol, a 35-year-old primipara, had an infant daughter by cesarean birth after failure to progress in labor. Carol is very tired, although she is relatively comfortable. Her husband was present during the labor and birth and is excited about being a father. He has no experience with children, and his job requires almost constant travel. Although Carol has two nephews, she has never taken care of a newborn.

The first postpartum day, Carol readily accepts attention and assistance with hygiene. She passively follows the nurse's suggestions to turn, cough, and breathe deeply. She recounts the details of her labor and wonders why the physician did not proceed with a cesarean birth earlier. She examines her baby girl closely and touches the face and hands gently with her finger tips. She remarks that she plans to breastfeed and is surprised that the infant sleeps so much.

Q:
1. What are Carol's priority needs at this time?
2. What phase of recovery is she manifesting? Why does she "finger-tip" the infant?

The second postpartum day, Carol's indwelling catheter and intravenous fluids are discontinued. Carol ambulates with minimal assistance and announces proudly that she is able to urinate without difficulty. She asks about bowel function and requests the prescribed stool softener. She requests that the infant be left with her and spends a great deal of time getting the baby to breastfeed. She is very frustrated that the infant does not breastfeed well and asks for assistance from the lactation educator.

Q:
3. What are Carol's priority needs now?
4. How have her behaviors changed?

Before discharge on the fourth postpartum day, Carol is breastfeeding well. The infant latches on and nurses for 10 to 15 minutes, and Carol's nipples are free of tenderness or signs of trauma. Carol has no relatives in the area, and her husband is home for the weekend only. She states that she will just have to get along by herself after that.

Q:
5. What anticipatory guidance should Carol receive about her own care? About the infant's care?
6. What further nursing interventions would be most helpful to her and the baby?

A:
1. Carol's priority needs are for physical care and comfort. She also has a need to make the experience of childbirth part of her reality; she does this by recounting the details of her birth experience to anyone who will listen and by trying to fill in the missing pieces about the cesarean birth.
2. Carol is in the taking-in phase. She is getting acquainted with her "real" baby by exploring with her finger tips. This is usually the first maternal touch observed.
3. Carol's priorities are to assume control of her own body functions and to manage her care so that she can "take hold" and assume care of the baby.
4. Carol has become more independent and now initiates breast-feeding. She demonstrates readiness to learn by requesting the assistance of the lactation educator.
5. Anticipatory guidance should focus on how she can manage the care of the infant while still getting adequate rest and nutrition. A flexible schedule, resting while the infant rests, and preparing simple meals are some of the most important items to emphasize.
6. It would be most helpful to assist her in identifying other individuals who could provide some support while her husband is away, perhaps a friend or neighbor. If this is not possible, she should have telephone numbers for community resources, such as the hospital "baby line."

or meticulous environment increase tension within the family.

- Emphasize that the priority during the first 4 to 6 weeks should be caring for mother and baby; encourage the family to accept assistance with shopping and meal preparation.
- Recommend that the mother sleep when the infant sleeps and that she conserve her energy for care of the baby.
- Encourage family members to let friends and relatives know sleep-nap times and request they telephone or visit at other times. Adequate rest is necessary for mental restoration, release of tension, and integration of new information into the memory.
- Advise parents to place a "Do Not Disturb" sign on the door; recommend that they sleep when the infant sleeps, regardless of household chores that need to be done.
- Instruct the family about the need to restrict coffee, tea, colas, and chocolate because they contain the stimulant caffeine.
- Teach breathing exercises and progressive relaxation to reduce stress and to energize and refresh, especially when a nap is not possible.
- Encourage both parents to delay tiring projects until the infant is older. Remind them that although schedules are chaotic for awhile, the infant's behavior is generally more predictable by 12 to 16 weeks.

Text continues on page 472

Nursing Care Plan 18–1

Adaptation to the Birth of Twins

Assessment:
Maureen Parry, a primipara 32 years old, gave birth to twin girls 22 hours ago. Her labor was induced at term, and she was able to deliver vaginally. She and her husband knew to expect twins for several months; however, neither has experience with infants. Maureen took breastfeeding classes, and both she and her husband attended parenting classes during her pregnancy. Both infants are in the room, and she moves anxiously from one to the other. She has examined both infants; however, she has not had individual time with each infant. She touches the infants cautiously and asks, "How in the world will I be able to care for two babies?"

Nursing Diagnosis:
High Risk for Altered Parenting related to inadequate bonding with individual infants and lack of confidence in ability to provide care for two infants.

Goals:
Maureen will:
1. Demonstrate progressive bonding behaviors with each infant before discharge.
2. Collaborate to devise a plan for caring for the infants during the early weeks at home.
3. Verbalize increased confidence in her ability before discharge.

Intervention:	Rationale:
1. Promote bonding and attachment with individual infants by allowing separate time with each infant and pointing out the unique characteristics of each child. For instance, Baby Girl A is larger, she has less hair, and she looks directly at her mother. Baby Girl B is small but alert, and she enjoys cuddling.	1. It is believed that parents can become attached to only one infant at a time. They must go through the getting acquainted phases separately and progress with individual infants rather than with both twins at the same time.
2. Make sure that the parents have contact with the infant who is awake and responsive.	2. It is necessary for the infant to respond to the parent by some signal, such as eye contact, gazing, or responding to the parent's voice (entrainment) for attachment to occur.
3. Foster a relaxed atmosphere that permits unlimited contact between parents and the twins; use some of the time to model behaviors such as holding, consoling, and talking to the infants.	3. A relaxed atmosphere and prolonged contact with the twins provide the best opportunity for interaction that promotes bonding. Modeling is one of the most effective teaching strategies for demonstrating appropriate interactions.
4. Encourage participation in infant care. Model infant care, and praise all maternal efforts to provide care.	4. Caring for the infant or successfully consoling a crying infant elicits powerful feelings of nurturing and responsibility and greatly increases the feelings of confidence and competence.
5. Assist Maureen in making a plan for caring for the twins. a. Provide instruction and encouragement with breastfeeding; if necessary, refer parents to a lactation educator for continuing support. (See Chapter 21 for detailed information about breastfeeding twins.) b. Suggest that the parents keep a record of care for each baby for the first few days at home so that they do not become confused; include feeding times, elimination, and baths. c. Reassure parents that it is not necessary to bathe and shampoo the infants each day; bathing every other day is adequate because the face, neck, and buttocks are bathed as necessary.	5. Breastfeeding is usually established within 2 weeks, and during this time, the mother needs information and encouragement. Collaborating on a plan for providing and recording care increases the parents' confidence in their ability to care for the infants. This is particularly true when the parents receive reassurance that care does not have to be on a strict schedule.

Nursing Care Plan continued on following page

Nursing Care Plan 18–1 Continued

Adaptation to the Birth of Twins

6. Emphasize the importance of obtaining adequate rest. Suggest that the mother sleep when the infants sleep, and suggest that the parents take turns caring for the infants. Recommend that they accept assistance with all household tasks from family and friends so that they can concentrate on care of the twins.

6. Sleep deprivation and chronic fatigue can interfere with the joys of parenting unless the parents anticipate the problem and make plans to deal with it.

Evaluation:
Maureen progressed from finger-tipping to a full range of consoling behaviors with the twins and selected names for the baby girls. By discharge on the third postpartum day, she was breastfeeding with some confidence but continued to need encouragement. Both parents participated in infant care and collaborated to identify family members they could count on for support and assistance during the early weeks at home. Maureen verbalized increased confidence in their ability to provide care.

Assessment:
During discharge teaching, Maureen states that she does not work outside the home and has always assumed total responsibility for household tasks. She reveals that a perfectly maintained home is important to her and especially to her husband. She wonders how he will react to the disruption that the twins will create.

Nursing Diagnosis:
High Risk for Altered Family Processes related to impact of twins on family functioning.

Goals:
The couple will:

1. Share concerns with each other and identify family strengths by (date).
2. Identify measures that reduce stress and promote family adjustment to the birth of twins by discharge.
3. Renegotiate responsibilities for the first few weeks at home by (date).

Intervention:	Rationale:
1. Determine whether Maureen has shared her concerns with her husband; if she has not, advise her to tell him that she is worried that he does not understand how much the twins will disrupt the routine and make meticulous housekeeping impossible during the first weeks at home.	1. Open communication is the first step in identifying stressors and clarifying feelings.
2. Attempt to determine overlooked family strengths, such as the availability of funds to hire help with the housework for a few weeks. Family members are often willing to shop, do laundry, and help with other household tasks.	2. Many families develop a higher level of functioning during times of stress, and individual members participate actively for as long as they are needed. Many families also overlook community resources, such as neighbors and friends.
3. Assist the family in identifying measures to reduce stress that may occur when family patterns are disrupted: a. Recommend simple meals that are easy to prepare, and suggest using disposable dishes for a few weeks. b. Emphasize the importance of good nutrition; a supply of fruits, vegetables, whole grain breads, and cereals is particularly important. Also emphasize the need for daily exercise and recreation. c. Review measures to obtain rest; however, fatigue is a problem likely to persist until the twins sleep through the night. d. Recommend both parents continue to participate in activities that provide recreation and relaxation; Maureen enjoys walking and listening to music, and her husband plays tennis.	3. During times of stress, many parents overlook the benefits of good nutrition, exercise, and recreation; even a few moments of listening to music or indulging in a favorite pasttime can refresh the spirits and replenish energy.

Nursing Care Plan 18–1 *Continued*

Adaptation to the Birth of Twins

Intervention	Rationale
4. Suggest that the couple negotiate sharing household tasks for the first few weeks, although this is not part of their usual responsibilities. This is particularly important for tasks that must be done daily, like meal preparation and some housecleaning.	4. It will take both partners to maintain the home and to care for the twins without undue stress on either. Sharing tasks reduces fatigue and helps to prevent frustration and arguments during this time of stress.

Evaluation:
Maureen shared her concerns about the effect of the twins on the usual pattern of family life and was surprised to learn that her husband had made plans to assume many of the household tasks while the infants require so much care. Maureen's mother is available to babysit, so the couple can have some time for exercise and recreation.

Additional Nursing Diagnoses to Consider:
Ineffective Breastfeeding
High Risk for Parental Role Conflict.
Diversional Activity Deficit

Nursing Care Plan 18–2

Adaptation to Career Plus Motherhood

Rebecca Sanders, a 30-year-old single mother, gave birth to a baby boy by cesarean delivery 2 days ago. Rebecca must return to work as a sales executive in 6 weeks. She is concerned about her appearance. "How can I go back looking like this? I look worse than I did when I was pregnant, and I'm so flabby. This weight is coming off, that's for sure, and I'm going to get rid of this tummy." She plans to breastfeed the baby at least until she returns to work and for a longer time if she can find a place to pump her breasts during the day.

Nursing Diagnosis:
Body Image Disturbance related to perceived negative effects of changed appearance.

Goals:
Rebecca will:
1. Verbalize concerns about her appearance by (date).
2. Describe a realistic plan for weight loss and exercise by discharge.

Intervention:	Rationale:
1. Listen for any comments that indicate a negative assessment of her appearance, and guide the interaction to specific concerns. For example, "You're disappointed that you didn't lose more weight?" "You're anxious to begin exercises to tighten the abdomen?"	1. Rebecca's concerns and feelings must be clarified and validated before effective teaching can take place. Messages conveyed in guided interactions are that (a) someone is interested in her concerns and (b) there are measures that can help her improve her body image.
2. Encourage Rebecca to discuss her expectations for a return to her pre-pregnancy size and shape and her plans to achieve this.	2. Her plans may be unrealistic or may include excessive dieting or a rigorous exercise program, or both, before she is fully recovered from the cesarean birth.
3. Determine her knowledge of the nutrition needed during breastfeeding, and provide additional information if necessary. For instance, it takes about 500 additional calories per day to maintain a mother's energy and produce an adequate milk supply for the infant.	3. Prolonged undernutrition results in the production of less milk every day. Eliminating "empty" calories (simple sugars, excessive fat) and including more fruits, vegetables, and whole grains provide both the energy and nutrients needed.
4. Emphasize that weight loss should be gradual and that about 6 months is usually required.	4. Rigid restriction of calories can lead to depleted energy and decreased immunity as well as decreased production of milk.

Nursing Care Plan continued on following page

Nursing Care Plan 18–2 *Continued*

Adaptation to Career Plus Motherhood

Intervention	Rationale
5. Recommend that Rebecca seek the advice of her health care provider before initiating a rigorous exercise program. Emphasize the importance of graduated exercises to regain muscle tone. (See also Chapter 17.)	5. A program of graduated exercises restores function of the abdominal muscles in about 8 weeks.
6. Recommend that Rebecca try safe activities, such as walking, that maintain her perception of her body as strong and healthy; recommend that she increase the distance walked each day.	6. Body function is a major part of body image. Continued activity confirms that her body is functioning at a higher level as time passes.
7. Reassure Rebecca that some skin changes are temporary (chloasma and linea nigra) and that they will disappear.	7. Most skin changes are due to increased estrogen; when estrogen levels decline following delivery of the placenta, the areas of hyperpigmentation begin to fade.

Evaluation:
Rebecca verbalized her concern about how her changed appearance might affect her confidence in her ability to interact with clients in her job as sales executive. She is committed to breastfeeding for as long as possible and has worked out a plan to lose weight over a 6-month period. She plans to walk each day but will consult with her physician before beginning an exercise program for strengthening the abdominal muscles.

Assessment:
Rebecca is discharged to go home 4 days after the birth. She cares for herself with minimal assistance and demonstrates confidence in breastfeeding. Her mother will be with her for 2 weeks, and Rebecca will have another month before she must return to work. She states that she does not want to leave the baby with someone else while she works. "My mother was always there for me and I want to be with Derrek but it is just impossible. How can I be a mother and work full time?"

Nursing Diagnosis:
Anticipatory Grieving related to inability to perform role of mother as she wishes because of the need to place the infant with another care provider and return to full-time employment.

Goals:
Rebecca will:

1. Describe concerns and feelings that result from need to leave infant with secondary caregiver by (date).
2. Verbalize plans to achieve maximum satisfaction in her role as mother by the time she returns to work.

Intervention:	Rationale:
1. Allow Rebecca to describe her perception of her role as mother and to express concerns about how employment will interfere with her ability to fulfill this role.	1. When a mother envisions the role of mother as the primary caregiver who is always available, yet faces the need to leave the infant with another caregiver, role conflict, stress, and grief can result.
2. Recommend free expression of feelings to significant others and to the care provider who is selected. Many mothers experience intense "separation grief" as well as anxiety, guilt, and jealousy when they leave the infant with a care provider.	2. Candid expression of feelings helps to resolve them and opens the way for a discussion of measures that will help to overcome the intense feelings that cause so much mental conflict.
3. Acknowledge the feelings Rebecca expresses, and reassure her that the feelings are common.	3. Knowledge that the feelings are not trivial and that they are common is sometimes the most helpful intervention.

Nursing Care Plan 18–2 *Continued*

Adaptation to Career Plus Motherhood

4. Help Rebecca develop a schedule that allows her maximum time with the infant: a. Make a list of errands and supplies needed to avoid frequent stops that delay getting home from work. b. Double the recipe when cooking, and freeze half for future use. c. Pick up nutritious take-out meals to avoid cooking each evening. d. Schedule appointments on the same day when possible. e. Work out plans that include the baby in daily walks, exercise, or social visits.	4. Feelings of frustration and stress can be alleviated if the mother has a plan that allows her long periods of uninterrupted time with the infant.
5. Recommend that Rebecca allow 30 to 45 minutes when she first gets home to hold the infant. Delay all other activities until this need is satisfied for both mother and infant.	5. Time is needed to re-establish feelings of closeness, comfort, and attachment.
6. Suggest that Rebecca delay her return to employment, if possible, until the infant is at least 16 weeks old.	6. By this time, most infants are able to sleep through the night; this reduces the chance that sleep deprivation will add to the stress of working, caring for the infant, and leaving the infant with a secondary care provider.
7. Recommend that Rebecca investigate several day care providers before choosing and that she check references, make unannounced visits, insist on seeing required licenses and certification, discuss number and ages of children cared for, request a schedule of planned care, determine the provider's philosophy of infant care (rigid schedule, predictable environment, or no planned schedule), determine whether the care provider is trained in cardiopulmonary resuscitation (CPR), and know what plans are in place if a fire or disaster occurs.	7. A great deal of stress is eliminated if parents feel confident that a competent and nurturing day care provider has been found.
8. Suggest that Rebecca leave the infant with the chosen day care provider for 2 to 3 days prior to resuming full-time employment.	8. This allows both mother and infant to "practice separating" while there is still some flexibility in their schedules, and the first day back at work will be less traumatic.
9. Recommend that Rebecca pump her breasts and feed the infant by bottle at least once a day for several weeks before returning to work.	9. This gives her a chance to become proficient at pumping the breasts and introduces the infant to bottle feeding before all-day separation is necessary.

Evaluation:
Rebecca freely expressed her feelings of guilt, anxiety, and concern about leaving her infant. She has organized a plan to investigate day care in her area and verbalized plans to reorganize her work and social schedule so that she can spend as much time as possible with her son.

Additional Nursing Diagnoses to Consider:
- Diversional Activity Deficit
- Parental Role Conflict
- Sleep Pattern Disturbance

- Encourage open expression of feelings between parents as a first step in coping with stress.
- Remind parents of the need for healthy nutrition and for favorite recreation. It is easy for fatigue and tension to overwhelm the anticipated joys of parenting if there is no respite from constant care.
- Suggest that new parents enlist grandparents, other relatives, and friends to help with meal preparation and shopping.

Providing Ways to Reduce Sibling Rivalry. Suggest that parents plan time alone with the older child and that they praise and reassure the child frequently of his or her place in the family. The parents should try to offer frequent expression of love and affection. It is also helpful if visitors and family do not focus exclusively on the infant but also include the older child in their gift giving and exclamations about the newborn.

Emphasize the importance of responding calmly and with understanding when the child regresses to more infantile behaviors or expresses hostility toward the infant. Acknowledging the child's feelings and offering prompt reassurance of continued love are most valuable.

Some children, particularly those older than 3 years of age, enjoy being a big brother or big sister and respond well when they are included in infant care. This may not be possible with younger children, and it may be more worthwhile for the parents to set aside separate time to participate in a favorite activity with them.

Assist in Identifying Resources. Many women assume the major responsibilities of day-to-day homemaking. With the birth of an infant, this task becomes more difficult. A division of labor must be negotiated to prevent undue stress and fatigue. This is particularly important if there are young children whose needs for time, attention, and comfort must also be met.

The mother's primary support is often the father of the baby; however, extended family members, particularly grandmothers and sisters, also provide valuable support. Community resources should not be overlooked—day care centers, parenting classes, and breastfeeding support are available in many areas. In addition, close friends and neighbors often share solutions they have found for specific problems. Remind the mother that there are resources available when she begins to feel isolated and exhausted.

Evaluation

A prompt, gentle response to infant crying or fussing indicates an understanding of the infant's need. Devising a plan for obtaining rest and reducing anxiety in siblings is a first step in reducing stress. Identifying external resources in the family, neighborhood, and community may help the family function to meet its needs during the early weeks at home.

Summary Concepts

- Bonding and attachment are gradual processes that begin before childbirth and progress to feelings of love and deep devotion that last all through life. Nurses foster bonding and attachment by providing early, unlimited contact between the parents and infant and by modeling attachment behaviors.
- For bonding and attachment to occur, interaction between parents and the infant is required. Contact is particularly important during the "sensitive period," when the infant is awake and alert and able to interact with the parents. Nurses often delay care that can be postponed so that the parents and infant can have this time together.
- Maternal touch changes over time as the mother progresses from the getting-acquainted phase of exploring by "finger-tipping" to enfolding and finally demonstrating a full range of comforting behaviors.
- Verbal behaviors are important indicators of maternal attachment as mothers progress from referring to the infant as "it" to calling the infant by name, and finally identifying his or her unique characteristics. Nurses often model how to speak to the infant and point out the infant's response to the verbal stimulation.
- Maternal adjustment to parenthood is a gradual process that involves restorative phases that allow the mother to replenish her energy, relinquish her role as a woman without a child, and develop attachment to the infant. Nurses play a valuable role in the process by first "mothering the mother" and fostering independence as the mother becomes ready.
- Postpartum blues, a temporary, self-limiting period of weepiness, is often ignored by the health care team. Explanations and support are generally all that are required to assist the mother through this distressing episode.
- Parents usually progress through four stages before they attain a sense of harmony in the role of parent when they structure their parenting behaviors to mesh with the unique needs of their child.
- Many women experience role conflict when they

must leave the infant with a caregiver and return to work. Nurses can offer anticipatory guidance that will make the conflict less difficult.

- The birth of a baby necessitates reorganization of family structure and renegotiation of family responsibilities; nurses can make the process easier by assisting the father in co-parenting the infant and helping the new parents identify family resources.
- Siblings feel jealousy and fear that they will be replaced by the newborn in the affection of the parents. Nurses can reduce the negative feelings by providing information about how to reduce sibling rivalry.

References and Readings

Ament, L.A. (1990). Maternal tasks of the puerperium reidentified. *Journal of Obstetric, Gynecologic, and Neonatal Nursing*, 19(4), 330–335.

Anderson, J.M. (1990). Health care across cultures. *Nursing Outlook*, 36(3), 136–139.

Ball, J.A. (1988). Mothers need nurturing, too. *Nursing Times*, 84(17), 29–31.

Beck, C.T., Reynolds, M.A., & Rutowski, P. (1992). Maternity blues and postpartum depression. *Journal of Obstetric, Gynecologic, and Neonatal Nursing*, 21(4), 287–293.

Brouse, A.J. (1988). Easing the transition to the maternal role. *Journal of Advanced Nursing*, 13, 167–172.

Busch, P., & Perrin, K. (1989). Postpartum depression: Assessing risk, restoring balance, RN, August, 46–49.

Comfort, M., Wulff, L.M., & Smeriglio, V.L. (1987). Adolescent parenthood: Implications for care of the mother and child. *Maryland Medical Journal*, 36(11), 955–959.

Culp, R.E., & Osofsky, H.J. (1989). Effects of cesarean delivery on parental depression, marital adjustment, and mother-infant interaction. *Birth*, 16(2), 53–56.

Donaldson, N.E. (1991). A review of nursing intervention research on maternal adaptation in the first 8 weeks postpartum. *Journal of Perinatal Neonatal Nursing*, 4(4), 1–9.

Dormire, S.L., Strauss, S.S., & Clarke, B.A. (1989). Social support and adaptation to the parent role in first-time adolescent mothers. *Journal of Obstetric, Gynecologic, and Neonatal Nursing*, 18(4), 327–337.

Errante, J. (1985). Sleep deprivation or postpartal blues. *Topics in Clinical Nursing*, 6(4), 9–18.

Flagler, S. (1990). Relationships between stated feelings and measures of maternal adjustment. *Journal of Obstetric, Gynecologic, and Neonatal Nursing*, 19(5), 411–416.

Fortier, J.C., Carson, V.B., Will, S., et al. (1991). Adjustment to a newborn: Sibling preparation makes a difference. *Journal of Obstetric, Gynecologic, and Neonatal Nursing*, 20(1), 73–79.

Gardner, D.L., & Campbell, B. (1991). Assessing postpartum fatigue. *Maternal-Child Nursing Journal*, 16(5), 264–266.

Hacker, N., & Moore, G. (1992). *Essentials of obstetrics and gynecology* (2nd ed.). Philadelphia: W.B. Saunders.

Hall, L.A., Gurley, D.N., Sachs, B., & Kryscio, R.J. (1991). Psychosocial predictors of maternal depressive symptoms, parenting attitudes, and child behavior in single-parent families. *Nursing Research*, 40(4), 214–220.

Hampson, S.J. (1989). Nursing interventions for the first three postpartum months. *Journal of Obstetric, Gynecologic, and Neonatal Nursing*, 18(2), 116–122.

Hans, A. (1986). Postpartum assessment: The psychological component. *Journal of Obstetric, Gynecologic, and Neonatal Nursing*, 15(1), 49–51.

Jordan, P.L. (1990). Laboring for relevance: Expectant and new fatherhood. *Nursing Research*, 39(1), 11–16.

Klaus, M., & Kennell, J. (1982). *Maternal-infant bonding*. St. Louis: C.V. Mosby.

Landry, S., Montgomery, J., & Walsh, S. (1989). Postpartum depression: A clinical view. *Maternal-Child Nursing Journal*, 18(1), 1–29.

Manio, E.B., & Hall, R.R. (1987). Asian family traditions and their influence in transcultural health care delivery. *Children's Health Care*, 15(3), 172–177.

Marecki, M., Powhatan, W., Dow, A., et al. (1985). Early sibling attachment. *Journal of Obstetric, Gynecologic, and Neonatal Nursing*, 14(5), 418–423.

Martell, L.K. (1990). Postpartum depression as a family problem. *Maternal-Child Nursing Journal*, 15(2), 90–93.

Martell, L.K., & Mitchell, S.K. (1984). Rubin's puerperal change reconsidered. *Journal of Obstetric, Gynecologic, and Neonatal Nursing*, 13(3), 145–148.

Mattson, S., & Lew, L. (1991). Culturally sensitive prenatal care for Southeast Asians. *Journal of Obstetric, Gynecologic, and Neonatal Nursing*, 21(1), 48–54.

May, K., Perrin, S. (1985). The father in pregnancy and birth. In S. Hanson & F. Bozett (Eds.). *Dimensions of fatherhood*. Beverly Hills: Sage Publishing.

Mercer, R.T. (1985). The process of maternal role attainment. *Nursing Research*, 34(4), 198–204.

Mercer, R.T. (1986). Predictors of maternal role attainment at one year postbirth. *Western Journal of Nursing Research*, 8(1), 9–32.

Mercer, R.T. (1990). *Parents at risk*. New York: Springer Publishing.

Mercer, R.T., & Ferketich, S.L. (1990a). Predictors of family functioning eight months following birth. *Nursing Research*, 39(2), 76–82.

Mercer, R.T., & Ferketich, S.L. (1990b). Predictors of parental attachment during early parenthood. *Journal of Advanced Nursing*, 15, 268–280.

Morrow, K. (1986). Transcultural midwifery: Adapting to Hmong birthing customs in California. *Journal of Nurse-Midwifery*, 31(6), 285–288.

Murray, R.B., & Zenter, J.P. (1989). *Nursing assessment and health promotion strategies through the life span* (4th ed.). Norwalk, Conn.: Appleton & Lange.

Norr, K.F., Roberts, J.E., & Freese, U. (1989). Early postpartum rooming-in and maternal attachment behaviors in a group of medically indigent primiparas. *Journal of Nurse-Midwifery*, 34(2), 85–91.

Pridham, K.F., Lytton, D., Chang, A.S., et al. (1991). Early postpartum transition: Progress in maternal identity and role attainment. *Research in Nursing and Health*, 14(1), 21–31.

Rubin, R. (1961). Puerperal change. *Nursing Outlook*, 9(12), 743–755.

Reichert, J.A., Baron, M., & Fawcett, J. (1993). Changes in attitude toward cesarean birth. *Journal of Obstetric, Gynecologic, and Neonatal Nursing*, 22(2), 159–167.

Rubin, R. (1977). Binding-in in the postpartum period. *Maternal-Child Nursing Journal*, 6(1), 65–75.

Rubin, R. (1984). *Maternal identity and the maternal experience*. New York: Springer Publishing.

Schachere, K. (1990). Attachment between working mothers and their infants: The influence of family processes. *American Journal of Orthopsychiatry*, 60(1), 19–34.

Symanski, M.E. (1992). Maternal-infant bonding: Practice issue for the 1990s. *Journal of Nurse-Midwifery*, 37(2), (Supplement), 67–73.

Tomlinson, P.S. (1990). Verbal behavior associated with indicators of maternal attachment with the neonate. *Journal of Obstetric, Gynecologic, and Neonatal Nursing*, 19(1), 76–81.

Trip-Reimer, T., & Afifi, L.A. (1989). Cross-cultural perspectives on patient teaching. *Nursing Clinics of North America*, 24(3), 613–619.

Ugarriza, D.N. (1992). Postpartum affective disorders: Incidence and treatment. *Journal of Psychosocial Nursing*, 30(5), 29–32.

Williams, K.J., Suls, J., Alliger, G.M., et al. (1991). Multiple role juggling and daily mood states in working mothers: An experience sampling study. *Journal of Applied Psychology*, 76(5), 664–674.

Williams, L.R., & Cooper, M.K. (1993). Nurse-managed home care. *Journal of Obstetric, Gynecologic, and Neonatal Nursing*, 22(1), 25–31.

19

Normal Newborn:

The Processes of Adaptation

Objectives

1. Explain the physiological changes that occur in the respiratory and cardiovascular systems during the transition from fetal to neonatal life.
2. Describe thermoregulation in the newborn.
3. Identify newborn reflexes and sensory ability.
4. Describe common variations of the musculoskeletal system.
5. Compare gastrointestinal functioning in the newborn and adult.
6. Explain the causes, effects, and treatment of hypoglycemia.
7. Describe the steps in normal bilirubin excretion and the development of physiologic, pathologic, and breast milk jaundice.
8. Describe kidney functioning in the newborn.
9. Discuss potential benefits, risks, and methods of circumcision.
10. Explain the functioning of the newborn's immune system.
11. Describe the periods of reactivity and the six behavioral states of the newborn.

Definitions

Acrocyanosis • Bluish discoloration of the hands and feet due to reduced peripheral circulation.

Asphyxia • A condition in which there is deficient oxygen in the blood and excess carbon dioxide in the blood and tissues.

Bilirubin • Unusable component of hemolyzed erythrocytes.

Brown fat (or **brown adipose tissue**) • Fat that is metabolized to provide heat in the newborn.

Caput succedaneum • Area of edema over the presenting part resulting from pressure against the cervix. Often simply called "caput."

Cephalohematoma • Bleeding between the newborn's periosteum and a skull bone from pressure during birth.

Choanal atresia • Abnormality of the nasal septum that obstructs one or both nasal passages.

Craniosynostosis • Premature closure of the sutures of the infant's head.

Cryptorchidism • Failure of one or both testes to descend into the scrotum.

Epispadias • Abnormal placement of the urinary meatus on the dorsal penis.

Fetal lung fluid • Fluid that fills the lungs during prenatal life, expanding the alveoli and promoting normal development of the lungs.

First period of reactivity • Period from birth until the infant first falls asleep.

Hyperbilirubinemia • Excessive amount of bilirubin in the blood, often leading to jaundice.
Hypospadias • Abnormal position of the urinary meatus on the ventral side of the penis.
Jaundice • Yellow discoloration of the skin caused by excessive bilirubin in the blood.
Molding • Shaping of the fetal head during movement through the birth canal.
Neutral thermal environment • Environment in which body temperature is maintained without an increase in oxygen use or in metabolic rate.
Nonshivering thermogenesis • Heat production, without shivering, by oxidation of brown fat.
Periodic breathing • Cessation of breathing lasting no more than 10 seconds without changes in color or heart rate.
Polycythemia • Abnormally high number of erythrocytes.
Polydactyly • More than ten digits on the hands or feet.
Pseudomenstruation • Vaginal bleeding in the newborn, resulting from withdrawal of placental hormones.
Second period of reactivity • Period after the first sleep following birth, when the infant is approximately 4 hours old.
Strabismus • A turning inward or outward ("crossing") of the eyes.
Surfactant • A combination of lipoproteins produced by the lungs of the mature fetus to reduce surface tension in the alveoli, thus promoting lung expansion after birth.
Syndactyly • Webbing between fingers or toes.
Tachypnea • Respiratory rate above 60 breaths per minute in the newborn after the first hour of life.
Thermogenesis • Heat production.
Thermoregulation • Maintenance of body temperature.

At birth, the neonate must make profound physiological changes to adapt to extrauterine life. The fetus does not have to breathe, take in and digest food, or maintain temperature because the placenta, amniotic fluid, and mother's body perform these functions. The newborn must make immediate changes to meet respiratory, digestive, and regulatory needs. Nurses must be aware of the normal physiological changes occurring during the early hours and days after birth so that they can identify behaviors signifying problems or abnormalities. This chapter discusses the physiological adaptation of the newborn.

Initiation of Respirations

The first vital task that the infant must accomplish at birth is initiation of respirations. Many forces work together throughout pregnancy and at the time of birth to bring about this change.

Development of the Lungs

During fetal life, the respiratory tract produces a fluid that fills the lungs. Fetal lung fluid expands the alveoli and is essential for normal development of the lungs. Some of the fluid empties from the lungs into the amniotic fluid.

As the lungs mature, they begin to produce surfactant, a slippery, detergent-like lipoprotein substance. Surfactant reduces surface tension within the alveoli, which allows them to remain partially open when the infant begins to breathe at birth. Without surfactant, the alveoli collapse as the infant exhales and must be reopened with each breath. This greatly increases the work of breathing.

Causes of Respirations

The infant's first breath at birth must force the fetal lung fluid into the interstitial spaces around the alveoli so that air can enter the respiratory tract. This requires a much larger negative pressure (suction) for the first breath than for subsequent breathing. Initiation of breathing is due to chemical, thermal, and mechanical factors that stimulate the respiratory center in the medulla of the brain and trigger respirations. All of these factors are significant, and they are discussed in order of importance (Fig. 19–1).

CHEMICAL FACTORS

Chemoreceptors in the carotid arteries and the aorta respond to changes in blood chemistry brought about by the hypoxia that is part of normal birth. A decreased blood oxygen level (Po_2) and an increased blood carbon dioxide level (Pco_2), along with a decreased pH, cause impulses from these receptors to stimulate the respiratory center in the medulla. A forceful contraction of the diaphragm results, causing air to enter the lungs. However, if the period of hypoxia is prolonged, stimulation of the respiratory center and breathing will not occur because of central nervous system depression.

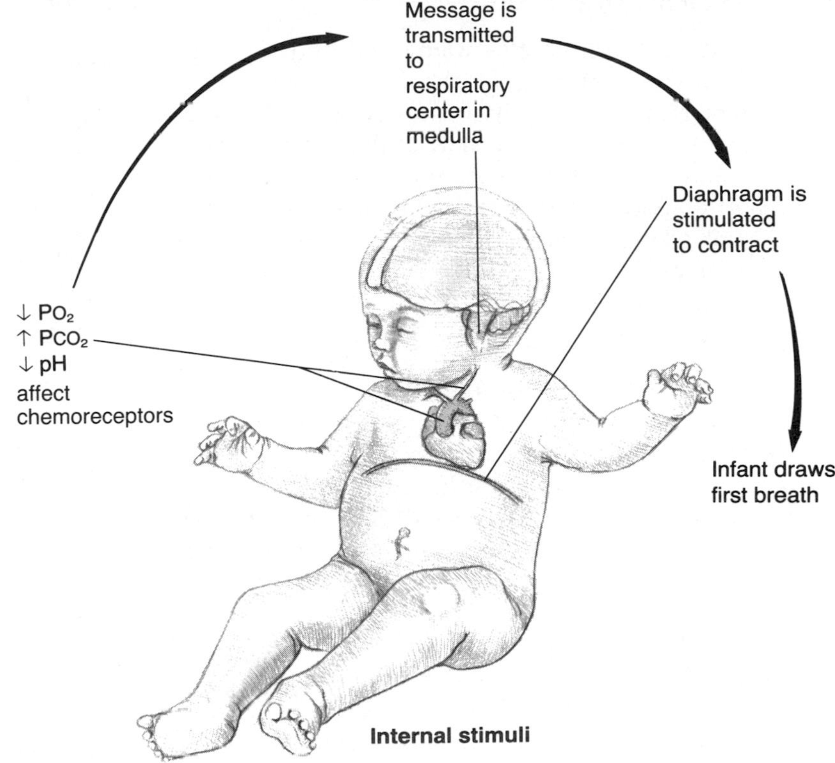
Message is transmitted to respiratory center in medulla
Diaphragm is stimulated to contract
↓ PO_2
↑ PCO_2
↓ pH
affect chemoreceptors
Infant draws first breath
Internal stimuli

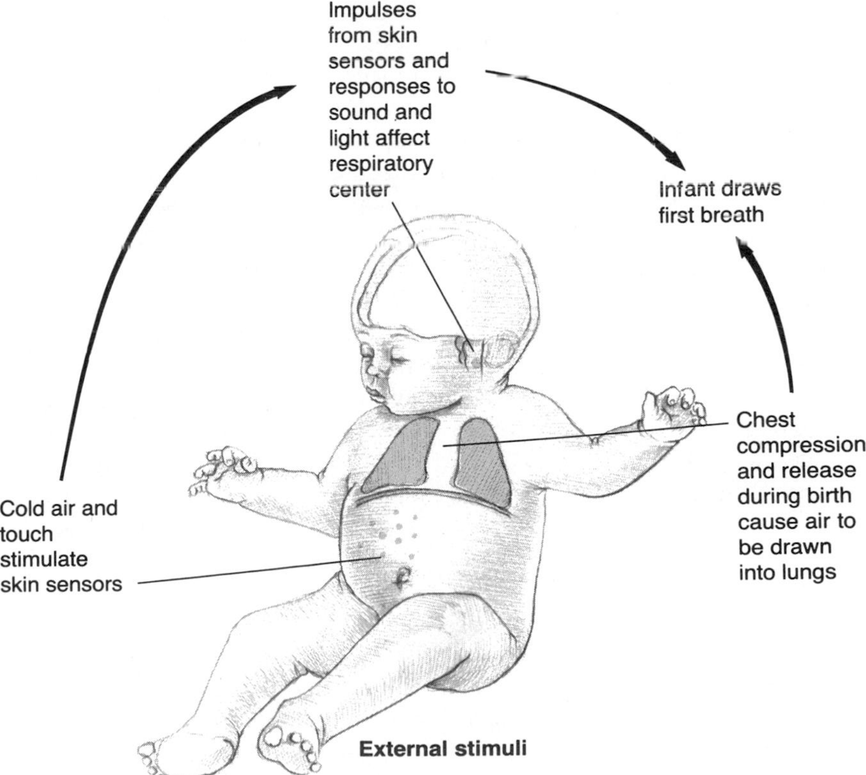
Impulses from skin sensors and responses to sound and light affect respiratory center
Infant draws first breath
Chest compression and release during birth cause air to be drawn into lungs
Cold air and touch stimulate skin sensors
External stimuli

Figure 19–1

Internal causes of the initiation of respirations are the chemical changes that take place at birth. External causes of respirations include thermal and mechanical factors.

THERMAL FACTORS

The infant comes from the warm, fluid-filled uterus into an environment in which the temperature is more than 20°F lower. Skin sensors react to this sudden change in temperature and stimulate the respiratory center. The temperature change is a major stimulus to respirations. Yet, if the infant's temperature drops too low, respirations are depressed rather than stimulated.

MECHANICAL FACTORS

During a vaginal birth, the fetal chest is compressed by the narrow birth canal. Approximately one third of the fetal lung fluid is forced out of the lungs into the upper air passages during birth. The fluid passes out of the mouth or nose or is suctioned as the head emerges from the vagina. As the chest wall recoils when the pressure against it is released, a small amount of air is drawn into the lungs.

Skin sensors respond to tactile stimuli that occur at birth. Nurses hold, dry, and wrap infants in blankets, providing further stimulation to skin sensors. The stimulation of the sounds and lights of the delivery room may also aid in initiating respirations.

Continuation of Respirations

Once the alveoli expand, surfactant acts to keep them partially open between respirations. About half of the first breath of air remains in the lungs to become the functional residual capacity. Because the alveoli remain partially expanded with this residual air, subsequent breaths require much less effort than the first one. With each of the first few respirations, more alveoli are opened.

The remaining fetal lung fluid is forced into the interstitial spaces, where it is absorbed by the circulatory and lymphatic systems. Reabsorption is accelerated by the process of labor and may be delayed after cesarean birth. It may take as long as 24 hours, although most is absorbed within a few hours. This explains why the lungs may sound moist when first assessed but become clear a short time later.

Normal Respiratory Status

RESPIRATORY RATE

The normal newborn respiratory rate ranges between 30 and 60 breaths/minute, with an average rate of 30 to 40. The infant may breathe faster immediately after birth, during crying, and during the first and second periods of reactivity. Because the pattern and depth of respirations are irregular, they must be counted for a full minute for accuracy.

Apnea lasting up to 10 seconds may occur in the normal newborn, usually after the first 24 hours of life. This is known as periodic breathing and is normal. There are no changes in color or heart rate with periodic breathing. Apnea lasting longer than 15 seconds, or accompanied by cyanosis or other signs of difficult breathing, is abnormal.

BREATH SOUNDS

Breath sounds should be present equally throughout all lobes of the lungs. They should be clear over most areas, but it is not unusual to hear sounds of fluid in the lungs from the incompletely absorbed fetal lung fluid. The lungs should clear rapidly during the first hours after birth. Infants of cesarean births miss the pressure on the chest during vaginal birth that causes expulsion of some of the fetal lung fluid. Therefore, they are more likely to have coarse breath sounds at birth.

NASAL PASSAGES

Newborns are obligate nose breathers for approximately the first 3 weeks of life. This means that they breathe mostly through the nose, except when crying. If the nose becomes obstructed, the infant will have difficulty getting enough oxygen. Choanal atresia is a condition in which one or both nasal passages are blocked by an abnormality of the septum. Bilateral choanal atresia causes severe respiratory distress and necessitates surgery. Blockage of one side puts the infant at risk for respiratory distress should the other side become occluded by mucus or edema.

Respiratory Distress

Signs of respiratory distress may be present at birth or may develop later. These are discussed next.

Tachypnea. This is the most common sign of respiratory distress. Tachypnea, a respiratory rate above 60 breaths/minute, is not unusual during the first hour after birth and during the second period of reactivity. However, continued tachypnea is abnormal.

Retractions. When the infant's weak chest wall muscles are used to help draw air into the lungs, retractions result. The tissue around the bones of the chest is drawn in with the effort of pulling air into the lungs. Substernal or xyphoid retractions occur when the area under the sternum retracts each time the infant inhales. When the muscles between the ribs are pulled in so that each rib is outlined, intercostal retractions are present. The muscles above the sternum and around the clavicles may also be used to aid in respirations. Retractions may be mild or severe, depending on the degree of respiratory difficulty. Occasional mild retractions are not uncommon immediately after birth but should not continue after the first hour.

Flaring of the Nares. A reflex widening of the nostrils occurs when there is insufficient oxygen. Intermittent flaring may occur in the first hour after birth. Continued flaring indicates a more serious respiratory problem.

Cyanosis. Cyanosis is an important indication of hypoxia. Central cyanosis involves the lips, tongue, and trunk and indicates true hypoxia. It must be differentiated from peripheral cyanosis, or acrocyanosis, which involves just the extremities. Acrocyanosis is normal in the first few hours after birth or if the infant becomes cold. It is due to poor perfusion of blood to the periphery of the body.

Grunting. Grunting describes a noise made on expiration when pressure is increased within the alveoli to help keep them open. Grunting may be very mild and heard only with a stethoscope, or it may be loud enough to hear unaided in an infant having severe difficulty. Grunting is a common sign of respiratory distress syndrome and necessitates expanded assessment and referral for treatment.

Seesaw Respirations. Normally, the chest and abdomen rise and fall together during respiration. When the infant is having severe respiratory difficulty, the chest falls when the abdomen rises and the chest rises when the abdomen falls, causing a seesaw effect. This is a sign of severe respiratory difficulty.

✔ *Check Your Reading*

1. How do hypoxia during birth, a cool delivery room, and handling at birth stimulate the newborn to breathe?
2. Why is surfactant important to the newborn's ability to breathe easily?
3. How is the fluid that fills the lungs during fetal life removed after birth?

Cardiovascular Adaptation

Transition from Fetal to Neonatal Circulation

Knowledge of fetal circulation is necessary to understand the circulatory changes that occur at birth. It may be helpful to review this material in Chapter 6 (p. 112) before beginning to read this section. During fetal life, most of the blood flow bypasses the nonfunctional lungs and liver. At birth, the infant's blood must begin to circulate to the lungs for oxygenation and to the liver for filtration.

In order for these changes to occur, three shunts that existed before birth, the ductus arteriosus, foramen ovale, and ductus venosus, must close. These closures occur in response to increases in blood oxygen level, in response to shifts in pressure in the heart, and as a result of cord clamping. The changes necessary for transition from fetal to neonatal circulation occur simultaneously within the first few minutes after birth. Table 19–1 summarizes these changes.

DUCTUS ARTERIOSUS

In the fetus, the widely dilated ductus arteriosus carries most of the blood flow away from the narrow pulmonary arteries and into the aorta, bypassing the non-functioning lungs. When the newborn begins to breathe, the ductus arteriosus constricts in response to the higher level of oxygen in the blood. The vessel becomes almost or completely closed, forcing blood flow through the pulmonary artery to the lungs for oxygenation.

Although the ductus arteriosus constricts in response to increased oxygen, the vessels within the lungs dilate. This allows them to accommodate to the suddenly increased blood flow. As fetal lung fluid moves into the interstitial spaces and is removed by the blood and lymph system, there is more room for dilation of the pulmonary blood vessels.

The closure of the ductus arteriosus is at first functional rather than permanent and may be reversed. If there is not enough oxygen in the blood, the ductus arteriosus will dilate and the pulmonary vessels will constrict. A patent ductus arteriosus may occur in the infant who is preterm, who experiences asphyxia at birth, or who becomes hypoxic later (see Chapter 29, p. 871) for a discussion of this condition). Although the ductus arteriosus is functionally closed 15 to 24 hours after birth, it is not permanently closed for 3 to 4 weeks (Lott, 1993). Once closed, it is called the ligamentum arteriosum.

FORAMEN OVALE

The foramen ovale is a flap in the septum between the right and the left atria of the fetal heart. The flap opens only from right to left and shunts blood away from the lungs to the aorta before birth. This right-to-left shunt operates because the pressure in the

Table 19–1. CIRCULATORY CHANGES AT BIRTH

Purpose in Fetal Life	Change at Birth	Cause of Change at Birth	Results of Change at Birth	Time of Functional and Permanent Change
		Ductus Arteriosus		
Widely dilated; carries blood from pulmonary artery to aorta and avoids non-functioning lungs	Constricts almost completely	Increased oxygen level in blood	Blood in pulmonary artery directed to lungs for oxygenation	Functional: from within minutes after birth to complete closure in 10–15 hours. Permanent: 3 weeks. Becomes ligamentum arteriosum.
		Pulmonary Blood Vessels		
Narrowed vessels increase resistance in lungs to blood flow	Dilation of all vessels in lungs	Elevated blood oxygen level and removal of fetal lung fluid	Decreased resistance in lungs allows blood to enter freely to be oxygenated	Begins with first breath
		Foramen Ovale		
Provides one-way opening between R and L atria so that blood can avoid non-functioning lungs and go directly to LV and aorta. Opens only in R-to-L direction because of high R atrial pressure and low L atrial pressure.	Closes when pressure in LA becomes higher than pressure in RA	Cord clamping elevates systemic resistance. Blood returns from pulmonary veins to LA. Both increase L heart pressure. Decreased pulmonary resistance allows free flow of blood into lungs and decreased pressure in RA. Low R atrial pressure and high L atrial pressure causes foramen ovale to close.	Blood entering RA can no longer pass through to LA. Instead, it goes to RV and through pulmonary arteries to the lungs.	Functional: within minutes. Permanent: 3 months. Becomes fossa ovale.
		Ductus Venosus		
Shunts blood from umbilical vein to inferior vena cava and away from immature liver	Closed by cord clamp	Clamping of cord stops flow of blood from placenta through umbilical vein to ductus venosus	Blood travels through liver to be filtered as in adult circulation	Functional: when cord is clamped. Permanent: fibrosed in 1 week. Becomes ligamentum venosum.

Abbreviations: R, right; L, left; RV, right ventricle; LA, left atrium; RA, right atrium.

right atrium is higher than that in the left atrium. Resistance to blood flow through the pulmonary artery elevates the pressure in the right heart. Pressure is low on the left side of the heart because there is no resistance to blood leaving the left ventricle. This blood travels to the rest of the body and then to the placental vessels, which are widely dilated to ensure adequate blood flow into the intervillous spaces.

At birth, pressures are reversed between the right and the left atria. The free flow of blood from the right ventricle to the lungs and the decreased blood return to the right atrium after clamping of the umbilical cord combine to decrease pressure in the right heart. Pressure in the left heart builds when blood enters the left atrium from the pulmonary veins and blood flow to the placenta ceases. Because the foramen ovale can open only from right to left, it closes when the pressure in the left heart is higher than that in the right heart.

Closure of the foramen ovale prevents blood flow from the right to the left atrium and forces the blood into the right ventricle and pulmonary artery. With the ductus arteriosus closed, the blood continues on into the lungs for oxygenation and returns to the left atrium through the pulmonary veins. It enters the left ventricle and leaves through the aorta to circulate to the rest of the body. Thus, blood flow through the heart and lungs changes from fetal to neonatal circulation and is similar to that in the normal adult (see Fig. 6–9, p. 113, and Table 19–1).

The foramen ovale is functionally closed soon after

birth because the pressure changes within the heart prevent it from opening. Conditions such as asphyxia may reverse the pressures in the heart and cause the foramen ovale to reopen. It becomes permanently closed several months after birth, when it is called the fossa ovale.

DUCTUS VENOSUS

In fetal life, the ductus venosus directs most of the blood flow away from the liver and on into the rest of the body because it is not necessary for the liver to filter the blood as it does after the infant is born. Once the cord is cut, very little blood enters the ductus venosus. Fibrosis of the ductus venosus occurs by the end of the first week of life, and it is then called the ligamentum venosum.

✔ *Check Your Reading*

4. What brings about the closure of the ductus arteriosus, foramen ovale, and ductus venosus at birth?

Neurological Adaptation

Thermoregulation

An important task that the infant must take on at birth is thermoregulation, or the maintenance of body temperature. Although the fetus produces heat in utero, the consistently warm temperature of the amniotic fluid makes thermoregulation unnecessary. However, the temperature of the delivery room may be as much as 20°F lower than that of the uterus. Neonates must produce and maintain enough heat to prevent cold stress, which can have serious and even fatal effects.

NEWBORN CHARACTERISTICS LEADING TO HEAT LOSS

Some characteristics of newborns predispose them to lose heat. The skin is thin, and blood vessels are close to the surface. There is little subcutaneous fat to serve as a barrier to heat loss. Heat is readily transferred from the warmer internal areas of the body to the cooler skin surfaces and then to the surrounding air. Newborns have three times more surface area to weight than the adult, which provides more area for heat loss. They lose heat at a rate four times greater than adults do (Behrman, 1992).

The healthy full-term infant remains in a position of flexion, which helps to reduce the amount of skin surface exposed to the surrounding temperatures and prevents heat loss. This is not the case for the sick or preterm infant, who has decreased muscle tone and does not maintain a flexed position. These infants are at increased risk for cold stress.

METHODS OF HEAT LOSS

There are four methods of heat loss in the neonate: evaporation, conduction, convection, and radiation (Fig. 19–2). The nurse can prevent heat loss by each method and must be watchful for situations in which intervention is needed.

Evaporation. Evaporation occurs when wet surfaces are exposed to air. As the surfaces dry, heat is lost. At birth, the infant loses heat when amniotic fluid on the skin evaporates. Evaporation also occurs during bathing. Drying the infant as quickly as possible at birth and after bathing helps prevent excessive heat loss. Insensible water loss from the skin and respiratory tract increases heat loss by evaporation.

Conduction. Conduction of heat away from the body occurs when newborns come in direct contact with objects that are cooler than their skin. Placing infants on cold surfaces, such as scales or circumcision restraint boards, or touching them with cold hands or a cold stethoscope causes this type of heat loss. The reverse is also true. That is, wrapping newborns in warm blankets or placing them against the mother's skin can warm them.

Convection. Convection occurs when heat is transferred to air surrounding the infant. Air currents from air conditioning or people moving around increase the loss of heat. Keeping the newborn out of drafts and maintaining warm environmental temperatures help prevent this type of heat loss. Oxygen should be warmed before administration. Newborns are often placed in radiant warmers or incubators, in which the surrounding temperature can be controlled to prevent convective heat loss. Once their temperature is stable, they are moved to open cribs (Fig. 19–3).

Radiation. Radiation is the transfer of heat to cooler objects that are not in direct contact with the infant. For example, if the crib is near cold windows, heat is lost by radiation. Infants in incubators transfer heat to the walls of the incubator. If the walls of the incubator are cold, the infant will be cooled, even when the temperature inside the incubator is warm. Therefore, cribs and incubators should be kept away from windows and outside walls to minimize radiant heat loss.

NONSHIVERING THERMOGENESIS

When adults are cold, they shiver, increasing muscle activity to produce heat. Newborns do not normally shiver and have no voluntary control of their mus-

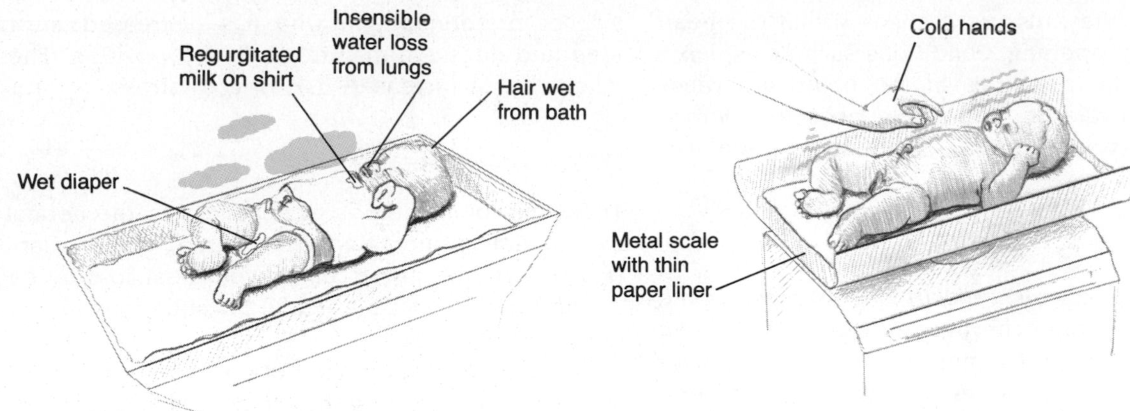

Evaporation can occur during birth or bathing from moisture on skin, as a result of wet linens or clothes, and from insensible loss

Conduction occurs when the infant comes in contact with cold objects or surfaces such as a scale, circumcision restraint board, cold hands, or a stethoscope

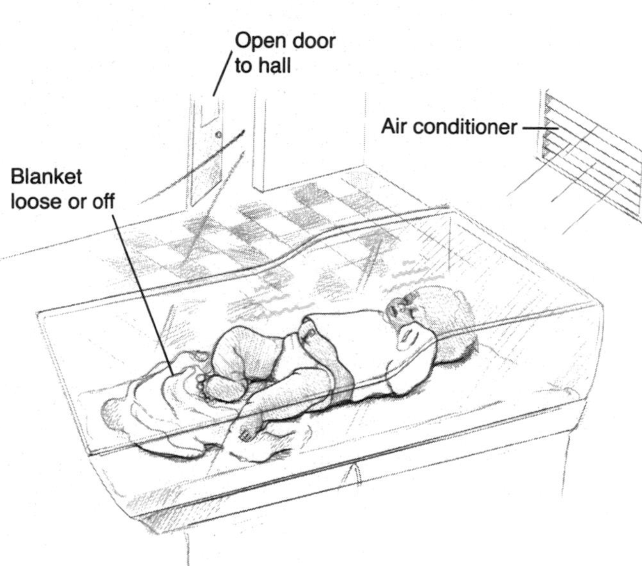

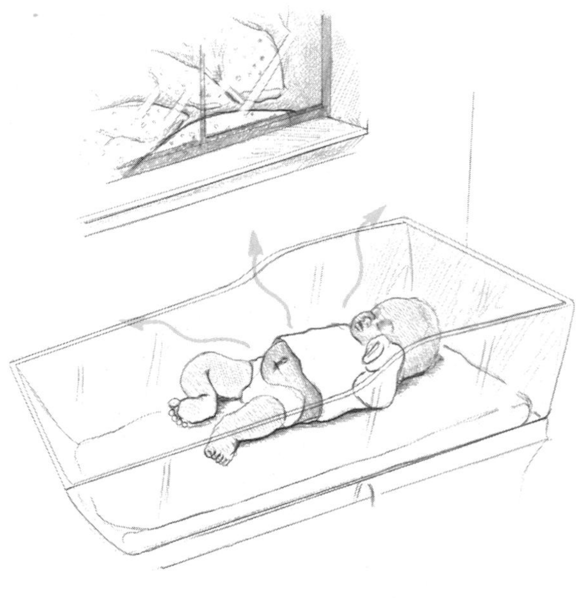

Convection occurs when drafts come from open doors, air conditioning, or even air currents created by people moving about

Radiation heat loss occurs when the infant is near colder surfaces. Thus, heat is lost from the infant's body to the side of the crib and to the outside walls and windows

Figure 19–2

Methods of heat loss.

cles. Instead, a neonate's metabolic rate increases in response to falling skin temperature. Heat is a byproduct of metabolic activity. Thus, increased metabolism leads to increased heat produced within the body.

If a higher metabolic rate does not provide enough heat, nonshivering thermogenesis, the oxidation of brown fat to produce heat, begins in the infant. Brown fat (also called brown adipose tissue) is a special kind of highly vascular fat found only in newborns. It contains an abundant supply of blood vessels, which cause the brown color. Brown fat is located primarily around the back of the neck; in the axillae; around the kidneys, adrenals, and sternum; between the scapula; and along the abdominal aorta (Fig. 19–4). As brown fat is metabolized, the heat produced is carried by the blood vessels within it to the rest of the body.

Brown fat may not be present in adequate amounts in the preterm infant or the neonate with

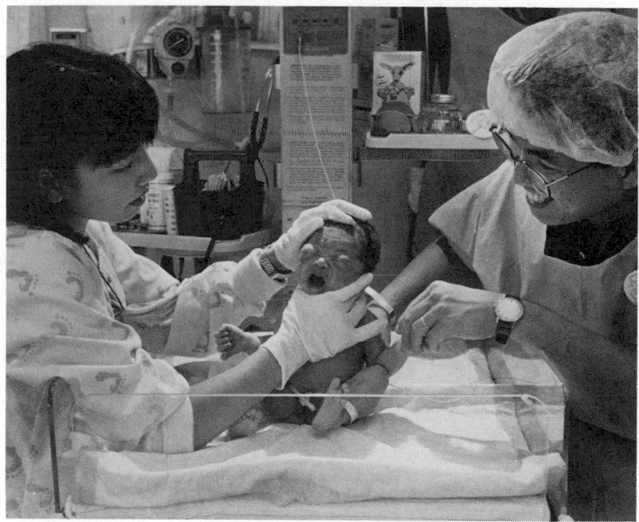

Figure 19–3

Radiant warmers allow easy access to the infant without increasing heat loss due to exposure. The nurse should be careful not to come between the infant and the overhead source of heat when caring for the infant.

intrauterine growth retardation. The fat may be consumed in newborns exposed to prolonged cold stress, and their body temperature cannot rise if they are subjected to further episodes of cold stress. Brown fat is used up during the early weeks after birth and is not present in the older infant.

Nonshivering thermogenesis begins when thermal receptors in the skin detect a drop in skin temperature. It goes into effect even before there is a change in core or interior body temperature, as measured with a rectal thermometer. Activating thermogenesis before core temperature decreases allows the body to maintain internal heat at an even level. Therefore, nonshivering thermogenesis may begin in an infant when skin temperature is cool, even though a temperature taken rectally shows a normal reading.

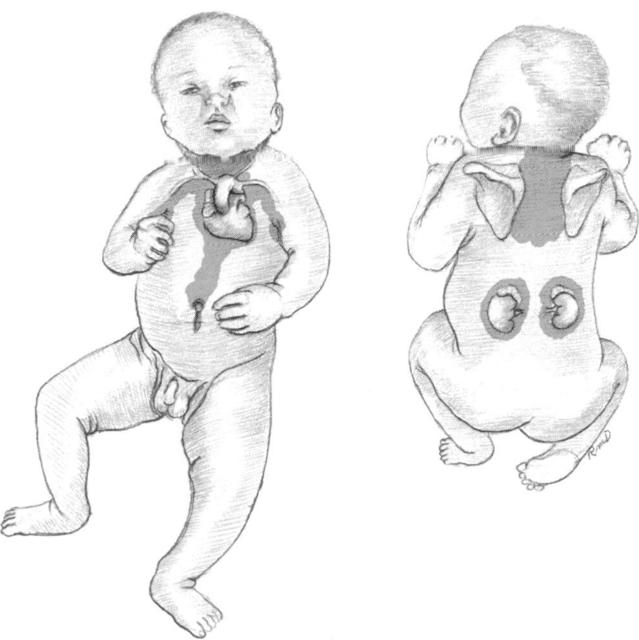

Figure 19–4

Sites of brown fat in the neonate.

EFFECTS OF COLD STRESS

When newborns experience a drop in body temperature, their metabolism increases to produce heat (Fig. 19–5). This results in an increased need for oxygen and glucose. A small increase in metabolic rate can lead to a significant rise in the need for oxygen. Even during mild respiratory distress, the infant may experience severe hypoxia as oxygen is used for heat production. The infant may not have sufficient oxygen for the metabolic rate to increase. Prolonged cold stress can cause respiratory difficulty even in a healthy full-term infant. Another result of cold stress is decreased production of surfactant, which increases the work of the lungs even more.

Glucose is necessary in larger amounts when the metabolic rate rises to produce heat. When the infant's temperature drops, glycogen stores are converted to glucose. The stores may be quickly depleted, causing hypoglycemia. Metabolism of glucose in the presence of insufficient oxygen causes increased production of acids.

Metabolism of brown fat also releases fatty acids. This increased production of acids can cause metabolic acidosis, which can be life-threatening. Elevated fatty acids in the blood stream can also interfere with transport of bilirubin to the liver, increasing the risk of jaundice.

As part of the body's effort to conserve heat, vasoconstriction of the peripheral blood vessels occurs. This helps reduce heat loss from the skin's surface. Decreased oxygen levels in the blood may also cause vasoconstriction of the pulmonary vessels and a return to fetal circulation patterns. This further increases the infant's respiratory distress.

NEUTRAL THERMAL ENVIRONMENT

A neutral thermal environment helps prevent heat loss in newborns. This is an environment in which an increase in the infant's use of oxygen or in the metabolic rate is not needed to maintain body temperature. In newborns, a temperature of 32 to 34°C (89.6 to 93.2°F) will provide a neutral thermal environment.

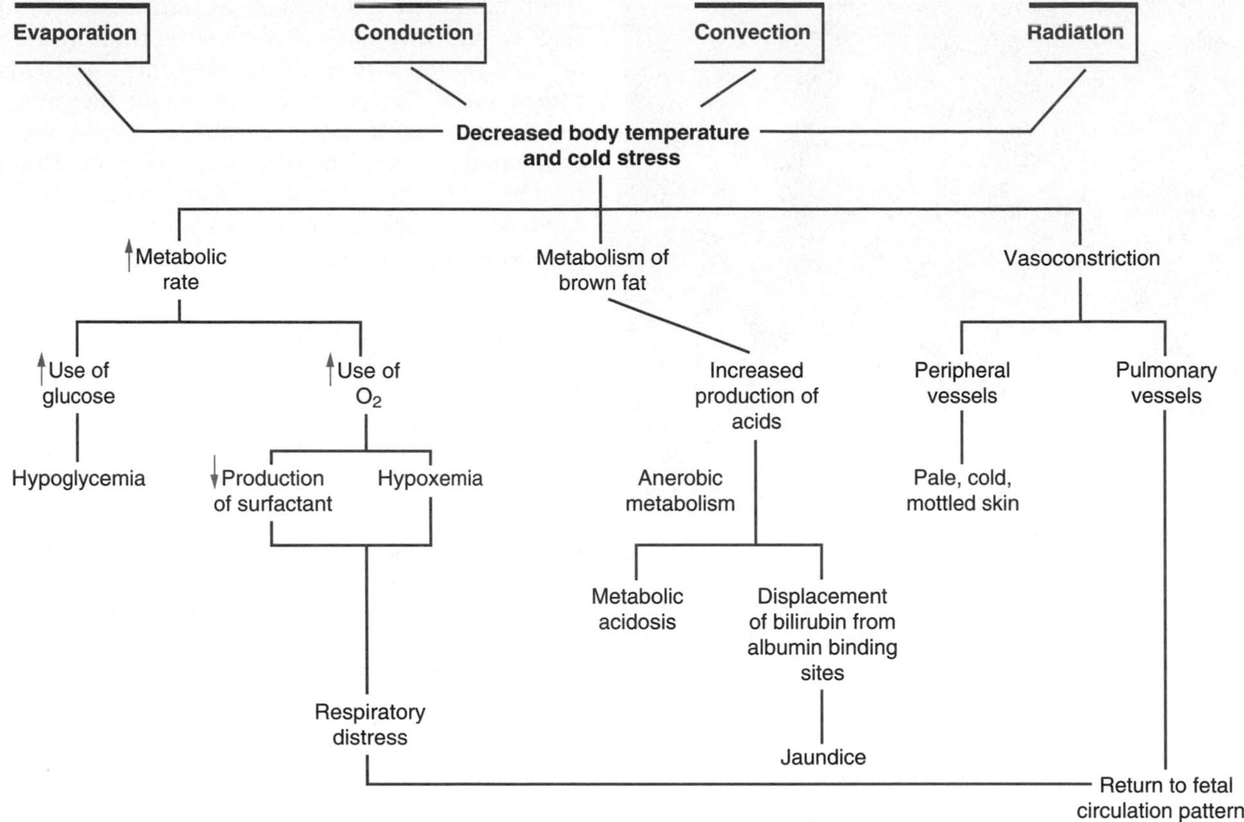

Figure 19–5

Effects of cold stress.

Critical to Remember

Hazards of Cold Stress

- Increased oxygen need
- Respiratory distress
- Decreased surfactant production
- Hypoglycemia
- Metabolic acidosis
- Jaundice

HYPERTHERMIA

Infants also respond poorly to hyperthermia. With an increase in temperature, the metabolic rate rises and with it the need for oxygen and glucose. In addition, vasodilation leads to increased insensible fluid losses. The most frequent cause of hyperthermia in newborns is overheating by equipment designed to keep them warm. When infants are under radiant warmers or warming lights, or in warmed incubators, the temperature mechanism must be set to vary the heat according to the infant's skin temperature.

✔ Check Your Reading

5. Why are neonates more prone to heat loss than older children or adults?
6. What are the effects of low temperature in newborns?

Reflexes

The presence and strength of the reflexes can be assessed to determine the health of the newborn's central nervous system (common reflexes are summarized in Table 19–2). The reflexes should be equal on both sides of the body. Asymmetry may indicate nerve damage or paralysis. Absence of a reflex may be a sign of serious pathology of the central nervous system. Some reflexes, such as the blink, swallow, or gag responses, remain the same throughout life. However, many of those characteristic of the newborn gradually weaken and disappear.

Retention of reflexes beyond the age when they should disappear indicates pathology and should prompt further investigation. Failure of the reflexes to fade on schedule may interfere with normal de-

Table 19–2. SUMMARY OF NEONATAL REFLEXES

Reflex	Method of Testing	Expected Response	Comments
Babinski	Stroke lateral sole of foot from heel to across base of toes	Toes flare with dorsiflexion of the big toe	Disappears by 8–9 months
Gallant (trunk incurvation)	Lightly stroke the back lateral to the vertebral column	Entire trunk flexes to side stimulated	Disappears by 1 month
Grasp reflex (palmar and plantar)	Press finger against base of fingers or toes	Fingers curl tightly, toes curl forward	Palmar grasp lessens in 3–4 months, disappears by 5–6 months. Plantar disappears by 8–9 months.
Moro	Let infant's head drop back approximately 30 degrees	Sharp extension and abduction of arms followed by flexion and adduction to "embrace" position. Legs follow similar pattern.	Asymmetry may indicate damage to brachial plexus, paralysis, or fractured clavicle. Weakens progressively and disappears by 6 months.
Rooting	Touch side of cheek near mouth	Infant turns to side touched. May begin to suck if finds nipple.	Difficult to elicit if infant sleeping or just fed. Disappears by 3 months.
Stepping	Hold infant so feet touch solid surface	Infant alternately lifts feet as if walking	Lasts about 1 month
Suck	Place nipple or finger in mouth, rub against palate	Infant begins to suck	Well coordinated with swallow by 34–36 weeks' gestation. Weak if recently fed.
Tonic neck reflex	Gently turn head to one side	Extension of extremities on side to which head turned, with flexion on opposite side	May be weak at birth and increase to 1 month, then disappears by 4 months

velopment. For example, the palmar grasp reflex must disappear so that the infant can learn to grasp voluntarily and later to release objects at will. Persistence of the plantar reflex would interfere with walking. Some of the reflexes are shown in Figure 19–6.

Sensory Adaptation

EARS

A newborn's ears are normally placed in such a way that they join the head on a line even with the middle of the eye. Abnormally placed ears or defects such as skin tags or preauricular sinuses may occur with other anomalies such as chromosomal abnormalities, mental retardation, or kidney defects. The stiffness of the cartilage and the degree of incurving of the pinna help determine the gestational age.

Infants can hear by the last trimester of pregnancy. Their hearing is very good after birth, once fluid drains from the middle ear and the eustachian tubes fill with air. The newborn shows preference for interesting sounds, such as his or her mother's voice, by turning toward the source.

EYES

The eyes should be symmetrical and of the same size. The usual slate-gray-blue color gradually changes to the true color by 3 to 12 months of age. The eyelids may be edematous, and subconjunctival hemorrhages may appear as reddened areas in the sclera. They result from pressure on the head during birth, which causes capillary rupture in the sclera.

The pupils should be equal in size and react to light. Cataracts (opacities of the lens) appear as white areas over the pupils. They may develop in infants of mothers who had rubella or other infections during the pregnancy. Tears are very scant or absent for the first 2 to 4 weeks of life. Excessive tearing may indicate a plugged lacrimal duct, which is treated with massage or surgery.

Figure 19–6. Reflexes.

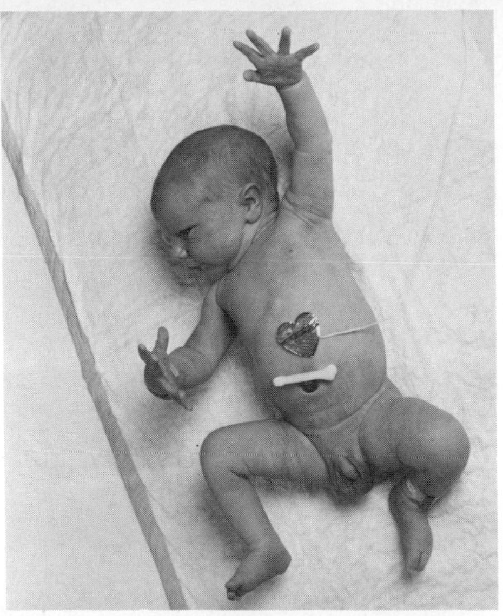

MORO REFLEX

The Moro reflex is the most dramatic reflex. It occurs when the infant's head is allowed to drop back 30 degrees or when the infant is startled. The infant's arms and legs extend and abduct, with the fingers fanning open and thumb and forefinger forming a "C" position. The arms then return to their normally flexed state with an embracing motion. The legs may also extend and then flex.

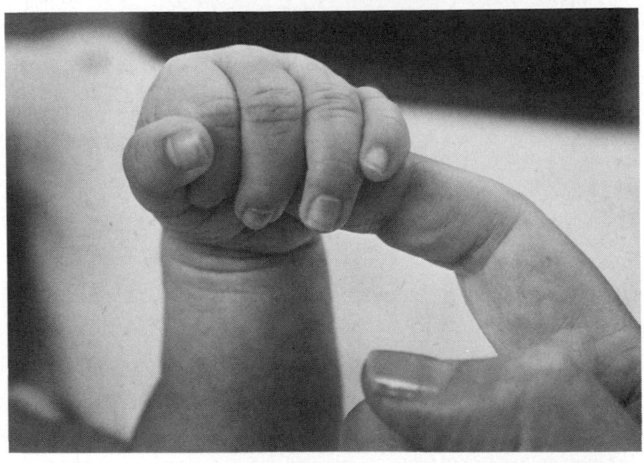

PALMAR GRASP REFLEX

The palmar grasp reflex occurs when the infant's palm is touched near the base of the fingers. The hand closes into a tight fist. The grasp reflex may be weak or absent if the infant has damage to the nerves of the arms.

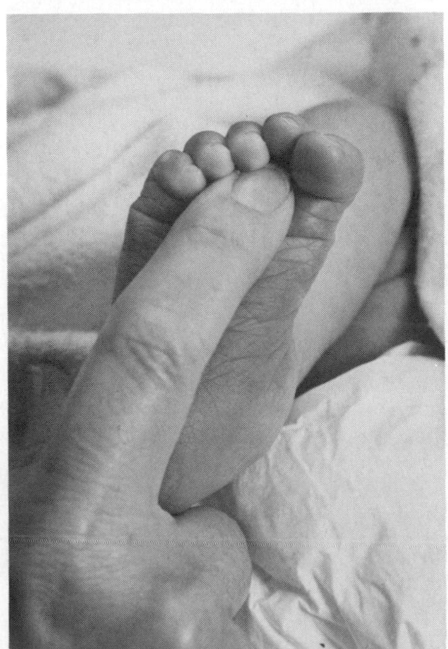

PLANTAR GRASP REFLEX

The plantar grasp reflex is similar to the palmar grasp reflex. When the area below the toes is touched, the infant's toes curl over the nurse's finger.

Figure 19–6. Reflexes *Continued*

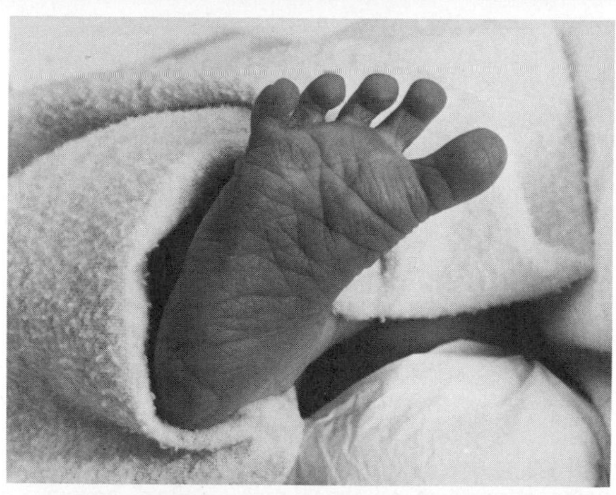

BABINSKI'S REFLEX

The Babinski reflex is elicited by stroking the lateral sole of the infant's foot from the heel forward and across the ball of the foot. This causes the toes to flare outwards and the big toe to dorsiflex.

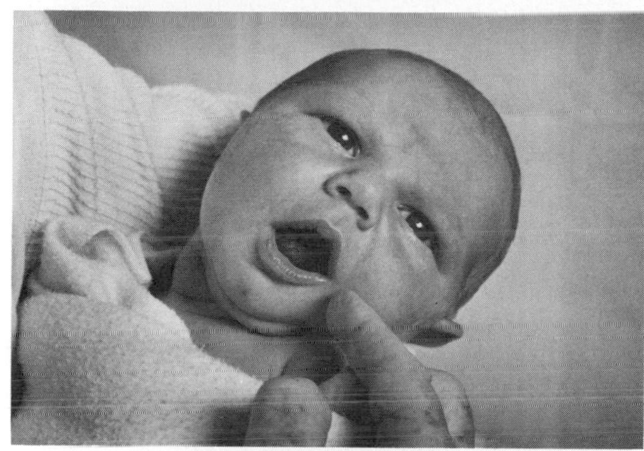

ROOTING REFLEX

The rooting reflex is important in feeding. When the infant's cheek is touched near the mouth, the head turns toward the side that has been stroked. This helps the infant find the nipple for feeding. The reflex occurs when either side of the mouth is touched. Touching the cheeks on both sides at the same time confuses the infant. Infants who are hungry are more likely to demonstrate the rooting reflex.

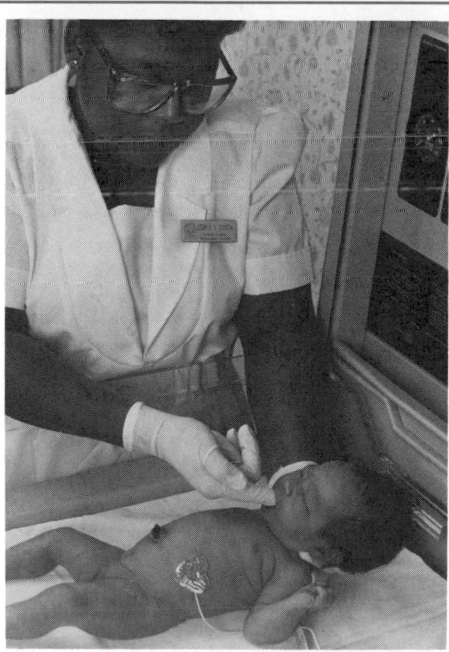

SUCKING REFLEX

The sucking reflex is essential to life. When the mouth or palate is touched by the nipple or a finger, the infant begins to suck. The sucking reflex is assessed for its presence and strength. Feeding difficulties may be related to problems in the infant's ability to suck and to coordinate sucking with swallowing.

Figure continued on following page

Figure 19–6. Reflexes *Continued*

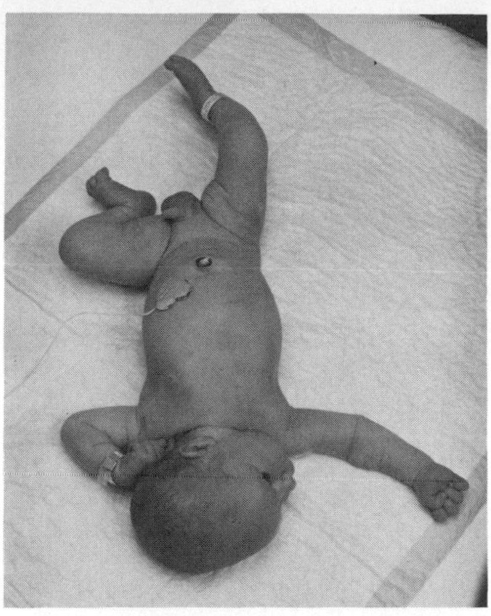

TONIC NECK REFLEX

The tonic neck reflex refers to the posture assumed by newborns when in a supine position. The infant extends the arm and leg on the side to which the head is turned and flexes the extremities on the other side. This is sometimes referred to as the "fencing reflex" because the infant's position is similar to that of a person engaged in a fencing match.

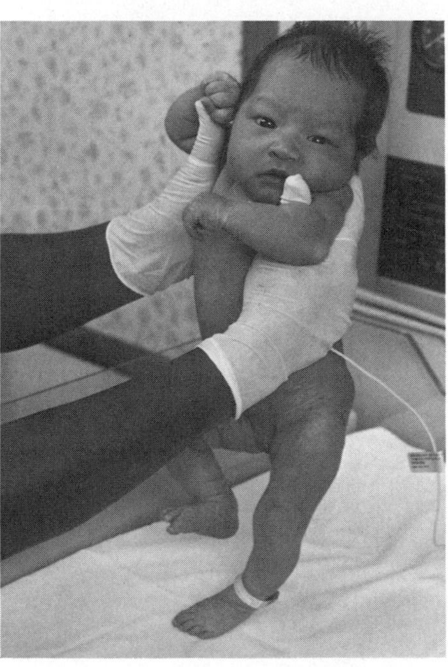

STEPPING REFLEX

The stepping reflex occurs when infants are held upright with their feet touching a solid surface. They lift one foot and then the other, giving the appearance that they are trying to walk.

Although visual acuity is not well developed and the eyes cannot accommodate for distance, the newborn is able to fixate for a short period of time. Neonates focus best on objects that are 8 to 9 inches away (Blackburn and Loper, 1992). Infants can follow interesting objects horizontally 180 degrees and vertically 30 degrees. They respond well to the human face and geometrical patterns of black and white or medium-bright colors. Infants show little interest in pastel colors.

Transient strabismus ("crossed eyes") is common for the first 3 to 4 months after birth because infants have poor control of the eye muscles until the 2nd month. The doll's eye sign is a normal finding in the newborn: when the head is turned quickly to one side, the eyes move toward the other side. The setting-sun sign—the iris appears low in the eye and part of the sclera can be seen above the iris—may be an indication of hydrocephalus.

Conjunctivitis may result from infection or a chemical reaction to medications. *Staphylococcus*, *Chlamydia*, and *Neisseria gonorrhoeae* are common organisms that cause infection. Gonorrhea in the mother can cause infection of the infant during birth. The resulting ophthalmia neonatorum may cause blindness. In order to prevent this condition, all infants are treated prophylactically. Silver nitrate was once the major form of prophylaxis but frequently caused a chemical conjunctivitis. Most hospitals now use antibiotic ointment or drops such as erythromycin. Erythromycin is also effective for the infant infected with *Chlamydia* (see Drug Guide: Erythromycin Ophthalmic Ointment, Chapter 20, p. 516).

OTHER SENSES

Newborns have a good sense of smell, and discrimination develops quickly. They prefer odors belonging to the mother and can smell breast milk within a few days after birth (Blackburn and Loper, 1992). The ability of infants to distinguish taste is shown by their increased suck when given sweet liquids and rejection of those that are sour or bitter.

Infants respond to soothing, gentle touch by quieting down. They react to painful stimuli by crying, and there is an increase in vital signs. The infant's response to the mother's touch is an important part of the bonding process. Rocking motions are often used as an effective method of quieting an irritable infant.

Other Neurological Signs

Tremors or jitteriness may signify a variety of conditions. Hypoglycemia is probably the most common cause. Deficiency of calcium and prenatal exposure to drugs also cause tremors and should be suspected in the jittery infant who does not have a low blood glucose level. Tremors increase each time the infant is touched or moved but will stop briefly if the extremity is flexed and held firmly.

Seizures indicate central nervous system abnormality. They are not affected by disturbances and cannot be stopped by flexing or holding the extremities. Seizure activity may also include abnormal movements of the eyes or mouth and other subtle signs. Any infant thought to be having seizures should be referred for further assessment and treatment.

The normal infant "molds" his or her body to that of the caretaker when held. The infant who seems stiff or arches the back when disturbed may have neurological damage. Excessive irritability or a high-pitched cry may also be a sign of damage to the nervous system.

Hematological Adaptation

Factors Affecting Blood Composition

The volume of the blood and the quality of its various components in the newborn are dependent on the site from which the blood is drawn, whether clamping of the cord occurs immediately after birth or is delayed, and the position of the infant just before the cord is clamped (see Appendix C, p. 972). For example, blood samples drawn from the heel, where the circulation is sluggish, will result in higher measurements of hemoglobin and hematocrit than samples from central areas. Venous blood samples are more accurate and are taken when it is essential to be precise.

The average blood volume of the newborn is 80 to 85 ml/kg. Whether or not to encourage blood flow from the placenta to the infant at birth is controversial. The infant held below the level of the placenta for 1 minute before the cord is clamped may have as much as a 50-ml increase of blood volume (Glader and Naiman, 1991). The extra blood volume may increase the workload of the heart excessively. As the added red blood cells break down, they release bilirubin, increasing the risk of jaundice. Although nurses do not make the decision as to when clamping should occur, they must watch for possible adverse effects of the technique used.

Blood Values

RED BLOOD CELLS

At birth, the infant has comparatively more red blood cells (erythrocytes) and a higher hemoglobin and hematocrit level than the adult. This is necessary because the partial pressure of oxygen of fetal blood in the umbilical vein is only about 30 mmHg (Guyton, 1991). The large number of red blood cells and higher hemoglobin level enable the fetal cells to receive enough oxygen. Fetal hemoglobin, which makes up 90 to 95 per cent of the newborn's hemoglobin level, carries greater amounts of oxygen than adult hemoglobin (Blackburn and Loper, 1992). Erythrocytes in the newborn have a shorter life span than those in the adult and break down soon after birth. When this happens, hemoglobin is broken down, releasing bilirubin. Excess amounts of bilirubin due to hemolysis of large numbers of red blood cells may lead to jaundice. (See discussion of hyperbilirubinemia, p. 496.)

HEMATOCRIT

The hematocrit level in the normal infant is 48 to 69 per cent from peripheral sites (Nicholson and Pesce, 1992). A level above 65 per cent from a central site indicates polycythemia, an abnormally high erythrocyte count. Polycythemia increases the risk of jaundice and damage to the brain or other organs as a result of blood stasis.

LEUKOCYTES

The leukocyte count in the newborn is 9000 to 30,000/mm^3. In newborns, an elevated white blood cell count does not necessarily indicate infection. In fact, the white blood cell count may decrease in infections. Increased numbers of immature leukocytes are a sign of infection or sepsis in the neonate. Platelets may also decrease as a result of infections. (See discussion of sepsis in Chapter 29, p. 853.)

Risk of Clotting Deficiency

Newborns are at risk for clotting deficiency during the first few days of life because they lack vitamin K, which is necessary to activate several of the clotting factors (factors II, VII, IX, and X.) Vitamin K is synthesized in the intestines, but food and normal intestinal flora are necessary for this process. At birth, the intestines are sterile and therefore unable to produce vitamin K. To decrease the risk of hemorrhage, intramuscular vitamin K is administered to most infants during the initial assessment and care. Drugs such as phenytoin (Dilantin), phenobarbital, or aspirin taken during pregnancy interfere with clotting ability in the infant after birth.

✔ Check Your Reading

7. Why are newborn reflexes important?
8. Why do newborns have higher levels of red blood cells, hemoglobin, and hematocrit than adults?

Musculoskeletal System

Activity and Muscle Tone

The normal infant should actively move the extremities in a random manner. Movement of all extremities should be equal. In utero, the fetus is in a position of flexion. After birth, the newborn's extremities should remain sharply flexed and resist extension during examination. Poor muscle tone results in a limp or "floppy" infant. This may be due to inadequate oxygen during birth but often resolves within a few minutes as the infant increases oxygen intake. Continued poor muscle tone is common in the preterm infant but may indicate neurological damage in the term infant. Infants with previously good muscle tone may show decreased flexion if they become hypoglycemic or experience respiratory difficulty.

Head

The head is the heaviest part of the newborn and constitutes one fourth of the body length. It is much larger in proportion to body size than in the adult. The head is assessed for abnormalities and changes that may be due to the trauma of birth.

MOLDING

Molding refers to changes in the shape of the head that allow it to pass through the birth canal. It is caused by overriding of the sutures and is common, especially following a long labor and/or second stage labor. Molding generally resolves within a few days of birth.

Normal molding must be differentiated from abnormalities of the skull. Widening of the sutures may indicate increased intracranial pressure. If there is no space between suture lines, they may be prematurely closed. This condition, called craniosynostosis, may impair brain growth and the shape of the head and necessitates surgery.

FONTANELLES

The fontanelles are the areas of the head where the bones come together. They are not calcified in the newborn but, rather, are covered by membrane. This allows space for the brain to grow. The fontanelles close and the sutures calcify during early childhood.

The anterior fontanelle is a diamond-shaped membrane where the frontal and parietal bones come together (see Fig. 12–4, p. 271). It measures 3 to 4 cm in length by 2 to 3 cm in width. Molding may alter the size and shape of the anterior fontanelle for the first few days of life. It closes between 12 and 18 months of age.

The posterior fontanelle is a triangular membrane where the occipital and parietal bones are joined. It is much smaller than the anterior fontanelle, measur-

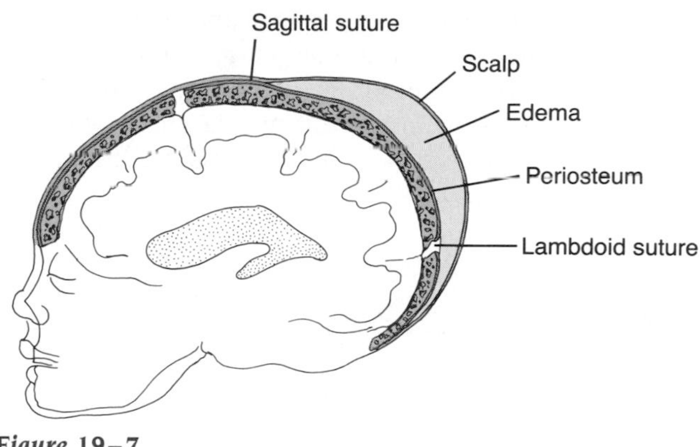

Figure 19–7

Caput succedaneum is an edematous area on the head from pressure against the cervix.

ing 1 to 2 cm. This fontanelle closes by the time the infant is 2 to 3 months old.

CAPUT SUCCEDANEUM

Caput succedaneum is a common variation of the normal skull (Fig. 19–7). It is an area of edema under the scalp from pressure against the cervix during labor. The pressure against the presenting part interferes with blood flow from the area, causing edema. This is especially common after a long labor. The edematous area is soft and varies in size. Caput may also occur when a vacuum extractor is used to hasten the second stage of labor. When the vacuum is used, the caput corresponds to the area where the extractor was placed on the skull. Caput succedaneum may cross over suture lines and is present at birth. It usually reabsorbs within a day or two after birth.

CEPHALOHEMATOMA

A cephalohematoma occurs when there is bleeding between the periosteum and a bone of the skull due to pressure during birth (Fig. 19–8). It is usually over the parietal bones, although occasionally it may form over the occipital bone. Although it is not present at birth, a firm swelling develops within the first 24 to 48 hours. A cephalohematoma does not cross suture lines as caput succedaneum does because it is held between the bone and its covering, the periosteum. It reabsorbs slowly and is generally gone within a few weeks after birth. Because of the breakdown of the red blood cells within the hematoma, the affected infant is at greater risk for jaundice or hyperbilirubinemia.

Neck and Clavicles

The newborn has a very short neck. Webbing of the neck and an unusually large fat pad between the occiput and the shoulders may indicate a chromosomal anomaly. The head should turn easily to each side. Fracture of the clavicle may be present if shoulder dystocia occurred. Damage to the brachial plexus may cause paralysis of the arm on the side of the fracture.

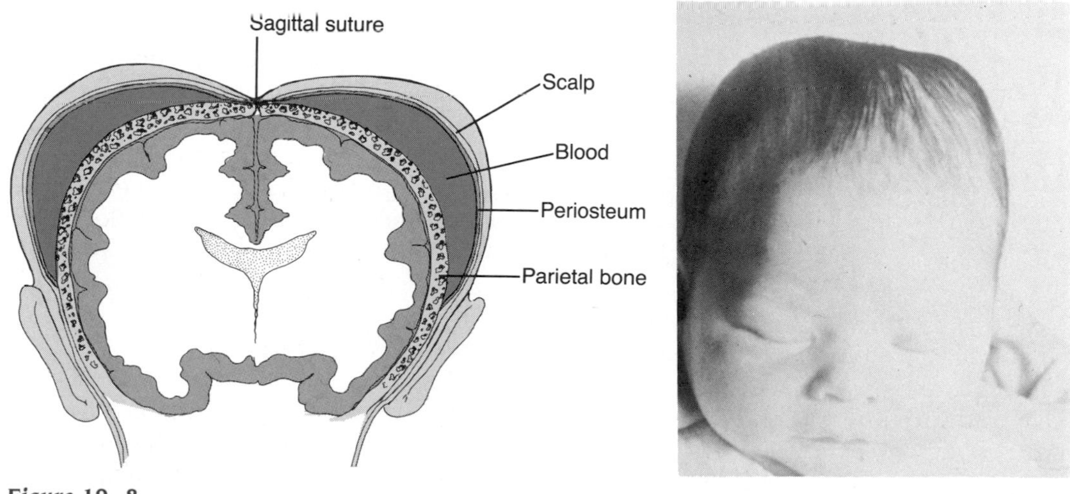

Figure 19–8

A cephalohematoma is characterized by bleeding between the bone and its covering, the periosteum. It may occur on one or both sides.

Extremities

FRACTURES

Although the clavicle is the bone most often broken, fractures of other bones may also occur during birth. Injury to the brachial nerve plexus may cause Erb's palsy (Erb-Duchenne paralysis). In this condition, there is paralysis of the shoulder and arm muscles. Instead of the usual flexed position, the affected arm is extended at the infant's side with the forearm prone. Movement is diminished during the Moro reflex. The condition is treated by exercise and/or splinting.

POLYDACTYLY AND SYNDACTYLY

Polydactyly is the presence of more than ten fingers or ten toes. Often the extra digit is smaller than the others and may not have a bone inside. In these cases, it can be tied off and will atrophy and eventually drop off. If there is a bone, surgery will be necessary to remove it.

Syndactyly occurs when fingers or toes are joined together. They may be joined by just a web of skin, which is easily remedied with minor surgery, or they may be partially or completely fused.

PALMAR CREASES

Normally, there are several creases partially crossing the palm. A simian line is a single crease that crosses the palm without breaking. This may be seen with an incurving of the little finger in Down syndrome. The simian line alone is not diagnostic of Down syndrome, however, and may occur in normal infants.

HIPS

Congenital hip dysplasia is incomplete development of the acetabulum, which allows the head of the femur to slip out of the acetabulum and become dislocated. Infants who were in a breech position at birth are at increased risk for hip dysplasia. Although the hip is usually not actually dislocated at birth, it will become dislocated and permanently damaged if the infant is allowed to walk. Therefore, early identification and treatment are important. Treatment consists of immobilizing the leg in a flexed, abducted position, usually with a harness. Sometimes, the use of double or triple diapers is sufficient.

FEET

Talipes equinovarus, or clubfoot, is a common malformation of the feet. In true clubfoot, the foot turns inward and cannot be moved to a midline position. Casting is used, and sometimes surgery may be necessary. Positional clubfoot is a temporary result of the infant's position in the uterus. In this case, the foot can be manipulated back to normal position and casting is unnecessary.

Gastrointestinal System

At birth, the infant must begin to take in, digest, and absorb food, as the placenta no longer performs these functions.

Stomach

The stomach capacity is only about 40 to 60 ml at birth but expands to 90 ml within the first few days of life. The stomach begins to empty during feeding and is completely empty within 2 to 4 hours. Peristalsis is rapid and is increased by feeding. The gastrocolic reflex is stimulated when the stomach fills, causing increased intestinal peristalsis. Infants frequently pass a stool during or following a feeding. The cardiac sphincter between the esophagus and the stomach is relaxed in the newborn, which explains the tendency to regurgitate feedings easily.

Intestines

The intestines are long in proportion to the infant's size compared with those of the adult. The added length allows more surface area for absorption. However, it makes infants more prone to water loss should diarrhea develop. Air enters the gastrointestinal tract soon after birth, and bowel sounds are present within the first hour.

The digestive tract is sterile at birth. Once the infant is exposed to the external environment and begins to take in fluids, bacteria enter the gastrointestinal tract. Normal intestinal flora is established within the first few days of life.

Digestive Enzymes

The enzymes that are necessary to digest simple carbohydrates, proteins, and fats are present by 36 to 38 weeks of gestation. Pancreatic amylase is not present for the first 3 to 6 months after birth. As a result, the newborn cannot digest complex carbohydrates such as those in cereals. Amylase is also produced by the salivary glands, but saliva is not secreted in adequate amounts until about the 3rd month of life.

Lactose is the major carbohydrate in the infant's milk diet and is easily digested. Protein is also well digested. Fat is not absorbed as completely as lactose and protein because the newborn is deficient in pancreatic lipase. Breast milk contains lipase to aid in fat digestion. Fats in breast milk are in a form that the infant can use more readily than the fat in formula.

Stools

Meconium is the first stool excreted by the newborn. It consists of particles from amniotic fluid such as skin cells and hair, along with cells shed from the intestinal tract, bile, and other intestinal secretions. Meconium, which is greenish-black in color with a thick, sticky, tar-like consistency, accumulates in the fetus's intestines throughout gestation. The first meconium stool is usually passed within the first 24 hours of life. If none is passed within 36 to 48 hours, obstruction is suspected.

The second type of stool excreted by the newborn is called transitional stool and is greenish-brown and of a looser consistency than meconium. These stools are a combination of meconium and milk stools. They are followed by the stool that is characteristic of the type of feeding that the infant receives.

The stools of infants on breast milk are the color and consistency of mustard with a sweet-sour smell. The breastfed infant generally has more frequent stools than the infant who is formula-fed. Breastfed infants may excrete as many as ten small stools each day, although some pass only one stool every 2 to 3 days. Parents should be taught that either pattern can be normal as long as the stools are neither watery nor hard in consistency.

The formula-fed infant excretes light-yellow stools. They are firmer in consistency than those of the breastfed infant. The infant may excrete several stools daily or only one or two. The stools have the characteristic odor of feces.

✔ Check Your Reading

9. What is the difference between molding, caput succedaneum, and cephalohematoma?
10. How do the stools change over the first few days after birth?

Hepatic System

The liver assumes many different functions after birth. Some of the most important include maintenance of blood glucose levels, production of factors necessary for blood coagulation, storage of iron, metabolism of drugs, and conjugation of bilirubin.

Blood Glucose Maintenance

Throughout gestation, glucose is supplied to the fetus by the placenta. During the last 4 to 8 weeks of pregnancy, glucose is stored in the fetal liver as glycogen for use after birth. Glucose is used more rapidly in the newborn than in the fetus because energy is needed during the stresses of delivery and for breathing, heat production, movement against gravity, and activation of all the functions that the neonate must take on at birth. In addition, glucose must be readily available for use by the brain, which needs a constant supply. Without adequate glucose, the brain may be damaged. Therefore, the liver's ability to convert glycogen to glucose is essential.

Until newborns begin regular feedings and their intake is adequate to meet energy requirements, the glucose that is present in the body is used. As the blood glucose level falls, the liver begins to convert glycogen to glucose, which is made available for the rest of the body. In the term infant, glucose levels should stabilize at 50 to 60 mg/dl during the early hours after birth (Blackburn and Loper, 1992). A blood glucose level below 40 mg/dl in the term infant indicates hypoglycemia (Behrman, 1992).

INFANTS AT RISK

Many newborns are at increased risk for hypoglycemia. The newborn may have inadequate glycogen stores, and early needs cannot be met. In the preterm and small-for-gestational-age infant, adequate stores of glycogen or even fat for metabolism may not have accumulated. Stores of glycogen may be used up before birth in the postterm infant because of poor intrauterine nourishment from a deteriorating placenta.

Large-for-gestational-age newborns may produce excessive insulin that consumes available glucose quickly. This is particularly true if the mother is diabetic. These infants receive large amounts of glucose from the mother throughout pregnancy and must produce enough insulin to use the glucose. Although the supply of glucose is cut off at birth, the infants still produce more insulin than needed, which results in hypoglycemia soon after birth. (See Chapter 29, p. 856, for a discussion of the infant of a diabetic mother.)

Almost any stress can predispose a newborn to hypoglycemia. When infants are exposed to such stressors as asphyxia, which results in rapid use of glucose, the glycogen in the liver may quickly be exhausted, and they show signs of hypoglycemia. In newborns who are not kept warm, glucose may be used up to increase metabolism and raise body temperature.

SIGNS OF HYPOGLYCEMIA

Early signs of hypoglycemia include jitteriness and poor muscle tone. Other signs include respiratory difficulty, such as tachypnea, dyspnea, apnea, and cyanosis. Perspiration rarely relates to temperature but may indicate hypoglycemia. Hypothermia may result when there is not enough glucose to maintain a metabolic rate sufficient to maintain body temperature. The infant may suck poorly. Central nervous system signs of lack of glucose include high-pitched cry, lethargy, seizures, and eventually coma.

TREATMENT

Infants with hypoglycemia are fed to provide the needed glucose. If the blood glucose does not remain at an adequate level, other causative factors are investigated. Infants may receive intravenous feedings until blood glucose is regulated with oral feedings.

Conjugation of Bilirubin

A major function of the liver is the conjugation of bilirubin (Fig. 19–9). Although the newborn's liver is able to perform this function, it may not be mature enough to prevent the development of jaundice during the first week of life. Jaundice occurs in 60 per cent of term newborns (Behrman, 1992).

SOURCE AND EFFECT OF BILIRUBIN

The principal source of bilirubin is the hemolysis of erythrocytes. This is a normal occurrence after birth, when fewer red blood cells are needed than during fetal life. The breakdown of erythrocytes releases their components into the blood stream to be reused by the body. Only bilirubin remains as an unusable residue in the blood. It is toxic to the body and must be excreted.

Bilirubin is released in an unconjugated form. Unconjugated bilirubin, also called indirect bilirubin, is

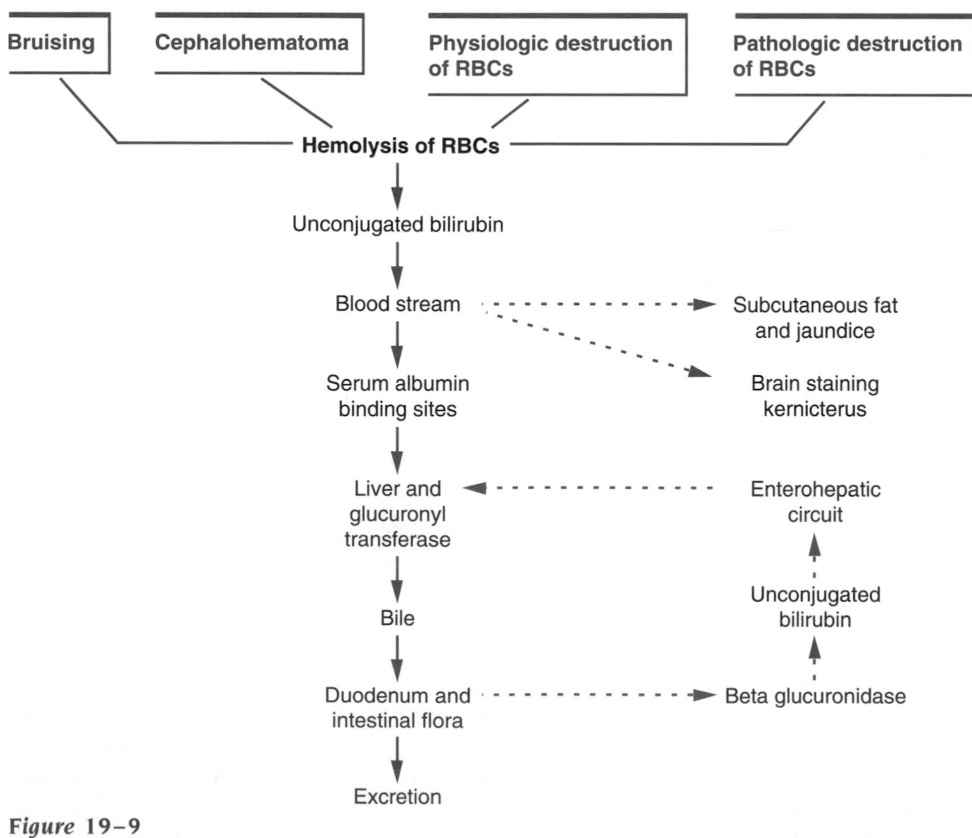

Figure 19–9

Diagram showing sources of bilirubin and how it is removed from the body.

not soluble in water. The liver must change it to a water-soluble form by a process called conjugation before it can be excreted. The bilirubin is then known as conjugated or direct bilirubin.

Because unconjugated bilirubin is fat-soluble, it may be absorbed by the subcutaneous fat, causing the yellowish discoloration of the skin called jaundice. If enough unconjugated bilirubin accumulates in the blood, staining of the tissues in the brain may occur. This is known as kernicterus and may result in severe brain damage. The infant afflicted with kernicterus has a 75 per cent chance of dying from the condition. Those who survive may have cerebral palsy, hearing loss, and/or mental retardation (Behrman 1992).

NORMAL CONJUGATION

When unconjugated bilirubin is released into the blood stream, it attaches to binding sites on albumin in the plasma and is carried to the liver. There, the enzyme glucuronyl transferase changes it to the conjugated form. It is excreted into the bile and then into the duodenum. In the intestines, the normal flora acts on bilirubin to reduce it to stercobilin, which is excreted in the stool.

A small percentage of conjugated bilirubin may be converted back to the unconjugated state by the intestinal enzyme β-glucuronidase. It is reabsorbed into the blood stream and carried back to the liver, where it once again undergoes the conjugation process. This recirculation of bilirubin is called the enterohepatic circuit, and it is added work for the liver.

FACTORS IN INCREASED BILIRUBIN

A number of factors in the newborn lead to the production of excessive amounts of bilirubin or interfere with the normal process of conjugation (Table 19–3), resulting in an increased incidence of jaundice in the first week of life.

Excess Production. Bilirubin is produced in newborns at a rate twice that in adults (Oski, 1991b). Newborns have more red blood cells per kilogram of weight than adults. This is because oxygen levels are low during fetal life and more erythrocytes are needed to carry enough oxygen to the cells.

Red Blood Cell Life. Fetal red blood cells last only two thirds as long as adult erythrocytes before hemolysis. For their size, neonates have more red blood cells breaking down faster and producing greater amounts of bilirubin to excrete when compared with adults.

Liver Immaturity. The newborn's immature liver may not produce adequate amounts of glucuronyl transferase. Insufficient availability of this enzyme limits the amount of bilirubin that can be conjugated. The liver usually matures after the first few days of life and is then able to perform this function adequately for normal needs.

Intestinal Factors. The intestines of the newborn are sterile at first. Conjugated bilirubin cannot be reduced to stercobilin for excretion without the action of intestinal flora. In addition, the newborn intestines have a large amount of the enzyme β-glucuronidase, which changes bilirubin back to the unconjugated state. These two factors may result in high levels of unconjugated bilirubin, which are reabsorbed back into the blood circulation.

Delayed Feeding. Feeding the newborn helps establish the normal intestinal flora and promotes passage of meconium, which is high in bilirubin. When feeding is delayed or stools are not passed, the chance of conversion of conjugated bilirubin to the unconjugated state and reabsorption into the blood increases.

Trauma. Trauma during birth may result in increased hemolysis of red blood cells. This is particularly true when there is bruising, which may be caused by use of forceps or the vacuum extractor. The infant born in a breech position may also have bruising. In newborns with cephalohematoma, a large number of erythrocytes may have been removed from the circulation. As the red blood cells in the bruised areas break down, they add to the bilirubin load.

Fatty Acids. Fatty acids have a greater affinity than bilirubin for the binding sites on albumin and will bind to albumin in place of bilirubin. They are released when brown fat is used to increase heat during cold stress. During asphyxia, anaerobic metabolism also produces fatty acids. Thus, in infants who suffer cold stress or asphyxia, unbound unconjugated bilirubin is in the circulation and jaundice may develop.

Table 19–3. FACTORS THAT INCREASE HYPERBILIRUBINEMIA

Hemolysis of excessive erythrocytes
Short red blood cell life
Liver immaturity
β-Glucuronidase in large amounts
Lack of intestinal flora
Delayed feeding
Trauma resulting in bruising or cephalohematoma
Fatty acids from cold stress or asphyxia

Hyperbilirubinemia

PHYSIOLOGIC JAUNDICE

Physiologic jaundice is due to the transient hyperbilirubinemia that occurs for any of the reasons already discussed. It is never present during the first 24 hours of life but, rather, appears on the 2nd or 3rd day after birth. Physiologic jaundice becomes visible when the bilirubin in the serum reaches 5 to 7 mg/dl and is considered a normal phenomenon in newborns.

The rate at which bilirubin in the blood rises and falls is important because it helps one to estimate whether the rate for a particular infant is following the expected curve for age and birth weight. Cord blood has an average bilirubin level of 1.5 mg/dl. In physiologic jaundice, the serum bilirubin rises rapidly, peaking at 6 to 7 mg/dl on the 3rd day of life. It then begins to fall, reaching 3 mg/dl by day 5, and is back to a normal level of 1 mg/dl by the end of the 2nd week (Oski, 1991b).

Physiologic jaundice may be treated with phototherapy when the bilirubin levels rise faster or to higher levels than expected. Because preterm and low-birth-weight infants are more susceptible to kernicterus at lower bilirubin levels, phototherapy may be used sooner than in the full-term infant. (Nursing care of the infant needing phototherapy is discussed in Chapter 29, p. 846.)

PATHOLOGIC JAUNDICE

Physiologic jaundice must be differentiated from pathologic jaundice, which is abnormal and necessitates further investigation. One of the most important differences is the time the jaundice appears. Pathologic jaundice occurs in the first 24 hours after birth, whereas physiologic jaundice never occurs that early. If the bilirubin concentration increases by more than 5 mg/dl/day, or the level reaches 13 mg/dl, the jaundice is considered pathologic (Oski, 1991a).

Pathologic jaundice is due to abnormalities causing excessive destruction of erythrocytes. These include infection, incompatibilities between the mother's and infant's blood types (see Chapter 24, p. 691), or metabolic disorders (see discussion of pathologic jaundice in Chapter 29, p. 845).

BREAST MILK JAUNDICE

Jaundice in breastfed infants may develop because of insufficient intake during the first few days of life to cause the elimination of meconium, which is high in bilirubin. A sleepy infant, one who has a poor suck, or one who nurses on an infrequent schedule may not receive enough colostrum, the substance that precedes true breast milk, to take advantage of its normal laxative effect. Lack of adequate suckling depresses production of breast milk and increases the problem further. Helping the mother with breastfeeding to increase the infant's intake and stimulate milk production may be the most important treatment.

In true breast milk jaundice, bilirubin levels begin to rise between the 4th and 7th day of life, after the time of onset of physiologic jaundice. Bilirubin levels peak at 2 weeks at 15 to 20 mg/dl and take as long as 16 weeks to fall to normal levels (de Steuben, 1992). Although the exact cause of breast milk jaundice is unknown, it is thought to be related to the presence of pregnanediol and free fatty acids in the milk. These substances interfere with enzyme activity in the liver.

Treatment of breast milk jaundice includes close monitoring of bilirubin levels in the blood. Although the levels are higher and last longer than in physiologic jaundice, there are no reported cases of kernicterus from this type of jaundice (Shoptaugh, 1992). If bilirubin levels become too elevated, breastfeeding may be discontinued for 24 to 48 hours. This causes a rapid drop in bilirubin. The level may rise again when breastfeeding is resumed but generally not enough to interfere with further breastfeeding.

Blood Coagulation

Prothrombin and coagulation factors II, VII, IX, and X are produced by the liver and activated by vitamin K, which is deficient in the newborn. This is discussed under hematologic adaptation (p. 490).

Iron Storage

Iron is stored in the liver during the last weeks of pregnancy. If the infant is born at full term and the mother's diet was adequate in iron, there will be enough stored iron to prevent anemia during the infant's early months, when the diet is poor in iron. The infant whose prenatal stores may be inadequate is given iron-fortified formula.

Metabolism of Drugs

One function of the liver is to metabolize drugs. In the newborn, this function is inefficient. This is taken into consideration when drugs are given to the neonate. A breastfeeding mother should alert her physician before taking medications, which may be transferred to the infant via the breast milk.

✔ Check Your Reading

11. Why is hypoglycemia a problem for the newborn?
12. What are some signs of hypoglycemia?
13. What are the differences between physiologic, pathologic, and breast milk jaundice?

Genitourinary System

Kidneys

The kidneys remove waste products from the blood stream and maintain fluid and electrolyte balance.

DEVELOPMENT

The kidneys begin to produce urine at about the 12th week of gestation. Fetal urine is not actually a waste product because the placenta eliminates wastes for the fetus. It becomes the major source of amniotic fluid by the second half of pregnancy. Failure of the kidneys to produce urine will cause oligohydramnios, or lack of sufficient amniotic fluid.

The kidneys are completely developed at 35 weeks of gestation. Full kidney function does not occur until after birth, when the kidneys take over the elimination of wastes from the blood. Blood flow to the kidneys increases after birth because of decreased resistance in the renal vessels. The improved perfusion results in a steady improvement in kidney function during the first few days of life.

KIDNEY FUNCTION

Although the formation of nephrons is complete by birth, kidney function is immature when compared to that in the adult. The ability of the glomeruli to filter and the renal tubules to reabsorb is considerably less than in adults. The glomerular filtration rate at birth is as little as half that in the adult but reaches adult levels by 1 to 2 years of age (Anand, 1991b).

Substances such as glucose and protein may escape into the urine of the neonate. These substances disappear within the first 3 days of life as kidney function improves. Urate crystals may give a pink color to the urine that is sometimes mistaken for blood.

The first voiding occurs within 24 hours of birth in most newborns. The newborn who does not void within 48 hours may lack kidneys or have hypovolemia, obstructions of the urinary tract, or other abnormalities. Only 2 to 6 voidings occur during the first 2 days of life, but urine output then increases to 5 to 25 voidings daily (Anand, 1991b).

FLUID BALANCE

Newborns have a lower tolerance for changes in total volume of body fluid than older infants. This is because of the location of water within the newborn's body and the inability of the kidneys to adapt to large changes in body fluids.

Water Distribution. A large percentage of the infant's body is composed of water, which is distributed differently than in the adult (Fig. 19–10). Water constitutes 78 per cent of the infant's body weight. It takes approximately 1 year for body fluid to decrease to the adult level of 60 per cent of body weight (Behrman, 1992).

In the adult, 20 per cent of body weight is composed of extracellular water located in the interstitial or intravascular spaces. The percentage of extracellular water in newborns is more than twice as high as in adults. Although fluid within the cells is relatively stable, extracellular water is easily lost from the body. Because infants have more fluid for their size than adults, and because a larger proportion of it is located outside the cells, total body water is easily depleted. Conditions such as vomiting or diarrhea can quickly result in life-threatening dehydration.

Insensible Water Loss. Water lost from the skin and respiratory tract contributes to insensible water loss. Insensible water losses are increased in the newborn because of the large surface area of the body and the rapid respiratory rate. Fluid losses increase greatly when infants are under radiant heaters, which accelerate evaporation from the skin. An elevated respiratory rate or low humidity in the air surrounding the infant raises insensible water losses even further.

Urine Dilution and Concentration. The ability of a newborn's kidneys to dilute urine is relatively good, to a specific gravity of 1.001 to 1.005. However, a newborn's kidneys cannot handle large increases in fluids, which results in fluid overload. This is most likely to happen when infants receive intravenous fluids.

Newborns have more difficulty preventing loss of fluid in the urine than adults because they have only half the adult's ability to excrete concentrated urine (Guyton, 1991). Neonates can concentrate urine only to a specific gravity of 1.015 to 1.020 (Portman et al, 1989) as compared to the adult level of 1.040. It takes 3 to 6 months for concentrated urine to reach adult levels. When abnormal conditions such as diarrhea cause excessive loss of fluid, the newborn's

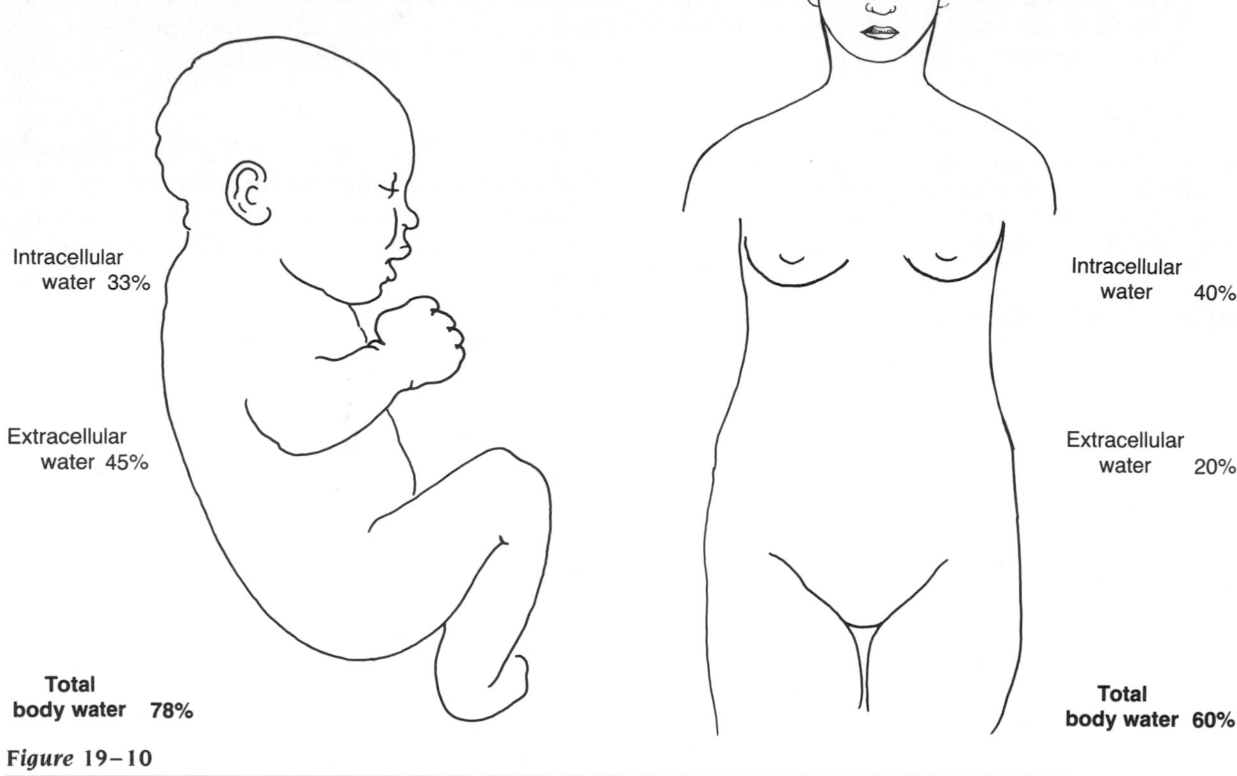

Figure 19–10

Comparison of distribution of body water in newborns and adults as a percentage of body weight.

limited ability to conserve water may result in dehydration more quickly than in the older infant or child.

ACID-BASE AND ELECTROLYTE BALANCE

The maintenance of acid-base and electrolyte balance is a primary function of the kidneys and may be precarious in neonates. They tend to lose bicarbonate at lower levels than adults, increasing their risk for acidosis. The excretion of solutes is less efficient in newborns as well. Although newborns conserve needed sodium well, they are less able to excrete it efficiently if they receive excessive amounts (Anand, 1991b).

Genitals

FEMALE

In the full-term female infant, the labia majora should be large and should completely cover the clitoris and labia minora. The labia majora may be darker than the surrounding skin, especially in newborns with dark skin tones. This is a normal response to exposure to the mother's hormones before birth. A white mucus vaginal discharge is normal. A small amount of vaginal bleeding, known as pseudomenstruation, may be noted. It is due to the sudden withdrawal of the mother's hormones at birth. Hymenal tags are small pieces of tissue at the vaginal orifice. They are normal and disappear in a few weeks.

MALE

The testes begin to descend through the inguinal canal at about 30 weeks of gestation and should be within the scrotal sac at 36 weeks. Cryptorchidism, or undescended testes, occurs in approximately 10 per cent of full-term newborns (Behrman, 1992). If the testes do not descend soon after birth, the condition must be treated surgically to preserve fertility.

In the term infant, the scrotum is pendulous and covered with wrinkles called rugae. A hydrocele is a collection of fluid around the testes and may occur on one or both sides. Hydroceles usually reabsorb within a year, although some necessitate surgery.

The prepuce, or foreskin, of the penis covers the glans and is adherent to it. Attempts to retract it in the newborn are unnecessary and can cause damage. The foreskin may be incompletely formed when the urinary meatus is abnormally placed.

The meatus should be at the tip of the glans penis. It may be abnormally located on the ventral or underside of the penis (hypospadias). Hypospadias may be accompanied by chordee, a condition in which fibrotic tissue causes the penis to curve downward. Epispadias exists when the meatus is on the dorsal or upper side of the penis. The meatus may also be located on the perineum. These abnormalities are later corrected by surgery.

Circumcision

Circumcision is the surgical removal of the prepuce of the glans penis. The prepuce is a fold of skin that covers the glans. Although it can be retracted easily for cleaning in the older child, the prepuce is not retractable in most newborns because it has not yet separated completely from the glans. It may not become fully retractable until age 3 or older (American Academy of Pediatrics, 1989). The prepuce should never be forcibly retracted in any infant as part of routine care because trauma and adhesions can result.

Until 1988, the American Academy of Pediatrics (AAP) issued a number of position statements noting that there were no absolute medical indications for circumcision of newborns as a routine procedure. However, in 1988 and 1989, the AAP issued a statement that "new evidence has suggested possible medical benefits from newborn circumcision." The report concluded that "newborn circumcision has potential medical benefits and advantages as well as disadvantages and risks" (American Academy of Pediatrics, 1989).

POTENTIAL BENEFITS

The major potential benefit of circumcision of newborns may be reduction of urinary tract infections. Inflammation of the glans (balanitis), prepuce, or urinary meatus as well as cancer of the penis, although not common, occurs more frequently in uncircumcised males. Some studies indicate that there may be an increased incidence of sexually transmitted diseases (herpes genitalis, candidiasis, gonorrhea, and syphilis) in uncircumcised males. However, there is disagreement as to whether this relates to poor hygiene or circumcision status because poor hygiene is associated with each of these conditions. Claims that circumcision of the male decreases the incidence of cervical cancer in his partner are not conclusive. Cervical cancer is strongly correlated with sexually transmitted diseases, early intercourse, and multiple partners.

Some parents have other reasons for circumcising their sons. The oldest reasons are religious and cultural. Jewish parents may have their infants circumcised on the 8th day after birth as part of a special ceremony. Some parents choose circumcision so that their son will look like his father or peers. Others feel that it is an expected part of newborn care, and some do not realize that they have a choice in the matter.

Some parents are concerned that later in life the infant might develop a problem such as phimosis, a tightening of the prepuce that prevents its retraction, necessitating circumcision. Although the number of such cases is very small, surgery after the newborn period involves hospitalization and anesthesia and can be psychologically disturbing to the young child. However, performing surgery because a need might later arise may subject the majority of infants, who will never have a problem, to unnecessary surgery.

Lack of knowledge about the care of the prepuce is the reason some parents choose to have it removed. Poor hygiene may increase the risk of infections and other problems. Teaching the proper care of the uncircumcised penis to the parents and child can prevent surgery and complications related to inadequate cleanliness.

POTENTIAL RISKS

The most common complications of circumcision are hemorrhage and infection. Other complications include the removal of too much or too little of the prepuce, stenosis or fistulas of the urethra, and adhesions, necrosis, or other damage to the glans. The glans unprotected by the prepuce may be more prone to irritation from constant exposure to urine and rubbing against diapers.

Only healthy newborns should undergo circumcision. The preterm or sick infant should not be circumcised until he is healthy enough to tolerate the procedure. Infants with blood dyscrasias may have excessive bleeding if circumcised. For the repair of anatomical abnormalities of the penis, such as hypospadias or epispadias, an intact prepuce may be needed for use in plastic surgery.

PAIN RELIEF

Circumcision is often performed without giving the infant an anesthetic. Although at one time it was commonly thought that newborns did not feel pain, this is no longer considered accurate. By the third trimester, the fetus is able to perceive pain (Lund,

1990). During circumcision, newborns show changes in vital signs, oxygen saturation levels, and responses by the adrenals, indicating that they feel pain. After the procedure, many infants exhibit changes in eating and sleeping behavior. The infant may be more irritable and cry more often during the first day after the procedure.

Injection of the dorsal penile nerves or the area around the foreskin with an anesthetic drug such as lidocaine reduces or eliminates pain during circumcision. Complications of anesthesia include hematomas, local skin necrosis, and absorption into the blood stream. Anesthetic cream may be somewhat less effective, but its use avoids the pain of injection (Mudge and Younger, 1989).

Non-pharmacological pain relief methods include pacifiers, soothing music, recordings of intrauterine sounds, and talking softly to the infant. All have shown some success in reducing an infant's pain responses to circumcision (Marchette et al, 1991). The effect of these measures is distraction from rather than actual elimination of pain.

METHODS

The Gomco (Yellen) clamp (Fig. 19–11) and the Plastibell (Fig. 19–12) are two commonly used devices for performing circumcisions. In each method, the prepuce is first separated from the glans with a probe and incised to expose the glans.

✔ *Check Your Reading*

14. How does the distribution of fluid in the newborn compare with that in the adult?
15. What are the reasons parents decide for or against circumcision?

Immune System

Full-term newborns receive antibodies from the mother during the last trimester of pregnancy and in breast milk, if fed by that method. However, the neonate's ability to fight off infection is less than that of the older infant or child. The various white

Glans

Prepuce

Prepuce is slit

Prepuce is drawn over a metal cone

Clamp is applied for 3 to 5 minutes, then excess prepuce is cut away

Figure 19–11

Circumcision using the Gomco (Yellen) clamp. The physician pulls the prepuce over a cone-shaped device that rests against the glans. A clamp is placed around the cone and prepuce and is tightened to provide enough pressure to crush the blood vessels. This prevents bleeding when the prepuce is removed after 3 to 5 minutes.

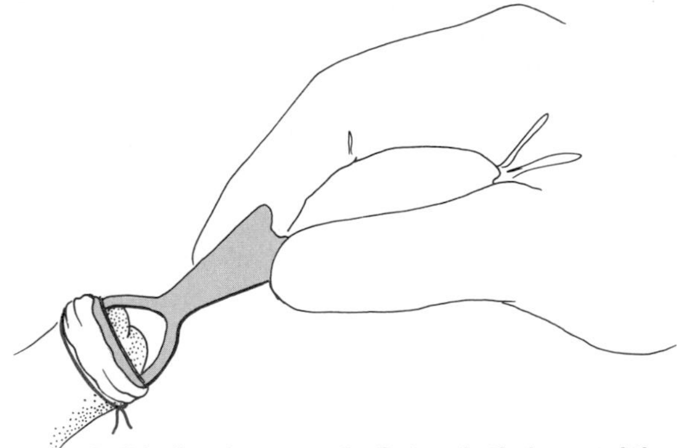

Bell is fitted over penis. Suture is tied around the rim of the bell, and excess prepuce is cut away

The plastic rim remains in place until healing occurs

Figure 19–12

Circumcision using the Plastibell. The physician places the Plastibell, a plastic ring, over the glans, draws the prepuce over it, and ties a suture around the prepuce and Plastibell. This prevents bleeding when the excess prepuce is removed. The Plastibell remains in place until it falls off in 3 to 4 days.

blood cells respond slowly and inefficiently when there is an invasion by organisms, both in moving to the site of invasion and in destroying the invader. Fever and leukocytosis, which normally occur during infection of the older child, are often not present in the newborn with infection because the inflammatory response is immature.

Immunoglobulins are serum globulins that have antibody activity and help protect the newborn from infection. The major immunoglobulins are IgG, IgM, and IgA, each of which performs a different function.

IgG

IgG from the woman crosses the placenta readily and provides the fetus with passive immunity to bacteria and viruses to which the mother has been exposed during her lifetime. Thus, if the mother has developed immunity to an organism, that immunity is temporarily passed on to her fetus. IgG also protects the fetus from bacterial toxins. IgG begins to cross the placenta during the first trimester, but most of the transfer occurs in the third trimester. A preterm infant born before 32 weeks of gestation will have received less than half the IgG of the infant born at full term.

Although the fetus begins to make its own IgG at 20 weeks of gestation, very little is produced until 3 to 4 weeks after birth. At that time, it is gradually produced in greater quantities to replace IgG from the mother, which is being catabolized. The passive immunity lasts for varying amounts of time. Although much of it is gone by about 3 months of age, the antibodies to measles may last much longer. Administration of the measles vaccine is delayed until about 15 months of age so that the passive immunity will not interfere with the infant's ability to form active immunity to measles.

IgM

IgM is the first immunoglobulin produced by the body when it is challenged. It helps protect against gram-negative bacteria. Small amounts of IgM are produced beginning at 20 weeks of gestation, and it is rapidly produced beginning a few days after birth. IgM cannot cross the placenta because the cells are too large. Therefore, any IgM in the cord blood is most likely produced by the fetus. If IgM is found in larger than normal amounts, exposure to infection in utero is probable. Exposure to the TORCH infections is suspected when IgM is elevated. (Fetal-neonatal effects of TORCH are discussed in Chapter 25, p. 720 and Chapter 29, p. 853.)

IgA

IgA is not produced until about 4 weeks after birth. Because IgA is important in protection of the respiratory and gastrointestinal systems, newborns are particularly susceptible to respiratory and gastrointestinal infection. A form of IgA is included in colostrum and breast milk. Therefore, breastfed infants receive protection from intestinal infection.

Psychosocial Adaptation

Periods of Reactivity

In the early hours after birth, the infant goes through changes called the periods of reactivity. There are two periods of reactivity and a period of sleep in between.

FIRST PERIOD OF REACTIVITY

The first period of reactivity begins at birth. Infants are very active at this time and appear wide awake, alert, and interested in their surroundings. Parents enjoy this phase, as the infant gazes directly at them when held in the *en face* (face-to-face) position. Infants move their arms and legs energetically, root, and appear hungry. If allowed to nurse, many infants will latch on to the nipple and suck well.

Respirations during the first period of reactivity may be as high as 80 breaths/minute. The heart rate may be elevated to 180 BPM (beats per minute). There may be crackles, retractions, nasal flaring, and increased mucus secretions. The pulse and respirations gradually slow, and the infant becomes sleepy after about 30 minutes.

PERIOD OF SLEEP

After the first period of reactivity, infants become quiet and eventually fall into a deep sleep, which lasts 2 to 4 hours. During this time, the pulse and respirations drop to the normal range but the temperature may be low.

SECOND PERIOD OF REACTIVITY

When infants waken from the period of sleep, they enter the somewhat unstable second period of reactivity. During this time, the pulse and respiratory rates again increase. Some infants become cyanotic or have periods of apnea. Mucus secretions increase, and infants may gag or regurgitate. Infants may pass meconium and become interested in feeding at this time.

The second period of reactivity may last for 4 to 6 hours, although there is much individual variation. Many infants pass through both stages within 8 hours. Once the second period of reactivity is over, the infant is relatively stable.

Behavioral States

There are six gradations in the behavioral state of the infant, ranging from deep sleep to crying. The amount of time infants spend in the different sleep-wake states will vary and is a key to their individuality. Infants tend to move from one state to the next in the following sequence.

Sleep State. In the quiet sleep state, the infant is in a deep sleep with closed eyes and no eye movements. Respirations are quiet, regular, and slower than in the other states. Although there are startles at intervals, the infant's body is quiet. There is little or no response to noise or stimuli, and the infant returns to deep sleep quickly if not disturbed.

Active Sleep State. In the active sleep state, infants move their extremities, stretch, change facial expressions, and may fuss briefly. During this period, respirations tend to be more rapid and irregular and rapid eye movement (REM) is seen. Infants are more likely to startle from noise or disturbances and may return to sleep or move to an awake state.

Drowsy State. The drowsy state is a transitional period between sleep and waking similar to that experienced by adults as they wake. The eyes may remain closed or, if open, appear glazed and unfocused. Infants startle and move their extremities slowly. They may go back to sleep or, with gentle stimulation, gradually awaken.

Quiet Alert State. In the quiet alert state, infants appear bright and interested in their surroundings. Body movements are minimal as they seem to concentrate on the environment. Because this is such an excellent time to increase bonding, this state should be pointed out to parents. Infants focus on objects or people and respond to the parents with intense gazing.

Active Alert State. The active alert state is one in which infants are often fussy. They seem restless, respirations become faster and more irregular, and they seem more aware of feelings of discomfort from hunger or cold. Although their eyes are open, they seem less focused on visual stimuli than during the quiet alert state.

Crying State. The crying state may quickly follow the active alert state if there is no intervention to comfort the infant. The cries are continuous and lusty, and the infant does not respond well to stimulation. It may take a period of comforting to move the infant to a state in which feeding or other activities can be accomplished.

✔ Check Your Reading

16. Why are IgG, IgM, and IgA important to the newborn?
17. What are newborns like during the first and second periods of reactivity?
18. How do infant behavioral states vary?

Summary Concepts

- Chemical, thermal, and mechanical factors combine to stimulate the respiratory center in the brain and initiate respirations at birth.
- Surfactant lines the alveoli and reduces surface tension to keep the alveoli open. Fetal lung fluid is removed during birth or by the lymphatic and vascular systems.
- Signs of respiratory distress include tachypnea, retractions, flaring nares, central cyanosis, grunting, and seesaw respirations.
- Increases in blood oxygen levels, shifts in pressure in the heart, and cord clamping cause closure of the ductus arteriosus, foramen ovale, and ductus venosus at birth.
- Infants are predisposed to heat loss because they have thin skin with little subcutaneous fat, blood vessels close to the surface, and a large skin surface area. They lose heat by evaporation, conduction, convection, and radiation.
- Heat is produced in newborns by an increase in metabolism, vasoconstriction, and nonshivering thermogenesis. These increase oxygen and glucose consumption and may cause respiratory distress, hypoglycemia, acidosis, and jaundice.
- Reflexes are an indication of the health of the central nervous system. Asymmetry or retention of reflexes beyond the time when they should disappear is abnormal.
- Laboratory values for red blood cells, hemoglobin, and hematocrit are higher for newborns than for adults because oxygen available to them in fetal life was less than after birth.
- Molding of the head is normal during birth and may cause the head to appear misshapen. There may be caput succedaneum (localized swelling

from pressure against the cervix) or a cephalohematoma (bleeding between the periosteum and the bone).

- After birth, the stools progress from thick, greenish-black meconium to loose greenish-brown transitional stools to milk stools. Stools of breastfed infants are frequent, soft, and mustard-colored, whereas those of formula-fed infants are brown, firmer, and less frequent.
- The brain needs a constant supply of glucose and may be damaged without it. Early signs of hypoglycemia include jitteriness, poor muscle tone, respiratory distress, perspiration, low temperature, and poor suck.
- Physiologic jaundice occurs in normal newborns after the first 24 hours of life as a result of hemolysis of red blood cells and immaturity of the liver. Pathologic jaundice is abnormal, begins within the first 24 hours, and often necessitates treatment with phototherapy. Breast milk jaundice begins later than physiologic jaundice and is thought to be due to enzymes in the milk.
- The ability of the newborn's kidneys to filter, reabsorb, and monitor fluid and electrolyte balance is less than that of the adult's. The newborn's body is composed of a greater percentage of water, with more located in the extracellular compartment, than the adult's.
- Potential benefits of circumcision may include decreased incidence of urinary tract infections and inflammation of the glans, prepuce, or meatus. Other reasons for circumcision include religious dictates, parent preference, and lack of knowledge about care of the foreskin. Potential risks of circumcision include hemorrhage, infection, overremoval, urethral stenosis or fistula, adhesions, and damage to the glans.
- Newborns receive passive immunity when IgG crosses the placenta in utero. After birth, IgM and IgA are produced to protect against infection.
- During the first and second periods of reactivity, newborns are active and alert and may be interested in feeding. Their pulse and respiratory rates may be elevated, and they may show some transient signs of respiratory distress.
- Newborns progress through six behavioral states: quiet sleep, active sleep, drowsy, quiet alert, active alert, and crying.

References and Readings

American Academy of Pediatrics. (1989). Report of the AAP Task Force on Circumcision. *Pediatrics,* 84(4), 388–391.

American Academy of Pediatrics and American College of Obstetricians and Gynecologists. (1992). *Guidelines for perinatal care* (3rd ed.). Elk Grove, Ill.: American Academy of Pediatrics.

Anand, S.K. (1991a). Clinical evaluation of renal disease. In H.W. Taeusch, R.A. Ballard, & M.E. Avery (Eds.), *Schaffer's diseases of the newborn* (6th ed.). Philadelphia: W.B. Saunders.

Anand, S.K. (1991b). Maturation of renal function. In H.W. Taeusch, R.A. Ballard, & M.E. Avery (Eds.), *Schaffer's diseases of the newborn* (6th ed.). Philadelphia: W.B. Saunders.

Avery, G.B. (1987). *Neonatology: Pathophysiology and management of the newborn* (3rd ed.). Philadelphia: J.B. Lippincott.

Behrman, R.E. (1992). *Nelson textbook of pediatrics* (14th ed.). Philadelphia: W.B. Saunders.

Blackburn, S.T., & Loper, D.L. (1992). *Maternal, fetal, and neonatal physiology: A clinical perspective.* Philadelphia: W.B. Saunders.

Creasy, R.K., & Resnik, R. (1989). *Maternal-fetal medicine: Principles and practice* (2nd ed.). Philadelphia: W.B. Saunders.

de Steuben, C. (1992). Breast-feeding and jaundice: A review. *Journal of Nurse-Midwifery,* 37(Suppl. 2), 59S–66S.

Foster, R.L.R., Hunsberger, M.M., & Anderson, J.J.T. (1989). *Family-centered nursing care of children.* Philadelphia: W.B. Saunders.

Glader, B.E., & Naiman, J.L. (1991). Erythrocyte disorders in infancy. In H.W. Taeusch, R.A. Ballard, & M.E. Avery (Eds.), *Schaffer's diseases of the newborn* (6th ed.). Philadelphia: W.B. Saunders.

Guyton, A.C. (1991). *Textbook of medical physiology* (8th ed.). Philadelphia: W.B. Saunders.

Kenner, C., Brueggemeyer, A., & Gunderson, L.P. (1991). *Comprehensive neonatal nursing.* Philadelphia: W.B. Saunders.

Klaus, M.H., & Fanaroff, A.A. (1993). *Care of the high-risk neonate* (4th ed.). Philadelphia: W.B. Saunders.

Lott, J.W. (1993). Assessment and management of cardiovascular dysfunction. In C. Kenner, A. Brueggemeyer, & L.P. Gunderson, (Eds.), *Comprehensive neonatal nursing: A physiologic perspective.* Philadelphia: W.B. Saunders.

Lund, M. (1990). Perspectives on newborn male circumcision. *Neonatal Network* 9(3), 7–11.

Marchette, L., Main, R., Redick, E., Bagg, A., & Leatherland, J. (1991). Pain reduction interventions during neonatal circumcision. *Nursing Research,* 40(4), 241–244.

Mattson, S., & Smith, J.E. (1993). NAACOG *core curriculum for maternal-newborn nursing.* Philadelphia: W.B. Saunders.

Mudge, D., & Younger, J.B. (1989). The effects of topical lidocaine on infant response to circumcision. *Journal of Nurse-Midwifery,* 34(6), 335–340.

Nicholson, J.F., & Pesce, M.A. (1992). Laboratory medicine and reference tables. In R.E. Behrman (Ed.), *Nelson textbook of pediatrics* (14th ed.). Philadelphia: W.B. Saunders.

Oski, F.A. (1991a). Differential diagnosis of jaundice. In H.W. Taeusch, R.A. Ballard, & M.E. Avery (Eds.), *Schaffer's diseases of the newborn* (6th ed.). Philadelphia: W.B. Saunders.

Oski, F.A. (1991b). Disorders of bilirubin metabolism: General considerations. In H.W. Taeusch, R.A. Ballard, & M.E. Avery (Eds.), *Schaffer's diseases of the newborn* (6th ed.). Philadelphia: W.B. Saunders.

Portman, R., Browder, S., & DiStefano, S.M. (1989). Neonatal nephrology. In G.B. Merenstein & S.L. Gardner (Eds.), *Handbook of neonatal intensive care.* St. Louis: C.V. Mosby.

Shoptaugh, G.M. (1992). Hyperbilirubinemia. In T.L. Gomella (Ed.), *Neonatology: Management, procedures, on-call problems, diseases, drugs.* Norwalk, Conn.: Appleton & Lange.

Whaley, L.F., & Wong, D.L. (1991). *Nursing care of infants and children* (4th ed.). St. Louis: C.V. Mosby.

Wilkerson, N.N. (1989). A comprehensive look at hyperbilirubinemia. MCN: *American Journal of Maternal Child Nursing,* 14(1), 32–36.

20

Normal Newborn:

Assessments and Care

Objectives

1. Describe the assessments that the nurse makes during the initial and ongoing care of the neonate.
2. Explain the nurse's responsibility in cardiorespiratory and thermoregulatory assessments and care.
3. Describe nursing assessments and interventions regarding feeding and urine and stool excretion.
4. Explain the assessments included in gestational age assessment.
5. Explain the information that new parents need about infant care.
6. Describe methods of protecting newborns from infection and kidnapping.

Definitions

Café au lait spots • Light-brown birthmarks.

Erythema toxicum • Benign maculopapular rash of unknown cause in newborns.

Lanugo • Fine hair covering the fetus.

Milia • Distended sebaceous glands.

Mongolian spots • Bruise-like marks that occur mostly in newborns with dark skin tones.

Nevus flammeus • Permanent purple birthmark.

Nevus vasculosus • Rough red collection of capillaries with a raised surface that disappears with time.

Point of maximum impulse • Area of the chest where the heart sounds are loudest when auscultated.

Telangiectatic nevi (stork bites) • Flat red areas on the nape of the neck and over the eyelids resulting from dilation of small blood vessels.

Vernix caseosa • Thick white substance that protects the skin of the fetus.

△ Alert for a high risk of exposure to substances to which universal precautions apply. See Appendix B for additional information about infection control.

The role of the nurse in caring for the newborn is to (1) identify abnormalities or problems of the infant in adapting to life outside the uterus, (2) keep the infant safe, and (3) teach the parents how to provide care. To fulfill this role, nurses must understand the normal physiological changes discussed in Chapter 19. A brief discussion of the immediate assessment, such as assigning an Apgar score, and care of the infant after birth is included in Chapter 13, p. 318. This chapter builds on that information. Table 20–1 provides a summary of all newborn assessments. In addition, Keys to Clinical Practice (Appendix E, p. 978) provides order of assessments and care during admission.

Early Assessments and Care

Scanning for Anomalies

Immediately after birth, the infant is quickly scanned for respiratory problems and obvious anomalies. The nurse determines whether resuscitation (see Chapter 29, p. 840) or other immediate intervention is necessary. When it is apparent that the infant is stable and oxygenating well, a more careful scanning can be performed. However, the nurse must be vigilant for any changes in condition during the initial assessments and during routine care following birth.

If there are abnormalities, maintain a calm, quiet demeanor to avoid frightening the parents. Quietly alert the physician, who will explain the problem to the parents.

HEAD

Palpate the infant's head thoroughly to note its shape and to identify abnormalities. The newborn who was in a breech position or was delivered by cesarean procedure will have a round head, whereas the infant born vaginally will probably have some molding. Note the degree of molding, size of the fontanelles, and presence of caput succedaneum or cephalohematoma. Separate the hair, if necessary, to look for marks on the scalp. Note bruises, rashes, or other marks. A small red mark will be apparent if a fetal monitor electrode was inserted into the skin of the scalp. Later a small scab will form. Occasionally, these areas become infected.

Molding. The normal changes in head shape that allow the head to fit through the birth canal may be frightening to parents. Reassure them that the infant's head will return to its normal shape within a few days. Often dramatic improvement is seen by the end of the first day of life. Note the space between suture lines. Report abnormally wide or completely closed suture lines, as they may signify increased intracranial pressure or premature fusing of the sutures.

Fontanelles. Palpate the anterior and posterior fontanelles, noting their position in relation to the other bones of the skull. When palpating the anterior fontanelle, elevate the infant's head for accurate assessment. The infant can be placed in a sitting position or held in an upright position.

Each fontanelle should be flat or level with the bones around it and should feel soft. Although the anterior fontanelle may bulge slightly when the infant cries, bulging when at rest may indicate increased intracranial pressure. A fontanelle that is between flat and bulging is often termed "full." A larger-than-normal fontanelle may also be a sign of increased pressure within the skull. A depressed fontanelle is unusual in a newborn unless it is due to molding. After molding resolves, a depressed fontanelle is a sign of dehydration. Report any of these abnormal signs to the physician or nurse practitioner.

Parents have many questions about care of the anterior fontanelle, or "soft spot" as it is commonly called. They may be frightened by seeing the normal pulsations in this area and worry that they might injure the infant during normal care. Reassure them that normal handling of the infant, including washing the head, will not harm the fontanelle.

Locate the posterior fontanelle, which feels like a dimple at the juncture of the occipital and parietal bones. Molding may make it difficult to identify because the overlapping bones impinge on that space. Careful palpation will help the nurse to identify the posterior fontanelle.

Caput Succedaneum and Cephalohematoma. The swelling of a caput succedaneum often appears over the vertex of the newborn's head as a result of having been pressed against the mother's cervix. The edema, which crosses suture lines, resolves quickly and may almost disappear within 24 hours after birth. Palpate the head to determine the amount of edema and observe whether there is bruising as well.

A cephalohematoma may occur on one or both sides of the head. It appears later than a caput succedaneum and is firmer to touch. It does not cross the suture lines.

Both caput succedaneum and cephalohematoma are frightening to parents. Reassure them that these conditions are not harmful to the infant. Discuss the causes and how long it takes for the areas to normalize. Some parents do not ask questions about these conditions even though they are worried. In these cases, address the conditions openly rather than assume that the parents are not concerned.

Table 20–1. SUMMARY OF NEWBORN ASSESSMENTS

Normal	Variations	Nursing Considerations
	Respiratory	
Rate 30–60 breaths/minute. Chest movements symmetrical. Respirations irregular, shallow. Breath sounds present and clear bilaterally. Both nostrils open to air flow.	Retractions, nasal flaring, grunting, tachypnea, slow respirations, moist breath sounds, periods of apnea, seesaw respirations. Lack of air passage through one or both nostrils (choanal atresia). Excessive mucus.	Mild variations necessitate continued monitoring. If more than mild, suction as needed, give oxygen, and refer for more intensive care.
	Cardiovascular	
Heart rate and rhythm regular at 120–160 BPM (100 sleeping, 180 crying). Color pink with acrocyanosis. Brachial and femoral pulses present and equal bilaterally. Pedal pulses present. Blood pressure average 65/41.	Tachycardia or bradycardia. Murmurs and arrhythmias should be assessed by skilled practitioners. Cyanosis (differentiate from facial bruising). Absent or unequal pulses or blood pressure (coarctation of the aorta).	Central cyanosis necessitates oxygen and further treatment with continued monitoring. Refer abnormal rates, rhythms and sounds, pulses.
	Neurological	
Temperature 36.5–37.6°C (97.7–99.7°F) rectal; 36.5–37.5°C (97.7–99.5°F) axillary.	Low or high temperature.	If low, institute warming measures and retake in 30 minutes. Watch for symptoms of hypoglycemia and check blood glucose. If high, check warmer temperature setting. Look for signs of infection for low or high temperature.
Reflexes Moro, palmar and plantar grasp, rooting, sucking, tonic neck, and stepping reflexes present.	Absent, asymmetrical, or weak reflexes.	Observe for signs of fractures, nerve damage, or injury to central nervous system.
Sensory **Ears:** well formed and complete. Notch where ear meets head is even with line drawn from inner to outer canthus of eye. Responds to sounds. **Eyes:** clear, transient strabismus, scant or absent tears. Pupils equal and react to light. Follows objects to midline.	**Ears:** skin tags on ears or preauricular sinuses. Low set (chromosomal disorders). **Eyes:** Inflammation or drainage (chemical or infectious conjunctivitis). Constant tearing (plugged lacrimal duct). Unequal pupils. Failure to follow objects (blindness). Subconjunctival hemorrhage or edema of eyelids (pressure during delivery).	Kidney anomalies may accompany abnormalities of ear; check voiding. Look for signs of chromosomal abnormality if ears abnormally positioned. Clean and monitor any drainage; seek cause. Reassure parents that subconjunctival hemorrhage and edema will clear. Refer other abnormalities.
Other Minimal tremors of extremities. Infant "molds" body to caretaker's when held and responds by quieting down when needs met.	Jitteriness or tremors. Seizures. Arching of back or failure to mold. Excessive irritability or high-pitched cry.	Check for hypoglycemia or hypocalcemia. Monitor for signs of neurological damage or prenatal drug exposure.
	Musculoskeletal	
Muscle Tone Flexed extremities that resist when extended and return quickly to flexed state.	Limp, flaccid, "floppy" extremities, indicating poor tone.	Seek cause: need for oxygen, drugs given mother near birth, etc.
Measurements **Weight:** 2700–4000 g (6–9 pounds). **Length:** 48–53 cm (19–21 inches). **Chest circumference:** 30.5–33 cm (12–13 inches).	Above or below normal range.	Seek cause: gestational age, large or small for gestational age, size of parents, medical conditions in mother that would affect intrauterine growth. Monitor for complications common to cause.

Table continued on following page

Table 20–1. SUMMARY OF NEWBORN ASSESSMENTS *Continued*

Normal	Variations	Nursing Considerations
Head		
Head circumference: 33–35.5 cm (13–14 inches). Head length is approximately one fourth of infant's length. Sutures palpable, with small separation between each. Anterior fontanelle diamond-shaped, 3–4 × 2–3 cm in size, soft and flat. Posterior fontanelle triangular-shaped, 1–2 cm in size. Face symmetrical.	Head large (hydrocephalus) or small (microcephaly). Sutures overriding from molding, widely separated (hydrocephalus), or not palpable (craniosynostosis). Anterior fontanelle depressed (dehydration), full or bulging (increased intracranial pressure or overhydration). Caput succedaneum or cephalohematoma. Drooping of mouth on one side of face, "one-sided cry" (facial nerve damage).	Seek cause of variations. Monitor for signs of dehydration for depressed fontanelle, increased intracranial pressure for bulging of fontanelle or wide separation of sutures. Refer for treatment. Differentiate caput succedaneum from cephalohematoma and teach/reassure parents of normal outcome. Check delivery history for possible cause of damage to facial nerve.
Neck/Clavicles		
Short neck turns easily side to side. Infant able to raise head when prone. Clavicles intact.	Muscle weakness or contractures leading to interference with movement of head. Webbing of neck or large fat pad at back of neck (chromosomal disorders). A lump, movement, or crepitus when clavicle palpated, with diminished or absent movement of arm on that side (fractured clavicle).	Refer any abnormalities. Look for other signs. Fracture of clavicle occurs especially in large infant with history of shoulder dystocia. Look for other injuries.
Upper Extremities		
Correct number and formation of fingers. Equal and bilateral movement of extremities. Palm creases normal.	Crepitus, redness, swelling (fracture). Diminished or lack of movement of extremity (seen especially during Moro reflex). Polydactyly (note presence or absence of bone in extra digits). Syndactyly (webbing) or fusing of digits. Absent digits. Simian crease (Down syndrome).	Refer all anomalies and look for others.
Lower extremities		
Correct number and formation of toes. Legs equal in length, abduct easily and equally; gluteal and thigh creases equal; no hip click. Normal position of feet.	Difference in leg length, resistance when one leg is abducted, unequal thigh or gluteal creases, hip click, movement of head of femur (Ortolani's sign). All may indicate congenital dysplasia of hip. Malposition of feet, which may or may not be manually manipulated into normal position (talipes equinovarus).	Refer all anomalies, look for others.
Vertebral Column		
No openings observed or felt.	Failure of vertebra to close (spina bifida), with or without sac with spinal fluid and meninges (meningocele) and/or cord (myelomeningocele) enclosed.	Refer abnormalities. Observe for movement below level of defect. If sac present, cover with sterile dressings moistened with sterile saline. Protect from injury.
	Gastrointestinal	
Mouth		
Mouth, gums, tongue pink. Tongue normal in size and movement. Lips and palate intact. Sucking reflex strong.	Precocious teeth. Epstein's pearls. Cyanosis of tissues. White patches in mouth (*Candida albicans* or thrush). Protruding tongue (Down syndrome). Diminished movement of tongue (facial nerve paralysis). Unilateral or bilateral cleft lip and/or palate. Absent or weak sucking reflex.	Refer anomalies. Expect loose teeth to be removed. Oxygen for cyanosis. Expect nystatin medication for *Candida.* Check mother for vaginal or breast infection.
Abdomen		
Rounded, soft. Bowel sounds present soon after birth. Liver palpable 1–2 cm below costal margin.	Sunken abdomen (diaphragmatic hernia). Distended abdomen or loops of bowel visible (possible obstruction). Masses felt on palpation. Umbilical hernia.	Refer abnormalities.

Table 20–1. SUMMARY OF NEWBORN ASSESSMENTS *Continued*

Normal	Variations	Nursing Considerations
Feeding		
Takes feeding with good suck/swallow coordination and retains well.	Poorly coordinated suck and swallow. Choking, gagging, duskiness, or cyanosis during feeding. Excessive drooling with difficulty with feeding (tracheoesophageal fistula).	Feed slowly. Stop frequently if difficulty. Suction and stimulate if necessary. Do not feed if tracheoesophageal fistula suspected. Remove stomach contents if infant has distended stomach and may have swallowed blood, amniotic fluid, or meconium. Refer infants with continued difficulty for further investigation.
Stools		
Meconium passed within 24–48 hours. Transitional stool progressing to formula or breast milk stools. One to ten passed a day, depending on type of feeding. Soft in consistency.	No passage of meconium (imperforate anus or obstruction). Hard, marble-like stools or watery stools with water ring.	Note type and amounts of previous feedings, abdominal distention, and signs of infection and refer for treatment.
	Genitourinary	
Urine passed within 24 hours. Urinates 2–6 times first 2 days, 5–25 times a day thereafter. **Male:** Testes within scrotal sac, rugae on scrotum, prepuce—nonretractable. Meatus at tip of penis. **Female:** Labia majora covers clitoris and labia minora. Small amount of white mucus vaginal discharge.	Lack of urinary output or inadequate amounts. Brick dust staining. **Male:** Testes in inguinal canal or abdomen (cryptorchidism). Lack of rugae on scrotum. Edema of scrotum (pressure especially in breech birth). Hydrocele. Urinary meatus located on dorsum of penis (epispadius), ventral penis (hypospadius), or perineum. **Female:** Clitoris and labia minora larger than labia majora. Vaginal bleeding (pseudomenstruation). Hymenal tags. Edematous labia (breech birth).	Increase fluids if lack of output. Check to see if a voiding was missed. Check gestational age for immature genitalia. Refer anomalies. Explain to parents why no circumcision can be done if abnormal placement of meatus.
	Integumentary	
Color pink with some acrocyanosis. Vernix caseosa in creases. Small amounts of lanugo over shoulders, sides of face or forehead, upper back. Nipples present and located properly. Three vessels in cord. Clamp tight and cord drying. Skin turgor good with quick recoil. Some cracking and peeling of skin. Hair silky and soft, with individual hair strands. Nails to end of fingers or slightly beyond.	Cyanosis. Differentiate facial bruising from cyanosis. Jaundice (pathologic if appears in first 24 hours). Very thick vernix caseosa or excessive lanugo (preterm infant). Forceps marks. Puncture on scalp from electrode. Petechiae. Telangiectatic nevi ("stork bites"). Nevus flammeus (port-wine stain), Nevus vasculosus (strawberry hemangioma). Milia. Mongolian spots, café au lait spots, erythema toxicum. Supernumerary or improperly placed nipples. Two vessels in cord, loose clamp, bleeding or other drainage from cord. Skin turgor poor with "tenting." Excessive peeling (postterm infant). Wooly, bunchy hair (preterm infant).	Suction and give oxygen for cyanosis. Refer jaundice in first 24 hours. Look for other signs and complications of preterm or postterm birth. Point out and explain normal skin variations to parents. Look for other anomalies if only two vessels in cord. Tighten or replace loose cord clamp. Refer continued bleeding, oozing, or other drainage from cord.

NECK AND CLAVICLES

Assess the infant's neck for webbing and ability to turn the head from side to side. When lying in a prone position, the newborn should be able to raise the head enough to turn it from side to side. Observe the back of the neck for an unusually large fat pad, which may be a sign of Down syndrome.

Palpate the clavicles to assess for fractures, which are more likely to occur in large infants. If a fracture is present, a lump, movement, or crepitus (grating of the bone) is noted. There may also be tenderness, swelling of the area, and lack of motion of the arm on the affected side. A difference in the movement of the arms is especially noticeable when the Moro reflex is elicited.

CORD

Count the vessels in the cord. There should be two arteries, which are small and may stand up at the cut end. There is one vein, which is larger than the arteries and resembles a slit because its walls are more easily compressed. If there is only one artery, assess carefully for other anomalies. A two-vessel cord often signals defects of other structures that formed early in fetal life. Note the amount of Wharton's jelly in the cord. If the cord appears thin, the infant may have been poorly nourished. Look for a green tinge to the cord, which indicates that there was a release of meconium and fetal distress before birth.

EXTREMITIES

Examine the neonate's extremities to identify abnormalities. Palpate the bones of the arms and legs to see that they are intact. Crepitus, redness, swelling, and lack of use of the extremity are signs of fractures. Determine that each extremity moves independently to identify possible damage to nerves that may occur with or without fractures.

Hands and Feet. Count the fingers and toes and note the presence of an excess number (polydactyly) or webbing between digits (syndactyly). Check the palms for a simian line or crease. Although some normal newborns have a simian line, it may be an indication of chromosomal disorders such as Down syndrome. Examine the feet to identify clubfoot (talipes equinovarus). Gently manipulate the foot to see if it will move to normal position. If it will, the abnormal position is probably temporary, resulting from the position of the infant in the uterus.

Hips. Examine the hips for congenital hip dysplasia and dislocation. Extend the legs to determine if they are equal in length and if thigh and gluteal creases are symmetrical. If there is a dislocation of the hip, the leg on that side is shorter and the creases are asymmetrical. With the infant's feet flat on the bed, bend the knees to see whether they are of equal height. If the hip is dislocated, the knee on the affected side will be lower. Determine whether both legs abduct equally. It may be more difficult to abduct the affected hip. Because the hip may be unstable, but not yet dislocated, these signs may not be present at birth.

Eliciting Ortolani's sign is a method of assessing for hip instability due to dysplasia (Fig. 20–1). If the hip is dislocated, a click is heard and the head of the femur is felt to slip over the edge of the acetabulum.

VERTEBRAL COLUMN

Palpate the entire length of the newborn's vertebral column to discover any defects in the vertebrae. An indentation is a sign of spina bifida occulta, a failure of a vertebra to close. The defect is not obvious on visual inspection because it is covered with skin, but sometimes a tuft of hair grows over the area. Other, more obvious neural tube defects include a meningocele or myelomeningocele. These are protrusions of nerves and/or the spinal cord through the defect in the vertebrae. They appear as a sac on the back and may be covered by skin or just the meninges. Cover a meningocele or myelomeningocele with sterile dressings moistened with sterile saline immediately after birth (see Chapter 29, p. 869).

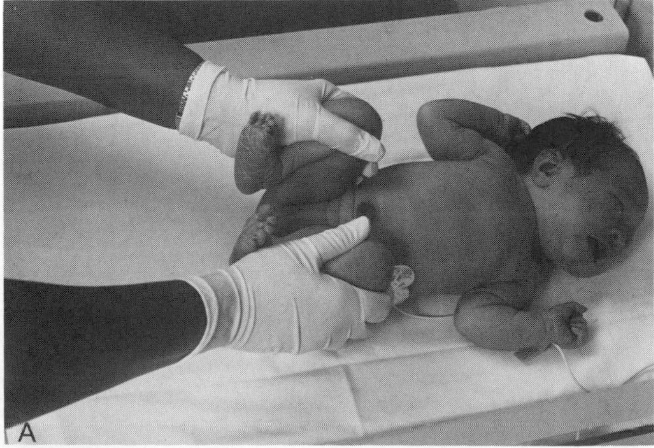

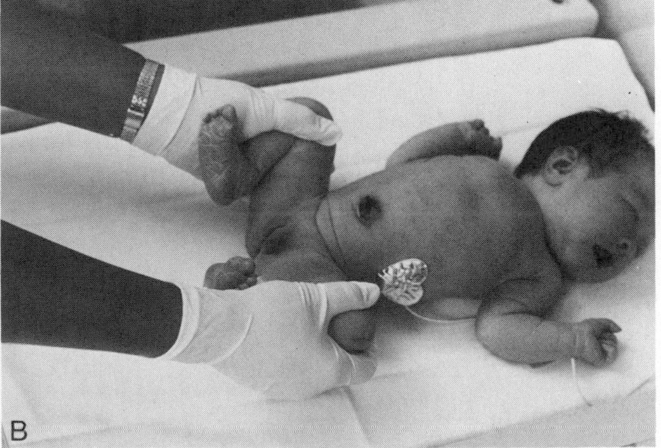

Figure 20–1

Ortolani's maneuvers to assess the hips. **A**, Place the fingers over the infant's greater trochanter with the thumbs holding the femur and bend the infant's knees and hips at a 90-degree angle. **B**, Abduct the thighs, and apply gentle pressure downward. A click and movement of the femur in the acetabulum denote dislocation of the hip.

Procedure 20–1 Identifying Infants

Purpose: To ensure that each infant is *always* given to the correct mother.

1. **Identify infants and mothers with identification bands whenever reuniting them, even after a brief separation.** *Ensures that the correct infant is always given to the correct mother.*

2. **When taking an infant into the mother's room, unwrap the blankets enough to expose the identification band on the infant's wrist or ankle. Do *not* rely on memory of the number.** *Allows visualization of the band to check the numbers.*

3. **Explain the identification procedure and its purpose to the mother. Show the mother the number on her band and the number on the infant's bands that are used for identification.** *Ensures the mother's understanding and cooperation.*

4. **Look at the number on the infant's band and ask the mother to read off the preprinted number on her identification band. Do *not* reverse the process by reading off the infant's number to the mother.** *Allows the nurse to be certain that the numbers match. If the numbers are read to a mother who does not understand the process, she might indicate that the numbers are correct when they are not.*

5. **An alternative procedure is for the nurse to compare both the infant's and the mother's bands visually.** *If the mother does not speak English or there is any other reason she might have difficulty with the process, the nurse can be sure that the infant is identified without error.*

6. **In some situations, the infant may be released to the father or other support person who is wearing an identification band. Follow the same identification procedure.** *Ensures that the correct infant is given to the correct support person.*

Identification

It is essential to implement a method to identify newborns immediately after birth, before mothers and infants are separated. Identification is important to ensure that the wrong infant is never given to a mother. This could result in interference with bonding, lack of confidence in the reliability of the staff, and lawsuits.

The most common method of identifying infants is the use of identification bands, which are placed on both the mother and the infant. The father or other support person may also receive an identification band. Information on each band is identical. It includes the mother's name, identification number, and physician. the infant's sex and the date and time of birth, and a number that is preprinted on the plastic band. The preprinted number is used to identify the mother and the infant every time the infant is brought to the mother after a period of separation, however brief (Procedure 20–1). The identification of the infant and the mother by identification bands ensures that the correct infant is always given to the mother.

Other methods of identifying infants include taking footprints of the infant and a fingerprint or thumbprint of the mother. Taking a picture of the infant is another means of identification. Note any birthmarks or other distinguishing features on the admission notes.

Measurements

Measurements provide information about the infant's growth in utero. Abnormal measurements alert the nurse that complications may occur. Measure the weight, length, and circumference of the head and chest as part of the initial assessment. Compare this information with the norms expected for the infant's gestational age. When there is a difference between what is expected and what is found, expanded assessments are necessary. For example, a newborn may be larger or smaller than expected because there was an error in calculating the length of the pregnancy (Procedure 20–2).

WEIGHT

Weigh the infant as part of the initial assessment. The average weight of a full-term newborn is 3400 g (7.5 pounds), with a range from 2700 to 4000 g (6 to 9 pounds). If the infant's weight is outside the average range, assess the cause. Factors determining weight include gestational age, placental functioning, maternal diabetes, and genetic factors such as race and parental size.

Procedure 20–2

Weighing and Measuring the Newborn

Purpose: To obtain accurate measurements of the newborn.

1. **Cover the scale with a blanket. Place a paper cover over the blanket if desired.** *Prevents conductive heat loss from contact between the infant and a cold surface, helps prevent cross-contamination, and makes cleaning easier.*

2. **Balance or adjust the scale to zero after the covering is placed. Electronic scale: push the "on" button and check to see that the digital readout is at zero. The electronic scale is usually self-adjusting. Balance scale: adjust until the balance arm is horizontal.** *Results in accurate weight of the infant without including weight of the scale covering.*

3. **Place the infant in supine position on the scale. Keep one hand just above the infant and watch carefully throughout the procedure.** *Infants are frequently startled when first placed on the scale, and the Moro reflex may occur. There is a danger that they might slide off the scale.*

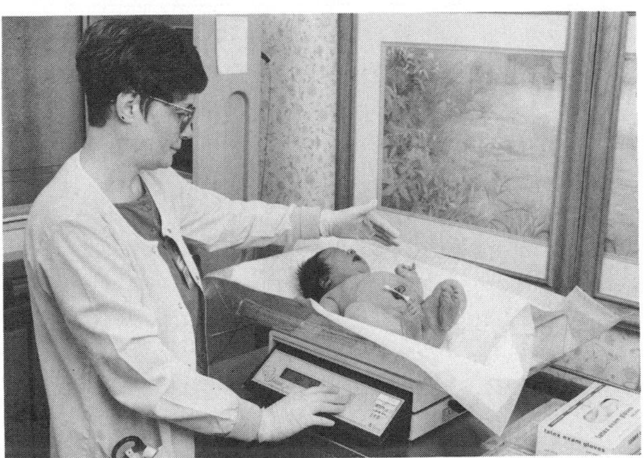

4. **Wait until the infant is somewhat quieted down. The electronic scale displays weight in pounds and ounces or in grams. Some electronic scales read "stable" when an accurate weight has been obtained. For a balance scale, move weights slowly until the arm is level.** *Increases accuracy to wait until the infant is quiet.*

5. **Write the numbers down immediately. If the scale is covered with paper, the weight can be written on the paper and taken with the infant to the warmer. Write it on the chart or admission forms when the infant is safely settled.** *Prevents forgetting the weight.*

6. **Compare weight with the normal range of 2700 to 4000 g (6 to 9 pounds).** *Shows whether or not the infant is within expected range.*

LENGTH

Ruler Printed on Scale or Crib

1. **Place the infant in supine position with the head at the upper edge of the ruler on the scale.** *Places the infant in the proper position.*

2. **While holding the infant with one hand so that the head does not move, use the other hand to extend the infant's leg along the ruler. Note the length at the bottom of the heel.** *Holding the infant firmly ensures safety and allows an accurate measurement.*

Tape Measure

1. **When using a paper tape, be sure it has no partial tears in it.** *A torn measuring tape would give an inaccurate measurement.*

2. **Place tape beside the infant, with the upper end at the top of the head. Tuck it beneath shoulder, and extend it down to the feet.** *Prevents movement of the tape and helps ensure accurate measurements.*

3. **Hold the tape straight alongside the infant's body while extending one leg full length. Be sure tape has not moved from the top of the head.** *Careful attention to tape placement ensures accurate measurement.*

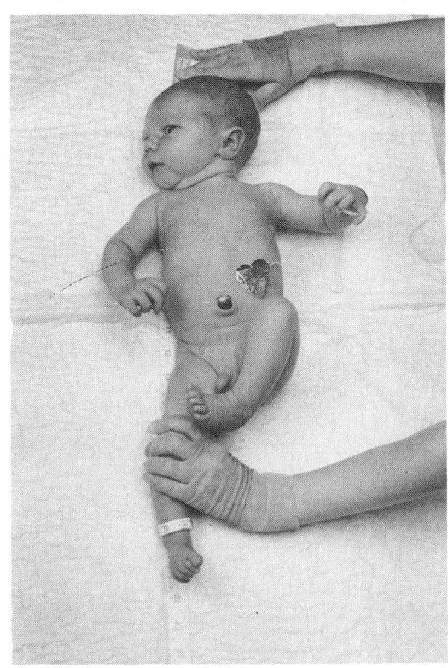

Weighing and Measuring the Newborn *Continued*

4. **Another method is to mark the paper on which the infant is lying at the top of the head and the end of the extended leg. Then measure the distance between the two marks.** *Makes it easier to measure accurately when the infant is very active.*

5. **Compare with normal range of 48 to 53 cm (19 to 21 inches).** *Helps determine abnormalities.*

HEAD AND CHEST CIRCUMFERENCE

1. **Place tape under the head and measure around the occiput and just over the eyebrows.** *Allows measurement of the largest diameter of the head.*

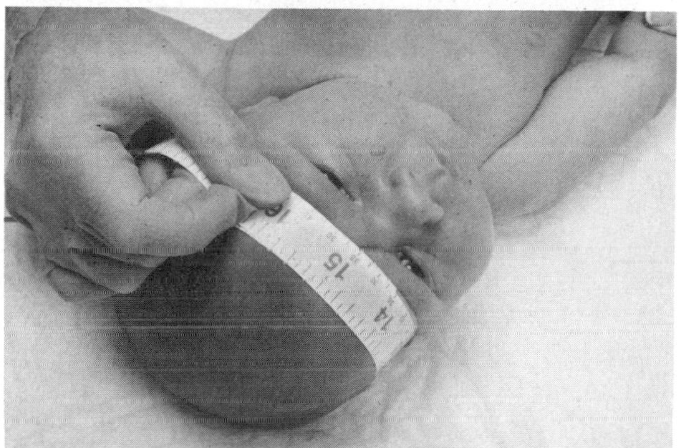

2. **Move tape down to measure chest at the level of the nipples. Be sure tape is even and taut.** *Ensures accurate measurement.*

3. **Remove tape by lifting or rolling the infant instead of pulling tape.** *Pulling tape can cut the infant's skin.*

4. **Compare measurements with normal range. Head: 33 to 35.5 cm (13 to 14 inches). Chest: 30.5 to 33 cm (12 to 13 inches).** *Determines if the infant's measurements are normal.*

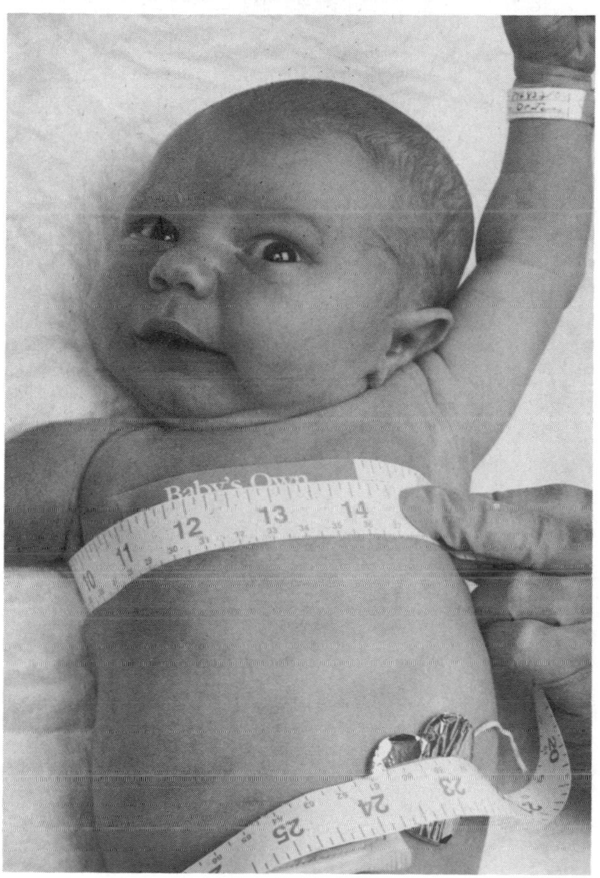

Procedure 20–3 Administering Intramuscular Injections to Newborns

Purpose: To place medication in the muscle without injury.

1. **Prepare medication for injection. A 1-ml syringe with a 5/8-inch 25-gauge needle is commonly used. A filter needle may be used to draw up medication from a glass ampule. After drawing up the medication, replace the filter needle with the original sterile needle to give the injection.** *A small needle reaches the newborn's muscle but avoids the possibility of striking the bone. Use of a filter needle prevents the possibility of particles of glass being drawn into the syringe.*

2. **Put on gloves.** *Protects the nurse against contamination with blood.*

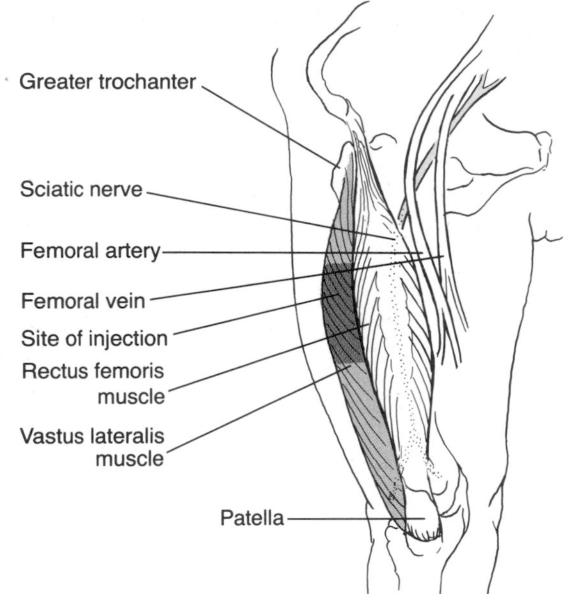

3. **Locate the correct site. Intramuscular medication for an infant is given in the vastus lateralis muscle or, if necessary, the rectus femoris muscle. Divide the area between the greater trochanter of the femur and the knee into thirds. Give the injection in the middle third of the muscle, lateral to the midline of the anterior thigh.** *The large vastus lateralis muscle is located away from the sciatic nerve, femoral artery, and femoral vein. The rectus femoris muscle is located nearer to these structures and poses more of a danger.* (Note: *The gluteal muscles are never used until a child has been walking for at least a year. These muscles are poorly developed and dangerously near the sciatic nerve.*)

4. **Cleanse the area with an alcohol wipe.** *Removes organisms and prevents infection. (If the area is covered with thick vernix caseosa and/or blood, wash the area first.)*

5. **Stabilize the leg firmly while grasping the thigh between the thumb and fingers.** *Prevents sudden movement by the infant and possible injury.*

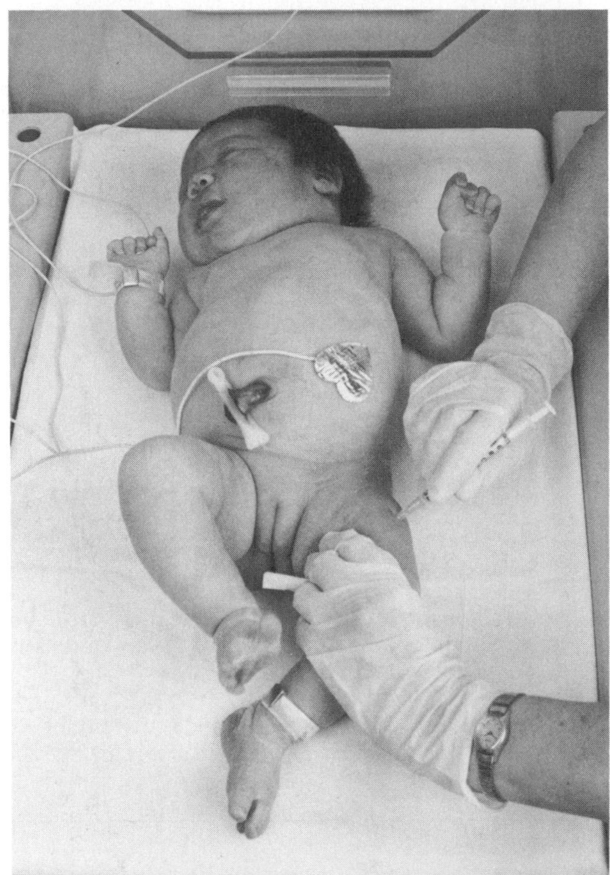

6. **Inject needle at a 90-degree angle.** *Places the medication into the muscle rather than the subcutaneous tissue.*

7. **Aspirate and inject the medication slowly if there is no blood return. If blood returns, withdraw the needle. Discard the medication and syringe and prepare new medication.** *Aspirate to see if the needle has entered a blood vessel. Blood return indicates that the needle is in a blood vessel. Slow injection reduces discomfort.*

8. **Withdraw needle quickly and massage the site with alcohol wipe.** *Both increase comfort. Massage helps medication absorb.*

Weigh the infant once each day to keep track of weight loss. Infants can be expected to lose 5 to 10 per cent of their birth weight during the first few days of life because they generally do not take in adequate calories to maintain their weight during this period. Excretion of meconium from the bowel and normal loss of extracellular fluid also contribute to early weight loss. Infants normally regain birth weight by the 10th day of life. Thereafter, they gain about half a pound a week for the first 6 months.

LENGTH

Measure the infant's length from the top of the head to the end of the outstretched leg. The average length of a full-term newborn is 48 to 53 cm (19 to 21 inches). Some agencies record the crown-to-rump measurement as well, which is approximately equal to the head circumference.

HEAD AND CHEST CIRCUMFERENCE

Measure the diameter of the head around the occiput and just above the eyebrows. The average head circumference of the term newborn is 33 to 35.5 cm (13 to 14 inches). The measurement may be affected by molding of the skull during the birth process. If there is a large amount of molding, remeasure the head when it has returned to its normal shape. An abnormally small head may indicate poor brain growth and microcephaly. A very large head may be a sign of hydrocephalus.

Measure the chest at the level of the nipples. It is usually 2 to 3 cm smaller than the head. The average circumference of the chest is 30.5 to 33 cm (12 to 13 inches). If there is molding of the head, the head and chest measurement may be equal at first.

Administering Prophylactic Medications

Two prophylactic medications are administered to the infant soon after birth. They are vitamin K, to prevent hemorrhagic disease of the newborn, and erythromycin, to prevent ophthalmia neonatorum.

VITAMIN K

Give vitamin K intramuscularly to the neonate within the first hour after birth (see Procedure 20–3 and Drug Guide: Vitamin K_1 [Phytonadione]). Because infants cannot synthesize vitamin K in the intestines without bacterial flora, they are deficient in clotting factors. The one dose of vitamin K prevents bleeding problems until the infant is able to produce it on his or her own.

EYE TREATMENT

All infants receive prophylactic treatment to prevent ophthalmia neonatorum in case the mother is infected with gonorrhea. Currently, the most common medication for eye prophylaxis is erythromycin (see Fig. 20–2 and Drug Guide: Erythromycin Ophthalmic Ointment).

A mild inflammation develops in some infants a few hours after prophylactic treatment at birth. As-

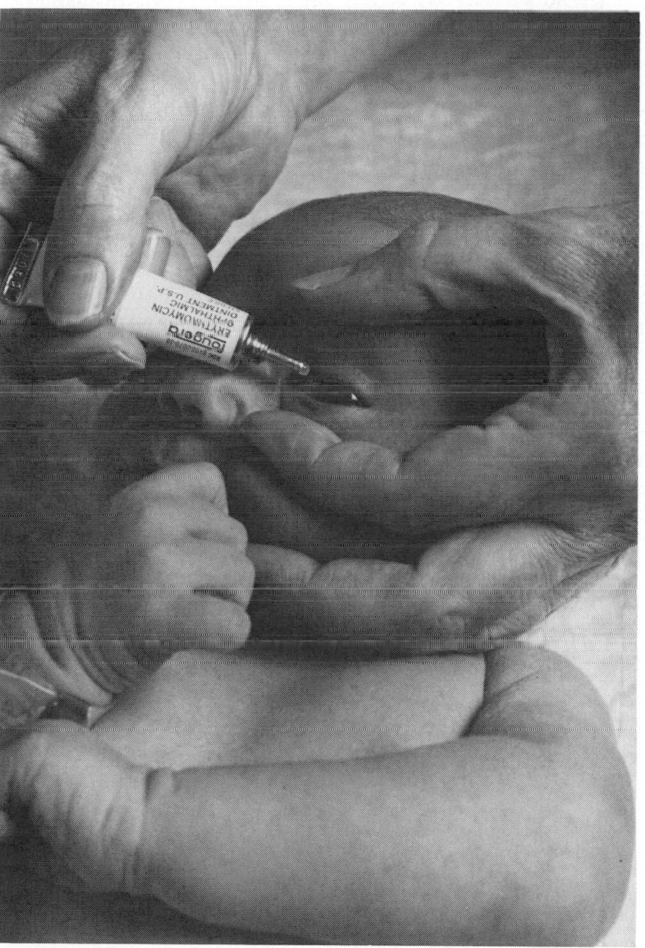

Figure 20–2

Administration of ophthalmic ointment. The nurse gently cleans the eyes of blood or vernix using sterile saline. Then, placing a finger and thumb near the edge of each lid, the nurse gently presses against the periorbital ridges to open the eyes, avoiding pressing on the eye itself. A ribbon of ointment is squeezed into each conjunctival sac. (Gloves are worn if the infant has not yet been bathed.)

Drug Guide

VITAMIN K_1 (Phytonadione)

Classification: Fat-soluble vitamin.

Other Names: AquaMEPHYTON, Konakion.

Action: Promotes the formation of factors II (prothrombin), VII, IX, and X by the liver for clotting. Provides vitamin K, which is not synthesized in the intestines for the first 5 to 8 days after birth because of the newborn's lack of intestinal flora necessary for vitamin K production.

Indication: Prevention or treatment of hemorrhagic disease of the newborn.

Neonatal Dosage and Route: Neonatal dosage: 0.5 to 1 mg (0.25 to 0.5 ml) given once intramuscularly within 1 hour of birth for prophylaxis. (The lower dose may be used for small infants weighing less than 2500 g.) Repeat the dose in 6 to 8 hours, if necessary, for infants of mothers on oral anticoagulants or anticonvulsants during pregnancy. The dose is repeated if the infant shows bleeding tendencies.

Absorption: Readily absorbed after intramuscular injection. Effective within 1 to 2 hours.

Adverse Reactions: Pain and edema at site of administration. Hemolysis or hyperbilirubinemia, especially in a preterm infant or when large doses used.

Nursing Considerations: Protect the drug from light until just before administration, as it decomposes and loses potency on exposure to light. Incompatible with other drugs. Observe all infants for signs of vitamin K deficiency: ecchymoses or bleeding from any site.

sess their eyes frequently and remove any drainage with sterile saline and cotton. Any drainage from the eyes, especially if it is purulent, should alert the nurse to the possibility of infection. If the mother is known to have gonorrhea or chlamydia, the infant will need additional antibiotic treatment. The prophylactic treatment routinely given to all infants may not be enough to completely treat the infection.

Explain to the parents why eye medication is necessary. Because the ointment may temporarily blur the infant's vision, parents may wish to delay treatment for a short time during initial bonding. The medication may be delayed for as long as an hour after birth without adverse effects.

✔ Check Your Reading

1. What is the purpose of scanning after birth?
2. Why are measurements of the neonate important?
3. Why are prophylactic medications given to all newborns?

Drug Guide

ERYTHROMYCIN OPHTHALMIC OINTMENT

Classification: Antibiotic.

Action: Inhibits cell wall replication in bacteria.

Indications: Prophylaxis against the organisms *Neisseria gonorrhoeae* and *Chlamydia trachomatis.* Prevents ophthalmia neonatorum in infants of mothers infected with gonorrhea, and conjunctivitis in infants of mothers infected with *Chlamydia.* Prophylaxis against gonorrhea is required by law for all infants whether or not the mother is known to be infected.

Neonatal Dosge and Route: A "ribbon" of 0.5 per cent erythromycin ointment, 0.5 to 1 cm (0.25 to 0.5 inch) long, is applied to the lower conjunctival sac of each eye no later than 1 hour after birth. May also be used in drop form.

Adverse Effects: Irritation may result in chemical conjunctivitis, which may last 24 to 48 hours. Ointment may cause temporary blurred vision.

Nursing Considerations: Cleanse the infant's eyes before application, as needed. Hold the tube in a horizontal rather than a vertical position to prevent injury to the eye from sudden movement. Administer from the inner canthus to the outer canthus. Do not touch the tip of the tube to any part of the eye, as this may spread infectious material from one eye to the other. Do not rinse or wipe ointment from conjunctiva. Observe for irritation. Do not use tube on another infant, as this may spread infection. Other medications used for prevention of gonorrhea include tetracycline and silver nitrate solution.

Cardiorespiratory Status: Application of Nursing Process

Assessments of respiratory and cardiovascular status are performed together because transitional changes take place in both systems at birth. Problems in adaptation in one system will most likely result in problems in the other system as well (see Nursing Care Plan 20–1, p. 554).

Assessment

HISTORY

Information about the pregnancy, labor, and delivery is important in assessing the infant's cardiovascular and respiratory status and the likelihood of problems at birth. For example, if the mother received narcotic analgesics late in labor, depression of the fetal central nervous system may interfere with initiation of respirations in the neonate. Although a certain amount of hypoxia enhances the stimulation of respirations, severe asphyxia throughout labor or delivery results in depression at birth. Infants who are preterm may not produce adequate amounts of surfactant, and atelectasis will occur because the alveoli do not remain open.

AIRWAY

During birth, fetal lung fluid is forced into the upper airways. Determine whether there is excessive fluid or mucus in the infant's respiratory passages. There may continue to be fluid in the respiratory tract for several hours after birth.

Signs of Respiratory Distress. Throughout the assessment, be alert for signs of respiratory distress. They include tachypnea, retractions, flaring nares, central cyanosis, grunting, and seesaw respirations. Whenever one sign of labored breathing is present, carefully expand the assessment to look for others.

Respiratory Rate. Assess respirations every 15 minutes for the first hour and, if stable, every hour for the next 4 hours after birth. If abnormalities are noted, assess respirations more often. The normal respiratory rate is 30 to 60 breaths/minute, although it may be faster during the early hours after birth. Respirations should not be dyspneic, and the chest movements should be symmetrical.

Counting the rapid, shallow, irregular respirations of a newborn can be difficult at first. Some nurses count while observing the infant's chest. If the infant is dressed, lift the shirt and blanket to visualize the chest and abdomen. Sometimes it is hard to differentiate the respirations from other movement if the newborn is very active. Use observation, palpation, or auscultation, alone or in combination, to obtain a respiratory rate (see Procedure 20–4).

Observe for apnea, which may occur in the normal infant for up to 10 seconds. This is known as periodic breathing and is considered normal as long as there are no changes in color or heart rate. Any apnea lasting longer than 15 seconds, or accompanied by cyanosis or other signs of difficult breathing, is abnormal.

Breath Sounds. Auscultate the entire anterior and posterior lung fields for breath sounds. They should be clear over most areas, but it is not unusual to hear sounds of moisture in the lungs during the first hour or two after birth because fetal lung fluid has not been completely absorbed. Breath sounds may be coarse in infants born by cesarean delivery. This is because they do not receive pressure on the chest from passage through the birth canal, which squeezes out part of the fetal lung fluid.

When the listener is not experienced in assessing the lungs of a newborn, distinguishing between clear breath sounds and coarse or moist sounds is less difficult than trying to describe crackles or wheezes. Abnormal or diminished sounds should always be verified by an experienced nurse and reported to the physician or nurse practitioner if they continue.

Choanal Atresia. Because the nasal passages of infants are so small and easily occluded, it is important that they remain clear. Should one side be blocked congenitally, the infant is at risk for complete obstruction. Assess the infant for choanal atresia, in which one or both nasal passages are obstructed. Close the infant's mouth and occlude one nostril at a time. Observe whether the infant can breathe through each side individually. Another method of assessment for choanal atresia is to pass a catheter through each nostril to check for patency. Infants with choanal atresia may become cyanotic when quiet but pink when crying, as air is then drawn in through the mouth.

Bilateral choanal atresia causes severe respiratory distress and necessitates surgery. Blockage of one side puts the infant at risk for respiratory distress should the other side become occluded by mucus or edema.

HEART SOUNDS

Auscultate the heart for rate, rhythm, and the presence of murmurs or abnormal sounds. The rate should range between 120 and 160 BPM with normal activity. It may elevate to 180 BPM when infants are crying or drop to as low as 100 BPM when they are in a deep sleep.

Count the apical pulse for a full minute for accuracy and to listen for abnormalities. Because the heart beat is so rapid, it is difficult for the inexperienced listener to count it at first. Listening to the pattern of the heart beat for a short time before attempting to count it may make counting easier.

The chest of the infant is small, and it is easy to hear other noises, such as breath sounds or even bowel sounds, when trying to listen to the heart. A pediatric-sized stethoscope is preferable to the adult-sized one, which tends to pick up more extraneous sounds. Move the stethoscope over the entire heart area to listen to all sounds.

An experienced examiner can determine the position of the heart in the chest by the location of the heart sounds and the point of maximum impulse. The apex of the heart is located at the point of maximum impulse, where the pulse is most easily felt and the sound is loudest. This is at the 4th intercostal space, slightly left of the midclavicular

Procedure 20–4

Assessing Vital Signs in the Newborn

Purpose: To obtain an accurate measurement of newborn vital signs.

RESPIRATIONS

1. **Assess respirations when the infant is quiet or sleeping if possible. Count the respirations (and apical pulse) before disturbing the infant for other assessments.** *Allows for easy assessment and prevents crying.*

2. **Assess respirations by observing, palpating, and/or auscultating the chest and abdomen.** *Increases accuracy of the assessment.*

3. **To observe respirations, lift the infant's shirt and blanket so that the chest and abdomen can be seen. Observe the pattern of respirations before beginning to count.** *Respirations are often irregular, but there is a basic pattern. Observation of the pattern makes it easier to count the rate.*

4. **If desired, place a hand lightly over the infant's chest or abdomen to feel the movement.** *Palpation helps keep track of the rate.*

5. **To auscultate respirations, place a stethoscope on the right side of the infant's chest.** *Allows the sounds of the lungs to be heard with less interference from heart sounds. Allows the nurse to hear breath sounds too. The completion of assessment of breath sounds can be done as soon as respirations are counted.*

6. **Count for a full minute.** *Respirations are normally irregular in the newborn. Counting for a full minute increases accuracy.*

7. **If the infant is crying, continue to count.** *Although it is easiest to assess respirations on a quiet infant, they can be counted when the infant is crying. (Remember, the infant breathes while crying!) The rate may be faster than when the infant is quiet and should be charted as crying.*

8. **Observe the infant for signs of respiratory distress, including tachypnea, retractions, flaring, cyanosis, grunting, or seesawing.** *Expect the respiratory rate to be 30 to 60 breaths/minute when the infant is at rest. Allows identification and follow-up of abnormalities.*

PULSE

1. **Listen to the apical pulse on a quiet or sleeping infant if possible. Begin with this assessment before disturbing the infant for other assessments and care.** *Allows one to hear heart sounds more clearly.*

2. **Use a pediatric head on the stethoscope to listen to apical pulse.** *Although the larger head may be used if necessary, the small head allows better contact between the stethoscope and the chest wall and eliminates some of the noises of the lungs and intestines.*

3. **If the infant is crying, insert a pacifier or a gloved finger into the mouth.** *Stimulates the sucking reflex and often quiets infants.*

4. **If the infant cannot be quieted, increase concentration and time spent listening.** *Helps separate the sounds heard and to focus in on the heart beat.*

5. **Listen briefly before beginning to count. Tapping a finger in rhythm with the beat may be helpful. Expect heart rate to be 120 to 160 BPM at rest.** *Allows time to get used to the pattern of the heart beat before beginning to count.*

6. **Move stethoscope over the entire heart area to listen to all sounds. Assess for arrhythmias, murmurs, or other abnormal sounds. Refer any abnormal sounds for follow-up.** *Listening over the entire area increases chances of hearing abnormal sounds. Reporting abnormalities to the pediatrician allows further investigation.*

TEMPERATURE

Axillary

1. **Hold the thermometer in the center of the axillary space with the infant's arm firmly over the thermometer.** *If the thermometer protrudes behind the axilla, it gives an inaccurate reading. Holding the arm keeps the thermometer positioned correctly and prevents accidental injury if the infant moves unexpectedly.*

2. **Read thermometer at the proper time: glass, 5 minutes; plastic strip, 1 to 1.5 minutes (with a 10-second wait before reading); electronic, when indicator sounds. Normal range: 36.5° to 37.5°C (97.7° to 99.5°F).** *Ensures an accurate reading.*

Assessing Vital Signs in the Newborn *Continued*

Rectal

1. **Take a rectal temperature when birth facility policy states that this method is to be used for the first temperature taken. It may also be used to confirm axillary measurements because the readings for both methods are very similar. However, use the axillary method whenever possible.** *Rectal temperature involves the potential risk of perforation of the rectum, which can be life-threatening.*
2. **Lubricate the tip of the thermometer with water-soluble lubricant.** *Allows the thermometer to be inserted without irritation to sphincter. Water-soluble lubricant dissolves and washes away.*
3. **Place the infant in a supine or side position and hold the ankles firmly in one hand. Bend the infant's knees against the abdomen and raise the legs to expose the anus, or place the infant prone and separate the buttocks.** *Provides visualization while preventing excessive movement that might dislodge the thermometer or cause it to break (if glass), resulting in injury to delicate tissues.*
4. **Insert the thermometer carefully and gently no more than 0.5 inch into the rectum.** *The rectum turns to the right 1 inch from the sphincter. Inserting the thermometer farther may cause perforation.*
5. **Do *not* force the thermometer if it does not insert easily.** *There may be an obstruction preventing insertion of the thermometer.*
6. **Hold the thermometer securely near the buttocks throughout the time it remains in the rectum.** *Maintains control over the thermometer to avoid inserting it too far and prevents injury if the infant moves.*
7. **Read thermometer at the proper time: glass, 5 minutes; electronic, when indicator sounds. Normal range: 36.5 to 37.6°C (97.7 to 99.7°F).** *Ensures accurate reading.*

Tympanic

1. **Cover the probe according to directions from the manufacturer.** *Prevents contamination of probe and cross-contamination between infants.*
2. **Gently insert the probe into the external auditory canal.** *Prevents injury to the ear.*
3. **Read the thermometer at 1 second or as directed by the manufacturer.** *Ensures accurate measurement.*

line (a line drawn from the middle of the left clavicle). Conditions that affect the position of the heart include pneumothorax and dextrocardia (in which the heart position is reversed from normal).

The rhythm of the heart should be regular, and the first and second sounds (the lub and dub) of the heart beat should be clearly heard. Note abnormalities in rhythm or sounds such as murmurs. Murmurs are sounds of abnormal blood flow through the heart and may indicate openings in the septum of the heart or problems with blood flow through the valves. Most murmurs in the newborn are temporary and due to incomplete transition from fetal to neonatal circulation. For example, because the ductus arteriosus may not be functionally closed for the first few hours after birth, a murmur may be heard when the heart sounds are auscultated. The murmur will disappear when complete functional closure occurs. Although this may be a "normal" murmur, any abnormal sounds of the heart should be investigated further, as they may be signs of cardiac defects.

Auscultate the heart once every 15 minutes for 1 hour and every hour for the next 4 hours after birth, or more often if there are abnormalities. Once stable, the vital signs are checked once every 8 hours unless there is a reason to assess them more frequently.

COLOR

Note the newborn's overall color, because it is an important indication of both cardiovascular and respiratory status.

Cyanosis. Cyanosis is a purplish-blue discoloration that indicates that the infant is not getting enough oxygen. It may be preceded by a dusky or gray hue to the skin.

In cyanosis, it is important to note which parts of the body are involved. Cyanosis of the hands and feet is acrocyanosis, or peripheral cyanosis. Acrocyanosis is normal in the newborn because circulation to the ends of the extremities is not completely established at first. Central cyanosis involves the center areas of the body and the mucus membranes. It indicates that not enough oxygen is getting to the vital organs and necessitates immediate attention.

Note when cyanosis occurs. Cyanosis may be present at birth or become apparent later. It is not unusual to see a purplish-blue discoloration at birth that quickly turns pink as the infant begins to breathe. Cyanosis occurs anytime the infant's breathing is impaired as a result of secretions. It may occur during feedings because of difficulty in coordinating sucking and swallowing with breathing. Infants who become cyanotic on exertion or crying may have a congenital heart defect.

Pallor. Some infants have a pale skin color. Pallor can indicate that the infant is slightly hypoxic or anemic. A laboratory examination of hemoglobin and hematocrit or a complete blood count may be ordered by the physician.

Ruddy Color. In contrast to pallor, a ruddy color is observed in some infants. These infants may have a polycythemia, an excessive number of red blood cells. A hematocrit determination will confirm polycythemia. Infants with elevated hematocrits are at increased risk for jaundice during the normal destruction of excessive red blood cells that occurs after birth. Watch for jaundice in infants with hematocrits above 65 per cent.

BRACHIAL AND FEMORAL PULSES

Palpate the neonate's brachial and femoral pulses as part of the initial assessment. They should be present and equal bilaterally. The brachial pulse is located over the antecubital space, whereas the femoral pulse is located at the groin. Differences between the brachial and the femoral pulses may be due to impaired blood flow in coarctation of the aorta, a congenital heart defect. In this condition, a narrowed area of the aorta impedes blood flow to the lower part of the body.

BLOOD PRESSURE

Measure blood pressure on the arm, leg, or both as part of the initial assessment of the newborn. Doppler ultrasonography or other electronic measurement makes it easier to obtain an accurate blood pressure. The average blood pressure is 65 systolic and 41 diastolic (Park and Lee, 1989). If the pressure of the lower extremities is less than that of the upper extremities, coarctation of the aorta may be present. Hypotension may be present in the sick infant.

Analysis

Whereas some infants experience an actual problem with excessive airway secretions, almost all infants must undergo fluid removal from the respiratory passages during the early hours after birth. Therefore, one of the most common nursing diagnoses for the newborn is: *Ineffective Airway Clearance related to excessive secretions in respiratory passages.*

Planning

The goals for this nursing diagnosis are that the newborn:

- Will maintain a patent airway with a respiratory rate within the normal range of 30 to 60 breaths/minute.
- Will show no signs of respiratory distress.

Interventions

POSITIONING THE INFANT

Position the infant with the head slightly lower than the extremities to aid in draining fluid from the respiratory passages immediately after birth. Use this position briefly whenever the infant is having difficulty clearing the airways, such as during regurgitation. Do not leave the infant in a head-dependent position longer than necessary because pressure from the intestines may interfere with movement of the diaphragm.

SUCTIONING SECRETIONS

Use the bulb syringe frequently to suction secretions as they drain into the infant's mouth or nose (see Procedure 20–5). Suction the mouth first because the infant may gasp when the nose is suctioned, and aspiration could occur if there is mucus or fluid in the mouth. Then gently suction the nose, taking care to avoid trauma to the delicate mucus membranes. Keep the bulb syringe in the crib near the infant's head, where it will be available if needed quickly. Teach both parents how to use the bulb syringe correctly. Send it home with the infant so that the parents will be able to use it if the infant experiences a problem.

If mechanical suctioning is necessary to remove deeper secretions, choose a small catheter to avoid damaging the tissues of the respiratory tract. Suction for no more than 5 seconds at a time using minimal negative pressure to avoid trauma, laryngospasm, and bradycardia.

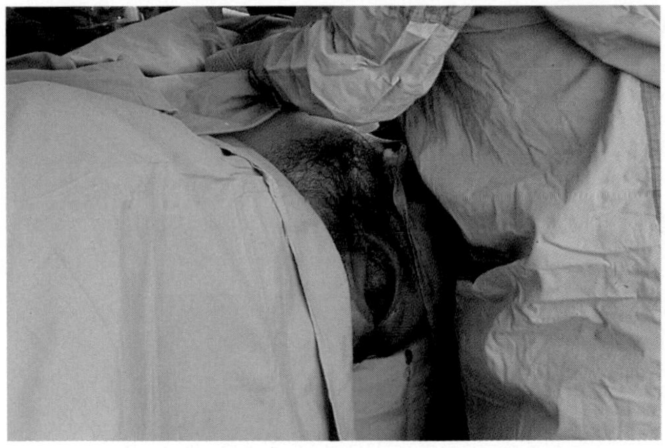

I. Crowning begins

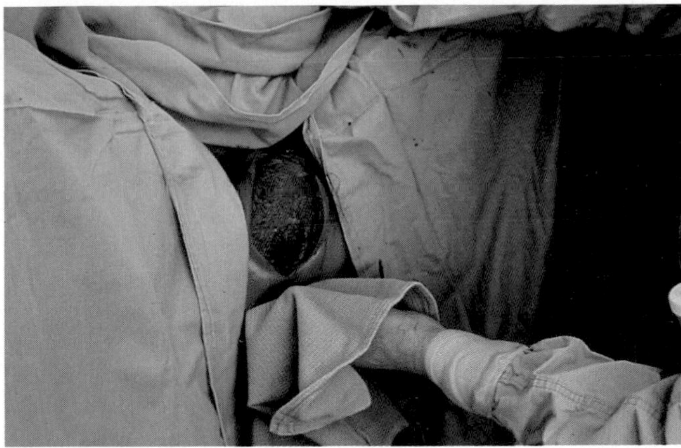

II. Crowning

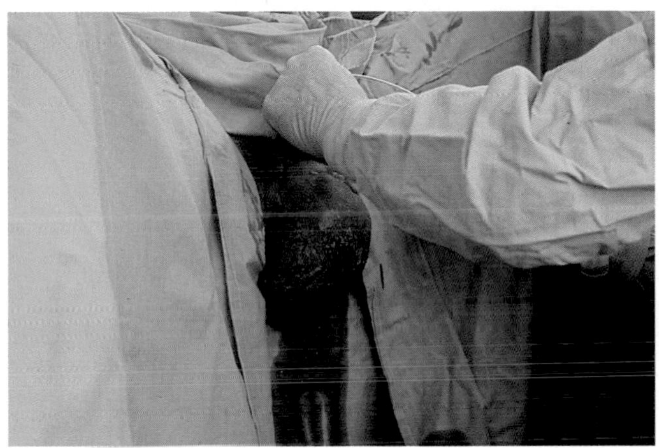

III. The head is delivered

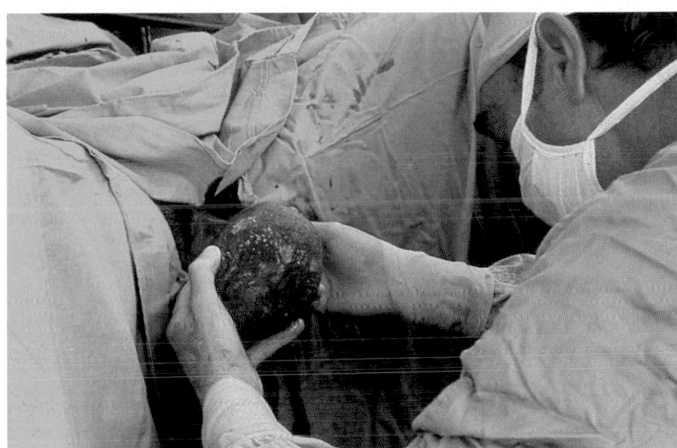

IV. External rotation

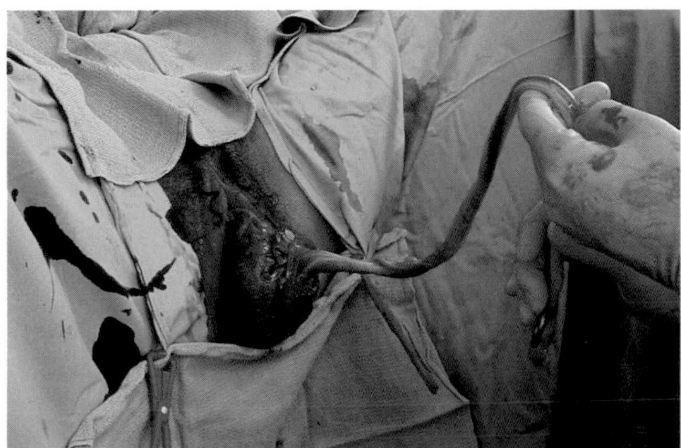

V. The placenta is delivered

Plates I–V courtesy of Long Beach Memorial Medical Center, Long Beach, California

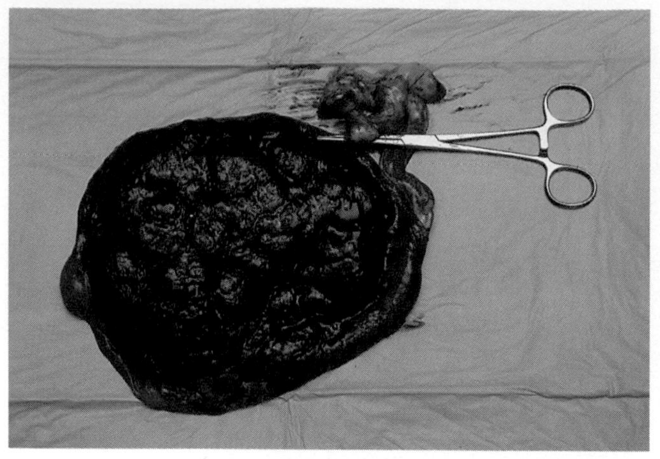

VI. Placenta: maternal side

VII. Placenta: fetal side

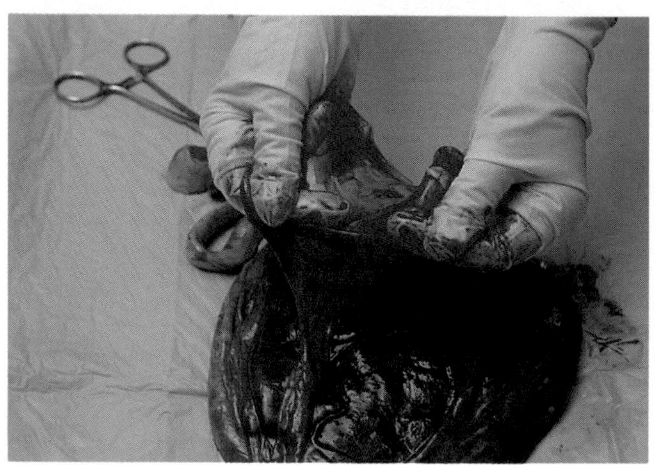

VIII. Placenta: separating membrane

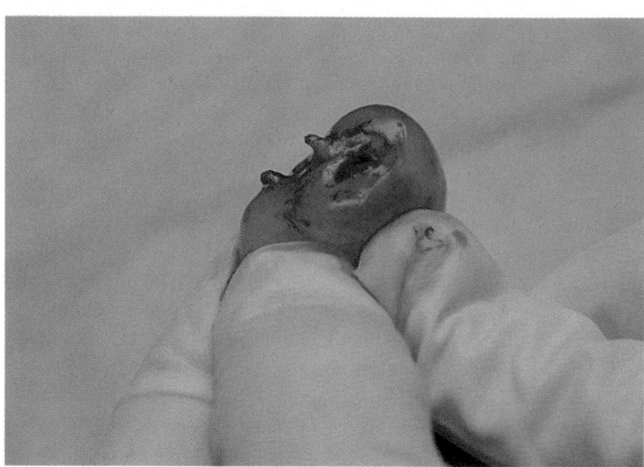

IX. Umbilical cord vessels

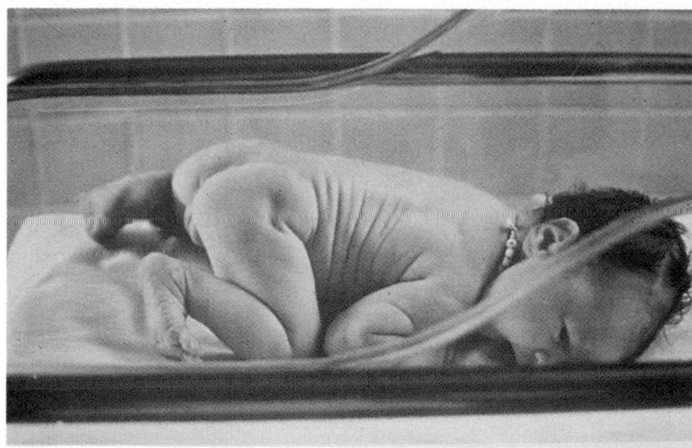

X. Acrocyanosis

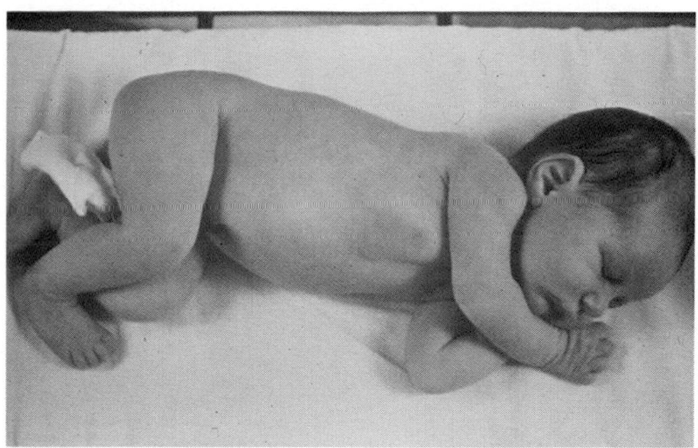

XI. Jaundice

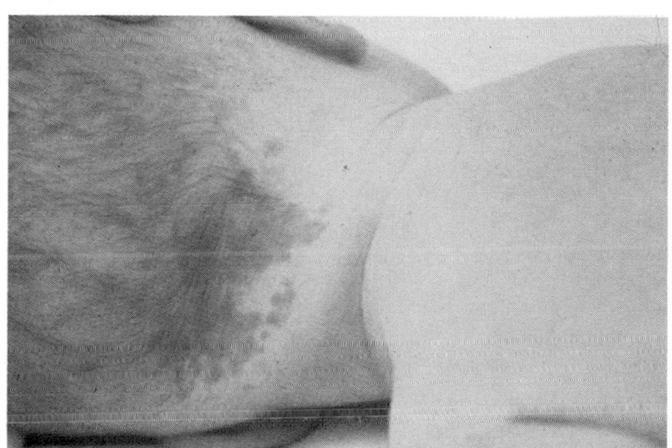

XII. Stork bite

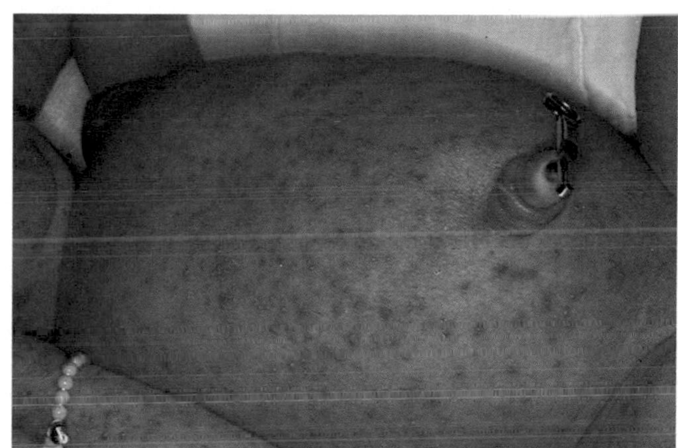

XIII. Erythema

Plates X–XII courtesy of Jane Deacon, MS, RN, NNP, The Children's Hospital, Denver, Colorado

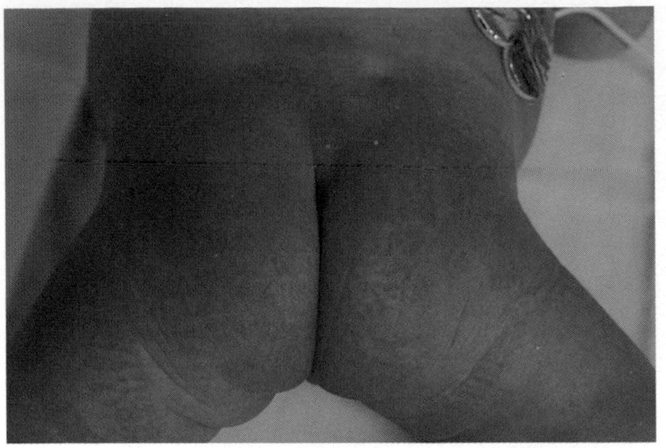

XIV. Mongolian spots

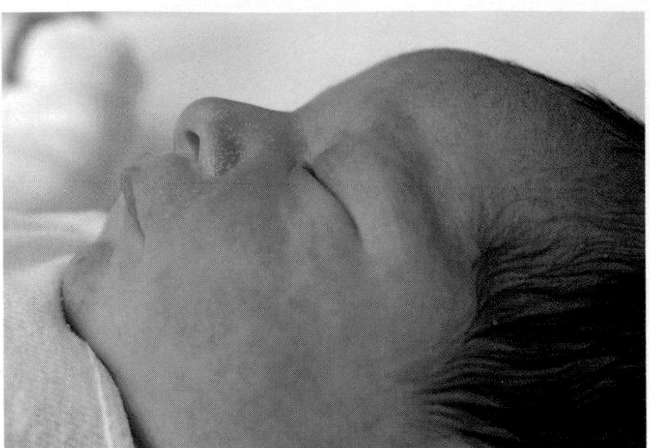

XV. Milia

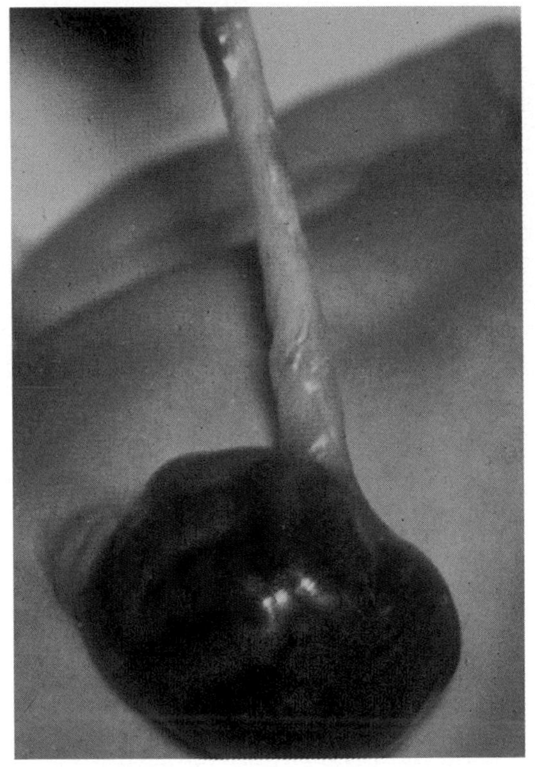

XVI. Omphalocele

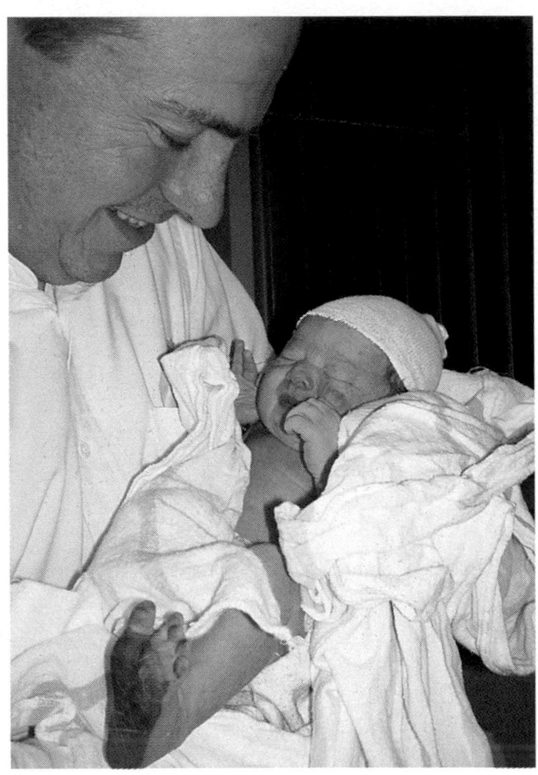

XVII. Father greets daughter

Plate XVI courtesy of Jane Deacon, MS, RN, NNP, The Children's Hospital, Denver, Colorado

Procedure 20–5 Using a Bulb Syringe

Purpose: To provide an open airway by removing secretions from the infant's mouth and nose.

1. **When an infant needs suctioning because of excessive mucus or regurgitation of a feeding, position the infant's head to the side or pick up the infant and hold with the head lower than the rest of the body.** *Allows for drainage of mucus from the mouth to prevent aspiration.*

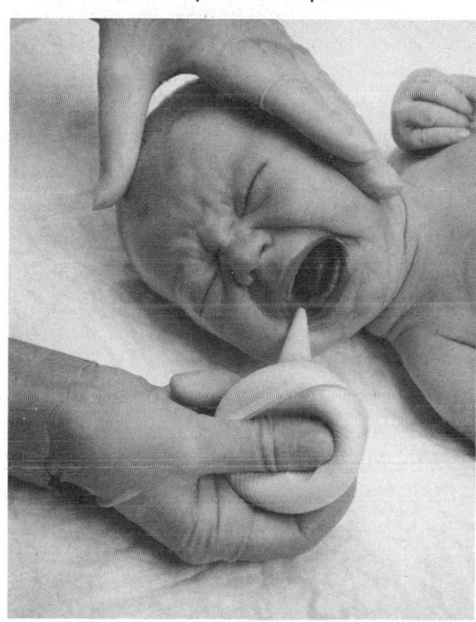

2. **Compress the bulb before inserting it into the infant's mouth.** *Removes the air from the syringe so that it will suction. (Be sure not to compress the bulb while it is in the infant's mouth, or secretions in the bulb could be squirted back into the mouth.)*

3. **Insert the bulb into the side of the infant's mouth. Do not insert it straight to the back of the throat.** *A vagal response could be stimulated, with bradycardia or even apnea resulting. The infant might gag as well.*

4. **Release the bulb slowly while it is in the mouth. Remove the syringe and empty it by compressing it several times before using again as needed.** *Release the bulb to draw the secretions from the infant's mouth into the bulb. Empty it to prepare it for use again.*

5. **Suction the nose if necessary after the mouth is cleared.** *Infants often gasp when the nares are suctioned and might aspirate secretions in the mouth if the mouth is not cleared out first.*

6. **Suction the nose carefully and gently.** *Trauma could cause edema to the delicate tissues and lead to obstruction. Infants are obligate nose breathers and will have respiratory difficulty if the nasal passages are blocked.*

Evaluation

The normal newborn has little difficulty clearing the airway after the first few hours of life. Goals are met if:

- The infant is stable.
- The respiratory rate between 30 and 60 breaths/minute.
- There are no signs of respiratory distress.

Thermoregulation: Application of Nursing Process

Understanding the process of heat loss and production in the newborn can help the nurse in the assessment and care related to this vital function (see Nursing Care Plan 20–1, p. 554).

Assessment

Assess the neonate's temperature soon after birth. Place the infant in a radiant warmer and attach a skin probe to the abdomen. The probe allows the warmer to measure and display the infant's temperature continuously. It is set to regulate the amount of heat produced by the warmer according to the infant's skin temperature. The temperature should be noted every 15 minutes during the first hour, and hourly during the next 4 hours. At that point, the temperature can be assessed every 8 hours as long as it remains stable.

In some agencies, the first temperature is taken rectally. This provides information about the neonate's core temperature as well as patency of the anus. Insert the thermometer no more than 0.5 inch into the anus when taking a rectal temperature. The colon turns at a sharp right angle approximately

1 inch from the anal sphincter. Inserting the thermometer farther might result in potentially fatal perforation of the intestinal wall. Never force a thermometer into the rectum, because there may be an imperforate anus. The normal range of rectal temperature is 36.5° to 37.6°C (97.7° to 99.7°F) (Whaley and Wong, 1991) (see Fig. 20–3 and Procedure 20–4).

Taking axillary temperatures is safer than taking rectal temperatures because it avoids the possibility of damage to the rectum. Axillary temperatures provide a reading very close to rectal measurements. The normal range for axillary temperature is 36.5° to 37.5°C (97.7° to 99.5°F) (Merenstein et al, 1989).

Measure temperatures with an electronic or glass thermometer, a disposable plastic strip, or a tympanic thermometer. Disposable plastic strips change color to indicate temperature change. Insert the covered plastic probe of a tympanic thermometer into the auditory canal. An infrared sensor determines temperature within 1 second. Although these devices are expensive, they are quick, easy, and accurate even when the infant has an ear infection.

Analysis

Any newborn may have difficulty maintaining a stable temperature. Therefore, an appropriate nursing diagnosis is: *High Risk for Ineffective Thermoregulation related to immature compensation for changes in environmental temperature.*

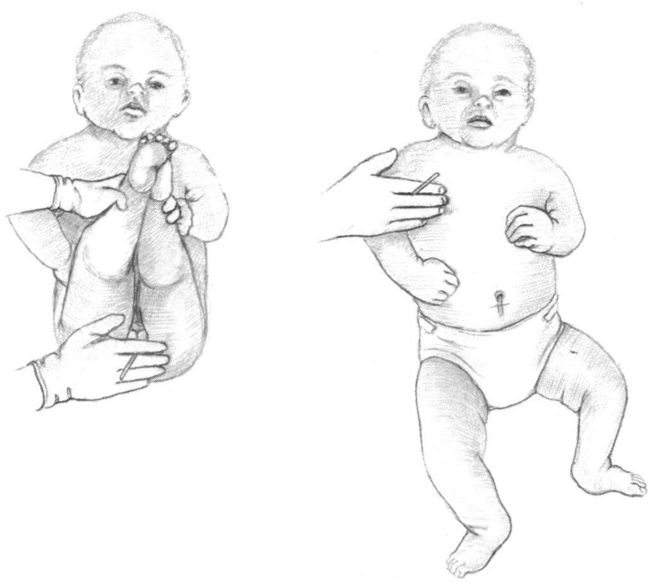

Figure 20–3

A rectal or axillary temperature may be taken. The infant is held securely to prevent injury and obtain an accurate reading.

Planning

The goal for this diagnosis is that the infant will maintain body temperature within the normal ranges:

- Rectal, 36.5° to 37.6°C (97.7° to 99.7°F)
- Axillary, 36.5° to 37.5°C (97.7° to 99.5°F).

Interventions

PREVENTING HEAT LOSS

Begin preventive measures before the infant is born. Provide a neutral thermal environment with a radiant warmer during initial assessments. This ensures that the infant's metabolic rate does not have to increase and that excess oxygen and glucose do not have to be used to maintain body temperature. Check the radiant warmer to be sure that it is functioning properly before the delivery. Turn it on early enough so that the bed is ready and warm for the newborn.

Immediately after birth, place the infant on the mother's abdomen or under the radiant warmer to counteract the cool temperature of the delivery room. Dry the wet infant quickly with warm towels to prevent heat loss by evaporation. Pay particular attention to drying the hair because the head is a large surface area and hair that remains damp increases heat loss. Remove towels or blankets as soon as they become wet and replace them with dry, warmed linens.

Warm anything that comes in contact with the infant to avoid conduction of heat away from the body. Pad cool surfaces such as scales before placing infants on them. Warm stethoscopes and clothing before using them on the infant. Run warm water over your hands if they are cold.

To prevent heat loss by radiation, position the newborn's crib or incubator away from walls or windows that are part of the outside of the building. It is easy to overlook this source of heat loss when the objects and air around the infant seem warm, but infants may lose heat to objects not in close contact with them. Keep this in mind when positioning cribs in mothers' rooms, which are often short of space. Place the crib at the end of the mother's bed or between the beds (in a two-bed room) rather than next to the windows. Avoid areas where there is a draft.

When assessing or caring for newborns, avoid exposing more of their bodies than necessary. Remove clothing and blankets only from the areas being assessed. Keep the upper part of the infant covered when changing diapers. Wrap them in blankets and use a stockinette or insulated hat to prevent heat loss from the large surface area of the head.

RESTORING THERMOREGULATION

When an infant's temperature drops, institute nursing measures to assist thermoregulation immediately. If the axillary temperature is low, some nurses check the rectal temperature. However, do not wait for the rectal temperature to drop. The process of nonshivering thermogenesis will begin in the infant before the core temperature becomes abnormal.

First look for obvious causes for the infant's low temperature. Perhaps the infant is unwrapped or is wearing wet diapers or clothing. The mother's room may be cold, or the crib may be placed near the air conditioner. These causes can easily be corrected.

A slight drop in temperature may require only the addition of extra clothing. Use two blankets, each wrapped separately around the infant to increase insulation of heat by trapping air between the layers. Place another blanket over the infant in the crib and be sure that a hat is on the head. Place linens in a warmer prior to use if added warmth is desired.

A greater drop in temperature necessitates additional measures. Place the infant under a radiant warmer for a short time. For an infant with a markedly decreased temperature, set the temperature control on the warmer to warm the infant slowly. Too rapid warming can cause complications, including apnea.

PERFORMING EXPANDED ASSESSMENTS

Expanded assessments are necessary whenever there is a decreased temperature in a newborn. Assess the respiratory rate because nonshivering thermogenesis increases the need for oxygen. Observe for signs of respiratory distress brought on by the additional oxygen requirement.

Because the cold infant uses more glucose to produce heat, test the blood glucose level when temperature is abnormal. A reading of 45 mg/dl or less necessitates feeding.

Infants who do not respond to these simple measures need additional treatment. Notify the physician or nurse practitioner, and keep the infant in an incubator in the nursery for close observation until the temperature stabilizes. Observe for signs of infection, of which low temperature is one indication.

Evaluation

When a temperature within the normal ranges has been maintained for several hours, the infant can be considered stable in thermoregulation. Assess the infant's temperature according to agency routine, generally every 8 hours unless further problems develop.

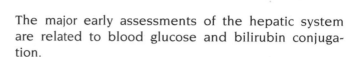

✔ Check Your Reading

4. What is included in assessment of the newborn's cardiovascular status?
5. How can nurses prevent heat loss in newborns?

Hepatic Function: Application of Nursing Process

The major early assessments of the hepatic system are related to blood glucose and bilirubin conjugation.

Blood Glucose

Assessment

Be alert for newborns at increased risk for hypoglycemia, which can cause damage to the brain. Ask questions about factors that might have caused the infant to use up available glucose (Table 20–2). When the infant is born, do a quick estimate to determine whether the newborn appears to be near-term and of appropriate size for gestational age. This estimate will be verified when the gestational age assessment is completed. Observe for signs of hypoglycemia throughout routine assessment and care (see Critical to Remember: Signs of Hypoglycemia in the Newborn).

Screen for blood glucose level as appropriate. In some agencies, the admission for all newborns includes a test for blood glucose with a glucose screening strip. In others, the usual procedure is to test only infants in risk categories or those showing early signs of hypoglycemia. Dextrostix and Chemstrip reagent strips are commonly used to screen for hypoglycemia.

The tests involve placing a drop of blood from the infant's heel onto a treated paper strip for 1 minute and comparing it with a color chart after the blood is

Table 20–2. RISK FACTORS FOR HYPOGLYCEMIA

Prematurity
Postmaturity
Intrauterine growth retardation
Asphyxia
Cold stress
Large for gestational age
Infant of diabetic mother
Maternal intake of ritodrine or terbutaline

Critical to Remember

Signs of Hypoglycemia in the Newborn

- Jitteriness
- Poor muscle tone
- Increased pulse and respiration
- Respiratory distress
- Cyanosis
- Apnea
- Diaphoresis
- Low temperature
- Poor suck
- High-pitched cry
- Lethargy
- Irritability
- Seizures

removed. Reagent strips can also be used with blood glucose meters that electronically determine the amount of glucose in the blood sample. Carefully follow the manufacturer's directions for each method to obtain accurate results (see Procedure 20–6).

Take care to avoid injuring the foot during heel sticks. Do not make the heel puncture deep enough to go into the calcaneus bone, as osteomyelitis may result. Choose a site that avoids the major nerves and arteries of the area.

Because capillary blood is used in screening tests, these are less accurate than laboratory tests for which venous blood is used. Therefore, obtain a laboratory analysis (per agency policy) to verify low readings on glucose strips.

Analysis

For infants who have glucose levels of 40 mg/dl by laboratory analysis or 45 mg/dl by screening tests, the following collaborative problem may be used: Potential complication: *Hypoglycemia*.

Planning

Client-centered goals for hypoglycemia are inappropriate because this problem requires collaboration between the nurse and the physician. Planning revolves around the nurse's role in:

- Monitoring for signs of hypoglycemia
- Notifying the physician about signs of hypoglycemia or determining whether routine orders have been left by the physician for infants with hypoglycemia
- Intervening to minimize hypoglycemia

Interventions

MAINTAINING SAFE GLUCOSE LEVELS

If glucose is not constantly available to the brain, permanent damage may occur. To prevent this, follow agency policy and physician orders regarding feeding infants with low glucose levels. A common practice is to feed the newborn if the glucose strip shows a level of 45 mg/dl or less to prevent further depletion of glucose. If this is the infant's first feeding, glucose water or breast milk may be given. Follow the water with formula 1 hour later. If the mother plans to breastfeed, help her begin the first feeding. If she is unable to nurse the infant immediately (because of pain or exhaustion from delivery), feed the infant glucose water to prevent continued insufficient levels of blood glucose. Follow with formula 1 hour later if the mother is still unable to breastfeed.

REPEATING GLUCOSE TESTS

Observe newborns who have shown signs of hypoglycemia closely until glucose levels are stable. A schedule for retesting is routine in many agencies. An example of such a routine is a second screening an hour after the first test, and another screening every 2 hours for the next 6 hours. If the tests are normal at that time, further testing is unnecessary unless further indications of hypoglycemia develop.

Keep the physician or nurse practitioner aware of the newborn's status. If the glucose problem continues, the infant may be transferred to a nursery for more intensive treatment.

Parents may be distressed over the multiple heel sticks their infant must endure. Explain the importance of adequate blood glucose levels and why the tests and frequent feedings are necessary. Encourage parents to feed the newborn according to suggestions so that enough glucose is available to meet the infant's needs. Discuss the routine for blood testing and when the infant will no longer require it.

Evaluation

In evaluating collaborative interventions for hypoglycemia, the nurse notes the presence or absence of continued signs of hypoglycemia and compares blood glucose screening with normal values. The blood glucose should remain above 45 mg/dl on screening.

Procedure 20–6

Assessing Blood Glucose in the Newborn

Purpose: To accurately measure the infant's blood glucose by heel puncture.

Note: The instructions for obtaining a blood sample for glucose are also appropriate for taking blood samples for other tests.

1. **Wash hands.** *Helps prevent spread of infection.*

2. **Gather supplies needed: gloves, alcohol wipe, sterile 2×2 gauze, lancet, cotton ball, adhesive bandage, diaper or commercial warming pack to warm heel, and bottle of glucose screening strips (Chemstrip or Dextrostix). Do not remove strip from container until just before use. Include automatic heel puncturing device and glucose monitoring meter if used.** *Having all supplies ready allows efficient performance of procedure. Bottle or bottle cap may contain preservative. Removing reagent strip too early can result in a false reading.*

3. **Warm foot for a few minutes if it is cold or if blood is needed for other tests as well. Dampen a disposable diaper with warm water and fasten it over the heel, or use a commercial heel warming pack according to directions.** *Warming causes vasodilation and allows blood to flow more easily. This avoids having to make more than one puncture as a result of insufficient blood flow.*

4. **Apply gloves.** *Prevents contamination of hands with blood and is part of universal precautions.*

5. **Clean lateral heel with alcohol. Wipe dry with sterile gauze.** *Alcohol removes contaminants. Drying prevents diluting specimen with alcohol.*

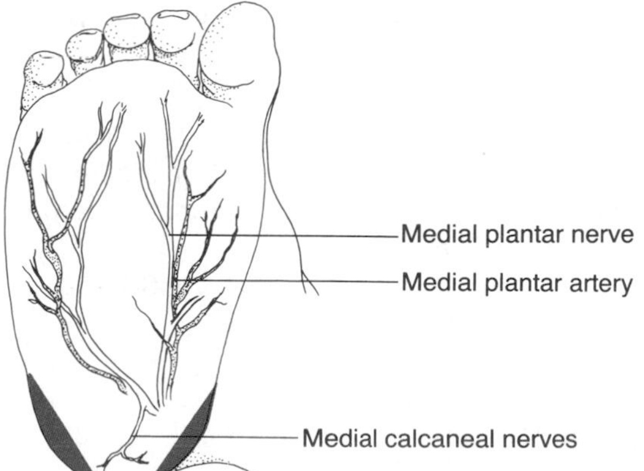

6. **Hold heel in one hand and locate site. Feel the bone of the heel. Place the thumb or finger over the walking surface to shield this area. Determine area for puncture.** *Stabilizes heel so that infant cannot move it and cause inadvertent injury from lancet. Locating the bone and covering the walking surface helps avoid puncturing the calcaneus bone, which might result in infection. Also avoids damage to nerves and arteries of area.*

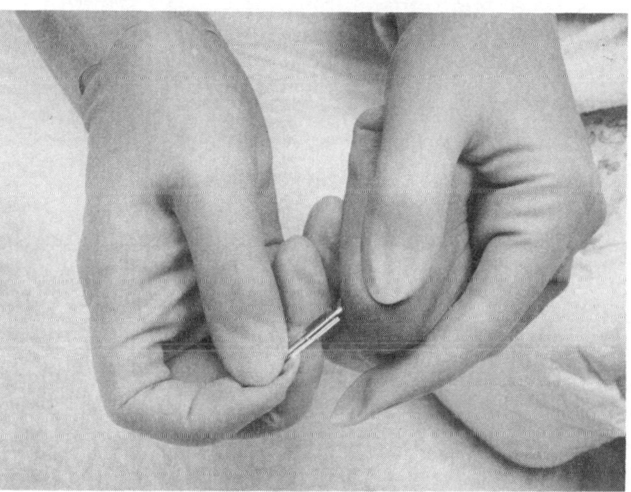

7. **Puncture side of heel with lancet. Place lancet in a safe place outside the crib until the test is completed, then dispose of lancet in sharps container.** *Prevents injury to infant and injury or unnecessary exposure of nurse and others to infant's blood.*

8. **If automatic puncture device is used, place over appropriate site and activate according to manufacturer's directions.** *Ensures proper use of device.*

9. **Wipe away first drop of blood with sterile gauze. Collect a large "stand-up" drop of blood at the puncture site and place it on end of screening strip over treated area. The entire treated area of the strip should be covered. Avoid excessive squeezing of the foot.** *First drop may be diluted with fluid from the area of the puncture. Enough blood must be applied to the strip so that it will not dry during the waiting time and will provide an adequate sample for accuracy. Excessive squeezing causes dilution of the sample with fluid from the tissues.*

Procedure continued on following page

Assessing Blood Glucose in the Newborn *Continued*

10. **Wait exactly 60 seconds before removing blood from the strip.** *Allows treated area of strip to change color. More or less time will affect accuracy of reading.*

11. **Remove blood by the method appropriate for the type of screening strip used. Dextrostrix: run cold water slowly over the end of the strip to wash away the blood. Chemstrip: wipe away blood with cotton.** *Correct procedure promotes accuracy. Water flowing with too much force can wash away color change. Warm water may affect color.*

12. **Compare strip with color chart on bottle at time appropriate for brand used. Dextrostix: read immediately. Chemstrip: read after 60 seconds.** *Gives accurate results.*

13. **If using glucose meter, insert strip into machine and read according to manufacturer's directions.** *Promotes accurate use of machine.*

14. **Apply adhesive bandage.** *Prevents infection of site.*

15. **Record results. Report readings below 45 mg/dl. Have laboratory draw blood for verification of abnormal results. Feed infant if reading below 45 mg/dl.** *More intensive treatment may be necessary for more abnormal results. Feeding infant with low glucose level provides calories needed for metabolism and prevents further decrease.*

Bilirubin

Assessment

Bilirubin levels may become elevated when there is hemolysis of erythrocytes or interference with the normal process of bilirubin conjugation. Hyperbilirubinemia results in deposits of bilirubin in the subcutaneous fat, resulting in jaundice. Assess for jaundice: Press the infant's skin over a firm surface, such as the end of the nose or the sternum. The skin blanches as the blood is pressed out of the tissues, making it easy to see the yellow color that remains. When jaundice is present in one area, determine what other areas are involved. Because the progression starts at the head and moves down the body, one can make a rough estimate of the severity of the problem.

In physiologic jaundice, the bilirubin level peaks at 6 to 7 mg/dl on the 3rd day of life and then begins to drop. Jaundice becomes visible when the bilirubin level reaches 5 to 7 mg/dl. Therefore, jaundice that appears before the 3rd day of life may indicate that the bilirubin is rising more quickly and to higher levels than normal. Alert the physician or nurse practitioner about infants who have jaundice so that they can order laboratory determinations of the bilirubin level if necessary. If serial bilirubin assays are ordered, note changes from one reading to the next and correlate them with the infant's age.

Analysis

A common collaborative problem used for hepatic dysfunction in the neonate is Potential complication: *Hyperbilirubinemia.*

Planning

Client-centered goals for hyperbilirubinemia are inappropriate because this problem requires collaboration between the nurse and the physician. Planning for the nurse includes:

- Identifying infants at increased risk for hyperbilirubinemia
- Noting the presence of jaundice early so that measures to decrease it can be implemented
- Notifying the physician about infants with jaundice and the results of ordered laboratory tests for bilirubin
- Planning appropriate intervention to minimize further hyperbilirubinemia

Interventions

During assessment and care of newborns, be aware of which infants are at increased risk for hyperbilirubinemia. Table 20–3 lists common risk factors for jaundice. By using extra vigilance in caring for infants

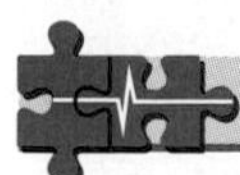

Clinical Situation

You are caring for Nancy Belinsky and her son, Andy, who have both been doing well since Andy was born early this morning. As you enter the room after lunch, Nancy says, "Andy's hands and feet are so cold! But I've heard that all babies have cold hands and feet. Are they always so shaky too?"

Q:
1. What are the nursing priorities in this situation?
2. What expanded assessments are necessary?
3. What interventions are necessary?
4. How will you respond to Nancy?

A:
1. Determine whether Andy is showing signs of hypothermia and/or hypoglycemia. Reassure and teach Nancy as assessments and interventions are completed.
2. While taking the infant's temperature, assess for skin temperature, jitteriness, and general behavior. Check the blood glucose level.
3. If temperature is low, intervene by changing wet linens, double wrapping, and applying hat. Feed Andy if the blood glucose level is low. Recheck temperature in 30 minutes. If it is still low, place Andy under a radiant warmer. Notify the physician if Andy is still having difficulty maintaining temperature. (See Nursing Care Plan 20–1 for other interventions.)
4. Praise Nancy for being so observant of her son. If Andy's temperature is normal and he is not jittery, discuss the fact that peripheral circulation is sluggish in newborns and that their hands and feet tend to be cool. If "shakiness" is the Moro reflex or normal newborn behavior, discuss the reflex and the immaturity of the central nervous system. Show Nancy how to wrap Andy so that he stays warm and the Moro reflex is not elicited. Discuss methods of temperature control, and be sure that Nancy knows how to read a thermometer. Explain all interventions.

at higher risk, nurses can detect jaundice earlier and measures can be taken to decrease it.

Make sure that infants take adequate feedings to ensure prompt passage of meconium, which has a high bilirubin content. When a newborn is feeding poorly, determine the reasons and intervene appropriately. Help mothers to wake sleepy infants to feed, spend extra time with an infant with a poor suck, or teach the mother how much is appropriate to feed the infant at each feeding. Ensuring adequate feedings can stimulate passage of stools. This decreases the chance that the enzyme β-glucuronidase will deconjugate the bilirubin and increase the work of an already overworked liver.

Table 20–3. COMMON RISK FACTORS FOR HYPERBILIRUBINEMIA

Prematurity
Cephalohematoma
Bruising
Delayed or poor intake
Cold stress
Asphyxia
Rh incompatibility
ABO incompatibility
Sepsis

Discuss jaundice with the parents. Explain the significance of the color change in the skin and why blood testing is necessary. Answer questions that they may have, especially if their infant may need phototherapy (see Nursing Care Plan 29–1, p. 851).

True breast milk jaundice does not develop until 4 to 7 days after birth, when the infant is at home. If the mother must discontinue breastfeeding for a day or two, she may become very concerned. Provide her with information about this type of jaundice, and reassure her that her milk is adequate and not harmful to the infant. Help her maintain her milk supply by using a manual or electric breast pump during the time the infant is taking formula.

Evaluation

The nurse compares data for hyperbilirubinemia by noting changes in bilirubin levels and changes in skin color as a result of collaborative interventions. The jaundice should steadily decrease in the infant.

✔ Check Your Reading

6. Why is it important for the nurse to use the correct site for heel punctures to obtain blood samples?
7. What are some of the interventions used when the infant has jaundice?

Assessment and Care of Body Systems

Neurological System

REFLEXES

Note the strength of the reflexes and whether both sides of the body respond symmetrically. A diminished overall response occurs in preterm or ill infants. Absence of reflexes may indicate a serious neurological problem. An asymmetrical response may indicate that trauma during birth has caused nerve damage or fracture of a bone. For example, trauma to the facial nerve from forceps or pressure during birth may cause drooping of the mouth. The infant may appear to have a one-sided cry and may have no rooting reflex on that side. A Moro response in which there is little movement of one arm may indicate a fractured clavicle or damage to the brachial nerve.

SENSORY ASSESSMENT

Ears. Assess the ears for placement, overall appearance, and maturity. A line drawn from the inner to the outer canthus of the eye should be even with the notch where the ear joins the head (Fig. 20–4). Examine the ears for skin tags and preauricular sinuses or dimples. If there are abnormalities of the ear, the newborn may have other anomalies, particularly of the kidneys.

Assess hearing by noting the infant's reaction to sudden loud noises, which should cause a Moro response. Also observe the neonate's response to the sound of voices. Infants prefer a high-pitched tone of voice and will respond to the sound of the mother's voice over that of another person.

Eyes. Examine the eyes for placement, abnormalities, and signs of inflammation. Edema of the eyelids or subconjunctival hemorrhages may be frightening to parents. Explain that they are temporary effects of birth. The edema will diminish in a few days, and the hemorrhages will take a week or two to resolve. Check the pupils for equality of size and reaction to light. Observe for cataracts, which appear as white areas over the lens. When a light is directed into the eyes, the normal red reflex may not be present if large cataracts are present.

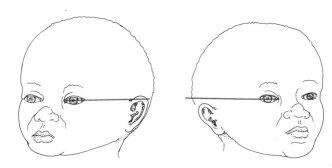

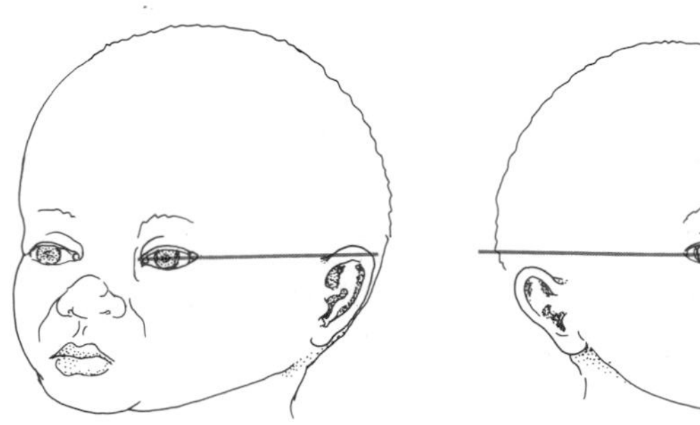

Figure 20–4

To determine whether the ears are in the correct position, an imaginary line is drawn from the inner to the outer canthus of the eye and then to the ear. The line should intersect with the notch where the ear joins the head. A low-seated (low-set) ear may indicate other abnormalities.

Note the infant's visual response to the environment. Newborns should make eye contact when held in a cradle position during a period of alertness. Bright lights cause them to blink or close their eyes. Report any infant who does not respond to visual stimuli to the physician or nurse practitioner for further investigation.

OTHER SIGNS

Assess the newborn for jitteriness or tremors. If jitteriness is present, assess the blood glucose level. If blood glucose is within normal range, consider low calcium levels or prenatal exposure to drugs.

Some infants have seizures. To differentiate jitteriness from seizures, hold the infant's extremities in a flexed position. This will cause the tremors to stop, but a seizure will continue.

Note the pitch of the cry. A shrill or high-pitched cry, a cat-like "mewing," or a hoarse cry is abnormal. They may indicate a neurological or other problem.

Determine the newborn's responses to touch and holding. Normal infants are quiet and appear content when their needs are met. Most infants "mold" their body to that of the person holding them, making them easy to hold and cuddle. The neonate who stiffens the body, seems to pull away from contact, or arches the back when picked up is showing signs of central nervous system abnormalities. Report all such abnormal signs for further neurological assessment.

Gastrointestinal System

The initial assessment of the gastrointestinal tract occurs during the first hours after birth, as the nurse visualizes the parts that can be seen and gives the infant the initial feeding. Abnormalities and normal variations in structure and function are identified.

MOUTH

Inspect the mouth visually and by palpation. Some infants are born with precocious teeth, usually incisors. If they are loose, the physician usually removes them to prevent aspiration. Note the presence of Epstein's pearls, the small, white, hard cysts on the palate that disappear without treatment.

Examine the tongue for size and movement. A large protruding tongue is present in some chromosomal disorders such as Down syndrome. Paralysis of the facial nerve causes drooping of the mouth and affects the movement of the tongue. The tongue may appear to be tongue-tied because of the short frenulum, but this is normal and has no effect on the infant's ability to feed. Clipping of the frenulum is no longer practiced because of the potential for infection.

Although candidiasis (thrush) is not apparent in the mouth immediately after birth, it may appear a day or two later. The lesions resemble milk curds on the tongue and cheeks, but they bleed if attempts are made to wipe them away. Newborns may become infected with *Candida albicans* during passage through the birth canal if the mother has a candidal vaginal infection. The infant is treated with nystatin suspension.

A cleft lip or palate results if the lip or palate fails to close during fetal life. Cleft palate may involve the hard and/or soft palate and may appear alone or with a cleft lip. Observe the palate when the infant cries. Insert a gloved finger into the mouth and palpate both the hard and the soft palate. A very small cleft of the soft palate might be missed if only a visual examination is done (see Chapter 29, p. 867, for a discussion of cleft lip and palate).

SUCK

The normal full-term infant should have a strong suck reflex, which is elicited when the lips or palate are stimulated. It is weaker in the neonate who is preterm or ill or who has just been fed. The newborn's cheeks have well-developed muscles and sucking pads that enhance the ability to suck. These fatty sucking pads last until late in infancy, when sucking is no longer essential. There may be blisters on the newborn's hands or arms because of strong sucking before birth.

ABDOMEN

The abdomen should be rounded and protrude slightly but should not be distended. A distended abdomen with stretched, shiny skin may indicate obstruction. Loops of bowel should not be visible through the abdominal wall. Bowel loops may indicate that air and/or meconium is not passing through the intestines normally.

A sunken or scaphoid appearance of the abdomen occurs in diaphragmatic hernia, in which the intestines are located in the chest cavity instead of the abdomen. This interferes with development of the lungs, resulting in respiratory difficulty at birth. Listen over the abdomen for bowel sounds, which usually appear within the first hour after birth. Bowel sounds heard in the chest may indicate diaphragmatic hernia.

An umbilical hernia occurs when the intestinal muscles fail to close around the umbilicus, allowing the intestines to protrude into the weaker area. It is more common in African-American infants. By the time the infant is walking well, the muscles are usually strong enough that the hernia is no longer present. Some umbilical hernias necessitate surgical repair.

Palpating the abdomen is easiest when the infant is relaxed and quiet. The abdomen should feel soft because the muscles are not yet well developed. Masses may indicate enlargement of tumors of the kidneys. Although palpation of the liver and kidneys may not be part of the usual nursing assessment of the abdomen, be aware that the newborn's liver could be enlarged. The liver is normally felt no more than 1 to 3 cm below the right costal margin. If it seems large, report it to the physician or nurse practitioner.

INITIAL FEEDING

The initial feeding is an opportunity to further assess the newborn. As the mother continues feedings, note how well she increases in ability and confidence. Continue teaching as appropriate (see Chapter 21).

Position. Hold the infant so that the head is elevated. If feeding a newborn under a radiant warmer, place one hand under the head and raise the infant to a semi-Fowler's position. This helps prevent aspiration and allows assessment of the infant's feeding behavior.

Observations. Observe carefully during the feeding to assess the infant's ability to suck, swallow, and breathe in a coordinated manner. Although the fetus sucks and swallows in utero, these acts may not have been performed together. The addition of breathing to sucking and swallowing is a new experience.

Some newborns choke or gag during the first feeding. Others may become dusky or cyanotic because they "forget" to breathe while they are feeding. In either case, stop the feeding immediately and stimulate the infant to cry. Allow a moment of rest before resuming the feeding.

Most infants learn to coordinate sucking, swallowing, and breathing by the time the first feeding is finished. Neonates who continue to have difficulty may have a cardiac anomaly or a connection between the esophagus and the trachea, such as tracheoesophageal fistula (see Chapter 29, p. 867). Infants with tracheoesophageal fistulas may also drool excessively. Further assessment and referral are necessary.

Breastfeeding. Assist the mother who wishes to breastfeed immediately after birth. Many newborns are able to breastfeed well at this time. Others may simply nuzzle or "mouth" the breast. Reassure the mother that this is normal and that the infant will suck better later. Watch unobtrusively as the infant nurses to see how the feeding is tolerated.

Formula Feeding. If the initial feeding is by bottle, the newborn is usually given plain water first. Plain water is less irritating to the lungs than dextrose water or formula, should aspiration occur. If the infant tolerates a few sips of plain water without difficulty, switch to 5 per cent dextrose water or formula for more nourishment.

Regurgitation. Infants who regurgitate have an increased risk of aspirating the fluid. Therefore, keep a bulb syringe nearby in case the neonate needs suctioning. Take measures that help prevent regurgitation during and after the feeding. Limit the initial feeding to no more than 1 ounce. Burp the infant midway in the feeding and again when the feeding is finished. This decreases the risk of regurgitation by avoiding overdistention of the stomach.

After the feeding, position newborns to promote emptying of the stomach. That is, place them on their side and prop them with a rolled blanket. This allows regurgitated fluid to run out of the mouth and decreases chances of aspiration. Because the lower end of the stomach is on the right side, turning the infant to the right allows gravity to help empty the stomach more quickly. The head of the bed may be elevated for a short time after the feeding. This helps keep stomach contents from flowing into the esophagus through the relaxed cardiac sphincter.

Excess Fluids in Stomach. Some newborns swallow mucus, blood, and amniotic fluid during the birth process. This is especially true after cesarean birth. It may cause abdominal distention and regurgitation. If the infant swallows meconium with the amniotic fluid, it may be regurgitated and cause lung inflammation if aspirated. In some agencies, it is routine to empty the stomach soon after birth by feeding tube to prevent aspiration (Behrman, 1992).

STOOLS

Observe the stools for normal color and consistency. Meconium stools are dark greenish–black. They are soft but thick and tend to adhere to the skin. The infant may pass meconium at delivery, when a rectal temperature is taken, or after the initial feeding. Meconium stools are followed by transitional loose greenish-brown stools.

Breastfed infants pass very soft, mustard-yellow stools after transitional stools. Formula-fed infants excrete stools that are more solid and light yellow. There should never be a "water ring" around the solid part of any stool. This indicates passage of a diarrhea stool, the watery part of which has absorbed into the diaper.

It is important to be aware of when the infant's last stool occurred and whether or not there have been any stools since birth. Most newborns pass the first meconium stool within 24 hours of birth. If there is a question about whether the infant has excreted a stool, investigate further. Read through the chart to be sure that there is no stool recorded. Because the infant may have passed meconium at delivery, check the charting done at that time as well. Ask the mother if she has changed a diaper with stool in it and ask her to notify a nurse if she does.

If the agency routine is to take one rectal temperature on all newborns after birth, check the chart to see if this was recorded as rectal. This ensures that the anus is patent, although there may be an obstruction of the intestine above the anus. Taking a rectal temperature may stimulate peristalsis and passage of meconium.

When assessment shows that there has not been a stool and that all other areas of assessment are normal, consider the infant's intake. If the infant has been sleepy and has fed poorly, increase the feedings. Offering the neonate extra fluid or asking a nursing mother to feed more often may make the difference. Although some infants do not pass a stool for as long as 48 hours, notify the physician or nurse practitioner when 24 hours have elapsed. If there has been no stool within 48 hours, there is probably an obstruction in the gastrointestinal tract.

✔ Check Your Reading

8. Why is it important for the nurse to observe the first feeding carefully?
9. When will newborns pass the first stool? What can be done to stimulate stool passage?

Genitourinary System

Assess the genitourinary system for kidney function and anomalies of the genitalia.

KIDNEY PALPATION

Palpation of the kidneys is not usually part of the routine nursing assessment of the newborn. However, the kidneys may be felt in the newborn during the first hours after birth just above the level of the umbilicus on each side of the abdomen. Suspect enlargement or tumors of the kidneys if masses are palpated in the abdomen during the initial assessment. Anomalies of the kidney may accompany other defects because an insult early in fetal development often affects all organs being formed at that time. For example, an infant with only one umbilical artery or defects involving the ears may have renal anomalies. Observe carefully for urinary output in these infants to determine if the kidneys are functioning.

URINE

Most newborns void within 24 hours of birth, with a few voiding within 48 hours. Because absence of urine output during this time may indicate anomalies, note the time of the first void on the chart. The newborn's bladder empties as little as two to six times during the first 2 days, and the first void may be missed. Sometimes it occurs in the delivery room but goes unnoticed because attention is focused on the infant's overall condition.

If there is concern over whether the newborn has urinated, read the chart carefully to see if a void was noted in delivery room notes or elsewhere. Ask the mother if she has changed a wet diaper. Increasing the infant's fluid intake can often initiate urination. If there is no void in the expected time, alert the physician or nurse practitioner.

After the first 2 days of life, the newborn's bladder empties 5 to 25 times each day. This is usually recorded by a check mark on the chart each time a wet diaper is changed. Ask the mother the number of wet diapers she has changed, and correlate the total number with what is appropriate for the age of the infant. Teach mothers that approximately six to ten wet diapers, after the first 2 days, indicate that the infant is taking adequate fluid.

If an infant is having feeding difficulties, it is especially important to note the number of wet diapers. Disposable diapers may be very absorbent, and it is sometimes difficult to tell whether the diaper is wet. The pale color of the newborn's urine may cause very little color change on the diaper. Wet diapers generally feel heavier than dry ones. If necessary, put on gloves and take the diaper apart to examine it. The absorbent inner lining will be damp if urine is present.

The newborn's urine may contain urate crystals that cause a reddish or pink stain on the diaper. This is known as "brick dust staining" and may be frightening to parents, who may think the infant is bleeding. Explain that this will not continue beyond the first few days as the kidneys mature.

GENITALIA

Examine the newborn's genitalia for size, maturation, and presence of any abnormalities.

Female. In the full-term female infant, the labia majora should be large and completely cover the clitoris and labia minora. The labia may be darker than the surrounding skin, especially in infants with dark skin tones. This is a normal response to exposure to the mother's hormones before birth. A white mucous vaginal discharge is normal in the newborn girl. A small amount of vaginal bleeding, known as pseudomenstruation, may be noted. It is due to the sudden withdrawal of the mother's hormones at birth. Hymenal tags are small pieces of tissue at the vaginal orifice. These are normal and disappear in a few weeks.

Male. Examine the scrotum and penis for maturity and abnormalities. Check the scrotum for rugae (creases in the scrotum) and presence of the testes. The rugae should be deep and cover the entire scrotum in the full-term infant. The scrotum may be dark brown from maternal hormones. Pressure during a breech delivery may cause it to be edematous.

Palpate the scrotal sac on each side to determine if the testes have descended. The testes feel like small, round, movable objects that "slip" between the fingers (Fig. 20–5). If the testes are not present in the scrotal sac, palpate the inguinal canal to see whether they can be located. Undescended testes may occur on one or both sides. An empty scrotal sac will appear smaller than one in which the testes are present.

Enlargement of one or both sides of the scrotum may be due to a hydrocele. This collection of fluid around the testes may make palpating the testes difficult. Placing a flashlight against the sac may allow one to see the outline of the testes. Explain to parents that hydroceles are not painful and often reabsorb within a year. Some necessitate later surgery.

Examine the penis to determine the location of the urinary meatus. The meatus may appear on the upper part of the penile shaft in an epispadias or,

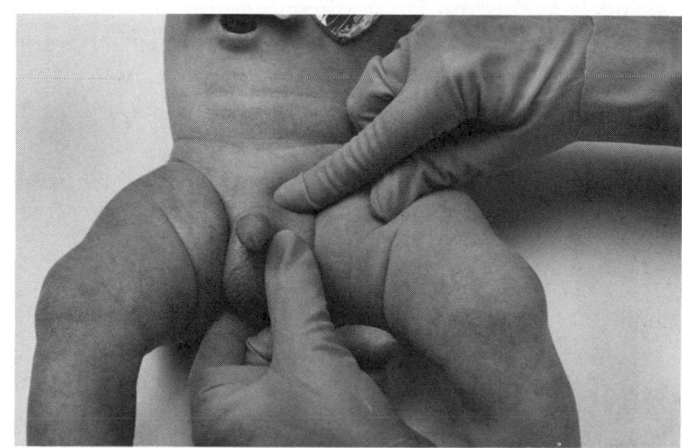

Figure 20–5

The testes are most easily located by palpating from front to back with the thumb and forefinger. If necessary, placing another finger over the inguinal canal during palpation holds the testes in place for palpation.

more often, on the lower part of the shaft in a hypospadias. An abnormal opening may not be visible because it is covered by the prepuce or foreskin, but more often the foreskin is not completely formed. If the penis is bent downward, a chordee is present.

Support the parents, who will be very concerned if there are abnormalities of the genitalia. Explain to them why the infant may not be circumcised if an abnormally positioned meatus is identified. The foreskin may be needed for later plastic surgery to repair the defect.

CIRCUMCISION

Nursing Considerations

Circumcision is a somewhat controversial procedure with which the nurse must be familiar. Parents may ask for information when they are deciding whether or not to have their son circumcised. They will need information about caring for the infant after the procedure if they decide to have it done.

Assisting in Decision Making

Ideally, parents make the decision about circumcision early in pregnancy on the basis of careful consideration of the risks and benefits. However, this is not always the case. Some parents are not well informed about circumcision. The physician is responsible for explaining the risks and benefits to the parents, but the nurse may be called on to answer questions or clarify misconceptions that the parents may have.

Nurses must be certain that their own biases about circumcision do not interfere with their ability to give objective information to parents. Once the parents have come to a decision, the nurse should support it. Although nurses generally teach parents of circumcised infants how to care for the penis, they may not think about providing teaching for parents who decide against circumcision. Include care of the intact penis in the teaching plan for these parents. (see Parents Want to Know: How to Care for the Uncircumcised Penis).

Preparation and Care

As with any surgical procedure, obtain a signed consent from the parents before the circumcision is performed. The nurse sees that the consent has been signed and should be aware of any problems that might impair the infant's ability to withstand circumcision. The infant should be at least 12 hours old so that he has recovered from the stress of birth.

Parents Want To Know

Caring for the Uncircumcised Penis

Wash your son's penis daily and when soiled diapers are changed. There is no need to retract the foreskin because it is still attached to the glans, or end of the penis. It will gradually separate from the glans over a period of time. It may take 3 years or even longer for complete separation to occur.

You can occasionally gently pull back on the foreskin to see how much separation has occurred during this time. However, *never* force the foreskin to retract. This will be painful and may cause bleeding, infections, and adhesions.

As your son gets older and takes over his own care, teach him to wash the area during his daily bath or shower. He should do this by gently pulling the foreskin back only as far as it retracts easily. This should become a daily routine, much like washing his face or hands.

Prepare the infant for the procedure. To prevent regurgitation, do not feed the infant for 2 to 4 hours before the circumcision. Because he is restrained in a supine position, regurgitation may cause aspiration. Keep a bulb syringe nearby in case suction is necessary. Gather the equipment and supplies prior to the procedure.

When the physician and equipment are ready, place the infant on a circumcision board. This is a plastic holder that is molded to fit the infant's body and has restraints for his arms and legs (Fig. 20–6). Place a blanket under the infant, and remove only the diaper. A drape is used to provide warmth and maintain sterility. Position a heat lamp over the infant to prevent cold stress.

Comfort the infant during the procedure, especially if no anesthesia is used. Talk to the infant and provide a pacifier. Soft music or tapes of intrauterine sounds may also be effective in distracting the infant from pain.

Post-procedure Care

Remove the infant from the restraints immediately after the circumcision is completed. If the Gomco clamp was used, squeeze petroleum jelly over the circumcision site to prevent the diaper from sticking to it. A 2 × 2 piece of gauze may be placed over the area. In some institutions, an antibiotic ointment is used instead of petroleum jelly. Petroleum jelly is not necessary when a Plastibell is used. Comfort the infant and return him to his mother, who may be anxious about her son.

Monitor for signs of complications following the circumcision. Check the wound for bleeding every 15 minutes for the first hour, and every half hour for the next hour. If the infant is to be discharged after the circumcision, observe him for at least an hour before

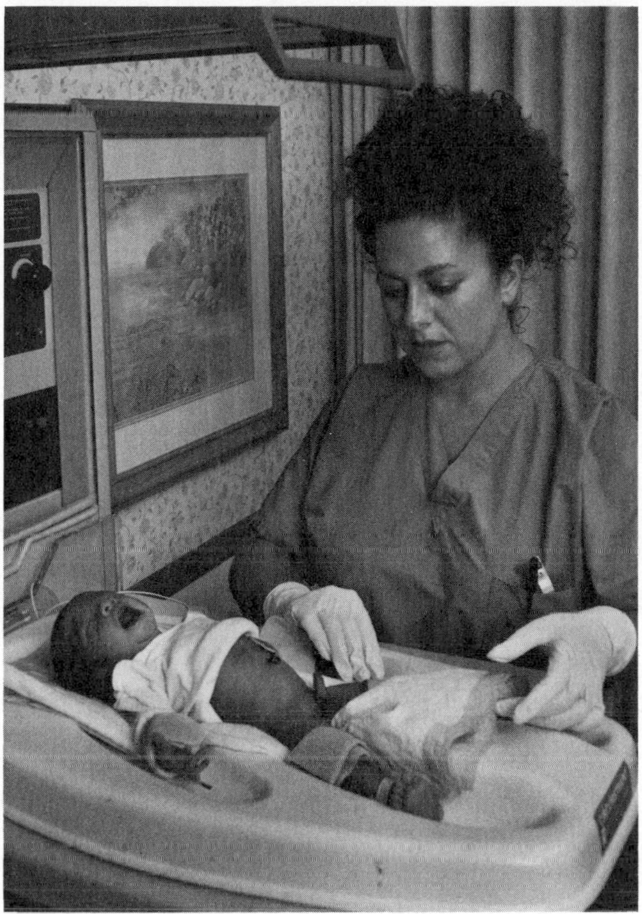

Figure 20–6

The infant is placed on the circumcision board just before the procedure is begun. The nurse stands nearby because the siderails are down. The radiant warmer provides heat.

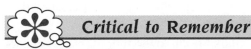

releasing him (see Critical to Remember: Signs of Complications After Circumcision).

If excessive bleeding occurs, apply steady pressure to the penis with a sterile piece of gauze. Notify the physician if bleeding continues. A small amount of blood loss may be significant in an infant, who has a small total blood volume. The physician may apply Gelfoam sponge or suture the small blood vessels.

Critical to Remember

Signs of Complications After Circumcision

- Bleeding more than a few drops with first diaper changes
- Failure to urinate
- Signs of infection: fever or low temperature, purulent or foul-smelling drainage
- Displacement of the Plastibell
- Scarring (after healing)

Parents Want To Know

How to Care for the Circumcision Site

Observe the circumcision site at each diaper change. Note the amount of bleeding. Call the physician if there is more than a few drops of bleeding with diaper changes during the first day or any bleeding thereafter.

Continue to apply petroleum jelly to the penis with each diaper change for the first 24 to 48 hours. If a Plastibell was used, petroleum jelly is not necessary.

Keeping the circumcision site clean is important for healing. Squeeze warm water from a clean washcloth over the penis to wash it. Fasten the diaper loosely to prevent excessive rubbing or pressure on the incision site.

Expect a yellow crust to form over the circumcision site. This is a normal part of healing and should not be removed. Watch for signs of infection such as fever or drainage that smells bad or has pus in it. *Call your physician if you suspect any abnormalities.* The circumcision site should be fully healed in approximately 10 days.

Note the first urination after circumcision because edema could cause an obstruction. If the infant goes home before voiding, instruct the mother to call the physician if there is no urinary output within 6 to 8 hours.

Parent Teaching

Because circumcision is often performed on the day of discharge, the parents will have to take over care of the site. Provide teaching during the time the circumcision site is being observed before discharge. Each time the site is checked for bleeding, show the parents the amount of blood on the diaper to help them understand how much to expect. Describe the yellowish exudate that will form over the site and differentiate it from purulent drainage (see Parents Want to Know: How to Care for the Circumcision Site).

✔ Check Your Reading

10. When should the first void occur? How often do infants void?
11. What information do parents need about care of the intact and circumcised penis?

Integumentary System

SKIN

The skin of the newborn is fragile and easily shows marks, especially in infants with fair coloring. Because the skin is so sensitive, reddened areas or rashes may develop during the early days of life.

These can be alarming to parents, who may have many concerns about any apparent abnormalities. Examine every inch of skin surface carefully during the initial assessment at birth and at the beginning of each shift.

Color. Observe the color of the newborn's skin, which should be pink or tan. Acrocyanosis is common during the first day or two as a result of poor peripheral circulation. The infant's mouth and central body areas should not be cyanotic at any time. Blanch the skin over the nose or chest to check for jaundice. Jaundice is abnormal during the first day of life but not uncommon during the first week.

A greenish-brown discoloration of the skin, nails, and cord results if meconium was passed before birth. This indicates that the infant was stressed at some time before birth, and it is more common in the postterm infant. Observe these infants for other complications, such as respiratory difficulty.

Vernix Caseosa. Note the amount of vernix on the skin. This thick white substance resembles cream cheese and provides a protective covering for the fetal skin in utero. The full-term infant has very little vernix left on the body but has small amounts in the creases. A thick covering of vernix may indicate a preterm infant, whereas a postterm infant may have none at all. Most of the vernix is removed when the infant is dried at birth or during the first bath. The rest is absorbed by the skin.

Lanugo. Lanugo is fine hair that covers the fetus during intrauterine life. As the fetus nears term, the lanugo becomes thinner. Observe the amount of lanugo on the newborn's body. The infant may have a small amount of lanugo on the shoulders, forehead and sides of the face, and upper back. Dark-skinned infants have more lanugo than infants with lighter coloring, and their darker hair is more visible.

Milia. Milia are distended sebaceous glands (oil glands) that are not yet functioning properly. Milia occur on the face over the forehead, nose, and chin and disappear without treatment (see Color Plate XV). Because milia resemble whiteheads, some parents try to squeeze them. Caution them that this is unnecessary and can cause an infection.

Erythema Toxicum. Note the presence of erythema toxicum, a maculopapular rash with a red base and a small white papule in the center. It is commonly called "flea bite" rash and resembles small bites or acne. It appears during the early days after birth (see Color Plate XIII). The rash is most common over the back, shoulders, and chest. It is not due to infection and is not harmful but should be differentiated from a pustular rash caused by infection with staphylococcus. The cause of erythema toxicum is unknown, and it disappears within a few days.

Birthmarks. Note the size and location of any birthmarks. Some of the more common birthmarks are listed here.

- Mongolian spots are bluish-black marks that resemble bruises (see Color Plate XIV). They are located on the sacral area most frequently but can be found on the buttocks, arms, shoulders, or other areas. Mongolian spots occur most often in newborns with dark skin and disappear after the first few years of life.
- Telangiectatic nevi are sometimes called "stork bites" or "angel kisses" (see Color Plate XII). They are flat pink or red discolorations from dilated capillaries that occur over the eyelids, above the bridge of the nose, or at the nape of the neck. Press the area with a finger and the color blanches. Stork bites disappear by age 2 years.
- Nevus flammeus (port-wine stain) is a permanent, flat, dark reddish–purple mark. It varies in size and location and does not blanch with pressure. If it is large and in a visible area, it can be removed by lasar surgery.
- Nevus vasculosus (strawberry hemangioma) consists of enlarged capillaries in the outer layers of skin. It is dark red and raised with a rough surface, giving it a strawberry-like appearance. The hemangioma is usually located on the head and may grow larger for a time. Inform parents that it eventually shrinks and usually disappears by the early school years. Although parents may wonder about plastic surgery for this birthmark because it is so visible, reassure them that it will resolve by itself.
- Café au lait spots are light brown areas that may occur anywhere on the body. Although they are harmless, carefully note the number and size. More than six spots or spots larger than 1.5 cm are associated with neurofibromatosis, a genetic condition of neural tissue.

Marks from Delivery. Inspect the infant for marks that may have occurred from injury or pressure during labor or delivery.

- Forceps marks occur over the cheeks and ears where the instruments were applied. They should be carefully documented as to size, color, and location. Observe for facial symmetry and movement when forceps have been used.
- Bruises may occur on any part of the body where there was pressure during delivery. This is especially true when there was a difficult second-stage labor. Bruising of the face may be present if the cord was wrapped around the neck during birth.
- Petechiae, pinpoint bruises that resemble a

rash, may appear over areas such as the back or face. They are due to increased intravascular pressure during the birth process, such as occurs when there is a nuchal cord during delivery. Widespread petechiae or continued formation of petechiae may indicate infection or a low platelet count.

- A small puncture mark will be present on the newborn's head if a fetal monitor scalp electrode was attached. A scab will form. This area should heal normally but may become infected.

Other Aspects. Note other aspects of the skin that may indicate abnormalities. Localized edema may be due to trauma of delivery. Generalized edema indicates more serious conditions, such as heart failure. The cause should always be explored. Peeling of the skin is normal in full-term newborns. Excessive amounts of peeling may indicate a postterm infant.

BREASTS

Note the placement of the nipples, and look for extra (or supernumerary) nipples, which may appear on the chest or in the axilla. Occasionally, the breasts become engorged 2 or 3 days after birth and secrete a small amount of white fluid (sometimes called "witch's milk") a few days later. This is due to the hormones that passed from the mother to the infant during the pregnancy. Reassure the parents that the condition will resolve by itself within a few weeks and that no treatment is necessary. Advise against manipulation of the breasts, as it could result in mastitis.

HAIR AND NAILS

The hair on the full-term infant should be silky and soft, whereas that on the preterm infant is woolly or fuzzy. The nails come to the end of the fingers or beyond. Very long nails may indicate a postterm infant. Cover the infant's hands with his or her shirt to prevent scratches.

DOCUMENTATION

Document any marks, bruises, rashes, or other abnormalities of the skin in the nurses' notes. Describe the location, size, color, elevation, and texture of each mark. Describe changes in their appearance from previous descriptions noted on the chart.

One may not always know the proper name for each of the different types of marks. Most agencies have books with pictures of the common skin variations.

When in doubt about the name of a mark, a description will be sufficient. For example, a stork bite (telangiectatic nevus) might be described as a "flat, reddened area 1 × 2 cm in size over right eyelid that blanches with pressure."

Assessment of Gestational Age

The gestational age assessment is an examination of the newborn to determine the amount of time spent in the uterus (number of weeks from conception to birth). The determination is based on physical and neurological characteristics. It is an important determination because neonates born before or after term are at increased risk for complications. Both medical and nursing care are determined by the gestational age of the infant. The gestational age may be calculated from the mother's last menstrual period. However, this is not always accurate and does not provide information about how well the infant has grown during intrauterine life.

Because it is known when various characteristics develop in the fetus, their presence or absence can be used to estimate gestational age. The estimated age can then be compared with the newborn's weight, length, and head circumference to decide whether the neonate is large, appropriate (or average), or small in size for gestational age.

The nurse performs the gestational age assessment in the early hours after the infant's birth. The actual timing varies in different birth facilities. In some, it is part of the initial assessment of the infant; in others, it may be delayed for a short time. The physical characteristics are often examined within the first hours after birth, but the neurological examination may be delayed until after the first 24 hours. This allows the infant to recover from the stress of birth.

Assessment Tools

Several different tools are used to assess gestational age. The Dubowitz scoring system is an in-depth, detailed assessment tool that includes examination of physical, neurological, and behavioral characteristics. The Ballard scoring system (Fig. 20–7) is a condensed and simplified adaptation of the Dubowitz tool that is often used because it can be performed quickly, yet provides an accurate estimate of the gestational age. The Ballard tool focuses on physical and neuromuscular aspects, eliminating the behavioral characteristics. With each tool, a score is given to each assessment and the total score is used to determine the gestational age of the infant. The Ballard scoring system is described as an example.

Neuromuscular Characteristics

Refer to the diagrams in Figure 20–7, Ballard Estimation of Gestational Age by Maturity Rating, and

NEWBORN MATURITY RATING and CLASSIFICATION

ESTIMATION OF GESTATIONAL AGE BY MATURITY RATING

Side 1

Symbols: X - 1st Exam O - 2nd Exam

NEUROMUSCULAR MATURITY

	0	1	2	3	4	5
Posture						
Square Window (Wrist)	90°	60°	45°	30°	0°	
Arm Recoil	180°		100°-180°	90°-100°	< 90°	
Popliteal Angle	180°	160°	130°	110°	90°	< 90°
Scarf Sign						
Heel to Ear						

PHYSICAL MATURITY

	0	1	2	3	4	5
SKIN	gelatinous red, transparent	smooth pink, visible veins	superficial peeling &/or rash, few veins	cracking pale area, rare veins	parchment, deep cracking, no vessels	leathery, cracked, wrinkled
LANUGO	none	abundant	thinning	bald areas	mostly bald	
PLANTAR CREASES	no crease	faint red marks	anterior transverse crease only	creases ant. 2/3	creases cover entire sole	
BREAST	barely percept.	flat areola, no bud	stippled areola, 1–2 mm bud	raised areola, 3–4 mm bud	full areola, 5–10 mm bud	
EAR	pinna flat, stays folded	sl. curved pinna, soft with slow recoil	well-curv. pinna, soft but ready recoil	formed & firm with instant recoil	thick cartilage, ear stiff	
GENITALS Male	scrotum empty, no rugae		testes descending, few rugae	testes down, good rugae	testes pendulous, deep rugae	
GENITALS Female	prominent clitoris & labia minora		majora & minora equally prominent	majora large, minora small	clitoris & minora completely covered	

Gestation by Dates ______________ wks

Birth Date __________ Hour __________ am pm

APGAR __________ 1 min __________ 5 min

MATURITY RATING

Score	Wks
5	26
10	28
15	30
20	32
25	34
30	36
35	38
40	40
45	42
50	44

SCORING SECTION

	1st Exam=X	2nd Exam=O
Estimating Gest Age by Maturity Rating	______ Weeks	______ Weeks
Time of Exam	Date ______ Hour ______ am pm	Date ______ Hour ______ am pm
Age at Exam	______ Hours	______ Hours
Signature of Examiner	______ M.D.	______ M.D.

Figure 20–7

Ballard assessment tool. (Courtesy of Bristol-Myers Company, Evansville, Ind.) (From Ballard J.L., et al (1977). A simplified assessment of gestational age. *Pediatric Research*, 11, 374. Adapted from Sweet, A.Y. (1977). Classification of the low-birth-weight infant. In Klaus, M.H., Fanaroff, A.A. [Eds.] *Care of the high-risk infant* [p. 47]. Philadelphia: W.B. Saunders.)

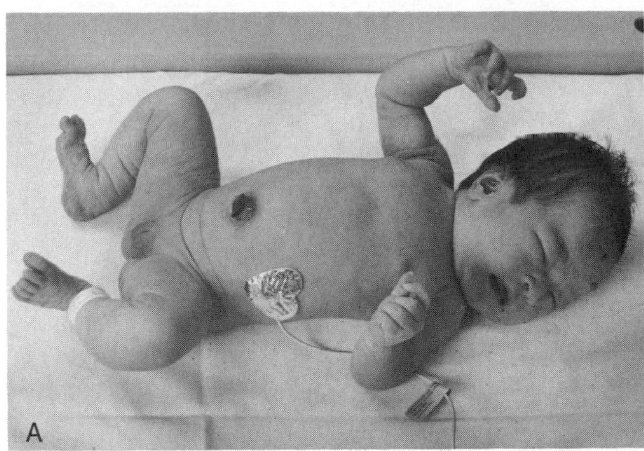

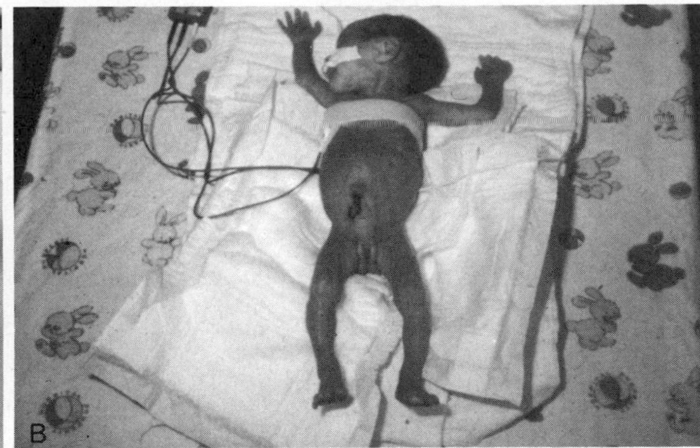

Figure 20–8

Posture in newborns. **A**, The healthy full-term infant remains in a strongly flexed position. **B**, The preterm infant's extremities are extended.

Figures 20–8 to 20–20, which correlate with each part of the assessment.

POSTURE

Note the posture and degree of flexion of the extremities before disturbing the quiet infant to perform the remainder of the examination (Fig. 20–8). The preterm neonate will not have the energy or muscle tone to keep the extremities fully flexed but will have partially extended, limp arms and legs that offer little resistance to movement by the examiner. The full-term infant holds the arms close to the body with the elbows sharply flexed. The legs should be flexed at the hips, knees, and ankles. Posture is scored from zero (0) for a limp, flaccid posture to 4 if the newborn demonstrates good flexion of all extremities.

SQUARE WINDOW

Elicit the square window sign by bending the hand at the wrist until the palm is as flat against the forearm as possible with gentle pressure (Fig. 20–9). Measure the angle between the palm and the forearm. If the palm bends only to 90 degrees (which is the extent of flexion of the adult wrist and looks like a square window), the score is zero. The gestational age of the infant is probably 32 weeks or less. The more mature the neonate, the smaller the angle, until the palm folds flat against the forearm at term.

ARM RECOIL

In testing for arm recoil, hold the neonate's arms fully flexed at the elbows for 5 seconds, then pull the hands straight down to the sides (Fig. 20–10). Quickly release the hands and measure the degree of flexion as the arms return to their normally flexed position. The preterm infant may not move the arms at all and receives a score of zero. A somewhat older infant may have a sluggish recoil with only partial return to flexion. If the arms move quickly to an angle of less than 90 degrees at the elbows, a score of 4 is given.

POPLITEAL ANGLE

In measuring the popliteal angle, fold the newborn's lower leg against the thigh, with the thigh on the abdomen (Fig. 20–11). Keep the infant's hips flat on the bed. With the thigh still flexed on the abdomen, straighten the lower leg until resistance is met. The angle at the popliteal space is scored, with a range of no (zero) points when the leg can be fully extended, to a score of 5 if the angle at the popliteal space is less than 90 degrees. Score the angle when resistance is first felt. Continued pressure will cause the infant to further extend the leg and will result in an inaccurate score.

SCARF SIGN

In eliciting the scarf sign, grasp the infant's hand and bring the arm across the body to the opposite side (Fig. 20–12). Take care not to lift the shoulder from the surface upon which the infant is lying. Note the position of the elbow in comparison to the midline of the infant's body. Give a score of zero to the infant who has such poor muscle tone that the arm wraps across the body much like a scarf. Give a full score (4) when the elbow fails to reach midline.

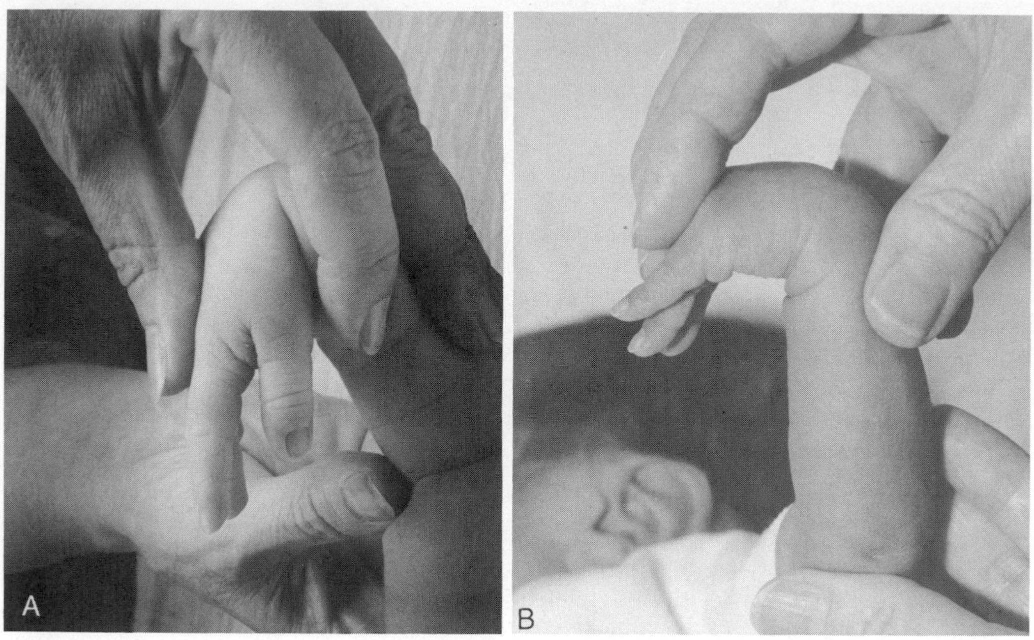

Figure 20–9

The square window sign is performed on the arm without the identification bracelet. The nurse bends the wrist and measures the angle. **A**, Infant near full term. **B**, Preterm infant.

Figure 20–10

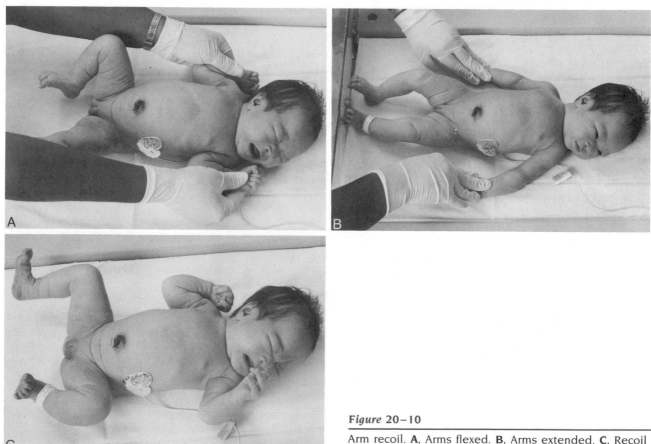

Arm recoil. **A**, Arms flexed. **B**, Arms extended. **C**, Recoil for the full-term infant.

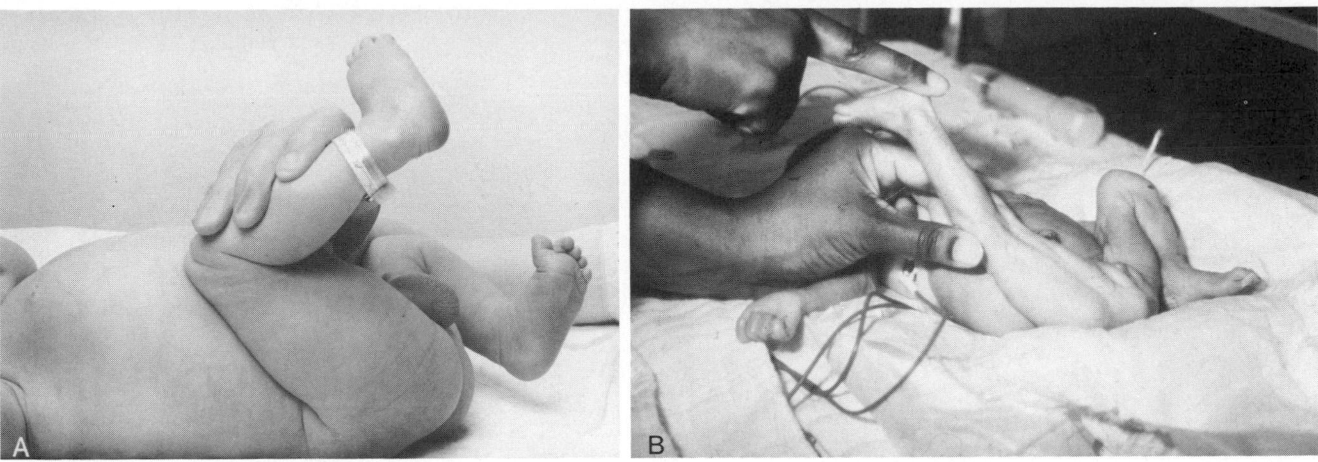

***Figure* 20–11**

The popliteal angle is measured by flexing the thigh against the abdomen and extending the lower leg to the point of resistance. **A**, Full-term infant. **B**, Preterm infant

HEEL TO EAR

The heel-to-ear assessment is similar to the measurement of the popliteal angle. However, in this case, the nurse grasps the infant's foot and pulls it straight up toward the ears while the hips remain flat on the surface of the bed (Fig. 20–13). When resistance is felt, the position of the foot in relation to the head and the amount of flexion of the leg are compared to the diagrams. The more resistance and flexion, the more mature the infant.

Record the position when resistance is first felt, as the neonate may relax the leg if pressure continues. This assessment may be inaccurate in infants who were in a breech position at delivery because they may lie with the legs extended toward the head. It may be necessary to omit this part of the examination until later or to estimate the score temporarily.

Physical Characteristics

SKIN

Examine the neonate's skin for color, visibility of veins, and peeling and cracking. The preterm infant's skin appears almost transparent because of its thinness and the small amount of subcutaneous fat beneath the surface. The skin is red, and veins are easily visible; the skin seems very fragile. In the

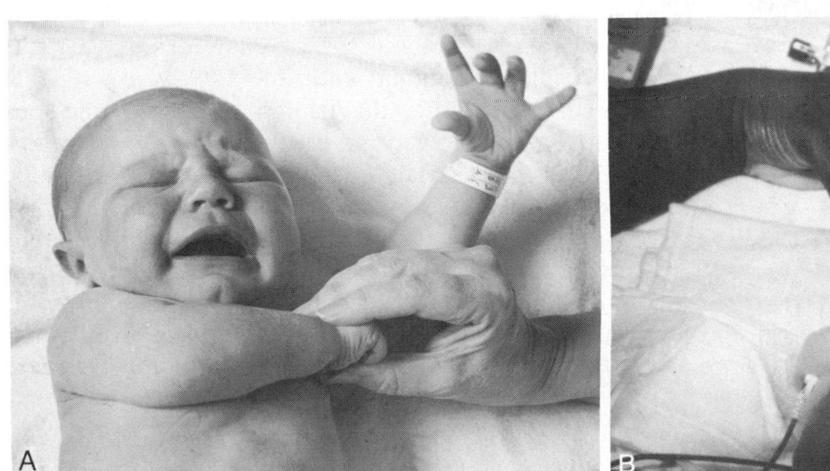

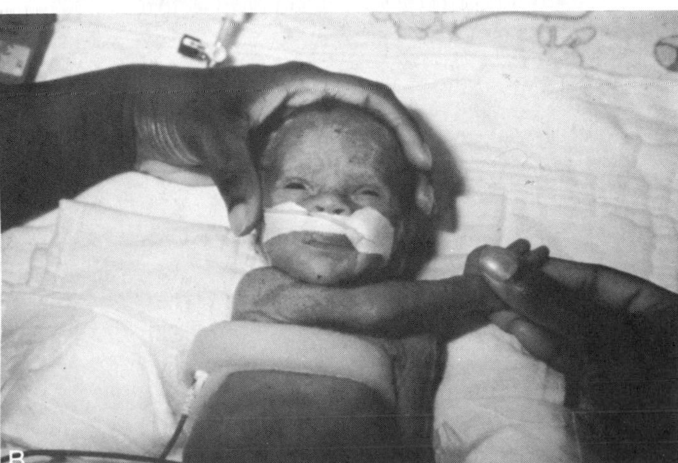

***Figure* 20–12**

Scarf sign. The nurse determines how far the arm will move across the chest and observes the position of the elbow when resistance is felt. **A**, Full-term infant. **B**, Preterm infant.

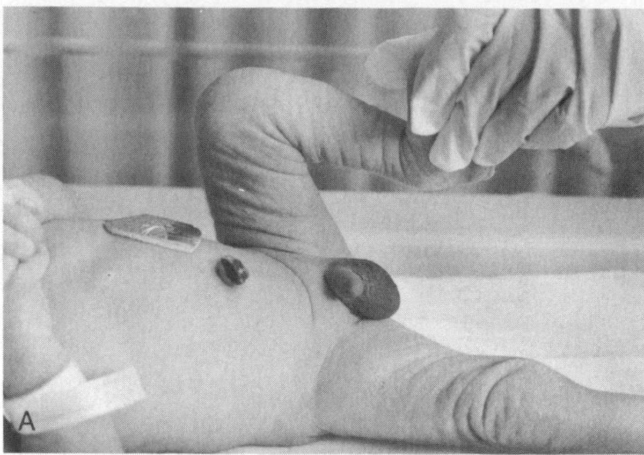

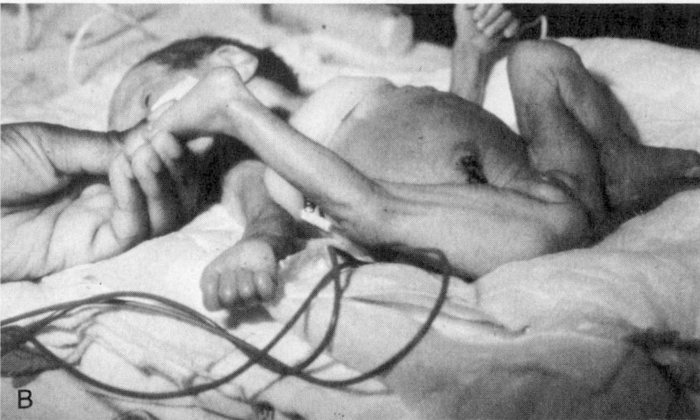

***Figure* 20–13**

Heel to ear. The nurse grasps the foot and brings it up toward the ear, keeping the hips flat. The score is recorded when resistance is felt. **A**, Full-term infant. **B**, Preterm infant.

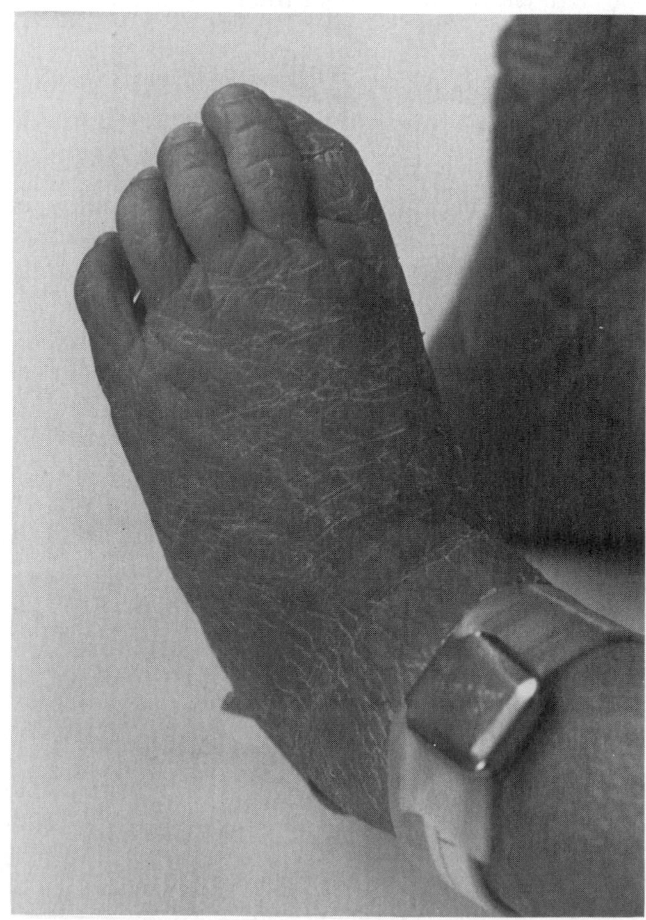

***Figure* 20–14**

The postterm infant has dry, leathery, peeling skin.

mature newborn, the skin color is paler and there are only a few veins visible, usually over the chest and abdomen. As the fetus matures, the skin gradually loses vernix; at term, vernix is present only in the creases.

The full-term infant will exhibit some peeling and cracking of the skin, especially around areas where there are creases, such as the ankles and feet. The postmature infant will have deeply cracked skin that appears as dry and thick as leather (Fig. 20–14). Peeling becomes even more apparent during the hours after birth as the skin loses moisture.

LANUGO

Lanugo covers the fetus at 20 weeks of gestation, increasing in amount until 28 to 30 weeks (Fig. 20–15). At that time, the lanugo begins to disappear, until it is almost completely gone at term. A small amount may remain over the upper back and shoulders, over the ears, or at the sides of the forehead. Newborns with dark coloring may have more lanugo (which is dark and more easily noticed) than infants with fair skin and very light hair even though they are the same gestational age. Assign a score to the newborn according to the amount of lanugo present.

PLANTAR CREASES

Plantar creases begin to appear at 32 weeks of gestation (Fig. 20–16). Although they are only red lines near the toes at first, they gradually become deeper

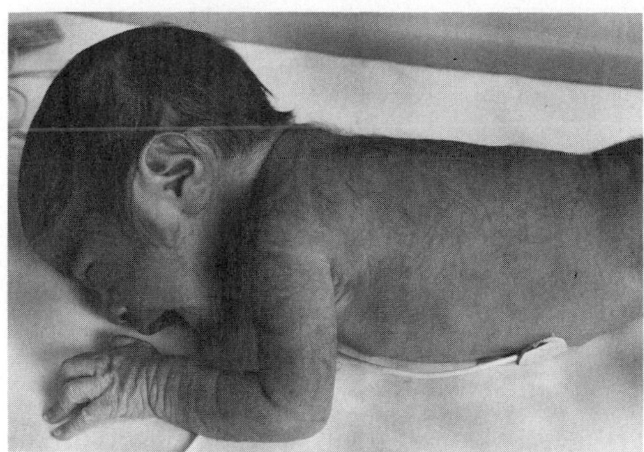

***Figure* 20–15**

Lanugo is abundant on this slightly preterm infant.

and spread down toward the heel. At 37 weeks, creases cover the anterior two thirds of the sole; by 40 weeks, the entire sole is covered with deep creases. The plantar creases must be assessed during the early hours after birth because, as the infant's skin begins to dry, the creases will appear more prominent.

BREASTS

Assess the nipples, areolae, and subcutaneous fat pads (or breast buds). In the very preterm infant, the structures are hardly visible. Gradually they become more noticeable, and the areolae become raised above the chest wall. The fat pads or buds enlarge, until they are approximately 1 cm at term. To determine their size, place a finger on each side and measure the diameter (Fig. 20–17). Use of the thumb and forefinger may cause excess tissue to be drawn together, possibly resulting in an inaccurate score.

EAR

At about 33 to 34 weeks of gestation, the upper pinnae, which have been flat, begin to curve over. The incurving continues downward until the pinnae are curved down to the earlobe at 39 to 40 weeks. The amount of cartilage present in the ears is a more accurate guide to gestational age than the curving of the pinnae because of individual differences in ear shape. As cartilage is deposited in the pinnae, the ears become stiff and stand away from the head.

In assessing the ear, observe the incurving and thickness of each pinna (Fig. 20–18). Fold the ear over longitudinally and horizontally to assess the resistance to folding and how fast the ear returns to its original state. In the preterm infant less than 32 weeks gestational age, the ear has little cartilage to keep it stiff. When folded, the ear remains folded over or returns slowly. In the term neonate, the

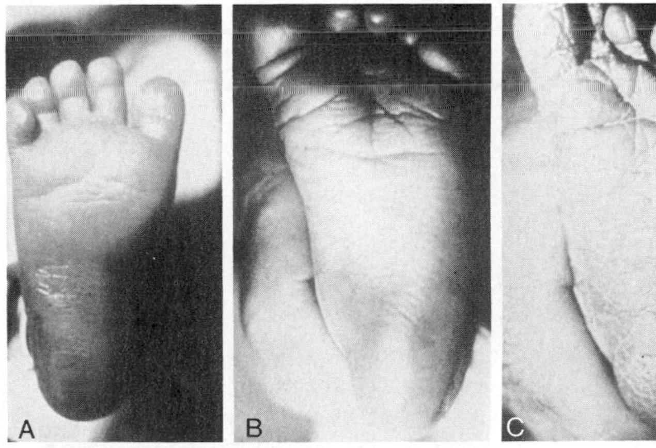

***Figure* 20–16**

Plantar creases begin to develop at the base of the toes and extend to the heel. **A**, The preterm infant has few creases on the entire foot. **B**, As the infant nears term, deeper creases cover more of the foot. **C**, The postterm infant has deep creases.

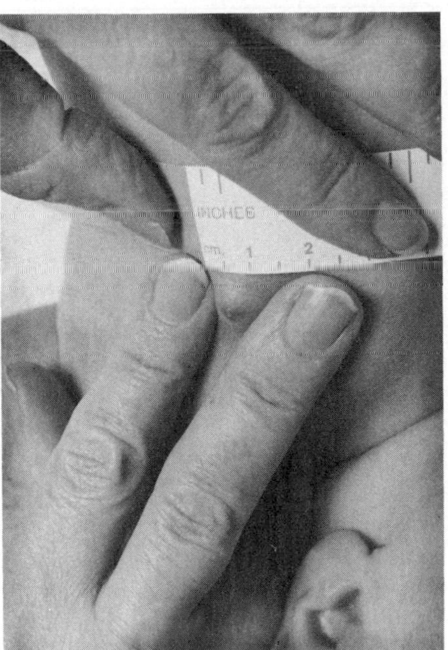

***Figure* 20–17**

The nurse places a finger on either side of the areola and measures the breast tissue. In the full-term infant, breast tissue is raised and the nipple is easily distinguished from surrounding skin.

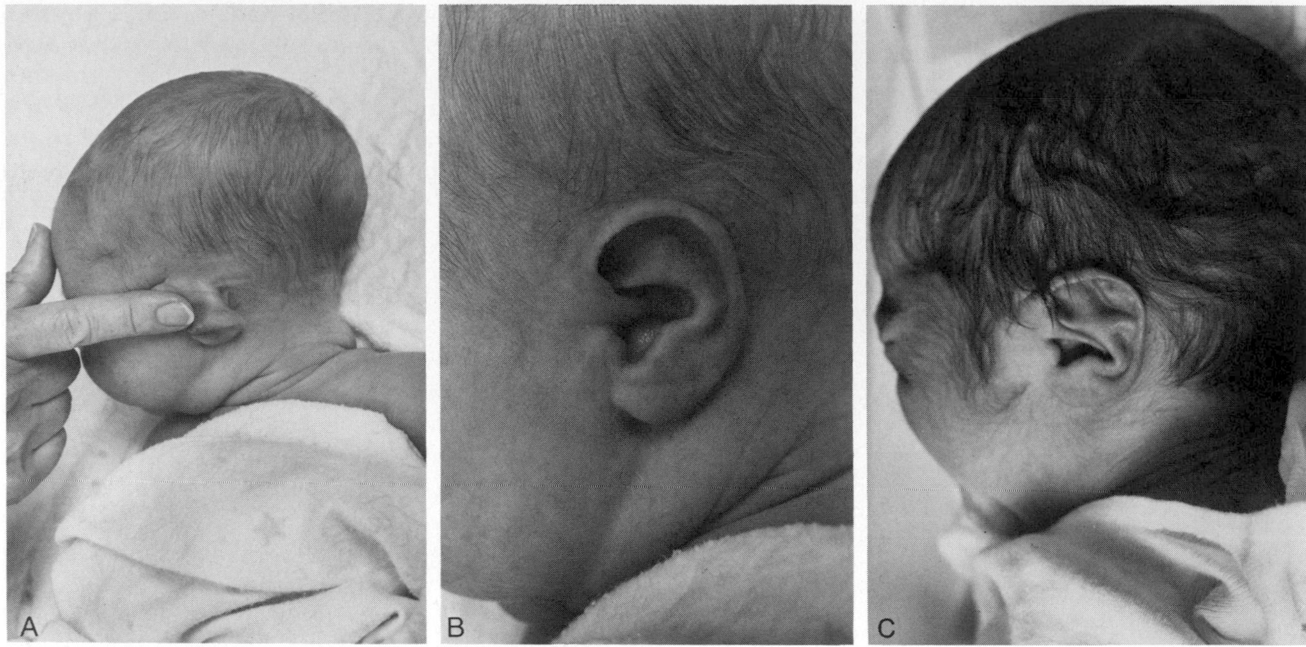

Figure 20–18

Ear maturation. **A**, The nurse folds the ears and notes how quickly they return to position. **B**, Ears in the full-term infant are well formed and have instant recoil. **C**, In the preterm infant, ears show little curving of the pinna and recoil slowly or not at all.

folded ear springs back to its original position immediately.

GENITALS

In the female infant, assess the relationship in size of the clitoris, labia minora, and labia majora (Fig. 20–19). In the preterm infant, the labia majora are small and separated, whereas the clitoris and labia minora are large by comparison. As the infant nears term, the labia majora gradually enlarge, until the clitoris and labia minora are completely covered. Because the size of the labia majora is affected by the amount of fat deposited, the infant who is malnourished in utero may have genitalia with an immature appearance.

In the male infant, assess the location of the testes and the rugae (ridges or wrinkles) on the scrotum (Fig. 20–20). The testes originate in the abdominal cavity but move down into the inguinal ring at 30 weeks of gestation. By 37 weeks, they are located high in the scrotal sac, and they are generally completely descended by term. Rugae form on the surface of the scrotum beginning at about 36 weeks of gestation and cover the sac by 40 weeks. Once the testes are completely down into the scrotum, it appears large and pendulous.

Scoring

As each part of the assessment is performed, match the infant's response with the diagrams and explanations on the assessment tool. After completing the assessment, total the points and compare the score

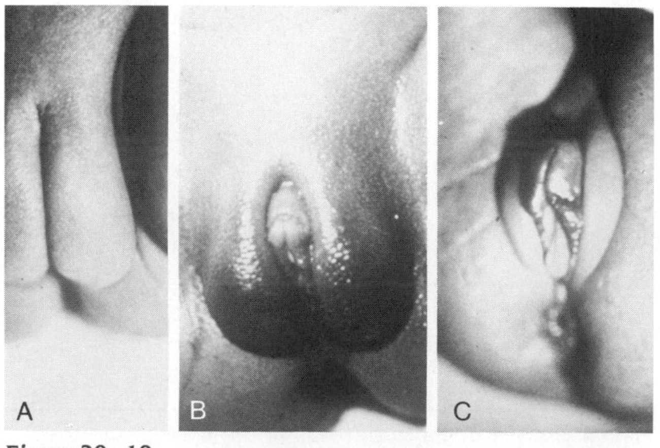

Figure 20–19

Female genitals. As the female matures, the labia majora cover the labia minora and clitoris completely; in the preterm infant, these structures are not covered. **A** Full-term infant. **B**, Near-term infant. **C**, Preterm infant.

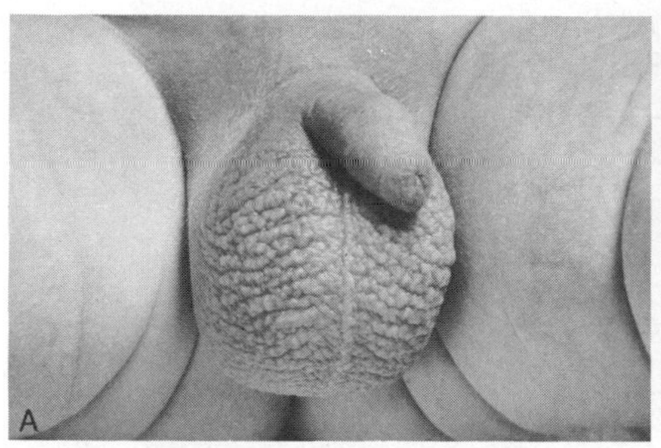

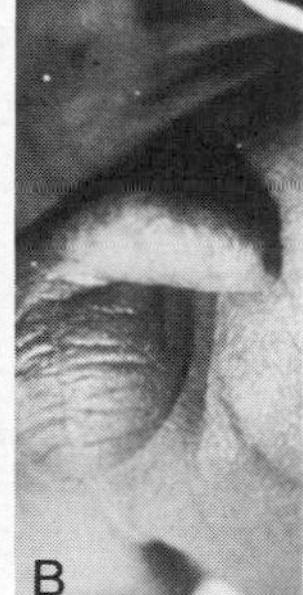

Figure 20–20

Male genitals. **A**, The full-term infant has a pendulous scrotum with deep rugae. **B**, In the preterm infant, the testes may not be descended and there are few rugae.

with the corresponding gestational age. Although slight differences in the scores may be obtained by different examiners, a difference of 2.5 points would be necessary to change the gestational age by 1 week. Therefore, slight differences in the scores of different examiners are not likely to cause significant differences in outcome of the examination.

Gestational Age and Infant Size

Once the gestational age of the newborn is determined, plot it on a graph of the intrauterine development curve (Fig. 20–21) along with the neonate's weight, length, and head circumference to determine the appropriateness for gestational age. This score determines how well the infant has grown for the amount of time spent in the uterus. An infant may be small, large, or appropriate (average) for gestational age. The infant who is appropriate for gestational age falls between the 10th and the 90th percentile on the graph. The large-for-gestational-age (LGA) infant is above the 90th percentile, whereas the small-for-gestational-age (SGA) infant is below the 10th percentile.

Although the SGA infant is often thought to be born before term, the preterm infant can be appropriate or LGA. Similarly, the LGA infant can be born before term, at term, or beyond term. For example, an infant born at 28 weeks of gestation may have measurements that correspond to the 92nd percentile on the intrauterine growth curve chart. The infant would be LGA even though born before term. An infant judged to be 43 weeks gestational age may have measurements that correspond to the 7th percentile on the growth curve. The infant would be SGA.

Nursing Considerations

The results of the gestational age assessment determine the nursing care needed by the infant. When an infant's gestational age or measurements fall outside the range expected, the nurse monitors for complications that might occur. Some specific complications are common to the preterm, postterm, SGA, and LGA infant. For example, the SGA infant may not have received adequate nutrients during intrauterine life as a result of abnormal conditions of the pregnancy. Such an infant is more prone to hypoglycemia, difficulty maintaining thermoregulation, and respiratory problems.

The most common causes of an LGA infant are diabetes in the mother or very large parents. The most common complications that the nurse will monitor for include birth injuries, due to difficulty of the large infant passing through the birth canal, and hypoglycemia.

✔ Check Your Reading

12. What is the nurse's responsibility regarding marks on the newborn's skin?
13. Why is the gestational age assessment important?

Assessments and Care Related to Behavior

Assessment of the infant's behavior helps determine intactness of the central nervous system and provides information about ability to respond to caretaking activities. Because behavior differs at various times after birth, it is important for the nurse to be aware of the periods of reactivity and the six different states of behavior so that nursing care can be adapted appropriately.

Periods of Reactivity

ASSESSMENT

During the first and second periods of reactivity, newborns may have elevated pulse and respiratory rates and low temperature. During the sleep period between the first and second periods of reactivity, newborns cannot be awakened easily and are not interested in feeding. It is important to observe infants carefully during this time, but it can usually be done unobtrusively so that parents can continue to enjoy them.

CLASSIFICATION OF NEWBORNS – BASED ON MATURITY AND INTRAUTERINE GROWTH

Symbols: X - 1st Exam O - 2nd Exam

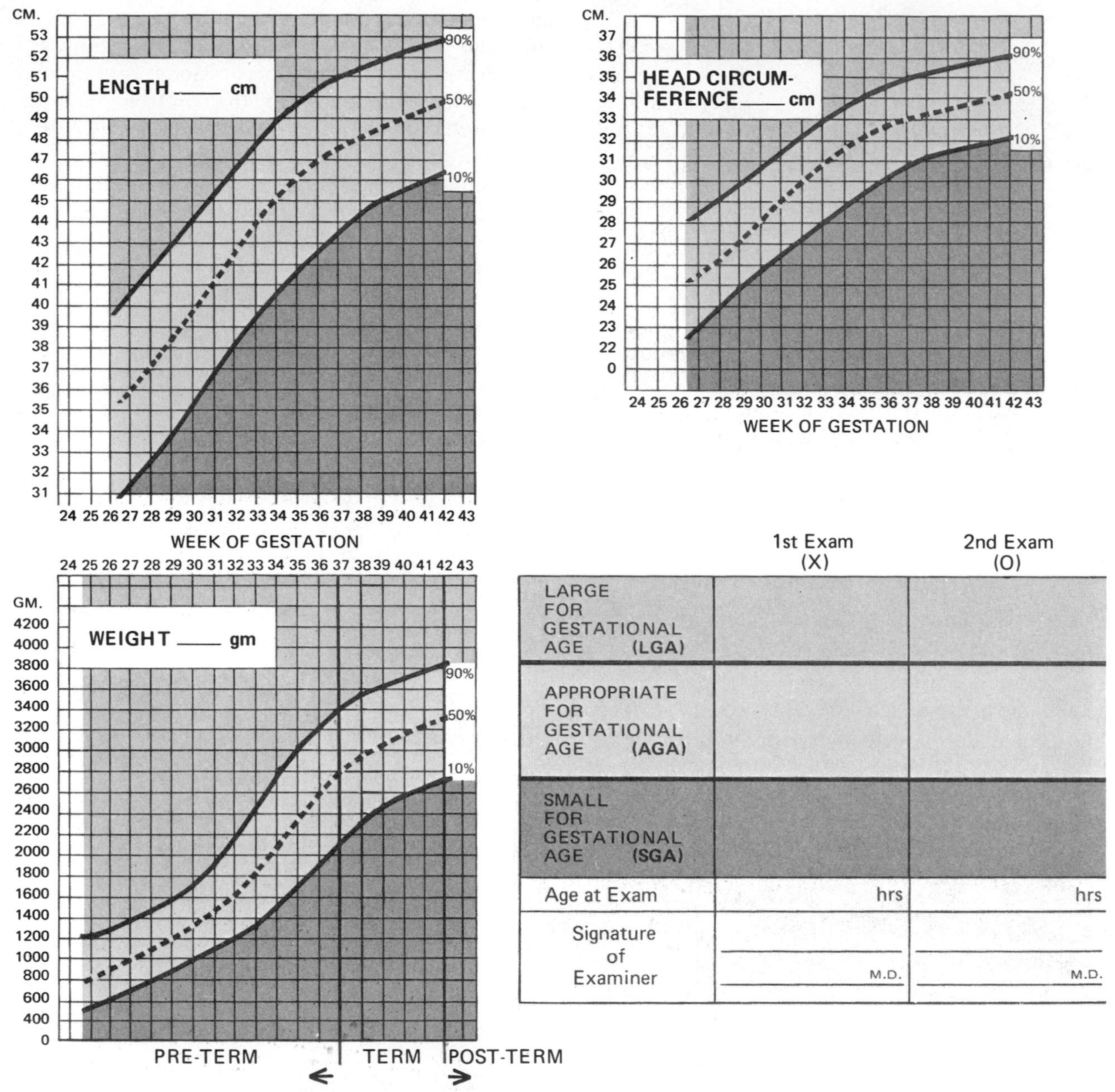

Adapted from Lubchenco LC, Hansman C, and Boyd E: Pediatr 37:403, 1966; Battaglia FC, and Lubchenco LC: J Pediatr 71:159, 1967.

Figure 20–21

Intrauterine growth grids. (Courtesy of Bristol-Myers Company, Evansville, Ind.) (Adapted from Lubchenko, L.C., Hansman, C, & Boyd, E. (1966). *Pediatrics,* 37,403; and from Battaglia, F.C., & Lubchenko, L.C. (1967). *Journal of Pediatrics,* 71, 159.)

NURSING CONSIDERATIONS

During the first period of reactivity, encourage parents to take advantage of the newborn's alert behavior, which enhances bonding. If the mother wishes to breastfeed, help her position the infant. Although many neonates nurse well at this time, others may not. Reassure the mother that the infant who only nuzzles or licks the nipple at first will nurse well later.

Suction the mouth and nose as necessary. Use warmed blankets and replace them as needed if the infant is no longer under a warmer. The gestational age assessment is completed during the first hours after birth. Infants in the sleep phase will have relaxed muscle tone. Take this into consideration, or the score will not be accurate. Infants who previously were sucking vigorously on their hands may have a poor suck if attempts to feed them are made.

By the time of the second period of reactivity, the infant may be alone with the mother without constant attendance by the nurse. Whereas nurses know that regurgitation, gagging, and episodes of cyanosis are normal during the first and second periods of reactivity, these may be very frightening to the mother. Teach the appropriate responses to the behaviors common to this phase. Demonstrate use of the bulb syringe to mothers and instruct them to call for help as needed. Check frequently with the mother to see if the infant is having difficulty. Explanations of the infant's behavior, along with reassurance and praise for the mother's handling, are important nursing interventions.

Behavioral Changes

Assess the infant's behavioral changes. Note the six different behavioral states: deep sleep, active sleep, drowsy, quiet alert, active alert, and crying. A number of special tools are available for the assessment of newborn behavior. The Brazelton neonatal behavioral assessment scale is often used when detailed knowledge about the infant is needed. Extensive education is required in its use. Although nurses do not use these special tools during routine nursing care of the newborn, they should be aware that the tools are available and that they can assess the infant's behavioral states informally.

In addition to their use in assessing the behavioral states, special tools are used to analyze other aspects of the newborn's behavior, such as habituation, orientation, self-consoling behaviors, social behaviors, and the appropriateness of the amount of time in each of these activities.

HABITUATION

Note the infant's response to a visual, auditory, or tactile stimulus. Generally, the first response in a healthy newborn is a period of alertness to an interesting stimulus, such as a brightly colored object or a bell. If the stimulus is disturbing, like a bright light flashed in the eyes or a pinprick to the foot, the infant startles and attempts to escape by averting the eyes or pulling the foot away.

Infants will gradually lose interest in and stop responding to continued noxious stimuli. This allows infants to ignore the stimuli and save energy for physiological needs. They may go into a dull drowsy state or fall into a deep sleep. Infants who seem unresponsive in a bright, noisy nursery may be in a state of habituation. The preterm infant or one with damage to the central nervous system may not be able to habituate.

ORIENTATION

Orientation is the infant's ability to pay attention to an interesting visual or auditory stimulus. It is most prominent during the quiet alert state. Infants will focus their eyes and turn their heads toward stimuli in an attempt to prolong contact with it. Preterm or ill neonates have less ability to orient to stimuli. Attempts to stimulate them may result in overfatigue.

SELF-CONSOLING ACTIVITIES

Normal newborns are able to console themselves for short periods of time. They attempt to bring their hands to their mouth and suck on their fists, and they watch objects in the environment to meet their needs for comfort. Infants who are ill, preterm, or exposed to drugs prenatally have less ability to console themselves.

NURSING CONSIDERATIONS

Explain the infant's behavioral changes to the parents to help them learn how to interpret the infant's cues and facilitate bonding. Point out examples of the changes in the infant's behavior and suggest methods of responding. Assess the parents' growing ability to respond to the infant's behavioral cues.

✔ *Check Your Reading*

14. How do the periods of reactivity affect nursing care?

Daily Assessments and Care

Keys to Clinical Practice: Daily Assessments and Care provides a summary of daily nursing activities in meeting newborn needs (see Appendix E, p. 978). Certain areas are discussed more fully here.

Continuing Assessments

Assess vital signs once every 8 hours or more often if they are abnormal. Weigh the infant once daily and note weight loss or gain. Perform a complete assessment every 8 hours according to the birth facility's routine but be alert at all times for signs of change in the newborn's condition.

Assess the skin for new marks or changes in old ones. The scalp should be carefully assessed for marks that may not be obvious because they are covered by abundant hair. Assess skin turgor and presence of edema. To assess skin turgor, pinch up a small area of skin over the chest or abdomen and note how quickly it returns to its normal position. The return should be immediate in the normal newborn, with no "tenting."

Observe the cord for bleeding or oozing during the early hours after birth. Be certain that the cord clamp is securely fastened and that no skin is caught in it. Look for serosanguinous or purulent drainage and other signs of infection such as redness or edema at the base. The cord begins to dry shortly after birth. It becomes brownish-black within 2 to 3 days and falls off at 10 to 14 days.

Nursing Considerations

SKIN CARE

Bathing. Give the infant a bath as soon after birth as the temperature is stable. The bath removes blood and excessive vernix. While shampooing the hair, comb through it to help to remove clots of blood. Return the infant to the radiant warmer quickly to minimize heat loss. Dry the infant thoroughly, paying special attention to creases. Blot the hair well and comb it out to hasten drying.

After the initial bath, the infant may not receive another full bath during the birth facility stay. However, cleanse the infant's skin as necessary, usually at diaper changes and to remove regurgitated milk. Use clear water only or a mild soap solution according to agency policy.

Cord Care. The cord may be treated with a bactericidal substance such as triple dye solution, Betadine, an antibiotic ointment, or alcohol. In some agencies, triple dye solution may be applied after the admission bath and alcohol used once or twice a shift to assist with drying. Teach parents how to apply alcohol to clean the cord. They should continue this at home until the cord falls off. Fold the diaper down below the cord in order to keep it dry and free from contamination.

Remove the cord clamp when the end of the cord is dry, usually about 24 hours after birth (Fig. 20–22). The base of the cord will still be moist when the clamp is removed, but as long as the end is dry and crisp, there is no danger of bleeding from the now-closed umbilical vessels. It is important to be sure that the cord clamp is removed before the infant is discharged. If the neonate is taken home before the cord is dry enough for the clamp to be removed, the cord may be tied or the clamp left for the physician to remove later. In some birth facilities, early discharge is followed by a home visit by a nurse, who assesses the infant and removes the clamp at that time.

Diaper Area. Wear non-sterile gloves because contact with body fluids is likely while changing a diaper. Clean the infant well after each stool. Meconium is very thick and sticky and can be difficult to remove from the skin. Plain water can be used for cleaning, or a special soap solution may be preferred in some agencies. Petroleum jelly or other skin preparations are sometimes used to make cleaning

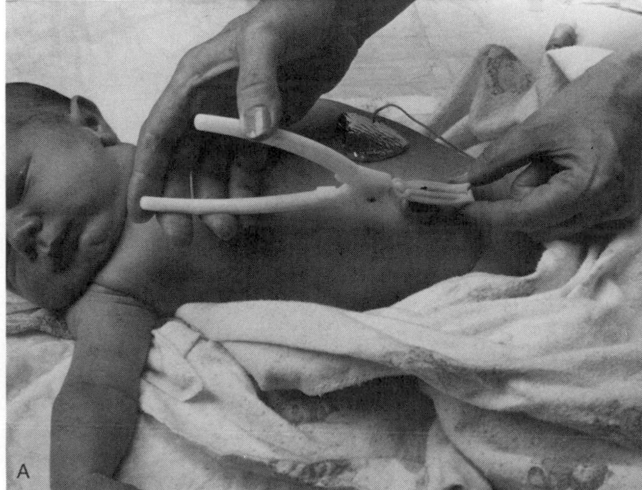

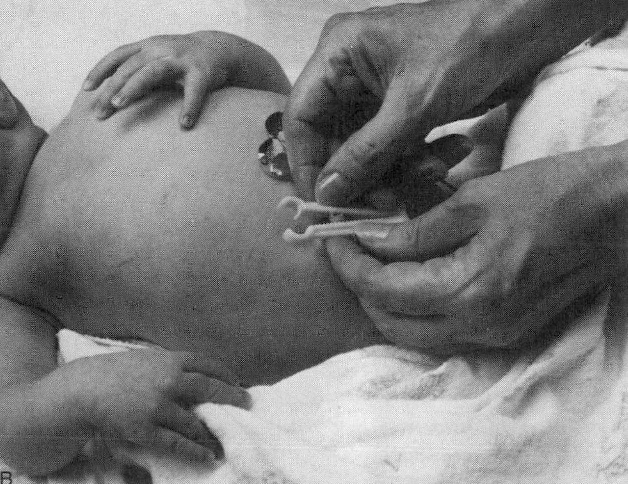

Figure 20–22

The cord clamp is removed when the end of the cord is dry and crisp. The clamp is **(A)** cut and **(B)** separated.

meconium stools easier and to prevent skin irritation.

Clean all creases well. Rinse the skin well if using soap. Demonstrate diaper care to the parents and answer their questions. Encourage parents to change diapers and to perform other care for the infant so that the nurse can assess their knowledge and make suggestions.

OTHER CARE

Ensure that the infant is eating well and that the parents understand their chosen feeding method. Provide teaching about all areas of newborn care during every contact with the parents. Determine whether they appear to be bonding with their infant (see Chapter 18, p. 450, for more information about bonding).

Because any marks on the skin are a source of concern to parents, explain their significance. Usually, they need only reassurance that the spots are normal in newborns and information about when they will disappear. However, parents should be allowed to express their anxieties fully. What may seem of no importance to a nurse who has worked with many neonates may be of major concern to a mother who has never seen a newborn.

Protecting the Infant

Safeguarding the infant is a major role of the nurse. Two primary ways nurses protect newborns are by (1) prevention and early recognition of infection and (2) taking precautions to prevent kidnapping.

INFECTION

Because the newborn has limited ability to respond to infection, prevention is of utmost importance throughout the birth facility stay and constitutes a major part of parent teaching.

Prevention. A number of nursing actions are designed to prevent infection. At the beginning of their shift, nurses in many agencies perform a scrub of the hands and arms. Throughout the day, hand washing is important before and after touching any infant. It is essential not to handle one neonate and then go to another without again washing one's hands. An infection that develops in one infant could quickly spread to others if these precautions are not taken.

Encourage parents to wash their hands before handling their infant. Also instruct visitors to wash their hands before they hold infants. Discourage visitors with colds or other infections from coming in contact with the mother or newborn. Explain the importance of this to the parents.

Avoid cross-contamination by keeping each infant's supplies separate. Use materials in drawers or cupboards of the crib unit belonging to one infant only for that infant, because they are likely to be touched by the nurse as she or he is caring for the infant. Using them for another neonate could result in the transfer of infectious organisms.

When the mother has an infection, consult with the physician or nurse practitioner as to whether it is safe for the newborn to remain with her. Although mother and infant may well share the same organisms, if the mother is acutely ill, the infant may need to stay in the nursery until the mother is no longer contagious and feels able to perform infant care.

Some birth facilities have a policy governing when separation of mother and newborn is necessary. Often the degree of the mother's fever is one of the determining factors. The separation of mother and infant should be as short as possible, of course, to promote bonding.

Recognizing Signs of Infection. Be vigilant for signs of infection during assessment and care of the infant. These signs are often different from those of the older infant or child and may be very subtle. Instead of a fever, there may be a decrease in temperature. The infant may feed poorly or be lethargic. Periods of apnea sometimes occur without obvious cause. Any change in behavior that is unexplained should be recorded and investigated. The same holds true, of course, for the more obvious signs of infection such as drainage from the eyes, cord, or circumcision site (see discussion of sepsis, p. 853, in Chapter 29; see Critical to Remember: Signs of Sepsis, p. 855, Chapter 29).

KIDNAPPING

An unfortunate but essential role of the nurse is protection of the infant against kidnapping (Table 20–4). Precautions include providing a means to differentiate birth facility personnel from visitors. Teach parents how to recognize birth facility personnel, whether by a picture identification badge or by other means. Caution them never to give their infant to anyone who does not have proper identification.

In some agencies, an electronic device is attached to each infant's wrist, ankle, or clothing. The facility's exits are wired so that an alarm is triggered when the device is near.

Entrances to the maternity unit should be in areas where staff can watch those entering and leaving. Remote exits are often locked or equipped with an alarm to prevent use. Respond quickly anytime a door alarm sounds. Although alarms are usually trig-

Table 20–4. PRECAUTIONS TO PREVENT INFANT KIDNAPPING

1. All birth facility personnel must wear appropriate identification at all times.
2. Enlist parents' help in preventing kidnapping. Teach them to allow only birth facility staff with proper identification to take their infants from them.
3. Teach parents and staff to transport infants only in their cribs and never by carrying them. Question anyone walking in the hallway carrying an infant.
4. Question anyone with a newborn in an unusual part of the hospital, especially if near an exit.
5. Be suspicious of anyone who does not seem to be visiting a specific mother or who asks questions about nursery or discharge routines.
6. Respond immediately when an alarm sounds signaling that a remote entrance has been opened or that an infant has been taken into an unauthorized area.
7. Never leave infants unattended at any time. Teach parents that infants must be attended at all times. Suggest that they send the infant to the nursery if they or a family member cannot watch the infant.
8. Take infants to mothers one at a time. This avoids having an infant in a crib waiting outside in the hall while the nurse is in a room with another mother.
9. Identification bracelets are often given to a mother's support person so that he or she can come to the nursery to get the infant. When a parent or family member comes to the nursery to take an infant, always match the infant and adult identification bracelet numbers.
10. Alert birth facility security when any suspicious activity occurs.

gered accidentally, it is always possible that a kidnapper is using a remote exit for a quick getaway.

Many agencies take pictures of newborns soon after birth. The pictures and footprints can be used later should it become necessary to identify the infant. Note any marks that could also help prove the identity of an infant.

Newborns are usually abducted by women who are familiar with the birth facility and its routines. They usually visit several times to learn the routines so that they can impersonate birth facility staff to gain access to a newborn. The woman may have lost an infant or has been unable to have a child of her own. Although the woman plans the kidnapping, she waits for an appropriate opportunity to take any infant.

✔ Check Your Reading

15. What is the most important method of preventing infection in newborns?
16. How can kidnapping be prevented?

Parents' Knowledge of Newborn Care: Application of Nursing Process

The needs of every infant and family differ. Nurses must assess and identify the particular needs of each family so that they can plan and carry out care appropriately (see Nursing Care Plan 20–1, p. 554). Although inexperienced nurses may have little personal experience with infants, they can draw on a number of resources to help them teach new parents. Table 20–5 discusses concerns that are common to many student nurses.

Assessment

Assess parents' learning needs during every contact with them. Determine initial as well as ongoing understanding and how well they are able to use the information taught. Consider the mother's and infant's physical conditions and any special concerns that the mother may have. Review the principles of teaching discussed in Chapter 2 for special considerations when planning teaching sessions.

Assess the father's learning needs and his plans for involvement with infant care. Whether or not the father participates in care of the infant may depend on cultural beliefs about the role of the father. In some cultures, the father participates very little in the care of the young infant. He may become more involved as the children get older. In other families, the father actively takes part in care of the children from the time of their birth. These fathers may care for the newborn even during the birth facility stay. They often have many questions and are very eager to learn about care of their infant.

Determine learning needs for experienced mothers. They may not be aware of the latest information on certain aspects of child care that has come about since the birth of their last infant. Differences in physical requirements or even in temperament between siblings may be a cause for concern for a mother. She may need information about helping other children adjust to the newborn.

Analysis

A nursing diagnosis that is appropriate for the family with learning needs is: *Health Seeking Behaviors related to the desire for information about infant care.*

Planning

The primary goals for this diagnosis are that the parents will:

- Correctly demonstrate infant care before discharge.
- Express confidence in their ability to meet their infant's needs.

Interventions

DETERMINING WHO TEACHES

In many agencies, one nurse is responsible for care of both mother and infant. This extended contact helps the nurse gain a more complete understanding of the mother's learning needs. There is more time for teaching as additional learning needs become apparent.

If the mother and infant are cared for by separate nurses, be sure that all learning needs are met. Traditionally, postpartum nurses teach mothers how to care for themselves, and nursery nurses teach them how to care for their newborn. However, nurses from both areas must be able to teach about both subjects to be certain that all the concerns of mothers are addressed.

MODELING BEHAVIOR

Modeling by the nurse is an important teaching tool. Mothers watch closely when nurses handle infants. The nurse demonstrates mothering behavior by the way the infant is held and by talking to the infant as daily care is given. This is particularly important for the mother with no experience in child care.

TEACHING INTERMITTENTLY

Plan teaching in small segments that are interspersed with the care of the infant. Check the parents' understanding frequently. Ask them to give return demonstrations throughout the day. Gradually allow them to take over until they are doing all of the infant's routine care. Use Parents Want to Know: Techniques for Infant Care to determine what subjects to include. Demonstrate positions for holding, burping, and wrapping and how to read a thermometer.

INCLUDING THE FATHER

Identify fathers who would like to participate in care of their infants but who hesitate because of lack of experience. Offer them the same teaching given the inexperienced mother. Give praise liberally whenever mothers and fathers practice their new infant care skills. This increases their self-confidence and skill.

Evaluation

Ongoing evaluation of parents' learning is necessary throughout the birth facility stay. Determine whether they can demonstrate important aspects of infant care safely and correctly. As they learn more caregiving skills, their confidence should increase as well.

Newborn Screening Tests

Most states require that certain screening tests be performed on the blood of all newborns before they are discharged from the birth facility. Blood is taken from the heel of the infant for these tests, which are usually performed on the day of discharge. Parents may have questions about the purpose of the tests that the nurse will need to answer.

Newborn screening tests are done to detect conditions that result from inborn errors of metabolism or other genetic conditions. The disorders may result in mental retardation if not treated early. The tests are easy and inexpensive. More thorough testing is necessary to confirm any abnormal test results. Although each state determines which conditions will be tested, those most commonly included are for phenylketonuria, hypothyroidism, and galactosemia.

Phenylketonuria

Phenylketonuria (PKU) is a condition in which the infant cannot metabolize the amino acid phenylalanine, which is common in protein foods such as milk. Although some phenylalanine is essential to growth, accumulations of it can result in mental retardation. If treatment for the condition is begun in the first 2 months of life, retardation can be prevented. PKU is treated with a special low-phenylalanine diet, in which the amount of the amino acid is carefully regulated.

The screening test is often performed on the day of discharge so that the infant will have received formula or breast milk and the phenylalanine. It is best to perform the test after milk ingestion, but preliminary results may be accurate even if the infant has fed poorly. Positive tests require further testing.

Hypothyroidism

One in 4000 newborns has hypothyroidism (Gomella, 1992). In this condition, the thyroid produces inadequate amounts of the hormone thyroxine. Thyroid hormones affect the entire body, and the symptoms in an untreated infant include respiratory, feeding, growth, and neurological problems due to damage to the brain. Early and consistent treatment with thy-

Text continued on page 557

Table 20–5. COMMON CONCERNS OF STUDENTS WHEN TEACHING PARENTS

Students with no experience in care of the newborn often have concerns about their ability to teach new parents. Concerns commonly include lack of experience, fear of giving inaccurate information, and dealing with the mother who is more experienced in infant care than the student.

Although students may begin maternity nursing with little understanding of newborn care, that changes quickly. Many methods of increasing knowledge and confidence are available so that parent teaching can become one of the most enjoyable aspects of nursing care.

Taking Stock

First, take stock of the knowledge possessed. Classes taken previously in normal anatomy and physiology and in pathophysiology will be helpful in answering parents' questions. Nursing theory classes will provide new information. Learning will increase daily with thorough reading of the textbook and experience in the clinical area.

Resources Available to Students

Take advantage of available resources. In addition to using the assigned maternity and pediatric nursing textbooks, visit college and hospital libraries for nursing journals with articles on newborn nursing care. Read parent education materials available on the maternity unit such as pamphlets and baby magazines. Because these publications are written for parents of various reading skills, nursing students will generally find them easy to read and a source of quick information.

Seek out resource people who can help with teaching skills. Nursing instructors and clinical nurses are excellent resources for infant care. Most staff nurses enjoy sharing their knowledge with students and can offer practical advice about parent education. Listen to an instructor or staff nurse teach parents—these professionals are role models who can provide examples of approaches to use and answers to questions that may arise.

Many units have staff members who are involved primarily in parent education. There may be a lactation educator helping mothers learn the basics of breastfeeding or an instructor who teaches prenatal classes on infant care and feeding. Some agencies hold classes on the maternity unit to teach mothers to care for themselves and their newborns. Students are generally welcome to observe and participate in these classes, where they can learn about both infant care and teaching techniques.

Make use of audiovisual materials for parent education that are available on maternity units. Watching a video with parents helps both students and parents learn the material. It also provides a starting place for clarifying parents' questions and concerns.

Repetitive Teaching

Keep in mind that much of the teaching required is repetitive. Although there are individual differences, all parents need basic information such as care of the cord, reading a thermometer, and infant feeding. Material that is at first new will quickly become familiar to the student who has taught it to several parents. With practice, students will become polished in their presentations and even develop a variety of ways to teach the same information.

The Experienced Mother

What does one teach the mother having her fourth (or eighth) baby? Begin by assessing the state of the mother's knowledge. If her youngest child is older than a year or two, she has probably forgotten some of the details of infant care. It is often helpful to review the material that is routinely given to first-time mothers to assess whether there are any gaps in the experienced mother's knowledge. For example, the mother of girls may need information about care of the penis (circumcised or uncircumcised). The mother who bottle-fed her last infant will have many questions if she chooses to breastfeed this time.

As you teach, acknowledge that the mother has knowledge by affirming her experience. For example, you may say, "You probably remember much of this information from when your last baby was born. But let me review it with you briefly to see if anything has changed or if you have any questions." Then begin the list of topics. Insert phrases like "As you remember . . . —" or "And you probably know about . . . —" as new topics are introduced. This provides recognition that the mother has experience but allows her to refresh her memory.

Some experienced mothers hesitate to ask questions about topics that they feel that the nurse might expect them to know. Reviewing all material will provide an opportunity for the mother to ask questions without feeling foolish. Providing an environment that is warm and accepting will help the mother feel that it is "safe" to ask questions.

Another method is to ask the mother what techniques she used with her last baby or if she had any problems with a certain aspect of infant care. Ask for her opinions about specific topics. For example, "When did you decide to give your last baby the first bath? How did it go?" Or, "What do you think is the best kind of diaper to use—cotton or disposable?" Not only does this provide an opportunity for discussion, but the nurse may learn more about infant care from the mother's experience!

Sometimes the experienced mother's concerns are not centered on the new baby but on her other children. She may wonder how her 2-year-old will feel about the newborn or how she'll be able to stretch her time to meet the needs of each child when she feels so fatigued. Help the mother problem-solve in these areas by using therapeutic communication techniques. Acting as a "sounding board" for the mother as she sorts out priorities and makes plans may be all that is necessary.

The Experienced Nurse/Parent

A word of caution is necessary for the nursing student who is also an experienced parent. It's easy to compare a situation with one's own personal experiences. Sometimes this increases empathy, but personal experiences should seldom be shared with clients. Clients want to talk about their own present experience and may not feel that the nurse's experiences are applicable in their situation. Often, current philosophy and knowledge about infant care may have changed, and nurses who rely on experience with their own children may pass along incorrect information.

Parents Want To Know

Techniques for Infant Care

This guide is written in language that the nurse might use when teaching parents about infant care. Adapt the subjects to meet the needs of individual parents.

Handling the Infant:

Head Support: An infant's head is the heaviest part of the body and makes up a quarter of the total body length. Because the head is so heavy, infants are unable to support their head when held in an upright position. Place your hand behind the baby's head whenever you hold him or her to help support the head. Babies' muscles become strong enough to support the head after the first few months of life.

Positions: Most mothers hold the infant in the cradle position. In the "football" position, the baby's head is supported in the palm of the hand and the body is held along the arm and supported against your side. This position is useful when washing the baby's hair or breastfeeding. It allows the other hand to be free.

The shoulder hold is familiar to most mothers and is often used in burping the baby. Another position for burping is to sit the baby on your lap. Support the head and chest with one hand while gently patting or rubbing the infant's back with the other hand. This allows you to see the baby's face in case of "spit ups."

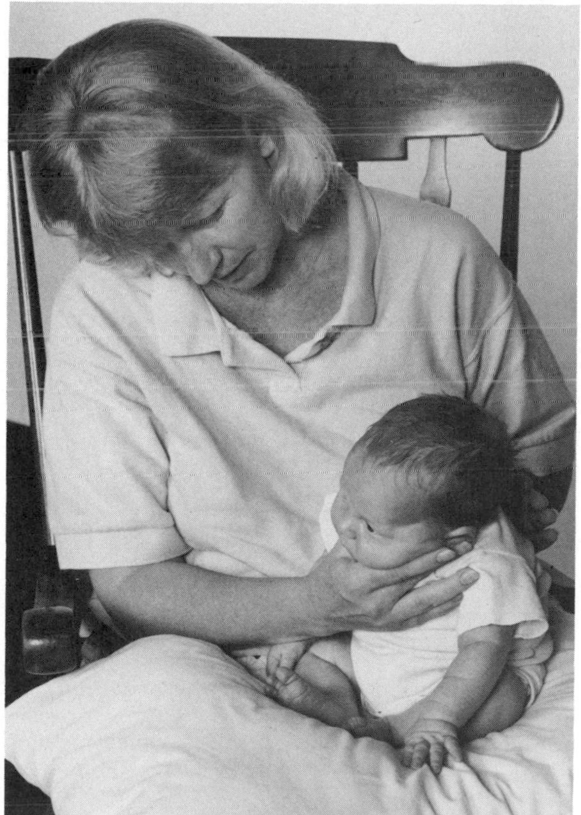

Wrapping: Young infants seem to feel more secure when wrapped firmly in a blanket, which may simulate the enclosed space of the uterus. A fussy baby often responds well to swaddling. To swaddle the infant, turn down one corner of the blanket and position the infant with the head there. Fold one side of the blanket over the body and arm. Bring the lower corner up and fold it over the chest. Then bring the other side around the infant and tuck it underneath.

Normal Body Processes:

Breathing: Newborns normally breathe more than twice as fast as adults, about 30 to 60 times a minute. Their breathing is irregular and may vary from loud to very soft. Sometimes babies breathe so quietly that mothers wake them to be sure that they actually are breathing. Sneezing is usually a normal response to lint from new baby clothes rather than a sign of a cold developing.

Using a Bulb Syringe: Use the bulb syringe when the infant has excessive mucus in the mouth or nose or spits up milk during the early days. Squeeze the bulb before you insert it into the mouth and aim it to the side of the mouth rather than to the back. Extra mucus is common in the first days of life but is usually not a problem thereafter unless a cold develops. *Call your physician if the baby's skin becomes blue or if the baby stops breathing for more than 15 seconds, has difficulty breathing, or has yellow or green drainage from the nose.*

Temperature: Newborns have difficulty in the early weeks regulating their temperature. If they become cold, more calories and more oxygen are used than they would otherwise need. This can be dangerous for them but can be prevented by making sure that the infant is kept warm enough. Dress your baby as you would like to be dressed. Place a light receiving blanket over the young infant, except in very hot weather.

Using a Thermometer: You need to learn to use a glass thermometer correctly so that you can check the baby's temperature during illness. It is best to take the temperature by the axillary method, that is, by placing the thermometer under the infant's arm. This avoids injury to the rectum. Place the thermometer in the space under the arm, making sure that the bulb does not protrude behind the arm. Hold the arm firmly over the thermometer and read it at 5 minutes. *Call your physician if the baby has a temperature higher than 100°F axillary or lower than 97.7°F.*

Urine Output: Your baby will have a minimum of two to six wet diapers a day during the first day or two and six to ten wet diapers a day thereafter. Counting the number of wet diapers is one way to tell if the baby is getting enough milk to drink. *Call your baby's doctor if the infant doesn't void for over 12 hours.*

Stool Output: The baby's bowel movements will vary according to the type of feeding given. Formula-fed infants pass one to several stools each day that are light yellow–brown and formed. Breastfed infants pass very soft stools that have a sweet-sour odor and are mustard yellow. The number varies from one movement every few days to as many as ten a day.

Because infants often turn red in the face and seem to strain when passing a stool, mothers may think they are constipated. However, a constipated infant passes a dry stool, and there may be small, hard pieces. There are usually fewer stools per day than is average. If the movement is soft, you do not need to worry if the baby seems to strain while passing stools.

Parents Want to Know continued on following page

Diarrhea**:** Babies with diarrhea will pass an increased number of stools, and the color and consistency will change. Because the contents move through the intestines more quickly than normal, the color will be greener and the stools will be more liquid than usual. There may be a water ring—an area in the diaper where the liquid has absorbed, sometimes around an area of more solid stool. *Call your physician for further instructions if the infant passes more than two diarrhea stools.*

Skin Care:
A number of normal marks occur on the newborn's skin. One is a rash called erythema toxicum that resembles small insect bites. Another is small whiteheads called milia. These are normal and disappear without treatment. Do not squeeze them or they may become infected and will last longer.

Newborns have very dry skin, and they peel all over during the first few weeks of life. This is because they were surrounded by water for 9 months and the outer layers of the skin were not shed. After peeling, the baby will have the soft skin one associates with newborns. It is not necessary to put lotions or creams on the skin, as they may cause irritation.

Cord**:** Clean the cord about three times a day. Use a cotton swab to clean the cord and the crevices at the base of the cord. This will not hurt the baby, as there are no nerves in the cord. *Notify your physician if you see bleeding or signs of infection, such as redness, drainage, or a foul odor.*

Keep the cord dry by folding the diaper below the cord so that it is not wet by urine. The cord generally falls off in about 10 days to 2 weeks. Sometimes it is attached by just a few strands on the last day and may bleed a few drops when it does detach. Do not start tub baths until the cord is off and the area is well healed.

Diaper Area**:** Clean the diaper area with each diaper change. Washing with soap and water is usually sufficient. For girls, separate the labia (folds) and cleanse of all stool. For boys, wash under the scrotum to help prevent rashes. If the diaper area becomes red, increase the frequency of diaper changes. Leaving the diaper off to expose the area to air is also helpful. If an ointment is needed, petroleum jelly or a barrier-type ointment may be used. *If redness persists, ask your baby's doctor for suggestions.*

Bathing:
Give your baby a sponge bath until the navel and circumcision sites are healed. At that time, tub baths can begin. Give the bath at any time of day that is most convenient. Because infants are washed as needed after regurgitation and with diaper changes, it isn't necessary for the infant to receive a bath every day. Fathers often enjoy giving the infant a bath, and some make this their special time with the baby.

Sponge Baths**:** Before beginning a sponge bath, gather all the supplies together. You will need a container for the warm water (or use a sink), washcloth and towel, baby shampoo, alcohol and cotton or cotton-tipped swabs for cord care, and clean clothes. Soap is not necessary for the young infant, but if it is used, it should be gentle and non-alkaline to protect the natural acid mantle of the infant's skin.

Give the bath in a room that is warm and free of drafts. Bathe the baby on a surface that is comfortable and safe. If you use a counter, you can pad it with blankets or towels.

NEVER *leave the infant alone on an unprotected surface, even for a minute.* Keep one hand on the infant at all times to prevent falls. Some mothers find that taking the phone off the hook during the bath prevents distractions. If you must leave the room for any reason during the bath, take the baby along or place him or her in the crib.

As you give the sponge bath, keep the baby warm by exposing only the area you are washing. Carefully wash and dry each area to prevent heat loss by evaporation. Wash and dry the baby's body, one part at a time, to prevent chilling. Cord care can be done at this time. Clean the diaper area last, using the principle of "clean to least clean." Start by washing the face with clear water. Use a separate clean area of the washcloth to wipe each eye. Use a washcloth to clean the ears. Wash carefully behind the ears, where regurgitated milk may accumulate. Do not use cotton-tipped swabs in the infant's ears or nose, as injury may occur if the baby moves suddenly. Using a corner of the washcloth is sufficient.

Infants have very short necks, and it's sometimes difficult to clean the neck folds. Put one hand under the baby's shoulders and lift slightly. This causes the head to drop back enough that the creases in the neck can be washed.

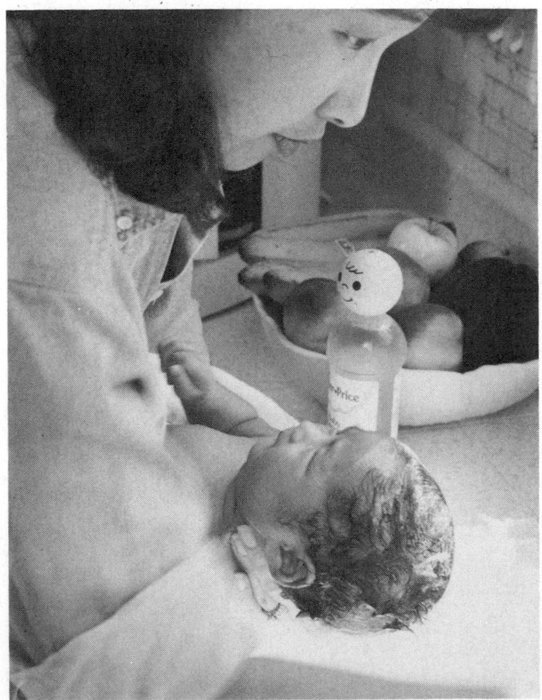

Shampoo the head while holding the baby in a football position, which allows one hand to be free to wash the hair. Although the fontanelle or "soft spot" may seem delicate, it is covered with a tough membrane. The area will not be injured by washing over it. Use a towel to dry the hair well to prevent heat loss. Combing out the hair will hasten drying.

Tub Bath**:** The procedure for a tub bath is very similar to that for a sponge bath. First, gather all equipment in a warm room. Use a small plastic tub or a clean sink for the bath. Pad the bottom with a towel to make it more comfortable. Place approximately 3 inches of warm water in the tub. Wash the face and hair before placing the baby in the tub. Keeping the baby dressed until after the hair is washed helps prevent chilling.

The first few times you are giving a tub bath, you may find it easier to lather your hands with soap and water and then lather the infant's body. You can then immerse the baby in the tub for rinsing. This shortens the time that the infant is in the tub and allows you to wash each area well. It is not unusual for young infants to be frightened when they are first put in water. Talk to your baby softly and calmly while holding him or her securely to help the baby adjust to this new experience.

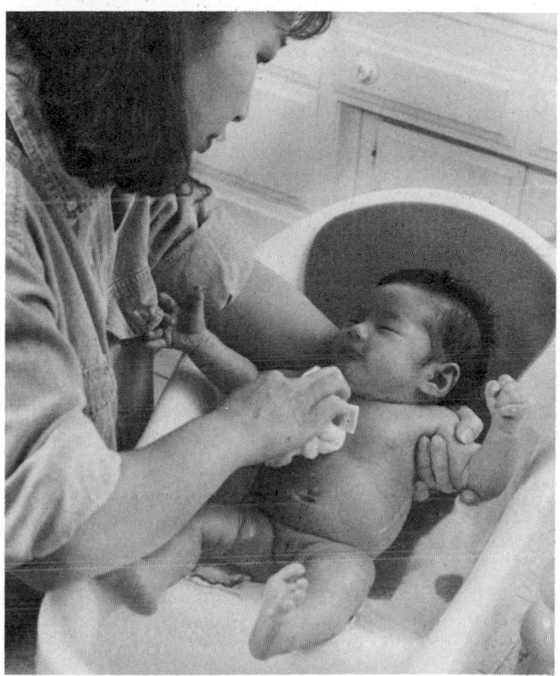

Feeding

Breastfeeding, Formula Feeding: *See Chapter 21, Infant Feeding.*

Bottle Feeding: Hold the bottle so that the nipple is filled with milk to prevent the infant from swallowing air. Gently rubbing the palate with the nipple encourages the infant to begin sucking. However, excessive movement of the nipple in the baby's mouth is distracting to the baby.

Burp the baby once midway during the feeding, using the shoulder or the sitting position. After feeding, always place the baby on his or her side with a rolled blanket behind the back to prevent choking if the baby spits up.

Behavior:
Knowing that infants have six different behavioral states will help you learn about your baby's individual characteristics.

Quiet Sleep: During the quiet sleep phase, the infant sleeps soundly with quiet breathing and little movement. Your baby will not be disturbed by noises of appliances or other children at this time.

Active Sleep: Babies spend more time in the active sleep state. Because the baby moves or fusses during sleep, you may think that he or she is awake. If your baby sleeps in your room, you may have difficulty sleeping because of the noises and movement made during this phase.

Drowsy State: During the drowsy state, the baby is beginning to wake but may go back to sleep if not disturbed. However, if it is time for feeding or other activities, talk softly to help movement to a more awake state.

Quiet Alert State: The quiet alert state is the one that parents enjoy most because the infant seems so intent on studying the objects and people nearby. This is a good time for infant stimulation and "play time."

Active Alert State: Parents soon learn to recognize the active alert or "fussy" state in their infants. The infant may be signaling hunger or discomfort from wet and cold diapers.

Crying: If you do not intervene during the active alert state, the baby will soon move to the crying state. If the baby cries too long, he or she may not respond at first to care activities. A few minutes of rocking and holding close may be necessary before the infant settles down.

Socialization:
Infants are social beings who enjoy contact with people. Because infants hear their mothers' voices in utero, they are likely to respond with interest when their mothers talk to them after birth. The baby should be part of the life of the family. Use an infant seat or an infant carrier to keep the baby near you and the rest of the family yet allow you to have your hands free to do other things.

Infants enjoy watching the human face. Most mothers use a cradle hold so that the baby can see the face. Spend time holding your baby close and talking to him or her to provide social stimulation. This is one way the baby will eventually learn to talk.

Stimulation:
In addition to social stimulation, you can use other types of stimulation.

Sounds: Play music of different types to provide auditory stimulation. Infants prefer music that is not too loud. Music boxes, tapes, or the radio can provide a variety of sound.

Sights: Because babies can focus their eyes best at a distance of 7 to 12 inches, items to be used for visual stimulation should be placed within this range. Be sure that mobiles are not placed too high over the crib for infants to focus on them. Babies especially like black-and-white geometric figures. They enjoy bright colors very early but are not particularly interested in pastels.

Variety: Place the baby in an infant seat in the kitchen while you prepare meals to stimulate the senses of sight, hearing, and smell. An infant carrier pack provides the stimulation of motion as well.

Timing: Stimulation is best used during the baby's quiet alert state. Do not try to use stimulation techniques with a fussy infant because, when tired or hungry, an infant can become overstimulated easily. This causes the baby to be irritable and have difficulty going to sleep.

Nursing Care Plan 20–1

The Normal Newborn

Assessment: Molly is a full-term newborn who was delivered after 18 hours of normal labor. She weighs 7 pounds, 8 ounces, and is 20 inches long. Her parents, Catherine and Bill, are very happy and excited about their first baby. Molly's Apgar score is eight at 1 minute and nine at 5 minutes. During the admission procedures, Molly seems to have an excessive amount of mucus. Her respiratory rate is 62, apical pulse 156, and breath sounds slightly moist. She has mild substernal retractions but no flaring of the nares or grunting respirations. Her color is pink with acrocyanosis.

Nursing Diagnosis: High Risk for Ineffective Airway Clearance related to excessive secretions in airways.

Goals:

Molly will maintain a patent airway and no respiratory distress throughout birth facility stay as demonstrated by respiratory rate of 30 to 60, clear breath sounds, and no cyanosis, retractions, flaring, or grunting.

Before discharge, Catherine and Bill will demonstrate correct usage of the bulb syringe and verbalize the appropriate times to use it.

Intervention:	Rationale:
1. Place Molly in a side-lying position with her head slightly lower than the rest of her body.	1. Facilitates drainage of secretions from the airways.
2. Use a bulb syringe to suction mouth. If the nose also requires suctioning, suction it after suctioning the mouth.	2. As secretions drain into the mouth and nose, suctioning removes them. Suctioning the mouth first prevents aspiration of oral secretions should Molly gasp when her nose is suctioned.
3. Change Molly's position frequently.	3. Position changes promote expansion and drainage of all parts of the lungs.
4. Demonstrate and explain use of the bulb syringe to Catherine and Bill. Ask them to do a return demonstration.	4. Demonstration and return demonstration help ensure that parents learn correct techniques.
5. Continue to observe Molly for signs of respiratory distress. Count pulse and respirations every 15 minutes for first hour, every hour for 4 hours, and then every 8 hours if there is no further problem. Continue to assess for other signs of ineffective airway clearance and respiratory difficulty, such as cyanosis, retractions, flaring, and grunting.	5. Monitoring should be based on history of excessive mucus, ability to deal with mucus, and other signs of respiratory difficulty.

Evaluation:

Molly maintains a patent airway throughout her birth facility stay. Her breath sounds are clear within 3 hours of birth, and her respiratory rate stays within normal limits. She has no signs of respiratory difficulty. Catherine and Bill demonstrate correct use of the bulb syringe and can verbalize when the syringe should be used.

Assessment: Molly's first temperature after birth is 36.5°C (97.7°F). After the first rectal temperature, axillary temperatures are taken. They range from 36.2° to 36.8°C (97.2° to 98.2°F) over the first 2 hours of life.

Nursing Diagnosis: High Risk for Ineffective Thermoregulation related to immature compensation for changes in environmental temperature.

Goals:

Molly will maintain a temperature within the normal range of 36.5° to 37.6°C (97.7° to 99.7°F) rectal, or 36.5° to 37.5°C (97.7° to 99.5°F) axillary, throughout her birth facility stay.

Nursing Care Plan 20–1 *Continued*

The Normal Newborn

Intervention:	Rationale:
1. Place Molly under a radiant warmer at birth with a skin probe on the abdomen. Keep her under the warmer until her temperature is stable.	1. The radiant warmer provides heat according to infant's temperature as detected by the skin probe. It also displays skin temperature.
2. Dry wet skin promptly at birth, when bathing, or when changing wet diapers or clothing. Replace any wet clothing or linens promptly.	2. Heat loss from evaporation occurs when the infant's skin is wet.
3. Keep warmer or crib away from cold walls, windows, or drafts from air conditioners and open doors or windows.	3. Heat loss by radiation and convection occurs from exposure to cold objects or air drafts.
4. Warm everything that comes into contact with Molly. Place warm blankets under her and warm your hands, stethoscope, and other equipment that touches her.	4. Heat can be gained or lost by conduction.
5. Assess axillary temperature every 15 to 30 minutes until stable, according to birth facility procedure and Molly's response.	5. Continued assessment shows response to interventions.
6. Check blood sugar according to birth facility routine, especially if Molly is jittery or lethargic. Feed her if blood sugar is at or below 45 mg/dl.	6. Nonshivering thermogenesis results in stores of glycogen being used. Infants may show tremors or lethargy as a result of hypoglycemia. Feeding provides calories for heat production.
7. Monitor for tachypnea or other signs of respiratory distress. Suction and apply oxygen if needed.	7. Nonshivering thermogenesis necessitates use of large amounts of oxygen, increases work of the respiratory system, and may lead to hypoxia.
8. If Molly is slow to warm or has repeated episodes of low temperature, alert physician or nurse practitioner.	8. Temperature instability is one sign of infection in newborns. Physician or nurse practitioner may order further tests, transfer to incubator, or other interventions.
9. When Molly is ready to go into an open crib, warm her clothes before dressing her. Place two warmed blankets, wrapped separately, around her. After she is swaddled, place one or two blankets over her.	9. Warming clothing and blankets keeps infant warm. Wrapping blankets separately permits air between layers, which acts as an insulating agent.
10. Remove extra blankets according to Molly's temperature.	10. Overheating causes use of oxygen and glucose and should be avoided.
11. Apply stockinette or insulated hat to head.	11. Covering the head prevents exposure of this large surface area, from which a great amount of heat can be lost.
12. After Molly is transferred to open crib, monitor for temperature changes every 30 to 60 minutes until stable.	12. Provides information about effectiveness of interventions and whether more intensive measures are needed.
13. Explain temperature maintenance and procedures to Catherine and Bill.	13. Explanations to parents provide reassurance and information.

Nursing Care Plan continued on following page

Nursing Care Plan 20–1 Continued

The Normal Newborn

14. Teach Catherine and Bill measures that can be taken to assist thermoregulation. Include sources of heat loss, how to avoid excessive exposure of infant during care, methods of wrapping and use of hat to prevent heat loss, and prompt changing of wet clothes and linens. Teach them how to take Molly's axillary temperature at home.	14. Teaching increases parents' competence in infant care.

Evaluation:
Molly's axillary temperature at 3 hours after delivery is 37°C (98.6°F). She has no further problems with temperature instability during her birth facility stay.

Assessment: Neither Catherine nor Bill have much experience with infants. They have many questions about how to take care of Molly.

Nursing Diagnosis: Health-Seeking Behaviors related to desire for information about infant care.

Goals:
Catherine and Bill will:
1. Identify their own information needs and seek assistance from nurses to meet those needs before discharge.
2. Correctly demonstrate safe infant care skills as appropriate to meet infant's needs before discharge.

Intervention:	Rationale:
1. Discuss areas of infant care to be taught with Catherine and Bill. Ask them to choose subjects about which they would like to learn more.	1. Involving parents in determining the learning content ensures their interest and cooperation. Determining their major concerns helps set priorities in the teaching plan. (Parents Want to Know Techniques for Infant Care can be used as a basis for teaching.)
2. Set the priorities in subject matter as determined by parents' concerns and observation of their needs. Start with a subject that is of most concern to them, even if it seems minor.	2. Discussing parents' most pressing needs first will enhance further learning by decreasing their anxiety so that they can concentrate on the information.
3. Use a variety of teaching methods.	3. Using a variety of teaching techniques increases effectiveness, makes the subject more interesting, and increases retention of the material.
4. Demonstrate infant care skills. Ask Catherine and Bill to do a return demonstration.	4. Demonstration allows parents to see the skill done correctly and then to practice it under supervision so that nurse can give suggestions and make corrections as needed.
5. Discuss information with Catherine alone or along with her family members, her roommate, or a group of mothers.	5. A woman may learn better having the complete attention of nurse to herself or may benefit from watching and listening to others. Group teaching allows nurse to make more efficient use of time.
6. Use audiovisual materials, including pamphlets, baby magazines, films or videos, and TV programs. Review the written material with Catherine to point out the most important parts, watch the videos with her, and clarify information as necessary.	6. Reviewing visual and written material with clients reinforces learning.
7. Explain rationale for each point made during teaching sessions.	7. Explanations about why information is important increase the likelihood that clients will follow nurse's instructions.

Nursing Care Plan 20–1 *Continued*

The Normal Newborn

Intervention:	Rationale:
8. Adapt routine teaching to meet the individual needs of Catherine and Bill. Refer to their baby by name, their home situation, and their wishes and plans.	8. Individualizing teaching makes it more relevant to parents' personal situation and avoids "canned" teaching. This increases parents' interest and retention because they feel that the material is pertinent to their own situation.
9. Use both planned teaching sessions and informal on-the-spot teaching throughout the day to meet needs as they are identified.	9. Use of planned teaching sessions allows nurse to prepare and set aside time for teaching. Teaching while other care is being given allows for reinforcement and addition of new material based on new needs and makes efficient use of nurse's time.
10. Ask questions often and encourage Catherine and Bill to ask questions.	10. Questions help clarify misconceptions and allow nurse to determine parents' understanding of the material.
11. Offer praise and encouragement frequently when Catherine and Bill ask questions, attempt to perform skills, etc. Make corrections gently by combining praise for what was done correctly with suggestions for improvement.	11. Praise helps parents feel that they are growing in ability to care for their baby, thus increasing their confidence. Parents are more likely to ask for additional help if they feel comfortable with nurse's response when they make mistakes.

Evaluation:

Catherine and Bill identify their learning needs and seek assistance as they need it from the staff. They are able to demonstrate safe infant care correctly and adapt care to meet Molly's needs. They express confidence in their ability to care for Molly when they go home.

Additional Nursing Diagnoses to Consider:

High Risk for Altered Parenting
High Risk for Infection

roid hormones allows normal growth and development of full intellect.

Galactosemia

Absence of the enzyme necessary for the conversion of the milk sugar galactose to glucose causes galactosemia. The condition results in damage to the liver, brain, and eyes and eventually causes death. Treatment includes elimination of milk from the diet.

Others

Screening may also be performed for sickle cell disease, thalassemia, maple syrup urine disease, homocystinuria, and other conditions. Knowing which conditions are included in testing will allow the nurse to include appropriate information in parent teaching.

Summary Concepts

- Nurses scan newborns for anomalies immediately after birth to detect serious abnormalities. If no problems are detected with quick scanning, a more detailed assessment is performed. Every part of the newborn must be carefully examined.
- Measurements are an important way to learn about growth before birth. Abnormal measurements alert the nurse that complications may occur.
- Prophylaxis against hemorrhagic disease of the newborn and ophthalmia neonatorum is prescribed by law. It is provided by an injection of vitamin K and erythromycin ophthalmic ointment.
- Assessment of cardiovascular status includes history, airway, heart sounds, color, pulses, and blood pressure.

- Nurses can prevent heat loss in newborns by keeping them dry and covered, avoiding contact between them and cold objects or surfaces, and keeping them away from drafts and outside windows and walls.
- Hypoglycemia can cause damage to the brain. In performing heel sticks for blood glucose, the nurse must choose the site carefully to avoid damage to the bone, nerves, or blood vessels of the heel.
- Important interventions for jaundice are to monitor for its occurrence, to be sure that the infant is feeding well, and to explain the process to the parents.
- The initial feeding provides information about the neonate's ability to coordinate sucking, swallowing, and breathing and tolerance to feeding.
- Newborns usually pass the first stool within 24 hours of birth. Feeding and taking a rectal temperature may stimulate stool passage. Absence of stool for 48 hours may signify an obstruction.
- The newborn's first void occurs within 24 to 48 hours. Infants void 2 to 6 times the first two days and 5 to 25 times daily thereafter.
- Teach parents with uncircumcised sons not to retract the foreskin until it becomes separate from the glans later in childhood.
- Teach parents of circumcised infants signs of complications and how to care for the area.
- Marks on the skin should be documented, including location, size, color, elevation, and texture. Explain marks to parents and offer emotional support if they are upset.
- The gestational age assessment provides an estimate of the infant's age since conception. It alerts the nurse to possible complications of age and development.
- Expect the infant to need nursing intervention for low temperature, elevated pulse and respirations, and excessive respiratory secretions during the first and second periods of reactivity. Between these periods, the infant will be in a deep sleep with relaxed muscle tone and no interest in feeding.
- Infection can best be prevented by scrupulous hand washing by staff and all who come in contact with newborns.
- Parents and nurses must work together to prevent kidnapping. Parents must know how to identify hospital staff. Nurses should be alert for suspicious behavior.

References and Readings

American Academy of Pediatrics and American College of Obstetricians and Gynecologists. (1992). *Guidelines for perinatal care* (3rd ed.). Elk Grove, Ill.: American Academy of Pediatrics.

Avery, G.B. (1987). *Neonatology: Pathophysiology and management of the newborn* (3rd ed.). Philadelphia: J.B. Lippincott.

Beachy, P., & Deacon, J. (1992). Preventing neonatal kidnapping. *Journal of Obstetric, Gynecologic, and Neonatal Nursing,* 21(1), 12–16.

Behrman, R.E. (1992). *Nelson textbook of pediatrics* (14th ed.). Philadelphia: W.B. Saunders.

Blackburn, S.T., & Loper, D.L. (1992). *Maternal, fetal, and neonatal physiology: A clinical perspective.* Philadelphia: W.B. Saunders.

Blackburn, S.T., & VandenBerg, K.A. (1993). Assessment and management of neonatal neurobehavioral development. In C. Kenner, A. Brueggemeyer, & L.P. Gunderson (Eds.), *Comprehensive neonatal nursing, a physiologic perspective.* Philadelphia: W.B. Saunders.

Cole, M.D. (1991). New factors associated with the incidence of hypoglycemia: A research study. *Neonatal Network,* 10(4), 47–50.

D'Avanzo, C.E. (1992). Bridging the cultural gap with Southeast Asians. *MCN: American Journal of Maternal Child Nursing,* 17(4), 204–208.

de Steuben, C. (1992). Breastfeeding and jaundice: A review. *Journal of Nurse-Midwifery,* 37(Suppl. 2), 59–66.

Dubowitz, L., & Dubowitz, V. (1977). *Gestational age of the newborn.* Reading, Mass.: Addison-Wesley.

Foster, R.L.R., Hunsberger, M.M., & Anderson, J.J.T. (1989). *Family-centered nursing care of children.* Philadelphia: W.B. Saunders.

Gomella, T.L. (Ed.). (1992). *Neonatology* (2nd ed.). Norwalk, Conn.: Appleton & Lange.

Gorrie, T.M. (1989). *A guide to the nursing of childbearing families.* Baltimore: Williams & Wilkins.

Harrison, L.L. (1990). Patient education in early postpartum discharge programs. *MCN: American Journal of Maternal Child Nursing,* 15(1), 39.

Kenner, C. (1990). Measuring neonatal assessment. *Neonatal Network,* 9(4), 17–22.

Kenner, C., Brueggemeyer, A., & Gunderson, L.P. (1993). *Comprehensive neonatal nursing, a physiologic perspective.* Philadelphia: W.B. Saunders.

Lund, M. (1990). Perspectives on newborn male circumcision. *Neonatal Network* 9(3), 7–11.

Marchette, L., Main, R., Redick, E., Bagg, A., & Leatherland, J. (1991). Pain reduction interventions during neonatal circumcision. *Nursing Research,* 40(4), 241–244.

Mattson, S., & Smith, J.E. (1993). *NAACOG core curriculum for maternal-newborn nursing.* Philadelphia: W.B. Saunders.

Merenstein, G.B., Gardner, S.L., & Blake, W.W. (1989). Heat balance. In G.B. Merenstein & S.L. Gardner (Eds.), *Handbook of neonatal intensive care.* St. Louis: C.V. Mosby.

Mudge, D., & Younger, J.B. (1989). The effects of topical lidocaine on infant response to circumcision. *Journal of Nurse-Midwifery,* 34(6), 335–340.

Park, M., & Lee, D. (1989). Normative oscillometric blood pressure values in the first five years in an office setting. *American Journal of Diseases of Children,* 143 (7), 860–864.

Vaughans, B. (1990). Early maternal-infant contact and neonatal thermoregulation. *Neonatal Network,* 8(5), 19–21.

Whaley, L.F., & Wong, D.L. (1991). *Nursing care of infants and children* (4th ed.). St. Louis: C.V. Mosby.

Wilkerson, N.N. (1989). A comprehensive look at hyperbilirubinemia. *MCN: American Journal of Maternal Child Nursing,* 14(1), 32–36.

21

Infant Feeding

Objectives

1. Identify the nutritional and fluid needs of the infant.
2. Compare the composition of breast milk with that of formula.
3. Explain important factors in choosing a method of infant feeding.
4. Explain the physiology of lactation.
5. Identify nursing management of initial and continued breastfeeding.
6. Describe nursing assessments and interventions for common problems in breastfeeding.
7. Describe nursing assessments and interventions in formula feeding.

Definitions

Colostrum • Breast fluid secreted during pregnancy and the first 2 to 3 days following childbirth.

Engorgement • Swelling of the breast resulting from increased blood flow and presence of milk.

Foremilk • First breast milk received in a feeding.

Hindmilk • Breast milk received nearer the end of a feeding; contains higher fat content than foremilk.

Latch-on • Attachment of the infant to the breast.

Let-down reflex • See **Milk-ejection** reflex.

Mastitis • Inflammation of the breast, usually caused by stasis of milk in the ducts or infection.

Mature milk • Breast milk that appears about 3 weeks after lactation begins.

Milk-ejection reflex • Release of milk from the alveoli into the ducts; also known as the **let-down reflex.**

Oxytocin • Hormone produced by the posterior pituitary gland that stimulates uterine contractions and the milk-ejection reflex; also prepared synthetically.

Prolactin • Anterior pituitary hormone that promotes growth of breast tissue and stimulates production of milk.

Transitional milk • Breast milk that appears between secretion of colostrum and mature milk.

Infant feeding is an important part of parenting. A large amount of time is spent feeding the infant, and a woman may derive much of her satisfaction as a mother from her perception of success with feeding. Helping the mother choose a feeding method and feel comfortable using it are important contributions of the nurse that require knowledge of the infant's nutritional needs and the techniques to meet those needs.

Nutritional Needs of the Newborn

Calories

The full-term newborn needs 110 to 120 kcal/kg (50 to 55 kcal/pound) of body weight each day. The infant must consume sufficient calories to meet energy needs, prevent use of body stores, and provide for growth. The diet should contain enough carbohydrate and fat so that dietary proteins are not used for energy, as this would decrease protein available for growth needs.

The average newborn weighs 3.4 kg (7.5 pounds). Breast milk and formulas used for the normal newborn contain 20 kcal/ounce. Therefore, the newborn requires approximately 19 to 21 ounces of breast milk or formula each day. Breastfeeding infants who feed every 2 to 3 hours need an average of 45 to 75 ml (1.5 to 2.5 ounces) at each feeding to meet caloric requirements. Formula-fed infants who feed every 3 to 4 hours need an average of 75 to 105 ml (2.5 to 3.5 ounces) at each feeding.

During the early days after birth, many infants lose 5 to 10 per cent of their birth weight. This is because of normal loss of extracellular water and because they frequently consume fewer than the number of calories required. The stomach capacity at birth is only 10 to 20 ml (⅓ to ⅔ ounces). This rapidly increases to 30 to 90 ml (1 to 3 ounces) by the end of the first week of life (Whaley and Wong, 1991). Therefore, the newborn's stomach is unable to hold the full amount required to meet calorie needs at first. In addition, newborns may fall asleep during feedings or sleep through feedings during the early days as they recover from birth. Infants usually regain the lost weight by age 10 days. This should be explained to parents.

Nutrients

The calories needed by the newborn are provided by carbohydrates, proteins, and fat in breast milk or formula. Full-term neonates digest simple carbohydrates and proteins well. Fats are less well digested because of the lack of pancreatic amylase in the newborn. Vitamins and minerals are provided by both breast milk and formula.

Water

The newborn needs much larger amounts of fluid in relationship to size than does the adult because body composition is 78 per cent water as compared to 60 per cent water in the adult. Infants also lose water more easily from the skin, kidneys, and intestines. As a result, they must take in fluids equal to 10 to 15 per cent of their body weight each day, whereas adults need a daily intake of only 2 to 4 per cent of their body weight (Behrman, 1992). The normal newborn needs 60 to 80 ml/kg (27 to 36 ml/pound) daily for the first 2 days of life, and then needs 100 to 150 ml/kg (45 to 68 ml/pound) a day (D'Harlingue and Byrne, 1991). Breast milk or formula supplies the infant's fluid needs. Additional water is unnecessary.

Breast Milk and Formula Composition

Breast Milk

Breast milk is species-specific for human infants and offers many advantages over formula. The nutrients in breast milk are proportioned appropriately for the neonate and change to meet the newborn's changing needs. Breast milk provides protection against infection and is easily digested. Table 21–1 compares breast milk and formulas according to the recommended nutrient intake for infants.

CHANGES IN COMPOSITION

The composition of breast milk changes in three phases: colostrum, transitional milk, and mature milk, which vary in makeup to meet the newborn's changing nutritional needs.

Critical to Remember

Daily Calorie and Fluid Needs of the Newborn

- Calories: 110 to 120 kcal/kg
- Fluid: 60 to 80 ml/kg (first 2 days of life)
  100 to 150 ml/kg (after first 2 days of life)

Table 21–1. COMPARISON OF RECOMMENDED DIETARY ALLOWANCES WITH INFANT MILKS PER DECILITER

Nutrient	Recommended Dietary Allowances (Infants to 6 Months)	Mature Human Milk	Cow's Milk	Modified Cow's Milk Formulas
Protein (g)	13	1	3.3	1.5
Fat (g)		4.5	3.3	3.6
Vitamin A (IU)	1238	190–240	310	203
Vitamin D (IU)	300	2.2	4.2	41
Vitamin C (mg)	30	4.3–5	0.8	5.4
Thiamin (mg)	0.3	0.14	0.04	0.06
Riboflavin (mg)	0.4	0.37	0.17	1.01
Niacin (mg)	5	0.15–0.18	0.08	0.7
Calcium (mg)	400	33	121	51
Phosphorus (mg)	300	15	95	39
Iron (mg)	6	0.02	0.04	0.12
Sodium (mg)	120	16	50	22

Data from Institute of Medicine, National Academy of Sciences, Food and Nutrition Board. (1991). *Nutrition during lactation.* Washington, D.C.: National Academy Press; Mahan, L.K., & Arlin, M.T. (1992). *Krause's food, nutrition, and diet therapy* (8th ed.). Philadelphia: W.B. Saunders; Merenstein, G. B., & Gardner, S.L. (1989). *Handbook of neonatal intensive care* (2nd ed.). St. Louis: C.V. Mosby.

Colostrum. The major secretion of the breasts during the first week of lactation is colostrum, a thick, yellow substance. Colostrum is higher in protein, fat-soluble vitamins, and minerals than mature milk but lower in calories, fat, and lactose. It is rich in immunoglobulins, especially secretory IgA, which helps protect the infant's gastrointestinal tract from infection. Colostrum helps establish the normal intestinal flora in the intestines, and its laxative effect speeds the passage of meconium.

Transitional Milk. Transitional milk appears by 7 to 10 days after lactation begins. Transitional milk is secreted during the period that the milk is changing from colostrum to mature milk. The composition changes to meet the infant's needs. Immunoglobulins and proteins decrease while lactose, fat, and calories increase. The vitamin content is approximately the same as that of mature milk.

Mature Milk. After the first 2 weeks of lactation, mature milk replaces transitional milk. Because breast milk is bluish and not as thick as colostrum, some mothers may think that their milk is not "rich" enough for the infant. Nurses should explain the normal appearance of breast milk to mothers. Mature milk contains approximately 20 kcal/ounce and nutrients sufficient to meet the infant's needs. In general, discussions of breast milk and its contents refer to mature milk unless otherwise stated.

NUTRIENTS

Although pure cow's milk is not given to infants in developed countries, it forms the base for most infant formulas. Comparing human milk with cow's milk demonstrates the adaptations that are necessary to produce infant formulas.

Protein. The concentrations of various amino acids in breast milk are suited to the infant's needs and ability to metabolize them. Breast milk contains a high level of taurine, which is important for bile formation and brain development. Tyrosine and phenylalanine are low in breast milk to correspond to the infant's low enzyme levels for digesting them. The proteins produce a lower solute load for the infant's immature kidneys than the proteins in cow's milk.

Casein and whey are the proteins in milk. Casein forms a large, insoluble curd that is harder to digest than the curd from whey, which is very soft. Breast milk is more easily digested because of the higher ratio of whey to casein in human milk than in cow's milk. The larger proportion of casein in cow's milk results in a curd that takes longer to digest and is less completely digested. Commercial formulas must be adapted so that the percentage of whey is increased to make the curd more digestible.

The body's immune system recognizes and may react to the protein in cow's milk, making it one of the most common allergens. Allergies develop in approximately 3 to 5 per cent of infants fed cow's milk formula (Adams, 1992). Because breast milk is made for the human infant, it will not cause allergies (Lawrence, 1989). This knowledge is of particular importance when there is a family history of allergies.

Carbohydrate. The major carbohydrate in breast milk is lactose. Its higher level in breast milk may improve absorption of calcium, which is necessary for the development of bones and teeth (Lawrence, 1989). Lactose also promotes growth of the normal bacterial flora in the intestines.

Fat. Thirty to fifty-five per cent of the calories in breast milk are from fat. The fat composition of human milk differs greatly from that of cow's milk. The majority of fat is in the form of triglycerides, with higher amounts of several essential fatty acids. Cholesterol is also higher in breast milk than in cow's milk. The high level may be necessary to aid in the development of the central nervous system.

The amount of fat in breast milk varies during the feeding and according to the time of day. There is more fat present in the hindmilk, the milk produced at the end of the feeding, than at the beginning. The hindmilk produces satiety and helps the infant gain weight. Fat is also increased in breast milk during the middle of the day.

Vitamins. The vitamin content varies between human and cow's milk as well. Vitamin C must be added to commercial formulas to match the levels in human milk, which meet the infant's needs if the mother has an adequate intake. Vitamin D may be inadequate if the mother's diet is poor and/or she is not exposed to the sun. The pediatrician may recommend supplementation of vitamin D for the breastfed infant.

Minerals. Although iron in breast milk is lower than in formula, approximately 50 per cent is absorbed, compared with only 7 per cent of that in iron-fortified formula (Institute of Medicine, 1991). The increased absorption may be due to the higher lactose and vitamin C content in breast milk. The infant who is breastfed exclusively maintains iron stores for the first 6 months of life. However, the addition of formula or other foods may decrease the absorption of iron, making supplementation necessary.

Sodium, calcium, and phosphorus are higher in cow's milk than in human milk. This could cause an excessively high renal solute load if formula is not diluted properly. The amount of fluoride in breast milk is not influenced by the mother's diet. Fluoride supplements are often given to all infants if the water supply does not have adequate amounts (Institute of Medicine, 1991).

ENZYMES

Breast milk contains enzymes that aid in digestion. For example, salivary and pancreatic amylase, which is necessary to digest fats, is not developed in the newborn, but the enzyme is present in breast milk. Lipase in the milk helps the infant to digest the fat almost completely.

INFECTION-PREVENTING COMPONENTS

Other factors present in human milk help prevent infection in the newborn. *Bifidus factor* promotes the growth of *Lactobacillus bifidus*, an important part of the intestinal flora that helps produce an acid environment in the gastrointestinal tract. This protects the infant against infection from common intestinal pathogens.

Leukocytes present in breast milk also help protect against infection. Macrophages are most abundant and secrete lysozyme and lactoferrin. *Lysozyme* is a bacteriolytic enzyme that acts against gram-positive and enteric bacteria. *Lactoferrin* is a protein that binds iron in iron-dependent bacteria, such as staphylococcus and *Escherichia coli*, preventing their growth. It also acts against *Candida albicans*. Giving infants supplementary iron may interfere with the effectiveness of lactoferrin.

Immunoglobulins are present in highest amounts in colostrum but are present throughout lactation. Higher levels occur when the infant is born prematurely. Lymphocytes in the milk produce secretory IgA, which helps prevent viral or bacterial invasion of the intestinal mucosa, resulting in fewer intestinal infections in breastfed than in formula-fed infants. This protection is especially important, as the infant does not produce adequate amounts of IgA in the intestinal tract until 4 to 6 weeks of age. IgA also prevents absorption of foreign molecules that might precipitate development of allergies.

EFFECT OF MATERNAL DIET

Although the fatty acid content of breast milk is influenced by the mother's diet, malnourished mothers have about the same proportions of protein, carbohydrates, and most minerals as those who are well nourished. However, levels of vitamins in breast milk are affected by the mother's intake and stores. It is important that breastfeeding women eat a well-balanced diet to maintain their own health and energy levels. (Nutrition for the lactating mother is discussed in Chapter 9, p. 205.)

Formulas

Commercial formulas are produced to replace or supplement breast milk. Manufacturers adapt commercial formulas to correspond with the components in breast milk as much as possible, although an exact match is not possible. A variety of formulas that differ in price and ingredients are available.

COW'S MILK

Modified cow's milk is the source of approximately 80 per cent of commercial formulas. Manufacturers specifically formulate it for infants by reducing protein to decrease renal solute load. Saturated fat is removed and replaced with vegetable fats. Vitamins and other nutrients are added to simulate the contents of breast milk. Examples of formulas are Similac (Ross), Enfamil (Mead Johnson), and SMA (Wyeth). These formulas are also available with added iron.

FORMULAS FOR ALLERGIC INFANTS

Infants who have formula intolerance or allergies or come from families in which allergies are prevalent are given soy or protein hydrolysate formulas. Soy milk is derived from the protein of soybeans and supplemented with amino acids. It is also used for infants unable to tolerate lactose. Examples of soy formulas are ProSobee (Mead Johnson) and Isomil (Ross)

Many infants with cow's milk allergy are also allergic to soy formulas. Protein hydrolysate formulas are more universally tolerated by infants with allergies. The protein in these cow's milk–based formulas is treated so that they are hypoallergenic. Nutramigen (Mead Johnson) is an example of a casein hydrolysate formula. These formulas are also used for infants with fat malabsorption.

SPECIAL FORMULAS

Some formulas are designed to meet the needs of infants with special problems. The preterm infant may require a more concentrated formula with more calories in less liquid, such as Enfamil Premature and Similac Special Care. Specific nutrients are added for the preterm infant's higher requirements in a more easily digestible form. Human milk fortifiers, such as Similac Natural Care, are designed to be added to human milk to adapt it to the special needs of preterm infants. Formulas such as Pregestimil (Mead Johnson) are produced for infants with gastrointestinal problems. Lofenalac (Mead Johnson) is low in the amino acid phenylalanine and is given to infants with phenylketonuria (PKU), who are deficient in the enzyme and cannot use phenylalanine found in standard formulas.

✔ Check Your Reading

1. Why do some newborns lose weight after birth?
2. What are the differences between colostrum, transitional milk, and mature breast milk?
3. How does breast milk compare to commercial formulas?
4. What factors does breast milk contain that help prevent infection?
5. What types of commercial formulas are available?

Considerations in Choosing a Feeding Method

Whereas some mothers decide on a feeding method well ahead of delivery, others may have questions until late in their pregnancy about which method is best for them and their families. The nurse plays a major part in helping mothers decide on a method and gain confidence in feeding their infants.

It is very important for nurses to be sensitive to mothers' feelings about feeding. Although nurses should encourage breastfeeding, they should be supportive of the mother's chosen method once the decision is made. The early days of parenting are a very vulnerable time for new mothers, who may feel that their feeding ability reflects on their mothering ability. The nurse's teaching and encouragement about the chosen feeding method will increase their self-confidence.

Breastfeeding

Breastfeeding offers many advantages, which are summarized in Table 21–2. Although it was once the major method of feeding, in 1988 only 54 per cent of mothers were breastfeeding at discharge from the birth facility and only 21 per cent were still breastfeeding at 5 to 6 months (U.S. Department of Health

Table 21–2. BENEFITS OF BREASTFEEDING

For the Infant

No allergic reaction to breast milk
Immunological properties help prevent infections; infant likely to have fewer respiratory and gastrointestinal infections and upsets
Composition meets infant's specific nutritional needs
Nutritional and immunological properties change according to infant's needs
Breast milk easily digested
Protein, fat, and carbohydrate in most suitable proportions
No possibility of improper (and potentially dangerous) dilution
Breast milk unlikely to be contaminated; not affected by water supply
Less likely to result in overfeeding

For the Mother

Oxytocin release enhances involution of uterus
She is more likely to rest while feeding
She is likely to eat balanced diet that improves healing
Helps with postpartum weight loss
Frequent, close contact may enhance bonding
Convenient: always available, no bottles to prepare, no formula to buy or heat
Economical: eliminates cost of formula and bottles
Traveling is easy: no bottles to prepare, carry, refrigerate or warm

and Human Services, 1991). The advent of refrigeration, the development of commercial formulas, and the increased incidence of maternal employment led to an increase in the number of mothers choosing formula feeding. In addition, advertisements by formula companies and formula gift packs given to mothers at hospital discharge, which may imply an expectation that nursing mothers will need formula, have aided the move away from breastfeeding.

Yet it has been increasingly recognized that formula feeding can never fully equal breastfeeding in terms of providing for the infant's optimal growth and development. Both the American Academy of Pediatrics and the U.S. Surgeon General recommend breastfeeding. A goal set by the U.S. Department of Health and Human Services (USDHHS) for the year 2000 is for 75 per cent of all new mothers to breastfeed at the time of birth facility discharge and for at least 50 per cent to continue breastfeeding for 5 to 6 months (USDHHS, 1991).

Formula Feeding

Mothers choose formula feeding for many reasons. Some mothers are embarrassed by breastfeeding, seeing the breast only in a sexual context. Many mothers have little experience with family or friends who have had positive breastfeeding experiences. Some women feel a need to maintain a strict feeding schedule and are uneasy not knowing exactly how much milk the infant will take at each feeding. A mother who has many other commitments may feel that formula feeding would meet her needs best. Some women may require medications that enter breast milk and are harmful to the infant. A frequent reason that mothers choose formula feeding instead of breastfeeding may be a lack of adequate knowledge about the two methods.

Combination Feeding

Some parents find that a combination of breastfeeding and bottle feeding works best. It is best to delay this until lactation has been well established at 3 to 4 weeks, if possible. Either breast milk or formula may be used when the infant is given a bottle. The mother may give a bottle routinely each day or only occasionally, such as when a baby-sitter is with the infant. This method allows the mother some freedom to be away from the infant for longer periods of time, yet allows the closeness with the infant that many mothers enjoy, as well as the physical advantages of breastfeeding, to continue.

Factors Influencing Choice

CULTURE

Cultural influences may dictate decisions about whether to breastfeed and how and when a mother feeds her infant. For example, many Mormon women believe that breastfeeding is an important part of motherhood. In some Asian and Latino cultures, mothers give their infants formula while in the birth facility and do not begin to breastfeed until at home. This may be due to modesty and embarrassment about nursing in front of others in the birth facility, as well as lack of understanding about the value of colostrum. Women in some cultures feel that colostrum may be "spoiled" because it has been in the breasts for a long time. They may manually express colostrum and discard it before they begin to breastfeed the infant.

Some mothers may be amenable to nursing the infant with help while in the birth facility, especially if the antibody and laxative properties of colostrum are explained. Breastfeeding involves a learning process for both mother and infant, and this is best started in the birth facility, where assistance is available. Nurses can help mothers learn by offering to help them "practice" breastfeeding at least a few times before discharge. This helps build their confidence and allows for early identification and correction of problems. If the mother is firm in her desire to wait until discharge to begin breastfeeding, nurses can support her by teaching her what she will need to know when she goes home. Cultural values about feeding, as about other areas of health care, must be respected.

Some women who are immigrants to the United States from countries where breastfeeding is the norm may breastfeed for shorter durations or not at all because they lack the support system they had in their own country. In addition, formula feeding may be seen as a symbol of the new way of life. For example, Southeast Asian mothers born in their own country are more likely to breastfeed their infants than those born in the United States (Serdula et al, 1991). Ethiopian women often breastfeed for more than a year in their home country but may breastfeed for much shorter periods when they come to the United States (Meftuh et al, 1991). Nurses should be particularly watchful for ways to help mothers from other cultures who might wish to breastfeed but fail to do so because of lack of support.

EMPLOYMENT

The need to return to work outside the home soon after birth may cause concern about feeding methods. The mother may feed the infant formula from the beginning, plan on a short period of breastfeeding before weaning the infant to formula, or use a combination of breastfeeding and bottle feeding. Nurses help mothers look at their options, if the decision is not firm, and support them once it is made. Mothers may need information about ways to combine breastfeeding and working, using breast pumps (see p. 585), and storage of breast milk. Pamphlets and books for the working breastfeeding mother will be particularly helpful.

SUPPORT FROM OTHERS

Friends and family members may also share in the decision-making process. The mother with little support or with active discouragement from her family will probably have a difficult time nursing. Involvement of the father in feedings is important in some families and may be thought possible only if he can give a bottle regularly. Nurses can suggest other ways that fathers can participate in infant care, such as holding and rocking.

The support that the mother receives from the nursing staff is also important in whether or not she feels comfortable with the feeding method she chooses. This is especially true for breastfeeding mothers. Those who do not feel confident in their ability to breastfeed before they leave the birth facility are less likely to continue breastfeeding if they encounter difficulties at home.

✔ Check Your Reading

6. What factors influence a woman's choice of feeding method?

Normal Breastfeeding

To be most helpful to lactating mothers, the nurse must have a good understanding of the physiology of lactation, including changes occurring during pregnancy and those which cause milk production after birth. The anatomy and physiology of the breast are discussed in Chapter 4 (p. 63), and breast changes occurring in pregnancy are discussed in full in Chapter 7 (p. 119) (see Figs. 4–8 and 7–3).

Breast Changes During Pregnancy

Breast changes begin early in pregnancy with development of the ducts, lobules, and alveoli in response to the hormones estrogen, progesterone, placental lactogen, prolactin, and chorionic gonadotropin. The breasts begin to secrete colostrum by the second trimester, and women who deliver infants after the 16th week of gestation will produce colostrum (Lawrence, 1989). During pregnancy, the anterior pituitary secretes high levels of prolactin, the hormone that causes the breasts to produce milk. However, milk production is prevented by estrogen, progesterone, and placental lactogen, which inhibit breast response to prolactin.

Milk Production

Milk is produced in the alveoli of the breasts through a complex process by which materials are removed from the mother's blood stream and reformulated into breast milk. Thus, amino acids, glucose, lipids, enzymes, leukocytes, and other materials are used to manufacture the various proteins, carbohydrates, fats, and other substances needed to nourish and protect the infant. Most milk is synthesized during the time that the infant is suckling, although a small amount is made between feedings and stored for the next feeding (Lawrence, 1989).

The milk is ejected from the secretory cells of the alveoli into the alveolar lumen by contraction of the myoepithelial cells. From there, it travels into the lactiferous ducts, which lead from the alveoli to the nipple. The ducts widen in the area of the areola to become the lactiferous sinuses (or ampullae), which the infant compresses during nursing to eject a stream of milk through pores in the nipple.

Hormonal Changes at Birth

PROLACTIN

Separation of the placenta and suckling of the infant are responsible for initiation of lactation. Loss of progesterone, estrogen, and placental lactogen from the placenta results in increasing levels and effectiveness of prolactin and brings about milk production. The tactile stimulation of suckling further increases prolactin output.

OXYTOCIN

The hormone oxytocin, from the posterior pituitary, increases in response to nipple stimulation as well. Oxytocin causes the milk ejection reflex, commonly known as the let-down reflex. The resulting contraction of myoepithelial cells around the alveoli releases milk into the ducts, making it available to the infant.

Oxytocin levels increase in some mothers when they see their infant or hear their infant's cry, bringing about a let-down of milk. Pain or lack of relaxation can inhibit oxytocin release. Helping the mother find a comfortable position and relieving her pain will help the let-down reflex occur more quickly. Oxytocin is also responsible for the uterine contractions mothers may feel at the beginning of nursing sessions, hastening involution of the uterus (Fig. 21–1).

Continued Milk Production

The amount of milk produced depends primarily on adequate stimulation of the breast by suckling or use of a breast pump, which causes production of prolactin. This "supply and demand" effect continues throughout lactation; that is, increased demand with more frequent and longer nursing results in more milk available for the infant.

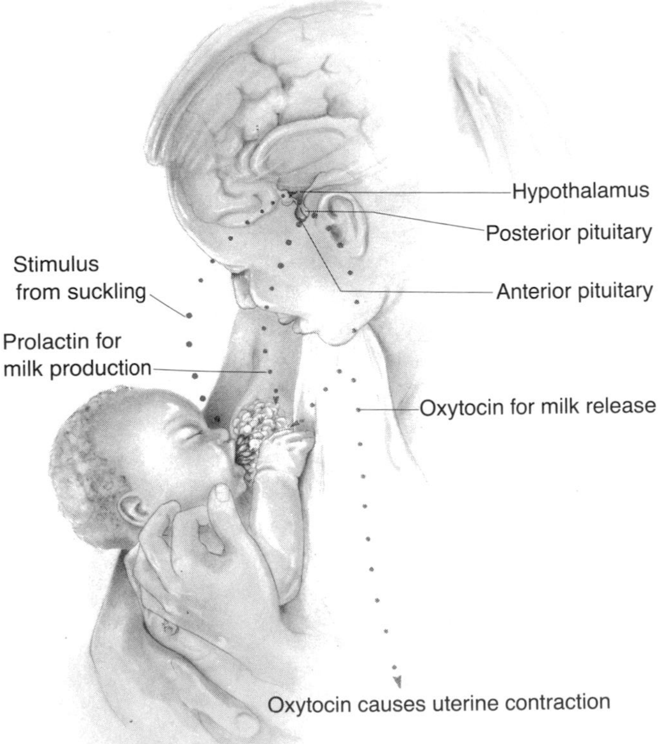

Figure 21–1

Effect of prolactin and oxytocin on milk production. When the infant begins to suckle at the breast, nerve impulses travel to the hypothalamus, which causes the anterior pituitary to secrete prolactin to increase milk production. Suckling also causes the posterior pituitary to secrete oxytocin, producing the let-down reflex, which releases milk from the breast. Oxytocin also causes the uterus to contract, which aids in involution.

If milk (or colostrum) is not removed from the breasts, the alveoli become very distended and blood flow is reduced as a result of pressure on the vessels. Diminished blood flow prevents prolactin from reaching the secretory cells and eventually prevents further milk production. The milk in the ducts is absorbed, the alveoli become smaller, and the cells return to a resting state.

Preparation of Breasts for Breastfeeding

Little preparation is needed during pregnancy for breastfeeding. The mother should avoid soap on the nipples to prevent removal of the natural protective oils from the Montgomery tubercles of the breasts. The use of creams, nipple rolling, pulling, and rubbing to "toughen" nipples will not necessarily decrease nipple pain after delivery and may cause irritation or uterine contraction from release of oxytocin. In addition, some women feel that extensive nipple preparation is too much trouble or distasteful, and they may decide not to breastfeed if they feel that this preparation is necessary.

The breasts should be assessed during pregnancy to identify flat or inverted nipples (Fig. 21–2). Normally, the nipples protrude. Flat nipples appear soft, like the areola, and do not stand erect unless stimulated by rolling them between the fingers. Nipples may also be inverted, or drawn into the breast tissue. Both conditions make it difficult for infants to draw the nipples into the mouth. Some nipples appear normal but draw inward when the areola is compressed. Compressing the areola between the thumb and the forefinger will determine whether the nipple projects normally or becomes inverted.

Women with flat or inverted nipples use breast shells (also called breast cups), which are worn in the bra with the opening over the nipple (Fig. 21–3). The shells exert pressure against the tissue around the nipples and help the nipples protrude. They can be used during pregnancy and after the birth. Hoffman's exercises may also be used to help loosen adhesions that cause inversion of the nipple (Fig. 21–4). These exercises can be used throughout pregnancy if there is no indication of preterm labor.

✔ Check Your Reading

7. What is the effect of suckling on the let-down reflex and milk production?
8. How does the principle of "supply and demand" apply to breastfeeding?
9. What preparation of the breasts is needed during pregnancy?

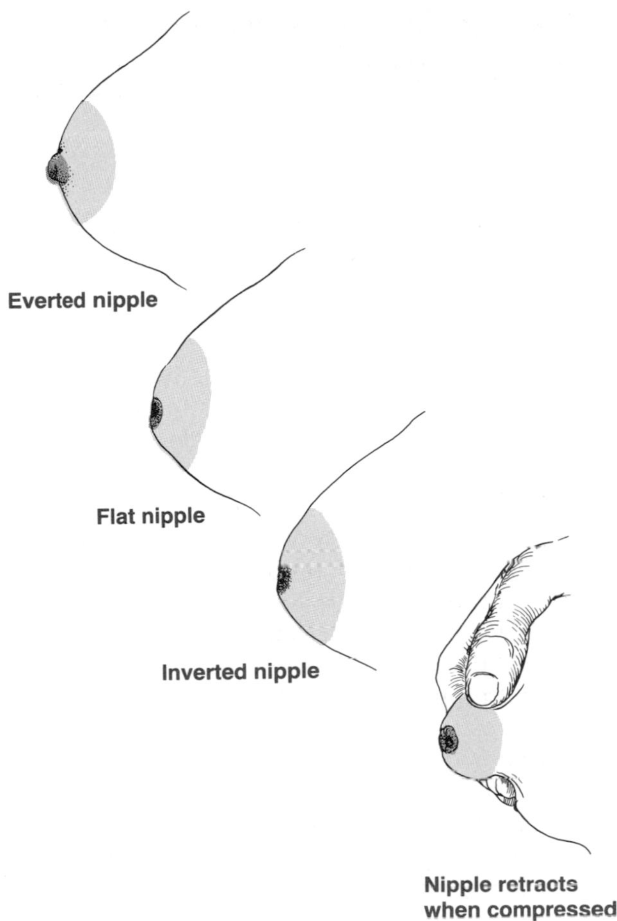

Figure 21–2

Protruding nipple and conditions that may cause the infant difficulty grasping the nipple.

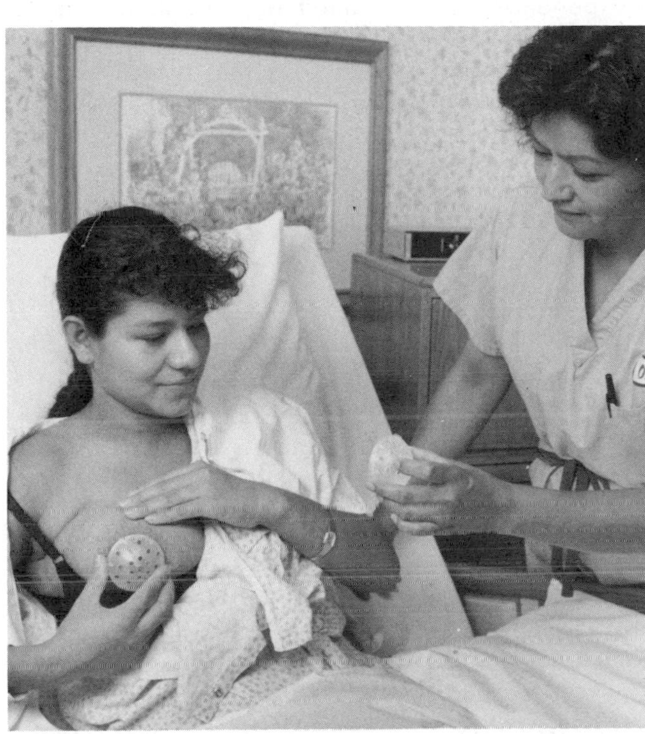

Figure 21–3

The nurse shows the mother how to position breast shells over her nipples to help them protrude.

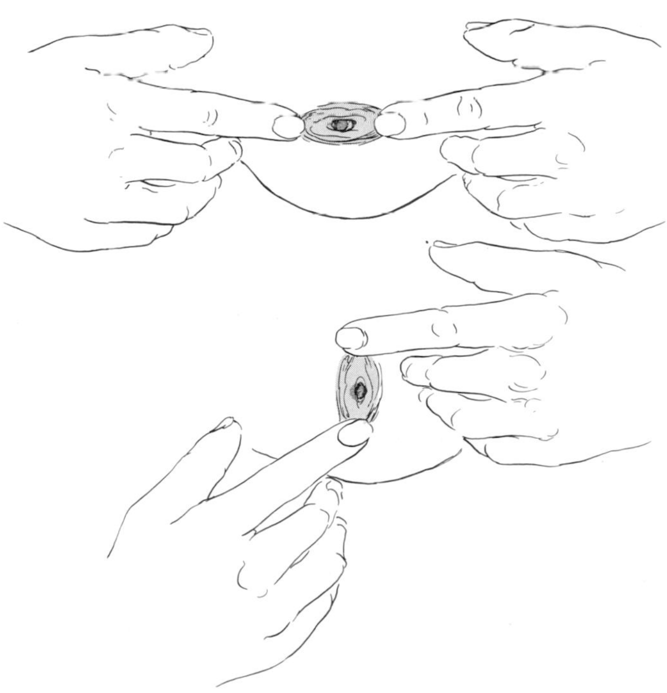

Figure 21–4

In Hoffman's exercise, the fingers are placed on the areola and gently pulled apart to stretch the tissue. This helps release adhesions that may cause the nipple to be inverted. The exercise is repeated with the fingers moved all around the areola.

Breastfeeding: Application of Nursing Process

Assessment

The nurse must assess both the mother and the infant during the breastfeeding process.

MATERNAL ASSESSMENT

Assess the condition of the breasts and nipples and the mother's knowledge of and experience with breastfeeding. The mother's needs for assistance can thus be determined.

Breasts and Nipples. Examine the breasts and nipples during pregnancy so that problems that might interfere with feeding can be corrected before delivery. However, if this has not occurred, examine the breasts and nipples before the initial feeding. Assess the protrusion of the nipples to identify flat or inverted nipples.

Ongoing assessments include identification of engorgement, the swelling of the breasts that may occur early in lactation as a result of increased blood circulation and the pressure of the newly produced milk. Engorgement may also occur if the infant is not fed frequently enough. Palpate the breasts to see if they are soft, filling, or engorged. Soft breasts feel like a cheek. If milk is beginning to come in, the breasts may be slightly firmer, which is charted as "filling." Engorged breasts are hard and tender, with taut, shiny skin. Note any redness, tenderness, or lumps within the breasts.

Assess the nipples for skin integrity. Nipples may be red, bruised, or blistered; may have fissures; or may bleed. Ask about tenderness of the nipples and when it occurs. Evaluate the breastfeeding techniques of the mother having problems with her nipples.

Knowledge. Assess the mother's knowledge of breastfeeding techniques. The mother breastfeeding her first infant may have many questions and may need substantial guidance during her first attempts. Although the mother who has nursed before may have a better understanding of breastfeeding, she may have questions or have forgotten some aspects. Current information about breastfeeding may have been unavailable when she breastfed her last infant.

INFANT FEEDING BEHAVIORS

Assess the infant's readiness for feeding before initiating a breastfeeding session. The infant should be awake and hungry. Trying to feed an infant in a deep sleep period will be frustrating to both mother and infant. On the other hand, waiting too long to start the feeding can cause the infant to be too upset to feed well. Sucking on the hands, rooting when the cheek or side of the mouth is touched, and slight fussiness are signs that the infant is ready for feeding.

Analysis

Inexperienced mothers need teaching about breastfeeding. In addition, mothers who have nursed before may have misconceptions that could result in ineffective breastfeeding if not corrected. Therefore, the most common nursing diagnosis for the breastfeeding mother is *High Risk for Ineffective Breastfeeding related to lack of knowledge of breastfeeding techniques.*

Planning

The goals for this nursing diagnosis are:

- The infant will breastfeed using nutritive suckling for at least 10 minutes at each breast at each feeding before discharge.
- The mother will demonstrate breastfeeding techniques as taught before discharge.
- The mother will verbalize satisfaction and confidence with the breastfeeding process before discharge.

Interventions

The interventions are centered around the teaching that nurses should provide to all inexperienced breastfeeding mothers and should be adapted as appropriate for mothers who have some knowledge of breastfeeding but need review or clarification. Interventions used for the first feeding session are summarized in Keys to Clinical Practice: Assisting the Inexperienced Breastfeeding Mother (see Appendix E, p. 984).

ASSISTING WITH FIRST FEEDING

The first feeding should take place within the first 1 to 2 hours after birth if both mother and infant are stable. Ideally, it occurs immediately after birth, when infants are in an alert state and many begin to nurse immediately. Others may nuzzle, lick, or suck intermittently at the breast, all of which stimulate production of prolactin necessary for lactation. Feed-

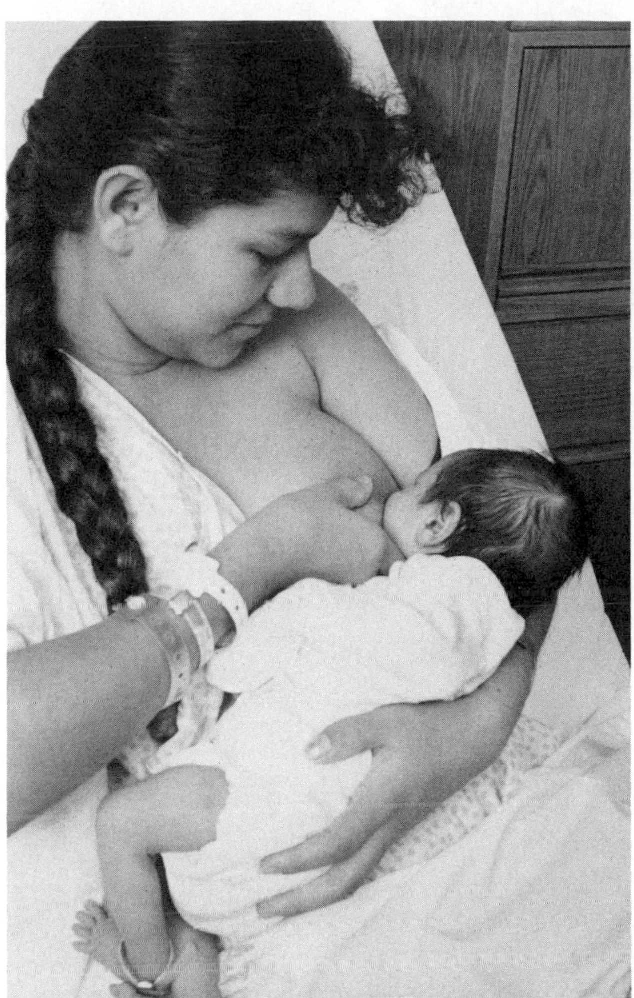

Figure 21–5

For the cradle hold, the mother positions the infant's head at or near the antecubital space and level with her nipple with her arm supporting the infant's body. Her other hand is free to hold the breast. Once the infant is positioned, pillows or blankets can be used to support the mother's arm, which may tire from holding the baby.

ing at this time also helps establish early bonding. It may be very gratifying to a mother to see her infant nurse immediately after birth.

Help the mother move to her side or into Fowler's position. Show her how to hold the breast and explain proper positioning of the infant. This will be a short session, and teaching should be repeated at the next feeding for reinforcement.

Some mothers are fatigued or uncomfortable after birth and prefer to wait until later to nurse. Mothers who have had a cesarean birth may prefer to postpone the first feeding for a short time. Breastfeeding should be initiated as soon as possible once the mother's needs for rest and comfort measures have been met. Whenever the first feeding occurs, it is a time for assessment of the mother's knowledge and technique. Teaching at this time will help prevent problems later.

TEACHING FEEDING TECHNIQUES

The nurse must teach the new mother many feeding techniques.

Position

Both the mother and the infant must be positioned properly for optimum breastfeeding. Make the mother as comfortable as possible before she begins to nurse. Pain or an awkward position may interfere with the let-down reflex and cause her to tire. Prevent interruptions and provide privacy so that the mother can concentrate on learning the techniques that she will need.

The side-lying position is the most common along with the cradle, football, and cross-cradle holds (Figs. 21–5 to 21–8). For each position, use pillows behind the mother's back to protect an abdominal incision or to increase her comfort. Arrange folded blankets or pillows to elevate the infant to the level of the nipple so that there is no pulling and tension on the nipple, which would causes it to become sore. The infant's head and body should directly face the breast (Fig. 21–9). If the infant must turn the head to reach the breast, swallowing is difficult. The neck should be flexed because hyperextension also makes swallowing difficult.

Hand Position

The mother's hand position is also important. She should hold her hand in a "C" position around her breast with the thumb on top behind the areola and the fingers against the chest wall and supporting the underside of the breast (Fig. 21–10). Be sure that her fingers are behind the areola. If they are on the areola, the infant may not be able to get enough of the areola into the mouth and will suck only on the nipple.

Some experienced mothers have used the "scissors hold" in the past. They use the forefinger and middle finger to support the breast during feedings. This increases the risk that the fingers will slip down the wet areola and interfere with the placement of the infant's mouth. However, if the mother prefers this position, show her how to do it correctly by placing her fingers well back on the breast.

Although mothers worry about the infant's ability to breathe while nursing, it is seldom necessary to

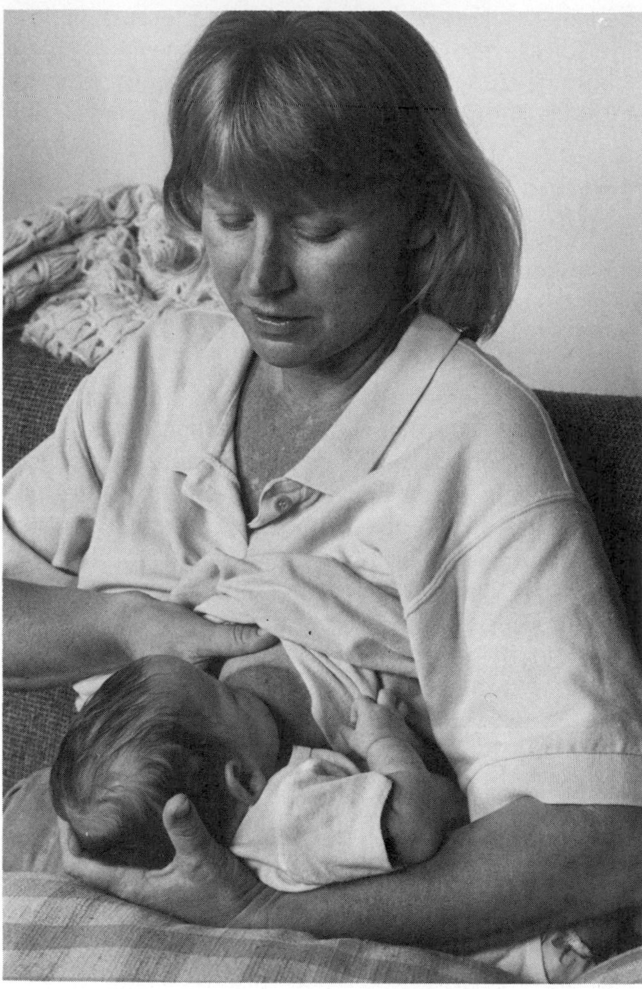

***Figure* 21–6**

For the football hold, the mother supports the infant's head in her hand, with the body resting on pillows alongside her hip. This method allows the mother to see the position of the infant's mouth on the breast, helps her control the head, and is especially helpful for mothers with heavy breasts. This hold also avoids pressure against an abdominal incision.

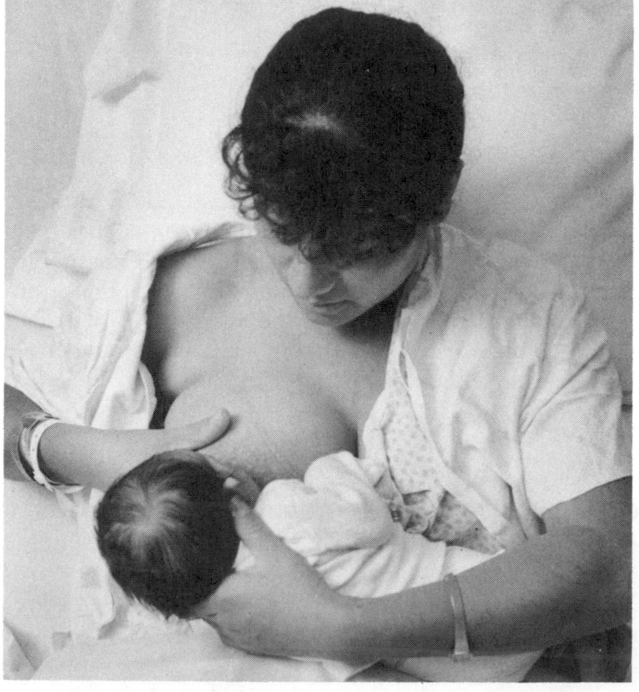

***Figure* 21–7**

The cross-cradle hold is helpful for the very small or preterm infant. The mother holds the infant's head in the hand opposite from the breast on which the infant will feed, with the arm supporting the infant's body across her lap. The other hand holds the breast. This position allows the mother to guide the infant's head to the breast, support it during the feeding, and see the infant's mouth on the breast.

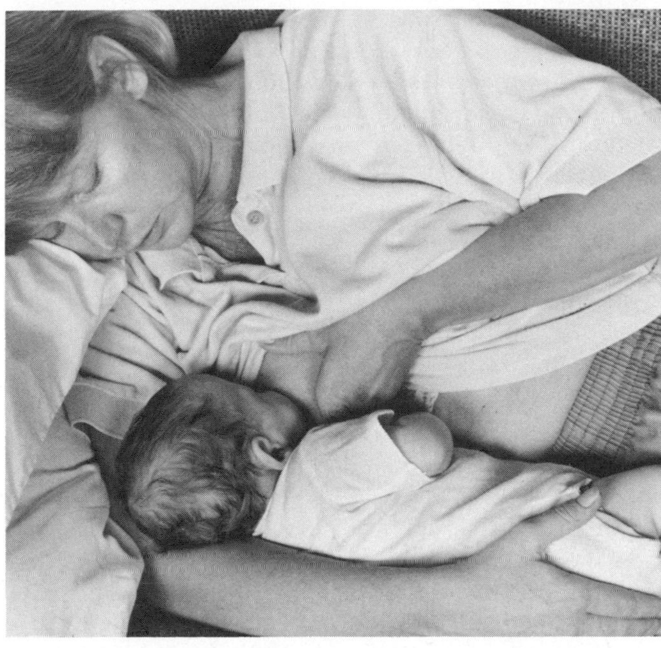

Figure 21–8

The side-lying position avoids pressure on episiotomy or abdominal incisions and allows the mother to rest while feeding. She lies on her side, with the lower arm supporting her head or placed around the infant. A pillow behind her back and between her legs provides comfort. Her upper hand and arm are used to position the infant on his side at nipple level and hold the breast. When the infant's mouth opens to nurse, the mother leans slightly forward or draws the infant to her to insert the nipple into the mouth.

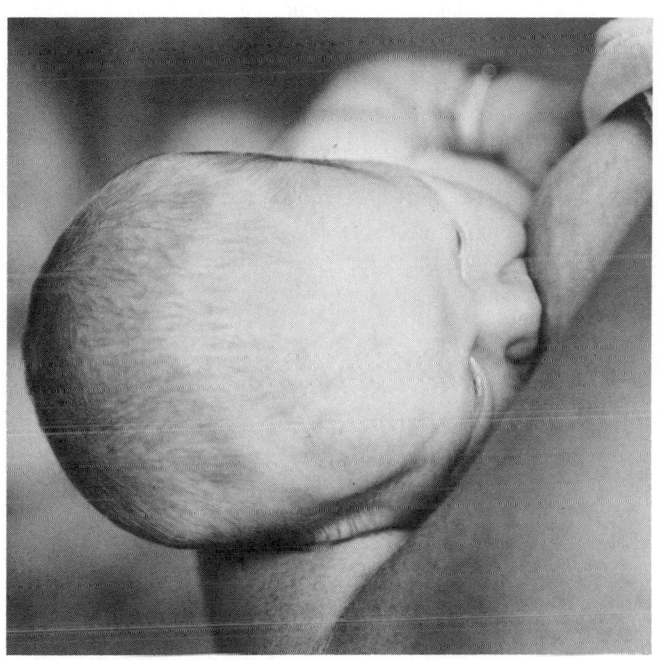

Figure 21–9

The infant is positioned facing the breast.

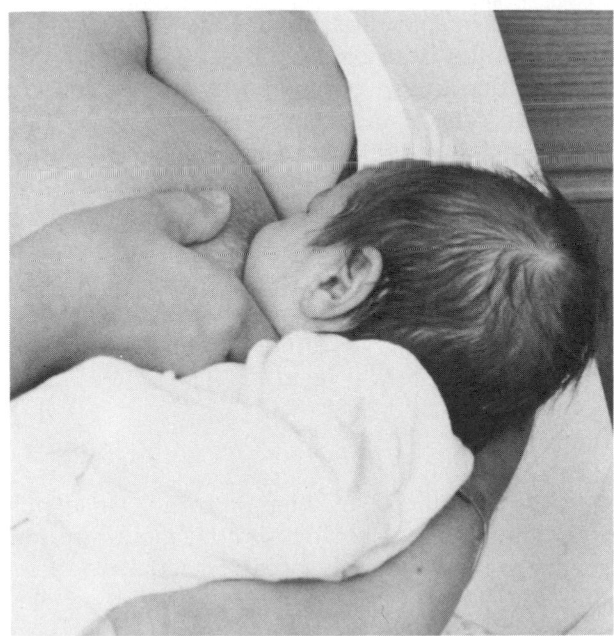

Figure 21–10

"C" position of hand on breast. The hand is positioned so the thumb is on top of the breast while the fingers support the breast from below.

indent the breast tissue near the infant's nostrils, which might interfere with milk flow. Unless the mother's breasts are very heavy and the infant buries the nose in the tissue, breathing will not be occluded. Lifting the infant's hips to a more horizontal position is usually sufficient if there appears to be a problem.

Latch-on Techniques

A number of techniques can be taught that help the infant latch on to the breast. The infant should be awake and ready to nurse. The mother can talk and cuddle with the infant to help prepare for nursing. This will help a sleepy infant awaken and will calm an upset infant.

Eliciting Latch-on. After positioning the infant to face the breast, the mother holds her breast so that the nipple brushes against the infant's lower lip. A hungry infant will usually open the mouth as soon as anything comes near it, but some need up to a minute of stroking the area around the mouth. The breast should not be inserted until the infant's mouth is opened wide, as the infant will compress the end of the nipple, causing pain and trauma and little milk flow. When the mouth opens wide, the mother should quickly bring the infant close to her so that the infant can latch on to the areola.

Position of the Mouth. Assess the position of the mouth on the breast (Fig. 21–11). As much of the areola as possible should be in the infant's mouth to allow the nipple to be drawn toward the back of the mouth. The infant's lips should be about 1 to 1.5 inches from the base of the nipple (Lawrence, 1989). This positions the gums over the milk sinuses just behind the areola and causes milk to be released into the infant's mouth each time the gums compress them.

Assess the position of the infant's tongue by gently pulling down on the lower lip. The tongue should be under the breast and over the top of the lower gums. The lips should be flared outward. Be sure that the lower lip is not turned in, as a friction burn on the lower nipple will result.

Suckling Pattern

Observe the infant's suckling pattern. During nutritive suckling, the infant sucks with smooth, continuous movements with only occasional pauses to rest. Each suck may be followed by a swallow or there may be two or three sucks before the swallow. Nonnutritive suckling often occurs when the infant is falling asleep. There may be a fluttery or choppy motion of the jaw that is not accompanied by the sound of swallowing. The mother should remove the infant from the breast when this occurs because her nipples may become sore. If she feels that the infant should feed longer, she can try burping the infant and switching him or her to the other breast, which will probably cause the infant to wake.

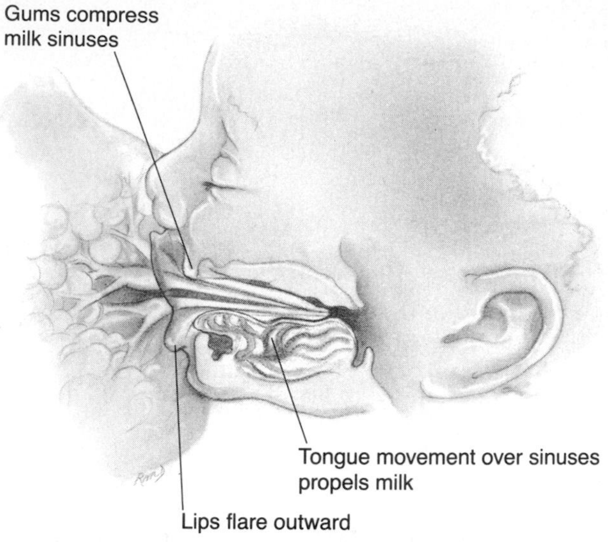
Gums compress milk sinuses
Tongue movement over sinuses propels milk
Lips flare outward

Figure 21–11

Position of infant's mouth while suckling. When the nipple and areola are properly positioned in the infant's mouth, the gums compress the milk sinuses behind the areola. The tongue is between the lower gums and the breast. The tongue moves over the sinuses like a peristaltic wave to bring the milk forward into the infant's mouth. The infant's lips are flared outward.

Explain the milk-ejection reflex to the mother. She will learn to recognize the feeling of tingling in her nipples as the let-down occurs. The reflex occurs several times throughout the feeding. She will see the infant begin to swallow more rapidly each time a new let-down brings more rapid expulsion of milk.

Mothers often wonder whether or not their infants are actually receiving milk from the breast. Call their attention to the sound of swallowing when it occurs. A soft "ka" or "ah" sound indicates that the infant is swallowing colostrum or milk. The infant will swallow a number of times in succession and then have a period of no swallowing until there is another let-down.

Short pauses are normal during nursing. Caution mothers not to jiggle the breast in the infant's mouth in an effort to start the suckling again. This may cause the infant to lose the grasp on the nipple and areola, resulting in "chewing" on the nipple and soreness. If necessary, she should take the infant off the breast to awaken him or her, then start again.

Removal from the Breast

Teach the mother to remove the infant from the breast for burping midway in the feeding and whenever suckling becomes non-nutritive. Show her how to avoid trauma to the breast by removing the infant properly. Have her insert her finger into the corner of the infant's mouth to break the suction, then remove the breast quickly before the infant begins to suck again. Another method is to indent the breast tissue with a finger near the infant's mouth and remove the infant when the suction is released.

Frequency of Feedings

Mothers are often concerned about how often they should feed. Because breast milk is digested more quickly than formula (within about 2 hours), the infant should be fed every 2 to 3 hours. Frequent feedings are especially important in the early days after birth, when lactation is being established and stomach capacity is small. Explaining that the hormone prolactin, which is responsible for milk production, is released in increased amounts while the infant is suckling will help mothers understand the relationship of frequent feeding to milk supply.

Infants who are fed frequently during the daytime will often sleep longer during the night. However, during the early weeks of life, the infant should not be allowed to sleep beyond 4 to 5 hours at a time. Long periods between feedings increase the likelihood of breast engorgement. The resulting decreased stimulation of prolactin may reduce milk supply. Generally, the mother should nurse 8 to 12 times in each 24-hour period. Strict scheduling of infant feedings is unnecessary and leads to frustration for both mother and infant. A mother should take her cues from her infant.

Length of Feedings

Although early feedings were once limited to only a few minutes per breast in an attempt to prevent sore nipples, improper positioning, rather than time at breast, is the usual cause of nipple trauma. It may take as long as 5 minutes for the milk ejection (letdown) reflex to occur during the early days after birth.

Instruct mothers to start with feedings lasting at least 10 minutes on each side. The mother should burp and awaken the infant after feeding on the first breast for 10 to 15 minutes. She should then feed the infant on the other breast until the infant falls asleep or begins non-nutritive suckling, generally at least 10 to 15 minutes.

Inform the mother about the differences between foremilk, the watery first milk that quenches the infant's thirst, and hindmilk, which is richer in fat, more satisfying, and leads to weight gain. Feeding for too short a time prevents the infant from getting the hindmilk. Although the infant may go to sleep for a brief time, hunger will cause early awakening. The frustration of having a fussy infant who "always wants to eat" may lead mothers to discontinue breastfeeding.

Preventing Problems

Once mothers leave the birth facility, they often have no one to advise them about breastfeeding. Nurses can help prevent problems by intensive teaching during the short time that the mother is in the birth facility. Include suggestions on how to improve positioning and techniques and common problems and their solutions. Allow ample time to answer questions. Give the mother breastfeeding pamphlets and review them with her. Breastfeeding videos provide another means of providing education. (Before using pamphlets or videos, review them to be sure that the information is correct.)

After discharge, mothers may continue to have questions. Provide them with the telephone number of the nursery as well as of local support groups, such as LaLeche League, or lactation educators or consultants in the area for more involved problems. Some birth facilities provide follow-up telephone calls or home visits to breastfeeding mothers.

Mothers may need help determining whether or not a problem exists. The most common concern is whether the infant is receiving enough milk. Methods of determining this are explained in Mothers Want to Know: Is My Baby Getting Enough Milk? Although mothers are not encouraged to weigh their infants at home because it focuses too much attention on weight gain, the physician or nurse practitioner will assess weight gain at well baby check-ups. After the initial weight loss following birth, infants generally gain approximately 15 to 30 g (0.5 to 1 ounce) each day during the early months of life.

Evaluation

Evaluation of interventions should be continued throughout the birth facility stay. Before discharge, the infant should be feeding at least 10 minutes at each breast. The mother should be able to demon-

Nursing Care Plan 21–1

Breastfeeding for the First Time

Assessment: Melinda Barber plans to breastfeed her first infant, David, but tells the nurse that she is afraid she won't be successful because she knows nothing about it except that "it is best for the baby." She asks many questions and appears unsure during her first feeding attempts.

Nursing Diagnosis: High Risk for Ineffective Breastfeeding related to lack of understanding of breastfeeding techniques.

Goals:

1. David will feed with nutritive suckling for at least 10 minutes at each breast before birth facility discharge.
2. Melinda will demonstrate breastfeeding techniques as taught before discharge.
3. Melinda will verbalize satisfaction and confidence with breastfeeding process before discharge

Intervention:	Rationale:
1. Assess Melinda's level of knowledge about breastfeeding techniques. Determine her special concerns.	1. Teaching should start with and build on mother's basic knowledge and focus on her perceived needs.
2. Demonstrate cradle and football holds, side-lying position, and use of pillows for support. Help Melinda try out each one. Place David on his side, facing the breast at nipple level.	2. Knowledge about a variety of positions to use will increase the mother's confidence.
3. Demonstrate "C" position of hand—hand cupped around breast with thumb and fingers behind areola.	3. Position allows infant to take enough of the nipple and areola into mouth without interference from mother's fingers, reduces trauma to the nipple, and provides support to the breast to keep it in place.
4. Elicit latch-on by rubbing nipple against David's lower lip and inserting it when he opens his mouth wide.	4. Rubbing lip stimulates infant to open mouth. Waiting for wide-open mouth allows insertion of nipple and areola and prevents infant from compressing nipple and causing trauma.
5. Assess position of mouth, suck, and swallow.	5. Prevents trauma to nipple from poor positioning and ensures that infant is receiving colostrum.
6. Demonstrate removal from breast.	6. Breaking suction before removal prevents trauma to the nipple.
7. Answer Melinda's questions about frequency and length of feedings. Ask her if she has other questions.	7. Eliciting questions gives mother the information that she needs for continued successful nursing.
8. Instruct Melinda to begin each feeding with the breast where the infant finished the last feeding. Suggest that she place a safety pin on her bra strap to help her remember which side to use first.	8. Even stimulation and emptying of each breast increases production of milk.
9. Observe Melinda and David at intervals throughout first feeding session and periodically during subsequent sessions.	9. Periodic reassessment helps determine if techniques are performed correctly, identifies problems, and allows the nurse to correct misconceptions and answer questions.
10. Encourage Melinda to feed David every 2 to 3 hours.	10. Frequent feeding provides adequate nourishment and stimulates milk production.

Evaluation:
Melinda and David seem satisfied with feedings that consist of approximately 10 to 15 minutes of nutritive suckling per side. Melinda verbalizes confidence and demonstrates techniques as taught.

Mothers Want To Know
Is My Baby Getting Enough Milk?

Ask yourself the following questions to determine if your baby is getting enough milk:

- Can you hear the baby swallow during feedings? It sounds like a soft "ka" or "ah" sound. You should hear it frequently during the feeding.
- Can you see nutritive suckling, a smooth series of sucking and swallowing with occasional rest periods? This is different than short, choppy sucks that occur when the baby is falling asleep and not getting milk. After rest periods, you may feel a tingling of your nipples as a new let-down reflex occurs. This will be followed by more nutritive suckling as the infant swallows the increased milk available.
- Is your breast getting softer during the feeding? If your breast is firm before feedings, you will notice that it is softer by the end of the feeding as milk is removed.
- How many times does your baby nurse each day? There should be 8 to 12 feedings each 24 hours. You will produce more milk when you nurse more often.
- How many wet diapers does your baby have each day? During the first 2 days of life, there should be two to six wet diapers each day. By the 3rd day, there should be at least six to eight wet diapers a day. Disposable diapers are very absorbant. If you are unsure whether the diaper is wet, take the lining apart to feel the inside layers.
- How many bowel movements does your baby have each day? Breastfed babies usually pass at least one stool daily and often more.
- Does your baby seem satisfied after feedings? Babies will remain quietly awake or go to sleep for at least an hour after most feedings. (An occasional fussy time is not unusual and does not mean that the baby is not getting enough to eat.)
- Has your baby gained weight at the first well baby check-up? Weight gain indicates that the baby is getting enough milk.

strate the feeding techniques taught by the nurses and should voice satisfaction with breastfeeding and confidence in her ability. This will be a major determinant of whether she will continue breastfeeding once she is home.

✔ Check Your Reading

10. How can the nurse help the mother establish breastfeeding during the initial feeding sessions?
11. What should the nurse teach the mother about frequency and length of feedings?

Common Breastfeeding Concerns

Many mothers experience problems while breastfeeding that nurses can help them solve. These problems may be divided into those originating with the infant and those having to do with the mother. Because mothers may be discharged from the birth facility before problems occur, nurses should teach them how to prevent and treat common problems. Prevention and solutions for some problems are addressed in Mothers Want to Know: Solutions to Common Breastfeeding Problems and in Nursing Care Plan 21–1.

Guidance for breastfeeding problems can be continued at home by referring the mother to lactation specialists or organizations such as LaLeche League, which is a support group designed to give ongoing assistance to breastfeeding mothers. LaLeche League chapters are available in most communities and are listed in the telephone book. Women with more serious breastfeeding problems need referral to a lactation consultant, a professional educated to deal with more complex situations. Some birth facilities provide one or two home visits for new mothers by a nurse who can assess both the mother's and the infant's progress and intervene appropriately.

Infant Problems

Infant problems are generally due to a sleepy infant, problems with suckling, or difficulties related to complications of the infant such as jaundice or prematurity. Crying or fussiness are common problems during the first weeks after birth for all infants and are discussed in Chapter 22 (p. 596).

SLEEPY INFANT

It is not unusual during the first few days after birth for infants to sleep longer than expected or fall asleep at the breast after feeding for only a short period. Infants may be tired from the birth process and may not recognize or respond appropriately to hunger. When infants fall asleep before they have fed adequately, they often wake up again within an hour, only to repeat the process. The mother should be informed that this is a common situation during the early days after birth and does not reflect on her ability or her breast milk.

The nurse should show mothers how to arouse sleepy infants for breastfeeding. If infants start the feeding fully awake, they are more likely to stay

Text continued on page 580

Nursing Care Plan 21–2

Positioning for Breastfeeding

Assessment: Maria Nunez complains of pain in her breasts and nipples. Her nipples are red but there are no blisters, fissures, or bleeding. Maria indicates that she prefers the cradle position. She positions Angelique so that the infant is lying on her back with her hips and legs lower than the rest of her body. Maria uses a scissors hold on the breast with her fingers resting on areola.

Nursing Diagnosis: Alteration in Skin Integrity related to incorrect positioning.

Goals: Maria will:

1. Have no redness of the nipples within 2 days.
2. Demonstrate correct positioning within 1 day.
3. Verbalize causes and care of sore nipples within 1 day.

Intervention:	**Rationale:**
1. Demonstrate correct positioning of the infant. Place Angelique on her side so that she faces the nipple with her body horizontal across Maria's lap.	1. Correct positioning prevents the infant from having to turn the head to feed, which interferes with swallowing and tends to cause traction on the nipple. Raising the lower body to horizontal position prevents the infant's weight from pulling on the nipple.
2. Change Maria's hand position from a scissors hold to cupping the breast with her hand in a "C" position, thumb and fingers behind the areola.	2. The scissors hold may cause fingers to slip down on the wet areola and interfere with the infant's ability to take enough of the areola into the mouth. This results in compression of the nipple instead of the milk sinuses under the areola, leading to trauma and decreased expulsion of milk.
3. Assess Angelique's mouth position on the nipple by gently pulling down the lower lip to see that her tongue covers the lower gum. If the lower lip is turned in, gently pull it out it so that the lips flare. The mouth should be 1 to 1.5 inches from the base of the nipple.	3. The tongue cushions the lower gum compression of the areola. A turned-in lower lip causes a friction rub on the nipple and areola. If the mouth is 1 to 1.5 inches from the base of the nipple, the nipple should be at the back of infant's mouth.
4. Assess the infant's mouth for signs of *Candida* infection (thrush): white patches that bleed if removed. Notify the pediatrician and obstetrician for treatment if found.	4. *Candida* infection of the infant can infect the mother's nipples, causing itching, burning, and stabbing pain. Usual treatment is nystatin drops for the infant and cream for the mother.
5. Have Maria begin the feeding on the less sore side.	5. The let-down reflex will occur in both breasts at same time. Vigorous suckling on the sore side before let-down reflex occurs will increase nipple trauma.
6. Suggest that Maria use a variety of positions for feeding and demonstrate each.	6. Changing the area of stress on the nipple allows healing of the sore area.
7. Teach Maria to leave the flaps of her nursing bra down between feedings. Instruct her to express colostrum at end of feedings and apply it to the nipples.	7. Increased air circulation promotes drying. Colostrum has lysozymes and other healing properties.
8. Teach Maria to avoid creams that must be removed before nursing or to which she may have allergies. If she uses breast pads, suggest that she change them frequently. Tell her to avoid using soap on her nipples.	8. Cream removal, allergies, or wet pads increase irritation. Prolonged exposure to wet pads can cause maceration of skin and cause it to break down. Soap removes protective oils from nipples.

Evaluation:
Maria's nipple redness and tenderness gradually decrease and are gone within 2 days. She demonstrates correct positioning at every feeding and can describe causes and care for sore nipples. Reassess for other causative factors if goals not met.

Nursing Care Plan 21–3

Engorged Breasts

Assessment: Sally Portner complains of painful breasts and asks that her infant, Grady, be fed formula by the nurses after this feeding and during the night because "I'm just too sore to nurse anymore today." Her breasts are engorged, hard, warm, and tender. Grady has difficulty grasping Sally's nipple and areola to feed. Sally says she has been breastfeeding for 3 minutes per side every 4 to 4½ hours. She fed the infant formula at the last feeding.

Nursing Diagnosis: Pain related to engorgement secondary to short, widely spaced feedings and skipped feedings.

Goals:
Sally will:

1. Report gradually decreasing breast pain until pain is minimal or absent by 2 days.
2. Describe prevention and treatment of engorgement within 1 day.
3. Describe soft breasts after feedings within 2 days.

Intervention:	Rationale:
1. Apply heat to Sally's breasts before feedings with warm compresses (such as wet disposable diapers) or by having Sally stand in a shower.	1. Heat dilates blood vessels and milk ducts, encourages the let-down reflex, and relieves pain.
2. Demonstrate gentle massage of the breasts before feedings.	2. Massage causes release of oxytocin, resulting in the let-down reflex. The infant will get milk more quickly, reducing non-productive time on a painful breast.
3. Demonstrate hand expression or use of a breast pump if necessary to soften the areola enough so that Grady can grasp it to suckle.	3. If the areola is hard, the infant will not be able to get it far enough into the mouth to compress the milk sinuses. The nipple will be compressed, leading to trauma. The breast will not be emptied adequately, and milk production will fall.
4. Instruct Sally to wear a well-fitting bra both day and night.	4. The bra will support mother's painful breasts.
5. Offer Sally ordered medication approximately 30 minutes before feedings. Be sure that the medication ordered is safe for the infant.	5. Medication will relieve pain that could interfere with the let-down reflex, yet only minimal amounts will reach breast milk within the feeding time.
6. Prevent further engorgement by teaching Sally to feed Grady every 2 to 3 hours during the day and at least every 4 hours at night (unless contraindicated for other reasons). She should feed at least 10 minutes per side initially.	6. Frequent feedings of adequate length can empty the breasts, prevent stasis, decrease congestion, and reduce the risk of mastitis. Frequent feedings also stimulate production of milk to meet the infant's needs. Feedings of adequate length allow time for the let-down reflex, which may be delayed at first, to occur so that the infant receives nourishment.

Evaluation:
Sally breastfeeds Grady every 2 to 3 hours for at least 10 minutes per side during the day and at least every 4 hours at night. Her breasts are soft after feedings, and her pain is relieved completely by the 2nd day. Sally verbalizes methods that she will use to prevent further engorgement.

Nursing Care Plan 21–4

Breastfeeding an Infant Who Has Complications

Assessment: Martha James' son John develops respiratory complications at birth and is admitted to the neonatal intensive care unit (NICU). Martha had looked forward to breastfeeding her infant, but John will probably not be able to feed at the breast for a few days. Although Martha understands the situation, she sounds disappointed and discouraged about whether or not she will be able to breastfeed at all. She states that she will probably have to use formula after John is better because "it will be too late to start breastfeeding."

Nursing Diagnosis: Interrupted Breastfeeding related to separation from infant secondary to illness.

Goals:

Martha will:

1. Verbalize the importance of breastfeeding her infant—her desire to maintain lactation.
2. Pump her breasts as taught.
3. Breastfeed John successfully when it becomes possible.

Intervention:	Rationale:
1. Explore Martha's perception of problem and her understanding of the cause for separation and the effect on breastfeeding.	1. Encouraging the mother to discuss the problem helps identify misconceptions she may have and determine the type of teaching and support that may be required.
2. Use therapeutic communication techniques to help Martha express her feelings of disappointment with the unexpected change in plans.	2. Helping the mother express her feelings and accepting them will help her deal with the situation.
3. Explain to Martha how valuable breast milk is for her infant and that she can use a breast pump to maintain lactation until John is able to breastfeed.	3. Reinforcing the value of breastfeeding and offering encouragement increase the chance of success.
4. Teach Martha to use a breast pump and store her milk. Instruct her to pump her breasts every 3 hours during the day and at least once at night, if possible.	4. Frequent use of a breast pump helps establish lactation by causing release of oxytocin and prolactin so that milk is produced and released from her breasts.
5. Feed John breast milk if possible, whether by bottle or gavage. Teach Martha how to store her milk and how to prepare it for hospital use for her infant.	5. Breast milk has properties especially valuable for the sick infant.
6. Arrange for Martha to spend as much time with John as possible. Accompany her during the early visits and when she begins to breastfeed to answer her questions and provide support.	6. Bonding will occur more easily if a mother is able to be with her baby. Accompanying mother during visits with infant allows nurse an opportunity to offer support, encouragement, and teaching as needed.
7. Offer praise and realistic encouragement frequently.	7. A mother needs reinforcement of her abilities to increase self-esteem as a mother. Encouragement must be suited to actual circumstances.

Evaluation:

Martha verbalizes her determination to provide breast milk for John. She maintains lactation and brings breast milk to the hospital at each visit. At 5 days of age, John is ready to begin breastfeeding. Martha is very patient in helping John learn to breastfeed with the nurses' help. John is able to nurse well at each feeding by discharge.

Mothers Want To Know

Solutions to Common Breastfeeding Problems

Problem: *Infant is sleepy at feeding time or falls asleep shortly after beginning feeding.*

Prevention:

- Gently awaken your baby at feeding time. Talk, gently move infant's arms and legs, and play with infant for a short time before beginning the feeding.
- Unwrap the baby's blankets and change the diaper. Swaddling infants by wrapping them tightly with blankets is a calming technique that often helps them sleep. Leave the blanket off as you begin the feeding. Your body and a blanket draped over both of you after your baby begins to nurse well will provide adequate warmth.

Solutions: If your baby goes to sleep during the feeding, try the following:

- Rub the baby's hair or cheeks gently, stroke around the mouth, or shift the baby's position slightly to see if infant will wake up.
- Remove the baby from the breast and rub the back to bring up bubbles of air that may cause a sensation of stomach fullness. Rubbing the back also stimulates the central nervous system and awakens the baby.
- Switch breasts each time the baby falls asleep. The movement and the new flow of colostrum will stimulate the infant.
- Express a few drops of colostrum onto the nipple. The baby tastes the colostrum as soon as the nipple is offered and often begins renewed sucking.
- Wash the baby's face with a lukewarm washcloth to help infant wake up.

If your baby cannot be aroused with a few of the above gentle techniques, a longer sleep period may be needed. Put the infant down and wait a half hour, then begin again.

Problem: *Infant who has taken bottles pushes the nipple out of the mouth and sucks poorly during breastfeeding. Infant has become confused about how to suck from the breast.*

Prevention:

- Avoid all bottles unless absolutely necessary. If they are necessary, stop as soon as possible.
- Do not give the baby formula during the night. Although the extra sleep is nice, it is seldom worth it if the infant develops later feeding difficulties.
- Avoid giving formula at the end of a breastfeeding session, as it is unnecessary for healthy newborns. It may cause the infant's stomach to become distended, may result in more "spitting up," and causes the infant to wait longer before nursing again. This will decrease milk production.

Solutions:

- Stop all bottle feeding and pacifier use so that the baby will get used to suckling from the breast instead of the bottle. Nurse more often to stimulate milk and help the baby learn what to do.

Problem: *Infant sucks on the end of the nipple or fails to open mouth widely enough.*

Prevention:

- Be sure that the baby has the nipple at the back of the mouth and 1 to 1.5 inches of the areola in the mouth.
- Do not insert the breast into the infant's mouth until the infant opens mouth wide.
- Pull down gently on the chin to help the infant open the mouth if necessary.

Solutions:

- Stop the feeding and start again if you see dimples in the infant's cheeks or hear "smacking" or clicking sounds. Short, choppy movement of the jaw means that the infant is going to sleep or finished with the feeding.
- If you feel that the infant should nurse longer, awake infant and begin again.

Problem: *Breasts are hard and tender from engorgement.*

Prevention:

- Breastfeed the infant every 2 to 3 hours day and night. Do not give a bottle during the night, as this often increases the risk of engorgement. Waiting even 4 hours between feedings may increase the risk of engorgement, but frequent breastfeeding can often prevent it.

Solutions:

- Apply ice packs to the breasts between feedings to reduce edema and pain. Make inexpensive ice packs from clean rubber gloves or plastic bags filled with crushed ice and covered with washcloths.
- Before feedings, apply heat with compresses or a shower to stimulate milk flow. Moisten disposable diapers with warm water and apply over each breast. Fasten the tabs to keep the diapers in place and prevent dripping.
- Massage the breasts before feedings to stimulate the let-down reflex so that the baby can nurse more easily. Massaging the breasts in the shower provides comfort and helps prepare for feeding.
- If the breasts are very hard and your baby cannot latch on, express a little milk by hand or with a breast pump. As soon as the areola is soft, begin to nurse.

Mothers Want To Know continued on following page

Mothers Want To Know

Solutions to Common Breastfeeding Problems *Continued*

Problem: *Nipples are sore and may be cracked, blistered, or bleeding.*

Prevention:

- Be sure that the baby is positioned properly at the breast and that enough of the areola is in the mouth so that the nipple is not compressed between the baby's gums during nursing.
- Avoid engorgement by nursing frequently. Express enough milk to soften the areola if engorgement occurs.
- Do not use soap on the nipples, as it removes the protective oils and causes drying.
- If you use breast pads for leaking milk, remove them when they become wet to prevent irritation of the skin. Avoid pads with plastic linings that will retain moisture. Cut a cotton diaper or handkerchief into squares and use as inexpensive, washable substitutes for commercial breast pads.
- Breast creams are unnecessary and may cause sensitivity and irritation. If you are allergic to wool, you may be allergic to lanolin. Creams that have to be removed before each feeding may increase soreness.

Solutions:

- Try applying a covered ice cube to the nipple just before feeding to lessen pain during latch-on.
- If one nipple is more uncomfortable than the other, begin each feeding with the least sore side first. The hungry baby nurses more vigorously at first, which may be painful. The let-down reflex will be started, causing milk to flow more quickly on the second breast.
- Do not use nipple shields (latex nipples that fit over your own nipples). They decrease milk flow so that the baby does not get enough milk and milk production is decreased.
- Vary the position of the infant during nursing. The area of the nipple directly in line with the infant's nose and chin is most stressed during the feeding.
- Apply colostrum or breast milk to the nipples after feedings, as it has healing properties.
- Expose the nipples to air between feedings by lowering the flaps of your nursing bra. Use a hair dryer held 6 to 8 inches from the breast to apply heat and dry the nipples.
- If you have burning, itching, or stabbing pain throughout your breast, look in the baby's mouth for the white patches of thrush, a yeast infection that can infect the nipples. Call the pediatrician and obstetrician for medication to treat both you and your baby.

Problem: *Flat or inverted nipples that the baby has difficulty drawing into mouth.*

Prevention: These cannot be prevented, but they can be treated during pregnancy or after birth with breast shells and exercises.

Solutions:

- Wear breast shells in your bra during pregnancy or as soon as flat or inverted nipples are discovered. They help make the nipples protrude.
- Just before beginning breastfeeding, roll the nipple between your thumb and forefinger to help it protrude.
- Use Hoffman's exercises for inverted nipples.
- Use a breast pump just before feedings to draw out inverted nipples. Put the baby to breast immediately after the pump causes the nipple to become erect. Once the infant gets the nipple in the mouth, the normal suckling process will usually cause the nipple to stay erect.

Critical to Remember

Infant Signs of Breastfeeding Problems

- Falling asleep during feedings
- Refusal to breastfeed
- Tongue thrusting
- Smacking or clicking sounds
- Dimpling of cheeks
- Failure to open mouth wide at latch-on
- Lower lip turned in
- Short, choppy motions of jaw
- Use of formula

awake to finish the feeding. Pointing out the various behavioral states to the mother helps her develop a greater understanding of her infant and recognize when attempts to feed will be most successful.

When infants fall asleep during feedings, the nurse should evaluate whether the infant has fed adequately or should be awakened to feed longer. Emphasizing that wake-up techniques should be done gently is important. Using excessively irritating techniques might cause the infant to associate them with feeding and be unwilling to breastfeed. Infants who continue to be excessively sleepy or to nurse poorly need further evaluation. Poor feeding may be an early sign of a complication such as sepsis (see Chapter 29, p. 853).

NIPPLE CONFUSION

Nipple confusion (or nipple preference) occurs when an infant who has received bottle feedings confuses the tongue movements necessary for bottle feeding with the suckling of breastfeeding. The infant may refuse to breastfeed or may use tongue movements that push the breast out of the mouth. Some infants develop a preference for the bottle, from which milk flows freely without effort.

A comparison of sucking during bottle feeding and suckling during breastfeeding aids in understanding. Infants who are bottle-fed must push their tongue over the latex nipple to slow the flow of milk and prevent choking (Fig. 21–12). This can be demonstrated by holding a bottle of formula upside down and watching the steady drip of milk flowing from the nipple. In bottle feeding, the infant's lips are relaxed because there is no need to hold the nipple in place. If the infant uses the same thrusting tongue motion and relaxed lips while nursing, the breast may be pushed out of the mouth.

Ultrasound studies have shown that the mouth is used differently during breastfeeding. Suction is necessary to hold the nipple in place near the back of the throat. The tongue cups around the nipple and areola with the tip over the lower gum. With each compression of the lower jaw over the milk sinuses behind the areola, the tongue presses against the breast like a peristaltic wave, causing the milk to move forward from the sinuses and into the infant's mouth for swallowing.

Mothers who supplement with bottles are more likely to stop breastfeeding early (Houston and Field, 1988). Nurses should discourage routine use of formula in breastfeeding infants. It reduces breastfeeding time and results in diminished production of prolactin and, therefore, milk supply. Formula takes longer to digest, and the infant will not be hungry again for about 4 hours, further decreasing breast stimulation and milk supply.

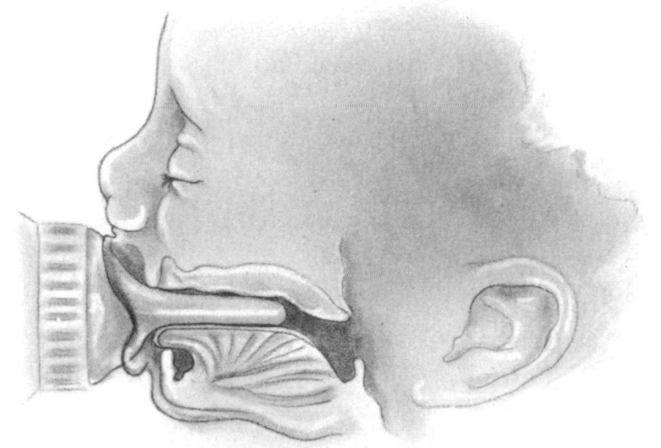
Tongue thrusts forward
to control milk flow

Figure 21–12

During bottle feeding, infants must thrust the tongue forward to slow the rapid flow of milk.

SUCKLING PROBLEMS

Suckling problems may occur when the nipple is poorly positioned in the mouth or when the infant is nipple-confused. Dimpling of the cheeks and smacking or clicking sounds may indicate that the infant needs more of the areola in the mouth and is sucking on the nipple only. Some infants do not open their mouth widely and suck on the end of the nipple. Short, choppy motions of the jaw signal nonnutritive suckling.

Suckling can be assessed by inserting a gloved finger into the infant's mouth. The peristaltic motion of the tongue should be felt as the infant sucks. The infant who is thrusting the tongue may have become confused by use of latex nipples, which should be avoided until the problem is resolved. If the infant tends to place the tongue on top of the nipple, placing a finger in the mouth and pressing the infant's tongue down just before latch-on may be effective. More complicated suckling problems may require assistance from a lactation educator or consultant.

✔ *Check Your Reading*

12. What wake-up techniques should the nurse teach the mother of a sleepy infant?
13. How does sucking from a bottle differ from suckling from the breast?

INFANT COMPLICATIONS

Infant complications may be minor and cause minimal interference with breastfeeding. However, the very preterm or ill infant may be unable to breastfeed for a long period of time.

Jaundice

Jaundice is discussed in detail in Chapters 19 (p. 496) and 29 (p. 845). Usually, jaundice (hyperbilirubinemia) need not interfere with breastfeeding. Even when infants receive phototherapy, they can usually be removed from the lights for feedings. Concern over adequate intake may be more prevalent in caring for the infant with jaundice. Insensible water loss from the skin is increased as a result of the heat and lights used in treatment and could lead to dehydration. Decreased intestinal motility from insufficient milk intake would allow reabsorption of bilirubin through the intestinal wall into the blood stream.

The policy in some birth facilities is to give extra water to infants receiving phototherapy. However, because albumin is necessary to bind bilirubin, frequent breastfeedings are often preferred to provide adequate intake of protein and stimulate the production of milk. In addition, breastfeeding will increase the number of stools and aid in excretion of bilirubin.

Preterm Infants

Breastfeeding the preterm infant is discussed in detail in Chapter 28, p. 827. If the preterm infant is unable to breastfeed immediately after birth, the mother needs encouragement and instruction to keep up her milk supply by using a breast pump. Breast milk offers immunological benefits to the preterm neonate and helps the mother feel that she is providing care for her infant even if she cannot take the infant home with her. The mother can pump her milk and take it to the nursery to be used for the infant's feedings. The nurse should provide sterile containers for the mother to take home and instruct her in special nursery requirements. She will need help in planning ahead for the time when the infant will be able to breastfeed.

Some preterm infants or those with breastfeeding problems respond well to the use of supplementary feeding devices. These consist of a container of milk with a small plastic feeding tube that is attached to the breast. When the infant begins to breastfeed, milk flows from the container as well as the breast, increasing the infant's motivation to continue suckling. As the infant's feeding ability increases, the amount of milk in the feeding apparatus is gradually decreased until the device can be discontinued completely.

Illness and Congenital Defects

Other conditions of the infant that may interfere with breastfeeding are those in which the infant is ill or has a congenital defect such as a cleft palate. Parents of these infants need the same type of assistance as parents of preterm infants. The focus is on helping the mother to maintain lactation until she is able to nurse the infant. Referral to support groups can be particularly helpful. Some groups focus on particular congenital defects, and others focus on breastfeeding infants with special problems.

Maternal Concerns

The most frequent breastfeeding problems of the mother involve problems of the breasts or nipples, although the ill mother may also need special help in continuing breastfeeding (see Critical to Remember: Maternal Signs of Breastfeeding Problems). Breastfeeding mothers may also have concerns about feeding after multiple birth, working, and weaning.

COMMON BREAST PROBLEMS

Engorgement, nipple trauma, flat or inverted nipples, plugged ducts, and mastitis are common problems involving the breasts.

Engorgement

Engorgement is a temporary swelling of the breasts in response to increased blood flow and rapid accumulation of milk when the milk begins to "come in" or change from colostrum to transitional breast milk. Engorgement does not usually occur until the 3rd day after birth but may occur earlier in multiparas who have nursed previously. Engorged breasts are edematous, hard, and tender, making feeding or even movement painful. The areola may become so hard that the infant cannot compress it for nursing. An engorged areola causes the nipple to become flat, making it more difficult for the infant to draw it into the back of the mouth. In addition to the discomfort engorgement causes the mother, the condition may lead to nipple trauma, mastitis, and even the discontinuation of breastfeeding.

Nurses can help prevent engorgement by assisting mothers to begin breastfeeding early and to feed frequently and for adequate lengths of time. The nurse should encourage mothers to breastfeed at night, unless there are extenuating circumstances, so that the breasts are emptied regularly.

The nurse should teach mothers with engorgement application of cold and heat, massage, and nursing

Critical to Remember

Maternal Signs of Breastfeeding Problems

- Hard, tender breasts
- Painful, red, cracked, blistered, or bleeding nipples
- Flat or inverted nipples
- Localized edema or pain in either breast
- Fever, generalized aching, or malaise

Therapeutic Communication

Jenny Lavelle breastfed her first infant for a week and then switched to bottle feeding because, she says, "I didn't have enough milk." Her second infant, Robin, is a sleepy baby but will nurse at times. Jenny's breasts are engorged, and her nipples are sore. Teresa Hernandez is her nurse.

Jenny: I really wanted to nurse Robin, but I don't know if it's worth the effort. My breasts hurt, and I don't know if he's getting enough milk. I'm beginning to feel like I should just use the bottle again.

Teresa: You sound really discouraged!

Reflecting the feelings expressed

Jenny: When I couldn't nurse my daughter, I was so disappointed. I had this "Mother Earth" view of the kind of mother I was going to be. But "Mother Earth's" baby wouldn't stop crying, so I went to the bottle.

Teresa: That must have been hard for you!

Reflecting the feelings expressed

Jenny: It was, and now it looks like I'm going to fail again. Robin doesn't cry much, but he won't nurse half the time. He'll probably start crying when I go home.

Teresa: Sounds like you're worried about what's going to happen when you go home.

Seeking clarification of mother's concerns

Jenny: What if he won't nurse when I get home? I feel so stupid! I hate asking for help. I should know what to do, this is my second baby. But I just don't!

Teresa: So when you don't know what to do, it makes you feel stupid, and you feel even more stupid when you ask for help.

Paraphrasing and clarifying

Jenny: That's right.

Teresa: You know, people think breastfeeding is an automatic process, but it isn't always easy. Mothers and babies both have to learn the process, and that takes time and a lot of patience. Robin's hungry now—would you like to try again? I'll stay with you and answer your questions. We can write down some of the techniques as we review so that you can remember them when you go home.

Offering realistic encouragement and assistance in techniques

Jenny: That would be great! Maybe I'll get the hang of this yet!

By allowing Jenny to express her feelings of discouragement and disappointment before beginning to teach, the nurse has a better idea of how important breastfeeding is to Jenny and how best to go about teaching her. Jenny feels accepted even though she feels she should know more because she is a second-time mother

techniques. Cold reduces edema and pain, whereas heat increases vasodilation and milk flow. Massage of the breasts causes release of oxytocin and increases the speed of milk release. This decreases the length of time that the infant nurses on painful breasts (Fig. 21–13).

If the areola is too engorged for the infant to compress it, the nurse should help the mother express milk by hand or with a manual or electric breast pump to soften the areola. Mothers with engorgement may need medication for discomfort so that they are comfortable enough to relax while breastfeeding. Medications that are safe for use during breastfeeding may be ordered by the physician. Medicating the mother 15 to 30 minutes before she feeds will decrease her pain, and she will be finished nursing before peak amounts reach the blood stream and enter the milk being produced.

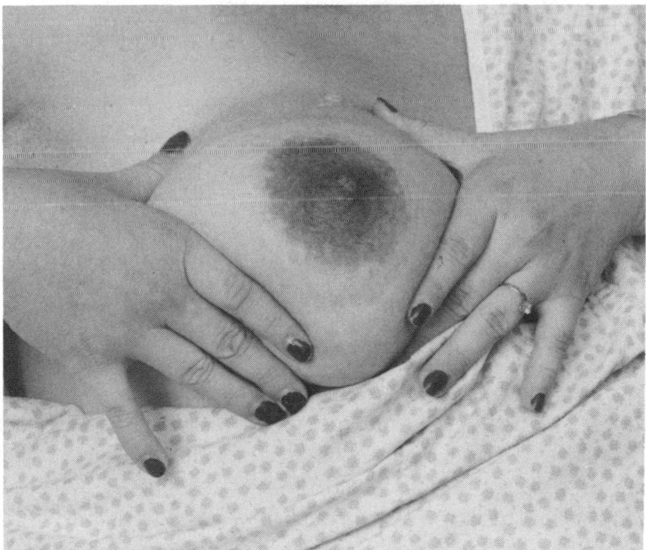

Figure 21–13

To massage the breasts, the mother places her hands against the chest wall with her fingers encircling the breasts. She gently slides her hands forward until the fingers overlap. The position of the hands is rotated to cover all breast tissue.

Nipple Trauma

Traumatized nipples appear red, cracked, blistered, or bleeding. Nipple redness alone can usually be treated by independent nursing interventions. When cracking, blisters, or bleeding occurs, the physician may order additional treatment. Redness of breast tissue, purulent drainage, and fever indicate mastitis or breast abscess and require antibiotic treatment (see discussion of mastitis in Chapter 27, p. 794).

Prevention. Nipple trauma can often be prevented by teaching the mother proper positioning and latch-on techniques and how to avoid common causes of nipple trauma. Exposure to soaps, prolonged moisture, or irritating creams may cause sore nipples. Some inflammation and skin changes of the nipple may result from suction during normal sucking (Ziemer & Pigeon, 1993). Prevention may not be entirely possible.

Mothers with vaginal candidiasis may transmit it to the infant during birth. If oral infection with *Candida albicans* (thrush) develops in the infant, the mother's nipples may become infected. The infant may or may not have visible white patches in the mouth, whereas the mother will have burning, itching, or stabbing pain throughout the breast. The obstetrician and the pediatrician should be notified, and both mother and infant are usually treated with nystatin.

Care. Teaching includes increasing air flow to the nipples, feeding with the less-inflamed side first, and varying positions for feeding to rotate strain on the nipples. The mother should apply breast milk to the nipples after feedings. Lysozymes, bacteriostatic enzymes in the milk, help prevent infection and aid in healing. Applying a covered ice cube to the nipple before feeding may decrease pain.

Mothers may ask about nipple shields, latex nipples with wide bases that are placed over a mother's own nipple to decrease pain during feedings. Nurses should caution against their use, which interferes with adequate emptying of the breast and markedly reduces the amount of milk that the infant receives. In addition, infants may become nipple-confused and have difficulty nursing from the breast alone.

Flat and Inverted Nipples

Nipple abnormalities should be treated during pregnancy, if possible, but interventions can begin after birth if the condition was not discovered before. Use of breast shells and Hoffman's exercises can be taught at this time. Some shells are solid, and milk may collect in them. Warn the mother that this milk should not be given to the infant because bacteria multiply rapidly in it.

Nipple rolling just before feeding helps flat nipples become more erect so that the infant can grasp them more readily (Fig. 21–14). A breast pump may help draw out inverted nipples.

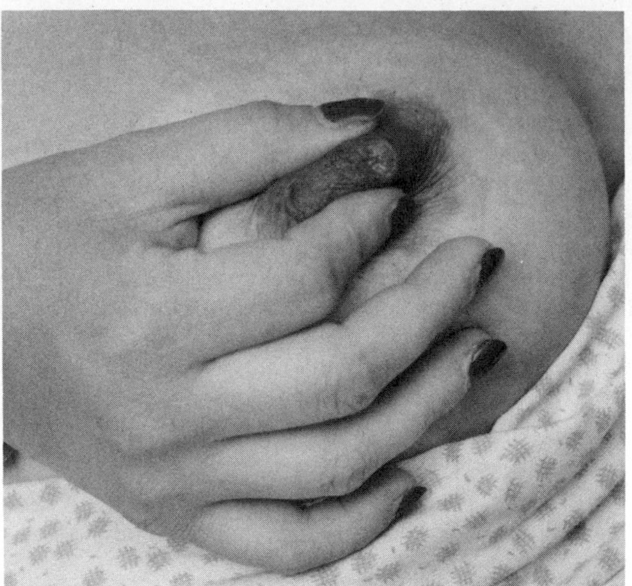

Figure 21–14

Rolling the nipples helps them to become erect in preparation for latch-on.

✔ *Check Your Reading*

14. How can the nurse help the mother who has engorged breasts?
15. How should the nurse advise the mother with sore nipples?

Plugged Ducts

A lactiferous duct may become occluded following engorgement or missed feedings, a condition called a plugged duct. There is localized edema and tenderness, and a hard area can be palpated. Massage of the area followed by heat will cause the duct to open. A plugged duct may progress to mastitis if not treated promptly. Mastitis involves localized pain accompanied by fever, generalized aching, and malaise. Nursing care of the mother with mastitis is discussed in Chapter 27, p. 794.

ILLNESS IN THE MOTHER

When the mother is ill, breastfeeding may have to be postponed temporarily because of the mother's condition or the drugs she receives. However, lactation should be continued when possible. Abrupt weaning may lead to mastitis as well as maternal depression from decreased prolactin, which has been associated with feelings of well-being (Lawrence, 1989). Another factor in depression may be the mother's emotional reaction to having to stop her chosen method of feeding (Nice, 1989). The nurse should explain the mother's condition to her and her family and help them explore appropriate options.

Conditions in Which Breastfeeding Should Be Avoided

Although breastfeeding is usually preferable to formula feeding, there may be some situations in which it is contraindicated. If the mother's illness is serious and can be transmitted to the infant, breastfeeding should be discontinued. An example is active tuberculosis or human immunodeficiency virus (HIV). Conditions such as cancer may be worsened by the hormonal changes of lactation.

Drug Transfer to Breast Milk

Most medications taken by the mother cross into the breast milk to some degree. Therefore, both prescription and over-the-counter drugs should be approved by a physician. Medications that can be safely used during breastfeeding should be chosen whenever possible. When a mother must take a drug that will be harmful to her infant, she should pump her breasts during the time that she is taking the medication. Once the drug clears her blood stream, she may resume breastfeeding (see Appendix E).

MILK EXPRESSION

When there is a need for milk expression, the nurse helps the mother use hand expression or a breast pump (Fig. 21–15). Hand expression can be done without other equipment. It is useful for the mother who wants to save breast milk for another feeding or whose areola is so engorged that the infant cannot grasp it. Use of massage and heat before expression helps the flow of milk begin.

The mother who needs to pump her milk for a prolonged period may prefer using a breast pump. Both manual and electric pumps are usually available. Large electric pumps can often be rented for home use. Small, relatively inexpensive battery-operated pumps are also available.

The mother should pump her breasts approximately every 3 hours during the day and once at night, if possible. The initial pumping session should be about 5 minutes on each breast. The mother should increase this time to 10 to 15 minutes at each breast over the next few days. The amount of suction should be set at a low level in the beginning and gradually increased. Too much negative pressure could traumatize the breast (Fig. 21–16).

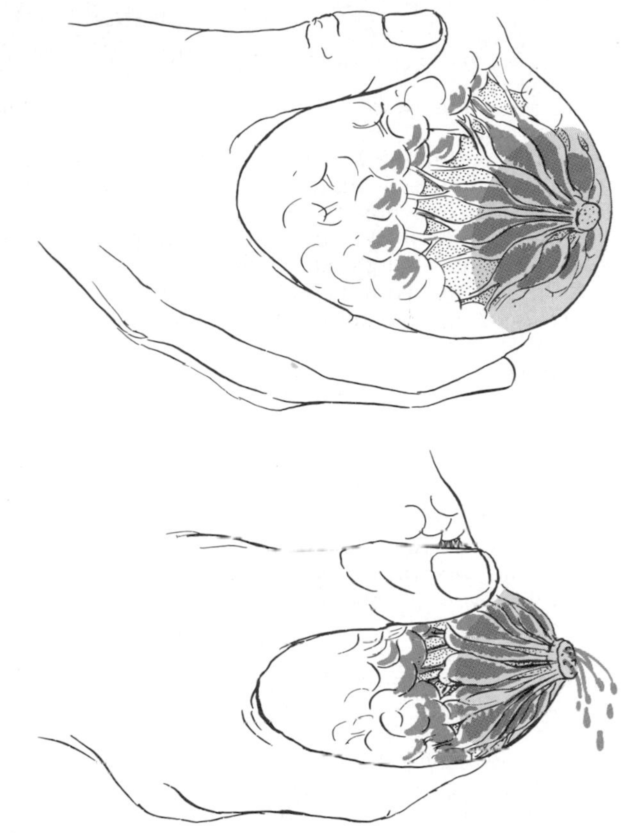

Figure 21–15

To express milk from the breast, the mother places her hand just behind the areola, with the thumb on top and the fingers supporting the breast. The tissue is pressed back against the chest wall, then the fingers and thumb are brought together while the hand moves toward the nipple. This compresses the milk sinuses and causes milk to flow. The action is repeated to simulate the suckling of the infant. Moving the hands around the areola allows compression of all sinuses and complete removal of milk from the breast. Compression should be gentle to avoid trauma.

BREASTFEEDING AFTER MULTIPLE BIRTH

Mothers who have multiple births may wish to breastfeed but may have many concerns about their ability to nurse more than one infant. They will need a great deal of help and support from nurses and family members. Common concerns of these mothers are addressed in Mothers Want to Know: Breastfeeding After the Birth of More than One Infant.

Mothers Want To Know

Breastfeeding After the Birth of More than One Infant

Mothers who wish to breastfeed after the birth of more than one infant may benefit from the following suggestions.

Ensuring Adequate Milk Production:
Mothers often wonder if they can produce enough milk to feed more than one infant. Because the amount of milk produced depends on the amount of suckling the breasts receive, providing enough milk should not be a problem. It is important that you nurse frequently, every 2 to 3 hours, to build up the milk supply. You may decide to have each infant nurse on the same breast at each feeding or to alternate breasts for each baby. It may be easier for you to keep track of feedings if infants nurse from the same breast each time. However, production of milk may be more evenly stimulated if you alternate breasts, especially if one infant has a weaker suck.

Using a Breast Pump:
If your infants are ill or too immature to be ready for breastfeeding, you can use a breast pump to provide milk for the infants to drink while still in the hospital and to build up your milk supply. Use the pump every 2 to 3 hours while you are awake for at least 5 minutes on each breast at first. Work up to pumping each breast for 10 to 15 minutes over the next 3 or 4 days. If possible, also use the pump once at night. Pumps that can be used on both breasts at the same time may decrease the time spent pumping and increase the production of milk. If one baby is ready to breastfeed before the other(s), nurse the baby and pump your breasts after each feeding to stimulate enough milk production to meet the needs of all infants. An alternative is to nurse the infant on one breast and to use a breast pump on the other at the same time.

Feeding Simultaneously or Individually:
You can feed each baby individually or feed two infants at once. Simultaneous nursing shortens feeding times, but both infants must be awake at once. You will need help positioning the infants at first. Individual feeding can be done without help and on each infant's own schedule, but a larger portion of your day will be spent feeding.

Positioning Infants for Simultaneous Feeding:
The infants may be placed in several different positions for breastfeeding. Changing positions may be helpful if your nipples become sore. Place pillows under both infants to bring them to the right height and to keep them in place. Use pillows under your arms and behind your back so that you are comfortable.

Football Hold: Place each infant's head on your lap and support each infant's body with pillows alongside your body. Support each infant's head in your hand and bring the infants to the nipples.

Football and Cradle Hold: Place one infant in a cradle position on pillows across your lap. Place the other in a football position with the body supported on pillows alongside you. Once the infants are in position, help one and then the other to latch on to the breast.

Criss-cross Hold: Place pillows on your lap and hold each baby in the cradle position. The infants' legs will criss-cross over each other.

Keeping Track:
Keep track of when and for how long each baby eats in the beginning, especially if you feed them individually. Also record the number of wet diapers each infant has each day. Six to ten wet diapers for each infant usually shows intake of enough breast milk.

Care for Yourself:
All new mothers need to be sure that they are eating well and getting enough rest. This is especially true for mothers who have had a multiple birth. Ask for help from family and friends during the early days after birth, which can be very hectic. Pamper yourself as much as possible and leave care of the house and cooking to others if you can. Your major responsibility during this time should be to take care of yourself and your new babies!

EMPLOYMENT

Mothers who plan to return to work soon after birth may have many questions about how to manage breastfeeding and employment. Working and breastfeeding can be combined very well. Although some advance planning may be necessary, many mothers feel that continuing the nursing relationship is gratifying to both mother and infant.

Whereas some mothers remain at home for the first 6 weeks after birth, others must return to work earlier. Milk supply can be well established by frequent breastfeeding during the time at home. About a week before she returns to work, the mother can begin using a breast pump once or twice a day to practice pumping her breasts and to build up a small supply of frozen breast milk. This avoids the stress of having to learn the technique or worry about having enough milk while adjusting to the work situation again.

Milk can be stored in plastic containers, as antibodies in the milk will adhere to glass. It can be kept in a refrigerator for 48 hours, a refrigerator freezer for up to 3 months, or a deep freeze at 0°F for 6 months. Leukocytes are destroyed by freezing, but most of the other immunological properties are preserved. Breast milk should be thawed by running the container under water rather than heating it and should not be refrozen. Refrigerated milk should be used as much as possible so that the lymphocytes are available for the infant, freezing some milk for a back-up supply.

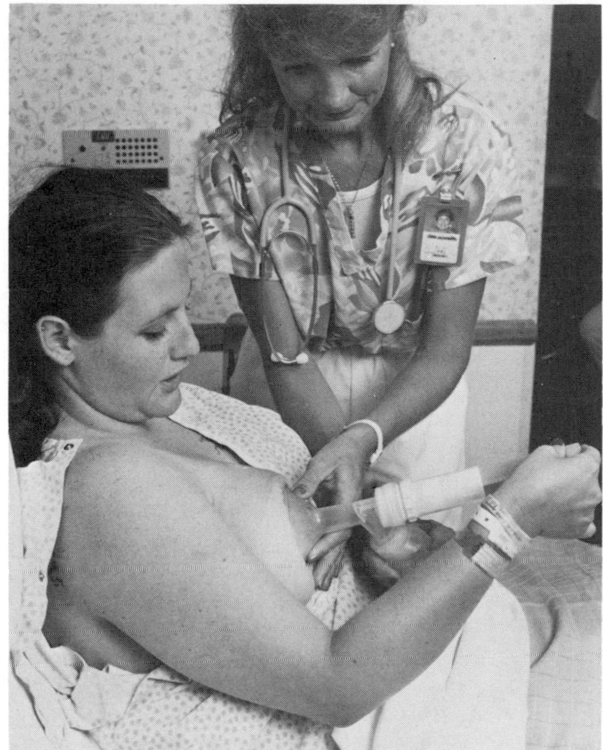

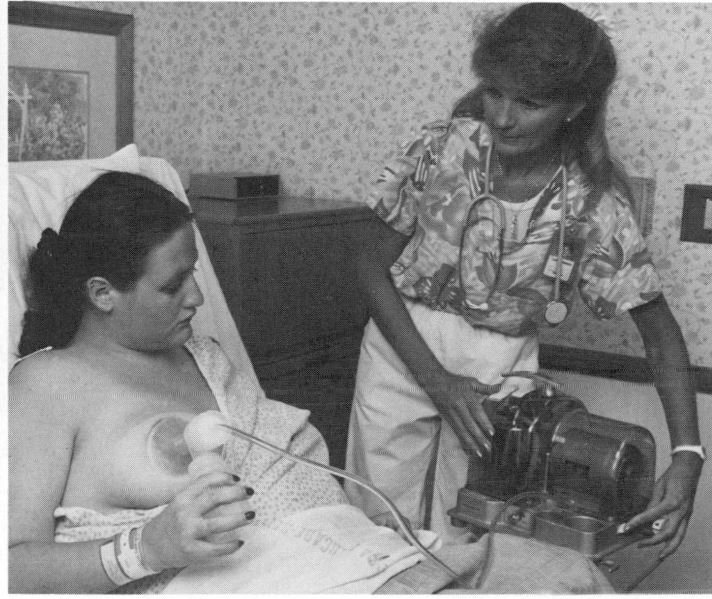

Figure 21–16

The nurse demonstrates methods of pumping breast milk. *Left,* Manual breast pump. *Right,* Electric breast pump.

Most mothers use a manual or battery-operated pump once or twice a day at work. This is often done during lunch or coffee breaks. The milk should be refrigerated and can be used for the next day's feeding. Breastfeeding just before leaving for work and again as soon as the mother returns home keeps the time between feedings at a minimum. The infant is breastfed frequently throughout the evening hours and on weekends to continue to build up the milk supply.

Some mothers choose to use formula during work hours but to breastfeed when at home. They should prepare for this by gradually eliminating the feedings that occur during work hours and substituting a bottle. Although the total milk supply will be diminished, breastfeeding can continue in the mornings and evenings and on weekends. This is sometimes called "minimal nursing." This is useful for the mother who is not able to pump her breasts at work but still wants to continue breastfeeding.

WEANING

Weaning is a subject of concern for many mothers. "When should I wean?" and "How do I go about it?" are common questions nurses are asked (see Mothers Want to Know: How to Wean from Breastfeeding). Because mothers are often subjected to pressure and opinions offered by family and friends about weaning, they benefit from the fact based information that nurses can offer.

There is no one "right" time to wean the infant. Weaning often depends on the infant's and mother's needs and desires. Although the introduction of solids should be delayed for the first 6 months of life, infants require more iron in the diet after that time. After 4 to 6 months, they take solids from a spoon without trying to suck them. Once teeth begin appearing, infants want to bite and become interested in chewing on finger foods. Although they receive antibodies and other protective substances from breast milk as long as they receive it, their immunological abilities increase as they get older.

Mothers choose to wean their infants for a number of reasons. The mother who wants to breastfeed for a short time but does not wish to continue when she returns to work may wean early. Some mothers feel that they need more freedom and decide to wean. Another pregnancy will necessitate a decision of whether to wean or to continue breastfeeding. The mother may feel that her older infant is mature enough to discontinue breastfeeding and to use a cup. If the mother becomes ill, she may have to stop breastfeeding.

The nurse should provide information so that mothers can make informed decisions about weaning

Mothers Want To Know

How to Wean from Breastfeeding

Deciding When to Wean:
Only you can make the decision about when to wean your baby from breastfeeding. Breastfeeding has many benefits, and you can continue to breastfeed as long as you are comfortable. However, you may decide at any time that weaning is appropriate for you and your baby. Look at all the reasons for continuing nursing or beginning weaning and then make your decision.

How to Proceed:
Gradual weaning is best for both you and your baby when you decide it is time to wean. Abrupt weaning can lead to engorgement and mastitis for you and can upset your baby. You both need to get used to this change slowly.

- Eliminate one feeding at a time. Replace it with a bottle for the younger infant who needs to continue sucking. Infants generally do not drink as much from a cup as they do from a bottle. They will need a bottle so that they drink enough milk to meet their nutritional requirements. The older infant who has learned to use a cup may not need to use a bottle at all.
- Wait several days before eliminating another feeding. This allows time for your milk production to adjust and for the baby to accept the changes.
- Omit daytime feedings first. Start with the feeding at which the baby seems least interested, probably during the day when the baby is busy with play.
- Eliminate the baby's favorite feedings last. Many infants are particularly fond of morning and bedtime feedings, so these should be the last feedings stopped. Many mothers will continue the bedtime feeding for some time, even though the infant is completely weaned during the day. This often helps the baby settle down for the night.
- Expect your infant to want to nurse again when tired, ill, or hurt during the weaning process. This is sometimes called "comfort nursing." A few minutes of nursing may be all that is necessary to comfort the baby.

and should support the mother once her decision is made. Explaining that even a short period of breastfeeding offers her infant many advantages is reassuring. Mothers may need help in planning a gradual weaning process, if it is possible. This allows the mother to avoid engorgement and the infant to get used to a bottle or cup over a period of time.

✔ Check Your Reading

16. What information should be taught to the mother who plans to return to work and continue breastfeeding?

Formula Feeding

Although formula feeding may require less knowledge and skill than breastfeeding, the inexperienced mother may have many questions and may need assistance in learning to use formula correctly. She may also need support from the nurse. Although breastfeeding is preferable, once the mother has made the choice to use formula she should receive support for her decision.

Formula Feeding: Application of Nursing Process

Assessment

Assess both the mother and the infant during the feeding process.

MOTHER'S KNOWLEDGE

Assess the mother's knowledge of bottle feeding. Ask her if she has fed an infant before and if she has questions. Observe her technique during the initial and subsequent feedings. Note how she holds the infant and the bottle, assess her burping technique, and identify areas in which she seems unsure. Determine whether she knows how to prepare formula for when she goes home.

INFANT FEEDING BEHAVIORS

Hungry infants show the same behaviors whether receiving breastfeeding or formula feeding. They may be fussy or crying, may suck on their hands or whatever is near the mouth, and may root for the nipple. Waiting until the infant is frantic may result in a feeding taken too fast, with excess swallowing of air or choking. Assess how the infant sucks during the feeding to identify sucking problems.

Analysis

The most common nursing diagnosis for the mother using formula feeding is: *Knowledge Deficit: Formula Preparation and Feeding Techniques.*

Planning

For this nursing diagnosis, the mother will:

- Demonstrate correct techniques in holding the infant and bottle during feedings.
- Describe how to prepare formula and the frequency of feedings.

Interventions

TEACHING FORMULA PREPARATION

The mother must learn what type of formula she is to use and how to prepare it. Improper preparation can cause problems for the infant. Infection may occur if the milk or water used for preparation is contaminated. Improper dilution of the formula may cause undernutrition or imbalances of sodium, which can be dangerous to the infant.

Types of Formula

Many types of formula are available, and the physician or nurse practitioner will prescribe the type of formula for the mother to use. If milk allergies are prevalent in the family, a soy-based or protein hydrolysate formula may be used from the start. Formula may be purchased in three different forms.

Ready-to-Use. This type of formula can be poured directly from the can into the bottle. Although expensive, it is especially practical when there is difficulty mixing the formula or the water supply is in question. Once the can is opened, it should be refrigerated and used within 24 hours.

Concentrated Liquid. This type must be diluted before use. Be sure that the mother understands the directions for dilution. The amount of concentrated liquid formula and water is specified on the label, but usually equal parts of each are used.

Powdered. Powdered formula is more economical and is particularly useful when a breastfeeding mother plans to give an occasional bottle. Usually one scoop of powder is added to each 2 ounces of warm water in a bottle.

Equipment

Many different types of bottles and nipples are available. Bottles may be glass or plastic, or a plastic liner that fits into a rigid container is used. The liners are designed to prevent swallowing of air from within the bottle. However, the infant will still swallow some air around the nipple. Some nipples are designed to simulate the human nipple to promote jaw development. Selection of type of bottles and nipples depends on individual preference.

Preparation

Discuss preparation of formula with the mother. The mother can prepare a single bottle or a 24-hour supply. If the water supply is safe, sterilization is no longer considered necessary. Bottles and nipples can be washed in hot, sudsy water, rinsed well, and allowed to air dry. Bottles may be washed in a dishwasher, but nipples tend to deteriorate quickly unless washed by hand. The top of the can and a can opener are washed just before opening the can. The formula and water are poured into the bottles, which are then capped. Be sure that the mother understands that the proportion of water and liquid or powdered formula must be adhered to exactly to prevent illness in the infant.

When safety of the water supply is questionable, sterilization, by aseptic or terminal method, is required. In both methods, all equipment is washed and rinsed well before beginning. In the aseptic method, everything needed for the procedure is boiled for 5 minutes in a sterilizer or deep pan. Water for diluting the formula is boiled separately. The bottles are then assembled, using sterilized tongs to avoid contamination by the hands. The formula and boiled water are added, and the bottles are capped and refrigerated until needed.

In the terminal sterilization method, the formula is prepared in the bottles, which are loosely capped. The bottles are then placed in the sterilizer or pan of water, where they are boiled for 25 minutes. After the bottles cool, the caps are tightened and the bottles refrigerated.

EXPLAINING FEEDING TECHNIQUES

The method for bottle feeding is similar to that for breastfeeding.

Positioning. The infant should be positioned in a cradle hold. This semi-upright position allows the mother to hold the infant close in a face-to-face position. The bottle is held so that the nipple is kept full of formula at all times to prevent excessive swallowing of air (Fig. 21–17).

Burping. The infant should be burped or "bubbled" after every half ounce for the first few days of life. The infant will gradually be able to take more milk before burping is necessary. Show the mother how to place the infant over her shoulder or in a sitting position with the head supported while she pats and rubs the infant's back. After the feeding, the infant should always be placed on the side and propped with a rolled blanket. This way aspiration is prevented should more bubbles of air come up with formula.

Frequency. The infant should be fed every 3 to 4 hours. Teach the mother to avoid rigid scheduling and to take her cues from the infant.

Amount. The appropriate amount for each feeding is a frequent concern of inexperienced mothers. The bottle-fed infant will take only 0.5 to 1 ounce per feeding during the first day of life but will increase to 2 to 3 ounces per feeding by the 3rd day. Again, it is important for the mother to adapt to her infant's

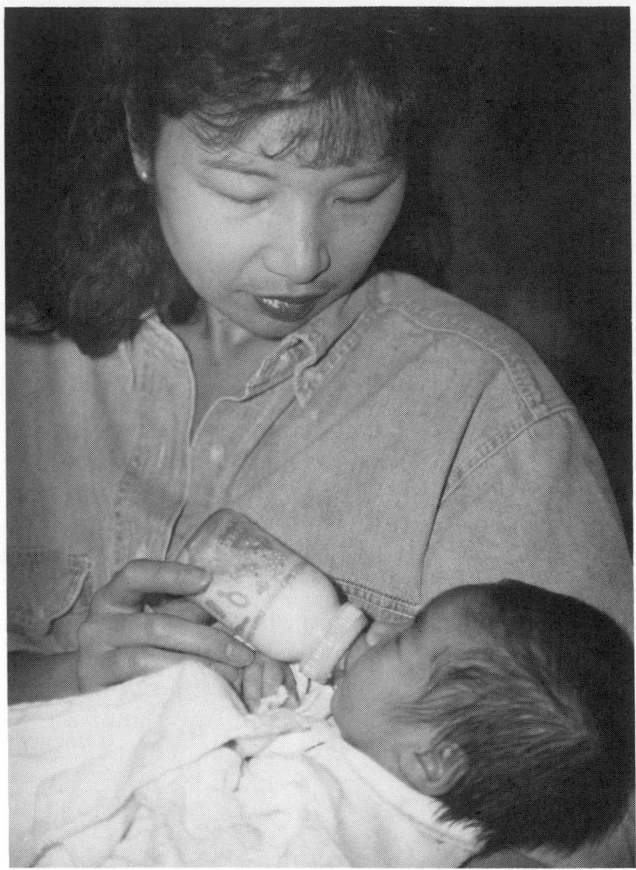

Figure 21–17

This mother holds her infant close during bottle feeding. The bottle is positioned so the nipple is filled with milk at all times.

needs. An infant who is satisfied will often go to sleep.

Cautions. Caution the mother not to prop the bottle. Propping eliminates the holding and cuddling that should accompany feeding and increases the likelihood of choking if regurgitation occurs. Some mothers put an infant to bed with a bottle propped. This not only increases the danger of aspiration but allows milk to stay in the mouth for prolonged periods. The milk may pool in the mouth, promoting growth of bacteria and leading to cavities once the teeth are in. Ear infections are also more common in infants who sleep with a bottle.

The mother should not try to coax the infant to finish the bottle at each feeding. This could result in regurgitation and excessive weight gain. Formula should not be saved from one feeding to the next because of the danger of rapid growth of bacteria in warm milk. Any formula not used within an hour should be discarded.

Formula should not be heated in a microwave oven because the heating is uneven and may result in some parts of the liquid being very hot even when the outside of the bottle feels only warm. Formula can be heated by placing it in a container of hot water until it is warm. The mother should test the formula by allowing a few drops from the bottle to fall on her inner arm to see if it is the right temperature.

Infant Variations. A mother may be concerned about variations in her infant's preference for feeding. Some infants drink from the bottle reluctantly. The mother of a sleepy infant will need to use the same wake-up techniques discussed for the breastfeeding mother.

Although formula is usually given at room temperature in the birth facility, some infants take heated formula better. Soft nipples may be helpful for the infant with a weak suck or small mouth. Angling the tip of the nipple so that it rubs the palate triggers the suck reflex in most infants. Placing a finger under the chin for support may help some infants to suck better. Often it takes patience and persistence to find the most effective techniques.

Evaluation

The mother should be able to:

- Demonstrate correct positioning of the infant and the bottle during feedings.
- Explain preparation of formula, the amount the infant should take, and the feeding techniques to be used.

✔ Check Your Reading

17. What questions might a mother have about formula feeding?

Summary Concepts

- The newborn may lose weight in the first few days after birth as a result of insufficient intake and normal loss of extracellular fluid.
- Colostrum is rich in protein, vitamins, minerals, and immunoglobulins. Transitional milk appears between colostrum and mature milk. Mature milk is present after the first 2 weeks of lactation.
- Breast milk has nutrients in proportions that the newborn requires and in an easily digested form. Commercial formulas are cow's milk adapted to simulate human milk.
- Breast milk contains factors that help establish the normal intestinal flora and prevent infection. These include *bifidus* factor, leukocytes, lysozymes, and immunoglobulins.

- A variety of commercial formulas are available. They include modified cow's milk formula for most infants, soy-based or casein hydrolysate formulas for infants with allergies, and special formulas for preterm infants or those with special problems.
- Factors that influence the mother's choice of feeding method include knowledge about each method, support from family and friends, cultural influences, and employment.
- Suckling at the breast causes the posterior pituitary to release oxytocin, which causes the let-down reflex. It also causes the anterior pituitary to release prolactin, which increases milk production.
- The principle of "supply and demand" applies to breastfeeding. Milk production increases when the infant feeds frequently. When breastfeeding ceases, prolactin is decreased and eventually the alveoli of the breasts atrophy and stop producing milk.
- Flat and inverted nipples should be identified during pregnancy, and the mother should use breast shells to correct them. Creams and methods to toughen the nipples are not necessary.
- The nurse can help the mother establish breastfeeding by initiating early feeding, helping to position the infant at the breast, and showing her how to position her hands. The nurse should teach the mother how to help the infant latch on to the breast, assess the position of the mouth on the breast, and remove the infant from the breast.
- The mother should feed the infant 8 to 12 times each day for 10 to 15 minutes at the first breast and until the infant is satisfied at the second breast (generally at least 10 minutes).
- Wake-up techniques that can be used for a sleepy infant include unwrapping the infant's blankets, talking to the infant, changing the diaper, rubbing the infant's back, expressing colostrum onto the breast, and switching the infant from one breast to the other.
- When infants suck from a bottle, they must push the tongue against the nipple to slow the flow of milk. When they suckle at the breast, they position the nipple far into the mouth so that the gums compress the areola as the tongue moves over the milk sinus in a wave-like motion.
- The nurse can help the woman with engorged breasts by encouraging frequent nursing, applying heat and cold, massaging, and expressing milk to soften the areola if necessary.
- The nurse should help the mother with sore nipples to check the positioning of the infant at the breast. The mother should vary the position of the infant at the breast, apply colostrum or breast milk to the nipples, and expose the nipples to air.
- Teaching for the mother who plans to work and breastfeed includes expression of breast milk by hand or pump and proper storage of the milk.
- Mothers who use formula need information about the types of formula available, how to prepare them correctly, and feeding techniques.

References and Readings

Adams, E.J. (1992). Nutritional care in food allergy and food intolerance. In L.K. Mahan & M.T. Arlin (Eds.), *Krause's food, nutrition, and diet therapy* (8th ed.). Philadelphia: W.B. Saunders.

Auerbach, K.G. (1990). Breastfeeding fallacies: Their relationship to understanding lactation. *Birth*, 17(1), 44–50.

Auerbach, K.G. (1990). The effect of nipple shields on maternal milk volume. *Journal of Obstetric, Gynecologic, and Neonatal Nursing*, 19(5), 419–427.

Behrman, R.E. (1992). *Nelson textbook of pediatrics* (14th ed.). Philadelphia: W.B. Saunders.

Bottorff, J.L. (1990). Mothers' perceptions of breast milk. *Journal of Obstetric, Gynecologic, and Neonatal Nursing*, 19(6), 518–527.

Bottorff, J.L. (1990). Persistence in breastfeeding: A phenomenological investigation. *Journal of Advanced Nursing*, 19(6), 201–209.

Bronner, Y.L., & Paige, D.M. (1992). Current concepts in infant nutrition. *Journal of Nurse-Midwifery*, 37(Suppl. 2), 43S–58S.

Conley, L.J. (1990). Childbearing and childrearing practices in Mormonism. *Neonatal Network*, 9(3), 41–47.

D'Avanzo, C.E. (1992). Bridging the cultural gap with Southeast Asians. MCN: *American Journal of Maternal Child Nursing*, 17(4), 204–208.

D'Harlingue, A.E., & Byrne, W.J. (1991). Nutritional needs in the newborn. In H.W. Taeusch, R.A. Ballard, & M.E. Avery (Eds.), *Schaffer and Avery's diseases of the newborn* (6th ed.). Philadelphia: W.B. Saunders.

Dix, D.N. (1991). Why women decide not to breastfeed. *Birth*, 18(4), 222–225.

Dungy, C.I., Christensen-Szalanski, J., Losch, M., & Russell, D. (1992). Effect of discharge samples on duration of breast-feeding. *Pediatrics*, 90(2), 233–237.

Edgehouse, L., & Radzyminski, S.G. (1990). A device for supplementing breast-feeding. MCN: *American Journal of Maternal Child Nursing*, 15(1), 34–35.

Foster, R.L.R., Hunsberger, M.M., & Anderson, J.J.T. (1989). *Family-centered nursing care of children*. Philadelphia: W.B. Saunders.

Frantz, K. (1991). Keep breastfeeding simple, keep it easy, keep it fun. *Birth*, 18(4), 228–229.

Harris, M.K.B. (1993). Breastfeeding. In S. Mattson & J.E. Smith (Eds.), NAACOG *core curriculum for maternal-newborn nursing*. Philadelphia: W.B. Saunders.

Heffern, D. (1990). Reminders for building confidence in breastfeeding moms. MCN: *American Journal of Maternal Child Nursing*, 15(4), 267.

Houston, R.J.R., & Field, P.A. (1988). Practices and policies in the initiation of breastfeeding. *Journal of Obstetric, Gynecologic and Neonatal Gynecologic Nursing*, 17(6), 418–424.

Hill, P.D. (1991). The enigma of insufficient milk supply. MCN: *American Journal of Maternal Child Nursing*, 16(6), 312–316.

Huggins, K. (1990). *The nursing mother's companion*. Boston: Harvard Common Press.

Institute of Medicine, National Academy of Sciences, Food and Nutrition Board. (1989). *Recommended dietary allowances* (19th ed.). Washington, D.C.: National Academy Press.

Institute of Medicine, National Academy of Sciences, Food and Nutrition Board. (1991). *Nutrition during lactation*. Washington, D.C.: National Academy Press.

Johnstone, H.A., & Marcinak, J.F. (1990). Candidiasis in the breastfeeding mother and infant. *Journal of Obstetric, Gynecologic, and Neonatal Nursing*, 19(2), 171–173.

Kearney, M.H., & Cronenwett, L.R. (1991). Breastfeeding and employment. *Journal of Obstetric, Gynecologic, and Neonatal Nursing*, 20(6), 471–480.

Kearney, M.H., Cronenwett, L.R., & Barrett, J. (1990). Breastfeeding problems in the first week postpartum. *Nursing Research*, 39(2), 90–95.

Kyenkya-Isabirye, M. (1992). UNICEF launches the Baby-Friendly Hospital Initiative. MCN: *American Journal of Maternal Child Nursing*, 17(4), 177–179.

Lawrence, R.A. (1989). *Breastfeeding: A guide for the medical profession* (3rd ed.). St. Louis: C.V. Mosby.

Meftuh, A.B., Tapsoba, L.P., & Lamounier, J.A. (1991). Breastfeeding practices in Ethiopian women in southern California. *Indian Journal of Pediatrics*, 58(3), 349–356.

Minchin, M.K. (1989). Positioning for breastfeeding. *Birth*, 16(2), 67–80.

Moore, E.R., Bianchi-Gray, M., & Stephens, L. (1991). A community hospital–based breastfeeding counseling service. *Pediatric Nursing*, 17(4), 383–389.

NAACOG. (1991). OGN *nursing practice resource: Facilitating breastfeeding*. Washington D.C.

NAACOG Executive Board. (1992). NAACOG position statement. Issue: Breastfeeding. NAACOG *Newsletter*, 19(1), 8.

Nice, F.J. (1989). Can a breastfeeding mother take medication without harming her infant? MCN: *American Journal of Maternal Child Nursing*, 14(1), 27–31.

Pipes, P.L. (1992). Nutrition in infancy. In L.K. Mahan & M.T. Arlin (Eds.), *Krause's food, nutrition, and diet therapy* (8th ed.). Philadelphia: W.B. Saunders.

Riordan, J. (1991). *A practical guide to breastfeeding*. St. Louis: C.V. Mosby.

Serdula, M.K., Cairns, K.A., Williamson, D.F., Fuller, M., & Brown, J.E. (1991). Correlates of breastfeeding in a low-income population of whites, blacks, and Southeast Asians. *Journal of the American Dietetic Association*, 19(1), 41–45.

Shrago, L., & Bocar, D. (1990). The infant's contribution to breastfeeding. *Journal of Obstetric, Gynecologic, and Neonatal Nursing*, 19(3), 209–215.

Sollid, D.T., Evans, B.T., McClowry, S.G., & Garrett, A. (1989). Breastfeeding multiples. *Journal of Perinatal Neonatal Nursing*, 3(1), 46–65.

Tiedje, L.B., & Collins, C. (1989). Combining employment and motherhood. MCN: *American Journal of Maternal Child Nursing*, 14(1), 9–14.

U.S. Department of Health and Human Services. (1991). *Healthy children* 2000. Washington D.C.

Walker, M. (1989). Management of selected early breastfeeding problems seen in clinical practice. *Birth*, 16(3), 148–158.

Walker, M., & Driscoll, J.W. (1989). Sore nipples: The new mother's nemesis. MCN: *American Journal of Maternal Child Nursing*, 14(4), 260–265.

Whaley, L.F., & Wong, D.L. (1991). *Nursing care of infants and children* (4th ed.). St. Louis: C.V. Mosby.

Williams, K.M., & Morse, J.M. (1989). Weaning patterns of first-time mothers. MCN: *American Journal of Maternal Child Nursing*, 14(3), 188–192.

Woldt, E.H. (1991). Breastfeeding support group in the NICU. *Neonatal Network*, 9(5), 53–56.

Worthington-Roberts, B. (1993). Lactation and human milk: Nutritional considerations. In B. Worthington-Roberts & S.R. Williams (Eds.), *Nutrition in pregnancy and lactation* (5th ed.). St. Louis: Times Mirror/Mosby.

Worthington-Roberts, B., & Williams, S.R. (1993). *Nutrition in pregnancy and lactation* (5th ed.). St. Louis: Times Mirror/Mosby.

Ziemer, M.M., & George, C. (1990). Breastfeeding the low-birth-weight infant. *Neonatal Network*, 9(4), 33–38.

Ziemer, M.M., & Pigeon, J.G. (1993). Skin changes and pain in the nipple during the first week of lactation. *Journal of Obstetric, Gynecologic, and Neonatal Nursing*, 22(3)247–256.

22

Parenting During the Early Weeks

Objectives

1. Explain why nurses need knowledge about care of the infant during the early weeks after birth.
2. Explain the safety features of infant equipment that parents must consider.
3. Explain methods of resolving common problems involving infant crying and sleep patterns during the early weeks of parenting.
4. Answer common questions that parents might have about care of the young infant.
5. Describe the normal changes in growth and development of the infant during the first 12 weeks of life.
6. Explain the purpose and importance of well baby check-ups and immunizations for infants.
7. List signs that indicate illness in the infant.
8. Discuss the current knowledge about sudden infant death syndrome.
9. Explain how home care of the high-risk infant differs from that of the normal infant.

Definitions

Attenuate • To weaken.

Extrusion reflex • Automatic nervous system response that causes an infant to push anything solid out of the mouth.

Miliaria (prickly heat) • Rash caused by heat.

Reflux • A condition in which stomach contents enter the esophagus and may be aspirated into the lungs.

Seborrheic dermatitis (cradle cap) • Yellowish, crusty area of the scalp.

Sudden infant death syndrome (SIDS) • Sudden unexplained death of an apparently healthy infant younger than 1 year of age.

Nurses are often called on to answer parents' questions about care of the infant during the early weeks after discharge from the birth facility. This chapter provides information to help nurses assist parents adjust to their new role and provide care for the well infant during the first 12 weeks of life. The focus is on teaching about well infants beyond the usual birth facility discharge teaching, which is included in Chapter 20. Information about the ill or older infant can be found in a pediatric textbook.

Information for New Parents

Needs

The early weeks after birth are often very stressful for new parents. This is particularly true for the first birth but also applies to families with other children. The mother is tired from the pregnancy and birth, both parents may be anxious about their new role, and the newborn may be awake much of the night or may behave in other unexpected ways. Parents have many questions not only about the newborn but also about adjustment to parenthood and ongoing care of the infant.

The need for information and support from nurses varies according to the experience, age, and individual concerns of parents. The very young mother may be most concerned about the physical care and medical needs of her infant, whereas the older mother may also be concerned about her own physical needs, including nutrition and exercise. Most mothers, regardless of age or experience, lack information about some aspects of infant care and psychosocial issues (Degenhart-Leskosky, 1989).

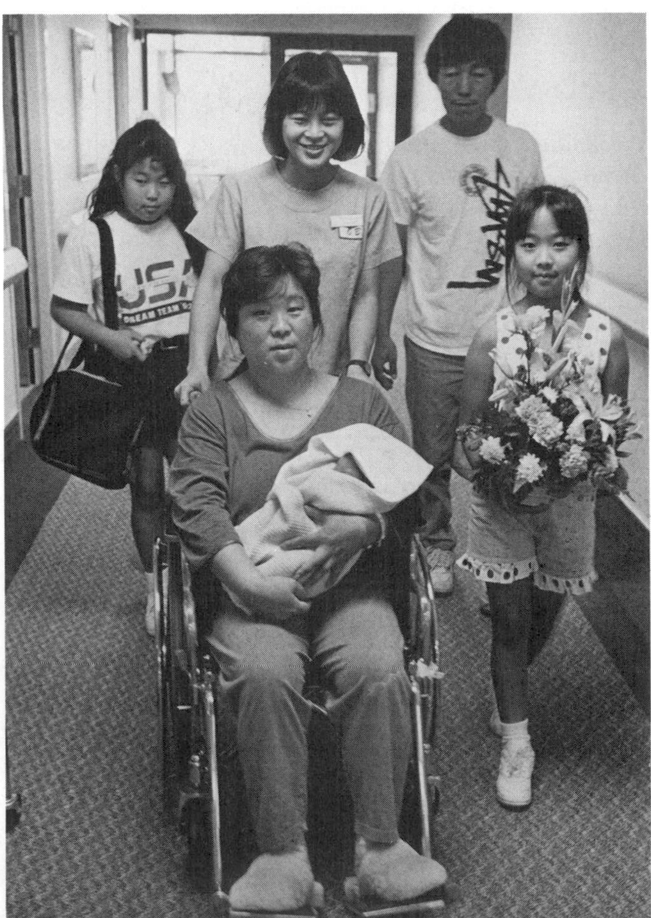

The homecoming can be a time of mixed emotions for all family members. Adjustments may cause the mother to become overwhelmed, the father may feel forgotten, and siblings may resent the changes a new baby brings.

Sources of Information

In the birth facility, parents may receive more information about care of the newborn than they can absorb in the very short time available. Birth facility stays now average 24 hours for mothers with normal vaginal births. Increasing numbers of women go home even before 24 hours after birth. Mothers who have cesarean deliveries generally remain in the hospital 3 to 4 days or less. This greatly limits the opportunity for nurses to offer teaching and support to new parents. During their time at the birth facility, new mothers may have physical needs and anxieties that interfere with their ability to learn. This leaves parents inadequately prepared to deal with the multiple demands of early parenting.

In the past, the extended family was the usual source of support and information for new parents. Today, family members are frequently widely separated and parents rely on friends and health care personnel. Friends can be important sources of support and information, but their knowledge may be incorrect or outdated. For example, they may not have accurate information about breastfeeding and the latest recommendations for immunizations. Nurses are ideal sources of assistance in these situations.

Because the nursery staff is available 24 hours a day, many hospitals encourage parents to call when they have questions about newborns. Others have instituted special hotlines for new parents. In some maternity units, nurses call all mothers within the first week after discharge, especially those who went home within 24 hours of birth or are at risk for problems. Home visits are provided as part of the maternity package in some birth facilities (Evans, 1991).

Nurses in pediatricians' offices sometimes fill this role. A few nurse entrepreneurs have started businesses to offer home visits to parents in the early days after birth.

Classes are often available to help parents during various stages of child development. Some of these classes, usually taught by nurses, focus primarily on the early weeks after birth. They provide an opportunity for parents to share feelings and experiences with each other while learning from a reliable source how to deal with areas of difficulty in infant care.

✔ Check Your Reading

1. Where do parents obtain information about caring for the infant during the early weeks after birth?
2. What are some ways in which nurses offer follow-up services to new parents?

Infant Equipment

Many parents have questions about choosing infant equipment. Ideally, they have obtained most of the equipment before the infant is born, but nurses may receive questions in the weeks after the birth. Although the nurse should never recommend specific brand names of equipment, guidance about features and safety is very helpful.

Safety Considerations

Parents, especially those of limited means, need to understand that there are few, if any, absolutely essential pieces of equipment for newborns. Infants sleep in padded dresser drawers and canopied cribs with equal comfort. Safety is the most important consideration.

New equipment sold in the United States is generally safe because manufacturers are required to follow certain governmental standards for safety. However, hand-me-down equipment may have been produced before newer requirements were in effect. Older equipment should be checked carefully to be certain that all parts are strong and working properly. See Table 22-1 for a summary of safety considerations.

Table 22-1. SAFETY CONSIDERATIONS FOR INFANT EQUIPMENT

Cribs

Crib slats must be no more than 2⅜ inches apart so that the infant's head cannot become wedged between them. Remove corner posts that extend more than 1/16 inch above the end panel to prevent strangulation if clothing catches on them. Plastic teething guards should be firmly attached to side rails.

Bumper pads prevent the infant from hitting against the side rails. They should fit well around the entire crib and must be anchored to keep them in place so that infants cannot get caught between the side rail and the bumper.

The crib mattress should fit snugly, with less than an inch between the mattress and the sides of the crib so that the infant cannot become wedged in that space. The mattress should be firm. There should be no soft pillows in the crib that would increase the risk of suffocation.

Crib toys or mobiles should be firmly attached, with no straps or strings in the infant's reach. Mobiles should be removed when the infant can reach them.

Cribs should be placed away from hanging cords of blinds or drapes, as these also could become wrapped around an active infant.

Other Equipment

Paint used to refurbish infant equipment should be marked lead-free and safe for children's equipment to prevent lead poisoning.

All parts should function properly: crib side rails must be secure, highchair trays must stay firmly in place, latches must remain fastened, etc. The frame and basic construction of all equipment should be sturdy.

All moving parts should be examined carefully to see whether little fingers could get caught or whether the infant could accidentally trigger a catch that would cause the equipment to become unsafe.

Safety straps for infant seats, swings, changing tables, high chairs, or other equipment in which the infant should be secured to prevent falling must be in good condition. Straps should fit around the infant but not be long enough that the infant could become entangled.

Automatic swings should have legs that are stable, without a tendency to tip over. Note how difficult it is to put the infant into the swing and to remove the infant from the swing safely.

All toys should be examined carefully for parts that can be removed and swallowed.

Car Seats

It is never safe for an adult to carry an infant while riding in a car because a sudden stop or accident can cause the infant to be hurled against the dashboard or crushed by the adult, who would be thrown forward by the force of the impact. Use of child safety seats in automobiles may reduce the chance of fatal injury to infants by as much as 69 per cent (Centers for Disease Control, 1991). In the United States, all states now require restraint of infants and young children in car seats when they are riding in automobiles. Generally, laws require that special seats be used for children under 4 years or 40 pounds. Discharge teaching should include information about state car seat laws. In some birth facilities, car seat rentals or loans are available.

Many different car seats are manufactured, and the array may be confusing to parents. Some car seats are designed for infants weighing up to 20 pounds. Others can be adapted to meet the needs of both newborns and young children. Seats for newborns face the rear of the car and recline at a 45-degree angle, whereas those for older children face forward and may allow the child to sit up or recline.

Parents should examine the harness restraint carefully before buying a car seat. Three-point and five-point harnesses are available. For very young infants, the five-point harness is safest (Fig. 22–1). It should firmly restrain the infant, yet be quick and easy to fasten. All car seats should be secured by the car seat belt so that there is no chance that the infant could be hurled forward on impact.

Preterm or very small infants may need special car seat adaptations because of their size. Blankets placed at the head, along the sides, and between the legs may improve the fit. Special seats or beds designed specifically for the very small infant are also available.

A large number of parents may use their car seats improperly. An incorrectly fastened harness may not restrain the infant in an accident or could cause damage, such as laceration of the liver. If the automobile seat belt is not routed through the correct area of the car seat, the seat may tip or become a flying missile during an accident. Asking parents if they have any problems with their car seat may provide an opportunity to encourage them to use it according to the manufacturer's directions so that the seats will function effectively. Car seats should be used only in cars and only according to manufacturer's directions. Safety considerations for car seat use are summarized in Table 22–2.

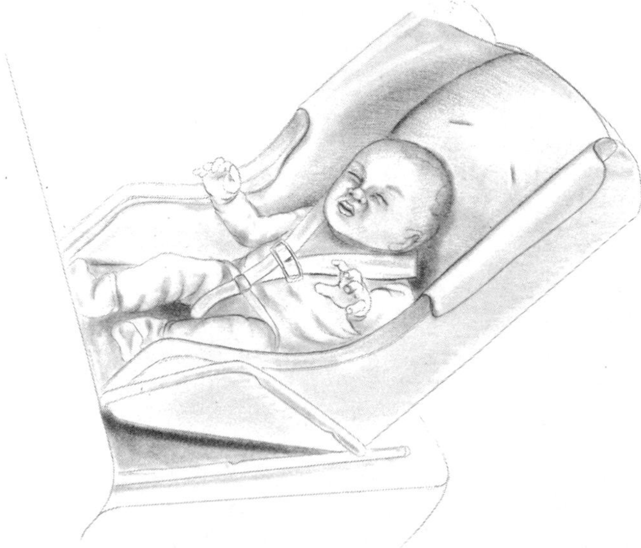

Figure 22–1

A car seat for an infant under 20 pounds should face the rear of the car. The restraint straps should fit snugly but should not be too high around the infant's neck.

Table 22–2. SAFETY CONSIDERATIONS FOR INFANT CAR SEATS

1. Use only car seats that are approved for use in automobiles. Seats designed for use in the home will not provide adequate protection in a car.
2. Use car seats that are appropriate for the infant's age and size. Infants weighing up to 20 pounds face the back of the car and recline.
3. Follow the manufacturer's directions for fastening the seat in the car and the infant in the car seat. Recheck the restraint straps each time the seat is used.
4. Be certain that the straps are tight enough to prevent the infant from getting out of the restraints or turning over in the seat. Infants who turn over can suffocate in the padding of the seat.
5. Check to see that the infant cannot become caught with the straps tightly around the neck.
6. Use car seats only in an automobile. Do not place them on a soft surface, such as a bed, where they might turn over and suffocate the infant. Do not place them on surfaces from which they might fall, such as grocery carts.
7. Never leave infants alone in a car, even for a few minutes. They could be kidnapped or injured in an accident involving the car even though it is parked. Cars quickly become very warm, and the infant could become dangerously overheated.

✔ Check Your Reading

3. What advice can the nurse offer about safety features of equipment used for infants?
4. What facts should parents consider when buying and using a car seat?

Early Problems

Infant Crying

Crying is one of the major concerns parents have during the early weeks after birth. Crying is most frustrating when parents cannot find a cause for it. Infants cry for many reasons, including hunger, discomfort, fatigue, overstimulation, and boredom. Sometimes no specific cause can be determined. Infants cry approximately 60 to 90 minutes a day during the first 3 weeks of life, then crying time increases to 2 to 4 hours a day by 6 weeks and gradually decreases by age 3 months (Whaley and Wong, 1991).

When there is not an obvious cause for crying, some parents are afraid that responding will spoil the infant. This concern may increase if the infant stops crying when picked up. However, changing the infant's position may help gas move in the intestines, relieve tired muscles, or distract the infant by

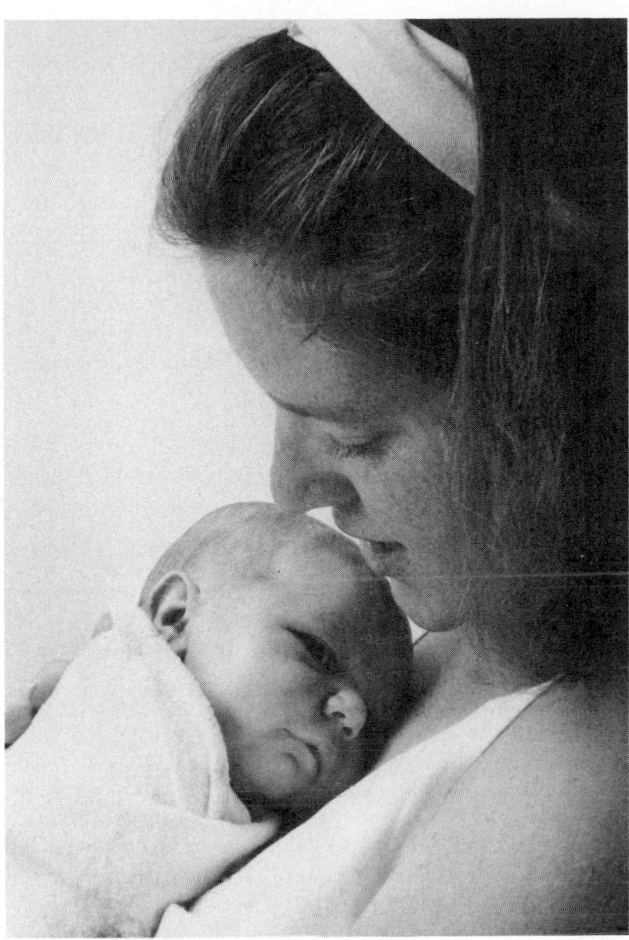

Many young infants prefer to be wrapped snugly in blankets. This infant is quiet when held against the mother's chest as she talks or sings softly.

changing the scenery, bringing about a temporary cessation of crying.

Infants cannot signal that they have unmet needs in any other way but crying and are unlikely to be spoiled by parents meeting their needs. In fact, it is essential that their needs be met in a consistent, warm, prompt manner for the development of trust to occur. Infants of parents who intervene appropriately for crying are less likely to cry excessively as they get older.

Some families develop quite original methods for dealing with crying infants. Others need help finding appropriate techniques to use. Parents Want to Know: Methods to Relieve Crying in Infants lists suggestions that nurses can make to frustrated parents.

When parents have searched for the usual causes for crying and tried the comfort techniques that are often successful to no avail, it may be necessary to let the infant "cry it out" alone. Some infants have a need to discharge excess tension by crying for a period of time before going to sleep. Although this is difficult for parents, leaving the infant safely in the crib for 15 minutes or so may be enough to allow the infant to fall sleep.

Some parents find that setting a timer is helpful. At the end of the period allowed, they can quietly check to be sure that the infant is all right. Changing the diaper or holding the infant for a few minutes before putting the infant back to bed may be all that is necessary. Talking softly to provide reassurance while patting the infant's back without picking the infant up may be effective. Occasionally, several 15-minute crying sessions are necessary before the infant drifts off to sleep.

Colic

DESCRIPTION

Colic is characterized by irritable crying for no obvious reason, which usually occurs during the late afternoon or early evening and lasts 3 to 4 hours or longer. It occurs in 10 to 20 per cent of all infants (Foye and Sulkes, 1990), beginning in the first 2 or 3 weeks of life. Although it usually ends about 3 months after birth, some infants continue to have colic until 6 months of age. The infant is in good health, eats well, and gains weight appropriately, despite the daily crying episodes.

Although many theories have been investigated, the cause of colic remains unknown. Allergies, poor feeding techniques, parental tension, and exposure to smoking have all been considered. Colic may be due to immaturity of the gastrointestinal tract or nervous system or to a combination of factors.

Infants with colic cry as though in pain, draw their knees onto the abdomen, and may pass flatus. The crying is intense and may last until the infant falls asleep exhausted. Because continuous crying causes a great deal of parental distress and may be a factor in parenting disorders or child abuse, it is important that nurses provide support to parents of colicky infants.

INTERVENTIONS

Nursing interventions consist of using therapeutic communication to help parents of colicky infants express their frustrations (see Therapeutic Communication) and teaching techniques for dealing with the problem. Parents should be reassured that the condition does not indicate poor parenting. They may feel inadequate about their failure to manage the problem and guilty if their frustration develops into

Parents Want To Know

Methods to Relieve Crying in Infants

Treating Common Causes:

***Hunger*:** Did the infant take the usual amount at the last feeding? Perhaps a bubble of air caused the infant to feel full at feeding time but hungry when it was expelled. Even when it seems too soon to feed again, the infant may be experiencing a "growth spurt," when more frequent feedings are needed for a day or two to provide necessary nutrients for rapid growth.

***Air Bubbles*:** Fussy infants may need more frequent burping during and after feedings than other infants. Burping is also appropriate during a crying spell, when the infant may swallow air.

***Diapers*:** Although most infants do not mind wet or soiled diapers, they may become cold or their skin may be irritated when diapers are not changed frequently enough.

***Clothing*:** Check the infant's clothing for anything that could cause discomfort. If pins are used, check that they are closed. Be sure that seams of plastic linings are not scratchy, elastic on sleeves too tight, or tags at the neck irritating.

***Warmth*:** Be sure that the infant is warm enough, yet not too warm. Feel the infant's abdomen to determine skin temperature. Dress the infant as an adult would want to be dressed, with a receiving blanket added. The abdomen should feel warm even if the hands and feet are cool. Infants who are overdressed rarely perspire but often cry because of their discomfort.

***Overstimulation*:** Too many visitors handling the infant or too much noise and commotion in the household may be overstimulating. A quiet environment, rocking, or just being left to work off excess tension alone in the crib may be necessary for the infant.

Quieting Techniques:

***Rocking*:** The gentle motion of rocking, reminiscent of intrauterine life, is often soothing for infants.

***Automatic Swings*:** Swings may be battery-operated or wind-up. If buying a wind-up swing, check the noise level to be sure that the winding does not wake the infant going off to sleep. Very small infants may need padding with blankets for safety and comfort.

***Walking, Jiggling, Swaying*:** Sometimes a newborn prefers a particular style of motion. Rocking sideways with the infant held in an upright position seems particularly helpful to some infants. Taking a walk outside may provide new sights and sounds and be distracting for both parents and infant.

***Swaddling*:** In the birth facility, infants are wrapped snugly because it is comforting to them and they are used to restricted activity in the uterus. During the first few weeks after birth, swaddling may be helpful when the infant is fussy.

***Stroller or Buggy Rides*:** The motion of a stroller or buggy may be soothing to some infants. The ride can be in or outside the house. A parent can move a stroller back and forth with one foot while doing chores or eating meals. The stroller should allow the infant to lie down rather than sit. Padding may increase comfort.

***Car Rides*:** Some infants go to sleep when in a moving car. A short ride around the block may put the infant to sleep. The infant may stay asleep when carried into the house.

***Music*:** The sound of a parent singing may be reassuring to the infant. Some newborns respond well to a music box, radio, or tape of music. Music with a steady beat or classical music may be particularly effective. Music should be played softly.

***White Noise*:** Background noise sometimes puts infants to sleep by diffusing other noises. A radio set on low, a clock ticking, the sound of a dishwasher, dryer, or even a vacuum cleaner may be effective. Tapes of sounds heard in utero are available and work best if introduced in the first week of life.

***Heat*:** A well-covered warm water bottle placed against the infant's abdomen may be soothing. (Take care not to burn the infant's skin.) A blanket warmed in the clothes dryer for a few minutes serves the same purpose. Placing the newborn in an infant seat on top of a dishwasher or clothes dryer provides heat and background noise. Be sure that the infant is well secured, of course. Do not use a heating pad.

***Bathing*:** Although older infants love baths, very young infants may not yet have reached that stage. However, giving a bath may be a distraction for both parent and infant, and the infant may sleep afterward.

***Water*:** An infant who has been crying for awhile may be thirsty even if not hungry. Although extra water is not a requirement for infants, some mothers like to give it on occasion. It may help bring up bubbles of air that the infant has swallowed while crying. The breastfed infant's thirst can be alleviated by nursing.

***Infant Carriers or Packs*:** Front carriers are designed for the young infant and may be especially helpful during crying episodes. A parent's warm body, soothing voice, and gentle swaying motion can often put an infant to sleep. At the same time, the parent can move around and accomplish other tasks. Backpacks should be used only for older infants who are able to support their head alone.

Parents Want To Know

Methods to Relieve Crying in Infants *Continued*

Pacifiers: Parents may find pacifiers useful for an irritable infant. The infant may be comforted by sucking even though not hungry.

Position Changes: Try varying the infant's position.

- Laying the infant prone across a parent's lap (or over a warmed blanket) may help expel flatus and be soothing.
- Using the "colic hold" works in some cases. Hold the infant upright in a forward-facing position. Place one arm under the infant's knees (Fig. 22–2). This may help the infant pass flatus. Placing the infant in a supine position and flexing the knees on the abdomen may also help.
- An alternate "colic hold" is to place the infant prone along the parent's arm with the infants head at the elbow and the body supported along the arm.

Mother's Diet: Breastfeeding mothers can review their diet to see if there is anything they have eaten that might cause a problem in the infant. Some infants react when mothers drink large amounts of cow's milk. Others react to highly acidic or spicy foods. Caffeine passes into breast milk and can cause wakefulness and irritability. Omitting the suspected food for 5 to 7 days, then trying the food again and watching for irritability after the next feedings may identify the cause of the crying.

Massage: Gentle massage may be soothing for some infants. Massage of the abdomen may help infants with colic.

anger. The nurse should let them know that it is not abnormal to feel ambivalent or even angry with the infant.

It is important for parents of colicky infants to talk about their feelings. Parents can talk to each other, to friends who have had colicky infants, as well as to nurses. The parents should be encouraged to take time away from the infant to rest and recoup the energy that is needed to deal with the demands of a crying infant, if possible. Leaving the infant with a baby-sitter or taking turns caring for the infant is vital.

All of the techniques listed in Parents Want to Know: Methods to Relieve Crying in Infants may alleviate crying from colic temporarily, but generally none gives prolonged relief. The colic holds may be

Therapeutic Communication

Shannon Gray tells the nurse, Mark Winston, about her daughter, Erin, who has been having crying spells every night lasting 4 hours or longer. Shannon looks tired and worried. Erin, age 4 weeks, eats well, shows good weight gain, and is developing appropriately for her age.

Shannon: It seems like I can't do anything at night anymore, except try to stop Erin's crying.

Mark: You spend a lot of time trying to find ways to comfort her.

Paraphrasing to encourage the mother to continue

Shannon: I've tried everything! I rock her, walk with her, try feeding and changing her. We go for car rides and put her in her swing, but nothing works for long. She just starts crying again.

Mark: How frustrating that must be for you when nothing works!

Reflecting mother's feelings shows that nurse is trying to understand them

Shannon: Sometimes I wonder why I ever wanted to have a baby. I never thought it would be like this. Isn't that an awful thing to say! But it's true! (Sounds defiant.)

Mark: Being a mother is so much harder than you expected that sometimes you aren't sure you made the right choice.

Reflects the content of what the mother said to help her focus. Shows acceptance.

Shannon: But I really do love her. I just don't know how to help her. I must be a terrible mother. (Becomes teary.)

Mark: Parents often feel guilty when they can't find a way to help an upset baby. And yet, we really don't know all the reasons babies cry. It sounds like you've tried very hard to help Erin. Maybe we can work together to think of some other techniques to use.

Gives reassurance that what the mother is feeling is normal, then offers information and further help.

Shannon: I'd love to find some other ways to help Erin. She really is a good baby, when she isn't crying so much. And it worries me to have her so unhappy. What else can I do for her?

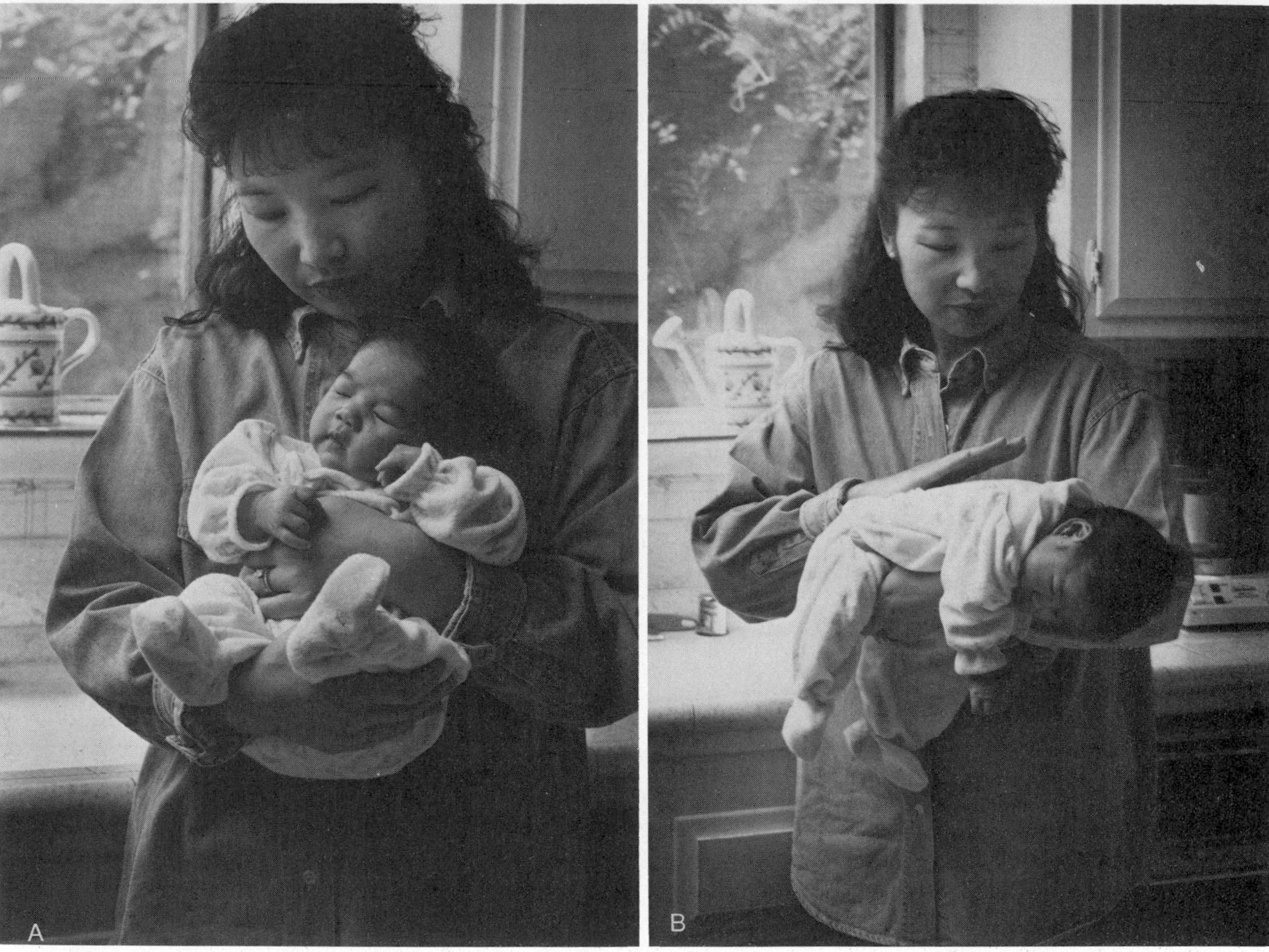

Figure 22–2

Positions for holding an infant with colic. **A,** The mother holds the infant facing forward. One hand creates slight pressure against the abdomen, while the other sharply flexes the knees. This position may help the infant expel flatus. **B,** The prone hold is also effective for some infants. The mother holds the infant in a horizontal position along her arm.

particularly effective for some infants (Fig. 22–2). Changing the bottle-fed infant's formula to one that is not cow's milk or to a soy derivative may help the infant with allergies. Breastfeeding mothers who drink large amounts of cow's milk should try eliminating it for 5 to 7 days to see if improvement occurs. (Other calcium-rich foods or a calcium supplement should be added to the mother's diet.)

A quiet environment, calm approach, and fairly regular schedule may help some infants with colic. Parents should be taught various methods to help crying infants. They should be encouraged to be creative in finding ways of soothing the infant. Parents should also be assured that spoiling will not result from responding to the infant's cries. In severe cases, the infant may be given a sedative, antispasmodic, antiflatulent, or antihistamine for a short time.

✔ Check Your Reading

5. Why should parents respond to crying without fear of spoiling the infant?
6. How can nurses help parents of crying infants?

Sleep

PARENTS

During the early months after birth, parents often wonder whether they will ever get a full night's sleep again. Because it is likely that they will be up during the night, they should try to make up lost sleep at other times. If the mother has not returned to work, she can sleep during the day when the infant naps. If she is working, parents can alternate responsibility for night or early-morning feedings. When mothers are breastfeeding, fathers can change the diaper, bring the infant to the mother for night feedings, and then settle the infant back in bed when the feeding is finished. This allows the mother more time to sleep, and some of the middle-of-the-night care of the infant is shared.

INFANT SLEEP PATTERNS

Infants spend less time than adults in deep sleep. They have a larger percentage of lighter rapid eye movement (REM) sleep. During this type of sleep, they may make noises loud enough to wake parents in the same room, and they move about as if awakening. Going to them at this time is likely to wake them, but, if left alone, they may return to deep sleep.

Infants should be positioned on the side for sleep. The nurse should explain to parents that this position prevents aspiration should regurgitation occur. No pillows or soft stuffed animals should be allowed in the crib, as they could cause suffocation. Some infants sleep better in an enclosed space and may scoot themselves into a corner of a large crib. The nurse should suggest to parents that they use rolled blankets around the infant to provide a "nest," which feels more like the circumscribed area of the uterus.

Parents Want To Know

How to Help Infants Sleep Through the Night

- Allow the infant to cry for a few minutes before responding. The infant may not be completely awake and may return to sleep if undisturbed.
- Keep nighttime feedings for feeding only. Avoid unnecessary activity, or the infant may eventually learn to think of this as a playtime.
- Use a soft light that provides only the amount of light essential for care.
- Give night feedings in the infant's room to further avoid stimulation.
- Keep sounds subdued. Soft music or humming may help the infant return to sleep, but talking should be kept to a minimum.
- Keep night feedings short and put the infant back to bed immediately.
- Change diapers in the middle of the feeding to prevent awakening the infant after feeding.
- As the infant nears the age when sleeping through the night is more likely, try patting him or her on the back instead of feeding. Offer water instead of milk.
- Allow the infant to fall asleep at bedtime on his or her own instead of always rocking and/or feeding the infant. This may help the infant go back to sleep alone after awakening in the night.

SLEEPING THROUGH THE NIGHT

Parents are often confused about when infants should sleep through the night. Newborns should not be expected to sleep through the night because they are neurologically unable to do so during the early weeks of life. By 12 weeks of age, 70 per cent of full-term infants are able to sleep at least 5 hours at night (Foye and Sulkes, 1990). Sleep lasting for 9 to 11 hours may begin by 12 to 16 weeks of age (Whaley and Wong, 1991).

Once infants establish longer sleep patterns, they often awaken at night again when they are teething or ill. Therefore, parents can expect to be awakened frequently during the early years. Methods of helping infants attain longer sleep periods at night once they are old enough to have more widely separated feedings are included in Parents Want to Know: How to Help Infants Sleep Through the Night.

Working Mothers

Many women must return to work after childbirth. Although it has been traditional for women to have at least 6 weeks of maternity leave, this is not always possible for all women. Some must return to work as early as 3 or 4 weeks after childbirth. Working mothers have a number of problems that are different from those of mothers who have a longer time at home. They must find adequate child care, identify methods of managing the household, and try to find enough time and energy to meet the needs of the infant, other family members, and themselves. (This topic is discussed in Chapter 18.)

It is important that working mothers do not become so involved in their many responsibilities that they have little time for their own needs. Some mothers regularly schedule time for themselves and for family activities. Many working mothers find that the time they can spend with their infant is particularly precious.

Adoptive Parents

Although adoptive parents have not experienced pregnancy and childbirth, they must make adjustments similar to those of biological parents. In some adoptive situations, the parents meet the biological

A working mother enjoys some quiet time with her infant after returning home.

mother during pregnancy and may even be with her during birth. In others, parents receive a call after months of waiting telling them that their new infant is ready for them. In either case, the lives of the parents will abruptly change.

In some agencies, adoptive parents receive the same teaching given to other parents. However, their ability to absorb information may be impaired by the excitement of the situation. Although adoptive mothers have not been pregnant nor undergone childbirth, they will still be very tired from the loss of sleep and sudden changes that they experience. This may be a surprise and very worrisome to some. They will have many questions that nurses can answer.

Nurses must offer the same support to adoptive parents that they do to biological parents. Parents need information about infant care and parenting techniques. They also need reassurance and emotional support as they go through this happy but exhausting change in their lives (see Clinical Situation).

Clinical Situation

Mary and John Reynolds received their adoptive daughter, Ashley, 3 days ago. They bring the 6-day-old infant to the pediatrician's office and discuss their concerns with the nurse. Although they received basic discharge teaching at the hospital where Ashley was born, they have many questions about infant care. The last two nights Ashley slept very little, and both parents are exhausted. "We've waited so long to get Ashley," Mary says, "but I'm beginning to wonder if Ashley is all right and if I'll be a good mother."

Q:
1. What are the priorities in this situation?
2. What information should the nurse include in teaching these parents?
3. How should the nurse deal with Ashley's night wakefulness?
4. How should the nurse support Mary and John?

A:
1. The major priorities are to support the parents in their new role and to determine if Ashley is progressing normally.
2. Information should be based on the parents' concerns. Identify basic areas of infant care, such as feeding, sleeping, cord care, and signs of illness, and determine whether Mary and John need more information. Explain normal characteristics and behaviors of the newborn. Provide frequent opportunities for the parents to ask questions.
3. Obtain further information about Ashley's sleep patterns. Discuss normal sleep in newborns and methods of helping infants sleep. Offer suggestions for methods of dealing with crying. Help Mary and John work out a plan by which they share the burdens as well as the joys of parenthood.
4. Use therapeutic communication techniques to allow Mary and John to express their feelings adequately. If Ashley appears to be progressing normally, emphasize that she is doing well. Point out to Mary and John that the problems they are encountering are not unique to them but are quite common for both biological and adoptive parents.

Common Questions and Concerns

Parents often ask nurses or others questions about infant care. Some of the most common concerns are summarized here.

Dressing and Warmth

A room temperature of about 70°F is warm enough for the infant. The infant should be dressed as the parents would like to be dressed, with a receiving blanket added. The abdomen should be checked to see if the infant is warm enough. The hands and feet will be slightly cooler than the rest of the body but should not be mottled or blue. The infant's head should be kept warm because there are many thermal skin sensors in the scalp. A hat is appropriate if the infant is outside when it is cold or windy.

Stool Patterns

Formula-fed infants generally pass at least one stool each day, whereas breastfed infants may pass a stool after every feeding or, occasionally, only one every 2 to 3 days. Infants may get red in the face and appear to be straining when having a bowel movement, but this is normal behavior and does not indicate constipation. It is the consistency of stools rather than the number that is important. Stools that are dry, hard, and marble-like indicate constipation.

Watery stools indicate diarrhea. A watery stool is absorbed into the diaper with little or no solid material left at the surface. A "water ring" remains on the diaper, showing where the liquid was absorbed. Diarrheal stools occur more frequently than the infant's normal stools and are greenish from bile moving quickly through the intestines. Diarrhea in infants can be serious because life-threatening dehydration can develop very quickly. Infants with diarrhea should be taken to the pediatrician or nurse practitioner for treatment.

Smoking

Many mothers quit smoking before or during pregnancy but may not realize that it is just as important that infants not be exposed to smoke after birth as before. Infants exposed to smoke from parents' cigarettes are more likely to develop frequent respiratory infections (Whaley and Wong, 1991) or other health problems. Smoking is a risk factor in sudden infant death syndrome, and the risk increases according to the amount the mother smokes (Valdes-Dapena, 1991). Smoke absorption by infants occurs even when smoking is done in another room (Greenberg et al, 1989). Parents who continue to smoke should do it outside the house and away from the infant.

Eyes

If a small amount of mucus accumulates in the corner of the eyes, parents can wipe it away with a damp cotton ball or corner of a clean washcloth. A large amount of mucus, redness, or excessive tearing indicates an infection or a blocked lacrimal duct. The infant should be seen by the pediatrician or nurse practitioner.

Transient strabismus, or crossing of the eyes, can be frightening to parents. The nurse should tell them that this is normal for infants for the first few months, until they gain control of the small muscles of the eye. It does not indicate that the infant will have later problems.

Baths

Giving sponge and tub baths is discussed in Chapter 20, p. 552, as is care of the cord p. 546 and the circumcision site (p. 533). Remind parents that it is not necessary to give a bath every day if the infant is washed well at diaper changes and when milk is regurgitated. Bathing should be a time for infant stimulation and parent-infant interaction. It can be done at any time of the day that is most convenient for parents.

Nails

Nails should be cut straight across with either blunt-ended scissors or clippers. The edges can be carefully smoothed with an emery board. Mothers should not attempt to cut nails too short, as this increases the danger of cutting the infant's fingertip. Some mothers prefer to cut nails while the infant is sleeping. Others have someone else hold the hand steady while the mother cuts the nails. Nails grow rapidly and may need trimming twice a week.

Sucking Needs

Parents often have questions about pacifiers and thumb or finger sucking. Nurses should explain that all infants have an urge to suck, although the amount of sucking needed varies with individual infants. Some seem satisfied by feedings, but others suck their hands or a pacifier even when not hungry.

A major concern of parents is that sucking a pacifier or thumb will cause the teeth to become maloccluded. The nurse should reassure them that intermittent sucking that does not continue beyond age 4 years will not result in changes to the teeth (Whaley and Wong, 1991). When sucking continues after the permanent teeth erupt, malocclusion is more likely. Trying to stop an infant from sucking is difficult and may cause emotional problems if it becomes a major focus.

Some infants increase non-nutritive sucking because the time they spend sucking during feedings is too short. Using bottle nipples with small holes and replacing the nipples every couple of months before they get soft will increase the amount of sucking that feedings provide. Breastfed infants should be allowed to continue sucking at the breast long enough to meet basic sucking needs. A short time of sucking after the infant is finished feeding will generally satisfy sucking needs and increase production of milk. Breastfed infants will stop sucking when they have had enough.

When parents want to give their infant a pacifier, they should be instructed to examine it often to be sure that it is in good condition. If the nipple is cracked, torn, sticky, or can be pulled away from the shield, it should be discarded. Pacifiers should be replaced every month or two because they may come apart as they deteriorate and cause aspiration of parts.

Pacifiers should be kept clean by frequent washing, and parents should buy several so that one is always clean when needed. Pacifiers should never be placed on a string around the infant's neck. The string could become tangled tightly around the neck and cause strangulation. Clips with a short band to attach pacifiers to the infant's clothing without danger are available.

Some parents find an advantage to a pacifier is that the infant gives it up more quickly than a thumb or finger because it is not so easily accessible. Parents who resort to the pacifier as the first response when the infant is fussy are likely to reinforce its use and increase dependence on it. Pacifiers used only after other causes of distress are ruled out may be used for a shorter duration. Because the need for non-nutritive sucking begins to diminish between 4 and 6 months of age, pacifier use may begin to decrease at that time with parents' help.

Teething

There is much individual variation in the time frame for tooth eruption. An occasional infant may have a tooth as early as 3 months or as late as 13 months of age, but generally the two lower central incisors come through the gums at about 6 to 8 months. The average age for eruption of all deciduous teeth is 2½ years.

The actual time teeth appear has no relationship to the infant's development. Parents may think that teething has begun when the infant is about 3 months of age, when the normal increased production of saliva causes drooling. It takes time for the infant to learn to swallow the extra saliva without drooling.

Some infants show signs of teething for weeks before the first tooth comes through the gums. These signs include excessive salivation, biting, irritability, and decreased feedings. Many infants who were sleeping through the night begin to wake again as a result of teething discomfort. Some infants have looser stools, and diaper rash may develop. A rash around the mouth may result from drooling. The infant's gums may look red and swollen over the area where the tooth will erupt.

Instruct parents that fevers or other signs of illness are not normal symptoms of teething. Infants may be more susceptible to illness at the time of teething because of poor eating and sleeping. In addition, teething begins at about the time many of the antibodies received in utero are disappearing. Signs of illness should be treated as they would at any other time, with a visit to the pediatrician or nurse practitioner if necessary.

Some teething infants like to bite on hard objects such as rubber teething rings. Some can be refrigerated or put in the freezer so that when used they soothe inflammation of the gums. Over-the-counter local anesthetics or analgesics, such as acetaminophen, are safe in small amounts for teething discomfort. Alcoholic beverages should never be rubbed on the gums because infants will swallow the alcohol.

Common Rashes

DIAPER RASH

Diaper rash occurs as a result of prolonged exposure of skin to wetness combined with a chemical reaction between urine and fecal enzymes that increases skin sensitivity to irritation. Although some infants seem prone to diaper rash from birth, it is more likely to develop when they begin to sleep for longer periods and the time between diaper changes increases. Other causes include incomplete rinsing of home-laundered diapers and sensitivity to commercial disposable washcloths or components of paper diapers. Infants may get diaper rash with either cloth or disposable diapers.

Treatment of diaper rash centers around keeping the diaper area clean and dry. The nurse should instruct the parents to change diapers as soon as they are wet or soiled. They should gently wash the perineum with mild soap and warm water, then rinse and dry well. Plastic pants or coverings should be avoided except when taking the infant out, as they prevent air flow to the diapered area and keep it damp. Removing the diapers and exposing the perineum to warm air helps healing. Disposable diapers designed to draw the wetness away from the skin may provide relief.

Applying a thin layer of creams such as those with zinc oxide may speed healing and help prevent further outbreaks. The nurse may suggest that parents try several different creams to see which works best. They should be told not to apply the ointments too thickly, as they may be hard to remove. Ointments contaminated with fecal matter may accumulate in the skin folds and hold bacteria.

If the rash becomes severe or pustules or crusted areas develop, it is infected. The infant should be taken to a pediatrician or nurse practitioner for treatment. *Candida albicans* or *Staphylococcus* is a common cause of infections. Antibiotic creams may be necessary for infections.

MILIARIA (PRICKLY HEAT)

Although most common during hot weather, miliaria or prickly heat develops in infants who are too warmly dressed in any weather. This rash is due to occlusion and inflammation of the sweat (eccrine) glands. It has a red base with papules or vesicles in the center.

Treatment is cooling the infant by removing excess clothing or by giving a soothing lukewarm bath. The condition clears quickly with removal of the cause, and ointments or other skin preparations should be avoided. The nurse should discuss the amount of clothing appropriate for the weather with parents when infants develop prickly heat.

SEBORRHEIC DERMATITIS (CRADLE CAP)

Cradle cap is a chronic inflammation of the scalp or other areas of the skin, in which there are yellow, scaly, oily lesions. It sometimes results when parents do not wash over the anterior fontanelle carefully for fear that they will hurt the infant.

Treatment is application of oil to the area to help the lesions soften, then removal with a comb before shampooing the head. The nurse should teach parents how to shampoo the scalp and explain that they will not damage the fontanelle by normal gentle shampooing. The scalp should be rinsed well after shampooing to remove all soap, which may cause irritation if it remains.

Nutrition During the Early Weeks

Infant feeding is discussed in detail in Chapter 21. The discussion here addresses only the most frequent concerns parents have about feeding.

Formula Feeding

Mothers using formula may be unsure about how much to feed the infant during the early weeks after birth. Although the infant will only take an ounce at a time during the first day or two of life, this will rapidly increase to 2 or 3 ounces per feeding during the first 2 weeks. The amount will continue to increase gradually to approximately 5 to 6 ounces every 3 to 4 hours by the end of 12 weeks. There is considerable variation between infants, and mothers should be encouraged to adapt to their own infant's needs.

Formula-fed infants generally eat every 3 to 4 hours. However, mothers should be encouraged not to set a strict timetable for feedings. They should feed the infant when his or her behavior indicates hunger. Fussiness or crying, rooting, sucking on hands, and eagerly taking the milk when it is offered are all signs that the infant is hungry.

Mothers should not urge infants to take all of the bottle if they do not seem interested. Infants will vary, as adults do, in the amount taken at each meal. Encouraging the infant to complete all feedings places undue emphasis on the feeding and may lead to later feeding problems or obesity.

Breastfeeding

The mother of the breastfed infant should also avoid strict schedules but should know that her infant will want to feed more often than if formula-fed, generally about every 2 to 3 hours. Infants should nurse at least 10 to 15 minutes at each breast initially (see Chapter 21). As nursing becomes well established, mothers generally feed approximately 15 minutes on the first side and then on the second side as long as the infant continues to nurse. The feeding should be ended when the infant falls asleep or after a short period of non-nutritive suckling.

The total time for each breastfeeding session varies with individual infants and from feeding to feeding. The time may be as short as 20 minutes or as long as 40 minutes. As infants become older, they become more efficient at nursing and obtain all the milk they need in a shorter period of time.

Water

Both formula and breast milk contain enough water for infants who are eating well. There is no need to give additional water. Some mothers give water to formula-fed infants who are fussy and do not respond to other interventions. A sip of water can also be given to infants with hiccoughs. However, hiccoughs will go away shortly, with or without water.

Infants should not be given water with sugar added. Sugar only adds empty calories and accustoms them to the sweet taste. Honey should never be used for young infants because there is a risk of botulism. (*Note*: In the birth facility, dextrose water may be given to some newborns to provide calories before the first milk feeding.)

Regurgitation

Infants often regurgitate ("spit up") because they may eat more than their stomach can easily hold and because their normally relaxed cardiac sphincter allows the stomach contents to flow into the esophagus easily. "Wet burps" result when air is trapped under stomach contents. As the air is expelled, a small amount of milk comes with it.

The nurse should teach parents to differentiate normal spitting up from vomiting, which is a sign of illness. Regurgitation may occur frequently, but there is usually only a small amount at a time. Vomiting may involve the entire feeding, and it is expelled forcefully. Parents should always seek treatment for the infant with projectile vomiting, in which the vomitus is expelled with such force that it travels some distance. This is a sign of pyloric stenosis, which may necessitate surgery.

Positioning the infant on the right side and elevating the head of the bed or using an infant seat to keep the infant in a slightly upright position after feedings may help air rise and prevent regurgitation. All infants should be placed on the side for sleep to promote drainage of regurgitated fluids and prevent aspiration.

Some infants swallow excessive air because they eat very rapidly. Nurses should instruct parents to feed them before they get too hungry and to stop often for burping. Switching breasts every 5 minutes with a burp in between helps some nursing infants. If the hole in a bottle nipple is too small, an infant may swallow air around the nipple. Enlarging the nipple slightly with a hot needle may prevent this.

Some infants experience reflux due to the flow of liquids across a dilated lower esophageal sphincter. These infants may have vomiting, and aspiration pneumonia develops in as many as one third of afflicted infants (Behrman, 1992). The infant who has excessive regurgitation or vomiting should be referred for follow-up with the pediatrician or nurse practitioner.

Introduction of Solid Foods

Infants do not need solid foods until 4 to 6 months of age. However, some mothers may consider introducing solids earlier in hopes that the infant will sleep longer at night. This is seldom successful, as the infant receives no more calories from the small amounts of solids taken than from milk. In addition, early introduction of solids may cause other problems. Solid foods given before the infant is ready for them may precipitate allergies and may cause intestinal upsets because they are incompletely digested. When infants start solids, they drink less milk, thus replacing a food that meets their nutrient needs well with another food that is poorly digested.

The extrusion reflex, in which infants push the tongue out against anything that touches it, continues until approximately 4 months of age. This makes feeding a younger infant difficult, as the infant pushes almost all of every spoonful out of the mouth. The nurse should explain the problems involved with early introduction of solid foods and encourage parents to wait until the infant is physiologically ready, at 4 to 6 months of age. The concerns that made the parents consider changing the feeding routine should also be discussed.

Weaning

Some mothers decide to wean the infant from the breast to the bottle during the first 12 weeks after birth. Information about weaning is included in Chapter 21, p. 587. Weaning from bottle to cup generally takes place during the 2nd year of life. This information can be found in pediatric textbooks.

✔ Check Your Reading

7. What are common signs of teething?
8. How can parents prevent or treat diaper rash?
9. How much should infants eat during the early weeks after birth?
10. Why should solid foods be avoided until the infant is 4 to 6 months old?

Growth and Development

Anticipatory Guidance

Parents often have questions about normal patterns of growth and stages of development. Nurses should provide parents with anticipatory guidance about these areas to help them develop realistic expectations about infants' abilities at various ages. It can also help prepare parents for changes that they must make to keep the infant's environment safe, especially during the second half of the first year of life, when the infant begins to explore the house alone.

Growth and Developmental Milestones

A brief summary of the changes that can be expected, particularly during the infant's first 12 weeks, is included here. More in-depth information is included in pediatrics textbooks. The nurse should emphasize to parents that guidelines are only averages, that the range of normal is often broad, and that individual differences are expected.

During the first 6 months of life, growth proceeds at a very predictable rate in normal infants. The weight lost after birth is usually regained by 10 days of age. Each month, the average infant will gain 680 g (1.5 pounds), grow 2.5 cm (1 inch), and have an increase in head circumference of 1.5 cm (0.5 inch) (Whaley and Wong, 1991). The posterior fontanel closes by 6 to 8 weeks, whereas the anterior fontanel closes by 12 to 18 months of age. Tears appear at 2 to 4 weeks after birth.

The Moro, grasp, tonic neck, and rooting reflexes are especially noticed by parents. The nurse should point out that their gradual disappearance helps prepare the infant to learn new skills, such as voluntary grasping or turning over, which are impossible if the reflexes continue. The infant gradually develops more control of the heavy head and has little bobbing or head lag by the end of the 3rd month of life.

Infants are social beings. They will stare at objects of interest within a range of 8 to 12 inches as newborns and learn to follow objects by turning the head a full 180 degrees during the first 12 weeks of life. A social smile begins as early as 3 to 5 weeks and is well developed by 6 to 8 weeks. Infants make vowel sounds (cooing) by 2 months and begin some consonant sounds (babbling) and may even squeal with delight at 3 months.

Accident Prevention

Knowing what infants can do helps prevent accidents. In the first 3 months after birth, they are totally helpless. Although they can communicate their needs through crying, someone must be available at all times to care for them. Parents must be taught the dangers of leaving the infant on any unprotected surface even for seconds. In a very short time, an infant can wiggle from the middle to the edge of a double bed and fall. Crib sides should be raised whenever the infant is in bed. Cribs should be positioned away from hanging cords of blinds or drapes, as these could become wrapped around an active infant and cause strangulation.

Parents should keep one hand on an infant lying on an unprotected surface if they must turn away. Infants should never be left for an instant in even an inch of water because of the danger of drowning. Parents should take the telephone off the hook and ignore the doorbell when bathing the infant, or take the infant out of the water and with them if they must leave the room.

After infants learn to grasp objects with increasing accuracy, parents must be certain that there is nothing in the infant's reach that could be swallowed or otherwise harmful. Encourage parents to think ahead to the time that the infant will be crawling and walking and make plans for how they will "child proof" their home.

Well Baby Care

Well Baby Check-ups

Well baby check-ups are an opportunity for the pediatrician or nurse practitioner to assess the infant's growth and development, answer questions about feeding and infant care, observe for abnormalities, and give immunizations. These check-ups may be provided by a private practitioner or in a well baby clinic, where examinations and immunizations are free or provided at reduced cost. Infants are usually taken to their first well baby check-up at 2 to 3 weeks of age. They are brought back for well baby check-ups approximately every 4 to 8 weeks during the first 6 months of life and every 8 to 12 weeks until age 1 year.

Well baby check-ups are a good time for mothers to learn about what is normal for their infants in terms of growth and behaviors. Anticipatory guidance is a major part of well baby visits. Many mothers are reassured to find that the things they are dealing with, such as wakefulness at night or changes in feeding habits, are normal. Safety is discussed as the parents learn about what skills the infant will be learning soon that might place them in danger.

Immunizations

Nurses often receive questions about the necessity of immunizations for uncommon diseases, such as diphtheria, that parents have never seen. Parents might consider a condition such as measles to be a harmless childhood illness. They may be reluctant to have their infants undergo painful procedures when they do not understand the need for them.

The nurse must explain to parents the importance of immunizations. In the United States, national health objectives for the year 2000 include full immunization of at least 90 per cent of children by age 2 years. Currently, the immunization rate is believed to be only 70 to 80 per cent, with some areas of the United States having rates lower than 50 per cent (Public Health Service, 1991). When immunization rates decline, the occurrence of communicable diseases begins to rise, as happened in the late 1980s, when a resurgence of measles occurred in many U.S. communities. The same may happen with other diseases that are preventable with immunization.

The nurse should briefly describe each of the conditions for which infants receive immunizations to help parents understand their dangers. Discuss the age at which each immunization is given and when boosters are needed. (see Table 22–3)

Table 22–3. IMMUNIZATIONS

Immunization	Age for Original Immunization	Age for Booster
DTP (diphtheria, tetanus, pertussis)	2, 4, 6 months	15–18 months* 4–6 years*
HbCV (*Haemophilus influenzae* B conjugate vaccine)†	2, 4, 6 months‡ 2, 4 months§	12–15 months
Hib and DPT	2, 4, 6 months	15–18 months
TOPV (trivalent oral poliovirus vaccine)	2, 4 months	15–18 months 4–6 years
MMR (measles, mumps, rubella)	15 months (12 months if community outbreak)	11–12 years
Hepatitis	Before hospital discharge, 1–2 months, 6–18 months‖	
Tuberculin skin test (not an immunization but a test)	12–15 months	Every 1–2 years

* Acellular pertussis vaccine is now approved for doses four and five only. It is combined with diphtheria and tetanus and causes fewer side effects.
† Time of immunization for *Haemophilus influenzae,* type B, depends on the vaccine used. HibTITER and PedvaxHIB immunize against *Haemophilus influenzae* alone. Tetramune is a combination with DPT.
‡ HibTITER vaccine.
§ PedvaxHIB vaccine.
‖ An alternative schedule for hepatitis vaccine for infants whose mothers are not HBsAg-positive is 2, 4, and 6 to 18 months.

✔ Check Your Reading

11. How can parents make use of knowledge about infant development to prevent accidents in the first 12 weeks of life?
12. What is the importance of well baby check-ups?
13. Why are immunizations important?

Illness

Parents have many questions about illness in the infant. They are concerned about recognizing an illness and when to call the pediatrician or nurse practitioner.

Recognizing Signs

Parents may need help in recognizing signs of illness in infants (summarized in Table 22–4). The nurse should explain that anytime the infant appears sick or parents feel that something is wrong with the infant, they should call the pediatrician or nurse practitioner. Office staff are usually educated to help parents determine whether or not the infant is sick enough to be seen.

Table 22–4. COMMON SIGNS OF ILLNESS

Fever above 100°F axillary
Vomiting all of a feeding more than once or twice in a day
Watery stools or significant increase in number of stools over what is normal for the infant
Blisters, sores, or rashes that are unusual for the infant
Unusual changes in behavior: listlessness or sleeping much more than usual, irritability or crying much more than usual
Coughing, frequent sneezing, runny nose. (*Note:* Occasional sneezing may be due to lint from new clothes or blankets.)
Pulling or rubbing at the ear, drainage from the ear

Calling the Pediatrician or Nurse Practitioner

When calling the pediatrician or nurse practitioner to discuss an illness, parents should prepare ahead by writing down the information about the illness to avoid forgetting something. They should have the name and telephone number of a pharmacy ready in case a prescription drug is needed, and they should be prepared to write down instructions. Information about reporting an illness is summarized in Table 22–5.

Office staff are usually prepared to answer questions on the telephone about common concerns and simple illnesses. They can help determine if an infant should be brought into the office, but parents should be assertive in asking for an appointment if they feel that one is needed. They are with the infant and have a more complete picture of the illness than can be given over the telephone. If there is a real emergency, the parents should say so immediately so that the staff can act accordingly. Parents can expect the pediatrician or nurse practitioner to return calls about acute illness as soon as possible and those about other concerns near the end of the day.

Table 22–5. CALLING THE PEDIATRICIAN OR NURSE PRACTITIONER

Write down pertinent information before calling. Have your pharmacy name and telephone number handy and a pen and paper to write down instructions.

1. Give the infant's name and age first.
2. Describe the illness or problem.
   a. When did it start?
   b. How often does it occur? (Reporting the number of times the infant vomits or passes a stool gives the pediatrician or nurse practitioner a better idea of the problem.)
   c. How does this compare with the infant's normal patterns?
   d. What does it look like? Describe the rash; describe the color and consistency of the stools.
3. Describe any fever.
   a. How high is it?
   b. Was it taken by axillary or rectal method?
   c. How long has the fever been present?
   d. Has it been higher than it is now?
4. Describe other signs of illness.
   a. Are there changes in eating behavior?
   b. Have sleep patterns changed?
5. Describe the infant's behavior.
   a. Does the infant seem sick?
   b. Is the infant irritable, lethargic, acting differently from normal?
6. Describe what has been done so far to treat the condition and the results.
7. Discuss other relevant information.
   a. Is there a similar illness in family members?
   b. Was the infant treated recently for a similar or different illness?
   c. Does the infant take any other medications?

When to Seek Immediate Help

Parents should take the infant to the pediatrician or to an emergency room if there are signs of dyspnea. An infant from birth to 3 months of age should not have a sustained respiratory rate above 60 breaths/minute. If there are retractions, cyanosis, or extreme pallor, parents should get immediate help. If respiratory difficulty occurs suddenly in an infant who is well, the infant may have aspirated a feeding or small object. Parents should call paramedics. Nurses should encourage all parents to take classes in cardiopulmonary resuscitation (CPR).

If an infant's respiratory rate is below 30, parents should stimulate the infant and see if the respirations increase and stay within normal range of 30 to 60 breaths/minute. If the respiratory rate continues to be below normal, the infant should be seen by a pediatrician or nurse practitioner.

Parents should call the pediatrician if the infant is hard to arouse and keep awake. The infant could be semicomatose and showing signs of central nervous system disease such as meningitis or encephalitis.

Sudden Infant Death Syndrome

A condition that worries all parents is sudden infant death syndrome (SIDS), in which an infant's abrupt death is unexplained by autopsy, examination of the scene of death, or history. SIDS is the second leading cause of infant mortality in the United States (Centers for Disease Control, 1992c). It occurs in apparently healthy infants during sleep. The infants are most often male and 2 to 4 months of age. In the United States, American Indians and African-Americans have the highest rates of SIDS, whereas the lowest rates occur in Asians and Latinos (Li and Daling, 1991). The reasons for these differences are not known.

Although many studies have been done, the cause of SIDS remains unknown. Major risk factors seem to be maternal smoking and maternal age under 20 (Willinger et al, 1991). Low birth weight, low socioeconomic status, viral infections, maternal drug abuse, cardiorespiratory or neurological abnormalities, and subtle growth retardation are some of the factors that have been associated with SIDS.

There may be an association between SIDS and infants sleeping in the prone position. Therefore, healthy infants should be placed in a side-lying position for sleep. It may be necessary to place premature infants with respiratory distress or infants with reflux in the prone position to promote drainage. Parents should consult their caregiver about what is best for their infant (American Academy of Pediatrics Task Force on Infant Positioning and SIDS, 1992).

The most important role of the nurse in relation to teaching parents about SIDS is to provide reassurance and support. Although SIDS is a major cause of death, it affects only approximately 8.5 infants in every 100,000 live births each year (Centers for Disease Control, 1992c). Siblings of infants who die with SIDS are at little, if any, increased risk (Krongrad, 1991).

Parents should be told that, despite many sensationalized reports about the condition, the cause of SIDS is still unknown and only theories are available. They should be reassured that there is nothing that they can do or avoid doing (with the possible exception of smoking) to prevent death by SIDS. The nurse should use therapeutic communication to assist parents concerned about this condition to talk about their fears.

✔ Check Your Reading

14. When should immediate help be sought for an infant?
15. What should nurses teach parents about SIDS?

The High-Risk Infant

High-risk infants, those with prematurity, congenital anomalies, prenatal exposure to drugs, and other conditions, are discussed in Chapters 28 and 29. These infants often continue to need special care after discharge. Although all parents need education about home care, it is especially important for parents of high-risk infants. It is common for parents to have anxiety about their ability to take over infant care after a long hospitalization. After having nursing support readily available throughout their contacts with the infant, they may feel lost without that resource. Many hospital nurseries have a program that enables parents to take over their infant's care gradually before discharge. Follow-up telephone calls or home visits by a nurse, when available, may decrease the need for rehospitalization.

Some infants need continued special treatments such as oxygen or apnea monitors at home. Parents may have questions about how to adapt treatments or equipment use to the home. Knowing that they can call the nursery at any time will be reassuring to them. Other problems may also arise. Finding a baby-sitter who is qualified to care for an infant on oxygen or who might need CPR may be difficult.

Although parents' greatest concerns involve the infant's health, they will also have the same concerns about normal newborn care that other parents have. Dealing with the needs of their other children along with those of the newborn may bring up new issues. The nurse may be able to suggest parent groups that offer practical help in caring for a high-risk infant.

Infants with complications such as prematurity often need more frequent visits to the pediatrician or nurse practitioner or are rehospitalized during the early months after birth. Common problems include respiratory illness, infections (gastroenteritis, sepsis, urinary tract infections, otitis media), or need for surgery, such as umbilical hernia repair. These parents need more information on preventive measures and care of the infant with acute illness (Termini et al, 1990).

Summary Concepts

- New parents have a need for information about care of the infant and the mother during the early weeks after birth. Because of shorter hospital stays and decline of the extended family, the traditional sources from which to obtain this information are limited. Nurses assist parents during this time by telephone calls, home visits, and classes about parenting.
- All equipment, particularly older, used articles, should be checked by parents for safety. Car seats must be chosen according to the size of the infant and must be used correctly to maintain safety.
- Crying is a major source of concern for parents. They should be reassured that infants will not be spoiled by prompt attention to their needs. The nurse can help parents determine the cause and appropriate techniques for dealing with a crying infant. The nurse should use therapeutic communication techniques to help parents deal with negative feelings.
- Common signs of teething include drooling, irritability, decreased appetite and sleep, rash, loose stools, and red, swollen gums. Fever or other signs of illness are not due to teething.
- Diaper rash can be avoided by keeping the area clean and dry and avoiding plastic pants and products to which infants seem sensitive. If rash occurs, exposing the area to air and applying creams sparingly will help.
- Both breastfed and formula-fed infants will vary in amounts taken at each feeding but will average

about 1 ounce per feeding initially and 5 to 6 ounces per feeding at 12 weeks of age. There is enough water in both breast milk and formula to meet the infant's needs. Solid foods cannot be completely digested until the infant is 4 to 6 months old, and they may cause allergies, gastric upsets, and decreased intake of needed nutrients in a younger infant.

- Well baby check-ups are important for assessment of growth and development, guidance, and immunizations. Immunizations safeguard infants and communities from spread of communicable diseases.
- Parents should learn signs of illness in the infant and when immediate medical care is necessary. When calling the pediatrician or nurse practitioner, parents should think through the information before calling to be sure that all important facts are discussed. They should seek immediate medical attention when infants have difficulty breathing, show cyanosis, or are difficult to arouse from sleep.
- The nurse should teach parents about the current state of knowledge about sudden infant death syndrome (SIDS) and that the cause remains unknown. Provide reassurance and support using therapeutic communication techniques to help parents with their fears.
- Parents of high-risk infants have all the usual problems and concerns of other parents, with the added stress of an infant with special needs. They benefit from continued contact with nurses for teaching and support.

References and Readings

American Academy of Pediatrics. (1991). *Report of the Committee on Infectious Diseases* (22nd ed.). Elk Grove Village, Ill.

American Academy of Pediatrics Committee on Infectious Diseases. (1992). Universal hepatitis B immunization. *Pediatrics*, 89(4), 795–800.

American Academy of Pediatrics Task Force on Infant Positioning and SIDS. (1992). Positioning and SIDS. *Pediatrics*, 89(6), 1120–1126.

Behrman, R.E. (1992). *Nelson textbook of pediatrics* (14th ed.). Philadelphia: W.B. Saunders.

Centers for Disease Control. (1991). Child passenger restraint use and motor-vehicle-related fatalities among children—United States, 1982–1990. *Morbidity and Mortality Weekly Report*, 40(34), 600–602.

Centers for Disease Control. (1992a, February). Pertussis vaccination: Acellular pertussis vaccine for reinforcing and booster use—supplementary ACIP statement. Recommendations of the Immunization Practices Advisory Committee. *Morbidity and Mortality Weekly Report*, 41(RR-1), 1–9.

Centers for Disease Control. (1992b, April). Deaths associated with infant carriers—United States, 1986–1991. *Morbidity and Mortality Weekly Report*, 41(16), 271–273.

Centers for Disease Control. (1992c, July). Sudden infant death syndrome—United States, 1980–1988. *Morbidity and Mortality Weekly Report*, 41(28), 515–517.

Coffman, S., Levitt, M.J., & Deets, C. (1990). Personal and professional support for mothers of NICU and healthy newborns. *Journal of Obstetric, Gynecologic, and Neonatal Nursing*, 20(5), 406–414.

Covington, C., Cronewett, L., & Loveland-Cherry, C. (1991). Newborn behavioral performance in colic and noncolic infants. *Nursing Research*, 40(5), 292–296.

Degenhart-Leskosky, S.M. (1989). Health education needs of adolescent and non-adolescent mothers. *Journal of Obstetric, Gynecologic, and Neonatal Nursing*, 18(3), 238–243.

Evans, C.J. (1991). Description of a home follow-up program for childbearing families. *Journal of Obstetric, Gynecologic, and Neonatal Nursing*, 20(2), 113–118.

Foye, H., & Sulkes, S. (1990). Developmental and behavioral pediatrics. In R.E. Behrman (Ed.), *Nelson essentials of pediatrics*. Philadelphia: W.B. Saunders.

Greenberg, R.A., Bauman, K.E., Glover, L.H., et al. (1989). Ecology of passive smoking by young infants. *Journal of Pediatrics*, 14(5), 774–780.

Keefe, M.R., & Froese-Fretz, A. (1991). Living with an irritable infant: Maternal perspectives. MCN: *American Journal of Maternal Child Nursing*, 16(5), 255–259.

Kid Safe—Texas. (1990). *Car restraints for low birth weight or premature babies*. San Antonio: University of Texas Health Science Center.

Krongrad, E. (1991). Infants at high risk for sudden infant death syndrome? Have they been identified? A commentary. *Pediatrics*, 88(6), 1274–1278.

Li, D., & Daling, J.R. (1991). Maternal smoking, low birth weight, and ethnicity in relation to sudden infant death syndrome. *American Journal of Epidemiology*, 134(9), 958–964.

Newborn RN's find niche: Teaching how to parent. (1990). *American Journal of Nursing*, 90(11), 80–81.

Public Health Service. (1991). *Healthy people 2000: National health promotion and disease prevention objectives*. Washington, D.C.: U.S. Department of Health and Human Services, Public Health Service.

Termini, L., Brooten, D., Brown, L., Gennaro, S., & York, R. (1990). Reasons for acute care visits and rehospitalizations in very low-birthweight infants. *Neonatal Network*, 8(5), 23–26.

Valdes-Dapena, M. (1991). A pathologist's perspective on the sudden infant death syndrome—1991. *Pathology Annual*, 27(1), 133–164.

Vessey, I.A., & Ritchie, S.R. (1993). The who, what, and why of pediatric immunization. RN, 56(9), 42–48.

Whaley, L.F., & Wong, D.L. (1991). *Nursing care of infants and children* (4th ed.). St. Louis: C.V. Mosby.

Willinger, M., James, L.S., & Catz, C. (1991). Defining the sudden infant death syndrome (SIDS): Deliberations of an expert panel convened by the National Institute of Child Health and Human Development. *Pediatric Pathology*, 11(5), 677–684.

Part V

Families at Risk During the Childbearing Period

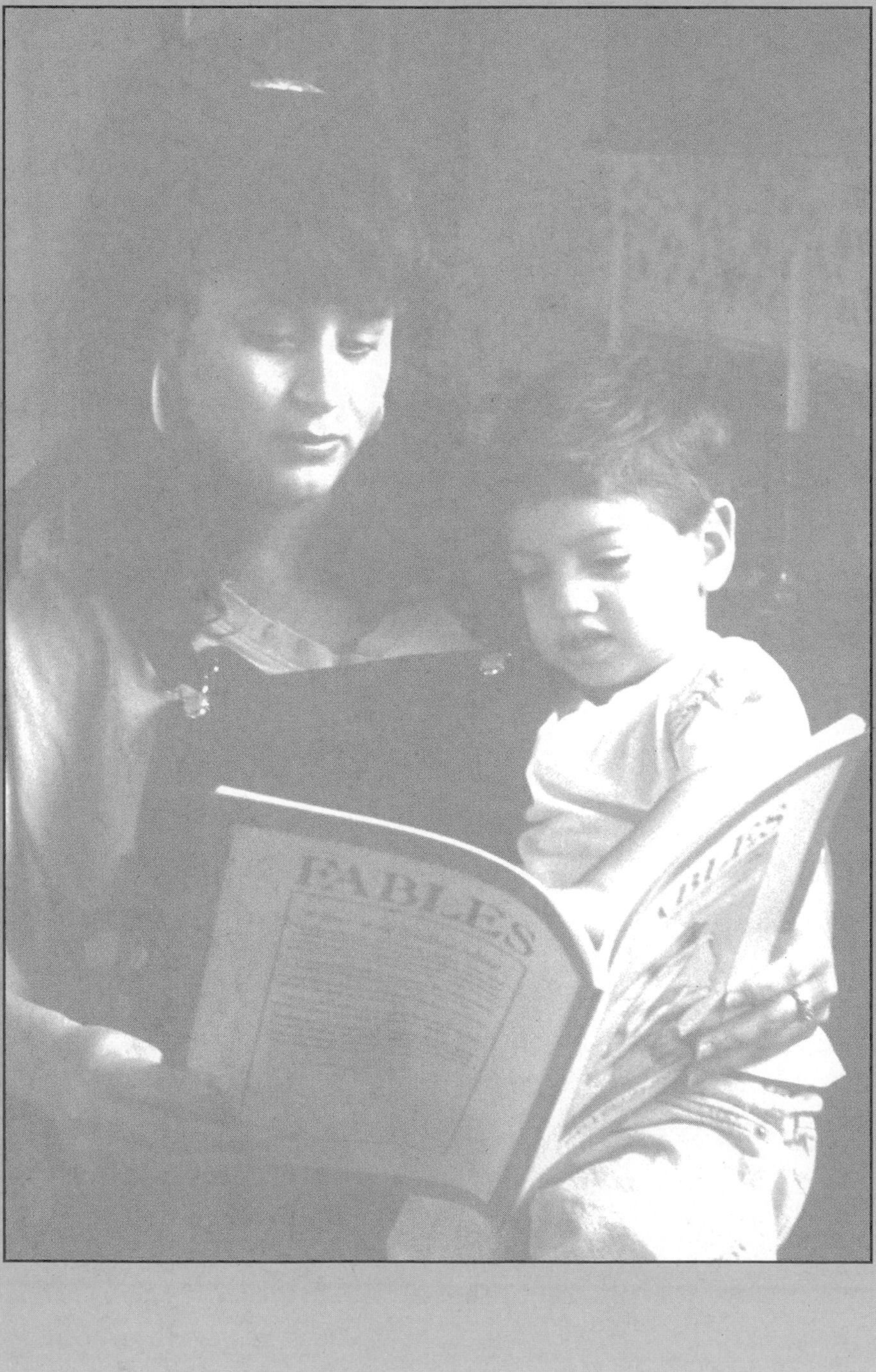

23

The Childbearing Family with Special Needs

Objectives

1. Describe the factors that contribute to teenage pregnancy as well as the effects of the pregnancy on the mother, infant, and family.
2. Discuss the role of the nurse in the prevention and management of teenage pregnancy.
3. Explain the major implications of delayed childbearing in terms of maternal and fetal health.
4. Describe the effects of substance abuse on the mother and the infant and identify nursing interventions to reduce or minimize the effects in the antepartal, intrapartal, and postpartal periods.
5. Discuss parental responses when an infant is born with congenital anomalies and identify nursing interventions to assist the parents.
6. Describe parental responses to pregnancy loss and identify nursing interventions to assist parents through the grieving process.
7. Describe the role of the nurse when the mother relinquishes the infant by adoption.
8. Identify the factors that promote violence against women and describe the role of the nurse in terms of assessment, prevention, and interventions.

Definitions

Abstinence syndrome • A group of symptoms that occur when a person who is addicted to a specific drug withdraws or abstains from taking that drug.

Addiction • Physical or psychological dependence on a substance such as alcohol, tobacco, or drugs, either legal or illicit.

Alcoholism • A chronic, progressive, and potentially fatal disease characterized by tolerance for and physical dependency on alcohol and/or by pathological organ changes due to alcohol abuse.

Amphetamines • Central nervous system stimulants that create a perception of pleasure that is unrelated to external stimuli.

Crack • A highly addictive form of cocaine that has been processed to be smoked.

Egocentrism • Interest centered on the self rather than on the needs of others.

Fetal alcohol syndrome • A group of physical and mental disorders of the offspring associated with maternal use of alcohol during pregnancy.

Methadone • A synthetic compound with opiate properties. Used as an oral substitute for heroin and morphine in the opiate-addicted person.

Neonatal abstinence syndrome • A cluster of physical signs exhibited by the newborn who was exposed in utero to maternal use of substances such as cocaine or heroin. See also **Abstinence syndrome.**

Withdrawal syndrome • See **Abstinence syndrome.**

Pregnancy and childbirth necessitate major adjustments in all families. However, some families are unable to make the adjustments without a great deal of assistance. Those with special needs include adolescent parents, parents who delayed childbirth, and families that have problems with substance abuse. In addition, many couples need assistance to cope with the birth of an infant with congenital abnormalities or with the unexpected loss of a pregnancy or neonate. Finally, many families exist in an atmosphere of continual violence and require multidisciplinary assistance to protect the safety of the mother and children. Perinatal nurses can make a difference in the lives of these families, particularly in the lives of infants born into them.

Adolescent Pregnancy

Incidence

The United States has one of the highest teenage pregnancy rates among developed nations. More than 1.2 million pregnancies occur each year in teenagers between the ages of 10 and 19, and the birth rate in females between the ages of 13 and 15 years is rising rapidly. Adolescents who become pregnant are likely to become pregnant again. The recurrent pregnancy rate within the first 12 months after giving birth is 20 per cent. Thirty-eight per cent are pregnant again within 24 months (Tuckson, 1991).

Factors Associated with Teenage Pregnancy

The high level of sexual activity among adolescents and the low incidence of contraceptive use are directly related to the incidence of teenage pregnancies. Of all students in grades 9 through 12, 54.2 per cent report having had sexual intercourse at least once and 39.4 per cent report having had sexual intercourse during the previous 3 months. Among sexually active high school students, 77.7 per cent report having used some form of contraception, such as birth control pills, condoms, or withdrawal some of the time (Centers for Disease Control, 1992). Factors that contribute to the high incidence of teenage pregnancy are listed in Table 23–1.

Table 23–1. FACTORS CONTRIBUTING TO TEENAGE PREGNANCY

Lack of accurate information about how to use contraceptives
Limited access to contraceptive devices
Fear of reporting sexual activity to parents
Ambivalence toward sexuality; intercourse not "planned"
Feelings of invulnerability
Peer pressure to begin sexual activity
Low self-esteem and consequent inability to set limits on sexual activity
Means to attain love or to escape present situation
Lack of appropriate role models
Low level of education correlated with incorrect use of contraceptives

Sex Education

Many adolescents acquire a large portion of their knowledge from peers, and the sex information they accumulate is often inaccurate and incomplete. Moreover, teenagers are often unprepared for puberty, when thoughts and fantasies about sexual activity accompany the development of primary and secondary sex characteristics and the increased sensitivity of the genitals. At the same time, adolescents are constantly exposed to sexually stimulating material from the mass media, receiving messages that sexual activity is not only condoned but expected.

Many educators believe that sex education should begin in elementary school and be continued until high school graduation. Within this context, information about prevention of pregnancy and sexually transmitted diseases (STDs), including HIV exposure, can be repeated on an ongoing basis. This information should be combined with other aspects of teenage sexuality, such as personal adjustments and attitudes, interpersonal associations, and the establishment of values.

TEACHING STRATEGY

Two major teaching strategies are often emphasized. First, teenagers are helped to understand how to set limits on sexual activity. Second, they are instructed in the effective use of contraception within a sexual relationship.

Setting limits on sexual behavior is particularly important for younger teenagers, who may be pressured to become sexually active before they have developed the maturity to deal responsibly with intercourse, contraception, or unplanned pregnancy. They need advice about how to handle the pressure so that they can postpone sexual intercourse until they are emotionally and physically ready. In clinical practice, adolescent females often say they wish they had been taught how to say "not now," "not yet," and "not you."

Nurses often counsel teenagers on an individual basis, in mixed groups, or in groups segregated by sex. Nurses must keep in mind that adolescent males and females mature at different rates and that it may be desirable to form segregated groups until the teenagers indicate that they would feel comfortable in a combined group. When providing sex education, nurses should use simple but correct language such as uterus, testicles, penis, and vagina. Once the meanings of the terms are understood, most teenagers prefer to use them in their discussions.

For complete information about appropriate contraceptive methods, see Chapter 31.

Options When Pregnancy Occurs

An adolescent who becomes pregnant must choose from the following options: (1) terminate the pregnancy, (2) continue the pregnancy and place the infant for adoption, or (3) continue the pregnancy and keep the infant. Almost 40 per cent (411,000) of all teenage pregnancies in the United States are terminated by legal abortion each year; however, termination of pregnancy is not an acceptable alternative for many families. Moreover, many teenagers do not acknowledge the pregnancy until late in the second trimester, when abortion is complicated.

The choice to continue the pregnancy and place the infant for adoption is not common for adolescents, even though there is a scarcity of infants available for adoption. Teenagers who do place their infant for adoption may have complicated feelings of grief, relief that a "bad" experience is over, and anger at parents who were unwilling to provide assistance and thus made adoption the only realistic option. On the other hand, the autonomous decision to relinquish the child "for the child's good" may be an important step toward maturity.

The choice of abortion or adoption leaves the adolescent with no tangible evidence of her pregnancy and with mixed messages from society regarding her decision. Unlike the teenager who decides to keep her infant, these adolescents receive less assistance about how to deal with their experience. They need help in understanding that their decision to terminate the pregnancy or to place the infant for adoption is an acknowledgment of a significant event, and they need assistance in dealing with their feelings. See the text on relinquishment by adoption, p. 649, for additional information.

Socioeconomic Implications

The financial cost of teenage pregnancy is enormous in the United States; however, the cost in human terms is often tragic. The developmental tasks of adolescence, such as achieving independence from parents and establishing a lifestyle that is personally satisfying, are interrupted. Educational goals are often curtailed, which limits employment opportunities and results in reliance on the welfare system. Children born into this situation do not escape unscathed. They show a higher incidence of impaired intellectual functioning and poor school adjustment. The negative cycle is usually repeated: a large percentage of teenage parents were children of teenage parents. As a result, children of adolescent parents are often among the poorest people in the United States. See Table 23–2 for a summary of the impact of pregnancy on the developmental tasks of adolescence.

Implications for Maternal Health

Pregnancy presents significant problems for the health of adolescent females. The maternal mortality rate for girls under the age of 15 years is 60 per cent higher than for women in their twenties (Tuckson, 1991). Adolescents are at increased risk for (1) cephalopelvic disproportion, (2) pregnancy-induced hypertension, (3) anemia, and (4) nutritional deficiencies.

An additional concern is the high incidence of STDs among pregnant teenagers. It is estimated that 86 per cent of all STDs occur between the ages of 15 and 24 years (Centers for Disease Control, 1992). Gonorrhea and chlamydial infection are particularly prevalent between the ages of 15 and 21 (McGregor, 1989).

The high incidence of complications of pregnancy among teenagers may be due to delayed prenatal care rather than to age. Some pregnant adolescents do not start prenatal care until the third trimester, and others receive none at all. Early prenatal care that includes counseling about nutritional needs and close observation of the client for the onset of pregnancy-induced hypertension can reduce the high rate of fetal and maternal death that occurs when the expectant mother is very young.

Implications for Fetal Health

The absence of adequate prenatal care puts the fetus at risk. There is an increased incidence of both

Table 23–2. IMPACT OF PREGNANCY ON THE DEVELOPMENTAL TASKS OF ADOLESCENCE

Developmental Task*	Impact of Pregnancy	Nursing Considerations
Achievement of a Stable Identity: how the person sees him/herself and how the person perceives that others see and accept him/her; peer group approval provides confirmation and is a major component of identity development.	The ability to adapt and respond to stress is a good indicator of identity development, and adolescents who become pregnant before a stable identity is developed may not be able to accept the responsibilities of parenthood and to plan for the future.	Explore the availability of a school-based mothers' program that will provide the peer support that is so important. Emphasize the importance of prenatal classes and the effect of prenatal care on the pregnancy. Encourage both parents to attend parenting classes and describe the expected growth and development of infants. Focus on the infant's need to develop trust and on the parenting behaviors that promote this. For instance, prompt, gentle, consistent responses to infant signals.
Achievement of Comfort with Body Image: requires internalization of mature body size, contour, and function.	The adolescent must learn to deal with body changes of pregnancy (increasing size, contour, increased pigmentation, and striae) before she has learned to accept the body changes associated with puberty. May deny pregnancy or severely restrict calories to prevent gaining weight. May be disgusted with the physical changes of pregnancy that make her look different from her peers.	Allow time for the teenager to verbalize her feelings about the body changes of pregnancy. Emphasize that dieting is harmful to the infant and will not stop the changes in body size and contour. Provide exercises that will help her regain her figure after the birth of the infant.
Acceptance of Sexual Role and Identity: requires internalization of strong sexual urges and achievement of intimacy with others.	The adolescent may need to achieve an intimate relationship with another and to form an exclusive relationship before ready. The pregnant teenager will also need to cope with changes in relationships with friends. She often has difficulty seeing herself as a sexual being or as a mother.	Allow the teenager to express her feelings about sexuality and about motherhood. Initiate classes designed specifically for adolescents and encourage all teenage expectant mothers to join a group with similar interests (childbirth education classes, parenting classes, or special groups that require nutrition counseling). This will help her deal with the changing relationship she has with her peers in school and move toward a mothering role.
Development of a Personal Value System: able to consider the rights and feelings of others.	Pregnancy occurs before the adolescent is able to move from following rules to considering the rights and feelings of others and developing ethical standards. May experience conflict when they must adjust to the responsibilities of premature motherhood.	Initiate a discussion of teenager's feelings of conflict about her role as mother versus her role as student. Explore her views about motherhood: How does she expect it to change her life? What are her future plans? Present options and assist her to explore her goals.
Preparation for Vocation or Career: completing educational or vocational goals; youths living in poverty may not have the means or encouragement to accomplish this.	Pregnancy often interrupts school for both parents; this may be a major frustration or it may result in permanent withdrawal from school and limited access to jobs that pay more than the minimum wage.	Discuss the importance of continued education and elicit teenager's feelings and plans to accomplish this. Determine the amount and availability of support from her parents. Refer her to social services for needed assistance.
Achievement of Independence from Parents: competent in social environment and able to function without parental guidance.	Must adjust to the need for continued financial assistance and dependence on parents at a time when achieving independence is a major priority.	Assist teenager to verbalize her feelings about continued dependence on parents. Discuss the reality of the situation—for instance, that she needs financial support and help with the care of the infant. Determine if she will continue to live at home and the reaction of her parents to the pregnancy. How much support will they provide? What are the conditions for her remaining at her parents' home with the infant?

* From Mercer, R. T. (1990). *Parents at risk.* New York: Springer.

premature and low birth weight (LBW; <2500 g) infants, particularly when the mother is younger than 15 years of age. Low-birth-weight infants are three times as likely to die within the first month of life, and they account for 27 per cent of all infant mortalities (Tuckson, 1991).

The cause of low birth weight may be intrauterine growth retardation, which means that the fetus does not grow as expected. This may be due to a variety of causes, such as poor placental perfusion, which occurs during pregnancy-induced hypertension, or the underdeveloped vasculature of the uterus in young primigravidas. When placental perfusion is decreased, the newborn may have a low birth weight even if the pregnancy goes to term because there has been inadequate transport of nutrients and oxygen to the placenta throughout the pregnancy.

Prematurity is also a major cause of low-birth weight infants. When the infant is born before 38 weeks of gestation, it is likely to weigh less than 2500 g, and in this case the newborn has the added risks associated with immature organs. Respiratory distress syndrome, which occurs as a result of immature lungs, is the leading cause of prolonged hospitalization and neonatal death. (For additional details about respiratory distress syndrome, see Chapter 29.) Other neonatal conditions that add to the high incidence of morbidity and mortality are birth trauma, congenital anomalies, and perinatal infections.

Psychological Implications

Not all adolescents react to unplanned pregnancy in the same manner. The reaction of the 13-year-old, who is in junior high school, will be very different from that of the 18 year old, who is at a totally different developmental stage. When nursing care is being planned, it is helpful to recognize that behavior, modes of thinking, and needs differ in early, middle, and late adolescence.

EARLY ADOLESCENCE

In early adolescence, from 12 to 15 years of age, a girl experiences a surge in physical growth and sexual maturation accompanied by an increase in hormones that leaves her dealing with an unfamiliar body and feelings that she never experienced before. If pregnancy occurs, she may be repulsed by changes occurring in her body and attempt to halt the increase in size by strict restriction of caloric intake. She may consciously or unconsciously deny pregnancy until it is so advanced that prenatal care is inadequate and her options are reduced.

Although she is about to become a mother, the early adolescent continues to need the parenting she receives from her own mother. This causes a great deal of ambivalence, because this is also the time during which adolescents begin to break away from the family. She is frightened by the desire for independence while longing for closeness with her mother. If her mother assumes care of the infant, the early adolescent may feel that the infant is stealing time and parenting that belong to her. She has no desire to move to a peer status with her mother.

Although the early adolescent may have some ability to problem solve, she is not ready for decision making or the responsibility that parenting involves. If she does not have the help of a stable adult, she cannot provide the care that an infant needs.

MIDDLE ADOLESCENCE

Roughly, the years from 15 through 17 are termed the middle stage of adolescence. At this age, the young woman is more able to plan for the future and to problem solve. The peer group is extremely important to her, and role models in the group set the standards of behavior. Teenage pregnancy is expected in some peer groups, and early motherhood may be viewed as a rite of passage into the adult world. Although the middle adolescent may see the

Pregnant adolescent. Thirty-eight per cent of teenage girls who become pregnant will be pregnant again within 24 months.

pregnancy as a way to become autonomous, she continues to require a great deal of assistance.

The middle adolescent continues to strive for independence and may show signs of open rebellion and antisocial behavior if conflicts with her parents are not resolved or if communication breaks down. She tends to be idealistic about motherhood and is often unprepared for the amount of time and attention that the infant requires.

Appearance is extremely important to young women of this age, and they may be unprepared for changes that occur in their bodies as pregnancy progresses. Increased size and change in body contour, "stretch marks," and increased skin pigmentation may cause acute distress.

LATE ADOLESCENCE

Ages 17 through 19 are the years of late adolescence, and this is a time when the young woman has achieved a degree of independence and problem-solving ability. Body image is fairly stable, and she usually has a positive image of herself. She is less self-centered and more able to give and to share. In late adolescence, the young woman is more likely to have a strong relationship with the father of the infant and a new level of understanding with her own family.

The older adolescent often assumes responsibility for obtaining prenatal care and participates in parenting classes. The family often accepts the pregnancy more easily than the family of a younger teenager, and the infant receives care that parallels that provided by older parents.

The Teenage Expectant Father

Almost all teenage expectant fathers indicate that they are not ready for fatherhood, and this attitude does not diminish as the pregnancy progresses. Many are depressed as they grapple with the conflicting roles of adolescence and fatherhood. Although some express interest in learning about childbirth and child care, those who do not want to be fathers are less likely to be supportive. Some do not wish to interact with the infant, leaving the pregnant girl to seek support elsewhere.

A disproportionate number of teenage expectant fathers are from environments of poverty and lack job skills or educational preparation. Many need job training before they are able to earn enough money to contribute to the support of their children.

Impact on Parenting

Adolescent mothers demonstrate significantly less empathy than older mothers to children's needs (Baranowski et al, 1990). Whether this is due to adolescence per se, the higher incidence of premature births, the lower socioeconomic status, or a particular home environment is difficult to determine. However, teenage mothers tend to be more insensitive to infant signals and needs and are often ambivalent about motherhood. Although adolescents may provide adequate physical care to infants, they appear to use less verbal interaction and to provide less stimulation than do older parents.

Teenage mothers often have unrealistic expectations about the mothering role and infant behaviors. They may expect too much too soon from their infants. For instance, adolescent mothers may expect that the infant will sleep through the night, smile, or be toilet trained before it is appropriate for infants to do these things.

Finally, young parents may become disenchanted quickly with parenting because they feel that it does not provide the rewards that they expected. Adolescents often become frustrated and tend to have more punitive child-rearing attitudes than older parents (Mercer, 1990). Clinical observations of parent-child interaction in adolescent mothers indicate inappropriate parental behaviors such as pinching, poking, or picking at the infant, although these behaviors are rare in older mothers.

The ability to deal with stress plays an important part in mothering skills and ability. Young adolescents have immature coping mechanisms, and they may be unable to separate the stress of other life events from the stress that occurs when the infant cries and cannot be consoled. They may respond with immature or punitive measures toward the infant when the source of stress is due to other factors, such as social isolation or inadequate financial resources.

✔ Check Your Reading

1. How does pregnancy affect the developmental tasks of adolescence?
2. What are the major problems associated with teenage pregnancy in terms of maternal and fetal health?
3. How does teenage parenting differ from that of older parents?

The Pregnant Teenager: Application of Nursing Process

Assessment

Physical Assessment

Although adolescents have special needs, assessment of pregnant teenagers is similar to that of older clients in many respects. At the initial visit, a thorough health history, family history, and physical examination are essential. Assessment focuses on signs that indicate the development of iron-deficiency anemia, pregnancy-induced hypertension (see Chapter 24), or preterm labor (see Chapter 26).

Because adolescents often have irregular menstrual periods, determining weeks of gestation based on last menstrual period may be complicated. Measure fundal height to determine as closely as possible the date of conception, based on fundal height in centimeters being equivalent to the number of gestational weeks. Report any signs of intrauterine growth retardation to the physician or nurse-midwife. (See Chapter 7 for a complete description of prenatal assessments.)

The incidence of STDs is high among adolescents. Elicit information about the teenager's number of sexual partners so that therapeutic management can be initiated as necessary.

Teenagers are sometimes defensive and inconsistent in their responses. Because they may not volunteer information about nutrition, exercise, and the use of alcohol or other drugs, the nurse needs to press for details. The teenager's statement "I eat O.K. and I am pretty active" requires follow-up questions worded to obtain specific information: "What did you eat yesterday? Begin with when you first got up." "What activities do you enjoy most?"

Additional assessments are necessary, and they must be carried out in a different manner. Instead of a list of questions that may elicit short, meaningless answers, structure the interview so that questions can be interspersed in a more general conversation that focuses on the teenager's likes and concerns. For example, a question such as "So, you are a member of the choir, will you be able to continue with that after the baby is born?" may establish rapport and help determine if the teenager is making plans for the future.

KNOWLEDGE OF INFANT NEEDS

Knowledge of infant needs and parenting skills must also be assessed. How does the teenager plan to feed the infant? What will she do when the infant cries? How will she know when the infant is ill and should be taken to a pediatrician? Does she know how much the infant should sleep? What plans have been made to provide for the hygiene and safety needs of the infant?

COGNITIVE DEVELOPMENT

Assess the teenager's cognitive development and ability to absorb health counseling. The three most important areas of cognitive development are:

1. *Egocentrism*, which involves the ability to defer personal satisfaction to respond to the needs of the infant: "What would you do if the baby were sick?" "How would you make the baby better?"
2. *Present-future orientation*, which involves the ability to make long-term plans: "What are your plans for finishing high school?" "What will you and the infant need in the first year of the infant's life?"
3. *Abstract thinking*, which involves identifying cause and effect: "Why is it important to keep clinic appointments?" "Why should condoms be used during sexual intercourse?"

FAMILY ASSESSMENT

Begin assessment of the family unit by determining the degree of participation by the father of the infant. Some may plan to marry the expectant mother; others deny responsibility for the pregnancy; still others do not plan to marry the expectant mother but plan to participate in the pregnancy and rearing of the child.

It is important to assess the adolescent without the presence of her parents, yet it is also crucial to determine the availability and amount of family support. Will the pregnant teenager continue to live with her parents? How do her parents feel about the pregnancy? How will they incorporate the mother and her infant into the family?

Families generally respond in one of three ways:

1. A family member (often the adolescent's mother) assumes the mothering role, which the teenager may abdicate willingly.
2. All care and responsibilities are left to the adolescent mother, although shelter and food are provided.
3. The family shares care and responsibilities, which allows the teenager to grow in the mothering role while completing the developmental tasks of adolescence.

The pregnant teenager's mother is particularly important when assessing the family. How does she feel about becoming a grandmother? Many women feel embarrassed and disgraced. She may feel that she has "failed" as a mother, or she may resent the new cycle of child care in which the pregnancy involves her. Is communication with her daughter open? Is she aware of the difficult role conflict (as adolescent and mother) that her daughter will experience? If the family is unable or unwilling to provide care for an adolescent with an infant, what other social support can be located?

Nursing Care Plan 23–1

Adolescent's Responses to Pregnancy and Birth

Assessment: Ann Killian, a 16-year-old Caucasian female, presented at the neighborhood health clinic during the 20th week of her pregnancy. She lives with her mother and father and a younger sister. Her father works full time in a food processing plant. Her mother works part time as a gardener's helper. Ann remains in school but verbalizes concern about how she looks and feels: "How much bigger am I going to get?" "Why is my face so blotchy?" "My feet swell and it looks gross."

Nursing Diagnosis: Body Image Disturbance related to perceived negative effects of pregnancy as evidenced by verbalized concern about appearance.

Goals:

Ann will:

1. Verbalize her feelings about pregnancy and her perception of self during each antepartal visit.
2. Make decisions about times for follow-up appointments by end of current visit.
3. Make two positive statements about herself during next antepartal visit.

Intervention:	Rationale:
1. Allow time at each prenatal visit for Ann to express concerns about weight gain and other physiological changes of pregnancy, such as hyperpigmentation and stretch marks.	1. The adolescent is often ashamed and uncomfortable with her pregnant body, and she must be helped to share these feelings and be reassured that they are a normal part of pregnancy.
2. Initiate interaction about body changes by asking open-ended questions such as "How do you feel about needing to wear maternity clothes?"	2. Adolescents are often intimidated by health care professionals and may think that their own feelings are not important enough to discuss.
3. Provide anticipatory guidance about expected changes during pregnancy; for example, the pattern of weight gain during pregnancy and the rate of weight loss following childbirth.	3. Most adolescents do not know what to expect during pregnancy, and their fears are often unexpressed. Anticipatory guidance reduces fear and provides information about expected changes.
4. Explain the reason for changes that are most troublesome at each prenatal visit (weight gain, hyperpigmentation, stretch marks, breast changes).	4. It is often helpful for the adolescent to know that some changes are temporary and that increasing weight indicates that the fetus is growing and developing. This often becomes a source of pride for the young teenager as well as for the older woman.
5. Involve Ann in scheduling follow-up prenatal appointments and other activities related to the birth of the infant (classes, plans for childbirth).	5. Participation in decision making promotes a positive sense of self.
6. Promote positive self-image by praising grooming, posture, and responsible behavior such as keeping prenatal appointments and following recommendations: "You have never missed an appointment, and your baby is growing so well."	6. Positive reinforcement is particularly important to assist the adolescent meet the developmental tasks of developing a sense of identity and self-worth.

Evaluation:

The plan of care can be considered successful if Ann verbalizes her concerns about how she looks and feels about herself, makes positive statements about herself, and participates in planning future appointments.

Nursing Care Plan 23–1 *Continued*

Adolescent's Responses to Pregnancy and Birth

Assessment: Ann reveals that her father has said that she has "shamed the family," and she is worried that her friends will reject her when they learn that she is pregnant. Ann states that she will have to "drop out of everything." She confides, in a trembling voice, that she feels guilty for putting her family "through this."

Nursing Diagnosis: Anxiety related to feelings of rejection by family and friends as manifested by statements indicating uncertainty about future support for self and infant.

Goals:
Ann will:
1. Identify at least two new measures to cope with anxiety by end of current antepartum visit.
2. Demonstrate ability to implement these measures during subsequent antepartum visits.

Intervention:	Rationale:
1. Help Ann identify what she can do to overcome anxiety about rejection of family and friends before next prenatal appointment.	1. Planning how to approach family and friends reduces anxiety.
a. Role play how Ann can initiate a conversation with friends to discuss activities that they can continue to share.	a. Acceptance by peer group and participation in peer group activities are primary concerns of the adolescent, and a change in the status within the group is a threat to self-concept that precipitates acute anxiety.
b. Suggest that she request a family meeting and acknowledge to them how she feels (guilty for the unhappiness that she is causing them and fearful that they will not assist her through the pregnancy and birth).	b. Although adolescents strive for independence, family values continue to be a significant influence. Rejection by the family at this time would leave her vulnerable to stress that is beyond her ability to cope.
c. Recommend that she share her feelings with the father of the infant if she continues to see him.	c. Expectant fathers may be a source of emotional and financial support.
2. Encourage Ann to discuss her economic needs as well as her plans for continuing school when the infant is born.	2. Beginning to develop plans for her future provides some sense of control over the situation and increases her feelings of competency.
3. Assist Ann in locating and joining the school-aged mothers' program if available through her school.	3. This peer group (teenagers who are either mothers or expectant mothers) often replaces the pregnant teenager's previous peer group. The shared concerns and activities provide an opportunity for growth.

Evaluation:
The plan of care can be considered successful if Ann identifies and follows up on suggested measures that may reduce her anxiety and if she begins to make future plans.

Assessment: Ann has given birth to a 6-pound, 3-ounce, girl at 38 weeks' gestation. She had a difficult labor and received continuous epidural anesthesia. She has decided not to breastfeed because she plans to go back to school as soon as possible. Ann will live at home, and her mother has agreed to care for the infant while Ann is in school. Ann is very concerned about caring for the newborn. She seems unsure how to respond when the infant cries and handles her only during feedings.

Nursing Diagnosis: High Risk for Altered Parenting related to knowledge deficit of infant needs and lack of confidence in ability to care for infant, as evidenced by uncertain responses to infant.

Goals:
Ann will:
1. Demonstrate basic infant care (cord care, bathing, burping, feeding, swaddling) by discharge.
2. Verbalize infant needs for gentle, prompt response to crying.
3. Demonstrate attachment behaviors (eye contact, gazing, holding, verbal stimulation, and positive comments about infant) before discharge.

Nursing Care Plan continued on following page

Nursing Care Plan 23–1 Continued

Adolescent's Responses to Pregnancy and Birth

Intervention:	Rationale:
1. Demonstrate infant care on first postpartum day, and obtain a return demonstration on 2nd postpartum day prior to discharge. (For a complete description of infant care, see Chapters 19 and 22.)	1. Confidence is increased by returning the demonstration of infant care.
2. Role play for Ann how to respond when the infant cries, and emphasize the importance of promptness and gentleness.	2. Observing how nurses respond to the infant increases the likelihood that adolescents will respond in the same manner. Trust develops when needs are consistently met in a prompt and gentle manner.
3. Emphasize the importance of touch and verbal stimulation, and point out the reciprocal bonding behaviors that the infant exhibits. (See p. 451.)	3. Many teenage parents do not provide adequate tactile and verbal stimulation for their infants, which may result in the infant's decreased ability to learn and respond to the environment. The infant has a repertoire of behaviors that stimulate mutual attachment between parent and child.
4. Include the grandmother and the father of the infant in as many demonstrations as possible.	4. When all primary caregivers are included, family cohesiveness and consistency of care are enhanced.
5. Instruct Ann in early growth and development of the infant (how often infants need to eat, how much they sleep, what to do when they cry). (See Chapter 22.)	5. Some teenage parents expect "too much, too soon" from infants and become frustrated when the infant does not respond as expected. In addition, anticipatory guidance may reduce some of the stress that many new parents experience.

Evaluation:
Demonstration of basic care, prompt and gentle response to infant crying, and verbalization of the expected growth and development of infants indicate that the plan of care was successfully implemented.

Additional Nursing Diagnoses to Consider:
High Risk for Altered Family Processes
High Risk for Altered Health Maintenance
High Risk for Altered Growth and Development

Analysis

Many adolescents wait until the second or third trimester to seek prenatal care because either they do not realize that they are pregnant or they continue to deny that they are pregnant. Moreover, many teenagers have little information about the physiological demands that pregnancy imposes on their bodies, such as the increased need for nutrients. As a result, they may have a pattern of sporadic prenatal care and missed appointments (see Nursing Care Plan 23–1). One of the most relevant nursing diagnoses is *High Risk for Altered Health Maintenance related to lack of knowledge of measures to promote health during pregnancy and increased family stress.*

Planning

For this nursing diagnosis:

- The expectant mother will keep scheduled prenatal appointments and actively participate in recommended group classes.
- She will verbalize concerns and seek knowledge of measures that promote her health and the health of the fetus throughout the pregnancy.
- She will verbalize knowledge of infant needs and the expected pattern of infant growth and development before the end of the third trimester.
- The family will verbalize emotions and concerns

and maintain functional support of the expectant mother and her infant.

Interventions

ELIMINATING BARRIERS TO HEALTH CARE

Barriers to health care for pregnant adolescents include scheduling appointments at inconvenient times or locations, along with negative attitudes of health care workers. To overcome the barriers related to scheduling appointments, it is often necessary to help the adolescent locate the clinic closest to her and to provide information about public transportation to that location. Moreover, appointments must be available when the girl (and her partner, if he wishes) are not in school. Some clinics are open in the evening or on Saturday; however, this is not always the case, and alternative plans may have to be made.

Many health care workers, including nurses, physicians, and social workers, are described by clients and families as rude, insensitive, patronizing, judgmental, hostile, condescending, and racist (American Nurses Association, 1987). Nurses can be instrumental in finding ways to overcome the negative attitudes of health care workers that discourage many pregnant women, including teenagers, from returning to prenatal clinics for needed follow-up care. Recommended strategies include:

- Identifying pervasive attitudes of the health care team
- Acknowledging that frustration, stress, and staff burnout are common when health care workers attempt to provide care for families with multiple problems
- Acknowledging that many health care workers who are parents of teenagers may feel vulnerable and fearful about their own children and project these feelings onto clients
- Allocating time for staff development, planning programs, and stress reduction
- Finding ways to obtain increased assistance from clerical and support personnel
- Initiating a scheduling plan that allows health care workers to see the same families whenever possible so that a caring relationship can be established

APPLYING TEACHING/LEARNING PRINCIPLES

To be effective, teaching must consider the major concerns of adolescents and sessions must be structured to meet their primary needs. Review principles of teaching/learning and factors that influence learning presented in Chapter 2. Table 23–3 summarizes additional recommended methods for teaching adolescents.

Table 23–3. RECOMMENDED METHODS FOR TEACHING PREGNANT ADOLESCENTS

Identify and correct barriers to prenatal care
Communicate with kindness and respect
Form small groups with like concerns
Allow ample time for clarification and discussion
Use audiovisual materials
Provide information in appropriate language
Convey empathetic concern by non-verbal communication skills
Include other family members when appropriate

Adolescents accept information more readily when it is presented with kindness and respect. Maintain a nonjudgmental approach and avoid sounding like a parent. Avoid using the word "should" or "ought," offering unwanted advice, or making decisions for them.

Because peers are important to adolescents, they benefit from participating in small groups with common concerns. Specific needs that might be addressed are nutrition counseling or education to reduce or eliminate unhealthful habits such as smoking, drug use, or alcohol consumption. As pregnancy progresses, needs and group focus change. For example, how to prepare for labor and delivery and how to care for an infant become the priorities (see Chapters 11 and 22).

Repetition is an important method of teaching and clarifying misconceptions. Remember that "telling is not teaching," and ample time must be allowed for questions and discussions. Although teenagers do not read or benefit from printed materials to the same degree that older parents do, many learn well from audiovisual aids. Numerous well-made videos and slide presentations deal with all aspects of prenatal and infant care. Time spent waiting for clinic appointments can be used to view videos that reinforce information.

Above all, remember the importance of non-verbal communication. Maintain open, friendly posture and convey empathy by using attending behaviors such as eye contact, frequent nodding, and leaning toward the speaker. As with all expectant families, avoid closed posture (arms folded across the chest), finger pointing, and lack of attention to the person speaking.

COUNSELING

Allowing time to counsel teenagers about their specific problems is an important aspect of nursing care. The most common areas involve nutrition counseling, stress reduction, and how to provide care for the infant.

Nutrition. Nutrition counseling is one of the most effective means for reducing the incidence of low-birth-weight infants. Adapt information to the individual adolescent's likes and peer group habits. The pregnant adolescent often needs instruction in how to make the most nutritious selection from fast-food menus and how to select and plan for healthy snacks when she is away from home.

Referrals to food stamps, the Special Supplemental Food Program for Women, Infants, and Children (WIC), surplus food distributors, food banks, and food preparation equipment may be necessary because many teenagers have limited access to food and lack the ability to store or prepare food. Nutrition education must be socially and culturally appropriate. (For additional information about the nutritional needs of adolescents and how to help them make good choices, see Chapter 9.)

Stress Reduction. Stress is an important factor in perinatal outcome, and teenagers are vulnerable to many sources of stress. Stress may be related to basic needs such as food, shelter, and health care. Fear of labor and delivery and fear of being single, alone, and unsupported all create stress. Perhaps a major source of stress for teenagers occurs when they attempt to meet the developmental tasks of adolescence while working on the developmental tasks of pregnancy (overcoming ambivalence, attaining the role of parent). (See Chapter 8 for additional information about the developmental tasks of pregnancy.)

A variety of measures may be used to reduce stress, depending on the teenager's age, situation, and available support. Adolescents with chronic life stress may require the concentrated efforts of a social worker to achieve stabilization. The pregnant teenager often experiences stress because she has not told her parents or the father of the infant about the pregnancy. It may be helpful to explore her reluctance to do this and to role play the encounter so that she can work out a plan for breaking the news. If appropriate, encourage her to tell the prospective father so that he can work out his role. If the girl is very young or if the pregnancy occurred as a result of rape or incest, social service and law enforcement agencies must become involved to provide protection and assistance.

Infant Care. The priorities for teaching gradually change from maternal needs to providing information about infant needs and normal growth and development. Demonstrating infant reflexes and explaining the infant's diffuse and uncoordinated motor responses may reduce the worry that many mothers feel when the child trembles or startles in response to loud noises. Explaining that development proceeds from the head downward helps the young mother understand that the infant must learn to sit before walking and must walk before toilet training is possible.

Because adolescents tend to have a more rigid and punitive approach to child care, emphasize to them that infants grow and develop a sense of trust when their needs are met promptly and gently. Attaining a sense of trust is necessary for future development to occur. Emphasize that crying does not indicate that the infant is spoiled but simply that the infant has a need. Perhaps the need is for food, warmth, or comfort and love. Discuss the importance of eye contact, holding, and cuddling, as well as the importance of verbal stimulation.

PROMOTING FAMILY SUPPORT

The pregnant teenager needs encouragement to include her family in her decision making and problem solving. The involvement of her mother, older sister, or other close relative is particularly important in terms of future plans. Topics that should be discussed include who will care for the infant, will the teenager return to school, and what financial assistance is available from the family and from the father of the infant. However, if the family has multiple problems that include substance abuse or domestic violence, it may be inappropriate to involve them; the teenager should be encouraged to communicate instead with a family friend or other trusted adult.

PROVIDING REFERRALS

Nurses who are knowledgeable about national and community resources for pregnant adolescents can make referrals to the closest and most convenient locations. These include well baby clinics offered by the Public Health Service, programs for school-aged mothers offered by many high schools, Aid to Families with Dependent Children offered by state social service agencies, and WIC. Church and community organizations may also provide needed assistance. When incest or rape is suspected, law enforcement agencies must be notified.

Evaluation

Nursing care has been effective if the pregnant adolescent keeps clinic appointments and participates actively in her plan of care, as demonstrated by asking questions, sharing concerns, and adhering to the recommended program of care. Demonstrating knowledge of infant needs as well as the infant's expected pattern of growth and development by the end of the pregnancy increases the teenager's confidence in her ability to provide a nurturing environment for the infant. Family support is often available, but, if it is not, nurses must often make referrals to agencies that can provide assistance.

✔ Check Your Reading

4. What methods are effective for teaching pregnant teenagers?
5. What should prospective teenage parents be taught about infant growth and development? Why?

Delayed Pregnancy

Women in their twenties are considered to be in their prime childbearing years; however, delaying the first pregnancy until after the woman is 35 years of age is an emerging trend. Women may delay pregnancy for a variety of reasons, the most common being a desire to establish a career or to become financially secure before having children. Some women have difficulty conceiving, and pregnancy is delayed until this problem is corrected.

Although a 35-year-old woman can hardly be considered elderly, she is often referred to as an "elderly primigravida" or "older mother"; however, the term "mature primigravida" is preferred by some.

Maternal and Fetal Implications

Once the mature woman decides to conceive, she may experience a delay in becoming pregnant. This is particularly true after the age of 35 years because of the normal aging of the ovaries and the increased incidence in reproductive tract disorders, such as pelvic inflammatory disease, which can cause pelvic and tubal adhesions that interfere with fertilization and implantation.

Once the mature woman conceives, she is at increased risk for complications associated with pregnancy. After age 35, pre-existing illness such as diabetes or hypertension is related to a slight but significant increase in maternal mortality. The older primigravida is also at increased risk for preterm labor, and, as a result, the pregnancy may be costly because of the need for prolonged bed rest or even hospitalization to maintain the pregnancy until the fetus is mature. Cesarean delivery is more common if the woman is over 35 years because cervical dilation may not occur as spontaneously as in younger women. In all women, recovery from cesarean birth is more difficult and takes more time than recovery from vaginal birth.

The risk of pregnancy-induced hypertension as well as the risk of having an infant who is small for gestational age increases with maternal age, particularly if the woman is a primigravida. Uterine fibroids occur with greater frequency in women in their late thirties and increase the risk of postpartal hemorrhage. Other bleeding disorders, such as abruptio placentae, occur more often in women over 35 years of age.

The increased risk of fetal chromosomal abnormalities with advancing maternal age is well documented. Trisomy 21 (Down syndrome) is the most common example, occurring once in every 365 live births at 35 years of age and increasing to once in every 32 live births by the age of 45 years (Jones, 1989). The use of chorionic villus sampling or amniocentesis permits detection of some chromosomal abnormalities, and legalized abortion allows the woman to terminate the pregnancy if that is an option she would consider.

Advantages of Delayed Childbirth

Unlike adolescents, for whom pregnancy may be unplanned and unwanted, women over 35 years of age seldom make the decision to have a child without careful thought. These women come to the parenting role with a range of personal resources: psychosocial maturity, self-confidence, and a sense of control over their lives. They demonstrate a high level of empathy and flexibility in child-rearing attitudes. Their parenting is less affected by the infant's temperament, whether it be easy, slow to warm up, or difficult (Mercer, 1990).

In addition, mature primigravidas are capable of solving complex problems and are often adept at maintaining interpersonal relationships. Because they are more likely to be financially secure, they can afford excellent care for their infants. They are experienced at setting priorities and developing plans. Moreover, they are usually able to manage stress and will independently seek support and assistance.

Disadvantages of Delayed Childbirth

Mature primiparas need more time to recover from childbirth, and they have less energy than their younger counterparts. They may find child care an exhausting experience for the first few weeks. This is particularly true if they had a cesarean birth, or if they are meticulous housekeepers and spend time cleaning when they might be resting.

Some women plan to take an extended leave from work following the birth of the infant, but, although they enjoy parenting, they miss the stimulation of work. Conversely, those who return to work soon after the infant is born experience all the anxiety, grief, and guilt that younger women feel when they leave the infant.

Mature primiparas may lack peer support. Many of their friends have teenage children and do not relate to the concerns of a new mother. Younger mothers have some of the same concerns, but they often do not share the perspective of older mothers.

Family support may also be lacking for the older woman. Her parents are usually in their 60s or 70s and may have health problems or find child care exhausting.

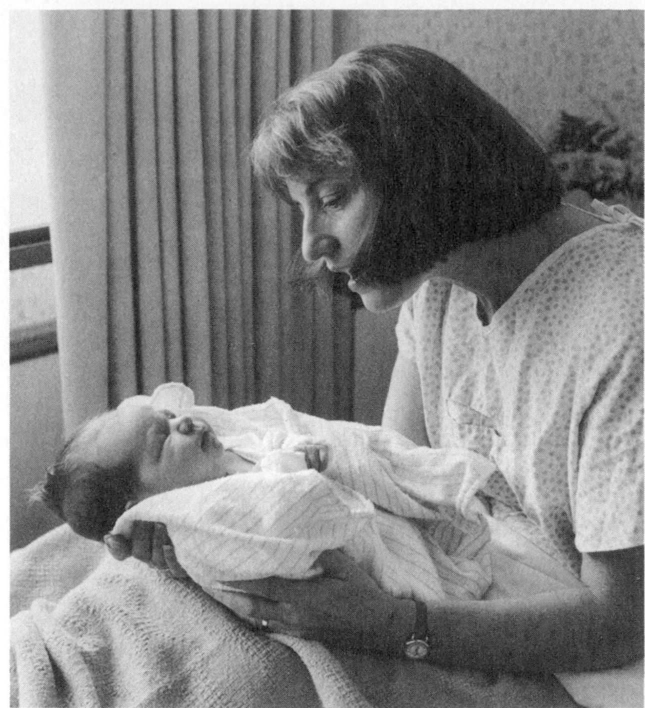

Although mature primigravidas bring maturity and self-assurance to the maternal role, they are at somewhat increased risk for physiological problems related to pregnancy and birth.

The Mature Primigravida: Application of Nursing Process

Assessment

Carefully assess the woman who is 35 years or older for pre-existing conditions, for example, diabetes, hypertension, heart disease, infections, and reproductive problems, such as uterine fibroids. In addition, carefully measure her fundal height at each prenatal visit for gestational age discrepancy; fundal height in centimeters should roughly correlate with weeks of gestation. Fundal height less than expected may indicate intrauterine growth retardation; fundal height greater than expected may indicate trophoblastic neoplasia (hydatidiform mole), which occurs more frequently in women older than 40 years of age.

The woman over 35 years may have advanced in her career to a high level of responsibility with associated stress. She often has a deep emotional commitment to her career. It is important to determine how she usually copes with stress and how she plans to balance the demands of her job with the demands of childbearing and infant care.

The mature primigravida often has little knowledge of infant needs, and she experiences a great deal of anxiety about her ability to parent. Determine her major concerns so that anticipatory guidance can be provided.

Because the fetus of a mature primigravida is at increased risk for chromosomal anomalies, the woman will most likely be informed about diagnostic tests that are available. The prospect of diagnostic tests is anxiety-provoking for many, and some women choose not to have the tests. (See Chapter 10 for detailed information about fetal diagnostic procedures.)

Analysis

Although a variety of nursing diagnoses are possible, the one most specific to the mature primigravida is *Anxiety related to possible abnormalities of the fetus and lack of confidence in ability to parent effectively*.

Planning

For this nursing diagnosis, the expectant parents will:

- Make an informed choice about whether to have genetic studies performed and will verbalize confidence in their decision.

- Verbalize their emotions while waiting for fetal diagnostic test results.
- Express confidence in their ability to care for the newborn.

Interventions

REINFORCING AND CLARIFYING INFORMATION

Only physicians, certified nurse-midwives, and nurses with special preparation in genetics should provide genetic counseling. All nurses, however, must be prepared to reinforce and clarify the information that has been provided. The tests most often recommended are alpha-fetoprotein, chorionic villus sampling, amniocentesis, and targeted ultrasonography. (See also Chapter 10.)

Beliefs and attitudes about abortion are related to the decision about whether to have the recommended tests. The family who would not consider abortion regardless of the condition of the fetus often decides to refuse the diagnostic studies. Respect the decision and acknowledge that it may have been a difficult one to make.

FACILITATING EXPRESSION OF EMOTIONS

Several days may pass between performance of diagnostic studies and when results of the tests are known. This is a particularly difficult time for many expectant parents.

Assist the couple to express their concerns and emotions. A broad statement such as "Many couples find it difficult to wait for the results" will often elicit free expression of how they feel. Follow-up questions such as "What concerns you most?" may reveal worry about the procedure itself or about the possible effects of the procedure on the fetus. Simply acknowledging that it is a stressful time helps the couple to cope with their emotions.

PROVIDING PARENTING INFORMATION

To prepare the mature primipara for effective parenting, point out her individual strengths and advantages. These often include financial security, a stable relationship, and personal maturity. The woman who delays childbearing may have unique needs. She often has less energy than younger mothers and must learn to conserve it, particularly during the early weeks following childbirth. Anticipatory guidance about measures that will help conserve energy following childbirth are very useful. This may involve meal planning or setting realistic housekeeping goals. In addition, encourage older mothers to mobilize all available support so that they can reserve their energy for care of the infant.

During the first weeks following childbirth, the mother may experience feelings of social isolation, particularly if her friends have children who are a great deal older. If she is accustomed to a great deal of mental stimulation, she may miss this while staying at home. If she elects to return to work, she is likely to experience guilt and grief because she must leave her infant. (See Chapter 18 for a discussion of this problem.)

First-time mothers over age 35 are especially receptive to prenatal classes. These include classes in childbirth education, preparation for cesarean birth, breastfeeding, and early parenting. When teaching infant care following childbirth, allow time for demonstrations and return demonstrations so that the expectant parents feel comfortable with routine care such as feeding, bathing, and diapering as well as care of the cord and circumcision site. The older couple is particularly interested in learning how the infant grows and develops and what they can do to provide nurturing care for the infant. They generally comprehend printed materials that can be used to reinforce teaching.

Evaluation

The decision of the couple to have or to refuse genetic testing should be based on a thorough understanding of the procedures offered as well as on their own beliefs and attitudes. This ensures a feeling of confidence that the right decision was made. Exposure to prenatal classes in breastfeeding and parenting as well as ample time for practice following childbirth increases confidence in the ability to provide care for the newborn.

✔ Check Your Reading

6. What special resources do mature primigravidas often have?
7. Why is it important to offer prenatal testing (alpha-fetoprotein, chorionic villus sampling, amniocentesis) to the mature primigravida?

Substance Abuse

Substance abuse has reached epidemic proportions in the United States and affects every socioeconomic group. Substance abuse includes not only illicit drugs, such as cocaine and heroin, but also legal substances, such as caffeine, tobacco, and alcohol. In the past, illicit drugs were largely confined to low-income urban areas; however, since the mid-1980s, the use of drugs, particularly cocaine, has risen dramatically in suburban and rural middle-class families.

Incidence

It is difficult to determine accurately the incidence of drug abuse during pregnancy. If the drugs used are illegal, the woman fears prosecution by the law and deliberately conceals her drug use. Many women also underreport the amount of legal and socially approved substances, such as alcohol, consumed because they know about the harmful effects of the substance on the fetus and feel guilty, or they fear reprisals by members of the health care delivery system.

Often drugs are used together, and abuse of one drug may indicate abuse of others. For example, cocaine is almost never used alone; alcohol, tranquilizers, and over-the-counter "downers," such as combination pain and sleep medications, are often used in conjunction with cocaine. This makes information about the incidence of drug abuse confusing and sometimes inaccurate.

It is estimated that more than 2.25 million women in the United States are problem drinkers. The incidence is highest among Native Americans and African-Americans and in homes where the parents or grandparents were alcoholics (Pietrantoni, 1991). Smoking is also prevalent; 20 to 30 per cent of women of childbearing age in the United States smoke cigarettes despite overwhelming evidence of the adverse effects of smoking on pregnancy outcomes. The frequency of cocaine use by pregnant women in the United States is estimated to approach 1 in 10, and the rate is significantly higher in some urban areas (Chasnoff et al, 1988). Additional illicit drugs that are commonly abused include marijuana, heroin, stimulants, and depressants.

Maternal and Fetal Effects

When the pregnant woman takes a substance, by drinking, smoking, snorting, or injecting it intravenously, the fetus receives the same substance. The fetus experiences the same systemic effects as the expectant mother but often more severely. While cocaine raises the blood pressure of the woman and puts her at risk of intracranial bleeding, it puts the fetus at the same risk. A drug that causes intoxication in the woman causes it in the fetus for prolonged periods. This is because the fetus is unable to metabolize drugs as efficiently as the expectant mother and will experience the effects long after they have abated in the woman. Therefore, substances taken by the woman can have great impact on the fetus and can interfere with normal fetal development and health. For a summary of the maternal and fetal effects of commonly abused substances, see Table 23–4.

SMOKING

The major consequences of smoking tobacco during pregnancy are low-birth-weight infants, prematurity, and increased perinatal loss. Maternal smoking decreases birth weight by approximately 290 g (Aaronson and Macnee, 1989). Infants born to women who smoke are symmetrically smaller in all areas, including head circumference (Creasy and Resnik, 1989). Smoking during pregnancy is also associated with delayed neurological and intellectual development of children. Examples include hyperactivity, shorter attention span, and lower reading and spelling scores during the primary grades. Smoking has the following adverse effects on the fetus:

- Nicotine causes vasoconstriction, resulting in reduced placental blood flow and decreased transport of oxygen and nutrients to the fetus.
- Elevated levels of carbon monoxide inactivate fetal and maternal hemoglobin and further reduce the amount of oxygen delivered to the fetus (Zuckerman, 1988).
- Toxic elements in tobacco smoke can cause abnormalities of the placenta.
- Indirect effects such as decreased maternal appetite result in inadequate intake of calories as well as increased difficulties in absorbing nutrients such as calcium and vitamins A, B, and C (Aaronson and Macnee, 1989).

ALCOHOL

Because alcohol is legal and socially accepted, it is one of the most commonly abused drugs during pregnancy. No safe level of alcohol consumption during pregnancy has been established. However, because it is known that alcohol retards growth and alters the development of the fetus, recommend that women consume no alcohol during pregnancy because of the risks to the fetus.

Fetal alcohol syndrome (FAS) is the name given to a set of abnormalities that occur in children who have been exposed to alcohol during the prenatal period. FAS is characterized by prenatal and postnatal growth retardation, central nervous system disor-

Table 23–4. MATERNAL AND FETAL/NEONATAL EFFECTS OF COMMONLY ABUSED SUBSTANCES

Substance	Maternal Effects	Fetal/Neonatal Effects
Caffeine (coffee, tea, cola, chocolate, cold remedies, analgesics)	Stimulates CNS and cardiac function, causes vasoconstriction and mild diuresis, half-life triples during pregnancy	Crosses placental barrier and stimulates fetus; teratogenic effects are undocumented
Tobacco	Decreased placental perfusion, anemia, PROM, preterm labor, spontaneous abortion	Prematurity, LBW, fetal demise, developmental delays, increased incidence of SIDS, pneumonia
Alcohol (beer, wine, mixed drinks, after-dinner drinks)	Spontaneous abortion	Fetal demise, IUGR, FAS (facial and cranial anomalies, developmental delay, mental retardation, short attention span), fetal alcohol effects (milder form of FAS)
Narcotics (heroin, methadone, morphine)	Spontaneous abortion, PROM, preterm labor, increased incidence of STDs, HIV exposure, hepatitis, malnutrition	IUGR, perinatal asphyxia, intellectual impairment, neonatal abstinence syndrome, neonatal infections, neonatal death (SIDS, child abuse and neglect)
Sedatives (barbiturates, tranquilizers)	Lethargy, drowsiness, CNS depression	Neonatal abstinence syndrome, seizures, delayed lung maturity, possible teratogenic effects
Cocaine ("crack")	Hyperarousal state, generalized vasoconstriction, hypertension, increased spontaneous abortion, abruptio placentae, preterm labor, cardiovascular complications (stroke, heart attack), seizures, increased STDs	Stillbirth, prematurity, IUGR, irritability, decreased ability to interact with environmental stimuli, poor feeding reflexes, nausea, vomiting, diarrhea, decreased intellectual development; distended, flabby, creased abdomen (prune-belly syndrome) due to absence of abdominal muscles
Amphetamines ("speed" or "ice" when processed in crystals to smoke)	Malnutrition, tachycardia, withdrawal symptoms (lethargy, depression)	Increased risk for cardiac anomalies and cleft palate (Rogers & Lee, 1988), IUGR, withdrawal symptoms
Marijuana ("grass" or "pot")	Often used with other drugs: alcohol, cocaine, tobacco; increased incidence of anemia and inadequate weight gain	Unclear, more study needed, believed related to prematurity, IUGR, neonatal tremors, sensitivity to light

CNS, central nervous system; PROM, premature rupture of membranes; LBW, low birth weight; SIDS, sudden infant death syndrome; IUGR, intrauterine growth retardation; FAS, fetal alcohol syndrome; STDs, sexually transmitted diseases; HIV, human immunodeficiency virus.

ders, and cranial and facial anomalies. Growth retardation includes retarded weight, length, and head circumference. The central nervous system injury is identified as mental retardation, shorter attention span, delayed motor development, hyperactivity, and irritability.

Common cranial and facial anomalies associated with FAS include microcephaly, short palpebral fissures (opening between the eyelids), flat midface, indistinct philtrum (median groove on the external surface of the upper lip), and a thin upper lip (Fig. 23–1). In addition, children with FAS are at increased risk for cardiac defects.

A second term, "fetal alcohol effects," is now being used to describe infants who exhibit mild or partial manifestations of FAS, such as low birth weight; developmental delay that may not be obvious for 1 to 2 years; and hyperactivity.

Researchers are unsure how alcohol causes damage to the fetus. However, it is known that alcohol passes easily through the placental barrier, and concentrations found in the fetus are believed to be at least as high as those found in the mother. During the first trimester, alcohol is believed to affect cell membranes and alter the organization of tissue. Throughout pregnancy, alcohol interferes with the metabolism of carbohydrates, lipids, and proteins and thus retards cell growth and division. The central nervous system is probably most vulnerable during the third trimester, which is a time of rapid brain growth; if alcohol consumption ceases during this time, the risk of further damage is reduced (Weiner and Larsson, 1987).

COCAINE

Cocaine can be inhaled, taken intravenously, or smoked, depending on how it is processed. Powdered cocaine is inhaled (snorted) or mixed with water and injected intravenously. Crack cocaine is smoked, and its availability, low cost, and highly addictive nature have led to a dramatic increase in its use.

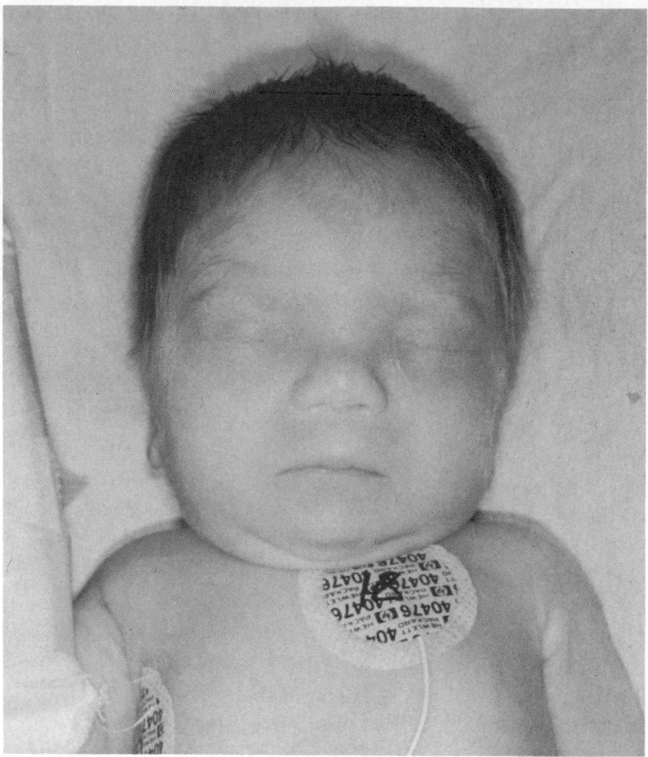

Figure 23–1

Infant with fetal alcohol syndrome. Subtle indicators that are present are flat midface, indistinct philtrum and low-set ears. (Courtesy of Trish Beachy, M.S., R.N., Perinatal Program Coordinator, University of Colorado Health Sciences, Denver.)

How Cocaine Works

Cocaine is a powerful, short-acting stimulant of the central nervous system. Chemically, cocaine works by blocking the presynaptic reuptake of the neurotransmitters norepinephrine and dopamine, producing an excess of these substances at nerve terminals. The excess of neurotransmitters acts on the cerebral cortex to produce a hyperarousal state that results in euphoria, physical excitement, reduced fatigue, and a heightened sense of well-being and power. Anorexia, hyperglycemia, hyperthermia, and tachypnea are among the array of side effects of cocaine use.

When the initial euphoria wears off, a period of irritability, fatigue, lethargy, depression, and impatience occurs, which elicits a strong desire for additional cocaine so that the initial feelings can be recaptured.

Physical effects of cocaine use are related to cardiovascular stimulation and vasoconstriction. The heart rate, systolic blood pressure, and demand for oxygen all increase. Complications of generalized vasoconstriction include myocardial ischemia, myocardial infarction, or cardiac arrhythmias. In addition, cocaine has been associated with stroke, subarachnoid hemorrhage, and temporal lobe seizures.

Maternal and Fetal Effects

Identifying a clear-cut, cause-and-effect relationship between cocaine use and perinatal morbidity is difficult. This is because many women who use cocaine have a lifestyle that includes the use of additional drugs, such as alcohol, tranquilizers, or marijuana, to "come down" from the superarousal state that cocaine produces. In addition, women who abuse cocaine are less likely to seek prenatal care or to eat a diet that contains adequate nutrition. Moreover, sex is often exchanged for drugs, which places the woman at increased risk for STDs.

Cocaine directly stimulates uterine contractions, and the most common problem attributed to cocaine use in the pregnant woman is premature delivery (Jones, 1989). There is also increased incidence of spontaneous abortion and abruptio placentae because of the cocaine-induced vasoconstriction of placental vessels. Additional complications include premature rupture of membranes, precipitous delivery, and stillbirths.

Cocaine crosses the placental barrier and causes the same physical stress on the fetus as on the expectant mother. Moreover, clearance of the drug takes a prolonged period of time in the fetus, and cocaine metabolites may persist in the fetus for as long as 7 days (Lynch and McKeon, 1990). Fetal effects have been documented extensively and include tachycardia, decreased beat-to-beat variability of the fetal heart rate baseline, fetal overactivity, and intrauterine growth retardation.

Neonatal Effects

Immediate Effects. Clinical symptoms observed in neonates exposed to cocaine in utero include tremors, tachycardia, marked irritability, muscular rigidity, hypertension, and exaggerated startle reflex. These infants are difficult to console and exhibit an inability to respond to voices or environmental stimuli. They are often poor feeders and have frequent episodes of diarrhea that may culminate in ischemic infarction of the bowel. Chasnoff et al (1988) also described an increase in genitourinary defects as well as absence of abdominal muscles that results in a flabby, distended, and creased abdomen known as *prune-belly syndrome*.

Long-Term Effects. The behavioral and developmental characteristics of cocaine-exposed infants may become lifelong disabilities, including both short-term and long-term learning problems, slower intellectual development, and delayed language and motor development. These infants may continue to be irritable and have limited interaction with people and objects in their environment (Lewis et al, 1989).

MARIJUANA

Estimates of marijuana use during pregnancy in the United States vary widely, from 10 to 42 per cent, and depend on the population being surveyed (Day and Richardson, 1991). However, very little research has been conducted on the effects of marijuana on the pregnant woman or fetus. One reason is that marijuana is often paired with other drugs such as cocaine or alcohol, making it difficult to determine the effects that are solely the result of marijuana use.

There appears to be an increased incidence in maternal anemia and inadequate maternal weight gain with increased incidence of intrauterine growth retardation if the use of marijuana is prolonged (Zuckerman et al, 1989). Clinically, the neonate exhibits hyperirritability, tremors, and increased sensitivity to light. Long term effects of marijuana on the development of the child deserve much more study before they can be ruled out or confirmed.

HEROIN

Heroin is an illegal narcotic agent derived from morphine that produces severe physical addiction. It may be taken intravenously, intranasally, or by smoking. Like all narcotics, heroin is a central nervous system depressant that soothes and lulls. It produces a feeling of mental dullness, drowsiness, and finally stupor ("on the nod"). Addiction may be said to exist when discontinuance causes abstinence or withdrawal symptoms that are quickly relieved by a dose of the drug.

Heroin use during pregnancy has been extensively studied, and the effects on the pregnant woman, the fetus, and the newborn have been repeatedly described. Women who abuse heroin have poor general health with multiple medical problems associated with their drug abuse and addicted lifestyle. Heroin is an appetite suppressant that also interferes with absorption of nutrients that are ingested, and many women start pregnancy malnourished and anemic. Additional problems include a high incidence of STDs such as gonorrhea, syphilis, and herpes. In addition, infections such as hepatitis and exposure to HIV occur frequently as a result of sharing unclean needles.

Fetal Effects

The fetus suffers both direct and indirect effects of heroin use by the expectant mother. The street supply of heroin is usually not steady, and direct effects on the fetus are due to frequent episodes of maternal overdose alternating with periods of withdrawal from the drug. This exposes the fetus to intermittent episodes of hypoxia in utero, which increases the risk of prematurity, growth retardation, and stillbirth. Indirect effects are due to maternal malnutrition and fetal exposure to STDs.

Neonatal Effects

Infants born to mothers who are addicted to narcotics, including heroin, methadone, meperidine, or morphine, exhibit a neonatal abstinence (withdrawal) syndrome. This syndrome affects all body systems; however, the most consistent symptoms described are neurological: tremors, jitteriness, restlessness, and, on occasion, seizures. Other manifestations include hypertonicity and prolonged continuous crying. The latter two symptoms are particularly difficult for nurses caring for the infant and for family members who are learning to provide for the special needs of the heroin-exposed neonate. Caretakers become frustrated because the infant's body is stiff and extended, and the newborn does not respond to cuddling or soothing behaviors that usually console a crying infant. Position and behavior for consoling drug-exposed infants are illustrated in Figure 23–2.

Figure 23–2

Consoling behaviors for a drug-exposed infant.

Additional symptoms of newborn abstinence syndrome include poorly coordinated sucking and swallowing reflexes, vomiting, and diarrhea, which may result in dehydration and failure to gain weight normally. Long-term developmental and learning problems are common. Moreover, the lifestyle of parents who are substance abusers is strongly associated with child neglect and abuse, which are major causes of infant death in this population.

✔ Check Your Reading

8. How does smoking affect the fetus? What are the long-term effects on the child?
9. How does fetal alcohol syndrome compare with fetal alcohol effects in terms of severity and physical effects?
10. What are the long-term effects of maternal cocaine use on the child?
11. How does neonatal abstinence syndrome affect the caregiver?

Therapeutic Management

In addition to toxicology screening, the pregnant woman who uses illicit drugs must be tested for STDs, hepatitis, and exposure to human immunodeficiency virus (HIV) throughout pregnancy. Physicians also use all available methods to assess the fetus. These methods include ultrasonography, non–stress tests, and biophysical profiles to help pinpoint problems. Nurses monitor weight gain and provide guidance in nutrition at each opportunity to prevent maternal anemia and inadequate weight gain.

Therapeutic management depends on the type of drug used. In the case of opioids, such as heroin, withdrawal during pregnancy has been associated with significant fetal stress and even fetal death due to the effects of abstinence syndrome (Hoegerman and Schnoll, 1991). One approach to treatment of the pregnant woman who uses heroin is to place her on an alternative drug such as methadone. Methadone is useful because it can be taken orally and is long-acting; therefore, the woman is able to maintain fairly consistent blood levels, in contrast to the use of heroin, which is short-acting and results in wide swings in blood level that can have severe adverse effects on the fetus.

Treatment for a great deal of substance abuse is aimed at establishing abstinence and preventing relapse. It is often helpful to combine education, individual and group therapy sessions, and peer support groups (Narcotics Anonymous, Alcoholics Anonymous, or Cocaine Anonymous). All members of the health care team must acknowledge that women have extremely positive memories associated with cocaine use, and thus relapse is common. Written contracts that focus on abstinence for one day at a time are often used to help the patient who has relapsed and experiences severe feelings of guilt and self-blame.

Most women are referred for additional treatment for substance abuse during pregnancy. The treatment may be conducted in outpatient clinics; however, residential treatment may provide the optimum setting for needed support.

Maternal Substance Abuse: Application of Nursing Process

Antepartum Period

Assessment

Multiple drug abuse appears to be the most common substance abuse problem among women, and all women must be screened at the first prenatal visit for nicotine, alcohol, and other drugs. Because substance abuse occurs in all populations, the nurse must not make assumptions based on class, race, or economic status.

Certain behaviors are strongly associated with substance abuse: seeking prenatal care late in the pregnancy, failing to keep appointments, and inconsistent follow-through with recommended regimens. Physical appearance offers additional clues. Poor grooming, inadequate weight gain, or a pattern of weight gain that does not correspond to the stated gestational age may be signs of a lifestyle that includes substance abuse. Intravenous drug users may have fresh needle punctures, thrombosed veins, or signs of cellulitis.

Defensive or hostile behaviors may be overt signs of substance abuse. Women who use drugs have low self-esteem, and they are dealing with conflicting issues: the physical or psychological need for the substance, the need to deny that the substance is harming the fetus, guilt that they may be responsible for harming the fetus, and, finally, fear that they will be prosecuted for use of illegal drugs. Moreover, many women with substance abuse problems face the discrimination and resentment of health care professionals who direct their frustration at the woman rather than at the problem.

Establishing past or current substance abuse is not a simple task because some substances are illegal and thus disclosure of their use may have serious consequences. In 1991, a woman in California was

Critical to Remember

Behaviors Associated with Substance Abuse

- Seeking prenatal care late in pregnancy
- Failure to keep prenatal appointments
- Inconsistent follow-through with recommended care
- Poor grooming, inadequate weight gain
- Needle punctures, thrombosed veins, cellulitis
- Defensive or hostile reactions
- Anger or apathy regarding pregnancy

prosecuted for murder when her newborn died as a result of cocaine exposure. Moreover, even when the substance is legal, such as alcohol or tobacco, women tend to deny the problem of dependence and conceal the frequency of use.

Given the powerful deterrents to self-disclosure, extensive history taking provides the best opportunity to determine current and past substance use. The nurse taking the health history must exhibit patience, empathy, and tolerance and must use a blend of approaches that reinforce concern for the woman and her infant.

MEDICAL HISTORY

The assessment focuses on medical conditions that are prevalent among women who use drugs: previous treatment for depression, seizures, hepatitis, pneumonia, cellulitis, STDs, hypertension, or suicide attempts. Current problems may include insomnia, panic attacks, exhaustion, or heart palpitations.

OBSTETRICAL HISTORY

An obstetrical history focuses on past and current complications of pregnancy. Spontaneous abortions, premature deliveries, abruptio placentae, and stillbirths are associated with substance abuse, although they also occur in the population that has never used drugs. Current complications may include STDs, vaginal bleeding, and an inactive or hyperactive fetus. Measurement of fundal height may be inconsistent with gestational age, suggesting intrauterine growth retardation.

Investigate emotional responses such as anger or apathy regarding the pregnancy. These feelings are particularly significant during the latter half of the pregnancy, when one would expect the normal feelings of ambivalence to be resolved. Negative feelings toward the pregnancy may interfere with prenatal compliance with follow-up care.

HISTORY OF SUBSTANCE ABUSE

Obtaining an accurate history of substance abuse is difficult and depends in large part on the way the health care worker approaches the woman. A sincere, nonjudgmental, empathetic approach promotes an open exchange of information.

Investigate all forms of drug use, including cigarettes, over-the-counter drugs, prescribed medications, and alcohol as well as illicit drugs such as cocaine, marijuana, and heroin. Examine patterns of drug use, which can range from occasional recreational use to weekly binges to daily dependence on a particular drug or group of drugs. Suggestions for interviewing are shown in Table 23–5.

Urine toxicology screening may also be useful to validate drug use. This is particularly important when the woman denies current use but presents with a group of symptoms that suggest that she is using one or more drugs.

Analysis

Data collected during the interview and during the physical examination are analyzed to formulate nurs-

Table 23–5. TECHNIQUES FOR INTERVIEWING A WOMAN ABOUT SUBSTANCE ABUSE

To determine whether the woman abuses substances:

Express an accepting and nonjudgmental attitude.

Explain why it is important to know about substance abuse: "We need to know about anything that might affect you or your baby during the pregnancy."

Acknowledge that women may be reluctant to disclose information: "I know it's difficult to talk to us about this, but we need to know so that we can give you and your baby the best care possible."

Begin with questions about over-the-counter or prescription drugs and lead up to use of tobacco, alcohol, and, finally, illicit drugs.

Demonstrate knowledge of types and forms of drugs commonly used in the community: "Do you see much cocaine in your neighborhood?" "Do you have friends who are having trouble with crack?"

When substance abuse is acknowledged, the important points in the drug history are

- The type of drug used
- The amount of drug used
- Frequency of use

The nurse can ask specific questions:

How often have you taken over-the-counter medications?

What drugs did you take last month? Were they prescribed?

How many cigarettes do you smoke on a daily basis? Are there times when you smoke more?

How many times a week do you drink alcoholic beverages (beer, wine, mixed drinks)? How many in a day? Are there times when you have more drinks?

How often did you use cocaine before becoming pregnant? How often do you use it now? Do you snort? Smoke crack? Shoot cocaine? How many lines or rocks do you use? How long do you stay high?

ing diagnoses. Some women acknowledge the use of harmful substances but have a lack of knowledge of their effects. Other women acknowledge the use of drugs and are aware of their harmful effects but are unable to stop using the substances. A nursing diagnosis that addresses both these factors is: *High Risk for Altered Health Maintenance related to lack of knowledge of the effects of substance abuse on self and fetus and inability to manage stress without the use of drugs.*

Planning

Realistic goals for this diagnosis are that the woman will:

- Identify harmful effects of substance on self and infant.
- Verbalize feelings related to continued use of harmful substances.
- Identify personal strengths and accept support offered by health care delivery system to stop using drugs.

Interventions

There are no simple answers to the problem of substance abuse. Effective interventions require the combined efforts of nurses, physicians, social workers, law enforcement, and numerous community and federal agencies. Nurses must be aware that progress is slow and frustrating. Keep in mind that the major priority is to protect the fetus and the expectant mother from the harmful effects of drugs.

PREVENTING SUBSTANCE ABUSE

Prevention is the most effective and ideal nursing intervention when dealing with substance abuse. Many pregnant women are not aware of the impact that their behavior has on the unborn infant, and they must be made aware of the dangers of substance abuse. The key to any preventive strategy is to provide accurate information in terms that the client can easily understand. Posters, diagrams, pamphlets, and other visual aids should be used to describe the effects of alcohol, tobacco, cocaine, and heroin on the fetus. The visual aids should be posted in high schools, colleges, supermarkets, shopping centers, and other areas where women of childbearing age will be exposed to them.

The nurse's approach should focus on the benefit of the woman's remaining drug free: a decrease in maternal medical and obstetrical complications and in neonatal complications. For example, fetuses exposed to cocaine only in the first trimester are less likely to experience growth retardation than fetuses exposed throughout pregnancy. Moreover, abstinence from alcohol after the second trimester decreases the risk of fetal alcohol syndrome (Chisum, 1990). The effects of smoking tobacco are potentially dose-related and cumulative, and nurses need to encourage and support cessation at any point during pregnancy.

PROVIDING FOLLOW-UP CARE

At each antepartum visit, consider the current status of substance use, social service needs, education needs, and compliance with treatment referrals. Particularly address current drug use because women may change their pattern of drug use during pregnancy. For instance, they may stop using cocaine but increase the use of marijuana or alcohol.

Because substance abusers have poor attendance rates at antepartum clinics as a result of their chaotic lifestyle, it is important to verify compliance with chemical-dependence referral programs. Often the nurse is responsible for verifying compliance with treatment recommendations and facilitating communication among various service providers, such as group therapy and prenatal classes.

Continuing education is essential to ongoing quality care for pregnant substance abusers. Prenatal education classes that include the anatomy and physiology of pregnancy, consequences of prenatal substance abuse, neonatal outcomes, and interventions for the neonate may prove helpful. In addition, education that stresses the benefits that abstinence will have on the expectant mother and the fetus is very important.

FACILITATING COMMUNICATION

The Nurse's Feelings. When working with substance-abusing pregnant women, nurses must first identify and acknowledge their own feelings and prejudices. One of the most common emotions expressed by nurses is anger at the woman who is not only engaging in self-destructive behavior but also may be inflicting harm on an innocent victim. Nurses may find it difficult to maintain feelings of empathy, concern, or helpfulness without becoming judgmental or even unknowingly punitive to the pregnant woman. Nurses may also feel helpless, incompetent, and discouraged when the pregnant woman continues to abuse drugs despite the best efforts of the health care team.

Inservice education, professional consultation, and peer support are all avenues to follow when working with pregnant women who abuse drugs. These processes can allow opportunities for discussion, sharing of feelings, problems, and particularly troublesome treatment issues.

Effective Communication with the Woman. If possible, allow time to get acquainted with the expectant mother. This often involves asking questions about various aspects of her life to obtain a better picture of what other stressors may be contributing to the pattern of substance abuse. Additional stressors may include inadequate housing, economic predicaments, family discord, and emotional or physical illness.

Continue to exercise patience because a hurried or impatient nurse may lose the trust of the expectant mother. Be honest at all times while displaying a non-judgmental attitude as well as genuine interest and concern. This is especially important when the woman relapses into substance-abusing patterns. Allow her to express guilt, and reassure her that abstinence is possible and that she must simply begin again.

HELPING THE WOMAN IDENTIFY STRENGTHS

Assist the substance-abusing pregnant woman in identifying personal strengths because she generally has a poor self-image. Stopping smoking and abstaining from the use of drugs or alcohol for even a short time should be acknowledged. Praise for maintaining an adequate weight gain and attending prenatal classes may increase self-esteem and increase compliance with the recommended regimen of care.

Evaluation

Interventions have been successful if the expectant mother:

- Identifies the harmful effects of substance abuse on her and on the fetus
- Verbalizes feelings engendered by continued use of substances that adversely affect her or the fetus
- Identifies personal strengths and accepts support from the health care team to stop using drugs

Intrapartum Period

Assessment

COCAINE

Nurses who work in labor and delivery units must become skilled at identifying drug-induced signs and symptoms. Behaviors associated with frequent or recent use of crack cocaine pose the greatest problems, including profuse sweating, high blood pressure, and irregular respirations, combined with a lethargic response to labor and lack of interest in the necessary interventions. Dilated pupils, increased body temperature, and sudden onset of severely painful contractions are often noted. Fetal signs often include tachycardia and excessive fetal activity.

Emotional signs of recent cocaine use may include angry, caustic, or abusive reactions to those attempting to provide care. Emotional lability and paranoia are signs of cocaine intoxication.

Critical to Remember

Signs and Symptoms of Recent Cocaine Use

- Diaphoresis, high blood pressure, irregular respirations
- Dilated pupils, increased body temperature
- Sudden onset of severely painful contractions
- Fetal tachycardia, excessive fetal activity
- Angry, caustic, abusive reactions and paranoia

HEROIN

Typically, the pregnant woman addicted to heroin comes to the labor and delivery unit intoxicated from a recent drug administration; well into her labor, she may request discharge shortly after delivery in order to avoid withdrawal symptoms. When the effects of the drug begin to wear off, withdrawal symptoms may be observed during labor. Early withdrawal symptoms may include yawning, diaphoresis, rhinorrhea, restlessness, and excessive tearing of the eyes.

Analysis

One of the most relevant nursing diagnoses during the intrapartal period is: *High Risk for Injury related to physiological and psychological effects of recent drug use.*

Planning

The major goal for this nursing diagnosis is that the woman and the fetus will remain free from injury during labor and childbirth.

Interventions

PREVENTING INJURY

When a laboring woman has recently used a substance such as cocaine, her life and the life of the fetus depend heavily on the nurse, who must intervene to meet the needs for safety, oxygen, and comfort.

Admitting Procedure. Two nurses may be needed to admit the woman into the labor unit and to persuade her to assume a safe position. One nurse helps the woman assume position, initiates electronic fetal monitoring, and begins administration of oxygen, as needed. The other nurse acts as communicator.

Because the woman who has recently used a drug such as cocaine often has difficulty following directions, she should hear only one voice telling her what to do. The second nurse states firmly what is happening and exactly what the woman must do: "Lie on your left side." "This helps us watch how the baby is doing." "This gives you more oxygen." This nurse maintains eye contact with the woman while giving her instructions.

Setting Limits. It is critical to realize the importance of setting limits to protect the safety of the mother and the fetus. For instance, the mother cannot smoke in most hospitals and certainly not when oxygen is in use. The nurse may say, "It must be difficult not to smoke, but there is real danger to you and to all of us if you do smoke." When the mother is in active labor or after the membranes are ruptured, she must remain in bed even though this may cause her to be agitated. The nurse may say, "I know it is hard to stay in bed, but we can't take good care of the baby when you walk." If it is safe for the woman to walk, the nurse must set limits about where she can walk (on the floor, not on the bed; in the labor room, not to the cafeteria).

Initiating Seizure Precautions. The laboring woman who recently used cocaine is at risk for hypertensive crisis and must be protected from injury in case of seizures. Seizure precautions include:

- Keeping the bed in a low, locked position
- Padding side rails and keeping them up at all times
- Making sure suction equipment functions properly to prevent aspiration
- Reducing environmental stimuli (lights, noise) as much as possible

MAINTAINING EFFECTIVE COMMUNICATION

Establishing a therapeutic pattern of communication is one of the primary methods of providing care for the patient who has recently used cocaine. Avoid confrontation; instead, acknowledge feelings: "I know you hurt, and I know how frightened you are. I will do everything I can to make you comfortable." When the woman is abusive, be careful not to take the abuse personally or react in a non-therapeutic manner. On the other hand, acknowledge the impact of abusive behavior: "I know this is so difficult for you, and I'm doing my best to take care of you. I feel sad and hurt when you talk to me like that."

Nurses must be aware of their own feelings when clients are abusive, and they must acknowledge when their own anger is getting in the way of providing care. Another nurse may need to assume care of the woman for a time to allow some relief from unrelenting abusive comments.

PROVIDING PAIN CONTROL

Pain control for women who are substance abusers poses a difficult problem because it is often impossible to determine the type or combination of drugs that were used prior to admission. If the woman has used opioids (heroin), drugs such as morphine, hydromorphine, and meperidine must be used with caution. Avoid some drugs, such as butorphanol, because they may cause acute withdrawal symptoms in the woman and the fetus (Kaye and Chasnoff, 1992). Comfort measures may require non-pharmacological nursing interventions, such as sacral pressure, back rubs, a cool cloth on the head, and continual support and encouragement. If medications can safely be administered, do not withhold them under the false assumption that their use will contribute to addiction.

PREVENTING HEROIN WITHDRAWAL

To prevent or stabilize heroin withdrawal during labor, methadone should be administered intramuscularly if the woman is nauseated or vomiting. Methadone should also be given to the woman who is receiving methadone as chemical-dependence treatment if she did not receive her daily dose. If signs of withdrawal are present, do not order narcotic agonists-antagonists, such as butorphanol (Stadol), because they may cause acute abstinence syndrome in the woman and fetus.

Evaluation

Both the expectant mother and the fetus may have experienced harmful effects of drugs throughout pregnancy. However, the interventions for this nursing diagnosis can be considered effective if neither the woman nor the fetus sustains additional injury during labor and childbirth.

Nursing Care Plan 23–2

Substance Abuse

Assessment: Nora Tanner is a 27-year-old gravida 2, para 1, who begins prenatal care during the 28th week of gestation. Nora is poorly groomed, lethargic, and very thin. She appears hostile during an attempt to complete the necessary history-taking interview. Nora states that her mother cares for her 3-year-old son but that she sees him "fairly often." Nora states that she smokes cigarettes "sometimes" and has "a drink or two now and then," but she denies that she uses cocaine often enough to "bother the baby."

Nursing Diagnosis: Ineffective Denial related to impaired ability to accept consequences of behavior as manifested by continued refusal to acknowledge effects of substance abuse.

Goals:

Nora will:

1. Keep prenatal appointments consistently.
2. Acknowledge effects of multidrug use (alcohol, tobacco, cocaine) on the developing fetus.
3. Abstain from alcohol, tobacco, or cocaine use during the remaining weeks of pregnancy.

Intervention:	Rationale:
1. Use a nonjudgmental, empathetic approach that demonstrates interest in Nora's health and the health of the unborn infant.	1. Demonstrating genuine concern and empathy may help to establish rapport and trust, which are essential to bring about a change in behavior.
2. Acknowledge Nora's reluctance to discuss drug use: "I know it is difficult to talk about this, but we need to know as much as possible so that we can provide good care for you and the baby."	2. Many women deny the frequency of use of both legal and illicit drugs because they fear accusations from health care workers or legal action if the drug used is illegal.
3. Acknowledge Nora's statements about irregular use of alcohol, tobacco, and cocaine and attempt to clarify the actual use: "How many times in a week do you use cocaine?" "Are there times when you use more?" "Do you always use alcohol when you use cocaine?"	3. Before treatment can be successful, it is necessary to know the type, amount, and frequency of drug use. This is in conflict with Nora's need to deny drug use as a way to protect her self-esteem—that is, she needs to feel that her actions are not jeopardizing the fetus. It will be very difficult for her to admit that they do.
4. Assist Nora in identifying the effects of substances on her health and the health of the fetus.	4. Knowledge of fetal harm is a powerful motivator to stop at least some substance abuse during pregnancy. For example, some women stop cocaine and alcohol use but continue to smoke.
a. Instruct her that whatever she drinks, smokes, or injects goes directly to the fetus. Remind her that the fetus is small and that substances remain in the fetal system far longer than in hers.	a. Health of the fetus is a major concern, and some women will change behaviors that they know to be harmful.
b. Offer hope by telling her that if she stops taking drugs now, the fetus has a better opportunity to grow and develop normally than if she continues to drink alcohol, smoke, and use cocaine.	b. The fetus has a better chance to survive without complications if substance abuse is stopped, even late in the pregnancy.
c. Measure the fundus and explain to her that this is how fetal growth is evaluated during pregnancy. Focus on the importance of the last trimester on fetal growth.	c. Knowledge that stopping substance abuse in the last trimester allows the fetus to grow bigger is a strong motivator for some women.
5. Help Nora recognize stressors that lead to substance abuse (boredom, unsatisfying personal relationships, low self-esteem): "So, you and your boyfriend use cocaine most weekends?" "What do you do when you have free time?"	5. It is extremely difficult to stop using substances such as alcohol or cocaine without changing an entire lifestyle, including friends and activities.

Nursing Care Plan continued on following page

6. Help Nora achieve abstinence. Acknowledge the difficulty of changing a lifestyle while emphasizing the benefits to the unborn infant.
   - a. Set short-term goals (stopping one day at a time).
   - b. Teach "thought stopping." (Visualize a stop sign, say "stop" aloud when thoughts of drug use come into the consciousness, then allow 30 seconds for conscious relaxation before continuing with previous activity.)
   - c. Recommend that she avoid high-risk places and people (bars, parties, friends who use drugs).
   - d. Promote involvement in rehabilitation programs (Cocaine Anonymous, Alcoholics Anonymous), and refer for long-term individual and group therapy.

6. Providing support and achievable abstinence measures may help the woman change her behavior.
   - a. Stopping substance one day at a time may seem less overwhelming than long-term plans.
   - b. Provides a concrete method to get through episodes when craving for the drug occurs.
   - c. Relapse is more common if she continues the same activities with friends who are using substances.
   - d. To obtain support from persons with similar problems.

Evaluation:
Nora demonstrates knowledge of the effects of alcohol, cocaine, and tobacco on the fetus and begins recommended drug rehabilitation several times. She is not able to abstain from use of the drugs; however, she states that the frequency of use has declined. Nora is not consistent in keeping prenatal appointments.

Assessment: Nora began labor abruptly in the 36th week of pregnancy and was admitted to the labor, delivery, recovery unit following recent use of both cocaine and alcohol. She is abusive, agitated, and in extreme discomfort from rapid, strong labor contractions. Multiple bruises are noted over her arms, legs, and shoulders. Membranes are ruptured, and particulate meconium is noted in amniotic fluid. Nora wants to smoke and insists that she be allowed to walk in the halls. The fetus demonstrates hyperactivity and tachycardia.

Nursing Diagnosis: High Risk for Maternal and Fetal Injury related to lack of awareness of measures needed to protect self and fetus during labor secondary to recent use of cocaine and alcohol.

Goals:
Nora will:
1. Remain free from injury throughout hospital stay.
2. Comply with necessary monitoring and treatment measures needed to protect her safety and the safety of the fetus.

Intervention:

1. Initiate care to protect the safety of Nora and fetus.
   - a. Arrange for two nurses to work with Nora during admission. Assign one nurse to provide information while another nurse assists Nora in complying. For example, help Nora get into bed, lie on her left side, allow electronic monitoring, and allow insertion of an intravenous line. Speak clearly and use short sentences when providing instruction or information.
   - b. Place bed in the lowest locked position; raise and pad side rails.
   - c. Take blood pressure, pulse, respiratory rate, and temperature at least every 2 hours or according to agency protocol.
   - d. Explain the necessity for continuous electronic monitoring.
   - e. Explain that smoking is not allowed in the hospital and emphasize the danger of smoking when oxygen is in use. Explain that bed rest is necessary because membranes have ruptured and labor is advancing rapidly.

Rationale:

1. The woman who recently took cocaine may be negative, unresponsive, angry, or abusive.
   - a. When "high," the woman has difficulty following directions and needs assistance to carry out even simple instructions. She responds better when only one person gives directions in a firm, clear, and directive manner.
   - b. Protects her from falls or from injury if she bangs into the side rails.
   - c. Crack cocaine produces diaphoresis, high blood pressure, irregular respirations, and hyperthermia.
   - d. Electronic fetal monitoring provides important data about the condition of the fetus. Particulate meconium indicates fetal distress.
   - e. Curtail smoking because of the risk of burns; this is particularly crucial if oxygen is in use. Insist on bed rest to protect the fetus from the danger of prolapsed cord when membranes are ruptured.

Nursing Care Plan 23–2 *Continued*

Substance Abuse

f. Consult with physician before administering pain medication and be certain that the physician realizes that the patient has recently taken cocaine and probably alcohol.

f. Use of some drugs (narcotics, sedatives) is contraindicated when cocaine or alcohol has been used because they may cause central nervous system depression.

2. Affirm Nora's feelings, and keep communication open: "I know you hurt and I know you are angry. I will do my best to take good care of you and your baby." "I understand how difficult it is to remain in bed. Let me help you turn to another position."

2. Although a trusting relationship is difficult to form under these circumstances, it provides the best opportunity to protect this woman and fetus during the hours of labor.

3. Use as many non-pharmacological measures as possible to reduce pain. (See also Chapter 15.)

3. Analgesics may cause drug interactions when the exact type and amount of drug taken before admission are unknown.

Evaluation:
Nursing interventions are successful if the woman remains free of injury and if the fetus experiences no additional trauma during the period of labor.

Assessment: Nora gave birth to a small-for-gestational-age girl at 36 weeks' gestation. Apgar scores were five at 1 minute and eight at 5 minutes. The infant's urine specimen was positive for cocaine metabolites and alcohol. Nora slept soundly for several hours following the birth, refused food, and demonstrated little interest in seeing the infant. Nora left the hospital with her boyfriend on the first postpartum day without waiting to see the physician and without the infant.

Nursing Diagnosis: Ineffective Family Coping: Disabling related to inability to manage life stress without the use of drugs as evidenced by neglectful relationship with infant.

Goals:
The infant will receive necessary care following discharge from the hospital.

Intervention:

Rationale:

1. Notify the hospital's social service department of the newborn's positive urine test for drugs so that plans can be made to place the infant in a foster home until long term care can be provided for Nora.

1. This diagnosis describes a family with a history of destructive behavior for which long-term care is required from a therapist with specialized education. Only interventions that focus on care that can be provided by a nurse in a short-term relationship and without specialized education are discussed in this chapter. Nurses must realize that they cannot meet all the needs of dysfunctional families and that referral to agencies that offer more options is often necessary.

2. Provide information about special care needed by the infant to those who will be assuming the infant's care. This includes frequent feeding, swaddling, and measures that help calm the difficult-to-console infant.

2. Knowledge of infant behaviors prepares caregivers to meet the needs of this infant.

Evaluation:
Interventions are effective if the infant is placed with a knowledgeable alternative caregiver until Nora receives rehabilitative treatment.

Additional Nursing Diagnoses to Consider:
Caregiver Role Strain
High Risk for Altered Growth and Development
Noncompliance

Postpartum Period

Assessment

In the postpartum unit, be aware of the signs of recent drug use and abstinence syndrome and continue to assess the vital signs and level of consciousness of the mother. Observe the mother-infant interaction so that bonding and attachment can be promoted (see Chapter 8). Observe the infant for signs of drug exposure or abstinence syndrome. Obtain a urine sample for toxicology on the newborn as soon after birth as possible. If metabolites of drugs are found in the urine, legal implications of illicit drug use must be addressed. In many areas, the infant is removed from the mother's care and the mother must complete a program of drug rehabilitation before she gains access to the infant. In addition, become aware of visitors who indicate a willingness to provide assistance when the mother and infant are discharged.

Analysis

A major concern for nurses is discharging an infant to a mother who is known to use drugs. The most worrisome nursing diagnosis is: *High Risk for Alteration in Parenting related to lack of knowledge of infant needs and inadequate family support.*

Planning

Goals for this nursing diagnosis are that:

- The mother (and at least one family member) will demonstrate effective feeding and appropriate consoling behaviors before discharge.
- The mother will verbalize plans to obtain the support of family members who are available to provide assistance before discharge.

Interventions

PROMOTING EFFECTIVE PARENTING

Child neglect, child abuse, and failure to respond to infant signals and cues are associated with alcohol and drug abuse. Anticipatory guidance should be started early in the pregnancy and repeated frequently. Provide information about the growth and development of infants, how much sleep they need, how often they need to eat, and when they can be expected to sleep through the night (see Chapter 19).

Parents Want To Know

Measures to Prevent Frantic Crying in a Drug-Exposed Infant

- Swaddle the infant with the hands brought to the midline and secured (Fig. 23–2).
- Provide a pacifier.
- Keep the infant's back toward you and support the head while flexing the knees. Slowly and smoothly rock in a vertical motion.
- Coo softly and gently.
- Place the infant over your shoulder and gently stroke the back.
- Keep the room fairly dark because some infants are particularly sensitive to light.
- Avoid simultaneous auditory and visual stimuli.
- Curtail stimulation if infant shows signs of stress (yawning, sneezing, jerky movements, or spitting up).

Parents of a drug-exposed infant need to know that they may experience feelings of rejection, frustration, and even hostility. These feelings are likely to occur when the infant stiffens while being held, cries after being fed, or looks away. Parents must also know that drug-exposed infants are easily stressed because of the decreased stability of their central nervous system, and they display stress in a variety of ways, such as yawning, sneezing, hiccoughing, furrowing their brow, wearing a worried look, grunting, gagging, and averting their gaze.

Because of their hyperexcitable nervous systems, most infants born to women who used cocaine or other drugs during pregnancy have very low thresholds for overstimulation. When they are unwrapped, or handled excessively, they often change color, begin thrashing about, and quickly escalate to frantic crying. Methods to avert this appear in Parents Want to Know: Measures to Prevent Frantic Crying in a Drug-Exposed Infant.

Emphasize that the infant needs gentle handling and that crying does not mean that the infant is spoiled but, rather, indicates a need. Teach parents that infants need physical contact and soft verbal stimulation; however, visual and auditory stimulation should not be presented simultaneously to these infants.

PROVIDING ASSISTANCE WITH FEEDING

Infants exposed to drugs prenatally often have uncoordinated sucking and swallowing reflexes, and parents need instruction in how to get the infant to feed. Some measures that promote effective feeding include:

- Holding the infant in a sitting position with the arms forward in slight trunk flexion
- Keeping the infant's chin tucked downward; drug-exposed infants often push the head back, which causes an abnormal swallowing pattern
- Supporting the infant's chin or chin and cheeks with the hand if the infant has trouble sucking

MOBILIZING A SUPPORT SYSTEM

It is essential for the mother to establish a support system that is knowledgeable and reliable because infants who experienced prenatal drug exposure are difficult to care for. Often the grandmother, a neighbor, or a friend will agree to stand by for times when the mother senses that she is about to lose control. It is most beneficial if the support person commits to providing care at a specified time so that the mother does not have to wait for assistance until she feels out of control.

Evaluation

Interventions are effective if the mother and at least one family member demonstrate how to feed and console the infant before discharge and if adequate family support is identified.

✔ Check Your Reading

12. What prenatal behaviors indicate substance abuse?
13. What signs and symptoms indicate recent cocaine use?
14. How does nursing care differ during the intrapartum period when the woman has recently taken cocaine?
15. How can nurses promote positive parenting of drug-exposed infants?

Birth of an Infant with Congenital Anomalies

When an infant is born, the physician usually announces the sex of the child—for example, "It's a boy." The first questions from the parents—"Is he all right?" "Does he have all his fingers and toes?" —convey the anxiety that they feel until they know that the infant is perfectly formed. If a defect is present, the question may be met with momentary silence as the physician and nurse attempt to formulate a response. The silence increases the anxiety that the parents feel and precipitates a grief response because the parents must grieve the death of the perfect or "fantasy" infant before they can begin to form an attachment to the newborn.

Factors Influencing Emotional Responses of Parents

TIMING AND MANNER OF BEING TOLD

Until the 1970s, it was common practice to wrap an infant born with anomalies and remove him or her from the delivery area. Parents were told of the anomalies at a later time, often after the physician had an opportunity to prepare them for the disturbing news. However, parents experience less anxiety when they are told about the condition of the infant as early as possible. In current practice, the parents are told at once and are permitted to hold the newborn if the physical status of the infant allows.

The manner in which the information is presented is equally important. Some physicians and nurses present the infant to the parents in a very sensitive manner.

A baby girl was delivered with a major irreparable anomaly: the right arm below the elbow was entirely missing. While the placenta was still intact and the cord attached, the physician placed the infant on the mother's abdomen and said, "Oh, we have a very special baby." As mother and father stroked the infant, the physician pointed out how healthy and beautiful the child was and allowed ample time for the parents to hold their child.

PRIOR KNOWLEDGE OF THE DEFECT

In this age of sophisticated prenatal examinations, the parents may be aware of the existence of a congenital anomaly before the infant is born. These parents may not experience the shock and disbelief that parents who are unprepared experience. This should not be interpreted to mean that they do not experience grief but, rather, that they have completed some of the early stages of grieving prior to the birth.

One young couple was aware from the 18th week of gestation that the fetus had hydrocephalus and protrusion of brain tissue from the skull. The mother elected to carry the fetus to term so that the infant would have "every chance at life." When the infant died within minutes after birth, the parents calmly held their child and called the infant by the name that they had selected several weeks previously. The only overt signs of grief were silent tears and a request to see their minister.

TYPE OF DEFECT

Although any defect in a newborn produces feelings of extreme concern and anxiety, certain defects are associated with long-term parenting problems. It is particularly difficult for the family and the community to accept an infant with facial or genital anomalies. The face is visible to everyone, and parents are fearful about whether the child will be accepted. If the defect is cleft lip and palate, the parents are extremely concerned about surgical repair. Common questions are: When can it be done? Will the child look normal? Will the child sound normal? Will the scars be obvious? Parents are often anxious about how grandparents and siblings will accept the child. With time and support, families often work out unique methods to help the family develop strong feelings of attachment.

One young father, profoundly disturbed about the birth of a daughter with a cleft lip and palate and extremely concerned about how his 6-year-old daughter would respond to the infant, took control of the situation. He carefully presented the infant to her sister and pointed out that the baby was small and had special problems; she would need the love of her big sister to overcome them. The 6-year-old held the infant and promised to help care for her. After a long talk, the older child, with the help of a nurse, fashioned a sign that was placed in the infant's crib. The sign said, "Hello, my name is Rachel. As you can see, I have a problem, but I am going to be fine."

Gender is at the core of a person's identity, and any defect of the genitals, however slight or correctable, arouses deep concern in both parents. Some anomalies, such as hypospadias (opening of the urethra on the underside of the penis), are repaired in early childhood. Other genital anomalies, such as ambiguous genitalia when assignment of gender is in doubt, cause extreme concern in the family and affect such basic things as what to name the infant, how to dress the infant, and how to respond to questions about the infant's sex.

IRREPARABLE DEFECT

Although the initial impact of any defect is profound disappointment and concern, when the defect is irreparable, the parents have no time limit to their endeavors. Eventually, they must grapple with the knowledge that the infant will have a lifelong handicap. Examples of irreparable defects include Down syndrome, microcephaly, and amelia (absence of an entire extremity).

Emotional Responses

Emotional responses to the birth of an infant with an anomaly can be viewed in the framework of the grief process. Emotions include shock, anger, fear, guilt, and depression. Shock, accompanied by expressions of disbelief, is the initial reaction of most parents to the birth of an infant with a congenital defect. Anger is often a pervasive response, and it may take the form of fault-finding or resentment. Anger may be directed toward the family, medical personnel, or the self, but it is seldom directed toward the infant. Fear may be expressed as concern about what must be done in the immediate or distant future (surgical procedures, complicated health care, the infant's potential for a normal life). Guilt may be expressed as a question of responsibility for the defect: "I shouldn't have taken that trip while I was pregnant." Depression is manifested by crying, withdrawal from relationships, lack of energy, inability to sleep, and decreased appetite. (See Chapter 27 for additional information about interventions for postpartum depression.)

✔ Check Your Reading

16. When and how should parents be told that the infant has anomalies?
17. What types of defects affect parenting most?

Birth of an Infant with Congenital Anomalies: Application of Nursing Process

Assessment

Parental age, experience, and responses to the infant's condition are priority assessments. Young or first-time parents may be overwhelmed by the experience. Carefully observe parental responses such as denial, anger, or guilt so that support and information can be provided that meet the needs of the parents at that particular time.

Recognize that responses can change rapidly. Physical signs of grief, such as sighing, crying, and withdrawal from family and staff, are important cues to the emotional state of the parents. Cultural and religious beliefs may affect the expression of grief. Some groups express grief openly; other groups (such as Chinese, Japanese, or Native Americans) do not. In some cultures (such as Latino), it is acceptable for women, but not for men, to grieve publicly.

Often an infant born with congenital anomalies requires specialized care in the neonatal intensive care unit (NICU). Note the parents' response to the equipment, treatment, and scheduled procedures so that information and anticipatory guidance can be provided. (See Chapter 29 for nursing care for infants and families when the infant must be transferred to the NICU.)

In addition, assess contact between the parents and the infant. If the infant is stable, do the parents participate in the care of the newborn? Are attachment behaviors, such as eye contact, prolonged gazing, holding, and talking to the infant, part of the parent's response? Is either the mother or father willing to learn special procedures, such as feeding the infant with a cleft palate or positioning the infant with a spinal defect?

Finally, observe the reactions of the extended family. Are the grandparents available to act as support for the parents? What are the concerns about siblings?

Analysis

A wide variety of nursing diagnoses are possible for the family when an infant is born with congenital anomalies. One of the most common diagnoses is *High Risk for Altered Parenting related to the grief process and lack of knowledge of special care required by infant.*

Planning

Realistic goals for this diagnosis are that the parents will:

- Verbalize feelings regarding the infant to each other and to the staff throughout the hospital stay.
- Request assistance with necessary infant care before discharge from the acute care setting.
- Respond promptly and gently when the infant signals a need.

Interventions

PROMOTING BONDING AND ATTACHMENT

A priority nursing intervention is to promote bonding and attachment, which may be disrupted when parents who expected a perfect infant give birth to an infant with an unexpected abnormality. Although parents should be told of the neonate's anomaly as early as possible, the means of telling them is critically important. The infant should be wrapped carefully and presented as something precious.

Communicate acceptance by handling the infant gently; parents are particularly sensitive to facial expressions of shock or distress. Emphasize the normal aspects of the infant's body: "She is so alert and she has the most beautiful eyes."

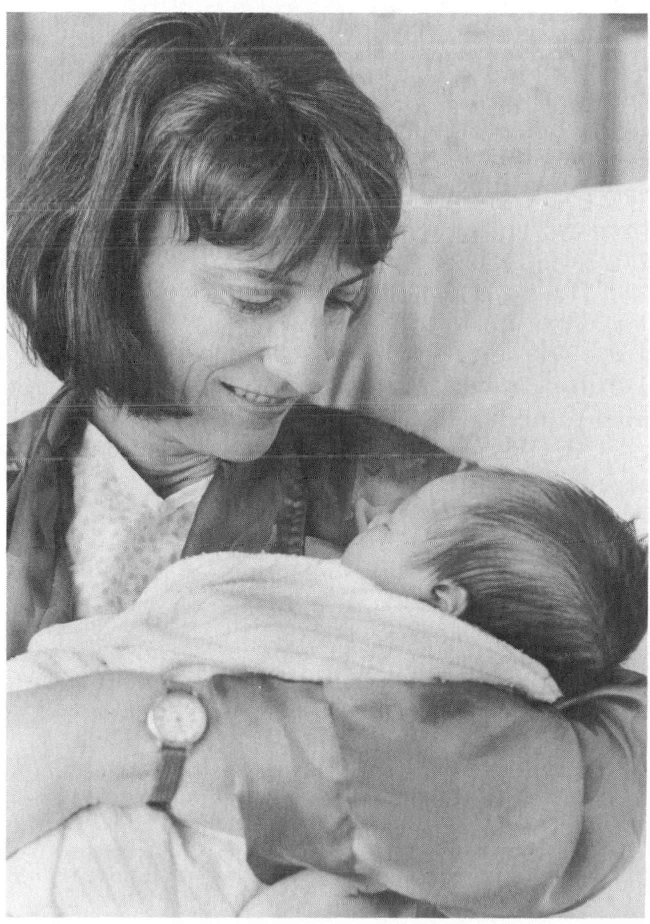

Bonding between parent and an infant born with a congenital anomaly is essential. As soon as the infant's condition allows, touching, cooing, and cuddling are encouraged.

Touching and cuddling are essential to caring. Help the parents hold and cuddle their infant as soon as the infant's condition allows.

ASSISTING WITH GRIEVING PROCESS

Remember that parents must grieve the loss of the perfect infant that they expected before they can form an attachment with the newborn. Remain with the parents through the initial phase of shock and disbelief, and maintain an atmosphere that encourages them to express their feelings. One way to do this is to listen carefully to what the parents say and to respond by reflecting the content and feelings that they express. For example, the mother of an infant girl with cleft palate says, "How could this happen? I should have gone to the doctor earlier." A helpful response might be, "Actually, we don't know what causes cleft palate, but let's talk about how you are feeling." This offers reassurance but keeps the interaction open to explore the underlying feelings of guilt that the mother may be expressing.

PROVIDING ACCURATE INFORMATION

Nurses who work in perinatal settings are responsible for becoming informed about follow-up treatment and timing of surgical procedures so that they can clarify and reinforce information provided by the physician. This involves discussing the plan of care with the physician as well as researching the nursing care that will be required. Parents develop trust in the health care team when consistent information is presented clearly and explained fully.

It may be wise to designate a primary nurse or team to work with the family throughout the hospital stay. Be prepared to repeat information frequently because it may be difficult for the grieving parents to retain it.

FACILITATING COMMUNICATION

Nurses are sometimes fearful of being asked questions that they are unable to answer, or they fear that they will say the wrong thing.

Answer questions as honestly as possible and, if unsure of information, say so: "I am not sure about that, but I will find someone with more experience than I have to answer." In addition to answers, parents need kindness, support, and genuine concern.

It is crucial that family members communicate with each other as well as with the health professionals. Include fathers in all discussion, handling, and care of the infant. Offer information and empathy consistently to both parents. Without this, the father cannot be expected to support his partner, explain the infant's condition to relatives and friends, or begin to deal with his own shock and sadness.

PLANNING FOR DISCHARGE

Often the parents need to learn the special feeding, holding, and positioning techniques that their infant needs; for example, how to feed an infant with cleft palate or how to hold and position the infant with meningocele (protrusion of meninges through a defect in the bony spine). Early participation in infant care fosters feelings of attachment and responsibility for the infant.

Anticipatory guidance may help prevent problems in the family when the infant is discharged to home care. Sibling reaction and behavior depend on their age and ability to understand the needs of the infant. Young children, who are often jealous of the attention and care that the infant requires, may regress to infantile behaviors, such as bed wetting or thumb sucking. Tell the parents that this indicates a need for attention rather than naughtiness (see Chapter 22).

Although grandparents can be a great source of strength and support, they may also have difficulty adjusting to the infant with an abnormality. When appropriate, or if the parents indicate their willingness, include grandparents when teaching special care that the infant will need.

PROVIDING REFERRALS

Finally, initiate referrals to national and community resources. Besides a referral to the social worker in the hospital, parents may also benefit from information about the National Easter Seal Society for Crippled Children, the March of Dimes–Birth Defects Foundation, or the Crippled Children's Services of the Public Health Department. In addition, organizations such as the Shriners provide funds for the care of children. Support groups vary from community to community, and perinatal nurses may wish to make a list of the names, addresses, and telephone numbers of these organizations.

Evaluation

Success of nursing care is indicated when parents

- Demonstrate appropriate attachment behaviors
- Participate in infant care
- Acknowledge feelings and communicate openly with family members

- Participate in plans to provide long-term care of the infant

✔ Check Your Reading

18. How do nurses promote bonding and attachment in families with an infant with congenital anomalies?
19. What should discharge planning for the family of an infant with congenital anomalies include?

Pregnancy Loss

Although pregnancy is an event that holds the promise of great joy, it also holds the potential for loss and, therefore, grief. Pregnancy loss can occur at any time. Early spontaneous abortion, fetal demise during the latter half of pregnancy, stillbirth, or neonatal death when the infant survives for a few days or weeks can be equally devastating for the family.

Despite advanced technology, approximately 33,000 infants are stillborn each year in the United States (Mercer, 1990). An additional 40,000 infants die within days or weeks following birth. The death of an anticipated infant, whether during pregnancy or following birth, is a tragedy for the parents. They experience shock, profound sadness, and grief.

Parents experiencing perinatal death often feel alone in their grief, however, because society in general does not consider perinatal loss to be on the same level as the loss of an older child or adult. Moreover, friends and family members are often hesitant to discuss the loss for fear of saying the wrong thing.

Fathers often feel a need to appear strong after the loss of a pregnancy or neonate so that they can support their partners. As a result, fathers often hold back their own feelings of grief and pain and are sometimes perceived as needing less support than the mother.

Early Pregnancy Loss

Parents who experience early pregnancy loss either by spontaneous abortion or by loss of an ectopic pregnancy often experience intense grief. However, many people, even health professionals, downplay the grieving that may accompany the loss. Comments such as "You shouldn't have any problems getting pregnant again" discount the feelings of expectant mothers and fathers who may already have heard fetal heart tones or viewed the fetus via ultrasonography and have begun to bond with the fetus.

A 40-year-old woman whose fetus died during the second trimester of pregnancy reported that when she saw her friends after delivery of the infant, they reacted as though she had never been pregnant. "I carried her for months, and we wanted her so much, but it was as though she had never existed."

When ectopic pregnancy is the reason for the loss, the woman has to deal with the loss of the pregnancy as well as with a surgical procedure, perhaps involving the loss of one fallopian tube, which decreases the probability of another pregnancy. Health care workers mean well when they say, "You still have one fallopian tube left, you'll get pregnant again," but this does not acknowledge the fact that a much desired child has been lost.

Early pregnancy loss is not simply a spontaneous abortion or loss of a fallopian tube but a grief-producing event that requires the same information and support as pregnancy loss at any stage.

Concurrent Death and Survival in Multifetal Pregnancy

Parents experience conflicting and complex feelings of joy and grief when one or more infants in a multifetal pregnancy survives and one or more infants in the same gestation dies. Contrary to common belief, parents do not grieve less for the dead infant because of the joy that they experience in the living child. They experience an acute sense of loss despite having an infant, and they grieve no less for the infant who did not survive.

For parents experiencing both survival and death of an infant, the grieving process may be more complicated. They may have fears about the health of the surviving infant, especially if the infant is preterm or ill. They may be unable to grieve for the dead child because of their concerns and responsibilities for the surviving child. They may also experience problems with attachment to the surviving infant because of grieving. Moreover, they may receive less support than parents who lost the only child in a single gestation.

One young woman who gave birth to twins, one living and one stillborn, sobbed uncontrollably when told by a well-meaning family member, "Well, you can't feel too bad, you have one beautiful baby." In a private moment with the nurse, the young mother asked, "What does he think, that they were interchangeable? What about my baby who never had a chance to live?"

For parents who experience the death of one infant and the survival of another, anticipate complex feelings of joy and grief and provide the same interventions as those offered for couples who lose the only child in a single gestation. These interventions include allowing the parents to hold the dead infant and gathering mementos. In addition, be prepared to confirm the cause of death, if known, and the health status of the surviving infant.

Pregnancy Loss: Application of Nursing Process

Assessment

Nursing assessment of the family who has experienced the loss of a fetus or infant requires a great deal of sensitivity. In the case of infant death, collect as much information as possible before meeting with the woman and her family for the first time so that hurtful mistakes can be avoided. Knowing the child's sex, weight, length, and gestational age and whether any abnormalities were noted will help the nurse communicate effectively.

Many perinatal units design a sticker to place on the door, chart, and Kardex so that all staff who come into contact with the family, including auxiliary, housekeeping, laboratory, and radiology personnel, will be alerted that the infant has not survived. Designs include a flower, a teardrop, or a rainbow. This visual symbol increases the chance that inadvertent comments that cause the family pain can be avoided.

Nurses are often unsure how to interact with a family that has experienced the loss of an infant. It is helpful for the nurse to acknowledge the situation and clarify her or his role at once: "I am Bette Turner, I will be your nurse for the next 8 hours. I am so sorry for your loss, let me know if there is any way I can be of help." This is not an appropriate time for self-disclosure or for false reassurance. Keep the focus on the family's response and their ability to support each other.

Keep in mind the initial grief responses, and observe for overt signs of grief, such as crying, anger, denial, withdrawal behaviors, and expressions of guilt or blame. In addition, be aware of subtle cues that indicate grief, such as sighing, excessive sleeping, apathy, poor hygiene, or loss of appetite. This is especially important when assessing members of cultural groups that do not display grief publicly.

Evaluate also the availability of a support system that includes family members or clergy. It may be necessary to ask whether a spiritual adviser would offer comfort. Many religions emphasize the acceptance of God's will and the immortality of the soul, and hearing these beliefs affirmed may help the family cope with the grief that they are experiencing. Some fathers focus all their energy on supporting the mother and may not acknowledge their own grief. As a result, they may not receive the support they need.

Analysis

Each woman whose infant or fetus dies experiences different responses, including denial, anger, guilt, placing blame, or profound sadness. Emotional responses are evidenced by crying, poor appetite, and sleeplessness. The most obvious nursing diagnosis is: *Grieving related to newborn (or fetal) death.*

Planning

Grief reactions are unique to each person, and it is inappropriate to assign a time frame in which parents will acknowledge or share their grief. Goals for this diagnosis are that the parents will:

- Acknowledge their grief and express the meaning of the loss.
- Share grief with significant others.

Interventions

ASSISTING TO CREATE MEMORIES

For many years, it was believed that when an infant was stillborn or died shortly after birth, the less parents knew of the infant, the less they would grieve. The infant was wrapped in a towel as soon as possible and whisked away so that the parents never saw their newborn. Relatives often disposed of the clothes and the bassinet of the expected infant before the mother returned home, and the parents were left with very few memories of the event.

Now it is acknowledged that the death of a newborn is a loss that must be mourned by the parents and that mourning requires memories. In this climate, nurses have been able to explore measures that assist the family create memories of an infant so that the existence of the child is confirmed and the parents can complete the grieving process.

Presenting the Infant to the Parents

Encourage the parents to see, touch, and hold the infant. Keep in mind that how the infant is presented to the parents is extremely important because these are the memories that they will retain. If necessary, wash the infant and apply baby lotion or powder. Wrap the infant in a soft, warm blanket. If possible, bring parents and infant together while the infant is still warm and soft. It may be necessary to keep the infant in a warmed incubator if some time elapses before the parents have contact with the infant. If this is not possible, tell the parents that the skin may feel cool. Allow parents to keep the infant as long as they wish, and make them feel free to unwrap the infant if they wish.

Many nurses are concerned about how to present the stillborn infant with severe deformities. Explain the defect briefly and gently. Wrap the infant to expose the most normal aspect. Use diapers to cover genital defects, and use booties and mittens to cover abnormalities of the hands and feet. However, it is not advisable to try to hide the defects completely. Allow parents to progress at their own speed in inspecting the infant. Clinical experience shows that many parents never unwrap the infant but, instead, quietly discuss positive features of the infant: "He has my father's eyes." "Look at the long fingers."

In one case, a stillborn infant had a severely deformed head and face. The nurse wrapped the infant loosely and draped a corner of the blanket over the part of the face that was most affected before giving the infant to the father and mother to hold. Neither parent lifted the blanket, although they did reach under the blanket to hold the infant's hands and feet.

Allow as much privacy and time as the parents and other family members need to be together. Avoid prying and remain sensitive to cues that members of the family want to talk or prefer not to. It is not necessary to keep up a flow of conversation. A sympathetic smile, a gentle touch of the hand, or a promise to return in a specific time and returning at that time are equally important. It is all right to ask, "Do you want to talk?" Then, listening quietly and reflecting the mother or father's feelings are all that is required.

Preparing a Memory Packet

Most parents treasure a memory packet that includes a photograph, footprints, a birth bracelet with the date and time of birth, the crib card with the infant's name, weight, and length, and, if possible, a lock of hair. Some parents and grandparents want pictures taken of themselves with the infant. The memory packet should be kept on file if the parents do not wish to take it home; they may change their minds later.

PROVIDING REFERRALS

Parents may find that friends and relatives expect them to recover quickly from perinatal loss and are unable to understand their continued grief. The greatest help often comes from contact with persons who have experienced similar loss, and a variety of support groups have been formed. These include Resolve through Sharing, AMEND (Aiding a Mother Experiencing Neonatal Death), SHARE (Source of Help in Airing and Resolving Experiences), and HAND (Helping After Neonatal Death).

Evaluation

Nursing care has been successful if the parents acknowledge their feelings of loss and grief and communicate them to significant others.

✔ *Check Your Reading*

20. How should the stillborn infant be presented to the parents? Why?
21. What is a memory packet and what should it include?

Relinquishment by Adoption

Women sometimes elect to carry a pregnancy to term even though they lack the financial or emotional means to provide a nurturing home for the infant. In this case, they may relinquish the newborn to the care of another family by adoption. The decision to place the infant for adoption is a painful one that can produce long-lasting feelings of ambivalence. On the one hand, the expectant mother may be satisfied that the infant is going into a stable home where a child is wanted and will receive excellent care, yet there are often intense social pressures against giving up one's child.

The process of adoption is relatively simple for the expectant mother. Each state and many organized churches have an adoption agency. In addition, private adoptions are becoming more common, although the legality of these adoptions may be called into question in some states. In private adoptions, an attorney acts as the intermediary between the expectant woman and the couple wanting to adopt the infant. The adoptive family usually agrees to pay the medical expenses of the woman, and sometimes a supportive relationship is established between the expectant mother and the adoptive family. Some adoptive mothers want to experience as much of the birth as possible and elect to act as coach or support person during the birth.

Nursing Considerations

Nurses are sometimes unsure of how to communicate with the woman who is relinquishing her infant. First, the nursing staff who come into contact with the woman must be informed of her decision to place the infant for adoption. This prevents inadvertent comments that could cause distress. Second, nurses must remember that adoption is an act of love, not one of abandonment, as the woman relinquishes the newborn to a family that is better able to provide financial and emotional support for the infant.

Nurses must also be prepared to respect any special wishes that the mother may have about the delivery. For instance, most birth mothers want to know all about the infant—how big he or she is, how healthy, how beautiful. They may want to see and hold the newborn. Some wish to name the infant or to give it a gift. Many take photographs or hold on to mementos such as the birth bracelet or crib card. Such actions provide memories of the infant and help the mother through the grieving process that may accompany relinquishment of the child.

After the delivery, the nurse should try to establish a rapport and a trusting relationship with the mother. The first step in this process is to acknowledge the situation at the initial contact with the woman: "Hello, my name is Denise, and I will be your nurse today. I understand the adoptive family is coming this morning, what can I do to help you get ready for that?" This is much more helpful than providing postpartum care without reference to an event that is of utmost concern to the mother. It also provides a broad opening for her to express feelings that may include strong attachment and love for the infant, ambivalence about her decision, and profound sadness. Therapeutic communication techniques, such as reflecting, paraphrasing, and summarizing, are useful to help the mother explore her feelings. Be careful not to offer advice, and remain nonjudgmental.

TEACHING ADOPTIVE PARENTS

Nurses also teach adoptive families how to care for the newborn. This requires that adequate time and a place that is private be provided. This family benefits from all the teaching that is provided for new parents. They may be anxious, and demonstrations as well as return demonstrations are appropriate. (See Chapters 21 and 22 for a complete discussion of infant care that should be taught.)

✔ Check Your Reading

22. What is meant by the phrase "adoption is an act of love"?

Violence Against Women

Violence against women, including both physical and sexual abuse, has a variety of names, such as spouse abuse, domestic violence, wife battering, marital rape, and, more recently, intimate violence. No matter what the name, it is a widespread problem. Ninety-five per cent of all spouse abuse cases involve women who are hurt by men. Each year, 3 to 4 million women in the United States are battered by the men with whom they live (March of Dimes, 1992). Battering is the single most common source of injury to women, more common than auto accidents, muggings, and rapes by a stranger combined (Stark and Flitcraft, 1988).

Battering is often associated with rape. In one study, more than one third of the women were beaten for refusing to engage in sex, and half who were beaten were forced to engage in sex immediately after beatings (Campbell and Alford, 1989). Remember, violence against women is deliberate, severe, and generally repeated.

Battering may start or become worse during pregnancy. Studies on domestic violence reveal an increase in the frequency and severity of attacks on the pregnant woman and note that the abdomen often replaces the face and breasts as the target for battery (Satin et al, 1991). Moreover, battering during pregnancy may be an indication of what life holds in store for the unborn child. The majority of men who batter the woman also batter the children, and some women who are battered will physically abuse the children.

Factors That Promote Violence

Family violence occurs in cultures in which the roles of males and females are gender-based and little

Table 23–6. MYTHS AND REALITIES OF VIOLENCE AGAINST WOMEN

Myths	Realities
The battered woman syndrome affects only a small percentage of the population	Battering is the single major cause of injury to women; 3–4 million women are battered each year by their partners
Battering of women occurs only in lower socioeconomic classes and in minority groups	Violence occurs in families from all social, economic, educational, racial, and religious backgrounds
The problem is really "spouse abuse," couples who assault each other	95 per cent of serious assaults are male against female; violence against women is about control and power
Alcohol and drugs cause abusive behavior	Substance abuse and violence against women are two separate problems: substance abuse is a disease, violence is a learned behavior; it can be unlearned
The abuser is "out of control"	He is not out of control; he is making a decision, because he chooses who, when, and where he abuses
The woman "got what she deserved"	No one deserves to be beaten. No one has the right to beat another person. Violent behavior is the responsibility of the violent person.
Women "like" it or they would leave	Women are threatened with severe punishment or death if they attempt to leave; many have no resources and are isolated, and they and their children are dependent on the abuser
Marriage counseling is a good recommendation for abusive relationships	Marriage counseling is not only ineffective for the couple, it can be dangerous for the abused woman

value is placed on the woman's role. Men hold power, and women are viewed as less worthy of respect than men. In these cultures, strength and aggression, the ability to "show her who is boss," are considered attractive and desirable in males.

In many cultures, women are treated as being relatively powerless. They earn less than men in the job market, and they are often victimized by marriage. For example, women who hold full-time jobs continue to carry the major responsibilities for housekeeping and child care. They often remain in unhealthy relationships because they are financially dependent on the man. If they divorce, most women become single parents with a standard of living much lower than that of their former husbands.

Stereotyping males as powerful and females as weak and without value has a profound effect on the self-esteem of women. Many women internalize the messages and come to believe that they are less worthy than their partner and that they are the cause of their own punishment. They accept the message from society that when women are battered or raped, "they got what they deserved." Furthermore, American culture accepts and condones violence. Movies, television, and sports such as football, hockey, and boxing glorify aggression, physical strength, and the ability to hurt and dominate the opponent.

Alcohol is often stated as a cause of violence against women; however, chemical dependence and domestic violence are two separate problems. Chemical dependency is a disease of addiction; abuse is a learned behavior that can be unlearned. However, violence may become more severe or bizarre when alcohol or drugs are involved. See Table 23–6 for a summary of the myths and realities of violence against women.

Characteristics of the Abuser

Physical abuse concerns power, and it is only one of many tactics that abusive men use to control their partners. Other tactics include isolation, intimidation, threats, and emotional, economic, and sexual abuse. Extreme jealousy and possessiveness are typical of the abuser. An abusive male often attempts to control every aspect of the woman's life, including where she goes, whom she speaks to, what she wears, and when the housework is done. He controls access to money and transportation and may force the woman to account for every moment spent away from him.

The abusive male often has a low tolerance for frustration and poor impulse control. He does not perceive his violent behavior as a problem and often denies responsibility for the violence by blaming the woman. Most abusive men come from homes where they witnessed the abuse of their mothers or were themselves abused as children. Although many abusive men have alcohol problems, many also batter their partners when they are sober.

Cycle of Violence

Violence occurs in a cycle that consists of three phases: (1) a tension-building phase, (2) a battering phase, and (3) a honeymoon phase. Being aware of behaviors that accompany each phase will enable the nurse to counsel the woman. Figure 23–3 depicts these behaviors.

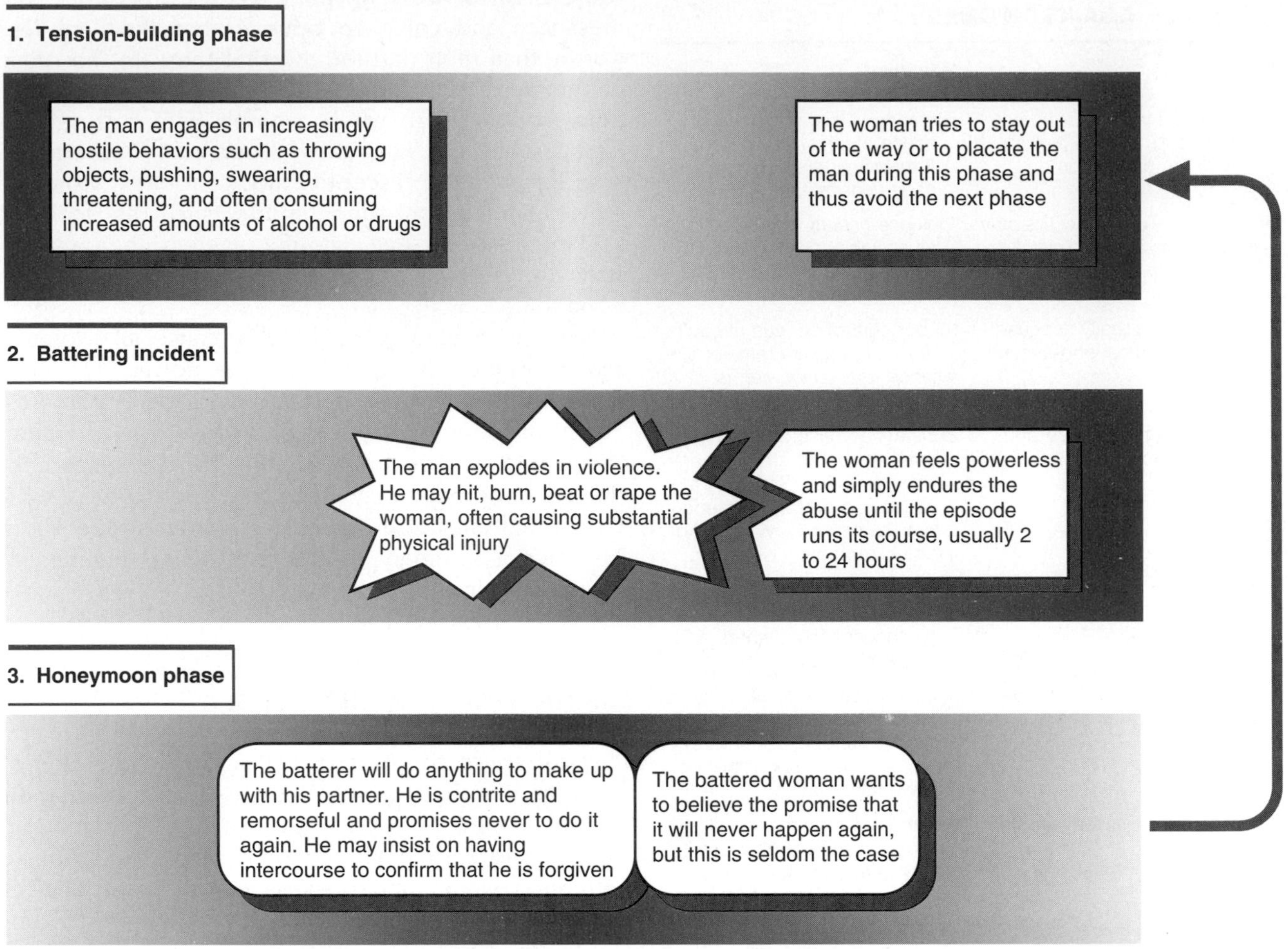

1. Tension-building phase

The man engages in increasingly hostile behaviors such as throwing objects, pushing, swearing, threatening, and often consuming increased amounts of alcohol or drugs

The woman tries to stay out of the way or to placate the man during this phase and thus avoid the next phase

2. Battering incident

The man explodes in violence. He may hit, burn, beat or rape the woman, often causing substantial physical injury

The woman feels powerless and simply endures the abuse until the episode runs its course, usually 2 to 24 hours

3. Honeymoon phase

The batterer will do anything to make up with his partner. He is contrite and remorseful and promises never to do it again. He may insist on having intercourse to confirm that he is forgiven

The battered woman wants to believe the promise that it will never happen again, but this is seldom the case

Figure 23–3

Types of behaviors that are evident in each step of the cycle of violence.

Battering During Pregnancy

Battering of a pregnant woman poses serious health consequences for the entire family. Women battered during pregnancy are more likely to have multiple injury sites (Bohn, 1990). Pregnant women in battering relationships face an increased risk of bearing low-birth-weight infants (<2500 g, or 5.5 pounds). Women who are battered during pregnancy are more likely to seek health care for injuries than women battered before pregnancy, and battering during pregnancy has been associated with subsequent homicide (women killing their abuser).

Nurse's Role in Prevention

Although the problem of physical abuse against women is immense and is becoming worse each year, nurses can do a great deal to prevent it by examining their own attitudes and altering their practice. First, they should examine their attitudes to determine whether they accept the prevailing attitude that blames the victim: "Why was she wearing that?" "She shouldn't have flirted with someone else." "Why does she stay with him?"

Second, nurses can consciously practice in ways that empower women and make it clear that the woman owns her body. Once the woman is clear about ownership of her body, she has the right to decide how it should be treated. Nurses must use language that indicates that the woman is an active partner in her care: "You understand your body, what do you think?" "How did your body respond when you tried that?"

During examinations, nurses can introduce aspects of care that increase the woman's control over the situation. For example, make sure that the woman, while seated and clothed, meets the physician or nurse practitioner who is to examine her, rather than while unclothed and in the lithotomy position. Nurses can place the examination table so that the

Critical to Remember

Cues Indicating Violence Against Women

Non-verbal. Facial grimacing, slow and unsteady gait, vomiting, abdominal tenderness, absence of facial response.

Injuries. Welts, bruises, swelling, lacerations, burns, vaginal or rectal bleeding. Evidence of old or new fractures of the nose, face, ribs, or arms.

Vague somatic complaints. Anxiety, depression, panic attacks, sleeplessness, anorexia.

Discrepancy between history and type of injuries. Wounds do not match woman's story, multiple bruises in various stages of healing, bruising on the arms (which she may have raised to protect herself), old, untreated wounds.

woman's head, and not her genitalia, meets the examiner's eye when he or she enters the room. When the woman is positioned for the examination, the table can be raised 45 degrees so that she has an opportunity to make eye contact with the examiner. Many nurses now provide the woman with a mirror so that she can view the examination and be fully informed about her body parts.

School nurses are in an excellent position to influence how teenagers define gender roles: "Real men don't beat up women." "Girls don't have to put up with verbal or physical abuse from anyone." "Use a condom; it's not cool to give someone you love sexually transmitted diseases or an unwanted pregnancy."

✔ Check Your Reading

23. What is the effect of pregnancy on battering behavior?
24. How can nurses alter their practice to help prevent violence against women?

The Battered Woman: Application of Nursing Process

Assessment

All nurses come into contact with women who are physically or sexually abused. Although many women who are abused are seen in the emergency department, perinatal nurses often suspect that a woman is being abused and become concerned. All women should be screened for physical abuse.

Nurses are often unsure of how to approach the issue of suspected abuse. Women often seek care and are assessed in the "honeymoon phase" of the violence cycle. It is during this phase that the man is often overly solicitous (hovering husband syndrome) and eager to explain any injuries that the woman exhibits. Introducing the subject of violence in the presence of the man places the woman in danger; it is absolutely essential to separate the woman from the man for the interview.

When a private, secure place has been found, reassure the woman that her privacy will be protected and that confidentiality will be absolute. Ask questions directly. If there is trauma, appropriate questions are, "Did someone hurt you?" "Did you receive these injuries from being hit?" The abused woman often appears hesitant, embarrassed, or evasive. She may be unable to look the nurse in the eye and appears guilty, ashamed, jumpy, or frightened.

Evaluate and document all signs of injury, both past and present. This includes areas of welts, bruising, swelling, lacerations, burns, and scars. Injuries are most commonly noted on the face, breasts, abdomen, and genitalia. Many women have new or old fractures. These are usually fractures of the face, nose, ribs, or arms. If there has been sexual abuse, a gynecological examination is necessary because there is often trauma to the labia, vagina, or cervix. The types of forced sex most frequently reported are vaginal stretching, vaginal intercourse, anal intercourse, and insertion of objects into the vagina and anus (Campbell and Alford, 1989). Vaginal or rectal bleeding or trauma must be documented according to hospital protocol.

Be particularly alert for non-verbal cues that indicate that abuse has occurred. Facial grimacing or a slow, unsteady gait may indicate pain. Vomiting or abdominal tenderness may indicate internal injury. A flat affect, that is, absence of facial response, is indicative of women who mentally withdraw from the situation to protect themselves from the horror and humiliation they experience during an abusive episode. Keep in mind that the woman may fear for her life because abusive episodes tend to escalate. Open-ended questions help prompt full disclosure and the expression of feelings.

Analysis

Nursing diagnosis depends on the data collected during the assessment. However, the most meaningful diagnosis for perinatal nurses to make may be *Fear related to possibility of severe injury to self and/or children during unpredictable cycle of violence.*

Planning

The abused woman may have difficulty developing a long-term plan of care without a great deal of specialized assistance. She is often unwilling to leave the abusive situation, and nurses must often focus on working with the woman to plan short-term goals that will protect her from future injury.

For realistic short-term goals, the woman will:

- Acknowledge the physical assaults.
- Develop a specific plan of action to implement when the abusive cycle begins.
- Identify community resources that provide protection for her and her children.

Interventions

DEVELOPING A PREVENTION PLAN

When physical abuse has been determined, assist the woman to make concrete plans to protect her safety and the safety of all children in the home. For example, if the woman insists on returning to the shared home, describe the cycle of behavior that culminates in physical abuse and instruct her in factors that precipitate a violent episode. These include the use of alcohol or other drugs and behaviors that indicate that the level of frustration and anger is increasing. Help her locate the nearest shelter or safe house, and make specific plans for going there once the cycle of violence begins. She should obtain extra keys to her car, and keep them as well as necessities packed and hidden until needed. Make sure that the woman pre-arranges with someone to respond to a call for help and stress that she must memorize the telephone number because time is often a crucial element in her decision.

The abused woman often believes that she is responsible for the abuse. Let her know that no one deserves to be hit for any reason. The one who hit her is the person responsible; she did not provoke it, and she did not cause it. Nurses are often responsible for teaching basic family processes, such as:

- Violence is not normal
- Violence is usually repeated and usually escalates
- Battering is against the law
- Battered women have alternatives

PROVIDING REFERRALS

When contact with the battered woman is short-term, acknowledge that many interventions are outside the

Clinical Situation

Joan Piszarek, a 28-year-old primigravida, is admitted to the labor, delivery, recovery unit in active labor. The right side of her face is swollen, there is evidence of old bruises on her upper arms that look like fingerprints, and there is a large bruised area on her abdomen. She is accompanied by her husband, who is very solicitous. He verbalizes concern about her labor status and remains close beside her at all times. Joan appears lethargic and avoids eye contact with the nurse who is admitting her. She states that she fainted at home and hurt herself when she fell against the bathtub.

Q:
1. What suspicious signs of battering does Joan exhibit?
2. How may the behavior of the husband be interpreted?
3. What action should the nurse take?

When time alone with Joan can be arranged, the nurse asks, "Did he hurt you? Did you get these injuries from being hit?" Joan appears extremely anxious and says, "Don't say anything; he got so mad when I was late getting home from shopping, it was my fault."

Q:
4. What should be the response of the nurse?
5. How can Joan be protected?

A:
1. Facial injury, signs of previous bruising that resemble "grab marks," and abdominal bruising. Joan's story of falling and hurting herself is not congruent with the location of abdominal injury and injuries on her arms. Joan's lethargy and avoidance of eye contact also suggest that she is afraid.
2. In the honeymoon phase of the cycle of violence, husbands (or male partners) are often overly solicitous and exhibit the "hovering husband syndrome."
3. The nurse should not question Joan's explanation of the injury in the presence of the husband because this can increase the danger of escalating violence when the mother and infant are discharged.
4. The nurse should respond, "No one deserves to be hurt; it's not your fault. How can I help you?"
5. Joan needs information about how to protect herself and the coming infant from future harm. However, this is not the appropriate time to give her this information. The nurse must inform the physician and the postpartum staff of the problem, and she must make the necessary referrals to the hospital's social service department for follow-up contact with the staff that intercedes for women who are admitted to the emergency department for injuries sustained during an episode of battering.

scope of nursing practice. As a result, be prepared to refer the family to community agencies that are available to the victim. These include the local police department, legal services, community shelters, counseling agencies that provide services for the entire family, including the abuser, and social service agencies.

It is essential to accept the decisions of the battered woman and acknowledge that she is on her own timetable. She may not contact the police, go to a shelter, or take any actions at the time that they are recommended. Therefore, listening to her, believing her, and providing information about resources may be the only help the nurse can provide.

Do not become negative or pass judgment on the partner of an abused woman. She is often tied to the man by both economic and emotional bonds and may become defensive if her partner is criticized. Tell her that resources are available for her partner but that it is necessary for him to admit abuse and seek assistance before help can be offered. To initiate referrals for the partner before he asks for help will increase the danger to the woman if her partner feels that he has been betrayed.

Evaluation

The plan of care can be judged successful if the woman:

- Acknowledges violent episodes in the home
- Makes concrete plans to protect herself and her children from future injury
- Uses the community resources available to her

✔ Check Your Reading

25. What are the major cues that a woman has been physically abused?
26. How can nurses intervene to help women protect their safety if they choose to remain in a home situation with a partner who physically abuses them?

Summary Concepts

- Teenage pregnancy is a major health problem in the United States that requires that adolescents receive not only accurate information about contraceptives but also how to set limits on sexual behavior.
- Pregnancy imposes serious physiological risks for the adolescent and the fetus that result in higher incidence of pregnancy-induced hypertension, anemia, and nutritional deficiencies for the expectant mother as well as prematurity and low birth weight for the infant.
- Teenage pregnancy interrupts the developmental tasks of adolescence and may result in childbirth before the parents are capable of providing a nurturing home for the infant without a great deal of assistance.
- The mature primigravida often has financial and emotional resources that younger women do not have; however, she may experience anxiety about recommended antepartum testing and her ability to parent effectively.
- Multidrug substance abuse is a widespread problem that can have devastating fetal and neonatal effects that may persist and become long-term developmental problems for the child.
- The lifestyle associated with illicit drug abuse includes inadequate nutrition, inadequate prenatal care, and increased incidence of sexually transmitted diseases and necessitates interdisciplinary interventions to prevent injury to the expectant mother and to the fetus.
- Birth of an infant with congenital anomalies produces strong emotions of shock and grief in the family and necessitates a sensitive response from the health care team to assist the family to grieve for the loss of the perfect or "fantasy" infant and to form attachment to the newborn.
- Pregnancy loss, at any stage of pregnancy, produces grief that must be acknowledged and expressed before it can be resolved. Nurses realize that mourning requires memories and intervene to arrange unlimited contact between the family and the stillborn infant and to gather a memento packet for the family.
- Nursing care for the mother who is placing her infant for adoption is based on the knowledge that relinquishment (adoption) is an act of love, not abandonment
- Multiple factors are associated with violence against women, which is deliberate, severe, and generally repeated in a predictable cycle of violence that often causes severe physical harm (or death) to the woman.
- All perinatal nurses come into contact with abused women who require assistance to protect themselves and their children from serious injury.

References and Readings

Aaronson, L.S., & Macnee, C.L. (1989). Tobacco, alcohol, and caffeine use during pregnancy. *Journal of Obstetric, Gynecologic, and Neonatal Nursing*, 18(4), 279–286.

Abel, E., Rockwook, G.A., & Riley, E.P. (1986). The effects of early marijuana exposure. In E. Riley & C. Vorhees (Eds.), *Handbook of behavioral teratology* (pp. 267–288). New York: Plenum Press.

Adams, C., Eyler, F.D., & Behnke, M. (1990). Nursing intervention with mothers who are substance abusers. *Journal of Perinatal and Neonatal Nursing*, 3(4), 43–52.

American Nurses Association. (1987). *Access to care: Key to preventing low birthweight*. Kansas City.

Baranowski, M.D., Schilomoeller, G.L., & Higgins, B.S. (1990). Parenting attitudes of adolescent and older mothers. *Adolescence*, 25(100), 781–790.

Bohn, D.K. (1990). Domestic violence and pregnancy: Implications for practice. *Journal of Nurse-Midwifery*, 35(2), 86–98.

Bullock, L.F., & McFarlane, J. (1989). Birth-weight/battering connection. *American Journal of Nursing*, 89(9), 1153–1156.

Byrne, M.W., & Lerner, H.M. (1992). Communicating with addicted women in labor. MCN: *American Journal of Maternal Child Nursing*, 17(1), 22–26.

Campbell, J.C., & Alford, P. (1989). The dark consequences of marital rape. *American Journal of Nursing*, 89(7), 946–949.

Centers for Disease Control. (1992). Sexual behavior among high school students. *Morbidity and Mortality Weekly Report*, 40,(51 and 52), 885–888.

Chasnoff, I.J. (1991). Cocaine and pregnancy: Clinical and methodologic issues. *Clinics in Perinatology*, 18(1), 113–123.

Chasnoff, I.J., Chisum, G.M., & Kaplan, W.E. (1988). Maternal cocaine use and genitourinary malformations. *Teratology*, 37(1), 201–204.

Chisum, G.M. (1990). Nursing interventions with the antepartum substance abuser. *Journal of Perinatal and Neonatal Nursing*, 3(4), 26–33.

Council on Scientific Affairs, American Medical Association. (1992). Violence against women: Relevance for medical practitioners. *Journal of the American Medical Association*, 267(23), 3184–3190.

Creasy, R.K., & Resnik, R. (1989). Intrauterine growth retardation. In R.K. Creasy & R. Resnik (Eds.), *Maternal-fetal medicine: Principles and practice* (2nd ed., pp. 547–564). Philadelphia: W.B. Saunders.

Day, N.L., & Richardson, G.A. (1991). Prenatal marijuana use: Epidemiology, methodologic issues, and infant outcomes. *Clinics in Perinatology*, 18(1), 77–91.

de Selincourt, K. (1991). Dignified in death. *Nursing Times*, 87(29), 16–17.

Dormire, S.L., Strauss, S.S., & Clarke, B.A. (1989). Social support and adaptation to the parent role in first-time adolescent mothers. *Journal of Obstetric, Gynecologic, and Neonatal Nursing*, 18(4), 327–337.

Dubiel, D. (1990). Action stat: Cocaine overdose. *Nursing 90*, 20(3), 33.

Forrest, J.D., & Silverman, J. (1989). What public school teachers teach about preventing pregnancy, AIDS, and sexually transmitted diseases. *Family Planning Perspective*, 21(2), 65–72.

Furrh, C.B., & Copley, R. (1989). One precious moment: What you can offer when a newborn infant dies. *Nursing 89*, 19(9), 52–54.

Hadley, S.M. (1992). Working with battered women in the emergency department: A model program. *Journal of Emergency Nursing*, 18(1), 18–23.

Herold, E.S., Fisher, W.A., Smith, E.A., & Yarber, W.A. (1990). Sex education and the prevention of STD/AIDS and pregnancy among youths. *Canadian Journal of Public Health*, 81(2), 141–145.

Hoegerman, G., & Schnoll, S. (1991). Narcotic use in pregnancy. *Clinics in Perinatology*, 18(1), 51–76.

House, M.A. (1990). Cocaine. *American Journal of Nursing*, 90(4), 41–45.

Jecker, N.S. (1993). Privacy beliefs and the violent family: Extending the ethical argument for physician intervention. *Journal of the American Medical Association*, 269(6), 776–780.

Jones, O.W. (1989). Basic genetics and patterns of inheritance. In R.K. Creasy & R. Resnik (Eds.), *Maternal-fetal medicine: Principles and practice*. (2nd ed., pp. 3–77). Philadelphia: W.B. Saunders.

Kaye, M.E., & Chasnoff, I.J. (1992). In R.A. Knuppel & J.E. Drukker (Eds.), *High-risk pregnancy: A team approach* (2nd ed., pp. 163–179. Philadelphia: W.B. Saunders.

Lewis, K.D., Bennett, B., & Schmeder, N.H. (1989). The care of infants menaced by cocaine abuse. MCN: *American Journal of Maternal Child Nursing*, 14(5), 224–332.

Little, B.B., & Snell, L.M. (1991). Brain growth among fetuses exposed to cocaine in utero: Asymmetrical growth retardation. *Obstetrics and Gynecology*, 77(3), 361–364.

Lynch, M., & McKeon, V.A. (1990). Cocaine use during pregnancy: Research findings and clinical implications. *Journal of Obstetric, Gynecologic, and Neonatal Nursing*, 19(4), 285–292.

Mallinson, G. (1989). When a baby dies. *Nursing Times*, 85(9), 31–34.

March of Dimes. (1992). Prevention of battering during pregnancy [Pamphlet].

McFarlane, J. (1989). Battering during pregnancy: Tip of an iceberg revealed. *Women & Health*, 15(3), 69–83.

McGregor, J.A. (1989). Chlamydial infection in women. *Obstetrics and Gynecology Clinics of North America*, 16(3), 565–592.

Mercer, R.T. (1990). *Parents at risk*. New York: Springer.

Parker, B., & McFarlane, J. (1991). Identifying and helping battered pregnant woman. MCN: *American Journal of Maternal Child Nursing*, 16(3), 161–164.

Pietrantoni, M., & Knuppel, R.A. (1991). Alcohol use in pregnancy. *Clinics in Perinatology*, 18(1), 93–111.

Ritchie, C.W. (1989). Adoption: An option often overlooked. *American Journal of Nursing*, 89(9), 1156–1157.

Rogers, B.D., & Lee, R.V. (1988). Drug abuse. In G.N. Burrow & T.F. Ferris (Eds.), *Medical complications during pregnancy* (3rd ed.). Philadelphia: W.B. Saunders.

Sampselle, C.M. (1991). The role of nursing in preventing violence against women. *Journal of Obstetric, Gynecologic, and Neonatal Nursing*, 20(6), 481–487.

Satin, A.J., Hemsell, D.L., Stone, I.C., Theriot, S., & Wendel, G.D. (1991). Sexual assault in pregnancy. *Obstetrics and Gynecology*, 77(5), 710–714.

Stark, E., & Flitcraft, A. (1988). Violence among intimates: An epidemiological review. In V.B. Van Haslett, R.L. Morrison, A.S. Bellack, & M. Hersen (Eds.), *Handbook of family violence* (pp. 293–318). New York: Plenum Press.

Sullivan, K.R. (1990). Maternal implications of cocaine use during pregnancy. *Journal of Perinatal and Neonatal Nursing*, 3(4), 12–23.

Tuckson, R.V. (1991). Special needs in adolescent pregnancy. *Perinatal Advocate*, 11(3), 25–26.

Weiner, L., & Larsson, G. (1987). Clinical prevention of fetal alcohol effects—a reality: Evidence for the effectiveness of intervention. *Alcohol Health Research World*, 11(1), 60–63, 92–93.

Zuckerman, B. (1988). Marijuana and cigarette smoking during pregnancy. In I.J. Chasnoff (Ed.), *Drugs, alcohol, pregnancy and parenting* (pp. 73–90). Boston: Kluwer Academic Publishers.

Zuckerman, B., Frank, D.A., Hingson, R., et al. (1989). The effects of maternal marijuana and cocaine use on fetal growth. *New England Journal of Medicine*, 320(12), 762–768.

24

Complications of Pregnancy

Objectives

1. Describe the hemorrhagic conditions of early pregnancy.
2. Explain disorders of the placenta that result in hemorrhagic conditions of late pregnancy.
3. Discuss the effects and management of hyperemesis gravidarum.
4. Describe the development and course of hypertensive disorders of pregnancy.
5. Compare Rh and ABO incompatibility in terms of etiology and fetal-neonatal complications.

Definitions

Abortion • A pregnancy that ends before 20 weeks gestation, either spontaneously or electively. *Miscarriage* is a lay term for spontaneous abortion.

Abruptio placentae • Premature separation of a normally implanted placenta.

Cerclage • Encircling of the cervix with suture to prevent recurrent spontaneous abortion caused by early cervical dilation.

Culdocentesis • Needle puncture through the upper posterior vaginal wall (**cul-de-sac** of Douglas) to aspirate blood from the pelvic cavity.

Dilatation and curettage (D & C) • Stretching the cervical os to permit scraping of the walls of the uterus. The procedure is performed in abortion, to obtain samples of uterine lining tissue for laboratory examination, and during the postpartum period to remove retained fragments of placenta.

Eclampsia • Convulsive form of pregnancy-induced hypertension.

Ectopic pregnancy • Implantation of a fertilized ovum in any area other than the uterus; the most common site is the fallopian tube.

Erythroblastosis fetalis • Agglutination and hemolysis of fetal erythrocytes due to incompatibility between maternal and fetal blood. In most cases, the fetus is Rh-positive and the mother is Rh-negative.

Hypovolemic shock • Acute peripheral circulatory failure due to loss of circulating blood volume.

Kernicterus • Accumulation of unconjugated bilirubin in the brain causing neurological damage; also called **bilirubin encephalopathy.**

Laparoscopy • Insertion of an illuminated tube into the abdominal cavity to visualize contents, locate bleeding, and perform surgical procedures.

Linear salpingostomy • Incision along the length of a fallopian tube to remove an ectopic pregnancy and preserve the tube.

Maceration • Discoloration and softening of tissues and eventual disintegration of a fetus that is retained in the uterus after its death.

Perinatologist • A physician who specializes in the care of the mother, fetus, and infant during the perinatal period (from the 20th week of pregnancy to 4 weeks following childbirth).

△ Alert for a high risk of exposure to substances to which universal precautions apply. See Appendix B for additional information about infection control.

Pre-eclampsia • A hypertensive disorder induced by pregnancy that includes a triad of signs and symptoms: hypertension, edema, and proteinuria.

Salpingectomy • Surgical removal of a fallopian tube.

Toxemia • A term occasionally used to denote pregnancy-induced hypertension (*pre-eclampsia* and *eclampsia*).

Vasoconstriction • Narrowing of the lumen of blood vessels.

Although childbearing is a normal process, there is a fine line between health and illness during pregnancy because of the numerous physiological adaptations that occur. Complications may arise that threaten the well-being of the expectant mother and/or the fetus. Family physicians or nurse-midwives may be responsible for co-managing women with complications of pregnancy; however, these women are often referred to a perinatologist or to a perinatal center for management.

Nurses who work at the primary care site or at the perinatal center frequently fill the role of case manager, or coordinator of services provided for the woman. Often the nurse is the only consistent provider involved in the client's care and therefore is the person whom the woman counts on to guide her through the system, answer questions and concerns, and explain the reasons for tests and procedures.

Conditions that complicate pregnancy are divided into two broad categories: (1) those related to pregnancy and not seen at other times, and (2) those that could occur at any time, but, when they occur concurrently with pregnancy, they may complicate the course of pregnancy. Concurrent conditions that affect pregnancy are considered in Chapter 25.

The most common pregnancy-related complications are hemorrhagic conditions that occur in early pregnancy, hemorrhagic complications of the placenta in late pregnancy, hyperemesis gravidarum, hypertensive disorders of pregnancy, and blood incompatibilities.

Hemorrhagic Conditions of Early Pregnancy

The three most common causes of hemorrhage during the first half of pregnancy are abortion, ectopic pregnancy, and hydatidiform mole.

Abortion

Abortion is the loss of pregnancy before the fetus is viable, that is, capable of living outside the uterus. The medical consensus today is that a fetus of less than 20 weeks' gestation, or weighing less than 500 g, is not viable; termination of pregnancy before this time is considered to be an abortion. Abortion may be either spontaneous or induced. Lay people often use the term "miscarriage" to denote an abortion that has occurred spontaneously as opposed to one that has been induced. Abortion is the accepted medical term for either, and this point should be clarified in discussions with clients to avoid misinterpretation or confusion.

Spontaneous abortion is defined as termination of pregnancy without action by the woman or any other person to initiate termination. Induced abortion is the interruption of pregnancy prior to the age of fetal viability at the request of the woman, or for reasons of maternal health or fetal disease. Induced abortion, often termed "elective" or "therapeutic" abortion, involves ethical and social implications (see Chapter 3).

Spontaneous Abortion

INCIDENCE AND ETIOLOGY

Determining the exact incidence of spontaneous abortion is difficult because unrecognized losses occur in early pregnancy. However, it is believed that from 10 to 20 per cent of all pregnancies end in spontaneous abortion (Bennett, 1992). The majority of spontaneous abortions occur in the first 12 weeks of pregnancy, with the rate declining rapidly thereafter.

The causes of spontaneous abortion are varied; however, the most common cause is significant genetic abnormalities that are incompatible with life or that would result in gross deformity of the fetus. Spontaneous abortion due to genetic abnormalities may reflect nature's way of extinguishing imperfect embryos. Additional causes include maternal infections, such as listeriosis, toxoplasmosis, brucellosis, rubella, and cytomegalic inclusion disease. There is inconclusive evidence that genital herpes and *Chlamydia trachomatis* also increase the risk of abortion. (See Chapter 25 for additional information about maternal infections.) In addition, maternal endocrine disorders, such as hypothyroidism, and abnormalities of the reproductive organs have also been implicated.

Spontaneous abortion is divided into six subgroups: threatened, inevitable, incomplete, complete, missed, and recurrent. Figure 24–1 illustrates threatened, inevitable, and complete abortion.

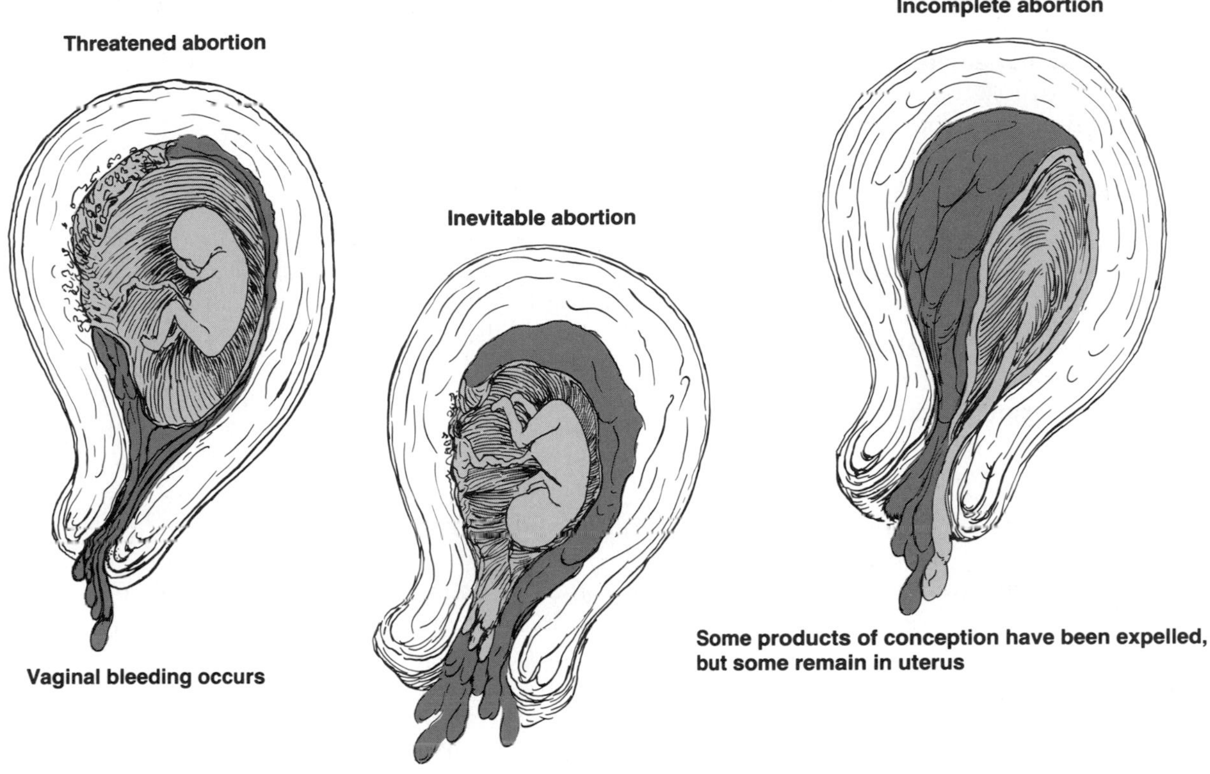
Threatened abortion
Vaginal bleeding occurs
Inevitable abortion
Membranes rupture and cervix dilates
Incomplete abortion
Some products of conception have been expelled, but some remain in uterus

Figure 24–1

Three types of spontaneous abortion.

THREATENED ABORTION

Clinical Manifestations. The first symptom is vaginal bleeding, which is rather common during pregnancy. Although from 10 to 30 per cent of all women experience "spotting" or bleeding in early pregnancy, about half of these pregnancies will end in spontaneous abortion whereas the remainder will progress to term (Cunningham et al, 1989).

Vaginal bleeding may be followed by rhythmic uterine cramping, persistent backache, or feelings of pelvic pressure. These symptoms increase the chance that the threatened abortion will progress to inevitable abortion.

Therapeutic Management. Bleeding in the first half of pregnancy must always be considered a threatened abortion, and women should be advised to notify their physician or certified nurse-midwife whenever vaginal bleeding is noted. When vaginal bleeding is reported, the nurse obtains a detailed history that includes length of gestation and the onset, duration, and amount of vaginal bleeding. Any accompanying discomfort, such as cramping, backache, or sharp abdominal pain, is also evaluated.

Ultrasound examination is often performed to determine whether the fetus is present and, if so, whether it is alive. When a live fetus is demonstrated, bed rest is sometimes recommended; the woman is advised to curtail sexual activity until bleeding has ceased and for 2 weeks following the last evidence of bleeding, or as recommended by the physician or certified nurse-midwife.

Bleeding episodes are frightening, and psychological support is very important. The woman often wonders whether her actions may have contributed to the situation and is anxious about her own condition and that of the fetus. The nurse should offer accurate information and avoid false reassurance, because the woman may lose her pregnancy despite every precaution.

INEVITABLE ABORTION

Clinical Manifestations. Abortion is usually inevitable (that is, it cannot be stopped) when there is gross rupture of the membranes and dilation of the cervix. Rupture of membranes is generally experienced as a sudden gush of fluid from the vagina followed by uterine contractions and bleeding. If complete evacuation of the products of conception does not occur spontaneously, excessive bleeding or infection can occur.

Therapeutic Management. Women must be admitted to the hospital for ultrasound evaluation to determine whether the process is inevitable or if it has progressed to an incomplete abortion. Analgesics should be administered to control pain, and evacuation of the uterus, usually by curettage, may be necessary.

All unsensitized Rh-negative women should receive Rh_0(D) immune globulin (RhoGAM) following abortion to prevent the development of Rh antibodies that would result in destruction of fetal erythrocytes in subsequent pregnancies.

INCOMPLETE ABORTION

Clinical Manifestations. Incomplete abortion occurs when some but not all products of conception are expelled from the uterus. The major symptom, and chief danger, is uterine hemorrhage, which occurs when the retained material prevents the uterus from contracting firmly, thus allowing profuse bleeding from uterine blood vessels.

Therapeutic Management. Hospital admission is necessary, and initial treatment should be focused on stabilizing the woman from a cardiovascular standpoint. A blood specimen is drawn for cross-matching and blood typing, and an intravenous line is inserted for fluid replacement. When the woman's condition is stable, a dilatation and curettage (D & C) is usually performed to remove remaining tissue. A D & C is a surgical procedure that involves dilating the cervical os and inserting instruments to scrape the lining of the uterus. This procedure may be followed by intravenous administration of oxytocin or intramuscular administration of methylergonovine (Methergine) to contract the uterus and control bleeding.

A D & C may not be performed if the pregnancy has advanced beyond 14 weeks because of the danger of excessive bleeding. In this case, oxytocin or prostaglandin is administered to stimulate uterine contractions until all products of conception (fetus, membranes, placenta, amniotic fluid) are expelled.

COMPLETE ABORTION

Clinical Manifestations. Complete abortion occurs when all products of conception are expelled from the uterus. After passage of all products of conception, uterine contractions and bleeding abate and the cervix closes. The uterus feels smaller than the length of gestation would suggest. The symptoms of pregnancy are no longer present, and the pregnancy test becomes negative.

Therapeutic Management. Once complete abortion is confirmed, no additional intervention is required unless excessive bleeding or infection develops.

MISSED ABORTION

Clinical Manifestations. Missed abortion occurs when the fetus dies during the first half of pregnancy but is retained in the uterus, usually for some weeks. When the fetus dies, the early signs of pregnancy (nausea, breast tenderness, urinary frequency) disappear. Moreover, the uterus not only stops growing but also decreases in size, reflecting the absorption of amniotic fluid and maceration of the fetus.

Therapeutic Management. The first step is to confirm death of the fetus by real-time ultrasound examination, which provides reliable information by the 6th week of pregnancy. Once fetal demise is confirmed, the usual management is to wait 3 to 5 weeks for spontaneous abortion, which occurs in 93 per cent of cases (Hayashi and Castillo, 1993). Waiting for the spontaneous expulsion of the pregnancy may be a trying time for the woman, particularly if it takes weeks.

Two major complications of missed abortion are infection and disseminated intravascular coagulation (DIC). If there are signs of uterine infection, such as elevations in temperature, vaginal discharge with a foul odor, or abdominal pain, evacuation of the uterus will be delayed until antibiotic therapy is initiated.

A life-threatening defect in coagulation, DIC may occur if the fetus is retained for a prolonged period. This defect is also associated with abruptio placentae (see also p. 672).

RECURRENT SPONTANEOUS ABORTION

Clinical Manifestations. Recurrent spontaneous abortion is sometimes referred to as "habitual" abortion; the current definition is three or more consecutive spontaneous abortions. The most common cause of recurrent abortions is an incompetent cervix, an anatomical defect that results in painless dilation of the cervix in the second trimester. Membranes prolapse through the open cervix and rupture, followed by expulsion of the products of conception. Systemic diseases, such as diabetes mellitus, systemic lupus erythematosus, and thyroid disease, are also associated with recurrent abortions, as are infectious diseases, such as toxoplasmosis, cytomegalic inclusion disease, and syphilis.

Therapeutic Management. The first step is a thorough examination of the cervix to determine whether anatomical defects are the cause. If the cervix is normal, the woman who has experienced three or more spontaneous abortions is often referred for genetic screening to determine the presence of genetic factors that would increase the possibility of recurrent abortions.

Additional therapeutic management of recurrent pregnancy loss depends on the cause. For instance, treatment may involve assisting the woman to develop a regimen to maintain normal blood glucose if diabetes mellitus is a factor; administration of appropriate antibiotics is necessary if the cause is syphilis.

Therapeutic management of cervical incompetence may involve procedures for suturing the cervix to keep it from opening. The most common procedures are cerclage, McDonald's procedure, or Shirodkar's procedure. These three procedures vary according to the type and placement of the sutures. Sutures are sometimes removed near term in preparation for vaginal delivery; however, they may be left in place if a cesarean birth is planned. Prophylactic antibiotics may be necessary if the woman is judged to be at high risk for infection.

Elective (Therapeutic) Abortion

Elective abortion is a voluntary method of terminating a pregnancy. The woman may choose to terminate her pregnancy for many reasons: to preserve her own health, to prevent the birth of an infant with severe genetic defects, or to end a pregnancy caused by rape or incest. She may also choose to terminate the pregnancy for economic or social reasons. Whatever the reason, the decision to terminate a pregnancy involves social and ethical conflicts (see Chapter 3).

METHODS OF ABORTION

Abortion can be performed by surgical or medical intervention. Surgical intervention includes vacuum curettage, D & C, and dilation and evacuation (D & E). Medical intervention includes prostaglandin suppository or injection, hypertonic saline injection, or hypertonic urea injection.

Vacuum Curettage. Early vacuum curettage accounts for 80 per cent of abortions performed in the United States. It should be performed within 8 to 10 weeks of the last missed menstrual period and involves dilation of the cervical os and aspiration of the contents of the uterus.

The cervix is dilated with metal dilators or with laminaria that have been set in place 6 to 24 hours prior to the procedure. Laminaria are short, rounded pieces of a Japanese seaweed that are hygroscopic (absorb water). When one or more of these small sticks of compressed seaweed are inserted into the cervix, they draw fluid from the cervical canal and expand, causing the cervix to dilate. Cervical dilation occurs slowly. This method is preferred by many physicians over the use of metal dilators because it is less traumatic to the cervix.

A suction tube is inserted into the uterus, and the uterine lining is aspirated. Usually, 3 to 5 minutes is required. A uterine curet may be used to scrape any remaining tissue from the uterine wall. Cramping may last 20 to 30 minutes after the procedure is completed. Complications may include uterine perforation, hemorrhage, cervical lacerations, or adverse reactions to the anesthetic agent.

Dilatation and Curettage. Currently, D & C is less frequently performed than vacuum curettage because it carries a relatively high risk of excessive blood loss and cervical or uterine trauma. In this procedure, the physician dilates the cervical os and scrapes the uterine walls with a metal curet to remove the products of conception.

Dilation and Evacuation. D & E is most appropriate when the pregnancy has advanced to the 13th to 16th week. It may require greater cervical dilation, crushing instruments, or a large-bore vacuum curet.

The cervix is dilated with laminaria. After removing the laminaria, the physician usually administers a paracervical block (see Chapter 15) or general anesthesia and further dilates the cervix. The products of conception are removed by vacuum curettage and other equipment as necessary.

Prostaglandin Suppository. A vaginal suppository of prostaglandin E_2 (PGE_2) may be used to induce an abortion when the pregnancy has progressed to the second trimester. PGE_2 produces uterine contractions, and the abortion generally occurs within 13 to 15 hours after insertion of the suppository. Many women experience adverse effects of prostaglandin, including nausea, vomiting, and fever. Occasionally, a live fetus is delivered.

Hypertonic Sodium Chloride Injection. This method is performed from the 14th to the 24th week of gestation. The physician inserts an 18-gauge, 7.5-cm (3-inch) needle into the amniotic sac, withdraws 150 to 250 ml of amniotic fluid, and injects an equal amount of a hypertonic solution of sodium chloride into the amniotic cavity. Uterine contractions usually begin from 10 to 24 hours after the sodium chloride injection, followed by expulsion of the fetus. Uterine contractions are sometimes weak and ineffective, and intravenous oxytocin may be used to augment the contractions.

Injection of hypertonic saline is used less frequently than other methods because most abortions are performed before the second trimester and because of the potential complications. Complications include infection, DIC, hypernatremia, and cerebral edema, and embolism if hypertonic sodium is injected directly into the circulation.

Hypertonic Urea Injection. Injection of hypertonic urea into the amniotic sac also produces second-trimester abortion. This procedure is similar to the injection of hypertonic saline, except hypertonic urea is injected following removal of 150 to 200 ml of amniotic fluid. This procedure results in fewer complications than injection of hypertonic saline; however, it is associated with a high failure rate when used alone. It is frequently combined with prostaglandin administration to overcome this disadvantage.

Combined Methods. Physicians often combine methods to ensure complete abortion. Laminaria or prostaglandin suppositories may be used to dilate the cervix, hypertonic sodium chloride or urea achieve feticidal results, and oxytocin or prostaglandins produce uterine contractions.

New Methods. RU-486 (mifepristone), a pill that induces early abortion, has been used effectively in France and China for several years. The pill works by blocking progesterone, a hormone that is vital for pregnancy to continue. RU-486 allows a client who is less than 5 weeks' pregnant to interrupt pregnancy without surgery. The drug is not yet available in the United States.

NURSING CONSIDERATIONS

The nurse's role in caring for women seeking elective abortion is one of physical and emotional support and providing information. History taking and collection of laboratory data depend on the routine of the health care setting in which the nurse is functioning. Counseling and lending emotional support are nursing responsibilities, unless a designated counselor performs these services.

Nurses are also responsible for providing information for self-care following an abortion. The major points are summarized in Women Want to Know: Self-Care Measures Following Induced Abortion.

✔ Check Your Reading

1. What are the signs of threatened abortion? What are the signs of inevitable abortion?
2. What self-care measures should be taught following elective abortion?

Women Want To Know

Self-Care Measures Following Induced Abortion

- Normal activities may be resumed, but strenuous work or exercise should be avoided for a few days.
- Bleeding or cramping may occur for a week or two. If either becomes severe, medical advice should be sought. Light "spotting" may occur for about a month.
- Sanitary pads rather than tampons should be used for the first week after the abortion to avoid possible infection.
- Douching should be avoided for at least 1 week to prevent infection.
- Intercourse should be curtailed for 1 week after the abortion because of the possibility of infection until the uterine lining heals.
- Birth control measures should be used if sex is resumed before menstruation begins because it is possible to become pregnant during this time. Menstruation usually resumes in 4 to 6 weeks.
- Temperature should be taken twice a day to detect possible infection; a temperature above 37.8°C (100°F) should be reported to the health care provider.
- It is important to keep the follow-up appointment in 2 weeks.

Ectopic Pregnancy

The term ectopic pregnancy refers to implantation of a fertilized ovum in an area outside the uterine cavity. Although implantation can occur in the abdomen or in the cervix, almost 95 per cent of ectopic pregnancies are in the fallopian tube (Palmieri and Moore, 1992). Figure 24–2 illustrates common sites of implantation.

Ectopic pregnancy has been called "a disaster of reproduction" for two reasons:

- It remains a leading cause of maternal death from hemorrhage.
- It sharply reduces the woman's chance of subsequent pregnancies because of damage or destruction of a fallopian tube.

INCIDENCE AND ETIOLOGY

The incidence of ectopic pregnancy has increased dramatically throughout the world in the last 15 years. In the United States, the rate has more than tripled, to 14 in every 1000 reported pregnancies. The highest rate is seen in non-Caucasian women over the age of 35 years (Doyle et al, 1991). The rapid increase in incidence is attributed to the grow-

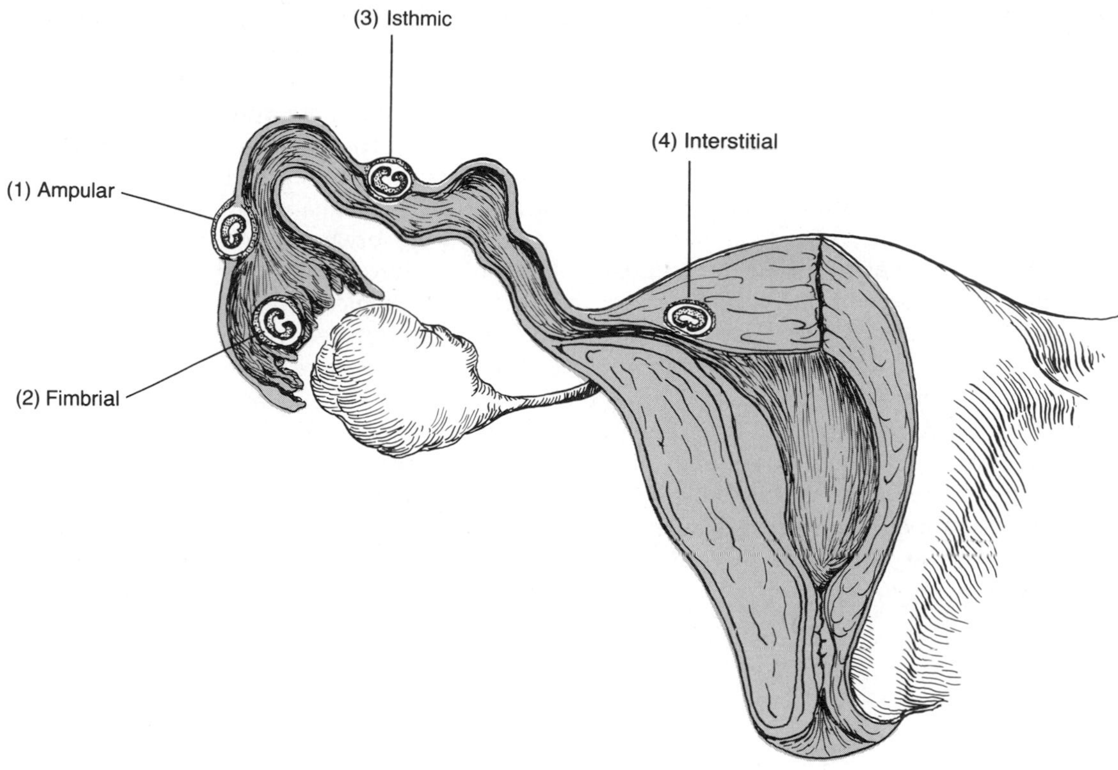

Figure 24–2

Sites of ectopic pregnancy. Numbers indicate the order of prevalence.

ing number of women of childbearing age who experience scarring of the fallopian tubes caused by pelvic infection, inflammation, or surgery. Pelvic infection is most often due to *Chlamydia*, *Neisseria gonorrhoeae* or mixed aerobe-anaerobe organisms. Failed tubal ligation and a history of previous ectopic pregnancy also increase the risk for an ectopic pregnancy that implants in the fallopian tube.

In addition, there is a significant risk of ectopic pregnancy when conception occurs while an intrauterine contraceptive device (IUD, IUCD) is in place. Whether this is due to latent infection or some other mechanism is unknown, but the risk appears to increase with the length of time the IUD has been in place. Risk appears to return to normal after the IUD is removed (Doyle et al, 1991).

Additional causes of ectopic pregnancy are delayed or premature ovulation, with the tendency of the fertilized ovum to implant before arrival in the uterus, and altered tubal motility in response to changes in estrogen and progesterone levels. Multiple previous induced abortions are associated with increased risk of tubal pregnancy, possibly due to salpingitis (infection of the fallopian tube) that has occurred following induced abortion. Table 24–1 summarizes the risk factors for ectopic pregnancy.

Regardless of the cause of ectopic pregnancy, the effect is that transport of the fertilized ovum through the fallopian tube is hampered.

CLINICAL MANIFESTATIONS

The classic signs of ectopic pregnancy are:

- Missed menstrual period
- Abdominal pain
- Vaginal "spotting"

More subtle signs and symptoms depend on the site of implantation. If implantation occurs in the distal

Table 24–1. RISK FACTORS FOR ECTOPIC PREGNANCY

History of sexually transmitted diseases (gonorrhea, chlamydial infection)
History of pelvic inflammatory disease
History of previous ectopic pregnancies
Failed tubal ligation
Intrauterine device
Multiple induced abortions
Maternal age over 35 years

end of the fallopian tube, which is able to accommodate the growing embryo for longer periods of time, the woman may at first exhibit the usual early signs of pregnancy and consider herself to be normally pregnant. Several weeks into the pregnancy, intermittent abdominal pain and small amounts of vaginal bleeding occur and initially could be mistaken for threatened abortion.

If implantation has occurred in the proximal end of the fallopian tube, rupture of the tube may occur within 2 to 3 weeks of the missed period. Symptoms include sudden, severe pain in one of the lower quadrants of the abdomen as the tube tears open and the embryo is expelled into the pelvic cavity, often with profuse hemorrhage. Pain in the shoulder may indicate bleeding into the abdomen. Hypovolemic shock is a major concern because systemic signs of shock may be rapid and extensive without obvious bleeding.

DIAGNOSIS

The combined use of transvaginal ultrasound examination (described in Chapter 10) and determination of the beta subunit of human chorionic gonadotropin (β-hCG) are helpful in early detection of ectopic pregnancy. The presence of β-hCG is a strong indication of pregnancy. If β-hCG is present but the gestational sac cannot be visualized, a diagnosis of ectopic pregnancy may be made with great accuracy. Visualization of an intrauterine pregnancy, however, does not absolutely rule out an ectopic pregnancy. It is possible for a woman to have an intrauterine pregnancy and concurrently to have an ectopic pregnancy.

A culdocentesis may be performed to determine whether there is blood in the cul-de-sac of Douglas (located between the rectum and the uterus). In this procedure, an aspiration needle is inserted through the posterior vaginal wall into the cul-de-sac. Aspiration of blood from the cul-de-sac may indicate bleeding from rupture of a fallopian tube. Laparoscopy (examination of the peritoneal cavity by means of a laparoscope) is often necessary before diagnosis of ectopic pregnancy can be made. A characteristic bluish swelling within the tube is the most common finding (Cartwright, 1991).

THERAPEUTIC MANAGEMENT

Management of tubal pregnancy depends on whether the tube is intact or ruptured. Expectant management may be possible if the tube is intact and serial hCG levels are declining, which indicates spontaneous regression of the tubal pregnancy (Stovall and Ling, 1991). Medical management may also be possible if the tube is unruptured. Methotrexate, a chemotherapeutic agent that interferes with cell reproduction, is currently recommended as a means for inhibiting cell division in the developing embryo. The primary impetus for medical management is preserving the tube and improving the chance of future fertility (Ory, 1991).

Surgical management of a tubal pregnancy that is unruptured may involve a linear salpingostomy to salvage the tube (Fig. 24–3). Linear salpingostomy may also be attempted if the tube is ruptured but damage to the tube is minimal. Salvaging the tube is particularly important to women who are concerned about future fertility.

When ectopic pregnancy results in rupture of the fallopian tube, the goal of therapeutic management is to control the bleeding and prevent hypovolemic shock. When the cardiovascular status is stable, a salpingectomy is performed to remove the affected tube and to ligate bleeding vessels. Future pregnancies can occur when only one tube is present; however, the incidence of pregnancy declines.

NURSING CONSIDERATIONS

Nursing care is focused on preventing hypovolemic shock, controlling pain, and providing psychological support for the woman who experiences an ectopic pregnancy. Nurses administer analgesics and evaluate their effectiveness so that pain can be controlled.

The client and her family will need psychological support to resolve intense emotions that may include anger, grief, guilt, and self-blame. The woman may also be anxious about her ability to become pregnant in the future, and it may be necessary for nurses to clarify the physician's explanation and to use therapeutic communication techniques that assist the woman to deal with her anxiety.

Hydatidiform Mole

Hydatidiform mole is a form of gestational trophoblastic neoplasia (abnormal growth of the peripheral cells that attach the fertilized ovum to the uterine wall) that involves abnormal development of the placenta as the fetal part of the pregnancy fails to develop. The condition is characterized by proliferation and edema of the chorionic villi. The fluid-filled villi form grape-like clusters that may grow large enough to fill the uterus to the size of an advanced pregnancy (Fig. 24–4).

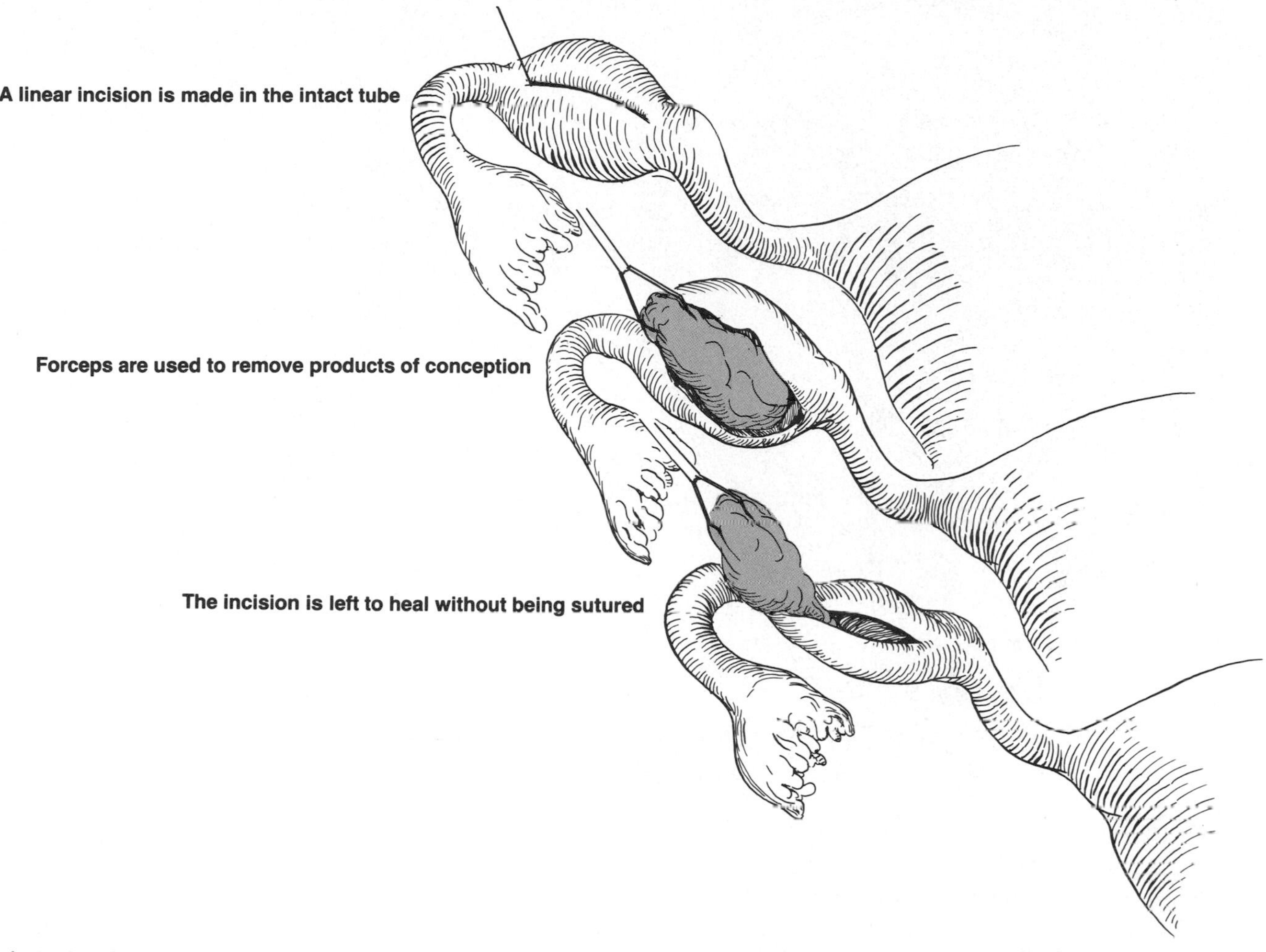
A linear incision is made in the intact tube
Forceps are used to remove products of conception
The incision is left to heal without being sutured

Figure 24–3

Linear salpingostomy.

Ultrasound examination allows a differential diagnosis to be made between two types of molar pregnancies: (1) a partial mole that includes some fetal tissue and membranes, and (2) a complete mole that is composed only of enlarged villi and contains no fetal tissue or membranes.

INCIDENCE AND ETIOLOGY

In the United States, the incidence of hydatidiform mole is 1 in every 2000 pregnancies (Berek, 1992). It is much more common in other countries, particularly Asia and Mexico. Age is also a factor, with the frequency of molar pregnancies ten times greater in women over the age of 45 years. Women who have had one molar pregnancy are at increased risk to have another. About 10 to 20 per cent of complete moles advance to invasive, potentially metastatic choriocarcinoma.

Although there are variations, *complete mole* is believed to occur when the ovum is fertilized by a sperm that duplicates its own chromosomes while the chromosomes of the ovum are inactivated. In a *partial mole*, the maternal contribution is usually present but the paternal contribution is double, and thus the karyotype is triploid (69,XXY or 69,XYY).

CLINICAL MANIFESTATIONS

In early pregnancy, the signs and symptoms of hydatidiform mole cannot be distinguished from normal pregnancy. As the pregnancy progresses, the following changes occur:

1. There is vaginal bleeding, which varies from dark-brown spotting to profuse hemorrhage.
2. The uterus is often larger than one would expect based on the duration of the pregnancy. For instance, at 10 weeks of gestation, the uterus may be palpated midway between the symphysis and the

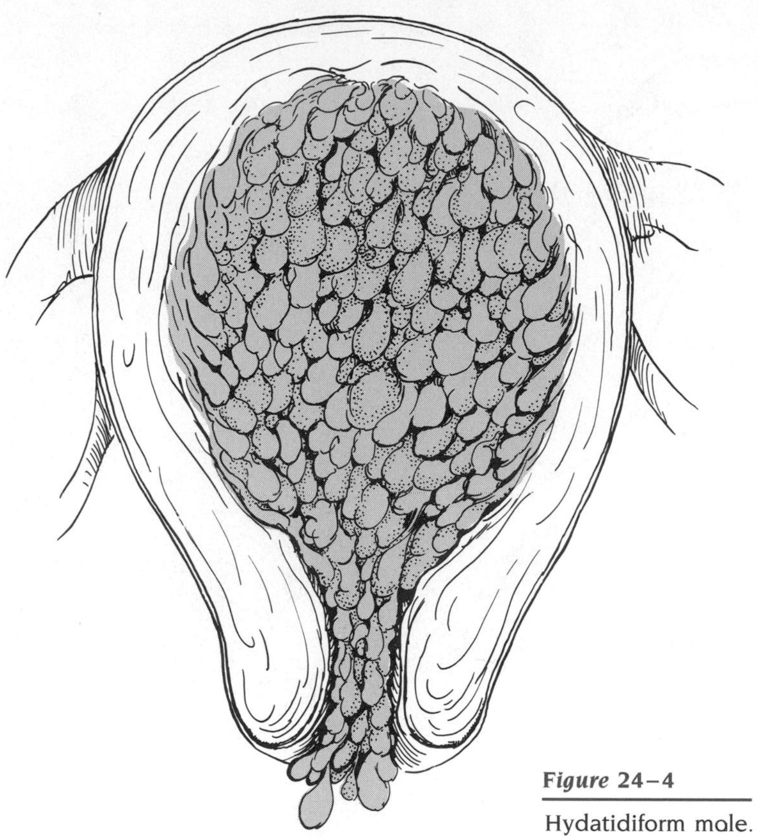

Figure 24–4

Hydatidiform mole.

umbilicus, which is consistent with a pregnancy of 16 weeks.

3. Fetal heart activity and fetal movement are not detected even with sensitive instruments and even when uterine size indicates that they should be present.

4. The woman has excessive nausea and vomiting (hyperemesis gravidarum), which may be related to excessive hCG from the proliferating trophoblasts.

5. The woman experiences early development of pregnancy-induced hypertension, which is rarely diagnosed before 24 weeks in a normal pregnancy.

THERAPEUTIC MANAGEMENT

Medical management includes two phases: (1) immediate evacuation of the mole and (2) continuous follow-up of the woman to detect any malignant changes of the remaining trophoblastic tissue. Prior to evacuation, a chest x-ray, computed tomography, or magnetic resonance imaging may be used to detect metastic disease. A complete blood count, laboratory assessment of clotting factors, and blood typing and crossmatching are also necessary in case a transfusion is needed.

Most often, vacuum aspiration is used to extract the mole; intravenous oxytocin is used to contract the uterus during the procedure. Curettage follows the evacuation, and the tissue obtained is sent for careful laboratory evaluation. This is extremely important because, although a hydatidiform mole is usually a benign process, choriocarcinoma is sometimes a complication.

Follow-up is critical to detect any changes suggestive of trophoblastic malignancy. Follow-up protocol involves evaluation of serum chorionic gonadotropin levels every 1 to 2 weeks until normal pre-pregnancy levels are attained. The test is repeated every 1 to 2 months for a year. Pregnancy must be avoided during the 1-year follow-up because it would obscure the evidence of choriocarcinoma. Affected women should also be advised that oral contraceptives are safe to use but that IUDs may cause irregular bleeding and should not be used.

NURSING CONSIDERATIONS

Women who have had a hydatidiform mole experience many of the same emotions as those who have had any other type of pregnancy loss. In addition, they may be anxious about follow-up evaluations and the need to delay pregnancy for at least a year.

✔ Check Your Reading

3. Why is ectopic pregnancy called a disaster of reproduction?
4. Why is the incidence of ectopic pregnancy increasing in the United States?
5. What are the two phases of treatment for hydatidiform mole?

Hemorrhagic Conditions of Early Pregnancy: Application of Nursing Process

Regardless of the cause of antepartum bleeding, nurses play a vital role in its management. Nurses are responsible for monitoring the condition of the pregnant woman and for collaborating with the physician to provide treatment. Nurses must also be aware of the emotional responses of the woman and her family, who may not only fear for the life of the woman but also grieve for the actual or anticipated loss of the unborn infant.

Physical Condition

Assessment

Physical assessment focuses on determining the amount of bleeding and the description, location, and severity of pain. Estimate the amount of vaginal bleeding by examining linen and peripads. If necessary, make a more accurate estimation by weighing the linen and peripads (1 g weight equals 1 ml volume).

When asking a woman how much blood she lost at home, ask her to compare the amount lost to a common measure such as a tablespoon or a cup. Ask also how long the bleeding episode lasted and what has been done to control the bleeding.

Bleeding may be accompanied by pain. Uterine cramping usually accompanies spontaneous abortion; deep, severe pelvic pain is associated with ectopic pregnancy. Remember, that in ectopic pregnancy, bleeding may be concealed and pain is the major symptom.

Assess vital signs to determine cardiovascular status. Moreover, because abortion may be associated with infections, assess the woman for fever, malaise, and prolonged vaginal discharge.

Confirmation of pregnancy is important. Does the woman know for certain that she is pregnant? How many weeks is the pregnancy? Hemoglobin and hematocrit levels may be decreased following an episode of prenatal bleeding, and these blood values should be evaluated and reported to the physician or nurse-midwife so that anemia can be treated. Determine Rh factor so that all women who are Rh-negative can receive $Rh_o(D)$ immune globulin. Additional information about $Rh_o(D)$ immune globulin appears in the discussion of Rh incompatibility (p. 691).

Analysis

Major hemorrhage is rarely associated with spontaneous abortion; however, ruptured ectopic pregnancy may produce serious hemorrhage that can progress to hypovolemic shock. (See p. 673 for information about the potential complication of hypovolemic shock.) All women who have experienced prenatal bleeding and invasive procedures are at increased risk for infection, and a commonly used nursing diagnosis is: *High Risk for Infection related to lack of knowledge of measures to prevent infection and dietary practices that increase hemoglobin and hematocrit.*

Planning

Goals for this nursing diagnosis are that the woman will:

- Verbalize measures that prevent infection.
- Verbalize signs of infection that should be reported to the health care provider.

Interventions

TEACHING MEASURES TO PREVENT INFECTION

The risk for infection is greatest during the first 72 hours following spontaneous abortion or operative procedures; however, many women are discharged within a few hours. Validate that the woman knows how to use a thermometer and instruct her to take her temperature every 8 hours for the first 3 days at home.

Personal hygiene should include careful hand washing before and after changing perineal pads, and daily showers. Perineal pads instead of tampons should be used until bleeding has subsided. The woman should obtain permission from the health care provider before sexual intercourse is resumed.

PROVIDING DIETARY INFORMATION

Nutrition plays a vital role in maintaining the body's defense against infection, and the nurse must promote adequate diet. The woman who is at risk for infection needs foods that are high in iron to increase hemoglobin and hematocrit values. These foods include liver, red meat, spinach, egg yolks, carrots, and raisins. In addition, she needs foods that are high in vitamin C, which increases the utilization of iron. These include citrus fruits, broccoli, strawberries, cantaloupe, cabbage, and green peppers.

Iron supplementation is also frequently prescribed, and the woman may require information to lessen the gastrointestinal upsets that many people experience when iron is administered. Less gastric upset is experienced when iron is taken with meals, and a diet that is high in fiber and fluid helps to reduce constipation that is an associated problem for many.

TEACHING SIGNS OF INFECTION TO REPORT

Instruct the woman to seek medical help if her temperature goes above 37.8°C (100°F). She should also report additional signs of infection, such as vaginal discharge with foul odor, pelvic tenderness, or general malaise, to the health care provider so that treatment can be initiated.

Evaluation

Interventions are judged successful if the woman:

- Verbalizes hygienic and dietary measures that reduce the risk of infection.
- Verbalizes signs of infection that should be reported to a health care professional.

Psychosocial Responses

Assessment

The woman's response to early pregnancy loss is particularly complex. The unique relationship between expectant mother and fetus and the attachment that evolves has deep psychological roots. This special relationship comes to an abrupt end and may initiate an emotional upheaval for the woman and her family.

Note both subjective and objective signs of grieving. Subjective signs include expressions of sadness, depression, shock, fear, denial, guilt, and anxiety. Objective signs include crying, inability to cry, withdrawal behavior, apathetic behavior, changes in grooming or hygiene, anorexia, or inability to sleep.

Analysis

Grieving may occur in anticipation of a loss or as a result of actual loss. A nursing diagnosis that is relevant to early hemorrhagic conditions of pregnancy is: *Grieving related to expected or actual loss of pregnancy.*

Planning

Goals for this nursing diagnosis are as follows:

- The woman and her family will express emotions in the days following the pregnancy loss.
- The woman will share emotions with significant others (spouse, parents) throughout the period of grieving.

Interventions

ACKNOWLEDGING THE PARENTS' EMOTIONS

There is often an erroneous belief that early pregnancy loss does not produce the grieving that accompanies loss at a later stage of gestation. Friends and family may unknowingly compound the grief that the woman experiences by making comments that belittle her emotions. The two most common remarks are: "These things happen for the best" and "You can have other children." Prepare the parents for the fact that some persons may not understand the depth of their grief or may think that reassurances about future pregnancies will lessen the grief that they feel.

As part of the grief reaction, many women experience a sense of guilt, and they wonder how they could have prevented spontaneous abortion. The nurse must carefully acknowledge and reflect the woman's feelings. When feelings have been expressed and reflected, it may be appropriate to explain that the cause of a spontaneous abortion is often unknown and that most cannot be prevented.

Allow adequate time for the family to express the strong emotions that they are feeling and then acknowledge the emotions expressed. The family may be disappointed or disheartened by the experience.

SUPPORTING GRIEF REACTIONS

Anger often replaces denial in the grieving process, and it is one of the earliest signs of grief when pregnancy loss occurs. Therapeutic communication techniques, such as paraphrasing, reflecting, and summarizing, allow the family to express their feeling of anger and to progress in the grieving process.

Many parents want to share the hopes and dreams that they had for the child, and nurses should be prepared to allow this. Some parents benefit from contact with the hospital chaplain or their own religious leader.

Evaluation

Interventions can be judged successful if the woman and her family express their emotions to each other as well as to the health care provider.

Hemorrhagic Conditions of Late Pregnancy

After 20 weeks of pregnancy, the two major causes of hemorrhage are the disorders of the placenta called placenta previa and abruptio placentae. Abruptio placentae may be further complicated by DIC, which can culminate in hemorrhagic shock.

Placenta Previa

Placenta previa is defined as implantation of the placenta in the lower uterine segment in advance of the fetal presenting part. The three classifications of placenta previa (total, partial, and marginal) depend on how much of the cervical os is covered by the placenta (Fig. 24–5).

Marginal or low-lying placentas (implanted in the lower uterine segment but not extending to the cervical os) that are found on early ultrasound examinations frequently "move" upward and away from the internal cervical os as the pregnancy develops. Follow-up ultrasonography is performed to locate the placenta and to determine whether the problem of marginal or low-lying placenta resolves during the last weeks of pregnancy.

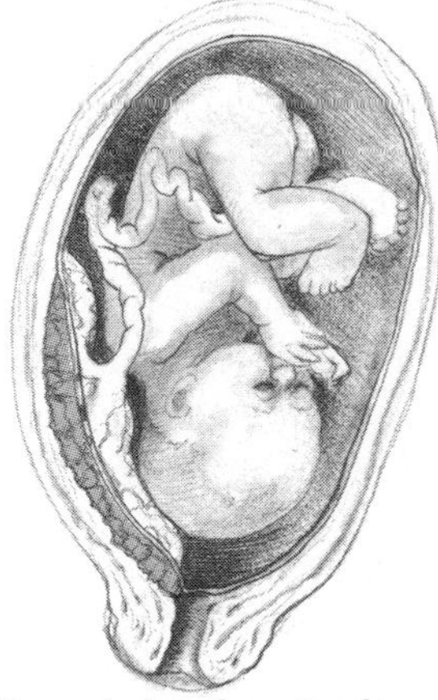
Marginal
Placenta barely extends to cervical os

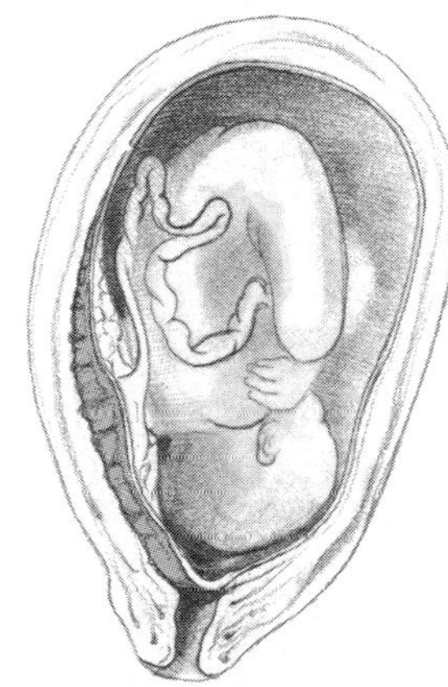
Partial
Placenta partially covers cervical os

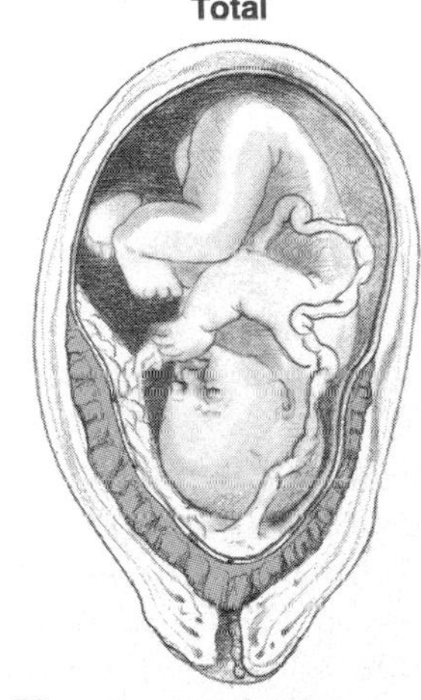
Total
Placenta completely covers cervical os

Figure 24–5

The three classifications of placenta previa.

INCIDENCE AND ETIOLOGY

In the United States, the incidence of placenta previa averages 1 in 200 to 250 pregnancies. It is much more common in multiparas, in women who have had a cesarean birth, and in women who have had multiple early pregnancy terminations. The groups at highest risk are those who have had previous placenta previa and those who have had multiple prior cesarean births (Green, 1989).

CLINICAL MANIFESTATIONS

The classic sign of placenta previa is painless uterine bleeding that occurs in the latter half of pregnancy; however, many cases of placenta previa are diagnosed by ultrasound examination before the onset of bleeding. Bleeding occurs when the placental villi are torn from the uterine wall, resulting in hemorrhage from the uterine vessels. Bleeding is painless because it is not occurring in a closed cavity and does not cause pressure on adjacent tissue; it may be scanty or profuse, and it may cease spontaneously, only to recur later.

Bleeding may not occur until labor starts, when cervical changes disrupt placental attachment. The admitting nurse may be unsure whether the bleeding is heavy "bloody show" or sign of a placenta previa.

If there is any doubt, the nurse never performs a vaginal examination or takes any action that would stimulate uterine activity. Digital examination of the cervical os when a placenta previa is present can cause additional placental separation or tear the placenta itself, causing severe hemorrhage and extreme risk to the fetus. Until the location and position of the placenta are verified by ultrasonography, no manual examinations should be performed, and administration of oxytocin should be postponed to prevent strong contractions that could result in sudden placental separation and rapid hemorrhage.

THERAPEUTIC MANAGEMENT

When the diagnosis of placenta previa is confirmed by ultrasonography, medical interventions are based on the condition of the expectant mother and fetus. The woman is carefully evaluated to determine the amount of hemorrhage, and electronic fetal monitoring is initiated to determine the condition of the fetus. If her cardiovascular status is stable and if the fetus is immature and shows no signs of distress, conservative treatment may be initiated. The woman may be hospitalized, or she may be discharged and advised to rest in bed, curtail sexual intercourse, and report at once any signs of vaginal bleeding. Conservative treatment may provide valuable time for the fetus to mature. If the fetus is over 36 weeks' gestation, lung maturity may be confirmed by amniocentesis, and delivery may be planned.

If bleeding is excessive, or if the expectant mother demonstrates signs of hypovolemia, delivery must be accomplished immediately regardless of fetal immaturity. Cesarean delivery has largely replaced attempts at vaginal delivery, even when the previa is partial or marginal.

NURSING CONSIDERATIONS

Nursing care for the woman with placenta previa depends on the course of medical management that is prescribed. The woman may be discharged after the initial episode of bleeding, and nurses are responsible for helping the family develop a plan that will allow her to remain on bed rest for a prolonged period. Moreover, many families are deeply concerned about the fetus.

The concerned family feels reassured when they receive specific, accurate information about the condition of the fetus. For example, tell the parents that the fetal heart rate is within the expected range and that the electronic fetal monitoring strip indicates that the fetus is not in distress.

Women with placenta previa are often admitted to the antepartum unit so that constant assessment and care can be provided. When the expectant mother is confined to the hospital, nursing assessments are focused on determining whether she experiences bleeding episodes and monitoring the condition of the fetus. Periodic electronic fetal monitoring is necessary to determine whether there are changes in fetal heart activity that indicate fetal distress. Any significant change in fetal heart activity or any episode of vaginal bleeding should immediately be reported to the physician.

If bleeding does not subside or if there are signs of fetal distress, the fetus will be delivered immediately by cesarean procedure. Nurses should prepare the expectant mother for surgery: abdominal preparation, insertion of an indwelling catheter, confirming that appropriate preoperative permission forms are signed, validating that blood typing and crossmatching have been done, and starting intravenous fluids as directed by the physician.

The preoperative procedures are often performed quickly, and the family may become anxious and concerned about the condition of the fetus and the expectant mother. Nurses must use whatever time is available to keep the family informed.

During the rapid preparations for surgery, the nurse can reassure both the client and the family by briefly describing the necessary preparations: "I'm sorry we have to rush, but we need to start the IV in case she needs extra fluids." "Do you have questions I might answer as we prepare for the cesarean?"

Abruptio Placentae

Separation of a normally implanted placenta before the fetus is delivered (called abruptio placentae, placental abruption, or premature separation of the placenta) occurs when there is bleeding and formation of a hematoma (clot) on the maternal side of the placenta. Blood may either extend upward toward the fundus, resulting in concealed hemorrhage, or extend downward toward the cervix, resulting in external bleeding. The severity of the complication depends on the amount of bleeding and the size of the hematoma. If there is continued bleeding, the hematoma expands and obliterates intervillous spaces. When this occurs, fetal vessels in the placenta are not perfused with maternal blood, and fetal oxygen is severely compromised. Moreover, fetal vessels are sometimes damaged and there is fetal as well as maternal bleeding.

Abruptio placentae is a dangerous condition for both the expectant mother and the fetus. The major danger for the woman is hemorrhage and consequent hypovolemic shock. The major dangers for the fetus are anoxia, excessive blood loss, or delivery before the fetus is mature enough to survive.

INCIDENCE AND ETIOLOGY

Published incidence of abruptio placentae varies widely; however, it probably occurs in less than 1 per cent of all pregnancies in the United States (Green, 1989). Placental abruption extensive enough to cause the death of the fetus is reported to occur once in 850 deliveries (Cunningham et al, 1989).

The cause is unknown; however, several factors that increase the risk have been identified. The risk factors include maternal hypertension, multigravida, short umbilical cord, abdominal trauma, and history of previous premature separation of the placenta. Maternal use of cocaine, which causes vasoconstriction in the endometrial arteries, is one of the leading causes of abruptio placentae.

CLINICAL MANIFESTATIONS

The four classic signs and symptoms of abruptio placentae are:

- Vaginal bleeding
- Abdominal pain
- Uterine hyperactivity with poor relaxation between contractions
- Uterine tenderness

Additional signs include back pain, fetal distress, signs of hypovolemic shock, and fetal death.

Cases of abruptio placentae are divided into 2 main types: (1) those in which hemorrhage is concealed and (2) those in which hemorrhage is apparent. In either type, the placental abruption may be complete or partial. Concealed hemorrhage occurs when there is bleeding behind the placenta but the margins remain intact, causing formation of a hematoma. The hemorrhage is apparent when bleeding separates or dissects the membranes from the endometrium and blood flows out through the vagina. Figure 24–6 illustrates abruptio placentae with external and concealed bleeding. It must be emphasized that apparent bleeding does not indicate the actual amount of blood lost, and signs of shock (tachycardia, hypotension, pale color, and cold, clammy skin) may be present when there is little or no external bleeding.

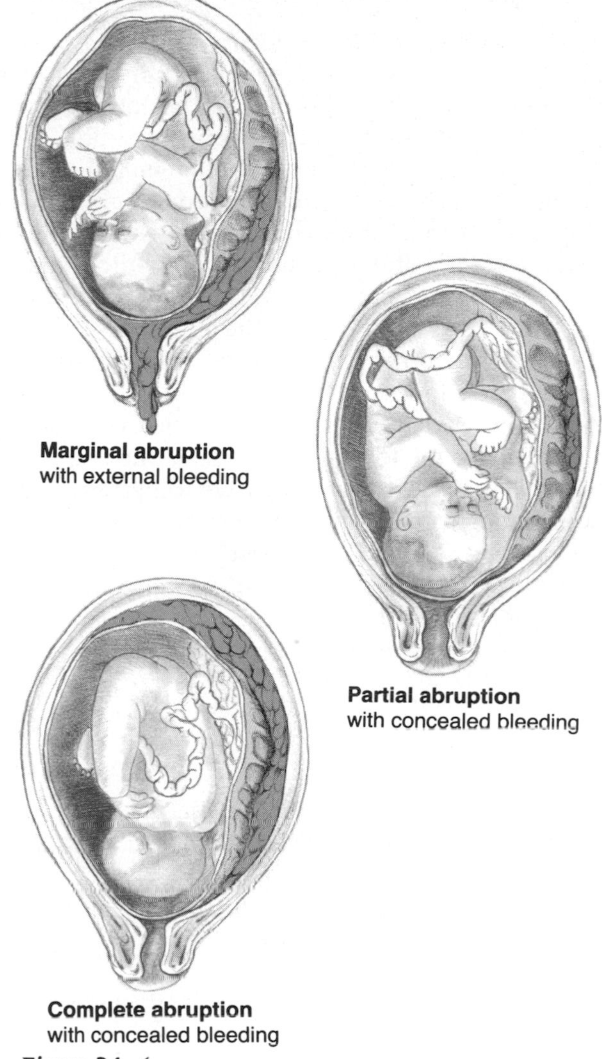

***Figure* 24–6**

Types of abruptio placentae.

Abdominal pain is also related to the type of separation. It may be sudden and severe when there is bleeding into the myometrium (uterine muscle), or intermittent and difficult to distinguish from labor contractions. The abdomen may become exceedingly firm (board-like) and tender, making palpation of the fetus difficult. Ultrasound examination is helpful to rule out placenta previa as the cause of bleeding, but it cannot be used to diagnose abruptio placentae because the separation and bleeding may not be obvious on ultrasonography.

THERAPEUTIC MANAGEMENT

Any woman who exhibits signs of abruptio placentae should be hospitalized and evaluated at once. Evaluation focuses on the condition of the fetus and the cardiovascular status of the expectant mother. If the condition is mild and the fetus is immature and shows no signs of distress, conservative management may be initiated. This includes bed rest and may include administration of tocolytic medications to decrease uterine activity (Green, 1989). Conservative management is rare owing to the great risks of fetal death and maternal hemorrhage associated with abruptio placentae.

Immediate delivery of the fetus is necessary if there are signs of fetal distress or if the expectant mother exhibits signs of excessive bleeding, either obvious or concealed. Intensive monitoring of both the woman and the fetus is essential because rapid deterioration of either can occur. Blood products for replacement should be available, and two large-bore intravenous lines should be secured for replacement of fluid and blood.

NURSING CONSIDERATIONS

Abruptio placentae is extremely frightening for the woman. She experiences severe pain and is aware of the danger to her and to the fetus. She must be carefully assessed for signs of concealed hemorrhage. See Critical to Remember: Signs of Concealed Hemorrhage.

If immediate cesarean delivery is necessary, the woman may feel powerless as the health care team hurriedly prepares her for surgery. If it is at all possible in the time available, nurses must explain anticipated procedures to the client and her family to reduce their feelings of fear and anxiety.

Excessive bleeding and fetal distress are always major concerns with abruptio placentae, and nurses are responsible for continuous monitoring of both the expectant mother and the fetus so that problems can be detected early before the condition of the woman or the fetus deteriorates.

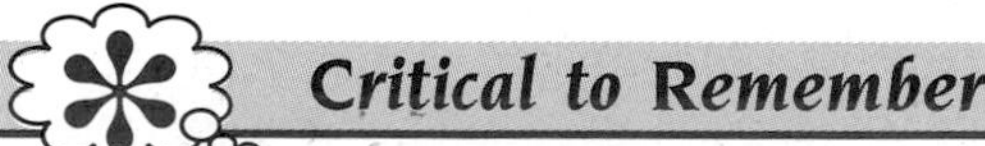

Signs of Concealed Hemorrhage

- Increase in fundal height
- Hard, board-like abdomen
- High uterine base tone on electronic monitoring strip
- Persistent abdominal pain
- Systemic signs of early hemorrhage (tachycardia, falling blood pressure, restlessness)
- Progressive late deceleration in fetal heart rate or decreasing baseline variability
- Vaginal bleeding may be slight or absent

COMPLICATION: DISSEMINATED INTRAVASCULAR COAGULATION

Abruptio placentae is sometimes associated with DIC, a life-threatening and confusing disorder in which anticoagulation and procoagulation factors are activated simultaneously. DIC develops when the clotting factor thromboplastin is released into the maternal blood stream as a result of placental bleeding and consequent clot formation. The circulating thromboplastin activates widespread clotting in small vessels throughout the body. This process consumes or "uses up" other clotting factors such as fibrinogen and platelets. The condition is further complicated by activation of the fibrinolytic system to lyse, or destroy, clots. The net result is a simultaneous decrease in clotting factors and increase in circulating anticoagulants that leaves the circulating blood unable to clot. This allows profuse bleeding to occur from any vulnerable area, such as intravenous sites, incisions, or the gums or nose, as well as from expected sites such as the site of placental attachment during the postpartum period.

Laboratory studies are helpful to establish a diagnosis. Fibrinogen and platelets are usually decreased, prothrombin and partial thromboplastin time may be prolonged, fibrin degradation products (FDP), the most sensitive measurement, are increased.

The priority in treatment of DIC is delivery of the fetus and placenta so that the production of thromboplastin, which is fueling the process, is stopped. In addition, blood replacement products, such as whole blood, packed red blood cells, and cryoprecipitate, are administered to maintain the circulating volume and to transport oxygen to body cells.

✔ Check Your Reading

6. What are the signs and symptoms of placenta previa? What are the signs and symptoms of abruptio placentae?
7. What is the major danger to the expectant mother and the fetus during placental abruption?

Hemorrhagic Disorders of Late Pregnancy: Application of Nursing Process

Nurses are responsible for monitoring the condition of both the expectant mother and the fetus and for collaborating with the physician to provide treatment when the woman experiences hemorrhagic disorders of the placenta. This often involves preparing her for a surgical procedure or for delivery of a fetus that may or may not be mature.

Furthermore, nurses must be aware of the emotional responses of the client and her family to antepartum bleeding. They may not only fear for the life of the woman but may also grieve for the actual or anticipated loss of the unborn infant.

Assessment

Some nursing assessments should be performed immediately, and others can be deferred until initial measures have been taken to stabilize the cardiovascular status of the woman. The priority nursing assessments are:

- *Amount and nature of bleeding*. Time of onset, estimated loss before admission to hospital, and description of tissue or clots passed. Peripads and linen savers should be retained so that blood loss can be accurately estimated.
- *Pain*. Type (constant, intermittent, sharp, dull, severe); onset (sudden, gradual); location (generalized over abdomen, localized). Is the uterus tender to gentle palpation?
- *Maternal vital signs*. Within normal limits, deviation from baseline.
- *Condition of the fetus*. Application of an external monitor to determine fetal heart rate, baseline variability, and fetal response to uterine activity (late decelerations are of particular concern).
- *Uterine contractions*. Application of a tocotransducer to the fundus to determine uterine resting tone and frequency and duration of contractions. A high uterine resting tone and frequent, long contractions are associated with abruptio placentae.
- *Obstetrical history*. Gravida, para, previous abortions, preterm infants, previous pregnancy outcomes.
- *Length of gestation*. Date of last menstrual period, fundal height, correlation of fundal height with estimated gestation. *If there is bleeding into the myometrium, the fundus extends rapidly as bleeding progresses*. Some nurses use a piece of tape to mark the top of the fundus at a given time and then observe and report increasing fundal size, which indicates that bleeding into uterine muscles is occurring.
- *Laboratory data*. Hemoglobin, hematocrit, clotting factors, blood type, partial thromboplastin time, clotting time. Laboratory data are obtained to prepare for transfusions should they become necessary and to determine whether signs of DIC are developing.

Despite the emphasis on physical assessment, the emotional response of the expectant mother and her partner must also be noted. They will most likely be anxious, fearful, confused, and overwhelmed by the activity. They may have very little knowledge of expected medical management and may not realize that the fetus will need to be delivered as quickly as possible and that a surgical procedure is necessary. Moreover, they may fear for the life of the woman and the fetus.

Analysis

Nursing diagnoses vary, depending on the cause and severity of the bleeding. The most commonly used nursing diagnoses for antepartum bleeding appear in Nursing Care Plan 24–1. The most dangerous potential complication is: *Hypovolemic Shock*, which jeopardizes the life of the mother as well as the fetus.

Planning

Client-centered goals are inappropriate for the potential complication of hypovolemic shock because the nurse cannot independently manage this condition but must confer with physicians for medical orders for treatment. Planning should reflect the nurse's responsibility to:

- Monitor for signs of hypovolemic shock
- Consult with the physician if signs of hypovolemic shock are observed
- Perform actions that will minimize the effects of hypovolemic shock

Interventions

MONITORING FOR SIGNS OF HYPOVOLEMIC SHOCK

Assess bleeding from the vagina as well as from any surgical sites or puncture wounds (epidural or intra-

Nursing Care Plan 24–1

Antepartum Bleeding

Assessment: Bette Nayed, 25-year-old gravida iii, para ii, of 33 weeks' gestation is admitted to the antepartal unit following an episode of vaginal bleeding that has been diagnosed as total placenta previa. Vital signs are stable and fetal heart rate is 140 with good variability and accelerations with fetal activity. Bette and her husband, Tom, appear anxious, and they have many questions about how the bleeding affects Bette and the fetus and how long Bette will have to remain in the hospital.

Nursing Diagnosis: Anxiety related to unknown effects of bleeding and lack of knowledge of predicted course of management.

Goals:

1. The couple will verbalize expected routines and projected management by the end of the first day following admission.
2. The couple will relate less anxiety following teaching.

Intervention:	Rationale:
1. Remain with the couple and acknowledge the emotions that they exhibit: "I know this is unexpected and you must have many questions; perhaps I can answer some of them."	1. The nurse's presence and empathetic understanding are potent therapeutic tools to prepare the family to cope with the unexpected situation.
2. Determine the level of understanding of the situation and the projected management: "Tell me what you've been told to expect."	2. Allows the nurse to reinforce the physician's explanations and to notify the physician if additional explanations are necessary.
3. Provide the couple with factual information about projected management. a. Explain that Bette will need to remain in the hospital so that her condition and the condition of the fetus can be closely watched. b. Explain why a cesarean birth is necessary this time even though she delivered vaginally before. c. Provide information about hospital routines (meals, visiting hours) and monitoring techniques that will be used (electronic fetal monitoring, nonstress tests).	3. Patient education has proved to be an effective measure for preventing and reducing anxiety.
4. Allow Bette and her family to participate in the routine as much as possible. This may mean scheduling procedures around times when Tom and the children can visit.	4. Overcomes the feeling of powerlessness that many women feel when they are confined to bed and a course of treatment is prescribed without consultation.

Evaluation:
The interventions are judged to be successful if the couple demonstrates knowledge of the projected management and why it is necessary and verbalizes reduced anxiety.

Assessment: Bette has no further episodes of vaginal bleeding, and the fetus demonstrates no sign of distress; however, 3 days after admission, Bette is observed to be crying while she talks on the telephone with her children. She tells the nurse, "Things are just going to pieces at home and I'm so useless; I feel so guilty for not being there." The children are 6- and 7-year-old girls.

Nursing Diagnosis: Situational Low Self-Esteem related to temporary inability to provide care for family.

Nursing Care Plan 24–1 Continued

Antepartum Bleeding

Goals:

1. Bette will: Identify positive aspects of self during hospitalization.
2. Identify ways of providing comfort and affection for her children during the hospital stay.

Intervention:	Rationale:
1. Encourage Bette to express her concerns about the need for hospitalization: "What bothers you most about being away from the girls?"	1. Major concerns may not be identified or may be misunderstood unless they are clarified by the client.
2. After acknowledging feelings, encourage examination of the need for hospitalization and its consequences, that is, it provides time for the fetus to mature.	2. Assists Bette to identify positive aspects of the situation and her important role.
3. Explore reality of Bette's self-appraisal ("I'm so useless") by assisting her to investigate ways to provide nurturing care for her children while she is hospitalized: a. Making wake-up and goodnight telephone calls b. Writing daily cards or clipping pictures from magazines c. Making small hand-made items such as book marks or hair bands d. Helping with homework during daily visits	3. Daily involvement in the lives of the children helps Bette to reduce feelings of isolation and failure to meet obligations to her family.
4. Assist Bette to involve the children in plans for the newborn. The children might benefit from sibling classes or playtime with the mother that involves caring for dolls.	4. Provides goals for combined family interaction that increase Bette's feeling of self-worth.

Evaluation:
Bette is able to make positive comments about the importance of bed rest to the health of the fetus, and she initiates numerous activities that permit her to continue close, comforting contact with her children during the period of hospitalization.

Assessment: Eleven days after admission, Bette experiences a profuse episode of vaginal bleeding. Vital signs remain relatively stable, although the pulse rate is 110. The skin is warm and dry, and Bette is alert and frightened. The fetal heart rate remains at 140 without signs of distress. The physician is notified of the bleeding episode and is en route to the hospital to assess Bette's condition.

Potential Complication:
Hypovolemic shock.

Goals:
Client-centered goals are inappropriate for the potential complication of hypovolemic shock because the nurse cannot independently manage this condition but must confer with physicians for medical orders for treatment. Planning should reflect the nurse's responsibility to:

1. Monitor for signs of hypovolemic shock
2. Consult with the physician if signs of hypovolemic shock are observed
3. Perform actions that minimize the risk of hypovolemic shock

Nursing Care Plan continued on following page

Nursing Care Plan 24–1 *Continued*

Antepartum Bleeding

Intervention:	Rationale:
1. Monitor for signs and symptoms of shock: a. Increased pulse rate (may be due to blood loss or fear) b. Decreased peripheral pulses c. Decreased blood pressure d. Changes in skin temperature from warm and dry to cool or cold and clammy e. Increased respiratory rate f. Restlessness or agitation g. Urinary output less than 30 ml/hour	1. The compensatory response to decreased blood volume is to increase the heart and respiratory rates to provide oxygen to essential organs. Blood is shunted from peripheral vessels to essential organs such as the kidneys, liver, and brain, resulting in decreased peripheral pulses and changes in skin temperature and color. Decreased circulation to the brain results in altered mentation. Decreased circulation to the kidneys results in decreased urinary output.
2. Initiate a "pad count" and save all peripads, linen savers, or linen so that blood loss can be accurately estimated by weighing the items.	2. Visual estimation of blood loss is often inaccurate.
3. If not already initiated, begin continuous electronic fetal monitoring.	3. The fetus may experience hypoxia and exhibit signs of distress such as decreasing baseline variability or tachycardia.
 4. Insert intravenous lines and begin fluid replacement as directed by the physician.	4. Fluid replacement is one of the primary measures (along with controlling bleeding) for preventing hypovolemic shock.
 5. Prepare for cesarean delivery as directed by the physician: a. Abdominal preparation b. Insertion of indwelling catheter c. Validation that necessary permits are signed d. Validation that appropriate laboratory data are available (CBC, blood type and crossmatch, urinalysis) and that whole blood is available if needed	5. Prompt delivery by cesarean procedure is necessary to prevent fetal hypoxia and to prevent excessive blood loss from the mother.

Evaluation:
Although client-centered goals are not developed for potential complications, the nurse collects and compares data with established norms and then judges whether the data are within normal limits. For hypovolemic shock, vital signs remain near baseline, skin remains warm and dry, fetal heart rate remains between 120 and 160 with adequate variability, bleeding episode subsides.

Additional Nursing Diagnoses to Consider:
High Risk for Altered Family Processes
Fear
High Risk for Altered Parenting
Powerlessness

venous sites) so that uncontrolled bleeding or bleeding from unexpected sites, which may indicate DIC, can be reported to the physician for immediate, aggressive medical management.

Assess for any sign of developing hypovolemic shock. The body attempts to compensate for decreased blood volume and to maintain oxygenation of essential organs by increasing the rate and effort of the heart and lungs and by shunting blood from less essential organs, such as the skin and the extremities, to more essential organs, such as the brain and kidneys. This compensatory mechanism results in the early signs and symptoms of hypovolemic shock:

- Tachycardia, diminished peripheral pulses
- Normal or slightly decreased blood pressure
- Increased respiratory rate
- Cool, pale skin

The compensatory mechanism fails if hypovolemic shock progresses and there is insufficient blood to perfuse the brain and kidneys. Later signs of hypovolemic shock include:

- Falling blood pressure
- Pallor, skin becomes cold and clammy
- Urine output less than 30 ml/hour
- Restlessness, agitation, decreased mentation

MONITORING THE FETUS

If possible, initiate continuous electronic fetal monitoring so that signs of fetal distress, such as decreasing baseline variability or late deceleration, can be seen. If fetal distress is noted, contact the physician at once because the fetus sometimes experiences distress before maternal signs of hemorrhage or hypovolemia are obvious.

PROMOTING TISSUE OXYGENATION

To promote oxygenation of tissues:

- Place the woman in a lateral position, with the head of the bed lowered to increase cardiac return and thus to increase circulation and oxygenation of the placenta and other vital organs.
- Restrict maternal movements and activity to decrease the tissue demand for oxygen.
- Provide simple explanations, reassurance, and emotional support to the woman to help reduce anxiety, which increases the metabolic demand for oxygen.

COLLABORATING WITH PHYSICIAN FOR FLUID REPLACEMENT

To replace fluids:

- Obtain an order for blood typing and cross-matching so that whole blood is available for replacement if necessary.
- Insert intravenous lines according to hospital protocol; usually two lines that use large-bore catheters are recommended so that whole blood can be administered if necessary.
- Administer fluids for replacement as directed by the physician to maintain a urinary output of at least 30 ml/hour.

PREPARING FOR SURGERY

It may be necessary to prepare the client quickly for cesarean delivery. The nurse is responsible for:

- Surgical preparation and insertion of indwelling urinary catheter
- Validating that preoperative permits have been correctly signed
- Validating that appropriate laboratory work has been done
- Administering non-particulate antacid as ordered by the anesthesiologist
- Remaining with the woman and providing information and reassurance to the family (this is particularly important because the hurried activity and unusual procedures provoke fear and anxiety in the family)

PROVIDING EMOTIONAL SUPPORT

Once the safety of the woman and the fetus is assured, nursing interventions are aimed at promoting comfort and providing emotional support. Explain what is causing the discomfort, and reassure her that pain relief measures will be initiated as soon as possible without causing harm to the fetus. Although it is unwise to offer false reassurance about the condition of the fetus, it is important to remain with the client and to provide accurate and timely information.

Find time to explain what is going on to the woman and her family. They can feel overwhelmed by all of the activity and the sense of haste. When possible, allow time for the woman to express her feelings, which usually include fear about the condition of the fetus.

Evaluation

Although client-centered goals are not developed for collaborative problems, the nurse collects and compares data with established norms and judges whether the data are within normal limits. For hypovolemic shock, the maternal vital signs remain within normal limits and the fetal heart demonstrates no

Critical to Remember

Signs and Symptoms of Impending Hypovolemic Shock

- Increased pulse rate, falling blood pressure, increased respiratory rate
- Weak, diminished, or "thready" peripheral pulses
- Cool, moist skin, pallor or cyanosis (late sign)
- Decreased urinary output (<30 ml/hr)
- Decreased hemoglobin, hematocrit levels
- Change in mental status (restlessness, agitation, difficulty concentrating)

signs of compromise, such as late decelerations or decreasing baseline variability.

Hyperemesis Gravidarum

Hyperemesis gravidarum is a condition of persistent, uncontrollable vomiting that begins in the first weeks of pregnancy and may continue throughout pregnancy. Unlike so-called "morning sickness," which is self-limiting and causes no serious complications, hyperemesis gravidarum has serious consequences. It can lead to severe weight loss, dehydration, and electrolyte imbalance (both sodium and potassium are lost from gastric fluids). Metabolic alkalosis may develop because large amounts of hydrochloric acid are lost in the vomitus. If the intractable vomiting persists and the woman is unable to retain food, metabolic acidosis may develop as a result of starvation. This partially obscures the alkalosis of vomiting and can give rise to a mixed acid-base disorder.

Etiology

Although the cause of hyperemesis gravidarum is not known, some demographic factors have been studied. It is more common among unmarried, Caucasian women and during first pregnancies. For many years it was believed to be related to neurosis of the expectant mother. Women with infantile personalities or women who did not want to be pregnant were sometimes said to be experiencing unconscious rejection of the pregnancy by attempting to "throw up" or disgorge the pregnancy. Although it has not been investigated or confirmed by research, this false belief persists in the minds of some health care workers.

THERAPEUTIC MANAGEMENT

The priorities of management are to:

- Maintain hydration
- Replace electrolytes
- Maintain adequate nutrition
- Provide emotional support

Initial treatment occurs in the home, where the woman attempts to control the nausea by the palliative methods that are used for morning sickness (see Chapter 7). In addition, some physicians prescribe vitamins, such as pyridoxine (vitamin B_6), that may provide some relief. The use of antiemetic medications is controversial because reported fetal anomalies associated with them have been widely circulated; however, the evidence is in question, and some physicians elect to prescribe antiemetics when nausea does not respond to other management (Key, 1989).

If home treatment is unsuccessful and weight loss or electrolyte imbalance persists, the woman must be hospitalized for intravenous fluid and electrolyte replacement and/or hyperalimentation.

Hyperemesis Gravidarum: Application of Nursing Process

When the pregnant woman is admitted to the antepartum unit at the hospital for hyperemesis gravidarum, nursing is directed at monitoring her physical and psychological status and providing physical care and psychological support.

Assessment

Physical assessment focuses on determining the intake and output of the woman with excessive vomiting. Intake includes intravenous fluids and parenteral nutrition, which are administered, as well as oral nutrition, which is allowed once vomiting is controlled. Output includes the amount and character of emesis and urinary output. As a rule of thumb, the normal urinary output is about 1 ml/kg/hr (2.2 pounds) of body weight. A record of bowel elimination also provides significant information about oral nutrition.

Evaluate laboratory data to determine whether hemoglobin and hematocrit levels are elevated as a result of inability to retain fluid, which has resulted in hemoconcentration. Concentrations of sodium, potassium, and chloride may be reduced, resulting in hypokalemia and alkalosis.

For the woman with pernicious vomiting, weigh her daily and test her urine for ketones. Weight loss and presence of ketones in the urine suggest that fat stores and protein are being metabolized to meet energy needs.

Note signs of dehydration. These include decreased fluid intake ($<$2000 ml/day), decreased urinary output, increased specific gravity of urine ($>$1.025), dry skin or dry mucous membranes, and poor skin turgor.

Analysis

The major danger of hyperemesis gravidarum is that the woman will become dehydrated and no longer be able to provide the fetus with essential nutrients for growth. Prolonged hospitalization for this condition may result in the diagnoses of Situational Low Self-esteem or Diversional Activity Deficit. A commonly used nursing diagnosis is: *High Risk for Fluid Volume Deficit related to excessive fluid loss secondary to vomiting and decreased fluid intake.*

Planning

For this nursing diagnosis, the woman will:

- Remain free of signs of dehydration throughout pregnancy.
- Experience fewer episodes of vomiting each day.

Interventions

REDUCING NAUSEA AND VOMITING

When food is offered to the woman, keep portions small so that the amount does not appear overwhelming. Food should be attractively presented, and foods with strong odors should be eliminated from the diet because nausea is often associated with food smells.

Empty emesis basins at once, and keep them out of the woman's sight so that she is not constantly reminded of vomiting. Offer her favorite fluids in small amounts as directed by the physician.

MAINTAINING NUTRITION AND FLUID BALANCE

Administer intravenous fluids and total parenteral nutrition as directed by the physician. Small oral feedings of clear liquids are often begun within 1 to 2 days of admission. As oral fluids are tolerated, the diet is progressed to a soft diet and then to a regular diet as tolerated. As oral nutrition improves, parenteral nutrition is gradually discontinued. Report any inability to tolerate oral feedings or continued episodes of vomiting to the physician so that continued parenteral fluids and nutrition are prescribed.

PROVIDING EMOTIONAL SUPPORT

There is often a curious lack of sympathy and support for the woman who experiences hyperemesis gravidarum. The underlying reason for this is obscure; however, it may be because the reported cause has been termed psychogenic. Whatever the cause, nurses must examine their own beliefs and biases so that they can provide comfort and support, which are essential. It may be necessary to have case conferences or inservice educational programs to overcome pre-set beliefs and to establish a level of care that meets the needs of the client.

The woman with hyperemesis gravidarum needs the opportunity to express how it feels to be pregnant and to live with ever-present nausea. At times, counseling may be necessary to help her decide whether to terminate the pregnancy or allow it to progress to term.

Evaluation

Interventions have been successful in the following situations:

- Absence of signs of dehydration indicates that fluid intake and output are in balance.
- Fewer episodes of vomiting suggest that progress is being made in reducing nausea.

✔ Check Your Reading

8. How do "morning sickness" and hyperemesis gravidarum compare in terms of onset, duration, and effect on the client?
9. How can either metabolic alkalosis or metabolic acidosis develop as a result of hyperemesis gravidarum?

Hypertensive Disorders of Pregnancy

Hypertension, along with hemorrhage and infection, is one of the leading causes of maternal and neonatal death in the United States.

Classification

The classification of hypertensive disorders is confusing and necessitates definition of six forms of pregnancy-related hypertension, including pregnancy-induced hypertension (PIH), which includes pre-eclampsia and eclampsia. The classification system recommended by the American College of Obstetricians and Gynecologists is outlined in Table 24–2. In clinical practice, the terms pregnancy-induced hypertension and pre-eclampsia are often used interchangeably.

PREGNANCY-INDUCED HYPERTENSION

PIH usually develops in the third trimester and usually recedes within 48 hours after the birth of the

Table 24–2. CLASSIFICATIONS OF HYPERTENSIVE DISORDERS OF PREGNANCY

Pregnancy-induced hypertension (PIH)	Development of hypertension (BP >140/90 during second half of pregnancy in previously normotensive woman)
Pre-eclampsia	Type of PIH accompanied by proteinuria and edema
Eclampsia	Pre-eclampsia that progresses to include maternal convulsions
Chronic hypertension	Hypertension present prior to 20th week of gestation
Pre-eclampsia superimposed on chronic hypertension	Increase in pre-existing hypertension with proteinuria or generalized edema
Transient hypertension	Development of elevated blood pressure during pregnancy without additional signs of proteinuria or edema

fetus. The only known cure is delivery of the fetus; however, if the fetus is immature, this may not be practical. Although the disease cannot be cured, it can be controlled if detected early and managed carefully.

At one time, the entire pathological process of PIH was referred to as *toxemia* because it was believed to be caused by a toxin that resulted from pregnancy, and this word is still used occasionally.

Incidence and Risk Factors

PIH is relatively common. Seven per cent of all pregnancies that progress to the second trimester are affected (Roberts, 1989). It is the major cause of perinatal mortality, and it is often associated with intrauterine fetal growth retardation. (See Chapter 28 for additional information on fetal growth retardation.)

Although the cause of PIH is not understood, several factors have been identified that are known to increase a woman's risk that the condition will develop. It is much more common in the first pregnancy, and it is more common in adolescents and women over the age of 35 years. A family history of PIH increases the risk, as do diabetes mellitus and multifetal pregnancy. There is a higher incidence among poor women; this may be related to a diet that is deficient in protein or to inadequate prenatal care. There is a strong correlation between eclampsia (severe disease that includes convulsions) and lower socioeconomic status. This suggests that the disease may not be diagnosed until it is far advanced in women who do not have early prenatal care. Race has also been identified as a factor, with non-Caucasians at a much higher risk. However, these data are difficult to interpret because they may reflect economic factors rather than a predisposition of non-Caucasian races for development of the disease.

PIH is sometimes considered an autoimmune disease, and immunoglobulins have been identified in tissue of affected women. This discovery provides one of the most promising research frontiers for finding the direct cause of PIH. See Table 24–3 for a summary of factors that increase the risk of PIH.

Pathophysiology

PIH is due to generalized vasospasm. The underlying cause of the vasospasm remains a mystery; however, some of the physiological processes are known. In normal pregnancy, there is a significant increase in vascular volume as well as increased production of renin, which is ultimately involved in the production of angiotensin II, a powerful vasoconstrictor. Despite these factors, blood pressure does not rise in normal pregnancy because pregnant women develop a resistance to the effects of angiotensin II. This is probably due to the effects of certain prostaglandins that act as vasodilators. As a result, in normal pregnancy, peripheral vascular resistance decreases and blood pressure remains normal.

However, in PIH, total peripheral vascular resistance increases. This is believed to be due to increased sensitivity of some women to angiotensin II as well as due to a decrease in vasodilators, such as prostaglandin PGE_2 and prostacyclin, and an increase in vasoconstrictors, such as thromboxane.

Vasospasms decrease the diameter of blood vessels, which results in endothelial cell damage, impeded blood flow, and elevated blood pressure. As a result, circulation to all body organs, including the kidneys, liver, brain, and placenta, is decreased. The following changes are most significant:

1. Decreased renal perfusion causes decreased glomerular filtration rate; consequently, blood urea

Table 24–3. RISK FACTORS FOR PREGNANCY-INDUCED HYPERTENSION

First pregnancy
Non-Caucasian
Younger than 18 years of age, older than 35 years of age
Multiple gestation
Lower socioeconomic status
Poor diet
Inadequate or late prenatal care
Diabetes mellitus
Underlying (chronic) hypertension
Hydatidiform mole
Family history (mother or sister) of PIH

nitrogen, creatinine, and uric acid levels begin to rise.

Reduced blood flow to the kidneys also results in glomerular damage, which allows protein to leak across the glomerular membrane, which is usually impermeable to large protein molecules. This reduces colloid osmotic pressure and allows fluid to shift to interstitial spaces. This results in edema and relative hypovolemia, which causes increased viscosity of the blood and a rise in hematocrit. In response to hypovolemia, additional angiotensin II and aldosterone are secreted to trigger the retention of both sodium and water. It is obvious that the pathological processes spiral: additional angiotensin II results in further vasospasm and hypertension; aldosterone increases fluid retention, and edema is worsened.

2. Decreased circulation to the liver leads to impaired liver function as well as to hepatic edema and subcapsular hemorrhage, which can result in hemorrhagic necrosis. This is manifested by elevation of liver enzymes in maternal serum.

3. Decreased perfusion to the brain leads to cerebral edema and small cerebral hemorrhages. Symptoms of arterial vasospasms and cerebral edema include headache and visual disturbances, such as blurred vision and "spots" before the eyes.

4. Decreased placental circulation has serious consequences. Placental ischemia results in infarctions that increase the risk of abruptio placentae and DIC. In addition, when maternal blood flow through the placenta is decreased, the fetus is likely to experience intrauterine growth retardation and persistent fetal hypoxemia, which can result in fetal acidosis, mental retardation, or death. See Figure 24–7 for a summary of the pathological processes of PIH.

Preventive Measures

In recent years, low doses of aspirin (40 to 100 mg/day) have been suggested as a means to prevent the

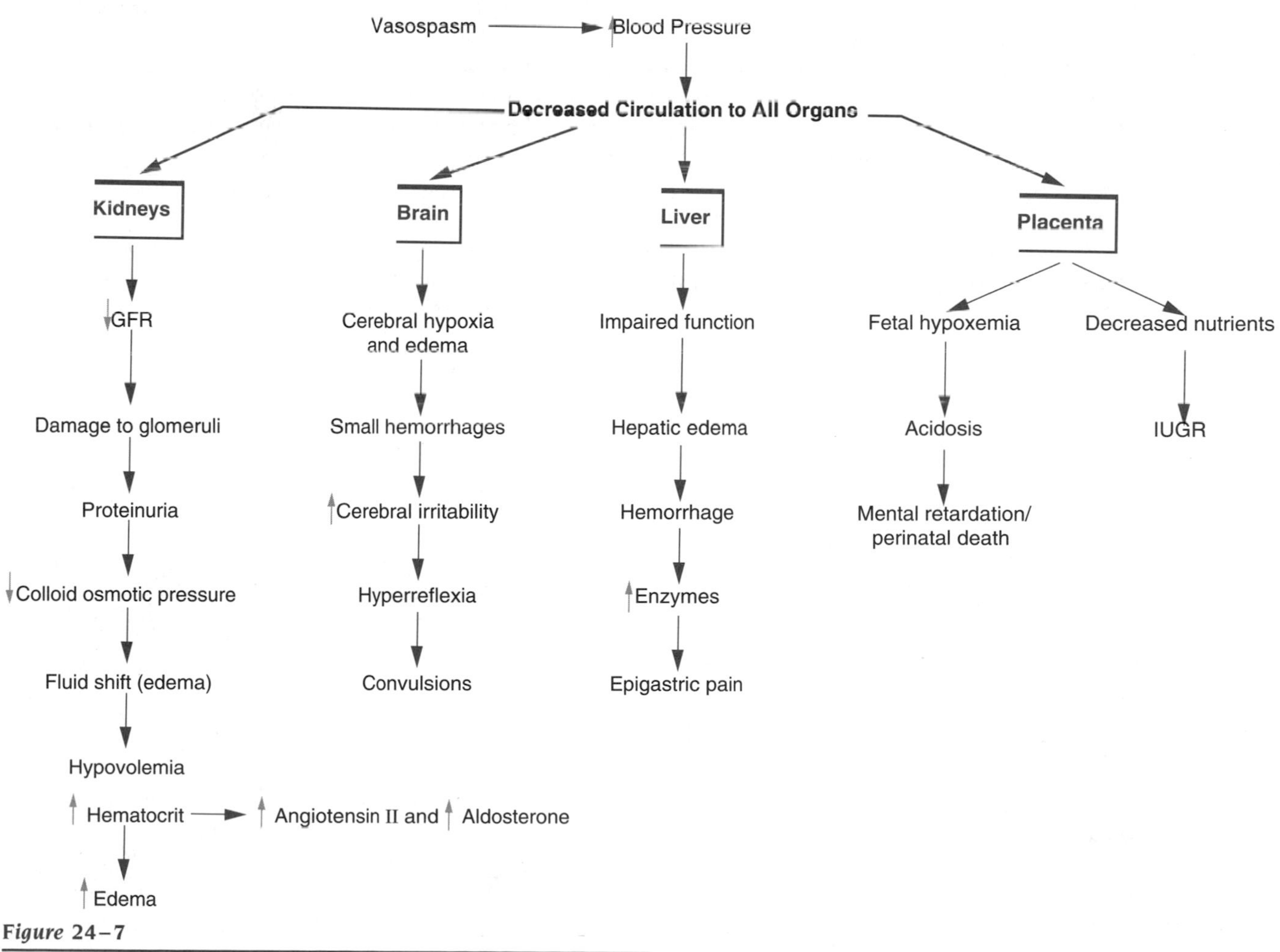

Figure 24–7

The pathological processes of pregnancy-induced hypertension.

development of PIH (Repke, 1991). The rationale for aspirin therapy is that it helps to prevent injury to endothelial cells that line the blood vessels and thus reduces an aggregation of platelets. In addition, aspirin suppresses synthesis of thromboxane, a potent vasoconstrictor.

Another method that has been suggested for the possible prevention of PIH is dietary calcium supplementation. Some evidence suggests that women who receive calcium supplementation are less sensitive to the pressor effects of angiotensin II and have a lower overall incidence of hypertension (Repke, 1991).

Clinical Manifestations of Pre-eclampsia

Classic Signs. When hypertension is accompanied by generalized edema and proteinuria, the disease is termed pre-eclampsia. The first indication of pre-eclampsia is usually hypertension; however, the first sign that the pregnant woman may notice is a rapid weight gain, which is due to fluid retention and consequent generalized edema. Edema is obvious not only in the lower legs, as is common in pregnancy, but also in the hands and face (Fig. 24–8).

Blood pressure equal to or above 140/90 indicates hypertension whether or not the baseline blood pressure is known. If the baseline is known, an elevation of 30 mmHg in systolic pressure or 15 mmHg in diastolic pressure indicates hypertension. Thus, if the baseline pressure is 100/60 and there is an elevation to 130/75, hypertension might be diagnosed if two blood pressure readings, taken at least 6 hours apart, are abnormal.

Because of the potential errors associated with determination of blood pressure, it is recommended that blood pressure be taken in the sitting position and that the fifth Korotkoff sound (disappearance) be used for determining diastolic pressure (Brinkman, 1992).

It is necessary to obtain a clean-catch or catheterized urine specimen to avoid contamination of the specimen by vaginal discharge. Proteinuria usually develops later than hypertension and edema, and the combination of proteinuria and hypertension increases the possibility of fetal jeopardy.

Additional Signs. Careful assessment may reveal additional signs of pre-eclampsia. For instance, when the retina is examined, vascular constriction and narrowing of the small arteries are obvious in a majority of clients. It is important to realize that the vasoconstriction that can be seen in the retina is occurring throughout the body. If deep tendon reflexes are elicited, they may be very brisk (hyperreflexia). This suggests cerebral irritability secondary to decreased circulation and edema.

Symptoms. Pre-eclampsia is particularly dangerous for the expectant mother and fetus for two reasons: (1) it develops and progresses rapidly and (2) the early signs are not noticed by the woman. By the time she experiences symptoms, the disease has progressed to an advanced state and valuable treatment time has been lost.

Certain symptoms, such as continuous headache, drowsiness, or mental confusion, indicate poor cerebral perfusion and may be precursors of convulsions. Visual disturbances, such as blurred or double vision or spots before the eyes, indicate arterial spasms

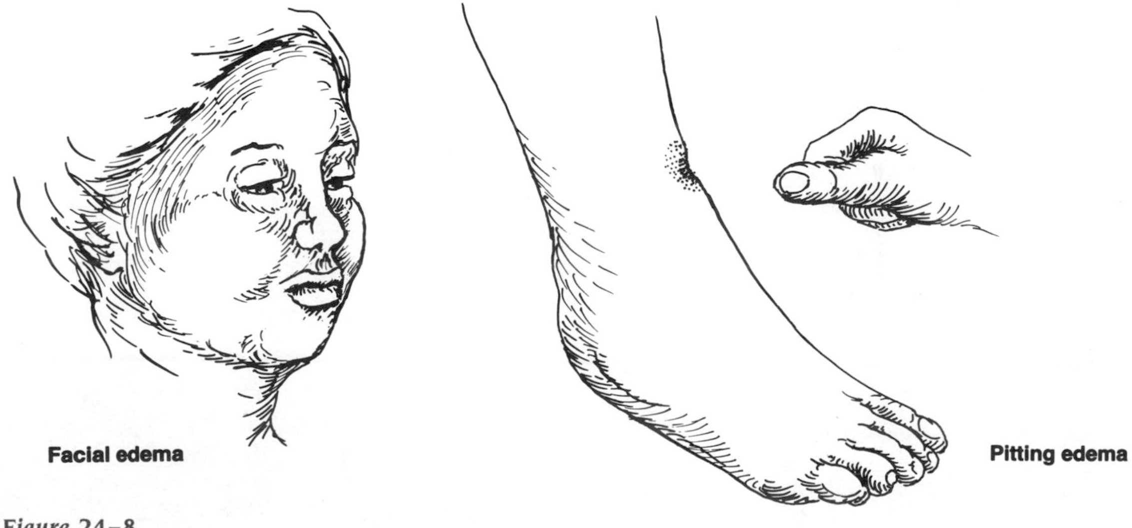

Figure 24–8

Generalized edema is a classic sign of pre-eclampsia.

and edema in the retina. Numbness or tingling of the hands or feet occurs when nerves are compressed by retained fluid. Some symptoms, such as epigastric pain or "upset stomach," are particularly ominous because they indicate distention of the hepatic capsule and often warn that a convulsion is imminent. Decreased urinary output indicates poor perfusion of the kidneys and may precipitate acute renal failure.

Mild Versus Severe Pre-eclampsia

Pre-eclampsia continues to be categorized as either mild or severe, depending on the frequency and intensity of presenting signs and symptoms. However, the disease may progress rapidly, and an apparently mild condition can become severe in a very short time. Pre-eclampsia is considered mild when the diastolic blood pressure is under 100 mmHg, proteinuria is trace to 1 +, and there are no symptoms (headache, visual disturbances, abdominal pain). In addition, signs of kidney or liver involvement are absent, and the fetus demonstrates normal growth.

The disease is considered severe when diastolic blood pressure is above 110 mmHg, proteinuria is 2 + or more, and the client reports symptoms that were absent in the mild form of the disease. If laboratory findings indicate liver involvement (elevated enzymes or hyperbilirubinemia) or kidney damage (elevated creatinine), the disease is judged to be severe. See Table 24–4 for a comparison of mild and severe pre-eclampsia.

Therapeutic Management of Mild Pre-eclampsia. Home management may be possible for selected women if the condition is mild, although many physicians are wary about home management for any woman with signs of pre-eclampsia. Management includes restricting the expectant mother's activity, providing an adequate diet, and checking fetal movements.

Table 24–4. MILD VERSUS SEVERE PRE-ECLAMPSIA

	Mild	Severe
Diastolic blood pressure	<100 mmHg	>110 mmHg
Proteinuria	Trace to 1+ (<5 g/24 hr)	>2+ (>6 g/24 hr)
Headache	Absent	Present
Visual disturbances	Absent	Present
Urinary output	>30 ml/hr	<30 ml/hr
Fetal growth	At expected level	Below expected level
Liver enzymes	Normal	Elevated
Creatinine	Normal	Elevated

Maternal Restrictions. Bed rest is prescribed with bathroom privileges only. The expectant mother is instructed to rest in the left lateral position as much as possible. This position decreases pressure on the vena cava, thereby increasing cardiac return and circulatory volume and thus improving perfusion of vital organs. Increased renal perfusion decreases angiotensin II levels, promotes diuresis, and lowers the blood pressure. The woman is advised to remain quiet and calm. This may involve restricting visitors or telephone calls that cause agitation.

Diet. A diet that is moderate to high in protein (1.5 g/kg) is recommended to replace protein that is lost in the urine. A diet that contains adequate fiber and fluid helps to maintain hydration and prevent constipation, which can become a problem owing to restricted activity.

In the past, sodium was restricted to decrease fluid retention; however, this is no longer believed to be beneficial, and the woman is advised to eat a well-balanced diet that contains adequate sodium but to avoid foods that are very high in sodium, such as chips, pickles, and canned foods. Diuretics are no longer recommended for treating edema associated with PIH because they may cause increased loss of intravascular volume, which is already deficient as a result of escape of intravascular fluid to interstitial spaces.

Fetal Activity. While home management is in effect, the expectant mother is asked to keep a record of fetal movements, commonly called a "kick count." She is asked to count the number of times the fetus moves in a 60-minute period, three times a day. If there is no movement in one 60-minute period, she should wait for 1 hour and begin the count again. No movement during the second counting period should be reported at once. No movement during any 4-hour period or a decrease in the number of movements should be reported as well.

Weekly non-stress testing of the fetus should begin at 30 to 32 weeks' gestation to observe for fetal compromise. If the non-stress test indicates that there is no fetal compromise, the test is repeated in 1 week. If the test indicates the possibility of fetal compromise, additional tests, such as a contraction stress test or biophysical profile, are prescribed by the physician. If not already hospitalized, the mother will be admitted for continuous monitoring of her condition and the condition of the fetus. (See Chapter 10 for a complete description of antepartal tests.)

Therapeutic Management of Severe Pre-eclampsia. Goals of management are to prevent convulsions and to maintain the pregnancy until it is safe to deliver the fetus. Hospitalization is necessary if pre-eclampsia does not respond to home management.

Bed Rest. As during home management, the hospitalized woman is kept on bed rest and her environment is kept quiet. External stimuli (lights, noise) that might precipitate a convulsion should be reduced.

Diet. A diet that supplies adequate calories, protein, fluids, and sodium is essential. Foods that are excessively high in salt should be avoided.

Antihypertensive Medications. Blood pressure control does not improve fetal oxygenation, and thus the use of antihypertensives is usually reserved for severe hypertension when there is the possibility of intracranial bleeding (Roberts, 1989). When necessary, hydralazine (Apresoline, Neopresol) is the antihypertensive most often used to control blood pressure (see Drug Guide on hydralazine for additional information).

Sedatives. Sedatives such as phenobarbital or diazepam (Valium) are sometimes used to encourage quiet bed rest. However, they are not helpful in preventing convulsions, and many physicians are reluctant to administer barbiturates that cross the placental barrier; prolonged use may result in fetal addiction (Deglin and Vallerand, 1993).

Anticonvulsants. In the United States, magnesium sulfate ($MgSO_4$) is the drug of choice to prevent convulsions; however, phenytoin (Dilantin, Diphenylan) is occasionally used. Magnesium acts as a central nervous system depressant by blocking neuromuscular transmission and decreasing the amount of acetylcholine liberated. Magnesium is not an antihypertensive medication, but it relaxes smooth muscle and thus reduces vasoconstriction. Decreased vasoconstriction promotes circulation to the vital organs of the expectant mother and increases placental circulation. Increased circulation to the maternal kidneys leads to diuresis, as interstitial fluid is shifted into the vascular compartment and excreted.

One of the major advantages of magnesium is that it can safely be used to prevent convulsions without harming the fetus or neonate. Fetal magnesium levels are nearly identical with those of the expectant mother. There is not a cumulative effect because the fetal kidneys effectively excrete magnesium (Roberts, 1989).

Significant adverse reactions and side effects are associated with parenteral administration of magnesium. The most important is central nervous system depression, including depression of the respiratory center. It must also be remembered that magnesium is excreted solely by the kidneys, and administration of parenteral magnesium depends on kidneys that function effectively.

Drug Guide

HYDRALAZINE (Apresoline, Alazine, Dralzine)

Classification: Antihypertensive.

Action: Relaxes arterial smooth muscle to reduce blood pressure.

Indications: Used in obstetrics to lower blood pressure in severe pregnancy-induced hypertension or pre-eclampsia when blood pressure is elevated to a degree that might be associated with intracranial bleeding.

Dosage and Route: For obstetrical use, 10 to 50 mg is administered intramuscularly. Following a test dose to determine hypotensive effects, 5 to 25 mg may be administered by intravenous bolus infusion. Interval between doses should be 3 to 6 hours.

Absorption: Well absorbed from intramuscular sites. Widely distributed, crosses the placenta; enters breast milk in minimal concentrations.

Excretion: Metabolized and excreted by the liver.

Contraindications and Precautions: Contraindicated in coronary artery disease, cerebrovascular disease, and hypersensitivity to hydralazine. Used cautiously in obstetrics because safety during pregnancy and lactation has not been established.

Adverse Reactions: Headache, dizziness, drowsiness, hypotension that can interfere with uterine blood flow, epigastric pain, which may be confused with worsening pre-eclampsia.

Nursing Implications: Obstetrical clients are hospitalized prior to initiation of hypertensive medications. Blood pressure and pulse must be monitored every 2 to 3 minutes for 30 minutes after initial dosage and periodically throughout the course of therapy. Therapy is repeated only when diastolic pressure exceeds limits set by physician or facility protocol (usually >110 mmHg).

Magnesium is generally administered by intravenous infusion, which allows for immediate onset of action and avoids the discomfort associated with intramuscular administration. Intravenous magnesium is administered via a secondary line ("piggyback" line) so that the medication can be discontinued at any time while the primary line remains open and functional. See Drug Guide on magnesium sulfate for additional information.

Therapeutic Management of Eclampsia

Eclampsia is marked by a tonic-clonic convulsion that may be preceded by facial twitching that lasts a

Drug Guide

MAGNESIUM SULFATE

Classification: Miscellaneous anticonvulsant.

Action: Decreases acetylcholine released by motor nerve impulses, thereby blocking neuromuscular transmission. Depresses the central nervous system to act as an anticonvulsant; also decreases frequency and intensity of uterine contractions. Produces flushing and sweating due to decreased peripheral blood pressure.

Indications: Prevention and control of seizures in severe pre-eclampsia. Prevention of uterine contractions in preterm labor.

Dosage and Route: Two regimens are used extensively; 2 to 4 g loading dose is administered intravenously over 15 minutes, with 10 g administered intramuscularly at the same time. Intravenous magnesium results in an immediate elevation of serum magnesium, which falls rapidly, and the absorption of intramuscular magnesium keeps a relatively constant level.

A second regimen is to administer 2 to 4 g of magnesium intravenously over 15 minutes, followed by a controlled continuous infusion of 1 to 2 g/hour by constant infusion pump in piggyback fashion.

Absorption: Immediate onset following intravenous route, within 1 to 2 hours if given intramuscularly. Duration of action is 3 to 4 hours.

Excretion: Excreted by the kidneys.

Contraindications and Precautions: Contraindicated in persons with myocardial damage, heart block, or impaired renal function.

Adverse Reactions: Result from magnesium overdose and include flushing, sweating, hypotension, depressed deep tendon reflexes, central nervous system depression, including respiratory depression.

Nursing Implications: Monitor blood pressure closely during administration. Assess client for respiratory rate above 12/minute, presence of deep tendon reflexes, and urinary output greater than 30 ml/hour before administering magnesium. Place resuscitation equipment (suction, oxygen) in the room. Keep calcium gluconate, which acts as an antidote to magnesium, in the room along with syringes and needles.

---

few seconds. The tonic phase refers to prolonged contraction of the muscles of the entire body, and it generally lasts about 20 seconds. The clonic phase of the convulsion refers to alternate contraction and relaxation of the muscles, which generally lasts about a minute. An eclamptic seizure is an emergency that is associated with cerebral hemorrhage, premature separation of the placenta, and severe fetal hypoxia. Uterine irritability often follows and results in premature rupture of membranes or onset of labor.

Magnesium may be given intravenously to control the convulsions. Sedatives such as phenobarbital or diazepam are used only if magnesium fails to bring the seizures under control. Sedatives should not be given if birth is expected within an hour or two because of their depressant effects on the fetus.

Pulmonary edema, circulatory or renal failure, and cerebral hemorrhage are complications that may occur with eclampsia. The woman's lungs should be auscultated frequently, and furosemide (Lasix) may be administered if pulmonary edema develops. Digitalis may be needed to strengthen the heart beat if circulatory failure results. Urine output should be assessed hourly; if output drops below 30 ml/hour, renal failure should be suspected.

The woman should be carefully monitored for ruptured membranes, signs of labor, or abruptio placentae because eclampsia stimulates uterine irritability. While the woman is comatose, she should be kept on her side to prevent aspiration and to improve placental circulation. The side rails should be kept up to prevent a fall and possible injury. When vital signs have stabilized, delivery of the fetus should be considered.

Intrapartum Management. The majority of seizures occur during labor and the postpartum period (Roberts, 1989), suggesting that these are the times when continued assessment and therapy are most important. During labor, the fetus as well as the expectant mother must be continuously monitored to detect signs of imminent convulsions. The woman should be kept in a lateral position to promote circulation through the placenta, and efforts should be focused on controlling pain that may cause agitation and precipitate seizures.

Induction of labor by intravenous oxytocin is often planned once the fetus is mature. Oxytocin to stimulate uterine contractions and magnesium sulfate to prevent convulsions are often administered simultaneously during labor. Infusion pumps should be used to ensure that the medications are administered at the prescribed rate, and equipment and intravenous lines should be carefully checked for correct placement and function.

Narcotic analgesics are sometimes administered, and epidural anesthesia may be administered to provide comfort and to reduce painful stimuli that could precipitate a convulsion.

Continuous fetal electronic monitoring is necessary to determine any change in fetal heart activity that could indicate fetal hypoxia. Oxygen is administered to the expectant mother if fetal compromise is noted.

A pediatrician, neonatologist, or neonatal nurse practitioner must be available to care for the newborn at birth.

Postpartum Management. Following delivery, careful assessment of blood loss and signs of shock are essential because the hypovolemia caused by PIH may be aggravated by blood loss during the delivery. Assessments for signs and symptoms of PIH must be continued for at least 48 hours, and magnesium may be continued to prevent seizures.

Signs that the patient is recovering from PIH are:

- Urinary output of 4 to 6 L/day, which causes a rapid reduction in edema and rapid weight loss
- Decreased protein in the urine
- Return of blood pressure to normal, usually within 2 weeks

✔ Check Your Reading

10. What are the effects of vasospasm on the fetus?
11. Why is bed rest recommended for management of PIH?
12. What is the effect of vasospasm on the brain?
13. What are the effects of magnesium sulfate, including the primary adverse effect?

HELLP SYNDROME

The acronym HELLP (*h*emolysis, *e*levated liver enzymes, *l*ow *p*latelets) is used to identify a potentially life-threatening complication or variation of PIH. Hemolysis is believed to occur as a result of the fragmentation and distortion of erythrocytes during passage through small damaged blood vessels. Elevated liver enzymes occur when hepatic blood flow is obstructed by fibrin deposits. Hyperbilirubinemia and jaundice may also be observed. Low platelets are due to vascular damage resulting from vasospasm; platelets aggregate at sites of damage, resulting in thrombocytopenia.

Signs and symptoms of HELLP syndrome include right upper quadrant pain and tenderness due to liver distention. Additional signs include nausea, vomiting, and severe edema. Laboratory data include irregular, damaged red blood cells, progressive anemia, thrombocytopenia, and elevated liver enzymes.

The syndrome is associated with poor maternal and perinatal outcomes. The maternal mortality rate ranges from 0 to 24 per cent, and the perinatal mortality rate from 7.7 to 60 per cent (Sibai, 1990).

Treatment includes hospitalization with strict bed rest, administration of volume expanders, and antithrombic medications.

CHRONIC HYPERTENSION

Chronic hypertension indicates that the woman's blood pressure was elevated to 140/90 before pregnancy, and the condition persists during pregnancy. Treatment is aimed at preventing pre-eclampsia or eclampsia. The woman is evaluated at least every 2 weeks, and ultrasound examination is performed frequently to detect intrauterine growth retardation of the fetus.

A high-protein diet with adequate but not excessive salt is recommended, and the woman is advised to weigh herself every 3 days to detect abnormal weight gain. Antihypertensive medication should be continued if already in use. If not in use, antihypertensive medication should be initiated once the diastolic pressure is consistently higher than 90 mmHg (Brinkman, 1992). The choice of antihypertensive medication is of great concern because of the possible teratogenic effects of these medications. Alpha-methyldopa (Aldomet) is one of the most commonly prescribed antihypertensives during pregnancy, and long-term follow-up evaluations of children whose mothers took alpha-methyldopa indicate no signs of teratogenic effects (Roberts, 1989).

✔ Check Your Reading

14. What do the initials HELLP stand for?
15. Compare pregnancy-induced hypertension with chronic hypertension in terms of onset.

Pregnancy-Induced Hypertension: Application of Nursing Process

Assessment

PRENATAL ASSESSMENT

Successful management depends on early identification of PIH. Assess all expectant women at each prenatal visit for signs and symptoms of the disease. Although the assessments may seem routine to the client, a check of weight gain, blood pressure, and urinalysis provides the basic information. Sudden weight gain of more than 1.4 kg (3 pounds) per month in the second trimester or 0.5 kg (1 pound) per week in the third trimester is considered excessive and may indicate fluid retention.

Check the woman for edema. Dependent edema, that is, of the feet and lower legs, is a common finding in normal pregnancy. However, edema of the hands or face (of the eyelids and cheekbone area) or pitting edema must be carefully evaluated. Pitting edema occurs when fluid moves to adjacent tissue and away from the point of pressure, creating a small pit. The pit usually disappears within 15 to 30 seconds.

Blood pressure elevation of 30 mmHg systolic or

15 mmHg diastolic or a reading of 140/90 or higher indicates hypertension.

Obtain a clean-voided midstream urine specimen, and check with standard dipstick for urinary protein. Concentrations greater than 1 + on two or more occasions at least 6 hours apart indicate proteinuria. Proteinuria is often the last of the triad of signs (hypertension, edema/weight gain, proteinuria) to appear, and it may be the most ominous sign of pre-eclampsia.

Further assessment focuses on the symptoms that may be present. Ask the woman to describe headaches, visual problems, or abdominal discomfort. Funduscopic examination of the retina may confirm vasoconstriction. Laboratory data, such as a complete blood count, liver enzymes (SGOT, SGPT), blood chemistry (blood urea nitrogen, creatinine, and glucose), and clotting studies (prothrombin time, partial thromboplastin time, platelets), may indicate clotting disorders, liver damage, or renal impairment.

ASSESSMENT OF HOSPITALIZED CLIENT

Nursing assessment is one of the most important components of successful management of PIH. Assess the client to determine whether the condition is responding to medical management or whether the disease is worsening. Many hospitals assign nurses to clients on a "one-to-one" basis or admit the woman to the antepartal intensive care unit.

Weigh the client on admission and daily after that. Insert an indwelling catheter, and monitor urinary output hourly. Check urine for protein every 4 hours. Assess vital signs, and the location and severity of edema, at least every 4 hours. The amount of edema is difficult to determine; however, Table 24–5 provides a useful method for describing edema.

Table 24–5. ASSESSMENT OF EDEMA

Minimal edema of lower extremities:	+1
Marked edema of lower extremities:	+2
Edema of lower extremities, face, hands, and sacral area:	+3
Generalized massive edema that includes ascites (accumulation of fluid in peritoneal cavity):	+4

Auscultate the chest for moist breath sounds that are indicative of pulmonary edema. Monitor fetal heart rate continuously if intravenous magnesium is infusing. Assess and document levels of consciousness (alert, drowsy, confused, oriented). Question the client carefully about symptoms that she may be experiencing. An open-ended question such as "How do you feel?" may not be adequate, and detailed questions should follow if the woman states that she feels "fine." Ask targeted questions, such as: "Do you have a headache? Describe it for me." "Do you have any pain in the abdomen? Show me where it is and describe it." "Do you see spots before your eyes? Flashes of light? Double vision?" "Is your vision blurred?" "I see you have removed your rings, did you do that because your hands were swollen? When was that?" See Table 24–6 for a summary of nursing assessments.

Assess the woman also for evidence of hyperreflexia in the brachial and patellar tendons, which

Table 24–6. NURSING ASSESSMENTS FOR PREGNANCY-INDUCED HYPERTENSION

Assessment	Implications
Daily weight	Provides estimate of fluid retention
Blood pressure	To determine response to treatment
Respiratory rate	Drug therapy ($MgSO_4$) causes respiratory depression, and drug should be held if respiratory rate is $<$12/minute
Breath sounds	To detect onset of pulmonary edema
Deep tendon reflexes	Hyperreflexia indicates increased cerebral edema; hyporeflexia indicates magnesium excess
Edema	For estimation of interstitial fluid
Urinary output	More than 30 ml/hr indicates adequate perfusion of the kidneys
Level of consciousness	Drowsiness, dulled sensorium indicate therapeutic effects of magnesium; non-responsive behavior or muscle weakness indicates magnesium excess
Headache, epigastric pain, visual problems	Indicate increasing severity of condition and development of eclampsia
Fetal heart rate and baseline variability	Rate should be between 120 and 160; decreasing baseline variability may be due to magnesium or to continuous fetal hypoxemia and fetal distress
Laboratory data	Elevated serum creatinine, elevated liver enzymes, or decreased platelets (thrombocytopenia) are significant signs of increasing severity of disease; serum magnesium levels should be in therapeutic range designated by physician

Procedure 24–1 Assessing Deep Tendon Reflexes

Purpose: To determine if there are exaggerated reflexes (hyperreflexia) or diminished reflexes (hyporeflexia).

Assess both the biceps and the quadriceps reflex, plus clonus. Equipment: reflex hammer.

1. **To assess the biceps reflex, support the woman's arm and instruct her to let it go totally limp while it is being held.** *This position partially relaxes and partially flexes the person's arm.*

2. **Place the thumb over the tendon, as illustrated, and strike the thumb with the small end of the reflex hammer. The normal response is slight flexion of the forearm.** *The tendon response can be felt as well as seen when the tendon is tapped.*

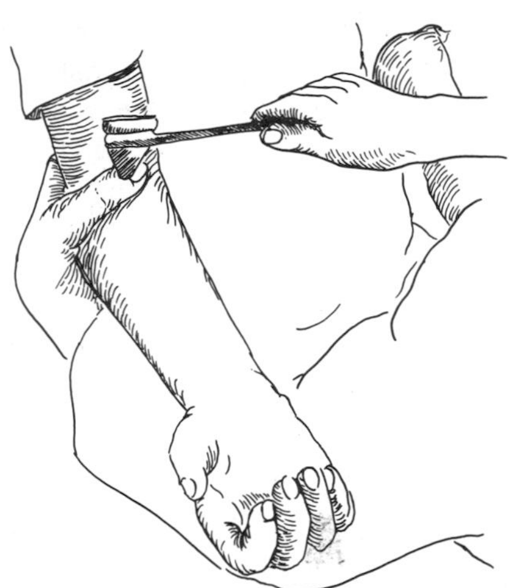

3. **The quadriceps reflex can be assessed in two positions—sitting or lying. When the woman is sitting, allow the lower legs to dangle freely to flex the knee and stretch the tendons. Strike the tendon with the reflex hammer just below the patella.** *To determine deep tendon reflexes in the lower extremities when the person is sitting.*

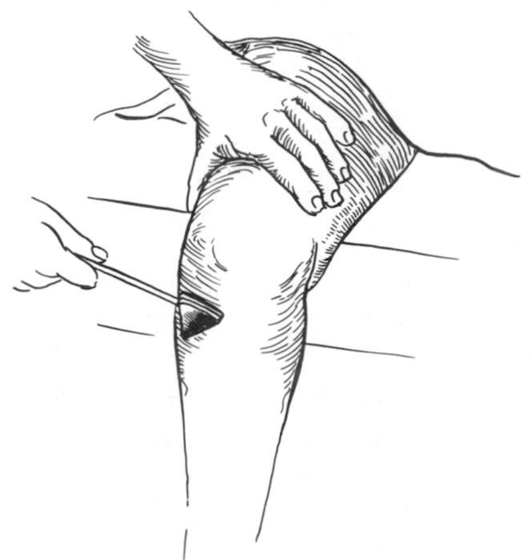

4. **When the woman is in the supine position, the weight of the leg must be supported to flex the knee and stretch the tendons. Strike the partially stretched tendons just below the patella. Extension of the leg is the expected response.** *It is necessary to support the leg because an adequate response requires that the limb be relaxed and the muscle partially stretched.*

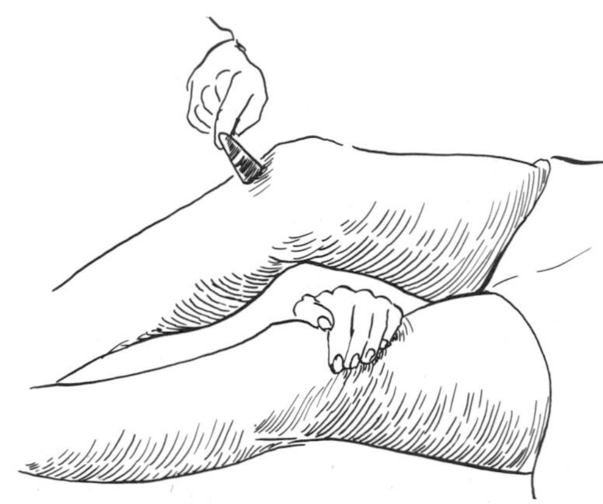

5. **Clonus should be tested, particularly when the reflexes are hyperactive. The lower leg should be supported, as illustrated, and the foot sharply dorsiflexed. Hold the stretch. With a normal response, no movement will be felt. When clonus is present, rapid rhythmic jerking motions of the foot are obvious.** *Dorsiflexion stretches the muscle, and rapid rhythmic contractions indicate hyperreflexia.*

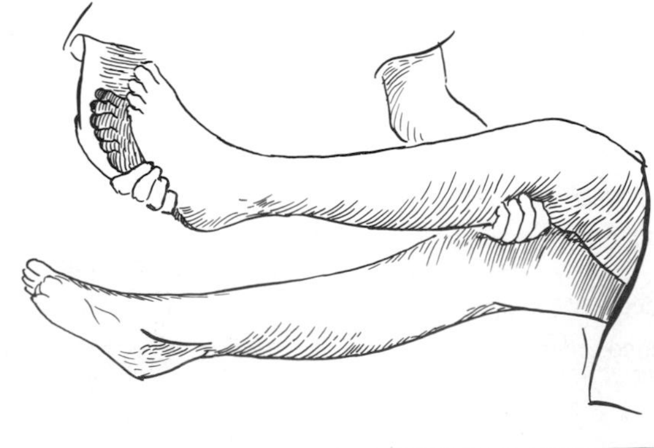

DEEP TENDON RATING SCALE

0 = Reflex absent
+1 = Reflex present, hypoactive
+2 = Normal reflex
+3 = Hyperactive reflex
+4 = Hyperactive reflex with clonus present

indicates increasing cerebral irritability. Clonus should also be assessed by sharply dorsiflexing the foot while the knee is held in a flexed position. Normally, no clonus is present; however, if oscillations or "jerking" motions occur as the foot drops, clonus is present and should be reported to the physician. Procedure 24–1 illustrates how to assess and rate levels of deep tendon reflexes.

Assess deep tendon reflexes to determine as well whether central nervous system depression is occurring as a result of magnesium toxicity.

PSYCHOSOCIAL ASSESSMENT

The development of PIH places a great deal of stress on the childbearing family. The woman may be on bed rest or hospitalized for some time. This creates anxiety about the condition of the fetus as well as the expectant mother. Moreover, many families do not understand the seriousness of the disease; after all, the woman feels well for some time after its onset.

Investigate how the family will function while the expectant mother is hospitalized. Determine how the woman is adapting to the "sick role" and the necessity to be dependent on others instead of functioning in her primary role. Ask how much support is available and who is willing to participate. Finally, determine the major concerns of the family.

Analysis

Analysis of the data collected during assessment leads to both nursing diagnoses and collaborative problems or potential complications. A wide variety of nursing diagnoses may be obvious (see Nursing Care Plan 24–2). Potential complications necessitate that nurses monitor to detect onset or changes in status. Both physician-prescribed and nurse-prescribed interventions are used to minimize the complication. A common potential complication for the woman with PIH is: *Magnesium Toxicity.*

Planning

Client-centered goals are inappropriate for the potential complication of Magnesium Toxicity because the nurse cannot independently manage this condition but must confer with physicians for medical orders for treatment. Planning should reflect the nurse's responsibility to:

- Monitor for signs of magnesium toxicity
- Consult with the physician if signs of magnesium toxicity are observed
- Perform actions that will minimize the possibility of magnesium toxicity

Interventions

MONITORING FOR SIGNS OF MAGNESIUM TOXICITY

Magnesium excess depresses the entire central nervous system, including the brain stem, which controls respirations and cardiac function, and the cerebrum, which controls memory, mental processes, and speech. Carbon dioxide accumulates if the respiratory rate is reduced, leading to respiratory acidosis and further central nervous system depression, which could culminate in respiratory arrest.

Signs of magnesium toxicity include:

- Respiratory rate under 12 breaths/minute
- Absence of deep tendon reflexes
- Sweating, flushing
- Altered sensorium (confused, lethargic, slurring of speech, drowsiness, disorientation)
- Hypotension

Check magnesium levels before administering magnesium sulfate to determine whether the therapeutic range ordered by the physician has been exceeded.

RESPONDING TO SIGNS OF MAGNESIUM TOXICITY

Discontinue magnesium if the respiratory rate is below 12 breaths/minute or if deep tendon reflexes are not present. These are signs of magnesium toxicity, and administration of additional magnesium will make the condition worse. Notify the physician of the woman's condition so that additional orders can be received. Magnesium is excreted by the kidneys, and if the urinary output falls below 30 ml/hour, the physician should be notified before magnesium is administered.

Calcium gluconate is the antidote for magnesium sulfate, because it effectively antagonizes the effects of magnesium at the neuromuscular junction, and it should be readily available whenever magnesium is administered.

Evaluation

Although client-centered goals are not developed for collaborative problems, the nurse collects and compares data with established norms and then judges whether the data are within normal limits. For magnesium toxicity, respiratory rates remain above 12 breaths/minute and deep tendon reflexes are present.

Analysis

A second common collaborative problem for the woman with PIH is: *Potential Complication: Eclamptic Seizures.*

Planning

Client-centered goals are inappropriate for the potential complication of Eclamptic Seizures because the nurse cannot independently manage this condition but must confer with physicians for medical orders for treatment.

Planning should reflect the nurse's responsibility to:

- Monitor for signs of impending seizures
- Consult with the physician if signs of impending seizures are observed
- Perform actions that will minimize the risk of seizures occurring and prevent injury if seizures do occur

Interventions

MONITORING FOR SIGNS OF IMPENDING SEIZURES

Signs of impending seizures include:

- Hyperreflexia and or the presence of clonus
- Increasing signs of cerebral irritability (headache, visual disturbances)
- Epigastric pain

INITIATING PREVENTIVE MEASURES

In the presence of cerebral irritability, seizures may be precipitated by excessive visual or auditory stimuli. Nurses should reduce external stimuli by:

- Admitting the woman to a private room in the quietest section of the unit and keeping the door to the room closed
- Padding the door to reduce noise when the door must be opened and closed
- Keeping the lights low and noise to a minimum; this may include blocking incoming telephone calls
- Grouping nursing assessments and care to allow the woman long periods of undisturbed quiet
- Moving carefully and calmly around the room and avoiding bumping into the bed or startling the woman
- Collaborating with the woman and her family to restrict visitors

PREVENTING SEIZURE-RELATED INJURY

The bed side rails should be padded and the bed kept in the lowest position with the wheels locked to prevent trauma should the woman hit the side rails or fall from the bed during a convulsion.

Oxygen and suction equipment should be assembled and ready to use to prevent aspiration and to provide oxygen as necessary. Check equipment at the beginning of each shift because there will not be time to set up equipment if convulsions occur.

A PIH tray, sometimes called a "toxemia tray," should be in the room; it should contain an ophthalmoscope, syringes, needles, tourniquet, Doppler fetoscope, antihypertensive medications, airway, and reflex hammer. Additional medications that should be on hand include magnesium sulfate, sodium bicarbonate, heparin sodium, epinephrine, phenytoin, and calcium gluconate.

PROTECTING CLIENT DURING A CONVULSION

Nurses must protect the woman and the fetus during a convulsion. The nurse's primary responsibilities are the following:

- Remain with the client and press the emergency bell for assistance.
- If there is time, attempt to turn the woman on her side when the tonic phase begins.
- Note the time and sequence of the convulsion. Eclampsia is marked by a tonic-clonic convulsion that may be preceded by facial twitching that lasts for a few seconds. A tonic contraction of the entire body lasts about 20 seconds and is followed by the clonic phase, which may last about a minute. A Sims position permits greater circulation through the placenta; it may also help prevent aspiration.
- Insert an airway following the convulsion, and suction the mouth and nose to prevent aspiration; administer oxygen by mask to increase oxygenation of the placenta and all maternal body organs.
- Notify the physician as soon as possible that a convulsion has occurred. This is an obstetrical emergency that is associated with cerebral

hemorrhage, premature separation of the placenta, severe fetal hypoxia, and death.
- Administer medications and prepare for additional medical interventions as directed by the physician.

PROVIDING INFORMATION AND SUPPORT FOR THE FAMILY

Explain to the family what has happened, but do not minimize the seriousness of the situation. A convulsion is very frightening for anyone who witnesses it, and the family is often reassured when the nurse explains that the convulsion lasts for only a few minutes and that the woman will probably not be conscious for some time. Acknowledge that the convulsion indicates worsening of the condition and that it will be necessary for the physician to determine future management, which may include delivery of the infant as soon as possible.

Evaluation

The nurse collects and compares data with established norms and then judges whether the data are within normal limits. Interventions are judged to be successful if:

- Deep tendon reflexes remain within normal limits (+1 to +3).
- Clonus is absent.
- The woman is free of visual disturbances, headache, and epigastric pain.

✔ Check Your Reading

16. Why is it important to assess deep tendon reflexes?
17. Why is it important to reduce environmental stimuli when the woman is hospitalized for PIH?

Incompatibility Between Maternal and Fetal Blood

Rh Incompatibility

Rhesus (Rh) factor incompatibility during pregnancy is possible only when two specific circumstances coexist: (1) the expectant mother is Rh-negative and (2) the fetus is Rh-positive. For such a circumstance to occur, the father of the fetus must be Rh-positive. Rh incompatibility is basically a problem that affects the fetus; it causes no harm to the expectant mother.

Rh-negative blood is a recessive trait; therefore, a person must inherit the same gene from both parents to be Rh-negative. This is why only about 15 per cent of the Caucasian population in the United States is Rh-negative. The incidence is lower in the African-American population (8 per cent) and the Asian population (1 per cent) (Tabsh and Theroux, 1992).

PATHOPHYSIOLOGY

People who are Rh-positive have the Rh antigen on a portion of their red blood cells, whereas people who are Rh-negative do not have the antigen. When blood from a person who is Rh-positive enters the blood stream of a person who is Rh-negative, the body reacts as it would to any foreign substance: it develops antibodies to destroy the invading antigen. To destroy the Rh antigen, which exists as part of the red blood cell, the entire red blood cell must be destroyed.

Theoretically, there is no mixing of fetal and maternal blood during pregnancy. In reality, small placental accidents may occur that allow a drop or two of fetal blood to enter the maternal circulation and initiate the production of antibodies to destroy the Rh-positive blood. Sensitization can also occur during a spontaneous or elective abortion, during antepartal procedures such as amniocentesis, or in the unlikely event that the expectant mother is transfused with Rh-positive blood. Figure 24–9 illustrates the process of maternal sensitization.

Most exposure of maternal blood to fetal blood occurs during the third stage of labor, when there may be active exchange of fetal and maternal blood from damaged placental vessels. In this case, the woman's first child is not affected because antibodies are formed following the birth of the infant. Subsequent Rh-positive fetuses may be affected, however, unless the mother receives anti-Rh_0(D) gamma globulin (RhoGAM) to prevent antibody formation after the birth of each Rh-positive infant.

The incidence of maternal sensitization has decreased greatly as a result of the common practice of administering RhoGAM to unsensitized Rh-negative women following all abortions at any stage of gestation, whether induced or spontaneous, following amniocentesis, following childbirth, and at the 28th week of gestation.

FETAL-NEONATAL IMPLICATIONS

If antibodies to the Rh factor are present in the expectant mother's blood, they cross the placental

Nursing Care Plan 24–2

Pregnancy-Induced Hypertension

Assessment: Julie Frost, a 16-year-old primigravida, is seen in the prenatal clinic at 26 weeks of gestation. She exhibits signs of mild hypertension (from a baseline BP of 110/70 to 130/82). She is instructed to go home and rest in bed (on her left side as much as possible) and to come back to the clinic in 3 days. Julie states that she feels fine and doesn't want to miss school. She says that she doesn't see the reason for bed rest.

Nursing Diagnosis: High Risk for Non-compliance related to knowledge deficit of the importance of treatment regimen.

Goals:

1. Julie will: Verbalize benefits of bed rest and frequent prenatal evaluations by the end of the first prenatal appointment.
2. Verbalize intent to comply with recommended regimen of bed rest and will keep prenatal appointments.

Intervention:	**Rationale:**
1. Initiate an interaction that allows Julie to verbalize feelings about recommended regimen: "How do you feel about staying in bed and having to come back to the clinic twice each week?" "What concerns you most about missing school?" Acknowledge her feelings as important: "It must be difficult to think of falling behind in your schoolwork." "It isn't any fun to miss all the after-school activities."	1. If Julie identifies her feelings and they are acknowledged as important, anxiety will decrease and teaching/learning can begin.
2. Describe in general terms the physiological processes that are occurring and their effect on her and the fetus: "The small blood vessels in your body are constricted so they don't carry enough blood to your vital organs or to the baby." "Staying in bed on your left side helps the blood to circulate to all parts of your body and to carry oxygen to the baby."	2. Expectant mothers are highly motivated to comply with a therapeutic management that will benefit the fetus, and knowledge of how the planned program provides the fetus with oxygen improves the possibility of compliance with bed rest and frequent assessments.
3. Explain that she may feel well even when the condition worsens and that the painless symptoms can be checked only at the clinic.	3. Hypertension and proteinuria are not noticed by the expectant mother. Edema is considered normal by many clients, and they may not identify edema above the waist as more significant than dependent edema.
4. Instruct Julie to call the clinic if she notices headache, double vision, or spots before her eyes.	4. These signs indicate rapid progression of the disease and that additional management is needed.
5. Collaborate with Julie to arrange for contact with her boyfriend or selected friends and to arrange for ongoing homebound classes.	5. Such an agreement will allow a schedule to be developed that provides Julie with peer support but that allows for prolonged periods of quiet. Homebound classes alleviate the concern that she is falling behind with schoolwork, and related anxiety will decrease.

Evaluation:
Keeping clinic appointments twice each week is an important way to evaluate compliance. Signs and symptoms that do not increase may indicate adherence to bed rest regimen; however, the disease may progress despite careful home management.

Nursing Care Plan 24–2 Continued

Pregnancy-Induced Hypertension

Assessment: Julie is admitted to the hospital at 31 weeks of gestation with blood pressure 160/110, heart rate 92, and respirations 22. There is 2+ proteinuria and marked edema of the hands and face. She is started on continuous intravenous infusion of magnesium sulfate ($MgSO_4$), seizure precautions are initiated, and environmental stimuli are carefully monitored. The condition of the fetus is assessed by electronic fetal monitoring and daily non-stress tests. Julie is agitated and verbalizes concern that the procedures are going to hurt her or the fetus. She frequently asks, "How sick am I?" "Is the baby going to be O.K.?" Her hands are perspiring, and her hands shake when she reaches for a tissue.

Nursing Diagnosis: Anxiety related to hospitalization and concern about her health and the health of the fetus.

Goals:
1. Julie will: Verbalize her concerns and describe the benefits of the treatment while her family is present.
2. Manifest less anxiety (agitation, physiological signs such as tremors, tachycardia, and perspiration).

Intervention:	Rationale:
1. Initiate measures to reduce anxiety. a. Provide positive reassurance that a solution to anxiety can be found: "I can see you are really worried, and I will try to answer all your questions." b. Allow her to cry, get angry, or express any feeling that is present. c. Encourage a discussion of feelings: "Tell me more about how you feel." d. Reflect observations: "I see you wringing your hands, do you want to tell me about it?" e. Convey empathy and positive regard; use nonverbal behavior, including touch, when appropriate.	1. Anxiety is an ominous feeling of tension resulting from a physical or emotional threat to the self. It is a global, often unnamed sense of doom, a feeling of helplessness, isolation and insecurity. Anxiety needs to be ventilated and then addressed by conveying that the person is not alone and that they will be protected.
2. Provide information about hospital routines and procedures when anxiety is diminished enough for learning to take place. a. Be very specific about procedures, such as fetal monitoring, assessment of deep tendon reflexes, and vital signs. Explain what they are for, who will do them, and how long they will be maintained. b. Focus on Julie's present concerns; she is not able to be future-oriented at this time. c. Speak slowly and calmly, give very short directions, and do not ask Julie to make decisions: "Turn on your side." "Breathe slowly." d. Allow a friend or family member to remain with Julie and instruct them in the necessity for a low-stimulus environment.	2. Knowledge of the procedures that will be performed and the purpose of the procedures provides a sense of control that reduces anxiety. Perception is somewhat narrowed when anxiety is high; therefore, short, brief instructions are easier for the anxious person to understand than long explanations.

Evaluation:
Julie feels free to discuss feelings with the nurse and with support person. She feels in control of anxiety as manifested by a decrease in signs of agitation and physiological signs (tachycardia, tachypnea) and by the ability to use relaxation techniques.

Nursing Care Plan continued on following page

Nursing Care Plan 24–2 Continued

Pregnancy-Induced Hypertension

Assessment: Julie's blood pressure continues to rise, and she exhibits symptoms of increased cerebral irritability (headache, double vision, hyperreflexia) despite intravenous administration of magnesium sulfate.

Potential Complication:
Seizures.

Intervention:	Rationale:
1. Reduce environmental stimuli. a. Lower lights, pull curtains, keep door closed, restrict visitors, block incoming telephone calls, and group physical assessments and care to allow for prolonged periods of quiet. b. Move quietly around the room, avoid bumping the bed.	1. Environmental stimuli increase cerebral irritability and accelerate the risk of seizures.
2. Monitor blood pressure, urinary output, urine for protein, deep tendon reflexes, and clonus every 2 hours or according to hospital protocol.	2. Rising blood pressure suggests increasing vasospasm; decreased urinary output and proteinuria indicate decreased renal perfusion; hyperreflexia and the presence of clonus indicate cerebral irritability.
3. Assess for headache, visual disturbances, increasing edema, and epigastric pain every 2 hours or according to hospital protocol.	3. Headache and visual disturbances suggest cerebral edema; epigastric pain is caused by hepatic edema and suggests that a convulsion is imminent.
4. Prepare to intervene if a convulsion occurs. a. Assemble suction and oxygen equipment in the room and have it ready for use. b. Place a "toxemia tray" containing syringes, needles, antihypertensive medications, airway, reflex hammer, tourniquet, and alcohol wipes in the room. Be certain that medications such as magnesium sulfate, calcium gluconate, sodium bicarbonate, and epinephrine are in the room. Sterile water and sterile saline may also be needed for flushing intravenous tubes or mixing medications.	4. If a convulsion occurs, the client should be suctioned to prevent aspiration; administration of oxygen increases the Po_2 that is available to the placenta and vital organs of the expectant mother. Calcium gluconate is an antidote to magnesium sulfate and should always be available when the client is receiving intravenous magnesium.
5. Make arrangements to protect the client from injury should a convulsion occur. a. Keep the bed at the lowest level and in a locked position. b. Pad the side rails and keep them raised at all times. c. Remain with the client; she should not be unattended.	5. During the uncontrolled movements of a tonic-clonic convulsion, the client is at risk for falling or for injury as the arms thrash against unpadded side rails.

Evaluation:
Although client-centered goals are not developed for potential complications, the nurse collects and compares data with established norms and then judges whether the data are within normal limits. Hyperreflexia and the presence of other signs of cerebral irritability are not within expected limits and must be reported to the physician.

Additional Nursing Diagnoses to Consider:
High Risk for Ineffective Airway Clearance
High Risk for Injury
High Risk for Aspiration

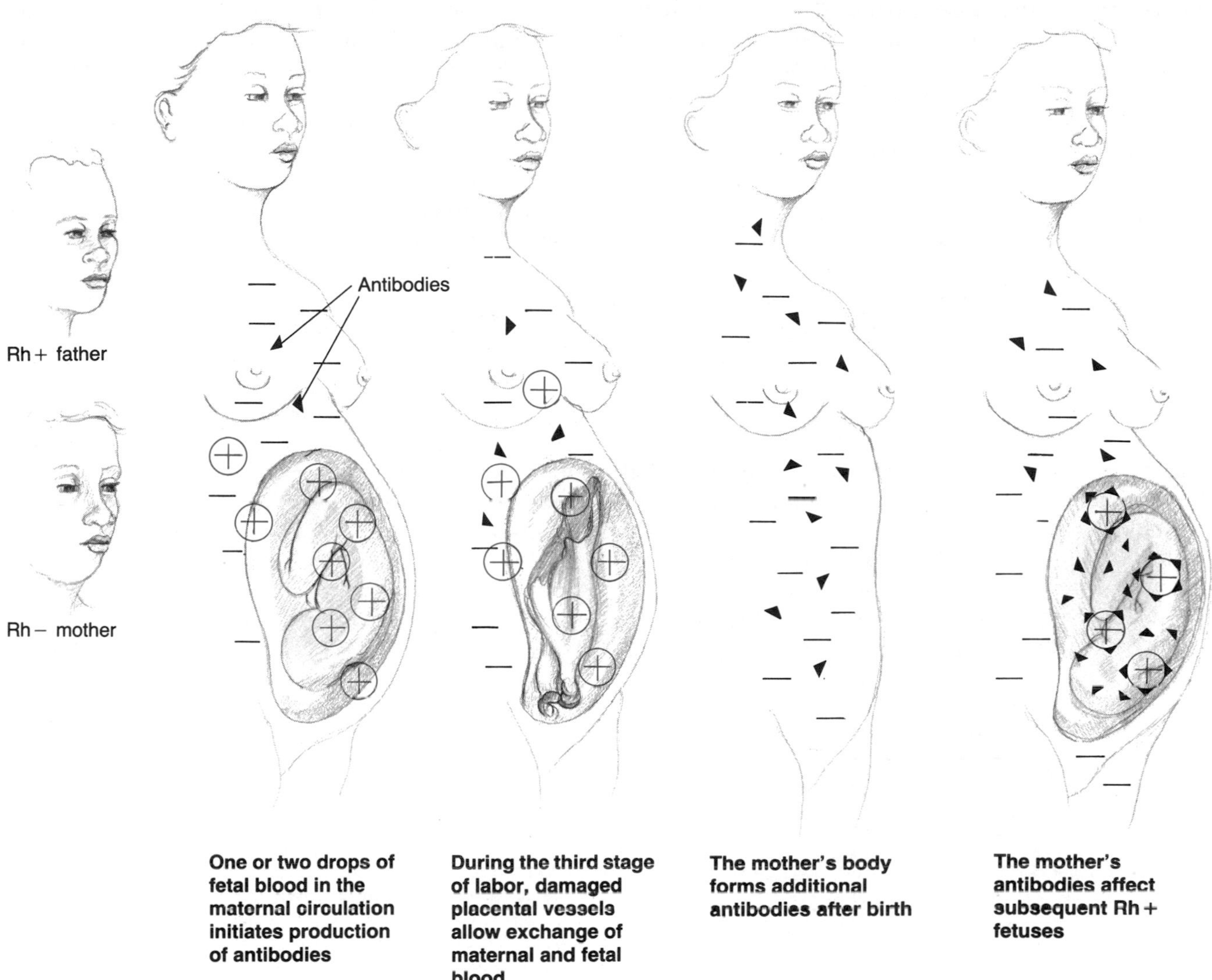

Rh+ father
Rh– mother
Antibodies
One or two drops of fetal blood in the maternal circulation initiates production of antibodies
During the third stage of labor, damaged placental vessels allow exchange of maternal and fetal blood
The mother's body forms additional antibodies after birth
The mother's antibodies affect subsequent Rh+ fetuses

Figure 24–9

The process of maternal sensitization to the Rh factor.

barrier and cause massive destruction of fetal red blood cells. The fetus becomes deficient in red blood cells, which are needed to transport oxygen to fetal tissue. As fetal red blood cells are destroyed, fetal bilirubin levels increase (icterus gravis), which can lead to severe neurological disease (kernicterus). This hemolytic process results in rapid production of erythroblasts (immature red blood cells), which cannot carry oxygen, and the entire syndrome is termed erythroblastosis fetalis. The fetus becomes so anemic that generalized fetal edema (hydrops fetalis) results and can terminate in fetal congestive heart failure.

Management of the infant born with erythroblastosis fetalis is discussed in Chapter 29.

PRENATAL ASSESSMENT AND MANAGEMENT

All pregnant women should have a blood test to determine blood type and Rh factor at the initial prenatal visit. Rh-negative women should have an antibody titer (indirect Coombs' test) to determine if they are sensitized (have developed antibodies) as a result of previous exposure to Rh-positive blood. If the indirect Coombs' test is negative, it is repeated at 28 weeks of gestation in case of subsequent sensitization. A negative indirect Coombs' test accurately identifies the fetus as not at risk for hemolytic disease of the newborn.

RhoGAM, an anti-Rh_o(D) gamma globulin, is administered to the unsensitized, Rh-negative woman at 28 weeks of gestation as a preventive measure. RhoGAM is a commercial preparation of passive antibodies against Rh factor. It effectively prevents the formation of antibodies if there is accidental transport of fetal Rh-positive blood into the circulation of an Rh-negative mother during the remainder of the pregnancy.

If the indirect Coombs' test is positive, that is, if it indicates maternal sensitization and the presence of antibodies, it is repeated at frequent intervals throughout the pregnancy to determine if the antibody titer is rising. An increase in titer indicates that the process is continuing and that the fetus will be in jeopardy.

Amniocentesis may be performed to evaluate change in the optical density (delta OD) of amniotic fluid. This reflects the amount of bilirubin (residue of red blood cell destruction) that is present in the amniotic fluid. If the fluid optical density remains low, it may indicate that the fetus is Rh-positive but in no jeopardy or, more likely, that the fetus is Rh-negative. If the optical density is elevated, indicating fetal jeopardy in a hostile environment, intrauterine transfusion may be planned. If the fetal age is more than 32 weeks, early delivery may provide the best opportunity for survival.

Ultrasound examination is also used to evaluate the condition of the fetus. Generalized fetal edema, ascites, enlarged heart, or hydramnios indicates serious fetal compromise. See Figure 24–10 for a summary of assessments.

POSTPARTUM MANAGEMENT

If the mother is Rh-negative, umbilical cord blood is taken at delivery to determine blood type, Rh factor, and antibody titer (direct Coombs' test) of the newborn. Rh-negative, unsensitized (negative indirect Coombs' test) mothers who give birth to Rh-positive infants are given an intramuscular injection of RhoGAM within 72 hours following delivery. If RhoGAM is given to the mother in the first 72 hours following delivery of an Rh-positive infant, any Rh antigens present are destroyed, and therefore the mother

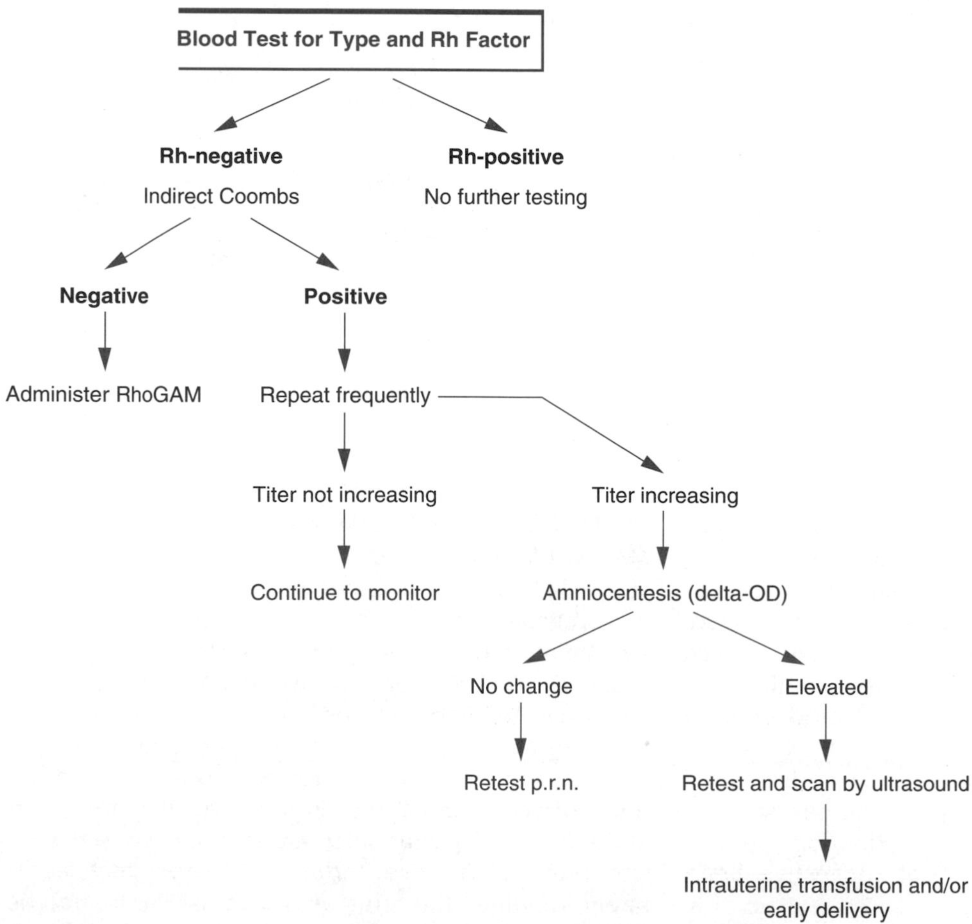

Figure 24–10

Sequence of assessments for Rh sensitization. p.r.n., as needed; delta = OD.

Parents Want To Know
About Rh Incompatibility

What does it mean to be Rh-negative?
Those who are Rh-negative lack a substance that is present on the red blood cells of those who are Rh-positive.

How can the expectant mother be Rh-negative and the fetus Rh-positive?
The fetus can inherit the Rh-positive factor from the father.

What does sensitization mean?
Sensitization means that the expectant mother has been exposed to Rh-positive blood and has developed antibodies against the Rh-positive factor.

Do the antibodies harm the expectant mother?
No, because she does not have the Rh-positive factor.

Do Rh-positive men always father Rh-positive children?
No. Rh-positive men who have an Rh-positive gene and an Rh-negative gene can father Rh-negative children.

Why is RhoGAM necessary during pregnancy and following childbirth?
RhoGAM prevents the development of Rh antibodies, which might be harmful to subsequent fetuses.

Why will the next fetus be jeopardized if RhoGAM is not administered?
If RhoGAM is not administered when the fetus is Rh-positive, the expectant mother may develop antibodies that cross the placental barrier and affect the next Rh-positive fetus.

forms no natural antibodies. (See Drug Guide for Rh_o(D) immune globulin [RhoGAM].)

If the infant is Rh-negative, there is no possibility of antibody formation, and RhoGAM is not necessary. As stated previously, RhoGAM is also administered following abortion, either induced or spontaneous, following amniocentesis when fetal-to-maternal transfusion is possible, and at 28 weeks of gestation if the mother is Rh-negative and unsensitized.

Nurses must be prepared to reassure the expectant parents that the medical management is generally effective and to answer questions that are commonly asked. See Parents Want to Know: Answers to Common Questions About Rh Incompatibility.

Families are often very concerned about the fetus, and nurses must be sensitive to cues and signals that indicate that the family is anxious and to offer honest reassurance. This is especially important if the expectant mother is sensitized and fetal testing is necessary throughout pregnancy.

During labor, the nurse is often responsible for reminding the physician that cord blood is needed to determine the blood type and Rh factor of the newborn. During the postpartum period, nurses are responsible for follow-up to determine if RhoGAM is necessary and for administering the injection within the prescribed time.

Drug Guide

Rh_o(D) IMMUNE GLOBULIN (HypRho-D, Gamulin Rh, RhoGAM)

Classification: Concentrated immunoglobulins directed toward the red blood cell antigen Rh_o(D).

Action: Prevents production of anti-Rh_o(D) antibodies in Rh-negative women who have been exposed to Rh-positive blood by suppressing the immune reaction of the Rh-negative woman to the antigen in Rh-negative blood. Prevents antibody response and subsequently prevents hemolytic disease of the newborn in future pregnancies of women who have conceived an Rh-positive fetus.

Indications: Administered to Rh-negative clients who have been exposed to Rh-positive blood by:
1. Delivering an Rh-positive infant.
2. Aborting an Rh-positive fetus.
3. Having amniocentesis or intra-abdominal trauma while carrying an Rh-positive fetus.
4. Following accidental transfusion of Rh-positive blood to Rh-negative client.

Dosage and Route: One vial standard dose administered intramuscularly at:
1. 28 weeks of pregnancy and within 72 hours of delivery.
2. Within 72 hours following termination of pregnancy >13 weeks' gestation.

One vial *microdose* within 72 hours following termination of pregnancy <13 weeks' gestation.

Dose is calculated based on the volume of blood erroneously administered in transfusion accidents.

Absorption: Well absorbed from intramuscular sites.

Excretion: Metabolism and excretion unknown.

Contraindications and Precautions: Women who are Rh-positive or women previously sensitized to Rh_o(D) should not receive Rh_o(D) immune globulin. Used cautiously for clients with previous hypersensitivity reactions to immune globulins.

Adverse Reactions: Local pain at intramuscular site and/or fever.

Nursing Implications: Type and crossmatch of mother's blood and cord blood of the newborn must be performed to determine the need for the medication. Mother must be Rh-negative and negative for Rh antibodies; the newborn must be Rh-positive. If there is doubt regarding the fetus's blood type following termination of pregnancy, the medication should be administered. The drug is administered to the mother, not the infant. The deltoid muscle is recommended for intramuscular administration.

ABO Incompatibility

ABO incompatibility occurs when the expectant mother is blood type O and the fetus is blood type A or B. Type A and B blood contains a protein component (antigen) that is not present in type O blood.

People with type O blood develop anti-A or anti-B antibodies naturally as a result of exposure to antigens in the foods that they eat or to infection by gram-negative bacteria. As a result, some women with blood type O have developed high serum anti-A and anti-B antibodies titers before they become pregnant for the first time, and the first fetus can be affected. When the woman becomes pregnant, anti-A and anti-B antibodies cross the placental barrier and cause hemolysis of fetal red blood cells. Fortunately, ABO incompatibility is less severe than Rh incompatibility because fewer antibodies cross the placental barrier.

No specific prenatal care is needed; however, the nurse must be aware of the possibility of ABO incompatibility. During the delivery, cord blood is taken to determine the blood type of the newborn and the antibody titer (direct Coombs' test). The newborn is carefully screened for jaundice, which indicates hyperbilirubinemia. See Chapter 29 for medical and nursing management of hyperbilirubinemia in newborns.

✔ Check Your Reading

18. Why do unsensitized Rh-negative expectant mothers receive RhoGAM during pregnancy and following an abortion, amniocentesis, and childbirth?
19. Why is the first fetus sometimes affected if there is ABO incompatibility?

Summary Concepts

- Spontaneous abortion is one of the leading causes of pregnancy loss. Treatment is aimed at preventing complications, such as hypovolemic shock and infection, and providing emotional support for grieving, which accompanies any pregnancy loss.
- Both surgical and medical methods are used to induce elective abortion. Nurses are often responsible for providing self-care information for women who have had an elective abortion to prevent infection or other complications.
- The incidence of ectopic pregnancy is increasing in the United States as a result of pelvic inflammation associated with sexually transmitted diseases. The goals of therapeutic management are to prevent severe hemorrhage and to preserve the fallopian tube so that future fertility is retained.
- Management of hydatidiform mole involves two stages: (1) evacuation of the molar pregnancy and (2) continuous follow-up to detect malignant changes in the remaining trophoblastic tissue.
- Disorders of the placenta (placenta previa and abruptio placentae) are responsible for hemorrhagic conditions of the last half of pregnancy. Either condition may result in maternal hemorrhage and fetal or maternal death.
- Disseminated intravascular coagulation is a life-threatening complication of abruptio placentae, in which procoagulation and anticoagulation factors are simultaneously activated.
- The cause of hyperemesis gravidarum remains obscure, but the goals of management are to prevent dehydration, malnutrition, and electrolyte imbalance. Emotional support is a most important therapy and a responsibility of nurses.
- Hypertensive disorders of pregnancy may include pre-existing (chronic) hypertension or pregnancy-induced hypertension. The underlying process is generalized vasospasm, which decreases circulation to all organs of the body, including the placenta. Major maternal organs affected include the liver, kidneys, and brain.
- Treatment of pregnancy-induced hypertension includes bed rest, reduction of environmental stimuli, and administration of anticonvulsants.
- Magnesium sulfate, an anticonvulsant used to prevent pregnancy-induced hypertension from progressing to eclamptic convulsions, is associated with adverse effects, the most serious being central nervous system depression, which includes depression of the respiratory center.
- Nurses monitor the woman to determine the effectiveness of medical therapy and to identify signs that the condition is worsening, such as increasing hyperreflexia. Nurses also control external stimuli and initiate measures to protect her in case of eclamptic seizures.
- Rh incompatibility can occur when an Rh-negative woman conceives a child who is Rh-positive. As a result of exposure to the Rh-positive antigen, maternal antibodies may develop that cause hemolysis of fetal red blood cells in subsequent pregnancies.
- The incidence of serious problems that can result from Rh incompatibility has greatly decreased as a result of RhoGAM, administered during pregnancy and following abortion, amniocentesis, and childbirth.

- ABO incompatibility usually occurs when the mother has type O blood and naturally occurring anti-A and anti-B antibodies, which cause hemolysis if the fetus' blood is not type O. ABO incompatibility may result in hyperbilirubinemia of the infant, but it usually presents no serious threat to the health of the child.

References and Readings

Appleton, M.P., Kuehl, T.J., Raebel, M.S., et al. (1991). Magnesium sulfate versus phenytoin for seizure prophylaxis in pregnancy-induced hypertension. *American Journal of Obstetrics and Gynecology*, 165(4, Pt. 1), 907–913.

Barton, J.R., & Sibai, B.M. (1991). Care of pregnancy complicated by HELLP syndrome. *Obstetrics and Gynecology Clinics of North America*, 18(2), 165–180.

Bennett, M.J. (1992). Abortion. In N.F. Hacker & J.G. Moore (Eds.), *Essentials of obstetrics and gynecology* (2nd ed., pp. 415–424). Philadelphia: W.B. Saunders.

Berek, J.S. (1992). Gestational trophoblastic neoplasia. In N.F. Hacker & J.G. Moore (Eds.), *Essentials of obstetrics and gynecology* (2nd ed., pp. 626–634). Philadelphia: W.B. Saunders.

Bowman, J.M. (1989). Hemolytic disease (erythroblastosis fetalis). In R.K. Creasy & R. Resnik (Eds.), *Maternal-fetal medicine: Principles and practice* (2nd ed., pp. 613–655). Philadelphia: W.B. Saunders.

Brinkman, C.R. (1992). Hypertensive disorders of pregnancy. In N.F. Hacker & J.G. Moore (Eds.), *Essentials of obstetrics and gynecology* (2nd ed., pp. 163–174). Philadelphia: W.B. Saunders.

Carpenito, L.J. (1992). *Nursing diagnosis: Application to clinical practice* (4th ed.). Philadelphia: J.B. Lippincott.

Cartwright, P.S. (1991). Diagnosis of ectopic pregnancy. *Obstetrics and Gynecology Clinics of North America*, 18(1), 19–39.

Catlin, A.J. (1989). Early pregnancy loss: What you can do to help. RN, 52(8), 56.

Cunningham, F.G., MacDonald, P.C., & Gant, N.F. (1989). *Williams obstetrics* (18th ed.). Norwalk, Conn.: Appleton & Lange.

Deglin, J.H., & Vallerand, A.H. (1993). *Davis's drug guide for nurses* (3rd ed.). Philadelphia: F.A. Davis.

Doan Wiggins, L. (1990). PIH: Combating the dangers. *Emergency Medicine*, 22(6), 29–31, 34–36.

Doyle, M.B., DeCherney, A.H., & Diamond, M.P. (1991). Epidemiology and etiology of ectopic pregnancy. *Obstetrics and Gynecology Clinics of North America*, 18(1), 1–18.

Green, J.R. (1989). Placenta previa and abruptio placentae. In R.K. Creasy & R. Resnik (Eds.), *Maternal-fetal medicine: Principles and practice* (2nd ed., pp. 592–613). Philadelphia: W.B. Saunders.

Hayashi, R.H., & Castillo, M.S. (1993). Bleeding in pregnancy. In R.A. Knuppel & J.E. Drukker (Eds.), *High-risk pregnancy: A team approach* (2nd ed., pp. 539–560). Philadelphia: W.B. Saunders.

Key, T.C. (1989). Gastrointestinal diseases. In R.K. Creasy & R. Resnik (Eds.), *Maternal-fetal medicine: Principles and practice* (2nd ed., pp. 1032–1047). Philadelphia: W.B. Saunders.

Knuppel, R.A., & Drukker, J.E. (1993). Hypertension in pregnancy. In R.A. Knuppel & J.E. Drukker (Eds.), *High-risk pregnancy: A team approach* (2nd ed., pp. 468–575). Philadelphia: W.B. Saunders.

Lockwood, C.J. (1991). Preeclampsia and hypertensive disorders of pregnancy. In S.H. Cherry & I.R. Merkatz (Eds.), *Complications of pregnancy: Medical, surgical, gynecologic, psychosocial, and perinatal* (4th ed., pp. 476–494). Baltimore: Williams & Wilkins.

McHugh, J., & McHugh, W. (1990). How to assess deep tendon reflexes. *Nursing 90*, 20(8), 62–64.

Palmieri, A., & Moore, J.G. (1992). Ectopic pregnancy. In N.F. Hacker & J.G. Moore (Eds.), *Essentials of obstetrics and gynecology* (2nd ed., pp. 425–435). Philadelphia: W.B. Saunders.

Ory, S.J. (1991). Chemotherapy for ectopic pregnancy. *Obstetrics and Gynecology Clinics of North America*, 18(1), 123–135.

Palmieri, A., & Moore J.G. (1992). Ectopic pregnancy. In N.F. Hacker & J.G. Moore (Eds.), *Essentials of obstetrics and gynecology* (2nd ed., pp. 425–435). Philadelphia: W.B. Saunders.

Poole, J.H. (1988). Getting perspective on HELLP syndrome. *American Journal of Maternal-Child Nursing*, 13(6), 432–437.

Remich, M.C., & Youngkin, E.Q. (1989). Factors associated with pregnancy induced hypertension. *Nurse Practitioner*, 14(1), 20–24.

Repke, J.T. (1991). Prevention and treatment of pregnancy-induced hypertension. *Cardiovascular Diseases*, 17(5), 25–31.

Ricci, J.M. (1992). Antepartum hemorrhage. In N.F. Hacker & J.G. Moore (Eds.), *Essentials of obstetrics and gynecology* (2nd ed., pp. 154–162). Philadelphia: W.B. Saunders.

Roberts, J.M. (1989). Pregnancy-related hypertension. In R.K. Creasy & R. Resnik (Eds.), *Maternal-fetal medicine: Principles and practice*, (2nd ed., pp. 777–823). Philadelphia: W.B. Saunders.

Sharts-Engel, N.C. (1992). Aspirin for prevention of pregnancy-induced hypertension MCN: *American Journal of Maternal Child Nursing*, 17(3), 168.

Sibai, B. (1990). The HELLP syndrome: Much ado about nothing? *American Journal of Obstetrics and Gynecology*, 162(2), 311–316.

Siskind, J. (1990). Handling hemorrhage wisely. *Nursing 90*, 20(3), 137–143.

Stovall, T.G., & Ling, F.W. (1991). Expectant management of ectopic pregnancy. *Obstetrics and Gynecology Clinics of North America*, 18(1), 135–145.

Tabsh, K., & Theroux, N. (1992). Rhesus isoimmunization. In N.H. Hacker & J.G. Moore (Eds.), *Essentials of obstetrics and gynecology* (2nd ed., pp. 299–307). Philadelphia: W.B. Saunders.

Thornton, K.L., Diamond, M.P., & DeCherney (1991). Linear salpingostomy for ectopic pregnancy. *Obstetrics and Gynecology Clinics of North America*, 18(1), 95–110.

Trustem, A. (1991). When to suspect ectopic pregnancy. RN, 54(8), 22–25.

Vancaillie, T.G. (1991). Salpingectomy. *Obstetrics and Gynecology Clinics of North America*, 18(1), 111–122.

25

Concurrent Disorders During Pregnancy

Objectives

1. Compare the effects and management of gestational diabetes with pre-existing diabetes mellitus during pregnancy.
2. Describe the major effects of pregnancy on the woman who has heart disease, and identify the goals of therapy.
3. Explain the maternal and fetal effects of specific anemias and the required management during pregnancy.
4. Identify the effects of some uncommon pre-existing conditions and the nursing considerations during pregnancy.
5. Discuss maternal, fetal, and neonatal effects of some common infections that may occur during pregnancy.

Definitions

Acquired immunodeficiency syndrome (AIDS) • Syndrome caused by the human immunodeficiency virus (HIV), resulting in loss of defense against malignancies and opportunistic infections.

Cardiac decompensation • Failure of the heart to maintain adequate circulation to the tissues. See also **Congestive heart failure.**

Caudal regressive syndrome • A severe malformation that results when the sacrum, lumbar spine, and lower extremities fail to develop.

Congenital anomaly • Abnormal intrauterine development of an organ or structure.

Congestive heart failure • Condition resulting from failure of the heart to maintain adequate circulation; characterized by weakness, dyspnea, and edema in body parts that are lower than the heart.

Diabetes mellitus • A disorder of carbohydrate metabolism caused by a relative or complete lack of insulin secretion. Characterized by *glycosuria* (glucose in the urine) and **hyperglycemia** (see below).

Dystocia • Difficult or prolonged labor. Often associated with abnormal uterine activity and **cephalopelvic disproportion.**

Euglycemia • Normal blood glucose level.

Gestational diabetes • Impaired glucose tolerance that is induced by pregnancy and diagnosed during pregnancy. Usually disappears after childbirth.

HIV • An acronym for *h*uman *i*mmunodeficiency *v*irus, which eventually results in the development of **AIDS.**

Hydramnios • Excessive volume of amniotic fluid (more than 2000 ml at term). Also called **polyhydramnios.**

△ Alert for a high risk of exposure to substances to which universal precautions apply. See Appendix B for additional information about infection control.

Hyperglycemia • An abnormally high blood glucose level.

Hypoglycemia • An abnormally low blood glucose level.

Ketosis • Accumulation of ketone bodies (metabolic products) in the blood; frequently associated with acidosis.

Macrosomia • Abnormally large fetal size; infant birth weight over 4000 grams.

Neonatologist • A physician who specializes in the care of newborn infants (from birth until the 29th day of life).

Osmotic diuresis • Secretion and passage of large amounts of urine as a result of increased osmotic pressure that results from **hyperglycemia.**

Perinatologist • A physician who specializes in the care of the mother, the fetus, and the infant during the perinatal period (from the 20th week of pregnancy to 4 weeks following childbirth).

Polydipsia • Excessive thirst.

Polyphagia • Excessive ingestion of food.

Polyuria • Excessive excretion of urine.

Seroconversion • Change in a blood test from negative to positive, indicating the development of antibodies in response to infection or immunization.

A woman with a medical condition who becomes pregnant may require a variation of her usual treatment because of the pregnancy and antepartum care may have to be adapted to safeguard her health and that of the fetus. Some disorders that are mild or even subclinical in the pregnant woman can produce massive damage to the fetus. Moreover, treatment of pre-existing disorders can be complicated because of the teratogenic effects of some drugs. This chapter describes disorders that most commonly pose significant fetal jeopardy.

Diabetes Mellitus

In the years before the discovery of insulin, fetal or neonatal death was the rule and maternal morbidity (illness) was greatly increased when women with diabetes mellitus became pregnant. Today, techniques such as multiple doses or constant infusion of insulin, home glucose testing, dietary counseling, and advanced methods of fetal surveillance most often result in the birth of a healthy infant. Moreover, such measures permit the expectant mother to be an active participant in her own care that may reduce the risks of long-term complications from diabetes mellitus.

Pathophysiology

ETIOLOGY

Diabetes mellitus is a complex disorder of carbohydrate metabolism caused primarily by a partial or complete lack of insulin secretion by the beta cells of the pancreas. Without insulin, the body's cells are unable to transport glucose across the cell membranes. Therefore, glucose accumulates in the blood, resulting in hyperglycemia. The body attempts to dilute the glucose load by any means possible. The first strategy is to increase thirst (polydipsia), one of the classic symptoms of diabetes mellitus. Next, fluid from the intracellular spaces is drawn into the vascular bed, resulting in dehydration at the cellular level but fluid volume excess in the vascular compartment. The kidneys attempt to secrete large volumes of this fluid plus the heavy solute load of glucose (osmotic diuresis). This produces the second symptom of diabetes, polyuria, as well as *glycosuria* (glucose in the urine). Without glucose, the cells starve, so that there is weight loss even though the person ingests excessive amounts of food (polyphagia).

Weight loss and polyphagia are also common symptoms of diabetes mellitus. Because the body is unable to metabolize glucose, it begins to metabolize protein and fat to meet energy needs. Metabolism of protein produces a negative nitrogen balance, and the metabolism of fat results in the buildup of ketone bodies (such as acetone, acetoacetic acid, or beta-hydroxy-butyric acid) or ketosis (accumulation of acids in the body).

If the disease is not well controlled, serious complications may occur. Either hypoglycemia or hyperglycemia can result if the amount of insulin administered is not matched to the diet. Moreover, fluctuating periods of hyperglycemia and hypoglycemia damage small blood vessels throughout the body. This can cause serious impairment, especially in the kidneys, eyes, and heart.

EFFECT OF PREGNANCY ON GLUCOSE METABOLISM

Pregnancy has a profound effect on glucose metabolism in women who do not have pre-existing diabetes as well as in those who do. During pregnancy, glucose is continuously transferred from maternal circulation to the fetus for growth and development. Maternal insulin does not cross the placental barrier and the fetus must produce insulin to metabolize the glucose received.

As pregnancy progresses, placental hormones—

Table 25–1. CLASSIFICATION OF DIABETES MELLITUS

Type I: Insulin-dependent (prone to ketosis)

Type II: Non–insulin-dependent (ketosis-resistant)
1. Non-obese
2. Obese

Secondary diabetes (associated with certain conditions or syndromes)

Impaired glucose tolerance

Gestational diabetes
1. Diet-controlled
2. Insulin required

From Classification of diabetes mellitus and other categories of glucose intolerance (1979). *Diabetes,* 28:1039. Reprinted with permission from National Diabetes Data Group.

estrogen, progesterone, and particularly human chorionic somatomammotropin (hCS), also known as human placental lactogen (hPL)—create resistance to insulin in maternal cells. In addition, placental insulinase accelerates the breakdown of insulin and increased cortisol from the adrenal glands accelerates *gluconeogenesis* (formation of glycogen from noncarbohydrate sources, such as amino or fatty acids). These metabolic changes have two major effects: (1) they allow an abundant supply of glucose for the fetus, and (2) they may leave the woman with insufficient insulin and episodes of hyperglycemia. For many women, this is not a problem; the pancreas responds by simply increasing the production of insulin. If the pancreas is unable to respond, however, the woman will experience fluctuating periods of hyperglycemia (gestational diabetes, or pregnancy-induced glucose intolerance).

Classification

Clinically, diabetes is classified in two ways:

Non–insulin-dependent diabetes—The beta cells of the pancreas function but secrete inadequate amounts of insulin.

Insulin-dependent diabetes—Because no insulin is secreted by the pancreas, insulin must be administered daily to maintain normal blood glucose levels.

The general classifications of diabetes mellitus are listed in Table 25–1.

In addition to the general classification, the classification of diabetes during pregnancy considers onset, duration, and the presence of vascular or renal impairments that may complicate diabetes (Table 25–2).

Incidence

Diabetes mellitus is one of the major health problems facing the United States population. Type II (non–insulin-dependent) diabetes, previously called *maturity-onset diabetes,* is the most common form of diabetes in the United States. The incidence increases with age, and one of every four families has a history of the disease. Non–insulin-dependent diabetes is treated with diet and with oral hypoglycemic agents except when pregnancy exists. Oral hypoglycemic agents are never used during pregnancy because of the known teratogenic effects. Type I (insulin-dependent) diabetes, formerly called *juvenile-*

Table 25–2. CLASSIFICATION OF DIABETES COMPLICATING PREGNANCY

Pre-gestational Diabetes

Class	*Age of Onset*		*Duration (years)*	*Vascular Disease*	*Therapy*
A	Any		Any	None	A-1 Diet only
B	>20	*or*	<10	None	Insulin
C	10–19	*or*	10–19	None	Insulin
D	<10		>20	Benign retinopathy	Insulin
F	Any		Any	Nephropathy	Insulin
R	Any		Any	Proliferative retinopathy	Insulin
H	Any		Any	Heart disease	Insulin

Gestational Diabetes

Class	*Fasting Plasma Glucose*	*Postprandial Plasma Glucose*
A-1	<105 mg/dl	<120 mg/dl
A-2	>105 mg/dl	>120 mg/dl

Reprinted with permission from the American College of Obstetrics and Gynecology (1986). ACOG Technical Bulletin No. 92. Washington, D.C.

onset diabetes, complicates 0.2 to 0.8 per cent of all pregnancies (Kappy, 1991). Gestational diabetes occurs in 2 to 4 per cent of all pregnancies.

Gestational Diabetes

RISK FACTORS

Gestational diabetes is described as a carbohydrate intolerance of variable severity that develops or is first recognized during pregnancy, usually in late second trimester. Factors known to increase the risk include:

- Obesity
- Chronic hypertension
- Maternal age over 30 years
- Family history of diabetes
- Prior birth of a large infant
- Prior birth of an infant with congenital anomalies
- Prior stillborn infant
- Gestational diabetes in previous pregnancy

The incidence is not always comparable for different geographic areas. For example, in areas with a specific ethnic group, such as Latinas, or in populations in which a specific health problem, such as obesity, is prevalent, the incidence is as high as 7 to 9 per cent (Langer, 1991).

SCREENING

Urine. Urine testing is performed at each prenatal visit, although measuring for glycosuria is a simple screening test only and the presence of glycosuria is not diagnostic for diabetes. Glycosuria can be detected with Diastix or Testape, which is specific for glucose and does not reflect lactose or fructose. Glycosuria is often related to recent intake of foods high in sugar and is a common finding in pregnancy, even in women without gestational diabetes.

Plasma Glucose. Additional laboratory tests are necessary for diagnosis of gestational diabetes. A 50 g glucose tolerance test (GTT) is often routinely performed at 24 to 28 weeks' gestation. This is a convenient test because it can be done at a regular clinic visit. The woman does not need to fast, and the test need not follow a meal. The woman ingests 50 g of oral glucose solution; 1 hour later, a blood sample is taken. If the blood glucose exceeds 140 mg/100 ml (140 mg/dl), a 3-hour oral GTT is recommended (Harris, 1992).

Plasma glucose is often tested at the first prenatal visit if the woman has the high-risk factors mentioned earlier. If findings are normal, the test is repeated at 28 weeks' gestation. If values exceed 140 mg/dl, a 3-hour GTT is necessary.

Glucose Tolerance Test. A 3-hour GTT is more complicated and involves the woman's participation. She eats a high-carbohydrate diet for 2 days before the scheduled test and fasts from midnight on the day of the test. A fasting plasma glucose level is obtained. She then ingests 100 g of oral glucose solution. Plasma glucose levels are obtained at 1, 2, and 3 hours. Gestational diabetes is the diagnosis if the fasting blood glucose is abnormal or if two or more of the following values are found:

Fasting, >105 mg/dl
1 *hour,* >190 mg/dl
2 *hours,* >165 mg/dl
3 *hours,* >145 mg/dl

Glycosylated Hemoglobin. Long-term assessment is based on the glycosylated hemoglobin (HbA1c) level, which reflects the amount of hemoglobin that is saturated with glucose. The test is particularly useful because it can accurately indicate serum glucose levels for the past 4 to 6 weeks. Other tests reflect the amount of glucose in the plasma at that moment and are influenced by the recent intake of food. The HbA1c value is not affected by recent intake or restriction of food.

MATERNAL EFFECTS

Significant maternal effects are associated with gestational diabetes. These include:

- Increased incidence of urinary tract infections, possibly due to spilling of glucose into the urine, which provides a nutrient-rich medium for bacterial growth
- Increased incidence of hydramnios, which may result from fetal hyperglycemia and consequent fetal diuresis
- Increased risk of premature rupture of membranes and preterm labor, which may be due to overdistention of the uterus by hydramnios and the large infant
- Increased risk for the development of pregnancy-induced hypertension; the reason for this is unclear
- Increased incidence of shoulder dystocia (delayed or difficult birth of fetal shoulders after the head is born) and consequent injury to the vaginal canal during birth because the fetus is frequently large (>4000 g). Large fetal size also increases the likelihood that a cesarean birth will be necessary and makes the possibility of postpartum hemorrhage more likely.

FETAL-NEONATAL EFFECTS

Because gestational diabetes develops after the first trimester—the critical period of major fetal organ development (organogenesis)—it is not usually associated with an increased risk of major congenital malformations. Nevertheless, gestational diabetes characterized by maternal hyperglycemia during the third trimester is associated with increased neonatal morbidity and mortality.

Macrosomia. Macrosomia results when elevated levels of blood glucose stimulate excessive production of fetal insulin, which acts as a powerful growth hormone. This is a major neonatal effect (birth weight above 4000 g), with consequent increase in birth injury due to shoulder dystocia or cesarean birth.

Hypoglycemia. The neonate is also at increased risk for hypoglycemia because fetal insulin production was accelerated during pregnancy to metabolize excessive glucose received from the expectant mother. The constant stimulation of hyperglycemia leads to both hyperplasia and hypertrophy of the islets of Langerhans in the pancreas. At birth, when the maternal glucose supply is withdrawn, the level of neonatal insulin exceeds the available glucose and hypoglycemia develops rapidly. Additional metabolic disorders may include hypocalcemia (diminished calcium in the blood) and hyperbilirubinemia (excess levels of bilirubin).

Respiratory Distress Syndrome. Fetal hyperinsulinemia retards cortisol production, which is necessary for synthesis of surfactant (lipoproteins that prevent collapse of alveoli) and the inadequate production of surfactant increases the risk that the newborn will experience respiratory distress syndrome. (See Chapter 29 for additional information about neonatal complications.)

THERAPEUTIC MANAGEMENT

Gestational diabetes is usually controlled by a regular pattern of physical activity and dietary management. The diet is individualized to provide 30 to 40 kcal/kg of body weight, and the calories are best divided among three meals and at least two snacks (Mahan and Arlin, 1992). Fasting and postprandial (after-meal) glucose levels are evaluated at least every 2 weeks to confirm the effectiveness of the dietary regimen (Rotondo and Coustan, 1993). Insulin is added to the treatment regimen if fasting glucose levels are greater than 120 mg/dl (Kappy, 1991).

Early delivery is not usually required; however, labor is often induced at term. Antepartum fetal testing is usually initiated if the mother requires insulin, if hypertension develops, or if there is a history of prior stillbirth. The most common fetal surveillance techniques of the third trimester include fetal movement counts ("kick counts"), the non-stress test, amniotic fluid index, and biophysical profile. (See Chapter 10.)

Pre-Existing Diabetes Mellitus

The course of pregnancy for women with diabetes mellitus has improved greatly as a result of newer treatments and more effective methods of fetal surveillance. However, the incidence of complications that affect both the mother and fetus remains higher than that experienced by the general population.

For the woman with pre-existing diabetes mellitus, diabetes may have developed many years before she became pregnant. Generally, she uses a combination of diet, planned exercise, and insulin to maintain normal blood glucose levels. Vascular complications depend on how long she has had the disease and how well the blood glucose level has been maintained.

MATERNAL EFFECTS

Diabetes adversely affects pregnant women in a number of ways. The risk of pregnancy-induced hypertension is four times greater than in the normal population even if there is no evidence of vascular or renal complications (Cunningham et al, 1989). Maternal infections, such as cystitis and pyelonephritis, are more common and more severe. The development of ketoacidosis is a threat to women with insulin-dependent diabetes and is most often precipitated by infection or missed insulin doses. Moreover, ketoacidosis may develop during pregnancy at lower thresholds of hyperglycemia than those seen in non-pregnant individuals. Untreated ketoacidosis can progress to fetal and maternal death. See Table 25–3 for a summary of the effects of diabetes mellitus in pregnancy.

During the first trimester, when major fetal organ development is occurring, the effects of the abnormal metabolic environment, such as hypoglycemia, hyperglycemia, and ketosis, may also lead to increased incidence of spontaneous abortion or major fetal malformations.

FETAL-NEONATAL EFFECTS

Fetal and neonatal effects of pre-existing diabetes include those associated with gestational diabetes. There are also problems that depend on the timing and severity of maternal hyperglycemia and the degree of vascular impairment that has occurred.

Congenital Malformation. The most common major congenital malformations associated with pre-existing diabetes are neural tube defects (caudal re-

Table 25–3. SUMMARY OF THE EFFECTS OF DIABETES ON PREGNANCY

Increased Maternal Risks
Pregnancy-induced hypertension
Urinary tract infections
Hydramnios
Preterm labor
Premature rupture of membranes
Difficult labor
Injury to birth canal
Cesarean birth
Postpartum hemorrhage
Development of ketoacidosis
Increased Fetal Risks
Perinatal death
Congenital anomalies
Large infant (>4000 g)
Birth injury
Intrauterine growth retardation
Polycythemia
Hyperbilirubinemia
Neonatal respiratory distress syndrome
Neonatal hypoglycemia

gression, anencephaly, spina bifida) and cardiac defects. Infants of diabetic mothers have a twofold to threefold greater frequency of severe malformations than women without diabetes. The incidence correlates directly with the degree of maternal hyperglycemia during the first trimester and may be decreased considerably if maternal blood glucose levels are normalized early in the pregnancy or before conception (Kappy, 1991).

Variations in Fetal Size. Fetal size is related to maternal vascular integrity. In women without vascular impairment, glucose is easily transported to the fetus; if the woman is hyperglycemic, so is the fetus. Glucose stimulates the secretion of fetal insulin (a potent growth factor) and results in macrosomia.

If there is vascular impairment, placental perfusion may be compromised and the supply of glucose as well as oxygen to the fetus will be decreased. As a result, the newborn is likely to be small for gestational age. This condition is frequently called intrauterine growth retardation (IUGR).

Fetal Hypoxia. Persistent fetal hypoxia (lessened availability of oxygen) causes two additional interrelated problems: polycythemia (increased red blood cell volume) and hyperbilirubinemia. When oxygen concentration is low, additional erythrocytes (red blood cells) are produced to transport all available oxygen to fetal tissue. Following delivery, the erythrocytes are broken down and bilirubin (the residue from red blood cell destruction) builds up in the blood of the newborn, causing neonatal jaundice. (See Chapter 29 for additional information about hyperbilirubinemia.)

The occurrence of maternal and fetal-neonatal complications can be greatly diminished by maintaining normal blood glucose levels. The objective of the team providing treatment is to devise a plan that allows the woman to maintain a level as close to normal as possible.

THERAPEUTIC MANAGEMENT

The goals of therapeutic management for a pregnant woman with diabetes are to: (1) maintain normal blood glucose levels, (2) give birth to a healthy baby, and (3) avoid accelerated impairment of blood vessels and other major organs. The improved outcome for women with diabetes mellitus is due to the advent of the *team approach to management* and the widespread use of home glucose monitoring (Kappy, 1991).

Members of the team include:

- A perinatologist-obstetrician, skilled in the management of diabetes in pregnancy, who performs screening procedures in the fetus, monitors the general health of the expectant mother, and determines the optimal time for delivery
- A diabetologist, who assists in the regulation of maternal blood glucose levels before conception and throughout the pregnancy
- A nurse, who provides ongoing education and additional support, which are often necessary to help the woman maintain normal blood glucose levels
- A dietitian, who provides a balanced meal plan that minimizes the risk of hypoglycemia or hyperglycemia
- A neonatologist, who is an important member of the management team around the time of the delivery and who should be apprised of the mother's course throughout her pregnancy
- A family physician and the pediatrician, who provide primary care for the baby and the mother. They also receive information about the plan of care, since they will be providing care on an ongoing basis following discharge from the hospital

Pre-conception Care

Ideally, the team approach should begin before conception and both prospective parents should participate in care sessions to learn more about the following issues:

- Establishing the optimal time for pregnancy on the basis of maintenance of normal maternal blood glucose levels so that the risk of major fetal malformations can be reduced
- Evaluating the degree of maternal vascular complications

- Providing information about the importance of maintaining normal blood glucose levels throughout the pregnancy; this is particularly important if excellent control has not been accomplished prior to conception
- Providing instruction, if necessary, in the use of home glucose monitoring techniques

Diet. The guidelines for dietary regulation of diabetes during pregnancy are similar to those recommended generally for persons with diabetes and for the general population. Namely 50 to 60 per cent of calories should be derived from carbohydrates, 25 per cent from protein, and 20 to 30 per cent from fat. On the average, the pregnant woman with diabetes requires a total of 2000 to 2400 kcal/day (Kappy, 1991). Food intake is divided throughout the day as three meals and two to four snacks.

Insulin. The need to maintain rigorous control of the maternal metabolism during pregnancy necessitates more frequent doses of insulin than usual. Most treatment regimens rely on three daily injections, with a combination of short-acting (Regular) insulin and intermediate-acting (NPH) insulin given before breakfast, regular insulin before dinner, and NPH insulin at bedtime. Some regimens call for long-acting (Ultralente) insulin to be given once or twice daily, supplemented by regular insulin before meals (Kappy, 1991).

Because insulin needs change throughout pregnancy owing to the effect of the placental hormones, insulin coverage will need to be adjusted as pregnancy progresses.

First Trimester. Insulin needs generally decline during the first trimester. This is because the secretion of placental hormones that are antagonistic to insulin are low and because the woman often experiences nausea, vomiting, and anorexia; this results in decreased intake of food, and thus less insulin is needed. Moreover, the fetus receives its share of glucose, and this reduces maternal plasma glucose levels and decreases the need for maternal insulin.

Second and Third Trimesters. Insulin needs increase markedly during the second and third trimesters, when placental hormones, which increase maternal resistance to the effects of insulin, reach their peak. In addition, the nausea of early pregnancy usually resolves and the diet includes at least 300 additional calories per day, which is necessary to meet the increased metabolic demands of pregnancy.

During Labor. Insulin needs during labor are based on the blood glucose level. The vigorous muscular exertion and lack of oral intake should decrease the amount of insulin needed; however, glucose is sometimes administered intravenously, which may make administration of insulin necessary. The only accurate way to determine insulin needs is to evaluate blood glucose levels. This should be done hourly during labor (Rotondo and Coustan, 1993). If insulin is needed, regular insulin may be added to the intravenous solution and is infused at a rate to maintain normal levels.

Post Partum. Insulin needs should decline rapidly following delivery of the placenta and the abrupt cessation of placental hormones. Blood glucose levels should be monitored at least four times daily, however, so that insulin dose can be adjusted to meet individual needs.

Timing of Delivery. If possible, pregnancies are usually allowed to progress to term so that the fetal lungs have a chance to mature and so that the risk of neonatal respiratory distress syndrome can be reduced. However, if there is evidence of fetal compromise, such as non-reactive non–stress tests or late decelerations on a contraction stress test, an amniocentesis may be performed to evaluate the ratio of lecithin to sphingomyelin (L/S). If the L/S ratio is at least 2.0 and the phospholipid phosphatidyl-glycerol (PG) is present, the lungs are judged to be mature and early delivery may be planned.

✔ Check Your Reading

1. What effects do placental hormones have on maternal glucose metabolism?
2. What are the major effects of gestational diabetes on the mother and fetus?
3. How is gestational diabetes usually treated?
4. What are the possible effects of hyperglycemia during the first trimester?
5. How do insulin needs change throughout pregnancy, during labor, and in the postpartum period?
6. Why might the fetus be either large or growth-retarded when the mother has diabetes mellitus?

The Pregnant Woman with Diabetes Mellitus: Application of Nursing Process

Learning Needs

Assessment

Determine how well the woman understands the prescribed management and how the family plans to carry out the recommended regimen. This involves evaluating her experience with management of diabetes. She may be newly diagnosed and may have no experience in the necessary skills and procedures. On the other hand, she may be very experienced with glucose monitoring and insulin injections but may have no knowledge of the effects that pregnancy has on her condition.

Ask the expectant mother to demonstrate her skill in blood glucose monitoring and in mixing and injecting insulin to verify that her techniques are accurate. Determine also if the woman and her family are aware of the need to select appropriate sites and injection procedures that prevent insulin leakage.

Diet is prescribed by a dietitian. However, it is necessary to assess how well the woman and her family understand the diet and to determine whether there are special problems with food preferences or availability of recommended foods. It may be necessary to review the exchange list and ask the woman how she plans to substitute and exchange foods.

Identify the woman's knowledge of potential complications, such as hypoglycemia and hyperglycemia, so that she and her family can be provided with pertinent information.

Analysis

One of the priority nursing diagnoses is: *High Risk for Altered Health Maintenance related to lack of knowledge of specific measures to maintain normal blood glucose levels and signs of hypoglycemia and hyperglycemia.*

Planning

For this nursing diagnosis, the expectant mother (and her family):

- Will demonstrate competence in home glucose monitoring and administration of insulin before home management is initiated.
- Will describe a plan for meeting dietary recommendations.
- Will identify signs and symptoms of hypoglycemia and hyperglycemia and the necessary management required in each.

Interventions

Although management of diabetes mellitus during pregnancy is a team effort, the major responsibility of the nurse is to provide accurate information about the recommended therapeutic regimen and to offer consistent support for the patient's efforts to comply with the recommendations. It may be necessary to demonstrate specific skills that the woman and her family must master and to review and reinforce information that comes from other members of the health care team.

TEACHING SELF-CARE SKILLS

Before beginning any teaching session, find a private location that is free of interruptions or distractions and assess the patient's knowledge. Determine the teaching method to be used; demonstration and return demonstration are the most effective ways to teach and evaluate psychomotor skills. The patient (and her family) must learn to mix and inject insulin and to obtain a small sample of blood to test for glucose. Both of these procedures will be performed several times each day, and the nurse is responsible for teaching them and for evaluating the patient's skill in performing them. Both procedures are invasive and cause mild discomfort; this may make the client reluctant to start. Acknowledge these feelings before teaching begins.

Home Blood Glucose Monitoring. The blood glucose level is monitored several times a day, and the patient must be comfortable with the procedure.  Spring devices, available for sticking the finger, make the procedure easier and less painful. Recommend that the expectant mother use the side of the finger that is less sensitive than the tip. Teach her to cleanse the area to prevent infection. Each home monitoring kit contains specific instructions for timing and washing or blotting the blood from the reagent strip, and these directions must be followed exactly to obtain an accurate reading.

Administration of Insulin. Two types of insulin are usually prescribed: intermediate-acting and short-acting (regular) insulin. Teach the expectant mother the difference in onset, peak, and duration of each type of insulin. She also needs to learn how to mix the two insulins in the same syringe.

Insulin is administered subcutaneously. Common sites include the upper thighs, abdomen, and upper arms. Aseptic technique is recommended to prevent infection.

Because the pregnant woman is injecting insulin frequently, emphasize these precautions:

- To prevent hypoglycemia, a meal should be taken 30 minutes after insulin is injected.
- Unless the woman is very thin, insulin should be injected at a 90-degree angle. If she is thin, a 45-degree angle is appropriate to ensure the most effective absorption.
- The needle should be inserted quickly to minimize discomfort.
- The tissue pinch, if used, is released after in-

- serting the needle and before injecting insulin because pressure from the pinch can promote insulin leakage from the subcutaneous tissue.
- It is not necessary to aspirate; doing so may cause tissue damage.
- Insulin is injected slowly (over 2 to 4 seconds) to allow tissue expansion and to minimize pressure, which can cause insulin leakage.
- The needle is withdrawn quickly to minimize the formation of a track, which might permit insulin to leak out.

Emphasize the importance of administering the correct dose at the correct time. Teach the woman and her family the function of insulin and the importance of following the directions of the physician in regard to coordinating meals with the administration of insulin.

INSTRUCTING IN DIETARY MANAGEMENT

Although a dietitian prescribes the recommended diet, the nurse must be aware of the general requirements and must be sensitive to the expectant mother's dietary habits and preferences. There is often a need to review and clarify how the exchange lists are used to plan meals and snacks. Encourage the patient to avoid simple sugars (candy, cake, cookies), which raise the blood glucose levels quickly, and to include foods high in fiber, which are believed to help reduce glucose levels.

Finances are often a problem, and it may be necessary to help the woman select foods that are high in nutrients but low in cost. Animal protein is especially expensive, and alternative sources of protein (beans, peas, corn, grains) can be substituted to meet some of the protein needs.

Allow the expectant mother to verbalize her frustrations or problems with the diet, and collaborate with the dietitian if she has a particular problem.

RECOGNIZING AND CORRECTING HYPOGLYCEMIA AND HYPERGLYCEMIA

Every woman and her family must be aware of the signs and symptoms that indicate abnormal blood glucose levels. Both hypoglycemia and hyperglycemia pose a threat to both mother and fetus if they are not identified and corrected quickly.

Hypoglycemia. The most obvious signs and symptoms of hypoglycemia are listed in Critical to Remember: Signs and Symptoms of Maternal Hypoglycemia. Treat hypoglycemia at once to prevent damage to the brain, which is dependent on glucose. If the woman is able to swallow, have her drink 8 ounces of milk and eat two crackers. Repeat the snack in 15 minutes if symptoms persist or blood glucose level is between 40 and 80 mg (Hollingsworth and Moore, 1989). Follow this within 10 to 15 minutes with a well-balanced meal.

Critical to Remember

Signs and Symptoms of Maternal Hypoglycemia

- Shakiness (tremors)
- Sweating
- Pallor; cold clammy skin
- Disorientation; irritability
- Headache
- Hunger
- Blurred vision

Teach family members how to inject glucagon in the event that the woman cannot swallow or retain food. Notify the physician at once and give intravenous glucose if she is hospitalized. If untreated, hypoglycemia can progress to convulsions and death.

To prevent episodes of hypoglycemia, instruct the woman to have meals at a fixed time each day and to plan snacks at 10 a.m., 3 p.m., and at bedtime. Suggest that she carry a thermos of milk and some dry crackers at all times.

Hyperglycemia. Because infection is the most common cause of hyperglycemia, pregnant women must be instructed to notify the physician whenever they have an infection of any type. See Critical to Remember: Signs and Symptoms of Maternal Hyperglycemia.

If untreated, hyperglycemia can lead to ketoacidosis, coma, and maternal and fetal death. If signs and

Critical to Remember

Signs and Symptoms of Maternal Hyperglycemia

- Fatigue
- Flushed, hot skin
- Dry mouth; excessive thirst
- Frequent urination
- Rapid, deep respirations; odor of acetone on the breath
- Drowsiness; headache
- Depressed reflexes

symptoms occur, notify the physician at once so that treatment can be initiated. Hospitalization is often necessary for monitoring blood glucose levels and intravenous administration of insulin.

Evaluation

- The expectant mother and one family member demonstrate competence in blood glucose monitoring and administration of insulin.
- She verbalizes the function of insulin and the importance of coordinating insulin injection and meals.
- The family describes a plan for meeting dietary requirements.
- The woman and her family list the signs and symptoms of hypoglycemia and hyperglycemia.
- They describe the initial management of these conditions.

Emotional Needs

Assessment

Pregnancy presents a stressful situation for some women with pre-existing diabetes, because to a large extent a successful outcome depends on their ability to maintain blood glucose levels as close to normal as possible. Some women respond calmly when their pregnancy is designated "high-risk"; others respond with anxiety, fear, denial, or anger and feel inadequate or unable to control the diabetes to the degree expected by the health care team. These feelings may not be shared spontaneously, but they may affect the woman's ability to achieve the desired outcomes.

A woman often does not volunteer information about her feelings and concerns, especially if she has negative feelings about her care. Moreover, both the woman and the nurse may be unaware of the misunderstandings or conflicts regarding the plan of care.

Ask specifically about the feelings and concerns the woman and her family have about the pregnancy. Use broad opening questions, such as, "What are your major concerns?" "How do you feel about the plan of care?" Follow with more specific questions, such as, "How do you feel about the fetal testing?" "What would you like to change about the diet?" The woman's comments can provide valuable information about her emotional response to the care plan. One woman remarked, "I can tell you one thing, I don't feel like a person; I feel like an incubator, a faulty incubator." Another woman, who had a difficult time achieving the desired blood glucose level, said: "I feel as if my whole life has been taken over by diabetes. I'm tired of feeling like a sick person."

Some women look forward to fetal surveillance and feel relieved and highly motivated to continue the treatment regimen when the test results indicate that the fetus is thriving. Other women dread the tests and feel anxious whenever they are necessary. When this information is revealed, clarify the woman's feelings.

Analysis

Anger, apathy, uneasiness, or expressions of dissatisfaction about their ability to maintain strict control over their diabetes may indicate a sense of powerlessness in some pregnant women. The most troubling problem and its cause are identified in the nursing diagnosis *Powerlessness related to ineffective communication between person and health care team and inadequate opportunity to make decisions about plan of care.*

Planning

Goals for the nursing diagnosis are as follows:

- The expectant mother will verbalize feelings on a continuing basis to health care team.
- She will verbalize knowledge of reasons for fetal surveillance and blood glucose monitoring throughout pregnancy.
- She will make decisions regarding her care when possible.

Interventions

INCREASING EFFECTIVE COMMUNICATIONS

The nurse must be an active listener and allow time for the woman and her family to express concerns and feelings. Convey acceptance of feelings that are expressed whether they are negative or positive. Many women are reassured to hear that their feelings of stress or anger are normal and to know that the health care team understands those feelings. Sharing of emotions will help her prevent or diminish unnecessary guilt, anxiety, or frustration and thus promote positive feelings about her ability to participate successfully in her plan of care.

Most women benefit from praise when diabetic control is well maintained; they feel competent and trusted by the health care team and are motivated to continue their efforts.

EXPLAINING PROCEDURES, TESTS, AND PLAN OF CARE

Explain the schedule and the reasons for frequent check-ups and tests that are necessary. Encourage the woman and her family to ask questions if any part of the schedule is confusing. This is particularly important for women who are aware that their prenatal care differs significantly from that of their friends who do not have diabetes. Knowing that the tests provide information about the condition of both mother and fetus reduces frustration and anxiety. Specifically, pregnant women and their families need to know why weekly (or daily) non–stress tests are necessary. Moreover, inform them why it is necessary to perform contraction stress tests, an amniotic fluid index, and amniocentesis. (See Chapter 10 for additional information about prenatal testing.) Clients may be especially concerned if they think that the test results have changed because the condition of the fetus is deteriorating. Women need to know that their diabetic care will require more of their time and effort than it did before pregnancy but that this care greatly improves the likelihood that they will have healthy infants.

PROVIDING OPPORTUNITIES FOR CONTROL

Allowing the woman to make as many decisions as possible increases her sense of being in control. For instance, she can select foods from the exchange list that provide the necessary nutrients but still allow her some choice. She may also work out a regular schedule of exercise and sleep that help to keep the blood glucose level under control. Allow as much flexibility as possible when scheduling stressful events, such as fetal monitoring tests and amniocentesis.

Some women resent being "treated as though ill" even though their diabetic control is excellent. These women may be capable of making more decisions regarding their care during pregnancy, but they need the support of an understanding team to do this.

PROVIDING NORMAL PREGNANCY CARE

Some women express a need for normal pregnancy care that is sometimes ignored because of the focus on preventing complications that might occur as a result of diabetes. Women with diabetes also experience the discomforts that non-diabetic women experience during pregnancy, such as morning sickness, fatigue, backache, and difficulty sleeping. The nurse caring for women with high-risk pregnancies should provide education and counseling regarding normal pregnancy discomforts. Also, because women with diabetes are concerned about how they will manage during labor and delivery, nurses should offer childbirth preparation classes and discuss with them the experiences that are common to all pregnant women.

Evaluation

Interventions are successful when:

- The expectant mother and her family verbalize their feelings and ask questions about any part of the treatment plan that is not understood. Verbalized knowledge of the reasons and importance of prenatal tests often increases the feeling of control.
- They can make appropriate decisions independently, whenever possible; this also reduces feelings of powerlessness.

Heart Disease

Alterations in cardiovascular function are necessary in every pregnancy to meet increased maternal metabolic demands and to meet the needs of the fetus. Plasma volume, venous return, and cardiac output all increase, and there is a significant change in clotting factors. (See Chapter 7 for more complete details of cardiovascular changes in normal pregnancy.)

A normal heart can adapt to the changes so that pregnancy and delivery are tolerated without difficulty. If there is pre-existing or underlying heart disease, however, the changes can impose an additional burden on an already compromised heart, and cardiac decompensation and congestive heart failure can result.

Incidence and Classification

Heart disease complicates about 1 per cent of pregnancies, and despite advances in diagnosis and treatment, maternal cardiovascular disease continues to account for up to 30 per cent of all maternal deaths (Clark, 1991).

The two major categories are rheumatic heart

Text continued on page 715

Nursing Care Plan 25–1

Pregnancy and Diabetes Mellitus

Assessment: Kathy Ringold is a 24-year-old primigravida of 9 weeks' gestation who was diagnosed with insulin-dependent diabetes mellitus 6 years ago. She has been on a daily regimen of insulin and is comfortable with insulin administration and blood glucose monitoring. She is experiencing daily nausea and vomiting. Kathy states that she is concerned because she is not eating as much as before becoming pregnant. She also reveals that she had sometimes "binged" on food before becoming pregnant and didn't always monitor blood glucose as often as directed. She does not see why her blood glucose has to be so carefully watched.

Nursing Diagnosis: High Risk for Altered Health Maintenance related to knowledge deficit of the effects of pregnancy on diabetes control.

Goals:
Kathy will:

1. Describe predicted changes in insulin needs throughout pregnancy and will follow prescribed schedule of blood glucose monitoring, insulin administration, diet, and exercise.
2. Describe the importance of frequent fetal surveillance and will follow the prescribed schedule.

Intervention:	Rationale:
1. Reduce barriers to learning a. Allow her to express emotions and concerns prior to teaching. b. Examine her beliefs and past experiences related to diabetes. c. Assess readiness to learn, based on interest, attention, and participation in scheduled learning sessions.	1. Motivation and readiness to learn are essential for permanent learning to occur. She will learn only if she sees the value of the information.
2. Instruct Kathy about the predicted changes in insulin needs during pregnancy. a. Explain the importance of blood glucose testing; Kathy will need less insulin because of the nausea and vomiting occurring in the first trimester. b. Emphasize that later (during the second and third trimesters) she will probably require more insulin because of the effects of the placental hormones. Re-emphasize the importance of glucose monitoring. c. Describe the importance of following the prescribed diet and exercise regimen to maintain normal blood glucose.	2. Behaviors change when learning occurs, and understanding how insulin needs change throughout pregnancy, labor, and the postpartum period increases the likelihood that Kathy will follow the recommended regimen even when it is inconvenient or time-consuming.
3. Inform Kathy about specific fetal surveillance techniques recommended during pregnancy (serial non–stress tests, contraction stress tests, biophysical profiles), and explain the importance of the tests.	3. Some frequently ordered tests are time-consuming and expensive. The client is more likely to comply if she understands the importance of monitoring the fetal condition at frequent intervals.
4. Allow time for Kathy to focus on her feelings and concerns at each teaching session; offer praise and encouragement for her adherence to the prescribed regimen.	4. Motivation to comply with the regimen is strengthened by praise and the awareness that the client's feelings are important.
5. Explain in simple, positive terms the advantages to the fetus of maintaining a normal, maternal blood glucose level, especially an optimal pattern of growth, the increased likelihood that the baby will be born near term, and fewer complications associated with prematurity.	5. Although Kathy has had diabetes for 6 years, this is the first pregnancy and she may not understand the relationship between maternal hyperglycemia and fetal condition. Presenting easy-to-comprehend information lessens the chance of the client's experiencing undue anxiety.

Nursing Care Plan 25–1 *Continued*

Pregnancy and Diabetes Mellitus

6. Review the recommended plan for diet and exercise during pregnancy, and determine whether Kathy knows the importance of these factors in her care.

6. Maintenance of normal blood glucose depends on coordinating the amount of food, insulin, and exercise. If any of these is altered, the others must also be altered to prevent either hypoglycemia or hyperglycemia.

Evaluation:
Kathy verbalizes her understanding of changing insulin needs and the importance of glucose monitoring. She states that she feels in better control of the diabetes and plans to comply with recommended schedule of fetal surveillance, diet, and exercise.

Assessment: When Kathy is 24 weeks' pregnant, she states that she is "hungry all the time" and wonders if it really matters if she gains a few extra pounds during pregnancy. She states that her mother gained 50 pounds and she had a healthy baby. Kathy craves ice cream and enchiladas, which are high in dairy fat. Kathy is 5 feet 2 inches tall, and she weighed 145 pounds when she became pregnant. She has gained 19 pounds to date. She seldom walks, although this is part of her recommended plan of care.

Nursing Diagnosis: Altered Nutrition: More Than Body Requirements related to reported belief that weight gain during pregnancy is not a problem, and lack of exercise.

Goals:
1. Kathy will describe nutritional needs during pregnancy.
2. She will describe the effect of exercise on insulin requirements.
3. She will plan food intake that satisfies her hunger but limits the intake of fats and "empty calories."

Interventions:

1. Explore beliefs about weight gain during pregnancy and the relationship of weight gain to maternal and fetal health.
2. Briefly review the nutritional needs of pregnancy in terms that the client can understand.
   a. Avoid technical terms, and relate nutrients to food sources that are common to her. For example, avoid terms like "ascorbic acid" and "riboflavin" in favor of food sources (oranges, milk products, and green leafy vegetables).
   b. Reinforce that only about 300 additional calories are needed to meet the daily energy needs of pregnancy. Provide some perspective about what constitutes these 300 calories; for instance, a cup of yogurt with an apple.
   c. Review foods that are high in unwanted fat (ice cream, cheese) and suggest low-fat yogurt, ice milk, and skim milk cottage cheese to reduce the number of calories consumed.
   d. Review foods that are high in simple sugars, and suggest foods high in fiber and complex carbohydrates (whole grain bread, cereal, pasta).
   e. Recommend fresh fruits as substitutes for candy and cakes.

Rationale:

1. Family and cultural values exert a strong influence on how the patient feels about dietary management.
2. Simple sugars raise the blood glucose level and often stimulate desire for additional sweets. Substituting low-fat foods reduces the caloric intake while satisfying the desire for ice cream and cheese.

Nursing Care Plan continued on following page

Nursing Care Plan 25–1 *Continued*

Pregnancy and Diabetes Mellitus

Intervention	Rationale
3. Attempt to motivate Kathy to exercise as directed. a. Encourage her to walk the distance recommended; suggest that she walk early and walk with a friend. b. Recommend that she take a walk and eat an apple when she is bored or when she usually overeats. c. Suggest that she set small goals and to increase the destination each day until the recommended distance is covered. d. Explain that muscles use glucose for energy and daily exercise helps to keep blood glucose levels under control.	3. Insulin is prescribed on the basis of the amount of planned exercise as well as type of diet. If the client does not exercise, adjust the insulin dose. Walking with a friend can make exercise more pleasant, and incremental goals may motivate her to continue.

Evaluation:
Kathy accurately verbalizes nutritional needs and sources of nutrients. She reports that her hunger is satisfied by substitutions that are lower in fat and simple sugars. She has begun to walk with a neighbor and plans to continue.

Assessment: At 32 weeks' gestation, Kathy's blood glucose is consistently above the desired level and daily non–stress tests are prescribed. The tests are reactive, indicating no present fetal compromise; however, Kathy verbalizes anxiety about the condition of the fetus and asks when it will be safe for the baby to be born.

Nursing Diagnosis: Anxiety related to perceived threat to the health of the fetus and lack of knowledge about the timing of the delivery.

Goals:
1. Kathy will relate her perception of the condition of the fetus and the significance of the reactive non–stress test as the tests are performed.
2. She will describe her concerns about timing of the delivery at the conclusion of the next non–stress test.

Intervention:	Rationale:
1. Ask Kathy to describe her concern about the fetus, and clarify her feelings.	1. Her concerns must be identified and clarified so that misconceptions do not occur. For example, Kathy may begin to be anxious about labor and delivery or she may worry that the elevated blood glucose level poses an immediate threat to the baby.
2. Explain that a reactive non–stress test indicates that the fetal heart rate accelerates whenever the fetus moves; this is a good sign that the fetus is not in immediate jeopardy.	2. Reassurance that the fetus is not in jeopardy and that the daily tests will detect early signs if a problem develops reduces anxiety about the fetal condition.
3. Ask Kathy how she feels about the labor and delivery; determine whether she is taking childbirth education classes and whether she has selected her coach.	3. It is normal for women to become concerned about the birth process and how they will cope with labor during the last few weeks of pregnancy. The need for normal pregnancy care is sometimes neglected for women with a high-risk pregnancy.
4. Assist her in investigating a childbirth education class if she has not done so previously, and suggest that she and her coach begin classes.	4. Knowledge learned at childbirth classes may reduce the anxiety about the birth processes.
5. Acknowledge that the prospect of labor and delivery causes many women some anxiety even when the condition of the infant is not in question.	5. Knowledge that her feelings are common to most women may provide some relief from anxiety.

Nursing Care Plan 25-1 *Continued*

Pregnancy and Diabetes Mellitus

Evaluation:
Kathy has been reassured by explanations regarding the reactive non–stress test, but is concerned about how she will do in labor. She initiates plans to attend a childbirth education class with her sister as the coach.

Additional Nursing Diagnoses to Consider:
High Risk for Altered Family Processes
High Risk for Altered Parenting
High Risk for Injury

disease and congenital heart disease. Mitral valve prolapse (MVP) is a benign developmental condition that does not fit into either category; generally, it does not pose a threat to the mother or fetus (Meller and Goldman, 1991).

RHEUMATIC HEART DISEASE

There has been a remarkable decline in rheumatic heart disease as a result of early treatment of streptococcal pharyngitis ("strep throat"), which often precedes the onset of rheumatic fever. Even one bout of rheumatic fever may cause scarring of the valves in the heart. This results in narrowing (stenosis) of the openings between the chambers of the heart. The mitral valve is the most common site of stenosis. Mitral stenosis obstructs free flow of blood from the left atrium to the left ventricle and greatly increases the cardiac workload and predisposes to the development of congestive heart failure.

CONGENITAL HEART DISEASE

The incidence of pregnancy complicated by congenital heart disease is increasing because more women with congenital cardiac defects now survive to reproductive age. The most common congenital defects include atrial or ventricular septal defects, patent ductus arteriosus, cyanotic heart defects (such as tetralogy of Fallot), and pulmonary hypertension.

Septal Defects. When there is a septal defect, blood is shunted from the left side of the heart to the right side of the heart because pressure in the left side of the heart is higher than it is in the right side. Left-to-right shunting increases the chance of pulmonary hypertension because the additional blood that moves to the right side of the heart is transported to the lungs via the pulmonary artery. When pulmonary vascular resistance rises to exceed peripheral vascular resistance, right-to-left shunting may occur through septal defects. Right-to-left shunting imposes a significant burden on the right ventricle, and the risk of arrhythmias and right ventricular failure is increased.

Tetralogy of Fallot. The primary cause of right-to-left shunting is tetralogy of Fallot, a combination of four defects (ventricular septal defect, pulmonary valve stenosis, right ventricular hypertrophy, and rightward displacement of the aorta). Untreated patients with tetralogy of Fallot have obvious symptoms of heart disease that include (1) cyanosis; (2) clubbing of the fingers, which indicates proliferation of capillaries to transport blood to the extremities; and (3) inability to tolerate activity.

Effect of Pregnancy. The ability of the woman with a congenital heart defect to withstand the stress of pregnancy depends on the specific defect and treatment of the defect before pregnancy. If she has undergone successful surgical repair with no residual effects, she can usually expect an uncomplicated pregnancy. Women with untreated cyanotic heart defects or pulmonary hypertension should be counseled to avoid pregnancy because the risk to both mother and fetus is high.

MITRAL VALVE PROLAPSE

Mitral valve prolapse is one of the most common cardiac conditions among the general population. The incidence is 5 to 15 per cent in all women (Meller and Goldman, 1991). The leaflets of the mitral valve prolapse into the left atrium during ventricular contraction. MVP is considered a benign condition, and most women with MVP are asymptomatic. Some women experience arrhythmias or chest pain; however, most women with MVP tolerate pregnancy well. The condition is considered by some to be a significant risk factor for bacterial endocarditis, and some physicians administer prophylactic antibiotics before and during labor and delivery. If arrhythmia or chest pain occurs, beta-blockers, such as propranolol hydrochloride (Inderal), are administered to prevent stimulation of myocardial, vascular, and pulmonary receptor sites.

PERIPARTUM AND POSTPARTUM CARDIOMYOPATHY

Cardiomyopathy in the peripartum or postpartum period is a very rare condition that is exclusively associated with pregnancy. Women with this condition have no underlying heart disease, but symptoms of cardiac decompensation appear during the last weeks of pregnancy or 2 to 20 weeks post partum. The symptoms are those of congestive heart failure: dyspnea, edema, weakness, chest pain, and heart palpitations. The condition is treated with digitalis, diuretics, sodium restriction, and prolonged bed rest. Peripartum cardiomyopathy tends to recur with subsequent pregnancies, and prognosis for future pregnancies is related to heart size. Future pregnancies are definitely contraindicated if the heart remains enlarged following the initial episode.

Diagnosis and Classification

Early recognition of underlying heart disease is essential, and careful assessment for specific signs and symptoms of heart disease is part of every initial prenatal visit. Signs and symptoms include dyspnea, syncope (fainting) with exertion, hemoptysis, paroxysmal nocturnal dyspnea, and chest pain with exertion. Additional signs that confirm the diagnosis are: (1) diastolic, presystolic, or continuous heart murmur, (2) cardiac enlargement, (3) a loud, harsh systolic murmur associated with a thrill, or (4) serious arrhythmias (Cunningham et al, 1989, p. 797).

Diagnosis of heart disease may be made from clinical signs and symptoms and physical examination. It is often confirmed by chest x-ray, electrocardiogram, or echocardiogram.

Once the diagnosis is made, the severity of the disease can be determined by the client's ability to endure physical activity. A clinical classification based on the effect of exercise on the heart has been developed by the New York Heart Association (Table 25–4).

Table 25–4. FUNCTIONAL CLASSIFICATION OF HEART DISEASE

Class I. Uncompromised. No limitation of physical activity. Asymptomatic with ordinary activity.

Class II. Slightly compromised, requiring slight limitation of physical activity. Comfortable at rest, but experience fatigue, dyspnea, palpitations, or anginal pain with ordinary physical activity.

Class III. Marked limitation of physical activity. Comfortable at rest, but less than ordinary activity causes excessive fatigue, palpitation, dyspnea, or anginal pain. Markedly compromised.

Class IV. Inability to perform any physical activity without discomfort. Symptoms of cardiac insufficiency even at rest. In general, maternal and fetal risks for Class I and II disease are small but are greatly increased with Class III and IV.

Therapeutic Management

The primary goal of management is to prevent cardiac decompensation and the development of congestive heart failure. Moreover, every effort is also made to protect the fetus from hypoxia and IUGR, which can occur if placental perfusion is inadequate.

ANTEPARTUM MANAGEMENT

All pregnant women with heart disease should:

- Limit physical activity so that cardiac demand does not exceed cardiac capacity.
- Avoid excessive weight gain, which places further demands on the heart. A diet adequate in protein, calories, and sodium is necessary; however, a low-sodium diet (2 g/day) prevents excessive expansion of blood volume (Nuwayhid and Khalife, 1992).
- Prevent anemia, which decreases the oxygen-carrying capacity of the blood and results in a compensatory increase in heart rate.
- Prevent infection; this may include administration of prophylactic antibiotics every 4 weeks (Ueland, 1989).
- Undergo careful assessment for the development of congestive heart failure, pulmonary edema, or cardiac arrhythmias.

DRUG THERAPY

Anticoagulants. During pregnancy, clotting factors normally increase and thrombolytic activity decreases. These changes may predispose the pregnant woman to thrombus formation. Superimposed cardiac problems, such as mitral valve stenosis, may necessitate anticoagulant therapy during pregnancy. There is no completely safe anticoagulation regimen during pregnancy: Warfarin is associated with fetal malformations; heparin, which does not cross the placental barrier, is associated with lack of adequate anticoagulation or excessive anticoagulation (Meller and Goldman, 1991). When anticoagulation therapy is required, heparin is generally prescribed. Careful monitoring of partial thromboplastin time is essential to achieve effective anticoagulation.

Antiarrhythmic Therapy. When medication to control arrhythmias is necessary during pregnancy, the effect on the fetus must be considered. Digoxin, quinidine, and procainamide are not harmful to the fetus, and despite early concerns, beta-blocker therapy is not associated with adverse fetal outcomes (Clark, 1991).

Anti-infectives. Anti-infectious agents, such as ampicillin and gentamicin, may be administered as prophylaxis against bacterial endocarditis.

INTRAPARTUM MANAGEMENT

During labor, every effort is made to minimize the effect and prevent decompensation of the maternal heart. With every uterine contraction, 300 to 500 ml of blood is shifted to central circulation, greatly increasing cardiac output. Careful management of intravenous (IV) fluid administration is essential to prevent fluid overload. The woman is positioned on her side, with the head and shoulders elevated. Oxygen is administered to increase the oxygen-carrying capacity of the blood. Sedation and epidural anesthesia are recommended early in labor to reduce discomfort. The environment is kept as quiet and calm as possible to decrease anxiety.

The fetus is electronically monitored, and signs of fetal distress as well as maternal signs of cardiac decompensation (tachycardia, rapid respirations, moist rales, exhaustion) should be reported immediately to the physician.

If cardiac disease is severe, a Swan-Ganz flow-directed pulmonary artery catheter is inserted to measure central venous pressure, right atrial pressure, and pulmonary wedge pressure. Cardiac rhythm is monitored continuously, and fluid intake and output, blood gases, hemoglobin, and electrolytes are also monitored.

A vaginal delivery is recommended for the woman with heart disease unless there are indications for cesarean birth. Outlet forceps are often used to shorten the second stage of labor.

The fourth stage of labor is associated with special risks. After delivery of the placenta, when the uterus contracts, about 500 ml of blood is added to the intravascular volume. To minimize the risks of overloading the circulation, her legs are kept level with the body by lowering of the stirrups during the third stage of labor and not massaging the uterus to expedite separation of the placenta. Careful assessment for signs of circulatory overload, such as bounding pulse, distended neck, peripheral veins, and moist rales in the lungs, is performed during the third and fourth stages of labor.

The Pregnant Woman with Heart Disease: Application of Nursing Process

Assessment

Begin with a review of the woman's medical record to determine the functional classification assigned (see Table 25–4). Assess the woman at each prenatal appointment to determine how pregnancy affects the functional capacity of the heart.

- Take vital signs, and compare them to pre-conception levels; note any changes since the last prenatal appointment.
- Assess the level of fatigue and any changes in fatigue level since the last prenatal appointment; this is especially important when fluid volume peaks and the chance of cardiac decompensation is greatest (18 to 32 weeks' gestation).
- Observe for signs or symptoms of congestive heart failure. (See Critical to Remember: Signs and Symptoms of Congestive Heart Failure.)
- Note additional factors that may increase the workload on the heart (anemia, infections, anxiety, lack of adequate support to manage the activities of daily living).
- Weigh the client, and compare the desired pattern of weight gain with the actual one to detect excessive weight gain or fluid retention.
- Assess the woman's knowledge of the prescribed regimen of care and her ability to comply with it.

Analysis

The pregnant woman with a cardiac defect may be unable to tolerate activity to the same degree as before pregnancy because of the stress imposed on the cardiovascular system. Arriving at the nursing diagnosis *Activity Intolerance related to insufficient knowledge of measures that reduce cardiac stress* is a priority.

Planning

Goals are as follows:

- The woman (and her family) will identify factors that increase cardiac workload.

- They will describe measures that promote adaptation to activity restrictions.

Interventions

Management of the pregnant woman with heart disease requires a team effort, and the nurse is a vital member of the team. Prenatal nursing care focuses on teaching the woman and her family how the disease may affect their lives. This may include specific instructions about factors that increase the workload of the heart and measures that promote adaptation to restrictions in activity.

TEACHING ABOUT INCREASED CARDIAC WORKLOAD

Excessive Weight Gain and Edema. Excessive weight gain and edema increase the workload of the heart and should be avoided. A well-balanced diet that contains approximately 2200 calories is recommended, with adequate high-quality protein and no added salt, which leads to water retention and increased vascular volume. Monitor the pattern of weight gain, and help the woman not to exceed the weight gain recommended by the physician in order to avoid additional strain on the heart.

Exertion. Instruct the woman to modify approaches to activities to regulate energy expenditures and to reduce cardiac workload. For instance, she might take rest periods during the day and for an hour after meals. She can sit rather than stand, if possible, when performing activities. She should rest every few minutes when performing an activity that increases the heart rate to allow the heart time to recover. Emphasize that she should stop an activity if she experiences dyspnea, chest pain, or tachycardia.

Critical to Remember

Signs and Symptoms of Congestive Heart Failure

- Cough (frequent, productive, hemoptysis)
- Progressive dyspnea with exertion
- Orthopnea
- Pitting edema of legs and feet or generalized edema of face, hands, sacral area
- Palpitations of heart
- Progressive fatigue or syncope with exertion
- Moist rales in lower lobes, indicating pulmonary edema

Exposure. Instruct the woman to avoid unnecessary exposure to environmental extremes. She should dress warmly during cold weather and create a barrier to cold temperatures by wearing layers of clothing. She must become aware that exertion in hot, humid weather or during extreme cold places additional demands on the heart and should be avoided.

Emotional Stress. Help the woman to identify areas of stress in her life, if applicable, and explain the effects of emotional stress on the cardiovascular system (increased blood pressure, heart rate, and respiratory rate). Discuss various methods for stress management, such as meditation, progressive relaxation of muscles, and biofeedback.

HELPING THE FAMILY ACCEPT RESTRICTIONS ON ACTIVITY

Assist family members to accept the need for activity restriction. The amount of activity that can be tolerated depends on the severity of the disease; however, all women with heart disease require 8 to 10 hours of sleep each night, with a period of morning and afternoon rest. For some women, complete bed rest (with bathroom privileges only) is necessary during the last half of pregnancy and this may create special problems for the family. Nurses often help the family plan how to meet their needs while the expectant mother remains on bed rest. See Chapter 26 and the Nursing Care Plan for Preterm Labor (p. 758) for additional interventions when a prolonged period of bed rest is required.

PROVIDING CARE POST PARTUM

After childbirth, the mother may be unable to assume care of the newborn; however, every effort should be made to promote contact between the mother and baby. Many nurses assess the baby and perform the necessary newborn care at the bedside, then allow the mother ample time to hold the infant. The father and other family members should be included in the care of the infant whenever possible.

Breastfeeding may not be recommended because of the demands on the mother's energy. However, she should be allowed to feed the infant, whenever possible, to promote maternal-infant attachment. Consult with physicians, and make referrals as necessary for follow-up care, which may include home nursing. Be certain that the family understands the signs and symptoms of cardiac complications and when to notify the physician that problems have developed.

Evaluation

Being able to identify the factors that increase cardiac workload offers reassurance that the family will initiate measures that promote adaptation to restricted activity.

✔ Check Your Reading

7. How do the cardiovascular changes of pregnancy affect the condition of the woman who has a cardiac defect?
8. What are the two major categories of heart disease? What is the functional classification of heart disease?
9. What are the primary goals for management of heart disease in terms of diet, activity, and weight gain?

Anemias

Folic Acid Deficiency Anemia

Folic acid is a nutrient that is essential for the formation of both red and white blood cells in the bone marrow and for their maturation.

MATERNAL EFFECTS

Maternal needs for folic acid increase during pregnancy in response to the need for greater production of erythrocytes and for fetal and placental growth. A deficiency in folic acid results in a reduction in the rate of deoxyribonucleic acid (DNA) synthesis and mitotic activity of individual cells, resulting in the presence of large, immature erythrocytes (megaloblasts).

Non-nutritional factors that contribute to folic acid deficiency include hemolytic anemias with increased red blood cell turnover; some medications, such as phenytoin (Dilantin); and malabsorption entities. Folic acid deficiency is often present in association with iron-deficiency anemia (see Chapters 7 and 9).

FETAL-NEONATAL EFFECTS

Folate deficiency is associated with increased risk of spontaneous abortion, abruptio placentae, and fetal anomalies. There is particular interest in the relationship between folic acid–deficiency anemia and an increase in neural tube defects.

THERAPEUTIC MANAGEMENT

The Recommended Daily Allowance (RDA) for folic acid doubles during pregnancy, and some women have difficulty ingesting the amount needed even though it does occur widely in foods. The best sources of folic acid are liver, kidney beans, lima beans, and fresh dark-green leafy vegetables. For prevention of deficiency, a dietary supplement is often recommended.

Sickle Cell Anemia

Sickle cell anemia occurs when the gene for the production of S hemoglobin is inherited from both parents. When the S hemoglobin gene is transmitted from only one parent, the child receives the sickle cell trait but not the disease. The defect in the hemoglobin causes erythrocytes to be shaped like a sickle, or crescent. Because of their distorted shape, the erythrocytes have difficulty passing through small arteries and capillaries and tend to clump together and occlude the blood vessel.

The disease is characterized by chronic anemia, increased susceptibility to infection, and intermittent episodes of occlusions of blood vessels by the abnormally shaped erythrocytes. Sickle cell anemia occurs most often in people of African-American or Mediterranean ancestry. The incidence is 1 in 2000 persons in African-Americans (Nuwayhid and Khalife, 1992).

MATERNAL EFFECTS

Pregnancy may exacerbate sickle cell anemia and bring on "sickle cell crisis." Sickle cell crisis is a broad term that describes several different conditions, particularly temporary cessation of bone marrow function, hemolytic crisis with massive erythrocyte destruction resulting in jaundice, and vaso-occlusive crisis—severe pain caused by infarctions located in the joints and all the major organs. In addition, expectant mothers with sickle cell anemia are prone to pyelonephritis, bone infection, heart disease, and pregnancy-induced hypertension.

FETAL-NEONATAL EFFECTS

The fetus is prone to serious complications, including prematurity and IUGR. The incidence of fetal death is particularly high in the presence of sickle cell crisis.

THERAPEUTIC MANAGEMENT

Women with sickle cell disease should seek early prenatal care and should be informed of the maternal and fetal risks associated with the pregnancy. Frequent evaluations of hemoglobin, complete blood count, serum iron, total iron-binding capacity, and serum folate are necessary to determine the degree of anemia and iron and folic acid stores.

Fetal surveillance studies (ultrasonography, non-stress tests, contraction stress tests) are necessary to assess fetal growth and development.

When the woman is hospitalized, nurses must be alert for signs of sickle cell crisis. The most common indications are pain in the abdomen, chest, vertebrae, joints, or extremities; pallor; and signs of cardiac failure. Nurses must also provide comfort measures, such as repositioning, good skin care, assisting with ambulation and movement in bed, and assisting the woman to splint the abdomen with a pillow when she must cough or breathe deeply.

Intrapartum care focuses on preventing the development of sickle cell crisis. Oxygen is administered continuously, and fluids should be administered to prevent dehydration because both hypoxemia and dehydration, as well as exertion, infection, and acidosis, stimulate the sickling process.

✔ Check Your Reading

10. What are the maternal and fetal effects of folic acid anemia?
11. What is the effect of pregnancy on sickle cell anemia?

Less Common Medical Conditions

Women with a pre-existing medical condition should be aware of the effect that the pregnancy will have on the condition and the impact that the medical condition will have on the pregnancy outcome. Table 25–5 describes the maternal, fetal, and neonatal effects of some of the less common conditions and the relevant nursing considerations.

Infections During Pregnancy

Pregnant women are vulnerable to the same infectious diseases as other women, but during pregnancy a disease may have profound effects on the health of the fetus. In some cases, the disease can be prevented. For example, vaccination against rubella (German measles) before pregnancy offers complete protection against the devastating effects of this disease. Prevention of communicable infections is a major focus for all nurses, and they must be prepared to provide information and guidance to women throughout their reproductive years.

When infection occurs, nurses are responsible for collaborating with physicians so that the most effective therapeutic management can be provided. In some cases, there is no known treatment. Nurses help the family in preparing to deal with maternal and fetal complications.

TORCH

The acronym TORCH* denotes a group of infections that do not seriously impair the health of the mother but can cause massive damage to the fetus. Some sources consider the O in TORCH to represent other infections, such as varicella or group B streptococcus infection; other sources add an S (TORCHS), with S representing syphilis.

TOXOPLASMOSIS

Toxoplasmosis is a protozoal infection caused by *Toxoplasma gondii*. Infection is transmitted through organisms in raw or undercooked meat, through contact with infected cat feces, or across the placental barrier to the fetus if the expectant mother acquires the infection during pregnancy.

Toxoplasmosis is often subclinical; the woman may experience a few days of fatigue, muscle pains, and swollen glands but may be unaware of the disease. If the infection is suspected, diagnosis can be confirmed by positive serologic tests, which include indirect fluorescent antibody tests for immunoglobulins IgG and IgM.

Fetal-Neonatal Effects. Although toxoplasmosis may go unnoticed in the pregnant woman, infection during pregnancy may cause abortion or result in the birth of a live-born infant with the disease. About 50 per cent of the infants born to mothers who were infected during pregnancy will acquire congenital toxoplasmosis. Affected infants may be asymptomatic at birth or may present with low birth weight, enlarged liver and spleen, jaundice, and anemia. Complications, usually chorioretinitis, or signs of neurological damage may develop several years later.

Therapeutic Management. Prevention is the most desirable action, and nurses must teach expectant mothers about the source of the disease. All pregnant women should be advised to:

- Cook meat thoroughly, particularly pork, beef, and lamb
- Avoid touching mucous membranes of the mouth or eyes while handling raw meat

* TO, toxoplasmosis; R, rubella; C, cytomegalovirus infection, H, genital herpes.

Table 25–5. INFREQUENT CONDITIONS AND THEIR EFFECT ON PREGNANCY

Condition	Maternal-Fetal Effects	Nursing Considerations
	Epilepsy	
A chronic seizure disorder that may be idiopathic or secondary to other disorders, such as head injury, infections, or vitamin deficiency. Most commonly used drugs to control seizures are phenytoin (Dilantin) and phenobarbital (Nuwayhid and Khalife, 1992).	Seizure activity may increase, decrease, or remain the same during pregnancy. Expectant mothers with epilespy have an increased risk of pre-eclampsia, hyperemesis, and premature labor. Teratogenic effects of drugs needed to control seizures in the mother may account for the increase in congenital anomalies. In addition, anticonvulsants decrease clotting factors and the newborn is at increased risk for hemorrhage.	Refer the expectant mother for counseling that includes the teratogenic risks of her medication and the risk of seizures during pregnancy. From a medical standpoint, the benefits of seizure prevention must be weighed against the teratogenic effect of the anticonvulsant.
	Hyperthyroidism	
An overactive, enlarged thyroid gland that is difficult to diagnose and manage during pregnancy because the normal changes of pregnancy increase the metabolic rate and mimic hyperthyroidism. Graves' disease is the most common cause during pregnancy.	Increased incidence of pregnancy-induced hypertension and postpartum hemorrhage if not well controlled during pregnancy. Treatment is complicated by the presence of the fetus, who may be jeopardized by surgery or antithyroid medications. Propylthiouracil has limited placental transfer and is widely used during pregnancy to control thyroid function.	Be aware of the major signs that should be reported. These include a resting pulse rate greater than 100/minute, loss of weight, or failure to gain weight in spite of normal intake of food, heat intolerance, and abnormal protrusion of the eyes (exophthalmos).
	Hypothyroidism	
Characterized by inadequate thyroid secretion; confirmed by an elevated level of thyroid-stimulating hormone (TSH) and low levels of triiodothyronine (T_3) and thyroxine (T_4).	If the expectant mother is untreated, there is an increased risk of neonatal goiter and congenital hypothyroidism; severity of symptoms depend on time of onset and severity of the deprivation.	Suspect neonatal hypothyroidism when the infant is large for gestational age, with respiratory and feeding difficulties, rough dry skin, and an umbilical hernia.
	Maternal Phenylketonuria (PKU)	
Inherited single gene recessive anomaly leading to an inability to metabolize the amino acid phenylalanine, resulting in high serum levels of phenylalanine. Irreparable mental retardation occurs if the pregnant woman is not treated early with a diet that provides adequate protein but restricts phyenylalanine.	The woman must be on a low-phenylalanine diet prior to conception and pregnancy. If not, there is an increased fetal risk of microcephaly, mental retardation, heart defects, and intrauterine growth retardation.	Advise women that the child will either be a carrier of the gene or will inherit the disease, depending on the presence of the gene in the father of the child. Treatment at a PKU center is recommended.
	Systemic Lupus Erythematosus (SLE)	
A chronic autoimmune disease affecting connective tissue, characterized by multiple system involvement and exacerbations and remissions. Symptoms include a "butterfly" rash on the face, photosensitivity, joint inflammation, fever, nephritis, arthritis, and nerve disorders.	If SLE is mild or quiescent, there may be little risk to mother or fetus. The abortion and stillbirth rates are increased, and inflammation of small arteries may result in intrauterine growth retardation. Fetal-neonatal cardiac complications are increased and are believed to be due to the presence of maternal antibodies (anticardiolipins) to the fetal heart.	Advise women to avoid fatigue, infection, and strong sunlight. Fetal surveillance will probably begin when the fetus is viable and will continue until delivery. Low-dose steroids and heparin may be continued throughout pregnancy.

- Wash all kitchen surfaces that come into contact with uncooked meat
- Wash the hands thoroughly after handling raw meat
- Avoid uncooked eggs and unpasteurized milk
- Wash fruits and vegetables before consumption
- Avoid contact with materials that are possibly contaminated with cat feces (cat litter boxes, sandboxes, or garden soil)

Toxoplasmosis is a self-limiting infection. Pharmacological therapy with pyrimethamine, sulfadiazine, and folinic acid is available; however, the drugs carry potential fetal risks and their use in pregnancy is controversial (Ricci, 1992). Because the most serious fetal effects occur if the disease is contracted during the first 20 weeks of pregnancy, abortion may be presented as an option for the parents to consider.

RUBELLA

Rubella is caused by a virus that is transmitted from person to person by droplets or through direct contact with articles contaminated with nasopharyngeal secretions. Rubella is a mild disease; fever, general malaise, and a characteristic maculopapular rash that begins on the face and migrates over the body are the major symptoms.

Fetal-Neonatal Effects. Rubella remains a serious concern because the virus crosses the placental barrier and can infect the fetus. The greatest risk to the fetus occurs during the first trimester, when fetal organs are developing. If maternal infection occurs during this time, approximately one third of these cases will result in spontaneous abortions and the surviving fetuses may be seriously compromised. Deafness, mental retardation, cataracts, cardiac defects, IUGR, and microcephaly are the most common fetal complications. Moreover, infants who are born to mothers who had rubella during pregnancy shed the virus for many months and thus pose a threat to other infants as well as to susceptible adults who come in contact with them.

Therapeutic Management. Prevention is the only effective protection for the fetus. Since women who are immune do not become infected, it is critical to determine the immune status of all women of childbearing age. A serologic test, hemagglutination inhibition (HAI), determines rubella titers. A titer of 1:8 provides evidence of immunity (Gibbs and Sweet, 1989). Women who are not immune should be vaccinated before they become pregnant, and they should be advised not to become pregnant for 3 months following vaccination because there is a possible risk to the fetus from the live-virus vaccine. Many women are vaccinated during the postpartum period so that they will be immune before becoming pregnant again. In some facilities, women of childbearing age must read and sign a document indicating that they understand the risks to the fetus if they become pregnant before 3 months.

CYTOMEGALOVIRUS INFECTION

Cytomegalovirus (CMV), a member of the herpesvirus group, causes the initial infection and then may invade the host's cells and remain latent for many years before reactivation. Although the individuals may have no symptoms, they may shed the virus continually during this time. CMV has been isolated from urine, saliva, blood, cervical mucus, semen, breast milk, and stool. Transmission may occur from contamination of any of these bodily fluids. CMV is often transmitted as a "kissing disease" among a fairly young population. The highest rate of infection occurs between the ages of 15 and 35 years; thus, the possibility of CMV infection occurring during pregnancy is high, although 50 per cent of all women show positive antibodies from previous exposure by the time they become pregnant.

Diagnosis can be confirmed by the isolation of CMV in the urine, although this does not differentiate primary infection from recurrent infection. Recurrent infection can occur in some women during pregnancy, enabling them to transmit the disease to the fetus.

Although CMV infection is widespread, it produces serious illness only in the fetus. During pregnancy, the disease is transmitted across the placental barrier as well as through contact with contaminated vaginal secretions, urine, or feces. Cytomegalovirus infection may also be transmitted through blood transfusions or through breastfeeding.

Fetal-Neonatal Effects. Cytomegalovirus infection is the most common perinatal infection. Of all live neonates, 2.5 per cent are infected with the virus; about 10 per cent of this number experience serious complications, including mental retardation, blindness, epilepsy, and deafness (Ricci, 1992). Some of these conditions may not be obvious for several months or even years.

Therapeutic Management. Treating CMV infection is frustrating because there is no effective remedy and no vaccine to prevent it. It is a common disease in the reproductive years, yet there is no practical way to prevent exposure. Although it is a benign, often subclinical disease in adults, there may be serious consequences for the fetus. Infected infants may be asymptomatic, but they should be isolated in the nursery because the virus is shed in saliva and urine. Moreover, because complications of the disease may not be obvious for several years, the family must be instructed about the importance of careful follow-up for neurological problems that can develop later.

HERPES GENITALIS

Genital herpes is one of the most common sexually transmitted diseases. It is caused by herpesvirus serotype 2 (HSV-2). Primary infection occurs as a result of direct contact of the skin or mucous membrane with an active lesion. Lesions form at the site of contact and begin as a group of painful papules that progress rapidly to become vesicles, shallow ulcers, pustules, and crusts. The patient sheds the virus until the lesions are completely healed. The virus then migrates along the sensory nerves to reside in the sensory ganglion, and the disease enters a latent phase. It can be reactivated later as a recurrent infection.

Vertical transmission (from mother to infant) generally occurs in two ways: (1) after rupture of membranes, when the virus ascends from active lesions, and (2) during birth, when the fetus comes into contact with infectious genital secretions.

Diagnosis is usually based on clinical signs and symptoms; however, definitive diagnosis involves isolation of the virus from a lesion. (See Chapter 32 for implications of herpes genitalis in non-pregnant women.)

Fetal-Neonatal Effects. Effects depend on whether a primary or recurrent infection occurs during pregnancy. If primary infection occurs during the first 20 weeks, there is an increase in the rate of spontaneous abortions, IUGR, and preterm labor. Complications from recurrent infections are rare; however, 4 per cent of infants born to mothers with recurrent infections at the time of delivery have HSV infection. Symptoms are usually present within 2 to 3 days of birth, and the disease progresses rapidly. The mortality rate for infants with disseminated herpes infection is approximately 60 per cent, with as many as 50 per cent of the surviving infants suffering severe neurological complications (Ricci, 1992).

Therapeutic Management. There is no known cure for herpes infection, although antiviral chemotherapy (acyclovir) is prescribed in non-pregnant women to reduce symptoms and shorten the duration of the lesions. The safety of acyclovir has not been established during pregnancy and should be used for a pregnant woman only when there is a life-threatening disseminated infection, such as pneumonitis or encephalitis.

For women with a prior history of genital herpes, vaginal delivery is allowed if there are no genital lesions at the time of labor. For women with active lesions, either recurrent or primary, at the time of labor, delivery should be cesarean. After delivery, isolation of the mother from her infant is not necessary as long as direct contact with lesions is avoided and mothers are instructed in careful hand-washing techniques. Mothers may breastfeed if there are no lesions on the breasts.

The infant is carefully observed for signs of infection, including temperature instability, lethargy, poor sucking reflex, jaundice, seizures, and herpetic lesions.

Expectant mothers need information about effective ways to deal with the emotional as well as the physical effects of herpes. Many women are concerned about privacy and do not want family members to be told why cesarean birth is necessary. Such women must be assured that their wishes will be

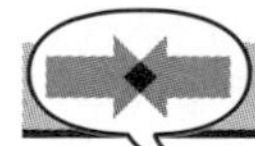

Therapeutic Communication

Mary Post, who had a cesarean delivery because of an active herpes lesion, appears anxious and uncomfortable during the morning assessment by nurse Eileen Sinclair.

Mary: Why does everyone wear gloves whenever they come near me?

Eileen: You wonder why we wear gloves when we care for you?

Reflecting content

Mary: Well, it bothers me that you think I am so contagious.

Eileen: You think we wear gloves because you have a herpes outbreak and that upsets you?

Clarifying both content and feeling

Mary: Yes, why else would it be necessary?

Eileen: We wear gloves when we care for all patients, whenever there is a chance that we will come into contact with body fluids. I'm sorry you thought it was because of the herpes.

Providing information and conveying empathy

Mary: I'm just so touchy about having my family find out I have herpes.

Eileen: You don't want your family to know why you had a cesarean?

Clarifying and reflecting feelings

Mary: Yes, I'm so embarrassed. I wish they didn't have to know.

Eileen: They will know only if you tell them. We do everything possible to protect your privacy. I'd like to come back in a few minutes and we can talk more about how you feel.

Offering reassurance about Mary's privacy and leaving the door open so that she can express her feelings more completely at a later time

respected. Many women need an opportunity to discuss their feelings of shame, anger, or anxiety about the disease.

Hepatitis B

Hepatitis B, also known as serum hepatitis, is caused by a virus that is transmitted via blood, saliva, vaginal secretions, semen, or breast milk and across the placental barrier. The disease is prevalent in certain population groups, such as Asians, Native Americans, Eskimos, Southeast Asian immigrants, and intravenous drug users.

FETAL-NEONATAL EFFECTS

There is an increased incidence of prematurity, low birth weight, and neonatal death when the mother has hepatitis B infection during pregnancy. Moreover, infants born to mothers who acquire hepatitis B during pregnancy or who are chronic carriers of hepatitis B surface antigen (HBsAg) are at risk for the development of acute infection at birth.

THERAPEUTIC MANAGEMENT

All pregnant women should be screened for hepatitis B surface antigen (HBsAg). Women at high risk for hepatitis should be rescreened in the third trimester if the initial screen is negative. Household members and sexual contacts should be tested and offered vaccination if they are susceptible. The Centers for Disease Control (CDC) recommends that newborns of HBsAg-positive mothers receive passive immunization with a single dose (0.5 ml intramuscularly) of specific hepatitis B immune globulin (HBIG, Hep-B-Gammagee), and hepatitis B vaccine (Heptavax-B) soon after birth. *The newborn must be carefully bathed before any injections are given to prevent infections from skin surface contamination.*

Breastfeeding is considered safe as long as the newborn has received the above treatment. Vaccination is recommended for any population at risk; this includes nurses who frequently come into contact with blood.

Varicella

Varicella infection (chickenpox) is caused by the varicella-zoster virus (VZV), a herpesvirus that is transmitted by direct contact or via the respiratory tract. The varicella virus has the ability to become latent in nerve ganglia. When the virus is reactivated, herpes zoster (shingles) results. Potential maternal complications of acute varicella infection may include preterm labor, encephalitis, and varicella pneumonia, which is the most serious complication associated with VZV.

FETAL-NEONATAL EFFECTS

Fetal-neonatal effects depend on the time of maternal infection. If the infection occurred during the first trimester, the fetus is at risk for congenital varicella syndrome; clinical findings include limb hypoplasia, cutaneous scars, chorioretinitis, cataracts, microcephaly, and symmetric IUGR. In later pregnancy, transplacental passage of maternal antibodies usually protects the fetus. If the fetus is exposed to the virus in utero and is born prior to the development of maternal antibodies, however, the infant is at risk for development of life-threatening neonatal varicella infection.

THERAPEUTIC MANAGEMENT

Pregnant women should be advised to avoid contact with persons infected with chickenpox and should be educated about the symptoms of the disease. Those infected with chickenpox during pregnancy should be instructed to report pulmonary symptoms immediately. Hospitalization, fetal surveillance, full respiratory support, and hemodynamic monitoring should be available for women diagnosed with varicella pneumonia.

For infants born to mothers with varicella, authorities recommend immunization with varicella-zoster immune globulin (VZIG) within 72 hours of birth. Women and infants with varicella are highly contagious and should be placed in strict isolation. Only staff known to be immune to varicella should come in contact with these clients.

Erythema Infectiosum (Fifth Disease)

Erythema infectiosum, caused by human parvovirus B19, is an acute, communicable disease that is characterized by a highly distinctive rash. The rash starts on the face with a "slapped-cheeks" appearance, followed by a generalized maculopapular rash. Erythema infectiosum is more common among children and often occurs in community epidemics. The prognosis is excellent; however, if the disease occurs in pregnancy, there are potential fetal and neonatal effects.

FETAL-NEONATAL EFFECTS

If the expectant mother experiences erythema infectiosum during pregnancy, the major risks to the fetus are hemolysis and inadequate production of erythrocytes. She should be assessed for elevated levels of alpha-fetoprotein; if elevated levels are found, serial ultrasonography can be performed to detect hydrops fetalis (generalized edema), which occurs when the fetus suffers severe anemia. At delivery, the umbilical cord blood should be examined for virus or IgM antibody, which reveals whether or not the virus has crossed the placenta and infected the fetus. If this has occurred, the infant is examined for any defect and is followed up for several years to exclude the possibility of delayed complications.

THERAPEUTIC MANAGEMENT

There is no specific treatment. Starch baths may be helpful in reducing pruritus, and analgesics may be necessary for adults who experience mild joint pain.

Group B Streptococcus Infection

Group B streptococci are normally found in humans, particularly in the gastrointestinal tract. The streptococcus has also been isolated from the vaginal and cervical canals as well as the throat, skin, and urine of healthy individuals. Group B streptococci may be transferred from mother to infant during childbirth. Risk factors include premature labor, premature rupture of membranes, and a prolonged period between rupture of membranes and the beginning of labor.

Group B streptococcus is one of the most common causes of bacteriuria in pregnancy and is a major cause of puerperal infection (see Chapter 27).

FETAL-NEONATAL EFFECTS

Group B streptococcal infection is the most common cause of neonatal sepsis in the United States. The infant exhibits signs of sepsis, which include meningitis, within a few days following birth. (See Chapter 29 for additional information about the manifestations and recommended management of neonatal sepsis.)

THERAPEUTIC MANAGEMENT

Many treatment programs focus on intrapartum management to prevent transmission to the infant during labor. Culture for group B streptococcus requires 24 to 48 hours and is not practical for women in labor. In some facilities, a specimen for culture may be obtained for women at high risk (prior history of preterm labor, premature rupture of membranes, or previous birth of an infant with neonatal sepsis) in the last trimester; treatment may be initiated with ampicillin, depending on the results of the culture.

Tuberculosis

Tuberculosis results from infection by *Mycobacterium tuberculosis*. It is transmitted by aerosolized droplets of liquid containing the bacterium, which is inhaled by a non-infected individual and taken into the lung. Initially, most individuals are asymptomatic. Women obtaining prenatal care or appearing for a delivery without prenatal care should be screened for tuberculosis. This involves an intradermal injection of mycobacterial protein (PPD, purified protein derivative). If the reaction is positive, a chest x-ray and additional follow-up are necessary. Diagnosis is established by isolating and identifying the bacterium in the sputum.

Symptomatic patients present with general malaise, fatigue, loss of appetite, weight loss, and fever, which occurs in the late afternoon and evening and is accompanied by night sweats. As the disease progresses, a chronic cough develops and a mucopurulent sputum is produced.

Tuberculosis is associated with poverty, malnutrition, and acquired immunodeficiency syndrome (AIDS), and the incidence is increasing in inner city areas and among the homeless. It is also present among immigrants from Southeast Asia and Central and South America, where tuberculosis is prevalent.

FETAL-NEONATAL EFFECTS

Although congenital infection is rare, if the infectious mother remains untreated, the newborn is at high risk for acquiring tuberculosis by inhalation of infectious respiratory droplets from the mother.

THERAPEUTIC MANAGEMENT

Treatment during pregnancy may be complicated by concern about fetal effects. Isoniazid (INH) with ethambutol has been used to treat tuberculosis in pregnant women without harm to the fetus (Deglin and Vallerand, 1991). Pyridoxine (vitamin B_6) is often administered with INH to prevent fetal neurotoxicity.

Additional Sexually Transmitted Diseases, Vaginal Infections, and Urinary Tract Infections

Table 25–6 indicates nursing considerations of sexually transmitted diseases and vaginal infections. Table 25–7 provides a summary of urinary tract infections and their effect on pregnancy. (See also Chapter 32.)

Text continued on page 728

Table 25–6. SEXUALLY TRANSMITTED DISEASES AND VAGINAL INFECTIONS: THEIR IMPACT ON PREGNANCY

	Fetal-Neonatal Effects	Nursing Considerations
Sexually Transmitted Diseases		
Syphilis (Causative Organism Spirochete *Treponema Pallidum*)		
	If untreated, the infection may be passed across the placenta to the fetus and result in spontaneous abortion, a stillborn infant, premature labor and birth, or possibly, congenital syphilis. Major signs of congenital syphilis are enlarged liver and spleen, skin lesions, rashes, osteitis, pneumonia, and hepatitis.	Check for allergies before administering penicillin, the usual treatment. Erythromycin is sometimes used when there is an allergy to penicillin. Advise the woman to return for prenatal visit every month to be certain that the treatment is successful. Reassure her that with adequate treatment the risk to the neonate is decreased. Refer sexual contacts for treatment. Emphasize that it is possible to become reinfected.
Gonorrhea (Causative Organism Bacterium *Neisseria Gonorrhoeae*)		
	Not transmitted via the placenta; vertical transmission from mother to infant during birth may cause ophthalmia neonatorum. Endocervicitis and weakening of the fetal membranes increase the risk of premature rupture of membranes and preterm labor.	Most gonococcal strains are sensitive to penicillin and are eradicated by a single dose. The partner must also be treated because reinfection is possible. All infants are treated with erythromycin ophthalmic ointment at birth to prevent serious eye infection that can result in blindness.
Chlamydial Infection (Causative Organism Bacterium *Chlamydia Trachomatis*)		
	The fetus may be infected during birth and may suffer neonatal conjunctivitis or pneumonitis, which manifests within 4 to 6 weeks. Conjunctivitis is prevented by erythromycin ophthalmic ointment. *Chlamydia* may also be responsible for premature labor, premature rupture of membranes, and chorioamnionitis.	Education is particularly important because *Chlamydia* is the most common sexually transmitted organism in the United States. Infection is usually asymptomatic. Treat both partners to prevent recurrent infection. As with all sexually transmitted diseases, the use of condoms decreases the risk of infection.
Trichomoniasis (Causative Organism Protozoaon *Trichomonas Vaginalis*)		
	Not transmitted across placental barrier; the organism cannot survive in the infantile, non-estrogenized vagina. Trichomoniasis acquired at birth is short-lived.	Use metronidazole (Flagyl) during the second and third trimesters; safety has not been established (Deglin and Vallerand, 1993). Treat the partner to prevent partners from reinfecting each other ("ping-pong" effect).
Condylomata Acuminata (Causative Organism Human Papillomavirus)		
	Transmission of condylomata acuminata, also called venereal warts, may occur during vaginal birth and may be associated with the development of epithelial tumors of the mucous membranes of the larynx in children under the age of 4 years (Koutsky and Welner-Hanssen, 1989).	Do not use podophyllin, sometimes used for treatment in non-pregnant women, during pregnancy because of possible teratogenic effects. Applications of trichloracetic acid may be prescribed, or treatment may be delayed during pregnancy, making cesarean birth necessary if the birth canal is obstructed.

Table 25–6. SEXUALLY TRANSMITTED DISEASES AND VAGINAL INFECTIONS: THEIR IMPACT ON PREGNANCY *Continued*

	Fetal-Neonatal Effects	Nursing Considerations
Vaginal Infections		
Candidiasis (Causative Organism Yeast *Candida Albicans*)		
	Oral candidiasis (thrush) may develop in newborns if infection is present at birth. Treat the newborn with thrush with 1 ml of nystatin (Mycostatin) over surfaces of the oral cavity four times a day for several days.	Candidiasis (previously called monilia), is a persistent problem for many women during pregnancy. Characteristic "cottage cheese" vaginal discharge with vulvar pruritus, burning, and dyspareunia. The vagina and vulva may be tender, red, and edematous. Effective treatment may be obtained with miconazole nitrate (Monistat) or clotrimazole (Gyne-Lotrimin), both available over the counter.
Bacterial Vaginosis (Causative Organism *Gardnerella Vaginalis)**		
	No known fetal effects; however, treatment with metronidazole has potential teratogenic effects.	Causes profuse, malodorous, "fishy" vaginal discharge, itching, and burning. Metronidazole (Flagyl) is the most effective treatment, and may be used in the second and third trimesters. The alternative treatment is ampicillin.

* In the presence of anaerobic bacteria (*Bacteroides,* Peptococcus). Formerly called nonspecific vaginitis or *Gardnerella* vaginitis.

Table 25–7. URINARY TRACT INFECTIONS AND THEIR EFFECT ON PREGNANCY

Fetal-Neonatal Effects	Nursing Considerations
Asymptomatic Bacteriuria (Causative Organisms *Escherichia coli, Klebsiella, Proteus*)	
Fetal effects are due to ascending bacteria that can result in cystitis or pyelonephritis in later pregnancy if condition remains untreated.	Defined as recovery of the same pathogen from two consecutive urine samples of 100,000 colony-forming units per milliliter of urine. Usually asymptomatic; diagnosed by midstream, clean-catch specimen. Treat with oral sulfonamides or ampicillin in early pregnancy; sulfonamides displace bilirubin from albumin in fetal circulation in late pregnancy and can result in neonatal hyperbilirubinemia.
Cystitis (Causative Organisms *E. Coli, Klebsiella, Proteus*)	
Ascending infection may lead to acute pyelonephritis, which is associated with preterm labor and premature birth.	Emphasize importance of reporting signs of urinary tract infection to prevent spread of infection. Stress the importance of taking all the medication prescribed even if symptoms abate. Provide information about hygiene measures (see Chapter 27, pp. 796).
Acute Pyelonephritis (Causative Organisms *E. Coli, Klebsiella, Proteus*)	
Increased risk of preterm labor and premature delivery.	Inform women with asymptomatic bacteriuria or cystitis of signs and symptoms, such as sudden onset of fever, chills, flank pain or tenderness, nausea, and vomiting so that treatment can begin promptly.

✔ Check Your Reading

12. How can toxoplasmosis and rubella be prevented?
13. How is herpes genitalis transmitted to the fetus?
14. What is the recommended treatment for neonates when the mother is a carrier of hepatitis B?

Acquired Immunodeficiency Syndrome (AIDS)

AIDS is caused by a retrovirus known as human immunodeficiency virus (HIV). Transmission of HIV infection is predominantly through three modes: (1) sexual exposure to genital secretions of an infected person, (2) parenteral exposure to infected blood or tissue, and (3) perinatal exposure of an infant to an infected mother. The virus must enter the recipient's blood stream to produce infection.

RISK FACTORS

In the past, the populations at highest risk for HIV exposure included homosexual and bisexual men, intravenous drug users (who often share contaminated needles), and inhabitants of West Africa and Haiti (where heterosexual transmission is common). In inner city areas, the incidence is increasing rapidly among young, disadvantaged African-Americans and Latinos. Heterosexual transmission is becoming more common, and HIV can be transmitted from female to male as well as from male to female. Among an estimated 1 million to 1.5 million Americans infected with HIV, about 10 per cent (100,000 to 150,000) are women (Nanda, 1990).

PATHOPHYSIOLOGY

Like other retroviruses, HIV has the unique ability, when infecting a cell, to integrate its viral genetic makeup into the genetic makeup of the cell. This results in an abnormal cell, one that cannot perform its functions properly. At the same time, this cell replicates and produces more viruses that invade more cells. The disease worsens as more and more cells cease to function, while at the same time a greater number of viruses are produced. $CD4^+$ ("helper"-inducer) T lymphocytes plus neurons and glial cells in the human brain are the principal hosts for HIV because they all have the CD4 receptor molecule on their surface.

HIV destroys the helper (T4) subset of T lymphocytes, which are critical in maintaining an adequate immune response. Over time, the individual has fewer and fewer T4 cells; the normal range is 800 to 1200/mm. The ratio of T4 to T8 ("suppressor") cells is also lower. T8 cells suppress continuous overreactions, or hypersensitivity, in the immune system. Because these cells directly oppose the activity of helper cells, a balance is necessary to maintain optimal functioning of the immune system. As the number of T4 cells declines and the number of T8 cells remains normal, the ratio of helper to suppressor cells decreases and immune function is profoundly suppressed. In time, the immune response is so inadequate that opportunistic infections overwhelm the person who is HIV-positive.

COURSE OF THE DISEASE

Clinicians now recognize four relatively distinct stages of HIV infection (Barrick, 1991):

1. An early, or acute, stage, which produces high-level viral replication and may include flu-like symptoms lasting a few weeks.
2. A middle, or asymptomatic, period of minor or no clinical problems, characterized by continuous, low-level viral replication and T4 cell loss, lasting for years.
3. A transitional, intermediate-length period of symptomatic disease (previously referred to as AIDS-related complex, or ARC).
4. A late, or crisis period, of symptomatic disease lasting months or years.

During stages 1 and 2, the infected person is termed HIV-positive; during stages 3 and 4, the immune system no longer offers adequate protection, and opportunistic diseases occur. The person is then said to have AIDS.

DIAGNOSIS

Some persons experience a brief febrile illness after exposure, with symptoms of fatigue, and lymphadenopathy similar to mononucleosis. Most people, however, do not have any immediate symptoms, and diagnosis depends on serological studies to detect HIV antibody. Antibodies to HIV can usually be detected within 3 to 12 months following exposure.

The most commonly used test is performed by enzyme-linked immunosorbent assay (ELISA), with the Western blot test used for confirmation. Persons must be considered contagious from the initial exposure, before HIV antibodies can be detected, as well as after seroconversion (becoming positive for HIV antibodies), even though they may remain asymptomatic for many years.

FETAL-NEONATAL EFFECTS

Although techniques for diagnosis are not standardized, an infant born to an HIV-positive mother has a 20 to 40 per cent risk for developing the disease (Mendez and Jule, 1990). Characteristically, the newborn is asymptomatic at birth but signs and symptoms usually become obvious during the first year of life. The most common early signs are enlargement of the liver and spleen, lymphadenopathy, failure to thrive, persistent thrush, and extensive seborrheic dermatitis (cradle cap). Unlike adults, infants frequently experience chronic bacterial infections, such as meningitis, pneumonia, osteomyelitis, septic arthritis, and septicemia.

THERAPEUTIC MANAGEMENT

Prevention

Education remains the most powerful tool available in the battle to control HIV infection. Nurses must be prepared to teach everyone how HIV is transmitted and how to protect themselves and others from the disease. Because there is no vaccine to prevent HIV infection and no effective treatment for AIDS exists, prevention of HIV transmission must be aimed at person-to-person spread by sexual activity, blood-borne routes, and perinatal routes.

Sexual Transmission

Sexual transmission can be avoided by several means. Abstinence would render a person safe from all sexually transmitted diseases, including HIV; however, for many people sexual expression adds to the quality of life, and many are not willing to practice total abstinence. HIV transmission can also be prevented if infected persons do not have vaginal or anal intercourse with susceptible persons. If intercourse does occur, barrier methods, such as latex condoms in conjunction with spermicidal jellies containing nonoxynol-9, have been demonstrated to be effective. A rubber dam or plastic wrap (condom) offers protection from transmission through cunnilingus or fellatio (oral sex).

Nurses must teach people to use barriers and lubricants correctly and explain the importance of limiting the number of partners with whom they have vaginal or rectal intercourse. Nurses must also promote discretion in the use of alcohol and drugs, which may decrease sexual inhibition and lead to unsafe sex. They must counsel IV drug users to seek rehabilitative treatment. If IV drug use is continued, IV drug users must be taught to wash the equipment with water, soap, and bleach before each use to prevent transmission of the virus from one person to another via a soiled needle.

Critical to Remember

Facts About HIV

- Following initial exposure, there is a period of from 3 to 12 months before seroconversion; the person is considered infectious during this time
- There is a long period of time (often years) from seroconversion to development of AIDS; persons must be considered infectious during this time
- As of now, AIDS will eventually develop in all those who are HIV-positive
- There is no cure for AIDS; however, certain medications slow replication of the virus and delay onset of opportunistic diseases. Effects of these medications on the fetus are not completely understood
- HIV is transmitted by sexual contact with an infected person, by contact with infected body fluids, and through the placenta from mother to fetus

Medical Management

Unlike other sexually transmitted diseases, HIV infection is almost always universally fatal. After the development of AIDS and the onset of opportunistic diseases, the average survival time is 10 months (Allen, 1990).

Zidovudine (azidothymidine, AZT) is the first drug that shows promise. AZT is thought to act by inhibiting the replication of the virus. Benefits may include a longer life span for those infected with HIV, a decreased incidence of opportunistic diseases, and an increase in T-helper cell number. Side effects include a lowered hemoglobin level and white blood cell count. There has been little reported experience with its use in pregnancy.

Didanosine (ddI) is used to treat symptomatic HIV infection in patients who are unable to tolerate zidovudine.

Prophylaxis against *Pneumocystis carinii* pneumonia, one of the leading causes of death as a result of immunodeficiency, includes aerosolized pentamidine and trimethoprim-sulfamethoxazole.

The safety of these treatments in pregnancy is not known and should be considered only in consultation with an infectious disease specialist.

✔ *Check Your Reading*

15. What are three ways in which HIV infection is transmitted, and what are the possible effects on the fetus?
16. How does HIV produce AIDS?

17. How does the client who is HIV-positive compare with one who has AIDS in terms of ability to transmit the virus and clinical manifestations?

The HIV-Positive Pregnant Woman: Application of Nursing Process

Assessment

A careful and comprehensive assessment of the woman who is suspected of being HIV-positive or who has AIDS is crucial during pregnancy. History taking requires great sensitivity because it focuses on areas the patient may be reluctant to discuss: sexual practices, a history of sexually transmitted diseases, and exposure to infected blood during intravenous drug use. For women who are victims of sexual abuse or who have had blood transfusions, assess for the possibility that they are HIV-positive. Here are some sample questions to ask:

- Have you or your partner received blood or blood products between the years 1977 and 1985?
- Have you had sex with someone who is a bleeder (a person with hemophilia)?
- Have you ever had sex with someone who uses needles to "shoot" drugs?
- Do you ever inject drugs into your veins?
- Have you ever had sex with a man who also has sex with other men or prostitutes?
- Have you ever had sex in order to obtain drugs?
- Have you been treated for sexually transmitted diseases?
- Have you had sex with more than five different people in the last year?

Assess the patient's level of knowledge regarding modes of transmission, effects of the disease, diagnostic tests, recommended treatment, and community resources. During pregnancy, it is especially important to assess the client's knowledge of the risks associated with childbearing.

PHYSICAL ASSESSMENT

Because the woman who is HIV-positive is susceptible to a variety of opportunistic infections, the nurse must look for many different signs and symptoms, including fatigue, fevers of undetermined origin, weight loss, skin rashes, and night sweats.

Pregnant women who are HIV-positive should also be tested for toxoplasmosis, cytomegalovirus, persistent candidiasis, and recurrent herpes infections because these infections proliferate when the immune response is deficient.

Examine all laboratory data. This includes antibody titer, white blood cell count, number of lymphocytes, number of T4 cells, ratio of T4 to T8 cells, red blood cell count, and hemoglobin value. Such information is valuable for determining immune system status and the woman's overall condition.

PSYCHOSOCIAL ASSESSMENT

A psychosocial assessment is equally important. Assess family structure and significant, available support. Moreover, assess which family members and friends are aware of the diagnosis and are prepared to assist the woman during the pregnancy and the infant later.

Learning of HIV infection during pregnancy can have a devastating and immobilizing effect on the entire family. Crisis intervention may be necessary to help the family cope. To determine the most pressing needs, assess the perception of the woman and her family about the pregnancy. What are their major concerns, worries, problems? Determine how they cope with stress and problems. Which coping mechanisms are most successful?

Obtain information about the woman's employment status, activities of daily living, and financial resources to help in determining her ability to secure assistance during and after the pregnancy. Assess the expectant mother's mood, cognitive ability, and level of anxiety to help in planning care and monitoring changes that will occur during pregnancy.

Analysis

Several nursing diagnoses are relevant for the woman who is pregnant and infected with HIV: (1) High Risk for Infection related to altered immune response and (2) Altered Family Processes related to increased needs for family support during illness. For the woman with AIDS, a common nursing diagnosis is Alteration in Nutrition: Less than Body Requirements related to anorexia and fatigue that is secondary to pregnancy and the effects of recurrent illness.

(Goals and interventions for this diagnosis are similar to those presented for the common discomfort nausea and vomiting during pregnancy and hyperemesis gravidarum; see pp. 150 and 678 and 679.)

Nurses must collaborate with the expectant mother to work out a plan of care that affords a degree of control over her life and that is realistically based on available resources. (See Nursing Care Plan 25–2, p. 732.)

Anticipatory grief occurs when a life-threatening situation gives the family time to prepare for a loss. Therefore, a priority nursing diagnosis for the pregnant woman with HIV infection is: *Anticipatory Grieving related to decreased quality of life and near-certain death of the woman, her partner, or the infant* (Jones, 1991).

Planning

For this nursing diagnosis, the woman will:

- Express her grief to family and significant others as well as to the health care team.
- Participate in decision making for the future.

Interventions

PROVIDING EMOTIONAL SUPPORT

Nursing interventions include supporting the woman and her family with the emotional changes they will experience because of the anticipated losses. Responses vary from shock and disbelief to awareness of the eventual losses, which can precipitate sadness and depression. Allow time for the woman to express her feelings, and convey a sense of empathetic concern for her feelings. Unless nurses are prepared, they may be overwhelmed by the intensity of the emotions revealed by the woman and by the depth of her concern.

Reassuring the family that it is normal to mourn may be helpful. It is often necessary to point out that family members may mourn in different ways. Some may deny the seriousness of the situation longer than others. Some become angry until they can deal with the grief that will follow. Focus on the expectant mother's concerns and fears, and assist her in dealing with them. Some of the most common fears are loss of control, loss of support and love, social isolation, and loss of privacy. The nurse's response may involve finding ways for the woman to retain control while she is physically able and to assist her in selecting those in her family who will provide continued love and emotional support. Above all, reassure the woman that her right to privacy will not be violated.

FACILITATING WELLNESS

Nurses help the woman maintain the highest level of wellness possible. Adequate, high-quality nutrition decreases the risk of opportunistic infections and promotes vitality. A daily regimen should include sufficient rest and activity. Avoidance of large crowds, travel to areas with poor sanitation, or exposure to infected individuals is important. Meticulous skin care is essential, especially during recurrent herpes infections.

PRESERVING AUTONOMY

A major concern for nurses is helping the woman remain autonomous and involved in decision making regarding her care for as long as possible. This involves respecting her wishes about who should be told and limiting access to information as directed. She has the right to decide who in her family and among her friends will be given details of her illness and to make plans for her future needs.

Many health care professionals are concerned about how to present options for the HIV-negative woman who is pregnant by an HIV-positive man. Such a woman obviously has been exposed to the virus; however, it may be impossible to determine for several weeks whether the virus has been transmitted because it takes from 3 to 12 months for seroconversion. Many physicians believe that it is essential to provide information early enough so the woman can choose abortion or continue the pregnancy with complete information about the risks to the infant if future tests confirm that she is HIV-positive.

Since expectant mothers cannot participate in their care without adequate knowledge, be prepared to explain the necessity for frequent blood tests and to answer questions about the possible course of the disease. The woman will need to know that breastfeeding is contraindicated but that she can provide all other care for her infant. She will almost certainly experience a great deal of anxiety about whether the infant will be HIV-positive. Explain that the fetus receives antibodies from her and may be antibody-positive for the first few weeks following birth, but this does not necessarily indicate that the infant is HIV-positive; additional testing will be required. Moreover, teach about medication, such as AZT, that may slow the progression of the disease but that may have teratogenic effects.

PROVIDING INFORMATION ABOUT RESOURCES

Community resources vary from area to area; however, some national resources include:

1. AIDS hotline (1-800-342-AIDS; 1-800-344-7432, Spanish; 1-800-AIDS-TTY, (hearing impaired)

Text continued on page 734

Nursing Care Plan 25–2

Pregnancy and HIV

Assessment: Nancy Pinchon, a 29-year-old woman who is 8 weeks' pregnant, has had recurrent fevers with night sweats for the past several months; she also has persistent candidiasis. She agreed to be tested for HIV, and the test is positive; her husband is HIV-negative. Nancy has never used intravenous drugs, nor has she had a blood transfusion. She was sexually active for several years before marriage and used birth control pills to protect herself from unwanted pregnancy.

Nancy says she cannot believe this is happening to her. She still feels fairly well and is angry that she will not be able to see the infant grow up. At times she weeps as she describes her overwhelming feelings of sadness and shock when she contemplates the loss of her health, her independence, and her life as well.

Nursing Diagnosis: Anticipatory Grieving related to multiple losses that include the near-certain loss of her life and possible death of the infant

Goals:

Nancy will:

1. Express her grief to significant others as well as to the health care team.
2. Continue to make decisions about her care.

Intervention:	Rationale:
1. Promote support for grief responses. a. Provide a quiet private environment and ample time for her to express her emotions and concerns. b. Demonstrate empathetic interest, and use therapeutic communication skills, such as active listening, paraphrasing, and reflection to assist her to verbalize her feelings. c. Assure her that it is normal to experience strong emotions and that the emotions change from day to day. d. Promote grief responses (denial, anger, depression, isolation) as they occur, and acknowledge that individuals differ in the stage of grief they are experiencing.	1. Shock and disbelief are characteristic responses during the period of recognizing the anticipated loss. Denial is one of the earliest responses, and it may be replaced by anger as a person attempts to deal with the anticipated losses. Reassurance that the strong emotions are normal gives the client permission to continue to express feelings and concerns.
2. Promote family cohesiveness. a. Encourage Nancy to describe her perceptions of the anticipated loss and to discuss her feelings with significant family members. b. Identify and reinforce the strengths of each family member. c. Explain the need to discuss changes in relationships and to identify behaviors that interfere with family function, for example, the fear that the disease can be spread by casual contact or a lack of awareness of the expectant mother's sense of isolation and dread. d. Explain the use of denial and anger by one family member to other members. e. Avoid pushing the client or family to move past denial without emotional readiness.	2. Family members may not be aware of the stress that the woman is experiencing, and misunderstandings can occur because responses to the anticipated loss differ. Relationships will change as the patient requires more physical and emotional support. This is often a major role change for women who have been independent. In addition, the sexual relationship changes when women worry about transmitting the disease to their partner.
3. Help Nancy describe her understanding of the current health situation and to verbalize fears and concerns. Facilitate exploration of available assistance from family, friends, clergy, and community resources.	3. This helps her verbalize information needs, begin to make informed decisions, and use appropriate resources.
4. Encourage the couple to join support groups with others who are in a similar situation. Inform the woman and her family of available community resources.	4. Groups are often able to provide information, comfort, and support that others who are not in the same situation cannot supply.
5. Foster an environment in which the loss can be experienced within a spiritual context if this is appropriate.	5. Many people find great comfort in their spiritual beliefs or in a philosophy of life that has helped them to cope with crises in the past.

Nursing Care Plan 25–2 *Continued*

Pregnancy and HIV

Evaluation: Nancy has verbalized fear of her own death and extreme anxiety about the condition of the fetus. Three family members were aware of her diagnosis and offered consistent support. Nancy has joined a women's support group. She states that the group "opened their hearts" and provided a lot of comfort.

Assessment: At 20 weeks, Nancy's T cells are under 200, and she has experienced an episode of shingles and one severe episode of gastroenteritis within the last few weeks. She and her husband ride bikes, but Nancy is concerned that any small injury might become infected.

Nursing Diagnosis: High Risk for Infection related to altered immune response

Goals:
Nancy will:
1. Demonstrate knowledge of factors that increase risk of infection.
2. Verbalize a plan to reduce exposure to infections.

Intervention:	Rationale:
1. Instruct Nancy in measures to decrease risk of infection. She can: a. Avoid persons with colds, flu, or other infectious diseases. b. Avoid large crowds, places with unsanitary conditions, and contact with pet waste. c. Wear protective gear when exercising. d. Treat each small abrasion as soon as possible. e. Practice meticulous hand washing, particularly after touching pets or uncooked fish, chicken, or meat. f. Avoid eating raw or undercooked meat. g. Wash vegetables and fruit thoroughly if they are to be eaten raw.	1. The pregnant woman who is HIV-positive is highly susceptible to infectious agents in the environment for two reasons: a. The immune response is inadequate because the T4 cells offer little protection. b. Pregnancy increases vulnerability to infection; one way to decrease the risk of infection is to avoid contact with pathogens whenever possible.
2. Instruct Nancy in measures to reduce susceptibility to infection. a. Encourage her to maintain adequate caloric and protein intake. b. Emphasize the importance of getting adequate rest and engaging in a program of physical activity designed to provide adequate exercise but not overtax physical reserves. c. Emphasize the importance of curtailing alcohol and drug use and avoiding excessive stress.	2. Alcohol, drugs, and stress may damage the immune system. Adequate calories and protein are required for energy and tissue repair.
3. Identify the specific signs and symptoms that require prompt medical attention (fevers, night sweats, weight loss, diarrhea, rashes, skin lesions).	3. These are signs of opportunistic infection. Progress is rapid without immediate medical attention.

Evaluation:
Nancy and her husband demonstrate knowledge of measures to reduce contact with infectious organisms. They verbalize a plan to increase her resistance as much as possible. She is familiar with signs and symptoms warranting immediate medical attention.

Additional Nursing Diagnoses to Consider:
- Altered Family Processes
- Fear
- Altered Sexuality Patterns
- Altered Parenting
- High Risk for Injury
- Powerlessness

2. Foundation for Children with AIDS (617-783-7300)
3. National Self-Help Clearinghouse (212-840-1258)

Evaluation

Continued communication and free expression of emotions to health care workers and to selected family members confirm that the woman is able to share and thus to cope with her grief. Participation in health care decisions provides a sense of control and promotes commitment to high-level wellness for as long as possible.

Summary Concepts

- Placental hormones, which reach their peak during the second and third trimesters, create resistance to insulin in maternal cells and precipitate changes in insulin needs throughout pregnancy.
- Fetal effects of maternal hyperglycemia include increased production of fetal insulin (a powerful growth hormone), which results in fetal macrosomia, and neonatal hypoglycemia when the maternal source of glucose is abruptly withdrawn while the neonate's production of insulin remains high for a few days.
- Gestational diabetes is induced by pregnancy and can usually be treated by diet and exercise. Women with pre-existing diabetes require administration of insulin and frequent home glucose monitoring.
- Because maternal hyperglycemia during the first trimester increases the risk for congenital anomalies in the fetus, a major goal of management is to establish normal blood glucose levels before pregnancy occurs.
- Fetal growth depends on the condition of maternal blood vessels; if there is no vascular impairment, placental perfusion is adequate and the infant is likely to be large for gestational age. If there is vascular impairment, placental perfusion may be compromised and the fetus may experience intrauterine growth retardation.
- Cardiovascular changes that occur in normal pregnancy impose an additional burden that may result in cardiac decompensation if the expectant mother has pre-existing heart disease.
- Rheumatic and congenital heart disease are the two major categories of cardiac disease, and the severity of the condition can be determined by the woman's ability to endure physical activity.
- The primary goal of management of the pregnant woman with heart disease is to prevent cardiac decompensation and the development of congestive heart failure by restricting activity so that cardiac demand does not exceed cardiac reserves.
- Obtaining sufficient folic acid to prevent megaloblastic anemia is a problem for some women. A folic acid supplement may be necessary to prevent both maternal and fetal effects.
- Sickle cell anemia is exacerbated by pregnancy, and a primary goal is to prevent sickle cell crisis during pregnancy.
- Management of less common conditions, such as epilepsy, is complicated by teratogenic effects of certain medications.
- Infections that occur during pregnancy can be transmitted to the fetus in two ways: across the placental barrier or by exposure to organisms during birth.
- Many infections, such as rubella, toxoplasmosis, and AIDS, are preventable, and education is a major focus of the health care team. Others, such as syphilis, gonorrhea, and chlamydial infection, are treatable, and fetal effects can be prevented.
- HIV is a retrovirus that invades the T4 subset of lymphocytes and destroys them, producing AIDS, which allows opportunistic infections to overwhelm the immune system.
- Pregnant women who are HIV-positive or who are at risk for HIV-positive status experience anxiety, fear, and grief as they contemplate the losses they will experience as a result of the disease. Nurses must provide emotional support, information, and counseling, which will help the woman cope with her emotions and retain control of her care for as long as possible.

References and Readings

Allen, M.H. (1990). Primary care of women infected with human immunodeficiency virus. *Obstetrics and Gynecology Clinics of North America*, 17(3), 557–569.

Barrick, B. (1991). Light at the end of the decade. *American Journal of Nursing*, 91(11), 37–40.

Becerra, J.E., Khoury, M.J., Cordero, J.F., & Erickson, J.D. (1990). Diabetes mellitus during pregnancy and the risks for birth defects: A population-based case-control study. *Pediatrics*, 85(1), 1–9.

Cherry, J.D. (1992). Parvoviruses. In R.D. Feigin & J.D. Cherry (Eds.), *Textbook of pediatric infectious diseases* (3rd ed., pp. 1626–1633). Philadelphia: W.B. Saunders.

Clark, S.L. (1991). Cardiac disease in pregnancy. *Obstetrics and Gynecology Clinics of North America*, 18(2), 237–256.

Cunningham, F.G., MacDonald, P.C., & Gant, N.F. (1989). *Williams obstetrics* (18th ed.). Norwalk, Conn.: Appleton & Lange.

Deglin, J.H., & Vallerand, A.H. (1993). *Davis' drug guide for nurses* (3rd ed.). Philadelphia: F.A. Davis.

Elderbrock, T.V., & Rogers, M.F. (1990). Epidemiology of human immunodeficiency virus infection in women in the United States. *Obstetrics and Gynecology Clinics of North America*, 17(3), 523–544.

Forrest, J.D., & Silverman, J. (1989). What public school teachers teach about preventing pregnancy, AIDS, and sexually transmitted diseases. *Family Planning Perspective*, 21(2), 65–72.

Gibbs, R.S., & Sweet, R.L. (1989). Clinical disorders. In R.K. Creasy & R. Resnik, *Maternal-fetal medicine: Principles and practice* (2nd ed., pp. 656–725). Philadelphia: W.B. Saunders.

Glenn, P.S.F., Nance-Spronson, L.E., McCartney, M., & Yesalis, C.E. (1991). Attitudes toward AIDS among a low-risk group of women. *Journal of Obstetric, Gynecologic, and Neonatal Nursing*, 20(5), 398–405.

Grau, P.A. (1991). Are you at risk for hepatitis B? *Nursing 91*, 21(3), 45–46.

Greene, M.F., & Benacerraf, B.R. (1991). Prenatal diagnosis in diabetic gravidas: Utility of ultrasound and maternal serum alphafetoprotein screening. *Obstetrics and Gynecology*, 77(4), 520–524.

Harris, J.L. (1992). Diabetes mellitus in pregnancy. *Western Journal of Medicine*, 156(6), 647–648.

Herold, E.S., Fisher, W.A., Smith, E.A., et al. (1990). Sex education and the prevention of STD/AIDS and pregnancy among youths. *Canadian Journal of Public Health*, 81(2), 141–145.

Hohlfeld, P., Vial, Y., Maillard-Brignon, C., et al. (1991). Cytomegalovirus fetal infection: Prenatal diagnosis. *Obstetrics and Gynecology*, 78(4), 615–618.

Hollingsworth, D.R., & Moore, T.R. (1989). Diabetes and pregnancy. In R.K. Creasy and R. Resnik (Eds.), *Maternal-fetal medicine: Principles and practice* (2nd ed., pp. 925–989). Philadelphia: W.B. Saunders.

Isada, N.B., Parr, D.P., Grossman, J.H., & Straus, S.E. (1992). TORCH infections: Diagnosis in the molecular age. *Journal of Reproductive Medicine*, 37(6), 499–507.

Jones, D.A. (1991). HIV-Seropositive childbearing women: Nursing management. *Journal of Obstetric, Gynecologic, and Neonatal Nursing*, 20(6), 446–452.

Kappy, M.S. (1991). Diabetes in pregnancy: Rationale and guidelines for care. *Comprehensive Therapy*, 17(7), 50–56.

Koutsky, L.A., & Welner-Hanssen, P. (1989). Genital papillomavirus infections: Current knowledge and future prospects. *Obstetrics and Gynecology Clinics of North America*, 16(3), 541–564.

Landy, H.J., & Grossman, J.H. (1989). Herpes simplex virus. *Obstetrics and Gynecology Clinics of North America*, 16(3), 495–516.

Langer, O. (1991). Diabetes in pregnancy. In S.H. Cherry & I.R. Merkatz (Eds.), *Complications of pregnancy: Medical, surgical, gynecologic, psychosocial, and perinatal* (4th ed.). Baltimore: Williams & Wilkins.

Leff, E.W., Gagne, M.P., & Jefferis, S.C. (1991). Type I diabetes and pregnancy. . . are we hearing women's concerns? *Maternal-Child Nursing Journal*, 16(2), 83–87.

Mahan, L.K., & Arlin, M. (1992). *Krause's food, nutrition, and diet therapy* (8th ed.). Philadelphia: W.B. Saunders.

Martens, M.G. (1989). Pyelonephritis. *Obstetrics and Gynecology Clinics of North America*, 16(2), 305–314.

McGregor, J.A. (1989). Chlamydial infection in woman. *Obstetrics and Gynecology Clinics of North America*, 16(3), 565–592.

McNicol, L.B., Hadersbeck, R.E., & Dickens, D.R. (1991). AIDS and pregnancy: Survey of knowledge, attitudes, beliefs, and self-identification of risk. *Journal of Obstetric, Gynecologic, and Neonatal Nursing*, 20(1), 65–72.

Meller, J., & Goldman, M.E. (1991). Cardiovascular disease in pregnancy. In S.H. Cherry & I.R. Merkatz (Eds.), *Complications of pregnancy: Medical, surgical, gynecologic, psychosocial, and perinatal* (4th ed., pp. 460–475). Baltimore: Williams & Wilkins.

Mendez, H., & Jule, J.E. (1990). Care of the infant born exposed to human immunodeficiency virus. *Obstetrics and Gynecology Clinics of North America*, 17(3), 637–650.

Nanda, D. (1990). Human immunodeficiency virus infection in pregnancy. *Obstetrics and Gynecology Clinics of North America*, 17(3), 617–626.

Nettina, S.L. (1990). Syphilis, a new look at an old killer. *American Journal of Nursing*, 90(4), 68–69.

Nuwayhid, B., & Khalife, S. (1992). Medical complications of pregnancy. In N.F. Hacker & J.G. Moore (Eds.), *Essentials of obstetrics and gynecology* (2nd ed., pp. 197–222). Philadelphia: W.B. Saunders.

Ricci, J.M. (1992). AIDS and infectious diseases in pregnancy. In N.F. Hacker & J.G. Moore (Eds.), *Essentials of obstetrics and gynecology* (2nd ed., pp. 175–188). Philadelphia: W.B. Saunders.

Rotondo, L., & Coustan, D. R. (1993). Diabetes mellitus in pregnancy. In R.A. Knuppel & J.E. Drukker (Eds.), *High-risk pregnancy: A team approach* (2nd ed., pp. 518–538). Philadelphia: W.B. Saunders.

Ucland, K. (1989). Cardiac diseases. In R.K. Creasy & R. Resnik (Eds.), *Maternal-fetal medicine: Principles and practice*. (2nd ed., pp. 746–763). Philadelphia: W.B. Saunders.

26

Intrapartum Complications

Objectives

1. Explain abnormalities that may result in dysfunctional labor.
2. Describe maternal and fetal risks associated with premature rupture of the membranes.
3. Analyze factors that increase a woman's risk for preterm labor.
4. Explain maternal and fetal problems that may occur if pregnancy persists beyond 42 weeks.
5. Describe common intrapartum emergencies.
6. Explain therapeutic management of each intrapartum complication.
7. Apply the nursing process to care of women with intrapartum complications and to their families.

Definitions

Abruptio placentae • Premature separation of a normally implanted placenta.

Amniotic fluid embolism • An embolism in which amniotic fluid with its particulate matter is drawn into the pregnant woman's circulation, lodging in her lungs.

Cephalopelvic disproportion • Fetal size that is too large to fit through the maternal pelvis at birth. Also called **fetopelvic disproportion.**

Chorioamnionitis • Inflammation of the amniotic sac (fetal membranes); usually caused by bacterial or viral infection. Also called **amnionitis.**

Dystocia • Difficult or prolonged labor; often associated with abnormal uterine activity and **cephalopelvic disproportion.**

Hydramnios • Excessive volume of amniotic fluid (more than 2000 ml at term). Also called **polyhydramnios.**

Hypertonic labor dysfunction • Ineffective labor characterized by irregular, short, and poorly coordinated contractions. **Uterine resting tone** is higher than normal.

Hypotonic labor dysfunction • Ineffective labor characterized by weak, infrequent, short, but coordinated contractions. **Uterine resting tone** is normal.

Macrosomia • Abnormally large fetal size; infant birth weight over 4000 grams.

Multifetal pregnancy • A pregnancy in which the woman is carrying two or more fetuses. Also called **multiple gestation.**

Occult prolapse • See **Prolapsed cord.**

Oligohydramnios • Abnormally small volume of amniotic fluid (less than 500 ml at term).

Placenta accreta • A placenta that is abnormally adherent to the uterine muscle. If the condition is more advanced, it is called **placenta increta** (the placenta extends into the uterine muscle) and **placenta percreta** (the placenta extends through the uterine muscle).

△ Alert for a high risk of exposure to substances to which universal precautions apply. See Appendix B for additional information about infection control.

Placenta previa • Abnormal implantation of the placenta in the lower uterus.
Precipitate birth • A birth that occurs without a trained attendant present.
Precipitate labor • An intense, unusually short labor (under 3 hours).
Preterm labor • Onset of labor after 20 weeks and before the beginning of the 38th week of gestation.
Prolapsed cord • An emergency in which the fetal umbilical cord slips down in front of or beside the presenting part. An **occult prolapse** is one that is suspected on the basis of fetal heart rate patterns; the umbilical cord cannot be palpated or seen.
Shoulder dystocia • Delayed or difficult birth of the fetal shoulders after the head is born.
Tocolytic • A drug that inhibits uterine contractions.
Uterine inversion • An emergency in which the uterus turns inside out after childbirth.
Uterine resting tone • Degree of uterine muscle tension when the woman is not in labor or during the interval between labor contractions.
Uterine rupture • A tear in the wall of the uterus.

For most women, childbirth is a normal process free of major complications. However, there may be complications that make childbearing hazardous for the woman or her baby. The nurse's challenge is to provide effective care for these mothers while nurturing the entire family during this significant life event.

The complications addressed in this chapter often interrelate. For example, a dysfunctional labor is likely to be prolonged, and the woman would be more vulnerable to infection and psychological distress. The nurse should select nursing care that relates to all problems experienced by the woman.

Dysfunctional Labor

Normal labor is characterized by progress. A dysfunctional labor is one that is ineffective because it fails to bring about cervical effacement, dilation, and/or fetal descent. Dystocia is another term often used to describe ineffective labor. Dysfunctional labor may result from problems with the powers of labor, the passenger, the passage, or the psyche. Dysfunctional labor also may be prolonged or unusually short.

A cesarean or forceps-assisted birth may be needed if dysfunctional labor does not resolve or if signs associated with fetal hypoxia occur. These signs include persistent non-reassuring fetal heart rate (FHR) patterns (see p. 346), fetal acidosis (see p. 348), and meconium passage.

Problems of the Powers

Powers that are inadequate to result in labor progress can occur because of (1) ineffective contractions, (2) ineffective maternal pushing efforts, and/or (3) a lax abdominal wall.

INEFFECTIVE CONTRACTIONS

Each labor contraction normally begins in the fundus of the uterus and spreads downward toward the cervix. Contractions are strongest in the fundus, where there are more muscle fibers, and gradually weaken as they reach the lower uterus.

Effective uterine activity is characterized by coordinated contractions that are strong and numerous enough to propel the fetus past the resistance of the maternal bony pelvis and soft tissues. It is not possible to say how frequent, long, or strong labor contractions must be. One woman may have normal labor progress with contractions that would be inadequate for another woman. Possible causes of ineffective contractions include:

- Maternal fatigue
- Fluid and electrolyte imbalance
- Hypoglycemia
- Excessive analgesia or anesthesia
- Maternal catecholamines secreted in response to stress or pain
- Cephalopelvic disproportion
- Uterine overdistention, such as with multiple gestation or hydramnios

Two patterns of ineffective uterine contractions are hypotonic and hypertonic dysfunction. Characteristics and management of each are different, but the result—arrest of labor progress—is the same if they persist. Cervical dilation, effacement, and fetal descent slow or cease entirely (Table 26–1).

Hypotonic Dysfunction. Hypotonic uterine dysfunction is more common than hypertonic. Contractions are coordinated but are too weak to be effective. They are infrequent and short, and can be easily indented with fingertip pressure at the peak.

Hypotonic dysfunction usually occurs during the active phase of labor. Labor begins normally, but contractions gradually weaken after the cervix is about 4 cm dilated. Uterine overdistention is associated with hypotonic dysfunction because the stretched uterine muscle contracts poorly.

The woman may be fairly comfortable because her contractions are weak. However, she is often frustrated because labor slows down at a time when she expects more rapid progress. Persistent hypo-

Table 26–1. PATTERNS OF LABOR DYSFUNCTION

Hypotonic Dysfunction	Hypertonic Dysfunction
Contractions	
Coordinated, but weak. Become less frequent and shorter in duration. Easily indented at peak. Woman may have minimal discomfort because the contractions are weak.	Uncoordinated, irregular. Short and poor intensity, but painful and cramp-like.
Uterine Resting Tone	
Not elevated.	Higher than normal. Important to distinguish from abruptio placenta which has similar characteristics (p. 670).
Phase of Labor	
Active. Typically occurs after 4 cm dilation. More common than hypertonic dysfunction.	Latent. Usually occurs before 4 cm dilation. Less common than hypotonic dysfunction.
Therapeutic Management	
Amniotomy (may increase the risk of infection). Oxytocin augmentation. Cesarean birth if no progress.	Correct cause if it can be identified. Sedation. Hydration. Tocolytics to reduce high uterine tone and promote placental perfusion.
Nursing Care	
Interventions related to amniotomy and oxytocin augmentation. Encourage position changes. A scultetus binder may help direct the fetus toward the mother's pelvis if her abdominal wall is very lax. Ambulation if no contraindication and if acceptable to the woman. Emotional support: Allow her to ventilate feelings of discouragement. Explain measures taken to increase effectiveness of contractions. Include her partner/family in emotional support measures as they may have anxiety that will heighten the woman's anxiety.	Promote uterine blood flow: side-lying position. Promote rest, general comfort, and relaxation. Pain relief. Emotional support: Accept the reality of the woman's pain and frustration. Reassure her that she is not being childish. Explain reason for measures to break abnormal labor patterns and their expected results. Allow her to ventilate her feelings during and after labor. Include partner/family (see hypotonic labor).

tonic dysfunction is fatiguing for the mother and may worsen the abnormal labor pattern.

Management depends on the cause. Some women respond to simple measures. Providing intravenous or oral fluids corrects maternal fluid and electrolyte imbalances or hypoglycemia. Maternal position changes may favor fetal descent and enhance contractions. Contractions are often stronger, though often less frequent, when the mother lies on her side.

Before more complex interventions are used, the physician or nurse-midwife verifies the gestational age to rule out preterm labor and obvious cephalopelvic disproportion. Amniotomy is often used to stimulate a labor that has slowed (see p. 390). Oxytocin augmentation of labor stimulates more powerful uterine contractions but can result in fetal or maternal injury, such as uterine rupture (see p. 766).

Hypertonic Dysfunction. Hypertonic dysfunction of labor occurs less frequently than does hypotonic. Contractions are uncoordinated, irregular, and short, and are of poor intensity. Despite their ineffectiveness, they are quite painful to the woman. Hypertonic dysfunction usually occurs during the latent phase of labor, before 4 cm cervical dilation.

Although each contraction is of low intensity, the uterine resting tone between contractions is high, reducing uterine blood flow. The resulting uterine ischemia decreases fetal oxygen supply and causes the woman to have almost constant cramping pain. Because high resting tone is also seen in abruptio placentae (see p. 670), this complication should be considered as well.

The mother may become quite fatigued because of near-constant discomfort. She may lose confidence in her ability to accomplish delivery and to cope with the discomfort of labor. She often thinks, "If it hurts this much early, I must be a real baby." Frustration and anxiety further reduce her pain tolerance and can interfere with normal processes of labor. The nurse should be accepting of this frustration and discomfort. It is important not to equate cervical dilation with the amount of pain a woman "should" experience.

As in hypotonic dysfunction, management depends on the probable cause. Sedation allows the expectant mother to rest, and many women will awaken having effective contractions. Oxytocin is not usually given because it can intensify the already high uterine resting tone. Tocolytic drugs, such as terbutaline, may be ordered to reduce uterine tone and improve placental blood flow.

INEFFECTIVE MATERNAL PUSHING

A reflex urge to push or bear down with contractions usually occurs as the fetal presenting part reaches the pelvic floor during second-stage labor. However, ineffective pushing may result from:

- Use of incorrect pushing techniques
- Fear of injury from pain and tearing sensations felt by the mother when she pushes
- Depressed or absent urge to push, with loss of sensation secondary to epidural anesthesia
- Maternal exhaustion

Management is supportive and focuses on correcting causes contributing to the dysfunction. If maternal and fetal vital signs are normal, there is no arbitrary maximum duration for the second stage. The physician or nurse-midwife clinically evaluates each woman to determine whether her labor should be terminated by cesarean or forceps birth. For most women, this will be after about 2 to 3 hours of *vigorous* pushing efforts that do not result in fetal descent to the pelvic floor.

Nursing care to promote correct pushing techniques helps the mother make each pushing effort more effective (see p. 319). The woman who fears injury because of the sensations she feels each time she pushes may respond to accurate information about the process of fetal descent. If she understands that sensations of tearing often accompany fetal descent but that her tissues can expand to accommodate the baby, she may be more willing to push with contractions.

If she has epidural anesthesia and cannot feel the urge to push, she can be coached to push as each contraction begins. Allowing the epidural block to wear off slightly may increase her sensation of the urge to push, yet continue providing adequate pain relief.

The woman who is exhausted may push more effectively if she is encouraged to rest, and to push only when she feels the urge, or she may push with every other contraction. Giving intravenous (IV) or oral fluids, as ordered, provides energy for strenuous work during second-stage labor.

LAX MATERNAL ABDOMINAL WALL

For the woman with a lax abdominal wall, usually a grand multipara (5 or more), labor may be dysfunctional because her uterus falls forward and displaces the fetal head from the pelvis. With loss of pressure from the fetal head, cervical effacement and dilation do not progress. A scultetus binder (Fig. 26–1) can support the uterus and align the fetal head with the pelvis, increasing pressure of the fetal head on the cervix during each contraction. Upright positioning adds gravity to the force of uterine contractions (Hall, 1985).

Problems with the Passenger

Fetal problems associated with dysfunctional labor are those related to:

- Fetal size
- Fetal presentation or position
- Multifetal pregnancy
- Fetal anomalies

These variations may cause mechanical problems and contribute to ineffective contractions.

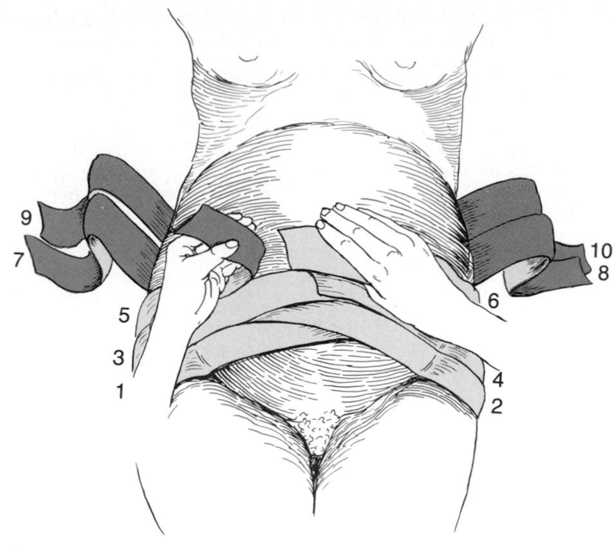

***Figure* 26–1**

Applying a scultetus binder to support the uterus and direct the fetal head toward the pelvis. Begin overlapping the binder's tails at the lower end, as numbered, alternating right and left sides. Secure the last tail with a safety pin.

FETAL SIZE

Macrosomia. The macrosomic infant weighs over 4000 g (8.8 pounds) at birth. The head may be too large to pass through the maternal pelvis and may be unable to mold enough to adapt to the pelvis. If the head makes it through the pelvis, the shoulders may be too large to pass. In addition, a very large fetus distends the uterus, reducing the strength of contractions both during and after birth.

Size is relative, however. The woman with a small pelvis or one that is abnormally shaped may not be able to deliver an average-sized or small infant. A woman with a large pelvis may easily give birth to an infant heavier than 4000 g.

Shoulder Dystocia. Delayed or difficult birth of the shoulders may occur as they become impacted above the maternal symphysis pubis. As soon as the head is born, it retracts against the perineum, much like a turtle's head drawing into its shell ("turtle sign"). Shoulder dystocia is more likely with a macrosomic fetus or with a maternal pelvis that is small relative to fetal size.

Shoulder dystocia is an urgent situation because the umbilical cord is easily compressed between the fetal body and the maternal pelvis. Although the infant's head is out of the vaginal canal, the chest is compressed, preventing respirations. The physician or nurse-midwife, with help from the experienced nurse, may use several methods to relieve the im-

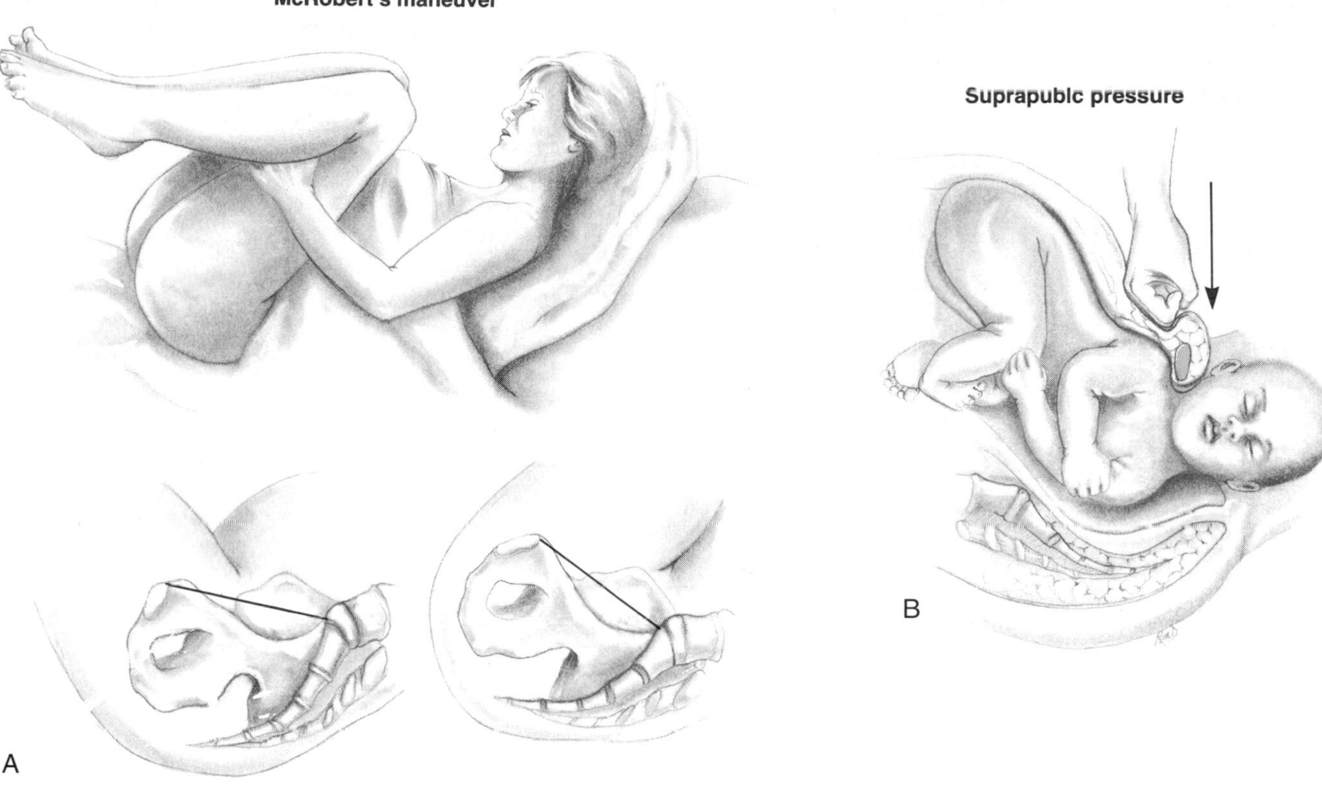

Figure 26–2

Methods that may be used to relieve shoulder dystocia. **A,** McRobert's maneuver. The woman flexes her thighs sharply against her abdomen, which straightens the pelvic curve somewhat. A supported squat has a similar effect and adds gravity to her pushing efforts. **B,** Suprapubic pressure by an assistant pushes the fetal anterior shoulder downward to displace it from above the mother's symphysis pubis. Fundal pressure should *not* be used, as it will push the anterior shoulder even more firmly against the mother's symphysis.

pacted fetal shoulders (Fig. 26–2). The infant's clavicles should be checked for crepitus, deformity, or bruising, each of which suggests fracture (see p. 509).

ABNORMAL FETAL PRESENTATION OR POSITION

An unfavorable fetal presentation or position may interfere with cervical dilation or fetal descent.

Rotation Abnormalities. Persistence of the fetus in the occiput posterior or occiput transverse position can contribute to dysfunctional labor. Persistence in these positions does not allow the mechanisms of labor (cardinal movements) to occur normally. Most fetuses that begin labor in an occiput posterior position will spontaneously rotate to an occiput anterior position, facilitating extension and expulsion of the head (see p. 281). The fetus may not rotate, or it may partly rotate and remain in an occiput transverse position. Although most women cannot readily accomplish vaginal birth when the fetus remains in the occiput posterior position, the woman with a large pelvis may be able to do so.

Labor is usually longer and more uncomfortable when the fetus remains in the occiput posterior or occiput transverse position. Intense back or leg pain that is poorly relieved with analgesia makes it difficult for the woman to cope with labor.

Maternal position changes may assist fetal head rotation to an occiput anterior position (see Table 13–4, p. 311). Examples are:

- Sitting or kneeling, leaning forward with support
- Using hands and knees
- Using the side-lying position (on her left side if the fetus is in a right occiput posterior [ROP] position and on her right side for a left occiput posterior [LOP] position)
- Squatting (for second-stage labor)

The first three positions favor rotation because the mother's abdomen is positioned somewhat dependent in relation to her spine. The convex surface of the fetal back tends to rotate toward the convex surface of the uterus, similar to nesting two spoons together (Fig. 26–3). Moreover, these positions decrease the mother's discomfort by letting the fetal head fall forward, away from her sacrum. The squatting position aids both rotation and fetal descent by straightening the pelvic curve and by slightly increasing pelvic diameters.

If spontaneous rotation does not occur, the physician may assist rotation of the head with forceps. If forceps rotation fails, a cesarean birth may be required.

Deflexion Abnormalities. The poorly flexed fetal head presents a larger diameter to the pelvis than if flexed with the chin on the chest (see Fig. 12–7, p. 274). In the *vertex presentation*, the head diameter is smallest; in the *military* and *brow presentations*, the head diameter is larger. In the *face presentation*, head diameter is similar to that of the vertex presentation, but the maternal pelvis can be negotiated only if the fetal chin (mentum) is anterior.

Breech Presentation. Cervical dilation and effacement are often slower when the fetus is in a breech presentation because the buttocks and/or feet do not form a smooth, round dilating wedge like the head. The greatest fetal risk is that the head—the largest fetal part—is the last to be delivered. By the time the buttocks are born, the umbilical cord is well into the pelvis and may be compressed. Thus, the shoulders, arms, and head must be delivered quickly so that the infant can breathe.

Although a breech presentation is common well before term, only 3 to 4 per cent of term fetuses remain in this presentation. Outcomes for infants remaining in the breech presentation are generally worse, often because of other complications associated with a breech birth:

- Fetal injury with a difficult vaginal birth
- Prolapsed umbilical cord

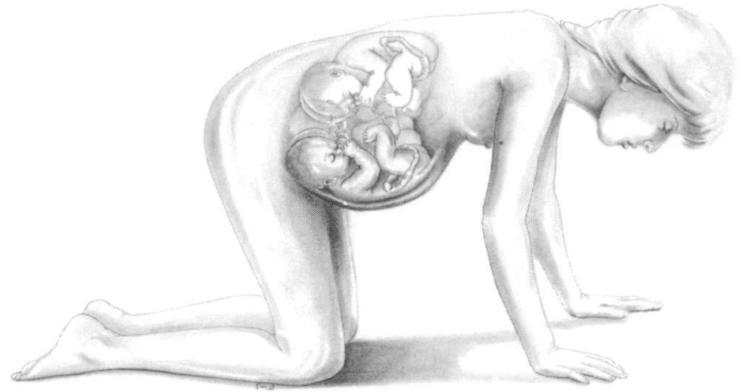

Figure 26–3

A "hands and knees" position helps the fetus rotate from a left occiput posterior (LOP) position to an occiput anterior position.

- Low birth weight caused by preterm gestation, multifetal pregnancy, or intrauterine growth retardation
- Fetal anomalies, such as hydrocephalus
- Complications secondary to placenta previa (see p. 669) or cesarean birth (see p. 403)

External version may be attempted to change the fetus in a breech presentation or transverse lie to a cephalic presentation (see p. 397). If the fetus remains in the abnormal presentation, cesarean birth is usually performed to avoid potential complications of a difficult vaginal birth. Delivery for the nulliparous woman with a fetus in a breech presentation is almost always cesarean. If the fetus remains in a transverse lie, delivery is always cesarean.

The physician may recommend that vaginal birth be attempted when the fetus is in a breech presentation if:

- The maternal pelvis is of normal size and shape (see p. 272)
- The estimated fetal weight is under 3600 g (8 pounds)
- Other complications, such as placenta previa or prolapsed cord, are not present

Because some women are admitted in advanced labor with the fetus in a breech presentation, physicians, nurse-midwives, and intrapartum nurses must be prepared to care for the woman having either a planned or an unexpected vaginal breech birth. Figure 26–4 illustrates the mechanisms of vaginal birth for an infant in a breech presentation.

MULTIFETAL PREGNANCY

Multifetal pregnancy may result in dysfunctional labor because of (1) uterine overdistention, which contributes to hypotonic dysfunction, and (2) abnormal presentation of one or both fetuses (Fig. 26–5). Additionally, the potential for fetal hypoxia during labor is multiplied because the mother must supply oxygen and nutrients to more than one fetus. She is also at greater risk for postpartum hemorrhage resulting from uterine atony because of uterine overdistention (see p. 776).

Because of these complications, delivery for a woman with a multifetal pregnancy is often cesarean. If triplets or more than three fetuses are involved, the birth is almost always cesarean. Some women having twins may have a safe vaginal delivery. The physician considers fetal presentations, maternal pelvic size, and presence of other complications, such as pregnancy-induced hypertension.

During labor, each twin's FHR must be monitored separately for non-reassuring patterns. The woman

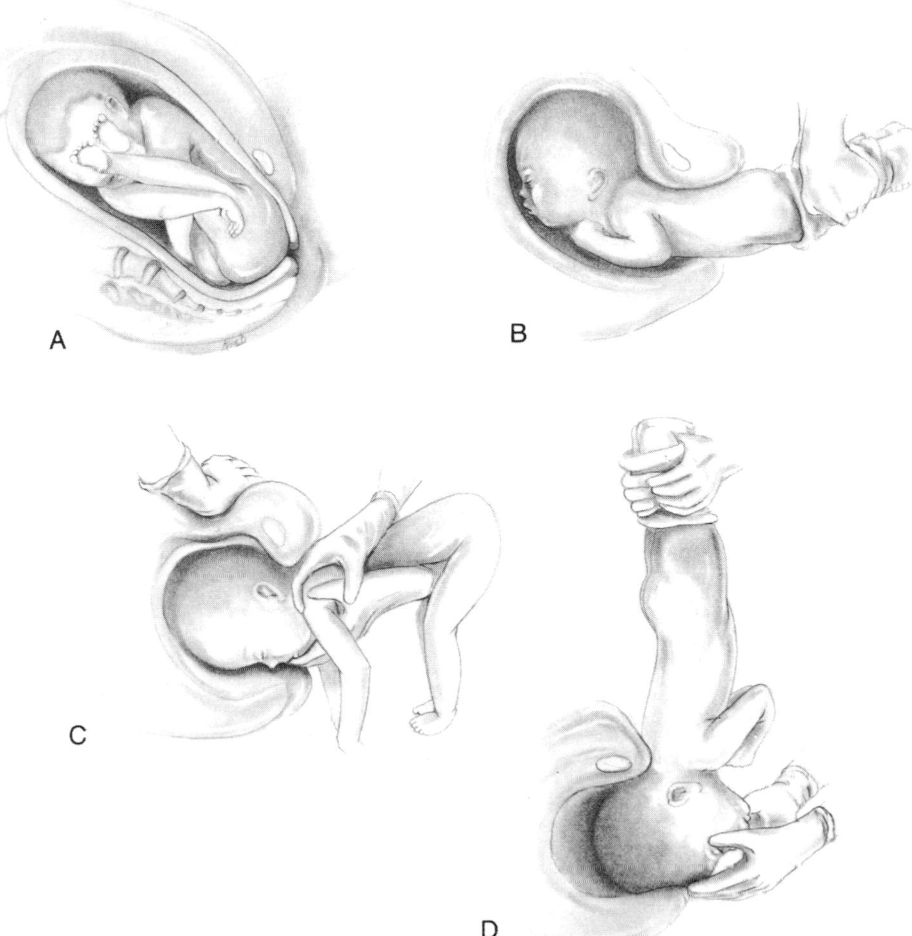

Figure 26–4

Sequence for vaginal birth in a frank breech presentation. **A,** Descent and internal rotation of the fetal body. **B,** Internal rotation complete; extension of the fetal back as the trunk slips under the symphysis pubis. The birth attendant uses a towel for traction when grasping the fetal legs. **C,** After birth of the shoulders, the attendant maintains flexion of the fetal head by using the fingers of the left hand to apply pressure to the lower face, the fetal body straddles the attendant's left arm. An assistant provides suprapubic pressure to help keep the fetal head well flexed. **D,** After the fetal head is brought under the symphysis pubis, an assistant grasps the fetal legs with a towel for traction while the attendant delivers the face and head over the mother's perineum.

should remain in a lateral position to promote adequate placental blood flow. After vaginal birth of the first twin, assessment of the second twin's FHR continues until birth. The nurse observes for signs of hypotonic labor dysfunction.

Whether the birth is vaginal or cesarean, the intrapartum staff must be prepared for the care and possible resuscitation of multiple infants. Cord clamps, bulb syringes, radiant warmers, and resuscitation equipment must be prepared for each infant. One nurse (or more), a pediatrician, and/or a neonatologist should be available to care for each infant. One nurse should be free to care for the mother. Another physician and an anesthesiologist may be present because the potential for maternal and infant complications is greater than with singleton (single infant) births.

FETAL ANOMALIES

Fetal anomalies, such as hydrocephalus, or a large fetal tumor may prevent normal descent of the fetus. Abnormal presentations, such as breech or transverse lie, are also associated with fetal anomalies. These abnormalities may be discovered by ultrasound examination before labor. A cesarean birth is scheduled if vaginal birth is not possible or if it is inadvisable.

Problems of the Passage

Dysfunctional labor may occur because of variations in the maternal bony pelvis or because of soft tissue problems that inhibit fetal descent.

PELVIS

A small (contracted) or abnormally shaped pelvis may slow down labor and obstruct fetal passage. The woman may experience poor contractions, slow dilation, slow or arrested fetal descent, and prolonged labor. There is a greater danger of uterine rupture with thinning of the lower uterine segment (see p. 766).

There are four basic pelvic shapes, each with different implications for labor and birth (Table 26–2). Most women do not have a pure pelvic shape but have mixed characteristics from two or more types.

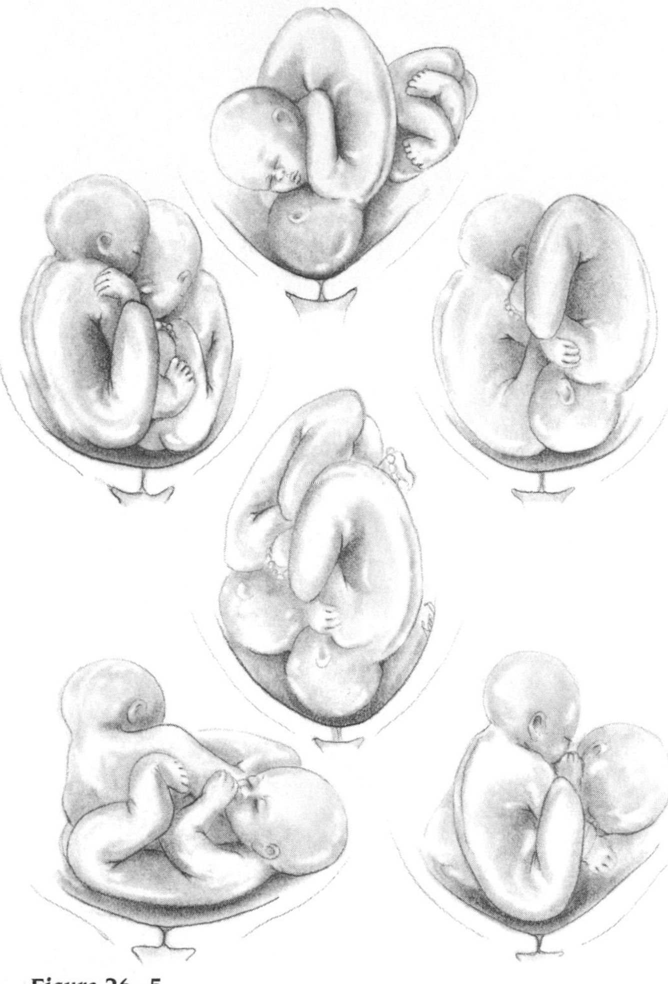

Figure 26–5

Twins can present in any combination.

Maternal Soft Tissue Obstructions

During labor, a full bladder is a common soft tissue obstruction. Bladder distention reduces available room in the pelvis, can prevent normal fetal descent, and intensifies maternal discomfort. The woman should be assessed for bladder distention regularly and encouraged to void every 1 to 2 hours. Catheterization may be needed if she cannot urinate.

Less common soft tissue obstructions are tumors, such as benign uterine fibroids. Invasive cervical carcinoma occasionally occurs during pregnancy and is a contraindication to labor and vaginal birth because of the increased risk for hemorrhage and infection. However, in many cases a diagnosis is not made until after the delivery and there is no evidence that vaginal birth alters the cancer prognosis (Savage and Parham, p. 600).

Problems of the Psyche

Labor is a stressful event for most women. However, a perceived threat caused by pain, fear, non-support, or one's personal situation can result in excessive maternal stress and interfere with normal labor progress. The woman's perception of stress—more than the actual existence of a threat—is important.

The body responds to stress, preparing itself for fight or flight. However, responses to excessive or prolonged stress interfere with labor in several ways:

- Increased glucose consumption by body cells reduces the energy supply available to the contracting uterus.
- Secretion of catecholamines (epinephrine and norepinephrine) by the adrenals stimulates uterine beta-receptors, which inhibit uterine contractions (an action similar to that of tocolytic drugs, such as terbutaline).
- Adrenal secretion of catecholamines diverts blood supply from the uterus and placenta to skeletal muscle.
- Effectiveness of labor contractions and maternal pushing efforts is reduced because these powers are working against the resistance of tense abdominal and pelvic muscles.
- Pain perception is increased and pain tolerance is decreased, which further increase maternal anxiety and stress.

Nursing care to help the woman relax helps her body work more efficiently with the forces of labor and promotes normal progress. General measures involve:

- Making the environment comfortable by adjusting temperature and light
- Promoting physical comfort, such as cleanliness
- Providing accurate information
- Implementing non-pharmacological and pharmacological pain management

Chapter 15 describes specific methods to encourage relaxation and promote comfort.

✔ Check Your Reading

1. How does hypotonic labor dysfunction differ from hypertonic labor in terms of: The most common labor phase when it becomes evident? Uterine contractions? Presence of pain? Therapeutic management?
2. How can maternal position changes favor rotation of the fetus from an occiput transverse or occiput posterior position to an occiput anterior position?
3. Why does a cesarean birth not eliminate all adverse outcomes for infants in a breech presentation?

Table 26–2. PELVIC SHAPES

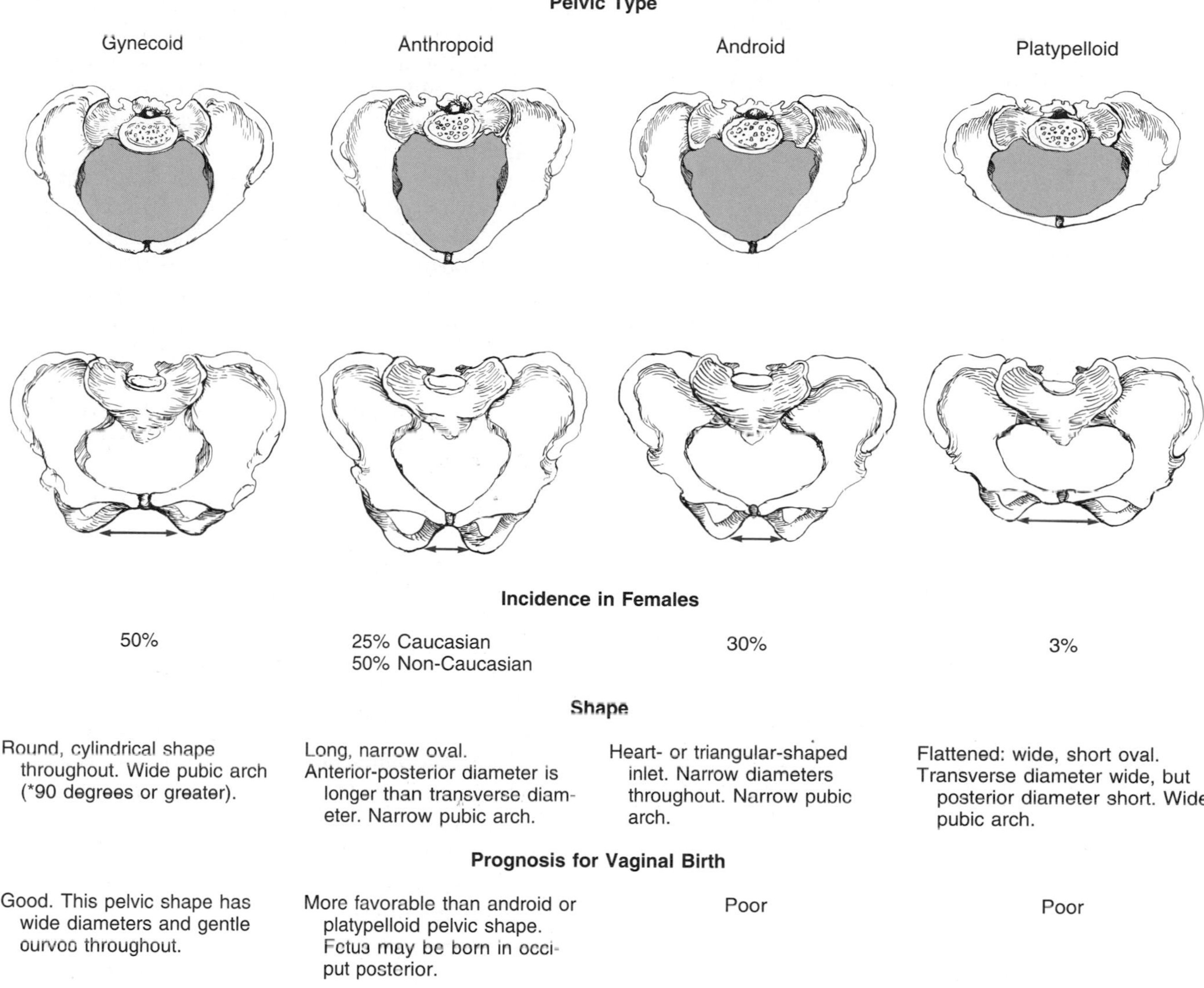

	Gynecoid	Anthropoid	Android	Platypelloid
Incidence in Females	50%	25% Caucasian 50% Non-Caucasian	30%	3%
Shape	Round, cylindrical shape throughout. Wide pubic arch (*90 degrees or greater).	Long, narrow oval. Anterior-posterior diameter is longer than transverse diameter. Narrow pubic arch.	Heart- or triangular-shaped inlet. Narrow diameters throughout. Narrow pubic arch.	Flattened: wide, short oval. Transverse diameter wide, but posterior diameter short. Wide pubic arch.
Prognosis for Vaginal Birth	Good. This pelvic shape has wide diameters and gentle curves throughout.	More favorable than android or platypelloid pelvic shape. Fetus may be born in occiput posterior.	Poor	Poor

4. How does preparation for the birth of twins (vaginally or cesarean) differ from preparation for a single infant's birth?
5. Why should the nurse observe the laboring woman's bladder frequently?
6. Why is psychological support during labor important for effective physiologic function?

Abnormal Labor Duration

An unusually long or short labor may result in maternal, fetal, or neonatal problems.

PROLONGED LABOR

Prolonged labor usually results if there are abnormalities of the powers, passenger, passage or psyche or combinations of these elements. After reaching the active phase of labor, cervical dilation should proceed at a rate of 1.2 cm/hour in the nullipara and 1.5 cm/hour in the multipara. Figure 26–6 is a graphic representation of a woman with prolonged cervical dilation in labor.

Potential maternal and fetal problems in prolonged labor include:

- Maternal infection, intrapartum or postpartum
- Neonatal infection, which may be severe or fatal (see p. 853).

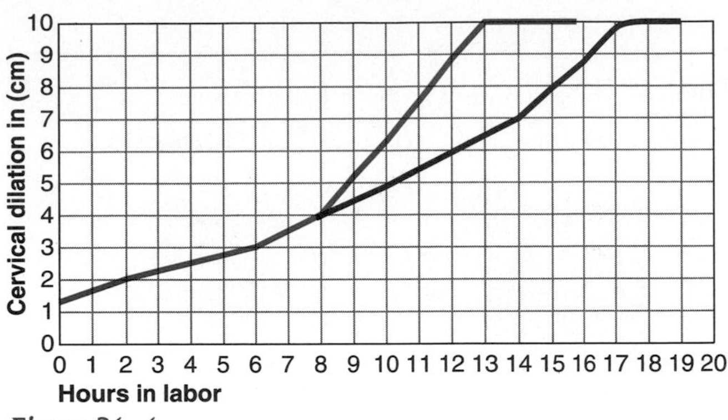

Figure 26–6

Graphic representation of cervical dilation in a normal nulliparous labor (*colored line*) and cervical dilation in the nulliparous woman who has prolonged dilation (*black line*).

- Maternal exhaustion
- Higher levels of anxiety and fear in the mother during a subsequent labor

Maternal and neonatal infections are more likely if the membranes have been ruptured for a prolonged time (see p. 749).

Priority nursing care for a woman in prolonged labor is essentially the same as that for a woman in dysfunctional labor. Nursing actions include promotion of the mother's comfort, conservation of her energy, position changes that favor normal progress, and assessments for infection.

PRECIPITATE LABOR

For a woman in precipitate labor, delivery occurs within 3 hours of its onset. Often there is an abrupt onset of intense contractions rather than the more gradual increase in frequency, duration, and intensity that characterize most other labors.

Precipitate labor is not the same as a precipitate birth. A precipitate birth occurs after a labor of any length, in or out of the hospital or birth center, when a trained attendant is not present. However, a woman in precipitate labor may also have a precipitate birth. Table 13–6 addresses the nurse's role in emergency birth (see p. 318). The nurse should never lock the mother's legs or otherwise hold the fetal head back to delay birth. Such actions can result in fetal hypoxia or other injury.

If the maternal pelvis is adequate and the soft tissues yield easily to fetal descent, little maternal injury is likely. However, if the soft tissues are firm and resist stretching, trauma (uterine rupture, cervical lacerations, hematoma) of the vagina or vulva may occur.

The fetus may suffer direct trauma, such as intracranial hemorrhage or nerve damage, during a precipitate labor. The fetus may become hypoxic because intense contractions with a short relaxation period do not allow the intervillous spaces of the placenta to refill with blood. Fetal bradycardia and late decelerations are probable electronic fetal monitor patterns (see p. 346).

Priority nursing care of the woman in precipitous labor includes promotion of fetal oxygenation and maternal comfort. The woman should remain in a side-lying position to enhance placental blood flow and reduce the effects of aortocaval compression. Additional measures to enhance fetal oxygenation include administering oxygen to the mother and maintaining adequate blood volume with non-additive IV fluids. If oxytocin is in use, it should be stopped. A tocolytic drug, such as terbutaline, may be ordered.

Promoting comfort is difficult in a precipitous labor because intense contractions give the woman little time to prepare and to use coping skills, such as breathing techniques. Pharmacologic measures (narcotic analgesia or regional block) may not be useful because rapid labor progression does not allow time for them to become effective. Also, possible newborn respiratory depression must be considered when narcotics are given near birth. Breathing with the woman throughout each contraction can help her focus on techniques to cope with pain. It is essential to remain with her, both to provide support and to assist with an emergency birth if it occurs.

✔ Check Your Reading

7. During the active phase of labor, what is the dilation rate for the average nulliparous woman? What is the dilation rate for the average multiparous woman?
8. What is the priority nursing care for a woman in prolonged labor?
9. What are the maternal and fetal risks when labor is unusually short?

Dysfunctional Labor: Application of Nursing Process

Several nursing diagnoses and collaborative problems may be appropriate in dysfunctional labor. The potential complication of fetal compromise should be part of all intrapartum management (see Chapter 14). Pain management (see Chapter 15) is especially important to women in dysfunctional labor because they may find that their coping skills are inadequate. Maternal or fetal injury may occur with dysfunctional labor (see Chapters 27 and 29).

Nursing care focuses on two problems: (1) possible intrauterine infection and (2) maternal exhaustion. Anxiety or fear is often higher with abnormal labor. Nursing management is similar to that for intrapartum emergencies (see p. 770).

Intrauterine Infection

Assessment

Infection can occur with both normal and dysfunctional labors. Assess the FHR and maternal vital signs for evidence of infection:

- Fetal tachycardia (>160/minute), often the first sign of intrauterine infection
- Maternal temperature; assess every 2 to 4 hours in normal labor and every 2 hours after membranes rupture; assess hourly if elevated (38°C, or 100.4°F) or if other signs of infection are present
- Maternal pulse, respirations, and blood pressure at least hourly to identify tachycardia or tachypnea, which often accompanies temperature elevation.

Assess amniotic fluid for normal clear color and mild odor. Yellow or cloudy fluid or fluid with a foul or strong odor suggests infection. The strong odor may be noted before birth or afterward on the infant's skin.

Analysis

Some women are admitted with signs of infection already present. In this case, a collaborative problem would be more appropriate than a nursing diagnosis.

For the woman without signs of infection but who does have risk factors, the nursing diagnosis selected is: *High Risk for Infection related to presence of favorable conditions for its development* (specify).

Planning

Goals appropriate to this nursing diagnosis relate to detection of a developing infection:

- Maternal temperature will remain below 38°C (100.4°F).
- The FHR will remain near the baseline and below 160 BPM.
- The amniotic fluid will remain clear and without a foul or strong odor.

Interventions

REDUCING THE RISK FOR INFECTION

Nurses should wash their hands before and after each contact with the woman and her infant to reduce transmission of organisms. Use gloves and other protective wear to prevent contact with potentially infectious secretions (universal precautions) both before and after birth. 

Limit vaginal examinations as much as possible to reduce transmission of vaginal organisms upward into the uterine cavity, and maintain aseptic technique during vaginal examinations. The intrapartum nurse learns to estimate a woman's progress with few vaginal examinations. For example, there may be increased bloody show and heightened anxiety when the cervix is about 6 cm dilated; she may become irritable and seems to lose emotional control at about 8 cm dilation.

Keep underpads as dry as possible to reduce the moist, warm environment that favors bacterial growth. Periodically clean excess secretions from the vaginal area in a front-to-back motion to limit fecal contamination. These actions also promote the mother's comfort. 

IDENTIFYING INFECTION

Assess the woman and fetus for signs of infection. Increase frequency of assessments if labor is prolonged. If signs are noted, report them to the physician or nurse-midwife for definitive treatment. Note the time at which the membranes have ruptured to identify prolonged rupture, which adds to the risk for infection.

The physician or nurse-midwife may collect specimens from the uterine cavity for culture to identify infectious organisms and determine antibiotic sensitivity. Both aerobic and anaerobic culture specimens may be collected in containers specifically made for these two types of organisms. Follow directions on the container for proper handling and to prevent contamination with extraneous organisms, which would result in inaccurate culture and sensitivity results. Transport specimens to the laboratory 

Critical to Remember

Signs Associated with Intrapartum Infection

Fetal tachycardia (over 160/minute)

Maternal fever (38°C or 100.4°F)

Foul or strong-smelling amniotic fluid

Cloudy or yellow appearance to amniotic fluid

promptly because living organisms are required for these studies.

Inform the newborn nursery staff and the pediatrician if signs of infection are noted or if increased maternal risk factors are present. Specimens of infant secretions may be obtained for culture for the same reason that maternal procedures are done. They should be cared for in the same manner.

The infant is often given prophylactic antibiotics to prevent neonatal sepsis (see p. 853). If results of infant cultures indicate no infection present, the antibiotic is usually discontinued. Culture and sensitivity may also reveal the presence of infection and indicate that a different antibiotic would be more effective.

Evaluation

If the goals are achieved

- The woman's temperature will remain below 38°C (100.4°F).
- The amniotic fluid will have normal characteristics.
- Fetal tachycardia, either sudden or gradual in onset, will be absent.

Even if the woman has no signs of intrapartum infection, she remains at higher risk for postpartum infection and should be observed for these signs and symptoms (see p. 790).

Maternal Exhaustion

Assessment

Many women begin labor with a sleep deficit because of fetal movement, frequent urination, and shortness of breath associated with advanced pregnancy. As labor drags on, the mother's reserves are further depleted.

Assess the mother for signs and symptoms of exhaustion:

- Verbal expression of tiredness, fatigue, or exhaustion
- Verbal expression of frustration with a prolonged, unproductive labor ("I can't go on any longer. Why doesn't the doctor just take the baby?")
- Ineffectiveness or inability to use coping techniques (such as patterned breathing) that she previously used effectively
- Changes in her pulse, respiration, and blood pressure (increased or decreased)

Analysis

The intense energy demands of a dysfunctional labor often exceed a woman's physical and psychological ability to meet them. The woman who displays any of the physical changes or behaviors listed under Assessment has likely reached or exceeded her tolerance for the physical requirements of labor. For this reason, the nursing diagnosis selected is: *Activity Intolerance related to depletion of maternal energy reserves.*

Planning

Contractions must continue for labor to progress. Throughout the remainder of labor, the woman will try to attain two realistic goals:

- Rest between contractions with her muscles relaxed
- Use coping skills, such as breathing and relaxation techniques

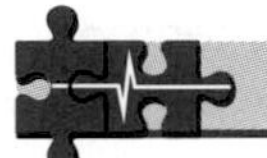

Clinical Situation

A woman having her first baby has been in labor for several hours. Her nurse-midwife performs a vaginal examination and says that the cervix is 6 cm dilated and completely effaced, with the fetus in right occiput posterior (ROP) position. The mother is having persistent back pain that worsens during contractions.

Q: Why is she having these symptoms? What nursing measures are appropriate for her and why?

A: When the fetus is in one of the occiput posterior positions, back pain is usually persistent because the fetal head presses on the mother's sacrum with each contraction, often called "back labor." Additionally, the fetal head has to internally rotate a wider arc to ultimately reach an occiput anterior position for birth; this process prolongs labor in most women.

To make the woman more comfortable and to promote rotation of the fetal head to an occiput anterior position, encourage her to change positions regularly. Positions that cause her uterus to fall forward reduce pressure on her sacrum and straighten the pelvic curve somewhat to encourage fetal rotation. Examples of these are leaning forward while sitting or standing and a hands-and-knees position. If she wants to lie in bed, a left side-lying position favors fetal rotation. Consult with her nurse-midwife if she wants analgesia or anesthesia.

Interventions

CONSERVING MATERNAL ENERGY

Reduce factors that interfere with the woman's ability to rest. Lower the light level, and turn off overhead lights that shine in her eyes. Reduce noise by closing the door or masking it with soft music or other comforting sounds. Maintain a comfortable maternal temperature with blankets or a fan.

Position the woman to encourage comfort and to promote fetal descent. Support her with pillows to reduce muscle strain and added fatigue. Avoid the supine position because it compresses the vena cava and reduces placental blood flow. Contractions are less effective and more uncomfortable in this position as well. Help her change positions regularly (about every 30 to 60 minutes) to reduce muscle tension from constant pressure.

A soothing back rub may reduce muscle tension, which contributes to fatigue. Firm sacral pressure may reduce back pain.

An intravenous infusion may be ordered to provide fluid, electrolytes, and sometimes glucose.  Maintain the IV fluids at the rate ordered, usually about 125 ml/hour. Assess intake and output to identify dehydration, which may accompany prolonged labor. Dehydration may be another cause of maternal fever. If there is no contraindication, provide juice, lollipops, or Popsicles, as ordered by the physician or nurse-midwife, to moisten the woman's mouth and replenish her energy.

PROMOTING COPING SKILLS

When position changes or medical therapy is used to enhance labor, explain their purpose and expected benefits. Generous praise and encouragement of the woman's use of skills, such as breathing techniques, motivate her to continue them even when she is discouraged. As with any laboring woman, tell her when she is making progress. Knowing that her efforts are having the desired results gives the woman courage to continue.

Evaluation

Goals are met if the woman:

- Can rest and relax between contractions. If she is unable to relax, discuss analgesia options with her. Inability to relax between contractions is associated with pain beyond the woman's tolerance.
- Continues to demonstrate adequate, if not optimal, physical and psychological energy to cope with labor.

Additionally, solicit the woman's perceptions of her ability to relax and cope with labor.

Premature Rupture of the Membranes

Rupture of the amniotic sac before onset of true labor, regardless of length of gestation, is called *premature rupture of the membranes* (PROM). A similar term, *preterm premature rupture of the membranes* (PPROM), describes ruptured membranes before term, with or without contractions. PPROM is strongly associated with preterm labor and birth.

Etiology

Several conditions are associated with premature membrane rupture, but the exact cause often remains unclear. Possible causes are:

- Infections of the vagina or cervix
- Chorioamnionitis
- Incompetent cervix
- Fetal abnormalities or malpresentation
- Hydramnios
- Amniotic sac with a weak structure
- Recent sexual intercourse
- Nutritional deficiencies

Complications

Both mother and newborn are at risk for infection during the intrapartum and post-birth periods. Chorioamnionitis can be both a cause and a result of prematurely ruptured membranes. The mother is at higher risk for postpartum infection, and the newborn is vulnerable to neonatal sepsis.

If chorioamnionitis does not precede PROM, it is more likely to occur if a long time elapses between membrane rupture and birth. The exact time at which infection occurs cannot be predicted, but the risk is known to be greatly increased after 24 hours have elapsed. However, infection may occur after just a few hours of ruptured membranes.

If preterm birth occurs, the infant is more likely to have respiratory distress syndrome and complications related to immaturity (see Chapter 28). The hazards of prematurity are greatest before 36 weeks' gestation. Other infant complications result from the loss of the amniotic fluid cushion (oligohydramnios). Umbilical cord compression, reduced lung volume, and deformities resulting from compression may occur.

Therapeutic Management

Management of prematurely ruptured membranes depends on duration of gestation and whether there is evidence of infection or other fetal or maternal compromise. For many women at term, PROM heralds the imminent onset of true labor. Usually, the cervix will be soft with some dilation and effacement. The fetal head is at or near a zero (0) station. If the woman is not at term or if her cervix is not soft and favorable for labor, therapeutic management is more complex. The risk of infection or preterm birth is weighed against the hazards of labor induction by oxytocin or cesarean birth.

DETERMINING TRUE MEMBRANE RUPTURE

First, determine whether the membranes are really ruptured. Women often think their membranes have ruptured if urinary incontinence, increased vaginal discharge, or loss of the mucus plug occurs. A vaginal examination is avoided, particularly if the gestation is preterm and there is no evidence of labor. Instead, the physician or nurse midwife performs a sterile speculum examination to identify a pool of fluid near the cervix and estimate dilation and effacement. Specimens of the fluid may be obtained for a Nitrazine or fern test (see p. 295), assessment of fetal lung maturity (see p. 225), Gram stain, and culture.

GESTATION NEAR TERM

If the woman is at or near term (about 36 weeks) and her cervix is soft, labor is usually induced if it has not started within 4 to 6 hours after membrane rupture. Walking may help stimulate contractions. If the cervix is not favorable, induction may be delayed up to 24 hours to allow cervical softening. If induction is unsuccessful or if infection develops during early labor, a cesarean birth is usual.

PRETERM GESTATION

If the gestation is preterm, the physician weighs the risks of maternal-fetal infection against the infant's risk for complications of prematurity. The cervix is usually not favorable for induction far from term. The physician considers factors such as gestational age, amount of amniotic fluid remaining, and fetal lung maturity.

Nursing Care

The woman may remain hospitalized until birth, or she may return home after a few days of hospital observation. If she is hospitalized, observe for signs of infection. Preparation for home management includes teaching the woman to:

- Avoid sexual intercourse
- Take her temperature at least four times a day, reporting any temperature over 37.8°C (100°F)
- Remain on bed rest in a lateral position (she may usually walk to the bathroom)
- Note uterine contractions

See care of the woman with preterm labor for additional care.

✔ Check Your Reading

10. How does premature rupture of the membranes (PROM) differ from preterm premature rupture of the membranes (PPROM)?
11. What is the relationship of infection to PROM?
12. What is the usual therapeutic management of PROM if the woman is at or near term?
13. What factors does the physician consider if the woman with PROM is not near term gestation?

Preterm Labor

Preterm labor begins after the 20th week but before the 38th week of pregnancy. The physical risks to the mother are no greater than labor at term unless there are other complications, such as infection. However, preterm labor may result in the birth of an infant who is ill equipped for extrauterine life.

Associated Factors

Just as the causes of labor's onset at term are not known, the causes of preterm labor are not known either. However, several factors are more likely to be associated with preterm labor: (1) medical conditions, (2) present and past obstetrical conditions, (3) social and environmental factors, and (4) demographic factors such as race and age. Each category of risk factors is presented in more detail in Table 26–3.

Table 26–3. MATERNAL RISK FACTORS FOR PRETERM LABOR

Medical History	Obstetrical History	Present Pregnancy	Lifestyle and Demographics
Uterine or cervical anomalies Diethylstilbestrol (DES) exposure as a fetus History of cone biopsy Low weight for height Chronic illness (such as cardiac, renal, hypertension)	Previous preterm birth Previous preterm labor Previous first trimester abortions (>2) Previous second trimester abortion History of previous pregnancy losses (2 or more) Incompetent cervix	Uterine distention (such as multifetal pregnancy or hydramnios) Dilated or effaced cervix at 32 weeks Abdominal surgery during pregnancy Uterine irritability Uterine bleeding Dehydration Infection Anemia Incompetent cervix Pre-eclampsia Premature rupture of membranes Fetal or placental abnormalities	Little or no prenatal care Poor nutrition Age under 15 First pregnancy after 35 Low education level Low socioeconomic status Smoking > 10 cigarettes daily Non-Caucasian Chronic physical or psychological stress Substance abuse

Signs and Symptoms

Signs and symptoms of early preterm labor are more subtle than those of labor at term. The woman may be only vaguely aware that something seems different, or she may not detect that anything is amiss. Only when preterm labor reaches the active phase is it likely to have the characteristics of term labor. Symptoms vary among women, but common ones are:

- Uterine contractions that may be uncomfortable but are often painless; the woman may not perceive contractions
- A sensation that the baby is frequently "balling up"
- Cramps similar to menstrual cramps
- Constant backache
- Sensation of pelvic pressure or a feeling that the baby is pushing down
- Change or increase in vaginal discharge (increased, watery, bloody)
- Abdominal cramps with or without diarrhea
- Thigh pain
- A sense of "just feeling bad" or "coming down with something"

Preventing Preterm Birth

BEFORE CONCEPTION

Prevention of a preterm delivery is cost-effective because of the substantial physical, emotional, and financial burdens involved. Nurses play an important role in preventing preterm birth. Ideally, strategies begin before conception, with community education of adolescent girls and women. Programs often include teaching about:

- Duration of a normal pregnancy
- Consequences of preterm birth
- Role of early and regular prenatal care in preventing preterm birth
- Conditions that increase risk for preterm birth

Women who are aware of the consequences of preterm birth may be more likely to take action to prevent it. If they recognize that they have risk factors, they may seek prenatal care earlier in gestation than they otherwise might.

AFTER CONCEPTION

Preventing preterm birth during pregnancy includes:

- Reducing barriers and improving access to early prenatal care for all women
- Assessing for risk factors
- Promoting adequate nutrition during pregnancy
- Educating women about the subtle symptoms of preterm labor and how they differ from normal pregnancy changes
- Empowering women to take an active approach if they have symptoms of preterm labor

Improving Access to Care. Improving access to prenatal care must be customized for the community. What works in one area may be inappropriate for another. Difficult access is a significant problem for women who rely on public clinics for their care. Long waits, fragmented care, language barriers, and insensitivity of caregivers may discourage women from obtaining the care they need and want. Expanding the number of caregivers by using nurses with advanced education, such as certified nurse-midwives and nurse practitioners, can reduce waits for care significantly. Additionally, nurses can help coordinate various aspects of care to limit the number of different appointments a woman needs to obtain complete care.

Identifying Risk Factors. Women who have additional risk factors for preterm birth can benefit from programs to reduce the risk and identify preterm labor early. These women usually have more intense prenatal surveillance, including frequent prenatal care appointments, reinforcement of the symptoms of preterm labor, telephone contacts, and assessments of fetal growth and health.

Some risk factors can be reduced or eliminated, but substantial lifestyle changes are required. For example, women who smoke or use drugs are encouraged to stop. The woman may need additional rest or to stop working, and this may be difficult or impossible for many. Nurses can work with the woman to help reduce her risks as much as possible.

Infections of the urinary and reproductive tracts are associated with PPROM and preterm labor. Screening for abnormal microorganisms in the urine, vagina, or cervix identifies women who may benefit from antibiotic therapy.

Promoting Adequate Nutrition. An adequate maternal diet contributes positively to the length of gestation and the infant's weight. Every pregnant woman should be offered culturally sensitive diet counseling. The Women, Infants, and Children (WIC) program is available to supplement the diet of some low-income women. Anemia can be corrected with appropriate supplements. (See Chapter 9 for a discussion of prenatal maternal nutritional needs.)

Educating Women About Preterm Labor. All pregnant women should be taught about symptoms of preterm labor because half of preterm births occur in women who have no identified risk factors. Language barriers can be reduced by using fluent translators and printed materials in the woman's primary language. The symptoms of early preterm labor should be reinforced regularly for women who have additional risk factors.

Empowering Women. Delaying birth when preterm labor occurs critically depends on identifying it early. Women should be encouraged to seek treatment promptly if they detect symptoms that suggest preterm labor. They should be encouraged to be assertive in communicating their concerns when they arrive at the clinic or hospital. Otherwise, they may wait for hours to be seen in a public facility.

The nurse may need to role play to give a woman an example about being assertive if she thinks she is in preterm labor. For example, "I'm not due for 8 more weeks, but I think I may be in labor. It's important for the doctor (or nurse-midwife) to see me right away, or I might have a premature baby."

It is equally important not to make the woman feel foolish if she reports significant symptoms yet is not in labor. Otherwise, she may not seek care for recurrent symptoms and a preterm birth may result.

Therapeutic Management

Management focuses on (1) identifying preterm labor early, (2) stopping preterm labor and delaying birth, and (3) accelerating fetal lung maturity if preterm birth is inevitable.

IDENTIFYING PRETERM LABOR

Frequent Prenatal Visits. Women at risk for preterm labor are seen more frequently for prenatal care. At each visit, the woman is checked for symptoms of preterm labor and her ability to follow therapy to prevent it. Cervical examinations for dilation or effacement that may occur without symptoms may be recommended more frequently for these women. If infections occur, they can be treated promptly.

Home Uterine Activity Monitoring. Home uterine activity monitoring supplements other methods of identifying preterm labor by providing regular, objective information about uterine activity. An essential part of this service is 24-hour phone availability of experienced perinatal nurses to (1) evaluate uterine activity, (2) determine symptoms that may be present, (3) reinforce symptoms she should report, and (4) notify the woman's physician of significant signs or symptoms.

The home uterine activity monitor is different from the fetal monitor used during labor (Fig. 26–7). It uses a device that is sensitive to less-intense contractions and functions better when the fetus is small and active. The sensor is applied to the maternal abdomen with a belt and attached to a small battery-powered recording device. Monitoring is done twice a day for 60 minutes, but it can be done any time the woman detects symptoms. After the monitoring session, data are transmitted to a central nursing service by telephone for evaluation on a computer screen. The devices in the home do not have a screen or paper chart to indicate uterine activity and do not detect the fetal heart rate.

After evaluating the data, the nurse contacts the woman by phone and asks her about symptoms of preterm labor. Depending on the data and the physician's orders, the nurse instructs the woman to monitor at the next scheduled time or remonitor

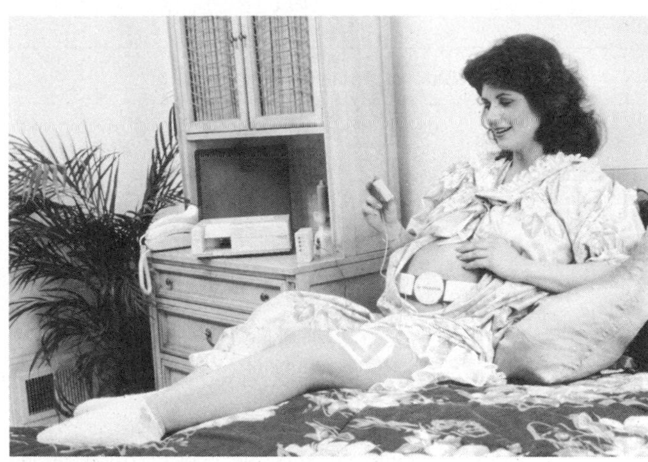

Figure 26–7

The home uterine activity monitor. This woman is also receiving terbutaline with a continuous low dose infusion pump. Note the needle insertion site on her left thigh. (Courtesy of Healthdyne Perinatal Services, Marietta, Ga.)

after emptying her bladder and drinking two glasses of water. (Dehydration and a full bladder can increase uterine activity.) The nurse immediately informs the physician of any uterine activity that exceeds a prescribed limit and discusses the physician's recommendation with the mother.

STOPPING PRETERM LABOR

The entire reason for preventing and identifying preterm labor early is to prolong pregnancy, giving the fetus added time to mature. Once diagnosis of preterm labor is made, management focuses on stopping the uterine activity before it reaches the point of no return, usually about 4 cm dilation. If preterm delivery is inevitable, therapy is directed toward reducing the infant's risk for respiratory distress.

Several criteria are used to distinguish preterm labor from other uterine activity that occurs between 20 to 37 weeks' gestation:

1. Uterine contractions (four in 20 minutes or eight in 60 minutes) and ruptured membranes
2. Uterine contractions as above with intact membranes and:
   a. Change in the cervical dilation and/or effacement.
   b. Cervical effacement of 80 per cent or more
   c. Cervical dilation of 2 cm or more

Initial Measures

Initial measures to stop preterm labor include hydrating the woman and placing her on bed rest. The posterior pituitary gland responds to dehydration by secreting antidiuretic hormone. Oxytocin may be secreted along with it, increasing uterine contractions. Rest promotes placental blood flow and reduces fetal pressure against the cervix.

Tocolytics

Most tocolytic drugs are used primarily for conditions other than premature labor and are only investigational when used for this condition. They have potentially adverse effects because they affect systems other than the uterus. Four types of drugs are used: (1) beta-adrenergics, (2) magnesium sulfate, (3) prostaglandin synthesis inhibitors, and (4) calcium antagonists. Table 26–4 summarizes doses and routes of administration for each of these drugs.

Successful tocolysis depends on early identification of preterm labor. Tocolysis is usually not ordered after the cervix is 4 cm dilated because it is unlikely to delay preterm birth for a significant time once this point is reached. Tocolysis is not usually recommended after 37 weeks' gestation because the infant's risk for respiratory distress is relatively low if birth occurs then. However, the physician assesses each woman individually to evaluate whether she may benefit from tocolysis.

Maternal or fetal contraindications to prolonging the pregnancy are also contraindications for tocolysis. Examples of these are pregnancy-induced hypertension, maternal hypovolemia, chorioamnionitis, or fetal distress. Other precautions and contraindications vary with the tocolytic drug. Urinary tract infections reduce the likelihood of stopping preterm labor and are treated concurrently.

Beta-Adrenergic Drugs. Ritodrine (Yutopar) is the only beta-adrenergic presently approved by the U. S. Food and Drug Administration (FDA) for tocolysis, although terbutaline (Brethine) is widely used. However, a Canadian study has concluded that ritodrine did not significantly prolong pregnancy or increase infant birth weights (Canadian Preterm Labor, Investigators Group, 1992).

The main side effects involve the cardiopulmonary system. Maternal and fetal tachycardia are common; other side effects include an altered blood pressure, wide pulse pressure, arrhythmias, myocardial ischemia, chest pain, and pulmonary edema. Beta-adrenergics can cause hyperglycemia and may be inappropriate for the diabetic woman or may require an increase in her insulin dose. Hypokalemia accompanies hyperglycemia and increases the risk for cardiac arrhythmias. Tremors and restlessness are bothersome side effects. See the Drug Guide on p. 755 for nursing care related to terbutaline tocolysis.

Table 26–4. DRUGS USED IN PRETERM LABOR

Drug/Purpose	Common Doses*	Side or Adverse Effects
Beta-adrenergics (tocolysis) Ritodrine	IV: Start at 0.05–0.1 mg/minute. Increase by 0.05 mg/minute q 30 minutes until contractions stop or significant side effects develop. Maximum dose: 0.35 mg/minute. p.o.: 10 mg q 2 hour. Give first dose 30 minutes before stopping IV infusion. Maintenance dose: 10–20 mg q 4–6 hours	Side effects are dose-related and more prominent during increases in the infusion rate than during maintenance therapy. Cardiovascular: maternal and fetal tachycardia. Wide pulse pressure. Pulmonary: Shortness of breath, chest pain. Gastrointestinal: Nausea, vomiting, diarrhea, ileus. Tremors, jitteriness, restlessness, feeling of apprehension. Metabolic alterations: hyperglycemia; hypokalemia. Pulmonary edema (more likely if the woman receives corticosteroids at the same time). Infection at injection site (subcutaneous terbutaline pump).
Terbutaline	See Drug Guide: Terbutaline (p. 755)	
Magnesium sulfate (tocolysis)	IV: Loading dose: 4–6 g; continue at 2–4 g/hour	Side and adverse effects are dose-related, occurring at higher serum levels. Depression of deep tendon reflexes. Respiratory depression. Cardiac arrest (usually at serum levels above 12/mg/dl). Less serious side effects include: Lethargy, weakness, visual blurring, headache, sensation of heat, nausea, vomiting, constipation. Fetal-neonatal effects: Reduced FHR variability. Hypotonia.
Indomethacin (tocolysis)	p.o.: 25–50 mg q 6 hours for 48 hours. Rectal suppository: same as p.o. dose.	Gastrointestinal: Epigastric pain, gastrointestinal bleeding. Fetus: May have constriction of the ductus arteriosus and decreased urine output. Decreased urine output is associated with oligohydramnios, which may result in cord compression. Adverse fetal effects usually resolve within a day after treatment is stopped.
Nifedipine (tocolysis)	p.o.: Initial dose: 30 mg. Maintenance dose of 20 mg q 8–12 hours for 3 days.	Maternal flushing. Transient maternal tachycardia. Maternal hypotension.
Corticosteroids (accelerating fetal lung maturation and production of surfactant) *Betamethasone *Dexamethasone	Same dose/route for both drugs. IM: 12 mg initially. Repeat 12 mg in 12–24 hours. Repeat treatment course weekly until 34 weeks' gestation.	Concurrent administration with beta-adrenergics and corticosteroids has been associated with development of pulmonary edema. May worsen conditions such as diabetes and hypertension and may delay wound healing.

* Doses and frequency of administration are common, but protocols do vary.

Therapy with beta-adrenergics is usually begun by the IV route, although terbutaline may begin with subcutaneous (SC) administration. The rate is increased until uterine activity stops or adverse maternal or fetal effects occur (primarily tachycardia and hypotension). After contractions stop, therapy shifts to the intramuscular (IM), SC, or oral (p.o.) route. To maintain adequate blood levels, the drug is given by the new route 30 minutes before stopping the IV drug and it must be given at evenly spaced intervals.

Terbutaline is often given subcutaneously, with a continuous, low-dose infusion pump at home or in the hospital to maintain tocolysis. The constant low infusion of medication reduces the incidence of recurrent preterm labor that is more likely with intermittent subcutaneous or oral doses.

Magnesium Sulfate. Magnesium sulfate is used in

Drug Guide

TERBUTALINE

Classification: Beta-adrenergic agent.

Action: Stimulates beta-adrenergic receptors of sympathetic nervous system. Action primarily results in bronchodilation and inhibition of uterine muscle activity. Increases pulse rate and widens pulse pressure.

Indications: Stop preterm labor. Reduce or stop hypertonic labor contractions that may contribute to placental insufficiency or cord compression.

Dosage and Route:

1. *Intravenous (IV) infusion.* Begin at 0.01 mg/minute. Increase by 0.005 mg/minute at 10- to 20-minute intervals until contractions stop (maximum of 0.080 mg/minute). Maintain this dose for 30 to 60 minutes, then reduce rate at increments of 0.005 mg/minute every 30 minutes to reach minimum maintenance dose. Continue maintenance dose at least 8 hours after contractions stop before changing route of administration.
2. *Subcutaneous (SC).* 0.25 mg every 1 to 3 hours.
3. *Oral.* 2.5 to 5 mg every 2 to 4 hours.
4. *Continuous subcutaneous infusion pump.* Basal rate of 0.02 to 0.09 mg/hour, with boluses individualized according to the woman's uterine activity pattern.

When changing from IV to SC therapy, give the SC dose as soon as the infusion is discontinued. When changing from IV to oral therapy, give oral dose 30 minutes before discontinuing infusion.

Absorption:

1. *Intravenous.* Prompt; duration about 2 hours.
2. *Subcutaneous.* 6 to 15 minutes; duration 1.5 to 4 hours.
3. *Oral.* 1 to 2 hours; duration 4 to 8 hours.

Excretion: Metabolized in the liver. Excreted in urine.

Contraindications: Hypersensitivity. Contraindicated before 20 weeks' gestation and if continuing the pregnancy is hazardous to the mother or fetus, as in fetal distress, hemorrhage, chorioamnionitis, or intrauterine fetal death. Contraindicated in conditions that may be adversely affected by beta-adrenergic agents (uncontrolled diabetes, hyperthyroidism, bronchial asthma treated with other beta-mimetic agents or steroids, cardiac arrhythmias, hypovolemia, or uncontrolled hypertension).

Precautions: Terbutaline is not approved by the United States Food and Drug Administration for inhibiting uterine activity, although it is widely used internationally for this purpose. Because its use is investigational, the hospital may require a signed informed consent. Most effective if begun as soon as a diagnosis of preterm labor is made.

Adverse Reactions:

1. *Cardiovascular:* Maternal and fetal tachycardia, palpitations, cardiac arrhythmias, chest pain, wide pulse pressure.
2. *Respiratory:* Dyspnea, chest discomfort.
3. *Central Nervous System:* Tremors, restlessness, weakness, dizziness, headache.
4. *Metabolic:* Hypokalemia, hyperglycemia, hyperinsulinemia.
5. *Gastrointestinal:* Nausea, vomiting.
6. *Skin:* Flushing, diaphoresis.

Nursing Implications: Diagnostic studies that may be ordered related to terbutaline therapy: electroencephalogram, blood glucose, electrolytes, urinalysis. Explain common side effects that are usually well tolerated, such as palpitations, tremors, restlessness, weakness, headache. Assess fetal heart rate (FHR), usually with continuous electronic fetal monitoring, recording rate and patterns every 15 minutes during IV dose increases. Assess maternal pulse, respirations, and blood pressure by same schedule as for FHR. Maintain adequate IV or oral hydration. Encourage the woman to empty bladder every 2 hours. Notify physician for significant or unacceptable side effects (maternal heart rate above 120/minute, respirations over 24/minute, systolic blood pressure lower than 90 mmHg, FHR over 160/minute, chest pain, dyspnea). Report continuing or recurrent uterine activity. Teach the woman to take oral medication evenly spaced around the clock and to take her pulse before each new dose (notify physician if rate is higher than 120/minute). Teach signs and symptoms of infection at insertion site of continuous SC pump. Teach signs and symptoms of recurrent preterm labor and follow-up medical care after discharge.

---

pregnancy primarily for its anticonvulsant effects when pregnancy-induced hypertension is present (see the Drug Guide on p. 685). Because of its added effect of quieting uterine activity, it is often used to inhibit preterm labor. Magnesium sulfate therapy has a well-established record of safety during pregnancy. If there are contraindications or if the pregnant woman does not tolerate other drugs, she may benefit from magnesium sulfate tocolysis.

Magnesium sulfate for tocolysis is given IV using a similar protocol as that for pregnancy-induced hypertension. A higher serum level (5 to 7 mg/dl) may be needed to inhibit contractions. Nursing care focuses on observing for these criteria needed to continue magnesium sulfate therapy:

- Urine output of at least 30 ml/hour
- Presence of deep tendon reflexes
- Respirations of at least 12/minute

Calcium gluconate, 10 per cent, should be available to reverse magnesium toxicity and prevent respiratory arrest.

The woman is usually switched to an oral beta-adrenergic drug or to terbutaline, administered by pump, for maintenance of tocolysis after contractions are stopped.

Prostaglandin Synthesis Inhibitors. Because prostaglandins stimulate uterine contractions, drugs may be used to decrease their synthesis. Indomethacin is the drug in this class that is most often used for tocolysis. Constriction of the fetal ductus arteriosus and inhibited platelet function in mother and infant are concerns, however.

Calcium Antagonists. Nifedipine is a calcium antagonist usually given to persons with cardiovascular problems. Because calcium is essential for smooth muscle contraction and because the uterus is a smooth muscle, nifedipine shows promise as an effective tocolytic drug. Flushing of the skin and a transient increase in the maternal and fetal heart rates are common side effects. Postural hypotension may occur with sudden position changes.

ACCELERATING FETAL LUNG MATURITY

If preterm birth seems inevitable, the physician may order corticosteroids to speed fetal lung maturation. Steroid therapy may reduce the incidence and severity of respiratory distress in the preterm infant, but it has no effect on other complications of prematurity. Betamethasone and dexamethasone are common drugs for this purpose.

Corticosteroids are of most benefit between 30 and 34 weeks of gestation. For greatest effectiveness in reducing respiratory distress syndrome, delivery must occur no sooner than 24 hours but within 7 days after the drug is given. Additional weekly doses may be given if birth does not occur within 7 days after the last dose.

Preterm Labor: Application of the Nursing Process

Much of the nursing care for the woman who is hospitalized with preterm labor relates to tocolytic drug therapy. If labor cannot be halted, care is similar to that for other laboring women related to fetal observations and pain management, with additional care to prepare for the preterm infant's needs. Support for anticipatory grieving may be needed if the infant is very immature and is expected to die.

Nursing care that is specifically appropriate for the woman at risk for preterm labor or who is receiving long-term therapy to prevent it relates to these three problems: (1) psychosocial concerns, (2) management of home care, and (3) boredom.

Psychosocial Concerns

Assessment

The entire family is affected by stressors associated with a complicated pregnancy. Assess how the woman and her family usually cope with crisis situations and how they are coping with the problem pregnancy. Determine their greatest concerns. For example, the nurse might say, "This development in your pregnancy must have been a shock. How are you handling things? What concerns you the most right now?"

The woman or her family may have physical, emotional and cognitive impairments because of the unexpected problems. Physical signs of emotional distress, such as tremulousness, palpitations, and restlessness, are also associated with many tocolytic drugs. The woman may express fear, helplessness, or disbelief. She may be irritable and tearful. Her ability to concentrate may be impaired at a time when she needs to learn new self-care skills.

Her partner often feels that he is at loose ends. He struggles to do something productive and to keep the household running while she must be inactive. Young children pick up on their parents' anxiety and may misbehave or regress. They do not understand why their mother cannot pick them up or play with them as they expect.

The family may be under financial strain. The woman must usually curtail or stop working. If she does not have adequate sick time or other benefits, the family sustains an abrupt drop in income. At the same time, medical expenses are mounting.

Analysis

The sudden and unexpected development of complications during pregnancy can prevent a woman and her family from using their normal coping mechanisms. Therefore, the nursing diagnosis selected is: *Anxiety related to uncertain outcome of the pregnancy, disruption of family relationships, and financial concerns.*

Planning

The outcome of any pregnancy is never certain, and this is especially true when the pregnancy is a high-risk one. Goals focus on the family's ability to cope with the crisis of preterm labor. One appropriate goal is: The family will identify methods to cope with the disruption in their lives.

Interventions

PROVIDING INFORMATION

Knowledge decreases anxiety and fear related to the unknown. Include her partner and other family members so that they are more likely to be supportive. Determine what the woman knows about preterm labor and birth and about the specific therapy that is recommended. Determine whether she understands problems that a preterm infant may face. Use this opportunity to correct any misinformation, and reinforce accurate information.

Initially, the woman may be highly motivated to maintain activity restrictions. However, because she usually feels well, she may begin to feel lazy and unproductive. Continue to reinforce how physical inactivity benefits her baby and that she is indeed doing an important job. Emphasize that carrying her baby closer to term is a full-time job when preterm labor threatens.

PROMOTING EXPRESSION OF CONCERNS

Encourage the woman and her family to express their concerns. Begin by exploring common concerns of women with problem pregnancies. For example, say, "Most women are worried when they have to stop working. How has this affected your family?" An open question gives them a chance to ventilate their feelings so they can take the next step: identifying constructive methods to cope with the situation. Collaboration with a social worker may identify financial or other community resources available.

EXPLAINING WHAT MAY OCCUR DURING A PRETERM BIRTH

Because preterm birth can occur despite all interventions, a pregnant woman should be prepared for that possibility. In hospitals with neonatal intensive care units, one or more nurses and often a physician are present at birth to care for the infant. The woman who has planned to give birth in a hospital without a neonatal intensive care unit may be transferred to a facility with this type of unit before the birth to allow immediate care and stabilization of her newborn. The infant may also be transferred after birth if there is no time to transfer the woman before birth or if the infant has more problems than were anticipated. Hospitalization of the mother and/or infant at a distant location adds to the stress on the family.

Evaluation

The goal for this nursing diagnosis is achieved if the woman and her family can identify constructive methods to deal with their anxiety. The nursing diagnosis should be re-evaluated periodically because anxiety may be chronic and its source may change as time goes by. A nursing diagnosis of Altered Family Processes may be more appropriate if the family has problems adapting constructively after the initial period of anxiety and disorganization.

Management of Home Care

Assessment

Long-term care of women at risk for preterm birth most often occurs in the home. In many families, the daily household activities are managed by the woman. When she is disabled, even temporarily, the usual roles of family members are disrupted. Moreover, therapy for preterm labor, such as tocolytic drugs or home monitoring, adds new demands for learning.

Determine the level of activity prescribed by the physician. Identify roles of each family member. A good way to do this is to have the woman describe a usual day before activity restrictions were instituted. Ask how many children are in the family and their ages.

Evaluate the home itself, either by visual inspection or by questioning the family. Ask whether the home is on more than one level or if it is an apartment and whether it is upstairs or downstairs. Ask whether there is a telephone for emergency contact and home monitoring if that is instituted. If the woman is to take medication, determine whether there is a place where it is easily available for access but out of reach of small children. Learn whether there are two or more areas where she can maintain bed rest, such as a sofa in the living room and a bed in the bedroom.

Evaluate resources. Ask whether there are family members and friends in the area who are available to help. Explore local support groups, such as churches or mother-to-mother networks, that the family might contact for assistance.

Text continued on page 762

Nursing Care Plan 26–1

Preterm Labor

Assessment: Rhonda Ellis is a 28-year-old gravida IV, para III. Her first child was born at 40 weeks of gestation, the second at 28 weeks, and the third at 32 weeks. Her oldest child is a second grader, the second is 4 years old, and the youngest is 18 months old. She is having her regular prenatal appointment today. Her pregnancy has progressed normally, with normal weight gain. Rhonda tells the nurse she is anxious to avoid having another premature baby. Rhonda is married to Carl.

Nursing Diagnosis: Health Seeking Behaviors related to Rhonda's desire for a full-term pregnancy as manifested by her verbal comments.

Goals:
At the end of teaching, Rhonda will restate:
1. Actions that may prevent preterm labor.
2. Symptoms that may be early indicators of early preterm labor.
3. What to do if she has symptoms of preterm labor.

Intervention:	**Rationale:**
1. Ask Rhonda what she already knows about preterm labor. For example: a. How long pregnancy should last for the baby to have minimal problems. b. How serious she believes preterm labor and birth are. c. How likely it is to recur. d. Whether preterm labor can be detected and stopped.	1. Knowledge is best retained if it is related to something the learner already knows. Rhonda must perceive her risk for preterm labor to be real and the consequences serious enough for her to be motivated to take action to prevent it.
2. Discuss methods to prevent preterm labor that are appropriate for Rhonda's present situation. Rhonda should:	2. Rhonda is in a high-risk group because she has already had two preterm infants. Since she has not yet had symptoms of preterm labor, she has no strict activity limits. Prevention focuses on usual health-promoting activities, with preparation for other restrictions that may be needed.
a. Avoid physically or psychologically stressful activities.	a. Physical or psychological stress increases the risk for preterm labor. Rhonda has 3 young children, including two preschoolers.
b. Plan several rest periods during the day. A side-lying position is preferable.	b. Rest promotes uterine blood flow and relieves some of the stress of everyday life.
c. Eat a well-balanced diet so that she gains about 1 pound per week.	c. A high-quality diet and adequate weight gain have a positive effect on pregnancy outcomes. Low pre-pregnancy weight and inadequate weight gain are associated with preterm labor and birth.
d. Drink at least eight large glasses of fluid each day, excluding caffeine-containing beverages.	d. Dehydration causes the pituitary to secrete antidiuretic hormone. Oxytocin, a stimulant of uterine activity, may be released along with it.
e. Avoid breast stimulation during sexual activity, in bathing, and in preparing for breastfeeding.	e. Breast stimulation may cause release of oxytocin from the posterior pituitary.
f. Avoid sexual intercourse until 37 weeks (or as recommended by the physician). Discuss other methods of sexual satisfaction that do not involve intercourse.	f. Mechanical stimulation of the cervix during intercourse can start uterine contractions. If Rhonda and her partner know non-intercourse options for sexual activity, they may be more willing to accept this restriction.

Nursing Care Plan 26–1 *Continued*

Preterm Labor

3. Ask Rhonda how labor started in her other preterm births and how these differed from her term birth. Explain that she should promptly go to the hospital if she has any of these symptoms of preterm labor:
   a. Uterine contractions, painful or painless. These may feel like the baby is "balling up."
   b. Cramping similar to menstrual cramps.
   c. A constant backache.
   d. A sensation of pelvic pressure or thigh pain.
   e. A change or increase in vaginal discharge.
   f. Abdominal or intestinal cramps, with or without diarrhea.
   g. A sense of "feeling bad" or that something is not quite right.

3. Symptoms of early preterm labor are often vague and not as obvious as signs of early term labor. Relating common symptoms to what Rhonda experienced before enhances her understanding and retention of the material. However, because her symptoms with a third preterm labor may be different, all should be emphasized so that she will consider the possibility. If she recognizes possible preterm labor, Rhonda is more likely to seek early therapy, which is more likely to be effective.

4. Teach Rhonda signs of a urinary tract infection:
   a. Fever (low-grade or very high).
   b. Burning or pain on urination.
   c. Unusual urinary frequency.
   d. Flank pain.
   e. Strong-smelling or cloudy urine.

4. Urinary tract infection is associated with onset of preterm labor. Treatment of the infection improves effectiveness of other measures to halt preterm labor and birth.

Evaluation:
Rhonda already knows about the need for rest but acknowledges that this is difficult with small children. She tries to eat a well-balanced diet but is often rushed during meals because of the demands of her family. She dislikes water and prefers colas but says she will try to drink more water and fewer caffeinated drinks. Rhonda discusses several early symptoms of preterm labor, including those she had with her other pregnancies. She says she will come to the hospital right away if she suspects labor is beginning before 37 weeks.

Assessment: Rhonda has light cramping and pelvic pressure at 28 weeks and comes to the hospital right away. The physician does a speculum examination of her cervix and finds that it is dilated 1 to 2 cm and is beginning to efface. She is placed on intravenous magnesium sulfate to stop her contractions. Rhonda is started on oral terbutaline to maintain tocolysis after the magnesium sulfate is discontinued. She will be discharged home in a few days if no recurrent symptoms develop. Rhonda did not have either of these therapies with her other preterm labors because labor was too advanced to stop when she entered the hospital. Rhonda seems confused about why she must be awakened at night for her oral terbutaline. She says, "I need all the sleep I can get."

Nursing Diagnosis: High Risk for Non-compliance (medication regimen) related to knowledge deficit about medication and negative effects of sleep disruption.

Goals:
After instructions Rhonda will:
1. Restate the reason for taking terbutaline around the clock and the side effects that should be reported.
2. Verbalize signs and symptoms that may indicate preterm labor is recurring.

Intervention: / **Rationale:**

1. Teach Rhonda the prescribed method for taking oral terbutaline:
   a. Take one 2.5-mg tablet by mouth every 3 hours.
   b. Set alarm clock at 3-hour intervals to take medication.

1. For most effective inhibition of preterm uterine activity, a constant blood level of the chosen tocolytic should be maintained. Setting an alarm for the next dose on an every 3-hour schedule reduces the risk that Rhonda will forget or be late with a dose.

2. Teach Rhonda side effects of terbutaline that she should report:
   a. Take pulse before each dose and report any rate over 120/minute, or as prescribed.
   b. Report any chest pain or difficulty breathing immediately or come to the hospital.

2. These are significant side effects that may warrant discontinuing or reducing the dosage of terbutaline. Maternal tachycardia above 120/minute can reduce cardiac output and oxygenation. Chest pain and dyspnea may be symptoms of pulmonary edema, an unlikely but serious complication.

Nursing Care Plan 26–1 *Continued*

Preterm Labor

Intervention	Rationale
3. Teach Rhonda common side effects that may be bothersome but that usually do not require that the drug be stopped. Explain that these will subside soon after the drug is stopped permanently. a. Tremors and shakiness. b. Restlessness and difficulty sleeping. c. Feelings of anxiety or apprehension. d. Headache.	3. Knowing common side effects increases the likelihood that Rhonda will not interpret them as dangerous. She may then be more likely to tolerate them during the short-term use of terbutaline.
4. Review signs and symptoms of preterm labor with Rhonda, and ask her to restate them. Emphasize that she should promptly return to the hospital if any of these occur.	4. Preterm labor often recurs despite tocolytic therapy. Repeating intravenous tocolytic therapy may stop contractions again, prolonging Rhonda's pregnancy and giving her fetus more time to mature. Reinforcing previously learned information increases its retention.

Evaluation:
Rhonda says that she dislikes having to be so careful to maintain her medication evenly spaced around the clock, but she prefers this small inconvenience if it will help her carry her baby longer. She also says that the bothersome side effects will be worth it if she can avoid another premature baby. Rhonda correctly restates each significant side effect of terbutaline that should be reported. She says she remembers signs and symptoms of preterm labor as well.

Assessment: When Rhonda's uterine activity has remained quiet for 2 days on bed rest and oral terbutaline, she is to be discharged home the following day. She is to remain on bed rest (side-lying) except for going to the bathroom and taking a quick shower each day. Rhonda will have home uterine activity monitoring, which will be managed by an outside company. She says she is worried about how she can stay in bed with three children to care for. Her mother-in-law lives nearby but works part-time.

Nursing Diagnosis: Impaired Home Maintenance Management related to activity restrictions and family demands as manifested by Rhonda's statement of concern.

Goal:
By hospital discharge, Rhonda will relate ways that she can maintain prescribed bedrest.

Intervention:	Rationale:
1. Assess what support systems are available and financially feasible to help Rhonda with child care and transportation. a. Day care center. b. Mothers' day out at church nursery. c. College student. d. Friends. e. Relatives, including her mother-in-law. f. Husband (Carl).	1. Rhonda's responsibilities to her other three children could easily impede her ability to maintain bed rest nearly 24 hours a day. Coordination among several resources helps provide all-day coverage for child care.
2. Encourage Rhonda to temporarily lower her standards for home management: a. Eat nourishing take-out or fast food. b. Prioritize household tasks that must be done. c. Let her children do tasks that are within their abilities. d. Make lists of tasks that need to be done for different people who will be available to help her.	2. Most of Rhonda's usual roles must be reallocated during this time and will not be done as she usually does them. For her to maintain bed rest, which is essential to curb uterine activity, she must resist the temptation to do seemingly simple and non-strenuous chores.
3. Encourage Rhonda to accept help from others. Remind her that this situation is temporary and that she may be able to help someone else at another time.	3. Women often feel like a burden if they must rely on others for assistance. If Rhonda feels that she can return the favor some day, she may be more willing to accept help. This also increases her sense of control over the situation.

Nursing Care Plan 26–1 *Continued*

Preterm Labor

Evaluation:
Rhonda identifies three friends in addition to her mother-in-law who may be able to help with child care. She says she cannot afford to continue sending her children to their day care center. She feels that if her children are cared for, her husband can handle her home management needs.

Assessment: Rhonda says, "With three young children, the idea of lying around all day sounds great! I wonder how it will be in a week or two? I don't watch much television or anything like that."

Nursing Diagnosis: Diversional Activity Deficit related to activity restrictions as manifested by Rhonda's comments about what she will do during this time.

Goal:
Rhonda will identify appropriate activities that she can do while on bed rest by the time she is discharged.

Intervention:	Rationale:
1. Determine Rhonda's usual activities when she is not working. Ask her about household duties that can be done in bed and about quiet leisure activities she enjoys. Ask about hobbies that she may have had in the past that she would like to reactivate or new ones she would like to learn.	1. Assessing common activities identifies those that can still be done within activity restrictions. It also gives the nurse a better understanding of Rhonda's personality so suggestions for appropriate activities can be individualized.
2. Encourage Rhonda to schedule specific activities for different times of the day.	2. Varying activities with a non-rigid schedule gives the day structure and helps her not to become tired of a single activity.
3. Advise Rhonda to set up at least two areas of her home where she can lie down. Tell her to have pillows, a blanket, writing materials, hobby supplies, a telephone, and a television nearby. Suggest that Carl or another helper stock a small picnic cooler with sandwiches and drinks, keeping it near Rhonda's "nest."	3. Having adequate activities, food, and drinks at hand limits the temptation to walk around, reduces boredom, gives Rhonda a change of scenery, and makes her feel more a part of family activities.
4. Encourage Rhonda to write down a list of possible activities that she can do while on bed rest. Encourage her to add to the list and share it with nurses who work with other women in her situation.	4. Making a list helps Rhonda focus on specific activities and helps her feel productive by contributing to the health of other women.
5. If there is another mother who has successfully handled a similar situation, ask her if she would be willing to share her tips for coping with therapy for preterm labor.	5. Interacting with another gives Rhonda a role model, helps remind her that her temporary inactivity is vital to her baby's health, and helps her further identify practical suggestions for coping with the situation.

Evaluation:
Rhonda plans to continue her role as the family financial manager. She has few hobbies but says that she has always wanted to crochet. Her mother-in-law crochets and will get Rhonda supplies for a baby blanket and teach her. Another woman who has recently been through a similar situation has volunteered to be a telephone contact to give advice and encouragement to Rhonda and others like her.

Additional Nursing Diagnoses to Consider:
Anxiety
Family Processes, Altered
Health Maintenance, Altered
Ineffective Individual or Family Coping

Analysis

The diagnosis is: *Altered Home Maintenance Management related to change in usual roles and responsibilities.*

Planning

Two goals are appropriate for this nursing diagnosis:

- *Short-term*: The family will identify methods for management of daily household routines.
- *Long-term*: The woman will be able to maintain the prescribed level of activity, drug therapy, and home monitoring (if applicable).

Interventions

The pregnancy threatened by preterm labor is a relatively long-term, but self limiting situation. Changes in home routines and therapy usually extend over several weeks. However, it is a self-limiting situation, making temporary adjustments somewhat easier.

CARING FOR CHILDREN

The woman who has children has different concerns than the woman who does not. Knowledge of growth and development helps the nurse identify the most appropriate way to ensure adequate care for the children and strengthen family relationships.

Toddlers and preschoolers rarely understand why their mother cannot play with them and why she spends most of the time lying down. If they are already in day care, this may continue if the family can afford it. They may live with a relative or friend temporarily. Toddlers may feel that their parents have abandoned them if they are sent away, although this may be the only realistic solution if there is no one besides the mother to supervise them.

School-aged children usually understand the situation better and are often quite helpful. Older school-aged children are usually interested in any technical devices, such as infusion and monitoring equipment. They may be helpful with care of other children, but they should not be put into the role of an adult. They may resent responsibility that is excessive for their age.

Adolescents may welcome the trust their parents have in them, but they also may resent the intrusion on independent activities with their peers. Teenagers who drive can be very helpful in taking younger siblings to school and to other activities. They may be enlisted for grocery shopping and meal preparation. If resentment flares, the parents and nurse can remind teenagers that the situation is temporary and that they are valuable contributors to the health of the new baby.

MAINTAINING THE HOUSEHOLD

The first step to home maintenance during this time may be for the woman to lower her standards of housekeeping. Things will not be as clean and neat as she might like. The father may take over many household tasks, but these compete with his other responsibilities outside the home.

Women who feel well but are on bed rest often feel unproductive and burdensome. Small tasks like dusting or emptying the dishwasher seem harmless enough. If she is on bed rest, emphasize to her and her family that all activity may increase contractions and the risk of preterm labor and birth. If she is rehospitalized, avoid making her feel guilty if she mentions doing any unprescribed activity.

Advise the woman to have a list of tasks ready when friends and family ask, "Can I do anything to help?" If they offer to bring a meal or do laundry, encourage her to accept. Remind her that people who offer to help really mean it and that she may be able to return the favor to someone else. Encourage the family to spread the load of household management so that helpers do not become "burned out." Many families find it difficult to ask for help from others, particularly non-relatives.

Transportation of school-aged children may be a concern. If no family or friends are available, the school nurse or Parent-Teacher Association (PTA) may help find someone willing to take the children to school each day.

Evaluation

Goals are met under the following conditions:

- The short-term goal may be met while the mother is in the hospital if she and her family can identify several methods for managing minimum household responsibilities.
- The long term goal is met if she can maintain the prescribed therapy.

Boredom

Assessment

Because prevention of preterm birth usually involves significant long-term activity restrictions, determine what skills the woman has for coping with boredom. Most women at risk for preterm labor must remain lying down virtually all day, although they may usually walk to the bathroom, take a shower, and sometimes eat their meals at the table. At first, the prescription for bed rest may sound wonderful, but after a short while, it can become trying.

Ask about a usual day to identify activities that are still appropriate within the restrictions prescribed. Ask about hobbies, present or past. What type of leisure activities does the woman enjoy? Which activities are available or possible?

Assess her personality. Is she calm and composed, taking whatever comes with serenity? Or does she need to be busy most of the time? No matter how motivated, the woman who finds inactivity tiresome will find bed rest difficult to maintain.

Analysis

The nursing diagnosis is: *Diversional Activity Deficit related to activity limitations.*

Planning

Two goals are appropriate for this nursing diagnosis. The woman will:

- Identify activities that are appropriate for her level of activity restriction.
- Pursue (with help of others) activities to relieve boredom.

Interventions

IDENTIFYING APPROPRIATE ACTIVITIES

Determine the woman's level of understanding about her activity restrictions to identify misunderstandings and reinforce correct information. Help her identify which usual activities are permitted and which ones should not be done and why. If she understands the rationale, she may be more willing to comply with restrictions.

Some women continue work activities, such as paperwork or phone calls, that can be accomplished lying down. The woman should avoid emotional strain and tension, which add to the strain already present because of her high-risk situation. Workplace deadlines can increase stress, even if she works at home. However, the feeling of usefulness gained by such activities may be beneficial because she is willing to maintain activity restrictions. Moreover, work-related activities can help reduce some of the family's financial concerns.

Suggest activities to help women keep busy and productive. These may include (1) household activities that can be done lying down, (2) volunteering for activities such as phone calls, and (3) leisure activities, such as puzzles, games, and hand needlework. Help her identify someone who can help her get the necessary supplies. This might be a good time to reactivate an old hobby.

The expectant mother can participate in some activities with her children while she is in bed. She can read to them and play board or card games. Encourage her to help the children with their homework and stimulate their development with thought-provoking discussions.

CHANGING THE PHYSICAL SURROUNDINGS

When assessing the home, encourage the woman to identify two areas where she can stay in bed. Many women choose one area in the bedroom and the other in the living area. This gives them a change of scene and helps them feel more a part of the family activities. Each area should include pillows, blankets, and a clipboard with writing materials. Ideally, the telephone is within reach and there is a television with a remote control unit.

Evaluation

The first goal is short term and may be met when activity restrictions are first instituted: The woman can accurately discriminate between appropriate and inappropriate activities. The second goal is met if she actually pursues appropriate activities.

✔ Check Your Reading

14. What symptoms of preterm labor should be taught to women at risk?
15. Why is it important to identify preterm labor early?
16. What is an appropriate response if a woman on bed rest at home asks, "Will it hurt anything if I do one or two loads of laundry?"

Prolonged Pregnancy

The duration of a prolonged pregnancy (often called postmature, postdate, or postterm) is longer than 42 weeks. Some apparent cases of prolonged pregnancy may only be miscalculation of the estimated date of delivery (EDD) because the woman has had irregular menstrual periods or has forgotten the date of her last normal one. Inadequate prenatal care limits the use of clinical methods such as ultrasonography, which might otherwise be used to pinpoint her EDD.

The main physical risk in prolonged pregnancy is to the fetus or newborn. Insufficiency of the placenta secondary to aging and infarction reduces transfer of oxygen and nutrients to the fetus and removal of waste. Because the fetus often has less reserve to tolerate uterine contractions, signs of fetal compromise, such as late decelerations and decreased variability, may develop during labor (see Chapter 14). Additionally, a reduced amniotic fluid volume (oligohydramnios) can result in umbilical cord compression. Meconium-stained amniotic fluid may cause respiratory distress in the newborn. The infant may be growth-retarded and may appear to have lost weight (see Chapter 29).

Some fetuses do not suffer from placental insufficiency and may continue growing. The woman and fetus then may suffer complications related to dysfunctional labor, inadequate postpartum uterine contraction to control bleeding, and injury if the birth is traumatic.

Psychologically, the expectant mother often feels as if her pregnancy will never end. She may fear induction of labor, a possible cesarean birth, and potential problems with her baby. The added fatigue imposed by prolonged pregnancy diminishes her resources for tolerating the added stress and anxiety. She may be more acutely perceptive of pain during labor and may need added measures to cope with it (see Chapter 15).

Intrapartum Emergencies

Placental Abnormalities

Women with placental abnormalities may experience hemorrhage during the intrapartum period. Placenta previa and abruptio placentae may cause bleeding anytime, most often during the third trimester. Placenta previa is sometimes associated with an abnormally adherent placenta (placenta accreta). Placenta accreta may cause immediate or delayed hemorrhage immediately after birth because the placenta does not separate cleanly, often leaving small fragments that prevent full uterine contraction. More extreme degrees of abnormal adherence occur when the placenta penetrates into the uterine muscle itself (placenta increta) or even all the way through the uterus (placenta percreta). All or only part of the placenta may be involved. A hysterectomy is often required if a large portion of the placenta is abnormally adherent. Placental abnormalities also may be associated with uterine rupture or uterine inversion.

Prolapsed Umbilical Cord

A prolapsed umbilical cord slips downward after the membranes rupture, subjecting it to compression between the fetus and pelvis (Fig. 26–8). It may slip down with the fluid gush immediately or long after the membranes rupture. Interruption in blood flow through the cord interferes with fetal oxygenation and is potentially fatal.

SIGNS OF PROLAPSE

Prolapse may be complete, with the cord visible at the vaginal opening. A prolapsed cord may not be visible but may be palpated on vaginal examination as it pulsates synchronously with the fetal heart. An occult prolapse of the cord is one that is suspected because of changes in the fetal heart, although it cannot be palpated or seen. The cord slips alongside the fetal head or shoulders. Fetal heart rate changes that suggest cord compression may involve variable decelerations or bradycardia if the compression is prolonged (see p. 345).

CAUSES

A prolapsed umbilical cord is more likely when there is a poor fit between the fetal presenting part and the maternal pelvis. When the fit is good, the fetus fills up the pelvis, leaving little room for the cord to slip down. Although a prolapsed cord is possible during any labor, it is more likely when these conditions are present:

- A fetus that remains at a high station
- A very small fetus
- Breech presentations (the footling breech is more likely to be complicated by a prolapsed cord because the feet and legs are small and do not fill the pelvis well)
- Transverse lie
- Hydramnios (often associated with abnormal presentations; also, the unusually large amount of fluid exerts more pressure to push the cord out)

THERAPEUTIC MANAGEMENT

Medical and nursing management often overlap, as they do in many emergency situations. Either the nurse or the physician may be the first to discover

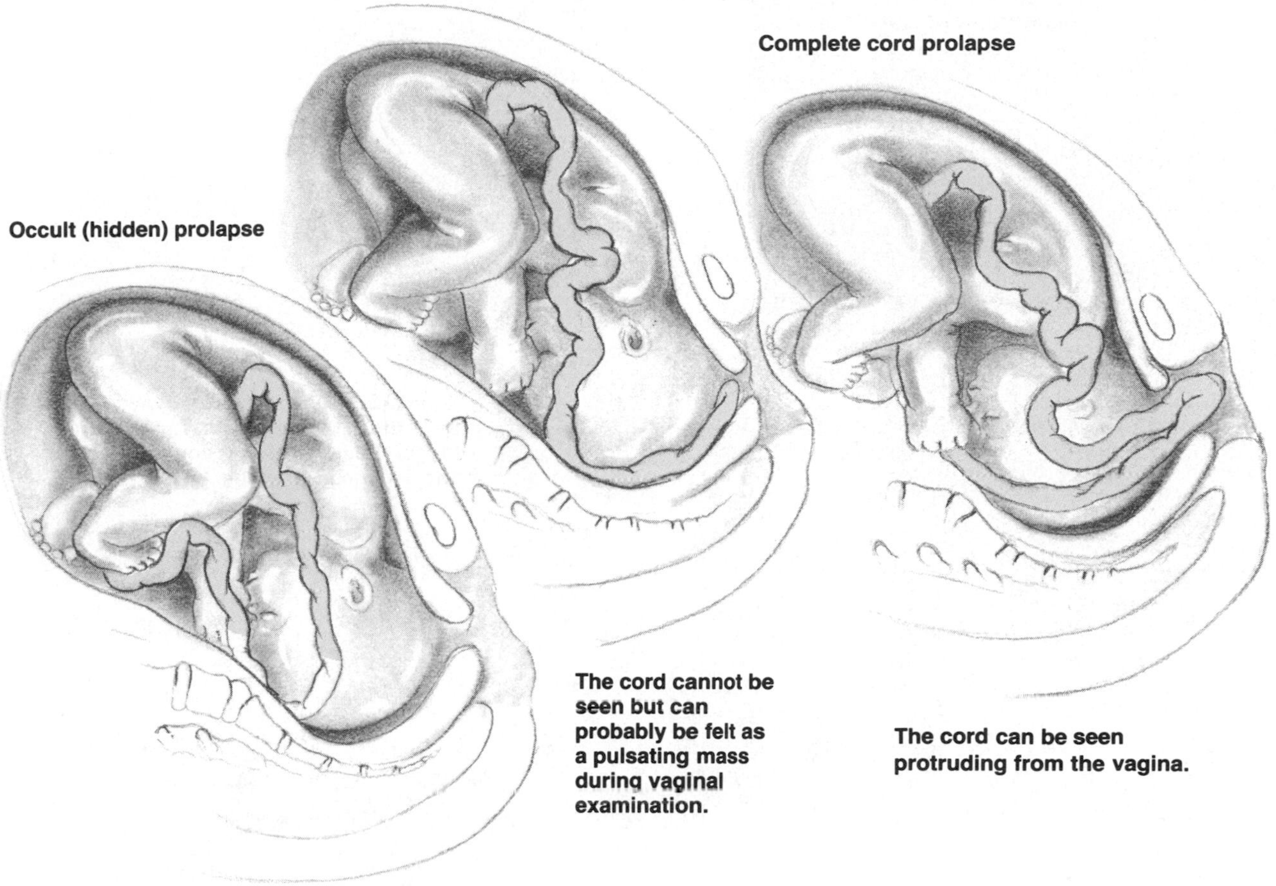

Cord prolapsed in front of the fetal head

Complete cord prolapse

Occult (hidden) prolapse

The cord cannot be seen but can probably be felt as a pulsating mass during vaginal examination.

The cord can be seen protruding from the vagina.

The cord is compressed between the fetal presenting part and pelvis but cannot be seen or felt during vaginal examination.

Figure 26–8

Variations of prolapsed umbilical cord.

umbilical cord prolapse. Birth is almost always cesarean unless vaginal delivery can be accomplished more quickly and less traumatically.

When cord prolapse occurs, the priority is to relieve pressure on the cord to restore blood flow through it until delivery. None of these interventions should delay the promptest possible delivery. Push the call light to summon help. Others should call the physician and prepare for delivery. Notify the nursery and pediatrician and prepare for possible neonatal resuscitation.

Prompt actions to relieve cord compression and increase fetal oxygenation are taken by the experienced intrapartum nurse, the nurse-midwife, and/or the physician (Fig. 26–9):

1. Position the expectant mother's hips higher than her head by any of these methods:
   a. Knee-chest position.
   b. Trendelenburg position.
   c. Hips elevated with pillows, with side-lying position maintained.
2. With a gloved hand, push the fetal presenting part upward. Maintain this position until the physician orders it stopped, which may not be until a cesarean incision is made.

While relieving cord compression, give oxygen at 8 to 10 L/minute by face mask to increase maternal blood oxygen saturation, making more available for the fetus.

Other actions may enhance fetal oxygenation, but prompt delivery is the priority and often there is no time for these measures. A tocolytic drug, such as terbutaline, may be ordered to inhibit contractions, increasing placental blood flow and reducing intermittent pressure of the fetus against the pelvis and cord. Warm saline moistened towels may be used to

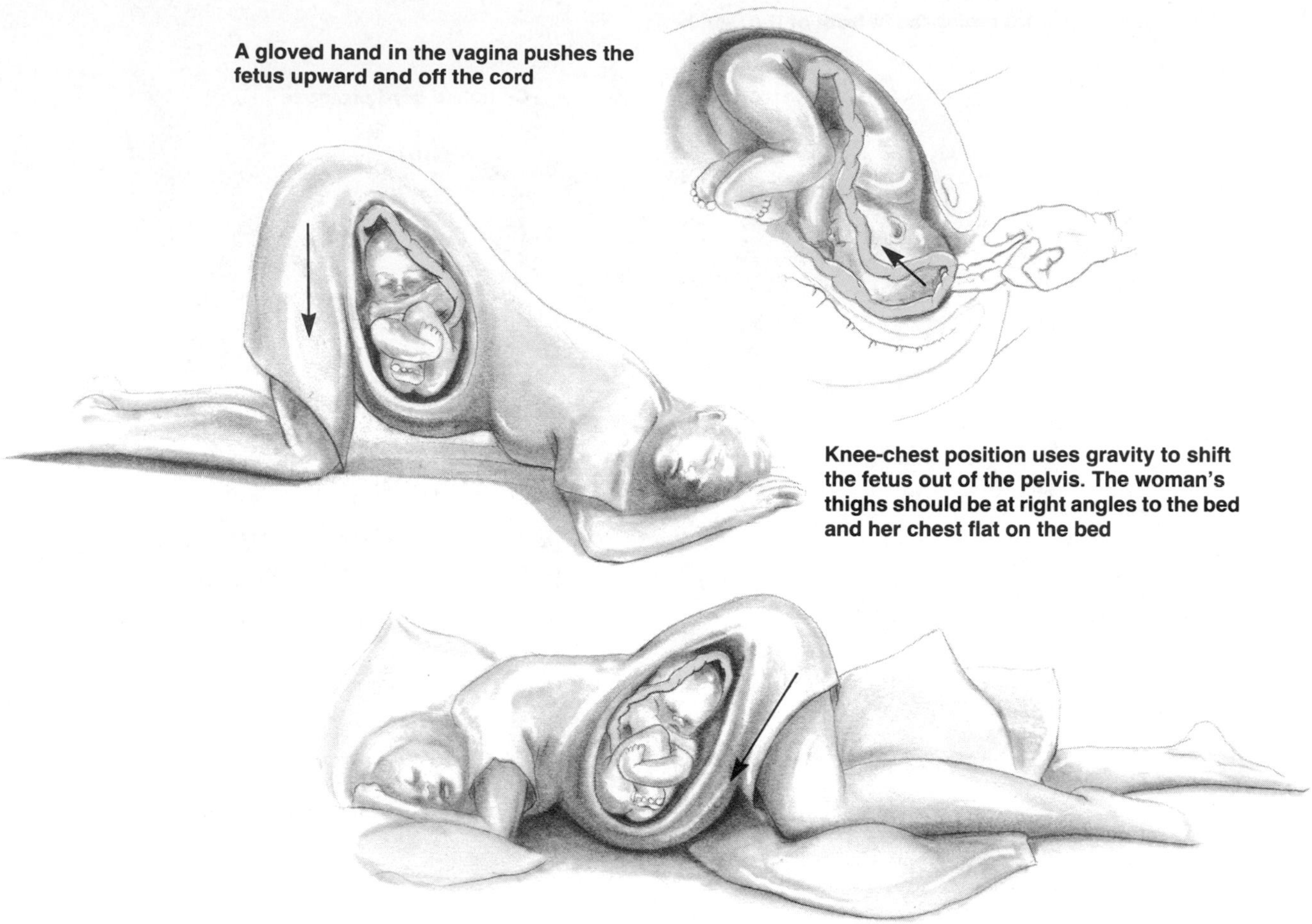

A gloved hand in the vagina pushes the fetus upward and off the cord

Knee-chest position uses gravity to shift the fetus out of the pelvis. The woman's thighs should be at right angles to the bed and her chest flat on the bed

The woman's hips are elevated with two pillows; this is often combined with a Trendelenburg (head down) position

Figure 26–9

Measures that may be used to relieve pressure on a prolapsed umbilical cord until delivery can take place.

retard cooling and drying of the cord. If the cord is protruding from the vagina, there should be no attempt to replace it because to do so could traumatize it and further reduce blood flow through it.

Prognosis for the woman is good because the only additional risks are those associated with cesarean birth. Prognosis for the infant depends on how long and how severely blood flow through the cord has been impaired. With prompt recognition and corrective actions, the infant usually does well.

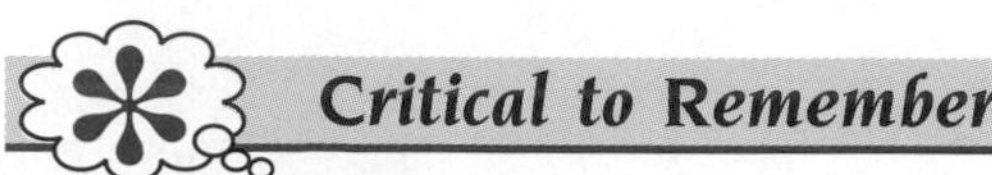

Critical to Remember

Factors That Increase a Woman's Risk for a Prolapsed Umbilical Cord

Ruptured membranes *and:*

- The fetal presenting part at a high station
- A fetus that poorly fits the pelvic inlet because of small size or abnormal presentation
- Excessive volume of amniotic fluid (hydramnios)

NURSING CONSIDERATIONS

In addition to prompt corrective actions, the nurse must consider the woman's anxiety. The nurse must remain calm during this time and acknowledge the woman's anxiety. Explanations must be simple because anxiety interferes with the client's ability to comprehend them. Her partner and family should be included as much as possible.

Uterine Rupture

Sometimes a tear in the wall of the uterus occurs because the uterus cannot withstand the pressure against it (Fig. 26–10). There are three variations of uterine rupture:

Complete rupture–a direct communication between the uterine and peritoneal cavities.

Incomplete rupture–rupture into the peritoneum covering the uterus or into the broad ligament but not into the peritoneal cavity.

Dehiscence–a partial separation of an old uterine scar. There may be little or no bleeding. There may be no signs or symptoms, and the rupture may be found incidentally during a subsequent cesarean birth or other abdominal surgery.

CAUSES

Although uterine rupture is rare (1 in 1500), dehiscence is not unusual. Uterine rupture is associated with previous uterine surgery, such as cesarean birth or surgery to remove fibroids. The risk for rupture in a woman who has had a prior cesarean birth depends on the type of uterine incision. The risk for rupture is ten times greater in women with a classic incision (vertical into the upper uterine segment) than in women with a low transverse incision. For this reason, vaginal birth after cesarean (VBAC) is not recommended for women who have had a previous classic cesarean birth.

Rupture of the unscarred uterus is unusual but is more likely for (1) women of high parity with a thin uterine wall, (2) women sustaining blunt abdominal trauma, and (3) women having intense contractions, especially if there is fetopelvic disproportion. Excessively strong contractions may cause the intrauterine pressure to exceed the tensile strength of the uterine wall. If the fetus cannot be expelled downward through the pelvis, contractions may push it through the lower uterine segment. Intense contractions are more likely to occur when oxytocin is administered for induction or augmentation of labor, but they also may occur spontaneously.

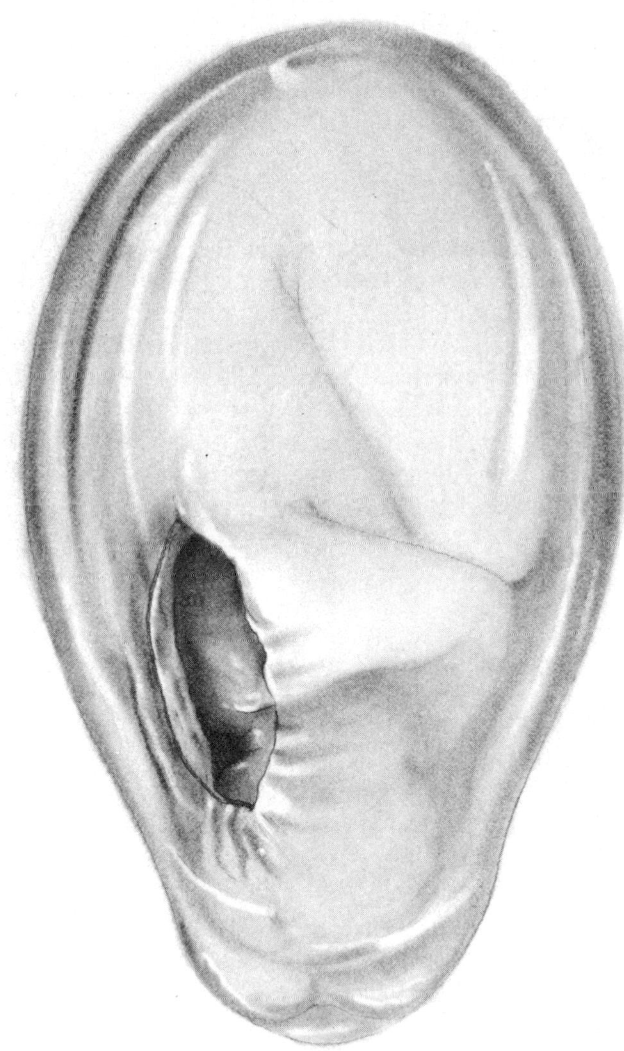

***Figure* 26–10**

Uterine rupture in the lower uterine segment.

SIGNS AND SYMPTOMS

Dehiscence is not usually associated with signs or symptoms and may not interfere with labor or vaginal delivery. Manifestations of uterine rupture vary with the degree of rupture and may mimic other complications. Possible signs and symptoms of complete or incomplete uterine rupture are:

- Hypovolemic shock caused by hemorrhage: falling blood pressure, tachycardia, tachypnea, pallor, cool and clammy skin, anxiety. Signs of shock may not occur until after birth.
- Abdominal pain and tenderness. The pain may not be severe; it may occur suddenly at the peak of a contraction. The woman may describe a feeling that something "ripped."
- Chest pain, pain between the scapulae, or pain on inspiration. Pain occurs because of the irritation of blood below the woman's diaphragm. These symptoms are similar to those of pulmonary embolism.
- Signs associated with impaired fetal oxygenation, such as late decelerations, reduced variability, tachycardia, or bradycardia.
- Absent fetal heart tones with disruption of the placenta.
- Cessation of uterine contractions.
- Palpation of the fetus outside the uterus, (usually occurs only with a large complete rupture). The fetus is likely to be dead.

If the rupture is incomplete, blood loss is slower and signs of shock, chest pain, or intrascapular pain may be delayed. Complete rupture results in massive blood loss into the abdominal cavity. Signs of shock and pain develop quickly.

THERAPEUTIC MANAGEMENT

Management depends on the status of mother and fetus when rupture is suspected. If the rupture is small and recognized quickly, laparotomy may save the fetus and prevent undue maternal blood loss. If the rupture is small and the woman wants other children, it may be repaired. A woman with a large uterine rupture will require hysterectomy. Blood is replaced if needed.

NURSING CONSIDERATIONS

Because the nurse is the professional who attends the woman most closely during labor, the chance of uterine rupture should always be considered. Be aware of women who are at increased risk, and stay alert for the signs and symptoms. Administer oxytocin cautiously to reduce the likelihood of excessive contractions (see p. 393). Be aware that hypertonic contractions can occur in either a stimulated or an unstimulated labor. Notify the physician or nurse-midwife if this occurs. A tocolytic drug may be ordered to reduce the intensity of hypertonic contractions.

Uterine rupture may not be detected before birth. If postpartum bleeding is excessive and the fundus is firm, injury to the birth canal, including uterine rupture, is possible. Bleeding may be concealed if the ruptured area bleeds into the broad ligament. In this case, signs of hypovolemic shock are likely to develop quickly.

Uterine Inversion

An inversion occurs when the uterus completely or partly turns inside out, usually during the third stage of labor. Such an event is uncommon, but potentially fatal.

CAUSES

Often no single cause is identified. Predisposing factors are:

- Pulling on the umbilical cord before the placenta detaches from the uterine wall
- Fundal pressure during birth
- Fundal pressure on an incompletely contracted uterus after birth
- Increased intra-abdominal pressure
- An abnormally adherent placenta
- Congenital weakness
- Fundal placenta implantation

SIGNS AND SYMPTOMS

The physician notes that the uterus is either absent from the abdomen or has a depression in the fundal area. The interior of the uterus may be seen through the cervix or protruding into the vagina. Massive hemorrhage, shock, and pain quickly become evident. Shock is often out of proportion to the blood lost because traction of the inverted uterus on the expectant mother's abdominal organs causes a neurogenic fall in blood pressure (vasovagal reaction).

MANAGEMENT

Management is urgent and involves nursing and medical personnel simultaneously. The physician will try to replace the uterus through the vagina into a normal position. If that is not possible, laparotomy with replacement is done. Hysterectomy may be required.

Uterine inversion usually occurs while the woman is in the delivery or birthing room and the physician or nurse-midwife is still present. General anesthesia is often needed to relax the uterus enough to replace it. Tocolytic drugs also may be ordered for this purpose. Usually, two IV lines are established to allow rapid volume replacement. After the uterus is replaced, oxytocin is given to contract the uterus and control blood loss. Oxytocin is not given until the uterus is repositioned to avoid trapping the inverted fundus in the cervix.

NURSING CONSIDERATIONS

Nursing care during the emergency supplements that of other staff members. Postpartum nursing care is directed toward observing and maintaining maternal blood volume and correcting shock. The woman may be transferred to the intensive care unit.

Assess the uterine fundus for firmness, height, and deviation. Assess vital signs every 15 minutes or more frequently until stable, then according to recovery room routine. Observe for tachycardia and a falling blood pressure, which are associated with shock. A cardiac monitor may be used to identify dysrhythmias, which may occur with shock. Invasive monitoring, such as central venous pressure lines, are common.

An indwelling catheter is often inserted to monitor fluid balance and to keep the bladder empty so that the uterus can contract well. Assess the catheter for patency, and record intake and output. Urine output should be at least 30 ml/hour. A fall in urine output may indicate hypovolemia or an obstructed catheter.

The woman remains on NPO status until her condition is stable. She can usually receive fluids and progress to solid foods quickly, since uterine inversion does not usually recur. However, it may recur in a future pregnancy if conditions that favor its development are present.

Amniotic Fluid Embolism

Amniotic fluid embolism occurs when amniotic fluid is drawn into the maternal circulation and carried to the woman's lungs. Fetal particulate matter (skin cells, vernix, hair, meconium) in the fluid obstructs pulmonary vessels. Abrupt respiratory distress, heart failure, and circulatory collapse quickly occur. Disseminated intravascular coagulation (see p. 672) is likely because thromboplastin-rich amniotic fluid interferes with normal blood clotting. This rare disorder is often fatal. Survivors may have neurologic deficits.

Amniotic fluid embolism is more likely when the labor is very strong. High intrauterine pressure forces amniotic fluid into open uterine or cervical veins. Meconium that often accompanies a stressed fetus in such a labor adds to the particulate matter forced into the woman's circulation and increases the likelihood of death from this embolism.

Therapeutic management of amniotic fluid embolism is primarily medical and includes:

- Cardiopulmonary resuscitation
- Oxygen with mechanical ventilation
- Blood transfusion
- Correction of coagulation deficits with platelets or fibrinogen

✔ Check Your Reading

17. What are three risks to the fetus or neonate when pregnancy lasts longer than 42 weeks?
18. What is the priority of care if a prolapsed umbilical cord occurs? What is its immediate management?
19. How can oxytocin-stimulated contractions increase the risk for uterine rupture?
20. What is the primary complication if a uterine inversion occurs? How is it managed?
21. Under what circumstances does a woman have an increased risk for amniotic fluid embolism?

Trauma

Trauma during pregnancy occurs because of accidents, assault, and suicide. Battering is a significant cause of maternal-fetal trauma during pregnancy. (The social and emotional issues of battering are addressed in Chapter 23.)

Most trauma during pregnancy is blunt trauma, but penetrating trauma, such as gunshot or knife wounds, also may occur. The pregnant trauma victim may be cared for in the emergency department, the intrapartum area, or the critical care area. Collaboration among specialists in maternal-fetal and trauma care improves outcome for the woman and fetus.

Although fetal injury may not be fatal, later neurologic deficits are sometimes found. Direct fetal trauma, such as skull fracture or intracranial hemorrhage, may occur from pelvic fracture, penetrating wounds, or blunt trauma. Indirect causes of fetal injury or death include abruptio placentae and disruption of the placental blood flow secondary to maternal hypovolemia or uterine rupture. The most common cause of fetal death is death of the mother.

Anatomical and physiological changes of pregnancy (see Chapter 7) make trauma care unique. During early pregnancy, the uterus is surrounded by the pelvis and is well protected from direct damage. As the uterus grows it protrudes and becomes a large target for trauma. At the same time, it acts as a shield for other maternal organs such as the kidneys, often protecting them from direct trauma.

Normal alterations of pregnancy can affect the maternal and fetal outcomes following traumatic injury and can affect interpretation of diagnostic studies that may be done. Pregnant women have an increased blood volume compared with that in nonpregnant women which gives them a cushion against blood loss (see p. 120). However, the fetus may suffer if the woman hemorrhages because maternal blood is diverted from the placenta. This can lead to fetal hypoxia, acidosis, and death of the fetus.

Maternal fibrinogen levels are also higher during pregnancy (350 to 400 mg/dl). A decrease to lower levels is associated with abruptio placentae and may indicate that disseminated intravascular coagulation is developing.

MANAGEMENT

Care of the pregnant trauma victim first focuses on injuries that threaten her life. Management of the fetus depends on the gestational age and on whether the fetus is living. The fetus may be delivered by cesarean birth if mature enough to survive and if the maternal or fetal condition is likely to be improved by prompt delivery. The fetus that is too immature to survive will not usually be delivered unless delivery will likely improve the outcome for the mother. There is no urgency to deliver a dead fetus unless this improves the woman's status.

NURSING CONSIDERATIONS

Nursing care of the pregnant trauma victim also focuses first on maternal, then fetal stabilization. A wedge is placed under her right side to prevent supine hypotension and further hemodynamic instability and to improve placental blood flow. Vital signs are noted as often as necessary based on her condition, usually at least every hour at first. An automatic blood pressure monitor, such as a Dinamap, is useful when vital signs must be assessed every 15 minutes or more often. Vital signs and urine output (at least 30 ml/hour) provide information about the adequacy of her blood volume. Bloody urine may indicate bladder or renal damage. Other nursing care is directed toward the specific injuries that have been suffered and toward implementation of medical care.

Observe for signs that may indicate abruptio placentae because this complication may occur with abdominal trauma: vaginal bleeding with uterine pain and tenderness. The uterine height may also increase as it fills with blood.

Once the woman's condition is stable, nursing care includes the fetus. External monitoring of the fetus is appropriate if it has reached a viable gestational age. Preterm labor may occur but may not be recognized if the woman is unconscious or if pain from injuries overshadows discomfort from contractions. Observe for recurrent restlessness or moaning, and palpate her uterine fundus for contractions.

✔ Check Your Reading

22. What is the primary focus of medical and nursing care of the pregnant trauma victim?
23. What are common causes of fetal injury and death when a pregnant woman suffers trauma?
24. What are important nursing considerations for each kind of intrapartum emergency?

Intrapartum Emergencies: Application of the Nursing Process

Nursing care of the woman with intrapartum emergency overlaps with care in other situations discussed elsewhere. Much of the nursing care is collaborative and supports medical management. The fetus is at greater risk for compromise when many intrapartum emergencies occur (see Chapter 14). Parents may suffer loss if the fetus dies or if the mother loses her ability to bear future children, as may occur with uterine rupture. One problem that is expected in any emergency situation is the emotional distress of the woman and her family.

Assessment

When any emergency occurs, simply because of its suddenness, the woman and her family have little time to absorb what has happened. In cord prolapse, for example, labor has often been uneventful up to that point. Suddenly, a room full of nurses place the woman in a strange position, apply oxygen, and pull her toward the operating room.

Under such circumstances, the woman and her family have a very narrow focus. They are obviously apprehensive and may lose control. The woman or her partner may seem to freeze, immobilized by fear. Reactions are similar for other emergency situations.

Analysis

The nursing diagnosis is: *Anxiety related to knowledge deficit secondary to sudden development of complications.* This diagnosis is expected to differ from the anxiety associated with preterm labor because the onset is acute; the anxiety also may lessen more quickly because the emergency is usually resolved within minutes.

Planning

The focus of a goal is very narrow in an emergency situation. Two appropriate goals, during and after the emergency, are that the woman and her family will:

- Indicate an understanding of emergency procedures.
- Express their feelings about the complication.

Interventions

Although there is little time for discussion, explain honestly and simply what is occurring. Tell the woman what is happening and why, in order to reduce fear and anxiety related to the unknown. Include her partner and family if appropriate. Provide continued reassurance and support to the woman because her partner must often be excluded from the delivery or operating room when an emergency occurs.

The infant born in an emergency situation may need resuscitation or other supportive measures. Nurses and a physician from the neonatal intensive care unit, if there is one, are usually present at the birth to attend the infant. Explain to the family who the other professionals are and what their roles are. If possible, explain what is being done to care for the baby.

After the emergency, give the woman and her family a chance to ask questions. The ability to absorb new knowledge during periods of severe anxiety is very limited. Adequate explanations afterward help them understand and assimilate the experience.

Although the nurse is usually anxious in an emergency situation too, it is important to keep a calm attitude. The woman and her family quickly pick up on the staff's anxiety, and consequently theirs will escalate. Remain with the woman to reduce fears of abandonment. If possible, hold her hand. Speak in a low, calm voice.

Evaluation

Evaluation of the goals will probably be impossible until the emergency is over and the woman's physical condition stabilizes. Goals for this nursing diagnosis are achieved if the woman and her family:

- Indicate that they understand the problem and the rationale for emergency procedures.
- Express, over several days, their feelings about what has occurred.

Summary Concepts

- Dysfunctional labor may occur because of abnormalities in the powers, the passenger, or the passage. Combinations of abnormalities are common.
- Nursing care in dysfunctional labor focuses on prevention or prompt identification and action to correct additional complications: fetal hypoxia, infection, injury to the mother or fetus, and postpartum hemorrhage.
- Premature rupture of the membranes is associated with infection as both a cause and an effect.
- The early indications of preterm labor are often subtle. Prompt identification of preterm labor enables the most effective therapy to stop it.
- Nursing care for the woman at risk for preterm birth focuses on helping her implement therapy to prolong her pregnancy. The goal is for the gestation to reach a point at which the infant's problems with immaturity are minimal.
- The main risk in prolonged pregnancy is reduced placental function. This may compromise the fetus during labor and may result in meconium aspiration in the neonate. Dysfunctional labor may occur if the fetus continues growing during the prolonged pregnancy.
- If the umbilical cord becomes prolapsed, the key intervention is to relieve pressure on it and to expedite delivery.
- Be aware of women at risk for uterine rupture, and observe constantly for signs and symptoms: Signs of shock, abdominal pain, a sense of tearing, chest pain, pain between the scapulae, abnormal fetal heart rate patterns, cessation of contractions, and palpation of the fetus outside the uterus.
- Uterine inversion is often accompanied by shock that is out of proportion to the amount of blood lost. Recovery care promotes uterine contraction and maintenance of adequate circulating volume.
- Amniotic fluid embolism is more likely to occur when labor is intense and the membranes have ruptured.
- Medical and nursing care of the pregnant trauma victim focuses on stabilization of the mother first. Management of the fetus depends on gestational age and whether or not the fetus is alive. Abruptio placentae and uterine rupture are obstetrical complications that may occur with direct abdominal trauma.

References and Readings

Alexander, G. R., Weiss, J., Hulsey, T. C., & Papiernik, E. (1991). Preterm birth prevention: An evaluation of programs in the United States. *Birth*, 18(3), 160–169.

American College of Obstetricians and Gynecologists. (1990). *Precis IV*. Washington, D. C.

Arnone, B. (1989). Amniotic fluid embolism: A case report. *Journal of Nurse-Midwifery*, 34(2), 92–94.

Bashore, R. A. (1992). Dystocia. In N. F. Hacker & J. G. Moore (Eds.), *Essentials of obstetrics and gynecology* (2nd ed., pp. 261–269). Philadelphia: W. B. Saunders.

Bennet, N. L., & Botti, J. J. (1989). New strategies for preterm labor. *Nurse Practitioner*, 14(4), 27–38.

Bentley, D. L., Bentley, T. L., Watson, D. L., et al. (1990). Relationship of uterine contractility to preterm labor. *Obstetrics and Gynecology* (Supplement), 76(1), 36S–38S.

Biancuzzo, M. (1993). Six myths of maternal posture during labor. *MCN: American Journal of Maternal-Child Nursing*, 18(5), 264–269.

Biancuzzo, M. (1991). The patient observer: Does the hands-and-knees posture during labor help to rotate the occiput posterior fetus? *Birth*, 18(1), 40–47.

Blackburn, S. T., & Loper, D. L. (1992). *Maternal, fetal, and neonatal physiology: A clinical perspective*. Philadelphia: W. B. Saunders.

Bowes, W. A. (1989). Clinical aspects of normal and abnormal labor. In R. K. Creasy & R. Resnick, *Maternal-fetal medicine: Principles and practice* (pp. 510–546). Philadelphia: W. B. Saunders.

Brustman, L. E., Langer, O., Anyaegbunam, A., (1990). Education does not improve patient perception of preterm uterine contractility. *Obstetrics and Gynecology* (Supplement), 76(1), 97S–101S.

Canadian Preterm Labor Investigators Group. Treatment of preterm labor with the beta-adrenergic agonist ritodrine. *New England Journal of Medicine*, 327(5), 308–312.

Chibber, G. (1990). Patient attitude toward home uterine activity monitoring. *Obstetrics and Gynecology* (Supplement), 76(1), 90S–92S.

Cibils, L. A. (1990). Dysfunctional labor. In E. J. Quilligan & F. R. Zuspan F. R. (Eds.), *Current therapy in obstetrics and gynecology* (Vol. 3, pp. 222–226). Philadelphia: W. B. Saunders.

Cowan, M. (1993). Home care of the pregnant woman using terbutaline. MCN: *American Journal of Maternal-Child Nursing*, 18(3), 99–105.

Creasy, R. K. (1989). Preterm labor and delivery. In R. K. Creasy & R. Resnick (Eds.), *Maternal-fetal medicine: Principles and practice* (pp. 477–504). Philadelphia: W. B. Saunders.

Creasy, R. K., & Merkatz, I. R. (1990). Prevention of preterm birth: Clinical opinion. *Obstetrics and Gynecology* (Supplement), 76(1), 2S–4S.

Cunningham, F. G., & MacDonald, P. C. (1989). *Williams obstetrics* (18th ed.). Norwalk, Conn.: Appleton and Lange.

Dineen, K., Rossi, M., Lia-Haogberg, B., & Keller, L. O. (1992). Antepartum home-care services for high-risk women. *Journal of Obstetric, Gynecologic, and Neonatal Nursing*, 21(2), 121–125.

Driscoll, M., Gilbert, D., Dennis, G., & Bukowy, D. (1990). Prevention of Preterm Labor Project in a public hospital: Breaking down barriers to prenatal care. *Journal of Perinatal and Neonatal Nursing*, 4(3), 44–55.

Fenwick, L., & Simkin, P. (1987). Maternal positioning to prevent or alleviate dystocia in labor. *Clinical Obstetrics and Gynecology*, 30(1), 83–90.

Few, B. J. (1988). Corticosteroids and respiratory distress syndrome. MCN: *American Journal of Maternal Child Nursing*, 13(1), 17.

Freda, M. C., Damus, K., Anderson, H. F., Brustman, L. E., & Merkatz, I. R. (1990). A "PROPP" for the Bronx: Preterm birth prevention education in the inner city. *Obstetrics and Gynecology* (Supplement), 76(1), 93S–96S.

Freda, M. C., Damus, K., & Merkatz, I. (1991). What do pregnant women know about preventing preterm birth? *Journal of Obstetric, Gynecological, and Neonatal Nursing*, 20(2), 140–145.

Gilbert, E. S., & Harmon, J. S. (1993). *Manual of high risk pregnancy and delivery*. St. Louis: Mosby.

Gill, P., Smith, M., & McGregor, C. (1989). Terbutaline by pump to prevent recurrent preterm labor. MCN: *American Journal of Maternal Child Nursing*. 14(3), 163–167.

Gonik, B. (1989). Intensive care monitoring of the critically ill pregnant patient. In R. K. Creasy & R. Resnick (Eds.), *Maternal-fetal medicine: Principles and practice* (pp. 845–874). Philadelphia: W. B. Saunders.

Graham, A. D. M. (1992). Preterm labor and premature rupture of the membranes. In N. F. Hacker & J. G. Moore (Eds.), *Essentials of obstetrics and gynecology* (2nd ed., pp. 270–280). Philadelphia: W. B. Saunders.

Griese, M. E., & Prickett, S. A. (1993). Nursing management of umbilical cord prolapse. *Journal of Obstetric, Gynecologic, and Neonatal Nursing*, 22(4), 311–315.

Hall, G. P. (1985). The scultetus binder. *Journal of Nurse-Midwifery*, 30(5), 290–292.

Hamilton, L. A., & Hobel, C. J. (1992). Intrauterine growth retardation, intrauterine fetal demise, and post-term pregnancy. In N. F. Hacker & J. G. Moore (Eds.), *Essentials of Obstetrics and Gynecology* (2nd ed., pp. 281–288). Philadelphia: W. B. Saunders.

Harvey, M. (1992). OB critical care: Beyond high-risk pregnancy. MCN: *American Journal of Maternal Child Nursing*, 17(6), 296–309.

Hill, W. C., Fleming, A. D., Martin, R. W., Hamer, C., Knuppel, R. A., Lake, M. F., Watson, D. L., Welch, R. A., Bentley, D. L., Gookin, K. S., & Morrison, J. C. (1990). Home uterine activity monitoring is associated with reduction in preterm birth. *Obstetrics and Gynecology* (Supplement), 76(1), 13S–17S.

Holbrook, R. H., Laros, R. K., & Creasy, R. K. (1989). Evaluation of a risk-scoring system for prediction of preterm labor. *American Journal of Perinatology*, 6(1), 62–68.

Holohan, T. V., & Green, I. (1992). Home uterine monitoring. *Health Technology Review*, No. 1, July 1992.

Iams, J. D. (1990). Prevention and management of preterm birth. In E. J. Quilligan & F. R. Zuspan (Eds.), *Current therapy in obstetrics and gynecology* (Vol. 3, pp. 264–268). Philadelphia: W. B. Saunders.

Iams, J. D., Stilson, R., Johnson, F. F., Williams, R. A., & Rice, R. (1990). Symptoms that precede preterm labor and preterm premature rupture of the membranes. *American Journal of Obstetrics and Gynecology*, 162(2), 486–490.

Iams, J. D., Johnson, F. F., & Hamer, C. (1990). Uterine activity and symptoms as predictors of preterm labor. *Obstetrics and Gynecology* (Supplement), 76(1), 42S–46S.

Jackson, V. M. (1989). Delivery of the second twin. *Journal of Perinatal-Neonatal Nursing*, 3(1), 22–34.

Johnson, F. F. (1989). Assessment and education to prevent preterm labor. MCN: *American Journal of Maternal Child Nursing* 14(3), 157–160.

Kosasa, T. S., Abou-Sayf, F. K., Li-Ma, G., & Hale, R. W. (1990). Evaluation of the cost-effectiveness of home monitoring of uterine contractions. *Obstetrics and Gynecology* (Supplement), 76(1), 71S–75S.

Knuppel, R. A. (1990). Preventing preterm birth in twin gestation: Home uterine activity monitoring and perinatal nursing support. *Obstetrics and Gynecology* (Supplement), 76(1), 24S–27S.

Lake, M. F. (1992). Prolonged pregnancy. In L. K. Mandeville & N. H. Troiano (Eds.), *High-risk intrapartum nursing* (pp. 83–99). Philadelphia: Lippincott.

Lynam, L. E., & Miller, M. A. (1992). Mothers' and nurses' perceptions of the needs of women experiencing preterm labor. *Journal of Obstetric, Gynecologic, and Neonatal Nursing*, 21(2), 126–136.

Lynch, M., & McKeon, V. A. (1990). Cocaine use during pregnancy: Research findings and clinical implications. *Journal of Obstetric, Gynecological, and Neonatal Nursing*, 19(4), 285–292.

MacLennan, A. H. (1989). Multiple gestation: Clinical characteristics and management. In R. K. Creasy & R. Resnick (Eds.), *Maternal-fetal medicine: Principles and practice* (pp. 580–591). Philadelphia: W. B. Saunders.

Makowski, E. L. (1990). Twin pregnancy. In E. J. Quilligan & F. R. Zuspan (Eds.), *Current therapy in obstetrics and gynecology* (Vol. 3, pp. 290–292). Philadelphia: W. B. Saunders.

Marshall, V. A. (1991). Maternal health practices and complications of term labor. *Journal of Nurse-Midwifery*, 36(3), 168–173.

Martin, J. N., McColgin, S. W., Martin, R. W., Roach, H., & Morrison, J. C. (1990). Uterine activity among a diverse group of patients at high risk for preterm delivery. *Obstetrics and Gynecology* (Supplement), 76(1), 47S–51S.

Martin, R. W., Gookin, K. S., Hill, W. C., Fleming, A. D., Knuppel, R. A., Lake, M. F., Watson, D. L., Welch, R. A., Bentley, D. L., & Morrison, J. C. (1990). Uterine activity compared with symptomatology in the detection of preterm labor. *Obstetrics and Gynecology* (Supplement), 76(1), 19S–23S.

Mashburn, J. (1988). Identification and management of shoulder dystocia. *Journal of Nurse-Midwifery*, 33(5), 225–231.

McShan, M. W. (1992). Current concepts: Neonatal group-B streptococcal infection. *Perinatal Advocate*, 12(2), 10.

Monahan, P. A., & DeJoseph, J. F. (1991). The woman with preterm labor at home: A descriptive analysis. *Journal of Perinatal and Neonatal Nursing*, 4(4), 12–20.

Moore, J. G. (1992). Surgical conditions in pregnancy. In N. F. Hacker & J. G. Moore (Eds.), *Essentials of obstetrics and gynecology* (2nd ed., pp. 223–229). Philadelphia: W. B. Saunders.

Moretti, M. L., & Sibai, B. M. (1990). Peripartum emergencies. In G. I. Benrubi & A. Harwood-Nuss (Eds.), *Obstetric emergencies* (pp. 153–170). New York: Churchill Livingstone.

Morrison, J. C., Pittman, K. P., Martin, R. W., & McLaughlin, B. N. (1990a). Cost/health effectiveness of home uterine activity monitoring in a medicaid population. *Obstetrics and Gynecology* (Supplement), 76(1), 76S–81S.

Morrison, J. C. (1990b, April 15). Is tocodynamometry useful? Yes. *Contemporary OB/GYN*, 35 96–112.

Morrison, J. C. (1990c). Preterm birth: A puzzle worth solving. *Obstetrics and Gynecology* (Supplement), 76(1), 5S–12S.

Neal, A. D., & Bockman, V. C. (1992). Preterm labor and preterm premature rupture of membranes. In L. K. Mandeville & N. H. Troiano (Eds.), *High-risk intrapartum nursing* (pp. 57–81). Philadelphia: Lippincott.

Nelsson-Ryan, S. (1988). Positioning: Second stage labor. In S. S. Humenick & F. H. Nichols (Eds.), *Childbirth education: Practice, research, and theory* (pp. 256–274). Philadelphia: W. B. Saunders.

Newman, R. B., Richmond, G. S., Winston, Y. E., Hamer, C., & Katz, M. (1991). Antepartum uterine activity characteristics differentiating true from threatened preterm labor. *Obstetrics and Gynecology* (Supplement), 76(1), 39S–41S.

O'Grady, J. P. (1991). Twins and beyond: Management guide. *Contemporary OB/Gyn*, 36(2), 45–64.

Pavlk, M. (1988). Positioning: First stage labor. In S. S. Humenick & Nichols, F. H. (Eds.) *Childbirth education: Practice, research, and theory* (pp. 234–255). Philadelphia: W. B. Saunders.

Penney, D. S., & Perlis, D. W. (1992). Shoulder dystocia: When to use suprapubic or fundal pressure. MCN: *American Journal of Maternal Child Nursing*, 17(1), 34–36.

Porto, M. (1990, April 15). Home uterine activity monitoring: Essential tool or expensive accessory? *Contemporary OB/Gyn*, 35, 114–123.

Resnik, R. (1992). Post-term pregnancy. In R. K. Creasy & R. Resnick, (Eds.), *Maternal-fetal medicine: Principles and practice* (pp. 505–509). Philadelphia: W. B. Saunders.

Reynolds, H. D. (1991). Bacterial vaginosis and its implication in preterm labor and premature rupture of membranes: A review of the literature. *Journal of Nurse-Midwifery*, 36(5), 289–296.

Romero, R., Avilia, C., Mazor, M., & Oyarzun, E. (1989). Can antimicrobials prevent preterm delivery? *Contemporary OB/Gyn*, 34(5), 81–92.

Rubinstein, T. H., & Schifrin, B. S. (1992). Prolonged labor with persistent occiput-posterior position in postterm pregnancy. *Journal of Perinatology*, 12(2), 181–184.

Sala, D. J., & Moise, K. J. (1990). The treatment of preterm labor using a portable subcutaneous terbutaline pump. *Journal of Gynecological, Obstetrical, and Neonatal Nursing*, 19(2), 108–115.

Savage, E. W., & Parham, G. P. (1992). Cervical dysplasia and cancer. In N. F. Hacker & J. G. Moore (Eds.), *Essentials of obstetrics and gynecology* (pp. 587–601). Philadelphia: W. B. Saunders.

Shields, J. R., & Medearis, A. L. (1992). Multiple gestation. In N. F. Hacker & J. G. Moore (Eds.), *Essentials of obstetrics and gynecology* (2nd ed.), (pp. 241–249). Philadelphia: W. B. Saunders.

Stanton, R. J. (1991). Comanagement of the patient on subcutaneous terbutaline pump therapy. *Journal of Nurse-Midwifery*, 36(3), 204–208.

Thomson, M. (1988). Different rates of prolonged first-stage labor in primiparas at two hospitals. *Birth*, 15(4), 209–212.

Throckmorton, K., & Placido, J. D. (1988). Amniotic fluid embolism. *Emergency Medical Services*, 17(5), 43.

U. S. Preventive Services Task Force. (1993). Home uterine activity monitoring for preterm labor. *Journal of the American Medical Association*, 270(3), 371–376.

Watson, D. L., Welch, R. A., Mariona, F. G., Lake, M. F., Knuppel, R. A., Martin, R. W., Johnson, C., Bentley, D. L., Hill, W. C., Fleming, A. B., & Morrison, J. C. (1990). Management of preterm labor patients at home: Does daily uterine activity monitoring and nursing support make a difference? *Obstetrics and Gynecology* (Supplement), 76(1), 32S–35S.

Wingeier, R., & Griggs, R. (1991). Management of retained placenta using intraumbilical oxytocin injection. *Journal of Nurse-Midwifery*, 36(4), 240–244.

27

Postpartum Maternal Complications

Objectives

1. Describe postpartum hemorrhage in terms of predisposing factors, causes, clinical signs, and therapeutic management.
2. Identify complications of postpartum hemorrhage.
3. Explain major causes, clinical signs, and therapeutic management of subinvolution.
4. Describe three major thromboembolic disorders (thrombophlebitis, deep vein thrombosis, pulmonary embolism) in terms of predisposing factors, causes, clinical signs, and therapeutic management.
5. Discuss puerperal infection in terms of location, predisposing factors, causes and therapeutic management.
6. Describe two major affective disorders (postpartum depression and psychosis).

Definitions

Atony • Absence or lack of usual muscle tone.

Dilation and curettage (D & C) • Stretching of the cervical os to permit scraping of the walls of the uterus. The procedure is performed in abortion, to obtain samples of uterine lining tissue for laboratory examination, and during the postpartum period to remove retained fragments of placenta.

Embolus • A clot, usually part or all of a **thrombus**, brought by the blood from another vessel and forced into a smaller one, thus obstructing circulation.

Hematoma • Localized collection of blood in a space or tissue.

Hydramnios • Excess volume of amniotic fluid (more than 2000 ml at term). Also called **polyhydramnios.**

Hypovolemia • Abnormally decreased volume of circulating plasma in the body.

Hypovolemic shock • Acute peripheral circulatory failure due to loss of circulating blood volume.

Placenta accreta • A placenta that is abnormally adherent to the uterine muscle. If the condition is more advanced, it is called **placenta increta** (the placenta extends into the uterine muscle) or **placenta percreta** (the placenta extends through the uterine muscle).

Psychosis • Mental state in which a person's ability to recognize reality, communicate, and relate to others is impaired.

Thrombus • Collection of blood factors, primarily platelets and fibrin, that may cause vascular obstruction at the point of formation.

△ Alert for a high risk of exposure to substances to which universal precautions apply. See Appendix B for additional information about infection control.

Most mothers recover from the stress of pregnancy and childbirth without complication. However, nurses must be aware of problems that may occur and their effect on the family. The most common physiologic complications are hemorrhage, thromboembolic disorders, and infection. Complications that are psychogenic in origin include postpartum depression and postpartum psychosis.

Postpartum Hemorrhage

Postpartum hemorrhage is defined as blood loss that exceeds 500 ml following vaginal childbirth or 1000 ml following cesarean birth (Hayashi, 1992). Blood loss to this extent in the first 24 hours following childbirth is termed *early* postpartum hemorrhage; such blood loss occurring after 24 hours is called *late* postpartum hemorrhage.

Visual estimation of blood loss is not reliable, especially when bleeding is brisk or when hemorrhage is concealed. Estimated blood loss during delivery frequently constitutes only about half the actual loss (Cunningham et al, 1989). This is important to remember when total blood loss is being analyzed.

Postpartum blood loss of more than 500 ml is relatively common, occurring in one of every 25 deliveries, whereas bleeding in excess of 1000 ml occurs once in every 75 deliveries (Cunningham et al, 1989). Hemorrhage, along with infection and hypertensive disorders, is one of the three leading causes of maternal morbidity and mortality. Common predisposing factors are listed in Table 27–1.

Table 27–1. COMMON PREDISPOSING FACTORS FOR POSTPARTUM HEMORRHAGE

Overdistention of the uterus (multiple gestation, large infant, hydramnios)
Multiparity (>5)
Precipitate labor or delivery
Prolonged labor
Use of forceps, vacuum extractor
Cesarean birth
Manual removal of placenta
Previous postpartum hemorrhage
General anesthesia
Additional factors
Low implantation of placenta
Administration of magnesium sulfate
Clotting disorders

Early Postpartum Hemorrhage

There are two major causes of early postpartum hemorrhage: (1) uterine atony and (2) trauma to the birth canal during labor and delivery. Abnormalities of the third stage of labor, such as placenta accreta (abnormal adherence of the placenta to the uterine wall), and inversion of the uterus are described in Chapter 26. Clotting disorders, such as disseminated intravascular coagulation, are described in Chapter 24.

UTERINE ATONY

Approximately 75 per cent of cases of early hemorrhage are due to uterine atony (Hayashi, 1992). Atony refers to lack of muscle tone that results in failure of the uterine muscle fibers to contract firmly around myometrial blood vessels when the placenta separates. The relaxed muscles allow rapid bleeding from the endometrial arteries at the placental site. Bleeding continues until the uterine muscle fibers contract to stop the flow of blood.

Figure 27–1 illustrates the effect of uterine contraction on the size of the placental site and the amount of bleeding that occurs.

Clinical Signs. For the first 24 hours after birth, the uterus should feel like a firmly contracted ball roughly the size of a large grapefruit. It should be easily located at about the level of the umbilicus. If the uterus is without tone, it is difficult to locate, and when it is located, it feels soft or "boggy." It may become firm with uterine massage but may lose its tone when massage is stopped.

If the uterus is firmly contracted, lochia should be dark red and moderate in amount. Saturation of more than one peripad per hour is considered excessive, even in the early postpartum period. The nurse must realize that although bleeding may be profuse and dramatic, a constant steady trickle is just as dangerous. (Refer to Chapter 17 for additional information about assessing the uterus and lochia.)

Predisposing Factors. Knowledge of factors that increase the risk of uterine atony can be used to anticipate and thus to prevent excessive bleeding. Overdistention of the uterus from any cause (multiple gestation, a large infant, polyhydramnios) makes it more difficult for the uterus to contract with enough firmness to prevent excessive bleeding. Multiparity (more than five births) results in muscle fibers that have been stretched repeatedly, making it difficult for muscle fibers to remain contracted following birth (Hayashi, 1992). Intrapartum factors include contractions that were barely effective, resulting in *prolonged labor,* or contractions that were very vigorous, resulting in *precipitate labor.* Labor that was either induced or augmented with oxytocin is more likely to be followed by post-delivery uterine atony and hemorrhage. Retention of a large segment of the

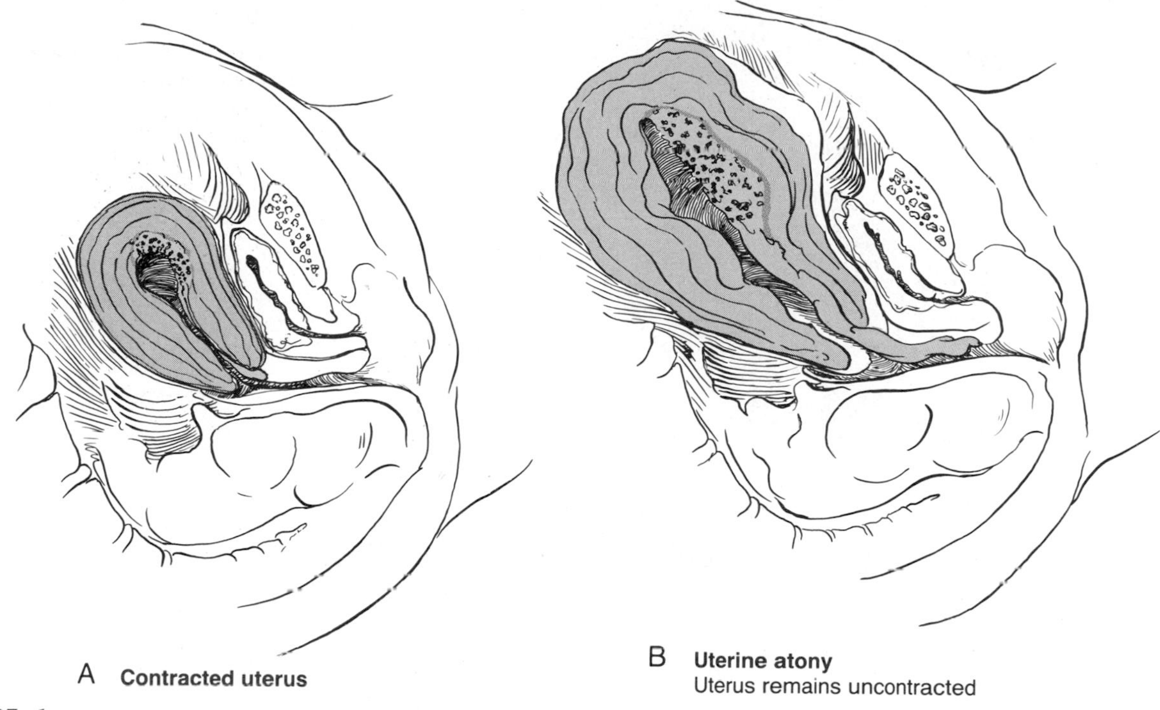

Figure 27–1

A, When the uterus remains contracted, the placental site is smaller, so bleeding is minimal. **B,** If uterine muscles fail to contract around the endometrial arteries at the placental site, hemorrhage occurs.

placenta does not allow the uterus to contract firmly and can result in uterine atony.

Therapeutic Management. Initial management focuses on measures to contract the uterus and to provide fluid replacement. If the uterus is not firmly contracted, the initial intervention is to massage the fundus until it is firm and to express clots that may have accumulated in the uterus. One hand is placed just above the symphysis pubis to support the lower uterine segment while the fundus is gently but firmly massaged in a circular motion. Clots that may have accumulated in the uterine cavity are expressed by applying firm but gentle pressure on the fundus in the direction of the vagina. *It is critical not to attempt to express clots until the uterus is firmly contracted.* Pushing on an uncontracted uterus could invert the uterus and cause massive hemorrhage. Figure 27–2 illustrates correct hand placement for fundal massage.

If the uterus does not remain contracted as a result of uterine massage, pharmacological measures are ordered. A rapid intravenous infusion of dilute oxytocin (40 to 80 units in 1000 ml of normal saline) often increases uterine tone and controls bleeding (Hayashi, 1992). If the uterus remains atonic and bleeding continues, methylergonovine (Methergine) may be given by intramuscular (IM) or intravenous (IV) injection (Deglin and Vallerand, 1993). Methylergonovine has the side effect of elevating blood pressure and should not be given to a woman who is hypertensive. Analogs of prostaglandin F2-alpha ($PGF_{2\alpha}$) given IM or by IV bolus are sometimes effective in controlling postpartum hemorrhage caused by uterine atony.

If uterine massage and pharmacological measures are ineffective in stopping uterine bleeding, bimanual compression of the uterus with one hand inserted in the vagina and the other compressing the uterus through the abdominal wall is usually effective (Figure 27–3). It may also be necessary to return the woman to the delivery area so that the physician can explore the uterine cavity and remove retained placental fragments that are interfering with uterine contraction.

Fluid replacement with normal saline, lactated Ringer's solution, and whole blood may be necessary. The nurse may need to obtain an order for type and cross-matching so that the desired blood type can be available.

Operative procedures are the last resort. A hysterectomy may be necessary to save the life of a woman with uncontrollable postpartum hemorrhage.

TRAUMA

The second most common cause of early postpartum hemorrhage is trauma to the birth canal. Trauma can include vaginal, cervical, or perineal lacerations as well as hematomas.

Lacerations. The most common sites for lacerations are the perineum, the vagina, or the cervix or

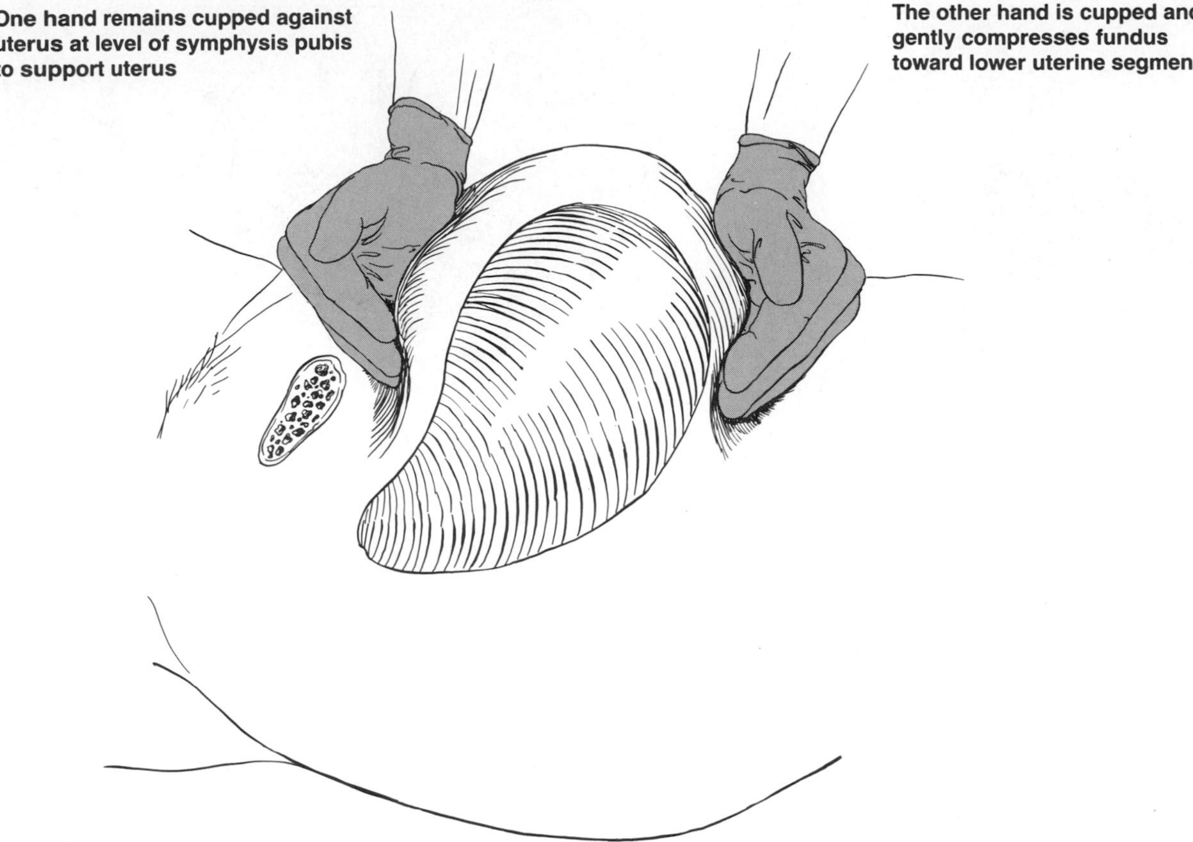
One hand remains cupped against uterus at level of symphysis pubis to support uterus
The other hand is cupped and gently compresses fundus toward lower uterine segment

Figure 27–2

Technique for fundal massage.

the area around the urethral meatus. Cervical lacerations occur most often when the cervix dilates rapidly during the first stage of labor. Lacerations of the vagina, perineum, and periurethral area occur most often during the second stage of labor, when the fetal head descends rapidly or when assistive devices, such as forceps or a vacuum extractor, are used to assist in delivery of the fetal head.

Clinical Signs. Lacerations of the birth canal should always be suspected if excessive uterine bleeding continues when the fundus is contracted firmly and at the expected location. Bleeding from lacerations of the genital tract is often bright red, in contrast to the darker red color of lochia.

Hematomas. Hematomas occur when there is bleeding into loose connective tissue while overlying tissue remains intact. Hematomas develop as a result of injury to soft tissue in spontaneous deliveries as well as in deliveries where forceps or vacuum extractors are used. Hematomas generally develop in the vulvar tissue or inside the vagina.

Clinical Signs. Visible vulvar hematomas appear as a discolored bulging mass that is caused by rapid

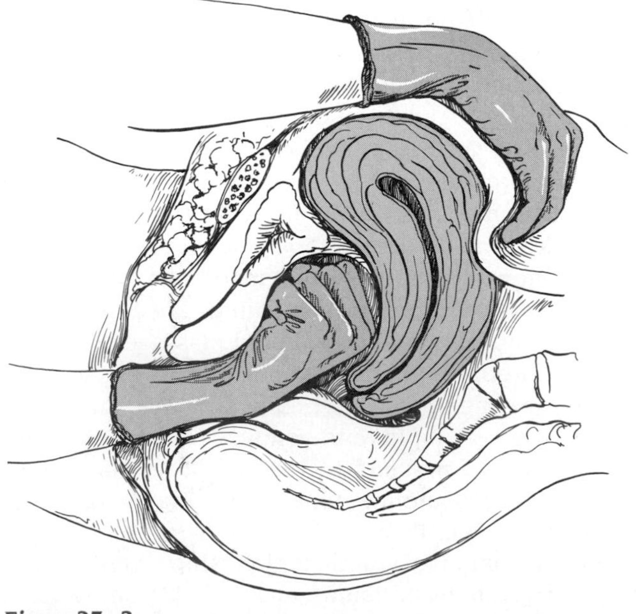

Figure 27–3

Bimanual compression. One hand is inserted in the vagina, and the other compresses the uterus through the abdominal wall.

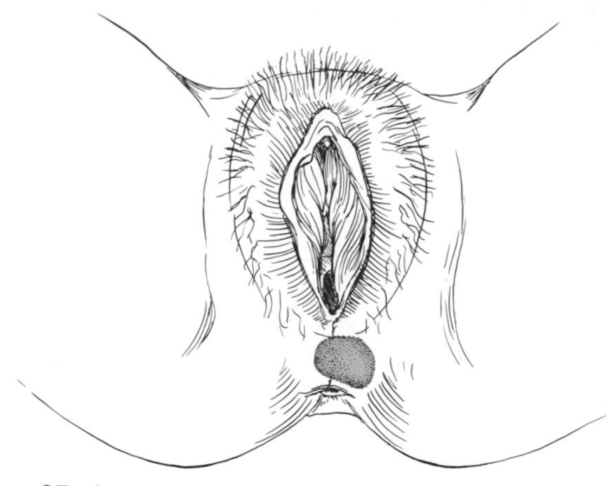

Figure 27–4

A vulvar hematoma is caused by rapid bleeding into soft tissue, and it causes severe pain and feelings of pressure.

bleeding into soft tissue. Both vulvar and vaginal hematomas produce deep, severe, unrelieved pain and feelings of pressure. Formation of a hematoma should also be suspected if the mother demonstrates systemic signs of concealed blood loss, such as falling blood pressure or tachycardia while the fundus is firm and lochia is within normal limits. Figure 27–4 illustrates a vulvar hematoma.

Predisposing Factors. Many of the same factors that increase the risk of uterine atony also increase the risk of soft tissue trauma during childbirth. For example, trauma to the birth canal is more likely to occur if the infant is large or if labor and delivery occur rapidly. Induction and augmentation of labor increase the risk of tissue trauma, as does the use of assistive devices.

Therapeutic Management. When postpartum hemorrhage is due to trauma of the birth canal, surgical repair is often necessary. It is difficult to visualize lacerations of the vagina or cervix, and it is necessary to return the mother to the delivery area, where surgical lights are available. She is placed in a lithotomy position and carefully draped. Surgical asepsis is required while the laceration is being visualized and repaired.

Small hematomas usually reabsorb naturally; however, large hematomas may require incision, evacuation of the clots, and location of the bleeding vessel so that it can be ligated. See Table 27–2 for a summary of therapeutic management for early postpartum hemorrhage.

Table 27–2. THERAPEUTIC MANAGEMENT FOR EARLY POSTPARTUM HEMORRHAGE

Cause	Treatment
Uterine atony	Massage of the uterus to stimulate contraction and control bleeding from placental site
	Pharmacologic measures:
	Rapid infusion of intravenous oxytocin (40–80 units per 1000 ml of normal saline or lactated Ringer's solution)
	Methylergonovine 0.2 mg IM or IV bolus (Hayashi, 1992) or Ergonovine maleate
	Analogs of prostaglandin F2-alpha ($PGF_{2\alpha}$)
	Bimanual compression and massage of the uterus
	Abdominal hysterectomy if all other interventions fail to control bleeding
Trauma	Location and repair lacerations and hematomas in the genital tract
Retained placental fragments	Oxytocin, methylergonovine, or curettage if hemorrhage continues.

Late Postpartum Hemorrhage

The major cause of late postpartum hemorrhage is retained placental fragments. If the fragments are small, clots form around the retained fragments that remain attached to the myometrium when the placenta is delivered. When the clots slough, several days after delivery, excessive bleeding may occur.

To prevent late postpartum hemorrhage from retained placental fragments, the placenta is inspected by the nurse-midwife or physician for evidence of missing pieces. The uterine cavity may also be checked for retained placental fragments. 

Late postpartum hemorrhage, which typically occurs after discharge and without warning, can be dangerous for the unsuspecting mother. Families must be taught how to assess the fundus and the normal duration of lochia. Moreover, they must be instructed to notify their health care provider if bleeding persists or becomes unusually heavy.

Predisposing Factors. Attempts to deliver the placenta before it separates from the uterine wall, manual removal of the placenta, and placenta accreta are the primary predisposing factors for retention of placental fragments.

Therapeutic Management. Initial treatment for late postpartum hemorrhage is directed toward control of the excessive bleeding by using IV oxytocin, ergonovine, methylergonovine, or prostaglandins. The placental fragments are often dislodged and swept out of the uterus by the bleeding, and if the bleeding subsides when oxytocin is administered, no other treatment is necessary (Cunningham et al, 1989). If bleeding continues or recurs, curettage may be carried out to remove placental fragments and antibiotic therapy is often administered to prevent infection.

Complications

EXHAUSTION

Women who experience postpartum hemorrhage are subject to a variety of complications. In general, they are exhausted and it may take weeks for them to feel well again. Anemia often results, and blood transfusions or a course of iron therapy may be prescribed to restore a functioning hemoglobin level. Activity may be restricted until the strength returns. Some women need extra assistance with housework and care of the new infant. Exhaustion may interfere with bonding and attachment. Moreover, extensive blood loss increases the risk of postpartum infection.

HYPOVOLEMIC SHOCK

The most severe complication of postpartum hemorrhage is hypovolemic shock, which may develop quickly when circulating blood volume is depleted. The loss of adequate blood volume endangers vital organs by depriving them of oxygen. The brain, heart, and kidneys are especially vulnerable to hypoxia and may suffer damage in a brief period.

Recognition of hypovolemic shock may be delayed because the body activates compensatory mechanisms that mask the severity of the problem. For example, carotid and aortic baroreceptors are stimulated to constrict peripheral blood vessels. This shunts blood to the central circulation and away from less essential organs, such as the skin and extremities. This causes the skin to become pale and cold but maintains cardiac output and perfusion of vital organs.

In addition, the adrenal glands release catecholamines, which compensate for decreased blood volume by promoting vasoconstriction in non-essential organs, increasing the heart rate, and raising the blood pressure. As a result, blood pressure remains normal initially, but the tachycardia that develops is an early sign of compensation for excessive blood loss.

As shock worsens, the compensatory mechanisms fail and physiological insults spiral. Inadequate organ perfusion and decreased cellular oxygen for metabolism result in a buildup of lactic acid and the development of metabolic acidosis. Decreased serum pH (acidosis) results in vasodilation, which further increases bleeding. In this instance, the effects of hemorrhage now become additional causes of further blood loss.

Eventually, circulating volume becomes insufficient to perfuse cardiac and brain tissue; cellular death occurs as a result of anoxia, and the mother dies.

Postpartum Hemorrhage: Application of Nursing Process

Assessment

Conditions that predispose a woman to postpartum hemorrhage appear in Table 27–1. The initial postpartum assessment includes a chart review to determine whether such predisposing conditions exist. For example, a prolonged labor or a large infant put the mother at increased risk for excessive bleeding. Postpartum assessments and signs that warrant further management appear in Table 27–3.

UTERINE ATONY

Priority assessments include the fundus, lochia, vital signs, skin temperature, and color. The fundus should be firmly contracted at or near the level of the umbilicus and midline. If the uterus is not firmly contracted, the fundus feels soft (boggy), and bleeding from the placental site is rapid and continuous. If the fundus is above the level of the umbilicus and displaced, usually to the right, assess the bladder. A full bladder lifts the uterus and impedes contraction, which allows excessive bleeding. See Procedure 17–1 (p. 426) for complete information about assessing the fundus.

It is difficult to estimate the volume of lochia by visual examination of peripads (see Fig. 17–2, p. 418). More accurate information is obtained by weighing peripads and bedliners before and after

Table 27–3. POSTPARTUM HEMORRHAGE

Assessment	Signs Warranting Further Management
Fundus	Soft, "boggy," difficult to locate, above umbilicus, displaced from midline
Lochia	Saturating more than 1 pad per hour, constant trickle, large clots
Vulva	Bulging mass, discoloration, intense pain
Vital signs	Tachycardia, tachypnea, falling blood pressure, narrowing pulse pressure
Skin changes	Cool, cold, pale, clammy, delayed capillary refill
Urine output	Below 50 ml/hour
Central nervous system	Anxiety, confusion, lethargy

use and subtracting the difference. One gram (weight) equals 1 ml (volume). When inspecting for  blood loss, always ask the woman to turn on her side to be certain that large amounts of blood are not pooling undetected underneath her. Although bleeding may be profuse and dramatic, a constant, steady trickle may lead to significant blood loss that becomes increasingly life-threatening.

Measure vital signs regularly to detect trends that may reveal a deteriorating status in a woman with significant blood loss. Compensatory mechanisms (described earlier) maintain the blood pressure and produce a rise in the heart rate until more than 15 per cent of the total circulating volume is lost. If more than 15 per cent is lost, compensatory mechanisms begin to fail and hypovolemic shock ensues (McCormac, 1990).

The skin should be warm and dry, mucous membranes of the lips and mouth should be pink, and there should be prompt capillary return when the nails are blanched. These signs confirm that there is adequate circulating volume to perfuse the peripheral tissue.

TRAUMA

If the fundus is firm but bleeding is excessive, the cause may be lacerations of the cervix or birth canal.  Inspect the perineum to determine whether a laceration is visible in that area. Lacerations of the cervix or vagina are not visible, but bleeding in the presence of a contracted uterus is suggestive of a laceration; this sign warrants examination of the vaginal walls and the cervix by the health care provider.

If the mother complains of deep, severe pelvic or rectal pain or if vital signs or skin changes suggest hemorrhage but excessive bleeding is not obvious, the cause may be concealed bleeding and the formation of a hematoma. Examine the vulva for bulging masses or discoloration of the skin. However, a hematoma may be developing in the vagina or in the retroperitoneal area and will not be obvious when the vulva is examined.

HYPOVOLEMIC SHOCK

Observe vigilantly for signs of hypovolemic shock. Tachycardia is one of the earliest signs, and even, gradual increases in the pulse rate should be noted. A decrease in blood pressure and narrowing of pulse pressure (difference between systolic and diastolic blood pressure) occurs when the circulating volume of blood is sufficiently decreased. The respiratory rate increases as the woman becomes more anxious and also as she attempts to take in more oxygen to overcome the need created when hemoblobin is inadequate to transport oxygen to all organs.

Skin changes also provide early cues. Increased catecholamine levels initiate vasoconstriction in the skin, and the skin becomes pale and cool to the touch. As hemorrhage worsens, the skin changes become more obvious; pallor increases, and the skin temperature changes from warm and dry to cold and clammy.

As shock progresses, changes also occur in the central nervous system. The mother becomes anxious, then confused, and finally lethargic when blood loss totals 30 to 40 per cent of the total blood volume. Urine output also progressively decreases from more than 30 ml/hour in early shock to less than 5 ml/hour when more than 40 per cent of the blood is lost.

Critical to Remember

Early Signs of Postpartum Hemorrhage

- An uncontracted uterus
- Large gush or slow, steady trickle of blood from the vagina
- Saturation of more than one peripad per hour
- Severe, unrelieved perineal or rectal pain
- Tachycardia

Analysis

Postpartum hemorrhage is a potential complication that requires the efforts of both nurses and physicians to control the hemorrhage and to prevent hypovolemic shock.

Planning

Client-centered goals are inappropriate for this potential complication because the nurse cannot independently manage postpartum hemorrhage but must confer with the physicians or nurse-midwives for medical orders to treat the condition. Planning should reflect the nurse's responsibility to:

- Monitor for signs of postpartum hemorrhage
- Consult with the health care provider if signs of postpartum hemorrhage are observed
- Perform actions that will minimize postpartum hemorrhage and prevent hypovolemic shock

Interventions

PREVENTING HEMORRHAGE

Every nurse should be aware of factors that put the new mother at risk for postpartum hemorrhage. This knowledge alerts the nurse to be particularly vigilant in monitoring these women so that postpartum hemorrhage can be anticipated and prevented.

When predisposing factors are present, initiate frequent assessments. Many hospitals and birth centers have a standard of care that calls for assessments every 15 minutes during the first hour following delivery, every 30 minutes for the next 2 hours, and hourly for the next 4 hours. However, this may not be adequate for the woman at known risk for postpartum hemorrhage because bleeding occurs rapidly and a delay in assessment may result in a great deal of blood loss.

Signs of hemorrhagic shock are progressive, and they depend on the amount of blood lost. Early recognition of excessive bleeding is essential so that prompt intervention can control the bleeding before hypovolemic shock develops.

COLLABORATING WITH THE HEALTH CARE PROVIDER

Notify the physician or nurse-midwife when excessive bleeding is suspected. In addition, initiate actions, such as uterine massage, to control bleeding. In some hospitals or birth centers, protocols also permit nurses to initiate specific laboratory studies, such as typing and cross-matching blood, and to start IV fluids while the health care provider is being informed of the mother's condition. These actions do not substitute for notifying the health care provider, but they do allow nurses to make initial interventions quickly.

Maintain the woman on bed rest to increase venous return and maintain cardiac output. Trendelenburg's position may interfere with cardiac function and is not advised. Continue the assessments described earlier, call for assistance, and save all pads, linen savers, and linen so that an accurate estimation of blood loss can be made. Assistance is necessary because one nurse must continue to massage the uncontracted uterus and perform and record assessments while the other notifies the health care provider of the mother's condition.

When the health care provider is notified, the time and content of each communication must be documented. For example, on 2/1/93 at 1300 hours (1 p.m.), Dr. X was notified of difficulty maintaining uterine contraction and continued excessive bleeding. Requested Dr. X to see client. Orders for 1000 ml of normal saline with 20 units of oxytocin to infuse at 120 gtts (drops)/minute received.

Administer medications and fluids ordered by the health care provider, and evaluate their effect. For example, add the prescribed amount of oxytocin to the IV solution and infuse the solution at the prescribed rate. Evaluate the effect of the medication on the uterus, and relay this information to the health care provider. The physician or nurse-midwife depends on the nurse for accurate information, and they base medical management on information relayed by the nurse.

If measures fail to control bleeding, notify the health care provider so that additional procedures can be initiated. These may include preparation for operative intervention (surgical prep, consent signed for operative procedure, or confirmation that blood replacement is available).

TREATING HYPOVOLEMIC SHOCK

If excessive bleeding continues, initiate constant evaluation of vital signs if equipment is available. If not, one person should be assigned to evaluate and record vital signs, skin temperature, and color as well as capillary return every 3 to 5 minutes. The purpose of the assessments is to determine if signs of hypovolemic shock (tachycardia, falling blood pressure, cool skin temperature, pallor) are developing.

If an indwelling catheter has not been inserted and progressive changes indicate impending shock, insert the catheter so that the hourly urinary output can be measured. The indwelling catheter is necessary if the woman requires a surgical procedure to control the hemorrhage.

A second IV line may be inserted with a large-bore (No. 16) catheter to maintain fluid a sufficient fluid volume to produce a urinary output of at least 30 ml/hour. A large bore is essential if whole blood is given. Oxygen may be needed to increase the saturation of fewer red blood cells; administer the oxygen by tight face mask at 6 L/minute or as directed by the health care provider.

The unusual activity of the hospital staff may make the mother and her family anxious. Be alert to their non-verbal cues, and when they appear frightened, acknowledge their feelings. Moreover, keeping them informed is one of the most effective ways of reducing anxiety.

Acknowledge the anxiety, and provide simple appropriate explanations of the activity. "I know all this activity must be frightening; she is bleeding a little more than we would like, and we are doing several things at once."

Nursing Care Plan 27–1

Postpartum Hemorrhage

Assessment: Dolores Navarra, a 26-year-old multipara, is admitted to the postpartum unit following rapid labor and the birth of her fourth infant. The baby weighed 4000 g (8 pounds, 12 ounces) 2 hours ago. At the initial assessment, Dolores' fundus is firm, at the level of the umbilicus. Lochia is heavy, with occasional small clots expressed. Vital signs are unchanged from prenatal norms.

Potential complication: Postpartum hemorrhage.

Goals:
Client goals are inappropriate because the nurse cannot independently manage postpartum hemorrhage. Planning reflects the nurse's responsibilities:

1. Monitor for signs of postpartum hemorrhage.
2. Consult with the physician if signs of postpartum hemorrhage are observed.
3. Perform actions that will minimize the risk of postpartum hemorrhage.

Intervention:	Rationale:
1. Monitor Dolores' blood pressure, pulse, skin color, and uterine tone every 15 minutes for the first hour; assess more often if signs of hemorrhage develop.	1. Detect early signs of excessive bleeding so that bleeding can be controlled before signs of shock develop.
2. Assess lochial flow and uterine position every 15 minutes; massage fundus, as necessary, to maintain firmness; administer oxytocin as ordered.	2. Bleeding from the placental site is controlled by effective uterine contraction that compresses torn vessels; oxytocin stimulates uterine contraction.
3. Assess for signs of trauma, such as deep, severe, unrelieved perineal or rectal pain or a discolored bulging hematoma of the perineum.	3. Rapid labor and delivery are associated with trauma, which may include hematoma formation and concealed bleeding that can be significant.
4. Notify the physician or nurse-midwife if signs of hemorrhage develop (uncontracted uterus, saturation of more than one pad per hour, changes in vital signs, skin color, or skin temperature).	4. The presence of hemorrhage requires the combined efforts of primary health care providers and nurses to prevent hypovolemic shock, a potentially life-threatening condition.

Evaluation:
Because client-centered goals are not developed for potential complications (collaborative problems), the nurse collects and compares data to established norms for postpartum bleeding and judges whether the bleeding is within normal limits: the fundus remains firm, bleeding does not saturate more than one pad per hour, and vital signs remain stable at pre-delivery norms.

Assessment: Despite close monitoring, Dolores experienced a postpartum hemorrhage that required a dilation and curettage (D & C) to remove placental fragments. She states that she is exhausted and can hardly find the energy to care for herself. She verbalizes concern about how the family will be able to provide care for the new baby and three other children until she feels better.

Nursing Diagnosis: High Risk for Altered Family Processes related to mother's fatigue that is secondary to childbirth and postpartum hemorrhage.

Goals:
The family will describe a specific plan to provide care for family members by the time of Dolores' discharge from the facility.

Intervention:	Rationale:
1. Help the family acknowledge the impact of Dolores' fatigue on family functioning.	1. The mother's illness is particularly difficult because she is generally the primary caregiver; the first task of the family is to acknowledge the problem.

Nursing Care Plan continued on next page

Nursing Care Plan 27–1 *Continued*

Postpartum Hemorrhage

2. Help the family to identify members who are available to provide assistance and to work out a concrete plan that includes specific persons and specific times.	2. Following a schedule of rotating family members or friends is less stressful than calling for spur-of-the-moment assistance.
3. Encourage Dolores to conserve her energy for breastfeeding and maintaining close contact with the siblings; suggest that other activities be temporarily taken over by family members.	3. Close contact with the children meets their needs for Dolores' affection and reduces anxiety and sibling rivalry. It also meets her need to provide care and nurturing for the children.

Evaluation:
Extended family members, friends, and Dolores' husband have worked out a rotating schedule for meal preparation, laundry, and essential household tasks until Dolores regains her energy.

Additional Nursing Diagnoses to Consider:
Fatigue
High Risk for Infection
High Risk for Altered Health Maintenance
High Risk for Impaired Home Maintenance Management

Evaluation

Although client-centered goals are not developed for potential complications (collaborative problems), the nurse collects and compares data to established norms and judges whether the data are within normal limits. For postpartum bleeding:

- The fundus remains firm.
- Lochia is moderate.
- Vital signs remain near pre-delivery levels.

✔ Check Your Reading

1. Why does the nurse examine the mother's prenatal record as well as her labor and delivery record?
2. Why is a mother who has given birth to twins at increased risk for postpartum hemorrhage?
3. Can the nurse be positive that bleeding is controlled when the fundus is firm and the lochia is moderate? Why or why not?
4. Why does the blood pressure remain normal in early postpartum hemorrhage?

Subinvolution of the Uterus

Subinvolution refers to a slower than expected return of the uterus to its pre-pregnancy size following childbirth. Normally, the uterus descends at the rate of about 1 cm or one fingerbreadth per day, and by 2 weeks it is no longer palpable above the symphysis pubis. The endometrial lining has sloughed off as part of lochia, and the site of placental attachment is well healed by 6 weeks after childbirth if involution progresses as expected. (See Chapter 17 for additional information about involution.)

The most common causes of subinvolution are retained placental fragments and endometritis (inflammation of the endometrium, the inner lining of the uterus). Signs and symptoms of subinvolution include uterine tenderness, fundal height that remains unchanged, pelvic pain or feelings of pelvic heaviness, backache, lochia that varies from expected pattern or duration, fatigue, and persistent general malaise.

THERAPEUTIC MANAGEMENT

Treatment is tailored to correct the cause of subinvolution. Oral methylergonovine maleate (Methergine), 0.2 mg every 3 to 4 hours for 24 to 48 hours, provides long, sustained contraction of the uterus (Drug Guide, p. 785). If infection is the cause, antibiotics are also administered. If this treatment is not effective or if the cause is believed to be adherent placental fragments, cervical dilatation and curettage (D & C) of the uterus may be indicated.

NURSING CONSIDERATIONS

In most cases, subinvolution is not obvious until the mother has returned home following childbirth. For

Drug Guide

METHYLERGONOVINE

Classification: Oxytocic.

Action: Directly stimulates contraction of the uterus.

Indications: Used for the prevention and treatment of postpartum or post-abortion hemorrhage caused by uterine atony or subinvolution.

Dosage and Route:

Usual dosage is 0.2 mg IM every 2 to 4 hours for up to five doses. Change to oral route 0.2 to 0.4 mg every 6 to 12 hours for 2 to 7 days.

Absorption: Well absorbed following oral or IM route.

Excretion: Metabolic fate unknown, probably metabolized by the liver.

Contraindications and Precautions: Do not use to induce labor; do not use IM if the mother is hypersensitive to phenol. Use caution in hypertensive women, in those with severe hepatic or renal disease, and in women in the third stage of labor.

Adverse Reactions: Dizziness, headache, dyspnea, palpitations, hypertension, nausea, uterine and gastrointestinal cramping

Nursing Considerations: Before administering medication, check expiration date and monitor blood pressure. Follow facility protocol if medication must be withheld (usually a reading of 136/90). Caution the mother to avoid smoking because nicotine constricts blood vessels. Remind her to report any adverse reactions.

---

this reason, nurses must teach the mother and her significant other how to assess for the condition and how to recognize its occurrence.

The nurse demonstrates how to locate and palpate the fundus and how to estimate fundal height in relation to the umbilicus. The nurse requests return demonstrations until the mother is confident of her skill. The uterus should become smaller each day (by approximately one fingerbreadth). The nurse also explains the progressive changes from lochia rubra, to lochia serosa, and then to lochia alba (see Chapter 17).

The mother is instructed to report any deviation from the expected pattern or duration of lochia. A foul odor often indicates uterine infection, for which treatment must be sought. Additional signs must be reported to the physician or midwife, such as pelvic or fundal pain, backache, or feelings of pelvic pressure or fullness.

✔ Check Your Reading

5. What are the major signs of subinvolution?
6. What is the nurse's primary responsibility in the management of subinvolution?

Thromboembolic Disorders

There are three thromboembolic disorders most frequently encountered during the postpartum period. *Superficial thrombophlebitis* generally involves the saphenous venous system and is confined to the lower leg. *Deep venous thrombosis* involves the venous system from the foot to the iliofemoral region and is a major concern because it predisposes to *pulmonary embolism,* a dangerous and potentially fatal complication that occurs when a pulmonary artery is obstructed by a blood clot that was swept into circulation from a vein. Figure 27–5 illustrates the venous system of the leg.

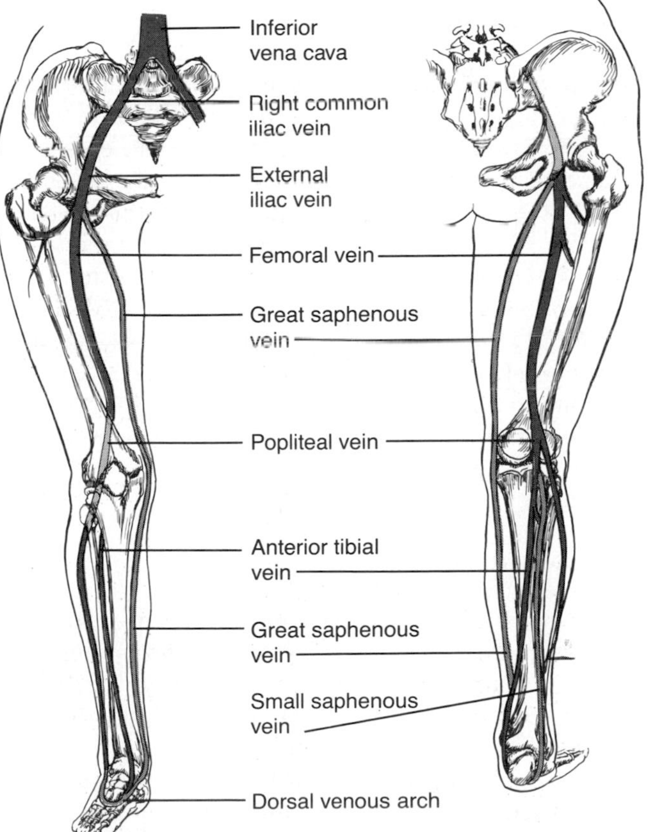

Figure 27–5

The venous system of the leg is affected when deep venous thrombosis occurs.

Incidence and Etiology

The incidence of superficial thrombophlebitis is 1 in 95 in the postpartum period; the incidence of deep venous thrombosis is less than 1 in 700 (Nuwayhid and Khalife, 1992). It is generally accepted that the low incidence is due to the practice of early ambulation and the reduction in traumatic deliveries.

A *thrombus* is a collection of blood factors, primarily platelets and fibrin, on a vessel wall. Thrombus can form whenever the flow of blood is impeded. Once started, the thrombus can enlarge with successive layering of platelets, fibrin, and blood cells as the blood flows past the clot. Thrombus formation is often associated with an inflammatory process in the vessel wall and is then termed *thrombophlebitis*.

There are three major causes of thrombophlebitis: venous stasis, hypercoagulable blood, and injury to the intima (the innermost layer) of the blood vessel. At least two of these conditions—venous stasis and hypercoagulable blood—are present in all pregnancies.

VENOUS STASIS

Pregnancy is characterized by an increase in venous stasis in the lower extremities and pelvis as a result of compression of the large vessels by the enlarging uterus. Stasis is most pronounced when the pregnant woman stands for prolonged periods of time. Stasis of blood in the lower extremities during pregnancy results in dilated vessels and the potential for continued pooling of blood post partum. Relative inactivity during pregnancy also leads to venous pooling and stasis of blood in the lower extremities.

Prolonged time in stirrups for delivery and repair of the episiotomy may also promote venous stasis and increase the risk of thrombophlebitis.

HYPERCOAGULATION

Pregnancy is also characterized by changes in the coagulation and fibrinolytic systems that persist in the postpartum period. During pregnancy, the levels of most coagulation factors (particularly fibrinogen and factors III, X, and VIII) are elevated. In addition, there is also a suppression of the fibrinolytic system (plasminogen activator and anti-thrombin III) which causes clots to disintegrate (lyse). The net result is that factors that promote clot formation are increased to prevent maternal hemorrhage, whereas factors that prevent clot formation are decreased, resulting in a higher risk for thrombus formation during pregnancy and particularly during the postpartum period.

BLOOD VESSEL INJURY

Injury to the intima of the blood vessel probably plays no role in initiation of thrombosis in pregnancy except for the possibility of injury during cesarean births, which could conceivably trigger a pelvic vein thrombosis. Thrombophlebitis is three times more likely to occur if the birth was cesarean (Ingardia and Pitcher, 1993).

ADDITIONAL PREDISPOSING FACTORS

Certain factors create additional risk for some women. These factors include varicose veins, obesity, a history of thrombophlebitis, and smoking. Women older than 35 years of age or who have had more than three pregnancies, as well as women who had a cesarean birth, are also at increased risk.

Superficial Thrombophlebitis

CLINICAL SIGNS AND SYMPTOMS

Superficial thrombophlebitis can usually be diagnosed by clinical signs and symptoms. In most people, superficial thrombophlebitis is limited to the calf area. Symptoms include swelling and tenderness of the involved extremity. On physical examination, there is redness, tenderness, and warmth. It may be possible to palpate the enlarged, hardened vein. Patients sometimes experience pain when they walk.

THERAPEUTIC MANAGEMENT

Superficial thrombophlebitis is not life-threatening, but if it is not treated promptly, the inflammatory process can extend to the deep veins. Analgesics, local application of heat (a thermal blanket), and elevation of the lower extremity to promote improved venous return are often sufficient treatment. There is no need for anticoagulants or anti-inflammatory agents (Nuwayhid and Khalife, 1992). After 5 to 7 days of bed rest and when symptoms disappear, the woman may ambulate gradually. She should avoid standing for long periods of time and wear support hose to help prevent venous stasis and a subsequent episode of superficial thrombophlebitis.

Deep Vein Thrombosis

Deep vein thrombosis is much more difficult to diagnose on the basis of clinical manifestations because signs and symptoms are often absent or diffuse. If they are present, they are due to an inflammatory process and obstruction of venous return; calf swelling, erythema, heat and tenderness, and pedal edema are the most common signs.

It is a common belief that a positive Homans' sign (presence of pain behind the knee when the foot is dorsiflexed) is an indicator of deep vein thrombophlebitis; however, Homans' sign has proved to be of little value in the diagnosis of deep vein thrombophlebitis; (Sternbach, 1989). Reflex arterial spasms may cause the leg to become pale and cool to the touch with decreased peripheral pulses. At one time, this condition was called "milk leg."

Additional symptoms may include pain on ambulation, chills, general malaise, and stiffness of the affected leg.

DIAGNOSIS

Clinical signs and symptoms arouse suspicions of deep vein thrombophlebitis; however, diagnosis depends on additional testing. Non-invasive tests include real-time ultrasonography and continuous-wave and duplex Doppler examinations, which detect alterations in blood flow. Impedance plethysmography measures results of changes in venous volume of a leg. Venography is the most accurate method for diagnosing deep vein thrombophlebitis; however, there are significant risks and side effects. The most common are reactions to the contrast dye, muscle pain, leg swelling, tenderness, and erythema (Rutherford and Phelan, 1991).

THERAPEUTIC MANAGEMENT

Initial Treatment. Initial treatment of deep vein thrombophlebitis consists of:

- Bed rest, with the affected leg elevated to decrease interstitial swelling and to promote venous return from that leg
- Anticoagulant therapy, which usually begins with continuous infusion of intravenous heparin to prevent extension of the thrombus by delaying the clotting time of the blood
- Analgesics, as necessary, to control pain
- Antibiotic therapy, if necessary, to prevent or control infection

Subsequent Treatment. After signs and symptoms have completely abated, well-fitting elastic stockings should be applied and gradual ambulation may be started while heparin is continued (Cunningham et al, 1989). Recovery to this stage usually takes several days. The prothrombin time (PT) is evaluated daily when IV heparin is administered.

When the woman is symptom-free and fully ambulatory, anticoagulant therapy is usually changed to sodium warfarin, which is continued for 2 to 6 months at home. During this time, the partial thromboplastin time (PTT) is assessed periodically to maintain correct dosage levels (Nuwayhid and Khalife, 1992).

NURSING CONSIDERATIONS

When strict bed rest is required, care must be taken to prevent flexion of the knees or hips, which can cause pressure and obstruction of blood flow from the legs. The nurse must remind the mother to change positions every 2 hours, and she will need assistance to perform prescribed range of motion exercises.

The nurse must inform the mother and her family that massage is prohibited because of the danger of dislodging the clot. (See also nursing interventions for preventing excess anticoagulant therapy (p. 790)).

Pulmonary Embolism

PATHOPHYSIOLOGY

Pulmonary embolism is a rare but dreaded complication of deep vein thrombosis. It occurs when fragments of a blood clot dislodge and are carried to the pulmonary artery or one of its branches. The embolus occludes the vessel and obstructs the flow of blood into the lungs, either entirely or partially. If pulmonary circulation is severely compromised, death may occur within a few minutes. If the embolous is small, adequate pulmonary circulation may be maintained until treatment can be initiated.

CLINICAL SIGNS AND SYMPTOMS

Clinical signs and symptoms depend on how much the flow of blood is obstructed. Sudden, sharp chest pain, tachycardia, syncope, tachypnea, pulmonary rales, cough, and hemoptysis are the most common signs. Arterial blood gas determinations show decreased partial pressure of oxygen, and chest x-ray studies reveal areas of atelectasis and pleural effusion.

Thromboembolic Disorders: Application of Nursing Process

The Mother at Risk for Thrombophlebitis

Assessment

Begin with a thorough chart review to determine the existence of factors, such as age over 35 years or

Table 27–4. FACTORS THAT INCREASE THE RISK OF THROMBOPHLEBITIS

Inactivity
Obesity
Cesarean birth
Smoking
History of previous thrombophlebitis
Varicose veins
Diabetes mellitus
Prolonged time in stirrups in second stage of labor
Maternal age >35 years
Parity >3

smoking, that increase the risk for decreased tissue perfusion as a result of venous stasis (Table 27–4).

All women are at increased risk for thrombophlebitis following childbirth. Assess the new mother at every shift for any signs or symptoms: localized areas of warmth, redness, or tenderness. Inspect the legs for the location and degree of edema. Palpate the pedal pulses, which should be easily palpable and equal. Have the mother sharply dorsiflex each foot, and report the presence of a positive Homans' sign.

Analysis

A clinically useful nursing diagnosis will generate interventions to decrease venous stasis or provide information that may prevent the development of thrombophlebitis. If thrombophlebitis develops, medical as well as nursing interventions are necessary. Therefore, the most relevant nursing diagnosis is: *High Risk for Altered Peripheral Tissue Perfusion related to venous stasis and lack of knowledge of preventive measures.*

Planning

Goals for this nursing diagnosis are as follows:

- The mother will remain free of signs and symptoms of altered tissue perfusion.
- The mother (and her family) will identify factors that improve peripheral circulation.
- The mother will describe a plan to make necessary lifestyle changes to reduce the risk of thrombophlebitis.

Interventions

IMPROVING VENOUS CIRCULATION

To prevent thrombophlebitis, assist the mother with early, frequent ambulation to promote circulation in the lower extremities. If she is unable to ambulate, begin range of motion and gentle leg exercises, such as flexing and straightening the knee and raising one leg at a time within 8 hours following childbirth.

Suggest that the mother avoid using pillows or the knee gatch to prevent sharp flexion at the knees and consequent pooling of blood in the lower extremities.

Obtain an order for anti-embolus stockings for mothers with varicose veins or a history of thrombophlebitis, or for those who had a cesarean delivery. Apply the stockings before the mother rises in the morning to prevent venous congestion, which begins as soon as she gets up. Teach the correct way to put on the anti-emboli stockings; improperly applied stockings can roll or bunch and may cause slower venous return from the legs.

During childbirth, pad the stirrups to prevent prolonged pressure against the popliteal angle during the second stage of labor. Try to restrict the time in stirrups to no more than 1 hour.

TEACHING PREVENTIVE MEASURES

Before hospital discharge, inform the mother about lifestyle changes that can improve peripheral circulation. Specific suggestions appear in Women Want to Know: How to Prevent Thrombophlebitis.

Evaluation

Assessment prior to discharge determines if the mother is free of the signs and symptoms of altered tissue perfusion. Interventions have been successful if she (and her family) can:

- Describe measures that improve peripheral circulation
- Describe a plan to initiate lifestyle changes (stopping smoking, increasing ambulation, maintaining an adequate fluid balance)

The Mother with Thrombophlebitis

Assessment

Assessment focuses on determining the status of the venous thrombosis. Palpate pedal pulses to determine whether they are absent, diminished, or easily palpable and equal. Inspect the affected leg for

Women Want To Know

How to Prevent Thrombophlebitis

Methods to improve peripheral circulation will help prevent the occurrence of thrombophlebitis:

- Improve your circulation with regular schedule of activity, preferably walking.
- Avoid prolonged standing or sitting in one position.
- When sitting, elevate your legs and avoid crossing them. This will increase the return of venous blood from the legs.
- Maintain a fluid intake of at least 2500 ml (approximately 2½ quarts) to prevent dehydration and consequent sluggish circulation.
- Stop smoking. Not only is smoking a risk factor for thrombophlebitis, but it can cause respiratory problems in both you and your newborn.

unusual warmth or redness, which indicates inflammation, or for unusual coolness or cyanosis, which indicates venous obstruction. Compare the affected and unaffected leg for size and color. Sometimes the nurse measures the legs and compares the circumference to obtain an accurate estimation of the edema that is present in the affected leg.

Determine the degree of discomfort present. Pain is caused by tissue hypoxia, and increasing pain indicates increased obstruction.

If the mother is taking anticoagulants, evaluate the laboratory report of PT or PTT before administering the medication.

Observe for signs of pulmonary embolism, such as coughing, dyspnea, tachypnea, or chest pain. Report these signs immediately because pulmonary embolism is a life-threatening complication of deep vein thrombosis that requires immediate attention.

Assess family structure to determine how prepared the family is to cope with the mother's illness. How many children are in the family? What are their ages? Who is usually the primary caregiver? Are family members available to provide care while the mother is confined to bed or on limited activity? Who helps the family in times of need?

Note interactions between the mother and the newborn as well as between the father and the newborn. If the father is not present, determine who else will be available to support the mother during the next weeks. For additional information and for nursing interventions for the nursing diagnosis *High Risk for Altered Family Processes*, see Nursing Care Plan 27–1.

Analysis

Two potential complications are most troublesome for the woman with thrombophlebitis:

- *Hemorrhage* secondary to excessive anticoagulant therapy
- *Pulmonary embolism*

Planning

Client-centered goals are inappropriate for potential complications because the nurse cannot independently manage them but must confer with physicians for medical orders to treat the condition. Planning should reflect the nurse's responsibility to:

- Monitor for signs of pulmonary embolism and hemorrhage
- Consult with the physician if signs of pulmonary embolism or hemorrhage are observed
- Perform actions that will minimize the risk of hemorrhage or pulmonary embolism

Interventions for Pulmonary Embolism

MONITORING FOR SIGNS OF PULMONARY EMBOLISM

When caring for a woman with thrombophlebitis, be aware of the danger of pulmonary embolism and focus the assessment for early signs and symptoms. Note any increase in respiratory rate, and auscultate the breath sounds carefully for abnormal breath sounds. Make note of coughing, and notify the physician at once if it occurs. Observe for signs of air hunger, dyspnea, tachycardia, pallor, or cyanosis. Above all, be able to recognize the development of pulmonary embolism and notify the physician.

FACILITATING OXYGENATION

Administer oxygen without delay, and remain with the mother to allay fear and apprehension. Raise the head of the bed to facilitate breathing and begin oxygen if she is experiencing dyspnea. Keep her warm, and be prepared to administer medication to relieve pain. Call for assistance to keep the family informed about any needed emergency procedures. The woman's condition is precarious until the clot is lysed or until it adheres to the pulmonary artery wall and is reabsorbed. A woman with this degree of postpartum complication is usually transferred to an intensive care unit for continuing care.

Treatment of pulmonary embolism is aimed at dissolving the clot and maintaining pulmonary circulation. Heparin therapy is initiated and may be continued for many months to prevent further emboli. Streptokinase or urokinase may be used for massive pulmonary emboli. Embolectomy (surgical removal of the embolus) may be attempted if there is no time to allow the clot to dissolve.

Interventions to Prevent Excess Anticoagulant Therapy

Check laboratory reports daily to determine PT or PTT. Hold the dose of anticoagulation medication, and notify the physician if clotting time is beyond prescribed therapeutic levels because prolonged clotting times increase the risk of bleeding.

Verify that medications containing aspirin are not given in combination with anticoagulants. Aspirin has an anti–vitamin K effect that inhibits synthesis of clotting factors, including prothrombin. This can lead to prolonged clotting times, which increases the risk of bleeding.

MONITORING FOR SIGNS OF BLEEDING

At least twice a day, visually inspect the mother for the appearance of bruising or petechiae. Instruct her to report the appearance of any bleeding: bloody nose, blood in urine, bleeding gums, or increased vaginal bleeding.

Be alert to signs of hemorrhage, such as tachycardia, falling blood pressure, or other signs of shock.

Unless frank hemorrhage is present, the usual treatment for excessive anticoagulation is temporary discontinuance of heparin. However, keep protamine sulfate, the antidote for heparin, available.

EXPLAINING CONTINUED THERAPY

Women with thrombophlebitis are usually discharged on oral anticoagulants and must be instructed in measures to prevent excessive anticoagulation. Carefully explain the treatment regimen, including the schedule of medication and possible side effects, such as unexplained fever, unusual fatigue, or sore throat (signs of agranulocytosis or diminished number of neutrophils). Assist the mother to devise a method for remembering to take the medication as directed, for example, marking a calendar each time the drug is taken. Caution her not to "double up" if a dose is missed.

Emphasize the importance of keeping the health care provider informed about any medications the mother takes because oral anticoagulants are associated with many clinically significant drug interactions. Also emphasize the importance of reporting unusual bleeding.

Suggest that the mother use a soft toothbrush and floss her teeth gently to prevent bleeding from the gums. She should postpone dental appointments until the therapy is completed. Recommend a depilatory to remove unwanted hair; this is safer than a razor during anticoagulant therapy.

Caution the new mother against going barefoot, about the importance of avoiding activities that may cause injury, and against the use of alcohol, which inhibits the metabolism of oral anticoagulants.

Evaluation

Although client-centered goals are not developed for potential complications, the nurse collects and compares data to established norms and judges whether the data are within normal limits:

- The new mother, even one with thrombophlebitis, remains free of signs of respiratory distress, which suggests pulmonary embolism.
- Mothers receiving anticoagulant therapy maintain ordered therapeutic levels.
- The mother demonstrates no signs of unusual bleeding or other side effects of the medication.

✔ Check Your Reading

7. Why is the risk of thrombophlebitis increased in the postpartum period?
8. Why is strict bed rest prescribed for the woman with deep vein thrombosis?
9. What additional nursing assessments are necessary when the mother is receiving anticoagulation medication?

Infection

Infection is always a major concern in the new mother. It occurs in 6 to 7 per cent of all women who have had vaginal deliveries and twice as often in women who have had cesarean deliveries (Hayashi, 1992). Until the advent of antibiotics, *puerperal infection* (infection of the reproductive tract following childbirth) resulting in death was not uncommon. Even today, it is one of the three leading causes of maternal deaths.

The postpartum woman is subject to infection in a number of sites: the interior of the uterus, the episiotomy incision, the cesarean incision, the urinary tract, and the breasts. Endometritis can become the most serious, as it can spread throughout the reproductive tract and even cause generalized sepsis.

Definition

The definition of puerperal infection, according to the Joint Committee on Maternal Welfare, is a fever of 38°C (100.4°F) or higher after the first 24 hours following childbirth, occurring on at least 2 days during the first 10 days. Although a slight fever may occur during the first 24 hours because of dehydration or the exertion of labor, any mother with fever should be assessed for other signs of infection.

Effect of Normal Anatomy and Physiology on Infection

To understand the seriousness of infection of the reproductive tract, it is important to consider the anatomy of the region. Every part of the reproductive tract is connected to every other part, and organisms can move from the vagina, through the cervix, into the uterus, up the fallopian tubes, and out the tubes to infect the ovaries and the peritoneal cavity. Moreover, the entire reproductive tract is particularly well supplied with blood vessels during pregnancy and after delivery. Bacteria, which invade or are picked up by the blood vessels or lymphatics, can carry the infection to the rest of the body and can result in life-threatening septicemia.

The normal physiological changes of childbirth increase the risk of infection. During labor, the acidity of the vagina is reduced by the amniotic fluid, blood, and lochia, which are alkaline. An alkaline environment encourages growth of bacteria.

Necrosis of the endometrial lining and the presence of lochia provide a favorable environment for the growth of anaerobic bacteria. Many small lacerations, some microscopic in size, occur in the endometrium, cervix, and vagina during birth and allow bacteria to enter the tissue. Although the uterine interior is not sterile until 3 to 4 weeks after delivery, infection does not develop in most women. This is partly due to the presence of granulocytes, in the lochia and endometrium, which prevent infection. Scrupulous aseptic technique during labor and birth and careful hand washing during the postpartum period are also major preventive factors.

Other Risk Factors

In addition to the normal physiological changes of the puerperium, a number of other factors may predispose a woman to infection (Table 27–5). A cesarean procedure, a major predisposing factor, increases the risk five to 30 times above that for vaginal delivery (Gibbs and Sweet, 1989). This is because of the trauma to the tissue that occurs in surgery, the incision which provides an entrance for bacteria, the possibility of contamination during surgery, and the presence of foreign bodies such as sutures. In addition, women who must have a surgical delivery because of a problem that develops during labor may have other risk factors, such as prolonged labor, that raise the chances of infection.

Any trauma to maternal tissues increases the hazard of infection. Trauma may occur with rapid delivery, delivery of a large infant, use of forceps or a vacuum extractor, or the need for manual delivery of the placenta as well as lacerations and episiotomies. Catheterization during labor increases the chance of introduction of organisms into the bladder and adds to the trauma of the urinary tract that occurs during normal delivery.

When there is prolonged rupture of membranes during labor, organisms from the vagina are more likely to ascend into the uterine cavity. This is especially true if more than 24 hours passes before delivery, but infection may develop even when rupture of membranes has occurred in a much shorter time. A long labor or many vaginal examinations during labor increase the danger of infection. Each vaginal examination increases the possibility of contamination from gloves or from organisms in the vagina being pushed through the open cervix. If part of the placenta remains inside the uterus after delivery, the tissue becomes necrotic and provides a good place for bacteria to grow.

Additional factors include postpartum hemorrhage, which causes loss of some of the infection-fighting components of the blood, such as leukocytes, and leaves the mother in a weakened condition. Prenatal conditions (poor nutrition, anemia) interfere with the mother's ability to resist infection. Lack of knowledge of hygiene or lack of access to facilities that permit adequate hygiene increases the risk of postpartum infection.

Specific Infections

ENDOMETRITIS

Endometritis is an inflammation of the endometrium of the uterus, often at the placental site. It is the most common of the postpartum infections and is the one considered first when signs of infection develop.

Etiology. Endometritis is usually due to organisms

Table 27–5. RISK FACTORS FOR PUERPERAL INFECTION

Risk Factor	Reason
Surgical delivery (cesarean birth is consistently associated with higher rates of infection)	Causes break in skin and increases portals of entry for bacteria
Trauma (rapid delivery, large infant, forceps, vacuum extractor, lacerations)	Provides entrance for bacteria and makes tissues more susceptible
Prolonged rupture of membranes	Removes barrier of amniotic membrane and allows access for organisms to interior of uterus
Prolonged labor	Increases number of vaginal examinations done and possibility that other invasive measures will be necessary
Catheterization	Possibly introduces organisms into bladder; added trauma makes woman more susceptible to infection
Excessive number of vaginal examination	Increases chance that organisms from vagina or outside sources are carried into the uterus
Retained placental fragments	Provides growth medium for bacteria and may interfere with flow of lochia
Hemorrhage	Loss of infection-fighting components of blood and general weakening
Poor general health (excessive fatigue, anemia, frequent minor illnesses)	Mother more susceptible to infections and complications in labor
Poor nutrition (decreased intake of protein, vitamin C)	Mother less able to defend against infection
Poor hygiene	Excessive exposure to organisms
Other medical conditions, especially diabetes	Mother susceptible to infection of any kind
Low socioeconomic status	Mother likely to have poor nutrition, poor health, and little or no prenatal care

that are normal inhabitants of the vagina and cervix. More than one organism is responsible for most infections. Organisms most often involved include gram-negative coliform bacteria, such as *Escherichia coli*, *Bacteroides*, *Staphylococcus*, and anaerobic non-hemolytic *Streptococcus*. Although group A hemolytic streptococcal infections were once the source of epidemics of puerperal infections (then known as "childbed fever"), improved routine care has made it uncommon today. Group B *Streptococcus* is involved in as many as 30 per cent of endometritis cases today. This organism is also the major cause of sepsis in the newborn.

Clinical Signs and Symptoms. The major signs and symptoms of endometritis are fever, malaise, uterine tenderness, and purulent, foul-smelling lochia. Additional signs include tachycardia, either scant or profuse lochia, and subinvolution. In most cases, the signs and symptoms occur within the first 2 to 7 days (Gibbs and Sweet, 1989). Not all patients show the complete picture. When the causative organisms are group A or group B streptococci, the woman may exhibit no signs except fever.

The mother with severe endometritis looks sick. She may have generalized malaise and aching. She presents a very different picture from the typical happy new mother.

Laboratory data may be ordered to confirm the diagnosis. The results of a complete blood count may show an elevation of leukocytes. However, leukocytes are normally elevated to 20,000 or as high as 30,000 during labor and for a short time afterward. Elevations in the upper ranges of normal should cause suspicion.

Two aerobic and anaerobic specimens may be taken from the blood, endocervix, and uterine cavity for cultures. A catheterized urine specimen should also be obtained. The antibiotic sensitivity from these cultures may be used to determine the appropriate second-line antibiotic therapy in case the broad-spectrum therapy is unsuccessful in halting the infection.

Therapeutic Management. The initial treatment of endometritis usually includes intravenous administration of antibiotics. This is done to confine the infectious process to the uterus and to prevent spread of the infection throughout the body. Broad-spectrum antibiotics, such as ampicillin and cephalosporins, are usually effective for mild to moderate infection. A penicillin-aminoglycoside combination may be used for moderate to severe infection (Hayashi, 1992). Improvement in clinical signs usually follows within 48 to 72 hours. If the symptoms persist, additional investigation is needed to determine

Critical to Remember

Signs and Symptoms of Postpartum Infection

- Fever, chills
- Pain or redness of wounds
- Purulent wound drainage
- Tachycardia
- Uterine subinvolution
- Abnormal duration of lochia, foul odor
- Elevated white blood cell count
- Frequency or urgency of urination, dysuria, hematuria
- Suprapubic pain
- Localized area of warmth, redness, or tenderness in the breasts
- Body aches, general malaise

the cause and precise location. Oral antibiotics may be used after completion of an IV course of treatment. Some physicians give prophylactic antibiotics intravenously and/or orally for any woman who is having a cesarean procedure or who is particularly at risk for infection. Other drugs include antipyretics for fever and oxytocics, such as Methergine, to increase drainage of lochia and promote involution.

Complications. If the infection spreads outside the uterine cavity, there may be infection of the fallopian tubes (*salpingitis*) or the ovaries (*oophoritis*), which could result in sterility. Pelvic cellulitis (*parametritis*) results from spread of infection via lymphatics through the uterine wall to the connective tissue of the broad ligament or the entire pelvis. *Peritonitis* (inflammation of the membrane lining the walls of the abdominal and pelvic cavities) may occur and lead to formation of a pelvic abscess. In addition, the risk of pelvic thrombophlebitis is increased when pathogenic bacteria enter the blood stream during episodes of endometritis. Figure 27–6 illustrates complications of endometritis.

Signs and symptoms that the infection is spreading (or extending) may be similar to those in endometritis, but more severe. Fever and abdominal pain will be particularly pronounced. Peritonitis may result in paralytic ileus and a distended, board-like abdomen with absent bowel sounds.

Nursing Considerations. The mother with endometritis is placed in a Fowler's position to promote drainage of lochia. She is medicated as needed for abdominal pain or cramping, which may be severe. The nurse gives the medications as directed and observes the mother for signs of improvement or

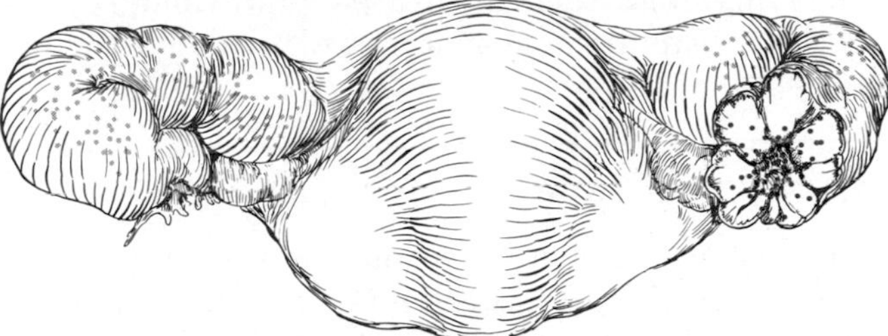

Salpingitis: Infection in fallopian tubes causes them to become enlarged, hyperemic, and tender

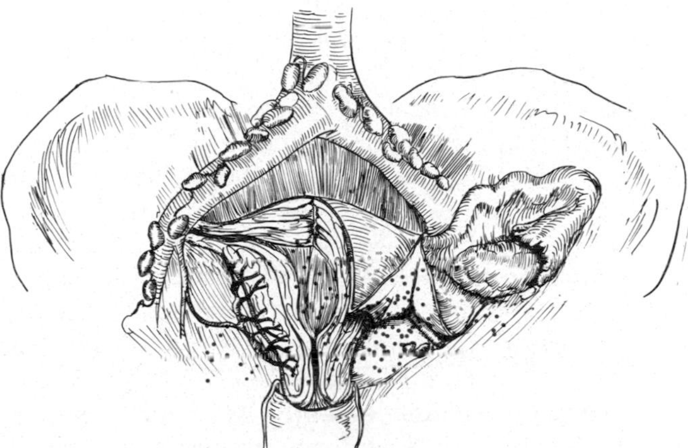

Parametritis: Infection spreads via lymphatics through uterine wall to connective tissue of broad ligament or entire pelvis

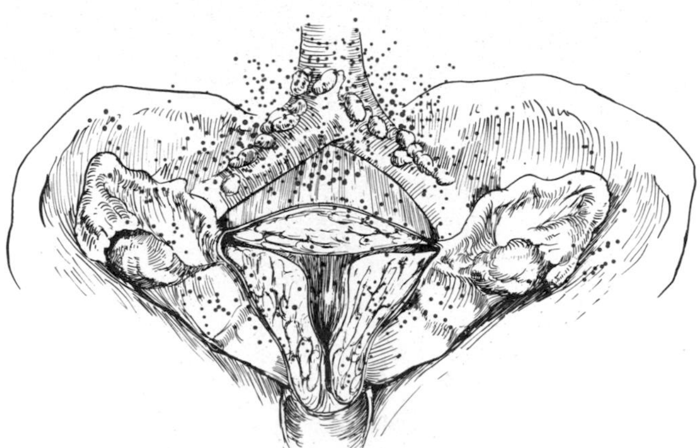

Peritonitis: Infection spreads via lymphatics to peritoneum; formation of a pelvic abscess may occur

Figure 27–6

Areas of spread of endometrial infection.

new symptoms, such as nausea and vomiting, abdominal distention, absent bowel sounds, and severe abdominal pain.

WOUND INFECTION

Any break in the skin or mucous membrane provides a portal of entry for bacteria and can result in a localized infection. The most common sites are the perineum, where episiotomies and lacerations are common (Fig. 27–7), the vagina, or the cesarean surgical incision. Localized infections can spread to other areas as well.

Clinical Signs and Symptoms. The signs of infection are edema, redness, and pain. In addition, the edges of the wound may pull apart and there may be purulent drainage from the wound. If the wound remains untreated, generalized signs of infection, such as fever and malaise, may develop as well.

Fortunately, perineal infections are rare because of improved methods during childbirth and improved hygiene during the puerperium. When they do occur, they are painful and annoying to the mother out of proportion to their size. Perineal infections cause discomfort during many activities, such as walking, sitting, or defecating, and are particularly troublesome because they are not expected by the new mother.

Therapeutic Management. The physician or nurse-midwife may decide to remove some sutures to open the area and allow for drainage. Packing, such as iodoform gauze, may be placed in the open lesion to keep it open and to facilitate drainage. Broad-spectrum antibiotics will be ordered until a report of the antibiotic sensitive organism is returned. Analgesics are often necessary, and warm compresses or sitz baths may be used to provide comfort and to promote healing by increasing circulation to the area.

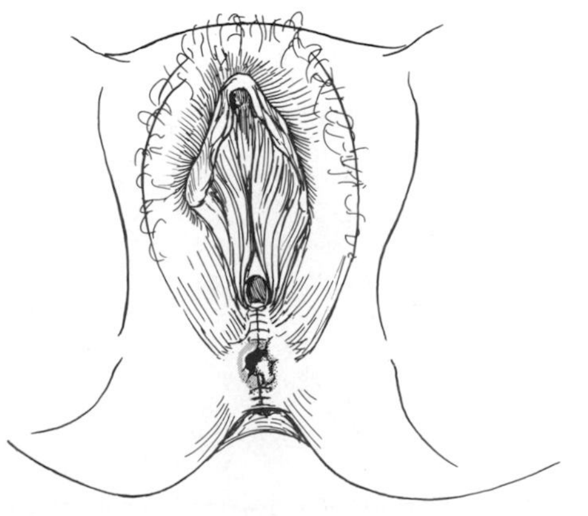

Figure 27–7

Any break in the skin, such as the episiotomy site, provides a portal of entry for bacteria and can result in localized infection.

URINARY TRACT INFECTIONS

Etiology. Trauma during birth and stasis of urine after birth contribute to the development of urinary tract infections. During delivery, the bladder and urethra are traumatized by the pressure from the descending fetus. Insertion of a catheter, with its risk of infection, occurs at least once during many labors. Following birth, the bladder and urethra are hypotonic, with stasis of urine and urinary retention common problems. Moreover, there may be residual urine and reflux of urine during voiding.

Women who had bacteria in the urine during pregnancy are at increased risk. Urinary tract infections are usually due to coliform bacteria, such as E. *coli*.

Clinical Signs and Symptoms. Symptoms typically begin on the first or second postpartum day. They include dysuria (a burning pain on urination), urgency, and frequency of urination. A low-grade fever is sometimes the only symptom. In some women, an upper urinary tract infection, such as pyelonephritis, may develop the third or fourth day with chills, spiking fever, costovertebral angle tenderness, flank pain, and nausea and vomiting. This infection of the kidney pelvis may result in permanent damage to the kidney if not promptly treated.

Therapeutic Management. Cystitis is usually treated with oral antibacterial therapy. If the mother is breastfeeding, the most commonly prescribed medication is ampicillin, which can safely be taken during pregnancy and lactation (Deglin and Vallerand, 1993). Sulfonamides, nitrofurantoin, or cephalosporin should be used cautiously during lactation.

Pyelonephritis warrants IV hydration and IV administration of broad-spectrum antibiotics until the causative organism and its sensitivity are known; then the antibiotic therapy can be adjusted.

Nursing Considerations. The woman with a urinary tract infection must be instructed to take the medication for the entire time it is prescribed and not stop when symptoms abate. In addition, she must drink at least 3000 ml of fluid each day to help dilute the bacterial count and flush the infection from the bladder. Acidification of the urine inhibits multiplication of bacteria. Apricot, plum, prune, or cranberry juice is often recommended. Some physicians recommend 500 mg of ascorbic acid twice each day to acidify the urine (Bhatia, 1992).

MASTITIS

Mastitis is a breast infection that is not usually seen in the hospital setting. It occurs most often during the 2nd and 3rd weeks following birth, although it may develop at any time during breastfeeding (Lawrence, 1989). It is more common in mothers nursing for the first time and usually affects only one breast.

Etiology. Mastitis is generally caused by S. *aureus*, although E. *coli* may also be involved. The bacteria are most often carried on the hands of the mother or staff; however, the mouth of the newborn is also an important source. The organism may enter through an injured area of the nipple, such as a crack or blister, although there may be only redness or no obvious signs of injury. Soreness of a nipple may result in insufficient emptying of the breast due to pain during breastfeeding. Engorgement and stasis of milk frequently precede mastitis. This may happen when a feeding is skipped, when the infant begins to sleep through the night, or when breastfeeding is suddenly stopped. Constriction of the breasts from a bra that is too tight may interfere with emptying of all the ducts and may lead to infection. The mother who is fatigued or stressed or who has other health problems that might lower her immune system is also at increased risk for mastitis.

Clinical Signs. At first, the mother may think that she has the flu because of fatigue and aching muscles. Symptoms progress to include fever of 38.4°C (101.1°F) or higher, chills, malaise, and headache. The breast is reddened, edematous, hot, and tender. There may be purulent drainage. Untreated mastitis may progress to breast abscess. Figure 27–8 illustrates mastitis.

Therapeutic Management. With early antibiotic treatment, mastitis usually resolves within 24 to 48 hours and abscess formation is unusual. Antibiotics are usually given orally. In most cases, the mother can continue to breastfeed from both breasts (Gibbs and Sweet, 1989). If an abscess forms and ruptures into the ducts of the breasts, breastfeeding should be discontinued and a mechanical pump used to empty the breast. Milk obtained should be discarded.

Nursing Considerations. Once mastitis occurs, nursing measures are aimed at increasing comfort and helping the mother maintain lactation. Moist heat promotes comfort and increases circulation. A shower or hot packs should be used before feeding or emptying the breasts. One way to apply heat to the breast is to use a disposable diaper moistened with hot water. The thickness helps to retain heat, and the plastic cover prevents dripping.

The breast should be completely emptied at each feeding to prevent stasis of milk, which can result in an abscess. If the mother is too sore to breastfeed on the affected side or if she is taking antibiotics that should not be given to the infant, instruct her in how to empty the breasts by expressing the milk or using a mechanical pump. Breastfeeding or pumping every 1½ to 2 hours makes the mother more comfortable and prevents stasis. Starting the feeding on the unaffected side causes the milk-ejection reflex to occur in the painful breast and make the process more efficient. Massage over the affected area before and during the feeding helps to ensure complete emptying. The mother should stay in bed during the acute phase of her illness. Her fluid intake should be at least 3000 ml/day. Analgesics may be required to relieve discomfort.

The mother with mastitis is likely to be very discouraged. Some mothers decide to stop breastfeeding because of the discomfort involved. However, weaning during an episode of mastitis may increase

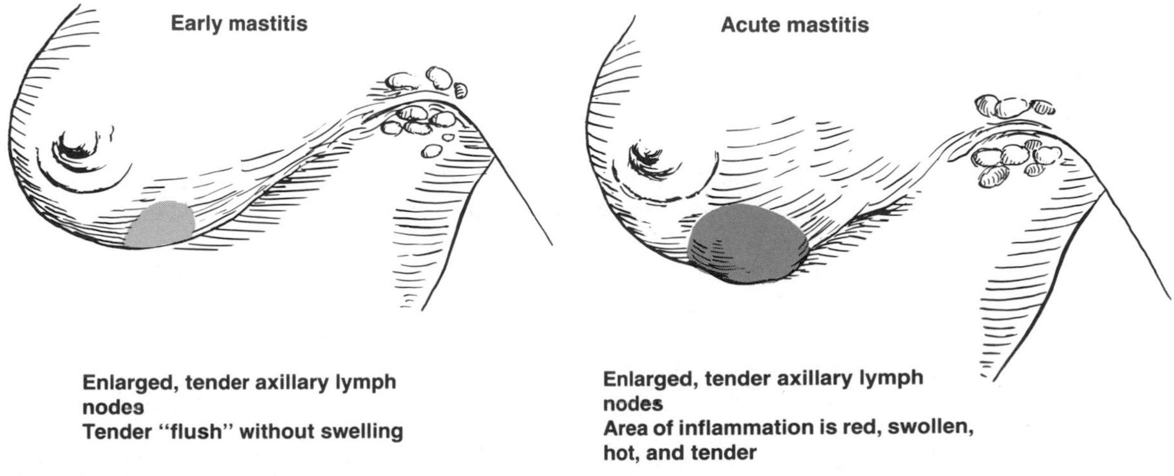

Figure 27–8

Mastitis is an infection that usually occurs 2 to 3 weeks after birth in the breast of a woman who breastfeeds.

engorgement and stasis, leading to abscess formation or recurrent infection. The mother may need much encouragement, and she will need help in arranging care for other children or with other responsibilities so that she can remain in bed.

Infection: Application of Nursing Process

Assessment

Begin with a careful chart review to identify the woman with factors that increase the risk for infection (see Table 27–5). Although all women are observed for indications of infection as part of the routine nursing assessments, the nurse must practice increased vigilance for mothers who are at increased risk of infection.

Pay particular attention to signs that may be expected in infection, such as fever; tachycardia; pain; or unusual amount, color, or odor of lochia. Generalized symptoms of malaise and muscle aching may also be significant. Examine all wounds each shift for the presence of signs of localized infection, such as redness, edema, tenderness, discharge, or pulling apart of incisions or sutured lacerations. Particularly note whether the mother experiences difficulty emptying her bladder or discomfort related to urination.

Assess the mother's knowledge of hygiene practices that prevent infections, such as proper hand washing, perineal care, and handling of perineal pads. Evaluate her knowledge of breastfeeding and any problems that might result in breast engorgement and stasis of milk in the ducts. Assess the nipples for signs of injury that might provide a portal of entry for organisms.

Analysis

All women are at risk for infection following childbirth because of the presence of conditions that favor infection (see effect of reproductive anatomy and physiology, p. 791). Additional factors increase the chance of infection in some women. Significant risk factors might be prolonged labor, prolonged rupture of membranes, cesarean birth, history of frequent urinary tract infection, nipple trauma, knowledge deficit of hygiene practices, or any number of risk factors discussed earlier. The most relevant nursing diagnosis is: *High Risk for Infection related to the presence of significant risk factors.*

Therapeutic Communication

Valerie Nunez, a 28-year-old multipara, has endometritis after the birth of her second baby. She is over the acute phase of the illness but must remain in the hospital for treatment. She still feels tired and weak. Sharon Greenspan is her nurse.

Valerie: I can't believe how different this baby's birth was from my last one. It's been just awful.

Sharon: Things haven't gone as you expected, have they? It's been a very difficult time for you.

Reflecting Valerie's feelings

Valerie: With my 2-year-old, I was home and back to normal by this time. I really miss her. And I feel that I haven't had a chance to get to know my son.

Sharon: Being sick has prevented you from being with both your children. It must be really frustrating.

Paraphrasing and acknowledging feelings

Valerie: It is frustrating. But I guess I wouldn't have been much use to either of them the way I felt these last few days. The doctor says my baby can come to see me now and I can start breastfeeding him. And my husband is bringing my daughter to see me this afternoon. I'll just have to make up for lost time.

Sharon has allowed Valerie time to verbalize her feelings; Valerie feels more ready to meet the challenges of parenting

Planning

Goals for this nursing diagnosis are as follows. The mother will:

- Remain free of signs of infection during the postpartum period.
- Verbalize methods of prevention of infection and signs of infection that should be reported immediately.

Interventions

PREVENTING INFECTION

Promoting Hygiene. Nursing responsibilities for the woman at risk for puerperal infection focus on prevention of initial infection. Preventive measures include aseptic technique for all invasive procedures and meticulous attention to hand washing. Hand washing is important not only for the nursing staff but also for the mother. She should wash her hands before and after changing pads or touching the perineum. Instruct her on care of the perineum and episiotomy site (see Chapter 17), making sure that she can demonstrate cleansing methods before she is discharged.

Nursing Care Plan 27–2

Postpartum Infection

Assessment: Lisa Pyle, a thin, pale, 16-year-old primipara, is admitted to the postpartum unit after a cesarean birth. Her membranes were ruptured for 14 hours, and she was in labor for 16 hours before the birth. She was catheterized twice during labor and now has an indwelling catheter.

Nursing Diagnosis: High Risk for Infection related to presence of favorable conditions for infections (prolonged labor, prolonged rupture of membranes, cesarean birth, catheterizations).

Goals:
Lisa will:

1. Remain free of signs of infection during the postpartum period.
2. Verbalize methods of prevention of infection and signs that infection may be present.

Intervention:	Rationale:
1. Assess vital signs every 4 hours.	1. Temperature above 38°C (100.4°F) or tachycardia suggests an infectious process and should be reported.
2. Observe the surgical incision for redness, tenderness, or edema every 4 hours; note odor of lochia at each assessment; determine whether Lisa experiences frequency, urgency, or pain with urination when the catheter is removed.	2. Redness, pain, or swelling of the incision suggests wound infection; foul odor of lochia suggests endometrial infection; frequency, urgency, or painful urination may indicate urinary tract infection.
3. Instruct Lisa in hygienic practices to prevent infection:	3.
a. Careful hand washing before and after perineal care	a. Hand washing is the most important defense against infection and its spread.
b. Perineal cleansing following elimination	b. Perineal cleansing helps prevent growth of bacteria.
c. Changing peripads frequently	c. Frequent pad changes remove accumulated lochia, which provides an excellent culture for bacteria.
d. Wiping the perineum from front to back	d. Wiping from front to back prevents fecal contamination of the vagina.
4. Initiate measures to reduce the risk of urinary tract infection. a. Provide fluids of Lisa's choice when she is able to take them, and emphasize the importance of drinking at least 2000 ml/day. b. Monitor bladder distention to prevent overfilling; teach Lisa the importance of emptying her bladder every 2 hours during the first days after childbirth. c. Use methods to promote bladder emptying, such as running water in the shower or sink, running warm water over the perineum, and providing pain medication as needed.	4. Adequate hydration and frequent emptying of the bladder help prevent stasis of urine, which increases the risk of urinary tract infection; relief of pain may allow the mother to relax enough to void.
5. Offer and encourage Lisa to eat well-balanced meals when she progresses to a regular diet. Emphasize the importance of a diet high in protein and vitamin C.	5. Adequate protein and vitamin C are necessary for healing tissues that were damaged during childbirth.

Evaluation:
Interventions have been successful if Lisa remains free of the signs and symptoms of infection throughout her hospital stay and if she verbalizes measures that reduce the risk of infection when she is discharged from the hospital.

Additional Nursing Diagnoses to Consider:
Activity Intolerance
Pain
Fatigue
High Risk for Altered Parenting

Preventing Urinary Stasis. An adequate supply of fluids (at least 2500 to 3000 ml/day) is important for preventing stasis of urine. Encourage the woman to empty her bladder at least every 2 to 3 hours during the day. Measure the first two voidings after delivery or removal of an indwelling catheter, and assess the bladder and fundus to be certain the bladder is empty. Instruct her to report any signs of urinary tract infection immediately so that early treatment can be obtained. Use appropriate measures to promote bladder emptying if she has difficulty. Drinking hot fluids, such as tea, helps some mothers to void. Running water or having the mother blow bubbles in a glass of water uses the sound of water to stimulate the urge to urinate. Pouring warm water over the perineum or having the mother void in a sitz bath or shower may help relax the urinary sphincter. Administration of analgesics may help her relax enough to urinate.

Teaching Breastfeeding Techniques. Mothers often need assistance in establishing an effective pattern of breastfeeding that results in complete emptying of the breasts at each feeding and that reduces the risk of nipple trauma (see Chapter 21).

Providing Information. Advise mothers to obtain adequate rest and sufficient food of high nutritive value to replenish their energy and prevent infection. It may be necessary to identify foods high in protein, which is necessary for repair of damaged tissue. Whole grain breads, cereals, or pasta, cheese, eggs, chicken, fish, and meat are some of the best sources of protein. This is particularly important if the mother is breastfeeding.

Obtaining adequate rest is a problem for many mothers. Nursing interventions focus on helping them plan a schedule that allows them to rest while the infant sleeps and to identify family members or friends who are available to provide support and assistance.

TEACHING SIGNS AND SYMPTOMS THAT SHOULD BE REPORTED

With many women being discharged in less than 24 hours following childbirth, they must be taught signs and symptoms of infection that should be reported to their health care provider. These include fever, chills, dysuria, and redness and tenderness of a wound.

Evaluation

The interventions can be judged to be successful if:

- The mother remains free of signs of infection during the puerperium.
- She identifies signs and symptoms that should be reported to the health care provider as soon as possible.

If infection actually occurs, the problem is no longer amenable to independent nursing actions but becomes a collaborative problem requiring both medical and nursing interventions.

✔ *Check Your Reading*

10. Why is the woman who had an assisted birth or cesarean birth at increased risk for postpartum infection?
11. Why do the normal physiologic changes of childbearing make a mother especially susceptible to infection?
12. Why is mastitis more likely to develop in a mother who skips feedings?
13. What measures can the nurse take to decrease the risk of urinary tract infection?

Affective Disorders

Affective (mood) disorders are disturbances in function, affect, or thought processes that can impact on the family following childbirth as severely as physiologic problems. However, one of the difficulties in dealing with affective disorders is that there is no consensus on how to define the disorders. Some practitioners view postpartum "blues," postpartum depression, and postpartum psychosis as part of a continuum of the same disorder, with postpartum blues being the mildest form and postpartum psychosis the most severe form. Others view affective disorders as three separate entities.

Postpartum blues is a transient, self-limiting mood disorder that affects 75 to 80 per cent of new mothers. It is believed to be related to hormonal fluctuations following childbirth (see Chapter 18). Postpartum depression and postpartum psychosis are more serious disorders that disrupt the family and require intervention to resolve.

Postpartum Depression

INCIDENCE

In the United States, the reported incidence of postpartum depression has ranged from 3 to 30 per cent in mothers during the first 3 months after childbirth. However, postpartum depression is believed to be underdiagnosed and underreported (Ugarriza, 1992).

CLINICAL SIGNS AND SYMPTOMS

The onset is insidious rather than sudden. The woman experiencing depression shows less interest in her surroundings and a loss of her usual emotional response toward her family. Even though she cares for the infant in a loving manner, she is unable to feel pleasure or love. She may have intense feelings of unworthiness, guilt, and shame, and she often expresses a sense of loss of self. Generalized fatigue, complaints of ill health, and difficulty in concentrating are also present. The illness differs from postpartum blues in that it is not transitory; also, all women who experience the condition feel disabled by it.

A list of symptoms does not convey the turmoil associated with postpartum depression. More graphic descriptions have been obtained from women experiencing the condition. According to Beck (1992),

> Postpartum depression is a living nightmare in which severe, uncontrollable anxiety causes the mother to feel she is teetering on the edge of insanity. Loss of control over the emotions prevails as overwhelming insecurities suffocate independence. Obsessive thoughts of failure as a mother and questioning what is wrong with herself bombard the mother's waking hours. All-consuming guilt and fear are experienced as the horror of thoughts of harming the infant are pondered. Enveloped in loneliness, the mother loses all previous interests and goals. Postpartum depression is associated with a vision of self as a robot devoid of all feelings. While grieving the loss of self, fear is all-encompassing that prior normalcy in life will never return.

IMPACT ON THE FAMILY

Postpartum depression will have an impact on the entire family. It creates strain on each member's usual methods of coping and often causes difficulties in relationships. Stressors tend to be magnified, and the family tends to decrease their interactions with the depressed mother when she needs support the most. Communication is impaired because she gradually withdraws from contact with others. Moreover, decreased libido commonly associated with depression may also affect the relationship with the significant other.

Depressed mothers interact differently with their infants than women who are not depressed; they appear tense, are more irritable, and feel less competent as mothers.

PREDISPOSING FACTORS

The cause of postpartum depression is unknown; however, factors believed to increase the risk of its occurrence have been grouped into three areas: biological, psychological, environmental-cultural (Boland, 1992).

Biological Factors. These include the hormonal fluctuations that follow childbirth. There is a rapid decline in estrogen, progesterone, and a transient decline in thyroid function. Medical problems during pregnancy, such as pregnancy-induced hypertension and pre-existing diabetes mellitus, may also be related to increased incidence.

Psychological Factors. Psychological factors, such as a history of depression, mental illness, or alcoholism, either in the woman or in her family, predispose to postpartum depression. Personality characteristics, such as immaturity and low self-esteem, are also associated with increased risk.

Environmental and Cultural Factors. These include marital dysfunction, difficult relationship with significant others, and anger at the pregnancy. Isolation is another important factor, but whether isolation causes or results from the depression is unknown. A strong support system can help make the transition to parenting, but childbearing families are often preoccupied and, as a result, separated from other family members and friends who might help. A family that usually plans all activities and responsibilities may feel out of control because of the erratic schedule in the early weeks at home and is more likely to experience postpartum depression. Fatigue, sleep deprivation, financial worries, and birth of an ill infant or an infant with anomalies are additional factors. The lack of a clearly defined ritual designed to provide support to all postpartum women and their families may contribute to the occurrence of postpartum depression.

Postpartum Depression: Application of Nursing Process

Assessment

Be a careful listener, and observe for subjective symptoms, such as apathy, lack of interest or energy, anorexia, or sleeplessness. The mother's verbalizations of failure, sadness, loneliness, anxiety, or vague confusion are also important cues. Objective data, such as crying, poor personal hygiene, or inability to follow directions or to concentrate may be present.

Observe the family and determine the support available as part of each assessment. Single mothers or mothers with absent or unavailable support system may feel increasingly isolated; this may lead to stress that they are unable to manage. Inappropriate expressions of blame or anger toward the partner and unmet expectations of the baby or the parenting role are sometimes present.

Analysis

A likely nursing diagnosis, particularly if predisposing factors are present, is: *High Risk for Ineffective Individual Coping related to depression in response to stressors associated with childbirth and parenting.*

Planning

To achieve the goals for this nursing diagnosis, the new mother will:

- Identify factors associated with her emotional state by discharge.
- Make plans to verbalize feelings with the health care provider and significant other throughout the postpartum period.
- Identify strengths and resources that are available during the postpartum period.

Interventions

ASSISTING THE MOTHER IN IDENTIFYING CONTRIBUTING FACTORS

Some mothers, particularly young mothers, are unprepared for the rapid change in lifestyle that follows the birth of an infant. Initiate a discussion of the changes in order to present anticipatory guidance about the early weeks at home. Discuss the need for frequent contact with other adults so that the new mother does not become isolated. Emphasize the need for continued communication with the partner or with a close friend who is available to provide support when loneliness or anxiety becomes a problem. Explain the importance of adequate rest and nutrition for maintaining energy and a feeling of health and well-being.

HELPING THE MOTHER VERBALIZE FEELINGS

Once specific contributing factors are identified, help the mother find ways to accomplish problem solving. Emphasize the necessity of acknowledging the importance of her feelings. Many women and their families minimize depression because they cannot find the exact cause. Moreover, many in the health care delivery system also trivialize the problem by making comments such as, "You'll get over it; after all, you have a beautiful baby."

Recommend that although some of her feelings may seem "unreasonable" (anger, guilt, shame), she should acknowledge these feelings to herself and insist that others acknowledge them too. It may be helpful to rehearse some of the situations that may occur, such as a fussy baby or being home alone and feeling lonely, as a means to develop perspective and to find solutions before the situation occurs.

DISCUSSING OPTIONS AND RESOURCES

Assist the new mother in identifying those persons who are available to provide support. Suggest that she explain her anticipated needs to those persons before the development of symptoms. In addition, provide her with telephone numbers for support groups in the area. In some areas, telephone support is termed "warm minds" rather than a "hotline."

Additional information and support are supplied by national and international programs:

Depression after Delivery (DAD)
Morrisville, PA 19067
215-295-3994
Provides families with excellent information.

Postpartum Support International
927 N. Kellogg Ave.
Santa Barbara, CA 93111
805-967-7636
Provides information and demonstrates that depression is widespread.

Health Science Consortium
201 Silver Cedar Court
Chapel Hill, NC 27514-1517
Markets a video that provides a great deal of support: "Postpartum Depression: You Are Not Alone."

Evaluation

The interventions have been successful if:

- The mother identifies those stressors in her life that contribute to postpartum depression. Each woman is unique, and the factors will vary from person to person.
- She is able to verbalize her feelings and insist that others acknowledge the feelings and their impact on her. By achieving this goal, she may be able to reduce the severity of the depression. Family and community resources vary, but knowing that she is not alone and that there are support groups is very helpful.

Postpartum Psychosis

Postpartum psychosis is a rare condition that affects about 1 in 1000 postpartum women. It generally surfaces within 3 weeks of delivery. There are two categories: (1) *bipolar disorder* is characterized by the occurrence of both manic and depressive episodes; (2) *major depression* is characterized by depression without manic episodes.

Women experiencing bipolar depression suffer from irritability, hyperactivity, euphoria, and grandiosity. They exhibit little need for sleep and are seldom aware they have a problem. The poor judgment and confusion they experience make self-care and infant care impossible and can create a dangerous, even life-threatening set of conditions for both mother and infant. The depressions of the bipolar disorder and major depression are similar and are characterized by tearfulness, preoccupations of guilt, feelings of worthlessness, sleep and appetite disturbances, and an inordinate concern with the baby's health. Delusions about the infant being dead or defective are common (Ugarriza, 1992).

THERAPEUTIC MANAGEMENT

Assessment and management of postpartum psychosis are beyond the scope of maternity nurses, and mothers who experience these conditions must be referred to specialists for comprehensive therapy.

Hospitalization is usually necessary to treat women suffering from postpartum psychosis, and treatment is aimed toward the particular disorder. Women who present with manic symptoms are usually treated with the standard medications (lithium, antidepressants, antipsychotics). Women who present with depressive symptoms must be assessed for suicidal potential and treated according to the severity of the threat. Antipsychotics and antidepressants are used for treatment, and careful monitoring is required because of the effect of hormonal imbalances on the mother's reaction to the prescribed medication.

✔ Check Your Reading

14. Describe the symptoms of postpartum depression and their impact on the family.
15. Identify community resources that are available for postpartum depression.

Summary Concepts

- Postpartum hemorrhage can sometimes be anticipated and prevented by careful examination of antepartum and intrapartum factors that predispose to excessive bleeding.
- Overstretching of the muscle fibers during pregnancy or repeated stretching during past pregnancies predispose to uterine atony and excessive uterine bleeding.
- Uterine atony is not the only cause of hemorrhage; soft tissue trauma (lacerations, hematomas) can also cause rapid loss of blood even when the uterus is firmly contracted.
- Initial management of uterine atony focuses on measures to contract the uterus and provide fluid replacement.
- Management of trauma of the reproductive tract involves locating the trauma and repairing it before excessive blood loss occurs.
- Compensatory mechanisms maintain the blood pressure in early hemorrhage so that vital organs, such as the brain, heart, and kidneys, receive adequate oxygen.
- The process of uterine involution is delayed (subinvolution) when placental fragments are retained or when the inner lining of the uterus is infected (endometritis).
- Subinvolution of the uterus develops after the mother has been discharged from the hospital. The nurse teaches the family the process of normal involution and the signs and symptoms that should be reported to the health care provider.
- Venous stasis that occurs during pregnancy, as well as increased levels of coagulation factors that persist into the postpartum period, increases the risk of thrombus formation during the puerperium.
- Treatment for deep vein thrombophlebitis includes anticoagulants, analgesics, and bed rest, with the affected leg elevated to decrease interstitial edema and improve venous return.
- Pulmonary embolism is a complication of deep vein thrombophlebitis that occurs when a clot is partially or completely dislodged from the vein and carried by the blood to a pulmonary artery, which may be completely or partially occluded by the clot.
- Nurses who administer anticoagulant therapy are responsible for assessing the mother to determine whether her clotting time is within the recommended therapeutic level so that overmedication with anticoagulants does not result in bleeding from unusual sites.

- The risk of postpartum infection is increased because the anatomy of the reproductive tract provides open access to bacteria from the vagina through the fallopian tubes and out into the peritoneal cavity. Increased blood supply to the pelvis and the alkalinization of the vagina by the amniotic fluid further increase the risk of infection in the inner lining of the uterus (endometritis).
- Any break in the skin or mucous membranes during childbirth provides a portal of entry for pathogenic organisms and increases the risk of puerperal infection. Nurses must assess women with an incision or laceration for signs of localized wound infections.
- Urinary stasis and trauma to the urinary tract increase the risk of postpartum urinary tract infection. Nurses must initiate measures to prevent urinary stasis.
- Nurses must provide information about the importance of completely emptying the breasts at each feeding and about measures to prevent nipple trauma to prevent mastitis.
- Postpartum depression is a disabling affective disorder that affects the entire family. It is often underdiagnosed and underreported. Nurses must help the woman to acknowledge her feelings and assist her in identifying measures that will help her cope with the condition.

References and Readings

Affonso, D.D., Lovett, S., Paul, S.M., & Sheptak, S. (1990). A standardized interview that differentiates pregnancy and postpartum symptoms form clinical depression. *Birth*, 17(3), 121–130.

Bastin, J.P. (1989). Action stat: Postpartum hemorrhage. *Nursing 89*, 19(2), 33.

Beck, C.T. (1992). Postpartum depression: A phenomenological study. Presented at the National NAACOG Conference. Minneapolis, May 31–June 4.

Beck, C.T., Reynolds, M.A., & Rutowski, P. (1992). Maternity blues and postpartum depression. *Journal of Obstetric, Gynecologic, and Neonatal Nursing*, 21(4), 287–293.

Berchtold, N., & Burrough, M. (1990). Reaching out: Depression after delivery support group network. *Clinical Issues in Perinatal and Women's Health Nursing*, 1(3), 385–395.

Bhatia, N.N. (1992). Pelvic relaxation and urinary problems. In N.F. Hacker & J.G. Moore (Eds.), *Essential of obstetrics and gynecology*. Philadelphia: W.B. Saunders.

Boland, L. (1992). Postpartum depression: The silent disabler. Presented at NAACOG National Conference. Minneapolis, May 31–June 4.

Boyer, D.B. (1990). Prediction of postpartum depression. *Clinical Issues in Perinatal and Women's Health Issues*, 1(3), 359–369.

Busch, P., & Perrin, K. (1989). Postpartum depression: Assessing risk, restoring balance. RN, August, pp. 46–49.

Culp, R.E., & Osofsky, H.J. (1989). Effects of cesarean delivery on parental depression, marital adjustment, and mother-infant interaction. *Birth*, 16(2), 53–58.

Cunningham, F.G., MacDonald, P.C., & Gant, N.F. (1989). *Williams obstetrics* (18th ed.). Norwalk, Conn.: Appleton & Lange.

Deglin, J.H., & Vallerand, A.H. (1993). *Davis's drug guide for nurses* (3rd ed.). Philadelphia: F.A. Davis.

Gibbs, R.S., & Sweet, R.L. (1989). Clinical disorders. In R.K. Creasy & R. Resnik (Eds.), *Maternal-fetal medicine: Principles and practice* (2nd ed.). Philadelphia: W.B. Saunders.

Hall, L.A., Gurley, D.N., Sachs, B., & Kryscio, R.J. (1991). Psychosocial predictors of maternal depressive symptoms, parenting attitudes, and child behavior in single-parent families. *Nursing Research*, 40(4), 214–220.

Hayashi, R.H. (1992). Postpartum hemorrhage and puerperal sepsis. In N.F. Hacker & Moore, J.G. (Eds.), *Essentials of obstetrics and gynecology* (pp. 289–307). Philadelphia: W.B. Saunders.

Ingardia, C.J., & Pitcher, E.F. (1993). Additional medical complications in pregnancy. In R.A. Knuppel & J.E. Drukker (Eds.), *High-risk pregnancy: A team approach* (pp. 597–618). Philadelphia: W.B. Saunders.

Landry, S., Montgomery, J., & Walsh, S. (1989). Postpartum depression: A clinical view. *Maternal-Child Nursing Journal*, 18(1), 1–29.

Lawrence, R.A. (1989). *Breastfeeding: A guide for the medical profession* (3rd ed.). St. Louis: C.V. Mosby.

LeClerc, J.R., & Hirsh, J. (1988). Venous thromboembolic disorders. In G.N. Burrow & T.F. Ferris (Eds)., *Medical complications during pregnancy* (3rd ed.). Philadelphia: W.B. Saunders.

Martell, L.K. (1990). Postpartum depression as a family problem. *Maternal-Child Nursing Journal*, 15(2), 90–93.

McCormac, M. (1990). Managing hemorrhagic shock. *American Journal of Nursing*, 90(8), 22–29.

Nuwayhid, B., & Khalife, S. (1992). Medical complications of pregnancy. In N.F. Hacker & J.G. Moore (Eds.), *Essentials of obstetrics and gynecology* (pp. 197–222). Philadelphia: W.B. Saunders.

Rutherford, S.E., & Phelan, J.P. (1991). Deep venous thrombosis and pulmonary embolism in pregnancy. *Obstetrics and Gynecology Clinics of North America*, 18(2), 345–370.

Siskind, J. (1990). Handling hemorrhage wisely. *Nursing 90*, 20(3), 137–143.

Sternbach, G. (1989). John Homans: The dorsiflexion sign. *Journal of Emergency Medicine*, 7, 287–290.

Sweet, R., & Gibbs, R. (1990). *Infectious diseases of the female genital tract* (2nd ed.). Baltimore: Williams & Wilkins.

Taylor, E. (1989). Postnatal depression. What can a health visitor do? *Journal of Advanced Nursing*, 14, 877–886.

Ugarriza, D.N. (1992). Postpartum affective disorders: Incidence and treatment. *Journal of Psychosocial Nursing*, 30(5), 29–32.

28

High-Risk Newborn:

Complications Associated with Gestational Age and Development

Objectives

1. List risk factors that may lead to complications of gestational age and development in the newborn.
2. Explain the special problems of the preterm infant.
3. Identify common nursing diagnoses for preterm infants, and explain the nursing care for each.
4. Describe the complications that may result from premature birth.
5. Describe the characteristics and problems of the infant with postmaturity syndrome.
6. Explain the effects of intrauterine growth retardation.
7. Compare the problems of the large-for-gestational-age infant with those of the small-for-gestational-age infant.

Definitions

Apneic spells • Cessation of breathing for more than 15 seconds, accompanied by cyanosis or bradycardia.

Bronchopulmonary dysplasia (BPD) • Chronic pulmonary condition in which damage to the infant's lungs necessitates prolonged dependence on supplemental oxygen.

Compliance • Ability of the lungs and thorax to distend with air without resistance during respirations.

Enteral feeding • Nutrients supplied to the gastrointestinal tract orally or by feeding tube.

Intrauterine growth retardation (IUGR) • Failure of a fetus to grow as expected for gestational age.

Intraventricular hemorrhage (IVH) • Bleeding into the ventricles of the brain.

Large-for-gestational-age (LGA) infant • An infant whose size is above the 90th percentile for gestational age.

Low-birth-weight (LBW) infant • An infant weighing 2500 grams or less at birth.

Macrosomia • Abnormally large fetal size; infant birth weight over 4000 grams.

Necrotizing enterocolitis (NEC) • A condition of injury, invasion by bacteria, and possible necrosis of the intestines.

Non-compliance • Resistance of the lungs and thorax to distend with air during respirations.

Persistent fetal circulation • Failure of the pulmonary vessels to dilate and the ductus arteriosus to close; caused by low blood oxygen levels.

Postmaturity syndrome • Condition in which a

△ Alert for a high risk of exposure to substances to which universal precautions apply. See Appendix B for additional information about infection control.

postterm infant shows characteristics indicative of poor placental functioning before birth.

Postterm infant • An infant born at 42 or more weeks of gestation.

Preterm infant • An infant born before the beginning of the 38th week of gestation. Also called **premature infant.**

Pulse oximetry • Method of determining the level of blood oxygen saturation by sensors attached to the skin.

Respiratory distress syndrome (RDS) • Condition caused by insufficient production of surfactant in the lungs; results in atelectasis (collapse of the lung alveoli), **hypoxemia**, and **hypercapnia.**

Retinopathy of prematurity (ROP) • Condition in which interference with blood supply to the retina may cause decreased vision or blindness.

Small-for-gestational-age (SGA) infant • An infant whose size is below the 10th percentile for gestational age.

Total parenteral nutrition (TPN) • Intravenous infusion of all nutrients needed for metabolism and growth.

Transcutaneous oxygen/carbon dioxide monitoring • Method of continuous non-invasive measurement of oxygen and carbon dioxide levels in the skin.

Very-low-birth-weight (VLBW) infant • An infant weighing 1500 grams or less at birth.

Complications of the newborn may be obvious at birth or may become apparent later. The maternity nurse must recognize when risk factors for newborn problems are present and identify signs of complications to ensure immediate treatment. When complications are identified, the initial nursing care falls to the maternity nurse until the infant is transferred to the care of neonatal nurses in the neonatal intensive care unit (NICU) in the same or another facility. Parents of such infants ask nurses many questions about the infant's condition and care. This chapter is designed to provide nurses with knowledge of gestational complications of the newborn sufficient to deal with immediate nursing care needs and to form a basis for further study.

Care of High-Risk Newborns

Approximately 5 to 10 per cent of all newborns have some kind of illness, such as prematurity, congenital defects, or respiratory distress (Pettett et al, 1989). Nurses care for minor illness in the normal newborn nursery, but more serious problems necessitate care in specialized nurseries designed for that purpose. Nurses who work in NICU nurseries have additional education and experience to prepare them for this special role.

Regionalization of Care

Not every hospital is equipped to care for newborns who need complex treatment. Facilities offering such care use very expensive technical equipment and employ staff with specialized clinical expertise. The need for cost containment in health care prevents the feasibility of all hospitals providing neonatal intensive care.

Regionalization is a system whereby certain hospitals within a geographical area are designated to provide intensive care needed by sick newborns, and other hospitals within the area care for infants with less specialized needs. Hospitals are divided into three different levels (facilities at each level are able to provide care for infants with less acute needs as well):

- *Level* I facilities treat normal, low-risk mothers and newborns, who are the majority. They perform immediate resuscitation of infants with respiratory depression, treat physiologic jaundice and preterm infants weighing over 2000 g, and care for sick newborns until they can be transferred to a level II or III facility.
- *Level* II facilities provide care for infants with moderate- to high-risk problems. They may also serve as "step down" units for infants who have been in level III nurseries in the same or another hospital but no longer need that level of care. Examples of infants cared for in level II facilities are those with mild respiratory distress syndrome or suspected sepsis.
- *Level* III facilities offer services necessary for extremely high-risk infants. They are also called tertiary care centers. Examples of infants cared for in a level III facility are those who need prolonged treatment with ventilators or those with symptomatic congenital heart conditions (American Academy of Pediatrics and American College of Obstetricians and Gynecologists, 1992) (Fig. 28–1).

Transport

When the birth of an infant with a serious complication is suspected, the woman may be transferred to a tertiary care center before birth. This enables the

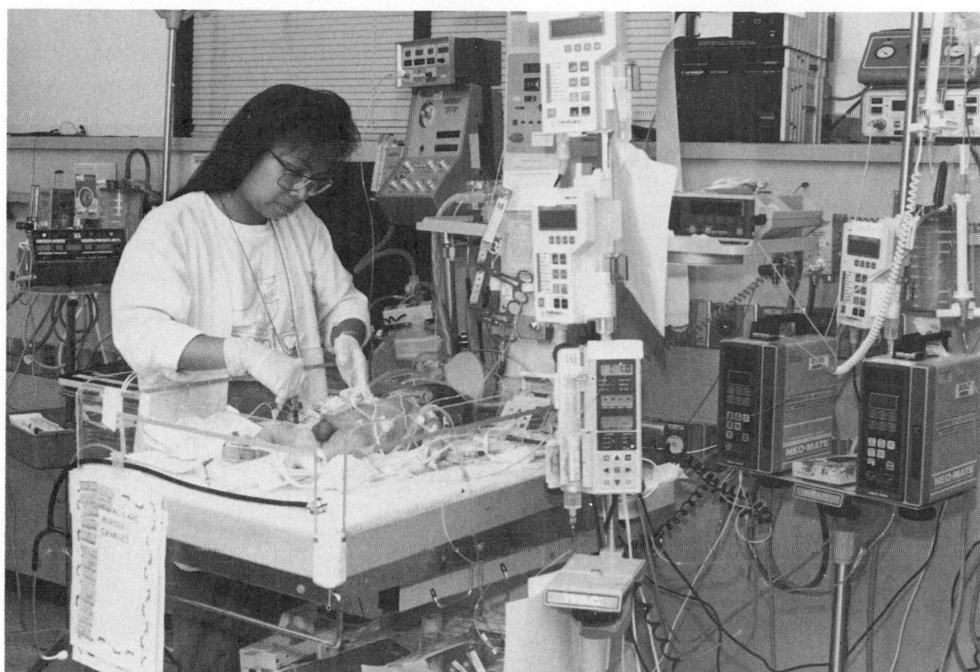

Figure 28–1

The infant in a neonatal intensive care nursery is cared for by nurses with highly specialized skills.

infant to receive essential highly technical care immediately and avoids the necessity of transporting a sick newborn in the critical hours after birth. It also prevents separating mothers from their sick newborns. When transfer before birth is impossible, care is provided for infants at the birth facility until they are stable enough to be transferred.

Not all infants with complications can be identified before birth. Women who have had normal pregnancies may experience unexpected problems during labor or delivery. Therefore, all maternity nurses must be prepared to give immediate care to the unexpectedly compromised newborn.

A special transport ambulance may take the infant to the new hospital. When traffic conditions or distance are a problem, an airplane or helicopter moves the infant. A team of specially prepared nurses, physicians, and respiratory therapists care for the infant during transit. In some situations, nurses manage transports alone.

When preparation is made for transferring an infant to another hospital, the nurse at the birth facility provides information about the infant's condition to nurses at the receiving agency. Thus, good assessment skills are essential for nurses to identify and communicate the infant's needs to other nurses who will assume care. If the nurses who will receive the infant have adequate information, they will be prepared to transfer the infant safely and there will be continuity of care.

Multidisciplinary Approach

The care of infants with problems at birth often necessitates collaboration between staff specialized in many different areas. In the hospital setting, this care may include nurses, nurse practitioners, physicians with different specialties, respiratory therapists, laboratory personnel, and pharmacists on a daily basis. Care from other professionals, including social workers, physical therapists, feeding specialists, psychologists, and infant development experts, may begin during the hospital stay and continue after the infant is discharged. Nurses must often coordinate this care and explain or clarify to parents what is being done.

Preterm Infants

Preterm infants are those delivered before the beginning of the 38th week of gestation. They are also called premature infants. Although these infants are born early, a gestational age assessment of their size and development may show that they are small, appropriate, or large for the amount of time that they have spent in the uterus. Most preterm infants are appropriate for their gestational age. (See Chapter 20 for a discussion of gestational age assessment.)

The word "preterm" can sometimes be confused

with the term "low birth weight" (LBW), which refers to infants weighing 2500 g (5 pounds, 8 ounces) or less at birth. Very-low-birth-weight (VLBW) infants weigh 1500 g (3 pounds, 5 ounces) or less at birth. Although most of these infants are preterm, others are full-term and have failed to grow normally while in the uterus, a condition called intrauterine growth retardation (IUGR).

Incidence and Etiology

SCOPE OF PROBLEM

More than 9 per cent of live births in the United States occur before the end of 37 weeks' gestation. Recent advances in technology have resulted in survival of more preterm infants at much lower birth weights than ever before. More than 90 per cent of infants weighing over 1500 g at birth, and 40 per cent of infants who weigh 750 g (1 pound, 10.5 ounces) at birth, now survive (Kliegman, 1990).

Although increased technology has allowed very small preterm infants to survive, the number of early births does not seem to be decreasing. In fact, the preterm birth rate has remained almost the same since the early 1960s (Main, 1991). In terms of medical expense, lost potential, and suffering of infants and their parents, preterm birth is extremely costly.

Care of very preterm infants raises ethical questions concerning the benefit of saving them at great expense versus the risk that they may have permanent, serious disabilities that may impair their chances to live normal, quality lives. Preterm infants may have long-term health problems, such as blindness, damage to the lungs and intestines, and mental retardation. Mild problems in development occur in 10 to 25 per cent of preterm infants, whereas 5 to 10 per cent have severe problems (Kliegman, 1990).

CAUSES

The exact causes of preterm birth are not known. All of the factors that place a pregnancy at risk should be considered potential causes of complications for the newborn as well. Difficulty during pregnancy may lead to preterm birth, and complications during labor or delivery may result in decreased oxygenation of the fetus or trauma during delivery.

One of the major factors associated with prematurity is low socioeconomic status of the pregnant woman, because a combination of risk factors are often present in women who are poor. These women are more likely to be malnourished, young, unmarried, and have frequent, closely spaced pregnancies. Poor women have little money and inadequate transportation for health care before or during pregnancy. As a result, they may begin pregnancy in poor health and may receive little or no prenatal care. Complications may not be discovered until late in the pregnancy or in labor, when they may be more difficult to treat. Substance abuse may occur more often among (but certainly is not limited to) the poor. All of these factors together increase the risk of complications of all kinds for women who live in poverty.

PREVENTION

Prevention of preterm birth is best accomplished by provision of adequate prenatal care for every pregnant woman to identify and treat risk factors as early as possible. Teaching women signs of preterm labor will help them seek care when halting the labor is still a possibility (see Chapter 26, p. 750).

Characteristics of Preterm Infants

Although the estimated due date is used before delivery to determine whether or not labor is preterm, the gestational age assessment made after birth is the most accurate method of computing the number of weeks that the infant spent in the uterus (see Chapter 20, p. 535). Characteristics of preterm infants vary by gestational age. For example, the appearance and problems of infants born at 36 weeks' gestation are different from those of infants born at 26 weeks' gestation. However, some characteristics are common to all preterm infants.

APPEARANCE

Preterm infants appear frail and weak. Not only are they smaller than full-term infants, they have underdeveloped flexor muscles and muscle tone. Their extremities are limp and remain extended, offering little or no resistance when moved. Premature newborns typically lie in an extended position (see Fig. 20–8B, p. 537). The head of the normal preterm infant is large in comparison to the rest of the body.

Preterm infants lack subcutaneous fat, which makes their thin skin appear red and almost transparent, with blood vessels clearly visible. The nipples and areola may be barely perceptible, whereas vernix caseosa and lanugo may be abundant. Plantar creases are absent in infants less than 32 weeks' gestation. As gestational age progresses, faint lines appear at the top of the sole first, then deeper lines appear that eventually cover the entire sole (see Fig. 20–16, p. 541).

The pinna of the ear may appear flat, lacking the rolled-over look of full-term ears (see Fig. 20–18C, p. 542). When folded, the ears are soft and may remain folded or return slowly to the original position because there is little cartilage. The male infant may have undescended testes, with a small, smooth scrotal sac. In the female infant, the clitoris and labia minora are large and uncovered by the small, separated labia majora (see Figs. 20–19 and 20–20, pp. 542 and 543).

BEHAVIOR

The behavior of preterm infants differs from that of full-term infants because of the stress of having to adjust to extrauterine life before they are ready. They have little excess energy for maintaining muscle tone. Premature newborns are easily exhausted from noise and routine activities. Their response is varied, including lowered oxygenation levels and behavior changes. The cry is feeble and seldom heard because the infant is too weak to cry.

✔ Check Your Reading

1. Why are poor women at increased risk of having preterm infants?
2. How does the appearance of a preterm infant differ from that of a full-term infant?

Common Problems of Preterm Infants

Because preterm infants are "unfinished" in their growth and development, they are prone to a number of problems.

RESPIRATORY PROBLEMS

Problems of the respiratory system are a major concern because preterm newborns must go through the same processes as the full-term infant to begin breathing, but with less mature lungs.

Surfactant. The presence of surfactant in adequate amounts is of primary importance. Surfactant reduces surface tension in the alveoli during inspiration and allows them to remain partially open during expiration. This decreases the amount of negative pressure necessary for each breath. When sufficient surfactant is not present, the lungs are stiff and non-compliant, and each breath requires a large amount of energy. On expiration, alveoli without enough surfactant will collapse.

Surfactant is first produced in the alveoli at 22 weeks of gestation. By 34 to 36 weeks, production of surfactant is usually mature enough to enable the infant to breathe normally outside the uterus (Hagedorn et al, 1993). If an infant is born before surfactant production is adequate, respiratory distress syndrome may develop (see Chapter 29, p. 842).

Surfactant is a composite of a number of different substances. Three of the components are lecithin, sphingomyelin, and phosphatidyglycerol, which can be detected by tests on amniotic fluid. These tests can predict whether the fetal lungs are mature enough so that survival outside of the uterus is possible. Tests for fetal lung maturity are discussed in Chapter 10.

Periodic Breathing and Apneic Spells. Although periodic breathing occurs occasionally in the full-term infant, it occurs more often in premature infants, especially those less than 36 weeks of gestation. It consists of an apneic period of 5 to 10 seconds followed by normal respirations for 10 to 15 seconds, with an overall respiratory rate of 30 to 40 breaths/minute. Other signs of distress, such as tachycardia or cyanosis, do not result from the short period of apnea.

Anytime bradycardia or cyanosis occurs during a period without breathing, the episode is called an apneic spell. Apneic spells occur in about a quarter of preterm infants. Generally, breathing stops for longer than 15 seconds and is accompanied by bradycardia and cyanosis. The spells may occur along with periodic breathing, and the infant may require stimulation.

Other Respiratory Problems. The weak or absent cough reflex and the very small air passages make the preterm infant susceptible to obstruction by mucus. Preterm infants, like full-term newborns, are obligate nose breathers. Therefore, obstruction of the nasal passages may lead to respiratory distress.

Signs of respiratory distress are common in preterm infants. They are similar to those for the normal newborn (see Chapter 19, p. 478). Retractions are particularly noticeable in the preterm infant, whose weak chest wall is drawn in with each inspiration. The excessive compliance of the chest cage during retractions may interfere with full expansion of the lungs. Grunting increases the pressure within the alveoli so that more oxygen can be absorbed and may be an early sign of respiratory distress syndrome. The Silverman-Andersen index is a useful tool for evaluating the degree of respiratory distress (Fig. 28–2).

CIRCULATORY PROBLEMS

Preterm infants may not make the changes from fetal to neonatal circulation that are necessary if their lungs do not remain fully expanded and blood oxygen levels do not rise normally. This is because inadequate oxygenation results in vasoconstriction, in-

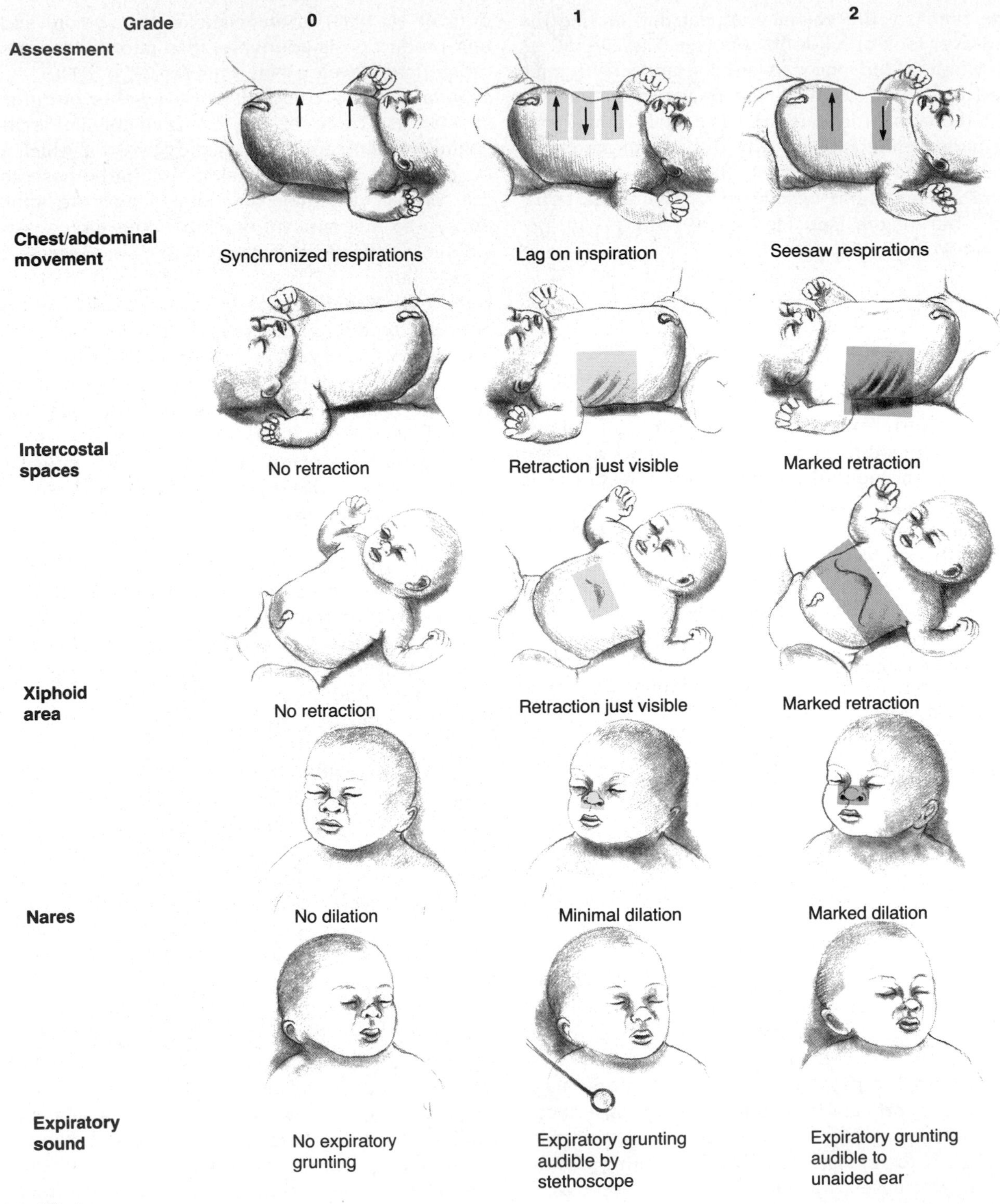

Figure 28–2

Assessment of respiratory distress. The Silverman-Andersen index is used to score the infant's degree of respiratory difficulty. The score for individual criteria matches the grade, with a total possible score of 10 indicating severe distress. (Modified from Silverman, W., & Andersen, D. [1956]. A cold clinical trial of effects of water mist on obstructive respiratory signs, death rate and necropsy findings among premature infants. *Pediatrics*, 17,4.)

stead of the normal dilation, of the pulmonary vessels and produces increased resistance of the lungs. At the same time, hypoxia brings about relaxation, instead of constriction, of the ductus arteriosus, allowing blood from the aorta to return to the lungs. This further increases pulmonary resistance. Thus, the effects of hypoxia are changes that result in more hypoxia. This is called persistent fetal circulation.

✔ Check Your Reading

3. How does surfactant affect the preterm infant's ability to breathe?
4. What other factors contribute to respiratory problems in preterm infants?

THERMOREGULATORY PROBLEMS

Although heat loss can be a problem for full-term infants, it is even more significant in those who are born preterm. Because the skin is thin with blood vessels near the surface, and scant subcutaneous fat is present to serve as insulation, rapid heat loss results. The shorter time in the uterus allows for less brown fat accumulation before birth, impairing the preterm infant's ability to produce heat by thermogenesis (brown fat is discussed in Chapter 19).

The preterm infant has a large head and more body surface area in proportion to size than the full-term infant. Although the term infant maintains heat by flexion of the extremities, the limp, extended body of the preterm newborn exposes a greater surface area to the air for heat loss. The temperature control center of the brain of preterm infants is less mature and may be further impaired by asphyxia.

Whereas full-term newborns increase metabolism to produce heat, preterm infants are less able to do this. Hypoglycemia and respiratory problems are more likely to develop. This limits the glucose and oxygen available to increase metabolism as a method of heat production. Vasoconstriction, which occurs when body temperature drops, may lead to metabolic acidosis, pulmonary vasoconstriction, interference with production of surfactant, and more respiratory difficulty.

NUTRITIONAL PROBLEMS

The need for adequate nutrition in the preterm newborn is especially acute because the infant is born before the full accumulation of nutrient stores during the last trimester of pregnancy. Full-term newborns have reservoirs of calcium, iron, and other substances, but these are lacking in preterm infants. Fat stores may be minimal or absent, and glucose reserves are used up soon after birth.

Nutrients are needed not only to promote growth but to prevent injury to the brain. Hypoglycemia is a major concern because of the lack of glucose and fat reserves. Low blood glucose develops very quickly and must be prevented or treated quickly because the brain needs a steady supply of glucose.

Preterm infants need 120 to 150 kcal/kg/day, which is higher than the 110 to 120 kcal/kg/day needed by the full-term newborn. They also need more protein, iron, calcium, and phosphorus. Preterm infants may be given special formulas designed to meet these needs.

The gastrointestinal tract of preterm infants does not absorb nutrients as well as that of full-term infants. Although they digest protein and carbohydrate fairly well, preterm newborns have insufficient bile acids and pancreatic lipase to absorb fat adequately. Their smaller stomach capacity limits the volume that they can tolerate at each feeding.

Coordination of sucking and swallowing usually occurs at about 32 to 34 weeks of gestation (Price and Kalhan, 1993). Infants less than 34 weeks' gestation or weighing under 1600 g generally have difficulty coordinating sucking, swallowing, and breathing. The gag reflex, which helps prevent aspiration, is not functional until about 36 weeks. Oral feeding may cause the very weak infant to expend too much oxygen and glucose. When sucking is uncoordinated or takes too much energy, the infant must receive intravenous or gavage feedings.

PROBLEMS WITH FLUID AND ELECTROLYTE BALANCE

Preterm infants lose fluid more easily than full-term newborns, through thin skin that has little protective subcutaneous fat. Their skin has a greater water content and is more permeable than the skin of the term infant. The large surface area in proportion to body weight and lack of flexion further increase insensible water losses. Radiant warmers and the heat from phototherapy lights may cause even more fluid loss through the skin. Radiant warmers may heighten insensible water losses enough to result in a 40 to 100 per cent increase in fluid needs (Blake and Murray, 1993). Water loss also occurs through the respiratory and gastrointestinal tracts. The rapid respiratory rate and the use of oxygen can increase fluid loss from the lungs. Loose stools will lead to rapid dehydration.

Development of the kidneys is not complete until approximately 35 weeks of gestation. The ability of the kidneys to concentrate or dilute urine is poor before that time, causing a fragile balance between dehydration and overhydration. Although there is variation according to size and gestational age, the fluid needs of preterm infants average 110 to 140 ml/kg/day after the first 2 days of life (Price and Kalhan, 1993). Monitoring intake and output of fluids is important in determining fluid balance. Normal urinary output is 1 to 3 ml/kg/hour.

Regulation of electrolytes by the kidneys is also a problem. Preterm infants need higher intakes of sodium because the kidneys do not reabsorb it as well as in full-term infants. However, if they receive sodium, they may be unable to increase sodium excretion adequately and are susceptible to sodium and water overload as a result.

PROBLEMS WITH INFECTION

The incidence of infection in preterm infants is three to ten times greater than that in full-term newborns (Behrman, 1992). Many preterm infants have one or more episodes of sepsis during their hospital stay. They have a large number of risk factors for infections. The mother may have had an infection that caused labor to begin prematurely. This exposed the infant to the same infection. The infant may not have been in the uterus long enough to receive passive immunity from the transfer of antibodies from the mother during the third trimester. In addition, the immune response is less mature than that of the full-term newborn.

Preterm infants are often exposed to situations that may cause infection. Their skin is fragile, permeable, and easily damaged by removal of tape or by pressure from equipment. They are subject to invasive procedures such as insertion of intravenous lines and drawing of blood specimens. Infections may develop from exposure to family members or staff members who have contagious diseases. Even the normal flora on the hands of caretakers may cause sepsis. Great caution must be taken at all times to protect the preterm infant from infection as much as possible.

Therapeutic Management of Preterm Infants

Therapeutic management of the preterm neonate immediately after birth focuses on respiratory care as necessary. If resuscitation measures are needed, they are essentially the same as for the full-term infant (see Chapter 29). The infant may need an endotracheal tube and mechanical ventilation. Continuous positive airway pressure may be necessary to keep the alveoli open and improve expansion of the lungs. High-frequency jet ventilation may be used to provide very fast, frequent respirations with less pressure than other methods.

A hood is often used for infants who are able to breathe alone but who need extra oxygen. The hood is a plastic box-like device that fits over the infant's head. The infant breathes the higher levels of oxygen surrounding the head, and there is no interference with access to the rest of the infant's body for care (Fig. 28–3).

Oxygen may also be given by nasal cannula for the infant who breathes well alone. The cannula must be kept in place by tape or ties. Many infants go home with oxygen delivered via nasal cannula. Oxygen must be humidified to prevent insensible water loss and drying of the delicate mucous membranes. It is warmed to maintain body temperature.

When oxygen is administered, the level of oxygen in the infant's blood is monitored. Arterial blood may be drawn for testing arterial oxygen levels. Pulse oximetry or transcutaneous monitoring may also be used. They are less invasive and provide continuous information about Po_2 levels through sensors attached to the skin.

Total parenteral nutrition (TPN) may be necessary for infants unable to take nutrients orally. TPN is the intravenous infusion of a solution containing all the nutrients needed for metabolism and growth. It provides calories, amino acids, fatty acids, vitamins, and minerals in amounts adapted to infants' specific needs.

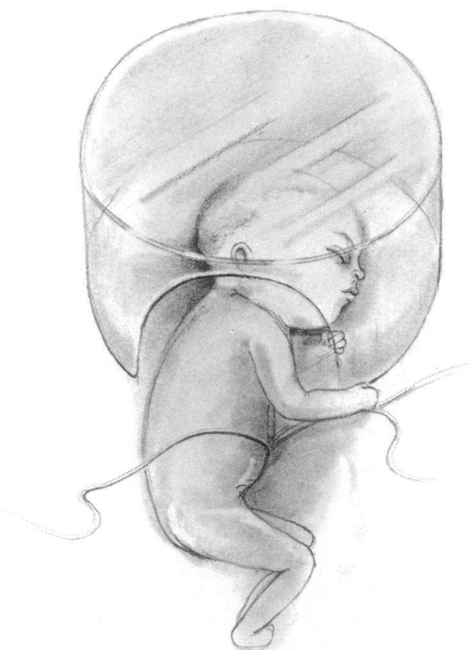

Figure 28–3

The oxygen hood is one way of delivering oxygen to an infant who can breathe unassisted.

Enteral feedings (feeding into the gastrointestinal tract given orally or by feeding tube) are started as soon as possible because they may help promote intestinal growth and maturity (Townsend et al, 1993). Although infants more than 34 weeks' gestation or weighing over 1800 g (4 pounds) are usually fed the same formulas as term infants, less mature infants may need special formulas. These formulas are adapted to meet the need for easily digestible, concentrated nutrients in a smaller volume of fluid. They often have 24 or 27 kcal/ounce (instead of 20 kcal/ounce used for the full-term infant) to meet the requirement for 120 to 150 kcal/kg/day. They contain added calcium, phosphorus, and vitamins needed by the preterm infant.

Other therapeutic management includes the regulation of intravenous fluids and treatment of complications that may arise. Common complications are respiratory distress syndrome, shock, sepsis, and hyperbilirubinemia (see Chapter 29).

Nursing Considerations

The nurse has an important collaborative role in care of the preterm infant. The nurse's role is to:

- Observe for changes in the infant's condition and responses to treatment
- Carry out the physician's or nurse practitioner's orders
- Monitor machinery to see that it is functioning properly

An important nursing responsibility is coordinating care by different health care workers. For example, many different tests are often needed, and the nurse must see that they are done properly, yet protect the infant from overstimulation.

OXYGENATION

Observe for changes in respiratory status at all times. Note the infant's response to various procedures, increasing or decreasing dependence on assistance in breathing, or need for oxygen. Ventilators and other respiratory equipment are often managed by the respiratory therapist, but the nurse must be knowledgeable about them as well. In some hospitals, the nurse adjusts the respiratory equipment according to the infant's responses.

Listen carefully for abnormal sounds of the heart and lungs when the infant is first admitted. Note changes in sounds that indicate improvement or deterioration in the infant's condition. A patent ductus arteriosus may cause a murmur at first, but it may close without treatment. Changes in breath sounds may indicate resolving atelectasis or a pneumothorax.

Note the presence of peripheral cyanosis (involving the hands and feet), which is normal, or central cyanosis (of the mucous membranes and trunk), which is abnormal. If cyanosis occurs, determine whether it is present at all times or only at certain times, such as during feeding or crying. Note changes in pulse oximeter readings during rest and activities like feeding that may result in increased oxygen need.

FLUID BALANCE

The nurse's role in maintenance of fluid balance is crucial. Because of the infant's small size, immature kidney function, and increased insensible water loss, fluid balance may be easily upset. Observe for and prevent fluid overload or deficit. Assess the infant's intake and output by all routes. Parenteral, feeding tube, or oral fluids are included when measuring intake. Carefully measure output from drainage tubes and urine. A urine output of less than 1 ml/kg/hour may indicate inadequate fluid intake, whereas more than 3 ml/kg/hour is a sign of overhydration (Gomella, 1992).

Intravenous Fluids. Regulate intravenous fluids carefully. Prevent fluid volume overload by maintaining parenteral fluids at the proper rate with an infusion control device. Dilute intravenous medications in as little fluid as is consistent with safe administration of the drug, and include this fluid when measuring intake. Starting intravenous lines on infants with  poor veins is a lengthy, difficult procedure. Restrain infants as necessary to prevent infiltration. Some fluids will cause extensive damage as a result of tissue sloughing if they infiltrate.

Urinary Output. There are several methods of measuring urinary output. Plastic bags that adhere to the perineum are often not suitable for the preterm infant because they may damage the fragile skin. Weighing diapers is less invasive to the infant. Subtract the weight of dry diapers from the weight when they are wet to determine the amount of urine excreted. One gram is equivalent to 1 ml of urine. However, humidification may add moisture to the diaper, whereas a radiant warmer may cause evaporation of urine on the diaper. When precise measurement is essential, fasten superabsorbent diapers around the infant (rather than placing open diapers under the infant) and check for urine output at least every 30 minutes (Fox, 1992).

Check specific gravity to determine if urine is more concentrated or dilute than expected. While wearing clean gloves, squeeze drops of urine from the diaper into a container. If the amount of urine in the diaper is small, place bits of the inner diaper lining into a syringe, and use the plunger to squeeze out a sample of urine for testing. Another method of collecting urine is by placing cotton balls at the perineum. The specific gravity should range between 1.002 and 1.010 (Adcock and Consolvo, 1993).

Weight. Changes in the infant's weight can give an indication of fluid gain or loss, especially when they are sudden and greater than would be expected from feeding changes. Weigh the undressed infant daily at the same time of day with the same scale. Very small infants are often placed in a bed that has a scale on it so that they do not have to be disturbed for daily weighing.

Signs of Dehydration or Overhydration. Observe for signs that indicate that the infant has received too little or too much fluid. Early signs of dehydration include decreased urine output and increased specific gravity. Weight loss may exceed that expected for the infant's age and general condition. Dry skin or mucous membranes, sunken anterior fontanelle, and poor tissue turgor are late signs.

Critical to Remember

Signs of Fluid Imbalance in the Newborn

Dehydration

- Urine output < 1 ml/kg/24 hours
- Urine specific gravity > 1.010
- Weight loss
- Dry skin and mucous membranes
- Sunken anterior fontanelle
- Poor tissue turgor
- Blood: elevated sodium, protein, and hematocrit levels

Overhydration

- Urine output > 3 ml/kg/24 hours
- Urine specific gravity < 1.002
- Edema
- Weight gain
- Bulging fontanelles
- Blood: decreased sodium, protein, and hematocrit levels
- Moist breath sounds
- Difficulty breathing

Changes in the blood include increased sodium, protein, and hematocrit levels due to decreased plasma volume.

Signs of overhydration include increased output of urine with a below-normal specific gravity. Edema and weight gain occur from retention of fluids. Bulging fontanelles and decreased blood sodium, protein, and hematocrit levels are also present. Complications of excess fluid may include patent ductus arteriosus and congestive heart failure. (See Critical to Remember: Signs of Fluid Imbalance.)

✔ Check Your Reading

5. Why are preterm infants more likely to experience cold stress than full-term infants?
6. What special problems related to feeding, fluid balance, and infections occur in preterm infants?

Common Complications of Preterm Infants

Complications of the preterm infant vary widely, according to the infant's gestational age at birth and the treatment required to support life. Respiratory distress syndrome is a common complication of the lungs. Hyperbilirubinemia and patent ductus arteriosus may also occur. Because these conditions are also found in full-term infants, they are discussed in Chapter 29. However, four complications that commonly occur in preterm infants are discussed here: intraventricular hemorrhage, retinopathy of prematurity, necrotizing enterocolitis, and bronchopulmonary dysplasia. The incidence of each of these conditions increases as the gestational age and the birth weight of the infant decrease.

INTRAVENTRICULAR HEMORRHAGE

Intraventricular hemorrhage (IVH) results from rupture of the fragile blood vessels in the germinal matrix, located around the ventricles of the brain. It occurs most often during the first 2 days of life in 20 to 30 per cent of infants less than 32 weeks of gestation or weighing under 1500 g (Minarcik and Beachy, 1993). IVH is most often associated with respiratory difficulty and hypoxia, resulting in increased blood pressure, vasodilation, and rupture of blood vessels.

Hemorrhage is graded 1 through 4, according to the amount of bleeding. Grade 1 is a very small bleed outside ventricle walls, producing few, if any, clinical changes. Grade 2 hemorrhage extends into the lateral ventricles, and grade 3 distends at least one ventricle. Grade 4 hemorrhage causes ventricular dilation and damage to brain tissue. Whereas there is no increase in complications or mortality with grade 1 or 2 hemorrhages, infants with grade 3 and 4 hemorrhages are likely to have neurological abnormalities and developmental delays. Those with grade 4 hemorrhage have a poor survival rate. The mortality rate for all infants with IVH is 25 to 50 per cent (Blackburn, 1993).

Signs of IVH are determined by the severity of the hemorrhage. They may include lethargy, poor muscle tone, deterioration of respiratory status with cyanosis or apnea, drop in hematocrit level, decreased reflexes, full or bulging fontanelle, and seizures. Because some infants show no signs, screening by ultrasonography, magnetic resonance imaging, or computed tomography is generally performed on preterm infants.

Treatment is supportive and focuses on maintaining respiratory function and dealing with other complications. Lumbar taps to drain the blood may be

necessary, or the bleeding may be left to resolve on its own. Hydrocephalus may develop, necessitating a shunt to drain cerebrospinal fluid. The nurse should measure the head circumference daily and observe the infant for changes in neurological status.

RETINOPATHY OF PREMATURITY

Retinopathy of prematurity (ROP), also called retrolental fibroplasia (RLF), is a condition that may result in visual impairment or blindness in preterm infants. ROP usually occurs in infants less than 36 weeks of gestation or weighing under 1500 g.

ROP is due to damage to immature blood vessels in the retina of the eye. Although the exact cause of the damage is unknown, it is thought to result partly from high arterial blood oxygen levels. It is the level of oxygen in the blood rather than the amount of oxygen that the infant receives that is important. Because ROP has developed in some infants who have not received oxygen, other causative factors are now being considered.

The incidence of ROP decreased when accurate monitoring of PaO_2 levels became available, but it has become more common since treatment and survival of VLBW infants have become possible. These infants may need higher levels of oxygen and have a variety of other problems that affect oxygen levels and necessitate intensive treatments. This combination of factors may be the cause of the increased incidence of ROP to these very immature infants.

In ROP, immature blood vessels in the retina of the eye constrict and become permanently occluded. New vessels proliferate, extending throughout the retina and into the vitreous of the eye. There may be hemorrhages from the fragile vessels, causing scarring, traction on the retina, and retinal detachment. On the other hand, there may be a spontaneous regression without impairment of vision.

Treatment involves screening of LBW infants between 4 and 8 weeks after birth to detect whether changes of the eye are occurring. Cryotherapy and laser surgery have been used to destroy the proliferating blood vessels or to reattach the retina.

NECROTIZING ENTEROCOLITIS

Necrotizing enterocolitis (NEC) is a serious condition of the intestinal tract with a 20–40 per cent mortality rate (Byrne, 1991). Although the exact causes are unknown, the condition seems to be preceded by injury to the intestinal mucosa from interference with blood supply. When asphyxia or other conditions decrease flow of blood to the intestines, the resulting ischemia of the tissue may make it more susceptible to invasion with bacteria. When infants are fed, bacteria may proliferate, and gas-forming organisms may invade the intestinal wall. Eventually, necrosis, perforation, and peritonitis may occur.

Signs of NEC are abdominal distention, increased gastric residuals, decreased or absent bowel sounds, vomiting, and blood in the stools. On x-rays, loops of bowel dilated with air and layers of gas in the intestinal wall may be seen. Free air in the peritoneum indicates that perforation has occurred.

Treatment includes antibiotics, discontinuation of oral feedings, and use of parenteral nutrition to rest the intestines. Surgery may be necessary if there is perforation. The necrotic area is removed, and an ostomy may be performed.

BRONCHOPULMONARY DYSPLASIA

Bronchopulmonary dysplasia (BPD) is a chronic condition occurring in as many as 30 per cent of infants treated with mechanical ventilation (Hagedorn et al, 1993). A combination of factors probably cause the condition. Part of the cause is damage to the alveoli and lining of the respiratory tract from oxygen and high pressures of pulmonary ventilation that may be necessary to keep very immature infants alive.

The major sign of BPD is inability of the infant to be weaned from oxygen as quickly as expected. The infant becomes cyanotic and has other respiratory difficulty if oxygen is decreased. Characteristic changes in the lungs are seen on x-rays.

Treatment is supportive with gradual decrease in the amount of oxygen, bronchodilators, and antibiotics as necessary. The infant may go home on long-term oxygen therapy, and some need frequent rehospitalization for respiratory infections.

Formation of new alveoli, which take the place of those destroyed by BPD, brings about gradual im-

Text continued on page 818

Nursing Care Plan 28–1

The Preterm Infant

Assessment: Juan was born at 33 weeks' gestation and weighs 1800 g (4 pounds). He breathes on his own with oxygen by hood. He has increased secretions and tends to regurgitate small amounts of gavage feedings. He shows nasal flaring and moist respirations before suctioning. He becomes fatigued easily, and, when fatigued, has increased respiratory distress.

Nursing Diagnosis: Ineffective Airway Clearance related to inability to manage own secretions secondary to weakness and fatigue.

Goals:
Juan will attain and maintain a patent airway with respiratory rate of 30 to 60 breaths/minute and clear breath sounds throughout hospital stay.

Intervention:	Rationale:
1. Keep Juan in a side-lying or prone position, or raise head of bed and place a diaper roll under shoulders.	1. Positions promote drainage of secretions or regurgitated formula. Prone position decreases respiratory effort. Slight elevation of shoulders with diaper roll straightens airway.
2. Plan to vary Juan's position every 1 to 2 hours when care is given.	2. Clustering nursing care prevents disturbing infant unnecessarily. Position variation provides for drainage of all airways.
3. Keep suction available at all times. Keep bulb syringe in crib. Check wall suction at beginning of shift to be sure that it functions properly. Have the proper size oxygen mask available at all times.	3. Suction or an oxygen mask may be needed unexpectedly. Having equipment available and functioning prevents delays.
4. Suction gently every hour or as indicated by accumulation of secretions in upper airways. If suctioning of nose is necessary, suction mouth first.	4. Gentle suction avoids trauma to airways. Removal of secretions increases air flow into the lungs. When the nose is suctioned, infants may gasp. Suctioning mouth before nose ensures that there are no fluids in the mouth that might be aspirated when the infant gasps.
5. Observe for fatigue, drop in oxygen saturation levels, and color or heart rate changes during any treatments given as part of Juan's care. Stop briefly to allow Juan to recover if they occur.	5. These signs show that infant may need rest or suctioning. Treatment can be fatiguing to infant.
6. Maintain adequate hydration. (Infants weighing 1800 g need an intake of 198 to 252 ml of fluid per day as ordered by the physician.) Observe for signs of dehydration, including thickened respiratory secretions, urine output of less than 1.8 ml/hour, specific gravity over 1.010, or dry mucous membranes.	6. Adequate hydration helps liquefy secretions so that they can be removed more easily. Thick, dry secretions could obstruct air passages.

Evaluation:
Juan attains and maintains patent airway with a respiratory rate between 30 and 60 breaths/minute and clear breath sounds.

Nursing Care Plan 28–1 Continued

The Preterm Infant

Assessment: Juan needs many treatments throughout the day. He demonstrates pallor and increased respiratory rate when tired. Noises tend to cause a drop in oxygen saturation. When held or disturbed for care, Juan may stiffen and extend his arms with the fingers splayed. He sleeps most of the time when he is undisturbed.

Nursing Diagnosis: Activity Intolerance related to weakness, fatigue, and possible overstimulation.

Goals:

1. Juan will not show signs of overstimulation (increased respirations, pallor, decreased oxygen saturation level, stiffening of arms and legs, or splaying of fingers) as a result of normal activity.
2. Juan will increase tolerance to activity gradually as demonstrated by fewer signs of fatigue or stress.

Intervention:	Rationale:
1. Schedule routine care to correspond to Juan's natural awake periods, whenever possible.	1. Preterm infants need undisturbed sleep to promote growth.
2. Schedule periods of uninterrupted rest, especially before and after energy-draining activities.	2. Infants tolerate activities best when they begin in a rested state and are allowed to recover from them before other activities are necessary.
3. Experiment with grouping care to determine the number and combination of care activities that Juan tolerates best.	3. Allows flexible nursing care, individualized to meet the infant's needs. Grouping accomplishes more tasks at once so that longer rest periods are possible between tasks. However, too many activities may cause too much fatigue.
4. Assess carefully to determine what activities bring about signs of overstimulation and fatigue: changes in color, respirations, or pulse; stiff, extended extremities; worried, hyperalert expression. Stop activity and allow short period of rest, if possible.	4. Allows infant to recover at first sign of distress before fatigue level becomes excessive.
5. Keep noise level around Juan as low as possible. Avoid talking unnecessarily (except talking gently to Juan during care), open and close doors softly, reduce volume on alarms and respond to them quickly.	5. Noise may be overstimulating and result in increased oxygen need.
6. Reduce non-essential lighting. Place Juan's bed facing away from bright lights. Partially cover incubator over Juan's head to keep out light, but allow visualization of infant. Place Juan in a prone position.	6. Continuous lighting interferes with infant's sleep. Reducing light in infant's face will increase rest.
7. Use blanket rolls to form "boundaries" around Juan.	7. Enclosed space promotes rest and comfort by preventing rubbing against hard walls of bed. Similar to small space of uterus.
8. Inform others of what works best in decreasing fatigue and stimulation for Juan. Tape signs on the bed to provide this information to parents and others.	8. All caregivers should have information available to help meet the infant's needs consistently.
9. Explain Juan's needs for rest and low stimulation to parents. Suggest ways that they can interact appropriately to meet Juan's needs, and point out signs that he is receiving too much stimulation.	9. Parents who are informed can care for infant appropriately and feel that they are members of the team and parenting their child by learning his needs.

Evaluation:
Juan gradually shows increased ability to tolerate progressive activity with fewer episodes of overstimulation. His respirations and oxygen saturation levels remain stable, and he rarely stiffens his arms and legs during activity.

Nursing Care Plan continued on following page

Nursing Care Plan 28–1 *Continued*

The Preterm Infant

Assessment: Juan begins to take feedings by nipple supplemented by gavage when he becomes too tired. He has occasional episodes of increased respirations or short cyanotic spells when fed. He sometimes takes only half the feeding before falling asleep and must receive the rest by gavage. Juan's mother has decided to formula feed.

Nursing Diagnosis: High Risk for Altered Nutrition: Less Than Body Requirements related to fatigue during feedings.

Goals:
Juan will:

1. Take in 264 to 330 kcal/day to meet his needs at a weight of 2200 g.
2. Gain approximately 30 g daily.
3. Complete nipple feedings without signs of excessive fatigue (such as increased respiratory rate or falling asleep during feeding).

Intervention:	**Rationale:**
1. Schedule nursing care to provide for a rest period before and after nipple feedings.	1. Nippling consumes a great deal of energy. Rest helps prevent excessive fatigue that might prevent infant from completing the feeding.
2. Gather equipment. Use a feeding container (such as a Volutrol) on which each milliliter is marked. Warm milk to room temperature or slightly warmer. Place container in warm water to warm. Do not use microwave ovens to warm.	2. Having all equipment ready prevents wasted motion and ensures that infant is fed without interruption. A preemie nipple requires less energy for sucking. Exact measurement of the amount taken is important to ensure that infant receives required nutrients. Some infants will take slightly warmed milk better than milk at room temperature. Microwaving provides uneven heating of formula and may cause infant to be burned.
3. Wrap Juan in warmed blankets and place a hat on his head. Feed him in incubator or under warmer if needed.	3. Hat and blankets help maintain temperature during time infant is out of incubator. If infant has difficulty maintaining temperature, incubator or warmer provides warmth during feedings.
4. Position Juan facing the nurse. Feed slowly, with frequent stops to burp gently.	4. Position allows nurse to watch infant suck, note response to feeding, and see regurgitation immediately. Slow feeding is necessary because of infant's decreased energy. The preterm infant may swallow more air than the full-term infant because sucking is less efficient.
5. Observe for coughing, gagging, cyanosis, bradycardia, apnea, increased respirations, or falling asleep before feeding is finished. Finish feeding by gavage if necessary.	5. These signs show difficulty coordinating sucking, swallowing, and breathing and possibility of aspiration or excess fatigue. Finishing the feeding by gavage conserves energy and prevents aspiration.
6. Position Juan on the right side or prone, with his head elevated approximately 30 degrees after feeding.	6. If regurgitation occurs, fluid will run out of mouth easily so that infant will not aspirate it. The right-side position and elevation of the head allow gravity to help empty the stomach.

Evaluation:
Juan consumes an average of 300 calories and gains an average of 31 g daily. He gradually takes more of his feeding by nipple and rarely needs gavage feeding to finish it. His respiratory rate remains under 60 breaths/minute, and he stays awake for the entire feeding.

Nursing Care Plan 28–1 Continued

The Preterm Infant

Assessment: As Juan progresses, he is able to be taken out of the incubator for short periods of time. However, his axillary temperature drops below 36.5°C (97.7°F) sporadically when he is removed from the incubator. As his weight nears 2000 g, plans are made to wean him gradually from added heat.

Nursing Diagnosis: Ineffective Thermoregulation related to exaggerated heat loss secondary to lack of subcutaneous fat and immature temperature control center in brain.

Goals:
Juan will:

1. Maintain axillary temperature between 36.5° and 37.5°C (97.7° and 99.5°F) throughout hospital stay.
2. Need gradually decreasing amounts of added heat to maintain his body temperature until he moves to an open crib.

Intervention:	Rationale:
1. Wrap Juan with warm blankets, and apply a hat when taking him from the incubator. Wrap each blanket individually.	1. Heat from the blankets helps infant withstand the change in environmental temperature. Wrapping blankets separately uses air to increase insulation.
2. Check Juan's axillary temperature every 30 to 60 minutes when he is taken out of incubator. Slip the thermometer under his coverings to avoid exposing his body while checking temperature.	2. Ongoing assessment determines how well infant maintains body heat and whether he must go back into the incubator or needs other measures to regulate temperature.
3. Keep Juan out of the incubator for only a few minutes at first. Increase the time allowed outside according to his ability to maintain his temperature within normal limits.	3. Adjusts demands for thermoregulation to infant's ability to manage this function alone.
4. Gradually wean Juan from heat source by lowering the temperature of the incubator a degree at a time until it is at room temperature. Check Juan's temperature every 30 to 60 minutes during this process.	4. A gradual change in environmental temperature gives the infant time to adjust while being carefully monitored.
5. When Juan is ready to be moved to an open crib, double-wrap him and provide hat. Assess temperature every 30 to 60 minutes at first, and gradually increase time intervals to an every 4-hour schedule.	5. Wrapping provides extra insulation to maintain body heat. Close monitoring helps determine if infant is able to retain body heat without outside help.
6. Assess for signs of complications if Juan's temperature falls below normal. Watch for respiratory distress and test for hypoglycemia.	6. Cold stress causes an increased need for oxygen and glucose. Discovering complications of cold stress immediately ensures that early treatment can be instituted.

Evaluation:
Juan gradually maintains his temperature between 36.5° and 37.5°C (97.7° and 99.5°F) as the heat in his incubator is turned down. He spends more time outside the incubator and eventually moves to an open crib. Juan shows no signs of cold stress throughout hospital stay.

Additional Nursing Diagnoses to Consider:

Altered Family Processes
High Risk for Caregiver Role Strain
High Risk for Altered Parenting
Potential Complication: Infection

provement in the condition. The alveoli normally increase in number from 20 million at birth to as many as 300 million at 8 years of age, when the lungs reach adult size (Lapido, 1989). Infants with BPD may experience resolution of the condition by age 3 years.

Preterm Infant: Application of Nursing Process

Preterm infants commonly have problems relating to maintenance of the airway, ability to tolerate activity, temperature regulation, and obtaining adequate nutrition. Their parents may have difficulty with bonding. Although these are concerns for all newborns, preterm infants are especially vulnerable.

Airway

Assessment

Observe the infant continuously for presence, increase, or decrease of respiratory distress. Determine frequency of assessments according to nursery policy and the infant's condition.

Count the respiratory rate for a full minute to allow for the normal irregularity of breathing. Differentiate periodic breathing from apneic spells. Periodic breathing involves cessation of breathing for 5 to 10 seconds without other changes, whereas apneic spells generally last more than 15 seconds and/or are accompanied by cyanosis and bradycardia. Note the presence of tachycardia, which may indicate inadequate oxygen intake. Assess for presence of cyanosis at all times.

Assess the effort required for breathing. Note location and severity of retractions, which may be substernal, supraclavicular, or intercostal. Retractions and nasal flaring demonstrate that the infant is having to use accessory muscles to breathe. Listen for grunting, which may be loud or audible only with a stethoscope. Assess for adventitious breath sounds or absence of breath sounds in any areas of the lungs.

Assess the infant's respiratory response to activity such as handling, feeding, and linen changes. Preterm infants are too weak to cough up mucus and are in danger of airway obstruction. They cannot move or turn their heads and can easily aspirate regurgitated formula. When they are overtired, the work of breathing becomes even more difficult.

Analysis

A common nursing diagnosis for the preterm infant is: *Ineffective Airway Clearance related to inability to manage own secretions secondary to weakness and fatigue*. Because preterm infants are unable to keep their respiratory passages clear, they must have assistance from the nurse.

Planning

The major goals for this nursing diagnosis are that the infant will:

- Maintain a patent airway with normal respiratory rate of 30 to 60 breaths/minute.
- Maintain clear breath sounds throughout hospital stay.

Interventions

Nursing interventions are similar to those used for the full-term newborn having temporary respiratory problems with excessive mucus. However, for the preterm infant, the problem will continue for a longer period of time. The infant's ability to withstand vigorous treatment is decreased, and all care must be performed very gently.

POSITIONING THE INFANT

Position the infant to facilitate drainage of respiratory secretions at all times. The side-lying or prone position allows regurgitated feedings to drain easily from the mouth. Although the prone position is not recommended for normal newborn infants because it may be associated with increased incidence of sudden infant death syndrome (SIDS), it is often necessary for the preterm infant. The prone position allows more efficient use of the respiratory muscles and decreases respiratory effort. Better oxygenation and lung compliance also occur when the infant is in the prone position (Lefrak-Okikawa and Lund, 1993).

Elevate the head of the bed, and turn the infant's head to the side when the infant is in the supine position. Place diaper rolls by the infant's head if movement is not desired. Put a small roll under the shoulders to straighten the airway. Change the infant's position frequently to help air passages drain and to prevent stasis of secretions.

SUCTIONING SECRETIONS

Have suction equipment available at all times. Check the equipment at the beginning of each shift to ensure that it is functioning properly. A bulb syringe is less likely to be traumatic than wall suction but may not reach mucus deep in the respiratory tract.

Suction mucus as it becomes apparent, and be ready to suction quickly if the infant regurgitates during or after feedings. Always suction the mouth before the nose to prevent aspiration of fluids if the infant gasps when the nose is suctioned.

WORKING WITH THE RESPIRATORY THERAPIST

The duties of the nurse and respiratory therapist vary according to hospital policy, with some overlap in care given. The therapist may do almost all the respiratory care, or the nurse may give some care while the therapist concentrates on managing the equipment. It is essential to maintain open communication and coordination of care.

PERFORMING CHEST PHYSIOTHERAPY

Chest physiotherapy (postural drainage, percussion, and vibration) and suctioning are used in some hospitals to help keep the airway clear. Plan a short period of postural drainage before beginning chest physiotherapy. Vary the infant's position so that affected areas can drain into the major bronchi. Repositioning during the treatment increases effectiveness.

Percussion helps loosen secretions and bring them into the bronchi, where they can be removed by suction. The procedure may not be used for the VLBW infant, as the stimulation causes too much stress. When it is a part of the treatment plan for a larger infant, percuss gently for 30 to 60 seconds at a time with a special rubber instrument, a nipple, or a padded medicine cup. Follow percussion with gentle vibration with fingertips or a special mechanical device designed for that purpose.

Suction at the end of the treatment to remove loosened secretions. Suction should always be gentle to avoid traumatizing the delicate mucous membranes. Trauma could cause edema, which could further decrease the size of the air passages and lead to more respiratory difficulty.

Observe the infant's response to chest physiotherapy. Stop the treatment immediately if lowered blood oxygen levels, bradycardia, or cyanosis occurs. Following the procedure, check respiratory rate and breath sounds. Increase oxygen if necessary before, during, or after the treatment. After chest physiotherapy, provide a period of rest.

MAINTAINING HYDRATION

Adequate hydration is essential to keep secretions thin so that they can be removed by drainage or suction. If infants become dehydrated, secretions will become thick and viscous and could obstruct tiny air passages. Increase fluid intake, within the limits of the overall treatment plan, if secretions seem to indicate even minimal dehydration. Small amounts of saline may be administered through endotracheal tubes just before suctioning in order to thin secretions.

PREVENTING INFECTION

Staff with respiratory infections or any other communicable disease should not be assigned to take care of the preterm infant. The infant's ability to avoid or respond to infection is limited and may cause quick development of further complications.

Evaluation

The goals have been met if:

- The infant maintains a patent airway throughout the hospital stay.
- The respiratory rate remains between 30 and 60 breaths/minute.
- Breath sounds are clear.

Activity

Not only are preterm infants very fragile, they are subject to numerous daily treatments in a bright, loud environment. The sounds of monitors, alarms, ventilators, opening and closing doors, and people talking create a noise level above that of loud traffic.

During uterine life, the fetus may have slept as much as 80 to 90 per cent of the time. The number of assessments and treatments necessary to care for preterm infants results in frequent interruptions of sleep and may interfere with the development of normal sleep-wake cycles. Although touch is generally thought to be comforting to infants, to preterms it is often associated with painful events. Even turning and handling involve the use of energy.

Stimulation of any kind can cause increased energy expenditure by the preterm infant. A drop in blood oxygen level is a common indication of the detrimental effect of overstimulation. The role of the nurse is to help the infant conserve energy needed for normal body function and growth.

Assessment

Assess the amount of noise to which the infant is exposed. Determine how often interruptions occur and how the infant responds to different types of care.

Assess the infant's ability to tolerate activity and noise. Overstimulation results in changes in oxygenation and behavior. Signs of alteration in oxygenation include pulse and respiratory rate variations from baseline, apnea, rapid color changes and cyanosis, flaring, and drop in oxygen saturation levels.

Behavioral indications of stress from stimulation include stiffening and extension of arms and legs with fisting or splaying (spreading) of the fingers. The infant may appear hyperalert with a worried facial expression or may turn away from eye contact. Coughing, yawning, hiccoughing, and regurgitation may also be signals that infants are receiving more stimulation than they can tolerate. All signs may be accompanied by increased fatigue. (See Critical to Remember: Signs of Overstimulation in Preterm Infants.)

Analysis

The nursing diagnosis appropriate for preterm infants having difficulty enduring the multiple stimuli in their environment is: *Activity Intolerance related to weakness, fatigue, and potential overstimulation.* Use of this nursing diagnosis can help the nurse to plan ways to increase the infant's ability to tolerate interventions.

Critical to Remember

Signs of Overstimulation in Preterm Infants

Oxygenation Changes

- Increase or decrease in pulse and respiratory rate
- Cyanosis, pallor, or mottling
- Flaring nares
- Drop in oxygen saturation levels
- Coughing
- Yawning
- Hiccoughing

Behavior Changes

- Stiff, extended arms and legs
- Fisting of the hands or splaying of the fingers
- Alert, worried expression
- Turning away from eye contact
- Regurgitation
- Fatigue

Planning

The goals for this nursing diagnosis are that the infant will:

- Show decreased signs of overstimulation as a result of routine activity.
- Gradually show an increased tolerance to activity, as demonstrated by ability to withstand more activity before showing signs of overstimulation.

Interventions

Nursing interventions are focused on providing developmentally supportive nursing care that meets the preterm infant's ability to tolerate stimulation.

SCHEDULING CARE

Schedule periods of undisturbed rest throughout the day to allow the infant to recover from treatments. Whenever possible, arrange routine care to correspond with the infant's awake periods to avoid disturbing rest. Group care activities so that several tasks are performed at one time to allow for more rest between interruptions. However, be alert to the infant's signs of stress. Grouping care activities may result in more activity than the infant can tolerate without rest. Be flexible in pacing care to adapt to the infant's response.

REDUCING STIMULI

Keep noise around the infant as low as possible. Avoid talking near the incubator. Even talking softly while giving care may overstimulate the infant. Set volume on alarms on low and respond quickly when they sound. Open and close doors on the incubator and on cupboards softly and gently. Avoid placing things on top of the incubator or using it as a writing surface, as this increases the noise inside. Implement "quiet hours," when all noise in the unit is kept to a minimum, to provide rest periods.

Lights are on 24 hours a day in the nursery. The constant light may interfere with the development of sleep cycles. Position the incubator so that the infant is not facing bright lights, and drape a blanket over one end to decrease light further. Place infants in a prone position to help them avoid looking at ceiling lights. This will promote sleep and improve oxygenation. When possible, have "low-light periods," when lights in the nursery are turned down.

PROMOTING REST

Place boundaries around the infant with rolled blankets. This provides a "nest" that promotes rest by keeping the infant in place and is more comforting to the infant, who is used to the enclosed space of the uterus. Use the prone position to increase quiet sleep periods.

Any change, such as moving from assisted to more independent breathing or introduction of new feeding methods, may require the infant to expend more energy during the adjustment period. Observe how well the infant tolerates these new situations. Allow increased rest periods during the time that the infant is adapting to changes.

COMMUNICATING INFANTS' NEEDS

Use the nursing care plan to inform other caregivers of techniques that are especially effective for certain infants. Tape notes on the incubator as reminders of needs that may be different from those of other infants. This also alerts parents to the methods that are being used to help their infant.

Let parents know that the infant born at less than 34 weeks of gestation may not be able to deal with socialization. The talking, smiling, and eye contact so effective with the full-term infant may be too stimulating with the very young or sick preterm. Encourage forms of touch and interaction based on the individual infant's capacity. Quiet holding or gentle stroking may be better until the infant is able to tolerate more. Teach parents signs of overstimulation so that they can adapt their interaction to meet the infant's needs.

Evaluation

As a result of interventions, the infant:

- Shows fewer episodes of overstimulation resulting from routine nursing care.
- Gradually shows increasing tolerance for more activity before demonstrating signs of overstimulation.

✔ Check Your Reading

7. What positions aid the respiratory status of the preterm infant?
8. How does the preterm infant show activity intolerance?
9. What can the nurse do for the infant at risk for activity intolerance?

Temperature Regulation

Preterm infants have more difficulty maintaining a stable body temperature than do full-term infants. They are more subject to decreased temperature because so many factors contribute to increased heat loss. However, they are also prone to elevated temperature, particularly when heating devices such as radiant warmers are set too high.

Assessment

Monitor the infant's temperature continuously by a skin probe on the infant's abdomen, which is attached to the heat control mechanism of the radiant warmer or incubator. Note and record the infant's temperature as shown on the monitor at least every hour initially, and every 4 hours when the infant is stable. Take the axillary temperature every 4 to 8 hours, and compare with the heat control reading to ensure that the machinery is functioning properly.

Expect the axillary temperature to remain between 36.5° and 37.5°C (97.7° and 99.5°F) and the abdominal skin temperature between 36° and 36.5°C (96.8° and 97.7°F). If the axillary temperature remains normal but the monitor shows a decreased temperature, this may indicate that brown fat in the axillary space is being used to maintain the infant's core temperature.

Check the temperature of any infant with indications of inadequate thermoregulation. These include poor feeding or intolerance to feedings in an infant who previously had little difficulty, lethargy, irritability, poor muscle tone, cool skin temperature, and mottled skin. Hypoglycemia and respiratory distress may be the first signs that the infant's temperature is low. Because hypothermia may be an early sign of infection, assess for other evidence that infection may be present. (See Critical to Remember: Signs of Inadequate Thermoregulation.)

Analysis

The most common nursing diagnosis dealing with temperature regulation in the preterm infant is: *Ineffective Thermoregulation related to exaggerated heat loss secondary to physiological characteristics of the preterm infant.*

Critical to Remember

Signs of Inadequate Thermoregulation

- Axillary temperature < 36.5°C or > 37.5°C
- Abdominal skin temperature < 36°C or > 36.5°C
- Change in feeding behavior
- Lethargy
- Irritability
- Decreased muscle tone
- Cool skin temperature
- Mottled skin
- Signs of hypoglycemia
- Signs of respiratory difficulty

Planning

The goal for this nursing diagnosis is that the infant will maintain axillary temperature between 36.5° and 37.5°C (97.7° and 99.5°F) throughout hospital stay with no other signs of inadequate thermoregulation.

Interventions

Maintenance of heat in preterm infants involves the same basic nursing care principles as for full-term newborns, including keeping the skin dry, avoiding contact with cold surfaces or drafts, and keeping the infant away from windows (see Chapters 19 and 20). Adapt implementation of these principles to meet the special needs of the preterm infant and the equipment used for care.

MAINTAINING NEUTRAL THERMAL ENVIRONMENT

A neutral thermal environment is especially important to avoid increased oxygen needed to maintain body temperature. Place preterm infants in radiant warmers or incubators until they are able to maintain normal body temperature alone. Charts are available that indicate the appropriate temperature setting to maintain a neutral thermal environment according to the infant's size and maturity. Smaller, less mature infants will need more warmth to maintain body heat than larger or older preterm infants because they lose more heat and produce less.

Infants needing many procedures are usually placed under the open radiant warmer to make it easier to see them and work with equipment. However, air currents around an unclothed infant can cause heat loss by convection despite the heat generated by the warmer. Keep doors near the warmer closed and traffic to a minimum to further decrease convective heat loss. Give the infant only warmed oxygen, because thermal receptors in the face are very sensitive to cold. Cold oxygen could quickly lead to cold stress.

Be sure that equipment or caregivers do not come between the infant and the heat source, preventing heat from reaching the infant. Place plastic barrier sheeting over the infant to allow heat from the warmer to pass across to the infant and to decrease insensible water loss while maintaining visibility of the infant's body parts.

When infants are in an incubator, keep portholes and doors closed as much as possible. A significant amount of heat is lost every time the incubator is opened, and it takes time to build up again. Wrap infants in heated blankets, and cover the head when removing the infant from the incubator for procedures or holding. Keep the doors closed while the infant is out of the incubator to retain heat inside. If a procedure cannot be done inside the incubator, place the infant under a radiant warmer or on a surface padded with warm blankets. Use a heat lamp over the infant for an alternative source of heat.

HELPING INFANTS ADJUST TO NORMAL ENVIRONMENT

Assist infants to gradually adjust to maintaining their own temperature without added heat. Lower the temperature of the incubator a degree at a time, and take the infant's temperature every 30 to 60 minutes. Do not lower the temperature further until the infant's temperature remains within normal limits.

Plan to transfer infants to an open crib when they reach approximately 2000 g, if possible. When they are ready for transfer, double-wrap them with warm blankets at first to help insulate body heat. Monitor their temperature at gradually increasing intervals until they are on a routine schedule.

Watch the infant carefully during the first few days following transfer to an open crib. Note signs that may indicate inadequate thermoregulation, such as decreased weight gain or poor feeding. When the infant's temperature is lower than normal, be alert for signs of complications. These include hypoglycemia, respiratory difficulty, and acidosis.

Evaluation

If nursing interventions have been successful:

- The infant's temperature is maintained between 36.5° and 37.5°C (97.9° and 99.5°F).

- There are no other signs indicating inadequate thermoregulation.

Nutrition

Because the preterm infant has special nutritional demands, the physician or nurse practitioner orders the type and amount of feedings. The nurse is responsible for assessment and management of the feeding, as well as evaluation of the infant's responses, regardless of the feeding method.

Assessment

The focus of assessment in nutrition is on infant tolerance and readiness for progress. Feedings are often changed according to nurses' assessment of how infants are adjusting to feedings and assessment of signs indicating complications or readiness for change.

READINESS FOR NIPPLE FEEDING

Preterm infants are often fed parenterally (intravenously) or by gavage (feeding tube) initially to conserve energy for growth and basic functioning. During feedings, watch for signs that nipple feeding by breast or bottle may soon be possible. These signs include rooting when the area around the mouth is stroked, sucking on the gavage tube, a finger, or a pacifier, and increasing ability to tolerate holding and handling. Note if the infant gags on the tube or a gloved finger inserted into the mouth. The presence of the gag reflex is essential before beginning oral feedings. Infants who do not have a gag reflex are more likely to aspirate feedings.

When the infant begins to feed by nipple, assess coordination of suck and swallow and observe for aspiration. Frequent choking, gagging, or cyanosis during feedings may indicate that the infant is unable to coordinate sucking, swallowing, and breathing well enough for nipple feeding. Some infants are so weak that the usual signs of aspiration are minimal or absent. (See Critical to Remember: Signs Indicating Feeding Readiness.)

Assess respiratory rate before and during feedings. When the respiratory rate is above 60 to 70 breaths/minute before feedings, gavage feed to prevent aspiration. An increase in respiratory rate, tachycardia, bradycardia, or excessive fatigue may indicate that the effort of nipple feeding involves the use of excessive energy and oxygen.

Critical to Remember

Signs of Feeding Readiness in an Infant

Signs of Readiness for Nipple Feedings

- Rooting
- Sucking on gavage tube, finger, or pacifier
- Able to tolerate holding
- Respiratory rate < 60 breaths/minute
- Presence of gag reflex

Signs of Non-readiness for Nipple Feedings

- Respiratory rate > 60 breaths/minute
- No rooting or sucking
- Absence of gag reflex
- Excessive gastric residuals

Adverse Signs During Nipple Feedings

- Tachycardia
- Bradycardia
- Increased respiratory rate
- Apnea
- Coughing
- Gagging
- Falling asleep early in feeding
- Feeding time beyond 25–30 minutes

FEEDING TOLERANCE

Assess how well the infant tolerates feedings, whether by feeding tube or nipple. Before beginning a gavage feeding, withdraw the gastric contents to measure the amount of the previous feeding left in the stomach. This helps determine if the stomach is emptying and prevents overdistention. Return the amount withdrawn to the stomach, and subtract that amount from the next feeding. A gastric residual of more than 30 per cent of the previous feeding shows that the infant is not digesting the formula as fast as expected. The amount or type of formula may need to be changed. Observe for other signs of intestinal complications.

Obtain objective data about abdominal distention by using a tape measure to check abdominal girth. Place the tape at the level of the umbilicus, and note placement on the nursing care plan to ensure consistency. Test stools for occult blood and reducing substance, which may indicate development of intestinal complications. Reducing substance is detected by dissolving stool in water and mixing with a

Clinitest tablet. Presence of reducing substance indicates malabsorption of carbohydrates.

Vomiting or frequent regurgitation may indicate that the amounts fed are too large. Vomitus containing bile may be a sign of intestinal obstruction. Diarrhea may be due to rapid advancement of the feeding or intolerance to the type of formula. Report signs of feeding intolerance to the physician or nurse practitioner, as they may be early indications of complications, such as ileus, sepsis, obstruction of the gastrointestinal tract, or necrotizing enterocolitis.

Analysis

When the infant's nutritional needs are met by parenteral methods, the nursing care is mainly collaborative. However, once the infant is able to take formula or to breastfeed, many nursing interventions are involved. These are designed for the nursing diagnosis *High Risk for Altered Nutrition: Less Than Body Requirements related to uncoordinated suck and swallow and fatigue during feedings.*

Planning

Goals written for an individual infant with this nursing diagnosis take into consideration the specific needs of that infant. The infant will:

- Take in adequate amounts of formula and/or breast milk to meet nutrient needs for age and weight.
- Gain weight as appropriate for age.

The actual amount of feedings and weight gain will vary according to the infant's gestational age and other conditions. What is appropriate for a particular infant can be discussed with the physician or nurse practitioner.

Interventions

ADMINISTERING GAVAGE FEEDINGS

Enteral feedings are those that go into the stomach by gavage or nipple. Gavage feedings of formula or breast milk are usually started before bottle feedings or breastfeedings for preterm infants. A small, soft catheter is inserted into the stomach at each feeding for intermittent (bolus) feedings. Alternatively, a catheter may be inserted into the stomach, duodenum, or jejunum and left in place for a period of time to provide for continuous feedings. Because the preterm infant's nasal passages are so small and the infant is an obligate nose breather, the tube is usually inserted through the mouth to avoid interfering with air flow through the nose (see Procedure 28–1).

Gavage feedings are begun in small amounts, with gradual increases as tolerated by the infant. Only a few milliliters of feeding are given at first. Carefully observe the infant's tolerance at each feeding to determine when the formula type or amount can be changed.

Give tube feedings at room temperature. For continuous feedings, place no more than a 4-hour supply of formula in a feeding bag or syringe at a time to prevent excessive growth of bacteria in the milk. Use an infusion pump to regulate the flow of solution at a constant, measured rate. Tape the feeding tube securely to the infant's face, and change the bag or syringe and its tubing every 4 hours, or according to hospital policy.

Check placement of the feeding tube before beginning bolus feedings or at least once a shift for continuous feedings. Insert 0.5 to 1 cc of air while listening over the stomach with a stethoscope to be sure that the tube is actually in the stomach. Withdraw stomach contents as another method of checking for placement.

Measure the gastric residual in the syringe, and return it to the stomach to prevent loss of electrolytes. Deduct the amount of formula left in the stomach from the amount to be given to avoid overdistending the stomach. During continuous feedings, check the gastric residual every 2 to 4 hours, and return it to the stomach. Compare the amount of gastric aspirate with the hourly rate of feeding. A residual equal to 2 to 3 hours of infusion volume may be normal if there are no other signs of feeding intolerance, such as emesis (Estrada and Brennan-Behm, 1992).

If the infant is able to suck, use a pacifier during feedings to help associate the comfortable feeling of fullness with sucking. This also helps prepare the infant for nippling, improves weight gain, and decreases oxygen consumption (Estrada and Brennan-Behm, 1992). A pacifier may help quiet the fussy infant as well.

ADMINISTERING BOTTLE FEEDINGS

Bottle feedings can begin when the infant reaches what would be 34 to 36 weeks of gestation if still in utero. At this time, most healthy preterm infants are able to coordinate sucking with swallowing and breathing, have a functional gag reflex, and have enough energy to feed orally without compromising oxygenation.

Preparing for Feedings. Provide for maintenance of heat during feeding times. When infants have

Procedure 28–1 Administering Gavage Feeding

Purpose: Gavage feeding is used for infants who are unable to take the full amount of formula by nipple. It may be used alone or along with nipple feedings.

1. **Wash hands and gather equipment, including gavage tube of proper size (usually 5 to 8 French, depending on size of the infant), medicine cup or other measured container, and 20-ml syringe. These may be available in a kit. Also obtain formula or breast milk, warmed to room temperature. Check the chart to determine the amount that the infant is to have and how previous feedings have been tolerated.** *Having all equipment ready makes the procedure go smoothly and quickly and avoids disturbing the infant or delaying feedings. Information about previous feedings will help meet the infant's needs.*

2. **Elevate the head of the bed approximately 30 degrees. If the infant has a tendency to regurgitate when moved after feedings, position on the right side or prone. If parents are present, they may be allowed to hold the infant in their arms once the tube is inserted or hold the hands if the infant cannot be held.** *Positioning uses gravity to help avoid reflux of formula into the trachea and promotes emptying of the stomach. Feeding is important to parents, and including them in the process increases their self-concept as parents.*

3. **Determine the length of catheter to insert by measuring from the infant's mouth to the earlobe and then to the xyphoid process. Mark the tube at the proper point with a piece of tape.** *The distance from the mouth to the earlobe to the xyphoid process is equal to the distance from the mouth to the stomach.*

4. **Moisten the tip of the catheter with water, and shake off any excess. While holding the infant's head steady, gently insert the tube through the mouth to the point marked. Remove the tube immediately if persistent coughing, choking, cyanosis, apnea, or bradycardia occurs.** *Moistening the tip provides lubrication. Signs may indicate that the tube is entering the trachea instead of the esophagus. Apnea or bradycardia may be caused by stimulation of the vagus nerve.*

5. **Check for placement. Attach a syringe to the tube and insert 0.5 to 1 cc of air through the tube while listening over the stomach with a stethoscope. Gently draw back on the plunger to withdraw the inserted air.** *Hearing air enter the stomach ensures that the catheter is in place. Withdrawing the inserted air provides more room for feeding and helps prevent regurgitation.*

6. **Gently aspirate stomach contents. Move or rotate the tube slightly if the plunger does not withdraw easily.** *Aspirating stomach contents provides further proof that the feeding tube is in the proper place. Use of force could traumatize the stomach lining if the end of the tube is resting against it. Moving the tube may draw it away from the stomach lining.*

7. **Tape the tube in place.** *This prevents dislodging during feeding.*

8. **Withdraw all of stomach contents. Observe amount, color, and consistency of the aspirate. Do not feed the infant if the aspirate is abnormal. Report abnormal appearance or amount of stomach contents.** *Allows assessment for abnormalities. Stomach contents that are red or dark brown may indicate blood. If the aspirate is green with bile or brown with feces, there may be an intestinal obstruction. An excessive amount may mean that the infant is receiving too much formula or that stomach emptying is delayed.*

9. **Replace the aspirate before beginning feeding. Subtract the amount of gastric residual from the amount of formula to be given.** *Replacement of aspirate prevents loss of electrolytes. Overdistention of the stomach is avoided by subtracting the residual from the formula to be given.*

10. **Remove the plunger and attach the syringe to the feeding tube. Pour the correct amount of formula into the syringe. If it does not begin to move down the tube, insert the plunger just far enough to get the flow started, then withdraw it. Do not use the plunger to force the formula through the tube. Allow feeding to flow by gravity or attach to a feeding pump that will regulate the amount of flow.** *Using the plunger to force the entire feeding may cause damage to the stomach mucosa from too much pressure. A gravity flow or regulation of the flow by pump causes less trauma and prevents filling the stomach too fast.*

11. **If using gravity flow, raise or lower the syringe to increase or decrease the rate of flow so that formula moves slowly into stomach over 15 to 30 minutes.** *The higher the syringe, the faster the flow of formula and the greater the pressure. Formula should be given slowly to prevent sudden distention or trauma from pressure.*

Procedure continued on following page

Administering Gavage Feeding *Continued*

12. **Give the infant a pacifier during the feeding.** *This stimulates the sucking reflex, helps prepare the infant for nippling, is comforting, and helps the infant associate sucking with feeding.*

13. **When feeding is complete, pinch the tube and withdraw quickly.** *Pinching prevents drops of formula from entering the trachea as the tube is removed, and quick removal decreases irritation.*

14. **Burp the infant, and position on right side or prone, with the head of the bed elevated. If movement tends to cause regurgitation, omit burping. Allow the infant to remain on the right side or prone.** *Air is swallowed around the tube and can cause the infant to regurgitate and aspirate. Position helps prevent reflux of feeding into the esophagus and promotes emptying of the stomach by gravity. If regurgitation occurs, the formula will flow out of mouth.*

15. **Record time, amount, and characteristics of gastric residual, type and amount of formula given, and how the infant tolerated feeding.** *Documentation allows monitoring of infant's ability to tolerate feedings and meet nutritional needs.*

stable temperature maintenance, wrap them in warm blankets and hold for feedings. If thermoregulation is a problem, use a heat lamp over the infant during the feeding or feed the infant in the radiant warmer or incubator.

Nipple feedings involve a greater expenditure of energy by the infant than gavage feedings. Arrange nursing care to allow for a period of rest before and after feedings. Use of a pacifier before feedings helps bring preterm infants to an inactive awake state that enhances oral feeding success (McCain, 1992). Infants may be fed according to a feeding schedule or at times when they demonstrate cues that they are ready. Preterm infants fed on demand may feed less often than those with scheduled feedings but gain weight as well (Saunders et al, 1991).

Some infants eat best using special "preemie" nipples, which are more pliable than regular nipples so that less energy is necessary for sucking. In other infants, soft nipples allow milk to flow too fast and cause choking. These infants can control the flow better with firmer nipples. Smaller nipples are available for the infant with a very small mouth.

Giving the Feeding. Position the infant at a 45- to 60-degree angle during the feeding, and hold so that observation of the infant's mouth is facilitated. Many nurses hold the infant facing them, with the head in the nurse's hand. The infant's head should be slightly forward, with the chin slightly down to provide support during sucking. Placing a finger on each cheek helps increase sucking strength. A finger under the jaw at the base of the tongue (midway between the chin and the throat), providing gentle upward pressure, helps support the tongue (Shaker, 1990) (Fig. 28–4).

Begin nipple feeding with small amounts to prevent overtiring the infant. The first nipple feedings may be only a few milliliters once a day, with the feeding completed by gavage. Placing the gavage tube before beginning oral feedings helps prevent regurgitation stimulated by passing the catheter. Gradually increase the amount and frequency of oral feedings until the infant feeds by bottle once a shift, then every 2nd or 3rd feeding, and eventually every feeding.

Feed slowly, and burp the infant well halfway through the feeding and at the end. Allow a longer time for feeding than for the full-term infant, but finish the feeding by gavage if the infant becomes too tired. Do not allow caloric intake to decrease because of fatigue.

Assessing Responses. Assess response to early nipple feedings especially carefully, as infants may aspirate easily. Observe for choking, gagging, in-

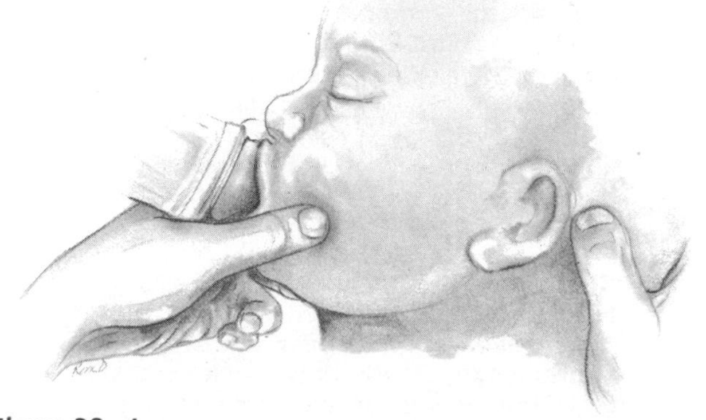

Figure 28–4

Method of positioning the nurse's hands to provide cheek and jaw support for feeding preterm infants.

crease or decrease in heart rate or respirations, or apnea during all feedings. Stop the feeding and allow the infant to recover, then evaluate the infant's ability to continue.

Determine if the infant becomes overfatigued during feedings. Falling asleep during the feeding, feeding more slowly than usual, or increased respiratory rate may indicate that the infant does not yet have the energy to feed by nipple. (See Critical to Remember: Signs of Feeding Readiness.) Feedings that last longer than 25 to 30 minutes may take too much energy and make the infant more likely to aspirate because of fatigue (Shaker, 1990).

Including Parents in Bottle Feeding. Teaching parents is a major part of nursing care, but it is especially important when they attempt to feed the preterm infant. Both parents should have an opportunity to feed the stable infant by bottle. They may need encouragement to feel comfortable holding the infant, and they should be taught what observations the nurse is making during the feeding. If they have held the infant during gavage feedings and at other times, they will feel more comfortable with holding for bottle feedings (Fig. 28–5).

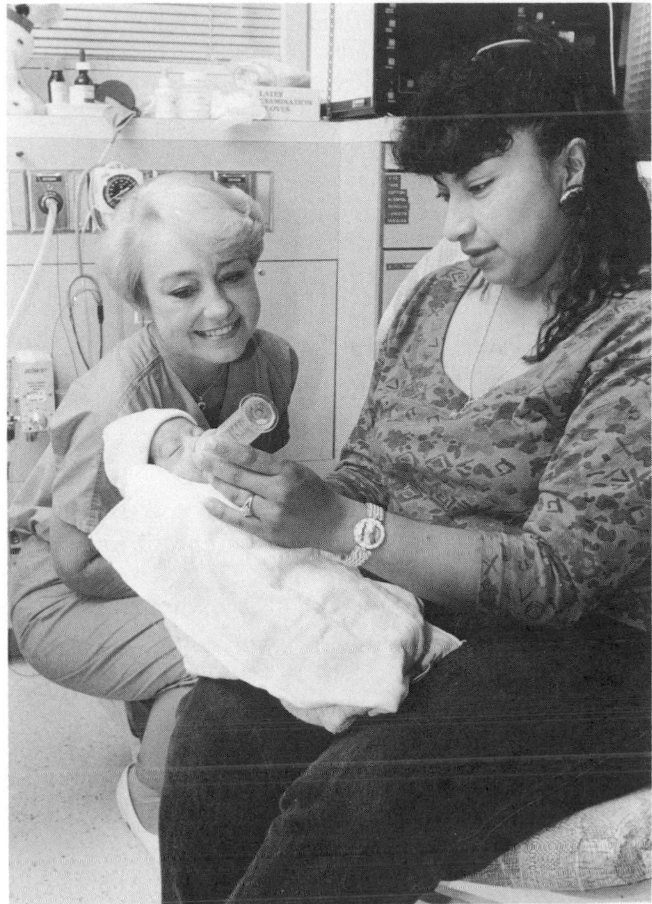

Figure 28–5

The nurse offers encouragement to a mother learning to feed her preterm infant.

FACILITATING BREASTFEEDING

Encourage mothers who would like to breastfeed. Breast milk has all of the advantages for the preterm infant that it has for the full-term newborn. The immunological benefits are particularly important to the preterm infant who did not receive passive immunity during fetal life. Contributing her milk to nourish the infant helps the mother feel that she is participating in an important way and enhances her self-esteem.

It may be necessary to add special fortifiers to breast milk to meet total nutrient needs, especially if the infant is very small. The fortifiers are added to the breast milk, which is then given by gavage or bottle. Explain the reasons for this to the mother so that she does not feel that there is something wrong with her milk.

When the mother plans to breastfeed, she will need special help in maintaining lactation until the infant is able to suckle. Teach her how to use a breast pump so that her milk can be used for gavage or bottle feedings until the infant is mature enough to suckle at the breast. Give her sterile containers to store her milk and tell her to place it in a refrigerator or freezer until she brings it to the NICU for the infant.

Generally, the mother may begin to breastfeed when the infant weighs about 2000 g (4 pounds, 6.5 ounces) and tolerates oral feedings (Ziemer and George, 1990). In some situations, breastfeeding may be started when the preterm is mature enough to take oral feedings, generally at 34 to 36 weeks, without giving the infant bottle feedings first. It has been used successfully with some infants weighing under 1500 g.

Breastfeeding may be less stressful than bottle feeding for preterm infants because the mother's body temperature helps keep the infant warm and the slower gastric filling prevents stomach distention. The infant should be able to coordinate sucking and swallowing with breathing successfully before breastfeeding is initiated.

Support the mother in her efforts in feeding, which may be difficult at first. Remind her that even full-term infants must learn how to breastfeed. Relaxation needed for feeding is difficult in the very busy NICU nursery. Provide as much privacy as possible, using a separate room or screens if necessary. The mother will need the same breastfeeding teaching as the mother of a full-term infant. In addition, help her to feel comfortable holding the tiny infant and any attached equipment, such as monitor leads. Use of the football hold allows the mother to see the infant well as she helps him or her latch on to the breast.

Make the same observations of the infant during breastfeeding as during bottle feeding. Signs of fatigue, bradycardia, tachypnea, or apnea may show lack of readiness for breastfeeding. Be sure that the infant stays warm. The mother's body heat should help maintain the infant's temperature during feedings. A warm blanket can be placed over mother and infant if necessary.

MAKING ONGOING ASSESSMENTS

Continuously assess the infant's responses to all feeding methods. Record the amount of formula or breast milk that the infant takes by gavage or bottle feeding and compare it with the amount needed to meet nutrient needs for the infant's age and weight. For breastfed infants, record the amount of actual suckling time for a rough idea of intake, and correlate this with weight gain.

Weigh the infant daily at the same time of day and using the same scale. Record the length and head circumference each week. Plot weight, length, and head circumference on a growth chart for preterm infants to see if changes are within expected ranges. Weight increase not accompanied by increased length may be due to edema and may be a sign of a complication such as congestive heart failure.

Observe changes in the infant's ability to take feedings. The suck and swallow coordination should gradually improve with maturity and practice. As the infant becomes more mature, less energy should be expended during the feeding sessions. The infant will take the feedings more quickly and show fewer signs of fatigue, such as falling asleep during feedings.

Evaluation

If the goals have been met, the infant will:

- Consume adequate amounts of formula or breast milk to meet nutrient needs for age and weight.
- Show a pattern of weight gain that is appropriate for age.

✔ Check Your Reading

10. How can the nurse prevent heat loss in preterm infants?
11. What signs indicate that the infant may be ready for nipple feeding?
12. How can the nurse help the mother who wants to breastfeed her preterm infant?

Parenting

The birth of a preterm infant is generally unexpected and always emotionally traumatic to parents who wanted a normal birth experience and a healthy newborn. Parents usually begin the process of getting to know their infant moments after birth. However, parents of a preterm infant must often postpone this initial period of interaction with their newborn. When they are allowed contact, they may have difficulty developing a feeling of attachment for the tiny infant, who looks so different from what they expected and is attached to an array of machines and equipment. (Further information on parental grieving is in Chapter 23.)

The extended hospitalization of the preterm infant results in separation of the parents from their newborn and disrupts family life. Some parents feel that they play such a small part in the preterm's life that the infant almost belongs to the hospital. The nurse must evaluate the progress of bonding and assist the parents to feel involved and important in caring for their infant. Parents need an understanding of the infant's condition and what is expected to occur throughout the hospital stay to help them adjust to the changes that they will need to make (Fig. 28–6).

Assessment

Assess for signs of parental attachment on the first and subsequent visits to the NICU nursery. Expect parents to be fearful at first but more able to focus on the infant as they get over the initial shock of preterm birth. Although parents show attachment to their infants in individual ways, there are some common behaviors that may show that bonding is progressing normally. These behaviors may include talking about the infant in positive terms, pointing out physical characteristics, naming the infant, making eye contact, and calling the infant by name. Parents should ask questions about the infant and the infant's needs. When parents are able to hold and participate in the care of the infant, observe for gradual increase in comfort and skill. The parents should smile and talk to the infant and verbalize increasing confidence in their caretaking abilities.

Watch for signs that bonding is not occurring as expected. (See Critical to Remember: Signs That Bonding Might Be Delayed.) These include failure to perform usual bonding behaviors or a decrease in behaviors that were previously present. Parents who

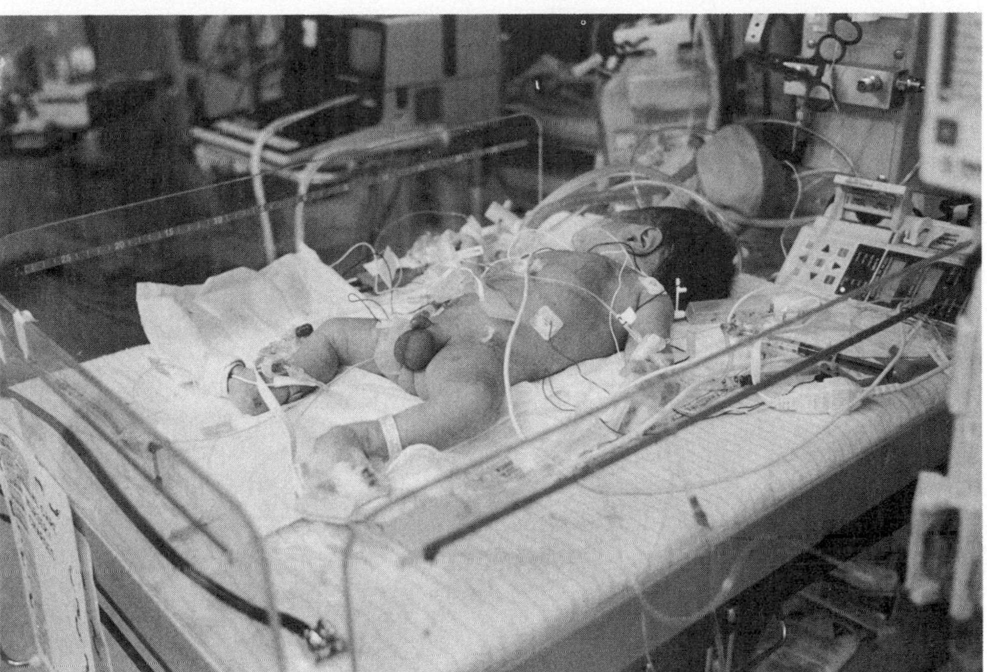

Figure 28–6

An infant in neonatal intensive care unit is surrounded by highly technological equipment. This can be very frightening to parents at first. Preparation of parents before they visit is an important nursing responsibility.

seem as interested in other infants in the NICU as their own or who talk about the infant in an impersonal way may be having difficulty. Note how often the parents make visits or calls to the NICU and watch for changes that may indicate a need for support. Determine if there are other stressors in the parents' lives that may interfere with their ability to visit and attach to the infant.

After the critical period soon after birth, healthy preterm infants move into a more stable condition. They still require specialized nursing care and hospitalization but gradually need less technological interventions. They are sometimes called "growers" at this time. Observe the parents' response to determine if they seem aware of the changes and the improved outlook. This is a time when their participation in the infant's care should increase (Fig. 28–7).

Critical to Remember

Signs That Bonding May Be Delayed

- Using negative terms to describe the infant
- Discussing the infant in impersonal or technical terms
- Failing to give the infant a name or to use the name
- Visiting or calling infrequently or not at all
- Decreasing the number and length of visits
- Showing interest in other infants equal to that in their own infant
- Demonstrating a lack of interest in holding and caring for the infant
- Showing a decrease in or lack of eye contact, in time spent talking to the infant, or in smiling at the infant

Analysis

Altered parenting is a potential problem in the development of parent-infant attachment for parents of any infant who has a problem at birth. It may occur whenever parents and infants must be separated because of hospitalization during the newborn period. One nursing diagnosis that is appropriate for the parents of preterm infants is *High Risk for Altered Parenting related to separation of parents from hospitalized infant and lack of understanding about the preterm infant's condition and characteristics.*

Planning

The goals for this nursing diagnosis are that the parents will:

- Demonstrate progressive evidence of bonding with infant by verbalizing concerns, visiting fre-

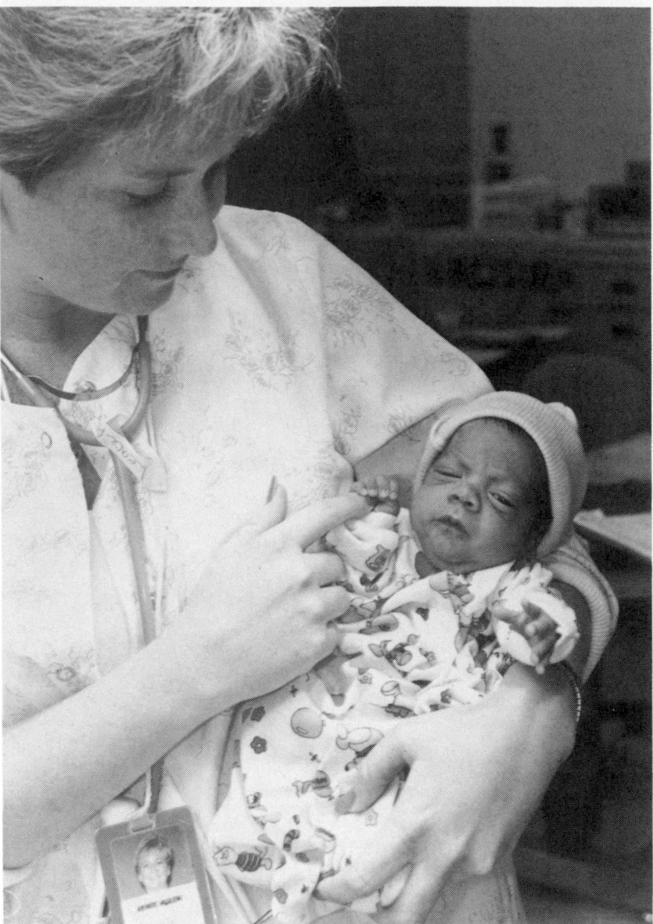

Figure 28–7

This growing preterm infant is almost ready to go home.

quently, and interacting as appropriate for infant's condition.

- Verbalize understanding of preterm infant's condition and characteristics and express increasing comfort in caring for infant.

Interventions

MAKING ADVANCE PREPARATIONS

Being able to prepare for threatening situations like preterm birth helps parents cope with the actual event. Parents expected to have a preterm birth should visit the NICU nursery before delivery, whenever possible. If the mother is confined to bed, arrange for a nurse from the NICU to visit her so that she feels a link with the nursery and can ask questions. The father or another support person should have a tour of the nursery so that he will know where to go and can discuss the nursery environment with the mother.

ASSISTING PARENTS AT BIRTH

After the birth, allow the mother to see the newborn in the delivery room, even if for only a few moments, so that she has a realistic idea of the infant's appearance and condition. If possible, allow the father to be present for initial care in the NICU nursery. If space is too crowded, perhaps he can watch from a window. Explain what is happening and why. This allows him to see the intensive efforts made on behalf of his infant, increases his confidence in the staff, and enables him to give the mother a full description later. Support the father, as well as the mother, by using therapeutic communication techniques during this difficult time.

If the infant must be transported to another facility, it is important to have the transport team go to the mother's room just before they leave, if possible. This helps the mother feel connected to her infant and to the staff providing care. Leaving photographs with the mother is one way of helping her bond even though the infant is not with her. It also helps prepare her for when she is able to go to see her infant.

SUPPORTING PARENTS DURING EARLY VISITS

Take the mother to the NICU nursery as soon as she is able. If she is too sick to be with her infant, bring her photographs. Before parents first visit the infant, prepare them for what they will see by describing the equipment and its purposes, the various attachments to the infant, and the sounds of alarms. Explain how the infant will look and behave. Table 28–1 provides specific steps that the nurse can follow to help parents become familiar with the NICU setting.

At first, stay with the parents during visits. When they are comfortable, allow them time alone with the infant so that they can interact in private. Answer questions and explain changes in the infant's condition and treatment. Use therapeutic communication as the parents deal with their grief, guilt, and emotional turmoil (see Therapeutic Communication).

Although too much handling overstimulates infants, parents should touch the infant as soon as possible because this helps promote the development of attachment. They may be hesitant initially because of fear that they will interfere with equipment. The smaller the infant, the more reluctant some parents may be. Show them how to touch in ways appropriate for the infant, such as holding the infant's hand

Table 28–1. INTRODUCING PARENTS TO THE NEONATAL INTENSIVE CARE UNIT (NICU) SETTING

Before Parents Visit the NICU

Describe the NICU environment. Include the noise of alarms, the busyness of the staff, the number of people and sick infants.

Show parents photographs of the infant. This helps prepare them, but it is not as overwhelming as seeing the infant in person.

Describe the infant. Include the size, the lack of fat, the breathing, the weak cry. Explain that no sound of crying can be heard if the infant is intubated. Include some human aspects: "He's a real fighter" or "She makes the funniest faces during her feedings."

Describe the equipment. Include ventilators, intravenous lines, monitors. Explain how they look and how they are attached to the infant. Keep the explanations simple, without technical details.

When Parents Visit the NICU

Help parents perform scrubbing and gowning procedures while explaining their purpose.

Stay with the parents during their visit. Having a familiar person nearby will help them feel more comfortable while they adjust to this unfamiliar environment.

Introduce them to their infant's nurse. Ask the NICU nurse to explain some of the things being done for the infant.

Provide parents with written information about the NICU so that they can take it home with them to read later. This usually includes visiting hours, calling for updates about the infant, availability of classes on infant care, and support groups.

Tell the parents that they will receive instruction on how to care for their infant in time. Encourage them to visit the infant as much as they are able. Emphasize how important they are to their infant.

Offer realistic encouragement based on the infant's condition.

Provide an opportunity for the parents to express their concerns and feelings and to ask questions.

through the portholes of the incubator or stroking the small areas of skin not encumbered by equipment. Some parents may hesitate to touch because they are afraid of becoming attached to an infant whom they may lose. They will need sensitive support from the nurse until they are ready to progress in their relationship with the infant.

PROVIDING INFORMATION

One of the most important ways nurses can help parents is meeting their need for information about their infant. Explain all nursing care, its purpose, and the expected response. Point out how preterm infants are similar to and different from full-term infants to help parents develop a realistic understanding of the infant's capabilities.

Offer realistic reassurance about the infant's condition. This means emphasizing positive aspects, yet being truthful in all communication with the parents. If they have misconceptions or did not understand a physician's explanations, clarify or ask the physician to go over specific information again. Translate medical terms into ones that the parents can understand. Use an interpreter if the parents do not understand English.

Repeat explanations, especially at first. Because of their emotional distress, parents are often unable to fully comprehend or remember what is said to them.

Therapeutic Communication

Ann Gibson gave birth to a preterm infant, Laura, at 30 weeks' gestation. Ann is visiting the NICU for the first time the day after the birth. The nurse, Lee Wills, has talked to her about what to expect and stays with her during the visit.

Ann: Oh, she looks so tiny. I saw her for only a minute after she was born, and I didn't really get a good look. How can she ever survive when she's so small and covered with tubes?

Lee: So far, Laura is doing very well. Her vital signs are stable, and she's holding her own. But it is frightening when she looks so small and vulnerable, isn't it?

Offering realistic reassurance and reflecting Ann's fearful feelings. Using infant's name to promote bonding.

Ann: I stayed in bed like they told me to do. I thought she wouldn't be born so soon if I stayed in bed.

Lee: It must have been a shock when you realized you were going to have her early even when you did all the things you were supposed to do.

Reflecting feelings and acknowledging that Ann did what she should have to prevent early birth.

Ann: I couldn't believe it. But the contractions just got harder and harder. Why didn't they stop?

Lee: Sometimes we just can't stop labor, and we don't always know why. That may happen even when mothers do everything they can to prevent having the baby early.

Offering information while again acknowledging Ann's attempts to stop labor.

Ann: Now she's so tiny and so sick! She looks so different from how I thought my baby would look.

Lee: She is tiny, but babies her size grow very quickly. Would you like to touch her?

Offering realistic reassurance and attempting to bring Ann closer to infant.

Ann: Oh, I don't know. I'd be afraid of hurting her. Maybe I should wait until she's bigger.

Lee: Even tiny babies like to have their mothers stroke their skin and talk to them. Why don't you hold her hand while I do some things to take care of her? And at the same time, I can tell you about all this equipment and what we are doing for Laura.

Emphasizing the mother's importance, involving her in care being given, and offering information about infant's equipment and care.

Offer written information about NICU policies and procedures in the language of the parents. Explanations about visiting hours, who can visit, routines for scrubbing and wearing cover gowns, and the role of parents can be reinforced in writing and available for later reading for parents who feel overwhelmed.

FACILITATING INTERACTION

As the infant progresses, point out small signs of improvement that may not be obvious to parents. Use positive phrases to point out even minor strengths. Explain that preterm infants are not able to respond to social interaction in the same way that full-term infants do. Call attention to indications that the infant is able to progress in socialization so that the parents can take advantage of the opportunity. Talk about individual characteristics that make this infant different from all others. The way the infant eats, reacts to sounds, or even how the infant seems to get tangled in the monitor leads may help parents feel closer to their newborn and understand the infant's special characteristics.

Involve the parents in care of the infant as soon as possible. As they become familiar with the NICU nursery setting and the equipment, more involvement will help them to feel a sense of control. At first, plan to change the linens in the incubator or radiant warmer when the parents are there so that they can hold their infant, even if for only a few moments. As the infant's condition improves, parents can develop skill in caring for a tiny infant by changing diapers, feeding, and bathing during the infant's hospitalization.

INCREASING PARENTAL DECISION MAKING

Encourage parents to help make large and small decisions about care of the infant. Consult them, when possible, about scheduling care of the infant around the times that they are able to visit. Give them the information they need to take an active part in decisions made about the infant's treatment plan. This will increase their feelings of control over a situation in which many parents feel they have little power.

ALLEVIATING CONCERNS

Encourage parents to call the NICU at any time for information about their infant. This helps allay worry when parents wake up at night and wonder how the infant is doing. Parents not able to visit the infant because of distance or other reasons will especially benefit by feeling free to call and talk to the nurse caring for their infant.

The need for support from others besides nursing staff is also important. Put parents in touch with other parents who have had a preterm infant. Talking with those who have faced the same problems can be very comforting. They can compare notes and get down-to-earth suggestions from an experienced parent's point of view.

PREPARING FOR DISCHARGE

To help parents plan for taking the infant home, teach them any special procedures that the infant will need after discharge. Begin early to show the parents how to manage treatments and describe what adaptations they will need to make at home. Observe the parents perform the care until they feel comfortable and can do it safely. Some hospitals have parents spend a night in a special "parent room," where they take over full 24-hour care of the infant. This provides an opportunity to practice assuming complete care of the infant in an environment where help is available if needed.

Assist the parents in planning for integrating the new infant into the family. Listen to their concerns about other children, and encourage siblings to visit, if possible. Caution parents that siblings with infections should not visit the infant who cannot fight off infections well. Help parents explain to the other children what they will see when they visit the infant. Siblings should touch or hold the infant, if possible, to help them bond. Taking photographs of the siblings with the infant will help them remember the visit.

These interventions help parental bonding by relieving some of the parents' concerns about their other children. Meeting the needs of their other children, in addition to the new responsibilities of caring for the preterm, is a major source of worry. Give frequent praise for their attempts to solve their problems and the care that they give the infant.

Evaluation

Goals are met if parents:

- Demonstrate bonding behaviors, including positive verbalization about the infant, frequent visiting, and interacting with the infant as appropriate for the infant's condition.
- Demonstrate understanding of the preterm infant's special needs and the treatment given throughout the hospital stay.
- Take an increasingly active role in care of the infant.

✔ Check Your Reading

13. How can the nurse help parents feel comfortable with their preterm infant?
14. How should the nurse prepare parents for the discharge of their preterm infant?

Postterm Infants

Postterm infants are those who are born after the 42nd week of gestation. Their longer-than-normal gestation places them at risk for a number of complications.

Scope of Problem

Approximately 6 to 12 per cent of all pregnancies are considered postterm. Postterm infants have a two to three times higher perinatal mortality rate (Hamilton and Hobel, 1992). The major concern with postmaturity is how well the placenta functions during the last weeks of pregnancy. In most cases, the fetus continues to be well supported by the placenta. Some may grow to over 4000 g (8 pounds, 13 ounces) and are at risk for birth injuries or the need for cesarean birth because of their size. However, in 20 to 30 per cent of postterm pregnancies, placental function has deteriorated, causing interference with oxygen and nutrient supply. This results in hypoxia and malnourishment and is called postmaturity (or dysmaturity) syndrome (Hamilton and Hobel, 1992).

Assessment

Signs of postmaturity syndrome may occur during pregnancy, during labor, or after birth. Diminished fetal growth or oligohydramnios may cause decreased uterine size during the last weeks of pregnancy. When labor begins, poor oxygen reserves may cause fetal distress. The fetus may pass meconium as a result of hypoxia before or during labor, increasing the chance of meconium aspiration at delivery.

At birth, the cord, skin, and nails may be stained, indicating that meconium was present for some time. The hyperalert, wide-eyed, worried look common to these infants is a sign of chronic intrauterine hypoxia. A hematocrit above 65 per cent shows polycythemia, a response to inadequate oxygen in utero.

A poorly nourished fetus has wasting and growth retardation. The infant is thin and has loose skin with little subcutaneous fat. Lanugo and vernix caseosa are minimal or absent in the postterm infant, and there is usually abundant hair on the head and long nails. The skin is dry, cracked, and peeling.

Therapeutic Management

Therapeutic management focuses on prevention and symptomatic treatment. Expectant mothers who are "overdue" are scheduled for tests of placental functioning (see Chapter 10), and labor is induced if there are signs of placental deterioration (see Chapter 16). During labor, fetal distress may necessitate a cesarean birth. Apgar scores less than seven are more likely in postterm infants. In cases of asphyxia or meconium aspiration, respiratory support is needed at birth. (See discussion of these complications in Chapter 29, pp. 840 and 844.)

During the nursery stay, respiratory problems may necessitate continued assessment and care. The infant is prone to hypoglycemia because of poor stores of glycogen at birth. Thermoregulation is a problem because the infant has little subcutaneous fat to act as insulation. Polycythemia makes the infant prone to hyperbilirubinemia.

Nursing Considerations

The nurse's role is primarily one of prevention of complications, where possible, and monitoring for changes in status. During labor and delivery, the nurse assists in correcting fetal distress, prepares for and assists in emergency delivery, and cares for respiratory problems at birth.

Be alert for signs of postmaturity syndrome in infants during the initial assessment. The condition may not have been diagnosed before birth if there was an error in calculating the mother's due date. Infants with any indications of postmaturity should be tested for blood glucose level soon after birth and again an hour later. Feed these infants early and more often to help compensate for the period of poor nutrition in utero.

Expect temperature regulation to be poor because fat stores have been used for nourishment in utero. The infant may need more time in a radiant warmer or incubator before thermoregulation is stable. Extra blankets, frequent monitoring of temperature, and teaching parents about prevention of cold stress may be necessary throughout the hospital stay.

Small-for-Gestational-Age Infants

The small-for-gestational-age (SGA) infant falls below the 10th percentile on growth charts. The infant may be preterm, full-term, or postterm but has failed to grow at the rate expected for the time spent in utero. For example, approximately one third of all infants who have a low birth weight are full term but small for gestational age (Pittard, 1993). Another name for the condition is intrauterine growth retardation (IUGR), and the terms are used interchangeably.

Causes

Many of the risk factors for neonatal complications may also cause an infant to be small for gestational age. Congenital malformations, chromosomal anomalies, and fetal infections from rubella or cytomegalovirus may cause IUGR. Poor placental function due to aging, small size, separation, or malformation may interfere with fetal growth. Illness in the expectant mother, including pregnancy-induced hypertension or severe diabetes, restricts uteroplacental blood flow and decreases fetal growth. Smoking and drug or alcohol abuse also impair fetal growth, as does severe maternal malnutrition.

Scope of Problem

Intrauterine growth retardation occurs in 3 to 10 per cent of all pregnancies, and affected infants have a four to eight times higher perinatal mortality rate than infants who are not growth retarded (Gomella, 1992). Death may occur from asphyxia before or during labor because of poor placental functioning. Infants who are small for gestational age are subject to many of the same complications as those who are preterm or postterm. The specific complications and their severity depend on the cause and degree of growth retardation. Infants with congenital defects will also have problems at birth that are associated with the anomaly. Drug-exposed infants may have the added complication of drug withdrawal.

Low Apgar scores, meconium aspiration, and polycythemia are increased in the SGA infant as in the postterm infant. Hypoglycemia occurs in as many as 67 per cent of infants with IUGR (Behrman and Kliegman, 1992) because there is little storage of glycogen in the liver. Although muscle tone enables the SGA infant to maintain better flexion than the preterm infant, SGA infants are prone to inadequate thermoregulation because subcutaneous and brown fat stores have been used to survive in utero. If hypoglycemia develops, there is inadequate glucose for increased metabolism to produce heat, increasing the problem.

Characteristics of SGA Infants

The appearance of the SGA infant may vary, according to whether the cause of growth retardation began early or late in the pregnancy:

- *Symmetric* growth retardation occurs in about 20 per cent of cases and involves the entire body. It is caused by congenital anomalies or exposure to infections or drugs early in pregnancy. Although the infant is small, the body is proportionate and appears normally developed for size. There is a decrease in the total number of cells, and the infant may have long-term complications.
- *Asymmetric* retardation begins late in pregnancy and accounts for approximately 80 per cent of infants with IUGR (Leake, 1991). The head is normal in size but seems large for the rest of the body, which appears long and thin. The loose skin has longitudinal thigh creases from loss of subcutaneous fat. The infant has sparse hair, a thin cord, dry skin, and the wide-eyed look associated with intrauterine hypoxia. These infants generally "catch up" in growth if they are adequately nourished after birth.

Therapeutic Management

Therapeutic management is focused on prevention by good prenatal care to identify and treat problems early. When growth retardation cannot be prevented, ultrasound examination may permit early discovery of the condition so that the infant can be delivered early, if necessary, and preparation can be made for the expected complications at birth. Problems after birth are treated as they occur.

Nursing Considerations

Because the causes of growth retardation are so varied, the care of the SGA infant must be adapted to meet the specific problems that the infant demonstrates. Monitor for signs of growth retardation and the complications that commonly accompany it. Examine SGA infants carefully for congenital anomalies. The general appearance and measurements will give an indication of the type of retardation that has occurred. Measurements of the head, chest, length, and weight will all be below normal in the infant with symmetric growth retardation. If the retardation is asymmetric, the head circumference and length will be normal and the chest circumference and weight will be low.

Watch for hypoglycemia, especially in the asymmetric growth-retarded infant. The brain of the infant is normal and needs large amounts of glucose, but the liver is small and has inadequate stores of glycogen. Calorie needs for this infant will be higher than for a normal infant. Initiate early and more frequent feeding as appropriate. Temperature regulation and respiratory support are added nursing concerns. Care is generally similar to that of the preterm or postterm infant, depending on the problems present.

Large-for-Gestational-Age Infants

Large-for-gestational-age (LGA) infants are those who are above the 90th percentile on intrauterine growth charts. They are usually born at term, although they may be preterm or postterm and may weigh more than 4000 g (8 pounds, 14 ounces).

Causes

LGA infants may be born to multiparas, large parents, and certain ethnic groups known to have large infants. Diabetes in the mother may cause increased size (see Chapter 29, p. 856), as may erythroblastosis fetalis (see Chapter 29, p. 846).

Scope of Problem

The LGA infant is more likely to go through a longer labor, be injured during birth, or be born by cesarean delivery. Shoulder dystocia may occur because the shoulders are too large to fit through the pelvis. Fractures of the clavicle or skull, damage to the brachial plexus or facial nerve, cephalohematoma, and bruising occur more often in these infants than in those of normal size. Congenital heart defects, lower Apgar scores, and a higher mortality rate are also more common.

Therapeutic Management

Therapeutic management is based on identification of macrosomia (large size) during pregnancy by measurements of fundal height and ultrasound examination. Delivery problems may lead to use of forceps, vacuum extraction, or cesarean delivery. Specific treatment involves identification and treatment of birth injuries and complications as they arise.

Nursing Considerations

Be prepared to assist in a difficult delivery or cesarean birth due to dystocias. After birth, assess the infant carefully for injuries or other complications such as hypoglycemia or polycythemia. (See care of the infant of a diabetic mother, Chapter 29, p. 856.)

✔ Check Your Reading

15. What is the typical appearance of the infant with postmaturity syndrome?
16. What special problems might a postmature infant have?
17. How are symmetric and asymmetric intrauterine growth retardation different?
18. What problems may occur in infants who are large for gestational age?

Summary Concepts

- Low socioeconomic status increases risk of preterm birth because of possible decreased general health, nutrition, and medical care and lack of economic, social, and emotional support.
- Preterm infants differ in appearance from full-term infants. Some differences include small size, limp posture, red skin, abundant vernix and lanugo, and immature ears and genitals.
- Preterm infants' lungs may lack adequate surfactant, which may cause the lungs to be non-compliant, increase the amount of energy necessary for breathing, and lead to atelectasis.
- Other factors that may increase respiratory problems are poor cough reflex, narrow respiratory passages, and weak muscles.
- Preterm infants are prone to cold stress because they have thin skin with blood vessels near the surface, little subcutaneous or brown fat, a large surface area, a limp position, and an immature temperature control center.
- Preterm infants are lacking in nutrient stores and need more nutrients but do not absorb them well. They lack coordination in sucking and swallowing and fatigue easily.
- Preterm infants are subject to increased insensible water losses and have difficulty maintaining fluid balance. Their kidneys do not concentrate or dilute urine as well as those of full-term infants.
- Preterm infants are subject to infections because they lack passive antibodies from the mother, have an immature immune system, have fragile

skin, and are subjected to many invasive procedures.

- Position preterm infants on the side or prone to increase drainage of respiratory secretions. Prone position decreases breathing effort because respiratory muscles are used efficiently. In the supine position, place a small roll under the shoulders to straighten the airway.

- Infants demonstrate that they are receiving too much stimulation by changes in oxygenation and behavior. The nurse should schedule care to allow rest periods, keep noise to a minimum, and teach parents how to interact with the infant appropriately.

- It is important to maintain a neutral thermal environment at all times for infants. Prevent air drafts, use warmed oxygen, and keep incubator doors and portholes closed. When the infant is taken out of heating devices, wrap in warmed blankets and use a hat.

- Signs indicating that an infant may be ready for feeding include rooting, sucking on gavage tube or pacifier, presence of gag reflex, respiratory rate below 60 breaths/minute.

- The nurse can help the mother who wishes to breastfeed her preterm infant by teaching her how to use a breast pump and store her milk until the infant is ready to breastfeed. Provide privacy, give support and encouragement, explain the infant's behavior, and answer general questions about breastfeeding.

- Nurses can increase parents' comfort with their preterm infant by providing information about the NICU environment, the infant's condition and characteristics, and the equipment and care. Spending time with parents during visits, offering therapeutic communication and realistic encouragement, and involving parents in care of the infant will also help with bonding.

- Preparation for discharge should be started early in the infant's hospital stay. This allows parents to gradually learn about and take on increasing responsibility in the care of the infant until they are comfortable with complete care.

- Infants with postmaturity syndrome may appear thin, with loose skin folds, cracked peeling skin, and meconium staining. They appear hyperalert and worried. They may have respiratory difficulties at birth and suffer hypoglycemia and inadequate temperature regulation.

- Infants with intrauterine growth retardation may be small for gestational age at birth. In symmetric growth retardation, the infant is proportionately small; in asymmetric growth retardation, the head is normal in size and the body is thin.

- Large-for-gestational-age infants may have birth injuries, such as fractures, nerve damage, or bruising, as a result of their size. They may have hypoglycemia or polycythemia.

References and Readings

Adcock, E.W., & Consolvo, C.A. (1993). Fluid and electrolyte management. In G.B. Merenstein & S.L. Gardner (Eds.), *Handbook of neonatal intensive care* (2nd ed.). St. Louis: C.V. Mosby.

Affonso, D.D., Hurst, I., Mayberry, L.J., Haller, L., Yost, K., & Lynch, M.E. (1992). Stressors reported by mothers of hospitalized premature infants. *Neonatal Network*, 11(6), 63–70.

American Academy of Pediatrics and American College of Obstetricians and Gynecologists. (1992). *Guidelines for perinatal care* (3rd ed.). Elk Grove Village, Ill.: American Academy of Pediatrics.

Bass, L.S. (1991). What do parents need when their infant is a patient in the NICU? *Neonatal Network*, 10(4), 25–33.

Beachy, P., & Deacon, J. (1992). *Core curriculum for neonatal intensive care nursing*. Philadelphia: W.B. Saunders.

Becker, P.T., Grunwald, P.C., Moormer, J., & Stuhr, S. (1991). Outcomes of developmentally supportive nursing care for very low birth weight infants. *Nursing Research*, 40(3), 150–155.

Behrman, R.E. (1992). *Nelson textbook of pediatrics* (14th ed.). Philadelphia: W.B. Saunders.

Blackburn, S.T., & Loper, D.L. (1992). *Maternal, fetal, and neonatal physiology: A clinical perspective*. Philadelphia: W.B. Saunders.

Blackburn, S.T., & VandenBerg, K.A. (1993). Assessment and management of neurologic dysfunction. In C. Kenner, A. Brueggemeyer, & L.P. Gunderson (Eds.), *Comprehensive neonatal nursing, a physiologic perspective*. Philadelphia: W.B. Saunders.

Blake, W.W., & Murray, J.A. (1993). Heat balance. In G.B. Merenstein & S.L. Gardner (Eds.), *Handbook of neonatal intensive care* (3rd ed.). St. Louis: C.V. Mosby.

Byrne, W.J. (1991). Disorders of the intestines and pancreas. In H.W. Taeusch, R.A. Ballard, & M.E. Avery (Eds.), *Schaffer and Avery's diseases of the newborn* (6th ed.). Philadelphia: W.B. Saunders.

Cole, J.G., Beglish-Duddy, A., Judas, M.L., & Jorgensen, K.M. (1990). Changing the NICU environment: The Boston City Hospital model. *Neonatal Network*, 9(2), 15–23.

Estrada, E.A., & Brennan-Behm, M. (1992). Neonatal nutrition. In P. Beachy & J. Deacon (Eds.), *Core curriculum for neonatal intensive care nursing*. Philadelphia: W.B. Saunders.

Fox, M.D. (1992). Measurement of urine output volume: Accuracy of diaper weights in neonatal environments. *Neonatal Network*, 11(2), 11–18.

Fox, M.D., & Molesky, M.G. (1990). The effects of prone and supine positioning on arterial oxygen pressure. *Neonatal Network*, 8(4), 25–29.

Gomella, T.L. (Ed.). (1992). *Neonatology: Management, procedures, on-call problems, diseases, drugs* (2nd ed.). Norwalk, Conn.: Appleton & Lange.

Griffin, T. (1990). Nurse barriers to parenting in the special care nursery. *Journal of Perinatal and Neonatal Nursing*, 4(2), 56–67.

Hagedorn, M.I., Gardner, S.L., & Abman, S.H. (1993). Respiratory diseases. In G.B. Merenstein & S.L. Gardner (Eds.), *Handbook of neonatal intensive care* (2nd ed.). St. Louis: C.V. Mosby.

Hamilton, L.A., & Hobel, C.J. (1992). Intrauterine growth retardation, intrauterine fetal demise, and postterm pregnancy. In N.F. Hacker & J.G. Moore (Eds.), *Essentials of obstetrics and gynecology* (2nd ed.). Philadelphia: W.B. Saunders.

Haney, C., & Allingham, T.M. (1992). Nursing care of the neonate receiving high-frequency jet ventilation. *Journal of Obstetric, Gynecologic, and Neonatal Nursing*, 21(3), 187–194.

Harrison, L.L., & Woods, S. (1991). Early parental touch and preterm infants. *Journal of Obstetric, Gynecologic, and Neonatal Nursing*, 20(4), 299–306.

Jensen, D.J.H. (1990). The applicability of nursing diagnoses in the neonatal intensive care unit. *Neonatal Network*, 9(2), 25–29.

Kenner, C., Brueggemeyer, A., & Gunderson, L.P. (1993). *Comprehensive neonatal nursing: A physiologic perspective*. Philadelphia: W.B. Saunders.

Klaus, M.H., & Fanaroff, A.A. (1993). *Care of the high-risk neonate* (4th ed.). Philadelphia: W.B. Saunders.

Kliegman, R.M. (1990). Fetal and neonatal medicine. In R.E. Behrman (Ed.), *Nelson essentials of pediatrics*. Philadelphia: W.B. Saunders.

Lapido, M. (1989). Respiratory distress revisited. *Neonatal Network*, 8(3), 9–14.

Leake, R. (1991). Growth disorders. In H.W. Taeusch, R.A. Ballard, & M.E. Avery (Eds.), *Schaffer and Avery's diseases of the newborn* (6th ed.). Philadelphia: W.B. Saunders.

Lefrak-Okikawa, L., & Lund, C.H. (1993). Nursing practice in the neonatal intensive care unit. In M.H. Klaus & A.A. Fanaroff (Eds.), *Care of the high-risk neonate*. Philadelphia: W.B. Saunders.

Main, D.M. (1991). Prevention of preterm birth. In H.W. Taeusch, R.A. Ballard, & M.E. Avery (Eds.), *Schaffer and Avery's diseases of the newborn* (6th ed.). Philadelphia: W.B. Saunders.

Mattson, S., & Smith, J.E. (Eds). (1992). NAACOG *core curriculum for maternal-newborn nursing*. Philadelphia: W.B. Saunders.

McCain, G.C. (1992). Facilitating inactive awake states in preterm infants: A study of three interventions. *Nursing Research*, 41(3), 157–160.

McLean, F.H., Boyd, M.E., Usher, R.H., & Kramer, M.S. (1991). Postterm infants: Too big or too small? *American Journal of Obstetrics and Gynecology*, 164(2), 619–624.

Meier, P. (1988). Bottle and breast-feeding: Effects on transcutaneous oxygen pressure and temperature in preterm infants. *Nursing Research*, 37(1), 36–41.

Minarcik, C.J., & Beachy, P. (1993). Neurologic disorders. In G.B. Merenstein & S.L. Gardner (Eds.), *Handbook of neonatal intensive care* (2nd ed.). St. Louis: C.V. Mosby.

Newman, C.B., & McSweeney, M. (1990). A descriptive study of sibling visitation in the NICU. *Neonatal Network*, 9(4), 27–31.

Novak, J.C. (1990). Facilitating nurturant fathering behavior in the NICU. *Journal of Perinatal and Neonatal Nursing*, 4(2), 68–77.

Pettett, G., Bonnabel, C., & Bird, C. (1989). Regionalization and transport in perinatal care. In G.B. Merenstein & S.L. Gardner (Eds.), *Handbook of neonatal intensive care* (2nd ed.). St. Louis: C.V. Mosby.

Pittard, III, W.B. (1993). Classification of the low-birth-weight infant. In M.H. Klaus & A.A. Fanaroff (Eds.), *Care of the high-risk neonate*. Philadelphia: W.B. Saunders.

Price, P.T., & Kalhan, S.C. (1993). Nutrition and selected disorders of the gastrointestinal tract. In M.H. Klaus & A.A. Fanaroff (Eds.), *Care of the high-risk neonate* (4th ed.). Philadelphia: W.B. Saunders.

Richardson, S. (1991). Renal function in the preterm neonate: An overview. *Neonatal Network*, 10(4), 17–23.

Saunders, R.B., Friedman, C.B., & Straoski, P.R. (1991). Feeding preterm infants: Schedule or demand? *Journal of Obstetric, Gynecologic, and Neonatal Nursing*, 20(3), 212–218.

Shaker, C.S. (1990). Nipple feeding premature infants: A different perspective. *Neonatal Network*, 8(5), 9–17.

Shellabarger, S.G. (1993). The critical times: Meeting parental communication needs throughout the NICU experience. *Neonatal Network*, 12(2), 39–44.

Silverman, W.A., & Andersen, D.H. (1956). A controlled clinical trial of effects of water mist on obstructive respiratory signs, death rate, and necropsy findings among premature infants. *Pediatrics*, 17(1), 1–9.

Strauch, C., Brandt, S., & Edwards-Beckett, J. (1993). Implementation of a quiet hour: Effect on noise levels and infant sleep states. *Neonatal Network*, 12(2), 31–35.

Thomas, K.A. (1989). How the NICU environment sounds to a preterm infant. *Maternal-Child Nursing Journal*, 14(4), 249–251.

Townsend, S.F., Johnson, C.B., Hay, Jr., W.W. (1993). Enteral nutrition. In G.B. Merenstein & S.L. Gardner (Eds.), *Handbook of neonatal intensive care* (3rd ed.). St. Louis: C.V. Mosby.

Weaver, L.J. (1991). Issues in nursing care of the newborn. In H.W. Taeusch, R.A. Ballard, & M.E. Avery (Eds.), *Schaffer and Avery's diseases of the newborn* (6th ed.). Philadelphia: W.B. Saunders.

Weibley, T.T. (1989). Inside the incubator. *Maternal-Child Nursing Journal*, 14(2), 96–100.

Whaley, L.F., & Wong, D.L. (1991). *Nursing care of infants and children* (4th ed.). St. Louis: C.V. Mosby.

Ziemer, M.M., & George, C. (1990). Breastfeeding the low-birth-weight infant. *Neonatal Network*, 9(4), 33–38.

29

High-Risk Newborn:

Acquired and Congenital Conditions

Objectives

1. Describe the steps involved in neonatal resuscitation.
2. Explain the common respiratory problems in the newborn.
3. Explain the causes and significance of pathologic jaundice.
4. Describe the nursing care of the infant with pathologic jaundice.
5. Explain the effect of maternal diabetes on the newborn.
6. Describe the effect of maternal substance abuse on the newborn.
7. Describe common congenital anomalies.

Definitions

Asphyxia • A condition in which there is deficient oxygen in the blood and excess carbon dioxide in the blood and tissues.

Erythroblastosis fetalis • Agglutination and hemolysis of fetal erythrocytes due to incompatibility between the maternal and fetal blood. In most cases, the fetus is Rh-positive and the mother is Rh-negative.

Esophageal atresia • Condition in which the esophagus is separated from the stomach and ends in a blind pouch.

Gastroschisis • Condition in which the intestines protrude through a defect in the abdominal wall.

Hydrops fetalis • Heart failure and generalized edema in the fetus secondary to severe anemia resulting from destruction of erythrocytes.

Kernicterus • Accumulation of unconjugated bilirubin in the brain causing neurological damage. Also called **bilirubin encephalopathy.**

Meconium aspiration syndrome • Obstruction and air trapping due to meconium in the lungs, causing severe respiratory distress.

Meningocele • Protrusion of the meninges through a defect in the bony spine; a form of **neural tube defect.**

Myelomeningocele • Protrusion of the meninges and spinal cord through a defect in the vertebrae; a form of **neural tube defect.**

Neonatal abstinence syndrome • A cluster of physical signs exhibited by the newborn who was exposed in utero to maternal use of substances such as cocaine or heroin. See also **Abstinence syndrome.**

Omphalocele • Protrusion of the intestines through a defect in the abdominal wall at the umbilicus.

Persistent pulmonary hypertension • Vasoconstric-

△ Alert for a high risk of exposure to substances to which universal precautions apply. See Appendix B for additional information about infection control.

tion of the pulmonary vessels after birth; may result in right-to-left shunting of blood flow through the ductus arteriosus and/or the foramen ovale.

Respiratory distress syndrome (RDS) • Condition caused by insufficient production of surfactant in the lungs; results in atelectasis (collapse of the lung alveoli), **hypoxemia**, and **hypercapnia.**

Spina bifida • Defective closure of the bony spine that encloses the spinal cord; a type of **neural tube defect.**

Tracheoesophageal fistula • Abnormal connection between the esophagus and the trachea.

Transient tachypnea of the newborn • Condition of rapid respirations due to inadequate absorption of **fetal lung fluid.**

In addition to the high-risk conditions related to gestational age discussed in Chapter 28, the newborn at risk may have acquired or congenital complications. Acquired conditions may be associated with prenatal complications, or they may occur at birth or shortly thereafter. These complications include respiratory problems, hyperbilirubinemia, infections, effects of prenatal exposure to drugs, and other conditions.

Respiratory Complications

Respiratory distress is one of the most common problems of the neonate. It may be due to asphyxia before or during birth, disease of the respiratory system, or diseases of other organs that affect the infant's respiratory ability. The nurse is responsible for identification and evaluation of respiratory status at birth and throughout the hospital stay. The degree of respiratory distress must be monitored for change, the need for intervention, and the effectiveness of treatment. Use of scales such as the Silverman-Andersen index helps evaluate the degree of respiratory distress (see Fig. 28–2, p. 808).

Asphyxia

Asphyxia is a lack of oxygen and increase of carbon dioxide in the blood. It may occur in utero, at birth, or later. When there is interference with oxygen supply to the fetus, a fetal monitor tracing may show tachycardia followed by bradycardia or decelerations. Asphyxia may cause the fetus to pass meconium and may lead to reflex gasping, which draws meconium deep into the air passages. (See meconium aspiration syndrome, p. 844.)

When asphyxia occurs at birth, it may be a continuation of asphyxia that began in utero, or it may be due to other factors, such as preterm lungs having insufficient surfactant to function adequately. The infant may have primary apnea, in which a few gasping breaths at birth are followed by cessation of respirations with a rapid fall in heart rate. Stimulation at this time may be all that is necessary to restart respirations. If asphyxia continues without intervention, gasping respirations may resume weakly until the infant enters a period of secondary apnea. In secondary apnea, the oxygen levels in the blood continue to decrease, the infant loses consciousness, and stimulation is ineffective. Resuscitative measures must be initiated immediately to prevent permanent damage to the brain or death.

Lack of oxygen to the cells leads to anaerobic metabolism and the production of acids. Metabolic acidosis develops when available bicarbonate is no longer able to buffer the accumulating acids. The blood shows a high $Paco_2$ and a low Po_2, pH, and bicarbonate. Vasoconstriction decreases blood flow to all organs except the brain, myocardium, and adrenal glands. The ductus arteriosus and foramen ovale may remain open because of the low oxygen in the blood, high resistance to blood flow through constricted pulmonary vessels, and elevated pressure on the left side of the heart. Thus, even circulating blood remains low in oxygen. Progress toward brain damage and death is rapid unless intervention is prompt.

INFANTS AT RISK

Whenever there are complications during pregnancy, labor, or birth, the infant may be at risk for asphyxia. In addition, if the expectant mother receives narcotics for analgesia shortly before delivery, the infant may be too depressed at birth to breathe spontaneously. Naloxone (Narcan) is given to these infants, (see Drug Guide, p. 843).

NEONATAL RESUSCITATION

Although asphyxia can sometimes be predicted, it may develop unexpectedly. Therefore, all personnel involved in deliveries should receive education on performance of resuscitative measures. A nurse, physician, or respiratory therapist may perform resuscitation if they have been educated in the technique. Equipment must be readily available and functioning properly in the delivery room at all times so that there is no delay in starting resuscitation. Neonatal resuscitation is presented in Procedure 29–1.

The nurse's role in asphyxia varies according to

Procedure 29–1

Performing Resuscitation in Newborns

Purpose: To ensure adequate oxygenation to the neonate with asphyxia.

1. **Determine whether resuscitation is necessary. Place the infant immediately under a preheated radiant warmer, and dry thoroughly.** *Prevention of cold stress is important to prevent increased oxygen need.*

2. **Position the infant with the infant's neck only slightly extended, in a "sniffing" position, so that the airway is open. Avoid hyperextension or flexion of the neck. Place a small blanket under the shoulders.** *Proper positioning will help maintain an open airway. Hyperextension or flexion may obstruct the airway.*

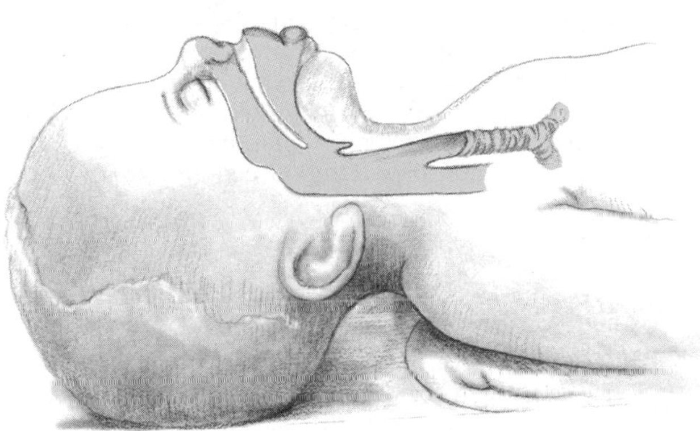

3. **Suction the mouth and then the nose.** *Suctioning removes mucus from the airways. Infants often gasp when the nose is suctioned and may aspirate secretions from the mouth into the lungs.*

4. **Stimulate the infant if necessary. Rub the infant's back or slap the soles of the feet if additional stimulation is needed.** *Spontaneous respirations should begin within the first 30 to 45 seconds after birth. The tactile stimulation of drying the infant and suctioning the mouth and nose may cause spontaneous respirations. If not, additional stimulation may be needed.*

5. **If there is no response after stimulating once or twice, do not continue to stimulate but initiate immediate resuscitation. Do not delay resuscitation until the Apgar scores are given.** *Resuscitation becomes more difficult the longer it is delayed. Immediate resuscitation is necessary to prevent brain damage.*

6. **Begin positive-pressure ventilation with a bag and mask if the infant fails to breathe spontaneously with initial stimulation or the heart rate is less than 100 BPM when respirations have begun.** *Positive-pressure ventilation ensures oxygen entry into the lungs.*

7. **Attach the bag to an oxygen source with 100 per cent oxygen. Place the mask snugly over the infant's nose and mouth. Squeeze the bag gently to force air into the infant's lungs with a pressure that will deliver 20 to 30 ml of air. If possible, use a bag with a gauge, to show the amount of pressure being used, and a "pop-off" valve, which releases if the pressure is high enough to cause lung damage.** *Great care must be taken to use a pressure that will deliver the 20 to 30 ml of air necessary to inflate the lungs without causing damage from overinflation.*

8. **Observe the rise and fall of the chest during ventilation. If the chest does not move, suction secretions and reposition the head and the mask. Ventilate the infant at a rate of 40 to 60 breaths/minute until the infant is breathing spontaneously and the heart rate is above 100 BPM.** *The airway must not be occluded by positioning or secretions.*

9. **Pause after 15 to 30 seconds of ventilation to take a 6-second heart rate, using a stethoscope or by feeling pulsations at the base of the cord. Multiply the rate by ten to get the heart rate per minute. If the rate is less than 60 BPM or between 60 and 80 BPM and not increasing, a second person should begin chest compressions while the first continues to ventilate the infant.** *Adequate ventilation causes improvement of bradycardia in most infants. Evaluation of the infant's status determines whether ventilation can be discontinued or chest compressions must be added for the infant to survive.*

Procedure continued on following page

Performing Resuscitation in Newborns Continued

10. Compress the chest by placing the hands around the infant's chest with the fingers under the back for support and the thumbs over the sternum. Position the thumbs just below the nipple line but above the xyphoid process. *Fingers under the infant's back provide support. Correct hand position compresses the heart but avoids or minimizes injury to the liver or spleen, fractures of the ribs, or pneumothorax.*

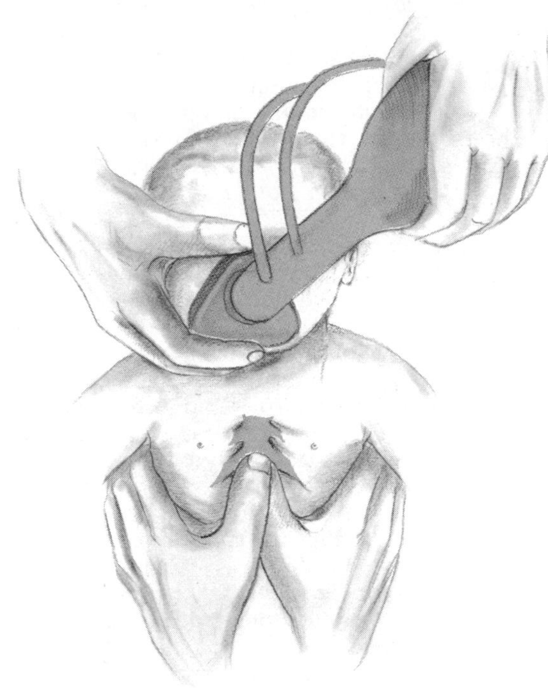

11. Compress the sternum ½ to ¾ inch, with three compressions followed by one ventilation, for a combined rate of compressions and ventilations of 120 each minute. This is 90 compressions and 30 ventilations each minute. *Simultaneous compression and ventilation may interfere with adequate ventilation, which is of primary importance for the neonate.*

12. Stop compressions after 30 seconds to check the heart rate for 6 seconds. If it is above 80 BPM, discontinue compressions but continue ventilation until spontaneous breathing begins. If the heart rate is below 80 BPM, continue compressions with rechecks of the heart rate periodically. *Periodic evaluation is necessary to ensure that treatment appropriate to the infant's status is used.*

13. Prepare medications as needed. They may include epinephrine given through an umbilical vein catheter or through an endotracheal tube, volume expanders, and naloxone. *Epinephrine is used to stimulate the heart. Volume expanders may be used for bleeding. Naloxone is used to counteract the effects of narcotics given to the mother in labor.* *(See Drug Guide on naloxone, p. 843.)*

Data from Neonatal resuscitation. (1992). *Journal of the American Medical Association, 268*(16), 2276–2281.

the agency, the other staff available, and the situation. Nurses must be alert for situations in which asphyxia may develop. They may begin resuscitation measures with positive-pressure ventilation with bag and mask and cardiac compression. Some nurses are educated to intubate infants in emergency situations. The physician or nurse practitioner may insert umbilical vein catheters and give medications through them. The nurse may assist in these procedures.

Once the infant is stabilized, the nurse will assess for further change when the infant is transferred to the regular or intensive care nursery. Infants with asphyxia often have other complications as well. Communication with the parents is a vital nursing function. They will be confused and frightened by the activity that they see in the delivery room and will need explanation and realistic reassurance. Parents often need continued support after the crisis to talk about their fears and concerns.

Respiratory Distress Syndrome

SCOPE OF PROBLEM

Respiratory distress syndrome (RDS) accounts for 20 per cent of all neonatal deaths in the United States, with 40,000 newborns affected each year (Gomella, 1992). It is most common in preterm infants, especially those less than 30 weeks gestational age and weighing less than 1200 g (2 pounds, 10 ounces) (Hagedorn et al, 1993). RDS also occurs in some

Drug Guide

NALOXONE HYDROCHLORIDE (Narcan)

Classification: Narcotic antagonist.

Action: Reverses central nervous system and respiratory depression caused by narcotics (opiates). Competes with narcotics at receptor sites.

Indications: Severe respiratory depression when the mother has received narcotics within 4 hours of delivery.

Dosage and Route:

Available in 0.4 mg/ml and 1 mg/ml. Dosage is 0.1 mg/kg. Given IV, IM, SC, or into an endotracheal tube.

Absorption: Well absorbed by all routes. Onset of action is 1 to 2 minutes if given IV.

Excretion: Metabolized by the liver and excreted by kidneys.

Contraindications and Precautions: Duration of effect is 1 to 4 hours. The dose may need to be repeated. If given to an infant of a mother addicted to drugs, it will cause withdrawal and may cause seizures. Resuscitative measures should be used as necessary.

Nursing Implications: Note the strength of the medication available when calculating the dose. Prepare the syringe before birth with 1 ml of the drug. After birth, the excess is removed from the syringe, and the amount is given according to the estimate of the infant's weight. Inject rapidly. Monitor for response, and be prepared to give repeated doses if necessary.

infants born to diabetic mothers and in those who were hypoxic during labor or had birth asphyxia, because these conditions interfere with surfactant production. However, conditions in which there is chronic fetal stress, such as pregnancy-induced hypertension, heroin addiction, or rupture of membranes over 48 hours, cause the lungs to mature more quickly. These infants are unlikely to have RDS.

CAUSES

RDS is caused by insufficient production of surfactant, a phospholipid that lines the alveoli, decreasing surface tension to allow them to remain open when air is exhaled. Surfactant must be continuously created as it is being used. When there is not enough surfactant, the alveoli collapse each time the infant exhales. The lungs become non-compliant, or "stiff," and resist expansion. Non-compliant lungs need a much higher negative pressure for the alveoli to open each time the infant inhales. Severe retractions occur with each breath, drawing the weak muscles of the chest wall inward. The resulting pressure on the lungs further interferes with expansion. As fewer alveoli expand, atelectasis results.

MANIFESTATIONS

Signs of RDS begin during the first hours after delivery, often become worse on the next day, and may begin to improve within 72 hours after birth. They include tachypnea, nasal flaring, retractions, and cyanosis. Grunting on expiration is characteristic and signifies physiological efforts to maintain lung expansion. Grunting closes the glottis and increases the pressure within the alveoli between breaths so that they remain partially open. Breath sounds may be decreased or wet. Acidosis develops as a result of hypoxemia. A chest x-ray shows a "ground glass" appearance of the lungs that is characteristic of RDS. Areas of atelectasis are present.

THERAPEUTIC MANAGEMENT

Treatment is supportive, with mechanical ventilation, correction of the acidosis, intravenous feedings, and care of developing complications.

A relatively new development is surfactant replacement therapy. Surfactant (obtained from calves' lungs or synthetic sources) is instilled into the infant's trachea immediately after birth or as soon as signs of RDS become apparent. Improvement in breathing occurs in minutes. Doses may be repeated, if necessary. This treatment may be used prophylactically to prevent RDS or as "rescue" treatment once RDS has occurred. Infants treated with surfactant have higher survival rates and fewer complications associated with RDS, although they may have other complications resulting from their prematurity.

NURSING CONSIDERATIONS

The nurse observes for signs of developing RDS at birth and during the early hours after the delivery. Changes in the infant's condition are constantly assessed. Other care is similar to the respiratory care for the preterm infant discussed in Chapter 28.

Transient Tachypnea of the Newborn

Infants who experience transient tachypnea of the newborn (TTN) have rapid respirations soon after birth that last a few hours or days. These neonates are usually full-term or near-term at birth and are frequently delivered by cesarean section. The condition occasionally occurs in infants born by rapid vaginal birth.

CAUSES

Although the exact cause of TTN is unknown, it is thought to be due to a delay in absorption of fetal lung fluid or aspiration of amniotic fluid. During vaginal birth, pressure on the chest causes expulsion of approximately one third of the fluid filling fetal lungs. When the birth is cesarean, this fluid remains in the lungs and must be absorbed by the blood and lymph vessels. The fluid moves from the alveoli to interstitial spaces around the alveoli and bronchioles and may cause compression and interference with air flow. The result is TTN.

MANIFESTATIONS

Although TTN initially appears similar to RDS, the condition is self-limited and generally resolves in 72 hours if no other problems are present. The infant may have no difficulty at birth, but tachypnea, retractions, nasal flaring, grunting, and mild cyanosis soon develop. The chest x-ray shows hyperinflation and presence of fluid in the fissures between the lobes and in the pleural space.

THERAPEUTIC MANAGEMENT

Treatment is supportive. Usually, moderate amounts of oxygen are sufficient to prevent cyanosis. Intravenous or gavage feeding may be necessary while the respiratory rate is high to prevent aspiration and conserve energy. The infant is carefully monitored for improvement or development of other complications.

NURSING CONSIDERATIONS

The nurse may be the first person to see signs of TTN, especially if they are not apparent at birth. After identifying signs, the nurse notifies the appropriate caregiver and carries out treatment. General nursing care is similar to that of the preterm infant discussed in Chapter 28.

Meconium Aspiration Syndrome

Meconium aspiration syndrome (MAS) occurs most often in postterm infants, although it may be present in other infants who have suffered intrauterine asphyxia. It results in mechanical obstruction of the airways, chemical pneumonitis, and air trapping.

CAUSES

The fetus passes meconium when hypoxia is severe enough to cause relaxation of the anal sphincter. Meconium aspiration syndrome develops when meconium enters the lungs during fetal life or at birth. The meconium may be drawn into the lungs if gasping movements occur in utero as a result of asphyxia and acidosis, or the meconium in the upper airways may be pulled deep into the respiratory passages when the infant takes the first breaths after birth.

MANIFESTATIONS

If meconium in the amniotic fluid is light, respiratory problems usually do not develop in the infant. However, thick meconium is likely to be associated with serious respiratory pathology. Signs of mild to severe respiratory distress are present at birth, with tachypnea, cyanosis, retractions, nasal flaring, grunting, and coarse breath sounds.

Meconium causes direct airway obstruction, allowing the entrance but not the escape of air in the alveoli. The bronchioles expand slightly during inhalation as air flows into them. However, they constrict during exhalation, and the meconium blocks the passage of air out of the lungs. This ball-valve mechanism results in air trapping. The overdistended alveoli may develop an air leak, with escape of air into the pleural cavity (pneumothorax) or mediastinum (pneumomediastinum). In addition, meconium is irritating to lung tissue and causes a chemical pneumonitis.

A common complication of MAS is persistent pulmonary hypertension. Low levels of oxygen in the blood from interference with gas exchange cause continued pulmonary vasoconstriction after birth. The ductus arteriosus remains open as well. The increased pressure in the lung from vasoconstriction and increased congestion causes a rise in pressure on the right side of the heart. This results in shunting of blood through the foramen ovale to the left side of the heart, as occurs during fetal circulation. Blood flow through the ductus arteriosus from the pulmonary artery to the aorta may also occur. The diversion of blood flow away from the lungs results in poor systemic oxygenation (Fig. 29–1).

THERAPEUTIC MANAGEMENT

Anytime meconium is noted in the amniotic fluid, preparation for appropriate care at birth must be made to minimize meconium aspiration. The infant's mouth and pharynx are suctioned as soon as the head is delivered and before delivery of the rest of the body. This helps prevent drawing the meconium

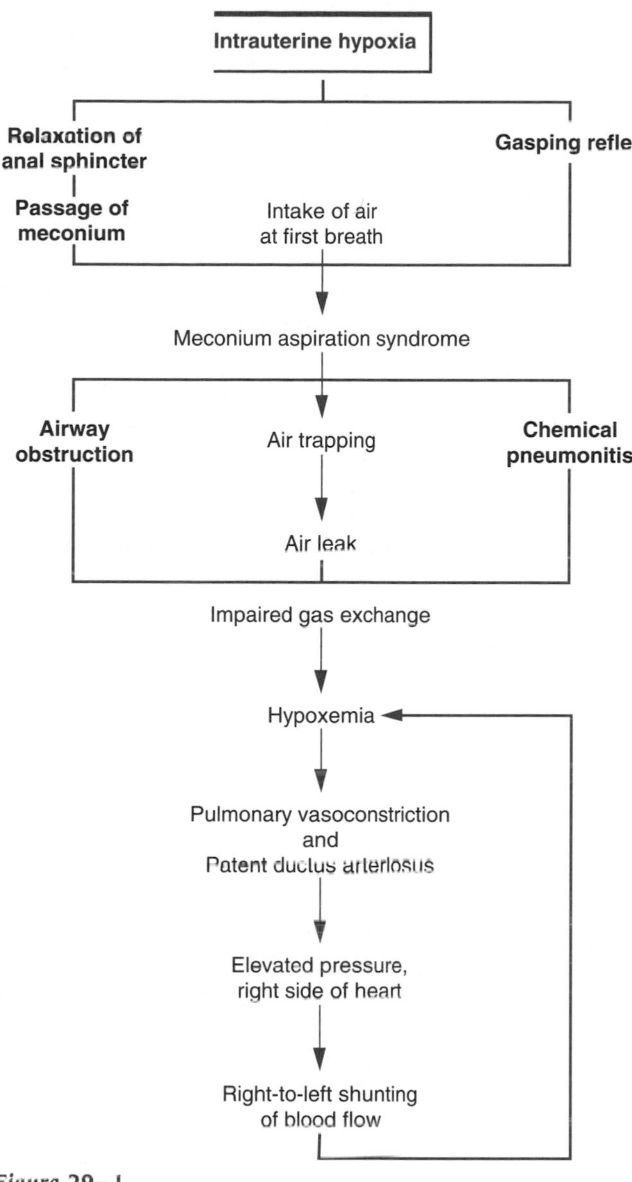

Figure 29–1

Flow chart of meconium aspiration syndrome.

from the upper air passages deep into the lungs during the infant's first breath.

Immediately after birth and before the infant takes the first breath, the vocal cords are visualized with a laryngoscope. If meconium is present below the area of the vocal cords, the infant can be expected to have it in the air passages below. An endotracheal tube is inserted to allow deep suction of meconium and ventilation, if necessary.

Infants may need only warmed, humidified oxygen, or extensive respiratory support with a ventilator may be required. High-frequency ventilation may be used. Supportive care to meet the problems presented makes up ongoing management.

Infants with severe MAS who do not respond to conventional treatment may benefit from extracorporeal membrane oxygenation (ECMO). This is a method available in some large hospitals to oxygenate the blood while bypassing the lungs, much like heart-lung machines used during heart surgery. It allows the infant's lungs to rest temporarily and recover.

NURSING CONSIDERATIONS

When meconium is noted in the amniotic fluid during labor, the nurse notifies the appropriate physicians of the amount of meconium present so that delivery care can be adapted as necessary. The nurse ensures that equipment is available and functioning and assists with care at delivery. After the infant's birth, nursing care is adapted to the problems presented. Because the meconium in the lungs promotes the growth of bacteria, infants should be closely observed for infection, which may further complicate the condition.

✔ Check Your Reading

1. What is the result of asphyxia before or during birth?
2. What is the role of the nurse in care of the infant with asphyxia?
3. Which infants are at risk for respiratory distress syndrome?
4. How is transient tachypnea of the newborn different from respiratory distress syndrome?
5. How does meconium get into an infant's respiratory tract? Why is it a problem?
6. What is the role of the nurse when meconium is discovered in amniotic fluid?

Hyperbilirubinemia (Pathologic Jaundice)

Conjugation of bilirubin and physiologic jaundice are discussed in Chapters 19, p. 496, and 20, p. 526. This discussion focuses on pathologic jaundice. When the bilirubin level reaches 5 to 7 mg/dl, jaundice begins to be visible in the skin (Gomella, 1992). Jaundice is considered pathologic when (1) it appears in the first 24 hours after birth; (2) the total bilirubin rises above 12.9 mg/dl in the full-term infant or 15 mg/dl in the preterm infant, or more than 5 mg/dl in 24 hours; (3) the direct bilirubin is above 1.5 to 2 mg/dl; or (4) it continues beyond the first week of life in the full-term infant or the second week in the preterm infant (Maisels, 1987).

Jaundice is a concern because it demonstrates rising levels of bilirubin that may lead to kernicterus or bilirubin encephalopathy. When kernicterus occurs, bilirubin deposits cause yellowish staining of the brain, especially the basal ganglia, cerebellum, and hippocampus. It is more likely to occur in infants who have suffered sepsis, hypoxia, or respiratory acidosis, which impairs the blood-brain barrier and allows unconjugated bilirubin to enter the brain.

Although kernicterus is rare today because of improved treatment measures, the mortality rate of affected infants is 50 per cent (Oski, 1991). Those who survive may suffer from cerebral palsy, mental retardation, hearing loss, or more subtle long-term neurological and developmental problems. The exact level at which bilirubin toxicity and kernicterus begin to develop is not known, but they may occur when total bilirubin levels reach 20 mg/dl in full-term infants and lower levels in preterms or neonates with other complications.

Causes

The most common cause of pathologic jaundice is incompatibility between the blood of the mother and that of the fetus. The best known cause is Rh incompatibility, in which the Rh-negative mother forms antibodies when Rh-positive blood from the fetus enters her circulation. Antibodies may have developed during a previous pregnancy or after injury, abortion, or amniocentesis. A transfusion with Rh-positive blood, although unlikely, would also result in the development of antibodies. The antibodies cross the placenta and attach to fetal red blood cells and destroy them. This condition is called erythroblastosis fetalis.

Infants with erythroblastosis fetalis are anemic as a result of loss of red blood cells, but jaundice usually does not develop until soon after birth because bilirubin crosses the placenta and is excreted by the mother. Severely affected infants may experience hydrops fetalis, a severe anemia that results in heart failure and generalized edema. Use of Rh immune globulin (Rh IgG), such as RhoGAM, to prevent the mother from forming antibodies against Rh-positive blood has greatly decreased the incidence of erythroblastosis fetalis. (Rh incompatibility is discussed further in Chapter 24, p. 691.)

ABO incompatibility also causes pathologic jaundice. Mothers with type O blood have natural antibodies to type A or B blood. The antibodies cross the placenta and cause hemolysis of fetal red blood cells. However, the destruction is much less than with Rh incompatibility and causes milder symptoms.

Other causes of pathologic jaundice include infection, hypothyroidism, inherited glucuronyl transferase deficiency, and biliary atresia. Any condition that causes destruction of erythrocytes or impairment of the liver may result in hyperbilirubinemia that may result in pathologic bilirubin levels.

Therapeutic Management

Therapeutic management is focused on determining the cause of the jaundice, following the course of bilirubin elevation by laboratory work, and treating the condition to prevent the development of kernicterus. The cause is determined by history and diagnostic tests to eliminate infections or blood abnormalities. During pregnancy, a positive Coombs' test of the expectant mother's blood shows the presence of antibodies against the fetus' blood. Amniocentesis may be performed to determine the degree of hyperbilirubinemia in the fetus. A positive direct Coombs' test (performed on cord blood at birth) indicates that antibodies from the mother have attached to the infant's red blood cells. Bilirubin levels are followed closely for changes that indicate that treatment should be initiated or changed.

PHOTOTHERAPY

The most common treatment of jaundice is phototherapy or "bili" lights. These are special fluorescent lamps placed over the infant at a distance determined by the type of bulb used (usually 12 to 30 inches) (Fig. 29–2). Fiberoptic phototherapy blankets may also be used.

During phototherapy, bilirubin in the skin absorbs the light and changes into water-soluble products (photobilirubin and lumirubin), which do not require conjugation by the liver and can be excreted in the bile and urine. Because kernicterus develops in preterm infants at lower bilirubin levels than in full-term infants, phototherapy is begun at lower levels for them. More than one light may be used if the bilirubin level is high.

Side effects of phototherapy include frequent loose green stools due to increased bile flow and peristalsis. This causes more rapid excretion of the bilirubin but may be damaging to the skin and result in fluid loss. African-American infants may experience a tanning effect from the light. Bronze baby syndrome, a grayish-brown discoloration of the skin, occurs in infants with cholestatic jaundice, in whom liver function and production or flow of bile are impaired. A skin rash similar to erythema toxicum may also occur. The color changes and rash disappear when phototherapy is ended. Some infants experience a temporary lactose intolerance during therapy and are fed a formula without lactose.

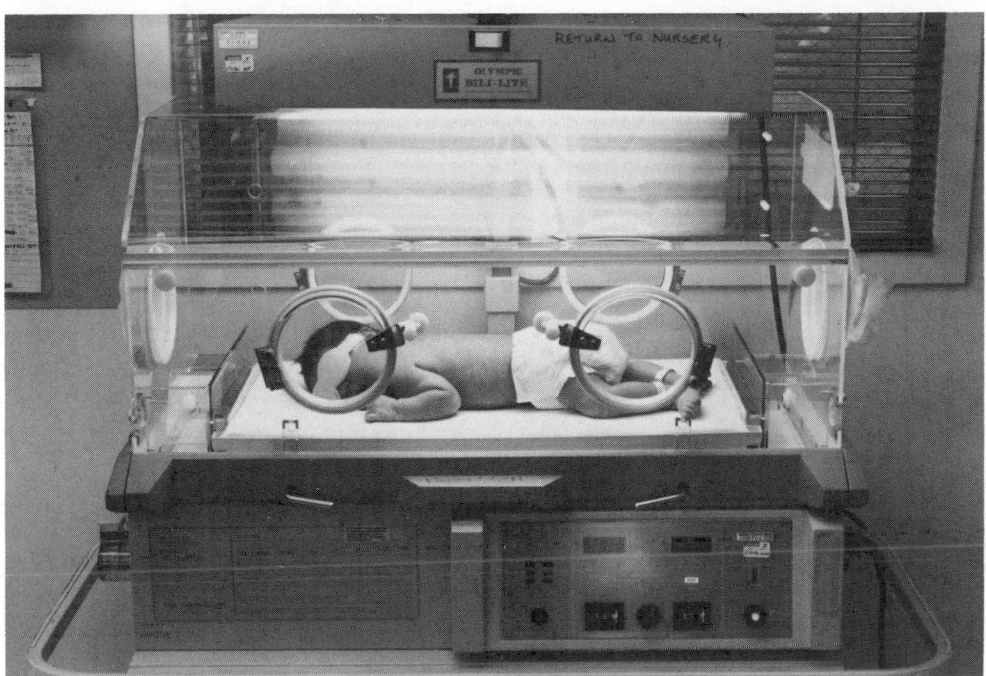

***Figure* 29–2**

The infant receiving phototherapy is wearing eye patches to protect the eyes and a diaper to protect the gonads.

Home phototherapy may be used to prevent prolonged hospitalization and separation from the parents. Parents using phototherapy at home need extensive teaching on how to manage the equipment and the infant's requirements. (See Parents Want to Know: Home Care for the Infant Receiving Phototherapy.) Home visits by nurses may be available to supervise use of equipment and help ensure that the infant is making adequate progress and that the parents understand how to provide care.

EXCHANGE TRANSFUSIONS

Although the use of phototherapy has decreased the need for exchange transfusions, they may be necessary when bilirubin levels become dangerously high. An exchange transfusion removes sensitized red blood cells before they break down and release large amounts of unconjugated bilirubin. The transfusion also removes antibodies and unconjugated bilirubin in the blood and corrects severe anemia. If the problem is Rh incompatibility, type O Rh-negative blood, crossmatched against the mother's and infant's blood, is used so that circulating antibodies will not destroy the erythrocytes.

Procedure. During the exchange transfusion, 5- to 10-ml portions of blood are removed and replaced with an equal amount of donor blood. Because the donor blood mixes with the infant's blood, it is necessary to administer approximately twice the infant's blood volume. Normal blood volume in a full-term infant is 80 to 85 ml/kg and in a preterm infant is 100 ml/kg. In an infant weighing 3000 g (6 pounds, 10 ounces), the normal blood volume is 255 ml. In an exchange transfusion, 510 ml of donor blood would be given.

At the end of the transfusion, approximately 85 per cent of the infant's red blood cells have been replaced. The bilirubin level after transfusion is about 45 per cent of this pre-exchange level. When the level in the blood decreases, bilirubin from the tissues moves into the plasma. This may increase the blood level to 60 per cent or more of the original level (Frank et al, 1993). This rebound elevation of bilirubin may necessitate repeat transfusions, but phototherapy is generally adequate to resolve it.

Complications. Many complications may occur during exchange transfusion, including infection, hypervolemia or hypovolemia, cardiac arrhythmias, and air embolism. Hypocalcemia is also a problem because preservatives in the blood lower the infant's blood calcium level. Signs of hypocalcemia include jitteriness, irritability, tachycardia, and ECG changes. Samples of blood are analyzed before and after the exchange, including a complete blood count, bilirubin and calcium levels, and other tests as needed.

Role of the Nurse. The nurse's role during exchange transfusion is to prepare equipment, assess the infant during and after the procedure, and keep accurate records. A cardiac monitor is attached to the infant, and adequate warmth is provided by a radiant heater. The nurse must also clarify any misun-

Parents Want To Know

Home Care for the Infant Receiving Phototherapy

- Position the phototherapy or "bili" light at the proper distance from your baby according to the manufacturer's direction. Placing it too close to the infant could result in fever or burns. Placing it too far away will make the treatment ineffective.
- Close the baby's eyes, and place patches over the eyes before placing the infant under the lights. Check at least every hour to see that the patches remain in place. They must cover the eyes but not press on the nose because they can interfere with breathing.
- The infant may be taken out from under the lights for feedings, diaper changes, and other general care but should receive phototherapy for 18 hours every day (or number of hours ordered by physician). Hold and cuddle your infant during the time that he or she is out of the lights. You can talk to the infant while he or she is under the lights so that the baby hears your voice and knows you are there. This may be very comforting.
- Check your infant's temperature under the arm before every feeding. The temperature should remain between 97.7 and 99.5°F. If it is abnormal, check to see that the heat in the room is not too low or too high. Be sure that the "bili" light is positioned correctly. Wrap your baby in warm blankets when removing him or her from the warmth of the light. Call the physician if the temperature is less than 97.7 or above 100°F.
- Change your baby's position approximately every 2 hours so that the light reaches all areas of the body. Keep diapers on your infant at all times, but no other clothing is necessary, as it would prevent exposure of the skin to the light. The temperature in the room may have to be higher than you would normally have it because the infant is undressed under the light.
- It is important for the infant to eat well while under the "bili" light. The infant is losing fluid because of the heat and because the light causes stools to be loose. This could lead to dehydration. The infant needs enough protein because it helps in the elimination of the bilirubin that causes the jaundice. Feed your baby every 2 to 3 hours.
- Keep a list of your baby's wet diapers and stools. The infant should have six to ten wet diapers a day. If there are less, or if the urine appears dark, increase the feedings.
- Call the physician or nurse practitioner if the infant has a fever, the mouth seems dry, the urine is dark or less than normal, or if the infant appears to be sick to you. Also call if you have any other questions about care.

derstandings that the parents may have about the treatment and help allay their anxiety.

Hyperbilirubinemia: Application of Nursing Process

Although collaborative care of the infant with jaundice is an important part of the nurse's role, a number of nursing diagnoses are appropriate. The nurse's role during phototherapy is particularly important. The infant may be at risk for injury associated with bilirubin increases and phototherapy and for fluid volume deficit.

Injury

The nurse must be alert for factors that might result in injury due to use of phototherapy and intervene appropriately.

Assessment

Assess the level of jaundice at the initial assessment each shift. Press the skin over a bony prominence, and note the color in the area before the blood returns. Determine the areas of the body affected by the jaundice, and document carefully to use for comparison during future assessment. Jaundice begins at the head and moves down the body as the bilirubin levels rise. Monitor laboratory bilirubin levels for change, especially because visibility of jaundice in the skin may be affected by phototherapy.

Assess for risk factors that might further increase bilirubin levels. Note temperature fluctuations, hypoglycemia, or infection. Determine the infant's oral intake and number of stools as an indication of gastrointestinal motility.

Analysis

Nurses can do many things to prevent situations that might cause further rises in bilirubin. They must also protect the infant from injury from the light during phototherapy. Therefore, an appropriate nursing diagnosis is: *High Risk for Injury related to preventable causes of further elevation of bilirubin and damage to the eyes or gonads secondary to phototherapy.*

Planning

The goals for this nursing diagnosis are that the infant will not:

- Experience injury due to increased bilirubin
- Experience exposure of the eyes or gonads to phototherapy lights

Interventions

Interventions are designed to prevent situations that might cause injury to the infant from rising bilirubin levels or effects of treatment.

MAINTAINING NEUTRAL THERMAL ENVIRONMENT

Prevent situations, such as cold stress or hypoglycemia, that could result in increased fatty acids in the blood due to acidosis, thereby decreasing the availability of albumin-binding sites for unconjugated bilirubin. Prevent cold stress at birth and during all care by maintaining the infant in a neutral thermal environment. Use a temperature probe to monitor the temperature, and check the axillary temperature every 2 to 4 hours to identify an early decrease before it becomes a problem. Dress the infant in warmed clothes and blankets when removing from phototherapy lights. (See Nursing Care Plan 28–1, p. 814, for more interventions for thermoregulation.)

Prevent elevation of the infant's temperature from exposure to the heat of the "bili" lights. Use a skin probe if the infant is in an incubator to maintain the environmental temperature appropriately. Position the lights the correct distance from the infant (as suggested by the manufacturer's guidelines) to prevent overheating or burning the skin.

PROVIDING OPTIMAL NUTRITION

See that the infant receives feedings every 2 to 3 hours, whether by breast or bottle. This prevents hypoglycemia, provides protein to maintain the albumin level in the blood, and promotes gastrointestinal motility and prompt emptying of bilirubin from the bowel.

PROTECTING THE EYES

Provide patches to protect the eyes from retinal damage from the phototherapy lights. Close the infant's eyes before placing the patches to avoid abrasions to the cornea. Be sure that the patches are in the proper position at all times. Infants often wiggle enough to push the patches above or below the eyes, leaving them exposed. The edges of the patches can dig into the eyes or compress the nose and interfere with breathing. Because the patches hide the eye area, an infection might not be noticed immediately. Remove the patches at each feeding, and inspect the eyes carefully for redness, edema, and drainage.

ENHANCING RESPONSE TO THERAPY

Expose as much skin as possible to the light. Turn the infant frequently to prevent irritation of the skin from lack of position change and to expose the areas evenly. Remove all clothing except a diaper. Use a face mask for a diaper if diapers cover too much skin. If the face mask has a metal strip to go over the nose, remove it so that it does not retain heat and burn the infant. Be sure that the testes or ovaries are covered, because there is a possibility that damage to DNA may occur from exposure of the gonads to phototherapy. Turn the light off when changing diapers.

The amount of time that the infant can be removed from phototherapy lights without decreasing the effectiveness is controversial. The lights are most effective during the first hour of exposure, and short periods of time out of the lights do not decrease effectiveness. The policy in most nurseries is to keep infants under the lights except during feedings. When bilirubin levels are high, some feedings may be given while the infant remains under the lights.

Observe for other complications. Although kernicterus is rare today, monitor for signs that indicate its presence. These include lethargy, poor muscle tone, decreased or absent Moro reflex, high-pitched cry, opisthotonos, and seizures. Note the presence of rashes or changes in the color of the skin, and inform parents that they are not harmful and will disappear when phototherapy is discontinued.

Evaluation

- The infant's bilirubin levels should gradually decrease.

- There should be no signs of injury, such as kernicterus.
- The eyes and gonads will not have been exposed to the phototherapy lights.

Hydration

Infants undergoing phototherapy may have increased insensible water losses and loose stools. The nurse must maintain the infant's hydration to compensate for this.

Assessment

Assess for signs of dehydration, including dry skin and mucous membranes. Decreased tissue turgor and a depressed anterior fontanelle are late signs. Note the intake of fluids, and compare this to the infant's need for 60 to 80 ml/kg/day (27 to 36 ml/pound/day) during the first 2 days of life and 100 to 150 ml/kg/day (45 to 68 ml/pound/day) thereafter.

Note the color and consistency of stools. Loose green stools are common during phototherapy, which increases intestinal motility. Look for a water ring, a discolored area around a bit of semisolid stool, which indicates that water has soaked into the diaper.

Note the color of the urine, which should be straw-colored. Count the number of wet diapers daily. Weigh diapers to determine the amount of urine excreted if water loss appears to be excessive or if urine appears dark and concentrated (1 g = 1 ml). Check specific gravity, which should range between 1.001 and 1.020 for the full-term infant (Anand, 1991).

Analysis

The infant receiving phototherapy is at risk for dehydration. An appropriate nursing diagnosis is: *High Risk for Fluid Volume Deficit related to increased insensible water loss, frequent stools, and inadequate intake of fluids to meet losses.*

Planning

The goals for this nursing diagnosis are that the infant will:

- Take in fluids at least equal to normal daily requirements for weight (100 to 150 ml/kg)
- Show no signs of dehydration

Interventions

Interventions are aimed at providing adequate hydration.

MAINTAINING HYDRATION

Feed the infant formula, or have the mother breastfeed every 2 to 3 hours, to ensure adequate intake of fluid and nutrients. Explain to the mother the need for more protein and fluid, as well as other nutrients, because of increased loss of fluids, the need for adequate albumin to carry bilirubin to the liver, and the fact that heightened intestinal motility decreases the absorption of nutrients. Avoid offering dextrose water because it interferes with intake of milk, which provides nutrients as well as fluid. Give formula if there is difficulty in breastfeeding and the infant must receive a supplement.

Evaluation

The infant takes in adequate fluids (100 to 150 ml/kg) and shows no signs of dehydration, such as decreased urine output and increased urine specific gravity, weight loss, or dry skin or mucous membranes.

✔ Check Your Reading

7. How is pathologic jaundice different from physiologic jaundice?
8. What is the role of the nurse in caring for the infant receiving phototherapy?

Infection

Neonatal infection is responsible for approximately 30 per cent of all neonatal deaths (Lott et al, 1993). The nurse must be constantly alert for this condition.

Transmission of Infection

Newborns acquire infection in two general ways: vertical transmission, which occurs in utero or during birth, and horizontal transmission, which occurs after birth.

VERTICAL TRANSMISSION

In vertical transmission, the fetus becomes infected from the expectant mother by transfer of organisms across the placenta during pregnancy, by contact

Nursing Care Plan 29–1

The Infant with Jaundice

Assessment: Holly is a full-term newborn who has developed jaundice secondary to ABO incompatibility and is receiving phototherapy.

Nursing Diagnosis: High Risk for Injury related to exposure of the eyes and gonads to phototherapy lights.

Goals:
There will be no exposure of the eyes or gonads to phototherapy lights.

Intervention:	Rationale:
1. Place eye patches on Holly before turning on the phototherapy lights.	1. Retinal damage can result if eyes are uncovered under lights.
2. Attach eye patches firmly so that they stay in place. Close Holly's eyes before applying patches.	2. Abrasions to the corneas may occur if eyes are open under the patches.
3. Check position of patches at least every hour.	3. Pressure from slipped patches can traumatize eyes or occlude nares and cause respiratory distress.
4. Remove patches before every feeding and inspect eyes for redness, edema, drainage, or trauma.	4. Infection or trauma that occurs under the patches may not be immediately identified if patches are not periodically removed.
5. Cover ovaries (or testes) with diaper or face mask (with metal removed). Turn off light when changing diapers.	5. Phototherapy light may damage the gonads.

Evaluation:
Holly has no exposure of the eyes or gonads to phototherapy lights.

Assessment: At 3 days of age, Holly weighs 3.2 kg (7 pounds, 1 ounce). She is a sleepy infant who takes formula poorly. Her skin is very dry, and her mucous membranes appear slightly dry. Skin turgor is good, and the anterior fontanelle is flat. Urine appears slightly concentrated. She has passed three loose green stools with no water ring on this shift. Holly was delivered by cesarean section, and her mother, Valerie, is very tired and appears frustrated with Holly's slow eating behavior.

Nursing Diagnosis: Fluid Volume Deficit related to inadequate oral intake to meet needs of increased insensible water loss and frequent loose stools.

Goals:
Holly will take in at least 320 to 480 ml of fluid per day to meet normal needs and will not show increased signs of dehydration (dry mucous membranes, poor skin turgor, sunken fontanelles, inadequate urine output, urine specific gravity >1.020).

Intervention:	Rationale:
1. Have Valerie feed Holly every 2 to 3 hours. Feed Holly in nursery at night or when Valerie needs rest, if she prefers.	1. Adequate intake of formula is necessary to meet infant's nutrient and fluid needs and ensure excretion of bilirubin in the stools. The mother's need for rest must be met without interfering with infant's needs.
2. Explain Holly's need for frequent feeding to Valerie.	2. Mother's understanding of need will increase her willingness to work with infant.

Nursing Care Plan continued on following page

Nursing Care Plan 29–1 Continued

The Infant with Jaundice

Intervention	Rationale
3. Observe Holly and Valerie during feeding and offer suggestions as needed. Show her how to waken the infant, if necessary, by unwrapping and gentle stimulation. Try warming formula slightly. Stroke around Holly's mouth, and insert finger to elicit suck reflex before feedings.	3. Observation of feeding may identify problems and interventions that work for this situation. A wide-awake infant is more likely to feed well. Some infants prefer warm milk. Oral exercises may help infant suck effectively.
4. Avoid offering dextrose water. Use formula instead.	4. Infants who are given dextrose water may decrease intake of formula, with its needed nutrients. Protein is especially important to maintain serum albumin. Formula increases motility of intestines and expedites excretion of bilirubin in stools.
5. Use therapeutic communication techniques to help Valerie vent her frustrations. Offer praise for her attempts to feed Holly.	5. Helping the mother deal with her feelings helps her meet the infant's needs. Feeding difficulties often interfere with the mother's view of herself as a "good" mother. Praise increases her self-concept and sense of adequacy.

Evaluation:
Holly drinks a total of 510 ml (17 ounces) of formula during 24 hours. Valerie is able to wake Holly, who begins to suck more vigorously. Holly's skin remains dry, which is normal for age. Mucous membranes are moist; there are ten wet diapers during the 24 hours.

Assessment: Holly's diaper area is slightly red and irritated from her frequent loose stools.

Nursing Diagnosis: Altered Skin Integrity related to frequent loose stools.

Goals:
Skin will return to normal within 2 days without further signs of irritation or breakdown.

Intervention:	Rationale:
1. Check diapers at least every hour. Cleanse diaper area with soap and water after each stool.	1. Extended exposure of the skin to stool and urine may cause skin breakdown. Thorough cleansing removes irritating substances from skin.
2. Place Holly prone, and expose diaper area to light and air. Place a diaper under Holly (for male infants, use a face mask to cover the scrotum). Expose entire diaper area to air for short periods when phototherapy light is off.	2. Exposure to air helps keep area dry and aids healing.
3. Avoid lotions, powders, or ointments.	3. These may increase the risk of burns from the phototherapy lights.
4. Use cloth diapers if paper disposable diapers seem to cause more irritation.	4. Cloth diapers are softer on irritated skin than paper diapers.
5. Explain reason for loose stools and methods of treatment of skin irritation to Valerie.	5. The mother may need help to understand that the condition is not the result of poor care. She should learn how to care for diaper rash at home.

Evaluation:
Holly's diaper area returns to normal within 1 day.

Additional Nursing Diagnoses to Consider:

Anxiety
Altered Parenting
Ineffective Thermoregulation

with organisms present in the vagina during birth, or by ascending infection after rupture of membranes. Infections that are acquired by vertical transmission include TORCH (toxoplasmosis, rubella, cytomegalovirus, and herpes) and hepatitis. Vertically transmitted infections may cause defects in the fetus and long-term consequences for the newborn and the family. Some of the most common of these infections and their effects on the neonate are listed in Table 29–1. Their effects on the expectant mother during pregnancy are discussed in Chapter 25, p. 720.

HORIZONTAL TRANSMISSION

In horizontal transmission, the infant acquires infection after birth from the mother or other family members, agency staff, or contaminated equipment. A common example is staphylococcal infection. Transmission of some organisms such as cytomegalovirus or *Streptococcus*, may occur either vertically or horizontally.

Sepsis Neonatorum

Infection that occurs during or after birth may result in sepsis neonatorum, systemic infection with bacteria in the blood stream. Bacterial sepsis occurs in 1 in 1000 full-term infants and in 1 in 250 preterm infants (Paxton, 1992).

Newborns are particularly susceptible to sepsis because their immune system is immature and they react more slowly to invasion by organisms. They fail to localize infection as well as older children, and

Table 29–1. COMMON VERTICAL INFECTIONS IN THE NEWBORN

Transmission	Effect on Newborn	Nursing Considerations
	Toxoplasmosis	
Transplacental	Asymptomatic or LBW, rash, enlarged liver and spleen, jaundice, anemia, seizures, microcephaly, hydrocephalus. Signs may not develop for years.	Consider in infants with IUGR with other signs. Confirmed by serum tests.
	Rubella	
Transplacental	If woman infected in first trimester, neonate may have deafness, cataracts, cardiac defects, IUGR, mental retardation, microcephaly.	Body fluid precautions. Infant may shed virus for months after birth and infect others. Diagnosed by presence of antibody.
	Cytomegalovirus	
Transplacental	LBW, IUGR, enlarged liver and spleen, jaundice, mental retardation, blindness, epilepsy, hearing loss. May not have signs for months or years.	Most common perinatal infection. Diagnosed by urine culture. May shed virus for months. Universal and body fluid precautions. △
	Herpes	
Usually during passage through infected vagina or ascending infection after rupture of membranes	Clusters of vesicles, temperature instability, lethargy, poor suck, seizures, jaundice, purpura. Mortality rate of untreated infection 50%, with ½ of survivors having severe neurological involvement.	Universal and body fluid precautions. Obtain lesion specimens for culture. Observe for side effects of antiviral medications. △
	Hepatitis B	
Usually during birth from contact with maternal blood	Asymptomatic at birth. At risk for chronic hepatitis or carrier state.	Universal precautions. Wash well to remove all blood before skin is pierced for any reason. After cleaning, administer hepatitis B immune globulin and hepatitis B vaccine to prevent infection. △
	Syphilis	
Transplacental after 18th week of pregnancy	Asymptomatic or copper-colored rash, enlarged liver and spleen, jaundice, petechiae, osteochondritis, pneumonitis, rhinitis, respiratory distress, CNS involvement, mental retardation.	Universal precautions. Diagnosed by blood and cerebrospinal fluid testing. Administer penicillin as ordered. △

Table continued on following page

Table 29–1. COMMON VERTICAL INFECTIONS IN THE NEWBORN *Continued*

Transmission	Effect on Newborn	Nursing Considerations
	Gonorrhea	
Usually during birth	Conjunctivitis (ophthalmia neonatorum), with red, edematous lids and purulent eye drainage. May result in blindness if untreated.	Universal and body fluid precautions. All infants treated with silver nitrate or erythromycin eye ointment or other antibiotic at birth. 
	Chlamydial Infection	
During birth	Conjunctivitis, pneumonia, otitis media	Universal and body fluid precautions. Erythromycin eye ointment for prevention of conjunctivitis. 
	Candidiasis	
During birth	White patches in mouth (thrush) that bleed if removed. May also have infection of perineal area or systemic infection with signs according to areas involved.	Body fluid precautions. Administer nystatin drops or cream and teach mother technique. Assess mother for *Candida* infection of vagina or breasts.
	HIV Infection, AIDS	
Transplacental; during birth from infected blood and secretions; breast milk.	Approximately 20–40% of infants of mothers with HIV are infected. Asymptomatic at birth, signs apparent at 4–12 months. Enlarged liver and spleen, lymphadenopathy, failure to thrive, persistent thrush *(Candida),* diarrhea, chronic bacterial infections.	Universal precautions. May have antibodies to HIV from mother. If uninfected will revert to negative after passive antibodies are gone (by age 2 years). Bathe early after birth to remove maternal blood. Do not puncture skin until bathed. Observe for side effects of medications. 
	Group B Streptococcal Infection	
During birth	Sudden onset of respiratory distress in infant usually well at birth: tachypnea, apnea, shock, pneumonia. May have late onset, more than a week after birth, with meningitis.	Carried in vagina of asymptomatic women. Diagnosed by cultures of organism from mother or infant. Early identification essential to prevent death. Body fluid precautions.

LBW, low birth weight; IUGR, intrauterine growth retardation; CNS, central nervous system; HIV, human immunodeficiency virus; AIDS, acquired immunodeficiency syndrome.

this allows it to spread easily from one organ to another. The blood-brain barrier is less effective in keeping out organisms, and central nervous system infection may occur. The preterm infant is especially susceptible to infection. (Infection in the preterm infant is discussed in Chapter 28.)

CAUSES

Although almost any bacteria may cause sepsis in the newborn, the common causative agents include group B β-hemolytic streptococcus, *Escherichia coli, Haemophilus influenzae, Klebsiella, Staphylococcus,* and *Listeria* (O'Donnell and Merenstein, 1993). Sepsis may be divided into early onset and late onset, according to when signs of disease begin.

Early-onset sepsis is often due to complications of labor such as prolonged rupture of membranes, prolonged labor, chorioamnionitis, or other infection in the mother. It has a higher mortality rate and more rapid progression than late-onset sepsis. It often involves the respiratory system.

Late-onset sepsis generally develops after the first week of life from exposure to organisms after birth and usually involves the central nervous system. Reasons for the differences between early- and late-onset sepsis are unknown.

Infection: Application of Nursing Process

Assessment

SIGNS OF INFECTION

In the newborn, signs of infection are not as specific or obvious as those in the older infant or child. Instead, they tend to be subtle and could indicate other conditions. There may be temperature instability, respiratory problems, and changes in feeding habits or behavior. (See Critical to Remember: Signs

Critical to Remember

Signs of Sepsis in the Newborn

General Signs

- Temperature instability (usually low)
- Nurse's feeling that infant is not doing well
- Rash

Respiratory Signs

- Tachypnea
- Apnea
- Respiratory distress—nasal flaring, retractions, grunting

Cardiovascular Signs

- Color changes—cyanosis, pallor, mottling
- Tachycardia
- Hypotension
- Decreased peripheral perfusion

Gastrointestinal Signs

- Decreased oral intake
- Vomiting
- Gastric residuals over half previous feeding
- Diarrhea
- Abdominal distention
- Hypoglycemia or hyperglycemia

Central Nervous System Signs

- Decreased muscle tone
- Lethargy
- Irritability
- Bulging fontanelle

Signs That May Indicate Advanced Infection

- Jaundice
- Evidence of hemorrhage (petechiae, purpura, pulmonary bleeding)
- Anemia
- Enlarged liver and spleen
- Respiratory failure
- Shock
- Seizures
- Death

of Sepsis.) It is often the nurse who notices the early, subtle changes that indicate sepsis. Experienced nurses may have a feeling that the infant is not doing well even before specific signs of infection are present. When this occurs, the nurse expands the assessment and watches carefully for the development of other signs. Early identification and reporting to the pediatrician or nurse practitioner will speed the beginning of treatment.

TESTING

Neonatal sepsis may be confused with other illnesses. For example, group B streptococcal pneumonia has the same symptoms as respiratory distress syndrome at first. Therefore, a variety of tests are ordered.

The nurse is responsible for obtaining or helping to obtain specimens for laboratory analysis and for seeing that other tests ordered by the physician are completed. Specimens of the blood, urine, gastric aspirate, and sometimes the cerebral spinal fluid are obtained for culture to determine areas infected. Although specimens of the nose, throat, cord, and skin surfaces may also be obtained for culture, these are not as reliable in determining the cause of the sepsis because they are contaminated by environmental organisms.

A complete blood count may show decreased neutrophils, increased bands (immature neutrophils), and decreased platelets. Presence of elevated IgM levels in cord blood or shortly after birth may indicate that infection was acquired in utero, as this immunoglobulin does not cross the placenta. It often indicates transplacental infection. A chest X-ray will help differentiate between respiratory distress syndrome and sepsis. Blood glucose levels should be checked, as they may be unstable in sepsis.

Analysis

When infants are at risk for infection, the nursing diagnosis *High Risk for Infection* is appropriate. When infants demonstrate signs of actual infection, the nurse will work with the potential complication: *Sepsis*.

Planning

Goals are not written for potential complications. The nurse's role is to identify early signs of sepsis, notify the physician or nurse practitioner, coordinate treatment, observe for change, and provide supportive care to the infant and family.

Interventions

PROVIDING ANTIBIOTICS

Because the signs of sepsis are non-specific and the disease can be fatal, physicians may order antibiotics before an actual diagnosis is made for infants who are at high risk or who show early signs. Broad-spectrum antibiotics are given intravenously until culture and sensitivity results are available. Continued antibiotic therapy is based on the organisms that are positive on culture.

Start the intravenous fluids, and see that the medications are administered on time. If more than one antibiotic is ordered, coordinate the timing of administration to increase effectiveness. Laboratory analysis of peak and trough levels may be ordered to determine when the blood levels of the medications are at their highest and lowest. This requires coordinating with the laboratory so that blood is drawn at the correct time in relation to medication administration. Expect antibiotic therapy to be necessary for 10 to 14 days or longer.

PROVIDING OTHER SUPPORTIVE CARE

Oxygen or other respiratory support is used if needed. The infant may need treatment for shock, hypoglycemia, electrolyte imbalances, and problems in temperature regulation. Intravenous immune globulin may be given prophylactically or as treatment to enhance the infant's ability to fight infection. Gavage feeding may be necessary if the infant is unable to take oral feedings.

Infants with sepsis may have other problems as well. They may be premature or have transplacentally acquired infections. These may require other intensive nursing care.

PREVENTING SPREAD OF INFECTION

Prevent transmission of infection to other infants in the nursery. Employ the same techniques that are used to prevent cross-contamination between normal infants (such as hand washing and separation of supplies) and ensure that they are conscientiously performed by all who come in contact with the infant. Placing the infant in an incubator provides a physical separation between infected and well infants similar to placing adults in isolation in private rooms. The nurse can observe the infant in an incubator at all times.

SUPPORTING PARENTS

Support parents of newborns with sepsis, and help them understand their infant's illness and treatment. The infant with sepsis often appears healthy at birth but suddenly becomes critically ill. Parents have feelings of shock, fear, and disappointment when their apparently healthy newborn is suddenly moved to the intensive care nursery. They will benefit from a chance to talk about their feelings with an understanding nurse who can explain the infant's treatment and care. Keeping the parents informed of the infant's changes in condition and involving them in care is essential.

Evaluation

An evaluation is not written for potential complications. The nurse manages the nursing aspects of the treatment program and monitors for change in the infant. The infant is expected to show steady improvement during treatment.

Infant of a Diabetic Mother

Scope of Problem

Maternal diabetes is a problem for the mother and the neonate. The effect of diabetes on the pregnancy is discussed in Chapter 25. The infant of a diabetic mother (IDM) faces a number of risks, which depend on the type of diabetes that the mother has and how well it is controlled. Infants of mothers with long-term diabetes and vascular changes may have intrauterine growth retardation due to decreased placental blood flow. Hypertension occurs more often in diabetic mothers and further compromises uteroplacental blood flow. Infants born to women with gestational diabetes or diabetes without vascular changes may be large for gestational age, particularly if the diabetes is not well controlled during the last trimester (Fig. 29–3).

When the mother is hyperglycemic, large amounts of amino acids, free fatty acids, and glucose are transferred to the fetus. Although maternal insulin does not cross the placenta, the fetal pancreas responds by hypertrophy of the islet cells of the pancreas. The islet cells produce large amounts of insulin, which acts as a growth hormone. The accelerated protein synthesis and the deposit of fat and glycogen in fetal tissues result in an infant with macrosomia. There may be other factors involved that cause macrosomia in the IDM, even if the mother's dia-

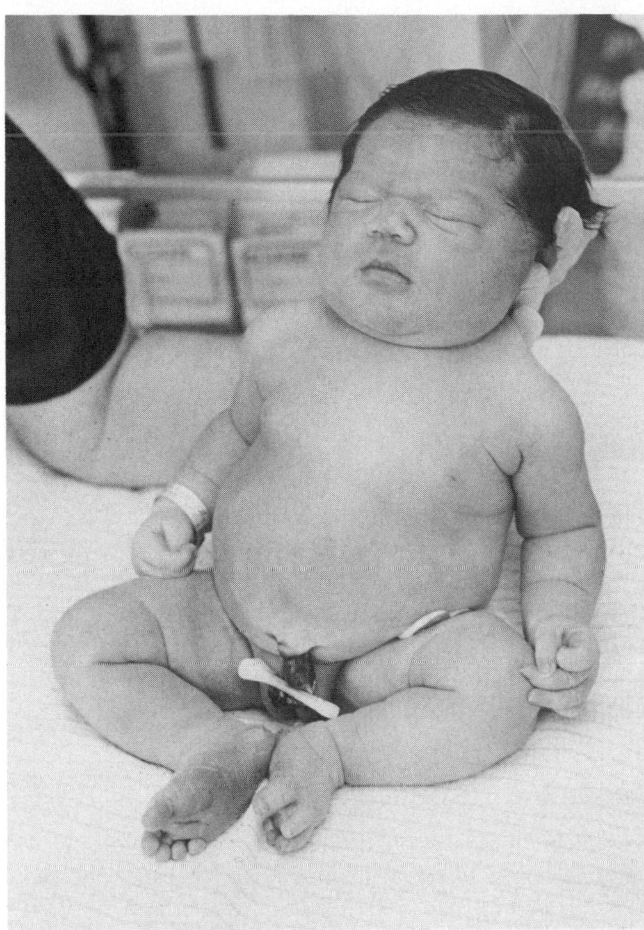

Figure 29–3

Macrosomia is common in infants of diabetic mothers. In response to large amounts of amino acids, free fatty acids, and glucose, the fetal pancreas produces large amounts of insulin which acts as a growth hormone in utero.

betes is well controlled. The large infant is more likely to suffer trauma during birth, including fractures or nerve damage.

Congenital anomalies are three to five times more likely in IDMs, with heart, vertebral, central nervous system, and kidney defects being most common (Ballard, 1991). The incidence of anomalies is less if blood glucose levels remain within normal limits, especially in the early weeks of gestation, when organs are forming.

Infants of diabetic mothers have a higher risk of RDS than normal infants because high levels of insulin interfere with the production of surfactant in the lungs. The lecithin/sphingomyelin (L/S) ratio may be inaccurate in predicting lung maturation in the IDM. Generally, an L/S ratio for these infants must be above 3:1, as compared to an L/S ratio above 2:1 for the normal infant, before lung maturation can be considered complete enough to prevent RDS. Presence of phosphatidylglycerol in the amniotic fluid usually indicates that adequate amounts of surfactant are present. Strict control of the diabetes and allowing the pregnancy to progress to full term reduces the incidence of RDS.

Other complications for which the IDM is at risk include hypoglycemia after birth, when the maternal supply of glucose ends but the infant's high level of insulin production continues. Hypocalcemia may occur as a result of decreased parathyroid hormone production, especially when the mother's diabetes was poorly controlled. Polycythemia (hematocrit level above 65 per cent) may be a problem because infants have decreased extracellular fluid and may have produced more erythrocytes than normal owing to poor oxygenation during fetal life. Organ damage from decreased blood flow and renal vein thrombosis are possible effects of polycythemia. Polycythemia also results in hyperbilirubinemia as the excessive red blood cells break down after birth.

Characteristics of IDMs

The small-for-gestational-age (SGA) infant of a diabetic mother is similar to SGA infants from other causes, but is more likely to have congenital anomalies. The macrosomia of the infant of a diabetic mother is different from other large-for-gestational-age (LGA) infants. The infant's size is due to fat deposits and hypertrophy of the liver, adrenals, and heart. All organs except the brain are larger than normal. The length and head size are generally within normal range for gestational age. Other LGA infants do not have enlargement of the organs and tend to be long with large heads to match the rest of the body. IDMs have a characteristic appearance. The face is round and red, and the body is obese. There is poor muscle tone at rest, but the infant becomes irritable and may have tremors when disturbed.

Infant of a Diabetic Mother: Application of Nursing Process

Assessment

Assess infants of diabetic mothers for signs of complications, trauma, and congenital anomalies at delivery and during the early hours after birth. Hypoglycemia may be present without observable signs.

Therefore, it is important to screen the blood glucose according to hospital protocol (Fig. 29–4). An example is screening within the first hour after birth and 1, 2, 4, 6, and 12 hours later. In infants with abnormal results, levels may be checked every 30 to 60 minutes until stable and then before feedings for 24 hours. Glucose levels of less than 45 mg/dl measured with glucose screening reagent strips should be reported and may be verified by the laboratory (see Procedure 20–6, p. 525).

Assess infants frequently for signs indicating hypoglycemia, which generally develops 1 to 2 hours after birth. The most frequent sign is jitteriness or tremors. Diaphoresis is uncommon in newborns and may be due to hypoglycemia. (Other signs are listed in Critical to Remember: Signs of Hypoglycemia, p. 524.) Because these signs are not specific for hypoglycemia, be alert for other complications, particularly if signs continue after feeding.

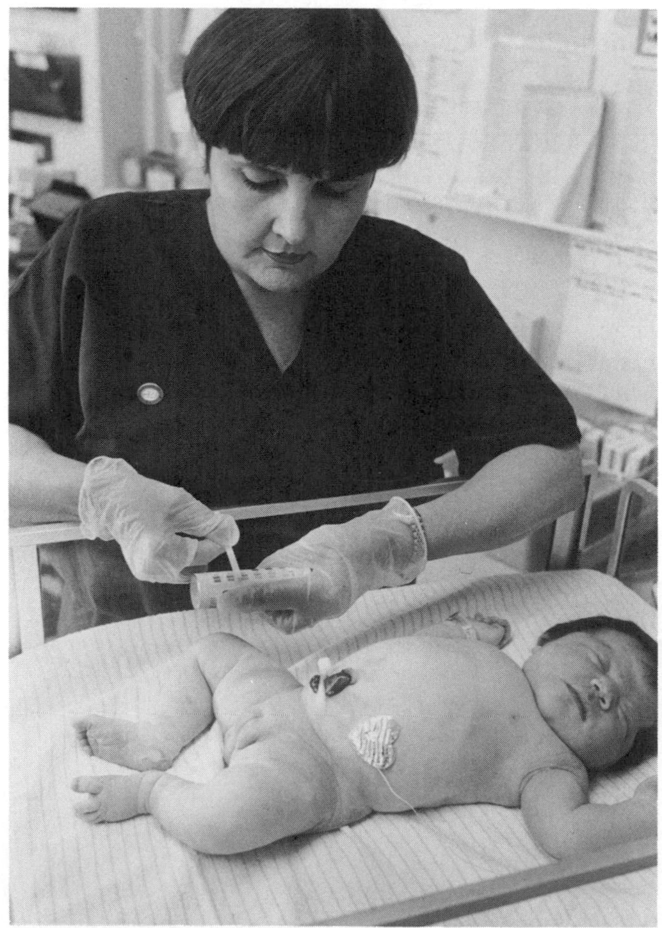

Figure 29–4

Frequent screening of blood glucose levels may be needed to detect hypoglycemia in the infant of a diabetic mother.

Analysis

Infants of diabetic mothers are prone to the potential complication: *Hypoglycemia.*

Planning

Goals are not written for potential complications. The nurse's role is to help identify the problem, assist in carrying out the treatment, and monitor for changes.

Interventions

Therapeutic management includes controlling the mother's diabetes throughout the pregnancy to decrease complications of the fetus (see Chapter 25). If the infant is LGA, delivery may be difficult and a cesarean birth may be required. Immediate care of respiratory problems and continued observation for complications determine treatment.

PROVIDING A SOURCE OF GLUCOSE

Feed the infant early if hypoglycemia develops. Although some institutions use 5 or 10 per cent dextrose water for the first feeding, a rebound hypoglycemia may occur. If dextrose water is given, it should be followed within an hour by breast milk or formula. Many institutions give breast milk or formula immediately when infants have low blood glucose levels to avoid rebound hypoglycemia and to provide longer normal glucose levels. Gavage feeding may be used if the infant does not suck well or if the respirations are high. Some infants may need intravenous glucose to maintain balance and prevent damage to the brain.

OBSERVING FOR OTHER COMPLICATIONS

Check the hematocrit level to determine if the infant has polycythemia. Hydrate the infant adequately to prevent sluggish blood flow and ischemia to vital organs. Expect an increased incidence of jaundice as blood cells break down.

Infants are at increased risk for low calcium levels. If jitteriness occurs and the glucose levels are normal, the infant may have hypocalcemia.

Observe for signs of respiratory distress, which may occur in IDMs even though they are not preterm. Prevent cold stress, which would increase the metabolic rate. Increased metabolism uses both oxygen and glucose more rapidly and could increase respiratory problems as well as exacerbate hypoglycemia.

PROVIDING SUPPORT TO PARENTS

Explain to parents why their infant, who appears fat and healthy to them, needs close observation and frequent blood tests. The mother may have had a difficult pregnancy and may feel guilty, even if she followed a program of good diabetic control. Provide ample opportunity for discussion of feelings as well as information about the care of the infant.

Evaluation

Although an evaluation is not written for collaborative problems, the infant will be expected to have blood glucose levels that remain within normal limits after collaborative care is given.

✔ Check Your Reading

9. What is the difference between vertical and horizontal transmission of infection?
10. What is the role of the nurse in caring for the infant with sepsis?
11. What problems occur in infants of diabetic mothers?
12. What are the major nursing responsibilities in caring for infants of diabetic mothers?

Prenatal Drug Exposure

The infant who is exposed to drugs before birth is subject to many problems. This is especially true for the infant whose mother abuses drugs. Substance abuse affects the fetus at any time during pregnancy because most drugs readily cross the placenta. Abuse during the first 2 months of pregnancy may cause congenital anomalies, whereas later abuse may interfere with development or functioning of organs already formed. Abuse of more than one substance is common, making it difficult to determine the exact cause of any one effect.

The effects of substance abuse on the pregnancy and on the fetus and neonate are discussed in Chapter 23. This discussion focuses on nursing care for infants with neonatal abstinence syndrome, the disorder in which neonates demonstrate signs of drug withdrawal.

Identification of Drug-Exposed Infants

Maternal substance abuse may be known before an infant is born, but many infants are born to women whose use is not known to the health professionals caring for them during labor and delivery. A history of no prenatal care or behaviors during labor and delivery that may indicate substance abuse may raise suspicion. When this occurs, the infant is observed closely for signs of prenatal drug exposure.

Neonatal abstinence syndrome occurs in infants who have suffered prenatal drug exposure sufficient to cause withdrawal signs after birth. It usually begins during the first 48 to 72 hours after birth, depending on the time of the mother's last drug dose. Signs may vary according to the drug but often include neurological and gastrointestinal abnormalities. Some infants with prenatal drug exposure present no abnormal signs at all. Common signs are listed in Critical to Remember: Signs of Intrauterine Drug Exposure.

Although some signs are similar to those of hypoglycemia, the blood glucose level is normal. Infants appear hungry and suck vigorously on their fists but have poor coordination of suck and swallow, with frequent regurgitation, vomiting, and diarrhea. They

Critical to Remember

Signs of Intrauterine Drug Exposure

Behavioral Signs

- Irritability
- Jitteriness
- Muscular rigidity, increased muscle tone
- Restless, excessive activity
- Exaggerated startle reflex
- Prolonged high-pitched cry
- Difficult to console

Signs Relating to Feeding

- Incoordinated sucking and swallowing
- Frequent regurgitation or vomiting
- Diarrhea

Other Signs

- Poor sleeping patterns
- Yawning, sneezing
- Nasal stuffiness
- Tachypnea
- Apnea
- Seizures
- Diaphoresis

Note: Some infants with prenatal drug exposure will present no abnormal signs at all.

are restless, and their excessive activity, coupled with poor feeding ability, results in failure to gain weight. Special scoring systems may be used to determine the number, frequency, and severity of behaviors that may indicate neonatal abstinence syndrome.

Congenital anomalies and other effects of prenatal drug exposure may be apparent at birth. For example, many of these infants are small for gestational age. Infants with fetal alcohol syndrome have a characteristic appearance (see Fig. 23–1, p. 632.)

When there is suspicion that exposure may have occurred, a urine specimen is collected from the infant for analysis. Drugs are present in the newborn's urine for various lengths of time after the mother has used them. Some drugs last several days because of the infant's difficulty in excreting them, whereas others disappear very soon. Therefore, it is important to obtain the first urine output from the infant, if possible. Meconium may also be tested for some drugs. (See Procedure 29–2.)

Therapeutic Management

Therapeutic management includes dealing with the complications common to drug-exposed infants during and after birth. Respiratory problems are treated as for other infants. Sedatives may be necessary for severe irritability. Drugs commonly used include tincture of opium, tincture of paregoric, phenobarbital, and diazepam (Valium). Use of gavage or intravenous feeding may be required at times because the infant's suck and swallow is uncoordinated. Follow-up care by social services both in and out of the hospital is important to deal with the long-term effects of the drugs, placement of the infant after hospitalization, and follow-up of the mother or other caretaker to help provide for the infant's needs.

Prenatal Drug Exposure: Application of Nursing Process

The infant who has been exposed to drugs prenatally will need special care to cope with drug withdrawal. Care is focused on feeding, rest, and enhancing parental attachment, if possible.

Feeding

Feeding the infant suffering from drug withdrawal is a special challenge.

Assessment

Note the infant's ability to coordinate sucking and swallowing. Infants often suck frantically on their fists or a nipple but are unable to coordinate feeding behaviors well. Determine the frequency and amount of regurgitation and vomiting and the length of time it takes infants to finish feedings.

Analysis

A nursing diagnosis for the drug-exposed infant is: *High Risk for Altered Nutrition: Less Than Body Requirements related to excessive activity and difficulty coordinating sucking and swallowing.*

Planning

The goals for this nursing diagnosis are that the infant will:

- Take in at least 110 to 120 kcal/kg/day to meet growth needs
- Lose no more than 5 per cent of birth weight
- Gain ½ to 1 ounce daily

Some infants may need more than the normal caloric requirements because of their excessive activity. Caloric intake should be adjusted to meet individual requirements.

Interventions

Interventions are directed at preventing distractions during feedings and enhancing feeding retention.

PREVENTING DISTRACTIONS

Choose an area of the nursery where noise and activity are low for feedings. Swaddle the infant tightly to prevent the startling that occurs when drug-exposed infants are handled. Talk to the infant softly, and keep movements smooth and slow.

ENHANCING FEEDING RETENTION

Use gavage feedings to save the infant's energy and prevent risk of aspiration if the infant is excessively agitated, is unable to suck and swallow adequately, or has rapid respirations. Aspirate gastric contents before feeding to determine if formula is passing from stomach to intestines between feedings. Subtract the amount of gastric aspirate from the next feeding.

Procedure 29–2

Applying a Pediatric Urine Collection Bag

Purpose: To collect a non-sterile urine specimen from an infant.

1. **Wash and dry the genitalia. Apply tincture of benzoin according to hospital policy. Allow to dry until "tacky."** *Gross contaminants should be removed from the skin to prevent contamination of the specimen. The bag will adhere to a clean, dry surface best. Tincture of benzoin increases adherence of the bag to the skin.*

2. **Remove the paper covering the posterior adhesive tabs first.** *Covering the perineum with the posterior tabs first helps ensure smooth fit at this area, where leakage of urine may occur in the female infant especially.* **To apply to female infants, fold the bag in half and apply smoothly over the perineum, extending the tabs to the side.**
For male infants, place the penis and scrotum inside the bag (if possible) and apply the posterior adhesive taps to the perineum. If the scrotum will not fit in the bag, apply the tabs smoothly over the scrotum.

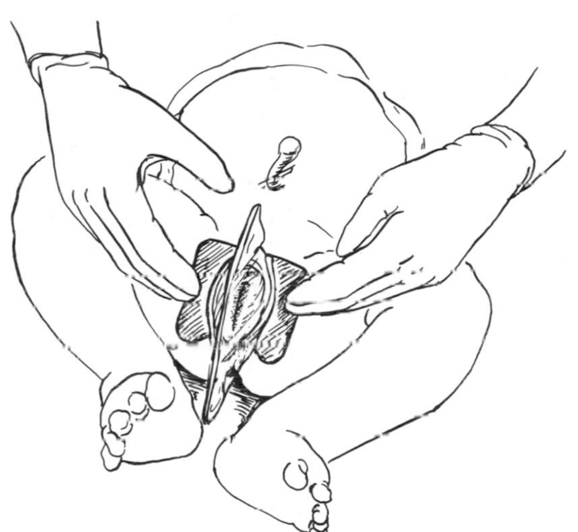

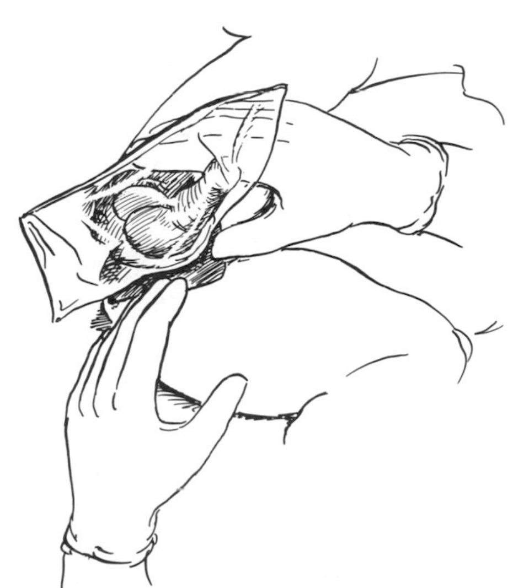

3. **Remove the paper covering the anterior adhesive tabs, and apply to cover genitalia. Be sure that there are no wrinkles in the tabs.** *Wrinkles allow openings for urine to leak out of the bag.*

4. **Leave the diaper off if warmth can be maintained. If the infant is to be diapered, place the diaper loosely over the bag or cut a slit in the diaper and gently pull the bag through the slit.** *Leaving the diaper off or cutting a slit in the diaper allows visualization of the bag. Placing the diaper too tightly over the bag might cause a pull against the adhesive, causing trauma to the skin and providing an opening through which the specimen might be lost.*

5. **Check the bag for urine frequently. Transfer the urine to a specimen cup by removing the tab over the hole in the bottom or cutting the lower corner and pouring. The specimen can also be aspirated with a syringe. Some laboratories prefer that the entire bag be placed in the specimen cup.** *Ensures removal of the bag before urine loosens the adhesive. Prepares the specimen to be sent to the laboratory for analysis.*

6. **Clean the genitalia, and observe for irritation.** *Removes urine and adhesive from the skin.*

When oral feedings are begun, feed the infant slowly and burp often to help prevent regurgitation. Provide chin and cheek support as for the preterm infant, if necessary, to help the infant suck more efficiently. After feedings, position the infant on the right side with the head of bed elevated 30 to 45 degrees.

Evaluation

The infant takes and retains feedings to provide 110 to 120 kcal/kg/day and gains ½ to 1 ounce daily.

Rest

The excessive activity and irritability of the infant with neonatal abstinence syndrome make obtaining adequate rest difficult.

Assessment

Assess the infant's muscle tone, tremors, and tendency for excessive activity with and without being disturbed. Note the degree of tremors and what increases or decreases irritability. Keep track of the number of hours that the infant sleeps.

Analysis

The infant may have difficulty falling asleep and maintaining sleep. An appropriate nursing diagnosis is: *Sleep Pattern Disturbance related to excessive irritability and activity.*

Planning

The goal for this nursing diagnosis is for the infant to have gradually increasing sleep periods and a decrease in excessive activity.

Interventions

Keep all stimulation of the drug-exposed infant to a minimum, especially at first, when the infant is excessively irritable. Reduce bright lights by placing a blanket over the head of the crib or incubator. Place the infant in the quietest corner of the nursery, and organize nursing care to reduce handling and noise. A calm approach and slow, smooth movements during care help avoid startling the infant.

Keep the infant swaddled tightly in a flexed position at all times. This prevents the infant from startling and becoming agitated. Use a pacifier if it helps quiet the infant. Organize nursing care so that the infant is not awakened from sleep.

Evaluation

The infant begins to sleep longer and have more periods when activity levels are less.

Bonding

Infants who test positive for drugs may not be released to the mother until her ability to care for her infant safely has been assessed by a court. She may be required to enter a drug rehabilitation program before she can obtain custody of the infant. The infant may receive care in an institution, in a foster home, or by family members approved by the court after hospital discharge. However, the mother will most likely gain custody of the infant eventually, and mother-infant bonding must be encouraged.

Assessment

Assess the mother's apparent interest in the infant by determining the frequency of her visits and her response when she is with the infant. Although some substance-abusing mothers are uninterested in their infants, for others the infant provides a reason to attempt to overcome their addiction. Assess the infant's response to interacting with others. Infants exposed to drugs prenatally may turn away from eye contact and are very difficult to console, making them demanding to care for and increasing the likelihood of inadequate mother-infant bonding.

Analysis

The mother who is a substance abuser has to cope not only with her own recovery but also with an infant who is difficult to care for and who does not inspire attachment in others. In order to help promote mother-infant attachment, the nursing diagnosis: *High Risk for Altered Parenting related to lack of understanding of infant characteristics* is appropriate.

Planning

The goals for this nursing diagnosis are that the mother will:

- Demonstrate interest in the infant by visiting the nursery
- Begin to participate in care of the infant

Interventions

Interventions are aimed at making the mother feel welcome in the nursery, including her in care, and providing her with information so that she will learn to care for the infant. If the mother is unable to care for the newborn, the same interventions can be used to help the person who will take over care of the infant on hospital discharge.

MAKING THE MOTHER COMFORTABLE

Because the mother will probably gain custody of the infant eventually, it is vital that nurses do whatever they can to enhance mother-infant bonding. The mother should be made to feel welcome whenever she comes to visit the infant. This provides one of the most challenging aspects of nursing care because it is sometimes easy to be judgmental and difficult to be accepting when the mother's behavior has been harmful to her infant. A friendly approach to the mother will make her more likely to visit the infant and to accept teaching from the nurse.

INCLUDING THE MOTHER IN INFANT CARE

Promote bonding by encouraging mothers to participate actively in infant care during visits. Including the mother will help her feel that the nurses trust her to care for the infant. This may help increase her determination to go through recovery to regain her newborn.

The mother's participation also provides a chance to assess the mother's infant care skills and areas in which further discussion of the newborn's needs will be helpful. In addition, it provides an opportunity for the nurse to demonstrate parenting skills. Many mothers who use drugs have not had good parenting role models and do not know what to do. Frequent positive feedback about the mother's participation is also important.

PROVIDING INFORMATION

The mother needs the same teaching given to all new parents, plus special techniques necessary to meet the needs of drug-exposed infants. Help her hold and feed the infant, and teach her about her newborn's special characteristics. Show her how to swaddle the infant in a flexed position to prevent excessive startles and tremors. (See Fig. 23–2, p. 633, and Parents Want to Know, p. 642.)

Drug-exposed infants may not make eye contact or may avert their eyes after 30 to 60 seconds of social interaction. This "time out" period is necessary because they cannot tolerate longer periods of interaction. Teach the mother that the infant responds poorly to everyone so that she does not think that only she is being rejected. Provide information and referral to any special programs available to help parents learn special stimulation techniques appropriate for drug-exposed infants.

Cocaine, amphetamines, and other drugs pass into breast milk. Trying to breastfeed an infant with poorly developed feeding skills may be too much stress for the mother who is trying to recover from her addiction. Therefore, discourage mothers likely to continue drug use after delivery from breastfeeding. However, there are situations in which breastfeeding may be allowed. Consult with the physician about the woman who has a strong desire to breastfeed.

Evaluation

The mother visits the infant regularly and gradually takes over greater amounts of infant care.

✔ Check Your Reading

13. What are common problems of infants with prenatal exposure to drugs?
14. What special nursing care measures are needed for drug-exposed infants?

Congenital Anomalies

Although only 2 to 3 per cent of newborns are reported to have major congenital anomalies, 14 per cent have some type of defect at birth. These defects are responsible for approximately 20 per cent of all neonatal deaths (Lott, 1993). Some infants have more than one anomaly, which may be part of a syndrome or be due to separate causes. Although congenital anomalies are generally treated in the pediatrics setting, they are usually identified soon after birth. Common congenital anomalies are noted in Table 29–2. (See a pediatric nursing textbook for more detailed information about care of infants with these conditions.) Congenital cardiac conditions are discussed here.

Nursing Care Plan 29–2

The Drug-Exposed Infant

Tracy was born at 38 weeks' gestation to Gloria, who was on a methadone maintenance program. However, Tracy tested positive not only for methadone but also for heroin, which Gloria admitted using several times in the days just before she began labor.

Assessment: Tracy weighs 2240 g (4 pounds, 15 ounces) and is small for gestational age. She is jittery, becomes agitated easily, and has poor suck and swallow coordination. Tracy regurgitates her feedings frequently. She has been fed by gavage but is now taking feedings orally.

Nursing Diagnosis: Altered Nutrition: Less Than Body Requirements related to abnormal coordination of suck and swallow and excessive activity.

Goals:
Tracy will take and retain 246 to 269 calories daily (110 to 120 kcal/kg/day) and will gain at least ½ ounce each day.

Intervention:	Rationale:
1. Feed Tracy as soon as she begins to wake at feeding times.	1. Drug-exposed infants often move from sleeping to an agitated state very quickly. This would make feeding more difficult.
2. Swaddle Tracy with her arms in a flexed position during feeding.	2. Infants become more agitated if they are allowed to startle. Swaddling provides a sense of security and prevents excessive movement.
3. Try warming the formula slightly before feeding.	3. Some infants take warmed formula more readily.
4. Stop the feeding frequently and burp Tracy. If frantic sucking continues when the feeding is stopped, use a pacifier to soothe her.	4. Frequent burping may help prevent regurgitation. Keeping Tracy calm while burping may also prevent regurgitation.
5. Place Tracy on her right side with her head elevated 30 to 45 degrees after feedings. Keep environment as non-stimulating as possible after feedings.	5. Positioning can use gravity to promote gastric emptying and helps prevent aspiration during regurgitation. Quiet surroundings promote sleep and decrease agitation.

Evaluation:
Tracy's intake averages 250 calories each day. She gains slightly more than ½ ounce daily.

Assessment: Tracy sleeps less than an hour after feedings. When she awakens, her high-pitched cry and agitation begin immediately. She wiggles out of her blankets, and her activity elicits the Moro reflex, which leads to more agitation. She is irritable and does not respond to caretaking activities as quickly as other infants.

Nursing Diagnosis: Sleep Pattern Disturbance related to agitation from own activity and irritability.

Goals:
Tracy will lengthen sleep periods after feedings to 2 hours or more and will respond to caretaking activities by decreasing crying a total of 1 hour a day within the first week.

Intervention:	Rationale:
1. Place Tracy's crib in the quietest corner of the nursery. Place a sign nearby to remind others of the need for quiet in that area. For example: "Shh please! Tracy is resting!"	1. Drug-exposed infants are easily overstimulated by noise and activity.
2. Keep lights turned down as much as possible. Place a blanket over the head end of the crib to help prevent Tracy from looking into lights.	2. Lowered lighting provides a more restful environment.

Nursing Care Plan 29–2 *Continued*

The Drug-Exposed Infant

Intervention	Rationale
3. Keep Tracy tightly swaddled in a flexed position during sleep and feedings.	3. The drug-exposed infant's own movements can cause startling, awakening, and agitation.
4. Use a pacifier, and keep Tracy's hands near her mouth.	4. Sucking may have a calming effect on the infant.
5. Use a front infant carrier during Tracy's awake periods.	5. The carrier provides the same effect as swaddling. In addition, it provides warmth and a rocking motion from the caretaker's body that may be soothing.
6. Organize nursing care so that Tracy is not disturbed when sleeping.	6. Once the infant is asleep, she should not be disturbed because she may have difficulty going back to sleep.

Evaluation:
Tracy gradually lengthens her sleep periods to 2 hours and decreases crying episodes within the first week.

Assessment: Gloria visits Tracy sporadically. She seems hesitant when she comes into the nursery and afraid to touch or care for Tracy. She asks, "Why does she cry so much?" When the nurse helps her hold Tracy, Gloria states, "I don't think she likes me."

Nursing Diagnosis: Altered Parenting related to lack of understanding of the infant's characteristics and how to relate with irritable infant.

Goals:

1. Gloria will visit at least every other day and will participate in Tracy's care by holding and feeding her.
2. Gloria will make positive statements about Tracy and will verbalize increasing comfort with her daughter.

Intervention:	Rationale:
1. Show acceptance of Gloria when she comes to visit Tracy. Greet her and provide her with an update on Tracy's progress.	1. A mother is more likely to visit her infant if she feels accepted by staff. The more she visits, the more she is likely to learn to parent her infant.
2. Assist Gloria to hold and feed Tracy. Explain nursing actions such as placing the crib in a secluded corner and covering the top with a blanket.	2. Encouraging the mother to participate in care of the infant helps her get to know her infant and how to care for the infant more quickly.
3. Show Gloria how to make Tracy more comfortable. Demonstrate swaddling and rocking and explain the purpose. Show her how to place a rolled blanket around the infant to provide a feeling of security and help promote sleep.	3. When the mother learns ways to comfort her infant, the positive response from the infant may increase bonding.
4. Explain the behavioral characteristics of infants who are drug-exposed. Explain that the infant's stiff body posture and failure to "mold" to the mother's body are normal for her. Point out signs that Tracy is overstimulated, such as gaze aversion and increase in irritability. Explain that the high-pitched cry is common, and suggest ways that are effective in quieting Tracy.	4. The mother needs to learn that the infant's behavior is part of the infant's problem, not due to the mother's handling of her.
5. Point out positive points about Tracy, such as her long eyelashes or delicate fingers. Point out signs that show that Tracy is making progress.	5. The mother needs help to focus on positive aspects of the infant as well as the problems.
6. Explain the routine care of a newborn. Spread teaching out over Gloria's visits.	6. The mother needs to learn the usual care of any newborn as well as the infant's special needs.

Nursing Care Plan continued on following page

Nursing Care Plan 29–2 *Continued*

The Drug-Exposed Infant

7. Give praise and encouragement frequently as Gloria works with Tracy.	7. The mother needs positive reinforcement and help to feel that she is capable of mothering her infant.

Evaluation:
Gloria begins to visit more often, coming three to four times a week. She participates in care, begins to talk about her "pretty little girl," and discusses her plans for when she can take Tracy home with her.

Additional Nursing Diagnoses to Consider:
Altered Family Processes
Ineffective Individual Coping
Impaired Skin Integrity

Congenital Cardiac Defects

Approximately 1 per cent of newborns have a congenital heart defect (Daberkow and Washington, 1989). The exact cause is unknown in most cases, but genetics, teratogens, and viral infections such as rubella are all known to be possible factors. Often a genetic predisposition is combined with an environmental cause. The heart forms by the 6th week of gestation, and problems in development during this period may result in other structural anomalies as well.

TYPES OF HEART DEFECTS

The types of heart anomalies that occur can be divided into four categories:

1. There may be abnormal openings between chambers of the heart or between vessels. Examples are defects of the septum, which allow abnormal blood flow between chambers of the heart, or maintenance of the ductus arteriosus, which permits continued blood flow between the aorta and the pulmonary artery after birth.
2. Structures of the heart or major blood vessels may be positioned abnormally, interfering with normal circulation of blood. An example is transposition of the great arteries.
3. There may be abnormal narrowing of structures, such as heart valves or blood vessels, as in coarctation of the aorta or pulmonary stenosis.
4. A combination of several different anomalies may occur, as in tetralogy of Fallot.

CLASSIFICATION OF CARDIAC DEFECTS

Cardiac defects are generally categorized as cyanotic or acyanotic, according to whether or not they cause early cyanosis. Some of the most common defects are illustrated and discussed in Table 29–3.

Cyanotic Defects. In cyanotic defects, there is a decrease in blood flow to the lungs and/or mixing of venous and oxygenated blood into the general systemic circulation, decreasing the oxygen carried to the tissues and resulting in cyanosis. This is often called a right-to-left shunt because venous blood from the right side of the heart flows to the left side of the heart and into the systemic circulation. An example of a cyanotic condition is transposition of the great arteries.

In cyanotic defects, infants generally have serious problems from birth. In addition to the flow of venous blood into the arteries, less blood may be directed to the lungs, further limiting oxygen available to the tissues. Although the heart and lungs work harder, adequate oxygenation may be impossible, resulting in hypoxia of the major organs. The infant grows poorly, has frequent infections, and is easily fatigued. Heart failure may be an early complication.

Acyanotic Defects. In acyanotic defects, there may be no mixing of venous and unoxygenated blood, but a decrease in the blood flow through a narrowed vessel or valve may occur, as in coarctation of the aorta. Or venous and oxygenated blood mixes but is carried to the lungs rather than to the rest of the body—a left-to-right shunt. Examples are ventricular septal defects and patent ductus arteriosus.

Although cyanosis is not an immediate problem in these infants, the excessive congestion in the lungs eventually causes increased resistance of the pulmonary vessels and pulmonary hypertension. The infant is prone to respiratory infections because of the pulmonary congestion and increased work of the heart and lungs. Growth is slowed, and the infant fatigues easily. The heart may fail from overwork.

Table 29–2. COMMON CONGENITAL ANOMALIES

Gastrointestinal Tract

Cleft Lip and Palate

Among the most common congenital anomalies.

Occur together or separately, on one or both sides.

Lip: minor notching of the lip or all of lip and into floor of nose.

Palate: only the soft palate or division of entire hard and soft palate.

Both genetic and environmental factors are included in cause.

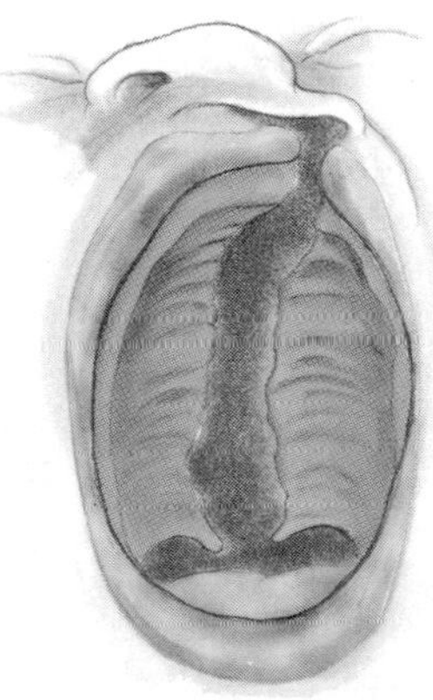

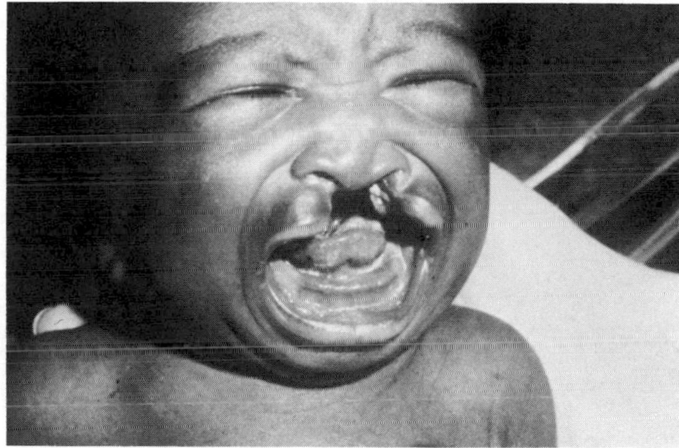

Assessment

Severe clefts obvious at birth.

Palpate hard and soft palate of all neonates during initial assessment.

Therapeutic Management

Lip surgery as soon as possible (usually at 10 weeks and 10 pounds with a hemoglobin of 10 g, if otherwise healthy) to enhance appearance and parental bonding.

Palate repair in stages, depending on the degree, beginning at about 1 year to minimize speech problems.

Long-term follow-up for orthodontia, speech therapy, and possible hearing problems.

Nursing Considerations

Degree of cleft determines approach to feeding.

Experiment to find method that works best for individual infant. Try:

1. Breastfeeding for cleft lip (soft breast tissue fills in the opening in the lip).
2. Soft preemie nipple directed away from a cleft palate.
3. Nipple with enlarged hole.
4. Compressible bottles.
5. Special long nipples that extend beyond cleft.
6. Nipples with extensions to cover cleft.
7. Medicine dropper.
8. Asepto syringe with soft tubing attached.

Feed infant in upright position, as milk enters nasal passages through palate, causing increased tendency to aspirate.

Feed slowly with frequent stops to burp, as infant tends to swallow excessive air.

Wash away milk curds with water after feeding.

Help parents deal with disappointment over infant with obvious anomaly.

Show "before" and "after" pictures of plastic surgery.

Reinforce physician's explanations of plans for surgery.

Teach parents feeding techniques. Have parents observe at first, then take over gradually. Discuss positioning infant upright during feedings, on side after feedings to prevent aspiration.

Prevent infections. Infants are especially susceptible to respiratory and ear infections, which can delay surgery. Ear infections may lead to hearing loss.

Emphasize the need for long-term follow-up. Refer to agencies that help with expense of long-term care and to support groups for help and emotional support from other parents.

Esophageal Atresia and Tracheoesophageal Fistula (TEF)

The esophagus is most commonly divided into two unconnected segments (atresia). There is a blind pouch at the proximal end, and the distal end is connected to the trachea, resulting in TEF. Cause is failure of normal development during 4th week of pregnancy. The cause is unknown but is probably environmental rather than genetic. Common variations of the condition are shown.

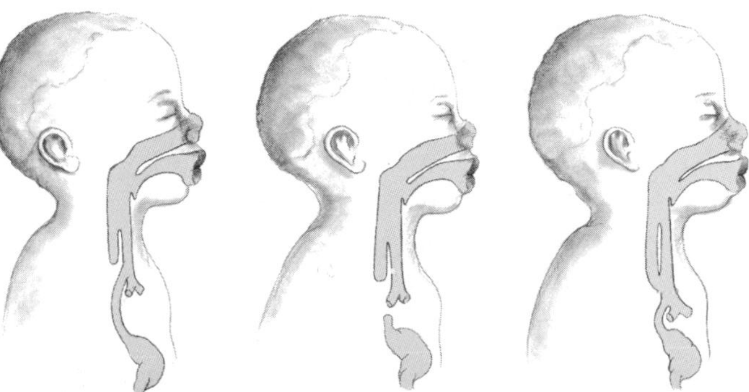

Table continued on following page

Table 29–2. COMMON CONGENITAL ANOMALIES *Continued*

Assessment

Watch for TEF when polyhydramnios occurs, because the excessive fluid may be due to fetal inability to swallow amniotic fluid.

Other defects (cardiovascular and gastrointestinal most common) occur in 30 to 50 per cent.

Symptoms vary by type of defect.

Suspect in infant with excessive drooling and needing more suctioning than usual. Regurgitation from pooling secretions in blind pouch. Catheter will not pass into stomach.

If upper esophagus connects with trachea, feedings enter lungs, causing immediate coughing, choking, and cyanosis.

If fistula is between distal esophagus and trachea, stomach becomes distended with air from trachea. Gastric secretions aspirate into the lungs, causing severe inflammatory reaction.

Therapeutic Management

Diagnosis by symptoms confirmed by x-ray studies.

Continuous suction to upper pouch and gastrostomy if infant too unstable for surgery.

Surgery to close fistula and join esophageal segments.

Long-term follow-up for esophageal reflux and dilation of strictures that form at surgical site.

Nursing Considerations

Observe all infants carefully during first feeding for respiratory difficulty or other signs. Sterile water usually given first to prevent aspiration of dextrose water or formula, if TEF is present.

If first feeding is by breast, observe carefully for respiratory difficulty.

Prevent aspiration by maintaining in a semi-upright position to prevent reflux of gastric fluids.

Maintain suction equipment.

Care after surgery involves ventilator, chest tubes, IV lines, and gastrostomy feedings.

Omphalocele and Gastroschisis

Both caused by congenital defects in the abdominal wall.

Omphalocele is a defect in which the intestines protrude into the base of the umbilical cord. Other anomalies often occur with omphalocele. (See Color Plate XVI.)

Gastroschisis is a defect to the side of the abdomen next to and not involving the cord. The intestines protrude through the defect and float freely in the amniotic fluid.

Assessment

Diagnosis is by prenatal ultrasound or obvious at birth.

Therapeutic Management

Surgery as soon as infant stable.

Intubation at delivery, with gastric tube placed to decrease air in stomach. Gastric suction, parenteral nutrition, antibiotics.

Nursing Considerations

Cover intestines with sterile saline dressings and plastic to prevent drying.

Prevent infection and trauma.

Diaphragmatic Hernia

Diaphragm fails to fuse during the 8th to 10th weeks of gestation. Large or small part of abdominal contents moves into the chest cavity, usually on the left side.

If herniation is large enough, lungs may fail to develop (hypoplastic lungs). When gas fills bowel, further pressure on heart and lungs results.

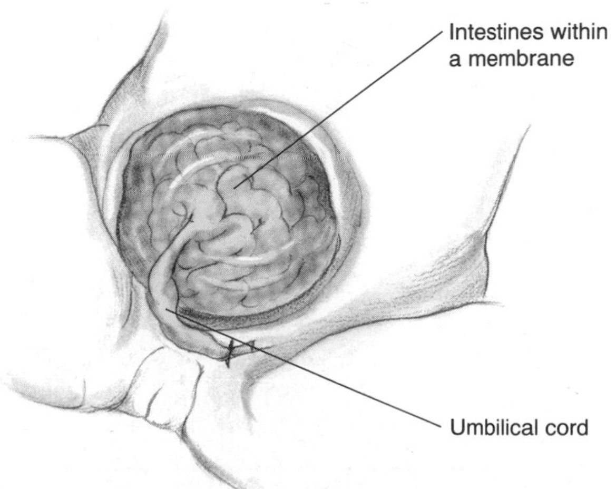

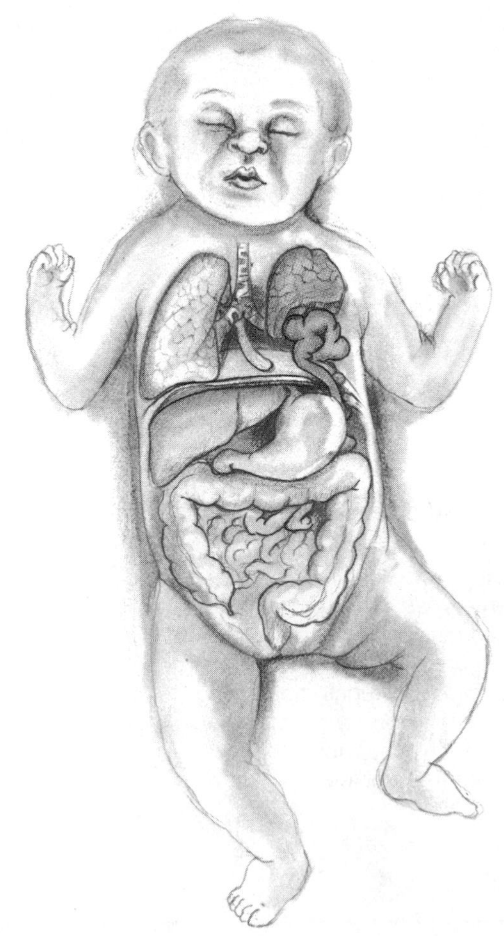

Table 29–2. COMMON CONGENITAL ANOMALIES *Continued*

Assessment

Mild to severe respiratory distress at birth.

Breath sounds diminished over the affected area.

Barrel chest.

Bowel sounds may be heard in the chest.

Heart beat may be displaced to the right.

Abdomen scaphoid (concave).

Therapeutic Management

Endotracheal tube for ventilation.

Gastric tube for decompression of stomach.

Surgery to replace intestines and repair defect in diaphragm.

Extracorporeal membrane oxygenation (ECMO) may be used.

Fetal surgery has been used.

Nursing Considerations

Position the infant on the affected side to allow unaffected lung to expand. Elevate the head to decrease pressure on the heart and lungs. Assist with ventilation, and monitor respiratory status. Expect surgery as soon as infant is stable.

Continue to monitor respiratory status after surgery to determine whether lung function will be adequate.

Central Nervous System

Forms of spina bifida most common CNS defects.

Spina bifida occulta is failure of the vertebral arch to close, usually without other anomalies. Seen by a dimple on the back, which may have a tuft of hair over it.

Meningocele is protrusion of meninges through the spina bifida, covered by skin or thin membrane. Since the spinal cord is not involved, there is no paralysis.

Myelomeningocele is protrusion of meninges and spinal cord covered with membrane through spina bifida. Degree of paralysis depends on location of defect. May also have hydrocephalus, or may develop after surgery.

Assessment

Note position and covering of defect at birth. Observe movement below the defect to determine degree of paralysis. Examine for relaxed anus and dribbling of stool and urine. Check for other anomalies.

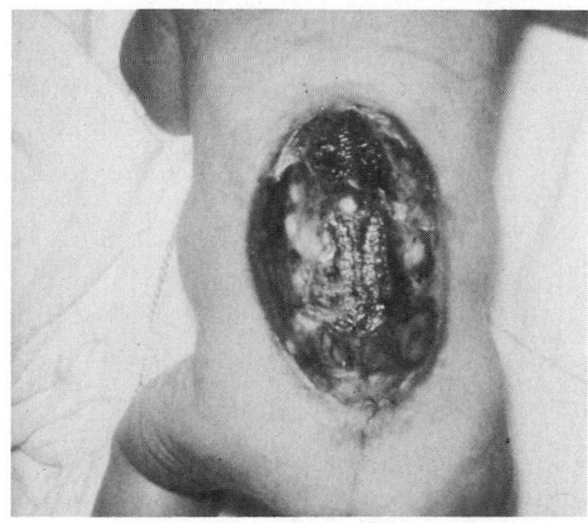

Meningocele.

Therapeutic Management

Surgery for meningocele and myelomeningocele.

Shunt to divert cerebrospinal fluid if hydrocephalus develops.

Antibiotics to prevent infection. Long-term follow-up with physical therapy and other care as needed.

Nursing Considerations

Apply sterile saline dressing and plastic over defect covered by membrane to prevent drying.

Handle infant carefully, and position prone or to side to prevent trauma to sac.

Prevent infection. Keep free of contamination from urine and feces.

Inspect sac for intactness before surgery. Monitor for signs of infection.

Check for increasing head circumference, bulging fontanelles, separation of sutures, intermittent apnea, and other signs of increased intracranial pressure every shift to identify early hydrocephalus.

May use Credé method (apply pressure) to prevent bladder distention.

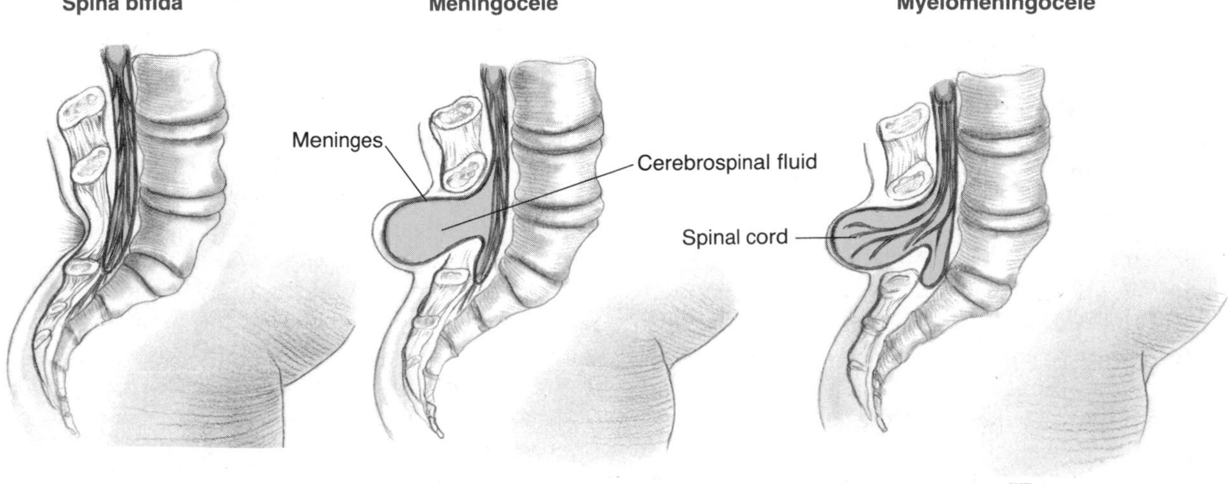

Table 29–3. COMMON CONGENITAL HEART DEFECTS

Acyanotic Heart Defects

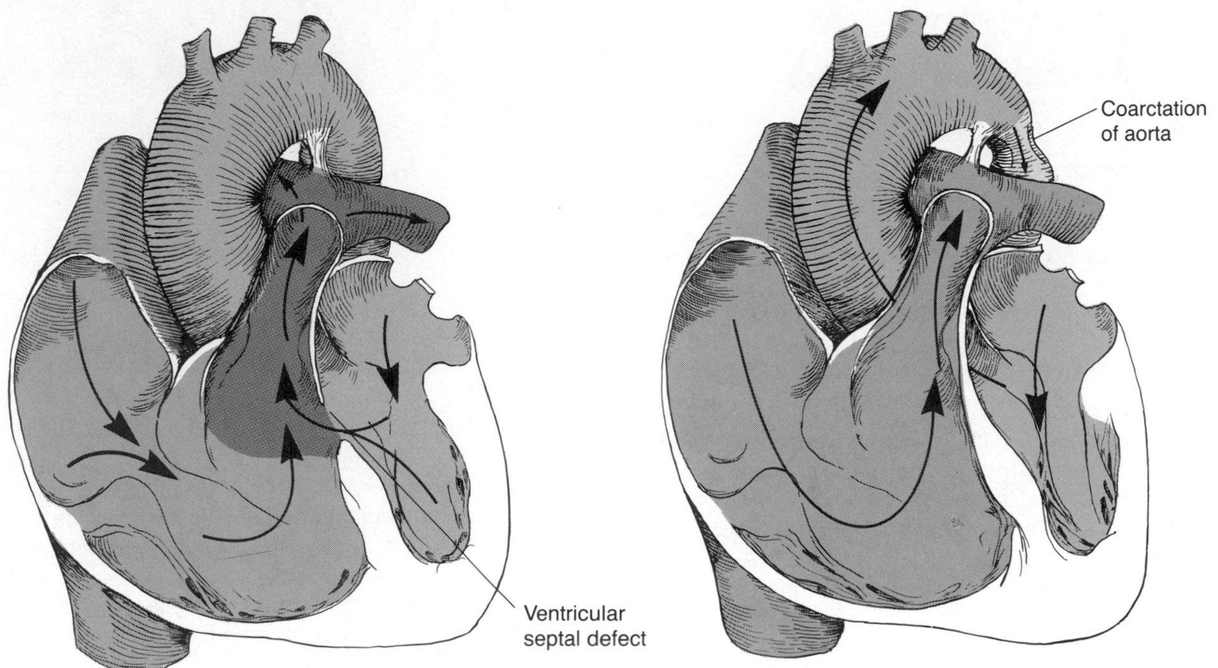

Ventricular Septal Defect

This is the most common type of congenital heart defect and may occur alone or with other defects. The size of the opening in the septum ranges from the size of a pin to very large. Fifty to 75% of small defects close spontaneously. When the pressure in the left ventricle increases after birth, oxygenated blood may be shunted through a large ventricular septal defect into the right ventricle and then recirculated to the lungs. Pulmonary resistance increases, leading to pulmonary hypertension and eventual heart failure. Surgery to correct the defect is necessary when it does not close spontaneously and symptoms increase.

Coarctation of the Aorta

In this condition, blood flow is impeded through a constricted area of the aorta while pressure behind the area and in the left ventricle is increased. The constriction may occur before or after the ductus arteriosus, determining where blood flow is decreased or increased. The blood pressure is >20 mmHg higher in the upper extremities than in the lower extremities. Carotid, brachial, and radial pulses are bounding, whereas pulses in the legs are weak or absent. The increased pressure in the left ventricle causes hypertrophy from the added work load. Congestive heart failure may result.

In some cases, pulmonary resistance increases sufficiently to change the pressures within the heart and reverse the shunting through an opening like a septal defect. Mixing of oxygenated and venous blood then causes cyanosis. Thus, many acyanotic conditions are potentially cyanotic.

MANIFESTATIONS

Congenital heart defects may present obvious signs at birth, or the indications may not become apparent until later, when changes from fetal to neonatal circulation are completed. Some infants have no difficulty for months or years, whereas others experience heart failure very early.

The most common indications of cardiac problems that may be discovered by the nurse on assessment are listed below. (See also Critical to Remember: Common Signs of Cardiac Anomalies.)

Cyanosis. Especially when there is no respiratory disease, cyanosis is a major sign of cardiac anomaly. It may be apparent in the delivery room or may develop slowly or suddenly later. If the cyanosis is due to a right-to-left shunt, giving oxygen will not improve the infant's color. Cyanosis increases with crying, feeding, or other activity. Pallor, mottling, or gray color may be present in infants who do not have cyanosis.

Heart Murmurs. Murmurs may be present at birth or may develop later. They may sound like clicks, machinery, rumbling, swishing, or other muffled noises. It takes much practice to detect heart mur-

Table 29–3. COMMON CONGENITAL HEART DEFECTS *Continued*

Cyanotic Heart Defects

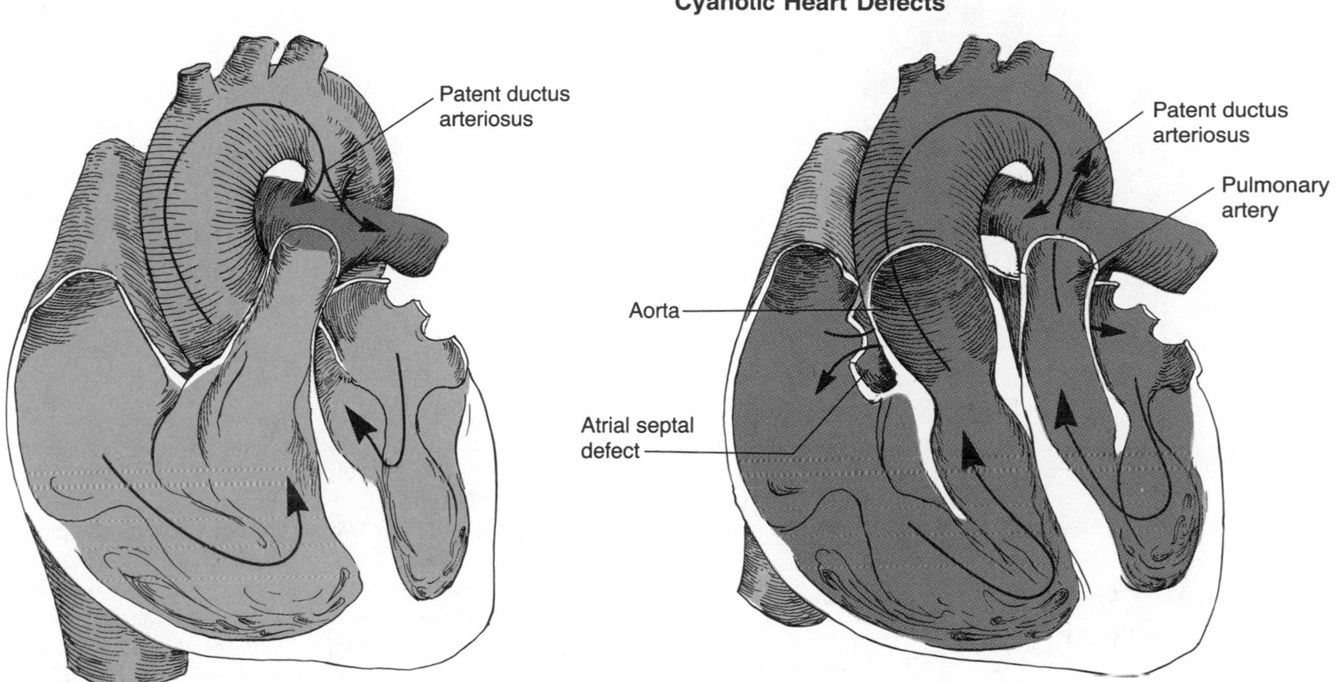

Patent Ductus Arteriosus
This condition is a failure of the ductus arteriosus, connecting the pulmonary artery and the aorta, to close after birth. Blood flows from the higher pressure of the aorta to the pulmonary artery and returns to the lungs—a left-to-right shunt. It may occur as a congenital defect of the vessel in the full-term infant but is more common in the preterm infant, especially those with respiratory distress syndrome. In preterms, the vessel is normal but immature and may close without treatment if arterial oxygen levels are kept high enough. Symptoms vary according to the size of the opening, from none to early congestive heart failure. Indomethacin, a prostaglandin inhibitor, may be effective in bringing about closure in some preterm infants. Prostaglandins cause vasodilation and may interfere with closure of the ductus arteriosus. Surgical ligation is used when necessary.

Transposition of the Great Arteries
In this condition, the aorta and pulmonary artery positions are reversed. The aorta carries venous blood from the right ventricle back to the general circulation from which it came. The pulmonary artery returns oxygenated blood from the left ventricle to the lungs. Unless there is another source for mixing oxygenated and venous blood, the infant gets no oxygen into the general circulation and dies. Generally, the ductus arteriosus and foramen ovale remain open for a time, or there is another defect that allows mixing of the circulations.

Table continued on following page

murs accurately. Although many infants have a temporary murmur until the fetal structures are closed, all abnormal sounds must be referred for follow-up.

Tachycardia and Tachypnea. These signs may occur anytime that the heart and lungs must work harder to provide sufficient oxygen to the body. Thus, they are present in respiratory conditions as well as in cardiac conditions. They may increase in congestive heart failure. Although retractions may be present at times, many infants with cardiac defects have no respiratory distress at all.

Feeding Difficulties. These may be due to the infant's fatigue. The infant may feed slowly or fall asleep before the feeding is finished. Although diaphoresis is not common in the newborn, it may appear during feedings in the infant with a heart defect.

THERAPEUTIC MANAGEMENT

Therapeutic management involves diagnosis of the specific defect and supportive and surgical treatment as indicated. Various tests, such as echocardiograms and cardiac catheterizations, confirm diagnosis. The decision for surgery depends on the status of the infant and whether surgery can be delayed safely.

Table 29–3. COMMON CONGENITAL HEART DEFECTS *Continued*

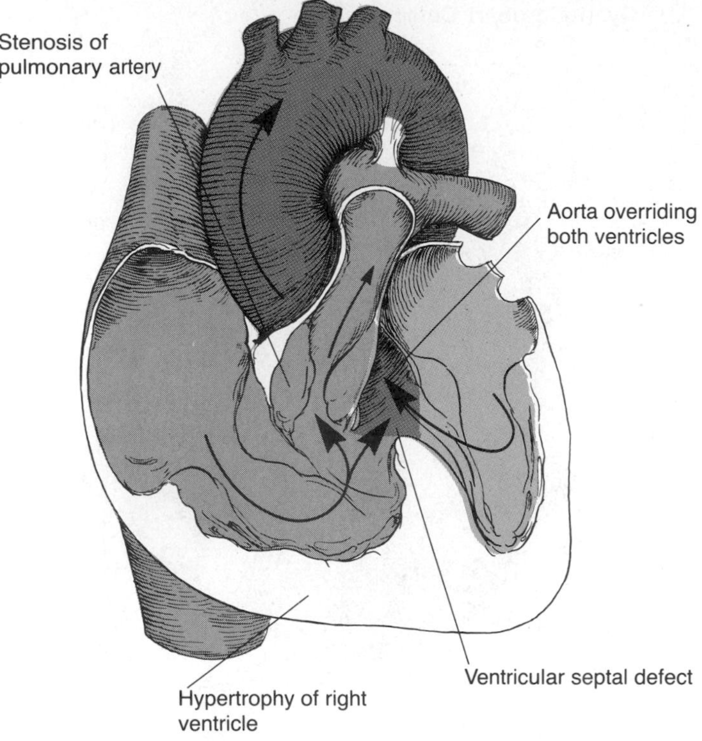

Tetralogy of Fallot

Tetralogy of Fallot has four characteristics: a ventricular septal defect, aorta positioned over the ventricular defect, stenosis of the pulmonary valve, and hypertrophy of the left ventricle. Cyanosis occurs because venous blood from the right ventricle flows through the septal defect and into the overriding aorta, and blood flow to the lungs is diminished because of the narrowed pulmonary valve. The amount of right-to-left shunting and cyanosis varies according to the degree and position of each defect.

Palliative surgery may be performed to correct a defect partially or to make another defect to allow greater amounts of oxygenated blood to get to the general circulation.

Oxygen and drugs such as digitalis, diuretics, potassium supplements, and sedatives may be prescribed. Prostaglandins may be given to prevent the ductus arteriosus from closing in some cases in which keeping it open will increase flow of oxygenated blood to the body.

Critical to Remember

Common Signs of Cardiac Anomalies

- Cyanosis—may increase with crying
- Pallor
- Murmurs
- Tachycardia
- Tachypnea
- Dyspnea
- Choking spells
- Falling asleep during feedings
- Diaphoresis

NURSING CONSIDERATIONS

Nursing care is focused on assessing for change in condition and reducing the infant's need for oxygen. The need for rest is especially important. Infants with rapid respirations are at risk for aspiration and may need feeding by gavage. Oxygen may be increased during feedings or other exertion, but only enough to maintain oxygen saturation levels adequately should be used.

Parent support and education about the infant's condition and expected treatment are important. The nurse uses drawings to help parents understand the defect. The parents are taught techniques for accurate administration of medications because the range between the therapeutic and the toxic dose of the drugs used is narrow.

✔ *Check Your Reading*

15. What types of defects of the heart can occur?
16. What is the difference between cyanotic and acyanotic heart defects?

Summary Concepts

- Asphyxia occurring before birth may cause release and possible aspiration of meconium. Asphyxia during birth causes apnea, acidosis, pulmonary hypertension, and possible death. Neonatal resuscitation must be initiated immediately.
- Nurses must identify conditions that increase the risk of asphyxia, begin resuscitation promptly, and assist other members of the team during treatment. Continued follow-up of the infant and parental support are also nursing responsibilities.
- Respiratory distress syndrome occurs in preterm infants, infants of diabetic mothers, and those suffering from asphyxia. It is characterized by respiratory difficulty because surfactant is not present in adequate amounts to keep the alveoli expanded.
- In transient tachypnea of the newborn, respiratory difficulty in full-term infants is caused by failure of fetal lung fluid to be absorbed completely. It occurs more often in infants delivered by cesarean section and usually resolves spontaneously with supportive care.
- In meconium aspiration syndrome, meconium enters the lungs before birth or during the first breaths after birth. It causes inflammation and blocks air flow
- The nurse's role in meconium aspiration syndrome is to prepare for care at birth by notifying the physician, seeing that equipment is available and functioning, assisting with care, and continuing aftercare.
- Pathologic jaundice appears in the first 24 hours of life and/or rises faster and to higher levels than physiologic jaundice. It may result in damage to the brain from kernicterus.
- The nurse's role in phototherapy includes decreasing situations such as cold stress or hypoglycemia that might further elevate bilirubin levels, seeing that lights are used properly, observing for excessive fluid loss or skin impairment, ensuring adequate oral intake, and teaching parents.
- Infection can be transmitted to neonates vertically (from mother to infant during pregnancy or birth) or horizontally (from family members or agency staff after birth).
- The infant of a diabetic mother may have congenital anomalies, may be large or small for gestational age, and may suffer from respiratory distress syndrome, hypoglycemia, hypocalcemia, and polycythemia.
- Nursing responsibilities in caring for infants of diabetic mothers include early identification and follow-up of complications, monitoring blood glucose levels, ensuring early and adequate feedings, and supporting parents.
- Infants with prenatal exposure to drugs may have congenital defects and behavioral and feeding abnormalities. They may fail to thrive and have difficulty relating to others.
- Nursing care for infants with neonatal abstinence syndrome includes decreasing stimuli from lights, noise, or handling, increasing feeding abilities, and fostering the mother's attachment to and ability to care for her infant.
- Heart defects may be due to abnormal openings in the heart, abnormal placement of structures, or impairment of blood flow.
- In cyanotic heart defects, unoxygenated blood flows into the systemic circulation, producing cyanosis. In acyanotic heart defects, there is impairment of blood flow or flow of oxygenated blood into the pulmonary system. Cyanosis does not occur with these conditions, or occurs only after other changes in pressures within the heart.

References and Readings

Anand, S.K. (1991). Clinical evaluation of renal disease. In H.W. Taeusch, R.A. Ballard, & M.E. Avery (Eds.), *Schaffer and Avery's diseases of the newborn* (6th ed.). Philadelphia: W.B. Saunders.

Ballard, R.A. (1991). Diabetes mellitus. In H.W. Taeusch, R.A. Ballard, & M.E. Avery (Eds.), *Schaffer and Avery's diseases of the newborn* (6th ed.). Philadelphia: W.B. Saunders.

Barbour, B.G. (1989). Is fetal alcohol syndrome completely irreversible? MCN: *American Journal of Maternal Child Nursing, 14*(1), 44–46.

Beachy, P., & Deacon, J. (1992). *Core curriculum for neonatal intensive care nursing.* Philadelphia: W.B. Saunders.

Behrman, R.E. (1992). *Nelson textbook of pediatrics* (14th ed.). Philadelphia: W.B. Saunders.

Blackburn, S.T., & Loper, D.L. (1992). *Maternal, fetal, and neonatal physiology: A clinical perspective.* Philadelphia: W.B. Saunders.

Bloom, R.S., & Cropley, C. (1990). *Textbook of neonatal resuscitation.* Dallas: American Heart Association and American Academy of Pediatrics.

Byrne, W.J. (1991). Disorders of the esophagus. In H.W. Taeusch, R.A. Ballard, & M.E. Avery (Eds.), *Schaffer and Avery's diseases of the newborn* (6th ed.). Philadelphia: W.B. Saunders.

Clark, R.D., & Eteson, D.J. (1991). Congenital anomalies. In H.W. Taeusch, R.A. Ballard, & M.E. Avery (Eds.), *Schaffer and Avery's diseases of the newborn* (6th ed.). Philadelphia: W.B. Saunders.

Cole, M.D. (1991). New factors associated with the incidence of hypoglycemia: A research study. *Neonatal Network, 10*(4), 47–50.

Composto, R., & Eichelberger, C. (1992). Congenital diaphragmatic hernia: Pathophysiology and nursing care. *Neonatal Network, 11*(6), 57–61.

Daberkow, E., & Washington, R.L. (1993). Cardiovascular diseases and surgical interventions. In G.B. Merenstein & S.L. Gardner (Eds.), *Handbook of neonatal intensive care* (2nd ed.). St. Louis: C.V. Mosby.

Fanaroff, A.A., Martin, R.J., & Miller, M.J. (1989). Identification and management of high-risk problems in the neonate. In R.K. Creasy & R. Resnik (Eds.), *Maternal-fetal medicine: Principles and practice* (2nd ed.). Philadelphia: W.B. Saunders.

Faro, S., & Pastorek, J.G. (1993). Perinatal infections. In R.A. Knuppel & J.E. Drukker (Eds.), *High-risk pregnancy: A team approach* (2nd ed.). Philadelphia: W.B. Saunders.

Flandermeyer, A.A. (1993). The drug-exposed neonate. In C. Kenner, A. Brueggemeyer, & L.P. Gunderson (Eds.), *Comprehensive neonatal nursing, a physiologic perspective*. Philadelphia: W.B. Saunders.

Frank, D.G., Turner, B.S., & Merenstein, G.B. (1993). Jaundice. In G.B. Merenstein & S.L. Gardner (Eds.), *Handbook of neonatal intensive care* (2nd ed.). St. Louis: C.V. Mosby.

Free, T., Russell, F., Mills, B., & Hathaway, D. (1990). A descriptive study of infants and toddlers exposed prenatally to substance abuse. MCN: *American Journal of Maternal Child Nursing*, 15(4), 245–249.

Freed, M.D. (1991). Congenital cardiac malformations. In H.W. Taeusch, R.A. Ballard, & M.E. Avery (Eds.), *Schaffer and Avery's diseases of the newborn* (6th ed.). Philadelphia: W.B. Saunders.

Glader, B.E., & Naiman, J.L. (1991). Erythrocyte disorders in infancy. In H.W. Taeusch, R.A. Ballard, & M.E. Avery (Eds.), *Schaffer and Avery's diseases of the newborn* (6th ed.). Philadelphia: W.B. Saunders.

Gomella, T.L. (Ed.). (1992). *Neonatology: Management, procedures, on-call problems, diseases, drugs* (2nd ed.). Norwalk, Conn.: Appleton & Lange.

Gorrie, T.M. (1989). *A guide to the nursing of childbearing families*. Baltimore: Williams & Wilkins.

Graves, B.W. (1992). Newborn resuscitation revisited. *Journal of Nurse-Midwifery*, 37(Suppl. 2), 36S–42S.

Hagedorn, M.I., Gardner, S.L., & Abman, S.H. (1993). Respiratory diseases. In G.B. Merenstein & S.L. Gardner (Eds.), *Handbook of neonatal intensive care* (2nd ed.). St. Louis: C.V. Mosby.

Hansen, T., & Corbet, A. (1991). Disorders of the transition. In H.W. Taeusch, R.A. Ballard, & M.E. Avery (Eds.), *Schaffer and Avery's diseases of the newborn* (6th ed.). Philadelphia: W.B. Saunders.

Hite, C., & Shannon, M. (1992). Clinical profile of apparently healthy neonates with in utero drug exposure. *Journal of Obstetric, Gynecologic, and Neonatal Nursing*, 21(4), 305–309.

Hodson, W.A., & Truog, W.E. (1989). *Critical care of the newborn* (2nd ed.). Philadelphia: W.B. Saunders.

Hoskins, S.K. (1990). Nursing care of the infant of a diabetic mother: An antenatal, intrapartal, and neonatal challenge. *Neonatal Network*, 9(4), 39–46.

Husser, D.A. (1992). New drugs. *Nursing* 92, 22(5), 55–61.

Ioli, J.G., & Richardson, M.J. (1990). Giving surfactant to premature infants. *American Journal of Nursing*, 90(3), 59–60.

Jones, M.B. (1990). A physiologic approach to identifying neonates at risk for kernicterus. *Journal of Obstetric, Gynecologic, and Neonatal Nursing*, 19(4), 313–317.

Kenner, C., Brueggemeyer, A., & Gunderson, L.P. (1993). *Comprehensive neonatal nursing, a physiologic perspective*. Philadelphia: W.B. Saunders.

Klaus, M.H., & Fanaroff, A.A. (1993). *Care of the high-risk neonate* (4th ed.). Philadelphia: W.B. Saunders.

Klaus, M.H., & Kennell, J.H. (1993). Care of the parents. In M.H. Klaus & A.A. Fanaroff (Eds.), *Care of the high-risk neonate*. Philadelphia: W.B. Saunders.

Krause, K.D., & Youngner, V.J. (1992). Nursing diagnoses as guidelines in the care of the neonatal ECMO patient. *Journal of Obstetric, Gynecologic, and Neonatal Nursing*, 21(3), 169–176.

Lapido, M. (1989). Respiratory distress revisited. *Neonatal Network*, 8(3), 9–14.

Lefrak-Okikawa, L., & Lund, C.H. (1993). Nursing practice in the neonatal intensive care unit. In M.H. Klaus & A.A. Fanaroff (Eds.), *Care of the high-risk neonate*. Philadelphia: W.B. Saunders.

Lewis, K.D., Bennett, B., & Schmeder, N.H. (1989). The care of infants menaced by cocaine abuse. MCN: *American Journal of Maternal Child Nursing*, 14(5), 324–329.

Lott, J.W. (1993). Fetal development: Environmental influences and critical periods. In C. Kenner, A. Brueggemeyer, & L.P. Gunderson (Eds.), *Comprehensive neonatal nursing: A physiologic perspective*. Philadelphia: W.B. Saunders.

Lott, J.W., & Kilb, J.R. (1992). The selection of antibacterial agents for treatment of neonatal sepsis, or which drug kills which bug? *Neonatal Network*, 11(6), 31–41.

Lott, J.W., Nelson, K., Fahrner, R., & Kenner, C. (1993). Assessment and management of immunologic dysfunction. In C. Kenner, A. Brueggemeyer, & L.P. Gunderson (Eds.), *Comprehensive neonatal nursing: A physiologic perspective*. Philadelphia: W.B. Saunders.

Ludwig, M.A. (1990). Phototherapy in the home setting. *Journal of Pediatric Health Care*, 4(6), 304–308.

Lynch, M., & McKeon V.A. (1990). Cocaine use during pregnancy: Research findings and clinical implications. *Journal of Obstetric, Gynecologic, and Neonatal Nursing*, 19(4), 285–292.

Maisels, M.J. (1987). Neonatal jaundice. In G.B. Avery (Ed.), *Neonatology: Pathophysiology and management of the newborn* (3rd ed.). Philadelphia: J.B. Lippincott.

Mattson, S., & Smith, J.E. (Eds.). (1992). NAACOG *core curriculum for maternal-newborn nursing*. Philadelphia: W.B. Saunders.

Mosijczuk, A.D., & Ellis-Vaiani, C. (1993). Hematologic diseases. In G.B. Merenstein & S.L. Gardner (Eds.), *Handbook of neonatal intensive care* (2nd ed.). St. Louis: C.V. Mosby.

Neonatal resuscitation. (1992). *Journal of the American Medical Association*, 268(16), 2276–2281.

Nora, J.G. (1990). Perinatal cocaine use: Maternal, fetal and neonatal effects. *Neonatal Network*, 9(2), 45–51.

O'Donnell, J.P., & Merenstein, G.B. (1993). Infection in the neonate. In G.B. Merenstein & S.L. Gardner (Eds.), *Handbook of neonatal intensive care* (2nd ed.). St. Louis: C.V. Mosby.

Oski, F.A. (1991). Kernicterus. In H.W. Taeusch, R.A. Ballard, & M.E. Avery (Eds.), *Schaffer and Avery's diseases of the newborn* (6th ed.). Philadelphia: W.B. Saunders.

Paxton, J.M. (1992). Neonatal infections. In P. Beachy & J. Deacon (Eds.), *Core curriculum for neonatal intensive care nursing*. Philadelphia: W.B. Saunders.

Peters, H., & Theorell, C.J. (1991). Fetal and neonatal effects of maternal cocaine use. *Journal of Obstetric, Gynecologic, and Neonatal Nursing*, 20(2), 121–126.

Rayburn, W., & Marsden, D. (1993). Medications in pregnancy. In R.A. Knuppel & J.E. Drukker (Ed.), *High-risk pregnancy, a team approach* (2nd ed.). Philadelphia: W.B. Saunders.

Ross, T., & Dickason, E.J. (1992). Nursing alert: Vertical transmission of HIV and HBV. MCN: *American Journal of Maternal Child Nursing*, 17(4), 192–195.

Rowe, M.A. (1990). Asphyxiated infants: Pathophysiologic consequences, parenting and nursing management. *Neonatal Network*, 9(4), 7–10.

Schuman, A.J., & Karush, G. (1992). Fiberoptic vs. conventional home phototherapy for neonatal hyperbilirubinemia. *Clinical Pediatrics*, 31(6), 345–352.

Sham, B. (1992). Perinatal substance abuse. In P. Beachy & J. Deacon (Eds.), *Core curriculum for neonatal intensive care nursing*. Philadelphia: W.B. Saunders.

Verklan, M.T. (1989). Safe in the womb? Drug and chemical effects on the fetus and neonate. *Neonatal Network*, 8(1), 59–65.

Whaley, L.F., & Wong, D.L. (1991). *Nursing care of infants and children*. St. Louis: C.V. Mosby.

Wilkerson, N.N. (1989). Treating hyperbilirubinemia. MCN: *American Journal of Maternal Child Nursing*, 14(1), 32–36.

Wiswell, T.E., Tuggle, J.M., & Turner, B.S. (1990). Meconium aspiration syndrome: Have we made a difference? *Pediatrics*, 85(5), 715–720.

Part VI

Other Reproductive Issues

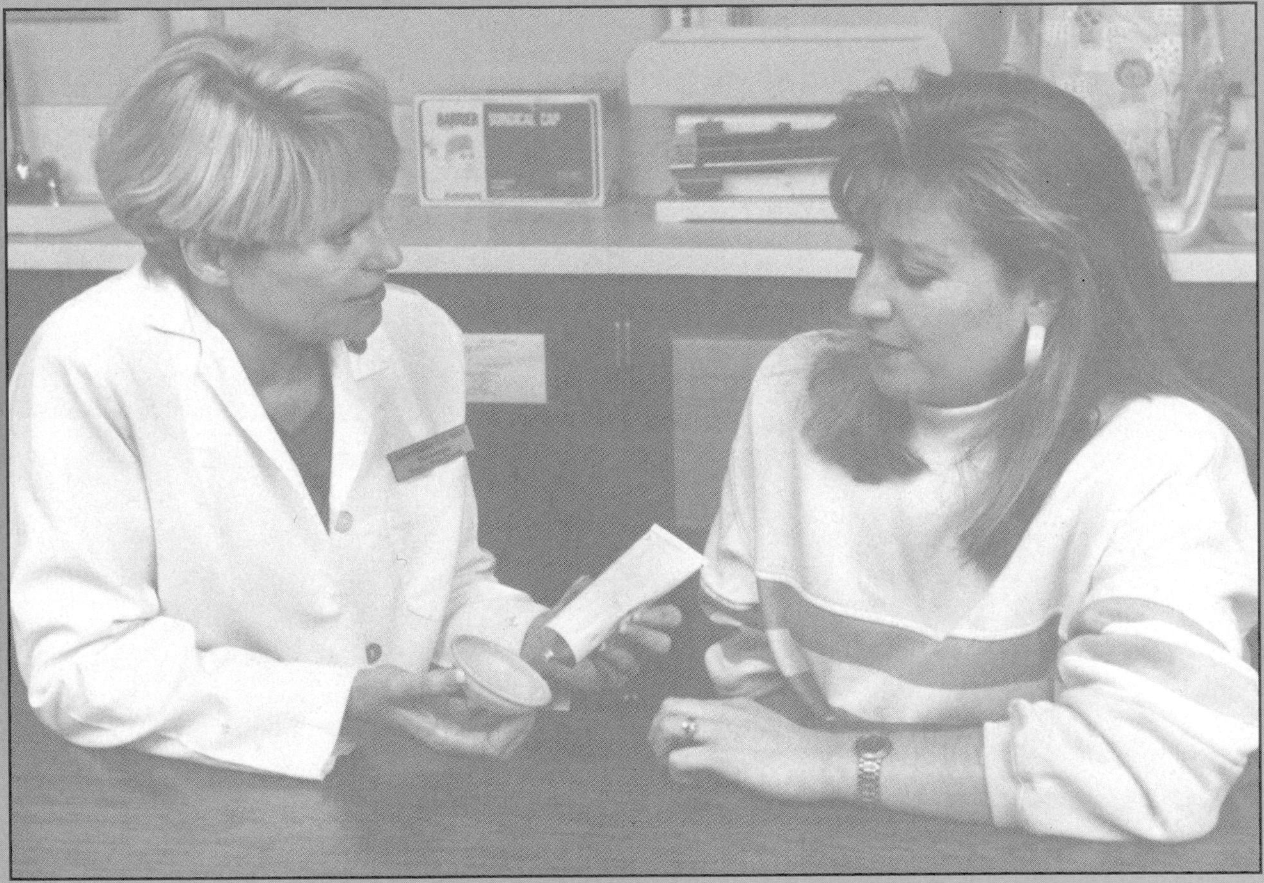

30

Family Planning

Objectives

1. Describe the role of the nurse in helping couples choose contraceptive methods.
2. Compare and contrast contraceptive methods in terms of safety, effectiveness, convenience, education needed, interference with spontaneity, availability, expense, and client preference.
3. Explain why informed consent is important for contraception.
4. Compare and contrast contraceptive needs of adolescent and perimenopausal women.
5. Explain the mechanism of action of each method of family planning available: natural family planning, barrier, hormonal, intrauterine devices, and sterilization.

Definitions

Basal body temperature • Body temperature at rest.

Cervical cap • A small cup-like device placed over the cervix to prevent sperm from entering, thus preventing pregnancy.

Coitus • Sexual union between a male and a female.

Coitus interruptus • Withdrawal of the penis from the vagina before ejaculation.

Condom • Latex shield covering the penis or lining the vagina to prevent sperm from entering the cervix and/or to prevent infection.

Contraception • Prevention of pregnancy.

Contraceptive sponge • Soft polyurethane disc containing **spermicide**, which forms a barrier over the cervix and kills sperm, thus preventing pregnancy.

Diaphragm • **Contraceptive** device consisting of a latex dome that covers the cervix and prevents entrance of sperm; must be used with **spermicide** to be effective.

Hormone implant • Small capsules of progestin inserted subcutaneously to provide contraception.

Intrauterine device (IUD) • A mechanical device inserted into the uterus to prevent pregnancy.

Libido • Sexual desire.

Mittelschmerz • Low abdominal pain that occurs at ovulation.

Natural family planning • Method of predicting ovulation based on normal changes in a woman's body.

Oral contraceptive • Drug that inhibits ovulation; contains progestins alone or in combination with estrogen.

Progestin • Any natural or synthetic form of progesterone.

Spermicide • A chemical, such as nonoxynol-9, that kills **sperm.**

Spinnbarkeit • Clear, slippery, stretchy quality of cervical mucus during ovulation.

Tubal ligation • Tying and/or ligating of the fallopian tubes to prevent passage of ova or sperm, thus preventing pregnancy.

Vasectomy • Tying and/or ligating of the vas deferens to prevent passage of sperm, thus preventing pregnancy.

Family planning involves choosing when and when not to have children. It includes contraception—the prevention of pregnancy—as well as methods to achieve pregnancy. Chapter 31 describes methods used by couples having difficulty attaining pregnancy. This chapter focuses on techniques used to avoid pregnancy.

Contraception cannot be left to chance if couples wish to control the timing of pregnancies, because 90 per cent of women will conceive within 1 year if no contraception is used and both partners are fertile (Cunningham et al, 1989). Ninety-five per cent of all sexually active women in the United States between the ages of 15 and 44 have used one or more contraceptive methods (Kaeser, 1990). Because the average woman bears only two children, she may make contraceptive decisions for more than 30 years.

The majority of contraceptive methods available must be practiced by women. Therefore, women most often make the decisions about which contraceptive methods to use. Most contraceptive choices are not final. During a woman's reproductive lifetime, her needs may change. Most women try a variety of methods before they reach menopause.

Information About Contraception

Common Sources

Women often obtain information about contraception from friends, relatives, newspapers, and magazines. They often seek answers to practical questions about comfort, partners' responses, and problems encountered. Although these sources are readily available, women may receive incomplete facts or misinformation when the source is not a health care professional.

Women frequently turn to nurses in clinics, physician's offices, birth settings, or even social settings for accurate information about contraception. Some women are more comfortable asking a nurse questions about contraception than a physician, particularly when they are unsure of what technique they desire.

Role of the Nurse

The nurse's role in family planning is that of counselor and educator. To fulfill this role, nurses must have current, correct information about contraceptive methods. Contraceptive failure would occur much less often if women had adequate education about their chosen method. The initial teaching that accompanies selection of the contraceptive technique may be insufficient to meet the woman's needs. Reinforcement of teaching and an opportunity to ask questions after initial use can help ensure that the woman is using her method correctly.

Nurses must be comfortable discussing contraception and sensitive to the client's concerns and feelings. In discussing family planning, the client's preferences take precedence. Nurses must be careful not to introduce their own biases toward or against specific methods. The nurse's personal experiences and choices regarding contraception should not be discussed. The woman and her partner will have different needs and feelings about contraception, and these must be the focus of the counseling session.

Nurses working in maternity settings should discuss family planning with every woman after birth to provide an opportunity to clarify misinformation and answer questions. Then, when the woman returns to her primary caregiver for the postpartum check-up, she will be ready to discuss contraception further, if necessary.

Considerations When Choosing a Contraceptive Method

There is no perfect contraceptive method. Each has advantages and disadvantages that may be more or less acceptable to various couples (Table 30–1). Finding the method that best suits a woman at various periods of her life may take time and diligence. A woman may try several methods before a satisfactory one is found. The nurse can help clients weigh factors involved in choosing the family planning method right for them. The importance of each factor will vary according to the circumstances of each client.

Safety

The safety of the method is a primary consideration. Although all contraceptives are tested before marketing, medical conditions may make some methods unsafe for certain women. For example, oral contra-

Table 30–1. ADVANTAGES AND DISADVANTAGES OF CONTRACEPTIVE METHODS

Advantages	Disadvantages
Barrier Methods (Spermicides, Condoms, Sponge, Diaphragm, Cervical Cap)	
Avoid systemic hormones Offer some protection from STDs	Most coitus-related (must be used just prior to coitus) May be messy May interfere with sensation Some people sensitive to components of spermicide or latex Most require new application for subsequent intercourse
Spermicides (Chemical Barrier)	
Quick and easy No prescription needed Inexpensive per single use	Films and suppositories must melt before effective Usually effective for only 1 hour
Condoms (Mechanical Barrier)	
Quick and easy No prescription needed Best protection available from STDs, especially if combined with spermicide Inexpensive per single use Can be carried discreetly Vaginal condoms increase women's control over contraceptive use and protection from STDs	Must be checked for expiration date and holes Can break or slip off Vaginal condom may seem unattractive
Sponge (Mechanical and Chemical Barrier)	
No prescription or fitting needed Can be carried discreetly Can be inserted as long as 24 hours before coitus Is effective for 30 hours No added spermicide necessary for repeated intercourse Relatively inexpensive per single use	Some women have difficulty placing and removing May cause discomfort or irritation Less effective for women who have had children Possibility of toxic shock syndrome
Diaphragm (Mechanical and Chemical Barrier)	
Can be inserted several hours before coitus	Initially expensive Must be fitted by NP or MD Education needed on proper use Some women have difficulty with correct insertion or removal Added spermicide necessary for repeated coitus Possibility of toxic shock syndrome Must be refitted after each birth or weight change of 10 or more pounds Pressure against bladder may cause infections
Cervical Cap (Mechanical and Chemical Barrier)	
Smaller than diaphragm and may fit women who cannot wear a diaphragm Requires less spermicide and no additional spermicide for repeated intercourse No pressure against bladder Can remain in place 48 hours Less noticeable than diaphragm	Sizes are limited Initially expensive Must be fitted by NP or MD Education needed on proper use Somewhat more difficult to insert than diaphragm Can be dislodged during intercourse Possibility of toxic shock syndrome Must be refitted each year and after birth
Oral Contraceptives	
Taken at time unrelated to coitus See Table 30–3	Must be taken at same time each day May cause side effects and complications Does not protect from STDs See Table 30–3

Table continued on following page

Table 30–1. ADVANTAGES AND DISADVANTAGES OF CONTRACEPTIVE METHODS *Continued*

Advantages	Disadvantages
Hormone Implant (Norplant System)	
In place at all times	Does not protect from STDs High initial cost, involves minor surgery Slightly visible Side effects similar to those of oral contraceptives
Hormone Injections (Depo-Provera)	
Unrelated to coitus	Must be repeated every 3 months Side effects similar to those of other progestion contraceptives
Intrauterine Devices	
In place at all times Low long-term cost	Does not protect from STDs High initial cost Can be expelled without woman's knowledge—must check for strings Potential side effects or complications—menorrhagia, infection, ectopic pregnancy, abortion, perforation
Natural Family Planning: All Methods	
Inexpensive No drugs or hormones Helps woman learn about her body Acceptable to most religions May be used to achieve pregnancy Can be combined with barrier methods to increase effectiveness	High level of motivation needed Extensive education needed Involves abstinence in large part of each cycle High risk of pregnancy if errors made Many factors may change ovulation time
Calendar	
Easy to calculate	Least reliable of natural methods
Basal Body Temperature	
Fairly easy to calculate	Temperature change shows ovulation has occurred, too late to prevent pregnancy Many other factors may affect temperature
Cervical Mucus	
Increased effectiveness over other natural methods	Depends on daily assessment of cervical mucus
Symptothermal	
More effective than most natural methods	Multiple daily assessments needed
Postovulation	
Most effective of all natural methods	Involves abstinence in at least half of cycle (until after ovulation)
Sterilization (Tubal Ligation and Vasectomy)	
Ends concern about contraception Tubal ligation can be done right after childbirth while woman still in hospital, or on outpatient basis at another time Vasectomy may be done in physician's office under local anesthesia Although expensive when done, long-term cost is low	Does not protect from STDs Expensive and potentially impossible to reverse should couple change their minds Involves surgery with potential complications of all surgeries After vasectomy, another contraceptive method must be used until no sperm are in semen

Table 30–1. ADVANTAGES AND DISADVANTAGES OF CONTRACEPTIVE METHODS *Continued*

Advantages	Disadvantages
Breastfeeding	
No expense or chemicals	Unreliable, especially if infant receives supplemental feedings Must continue night feedings as long as used for contraception
Coitus Interruptus*	
No expense or chemicals	Requires great control Unreliable, especially if there is semen spillage

* Not usually recommended as birth control method in the United States.

ceptives are contraindicated in women who have had thrombophlebitis or strokes because the hormones used may cause these conditions to recur. The contraceptive sponge, diaphragm, or cervical cap is unsafe for a woman with a history of toxic shock syndrome, which is a possible complication of these methods.

Effectiveness

The importance of avoiding pregnancy must be considered when choosing a contraceptive method. A couple may wish to put off pregnancy for a time but may be relatively unconcerned if pregnancy occurs before it was planned. Another couple may be extremely upset about an accidental pregnancy because it would affect the mother's health or have a major impact on their financial stability.

Effectiveness rates refer to how well pregnancy is prevented (Table 30–2). Two different effectiveness rates are often given:

1. The ideal, perfect, or theoretical effectiveness rate refers to perfect use of the method with every act of intercourse. Failures are due to a problem with the method itself rather than with the application of the method.
2. The typical, actual, or user effectiveness rate is taken from studies of occurrence of pregnancy in real people using the method. Failure is presumably due to incorrect or inconsistent use of the technique.

The difference between the two rates of failure shows how forgiving a method is, that is, how likely pregnancy is to occur if use is occasionally imperfect. The typical effectiveness rate is more meaningful when counseling clients (Franklin, 1990b). When comparing different methods, one must use the same method of analysis.

Effectiveness rates are listed as number of pregnancies in 100 women per year. Although a typical effectiveness rate of 88 per cent for a method might seem fairly good, it means that 12 of every 100 women using that method experience unintended pregnancies each year. For couples who feel that a one in eight yearly risk of pregnancy is too great, a method with a higher effectiveness rate is necessary.

Effectiveness varies according to accuracy of use. It diminishes greatly when the user does not understand how to use the method. The failure rate commonly decreases after the first year of use because experience with the method leads to more accurate use. Methods that are less reliable can sometimes be combined to increase effectiveness, such as using a condom with a spermicide.

The acceptability of the method to the couple must be balanced against the effectiveness. Surgical sterilization is the most effective method but is unacceptable to couples planning to have children at a later time. Oral contraceptives or intrauterine devices are also highly effective, but some women may dislike the side effects or have religious objections.

Convenience

Convenience is another important factor. If the woman perceives her contraceptive as difficult to use, time-consuming, or too much "bother," she is unlikely to use it consistently unless her level of motivation is very high. The education she receives about the method may affect her perception of its difficulty. Women knowledgeable about the contraceptive technique are less likely to feel that the contraceptive is difficult to use.

Contraceptives that are "messy" may seem inconvenient and unattractive. Spermicide may drip from

Table 30–2. CONTRACEPTIVE EFFECTIVENESS AND FAILURE RATES

Method	Effectiveness Rate: Typical or Actual Use (%)*	Failure Rate: Typical or Actual Use (%)*	Failure Rate: Ideal or Perfect Use (%)*
Sterilization			
Tubal ligation	99.6	0.4	0.2
Vasectomy	99.85	0.15	0.1
Hormone implant (Norplant)	99.96	0.04	0.04
Hormone injections (Depo-Provera)	99.7	0.3	0.3
Oral contraceptives	97	3	
Combined estrogen/progestin			0.1
Progestin only			0.5
Intrauterine devices	97	3	
Progestin			2
Copper			0.8
Condoms	88	12	2
Diaphragm	82	18	6
Cervical cap	82	18	6
Sponge			
Parous women	72	28	9
Nulliparous women	82	18	6
Spermicides	79	21	3
Natural family planning	80	20	
Calendar			9
Cervical mucus (ovulation)			3
Symptothermal			2
Postovulation			1
Coitus interruptus (withdrawal)	82	18	4
No contraceptive use	15	85	

Adapted from Trussell, J., Hatcher, R., Cates, W., Stewart, F.H., & Kost, K. (1990). Contraceptive failure in the United States: An update. *Studies in Family Planning, 21*(1), 51–54.

* Per cent of women who may be expected to avoid or to become pregnant with use of each method from typical or perfect use during the first year.

the vagina and decrease satisfaction for both the woman and the man. Less spermicide may decrease dripping but increases the risk of pregnancy.

Education Needed

Some methods of contraception involve very little education, whereas others depend on one or more teaching sessions to ensure adequate knowledge. For example, condoms are easy to use and involve less education than some other methods. Natural family planning methods rely on extensive education about anatomy and physiology and body changes that denote ovulation. Women using these methods need rather sophisticated information to practice them successfully.

Interference with Spontaneity

Coitus-related contraceptive methods, such as spermicides and barrier methods, must be used just prior to sexual intercourse. They interrupt lovemaking, increasing the chance that the method will not be used. Some couples remedy this by including placement of the contraceptive device, such as a condom, diaphragm, or cervical cap, as a part of foreplay. Others prefer methods such as oral contraceptives, intrauterine devices, or hormone implants that are used at times other than during sexual activity.

Availability

Condoms, spermicides, and sponges are readily available without prescriptions. They can be purchased anonymously at any time without a trip to a health care provider. This may be important to an adolescent who wants to hide her sexual activity or to any woman who is embarrassed to discuss contraception with a health care provider.

Expense

The cost of family planning methods per use must be compared with long-term expense. The price of a condom or sponge is relatively low, but frequent use makes them expensive over a period of years. Couples may find them economical for occasional sexual intercourse or until they can afford a more expensive method.

Any method that depends on periodic visits to a nurse practitioner or physician will be more expensive than an over-the-counter method. However, these more expensive methods include professional counseling, which may enhance contraceptive effectiveness. A visit to a health care provider for a contraceptive method also allows for screening for other health conditions and provides an opportunity for health teaching.

Contraceptive information and services are often available at family planning clinics at little or no cost. These clinics provide professional counseling about all contraceptive methods as well as follow-up services. However, women may object to a long wait and the fact that they may see a different health care provider at each visit.

Client Preference

The client makes the final decision about contraceptive method, and it is crucial that she be satisfied with it. Consistent use of any method depends on whether it meets the needs of the woman and her partner. If the woman feels pressured into choosing a method, or if the chosen method fails to live up to her expectations, use is likely to be inconsistent.

Some women are uncomfortable with their bodies and embarrassed by methods that involve touching the vagina. Inserting a diaphragm or cervical cap or performing a daily assessment of cervical mucus may be difficult for them. For these women, another technique would be preferable.

Religious or other personal beliefs also affect choice of contraceptives. Some clients' beliefs may allow them to use natural family planning methods only. Others are adverse to any method linked to abortion, such as post-coital contraception. The opinions of the woman's partner and friends may also influence what method she chooses.

Informed Consent

Because some methods have potentially dangerous side effects, it is necessary for the woman to sign an informed consent form to show that she received and understands information about risks and benefits. For example, written consent may be obtained from women choosing surgical sterilization, oral contraceptives, hormone implants or injections, or intrauterine devices. Of course, whether or not a formal consent form is used, every client should receive information about the chosen contraceptive method and its proper use, its risks and benefits, and alternative methods available.

✔ Check Your Reading

1. Why do women usually choose the method of contraception that a couple uses?
2. What is the role of the nurse in helping couples with contraceptive choices and use?
3. What are some important considerations in choosing a contraceptive technique?
4. Which contraceptive methods might involve an informed consent form?

Adolescents

Adolescent Knowledge

Many adolescents have little knowledge about their own anatomy and physiology, including how and when conception occurs. What they know about contraception is likely to be learned from other teenagers, who tend to pass on incorrect information. Even adolescents who have been pregnant misunderstand contraceptive techniques, and they may become pregnant again because of lack of information about family planning.

MISINFORMATION

Misinformation and erroneous beliefs cause adolescents to use ineffective methods of contraception or no method at all. Some teenagers think that it is impossible to become pregnant the first time that they have sexual intercourse unless they have an orgasm or have been menstruating a certain length of time. However, pregnancy can occur after any episode of intercourse if ovulation has occurred. Although many adolescents have anovulatory menstrual cycles during the early months after menarche, this cannot be depended on to prevent pregnancy.

Teenagers may douche (insert water into the vagina) after intercourse to prevent pregnancy. However, douching is ineffective because sperm may enter the cervix within 15 seconds after ejaculation (Hatcher et al, 1992). Coitus interruptus—withdrawal of the penis from the vagina before ejaculation—is another unreliable method used by teenagers. It requires more control than most adolescent boys have over timing of ejaculation. Semen spilled near the vagina can enter and cause pregnancy, even without penetration by the penis. In addition, pre-ejaculatory fluid may contain sperm.

RISK-TAKING BEHAVIOR

Adolescents are more likely to take risks in sexual activity because they feel that their chances of becoming pregnant are small. They often do not plan intercourse and therefore are not prepared with contraceptives. Their risk-taking behavior may lead to sexually transmitted diseases (STDs) as well as to pregnancy. Schools have helped increase birth control use among adolescents by offering information about family planning and prevention of STDs. Sometimes, contraceptive services are available on school campuses. Nevertheless, the number of adolescent pregnancies continues to be extremely large in the United States. (See Chapter 23 for more information about adolescent pregnancy.)

Counseling Adolescents

Nurses who counsel adolescents about sexuality must be sensitive to the feelings, concerns, and needs of the teenager. They must be prepared to be accepting of the teenager regardless of personal feelings about adolescent sexuality. For an adolescent to seek information about contraception, she must admit that she is and plans to continue to be sexually active. The teenager may be afraid to ask about contraception because she does not want anyone to know that she is sexually active or she fears that she will be lectured about her behavior. Her need for secrecy may cause her to miss appointments at a family planning clinic. The nurse must be adept at determining the adolescent's needs and must reassure her about confidentiality.

Because many teenagers forgo contraception rather than talk to their parents about it, family planning clinics in most states may provide information and supplies to minors without parental permission. Some family planning clinics are designed to meet the special needs of teenagers. For example, because adolescent girls may fear the pelvic examination, clinic staff may wait to perform it until the second visit. During the first visit, the teenager receives information about contraceptive techniques. Taking this extra time to explain different methods helps allay the common concern of adolescents about potential adverse health effects of contraceptives. It also helps the teenager to feel comfortable in the family planning clinic setting.

Because of her youth and probable lack of knowledge about anatomy and physiology, the adolescent needs more extensive teaching than the older woman. Liberal use of audiovisual materials, such as pictures, anatomical models, and samples of various methods, helps the teenager understand the information more easily (Fig. 30–1).

Using understandable terminology is especially important when teaching adolescents. The nurse must know street terms for body parts and sexual intercourse, as they may be the only words with which the teenager is familiar.

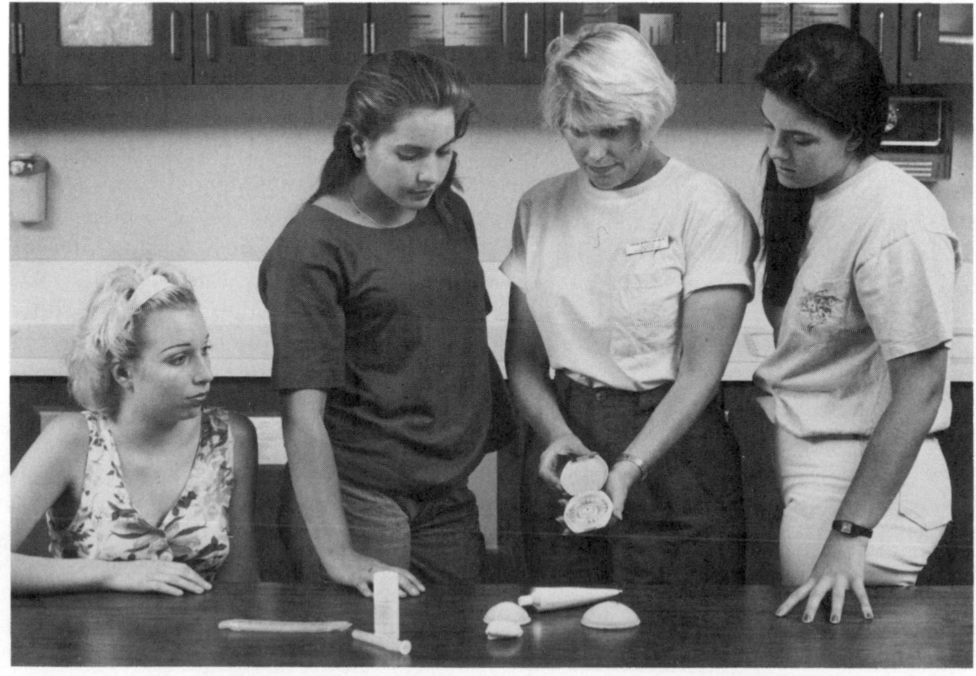

Figure 30–1

The nurse discusses a variety of contraceptives with adolescent girls. Here she is discussing oral contraceptives.

Adolescents are most successful when they choose contraceptive methods that are easy to use and that seem unrelated to coitus. Although they may use condoms for occasional sexual intercourse or to decrease the risk of STDs, many teenagers choose oral contraceptives. This method is safe, seems unrelated to sex, and is not difficult or messy. Long-term oral contraceptive use has not been found to cause problems in healthy women. However, adolescent females may be inconsistent in taking their pills every day. They should understand all aspects of management of missed pills and when there is need for a back-up method of contraception (see Women Want to Know: What to Do if an Oral Contraceptive Dose Is Missed, p. 891).

Perimenopausal Women

Perimenopausal women may continue to ovulate as long as they have regular menstrual periods, and some ovulate even when indications of menopause are present. Pregnancy is rare after age 50, and contraception can be discontinued sooner if menstruation has ceased for at least 2 years (Cunningham et al, 1989). The mature woman who does not smoke and has no other contraindications can use any method of contraception. It is important that she have regular physical examinations to identify any conditions that would necessitate a change in contraceptive method. Many couples who do not plan to have more children choose sterilization. This ends their concerns about contraception permanently.

✔ Check Your Reading

5. What are some erroneous beliefs about contraception commonly held by adolescents?
6. Why might teenagers be hesitant to seek contraceptive information?
7. How can the nurse increase effectiveness in teaching adolescents about contraception?
8. What special considerations are necessary in contraception for perimenopausal women?

Methods of Contraception

Barrier Methods

The barrier methods of contraception involve chemicals or devices that prevent sperm from reaching the cervix. The method may kill the sperm or place a temporary partition between the penis and the cervix. All of the barrier methods are coitus-related and may interfere with spontaneity. However, they avoid use of systemic hormones and provide some protection from STDs. Infection with human papillomavirus, an STD, may increase the risk of cervical cancer. Therefore, use of barrier contraceptives may lower the incidence of cervical cancer (Kost et al, 1991).

CHEMICAL BARRIERS

Chemicals that kill sperm are called spermicides and come in many forms. Creams and gels are generally used with mechanical barriers such as the diaphragm or cervical cap. Foams, suppositories, and vaginal film may be used alone. They are inserted into the vagina just before sexual intercourse and are effective for about 1 hour. Vaginal films and suppositories must melt before they become effective, which takes approximately 15 minutes. Nonoxynol-9 is used in many products containing spermicide and provides some protection against gonorrhea, genital herpes, trichomoniasis, syphilis, and human immunodeficiency virus (HIV) (NAACOG, 1991).

Women should avoid douching for at least 6 hours after intercourse and should add more spermicide if coitus is repeated. Sensitivity to the products may cause genital irritation. Some couples feel that spermicides are messy and interfere with sensation during intercourse. Spermicides, when used alone, are 70 per cent effective.

MECHANICAL BARRIERS

Mechanical barriers are devices placed over the penis or cervix to prevent passage of sperm into the uterus. They include the condom, contraceptive sponge, diaphragm, and cervical cap.

Male Condom. Condoms, the only male contraceptive device currently available, cover the penis and prevent sperm from entering the vagina. They are the third most popular method of contraception in the United States (Kaeser, 1990). Condoms are generally made of latex, and some are coated with spermicide.

Condoms provide the best protection available (other than abstinence) against syphilis, gonorrhea, herpes, chlamydia, trichomoniasis, and HIV. For this reason, they should be used during any possible exposure to an STD, even if another contraceptive technique is practiced or if the woman is pregnant.

Condoms are easily available, inexpensive, and can be carried inconspicuously. The typical failure rate of 12 per cent can be decreased by about half by using spermicide with the condom. Because condoms must be applied just before intercourse, some couples object to the interference with spontaneity. Others feel that condoms interfere with sensation. People who are allergic to latex should avoid use of

Couples Want To Know

What Is the Proper Way to Use Condoms?

Although condoms are easy to use, proper use increases their effectiveness.

- Condoms are available in a variety of colors, textures, and materials, but those made of latex are most effective. Others may not be effective for contraception or may not protect against sexually transmitted diseases.
- Check the expiration dates on packages because condoms may deteriorate after 2 years.
- Lubrication may increase comfort for the woman and reduce the risk of breakage. Use a water-soluble lubricant or a spermicide because oil-based products (such as petroleum jelly or baby oil) cause deterioration of the latex.
- Always apply the condom before there is any contact of the penis with the vagina because sperm content in pre-ejaculatory fluid may be high.

- Squeeze the air out of the tip of the condom, and leave a half inch of space at the tip as the condom is rolled onto the erect penis. This allows a place for sperm to collect and helps prevent breakage.
- The man should withdraw the penis from the vagina before it becomes soft and should hold the condom in place to prevent spilling semen into the vagina.
- Use a new condom each time intercourse is repeated.

latex condoms, as severe reactions are possible. (See Couples Want to Know: What Is the Proper Way to Use Condoms?)

Female Condom. The female condom (or vaginal pouch) is a polyurethane sheath, 7 inches long, inserted into the vagina. A flexible ring fits over the cervix like a diaphragm, and another ring extends outside the vagina so that the perineum is also covered. Another design is similar to a bikini panty with a pouch that is inserted into the vagina. The condom

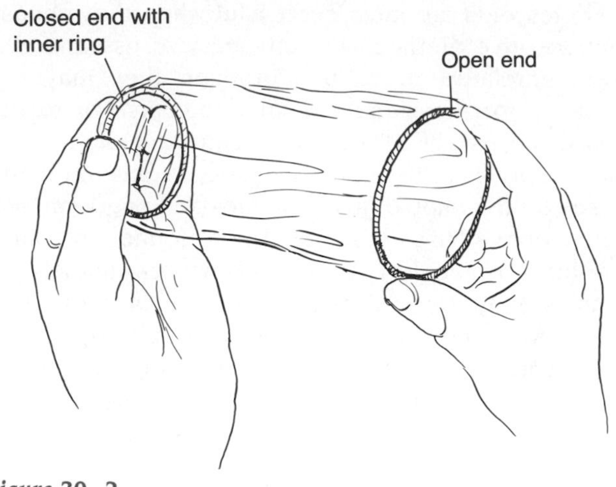

Figure 30–2

The female condom. A woman can protect herself from sexually transmitted diseases without relying on use of the male condom.

is lubricated with the spermicide nonoxynol-9 to help protect against STDs as well as pregnancy (Fig. 30–2).

The female condom is the first contraceptive device to allow a woman to protect herself from STDs without relying on the male condom. Like the male condom and the sponge, it is relatively inexpensive per single use but expensive with frequent use. It has a typical effectiveness rate of approximately 87.5 per cent.

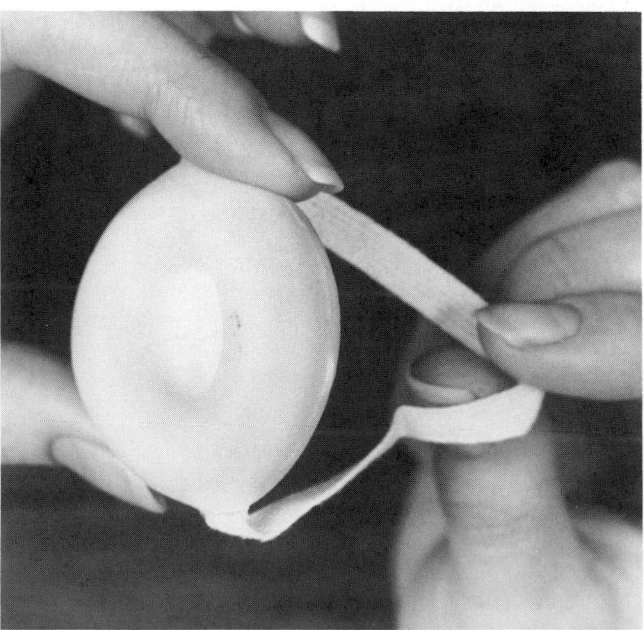

Figure 30–3

The contraceptive sponge can be purchased over the counter, and it can be used during the postpartum period.

Sponge. The contraceptive sponge is made of soft spermicide-impregnated polyurethane (Fig. 30–3). The woman inserts it into her vagina up to 24 hours before intercourse. The sponge traps and absorbs sperm, which are destroyed by the spermicide nonoxynol-9. No fitting, office visit, or prescription is needed, and sponges can be used during the postpartum period.

The typical effectiveness rate is 82 per cent for women who have never had children and 72 per cent for women who have had children. The lower rate for multigravidas is due to vaginal relaxation, which may interfere with the fit over the cervix. A particular advantage is that the sponge is effective for as long as 30 hours, and no added spermicide is necessary for repeated intercourse.

The sponge may cause discomfort or irritation in some women or their partners. It should never be used by women with a history of toxic shock syndrome, a possible complication of use (see Chapter 32). The sponge should not be left in place longer than 30 hours or used during menstruation, as the risk of toxic shock syndrome is increased (See Women Want to Know: How to Use a Contraceptive Sponge.)

Women Want To Know

How to Use a Contraceptive Sponge

- Plan to insert the sponge during lovemaking or as long as 24 hours before.
- Wet the sponge thoroughly, and squeeze to make it sudsy before inserting. This activates the spermicide.

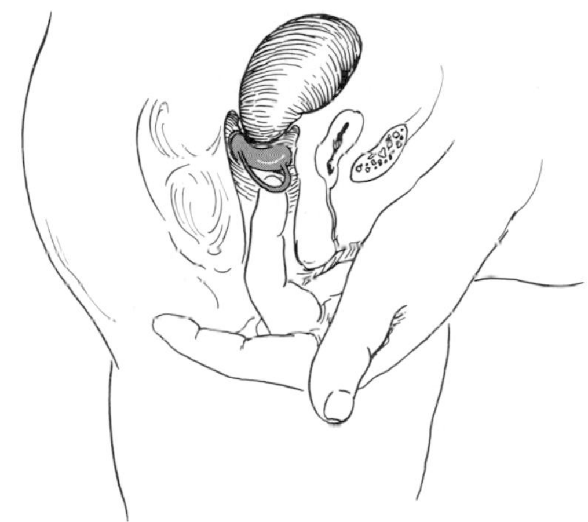

- To insert the sponge, assume a squatting position or place a foot on a chair. Fold the sponge, and insert it with the indentation against the cervix and the loop downward.
- No added spermicide is necessary for repeated intercourse.
- Leave the sponge in place at least 6 hours after intercourse. Earlier removal or douching may allow live sperm to enter the cervix. Do not leave it in the vagina for more than 30 hours.
- Remove the sponge by inserting a finger into the loop on the underside and pulling slowly. If you have any difficulty removing it, try bearing down while pulling the loop, taking a warm bath, or waiting a short time before making another attempt to remove it.
- Do not use the sponge during menstruation or if you have ever had toxic shock syndrome. Signs of toxic shock syndrome are fever, sunburn-like rash, vomiting, diarrhea, weakness, fainting, sore throat, and aching muscles or joints. If these signs develop, go to a physician immediately.

Diaphragm. The diaphragm is a latex dome surrounded by a spring or coil. The woman places spermicidal cream or gel into the dome and around the rim, then inserts it over the cervix by hand or with a plastic introducer. When folded, some models arc to form a half-moon shape, which assists in proper placement. Because it covers the cervix, the diaphragm prevents passage of sperm while holding spermicide in place for additional protection. It must be fitted by a nurse practitioner, nurse-midwife, or physician, and the woman should be checked for size changes after a weight gain or loss of more than 10 pounds and after each pregnancy. The correct size may not be available for all women.

Some couples object to the interference with spontaneity and feel that the diaphragm is messy. To eliminate interference with spontaneity, some women insert the diaphragm hours in advance of when intercourse is possible, although not necessarily planned. Future research may prove that use of spermicide with the diaphragm is unnecessary. Although some women cannot feel the diaphragm once it is in place, others find it noticeable or uncomfortable. Pressure on the urethra may cause irritation and urinary tract infections. Allergies to latex or history of toxic shock syndrome preclude use. (See Women Want to Know: How to Use a Diaphragm.)

Cervical Cap. The cervical cap is similar to the diaphragm but smaller. The flexible latex cup fits over the cervix and remains in place by suction (Fig. 30–4). Women who are difficult to fit with a diaphragm may be able to use the cervical cap. However, cap sizes are limited, and women with cervical abnormalities may not be able to use it.

Because it is smaller and requires less spermicide than the diaphragm, the cervical cap is less noticeable and causes no pressure on the bladder. It can remain in place for 48 hours, and more spermicide is not needed if intercourse is repeated. Insertion and removal are similar to diaphragm use but may be more difficult because the cap is smaller. The nurse should teach the woman to feel her cervix to check

Women Want To Know

How to Use a Diaphragm

Use of the diaphragm involves instruction at the time of fitting. Skill at insertion and removal increases with practice.

- Plan to insert the diaphragm during lovemaking or several hours before.

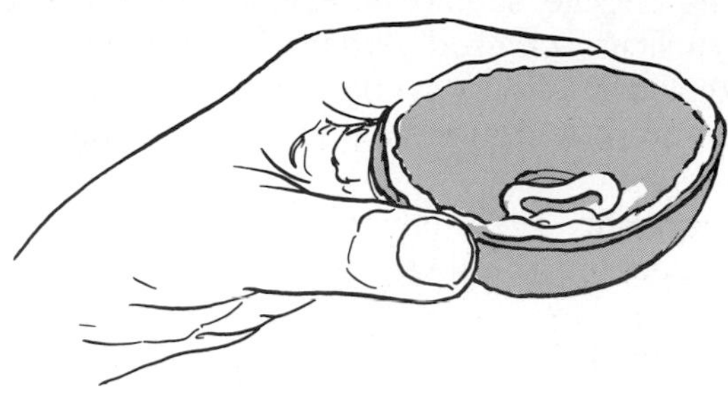

- Spread about a tablespoon of spermicidal cream or gel inside the dome and around the rim.

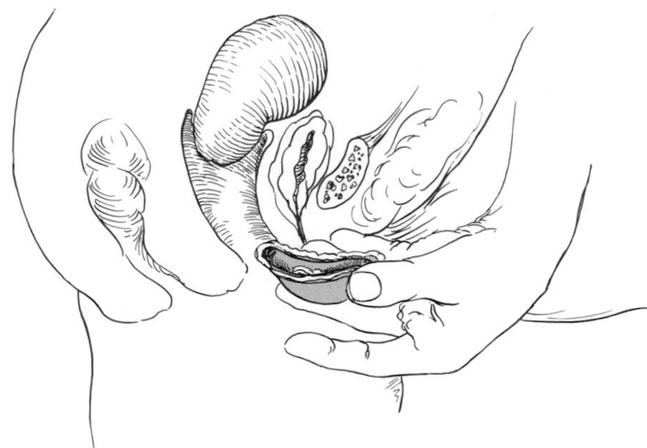

- Fold the diaphragm, and insert it into the vagina with the spermicide toward the cervix. A squatting position or placing one foot on a chair makes insertion and removal easier.

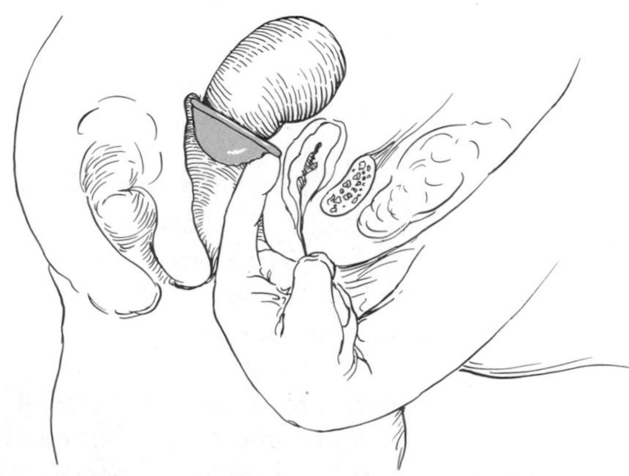

- Be sure that the front rim fits behind your pubic bone and that you can feel the cervix through the center of the diaphragm.
- If more than 6 hours elapse between insertion and intercourse or if you have intercourse again, insert more spermicide into the vagina without removing the diaphragm.
- Leave the diaphragm in place at least 6 hours after intercourse.
- Douching with the diaphragm in place is unnecessary and will lessen the effectiveness.
- Keep the diaphragm in place no longer than 24 hours, as risk of infection increases after that time.

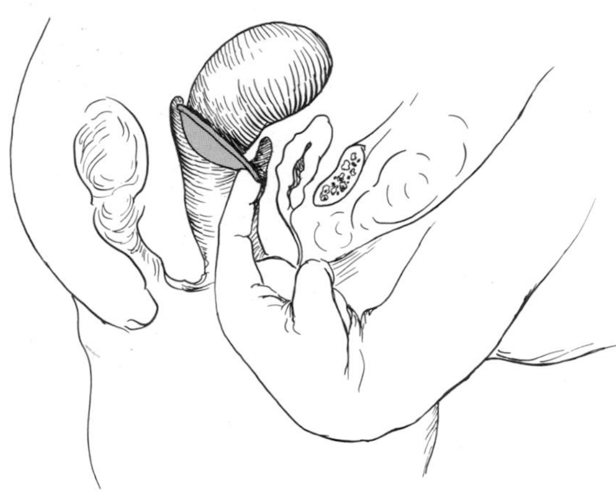

- To remove the diaphragm, assume a squatting position and bear down. Hook a finger under the front rim to break the suction, and pull down.
- Wash the diaphragm with mild soap, and dry well after each use. Inspect it occasionally for small holes by holding it up to a light. If you find one, use another contraceptive method and go to your physician or nurse practitioner for a new diaphragm.

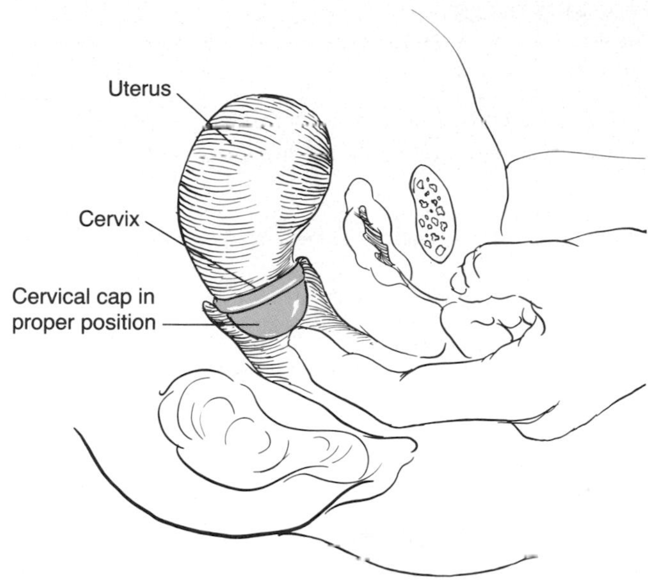

Figure 30–4

The cervical cap is inserted much like the diaphragm. The woman should check to be certain that it is placed over the cervix

placement before and after intercourse because the cap can be dislodged.

The cap fitting should be checked yearly, after abortion, childbirth, or surgery, or if it dislodges frequently. A second Pap smear is required 3 months after the original fitting because some users have had Pap smear changes indicating cervical neoplasia. If the Pap smear is normal at 3 months, only yearly examinations are necessary.

Hormonal Contraceptives

Administration of hormones alters the normal hormonal fluctuations of the menstrual cycle. This is the basis on which all hormonal contraceptives function to prevent pregnancy. Hormones may be given orally, by implant, or by injection.

ORAL CONTRACEPTIVES

Oral contraceptives are the most widely used reversible contraceptive method in the United States. Combination oral contraceptives contain both estrogen and progestin, whereas "mini-pills" contain only progestin. Both types contain much lower hormone levels than the original oral contraceptives, thus decreasing the risk of long-term side effects. Oral contraceptives have a 97 per cent typical effectiveness rate.

Combination. Estrogen and progestin combinations are the most commonly used oral contraceptives and have an action similar to pregnancy in preventing ovulation. The high level of estrogen and progestin prevents the discharge of gonadotropin-releasing hormone from the hypothalamus and follicle-stimulating hormone from the pituitary. Thus, maturation of the follicle and ovulation do not occur. (See Chapter 4 for information about the menstrual cycle.) In addition, the cervical mucus becomes too thick for sperm to penetrate, and the endometrium becomes less hospitable to implantation.

Combination oral contraceptives are available in packets of 21 or 28 tablets. With 21-tablet packets, the woman takes one pill daily for 3 weeks, then stops for a week, during which time menses occurs. Packets of 28 tablets include 7 tablets made of an inert substance that the woman takes during the 4th week. This avoids disrupting the everyday routine of taking pills.

Monophasic or multiphasic dosages are available. Monophasic pills have an estrogen and progestin content that remains constant throughout the cycle. There is a low-dose version for women who have difficulty with side effects such as nausea. A higher-dose version is given to women who have breakthrough bleeding.

With multiphasic pills, the estrogen dose may be constant or increased in the later part of the cycle, whereas the progestin is low at the beginning and increased later. This helps reduce side effects. Because there may be two or three phases of dose changes, it is important that women take the pills in the proper order.

Progestin. Oral contraceptives that contain progestin but no estrogen are called "mini-pills." They are less effective at inhibiting ovulation but cause thickening of the cervical mucus to prevent penetration by sperm and make the endometrial lining unfavorable for implantation. These pills have a lower dose of hormones and may avoid some of the side effects and risk factors associated with estrogen. Chance of breakthrough bleeding and risk of pregnancy are higher than with the combination hormones, however. If the woman misses any pills or does not take them at the same time each day, chances of pregnancy increase.

Benefits, Risks, and Contraindications. When choosing oral contraceptives, the balance between the benefits and the risks must be weighed for each individual (Table 30–3). Although there are risks in using oral contraceptives, it is important to know that the risks of complications during pregnancy and childbirth are greater (Hatcher et al, 1992). Hazards can be decreased by careful screening. Some women should not use oral contraceptives because they

Table 30–3. ORAL CONTRACEPTIVES: POTENTIAL BENEFITS AND RISKS

Benefits	Risks
Highly effective contraception	No protection against sexually transmitted diseases
Reduces ovarian and endometrial cancer by as much as 50%; protection continues for years after use	Affects carbohydrate metabolism and worsens diabetes
Regulates menstrual cycles; reduces cramping, menstrual blood loss, and associated anemia	Worsens conditions affected by fluid retention, such as migraine, asthma, epilepsy, kidney, or heart disease
Decreased incidence of: Benign breast disease Ovarian cysts Toxic shock syndrome Pelvic inflammatory disease Improves: Endometriosis Premenstrual syndrome Dysmenorrhea	Increased incidence of: Deep and superficial vein thrombosis Pulmonary embolism Myocardial infarction Stroke, especially in smokers and women over 35 Hypertension Migraines Cervical cancer Chlamydial infection Benign liver tumors Gallbladder disease Bleeding from existing fibroids

have histories of underlying conditions that make the hormones too dangerous. (See Critical to Remember: Contraindications to Oral Contraceptives.)

Although there has been concern about use of hormones in older women, studies now show that women in good health who do not smoke can continue to take oral contraceptives until menopause (NAACOG, 1991). Smoking increases the incidence of complications for women of all ages. Other factors that increase risk include hypertension, high cholesterol levels, obesity, and diabetes.

Critical to Remember

Contraindications to Oral Contraceptives

Oral contraceptives are contraindicated in women with a history of any of the following:

- Thrombophlebitis or thromboembolic disorders
- Cerebrovascular or cardiovascular diseases
- Any estrogen-dependent cancer or breast cancer
- Benign or malignant liver tumors

Oral contraceptives are contraindicated in women who currently have any of the following:

- Any of the above conditions
- Impaired liver function
- Suspected or known pregnancy
- Undiagnosed vaginal bleeding
- Heavy cigarette smoking (more than 15/day; any use of cigarettes is discouraged and should be evaluated individually)

Side Effects. Side effects of oral contraceptives are usually minor and include signs and symptoms often seen in pregnancy. Decreasing the amount of estrogen helps relieve nausea, headaches, or breast tenderness, whereas increasing the estrogen content prevents breakthrough bleeding. Other side effects include weight gain or loss, fluid retention, amenorrhea, mood changes or depression, acne, and chloasma. Side effects often decrease after the first few months of use.

Teaching. Education about proper use of oral contraceptives greatly increases their effectiveness. Teaching should be extensive when the woman begins to use the hormones, and follow-up is necessary to ensure that her questions and unanticipated problems are resolved. Because the instructions can be complicated, she should have them in simple written form in her own language, if she can read.

Blood Hormone Levels. Because maintaining a constant blood hormone level is important for effectiveness, the woman must take the pills at the same time each day. Many women make them a part of their bedtime routine, whereas others take them with a meal to avoid nausea. Breakthrough bleeding is more likely when there is a significant time variation between doses.

Missed Doses. Instructions for the woman who misses one or more doses are included in Women Want to Know: What to Do if an Oral Contraceptive Dose Is Missed. If a woman misses a period and thinks that there is a possibility that she may be pregnant because she missed one or more doses, she should stop taking the pills and get a sensitive pregnancy test immediately. It is essential that she use another contraceptive method during this time.

Women Want To Know
What to Do If an Oral Contraceptive Dose Is Missed

The following provides general information about what to do if you do not take one or more contraceptive tablets. Talk with your nurse practitioner, nurse-midwife, or physician for specific information suited to your needs.

If Any Pills Are Missed:
Use another form of contraception until a pill has been taken daily for the next 7 days. (Some practitioners say this is not necessary if only one pill is missed.)

One Pill Missed:
Take the pill as soon as you remember it. Take the next pill at the normal time, even if you take both pills together.

Two Pills Missed:
Take two pills as soon as you remember. Take the next pill at the normal time. (Some suggest taking two pills the next day also.)

Three Pills Missed:
Throw away all remaining pills. Start a new package of pills on the first day of menstrual flow.

Inactive Pills Missed Between Days 21 and 28:
Throw away pills missed, and continue to take the rest as scheduled. Contraception will not be affected.

Although there is no established association with fetal anomalies, continued use during pregnancy is not advisable.

Another contraceptive method is usually recommended when a dose is missed. The woman should use another method until seven tablets are taken consecutively after the missed dose, or for the rest of the cycle if more than one tablet is missed.

Nutrition. Nutrition may be affected by long-term oral contraceptive use. There may be some interference with use of vitamins A, B_6, B_{12}, folates, copper, and zinc (Cunningham et al, 1989). Whether or not supplementation is needed depends on the individual woman and her diet.

Lactation. Combination oral contraceptives reduce milk production in lactating women, and very small amounts may be transferred to the milk. If the combination forms are used during lactation, they should be started after milk production is well established. Progestin-only contraceptives do not affect milk production. Studies to date show no adverse effects on infants breastfed by mothers using oral contraceptives (Franklin, 1990a).

Other Medications. Oral contraceptives may interact with other medications, and the effectiveness of each may be changed. For example, some drugs used for epilepsy, and antibiotics such as ampicillin and tetracycline, decrease the effectiveness of oral contraceptives. Therefore, the woman should always tell the health care provider prescribing medications for her what other drugs she is taking.

Follow-up. The woman who takes oral contraceptives should have a yearly pelvic examination and Pap smear, breast examination, and blood pressure measurement. She should report any signs of adverse reaction immediately (Table 30–4). Return of fertility usually occurs soon after the pills are discontinued. However, the woman should wait until her menstrual cycle is re-established before conceiving so that she can date the beginning of her pregnancy more accurately.

HORMONE IMPLANT

The progestin implant (Norplant System) is the most effective reversible form of contraception available today (99.96 per cent). Six flexible capsules about 1.5 inches long (the size of a match) are inserted subcutaneously into the upper inner arm under local anesthetic (Fig. 30–5). This area is used because it is easily accessible and low in fat. The capsules are inserted in a fan-shaped configuration and are only slightly visible. They release progestin continuously, at a higher rate at first, then decreasing gradually over the 5 years that they are effective.

The progestin implant is expensive at the time of insertion, although the long-term cost is relatively low. Insurance coverage varies. Future improvements may decrease the number of capsules required and the costs.

Action. The action of the hormone implant is similar to that of progestin-only oral contraceptives. It causes cervical mucus changes that impede penetration by the sperm, affect sperm mobility, inhibit development of the endometrium, and prevent ovula-

Table 30–4. WARNING SIGNS OF COMPLICATIONS FROM ORAL CONTRACEPTIVE USE

Warning Sign	Possible Complication
Leg pain or swelling	Deep vein thrombosis
Chest pain, dyspnea, hemoptysis	Pulmonary emboli or myocardial infarction
Severe headache, visual changes such as blurred or double vision or visual loss, speech disturbance, weakness or numbness of extremities	Stroke
Abdominal pain, jaundice	Benign liver tumor, gallbladder disease

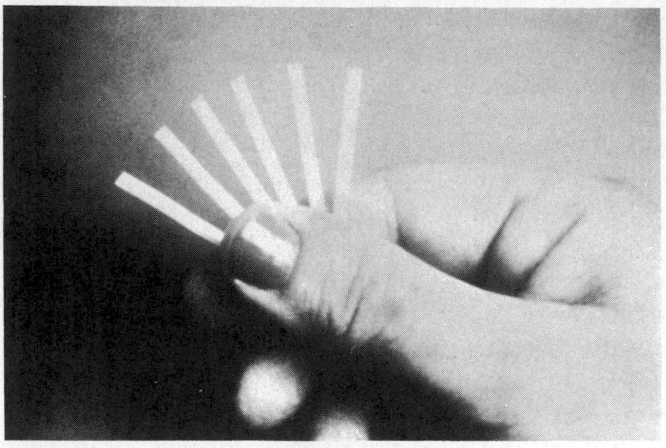

Figure 30–5

Norplant capsules are inserted under the skin of the upper arm and remain effective for 5 years. (Courtesy of Wyeth-Ayerst Laboratories, Philadelphia.)

tion at least half the time (Sharts-Engel, 1991). The implant provides continuous contraception without estrogens and without effort by the woman.

Side Effects. Side effects of the hormone implant include menstrual changes in up to 80 per cent of women, with irregular, midcycle, or prolonged bleeding a common cause of discontinuation of the method (Sharts-Engel, 1991). Some women have less bleeding than they did before the implants were inserted. Others have amenorrhea, and about a third experience other side effects common with oral contraceptives. Infection and expulsion of the implants are rare complications. Despite side effects, the continuation rate of hormone implants is high.

Women with conditions that would preclude using oral contraceptives generally should not use the implant. It is safe for use during lactation and can be inserted right after delivery. It may not be as effective in women weighing more than 150 pounds, as hormone concentration in the blood is less in heavier women.

HORMONE INJECTIONS

An injectable progestin (Depo-Provera) is now available and provides contraception for 3 months. Side effects are similar to other progestin contraceptives, primarily menstrual irregularities and weight gain. This method may be used during lactation and takes effect within 24 hours. It is 99.7 per cent effective.

Intrauterine Devices

Intrauterine devices (IUDs) are inserted into the uterus to provide continuous pregnancy prevention. The two types available in the United States are both shaped like the letter T. The Copper T 380A (ParaGard) IUD has copper wire wound around it, whereas the Progestasert IUD continuously releases small amounts of progestin (Fig. 30–6). They are 97 per cent effective. Although there was a concern about safety with early models, IUDs are considered very safe at this time.

Replacement of the IUD is necessary every year for those containing progesterone and every 8 years for the copper model. They are often inserted at the first postpartum check-up but may be placed even sooner. IUDs are expensive at the time of insertion but have a relatively low long-term cost.

ACTION

The mechanism of action varies for the two different IUDs. Copper IUDs cause inflammatory cells in the uterine cavity to release an endotoxin, which destroys sperm before they reach the fallopian tube (Chez et al, 1991). The steady release of progestin from the Progestasert prevents endometrial changes necessary for implantation and may inhibit ovulation.

SIDE EFFECTS

Side effects include cramping and bleeding with insertion. Menorrhagia (increased bleeding during menstruation) and dysmenorrhea (painful menstrua-

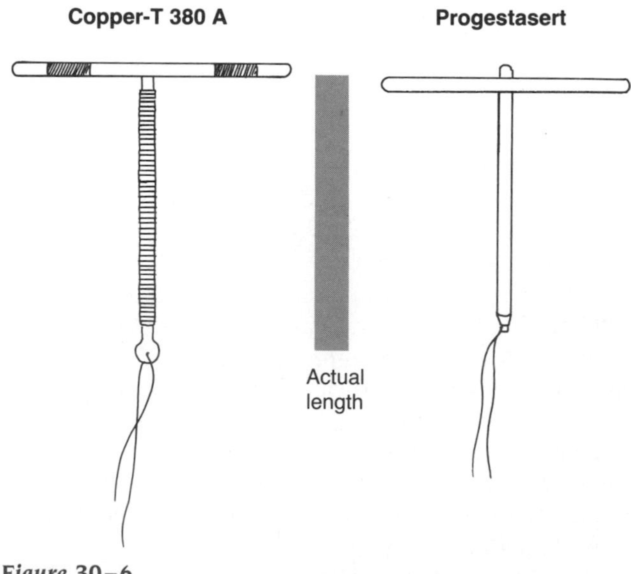

Figure 30–6

The Copper T 380A (ParaGard) and Progestasert intrauterine devices (IUDs). Currently, IUDs are considered a very safe method for preventing pregnancy.

tion) are common reasons for removal and may be more frequent with the copper device. Pelvic infections are less likely to occur than with the original models and are most often due to STDs. Therefore, only women in monogamous relationships and at low risk for STDs should use IUDs.

Other possible side effects include expulsion and perforation of the uterus. Women who become pregnant using the IUD are more likely to have ectopic pregnancies, spontaneous abortions, or preterm deliveries. Because of the known side effects, women with recent or recurrent pelvic infections, a history of ectopic pregnancy, bleeding disorders, or abnormalities of the uterus should choose another contraceptive method.

TEACHING

Teaching the woman about side effects and how to check for the presence of the strings or "tail" extending from the IUD into the vagina is important. The woman should feel for the strings once a week during the first 4 weeks, then monthly after menses, and if she has signs of expulsion (cramping or unexpected bleeding). If the strings are longer or shorter than previously, she should see her health care provider. Signs of infection, such as unusual vaginal discharge, pain or itching, low pelvic pain, and fever, should prompt a call to the physician. Any signs of pregnancy should be reported because of the danger of ectopic pregnancy. She should return yearly for a Pap smear and blood analysis to check for anemia if menses are heavy.

Natural Family Planning Methods

Natural family planning methods, also called fertility awareness or periodic abstinence methods, are based on using physiological cues to predict ovulation and avoiding coitus when fertilization is likely. The ovum can be fertilized for approximately 24 hours, and sperm can live up to 3 days in favorable conditions. Natural family planning methods are also used by women who wish to become pregnant to determine when sexual intercourse is most likely to achieve that goal (see Chapter 31).

Natural family planning allows a woman to learn about her body changes throughout her menstrual cycle. It is acceptable to most religions and avoids the use of drugs, chemicals, and devices. However, couples must be highly motivated because they must abstain from intercourse at certain times. Although natural family planning methods may be very effective if used perfectly, errors in predicting ovulation may result in pregnancy. Some women use the method to determine when they are fertile and use another contraceptive method at that time.

CALENDAR

The calendar method is based on the fact that ovulation occurs approximately 14 days before the onset of menses. This allows women with regular cycles to estimate when ovulation will occur. The woman keeps track of the length of her cycles for 6 months to determine the range in cycle length. She subtracts 18 days from the shortest cycle and 10 days from the longest cycle to predict the time when fertilization is possible. Thus, if her cycles varied from 28 to 32 days, she could be fertile between days 10 and days 22 ($28 - 18 = 10$, $32 - 10 = 22$). The calendar method is unreliable because many factors, such as illness or stress, can affect the time of ovulation.

BASAL BODY TEMPERATURE

In the basal body temperature method, the woman charts her oral temperature each morning before getting out of bed or increasing her activity, which would cause her temperature to rise. Her basal body temperature may drop slightly before ovulation and then rise approximately 0.2° to 0.45°C (0.4° to 0.8°F) when ovulation occurs (see Procedure 31–1, p. 909). The temperature remains higher throughout the second half of the cycle because of progesterone. The woman is no longer fertile on the 3rd day after the rise in temperature.

Used alone, this method is not reliable because temperature changes are very small and the rise in temperature indicates that ovulation has already occurred. If the woman has intercourse the day before her temperature rises, she may become pregnant. In addition, illness, a sleepless night, or stress could affect the temperature. To increase effectiveness, couples should avoid intercourse for several days before temperature changes are expected.

CERVICAL MUCUS

Also called the Billings or "ovulation" method, the cervical mucus technique is based on changes in cervical mucus due to rising estrogen levels during the follicular phase of the menstrual cycle. As estrogen increases, the mucus changes from thick and sticky to clear, slippery, and stretchy, like egg white. This condition is called spinnbarkeit (see Procedure 31–1, p. 910). The period of fertility lasts from the height of the mucus change (when it stretches at least an inch) to the evening of the 3rd day after the height of slippery mucus.

The woman assesses the cervical mucus by wiping it from the vaginal orifice with tissue each day. There is no mucus for the first 3 to 4 days after menses, then sticky mucus begins to appear. The mucus gradually increases and becomes clear and slippery. After ovulation, it decreases in amount and becomes thick and sticky again.

In addition to careful daily mucus assessment, strict adherence to the following rules is necessary to prevent pregnancy:

- During menstruation, intercourse is prohibited because some women with short cycles may enter the fertile period before the end of menses.
- Following menstruation, when there is no cervical mucus, intercourse is permitted only every other day because semen could interfere with assessment.
- From the appearance of sticky mucus until the evening of the 4th day after the height of slippery mucus, intercourse must be avoided.
- From the 4th day after the height of slippery mucus, intercourse is permitted.

Intercourse is safe for about 12 days of a 29-day cycle. It is not safe during periods of stress or cervical or vaginal infections, which can affect the quality of the mucus. Failure to follow the method perfectly increases the risk of pregnancy significantly. Intercourse during days of increased mucus, within 3 days of the height of slippery mucus, or during periods of stress may raise the risk of pregnancy to 28 per cent (Trussell and Grummer-Strawn, 1990).

SYMPTOTHERMAL

The symptothermal method combines the calendar, basal body temperature, and cervical mucus methods. In addition, other symptoms that occur near ovulation, such as weight gain, abdominal bloating, mittelschmerz (pain on ovulation), or increased libido, are noted. This increases awareness of when ovulation occurs and increases effectiveness.

POSTOVULATION

This method uses any combination of the above methods, but intercourse is avoided from the first day of the menstrual cycle until the end of the fertile period. Therefore, abstinence is necessary for more than half the cycle. Although this is the most effective of the natural techniques, it is difficult for many couples to achieve.

Sterilization

Sterilization is the most popular method of contraception (Franklin, 1990b). Although it is expensive at the time of surgery, it ends all contraceptive costs. It should always be considered a permanent end to fertility because restorative surgery is difficult, expensive, and usually not covered by insurance. Reversal surgery is not always successful and increases the risk of ectopic pregnancy.

Couples considering sterilization need counseling to ensure understanding of all aspects of the procedure. They should not have the surgery at a time of stress. When surgery is planned for immediately after childbirth, the decision should be made well before labor begins. Future divorce, remarriage, or death of a child may cause couples to regret their decision. Complications are those of any surgery, including hemorrhage, infection, and anesthesia complications.

TUBAL LIGATION

Female sterilization is the most frequently used method of family planning in the United States and the world, with more than 138 million women currently using this method (Church and Geller, 1990). The effectiveness rate is 99.6 per cent.

The surgery can be performed at any time but is easiest during the early postpartum period, when the fundus is located near the umbilicus and the fallopian tubes are directly below the abdominal wall. The procedure is scheduled on the day of birth or the next morning, if the mother and infant are stable. For the woman who is not postpartal, the procedure is often performed in an outpatient surgery department. General anesthesia is most common, but local anesthesia may also be used.

The procedure can be performed in two ways. A mini-laparotomy incision is made near the umbilicus in the postpartum period, and just above the symphysis pubis when surgery is not postpartal. The surgeon brings the tubes through the incision, where a piece is removed and the ends are tied.

In the second method, surgery is performed through a laparoscope inserted through a small incision. The surgeon visualizes the fallopian tubes and blocks them with clips or rings or destroys a portion of the tubes with electrocoagulation. Tubal ligation can be performed along with cesarean section when a woman is sure that she wants the procedure regardless of the outcome of the birth.

VASECTOMY

Vasectomy, the male sterilization procedure, is 99.85 per cent effective. It involves making a small incision in the scrotum and cutting the vas deferens, which carries sperm from the testes to the penis. After vasectomy, the semen no longer contains sperm.

Although performed less frequently than tubal ligation, vasectomy is a very popular method of contraception. It involves lower morbidity rates than tubal ligation and, because it can be performed in a physician's office under local anesthesia, it is less expensive as well. After surgery, the man applies ice to the area and watches for excessive swelling or bleeding.

The couple should understand that complete sterilization does not occur until all sperm has left the system, which may be a month or more. The man should submit sperm specimens for analysis until two specimens show no sperm present.

✔ Check Your Reading

9. How do barrier methods of contraception work?
10. What is the mechanism of action of hormonal contraceptives?
11. What education is important for the woman choosing an IUD?
12. What are the advantages and disadvantages of natural family planning methods?
13. What factors should a couple consider in deciding which method of sterilization to use?

Less Effective Methods of Contraception

The following methods of contraception are not considered reliable. However, they are used by women who lack information about their risks and other options or are unable to use other methods for medical or personal reasons. The nurse needs to be familiar with these methods to help clients who are adamant about not using other techniques.

BREASTFEEDING

Breastfeeding inhibits ovulation because suckling and prolactin interfere with secretion of gonadotropin-releasing hormone and luteinizing hormone. During lactation, the ovarian response to follicle-stimulating hormone and luteinizing hormone may be altered. The frequency, intensity, and duration of suckling are very important in inhibiting ovulation. Women who breastfeed completely are more likely to avoid ovulation and resumption of menstrual cycles than women who breastfeed partially.

Complete breastfeeding means feeding the infant at least ten times throughout the day and night. Supplemental feedings are withheld for 6 months because formula or solids decrease the frequency and duration of breastfeeding, increase the length of time between feedings, and reduce or end night feedings. This may cause ovulation and a return of menses.

Even with complete breastfeeding, prolactin levels eventually decrease and the menstrual cycle resumes, often after the first 6 months. Periods may be irregular, and ovulation may not occur consistently, depending on the amount and frequency of nursing that occurs. At this time, another method of contraception should be used.

COITUS INTERRUPTUS

Also called withdrawal, coitus interruptus is the removal of the penis from the vagina before ejaculation. It requires great control by the man and may be unsatisfying for both partners. Even a man who wishes to use the method may misjudge the timing and withdraw too late. Fluid that escapes from the penis before ejaculation contains sperm and should be wiped away before the penis is inserted into the vagina. Sperm spilled on the vulva may enter the vagina and cause pregnancy.

Future Methods

The development of new contraceptive technology involves extensive time, research, money, and risk. It takes approximately 10 years after a contraceptive is developed to gain approval from the U.S. Food and Drug Administration for general use in the United States. Some methods that may become available in the future are:

- Periodic testosterone injections for men to decrease sperm production temporarily.
- A device to plug, rather than cut, the vas deferens to allow long-term reversible sterilization.
- Contraceptive vaccines to cause temporary or permanent immunity to hormones.
- A vaginal hormonal ring that would release estrogen and progestin similarly to oral contraceptives, yet avoid the daily oral dose.
- Estrogen and progestin transdermal patches that would provide contraception with lower doses of hormones than oral contraceptives.

Choosing a Contraceptive Method: Application of Nursing Process

Contraceptive failure often occurs because women lack knowledge of how to use their contraceptive methods correctly or choose methods unsuited to their needs. When contraception fails, the woman is exposed to the physical, psychological, and social risks of unplanned pregnancy. Lack of understanding may also expose her to unnecessary side effects, possible complications, or STDs.

Assessment

Because contraception is a very private matter, approach it in a sensitive manner. Perform the assessment in a quiet area where interruptions are unlikely, and keep voices low to increase the woman's comfort. Assure the woman that her confidentiality will be maintained.

INTRODUCING THE SUBJECT

In the postpartum setting, introduce the subject by asking the woman if she plans to have more children. Most women indicate a desire to wait a period of time before the next pregnancy. Ask, "What method of family planning do you think you will use now?" or "How did you feel about the family planning method you used before pregnancy?" These kinds of questions may identify problems that the woman has had with contraception. In other settings, a woman may make some reference to her contraceptive method. The nurse can respond by asking, "How is (name method) working for you?" This shows that the nurse is interested if the woman wishes to pursue the topic.

UNDERSTANDING

Determine the woman's understanding of her contraceptive technique. For example, ask how she inserts her diaphragm, when and where she adds spermicide, or what time of day she takes her oral contraceptive. The woman should know how to use her technique effectively and what to do in special circumstances, such as when she misses on oral contraceptive pill or has difficulty removing her sponge or diaphragm. Explore any misinformation, concerns, or problems that the woman may have in regard to effectiveness, technique, or common side effects of the method.

SATISFACTION

Assess the woman's satisfaction with her contraceptive. The length of time that she has used the method may be important. Women may be unsure about their method in the early months until they gain comfort from repetitive use. Satisfaction, as well as effectiveness, increases with greater familiarity with the method. Side effects also affect satisfaction. They may be severe enough to cause the woman to consider another method, or they may be relieved by simple techniques. Be sure that what the woman considers simple side effects are not indications of complications that necessitate referral for treatment.

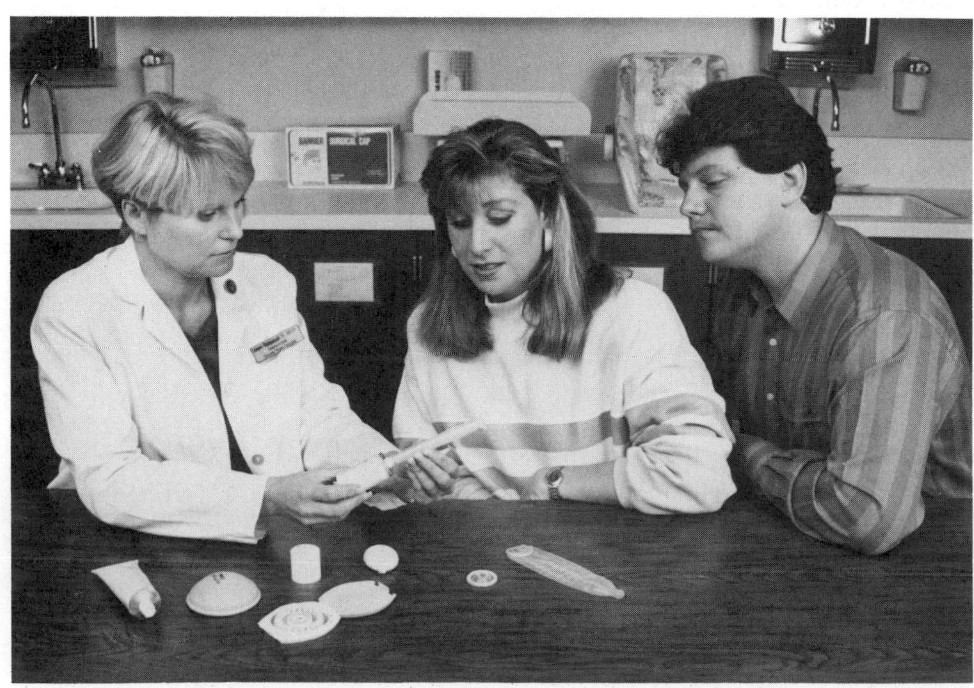

Success of contraception is more likely when both the woman and her partner are involved in discussions.

CHOICES

If the woman is considering a change in contraception, discuss available choices with her. Assess for factors that would help determine the best method for the individual woman. Include past history of medical conditions that might eliminate certain methods, childbearing history, cultural and religious beliefs, and the intensity of her desire to prevent pregnancy. The woman's ability to understand and follow complicated directions is important as well.

The type of relationship that a couple has is important in terms of contraceptive choice and protection against STDs. If the relationship is mutually monogamous, there is no risk of STDs if neither partner is infected. If either of the couple has more than one partner, protection against STDs is essential, even if the woman uses a contraceptive that is effective against pregnancy. A barrier method may be necessary in addition.

Frequency of coitus may help determine the best choice of contraception. For occasional sexual intercourse, a barrier method may be most satisfactory. If intercourse is frequent, the woman may desire a method that is always in place, such as an IUD or hormone implant. Explore her feelings about the methods that she has used in the past, what she considers important, and individual preferences. The woman who wants to avoid hormones that have a systemic effect is not a candidate for oral contraceptives or implants. Ask about beliefs and values that might eliminate certain choices.

Analysis

Lack of knowledge about family planning is common and can lead to physical, psychological, and social complications in a woman's life. A nursing diagnosis that addresses this problem is *High Risk for Altered Health Maintenance related to lack of understanding about contraceptive method chosen and/or others available.*

Planning

Goals for this diagnosis are that the woman will:

- Correctly describe how to use her contraceptive method, including solving common problems
- Describe common side effects, indications of complications, and correct follow-up
- Report that she and her partner are satisfied with their contraceptive method
- Describe other methods available and choose one if she is unsatisfied with her present form of contraception

Interventions

Interventions involve follow-up of problems identified during assessment that may interfere with the woman's ability to maintain health. Increasing the woman's understanding of her contraceptive technique will be the basis of the teaching plan.

INCREASING UNDERSTANDING OF METHOD

Fill in gaps in the woman's knowledge about how her contraceptive method works, its effectiveness, advantages and disadvantages, common side effects and complications, and when to seek help. Use demonstrations and return demonstrations of how to use the method (such as inserting a cervical cap or checking for IUD strings). Give suggestions on managing side effects and common problems.

TEACHING ABOUT OTHER METHODS

Provide information about other forms of contraceptives, if the woman wishes. Compare other methods with the one that the woman is using. Discuss aspects that are most important to the individual woman and her lifestyle. If a prescription or fitting is needed, discuss what is likely to happen during the visit.

PROTECTING AGAINST STDs

Address defense against STDs, particularly if the woman is using a method that does not provide protection. This, again, is a delicate subject. A way to approach the subject might be to say, "The method you are using is very effective against pregnancy but does not protect you against diseases you might catch from a partner. This is important because some diseases can never be cured, like HIV. Others can cause infections that could prevent you from having children later. If there is any chance that you or your partner might have sex with more than one person or that your partner might have an infection, you should protect yourself by using one of the barrier types of contraception along with the one you are using. Let me explain about those further."

INCLUDING THE WOMAN'S PARTNER

Invite the woman to include her partner in discussions, if possible. He may have a major impact on the woman's choice of contraception and whether or not she actually uses it and uses it correctly. If the partner understands how the method is properly used, he is more likely to take an active part in ensuring contraceptive success.

Evaluation

Evaluate the woman's understanding of the correct use of her contraceptive technique. She should correctly describe all aspects of her contraceptive method, including how to solve common problems and when to seek help for side effects or complications. Evaluate continued understanding, compliance with proper use, and satisfaction with the method at later visits. The woman who wishes to change her contraceptive method should describe other contraceptives available and how to use them. She should choose a new method and visit a nurse practitioner, nurse-midwife, or physician, if necessary, for further discussion, examination, fitting, or prescription.

Summary Concepts

- Because most contraceptive methods must be practiced by women, who are most affected by contraceptive failure, women usually choose the method used.
- The nurse plays an important role in educating women about contraceptive techniques available and their correct use.
- Safety, effectiveness, convenience, education needed, interference with spontaneity, availability, expense, and client preference must be considered in choosing the contraceptive method that is best for an individual woman.
- Because some methods have potential for serious complications, an informed consent form may be necessary.
- Adolescents often have erroneous beliefs and incorrect information about contraception that increase their risk of pregnancy and sexually transmitted diseases.
- Teenagers may avoid seeking contraceptive information because they do not want to admit that they are sexually active, are concerned about confidentiality, are afraid of a pelvic examination, or fear that contraception will have an adverse effect on their health.
- Adolescents feel more comfortable talking about contraception with a nurse who has an accepting attitude, provides extra time for education, and uses understandable terms and audiovisual materials.
- Contraception is necessary until menstruation has ceased for 2 years. The healthy woman who does not smoke or have contraindications can use any method of contraception safely.
- Barrier methods may be chemical or mechanical. They kill and/or prevent sperm from entering the vagina and provide some protection against sexually transmitted diseases.
- Hormonal contraceptives include oral contraceptives, hormone injections, and the progestin implant. They inhibit ovulation and make the cervical mucus unfavorable to sperm. Side effects and complications make these unsuitable for some women.
- Intrauterine devices prevent pregnancy by affecting sperm and implantation. Women must learn to check for the device's strings and when to seek medical treatment.
- Natural family planning methods involve avoidance of coitus when physiological cues suggest that ovulation is likely. They help a woman to learn about her body, avoid the use of chemicals, are inexpensive, and are acceptable to most religions. However, they involve extensive education and high motivation, and they have a high risk of pregnancy should error occur.
- Sterilization offers permanent contraception. A tubal ligation can be performed soon after birth or at any time. Vasectomy is less expensive and can be performed in an office under local anesthesia. Although surgery to reverse sterilization is possible, it is expensive and not always successful.

References and Readings

Ask the experts (1992). NAACOG *Newsletter*, No. 1, p. 15.

Chez, R.A., Grimes, D.A., & Tatum, H. (1991). IUD's: Underused and misunderstood. *Contemporary* OB/GYN, 36(10), 73–92.

Church, C.A., & Geller, J.S. (1990). *Voluntary female sterilization: Number one and growing* (Population Reports, Series C, No. 10). Baltimore: Johns Hopkins University, Population Information Program.

Church, C.A., & Rinehart, W. (1990). *Counseling clients about the pill* (Population Reports, Series A, No. 8). Baltimore: Johns Hopkins University, Population Information Program.

Contraception revolutionized for women (1991). NAACOG *Newsletter*, 18(3), 3.

Cunningham, F.G., MacDonald, P.C., & Gant, N.F. (1989). *Williams obstetrics*. Norwalk, Conn.: Appleton & Lange.

Darney, P.D., & Chez, R.A. (1991). Inserting Norplant capsules. *Contemporary* OB/GYN, 36(8) 40–41.

Fehring, R.J. (1991). New technology in natural family planning. *Journal of Obstetric, Gynecologic, and Neonatal Nursing*, 20(3), 199–205.

Fehring, R.J. (1990). Methods used to self-predict ovulation: A comparative study. *Journal of Obstetric, Gynecologic, and Neonatal Nursing*, 19(3), 233–237.

The female condom: On the market soon? (1992). *American Journal of Nursing*, 92(5), 12–13.

Franklin, M. (1990a). Reassessment of the metabolic effects of oral contraceptives. *Journal of Nurse-Midwifery*, 35(6), 358–364.

Franklin, M. (1990b). Recently approved and experimental methods of contraception. *Journal of Nurse-Midwifery*, 35(6), 365–376.

Hatcher, R.A., Stewart, F., Trussell, J., et al. (1992). *Contraceptive technology* 1990–1992 (15th ed.). New York: Irvington Publishers.

Hankinson, S.E., Colditz, G.A., Hunter, D.J., Spencer, T.L., Rosner, B., & Stampfer, M.J. (1992). A quantitative assessment of oral contraceptive use and risk of ovarian cancer. *Obstetrics and Gynecology*, 80(4), 708–714.

Harvey, S.M., Beckman L.J., & Murray, J. (1989). Factors associated with use of the contraceptive sponge. *Family Planning Perspectives*, 21(4), 179–183.

Jemmott, L.S., & Jemmott, J.B. (1991). Applying the theory of reasoned action to AIDS risk behavior: Condom use among black women. *Nursing Research*, 40(4), 228–234.

Kaeser, L. (1990). Contraceptive development: Why the snail's pace? *Family Planning Perspectives*, 22(3) 131–133.

Kestelman, P., & Trussell, J. (1991). Efficacy of the simultaneous use of condoms and spermicides. *Family Planning Perspectives*, 23(5), 226+.

King, J. (1992). Helping patients choose an appropriate method of birth control. MCN: *American Journal of Maternal Child Nursing*, 17(2), 91–95.

Kost, K., Forrest, J.D., & Harlap, S. (1991). Comparing the health risks and benefits of contraceptive choices. *Family Planning Perspectives*, 23(2), 54–61.

Lethbridge, D.J. (1991). Choosing and using contraception: Toward a theory of women's contraceptive self-care. *Nursing Research*, 40(5), 276–280.

Lethbridge, D.J. (1991). Coitus interruptus: Considerations as a method of birth control. *Journal of Obstetric, Gynecologic, and Neonatal Nursing*, 20(1), 80–85.

Lethbridge, D.J. (1989). The use of breastfeeding as a contraceptive. *Journal of Obstetric, Gynecologic, and Neonatal Nursing*, 18(1), 31–37.

Libbus, M.K. (1992). Condoms as primary prevention in sexually active women. MCN: *American Journal of Maternal Child Nursing*, 17(5), 256–260.

Loucks, A. (1989). A comparison of satisfaction with types of diaphragms among women in a college population. *Journal of Obstetric, Gynecologic, and Neonatal Nursing*, 18(3), 194–200.

Lynn, M.M., & Holdcroft, C. (1992). New concepts in contraception: Norplant subdermal implant. *Nurse Practitioner*, 17(3), 85–89.

NAACOG (1991). NAACOG OGN *nursing practice resource: Contraceptive options*. Washington, DC.

Panzarine, S., & Gould, C.L. (1988). Knowledge about contraceptive use and conception among a group of urban, black adolescent mothers. *Journal of Obstetric, Gynecologic, and Neonatal Nursing*, 17(4), 279–282.

Ross, J.A. (1989). Contraception: Short-term and long-term failure rates. *Family Planning Perspectives*, 21(6), 275–277.

Runner, J. (1992). If you're asked about Norplant. RN, 55(6), 44–47.

Schwarz, R.H., & Mead, P.B. (1991). A new look at IUD-associated infections. *Contemporary* OB/GYN, 36(10), 65–69.

Sharts-Engel, N. (1991). Levonorgestrel subdermal implants (Norplant) for long-term contraception. MCN: *American Journal of Maternal Child Nursing*, 16(4), 232.

Sharts-Engel, N. (1990). Update on cancer risk and oral contraceptives. MCN: *American Journal of Maternal Child Nursing*, 15(1), 37.

Sharts-Hopko, N. (1993). Depo-Provera. MCN: *American Journal of Maternal Child Nursing*, 18 (2), 128.

Trussell, J., & Grummer-Strawn, L. (1990). Contraceptive failure of the ovulation method of periodic abstinence. *Family Planning Perspectives*, 22(2), 65–75.

Trussell, J., Hatcher, R., Cates, W., Stewart, F.H., & Kost, K. (1990). Contraceptive failure in the United States: An update. *Studies in Family Planning*, 21(1), 51–54.

Winter, L., & Breckenmaker, L.D. (1991). Tailoring family planning services to the special needs of adolescents. *Family Planning Perspectives*, 23(1), 24–30.

Yuzpe, A.A. (1991). Current status of OC's. *Contemporary* OB/GYN, 36(3) 77–85.

31

Infertility

Objectives

1. Explain settings in which the nurse may encounter couples who have infertility problems.
2. Describe different factors that can impair a couple's ability to conceive.
3. Explain factors that may cause repeated pregnancy losses.
4. Specify evaluations that may be performed when a couple seeks help for their infertility.
5. Explain the use of procedures and treatments that may facilitate a couple's ability to conceive and carry the fetus to viability.
6. Analyze how infertility can affect a couple and others in their family.
7. Summarize the nurse's role when caring for couples experiencing problems with fertility.

Definitions

Anovulatory (or **anovular**) • Menstrual cycles occurring without ovulation.

Azoospermia • Absence of sperm in semen.

Climacteric • Endocrine, body, and psychic changes occurring at the end of a woman's reproductive period. Also informally called **menopause.**

Endometriosis • Presence of endometrial tissue (uterine lining) outside the uterine cavity.

Ferning (or **fern test**) • The microscopic fern-like appearance of dried cervical mucus that is most apparent at the time of ovulation.

Gametogenesis • Development and maturation of the **sperm** and **ova.**

Impotence • Inability of a man to achieve or maintain an erection of the penis that is sufficiently rigid to permit successful sexual intercourse.

Incompetent cervix • Inability of the cervix to remain closed long enough during pregnancy for the fetus to survive.

Infertility • Inability of a couple to conceive after 1 year of regular intercourse (two to three times weekly) without using contraception; also, the involuntary inability to conceive and produce viable offspring when the couple chooses. **Primary infertility** occurs in a couple who has never conceived; **secondary infertility** occurs in a couple who has conceived at least once before.

Oligospermia • A decreased number of sperm in semen, usually considered to be under 20 million per milliliter.

Retrograde ejaculation • Discharge of **semen** into the bladder rather than from the end of the penis.

Semen • **Spermatozoa** with their nourishing and protective fluid discharged at **ejaculation.**

Spinnbarkheit • Clear, slippery, stretchy quality of cervical mucus during ovulation.

Sterility • Total inability to conceive.

Varicocele • Abnormal dilation or varicosity of veins in the spermatic cord.

△ Alert for a high risk of exposure to substances to which universal precautions apply. See Appendix B for additional information about infection control.

Infertility care, or reproductive medicine, is a specialized area in the care of childbearing families. Although few nurses work directly in centers that provide infertility services, many nurses encounter persons who are seeking help for infertility or who have had treatment for it in other settings. Friends and family members often see the nurse as one who can answer questions and refer them to appropriate resources when they have problems conceiving. Nurses who work in the perioperative area often care for these couples as they have diagnostic or therapeutic surgery. Nurses who work with urology patients often see men who are being evaluated or treated for infertility. In the emergency department, nurses may care for women who are having a spontaneous abortion of a hard-won pregnancy.

Nurses who work in antepartum, intrapartum, and postpartum settings often encounter couples who have had successful infertility therapy. Additionally, parenthood after infertility is not always easy, and nurses who work in pediatric or psychosocial settings may counsel families needing help with parenting and changes in their personal relationships.

Extent of Infertility

The extent of infertility depends on how the problem is defined. Infertility is not an absolute condition; it is a reduced ability to conceive. Infertility is strictly defined as the inability to conceive after one year of unprotected regular sexual intercourse. A more workable definition does not specify a time limit but recognizes that infertility is any involuntary inability to conceive at the time desired. The definition is commonly expanded to include those couples who conceive but repeatedly lose a pregnancy (*pregnancy wastage*) before the fetus is old enough to survive. Couples may have primary infertility if they have never conceived. Couples with secondary infertility may have conceived before but are unable to conceive again.

About 10 to 15 per cent of couples wanting to have a baby experience infertility (ACOG, 1990a; Meldrum, 1992). Couples who delay childbearing until their mid to late 30s feel pressured by the approaching end of the woman's reproductive years. To older couples, delay in achieving pregnancy or having a viable baby is more significant than for young couples, who have more years available to pursue pregnancy.

Although the prevalence of infertility has not increased, more couples are seeking help for delayed conception. Additionally, couples needing infertility services make up a larger proportion of the childbearing population than in the past (Barad, 1991). Because of advances in diagnosis and treatment, couples who might have accepted childlessness may enter infertility therapy or resume therapy they had abandoned. Additionally, some women want to have a child without a male partner and may be served by infertility services.

Factors Contributing to Infertility

The ability to conceive depends not only on normal reproductive function in each partner but also on a delicate interaction between the partners. For some couples, identification and treatment of infertility are simple; for other couples, complex evaluation and treatment are required. (For a review of normal reproductive anatomy, physiology, and conception, see Chapters 4 and 6.)

The study of infertility underscores the delicacy of the reproductive process. Because some factors contributing to infertility may be unknown, identification and treatment of a problem do not always lead to its resolution or to a successful pregnancy. For example, some couples who seem likely to be infertile because of problems in either or both partners nevertheless have several children. Other couples may have no identified problem, yet they do not conceive despite having undergone all available treatments.

In couples with identified causes of infertility, about 35 per cent of the reasons are due to male factors, 35 per cent to female factors, and 30 per cent to combined male and female factors. Infertility remains unexplained after diagnostic testing in about 20 per cent of couples.

Factors in the Man

The test of a man's fertility is his ability to initiate pregnancy in a fertile woman. Few absolute criteria exist to distinguish normal from abnormal male fertility, although an adequate number of sperm having normal structure and function must be deposited near the woman's cervix. There may be problems with the sperm, the seminal fluid that carries them into the woman's reproductive tract, or with ejaculation.

PROBLEMS WITH THE SPERM

Many factors can impair the number, structure, or function of sperm. Some conditions are temporary, such as an acute illness; other conditions are permanent, such as a genetic disorder. A single finding may be abnormal, or there may be several. Further complicating evaluation of a man's fertility are the normal daily variations in semen.

Evaluation of the semen may reveal that the man has azoospermia or oligospermia. The average number of sperm released at ejaculation is 400 million. Twenty million sperm per milliliter of semen is considered to be the minimum number adequate for fertilization.

A sufficient number of normal sperm must move in a purposeful forward direction to reach the ovum in the fallopian tube. Abnormal sperm morphology (structure) or motility may reduce fertility, regardless of the actual number of sperm (Fig. 31–1). Inflammatory processes in the man's reproductive organs may cause the sperm to agglutinate (clump), inhibiting their motility and fertilizing ability. Other sperm may appear normal, yet may be unable to penetrate the ovum.

Many factors can impair the number and function of the sperm, such as:

- Acute or chronic illness
- Infections of the genital tract
- Anatomical abnormalities, such as a varicocele, or obstruction of the ducts that carry sperm to the penis
- Exposure to toxins, such as lead, pesticides, or other chemicals
- Therapeutic treatments, such as antineoplastic drugs or radiation for cancer
- Excessive alcohol intake
- Use of illicit drugs, such as marijuana or cocaine
- An elevated scrotal temperature resulting from febrile illness or repeated use of saunas or hot tubs
- Immunological factors, produced by the man against his own sperm (autoantibodies) or by the woman, causing the sperm to clump or be unable to penetrate the ovum

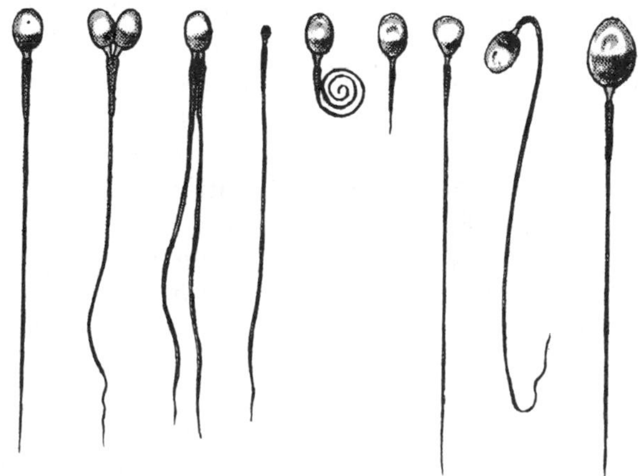

Figure 31–1

Abnormal infertile sperm, compared with a normal sperm on the right. (From Guyton, A.C. (1991). *Textbook of medical physiology* [8th ed., p. 890]. Philadelphia: W.B. Saunders.)

ABNORMALITIES OF SEMINAL FLUID

The seminal fluid nourishes, protects, and carries sperm into the vagina until they enter the cervix. Only sperm enter the cervix; the seminal fluid remains in the vagina. Semen coagulates immediately after ejaculation but liquefies within 30 minutes, permitting forward movement of sperm. Seminal fluid that remains thick traps the sperm, impeding their movement into the cervix. The pH of seminal fluid is slightly alkaline to protect the sperm from the acidic secretions of the vagina. Adequate fructose must be present to provide energy for the sperm.

The specific abnormality found in the seminal fluid suggests the cause of the abnormality, such as obstruction or infection in a specific area of the genital tract. Seminal fluid that is abnormal in amount, consistency, or chemical composition suggests obstruction, inflammation, or infection. The presence of large numbers of leukocytes suggests infection.

ABNORMAL EJACULATION

Abnormal ejaculation prevents deposition of the sperm in the ideal place to achieve pregnancy. Retrograde ejaculation is the release of semen backward into the bladder rather than forward through the tip of the penis. Conditions that may cause retrograde ejaculation are diabetes, neurological disorders, surgery that impairs function of the sympathetic nerves, and drugs such as antihypertensives and psychotropics.

Anatomical abnormalities, such as hypospadias (urethral opening on the underside of the penis), may cause deposition of semen near the vaginal outlet rather than near the cervix. Men who have suffered spinal cord injury may retain the ability to ejaculate, depending on the level of cord damage; however, this function may be ineffective in initiating pregnancy.

Excessive alcohol intake or use of illicit drugs can adversely affect ejaculation as well as sperm number and function. Ejaculation may be slow, absent, or retrograde when a man takes drugs that affect neurological coordination of this event.

✔ Check Your Reading

1. How is infertility defined? What is the difference between primary and secondary infertility?

2. What are normal characteristics of sperm and of the seminal fluid that carries them into the woman's vagina?
3. What problems in the man can occur with ejaculation of semen?
4. What can cause abnormalities in the sperm? In the seminal fluid? In ejaculation?

Factors in the Woman

A woman's fertility depends on:

- Regular production of normal ova
- An open and receptive path from her cervix to the fallopian tube to promote fertilization and movement of the embryo into the uterus for implantation
- An endometrium that supports the pregnancy after conception

Female factors may be the single or a contributing cause of infertility.

DISORDERS OF OVULATION

Normal ovulation depends on delicately timed and balanced secretions from the hypothalamus and pituitary and an ovarian response to mature and release an ovum. The hypothalamus secretes gonadotropin-releasing hormone (GnRH) beginning at puberty. GnRH, in turn, stimulates the pituitary to release follicle-stimulating hormone (FSH) and luteinizing hormone (LH). FSH stimulates maturation of several follicles in the ovary. While the follicles mature, the ovary secretes estrogen to thicken the endometrium. About 24 to 36 hours before ovulation, there is a marked increase of LH, which stimulates final maturation and release of one ovum from its follicle. The other follicles regress and will not mature. The collapsed follicle from which the ovum was released, now called a *corpus luteum*, produces progesterone and estrogen, which further prepare the endometrium for implantation and nourishment of the fertilized ovum. (See Chapter 4 for a complete discussion of the male and female reproductive systems.)

Ovulation can be disrupted by dysfunction in the hypothalamus or pituitary gland that alters the balanced secretion of GnRH, FSH, and LH. If the ovaries do not respond to FSH and LH, an ovum will not be matured or released. Disruption of hormone secretion or of the ovarian response to hormone secretion can be caused by cranial tumors, stress, obesity, anorexia, systemic disease, abnormalities in the ovaries or other endocrine glands (ACOG, 1990a).

A female has all the oocytes (immature ova) she will ever have before the 30th week of prenatal life. Her existing oocytes, therefore, are vulnerable to cumulative toxic effects from therapeutic drugs, social or abused drugs, and environmental agents until the end of her reproductive life. Examples of factors that may impair ovulation include cancer chemotherapeutic agents, excessive alcohol intake, and cigarette smoking.

Women with ovulation disorders often have abnormal menses because hormone levels do not permit normal development and shedding of the endometrium. The woman may have absent, scant, or heavy menstrual periods. However, other women may have no menstrual disorders; inability to conceive may be their only complaint.

A natural decline in ovulation occurs near the climacteric. As a woman approaches the end of her reproductive life, she ovulates and menstruates more erratically. Thus, her fertility naturally declines with age, falling dramatically after 40 years.

ABNORMALITIES OF THE FALLOPIAN TUBES

At least one patent (open) fallopian tube is needed for conception and implantation to occur (Fig. 31–2). Tubal obstruction commonly occurs because of scarring and adhesions following reproductive tract infections. Sexually transmitted diseases, such as chlamydial infection and gonorrhea, are responsible for many cases of infertility due to tubal obstruction. Prevention or prompt treatment and eradication of all pelvic infections can reduce the incidence of fallopian tube damage.

Endometriosis may cause tubal adhesions, painful menstrual periods, and painful intercourse (see Chapter 32). Small lesions are unlikely to affect tubal function, but large lesions may significantly distort tubal anatomy and lead to infertility.

Tubal obstruction also may occur if adhesions develop after pelvic surgery, ruptured appendix or peritonitis, or some ovarian cysts. The fallopian tubes and other reproductive organs may have congenital anomalies that interfere with normal function.

Conditions that cause obstruction also may interfere with normal motility within the fallopian tube. Poor movement of the fimbriated (distal) end of the tube may prevent pick-up of the ovum from the ovarian surface after ovulation. Abnormal action of the cilia within the tube prevents normal movement of the ovum toward the uterine cavity.

Depending on the extent and location of the blockage, fallopian tube obstructions can prevent fertilization of the ovum or may lead to an ectopic pregnancy. Complete tubal occlusion prevents fertil-

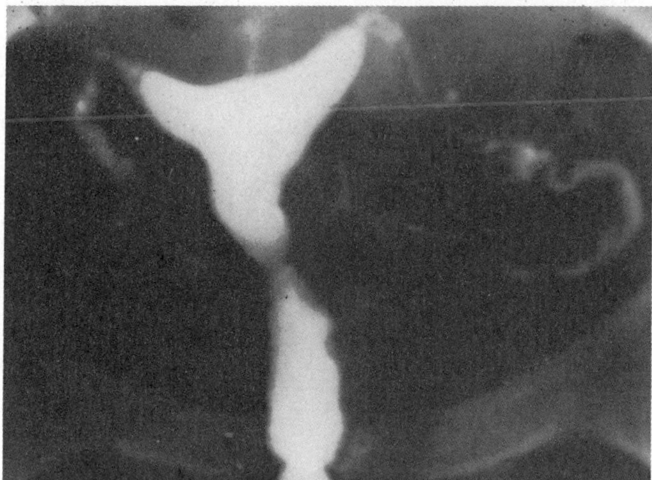

Figure 31–2

A hysterosalpingogram can determine whether fallopian tubes are patent. When tubes are open, as in this photograph, contrast medium that was injected through the cervix spills out of the fallopian tubes into the peritoneal cavity. (From Hacker, N.F., & Moore, J.G. (1992). *Essentials of obstetrics and gynecology* [2nd ed., p. 559]. Philadelphia: W.B. Saunders.)

izing sperm from reaching the ovum, and the woman will be sterile without advanced techniques such as in vitro fertilization (IVF). Partial obstruction may result in an ectopic tubal pregnancy, because sperm can reach the ovum to fertilize it but the fertilized ovum cannot reach the uterine cavity for implantation.

ABNORMALITIES OF THE CERVIX

Estrogen levels from the ovary peak twice during the menstrual cycle—once before ovulation and again about 1 week after ovulation. The first peak occurs about 2 days before ovulation and causes the woman's cervix to dilate slightly and produce a clear, thin, slippery mucus that is similar to egg white in consistency. This mucus facilitates passage of sperm into the uterus. Low estrogen levels prevent development of this mucus and are usually associated with anovulation.

Polyps or scarring from past surgical procedures, such as cauterization or conization, may obstruct the woman's cervix. Abnormal cervical mucus caused by estrogen deficiency, surgical destruction of the mucus-secreting glands, and cervical damage secondary to infection or other factors prevents normal movement of the sperm into the uterus and fallopian tubes for fertilization (ACOG, 1990a).

✔ Check Your Reading

5. What factors can result in abnormal ovulation?
6. Why does a woman who has ovulation problems often have abnormal menstrual periods?
7. What are some causes of fallopian tube obstruction?
8. How do abnormalities of cervical mucus contribute to infertility?

Repeated Pregnancy Loss

Couples who repeatedly lose pregnancies have the same outcome as those unable to conceive: no living child. Repeated losses may result from abnormalities in the fetus or placenta or from maternal factors.

ABNORMALITIES OF THE FETAL CHROMOSOMES

Errors in the fetal chromosomes may result in spontaneous abortion, usually in the first trimester. Chromosome abnormalities often severely disrupt growth and development during prenatal life, and the embryo or fetus cannot survive to live birth.

Most chromosome abnormalities are sporadic, occurring randomly. Others occur because one parent has a balanced chromosome translocation that is passed on to the offspring. The parent with the balanced translocation has a normal total amount of chromosome material; however, when the chromosomes are divided during gametogenesis, the resulting sperm or ovum may receive too much or too little chromosome material. The sperm or ovum also may receive a balanced translocation like the parent, or it may receive a totally normal chromosome complement with no translocation. (See Chapter 5 for further information about the role of chromosome abnormalities in pregnancy loss.)

ABNORMALITIES OF THE CERVIX OR UTERUS

Stenosis or congenital malformations of the cervix or uterine cavity may cause repeated loss of a normal fetus (Fig. 31–3). These malformations may prevent

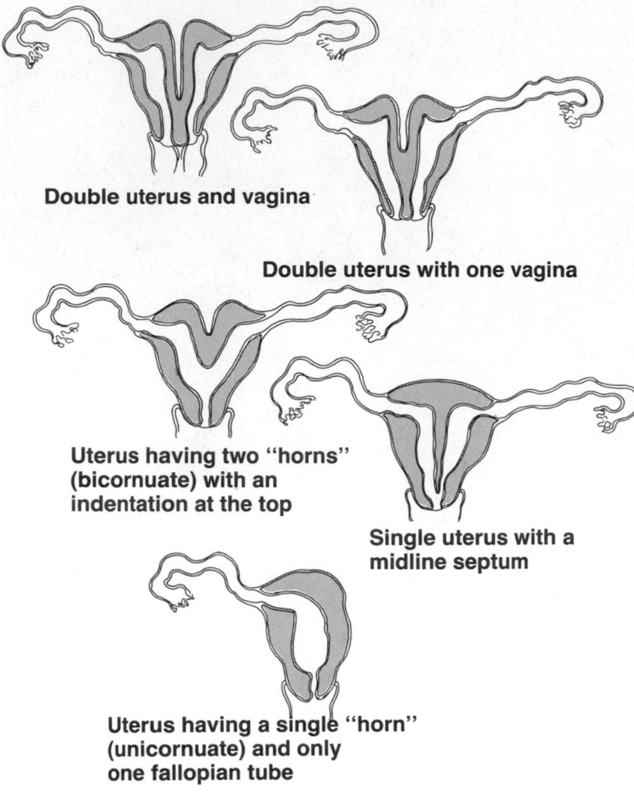

Figure 31–3

Types of uterine malformations that may cause infertility or repeated pregnancy loss.

normal implantation of the ovum or may prevent normal prenatal growth of the placenta or fetus.

Women who were prenatally exposed to diethylstilbestrol (DES) are more likely to have uterine malformations or an incompetent cervix. Cervical or uterine abnormalities also may occur after surgery or trauma from a previous birth. Painless and premature cervical dilation, often early in the second trimester, is characteristic in women with an incompetent cervix. Uterine malformations occur in many forms and may result in early spontaneous abortion or preterm labor.

Uterine myomas (benign tumors of the uterine muscle) and adhesions inside the uterine cavity may cause repeated fetal losses. These problems can alter the blood supply to the developing fetus or may cause uterine irritability that results in preterm labor and birth.

ENDOCRINE ABNORMALITIES

Inadequate progesterone secretion by the corpus luteum (luteal phase defect) prevents normal implantation and establishment of the placenta. The embryo may not implant, or it may implant poorly. In other cases, the corpus luteum may develop and function properly, but the woman's endometrium may not respond to its progesterone secretion.

Hypothyroidism and hyperthyroidism may be associated with the inability to conceive and with recurrent pregnancy loss. Poorly controlled diabetes can result in repeated pregnancy loss as well as many other complications of pregnancy (see p. 702). Mother and infant have the best outcomes if diabetes is well controlled before and throughout pregnancy.

IMMUNOLOGICAL FACTORS

Various immunological factors are implicated in some cases of recurrent pregnancy loss, although not all are conclusively established. The embryo has antigens different from those of the mother and would ordinarily be rejected as any other foreign tissue would be rejected. However, the mother's body normally blocks this rejection response and tolerates the developing baby. Some women respond inappropriately to the embryo, rejecting it as foreign tissue. These women often have recurrent spontaneous abortions.

Women with autoimmune disease, such as lupus erythematosus, are more likely to experience spontaneous abortion. The exact reason is unknown, but it appears related to thrombosis or other damage in placental blood vessels. Women with lupus usually have other complications in pregnancy, such as exacerbation of their symptoms, fetal heart block, fetal distress, and stillbirth.

ENVIRONMENTAL AGENTS

Some environmental agents have a well-established relationship to impairment of fertility and pregnancy loss (Table 31–1). Others are suspected to be damaging, but do not show a conclusive link to pregnancy loss. Additionally, the amount of exposure (dose) relates to the pregnancy outcome in most cases. For example, radiation exposure in the form of a chest x-ray might have no apparent adverse effect on pregnancy whereas the larger doses used for cancer therapy might be toxic.

Examples of established toxins are ionizing radiation, alcohol, and isotretinoin (Accutane). Suspected toxins are numerous, for example, cigarette smoke, anesthetic gas, chemicals such as organic solvents or pesticides, and lead and mercury in occupational settings. These agents may be directly toxic to the embryo or fetus, causing its death, or they may interfere with normal placental function that is necessary to sustain the pregnancy.

Table 31–1. ENVIRONMENTAL AND OCCUPATIONAL TOXINS THAT MAY AFFECT REPRODUCTIVE FUNCTION

Drugs	**Lifestyle Factors**
Amphetamines	Alcohol consumption
Antibiotics	Marijuana, LSD, cocaine use
Anticoagulants	Smoking
Anticonvulsants	Strenuous exercise
Antidepressants	Stress
Antidiabetics	
Antiemetics	**Biological Hazards**
Antihistamines	Cytomegalovirus
Antineoplastics	Herpes simplex virus
Antithyroid drugs	Immunizing agents (rubella, measles, mumps vaccines)
Digitalis	Lyme disease
Ganglionic blockers	Rubella virus
Hormones	Syphilitic infection
Narcotics	Toxoplasmosis
Sedatives	Varicella and herpes zoster
Chemical Agents	
Anesthetic gases	**Physical Agents**
Cadmium	Heat
Ethylene oxide	Microwaves
Herbicides	Radiation
Lead	X-rays
Methyl mercury	
Organic solvents	**Nutritional Factors**
Pesticides	Folate deficiency
Polycyclic aromatic hydrocarbons	Malnutrition
Styrene	
Vinyl chloride	

Modified from Shortridge, L. A. Advances in the assessment of the effect of environmental and occupational toxins on reproduction, in *Journal of Perinatal and Neonatal Nursing, 3*(4), 2, with permission of Aspen Publishers, Inc., Gaithersburg, Md. ©1990.

INFECTIONS

Infections of the reproductive tract are associated with poor pregnancy outcomes in general, and they may be related to early pregnancy losses as well. These infections are often asymptomatic, making their link to pregnancy loss difficult to establish.

✔ Check Your Reading

9. How can anatomical abnormalities of a woman's uterus or cervix cause her to lose a normal pregnancy?
10. What endocrine factors can cause repeated pregnancy loss?
11. What immunological factors may cause loss of a normal fetus?

Evaluation of Infertility

When a couple seeks help for their inability to conceive, both partners are evaluated in a systematic, timely, and cost-effective manner. Couples are often in a hurry for definitive therapy, but a thorough assessment of their problem is essential for appropriate treatment. Some tests, such as semen evaluation, must be repeated sequentially for an accurate picture. The prolonged evaluation process is frustrating to many couples, especially older ones who are anxious for a child before the end of the woman's reproductive years. Another frustration for couples undergoing an infertility work-up is that some diagnostic tests are investigational and their usefulness and normal values are not well established. Other tests are commonly used, but widely accepted normal values have not been established.

Many professionals are involved in evaluation and care of infertile couples: nurses, physicians specializing in reproductive medicine, gynecologists, urologists, microsurgeons, embryologists, and ultrasonographers. Additionally, general and specialized laboratory facilities may provide diagnostic services to enhance treatment. Nurses working in infertility clinics often coordinate communication among the many providers and help the couple negotiate the maze of evaluation and treatment.

History and Physical Examination

A thorough history and physical examination of each partner help to identify the appropriate diagnostic tests and therapy.

HISTORY

The reproductive history includes (1) the woman's menstrual pattern, (2) any pregnancies and their outcomes, (3) previous fertility with other partners, and (4) length of time the couple has had unprotected intercourse. Investigation of the couple's usual frequency and timing of intercourse may identify the need for a change in practice to facilitate conception.

The past medical history, including childhood illnesses and surgery, and a history of exposure to toxins provide more clues to the cause of infertility. The couple's past and present occupations may be associated with toxin exposure, stresses, or other adverse influences on reproduction.

PHYSICAL EXAMINATION

Couples who seek help for infertility are usually quite healthy. However, a thorough physical examination of each partner may suggest endocrine disturbances, cranial tumors, or undiagnosed chronic disease. Careful examination of the reproductive organs may identify structural defects, infection, cysts, or other abnormalities. Chromosome analysis may be performed for couples experiencing repeated pregnancy loss, especially if they have had a child with birth defects, whether or not the child is living at the time.

Diagnostic Tests

Each couple's evaluation is individualized, but testing generally proceeds from the simple and less expensive to the more complex and expensive diagnostics. Simple evaluations are done simultaneously, but more sophisticated tests are delayed until the need for them is established. Two methods of identifying ovulation—basal body temperature and assessment of cervical mucus—can be used as contraceptive measures in addition to their use in infertility care (Procedure 31–1). Table 31–2 summarizes diagnostic tests that may be recommended for the infertile couple.

Therapies to Facilitate Pregnancy

Evaluation of the couple identifies whether therapy might improve their chances to conceive and complete a pregnancy. A variety of procedures may be used, depending on the couple's initial and ongoing evaluations and on their personal choices. Some therapy is simple, like timing intercourse to coincide with ovulation; other procedures may involve considerable expense, discomfort, or unpleasant side effects. Many couples need a combination of treatments to improve their chances of conception.

Identification of appropriate infertility therapy is not always straightforward. Many factors must be considered, including the couple's history, their medical evaluations, financial resources, age and other time constraints, and religious and cultural values. Generally, simpler treatments are indicated before more complex ones, but the needs of each couple are considered individually. Infertility specialists may proceed more aggressively if the woman is in her mid-30s or older because she has less time before the end of her reproductive years than does the younger woman.

Statistical success rates for various procedures are often difficult for couples to evaluate and vary widely among facilities. Factors that affect a center's success rate for any procedure are numerous. For example, a referral center that accepts only couples with long-standing infertility may have lower success rates than one that accepts couples having fewer problems.

Medications

Hormones and other medications may be given to either the man or woman. A medication may be given to improve semen quality, induce ovulation, prepare the uterine endometrium, or support the pregnancy once it is established. Table 31–3 summarizes medications used in infertility therapy.

Ovulation Induction

Medications to induce ovulation may be prescribed for the woman who does not ovulate or who ovulates irregularly. Medications may also be given to provide multiple ova if a woman plans to have in vitro fertilization, gamete intrafallopian transfer (GIFT), or tubal embryo transfer (TET). The Drug Guide describes clomiphene citrate, the drug most commonly used to stimulate ovulation.

Ovulation induction increases the risk of multiple births because more than one ovum may be released and fertilized. Another serious complication is *ovarian hyperstimulation syndrome*, in which there is marked ovarian enlargement, with exudation of fluid into the woman's peritoneal and pleural cavities. Careful adjustment of medication dose and serial ultrasound examinations prevent most cases of high multifetal pregnancy (triplets or more) and ovarian hyperstimulation syndrome.

Surgical Procedures

In some men, correction of a varicocele may improve sperm quality and quantity. Endoscopic procedures may be used to correct obstructions, with minimal invasiveness, in either the man or the woman. The woman may need a laparotomy to relieve pelvic adhesions and obstructions caused by endometriosis, infection, or previous surgical procedures if these cannot be corrected via laparoscopy. Laser surgical techniques may be used to reduce adhesions; these techniques are precise and are less likely to cause formation of new adhesions. For surgical correction of obstructions in the fallopian tubes or tubal structures in the male genital tract, microsurgical techniques are needed because these structures are very narrow.

Transcervical balloon tuboplasty may be used to unblock a woman's fallopian tubes without more invasive procedures, such as laparoscopy or laparotomy. A thin catheter is threaded through the uterus into the fallopian tube, and the balloon is inflated to clear the blockage.

Procedure 31–1

Teaching Women Fertility Awareness

Purpose: To identify whether ovulation occurs and the probable time of ovulation. These techniques can be used in infertility care or as a minimally effective contraceptive method.

BASAL BODY TEMPERATURE

The basal body temperature (BBT) is designed to detect the slight elevation in temperature that accompanies increased progesterone secretion in response to the luteinizing hormone (LH) surge and ovulation.

1. **Teach the woman the relationship between her BBT and ovulation:**
   a. **Explain that the BBT is the lowest, or resting, temperature of the body.**
   b. **During the first half of the woman's menstrual cycle, her temperature is lower than during the second half of the cycle.**
   c. **The basal temperature often drops slightly at the time of ovulation. Not all women experience this fall in basal temperature.**
   d. **Progesterone is secreted during the second half of the cycle, rising just after ovulation. The BBT rises after the slight drop at ovulation and remains higher during the second half of the cycle.**
   e. **The BBT remains high if pregnancy occurs and falls about 2–4 days before menstruation if pregnancy does not occur.**

   This method of fertility awareness requires careful assessment and record keeping by the woman. She is more likely to have an accurate record if she understands the relationship between her basal temperature and ovulation.

2. **Explain the occurrences that can interfere with the accuracy of her BBT, for example, illness, restless or inadequate sleep, waking later than usual, traveling across time zones (jet lag), alcohol intake the evening before, sleeping under an electric blanket or on a heated water bed, or any activity before taking the temperature.** *Temperature changes are slight at ovulation; many factors can cause temperature to rise even if ovulation has not occurred.*

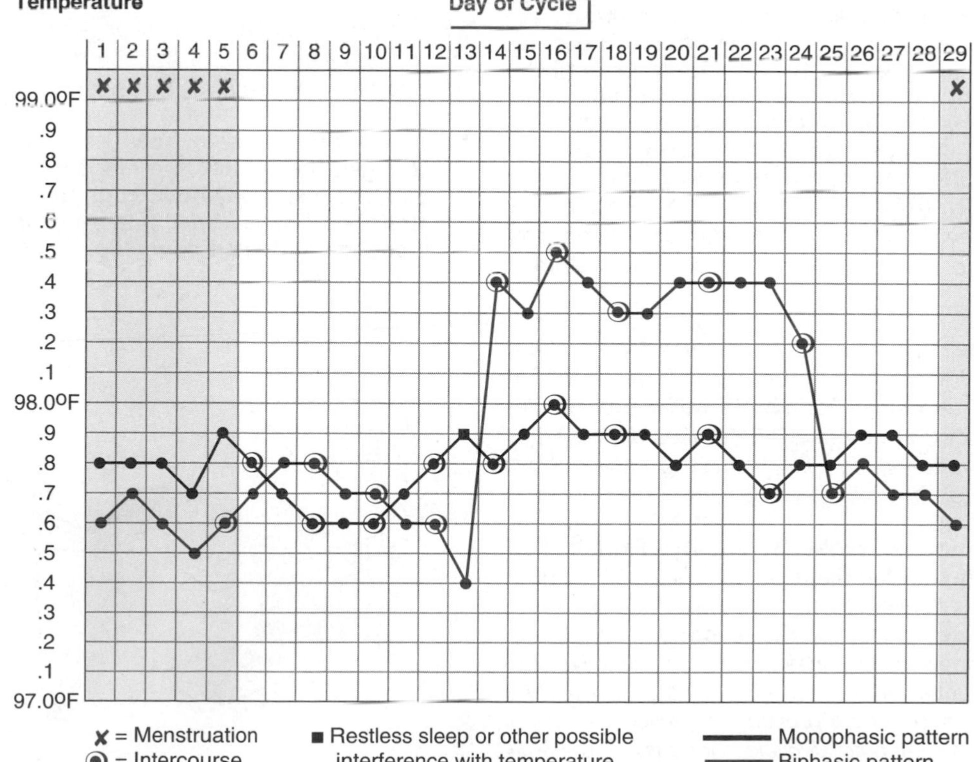

Procedure continued on following page

Teaching Women Fertility Awareness *Continued*

3. **Show the woman a fever thermometer and a basal thermometer. Explain that the range of temperatures on the basal thermometer is smaller (96° to 100°F) and is marked in tenths of a degree. Explain how to read the marks on the thermometer. Electronic thermometers that graph results are also available. The basal thermometer can be purchased at drugstores.** *Allows the woman to see the differences between the fever thermometer, which may be more familiar to her, and the special basal thermometer. The temperature rise is very slight (about 0.4°F higher than during the first half of the cycle). A special thermometer is needed to detect the change more accurately. Some women may not know how to read a mercury thermometer and should be taught.*

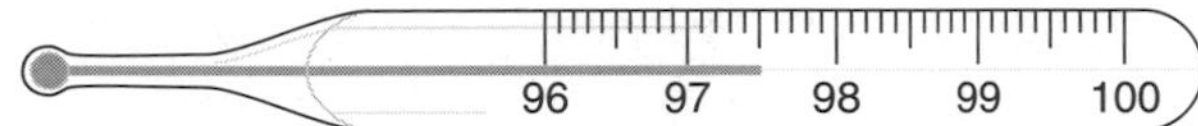

4. **Show the woman the chart for recording her BBT and the symbols for marking relevant events, such as menstrual periods, intercourse, illness or other occurrences, which may alter her BBT.** *Allows a consistent, more accurate interpretation of temperature fluctuations.*

5. **Teach the woman how to take her basal temperature:**
   a. **Shake the mercury thermometer down the night before.**
   b. **As soon as she awakens, but before any activity, place the basal thermometer under her tongue and leave it for 3 minutes or until the electronic thermometer beeps. Do not move the thermometer while it is in the mouth.**
   c. **After 3 minutes, read the thermometer and record the reading on the chart provided.**

   Any activity before taking the basal temperature, including shaking the thermometer down, can alter the reading enough to cause inaccurate interpretation.

6. **Encourage the woman to demonstrate taking her temperature and recording the result before leaving. Ask her to list events other than ovulation that can alter the BBT.** *Verifies that she has correctly understood the teaching and allows correction of misunderstandings.*

7. **As a method to avoid pregnancy: Explain that for greatest effectiveness, a woman should avoid intercourse from the onset of the menstrual period through the second day of elevated temperature.** *The most conservative approach requires a long period of abstinence while a viable ovum could be present, as much as half of the woman's menstrual cycle, because it primarily identifies that ovulation has already occurred. Not all women have a temperature drop at the time of ovulation, and the rise in BBT occurs after ovulation. Also, sperm can remain viable in the woman's reproductive tract for up to 72 hours, although most die within 24 hours. To reduce the time of abstinence, couples using fertility awareness as a method of contraception usually combine methods, such as BBT and the cervical mucus assessment.*

8. **To enhance the chances of conception, the couple should have intercourse when the temperature falls: Emphasize that the BBT primarily identifies that ovulation has already occurred and the adequacy of progesterone secretion to prepare her endometrium during the second half of her menstrual cycle. The BBT is less effective for timing intercourse to coincide with ovulation because of the short life span of the ovum after ovulation.** *Increases the likelihood that sperm will be available to fertilize the ovum while it is viable, no longer than about 12 hours after ovulation. The woman receiving infertility therapy should understand the limitations of the BBT in terms of enhancing conception.*

CERVICAL MUCUS ASSESSMENT

The cervical mucus normally changes just before ovulation to facilitate survival of the sperm and promote their passage into the woman's uterus.

1. **Teach the woman how her cervical mucus changes throughout the menstrual cycle. Spinnbarkheit describes how much the mucus can be stretched between her fingers or between a microscope slide and coverslip.**

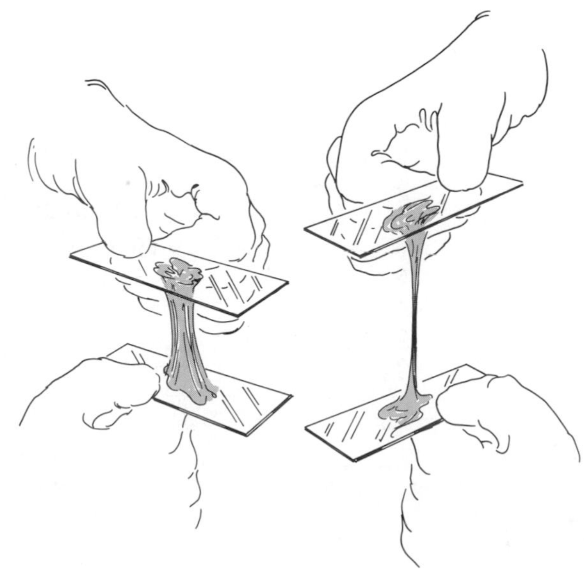

Teaching Women Fertility Awareness *Continued*

Before and after ovulation, the cervical mucus is scant, thick, sticky, and opaque. It stretches less than 6 cm.

Just before and for 2 to 3 days after ovulation, the cervical mucus is thin, slippery, and clear and is similar to raw egg white. It stretches 6 cm or more. When this ovulatory mucus is present, the woman has probably ovulated and could become pregnant. *As in the BBT, this method requires careful assessment and record keeping by the woman. She is more likely to perform the assessment and record changes in her cervical mucus accurately if she understands how the changes relate to fertility.*

2. **Explain the factors that can interfere with the accuracy of her assessment. The mucus may be thicker if she takes antihistamines. Vaginal infections, contraceptive foams or jellies, sexual arousal, and semen can make the mucus thinner even if ovulation has not occurred. Tell her to record these factors.** *Factors that interfere with the consistency of the cervical mucus may cause inaccurate identification of the fertile period.*

3. **Demonstrate how to stretch mucus between the thumb and forefinger by using raw egg white. Have the woman return demonstrate the process.** *Provides visual and tactile experiences to enhance learning. Return demonstration allows the nurse to determine whether the woman has misunderstood the teaching.*

4. **Teach the woman to wash her hands before and after assessing her mucus.** *Reduces the chance of introducing infection into the reproductive tract and of transferring infectious organisms from the vagina to other areas.*

5. **Teach the woman to obtain a small mucus sample several times a day from just inside her vagina and to note the following:**
   a. **The general sensation of wetness (around ovulation) or dryness (not near ovulation) on her labia.**
   b. **The appearance and consistency of the mucus: thick, sticky, and whitish or thin, slippery, and clear or watery.**
   c. **The distance the mucus will stretch between her fingers, usually at least 6 cm (2.3 inches) at the time of ovulation (see Figure on p. 910).**

   Allows the woman to identify cyclic changes in her mucus over the entire duration of her menstrual cycle.

6. **Have the woman record the day's typical mucus characteristics (often combined with her BBT recording).** *Provides a means of evaluating signs and symptoms associated with ovulation during the entire cycle.*

7. **As a method of contraception, the woman should avoid intercourse from the time the thin, stretchy ovulatory mucus appears until 48 to 72 hours after the mucus returns to its pre-ovulatory characteristics.** *Prevents sperm from being available for fertilization during the time the ovum is viable.*

8. **As a method to enhance conception, the couple should have intercourse every 2 days during the period of ovulatory mucus (approximately days 12 to 16 if the woman has a 28-day cycle).** *Makes sperm available to fertilize the ovum while it is viable.*

Therapeutic Insemination

The technique of therapeutic insemination (formerly called "artificial insemination") may use either the partner's semen or that of a donor to overcome a low sperm count. Donor insemination also may be used if the man carries a genetic defect or if a woman wants a biological child without having a relationship with a male partner. Intrauterine insemination is a variation that allows the sperm to bypass cervical mucus and reduces some immunological incompatibilities.

Sperm that are to be placed directly in the uterus or the fallopian tube are prepared by washing and spinning the semen in a centrifuge to remove seminal fluid. A technique called "sperm swim-up" uses a colloidal suspension to concentrate sperm having the best motility. Although the total number of sperm is lower, the remaining ones (those with normal morphology and highest motility) are more likely to fertilize the ovum.

Men who donate semen for therapeutic insemination are screened to reduce the risk of transmitting diseases or genetic defects. They are questioned about their personal and family health history, including genetic disorders or birth defects. Questions about their social habits and personality can disclose high-risk behaviors and also gives recipient parents information about traits their child might have. Physical and laboratory examinations are performed to evaluate the man's general health, determine his blood type and Rh factor, and screen for infections such as sexually transmitted diseases or human immunodeficiency virus (HIV). Carrier testing for rela-

Table 31–2. DIAGNOSTIC TESTS IN INFERTILITY

Test/Purpose	Nursing Implications
Male	
Semen Analysis Evaluates structure and function of sperm and composition of seminal fluid. Semen volume: 2.0 ml or more pH: 7.2–7.8 Sperm concentration: 20 million/ml or more Motility: 50% or more with rapid forward progression Morphology: 50% or more with normal forms Viability: 50% or more live White blood cells: Fewer than 1 million/ml Liquefaction: within 30 minutes	Explain purpose of semen analysis: three or more specimens are usually collected over several weeks' time for more accurate analysis. Explain to the man that he should collect the specimen by masturbation after a 2- to 3-day abstinence; semen may be collected in a condom if masturbation is unacceptable. Teach the man to note the time the specimen was obtained so that the laboratory can evaluate liquefaction of the semen; the specimen should arrive in the laboratory within 30 minutes.
Endocrine Tests Evaluates function of hypothalamus, pituitary gland, and the response of testicles. Assays are made to determine testosterone, luteinizing hormone (LH), and follicle-stimulating hormone (FSH) levels. Additional tests may be made on basis of history and physical findings.	Teach the man about the relationship between hypothalamic and pituitary function and sperm formation; LH stimulates testosterone production by Leydig cells of the testes, and FSH stimulates Sertoli cells of the testes to produce sperm.
Ultrasonography Evaluates structure of prostate gland, seminal vesicles, and ejaculatory ducts by use of a transrectal probe.	Teach the man that ultrasonography uses sound waves to evaluate these structures; no radiation is involved.
Testicular Biopsy An invasive test for obtaining a sample of testicular tissue; identifies pathology and obstructions.	Explain purpose of test; local anesthetic is used, and there should be little discomfort.
Sperm Penetration Assay Evaluates ability of sperm to penetrate a hamster ovum from which the zona pellucida has been removed.	Explain purpose of test; abnormal penetration does not necessarily mean that the sperm cannot fertilize a human ovum.
Female	
Ovulation Prediction Uses any of several methods to identify the surge of LH, which precedes ovulation by 24–36 hours; this enables timing of intercourse to coincide with ovulation and identifies absence of ovulation.	Explain purpose of tests (commercial ovulation predictor kits, basal body temperature, and cervical mucus assessment). Teach the woman to follow instructions on the commercial product. Teach her how to do the basal body temperature and cervical mucus assessment (see Procedure 31–1).
Ultrasonography Evaluates structure of pelvic organs. Identifies ovarian follicles and release of ova at ovulation. Evaluates for presence of ectopic or multifetal pregnancy.	Teach the woman that ultrasonography uses sound waves to evaluate these structures; no radiation is involved. Explain preparations needed for specific evaluations.
Post-coital Test Evaluates characteristics of cervical mucus and sperm function within that mucus at time of ovulation.	Explain that the test is performed 6 to 10 hours after intercourse; the woman may have to rearrange her personal or work commitments each time this test is done.
Endocrine Tests Evaluates functions of hypothalamus, pituitary gland, and ovary. Assays are made to determine LH, FSH, estrogen, and progesterone levels. Additional hormone evaluations may be done on basis of history and physical findings.	Explain purpose of each test: FSH and LH stimulate ovulation; estrogen and progesterone prepare uterine endometrium for implantation of a fertilized ovum.
Hysterosalpingogram X-ray that uses contrast medium to evaluate structure and patency of uterus and fallopian tubes.	Test is performed after menstrual period during first half of cycle to avoid flushing menstrual debris through tubes into the pelvic cavity and to avoid disrupting a pregnancy that might be in place. Explain purpose of test. Contrast medium is injected through the cervix, and x-ray films are made at the same time.

Table 31–2. DIAGNOSTIC TESTS IN INFERTILITY *Continued*

Test/Purpose	Nursing Implications
Female	
Endometrial Biopsy An invasive test for obtaining a small sample of endometrial tissue; determines whether endometrium is responding properly to estrogen and progesterone stimulation from ovary.	Explain purpose of test. Test is done 2–3 days before the woman expects her menstrual period; some cramping may occur, but it should be relieved with mild analgesics, such as ibuprofen. 
Hysteroscopy and Laparoscopy Examines uterine interior and pelvic organs with an endoscope; general anesthesia is used. Identifies abnormalities (polyps, endometrial adhesions). Some surgical procedures may be done via endoscope.	Explain purpose of test and any procedures that will be done at the same time. The woman takes nothing by mouth and should urinate before the procedure. Carbon dioxide gas, used to separate pelvic organs for better visualization, may cause temporary shoulder pain.

tively common genetic defects, such as sickle cell and Tay-Sachs diseases, reduces the risk for passing on these disorders. Donor sperm is frozen and held for 6 months before use to reduce the risk for transmitting diseases that may not be apparent at the initial screening.

Advanced Reproductive Techniques

In vitro fertilization, gamete intrafallopian transfer, and tubal embryo transfer are techniques that bypass many of the natural obstacles to conception. Each of these procedures begins with ovulation induction to permit retrieval of several ova, thus improving the likelihood of a successful pregnancy. Sperm are prepared and concentrated as they are for therapeutic insemination.

IN VITRO FERTILIZATION

The technique of in vitro fertilization involves bypassing blocked or absent fallopian tubes. The physician removes the ova by laparoscope and mixes them with prepared sperm from the woman's partner or a donor. Two days later, up to four embryos are returned to the uterus (Yee, 1991). Additional embryos may be transferred if the woman is older. The

Table 31–3. MEDICATIONS USED FOR INFERTILITY THERAPY

Drug	Use
Bromocriptine (Parlodel)	Corrects excess prolactin secretion by anterior pituitary, which causes inadequate progesterone production by corpus luteum, thus inhibiting normal implantation of embryo
Clomiphene (Clomid)	Induction of ovulation
Chorionic gonadotropin, human (hCG)	Used with menotropins to stimulate ovulation in the female or sperm formation in the male; stimulates progesterone production by corpus luteum
Gonadotropin-releasing hormone (GnRH; Lutrepulse)	Stimulates release of follicle-stimulating hormone (FSH) and luteinizing hormone (LH) from the pituitary gland in men and women who have deficient GnRH secretion by their hypothalamus; FSH and LH, in turn, stimulate ovulation in the female and stimulate testosterone production and spermatogenesis
Leuprolide (Lupron)	Reduces endometriosis
Menotropins (Pergonal)	Stimulates ovulation and spermatogenesis (given with hCG)
Nafarelin (Synarel)	Reduces endometriosis
Progesterone	Promotes implantation of embryo
Urofollitropin (Metrodin)	Stimulates ovulation (given in conjunction with hCG)

Drug Guide

CLOMIPHENE CITRATE (Clomid)

Classification: Ovarian stimulant.

Action: Stimulates pituitary gland to increase secretion of luteinizing hormone (LH) and follicle-stimulating hormone (FSH). LH and FSH stimulate maturation of the ovarian follicle, ovulation, and development of the corpus luteum.

Indications: Female infertility in which estrogen levels are normal.

Dosage and Route:

First course: 25–50 mg p.o. daily for 5 days.

Second course: Same dose if ovulation occurred with first dose. Increase to 100 mg daily for 5 days. Some women require up to 250 mg daily.

Absorption: Readily absorbed from the gastrointestinal tract. Time to peak effect is 4 to 10 days after last day of treatment.

Excretion: Excreted in the feces.

Contraindications and Precautions: Pregnancy, liver disease, abnormal bleeding of undetermined origin, ovarian cysts, neoplastic disease. Therapy is ineffective in women with ovarian or pituitary failure.

Adverse Reactions: Ovarian enlargement and symptoms, similar to premenstrual syndrome. Ovarian hyperstimulation. Multiple gestation, if more than one ovum is released. Visual disturbances. Abdominal distention, discomfort, nausea, vomiting. Abnormal uterine bleeding. Breast tenderness. Insomnia, nervousness, headache, depression, fatigue, lightheadedness, dizziness. Hot flashes, increased urination, allergic symptoms, weight gain, reversible alopecia.

Nursing Implications: Take history to determine whether the woman has a history of liver dysfunction or abnormal uterine bleeding. Rule out possibility of pregnancy. Teach the woman to report abdominal distention, pain in the pelvis or abdomen, or visual disturbances. Teach her to avoid tasks requiring mental alertness or coordination because the drug can cause lightheadedness, dizziness, and visual disturbances. Instruct her to stop taking clomiphene and report to the physician if she suspects that she might be pregnant. Teach the woman and her partner that she may notice irritability, mood swings, and other symptoms similar to those in premenstrual syndrome but that these are temporary.

---

woman receives supplemental progesterone to enhance the receptivity of her endometrium to implantation. Excess ova or embryos may be frozen for future attempts at in vitro fertilization or embryo transfer to the uterus.

In vitro fertilization is not always successful, although the rates vary among infertility centers. Bypassing the obstructions does not necessarily result in pregnancy. Not every ovum is successfully fertilized when this technique is used. Those embryos that are transferred to the woman's uterus may not implant.

GAMETE INTRAFALLOPIAN TRANSFER

For gamete intrafallopian transfer to take place, the woman must have at least one patent fallopian tube. The procedure begins in a fashion similar to that of in vitro fertilization, with retrieval of multiple ova and washed sperm. The ova are drawn into a catheter that also carries prepared sperm. Sperm and up to two ova per tube are injected into each fallopian tube, where fertilization occurs (Fig. 31–4). Progesterone is often given to enhance implantation.

TUBAL EMBRYO TRANSFER

Tubal embryo transfer, also called *zygote intrafallopian transfer* (ZIFT), is a hybrid of in vitro fertilization and gamete intrafallopian transfer. The woman's ova are fertilized outside her body, but the resulting fertilized ova are placed in the fallopian tubes and enter the uterus normally for implantation. The woman must have at least one patent fallopian tube.

RISKS AND BENEFITS

The primary advantage of gamete intrafallopian transfer and tubal embryo transfer (TET) over in vitro fertilization is that there is a higher pregnancy rate. The primary disadvantage is that the woman must have a minor surgical procedure (laparoscopy) to place the gametes (GIFT) or fertilized ova (TET) into the fallopian tube. When in vitro fertilization or tubal embryo transfer is used, there is evidence of fertilization before placement in the uterus or tubes. Either GIFT or TET may result in a tubal pregnancy if the embryo cannot reach the uterine cavity to implant.

Advanced reproductive techniques can result in multifetal pregnancy, sometimes greater than triplets. Pregnancies of more than twins carry a substantially higher risk to both mother and infants because of preterm labor and birth, placental insufficiency, and a high demand on maternal body systems. Selective reduction in the number of fetuses may be done to give the remaining ones a better chance to progress to a live birth. Such a procedure is, of course, heavily laden with emotional and ethical overtones.

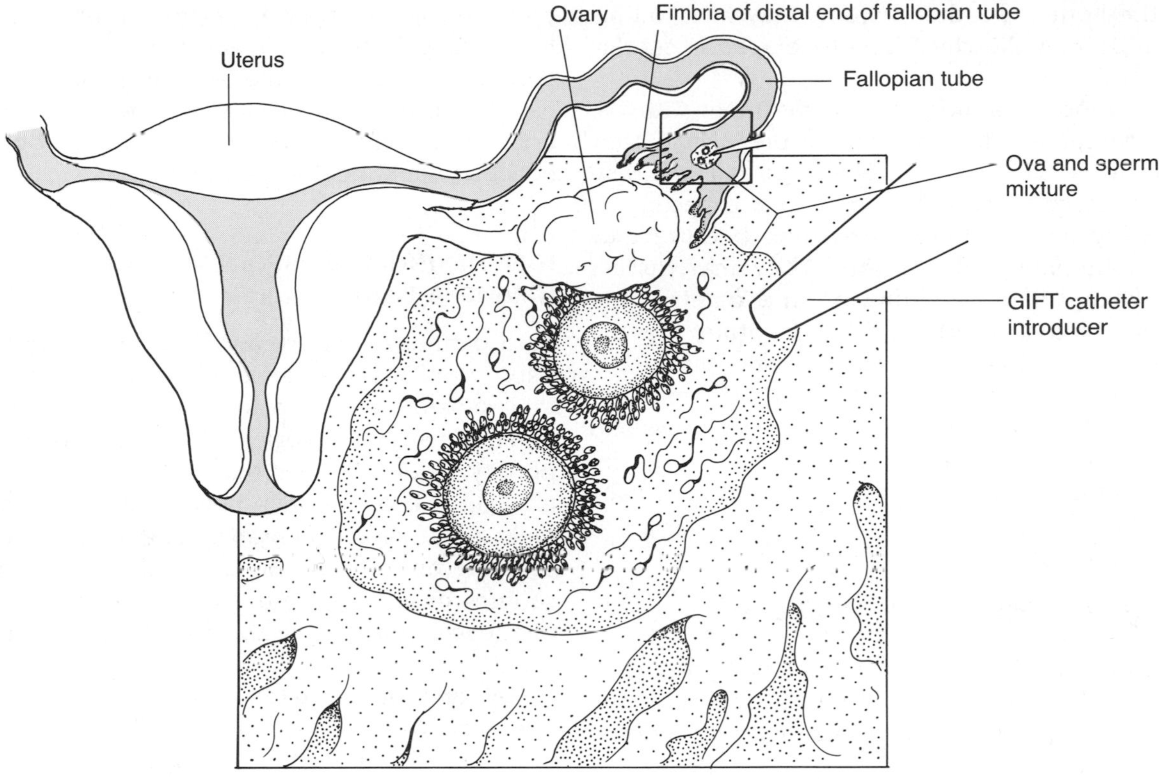

Figure 31–4

Gamete intrafallopian transfer (GIFT). Multiple ova and washed sperm are injected into the fallopian tube, where fertilization may occur.

✔ Check Your Reading

12. What elements are included in the history and physical examination for an infertility work-up?
13. What medications may be used to induce ovulation?
14. What screening tests are performed if donor sperm is used for therapeutic insemination or for gamete intrafallopian transfer?
15. What are the differences in technique between in vitro fertilization, gamete intrafallopian transfer, and tubal embryo transfer?

Responses to Infertility

The desire for children is strong in many couples. Even if they delay childbearing, most couples expect to have one or more children before the end of the woman's reproductive years. Some couples who chose childlessness earlier may re-evaluate their decision when they are older. If a couple does not achieve pregnancy or produce a living child as expected, they often experience psychological distress and a threat to their self-image. Either or both partners may feel like a failure. Their marital and family relationships may be stressed, and they may withdraw from relationships with others that they previously found satisfying. Every couple is unique, and many of their reactions depend on the importance of biological children in their lives. The following discussion describes how infertility can impact the lives of those affected.

Assumption of Fertility

Many couples practice contraception for a number of years before they decide to have a baby. They may want to establish a career and financial security, acquire a comfortable home and lifestyle, or perhaps travel and live freely without the responsibility of a child. They usually assume that they are fertile and must work hard to avoid pregnancy until they are ready.

When they do want a child, they discontinue contraception and assume that the woman will be pregnant within a few months at most. They may try to arrange conception so that the baby will be born at a certain time of year, such as avoiding pregnancy during the hottest weather. Parents may want to time the birth so that the child is not delayed in starting school.

Either or both partners may experiment with the role of parent as they anticipate pregnancy. They develop a heightened awareness of children and parenting. Being with others who are expecting or who already have children is exciting because they plan to join their ranks shortly. They may discuss issues like full-time parenting by one partner (usually the woman), child care, and future lifestyle changes. The woman often finds that she enjoys window shopping in the maternity and children's departments. The couple may begin acquiring toys and furnishings a child will need. Both partners may develop a fantasy child or a concept of what their baby will be like.

Growing Awareness of a Problem

As the months pass, the couple gradually becomes concerned about their inability to conceive. If the woman is older, in her mid to late 30s, they feel the urgency of the limited time before her reproductive years end. Older couples usually become distressed about the delay in conceiving sooner than younger ones. The plan to have a baby at a certain time of year is replaced by the desire for a baby anytime—and soon.

The couple begins to feel uneasy with child-related activities. Now they are not so sure when they will be parents. It begins to hurt when other family members or friends have babies. Events such as baby showers or christenings may become melancholy rather than joyful occasions, especially for the woman. They now bypass toy stores and children's departments. Family members and friends who are having children may feel guilty at their good fortune when they are around the couple who is unable to conceive.

The couple's own parents may be anxious as well. The potential grandparents may feel that their children are waiting too long to start a family or even that they are selfish. If they are aware that the couple is trying to conceive, they become even more worried as the months pass without the longed for announcement of a pregnancy. They are twice-saddened by the lack of a grandchild and by the hurt caused by their children's infertility.

Seeking Help for Infertility

Eventually, couples reach a point at which they decide whether they will seek help to conceive. They may reach this point after only a few menstrual cycles or, at the opposite extreme, may never seek help. Many factors enter into their decision, such as their age (especially the woman's), how long they have been unable to conceive, how much they want a biological child, how they regard adoption, and how they feel about a child-free life.

IDENTIFYING THE IMPORTANCE OF HAVING A BABY

Each partner may place a different value on having a baby. Conflicts may arise when one partner, often the woman, wants help to conceive sooner than the other. Having a biological child may be more of a priority to one partner than to the other. Additionally, cultural or religious beliefs influence how each feels about procreation and whether the couple will consider options such as assisted reproductive procedures or adoption. How the couple resolves these differences is crucial to the stability of their relationship.

Men and women often differ in their reactions to infertility. Women may want to talk about their feelings and frustrations, but men often internalize their feelings or feel as if they must be strong for their partner. The woman may interpret her partner's reluctance to express his feelings and his stoicism as disinterest or lack of concern and care for her. The two may withdraw from each other, further impairing communication and their relationship. On the other hand, Hirsch and Hirsch (1989) found that couples who shared their feelings and considered infertility a mutual problem emerged from the experience with a stronger bond.

SHARING INTIMATE INFORMATION

Although the infertility specialist will limit questions to the necessary ones, evaluation and treatment for infertility mandates that both partners reveal information about their sexual relationship, such as the frequency and timing of intercourse. This is difficult for those who regard this information as intimate. Additionally, the infertile couple may be highly sensitive and feel that the evaluation calls their sexual adequacy into question. They may feel defensive if they perceive a threat to their self-image.

CONSIDERING FINANCIAL RESOURCES

Financial concerns enter into the couple's decision about whether to seek treatment and how far to carry it. A technique such as basal body temperature assessment is inexpensive but has limited usefulness. Advanced techniques, like in vitro fertilization, are expensive and may have a low likelihood of success. Health insurance may not cover infertility treatment because it does not directly threaten the health of either partner. This restricts treatment choices for many low-income or middle-income couples. Indigent couples often have no real options for pursuing treatment. As a group, those who seek and pursue infertility treatment usually have greater financial resources than those who do not.

INVOLVEMENT IN CARE

Infertility evaluation and treatment require a great commitment from the couple in terms of time, energy, and money. Couples may be involved in this process for most or even all of a decade of their lives. They participate on a day-to-day basis as they do home assessments, take medications, and keep detailed records. For infertility diagnosis and therapy to be most effective, the couple must consider their ability and desire to be directly involved in the process over a long period of time.

Reactions During Evaluation and Treatment

Couples undergoing infertility evaluation and treatment have different reactions to the process. In addition, their reactions may change as infertility care progresses.

INFLUENCES ON DECISION MAKING

If their evaluation shows that a treatment or procedure may enable them to conceive, the couple must then decide whether to proceed. The decision-making process begins early and must be repeated during therapy if pregnancy does not occur. A complex array of factors enters into their decisions about beginning and continuing treatment or whether to end their pursuit of pregnancy. Although discussed separately, these factors interact dynamically as the couple makes each decision. The nurse helps them examine each factor and arrive at a decision that is best for them.

Social, Cultural, and Religious Values. Some medically appropriate options may not be acceptable to every couple. Surrogate parenting, in vitro fertilization, and therapeutic insemination (especially with donor sperm) are incompatible with the personal or religious beliefs of many people. If a procedure offers a couple hope for a child but is incompatible with their beliefs, their choices are two: use the technology despite their beliefs, or be willing to accept childlessness. Adoption may be a third alternative for some couples if the desire for a biological child is not absolute. As in other decisions, couples must work out conflicting personal values about what therapy is acceptable.

Difficulty of Treatment. The couple must consider how difficult, risky, and uncomfortable therapy will be. The level of difficulty involves physical, psychological, geographical, and time factors. Employment constraints may affect treatment decisions as well.

Many infertility treatments involve invasive procedures or surgery. Most of the invasive treatments involve the woman directly. The man or woman who undergoes the procedure must be the one who ultimately decides whether or not to do it. That person alone can decide whether the hope of a child is worth the risks and discomfort of the procedure.

Infertility treatment is stressful. Often partners feel or are willing to tolerate different levels of stress. To reduce the stress, they may abandon treatment completely or may take a vacation for a few months from the constant preoccupation with conceiving. Older women nearing or in their 40s often do not feel that they have the luxury of skipping a treatment cycle before their reproductive years end.

Some couples encounter geographical difficulties if they must travel a long distance for therapy. Time stresses are substantial. Many couples, particularly the woman, feel that achieving pregnancy is their new career. One or both of the partners may spend many hours every week in pursuit of pregnancy.

Employment constraints may be a barrier to infertility therapy because of the time required for treatment. The impact of time is usually greatest on the woman. Time away from work may burden the employer or co-workers. Stopping work may not be an option because the family needs the money and often needs the insurance coverage that comes with employment.

Probability of Success. Couples often have a biased interpretation of their statistical probability of success, especially when they begin treatment with a new procedure. For example, if a procedure has a 15 per cent likelihood of success with each cycle, they tend to expect that they will be in the successful group rather than in the 85 per cent who do not meet with success. As time goes by, however, they must weigh the likelihood of success of any therapy against financial concerns and their own willingness to accept the discomfort and difficulty associated with it.

Financial Concerns. Some couples, particularly those with ample resources and a strong desire for a biological child, pursue expensive treatments and pursue them longer than others of more limited means. They may do so despite a low probability of success. Couples with greater financial limitations find that they must abandon treatment sooner than they want. Other couples go heavily into debt, adding financial strain to the other stresses of treatment in their quest for a child of their own. Sandelowski et al. (1989) found that couples who pursue all avenues to achieve a biological child want to have no regrets, even if they are not successful and even if the treatment costs more than they can afford.

PSYCHOLOGICAL REACTIONS

A couple's initial reaction to infertility is often one of shock because they are usually healthy and often have had no idea that they might have problems conceiving. Their reactions vary according to how easily their infertility is alleviated, their personality and self-image, and the strength of their relationship.

Guilt. A partner having the only identified problem might feel that he or she is depriving the other of children. This feeling may be compounded if the "normal" partner has children from another relationship. It may be difficult for this person to understand that not all factors affecting fertility can be detected and that what seems like the problem of only one partner is often a couple problem.

Either partner may feel guilty about past choices that now affect fertility. A woman with adhesions resulting from a sexually transmitted infection may regret her past sexual choices. The man who wanted to delay pregnancy longer than the woman may feel guilty if her age is now affecting her fertility and limiting the length of time she has for achieving conception.

Isolation. Infertile couples often feel different from friends and relatives who do not have difficulty conceiving. They may withdraw from these relationships to insulate themselves from painful reminders of their infertility. Some couples develop supportive relationships with others who are also infertile, somewhat diminishing their sense of isolation.

Depression. One or both partners may experience depression as their sense of competence and control over their body is challenged, especially if therapy is not quickly successful. They often feel as if they are on a roller coaster of hope alternating with despair when the woman has her menstrual period each month. In an attempt to insulate themselves from disappointment, couples with long-term infertility try not to expect too much with each cycle.

The couple may feel envy at those who conceive easily. They may become judgmental and angry when they perceive those who seem to "have no business having a baby," such as an adolescent or a poor woman who has numerous children.

Stress on the Relationship. Because infertility can challenge one's identity and self-esteem, the couple may find less satisfaction in their relationship. They may feel unlovable or unappealing to their mate.

The man often finds it difficult to perform on demand for semen specimens and postcoital tests, feeling that others will judge his sexual function. The fact that semen samples are best obtained by masturbation may be unacceptable to some men because of religious prohibitions. Both partners may be stressed when intercourse must be scheduled to coincide with specific evaluations or with ovulation. Intercourse can become a chore more than an expression of love. It may come to be associated with failure rather than fulfillment.

If sperm from an anonymous donor is used for therapeutic insemination or other techniques, the man may feel that his masculinity is further threatened. He does not want to deprive his wife of a child, but he may be ambivalent about use of sperm from a third party. He may have difficulty distinguishing fatherhood as a biological achievement from fatherhood as a relationship.

The couple finds their relationship strained if they disagree on which treatments are appropriate and how long they should be pursued. One partner may want to keep trying "one more month," and the other may want to abandon treatment. If the couple is considering adoption, their relationship may be strained if they differ on whether to adopt and what kind of child they are willing to accept.

Outcomes After Infertility Therapy

After infertility therapy, three outcomes are possible. The couple may become parents, either biologically or through adoption. Infertility therapy may be unsuccessful, and the couple must decide whether or not to pursue adoption. The loss of a pregnancy may result in mixed emotions of grief and optimism.

Parenthood After Infertility

Couples who achieve conception often experience varied emotions. If they have been disappointed many times before, they may hardly believe the good news. They are often thrilled but worry about whether they can complete the pregnancy and take home a baby. Pregnancy after infertility is emotionally tentative for many infertile couples, especially those who have been trying to conceive for a long time or those who have lost a pregnancy. The couple may distance themselves from the reality of the pregnancy until much later in gestation than would fertile couples.

The previously infertile couple may find little sympathy from those who do not understand their fear of investing in the pregnancy. Others may be annoyed because they expect the couple to be overjoyed at a successful and apparently normal pregnancy. Outsiders may feel that the couple is self-centered and cannot decide what they want. Other infertile couples, who were previously a source of mutual support, may withdraw from the couple who achieves a pregnancy.

The woman who becomes pregnant after infertility treatment often continues care with the infertility center during the first trimester, when the risk for spontaneous abortion is highest. After this time, she is usually referred to her regular obstetrician for continuing care. The couple is often more anxious during pregnancy than couples who have not had problems conceiving. The woman has grown accustomed to sensing and reporting every symptom and may interpret normal physiological changes of pregnancy as a threat.

The parents' anxiety may be heightened during labor. They are afraid that something will go wrong at the last moment. Even after the birth of a healthy infant, some parents have difficulty relaxing and enjoying their baby.

Because they may have withdrawn from friends and family with children and because they delay investing emotionally in a pregnancy or the adoption process, the couple may have little experience with parental role models (Bernstein, 1990). These parents need much support as they gain experience with their child. Infertile couples who eventually have biological or adopted children may have unrealistic expectations about parenting. After investing so much financial and emotional resources in having a child, they may be reluctant to express any unhappiness or frustration over the realities of childrearing.

Choosing to Adopt

Not every couple who seeks treatment for infertility will achieve a "take-home" baby. Some couples discontinue treatment sooner than others, depending on their age and their tolerance for the fatigue, stress, and expense. Some couples investigate adoption early in infertility treatment because advanced age may make them ineligible to adopt through many agencies or because a non-biological child is acceptable to them.

Couples who consider adoption must confront their personal preferences, limitations, and even prejudices. As much as they want a child, many couples are not willing to adopt *any* child. Most couples prefer to adopt a newborn or an infant of their race. Some prefer an infant but are also willing to adopt an older child, one with special needs, one of a mixed or different race, or a group of siblings. Other couples, for a variety of reasons, will not consider adopting these children.

Some couples may fear adopting a child because the woman might become pregnant. Although pregnancy has been the goal for a long time, they may believe that they would love their adopted child differently from their biological child.

The couple who decides to adopt faces further scrutiny of their personal life. Agencies investigate their home, financial means (which may have been seriously drained), and their fitness as parents. Once again, they may feel that their personal competence is questioned.

The couple who decides on adoption may have emotions similar to those who achieve a pregnancy. They may be slow to invest in the process emotionally because they expect disappointment again. Additionally, the adopted child often comes to them suddenly and unexpectedly. Although they may have been waiting months for this happy event, they have little time to adjust to the reality that they are becoming parents.

Pregnancy Loss After Infertility

Harris et al. (1991) found that couples who suffer pregnancy loss after infertility may interpret the experience with mixed feelings of loss and gain. Couples undergoing infertility evaluation and treatment are often aware of a pregnancy much earlier than fertile couples. They want to hope, yet expect to be disappointed again. If a spontaneous abortion occurs, they may grieve profoundly for what they achieved and then lost.

Yet, despite their grief about the pregnancy loss, the couple may be encouraged because they have proved that they can achieve a pregnancy. They may feel that if they succeeded once, they can do it again. A spontaneous abortion may give them the courage to continue treatment.

✔ Check Your Reading

16. What factors does the couple consider when they are deciding whether to seek help for their infertility?

17. What factors must a couple consider when they reach decision points during infertility evaluation and treatment?
18. What are possible psychological reactions to infertility?
19. If the couple become parents, either through birth or adoption, how may they react to parenthood?
20. What are the issues couples must face if they consider adoption?
21. What emotions do couples often experience if they lose a pregnancy after infertility treatment?

Application of Nursing Process

Nurses may encounter couples facing infertility in many different settings and may identify numerous nursing care needs. Nursing care of the infertile couple is challenging, yet can be most satisfying. Regardless of the work setting, the nurse often addresses the couple's emotional needs associated with infertility evaluation, treatment, and outcomes of therapy.

Assessment

In many instances, infertile couples have previously had a positive self-image and feelings of competence about themselves. The diagnosis of infertility shakes their positive view of themselves. The nurse should be aware that these feelings may be present, regardless of the practice setting in which the couple is encountered.

Determine at what point the couple is in their infertility treatment. Couples who have just discovered that they may have difficulty conceiving may be shocked, yet optimistic that therapy will result in a baby for them. Couples with longstanding infertility may have a deeper sense of failure and a pessimistic outlook. Observe for remarks that are negative, expressing guilt or helplessness.

Evaluate how infertility has affected the couple's relationship with each other. Are there any conflicts or differences in values between the two partners? Observing their body language, such as eye contact, may provide clues about how similarly or differently they are committed to diagnosis and treatment. Ask them how their relationship has changed. Are they more or less satisfied with their marital relationship than they were before they had problems conceiving?

Ask about support systems. Couples suffering from infertility often withdraw from old relationships yet do not form other supportive ones. Do others who are significant in the couple's life know that they are trying to conceive? Are family members and friends nearby, and are they supportive? Ask whether they have encountered assumptions by others that infertility is the "fault" of one partner or the other. Are they subjected to questions that invade their privacy, such as "When are you two going to have a baby of your own?"

Elicit information about how the couple's culture or religion views infertility and the impact of these views on therapy. Are there potentially successful therapies that are unacceptable within one or both partners' beliefs and values? The partners may have differing views that can cause conflict during treatment, and they will need help to work these out.

Determine how the couple is coping with the stresses of treatment. How much has infertility cost them in terms of time, money, and discomfort? Identify the successes and failures they have experienced. Their age, especially the woman's, adds another stressor that they cannot avoid. Older couples may feel as though they must try to conceive with every menstrual cycle.

If the woman is pregnant or has recently given birth or if the couple has recently adopted a child, observe for high levels of anxiety in either or both parents. Assess them for negative behaviors and comments, such as reluctance to feel joy or a sense that they will "fail" again.

Analysis

A nursing diagnosis commonly encountered in most practice settings is: *Situational Low Self-Esteem related to perception of reproductive inadequacy.*

Planning

Three goals are appropriate for this nursing diagnosis, and they may apply to the man, the woman, or both partners. The person(s) will:

- Express feelings about infertility and its evaluation and treatment.
- Explore ways to increase control within the situation of infertility.
- Identify aspects of self that are positive.

Interventions

ASSISTING COMMUNICATION

Therapeutic communication is the primary technique for both assessment and intervention related to this nursing diagnosis. Use a variety of communication techniques, such as active listening and exploration, to encourage the partners to express their feelings honestly. Provide privacy and acceptance of their feelings. Nurses must recognize their personal biases and the validity of the couple's views and emotions.

Encourage the partners to accept their own feelings, both positive and negative. For example, the couple who has finally achieved pregnancy may be living a lie to some extent. They may act elated because they believe they should feel happy, yet inside they are cautious and hesitant to become attached to their baby. Explain that feelings are not right or wrong, they simply exist. It may be helpful to open the subject of negative feelings (fear of attachment) within a successful situation (pregnancy or birth) to reinforce the normality of their emotions. This technique gives them the opportunity to talk about emotional reactions that they or others feel are inappropriate and might otherwise be reluctant to discuss.

Discuss possible differences in how the man and the woman communicate. For example, explain that the woman may feel more comfortable than the man in talking about their problem and concerns about treatment. Explain that these differences in communication style can cause misunderstandings because one partner believes that the other does not care as much about their problem. Encourage them to be open with each other for the best mutual support.

INCREASING THE COUPLE'S SENSE OF CONTROL

Explore how the couple has dealt with stressors in the past and how these techniques might be used to cope with their present crisis. A couple's pattern of dealing with stress in other parts of their life is likely to carry over into infertility work-up and treatment and throughout pregnancy and parenthood. Reinforce coping skills that are positive, such as learning more about infertility and the proposed therapy for it.

Couples who experience undue stress may benefit from relaxation techniques, such as visualization and moderate exercise. Frequent strenuous exercise may reduce the woman's ability to ovulate. Although a hot tub is relaxing for many people, it should be avoided because the high temperatures may inhibit spermatogenesis. Additionally, the woman could become pregnant with any cycle and high temperatures have been associated with fetal anomalies (Jones, 1989).

Discuss behaviors that enhance the ability to handle stress and that provide a good environment for a pregnancy that might occur. Reinforce healthy choices, such as good nutrition and a balance between exercise and rest. Teach the couple ways to

Infertile Couples Want To Know
WHAT IS INFERTILITY TREATMENT LIKE?

General:

- Both members of the couple are evaluated.
- Simpler evaluations and therapies are done before more complex ones are undertaken.
- A complete medical history and physical examination are done for each partner.
- The ages of the partners, particularly the woman, are considered. Evaluations and therapy may be instituted more quickly if the woman is in her mid 30s or older.
- Costs may be partially covered by insurance; check to see what your insurance will cover.
- Difficult decisions may be required at different times during evaluation and treatment, for example, whether to proceed to more complex and expensive tests and therapies, whether to take a break from treatment, or whether to abandon treatment altogether.
- Infertility treatment is often stressful, can occupy as many hours per week as a full-time job, and requires a substantial commitment to self-care.
- Infertility remains unexplained in about 20 per cent of couples.

Men

- Semen analysis is usually the first test. Several semen specimens are obtained over a period of several weeks to obtain the best evaluation.
- Depending on your medical history, physical examination, and semen analysis, other diagnostic tests may be done (hormone assay, an ultrasonogram of your reproductive organs, a biopsy of your testicles, and specialized tests of sperm function).
- Corrective measures may include medications, surgery, and methods to reduce the scrotal temperature.

Women

- The first evaluation is usually to determine if you are ovulating each month. You may be taught to take your basal body temperature each morning and to assess your cervical mucus as the first step. These assessments are often done at the same time as other tests.
- Other evaluations may include a post-coital test to determine how your partner's sperm react in your cervix, an ultrasound examination, and a hysterosalpingogram (x-ray of your uterus and tubes).
- For some tests and therapies, an operative procedure may be required (hysteroscopy, laparoscopy, laser surgery, or microsurgery) on either an outpatient or inpatient basis.
- Typically, infertility evaluations and treatments require more of the woman's time, energy, physical discomfort, and risk than the man's.
- Corrective measures depend on the problem that is identified, for example, medications, surgery, and advanced reproductive techniques, such as in vitro fertilization.

enhance their general health if deficiencies are identified.

Explain any procedures and their purpose in language that the couple can understand. Reinforce any medical explanations that they may have been given. Encourage questions so that the couple is fully informed. Have them restate what was explained to reduce misunderstandings.

Help the couple explore their options at each decision point. No one else can decide the best course of action, but the nurse can help them identify pros and cons of each choice so that they can arrive at a decision appropriate for them. Be non-directive so that the choices are theirs and do not reflect the biases of the nurse or other caregivers.

REDUCING ISOLATION

Because couples often distance themselves from friend and family relationships that they find painful, they may have few social supports. Refer them to available support groups to provide emotional outlets, a sense of belonging, and a source of information. Lentner and Glazer (1991) reported that couples found support groups helpful in various degrees even when they were reluctant to attend at first.

The couple who achieves pregnancy or adopts a child may again find themselves isolated because they are now different from other infertile couples. Encourage them to take the initiative to re-establish ties with relatives and friends, who can be an important source of support during pregnancy and childrearing. Help them identify how they can improve communication with these significant others. Remind them that they have undergone significant shifts in self-image that have also affected those around them.

PROMOTING A POSITIVE SELF-IMAGE

Because infertility work is often such a dominant factor in their lives, a continuing inability to conceive erodes the couple's perception of themselves. Explore with them other areas of competence and activities that make them feel good about themselves. Reinforce positive attitudes and self-evaluations. Encourage them to maintain activities such as hobbies, sports, or volunteer work. The career of either partner may be a source of stress that needs relief, or it may be an avenue that fosters a positive self-perception.

Some people benefit from self-improvement activities, such as continuing education courses or enhancement of appearance. Encourage these activities if they help the individuals feel better about themselves. If the activity might impair fertility treatments, such as strict dieting, inform the person of this fact as well.

Evaluation

The goals established are achieved if the individual or couple:

- Can express their feelings about their situation, usually over a period of time.
- Can explore ways to increase personal control over their lives, evidenced by expressing feelings of reduced helplessness and dependence.
- Can identify one or more aspects of self perceived as positive and can identify areas of competence.

Summary Concepts

- Nurses may encounter persons having infertility problems in a variety of settings other than infertility clinics, for example, maternity and gynecology services, urology services, the perioperative area, and the emergency department. Friends and family members also see the nurse as an information resource about infertility care.
- About 20 per cent of couples have infertility that is unexplained by current evaluation techniques.
- Because there are many unknown factors in reproduction, identification and correction of problems in one or both partners do not necessarily resolve their infertility.
- A variety of structural and functional abnormalities may contribute to a couple's infertility. The man may have abnormalities of the sperm, the seminal fluid, or with ejaculation. The woman may have ovulation disorders; anatomical problems, such as fallopian tube occlusion; or physiological disorders, such as hormone imbalances.
- A systematic evaluation of both partners identifies therapy that is most likely to be successful and cost-effective.
- Infertility is a crisis for the couple and often for their extended family. Either or both partners may feel that the inability to conceive represents a personal failure. They may have a variety of psychological reactions.
- Infertile couples must make choices at many points before and during evaluation and therapy. Some major factors that enter into their decisions

involve social, cultural, and religious values; difficulty of treatment; probability of success; financial resources; and age, particularly the woman's.

- The possible outcomes after infertility may present new challenges to the couple and their families: unsuccessful therapy and the choice of whether to pursue adoption, pregnancy loss after infertility, and parenthood after infertility.
- Many nursing care needs may be identified as the couple negotiates infertility evaluation and treatment. Impairment of self-esteem in one or both partners is a problem that nurses can address.

References and Readings

American College of Obstetricians and Gynecologists (ACOG). (1990a). Infertility. *Precis IV: An update in obstetrics and gynecology* (pp. 349–364). Washington, D.C.

American College of Obstetricians and Gynecologists (ACOG) (1990b). In vitro fertilization and related reproductive technologies. *Precis IV: An update in obstetrics and gynecology* (pp. 364–367). Washington, D.C.

Barad, D.H. (1991). Epidemiology of infertility. *Infertility and Reproductive Medicine Clinics of North America*, 2(2), 255–266.

Bernstein, J. (1990). Parenting after infertility. *Journal of Perinatal-Neonatal Nursing*, 4(4), 11–23.

Bernstein, J., Mattox, J.H., & Kellner, R. (1988). Psychological status of previously infertile couples after a successful pregnancy. *Journal of Obstetric, Gynecologic, and Neonatal Nursing*, 17(6), 404–409.

Blackburn, S.T., & Loper, D.L. (1992). *Maternal, fetal, and neonatal physiology: A clinical perspective*. Philadelphia: W.B. Saunders.

Blenner, J.L. (1990a). Attaining self-care in infertility treatment. *Applied Nursing Research*, 3(3), 98–104.

Blenner, J.L. (1990b). Passage through infertility treatment: A stage theory. *Image: Journal of Nursing Scholarship*, 22(3), 153–158.

Blenner, J.L. (1991). Clomiphene-induced mood swings. *Journal of Obstetric, Gynecologic, and Neonatal Nursing*, 20(4), 321–327.

Carson, S.A. (1991). Nongenetic causes of recurrent fetal loss. *Contemporary OB/Gyn*, 36(2), 14–16, 21–23, 24, 26.

Cook, C.L. (1991). Luteal phase defect. In E.J. Quilligan & F.P. Zuspan (Eds.), *Current therapy in obstetrics* 3 (pp. 76–77). Philadelphia: W.B. Saunders.

Davis, D.C., & Dearman, C.N. (1991). Coping strategies of infertile women. *Journal of Obstetrics, Gynecologic, and Neonatal Nursing*, 20(3), 221–228.

Domar, A.D., & Seibel, M.M. (1990). Emotional aspects of infertility. In M.M. Seibel (Ed.), *Infertility: A comprehensive text*. Norwalk, Conn.: Appleton & Lange.

Dunnington, R.M., & Glazer, G. (1991). Maternal identity and early mothering behavior in previously infertile and never infertile women. *Journal of Obstetric, Gynecologic, and Neonatal Nursing*, 20(4), 5309–5318.

Fehring, R.J. (1991). New technology in natural family planning. *Journal of Obstetric, Gynecologic, and Neonatal Nursing*, 20(3), 199–205.

Francis, G.R., & Nosek, J.A. (1988). Ethical considerations in contemporary reproductive technologies. *Journal of Perinatal-Neonatal Nursing*, 1(3), 37–48.

Frank, D.I. (1989). Treatment preferences of infertile couples. *Applied Nursing Research*, 2(2), 94–95.

Frank, D.I. (1990a). Gender differences in decision making about infertility treatment. *Applied Nursing Research*, 3(2), 56–62.

Frank, D.I. (1990b). Factors related to decisions about infertility treatment. *Journal of Obstetric, Gynecologic, and Neonatal Nursing*, 19(2), 162–167.

Gangi, G.R., & Nagler, H.M. (1992). Clinical evaluation of the subfertile man. *Infertility and Reproductive Medicine Clinics of North America*, 3(2), 299–318.

Goode, C.J., & Hahn, S.J. (1993). Oocyte donation and in vitro fertilization. The nurse's role with ethical and legal issues. *Journal of Obstetric, Gynecologic, and Neonatal Nursing*, 22(2), 106–111.

Harris, B.G., Sandelowski, M., & Holditch-Davis, D. (1991). Infertility . . . and new interpretations of pregnancy loss. MCN: *American Journal of Maternal Child Nursing*, 16(4), 217–220.

Hirsch, A.M., & Hirsch, S.M. (1989). The effect of infertility on marriage and self-concept. *Journal of Obstetric, Gynecologic, and Neonatal Nursing*, 18(1), 13–20.

Hopkins, E. (1992, June 1). Behind the IVF hype: A shocking failure rate. *Medical Economics*, 69(11), 152–155, 159–160, 162–163.

Jacobs, M.H. (1991). Prediction of ovulation. *Infertility and Reproductive Clinics of North America*, 2(2), 287–306.

Jones, K.L. (1989). Effects of chemical and environmental agents. In R.K. Creasy & R. Resnick (Eds.), *Maternal-fetal medicine: Principles and practice* (pp. 180–192). Philadelphia: W.B. Saunders.

Lentner, E., & Glazer, G. (1991). Infertile couples' perceptions of infertility support group participation. *Health Care for Women International*, 12(3), 317–330.

Meldrum, D.R. (1992). Infertility. In N.F. Hacker & J.G. Moore (Eds.), *Essentials of obstetrics and gynecology* (2nd ed., pp. 551–562). Philadelphia: W.B. Saunders.

Millard, S. (1991). Emotional responses to infertility: Understanding patients' needs. AORN *Journal*, 54(2), 301–305.

Moghissi, K.S. (1990). Cervical factor in infertility. In E.J. Quilligan & F.P. Zuspan (Eds.), *Current therapy in obstetrics* 3 (pp. 12–19). Philadelphia: W.B. Saunders.

Moore, J.G. (1992). Contraception and sterilization. In N.F. Hacker & J.G. Moore (Eds.), *Essentials of obstetrics and gynecology* (2nd ed., pp. 453–467). Philadelphia: W.B. Saunders.

Moore, K.L. (1988). *The developing human: Clinically oriented embryology* (4th ed.) Philadelphia: W.B. Saunders.

Olshansky, E.F. (1988). Responses to high technology infertility treatment. *Image: Journal of Nursing Scholarship*, 20(3), 128–131.

Osborn, M.R. (1989). Selective reduction in multiple gestation. *Journal of Perinatal-Neonatal Nursing*, 3(1), 14–21.

Overstreet, J.W., Davis, R.O., & Katz, D.F. (1992). Semen evaluation. *Infertility and Reproductive Medicine Clinics of North America*, 3(2), 329–340.

Pace-Owens, S.(1989). Gamete intrafallopian transfer (GIFT). *Journal of Obstetric, Gynecologic, and Neonatal Nursing*, 18(2), 93–97.

Rabar, F.G. (1991). Gamete intrafallopian transfer: Another approach for the treatment of infertility. AORN *Journal*, 53(6), 1466–1475.

Sandelowski, M., Harris, B.G., & Holditch-Davis, D. (1989). Mazing: Infertile couples and the quest for a child. *Image: Journal of Nursing Scholarship*, 21(4), 220–226.

Sandelowski, M., Harris, B.G., & Holditch-Davis, D. (1990). Pregnant moments: The process of conception in infertile couples. *Research in Nursing and Health*, 13(5), 273–282.

Scoccia, B., & Scommegna, A. (1991). Induction of ovulation. In E.J. Quilligan & F.P. Zuspan (Eds.), *Current therapy in obstetrics* 3 (pp. 66–72). Philadelphia: W.B. Saunders.

Sharts-Engel, N.C. (1992). Nafarelin for endometriosis. MCN: *American Journal of Maternal Child Nursing*, 17(4), 224.

Shattuck, J.C., & Schwarz, K.K. (1991). Walking the line between feminism and infertility: Implications for nursing, medicine, and patient care. *Health Care for Women International*, 12(3), 331–339.

Sherrod, R.A. (1992). Helping infertile couples explore the option of adoption. *Journal of Obstetric, Gynecologic, and Neonatal Nursing*, 21(6), 465–470.

Shortridge, L.A. (1990). Advances in the assessment of the effect of environmental and occupational toxins on reproduction. *Journal of Perinatal-Neonatal Nursing*, 3(4), 1–11.

Shulman, S., & Shulman, J.F. Immunologic factors as a cause of infertility. *Infertility and Reproductive Medicine Clinics of North America*, 2(2), 351–369.

Speroff, L. (1991). Male infertility—intrauterine insemination. In E.J. Quilligan & F.P. Zuspan (Eds.), *Current therapy in obstetrics* 3 (pp. 78–80). Philadelphia: W.B. Saunders.

Stanton, A.L., Tennen, H., Affleck, G., and Mendola, R. (1991). Cognitive appraisal and adjustment to infertility. *Women and Health*, 17(3), 1–15.

Taymor, M.L. (1989). *Infertility: A clinician's guide to diagnosis and treatment*. New York: Plenum Medical Book Co.

Townsend, A.B. (1992). Ethical issues of gamete and embryo donation: Implications for nursing. *Journal of Perinatology*, 12(4), 359–362.

Wheeler, J.M. (1991). Epidemiologic aspects of recurrent pregnancy loss. *Infertility and Reproductive Medicine Clinics of North America*, 2(1), 1–17.

White, G.B. (1988). Infertility and ethical policy. *Nursing Connections*, 1(3), 16–22.

Woods, N.F., Olshansky, E., & Draye, M.A. (1991). Infertility: Women's experiences. *Health Care for Women International*, 12(2), 179–190.

Yee, B. (1991). In vitro fertilization. In E.J. Quilligan & F.P. Zuspan (Eds.), *Current therapy in obstetrics* 3 (pp. 74–76). Philadelphia: W.B. Saunders.

Zion, A.B. (1988). Resources for infertile couples. *Journal of Obstetric, Gynecologic, and Neonatal Nursing*, 17(4), 255–258.

32

Women's Health Care

Objectives

1. Explain examinations and various screening procedures that are recommended to maintain the health of women.
2. Define four benign disorders of the breast, relate them to expected age of onset, and describe the diagnostic procedures used to rule out cancer of the breast.
3. Describe the incidence, risks, pathophysiology, management, and nursing considerations of malignant tumors of the breast.
4. Discuss the four most common menstrual cycle disorders.
5. Explain nursing considerations for women who experience premenstrual syndrome.
6. Describe the physical and psychological changes associated with menopause and the risks versus benefits of hormonal replacement therapy.
7. Discuss preventive measures for osteoporosis.
8. Describe the major disorders associated with pelvic relaxation in terms of cause, treatment, and nursing considerations.
9. Discuss the most common benign and malignant disorders of the reproductive tract in terms of signs and symptoms, management, and nursing considerations.
10. Describe care of the woman with infectious disorders of the reproductive tract, including vaginitis, sexually transmitted diseases, pelvic inflammatory disease, and toxic shock syndrome.

Definitions

Adjuvant therapy • Additional treatment that increases or enhances the action of the primary treatment.

Amenorrhea • Absence of menses. **Primary amenorrhea** is a delay of the first menstruation. **Secondary amenorrhea** is cessation of menstruation after its initiation.

Adnexa • Accessory organs of the uterus, such as the fallopian tubes and ovaries.

Atrophic vaginitis • Inflammation that occurs when the vagina becomes dry and fragile, usually as a result of estrogen deficit after menopause.

Axillary tail • Wedge of tissue extending from the breast into the axilla (also called the *tail of Spence*).

Carcinoma in situ • Malignant neoplasm in surface tissue that has not extended into deeper tissue.

Climacteric • Endocrine, body, and psychic changes occurring at the end of the woman's reproductive cycle. Also called **menopause.**

Colposcopy • Examination of the vaginal and cervical tissue with a colposcope for magnification.

Condyloma • A wart-like growth of the skin seen on the external genitalia, in the vagina, on the cervix, or near the anus; may be caused by human papi-

△ Alert for a high risk of exposure to substances to which universal precautions apply. See Appendix B for additional information about infection control.

lomavirus (condyloma acuminata) or by syphilis (condyloma lata).

Cryotherapy • Treatment using extreme cold to destroy tissue.

Cystocele • Prolapse of the urinary bladder through the anterior vaginal wall.

Dysmenorrhea • Painful menstruation.

Dyspareunia • Difficult or painful coitus in women.

Dysplasia • Abnormal development of tissue.

Dysuria • Painful urination, often associated with urinary tract infection.

Endometrial hyperplasia • Excessive proliferation of normal cells of the uterine lining; may be due to administration of estrogen during the postmenopausal period.

Endometriosis • Presence of endometrial tissue (uterine lining) outside the uterine cavity.

Laparoscopy • Insertion of an illuminated tube into the abdominal cavity to visualize contents, locate bleeding, and perform surgical procedures.

Laparotomy • Incision through the abdominal wall to examine the abdominal or pelvic organs.

Mammogram • Study of breast tissue by means of very-low-dose x-ray; primary tool in the discovery of breast cancer.

Menarche • Onset of menstruation; average age is 12.8 years.

Menopause • Permanent cessation of menstruation during the climacteric.

Menorrhagia • Excessive bleeding at the time of menstruation, either in number of days or in amount of blood lost or both.

Metrorrhagia • Bleeding from the uterus at any time other than during the menstrual period.

Osteoporosis • Increased spaces (porosity) in bone; process greatly accelerates following menopause.

Peau d'orange • Dimpled skin condition that resembles an orange; associated with lymphatic edema and often seen over the area of breast cancer.

Rectocele • Herniation (protrusion) of the rectum through the posterior vaginal wall.

Toxic shock syndrome • Rare, potentially fatal disorder caused by toxin produced by *Staphylococcus aureus*; has been associated with improper use of tampons.

Nurses provide many services valued by women. Those with advanced education, such as nurse practitioners, provide primary care for many women throughout the life span. Nurses also act as educators and advocates for women and are responsible for explaining screening and diagnostic procedures. They clarify options so that clients can make informed decisions about care. Therefore, nurses must be well informed about measures that promote and maintain health and about the most common disorders that affect women. In addition, nurses traditionally offer support and comfort to women who experience disruptions in their health.

Health Maintenance

Health maintenance refers to measures that can be taken to prevent or detect specific diseases and includes periodic health examinations, immunizations, and screening procedures. Many women seek health care only when they have a problem, whereas others schedule yearly examinations with a gynecologist or nurse practitioner. Very often the only health care a woman receives comes from the gynecologist or nurse practitioner who conducts the annual gynecological examination. Therefore, it is important that those who provide health care for women are familiar with principles of screening and counseling in areas that are not traditionally associated with gynecology, for example, assessing risk factors for colon cancer and heart disease.

Health History

Nurses are frequently responsible for obtaining a complete health history. The health history of a well woman may be obtained through individual interviews or a combination of questionnaires, interviews, and previous records. Obviously, written methods cannot be used if the woman is unable to read or write, or if she is unfamiliar with the language.

The focus of a health history depends on the woman's age, but some topics need to be discussed with all women. Table 32–1 provides a summary of information that should be obtained. These topics include dietary intake, physical activity, habits, and sexual practices. When discussing drugs, it is important to include long-term use of prescription and over-the-counter medications.

Family history is essential to assess risk profiles. History of colon cancer, breast cancer, hyperlipidemia, heart disease, osteoporosis, and thyroid disease indicate which screening tests and examinations are needed. A list of family members who had cancer and their ages when it was discovered provides important information about the risk of cancer for a woman. For instance, a woman is at increased risk for colon cancer if a close relative (mother, father, sibling) had the disease, and a screening colonoscopy should be recommended.

Table 32–1. HEALTH HISTORY

Personal History
- Demographic data (name, age, marital status)
- Reason for seeking medical care (also termed chief complaint)
- Current and past state of health, previous surgeries
- Appetite, dietary intake
- Exercise pattern
- Habits (smoking, use of alcohol, drugs), allergies
- Sleep and rest patterns
- Patterns of elimination (current or chronic problems)
- Degree of stress and stress management techniques

Sexual History
- Sexually active (one partner, multiple partners, age when first sexually active)
- Method of contraception (satisfaction with method, adverse reactions)
- Knowledge/practice of measures to protect self from STDs

Menstrual History
- Age of menarche
- Regularity, duration of menstrual cycle
- Menstrual discomfort

Obstetrical History
- Gravida, para, length of gestation, weight of infant at birth
- Labor experience and method of delivery

Family History
- Cardiovascular problems (anemia, hypertension, clotting disorders, stroke, heart attacks)
- Cancer (breast, uterine, ovarian, bowel, lung)
- Osteoporosis

Psychosocial History
- Primary language, additional languages spoken or understood
- Marital status, employment, occupation, education (relevant to determine financial, social, and emotional support)

A family history of heart disease is especially important when the woman is postmenopausal, because estrogen, which protects against coronary heart disease, decreases after menopause. Therefore, a family history that includes myocardial infarctions increases the risk of coronary heart disease in a postmenopausal woman, particularly if she does not take estrogen replacement. In this case, a baseline electrocardiogram and periodic laboratory analysis of cholesterol and triglyceride levels may be necessary to identify additional risk factors.

✔ Check Your Reading

1. Why is a family history an important part of a health history?
2. What questions should be asked when taking a sexual history?

Physical Assessment

A thorough physical assessment is necessary to detect general health problems. Blood pressure, temperature, pulse, respirations, and weight are measured at each visit. Height is taken at the initial examination and yearly after that. Loss of height and abnormal curvature of the vertebral column (dorsal kyphosis or scoliosis) are important observations in evaluating osteoporosis in the postmenopausal woman.

The heart is generally auscultated at the initial visit to determine if a heart murmur is present. The extremities are observed for varicosities or edema, and pedal pulses are palpated. Palpation of the abdomen for tenderness, masses, or distention is an important part of the physical assessment.

Additional assessments are necessary if the woman is in other high-risk groups. For instance, if she smokes or drinks alcohol excessively, the oral cavity is examined for early signs of cancer. The skin is scrutinized to locate lesions suggestive of malignant melanoma, particularly if she tans frequently or has a history of frequent sunburns.

Screening Procedures

Relatively simple screening procedures are used to identify women who are at risk for a particular condition and who thus warrant more definitive diagnostic tests. The value of screening procedures is based on two assumptions: (1) prevention is better than cure, and (2) early diagnosis allows early treatment while the pathological process is still reversible.

A variety of screening procedures are recommended for all women, including three screening procedures for early detection of breast cancer as well as vulvar self-examination and screening for cervical cancer.

BREAST SELF-EXAMINATION

The National Cancer Institute, the American Cancer Society, and the American College of Radiology all recommend breast self-examination (BSE) as a supplement to, rather than as a substitute for screening by professional examination and mammography. In many parts of the world, BSE is the only realistic means of early cancer detection.

BSE should be performed monthly by all women after the age of 20 years. The first element in learning BSE technique is to perform it about a week following the onset of menses, when hormonal influences on the breasts are at a low level. If the woman no longer menstruates, she may choose a day that is easy to remember and perform the test on that day every month. An example would be the first day of the month or payday. (See Women Want to Know: How to Perform Breast Self-Examination.)

Women Want To Know

How to Perform Breast Self-Examination

1. Lie down. Flatten your right breast by placing a pillow under your right shoulder. If your breasts are large, use your right hand to hold your right breast while you do the exam with your left hand.
2. Use the sensitive pads of the middle three fingers on your left hand and a massaging motion to feel for lumps or changes in the breast tissue.
3. Press firmly enough to distinguish different breast textures.
4. Completely palpate or feel all parts of the breast and chest area. Be sure to examine the breast tissue that extends toward the shoulder. The amount of time required to completely palpate all the breast tissue depends on the size of the breast. Women with small breasts will need at least 2 minutes to examine each breast. Larger breasts will take longer.

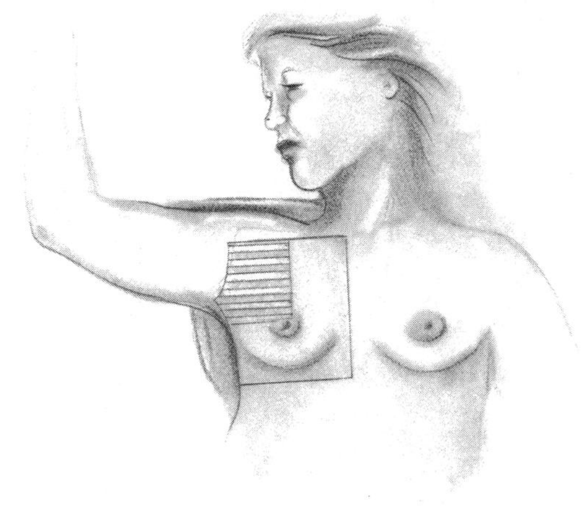

5. Use the same routine or pattern to feel every part of the breast tissue. Any of three patterns will help you to make sure you have covered your entire breast—the circular pattern, the vertical strip or the wedge. Choose the method you find easiest.

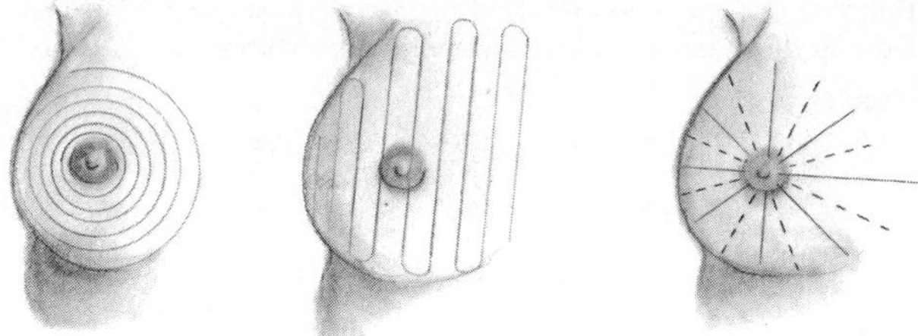

6. When you have completely examined your right breast, the left breast should be examined using the same method. Compare what you feel in one breast with the other.
7. You may also want to examine your breasts while bathing, when the skin is wet and lumps may be easily palpated.
8. You can check your breasts in a mirror by raising your arms and looking for an unusual shape, dimpling of the skin, and any changes in the nipple.

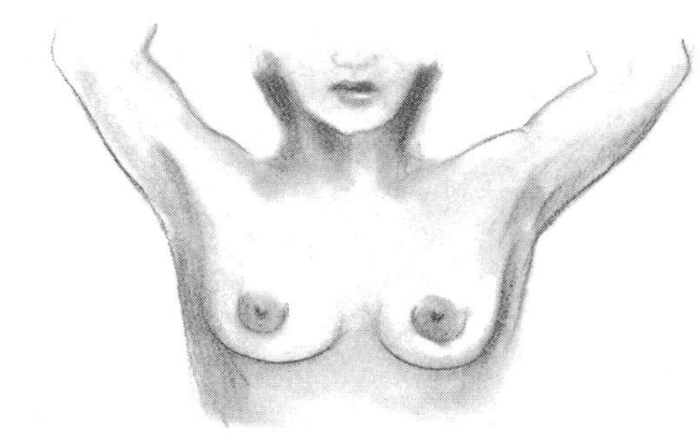

* Adapted from American Cancer Society. 1992. Special touch.

PROFESSIONAL BREAST EXAMINATION

Professional breast examination is a critical part of a gynecological examination. Professional breast examination is similar to BSE; however, professional examiners are more experienced and may detect questionable areas that individuals miss. The examination includes both inspection and palpation.

Inspection

1. While the woman is in an upright position, the examiner inspects the breasts for size, symmetry, color, or skin changes. The nipples and areola are inspected for differences in size, color, unilateral retraction of a nipple, or asymmetrical nipple direction, which may indicate an underlying tumor.
2. The woman raises her hands above her head, and the examiner inspects the sides and underneath portions of the breast for asymmetry or differences in color.
3. The woman places her hands on her hips and presses down; this action reveals skin dimpling or masses.

Palpation

1. With the woman in an upright position and while the arm is at the side and relaxed, each axilla is carefully palpated for enlarged or tender lymph nodes.
2. The woman lies in a supine position for palpation of the breasts. A small pillow or folded towel is placed under the shoulder to flatten the breast. The examiner uses the flat part of the first three fingers to palpate the breast, rotating the fingers against the chest wall. Tissue that extends into the axilla, the so-called tail of Spence, should also be palpated.

The procedure is repeated on the opposite side. Normal breast tissue is sometimes described as feeling like "lumpy oatmeal." Abnormal breast tissue is often likened to a raisin, watermelon seed, or a grape and requires further evaluation.

3. The nipples are compressed to detect the presence of discharge. If a suspicious area is found, follow-up by mammography is recommended.

MAMMOGRAPHY

Mammography is a vital tool in early detection of breast cancer. It can detect breast lumps long before they are large enough to be palpated. This allows early diagnosis and treatment and thus increases the chance of long-term survival. Table 32–2 lists the American Cancer Society guidelines for breast cancer detection. Women at high risk for breast cancer (see p. 933 for a summary of risk factors) may need earlier or more frequent evaluation.

The success of mammography depends on the equipment and the skill of the technologist performing the test. It is important that mammograms be performed in a facility that has been certified by the American College of Radiology. This ensures that the facility, staff, and equipment meet quality control standards. If the facility is not certified, women should be encouraged to ask the following questions (Morra and Blumberg, 1991):

1. Is the mammography unit dedicated? That is, is the machine used only for mammograms and not for any other type of x-ray? Women should select a dedicated unit, which provides more accurate information.

2. How many rads will each breast receive for two pictures? Newer machines emit considerably less than ½ rad per two pictures per breast. Selecting such a unit protects women from unnecessary exposure to x-rays.

3. Are specifically trained people performing and interpreting the test? Women should choose a unit where specially trained technologists perform the examination and where radiologists who read many mammograms each week interpret them.

4. Is there an ongoing quality assurance program that ensures the safest and most reliable screening methods and interpretation of results?

Despite the known value of mammography, many women have never had a mammogram. Reasons for this include expense, fear that x-ray exposure will cause cancer, fear of pain, and reluctance to learn that a problem exists.

Nurses provide information and reassurance whenever possible and, in this way, help the woman overcome her objections to the use of this valuable screening tool. Although mammography is relatively expensive, it is often covered by health insurance, and screening mammograms are frequently offered by the community at low cost. Knowledge that the risk of mammography is minimal to non-existent, because very-low-dose exposure to x-rays is used, may help women to overcome some of their fear. It is important to acknowledge that there is some discomfort when the breast is compressed between two x-ray films. Measures that reduce discomfort include scheduling the mammography following a menstrual period, when the breasts are less tender.

Table 32–2. GUIDELINES FOR SCREENING TESTS FOR BREAST CANCER

Breast Self-Examination	Age 20 and over: monthly
Professional examination	Age 20–39: every 3 years Age 40 and over: annually
Mammography	Age 35–39: baseline Age 40–49: every 1–2 years Age 50 and over: annually

Data from American Cancer Society. (1988). *Breast self-examination: A new approach.* Atlanta.

VULVAR SELF-EXAMINATION

Vulvar self-examination (VSE) should be performed monthly by all women over the age of 18 and by those under age 18 who are sexually active to detect signs of precancerous conditions or infections. VSE is visual inspection and palpation of the female external genitalia.

The woman is instructed to sit in a well-lighted area and to use a hand-held mirror to see the external genitalia. She is taught to examine the vulva in a systematic manner, starting at the mons pubis and then progressing to the clitoris, labia minora, labia majora, perineum, and anus. Palpation of the vulvar area should accompany visual inspection. New moles, warts or growths of any kind, ulcers, sores, changes in skin color, or areas of inflammation or itching should be reported to the woman's health care provider as soon as possible (Lawhead, 1990).

PELVIC EXAMINATION

Pelvic examination is scheduled between menstrual periods, and the woman is advised not to douche or have sexual intercourse for at least 48 hours prior to the examination (Rubin and Lauver, 1990). She is also advised not to use vaginal medications, sprays, or deodorants, which might interfere with interpretation of cytology specimens that are collected.

Before the pelvic examination is begun, the woman empties her bladder and the procedure is carefully explained. Although pelvic examinations are relatively painless, most women dread them and welcome sensitive, considerate support.

The pelvic examination is carried out with the client in a lithotomy position, with a pillow under her head. If she wishes, she may be placed in a semisitting position and offered a hand mirror so that she can observe the external genitalia and the examination. She is carefully draped so that only the parts being examined are exposed.

Necessary equipment to be assembled before the examination begins includes gloves, speculum, Pap smear slide, cotton swabs, and cytobrush and spatula for obtaining material for the Pap smear. A stool specimen may be obtained by the examiner during the rectal examination, and a slide for this specimen should also be available.

External Organs. The pelvic examination is conducted systematically and gently. The external organs are scrutinized for the degree of development or atrophy of the labia, the distribution of hair, and the character of the hymen. Any cysts, tumors, or inflammation of Bartholin's glands are noted. The urinary meatus and Skene's glands are inspected for purulent discharge. Perineal scarring resulting from childbirth is noted.

Speculum Examination. The vagina and cervix are inspected with an appropriately sized bivalve speculum. The speculum is warmed with tap water, and no other lubrication is used because it interferes with accurate Pap smear results. The size, shape, and color of the cervix are noted. A sample of any unusual discharge is obtained for culture.

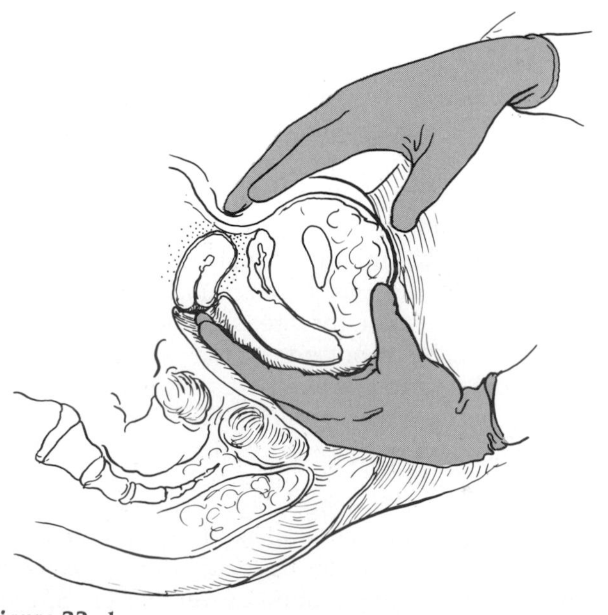

***Figure* 32–1**

Bimanual palpation provides information about the uterus, fallopian tubes, and ovaries.

Bimanual Examination. The bimanual examination provides information about the uterus, fallopian tubes, and ovaries. The labia are separated, and the gloved, lubricated index finger and middle finger of the examiner's non-dominant hand are inserted into the vaginal introitus.

The cervix is palpated for consistency, size, and tenderness to motion. The uterus is evaluated by placing the dominant hand flat on the abdomen with the fingers pressing gently just above the symphysis pubis so that the uterus can be felt between the examining fingers of both hands. The size, configuration, consistency, and motility of the uterus are evaluated (Fig. 32–1).

It is usually impossible to feel the fallopian tubes; however, the ovaries may be palpated between the fingers of both hands. Because ovaries atrophy following menopause, it is often impossible to palpate the ovaries of a postmenopausal woman.

THE PAPANICOLAOU TEST

Purpose

The Papanicolaou test (Pap smear) is a useful tool to detect precancerous and cancerous cells that may be shed by the cervix. It is less effective in detecting endometrial cancer. Cervical intraepithelial neoplasia (CIN) refers specifically to precancerous cellular development in the cervix. 

Procedure

With the speculum blades open and the cervix in view, samples of the superficial layers of the cervix and endocervix are obtained. Samples are best obtained with moistened cotton swabs, a spatula, or a cytobrush.

The cytobrush may cause bleeding, and it is used after other methods of sampling have been completed. Because of the potential to cause bleeding, the cytobrush is avoided during pregnancy. Most CIN lesions develop at the squamocolumnar junction (the border where developing squamous tissue meets the immature columnar epithelium). The cytobrush is most effective in obtaining an adequate specimen from this site, particularly in postmenopausal women, in whom the squamocolumnar junction recedes into the endocervix.

The material is placed on slides that are then either sprayed with or immersed in a fixative solution before being sent to the laboratory for analysis.

Classification of Cervical Cytology

The Bethesda system has replaced the previous numerical Papanicolaou class designation of cervical cytology (Solomon, 1989). In addition to eliminating the Papanicolaou class designation, the Bethesda system is also used to evaluate the specimen for adequacy and involves the use of descriptive terms to improve communication between the pathologist and the physician or nurse practitioner who performed the test.

The terminology for squamous epithelial lesions includes the following categories: (1) atypical squamous cells of undetermined significance; (2) squamous intraepithelial lesion (SIL), which is subdivided into low-grade SIL, mild, moderate, and severe dysplasia, or carcinoma in situ; and (3) squamous cell carcinoma.

RECTAL EXAMINATION

The anus is inspected for hemorrhoids, inflammation, or lesions. The lubricated index finger is gently inserted, and sphincter tone is noted. A slide may be prepared to test for the presence of occult blood in stool that may be present.

Fecal Occult Blood Testing

Screening for colorectal cancer should be part of every physical examination. Digital rectal examination detects less than 10 per cent of colorectal cancers and therefore is not a sufficient screening examination and should be combined with fecal occult blood testing (FOBT) (Rosen, 1990).

Special instructions are necessary to prevent false test results when materials for FOBT are sent home with the woman. She should be instructed to:

- Avoid vitamin C, acetylsalicylic acid, and nonsteroid anti-inflammatory drugs such as ibuprofen or naproxen for at least 48 hours prior to collecting the specimen
- Avoid red meat, turnips, beets, and horseradish for 48 hours before testing
- Collect a specimen from three consecutive stools
- Return slides as directed within 4 to 6 days after the specimens are collected

LABORATORY SCREENING TESTS

△ Additional laboratory tests depend on the history and risk assessment of the woman and might include:

- Testing for STDs, such as chlamydial infection, gonorrhea, syphilis, or HIV
- Testing for rubella antibodies to determine if the woman is immune; this is particularly important in the childbearing years
- Cholesterol testing of postmenopausal women, who do not have the protection that estrogen offers to prevent coronary heart disease
- A urinalysis, which is almost always done, to detect signs of infection in the urinary tract
- A thyroid function test, which may be indicated if the woman exhibits signs of thyroid dysfunction, such as heart palpitations or heat intolerance
- A serum test for CA 125, a tumor marker that may be elevated with ovarian cancer
- Transvaginal ultrasound, which may be recommended for women who are at increased risk for malignant disorders of the reproductive tract (see p. 949)

✔ Check Your Reading

3. What are the three screening procedures for cancer of the breast?
4. What is a Pap test, and why is it performed?
5. Why is fecal occult blood testing important?

Benign Disorders of the Breast

There are four relatively common benign disorders of the breast. The risk for each disorder is related to a specific age.

Fibroadenoma

Fibroadenomas are the most common benign tumors of the breast, and although they may occur at any age, they are most common during the teenage years and the twenties. Fibroadenomas are composed of both fibrous and glandular tissue; that is, they are felt as firm, hard, freely mobile nodules. They may or may not be tender when palpated. Fibroadenomas do not change during the menstrual cycle. They are generally located in the upper, outer quadrant of the breast, and it is not unusual for more than one to be present.

Treatment may involve careful observation for a few months, or the tumor may be excised and the specimen analyzed to rule out malignancy.

Fibrocystic Breast Changes

Fibrocystic breast changes, also called mammary dysplasia or chronic cystic disease, is the most common breast disorder in women between 30 and 50 years of age. Fibrosis, or thickening of the normal breast tissue, occurs in the early stages, whereas cysts form in the latter stages and are felt as multiple, smooth, well-delineated nodules that are usually tender and painful.

Discomfort is sometimes associated with the menstrual cycle and may be the result of a decrease in the production of progesterone or a relative increase in estrogen. Patients with fibrocystic breast changes improve dramatically during pregnancy and lactation because of the large amounts of progesterone produced. Generally, symptoms are more acute premenstrually and improve after menstruation.

Fibrocystic breast changes are not a disease but represent the way a woman's breasts respond to normal monthly hormonal fluctuation. These changes are not generally associated with an increased risk of breast cancer unless atypical cells are present (Morra and Blumberg, 1991). Needle aspiration biopsy may be performed to study cells in the aspirate. Open biopsy is mandatory if the fluid is bloody or if there is a residual mass following aspiration.

Medical treatment is rare because side effects of the drugs may be more distressing than the breast discomfort. If drugs are administered, they may include progesterone or tamoxifen (an antiestrogen) if an estrogen-progesterone imbalance is suspected to be the cause and if symptoms are severe. Bromocriptine (Parlodel), which inhibits the secretion of prolactin, may relieve breast discomfort. In severe cases, danazol (Danocrine), which suppresses gonadotropins and inhibits estrogen production, may be administered (Hacker, 1992).

Although it is controversial whether caffeine contributes to the development of fibrocystic breast changes, some physicians recommend limiting consumption of tea, coffee, colas, and chocolate. Some women also benefit from restricting sodium intake to reduce fluid retention the week before menstruation starts, when symptoms are often most acute.

Mastectomy is sometimes discussed if the fibrocystic breast changes are severe and if the patient is at increased risk of breast cancer because of family history or a previous episode of cancer of the reproductive system. This is a difficult decision for the woman, and she requires the opinion of at least two qualified physicians.

Ductal Ectasia

Ductal ectasia generally occurs as the woman approaches menopause. It is characterized by dilation of the collecting ducts, which become distended and filled with cellular debris. This initiates an inflammatory process that results in (1) a mass that feels firm and irregular, (2) enlarged axillary nodes, and (3) nipple retraction and discharge. These symptoms are similar to those of breast cancer, and accurate diagnosis is vital.

Once a surgical biopsy confirms that the condition is benign mammary duct ectasia, no further treatment is necessary.

Intraductal Papilloma

Intraductal papilloma develops most often just prior to or during menopause. It occurs when papillomas (small elevations or protuberances) develop in the epithelium of the ducts of the breasts. As the papilloma grows, it causes trauma and erosion within the ducts that result in serous or serosanguineous discharge from the nipple.

Treatment consists of excision of the mass and ductal area, plus analysis of nipple discharge to rule out a malignant tumor.

Diagnosis of Disorders of the Breast

When a lesion or lump is discovered in the breast, the physician must determine if it is benign or malignant. *Ultrasound* examination can be used to differentiate fluid-filled cysts from solid tissue that is potentially malignant. *Needle aspiration biopsy* can be performed to remove fluid from suspected cysts for analysis of the cells. *Surgical biopsy* is performed under these conditions (Hacker, 1992):

- If a suspicious mass persists throughout a menstrual cycle
- If the cystic mass does not collapse completely when needle aspiration is performed
- If the aspirate contains bloody fluid
- If serosanguineous nipple discharge is present
- If there are suspicious mammographic abnormalities.

Nursing Considerations

The discovery of any breast disorder creates great anxiety, and each woman responds to anxiety in a unique manner. Some women are relieved to learn that 90 per cent of all breast disorders are benign, but for some this information does not relieve their fear.

The nurse should explain the diagnostic procedures that are planned, such as ultrasound examination, mammography, needle biopsy, or surgical biopsy. The nurse acknowledges the woman's anxiety, as well as that her apprehension will continue while she awaits a final diagnosis. Nurses are uniquely qualified to help the woman express her concerns by focusing on the feelings that are expressed verbally or that are exhibited non-verbally.

✔ Check Your Reading

6. How are fibrocystic breast changes treated?
7. What three diagnostic procedures are used to determine if a breast disorder is benign or malignant?

Malignant Tumors of the Breast

Incidence

The incidence of breast cancer in the United States is staggering. It occurs in one in nine women, and it is second only to lung cancer as a cause of death from cancer among women. In 1991, 44,800 women died from the disease (American Cancer Society, 1991).

The incidence of breast cancer is approximately five times higher in the United States and northern Europe than in Asia and many African countries (Hacker, 1992). Possible reasons for the high incidence in these areas—high per capita consumption of dietary fat and smoking—are being studied.

Risk Factors

Although the actual cause of breast cancer remains unknown, several factors are known to increase the risk that breast cancer will develop (Table 32–3). The most significant risk factors for breast cancer are:

- *Gender*. The American Cancer society reports that of the 175,900 cases of breast cancer diagnosed in 1991, 175,000 were in women. Thus, being a woman is a significant risk factor.

Table 32–3. RISK FACTORS FOR BREAST CANCER

Female
Age over 50 years
History of breast cancer
Family history (grandmother, mother, sister, aunt)
Previous uterine, ovarian, or colon cancer
Nulliparity and first pregnancy after 30 years
Early menarche (< 12 years), late menopause (> 50 years)
Lifestyle factors: high intake of dietary fat, excessive consumption of alcohol, smoking

- *Age*. The risk of developing the disease is significantly increased after the age of 50 years.
- *Prior history*. A history of breast cancer is another factor increasing the risk of developing the disease.

Other factors that are believed to increase the risk of breast cancer include a family history of breast cancer as well as cancer of other organs, such as the uterus, ovaries, and colon.

Although risk factors are important, it is essential to understand that breast cancer develops in many women who do not fit into any high-risk category. Therefore, it is important that all women, not only those at "high risk," take advantage of all available screening procedures.

Pathophysiology

The most common type of breast cancer is infiltrating ductal carcinoma, which originates in the epithelium lining the mammary ducts. The rate of growth varies, but it is estimated to take from 5 to 9 years for the lesion to be large enough to be palpable. As long as the cancer remains in the duct, it is considered to be non-invasive. When it penetrates the duct into surrounding tissue, it is classified as invasive. Growth occurs in irregular patterns and invades the lymphatic channels, which eventually causes lymphatic edema and the dimpling of the skin that resembles an orange peel (peau d'orange).

Cancer cells are carried by the lymph channels to the lymph nodes, and metastasis occurs when the cells are spread by both blood and lymph systems. The most common sites of metastasis are the lungs, liver, bones, adrenal glands, and skin (Dow, 1991).

Staging

Although confirmation of malignancy is the first step in evaluating the client with cancer, staging is necessary to understand the severity of the cancer. Staging is generally based on the TNM (tumor, node, metastasis) system used to describe the cancer's anatomical extent. Stages of breast cancer progress from Stage 1, indicating a small tumor without lymphatic involvement or metastases, to Stage 4 that indicates spread to lymph nodes and metastases to other organs. The stages are often used to determine treatment, and they are useful guides as to prognosis. The type of cancer cell, the presence of hormone receptors, and the proliferative rate of the breast cancer cells are also important factors in the rate of recurrence.

Management

SURGICAL TREATMENT

Surgical treatment is recommended as soon as cancer is confirmed. The type of surgery depends on the type, stage, and location of the disease. The most common surgeries are:

- *Lumpectomy*, for removal of the lesion, usually with partial removal of the axillary lymph nodes for staging purposes
- *Simple mastectomy*, for removal of the lesion plus surrounding breast tissue; axillary lymph nodes are removed for staging purposes
- *Modified radical mastectomy*, for removal of breast tissue, axillary nodes, and some chest muscles; however, the pectoralis major muscles are preserved
- *Radical mastectomy*, for removal of all pectoral muscles; this surgery is less common

Breast reconstruction has been an integral part of the treatment of breast cancer, and an explanation of when the reconstruction is planned as well a description of the procedure should be discussed with the client prior to surgical treatment.

At present, reconstruction is complicated by controversy about the safety of silicone implants. Alternatives include saline implants and reconstruction using tissue from abdomen, hips, and thighs without relying on artificial implants.

ADJUVANT THERAPY

Adjuvant therapy is supportive or additional therapy that may be recommended following the surgical procedure. Radiation, chemotherapy, or hormonal therapy are adjuvant therapies that are currently recommended. The decision whether to use adjuvant therapy is based on the woman's age, the stage of the disease, the woman's preference, and the hormone receptor status of the lesion.

Radiation and chemotherapy are known to improve the chance of long-term survival, and one or the other may be recommended following surgical excision of the tumor. Because some tumors are estrogen-receptive, meaning that their growth is stimulated by estrogen, estrogen-blocking medications are administered. Tamoxifen is currently the hormonal therapy most recommended. Tamoxifen blocks estrogen by binding to estrogen receptors, thereby suppressing tumor growth by reducing the effects of estrogen. Side effects of tamoxifen include hot flashes, vaginal dryness or increased vaginal discharge, nausea, anorexia, and peripheral edema. Some women also experience depression, dizziness, and insomnia (Karb et al, 1989; Deglin and Vallerand, 1993). The side effects should be discussed with the client before tamoxifen is administered.

Psychosocial Consequences of Breast Cancer

The time from discovery to treatment of breast cancer is the most stressful time for many women. Factors that contribute to presurgery distress include a sense of uncertainty, inadequate information, the need to make difficult treatment decisions, and scheduling problems (Wainstock, 1991). Treatment usually involves consultations with at least one or more specialists, including a surgeron, a radiotherapist, a plastic surgeon, and a medical oncologist. Scheduling difficulties may create frustration that is compounded if conflicting opinions about primary treatment are presented.

Concerns frequently expressed during treatment for breast cancer include fear of death, uncertainty about the quality of life, changes in body image, the effect on sexuality, and side effects of recommended therapy.

Breast cancer can have psychological consequences not only for women but also for their husbands, significant others, and other family members. Among the difficulties reported by family members are sleep disturbances, eating disorders, and problems with work responsibilities (Northouse et al, 1991). Breast cancer can create strain on the marital relationship, primarily in the areas of sexual relations and communication about matters related to the illness. Women and their partners sometimes differ in regard to how much they want to discuss the illness. Some women have a great need to discuss their diagnosis, treatment, and fears of recurrence. Other women and many men view discussion of such fears as negative thinking that delays adjustment.

Nursing Considerations

The woman who is diagnosed with breast cancer depends on nurses for emotional support and accurate information. Allow time for the woman to express her feelings, and convey a sense of empathetic understanding by quiet presence, touch, and close attention to the woman's concerns. Many women feel that they have lost control and that their lives have been taken over by cancer and the recommended treatment. Some women are concerned about how the surgery will affect their relationship with a spouse or sexual partner. Allow each woman to express her fears and worries. In addition to providing time and demonstrating genuine interest in the woman's concerns, use communication techniques such as clarifying, paraphrasing, and reflecting feelings so that the woman can participate in decisions about her care.

The anxiety that most women experience is reduced when procedures and care are clearly understood. Preoperative teaching is often part of the nurse's responsiblity, and husbands and significant others should be included as much as possible in the teaching. Many women are relieved to learn that the hospital stay is short following mastectomy, and they may be relieved by knowing exactly what to expect. For instance, a pressure dressing may be applied over the wound to prevent further bleeding after surgery. Drainage tubes may be attached to portable suction apparatus (Hemovac) to prevent accumulation of fluid under the skin flaps. The incision may appear red and raised for the first few weeks. Edema of the arm on the same side as the mastectomy is possible, and specific exercises such as armlifts and pulley exercises may be necessary.

Discharge teaching focuses on the need for follow-up care and treatment. Some areas of concern include how to minimize the risk of wound infection, side effects of adjuvant therapy, and signs and symptoms that should be reported to the physician. Most women also benefit from information about such groups as Reach to Recovery and Encore, which provide support, information, and guidance following mastectomy.

✔ Check Your Reading

8. What are the major risk factors for breast cancer?
9. Why is staging for breast cancer important?
10. What is meant by adjuvant therapy, and why is it used?

Menstrual Cycle Disorders

Nurses are frequently asked about the four most common menstrual cycle disorders: (1) absence of menses (amenorrhea), (2) abnormal uterine bleeding, (3) pain associated with the menstrual cycle, and (4) cyclic mood changes, including premenstrual syndrome. Although most of the disorders are benign, all require comprehensive gynecological assessment. Nurses must be knowledgeable about underlying processes, diagnostic procedures, and expected treatment in order to fulfill the basic core of nursing activities, which includes client advocacy, education, and supportive counseling.

Amenorrhea

Amenorrhea is a symptom that can indicate either normal physiological processes or pathology in the reproductive system. Amenorrhea before menarche, during pregnancy, during the puerperium and lactation, and following menopause is normal. Amenorrhea at other times is abnormal, and it is called either primary or secondary amenorrhea, depending on when it occurs.

PRIMARY AMENORRHEA

Primary amenorrhea is the term used when menstruation fails to occur at puberty, or by the age of 16 years (Doody and Carr, 1990). This may be due to a variety of causes, including hormonal imbalances, congenital anomalies of the uterus or ovaries, chromosomal defects, systemic disease, or hypothalamic-pituitary abnormalities that result in inadequate secretion of gonadotropins. It may also be due to excessive exercise or eating disorders.

The condition causes a great deal of concern for the young woman and her family. Amenorrhea is a symptom, not a diagnosis, and they may worry that it indicates a serious disease. Moreover, menstruation is a unique function of women, and absence of menstruation may provoke concerns about femininity and the ability to have children. Concern increases if medical treatment is not successful.

The success of medical management depends on the cause. Counseling for eating disorders, such as anorexia nervosa, and reducing excessive exercise may prove helpful. Hormonal therapy may establish normal menses if the cause is hormonal imbalance; however, some conditions cannot be successfully treated. For example, if the cause is reproductive tract or congenital anomalies, normal menses and fertility may not be possible, and psychological support becomes the most important therapy.

SECONDARY AMENORRHEA

Secondary amenorrhea describes cessation of menstruation for a period of more than 6 months in a woman who has established a pattern of menstruation. It may be due to a variety of causes, including systemic diseases such as diabetes mellitus, tuberculosis, or hypothyroidism. Hormonal imbalances, strenuous aerobic exercise, poor nutrition, use of oral contraceptives, and ovarian tumors may also be the cause.

Assessment includes a thorough medical and obstetrical history, as well as questions about eating habits, history of dieting, and current exercise pattern. Women are also questioned about their uses of drugs, such as oral contraceptives, phenothiazines, and antihypertensives, which can cause secondary amenorrhea.

Medical treatment aims at identifying and correcting the underlying cause. Pregnancy testing is mandatory for any sexually active woman, and medications that are potentially teratogenic must be withheld until pregnancy is ruled out. Hormonal replacement therapy, ovulation stimulation, and periodic progesterone withdrawal often result in menstruation.

Abnormal Uterine Bleeding

Menstruation is considered normal when bleeding occurs every 21 to 35 days and lasts for 1 to 5 days (Kletzky, 1992). Although 75 per cent of abnormal bleeding in adult women results from non-organic causes, abnormal vaginal bleeding may be due to serious physical problems that must be investigated before a diagnosis can be made (Murata, 1990). The different types of abnormal bleeding are defined in Table 32–4.

ETIOLOGY

Abnormal vaginal bleeding may be due to a variety of causes, including systemic diseases such as thyroid dysfunction or diabetes mellitus, uterine myomas (fibroids), cervical polyps, genital infections, and cancer of the uterus or cervix. In addition, an imbalance in prostaglandins that initiate vasoconstriction and in those that cause vasodilation may result in abnormal bleeding at the time of menses.

Postmenopausal bleeding may be planned or unplanned. Planned postmenopausal bleeding occurs when the woman who takes estrogen and progesterone stops taking the drugs, usually once a month. This allows the uterine lining to be sloughed and prevents endometrial hyperplasia. Planned bleeding is generally not a cause for concern; however, unplanned postmenopausal bleeding should always be investigated as soon as possible because it is highly suggestive of endometrial cancer.

Table 32–4. TYPES OF ABNORMAL UTERINE BLEEDING

Menorrhagia. Excessive bleeding at the time of a menstrual period.

Metrorrhagia. Bleeding from the uterus between menstrual cycles.

Menometrorrhagia. Uterine bleeding that is irregular in frequency and also excessive in amount.

Postmenopausal bleeding. Any vaginal bleeding that occurs at least 1 year following cessation of spontaneous menstruation.

Dysfunctional uterine bleeding. Bleeding as a result of anovulation in the absence of any organic disease (Kletzky, 1992). Estrogen, which is secreted in the follicular part of the cycle, stimulates endometrial growth. However, if ovulation does not occur, inadequate progesterone is secreted during the luteal phase of the cycle, resulting in irregular shedding of the endometrium.

MANAGEMENT

Medical treatment for abnormal bleeding depends on the cause. Medications include the use of progestin-estrogen combination oral contraceptives, which suppress ovulation and allow a more stable endometrial lining to form. Non-steroidal anti-inflammatory drugs (NSAIDs) are sometimes used to block prostaglandin formation. Surgical therapy may include dilation and curettage (D & C) to remove polyps or to diagnose endometrial hyperplasia, which may be treated with progesterone. Hysterectomy is often performed if the uterus is enlarged as a result of fibroids or adenomyosis (benign invasive growth of the endometrium into the muscular layer of the uterus) and if the woman no longer wishes to bear children. Laser ablation is a new procedure that is used to permanently remove the endometrial lining.

Prolonged menorrhagia may result in decreased hemoglobin and hematocrit levels, and the woman may need treatment for iron-deficiency anemia.

NURSING CONSIDERATIONS

Although most nurses (with the exception of nurse practitioners) do not diagnose or treat abnormal or dysfunctional bleeding, they are often responsible for encouraging women to seek medical attention promptly when irregular bleeding occurs. Nurses also help the client keep a record of the bleeding episodes and the amount of blood lost. This involves keeping a calendar and noting any vaginal bleeding (spotting, menses) that occurs, as well as the number of pads and tampons saturated each day.

Nurses are also in a unique position to assist the woman to make necessary lifestyle changes. The nurse teaches the importance of adequate nutrition and discourages rigorous dieting. For women who are concerned about amenorrhea, the nurse should explain that, although exercise is beneficial, strenuous workouts or aerobic training can cause amenorrhea. In addition, the nurse teaches methods to reduce stress and promote relaxation. Finally, nurses must provide support for women who fear that irregular bleeding indicates a serious disease, such as cancer. It is unwise to offer false reassurance, but information about diagnostic procedures and expected medical management often reduces anxiety.

✔ Check Your Reading

11. How does primary amenorrhea differ from secondary amenorrhea in terms of onset, cause, and treatment?
12. What are possible causes of abnormal uterine bleeding, and why should it not be ignored?

Pain Associated with the Menstrual Cycle

Pelvic pain associated with the menstrual cycle (cyclic pelvic pain) must be distinguished from acute pelvic pain. Acute pelvic pain is sudden in onset, and it is not experienced with each menstrual cycle. Acute pelvic pain may indicate serious pathology, such as ectopic pregnancy or appendicitis. On the other hand, cyclic pelvic pain occurs repetitively and predictably in a specific phase of the menstrual cycle. The most common causes of cyclic pelvic pain are mittelschmerz, primary dysmenorrhea, and endometriosis.

MITTELSCHMERZ

Mittelschmerz ("middle" pain) refers to pelvic pain that occurs midway between menstrual periods, or at the time of ovulation. The pain is due to (1) growth of the dominant follicle within the ovary or (2) rupture of the follicle and subsequent spillage of follicular fluid and blood into the peritoneal space. The pain is fairly sharp and is felt on the right or left side of the pelvis. It generally lasts from a few hours to 2 days, and slight vaginal bleeding may accompany the discomfort. Generally, women do not need medical treatment beyond simple explanation of the discomfort or mild analgesics.

PRIMARY DYSMENORRHEA

Primary dysmenorrhea refers to menstrual pain without identified pathology. Commonly called "cramps," primary dysmenorrhea affects at least half of all women and causes 5 to 10 per cent to miss work or school (Muse, 1990). The pain begins within hours of the onset of menses, and it is spasmodic or colicky in nature. It is felt in the lower abdomen but often radiates to the lower back or down the legs. Primary dysmenorrhea occurs in ovulatory cycles, and it is most common in young nulliparous women.

One of the most confusing aspects of primary dysmenorrhea has been why it is experienced by some, but not all, women. It is now known that some women produce excessive endometrial prostaglandin during the late luteal phase of the menstrual cycle. The prostaglandins (particularly E_2 and $F_{2\alpha}$) diffuse into endometrial tissue and cause abnormal uterine muscle contractions, uterine ischemia, and hypoxia. This process accounts for the cramp-like uterine pain, as well as symptoms that often accompany it, such as diarrhea, nausea, and vomiting.

There are two recommended treatments of primary dysmenorrhea that provide marked relief: oral contraceptives and prostaglandin inhibitors. Oral contraceptives decrease the amount of endometrial growth that occurs during the menstrual cycle and thus reduce the production of endometrial prostaglandin. For women who do not wish to take oral contraceptives, prostaglandin inhibitors also offer relief. The most effective prostaglandin inhibitors include ibuprofen (Motrin, Advil) and naproxen (Naprosyn). To be effective, these must be taken before menses and the onset of cramps.

ENDOMETRIOSIS

Pathophysiology

Endometriosis refers to the presence of endometrial tissue outside the uterine cavity. The response of this tissue to the stimulation of estrogen and progesterone during the menstrual cycle is identical to that of the endometrium; that is, it grows and proliferates during the follicular and luteal phases of the cycle and then sloughs during menstruation. The menstruation from endometriosis lesions, however, occurs in a closed cavity, which causes pressure and pain on adjacent tissue. In addition, prostaglandins secreted by the endometriosis lesions irritate nerve endings and stimulate uterine contractions that further increase pain. Moreover, cyclic bleeding into the pelvic cavity initiates chronic inflammatory changes that may make conception and implantation difficult. The most common sites of endometriosis lesions are illustrated in Figure 32–2.

Although endometriosis occurs in 10 to 15 per cent of all women, the cause remains unknown (Metzger and Haney, 1989). One theory is that menstrual discharge contains viable endometrial cells that can attach to sites outside the uterus, where they grow and produce patches of endometrial tissue. It is possible that the endometrial cells are disseminated primarily by retrograde menstruation, that is, reflux of menstrual flow through the fallopian tubes. The cells attach to nearby structures and proliferate, creating spots of endometrial tissue.

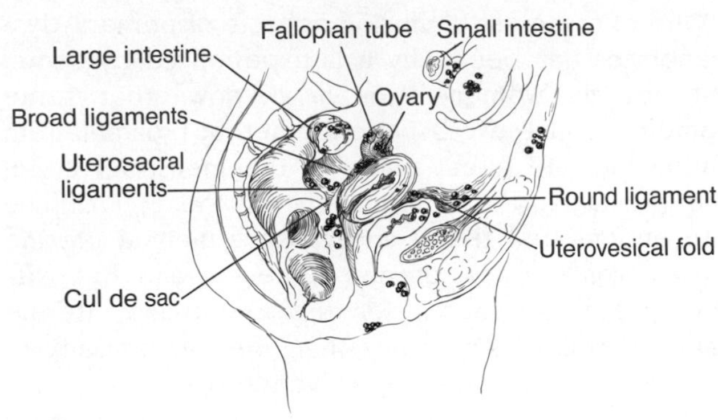

***Figure* 32–2**

Common sites of endometriosis.

Signs and Symptoms

The two major symptoms of endometriosis are pain and infertility. The pain of endometriosis differs from that of primary dysmenorrhea. Endometriosis pain is deep, unilateral or bilateral, and either sharp or dull. It is constant as opposed to the spasmodic or colicky pain of primary dysmenorrhea. Dyspareunia (painful intercourse) is typical, particularly with deep penetration. Rectal pain is common, especially during defecation. Diarrhea, constipation, and sensations of rectal pressure or urgency are other symptoms of endometriosis. Although the cause of infertility is not completely understood, pelvic adhesions and tubal pathology due to chronic inflammatory changes are certainly contributing factors.

Management

Treatment may be either medical or surgical, and the therapy chosen must weigh the need for relief of pain and the desire to maintain fertility against the side effects that accompany many treatment regimens. Because growth of endometriosis depends on the production of ovarian hormones (estrogen and progesterone) during the menstrual cycle, medical therapy is aimed at interrupting the menstrual cycle, thus leaving the woman in a state of "pseudomenopause." As a result, she experiences symptoms associated with estrogen deficit, such as hot flashes and vaginal dryness. Moreover, she is at increased risk for postmenopausal conditions, such as adverse serum lipid changes and osteoporosis (see menopause, p. 940).

Currently, danazol and analogues of gonadotropin-releasing hormone (GnRH) are the drugs of choice. Danazol is an androgen derivative that has been used for many years; GnRH agonists, such as leuprolide acetate (Lupron), are newer. Both drugs interfere with production of gonadotropins (follicle-stimulating hormone and luteinizing hormone) and thus stop the menstrual cycle, creating a "pseudomenopause." In addition, danazol often produces masculinizing effects, such as deepening of the voice, facial and body hair, and weight gain.

Pregnancy also interrupts menstruation, and if the woman wishes to conceive, she may be advised not to delay conception. If pregnancy is not an immediate option, continuous non-cyclic oral contraceptives are sometimes recommended, although the effectiveness in treating symptoms of endometriosis is not well documented.

Surgical treatment can take many forms. For the older woman with severe pain who no longer wishes to have children, a hysterectomy with bilateral salpingo-oophorectomy (removal of the uterus, both fallopian tubes, and both ovaries) and excision of all lesions offers the greatest chance for cure. This surgery results in early menopause with permanent estrogen deficit. Postoperative hormonal replacement therapy may be recommended if all lesions are removed. More conservative surgery includes laparoscopy for lysis of adhesions and laser vaporization of endometriosis lesions.

NURSING CONSIDERATIONS

Dysmenorrhea varies from mild "menstrual awareness" to incapacitating pain that affects the quality of life for many days out of each month. Too often the pain is belittled ("It's just cramps"). One of the most important nursing actions is to acknowledge the pain: "I understand this is really uncomfortable, and you are concerned that you have this much pain every month."

Women should be instructed in non-pharmacological measures to relieve pain, such as frequent rest periods, application of heat to the lower abdomen, moderate exercise, and a well-balanced diet. They should also be advised to schedule stress-provoking situations when they will not coincide with the menstrual period. NSAIDs provide relief for some women; they should be taken with meals to reduce gastrointestinal irritation. The woman should be counseled to report unusual side effects, such as headache, dizziness, or unusual fluid retention, to the physician or nurse practitioner.

Side effects of GnRh agonists depend on the degree of ovarian suppression and may include hot flashes, vaginal dryness, mood swings, bone loss, and irregular bleeding (Schmidt, 1991). Side effects of androgens may also include decreased libido, headache, dizziness, and irritability (Deglin and Vallerand, 1993). Time must be allowed for the woman to express her concerns about the therapy, and she should be instructed to use a form of contraception other than oral contraceptives during therapy. Some women benefit from information about measures that promote sleep and relaxation, and, most importantly, from the knowledge that someone is available to provide support and guidance when needed.

✔ Check Your Reading

13. What causes primary dysmenorrhea, and how may it be treated?
14. How does endometriosis cause dysmenorrhea, and how can it be treated?

Premenstrual Syndrome

Although millions of women experience some of the signs and symptoms of premenstrual syndrome (PMS), the following criteria must be met for the condition to be diagnosed as PMS:

- The signs and symptoms must be cyclical and recur in the luteal phase (after ovulation) of the menstrual cycle.
- The woman should be symptom-free during the follicular phase (prior to ovulation) of the menstrual cycle, and there must be at least 7 symptom-free days in the cycle.
- Symptoms must be severe enough to alter the lifestyle of the woman significantly.
- Diagnosis must be based solely on *prospective* symptom charting by the woman; that is, charting of symptoms as they occur rather than recall of symptoms that occurred in the past. There is no substitute for this time-consuming method (Chihal, 1990).

Several types of PMS diaries are available for symptom charting. Figure 32–3 illustrates one type of calendar or diary on which the woman records the symptoms that she experiences and the severity of the symptoms.

In general, women with PMS fall into one of three categories: those who experience (1) both physical and psychological symptoms, (2) predominantly psychological symptoms, or (3) predominantly physical symptoms. The most frequently reported symptoms have been classified as "tension states," such as anxiety, nervousness, irritability, frustration, agitation, and argumentativeness (Chihal, 1990). Table 32–5 lists the most common symptoms in approximate order of occurrence.

Calendar for PMS Symptoms

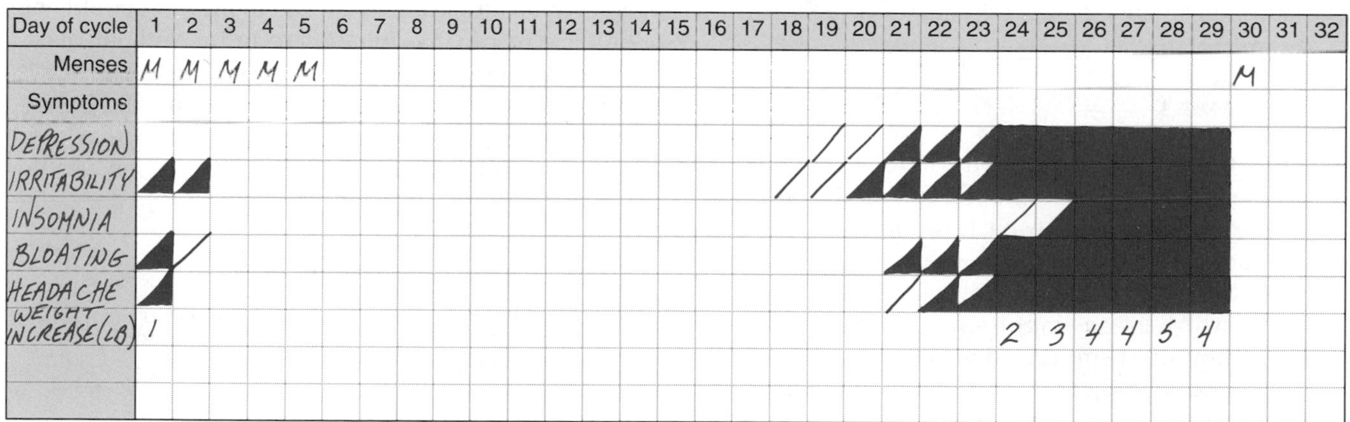

Name____________________
Month/year____________________

Severity of symptoms

- None
- Mild
- Moderate
- Severe

Figure 32–3

The woman uses a diary to record occurrence and severity of premenstrual symptoms.

Table 32–5. SYMPTOMS OF PREMENSTRUAL SYNDROME (PMS)

Physical Symptoms	Psychological Symptoms
Edema	Anxiety
Weight gain	Depression
Abdominal bloating	Irritabilty
Constipation	Mood swings
Hot flashes	Aggressive behavior
Breast pain	Increased appetite
Headache	Food cravings
Acne	Fatigue
Rhinitis	Inability to concentrate
Heart palpitations	Insomnia

ETIOLOGY

The cause of PMS is unknown, although well-known theories include (1) an imbalance between estrogen and progesterone, (2) low levels of β-endorphins, (3) abnormal production of prostaglandins, and (4) nutritional deficiency.

IMPACT ON FAMILY

Because symptoms recur every month, health care professionals must view PMS as a chronic disease that affects the functioning of the entire family (Lindow, 1991). Clinical descriptions of severe family disruptions include increased family conflict, disrupted communication, and decreased family cohesion. Of particular concern is the group of women who report symptoms of loss of control, child battering, self-injury, and increased accidents.

MANAGEMENT

Because the cause is unknown, there is no definitive treatment for PMS. Instead, treatment is based on the symptom profile of each woman. Mild potassium-sparing diuretics may be prescribed for women with fluid retention and weight gain. Vitamin B_6 (pyridoxine), which is an important co-factor in the synthesis of neurotransmitters that influence mood, may be prescribed. Progesterone supplementation is occasionally used, with reported improvement in hot flashes, peripheral edema, and abdominal bloating. Progesterone is less effective therapy for emotional symptoms such as depression and anxiety. Antianxiety medications are usually reserved for severe anxiety that does not respond to other therapy. Some studies indicate that oral administration of magnesium reduces premenstrual mood changes (Facchinetti, et al, 1991).

Nursing Considerations

Although the diagnosis of PMS is based on specific criteria, many women experience some of the symptoms and diagnose themselves. Discourage this practice because serious systemic disease can be missed if the criteria for diagnosis are ignored.

Once the diagnosis of PMS is confirmed, educate the family about lifestyle changes that are known to alleviate some symptoms of PMS and decrease the severity of others. (See Women Want to Know: How to Relieve Symptoms of PMS.) Acknowledge that dietary changes are particularly difficult because many women crave salty or sweet foods, which should be restricted. Women also benefit from education about expected cyclic changes. As they learn to predict the pattern of symptoms and gain a sense of control over them the symptoms often diminish.

Expand support and education to include the family. When the woman exhibits symptoms of PMS, family members often respond by withdrawing or confronting the woman. This increases the woman's feelings of anxiety and vulnerability. Help the family acknowledge feelings they believe the woman is experiencing. For instance, saying "It must be disturbing to feel so irritable. What can I do to help?" provokes a different emotional response than confronting or blaming comments. Try to allow family members to express their feelings so that anger and resentment within the family can be diminished.

Help the woman make concrete arrangements to obtain relief when she feels she is losing control or when she fears that she may harm herself or a child. A neighbor, friend, or family member should be identified to provide immediate relief, without questions or explanations, when the woman feels she is losing control. The telephone number of this important support person should be posted so that it is easily accessible, and the designated person should be called before symptoms are severe.

✔ Check Your Reading

15. What are the criteria for diagnosing PMS?
16. What lifestyle changes can be made to reduce the symptoms of PMS?

Menopause

Although "menopause" is commonly used to denote the total syndrome of endocrine, somatic, and psychic changes that occur at the end of the reproductive period, the term simply means the cessation of menstruation. The entire process, frequently called

Women Want To Know
How to Relieve Symptoms of PMS

Diet

- Decrease consumption of caffeine (coffee, tea, colas, chocolate), which increases irritability, insomnia, anxiety, and nervousness.
- Avoid simple sugars (cookies, cake, candy) to prevent abnormal elevations of blood glucose followed by a rapid decline and a period of low blood glucose (hypoglycemia).
- Decrease intake of salty foods (chips, pickles) to reduce fluid retention.
- Drink at least 2000 ml (2 quarts) of *water* per day, and do not include other beverages in this total.
- Eat six small meals a day to prevent hypoglycemia; meals should be well balanced, with emphasis on fresh fruits and vegetables, complex carbohydrates, and non-fat milk products.
- Avoid alcohol, which aggravates depression.

Exercise: Increase physical exercise to relieve tension and to decrease depression. Aerobic activity, such as jogging, fitness walking, or cycling, for at least 30 minutes four times a week is recommended (Chihal, 1990).

Stress Management: During the time when there are no symptoms of PMS, acknowledge the effect of PMS on daily life and make plans to avoid stressful situations during the premenstrual period when symptoms are acute.

Use guided imagery, conscious relaxation techniques, warm baths, and massage to reduce stress.

Sleep and Rest: To reduce fatigue and combat insomnia:

- Adhere to a regular schedule for sleep.
- Drink a glass of milk, which is high in tryptophan and is known to promote sleep, prior to bedtime.
- Schedule exercise in the morning or early afternoon rather than late afternoon.
- Engage in relaxing activities, such as reading, prior to bedtime, and avoid excitement at this time.

the "change of life," is correctly termed the *climacteric*. Premenopause refers to the early part of the climacteric, before menstruation ceases but after the woman experiences some of the climacteric symptoms, such as irregular menses. Perimenopause includes premenopause, menopause, and at least 1 year after menopause. Postmenopause refers to the phase following menopause.

Age of Menopause

In the United States, the average age for naturally occurring menopause is 50 to 51 years, and it generally takes place over 3 to 5 years (Wren, 1992). However, menopause can be induced or created artificially at any age. Surgical removal of the ovaries, or destruction of the ovaries by radiation, creates permanent cessation of ovarian function, including the production of estrogen. The most common reasons for performing these procedures are treatment of gynecological cancer or endometriosis. Young women who experience artificial menopause often have more symptoms associated with menopause than do women who go through the process naturally.

For the first time in history, women can expect to live another 30 years following menopause. It is during this period that they must deal with physical, psychological, and social changes that often require a re-evaluation of their primary roles and restructuring of personal goals.

Physiological Changes

Physiological changes in the reproductive cycle occur as women age. During the normal reproductive cycle, the ovaries respond to gonadotropins (follicle-stimulating hormone and luteinizing hormone) from the anterior pituitary in a predictable pattern: (1) a follicle matures, (2) the ovary secretes estrogen, (3) ovulation occurs, and (4) the corpus luteum produces progesterone. During the premenopausal period, the ovaries are less responsive to gonadotropins, and, although increased amounts of follicle-stimulating hormone are secreted, ovulation is sporadic and menstrual periods are irregular. With progressive aging, the ovaries become unresponsive, even to high levels of gonadotropins, and ovulation, menstruation, and the secretion of ovarian hormones (estrogen and progesterone) cease. Lack of estrogen has a significant effect on the health of women during the postmenopausal years.

Estrogen is responsible for the secondary sex characteristics of women; when estrogen levels decline, the organs of reproduction undergo regression. The labia become thin, pale, and flattened. The vaginal mucosa atrophies and becomes thin and fragile. Vaginal tissue loses its lubrication and is easily traumatized. Dyspareunia is not uncommon, and bacterial invasion of the epithelium may occur and lead to frequent vaginal infections. This entire process is referred to as atrophic vaginitis, which can be alleviated by either topical or systemic estrogen. Breasts become smaller, and there is atrophy of the uterus. However, a concurrent benefit is that uterine myomas (fibroids) and endometriosis lesions also atrophy. Estrogen deficit can also result in atrophic changes in the bladder and urethra that may give rise to loss of urethral tone and frequent atrophic cystitis.

In addition, absence of estrogen is associated with an adverse change in serum lipids. Low-density lipoproteins (LDLs) increase, and high-density lipoproteins (HDLs), which are known to carry cholesterol and to protect against the development of coronary heart disease, decrease.

Most menopausal women experience hot flashes or flushes, which are the result of vasomotor instability. The cause of vasomotor instability is not known; however, it is closely associated with increased secretion of gonadotropins. Hot flashes are characterized by a sudden feeling of heat or burning of the skin, followed by perspiration. They occur more frequently during the night, and fatigue, due to interrupted sleep, is a major problem for some women.

Psychological Responses

It is easy to understand why menopause is called the "change of life." It is accompanied not only by physical but also by psychological and social changes, and individual responses vary widely. Many women are relieved that their childbearing and child-rearing tasks are coming to an end. They look on this as an exciting time, when they can pursue personal development. Other women grieve that the possibility of childbearing is past; this may be particularly true for women who have never had a child. Menopause makes it necessary for women to come to terms with aging. It may be difficult to accept aging in a society that reveres youth, and many women become extremely concerned with measures that will slow the signs of aging. Moreover, many women become grandmothers during the same period, which also confirms aging and requires a major adjustment in how the woman views herself.

Other factors create personal stress at this time. Children leave home to complete their own development; aging parents may require increasing amounts of time and support; a husband may begin to examine his achievements and be dissatisfied with the results. These concurrent events may precipitate dissatisfaction with life during the years following menopause.

The fact that not all symptoms can be explained compounds the problem of providing care. Some symptoms do not have a physiological explanation, but they are no less real to women who experience them. Depression, mood swings, irritability, and agitation are common climacteric complaints. Insomnia and fatigue are frequently mentioned as major problems, even when hot flashes do not interfere with sleep.

One of the most puzzling aspects of menopause is the wide variation in both physical and psychological symptoms that women experience. For some women, the only changes are mild, infrequent hot flashes and amenorrhea. Other women experience severe, debilitating hot flashes, atrophic vaginitis, and multiple psychological symptoms, such as irritability and prolonged depression.

Hormonal Replacement Therapy

Hormonal replacement therapy is used to reduce symptoms of menopause and to protect women against the development of osteoporosis and coronary heart disease. The type of hormonal replacement, either estrogen only or estrogen in combination with progestin, depends on whether or not the woman has had a hysterectomy (removal of the uterus). Estrogen alone is prescribed for women who have had a hysterectomy (see Drug Guide on conjugated estrogens). Estrogen and progestin are prescribed for women who retain the uterus and are at risk for endometrial hyperplasia if unopposed estrogen is administered.

BENEFITS

Although hormonal replacement therapy is the primary medical treatment for the symptoms of menopause, the risks as well as the benefits of estrogen must be evaluated for each woman. There is ample evidence that estrogen controls hot flashes and alleviates genital atrophy, which is associated with atrophic vaginitis, atrophic cystitis, and urinary incontinence. Either oral or topical estrogen may be administered for atrophic vaginitis.

Estrogen also offers protection from cardiovascular disease, which increases dramatically in postmenopausal women. Women who take estrogen replacement therapy suffer half the risk of coronary heart disease as those who are untreated (Ettinger, 1990). Women who take both estrogen and progesterone may not experience the same protection from coronary heart disease as those who take estrogen alone. Estrogen is also known to protect against bone loss and the development of osteoporosis.

Many women expect more from estrogen than it can deliver. Estrogen does not prevent aging of the skin, and there is inconclusive evidence that it relieves depression or other psychological symptoms. However, some studies suggest that estrogen replacement relieves insomnia, promotes increased

Drug Guide

CONJUGATED ESTROGENS (Estrace, Premarin, Ogen)

Classification: Hormone—estrogen.

Action: Promotes the development and maintenance of secondary sex characteristics in women; restores hormonal balance in deficiency states; reduces blood cholesterol.

Indications: Treatment of vasomotor symptoms of menopause, such as hot flashes; prevention of postmenopausal osteoporosis; management of atrophic vaginitis.

Dosage and Route:

For relief of menopausal symptoms and for prevention of osteoporosis, 0.3 to 1.25 mg orally for 21 days, off for 7 days, and then repeated. Vaginal cream, 2 to 4 g of 0.0625 per cent applied daily for 21 days, off for 7 days, and then repeated, may be useful for atrophic vaginitis.

Absorption: Well absorbed following oral administration; readily absorbed through skin and mucous membranes.

Excretion: Metabolized largely by the liver; as hepatic recirculation occurs, more absorption occurs from the gastrointestinal tract.

Contraindications and Precautions: Contraindicated in thromboembolic disease, undiagnosed vaginal bleeding, pregnancy, and lactation. Used cautiously in underlying cardiovascular disease and severe hepatic or renal disease; unopposed use may increase the risk of endometrial carcinoma.

Adverse Reactions: Headache, dizziness, intolerance to contact lenses, nausea, jaundice.

Nursing Considerations: Assess blood pressure, pulse, and weight gain periodically throughout therapy; assess frequency and severity of hot flashes. Instruct the woman to report skin changes and to protect skin from excessive exposure to sunlight to prevent hyperpigmentation. Assess for vaginal bleeding, amenorrhea, or changes in menstrual flow, and instruct the woman to report these signs to her health care provider. Caution the woman to avoid use of any medication that has not first been approved by her health care provider.

Drug Guide

MEDROXYPROGESTERONE (Provera, Cycrin, Amen)

Classification: Hormone—progestin.

Action: A synthetic form of progesterone that transforms the endometrium from a proliferative to a secretory phase and promotes withdrawal bleeding when estrogen is also present. Promotes relaxation of uterine smooth muscle and growth of mammary alveolar tissue.

Indications: Used to reduce the risk of endometrial carcinoma when estrogen is administered to control postmenopausal symptoms or to prevent osteoporosis.

Dosage and Route:

For induction of secretory endometrium following estrogen priming, 5 to 10 mg orally for 10 days. Also used for secondary amenorrhea or abnormal uterine bleeding.

Absorption: Unknown; metabolized by the liver.

Excretion: Unknown.

Contraindications and Precautions: Contraindicated in pregnancy, thromboembolic disease, carcinoma of the breast, and liver disease. Used with caution with cardiovascular disease, seizure disorders, and mental depression.

Adverse Reactions: Depression, thrombophlebitis, edema, weight gain, dizziness, fatigue, headache, insomnia. Fluid retention may complicate other conditions such as asthma, heart disease, or renal disorders.

Nursing Considerations: Assess blood pressure throughout therapy. Monitor weight gain, and emphasize that steady weight gain should be reported to health care provider. Advise women to anticipate withdrawal bleeding 3 to 7 days after discontinuing medication. Emphasize the importance of reporting the following signs and symptoms: visual changes, sudden weakness, headache, leg or calf pain, shortness of breath, jaundice, depression, or skin rash.

energy, and improves the overall quality of life (Ditkoff et al, 1991).

RISKS

Administration of estrogen has been associated with an increased risk of endometrial cancer. To overcome this risk, small doses of progestin are given cyclically with estrogen (see Drug Guide on medroxyprogesterone). This eliminates the constant stimulation of the endometrium that occurs when estrogen alone is used and allows for periodic sloughing of the endometrium. Many women are unhappy with the monthly "period" that this involves, and alternative regimens that make periodic uterine bleeding unnecessary are being investigated.

Estrogen is contraindicated for some women. Growth of existing breast cancer may be stimulated by estrogen, and women who have had breast cancer usually do not take estrogen. Estrogen stimulates blood coagulation, and women who have developed a thrombosis should cease estrogen replacement therapy. Because estrogen is metabolized by the liver, it should not be taken by women who have hepatitis or liver disease. Not being able to take estrogen presents a dilemma for some women. Not only is osteoporosis an increased risk, but the atrophic changes of menopause and vasomotor instability remain major problems. When estrogen is contraindicated, women also have increased risk of coronary heart disease because they do not receive the protective effects of increased HDLs that estrogen provides. Table 32–6 summarizes contraindications for estrogen replacement therapy.

Alternative Medical Treatment

When hormonal replacement therapy is contraindicated, alternative therapy may be prescribed. Clonidine hydrochloride (Catapres, Dixarit), an antihypertensive, is sometimes prescribed to decrease the severity and frequency of hot flashes. Bellergal (a combination of phenobarbital, ergotamine tartrate, and belladonna) reduces hot flashes, but it is associated with unwanted side effects, such as drowsiness.

Nursing Considerations

Menopause is disturbing for many women because they have inadequate or inaccurate information and because many of the psychological symptoms they experience are not acknowledged by health care professionals. Nursing care focuses on helping the woman to understand the physical changes that occur and the psychological responses that vary widely. Clarify the individual regimen of hormonal replacement therapy as well as the risks and benefits of the therapy. For instance, point out that although hormonal replacement therapy effectively treats atrophic vaginitis and reduces dyspareunia, it may not overcome the loss of libido that some women experience. (See Women Want to Know: Recommendations for Taking Hormone Replacement Therapy.)

If hormonal replacement therapy is contraindicated, nurses are often the primary source of information about measures that mitigate symptoms. These measures include:

- Vitamin E, ginseng, and other herbs can be effective in relieving hot flashes.
- Water-soluble lubricants, such as Lubrin or Replens, provide relief from vaginal dryness and dyspareunia. Oil-based lubricants should not be used because they adhere to the mucous membrane for long periods of time and provide a medium for bacterial growth.
- Kegel exercises increase muscle tone around the vagina and urinary meatus and help counteract the effects of genital atrophy.
- Drinking at least eight glasses of water a day decreases the concentration of urine and reduces bacterial growth, thereby preventing atrophic cystitis.
- Wiping from front to back following urination or defecation reduces the transfer of bacteria from the anus to the urinary meatus and helps prevent cystitis.

Table 32–6. CONTRAINDICATIONS FOR ESTROGEN REPLACEMENT THERAPY

Thromboembolic disease
Undiagnosed vaginal bleeding
Previous episode of breast cancer or untreated uterine cancer
Diabetes mellitus
Gallbladder disease
Acute or chronic liver disease

Osteoporosis

The single greatest hazard of the postmenopausal years is osteoporosis, which occurs when bones lose mass and become porous, fragile, and susceptible to fractures. The vertebrae are the most common site of fractures. Twenty-five per cent, or one in four women, experience fractures of the vertebrae by the age of 60 years as a result of osteoporosis. Fractures

Women Want To Know
About Hormone Replacement Therapy

- Take the medication with meals to reduce nausea.
- If you miss a dose, take the medication as soon as you remember, but not immediately before the next scheduled dose. *Do not take double doses.*
- Expect withdrawal bleeding when estrogen and progestin are temporarily discontinued.
- Report unplanned or unanticipated bleeding to your health care provider.
- Stop smoking to reduce the risk of serious thrombotic disorders, such as thrombophlebitis.
- Use sunscreen and protective clothing to prevent increased pigmentation.
- Stop taking medication and notify your health care provider if pregnancy is suspected.
- Continue follow-up physical examinations, including blood pressure, measurements, Pap tests, and examinations of breasts, abdomen, and pelvis.

of the wrist, ribs, and hip are also common. About 200,000 women suffer fracture of the hip each year, and 15 to 20 per cent of these women die from complications, such as pneumonia (Wren, 1992).

RISK FACTORS

Small-boned, fair-skinned Caucasian women of Northern European extraction and Asian women are at greatest risk for osteoporosis. Other risk factors may include a family history of the disease, an oophorectomy before menopause, and a sedentary lifestyle. Women who smoke, drink alcohol, or take corticosteroids also have an increased risk for osteoporosis (Ettinger, 1990). African-American women, who have increased bone mass, experience less bone loss.

SIGNS AND SYMPTOMS

Osteoporosis causes no discomfort until there is a fracture or collapse of the vertebral column. Usually, the first signs are loss of height and back pain that occurs when the vertebrae collapse. Later, signs include the "dowager's hump," which occurs when the vertebrae can no longer support the upper body in an upright position. Figure 32–4 illustrates progressive changes in posture associated with osteoporosis.

Diagnosis of osteoporosis depends on a thorough history, physical examination, and bone mineral analysis. Conventional x-ray is of little help because more than 30 per cent of the bone mass must be lost before changes are apparent. Single-beam photon absorptiometry is the most available method; however, errors are common. Computed tomography (CT scan) is accurate but expensive and is not available to all.

PREVENTION AND MEDICAL MANAGEMENT

The major goal of treatment is to prevent the development of osteoporosis and to stabilize remaining bone mass. The most effective measures are (1) estrogen replacement, (2) supplemental calcium, and (3) exercise.

Estrogen Replacement. Estrogen halts bone loss and reduces the incidence of fractures. It is usually started in the perimenopausal period, and 0.625 mg/day is the usual recommended dose (Deglin and Vallerand, 1993). Once estrogen therapy is begun, it should be continued for life, because, when stopped, rapid bone loss begins.

Calcium. Although calcium cannot prevent bone loss, other therapies cannot be effective if calcium is deficient. Supplementation with calcium carbonate (1500 mg/day) is recommended for postmenopausal women (Wren, 1992). Vitamin D is necessary to absorb calcium from the intestine; however, an adequate amount is often obtained from food or from exposing the skin to sunlight, and supplemental vitamin D may be unnecessary.

Exercise. Exercises that are weight-bearing on the spine and the long bones appear to be most effective in preventing bone loss. Walking for 30 minutes a day is recommended (Wren, 1992). High-impact exercises should be avoided because of the risk to fragile vertebrae.

For women in whom osteoporosis has developed following menopause, etidronate and calcitonin can be administered as well as hormone replacement therapy and calcium (Wren, 1992).

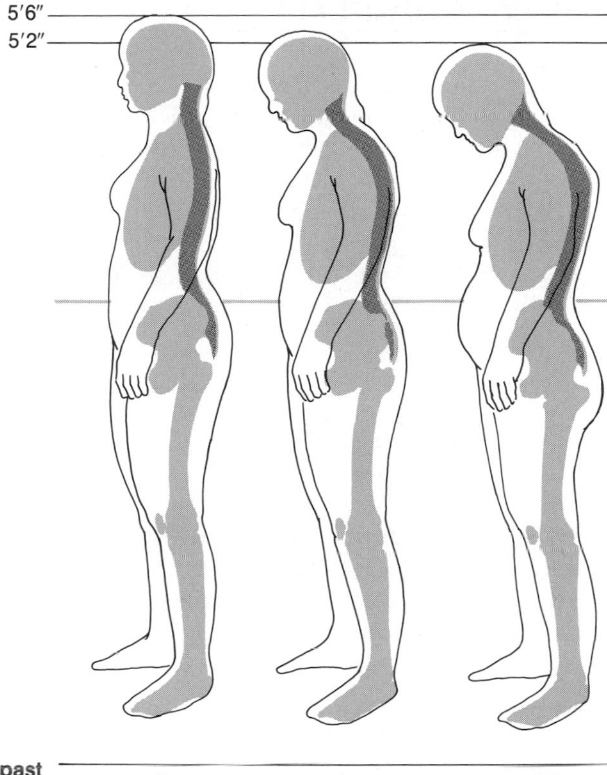

Figure 32–4

With progression of osteoporosis, the vertebral column collapses, causing loss of height and back pain. "Dowager's hump" is the term used for this curvature of the upper back.

✔ *Check Your Reading*

17. What are the physical effects of hormonal replacement therapy?
18. Hormonal replacement therapy is not recommended for women with which conditions?
19. How can osteoporosis be prevented?

Pelvic Relaxation

Pelvic relaxation occurs when muscles, ligaments, and fascia that support the pelvic organs become damaged or weakened, allowing the pelvic organs to prolapse into, and sometimes out of, the vagina. Although pelvic relaxation can occur in young nulliparous women, it generally occurs in the perimenopausal period and is the delayed result of traumatic childbirth. Prolapse may involve the vaginal wall or the uterus.

Vaginal Wall Prolapse

Prolapse of the vagina may occur at either the anterior or the posterior wall. Anterior vaginal wall prolapse involves the bladder and urethra and is referred to as cystocele. Prolapse of the posterior vaginal wall produces enterocele or rectocele.

CYSTOCELE

Cystocele develops when the weakened upper anterior wall of the vagina is no longer able to support the weight of urine in the bladder. The bladder protrudes downward into the vagina, resulting in incomplete emptying of the bladder and consequent cystitis. Urethral displacement, formerly termed urethrocele, may occur when the urethra bulges into the lower anterior vaginal wall, producing stress incontinence.

Stress incontinence is the loss of urine that occurs with a sudden increase in intra-abdominal pressure, such as that generated by sneezing, coughing, lifting, or sudden jarring motions. The two most common causes of stress incontinence are (1) damage to the normal supports of the bladder neck and urethra that occurs during pregnancy and childbirth, and (2) tissue atrophy that occurs following menopause.

ENTEROCELE

Enterocele refers to prolapse of the upper posterior vaginal wall between the vagina and rectum. This is almost always associated with herniation of the pouch of Douglas (a fold of peritoneum that dips down between the rectum and the uterus) and may contain loops of bowel. Enterocele often accompanies uterine prolapse.

RECTOCELE

Rectocele occurs when the posterior wall of the vagina becomes weakened and thin. Each time the woman strains at defecation, feces are pushed against the thinned wall, causing further stretching, until finally there is a protrusion of the rectum into the vagina. Many rectoceles are small and produce few symptoms. If the rectocele is large, the patient may have difficulty emptying the rectum. Some women learn to facilitate bowel elimination by applying digital pressure along the posterior vaginal wall to keep the rectocele from protruding during a

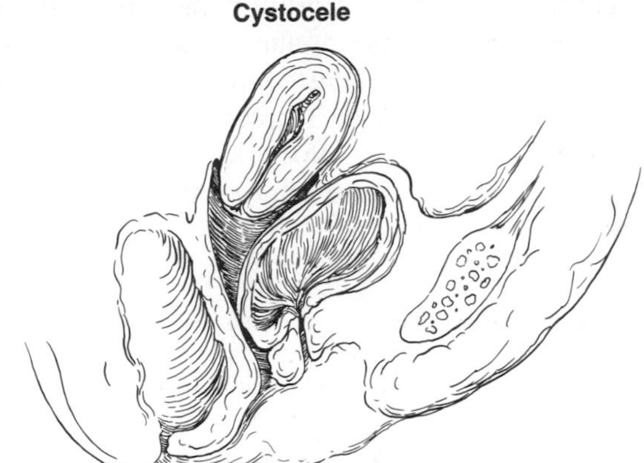

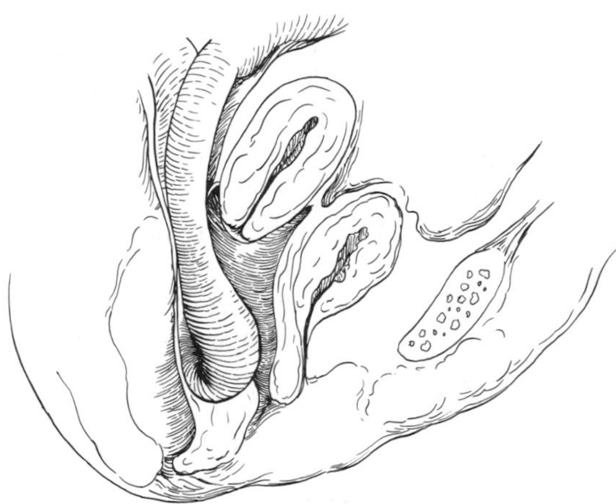

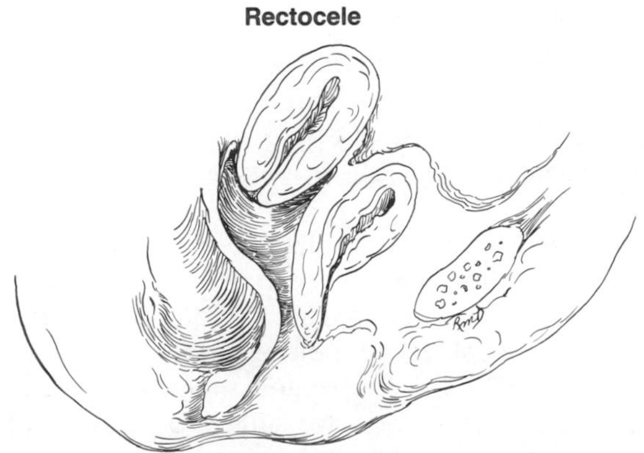

Figure 32–5

Three types of vaginal wall prolapse.

bowel movement. See Figure 32–5 for an illustration of various types of vaginal wall prolapse.

Prolapse of the Uterus

Uterine prolapse occurs when the cardinal ligaments, which support the uterus and vagina, are unduly stretched during pregnancy and do not return to normal following childbirth. This allows the uterus to sag backward and downward into the vagina. Uterine prolapse is less common than in the past, largely because of a decrease in traumatic vaginal deliveries; however, the condition continues to exist, particularly when the woman has had many vaginal deliveries or when the infants were large. Figure 32–6 illustrates three degrees of uterine prolapse from first degree, when the uterus remains in the vagina, to third degree, when the uterus protrudes through from the vagina.

SYMPTOMS

The degree of discomfort experienced by a woman with vaginal wall or uterine prolapse is extremely variable. Symptoms generally become obvious during the perimenopausal period, when estrogen, which maintained the tone of the pelvic tissue, diminishes. This results in atrophic changes in the supporting structures, and the symptoms of pelvic relaxation become troublesome.

The most common symptoms of vaginal wall prolapse are feelings of pelvic fullness, a dragging sensation, pelvic pressure, and fatigue. Low backache and a feeling that "everything is falling out" are sometimes described. Symptoms also relate to the structures involved. For instance, urinary frequency, urgency, and urinary incontinence are seen in patients with cystocele. Constipation, flatulence, and difficulty defecating are major symptoms of rectocele. Regardless of the location or structure involved, symptoms become worse after prolonged standing, and they are relieved by lying down.

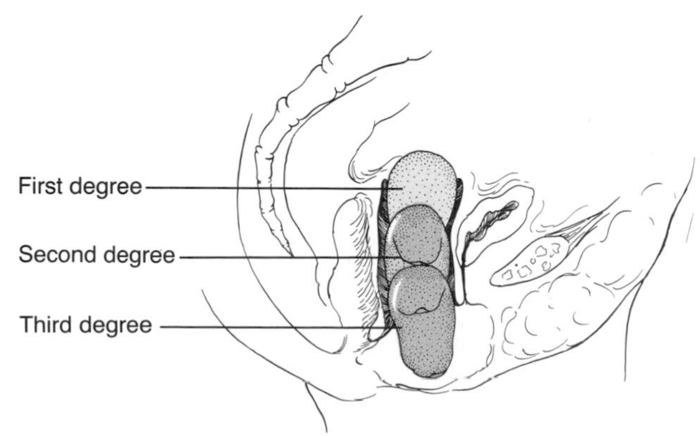

Figure 32–6

Three degrees of uterine prolapse.

Symptoms of uterine prolapse are produced by the weight of the descending structures and may include sensations of pelvic pressure, backache, and fatigue. Cervical ulceration and bleeding occur if the cervix protrudes from the vaginal introitus.

MANAGEMENT

Treatment of disorders related to pelvic relaxation depends on the client's age, physical condition, sexual activity, desire to have children, and degree of prolapse. Surgical procedures provide the most satisfactory therapy for women who have completed childbearing and who have significant discomfort.  The most common procedures are the anterior colporrhaphy and posterior colporrhaphy. The anterior colporrhaphy involves suturing of the pubocervical fascia to support the bladder and urethra when a cystocele exists. If a rectocele exists, a posterior colporrhaphy (suturing the fascia and perineal muscles that support the perineum and rectum) is performed.

Surgical treatment for prolapse of the uterus depends on the degree of prolapse. An anterior and posterior colporrhaphy may be effective for a first-degree prolapse. Treatment for more severe prolapse may include vaginal hysterectomy, in which the uterus is removed through the vaginal canal rather than through an abdominal incision. Vaginal hysterectomy may also be combined with anterior and posterior colporrhaphy.

If surgery is contraindicated, a pessary (a device to support pelvic structures) may be inserted into the vagina. The pessary must be inspected and changed frequently by a physician or nurse practitioner to prevent vaginal ulceration or infection.

Medical therapy may include hormonal replacement, which is beneficial in reducing the genital atrophy that contributes to pelvic relaxation. Some women have fears about hormonal therapy and are reluctant to take it. Nurses must be prepared to counsel women on an individual basis so that informed decisions about hormonal replacement therapy can be made. See p. 942 for additional information about the risks, benefits, and contraindications of hormonal replacement therapy.

NURSING CONSIDERATIONS

Research supports the effectiveness of Kegel exercises to strengthen the pubococcygeal muscle, which surrounds the urethra, vagina, and rectum and is the main support of the pelvic floor. Before teaching Kegel exercise, it is necessary to determine if the woman can contract the pubococcygeal muscle by asking her to sit with her legs apart while she urinates and to squeeze the muscles to stop the stream of urine. If this can be done, the muscle is contracted and it is possible for her to perform the exercise.

Some women mistakenly understand that Kegel exercise should be performed while urinating, and this idea should be corrected. The stream of urine is stopped only to determine if it is possible for the woman to contract the muscle; the exercise can be performed at any time. The woman must understand that for muscle tone to be maintained, the exercise must be continued for the rest of her life.

Measures that help reduce the symptoms of pelvic relaxation may also prove helpful. These include lying down with the legs elevated for a few minutes several times a day. Some women are relieved by assuming a knee-chest position for a few minutes. In addition, teaching may include measures to prevent constipation (see p. 151).

Nurses are often responsible for providing information about measures to alleviate problems with urinary incontinence. Many women believe that urinary incontinence is a part of aging and are unaware of measures, such as Kegel exercises, hormonal replacement therapy, or surgery, that can effectively reduce or control it. Acknowledge the awkwardness that women may feel about incontinence, and help them overcome their reluctance to seek medical attention. Moreover, women often benefit from knowing about some of the commercial products that protect the skin and prevent odor. These products are made of material similar to diapers that trap urine and prevent constant contact with the skin.

✔ *Check Your Reading*

20. How does cystocele differ from rectocele in terms of location? Symptoms? Treatment?
21. What causes uterine prolapse, and how is it treated?

Disorders of the Reproductive Tract

Benign Disorders

The most common benign conditions of the reproductive tract include cervical polyps, uterine leiomyomas (fibroids), and ovarian cysts.

CERVICAL POLYPS

Polyps are small tumors, usually only a few millimeters in diameter, that are generally on a pedicle (a stem-like structure). They are caused by proliferation of cervical mucosa, and they often cause intermittent vaginal bleeding.

Cervical polyps are surgically removed in an outpatient setting, and the specimen is sent for pathological examination to rule out the possibility of malignancy.

UTERINE LEIOMYOMAS

Leiomyomas, also called fibroids, are one of the most common gynecological conditions encountered. It has been estimated that 20 per cent of women have fibroids by 40 years of age (Moore, 1992). Although the cause of uterine fibroids is unknown, they develop from smooth muscle cells and are estrogen-dependent. They may grow rapidly during the childbearing years but begin to atrophy during menopause, unless growth is stimulated by estrogen replacement therapy. Fibroids may occur throughout the muscular layer of the uterus; Figure 32–7 illustrates the various locations.

Although uterine fibroids may produce no symptoms, increased uterine size and excessive menstrual

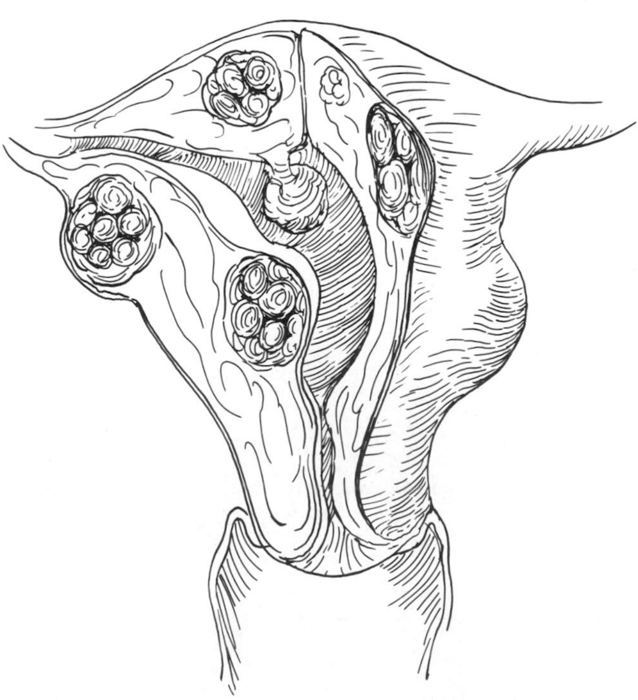

Figure 32–7

Sites within the uterus where fibroids commonly occur.

bleeding are the most common symptoms. Excessive bleeding may result in anemia, weakness, and fatigue. Additional symptoms include feelings of pelvic pressure, bloating, or urinary frequency that occurs when the tumor applies pressure on the bladder.

Treatment depends on the size of the fibroids and the symptoms experienced. In the absence of symptoms, treatment may consist of observation only. If abnormal bleeding is a problem, surgical intervention may be necessary. The most common surgical procedures are: (1) dilation and curettage (D & C), which is necessary to rule out endometrial cancer; (2) myomectomy, which consists of removal of the tumor; and (3) hysterectomy, or removal of the uterus, if the woman does not desire future childbearing. In addition, recent studies indicate the effectiveness of gonadotropin-releasing hormone agonists, such as leuprolide acetate, in reducing the size of the myomas and improving the symptoms of uterine fibroids (Schmidt, 1991).

OVARIAN CYSTS

Ovarian cysts may develop in either the follicular or the luteal phase of the menstrual cycle. A follicular cyst occurs when a follicle fails to rupture, and it generally regresses during the subsequent menstrual cycle. A lutein cyst may develop if the corpus luteum becomes cystic and fails to regress. As a result, it is likely to cause delay in the onset of menses and some alteration in the next menstrual cycle. Occasionally, an ovarian cyst can rupture or twist on its pedicle and become infarcted, causing pelvic pain and tenderness.

Treatment depends on differentiating a cyst from a solid ovarian tumor that may indicate cancer. If the patient is in her childbearing years, when the risk of ovarian cancer is less, and if the lesion is mobile and less than 6 cm in diameter, the physician may wait until after the next menstrual cycle and examine the woman again (Moore, 1992). Most ovarian cysts regress spontaneously. If there is question about the contents, transvaginal ultrasound examination is useful to determine if it is a fluid-filled cyst or a solid tumor. Laparoscopy may be helpful in ruling out endometriosis, and laparotomy may be necessary to resect the cyst from the ovary for examination by a pathologist.

Malignant Disorders

Cancer in the female reproductive organs occurs most often in the uterus, ovaries, or cervix. Cancer of the vagina, vulva, or fallopian tubes is relatively uncommon. Although cancer can occur at any age, the incidence increases with age.

Signs and Symptoms

Cancer of the reproductive organs may not be diagnosed until it is advanced because there are few symptoms in the early stages. When symptoms occur they are often non-specific and could be caused by infection or other benign conditions. Cancer of the ovaries is particularly difficult to diagnose because the condition may remain "silent" until far advanced, when the chance of long-term survival is greatly reduced.

Symptoms that should *always* be investigated include irregular vaginal bleeding, unexplained postmenopausal bleeding, unusual vaginal discharge, dyspareunia, persistent vaginal itching, elevated or discolored lesions of the vulva, abdominal bloating, persistent constipation, anorexia, or nausea.

RISK FACTORS

Risk factors as well as symptoms vary. Risk factors for cervical cancer include a history of STDs, particularly condyloma acuminata, or genital warts, caused by the human papillomavirus. Prolonged use of unopposed estrogen replacement therapy predisposes to overgrowth (hyperplasia) of endometrial tissue and is a significant risk factor for uterine cancer.

Family history is an important risk factor for ovarian cancer. Talcum powder and feminine hygiene products that contain talc have also been implicated in the development of this disease. Talc is composed of hydrous magnesium silicate, which is chemically related to asbestos. Women should be advised that products advertised to make women "feel fresh" are unnecessary and may pose a health hazard (Brucks, 1992).

See Table 32–7 for a summary of risk factors for cancer of the reproductive organs.

DIAGNOSIS

Long-term survival is strongly associated with early diagnosis of cancer of the reproductive organs, and a variety of screening and diagnostic procedures are useful in early detection. Screening tests include periodic pelvic examinations, Pap tests, ultrasonography, and serum tests for tumor markers such as CA 125, which may be increased with ovarian or other cancers. Diagnostic procedures include endometrial sampling, colposcopy, and biopsy.

Table 32–7. RISK FACTORS FOR CANCER OF THE REPRODUCTIVE ORGANS

Uterus
Obesity
Nulliparity
Late menopause
Diabetes mellitus
Hypertension
Gallbladder disease
Breast, colon, or ovarian cancer
Chronic unopposed estrogen stimulation
Cervix
First coitus before 20 years of age
Multiple sexual partners
Lower socioeconomic status (may be related to infrequent gynecological examinations)
Race (incidence higher in African-Americans)
History of sexually transmitted diseases (strong link with human papillomavirus)
Ovaries
Race (increased in Caucasion women)
Menopause > 52 years
Family history of ovarian or uterine cancer
Nulliparous women

MANAGEMENT

Treatment of cancer of the reproductive organs is based on location and extent of the disease as well as the age and desire of the woman to have children. Early treatment of cervical cancer may consist of cryosurgery, destruction of abnormal tissue by laser, loop electrodiathermy excision procedure (LEEP), or surgical conization of the cervix to remove the affected area.

Treatment for uterine, ovarian, or advanced cervical cancer usually consists of a total abdominal hysterectomy and bilateral salpingo-oophorectomy and may include adjuvant therapy with radiation or chemotherapy.

✔ Check Your Reading

22. What are the symptoms of leiomyomas (uterine fibroids), and how are they treated?
23. Why is ultrasound used to evaluate ovarian cysts?
24. What signs and symptoms are suggestive of cancer of the reproductive organs and should always be investigated?

Infectious Disorders of the Reproductive Tract

Despite advances in the development of antibiotics, infection continues to be a major health problem for women. One reason is the possibility of recurrent infection. Many infections are transmitted through sexual contact, and, unless both partners are treated simultaneously, reinfection occurs. Moreover, previous episodes offer no protection from future infection, and the same infection can occur repeatedly.

For discussion purposes, infectious disorders are divided here into (1) vaginitis that may or may not be transmitted by venereal contact, (2) infectious diseases that are sexually transmitted, and (3) other infections that are not transmitted by sexual contact. See Chapter 25 for the impact of these infections on pregnancy and the fetus.

Vaginitis

Vaginitis is an inflammation of the vagina and vulva that occurs when there is a disturbance in the resident flora or pH of the vagina that allows microorganisms to flourish. The most common symptom of vaginitis is a non-bloody vaginal discharge, and the characteristics of the discharge are often helpful in making a diagnosis. The three most common types of vaginitis are candidiasis, trichomoniasis, and bacterial vaginosis.

CANDIDIASIS

Candidiasis, also known as moniliasis and yeast infection, is the most common form of vaginitis. The cause is believed to be related to a change in vaginal pH that allows accelerated growth of *Candida albicans*, which is a gram-positive fungus that is commonly found in the digestive tract and on the skin. Some conditions, such as pregnancy, diabetes mellitus, oral contraceptive use, and systemic antibiotic therapy, result in changes in vaginal pH and flora that favor accelerated growth of *C. albicans*.

Vaginal discharge is white with a typical "cottage cheese" appearance; vaginal and perineal itching is common. Diagnosis is made by identifying the spores of *C. albicans* in a wet-mount preparation.

Treatment consists of vaginal application of miconazole nitrate (Monistat), clotrimazole (Gyne-Lotrimin), or nystatin (Mycostatin). These medications are available without prescription; however, women should be advised to seek medical attention if the infection persists or recurs frequently.

TRICHOMONIASIS

Trichomoniasis is caused by *Trichomonas vaginalis*, a microscopic protozoa that thrives in an alkaline environment. Most infections are believed to be transmitted by sexual contact. The typical vaginal discharge is thin, malodorous, and greenish-yellow in color. Vulvar itching, edema, and redness are often present. The diagnosis is made by identifying the organism in a wet-mount preparation.

The treatment of choice is metronidazole (Flagyl, Protostat), and concurrent treatment of all sexual partners is recommended, if possible.

BACTERIAL VAGINOSIS

This infection, previously referred to as non-specific vaginitis or Gardnerella vaginitis, is caused by the bacillus *Gardnerella vaginalis*, which inhabits the vagina of healthy women. At times, the organism proliferates or "overgrows" and produces an extremely contagious vaginitis. Cause of the proliferation is not known, although tissue trauma and vaginal intercourse have been identified as contributing factors. Chief symptoms are a thin grayish-white vaginal discharge that typically exudes a fishy odor. The diagnosis is made by preparing a saline wet mount and identifying characteristic clue cells (epithelial cells with numerous bacilli clinging to their surface).

Treatment is metronidazole, ampicillin, or tetracycline.

✔ *Check Your Reading*

25. What three conditions may change the normal flora and pH of the vagina and result in vaginitis?
26. How does the vaginal discharge of candidiasis differ from that of trichomoniasis?

Sexually Transmitted Diseases

Sexually transmitted diseases (STDs) include a variety of conditions that range from those that respond to treatment to those that are incurable. Moreover, STDs are extremely common and pose a significant health risk, particularly to the young.

Approximately two thirds of all STDs occur in clients between 16 and 24 years of age (Spence, 1989). There are many reasons for this. First, the age of the first sexual experience has been decreasing steadily, and sexual activity is high among this group. Multiple sexual partners and inadequate knowledge of transmission and prevention, as well as feelings of invincibility ("It won't happen to me") that are common among teenagers, have exacerbated the problem.

Methods of contraception can have a significant impact on the risk of sexually transmitted infection. Condoms provide protection in three ways:

1. Condoms prevent potentially infected ejaculate from gaining access to the female lower genital tract.
2. Condoms prevent small lesions on the penis from coming into contact with the labia, vaginal wall, and cervix.
3. Additional protection may be afforded by condoms that contain nonoxynol-9, which is an antimicrobial as well as a spermicidal.

Other barrier forms of contraception (diaphragm, contraceptive sponge, cervical cap, and spermicidal foams and jellies) do not offer the same degree of protection as the condom, although the devices can prevent cervical and upper genital tract infections. Use of oral contraceptives is associated with an increased risk of STDs, and some women have the mistaken belief that oral contraceptives *cause* infection. Nurses must explain that microorganisms transmitted by infected partners, not birth control pills, cause STDs.

CHLAMYDIAL INFECTION

Chlamydial infection, caused by the gram-negative bacteria *Chlamydia trachomatis*, is the most common STD in the United States, with a high incidence in the teenage population. Chlamydial infection is often asymptomatic in women, which makes diagnosis and control of the disease difficult. It should be suspected (1) when the male sexual partner is treated for non-gonococcal urethritis (NGU), or (2) when the culture results for gonorrhea are negative, yet the woman exhibits symptoms that are similar to gonorrhea, such as a yellowish vaginal discharge or painful urination. The most recent diagnostic research has been in the area of antigen detection. Two methods have been widely studied: (1) fluorescent antibody examination of a direct smear and (2) enzyme immunoassay (Martens, 1989).

Untreated, chlamydial infection ascends from the cervix to involve the fallopian tubes, and it is one of the chief causes of tubal scarring that results in infertility or ectopic pregnancy. The usual treatment is doxycycline hyclate or tetracycline, and concurrent treatment of all sexual partners is essential to prevent recurrence.

GONORRHEA

Gonorrhea is an infection of the genitourinary tract that is caused by the gonococcus *Neisseria gonorrhoeae*. Gonorrhea may be asymptomatic in women; however, when symptoms do occur, they usually include purulent discharge, dysuria, and dyspareunia. Diagnosis is based on a positive culture for the gonococcus. Similarly to chlamydial infection, gonorrhea is associated with pelvic inflammatory disease (PID), which increases the risk of tubal scarring and can result in infertility or ectopic pregnancy.

Currently, two factors influence the treatment of gonorrhea: (1) the high numbers of organisms that have become resistant to previously used antibiotics, such as penicillin and tetracycline, and (2) the high frequency of chlamydial infections in persons with gonorrhea. Norfloxacin or ceftriaxone, in combination with doxycycline, appears to be effective for treatment of all gonococcal infections and for treatment of chlamydial infection, which is often a simultaneous problem. If possible, all sexual partners should be treated simultaneously.

SYPHILIS

Syphilis is caused by the spirochete *Treponema pallidum*, and it is divided into primary, secondary, and tertiary stages. The first sign of primary syphilis is a painless chancre that develops on the genitalia, anus, lips, or in the oral cavity. At this time, diagnosis is made by identifying the spirochete on dark-field microscopy in material scraped from the base of the chancre. A serological test is generally negative in the primary stage. If untreated, the chancre will heal in about 6 weeks; the disease is highly infectious at this time.

Although the chancre disappears, the spirochete lives and is carried by the blood to all parts of the body. About 2 months after the initial infection, patients exhibit symptoms of secondary syphilis, including enlargement of the spleen and liver, headache, anorexia, and a generalized maculopapular skin rash. Skin eruptions, called condylomata lata, may develop on the vulva during this time. Condylomata lata resemble warts; they contain numerous spirochetes and are highly contagious. Serological tests are generally positive at this time.

If untreated, the disease enters a latent phase that may last for several years. Tertiary syphilis, which follows the latent phase, may involve the heart, blood vessels, and central nervous system. General paralysis and psychoses may result.

In addition to identification of the spirochete in material scraped from a chancre, diagnosis is also made by serology. The usual screening test is the Venereal Disease Research Laboratory (VDRL) serum test, which is based on the presence of antibodies produced in response to the infection. The rapid plasma reagin (RPR) and fluorescent treponemal antibody absorption (FTA-ABS) tests are more specific and are commonly performed.

Treatment of all stages of syphilis is with penicillin G; an alternative is tetracycline. In case of allergy, erythromycin may be administered.

HERPES GENITALIS

Herpes genitalis is an STD caused by the herpes simplex virus (HSV). Two types of HSV infections have been identified: type I and type II. Cold sores and other non-genital lesions are caused by HSV I. HSV II causes most genital lesions. However, either type can be transmitted through orogenital contact and cause either oral or genital lesions.

Within 2 to 20 days after the primary infection, vesicles (blisters) appear in a characteristic cluster on the vulva, perineum, or perianal area. The initial lesions may cause severe vulvar pain and tenderness as well as dyspareunia. Although they cannot be seen by the client, the lesion may also occur on the cervix or in the vagina. The vesicles rupture within 1 to 7 days and form ulcers that generally heal in 1 to 2 weeks, but they may last for up to 6 weeks if the infection is extensive (Gunning, 1992).

At the initial infection, the woman may also experience flu-like symptoms, including fever, general malaise, and enlarged lymph nodes. When symptoms abate, the virus remains dormant in the nerve ganglia and periodically reactivates, particularly in times of stress, fever, and menses. Recurrent episodes are seldom as extensive or painful as the initial episode; however, they are just as contagious. Diagnosis is often based on clinical signs and symptoms and confirmed by viral culture of fluid from the vesicle.

Because there is no permanent cure, treatment is focused on relieving discomfort and preventing complications from secondary infections. Acyclovir (Zovirax) may be administered either orally or topically to reduce the symptoms and shorten the duration of the infection. Clients should be advised to abstain from sexual contact while the lesions are present. If it is an initial infection, they should continue to abstain until they become culture-negative, because prolonged viral shedding may occur in such cases (Gunning, 1992). See Chapter 25 for management during pregnancy and delivery.

CONDYLOMATA ACUMINATA

Condylomata acuminata, also known as venereal or genital warts, is caused by the human papillomavirus (HPV). The dry wart-like growths may be small and discrete, or they may cluster and resemble cauliflower (Fig. 32–8). Common sites include the vagina, labia, cervix, and perineal area. A VDRL test must be done to distinguish them from condylomata lata (flat wart-like growths associated with syphilis). A culture to identify concurrent gonorrhea is also recommended.

Condylomata acuminata is of particular concern

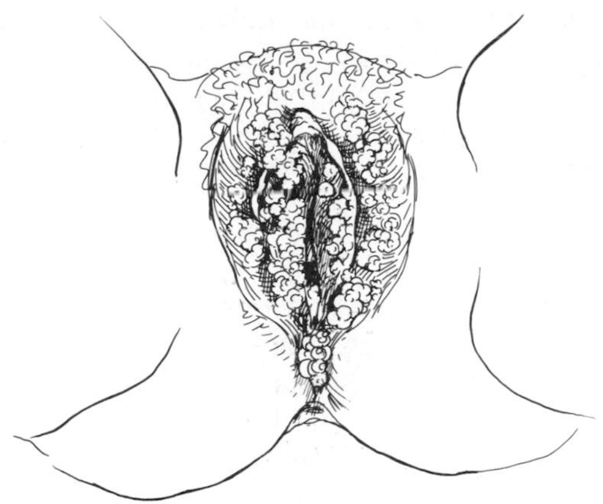

Figure 32–8

Condylomata acuminata, also called venereal warts, are caused by the human papillomavirus (HPV).

because of the increasing evidence of the association of HPV with cervical intraepithelial neoplasia (CIN), a precursor state of cervical cancer. Colposcopy, examination by a magnifying instrument called the colposcope, is generally recommended to evaluate CIN and to identify HPV. Women with condylomata acuminata should be advised to have semiannual or annual Pap tests to detect CIN.

The goal of treatment is to remove the warts, which easily transmit the virus back and forth between sexual partners. Weekly applications of 25 per cent trichloroacetic acid is the first line of treatment. Cryotherapy, electrocautery treatment, or laser therapy may be used to remove the warts. Podophyllin is sometimes used as an alternative therapy. It may be applied for 4 hours, and then the area must be carefully washed to prevent damage to surrounding tissue. Interferon, an antineoplastic drug, is sometimes used to treat condylomata acuminata in women who are more than 18 years of age who have not responded to conventional therapy. Interferon is injected at the base of each wart, and the woman should be advised to notify the physician if signs of hypersensitivity (hives, itching, wheezing, chest tightness) develop (Deglin and Vallerand, 1993).

It is important that the client understands that none of these treatments eradicate the virus and that there may be recurrences. Furthermore, all sexual partners must be treated. Sexual contact should be avoided until all lesions are healed, and the use of condoms is recommended to reduce transmission.

ACQUIRED IMMUNODEFICIENCY SYNDROME (AIDS)

AIDS is the most devastating STD in the world today, and the incidence in women and children is increasing annually. AIDS is caused by the human immuno-

Women Want To Know

About Sexually Transmitted Diseases

What are the most common symptoms of sexually transmitted diseases (STDs)?

Unexpected non-bloody vaginal discharge (increased amount, unusual color, or odor) or vaginal bleeding

Vulvar itching or swelling

Pelvic pain, including painful intercourse, painful urination, or abdominal tenderness

Skin eruptions or changes (rashes, chancres, warts, painful papules or vesicles)

Flu-like symptoms (fever, swollen or painful lymph glands, loss of appetite, nausea or vomiting)

Presence of symptoms in a sexual partner, even though symptoms are absent in the woman

What are the common methods of diagnosis?

Culture (vaginal discharge, cervix, lesions) to identify organism

Blood test (serology) to determine if antibodies for specific diseases are present (VDRL or FTA-ABS test for syphilis, HIV test for human immunodeficiency virus)

How can STDs be prevented?

Limit number of sexual partners

Establish monogamous relationship with uninfected partner

Use mechanical and chemical barriers (latex condoms in conjunction with nonoxynol-9)

Remember that one episode of an STD offers no protection from future infection

Make sure partner is simultaneously treated to prevent reinfection

What are the most important things to know about the treatment?

The entire course of medication must be completed even if symptoms subside

It is essential to comply with follow-up evaluation as recommended by health care provider

Sexual intercourse should be curtailed until free of infection

Partner must be examined and treated before sexual intercourse is resumed

Importance of reporting side effects of medications, such as skin rashes, difficulty breathing, or headaches

Not all STDs can be cured (herpes, AIDS, venereal warts), and treatment is aimed at slowing the disease and preventing complications

Are there measures that provide comfort and prevent secondary infections?

Keep the vulva clean but avoid strong soaps, creams, and ointments unless prescribed by health care provider

Keep the vulva dry; using a hair dryer turned on low is helpful

Wear absorbable cotton underwear and avoid pantyhose and tight pants as much as possible

Take analgesics (aspirin or acetaminophen) as directed by health care provider

Cool or tepid sitz baths may provide relief from itching

Wipe vulva from front to back following urination or defecation and then carefully wash hands

deficiency virus (HIV). HIV has been isolated from blood, semen, vaginal secretions, urine, saliva, tears, cerebrospinal fluid, amniotic fluid, and breast milk (Ricci, 1992). The primary modes of transmission are intimate contact with infected bodily secretions, exposure to infected blood and blood products, and perinatal transmission from mother to infant.

Currently, there is no cure for HIV-related disease, and the main focus of management is directed toward early detection and prevention of further transmission of the virus. See Chapter 25 for a complete discussion of HIV and AIDS.

NURSING CONSIDERATIONS

In their role as teachers and counselors, nurses can play a major part in preventing the spread of STDs. To fulfill this role, nurses must be prepared to:

- Teach the signs and symptoms that require medical attention
- Explain diagnostic or screening tests
- Teach preventive measures

See Women Want to Know: Answers to Questions About Sexually Transmitted Diseases.

✔ Check Your Reading

27. Why do barrier-type contraceptives reduce the risk of sexually transmitted diseases?
28. How do primary and secondary syphilis differ in terms of signs and symptoms and potential for transmitting the disease?
29. How is condylomata acuminata associated with CIN, a precursor state of cervical cancer?

Pelvic Inflammatory Disease

Pelvic inflammatory disease (PID), infection of the upper genital tract, is a serious health problem in the United States. Each year, more than 1 million women seek medical attention for acute pelvic pain, which is the primary symptom of PID (Washington et al, 1991). In addition, numerous other women with "silent" PID face the risk of chronic pelvic pain, infertility, and ectopic pregnancy, which are common sequelae.

ETIOLOGY

Although other organisms, such as *Escherichia coli* and gram-positive cocci, may cause PID, the primary infectious organisms are C. *trachomatis* and N. *gonorrhoeae*. These organisms invade the endocervical canal and cause cervicitis and a break down of the mucus plug that generally protects the upper reproductive organs from bacteria in the vagina. This allows bacteria to ascend and infect the endometrium, fallopian tubes, and pelvic cavity. The chronic inflammatory response is responsible for extensive tubal scarring and peritubal adhesions, which interfere with conception and with transport of the fertilized ovum through the obstructed fallopian tubes.

SYMPTOMS

Symptoms of PID vary widely. Some women are asymptomatic, whereas others experience pelvic pain, fever, purulent vaginal discharge, nausea, anorexia, and irregular vaginal bleeding. Findings during physical examination may include abdominal or adnexal tenderness, and tenderness of the uterus and cervix when they are moved during bimanual examination. Laboratory evaluation may reveal a marked leukocytosis and increased sedimentation rate. A urinalysis is needed to rule out urinary tract infection, and a cervical smear for N. *gonorrhoeae* helps to diagnose the disease.

MANAGEMENT

Current treatment of PID involves a combination of broad-spectrum antimicrobial therapy. The most effective combinations are cefoxitin-doxycycline and clindamycin-aminoglycoside (Peterson et al, 1991). If possible, the woman should be hospitalized so that medications can be administered intravenously. This is particularly important for women desiring future childbearing.

NURSING CONSIDERATIONS

Nurses can play an important role in preventing PID by teaching women how to prevent STDs in themselves and in their partners. Prevention can be thought of as occurring on two levels: primary and secondary. Primary prevention involves avoiding exposure to STDs or preventing acquisition of infection during exposure. Primary preventive measures include limiting the number of sexual partners and avoiding intercourse with those who have had multiple partners. Barrier methods (latex condoms with spermicide containing nonoxynol-9, diaphragm with spermicide) used consistently and correctly during all sexual activity help prevent STDs.

Secondary prevention involves keeping a lower genital tract infection from ascending to the upper genital tract or from being further transmitted within the community. This involves seeking medical attention promptly (1) after having unprotected sex with someone who is suspected of having an STD and (2) when vaginal discharge or genital lesions are apparent. Moreover, periodic medical assessment is necessary if the woman is not in a mutually monogamous relationship, even if she is asymptomatic.

Additional measures include taking medication as prescribed and returning for follow-up evaluation.

Toxic Shock Syndrome

Although toxic shock syndrome (TSS) is rare, it is a potentially fatal condition caused by toxin-producing strains of *Staphylococcus aureus*. The toxin that is produced alters capillary permeability, which allows intravascular fluid to leak from the blood vessels, leading to hypovolemia, hypotension, and shock. The toxin also causes direct tissue damage to organs and precipitates serious defects in coagulation.

If toxin-producing strains of S. *aureus* inhabit the vagina, certain factors increase the risk that the toxin will gain entry into the blood stream. These include the use of (1) high-absorbency tampons during menstruation and (2) barrier methods of contraception (cervical sponge, cervical cap, or diaphragm), both of which may trap and hold bacteria if left in place for a prolonged time.

Symptoms of TSS include a sudden spiking fever and flu-like symptoms (headache, sore throat, vomiting, diarrhea), hypotension, a generalized rash resembling sunburn, and skin peeling from the palms of the hands and the soles of the feet 1 and 2 weeks after the onset of the illness.

Treatment consists of fluid replacement and antimicrobial therapy. Corticosteroids may be used to treat skin changes, and naloxone hydrochloride is sometimes used to treat hypotension.

NURSING CONSIDERATIONS

Nurses are often responsible for providing information that may help to prevent TSS.

Tampon Use

- Wash the hands thoroughly to remove bacteria before inserting tampons.
- Change tampons at least every 1 to 4 hours to prevent excessive bacterial growth on a tampon that is left in place for a longer time.
- Do not use superabsorbent tampons at any time because they may be left in the vagina for a prolonged period, allowing bacteria to proliferate.
- Use pads rather than tampons during hours of sleep, which usually exceeds 6 to 8 hours.

Vaginal Sponge and Diaphragm Use

- Wash hands thoroughly before inserting diaphragm or sponge.
- Use only clean water to wet the sponge.
- Do not use the sponge or diaphragm during menstrual periods.
- Remove sponge and diaphragm within time recommended by health care provider (usually 24 hours).

✔ Check Your Reading

30. How can the risk of toxic shock syndrome be reduced?

Summary Concepts

- Health maintenance refers to examinations and screening procedures that allow early detection of specific conditions, such as breast or cervical cancer, and allow for early treatment that increases the chance of long-term survival.
- A major role of nurses is to explain screening procedures and to encourage women to have them on a regular basis. The most common screening procedures include breast self-examination, professional breast examination, and mammography for breast cancer; vulvar self-examination to detect precancerous conditions or infections; pelvic examination to detect abnormalities of the uterus or ovaries; Papanicolaou test for cervical cancer; and screening for fecal occult blood. Additional tests may include transvaginal ultrasound and CA 125 if the woman is at risk for ovarian cancer.
- Disorders of the breast may be benign, such as fibrocystic changes that occur in relation to the menstrual cycle, or malignant. The discovery of any breast disorder creates anxiety in women, and nurses must be prepared to explain diagnostic procedures such as ultrasonography, needle aspiration, and surgical biopsy.
- One in nine women in the United States develop breast cancer; besides gender, the greatest risk factors are advancing age and prior history of breast cancer. Additional factors include family history (grandmother, mother, sister) of breast cancer and previous uterine, ovarian, or colon cancer. Lifestyle factors such as a high intake of dietary fat, smoking, and consumption of alcohol are also suspected to increase risk.
- Management of breast cancer includes surgical removal of the tumor plus varying amounts of surrounding tissue and lymph glands. Adjuvant therapy includes radiation, chemotherapy, and hormonal therapy.
- Nursing care for women with cancer of the breast focuses on providing emotional support and accurate information.

- Menstrual cycle disorders include amenorrhea, abnormal uterine bleeding, cyclic pelvic pain, and premenstrual syndrome. Some of the disorders, such as premenstrual syndrome, respond to lifestyle alterations such as changes in diet, exercise habits, and stress management.
- Menopause, more correctly termed the climacteric, is a combination of endocrine, somatic, and psychic changes that occur at the end of the reproductive cycle. Women's responses to menopause vary widely; however, following menopause, all women are in a permanent state of estrogen deficit that can result in bone loss (osteoporosis) and increased incidence of coronary heart disease.
- Hormonal replacement therapy is commonly prescribed to manage the symptoms of estrogen deficit, such as hot flashes and atrophic vaginitis, and to prevent osteoporosis.
- Estrogen replacement has risks as well as benefits and is contraindicated for women who have thromboembolic disease, undiagnosed vaginal bleeding, previous episodes of breast cancer or untreated uterine cancer, or chronic liver disease. For these women, alternative measures are needed to control the symptoms of menopause.
- Relaxation of pelvic support structures occurs as a delayed result of traumatic childbirth and becomes troublesome when a deficiency in estrogen hastens genital atrophy.
- Although some infections of the reproductive tract are related to a change in the pH or the flora of the vagina, such as candidiasis, the majority are transmitted by sexual contact. The incidence of sexually transmitted diseases (STDs) is reduced by barrier methods of contraception, particularly the condom, which prevents potentially infected ejaculate from entering the lower genital tract.
- Barrier methods, such as the diaphragm, cervical sponge, or cervical cap are less effective than the condom in preventing STDs; however, they provide some protection for the upper genital tract. STDs, including AIDS, are caused by microorganisms, and the best means of protection are abstinence from sexual intercourse or an exclusive sexual relationship with an uninfected person.
- Pelvic inflammatory disease is often a complication of untreated STDs, particularly chlamydial infection or gonorrhea, which can result in infertility or ectopic pregnancy because of scarring of fallopian tubes resulting from inflammatory processes in the pelvic cavity.
- Toxic shock syndrome is a life-threatening condition resulting from infection with toxin-producing strains of *Staphylococcus aureus*. The infection is believed to be related to use of high-absorbency tampons that trap and hold bacteria in nutrient-rich menstrual blood for an extended time. Tampons should be removed every 1 to 4 hours, and other items that trap bacteria, such as cervical sponges, cervical caps, or diaphragms, should be removed as directed by the health care provider (usually within 6 to 24 hours).

References and Readings

American Cancer Society. (1988). *Breast self-examination: A new approach*. Atlanta.

American Cancer Society. (1991). *Cancer facts and figures—1991*. Atlanta.

Beahrs, O.H., Henson, D.E., Hutter, R.V., & Myers, M.H. (Eds.) (1988). *Manual for staging cancer* (3rd ed.). Philadelphia: J.B. Lippincott.

Bhatia, N.N. (1992). Pelvic relaxation and urinary problems. In N.F. Hacker & J.G. Moore (Eds.), *Essential of obstetrics and gynecology* (pp. 395–414). Philadelphia: W.B. Saunders.

Brown-Daniels, C.J., & Blasdell, A. (1990). Early-stage breast cancer: Adjuvant drug therapy. *American Journal of Nursing*, 90(11), 32–33.

Brucks, J.A. (1992). Ovarian cancer: The most lethal gynecologic malignancy. *Nursing Clinics of North America*, 27(4), 835–846.

Centers for Disease Control. (1992). Sexual behavior among high school students. *Morbidity and Mortality Weekly Report*, 40(5), 885–888.

Chihal, H.J. (1990). Premenstrual syndrome: An update for the clinician. *Obstetrics and Gynecology Clinics of North America*, 7(2), 457–479.

Cyr, M.G., & Moulton, A.W. (1990). Substance abuse in women. *Obstetrics and Gynecology Clinics of North America*, 17(4), 905–926.

Deglin, J.H., & Vallerand, A.H. (1993). *Davis's drug guide for nurses*. Philadelphia: F.A. Davis.

Ditkoff, E.C., Crary, W.G., Cristo, M., & Lobo, R.A. (1991). Estrogen improves psychological function in asymptomatic postmenopausal women. *Obstetrics and Gynecology*, 78(6), 991–996.

Doody, K.M., & Carr, B.R (1990). Amenorrhea. *Obstetrics and Gynecology Clinics of North America*, 17(2), 361–387.

Dow, K.H. (1991). Newer developments in the diagnosis and staging of breast cancer. *Seminars in Oncology Nursing*, 7(3), 166–174.

Drumm, D.L. (1992). Exploring misconceptions about breast cancer. *Nursing 92*, 22(6), 51–53.

Dulaney, P.E., Crawford, V.C., & Turner, G. (1990). A comprehensive education and support program for women experiencing hysterectomies. *Journal of Obstetric, Gynecological, and Neonatal Nursing*, 19(4), 319–325.

Eden, J.A. (1992). Dysmenorrhea and premenstrual syndrome. In N.F. Hacker & J.G. Moore (Eds.), *Essentials of obstetrics and gynecology* (2nd ed., pp. 332–337). Philadelphia: W.B. Saunders.

Ettinger, B. (1990). Hormone replacement therapy and coronary heart disease. *Obstetrics and Gynecology Clinics of North America*, 17(4), 741–758.

Ewing, J.A. (1984). Detecting alcoholism: The CAGE questionnaire. *Journal of the American Medical Association*, 254(16), 1905.

Facchinetti, F., Borella, P., Fioroni, L., et al. (1991). Oral magnesium successfully relieves premenstrual mood changes. *Obstetrics and Gynecology*, 78(2), 177–182.

Gossage, J. (1990). Early-stage breast cancer: How nurses help. *American Journal of Nursing*, 90(11), 31.

Gunning, J. (1992). Vaginal and vulvar infections. In N.F. Hacker & J.G. Moore (Eds.), *Essentials of obstetrics and gynecology* (2nd ed., pp. 377–386). Philadelphia: W.B. Saunders.

Hacker, N.F. (1992). Breast disease: A gynecologic perspective. In N.F. Hacker & J.G. Moore (Eds.), *Essentials of obstetrics and gynecology* (2nd ed., pp. 443–452). Philadelphia: W.B. Saunders.

Jutras, M.L., & Cowan, B.D. (1990). Abnormal bleeding in the climacteric. *Obstetrics and Gynecology Clinics of North America*, 17(2), 409–425.

Karb, V.B., Queener, S.F., & Freeman, J.B. (1989). *Handbook of drugs for nursing practice* (pp. 540–541). St. Louis: C.V. Mosby.

Kennedy, J. (1991). Health needs of midlife women. *Nurse Management*, 22(5), 62–66.

Kletzky, O.A. (1992). Amenorrhea and abnormal uterine bleeding. In N.F. Hacker & J.G. Moore (Eds.), *Essentials of obstetrics and gynecology* (2nd ed., pp. 522–534). Philadelphia: W.B. Saunders.

Knobf, M.T. (1990). Early-stage breast cancer: The options. *American Journal of Nursing*, 90(11), 28–30.

Kurman, R.J., Malkasian, G.D., Sedlis, A., et al. (1991). From Papanicolaou to Bethesda: The rationale for a new cervical cytologic classification. *Obstetrics and Gynecology*, 77(5), 779–782.

Landy, H.J., & Grossman, J.H. (1989). Herpes simplex virus. *Obstetrics and Gynecology Clinics of North America*, 16(3), 495–515.

Lauver, D., & Rubin, M. (1991). Women's concerns about abnormal Papanicolaou test results. *Journal of Obstetric, Gynecologic, and Neonatal Nursing*, 20(2), 154–159.

Lawhead, R.A., Jr. (1990). Vulvar self examination: What your patients should know. *The Female Patient*, 15(1), 33–38.

Lindow, K.B. (1991). Premenstrual syndrome: Family impact and nursing implications. *Journal of Obstetric, Gynecologic, and Neonatal Nursing*, 20(2), 135–138.

Long, C.A., & Gast, M.J. (1990). Menorrhagia. *Obstetrics and Gynecology Clinics of North America*, 17(2), 343–359.

Martens, M.G. (1989). Office diagnosis of sexually transmitted diseases. *Obsterics and Gynecology Clinics of North America*, 16(3), 659–678.

Metzger, D.A., & Haney, A.F. (1989). Etiology of endometriosis. *Obstetrics and Gynecology Clinics of North America*, 16(1), 1–14.

Morra, M.E., & Blumberg, B.D. (1991). Women's perceptions of early detection in breast cancer: How are we doing? *Seminars in Oncology Nursing*, 7(3), 151–160.

Moore, J.G. (1992). Benign diseases of the uterus. In N.F. Hacker & J.G. Moore (Eds.), *Essentials of Obstetrics and Gynecology* (2nd ed., pp. 347–355). Philadelphia: W.B. Saunders.

Murata, J.M. (1990). Abnormal genital bleeding and secondary amenorrhea. *Journal of Obstetric, Gynecologic, and Neonatal Nursing*, 19(1), 26–36.

Muse, K.N. (1990). Cyclic pelvic pain. *Obstetrics and Gynecology Clinics of North America*, 17(2), 427–440.

National Cancer Institute. (1988). *What you need to know about breast cancer* (88–1556). Bethesda, Md.: National Institutes of Health.

Newman, D.K., Lynch, K., Smith, D.A., & Cell, P. (1991). Restoring urinary continence. *American Journal of Nursing*, 91(1), 28–34.

Nielsen, B.B. (1991). Breast cancer screening. *Seminars in Oncology Nursing*, 7(3), 161–165.

Northouse, L.L., Cracchiolo-Caraway, A., & Appel, C.P. (1991). Psychologic consequences of breast cancer on partner and family. *Seminars in Oncology Nursing*, 7(3), 216–223.

Norwood, S.L. (1989). Fibrocystic breast disease: An update and review. *Journal of Obstetric, Gynecologic, and Neonatal Nursing*, 19(2), 116–121.

Peddicord, K. (1991). Strategies for promoting stress reduction and relaxation. *Nursing Clinics of North America*, 26(4), 867–874.

Peterson, H.B., Walker, C.K., Kahn, J.G., et al. (1991). Pelvic inflammatory disease: Key treatment issues and options. *Journal of the American Medical Association*, 266(18), 2605–2611.

Ricci, J.M. (1992). AIDS and infectious diseases in pregnancy. In N.F. Hacker & J.G. Moore (Eds.), *Essentials of obstetrics and gynecology* (2nd ed., pp. 175–188). Philadelphia: W.B. Saunders.

Rosen, M. (1990). Health maintenance strategies for women of different ages. *Obstetrics and Gynecology Clinics of North America*, 17(4), 673–694.

Rubin, M.M., & Lauver, D., (1990). Assessment and management of cervical intraepithelial neoplasia. *Nurse Practitioner*, 15(9), 23–31.

Sampselle, C.M. (1990). Changes in pelvic muscle strength and stress urinary incontinence associated with childbirth. *Journal of Obstetric, Gynecologic, and Neonatal Nursing*, 19(5), 371–377.

Schmidt, C. (1991). Applications of GnRH agonists for gyn patients. *Contemporary OB/GYN*, 36(10), 5050–5058.

Solomon, D. (1989). The 1988 Bethesda system for reporting cervical/vaginal cytologic diagnoses. *Diagnostic Cytopathology*, 5(3), 331–335.

Spence, M.R. (1989). Epidemiology of sexually transmitted diseases. *Obstetrics and Gynecology Clinics of North America*, 16(3), 453–466.

Stone, K.M. (1990). Avoiding sexually transmitted diseases. *Obstetrics and Gynecology Clinics of North America*, 17(4), 789–799.

Strong, B. (1992). The view from the mattress: How to care more sensitively for your cancer patients. *Nursing 92*, 22(5), 47–49.

Urrows, S.T., Freston, M.S., & Pryor, D.L. (1991). Profiles in osteoporosis. *American Journal of Nursing*, 91(12), 32–39.

Wainstock, J.M. (1991). Breast cancer: Psychosocial consequences for the patient. *Seminars in Oncology Nursing*, 7(3), 207–215.

Washington, A.E., Cates, W., & Wasserhelt, J.N. (1991). Preventing pelvic inflammatory disease. *Journal of the American Medical Association*, 266(18), 2574–2580.

Wren, B.G. (1992). The menopause. In N.F. Hacker & J.G. Moore (Eds.), *Essentials of Obstetrics and Gynecology* (2nd ed., pp. 543–550). Philadelphia: W.B. Saunders.

Glossary

Abortion A pregnancy that ends before 20 weeks gestation, either spontaneously or electively. **Miscarriage** is a lay term for spontaneous abortion.

Abruptio placentae Premature separation of a normally implanted placenta.

Abstinence syndrome A group of signs and symptoms that occur when a person who is addicted to a specific substance ceases or reduces ingestion of that substance.

Acidosis A condition resulting from accumulation of acid (hydrogen ions) or depletion of base (bicarbonate). The pH measures acid-base balance.

Acme Peak, or period of greatest strength, of a uterine contraction.

Acquired immunodeficiency syndrome (AIDS) Caused by the human immunodeficiency virus (HIV), resulting in loss of defense against malignancies and opportunistic infections.

Acrocyanosis Bluish discoloration of the hands and feet due to reduced peripheral circulation.

Addiction Physical or psychological dependence on a substance such as alcohol, tobacco, or drugs, either legal or illicit.

Adjuvant therapy Additional treatment that increases or enhances the action of the primary treatment.

Adnexa Accessory organs of the uterus, such as the fallopian tubes and ovaries.

Afterpains Cramping pain following childbirth caused by alternate relaxation and contraction of uterine muscles.

Agonist A drug or natural substance that causes a physiological effect.

Alcoholism A chronic, progressive, and potentially fatal disease characterized by tolerance for and physical dependence on alcohol and/or by pathological organ changes due to alcohol abuse.

Allele An alternate form of a gene.

Alpha-fetoprotein (AFP) Plasma protein produced by the fetus that crosses from amniotic fluid to maternal blood.

Ambivalence Simultaneous conflicting emotions, attitudes, ideas, or wishes.

Amenorrhea Absence of menses. **Primary amenorrhea** is a delay of the first menstruation. **Secondary amenorrhea** is cessation of menstruation after its initiation.

Amniocentesis Transabdominal puncture of the amniotic sac to obtain a sample of amniotic fluid that contains fetal cells and biochemical substances for laboratory examination.

Amnioinfusion Infusion of warmed isotonic saline into the uterine cavity during labor to reduce umbilical cord compression, also done to wash meconium out of the uterus, reducing the risk that the infant will aspirate meconium at birth.

Amnionitis See **Chorioamnionitis.**

Amniotic fluid embolism An embolism in which amniotic fluid with its particulate matter is drawn into the pregnant woman's circulation, lodging in her lungs.

Amniotomy Artificial rupture of the amniotic sac (fetal membranes)

Amphetamines Central nervous system stimulants that create a perception of pleasure that is unrelated to external stimuli.

Analgesic A systemic agent that relieves pain without loss of consciousness.

Anencephaly Absence of the cranial vault and all or most of the cerebral hemispheres; a form of neural tube defect.

Anesthesia Loss of sensation, especially to pain, with or without loss of consciousness.

Anesthesiologist A physician who specializes in administration of anesthesia.

Anorexia nervosa Refusal to eat because of a distorted body image and feeling of obesity.

Anovulatory (or Anovular) Female reproductive cycles occurring without ovulation.

Antagonist A drug that blocks the action of another drug or of body secretions.

Apneic spells Cessation of breathing for more than 15 seconds, accompanied by cyanosis or bradycardia.

Asphyxia A condition in which there is deficient oxygen in the blood and excess carbon dioxide in the blood and tissues.

Aspiration pneumonitis A chemical injury to the lungs that may occur with regurgitation and inspiration of acidic gastric secretions.

Atony Absence or lack of usual muscle tone.

Atrophic vaginitis Inflammation that occurs when the vagina becomes dry and fragile, usually as a result of estrogen deficit after menopause.

Attachment Development of strong affectional ties between an infant and a significant other (mother, father, sibling, caretaker).

Attenuate To weaken.

Attitude Relationship of fetal body parts to each other.

Augmentation of labor Artificial stimulation of uterine contractions that have become ineffective.

Autosome Any of the 22 pairs of **chromosomes** other than the **sex chromosomes.**

Axillary tail Wedge of tissue extending from the breast into the axilla (also called the *tail of Spence*).

Azoospermia Absence of sperm in semen.

Baroreceptors Cells that are sensitive to blood pressure changes.

Basal body temperature Body temperature at rest.

Baseline data Information that describes the status of the client before treatment begins.

Bilirubin Unusable component of hemolyzed erythrocytes.

Bilirubin encephalopathy See **Kernicterus.**

Bioethics Rules or principles governing right conduct, specifically that related to health care.

Biophysical profile (BPP) Method to evaluate fetal status during the antepartum period based on five variables originating with the fetus: heart rate, breathing movements, gross body movements, muscle tone, and amniotic fluid volume.

Birth defect An abnormality of structure, function, or body metabolism that often results in a physical or mental handicap, shortens life, or is fatal (according to the March of Dimes Birth Defects Foundation).

Birth plan A plan that a couple makes during pregnancy to identify their preferences for their birth experience.

Bloody show Mixture of cervical mucus and blood from ruptured capillaries in the cervix; often precedes labor and increases with cervical dilation.

Body image Subjective image of one's physical appearance and capabilities; derived from own observations and from the evaluation of significant others.

Bonding Development of a strong emotional tie to a newborn; also called *claiming* or *binding-in*.

Braxton-Hicks contractions Irregular, mild uterine contractions that occur throughout pregnancy; they become stronger and more evident in the last trimester.

Bronchopulmonary dysplasia (BPD) Chronic pulmonary condition in which damage to the infant's lungs necessitates prolonged dependence on supplemental oxygen.

Brown fat (or **brown adipose tissue)** Fat that is metabolized to provide heat in the newborn.

Bulimia Eating disorder characterized by ingestion of large amounts of food followed by purging behavior such as induced vomiting or laxative abuse.

Cafe au lait spots Light brown birthmarks.

Calorie See **Kilocalorie.**

Caput succedaneum Area of edema over the presenting part of the fetus or newborn resulting from pressure against the cervix. Often called simply *caput.*

Carcinoma in situ Malignant neoplasm in surface tissue that has not extended into deeper tissue.

Cardiac decompensation Failure of the heart to maintain adequate circulation to the tissues. See also **Congestive heart failure.**

Catabolism A destructive process that converts living cells into simpler compounds; process involved in **involution** of uterus after childbirth.

Caudal regressive syndrome A severe malformation that results when the sacrum, lumbar spine, and lower extremities fail to develop.

Cephalohematoma Bleeding between the newborn's periosteum and a skull bone due to pressure during birth.

Cephalopelvic disproportion (CPD) Fetal size that is too large to fit through the maternal pelvis at birth. Also called *fetopelvic disproportion.*

Cerclage Encircling of cervix with suture to prevent recurrent spontaneous abortion caused by early cervical dilation.

Cerebrospinal fluid (CSF) Clear fluid that bathes and cushions the brain and spinal cord.

Certified nurse-midwife (CNM) A registered nurse who has completed a nurse-midwifery program approved by the American College of Nurse-Midwives (ACNM) and passed the ACNM National Certification Examination.

Cervical cap A small cup-like device placed over the cervix to prevent sperm from entering, thus preventing pregnancy.

Cesarean birth Surgical delivery of the fetus through an incision in the lower abdominal wall and uterus.

Chadwick's sign Bluish discoloration of the cervix, vagina, and labia during pregnancy as a result of increased vascular congestion.

Chemoreceptors Cells that are sensitive to chemical changes in the blood, specifically changes in oxygen and carbon dioxide levels, and in acid-base balance.

Chignon Newborn scalp edema created by a vacuum extractor.

Chloasma Brownish pigmentation of the face during pregnancy; "mask of pregnancy."

Choanal atresia Abnormality of the nasal septum that obstructs one or both nasal passages.

Chorioamnionitis Inflammation of the amniotic sac (fetal membranes); usually caused by bacterial or viral infection. Also called **amnionitis.**

Chorionic villus sampling Transcervical or transabdominal sampling of chorionic villi (projections of the outer fetal membrane) for analysis of fetal cells.

Chromosomal sex See **Genetic sex.**

Chromosome Thread of DNA (deoxyribonucleic acid) in the cell nucleus that transmits genetic (hereditary) information.

Cilia Hair-like processes on the surface of a cell. Cilia beat rhythmically to move a cell or to move fluid or other substances over the cell surface.

Cleansing breath A deep breath taken at the beginning and end of each labor contraction.

Climacteric Endocrine, body, and psychic changes occurring at the end of a woman's reproductive period. Also informally called **menopause.**

Coitus Sexual union between a male and a female.

Coitus interruptus Withdrawal of the penis from the vagina before ejaculation.

Colostrum Breast fluid secreted during pregnancy and the first 2 to 3 days following birth.

Colposcopy Examination of the vaginal and cervical tissue with a colposcope for magnification.

Complete protein food Food containing all essential amino acids.

Compliance Ability of the lungs and thorax to distend with air without resistance during respirations. Also, adherence of the client to a therapeutic plan.

Conceptus Cells and membranes resulting from fertilization of the ovum.

Condom Latex shield covering the penis or lining the vagina to prevent sperm from entering the cervix and/or to prevent infection.

Condyloma A wart-like growth of the skin seen on the external genitalia, in the vagina, on the cervix, or near the anus; may be caused by human papillomavirus (condyloma acuminata) or by syphilis (condyloma lata).

Congenital Present at birth.

Congenital anomaly Abnormal intrauterine development of an organ or structure.

Congestive heart failure Condition resulting from failure of the heart to maintain adequate circulation; characterized by weakness, dyspnea, and edema in body parts that are lower than the heart.

Contraception Prevention of pregnancy.

Contraceptive sponge Soft polyurethane disc containing **spermicide** that forms a barrier over the cervix and kills sperm, thus preventing pregnancy.

Contraction stress test (CST) Method to evaluate fetal status during the antepartum period by observing response of the fetal heart to the stress of uterine contractions.

Cordocentesis See **Percutaneous umbilical blood sampling.**

Corpus luteum Graafian follicle cells remaining after ovulation that produce estrogen and progesterone.

Couvade Pregnancy-related rituals or a cluster of symptoms experienced by some expectant fathers during pregnancy and childbirth.

Crack A highly addictive form of cocaine that has been processed to be smoked.

Cradle cap See **Seborrheic dermatitis.**

Craniosynostosis Premature closure of the sutures of the infant's head.

Crowning Appearance of the fetal scalp or presenting part at the vaginal opening.

Cryotherapy Destruction of tissue using extreme cold.

Cryptorchidism Failure of one or both testes to descend into the scrotum.

Cul-de-sac See **Fornix.**

Culdocentesis Needle puncture through the upper posterior vaginal wall (**cul-de-sac** of Douglas) to aspirate blood or fluid from the pelvic cavity.

Culture Sum of values, beliefs, and practices of a group of people that are transmitted from one generation to the next.

Cystocele Herniation (protrusion) of the urinary bladder into the vagina.

Decrement Period of decreasing strength of a uterine contraction.

Delegated nursing interventions Physician-prescribed nursing actions that require nursing judgment because nurses are accountable for correct implementation. See also **Independent nursing interventions.**

Deontological theory Ethical theory holding that the right course of action is the one dictated by ethical principles and moral rules.

Developmental task A necessary step in growth and maturation that one must complete before additional growth and maturation are possible.

Diabetes mellitus A disorder of carbohydrate metabolism caused by a relative or complete lack of insulin secretion. Characterized by *glucosuria* (glucose in the urine) and **hyperglycemia.**

Diagnostic statement A phrase that describes a health problem; usually consists of a category label plus the etiology or contributing factors. It may also describe manifestations.

Diaphragm A contraceptive device consisting of a latex dome that covers the cervix and prevents entrance of sperm; must be used with **spermicide** to be effective.

Diastasis recti Separation of the longitudinal muscles of the abdomen (rectus abdominis) during pregnancy.

Dilation and curettage (D & C) Stretching of the cervical os to permit scraping of the walls of the uterus. The procedure is performed in abortion, to obtain samples of uterine lining tissue for laboratory examination, and during the postpartum period to remove retained fragments of placenta.

Diploid Having a pair of chromosomes (46 in humans). The diploid number of chromosomes represents one copy of every chromosome from each parent and is the number normally present in body cells other than **gametes.**

Disturbance in body image Negative feelings about characteristics, functions, or limits of one's body.

Duration Period from the beginning of a uterine contraction until the end of the same contraction.

Dysmenorrhea Painful menstruation.

Dyspareunia Difficult or painful coitus in women.

Dysplasia Abnormal development of tissue.

Dystocia Difficult or prolonged labor; often associated with abnormal uterine activity and **cephalopelvic disproportion.**

Dysuria Painful urination, often associated with urinary tract infection.

Early deceleration Slowing of the fetal heart rate that occurs during the uterine contraction.

Eclampsia Convulsive form of pregnancy-induced hypertension.

Ectopic pregnancy Implantation of a fertilized ovum in any area other than the uterus; the most common site is in the fallopian tube.

EDD Abbreviation for estimated date of delivery; also called **EDC** (estimated date of confinement).

Effleurage Massage of the abdomen or other body part performed during labor contractions.

Egocentrism Interest centered on the self rather than on the needs of others.

Ejaculation Expulsion of **semen** from the penis.

Embolus A clot, usually part or all of a **thrombus,** brought by the blood from another vessel and forced into a smaller one, thus obstructing circulation.

Embryo The developing baby from the 8th day through the 8th week after conception.

Endometrial hyperplasia Excessive proliferation of normal cells of the uterine lining; may be due to administration of estrogen during the postmenopausal period.

Endometriosis Presence of endometrial tissue (uterine lining) outside the uterine cavity.

Endometrium Lining of the uterus.

Endorphins Morphine-like substances that occur naturally in the central nervous system and modify pain sensations.

En face Position that allows eye-to-eye contact between the newborn and a parent; optimal distance is 20 to 22 cm (8 to 9 inches).

Engagement Descent of the fetal presenting part to at least a zero **station** (the level of the ischial spines in the maternal pelvis).

Engorgement Swelling of the breasts resulting from increased blood flow and presence of milk.

Engrossment Intense fascination and close face-to-face observation between father and newborn.

Enteral feeding Nutrients supplied to the gastrointestinal tract orally or by feeding tube.

Entrainment Newborn movement in rhythm to adult speech, particularly high-pitched tones, which are more easily heard.

Epidural space Area outside the dura, between the dura mater and the vertebral canal.

Episiotomy Surgical incision of the perineum to enlarge the vaginal opening.

Epispadias Abnormal placement of the urinary meatus on the dorsal penis.

Erythema toxicum Benign maculopapular rash of unknown cause in newborns.

Erythroblastosis fetalis Agglutination and hemolysis of fetal erythrocytes due to incompatibility between the maternal and fetal blood types. In most cases, the fetus is Rh-positive and the mother is Rh-negative.

Esophageal atresia Condition in which the esophagus is separated from the stomach and ends in a blind pouch.

Essential amino acids Amino acids that cannot be synthesized by the body and that must be obtained from foods.

Ethical dilemma A situation in which no solution seems completely satisfactory.

Ethics Rules or principles that govern right conduct and distinctions between right and wrong.

Ethnic Pertaining to religious, racial, national, or cultural group characteristics, especially speech patterns, social customs, and physical characteristics.

Ethnicity Condition of belonging to a particular **ethnic** group. Also refers to ethnic pride.

Ethnocentrism Opinion that one's own ethnic group is superior as related to its beliefs and customs.

Euglycemia Normal blood glucose level.

Extrusion reflex Automatic nervous system response that causes an infant to push anything solid out of the mouth.

Familial Presence of a trait or condition in a family more often than would be expected by chance alone.

Fantasy Mental images formed to prepare for the birth of a child.

Ferning (or **fern test)** Microscopic appearance of amniotic fluid that resembles fern leaves when the fluid is allowed to dry on a microscope slide. Also describes the microscopic fern-like appearance of dried cervical mucus that is most apparent at the time of ovulation.

Fertilization age Prenatal age of the developing baby calculated from the date of conception. Also called **post-conceptional age.**

Fetal alcohol syndrome A group of physical and mental disorders of the offspring associated with maternal use of alcohol during pregnancy.

Fetal lung fluid Fluid that fills the lungs during prenatal life, expanding the alveoli and promoting normal development of the lungs.

Fetus The developing baby from 9 weeks after conception until birth. In everyday practice, the term is often used to describe a developing baby during pregnancy, regardless of age.

FHR Abbreviation for fetal heart rate.

Finger-tipping First tactile (touch) experience between mother and newborn; the mother explores the infant's body with her finger tips only.

First period of reactivity Period from birth of infant until the infant first falls asleep.

Fontanelle Space at the intersection of sutures connecting fetal or infant skull bones.

Foremilk First breast milk received in a feeding.

Fornix (pl. **fornices)** An arch or pouch-like structure at the upper end of the vagina. Also called a **cul-de-sac.**

Fourth trimester First 12 weeks following birth; time of transition for parents and siblings.

Frequency Period from the beginning of one uterine contraction until the beginning of the next.

Fundus Part of the uterus that is farthest from the cervix, above the openings of the fallopian tubes.

Gamete Reproductive cell. The female gamete is an **ovum;** the male gamete is a **spermatozoon.**

Gametogenesis Development and maturation of the **sperm** and **ova.**

Gastroschisis Condition in which the intestines protrude through a defect in the abdominal wall.

General anesthesia Systemic loss of sensation with loss of consciousness.

Genetic Pertaining to the genes or chromosomes.

Genetic sex Sex determined at conception by union of two X chromosomes (female) or an X and a Y chromosome (male). Also called **chromosomal sex.**

Genogram See **Pedigree.**

Genotype Genetic make-up of an individual.

Gestational age Prenatal age of the developing baby (measured in weeks) calculated from the first day of the woman's last menstrual period. Also called **menstrual age.** About two weeks more than the **fertilization age.**

Gestational diabetes Impaired glucose tolerance induced by pregnancy and diagnosed during pregnancy. Usually disappears after childbirth.

Gonad Reproductive (sex) gland that produces gametes and sex hormones. The female gonads are **ovaries;** the male gonads are **testes.**

Gonadotropic hormones Secretions of the anterior pituitary gland that stimulate the gonads, specifically follicle-stimulating hormone (FSH) and luteinizing hormone (LH). Chorionic gonadotropin is secreted by the placenta during pregnancy.

Goodell's sign Softening of the cervix, a probable indication of pregnancy.

Graafian follicle A small sac within the ovary that contains the maturing ovum.

Gravida A woman who is or has been pregnant, regardless of the duration of the pregnancy(ies). Also refers to the number of pregnancies, including the one in progress, if applicable.

Gynecologic age Number of years since menarche.

Habituation Decreased response to a repeated stimulus.

Haploid Having one copy of each chromosome pair (23 in humans). **Gametes** normally have a haploid number of chromosomes.

Hematoma Localized collection of blood in a space or tissue.

Heme iron Iron obtained from meat, poultry, or fish sources; the form most usable by the body.

Heterozygous Having two different **alleles** for a genetic trait.

Hindmilk Breast milk secreted nearer the end of a feeding; contains higher fat content than **foremilk.**

HIV An acronym for human immunodeficiency virus, which eventually results in the development of AIDS (see **Acquired immunodeficiency syndrome**).

Homozygous Having two identical **alleles** for a genetic trait.

Hormone implant Small capsules of progestin inserted subcutaneously to provide contraception.

Hydramnios Excessive volume of amniotic fluid (more than 2000 ml at term). Also called **polyhydramnios.**

Hydrops fetalis Heart failure and generalized edema in the fetus secondary to severe anemia resulting from destruction of erythrocytes.

Hyperbilirubinemia Excessive amount of bilirubin in the blood, often leading to jaundice.

Hypercapnia Excess carbon dioxide in the blood, evidenced by an elevated Pco_2.

Hyperglycemia An abnormally high blood glucose level.

Hypertonic contractions Uterine contractions that are too strong, too frequent, or too long to allow optimum uteroplacental exchange.

Hypertonic labor dysfunction Ineffective labor characterized by irregular, short, and poorly coordinated contractions. **Uterine resting tone** is higher than normal.

Hypoglycemia An abnormally low blood glucose level.

Hypospadias Abnormal position of the urinary meatus on the ventral side of the penis.

Hypotonic labor dysfunction Ineffective labor characterized by weak, infrequent, short, but coordinated uterine contractions. **Uterine resting tone** is normal.

Hypovolemia Abnormally decreased volume of circulating plasma in the body.

Hypovolemic shock Acute peripheral circulatory failure due to loss of circulating blood volume.

Hypoxemia Reduced oxygenation of the blood, evidenced by a low Po_2.

Hypoxia Reduced availability of oxygen to the body tissues.

Iatrogenic An adverse condition resulting from treatment.

Impotence Inability of a man to achieve or maintain an erection of the penis that is sufficiently rigid to permit successful sexual intercourse.

Incompetent cervix Inability of the cervix to remain closed long enough during pregnancy for the fetus to survive.

Incomplete protein food Food that does not contain all essential amino acids.

Increment Period of increasing strength of a uterine contraction.

Independent nursing interventions Nurse-prescribed actions used in both nursing diagnoses and collaborative problems. See also **Delegated nursing interventions.**

Induction of labor Artificial initiation of labor.

Infant mortality rate Number of deaths per 1000 live births that occur within the first 12 months of life.

Infertility Inability of a couple to conceive after 1 year of regular intercourse (two to three times weekly) without using contraception. Also, the involuntary inability to conceive and produce viable offspring when the couple chooses. **Primary infertility** occurs in a couple who has never conceived; **secondary infertility** occurs in a couple who has conceived at least once before.

Intensity Strength of a uterine contraction.

Intermittent monitoring A variation of electronic fetal monitoring in which a 20-minute strip is obtained on admission. If patterns are reassuring, the woman is remonitored for 15 minutes at regular intervals (about every 30 to 60 minutes).

Interval Period between the end of one uterine contraction and the beginning of the next.

Intrauterine growth retardation (IUGR) Failure of a fetus to grow as expected for gestational age.

Intrauterine device (IUD) A mechanical device inserted into the uterus to prevent pregnancy.

Intraventricular hemorrhage (IVH) Bleeding into the ventricles of the brain.

Introversion Inward concentration on one's self and one's body.

Involution Retrogressive changes that return the reproductive organs, particularly the uterus, to their pre-pregnancy size and condition.

Jaundice Yellow discoloration of the skin caused by excessive bilirubin in the blood.

Karyotype A photomicrograph of a cell's chromosomes, arranged from largest to smallest.

Kegel exercises Alternate contracting and relaxing of the pelvic muscles; these movements strengthen the pubococcygeus muscle, which surrounds the urinary meatus and vagina.

Kernicterus Accumulation of unconjugated bilirubin in the brain causing neurological damage. Also called **bilirubin encephalopathy.**

Ketosis Accumulation of ketone bodies (metabolic products) in the blood; frequently associated with acidosis.

Kilocalorie Amount of heat necessary to raise the temperature of 1 gram of water 1 degree Celsius. Commonly called **calorie.**

Lactation Secretion of milk from the breasts; also describes the time in weeks or months during which a child is breastfed.

Lacto-ovovegetarian A **vegetarian** whose diet includes milk products and eggs.

Lactose intolerance Inability to digest most dairy products because of a lack of the enzyme lactase.

Lactovegetarian A **vegetarian** whose diet includes milk products.

Laminaria Slender cones of prepared seaweed or a similar substance inserted into the cervix to dilate it as they absorb water.

Lanugo Fine hair covering the fetus.

Laparoscopy Insertion of an illuminated tube into the abdominal cavity to visualize contents, locate bleeding, and perform surgical procedures.

Laparotomy Incision through the abdominal wall to examine the abdominal or pelvic organs.

Large-for-gestational-age (LGA) infant An infant whose size is above the 90th percentile for gestational age.

Latch-on Attachment of the infant to the breast.

Lecithin/sphingomyelin ratio (L/S ratio) Ratio of two phospholipids in amniotic fluid that is used to determine fetal lung maturity; an L/S ratio of 2:1 or greater indicates fetal lung maturity.

Late deceleration Slowing of the fetal heart rate after the onset of a uterine contraction that persists after the contraction ends.

Let-down reflex See **Milk-ejection reflex.**

Letting-go A phase of maternal adaptation that involves relinquishment of previous roles and assumption of a new role as parent.

Libido Sexual desire.

Lie Relationship of the long axis of the fetus to the long axis of the pregnant woman.

Lightening Descent of the fetus toward the pelvic inlet preceding labor.

Linear salpingostomy Incision along the length of a fallopian tube to remove an ectopic pregnancy and preserve the tube.

Lochia Vaginal drainage after birth.

Lochia alba Whitish or clear vaginal discharge that follows **lochia serosa;** occurs when the amount of blood is decreased and the number of leukocytes is increased.

Lochia rubra Reddish vaginal discharge that occurs immediately after childbirth; composed mostly of blood.

Lochia serosa Pinkish or brown-tinged vaginal discharge that follows **lochia rubra** and precedes **lochia alba;** composed largely of serous exudate, blood, and leukocytes.

Low-birth-weight (LBW) infant An infant weighing 2500 grams or less at birth.

Maceration Discoloration and softening of tissues and eventual disintegration of a fetus that is retained in the uterus after its death.

Macrosomia Abnormally large fetal size; infant birth weight over 4000 grams.

Malpractice Negligence by a professional person.

Mammogram Study of breast tissue using very-low-dose x-ray; primary tool in the discovery of breast cancer.

Mastitis Inflammation of the breast, usually caused by stasis of milk in the ducts or infection.

Maternal mortality rate Number of maternal deaths per 100,000 live births as a direct result of the reproductive process.

Mature milk Breast milk that appears about 3 weeks after lactation begins.

Meconium aspiration syndrome Obstruction and air trapping due to meconium in the lungs, causing severe respiratory distress.

Meiosis Reduction cell division in **gametes** that halves the number of chromosomes in each cell.

Menarche Onset of menstruation; average age is 12.8 years.

Meningocele Protrusion of the meninges through a defect in the bony spine; a form of **neural tube defect.**

Menopause Permanent cessation of menstruation during the **climacteric.**

Menorrhagia Excessive bleeding at the time of menstruation, in either number of days duration or amount of blood lost or both.

Menstrual age See **Gestational age.**

Methadone A synthetic compound with opiate properties. Used as an oral substitute for heroin and morphine in the opiate-addicted person.

Metrorrhagia Bleeding from the uterus at any time other than during the menstrual period.

Milia Distended sebaceous glands.

Miliaria (prickly heat) Rash caused by heat.

Milk-ejection reflex Release of milk from the alveoli into the ducts; also known as the **let-down reflex.**

Mimicry Copying the behaviors of other pregnant women or mothers as a method of "trying on" the role of advanced pregnancy or motherhood.

Miscarriage See **Abortion.**

Mitosis Cell division in body cells other than the **gametes.**

Mittelschmerz Low abdominal pain that occurs at **ovulation.**

Molding Shaping of the fetal head during movement through the birth canal.

Mongolian spots Bruise like marks that occur mostly in newborns with dark skin tones.

Monosomy Presence of only one of a chromosome pair in every body cell.

Motor block Loss of voluntary movement caused by **regional anesthesia.**

Multifetal pregnancy A pregnancy in which the woman is carrying two or more fetuses. Also called **multiple gestation.**

Multipara A woman who has given birth after two or more pregnancies of at least 20 weeks of gestation. Also may be used informally to describe a woman before the birth of her second child.

Multiple gestation See **Multifetal pregnancy.**

Mutation A permanent and transmissible change in a gene.

Myelomeningocele Protrusion of the meninges and spinal cord through a defect in the vertebrae; a form of **neural tube defect.**

Myometrium Uterine muscle.

Narcissism Undue preoccupation with one's self.

Natural family planning Method of predicting **ovulation** based on normal changes in a woman's body.

Necrotizing enterocolitis (NEC) A condition of injury, invasion by bacteria, and possible necrosis of the intestines.

Negligence Failure to act in the way a reasonable, prudent person of similar background would act in similar circumstances.

Neonatal abstinence syndrome A cluster of physical signs exhibited by the newborn who was exposed in utero to maternal use of substances such as cocaine or heroin. See also **Abstinence syndrome.**

Neonatal mortality rate Number of deaths per 1000 live births occurring at birth or within the first 28 days of life.

Neonatologist A physician who specializes in the care of newborn infants (from birth until the 29th day of life).

Neural tube defect A congenital defect in closure of the bony encasement of the spinal cord or of the skull. Includes **anencephaly, spina bifida, meningocele,** and **myelomeningocele.**

Neutral thermal environment Environment in which body temperature is maintained without an increase in oxygen use or in metabolic rate.

Nevus flammeus Permanent purple birthmark.

Nevus vasculosum Rough, raised, reddish collection of capillaries on the skin surface that disappears with time.

Nidation Implantation of the fertilized ovum **(zygote)** in the uterine endometrium.

Nitrazine paper Paper used to detect pH. Helps to determine whether the amniotic sac has ruptured.

Non-compliance Resistance of the lungs and thorax to distend with air during respirations. Also, failure of the client to adhere to a therapeutic plan.

Non-heme iron Iron obtained from plant sources.

Nonshivering thermogenesis Heat production, without shivering, by oxidation of **brown fat.**

Non–stress test (NST) A method to evaluate fetal status during the antepartum period by observing the response of the fetal heart rate to fetal movement.

Nuchal cord Umbilical cord around the fetal neck.

Nullipara A woman who has not completed a pregnancy to at least 20 weeks of gestation.

Nurse-anesthetist A registered nurse who has advanced education and certification in administration of anesthetics. Also *Certified Registered Nurse Anesthetist* (CRNA).

Nurse-midwife See **Certified nurse-midwife.**

Nurse Practice Acts Laws that determine the scope of nursing practice in each state.

Nutrient density Degree to which a food contains protein, vitamins, and minerals per 1000 calories.

Occult prolapse See **Prolapsed cord.**

Oligohydramnios Abnormally small volume of amniotic fluid (less than 500 ml at term).

Oligospermia A decreased number of sperm in semen, usually considered to be under 20 million per milliliter.

Omphalocele Protrusion of the intestines through a defect in the abdominal wall at the umbilicus.

Oogenesis Formation of female **gametes (ova)** in the female.

Oral contraceptive Drug that inhibits ovulation; contains progestins alone or in combination with estrogen.

Osmotic diuresis Secretion and passage of large amounts of urine as a result of increased osmotic pressure that results from hyperglycemia.

Osteoporosis Increased spaces (porosity) in bone; process greatly accelerates following menopause.

Ovovegetarian A vegetarian whose diet includes eggs.

Ovulation Release of the mature **ovum** from the ovary.

Ovum (pl. **ova)** Female **gamete,** or sex cell.

Oxytocin Hormone produced by the posterior pituitary gland that stimulates uterine contractions and the **milk-ejection reflex;** also prepared synthetically.

Paced breathing Learned breathing technique used during labor contractions to promote relaxation and increase pain tolerance.

Pain threshold (or **pain perception)** Lowest level of stimulus one perceives as painful. Pain threshold is relatively constant under different conditions.

Pain tolerance Maximum pain one is willing to endure. Pain tolerance may increase or decrease under different conditions.

Para A woman who has given birth after a pregnancy of at least 20 weeks of gestation. Also, the number of pregnancies that have ended after at least 20 weeks of gestation.

Peau d'orange Dimpled skin condition that resembles an orange; associated with lymphatic edema and often seen over the area of breast cancer.

Pedigree A graphic representation of a family's medical and hereditary history and the relationships among family members. May be called a **genogram.**

Percutaneous umbilical blood sampling (PUBS) Procedure for obtaining a fetal blood sample through ultrasound-guided puncture of an umbilical cord vessel to detect fetal problems such as blood disorders, acidosis, or infection. Also called *cordocentesis*.

Perinatologist A physician who specializes in the care of the mother, the fetus, and the infant during the perinatal period (from the 20th week of pregnancy to 4 weeks following childbirth).

Periodic breathing Cessation of breathing lasting no more than 10 seconds without changes in color or heart rate.

Persistent fetal circulation Failure of the pulmonary vessels to dilate and the ductus arteriosus to close; caused by low blood oxygen levels.

Persistent pulmonary hypertension Vasoconstriction of the infant's pulmonary vessels after birth; may result in right-to-left shunting of blood flow through the ductus arteriosus and/or the foramen ovale.

Phenotype The outward expression of one's genetic constitution.

Physiologic anemia of pregnancy Decrease in hematocrit values caused by dilution of erythrocytes by expanded plasma volume rather than by an actual decrease in erythrocytes or hemoglobin.

Phosphatidyglycerol (PG) A major phospholipid of **surfactant;** its presence in amniotic fluid indicates fetal lung maturity.

Phosphatidylinositol (PI) A phospholipid of **surfactant;** produced and secreted in increasing amounts as the fetal lungs mature.

Pica Ingestion of a non-food substance, such as laundry starch, dirt, or ice.

Placenta Fetal structure that provides nourishment and removes waste from the developing baby and secretes hormones necessary for the pregnancy to continue.

Placenta accreta A placenta that is abnormally adherent to the uterine muscle. If the condition is more advanced, it is called **placenta increta** (the placenta extends into the uterine muscle) or **placenta percreta** (the placenta extends through the uterine muscle).

Placenta previa Abnormal implantation of the placenta in the lower uterus.

Point of maximum impulse (PMI) Area of the chest where the heart sounds are loudest when auscultated.

Polycythemia Abnormally high number of erythrocytes.

Polydactyly More than ten digits on the hands or feet.

Polydipsia Excessive thirst.

Polyhydramnios See **Hydramnios.**

Polyphagia Excessive ingestion of food.

Polyploidy Having additional sets of chromosomes.

Polyuria Excessive excretion of urine.

Position Relation of a fixed reference point on the fetus to the quadrants of the maternal pelvis.

Post-conceptional age See **Fertilization age.**

Postmaturity syndrome Condition in which a **postterm infant** shows characteristics indicative of poor placental functioning before birth.

Post-neonatal mortality rate Number of deaths between 28 days and 1 year of life per 1000 live births.

Postpartum blues Temporary, self-limiting period of weepiness experienced by many new mothers within the first few days following childbirth.

Postterm birth A delivery that occurs later than 42 weeks of gestation.

Postterm infant An infant born after 42 weeks of gestation.

Precipitate birth A birth that occurs without a trained attendant present.

Precipitate labor An intense, unusually short labor (under 3 hours).

Pre-eclampsia A hypertensive disorder induced by pregnancy that includes a triad of signs and symptoms: hypertension, edema, and proteinuria.

Premature infant See **Preterm infant.**

Premature rupture of the membranes Spontaneous rupture of the membranes before the onset of labor. The gestation may be term, preterm, or postterm.

Presentation Fetal part that enters the pelvic inlet. Also, the **presenting part.**

Presenting part See **Presentation.**

Preterm birth A delivery that occurs after the 20th week and before the 38th week of gestation.

Preterm infant An infant born before the beginning of the 38th week of gestation. Also called **premature infant.**

Preterm labor Onset of labor after 20 weeks and before the beginning of the 38th week of gestation.

Primary infertility See **Infertility.**

Primigravida A woman who is pregnant for the first time.

Primipara A woman who has given birth after a pregnancy of at least 20 weeks of gestation.

Progestin Any natural or synthetic form of progesterone.

Prolactin Anterior pituitary hormone that promotes growth of breast tissue and stimulates production of milk.

Prolapsed cord An emergency in which the fetal umbilical cord slips down in front of or beside the presenting part. An **occult prolapse** is one that is suspected on the basis of fetal heart rate patterns; the umbilical cord cannot be palpated or seen.

Pseudomenstruation Vaginal bleeding in the newborn resulting from withdrawal of placental hormones.

Psychoprophylaxis Method of prepared childbirth that emphasizes mental concentration and relaxation to increase **pain tolerance.**

Psychosis Mental state in which a person's ability to recognize reality, communicate, and relate to others is impaired.

Puberty Period of sexual maturation accompanied by development of secondary sex characteristics and the capacity to reproduce.

Puerperium Period from the end of childbirth until **involution** of the uterus is complete; approximately 6 weeks.

Pulse oximetry Method of determining the level of blood oxygen saturation using sensors attached to the skin.

Reciprocal bonding behaviors Repertoire of infant behaviors that promote attachment between parent and newborn.

Recommended dietary allowances (RDA) Levels of nutrient intake considered to meet the needs of healthy individuals.

Rectocele Herniation (protrusion) of the rectum through the posterior vaginal wall.

REEDA An acronym for redness, ecchymosis, edema, discharge, and approximation; useful for assessing wound healing or the presence of inflammation or infection.

Reflux A condition in which stomach contents enter the esophagus and may be aspirated into the lungs.

Regional anesthesia Anesthesia that blocks pain impulses in a localized area without loss of consciousness.

Respiratory distress syndrome (RDS) Condition caused by insufficient production of **surfactant** in the lungs; results in atelectasis (collapse of the lung alveoli), **hypoxemia**, and **hypercapnia.**

Resting tone See **Uterine resting tone.**

Retinopathy of prematurity (ROP) Condition in which interference with blood supply to the retina may cause decreased vision or blindness.

Retrograde ejaculation Discharge of **semen** into the bladder rather than from the end of the penis.

Role transition Changing from one pattern of behavior and one image of self to another.

Ruga (pl. **rugae**) Ridge or fold of tissue, as on the male's scrotum and in the female's vagina.

Salpingectomy Surgical removal of a fallopian tube.

Seborrheic dermatitis (or **cradle cap**) Yellowish, crusty area of the scalp.

Second period of reactivity Period after the first sleep following birth, when the infant is approximately 4 hours old.

Secondary infertility See **Infertility.**

Secondary sex characteristics Physical differences between mature males and females that are not directly related to reproduction.

Semen The **spermatozoa** with their nourishing and protective fluid; discharged at **ejaculation.**

Sensory block Loss of sensation caused by **regional anesthesia.**

Seroconversion Change in a blood test from negative to positive, indicating the development of antibodies in response to infection or immunization.

Sex chromosomes The X and Y **chromosomes.** Females have two X chromosomes; males have one X and one Y chromosome.

Shoulder dystocia Delayed or difficult birth of the fetal shoulders after the head is born.

Sibling rivalry Feelings of jealousy and fear of replacement when a young child must share the attention of the parents with a newborn infant.

Small-for-gestational-age (SGA) infant An infant whose size is below the 10th percentile for gestational age.

Somatic cells Body cells other than the **gametes,** or sex cells.

Somatic sex Gender assignment as male or female on the basis of form and structure of the external genitalia.

Sperm See **Spermatozoon.**

Spermatogenesis Formation of male **gametes (sperm)** in the testes.

Spermatozoon (pl. **spermatozoa** or **sperm**) Male **gamete,** or sex cell.

Spermicide A chemical, such as nonoxynol-9, that kills **sperm.**

Spina bifida Defective closure of the bony spine that encloses the spinal cord; a type of **neural tube defect.**

Spinnbarkeit Clear, slippery, stretchy quality of cervical mucus during ovulation.

Standard of care Level of care that can be expected of a professional. This is determined by laws, professional organizations, and health care agencies.

Standardized procedures Procedures determined by nurses, physicians, and administrators that allow nurses to perform duties, usually part of medical practice.

Station Measurement of fetal descent in relation to the ischial spines of the maternal pelvis. See also **Engagement.**

Sterility Total inability to conceive.

Stork bites See **Telangiectic nevi.**

Strabismus A turning inward ("crossing") or outward of the eyes.

Striae gravidarum Irregular reddish streaks resulting from tears in connective tissue; during pregnancy they generally appear on the abdomen, breasts, or thighs.

Subarachnoid space Space between the arachnoid mater and the pia mater containing **cerebrospinal fluid.**

Sudden infant death syndrome (SIDS) Sudden unexplained death of an apparently healthy infant younger than 1 year of age.

Surfactant A combination of lipoproteins produced by the lungs of the mature fetus to reduce surface tension in the alveoli, thus promoting lung expansion after birth.

Sutures Narrow areas of flexible tissue that connect fetal skull bones, permitting slight movement during labor.

Syndactyly Webbing between fingers and toes.

Tachypnea Respiratory rate above 60 breaths per minute in the newborn after the first hour of life.

Taking-hold Second phase of maternal adaptation during which the mother assumes control of her own care and initiates care of the infant.

Taking in First phase of maternal adaptation during which the mother passively accepts care, comfort, and details of the newborn.

Telangiectatic nevi (or **stork bites**) Flat red areas on the nape of the neck and over the eyelids resulting from dilation of small blood vessels.

Telemetry Transmission with radio signals of electronic fetal monitoring data from another location to the bedside monitor unit.

Teratogen An agent that can cause defects in a developing baby during pregnancy.

Term A delivery that occurs between the 38th and 42nd week of gestation.

Thermogenesis Heat production.

Thermoregulation Maintenance of body temperature.

Thrombus Collection of blood factors, primarily platelets and fibrin, that may cause vascular obstruction at the point of formation.

Tocolytic A drug that inhibits uterine contractions.

Total parenteral nutrition (TPN) Intravenous infusion of all nutrients needed for metabolism and growth.

Toxemia A term occasionally used to denote pregnancy-induced hypertension (**pre-eclampsia** and **eclampsia**).

Toxic shock syndrome Rare, potentially fatal disorder caused by toxin produced by *Staphylococcus aureus*; has been associated with improper use of tampons.

Tracheoesophageal fistula Abnormal connection between the esophagus and the trachea.

Transcutaneous oxygen/carbon dioxide monitoring Method of continuous non-invasive measurement of oxygen and carbon dioxide levels using skin sensors.

Transducer A device that translates one physical quantity to another, such as fetal heart motion to an electrical signal, for rate calculation or generation of sound or of a written record.

Transient tachypnea of the newborn Condition of rapid respirations due to inadequate absorption of **fetal lung fluid.**

Transitional milk Breast milk that appears between secretion of **colostrum** and **mature milk.**

Translocation Attachment of all or part of one **chromosome** to another.

Trimester A division of pregnancy into three equal parts of 13 weeks each.

Trisomy Presence of three copies of a **chromosome** in each body cell.

Tubal ligation Tying and/or ligating of the fallopian tubes to prevent passage of **ova** or **sperm,** thus preventing pregnancy.

Ultrasonography Technique for visualizing deep structures of the body by recording the reflections (echoes) of sound waves directed into the tissue.

Uterine inversion An emergency in which the uterus turns inside out after childbirth.

Uterine resting tone Degree of uterine muscle tension when the woman is not in labor or during the interval between labor contractions.

Uterine rupture A tear in the wall of the uterus.

Uteroplacental insufficiency (UPI) Inability of the placenta to properly exchange oxygen, carbon dioxide, nutrients, and waste products between the maternal and fetal circulations.

Utilitarian theory Ethical theory stating that the right course of action is the one that produces the greatest good for the largest number of people.

Validate Make certain that the information collected during assessment is true.

Valsalva's maneuver Increasing pressure within the abdomen and thorax by holding the breath and pushing against a closed glottis.

Variable deceleration Slowing of the fetal heart rate having an inconsistent relationship to uterine contractions.

Varicocele Abnormal dilation or varicosity of veins in the spermatic cord.

Vasectomy Tying and/or ligating of the vas deferens to prevent passage of **sperm,** thus preventing pregnancy.

Vasoconstriction Narrowing of the lumen of blood vessels.

VBAC An acronym for vaginal birth after cesarean birth.

Vegan A complete **vegetarian** who does not eat any animal products.

Vegetarian An individual whose diet consists wholly or mostly of plant foods and who avoids animal food sources.

Vernix caseosa Thick white substance that protects the skin of the fetus.

Version Turning the fetus from one presentation to another before birth, usually from breech to cephalic.

Very-low-birth-weight (VLBW) infant Infant weighing 1500 grams or less at birth.

Vibroacoustic stimulation test Using sound stimulation to elicit acceleration (speeding up) of the fetal heart rate.

Withdrawal syndrome See **Abstinence syndrome.**

Zygote Developing baby from conception through the first week of prenatal life.

Appendix A

AWHONN Standards for the Nursing Care of Women and Newborns

Standard I: Nursing Practice

Comprehensive nursing care for women and newborns focuses on helping individuals, families, and communities achieve their optimum health potential. This is best accomplished within the framework of the nursing process. Nurses are responsible for integration of the components of nursing process (assessment, planning, diagnosis, implementation, and evaluation) in all areas of nursing practice.

Standard II: Health Education and Counseling

Health education for the individual, family, and community is an integral part of comprehensive nursing care. Such education is based on principles of teaching and learning and encourages participation in, and shared responsibility for, health promotion, maintenance, and restoration.

Standard III: Policies, Procedures, and Protocols

Written policies, procedures, and protocols clarify the scope of nursing practice and delineate the qualifications of personnel authorized to provide care to women and newborns within the health care setting. Policies and procedures should be developed by a multidisciplinary team and reviewed and revised on an annual basis. They should be readily accessible to the health care providers and should reflect the current standards of practice and local regulations.

Standard IV: Professional Responsibility and Accountability

Comprehensive nursing care for women and newborns is provided by nurses who are clinically competent and accountable for professional actions and legal responsibilities inherent in the nursing role. Nurses must be aware of changing practices and professional and ethical issues. In-service education, professional continuing education, research data, and professional literature provide nurses the opportunity to update knowledge and skills.

Standard V: Utilization of Nursing Personnel

Nursing care for women and newborns is conducted in practice settings that have qualified nursing staff in sufficient numbers to meet individualized needs. Nursing staff who provide direct care to women and newborns should be supervised by registered nurses who are clinically proficient in the specialty area of practice. In all practice settings, the nurse may practice independently or collaboratively with other health care team members. It is essential that nurses know both the responsibilities and the limita-

Modified from AWHONN. (1991). *Standards for the Nursing Care of Women and Newborns* (4th ed.) Permission granted by the Association of Women's Health, Obstetrical and Neonatal Nursing (formerly NAACOG).

tions of professional nursing practice specific to the practice setting.

Standard VI: Ethics

Ethical principles guide the process of decision making for nurses caring for women and newborns at all times and especially when personal or professional values conflict with those of the patient, family, colleagues, or practice setting. Nurses should clarify their own personal and professional values and recognize the difficulty in selecting a course of action that is morally and ethically acceptable to all parties. When confronted with an ethical dilemma, nurses must communicate openly and assertively, identify available options, and seek consultations.

Standard VII: Research

Nurses caring for women and newborns utilize research findings, conduct nursing research, and evaluate nursing practice to improve the outcomes of care.

Standard VIII: Quality Assurance

Quality and appropriateness of patient care are evaluated through a planned assessment program using specific, identified clinical indicators. The quality assurance plan should be written and should reflect a philosophy that is coordinated with the organization's mission and overall quality assurance plan.

Appendix B

Infection Control in Maternity and Women's Health Care

Universal Precautions to Prevent Transmission of Human Immunodeficiency Virus, Hepatitis B Virus, and Other Blood-Borne Pathogens*

Blood is the single most important source of hepatitis B virus (HBV) and human immunodeficiency virus (HIV) in the workplace. Both viruses have been transmitted in occupational settings by percutaneous inoculation (ie, needle sticks) or by contact of blood, blood-contaminated body fluids, or concentrated virus with an open wound, non-intact skin, or mucous membranes.

The concept of universal precautions stresses that *all patients should be assumed to be infectious for* HIV *and other blood-borne pathogens.* Universal precautions apply to these substances and to articles that may be contaminated with them: blood, amniotic fluid, pericardial fluid, peritoneal fluid, pleural fluid, synovial fluid, cerebrospinal fluid, saliva (in dental settings, because it may be contaminated with blood), semen, vaginal secretions, and any body fluid visibly contaminated with blood.

Universal precautions do not apply to feces, nasal secretions, saliva (other than in dental settings), sputum, sweat, tears, urine, and vomitus. *However, these substances may represent sources of other infections to the worker, client, and community. Use of general infection control measures is important to protect both workers and clients from a variety of infectious agents, not just* HBV *and* HIV.

Protection from blood-borne pathogens can be achieved by adhering to work practices that minimize or eliminate exposure and through use of personal protective equipment (ie, gloves, masks, and protective clothing). Gloves may reduce hand contamination. Masks and protective eye shields or face shields may reduce contamination of mucous membranes. Water-repellent gowns and aprons may reduce splash contamination of clothing.

Wash hands and other skin surfaces immediately and thoroughly if contaminated with blood, other body fluids to which universal precautions apply, or potentially contaminated items. Wash hands after gloves are removed.

Gloves cannot prevent injuries from needle sticks or sharp instruments. Do not recap needles, purposely bend or break them by hand, remove from disposable syringes, or otherwise manipulate used needles and other sharp instruments by hand. After use, place disposable syringes and needles, scalpel blades, and other sharp items in puncture-resistant containers for disposal.

* Modified from Centers for Disease Control. (1989). Guidelines for prevention of transmission of human immunodeficiency virus and hepatitis B virus to health care and public safety workers. *Morbidity and Mortality Weekly Report,* 38(S-6), 3–21.

Sources of Infection in Maternal, Newborn, and Women's Health Care

Because *all* body substances may contain pathogens, not just substances to which universal precautions apply, the nurse should use appropriate personal protective equipment whenever contact is possible. If the nurse considers all body substances to be infectious, those substances listed in universal precautions will automatically be included when wearing protective equipment. The nurse must take precautions when there is potential for contacting body substances directly, such as when changing a woman's perineal pad, and indirectly, such as handling contaminated objects.

Maternal, newborn, and women's health care nursing includes some unique situations in which the nurse must expect exposure to pathogens, both blood-borne and other infectious agents:

- Handling tissue specimens or specimens of body secretions, including but not limited to blood, amniotic fluid, urine, feces, respiratory secretions, cerebrospinal fluid, vaginal secretions, and semen (infertility studies)
- Surgical procedures, including circumcision of the neonate (scrub personnel near the operative site need more protective equipment than circulating personnel)
- Contact with non-intact skin, including surgical incisions
- Contact with mucous membranes, such as vaginal examinations or assessment of the infant's mouth
- Parenteral procedures, such as venipunctures, injections, finger-sticks and heel-sticks
- Application of medication to non-intact skin or mucous membranes, such as rectal or vaginal suppositories, topical analgesic preparations, infant eye prophylaxis, and care of the umbilical cord
- Perineal shave prep, enema, perineal care
- Handling linens, gowns, underpads, perineal pads, and dressings, especially during the intrapartum and postpartum periods, when these items are likely to be contaminated with amniotic fluid and/or blood
- Handling the infant after birth, before the first bath
- Changing diapers and cleaning the infant's diaper area
- Assessing breasts or assisting the mother to breastfeed, if contact with colostrum or breast milk is likely
- Suture or staple removal

Appendix C

Laboratory Values in Pregnant and Non-Pregnant Women

Value	Non-pregnancy	Pregnancy
Blood volume (ml)	4000	5600
Plasma volume (ml)	2400	3700
Red blood cell count (million/mm^3)	4.0–5.0	5.0–6.25
Hemoglobin (g/dl)	12–16	11–12
Hematocrit, packed cell volume (%)	37–48	32–46
White blood cell count	4500–10,000/mm^3	5000–16,000/mm^3
Neutrophils (%)	50–60	50–70
Lymphocytes (%)	25–35	25–44
Platelets	150,000–400,000/mm^3	Slight decrease (values < 100,000/mm^3 are considered abnormal); marked increase 3–5 days after delivery
Prothrombin time (seconds)	60–70	Slight decrease
Partial thromboplastin time (seconds)	12–14	Slight decrease
Glucose, serum		
Fasting (mg/dl)	70–80	65
2-hour postprandial (mg/dl)	60–110	<140 considered normal
Creatine, serum (mg/dl)	0.65 ± 0.14	0.46 ± 0.13
Creatinine clearance, urine (ml/minute)	85–120	120–180

Laboratory Values in the Newborn

Test, Specimen, and Unit of Measurement	Age	Normal Ranges (Conventional Units)	
		Preterm	*Full-Term*
Red blood cell count, whole blood (million/mm^3)	Cord	3.9–5.5	
	1–3 days	4.0–6.6	
	1 week	3.9–6.5	
	1 month	3.0–5.4	
Hemoglobin, whole blood (g/dl)	1–3 days (cap)	14.5–22.5	
	2 months	9.0–14.0	
Hematocrit, whole blood (g/dl)	1 day (cap)	48–69%	
	2 days	48–75%	
	3 days	44–72%	
	2 months	28–42%	
White blood cell count, whole blood (thousand/mm^3)	Birth	9.0–30.0	
	24 hours	9.4–34.0	
	1 month	5.0–19.5	
White blood cell differential count, whole blood			
Myelocytes		0%	
Neutrophils ("bands")		3–5%	
Neutrophils ("segs")		54–62%	
Lymphocytes		25–33%	
Monocytes		3–7%	
Eosinophils		1–3%	
Basophils		0–0.75%	
Platelet count, whole blood (thousand/mm^3)	Newborn	84–478	
Glucose, serum (mg/dl)	Cord	45–96	
	Newborn, 1 day	40–60	
	Newborn, >1 day	50–90	
Bilirubin, total serum (mg/dl)	Cord	< 2.0	2.0
	0–1 day	< 8.0	< 6.0
	1–2 days	<12.0	< 8.0
	2–5 days	<16.0	<12.0
	>5 days	< 2.0	0.2–1.0
Bilirubin, direct (conjugated) serum (mg/dl)	—	0–0.2	

Adapted from Behrman, R.E. (1992). *Nelson textbook of pediatrics* (14th ed.). Philadelphia: W.B. Saunders.

Appendix D

Effects of Drug Use During Pregnancy and Breastfeeding

FDA Pregnancy Risk Categories

The U.S. Food and Drug Administration (FDA) has assigned pregnancy risk categories to many drugs on the basis of their known relative safety or danger to the fetus and on whether safer alternative drugs exist. For many drugs, little is known about the fetal risk. The categories are:

A: No evidence of risk to the fetus.

B: Animal reproduction studies have not demonstrated a risk to the fetus. There are no adequate and well-controlled studies in pregnant women.

C: Animal reproduction studies have shown an adverse effect on the fetus but there are no adequate, well-controlled studies in humans. Potential benefits may warrant use of the drug in pregnant women despite fetal risks.

D: There is positive evidence of human fetal risk based on adverse reaction data, but potential benefits may warrant use of the drug in pregnant women despite fetal risks. Essentially, there are no safer alternatives to the drug.

X: There is positive evidence of human fetal risk based on animal or human studies and/or adverse reaction data. The risks of using the drug in pregnant women clearly outweigh potential benefits. There may be safer alternatives to these drugs.

Drug Use During Lactation

The effects of many drugs when used during lactation have not been studied. In general, if a drug is safe for use in infants, it is likely to be relatively safe for the lactating woman to take. Other drugs may be known not to be excreted in breast milk or to be excreted in an inactive form or in very low concentrations. As with drug use during pregnancy the benefits of the drug to the breastfeeding woman are weighed against possible risk to the infant.

Social and illicit drugs, such as alcohol and cocaine, are discussed in Chapters 23 and 29.

Drug	Use During Pregnancy	Use During Breastfeeding
	Analgesics	
Acetylsalicylic acid (aspirin)	Risk category C (D in late pregnancy). May prolong pregnancy because of its antiprostaglandin effects. May cause bleeding disorders in mother or newborn if used during late pregnancy.	Use cautiously. Rash or metabolic acidosis (high doses) may occur. Theoretically may result in platelet dysfunction.
Acetaminophen	Risk category B. Problems have not been documented, but drug does cross the placenta. Use with caution.	No adverse effects reported.
Ibuprofen	Risk category B (D in third trimester). Not recommended during the last trimester. May result in prolonged pregnancy or labor because of its antiprostaglandin effects.	Problems have not been detected in humans for most non-steroidal non-inflammatory drugs.
Narcotic analgesics	Most are risk category C. Neonatal respiratory depression is the most significant adverse effect when narcotic analgesics are used during labor (Chapter 15). Neonatal withdrawal may occur if the woman is addicted to the narcotic.	Most narcotics given in therapeutic doses are compatible with breastfeeding. Infant lethargy and poor feeding may be noted with large doses. Prolonged use may result in infant drug dependence and subsequent withdrawal when the mother no longer takes the drug.
	Anticoagulants	
Heparin	Risk category C. Does not cross the placenta, so is the anticoagulant of choice during pregnancy. The woman must be taught to self-inject the drug at prescribed intervals.	Not excreted in breast milk.
Warfarin derivatives (Coumadin)	Risk category X. Associated with nasal hypoplasia, skeletal abnormalities, eye abnormalities, microcephaly, and mental retardation.	Appears in breast milk in an inactive form. Does not appear to alter prothrombin time in the infant.

Table continued on following page

Drug	Use During Pregnancy	Use During Breastfeeding
	Anticonvulsants	
Carbamazepine (Tegretol)	Risk category C. May be associated with minor craniofacial abnormalities, underdeveloped fingernails, or developmental delay.	Excreted in breast milk, but considered compatible with breastfeeding.
Magnesium sulfate	Risk category B. Infants exposed to magnesium sulfate shortly before birth may exhibit respiratory depression, hypotonic muscle tone, depressed reflexes, hypocalcemia, or cardiac dysrhythmias. Calcium gluconate is the antidote to reverse these adverse effects. See Drug Guide, p. 685.	Problems have not been documented. Administration of the drug to the mother is usually discontinued about 24 hours after birth.
Phenobarbital	Risk category D. May also be used as a sedative. Fetal addiction with subsequent withdrawal is possible, but rare at the dose levels used for seizure control.	Use cautiously. Small amounts excreted in breast milk. Sedation, infantile spasms after weaning may occur.
Phenytoin or diphenylhydantoin (Dilantin)	Risk category D. The fetal hydantoin syndrome includes intrauterine growth retardation, small head, mental retardation, craniofacial abnormalities, underdeveloped nails or distal phalanges. Infants exposed in utero may exhibit none, some, or all of these characteristics.	Sedation and decreased sucking have been reported. The drug is probably safe for lactation if maternal serum levels are in the therapeutic range.
Trimethadione (Tridione)	Risk category D. Fetal risk for malformations is greater than with other anticonvulsants. Associated with developmental delay, craniofacial abnormalities, cardiovascular and other internal abnormalities.	Safety has not been established.
Valproic acid (Depakene)	Risk category D. Associated with neural tube defects, craniofacial abnormalities.	Excreted in breast milk. Use cautiously.
	Antidiabetic Agents	
Insulin	Risk category B. Insulin is the only appropriate drug to control diabetes during pregnancy because it does not cross the placenta. Women may have decreased insulin requirements during the first half of pregnancy, but their requirement increases during the second half of pregnancy.	Breastfeeding may decrease woman's insulin requirements.
Oral hypoglycemic agents	Risk factor X. Not recommended for use during pregnancy because insulin controls blood glucose levels without crossing the placenta. May cause prolonged neonatal hypoglycemia.	Use cautiously because infant hypoglycemia may occur.
	Antihistamines	
See next columns for specific drugs	Risk category B: brompheniramine, chlorpheniramine, cyproheptadine, dexchlorpheniramine, diphenhydramine, meclizine, triprolidine. Risk category C: astemizole, terfenadine. Contraindicated: cyclizine.	Cyclizine and promethazine are contraindicated. If reduced milk supply or infant drowsiness occurs, a different antihistamine may be tried.
	Antihypertensives	
ACE inhibitors (captopril, enalapril)	Risk category C (captopril) or D (enalapril). Hypotensive effects may reduce uteroplacental perfusion.	Use with caution.
Calcium channel blockers (nicardipine, nifedipine, verapamil)	Risk category C. Hypotensive effects may reduce uteroplacental perfusion and may lead to fetal heart failure and atrioventricular block. Nifedipine has been used on an investigational basis to inhibit preterm labor.	Drugs excreted in breast milk. Breastfeeding is contraindicated for nicardipine and nifedipine. The American Academy of Pediatrics considers verapamil compatible with breastfeeding.
Hydralazine (Apresoline)	Risk category C. No adverse fetal effects associated with long-term use.	No adverse effects reported.
Methyldopa (Aldomet)	Risk category C. May cause maternal sedation, a positive Coombs' test, and (rare) hemolytic anemia.	No adverse effects reported.
Propranolol (Inderal)	Risk category C.	No adverse effects reported.

Drug	Use During Pregnancy	Use During Breastfeeding
	Antimicrobials	
Aminoglycosides (gentamicin, kanamycin, neomycin, streptomycin)	Risk categories C and D. Associated with hearing loss.	Safety not established. Preterm infants and neonates may be especially susceptible to toxicity.
Cephalosporins	Most are risk category B.	Problems have not been documented.
Chloramphenicol	Risk category C. If given near term or during labor, may result in toxicity to the infant, resulting in the "gray syndrome" (rapid respiration, ashen and pale color, poor feeding, abdominal distention, vasomotor collapse, death).	Contraindicated. May cause bone marrow depression in infant.
Erythromycins	Risk category C. Very little transfer to fetus across placenta.	May cause alteration in GI flora, allergies, interference with infant's cultures for infection. The American Academy of Pediatrics considers the drug compatible with breastfeeding.
Fluoroquinolones (includes ciprofloxacin, norfloxacin, ofloxacin)	Risk category C.	Contraindicated.
Metronidazole (Flagyl)	Risk category B. However, not recommended to treat Trichomonas infections during the first trimester.	Contraindicated. Breastfeeding may be discontinued for 12–24 hours to allow the mother to excrete the last dose.
Nitrofurantoin (Macrodantin)	Risk category B. Should not be used near term because it may cause a hemolytic anemia in newborn.	Contraindicated in breastfeeding mothers and for use in infants younger than 1 month. Risk for hemolytic anemia if infant has an enzyme (G-6-PD) deficiency.
Penicillins (includes amoxicillin, ampicillin, penicillin G)	Most are risk category B. Most commonly prescribed antibiotic during pregnancy is ampicillin. No reported adverse fetal effects.	Same as erythromycins.
Sulfonamides	Risk category B (D in third trimester). Avoid use during the third trimester.	Should not be given to nursing mothers or infants younger than 2 months.
Tetracyclines	Risk category D. Can interfere with tooth enamel formation and cause discolored teeth, primarily during last trimester.	Excreted in breast milk. Same as erythromycins. Theoretically may cause tooth discoloration and inhibit bone growth, but little actual absorption by infant.
	Antineoplastics	
Few cases have been studied because of the relative rarity that these drugs are used in women of childbearing age. Therefore, their relative safety or danger cannot be accurately determined. Additionally, reported congenital defects may be more related to the mother's serious disease than to the drug itself.		
Alkylating agents	Probable association with fetal anomalies. Risk categories D or X.	Contraindicated.
Antimetabolites	Risk category D. Methotrexate is contraindicated for treatment of psoriasis or rheumatoid arthritis during pregnancy (risk category X).	Contraindicated.
Tamoxifen (Nolvadex)	Risk category D.	Contraindicated.
	Antituberculosis Agents (see also Antimicrobials)	
Ethambutol	Risk category B. No evidence of increased abnormalities. The fetal effects of combinations of ethambutol and other antituberculosis drugs are unknown.	Concentration of drug in breast milk is similar to that in maternal serum. Problems have not been documented.
Isoniazid	Risk category C. No evidence of increased abnormalities.	Excreted in breast milk. Infant should be observed for adverse drug effects.
Rifampin	Risk category C. No evidence of increased abnormalities.	Animal studies have shown a possible carcinogenic effect. The American Academy of Pediatrics considers rifampin to be compatible with breastfeeding.
	Antitussives and Expectorants	
Dextromethorphan	Risk category C.	Problems in humans have not been documented.
Guaifenesin	Risk category C.	Problems in humans have not been documented.

Table continued on following page

Drug	Use During Pregnancy	Use During Breastfeeding
	Antiviral Agents	
Acyclovir	Risk category C.	Use cautiously.
Ribavirin	Risk category X. Drug should not be administered to a woman of childbearing age.	Contraindicated. Not known if drug is excreted in milk.
	Bronchodilators	
Theophylline derivatives	Risk category C.	Excreted in milk. May result in infant irritability, insomnia, and fretfulness.
	Cardiac Glycosides	
Digoxin	Risk category C.	Digoxin levels in mother's serum and breast milk are similar, but the estimated daily infant dose is far below the usual infant maintenance dose. No adverse effects reported.
	Decongestants	
Ephedrine, epinephrine, oxymetazoline, phenylephrine	Risk category C. Should not be used during third trimester.	Use with caution. May cause irritability in infant.
Pseudoephedrine	Risk category B. Should not be used during third trimester.	The American Academy of Pediatrics considers pseudoephedrine compatible with breastfeeding.
	Diuretics	
Furosemide (Lasix)	Risk category C.	Appears in breast milk. Contraindicated.
Thiazides	Risk categories B and C. Decreased intravascular volume may reduce uteroplacental perfusion. Metabolic disturbances and thrombocytopenia may occur in the mother and fetus.	Use cautiously. May suppress lactation if used during first month.
	Hormones	
Adrenocorticotropins	Risk category C. Prednisone is the agent of choice for the asthmatic woman who needs steroids. Betamethasone and dexamethasone are used to accelerate maturation of the fetal lungs if preterm delivery is likely.	The following adrenocorticotropins are contraindicated for use during lactation: corticotropin, flunisolide, and prednisolone. The American Academy of Pediatrics considers prednisone compatible with breastfeeding.
Estrogens	Risk category X. Diethylstilbestrol (DES) is associated with development of vaginal cancer in female offspring during adolescence or adulthood.	Contraindicated. Excreted in breast milk.
Oral contraceptives (estrogen-progestin combinations)	Risk category X. Doses much higher than those used in oral contraceptives are associated with masculinization of the female fetus' genitalia.	Should not be used until lactation is well established, or drugs may decrease milk production.
Clomiphene citrate (Clomid)	Risk category C. Questionable association with chromosome abnormalities and increased spontaneous abortions. Drug should be discontinued if pregnancy is suspected. See Drug Guide, p. 914.	The woman is not usually breastfeeding when clomiphene is prescribed since it is given for infertility to stimulate ovulation.
	Psychoactive Drugs	
Benzodiazepines	Most are risk category D. The following benzodiazepines are risk category X and contraindicated for use during pregnancy: estazolam, quazepam, temazepam, and triazolam.	Diazepam and flurazepam may cause sedation and feeding problems. High doses of diazepam are contraindicated. Prazepam is concentrated in human milk.
Lithium	Risk Category D. Risk is primarily for cardiac abnormalities.	Present in breast milk. Contraindicated.
Meprobamate	Contraindicated. Associated with a significant increase in malformations. Equagesic contains meprobamate.	May cause sedation in infant. Concentrations in milk are higher than in maternal serum.
Phenothiazines (chlorpromazine, perphenazine, prochlorperazine, thioridazine, trifluoperazine)	Risk category C. Risk of malformations is uncertain. Continued use during pregnancy should be carefully evaluated.	Contraindicated.
Tricyclic antidepressants	Studies have failed to show a definite association with birth defects. Risk category B: maprotiline. Risk category C: clomipramine, desipramine, doxepin, trimipramine. Risk category D: amitriptyline, imipramine, nortriptyline.	Use with caution.

Drug	Use During Pregnancy	Use During Breastfeeding
	Thyroid Drugs	
Antithyroids (methimazole, propylthiouracil)	Risk category D. May result in neonatal goiter or hypothyroidism, which resolves within 2–6 weeks after birth. Methimazole is associated with scalp defects.	The American Academy of Pediatrics considers these drugs compatible with breastfeeding.
Iodine	Risk category C. Long-term exposure may produce massive fetal thyroid enlargement, which interferes with swallowing (thus resulting in hydramnios during pregnancy) and can compress the trachea.	Excreted in milk. May cause a rash or suppress infant's thyroid function.
Thyroid replacement hormone	Risk category A. Crosses placenta only to a limited extent.	Minimal amounts excreted in milk.
	Vitamins and Retinoids	
Etretinate (Tegison), isotretinoin (Accutane)	Risk category X. Related to vitamin A. Associated with severe fetal malformations (microcephaly, ear abnormalities, cardiac defects, central nervous system abnormalities). Etretinate has a long half-life and may have fetal effects 11 months after the drug is stopped.	Contraindicated.
Vitamin A	Risk category A (X if dose exceeds recommended RDA). Excess intake may lead to abnormalities noted for etretinate and isotretinoin.	Breast milk usually supplies sufficient vitamin A to infant.
Vitamin D	Risk category C (D if dose exceeds recommended RDA). Excess intake associated with malformations, including aortic stenosis, facial abnormalities, and mental retardation.	Breast milk usually supplies sufficient vitamin D to infant.

References

American Academy of Pediatrics Committee on Drugs (1989). Transfer of drugs and other chemicals into human milk. *Pediatrics*, 84(5), 924–936.

Brent, R.L., & Beckman, D.A. (1992). Prescribed drugs, therapeutic agents, and fetal teratogenesis. In E.A. Reece, J.C. Hobbins, M.J. Mahoney, & R.H. Petrie (Eds.), *Medicine of the fetus and mother* (pp. 300–316). Philadelphia: J.B. Lippincott.

Dallas County Hospital District. (1992). *Formulary and drug therapy guide* 1992. Hudson, Oh: Lexi-Comp.

Garber, A., Fox, M., & Tabsh, K. (1992). Genetic evaluation and teratology. In N.F. Hacker & J.G. Moore (Eds.), *Essentials of obstetrics and gynecology* (2nd ed., pp. 93–108). Philadelphia: W.B. Saunders.

Hodgson, B., Kizior, R., & Kingdon, R. (1993). *Nurse's drug handbook*. Philadelphia: W.B. Saunders.

Kuller, J.M. (1990). Effects on the fetus and newborn of medications commonly used during pregnancy. *Journal of Perinatal and Neonatal Nursing*, 3(4), 73–87.

Nichols, B.L. (1990). Pediatric nutrition and nutritional disorders. In R.E. Behrman & R. Kliegman (Eds.), *Nelson essentials of pediatrics* (pp. 57–90). Philadelphia: W.B. Saunders.

Rayburn, W., & Marsden, D. (1993). Medications in pregnancy. In R.A. Knuppel & J.E. Drukker (Eds.), *High-risk pregnancy: A team approach* (2nd ed., pp. 149–162). Philadelphia: W.B. Saunders.

Ross, M.G., & Hobel, C.J. (1992). Normal labor, delivery, and the puerperium. In N.F. Hacker & J.G. Moore (Eds.), *Essentials of obstetrics and gynecology* (2nd ed, pp. 119–133). Philadelphia: W.B. Saunders.

Simpson, J.L., & Golbus, M.S. (1992). Genetics in obstetrics and gynecology (2nd ed.). Philadelphia: W.B. Saunders.

Spratto, G.R., & Woods, A.L. (1993). RN's NDR-93: *Nurse's drug reference*. Albany, N.Y.: Delmar.

Wilton, J.M. (1988). Breastfeeding by the chemically dependent woman. In I.J. Chasnoff (Ed.), *Drugs, alcohol, pregnancy, and parenting* (pp. 149–157). Boston: Kluwer Academic Publishers.

Appendix E

Keys to Clinical Practice: Components of Daily Care

Intrapartum Care

Text to Prepare You for Clinical Practice

Chapter 11: Breathing techniques
Table 12–1: Pelvic divisions and measurements
Table 13–1: Intrapartum assessment guide
Table 13–2: Assessment and documentation of fetal heart rate
Table 13–3: Vaginal examination during labor
Table 13–5: Sequence for delivery
Table 13–7: Summary of intrapartum nursing care
Table 13–8: Apgar score

New Terms

Amniotomy
Bloody show
Crowning
EDD
Gravida
Lochia
Multipara
Nullipara
Para
Presentation
Station
VBAC

Equipment and Supplies

Sterile and nonsterile gloves
Lubricant
Urine specimen containers
Amniotic membrane perforator
Emesis basin
Bedpan
Disposable underpads
Extra linens
Fetal monitoring equipment and related supplies
Electronic fetal monitor
Doppler transducer
IV fluids, tubing, venipuncture supplies, IV pumps
Urinary catheters (indwelling and straight)
Oxygen equipment, including water, tubing, and face mask
Emergency cart
"Precip tray" (for emergency birth)

Normal Assessments

Fetus

Gestation. 38 to 42 weeks.

Fetal heart rate (FHR). 110 to 160/minute. The rate may slow during contractions but should return to its original level by the end of the contraction.

Amniotic fluid. Clear (may have particles of white vernix); no foul odor.

Woman

Temperature. Lower than 38°C (100.4°F).

Blood pressure. Near baseline levels established during pregnancy. (Report elevations of 140/90, or 30 mmHg systolic or 15 mmHg diastolic above baseline levels.)

Pulse. 60 to 100/minute.

Respirations. 12 to 20/minute.

Contractions. No more than 90 seconds in duration, with at least 60 seconds of uterine relaxation between the end of one contraction and the beginning of the next.

Bloody show. Dark blood mixed with mucus (has a distinct mucus component). The amount varies but increases as full dilation nears.

Lochia (fourth stage). No more than one saturated pad in 1 hour. (Perineal pads with cold packs in them absorb less and are saturated sooner than standard pads.)

Fundus (fourth stage). Firm, between the symphysis and the umbilicus, midline.

Nursing Care

The beginning nurse works with an experienced nurse in the intrapartum area and does not take full responsibility for the woman's care. Primary responsibilities of the novice in this area are to provide comfort and support to the woman and her family and to report maternal or fetal assessments that are not within normal limits.

△ Alert for a high risk of exposure to substances to which universal precautions apply. See Appendix B for additional information about infection control.

Personal protective equipment, such as gloves and water-repellent gowns or aprons, must be worn whenever the possibility of contact with body fluids (amniotic fluid, blood, lochia, colostrum, breast milk, urine, or stool) exists to conform with universal precautions. Protective eyewear also must be worn if splash or spray contamination of the eyes is a possibility.

ASSESSMENTS

Unless directed otherwise by the experienced nurse, assess the woman and fetus who do not have complications using the following guidelines:

1. FHR with continuous electronic fetal monitoring or intermittent auscultation: every hour during the latent phase; every 30 minutes during the active phase; every 15 minutes during the second stage.
2. The woman's temperature every 4 hours unless her membranes have ruptured, then every 2 hours.
3. The woman's blood pressure, pulse, and respirations every hour.
4. Contractions: assess at same time as FHR.

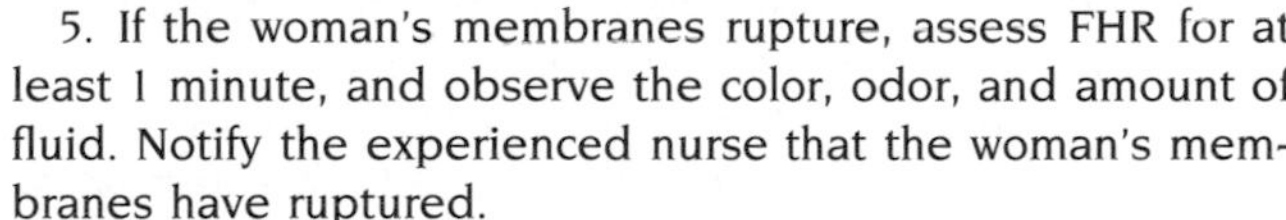

5. If the woman's membranes rupture, assess FHR for at least 1 minute, and observe the color, odor, and amount of fluid. Notify the experienced nurse that the woman's membranes have ruptured.

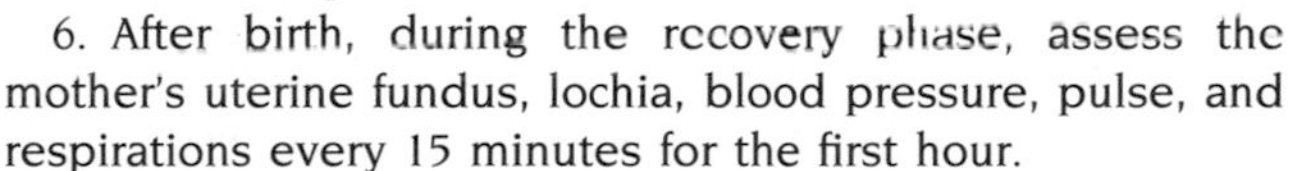

6. After birth, during the recovery phase, assess the mother's uterine fundus, lochia, blood pressure, pulse, and respirations every 15 minutes for the first hour.

INTERVENTIONS

1. Assess the woman and the fetus using the guidelines above or according to the facility's policy. Document all assessments, and *report any that do not fall within the normal limits.*
2. If there is no contraindication (ask the experienced nurse to be sure), give the woman ice chips, and encourage her to change position as much as she desires.
3. The woman can usually walk to the bathroom if she is not in late labor and has not had analgesia or anesthesia that impairs mobility. Record each time she voids or has a bowel movement.
4. Help the woman cope with labor:
   a. A cool, damp washcloth often feels good on her face, arms, and abdomen
   b. If her back hurts, offer to rub it, or apply firm pressure in the sacral area. Ask her where and how firmly to press.
   c. Give her generous praise and encouragement for her efforts to give birth. Praise the partner's efforts as a coach.
5. Offer a snack to the woman's partner, or encourage him/her to take a break and have a meal.
6. Look at the woman's perineum if she says that the baby is coming or begins making grunting sounds or bearing down. Summon the experienced nurse with the call bell immediately, but *do not leave the laboring woman.*
7. When the infant is born, focus on the respiratory efforts and maintain warmth. Use a bulb syringe (see Chapter 20, p. 521) to suction excess secretions. Keep the infant under a radiant warmer or wrap in warmed blankets. Be sure not to get between the radiant heat source and the infant.

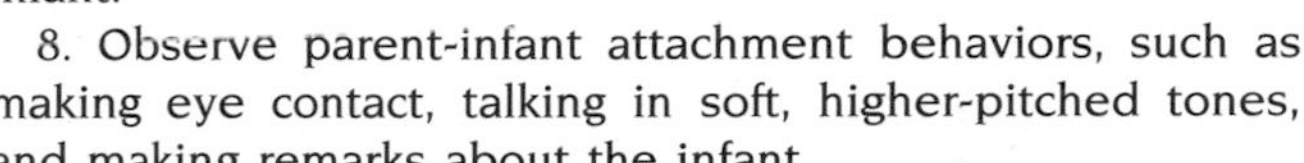

8. Observe parent-infant attachment behaviors, such as making eye contact, talking in soft, higher-pitched tones, and making remarks about the infant.
9. In many facilities, the infant remains with the parents during the recovery period, and the same nurse cares for both the mother and the newborn. If so, continue to observe the infant's respiratory effort and maintain the temperature.

Postpartum Care: Physiological Aspects

Text to Prepare You for Clinical Practice

Procedure 17–1: Assessing the uterine fundus
Procedure 17–2: Assessing the perineum
Figure 17–2: Estimating volume of lochia
Figure 17–7: Assessing Homans' sign
Table 17–1: Characteristics of lochia
Table 17–4: Observations of the fundus requiring nursing actions

New Terms

Afterpains
Atony
Colostrum
Engorgement
Episiotomy
Fundus
Lochia rubra, serosa, alba
Puerperium
REEDA (redness, edema, ecchymosis drainage, approximation)

Equipment and Supplies

Thermometer
Blood pressure equipment
Watch
Stethoscope
Flashlight
Non-sterile gloves
Peripads
Clean belt
Clean linen
Disposable underpads

Normal Assessments

Vital Signs

Temperature. Lower than 38°C (100.4°F).

Blood pressure. Near the baseline levels established during pregnancy.

Pulse. 50 to 60/minute is not unusual. Bradycardia reflects increased amount of blood returning to the central circulation.

Respirations. 16 to 20/minute. Should be unchanged from pre-conception levels; the lungs should be free of adventitious breath sounds.

Breasts

a. *First 24 hours.* Soft.

b. *Days 2 to 3.* Firm to very firm, as milk comes in.

Nipples. Free of redness, abraded areas, or fissures.

Gastrointestinal System

1. Mother hungry and thirsty.
2. Abdomen soft; temporary constipation may occur because of dehydration and decreased intake during labor.
3. Bowel sounds usually present within 24 to 36 hours after cesarean birth.
4. Hemorrhoids may be obvious, particularly during first 24 hours.

Genitourinary System

1. Diuresis normal for first 2 to 3 days; mother often unaware of need to urinate.
2. After voiding, bladder not palpable; fundus remains firm and at the level of the umbilicus.
3. Lochia rubra moderate to scant, with a fleshy, earthy odor.
4. Abdominal dressings for cesarean incision dry and intact until removed by physician or registered nurse.
5. Episiotomy or cesarean birth incision approximated; perineum free of severe edema, bruising, or severe discomfort.

Nursing Care

Preparation before approaching the new mother will help the beginning nurse to recognize unusual or abnormal data and to initiate the necessary nursing interventions. Moreover, it will build self-confidence that, in turn, inspires confidence in the new mother and sets the stage for individualized nursing care.

Non-sterile gloves must be worn whenever the possibility of contact with body fluids (blood, lochia, colostrum, breast milk, urine, or stool) exists.

The sequence in which postpartum assessments are performed is important because they should progress from areas that are least likely to be contaminated, such as the breasts, to areas that are associated with pathogenic organisms, such as the perineum and anal areas. The following sequence is recommended.

ASSESSMENTS

1. Explain the purpose of the assessments: "I know we do these assessments several times a day, but it is necessary to be sure everything is progressing as it should. It is also a good time for you to ask any questions you might have."
2. Assess vital signs, usually every 2 to 8 hours, depending on facility protocols and the condition of the mother.
3. Observe and report edema of the face or hands that may suggest pregnancy-induced hypertension.
4. Auscultate breath sounds and ability to deep breathe and cough if the woman had a cesarean birth, if she smokes, or if she has a history of respiratory disorders.
5. Ask the mother to unfasten her bra or to lower the bra flaps to assess the nipples for redness, fissures, or blisters that may occur with breastfeeding. Note nipple size and shape that may make breastfeeding more difficult (flat, retracted, inverted). Palpate the breasts; this is a good time to ask how well breastfeeding is progressing and if there are questions.
6. Lower the top of the bed, and ask the mother to flex her knees for comfort; palpate the abdomen (soft or distended?). If the woman had a cesarean birth, auscultate the abdomen for bowel sounds and ask if she is passing flatus.
7. Observe the dressing covering the incision for intactness or discharge; if the dressing has been removed, observe the cesarean incision for REEDA and note if staples, Steri-Strips, or skin clips remain in place.
8. Assess for bladder distention: time and amount of last voiding (can be validated from the chart before beginning the assessment), observable or palpable bulge above symphysis pubis. If an indwelling catheter is in place, note the color and amount of urine.
9. Palpate the lower extremities for the presence and extent of edema; press the thumb on the pretibial area and the feet to determine if pitting edema is present; note how long it takes for the pit to disappear.
10. Observe and palpate the lower extremities for signs of thrombophlebitis (areas of redness, tenderness, swelling). Sharply dorsiflex the foot to elicit Homans' sign.
11. Lower the perineal pad(s) and observe flow of lochia  while palpating the fundus for firmness and location.
12. Observe the perineal pad(s) for color and amount of lochia; ask how long since the peripad(s) was changed to determine the amount of flow; note unpleasant or foul odor.
13. Ask the mother to turn to her side to assess the perineum for REEDA. Note the number and size of hemorrhoids.
14. Evaluate the mother's ability to ambulate, and elicit information about dizziness, weakness, or lightheadedness during ambulation. Observe gait for steadiness and balance.
15. Ask the mother about particular problems and concerns. How is her appetite? How much rest is she getting? Does she have discomfort (where, when)? Does she require medication?

INTERVENTIONS

1. Changes in vital signs may be within expected limits or they may indicate the beginning of serious problems. Tachycardia or lower than expected blood pressure may indicate excessive bleeding and should be reported. When blood pressure is higher than expected, it may indicate pregnancy-induced hypertension. The blood pressure should be reassessed in both arms with the client in a left lateral recumbent position. *Temperature above 38°C (100.4°F) suggests infection rather than dehydration and should be reassessed and reported to the primary nurse. Diminished or abnormal breath sounds (wheezes or crackles), as well as difficulty breathing or coughing, should be reported at once.*

2. Nipple trauma provides a portal for entry of pathogenic organisms and creates discomfort during breastfeeding. The new mother often needs information, guidance, and encouragement with breastfeeding.

3. *Report at once if unable to locate the fundus, if the fundus feels soft (boggy), or if it is above the umbilicus or displaced from the midline.* Be prepared to assist the mother to void or to catheterize her if she is unable to empty her bladder. Use uterine massage to contract a boggy uterus.

4. *Report positive Homans' sign as well as areas of redness, edema, or tenderness of the legs.* Assist to ambulate if the gait is unsteady or the mother experiences lightheadedness when she ambulates.

5. If necessary, teach self-care measures, such as perineal care and sitz bath, to reduce perineal discomfort and to prevent infection.

6. Provide medication for afterpains or perineal discomfort according to the physician's orders; reassure the mother that very little of the medication administered for discomfort crosses into the breast milk and that the infant should not be affected.

Postpartum Care: Psychosocial Aspects

Text to Prepare You for Clinical Practice

Table 18–1: Assessing maternal adaptation
Table 18–2: Assessing family adaptation

New Terms

Attachment
Bonding
En face
Engrossment
Entrainment
Finger-tipping
Letting-go
Reciprocal bonding behaviors
Taking-hold
Taking-in

Normal Assessments

Maternal touch. During the first 24 hours, the mother progresses from the discovery phase, when she "finger-tips" the infant, to enfolding the infant and demonstrating a range of consoling behaviors.

Verbal expressions. The mother progresses from referring to the infant as "it" to "he" or "she" and finally to calling the infant by a given name.

Taking-in phase. Mothers are concerned with their own physical needs and the need to recount details of their labor and delivery.

Taking-hold phase. Mothers become more independent and focus on learning how to care for themselves and the infant.

Fathers. Fathers demonstrate intense fascination with the infant and are often observed to respond gently to infant signals, such as fussing or crying.

Family. Family support is obvious when the grandparents visit, offer to assist the mother, and demonstrate interest in the newborn.

Nursing Care

Although a psychological assessment is never as precise as a physical assessment, it is nevertheless essential, and a fairly systematic method can be developed. In order to sharpen observational skills, students should review expected maternal behaviors, progression of maternal touch, and verbal interactions before beginning a psychosocial assessment.

Pertinent observations may escape those who are unprepared and who make a casual, uninformed assessment. However, with preparation and careful practice, observational skills increase rapidly.

ASSESSMENTS

1. Collect data from the woman's chart (age, gravida, para, time and type of delivery, sex, and weight of infant, unusual characteristics or anomalies of infant, time mother was last medicated for discomfort) to identify factors that might affect adjustment.

2. Be prepared to begin a psychosocial assessment during the physical assessment, and continue to make observations throughout the day.

3. Observe maternal mood, general energy level, and activity.

4. Ask about the mother's comfort, how she slept, and whether she has special concerns.

5. Note the focus of the mother's attention—is it on

her needs or on care of the infant? Does she require assistance with hygiene and self-care measures? How much does she talk of the birth experience?

6. Observe the mother's interaction with the infant and her readiness to participate in infant care. Note voice tone and verbal interaction.

7. Watch how the mother touches the infant and how she responds to infant cues, such as crying or fussing.

8. Note the father's participation in infant care and his comfort handling the infant.

9. Notice infant behavior (awake, response to parents' voices, gazing); watch closely how the infant responds to the parents and whether the parents are successful in consoling the infant.

10. Observe visitors, particularly the grandparents and family who may provide assistance to the parents during the early weeks at home.

INTERVENTIONS

1. Anticipate needs and provide physical care and comfort measures that are particularly important in the early hours following childbirth.

2. Allow time to listen; this is very important in establishing rapport and assisting the mother to integrate the birth experience into her reality system.

3. Promote bonding and attachment by providing long periods of uninterrupted contact between the parents and the infant and by modeling behaviors, such as gentle response when the infant cries and talking to the infant in a high-pitched voice. Point out positive characteristics of the infant to the parents.

4. Prepare to teach basic infant care by observing videos and staff demonstrations. Clarify questions of care with instructor or primary nurse.

5. Answer questions or demonstrate care as the mother indicates a readiness to learn.

The Newborn: Care During Admission

Text to Prepare You for Clinical Practice

Procedure 20–2: Weighing and measuring
Procedure 20–3: Administering intramuscular injections to newborns
Procedure 20–4: Assessing vital signs in the newborn
Procedure 20–5: Using a bulb syringe
Procedure 20–6: Assessing blood glucose in the newborn
Table 20–1: Summary of newborn assessment

New Terms

Acrocyanosis
Caput succedaneum
Cephalohematoma
Hyperbilirubinemia
Lanugo
Milia
Molding
Mongolian spots
Vernix caseosa

Equipment and Supplies

Scale
Radiant warmer
Non-sterile gloves
Stethoscope
Thermometer
Tape measure
Vitamin K, syringe, filter needle, alcohol wipes
Eye medication
Bulb syringe

Normal Assessments

Vital Signs

Temperature:
a. Rectal—36.5° to 37.6°C (97.7° to 99.7°F).
b. Axillary— 36.5° to 37.5°C (97.7° to 99.5°F).
Heart rate. 120 to 160/minute.
Respirations. 30 to 60/minute.

Blood Glucose. Above 45 mg/dl by screening tests.

Measurements

Weight. 2700 to 4000 g (6 to 9 pounds).
Length. 48 to 53 cm (19 to 21 inches).
Head circumference. 33 to 35.5 cm (13 to 14 inches).
Chest circumference. 30.5 to 33 cm (12 to 13 inches).

Nursing Care

A typical order in which assessments and care are done in the labor, delivery, recovery unit or the admission nursery is given here. What is actually included and the order in which it is done will vary, depending on the facility's routine and the circumstances.

Adhere to universal precautions at all times. Wear non-sterile gloves at all times when handling the infant until the bath is given and all blood is removed from the skin. After the bath, wear gloves when soiling with body fluids is likely. 

Include family members who are present. They are often very interested in explanations of the assessments and care being given. Promote bonding by encouraging them to touch and talk to the infant.

ASSESSMENTS

Begin with a quick overall assessment of the infant's general condition before beginning a more detailed assessment. Attend to major problems, such as severe respiratory distress, before continuing the rest of the assessment and care. Observe for signs of distress or abnormality throughout the admission period, as this is the time when they are most likely to appear. Report and take action, as necessary, for any abnormal assessments.

1. Take weight and measure length and head and chest circumferences.
2. Assess vital signs. *Report and follow up on abnormalities immediately.*
3. Assess for and report gross abnormalities in any system. *Be constantly alert for signs of respiratory distress.*
4. Assess blood glucose according to signs of hypoglycemia and agency policy.
5. Perform overall assessment (see Table 20–4).
6. Continue monitoring vital signs every 15 minutes for the first hour, then hourly for the next 4 hours. Once stable, vital signs should be checked every 8 hours, and more frequently if abnormal.

INTERVENTIONS

1. Position the infant with the head lower than the body for a short time to drain airways. Suction as necessary. Return the infant to flat position as soon as drainage of airways is completed.
2. Take footprints, if not done previously.
3. Administer antibiotic to the eyes, and administer vitamin K injection. *Note*: do not give vitamin K until after the bath.
4. Allow the infant to rest quietly under radiant warmer when not being assessed or receiving care. Keep positioned on side with a rolled blanket to promote drainage of secretions.
5. Bathe the infant if the temperature is 37°C (98.6°F) axillary or above to remove blood and excess vernix. It is not necessary to remove all vernix. Keep the infant warm by drying as quickly as possible and removing wet linens. Dry the hair thoroughly to prevent heat loss.
6. Give first feeding. Give a few sips of plain sterile water to see if tolerated. Then change to dextrose 5 per cent in water or formula, according to facility policy. Give no more than 1 ounce. Assist breastfeeding mothers with the initial feeding. Burp the infant halfway through feeding.
7. Watch continuously for circumoral or other cyanosis, indicating that the infant is not breathing when sucking. Stop feeding and stimulate the infant by rubbing the back. Suction, if necessary, with bulb syringe. Continue feeding when the infant has regained color. Place the infant on right side with rolled diaper behind the back after feeding, or elevate head of bed slightly.
8. Complete gestational age assessment.
9. Prepare for transfer if the infant will be moved to another nursery or to the mother's room. Place clothing and blankets under the warmer to heat. Take last set of vital signs, dress, put on hat, wrap in two warmed blankets. Complete charting.
10. Give report if another nurse will take over care of the infant. Include gravida, para, length of labor, medications/anesthesia used in labor and delivery, time of rupture of membranes, any complications during birth, feeding, voids and stools, any problems in the nursery, and any other pertinent information.

The Newborn: Daily Care

Text to Prepare You for Clinical Practice

Procedure 20–1: Identifying infants
Procedure 20–4: Assessing vital signs in the newborn
Procedure 20–5: Using a bulb syringe
Parents Want to Know: Caring for the uncircumcised penis
Parents Want to Know: How to care for the circumcision site

New Terms

Erythema toxicum
Hypoglycemia
Nonshivering thermogenesis

Equipment and Supplies

Stethoscope
Thermometer
Alcohol wipes

Normal Assessments

Vital Signs

Temperature.
a. Rectal—36.5° to 37.6°C (97.7° to 99.7°F).
b. Axillary—36.5° to 37.5°C (97.7° to 99.5°F).
Heart rate. 120 to 160/minute.
Respirations. 30 to 60/minute.

Blood Glucose. Above 45 mg/dl by screening tests.

Nursing Care

Assess and care for infants using the following list as a guide. Keep in mind that the role of the nurse is to continue to observe for abnormalities and complications, as well as to assess progress of mother-infant bonding and the mother's ability to care for the infant.

ASSESSMENTS

1. *Vital signs.* Assess vital signs once every 8 hours and more often if there are any abnormalities. Begin with res-

pirations and pulse before disturbing the infant, if asleep. Temperature should be stable after the first day, and action is needed if not. Continue to listen for abnormal heart sounds. Murmurs heard earlier may disappear after the first day as transition to neonatal circulation becomes complete. Note acrocyanosis or other cyanosis. Listen to breath sounds, which should be clear.

2. *Weight.* Weigh infants once every 24 hours according to agency routine. Take weight at the same time each day.

3. *Skin.* Assess all skin areas to observe for new marks or changes in existing ones. Compare with previous assessments. Expect skin to be dry and peeling. Look for redness, scratches (keep hands covered), rashes, signs of skin breakdown or infection. Erythema toxicum may become more apparent. Caput succedaneum may be resolved by 2nd day, cephalohematoma resolves in several weeks. Physiologic jaundice may begin to develop after first 24 hours. Blanch skin over nose and bony prominences, and note color. Check cord and base of cord for redness, foul odor, serosanguineous or purulent drainage. Note how well cord is drying. Remove clamp when end of cord is dry and crisp (about 24 hours).

4. *Neurological.* Note state of alertness (six stages) and movement of extremities, reflexes (especially Moro, rooting, suck). Observe eyes for signs of inflammation (redness, drainage); may be due to reaction to eye medication or infection. Cleanse drainage with sterile water from inner to outer canthus, being certain no drainage from one eye gets into the other. Watch for signs of hypoglycemia ("jitteriness," tremors). Check fontanelle with the infant in upright position. Should be soft and flat. *Report fullness, bulging, depression.*

5. *Musculoskeletal.* Note movement of extremities and muscle tone. The infant should resist when extremities are extended. Note molding of the infant to the caregiver's body or arching of the infant's back.

6. *Gastrointestinal.* Abdomen should be soft, bowel sounds present. Observe part of feeding if the mother is doing all feedings. Assess for suck and swallow coordination, choking, length of time feeding lasts, amount taken, any regurgitation. Ask the mother how she feels the feedings are going. Note type and number of stools. Know if the infant has had stool on present shift and when last stool was. (First stool is generally within 24 hours of birth, usually sooner.)

7. *Genitourinary.* Note number of voidings, color of urine on diaper. Know if the infant has voided on present shift and when last voiding was. Expect the infant to have at least two to six wet diapers per day during the first 2 days of life and six to ten wet diapers per day thereafter. (First voiding should occur within 24 hours, usually sooner.) Observe circumcision site for drainage (purulent, serous, sanguineous—frank bleeding or oozing.) Determine if the infant is voiding after circumcision performed.

8. *Bonding.* Observe bonding behaviors in the mother and infant. Note how the mother holds the infant, whether she talks to infant, calls infant by name, etc. Note response of the infant to the mother's care.

9. *Teaching.* Assess in which areas the mother (or the parents) need teaching.

INTERVENTIONS

The following care of the infant is typical throughout the day. In addition, make rounds frequently (at least every hour) to monitor the progress of the mother in infant care and to determine the need for further interventions.

1. *Cord care.* Apply alcohol to the cord once or more each shift according to agency routine. Use an alcohol wipe or an applicator dipped in alcohol. Cleanse all parts of the cord and the crevices of the umbilicus. Do not apply alcohol to the skin around the cord because this is drying to the skin. Some units use "triple dye" or other bactericidal agents once daily.

2. *Care of circumcision site.* If a Plastibell was used, no special care is necessary other than observation for complications. If a Gomco clamp was used, squeeze petroleum jelly liberally over the circumcision site (and apply gauze if part of agency routine) at each diaper change for the first 24 hours. Assess the mother's knowledge of care of the circumcision site, and teach as necessary. Monitor incision throughout the day for redness, edema, purulent or sanguineous drainage, or odor.

3. *Identification.* If the mother and infant are separated at any time, use the proper identification process each time the infant is reunited with the mother.

4. *Protection.* Maintain vigilance against kidnappers at all times. Follow methods to provide for infant security.

5. *Feedings.* Determine if the infant is taking feedings adequately (every 2 to 3 hours if breastfed, every 4 hours if formula fed). Record each feeding with type, amount (or how long nursed at each breast), how feeding taken, and any regurgitation. Teach the mother as necessary.

6. *Elimination.* Record each wet diaper and stool. Note color, amount, consistency.

7. *Continue observation.* Observe for problems throughout the shift.

8. *Continue teaching.* Teach parents as needed along with the "scheduled" teaching that is part of the plan made at the beginning of the shift.

Assisting the Inexperienced Breastfeeding Mother

Text to Prepare You for Clinical Practice

Figure 21–5: Cradle hold
Figure 21–6: Football hold
Figure 21–7: Cross-cradle hold
Figure 21–8: Side-lying position
Figure 21–10: C position of hand on breast
Mothers Want to Know: Is my baby getting enough milk?

Mothers Want to Know: Solutions to common breastfeeding problems
Mothers Want to Know: Breastfeeding after the birth of more than one infant
Mothers Want to Know: How to wean from breastfeeding

New Terms

Latch-on
Nutritive suckling
Non-nutritive suckling

Normal Assessments

1. The infant is positioned facing the breast, and the body is well supported.
2. The mother is in a comfortable position and holds her breast so that the infant can take it into the mouth without interference.
3. The infant's mouth covers the nipple and as much of the areola as possible.
4. Suckling includes audible swallowing.

Nursing Care

This is a summary of information that nurses can use to help the inexperienced mother, especially during the first breastfeeding sessions.

Assessments

1. Assess the mother's knowledge about breastfeeding technique.
2. Assess the mother's nipples to identify flat or inverted nipples or nipple trauma.
3. Assess the infant's behavior state, sucking reflex, and coordination of sucking and swallowing.

INTERVENTIONS

1. Plan with the mother when the infant will be fed, and note any questions or concerns that she has about breastfeeding. Be sure that she is comfortable (pain relief needs met, etc.) and not in the middle of other care (a.m. care, meals). However, if the infant must eat immediately because of concerns about hypoglycemia, the mother's needs must be met quickly or postponed.
2. Explain that breastfeeding is a learned skill for both the mother and the infant and that practice is required to perfect the skill.
3. Bring the awake, hungry infant to the mother. Begin before the infant is ravenously hungry and upset.
4. Assist the mother to a sitting or side-lying position, and help her position the infant. Use pillows or bath blankets for comfort behind the mother's back, protecting any abdominal incision and raising the infant to nipple level.
   a. *Sitting.* Raise the head of the bed to a high Fowler's position. Place a pillow behind the mother's back and under elbow to support arm.
   b. *Cradle hold.* Place the infant in the mother's arms, with the head at the antecubital space (or at nipple level) and the mother's arm extending along the infant's body. The mother's other hand will position the breast. The infant should be totally on the side facing the breast so that no turning of the head is necessary.
   c. *Football hold.* Place the infant's head in the mother's hand, with the body extending along her side.
   d. *Side-lying.* Place pillows behind the mother's back and between her legs as she lies on her side. Her lower arm may go under her head or around the infant, while her upper hand positions the breast. Place the infant on the side, facing the breast, using pillows to pad siderails and to maintain position.
5. Demonstrate proper hand position, with the hand cupped around the breast with the thumb on top and with the fingers supporting the breast below. Keep the fingers and thumb behind the areola.
6. Elicit latch-on. Brush the nipple against the infant's lower lip until the infant opens the mouth wide. Then bring the infant toward the breast while inserting the nipple and as much of the areola as possible into the infant's mouth.
7. Assess the mouth position. The infant's mouth should be 1 to 1½ inches from base of the nipple with the lips flared outward. Remove the infant from the breast, and start over if dimpling of cheeks, clicking, or smacking sounds occur.
8. Assess the infant's suck. Nutritive suckling is smooth and continuous with occasional pauses. A swallow follows every one to three sucks and has a "ka" or "ah" sound. Non-nutritive suckling is choppy with no swallowing. Remove the infant from the breast and burp, change sides, awaken, or let sleep if feeding is finished. Do not jiggle the breast in the infant's mouth to stimulate suck or the infant may lose grip and chew on the nipple.
9. Demonstrate removal from the breast. Have the mother insert finger into corner of the infant's mouth to release suction. Remove the infant immediately.
10. Have the mother nurse at least 10 to 15 minutes per side at first. Burp the infant between breasts. Instruct her to nurse every 2 to 3 hours during the day and at least every 4 hours throughout the night to build the milk supply.
11. Observe the mother at intervals after the feeding begins. Help her switch sides to observe for difficulty. Then observe the mother at other feedings to give reinforcement and correct technique as needed. Offer praise generously because feeding the infant may affect the mother's view of her mothering abilities.

Appendix F

Answers to ✔Check Your Reading Questions

Chapter 1

1. Federal involvement and consumer demands.
2. Provides safe, quality care that adapts to both the physical and the psychosocial needs of the entire family during reproduction and greatly increases the responsibilities of nurses providing care.
3. Birthing centers provide professional care during pregnancy and childbirth in a home-like environment for women with low-risk pregnancies. They are associated with a nearby hospital in case of unexpected complications. The home setting, while providing comfort and closeness, may not have adequate equipment to handle unexpected developments.
4. Improved health of population, application of basic principles of sanitation, increase in medical knowledge, widespread availability of antibiotics, and improved prenatal care.
5. The higher incidence of poverty among African-American families is associated with inadequate prenatal care and the birth of low-birth-weight infants who are less likely to survive.
6. The United States ranks 21st in the world. Japan, Switzerland, and Canada all have lower infant mortality rates.
7. Mainstream families are headed by a husband and wife who view parenting as the major priority in their lives and whose energies are not depleted by poverty, illness, or substance abuse. Nontraditional families are defined by their unique structure and include single-parent families, blended families, extended families, homosexual families, and adoptive families.
8. Families below the poverty level; those headed by a single teenage parent; those with a preterm, ill, or handicapped infant; and those with lifestyle problems, such as substance abuse or family violence.
9. Ability to adapt, without undue stress, to the changes precipitated by childbirth. They communicate openly, volunteer assistance, and agree on basic principles of child care.
10. Lack of financial resources, absence of adequate family support, birth of an infant who requires specialized care, unhealthy habits (smoking, substance abuse), and the inability to make mature decisions.
11. To examine how their beliefs may generate conflict with those who hold different cultural beliefs.
12. The Western practice of dividing time into minutes and seconds and the emphasis on "being on time" creates conflicts with cultures that measure time in days or seasons and fail to understand the importance of precise time in the health care setting.
13. Prenatal care may be delayed when women who possess a feeling of fatalism do not plan for future events but leave them to the will of God.

Chapter 2

1. It is purposeful, goal-directed, and focused.
2. Conveying a lack of interest or haste; closed posture; interrupting; providing false reassurance; inappropriate self-disclosure; giving advice; failure to acknowledge comments or feelings.
3. Clarifying, paraphrasing, reflecting, silence, structuring, pinpointing, questioning, directing, summarizing.
4. Learning is increased when the learner demonstrates a readiness to learn, participates actively, is allowed to repeat a skill, and receives positive feedback, and when frustration is acknowledged and resolved before teaching begins. Effective methods of teaching include role modeling, presenting simple tasks before more complex material, and using a variety of teaching methods.
5. Developmental level, language, culture, previous experience, physical environment, and the organization and skill of the instructor.
6. The data base assessment gathers information about all aspects of the client's health. A focus assessment gathers information about an actual health problem.
7. Actual nursing diagnoses reflect health problems that can be validated by the presence of defining characteristics. High-risk nursing diagnoses indicate that risk factors are present that make the client vulnerable to the development of a particular health problem.
8. Goals should be stated in terms of the client; they should be observable and measurable; they must have a time frame; they should be realistic.
9. Nursing interventions that are not specific and do not clearly spell out exactly what is to be done are difficult to implement. Clearly written interventions that provide detailed instructions correct the problem.
10. Nursing diagnoses describe health problems that nurses can independently treat and for which they are legally accountable. Collaborative problems are potential complications that require physician-prescribed as well as nursing-prescribed interventions.
11. Goals for collaborative problems incorrectly imply accountability for problems that nurses cannot independently manage.

Chapter 3

1. Ethics examines conduct and distinctions between right and wrong. Bioethics applies only to the ethics of health care.
2. Deontological ethical theory applies ethical principles to determine what is right and does not vary the solution according to individual situations. Utilitarian theory analyzes the benefits and burdens to determine a course of action that provides the greatest amount of good for the greatest number of people.
3. Ethical principles of beneficence, non-maleficence, autonomy, and justice result in conflict in many situations.
4. Steps of the nursing process can be used to gather data from all concerned persons. Ethical theories and principles are analyzed to determine if an ethical dilemma exists. Planning involves identifying as many options as possible and choosing a solution. Interventions must be identified to implement the chosen solution, and the results are evaluated.

5. The Supreme Court decision of *Roe v. Wade* declared that abortion was legal anywhere in the United States and that existing state laws prohibiting abortion were unconstitutional because they interfered with the woman's right to privacy.
6. The belief that abortion is a private choice conflicts with the belief that abortion is taking a life.
7. States cannot give a husband veto power over his spouse's decision to have an abortion; states do not have an obligation to pay for abortions; physicians are given broad discretion to determine fetal viability; states may restrict abortions of viable fetuses. In addition, states may require parental consent for minors to obtain abortion as long as an alternative (judge's approval) is available; states may require a woman to wait 24 hours before seeking and obtaining an abortion; states may not require that a married woman must inform her husband before obtaining an abortion.
8. At the time they are hired, nurses must disclose their feelings about caring for women having an abortion.
9. Punitive approaches are against the principle of autonomy, bodily integrity, and personal freedom, and the resulting fear may jeopardize the health care of pregnant women.
10. Punishing the mother for fetal injury carries with it the danger of many women refusing to seek prenatal care, which becomes a cause of fetal injury.
11. Poverty is the underlying factor that causes many other problems, such as inadequate access to health care. The lack of access to health care is a major reason for the large number of low-birth-weight infants and the high infant mortality rate.
12. The focus has been on treatment and cure of illness; however, prevention is less expensive and provides care for greater numbers.
13. Standards of care are set by professional associations and describe the level of care that can be expected from practitioners.
14. Negligence is failure to perform the way a reasonable and prudent person of similar background would act in a like situation. Malpractice is negligence by professionals (including nurses) in the performance of their duties.
15. Nurses can prevent malpractice claims by following guidelines for informed consent, refusal of consent, and documentation and by maintaining their level of expertise.

Chapter 4

1. Development of the breasts is the first sign of puberty in girls. Appearance of pubic hair and a growth spurt occur at about the same time. In boys, growth of the testes is the first sign, followed by growth of the penis about a year later.
2. Usually, Asians and Native Americans have less and finer body hair than either Caucasians or African-Americans. African-Americans usually have body hair that is coarser and curlier than Asians, Native Americans, or Caucasians.
3. The female pelvis has a wide, rounded basin shape that favors childbearing. The male pelvis is heavier, narrower, and structurally suited for tasks requiring load-bearing.
4. Males generally attain a greater adult height than females because they begin their growth spurt about 1 year later than girls and continue growing for a longer period of time.
5. The female's secondary sex characteristics include round hips and breasts and the growth of pubic hair. Male secondary sex characteristics include presence of facial and pubic hair, a deeper voice, broader shoulders, and a greater muscle mass.
6. The female external reproductive organs are collectively called the vulva. The labia majora extend from the mons pubis to the perineum. The labia minora are within and parallel to the labia majora. The clitoris is at the anterior junction of the labia minora. The urinary meatus and vaginal introitus are found within the vestibule (the area enclosed by the labia minora). The hymen partly closes the vaginal opening. The perineum extends from the fourchette (posterior rim of the vaginal opening) to the anus.
7. The three divisions of the uterus are the corpus (body), isthmus, and cervix (neck).
8. The perimetrium is the outer peritoneal layer covering the uterus. Myometrium is the middle layer of thick muscle. The endometrium is the inner layer of the uterus.
9. The fallopian tubes are lined with cells that have cilia that beat rhythmically toward the uterine cavity to propel the ovum through the fallopian tube.
10. The two functions of the ovaries are to produce hormones (primarily estrogen and progesterone) and to mature on ovum for release during each reproductive cycle.
11. The pelvis is located at the lower end of the spine. The true pelvis is that part which is located below the linea terminalis.
12. Pelvic muscles enclose the lower pelvis and support internal reproductive, urinary, and bowel structures.
13. The ripening follicle secretes estrogen. After ovulation, the follicle (now called the corpus luteum) secretes large amounts of estrogen and progesterone.
14. Three ovarian phases of the female reproductive cycle are the follicular (maturation of an ovum), ovulation (release of the mature ovum), and luteal (secretion of estrogen and progesterone by the corpus luteum).
15. Three phases of endometrial changes occur with each female reproductive cycle. The proliferative phase occurs during the first half of the cycle and is when the endometrium becomes thicker. The secretory phase occurs during the last half of the cycle and is characterized by continued growth of the endometrium, growth of blood vessels and glands, and secretion of substances to nourish a fertilized ovum. If pregnancy does not occur, the endometrium becomes ischemic and necrotic and is shed in the menstrual phase.
16. The cervical mucus becomes thin, clear, and elastic during ovulation to facilitate entrance of sperm from the vagina into the uterus, thus enhancing the chances for conception.
17. Montgomery's tubercles secrete a substance during pregnancy and lactation that keeps the nipples soft.
18. A woman's breast size is not related to the amount of milk she can produce. It is influenced by the amount of fatty tissue in the breast.
19. Milk secretion does not occur during pregnancy because estrogen and progesterone produced by the placenta inhibit its production.
20. The penis has two functions. As a urinary organ, it transports urine from the bladder to outside the body during urination. As an organ of reproduction, it carries and deposits the semen into the vagina during coitus.
21. The two types of erectile tissue in the penis are the corpus spongiosum and the two columns of corpus cavernosum tissue on each side of the penis. The function of erectile tissue is to facilitate entry of the penis into the female's vagina.
22. The scrotum holds the testes away from the body to keep them cooler than the core body temperature, thus facilitating sperm production.
23. The testes function as endocrine glands, producing testosterone and the male gametes (spermatozoa).

Chapter 5

1. A gene is part of a chromosome. Each chromosome is composed of a varying number of genes.
2. Genes are too small to be seen under a microscope. They can be studied by analyzing the products they direct cells to produce, by direct study of the DNA, or by their close association with another gene that can be more easily studied.
3. Chromosomes can be seen under a microscope when living cells are dividing.
4. 46,XY is an abbreviation that describes the chromosome

makeup of a normal human male. 46,XX describes the chromosomes of a normal female.

5. The child of a parent who has an autosomal dominant disorder has a 50 per cent chance of having the same disorder.
6. Blood relationship (consanguinity) of parents increases the likelihood that both share some of the same harmful autosomal recessive genes, increasing the chance that their offspring will be affected with a disorder.
7. If both parents carry an abnormal gene for an autosomal recessive disorder, each of their children has a 25 per cent chance of receiving both copies of the defective gene and having the disorder. Each child also has a 50 per cent chance of receiving only one copy of the defective gene, thus being a carrier like the parents. Each child also has a 25 per cent chance of receiving the normal gene from each parent, thus being neither a carrier nor affected.
8. Males are more likely to have X-linked recessive disorders because they do not have a compensating X chromosome that has a normal gene. Sons of female carriers have a 50 per cent chance of having the trait and a 50 per cent chance of being unaffected. Daughters of the female carrier have a 50 per cent chance of being carriers and a 50 per cent chance of being unaffected.
9. A trisomy exists when each body cell contains an extra copy of one chromosome. Down syndrome is the most common trisomy.
10. A monosomy exists when each body cell is missing a chromosome. Turner's syndrome (a female with a single X chromosome) is the only monosomy compatible with life.
11. Genetic material can be lost or duplicated when a chromosome has a structural abnormality. Also, the position of genes on the chromosome may be altered, preventing them from functioning normally.
12. A parent with a balanced chromosome translocation may have a child with completely normal chromosomes, or the child may have a balanced chromosome translocation like the parent. The offspring may also receive an unbalanced amount of chromosome material, which often results in spontaneous abortion or birth defects.
13. Multifactorial disorders are typically present and detectable at birth. They are also isolated defects rather than being present with other unrelated defects.
14. Factors that may affect the likelihood that a multifactorial disorder will occur or recur include:
    a. The number of affected close relatives.
    b. The severity of the defect in those affected.
    c. The sex of the affected person.
    d. Geographical location.
    e. Seasonal variations.
15. The woman may be able to avoid exposing her fetus to teratogens by immunization against infections such as rubella, eliminating the use of nontherapeutic drugs such as alcohol or illicit drugs, changing therapeutic drugs to those having a lower risk to the fetus, and avoiding x-rays at a time when she may be pregnant.
16. A pregnant woman who has phenylketonuria (PKU) should return to her low-phenylalanine diet when she is pregnant so that toxic metabolic products do not build up and damage her fetus.

Chapter 6

1. Meiosis is a reduction in cell division that halves the number of chromosomes so that only one of each chromosome pair goes into each gamete. The union of male and female gametes at conception restores the number of chromosomes to 46 in the offspring.
2. One mature ovum results from meiosis of the oogonium.
3. Each spermatogonium produces four mature spermatozoa.
4. Fertilization usually occurs in the distal one third of the fallopian tube.
5. Seminal fluid nourishes and protects the sperm from the acidic environment of the woman's vagina.
6. When a spermatozoon penetrates the ovum, changes in the zona pellucida prevent other spermatozoa from entering. The ovum also completes its second meiotic division.
7. Fertilization is complete when the nuclei of the ovum and spermatozoon unite.
8. Implantation begins 6 days after conception and is completed on the 10th day.
9. The fundus, or upper uterus, is the ideal location for implantation for three reasons. It is rich with blood for fetal gas exchange and nutrition. The uterine lining is thick and prevents the placenta from attaching too deeply. The strong interlacing muscle fibers in the fundus contract to limit blood loss after birth.
10. Nutritive fluids produced in the thick endometrium pass to the conceptus by diffusion before a placental circulation is established.
11. During the first 8 weeks after conception, all major organ systems develop. The woman may be unaware that she is pregnant and inadvertently expose the embryo to harmful substances.
12. At 4 weeks, the trachea develops as a bud of the upper digestive tract and branches into the two bronchi. Branching continues until terminal air sacs develop.
13. The intestines are mostly contained within the umbilical cord until 10 weeks because they grow more rapidly than the abdominal cavity and because the liver and kidneys are relatively large. By 10 weeks, the abdominal cavity has caught up with the growth of its contents and can accommodate them.
14. Vernix caseosa protects fetal skin from constant exposure to amniotic fluid. Lanugo helps vernix adhere to the skin. Brown fat helps the newborn maintain temperature stability. Surfactant keeps the lung alveoli from collapsing with each expiration, thus making breathing easier after birth.
15. The fetus usually assumes a head-down position because this position fits the egg shape of the uterus best. Also, the head is heavier and tends to go downward in the pool of amniotic fluid.
16. Gestational age is calculated from the woman's last menstrual period and is about 2 weeks longer than fertilization age. Gestational age is the most commonly used because the menstrual period provides a specific marker.
17. The placenta gradually takes over the function of the corpus luteum and secretes estrogen and progesterone.
18. Exchange of oxygen, nutrients, and waste products between the woman and the fetus takes place in the intervillous spaces of the placenta.
19. It is important that the maternal and fetal blood do not mix because they may be of incompatible blood types.
20. The fetus can thrive in a relatively low-oxygen environment because:
    a. Fetal hemoglobin carries more oxygen than adult hemoglobin.
    b. The fetus has a higher hemoglobin and hematocrit level than does the newborn or adult.
    c. Rapid diffusion of carbon dioxide into the maternal blood causes her to give up oxygen more readily and causes oxygen to combine with fetal blood more readily.
21. The fetal membranes contain the amniotic fluid, which cushions the fetus, maintains a stable temperature, and promotes normal prenatal structural development.
22. Oxygenated blood enters the fetus through the umbilical vein. Half the blood goes to the liver, and the rest passes through the ductus venosus to the inferior vena cava. Blood enters the right atrium, where a small amount goes to the right ventricle, and the rest goes through the foramen ovale to the left atrium and then to the left ventricle. Some blood from the right ventricle goes to the lungs, and the rest goes through the ductus arteriosum, where it joins blood ejected from the left

ventricle. After circulation through the body, deoxygenated blood returns to the placenta through the two umbilical arteries.

23. Monozygotic twins occur when one spermatozoon fertilizes one ovum and the resulting conceptus later divides into two inner cell masses that will become two fetuses.
24. The placentas and chorions may fuse before birth, making it difficult to determine if the twins are monozygotic or dizygotic.
25. Dizygotic twins develop from two ova that are each fertilized by a spermatozoon and are like other siblings in a family.

Chapter 7

1. Uterine growth has generally reached the level of the umbilicus by 20 weeks' gestation; at 36 weeks, the uterus extends to the xiphoid process, the highest level of uterine growth.
2. Blocks ascent of bacteria from the vagina into the uterus, thereby protecting the membranes and fetus from infection.
3. The breasts enlarge and become more vascular; the areola increases in size and becomes more pigmented; the nipples increase in size and become more erect.
4. Physiologic anemia of pregnancy is caused by a greater increase in plasma volume than in red blood cells, resulting in a dilution but not inadequate hemoglobin concentration. Iron deficiency anemia is due to inadequate hemoglobin concentration.
5. Increased circulation through the kidneys is needed to remove metabolic wastes generated by the mother and fetus; increased circulation through the skin is necessary to dissipate heat that is generated by accelerated metabolism during pregnancy.
6. In a supine position, the weight of the gravid uterus on the vena cava and descending aorta impedes blood flow to and from the lower extremities, resulting in decreased cardiac output and a supine hypotensive syndrome.
7. The ribs flare, the substernal angle widens, and the circumference of the chest increases.
8. Nausea may be caused by increased levels of hormones (human chorionic gonadotropin, estrogen, progesterone) and relative hypoglycemia experienced by many women in early pregnancy.
9. Compression of the ureters between the uterus and the pelvic bones, resulting in dilation of the ureters and consequent stasis of urine, which allows prolonged time for bacterial growth.
10. Softening of pelvic ligaments and joints due to relaxin, a maternal hormone, creates instability and results in a wide stance and "waddling" gait. As the uterus increases in size, the woman must lean backward to maintain balance, which creates a progressive lordosis.
11. Progesterone maintains the uterine lining, prevents uterine contractions during pregnancy, and helps prepare the breasts for lactation.
12. Maternal hormones (human placental lactogen, estrogen, and progesterone) create increasing resistance of maternal tissues to insulin during the second and third trimesters.
13. Presumptive signs are subjective, probable signs are objective; both can be caused by conditions other than pregnancy.
14. Many things (gas, peristalsis, or pseudocyesis) can be mistaken by the woman for fetal movement.
15. Pregnancy tests performed too soon, or with other than the first urine of the day, or with urine that is allowed to stand for too long.
16. There is a gradual, predictable increase in uterine size as gestation advances; from approximately 22 weeks until term, fundal height in centimeters is nearly equal to gestational age in weeks.
17. Progesterone, which relaxes all smooth muscles, causes decreased motility of the bowel, resulting in constipation.
18. Allows palpation of the uterus for size, contour, tenderness, and position. Also permits internal pelvic measurements, described in Chapter 12.

Chapter 8

1. The fetus seems vague and unreal during the first trimester; gradually, physical changes (uterine growth, weight gain, "quickening") confirm that a fetus is developing, and the expectant mother begins to perceive the fetus as a separate, though dependent being.
2. Sexual responses vary according to the mother's body image, general health, and response of the expectant father to the physical changes of pregnancy.
3. The pregnant woman explores the role of mother to develop a sense of herself in the role and selects behaviors that confirm her sense of how she wants to fulfill the role.
4. The pregnant woman often experiences a sense of sadness when she realizes that she must give up certain aspects of her previous self when she moves into the role of mother.
5. She seeks the care of a physician or certified nurse-midwife and follows recommendations about diet, vitamins, rest, and subsequent prenatal care.
6. Experiences that make the child more real are "reality boosters"; the most frequently mentioned are hearing the fetal heart beats, feeling the fetus move, and seeing the fetus via ultrasound.
7. View the mother/father/fetus as their clients and focus on the father as well as the mother by encouraging the father's questions and including him in the plan of care.
8. A number of factors shape the way grandparents respond to a grandchild, including their own ages, the number and spacing of other grandchildren, and how they perceive their role as grandparents.
9. Toddlers may feel threatened and abandoned when attention must be shared with an infant. They may revert to infantile behaviors to gain the attention of their parents.
10. Make any changes in sleeping arrangements several weeks before the infant is born so that the toddler does not feel displaced by the newborn. Encourage family and friends to give as much time and attention to the child as they give to the infant. Arrange time alone with the older child, and frequently reassure the child of the parents' love and acceptance.
11. Priorities of the poor often focus on present needs (food, shelter) and less on preventive activities such as prenatal care.
12. Many health care workers are unsympathetic to the plights of poor families, who experience long delays at health care facilities, hurried examinations, and rudeness and arrogance from members of the health care team.

Chapter 9

1. Weight gain helps determine fetal growth. Too little may be associated with low birth weight, and too much with large infants.
2. 25 to 35 pounds. Underweight women and those carrying more than one fetus should gain more, and overweight women should gain less.
3. Approximately 3 to 4 pounds the first trimester, and 1 pound a week in the second and third trimesters.
4. 300 kcal/day.
5. 60 g/day, an increase of 10 to 16 g above pre-pregnancy needs.
6. Vitamins B_6, D, E, and folate.

7. Vitamins A, D, E, and K. They are stored in the fat and are available for longer periods than the water-soluble vitamins (B_6, B_{12}, folate, thiamin, riboflavin, niacin, and C), which must be replenished daily. Excessive intake of fat-soluble vitamins may cause toxicity.
8. Iron, calcium, zinc, and magnesium.
9. Excessive intake of vitamins and minerals may result in toxicity and may interfere with use of other vitamins and minerals.
10. Eight to ten 8-ounce glasses daily.
11. Whole grains: 7; fruits and vegetables: 5 (with 1 serving of vitamin A and 1 serving of vitamin C source); dairy products: 3; protein: 7 1-ounce servings.
12. Traditional foods for her culture, the degree to which she follows the traditional diet, and non-traditional foods she includes.
13. Both Southeast Asian and Latina women balance Yin and Yang or cold and hot food during pregnancy.
14. Financial resources for food purchase, need for financial assistance, and education.
15. Skipping meals, eating snacks and fast foods of low nutrient value, peer pressure.
16. Non-animal sources of iron, calcium, and vitamin B_{12} and methods of combining protein foods to ensure intake of all essential amino acids.
17. Choosing calcium-containing foods like leafy green vegetables, broccoli, corn tortillas, tofu, sunflower seeds, nuts, salmon, and sardines.
18. Abnormal pre-pregnancy weight, anemia, eating disorders, pica, grand multiparity, substance abuse, closely spaced pregnancies, and multiple pregnancy.
19. The lactating woman needs more of most nutrients than the woman who is not pregnant. She needs 200 more calories and a little more protein and vitamin C than the pregnant woman.
20. Alcohol, caffeine, and foods that seem to cause distress in the infant.
21. Decrease calories by 300 daily, continue to eat a well-balanced diet, and plan to lose extra weight slowly.

Chapter 10

1. Major reasons for level I ultrasonography during the first trimester are to confirm pregnancy, locate the fetus, determine multiple gestations, determine gestational age, and confirm fetal viability.
2. Level II ultrasound is "targeted" toward specific fetal anatomy when there is increased risk for fetal anomalies to occur.
3. MSAFP must be viewed as the first step in a series of diagnostic procedures that are necessary if abnormal concentrations are found.
4. Open neural tube defects, esophageal obstruction, abdominal wall defects, or undetected fetal demise. Additional causes include multiple gestation, inaccurate fetal age, or threatened abortion.
5. CVS is performed in the first trimester, and results are available in only 24 to 48 hours. Obtaining information about fetal anomalies in the first trimester instead of in the second trimester, when amniocentesis is performed, allows the woman to make an early decision about pregnancy termination.
6. Pregnancy loss remains a major concern for many women and physicians. Additional risks include maternal infection and Rh sensitization, which can be prevented by administration of Rh_O (D) immune globulin.
7. Maternal age of 35 years or more, chromosomal abnormality in close family member, elevated levels of MSAFP, and maternal Rh sensitization are the major indications for second-trimester amniocentesis.
8. Amniocentesis is performed in the third trimester to determine fetal maturity and to diagnose hemolytic disease of the fetus.
9. A non–stress test measures acceleration, or lack of acceleration, of the fetal heart beat in response to fetal movement. Acceleration provides reassurance of fetal health. It is so named because the fetus is not challenged or stressed to obtain data.
10. In a vibroacoustic stimulation test, unlike a non–stress test, it is necessary to use a false larynx to stimulate fetal movement.
11. To determine the response of the fetal heart rate to decreased fetal oxygenation that occurs when uterine contractions compress the arteries supplying the placenta with oxygenated blood.
12. Late decelerations indicate inadequate fetal oxygen reserves and inability of the fetus to tolerate the temporary hypoxia that contractions induce.
13. Loss of fetal tone indicates advanced asphyxia and fetal acidosis.
14. Decreased amniotic fluid volume is associated with long-term fetal hypoxemia, when blood is shunted away from the fetal lungs and kidneys, which produce amniotic fluid, and toward vital organs, such as the fetal heart and brain.

Chapter 11

1. To help women and their support persons to become knowledgeable consumers and active participants in pregnancy and childbirth.
2. Choosing a health care professional, birth setting, support persons for labor, and type of education for preparation (if any).
3. Early pregnancy: adapting to pregnancy, coping with common discomforts, learning what to expect in later pregnancy. Later classes: preparation for childbirth, postpartum, breastfeeding, parenting concerns.
4. The chance that a couple may experience cesarean birth is approximately 25 per cent.
5. Classes help ease family transition by providing information and opportunity for discussing common feelings.
6. They increase coping ability for childbirth by helping to decrease muscle and mental tension.
7. They send other messages to the brain so that pain messages are not recognized as strongly and perception of pain is reduced.
8. To increase relaxation during labor.
9. It increases a woman's satisfaction by helping her deal with stress, focus on her learned techniques, and feel that her experience is being shared.
10. Active assistance with coaching techniques, verbal encouragement, minimal physical assistance, being present without active involvement.
11. Assisting with relaxation, breathing, encouragement, sacral pressure, massage, comfort measures.

Chapter 12

1. Effacement and dilation of the cervix occur because contractions pull the cervix upward over the fetus and amniotic sac and, at the same time, push the fetus and amniotic sac downward against the cervix. The muscle fibers of the upper uterus become shorter to maintain these forces between contractions. Additionally, the uterus becomes smaller inside, maintaining pressure of the fetus and amniotic sac against the cervix.
2. The cervix of the nullipara effaces more completely before it dilates. The multipara's cervix does not usually efface as completely as the nullipara's cervix does.
3. Maternal changes that occur during labor include:
   a. Cardiovascular: Slight increase in blood pressure and decrease in pulse rate as each contraction temporarily stops

blood flow to her uterus. Supine hypotension may occur if she lies on her back because the heavy uterus compresses her inferior vena cava and reduces blood flow to her heart.
   b. Respiratory: Increased depth and rate of respirations.
   c. Gastrointestinal: Although a controversial belief, many authorities think that peristalsis slows during labor.
   d. Renal: Reduced sensation of a full bladder.
   e. Hematopoietic system: Leukocytes as high as 25,000 to 30,000. Elevated clotting factors.
4. Uterine contractions temporarily stop blood flow to the placenta. If the contractions were sustained, the fetus could not receive freshly oxygenated blood or dispose of waste products through the placenta.
5. Normal vaginal birth benefits the newborn after birth by compressing the chest, thus expelling excess lung fluid that might interfere with respirations. Labor also stimulates the fetus to secrete catecholamines, which help speed clearance of the lung fluid after birth and aid in temperature regulation.
6. The powers of labor during the first stage of labor are the uterine contractions. The powers during the second stage are uterine contractions, augmented by the woman's voluntary pushing efforts.
7. The three divisions of the true pelvis are the inlet, the midpelvis, and the outlet.
8. The vertex presentation, with the fetal head fully flexed forward, allows the smallest diameter of the fetal head to enter the pelvis.
9. ROP: The fetal landmark is the occiput, indicating a vertex presentation. It is located in the mother's right posterior pelvic quadrant. OA: The fetal landmark is the occiput, which is located in the mother's anterior pelvis and is not angled toward her left or her right. RSA: The fetal landmark is the sacrum, indicating that the fetus is in a breech presentation. It is located in the mother's right anterior pelvis. LMA: The fetal landmark is the mentum, or chin, indicating that the fetus is in a face presentation. The mentum is in the mother's left anterior pelvis.
10. If the fetus is in a face presentation, the occiput is not accessible by the examiner's fingers during vaginal examination. For this reason, the fetal chin (mentum) is used to describe position (ie, RMA or right mentum anterior).
11. The transverse diameter of the pelvic inlet is slightly larger than the inlet's anterior-posterior diameter. The anterior-posterior diameter of the fetal head (in line with the sagittal suture) is slightly larger than the transverse diameter. Therefore, the fetal head best fits the pelvis if the sagittal suture is aligned with the pelvic transverse diameter.
12. Because the woman's pelvic outlet is usually slightly larger in its anterior-posterior diameter than its transverse, the fetal head turns in the mechanism of internal rotation so that the sagittal suture aligns with the anterior-posterior diameter.
13. The woman may note any of several changes as labor approaches: increased strength and frequency of Braxton Hicks contractions, lightening, increased vaginal mucus, bloody show, ruptured membranes, an energy spurt, or a small weight loss.
14. False labor tends to differ from true labor in three major ways. True labor is characterized by contractions that become progressively more frequent, of longer duration, and of greater intensity. The discomfort of true labor begins in the lower back and sweeps to the lower abdomen. The key difference between true and false labor is that in true labor, progressive dilation and effacement of the cervix occur.
15. First stage, latent phase: The expectant mother is often sociable, excited, and somewhat anxious. First stage, active phase: The woman becomes less sociable and is inwardly focused. First stage, transition phase: The woman may become irritable and temporarily lose control. Second stage: The woman usually concentrates her energy toward pushing her baby out, interacting little with others. She often regains a feeling of being in control and an active participant in the birth.
16. Contractions vary among women, but there is a general pattern of increasing frequency, duration, and intensity throughout labor. First stage, latent phase: Contractions gradually increase until they are about 5 minutes apart, lasting for about 30 seconds with moderate intensity. First stage, active phase: Contractions increase to about 3 to 5 minutes apart, with a duration of about 45 seconds and a moderate to strong intensity. First stage, transition phase: Contractions are strong, with a frequency of 2 to 3 minutes and a duration of almost 90 seconds. Second stage: Contractions are about 3 minutes apart, strong, and have a duration of about 50 to 90 seconds.
17. Signs that the placenta may have separated include a spherical uterine shape; the uterus rises upward in the abdomen; the umbilical cord protrudes farther out from the vagina; and a gush of blood.
18. Hemorrhage may occur if the uterus does not remain contracted after birth of the placenta, because open blood vessels at the site will not be compressed by the interlacing muscle fibers of the uterus.

Chapter 13

1. The nurse should show warmth, concern, and friendliness when the woman and her family enter the hospital or birth center. In addition, a non-judgmental attitude facilitates communication and shows respect to the woman as an individual.
2. If a woman's cultural practices are not harmful to the woman or fetus, the nurse should try to identify and incorporate them into care during labor and birth. For example, ask if there are specific practices that are important during birth and facilitating communication by obtaining a fluent translator.
3. The nurse should promptly evaluate the maternal and fetal condition and the nearness of birth when a woman comes to the hospital or birth center.
4. The average fetal heart rate is 110 to 160 BPM.
5. Two tests may assist the nurse, nurse-midwife, or physician to determine if a woman's membranes have ruptured: the nitrazine test and examination of the amniotic fluid under a microscope for ferning.
6. Hypertonic contractions (too frequent, too long, or an inadequate rest period) reduce blood flow to and from the placenta. This interferes with fetal oxygenation and waste disposal.
7. The fetal heart rate should be assessed after the membranes rupture to detect whether the fetal umbilical cord was displaced with the gush of fluid and is being compressed between the fetal presenting part and the maternal pelvis.
8. Greenish amniotic fluid contains meconium, which may have been passed by the fetus in response to transient hypoxia. The newborn's airway should be thoroughly suctioned to remove meconium-stained amniotic fluid.
9. Frequent vaginal examinations may cause infection because microorganisms from the perineal area can be introduced into the uterus.
10. If the mother is unable to tolerate labor pain, she may be unable to use breathing techniques that she previously learned. She may have a tense facial and body posture both during and between contractions. She may verbally communicate pain or the desire for medication.
11. Hypotension reduces blood flow to the placenta (and therefore reduces fetal oxygenation) because it diverts blood away from the uterus to better supply the mother's brain, heart, and kidneys. Hypertension may result in vasospasm that can reduce exchange of oxygen, nutrients, and waste products in the placenta. Fetal hypoxia and acidosis can be the ultimate result of maternal hypotension or hypertension.
12. The mother can choose any position of comfort during labor except the supine. The supine position allows the heavy uterus to compress her vena cava, reducing blood flow to her heart and reducing placental blood supply. A small wedge under her side is effective to relieve vena cava compression.
13. General comfort measures during labor include soft, dim light-

ing; a comfortable temperature; maintaining cleanliness; mouth care; observations for a full bladder; positioning for comfort; and a warm bath or shower.

14. Shortly before birth, the woman's perineum bulges and the fetal head may become visible during contractions. At this time, she should be prepared for birth.

Chapter 14

1. Fetal oxygenation depends on normal maternal blood flow; normal oxygen saturation of the maternal blood; adequate oxygen-carbon dioxide exchange in the placenta; patent umbilical cord vessels; and normal fetal circulatory and oxygen-carrying function.
2. When the umbilical cord is compressed, the umbilical vein is compressed first, resulting in a slight fetal hypotension and acceleration of the fetal heart rate. Continued compression obstructs the umbilical arteries, resulting in fetal hypertension and slowing of the fetal heart rate. When compression is relieved, these changes are reversed.
3. The fetus increases cardiac output, and therefore oxygenation, primarily by increasing the heart rate. Rates lower than 50 or higher than 200 BPM (because of inadequate filling of the ventricles) may reduce fetal oxygenation.
4. Fetal monitoring should be done more frequently if there are risk factors present. These may include antepartal factors in the woman's history or course of pregnancy. They may also include problems in the woman or fetus that develop intrapartally. Although there are no absolute indications for continuous electronic fetal monitoring, most hospitals use it in both low- and high-risk intrapartal care.
5. Risk factors are sometimes associated with reduced fetal oxygenation.
6. Intermittent auscultation promotes the laboring woman's mobility and creates a more natural atmosphere. However, it can assess the fetus for only a small part of labor, may be distracting for some women, and generally requires more staff. Continuous electronic fetal monitoring provides more data, is often expected by parents, and can assist the nurse to better observe more than one laboring woman. Its primary drawback is reduced maternal mobility, adjustments to the equipment, and the technical atmosphere it lends to the birth process.
7. The upper grid records the constant changes in the fetal heart rate. The lower grid records contractions as a series of bell-shaped curves.
8. The Doppler ultrasound transducer senses fetal heart motion and translates the motion into a heart rate.
9. Four factors may affect the accuracy of the external uterine activity monitor: fetal size, abdominal fat thickness, maternal position, and where the transducer is located.
10. The two types of internal uterine activity catheters are the fluid-filled and the solid catheter. The fluid-filled catheter can be affected by its height in relation to the mother's transducer.
11. Fetal heart rate accelerations are a reassuring sign of fetal well-being.
12. In early decelerations, the fetal heart rate slows after the contraction begins and returns to the baseline rate by the end of the contraction. They are caused by fetal head compression and are a reassuring pattern. Late decelerations are characterized by slowing of the fetal heart rate late in the contraction cycle. They do not return to the baseline by the end of the contraction. Late decelerations are associated with decreased uteroplacental perfusion and are non-reassuring.
13. The fetal heart rate falls and rises abruptly in the variable deceleration. Variable decelerations do not have a consistent appearance to each other and may not occur at similar times in relation to the contractions. They are caused by compression of the umbilical cord.
14. Fetal scalp stimulation or vibroacoustic stimulation may be done to clarify fetal heart rate patterns as reassuring or non-reassuring when they are vague. The reassuring response to stimulation is an increase in the fetal heart rate of 15 BPM for 15 seconds. This suggests that the fetus has a normal oxygen and acid-base balance.
15. Cord blood gas and pH analysis assesses the newborn's oxygen and acid-base status immediately after birth and identifies if the fetus was adjusting to the stresses of labor.
16. Basic nursing actions for non-reassuring fetal heart rate patterns vary according to the pattern. They include identifying the cause of a non-reassuring pattern by vaginal examination, taking vital signs, checking medications, or applying internal monitoring; increasing placental perfusion by reducing excess uterine activity and positioning the woman on her side; giving the mother oxygen; and reducing cord compression by position changes and amnioinfusion.
17. A tocolytic drug reduces the force and frequency of uterine contractions, thus allowing more time for the placenta to be supplied with oxygen-rich maternal blood.
18. Amnioinfusion may be used to replace the fluid cushion around the umbilical cord, reducing compression. It may also be used to dilute thick meconium, which might otherwise cause respiratory distress in the newborn.

Chapter 15

1. Labor pain can be useful because it inspires the pregnant woman to seek shelter and help from others.
2. Childbirth pain differs from other painful experiences because it is part of a normal process, the woman has time to prepare for it, it is self-limited and intermittent, and it ends with the birth of an infant.
3. Excessive, unrelieved labor pain may result in a stress response (diverting blood flow from the uterus), maternal respiratory alkalosis and metabolic acidosis, and fetal acidosis. It may also increase the length of labor. Poor pain relief can lessen the joy of childbirth for the woman and her partner.
4. Physical and psychological factors interact to alter the ability to tolerate pain.
5. Four sources of pain present in most labor are cervical dilation, uterine ischemia, pressure and pulling on pelvic structures, and distention of the vagina and perineum.
6. Physical factors that influence pain include:
   a. A short, intense labor may be more painful because dilation, effacement, and fetal descent occur rapidly.
   b. A cervix that does not dilate or efface as readily is likely to be associated with a longer and more uncomfortable labor.
   c. An abnormal fetal position may cause a longer labor. Back pain is especially noticeable if the fetus is in an occiput posterior position.
   d. Variations in the mother's pelvic size or shape may result in abnormal fetal presentations or positions and in a longer labor because the fetus does not fit through the pelvis easily.
   e. Fatigue reduces the woman's pain tolerance and ability to use coping skills.
7. Psychosocial factors that influence labor pain include culture, anxiety and fear, previous experiences, preparation for childbirth, and the mother's support system.
8. Relaxation is a basic component of intrapartum nursing care because it promotes uterine blood flow, promotes efficient uterine contractions, reduces maternal tension that might increase pain perception, decreases pain tolerance, and inhibits fetal descent.
9. Nursing actions to promote relaxation include environmental comfort, maintaining the woman's personal comfort, reducing factors that cause anxiety and fear, and using specific directed relaxation techniques. Examples of these are light and noise adjustment, reducing intrusions, and helping the woman focus on relaxing specific tense muscles.
10. Accurate information and a focus on the normal aspects of

childbirth help reduce anxiety and fear. Avoid referring to the woman as a "patient," because this word is associated with illness.

11. Touch techniques include effleurage, firm palm or sole pressure, back rubs, and warm or cool applications. Firm pressure to the sacral area may help manage back pain during labor.
12. Drugs taken by the mother can affect the fetus directly, such as decreased fetal heart rate variability, or indirectly, such as hypotension that reduces placental blood flow and fetal oxygen supply.
13. Aortocaval compression should be offset by placing a wedge under the woman's right hip. She is more sensitive to general anesthesia and may have a greater fall in oxygenation when general anesthesia is induced. The reduced peristalsis and tone of the sphincter at the junction of the esophagus and stomach can lead to regurgitation and aspiration of gastric contents, primarily with general anesthesia. Additionally, lower doses of anesthetic agents will be needed for epidural or subarachnoid blocks.
14. Higher endorphin levels provide a natural analgesia and reduce the woman's requirements for pharmacological analgesia.
15. It is important to know what other drugs the laboring woman uses because drugs may interact with each other. These interactions may be harmful to the woman, fetus, or both. Knowledge of exactly what drugs she uses allows the safest choices in pharmacological pain relief methods.
16. Neonatal respiratory depression is the primary drawback to the use of narcotic analgesia. This effect can be reduced by timing the dose to reduce the amount transferred to the fetus (which varies according to the drug) and by giving the narcotic in small, frequent, intravenous doses at the beginning of the contraction. Naloxone (Narcan) is the drug given to reverse narcotic respiratory depression in the newborn.
17. Because naloxone's effects are shorter than those of the narcotic, the nurse must observe for a recurrence of respiratory depression.
18. The correct dose of naloxone for a 3178-g (7-pound) infant is 0.3 mg.
19. The major advantages of regional block is that the woman can have pain relief (sufficient also for cesarean birth) while remaining awake.
20. Epidural and subarachnoid blocks can cause maternal hypotension, which can reduce placental blood flow and fetal oxygen supply. This effect is reduced by giving the woman intravenous fluids before the block. Other less serious adverse effects are bladder distention, prolonged second stage of labor (epidural), and post-spinal headache (subarachnoid block only). Epidural narcotics, often given to the woman for long-lasting pain relief after cesarean birth, may result in delayed respiratory depression (up to 24 hours). They may also cause itching, which is annoying but not serious.
21. Maternal regurgitation with aspiration of acidic gastric contents is the major potential adverse effect of general anesthesia. The risk may be reduced by limiting intake to clear fluids, giving drugs to raise the gastric pH, giving drugs to reduce gastric secretions or speed emptying of the stomach, and using cricoid pressure (Sellick's maneuver) to block the esophagus while the endotracheal tube is being inserted. Respiratory depression, primarily in the infant, may also occur. It is minimized by delaying general anesthesia until the surgery team is prepared and by keeping the anesthesia level as light as possible until the umbilical cord is cut.

Chapter 16

1. Three major risks of amniotomy are prolapsed umbilical cord, infection, and abruptio placentae.
2. The fetal heart rate should be assessed after the membranes rupture to identify whether the umbilical cord has prolapsed and is being compressed.
3. Green amniotic fluid contains meconium, passed from the fetal intestines. It can be associated with fetal hypoxia or newborn respiratory distress.
4. Signs of chorioamnionitis include fetal tachycardia (often the first sign), elevated maternal temperature, and amniotic fluid that has a foul or strong odor or a cloudy or yellowish appearance.
5. Four precautions that promote safe oxytocin induction or augmentation of labor include:
   a. Dilution of the oxytocin.
   b. Piggybacking the oxytocin solution into the port nearest the venipuncture site.
   c. Starting the oxytocin infusion slowly.
   d. Increasing its rate gradually.
6. The woman whose labor is augmented with oxytocin usually needs less of the drug because her uterus is more sensitive to its effects.
7. The fetus may have an adverse reaction to oxytocin, manifested by non-reassuring fetal heart rate patterns: bradycardia, tachycardia, late decelerations, and decreased fetal heart rate variability.
8. Signs of uterine hyperactivity include incomplete relaxation of the uterus between contractions or a rest period shorter than 60 seconds, which may result in inadequate placental blood flow and a fall in fetal oxygenation.
9. Administration of oxytocin for a prolonged time may lead to postpartum hemorrhage because the fatigued uterus cannot contract properly to compress bleeding vessels at the placenta site (uterine atony).
10. Internal version is used only during the vaginal birth of a second twin to change the presentation of this fetus to one that can be born vaginally.
11. The fetal heart rate should be monitored before external version to identify abnormalities. It should be monitored as much as possible during, and for a short while after, to detect cord compression that can occur if the umbilical cord becomes entangled during change of the fetal presentation.
12. Uterine activity should be observed after external version for possible onset of labor because this procedure may cause uterine irritability and is done near term.
13. Both forceps and vacuum extractor can be used to provide traction to assist the mother in expulsion of the fetal head. Additionally, forceps can be used to rotate the fetal head position to one more favorable, and special forceps (Piper) can be used to deliver the aftercoming head of a breech.
14. The woman is usually catheterized before forceps are used to eliminate a full bladder, which could reduce available room in her pelvis, and to reduce the likelihood of injuring her bladder.
15. Use of cold following episiotomy reduces pain, edema, and formation of hematomas.
16. The infant with an asymmetrical facial appearance when crying may have facial nerve injury, a usually temporary condition that sometimes occurs when forceps are used to assist birth.
17. The low transverse uterine incision is preferred because it is less likely to rupture during another pregnancy than are either of the two vertical incisions. There are, however, valid reasons that demand the use of vertical incisions.
18. The woman expecting a cesarean birth should be taught the following about the operating room and recovery area:
   a. Preoperative procedures, such as the skin preparation and indwelling catheter.
   b. Personnel who will be present and their functions.
   c. The narrow table.
   d. When her partner or support person can come in.
   If a regional anesthetic is planned, explain that she will be awake and will feel pulling and pressure sensations but should not expect pain. If a general anesthetic is planned, explain that all preparations will be made before she is put to sleep, but that the surgery will not begin before she is asleep and that she will not awaken during it.
   e. In the recovery area, oxygen, pulse oximeter, and automatic blood pressure cuff will be in use.
19. The woman who has cesarean birth needs similar care to the

woman who delivers vaginally in terms of vital signs and fundus and lochia assessments. Additional care includes assessment of oxygen saturation, observation of urine output from the indwelling catheter, pain relief, and respiratory care (turning, coughing, deep breathing).

Chapter 17

1. Catabolism and contraction of muscle fibers.
2. One centimeter (approximately 1 fingerbreadth) per day so that, by the 10th postpartum day, it cannot be palpated abdominally.
3. Lochia rubra lasts for 3 days following delivery and consists mostly of blood and is therefore red. Lochia serosa is pinkish and usually lasts from the 4th to 10th day. Lochia alba is clear or colorless and may last from 3 to 6 weeks.
4. A temperature of 38°C (100.4°F) is common following delivery and may be caused by dehydration or normal postpartum leukocytosis.
5. Excitement, fatigue, dehydration, or hypovolemia may cause tachycardia.
6. Orthostatic hypotension, a drop in blood pressure when the mother goes from a supine to standing position quickly, produces symptoms of dizziness, lightheadedness, or feeling faint.
7. Approximately 7.5 to 9 kg (17 to 20 pounds) is lost following childbirth, accounting for the fetus, placenta, amniotic fluid, and blood loss during delivery; it also includes weight loss by diuresis, diaphoresis, and involution during the first few postpartum days.
8. The melanocyte-stimulating hormone, which causes hyperpigmentation, decreases rapidly as hormones decline following childbirth.
9. Breastfeeding delays the return of both ovulation and menstruation.
10. The best method for suppressing lactation is to prevent breast distention by binding the breasts or wearing a tight-fitting bra. Bromocriptine (Parlodel) is still used in some facilities.
11. Maternal vital signs must be stable; estimated blood loss during delivery should not exceed 250 to 300 ml; the fundus must be firm; lochia rubra must be scant and without offensive odor or clots; the mother must be able to ambulate and empty her bladder; and the perineum must be free of signs of infection. The infant must weigh more than 2500 g (5.5 pounds) and have a robust cry and normal reflexes. In addition, the infant must have voided, and the umbilical cord and circumcision site must be free of signs of bleeding or infection.
12. A great deal of teaching about self-care and infant care must be done in a short time when the family chooses early discharge.
13. Frequent respiratory assessments; auscultation of breath sounds; auscultation of bowel sounds; inspection of surgical dressing.
14. Early, frequent ambulation, pelvic lifts, and restriction of carbonated beverages and straws for drinking.

Chapter 18

1. The sensitive period is the first 30 to 60 minutes following birth, when the infant's eyes are open and the newborn responds physically to parental voice and touch, which fosters initial bonding.
2. Maternal touch progresses from finger-tipping in the discovery phase to enfolding the infant and a full range of consoling behaviors.
3. Parents progress from referring to the newborn as "it" to he or she and then to using the given name.
4. The mother is primarily focused on her own needs during the taking-in phase; she is often passive and dependent and repeatedly recounts her birth experiences. In the taking-hold phase, she becomes more independent and shifts her attention to the infant and exhibits a heightened readiness to learn.
5. Mothers and fathers relinquish previous lifestyle patterns to assume the parenting roles.
6. Postpartum blues is believed to be related to wide hormonal fluctuations that occur during labor, delivery, and the immediate postpartum period. It is helpful if nurses focus on how the mother is feeling and reassure her that what she is experiencing is normal and self-limited.
7. Transition to the parent role involves four stages (anticipatory, formal, informal, and personal) and generally lasts about 4 months.
8. Fathers who are sometimes ignored and not included in infant care may feel left out and unneeded.
9. Siblings may feel jealousy and fear that they will be replaced by the newborn in the affection of the parents.
10. Time must be allowed for parents to form attachment to each newborn individually.

Chapter 19

1. Chemical, thermal, and mechanical factors stimulate the respiratory center in the brain and initiate respirations at birth.
2. Surfactant reduces surface tension in the alveoli and allows them to remain partially open on expiration.
3. Part is squeezed out during birth, and the rest is absorbed by the lymphatic and vascular systems.
4. The ductus arteriosus closes as a result of increases in blood oxygen levels. The foramen ovale closes when pressure in the left atrium exceeds that in the right atrium. The ductus venosus closes when the cord is clamped.
5. They have thinner skin with less subcutaneous fat, blood vessels close to the surface, and a larger skin surface area.
6. Increased metabolism, vasoconstriction, and nonshivering thermogenesis, which increases oxygen and glucose consumption and may cause respiratory distress, hypoglycemia, acidosis, and jaundice.
7. They give one indication of the health of the central nervous system.
8. During fetal life, the available oxygen is lower than after birth, causing a need for increased red blood cells.
9. Molding of the head is change in shape due to normal temporary overriding of bones during birth. Caput succedaneum is localized swelling from pressure against the cervix. Cephalohematoma is bleeding between the periosteum and the bone that never crosses suture lines. Molding and caput disappear within a few days, whereas cephalohematoma may last for several weeks.
10. Stools progress from thick, greenish-black meconium, to loose greenish-brown transitional stools to milk stools that are frequent, soft, and mustard-colored if the infant is breastfed, and brown, firmer, and less frequent if formula fed.
11. The brain requires a constant supply of glucose and may be damaged without an adequate supply.
12. Jitteriness, poor muscle tone, respiratory distress, diaphoresis, low temperature, poor suck.
13. Physiologic jaundice occurs in normal newborns after the first 24 hours of life as a result of hemolysis of red blood cells and immaturity of the liver. Pathologic jaundice begins within the first 24 hours and may necessitate phototherapy. Breast milk jaundice begins later than physiologic jaundice and is thought to be due to enzymes in the milk.
14. The newborn's body is composed of a greater percentage of water, with more located in the extracellular compartment compared with that in adults.
15. Reasons parents choose circumcision: decreased incidence of urinary tract infections and inflammation of the glans, prepuce,

or meatus; religious dictates; parent preference; lack of knowledge about care of the foreskin. Reasons to avoid circumcision: risk of hemorrhage, infection, overremoval, urethral stenosis or fistula, adhesions and damage to the glans, pain, questions about need for surgery.

16. Newborns receive passive immunity to infections when IgG crosses the placenta in utero. After birth, infants produce IgM and IgA to protect against infection. IgA lines the gastrointestinal and respiratory tracts to prevent infection and is present in breast milk.
17. During both periods of reactivity, newborns are active and alert, may be interested in feeding, have elevated pulse and respiratory rates, may have transient signs of respiratory distress.
18. Newborns progress through six behavior states: quiet sleep, active sleep, drowsy, quiet alert, active alert, and crying.

Chapter 20

1. To detect serious abnormalities and anomalies.
2. They help determine if in utero growth was adequate and if complications may be present.
3. Prophylaxis against hemorrhagic disease of the newborn and ophthalmic neonatorum is prescribed by law.
4. History, airway, heart sounds, color, pulses, and blood pressure.
5. By keeping them dry and covered, away from cold objects or surfaces, drafts, and outside windows and walls.
6. To avoid damage to the bone, nerves, or blood vessels of the heel.
7. Monitor to detect early jaundice, ensure the infant is feeding well, and explain the process to parents.
8. It provides information about the neonate's coordination of sucking, swallowing, and breathing and tolerance to feeding.
9. Within 24 hours of birth. Feeding and taking a rectal temperature may stimulate stool passage.
10. Within 24 to 48 hours. Infants void 2 to 5 times the first day and 5 to 25 times daily thereafter.
11. Do not retract the foreskin on an uncircumcised penis until it becomes separate from the glans later in childhood. Teach child to retract to clean when separation occurs. Teach parents of circumcised infants signs of complications after the surgery and how to care for the area.
12. Document location, size, color, elevation, and texture; explain marks to parents; and offer emotional support as needed.
13. It provides an estimate of the infant's age since conception and alerts the nurse to possible complications of age and development.
14. The infant may need nursing intervention for low temperature, elevated pulse and respirations, and excessive respiratory secretions during the periods of reactivity and, between these periods, will be in a deep sleep with relaxed muscle tone and no interest in feeding.
15. Scrupulous hand washing by staff and all who come in contact with newborns.
16. Parents and nurses must be alert for suspicious behavior. Parents must know how to identify hospital staff and should never allow anyone without proper identification to take their infants.

Chapter 21

1. Because of insufficient intake and normal loss of extracellular fluid.
2. Colostrum is rich in protein, vitamins, minerals, and immunoglobulins. Transitional milk has less protein and immunogobulin but more lactose, fat, and calories than colostrum. Mature milk appears less rich than colostrum and transitional milk but supplies all nutrients needed.
3. Breast milk nutrients are in an easily digested form and in proportions required by the newborn. Commercial formulas are cow's milk adapted to simulate human milk.
4. Bifidus factor, leukocytes, lysozymes, and immunoglobulins.
5. Modified cow's milk formula, soy-based or casein hydrolysate formulas, and special formulas for preterm infants or those with special needs.
6. Knowledge about each method, support from family and friends, cultural influences, and employment demands.
7. It releases oxytocin from the posterior pituitary, which causes the let-down reflex and causes the anterior pituitary to release prolactin to increase milk production.
8. The more frequently the infant feeds, the more milk is produced, and vice versa.
9. Identification of flat and inverted nipples and use of breast shells to correct them.
10. By initiating early feeding, helping to position the infant at the breast, and showing the mother how to position her hands, help the infant latch on to the breast, assess the position of the mouth on the breast, and remove the infant from the breast.
11. The mother should feed the infant 8 to 12 times each day for 10 to 15 minutes at the first breast and until the infant is satisfied at the second breast (generally at least 10 minutes).
12. Unwrapping the infant's blankets, talking to the infant, changing the diaper, rubbing the infant's back, expressing colostrum onto the breast, and switching the infant from one breast to another.
13. Sucking from a bottle requires pushing the tongue against the nipple to slow the flow of milk. Suckling from the breast requires drawing the nipple far into the mouth so that the gums compress the areola as the tongue moves over the milk sinus in a wave-like motion.
14. Encourage frequent nursing, applying heat and cold, massaging, and expressing milk to soften the areola.
15. Ensure proper positioning of the infant at the breast, vary the position of the infant, apply colostrum or breast milk to the nipples, and expose the nipples to air.
16. Expression of breast milk by hand or pump, and proper storage of the milk.
17. The types of formula available, how to prepare it correctly, and feeding techniques.

Chapter 22

1. Friends, family, nurses, child care classes, and books.
2. Follow-up phone calls, home visits, and classes about parenting.
3. All equipment should be checked for safety, that parts are in good condition and functioning properly.
4. They must be chosen according to the size of the infant and must be used correctly to maintain safety.
5. Infants are not "spoiled" by prompt attention to their needs.
6. Help parents determine the cause and appropriate techniques for dealing with a crying infant, and use therapeutic communication techniques to help parents deal with negative feelings.
7. Drooling, irritability, decreased appetite and sleep, rash, loose stools, and red, swollen gums.
8. Prevent diaper rash by keeping the area clean and dry and avoiding plastic pants and products to which the infant seems sensitive. If rash occurs, expose the area to air and apply creams sparingly.
9. The amount will vary but will average about 1 ounce per feeding at first and 5 to 6 ounces per feeding at 12 weeks.
10. Solid foods cannot be completely digested until age 4 to 6 months and may cause allergies, gastric upsets, and decreased intake of needed nutrients.
11. Understanding the infant's changing capabilities helps parents assess situations to prevent accidents.
12. They provide for assessment of growth and development, guidance, and immunizations.

13. They safeguard infants and communities from spread of communicable diseases.
14. If infants have difficulty breathing, show cyanosis, or are difficult to arouse from sleep.
15. The cause of sudden infant death syndrome remains unknown, but the risk may be increased with maternal smoking, maternal drug abuse, or prone sleep position.

Chapter 23

1. Pregnancy interrupts the developmental tasks, such as the achievement of a stable identity, development of a personal value system, completing educational goals, and achievement of independence from parents.
2. Teenagers experience greater risk for cephalopelvic disproportion, pregnancy-induced hypertension, anemia, nutritional deficiencies, and sexually transmitted diseases. There is also increased risk for infants to be born prematurely and to be under 2500 g. Both infant and maternal mortality rates are higher during the teenage years.
3. Adolescent parents may have unrealistic expectations of infants; they demonstrate less empathy, tend to be less sensitive to infant signals, and provide less infant stimulation than older parents.
4. Teenagers may not benefit from printed materials to the same degree as older clients. A variety of teaching methods, such as visual aids, videos, group classes, and one-to-one counseling, may be effective.
5. Infants develop a sense of trust, which is necessary for future development, when their needs are met promptly and gently; crying indicates a need and does not mean that the infant is "spoiled"; physical growth and development proceed slowly from the head downward.
6. Emotional and financial resources that are still unavailable to younger women.
7. Women over the age of 35 years are at increased risk for chromosomal anomalies that may be detected by prenatal screening.
8. Low birth weight, prematurity, and increased perinatal loss as well as delayed neurological and intellectual development, including hyperactivity, shorter attention span, and lower reading and spelling scores during the primary grades.
9. Fetal alcohol syndrome is characterized by slow growth, central nervous system disorders, and cranial and facial anomalies. Fetal alcohol effect describes mild or partial manifestations of fetal alcohol syndrome.
10. Learning difficulties, slower intellectual development, delayed language and motor development, and limited interaction with people and objects in their environment.
11. Caretakers may be frustrated by the infant's hypertonicity and continuous crying and by their inability to console the infant during the abstinence syndrome.
12. Seeking prenatal care late in pregnancy, failing to keep appointments, inconsistent follow-through with recommended regimens, poor grooming, inadequate weight gain, needle punctures, thrombosed veins, or signs of cellulitis.
13. Profuse sweating, high blood pressure, irregular respirations, dilated pupils, increased body temperature, sudden onset of severely painful uterine contractions, fetal tachycardia, and excessive fetal activity. Emotional signs include anger, caustic or abusive reactions to caregiver, emotional lability, and paranoia.
14. Interventions are focused on preventing maternal or fetal injury and may require setting limits in a firm, non-judgmental manner with a client who may be abusive and in great pain.
15. Provide anticipatory guidance about the growth and development of infants, measures that prevent a frantic cry state, instruction in how to feed the infant with uncoordinated suck and swallow reflexes, and instruction in how to mobilize a support system that is knowledgeable and reliable.
16. Parents experience less anxiety when they are gently told the condition of the infant and allowed to hold their newborn as soon as possible.
17. Facial and genital defects are believed to affect parenting most.
18. Handling the infant gently, emphasizing normal traits, helping parents to hold and cuddle the infant, using communication skills to help parents come to terms with their feelings.
19. Special feeding, holding, and positioning techniques that the infant may require.
20. How the stillborn infant is presented creates memories that the parents will retain. If necessary, the infant should be washed; lotion or powder may be applied. If possible, the infant should be presented while still warm and soft, wrapped in a soft, warm blanket.
21. Most parents treasure a memory packet that includes a photograph, footprints, a birth bracelet, and crib card, and, if possible, a lock of hair.
22. Mothers see adoption as an act of sacrifice and love when they give up the child to those who can provide a better life.
23. Battering may start or become worse during pregnancy; the abdomen may replace the face and breasts as the target for battery.
24. Nurses can consciously practice in ways that empower women and make it clear that the woman owns her body and that no one deserves to be beaten.
25. The battered woman often appears hesitant, embarrassed, or evasive; she may avoid eye contact and appear ashamed, guilty, or frightened. There may be signs of present and past injury, such as bruising, swelling, lacerations, scars, and old fractures, as well as genital injuries.
26. Nurses can help establish short-term goals:
    a. Acknowledge the abuse.
    b. Develop a specific plan of action to implement when the abusive cycle begins.
    c. Identify community resources that provide protection for the woman and her children.

Chapter 24

1. Bleeding is the most common sign of threatened abortion; it may be accompanied by rhythmic uterine cramping, persistent backache, or feelings of pelvic pressure. When there is gross rupture of membranes followed by uterine contractions and bleeding, the abortion generally becomes inevitable.
2. Avoid strenuous exercise for several days; report prolonged or profuse bleeding; use sanitary pads rather than tampons for the first week; curtail intercourse and/or douching for at least 1 week; initiate birth control measures if intercourse is resumed before menstrual periods resume; take temperature twice a day and report a temperature above 37.8°C (100°F); keep follow-up appointment.
3. Ectopic pregnancy remains the leading cause of maternal death due to hemorrhage, and it sharply reduces the woman's chance of subsequent pregnancies because of damage to a fallopian tube.
4. As a result of pelvic inflammatory disease that may complicate untreated sexually transmitted diseases and result in scarring of the fallopian tubes, making it difficult for the fertilized ovum to pass through the obstructed tube.
5. The first phase is evacuation of the molar pregnancy; the second phase is follow-up to detect malignant changes in remaining trophoblastic tissue.
6. Placenta previa is characterized by painless vaginal bleeding in the last half of pregnancy due to implantation of the placenta in the lower uterine segment; abruptio placentae refers to premature separation of a normally implanted placenta and involves either obvious or concealed bleeding with severe abdominal pain.
7. The major danger of abruptio placentae for the mother is hemorrhagic shock; the major dangers for the fetus are anoxia, excessive blood loss, or delivery before the fetus is mature enough to survive.

8. Whereas morning sickness is self-limited and causes no serious complications, hyperemesis is persistent, uncontrollable vomiting that can result in dehydration and electrolyte or acid-base imbalance.
9. Metabolic alkalosis may develop when large amounts of gastric acid are lost in the vomitus. Metabolic acidosis may develop as a result of starvation.
10. Persistent vasospasm of the uterine arterioles may result in fetal hypoxemia, intrauterine growth retardation, or even death.
11. Bed rest in a side-lying position increases cardiac return and circulatory volume, thus improving perfusion of vital organs. Increased renal perfusion decreases angiotensin II levels, promotes diuresis, and lowers the blood pressure.
12. Vasospasm may result in maternal cerebral edema and small cerebral hemorrhages and may result in convulsions.
13. Magnesium prevents convulsions by reducing central nervous system instability and decreasing vasospasm. The primary adverse effect of magnesium is central nervous system depression, which includes depression of the respiratory center.
14. H—hemolysis, EL—elevated liver enzymes, LP—low platelets.
15. Pregnancy-induced hypertension occurs only during pregnancy and the early postpartum period; chronic hypertension is present before pregnancy and persists following delivery and the postpartum period.
16. Hyporeflexia indicates central nervous system depression (often as a result of magnesium toxicity); hyperreflexia indicates cerebral edema and worsening of pregnancy-induced hypertension.
17. When cerebral edema is severe, seizures may be precipitated by excessive environmental stimuli.
18. Administration of RhoGAM prevents the development of maternal Rh antibodies and is recommended following any procedure that includes the possibility of maternal exposure to Rh-positive blood.
19. Many women with blood type O have developed high serum anti-A or anti-B antibody titers before they become pregnant for the first time, and the first pregnancy may be affected.

Chapter 25

1. Placental hormones create resistance to insulin in maternal cells, resulting in the need for increased insulin as the pregnancy progresses.
2. Major maternal effects of gestational diabetes are increased incidence of urinary tract infections, hydramnios, premature rupture of membranes, preterm labor, and the development of pregnancy-induced hypertension. The fetus may be large for gestational age (>4500 g), resulting in dystocia, fetal injury, and injury to the maternal birth canal and making cesarean birth more likely. The newborn must be carefully observed for hypoglycemia and respiratory distress syndrome.
3. Usually controlled by a regular pattern of physical activity and dietary management.
4. Maternal hyperglycemia in the first trimester has been associated with increased risk for congenital anomalies.
5. Insulin needs generally decline during the first trimester because placental hormones are low and the woman often experiences nausea, vomiting, and anorexia. In addition, the fetus receives its share of glucose, which reduces maternal plasma glucose levels. Insulin needs increase during the second and third trimesters, when placental hormones reach their peak. Insulin needs during labor are based on blood glucose; however, they may decrease because of lack of oral intake and vigorous muscular exertion. Insulin needs should decline rapidly following delivery and the abrupt cessation of placental hormones.
6. Fetal size depends on maternal vascular impairment; if there is none, the fetus may be hyperglycemic at times, which produces macrosomia; if vascular impairment is present, the transport of glucose and oxygen may be decreased, resulting in a small-for-gestational-age fetus.
7. Cardiovascular changes of pregnancy (increased plasma volume and cardiac output) can impose an additional burden on a woman with pre-existing heart disease.
8. Rheumatic heart disease and congenital heart disease. The functional classification of heart disease (Class I to Class IV) depends on the ability to tolerate activity.
9. The primary goals of management are to prevent cardiac decompensation and the development of congestive heart disease by:
   a. Limiting physical activity so that cardiac demand does not exceed cardiac capacity.
   b. Avoiding excessive weight gain.
   c. Providing a diet that is adequate in protein, calories, and sodium.
10. Folic acid anemia is associated with increased risk of spontaneous abortion, abruptio placentae, and fetal anomalies (particularly neural tube defects).
11. Pregnancy may aggravate sickle cell anemia and bring on sickle cell crisis.
12. Toxoplasmosis can be prevented by thoroughly cooking meat, avoiding uncooked eggs and unpasteurized milk, washing the hands and cooking surfaces after touching raw meat, and avoiding materials contaminated with cat feces. Rubella can be prevented by vaccination during childhood or at least 3 months prior to becoming pregnant. The greatest danger to the fetus from rubella is during the first trimester, which is the period of organogenesis.
13. The fetus can become infected with herpes after rupture of membranes, when the virus ascends from active lesions, and during birth, when the fetus comes into contact with infected genital secretions.
14. Newborns should receive passive immunizations with a single dose of specific hepatitis B immune globulin and hepatitis B vaccine soon after birth.
15. HIV is transmitted by:
   a. Sexual exposure to genital secretions of infected person.
   b. Parenteral exposure to infected blood or tissue.
   c. Perinatal exposure of an infant to infected mother. It has been reported that an infant born to an HIV-infected mother has a 20 to 40 per cent risk of developing AIDS.
16. HIV is a retrovirus that invades and destroys the T4 subset of lymphocytes, resulting in inadequate immune response to infectious organisms.
17. Although HIV-positive persons may remain asymptomatic for many years until the immune system is depressed and opportunistic diseases prevail, they are infectious from the time they are infected with the virus.

Chapter 26

1. Hypotonic labor dysfunction usually occurs during the active phase of first-stage labor, whereas hypertonic dysfunction usually occurs during the latent phase. Uterine contractions become weaker, shorter, and less frequent in hypotonic dysfunction; in hypertonic dysfunction, they are painful but inefficient and the uterine resting tone is high. Hypotonic dysfunction is not painful because the contractions decline, although the woman may become tired; hypertonic dysfunction is characterized by a cramping type of pain. Management of both depends on the identified cause. Hypotonic dysfunction is often managed by ensuring adequate fluids and electrolytes, position changes, amniotomy, and oxytocin augmentation. Hypertonic dysfunction may be managed by mild sedation or tocolytic drugs to reduce excess uterine activity.
2. Maternal position changes encourage the fetus to roll from the occiput transverse or occiput posterior position to the occiput anterior position. The squatting position also increases pelvic

diameters and straightens the pelvic curve to facilitate both fetal rotation and descent.

3. Other complications are associated with a fetus in a breech presentation that may cause problems, regardless of the method of birth. These include low birth weight, fetal anomalies, and associated pregnancy complications.
4. The staff must be prepared for care of multiple infants. Duplicate staff and equipment should be prepared for every infant expected.
5. Bladder distention during labor can consume available room in the woman's pelvis, thus impeding labor progress and fetal descent. Additionally, it is a potential source of discomfort.
6. Psychological support helps reduce excess stress that can otherwise consume energy that the uterus needs, inhibit uterine contractions, reduce placental blood supply, impair the woman's pushing efforts, and increase the woman's pain experience.
7. The average nullipara's cervix dilates about 1.2 cm/hour; the average multipara's cervix dilates about 1.5 cm/hour.
8. Nursing care for the woman who has prolonged labor is similar to that for dysfunctional labor. Promoting comfort, energy conservation, position changes, and assessments for further complications, such as infection, should be done.
9. Trauma is the primary maternal risk of a precipitate labor, and may include uterine rupture, cervical lacerations, and hematomas. Fetal risks may include trauma, such as intracranial hemorrhage or nerve damage and hypoxia.
10. Premature rupture of the membranes occurs before true labor any time during pregnancy. Preterm premature rupture of the membranes (PPROM) occurs before term and may or may not be accompanied by contractions. PPROM is more likely to be associated with preterm labor and birth.
11. Infection may be both a cause of and a result of premature rupture of the membranes.
12. Labor is usually induced if a woman with ruptured membranes is near term, has a favorable cervix, and if labor does not spontaneously begin within about 4 to 6 hours.
13. The physician will balance the risks of prematurity against the risk for infection when deciding the best management of preterm premature rupture of the membranes.
14. Symptoms of preterm labor are often vague. They include uterine contractions that may often be painless; the fetus "balling up"; menstrual-like cramps; backache; pelvic pressure; change or increased vaginal discharge; abdominal cramps; thigh pain; a sense of "feeling bad."
15. Early identification of preterm labor enables management that may delay birth and allow further maturation of the fetus.
16. Any activity can increase uterine activity and thus increase the risk for preterm birth.
17. The three potential fetal/newborn risks are reduced placental function and umbilical cord compression before birth and meconium aspiration after birth.
18. The priority of care if umbilical cord prolapse occurs is to reduce compression of the cord and restore normal blood flow through it. At the same time, the nurse should summon help to expedite delivery.
19. Oxytocin-stimulated contractions are potentially more powerful than natural ones and may cause the pressure in the uterus to exceed the uterine wall's ability to withstand that pressure.
20. Shock and hemorrhage are rapidly developing complications of uterine inversion.
21. The risk for amniotic fluid embolism is greater if the woman has a very strong labor with ruptured membranes because the amniotic fluid can be forced into her blood vessels.
22. Care initially focuses on treatment of any life-threatening maternal injuries to stabilize her condition.
23. Maternal death is the most common cause of fetal death when trauma occurs. The fetus may also suffer direct blunt or penetrating trauma.
24. Prolapsed umbilical cord: Relieve pressure on the cord to restore adequate blood flow through it. *Uterine rupture*: Attempt to prevent by cautious intrapartal use of oxytocin and close monitoring of uterine contractions. *Uterine inversion*: Avoid pressure on the poorly contracted fundus after birth; assess for and correct shock. *Amniotic fluid embolism*: Respiratory support; observe for coagulation deficits. *Trauma*: Stabilize the mother's condition, and treat any life-threatening injuries; place wedge under right hip to improve hemodynamic stability.

Chapter 27

1. Postpartum hemorrhage can sometimes be anticipated and prevented by careful examination of the prenatal and intrapartal records that reveal predisposing factors for hemorrhage.
2. Overdistention of the uterus predisposes to uterine atony, which can result in excessive bleeding.
3. Trauma to the birth canal can cause rapid loss of blood even when the uterus is firmly contracted.
4. Compensatory mechanisms maintain the blood pressure when hemorrhage first occurs so that perfusion of vital organs, such as the kidneys, brain, and heart, continues as long as possible.
5. Uterine tenderness, a uterine fundus that does not descend as expected, pelvic pain or feelings of pelvic heaviness, backache, lochia that varies from expected pattern, and fatigue.
6. Nurses instruct mothers and significant others how to assess the fundus and lochia and how to recognize symptoms that indicate subinvolution and that must be reported to the health care provider.
7. During pregnancy, factors that promote clot formation are increased, whereas factors that prevent clot formation are decreased, resulting in a higher risk of thrombus formation. Additional factors include cesarean birth, obesity, varicose veins, and smoking.
8. To decrease interstitial swelling, to promote venous return from the affected leg, and to prevent stasis.
9. Prothrombin or partial thromboplastin time, bleeding from unusual sites (nose, gums, urine), signs of bruising or petechiae.
10. Trauma to tissues provides an entry for pathogenic organisms.
11. An alkaline environment, which promotes the growth of bacteria, occurs when the acidity of the vagina is reduced by amniotic fluid, blood, and lochia. Moreover, necrosis of the endometrial lining and the presence of lochia provide a favorable environment for anaerobic bacteria to grow.
12. Skipping feedings can result in engorgement and stasis of milk, which frequently precede mastitis.
13. Nurses should assist new mothers to empty their bladders every 2 to 3 hours during the day, encourage them to drink at least 3000 ml of fluid each day, and teach hygienic measures, such as hand washing and perineal care.
14. Gradual loss of interest in surroundings, loss of emotion toward the family, inability to feel pleasure or love, feelings of unworthiness, guilt, shame, loss of sense of self, and generalized fatigue and difficulty concentrating.
15. Depression After Delivery (DAD) and Postpartum Support International as well as local and community groups.

Chapter 28

1. Poor women may have impaired general health and may receive little or no prenatal care.
2. Preterm infants appear frail and weak and are small, with limp extremities, poor muscle tone, red skin, and immature ears, nipples, areola, and genitals.
3. Lack of surfactant makes the alveoli collapse on exhalation, increasing the energy needed for each breath.
4. Poor cough reflex, small air passages, and weak muscles.
5. They have thinner skin with blood vessels near the surface, little subcutaneous or brown fat, a larger head and body surface area, extended position, and an immature temperature control center.

6. They lack nutrient stores, need more calories, absorb nutrients poorly, and may be unable to coordinate sucking and swallowing. Their kidneys do not concentrate or dilute urine well, and they have greater insensible water losses. They lack passive antibodies from the mother and have an immature immune system.
7. The side-lying or prone position, or supine with a small roll under the shoulders.
8. By changes in respiratory and heart rate, apnea, color changes, stiffening of the extremities, hyperalert look, hiccoughs, and other behavioral changes.
9. Allow rest periods, reduce environmental stimuli, and communicate the infant's needs to others.
10. Avoid air drafts and exposure to cold oxygen or supplies, use plastic barrier sheeting, keep incubator doors and portholes closed.
11. Rooting, sucking, gag reflex, and respirations below 60.
12. Teach her how to pump and store her milk and breastfeeding techniques adapted to the preterm's needs, provide support and encouragement.
13. By providing warm support, realistic encouragement, and information about the NICU environment, the infant's condition and characteristics, and the equipment and care.
14. Help parents take on partial responsibility for care, beginning early in hospitalization and gradually increasing until discharge.
15. They may be thin, have loose skin folds, cracked and peeling skin, minimal vernix or lanugo, and meconium staining. They look hyperalert and worried.
16. Polycythemia, meconium aspiration, hypoglycemia, poor temperature regulation.
17. In symmetric growth retardation, all body parts are proportionately small. In asymmetric growth retardation, the head is normal in size but seems large for the small body.
18. Birth injuries, such as fractures, nerve damage, cephalohematoma, hypoglycemia, or polycythemia.

Chapter 29

1. Meconium aspiration, apnea, acidosis, failure of the ductus arteriosus and foramen ovale to close, brain damage, and death.
2. To identify high-risk situations, begin resuscitation promptly, assist the team, and provide follow-up and parental support.
3. Preterm infants, infants of diabetic mothers, and those with asphyxia because the amount of surfactant is inadequate to keep alveoli open.
4. Transient tachypnea of the newborn is caused by failure of fetal lung fluid to be absorbed completely in full-term infants often delivered by cesarean birth. Respiratory distress syndrome occurs in preterm infants as a result of inadequate surfactant.
5. Meconium in amniotic fluid enters the lungs before birth or is drawn in during the first breaths after birth, causing obstruction, air trapping, and inflammation.
6. To notify the physician, prepare equipment, assist with intubation, and observe for infection or other problems.
7. Pathologic jaundice appears in the first 24 hours of life and rises faster and to higher levels than physiologic jaundice. Physiologic jaundice appears after the first 24 hours of life as a result of normal erythrocyte breakdown.
8. To prevent cold stress, hypoglycemia, inadequate intake, and injury due to improper use of lights; monitor for complications.
9. Vertical infection is transmitted from the mother to the infant during pregnancy or birth. Horizontal infection is transmitted from other people to the infant after birth.
10. To identify early signs of sepsis, notify the physician, coordinate treatment, observe for change, and support the family.
11. Congenital anomalies, macrosomia or intrauterine growth retardation, respiratory distress syndrome, hypoglycemia, hypocalcemia, and polycythemia.
12. To identify complications, perform glucose screenings, feed early and adequately, and support parents.
13. Congenital defects, neonatal abstinence syndrome, behavior and feeding problems, failure to thrive, and abnormal social interaction.
14. Decreased environmental stimuli, assistance with feeding, and helping the mother bond and learn to care for the infant.
15. Abnormal openings in the heart, abnormal placement or narrowing of structures, or impairment of blood flow.
16. Cyanotic heart defects allow unoxygenated blood flow into the systemic circulation, producing cyanosis. Acyanotic heart defects cause impairment of blood flow or circulation of oxygenated blood into the pulmonary system, usually without cyanosis.

Chapter 30

1. Almost all contraceptive methods are used by women, and failure will affect them most.
2. To provide information so that women can choose appropriately and use contraceptives correctly.
3. Safety, effectiveness, convenience, education needed, interference with spontaneity, availability, expense, and client preference.
4. Surgical sterilization, hormone contraceptives, intrauterine devices.
5. That they cannot conceive during first intercourse, without orgasm, or without having menstruated a certain length of time, or that douching will prevent pregnancy.
6. They may fear loss of sexual privacy, the pelvic examination, and that contraception will adversely affect their health, and they may lack knowledge about effects of contraceptives.
7. By showing sensitivity to their feelings, being accepting, and providing extensive teaching without hurry, using understandable terms and audiovisual materials.
8. Women can conceive until menstruation has ceased for 2 years, but pregnancy is rare after age 50.
9. They kill and/or prevent sperm from entering the cervix.
10. They alter normal hormone changes, preventing ovulation and making the cervical mucus unfavorable to sperm.
11. Information about side effects, when and how to check the strings, and when to seek medical treatment.
12. They avoid drugs, chemicals, and devices; are inexpensive; and are acceptable to most religions. However, couples need extensive education and high motivation, and they risk pregnancy if they make an error.
13. The time, cost, and need for hospitalization, and whether reversal might later be desired.

Chapter 31

1. Infertility is strictly defined as the inability to conceive after 1 year of unprotected regular intercourse. Primary infertility is that which occurs in couples who have never conceived; secondary infertility occurs in those who have conceived before and are not able to conceive again.
2. The normal average number of sperm released at ejaculation is 400 million. At least half must be normal, have normal movement, and be living. The seminal fluid should liquefy within 30 minutes and should have few white blood cells.
3. Ejaculation abnormalities may result from retrograde ejaculation or hypospadias. Excessive alcohol intake or use of illicit drugs can cause delayed, absent, or retrograde ejaculation.
4. Abnormalities of the sperm, seminal fluid, or ejaculation can result from many factors, such as systemic illness, infections or abnormalities of the reproductive tract, exposure to toxins,

excessive alcohol consumption, illicit drug use, elevated scrotal temperature, obstruction, and immunological factors.

5. Abnormal ovulation can occur because of hormone disruptions caused by cranial tumors, stress, obesity, anorexia, systemic disease, and abnormalities in the ovaries or other endocrine glands.
6. Ovulation disorders are often associated with abnormal menstrual periods because hormone abnormalities do not promote normal buildup and decline of the woman's endometrium.
7. Some causes of fallopian tube obstruction include scarring or adhesions secondary to infections, endometriosis, and pelvic surgery.
8. Abnormal cervical mucus can trap sperm and prevent them from entering the uterus and fallopian tube.
9. Anatomical abnormalities of the woman's reproductive tract may prevent normal implantation or prevent normal placental or fetal growth.
10. Endocrine abnormalities associated with repeated pregnancy loss include inadequate progesterone secretion, inadequate endometrial response to progesterone, hypothyroidism and hyperthyroidism, and maternal diabetes.
11. Immunological causes of repeated pregnancy loss include an intolerance of the conceptus' foreign tissue and lupus erythematosus.
12. Elements included in the history and physical include a reproductive history, past medical history, examination for undiagnosed endocrine disturbances, tumors, chronic disease, and abnormalities of the reproductive organs. Chromosome analysis is sometimes done.
13. Medications used to induce ovulation include clomiphene, chorionic gonadotropin, gonadotropic-releasing hormone, menotropins, and urofollitropin. Clomiphene is a common drug for this purpose.
14. Screening tests related to donor sperm use include those for possible genetic defects and for infection.
15. In vitro fertilization mixes the male and female gametes outside the body and places embryos back into the uterus. Gamete intrafallopian transfer places the mixed ova and sperm into the fallopian tubes. Tubal embryo transfer mixes male and female gametes and places the fertilized ova into the fallopian tubes.
16. Factors couples will consider when seeking infertility help include their age, the length of their attempt to conceive, their desire for a biological child, and their feelings about adoption or a child-free life.
17. When deciding about infertility evaluations and treatments, the couple considers their social, cultural, and religious values; how difficult treatment may be; the probability of success with treatment; and financial concerns.
18. Psychological reactions to infertility include guilt, isolation, depression, and stress on the relationship.
19. Parenthood after infertility may be marked by anxiety about the pregnancy, lack of child care skills, loss of support from infertile couples, and unrealistic expectations about parenting abilities.
20. Couples considering adoption must confront their personal preferences, limitations, and prejudices.
21. Couples who lose a pregnancy after a period of infertility often experience grief, but sometimes the grief is mixed with optimism because they were able to achieve pregnancy.

Chapter 32

1. To assess risk factors for conditions such as heart disease, breast and colon cancer, and osteoporosis.
2. Sexual activity, number of partners, age when sexual activity began, method of contraception, and knowledge and practice of measures to protect self from STDs.
3. Breast self-examination, professional breast examination, and mammography.
4. A smear of the superficial layers of the cervix and endocervix to detect precancerous and cancerous cells of the cervix.
5. To detect colon or rectal cancer.
6. Medical treatment is rare because side effects of the drugs may be more distressing than the breast discomfort. If drugs are used, they may include progesterone, tamoxifen, or bromocriptine.
7. Ultrasound examination, needle aspiration biopsy, or surgical biopsy.
8. Gender (female), age (increases with age), and prior history of breast cancer.
9. To determine the extent of the breast cancer and to plan appropriate therapy.
10. Supportive or additional therapy recommended following surgery to improve the chance of long-term survival.
11. Primary amenorrhea describes menstruation that fails to occur by the age of 16 years; causes include hormonal imbalances, congenital anomalies, chromosomal defects, and systemic diseases as well as rigorous dieting and exercise; treatment is aimed at identifying and treating the underlying cause.

    Secondary amenorrhea describes cessation of menstruation for a period of 6 months in a woman who has an established pattern of menstruation; additional causes include use of drugs such as oral contraceptives, phenothiazines, and antihypertensives; once pregnancy is ruled out, treatment may include hormonal replacement therapy and ovulation stimulation.
12. Systemic diseases, uterine myomas, cervical polyps, genital infections, or cancer of the cervix or uterus, which must be investigated before diagnosis and treatment can be initiated.
13. Excessive endometrial prostaglandin that diffuses into endometrial tissue, causing abnormal uterine contractions, uterine ischemia, and tissue hypoxia. Effective treatment includes rest, application of warmth, oral contraceptives, and prostaglandin inhibitors.
14. Endometriosis lesions grow and proliferate during the follicular and luteal phases of the menstrual cycle and then slough during menstruation. The menstruation from endometriosis lesions occurs in a closed cavity, which causes pressure and pain on adjacent tissue. Endometriosis is often treated by interrupting the menstrual cycle and thus preventing bleeding into the pelvic cavity.
15. Symptoms must be cyclical and recur in the luteal phase of the menstrual cycle; the woman should be symptom-free during the follicular phase, and there must be at least 7 symptom-free days during the cycle; symptoms must be severe enough to alter the lifestyle of the woman.
16. Decreased consumption of caffeine, simple sugars, and salty foods; drinking at least 2000 ml of water per day; avoiding alcohol; eating six small meals per day to prevent hypoglycemia; increasing exercise; and using stress management techniques.
17. Controls hot flashes, alleviates genital atrophy, and protects against coronary heart disease and osteoporosis.
18. Hormonal replacement therapy is contraindicated for women with pre-existing breast cancer, liver disease, thrombophlebitis, or undiagnosed vaginal bleeding.
19. Estrogen replacement, supplemental calcium, and weight-bearing exercise.
20. Cystocele: the weakened upper anterior wall of the vagina cannot support the weight of urine, and the bladder protrudes downward into the vagina, resulting in incomplete emptying of the bladder and consequent cystitis and stress incontinence. Rectocele: the rectum protrudes into the vagina as the upper posterior wall of the vagina becomes weakened, which may result in difficulty emptying the rectum.
21. The cardinal ligaments are unduly stretched during pregnancy and do not return to normal; generally treated surgically according to severity.
22. Increased uterine size and excessive vaginal bleeding; treatment depends on size and symptoms and may include removal of the fibroid or hysterectomy.
23. To distinguish a fluid-filled ovarian cyst from a solid tumor, which necessitates additional evaluation.

24. Irregular vaginal bleeding, unexplained postmenopausal bleeding, unusual vaginal discharge, dyspareunia, persistent vaginal itching, elevated or discolored lesions of the vulva, abdominal bloating, persistent constipation, anorexia, or nausea.
25. Pregnancy, diabetes mellitus, oral contraceptive use, and antibiotic therapy.
26. Candidiasis causes a thick, white ("cottage cheese") discharge, whereas trichomoniasis causes a thin, malodorous, greenish-yellow discharge.
27. Barrier methods of contraception (particularly condoms) prevent potentially infected ejaculate from entering the genital tract.
28. The major symptom of primary syphilis is a painless chancre that disappears in about 6 weeks; the disease is highly infectious at this time. Symptoms of secondary syphilis are enlargement of the liver and spleen, headache, anorexia, and skin rash. Condylomata lata that contain numerous spirochetes and are highly contagious may develop.
29. Condylomata acuminata (genital warts) are caused by human papillomavirus (HPV), which is increasingly associated with cervical intraepithelial neoplasia (CIN).
30. By changing tampons every 1 to 4 hours, avoiding use of superabsorbent tampons, using pads rather than tampons during hours of sleep, and careful hand washing before as well as after inserting tampons or changing perineal pads.

Index

Note: Page numbers in *italics* indicate illustrations; page numbers followed by t indicate tables; page numbers followed by d indicate display material.

CONVERSION OF POUNDS AND OUNCES TO GRAMS

	Ounces																
Pounds	0	1	2	3	4	5	6	7	8	9	10	11	12	13	14	15	*Pounds*
0	—	28	57	85	113	142	170	198	227	255	283	312	430	369	397	425	0
1	454	482	510	539	567	595	624	652	680	709	737	765	794	822	850	879	1
2	907	936	964	992	1021	1049	1077	1106	1134	1162	1191	1219	1247	1276	1304	1332	2
3	1361	1389	1417	1446	1474	1503	1531	1559	1588	1616	1644	1673	1701	1729	1758	1786	3
4	1814	1843	1871	1899	1928	1956	1984	2013	2041	2070	2098	2126	2155	2183	2211	2240	4
5	2268	2296	2325	2353	2381	2410	2438	2466	2495	2523	2551	2580	2608	2637	2665	2693	5
6	2722	2750	2778	2807	2835	2863	2892	2920	2948	2977	3005	3033	3062	3090	3118	3147	6
7	3175	3203	3232	3260	3289	3317	3345	3374	3402	3430	3459	3487	3515	3544	3572	3600	7
8	3629	3657	3685	3714	3742	3770	3799	3827	3856	3884	3912	3941	3969	3997	4026	4054	8
9	4082	4111	4139	4167	4196	4224	4252	4281	4309	4337	4366	4394	4423	4451	4479	4508	9
10	4536	4564	4593	4621	4649	4678	4706	4734	4763	4791	4819	4848	4876	4904	4933	4961	10
11	4990	5018	5046	5075	5103	5131	5160	5188	5216	5245	5273	5301	5330	5358	5386	5415	11
12	5443	5471	5500	5528	5557	5585	5613	5642	5670	5698	5727	5755	5783	5812	5840	5868	12
13	5897	5925	5953	5982	6010	6038	6067	6095	6123	6152	6180	6209	6237	6265	6294	6322	13
14	6350	6379	6407	6435	6464	6492	6520	6549	6577	6605	6634	6662	6690	6719	6747	6776	14
15	6804	6832	6860	6889	6917	6945	6973	7002	7030	7059	7087	7115	7144	7172	7201	7228	15

Conversion formulas:
Pounds × 453.6 = grams
Ounces × 28.35 = grams
Grams ÷ 453.6 = pounds
Grams ÷ 28.35 = ounces

CONVERSION OF FAHRENHEIT TO CELSIUS

Fahrenheit (°)	Celsius (°)	Fahrenheit (°)	Celsius (°)	Fahrenheit (°)	Celsius (°)
96.1	35.6	99.3	37.4	102.6	39.2
96.4	35.8	99.7	37.6	102.9	39.4
96.8	36.0	100.0	37.8	103.3	39.6
97.2	36.2	100.4	38.0	103.6	39.8
97.5	36.4	100.8	38.2	104.0	40.0
97.9	36.6	101.1	38.4	104.4	40.2
98.2	36.8	101.5	38.6	104.7	40.4
98.6	37.0	101.8	38.8	105.2	40.6
99.0	37.2	102.2	39.0		

Conversion formulas:
Fahrenheit to Celsius: (°F − 32) × (5/9) = °C
Celsius to Fahrenheit: (°C) × (9/5) + 32 = °F